A Penguin Handbook
The Penguin Stereo Reco...

Edward Greenfield has been Record Critic of the *Guardian* since 1954 and from 1964 Music Critic too. At the end of 1960 he joined the reviewing panel of *The Gramophone*, specializing in operatic and orchestral issues. He is a regular broadcaster on music and records for the B B C, and in 1958 published a monograph on the operas of Puccini. More recently he has written studies on the recorded work of Joan Sutherland and André Previn.

Robert Layton studied at Oxford with Edmund Rubbra for composition and with the late Egon Wellesz for the history of music. He spent two years in Sweden at the universities of Uppsala and Stockholm. He joined the B B C Music Division in 1959, and as Music Talks Producer has been responsible for such programmes as *Interpretations on Record*. He has contributed 'A Quarterly Retrospect' to *The Gramophone* for a number of years, and he has written books on Berwald and Sibelius and has specialized in Scandinavian music. He has recently completed a monograph on the Dvořák symphonies and concertos for the B B C Music Guides, of which he is now series General Editor.

Ivan March is an ex-professional musician. He studied at Trinity College of Music, London, and later at the Royal Manchester College. After service in the R A F Central Band, he played the horn professionally for the B B C and has also travelled with the Carl Rosa and D'Oyly Carte opera company. Now director of the Long Playing Record Library, the largest commercial lending library for classical music on L P in the British Isles, he is a well-known lecturer, journalist, and personality in the world of recorded music. He is a regular contributor (as reviewer) to the new magazine *Cassettes and Cartridges*.

The Penguin Stereo Record Guide

Edward Greenfield
Robert Layton
Ivan March

Edited by Ivan March

Penguin Books

Penguin Books Ltd,
Harmondsworth, Middlesex, England
Penguin Books Inc.,
7110 Ambassador Road, Baltimore, Maryland 21207, U.S.A.
Penguin Books Australia Ltd,
Ringwood, Victoria, Australia
Penguin Books Canada Ltd,
41 Steelcase Road West, Markham, Ontario, Canada
Penguin Books (N.Z.) Ltd,
182–190 Wairau Road, Auckland 10, New Zealand

First published 1975

Copyright © The Long Playing Record Library Ltd, 1975

Made and printed in Great Britain by
Hazell Watson & Viney Ltd, Aylesbury, Bucks
Set in Monotype Times

Contents

The Stereo Record Guide Treasury

of Vocal, Instrumental and Orchestral Collections
plus a short selection of Humour on Record by

Edward Greenfield, Robert Layton, Ivan March

EDITED BY IVAN MARCH

To describe this survey as a 'Treasury' is apt, for within the wide repertoire covered there is a remarkable range of music and music-making of great distinction built up by the record industry over a period of a quarter of a century. Moreover, as is traditionally the way with real treasure, much of it is buried, away from easy access. Some of the records discussed here are not listed in any catalogue except the manufacturers' own lists (which are not in general circulation outside the record trade itself), and unless the collector maintains an indexed file of one of the major reviewing periodicals, going back well over twenty years, guidance as to what is precious and rewarding in a diverse musical cornucopia is even less easily discovered. The discerning will find an abundance of musical riches here. L P anthologies often provide an extremely worthwhile means of filling gaps in a serious record collection, simply because there is a vast range of great and beautiful music which can only be published in recorded form if gathered into a concert or recital.

'The Ninth Volume of the S.R.G. is devoted to records you may have searched for in vain . . . the increasingly valuable phenomenon, the L P anthology. We have orchestral concerts, collections of baroque and pre-classical music, choral records, instrumental and vocal recitals. It is a golden treasury, a modern Palgrave of the record world . . . enormously wide-ranging . . . a fascinating book, worthy to be called the S.R.G.'s *Ninth* . . . handsomely dressed in a jacket of pure gold.' *Gramophone*

'The collections are covered with the usual perspicacity, wisdom and enthusiasm that we have come to expect of this team. This is certainly a book to recommend to all discerning collectors . . . an ideal bedside book as well as an indispensable work of reference.' *Hi-Fi News and Record Review*

'These reviews take account only of musical worth, and refreshingly waste no space on waves of shifting (artists') popularity. I rate this an impressive book of its kind: the grouping of records does have a logic of its own. In short a book that works intelligently within its self-imposed limitations, to make ideal browsing material.' *Records and Recordings*

The Stereo Record Guide Treasury costs £2·75 (hardback edition).

It is published by the L P R L Ltd, not Penguin Books; it is available to order through any bookseller or record shop which sells books.

If in difficulty order direct from the publishers, enclosing remittance to include also carriage and packing of 50p. Please order from:

THE LONG PLAYING RECORD LIBRARY LTD

Squires Gate Station Approach, Blackpool, Lancs.

Preface

THE last decade has seen a remarkable
quickening of the expansion of the
available store of recorded music, and
this widening of repertoire – apparently
stimulated rather than heeded by
economic uncertainty – continues at
such a pace that it seems reasonable to
assume that the next few years will see
the availability of recordings of almost
every major work of significance. In
this way the gramophone is assuming
a role as fundamental as the printed
score for representing a composer's
wishes, a fact that both Britten and
Stravinsky (to say nothing of Elgar in
the 78 era) have recognized in a very
tangible way.

After a quarter of a century of LPs,
with stereo becoming available for
major projects from the mid-fifties
onwards, the achievement is considerable. Beethoven, Brahms, Britten,
Chopin, Debussy, Elgar, Mozart,
Puccini, Rachmaninov, Ravel, Tchaikovsky, Vaughan Williams, and Wagner are prominent among composers
who have already achieved a virtually
complete discography of their major
output, with many duplications of
works in the greatest public favour. The
list of modern recordings of Verdi's
operas is expanding apace, alongside
the music of Berlioz, and there is now
a choice of three different stereo
recordings of Wagner's complete *Ring*
cycle. There remain important gaps to
be filled, but all the Haydn symphonies
are recorded (and to listen to them in
sequence is to experience their historical impact in the way that Prince

Esterhazy and his court must have
done), and complete cycles of the
operas, string quartets and piano
sonatas are under way. It seems that
the record companies, having discovered that the public is attracted to
sets of works in albums, are showing
a remarkable penchant for issuing
complete series.

One area which is less well served is
the field of German Lieder and French
art song. The demand for such records
outside the 'popular' recital is apparently less easily sustained, and even
the integral recording of Schubert
songs by Dietrich Fischer-Dieskau for
DGG is currently withdrawn from the
British catalogue. It reappears sporadically, but its production, in albums of
too vast a proportion, seems wrongly
calculated to suit the larger musical
public. Some way needs to be found to
issue this kind of material in smaller
groupings, but so arranged that the
collector can avoid duplication. Then
the barrier to a wider appreciation of
this treasure may be broken, as has
already been achieved to a considerable extent in the field of chamber
music, not so long ago an extreme
minority interest.

With the high noon of our great
musical culture centred on Western
Europe now well past, the flow of new
masterpieces for the concert halls and
opera-houses is less readily perceived,
and we find ourselves turning back to
re-explore older and partly forgotten
second-line repertoire. But although
exciting discoveries are sometimes to

be made, as we listen even with an affectionate and indulgent ear we find that the reasons this music has fallen into disuse, with masterpieces ready to hand, are often too obvious. There are exceptions of course – one thinks of Monteverdi and Cavalli, or Vivaldi's *Four Seasons* – but not so many as to blunt the point that there are not inexhaustible resources of great music, and we are already in danger of over-familiarity with the readily accessible favourites.

A stale orchestra playing Beethoven's *Fifth* for the *n*th time is an unedifying experience for players and listeners alike. Yet the record collector, if he has purchased judiciously, is able to renew his experience of such masterpieces from a source that will communicate its balance of freshness and excitement, perception and bravura, with admirable consistency. Furthermore if the gramophone listener wants a change of approach to a favourite work, it is possible to possess for no more than the price of a concert ticket an alternative 'reading' of the score. If he is willing to use his imagination in terms of tonal truth and balance (and surely this is no more difficult than accepting a concert hall with an unsuitable acoustic) he has and will increasingly have access to the interpretative genius of musicians of other generations than his own.

One of the major functions of the gramophone is the constant renewal of the classical repertoire, and as the work of recording for each succeeding generation continues, recordings from the past must become easier to buy and cheaper too. Gramophone records, anyway, are almost unique among consumer durables in costing less (per minute of music) than they did twenty-five years ago. It is in the nature of things for any commercial organization to want to continue to make its past investment continually productive, and the surest way to market records of an earlier vintage is to reduce their cost. And, as our survey readily shows, from the point of view of the discerning consumer newest is not always best.

With the coming of quadraphony we are undoubtedly on the verge of a new era of recorded sound. Quadraphonic recording can add a new dimension to domestic listening, and there is no reason not to suppose that the next generation will see a further renewal of the repertoire. The not too distant future also holds fascinating possibilities of video, extending our experience still further. The fruits of advancing technology have a curious way of confounding advance criticism, and it is far too early for us to determine whether or not we shall welcome a picture to accompany our music. But meanwhile the musical riches available in terms of stereo sound alone are one of the great blessings of civilized society in the mid-seventies.

Stereo and Quadraphony –
A Historical Note

WHEN the long-playing record appeared in 1950 the technology of disc stereo had already existed for two decades. Its fundamentals had been established in 1931 by A. D. Blumlein, a brilliant engineer who worked for the British Columbia Gramophone Company (later to be amalgamated into EMI). However, besides setting out the basic principles of stereo recording (including microphone and reproducing techniques), Blumlein's early experiments showed – and actual stereo recordings were made – that the coarse-grained shellac used for 78 records was not refined enough to be a satisfactory medium for the system. It is probable too that the economic depression of the time contributed to the postponement of the development of stereo.

With the coming of the LP and the use of vinylite as its manufacturing material, Blumlein's obstacles were removed and by the mid-fifties the Decca company, under the technical leadership of another brilliant British audio engineer, Arthur Haddy, was already using experimental stereo for commercial recordings. One of the notable early instances was the 1955 Bayreuth Festival recording of *The Flying Dutchman* (only recently released, on Decca Eclipse, for the first time in the original stereo version); but Mozart's *Don Giovanni* appears to date from even earlier (1954/5). However, it was not until 1958 that the major British recording companies began to issue stereo recordings on a serious basis. The British record-buying public, perhaps wisely, refused at first to be over-impressed, and was slow to accept a conversion that involved considerable extra financial outlay and brought two speakers into the living-room where previously one had been sufficient.

This was advantageous in that it gave the manufacturers of pick-ups, playing arms and amplifiers a breathing space in which to redesign and improve their technology to match the new records. While this was happening the new sound started to percolate through to the public consciousness, and it began to be appreciated that there had been a step forward in the quality of recording comparable with the change from acoustic to electrical recording in the mid-twenties. However, the new records needed greater care in handling than their predecessors and it was soon found that, if record wear was not to become a serious problem, a fundamental improvement in pick-up design was needed, so that among other things the tracking weight at which the pick-up arm moved across the record could be greatly reduced. So began the remorseless progress towards lighter and lighter pick-ups (with improved playing arms to match), until the present situation was reached where it is possible to play a record at tracking pressures of less than one gramme. This is quite unrealistic in an age of atmospheric pollution and can produce a situation where dust adheres gently to the groove surface, and the pick-up cartridge, travelling across the disc almost like a feather, is too light to push the dust out of the way. The result is a series of unnerving clicks and pops.

Not all the faults on some modern records can reasonably be attributed to low tracking pressures, but it would seem likely that we have reached a situation where the 'best' modern equipment is so searching in its reproduction of what the record grooves contain that modern LP pressings, for the first time in the history of the gramophone, are of a lower level of technical refinement than the reproducer on which they may be played. This is frustrating for the perfectionist, but it is a state of affairs that is unlikely to improve. The modern LP pressing is already a miracle of twentieth-century mass-production techniques, and the manufacturers tell us that to ensure an absolutely perfect disc every time would need at least a threefold price increase. However, for those willing to make a sensible compromise in the matter of tracking pressures and who choose equipment designed to produce music rather than the X-ray effect, it is possible to obtain very satisfactory results indeed from modern records, although they need to be cared for and kept clean.

At the present time quadraphony is in a rather similar position to that of stereo at the end of the fifties, but the situation is doubly complicated by the existence of at least two competitive systems, neither of which is compatible with the other. It seems fair to state that *with the existing technology* the discrete CD4 system (represented in this book only by one or two RCA discs) has a marginal technical superiority in the matter of separation of the four channels over the alternative SQ matrix system, as represented by a more extensive, but still limited, range of discs on the CBS and EMI labels. The discrete CD4 system translates the two back channels into carrier waves above the range of human hearing, keeping the channel information totally separate at every stage. By the nature of things there is less chance of the channels feeding one to another with CD4 than with SQ matrix discs, where the four channels are encoded into two and the discs then pressed in the normal way.

However, the separation within the SQ system can still be very impressive, and in practice this system has certain other material advantages. For example one does not need a new pick-up, and if one buys an SQ record before adding a quadraphonic potential to the reproducing chain there is absolutely no danger of the disc deteriorating in use, for it is in every way compatible and gives perfectly good reproduction on normal stereo equipment. The SQ decoder plus second amplifier and additional speakers need not be excessively elaborate and expensive, for the rear channels are not normally as demanding as the front ones. In addition it is possible to transfer an SQ disc on to a cassette tape and retain the quadraphonic effect when the tape is replayed.

For the classical music lover the advantages of the SQ system as it stands are considerable. Certain kinds of music appear to gain more than others, but this may be a purely transitional effect while the aesthetics of the medium are developed to match the technology. String tone undoubtedly gains in richness and naturalness, and the effect of a brass tutti in a typical nineteenth-century score can be thrilling, while choral music shows a very striking gain in atmosphere. Even more in the field of opera does one have an increased sensation of realism; the stage image deepens and the singers appear to move within a genuine three-dimensional area. If the balance is correctly set one is not aware of the speakers at all. This especially applies to the best of the EMI records, which have a very natural balance, the back channels serving to increase the ambient effect, so that one is convincingly transported to where the music is being played or sung. Switch off the two back speakers and the atmosphere is almost cut by half – not quite the difference between monochrome and colour, but not far off. With CBS records the enhancement of the acoustic is similarly noticeable, but as American engineers seem unable to resist artificial balance techniques when any solo instruments are involved, the effect in concertante music is curiously ambivalent, the naturalness of the quadraphony if anything emphasizing the larger-than-life projection of the soloists.

It is a pity that public demonstrations of quadraphony are usually so unsatisfying. Only under domestic conditions can one fully experience the translation to another acoustic, but even then the surprising thing is how little directional effect matters. Of course there are fun records like the CBS *1812* with cannon to the right and left of you and echoing behind you, and the Mormon Tabernacle Choir thrown in for good measure, but even then it does not in the least matter where you sit.

Introduction

THE object of the *Penguin Stereo Record Guide* is to provide the serious collector with a comprehensive guide to the finest stereo records of permanent music available in the United Kingdom. Our survey covers records distributed through normal trade channels, and we have omitted specialist imports because their availability is much less certain. The American CBS and RCA companies, the Dutch Philips, and Deutsche Grammophon from Germany have their own British-based marketing organizations, while Telefunken records are distributed by Decca, an associate company. Alongside certain smaller labels there is also a long-standing British distribution arrangement for the Supraphon catalogue, and while supplies here are less reliable, it is generally possible for the patient collector to succeed eventually in obtaining most items from this Czech label.

Pressure of space forbids that every single obtainable LP is discussed within these pages; we have been consciously selective in trying to include virtually everything that is really important. For instance, in the case of Dvořák's *New World symphony* we have discussed rather more than half the available recordings, but even so more than a dozen records are involved, chosen because they seem to be competitive by reason of quality of performance, the interest of the artists involved, excellence of recording, and of course price. We have sometimes included records of comparatively indifferent quality if the music is not otherwise available, or if a lower price means that readers might reasonably expect to make some allowances.

Even allowing for any omissions we believe this is the most comprehensive coverage of the recorded repertoire in stereo ever attempted within the pages of a single volume. Because of the international character of the repertoire included, readers resident outside Britain should still find the survey useful, even if the listing does not exactly match the coverage of their own domestic catalogue.

The sheer number of available records of artistic merit offers considerable problems in any assessment of overall and individual excellence. While in the case of a single popular repertoire work it might be ideal for the discussion to be conducted by a single reviewer, it was not always possible for one person to have access to every version, and division of reviewing responsibility inevitably leads to some clashes of opinion. Also there are certain works and certain recorded performances for which one or another of our team has a special affinity. Such a personal identification can often carry with it a special perception too. We feel that it is a strength of our basic style to let such conveyed pleasure or admiration for the merits of an individual recording come over directly to the reader, even if this produces a certain ambivalence in the matter of choice between competing recordings. Where disagreement is profound (and this has rarely happened), then readers will find an indication of this difference of opinion in the text.

We have considered and rejected the use of initials against individual reviews, since this is essentially a team project. The occasions for disagreement generally concern matters of aesthetics, for instance in the manner of recording balance, where a contrived effect may trouble some ears more than others, or in the matter of style, where the difference between robustness and refinement of approach produces controversy, rather than any question of artistic integrity. As our survey is often based on reviews written at an earlier date (the hardback *Stereo Record Guide* originally extended to eight volumes, covering all the important issues made over a period of fifteen years), we have reserved the right to have second thoughts, sometimes finding that an earlier issue was overpraised in a less competitive market, sometimes showing that a record previously dismissed too summarily has genuine merit, especially when it is reissued on a bargain label.

EVALUATION

Unlike the early LPs, nearly all records issued now by the major companies are of a high technical standard, and most offer performances of a quality at least as high as is heard in the average concert hall. In deciding to adopt a starring system for the evaluation of records we have felt it necessary to use a wider margin than has sometimes been practised in the past, making use of from one to three stars.

The symbols (M) and (B) indicate whether a record is issued at medium

or bargain price. Where no bracketed initial precedes the starring it can be taken that the issue is on a premium-priced label (currently ranging up to about £3·25).

The key to our indications is as follows:

(M) Medium-priced label, usually below £2 in cost at present, although in the case of a boxed set some leeway may be given.

(B) Bargain-priced label, usually well below £1·50 (and just occasionally about £1).

(It is possible that a distribution change after we have gone to press could result in a price symbol being inaccurate, but this is likely only in limited instances.)

*** An outstanding performance and recording in every way.

** A good performance and recording of today's normal high standard.

* A fair performance, reasonably well or well recorded.

Brackets round one or more of the stars indicate some reservations about its inclusion and readers are advised to refer to the text.

Our evaluation is normally applied to the record as a whole, unless there are two main works, or groups of works, on each side of the disc, and by different composers. In this case each is dealt with separately in its appropriate place. In the case of a collection of shorter works we feel there is little point in giving a different starring to each item, even if their merits are uneven, since the record can only be purchased as a complete programme.

ROSETTES

To a very few records we have awarded a rosette: ❀.

Unlike our general evaluation, where we have tried to be consistent, a rosette is a quite arbitrary compliment by a member of the reviewing team to a recorded performance which he finds shows special illumination, a magic, or spiritual quality that places it in a very special class. The choice is essentially a personal one (although often it represents a shared view), and in some cases it is applied to an issue where certain reservations must also be mentioned in the text of the review. The rosette symbol is placed immediately before the normal evaluation and record number. It is quite small – we do not mean to imply an 'Academy award' but a personal token of appreciation for something uniquely valuable. We hope that once the reader has discovered and perhaps acquired a 'rosette' record, its special qualities will soon become apparent.

LAYOUT OF TEXT

We have aimed to make our style as simple as possible. All recordings are 12-inch LPs which play at $33\frac{1}{3}$ r.p.m. Immediately before the catalogue number, the record make and label are given in full, except for the familiar shortening of DGG for Deutsche Grammophon (Gesellschaft) and HMV for His Master's Voice. Few other abbreviations are used in indicating the contents of the record or the artists concerned, although for opera recordings only the principal artists are listed and we have, for space reasons, omitted details of the contents of operatic highlights collections. These can be found in the *Gramophone Classical Catalogue*, published quarterly by the *Gramophone* magazine.

We have followed common practice in the use of the original language for titles where it seems sensible. In most cases English is used for orchestral and instrumental music and the original language for vocal music and opera. There are exceptions, however; for instance, the Johann Strauss discography uses the German language in the interests of consistency.

ORDER OF MUSIC

The order of music under each composer's name broadly follows that adopted by the *Gramophone Classical Catalogue*: orchestral music, including concertos and symphonies; chamber music; solo instrumental music (in some cases with keyboard and organ music separated); vocal and choral music; opera.

The *Gramophone Classical Catalogue* now usually elects to include stage works alongside opera; we have not generally followed this practice, preferring to list, for instance, ballet music and incidental music (where no vocal items are involved) in the general orchestral group. Within each group our listing follows an alphabetic sequence, and couplings within a single composer's output are *usually* discussed together instead of separately with cross-references, although occasionally the alphabetical listing of contents makes this impossible.

CONCERTS AND RECITALS

Most collections of music now issued on LP are intended to be regarded as concerts or recitals. Often several composers are involved and it is quite impractical to deal with them within an alphabetical composer index. Reference is made to a number of such records within the pages of this book, usually when dealing with a short work found within such a collection. However, for reasons of space it has been impossible to include concert and recital discs within the present volume. They are dealt with in detail in a companion volume, *The Stereo Record Guide Treasury* (published as Volume 9); details of this book, which is only available in hardback form, are given on p. vi above. (NB. This is not published by Penguin Books but by the LPRL at Blackpool, and it can be ordered through any good bookseller.)

ACKNOWLEDGEMENTS

The editor and authors express herewith their gratitude to Mrs Judith Wardman, a member of Penguin's editorial staff, for her help in the preparation of this volume, and also to E. T. Bryant, M.A., F.L.A., and H. D. Goodwin, A.L.A., for their assistance with the task of proof-correcting.

RECORD NUMBERS

Enormous care has gone into the checking of record numbers to ensure that they are correct, but the editor and publishers cannot be held responsible for any mistakes that may have crept in despite all our zealous checking. When ordering records, readers are urged to provide their record-dealer with full details of the music and performers as well as the catalogue number.

Prices

It was originally intended to publish a list of record prices as part of this introduction, but over the past few years prices have seldom been completely stable for more than a couple of months at a time. The trend has been upwards, but often the alterations have been without a fixed pattern; sometimes the price of an individual label can alter if its distributor changes, to say nothing of the complications of tax changes. Rather than publish a list that would inevitably be at least partly out of date even before our survey was in print, we have preferred to let the basic price-range symbols (see under *Evaluation*, p. xiv) serve as an approximate guide. Readers are invited to inquire from their dealers about exact current prices of discs and of the many boxed sets which each have their own individual prices.

Deletions and Temporarily Unavailable Records

One of the problems inherent in the production of any discography is the permanent state of flux that exists in the record trade concerning the availability of records. L Ps are continually being deleted from their manufacturers' catalogues, often to reappear later, usually on a different label and often at a lower price. Sometimes EMI assemble a series of deleted records in album form, while Decca usually reissue distinguished full-price repertoire fairly promptly on their Ace of Diamonds (SDD or GOS), Eclipse (ECS), or *World of* . . . (SPA) labels. Thus (inevitably) a small number of the records reviewed in this book will prove currently unobtainable from their manufacturers; but this does not always mean that copies cannot still be found in the shops.

As we go to press, many of the Pye Collector series (prefix GSGC) are being remastered and reissued under new catalogue numbers (same prefix; series 15000). Where the new number is already known we have, of course, included it, but where the old catalogue number is given (series 14000) it is as well to check with your record-dealer to see whether it has been changed.

ADAM

Adam, Adolphe
(1803–56)

Le Diable à quatre (ballet in 2 acts): complete recording.
> *** Decca SXL 6188. London Symphony Orchestra, Richard Bonynge.

Le Diable à quatre was the seventh of Adam's thirteen ballets, arriving in 1845, four years after *Giselle*. We are reminded of the earlier work immediately at the opening by the typical 'hunting scene' music for the horns. Throughout the score Adam's felicitous sense of orchestral colouring (even more sophisticated here than in *Giselle*) adds to one's pleasure in the slight, but continuously melodic writing. This is a highly enjoyable disc, made the more so by Richard Bonynge's deliciously stylish pointing of the elegant writing for the upper strings. The familiar story of Countess and servant changing places (the former unwillingly) is strung out by rather slight incident, but one feels this might make a good ballet for television, with such reliably attractive music. The recording is up to Decca's superb ballet quality, with a slight pithiness to the upper strings which suits the brightness of the score.

Giselle (ballet): complete recording of original score.
> ** Decca SET 433/4. Monte Carlo Opera Orchestra, Richard Bonynge.

(i) *Giselle* (ballet): edited by Henri Büsser; (ii) *Si j'étais roi*: overture.
> (B) *** Decca SPA 384. Paris Conservatoire Orchestra, (i) Jean Martinon, (ii) Albert Wolff.

Giselle (ballet): older European score: highlights.

** (*) Decca SXL 6002. Vienna Philharmonic Orchestra, Herbert von Karajan.

Adam's famous score – the first of the great romantic ballets – has been heard in various forms since its first performance in 1841, but for the ordinary ballet-lover the various interpolations and alterations of orchestration will not be of prime importance. The Büsser version has the great advantage of fitting compactly on to a single disc and yet including all the important music. Martinon's performance is an ideal one, warm and full of poetry, with lovely string playing. The opening of Act 2 is enchanting. The recording here has splendid atmosphere and throughout has a fine tonal bloom and crispness of focus. Decca's alternative of the original score complete on two discs is much less desirable. The Monte Carlo Orchestra is competent enough, and so, of course, is Richard Bonynge, but the orchestral playing here does not really merit the SET price-range and the recording, although more modern than the Martinon issue, does not yield to it, except perhaps that this newer version is more ample in texture. In any case, apart from the price advantage, the inclusion of a stylish account of the *Si j'étais roi overture* (conducted by Albert Wolff) makes an attractive bonus, although, perhaps because of this, the recording on side one seems to have marginally less body than on side two.

Karajan's Vienna disc is lovingly played, with the suave blandishments of the Karajan baton guiding the famous orchestra to produce a reading of beauty and elegance. The glowing Decca recording is first-rate and as the legend of the Wilis (the ghosts of dead girls jilted by their lovers) on which *Giselle* is based is a German one, to have a distinct impression of Austrian peasantry and hunting music will seem to many very appropriate. But the lighter, French style of Martinon's account remains preferable.

P.S.R.G. –2

1

ALBÉNIZ

Albéniz, Isaac
(1860–1909)

Piano concerto No. 1, Op. 78.
(B) ** Turnabout TV 34372S. Felicja
Blumenthal (piano), Torino Orch-
estra, Alberto Zedda – LISZT:
Rapsodie espagnole. **

Albéniz's *Piano concerto* has little in
common with *Iberia.* The concerto is a
work of the composer's youth, and its
rhetorical brilliance shows the influence
of Liszt, with whom Albéniz studied in
1878. But it has a distinct melodic flair,
and the secondary themes of the first two
movements are attractive. The finale is
weaker, but the piece as a whole makes
pleasant listening. It is well played here,
and the recording is good, if not outstandingly rich.

Iberia (orchestrated by Arbós): excerpts; *Navarra* (completed by Séverac
and orchestrated by Arbós).
(M) ** (*) Decca Ace of Diamonds
SDD 180. Suisse Romande Orchestra, Ernest Ansermet – TURINA:
Danzas fantásticas. ** (*)

Albéniz wrote his piano suite *Iberia*
during the last three years of his life. It
consists of twelve terse yet evocative pictures of life in various parts of Spain. The
gaudy orchestral transcription of five of
these pieces was made by Albéniz's contemporary Enrique Arbós. *Navarra*, although a separate piece, which the composer did not finish himself, fits happily
after the suite and might well be part of it.
Ansermet's reading is distinguished and
in the quieter music his meticulous care
with inner colouring and balance creates
delicate pastel shading, which achieves
much of the restrained atmosphere of the
original piano writing. The conductor
recognizes the frank vulgarity of the

noisier passages, and plays them enthusiastically.

Suite española (arr. Frühbeck de
Burgos).
*** Decca SXL 6355. New Philharmonia Orchestra, Rafael Frühbeck de Burgos.

This is real light music of the best kind.
Tuneful, exotically scored (by the conductor, Rafael Frühbeck de Burgos), and
giving orchestra and recording engineers
alike a chance to show their paces,
Albéniz's *Suite española* makes highly
entertaining listening. We are given here
seven pieces from Albéniz's original piano
suite plus *Cordoba*, which is from the
same composer's *Cantos de España*. As
this has a very fetching tune, to end the
record graciously, no one is likely to
complain. But try the opening *Castilla* for
its glittering castanets or the *Asturias*
with its eloquent and sonorous brass
chords to offset the flurry of strings.

Iberia: complete recording; *Cantos de
España; Navarra.*
*** Decca SXL 6586/7. Alicia de
Larrocha (piano).

Miss de Larrocha brings a special
authority to this repertoire and has few
rivals here. Apart from the familiar
Evocación, Fête-Dieu à Séville, Triana
and one or two other pieces, there is a lot
of first-rate and highly colourful music
that will be new to many music-lovers.
Alicia de Larrocha's fingerwork invites
admiration for the clarity of her articulation and rhythmic attack. She plays
with full-blooded temperament and fire,
though there are occasionally touches of
wilful *rubato.* The piano recording has
extraordinary realism and range; on both
artistic and technical grounds this issue
is uncommonly rewarding.

2

d'Albert, Eugen
(1864–1932)

Scherzo in F sharp major, Op. 16/2.
*** RCA SB 6815. Earl Wild
(piano) – BALAKIREV: *Reminiscences;* MEDTNER: *Improvisation;*
SCHARWENKA: *Piano concerto
No. 1.******

D'Albert is remembered nowadays as
the composer of *Tiefland* and as one of
the great pianists of the early part of the
century. His piano music has more display than substance, but this *Scherzo* is
brilliantly played and the record is well
worth acquiring for the sake of the
Medtner and Scharwenka pieces.

Albert, Prince
(1819–61)

Songs: *Abendruhe; Einsamkeit; Gruss
aus der Ferne; Invocazione all'Armonia;
Klage der Liebe; Lebewohl; Die letzten
Worte eines Barden; Liebe hat uns nun
verient; Nichts Schöneres; Reiterlied;
Schmerz der Liebe; Ständchen; Trauerlied; Der Ungeliebte; Vereinigung; Die
Winterreise.*
(M) ******* Argo Ace of Diamonds SDD
370. Purcell Consort, Grayston
Burgess; Jennifer Partridge
(piano).

It is odd that the one major composer
eligible whose image is omitted from the
frieze of the Albert Memorial (good place
to visit before a Prom) is Schubert. Yet
Schubert is the very composer whose
music Prince Albert's own compositions
most closely resemble. Some of these
charming songs would have done credit
to the master himself, and though the

royal composer usually elects to stand or
fall by a simple idea not too elaborately
developed, the melodic lines are often
hauntingly memorable, with a flavour of
Mendelssohn added to that of Schubert.
German folk song was no doubt a common inspiration. With a leaflet of words
included and stylish singing from all the
soloists, notably the tenor, Ian Partridge,
brother of the excellent accompanist, it is
a delightful disc. First-rate recording.

Albinoni, Tommaso
(1671–1750)

Adagio for strings and organ (arr. from
Trio sonata in G minor by Giazotto).
(B) ****** Turnabout TV 34135S. Douglas Haas (organ), Württemberg
Chamber Orchestra, Joerg Faerber
– CORRETTE; HANDEL: *Concertos;* MOZART: *Sonata.*****

This is Albinoni's equivalent of Bach's
so-called *Air on the G string;* only the
lushness of the arrangement suggests the
twentieth rather than the nineteenth
century. The effect is vulgar but striking
too, and one can understand the piece
having considerable popular success. The
Turnabout version is played discreetly
and with taste.

Adagio in G minor (arr. Giazotto) *for
strings and organ; Oboe concerto in G
minor, Op. 9/8; Double oboe concerto
in F major, Op. 9/3; Violin concertos:
in B flat major, Op. 9/1; in G minor, Op.
10/8.*
(M) ****** Philips Universo 6580 001. I
Musici (with soloists).

The approach of I Musici to the infamous *Adagio* is to try and permeate it
with a genuine baroque sensibility. But
Giazotto's arrangement essentially needs

3

ALFORD

fuller textures than are provided here and the result is less happy than Faerber's version on Turnabout. The rest of the programme is much more successful, and as the disc is well filled it remains an excellent medium-priced anthology. The style throughout is vibrant and the recording vivid, if sometimes a little dry in texture. The two oboes are rather forwardly balanced in the *Double concerto*, but as Heinz Holliger is the principal the playing itself is distinguished. The quality of the presentation has the proper bright colouring, and the harpsichord comes through nicely without sounding artificially balanced. A fresh and enjoyable concert.

Oboe concertos, Op. 7, Nos. 3 in B flat major; 6 in D major.
- (B) *** Pye GSGC 15011. Evelyn Rothwell (oboe), Pro Arte Orchestra, Sir John Barbirolli – CIMAROSA and MARCELLO: *Concertos.****
- (B) ** Classics for Pleasure CFP 163. Sidney Sutcliffe (oboe), Virtuosi of England, Arthur Davison – VIVALDI: *Concertos.***

There are two outstanding collections of oboe concertos recorded by Evelyn Rothwell with her husband conducting, and while both are equally desirable they are also quite different in character. This is partly caused by the recording, which here balances Miss Rothwell fairly well forward, gives her a more ample tone than on the companion disc (Haydn; Corelli; Pergolesi) and reproduces the orchestra with a pithy athleticism. This suits Sir John's strong classical style and gives these two fine concertos greater stature than usual. Miss Rothwell's line in the two slow movements is ravishing without being too romantic, and the *spiccato* playing in the opening movement of Op. 7/6 and the crispness in the same work's finale are a joy.

Crisp, nicely stylish performances from Sidney Sutcliffe, with a beautifully sprung, crisp accompaniment from Davison. The recording is clean and clear to match the music-making, and with a fetching sleeve, this disc will give pleasure if not taken all at one sitting. Just a touch more flexibility and conveyed warmth in the slow movements would have made the music-making even more delightful, but Sutcliffe's pert characterizations are certainly effective.

Alford, Kenneth
(1881–1945)

Marches: *Army of the Nile; Cavalry of the Clouds; Colonel Bogey; Dunedin; The Great Little Army; H. M. Jollies; Holyrood; The Middy; Old Panama; On the Quarter Deck; The Standard of St George; The Thin Red Line; The Vanished Army; The Voice of the Guns.*
- *** Polydor 2383 153. Royal Marines Band, Portsmouth, Cpt. J. Mason.

Marches: *By Land and Sea; Colonel Bogey; Dunedin; Eagle Squadron; The Great Little Army; Holyrood; On the Quarter Deck; The Standard of St George; The Thin Red Line; The Vanished Army; The Voice of the Guns.* Novelty: *The Two Imps.* Waltz: *Thoughts.*
- *** HMV CSD 1282. Band of Royal Marines School of Music, Lt-Col. Vivian Dunn.

Kenneth Alford (otherwise Major Frederick Ricketts) was the British counterpart of John Philip Sousa. The relaxed swagger of his marches, the supreme self-confidence tempered with a characteristic dignified reticence, was as British as Sousa's extrovert exuberance was typically American. Here are two

4

collections of his work. The more famous marches are common to both, and each opens with the immortal *Colonel Bogey*. Both are excellently played and well recorded, although the HMV disc shows its age in a certain sharpness of focus in the percussion, which makes the prominent cymbals somewhat clattery. But Vivian Dunn was a very distinguished musician in the field of military music, and his performances show how well he was in sympathy with Alford's musical psychology. There is a subtle rhythmic lilt, so that his tempi seem fractionally more relaxed and the music-making has splendid assurance. But if you want the best sound the DGG disc is the one to go for.

Alfvén, Hugo
(1872–1960)

King Gustav II (suite): *Elegy. Swedish rhapsody No. 1 (Midsummer Watch), Op. 19.*

** HMV ASD 2952. Bournemouth Symphony Orchestra, Paavo Berglund – GRIEG: *Peer Gynt;* JÄRNEFELT: *Praeludium.***

Alfvén's *Rhapsody* has a justly famous principal theme, and apart from that is put together with imagination and skill, and the orchestration is delightful. Charm, however, does not seem to be Paavo Berglund's strong suit, and the recording too is brightly lit rather at the expense of warmth. The *Elegy* is affectionately done, however, and the disc is well planned.

Swedish rhapsody No. 1 (Midsummer Watch), Op. 19.

(M) (**) CBS Classics 61266. Philadelphia Orchestra, Eugene Ormandy – GROFÉ: *Grand Canyon suite.* (*)

Ormandy's performance is immensely vivid and likable. There is a superb sense of bravura from the orchestra, who obviously enjoy the folksy dance rhythms. Unfortunately the CBS recording is brittle and shrill, especially in the work's final climax. This can be recommended only to those wanting the *Grand Canyon suite*, which is rather better engineered.

Alkan, Charles
(1813–88)

Grande sonate (Les quatre âges), Op. 33.

(M) *** HMV HQS 1326. Ronald Smith (piano).

The *Grande sonate* dates from 1847, some six years before the Liszt *Sonata*, and is a rather extraordinary piece. Its four movements describe four decades of a man's life: his twenties, thirties, forties and fifties, each getting progressively slower. The first movement is a whirlwind of a scherzo whose difficulties Mr Smith almost nonchalantly bestrides; the second, *Quasi-Faust*, is the most Lisztian perhaps, while the last two are the most searching and individual. The piano sound is admirably realistic and clean (it could perhaps have done with a shade more resonance, though it is by no means dry) and it goes without saying that Mr Smith's performance is a remarkable piece of virtuosity.

Symphony for piano, Op. 39.

(M) * (*) Unicorn UNS 206. Ronald Smith (piano) – MUSSORGSKY: *Pictures.***(*)

Like his *Concerto*, Alkan's *Symphony for piano* is part of his *12 Studies*, Op. 39, the four movements comprising studies 4, 5, 6, and 7. But as music this is much less attractive than the *Concerto*, the outer movements tending to rhetoric. The most memorable is the second, a dark-hued little funeral march, and Ronald Smith, who gives a strong performance throughout, makes the very most of it. The recording is good, and so is the coupling, but this is essentially a record for the Alkan specialist rather than the ordinary collector.

Alwyn, William
(born 1905)

Symphony No. 3; The Magic Island: symphonic prelude.
*** Lyrita srcs 63. London Philharmonic Orchestra, the composer.

William Alwyn is perhaps best known for his film music but, as this record amply demonstrates, he is a composer of considerable substance. The symphony was the result of a BBC commission and first performed by the BBC Symphony Orchestra under Sir Thomas Beecham. It is a well-argued and imaginative score, richly coloured and at times even reminiscent of Bax. The scoring is opulent and masterly, and though the insistence on the four-note figure (D, E, F, A flat) is somewhat obtrusive and inhibiting, the work exhibits a genuine organic coherence. The performance is authoritative and the recording has enormous presence and clarity. The prelude is a fine piece, too, and the two works make a most welcome coupling.

(i) *Divertimento for solo flute;* (i; ii) *Naiades: Fantasy sonata for flute and harp;* (iii) *Mirages* (song cycle).
** (*) Lyrita srcs 61. (i) Christopher Hyde-Smith (flute); (ii) Marisa Robles (harp); (iii) Benjamin Luxon (baritone), David Willison (piano).

Two of these works are recent: the *Naiades*, which was written for Christopher Hyde-Smith and Marisa Robles in 1971, and the song cycle *Mirages*, from the previous year, settings of poems by the composer himself. (The record also presents Alwyn as an artist since the cover reproduces a self-portrait.) Though less immediately striking than the *Third Symphony*, the songs are rewarding pieces, not unreminiscent of Britten at times and Fauré at others (perhaps Berkeley too); and the *Naiades* is beguiling if unmemorable. Perhaps the least impressive item on the disc is the earlier *Divertimento for solo flute* (1939), which outstays its welcome. The exemplary performances and clean, well-defined recording make this a desirable disc: Alwyn is a civilized (and under-rated) composer.

String quartet in D minor; String trio.
(m) ** Unicorn uns 241. Gabrieli String Quartet – TURINA: *La oración.***

Although Alwyn scored some initial success with a *Piano concerto* which Clifford Curzon played at the Proms in 1930 and a set of *Five orchestral preludes* that were given three years earlier, he was side-tracked into film music. Yet his is a highly musical and civilized mind, as the other two works recorded here show. His musical craftsmanship is of the first order and his musical idiom readily accessible without ever being devoid of concentration and substance. The performances are thoroughly committed and polished, and the recording is both clean and truthful.

Arensky, Anton
(1861–1906)

Variations on a theme of Tchaikovsky, Op. 35a.

*** HMV ASD 2830. London Symphony Orchestra, Barbirolli – ELGAR: *Serenade*; R. STRAUSS: *Metamorphosen.****

(M) ** Vanguard VCS 10099. English Chamber Orchestra, Johannes Somary – PROKOFIEV: *Symphony No. 1*; TCHAIKOVSKY: *Serenade.***

Whereas Somary's performance, which is nicely made, tends to play up the unaffected charm of Arensky's pastiche-like variations, Sir John's reading shows the work's underlying emotional strength. His is a full-blooded, passionate reading which removes for ever the epithet 'slight' from a description of the score. The flexibility of phrasing and dynamic means that the slow variation, which is obviously modelled on the famous *Andante cantabile* from Tchaikovsky's *D major String quartet*, is gentle and moving in its unaffected simplicity. The sound is first-rate, at once spacious and brilliant, while the recording that Vanguard provide for Somary is rather dry in acoustic. However, the Vanguard disc is a fair recommendation at medium price if the couplings are attractive.

Arne, Thomas
(1710–78)

(i; ii) *Harpsichord concerto No. 5 in G minor;* (i) *Overture No. 1 in E minor;* (ii) *Harpsichord sonata No. 1 in F major.*

(M) *** Argo Ace of Diamonds SDD 336. (i) Academy of St Martin-in-the-Fields, Neville Marriner; (ii) George Malcolm (harpsichord) – C. P. E. BACH: *Collection.****

A highly attractive record. The Arne *Concertos* for organ or harpsichord were probably composed in the 1750s; the *Sonatas* date from the same time and are among the most advanced English keyboard music of the period. The music is beautifully played and the sound is crisp and elegant.

8 Overtures: Nos. 1 in E minor; 2 in A major; 3 in G major; 4 in F major; 5 in D major; 6 in B flat major; 7 in D major; 8 in G minor.

** Oiseau-Lyre DSLO 503. Academy of Ancient Music, dir. Christopher Hogwood (harpsichord).

Arne's *Overtures*, besides showing a pleasing individuality of invention, are formally imaginative too in not slavishly following either the traditional French or the newer Italian patterns. The performances here, recorded in a resonant but not inflated acoustic, are well made and spirited. However, while the use of authentic instruments (especially when skilfully played) has much in its favour, to offer an 'impossible' fanfare-like passage on open horn harmonics (as in *Overture No. 4*) seems grotesque when modern instruments could encompass the music without assaulting the ears of the listener. This blemish apart, the disc makes enjoyable listening. It is beautifully presented in a handsome sleeve with good insert notes.

Harpsichord sonatas Nos. 1 in F major; 2 in E minor; 3 in G major; 4 in D minor; 5 in B flat major; 6 in G minor; 7 in A major; 8 in G major.

*** Oiseau-Lyre DSLO 502. Christopher Hogwood (harpsichord).

A considerable part of the pleasure afforded by this record comes from the superb recording of the two harpsichords used, a 1766 Kirckman on side one, and a 1744 Blasser on side two. There are so few really truthful solo harpsichord records available that this one must be welcomed with open arms, particularly as Christopher Hogwood's playing is so spontaneous and full of character. The music itself, although rather eclectic in style, has plenty of personality; the *Sonata No. 7* is an especially vivid piece. *No. 8* is a set of variations on a very Handelian tune which is so familiar that one doubts the information in the insert note that it is 'reputedly taken from Rameau'. A most enjoyable record, presented in a delightful picture-sleeve which is the stylish format of this attractive Oiseau-Lyre Florilegium series.

Thomas and Sally (ballad opera): complete recording.
> (B) ** Pye GSGC 14125. Hazel Holt (soprano), Jean Temperley (mezzo-soprano), Paul Taylor, Philip Langridge (tenors), Northern Sinfonia, Simon Preston.

This is the most famous of ballad operas, and rightly so. Its fresh simplicity – both musical and dramatic – is hard to resist (sailor lover returns just in time to save his beloved from a fate worse than death), and since the early mono version disappeared from the catalogue many years ago, a stereo version is welcome. This one, recorded with excessive reverberation in a church, is not as polished as it might be, and the singing cast is not strong, but Simon Preston's direction is understanding, and with a libretto provided, it is well worth its bargain-label price.

Arnell, Richard
(born 1917)

Serenade for 10 wind instruments and double bass, Op. 57.
> (B) ** Pye GSGC 14040. London Baroque Ensemble, Karl Haas –

KAY: *Quartet*; R. STRAUSS: *Suite.**(*)

Arnell's *Serenade* begins with a most uncompromising cadence, but although the opening movement takes a little getting to know, the scherzo is vivacious, and the work as a whole is rewarding, in spite of its rather angular melodic lines. The finale has real charm. The recording is good but not outstanding.

Arnold, Malcolm
(born 1921)

Guitar concerto, Op. 67.
> *** RCA SB 6826. Julian Bream (guitar), Melos Ensemble, the composer – GIULIANI: *Concerto.****

Long available as a mono record this has only been issued in stereo comparatively recently. The recording has plenty of atmosphere, capturing the solo guitar most realistically, and the balance is good. Apart from what Arthur Jacobs has called the 'cream-puff' tune which forms the second subject of the first movement (which immediately stays in the memory), the concerto has less obvious melodic material than most Malcolm Arnold works. But the musing quality of the slow movement, imaginative in its texture, and the clever way the orchestral scoring throughout retains an orchestral presence, yet never swamps the soloist, recommend the concerto as one of the finest available for the instrument. The performance, with Julian Bream on top form and the composer directing, is first rate.

(i) *Little suite No. 2 for brass band, Op. 93; The Padstow lifeboat, Op. 94;* (ii) *Brass quintet, Op. 73;* (i; iii) *Song of freedom, Op. 109.*

(M) * (*) Decca SB 313. (i) City of London Brass, Geoffrey Brand; (ii) James Watson, Nigel Boddice (trumpets), Frank Lloyd (horn), Roger Harvey (trombone), Joan Smith (tuba); (iii) Harrow Schools Girls' Choir.

This is very much the curate's egg. The *Little suite*, written in 1967 for the Cornwall Youth Band, has a splendid finale with all the characteristic Malcolm Arnold inventive zest; the rest of the work is attractive but comparatively slight. *The Padstow lifeboat* has a foghorn (sounding D) as its dominating factor, which is effective but a little wearing on repetition. The *Brass quintet* is perhaps the most distinctive work here. It is skilfully written throughout, but it is again the finale that shows the composer's quirky rhythmic felicity at its most striking. The *Song of freedom* (which occupies all of side two) is a setting of children's poems. The words are direct and sincere, but the music seems aimed at a P T A audience and the effect is banal. The recording is good throughout, but studioish in atmosphere.

Symphony No. 3, Op. 63; Four Scottish dances, Op. 59.
 (M) ** Everest SDBR 3021. London Philharmonic Orchestra, the composer.

This well-recorded and mostly well-played disc begins with the four exuberant and typical *Scottish dances*. After this the *Symphony* comes as a shock. It is as if the composer, determinedly popular in his shorter works, is equally determined not to compromise himself in the least in the symphony. The two-part first movement – the scherzo section developing out of the opening material – reminds one often of Sibelius, but it lacks the conciseness and economy with which this great composer gathers together his fragments into a final

whole. Here the emotional atmosphere builds up oppressively but in the end peters out in a gentle second vein of lyricism. The second movement is even more forbidding, and it is difficult to reconcile the harshness of its climaxes with the composer's other work. The finale is looser but still pungent enough, and it makes a reasonably satisfying end.

Symphony No. 5, Op. 74; 4 Cornish dances, Op. 91; Overture Peterloo, Op. 97.
 ** (*) HMV ASD 2878. City of Birmingham Orchestra, the composer.

Malcolm Arnold directs characteristically alive and spontaneous performances of this well-contrasted group of his own works. It is arguable whether his symphonies contain his best music, but *No. 5* is fairly convincing, with an impressive slow movement. The *Peterloo overture*, a spectacular occasional piece, seems a trifle inflated, but the *Cornish dances* are tuneful and show the composer's marvellous feeling for orchestral colour. The recording is most vivid throughout.

Arriaga, Juan (1806–26)

String quartet No. 1 in D minor; String quartet No. 2 in A major.
 (B) *** Pye GSGC 14138. Fidelio Quartet.

Arriaga, the very talented Spanish composer who died when he was only twenty, has been known principally for his *Symphony*, recorded for H M V by the London Mozart Players. That recording, unfortunately, is currently unobtainable, but this excellent coupling of two of Arriaga's three string quartets serves admirably to demonstrate the strength of his musical personality. Like Mendelssohn's, his genius revealed itself at an early age; these two works were written when the composer was only sixteen, yet they are fully worthy of Haydn. The *First* has a memorable slow movement that immediately evokes that master, and the opening movement of the *Second* shows a quite remarkable impulse and maturity. Both quartets have gay finales, and neither has a bar of music not worthy of a musical mind of the highest order. The spontaneity and affection of the performances are matched by their polish and Pye's recording is excellent, offering a pleasingly homogeneous sound picture, yet no lack of detail. Highly recommended.

Auber, Daniel
(1782–1871)

Overtures: *The Black Domino; The Bronze Horse; The Crown Diamonds; Fra Diavolo; Masaniello (La Muette de Portici)*.

(B) ** Decca Eclipse ECS 695. Paris Conservatoire Orchestra, Albert Wolff.

Previously only available in mono, this collection is enhanced by the addition of *The Black Domino overture* (not previously included in either the original LXT or the Ace of Clubs format). It now opens the disc and is splendidly played and recorded. Elsewhere the recording is slightly marred in *tutti* by a too effusive bass drum (which sounded perfect in the old and much drier mono presentation). But the playing throughout is witty and idiomatic (*Fra Diavolo* comes off especially well) and the disc gives much pleasure.

Auric, Georges
(born 1899)

Overture.

*** Philips SAL 3637. London Symphony Orchestra, Antal Dorati – FRANÇAIX: *Concertino*; MILHAUD: *Le Bœuf*; SATIE: *Parade*.***

Georges Auric's *Overture*, although it seems to use part of a theme from Debussy's *Petite suite*, has more of the Montmartre atmosphere of Gershwin's *American in Paris*. It is irrepressibly gay, and its melodic freshness and a vivacious performance help to dispel the suspicion that it is a shade too long for its content. Vivid recording.

Avison, Charles
(1709–70)

Concertos, Op. 6, Nos. 1 in G minor; 2 in B flat major; 6 in D major; 8 in E minor; 9 in D major; 12 in A major.

(M) *** Oiseau-Lyre SOL 318. Hurwitz Chamber Ensemble, Emanuel Hurwitz; Charles Spinks (harpsichord).

Charles Avison was born in Newcastle upon Tyne. During the early part of his career he went to Italy and sojourned also in London, where he studied under the resident Italian composer, Francesco Geminiani. He returned in 1736 to his home city. There, besides teaching, playing and composing, he started a series of subscription concerts rather like Hallé was to do in Manchester more than a century later. Avison's music is written in a mature baroque style and some fifty concertos were published, which we are only just now beginning to re-explore (the Academy of St Martin-in-the-Fields have recorded several). Avison's concertos were widely popular in his day. They have a remarkable vitality of invention and it is no exaggeration to put the best of them on a level with Handel's Op. 6, although their style is more conventional, usually following a regular four-movement pattern. But within that form Avison wrote some highly original music and put a firm individual stamp of personality on it. The opening concerto here begins with a standard dotted adagio introduction, but when the fugato begins one is immediately aware of the liveliness of the composer's imagination and the freshness of his style. And as the record progresses the concertos become more and more attractive. The quirky rhythmic pattern of the main allegro of *Concerto No. 8* is balanced by an eloquent slow movement of Handelian grace; the nervous energy of the principal allegro of *Concerto No. 9* is matched by the vigour of the finale. This is a five-movement concerto and fully worthy of Handel. The playing here is marvellously live and committed, and the recording is superb.

Bacarisse, Salvador
(1898–1963)

Concertino in A minor for guitar and orchestra, Op. 72.
* (*) DGG 2530 326. Narciso Yepes (guitar), Spanish Radio and TV Orchestra, Odón Alonso – HALF-FTER: *Guitar concerto.***

Bacarisse, director of music of Spanish Radio in Republican days, was on this showing an uninspired composer. His *Concertino* is an unpretentious but dull little work, brilliantly played by Yepes. There is a cheaper version available on Contour (2870 365), played by Manuel Cubedo and coupled to the Rodrigo concerto, but it is poorly recorded.

Bach, Carl Philipp Emanuel
(1714–88)

(i; ii) *Harpsichord concerto in C minor, W. 43/4;* (i) *Sinfonia in B flat major, W. 182;* (ii) *Variations on Folies d'Espagne* (for harpsichord), *W. 118.*
(M) *** Argo Ace of Diamonds SDD 336. (i) Academy of St Martin-in-the-Fields, Neville Marriner; (ii) George Malcolm (harpsichord) – ARNE: *Collection.****

The *Sinfonia* is the second of a set of six and comes from the 1770s. It is a lively and thoroughly characteristic piece, with all the sudden and often disconcerting impetuosity that marks C. P. E. Bach's style. The *C minor Concerto* also comes from his Hamburg period and is highly inventive and brilliant; the structure of the piece is original, for when one expects the recapitulation the composer sets out on a slow movement in a remote key and completes the material of the first movement only after a minuet. The musical material is as interesting as its formal layout. The side also offers a set of variations on the famous *La Folia*, familiar from Corelli's set. The performances are extremely brilliant and the recording crisp and clear. This is an admirable introduction to the composer, and the attractive coupling enhances the interest of the record.

(i; iii) *Harpsichord concerto in D minor, W. 23;* (ii; iii) *Oboe concerto in E flat major, W. 165.*
** BASF BAC 3011/2. (i) Gustav Leonhardt (harpsichord); (ii) Helmut Hucke (oboe); (iii) Collegium Aureum – J. C. BACH: *Sinfonia concertante; Sinfonia.* (*)

In neither of these works is the invention especially memorable. The oboe

11

concerto is gracious in melodic style and, as it is beautifully played and very well recorded, it makes pleasant listening. The recording of the keyboard concerto does not entirely avoid the sewing-machine image, however, although the orchestral impulse is strong in character.

Concerto for 4 harpsichords and strings in F major (adapted and arr. Leppard).

(M) ** (*) Decca Ace of Diamonds SDD 451. George Malcolm, Valda Aveling, Geoffrey Parsons, Simon Preston (harpsichords), English Chamber Orchestra, Raymond Leppard – J. S. BACH: *Concertos* ** (*); MALCOLM: *Variations.***

This Decca record offers an interesting example of an attempt to record four harpsichords clearly and without jangle. In preventing the latter it has achieved its object but only at the expense of amplitude in the harpsichord tone. Thus the quieter keyboard figuration sounds insubstantial. The inability of present-day recording techniques to convey a four-dimensional effect is at fault, not the engineers, who do their best but do not quite bring the composite image off. But Raymond Leppard too must take some of the blame. His expansion of this work from a simple structure for two harpsichords and strings alone makes the orchestra sound very bold and full-blooded. In the days of C. P. E. Bach, orchestral tone was much less ample than it is today and the problems of balance with a harpsichord did not arise. Here they do, and one has to turn the volume well up to get the harpsichord image right. Having said this let it be added that this is a fine work, very appealing melodically with a splendid opening movement, and it is very well played indeed.

Sinfonias for strings and continuo: in E minor, W. 177; in B flat major, W. 182/2; in C major, W. 182/3; in B minor, W. 182/5.

*** Philips SAL 3689. English Chamber Orchestra, Raymond Leppard.

Most of the symphonies recorded here were composed between the birth of Mozart and the appearance of Haydn's *Sturm und Drang* symphonies, and they boast some wildly unpredictable modulations, many of them abrupt and by no means always convincing. The performances are full of drive and an alert intensity appropriate to this astonishing composer. The recordings are impeccable.

Sinfonias for strings and continuo: in B flat major, W. 182/2; in C major, W. 182/3; in A major, W. 182/4; in B minor, W. 182/5.

⊕ *** BASF BAC 3013. Collegium Aureum (using original instruments).

This is quite superb. If ever the use of original instruments was justified by the results, it is here. The resilient, slightly grainy sound has splendid virility and bite, yet the timbre has a strikingly fresh beauty too and the continuo comes through in perfect overall balance. The playing itself has tremendous conviction and impulse, bringing out the music's originality and power even more than Leppard's collection. The recording is resonant, clear and clean and of demonstration quality. An irresistible disc.

Sinfonias for strings and continuo: in D major, W. 183/1; in E flat major, W. 183/2; in F major, W. 183/3; in G major, W. 183/4.

*** Philips SAL 3701. English Chamber Orchestra, Raymond Leppard.

(M) ** Nonesuch H 71180. Little Orchestra of London, Leslie Jones.

Leppard's second record of C. P. E. Bach symphonies is devoted to four published in Hamburg in 1780. This music is not merely historically interesting but is often characterized by an emotional insistence that is disturbing and a capacity to surprise that is quite remarkable. The playing is every bit as lively and vital as on the companion disc and the recordings too are exemplary both in quality of sound and balance.

The Nonesuch performances are well recorded too, in a natural, open acoustic, with an agreeable resonance. The orchestral playing is excellent, and one often feels that the conductor's broad style is seeking parallels with the symphonies of Haydn. This is enjoyable and certainly good value for the price asked. But taken as a whole the performances have not the impulse and distinction of Leppard's set.

Magnificat.
   ** BASF BAC 3051. Elly Ameling (soprano), Maureen Lehane (contralto), Theo Altmeyer (tenor), Roland Hermann (bass), Tolzer Boys Choir, Collegium Aureum, Kurt Thomas.

This is the only performance of the *Magnificat* currently available in the British catalogues. The performance is a good one, Elly Ameling outstanding among the soloists. The splendour of the closing *Sicut erat* comes over impressively, but the recording does not provide much orchestral detail.

(i) *Sinfonia in F major, W. 183/3;* (ii) *Trio sonata in B minor;* (iii) *Duet for 2 violins in G major;* (iv) (Organ) *Fantasia and fugue in C minor;* (v) *Organ sonata in G minor.*
   ** Telefunken SAWT 9447. (i) Amsterdam Chamber Orchestra, André Rieu; (ii) Sextett Alma Musica; (iii) Herman Krebbers

and Theo Olof (violins); (iv) Piet Kee (organ); (v) Anthon van der Horst (organ).

An interesting anthology worth investigating for the sake of the *Sinfonia in F,* one of a set of four composed in the mid-1770s. There is no lack of expressive feeling here or of dramatic surprise, and the performance under André Rieu is both fresh and vital. The *G minor Sonata,* played by Anthon van der Horst, is less consistently interesting, though the instrument he uses (a 1760 chamber organ by Strümphfler) is a beautiful one. The other pieces are of varying interest and the recordings are eminently satisfactory.

Bach, Johann Christian
(1735–82)

Bassoon concerto in E flat major.
   (B) *(*) Turnabout TV 34278S. George Zukerman (bassoon), Württemberg Chamber Orchestra, Joerg Faerber (with GRAUN: *Bassoon concerto* (*)).

This work is inventive but not especially memorable. Both performance and recording are lively.

Fortepiano concertos: in B flat major, Op. 7/4; in E flat major, Op. 7/5; in D major, Op. 13/2; in G major, Op. 13/5.
   *** Philips 6500 847. Ingrid Haebler (fortepiano), Vienna Capella Academica, Eduard Melkus.
Fortepiano concertos: in G major, Op. 7/6; in C major, Op. 13/1; in F major, Op. 13/3; in E flat major, Op. 13/6.
   *** Philips 6500 041. Ingrid Haebler (fortepiano), Vienna Capella Academica, Eduard Melkus.

J. C. Bach composed three sets of clavier concertos, each comprising six works. The Op. 7 were published in or around 1780 and the Op. 13 set three years earlier. All the concertos here are in the major keys and are attractive, well-wrought compositions. It would be difficult to find a more suitable or persuasive advocate than Ingrid Haebler, who is excellently accompanied and most truthfully recorded. J. C. Bach is at his freshest and most beguiling in some of these concerto movements, and these records cannot be too strongly recommended.

Harpsichord concerto in A major.
>   *** Decca SXL 6385. George Malcolm (harpsichord), Academy of St Martin-in-the-Fields, Neville Marriner – HAYDN: *Concerto in D major.****

This is a delightful concerto, though its authenticity is doubtful. It was first published in Riga in the mid-1770s and attributed to Johann Christian though it is not very characteristic of his music of the period. At the same time it appeared in London in a somewhat mangled form with an attribution to the Berlin Bach, presumably Carl Philipp Emanuel. It is always possible that it may be a work composed by J. C. Bach when he was studying with his brother in Berlin. However, whatever the case may be, it is a particularly happy example of the keyboard concerto of the period: the invention is fresh and engaging. The playing is extremely crisp and vital, while the recording is a model of its kind: the harpsichord is not too forwardly balanced and sounds completely life-like, while the string tone is both realistic and firm. Strongly recommended.

(i; ii) *Sinfonia concertante in A major for violin, cello and orchestra;* (ii) *Sinfonia in E flat major for double orchestra, Op. 18/1.*
>   * (*) BASF BAC 3011/2. (i) Franz-josef Maier (violin), Angelica May (cello); (ii) Collegium Aureum, Rheinhold Peters – C. P. E. BACH: *Harpsichord and Oboe concertos.***

The *Sinfonia concertante* is rather dry as presented here. The style of the solo playing is not particularly expressive: the tone of the older instruments is rather husky and seems to detract from any lyrical quality in the music. The symphony is well played, but the acoustic is reverberant and the recording does not fully exploit the music's antiphonal possibilities, although the sound itself is good.

6 Sinfonias, Op. 3 (ed. Erik Smith): *Nos. 1 in D major; 2 in C major; 3 in E flat major; 4 in B flat major; 5 in F major; 6 in G major.*
>   *** Philips 6500 115. Academy of St Martin-in-the-Fields, Neville Marriner; Simon Preston (harpsichord).

These Op. 3 symphonies are recorded here for the first time. They were first played in 1765 'at Mrs Cornelys's' in Carlisle House, Soho Square, and are scored for strings with oboes and horns in subsidiary roles. Erik Smith, who has edited them, describes them as 'in essence Italian overtures, though with an unusual wealth of singing melody'. They are beguilingly played by the Academy of St Martin-in-the-Fields under Neville Marriner and beautifully recorded. None of this can be called great music but it has an easy-going and fluent charm.

Sinfonia in G minor, Op. 6/6; Sinfonia in D major, Op. 9/1; Sinfonia in B flat major, Op. 10/2 (Overture Lucio Silla); Sinfonia in B flat major (Overture Temistocle).
>   *** Philips SAL 3685. New Philharmonia Orchestra, Raymond Leppard.

If C. P. E. Bach's music has a disturbing emotional insistence, Johann Christian's is unfailingly ingratiating. He has none of the introspective temperament of his elder brother or the abundant humanity and inventive resource of his greater contemporaries, but he still has a rare feeling for proportion and great harmonic charm. The *G minor Symphony*, Op. 6/6, has genuine depths too, and the others have unfailing grace. The orchestral playing is buoyant and sensitive, rhythms are alert but never overemphasized, and the performances are smiling and enormously stylish. The recording, too, is musically balanced and fresh in quality.

Sinfonia in G minor, Op. 6/6; Sinfonia in D major, Op. 18/4; Sinfonia in D major, Op. 18/6.
* (*) BASF BAC 3014. Collegium Aureum (using original instruments).

The Collegium Aureum are less successful with the music of J. C. Bach than they were in their disc of sinfonias by Carl Philipp. But they are not helped by the recording, which though pleasant lacks brilliance and on side two seems not always absolutely secure in texture. The playing itself is gracious, but rather unsmiling. The slow movement of the *G minor Symphony*, which is the longest work, with a side to itself, has more emotional depth than is revealed here.

(i) *Sinfonia in B flat major* (for single orchestra), *Op. 9 (or 21)/3*; (ii) *Sinfonia in E flat major* (for double orchestra), *Op. 18/1* (English edition); *Sinfonia in D major* (for single orchestra), *Op. 18/1* (Dutch edition); *Sinfonia in D major* (for double orchestra), *Op. 18/3* (English edition).
(M) *** Oiseau-Lyre SOL 317. (i) Hurwitz Chamber Orchestra, Emanuel Hurwitz; (ii) English Chamber Orchestra, Colin Davis.

This makes an admirable introduction to this charming composer. Those who normally find the elegance and charm of the period eminently resistible should sample this collection. It is highly attractive. The *B flat Symphony*, Op. 9/3, is played by Hurwitz and is the overture to Bach's opera *Zanaida*. The other three works are all played by Colin Davis with the ECO and should give unfailing pleasure. The slow movement of the *E flat Symphony* is quite magical, and the spatial effects in both of the double orchestra works are well managed. The playing is vital and sensitive and the recording altogether exemplary. At Oiseau-Lyre price this is a bargain.

Sinfonia in E flat major, Op. 9/2; Sinfonia concertante in C major (for flute, oboe, violin, cello and orchestra).
** Decca SXL 6397. English Chamber Orchestra, Richard Bonynge (with SALIERI: *Sinfonia; Double-concerto**).

There is some careful attention to detail in these performances but they do not show the same sureness of style that marks Leppard's or Davis's recordings. A pity, since the works are not at present available in alternative versions and there is, of course, some fine playing from the soloists.

Sinfonias, Op. 18: Nos. 1 in E flat major; 3 in D major; 5 in E major.
*** Decca SXL 6638. Stuttgart Chamber Orchestra, Karl Münchinger.

Münchinger is not the most smiling or persuasive of conductors and charm is not, generally speaking, his strong suit. Yet these performances are among the most successful he has given us in recent years, and the slow movement of Op. 18/5 is beautifully done, even if it is slightly more matter-of-fact than Hurwitz's recording of the mid-1960s (ECS 741). Bright, well-detailed recording makes this disc an attractive proposition, and a useful alternative to Colin Davis's anthology on Oiseau-Lyre, though he and his players have more natural charm.

Flute sonatas (for flute and clavier), *Op. 16: Nos. 1 in D major; 2 in G major; 3 in C major; 4 in A major; 5 in D major; 6 in F major.*

   *** Philips 6500 121. Kurt Redel (flute), Ingrid Haebler (fortepiano).

The Op. 16 set of *Sonatas for flute and clavier* was published in 1776, five years or so before the composer's death. Like so much of Bach's music, these pieces are charming rather than profound, full of gracious sentiment and flowing melodies. What is so striking about this record is the superlative sound quality Philips have achieved (both flute and fortepiano seem to be in one's own room) and the excellence and liveliness of the playing. This is an outstanding issue in every way, and although great claims cannot be made for the music, it is always pleasing and full of charm.

Symphonies (for wind sextet) *Nos. 1 in E flat major; 2 in B flat major; 3 in E flat major; 4 in B flat major; 5 in E flat major; 6 in B flat major.*

   (M) ** Decca SDD 424. London Wind Soloists, Jack Brymer.

These six sextets were probably written for Vauxhall and they certainly would make attractive open-air music. The combination of clarinets, horns and bassoons was also that of many mid-18th-century military bands. This and the fact that marches replace minuets in a number of the works may indicate that Bach composed them for some regimental band. Attractive period music, but if the writing has plenty of surface charm there is little

real substance. However, for relaxed and undemanding listening it can be recommended: performances and recording are of a predictably high standard.

Keyboard sonatas, Op. 5: Nos. 1 in B flat major; 2 in D major; 3 in G major; 4 in E flat major; 5 in E major; 6 in C minor.

   *** Philips 6500 120. Ingrid Haebler (fortepiano).

J. C. Bach composed only two sets of solo keyboard sonatas, these in 1768 and another set, Op. 17, some ten years later. The music is hardly substantial but it is highly attractive, and Ingrid Haebler plays it with great clarity of articulation and delicacy of feeling. She uses a Neupert reconstruction of a fortepiano, and one can hardly imagine it being more vividly and realistically recorded. Both as a recording and as playing this disc is in the highest class.

Bach, Johann Sebastian (1685–1750)

ORCHESTRAL MUSIC

The Art of fugue (Die Kunst der Fuge), BWV 1080 (see also organ versions).

   (M) ** (*) Argo Ace of Diamonds SDD 356/7. Philomusica of London, George Malcolm.

   ** Decca SET 303/4. Stuttgart Chamber Orchestra, Karl Münchinger.

   (B) ** Oryx EXP 27/8. Kurpfalzische Chamber Orchestra, Hofmann; Heinz Göttsche (organ).

How to perform *The Art of fugue* has always presented problems, when the score left by Bach at his death gives few instrumental indications and is in any case incomplete. The great merit of Leonard Isaacs's arrangement on Argo is the clarity and variety of tone-colour, for with great taste he has varied the instrumental groupings for each of the numbers. It is only confusing when one of the parts changes its instrument, but at the lowest estimate listening is made twice as easy compared with, say, a performance on the organ. The playing by members of the Philomusica is as beautiful as the recording quality, and this set should go a long way towards dispelling the idea that Bach's most complex contrapuntal feat is too heavy for nonspecialist listening. For clearly expressed reasons Isaacs has left out the final, incomplete fugue, and concludes the work on the next most complex. This is disappointing, but otherwise Isaacs's order is exemplary in allowing contrast as well as a sense of logical development.

If the Isaacs arrangement seems too free in its approach to instrumentation, then Münchinger's set may be the right alternative. Contrapunctus I–XI are given to strings, sometimes, as in No. 8, to solo strings, but generally to the full chamber body. Contrapunctus XI makes a good half-way rounding-off point, and then follow the canons, given to solo woodwind varied with solo strings. After the canons come Contrapunctus XIII (flute, cor anglais and bassoon, followed by the two-harpsichord versions), Contrapunctus XII for the string band and finally the unfinished Contrapunctus XIV, which leaves off in mid-air. Münchinger then rounds things off with the chorale prelude *Vor deinen Thron*, in principle quite wrong but rather moving in practice. This order does at least avoid the anticlimactic effect of having the canons last, and includes everything Bach left in the score. Münchinger's performance is sound rather than inspired – his preference for square unrelieved rhythms does not help – but the very sobriety has a cumulative impact, and recording and playing is excellent. The album brings an interesting

booklet full of arguments as well as information, and an ingenious visual representation of one of the fugues.

The Hofmann version follows the same order as the Münchinger, finishing with the incomplete Contrapunctus XIV and *Vor deinen Thron* but not including the harpsichord versions of Contrapunctus XIII. When it comes to instrumentation, a simpler arrangement than Münchinger's is adopted, with plain string versions of the majority of numbers varied with versions for organ. All the canons are given to the organ, but otherwise the variation of instrumental tone is nicely judged to avoid monotony. Interpretatively the approach is similar to Münchinger's, rather square and solid but cumulatively compelling. Neither recording nor playing is quite up to that of the Decca set, but at the price few purchasers will object to the comparatively trivial discrepancy.

(i) *Brandenburg concertos Nos. 1–6, BWV 1046/51;* (ii) *Double harpsichord concertos Nos. 1 and 2, BWV 1090/1; Triple harpsichord concertos Nos. 1 and 2, BWV 1063/4; Quadruple harpsichord concerto in A minor, BWV 1065;* (i) *Double concerto for flute and violin in A minor, BWV 1044; Double concerto for oboe and violin in D minor, BWV 1060; Violin concertos Nos. 1 in A minor, 2 in E major, Double violin concerto in D minor, BWV 1041/3;* (i) *Orchestral suites Nos. 1–4, BWV 1066/9.*

* (**) Philips 6747 098 (9 discs). (i) I Musici with soloists; (ii) Raymond Leppard (harpsichord and cond.), English Chamber Orchestra (with other soloists).

The contributions of Raymond Leppard and the ECO in the *Suites* and *Harpsichord concertos* are outstandingly good, sparklingly played and brilliantly recorded. Those of I Musici and their associates are altogether more humdrum, though respectable enough, while the recording is on the dull side to match. But the exhilaration of Leppard in the keyboard concertos, particularly the multiple ones (where he is joined by such distinguished soloists as Philip Ledger and Andrew Davis), is irresistible, and may make the set a reasonable proposition for collectors willing to duplicate the other works. The album is to stay as a permanent special offer, and there is some hope, as we go to print, that the keyboard works may later be issued separately.

Brandenburg concertos Nos. 1 in F major; 2 in F major; 3 in G major; 4 in G major; 5 in D major; 6 in B flat major, BWV 1046/51. Orchestral suites Nos. 1 in C major; 2 in B minor; 3 in D major; 4 in D major, BWV 1066/9. The Musical Offering, BWV 1079.

   (M) ** (*) HMV SLS 831 (5 discs). Bath Festival Chamber Orchestra, Yehudi Menuhin.

HMV have now improved the quality of these recordings, which date from the early days of stereo. The *Brandenburgs* are outstanding, thoughtful, well-prepared readings, full of humanity. The *Suites* too are musically satisfying, and now that the set is competitively priced it makes a fine investment as a basis for a Bach collection, even though the sound in places begins to show the age of the originals.

Brandenburg concertos Nos. 1–6, BWV 1046/51 (complete recording).

   *** HMV ASD 327/8. Bath Festival Chamber Orchestra, Yehudi Menuhin.

   ** (*) Decca SET 410/11. English Chamber Orchestra, Benjamin Britten.

   (B) ** (*) Turnabout TV 34044/5S.

Württemberg Chamber Orchestra, Joerg Faerber.

   ** (*) Philips 6700 045 (2 discs). Academy of St Martin-in-the-Fields, Neville Marriner.

   ** Decca 5BB 130/1. Stuttgart Chamber Orchestra, Karl Münchinger.

   (M) ** HMV SXLP 20110/11. New Philharmonia Orchestra, David Littaur.

   ** BASF BAC 3007/8. Collegium Aureum (using original instruments).

   ** HMV SLS 866 (2 discs). London Philharmonic Orchestra, Sir Adrian Boult.

   * (*) DGG Archive 2708 013 (2 discs). Munich Bach Orchestra, Karl Richter.

   (B) * (*) Saga 5031/2. Hamburg Chamber Orchestra, Harry Newstone.

   (B) *(*) Classics for Pleasure CFP 40010/11. Virtuosi of England, Arthur Davison.

   * Philips 6700 013 (2 discs). I Musici.

Of some two dozen sets of *Brandenburg concertos* currently available, the Menuhin set holds its place as a fairly easy first recommendation. Fresh pressings from EMI yield very pleasing sound, although the hint of overloading from the horns in the first concerto has not entirely been cured. The playing, like the recording, is warm-hearted, musically satisfying, and authentic in the best possible way. Tempi are skilfully chosen, and with a front-rank team of soloists Menuhin achieves a freshness and spontaneity which are consistently satisfying. This set, with the Faerber as an excellent bargain alternative, has rightly dominated the catalogue for more than a decade.

Britten made his recording in the Maltings Concert Hall not long before the serious fire. The engineers had not quite accustomed themselves to the reverberant acoustic, and to compensate they put the microphones rather close to the players. The result is big beefy sound that in its way goes well with Britten's interpretations, which are not quite what one would expect. The disappointing element is the lack of delicacy in the slow movements of Nos. 1, 2, 4 and 6. Britten makes no concession to expansiveness of phrasing, so that coupled with close-up sound there is not as much relaxation as one ideally wants. But the bubbling high spirits of the outer movements are hard to resist, and Philip Ledger, the harpsichordist, follows the pattern he set in live Britten performances with extra Britten-inspired elaborations, a continual delight. Whatever the questions of balance, the sound is extraordinarily vivid, and for a virile, committed set of the *Brandenburgs* this is hard to beat, although not everyone will like the rather romantic flourishes on violin and viola that link the two movements of No. 3.

The Faerber performances are well made, spontaneous and musically convincing. The wind playing is generally excellent, and the harpsichord soloist distinguishes himself in No. 5, although the continuo playing is less imaginative elsewhere. The overall effect is of a small group of musicians playing with skill and conviction, and the recording has worn its years lightly, with good stereo separation. An excellent bargain set.

Marriner, one had predicted, would before long record a set of *Brandenburgs* to outshine all others. In some ways this Philips set does bear out one's expectations, for the stylishness of the playing, the point of phrasing, the resilience of rhythm, coupled with superb recording, are very satisfying. But, sadly, Marriner uses an edition prepared by the late Thurston Dart (here contributing to some of the concertos in the very last days before he died) which aims at

re-creating the first version of these works long before Bach thought of sending them to the Margrave of Brandenburg. So No. 1, for example, has only three movements, there is a horn instead of a trumpet in No. 2, and maddeningly squeaky sopranino recorders in No. 4. Often the sounds are delightful, but this is not a definitive set of *Brandenburgs* such as Marriner will one day make.

It was Münchinger and his Stuttgart Chamber Players who in the early days of LP revolutionized our ideas of Bach playing. After that in successive new versions of the *Brandenburgs* they seemed to grow more stolid, less imaginative. In this latest version their vitality seems restored, though this still does not have the detailed imagination of some of the finest rival versions, such as Britten's or Menuhin's. The recording is outstandingly fine. The box is offered at a price rather less than that for two premium discs.

Excellent Philharmonia playing and generally lively and colourful direction distinguish the Littaur set, together with first-rate, modern EMI recording. Raymond Leppard, as might be expected, provides an imaginative continuo, and Leppard's solo contribution to No. 5 is also notable. Not all the other solo playing is quite on this level, but generally this is an enjoyable pair of records. However, taken as a whole the Turnabout set remains better value for money, even though the continuo playing is comparatively unimaginative.

Of the two sets available on 'original instruments' (the alternative is on Telefunken), that by the Collegium Aureum is to be preferred. The use of older instruments often brings special rewards (the recorder playing creates some enchanting sounds), and No. 3 is very lively, with clean inner lines. No. 5 is strikingly fresh and clear, although the bravura harpsichord contribution which dominates the texture has a tendency to sound metronomic. In No. 2 the balance does not unduly favour the trumpet, and the piquant sounds provided by the other wind instruments contribute much to one's enjoyment.

Sir Adrian Boult, when recording his lively set of *Brandenburgs*, consciously turned back to the style of Bach playing he knew at the turn of the century, 'to the smooth and solid expression given by a far larger orchestra than Bach could ever contemplate'. In fact by the standards of 1900 or even 1939 these are authentic performances, smoother at times than usual but not always using a big orchestra. The speeds are often on the fast side, but with superb recording there is a place for this individual set, which is clearly preferable to other 'big orchestra' versions by Karajan and Klemperer.

Richter draws superb playing from his orchestra, and the recording is outstandingly clear. His admirers will be delighted with this set, but rhythmically Richter in his Germanic way puts the music rather into a straitjacket – witness the first movement of No. 6, which needs more persuasive handling. Fortunately in slow movements Richter allows a greater degree of expressive relaxation.

Newstone's famous early Saga recording was made with a first-rate chamber music group in Hamburg. Tempi, style and solo playing are excellent here and the balance is good, but the recording has an acid edge to the strings which not all will be willing to accept, even though the records are very cheap. Current pressings seem to show a considerable improvement in the matter of surface noise, pimples and dimples.

Arthur Davison gives a brisk, unfussy reading which has much to commend it, but even in this cheaper price category, there are more refined, more persuasive versions. The recording, however, is first-rate.

I Musici have made some excellent, stylish records in their time, but this set of *Brandenburgs* finds them rather stolid, generally slow of tempo, unresilient of rhythm. It is a reliable enough set, well recorded, but there are many better versions at half the price.

Harpsichord concertos Nos. 1 in D minor; 2 in E major; 3 in D major; 4 in A major; 5 in F minor; 6 in F major; 7 in G minor; 8 in D minor, BWV 1052/9.

(M) ** CBS SBRG 77335 (3 discs). Igor Kipnis (harpsichord), London Strings, Neville Marriner; Colin Tilney (harpsichord continuo).

With the London Strings – the St Martin's Academy under a pseudonym – Igor Kipnis undertook an intensive series of sessions, recording not merely the well-known keyboard concertos but the fringe works too, the arrangements of the *Violin concertos in E* and *A minor* and of the *Fourth Brandenburg concerto*, plus an eighth work reconstructed by Kipnis himself from a fragment of nine bars identical with the Sinfonia of *Cantata No. 35*. Kipnis has therefore scored that movement for concertante forces and added two other movements from the same cantata. That is typical of his eager approach to Bach. These are enjoyable performances, if not (from the soloist) the most refined available. The recording, made in E M I's St John's Wood studio, is better balanced than many from this source.

Harpsichord concerto No. 1 in D minor, B W V 1052.

** Decca SXL 6174. Vladimir Ashkenazy (piano), London Symphony Orchestra, David Zinman – CHOPIN: *Piano concerto No. 2.***

* (*) CBS Quadraphonic MQ 32300. Anthony Newman (harpsichord), Instrumental Ensemble – HAYDN:

Harpsichord concerto in D major.* (*)

Those who fancy their Bach on a piano rather than the harpsichord will find that Ashkenazy makes no concessions to the earlier instrument. This is no piano imitation of a plucked string instrument, but the piano on its own terms with a wide variety of colour in the first movement and gentle half-tones in the *Adagio*. Without preconceptions this can be successful and is especially so in the finale, where there are some surprisingly pianistic figurations. But in the opening movement such tonal sophistry does soften the forward momentum, and at the end of the second movement one feels the line of the melody suffers. David Zinman's accompaniment is most stylish, attentive to the soloist's needs and buoyantly rhythmic in the allegros, yet with nice light textures and no hint of heaviness. In its own way this is certainly enjoyable music-making and obviously sincerely felt. Excellent sound.

One has to take great care with the balance and volume settings of the CBS quadraphonic disc or the harpsichord jangles and the sound becomes oppressive. The dry, clear acoustic projects the performances well, although one is too conscious of the close microphones for the sound to be quite natural. The performance has plenty of cut and thrust in the outer movements, and the thoughtful account of the *Adagio* is impressive.

Harpsichord concertos Nos. 1 in D minor, BWV 1052; 2 in E major, BWV 1053.
   ** (*) HMV ASD 3007. George Malcolm (harpsichord), Menuhin Festival Orchestra, Yehudi Menuhin.

George Malcolm has recorded this coupling before for Decca with Münchinger and the Stuttgart Orchestra. On the whole, quite apart from the fuller recording quality, this version is pre-ferable for the more imaginative accompaniment from Menuhin. Malcolm is as brilliant as ever in his execution (registration sometimes controversial), at times to the point where his speeds run the risk of sounding rushed.

Harpsichord concertos Nos. 3 in D major, BWV 1054; 4 in A major, BWV 1055; 6 in F major, BWV 1057.
   *** HMV ASD 2713. George Malcolm (harpsichord), Menuhin Festival Orchestra, Yehudi Menuhin.

This *D major Concerto* is Bach's own arrangement of the great *E major Violin concerto*, with new touches of originality added in the transcription. *No. 6* is an even more striking transcription of a well-known work, the *Brandenburg concerto No. 4*, with the recorder parts superbly played here by David Munrow and John Turner. With fine recording quality and splendid balance, inspired performances from George Malcolm and sparkling accompaniment from Menuhin and the orchestra, this makes an outstanding recommendation.

Harpsichord concertos Nos. 5 in F minor, BWV 1056; 7 in G minor, BWV 1058; (i) Double harpsichord concertos Nos. 1 in C minor, BWV 1060; 2 in C major, BWV 1061.
   *** HMV ASD 2647. George Malcolm (harpsichord), Menuhin Festival Orchestra, Yehudi Menuhin, (i) with Simon Preston (harpsichord).

With two solo and two double concertos on a single disc this provides a generous and attractive sample of an inspired collaboration. George Malcolm's individuality is splendidly matched by Menuhin's warm and energetic conducting style. In the two *Double concertos* Simon Preston makes a brilliant partner, and the virtuosity in such movements as the finale of the *C major Concerto* is breathtaking. The degree of expressiveness in slow movements is entirely acceptable, unless you like your Bach very strait-laced. The *G minor Concerto* is Bach's own keyboard arrangement of the popular *A minor Violin concerto.* Warm, well-balanced recording.

Double clavier concerto in C major, BWV 1061.

(M) ** HMV SXLP 30175. Clara Haskil and Géza Anda (pianos), Philharmonia Orchestra, Alceo Galliera – MOZART: *Double concerto.***

One has to adjust to the sound of a modern piano in Bach, and even more so when there are two; but better clean, intelligent playing like this than the reverberant jangle we are offered on some harpsichord records. The whole performance is fresh and stylish, and the unexaggerated stereo makes the music's antiphonal effects within a slightly reverberant acoustic.

Quadruple harpsichord concerto in A minor (for 4 harpsichords and strings), *BWV 1065; Triple harpsichord concerto No. 1 in D minor* (for 3 harpsichords and strings), *BWV 1063; Triple harpsichord concerto No. 2 in C major* (for 3 harpsichords and strings), *BWV 1064.*

(B) *** Turnabout TV 34106S. Martin Galling, Hedwig Bilgram, Franz Lehrndorfer, Kurt-Heinz Stolze (harpsichords), Mainz Chamber Orchestra, Günter Kehr.

Recorded collections of music for several harpsichords are notorious for producing a jangling of plucked strings in profusion, but the present disc is engineered with skill, and the resonance of the stereo provides a most satisfactory sound. The performances are splendid, with Günter Kehr's masterly overall control of the music-making matched by fine solo playing. All three performances are truly excellent, and the *Quadruple concerto* is something of a *tour de force.*

Quadruple harpsichord concerto in A minor (for 4 harpsichords and strings), *BWV 1065; Triple harpsichord concerto No. 1 in D minor* (for 3 harpsichords and strings), *BWV 1063.*

(M) ** (*) Decca Ace of Diamonds SDD 451. George Malcolm, Valda Aveling, Geoffrey Parsons, Simon Preston (harpsichords), English Chamber Orchestra, Raymond Leppard – C. P. E. BACH: *Concerto* ** (*); MALCOLM: *Variations.***

As with the C. P. E. Bach concerto, the problems of clarity and balance are not entirely solved here, the harpsichords rather lacking substance. However, the recording is otherwise much better balanced than in the C. P. E. Bach work. The performances are excellent, displaying much more subtlety than one expects in a record of this nature.

Violin concertos Nos. 1 in A minor, BWV 1041; 2 in E major, BWV 1042; Double violin concerto in D minor, BWV 1043.

*** HMV ASD 346. Yehudi Menuhin, Christian Ferras (violins), Bath Festival Chamber Orchestra, Menuhin.

*** DGG Archive 2533 075. Eduard Melkus, Spiros Rantos (violins), Vienna Capella Academica.

** (*) DGG 138820. David and Igor Oistrakh (violins), Vienna Symphony and Royal Philharmonic Orchestras, Eugene Goossens.

(M) ** Philips Universo 6580 021. Felix Ayo, Roberto Michelucci (violins), I Musici.

* (*) DGG 2530 242. Zino Francescatti, Régis Pasquier (violins), Lucerne Festival Strings, Rudolf Baumgartner.

Double violin concerto in D minor, BWV 1043.

(M) ** (*) DGG Privilege 2726 008 (2 discs). David and Igor Oistrakh (violins), Royal Philharmonic Orchestra, Eugene Goossens – BEETHOVEN: *Triple concerto*; BRAHMS and VIVALDI: *Double concertos.*** (*)

(i) *Double violin concerto in D minor, BWV 1043*; (ii) *Double concerto in D minor, BWV 1060* (for violin, oboe, strings and continuo).

(M) ** (*) DGG Privilege 135082. (i) David and Igor Oistrakh (violins), Royal Philharmonic Orchestra, Eugene Goossens; (ii) E. Shann (oboe), O. Buchner (violin), Munich Bach Orchestra, Karl Richter – VIVALDI: *Double concertos.****

Menuhin's HMV disc (he directs the orchestra besides appearing as principal soloist in all three concertos) has long held a distinguished place in the catalogue. Recently HMV have freshened the recording, losing something in bass resonance but providing a sound picture which belies the record's age. The performances have warmth as well as spontaneity, and Menuhin was in good technical form when the disc was made. Ferras matches his playing to Menuhin's perfectly in the *Double concerto*, and the music-making cannot be faulted on minor points of style.

Melkus has the advantage of a first-rate modern DGG recording. He is not a soloist with a 'big' personality like Menuhin or Oistrakh, but he is a musician of uncommon sensibility, and the way the recording balance allows him to form part of the overall ensemble, rather than enjoy a spotlight, gives special character to the music-making. Although the production is concerned with authenticity, this is not achieved at the expense of spontaneity, as the lithe opening ritornello of the *Double concerto* immediately shows. Throughout one has the impression of a happy balance between scholarship and musical freshness. This is much preferable to a similar 'authentic' re-creation on Telefunken which suffers from under-characterization of the music itself.

The styles of David and Igor Oistrakh are different enough to provide a suitable contrast of timbre in their performance of the *Double concerto*; at the same time the musical partnership provided by father and son is an understanding one. The performance is available coupled to sympathetic versions of the solo concertos on an early full-priced issue. But with its somewhat dated sound this issue, for all its merits, seems less desirable than the Menuhin collection. However, the *Double concerto* is also available within a recommendable two-disc Privilege album of double and triple concertos, and on a single Privilege disc coupled to Vivaldi and the *Concerto for violin and oboe, BWV 1060*. The star here is the oboist, Edgar Shann. The violin soloist, Otto Buchner, supports him capably if with rather less distinction. The sound in both works is dated, but fully acceptable, when the somewhat fizzy treble is smoothed.

Francescatti's view of Bach is on the heavy side. In the *A minor Concerto* this works quite well, but the great *Largo* of the *Double concerto* – surely the movement on which any recommendation should rest – is a little stolid. This is much more successful on the Universo disc. Here Felix Ayo plays the *E major Concerto* with rather more flair than his colleague Roberto Michelucci shows in the

23

A minor; but the two players join for a spirited account of the *Double concerto*. The clear, unaffected approach to all three works gives pleasure, and the only snag is the dull, reverberant acoustic, which rarely allows the harpsichord continuo to come through with any bite. But the sound itself is pleasing, and at medium price this is good value.

(i; iii) *Violin concerto No. 2 in E major, BWV 1042;* (ii; iii) *Violin concerto in G minor, BWV 1056* (arr. of *Harpsichord concerto in F minor);* (i; ii; iii) *Double violin concerto in D minor, BWV 1043.*
> ** (*) HMV ASD 2783. (i) Itzhak Perlman (violin); (ii) Pinchas Zukerman (violin); (iii) English Chamber Orchestra, Daniel Barenboim.

Perlman and Zukerman with their friend and colleague are inspired to give a magic performance of the great *Double concerto*, one in which their artistry is beautifully matched in all its intensity. The slow movement in particular has rarely sounded so ravishing on record. Perlman is also most impressive in the slow movement of the *E major* solo *Violin concerto*, but neither he nor Zukerman in the *G minor Concerto* (arranged from the *F minor Harpsichord concerto* with its sublime *Arioso* slow movement) is quite so impressive without the challenge of the other. Nonetheless, with fine accompaniment from the ECO, this is a Bach record to cherish.

(i; ii; iv) *Double violin concerto in D minor, BWV 1043;* (i; iii; iv) *Double concerto in D minor for oboe, violin and strings* (reconstructed by Franz Giegling), *BWV 1060.*
> ** (*) Philips 6500 119. (i) Arthur Grumiaux (violin); (ii) Koji Toyoda (violin); (iii) Heinz Holliger

(oboe); (iv) New Philharmonia Orchestra, Edo de Waart —
VIVALDI: *Concerto, Op. 3/6.* ** (*)

In the *Double violin concerto* Grumiaux is very much the senior partner, but the purity of tone of his Japanese colleague still makes it a very satisfying reading, with a warm, expressive account of the slow movement. Just how Grumiaux responds to the challenge of working with another great artist comes over very clearly in the concerto with oboe reconstructed from the *Double harpsichord concerto in C minor*. There the interplay of phrasing is enchanting: this is far superior to the Privilege version listed above.

(i; iii) *Triple concerto for flute, violin and harpsichord in A minor, BWV 1044;* (ii; iii) *Triple violin concerto in D major* (arr. of *Triple keyboard concerto in C major, BWV 1064).*
> (M) ** (*) Philips Universo 6580 058. (i) Heinz Hörtzsch (flute), Gerhard Bosse (violin), Hannes Kästner (harpsichord); (ii) Gerhard Bosse, Günter Glass, Einhardt Nietner (violins); (iii) Leipzig Gewandhaus Orchestra, Bosse.

Both these concertos are arrangements. The first is by Bach himself, from the organ *Prelude and fugue in A minor* and the *Trio sonata in D minor*, and the performance here shows just how felicitous is Bach's rethinking. The slow movement is delightful, with lovely flute playing from Heinz Hörtzsch, while the first movement with its delicate textures sometimes reminds one of Mozart's *Flute and harp concerto*. The playing is alive, sensitive, and rhythmically flexible, without being in any way unstylish. The *Triple violin concerto* arrangement has the character of a concerto grosso, and the recording balance reflects this. It is not nearly so strong a work as its companion, but it makes agreeable listening in this accomplished but not outstanding performance, and the disc is worth exploring for *BWV 1044*.

Triple concerto in A minor for flute, violin and harpsichord, BWV 1044; Harpsichord concerto No. 4 in A major, BWV 1055; Sonata da chiesa in C major, BWV 1037 (first three movements only).

    (B) ** Oiseau-Lyre OLS 171. Richard Adeney (flute), Granville Jones (violin), Thurston Dart (harpsichord), Philomusica of London, Dart.

Though the sound shows its age a little, particularly in the upper strings, this is an attractive bargain record of stylish performances. The rarity is the orchestral version (devised by Thurston Dart) of the *Sonata da chiesa*. The last movement is omitted, because 'it seems so much more suitable for soloists'.

(i) *Triple concerto in A minor for flute, violin and harpsichord, BWV 1044;* (ii) *Suite No. 2 in B minor for flute and strings, BWV 1067.*

    (B) * (*) Turnabout TV 34219S. (i) Hans Möhring (flute), Susanne Lautenbacher (violin), Martin Galling (harpsichord), Stuttgart Soloists; (ii) Klaus Pohlers (flute), Mainz Chamber Orchestra, Günter Kehr.

The *Triple concerto* – not an easy work to bring off on record – is freshly played and recorded, the finale especially vivacious, the central movement musical rather than imaginative. The flautist in the famous *B minor Suite* is a nimble player, but some of his tempi are curious: the *Badinerie* is surely too fast. But these performances make a more than acceptable coupling and the recording is good.

The Musical Offering, BWV 1079.

    (M) ** Decca Ace of Diamonds SDD 310. Stuttgart Chamber Orchestra, Karl Münchinger.

    (B) ** Turnabout TV 34451S. Munich Instrumental Ensemble.

    ** Telefunken SAWT 9565. Vienna Concentus Musicus, Nikolaus Harnoncourt.

    ** DGG Archive 198320. Instrumental Ensemble, Karl Richter.

Although there are a number of good versions of Bach's masterly treatise, there is no really outstanding one. Karl Richter's Teutonic rendering on the Archive label, though it has good recording to commend it, is not an inspiring musical experience. Karl Münchinger's version has been in the catalogue for more than fifteen years now, though it wears its age lightly. One does not imagine that many will take exception to the instrumentation Münchinger chooses, and the sound is admirably clean. Denis Stevens spoke of it originally as 'a clean, scholarly performance' and readers are unlikely to quarrel with that verdict. At the same time, the upper strings sound a bit wiry now, and the performance itself is somewhat lacking in warmth. However, it has a competitive price tag and is probably better all-round value than either of the full-price versions by Richter and Harnoncourt.

Harnoncourt's version is a little wanting in vitality, though it is well recorded. In some ways the plain but musical account offered on Turnabout is a better proposition. It is serviceable as a recording, has the merit of being very cheap, and is musically very sound. At the bargain end of the spectrum, it offers a worthwhile alternative.

Orchestral suites Nos. 1 in C major; 2 in B minor (for flute and strings); *3 in D major; 4 in D major, BWV 1066/9.*

    ⊛ *** Argo ZRG 687/8. Academy

of St Martin-in-the-Fields, Neville Marriner.

*** Philips 6500 067 (Suites 1 and 4); 6500 068 (2 and 3). English Chamber Orchestra, Raymond Leppard.

** (*) BASF BAC 3009/10. Collegium Aureum (using original instruments).

** Telefunken SAWT 9509/10. Vienna Concentus Musicus, Nikolaus Harnoncourt.

(M) * (*) Decca Ace of Diamonds SDD 386/7. Stuttgart Chamber Orchestra, Karl Münchinger.

Enormous care went into the preparation of the Argo performances, with Thurston Dart's imaginative, scholarly mind searching always for a compromise between the truth of the original score and what is sensible in terms of modern re-creative performance. Hence not only the ornamentation comes into the picture but even the lightening of the scoring itself to favour the baroque practice of altering the colouring on repeats. This is especially noticeable in *Suites 3* and *4* in the use of the trumpets (which Thurston Dart tells us in his excellent notes did not appear in Bach's original). The set is a splendid memorial to Dart himself, and because the music-making is so exuberant and alive, it is the most joyous memorial; no one could ask for better. Indeed the playing throughout is quite marvellous, expressive without being romantic, buoyant and vigorous and yet retaining the music's strength and weight. William Bennett is the agile and sensitive flute soloist in the *Second suite*, even providing decoration in the famous *Badinerie*, with splendid bravura. Throughout the performances the baroque spirit is realized at its most colourful, and with tip-top Argo sound this is a fine set indeed.

Leppard's performances are both elegant and musical. Rhythms are alert, phrasing well shaped, and the playing has a welcome and refreshing enthusiasm. Moreover, it is given the benefit of excellent recording which has plenty of detail and yet preserves an overall perspective that is truthful and homogeneous. Although Marriner's set with the Academy of St Martin-in-the-Fields and the late Thurston Dart at the harpsichord is probably more highly characterized and is slightly more vividly recorded, the Leppard set has splendid style.

Two alternative re-creations of the 'original sound' are available, by the Collegium Aureum on BASF and by Harnoncourt and his Vienna Concentus Musicus. To say that stylistically and sonically they are very different is to emphasize how difficult it is to be definitive in instrumental authenticity. The BASF recording is spacious and reverberant, and the relatively small orchestral group is given an attractive richness and breadth. The resonant acoustic is not always caught with absolute clarity, but the sound is mostly very beautiful, especially in the *First* and *Second suites*. The Collegium Aureum's approach to the music itself is comparatively expressive – the famous *Air* in *Suite 3* is restrained but not played without feeling. Tempi are often similar to modern practice, although the slow introductions are not as crisply dotted and the pulse is less measured. The original woodwind instruments make some delightful baroque sounds, especially in *Suites 1* and *4*. With the early trumpets, however, one has to accept moments of poor intonation in the upper register. But despite any possible reservations this is a very enjoyable set.

Harnoncourt's approach is clean and literal, and the acoustic is brighter and harder than that given to the Collegium Aureum. The result is not always sweet on the ear, and the prevailing *mezzo forte* of the performances becomes monotonous. But these are livelier, more compelling performances than those of the *Brandenburgs* on the same label. Slow introductions are taken fast in allemande-style, minuets are taken slowly, and – hardest point to accept – there is no concession to expressiveness in the famous *Air* from *Suite 3*. The *Sarabande* of No. 2 may sound a little disconcerting, with its use of *notes inégales*, but the *Gigue* of No. 3 and for that matter all the fast movements and the fugues are splendidly alive. With good Telefunken recording this is preferable to the DGG Archive set from Richter, whose heavy-handed approach lacks spontaneity. Moreover Richter fails to observe the 'double-dotting' convention in the overtures, and this is surprising in a series dedicated to authenticity.

Unfortunately Münchinger's set, albeit competitive in price, cannot be enthusiastically recommended either. It has a heavy tread and is insensitively phrased, although the playing is alert and well disciplined. The Decca recording is bright, but all in all the set offers little musical pleasure.

Orchestral suites Nos. 2 in B minor, BWV 1067; 3 in D major, BWV 1068. Cantata No. 12: Sinfonia: 'Weinen, Klagen'. Cantata No. 131: Sonata: 'Der Himmel lacht'.
  (B) ** Decca Eclipse ECS 754. Suisse Romande Orchestra, Ernest Ansermet.

Orchestral suites Nos. 2 in B minor, BWV 1067; 3 in D major, BWV 1068.
  (B) * (*) Saga 5341. Netherlands Bach Orchestra, Jaap van Rhijn.

Ansermet's approach to Bach is surprisingly warm-hearted. Some might feel it a little too romantic, but it is easy to enjoy, particularly as the recorded sound is so beautiful. The acoustic is lively, but the focus is clean without being too clinical. The performances are fresh but with a full body of strings tending to swamp the harpsichord; however, the *Air* in No. 3 is played most expressively, and

only the out-and-out purist would cavil, especially with such elegant playing from the solo flautist in the *B minor Suite*. The bonuses are not memorable; Roger Reversy, the oboe soloist in the *Sinfonia* from *Cantata 12*, is accomplished but phrases rather stiffly. The acoustic of the encores is not as smooth as that managed for the *Suites*.

The Saga record makes a fair bargain at the modest price asked. The recording is somewhat thin and unsubstantial but can be made to sound reasonably well. The playing is quite stylish, with a good, unnamed flautist in the *Second suite*. There is also available a performance of the *Second suite* only, nimbly played by Claude Monteux on Decca Ace of Diamonds SDD 427, coupled to Gluck's *Dance of the blessed spirits* and Mozart's *Second Flute concerto*. The recording is perhaps a trifle over-rich in texture but is easy to enjoy.

CHAMBER AND INSTRUMENTAL MUSIC

(Guitar) Prelude in C minor, BWV 999; Violin partita No. 1 in B minor, BWV 1002: Sarabande and Double; Violin partita No. 2 in D minor, BWV 1004: Chaconne in D minor.
  *** DGG 2530 096. Narciso Yepes (guitar) – WEISS: *Fantasia; Suite.****

This playing has great clarity and tonal beauty to commend it, and is further evidence of Yepes's mastery. The *Suite* by Weiss is an inventive piece and further enhances the value of the disc. The recording is life-like and vivid.

Transcriptions for guitar: Violin partita No. 3 in E major, BWV 1006: Gavotte. Violoncello suite No. 5 in C minor, BWV 1011: Gavottes 1 and 2; Suite No. 6 in D major, BWV 1012:

Gavottes 1 and 2. (Clavier) *Prelude and Allegro. Well-tempered Clavier: Preludes 1, 6 and 9. Cantata 140: Chorale: Sleepers awake. Cantata 147: Chorale: Jesu, joy of man's desiring. Cantata 208: Chorale: Sheep may safely graze.*

(M) ** HMV HQS 1316. Christopher Parkening (guitar).

A most pleasant record, with bravura always subservient to musicianship. One wonders why the famous chorales should be transcribed at all (we are told the task was far from a simple one), but if *Jesu, joy of man's desiring* is not entirely successful, *Sleepers awake* (which closes the recital) is a *tour de force.* It sounds uncannily as though two guitars are being used, so cleverly is the chorale theme separated from its accompanying figuration. The result is most effective musically. The rest of the programme is of a popular nature, including many familiar tunes (not least the *First prelude* from the *Well-tempered Clavier*, which is the Bach original of the Bach/Gounod *Ave Maria*). Parkening's style sometimes seems slightly self-effacing, but this disc deserves to be a popular success.

Arrangements for harp: *French suite No. 3 in B minor, BWV 814; Partie in A major, BWV 832* (both for keyboard); *Partita No. 2 in D minor, BWV 1004* (originally for unaccompanied violin).

** DGG 2530 333. Nicanor Zabaleta (harp).

Whether you will enjoy this collection of harp arrangements will depend more on your regard for Zabaleta than for Bach. He is a fine artist who does his best not to offend good taste, and his harp-playing is ravishing, but – on record at least – why not have the original?

Complete works for lute: *Fugue in G minor, BWV 1000; Prelude in C minor, BWV 999; Prelude, fugue and allegro in E flat major, BWV 998; Suites: in G minor, BWV 995; in E minor, BWV 996; in C minor, BWV 997; in E major, BWV 1006.*

* DGG Archive 2708 030 (2 discs). Narciso Yepes (lute).

Although very clearly recorded in the best Archive manner (the sound is considerably superior to the Oryx record mentioned below), the performances are not convincing. Narciso Yepes is best-known as a guitarist of the romantic repertoire, and in the lute music of Bach he seems oddly ill at ease. The style is deliberate and the forward flow is interrupted by curious momentary pauses. This very free rhythmic manner in the end becomes irritating, although the fast movements go well. Given the attractive sound of the period instrument used, this could have been a fine set, but the playing as a whole is too mannered to be recommended with any enthusiasm.

(Lute) *Fugue in G minor, BWV 1000* (from *Violin sonata in G minor*); *Prelude in C minor, BWV 999; Suite in E minor, BWV 996: Allemande; Bourrée* (only); *Suite in E major, BWV 1006: Loure; Gavotte; Minuets 1 and 2; Gigue* (only); *Suite in A major, BWV 1007* (complete).

(B) ** (*) Oryx BACH 1202. Walter Gerwig (lute).

An excellent anthology, beautifully played. Walter Gerwig is recorded rather near the microphone, and the recorded focus is not clear-cut, but he manages, in spite of this, to provide light and shade. The recorded quality itself is pleasing. An enjoyable disc that is inexpensive too.

(i) *Lute suite No. 3 in G minor, BWV 995;* (ii) *Suite No. 6 in D major for viola pomposa, BWV 1012.*

(B) * (*) Turnabout TV 34430S. (i) Konrad Ragossnig (lute); (ii) Ulrich Koch (viola pomposa).

Both these works originate in the solo cello suites; the lute version of the *Cello suite No. 4* was by Bach himself. Konrad Ragossnig's performance is adequate, but rather lacking in character. The viola pomposa is an extra-large viola with five strings. It is played like a violin, although obviously a little awkward to hold. Its invention is attributed to Bach himself, but whether this suite was written for it is another matter. However, the history of the instrument adds some interest to this performance, which is quite a strong one, although the rather lugubrious tone quality sometimes gets in the way of the music.

Violin sonatas Nos. 1 in B minor; 2 in A major; 3 in E major; 4 in C minor; 5 in F minor; 6 in G major, BWV 1014/19.
  (M) ** DGG Privilege 2726 002 (2 discs). David Oistrakh (violin), Hans Pischner (harpsichord).
  * (*) Philips 6700 017 (2 discs). Henryk Szeryng (violin), Helmut Walcha (harpsichord).

The six Bach sonatas for violin and harpsichord are much less well known than the works for unaccompanied violin or cello, and their relative obscurity is quite undeserved. They contain music of great character and beauty: who can forget the beautiful *Siciliana* which opens *No. 4* or the more solemn dignity of the first movement of the *B minor Sonata*? The polyphony of the allegros is engagingly fresh and the continuo offers plenty of opportunities to the imaginative player. Oistrakh plays with his incomparable mastery, but his style is at variance with the music. His approach is that of the nineteenth-century concert hall, and his accompanist, Hans Pischner, is very much relegated to the background. Even so, at medium price, this seems the

set likely to give the most musical pleasure from those currently available. Szeryng's account calls for only a cautious recommendation. The balance between the parts is well preserved and the texture has admirable clarity. Walcha is too metronomically rigid and efficient for all tastes and the two artists do not always see eye to eye where the matching of phrases is concerned. We badly need a really first-class account of these fine sonatas, for neither this nor the Richter–Schneiderhan account on Archive is really ideal.

(Unaccompanied) *Violin sonatas Nos. 1 in G minor, BWV 1001; 2 in A minor, BWV 1003; 3 in C major, BWV 1005; Violin partitas Nos. 1 in B minor, BWV 1002; 2 in D minor, BWV 1004; 3 in E major, BWV 1006.*
  *** Philips SAL 3472 (Sonata 1; Partita 1); SAL 3473 (Sonata 2; Partita 2); SAL 3474 (Sonata 3; Partita 3). Arthur Grumiaux (violin).
  ** (*) DGG 2709 028 (3 discs). Henryk Szeryng (violin).
  (M) ** HMV SLS 818 (3 discs). Josef Suk (violin).

Arthur Grumiaux's fine performances were issued in mono over a decade ago but have not appeared in stereo until relatively recently. The recording, though less brilliant than Szeryng's on DGG, is still extremely fine and the performances are musically most satisfying. Grumiaux strikes just the right balance between expressive feeling and stylistic rectitude, and his readings of all six works are the product of superlative technique and a refined musical instinct.

Suk is, of course, a superb artist, but he approaches this music in much the same way as he would the virtuoso repertoire. There is a tendency to over-inflate that seems out of key. Though well recorded, these are not the searching performances one expects in this repertoire; Szeryng or, better still, Grumiaux remain the finest of the post-Heifetz versions.

(Unaccompanied) *Violoncello suites Nos. 1 in G major; 2 in D minor; 3 in C major; 4 in E flat major; 5 in C minor; 6 in D major, B W V 1007/12.*

> *** DGG Archive sᴀᴘᴍ 198186/7/8 (available separately). Pierre Fournier (cello).
> (ᴍ) *** HMV sʟs 798 (3 discs). Paul Tortelier (cello).

Fournier's richly phrased and warm-toned performances carry an impressive musical conviction. This is not refined, introvert playing – the cellist dwelling within himself – but a bold, vigorous reading obviously designed to convince a listener that this is music to be listened to and enjoyed. The recording, in a resonant, but not overblown ambience, is very satisfying. The records are available separately, but as such are more expensive than the Tortelier set.

Tortelier's rhythmic grip is strong, his technique masterly and his intonation true. Yet at the same time there are touches of reticence – one is tempted almost to say inhibition: it is as if he is consciously resisting the temptation to give full rein to his musical and lyrical instinct. Comparing his *Sarabande* from the *D minor Suite* (No. 2) with Casals leaves no doubts as to the greater freedom, range and inwardness of the latter. Tortelier sounds dull by comparison. Nonetheless the faster movements are splendidly played and the prelude to the *E flat major Suite* finds him at his most imposing. The set is good value and the recording, though made in the first half of the 1960s, is extremely fine.

Keyboard Music

Concertos (after Vivaldi): *Nos. 1 in D major, B W V 972; 2 in G major, B W V*

973; 4 in G minor, B W V 975; 5 in C major, B W V 976; 7 in F major, B W V 978; 9 in G major, B W V 980.

> (ᴍ) ** (*) Philips Universo 6580 017. Egida Giordani Sartori (harpsichord).

Vital, characterful readings that are probably the finest now available, even though the recording can be faulted (it is too closely balanced, as is Sebastyen on Turnabout), and the instrument itself could have been better chosen. But these are sensitive, intelligent performances and can be recommended.

French suites Nos. 1 in D minor; 2 in C minor; 3 in B minor; 4 in E flat major; 5 in G major; 6 in E major, B W V 812/17.

> (ᴍ) * (*) Oiseau-Lyre sᴏʟ 60039. Thurston Dart (clavichord).

French suites Nos. 1–4, B W V 812/15.

> * DGG Archive 2533 138. Huguette Dreyfus (harpsichord).

French suites Nos. 5 and 6, B W V 816/17; Capriccio in B flat major, B W V 992.

> (*) DGG Archive 2533 139. Huguette Dreyfus (harpsichord).

By cutting all the repeats Thurston Dart managed to get all six suites on to a single medium-priced LP. The choice of the clavichord for works of this scale is questionable, as its tiny voice has a restricted range of timbre as well as dynamic. The engineering too is not entirely successful in catching this very intimate sound. But Dart's playing is impeccable in style and has plenty of personality.

The manner of Huguette Dreyfus is by contrast painstaking and pedantic. At no point does it come to life, and in spite of vivid and lively recording it is not possible to recommend this set.

Goldberg variations, BWV 988.

(B) ** (*) Turnabout TV 34015S. Martin Galling (harpsichord).

(M) ** (*) Oiseau-Lyre SOL 261/2. George Malcolm (harpsichord).

** (*) Telefunken SAWT 9474. Gustav Leonhardt (harpsichord).

** (*) DGG SLPM 139455. Wilhelm Kempff (piano).

** DGG 2707 057 (2 discs). Karl Richter (harpsichord).

Martin Galling's account has integrity and power, and he is very well recorded, in a pleasingly warm but not too reverberant acoustic. With such obvious musicianship and taste and an inexpensive label this record seems to hold its place at the top of the list, even if the performance is not as individual as Malcolm's or Kempff's or as strong as Richter's.

Malcolm relaxes his tempi and takes the opportunity to make the very most of the colouristic possibilities of the modern Goff harpsichord, conveying his own pleasure in the music yet always retaining a sense of inner tension. The recording is vivid, sometimes a little close, but the result is exciting, the effect being of a modern virtuoso, well versed in matters of style, taking a fresh look at Bach's masterpiece and communicating very directly with the listener. At Oiseau-Lyre medium price this is well worth trying, although with repeats included it stretches to two discs.

Leonhardt offers a careful academic approach. He is beautifully recorded (this is perhaps the best-recorded of all), but the playing, although scholarly, has not quite the life of Galling or Malcolm.

Eyebrows will be raised by Kempff's DGG recording. Kempff ignores ornaments altogether in outlining the theme, and the instances of anachronisms of style are too numerous to list. Yet for all that the sheer musicianship exhibited by this great artist fascinates, and even where he seems quite wilfully nineteenth-century

in his approach, there is a musical impulse and conviction behind it. Readers should certainly hear this for themselves, and libraries should acquire it.

Richter's is a massive performance, maybe too massive, but his use of sixteen-foot tone is varied with a wide range of registrations, even if it is not so charming as George Malcolm's. This represents the modern German tradition at its most confident, the result recorded with fine clarity and balance.

Partitas Nos. 1 in B flat major; 2 in C minor; 3 in A minor; 4 in D major; 5 in G major; 6 in E minor, BWV 825/30.

(M) *** Telefunken KT 11012 (2 discs). Karl Richter (harpsichord).

(B) ** Oryx BACH 1200 (Partitas 1, 2 and 4); BACH 1201 (Partitas 3, 5 and 6). Derek Adlam (harpsichord).

(M) (*) CBS 77289 (2 discs). Glenn Gould (piano).

Admirers of Richter will find this set rewarding, and even those whose feelings for this artist are less warm can be assured that on grounds of both performance and recording these discs can be recommended. Richter is rarely dull here (he can so often be unimaginative and heavy-handed), and although none of these performances will command universal allegiance, they are the product of evident feeling and thought.

Derek Adlam's playing is fresh and intelligent and the music is well characterized. The instrument used is a British one, made by the Sevenoaks firm of Feldberg. It is strong in timbre, but as recorded is never oppressive. A highly spontaneous pair of discs.

Glenn Gould is as intelligent as he is eccentric. No records of his can be idly dismissed even if he is (at times infuriatingly) wilful. His phrasing and articulation compel admiration however much the results border on the perverse. Certainly the recording is lacking in timbre but its shallowness cannot be wholly blamed on the CBS engineers: Mr Gould admires this kind of sound. Many things here prompt one to think again about this music, but the performances are really too individual to encourage a recommendation, and the piano does not resemble any instrument that one is likely to encounter in real life.

The Well-tempered Clavier (48 Preludes and fugues), Book 1: Preludes and fugues Nos. 1–24, BWV 846/69.

> (M) * (*) CBS 77225 (2 discs). Glenn Gould (piano).

Glenn Gould is highly eccentric but undoubtedly a master pianist. There is ample evidence of his finger dexterity and control of touch on these two discs. Unfortunately the unappealing tone quality of the recording diminishes the value of this issue, and it must be recognized that Mr Gould's interpretations will not command undivided admiration.

Keyboard Collections

Capriccio in B flat major (On the departure of a beloved brother), BWV 992; Chromatic fantasia and fugue in D minor, BWV 903; Fantasia in C minor, BWV 906; 15 Two-part inventions, BWV 772/85; Italian concerto in F major, BWV 971; Partita No. 2 in C minor, BWV 826; Well-tempered Clavier: Prelude in C major BWV 846.

> (M) ** DGG Privilege 2726 016 (2 discs). Ralph Kirkpatrick (harpsichord or clavichord).

An uneven anthology. The *C minor Partita* has all the qualities of scholarship and discipline without stooping to pedantry. Sometimes the unrelenting rhythmic onflow and firmness of grip can strike one as too much of a good thing, as in the *Italian concerto.* The *Capriccio* is most

expressively played and with just the right amount of rhythmic licence. The *Two-part inventions* are played on the clavichord, though this is not stated on the label, and they are recorded at too high a level and are far too closely balanced to do justice to this most intimate of instruments. Nor is the playing particularly inspired here.

Capriccio in B flat major, BWV 992; Chromatic fantasia and fugue in D minor, BWV 903; Fantasia and fugue in A minor, BWV 904; Suite in E minor (for lute), BWV 996.

> ** Telefunken SAWT 9571. Gustav Leonhardt (harpsichord).

This recital is played on a modern harpsichord but one which is a reproduction of an mid-eighteenth-century instrument. The sounds here then are authentic and attractive, although slightly blown up by the recording style used. There is not the kind of contrast of colour and dynamic which George Malcolm finds in his exciting version of the *Chromatic fantasia and fugue.* But unquestionably Leonhardt's playing reflects what would have been possible in Bach's time, and with judicious ornamentation of repeated sections this playing has musical interest as well as scholarship. In the *Capriccio in B flat major (On the departure of a beloved brother)* the soloist announces the descriptive title of each section, and the playing has special colour.

Chromatic fantasia and fugue in D minor, BWV 903; English suite No. 5 in E minor, BWV 810; Fantasia in C minor, BWV 906; Two-part invention No. 1 in C major, BWV 772; Three-part invention No. 13 in A minor, BWV 799; Italian concerto in F major, BWV 971.

> (M) ** HMV SXLP 30141. George Malcolm (harpsichord).

By rights this disc should be a winner, but somehow the George Malcolm magic does not quite come over. Nonetheless on a mid-price label with an attractive selection of Bach's most accessible keyboard music, it can be confidently recommended.

Chromatic fantasia and fugue in D minor, BWV 903; Fantasia in C minor, BWV 906; French suite No. 6 in E major, BWV 817; Italian concerto in F major, BWV 971.

> (B) ** Classics for Pleasure CFP 40049. Leslie Pearson (harpsichord).

Leslie Pearson's disc is very well engineered; there are few more convincing records of a modern harpsichord. The playing itself is sometimes vivid but often too circumspect. The slow movement of the *Italian concerto* lacks spontaneity. But this prosaic quality is much less evident in the *French suite*, where some of the movements have real vivacity. The recital remains good value at the price asked.

Chromatic fantasia and fugue in D minor, BWV 903; French suite No. 5 in G major, BWV 816; Italian concerto in F major, BWV 971; Toccata in D major, BWV 912.

> (M) *** Decca Ace of Diamonds SDD 272. George Malcolm (harpsichord).

In 1955 George Malcolm made an outstanding record coupling a breathtakingly virtuoso performance of the *Chromatic fantasia* with a very lively *Italian concerto*. In his stereo re-make much of the flamboyance of that original *Chromatic fantasia* has disappeared, and the present reading is more considered. The result does not sound quite so spontaneous, and it reserves all its excitement for the cumulative climax of the Fugue. But Malcolm's rather more didactic approach to the *Italian concerto* achieves poise without loss of forward momentum, and the buoyant performance of the attractive *Toccata in D* is balanced on the second side with a genial, even lyrical, approach to the jolly *French suite*. The recording is outstandingly good (a trifle sharper in timbre than the original full-priced pressings), and this is currently the best Bach solo harpsichord collection in the catalogues at any price.

English suite No. 2 in A minor, BWV 807; Fantasia in C minor, BWV 906; French suite No. 6 in E major, BWV 817; Italian concerto in F major, BWV 971.

> ** Decca SXL 6545. Alicia de Larrocha (piano).

These days listeners who prefer their Bach keyboard music on a piano are not so well served, and this disc by a strikingly characterful artist fills an obvious need. She does not apologize for using the piano by attempting to imitate harpsichord tone, but translates such a work as the *Italian concerto* effectively into pianistic terms. Well recorded.

Organ Music

The Art of fugue, BWV 1080.

> (M) *** HMV SLS 782 (2 discs) (completed by Rogg). Lionel Rogg (organ of St Peter's Cathedral, Geneva).
>
> ** (*) DGG Archive 2708 002 (2 discs). Helmut Walcha (organ).

There seems little doubt that *The Art of fugue* was intended for the keyboard. Lionel Rogg gives a first-class reading of the work, with well-judged tempi and registration. The set includes his own completion of the work and has admirable notes by Basil Lam. The recording is impressively clear and truthful. Walcha's playing is a little dull at times, although the registration is quite varied, if somewhat restrained. Given the superiority of the newer HMV recording as well as the quality of Rogg's playing, his is probably the version to have.

Chorale preludes Nos. 1–45 (Orgelbüchlein), BWV 599/633 (complete recording).
  (M) ** (*) Telefunken SMT 1197/8. Robert Köbler (Silbermann organ, Freiberg Cathedral).
  (B) ** Oryx BACH 1013/14. Lionel Rogg (organ of Grossmünster, Zürich).
Chorale preludes Nos. 1–45 (Orgelbüchlein), BWV 599/633; Supplement: *Herr Jesu Christ, dich zu uns wend, BWV 709; Herzlich tut mich verlangen, BWV 727.*
  * (*) DGG Archive 2708 023 (2 discs). Helmut Walcha (Silbermann organ, St Pierre-le-Jeune, Strasbourg).

The forty-five *Chorale variations* which make up the *Orgelbüchlein* ('Little Organ Book') were devised by Bach to train organists in the working out of chorale themes. The set follows the Church calendar from Advent through to Easter, and so that the chorale is absolutely clear to the listener the melody invariably appears in the top line. Bach's elaborations are intended to illuminate the spirit of the text with which the tune is associated. Lionel Rogg observes the letter of Bach's intention, and the presentation and registration here are straightforward, the registration perhaps less imaginative than in some of Rogg's other recordings. But the simplicity of the approach is very effective, and the recording projects the music with admirable clarity.

Robert Köbler is also splendidly

recorded. The instrument at Freiberg has an exceptionally likable combination of clarity and sonority. Köbler's registration is more imaginative than Rogg's and he also shows himself much more personally involved in the music. Try *Das alte Jahr vergangen ist* at the end of side one to sample the restrained intensity characteristic of the gentle chorales. Köbler can also create a broad tapestry of genuine richness and weight, as in *Christus, der uns selig macht*, where the huge sound he conjures from the organ nearly defeats the pick-up. (A lower level of modulation would have been more sensible here.) But one hastens to add that the set as a whole reproduces easily and the glowing colours Köbler chooses are beautifully caught. There is sometimes a hint of rhythmic stodginess in the simpler hymn-like settings, but taken overall this well-presented album is excellent value.

Walcha's set offers considered, mellifluous playing and homogeneous textures. The sound lacks something in bite and detail, although Walcha makes sure that the chorale tune can always be heard. But in the last resort this is rather dull.

Chorale preludes, BWV 645/50 (Schübler chorales); 694; 710/13; 715; 717/18; 722; 722a; 724; 729; 732; 738; Chorale fughettas, BWV 695/704; Fugue on the Magnificat, BWV 733; Canonic variations on Vom Himmel hoch, BWV 769.
  ** Telefunken BC 25099 (1/2). Michel Chapuis (organs of St Paul's, Hamm, Westphalia; St Benedict's, Ringsted, Denmark).

Michel Chapuis follows a liturgical order for his extended recital, and the sequence is convincing both musically and ecclesiastically in opening with music associated with Christmas (the *Canonic variations*) and closing with chorales associated with Easter. The playing and registration are fresh and are helped by the characterful sound of the two chosen organs, which are splendidly recorded. The records are handsomely presented (as are the others of this series mentioned below) complete with pictures and specifications of the organs used plus miniature scores of the music.

Leipzig chorale preludes (Von verschiedener Art), BWV 651/68.
- (B) ** Oryx BACH 1017/18. Lionel Rogg (organ of Grossmünster, Zürich).
- (M) ** Vanguard VCS 10039/40. Anton Heiller (organ of Stiftskirche, Wilton, Innsbruck).

Lionel Rogg's integral set of Bach recordings for Oryx offers a high overall musical and technical standard at a very reasonable price. The playing on BACH 1017 and 1018 is very characteristic: cool, but always musical, detached and most effectively registered. Bach provides plenty of musical variety in these Leipzig chorales, particularly when he offers alternative settings in the same chorale, and sometimes a more flamboyant touch would not seem out of place. But Rogg is most impressive in the reflective music, which is never sentimentalized. The recording is nearly always excellent.

The Vanguard reissue of Heiller's performances seems to offer clearer sound than the original. Heiller is an excellent player, producing apt registrations, designed to clarify the chorale tune where appropriate. But in the last resort this set yields to Rogg, whose Zürich organ is used more imaginatively.

Chorale preludes 'for the Christmas season', BWV 599/612; 614; 659; 696/70; 703/4; 710; 722/4; 738.
- (B) *** Turnabout TV 34084S. Walter Kraft (organ).

Walter Kraft on Turnabout very generously gives us twenty-nine of Bach's *Chorale preludes* which have associations

with Christmas. In many cases there is more than one version of a single chorale, for instance *Gelobet seist du, Jesu Christ* is played in four versions, and both *Gottes Sohn ist kommen* and the well-known *Nunn komm der Heiden Heiland* each in three. However, this adds interest in showing Bach having second and sometimes third thoughts. Kraft uses six different organs, all dating from Bach's time and well suited to the texture of the writing. The recording is mostly excellent, with only the very slightest blurring on one or two tracks and some fascinating mechanical noises from the Silbermann organ in Ebermunster. The remarkable consistency of pitch – for nearly always there is a change of instrument at each item – is a tribute to organ builders and maintainers alike. A highly recommendable disc, very intelligently planned and well realized.

7 Chorale fughettas, BWV 696/9; 701; 703; 704; 8 Chorale variations, BWV 690/1, 706; 709; 711; 714; 731; 738; 6 Schübler chorales, BWV 645/50.
- (B) *** Oryx BACH 1006. Lionel Rogg (organ of Grossmünster, Zürich).

Lionel Rogg creates an unusually successful recital by his imaginative registration. In *Wachet auf*, the first of the Schübler set, he immediately establishes a practice he is to favour throughout the disc, separating the main chorale tune from its background by characterizing it on a strong, reedy stop. Throughout, his steady, relaxed style is never dull, and on side two, where the fifteen items are often quite short, he is ever ready to produce a fetching new mixture of colours to illuminate a quite simple piece.

Chorale partitas: Christ, der du bist der helle Tag, BWV 766; O Gott, du frommer Gott, BWV 767; Sei gegrüsset, Jesu gutig, BWV 768.

(B) *** Oryx BACH 1016. Lionel Rogg (organ of Grossmünster, Zürich).

This exceptionally well engineered disc again shows Lionel Rogg at his very best. The cool relaxed playing, the music unfolding with a gentle forward impetus, every detail clear, seems to provide exactly the right tapestry of colour for these early but felicitous sets of variations, which Bach wrote in his teens. In fact there is considerable evidence that Bach returned later to revise the masterly *Sei gegrüsset* set, and here Lionel Rogg's registration is particularly well judged. The sound itself is most beautiful.

Chorale variations: Allein Gott, BWV 717; Christ lag in Todesbanden, BWV 695 and 718; In dir hab ich gehoffet, BWV 712; Jesu meine Freude, BWV 713; Wir Christenleut, BWV 710; Wir glauben all'an einen Gott, BWV 740; Preludes and fugues in D minor, BWV 539; F minor, BWV 534.

(B) ** Oryx BACH 1004. Lionel Rogg (organ of Grossmünster, Zürich).

The performances of the two preludes and fugues are in Lionel Rogg's self-effacing manner and lack something in impact, but the *Chorale variations* have plenty of life and display the clear-timbred organ and Rogg's registration to good effect. The last item, *Wir glauben all'an einen Gott*, is played particularly beautifully. The sound is up to standard, although there was a touch of wow at the end of each fugue on our review copy.

Clavierübung, Part 3: *German organ mass* (complete recording).

(B) ** Oryx BACH 1007/8. Lionel Rogg (organ of Grossmünster, Zürich).

Bach's *Organ mass* is a fully-fledged mass conceived in terms of the solo organ. There are, of course, no words, but the composer uses as his basis both Gregorian melodies and Lutheran hymns. Within the variations Bach expresses his own emotional reactions and faith. The work opens with the *Prelude and fugue in E flat,* and Lionel Rogg gives it here a very measured account, setting the seal on the performance as a whole, which is restrained, and in the *Chorale variations* offers a simple devotional eloquence.

Concertos (for solo organ) *Nos. 1 in G major, BWV 592 (*after ERNST: *Concerto); 2 in A minor, BWV 593 (*after VIVALDI: *Concerto, Op. 3/8); 3 in C major, BWV 594 (*after VIVALDI: *Concerto, Op. 7/11); 5 in D minor, BWV 596 (*after VIVALDI: *Concerto, Op. 3/11).*

(M) *** Vanguard HM 35 SD. Anton Heiller (organ of Maria Kyrka, Hälsingborg, Sweden).

(M) ** HMV HQS 1293. Lionel Rogg (organ of St Nicholas, Aabenraa, Denmark).

This splendid record by Anton Heiller, made on the organ of Maria Kyrka, Hälsingborg, is one of about half a dozen discs of Bach's organ music which are among the most desirable on any label at any price. Heiller captures perfectly the extrovert quality of Bach enjoying himself, revelling in the music of others. Of the Vivaldi concertos the one in C major, BWV 594, is irresistible with its joyous and colourful opening *Toccata* (suggesting for a moment Handel's *Hallelujah chorus*). The short work based on a concerto by Prince Johann Ernst (formerly attributed to Vivaldi) has a gay opening movement, an expressive central section and a catchy finale. The recording is vivid and clear, and Heiller's registration in the slow movements creates some enchanting sounds.

Rogg's recording is made on an attractive Danish organ, with bright baroque timbres and slightly more depth of tone than is found on Heiller's Vanguard reissue. Rogg's playing is assured and lively but, compared with Heiller, somewhat inflexible and serious in manner: he is no match for Heiller in the *Toccata* which opens B W V 594. But this is a good disc of its kind, and well recorded too.

Fantasias and fugues: in C minor, B W V 537; in G minor, B W V 542; Preludes and fugues: in A major, B W V 536; in A minor, B W V 543; in C major, B W V 545; in C minor, B W V 546; in D minor, B W V 539; in F minor, B W V 534; in G major, B W V 541; Toccata and fugue in D minor (Dorian), B W V 538.

* (*) Telefunken BC 25100 (1/2). Michel Chapuis (organ of St Michael's, Zwolle).

Like the other issues in this Telefunken series, this album is impressively presented, but to gather together such a pantheon of masterpieces is to try the resources of the performing artist to the utmost. Michel Chapuis rises to the technical challenge with ease, indeed with consistent bravura, and he is recorded with admirable clarity and weight. But the music-making, although it does not lack spontaneity, often fails to probe beneath the surface. Chapuis can control a climax, but he does not always show a true sense of repose when the music is reflective.

Fantasia and fugue (fragment) *in C minor, B W V 562; Preludes and fugues: in B minor, B W V 544; in C major, B W V 531; in C major, B W V 547; in C minor, B W V 549; in D major, B W V 532; in E minor, B W V 533; in E minor, B W V 548; Prelude (toccata) and fugue in F major, B W V 540; in G major, B W V 550; in G minor, B W V 535.*

*** Telefunken BC 25101(1/2). Michel Chapuis (organ of St Michael's, Zwolle).

An excellent set in every way, splendidly recorded. The playing is considered, yet powerful, the tension controlled convincingly. There is a fine balance between a sense of architecture and the music's emotional demands. The registration too is well judged, and here the overall style shows a feeling for repose (without dullness) as well as bravura.

Pastorale in F major, B W V 590; Fugue in G minor, B W V 578; Preludes and fugues: in A major, B W V 536; in D major, B W V 532; in G major, B W V 550; in G minor, B W V 535.

** DGG Archive 2533 160. Helmut Walcha (organ of St Pierre-le-Jeune, Strasbourg).

The highlight of this collection is the *Pastorale*, but this delightful performance is currently available on an inexpensive sampler disc (2565 002; see p. 40, under Chorale preludes). Elsewhere on the present issue the registration is appropriately less piquant but still attractive. But the playing itself, relaxed and attentive to detail, does not generate a great deal of excitement.

Preludes and fugues: in A major, B W V 536; in B minor, B W V 544; in C major, B W V 545; in C minor, B W V 546.

(B) * (*) Oryx BACH 1012. Lionel Rogg (organ of Grossmünster, Zürich).

The opening C minor work is given a sense of massive authority in Rogg's account but the other performances on this disc are very relaxed, and, especially on the second side (containing B W V 536 and 544), the listener's concentration is tempted to falter, so mellifluous and uneventful is the playing. The engineering is excellent.

Preludes and fugues: in A minor, BWV 543; in C major, BWV 547; in E minor, BWV 548; in G major, BWV 541.

(B) * (*) Oryx BACH 1011. Lionel Rogg (organ of Grossmünster, Zürich).

The most enjoyable work here is the opening *A minor Prelude and fugue*, which is given a fairly light registration. The fugue is particularly effective. The long E minor piece which follows is less successful. The effect is heavy, and spontaneity is missing in Rogg's account. The C major and G major works on the reverse too lack the final spark that is needed to bring such conceptions fully to life. The engineering is consistent throughout.

Preludes and fugues: in C major, BWV 531; in C minor, BWV 549; in D major, BWV 532; in E minor, BWV 553; in G major, BWV 550; in G minor, BWV 535.

(B) *** Oryx BACH 1015. Lionel Rogg (organ of Grossmünster, Zürich).

This exhilarating record includes music Bach wrote in his teens and early twenties. The music has the hallmark of genius and the exuberance of youth. Lionel Rogg plays it with enthusiasm, and the spontaneity of the playing is matched by the excellence of the recording, which gives the Zürich organ a resplendent brightness most suitable for the glowing colours of the chosen registrations. The openings of BWV 532 and BWV 550 are particularly striking, and the C minor work, BWV 549 – the earliest work included here – makes a fascinating close to one of the most enjoyable Bach organ recitals in the catalogue. The extrovert flavour of the

music fires Rogg to obvious personal identification with the music.

Toccata, adagio and fugue in C major, BWV 564; Toccata and fugue in D minor (Dorian), BWV 538; Toccata and fugue in F major, BWV 540.

(B) *** Oryx BACH 1005. Lionel Rogg (organ of Grossmünster, Zürich).

The *Toccata and fugue in F major* begins with a lengthy discussion in canon, over a held pedal. This is the sort of exposition Lionel Rogg manages brilliantly. He maintains the tension throughout yet lets the music speak for itself without excess grandeur or trying to hurry it up. The *Toccata and fugue in D minor*, known as the *Dorian* to distinguish it from the more famous work in the same key (BWV 565), is hardly less effective, the *Toccata* (on side one) relaxed but strong, and the *Fugue* beautifully registered and allowed to grow naturally towards its own climax. There is little extrovert bravura in the famous *Toccata, adagio and fugue*, but plenty of inner power and fine, expressive playing in the second section.

Trio sonatas Nos. 1 in E flat major; 2 in C minor; 3 in D minor; 4 in E minor; 5 in C major; 6 in G major, BWV 525/30.

* (*) Philips 6700 059 (2 discs). Daniel Chorzempa (Schnitger organ, Meppel Reformed Church, Holland).

(i) *Trio sonatas 1–6;* (ii) *Allabreve in D major, BWV 589; Canzona in D minor, BWV 588; 4 Duets, BWV 802/5.*

** DGG Archive 2533 126 (Sonatas 2–5); 2533 140 (Sonatas 1 and 6 and *Allabreve; Canzona; Duets*). Helmut Walcha ((i) organ of St Laurenskerk, Alkmaar, (ii) organ of St Pierre-le-Jeune, Strasbourg).

Trio sonatas 1–6; Fantasias: in B minor, BWV 563; C major, BWV 570; Fugues: in C minor, BWV 575; G minor, BWV 578; Preludes: in A minor, BWV 569; G major, BWV 568; Trio in G major, BWV 584.

* (*) Telefunken BC 25098(1/2). Michel Chapuis (organ of Church of the Redeemer, Copenhagen).

Trio sonatas 1–6; Chorale variations: An Wasserflüssen Babylon, BWV 653b; Ein feste Burg, BWV 720; Fugue on the Magnificat, BWV 733; Herzlich tut mich verlangen, BWV 727; Nun freut euch, BWV 734; Valet will ich dir geben, BWV 736; Vater unser im Himmelreich, BWV 737.

(B) ** (*) Oryx BACH 1009 (Sonatas 1–4); BACH 1010 (Sonatas 5 and 6 and *Chorale variations*). Lionel Rogg (organ of Grossmünster, Zürich).

Chorzempa's set is disappointing. The playing is extremely relaxed, the registration subdued, and while the music-making is undoubtedly sensitive and technically immaculate, it seldom generates much tension. The mellifluous organ sound, with little bite in the reeds, does not help, and the whole effect too easily disengages the attention of the listener.

Walcha too leaves the music to speak for itself, but he holds the interest more readily than Chorzempa, although his advocacy of the shorter pieces which make the filler on 2533 140 is didactic rather than enthusiastic. Admirers of Walcha should find this a satisfactory investment, for the recording is excellent.

Michel Chapuis plays with clarity, even brilliance, helped by the bright organ sound. His registration is striking, but not varied very imaginatively, and the music-making itself suffers from a lack of flexibility, especially in the slow

movements. The chosen fillers, nearly all early works, are well done.

Rogg is less compelling in the first four *Sonatas* (on BACH 1009) than in the last two, but his musical skill is never in doubt and the registration produces sounds to charm the ear. Although the approach is scholarly the music is always alive. The *Chorale variations* are splendid and this puts BACH 1010 into the three-star class by its spontaneity and communicated pleasure. The engineering is excellent throughout.

Organ Recitals

Allabreve in D major, BWV 589; Canzona in D minor, BWV 588; Fugues in B minor, BWV 579; C minor, BWV 575; G major, BWV 577; G minor, BWV 578; Pastorale in F major, BWV 590.

(B) ** Oryx BACH 1002. Lionel Rogg (organ of Grossmünster, Zürich).

On BACH 1002 Rogg is at his best in the *Pastorale*, where his registrations give special pleasure, but there is a pervading seriousness in the fugues which does not relax into geniality, even for the *Fugue à la gigue* (BWV 577). The engineering is excellent.

5 Canonic variations on Vom Himmel hoch, BWV 769; Fantasia in C minor, BWV 562; Fantasia in G major, BWV 572; Toccata in E major, BWV 566; Trio in D minor, BWV 583.

(B) ** (*) Oryx BACH 1003. Lionel Rogg (organ of Grossmünster, Zürich).

BACH 1003 is notable for the brilliant feeling for colour Rogg shows in his registration at the opening of the *Fantasia in G major*. In the variations on *Vom Himmel hoch* the texture is laid out with remarkable clarity, which is absolutely essential if all the subtleties of Bach's writing are to be followed. The *Cantus firmus* can always be clearly heard. Rogg's approach to the *Toccata in E major* is characteristically relaxed but as the music jogs along the geniality (and Rogg's own affection) is communicated. This is one of Rogg's best performances, lacking exuberance perhaps, but very enjoyable in its own way.

Chorale partita on Sei gegrüsset, Jesu gütig, BWV 768; Fugue à la gigue, BWV 577; Toccata and fugue in F major, BWV 540.
  (B) *** Pye GSGC 14024. Ralph Downes (organ of the Royal Festival Hall, London) – WIDOR: *Toccata.*** (*)

This extraordinarily fine record dates from the very earliest days of stereo, being (in its original full-priced form) among the first disc-stereo pressings available in the United Kingdom. It would be impossible to guess from the sound, however, that it was not recorded relatively recently. Ralph Downes helped to design the Festival Hall organ, which because of its wide spatial layout is ideal for stereo recording. But it is not only the antiphonal and tonal qualities of the recording which recommend this bargain reissue, but the excellence of the performances too. The *Fugue 'à la gigue' in G major* is given a delightfully spirited reading; the elaborate *Toccata in F major* is spontaneous and invigorating; and the extended chorale variations are registered with flair and musicianship nicely balanced. It is a pity that the Widor coupling is somewhat too highly modulated, but in all other respects this is a most desirable disc.

Chorale preludes: Herzlich tut mich verlangen, BWV 727; Ich ruf' zu dir, BWV 639; In dulci jubilo, BWV 608; Nun freut euch, BWV 734; Valet will
ich dir geben, BWV 736; Vom Himmel hoch, BWV 700; Pastorale in F major, BWV 590; Prelude and fugue in G minor, BWV 535; Toccata and fugue in D minor, BWV 565.*
  (B) ** DGG Archive 2565 002. Helmut Walcha (organ of St Laurenskerk, Alkmaar).

An admirable and inexpensive sampler of Helmut Walcha's Bach style. The scholarly approach, the slight reticence and the keen feeling for registration within this ambience are well demonstrated. There are more dramatic performances of the famous *D minor Toccata and fugue* elsewhere, and the *Prelude and fugue in G minor* is relaxed too, but Walcha's skill with colour is shown in the chorale preludes and notably in the performance of the *Pastorale*. Here the piquancy of the chosen flute stops is delightful. The engineering is characteristically smooth.

Chorale prelude: Jesu, meine Freude, BWV 753; Clavierübung, Part 3: Wir glauben all'an einen Gott (Fugue on the Creed), BWV 680; Fantasia in G major, BWV 572; Fantasia and fugue in G minor, BWV 542; Preludes and fugues: in B minor, BWV 544; in C major, BWV 545.
  *** CBS Quadraphonic MQ 31424. E. Power Biggs (organ of Busch-Reisinger Museum, Harvard University).

Technically superb, this disc augurs well for the future of SQ quadraphony for organ recording. There is no sense of gimmickry: the listener's experience is of being actually in the Romanesque Hall at Harvard. The organ sound is thrilling, yet natural, and there is no sense of strain in the most spectacular moments. E. Power Biggs is not always the most imaginative of Bach players but here he is at his very best, presenting the music in a clear unforced manner, with vivid registration and letting the magnificent organ and Bach's music combine in the most positive way. An outstanding recital in every aspect.

Chorale and Chorale prelude: Liebster Jesu, BWV 373/633; Chorale preludes: Ich ruf' zu dir, BWV 639; Nun komm der Heiden Heiland, BWV 659; O Mensch, bewein, BWV 622; Vater unser in Himmelreich, BWV 762 and 737; Wer nur den lieben Gott, BWV 642; Prelude and fugue in A minor, BWV 543; Toccata and fugue in D minor, BWV 565.

(M) * (*) Decca Ace of Diamonds SDD 367. Ralph Davier (organ of Royal Albert Hall, London).

Without the advantages of quadraphony, this disc makes full use of the special dynamic and spatial range which is a feature of the Royal Albert Hall organ, and there are few ordinary stereo records engineered with such complete technical assurance. The placing of the swell and solo boxes behind the Great organ means the organist can readily create a distant effect along with a reduction of dynamic. This is shown in the opening *Toccata* (BWV 565), where the alternation of phrases is used almost to achieve a baroque echo effect. Whether this is entirely permissible in the context of Bach's music seems to matter less than whether it is musically effective. Unfortunately Ralph Davier sets a relaxed tempo and a low level of tension for his performance, and the receding effect decreases the tension still further. The chorales which follow are played in a very subdued manner so that the bright opening of the *Prelude and fugue in A minor* (which ends the recital) comes as something of a shock. In this work the use of the backwards antiphony is much more effectively integrated into the

work's structure, but one feels that the Swell could have been applied to even greater effect had the player been more daring. An interesting disc, then, but not one to recommend for the music-making alone.

Chorale variation: O Lamm Gottes unschuldig, BWV 656; Pastorale in F major, BWV 590; Prelude and fugue in D major, BWV 532; Trio sonata No. 2 in C minor, BWV 526.

(B) ** (*) Oryx EXP 51. Lionel Rogg (organ of Grossmünster, Zürich).

This recital begins most attractively with the early *Prelude and fugue in D major*. The spontaneous opening with its cheeky scale passage obviously catches Rogg's imagination, and he gives a splendid performance. The *Trio sonata* and *Pastorale* are characteristic, with nicely judged registration and a relaxed mood. The *Chorale variation* is brought to a striking climax, the recording here almost too brilliant. Taken as a whole this is a fair sampler of the diverse Rogg approach to Bach, and it is well engineered.

Fantasia and fugue in C minor, BWV 537; Fantasia and fugue in G minor, BWV 542; Passacaglia and fugue in C minor, BWV 582; Toccata and fugue in D minor, BWV 565.

(B) ** Oryx EXP 21. Lionel Rogg (organ of Grossmünster, Zürich).

At the price this collection is a remarkable bargain. The engineering is faultless, apart perhaps from a certain dryness in the deep bass: the pedals in the famous *D minor Toccata and fugue* lack something in depth and resonance. But the treble is bright without exaggeration, and the overall balance suits Rogg's relaxed approach, which lets the music unfold at a moderate pace and does not seek massive effects or spectacular registration. A musical disc, then, if not an especially exciting one.

Fantasia and fugue in G minor ('The great'), BWV 542; Passacaglia and fugue in C minor, BWV 582; Toccata, adagio and fugue in C major, BWV 564; Toccata and fugue in D minor, BWV 565.

  *** HMV CSD 1318. Fernando Germani (organ of the Royal Festival Hall, London).

This is another recital to show how well suited is the Festival Hall organ to stereo recording. Its 8,000 pipes are widely spread, and while there is only a suggestion here of point source in the sound, one can enjoy the impression of music originating from different sections of a broad area. The acoustic too means that the quality of the sound itself is clear, notably in the bass. The performances are first-class. The listener can hear every detail of the registration, and Germani's control of tension skilfully lets each fugue slowly build itself to an impressive climax.

Fantasia and fugue in G minor, BWV 542; Passacaglia and fugue in C minor, BWV 582; Prelude and fugue in G minor, BWV 542; Toccata and fugue in D minor, BWV 565.

  (M) ** Decca Ace of Diamonds SDD 258. Karl Richter (organ of Victoria Hall, Geneva).

An early stereo organ recording, one of the first to come from Decca. The sound is on the thick side, though acceptable enough for most of the time. Richter's tempi are characteristically steady (some will feel the famous D minor work is too relaxed); and this provides more clarity than would otherwise have been the case in the reverberant Victoria Hall, Geneva. The *Fantasia and fugue in G minor* is quite lively although it is slightly marred by touches of intermodulation distortion in the loudest moments. However, the climax of the *Passacaglia and fugue in C minor*, which Richter controls convincingly, is fairly impressive.

Fantasia and fugue in G minor, BWV 542; Prelude and fugue in E minor, BWV 548; Toccata, adagio and fugue in C major, BWV 564; Toccata and fugue in D minor, BWV 565.

  (M) ** (*) Philips 6599 368. Charles Benbow (organ of Chartres Cathedral).

This is an excellent bargain. A brilliant performance of *the* Toccata and fugue, both exciting and imaginatively registered, is followed by an equally impressive account of the large-scale *Toccata, adagio and fugue in C major*. Here Charles Benbow has considered both the overall shape and the proper element of contrast between the three sections. Side two offers some of the most massive organ sound ever put on record. The opening of the *Fantasia and fugue in G minor* is almost overwhelming, and by the end of the *Prelude and fugue in E minor*, a performance on the largest possible scale, the ear is virtually sated by the weighty registration. Those who revel in spectacular organ sound will surely be delighted (for pick-up and speakers seem to take it all with aplomb), but others might criticize Mr Benbow's overall judgement and feel that a little more light and shade would have made the culmination of BWV 548 even more devastating.

Passacaglia and fugue in C minor, BWV 582; Preludes and fugues: in A minor, BWV 543; in D major, BWV 582; Toccata and fugue in D minor, BWV 565.

  ** (*) Philips 6500 214. Daniel Chorzempa (organ of Our Lady's Church, Breda, Holland).

A beautifully recorded disc, with notable depth and resonance. Chorzempa's playing is impressive throughout and often stimulating, but his occasional dalliance with matters of colour can sometimes interfere with the music's forward impulse. Yet in the great *Passacaglia and fugue in C minor* it certainly adds to the interest and individuality of the performance. Sleeve-notes are provided by Chorzempa, who indicates the extent and reasons for his own elaboration of Bach's basic text. But in spite of this apparantly free approach the playing has a pontifical character in places. The titles on the record sleeve do not make it clear that the performances of both BWV 582 and 565 include the fugues.

Passacaglia and fugue in C minor, BWV 582; Preludes and fugues: in C minor, BWV 537; in G minor, BWV 542; Toccata and fugue in D minor, BWV 565.

(B) ** Oryx ORYX 1751. Lionel Rogg (Silbermann organ, Arlesheim).

This disc is from the 'Historic Organs of Europe' series, and the organ at Arlesheim is certainly a magnificent instrument, if not as clear-textured (as recorded) as Rogg's usual Zürich organ. The organ was carefully restored to its original pitch and timbre over a period from 1959 to 1962, when the pedal was strengthened, a weakness of the original specification. The new sound is impressive, as can be heard at the opening of the *Passacaglia and fugue*, where Rogg creates an ear-catching sombre colouring and matches it with a perfectly judged dignity of tempo. This is an excellent performance, characteristically without a slow cumulative effect, the tension instead held steadily throughout. The famous *D minor Toccata and fugue* also sounds well, but this is not a piece that responds especially well to Rogg's style – it needs more flair and flamboyance. The two *Preludes and*

fugues too tend to stay too much on one level; more variety of approach is surely desirable.

Prelude and fugue in C major, BWV 547; Toccata and fugue in D minor, BWV 565; Trio sonatas Nos. 1 in E flat major, BWV 525; 6 in G minor, BWV 530.

(M) *** DGG Privilege 135046. Helmut Walcha (organ of St Laurenskerk, Alkmaar).

This is a reissue of an early stereo LP, the first, in fact, released here in stereo of Walcha's famous Alkmaar recordings. The sound of the new transfer – rather more dry and compact than the original – is most satisfying, and Walcha's performances, with finely judged registration and an understanding of the differing stylistic demands of his programme, are first-rate.

Prelude and fugue in G minor, BWV 542; Trio sonata No. 5 in C major, BWV 529.

(B) *** DGG Début 2555 012. David Sanger (organ of Hercules Hall, Munich) – FRANCK: *Grande pièce symphonique.*** (*)

David Sanger is an impressive new talent. His playing is technically accomplished, and especially interesting in the control of light and shade. The *Prelude and fugue* is not played in a single cumulative forward sweep, but the tension is never allowed to drop too low. The *Trio sonata* is delightful, registered with an apt feeling for colour, the rhythmic pulse not too heavy. The organ itself is superbly recorded and seems to fit the music of Bach and Franck equally well. At the price this is an excellent bargain.

Toccata and fugue in D minor, BWV 565; Trio sonata No. 2 in C minor, BWV 526; Prelude and fugue in D

43

major, BWV 532; Prelude and fugue in G minor, BWV 534.

*** DGG SLPM 138907. Karl Richter (organ).

One of Karl Richter's very finest records and given a superlative recording, which is quite in a class of its own. Even a sustained pedal note (which usually causes a feeling of strain) is handled by the engineers with aplomb, and the sound remains clear in the spectacular cadences. The organ is a new one at Jaegersborg, near Copenhagen. The builders have attempted to simulate the principals and action of a baroque instrument, and the result is highly effective. Richter's registration is perceptive in its choice of the right timbres for each piece (notably so in the *Trio sonata*), and his control of the fugues is no less impressive. This is one of the finest available accounts of the famous *Toccata and fugue in D minor*, and if Richter does not show Rogg's exuberance in BWV 532, both this and BWV 534 have a splendid feeling of weight and power.

Orgelbüchlein (Chorale preludes) Books 1–3 (with original vocal chorales arr. Walter Emery), *BWV 599/644* (complete recording).

*** Argo ZRG 766/8. Peter Hurford (Sharp organs at Knox Grammar School Chapel, Sydney, and Wollongong Town Hall, Australia), with the Alban Singers.

The idea of recording Bach's *Chorale preludes* with each preceded by a vocal performance of the chorale itself has been previously tried by HMV with a fair degree of success, although the records are no longer available. The innovation of the present set is to use settings of the chorales by earlier composers. This has the double advantage of providing variety of style and throwing the Bach variants into relief, after first establishing the basic tune in the listener's consciousness. The success of this scheme is unqualified, helped by the expressive beauty of the singing and the way the lovely acoustic of the vocal recordings (made in St Alban's Abbey) matches the organs in Australia. Peter Hurford's playing is a model of style; his registration is apt without being flashy, and the music comes over with an admirable simple eloquence. These are records to be dipped into rather than played all at once, but for the lover of Bach and of distinctive choral singing they should provide very great satisfaction.

VOCAL MUSIC

Cantatas

Cantatas Nos. 1: Wie schön leuchtet der Morgenstern; 2: Ach Gott, vom Himmel; 3: Ach Gott, wie manches Herzeleid; 4: Christ lag in Todesbanden.

** (*) Telefunken SKW 1 (2 discs). Treble soloists from Vienna Boys' Choir, Paul Esswood (countertenor), Kurt Equiluz (tenor), Max van Egmond (bass), Vienna Boys' Choir, Chorus Viennensis, Vienna Concentus Musicus, Nikolaus Harnoncourt.

Telefunken have embarked on an enterprise as ambitious as Decca's Haydn symphonies and quartets; they aim to record all the Bach cantatas during the next decade with authentic instruments and scholarly performers. Each box includes notes by no less an authority than Alfred Dürr, the cantata texts in three languages, and miniature scores of the Bach Gesellschaft edition of the cantatas. These, it should be noted, use obsolete clefs – at least in the earlier volumes – and are in sepia print, but none the less they are an invaluable asset.

For all their scholarly rectitude, these performances are recorded in the order printed by the Bach Gesellschaft, that is to say, in the somewhat arbitrary order of publication chosen by the editors of the BGG rather than in any chronological order.

Boys' voices are used rather than female soloists, which will undoubtedly deter some collectors, though there are some very fine singers among those who have so far appeared in the series. The keen collector of Bach cantatas will invest either in all of this new series or in those cantatas he needs just for the sake of possessing an integral set. As only five boxes are scheduled per year, one is not confronted with too onerous a task in collecting the series, but readers wanting to be strictly selective will no doubt wish to know how the new survey compares with alternative records already in the catalogue.

Generally speaking there is a certain want of rhythmic freedom and some expressive caution. Rhythmic accents are underlined with some regularity, and the grandeur of Bach's inspiration is at times lost to view. Where there are no alternatives for outstanding cantatas, such as the marvellously rich and resourceful sonorities of the sinfonia to *Ach Gott, vom Himmel* (No. 2), with its heavenly aria, *Durchs Feuer wird das Silber rein*, choice is simple, and here the performance too is a fine one. There was slightly more grandeur to Richter's account of *Christ lag in Todesbanden* (No. 4), but there is so much fine music in Cantatas 2 and 3, not otherwise obtainable on record, that the first of these volumes is a must, even though the recording is not absolutely flawless; there is a trace of discoloration and discomfort. They appear occasionally to come close to overloading without ever doing so.

Cantatas Nos. 4: Christ lag in Todesbanden; 140: Wachet auf.

(M) ** Vanguard HM 20SD. Laurence Dutoit (soprano), Kurt Equiluz (tenor), Hans Braun (bass), Vienna Chamber Choir, Vienna State Opera Orchestra, Felix Prohaska.

These recordings are not of the most recent provenance but they are well worth considering, particularly as the disc is modestly priced. No. 4 has greater spontaneity and dramatic fire than the Harnoncourt, though it must of course yield to it in matters of authentic performance practice. *Wachet auf* has a warmth that is most appealing, and though fault can readily be found with the recording balance, the vigour and sincerity of these readings secure a recommendation for this disc.

(i) *Cantatas Nos. 5: Wo soll ich fliehen; 6: Bleib bei uns;* (ii) *7: Christ unser Herr zum Jordan kam; 8: Liebster Gott.*
** (*) Telefunken SKW 2 (2 discs). Paul Esswood (counter-tenor) Kurt Equiluz (tenor), Max van Egmond (bass), (i) Vienna Boys' Choir, Chorus Viennensis, Vienna Concentus Musicus, Nikolaus Harnoncourt, (ii) Regensburg treble soloists, King's College Chapel Choir, Leonhardt Consort, Gustav Leonhardt.

(i) *Cantatas Nos. 9: Es ist das Heil; 10: Meine Seele erhebt den Herren;* (ii) *11: Lobet Gott in seinen Reichen.*
** (*) Telefunken SKW 3 (2 discs). Esswood, Equiluz, Egmond, (i) Regensburg treble soloists, King's College Chapel Choir, Leonhardt Consort, Gustav Leonhardt, (ii) Vienna Boys' Choir, Chorus Viennensis, Vienna Concentus Musicus, Nikolaus Harnoncourt.

Although Richter's old recording of No. 8, *Liebster Gott*, on Archive (now deleted) was stiff and the tempi measured, it had greater breadth and vision than the Leonhardt version. Otherwise these two sets are well up to the standard of their predecessors, with good singing from the soloists and the King's College Choir adding extra colour to their choral contributions.

Cantata No. 10: Meine Seele erhebt den Herren.

*** Decca SXL 6400. Elly Ameling (soprano), Helen Watts (contralto), Werner Krenn (tenor) Marius Rintzler (bass), Vienna Academy Choir, Stuttgart Chamber Orchestra, Karl Münchinger – *Magnificat*.***

This performance is discussed under its coupling.

Cantatas Nos. 12: Weinen, Klagen; 13: Meine Seufzer, meine Tränen; 14: Wär Gott nicht; 16: Herr Gott, dich loben.

*** Telefunken SKW 4 (2 discs). Paul Esswood (counter-tenor), Kurt Equiluz, Marius Altena (tenors), Max van Egmond (bass), Walter Gampert, Peter Hinterreiter (trebles), King's College Chapel Choir, Leonhardt Consort, Gustav Leonhardt.

Cantatas Nos. 17: Wer Dank opfert; 18: Gleich wie der Regen; 19: Es erhub sich ein Streit; 20: O Ewigkeit, du Donnerwort.

*** Telefunken SKW 5 (2 discs). Esswood, Equiluz, Egmond, Vienna Boys' treble soloists, Vienna Boys' Choir, Chorus Viennensis, Vienna Concentus Musicus, Nikolaus Harnoncourt.

Two outstanding sets containing much wonderful music that is very little known. Performances and recordings are up to the highest standards of the series.

Cantatas for Advent and Christmas: Nos. 13, 28, 58, 61, 63–75, 81, 82, 111, 121, 124, 132, 171: complete recording.

** (*) DGG 2722 005 (6 discs). Edith Mathis, Sheila Armstrong (sopranos), Hertha Töpper, Anna Reynolds (contraltos), Peter Schreier, Ernst Haefliger (tenors), Dietrich Fischer-Dieskau (baritone), Theo Adam (bass), Munich Bach Choir and Orchestra, Karl Richter.

It is useful to have this anthology, which collects the Cantatas appropriate to the Christmas festival, and though there are some reservations to be made, there need be nothing but admiration for the purpose of the enterprise. The instrumental playing is extremely fine throughout, and much of the solo singing is of genuine distinction. There is a greater boldness about Richter's approach than, say, Harnoncourt's, but he is at times a little earthbound and not free from pedantry. However, in general this set will give pleasure. The acoustic is a pleasing one; it has warmth and clarity at the same time, but there are occasional traces of discomfort in tuttis which will worry some collectors more than others. But there is much noble music-making and noble music in this set.

Cantata No. 21: Ich hatte viel Bekümmernis.

(M) ** Supraphon 1120792. Nancy Burns (soprano), Libuše Márová (contralto), Friedrich Melzer (tenor), Günter Reich (bass), Stuttgart Bach Society, Helmuth Rilling.

Ich hatte viel Bekümmernis is one of the great tragic cantatas. The Supraphon performance is an imaginative one, and although the reverberant sound is not ideal it remains competitive in its price-range.

(i) *Cantatas Nos. 21: Ich hatte viel Bekümmernis;* (ii) *22: Jesus nahm zu sich die Zwölfe; 23: Du wahrer Gott.*

** (*) Telefunken SKW 6 (2 discs). Paul Esswood (counter-tenor), Kurt Equiluz (tenor), (i) Walker Wyatt (bass), Vienna Boys' Choir, Chorus Viennensis, Vienna Concentus Musicus, Nikolaus Harnoncourt, (ii) Walter Gampert (treble), Marius Altena (tenor) Max van Egmond (bass), King's College Chapel Choir, Leonhardt Consort, Gustav Leonhardt.

Cantatas Nos. 24: Ein ungefärbt Gemüte; 25: Es ist nichts gesundes; 26: Ach wie flüchtig; 27: Wer weiss, wie nahe mir.

*** Telefunken SKW 7 (2 discs). Esswood, Equiluz, Max van Egmond and Siegmund Nimsgern (basses), Vienna Boys' Choir, Chorus Viennensis, Vienna Concentus Musicus, Nikolaus Harnoncourt.

The magnificent *Ich hatte viel Bekümmernis* has greater sweep in the alternative version by Rilling on Supraphon. But the recording is better focused in this Telefunken set than in some of the first issues. Leonhardt is a little rigid in No. 22, *Jesus nahm zu sich die Zwölfe*; Harnoncourt tends in general to be freer, but a constant source of irritation throughout the series is the tendency to accent all main beats. The seventh volume is worth having in particular for the sake of the magnificent *Es ist nichts gesundes*, a cantata of exceptional richness of expression and resource. No. 27, *Wer weiss, wie nahe mir mein Ende*, is altogether magnificent too, and the performances are some of the finest to

appear in this ambitious and often impressive series. Certainly for those dipping into rather than collecting all this series, Volumes 1 and 7 would be good starting points, even though in the case of the latter all the cantatas are exceptionally short.

Cantatas Nos. 25: Es ist nichts gesundes; 103: Ihr werdet weinen und heulen.

(B) ** Oryx BACH 1107. Herrad Wehrung (soprano), Margarete Waldbauer (contralto), Raimund Gilvan (tenor), August Messthaler (bass), Stuttgart Motet Choir, Heidelberg Chamber Orchestra, Gunter Graulich.

Es ist nichts gesundes an meinem Leibe opens marvellously with some rich, strikingly sumptuous harmonies. Its text deals with the healing of the lepers as recorded in Luke XVII. The tenor is the best of the singers, though the others are by no means poor. The performance as a whole is good though the conductor is not a highly imaginative artist. The recording is clear: the balance is rather forward and the disc is cut at a very high level. However, it reproduces cleanly and with music of such quality, reservations are of small account. No. 103 is another superb cantata and one which is new to the catalogue. Written for the third Sunday after Easter, *Ye shall weep and howl but the world shall be glad* includes some of the finest of Bach's writing for chorus. The opening with sopranino recorder, flute, oboe d'amore and strings is particularly striking, and even if the performance is not always first class (the solo contralto is not particularly impressive), the tenor aria is marvellous. Again the recording is highly scored on its transcription to disc but there is no distortion. Bach lovers will find this a must. Choral tone could be firmer and their intonation more secure.

BACH, J. S.

Cantatas Nos. 27: Wer weiss, wie nahe mir; 59: Wer mich liebet; 118: O Jesu Christ, mein's Lebens Licht; 158: Der Friede sei mit dir.

*** Telefunken SAWT 9489. Rotraud Hansmann (soprano), Helen Watts (contralto), Kurt Equiluz (tenor), Max van Egmond (bass), Hamburg Monteverdi Choir, Concerto Amsterdam, Josef Schröder.

This is one of the most outstanding Bach cantata records on the market. Not only are the performances extremely sensitive yet vital, with excellent solo and choral singing as well as enthusiastic but disciplined instrumental support, but the cantatas themselves are among Bach's most inspired; Nos. 27 and 118 have great distinction and at times a visionary intensity that one finds in only the greatest Bach. A marvellous record and an indispensable one for serious collectors of the cantatas.

Cantatas Nos. 28: Gottlob! nun geht das Jahr zu Ende; 29: Wir danken dir, Gott; 30: Freue dich, erlöste Schar!

** (*) Telefunken SKW 8 (2 discs). Esswood, Equiluz, Egmond, Nimsgern, Vienna Boys' Choir, Chorus Viennensis, Vienna Concentus Musicus, Harnoncourt.

(i) *Cantatas Nos. 31: Der Himmel lacht, die Erde jubilieret;* (ii) *32: Liebster Jesu, mein Verlangen; 33: Allein zu dir, Herr Jesu Christ;* (i) *34: O ewiges Feuer, O Ursprung der Liebe.*

*** Telefunken SKW 9 (2 discs). (i) Esswood, Equiluz, Nimsgern, Vienna Boys' Choir, Chorus Viennensis, Vienna Concentus Musicus, Harnoncourt; (ii) Walter Gampert (treble), René Jacobs (counter-tenor), Marius Altena (tenor), Egmond (bass), Hannover Boys' Choir, Leonhardt Consort, Leonhardt.

Cantatas Nos. 35: Geist und Seele wird verwirret; 36: Schwingt freudig euch empor; 37: Wer da glaubet und getauft wird; 38: Aus tiefer Not schrei ich zu dir.

*** Telefunken SKW 10 (2 discs). Esswood, Equiluz, Ruud van der Meer (bass), Vienna Boys' Choir, Chorus Viennensis, Vienna Concentus Musicus, Harnoncourt.

These three albums continue the high standard that has distinguished this fine series. Of the new names in the roster of soloists one must mention the stylish singing of René Jacobs, and Walter Gampert is the excellent treble soloist in *Liebster Jesu.* No. 34 is an especially attractive cantata and here, as throughout, one notes the liveliness as well as the authenticity of the performances. SKW 10 is another set where the listener is struck again and again by the fertility of Bach's imagination. No. 35 features an outstanding concertante organ solo; No. 36 features a pair of oboi d'amore and there are oboes in duet in No. 38. Most enjoyable, with excellent solo singing.

Cantatas Nos. 45: Es ist dir gesagt; 105: Herr, gehe nicht in's Gericht.

(M) ** (*) Decca Ace of Diamonds SDD 384. Agnes Giebel (soprano), Helen Watts (contralto), Ian Partridge (tenor), Tom Krause (baritone), Suisse Romande and Lausanne Pro Arte Choirs, Suisse Romande Orchestra, Ernest Ansermet.

No. 45 is not one of Bach's most inspired cantatas but amends are more than made in 105, *Herr, gehe nicht in's Gericht.* This is of breath-taking sublimity of thought and the soloists respond to it with artistry and eloquence. Although this is not the most polished of performances, it has great directness of feeling and a sense of nobility. There is no current alternative recording to be had of No. 105, and it should be in every collection. The recording is eminently clean and well focused, and has admirable body and presence.

Cantata No. 50: Nun ist das Heil.
> (M) ** Vanguard HM 22SD. Vienna State Opera Chorus and Orchestra, Felix Prohaska – *Magnificat.***

Cantatas Nos. 50: Nun ist das Heil; 83: Erfreute Zeit; 197: Gott ist uns're Zuversicht (Wedding cantata).
> ** (*) Telefunken SAWT 9539. Treble and alto soloists from Vienna Boys' Choir, Kurt Equiluz (tenor), Max van Egmond (bass), Vienna Boys' Choir, Vienna Concentus Musicus, Nikolaus Harnoncourt.

These performances are all prepared with the utmost scrupulousness and use exactly the same forces as were used in Bach's day. All that remains of No. 50 is the opening chorus which celebrates the rejoicing in Heaven over Satan's fall. It is a muscular 8-part fugue and comes off splendidly. *Erfreute Zeit* (83), for three soloists, is well sung and performed; two of the movements are thought to be reworkings of a violin concerto. The natural horns produce some impressive sounds and tempi are convincing. The recording reproduces most smoothly. *Gott ist uns're Zuversicht* is a wedding cantata and an imposing work in two parts, the second of which was sung after the ceremony. It is on a large scale and the performance is fine, though the aria *Schläfert aller Sorgen* is a little sluggish. The use of boy soloists may not be to all tastes but they put up a good showing. Again the recording is not to be faulted.

Cantatas Nos. 51: Jauchzet Gott in allen Landen; 199: Mein Herze schwimmt im Blut.
> *** Philips 6500 014. Elly Ameling (soprano), German Bach Soloists, Helmut Winschermann.

Elly Ameling follows the example of the opening trumpets when she begins *Jauchzet Gott*, and her voice has an appropriate clarion ring to it. The opening of *Mein Herze schwimmt im Blut* is also strong and dramatic, and the intensity of the words comes over with commitment. The accompaniments to both cantatas are admirably done, and a beautifully balanced, crisp recorded sound projects both voice and instrumental group with great naturalness and realism. With such sensitive singing and playing this is a very enjoyable record indeed, and if Miss Ameling does not always convey the aching depth of feeling in the later cantata in the way a singer like Janet Baker can, her singing has a freshness and eloquence that tells in quite a different way. This is an outstanding coupling.

Cantatas Nos. 51: Jauchzet Gott in allen Landen; 202: Weichet nur (Wedding cantata).
> *** Telefunken SAWT 9513. Agnes Giebel (soprano), Concerto Amsterdam, Jaap Schröder.

Jauchzet Gott is one of the most brilliant of Bach's solo cantatas not only because of the virtuosity of the soprano part but the splendour of the trumpet obbligato. Agnes Giebel gives a dazzling account of the solo part. So for that matter does Maurice André, and in every respect their account is to be preferred to Richter's version on Archive which has just been deleted. The so-called *Wedding cantata* was also available sung by Maria Stader and accompanied by Richter in exactly the same coupling. If anything this is superior: Agnes Giebel sings superlatively and Gustav Leonhardt's continuo support is beyond praise, Jaap Schröder provides more sensitive direction than Richter and the recording has rather more detail and a livelier sound quality than the Archive disc. A superb issue.

Cantatas Nos. 53: Schlage doch; 54: Widerstehe doch der Sünde; 200: Bekennen will ich seinen Namen. St Matthew Passion: Erbarme dich.
   (M) ** Oiseau-Lyre SOL 60003. Helen Watts (contralto), Philomusica of London, Thurston Dart.

A most enjoyable anthology in which Helen Watts is heard in fresh voice and good artistic form. The accompaniment is stylish and the recording good, so that the disc tends to become more than the sum of its parts.

Cantatas Nos. 55: Ich armer Mensch; 160: Ich weiss, dass mein Erlöser lebt; 189: Meine Seele rühmt und preist.
   (B) ** Oryx BACH 1119. Raimund Gilvan (tenor), Mannheim Bach Choir, Heidelberg Chamber Orchestra, Heinz Göttsche.

These contrasted cantatas make an attractive anthology. No. 160, which is joyful and confident, follows No. 55, the cantata of the sinner seeking repentance, while No. 189, which is more ambitious in the matter of orchestral texture, has the theme of the human spirit rejoicing in the works of God. Raimund Gilvan shows sensitivity to the music's mood and line throughout the disc, and his singing is enjoyable also for its security and well-sustained tone. The accompaniments are generally sympathetic and the recording is pleasingly warm.

Cantatas Nos. 56: Ich will den Kreuzstab gerne tragen; 82: Ich habe genug.
   ** (*) DGG SAPM 198477. Dietrich Fischer-Dieskau (baritone), Munich Bach Choir and Orchestra, Karl Richter.

Perhaps Fischer-Dieskau is at times a little too expressive and over-sophisticated, but these are certainly sensitive performances, although Richter is sometimes a trifle heavy-handed. The recording is of excellent quality.

Cantata No. 60: O Ewigkeit, du Donnerwort.
   (M) * (*) Supraphon SUAST 50804. Marie Mrázová (contralto), Gerald English (tenor), Hermann Polster (bass), Musici Pragenses, Czech Philharmonic Chorus, Martin Turnovsky – BERG: *Violin concerto.****

It was a good idea to couple Suk's beautiful performance of the Berg *Violin concerto* with the Bach work from which Berg took his chorale theme, though in fact the Czech interpretation of Bach is far less stylish than the playing of the modern work. Turnovsky does not avoid rhythmic lumpiness with his slab-sided continuo-playing, and though the soloists are good, there is not enough variety of expression among the instrumentalists. The recording is well spread in stereo.

Cantatas Nos. 61: Nun komm, der Heiden Heiland; 132: Bereitet die Wege, bereitet die Bahn.
   (B) ** Oryx BACH 1117. Ingeborg Reichelt (soprano), Hildegard Rutgers (contralto), Theo Altmeyer (tenor), Eduard Wollitz (bass), Kantorei Barmen-Gemarke, German Bach Soloists, Helmut Kahlhofer.

Both these cantatas are worth acquiring and neither is otherwise available separately. True the performances are not especially distinguished, but both are eminently serviceable and the recording, though not outstanding, is fully acceptable and musically balanced.

Cantatas Nos. 62: Nun komm, der Heiden Heiland; 142: Uns ist ein Kind geboren.
- (B) * (*) Oryx BACH 1112. Petrina Kruse (soprano), Sabine Kirchner (contralto), Friedrich Melzer (tenor), Emund Illerhaus (bass), Mannheim Bach Choir, Heidelberg Chamber Orchestra, Heinz Göttsche.

No. 62 is not as well known as its immediate predecessor, which has the same title and is not as attractive. The performance both of the soloists and the chorus is not really very distinguished and Göttsche's direction could be firmer. The coupling, No. 142, is an early work dating from 1712, if indeed it is by Bach at all. Most authorities seem to doubt it and its invention is hardly worthy of him. The performance is adequate and the recording clear but, as so often in this series, cut a little too high.

Cantatas Nos. 74: Wer mich liebet; 147: Herz und Mund und Tat und Leben.
- *** Philips 6500 386. Ileana Cotrubas (soprano), Julia Hamari (contralto), Kurt Equiluz (tenor), William Reimer (bass), Netherlands Vocal Ensemble, German Bach Soloists, Helmut Winschermann.

Highly musical performances. For those wanting this particular coupling (*Herz und Mund und Tat und Leben* includes the famous *Jesu joy of man's desiring*) this is as good a choice as any. Indeed Winschermann's BWV 147 is far better than Richter's old Archive account and the cantata, though not without its (relatively speaking) less interesting numbers, be-longs on everybody's shelf. Winschermann varies the continuo, using harpsichord to provide contrast with organ when he feels it appropriate. Recording first-class.

Cantatas Nos. 80: Ein feste Burg; 140: Wachet auf.
- ** (*) HMV ASD 2381. Elly Ameling (soprano), Janet Baker (contralto), Theo Altmeyer (tenor), Hans Sotin (bass), South German Madrigal Choir and Consortium Musicum, Wolfgang Gönnenwein.
- ** DGG Archive SAPM 198407. Agnes Giebel (soprano), Hertha Töpper (contralto), Peter Schreier (tenor), Theo Adam (bass), Leipzig Thomanchor and Gewandhaus Orchestra, Rudolf Mauersberger.

A thoroughly reliable account of *Ein feste Burg* from Gönnenwein, and a useful alternative to the DGG version. Gönnenwein uses trumpets, which some authorities believe to have been added after Bach's death, whereas Mauersberger on the Archive record omits them. The singing is sensitive with the possible exception of the bass whose tone is not wholly pleasing. *Wachet auf* makes an attractive coupling. This performance is a fine one and Janet Baker's contribution, though small, is distinguished. The singing throughout is admirable and Gönnenwein secures highly musical results on the whole. And yet he misses the last ounce of inspiration, just as the HMV engineers, though admirable, fall short of producing an outstanding sound quality.

The DGG team of soloists too is a good one; their contribution is in the main sensitive and musical, if not rising to the greatest heights. The choral singing has life although it is not especially incisive. The recording is good, but generally the HMV disc is preferable.

Cantatas Nos. 82: Ich habe genug; 169: Gott soll allein mein Herze haben.
　** HMV ASD 2302. Janet Baker (contralto), Ambrosian Singers, Bath Festival Orchestra, Yehudi Menuhin.

Ich habe genug is one of the best-known of Bach's cantatas, while No. 169 is a comparative rarity. The performances are expressive and intelligent though Miss Baker does not achieve quite the same heights of inspiration as she does in her Oiseau-Lyre record of No. 159. Recording is admirably life-like and reproduces smoothly.

Cantatas Nos. 89: Was soll ich aus dir machen, Ephraim; 90: Es reifet euch ein schrecklich Ende; 161: Komm, du süsse Todesstunde.
　** Telefunken SAWT 9540. Sheila Armstrong (soprano), Helen Watts (contralto), Kurt Equiluz (tenor), Max van Egmond (bass), Hamburg Monteverdi Chorus, Concerto Amsterdam, Josef Schröder.

Komm, du süsse Todesstunde is the most substantial of the cantatas on this record and is also the best performed. As there are no alternatives at present in the catalogue of Nos. 89 and 90, this issue has the field very much to itself. The solo singing throughout is of a high standard and the flute obbligato in No. 161 is most sensitive. However, there is some routine playing from the Concerto Amsterdam and the disc is not their most inspired.

Cantatas No. 106: Gottes Zeit (Actus tragicus); 182: Himmelskönig, sei willkommen.
　*** Telefunken SAWT 9443. Julia Falk (contralto), Bert van t'Hoff (tenor), Jacques Villisech (bass), Hamburg Monteverdi Choir, Leonhardt Consort, Gustav Leonhardt (organ), Jürgen Jürgens.

Bach's *Funeral cantata* probably owes its existence to the death of Bach's uncle, Tobias Lämmerhirt, in 1707. Bach's feelings must have been mixed, as he was left a small legacy. At any rate, if this was for the uncle, Bach did him proud with writing of great poignancy. In fact *Gottes Zeit* is one of the most inspired of all Bach cantatas. Its opening sinfonia is positively sublime and it is played with great feeling and imagination here. It is no surprise to learn from the sleeve that Franz Brüggen is one of the recorder players. Throughout, the performance is as sensitive as it is stylish, and the recording is beautifully balanced and splendidly spacious. No. 182 is a Palm-Sunday cantata, not one of Bach's finest, but it is most persuasively performed and there are, of course, good things in the cantata. The recording is spacious yet well-defined and the disc is worth having for the coupling alone.

Cantata No. 110: Unser Mund sei voll Lachens (Christmas day cantata); Magnificat, BWV 243.
　* (*) BASF BAC 3067. Treble and alto solists from Tölz Boys' Choir, Theo Altmeyer (tenor), Siegmund Nimsgern (bass), Tölz Boys' Choir, Collegium Aureum (using original instruments), Gerhard Schmidt-Gaden.

This is the only available recording of the joyful Christmas day cantata, and it is given a serviceable performance here, well recorded. But use of authentic instruments does provide problems of intonation (and the solo singing is not immaculate in this respect either). The performance of the *Magnificat* shares this defect. Its style is robust, and the lack of refinement together with a jerky contribution from the chorus do not recommend it very highly.

Cantata No. 131: Aus der Tiefe rufe ich, Herr, zu dir.

** (*) HMV CSD 3741. Wendy Eathorne (soprano), Paul Esswood (counter-tenor), Neil Jenkins (tenor), John Noble (baritone), London Bach Society, Steinitz Bach Players, Paul Steinitz – HANDEL: *Sing unto God.* ** (*)

This early cantata is full of attractive music and inspired ideas. The performance is obviously dedicated – if anything a little too intense in mood. But with a very good recording, wide in range with plenty of detail and a warm acoustic, it makes enjoyable listening, and the Handel coupling is well worth having.

Cantatas Nos. 137: Lobe den Herren; 140: Wachet auf.

(B) * Decca Eclipse ECSR 729. Chloë Owen (soprano), Gert Lutze (tenor), Kieth Engen (bass), Munich Bach Choir, members of Munich State Opera Orchestra, Karl Richter.

Any Bach cantata on bargain label is welcome, as it increases the likelihood of this music's wider dissemination. These performances cannot, however, be recommended without some qualification. Richter is not the most fleet-footed or imaginative of conductors, though he is often deeply thoughtful. *Lobe den Herren* is probably the more successful of the two cantatas; but the recording as such is not sufficiently distinguished to make this disc strongly desirable.

Cantata No. 147: Herz und Mund und Tat und Leben. Motets: *Fürchte dich nicht, BWV 228; Der Geist hilft unsrer, BWV 226; Lobet den herrn, BWV 230.*

(M) *** HMV HQS 1254. Elly Ameling (soprano), Janet Baker (mezzo-soprano), Ian Partridge (tenor), John Shirley-Quirk (bass), King's College Chapel Choir, Academy of St Martin-in-the-Fields, David Willcocks.

The catalogue currently lists three recordings of *Herz und Mund und Tat und Leben*, now that Richter's pedantic account coupled with No. 60 is deleted. The Oiseau-Lyre version under Thomas is now past its prime, and the choice rests between this thoughtful version under David Willcocks and a no less refreshing account from Winschermann on Philips (see under No. 74). The HMV is cheaper and beautifully recorded; it also has on balance the finer solo singing. However, the Philips has the more successful coupling (the performance, not the music) and is no less well recorded.

Cantatas Nos. 159: Sehet, wir geh'n hinauf gen Jerusalem; 170: Vergnügte Ruh'.

⊕ (M) *** Oiseau-Lyre SOL 295. Janet Baker (contralto), Robert Tear (tenor), John Shirley-Quirk (baritone), St Anthony Singers, Academy of St Martin-in-the-Fields, Neville Marriner.

Sehet, wir geh'n hinauf gen Jerusalem is one of Bach's most inspired cantatas and surely ranks high on any short list of the essential Bach. Particularly glorious is the penultimate meditation, *Es ist vollbracht (It is finished)*, with its poignant oboe obbligato. Both Janet Baker and John Shirley-Quirk are in marvellous voice, and performance and recording are of high quality. The coupling, *Vergnügte Ruh', beliebte Seelenlust*, makes a worthy companion, and it is equally superbly performed. This is among the half dozen or so cantata records that ought to be in every collection.

Cantatas Nos. 172: Erschallet, ihr Lieder; 192: Nun danket alle Gott.

BACH, J. S.

(B) ** Oryx BACH 1111. Herrad Wehrung (soprano), Margarete Waldbauer (contralto), Raimund Gilvan (tenor), Hermann Achenbach (bass), Tübing Cantata Choir, South German Youth Symphony Orchestra, Hermann Achenbach.

No. 172 is a fine cantata and a newcomer to the catalogue. It is joyful in mood, being designed for performance at Whitsun. The performance, though not outstanding, is good on the whole, and the tenor soloist is particularly fine. No. 192 is attractive though it does not plumb the depths. The recording is loud and clear (as usual with records from this source, it is cut fairly high).

Cantata No. 198: Lass, Fürstin, lass noch einen Strahl.

*** Telefunken SAWT 9496. Rohtraud Hansmann (soprano), Helen Watts (contralto), Kurt Equiluz (tenor), Max van Egmond (bass), Hamburg Monteverdi Choir, Concerto Amsterdam, Jürgen Jürgens.

This ambitious work is not a church cantata but an ode mourning Queen Christiane Eberhardine of Saxony, whose death in 1727 caused a spontaneous expression of public sympathy. The libretto extols the queen's character, and Bach's especially imaginative scoring suggests he too had great affection and sympathy for her. After the impressive opening chorus, the soprano, contralto and tenor each sing the queen's praises, and the mood of the work at the close is happy and optimistic, the queen's translation to heaven obviously assured. The performance here is sensitive and spontaneous, as if the performers have been fired by such a rewarding and little-known masterpiece. First-rate recording, but poor presentation with no English translation.

Cantatas Nos. 202: Weichet nur (Wedding cantata); 209: Non sa che sia dolore.

*** HMV ASD 2876. Elly Ameling (soprano), Academy of St Martin-in-the-Fields, Neville Marriner.

No doubt the coupling will decide matters for most people, but in any event there is little to choose between Agnes Giebel's account of the *Wedding cantata* with Schröder conducting the Concerto Amsterdam (see under No. 51) and Elly Ameling's fine record with the Academy. Perhaps Miss Giebel gives the fresher and more invigorating reading but honours are fairly even, particularly when the admirable orchestral playing of the Academy of St Martin-in-the-Fields is so idiomatic and sympathetic. Either is worth the extra outlay when compared with the Turnabout disc, good though that is.

Cantatas Nos. 202: Weichet nur (Wedding cantata); 209: Non sa che sia dolore; 211: Schweigt stille (Coffee cantata); 212: Mer hahn en neue Oberkeet (Peasant cantata).

*** BASF BAC 3052/3. Elly Ameling (soprano), Gerald English (tenor), Siegmund Nimsgern (bass), Collegium Aureum (using original instruments).

One does not think of Bach primarily as an entertaining composer, but in these four secular cantatas he is shown in lighter vein than usual, and with such sensitive, spirited performances the ear is continually charmed. Elly Ameling is the star of the set and she sings delightfully throughout, notably in the *Wedding cantata*, where the obbligato oboist also contributes gainfully. The flautist in the other solo cantata, No. 209, has not as strong a personality as his colleague, and this work, which has an important solo flute (often very like the famous orchestral suite in B minor), is slightly affected by his reticence, although Miss Ameling is on top form. But the accompaniments in general are so stylish and alive that a strong recommendation is in order. Siegmund Nimsgern's contribution to the *Coffee cantata* has the proper *buffo* manner.

Cantatas Nos. 202: Weichet nur (Wedding cantata); 212: Mer hahn en neue Oberkeet (Peasant cantata).

(B) *** Turnabout TV 34042S. Ursula Buckel (soprano), Claus Ocker (bass), Württemberg Chamber Orchestra, Rudolf Ewerhart.

In both cantatas on the Turnabout disc the accent is on the solo voices; and thanks to the clarity and incisiveness of the soprano, Ursula Buckel, and the bass, Claus Ocker, the words are unusually audible. Excellent intonation and witty characterization (especially in the *Peasant cantata*) make this a most enjoyable disc, and since the orchestra is well up to standard and the sound full and realistic, this must be accounted a first-rate bargain.

Cantatas Nos. 203: Amore traditore; 209: Non sa che sia dolore.

** Telefunken SAWT 9465. Agnes Giebel (soprano), Jacques Villisech (bass), members of Leonhardt Consort, Gustav Leonhardt.

Cantatas Nos. 203: Amore traditore; 211: Schweigt stille (Coffee cantata).

(B) ** Turnabout TV 34071S. Elisabeth Speiser (soprano), Claus Ocker (bass), Martin Galling (harpsichord), Dieter Messlinger (cello), Württemberg Chamber Orchestra, Rudolf Ewerhart.

Doubts have been cast on the authenticity of the Italian cantata *Amore traditore*, and certainly if it is by Bach it is not one of his memorable works. The accompaniment is only a keyboard one with cello continuo (which the Turnabout sleeve-note writer seems not to have known was included) and the sparse textures do not add much in the way of colour to the vocal line, which Claus Ocker sings quite expressively. In the charming *Coffee cantata* he does not permit himself the full *buffo* style, but Elisabeth Speiser is delightful, if a little breathy in production. Taken as a whole this is a fair disc, and the recording is good.

Villisech is not quite as vivid as Ocker in *Amore traditore*, but in every other respect one could recommend the sensitive and attractive Telefunken performance. Agnes Giebel sings *Non sa che sia dolore* excellently, and she is most stylishly accompanied by the Leonhardt Consort and beautifully recorded.

Cantatas Nos. 204: Ich bin in mir vergnügt; 209: Non sa che sia dolore.

(B) ** Turnabout TV 34127S. Elisabeth Speiser (soprano), Württemberg Chamber Orchestra, Rudolf Ewerhart.

These two cantatas are sung very musically by Elisabeth Speiser, whose voice is smooth and well controlled as well as attractively fresh in timbre. The long melismas require good breath control, which this artist can manage also. The orchestral accompaniment is brightly projected and the various obbligato parts are sensitively played. One has, however, to comment finally that there is a lack of variety in the music itself: neither of these cantatas is among Bach's most memorable.

Cantata No. 206: Schleicht, spielende Wellen.

*** Telefunken SAWT 9425. Irmgard Jacobeit (soprano), Wilhelmine Mattès (contralto), Tom Brand

55

(tenor), Jacques Villisech (bass), Hamburg Monteverdi Choir, Amsterdam Chamber Orchestra, André Rieu.

Schleicht, spielende Wellen is one of Bach's secular cantatas and is noteworthy for a particularly fine opening chorus. The soloists are all admirable and the performance is vital and alive. The recording is as well-balanced and refined in tone as one has come to expect from this source.

Cantata No. 208: Was mir behagt (Hunting cantata).
*** Telefunken SAWT 9427. Erna Spoorenberg, Irmgard Jacobeit (sopranos), Tom Brand (tenor), Jacques Villisech (bass), Hamburg Monteverdi Choir, Amsterdam Chamber Orchestra, Jürgen Jürgens.

Was mir behagt, ist nur die muntre Jagd is a fine secular cantata and well worth acquiring. Its musical invention maintains a high standard and includes the famous *Sheep may safely graze*. The solo singing is on the whole quite admirable and the performances under Jürgens have both vitality and imagination to commend them.

Cantatas Nos. 211: Schweigt stille, plaudert nicht (Coffee cantata); 212: Mer hahn en neue Oberkeet (Peasant cantata).
(M) *** Telefunken SAW 9583. Rohtraud Hansmann (soprano), Kurt Equiluz (tenor), Max van Egmond (bass), Vienna Concentus Musicus, Nikolaus Harnoncourt.

These two cantatas are justly popular. This must surely be the most delightful record of the *Peasant cantata* in the catalogue; the performance is totally unselfconscious and uncondescending, while the singers are first-class. Harnoncourt uses authentic instruments or copies and infuses his players with enthusiasm and a genuine sense of enjoyment. The recording has an excellent ambience and space as well as focusing detail in the right perspective. The *Coffee cantata* is an obvious coupling and is no less well performed and sung. Max van Egmond's opening aria has great eloquence, and readers will hardly fail to respond to the splendid quality of both performance and recording. The reissue at medium price makes this coupling doubly attractive.

Tenor arias from Cantatas Nos. 36, 43, 75, 76, 103, 110, 134, 135, 177.
(B) *** Decca Eclipse ECS 737. Peter Schreier (tenor), Leipzig Gewandhaus Orchestra, Rudolf Mauersberger.

Some collectors, and especially those with limited resources, are reluctant to invest in the musical riches encompassed by the Bach cantatas, and for them (and indeed for small library collections) this admirable anthology offers a splendid sampler. The programme is exceptionally well chosen to show the emotional range of Bach's arias, from the stirring excerpt from the *Easter cantata* (No. 134) with its dramatic cries of *Auf, auf* (*Arise, arise*) to the heartfelt intensity of *Mein Jesus soll mein alles sein* from No. 75. Peter Schreier's singing throughout is notable for its freshness and eloquence, and the accompaniments are played with warmth (the many obbligati passages for the orchestral wind are sensitively realized). The recording too is excellent, clear but with plenty of atmosphere. An excellent bargain. Collectors who find this record to their liking might like to try a slightly more expensive DGG Privilege anthology (2538 231) which does not limit itself to tenor arias alone and features artists of the calibre of Edith Mathis, Ernst Haefliger and Dietrich Fischer-Dieskau.

Christmas oratorio, BWV 248.

** (*) Philips 6703 037 (3 discs). Elly Ameling (soprano), Brigitte Fass-baender (contralto), Horst Laub-enthal (tenor), Hermann Prey (baritone), Tölzer Knabenchor, Bavarian Radio Chorus and Orchestra, Eugen Jochum.

** (*) Telefunken SKH 25 (3 discs). Treble soloists from Vienna Boys' Choir, Paul Esswood (counter-tenor), Kurt Equiluz (tenor), Sieg-mund Nimsgern (bass), Vienna Boys' Choir, Chorus Viennensis, Vienna Concentus Musicus, Niko-laus Harnoncourt.

** Decca SET 346/8. Elly Ameling (soprano), Helen Watts (contral-to), Peter Pears (tenor), Tom Krause (bass), Lübecker Kan-torei, Stuttgart Chamber Orch-estra, Karl Münchinger.

* (*) DGG Archive 2710 004 (3 discs). Gundula Janowitz (sop-rano), Christa Ludwig (mezzo-soprano), Fritz Wunderlich (ten-or), Franz Crass (bass), Munich Bach Choir and Orchestra, Karl Richter.

Christmas oratorio, BWV 248: high-lights.

** Decca SET 423 (from above set cond. Münchinger).

Jochum, as in many of his other choral recordings, is searchingly dedicated. Like other conductors of his generation, he has little time for academic questions of orna-mentation and the like, but he brings to the performance a quality far more valuable, an ability to point Bach's rhythms in a way that gives unfailing resilience to the music, whether in fast numbers or slow. In this of all the Bach choral works, that quality is paramount, for the result with an excellent team of soloists has a genuinely celebratory

quality. Horst Laubenthal is a light-weight tenor, but that helps him to achieve sparkling precision. The record-ing of choir and orchestra is beautifully balanced and clear without being over-brilliant.

Harnoncourt in his search for authen-ticity in Bach performance has rarely been more successful than here. It will not be to everyone's taste to have a boy treble and male counter-tenor instead of women soloists, but the purity of sound of these singers is most affecting. Above all Har-noncourt in this instance never allows his pursuit of authentic sound to weigh the performance down. It has a lightness of touch which should please everyone. The sound, as usual from this source, is excellent.

Münchinger directs an admirably fresh performance, sharper in tone, brighter in recording than Jochum's set on Philips – a point that can be checked in the recording of Elly Ameling on both sets. With an excellent team of soloists and with Lübeck trebles adding to the fresh-ness, this is a good middle-of-the-road version that takes account of modern scholarship.

Richter has a high reputation in Ger-many for his Bach interpretations, yet here one notes his relative stiffness in comparison with Münchinger, let alone Jochum. He takes an unvarying view of the chorales; but fine solo singing and good choral work are some compensa-tion, with Christa Ludwig specially beau-tiful in the *Cradle song*. The contribution of the late Fritz Wunderlich too is glowingly beautiful, but Franz Crass, the bass, is coarse and unyielding.

Easter oratorio, BWV 249.

*** Decca SET 398. Elly Ameling (soprano), Helen Watts (contral-to), Werner Krenn (tenor), Tom Krause (bass), Vienna Academy Choir, Stuttgart Chamber Orchestra, Karl Münchinger.

Münchinger gives a spacious and impressive reading of the *Easter oratorio*, and is well served by his splendid team of soloists. Given such fine recording, too, this is a reliable recommendation for the work.

Magnificat in D major, BWV 243.

   *** Decca sxl 6400. Elly Ameling, Hanneke van Bork (sopranos), Helen Watts (contralto), Werner Krenn (tenor), Tom Krause (bass), Vienna Academy Choir, Stuttgart Chamber Orchestra, Karl Münchinger – *Cantata No. 10.****

   *** HMV asd 2533. Lucia Popp, Anne Pashley (sopranos), Janet Baker (contralto), Robert Tear (tenor), Thomas Hemsley, Don Garrard (basses), New Philharmonia Chorus and Orchestra, Daniel Barenboim – BRUCKNER: *Te Deum.*** (*)

(B) *** Oryx BACH 1183. Helen Donath, Gundula Bernat-Klein (sopranos), Birgit Finnila (contralto), Peter Schreier (tenor), Barry McDaniel (bass), South German Madrigal Choir, Stuttgart, German Bach Soloists, Wolfgang Gönnenwein.

(M) ** Vanguard HM 22sd. Mimi Coertse and Margaret Sjöstedt (sopranos), Hilde Rössl-Majdan (contralto), Anton Dermota (tenor), Frederick Guthrie (bass), Vienna State Opera Chorus and Orchestra, Felix Prohaska – *Cantata No. 50.***

The *Magnificat* receives a performance and recording from Münchinger and Decca as impressive as any in the catalogue. The soloists are uniformly good, and so are the contributions of the Vienna Academy Choir and the Stuttgart Orchestra. Münchinger tends to stress the breadth and spaciousness of the *Magnificat*, and the Decca engineers have captured the detail with admirable clarity and naturalness. The recording is finer than Barenboim's on HMV and the performance, though not as unfailingly musical, is more deeply considered. The *Cantata* too is very well performed and makes an excellent coupling.

Barenboim's way with Bach is nothing if not boisterous, and traditionalists will jib at the very fast tempo for the opening. But no one should miss the joyfulness of the music as presented here. Münchinger's is a fine, traditional version, but for those prepared to go along with Barenboim, this is a new youthful revelation. The solo singing too is more imaginative than in rival versions, and Janet Baker's singing of the two mezzo arias is intensely moving. Recording – made in a fairly small South London church – is agreeably warm without being startlingly brilliant.

A most beautiful performance too on the Oryx record, which has also the advantage of economy. Gönnenwein achieves a splendid forward momentum and freshness, without any sense of hurry, and he is helped by good choral singing and some excellent solo playing from his chamber orchestra. The soloists are a good team; both the tenor and the contralto make striking contributions, but the star of the performance is undoubtedly Helen Donath, the principal soprano, who sings with great beauty of tone and line. She seems a born Bach singer and her phrasing has the essential flexibility this music demands and a genuine nobility of conception. In addition this Oryx record is the only version including Bach's original Christmas interpolations.

Despite its age the Prohaska version is also competitive. The performance is vigorous and alive, and though the recording is perhaps wanting the same degree of freshness and detail as the Decca, it is still highly acceptable.

Mass in B minor, BWV 232.

(M) *** Vanguard VSD 71190 (3 discs). Felicity Palmer (soprano), Helen Watts (contralto), Robert Tear (tenor), Michael Rippon (bass), Amor Artis Chorale, English Chamber Orchestra, Johannes Somary.

** (*) Decca SET 477/8. Elly Ameling, Yvonne Minton (sopranos), Helen Watts (contralto), Werner Krenn (tenor), Tom Krause (bass), Stuttgart Chamber Chorus and Orchestra, Karl Münchinger.

** Telefunken SKH 20 (3 discs). Rohtraud Hansmann, Emiko Iiyama (sopranos), Helen Watts (contralto), Kurt Equiluz (tenor), Max van Egmond (bass), Vienna Sangerknaben, Chorus Viennensis, Vienna Concentus Musicus, Nikolaus Harnoncourt.

** DGG Archive 2710 001 (3 discs). Maria Stader (soprano), Hertha Töpper (contralto), Ernst Haefliger (tenor), Dietrich Fischer-Dieskau (baritone), Kieth Engen (bass), Munich Bach Choir and Orchestra, Karl Richter.

* (*) HMV SLS 930 (3 discs). Agnes Giebel (soprano), Janet Baker (contralto), Nicolai Gedda (tenor), Hermann Prey (baritone), Franz Crass (bass), BBC Chorus, New Philharmonia Orchestra, Otto Klemperer.

* (*) DGG 2740 112 (3 discs). Gundula Janowitz (soprano), Christa Ludwig (mezzo-soprano), Peter Schreier (tenor), Robert Kerns (baritone), Karl Ridderbusch (bass), Vienna Singverein, Berlin Philharmonic Orchestra, Herbert von Karajan.

More than any previous performance on record, Somary's conveys the feeling of a live performance, its tension and resolutions. Somary inspires his authentically small choir to superbly incisive singing. Recorded close, the result is bitingly dramatic, helped by Somary's brisk tempi and resilient rhythms, even if some of the more contemplative qualities of this sublime masterpiece are underplayed. The vocal soloists are as fine as on any rival set, and the ECO plays most stylishly. First-rate, bright recording.

Münchinger's is a strong, enjoyable performance with an exceptionally fine quintet of soloists and first-rate recording. That it comes on four sides instead of six adds to its attractiveness, and on balance it makes a good recommendation until a really great performance is recorded; but with fastish tempi and a generally extrovert manner, it is efficient rather than inspiring. The chorus sings well, but is placed rather backwardly.

As with Harnoncourt's other records of Bach, reactions will vary widely. Harnoncourt has very strictly rationed himself to authentic numbers as well as authentic instruments, and with boys' voices in the choir, the effect is more of a chamber performance – fatal in the great *Sanctus*. But Harnoncourt's dedication comes over, and in its way this is a successful issue. Good solo singing, particularly from Helen Watts.

Though Richter's performance dates from the early 1960s, it is still worth considering, for the choral work is well focused, firm and distinct. Among the soloists Hertha Töpper is disappointing, but the others, Fischer-Dieskau in particular, are most impressive.

Klemperer is disappointing. The sobriety of the reading, with plodding tempi, and a dogged observance of the *Neuen Bach-Ausgabe* (Bärenreiter) utterly unornamented, were no doubt predictable. Only when the drama of the mass takes over in the *Crucifixus* and *Et resurrexit* does the majesty of Klemperer's conception become apparent. Janet Baker stands out among the soloists, with superb accounts of the *Qui sedes* and *Agnus Dei*. Whatever the initial shortcomings, Klemperer's *Sanctus* (faster than usual) has wonderful momentum, the *Osanna* is genuinely joyful, and the concluding sections of the sublime work come vividly alive. The choral recording is, however, none too clear, and the quality overall is good rather than outstanding.

Karajan's performance is marked by his characteristic smoothness of Bach style. He conveys intensity, even religious fervour, but the sharp contours of Bach's majestic writing are often missing. The very opening brings an impressive first entry of the choir on *Kyrie*, but then after the instrumental fugue the contrapuntal entries are sung in a self-consciously softened tone. Karajan devotees will no doubt like it, but for all its polish it cannot be recommended widely.

Motets: *Fürchte dich nicht, BWV 228; Der Geist hilft unsrer, BWV 226; Jesu meine Freude, BWV 227; Komm, Jesu, komm, BWV 229; Lobet den Herrn, BWV 230; Singet dem Herrn ein neues Lied, BWV 225.*

(M) ** Supraphon SUAST 50821/2. Czech Philharmonic Chorus, Josef Veselka; Petr Sovadina (organ).

The Czech choir is rather bigger than we are used to in these glorious, often complex works. The incisiveness of the singing is enough to counter most objections, but the tempi too have been affected, often very expansive indeed.

Motets: *Fürchte dich Nicht, BWV 228; Der Geist hilft unsrer, BWV 226; Singet dem Herrn ein neues Lied, BWV 225; Sei Lob und Preis mit Ehren, BWV 231.*

(B) * (*) Decca Eclipse ECS 598. Aeolian Singers, Sebastian Forbes.

Motets: *Jesu meine Freude, BWV 227; Komm, Jesu, komm, BWV 229; Lobet den Herrn, BWV 230; O Jesu Christ, mein's Lebens Licht, BWV 118.*

(B) * (*) Decca Eclipse ECS 599. Aeolian Singers with instrumental group, Sebastian Forbes; Christopher Van Kampen (cello), Martin Neary (organ).

Bach's *Motets* are intricate in pattern, thus offering considerable technical problems to their interpreters, besides demanding also a strong and sympathetic emotional response and sense of line. On the whole the Aeolian Singers meet the latter requirements, but some motets show more technical assurance than others, and both intonation and pitch are not always absolutely secure. The more familiar items seem to come off best, suggesting greater familiarity; thus ECS 599 is a rather more satisfactory record than ECS 598. The recording is acceptable if not outstanding by Decca standards.

Motets: *Jesu meine Freude, BWV 227; Komm, Jesu, komm, BWV 229; Singet dem Herrn ein neues Lied, BWV 225.*

(M) *** HMV HQS 1144. King's College Choir, David Willcocks.

Three of the greatest pieces that Bach ever wrote for chorus sung by the Anglican world's leading choir in first-rate modern stereo and all on bargain-label: one hardly needs to say more, except that the Cambridge boys easily outshine any continental rivals and the spread of stereo is effective in catching the double-choir antiphony of *Singet dem Herrn*, with David Willcocks varying the mood and tone most stylishly. Whatever the scholarly arguments for or against accompaniment in these motets, Willcocks's avoidance of accompaniment brings greater clarity.

Motets: *Jesu meine Freude, BWV 227; Komm, Jesu, komm, BWV 231; Fan-*

tasia sopra Jesu meine Freude, BWV 713; 2 settings of Vom Himmel hoch: Fughetta, BWV 701; Chorus from Magnificat, BWV 243: Freut euch und jubiliert.

(M) ** Unicorn UNS 252. Louis Halsey Singers, Halsey; David Lumsden (organ).

Louis Halsey opts for organ accompaniment to works which as a rule have latterly been given unaccompanied. He justifies his decision in finely judged, intense performances of two of the finest motets, adding the other items for good measure, the organ pieces included as related postludes. The atmospheric recording was made in St Giles, Cripplegate.

Motet: *Jesu priceless treasure (Jesu meine Freude)*. Sacred part songs: *Die bitt're Leidenszeit; Brunnquell aller Güter; Es ist vollbracht; Gott lebet noch; Herr, nicht schicke deine Rache; Jesus ist das schönste Licht; O Jesuslein süss* (sung in English).

** Argo ZRG 5234. King's College Choir, David Willcocks.

There is a place in the catalogue for an English-language version of *Jesu meine Freude*, and this performance surpasses any German-text recordings made on the continent which have been available at various times. The famous King's atmosphere is caught in a characteristic Argo manner, yet the words are clear, and the balance with the continuo of organ, cello and bass is admirable. However, as can be seen above, David Willcocks and his choir have rerecorded the work in German on HMV bargain label coupled to other motets, and many will choose this (unaccompanied) version. The items from the Schemelli hymn-book which are included on the Argo disc are, however, not otherwise available in recommendable

versions. They are of fine musical quality and beautifully sung.

St John Passion, BWV 245 (sung in English).

*** Decca SET 531/3. Peter Pears (tenor), Heather Harper (soprano), Alfreda Hodgson (contralto), Robert Tear (tenor), Gwynne Howell (baritone), John Shirley-Quirk (bass), Wandsworth School Boys' Choir, English Chamber Orchestra, Benjamin Britten.

(M) ** (*) Argo Ace of Diamonds GOS 628/30. Peter Pears (tenor), Elizabeth Harwood (soprano), Helen Watts (contralto), Alexander Young (tenor), Hervey Alan (bass-baritone), David Ward (bass), King's College Choir, London Philomusica, David Willcocks.

St John Passion, BWV 245: highlights (in English): Nos. 1, 12, 13, 16–20, 28–31, 33–47, 49–52, 58, 67.

** (*) Decca SXL 6626 (from above set cond. Britten).

St John Passion, BWV 245 (sung in German).

** (*) Decca SET 590/2. Dieter Ellenbeck (tenor), Walter Berry (bass), Allan Ahrans (baritone), Elly Ameling (soprano), Julia Hamari (contralto), Werner Hollweg (tenor), Hermann Prey (baritone), Stuttgart Hymnus Boys' Choir, Stuttgart Chamber Orchestra, Karl Münchinger.

* (*) Telefunken SKH 19 (3 discs). Kurt Equiluz, Bert van t'Hoff (tenors), Max van Egmond, Jacques Villisech, Siegfried Schneeweis (basses), treble and alto soloists from chorus, Vienna Boys' Choir, Chorus Viennensis, Vienna

Concentus Musicus, Hans Gillesberger.

St John Passion, BWV 245: excerpts (in German): Nos. 1–5, 7, 16–20, 22–31, 35–8, 43–7, 49–54, 57–9, 63, 67–8.

** Telefunken SAWT 9479 (from above set cond. Gillesberger).

St John Passion, BWV 245; St Matthew Passion, BWV 244.

(M) ** DGG Archive 2722 010 (7 discs). Irmgard Seefried (soprano), Hertha Töpper (contralto), Ernst Haefliger (tenor), Hermann Prey or Dietrich Fischer-Dieskau (baritones), Kieth Engen (bass), Munich Bach Choir and Orchestra, Karl Richter.

At the Aldeburgh Festival and elsewhere Benjamin Britten directed live performances of this more dramatic of Bach's Passions, which culminated in this wonderfully vivid recording. Britten characteristically refuses to follow any set tradition, whether baroque, Victorian or whatever; and with greater extremes of tempo than is common (often strikingly fast), the result makes you listen afresh. The soloists are excellent, and though the Wandsworth School Boys' Choir has its rough edges, it reinforces the freshness of the interpretation. Excellent accompaniment from the English Chamber Orchestra, with outstanding continuo playing from Philip Ledger. The recording is vividly atmospheric.

Willcocks's version, much earlier than Britten's, is by no means superseded. The singing of the King's College Choir is far purer and fresher than that on the rival Decca set, and the soloists make an equally fine team, while the recording, always impressive, hardly sounds its age on this mid-price reissue. Only the big opening chorus falls a little short of the rest in intensity.

An excellent set of excerpts from Britten's performance is available on SXL 6626, giving a true representation of his fine interpretation. This includes the two great choruses at the beginning and end, plus a fair sample of the most dramatic sequences.

Münchinger's reading matches his other recordings of Bach choral works, with a superb line-up of soloists, all of them clear-toned and precise, and a fresh, young-sounding tenor as Evangelist, Dieter Ellenbeck. Though Münchinger does not equal a conductor like Britten in individuality of imagination, he points the musical balance of the score most satisfyingly without idiosyncrasy. For sound scholarly reasons he uses organ continuo with no harpsichord. The recording is excellent.

Though it uses original instruments most sensitively, Gillesberger's reading skates glibly over music that demands intense devotion. The *St John Passion* may seem less devotional than the *St Matthew* and much more intent on the dramatic impact of the Passion story, but it still has to have intensity. Readers wanting to sample Gillesberger's brand of authenticity might be better with the disc of excerpts, which is well chosen, but it takes some getting used to: no women's voices at all, either solo or choral, and the very characteristic timbre of the older stringed instruments. But once the adjustments have been made there is a certain compulsion about the performance, particularly when the boys' voices are recorded with bright fidelity. It is a pity that Kurt Equiluz has a curious, slightly tremulous tone which mars an otherwise sensitive performance. The chorales are taken at high speed, even the magnificent last one.

Richter's account is available only in a special edition coupled to the *St Matthew Passion* (see also below). It comes in the medium price-range and throws in a disc of keyboard music as a bonus. Admirers of Richter may feel the set is a good investment, even though the performance is not really a match for either of the

English-language ones. The choral contribution is quite strong, with a sense of drama, and the team of soloists is a good one, with Ernst Haefliger at his best. The recording, dating from the mid sixties, still sounds well.

St Matthew Passion, B W V 244.

*** H M V SLS 827 (4 discs). Peter Pears (tenor), Dietrich Fischer-Dieskau (baritone), Elisabeth Schwarzkopf (soprano), Christa Ludwig (mezzo-soprano), Nicolai Gedda (tenor), Walter Berry (bass), Boys of Hampstead Parish Church Choir, Philharmonia Choir and Orchestra, Otto Klemperer.

*** Decca SET 288/91. Peter Pears (tenor), Hermann Prey (baritone), Elly Ameling (soprano), Marga Höffgen (contralto), Fritz Wunderlich (tenor), Tom Krause (bass), Stuttgart Hymnus Boys' Choir, Stuttgart Chamber Orchestra, Karl Münchinger.

** Telefunken SAWT 9572/5. Kurt Equiluz (tenor), Paul Esswood, Tom Sutcliffe, James Bowman (counter-tenors), Nigel Rogers (tenor), Karl Ridderbusch, Max van Egmond, Michael Schopper (basses), Regensburger Domchor, solo trebles of Vienna Boys' Choir, King's College Choir, Vienna Concentus Musicus, Nikolaus Harnoncourt.

** D G G Archive 2712 001 (4 discs). Ernst Haefliger (tenor), Antoine Fahberg (soprano), Dietrich Fischer-Dieskau (baritone), Kieth Engen (bass), Munich Bach Choir and Orchestra with Boys' Choir, Karl Richter.

** D G G 2720 070 (4 discs). Peter Schreier (tenor), Dietrich Fischer-Dieskau (baritone), Gundula Janowitz (soprano), Christa Ludwig (mezzo-soprano), Anton Diakov, Walter Ludwig (basses), Vienna Singverein, Boys' Choir, German Opera Chorus, Berlin, Berlin Philharmonic Orchestra, Herbert von Karajan.

St Matthew Passion, B W V 244: excerpts.

** (*) Decca SXL 6272 (from above set cond. Münchinger).

* (*) Telefunken SAWT 9588 (from above set cond. Harnoncourt).

This is one of Klemperer's finest achievements on record, an act of devotion of such intensity that points of style and interpretation dwindle into insignificance. Klemperer's approach is, according to the latest dictates, old-fashioned. He takes the chorales slowly, with pauses at the end of each line; he makes no concessions to scholarship on the question of introducing ornamentation. On the face of it this could have been a very dull, plodding performance indeed, but instead, through Klemperer's genius, captured at white heat from first to last, we have a monument of the gramophone. The whole cast managed to share Klemperer's own intense feelings, and one can only sit back and share them too, whatever one's preconceptions. And if anyone at this date still wants convincing about the need for stereo, let him hear the first great chorus, *Kommt, ihr Töchter*, with the chorale *O Lamm Gottes unschuldig* given to trebles in ripieno. Stereo allows clear separation between the first and second choruses on left and right, while ringing out from the centre is the pure tone of the boys of the Hampstead choir. Klemperer's intensity is faithfully reflected in a matchless team of soloists, with Peter Pears at his peak in the role of Evangelist and Fischer-Dieskau deeply expressive as Jesus. The Philharmonia Choir (not the

63

amateur Philharmonia Chorus) sings with the finest focus, and in this reissue the recorded sound remains astonishingly vivid.

There is no direct conflict between Münchinger's version and Klemperer's colossal conception. Münchinger's direction does not reach such heights, but his performance is consistently fresh and alert, and above all has greater authenticity. All the soloists are excellent, with Peter Pears again showing that no tenor in the world today rivals him as the Evangelist. Elly Ameling, the soprano, is sweet-toned and sensitive. The recording is superlative, clear, brilliant and beautifully balanced, though some may object to the deliberate closeness with which the voice of Hermann Prey as Jesus has been recorded.

Harnoncourt's authentic approach means that his version of the *St Matthew Passion* can be compared with no other. The instrumental sound is different (the strings, for instance, use a vibrato-less tone production); the vocal sound is almost revolutionary in its total reliance on male voices (including boy trebles); the choral singing is incisive and lightweight. For many, the emotional kernel of Bach's work lies in the solo contributions and here these are variable, with Karl Ridderbusch (as Christus) and Paul Esswood outstanding. Some of the other contributions are less reliable. The use of solo boy trebles from the Vienna Choir for the soprano arias produces a strangely detached effect, although the singing itself is usually technically good.

Richter's recording dates from the earliest days of stereo, and very little attempt was made to give the listener an impression of antiphonal choruses. The sound is good for its time, but the balance is not always satisfactory and the overall quality cannot compare with more recent issues. Even so Richter's account is dedicated and often dramatic, and the soloists are good, with Fischer-Dieskau standing out. This set is available also in

an album together with the *St John Passion*, and Richter's admirers may feel this a good investment in the medium price-range (see above).

Karajan's Bach, always polished, grows smoother still with the years. His account of the *St Matthew Passion* is plainly aimed at devotees – of Karajan as much as of Bach. The result, concentrated in refinement, faithfully reflects the live performances which he has given in Berlin. With excellent singing and playing and with reverberant recording moulded to the interpretation, it represents an individual view pursued in the face of the current fashion, and many will enjoy it.

The selection from Münchinger's set has been well made, with the opening and closing choruses framing groups of numbers which are so arranged as to give the flavour of the whole work. Having selections from the dedicatedly authentic account of Harnoncourt, however, somehow only underlines the relative disappointment of the solo singing, technically fine, but at times sounding detached.

COLLECTIONS

Mass in B minor: Agnus Dei; Qui sedes. St John Passion: All is fulfilled. St Matthew Passion: Grief for sin.

(M) *** Decca Ace of Diamonds SDD 286. Kathleen Ferrier (contralto), London Philharmonic Orchestra, Sir Adrian Boult – HANDEL: *Arias.****

In the early days of stereo Sir Adrian Boult and the LPO with devotion and great skill rerecorded the accompaniments for these arias so that the new sound completely masked the old. It is splendid to hear Kathleen Ferrier's voice (and this was one of her finest records) enhanced by the greater warmth and beauty of the orchestra in stereo, and all who participated are to be congratulated on the complete artistic and technical success of this fine disc.

'The world of Bach': (i) *Brandenburg concerto No. 2 in F major, B W V 1047; Orchestral suite No. 2 in B minor, B W V 1067: Badinerie; Orchestral suite No. 3 in D major, B W V 1068: Air.* (ii) *Italian concerto, BWV 971:* 1st movement. (iii) *Toccata and fugue in D minor, B W V 565.* (iv) *Cantata No. 147: Jesu, joy of man's desiring.* (v) *Cantata No. 208: Sheep may safely graze.* (i; vi) *Christmas oratorio, B W V 248: Jauchzet, Frohlocket.* (vii) *Mass in B minor, B W V 232: Agnus Dei.* (i; viii) *St Matthew Passion, B W V 244: Wir setzen uns mit Tränen nieder* (chorus).

(B) *** Decca SPA 322. (i) Stuttgart Chamber Orchestra, Karl Münchinger; (ii) George Malcolm (harpsichord); (iii) Karl Richter (organ); (iv) St John's College, Cambridge, Choir, George Guest; (v) Kirsten Flagstad (soprano), London Philharmonic Orchestra, Sir Adrian Boult; (vi) Lübecker Cantorei; (vii) Kathleen Ferrier (contralto), London Philharmonic Orchestra, Sir Adrian Boult; (viii) Stuttgart Hymnus Boys' Choir.

A characteristically skilful Decca anthology that is even more than the sum of its parts, which itself is considerable. The juxtaposition of pieces is managed with perfect taste so that each seems to follow on spontaneously. The *Second Brandenburg concerto* and the other short orchestral items show the Stuttgart team at their best, but the real highlights here are vocal, notably Kathleen Ferrier's beautiful contribution, and the oratorio excerpts. The recording is consistently good throughout and often very good indeed. A most

satisfying concert in its own right, but one that should tempt inexperienced listeners to explore further.

ARRANGEMENTS

Chorale prelude: Wir glauben all'an einen Gott ('Giant' fugue), B W V 680. Easter cantata, B W V 4: Chorale. Geistliches Lied No. 51: Mein Jesu, B W V 487. Passacaglia and fugue in C minor, B W V 582. Toccata and fugue in D minor, B W V 565. Well-tempered Clavier, Book 1: Prelude No. 8 in E flat minor, B W V 853 (all orch. Stokowski).

** (*) Decca Phase 4 PFS 4278. Czech Philharmonic Orchestra, Leopold Stokowski.

Stokowski's flamboyant arrangements of Bach organ works inspired some of the Philadelphia Orchestra's ripest records in the old days of 78 discs. Here with flamboyant Phase Four sound to match, big, bold and reverberant, the results are massively satisfying for anyone prepared to forget his purist conscience for a moment. Stokowski, over ninety, challenges his players in expansive tempi, but the results are passionate in concentration.

Fugues: in A minor, B W V 543; in C major, B W V 564; in C minor, B W V 549; in D major, B W V 532; in E flat minor ('St Anne'), B W V 522; in G minor ('Great'), B W V 542; in G minor ('Little'), B W V 578 (all orch. Harris).

** RCA Quadradisc ARD 1 0026. Philadelphia Orchestra, Eugene Ormandy.

Orchestral arrangements of Bach organ music have long been popular in Philadelphia. If this collection of fugues is not so flamboyant as Stokowski's Phase Four record, the opulent Philadelphia sound is well suited to a quadraphonic demonstration disc.

'*Switched-on Bach*' (electronic realizations by Walter Carlos and Benjamin Folkman): *Brandenburg concerto No. 3 in G major. Cantata No. 29: Sinfonia. Cantata No. 147: Jesu, joy of man's desiring. Chorale prelude: Wachet auf. Suite No. 3 in D major: Air. 2-part inventions in B flat major; D minor; F major. The Well-tempered Clavier: Preludes and fugues Nos. 2 in C minor; 7 in E flat major.*
*** CBS Quadraphonic MQ 31018; Stereo 63501. Walter Carlos (Moog synthesizer).

The Moog Synthesizer has now become quite an accepted item in the recording studio, but this highly individual record was the one which above all established Moog's claims as a popularizer in the classical field. The purist will certainly wince, but almost any of these arrangements for computer sound has a hypnotic quality, attested by the phenomenal success the disc had in America and by the way that non-Bachians tend to take to it. The interpretation of the *Third Brandenburg* is allegedly based – with all the subtleties of *rubato* and phrasing – on two classic recordings of the past, though Mr Carlos rightly takes ultimate responsibility. The stereo effects are elaborate, many of them not just gimmicks but attempts to clarify what Bach wrote without altering his notes. In most ways this is a brilliantly successful record, the best of its kind.

If the ordinary stereo disc is entertaining, the new quadraphonic version is even more so. This is unashamed 'surround-sound', managed with great flair, particularly on side two where after an almost unnerving circular effect the *Fugue in C minor* (from the *Well-tempered Clavier*) makes its entry spectacularly with one entry to each loudspeaker. Later

the elaborate cadenza which forms the link between the two movements of the *Third Brandenburg concerto* shows just what quad can do when the creative artist in charge shows intelligence, wit and skill in equal proportions. A fascinating demonstration disc for the new medium.

'*Switched-on Bach*', *Vol. 2* (electronic realizations): *Brandenburg concerto No. 5 in D major. Suite No. 2 in B minor: Badinerie; Minuet; Bourrée. Two-part inventions in A minor, BWV 783 and 784. Anna Magdalena Notebook: Musette in D major; Minuet in G major; Bist du bei mir; March in D major. Cantata No. 308: Sheep may safely graze.*
** (*) CBS 65974. Walter Carlos (Moog synthesizer).

Walter Carlos was the first to use the Moog Synthesizer with real imagination, and Volume 2 of *Switched-on Bach* confirms that he remains unequalled by those who have followed the fashion he initiated, even if some of the slow items like *Sheep may safely graze* become too sweet for comfort. Once again stereo separation is wittily used in the recording.

'*Bach for band*': *Bist du bei mir. Cantata No. 29: Sinfonia. Cantata No. 80: Chorales. Chorale prelude: Wachet auf. Fugues: in E minor; G minor. Minuet in G major. Three-part invention in D major. Suite No. 2 in B minor: Badinerie. Suite No. 3 in D major: Air. Toccata and fugue in D minor, BWV 565* (all arr. Williams).
** CBS Quadraphonic MQ 31126. London Symphonic Band, Gerallt Williams.

There are some fascinating sounds here. The playing has great vigour and impulse, and if the wind sonorities have not the sumptuousness of Stokowski's orchestral Bach (partly because of a certain harshness in the CBS recording) the sheer colour of the sound is impressive. Perhaps surprisingly it is the gentler numbers one remembers most readily, although the greater part of the collection is loud and spectacular. The quadraphonic version is not gimmicky but adds to the resonance attractively.

The Bach family: collections

Bach, C. P. E.
(1714–88; see also above)

Bach, J. B.
(1715–39)

Bach, J. C.
(1735–82; see also above)

Bach, J. C. F.
(1732–95)

Bach, J. L.
(1677–1741)

Bach, W. F.
(1710–84)

BACH, C. P. E. *Double concerto for harpsichord, fortepiano and orchestra in E flat major.*

BACH, J. C. *Sinfonia concertante in F major for oboe, violoncello and orchestra.*

BACH, W. F. *Double concerto for 2 harpsichords and orchestra in E flat major.*

* (*) Telefunken SAWT 9490-A. Soloists with Leonhardt Consort, Gustav Leonhardt.

The best piece here is undoubtedly the C. P. E. Bach *Concerto for harpsichord*

and fortepiano. But this depends a good deal for its effect on a convincing balance between the soloists, and that has not been very well managed here. The harpsichord image tends to overwhelm its companion, except in the gentler musical exchanges. The balance is better in J. C. Bach's *Sinfonia concertante* in which the soloists are oboe and cello; it is played with some degree of charm, especially the final minuet. Unfortunately the longest work, W. F. Bach's *Double harpsichord concerto*, is square and uninspiring, and it is not helped by the jangly harpsichord recording and a tendency for over-bright strings. But the recording is generally good.

BACH, J. C. F. *Sinfonia in E flat major.*

BACH, J. L. *Suite in G major.*

BACH, W. F. *Harpsichord concerto in F minor; Sinfonia in F major.*

** (*) Philips 6500 071. English Chamber Orchestra, Raymond Leppard.

This came from a Philips album devoted to the Bach family. By far the most interesting pieces here are those by Wilhelm Friedemann; his *Harpsichord concerto* is impeccably played by Raymond Leppard and no less impeccably recorded. A useful disc, even if neither of the pieces by J. C. F. and Johann Ludwig are masterpieces.

BACH, J. C. F. (i) *Sextet in C major for oboe, violin, 2 horns, violoncello and harpsichord.*

BACH, J. C. (i) *Quintets: in E flat major, Op. 11/4; in D major, Op. 11/6* (for flute, oboe, violin, viola, cello).

BACH, W. F. (ii) *5 Polonaises for harpsichord.*

(B) ** Turnabout TV 34026S. (i) Günter Kehr Ensemble; (ii) Helma Elsner (harpsichord).

None of these works is well-known, but each shows originality of style and the independent musical personality of its composer. Johann Christian's *Quintets* have Italianate melodic felicity and Wilhelm's *Polonaises* have an improvisatory spontaneity. Johann Christoph's *Sextet* is forward-looking and strikingly diverse in content. All the works here are played with spirit, and the atmospheric stereo helps to recommend this excellent anthology.

Badings, Henk
(born 1907)

Octet.
  (M) *** Decca Ace of Diamonds SDD 316. Vienna Octet – WELLESZ: *Octet.****

The Dutch composer Henk Badings, much admired during the 1950s, has fallen out of favour. Though not a major figure, he is a composer of distinct talents, and this example of his art well rewards curiosity. It is expertly played and recorded, and the disc is of particular value in that it offers Egon Wellesz's inventive *Octet*, commissioned by these artists.

Baines, William
(1899–1922)

Coloured leaves; Paradise gardens; 7 Preludes; Silverpoints; Twilight pieces.
  ** Lyrita SRCS 60. Eric Parkin (piano).

William Baines came from Yorkshire and died in his early twenties. These small miniatures show a very considerable talent, with a refined harmonic palette. The influence of Delius, Cyril Scott and

others can be discerned, but some of these pieces deserve wider recognition and are quite powerful and individual. Eric Parkin plays persuasively but the recording is a little pale and shallow. None the less, this disc is well worth attention.

Balakirev, Mily
(1837–1910)

Symphony No. 1 in C major.
  (M) *** HMV SXLP 30171. Royal Philharmonic Orchestra, Sir Thomas Beecham – BORODIN: *Polovtsian dances.****

A welcome reissue of Beecham's fine performance, still on HMV's medium-price label, but now given the sizeable bonus of the *Polovtsian dances*. This is as fine a symphony as ever came from Russia, with a startlingly original first movement, a wonderfully lyrical slow movement, a sparkling scherzo and a breezy finale. It is an extended piece, but Balakirev's material and treatment can easily sustain the length, particularly when the performance is as glowing as Beecham's. Admittedly Karajan was more dynamic and passionate in his old recording, but Beecham offers just as many felicities and the recording has responded well to EMI's face-lift, which provides warm textures and a sparkle without edginess.

Thamar (symphonic poem).
  (B) ** Decca Eclipse ECS 642. Suisse Romande Orchestra, Ernest Ansermet – GLAZOUNOV: *The Seasons.** (*)

Balakirev's symphonic poem, based on a ballad by Lermontov, tells of the beautiful Queen Thamar who lives in a high castle built on the banks of a dangerous river torrent. Lured to the castle by the beauty of her siren call her lovers' bodies are cast to their fate in the raging waters as dawn breaks. Balakirev's piece is suitably melodramatic in character, but in the last resort it lacks melodic distinction. Ansermet's performance is characteristically atmospheric, and the recording, although dated, is more than adequate.

Islamey (oriental fantasy).
(M) *** Decca Ace of Diamonds SDD 181. Julius Katchen (piano) – RACHMANINOV: *Piano concerto No. 2.** (*)

Katchen's almost unbelievable technique is well demonstrated in Balakirev's fantasia. Even in an age of technicians few pianists could play the piece like this. The recording is clean and atmospheric in Decca's best manner.

Reminiscences of Glinka's opera 'A Life for the Tsar' (fantasy for piano).
*** RCA SB 6815. Earl Wild (piano) – D'ALBERT: *Scherzo*; MEDTNER: *Improvisation*; SCHARWENKA: *Piano concerto No. 1.***

A stunning performance of Balakirev's fantasy which does for Glinka what Liszt did for a host of operatic composers. Earl Wild's virtuosity seems to know no bounds, and his playing of the Scharwenka *Concerto* with which this is coupled is quite breathtaking.

Balfe, Michael
(1808–70)

The Bohemian Girl (opera in 3 acts): highlights.
** HMV CSD 3651. Veronica Dunne (soprano), Uel Deane (tenor), Eric Hinds (baritone), Orchestra,

Havelock Nelson – BENEDICT: *The Lily of Killarney*; WALLACE: *Maritana.***

This disc enterprisingly collects together music from three operas, two by Irish composers and the third set in Ireland, which some wag has cynically christened 'the Irish *Ring*'. It is proper that a whole side should be given to Balfe's *Bohemian Girl*, for this is the most famous of the three. First staged at Drury Lane in 1843, it has been often revived, and was a favourite of Sir Thomas Beecham. The music is corny but so sure of itself that when sung and played with gusto it has an undeniable success in the theatre. The conductor here well understands this and the *Overture, Waltz* and *Galop* are very successful indeed. The singing is more variable: Eric Hinds makes a suitably dolorous Count, Veronica Dunne is better in the second verse of the famous *I dreamt that I dwelt* than she is in the first (which she oversings), and the tenor is lyrically-minded if somewhat effete. But the anthology on this disc reminds us that these were the only British operas to hold the stage between Arne and Sullivan, and for those who can listen with tongue in cheek, this is irresistible. The recording, made in Dublin, has clarity and a splendid overall bloom.

Banks, Don
(born 1923)

Violin concerto.
*** Argo ZRG 715. Yfrah Neaman (violin), Royal Philharmonic Orchestra, Norman Del Mar – FRICKER: *Violin concerto.***

Don Banks is an Australian composer who lived for many years in London before recently returning to his homeland to take up an academic post. This enterprising British Council-sponsored disc rather appropriately couples his violin concerto with one by a British composer, Fricker, who has also spent a period of his musical life abroad, in America. Bank's *Concerto* is a strong and ambitious work. Although he is a committed serialist the genre is used as a basis for his own special brand of lyricism. A big orchestra is involved, but relatively gently, exploiting the most delicate textures, to which the conductor responds sensitively. The work is beautifully played by the soloist, Yfrah Neaman, whom we hear too seldom on disc, and with excellent recording this can be cordially recommended.

Barber, Samuel
(born 1910)

Adagio for strings, Op. 11.
(B) ** RCA Victrola VICS 1540. Strings of Boston Symphony Orchestra, Charles Munch – ELGAR: *Introduction and allegro*; TCHAIKOVSKY: *Serenade.***

The Boston performance is finely played and well recorded. It was Toscanini who made this movement of a string quartet famous in its present form for full string orchestra, and if Munch's account lacks the final intensity of Toscanini's own original record, it remains very effective when the stereo is so warm, and the playing so committed. Other versions of the work are available on Philips Universo 6580 045 (by I Musici, within a concert of twentieth-century string music) and Vanguard VSD 2126 (in a concert called *Nocturne*), although in the latter the performance is somewhat too relaxed.

(i) *Piano concerto, Op. 38;* (ii) *Violin concerto, Op. 14.*

(M) ** (*) CBS Classics 61621. (i) John Browning (piano), Cleveland Orchestra, George Szell; (ii) Isaac Stern (violin), New York Philharmonic Orchestra, Leonard Bernstein.

Barber's career has a number of parallels with that of William Walton: a vein of acid-tinged romanticism; comparatively sparse output, mainly of major works; a comparative failure to maintain full intensity in later work. The *Piano concerto*, written for John Browning, is one of those later works, and though technically it is most impressive and the seriousness cannot be denied, it never quite adds up to the sum of its parts. The seven-in-a-bar finale is the most immediately attractive movement, and will provide firm enjoyment from the start; the weighty first movement and intermezzo-like middle movement improve on acquaintance. The *Violin concerto* is more consistently inspired. It has warmth, freshness and humanity, and the slow movement is genuinely beautiful. Both performances here are of superlative quality, and if the characteristic CBS forward balance for the soloists is less than ideal, the recording is otherwise good. An impressive disc, recommended to all who care about twentieth-century music.

Bartók, Béla
(1881–1945)

Concerto for orchestra.
*** HMV ASD 3046. Berlin Philharmonic Orchestra, Herbert von Karajan.
*** CBS Quadraphonic MQ 32132; ** (*) Stereo 73161. New York Philharmonic Orchestra, Pierre Boulez.

** (*) DGG SLPM 139003. Berlin Philharmonic Orchestra, Herbert von Karajan.
(B) ** Classics for Pleasure CFP 176. London Philharmonic Orchestra, John Pritchard.

Comparison between Karajan's two performances (the earlier one made as recently as 1966) shows how little this conductor's view of the score has changed. The advantage of the new disc comes mainly in the recording. The earlier DGG was first-class by any standards, but the newer EMI sound is even more opulent and atmospheric. This suits Karajan's approach. The Berlin Philharmonic, in superb form on both discs, draws a performance that is rich, romantic and smooth – for some ears perhaps excessively so. Karajan is right in treating Bartók emotionally, but the comparison with Solti (see below) immediately points the contrast between Berlin romanticism and earthy red-blooded Hungarian passion. Both conductors allow themselves a fair degree of *rubato*, but Solti's is linked with the Hungarian folk-song idiom where Karajan's moulding of phrases is essentially of the German tradition. Yet with such magnificent recording (clearly superior to the Decca) the work's atmosphere comes over magically and there is rather more sparkle than in the earlier DGG version.

Though Boulez does not draw such precise ensemble from his New York players as many of his rivals do with other orchestras in this virtuoso music, this is an urgent, highly enjoyable performance, very much more consciously expressive than the accounts of the piece that he has directed live in London. The sessions were set up with quadraphonic sound very much in mind, and in the quadraphonic version the orchestra is made to completely surround the listener. But rather than sounding gimmicky or indeed oppressive, the effect is to increase one's involvement in the music. The internal orchestral clarity is achieved without even a hint of artificial separation, and in many places the double antiphony serves the composer admirably, not least in the finale, where it seems even to increase the tension. Whatever one's preconceptions, the end justifies the means and the result is enormously exciting. A pity the violin sound is a bit sharp-edged, for otherwise the orchestral quality is of the highest standard in the quadraphonic pressing.

Pritchard's is a clean, direct performance, very well played, if without any special sense of atmosphere. The brilliantly clear recording makes its effect and the confident wind playing is very striking in the *Allegretto*. But in the last resort the interpretation has not the subtlety and sense of mystery that make Haitink's Concertgebouw recording so memorable. This costs only slightly more and offers a bonus in the *Dance suite* (see below).

Concerto for orchestra; Dance suite.
*** Decca SXL 6212. London Symphony Orchestra, Sir Georg Solti.
(M) *** Philips Universo 6580 036. Concertgebouw Orchestra, Bernard Haitink.

Solti has become so much a part of the English musical scene one tends to forget his Hungarian upbringing. You could hardly ignore it after hearing this record, which gives Bartók's last-period lyricism the inflections of genuine Hungarian folk-song. This in effect means that Solti allows himself all sorts of *rubato* effects not strictly marked in the score, but the fire and intensity behind his interpretation come through in magnificent playing from the LSO from first bar to last. The inclusion of a fill-up, particularly one so generous as the *Dance suite*, is most welcome. The title *Dance suite* may suggest something rather trivial, but the beauty of Bartók's inspiration in this product of the early twenties (generally his most dissonant period) lies in the way that one can appreciate it on many different levels. Solti's performance has all the fire and passion one could want. The brilliant recording, outstanding in its day, shows its age a little in the string sound, but in all other respects is of high quality.

Haitink's record served to introduce Philip's excellent middle-price Universo label, and it made an auspicious start, for even at full price this had been near the top of the list of recommendations. The orchestral playing is of very high quality and the recording, always truthful and atmospheric, is now clear too, with a brighter texture than on the original, full-priced disc. Immediately at the opening of the *Concerto for orchestra* one is aware of the tension in the orchestral playing, and throughout Haitink shows subtlety as well as drama in his interpretation. His touch of emotional restraint brings a special character to the *Elegy* and the close of the *Allegretto*. Thus the contrasts of the furious bravura of the opening of the finale and the splendour of the work's closing pages are the more telling. There is superb playing and fine recording too in the *Dance suite*, which has a natural rhythmic impulse. A highly recommendable coupling and a genuine bargain.

Piano concertos Nos. 1 in A major; 2 in G major; 3 in E major; Rhapsody for piano and orchestra, Op. 1.
  (M) ** (*) DGG Privilege 2726 005 (2 discs). Géza Anda (piano), Berlin Radio Symphony Orchestra, Ferenc Fricsay.

Anda's performances of the Bartók *Concertos* have acquired something like classic status. In a bargain coupling like this they should not be missed – refined yet urgent, incisive but red-blooded too. The recording is excellent for its age, although the balance sometimes unduly favours the piano.

Piano concerto No. 1 in A major.
  (B) ** Turnabout TV 34065S. György Sándor (piano), South-West German Radio Orchestra, Rolf Reinhardt – STRAVINSKY: *Concerto.***

Sándor's is a highly idiomatic account of the *First Concerto*, with an excellent combination of Bartókian bite and sensitive phrasing. His fire carries one along in a work which is not the easiest to control. The playing of the South-West German Radio Orchestra is not always perfect in ensemble, but it has guts and that is what really matters. The recording favours the piano, but is far more vivid than one might expect.

Piano concerto No. 1 in A major; Piano concerto No. 3 in E major.
  *** HMV ASD 2476. Daniel Barenboim (piano), New Philharmonia Orchestra, Pierre Boulez.

CBS 'lent' Boulez to EMI for this record in repayment for the lending of Barenboim for Boulez's CBS record of Berg's *Chamber concerto*. EMI obviously had the better of that deal, and though these are not the most polished performances of the concertos ever recorded, they have a consistent dynamism stemming from a collaboration which brought mutual stimulus. In the event it is Barenboim who, rather surprisingly, seems to emerge the dominant partner. From Boulez one expects poised, clinical interpretations of Bartók, bitingly accurate, where here the orchestra enters with enormous gusto into the task of following the mercurial Barenboim. In the *First Concerto*, long regarded as barbaric, there is a striking element of humour entirely apt for Bartók's mellowed Indian summer, the jazz rhythms have a natural expressiveness, and again there is humour. The hymn-like slow movement has all the still intensity one expects of Barenboim, though in fact the tempo is not particularly slow. Warm EMI recording.

Piano concerto No. 2 in G major.
  (B) ** Turnabout TV 34036S. György
  Sándor (piano), Vienna Symphony
  Orchestra, Michael Gielen – *Sonata for two pianos and percussion.** (*)
  * (*) HMV ASD 2744. Sviatoslav
  Richter (piano), Orchestre de
  Paris, Lorin Maazel – PROKOFIEV: *Piano concerto No. 5.** (*)

Sándor (who was the first pianist ever to record the *Third Concerto* in the days of 78) gives a strong, idiomatic account of a concerto which if anything is even more difficult to interpret than No. 1. The coupling, a similarly compelling account of the *Sonata for two pianos and percussion*, would make a splendid bargain-label issue, but unfortunately the recording quality rather lets it down – too reverberant to allow Bartók's detail to bite properly.

Richter, playing here with less than his usual incisiveness, is less convincing than either Anda or Sándor, but with rich recording quality anyone who wants this particular coupling should not be too disappointed.

Piano concerto No. 3 in E major.
  *** Decca SXL 6209. Julius Katchen
  (piano), London Symphony Orchestra, Istvan Kertesz – RAVEL:
  *Concerto.****

Katchen first recorded the *Third Concerto* in the early days of LP, and very impressive his performance was, but this is finer still in every way, not least in the magnificent orchestral accompaniment provided by the LSO under Kertesz, here at his most compelling in his native Hungarian music. Katchen, who sometimes seemed a hard, even restless pianist, here matches the moods of the movements exactly. The night music of the middle movement is done with intensity but no mannerism, and the finale brings real exuberance. The recording is outstandingly good. With an outstanding version of the Ravel on the reverse it is one of the best records Katchen ever made.

(i) *Piano concerto No. 3 in E major;* (ii)
Viola concerto, Op. posth.
  (B) * (*) Turnabout TV 34483S. (i)
  György Sándor (piano), Vienna
  Pro Musica Orchestra, Michael
  Gielen; (ii) Ulrich Koch (viola),
  Radio Luxembourg Orchestra,
  Alois Springer.

Sándor is a Bartokian through and through, but he is let down here by indifferent accompaniment and mushy recording. The posthumous *Viola Concerto*, completed by Tibor Szerly, suffers from similar faults, and there the soloist – by no means as fine an artist as Sándor – is recorded unduly close. A possible recommendation at bargain price, but no more.

(i; iii) *Violin concerto No. 1, Op. posth.;*
(ii; iii) *Rhapsodies for violin and orchestra Nos. 1 and 2.*
  (B) (*) Turnabout TV 34484S. (i)
  Georg Egger (violin); (ii) Susanne
  Lautenbacher (violin); (iii) Radio
  Luxembourg Orchestra, Alois
  Springer.

The closeness of the soloists, noted on Turnabout's other Bartók concerto issues, is extreme enough here to preclude a recommendation, despite Lautenbacher's and Egger's warmly expressive playing. If the *First Violin concerto* is needed, there is a Hungarian import (SLPX 11314) which is much more recommendable than this.

Violin concerto No. 2 in B minor.
> *** HMV ASD 3014. Itzhak Perlman (violin), London Symphony Orchestra, André Previn.
> (M) *** Supraphon SUAST 50696. André Gertler (violin), Czech Philharmonic Orchestra, Karel Ančerl.

Perlman's is a superb performance, totally committed and full of youthful urgency, with the sense of spontaneity that comes more readily when performers have already worked together on the music in the concert hall. The contrasts are fearlessly achieved by both soloist and orchestra, with everyone relishing virtuosity in the outer movements. The slow movement is deliberately understated by the soloist, with the fragmentation of the theme lightly touched in, but even there the orchestra has its passionate comments. Though the disc is rather short measure with no coupling, no finer version of this masterly concerto has ever been available. The recording is rich and lively.

André Gertler's performance strikes a happy balance between romanticism and technical brilliance, and the Czech accompaniment is strikingly idiomatic. The opening is light in style with nice snapping rhythms and crisp accentuation, and in the slow movement Gertler – for long a dedicated Bartók interpreter – treats the music affectingly as a simple song. In the finale he is most successful in bringing out the scherzando humour. Though the shading of tone colour and the overall compulsion cannot quite compare with Perlman, this is in every way a keen competitor, even with no allowance made for price. At medium price – though with no fill-up – and with good atmospheric recording, no one should disregard it.

Violin concerto No. 2 in B minor; Rhapsody No. 1 for violin and orchestra.

> *** Philips 6500 021. Henryk Szeryng (violin), Concertgebouw Orchestra, Bernard Haitink.

Szeryng's recording of the *Concerto* is a strong one. The balance is not absolutely ideal (Szeryng is a bit forward in relation to the orchestra) but such is the conviction of his performance that reservations pale. Haitink keeps a firm grip on proceedings and there is a genuine sense of momentum and impetus about the performance that is really exciting. The orchestra play with their accustomed panache and brilliance, and yet there is no lack of mystery in the more reflective passages of the first movement or in the marvellously poetic slow movement. The recording is good.

(i; ii) Violin concerto No. 2 in B minor; (i; iii) Contrasts for clarinet, violin and piano.

> (B) * (*) Turnabout TV 34480S. (i) Susanne Lautenbacher (violin); (ii) Radio Luxembourg Orchestra, Alois Springer; (iii) Hans Lemser (clarinet), Bernard Kontarsky (piano).

Susanne Lautenbacher's playing of Bartók is warmly expressive, and the conviction of her playing is on the whole enhanced by the closeness of the violin in the recording. It is not always a subtle performance, but at bargain price it can be recommended, imaginatively coupled with the elusive but rewarding work that Bartók wrote at about the same time for Szigeti and Benny Goodman.

Dance suite; 2 Portraits, Op. 5; Rumanian dances, Nos. 1–7.

> ** Decca SXL 6121. Suisse Romande Orchestra, Ernest Ansermet.

If anything, Ansermet is too sensitive, too refined in the *Dance suite,* but it goes without saying that the Decca recording is excellent, and the *2 Portraits, Op. 5* (the first of which is now better known as the first movement of the rediscovered *Violin concerto No. 1*) plus the *Rumanian dances* make an excellent coupling.

Divertimento for strings.

(M) *** Decca Ace of Diamonds SDD 417. Moscow Chamber Orchestra, Rudolf Barshai – VIVALDI: *L'Estro armonico excerpts*.**

The Moscow Chamber Orchestra is a splendid group of players, and ensemble and intonation here are faultless. This is a performance of extreme brilliance, and if emotionally it is driven very hard, this is quite appropriate in such music. The recording is very bright, and can be made to yield realistic results.

Divertimento for strings; Music for strings, percussion and celesta.

*** Argo ZRG 657. Academy of St Martin-in-the-Fields, Neville Marriner.
** (*) HMV ASD 2670. English Chamber Orchestra, Daniel Barenboim.

Marriner and the St Martin's Academy provide a superlative Bartók record. The composer originally intended the *Music for strings, percussion and celesta* to be performed by a chamber-sized orchestra, and certainly, compared with the recorded performances using full orchestras (Solti's, Boulez's and Haitink's, all impressive), this one reveals extra detail, extra expressiveness, extra care for tonal and dynamic nuances. There is of course a comparative lack of body in some of the big climaxes, but that is not a big price to pay. Marriner, for example, observes meticulously in the slow opening fugue the instruction to keep the music down to a pianissimo as far as bar 26, and there is no sense of cold, uncommitted playing. Quite the opposite. In the second move-

ment the terracing of subtly different tempi is much more adeptly managed than usual, and all the playing reflects the working together beforehand in democratic conference which generally precedes a St Martin's performance. The *Divertimento* is given a similarly vivid performance, and the recording is outstandingly good.

The contrasts between Barenboim and Marriner are very clearly marked. They are most obvious in the *Divertimento*, where Barenboim's earthiness contrasts with the point and refinement of Marriner. Ensemble is wilder, but the results are just as convincing. In the *Music for strings* Barenboim's romanticism will be too extreme for some, with a very slow expressive opening fugue and wild urgency in second and fourth movements. If the *Divertimento* is your first concern, then this could be a first choice even over Marriner. The recording is rich and immediate.

2 Images, Op. 10; 4 Orchestral pieces, Op. 12; (i) 2 Portraits, Op. 5.

** (*) Philips 6500 781. Frankfurt Radio Symphony Orchestra, Eliahu Inbal, (i) with Andreas Röhn (violin).

The star of this record is Andreas Röhn, who plays with moving tenderness and intensity in the first of the *Two Portraits*. This is of course identical with the opening movement of the *First Violin concerto*. The other performances are all good ones. The wind playing is rather finer than the string sound, which is not so rich as some more famous orchestras, but with refined recording the *Two Images* are made to sound ravishingly atmospheric.

(i; ii) *The Miraculous Mandarin* (ballet): complete recording; (i) *Dance suite*.

** CBS Quadraphonic MQ 31368;
Stereo 73031. (i) New York Philharmonic Orchestra, Pierre Boulez; (ii) Schola Cantorum.

Here is clear proof of Boulez's remark
that whereas British players have to be
coaxed into playing with deep expressiveness, New York players do it with very
little encouragement indeed. This is a far
more romantic-sounding version of the
Miraculous Mandarin ballet than Dorati's
on Philips. Some will prefer it on that
account, though it has the disadvantage
of a poorly placed turnover, and the
Dance suite is given a markedly less
incisive performance than those of the
principal rivals, Solti and Haitink. The
quadraphonic version adds atmosphere
and sonority without altering the basic
sound picture.

(i; ii) *The Miraculous Mandarin* (ballet): complete recording; (i) *Divertimento for strings*.
** (*) Philips SAL 3569. (i) BBC
Symphony Orchestra, Antal Dorati; (ii) BBC Chorus.

The Miraculous Mandarin has always
been one of Dorati's favourite concert-
pieces, and during his regime at the
BBC he directed the orchestra in it many
times. Here, unlike many of his competitors on record, he gives the complete
ballet instead of the usual concert version
which omits much of the final scene.
Philips have even managed to include the
much longer work on a single side,
though the last degree of brilliance in
recording quality has been a little blunted.
The performance is as brilliant as anyone
could want, and on the reverse, apart
from a slightly too steady account of the
finale, the *Divertimento* is interpreted
with similar red-blooded Hungarian
passion. Whatever Dorati did not do for
the BBC Orchestra he certainly taught
them to play Bartók with an idiomatic
accent.

*The Miraculous Mandarin: suite; Music
for strings, percussion and celesta.*
*** Decca SXL 6111. London Symphony Orchestra, Sir Georg Solti.

Solti and the LSO at their very finest,
and how fine that is. The streak of
ruthlessness in Solti's make-up that sometimes mars performances of less barbaric
music is here given full rein in *The
Miraculous Mandarin suite*, and that same
unrelenting urgency makes this a most
exciting account of the *Music for strings,
percussion and celesta*. For all the nervous
drive Solti's control of dynamic and
rhythm is most precise, though he loses
some of the mystery of the weird third
movement. The recording is superb.

*The Miraculous Mandarin: suite; The
Wooden Prince: suite.*
(B) ** Turnabout TV 34086S. South-
West German Radio Orchestra,
Baden-Baden, Rolf Reinhardt.

A valuable coupling of the first recording in stereo of the *Miraculous Mandarin
suite* and the first version ever of the
Wooden Prince music. *The Wooden Prince*
was written soon after the opera *Bluebeard's Castle* and still reflects Bartók's
early dalliance with exotic orchestral
effects after Strauss and Debussy. This
suite, chosen by the composer himself,
provides about half the full ballet score,
and one suspects that but for the very
large orchestra it would have become a
popular repertory piece. The *Miraculous
Mandarin* is altogether tougher. Reinhardt's performance has not the bite and
attack of Solti's, but no one who fancies
the coupling need be deterred. Despite
some odd balance the recording is quite
acceptable.

*Music for strings, percussion and
celesta* (see also above under *Divertimento* and *Miraculous Mandarin*).
** (*) Philips 6500 015. Concertge-

76

bouw Orchestra, Bernard Haitink – KODÁLY: *Háry János*.** (*)

** (*) CBS 72652. BBC Symphony Orchestra, Pierre Boulez – STRAVINSKY: *Firebird suite*.***

** (*) DGG 2530 065. Berlin Philharmonic Orchestra, Herbert von Karajan – STRAVINSKY: *Apollo*.** (*)

* (*) HMV ASD 2964. Leningrad Philharmonic Orchestra, Yevgeny Mravinsky – HONEGGER: *Symphony No. 3*.** (*)

Boulez's version is one of his finest records. He gives an admirably hushed account of the opening and conveys its sense of mystery, while the quick movements have plenty of attack and rhythmic vitality. The BBC Symphony Orchestra respond with genuine enthusiasm and their playing is often most sensitive. Unfortunately the recording, though warm and lively, suffers from the artificial balance sometimes favoured by CBS, so that in the second movement a jumbo piano suddenly looms into the foreground, and the perspective elsewhere is not always ideal. However, for those who can overlook this, there are genuine rewards.

Haitink does not secure quite the same hushed intensity at the opening of the first movement as does Boulez. Nonetheless his performance as a whole is the more satisfying and musically perceptive. The splendid playing of the Concertgebouw Orchestra is an added inducement to investigate this account, and the Philips recording, though it robs the strings of some of their bloom (one feels the sound should expand a bit more), is still vastly superior to the CBS. The balance is musically judged and the detail is well placed. No doubt couplings will be the crucial issue for most collectors.

Karajan recorded this work originally in the days of 78, and since then his view of it has remained essentially romantic.

He avoids undue expressiveness in the opening slow fugue (except in a big *rallentando* at the end), but the third movement is given a performance in soft focus. Nonetheless the playing of the Berlin strings is a delight to the ear, and with an outstanding coupling – a luxuriant version of Stravinsky's *Apollo* – this is still a viable version, beautifully recorded.

For once Mravinsky and the Leningrad Orchestra give a disappointing performance. This recording, made live at a winter concert in Leningrad to the accompaniment of coughing, shows surprisingly slack ensemble, and even a lack of urgency – a feeling in the last movement that another rehearsal was needed. The Honegger coupling is far finer.

(i) *Music for strings, percussion and celesta*: (ii) *Cantata Profana (The Enchanted Stag)*.

(B) * (*) Turnabout TV 34382S. (i) Philharmonia Hungarica, Thomas Ungar; (ii) Murray Dickie (tenor), Edmond Hurshell (baritone), Vienna Chamber Choir, Vienna Symphony Orchestra, Heinrich Hollreiser.

This is a generous and convenient coupling on a cheap label of two important Bartók works, the cantata a rarity. Sung in English, it is effectively presented by Hollreiser, though the recording shows its age. The *Music for strings* is less successful, an indifferent performance when there are many fine ones available.

Rhapsody for piano and orchestra.

(B) ** Turnabout TV 34130S. György Sándor (piano), South-West German Radio Orchestra, Rolf Reinhardt – HONEGGER: *Concertino*; JANÁČEK: *Concertino*; STRAVINSKY: *Capriccio*.**

77

Bartók's *Rhapsody*, his Op. 1, shows him still influenced by Liszt's idea of Hungarian music. The warmly romantic orchestration is not given its full weight in a rather thin-sounding recording, but the reverberation helps to smooth things over, and Sándor's performance is magnificently virile. Like the other short piano concertos on this disc, this is a rarity that deserves wider circulation.

2 Rhapsodies for violin and orchestra.
*** HMV ASD 2449. Yehudi Menuhin (violin), BBC Symphony Orchestra, Pierre Boulez – BERG: *Violin concerto.****

There is an attractively earthy peasant manner in Menuhin's playing of the *2 Rhapsodies*, and rather surprisingly it is matched by Boulez's approach, warm rather than clinical. Menuhin's relaxedness and authentic 'tang' are matched by a vivid yet atmospheric recording.

The Wooden Prince (ballet): complete recording.
*** Philips SAL 3670. London Symphony Orchestra, Antal Dorati.

Bartók's music for his first ballet, *The Wooden Prince*, could hardly be more sharply contrasted with that for his other, biting allegory in ballet form, *The Miraculous Mandarin*. In *The Wooden Prince* he adopted his sweetest manner to match a fairy story which, for all its unintended Freudian overtones, has an essential warm simplicity. Though the climactic moments of both Stravinsky's *Firebird* and Ravel's *Daphnis et Chloé* are much more vividly memorable than anything here, Bartók's score is probably more consistent in its interest, rarely leaving one for long on mere filling-in material. Dorati's performance is brilliantly authentic, and the LSO responds in virtuoso style. This is one of Philips' brighter recordings.

CHAMBER MUSIC

(i; ii) *Contrasts for violin, clarinet and piano;* (ii) *Violin sonata* (for violin and piano).
(M) ** Supraphon SUAST 50740. (i) Milan Etlik (clarinet); (ii) André Gertler (violin), Diane Andersen (piano).

It was thanks to André Gertler, an ardent Bartókian from the days when this composer's music required active advocacy, that the *Violin sonata* here was rescued from oblivion. It was written in 1903 when the composer was twenty-two, and was influenced not just by Richard Strauss and Liszt (predictable enough) but by César Franck. The opening with its chains of thirds makes a good 'guess-what?'. Plainly youthful exuberance led Bartók to go on too long, but it is interesting to hear with what confidence he was developing.

Contrasts, written in 1938 for Benny Goodman and Josef Szigeti, is very refreshing in its sharp concise way. Gertler and his wife are joined by a slightly reticent clarinettist in a very enjoyable performance that does not quite catch the full bluffness of Bartók's humour. Good recording.

Sonata for two pianos and percussion.
(B) * (*) Turnabout TV 34036S. György Sándor, Rolf Reinhardt (pianos), Otto Schad, Richard Sohm (percussion) – *Piano concerto No. 2.***
* Decca SXL 6357. Bracha Eden, Alexander Tamir (pianos), Tristan Fry, James Holland (percussion) – POULENC: *Sonata for two pianos.* (*)

The excellent performance by Sándor and Reinhardt, marred by too reverberant recording, is discussed under its coupling. Eden and Tamir are formidable, conscientious artists, but they fail quite to appreciate the special, tough qualities of this Bartók work. For all their expressive intentions it becomes dull. Good recording.

String quartets Nos. 1 in A minor, Op. 7; 2 in A minor, Op. 17; 3 in C major; 4 in C major; 5 in B flat major; 6 in D major.

- (M) *** CBS Classics 61118 (Quartets 1 and 2); 61119 (3 and 4); 61120 (5 and 6). Juilliard Quartet.
- (B) *** Saga 5203 (1 and 2); 5204 (3 and 4); 5205 (5 and 6). Fine Arts Quartet.
- *** Telefunken SKH 25083 (1/3) (Quartets 1–6). Végh Quartet.
- (M) ** (*) DGG Privilege 2733 001 (3 discs; Quartets 1–6). Hungarian Quartet.

String quartets Nos. 3 in C major; 5 in B flat major.

- (M) *** Supraphon SUAST 50645. Prague City Quartet.

One can hardly go wrong with the Bartók quartets, for as well as the admirable Juilliard and Fine Arts series, the two boxes currently on the market – the first by the Végh Quartet on Telefunken and the other by the Hungarians on DGG's Privilege label – are both eminently satisfactory. The latter is cheaper, and has considerable authority: the Hungarians were the first to record Nos. 5 and 6, and their leader gave the première of the *Violin concerto*. But if they are more refined than their rivals, they do not quite convey the full, tearing intensity that both the American groups provide in their richly red-blooded performances. The DGG recording is excellent for its age (1962). The Véghs occasionally respond with more expressive warmth than some may like, but on the whole theirs are extremely perceptive performances, and they are very well recorded. They are, of course, the most expensive.

The Juilliard Quartet was the first group to record a complete cycle of the Bartók quartets on LP, and it was that early issue – appearing in Europe on Philips, in the United States on American Columbia – which alerted us to the arrival of a fine new quartet group. Since then the group's composition has altered, but the style in Bartók remains broadly the same. As the opening of the *Second Quartet* makes very plain, it is essentially a romantic style, full-blooded and warmly expressive rather than hushed and introspective. In the jerky rhythms of the scherzo of the same quartet, the Juilliard players convey the earthiness of Bartók's inspiration with little spurts of forward movement in a genuinely Hungarian manner. In the most difficult pair of quartets, Nos. 3 and 4 (coupled on the middle record of the three), this idiomatic, basically romantic and emotional approach makes the music sound less formidable even while the total impact is intensely sharp. As for the visionary passages of the *First Quartet* and the final quartet, No. 6, the Juilliard's warm style (not to mention the rather forward recording quality) takes something away from the music's hushed intensity, but there is no doubt whatever about the conviction behind the playing all through.

The Saga cycle by the Fine Arts Quartet (also of New York) provides performances at least as compelling, with recorded quality very nearly as vivid and wider in range. Current pressings are much better than those available in recent years, and the discs still cost under a pound each, but purchasers may still have to accept copies which are not immaculate from the point of view of bumps and clicks. Apart from this, and irrespective of price, the issue can be stated quite clearly: a choice between the Fine Arts' sharper-edged, almost Stravinskian approach, which reveals the musical emotional roots more and more on repetition, and the more obviously emotional approach of the Juilliard players. The Juilliard group displays marginally more brilliant virtuosity and precision of ensemble, but no one hesitating over price need worry about the cheaper records being inferior. Both sets are excellent by any standard.

The Supraphon record, made in Prague, has the disadvantage of cutting across the complete cycles, but for those attracted by this particular coupling the Prague City Quartet is a strong group that can play Nos. 3 and 5 (both difficult works) with the right idiomatic combination of incisiveness and red-blooded emotion. Their approach to Bartók is closer to that of the Juilliard Quartet than of the rival Fine Arts group, and as a mid-priced alternative it presents clear attractions. But both the Saga and CBS sets are available as separate records.

Violin sonata No. 1 (for violin and piano); *Violin sonatina* (for violin and piano); *Hungarian folk songs* (for violin and piano).

> (M) ** Supraphon SUAST 50650. André Gertler (violin), Diane Andersen (piano).

André Gertler has long been an outstanding Bartók interpreter – it was his quartet that made the first 78 recording of Bartók's *Sixth Quartet* – and this excellent Supraphon disc matches the quality of his coupling of the *Second Sonata* and *Solo violin sonata*. Gertler manages to be completely idiomatic while underlining the work's unexpected lyricism. With him it seems much less formidable – if still compelling – an argument than usual. After the sonata the remaining half-side is taken up with unpretentious folk material. The *Sonatina* is an adaptation made by Gertler in 1931 of an early (1915) piano work by Bartók, the three movements labelled *Bagpipers, Bear Dance* and *Finale.*

Violin sonata No. 2 (for violin and piano); *Solo violin sonata.*

> (M) ** Supraphon SUAST 50481. André Gertler (violin), Diane Andersen (piano).

Gertler is in his element here: Hungarian birth gains precedence over Belgian citizenship to reveal a passionate attachment to the disembodied lyricism of Bartók's *Second Sonata*, in which Diane Andersen is a first-rate partner. In the *Solo violin sonata*, Gertler achieves an overwhelming sense of drive, notably in the Fugue, and although the tone is on the shrill side throughout, the performances deserve the warmest commendation.

PIANO MUSIC

Collection: *Allegro barbaro; Three burlesques; Hungarian folk songs* (suite); *Out of Doors* (suite); *Rumanian Christmas carols; Rumanian folk dances; Sonatina.*

> (B) ** Turnabout TV 34167S. György Sándor (piano).

The manufacturers have rather hopefully subtitled this disc 'A timid soul's approach to Bartók'. But there is nothing timid about Sándor's playing, which brings out fully the percussive side to the composer's piano writing. Even so, much of this music is strong in personality, though a whole disc of it is a little wearing. Taken in sections it will make a valuable addition to any representative collection. The recording is clear and a little hard, but this suits the playing.

Allegro barbaro; Three rondos on folk tunes; Piano sonata.

> (M) ** Vanguard VCS 10048. Joseph Kalichstein (piano) – PROKOFIEV: *Sonata No. 9.***

Kalichstein, winner of the Leventritt Award in New York in 1969, gives aptly fiery performances of the *Piano sonata* and the smaller pieces. The recording copes very well with the percussive piano sounds.

Mikrokosmos, Volume 6 (complete) (i); *Out of Doors, Volumes 1 and 2* (complete); *Sonatina*.
  *** Philips 6500 013. Stephen Bishop (piano); (i) with Hiro Imamura (piano) in No. 145.

Quite outstandingly realistic piano tone here. Stephen Bishop gives splendidly idiomatic readings of these Bartók pieces, and plays with tremendous fire and intensity. This is a most satisfying anthology, a more sympathetic introduction to Bartók's keyboard music than the Turnabout disc.

OPERA

Bluebeard's Castle (opera in 1 act): complete recording (sung in Hungarian).
  *** Decca SET 311. Christa Ludwig (mezzo-soprano), Walter Berry (bass), London Symphony Orchestra, Istvan Kertesz.

Bartók's idea of portraying marital conflict in an opera was as unpromising as could be, but in the event *Bluebeard's Castle* is an enthralling work with its concentration on mood, atmosphere and slow development as Bluebeard's wife finds the key to each new door. With its comparative absence of action it is an ideal work for the gramophone, and there have been a surprising number of attempts to record it (so conveniently filling a single LP). None has achieved anything like the success of this magnificent version with Kertesz, the LSO and two soloists who have voices more beautiful and artistry more commanding than any recorded rivals. They may not be Hun-

garian-born (if they were their voices would probably wobble) but they cope with the Hungarian words most confidently, and it seems unlikely that their performance will be rivalled for a long time to come. The LSO under Istvan Kertesz (Hungarian influence there all right) is equally inspired, and the recording is superlative even by Decca standards.

Batten, Adrian
(dates uncertain; died probably 1627)

Fourth Evening Service. Anthems: *O sing joyfully; O Lord, Thou hast searched me out; Hear my prayer; Out of the deep; O clap your hands together*.
  (B) * (*) Argo Eclipse ECS 681. Richard Latham (organ), Choir of Peterborough Cathedral, Stanley Vann – DERING: *Anthems*.**

Batten's early training was as a chorister of Winchester Cathedral, and he was later to become choirmaster at Westminster Abbey and organist as well as vicar-choral at St Paul's Cathedral. He was a prolific composer and wrote a great deal of church music, most of it musical and accomplished rather than distinctive. The items here are quite typical, and the choral pieces are well sung, though the various solos by members of the choir leave something to be desired.

Bax, Arnold
(1883–1953)

The Garden of Fand (symphonic poem); *Mediterranean; Northern ballad No. 1; Tintagel* (symphonic poem).

*** Lyrita SRCS 62. London Philharmonic Orchestra, Sir Adrian Boult.

These are recordings of exceptional vividness, clarity and refinement; indeed, technically they must be numbered among the finest orchestral records Lyrita has given us. Sir Adrian Boult's reading of *The Garden of Fand* is full of poetry and almost erases memories of Beecham's magical account (HQM 1165), while the engineers capture so much detail and produce so natural a sound that for anyone wanting this imaginative and marvellous score, this is a first recommendation. *Tintagel* is no less voluptuous and beguiling and though more restrained in feeling than Barbirolli's, benefits by so being. The *Northern ballad No. 1*, though less memorable than either *Fand* or *Tintagel*, is worth having and only Bax's short *Mediterranean* fails to improve with the passage of time. This is an excellent record with which to begin a Bax collection.

November Woods (symphonic poem).
** (*) Lyrita SRCS 37. London Philharmonic Orchestra, Sir Adrian Boult – HOLST: *Fugal overture*; MOERAN: *Sinfonietta.****

A lush romantic score, regarded by some as one of Bax's finest tone poems. Others may feel that it misses the powerful atmosphere and imaginative distinction of the symphonies. However this may be, *November Woods* is a welcome addition to the growing representation of Bax on records; the LPO under Sir Adrian Boult give a good account of it and are well recorded.

Symphony No. 1 in E flat major.
** (*) Lyrita SRCS 53. London Philharmonic Orchestra, Myer Fredman.

Bax's symphonies remain controversial, and many listeners find their quality of invention and argument less intensely sustained than the composer's shorter orchestral tone poems. They nevertheless have a breadth of imagination which the smaller structures do not always carry. The *First Symphony* began life originally as a piano sonata. Bax wrote it in 1921–2, and the music has a certain Russian quality (Bax had been to Russia in 1910), especially noticeable in the finale. The first movement is a successful example of the composer's control of structure and it has a very striking and memorable secondary theme. The slow movement is impressive, if not as fine as that in the *Second Symphony*, and only the finale, with its touch of bombast, lets the work down. But the work as a whole is well worth exploring in the fine performance conducted by Myer Fredman. The recording is exceptionally vivid and clear.

Symphony No. 2 in E minor and C major.
*** Lyrita SRCS 54. London Philharmonic Orchestra, Myer Fredman.

The *Second* is arguably the most richly imaginative of all Bax's symphonies. The ideas are copious and vividly conceived, and the music has a wild, imaginative intensity that is wholly compelling. Its richness of texture and powerful sense of atmosphere are obvious from the very outset. Many Bax scores have suffered the handicap of indifferent performance or recording. Myer Fredman has secured a first-class account of the score: the LPO sound as if they have been playing it all their lives and the recording is in the demonstration class. Altogether outstanding.

Symphony No. 5 in C sharp minor.
*** Lyrita SRCS 58. London Philharmonic Orchestra, Raymond Leppard.

The *Fifth* is considered by some critics to be Bax's finest. Dedicated to Sibelius, it was first performed in January 1934 under the Finnish master's most eloquent champion, Sir Thomas Beecham. The symphony shows Bax holding in check the purely lyrical impulse to which he could give such generous vein in favour of a greater degree of motivic integration. In some ways this is the most symphonic of the seven, though it has the same brooding intensity and powerful atmosphere that distinguish the first three symphonies. Raymond Leppard gives a dedicated and indeed inspired account which should go far to persuade anyone who doubts the power of Bax's imagination or the strength of his symphonic instinct. The LPO are at their very best, and so too are the Lyrita engineers.

Symphony No. 6 in C major.
    ** (*) Lyrita SRCS 35. New Philharmonia Orchestra, Norman Del Mar.

The *Sixth Symphony* (1934) has some of the wild beauty of Inverness-shire, where Bax wrote it. He seems to have found his inspiration in the dark, brooding landscapes of the North and West, and there is a passionate fervour about it that offsets its somewhat sprawling architecture. Although the *Sixth* is not as imaginative as the *Second Symphony* or as fresh and original as the *Third*, it is a welcome addition to Bax's growing representation in the catalogue. Norman Del Mar's performance with the New Philharmonia is committed, though a greater attention to dynamic nuance would have been welcome. The balance, too, is less than ideal and far too close at times. Bax's woodwind writing is very distinctive and blends into the orchestral texture to highly personal ends: it is a pity that the aural perspective shifts to highlight it. The same happens to some of the delicate colouristic effects in the trio

section of the finale. Nonetheless, these are not major defects, and one hopes that readers will not be put off investigating this fine British symphony.

Tintagel (symphonic poem).
    *** HMV ASD 2305. London Symphony Orchestra, Sir John Barbirolli – DELIUS: *Collection;* IRELAND: *London overture.****

Barbirolli's performance of *Tintagel* was the first to be issued in stereo. It is a characteristically full-blooded account of Bax's most popular score. The sea vistas (with their musical reminders of Debussy as well as Wagner) are magnificently painted by players and recording engineers alike, and Sir John sees that the memorable principal tune is given a fine romantic sweep. If the couplings are attractive this is a highly recommendable disc.

Elegiac trio (for flute, viola and harp).
    ** Argo ZRG 574. Robles Trio – DEBUSSY: *Sonata;* RAVEL: *Introduction and allegro.* (*)

The Bax *Trio* is one of his less inspired works and cannot be compared with his finest chamber music. We badly need a new version of the *Nonet*. By its side this seems routine Celtic stuff. However, the Robles Trio play most sympathetically.

Piano sonata No. 2 in G major.
    (B) * (*) Pye GSGC 14085. Peter Cooper (piano) – TIPPETT: *Sonata;* MOZART: *Variations.* (*)

This is an acceptable but not especially imaginative performance. There is a finer version on Lyrita, but that is not available in stereo. The Pye recording, however, is much better than the Lyrita one, which is only fair.

The Beatles
(20th century)
(Music principally by **Paul McCartney**; words principally by **John Lennon**)

Collections:

*** Parlophone PCS 7009. '*Revolver*'.
** (*) Parlophone PCS 7016. '*Oldies*'.
*** Parlophone PCS 7027. '*Sgt. Pepper's lonely hearts club band*'.
*** Parlophone PCSP 717 (2 discs). '*1962–6*'.
** (*) Parlophone PCSP 718 (2 discs). '*1967–70*'.

Go to almost any one of the Beatles' LPs and the proportion of numbers with sharply conceived, tellingly executed invention is astonishingly high. Quite simply the Beatles – or more particularly Lennon and McCartney – can write first-rate tunes, and know how to present them imaginatively. From the purely musical point of view, *Revolver* is the gem of the Beatle collection with at least three McCartney solos that could readily stand among the work of classical song-writers – *Here, there and everywhere, For no one* and *Eleanor Rigby*. The following LP, *Sergeant Pepper*, develops not on those comparatively conventional lines but rather follows up the line of aural gimmickry which when you come down to it is not so far removed from the experimentation of Stockhausen, Boulez and others of the avant-garde. The theoretical basis may be less intellectual, but the joy in unconventional sound is the same.

Something must be said here about the Beatles' artistic catalyst, George Martin. Long before he met the Beatles, George Martin was a talented recording manager. When listening to these LPs the record-lover might well reflect on the relationship with Martin's earlier successes – classical issues on the Parlophone label and humorous records by Peter Sellers, Michael Bentine and others. The Beatles' records reflect both. Without Martin the group would probably have been a success, but might not have developed the degree of purely musical imagination that makes their best numbers stand out from anything else in the pop world. Martin was the Walter Legge to their Klemperer. That metaphor is closer than most record-lovers realize.

Oldies is, of course, a collection of the earlier singles, and as such has not the artistic unity of the later LPs; however, the two-disc anthology PCSP 717 has been cleverly arranged to include most of the favourites among the early numbers and this is the obvious way of sampling the unique individuality of the Lennon/McCartney team, together with the marvellous spontaneity of the first recordings. PCSP 718 shows how well the standard of sophistication was held at its peak, and how far the Beatles had come artistically since their early singles took the world by storm. But premier choice must remain with the first of the two composite albums and of course *Revolver*.

Bedford, David
(born 1937)

Music for Albion Moonlight.
** Argo ZRG 638. Jane Manning (soprano), members of BBC Symphony Orchestra, John Carewe – LUTYENS: *And suddenly*.**

David Bedford is one of the liveliest of the young composers who first started climbing inside their pianos or attacking them from underneath. He is now not to be counted among the wilder avant-garde, but he makes some extraordinary noises in his strange setting of words by

Kenneth Patchen. It is rather like a development of Schoenberg's *Pierrot Lunaire* that goes way beyond anything that the Second Viennese school ever conceived, and listeners should be warned of excruciating semi-tone glissandos on an instrument known as the alto-melodica. There are also sudden shrieks on the words 'Hell!' and 'Mad!' which are not recommended for the nervous. Beautifully performed and recorded.

The Tentacles of the Dark Nebula.
** (*) Decca Headline HEAD 3. Peter Pears (tenor), London Sinfonietta, the composer – BERKELEY: *Ronsard sonnets*; LUTOSLAWSKI: *Paroles.* ** (*)

Peter Pears was the inspirer of each of the three works on an unexpectedly varied disc coupling Bedford, Berkeley and Lutoslawski. The Bedford work presents the soloist in a narrative from a science-fiction story by Arthur C. Clarke, the images and situations vividly illustrated by Bedford's finely textured score. Whether the musical argument as such holds together is another matter, but on the level of illustration it is a more communicative piece than most. The performance and recording are excellent.

Beethoven, Ludwig van
(1770–1827)

Piano concerto in D major (in one movement)*; Piano concerto in E flat major* (1784).
(B) ** Turnabout TV 34367S. Martin Galling (piano), Berlin Symphony Orchestra, C. A. Bünte.

The *E flat concerto* is a reconstruction. All that survived was a soloist's hand-copied score of a concerto 'par Louis van Beethoven âgé de douze ans'. The solo part is complete with a piano transcription of the orchestral tuttis to link the separate solos. From this the Beethoven scholar Willy Hess deduced an orchestral part, and the work was given its first complete performance at the Queen Elizabeth Hall in London on 5 January 1968. It is a creditable work of Beethoven's early Bonn period (he was probably counting his age from the false birthdate given by his father, and so it is not necessarily the work of a twelve-year-old). The other work is more problematic, a solitary movement tentatively dated 1788–93 that was found in the last century and counted to be genuine Beethoven until someone found a score by the Czech composer Rössler containing the same movement. One Beethovenian touch is the weirdly unexpected modulation to the second subject in the recapitulation. Enjoyable performances from Galling, but rather dim recording.

Piano concertos Nos. 1–5 (complete recording); (i) *Choral fantasia in C minor, Op. 80.*
(M) ** (*) HMV SLS 941 (4 discs). Daniel Barenboim (piano), New Philharmonia Orchestra, Otto Klemperer, (i) with John Alldis Choir.

No more individual performances of the Beethoven concertos have ever been put on record, and not everyone will like them. But the combination of Barenboim and Klemperer is nothing if not inspired, and for every wilfulness of a plodding Klemperer there is a youthful spark from the spontaneously-combusting Barenboim. That may imply a lack of sympathy between conductor and soloist, but plainly this is not so. These recordings were made much more quickly than usual, with long takes allowing a sense of continuity rare on record. Some may not like an apparently spontaneous performance for repeated listening (in the *Emperor*, for example, Barenboim has some slight fluffs of finger) but the concentration is formidable and nowhere more compelling than in the slow movements, whether in the earliest concerto, No. 2 – here given an interpretation that is anything but Mozartian, and splendidly strong – or in the later concertos. No. 3 brings the most obviously wilful slow tempi, but, with fine rhythmic points from soloist and orchestra, the result is still vivid and compelling. No. 4 is anything but a delicate, feminine work, with basic tempi slow enough to avoid the need for much slowing when the lyrical counter-subjects emerge. The *Choral fantasia* too is given an inspired performance, with the weaknesses of Beethoven's writing wonderfully concealed when the music-making is so intense. Recording of good E M I vintage though not of ultimate refinement.

Piano concertos Nos. 1–5 (complete recording).

   ★ (M) *** D G G 2721 066 (4 discs). Wilhelm Kempff (piano), Berlin Philharmonic Orchestra, Ferdinand Leitner.

   ** (*) Decca S X L G 6594/7. Vladimir Ashkenazy (piano), Chicago Symphony Orchestra, Sir Georg Solti.

   (M) ** CBS 77371 (3 discs). Leon Fleischer (piano), Cleveland Orchestra, George Szell.

   (M) ** Decca Ace of Diamonds S D D E 304/7. Friedrich Gulda (piano), Vienna Philharmonic Orchestra, Horst Stein.

Kempff's cycle of the Beethoven concertos has never been surpassed for its consistent freshness of imagination. Individually there are weightier readings of each of these concertos, but none which more spontaneously captures the eager greatness of this music in its full range of expressiveness. The album is available at slightly more than medium price.

After Barenboim and Klemperer the partnership of Ashkenazy and Solti is no less fascinating. Where Solti is fiery and intense, Ashkenazy provides an introspective balance. No better example of this can be found than in the slow movement of the *Fourth Concerto*. The 'masculine/feminine' dialogue has rarely been so strongly contrasted on record, Solti strong and commanding, Ashkenazy's reply exquisitely gentle, yet never losing the argument. Ashkenazy brings a hushed, poetic quality to every slow movement, while Solti's urgency maintains a vivid forward impulse in the outer movements. Sometimes, as in the *C minor Concerto*, one feels that the music-making is too intense. Here a more relaxed, lyrical approach can find in the first movement a warmth of humanity that Solti misses. But for the most part the listener is given an overriding impression of vitality and freshness, and the *Emperor* performance, while on the grandest scale, has a marvellously individual moment in the first movement when Ashkenazy lingers over his presentation of the second subject. The Chicago orchestral playing is characteristically brilliant, and the very bright Decca recording (with not as rich piano tone as this company usually provides) is inclined to be fierce to emphasize the driving quality of the orchestral contribution.

Leon Fleischer is a pianist who worked with special understanding in the Szell regime at Cleveland. Fleischer has personality as an interpreter, but one suspects that, more than most pianists, he projects Szell's view of Beethoven, and so the advantages of youth and experience are combined with exceptional intensity. In the *First Concerto* the tempo for the first movement is unusually fast and Fleischer uses the longest of Beethoven's three cadenzas; the middle movement is unusually slow and nicely expressive in a Bellinian way. Where Fleischer falls short is in the finale, where he fails to give much of a spring to the rhythm. In the

Second Concerto there is a tendency to overdrive the music, which is after all very early Beethoven. This same vigorous hard-pressed manner informs the first movement of the C minor work; in the finale the brilliance is more effective, though again it is on the tense side. But there is good expressive playing from the soloist in the slow movement, not always matched by the orchestra. No. 4 is the finest performance of the set, opening with the genuine tension of a live performance and displaying throughout a commanding control of argument from soloist and conductor alike. Fleischer's half-tones are most beautiful and his fingerwork dazzling without ever giving the impression of mere slickness. The *Emperor* is impressive for its youthful, dramatic vigour. As elsewhere in these performances Fleischer (like Szell himself) sometimes finds it hard to relax naturally – as in the *espressivo* passages of the finale – but in one important detail this version relaxes more than its rivals. Szell noted that at the very end of the slow movement Beethoven's autograph asks for pizzicato strings half a bar after the point where the indication appears in printed scores. With Szell the first indication of the magical key-change comes gently on a sustained bowed note instead of with the usual 'plonk', quite an important point. The recording tends to be rather hard and unflattering, notably in the way it prevents the piano from ever sounding really soft, but these are very positive performances and the set is very competitively priced.

On the Ace of Diamonds set the orchestral recording is superb but the piano tone is curious. Gulda apparently insisted on using a Bösendorfer piano, with its characteristically light and velvety colouring which, as recorded, gives the ear the impression of a reduced tonal spectrum, limited at both top and bottom. Once one adjusts to this, the performances are most enjoyable, strong and direct and nearly always spontaneous. No. 2 is perhaps the least impressive, but No. 4 is particularly fine, with a really memorable slow movement. The *Emperor* too is another marked success, with tempi maintained consistently through each movement, and strength rather than inflexibility emerging, because of the compulsive quality of the playing.

Piano concerto No. 1 in C major, Op. 15.
   *** Philips 6500 179. Stephen Bishop (piano), BBC Symphony Orchestra, Colin Davis (with *Sonata No. 5***).

   *** DGG SLPM 138774. Wilhelm Kempff (piano), Berlin Philharmonic Orchestra, Ferdinand Leitner.

   *** HMV ASD 2616. Daniel Barenboim (piano), New Philharmonia Orchestra, Otto Klemperer.

   (M) *** Decca Ace of Diamonds SDD 227. Julius Katchen (piano), London Symphony Orchestra, Pierino Gamba – *Choral fantasia.****

   ** (*) Philips SAL 3712. Claudio Arrau (piano), Concertgebouw Orchestra, Bernard Haitink (with *Sonata No. 6***).

   ** DGG SLPM 139023. Christoph Eschenbach (piano), Berlin Philharmonic Orchestra, Herbert von Karajan.

   (M) ** Philips Universo 6580 086. Veronica Jochum von Moltke (piano), Bamberg Symphony Orchestra, Eugen Jochum – MOZART: *Piano concerto No. 14.** (*)

Piano concerto No. 1 in C major, Op. 15; Rondo in B flat major (for piano and orchestra), *G. 151.*
   (B) ** (*) Turnabout TV 34205S. Alfred Brendel (piano), Vienna Volksoper or Stuttgart Philharmonic Orchestra, Wilfried Boettcher.

The combination of Bishop and Davis rarely fails to produce an exceptionally satisfying reading, and this performance, which combines clarity of articulation and deep thoughtfulness, is among the very finest versions of this concerto. Maybe Bishop misses some of the exuberance of Kempff, but the unforced rightness of the interpretation may be judged from the fact that, though Bishop keeps the pulse remarkably steady in the slow movement, the result still conveys spontaneity with no feeling of rigidity. An advantage over Kempff and Barenboim (among others) is that Bishop uses the longest and most challenging of the cadenzas that Beethoven wrote for the first movement. The recording quality is beautifully refined in the Philips manner, and the fill-up brings another inspired interpretation of early Beethoven.

Kempff's sense of repose is remarkable in this concerto. The slow movement is in fact a shade faster than in Kempff's earlier version. Yet the very profundity of Kempff's sense of calm creates the illusion of something much slower. In the Finale, too, the playing sparkles joyously. The recording is good, with the piano balanced rather farther back than is common with DGG.

The first movement shows Klemperer in flexible mood. The opening is portentous yet noble in style, then the conductor relaxes for a beautifully lyrical and gentle treatment of the second subject. The *Largo* too finds a striking depth and intensity of expression. This is one of the very finest performances of the set and among the most compelling accounts available.

With its generous coupling Katchen's version has more music on it than almost any rival, but this does not inhibit him from using the longest and most impressive of the cadenzas that Beethoven provided for the first movement. The tempo for this movement is on the fast side, but Katchen keeps a classical firmness of control, and then provides the necessary

contrast in a relaxed, poetic account of the slow movement, and a sparkling reading of the finale. The orchestra's contribution is not quite so consistently successful – the slow movement could be more understanding – but with outstanding recording quality, it stands as one of the very best versions available.

Arrau's performance is the antithesis of the Barenboim/Klemperer approach. It is lightweight, fresh and lithe, essentially early Beethoven, almost Mozartian. The slow movement, however, has depth. The *Sonata* coupling is equally good, and with characteristic Philips Concertgebouw sound this is a strong competitor.

Like Barenboim and Klemperer, Eschenbach and Karajan choose a slow tempo for the first movement, and though, as on the EMI disc, the concentration holds the attention, the result here is closer to a chamber approach, where Barenboim and Klemperer are essentially working on a large scale. A beautiful performance of the slow movement and a lightweight finale. The performance is attractive and interesting, but in its concentration on refinement (Karajan's doing?) it misses any sort of greatness. Good recording.

Veronica Jochum von Moltke is the conductor's daughter, on this showing an urgent, intense performer who gives a strong, well-articulated account, helped by understanding accompaniment. With its unexpectedly generous Mozart coupling, excellent recording quality, and a mid-price label this makes a very acceptable recommendation.

Brendel's is one of the most satisfying readings of the *First Concerto* available at any price. His tempi for the outer movements are measured, but such is his rhythmic point (particularly in the dactylic rhythms of the finale) and such is his concentration that the result is never heavy. Similarly in the slow movement his tempo is rather slow for *Largo*, but the natural weight of expression has the immediacy of a live performance. The long cadenza in the first movement is interestingly confected from two of the cadenzas the composer himself wrote. The snag is the playing and recording of the orchestra – rather underpowered, with string-tone that often sounds seedy. Brendel's concentration turns the *B flat Rondo*, an early lightweight piece, into something genuinely bright and pointed. Despite the accompaniment this is an outstanding bargain.

Piano concertos Nos. 1 in C major, Op. 15; 2 in B flat major, Op. 19.

    ** Decca SXL 2178. Wilhelm Backhaus (piano), Vienna Philharmonic Orchestra, Hans Schmidt-Isserstedt.

In the *First Concerto* Backhaus's strength verges on coarseness (which was true of Beethoven in his later years) but it seems better to think of the C major work as more deserving of grace and charm, of subtlety of touch and tone. The account of No. 2 is distinctly better. More light comes through; the soloist is more generous in his variations of touch, and he succeeds in conveying something of the feeling of youthful freshness, though one could do with a little more wit and abandonment in the finale. The recorded sound, first-class in its day, still sounds well.

Piano concerto No. 2 in B flat major, Op. 19.

    *** DGG SLPM 138775. Wilhelm Kempff (piano), Berlin Philharmonic Orchestra, Ferdinand Leitner – *Concerto No. 4.***

    *** HMV ASD 2608. Daniel Barenboim (piano), New Philharmonia Orchestra, Otto Klemperer – *Choral fantasia.****

    ** (*) Philips SAL 3714. Claudio Arrau (piano), Concertgebouw Orchestra, Bernard Haitink (with *Sonata No. 1***).

    (M) ** (*) Decca Ace of Diamonds SDD 228. Julius Katchen (piano), London Symphony Orchestra, Pierino Gamba – *Concerto No. 4.* (*)

    (B) ** Turnabout TV 34206S. Alfred Brendel (piano), Vienna Volksoper Orchestra, Heinz Wallberg – *Choral fantasia.* (*)

Kempff's account of the *Second Concerto*, attractively coupled with the *Fourth*, has long been a favourite choice. Like No. 4 it is less individual a performance than on Kempff's earlier mono LP, but his playing is unmistakable in almost every bar and Leitner's conducting is both strong and sympathetic.

With its outstanding coupling of a superbly alive account of the *Choral fantasia*, ASD 2608 makes the best possible sampler for the Barenboim/Klemperer set of concertos. This early and least characteristic Beethoven concerto is given a reading of notable breadth, and here Klemperer's magisterial manner balances perfectly with the naturally expressive quality of Barenboim's playing.

Arrau's performance has a spontaneity and life not always present in his earlier records. Apparently at this set of sessions he was given longer takes than previously was customary, and the resulting gain in continuity and liveliness is readily apparent. This is a fresh, straightforward account, literal but strong, and it is sensitively accompanied by Haitink. The *Sonata* is more mannered in style but acceptable enough.

Katchen and Gamba offer a commanding and authoritative account of No. 2, but are less penetrating in No. 4. Katchen's virtuosity is remarkable but there is a lack of heart which can hardly be ignored, even if the coupling is attractive. The recording however is excellent.

As in his other Beethoven concerto

performances Brendel's concentration makes up for indifferent accompaniment thinly recorded. Fortunately the quality of the piano recording is far higher, so that Brendel's contribution at least can be appreciated to the full. Wallberg's conducting is lively and sympathetic, but on the reverse Boettcher is unimaginative in a work that is unusually difficult to hold together.

Piano concerto No. 3 in C minor, Op. 37.
   *** Philips 6500 315. Stephen Bishop (piano), BBC Symphony Orchestra, Colin Davis – *Sonata No. 8.*** (*)
   (M) ** (*) Philips Universo 6580 078. Claudio Arrau (piano), Concertgebouw Orchestra, Bernard Haitink.
   ** (*) HMV ASD 2579. Daniel Barenboim (piano), New Philharmonia Orchestra, Otto Klemperer.
   (B) ** (*) Turnabout TV 34207S. Alfred Brendel (piano), Vienna Pro Musica Orchestra, Heinz Wallberg (with *Sonata No. 26***).
   ** (*) DGG SLPM 138776. Wilhelm Kempff (piano), Berlin Philharmonic Orchestra, Ferdinand Leitner.
   ** Decca SXL 2190. Wilhelm Backhaus (piano), Vienna Philharmonic Orchestra, Hans Schmidt-Isserstedt (with *Sonata No. 14* (*)).
   * (*) DGG 2530 254. Christoph Eschenbach (piano), London Symphony Orchestra, Hans Werner Henze.

Piano concerto No. 3 in C minor, Op. 37; Rondo in B flat major (for piano and orchestra), *G. 151.*
   (M) ** (*) Decca Ace of Diamonds SDD 226. Julius Katchen (piano), London Symphony Orchestra, Pierino Gamba.

Like the other issues in the series with Bishop and Davis, this version of the *Third Concerto* is among the most satisfying available. If Bishop is less idiosyncratic than such rivals as Kempff, Barenboim and others, his concentration ensures that there is no lack of characterization. The first movement erupts in a superbly intense account of the cadenza, relishing the virtuosity of the conclusion. The central *Largo* is taken very slowly and intensely, and the Finale, relatively relaxed, allows Bishop to display the extraordinary clarity of his fingerwork. The recording of both the concerto and the sonata used as coupling is clear and refined.

Arrau's is an unusually distinguished performance, refreshingly unmannered. Though at the start the very refinement gives a Mozartian quality, and some will prefer a more powerful approach, the poetry of Arrau's playing is consistently satisfying. With mid-sixties recording that has been admirably refreshed on this medium-price reissue, it makes an excellent recommendation.

Barenboim's interpretation of the *Third Concerto* is the most controversial (as well as one of the most fascinating) of his set. The tempo for the first movement is very slow indeed, and only the high level of concentration holds the music's structure together. The slow movement too is relaxed. Here the opening cantilena is shaped most beautifully and persuasively. This disc will not appeal to everyone, but its degree of tension is high.

Brendel's account is among the finest of his Beethoven series, better balanced between piano and orchestra than some of the others, though still with some shrillness in the sound. The interpretation of the soloist is deeply satisfying, with the most delicate tonal and rhythmic control married to intellectual strength. The slow movement has depth as well as poetry and the Finale is beautifully jaunty. The *Sonata* is given an equally intense and alert performance.

Kempff is here in subdued mood compared with the other performances in his Beethoven cycle. The speed of the first movement is astonishingly slow, though the squareness conveys the architecture of the movement more effectively. For once in a DGG studio Kempff was not at his sprightliest. Yet even so the performance has rewards of its own, and the slow movement is most beautiful. The recording is very good.

In the medium price-range Katchen's account remains very competitive, parparticularly as the performance of the coupled *Rondo in B Flat* (an attractive, spontaneous piece) is of excellent quality. In the *Concerto* the first movement takes a little while to warm up, but when Katchen enters the performance comes fully to life. The slow movement is sustained with considerable tension, its beauty readily conveyed, and there is plenty of vigour and sparkle in the finale. With excellent recording this is a highly enjoyable disc.

Decca's earlier recording with Backhaus still remains a viable alternative. There is something of a rough-hewn quality about the first movement, with Backhaus magisterial, if seldom melting. The reading has a strong classical flavour and its uncompromising mood, the second movement rather baldly stated but without doubt compulsive, is matched by the clear, vivid recording.

Eschenbach in his reading is not well served by his accompanists, or at least not by Henze, who cannot produce more than the most routine conducting in Beethoven. Despite the imagination of the soloist and good recording, this is not a strong competitor.

Other currently available versions include a small-scale romantic account by Radu Lupu (Decca SXL 6503). Lupu's reading is individual but does not produce real concentration. It is mainly notable for its coupling, a fine performance of the *Variations in C minor, G.191.* A CBS issue by Glenn Gould and Bernstein

(72796) is hardly competitive. Though not wilful like Gould's reading of the *Emperor*, it suffers from forced brilliance, and there is little sense of feeling the music. A coupling by Rubinstein of the *Third* and *Fourth Concertos* on RCA SB 6787 is let down by poor recording. The performances show what natural insight this pianist has (few players find such unmannered depths in the slow movement of No. 3), but the sound is unacceptably shallow because of the long sides.

Piano concerto No. 4 in G major, Op. 58.

*** DGG SLPM 138775. Wilhelm Kempff (piano), Berlin Philharmonic Orchestra, Ferdinand Leitner – *Concerto No. 2.* ***

(M) *** HMV SXLP 30086. Emil Gilels (piano), Philharmonia Orchestra, Leopold Ludwig – MOZART: *Violin concerto No. 3.****

** (*) HMV ASD 2550. Daniel Barenboim (piano), New Philharmonia Orchestra, Otto Klemperer.

(B) ** Turnabout TV 34208S. Alfred Brendel (piano), Vienna Pro Musica Orchestra, Heinz Wallberg (with *Sonata No. 24***).

(M) * (*) Philips Universo 6580 060. Claudio Arrau (piano), Concertgebouw Orchestra, Bernard Haitink.

(M) * (*) Decca Ace of Diamonds SDD 228. Julius Katchen (piano), London Symphony Orchestra, Pierino Gamba – *Concerto No. 2.*** (*)

Although Kempff's delicacy of fingerwork and his shading of tone-colour are as effervescent as ever, this is not so personal a reading as his earlier mono LP. There were moments in that of the purest magic, provided one was ready to accept some waywardness. The stereo version also allows some speed variation, but the increased sense of unity owes much, it is plain, to the fine control of the conductor, Leitner.

Gilels's version, very competitively priced, may be regarded as an equally desirable alternative choice. This is a strong poetic reading of striking authority and eloquence. The poetry of the dialogue in the slow movement is finely realized and there is a rare combination of strength and sparkle in the finale. The recording is remarkably good: the piano tone is fresh and the orchestra cleanly focused.

Barenboim's account is issued without coupling and is thus comparatively expensive. But this is among the very finest current versions, with the deeply reflective quality of the solo playing – immediately noticeable by the searching quality of the opening bars – matched by Klemperer's broad wide-spun tempi and manner. This is very much an individual reading but immensely rewarding.

Brendel's interpretation is deeply satisfying, but as in the rest of the series he is hampered by unimaginative accompaniment thinly recorded. The first-movement tutti for example is rhythmically stodgy, and that detracts from the impact of the soloist in this work more seriously than in the other Beethoven concertos. It is interesting that Brendel uses the second of the cadenzas written for the work, not generally heard.

Arrau's is an unusually relaxed view of the first movement. But unlike some of the others in his cycle, it seems a relatively mannered performance, sounding unspontaneous. Katchen's version is discussed under its coupling.

(i) *Piano concerto No. 4 in G major, Op. 58;* Overture: *Leonora No. 3, Op. 72b.*
   *** Decca SXL 6654. Chicago Symphony Orchestra, Sir Georg

Solti, (i) with Vladimir Ashkenazy (piano).

The Ashkenazy/Solti performance of the *G major Concerto* is one of the finest of their complete series, the contrast between the musical personalities of soloist and conductor bringing new insights to this masterly score. The performance of the overture is fresh and dramatic, and this record can be recommended alongside those of Kempff, Gilels and Barenboim.

Piano concerto No. 4 in G major, Op. 58; Fantasia in G minor, Op 77.
   *** BASF BAC 3002. Paul Badura-Skoda (Hammerflügel piano), Collegium Aureum (using original instruments).

Paul Badura-Skoda's version is different from all others in that he uses a Viennese Hammerflügel fortepiano, built by Conrad Graf in 1820. Its tone is at once shallower and clearer in texture than the modern concert grand. The comparative lack of a rich sustained tone quality could easily produce a cold impression, but Paul Badura-Skoda shows himself a complete master of its technique, including the wide dynamic range possible with the 'soft' pedal without loss of brilliance. The effect of the performance is fresh and spontaneous, and the orchestral accompaniment is committed as well as polished. Once one has adjusted to the different sound, which is easy to do, especially on a second and subsequent listening, one can find a new dimension in the performance which is remarkably satisfying. The recording is vivid, although the balance tends slightly to enfold the piano into the orchestra. This seems eminently satisfactory when the musicians are making music as a group.

At the end of the first movement, separately banded, Beethoven's own cadenza is added as an appendix, a rather happy idea, especially as the orchestra then joins in to finish off the movement for the second time. The improvisatory *Fantasia* makes a good filler and rather suits the timbre of the period instrument. An excellent issue in every way.

Piano concerto No. 5 in E flat major (Emperor), Op. 73.

*** DGG SLPM 138777. Wilhelm Kempff (piano), Berlin Philharmonic Orchestra, Ferdinand Leitner.

*** Philips SAL 3787. Stephen Bishop (piano), London Symphony Orchestra, Colin Davis.

(M) *** Philips Universo 6580 094. Claudio Arrau (piano), Concertgebouw Orchestra, Bernard Haitink.

*** DGG 2530 438. Christoph Eschenbach (piano), Boston Symphony Orchestra, Seiji Ozawa.

(M) *** HMV SXLP 20104. Bruno-Leonardo Gelber (piano), New Philharmonia Orchestra, Ferdinand Leitner.

(B) ** (*) Classics for Pleasure CFP 40087. John Lill (piano), Scottish National Orchestra, Alexander Gibson.

(B) ** (*) Decca SPA 334. Clifford Curzon (piano), Vienna Philharmonic Orchestra, Hans Knappertsbusch.

** (*) HMV ASD 2500. Daniel Barenboim (piano), New Philharmonia Orchestra, Otto Klemperer.

(B) ** (*) Turnabout TV 34209S. Alfred Brendel (piano), Vienna Pro Musica Orchestra, Zubin Mehta (with *Fantasia, Op. 77*).

(M) ** Philips Universo 6580 005. Robert Casadesus (piano), Concertgebouw Orchestra, Hans Rosbaud.

(i) *Piano concerto No. 5 in E flat major (Emperor), Op. 73*; Overture: *Egmont, Op. 84.*

*** Decca SXL 6655. Chicago Symphony Orchestra, Sir Georg Solti, (i) with Vladimir Ashkenazy (piano).

(M) ** (*) Decca Ace of Diamonds SDD 225. London Symphony Orchestra, Pierino Gamba, (i) with Julius Katchen (piano).

Even amid the wealth of fine *Emperor* performances Kempff's version stands out as perhaps the most refreshing and imaginative of all. The interests of the musical argument always take precedence over the demands of virtuosity. Beside less thoughtful pianists Kempff's interpretation may at times sound comparatively small-scale: there is no attempt at the big bow-wow approach. But strength there is in plenty and excitement too. As ever Kempff's range of tone-colour is extraordinarily wide, from the merest half-tone as though the fingers are barely brushing the keys to the crisp impact of a dry fortissimo.

Bishop's too is one of the most deeply satisfying performances of this much-recorded concerto ever put on record. His is not a brash, extrovert way. With alert, sharp-edged accompaniment from Colin Davis, he gives a clean dynamic performance of the outer movements, then in the central slow movement finds a depth of intensity that completely explodes any idea of this as a central, lighter resting point. Even so he avoids weighing the simple plan down with unstylistic mannerisms; he relies simply on natural, unforced concentration in the most delicate, hushed tones. Fine clean recording to match.

Arrau's Universo version appeared first as part of a complete cycle, and it is remarkable how much more spontaneous he sounds here than in his previous account of the work, an early Columbia record (reissued on World Record Club). The slow movement in particular conveys the tension of a live performance – it sounds as though it might have been done in a single unedited take. Arrau is at his most commanding and authoritative in the outer movements, and the finale is most stylishly played. The recording is first-rate and, even without consideration of the reasonable price, this disc is one of the very finest available on all counts.

Eschenbach gives a deeply satisfying interpretation, helped by the equally youthful urgency of his accompanist. With thoughtfulness and bravura combined, it stands among the finest versions available, but the recording is reverberant even by Boston standards, which obscures a fair amount of inner detail. Even so, this remains a record that gives very great satisfaction.

Comparing Gelber – the young Buenos Aires pianist – directly with Kempff shows how astonishingly alike the two performances are. There is a wonderful hushed intensity in the slow movement and a willingness elsewhere to relax into half-tones whenever the music demands it. The bravura is clean and dramatic, the accompaniment first-rate and with excellent recording for its age this is an outstanding bargain.

Ashkenazy and Solti combine to give an excitingly dramatic performance on the largest possible scale, yet one which is imbued with considerable poetry. Alongside the *Fourth Concerto* this represents the peak of achievement of their complete cycle. With the *Egmont overture* a successful bonus, and brilliant recording, this can be cordially recommended as another very rewarding and individual performance of Beethoven's masterpiece.

Katchen's too is an excellent performance, full of characteristic animal energy and superbly recorded. The first and last movements are taken at a spanking pace but not so fast that Katchen sounds at all rushed. Plainly he enjoyed himself all through, and with this pianist, who had sometimes seemed too rigid in his recorded playing, it is good to find that here he seemed to be coaxing the orchestra to match his own delicacy. The slow movement is very relaxed – as in the *Third Concerto* – but with the tension admirably sustained, it contrasts well with the extreme bravura of the finale. The filler is a welcome and brightly-played performance of the *Egmont overture*.

John Lill has too often seemed inhibited by the recording process, but here, in the first offering of a projected Beethoven concerto cycle, his rare combination of power and poetry is captured with seeming spontaneity. With first-rate modern recording quality (only marred by a lack of edge on the violin tone) this is an outstanding version, even making no allowance for the modest price.

Curzon's is a refined, thoughtful reading of the *Emperor*, almost Mozartian in the delicacy of the finale but with keen intelligence and inner concentration working throughout. The recording, one of Decca's earliest stereo issues, has been revamped well, but on top there is a limited range, and the orchestral quality has moments of slight roughness. Even so this is a strongly competitive version and a great favourite of I.M.'s.

Barenboim's and Klemperer's account of the *Emperor* is individual almost to the point of perverseness. Many Beethovenians will resist it violently, but with its dry style and measured speeds coupled to a degree of concentration from pianist and conductor rarely caught on record, it provides an astonishingly fresh experience. The technical demands of the solo part, the sheer power, are somehow brought out more vividly, not less, when one has a pianist who, in the best sense, has to struggle to be master – no unthinking pile-driver but a searching voyager. The performance – with a number of unimportant 'fluffs' unedited – has the spontaneous quality of the rest of the cycle.

Brendel gives a splendidly bold and vigorous reading, and he is well supported by Zubin Mehta and the Vienna Pro Musica Orchestra. This is a performance without idiosyncrasy, yet strong in style and personality. Brendel's sense of line in the slow movement has a most compelling effect on the listener, so inevitable does his placing of the notes seem. The beginning of the finale is prepared most beautifully, and the main theme emerges vividly with great character. With a good balance between piano and orchestra, this too is recommended, even though the recording acoustic is rather dry.

Casadesus and Rosbaud give a most beautiful interpretation, satisfyingly detailed and refined with a wonderfully serene Adagio, though on the same midprice label Arrau is even more searching and better recorded.

Firkusny made an intensely refreshing recording of the *Emperor*, available first in mono on Music for Pleasure and later in stereo for CFP. The snag was the rather edgy recording. Now he has rerecorded the work in Decca Phase 4 (PFS 4291), and the new performance reveals the same concentration and thoughtfulness. But both the accompaniment by the New Philharmonia Orchestra under Uri Segal and the recording quality with its unexpected balances prevent it from being a competitive version.

Backhaus's account (on Decca SXL 2179) was perhaps the best performance of his integral set, made in the early days of stereo. The tension is held splendidly throughout with vigorous, forthright outer movements and a clear direct account of the Adagio which, although restrained, has real beauty. The recording, very good in its day, still sounds well. A much more recent issue (HMV ASD

3043) by Alexis Weissenberg with the Berlin Philharmonic under Karajan must be discounted as only a routine account in all respects, while a performance by Gould and Stokowski on CBS 72483 is quite unacceptable. This is arguably the most wilfully idiosyncratic *Emperor* ever recorded.

Violin concerto in D major, Op. 61.
*** Philips 6500 531. Henryk Szeryng (violin), Concertgebouw Orchestra, Bernard Haitink.
*** Philips SAL 3616. Arthur Grumiaux (violin), New Philharmonia Orchestra, Alceo Galliera.
*** Philips 6500 775. Arthur Grumiaux (violin), Concertgebouw Orchestra, Colin Davis.
(M) ** (*) DGG Privilege 135081. Wolfgang Schneiderhan (violin), Berlin Philharmonic Orchestra, Eugen Jochum.
(M) ** (*) CBS Classics 61598. Isaac Stern (violin), New York Philharmonic Orchestra, Leonard Bernstein.
(M) ** HMV SXLP 30168. David Oistrakh (violin), French National Radio Orchestra, André Cluytens.
(M) ** Philips Universo 6580 004. Henryk Szeryng (violin), London Symphony Orchestra, Hans Schmidt-Isserstedt.
(B) ** Classics for Pleasure CFP 139. Leonid Kogan (violin), Paris Conservatoire Orchestra, Constantin Silvestri.

(i) *Violin concerto in D major, Op. 61;* Overture: *Coriolan, Op. 62.*
** (*) HMV ASD 2667. New Philharmonia Orchestra, Sir Adrian Boult, (i) with Josef Suk (violin).

Beethoven's *Violin concerto* is well represented in each price-range, but opinions are divided over the relative merits of different interpretations and it is not easy to suggest a clear first choice. Certainly the newest record by Henryk Szeryng is highly recommendable, both for the outstanding excellence of the recording and for the quality of the partnership between soloist and orchestra. The opening is immediately riveting by its sense of scale and power, yet the music's lyrical feeling is fully revealed. In the *Larghetto* Szeryng does not create the withdrawn atmosphere of his earlier reading, but lets the music blossom fully with a richly drawn line. At its second appearance the glorious second subject is played straightforwardly, with great intensity, and after this emotional climax the link into the finale is managed with a fine sense of spontaneity. The dance-like mood which follows completes an interpretation that is as satisfying in its sense of overall shape as in its control of mood and detail, although for some ears this reading does not match Grumiaux in imaginative insight.

Grumiaux's earlier performance (SAL 3616) is imbued throughout with the spirit of classical serenity which is the essence of this concerto. There is, however, a touch more of personal temperament in the playing, noticeable especially in the slow movement, where the warmth given to the second subject suggests a conscious individual commitment – however restrained – and where the soloist's variation on the main theme, which follows, is given a quixotic lightness, even a suggestion of gaiety. This is one of the imaginative highlights of the reading, and Galliera's quickening of tempo here is pleasingly in sympathy with the soloist's mood. Indeed the orchestral contribution is modelled throughout with a professional's feeling for line and balance. Galliera is helped by a rich, sonorous recording, although the upper register has a slight tendency to fuzz.

Grumiaux's newer version (6500 775) provides fuller, richer, cleaner recording and sharper orchestral ensemble, to make the outer movements if anything even more impressive than in his version with Galliera. But in the slow movement there is not quite the same sense of repose, of spontaneous magic, as before. The balance of advantage between the two versions – both among the finest ever made – is impossible to resolve.

Schneiderhan's reading has now been reissued on DGG's mid-priced label. It makes a very considerable bargain. The serene spiritual beauty of the slow movement and the playing of the elusive second subject have never been surpassed on record, and the orchestra under Jochum provides a background tapestry of power and dignity. Against it Schneiderhan's small silvery tone and purity of style are so consistently poised and have such an innate sense of classicism that the senses and spirit alike are satisfied. The snag is the recording of the soloist, which makes the violin tone sound thin. But this remains one of the great readings of the greatest of all violin concertos. As an added point of interest Schneiderhan uses the cadenzas provided (by Beethoven?) for the transcription of the work for piano and orchestra. The first-movement cadenza is long and varied in mood and includes a solo part for the timpani.

Suk's performance too has been widely praised. In terms of sheer recorded sound his version has few rivals. The performance is more controversial. The first movement is taken at an unusually slow tempo, and neither E.G. nor I.M. finds that the playing has the kind of urgency and concentration to sustain the conception. But for R.L., Suk's playing is both noble and spacious. The performance is classical in style, although Suk, like Kreisler, pulls back at the G minor section in the development of the first movement. But it is the breadth and grandeur of design that emerge. Sir Adrian embodies the revisions in the score brought to light in Alan Tyson's edition, and the recording has exceptional body of tone and splendour. The eloquence of the slow movement and the lightness and sparkle of the finale are in no doubt, but both E.G. and I.M. find Grumiaux altogether more satisfying in the first movement, and his is a poetic and distinguished reading throughout. No one buys a record of the *Violin concerto* for the sake of the *Coriolan overture*, but were anyone to do so Boult's superbly recorded and impressively played account would almost be worth it. It is certainly among the finest on disc at present.

The reissue of Isaac Stern's performance on CBS Classics shows the intense creative relationship established between Stern and Bernstein. Stern's reading has a tremendous onward flow, his personality projected strongly, yet Bernstein keeps the orchestra well in the picture (in spite of the forward balance of the soloist), and the energy of the music-making is compulsive. The close CBS recording means that a real *pianissimo* in the slow movement is not possible, but the intensity is in no doubt, and the finale is comparably vigorous.

Among the other medium-priced reissues, choice between Szeryng's earlier recording on Universo and David Oistrakh's strong, aristocratic reading on HMV Concert Classics is not easy and must essentially be left to personal taste. The HMV recording is undoubtedly superior, with a spacious acoustic and warm, resonant orchestral tone. The balance, however, places the soloist unnaturally forward, although he is beautifully recorded. The reading is characteristically assured, the soloist's phrasing and sense of line impeccable, but there is a suggestion of aloofness in the slow movement. Szeryng is withdrawn in the *Larghetto*, but in a quite different way. He creates a dreamy, hushed atmosphere, and the gentle beauty of mood is a highlight of a performance that is strongly lyrical throughout. Where Cluytens provides a thoroughly musical accompaniment

for Oistrakh, Schmidt-Isserstedt seems rather too weighty and considered in the first movement, but he is sympathetic in the slow movement and he lightens the finale effectively. The Philips recording is full, but not so cleanly focused as the HMV, yet the overall effect is of a greater feeling of poetry in the Universo performance compared to the sense of the grand manner which permeates the Oistrakh account. Both are excellent value.

So too is the Classics for Pleasure version by Kogan. As in the Brahms *Concerto*, Kogan gives a fine performance that combines strength and poetry. The slow movement, taken sweetly and expansively, is particularly compelling, and with good stereo on one of the cheapest labels, this makes an excellent bargain version, missing only perhaps the extra degree of individuality that marks out the very finest versions.

Other readings of this concerto abound, including Ferras (with Karajan) on DGG and Francescatti (with Walter) on CBS's middle-priced label; but none of these seems really competitive with the records listed above. Menuhin's re-recording with Klemperer was generally less successful than his earlier account with Silvestri, currently unobtainable.

*Piano concerto in D major (*arr. of *Violin concerto, Op. 61).*
   *** DGG 2530 457. Daniel Barenboim (piano) with English Chamber Orchestra.

Whether or not Beethoven himself transcribed his *Violin concerto* into this piano version is in some dispute. What is certain is that whoever made the arrangement made little or no effort to rethink the solo part in pianistic terms. The result is to alter the character of the music entirely, bringing down the emotional scale and substituting charm where in the original there is great spiritual depth. The work could surely not receive

97

a more dedicated or affectionate performance than it does here. Barenboim makes the most of the limited piano part, and he is delightful in the slow movement. Incidentally the special cadenzas featuring the timpani can also be heard on the outstanding Schneiderhan version of the original.

Triple concerto for violin, violoncello, piano and orchestra in C major, Op. 56.
   ** (*) HMV ASD 2582. David Oistrakh (violin), Mstislav Rostropovich (cello), Sviatoslav Richter (piano), Berlin Philharmonic Orchestra, Herbert von Karajan.
   (M) ** (*) DGG Privilege 2726 008 (2 discs). Wolfgang Schneiderhan (violin), Pierre Fournier (cello), Géza Anda (piano), Berlin Radio Orchestra, Ferenc Fricsay – BACH, BRAHMS, VIVALDI: *Double concertos.* ** (*)
   ** DGG 136236. Schneiderhan; Fournier; Anda (as above).
   ** Philips 6500 129. Henryk Szeryng (violin), Janos Starker (cello), Claudio Arrau (piano), New Philharmonia Orchestra, Eliahu Inbal.
   (M) ** HMV SXLP 30080. David Oistrakh (violin), Sviatoslav Knushevitzky (cello), Lev Oborin (piano), Philharmonia Orchestra, Sir Malcolm Sargent – *Overtures.* **

Even in these days of star-studded recordings the roster of soloists on HMV is breathtaking (EMI plotted for a long time to capture the magic trio), and to have so spectacular a conductor as Karajan in addition is almost too good to be true. The results are aptly opulent, with Beethoven's priorities between the soloists well preserved in the extra dominance of Rostropovich over his colleagues. This is

warm, expansive music-making that confirms even more clearly than before that the old view of this as one of Beethoven's weaker works is wrong. The three Soviet soloists revel in the multiplicity of ideas, with Richter in the spare piano part providing a tautening influence. The recording is rather too reverberant, and suffers from distortion on some climaxes, but this is not too serious.

The recording is generally much better on the older DGG disc, with clever use of stereo in depth to solve the overall balance problems. The solo players are grouped well forward, and each is clearly separate from the other. The performance is a fine one, lacking a little in spontaneity (most noticeably in the first movement), perhaps because of the laudable desire of each player not to hog the stage to himself. Taken in all this is a most satisfying account and although it now seems too expensive in its single-disc, full-priced form, within the Privilege double album of concertante works it makes an excellent investment.

The performance on Philips matches the recording quality. In the outer movements it lacks the bite and bravura of the finest rivals, but the central brief slow movement is exquisitely done.

The HMV mid-price disc is a reissue of a very early stereo version and the recording is only fairly good, dry and without too much bloom. But the performance is authoritative, and if the coupled overtures are wanted (they are much better recorded) this makes a fair recommendation.

12 Contretänze; 12 German dances: Nos. 2, 3, and 8; Romances for violin and orchestra: (i) No. 1 in G major, Op. 40; No. 2 in F major, Op. 50; 11 Viennese dances (1819).
   ** Decca SXL 6436. Vienna Mozart Ensemble, Willi Boskovsky; (i) Willi Boskovsky (violin).

It is always a delight to catch Beethoven relaxing, and showing how warmly he felt towards the Viennese background against which he lived. Boskovsky and his players interpret these unpretentious dances to the manner born, and the recording is wonderfully vivid. Unfortunately Boskovsky's tone in the two violin *Romances* is sour and unattractive: they are more difficult than is sometimes realized, and it is a pity that an outside virtuoso was not brought in.

The Creatures of Prometheus: Overture and ballet music, Op. 43: complete recording.

> (B) * (*) Turnabout TV 34371S. Berlin Symphony Orchestra, Hans-Hubert Schönzeler.

The Creatures of Prometheus: Overture and ballet music, Op. 43: Nos. 1–5, 9, 10, 14–16.

> (M) ** (*) Vanguard VSD 71124. Utah Symphony Orchestra, Maurice Abravanel.

The Creatures of Prometheus: Overture and ballet music, Op. 43: Nos. 1–5, 8–10, 15, 16.

> ** (*) Decca SXL 6438. Israel Philharmonic Orchestra, Zubin Mehta.

Beethoven composed his ballet score during 1800–1801 for the Neapolitan dancer and choreographer Salvatore Viganó. The ballet was a distinct success, receiving nearly thirty performances during the following two years. It is a pity that Schönzeler's complete version is somewhat spoiled by the thin and edgy string sound of the Turnabout record, for the performance has a real feeling for the dance, with springy rhythms, and a sense of the dramatic (shown immediately at the opening chords after the Introduction), while the woodwind solos are shaped with pleasing romantic flexibility.

The Utah disc is infinitely better recorded, in a warm pleasing acoustic, and there is not the sense of crammed sides that one has with the Turnabout issue. This is achieved by omitting some of the less important sections of the score. Abravanel's style is broader, lyrical in a more symphonic way. The solo wind playing is delightful, but less romantic in flavour, notably so in No. 5 where Beethoven, rarely, uses the harp to introduce a forward-looking sequence for woodwind and solo cello. But the quick movements have no lack of spirit in Utah, and the Finale using the famous *Eroica* theme is well managed.

Mehta is perhaps not so natural a Beethovenian as Abravanel, who conducts on the rival disc of excerpts, but these are still excellent performances, with an extra persuasive manner in some of the comparatively un-Beethovenian dance movements. The lovely piece for cello and harp is beautifully played. Mehta makes a cut in his version of No. 8 and omits No. 14, so many may feel that the cheaper Vanguard disc is the better investment.

OVERTURES

Overtures: *The Consecration of the House, Op. 124; Coriolan, Op. 62; The Creatures of Prometheus, Op. 43; Egmont, Op. 84; Fidelio, Op. 72c; King Stephen, Op. 117; Namensfeier, Op. 115; Leonora Nos. 1–3, Opp. 138; 72a; 72b; The Ruins of Athens, Op. 113.*

> ** (*) DGG 2707 046 (2 discs). Berlin Philharmonic Orchestra, Herbert von Karajan.

These two records come from the box of three that DGG issued during the Beethoven Year under the title *Music for the stage.* The *Leonora No. 3* and *Fidelio* overtures come from the mid-sixties, however. There is a fastidiousness about some of the phrasing (for example in

99

Leonora No. 2) and a smoothness of texture that sometimes seem out of character and for this reason some readers might well prefer the plainer, graver readings of Klemperer. Nonetheless one cannot but marvel at the superlative playing of the Berlin Philharmonic and the no less excellent recorded sound. There are impressive and exciting things about these performances and they have undoubted atmosphere.

Overtures: *The Consecration of the House, Op. 124; Coriolan, Op. 62; The Creatures of Prometheus, Op. 43; Egmont, Op. 84; King Stephen, Op. 117.*
  *** Columbia SAX 2570. Philharmonia Orchestra, Otto Klemperer.
Overtures: *Fidelio, Op. 72c; Leonora Nos. 1–3, Opp. 138; 72a; 72b.*
  ** (*) Columbia SAX 2542. Philharmonia Orchestra, Otto Klemperer.

It was a good idea for Columbia to couple Klemperer's performances of the Beethoven overtures, previously available as fill-ups merely. This disc complements the one containing the four opera overtures, and has some really inspired playing. Even the trivial *King Stephen* overture is given strength and *The Consecration of the House* has never sounded so magnificent on record. Recordings of varying vintage come up well.

The second disc collects together Klemperer's performances of the four overtures written for *Fidelio* at various stages. The approach, as one expects with Klemperer, is on the staid side – even *Fidelio* is more serious than usual – but such is his control over tension, no unbiased listener could find the result dull or heavy. The recording is of fair EMI vintage of some years ago.

Overtures: *Coriolan, Op. 62; Egmont, Op. 84.*
  (M) ** HMV SXLP 30080. Berlin

Philharmonic Orchestra. Joseph Vandernoot – *Triple concerto.***

Vandernoot's performances are sensible and strong. This brings minor disappointments in a comparatively tepid ending to *Egmont* and a slow speed for the opening of *Coriolan,* but the playing of the Berlin Philharmonic is very good indeed and the recording is clear and atmospheric.

Overtures: *Coriolan, Op. 62; Egmont, Op. 84; Fidelio, Op. 72c; Leonora No. 3, Op. 72b; The Ruins of Athens, Op. 113.*
  *** DGG 2530 414. Berlin Philharmonic Orchestra, Herbert von Karajan.

Impressive performances that can stand comparison with the finest now in the catalogue. Karajan's accounts of all these overtures show an imposing command of structure and detail as well as the customary virtuosity one expects from him and the Berlin Philharmonic. The only reservation of note is in *Leonora No. 3,* where the tempo Karajan chooses in the coda strikes one as very brisk indeed. The recording is eminently acceptable even if it is not in the demonstration class.

Overtures: *Coriolan, Op. 62; Fidelio, Op. 72c; Leonora No. 3, Op. 72b.*
  ** (*) DGG SLPM 139001. Berlin Philharmonic Orchestra, Herbert von Karajan – SCHUBERT: *Symphony No. 8.****

Karajan gives characteristically brilliant performances of these three overtures, ending *Fidelio* and *Leonora No. 3* with bravura displays of virtuosity at speed. But most collectors will treat this merely as a coupling for Karajan's remarkably satisfying and beautifully controlled account of the Schubert *Unfinished.*

Overtures: *Egmont, Op. 84; Fidelio, Op. 72c; King Stephen, Op. 117; Leonora Nos. 1–3, Opp. 138; 72a; 72b.*
> (M) * (*) CBS Classics 61580. Cleveland Orchestra, George Szell.

Some of these performances by the Cleveland Orchestra were recorded in London when the players were on a European tour. The sound was originally good, but this reissue has made it harsher and more limited. In Szell's intense way the performances are excellent.

Overtures: *Fidelio, Op. 72c; Leonora Nos. 1–3, Opp. 138; 72a; 72b.*
> (M) * Decca Ace of Diamonds SDD 421. Israel Philharmonic Orchestra, Lorin Maazel.

The recording here is very good and so is the orchestral playing. But Maazel whips everything up into a frenzy, and in the end the ceaseless brilliance is self-defeating.

Romances for violin and orchestra Nos. 1 in G major, Op. 40; 2 in F major, Op. 50.
> (M) *** DGG Privilege 135039. David Oistrakh (violin), Royal Philharmonic Orchestra, Sir Eugene Goossens – BRUCH: *Violin concerto No. 1.***
> ** Philips 6500 137. Henryk Szeryng (violin), Concertgebouw Orchestra, Bernard Haitink – BRAHMS: *Double concerto.* * (*)

The performances on both these discs are of high quality, and those by Oistrakh are outstanding.

SYMPHONIES

Symphonies Nos. 1–9; Overtures: The Consecration of the House; Coriolan;

The Creatures of Prometheus; Egmont (with incidental music); *Fidelio; King Stephen; Leonora Nos. 1–3.*
> (B) ** (*) HMV SLS 788 (9 discs). Philharmonia Orchestra, Otto Klemperer (with soloists and chorus).

This set is priced very reasonably, and on any count it provides outstanding value for money in showing Klemperer's achievement in the Beethoven orchestral music. All these performances are reviewed individually elsewhere. Although there are some disappointments, notably in symphonies 1, 5, 7, 8 and 9 in varying degrees, Klemperer is never less than interesting. The performances of symphonies 2, 3, 4 and 6 are among the very finest ever recorded, and the overtures too are generally very successful in their magisterial way. The recordings have been freshened and generally sound well if inevitably sometimes slightly dated.

Symphonies Nos. 1–9; Overtures: The Creatures of Prometheus, Op. 43; Egmont, Op. 84; Leonora No. 3, Op. 72b.
> ** HMV Quadraphonic Q4 SLS 892 (8 discs). Munich Philharmonic Orchestra, Rudolf Kempe (with soloists and chorus).

Kempe's cycle had the distinction of being the first to be issued on disc in quadraphonic form. These were performances recorded over a relatively brief period, and they tend to reflect that in their merits as well as their limitations. Kempe as a Beethovenian believes in letting the music speak for itself at sensitive unexaggerated tempi. Plainly the orchestra has responded to this challenge, producing fresh, spontaneous-sounding playing, not always perfectly disciplined but natural and communicative. Not all the symphonies sound as intense as they might – No. 5, for example – but the cycle is rounded off by a splendid performance of the *Ninth*, in which Kempe more than elsewhere underlines the dramatic contrasts. The recording – whether on four channels or two – is vivid and atmospheric, although the string tone in tutti has a certain edge. The acoustic of the Munich studio does not seem so telling in quadraphonic terms as, for instance, the Great Hall of Birmingham University, where some of the most successful EMI quadraphonic discs have been made. The improvement in sound in quad is marginal, most striking, as might be expected, in the *Choral symphony*.

Symphony No. 1 in C major, Op. 21; Overtures: *Coriolan, Op. 62; Leonora No. 3, Op. 72b.*

(B) (*) ** Classics for Pleasure CFP 187. Berlin Philharmonic Orchestra, André Cluytens.

Symphonies Nos. 1 in C major, Op. 21; 2 in D major, Op. 36.

*** Philips 6500 113. Academy of St Martin-in-the-Fields, Neville Marriner.

** (*) DGG SLPM 138801. Berlin Philharmonic Orchestra, Herbert von Karajan.

** (*) Decca SXL 6437. Vienna Philharmonic Orchestra, Hans Schmidt-Isserstedt.

(M) ** CBS Classics 61150. Cleveland Orchestra, George Szell.

Symphonies Nos. 1 in C major, Op. 21; 8 in F major, Op. 93.

(B) ** (*) Decca Eclipse ECS 638. Vienna Philharmonic Orchestra, Pierre Monteux.

(M) ** (*) DGG Privilege 2538 074. Bavarian Radio or Berlin Philharmonic Orchestra, Eugen Jochum.

(B) ** Pye GSGC 14081. Hallé Orchestra, Sir John Barbirolli.

* (*) HMV ASD 2560. Philharmonia Orchestra, Otto Klemperer.

(M) * (*) Unicorn UNS 200. Little Orchestra of London, Leslie Jones.

Marriner presents the first two symphonies authentically with a Mozart-sized orchestra, and the result is lithe and fresh, with plenty of character but few if any quirks or mannerisms. Nor are the dramatic contrasts underplayed, for the chamber scale is most realistically captured in the excellent recording.

Karajan's refinement is shown in every movement of the *First Symphony*, yet the result is very far from being Mozartian and small-scale. The finale in fact is particularly exciting. Only the rather fast tempo for the slow movement is at all controversial, and there the moulding of phrase is so beautiful that Karajan's judgement is quickly justified. The approach to the *Symphony No. 2* is completely consistent with that to No. 1, refinement and strength combined. Again the slow movement is on the fast side.

For both symphonies 1 and 2 Schmidt-Isserstedt adopts unusually slow tempi, giving each movement a hint of ponderousness. In the finales of both symphonies the measured approach is a pure delight, revealing detail normally submerged and with nicely pointed playing from the Vienna Philharmonic. Though these are natural, unforced performances to give much pleasure, the Karajan coupling with its direct manners and crisp tempi is a safer recommendation than this for those not wanting Marriner's smaller scale.

The characteristic Cleveland sound with its absence of real *pianissimo* may for some listeners prove disconcerting in these early symphonies, but the clarity, the polish, the dynamism, the unfailing alertness of Szell's performances make up for any absence of charm. On a mid-price label this provides excellent value.

There is plenty of rhythmic life in Cluytens's account of the *First Symphony*, with no lack of vivacity in the outer movements and genuine high spirits in the finale. The *Andante* is kept moving, but the final impression here is of good musicianship rather than inspiration. The characteristic reverberant Berlin recording adds its own weight to the reading and tends to emphasize the conductor's accents. Of the two overtures, *Coriolan* is strongly dramatic, and *Leonora No. 3* has both breadth and excitement: it begins with a fine sweep, and if Cluytens then lets the tension drop marginally, the closing pages are really exciting.

Turning now to couplings of the *First* and *Eighth Symphonies*, one finds that the competition is keen. Monteux in his last years made a number of fine recordings of Beethoven, and his performance on Decca's cheapest label makes an outstanding recommendation. In both works Monteux steers an ideal course, neither underestimating the weight nor making the music too heavy. The first movement of the *Eighth* is specially exhilarating, and only the fast tempo of the *Allegretto* which follows (more scherzando in effect) might be regarded as at all controversial. First-rate recording for its early-sixties vintage.

Jochum too gives refreshingly unmannered readings of both symphonies, and the recordings – the Berlin Hall more spacious – sound very well indeed. As representative of the German tradition, these make a fine alternative to Monteux, although at medium price they are considerably more expensive.

Barbirolli's interpretation too stands the test of time. In Monteux's price-range, this Pye reissue bids for direct comparison, and the contest is certainly close. Against Monteux's more modern recording and slightly more polished string playing from the Vienna Philharmonic, you have Barbirolli's rather more stylish, more pointed way with Beethoven. The outer movements of the *First Symphony* have elegance but a sense of humour too, and the slow movement is most poetically phrased. Only the scherzo, with some less than perfect discipline, falls short. The *Eighth* is infectiously enjoyable, with sharper pointing and a more springy step in the first movement than Monteux gives. Barbirolli's speed for the *Allegretto* is more conventional than Monteux's scherzando and nicely shaped. The Hallé strings are less than immaculate in the minuet but make amends in the beautifully feathered opening of the finale, which is taken exhilaratingly fast. Recording good for its age and quite acceptable on a bargain-label issue.

Klemperer's coupling is disappointing. He takes a strangely ponderous view of the first and third movements of the C major work, and, as though to make up, the finale is taken fast, but even there the very precision of the playing, brilliant achievement though it is, gives the impression of excessive care when the music calls for infectious enjoyment. Klemperer's approach to the *Eighth* seems even more deliberately weighty. Weight there certainly should be, but it is very dubious whether slow speeds and a rather stiff beat will make it apparent in the right way. The Klemperer approach has its justification at the wonderful moment of the first-movement recapitulation. Riding on the climax of the development the main tune surges in on a towering *fortissimo*. But the *Allegretto* is too metronomic even for a movement intended as a playful portrait of that useful timepiece, and the finale plods for much of its length.

Like Marriner and the Academy, Leslie Jones presents Beethoven in a chamber scale, but the playing of the Little Orchestra, well pointed as it is, hardly compares with that of its rival. Even so, for anyone wanting this approach and this coupling rather than Marriner's it is a fair recommendation, helped by clean recording.

Symphony No. 2 in D major, Op. 36; Overtures: *The Creatures of Prometheus, Op. 43; Leonora No. 2, Op. 72a.*

** (*) HMV ASD 2561. Philharmonia Orchestra, Otto Klemperer.

Symphony No. 2 in D major, Op. 36; Overtures: *The Creatures of Prometheus, Op. 43; The Ruins of Athens, Op. 113.*

(M) ** (*) DGG Privilege 2538 075. Berlin Philharmonic or Bavarian Radio Orchestra, Eugen Jochum.

Symphony No. 2 in D major, Op. 36; Overture: *Egmont, Op. 84.*

(B) ** (*) Classics for Pleasure CFP 193. Berlin Philharmonic Orchestra, André Cluytens.

The weight of the slow introduction and the feeling of size in the main allegro mark Klemperer's performance out as a 'big' one. There is no feeling that this is an eighteenth-century work: it looks forward to Beethoven's later masterpieces rather than back to the symphonies of Mozart and Haydn. Klemperer carries this conception to an extreme, so that there are moments which verge on gruffness, particularly in the finale, which sounds rather stolid. The performances of the two overtures are outstanding.

Jochum gives a characteristically strong and refreshing reading of the *Second*, helped by beautifully balanced and pointed playing from the Berlin Orchestra. Though this Privilege issue is markedly more expensive than Cluytens's version with the same orchestra, and provides less good value than Szell's fine mid-price coupling of the *First* and *Second Symphonies*, it is still a good recommendation, with recording (late fifties) that hardly shows its age.

Cluytens characteristically directs a strong, urgent performance, marked by fine playing from the Berlin Philharmonic.

The ample Berlin acoustic makes up for any limitation in the recording. An excellent bargain with a welcome fill-up.

There is also available a very well recorded account by Ansermet on Ace of Diamonds (SDD 102), which now seems uncompetitive. The reading offers a straightforward no-nonsense approach, with a lack of real style about it.

Symphony No. 3 in E flat major (Eroica), Op. 55.

*** DGG SLPM 138802. Berlin Philharmonic Orchestra, Herbert von Karajan.

** (*) CBS 73154 (with discussion of first movement by conductor). New York Philharmonic Orchestra, Leonard Bernstein.

** (*) Decca SXL 6232. Vienna Philharmonic Orchestra, Hans Schmidt-Isserstedt.

(M) ** (*) CBS Classics 61151. Cleveland Orchestra, George Szell.

** (*) HMV ASD 2348. BBC Symphony Orchestra, Sir John Barbirolli.

(B) ** (*) Classics for Pleasure CFP 203. Berlin Philharmonic Orchestra, André Cluytens.

** DGG 2530 437. Vienna Philharmonic Orchestra, Karl Boehm.

(B) ** Decca SPA 123. Vienna Philharmonic Orchestra, Pierre Monteux.

(M) ** Philips Universo 6580 079. Concertgebouw Orchestra, Pierre Monteux.

Symphony No. 3 in E flat major (Eroica), Op. 55; Overture: *Coriolan, Op. 62.*

** (*) Philips 6500 141. BBC Symphony Orchestra, Colin Davis.

Symphony No. 3 in E flat major (Eroica), Op. 55; Overture: *Fidelio, Op. 72c.*

*** HMV ASD 2562. Philharmonia Orchestra, Otto Klemperer.

The *Eroica* is a symphony where only a handful of conductors have given their finest. Klemperer is certainly of their number. So is Karajan, and, perhaps more surprisingly, Bernstein. It is widely felt that Klemperer's stereo version of the *Eroica* failed quite to match the incandescence of his mono record with the same orchestra. In fact it is not quite so simple as that, for though characteristically Klemperer's tempi had grown slower over the years, only in the coda of the finale does this make for any degree of slackness. Otherwise the first movement is massively monumental, the *Funeral march* stoically intense, with a conclusion more poignant than before.

Karajan's is in some ways a safer, more straightforward recommendation, though it does not show quite the same individual imagination. The refinement of detail never gets in the way of the dramatic, dynamic urgency of the whole performance, and only in the *Funeral march* does Karajan give the music anything less than the weight one wants. The recording is good.

Bernstein, adopting a ferocious tempo for the first movement almost in the manner of Toscanini, completely justifies his decision to observe the exposition repeat – a strong point in favour of this version over most rivals. The close of the *Funeral march* is agonizingly poignant, while Bernstein's urgency of expression from first to last and his freedom from mannerism put this among the finest performances available. The recording is good but not outstanding. The explanatory talk makes an interesting extra.

Schmidt-Isserstedt's reading may not have quite the same power as some of the other symphonies in his cycle, but his is a very satisfying thoughtful reading, not lacking dramatic weight, and very well recorded. (It is a particular favourite with I.M.)

Szell's reading too is strong and dramatic in the Toscanini tradition. The first movement brings a taut control of argument over the longest span with few if any concessions to romanticism. No lack of feeling in the *Funeral march*, though the tempo is on the fast side. The Cleveland Orchestra's playing is deeply expressive, but the close-up recording marginally minimizes the effect of genuinely hushed *pianissimos*.

Barbirolli's is a spaciously conceived account in which Sir John secures excellent playing from the BBC Symphony Orchestra. Both the first and second movements are unhurried, yet well held together, and there is a genuine lyrical feel to the performance as well as spontaneity. The recording is a fine one, most musically balanced, and the disc deserves to be numbered among the more successful *Eroicas* in recent years.

A strong account from Davis, the conception broadly satisfying, and the playing excellent throughout. But with such an approach, and a very slow tempo for the *Funeral march*, a higher degree of concentration is needed, and good though this is, the sense of urgency here is lacking. The overture is a successful bonus, but this is not among the greatest available performances of the *Eroica*. It is, however, very enjoyable and splendidly recorded.

In the bargain category Cluytens should not be overlooked. Though his tempo at the start of the first movement sounds breathless, he quickly justifies it in strongly dramatic playing. The *Funeral march* is wonderfully hushed and intense, and the last two movements show the Berlin Orchestra in brilliant form, helped by warmly atmospheric recording. Make sure you get the pressing with the first two movements complete on the first side.

Except in the *Funeral march*, Boehm is not quite at his finest in the *Eroica*: later symphonies of his cycle have more intense playing. But the *Funeral march*

105

without undue moulding of phrase is still deeply devotional. Excellent recording.

Monteux's two performances have fine qualities, but by the best modern standards they both fall short. Broadly speaking the Vienna performance is the more satisfying interpretatively, the Amsterdam one the better played and recorded. If the SPA version, even with improved sound, now shows its age, the Philips issue is disappointing in the absence of real weight in the *Funeral march.*

Symphony No. 4 in B flat major, Op. 60.
   *** DGG SLPM 138803. Berlin Philharmonic Orchestra, Herbert von Karajan.
   (B) ** (*) Decca Eclipse ECS 671. London Symphony Orchestra, Pierre Monteux – *Ah perfido!* **
Symphony No. 4 in B flat major, Op. 60;
Overture: The Consecration of the House, Op. 124.
   *** Decca SXL 6274. Vienna Philharmonic Orchestra, Hans Schmidt-Isserstedt.
Symphony No. 4 in B flat major, Op. 60;
Overtures: The Creatures of Prometheus, Op. 43; Fidelio, Op. 72c; The Ruins of Athens, Op. 113.
   (B) ** Classics for Pleasure CFP 40001. Berlin Philharmonic Orchestra, André Cluytens.
Symphony No. 4 in B flat major, Op. 60;
(i) Egmont (incidental music), Op. 84: Overture; Die Trommel gerühret; Freudvoll und leidvoll; Klärchens Tod bezeichnend.
   *** HMV ASD 2563. Philharmonia Orchestra, Otto Klemperer; (i) Birgit Nilsson (soprano).
Symphony No. 4 in B flat major, Op. 60;
Overture: Leonora No. 2, Op. 72a.
   (M) *** DGG Privilege 2538 097. Berlin Philharmonic Orchestra, Eugen Jochum.

Symphonies Nos. 4 in B flat major, Op. 60; 5 in C minor, Op. 67.
   (M) ** CBS Classics 61152. Cleveland Orchestra, George Szell.
   (B) ** Contour 6870 583. Leipzig Gewandhaus Orchestra, Franz Konwitschny.

Klemperer's is a magnificent reading, one of his very finest Beethoven recordings. It is the strength which comes out more than anything, and the parallels with the *Seventh symphony* are reinforced much more strongly than usual – the monumental intensity of the slow introduction and the extended form for the scherzo. The superb polish of the Philharmonia playing prevents any feeling of heaviness in such an approach, and this now stands as a clear recommendation, with the *Egmont* incidental music as an attractive bonus.

Schmidt-Isserstedt's thoughtful, poetic style is well suited to the *Fourth* and provides a complete contrast to Klemperer. His account of the first movement has more relaxation in it than is common these days, and the very slow *Adagio* he chooses allows Beethoven's lyricism to flower in a comparatively gentle atmosphere. That does not mean that Schmidt-Isserstedt's is too small-scale or wayward a reading, but that he finds in this odd-man-out among the symphonies a different range of Beethovenian qualities. Excellent recording apart from rather dry timpani sound. For R.L. this is the finest version of all.

Karajan's too is a splendid interpretation, with the dynamic contrasts heavily underlined. In the slow movement there is a glow to the playing that almost makes it sound like Schubert, though Karajan's reading of the dotted rhythm is curiously unpointed. DGG, however, offer no coupling on this record, which becomes the most expensive way of acquiring this symphony.

Jochum's is a first-rate mid-price version, well played and well recorded. Anyone wanting this particular coupling can be safely recommended to Jochum's keenly alert interpretation. The hushed tension of the slow introduction (at least as impressive as on any rival version) leads to a thrilling account of the *Allegro vivace* and a beautifully poised reading of the slow movement. With a very good coupling this is a keen rival for any version at whatever price.

Monteux's is an excellent performance, well recorded. You have only to listen to the way Monteux leads into the second subject or the way he floats the high violin melody in the slow movement to realize that a master is at work. Some may find the finale too hectic in the fast, flying manner that Monteux tends to adopt in Beethoven finales, but it is very exciting. An unexpected but worthwhile fill-up on side two.

Cluytens and the Berlin Philharmonic give a vigorous performance, delightfully fresh and alert in the fast movements but marred by a somewhat pedestrian account of the sublime *Adagio*. A fair alternative as a bargain issue, if the three overtures are the coupling you want.

Ansermet's account (now available on Ace of Diamonds SDD 104) was the best of his early stereo cycle of the Beethoven symphonies, apart from the very successful *Choral*. It is a poised, controlled reading which has plenty of buoyancy too. The recording is excellent. This might be more competitive, but it is unfortunate that the filler is an undistinguished account of the *Coriolan overture* with no firm rhythmic pulse and the speed of the crescendos quickened.

The generosity of the coupling makes Szell's disc highly recommendable despite shortcomings in the performance of the *Fifth*. As the opening bars make plain, Szell does not believe in letting the first movement expand. His pauses are ruthlessly cut off, and at the end of the exposition the intense urgency is underlined by the omission of the exposition

repeat. The slow movement brings a degree of hardness, but the work's strength certainly comes over in all four movements; and the performance of No. 4 on the reverse, equally strong, is deeply satisfying all through. The slow movement shows Cleveland polish at its most poised and appealing, though the close-up recording does not do full justice to the quiet playing.

Konwitschny's version of No. 4 is another good one. The recording is weighty and this suits the character of a big if slightly phlegmatic performance in the German classical tradition. The opening is rather stolid but there is fine orchestral playing throughout and the scherzo's trio is notably gracious. No. 5, however, is much less successful. The first movement, taken slowly, does not have much lift, and the *Andante* too is pedestrian. NB. Fitting these symphonies on one record has necessitated the cutting of some repeats observed by Konwitschny at the original recording sessions.

Symphony No. 5 in C minor, Op. 67.
⊛ *** DGG 2530 516. Vienna Philharmonic Orchestra, Carlos Kleiber.
*** DGG SLPM 138804. Berlin Philharmonic Orchestra, Herbert von Karajan.
** (*) CBS 73045 (with lecture: see below). New York Philharmonic Orchestra, Leonard Bernstein.
(B) ** Philips 6833 102. Concertgebouw Orchestra, George Szell – MOZART: *Symphony No. 40.****
(M) ** DGG Privilege 135089. Berlin Philharmonic Orchestra, Lorin Maazel – SCHUBERT: *Symphony No. 8.***
(B) ** Music for Pleasure MFP 2104. Pittsburg Symphony Orchestra, William Steinberg.
** DGG 2530 062. Vienna Philharmonic Orchestra, Karl Boehm.

** Decca Phase 4 PFS 4197. London Philharmonic Orchestra, Leopold Stokowski – SCHUBERT: *Symphony No. 8.* (*)

Symphony No. 5 in C minor, Op. 67; Overture: *Coriolan, Op. 62.*

** HMV ASD 2564. Philharmonic Orchestra, Otto Klemperer.

Symphony No. 5 in C minor, Op. 67; Overture: *The Creatures of Prometheus, Op. 43.*

** (*) HMV ASD 2960. London Symphony Orchestra, André Previn.

Symphony No. 5 in C minor, Op. 67; Overture: *Fidelio, Op. 72c.*

(M) ** (*) DGG Privilege 2538 060. Bavarian Radio Orchestra, Eugen Jochum.

Symphonies Nos. 5 in C minor, Op. 67; 8 in F major, Op. 93.

*** Decca SXL 6396. Vienna Philharmonic Orchestra, Hans Schmidt-Isserstedt.

(B) ** (*) Classics for Pleasure CFP 40007. Berlin Philharmonic Orchestra, André Cluytens.

** Philips 6500 462. BBC Symphony Orchestra, Colin Davis.

Carlos Kleiber's *Fifth* stands out among all others, as did his father Erich's famous performance two decades earlier (still available as a stereo transcription: Decca ECS 518). On the new disc the first movement is electrifying, but has a hushed intensity too. Where Karajan, also outstanding, with a very similar overall approach suggests swaggering extroversion, the hero striding forward, Carlos Kleiber finds darker, more disturbed emotions. The slow movement is tender and delicate, with dynamic contrasts underlined but not exaggerated. The horns, like the rest of the VPO, are in superb form, and the finale, even more

than usual, releases the music into pure daylight.

Bernstein's is a strong, dramatic reading, not quite so distinguished as his account of the *Eroica* but very compelling. The disc also includes a fascinating lecture by Bernstein, which demonstrates with orchestrated illustrations how Beethoven's sketches developed. More atmospheric recording than one sometimes gets from CBS in New York.

Previn's is an unexpected reading, the opposite of what some of his admirers will expect. His view of the *Fifth* is essentially weighty and sober. His tempi are consistently slow (hence the extravagant layout), and there is no attempt to whip up excitement, although the fine playing of the LSO brings some striking dramatic moments, notably on the big crescendo from scherzo to finale. It is a rewarding, thoughtful reading that repays close listening. Excellent recording.

After an unexpectedly restrained opening Jochum launches into a finely vigorous reading unmarred by any romantic exaggeration, gripping in a totally natural, unforced way. The recording hardly shows its age.

Szell's Concertgebouw version, not quite so intense as his Cleveland version on CBS, is still strongly recommendable with fine playing, good recording and a first-rate coupling.

Maazel offers a hard-driven, exciting performance, and the warm playing of the Berlin Philharmonic Orchestra tempers the conductor's impetuosity. Thus although the slow movement is dramatic, with striking contrasts of dynamic, its opening lyrical theme is played with singing tone whenever it dominates the proceedings. The finale could perhaps do with a little more dignity, but those wanting a straightforward, exciting account should find this very acceptable if the coupling – a fresh but comparatively uneventful reading of Schubert's *Unfinished symphony* – is suitable.

Steinberg too gives a direct, straightforward performance, rather in the tradition of Toscanini. In the first movement the pressure is laid on too hard, with little breathing-space allowed, and the scherzo is lacking in lilt; but at its price with good stereo recording it has enough dramatic vigour to make it worth considering.

Klemperer's re-recording of Beethoven's *Fifth* in stereo was eagerly awaited, but when it arrived it proved something of a disappointment. It certainly offers a powerful, closely-knit reading, and the recorded sound is excellent. But somehow, in spite of fine playing and an indisputable feeling of strength in the shaping of the reading as a whole, the performance just refuses to catch fire as the earlier mono disc did. The overture is well done.

Boehm's is an enjoyable but underpowered reading of the *Fifth*. With excellent playing and recording, it may for some listeners make a good version to live with, not at all tense and nerve-racked, but Boehm's mood would be more apt for the *Pastoral symphony* rather than this essentially dramatic masterpiece.

Beethoven proves more resilient than Schubert on the reverse at resisting the effects of Stokowskification. This is a highly personal reading, but like Stokowski's magnificent *Ninth* it certainly has drama and magnetism. The first movement is splendidly strong, weakened neither by the expressive style for the second subject nor even by the absence of exposition repeat. The finale too is splendid, introduced by an unusually measured account of the scherzo – nicely pointed and therefore not sluggish. The *Andante*, however, is slow to the point of idiosyncrasy, and though once again the Stokowski magic works, not everyone will like it. The Phase Four glamour is well presented despite the great length of the side.

The coupling of symphonies 5 and 8 is a happy idea, and on Decca Schmidt-Isserstedt offers strong readings of both;

this is a splendid disc with generous sides and first-rate recording. Schmidt-Isserstedt makes no allowances and includes exposition repeats in both the first movements. The first movement of No. 8 is slower than usual in the interests of emphasizing that this is not simply Beethoven's '*Little one*' but a powerful, symphonic argument. A crisp, light *Allegretto* and a minuet more heavily pointed than usual, with a Brahmsian touch in the trio. But it is the performance of the *Fifth* – not a symphony that regularly gets good performances on record – that stands out in a first movement that has both bite and breathing space, a nicely measured *Andante* and a gloriously triumphant finale. Only the scherzo invites controversy in its slow tempo, but logic plays its part in the choice in that it allows the double basses in the trio to play their scampering part without either stumbling or having the conductor slow for them. Excellent recording considering the length of sides.

At bargain price Cluytens's disc is remarkable value, with very good sound, considering the length of sides. The *Fifth* is an admirably refreshing reading, direct and urgent, unforcedly compelling, and unlike most other versions on a single side it observes the exposition repeat. The Berlin horns in the finale are most exciting. The *Eighth* too is most satisfying: despite a slowish tempo for the first movement, the point of the Berlin playing keeps the performance alert all through.

Though there is much fine playing in Davis's coupling, the performances rarely take fire. The first movement of the *Fifth* has the disadvantage of omitting the exposition repeat, essential in this movement. First-rate recording.

Ansermet's similar coupling is reissued on Decca's cheapest label (SPA 326) and has the benefit of very good sound, but the interpretations hardly hold their own in so competitive a field. Cluytens is far preferable.

Symphony No. 6 in F major (Pastoral), Op. 68.

   *** DGG 2530 142. Vienna Philharmonic Orchestra, Karl Boehm.

   (B) *** Classics for Pleasure CFP 40017. Berlin Philharmonic Orchestra, André Cluytens.

   (B) *** RCA Victrola VICS 1449. Chicago Symphony Orchestra, Fritz Reiner.

   (B) ** (*) Music for Pleasure MFP 2112. Pittsburg Symphony Orchestra, William Steinberg.

   ** Decca Phase 4 PFS 4188. Royal Philharmonic Orchestra, Henry Lewis.

   * (*) DGG SLPM 138805. Berlin Philharmonic Orchestra, Herbert von Karajan.

   (B) * (*) Decca SPA 113. Vienna Philharmonic Orchestra, Pierre Monteux.

   (M) * CBS Classics 61153. Cleveland Orchestra, George Szell.

Symphony No. 6 in F major (Pastoral), Op. 68; Overture: *The Creatures of Prometheus, Op. 43.*

   (M) ** Philips Universo 6580 050. London Symphony Orchestra, Colin Davis.

Symphony No. 6 in F major (Pastoral), Op. 68; Overture: *Egmont, Op. 84.*

   ** (*) HMV ASD 2535. New Philharmonia Orchestra, Carlo Maria Giulini.

   ** Decca SXL 6329. Vienna Philharmonic Orchestra, Hans Schmidt-Isserstedt.

Symphony No. 6 in F major (Pastoral), Op. 68; Overture: *Leonora No. 1, Op. 138.*

   ⊛ *** HMV ASD 2565. Philharmonia Orchestra, Otto Klemperer.

Boehm gives a beautiful unforced reading of the *Pastoral*, one of the best played (even if Vienna violins are not quite as splendid on this showing as those of Berlin) and certainly one of the very best recorded. In the first movement he observes the exposition repeat (not many versions do); and though the dynamic contrasts are never underplayed and the phrasing is affectionate, there is a feeling of inevitable rightness about Boehm's approach, no sense of an interpreter enforcing his will. Only the slow movement with its even stressing raises any reservation, and that very slight.

Cluytens's recording is intensely warmhearted and atmospheric. On analysis alone one might object to the occasional idiosyncrasy, the very affectionate phrasing and a few speed changes. But the obvious spontaneity makes the whole performance most compelling, so that one finds oneself playing it again and again for sheer delight. Each movement has a glow which can only come from complete sympathy between players and conductor, and the final *Shepherds' hymn after the storm* shines out as an apotheosis. In the linking passage after the storm Beethoven's picture of a world freshened by rain is most vivid and from there to the end the sense of joyous release increases in triumphant crescendo. With good sound and at bargain price it should not be missed.

Reiner's disc in the same price-range also offers an outstandingly fresh and enjoyable performance. Throughout, Reiner adopts a straightforward, unmannered approach, his shading is subtle, and the recording, helped by the spacious Chicago acoustic, adds atmosphere without confusion of texture. The slow movement is particularly beautiful, but with the possible exception of a rather fast speed for the finale (justified in the firmness achieved) all the tempi sound utterly natural and unforced. The exposition repeat is observed in the first movement to add to the architectural strength which Reiner's freshness brings out.

Klemperer's *Pastoral* was one of the

very earliest stereo recordings, and although it still sounds well, the string tone is not as sweetly recorded as on the DGG Boehm disc, for instance. But this is a deeply satisfying, idyllic performance, much loved by E.G. and one of I.M.'s desert-island discs. It is a leisurely account, with a gently bucolic scherzo, taken slower, surely, than Beethoven intended, but falling naturally into place within the reading as a whole. The slow movement and the *Shepherds' hymn after the storm* are wonderfully beautiful, and the coda is inspired.

Giulini's is a lyrical approach to Beethoven's most relaxed symphony, and with fine playing from the New Philharmonia and rounded atmospheric recording, the result is warm and attractive. The generally slow tempi will not please everyone, and interpretatively at least the firmer Klemperer approach (also with slow tempi) is more consistently satisfying. But there is room for a relaxed version like Giulini's in the catalogue, though the fill-up with its limp, undramatic manner does nothing to add to the recommendation.

Steinberg's earlier version of the *Pastoral* was strikingly successful and so is the new one in stereo, also on MFP. The opening is this time markedly less genial, and the whole movement is a degree stiffer than before, but in the slow movement the contrast is the other way, with a marginally faster tempo allowing smoother phrasing. The *Peasants' merrymaking* is comparatively relaxed to allow for a genuine accelerando at the end before the storm. A fine horn in the transition into the finale. The stereo recording is very reverberant, with detail sometimes obscured and the violins not quite forward enough, but at the price (with an unusually attractive sleeve) it is an excellent bargain.

Widely separated Phase Four sound makes Henry Lewis's version one of the best recorded for small players, and very recommendable for hi-fi machines. The interpretation is fresh and unmannered, but with rather slower tempi than is usual with a direct approach. The *Peasants' merrymaking* of the scherzo is only a little faster than with Klemperer, and in the Storm (also treated expansively) the central lull comes out the more impressively in Phase Four. The finale is glowing and relaxed, though the RPO violins could be sweeter.

Davis's is a fresh, enjoyable performance, but next to more inspired readings it sounds understated. The recording is clean, but unexciting.

Schmidt-Isserstedt's Decca recording is in the last resort disappointing. It is beautifully recorded and offers a good, clean, straightforward classical account. But there is somehow a lack of atmosphere and warmth, in the approach rather than the playing, and certainly an absence of charm.

The Karajan version is the one real failure of his integral Berlin set. If he thought to imitate Toscanini he failed to note what importance Toscanini places on lyricism as well as hard driving. The impression from Karajan is hard and unyielding.

Monteux's version too is disappointing, in spite of good sound. Plainly the Vienna Philharmonic were not in the form they were for this conductor's account of the *Eroica*, and it is sad to find so little lilt in the first movement.

For all the firmness of style Szell is subtle in his control of phrasing, and it is a pity that the close-up sound robs the slow movement of any gentleness or delicacy of atmosphere. The finale, by contrast, is attractively relaxed.

There is also a CBS reissue from Bernstein, generously coupled to the *Choral fantasia*. But this has been provided at the expense of coarse, restricted sound. The first movement of the symphony is fast and unfeeling, the second sluggish and mannered. Not recommended.

Symphony No. 7 in A major, Op. 92.
(M) *** HMV SXLP 20038. Royal

Philharmonic Orchestra, Colin Davis.

*** DGG SLPM 138806. Berlin Philharmonic Orchestra, Herbert von Karajan.

(B) *** Classics for Pleasure CFP 40018. Berlin Philharmonic Orchestra, André Cluytens.

** (*) HMV ASD 2737. Chicago Symphony Orchestra, Carlo Maria Giulini.

** (*) DGG 2530 421. Vienna Philharmonic Orchestra, Karl Boehm.

(M) ** CBS Classics 61154. Cleveland Orchestra, George Szell.

Symphony No. 7 in A major, Op. 92;
Overture: *The Consecration of the House, Op. 124.*

* (*) HMV ASD 2566. Philharmonia Orchestra, Otto Klemperer.

Symphony No. 7 in A major, Op. 92;
Overture: *Egmont, Op. 84.*

** (*) Decca SXLN 6673. Los Angeles Philharmonic Orchestra, Zubin Mehta.

Symphony No. 7 in A major, Op. 92;
Overture: *Fidelio, Op. 72c.*

(B) ** (*) RCA Camden CCV 5026. Chicago Symphony Orchestra, Fritz Reiner.

Symphony No. 7 in A major, Op. 92;
Overture: *Leonora No. 3, Op. 72b.*

*** Decca SXL 6447. Vienna Philharmonic Orchestra, Hans Schmidt-Isserstedt.

Symphonies Nos. 7 in A major, Op. 92; 8 in F major, Op. 93.

(B) ** Contour 6870 582. Leipzig Gewandhaus Orchestra, Franz Konwitschny.

Schmidt-Isserstedt gives a glowing, magnetic performance of the *Seventh* that compels attention from first bar to last, and with outstandingly vivid recording quality this is one of the very finest Beethoven symphony records in the catalogue. Tempi are generally judged with perfect regard for the often conflicting requirements of symphony and dance – not too ponderous, not too hectic. The generous fill-up is most welcome, a splendidly dramatic performance of *Leonora No. 3*. For both symphony and overture the Vienna Philharmonic is in outstanding form.

Colin Davis's *Seventh* has long established itself as a firm recommendation. It may be on bargain label, but it rivals any performance ever recorded. Here is an ideal illustration of the difference between a studio run-through and a performance that genuinely takes one forward compellingly from bar to bar. Admittedly the opening of the slow introduction is a shade lacking in weight, but from there on there is barely a blemish. The first movement, with delicious pointing of the dotted rhythm, has both stylishness and strength. The slow movement, taken at a measured speed, is beautifully controlled not only in the detailed phrasing but over the architectural span of the whole movement. The scherzo, with all the repeats taken for once, is wonderfully rumbustious, with some superb woodwind playing. The finale, taken very fast indeed, barely allows one to breathe for excitement.

It is interesting to compare Karajan's Berlin account of the *Seventh* with his Vienna version of only a year or so before. Where the Vienna performance (available on Decca Ace of Diamonds SDD 232) failed to catch fire and the result was heartless, the Berlin performance tingles with excitement. It is hard-driven in the Toscanini manner, but in the last resort it does not quite have the lift to the dance-rhythms that the Italian Toscanini managed to retain, even when driving at his hardest.

The distinctive point about Cluytens's reading is his treatment of the main allegro on the first movement. He uses his relatively slow tempo to point the 6/8 rhythm with a delectable lilt – almost another *Pastoral* symphony – but there is no lack of Beethovenian drama, with Beethoven's characteristic sforzandos sharply underlined. The *Allegretto* is beautifully moulded, and more than is common Cluytens, in all four movements, combines Beethovenian unbuttonedness with the lilt of the dance. The recording, apart from some edginess on the violins – which helps to make this account of the finale the most exciting of any, if a little rough in places – is outstanding for its age. At bargain price this can hardly be matched, and the disc is very competitive irrespective of price.

With the Chicago Symphony Orchestra in commanding form and Giulini less mannered than he has sometimes been in Beethoven, his is a formidable version. The introduction is built up to a tremendous climax, and the 6/8 allegro skips nicely without lingering at the pivotal points. The *Allegretto* starts rather heavily, but Giulini's refinement gradually emerges. The last two movements are strong and brilliant, but there the reverberant recording quality masks much of the detail, notably the difficult violin semiquavers in the finale.

A powerful, understanding performance from Reiner, particularly impressive in the first and third movements, where the power is combined with fine rhythmic lift to confirm Wagner's 'apotheosis of the dance'. The fast tempo for the finale draws unscampering brilliance from the Chicago Orchestra. Marginally less impressive are the symphony's slow introduction and the *Allegretto* second movement, where Reiner's manner at fastish speeds is cooler. The atmospheric Chicago recording hardly shows its age (late 1950s).

Apart from a relatively slack performance of the *Egmont overture* as a fill-up, Mehta's is a thoroughly enjoyable disc. The reading of the *Seventh* is marked by fast speeds, which in fact sound slower than they are – sign of acute control. A bright, exciting reading, which falls short

only in the company of such interpreters as Davis, Schmidt-Isserstedt, Cluytens and Karajan. The recording is rather larger than life in the Los Angeles manner.

Boehm's account, splendidly recorded, has much in common with Schmidt-Isserstedt, but the style is marginally lighter, with speeds slightly slower, well-articulated playing throughout and an eloquent slow movement. The straight approach is most striking in the finale, a performance that keeps within itself, without the excitement of Cluytens or Davis. But on its own terms this is satisfying.

Szell's is a strong, finely wrought performance to match the rest of his series, but it is less buoyant than the best versions in this price-range, such as Davis's and Reiner's.

Klemperer on the whole is disappointing, but even when working at lower tension than usual he is intensely interesting. The speeds are slower than they were in his fine earlier mono version, and some of his idiosyncrasies which were vital and spontaneous-sounding then have come to sound like mannerisms. Whether or not he was dissatisfied with the first stereo version, Klemperer re-recorded the work for HMV (ASD 2537) before he died, but the result is in almost every way disappointing, lacking the verve essential in this symphony and without the incisiveness which can provide compensating weight. Two Decca performances by Abbado (SXL 6270) and Ansermet (reissued on SPA 327) fail to achieve enough distinction to be recommendable within their respective price-ranges.

Konwitschny's coupling of the *Seventh* and *Eighth Symphonies* is certainly good value for money (although, as in the similar coupling of Nos. 4 and 5, the repeats have been cut by the producers of the disc to make both works fit). Konwitschny's tempo for the first movement of the *Seventh* is characteristically broad, and the reading has plenty of weight. The

Allegretto is good, but the performance really begins to sparkle at the scherzo, which is splendidly vivacious. The finale too has an exhilarating forward impetus, without the music being rushed off its feet. *Symphony No. 8* is comparatively square throughout. The outer movements are taken steadily, the *Allegretto scherzando* makes a bright contrast, but the internal balance is less good in the minuet and trio, and the playing itself here is slightly below Konwitschny's usual standard.

Symphony No. 8 in F major, Op. 93 (see also under Symphonies 1, 5, and below).
> ** (*) Decca SXL 6549. Vienna Philharmonic Orchestra, Claudio Abbado – SCHUBERT: *Symphony No. 8.* ** (*)

Symphony No. 8 in F major, Op. 93; Overtures: *Coriolan, Op. 62; Fidelio, Op. 72c; Leonora No. 3, Op. 72b.*
> *** DGG SLPM 139015. Berlin Philharmonic Orchestra, Herbert von Karajan.

Abbado's fresh and alert performance underlines the sun in this symphony. The tempi are all well chosen, the rhythms beautifully sprung, and such key moments as the gentle pay-off to the first movement delicately pointed. Some of the abrasiveness of Beethoven is missing, but it makes an excellent coupling for an equally sunny account of Schubert's *Unfinished*. First-rate recording.

Karajan's *Eighth* (also available coupled to the *Ninth*) displays very much the same qualities as the other fine performances in his integral recording, hard-driving somehow combined with refinement. As in the *Seventh* there is a hint of over-driving, but the performance remains a strong recommendation. For those who have purchased an alternative version of the *Choral symphony*, this coupling should prove more than satisfactory.

Symphonies Nos. 8 in F major, Op. 93; 9 in D minor (Choral), Op. 125.
> *** DGG 2707 013 (2 discs). Janowitz, Rössl-Majdan, Kmentt, Berry, Vienna Singverein, Berlin Philharmonic Orchestra, Herbert von Karajan.
> *** HMV SLS 841 (2 discs). Armstrong, Reynolds, Tear, Shirley-Quirk, LSO Chorus, London Symphony Orchestra, Carlo Maria Giulini.
> *** DGG 2707 073 (2 discs). Jones, Troyanos, Thomas, Riddersbusch, Vienna State Opera Chorus, Vienna Philharmonic Orchestra, Karl Boehm.
> (M) ** (*) CBS 61155/6. Addison, Hobson, Lewis, Bell, Chorus and Cleveland Orchestra, George Szell.

Karajan gives one of the most completely satisfying performances of the *Ninth* available in stereo. It is strong, refined and has an urgency that carries the argument through from first to last with the vitality of a live performance. In the sessions for the integral Beethoven cycle the *Ninth* was left till last, and one senses the exhilaration of conductor and orchestra in achieving their goal with such outstanding success. The soloists are excellent, and the Vienna Singverein, taken specially to Berlin, sings with great passion, though the balance could be better. The slow movement is the only one which might cause any serious disappointment, for there Karajan does not quite achieve the spiritual quality one knows from live performances, though the sheer beauty of sound, particularly in the hushed playing, is magical.

Giulini's reading is positively affected by the recording acoustic, close, immediate and rich. His tempo in the first movement is unusually slow – like Solti (see below) he insists on precise sextuplets for the opening tremolo, with no mistiness – and he builds the architecture relentlessly, finding his resolution only in the concluding coda. The scherzo is lithe and powerful, with shattering timpani. The slow movement is warm and Elysian rather than hushed, while the finale, not always quite perfect in ensemble, is dedicatedly intense. The *Eighth Symphony* on the fourth side is less distinguished, but in its lyrical, moulded way is warmly enjoyable.

Boehm's reading makes a fine culmination to his cycle of the Beethoven symphonies with the Vienna Philharmonic. Even in this titanic work there is a natural, unforced quality about Boehm's interpretation, so that details are never distracting. In the slow movement you may well feel that his view is too straight – that quality is underlined when he chooses unusually slow tempi for both the *Adagio* and *Andante* themes, which are therefore given less contrast than usual. But the tone of voice is dedicated, and the work ends with a superbly dramatic yet controlled account of the finale, with excellent playing and singing all round. First-rate recording, except marginally for some forward balancing for soloists in the finale.

In first, second and fourth movements of the *Ninth*, Szell's performance is at least as satisfying as any put on record. The majesty of the argument as well as its intense drama is superbly registered, and though in the slow movement Szell, like Toscanini before him, failed to relax enough, skating over the deeper elements in the music at a fastish tempo, the beauty of phrasing from the Cleveland players helps to counteract this. In absolute terms this is the finest version on bargain label, though as it is on three sides instead of the more usual two the price is not equivalently cheap. Even so the absence of a break in the slow movement and the fill-up of a strong, attractive performance of the *Eighth* make it worth the extra. Recording of the best Cleveland vintage.

Symphony No. 9 in D minor (Choral), Op. 125.

- (M) *** Decca 6BB 121/2. Lorengar, Minton, Burrows, Talvela, Chicago Symphony Chorus, Chicago Symphony Orchestra, Sir Georg Solti.
- *** Decca SXL 6233. Sutherland, Horne, King, Talvela, Vienna State Opera Chorus, Vienna Philharmonic Orchestra, Hans Schmidt-Isserstedt.
- *** Decca Phase 4 PFS 4183. Harper, Watts, Young, McIntyre, LSO Chorus, London Symphony Orchestra, Leopold Stokowski.
- (B) *** Decca SPA 328. Sutherland, Suddaby, Dermota, Van Mill, Chorale du Brassus and Chœur des Jeunes de l'Église Nationale Vaudoise, Suisse Romande Orchestra, Ernest Ansermet.
- (B) ** (*) Classics for Pleasure CFP 40019. Brouwenstijn, Meyer, Gedda, Guthrie, St Hedwig's Cathedral Choir, Berlin Philharmonic Orchestra, André Cluytens.
- (M) ** Philips Universo 6580 006. Gueden, Heynis, Uhl, Rehfuss, Karlsruhe Oratorio Choir, Lamoureux Orchestra of Paris, Igor Markevitch.

Symphony No. 9 in D minor (Choral), Op. 125; Overtures: King Stephen, Op. 117; Leonora No. 3, Op. 72b.

- ** HMV SLS 790 (2 discs). Lovberg, Ludwig, Kmentt, Hotter, Philharmonia Chorus and Orchestra, Otto Klemperer.

The penny-in-the-slot criticism would be to suggest that Solti and the Chicago Symphony Orchestra skate over the surface of the *Ninth*, but the whole performance belies any such assumption. If you regard the sublime slow movement as

115

the key to this epic work, then Solti clearly is with you. With spacious, measured tempi he leads the ear on, not only with his phrasing but with his subtle shading of dynamic down to whispered *pianissimo*. Here is *Innigkeit* of a concentration rarely heard on record, even in the *Ninth*. Solti in the first movement is searing in his dynamic contrasts, maybe too brutally so, while the precision of the finale, with superb choral work and solo singing, confirms this as one of the very finest *Ninths* on record. Superb recording quality, clean yet coordinated.

Schmidt-Isserstedt, with no exaggeration and few if any high-flown purple passages, gives an intensely satisfying reading of the *Ninth*, which in many ways is easier to live with than more monumental, more obviously great performances. The approach associates the work more readily than most with Beethoven's earlier symphonic achievements – the link with the *Pastoral* at the end of the slow movement, for example – but it is the fine singing of soloists and chorus in the finale that above all makes this one of the keenest current recommendations. All four soloists are in peak form, and no rival version matches the beauty and balance of ensemble. Despite the length of sides the recording quality is outstandingly good.

Unmistakably Stokowski's is a great, compelling account of the *Ninth*. There is the sort of tension about this recorded performance which one expects from a great conductor in the concert hall, and that compulsion carries one over all of Stokowski's idiosyncrasies, including a fair amount of touching up in the orchestration. The first movement is strong and dramatic, taken at a Toscanini pace; the scherzo is light and pointed, with timpani cutting through; the slow movement has great depth and *Innigkeit*, and that perhaps more than anything confirms the greatness of the performance, for the finale with some strangely slow tempi is uneven, despite fine singing. Excellent

Phase Four recording, despite the length of sides.

Equally the most remarkable thing about Ansermet's *Ninth* is the quality of the recording; the transfer to a single disc has been achieved with complete success. The clarity of recording suits the interpretation, which lacks the weight of more traditional readings, but has a freshness which makes it consistently enjoyable and interesting. The first two movements are clear-cut and dramatic, and the slow movement is restrained. The finale, if a little lightweight, gains from the clarity of recording and the quality of the soloists, with Joan Sutherland at her most beautiful. The choir is energetic but not always perfectly disciplined.

Cluytens's version competes strongly. The glory of the performance is the hushed and intense account of the slow movement, which makes it the more irritating that because of the one-disc format that movement has to break in the middle. But the other movements are finely concentrated too, showing – as the rest of Cluytens's cycle does – that in his lifetime he was seriously underestimated as a Beethoven interpreter. Soloists and chorus are first-rate – with the possible exception of the cavernous-sounding Guthrie – and considering the length of sides the recording, with ample Berlin reverberation, is most acceptable.

Markevitch's is a strong, well argued performance with a very expansive, intense account of the slow movement. The singing in the finale is good, but even better on most counts is the Cluytens version on an even cheaper label.

The Klemperer set, originally issued on four full sides, has now been reduced to three, with the two overtures providing a fine bonus. But the performance of the symphony is disappointing. The detail of the first movement (very dramatically conceived) can seldom have emerged with more clarity, but Klemperer's characteristically slow tempo for the scherzo, coupled to a performance including every repeat, does seem to make the movement go on for ever. The *Adagio* is very beautiful and possesses a real spiritual quality. It is beautifully recorded, and one must remember that this set dates from the earliest days of stereo. This shows more readily in the finale, which is less successful. Klemperer's solo quartet is undistinguished, and Hans Hotter wobbles badly. The chorus is better disciplined than some, but as a whole Klemperer's conception, though always interesting, is in the last resort too austere, and the finale lacks the essential spirit of joyful exuberance.

There is also a CBS Bernstein set of the *Ninth* (on 78203) in an unusual two-disc format coupled with a characteristically vigorous account of the *Seventh.* Unhappily the recording quality, coarse and lacking in range, precludes a recommendation. In the outer movements of the *Ninth* Bernstein takes an urgently thrustful view, while the slow movement, with a moulded style initially at least, sounds mannered.

*Wellington's victory (*sometimes called *Battle symphony), Op. 91.*

(M) *** RCA LSB 4031. Philadelphia Orchestra, bands, electronic cannon and effects, Eugene Ormandy – TCHAIKOVSKY: *1812.****

(M) ** DGG Privilege 2538 142. Berlin Philharmonic Orchestra, Herbert von Karajan – TCHAIKOVSKY: *1812.*** (*)

Ormandy clearly takes this music seriously. He assembles his British and French armies at either side of the audio spectrum and lays out Beethoven's battle plan with enthusiasm. The battle itself is highly effective, with musketry and cannon blazing, and the culminating victory hymn has a Beethovenian grandeur. It is difficult to imagine this piece of musical hokum being presented with a better blend of dignity and histrionics.

The recording is splendid, especially during the opening drum and trumpet sections.

Karajan's performance is very professional and well recorded, but he does not display the flair in assembling his forces that Ormandy does, and generally the American conductor makes more of an occasion of the whole performance.

Wellington's victory, Op. 91. Musik zu einem Ritterballett: March; German song; Hunting song; Romance; War song; Drinking song; German waltz; coda. Jena symphony (attrib. Beethoven; probably by Friedrich Witt).

(B) ** Turnabout TV 34409S. Westphalian Symphony Orchestra, Hubert Reichert.

The main interest of this disc is the *Jena symphony*, which was wrongly attributed because of indications on the original set of orchestral parts that the composer was 'Louis van Beethoven'. The *galant* style of the piece should have given the truth away, but it is easy to be wise after the event, and it is true that the work's opening and certain other passages have some Beethovenian flavour; and the material and style are certainly not less characteristic than the *Ritterballett* also included here. This, like the symphony, makes pleasant listening and both are given quite accomplished performances. The account of *Wellington's victory* is serviceable and no more: the battle effects raise an unintentional smile by the lack of sophistication from the percussion department. But with surprisingly good recording and no lack of spontaneity throughout, this collection fills a useful gap in the catalogue.

CHAMBER MUSIC

Clarinet trio in B flat major, Op. 11 (for clarinet, piano and violoncello).

117

(B) ** Turnabout TV 34108S. David Glazer (clarinet), Frank Glazer (piano), David Soyer (cello) – BRAHMS: *Clarinet trio.** (*)

This is a successful performance in which good teamwork counts quite as much as the convincing style of the clarinet-player, David Glazer. The playing has plenty of lift and the finale is particularly spontaneous: it is one of those happy light-hearted inventions that remind one of the *Septet*. The recording is dry but projects the music-making well, whereas in the coupling it is less suitable.

Clarinet trio in B flat major, Op. 11; Piano trios Nos. 1–7; Trio No. 14 in E flat major (1784); *Trio in E flat major* (1790/1); *14 Variations in E flat major, Op. 44; 10 Variations on Müller's 'Ich bin der Schneider Kakadu', Op. 121a.*

(M) ** (*) HMV SLS 789 (5 discs). Daniel Barenboim (piano), Jacqueline du Pré (cello), Pinchas Zukerman (violin), Gervase de Peyer (clarinet).

The Barenboim/Zukerman/du Pré set of Beethoven's music for piano trio was recorded in an intensive series of sessions spread over a week at the EMI Abbey Road studios. Even more than usual for Barenboim, the individual takes involved long spans of music, often complete movements, sometimes even a complete work. The result is playing of rare concentration, spontaneity and warmth. Any tendency to self-indulgence (and this is an aspect of the playing R.L. finds obtrusive), plus a certain leaning towards romantic expressiveness, are counterbalanced by the urgency and intensity of the playing. Speeds tend to be extreme in both directions, and the *Innigkeit* of some of the slow movements, especially in the *Ghost trio*, Op. 70/1, has the depth of really mature artistry, extraordinary in

the work of such young musicians. The first movement of the *Archduke trio* offers the most controversial performance. The speed is uncharacteristically slow, and the music's weight seems minimized. But this is counterbalanced by a slow movement of great depth and eloquence and an exuberant finale. The extra items include an early work in E flat (1784) and another written in 1790–91. Of the variations, the *Kakadu* set is given a superlative performance, and Gervase de Peyer joins the team for the *Clarinet trio*, which is played most beautifully. The recording is excellent throughout, and although these performances will not suit all tastes (and at the moment one has to purchase the whole set, if at virtually bargain price), there is no question about their integrity.

Piano trio No. 1 in E flat major, Op. 1/1.

(M) *** Supraphon SUAST 50639. Prague Trio – SCHUMANN: *Trio, Op. 80.***

The twenty-three-year-old composer's first piano trio has not only facility but genuine musical spontaneity. It has been lucky on records and the present disc is no exception. The overall effect is highly exhilarating, but the playing is more than just buoyant and spirited. Each player not only conveys affection but shows, by his phrasing and control of dynamic and line, that he has thought carefully about the music. The result is entirely satisfying.

(i; ii) *Piano trio No. 3 in C minor, Op. 1/3;* (i) *Horn sonata in F major, Op. 17* (version for cello and piano).

(B) (**) Philips 6833 054. Pablo Casals (cello), with (i) Mieczyslaw Horszowski (piano), (ii) Sandor Végh (violin).

This performance was given in the Beethovenhaus, Bonn, in the late 1950s, and it has the spirit of live music-making in the home. The acoustic is uncomfortably dry and there is a small audience present. The recording is far from ideal; all three instruments in the *C minor Trio* sound a little starved of timbre and wanting in colour, while climaxes are not negotiated without some degree of discomfort. Add to this the fact that Végh is often under the note and one would think this hardly a recommendable disc. Yet the playing is so tremendously alive, the sense of real music-making so strong, and the warmth and humanity of these artists so great that one still derives artistic satisfaction from it. What a wonderfully sensitive pianist Horszowski was, by the way! There is something rather special about this playing, but would-be purchasers should be warned that this record is not the document of perfection so many collectors expect nowadays.

Piano trios Nos. 4 in D major (Ghost), Op. 70/1; 5 in E flat major, Op. 70/2.
  *** HMV ASD 2571. Daniel Barenboim (piano), Pinchas Zukerman (violin), Jacqueline du Pré (cello).
  ** DGG 2530 207. Wilhelm Kempff (piano), Henryk Szeryng (violin), Pierre Fournier (cello).

On the HMV disc the slow movement of the *Ghost trio* brings, from all three artists, playing of such hushed intensity that the result feels like a live performance. Some may find it a little self-indulgent, but anyone who responds to the emotional content of Beethoven on record will find it an enthralling experience. The complete cycle is available at a relatively more reasonable price, but this is an excellent sample.

Kempff and his colleagues are much more restrained than Barenboim and friends. These two *Trios*, sensibly coupled, illustrate the contrasts better than any. As a whole these are sweet and lyrical rather than dramatic readings, which some will prefer.

Piano trio No. 6 in B flat major (Archduke), Op. 97.
  ** DGG 2530 147. Wilhelm Kempff (piano), Henryk Szeryng (violin), Pierre Fournier (cello).
Piano trios Nos. 6 in B flat major (Archduke), Op. 97; 10 in B flat major, G. 154.
  ** (*) HMV ASD 2572. Daniel Barenboim (piano), Pinchas Zukerman (violin), Jacqueline du Pré (cello).

The outstanding quality of the performance by Barenboim, Zukerman and du Pré is its sense of spontaneity – not surprising when it was recorded in very long takes of more than one movement at a time. The slow movement, so hushed and intense one catches one's breath, provides the peak of the experience. The first movement is rather wayward, but rhythmic point grips the attention, and the second and fourth movements are nothing less than sparkling. The early *B flat Trio* makes a brief but worthwhile fill-up. Good recording.

Kempff and his colleagues give a crystalline reading of the *Archduke*. It is the clarity and imagination of Kempff's playing which set the tone of the whole performance. He it is who grips the listener's attention with his individual touches of genius, so that relatively Szeryng and Fournier sound less than inspired. An interesting but not a definitive version.

Piano and wind quintet in E flat major, Op. 16.
  *** Decca SXL 6252. Vladimir Ashkenazy (piano), London Wind Soloists – MOZART: *Quintet.***
  (M) *** Decca Ace of Diamonds SDD 256. Walter Panhoffer (piano), members of the Vienna Octet – SPOHR: *Octet.***
  * (*) Philips 6500 326. Ingrid

119

Haebler (piano), Bamberg Wind Quintet – MOZART: *Quintet.* (*)*

The Beethoven is less interesting than the Mozart *Quintet* which plainly inspired it, except from the pianist's standpoint. Of the two Decca versions, Ashkenazy and the London Wind Soloists secure the greater measure of brilliance, although both performances have great spontaneity, and the robust nature of the Panhoffer account is entirely in keeping with the spirit of the music. Both these recordings have admirable presence and immediacy, and if the attractive Spohr *Octet* is particularly wanted the Ace of Diamonds disc is excellent value for money. The Philips performance is disappointing. Ingrid Haebler makes a considerable contribution, but the supporting wind group are not especially imaginative and the finale lacks impetus. The slow movement comes off best.

Septet in E flat major, Op. 20.
- (M) *** Decca Ace of Diamonds SDD 200. Members of the Vienna Octet.
- (B) *** Classics for Pleasure CFP 40059. St James Ensemble.
- ** Philips 6500 543. Members of the Berlin Philharmonic Octet.

(i) *Septet in E flat major, Op. 20;* (ii) *Duo for clarinet and bassoon No. 1 in C major, G. 147.*
- (M) *** HMV HQS 1286. Melos Ensemble; (ii) Gervase de Peyer (clarinet), William Waterhouse (bassoon).

(i) *Septet in E flat major, Op. 20;* (ii) *3 Duos for clarinet and bassoon, G. 147.*
- (B) ** Turnabout TV 34076S. (i) Bamberg Chamber Ensemble; (ii) Jacques Lancelot (clarinet), Paul Hongne (bassoon).

The Decca recording of Beethoven's *Septet* is one of the most enchanting and desirable chamber music records ever made. The spontaneity of the playing helps a great deal towards this effect, and it will surely be a long time before Beethoven's attractive work receives a better all-round performance. The stereo too is notably realistic and clear and contributes much to the illusion of a live performance.

The St James Ensemble is made up of some of Britain's most famous orchestral players, and their flair, the bounce of exuberance, makes this too as enjoyable a version as there is in the catalogue at whatever price. It is not always quite so poised in ensemble as other more expensive accounts, but with first-rate stereo (and this a work which shows off directional effects very well), this is highly competitive. Whatever Beethoven felt about this work when it had been overplayed in his lifetime, it is ideal desert-island music for our gramophones today.

With Gervase de Peyer (whether intentionally or not) very much the dominant personality in a distinguished group, the Melos Ensemble gives a reading that brims with life and energy, wonderfully idiomatic and spontaneous-sounding. The recording is first-rate, more vividly modern than on the mid-price Vienna Octet version, though choice between this, the Vienna, and the St James Ensemble on CFP (cheaper still) could hardly be more difficult.

The tempi of the allegros in the Bamberg performance are brisk but not ungainly; this is why Turnabout can squeeze the complete work on a single side. The performance, if without the finesse of the other versions, is alive and spontaneous and has genuine high spirits. The recording is somewhat thick, and the stereo separation does not always bring a commensurate amount of inner detail. Nevertheless the sound itself is warm and pleasing, and the rich, bland textures make their own contribution to the character of the performance, particularly in the finale. With its attractive bonus this is an excellent bargain.

The Berlin players take a somewhat solemn view of the *Septet*. Theirs is a refined performance, beautifully recorded, but next to other cheaper versions it lacks wit and sparkle. There is also a well-played version on Oryx's bargain label (EXP 29) by the Consortium Classicum, but the lack of dynamic range in the sound (which is otherwise good) makes this uncompetitive.

Serenade in D major for flute, violin and viola, Op. 25.

(M) *** Oiseau-Lyre SOL 284. Melos Ensemble of London – WEBER: *Flute trio.****

The light and charming combination of flute, violin and viola inspired the youthfull Beethoven to write in an unexpectedly carefree and undemanding way. The sequence of tuneful, unpretentious movements reminds one of Mozart's occasional music, and this delectable performance brings out all its genial charm.

Serenade in D major for flute, violin and viola, Op. 25; Serenade in D major for violin, viola and violoncello, Op. 8.

** (*) Philips 6500 167. Grumiaux Trio, with Maxence Larrieu (flute).

This is a sensible coupling, as both works were probably composed at about the same time. The *Serenade* for strings alone does not match its better-known companion for charm, and the performance here, although polished, is not especially persuasive. The Op. 25, however, is freshly played and enjoyable, although it is not quite so spontaneous in effect as the Oiseau-Lyre version.

Sextet in E flat major, Op. 81b (for 2 horns and string quartet); *String quintet in C major, Op. 29.*

(M) ** (*) Decca Ace of Diamonds

SDD 419. Members of the Vienna Octet.

The *Sextet* is not one of Beethoven's greatest works, but it is a highly agreeable one. It is attractively played and recorded here. The *String quintet*, on the other hand, is a work of considerable substance, and although this performance is not ideal (it wants a certain tautness and power), it is far finer than any of its predecessors in the stereo catalogue. On the whole a worthwhile disc.

Wind Music

(i) *Flute trio* (for flute, bassoon and piano) *in G major;* (ii) *Horn sonata in F major, Op. 17;* (iii) *Quintet in E flat major for oboe, 3 horns and bassoon;* (iv) *Serenade in D major for flute, violin and viola, Op. 25;* (iii) *Trio for 2 oboes and cor anglais, Op. 87; Variations on Mozart's 'Là ci darem'* (from *Don Giovanni*).

(M) ** (*)DGG Privilege 2726 007 (2 discs). (i) Aloys Kontarsky (piano), Karlheinz Zöller (flute), Klaus Thunemann (bassoon); (ii) Gerd Seifert (horn), Joerg Demus (piano); (iii) members of Dresden State Orchestra; (iv) Karlheinz Zöller (flute), Thomas Brandis (violin), Siegbert Ueberschaer (viola).

Eminently musical playing here, and excellent recorded sound. There are more spontaneous and fresh accounts of the *Serenade*, Op. 25, in the catalogue, and there is a tendency for some of this music to sound a little wanting in character. It is not, of course, among Beethoven's greatest, but it can sound more winning in persuasive hands. However, there is no reason to withhold a recommendation, and the set will surely give pleasure.

*March in C major (Zapfenstreich); 2
Military marches for the Caroussel:
Nos. 1 in F major; 2 in F major, G.145;
Wind octet in E flat major, Op. 103;
Rondino in E flat major for wind octet,
G.146; Wind sextet in E flat major,
Op. 71.*

(B) ** Pye GSGC 14038. London
Baroque Ensemble, Karl Haas.

The marches are great fun. The one in
C major is especially bucolic (it is the
second in order, on the disc) and No. 2
in F major has a virtuoso bassoon part
which enlivens the texture agreeably. But
you have to listen for it through the
(quite proper) drums and cymbals.
Clearly Beethoven is enjoying himself.
The marches are played with great spirit,
but the performances of the chamber
works are more circumspect. The recording allows the instruments to blend
mellifluously and the playing is first-rate
but a little dry. The end of the *Rondino*,
however, which is gentle, is done most
affectingly. Excellent sound; limited
separation, but a very convincing overall
effect.

*Wind octet in E flat major, Op. 103;
Rondino in E flat major for wind octet,
G.146; Wind sextet in E flat major,
Op. 71; March in B flat major for two
clarinets, two horns and two bassoons;
Quintet for three horns, oboe and
bassoon.*

(M) *** Decca Ace of Diamonds
SDD 383. London Wind Soloists,
Jack Brymer.

This collection, described as 'Beethoven's complete music for wind ensemble', follows up the highly successful
series by the same players of Mozart's
complete wind music. Trivial and un-
exacting, it is a joy from beginning to
end. The *Octet* was written before Beethoven left Bonn for Vienna, and the

Sextet followed soon after he arrived
there. The *Quintet* is the mystery work.
Beethoven probably completed it, but the
only known score has the beginning and
end missing. But some astute analytical
work by the nineteenth-century scholar
Leopold Zellner brought a performable
version of the movements as far as the
minuet (trio missing). The work proves of
far more than antiquarian interest, and
the playing throughout the disc is
masterly, with Alan Civil gloriously confident on the horn. The recording is of
demonstration level.

*Wind octet in E flat major, Op. 103;
Rondino in E flat major for wind octet,
G.146; Wind sextet in E flat major,
Op. 71.*

(M) *** Supraphon 111 0703. Chamber Ensemble of the Czech Philharmonic Orchestra.

Although this record contains less
music than the outstanding Decca issue
listed above, it cannot be ignored. Czech
wind playing has always been famous for
its character, and there is no better example than this collection. The quirkiness
of rhythmic style brings delicious point to
the quick movements of the *Octet*; the
lyricism of the *Rondino* is a constant
delight, and the *Sextet* has marvellous
spontaneity and colour. The recording is
exceptionally life-like and natural in
timbre.

*Trio in G major for 3 flutes; Allegro and
minuet in G major for 2 flutes; 6
Themes and variations for flute and
piano, Op. 105.*

(B) *** Turnabout TV 34059S. Jean-
Pierre Rampal, Christian Larde,
Alain Marion (flutes), Robert
Veyron-Lacroix (piano).

With a disc like this you have to take a
certain amount of pleasing rather than
memorable music to secure the highlights,

but when the playing is so good, the recording excellent, and the price cheap, one can afford to do just this. Of the music for two and three flutes, delightful in its ocarina-like piping, but a little limited in colour range, the Rondo finale of the *Trio* is a winner. On the other side of the disc are the *Themes and variations*, Op. 105, an offshoot of Beethoven's arrangements of British folk-songs, inspired and commissioned by the Scottish publisher Thomson. Five of the six are based on Scots or Irish airs. Surprisingly, *The Last Rose of Summer* (with a slightly different melodic line to the format we know) is not entirely successful; the gems are the variations on *The Cottage Maid* (which begins the side with enchanting naïvety) and perhaps an even more ingenuous set on the Austrian tune *A Schüssel und a Reindel*. This is a disc for Beethoven connoisseurs.

String Quartets

String quartets Nos. 1–16; Grosse Fuge, Op. 133.
> (B) ** (*) HMV SLS 857 (10 discs). Hungarian Quartet.
> ** DGG 2721 071 (10 discs). Amadeus Quartet.

The Hungarian set of the quartets retails at less than two thirds the price of the Amadeus; it costs as little as £11·50 at the time of writing. But quite apart from considerations of cost, indeed even if it were more expensive, this would be the one to have. The Hungarians' readings are sound and unmannered and in the late quartets a good deal more perceptive than the Amadeus's. The recording too is lively and vivid, though where the alternative exists (in the late quartets, the *Harp* (Op. 95) and two of the Op. 18 set) the Italians are to be preferred both as performances and certainly as recordings.

The Amadeus are at their best in the Op. 18 quartets, where their mastery and polish are heard to good advantage. In the middle-period and late quartets their sumptuous tone and refinement of balance are always in evidence, but they do not always penetrate very far beneath the surface. Norbert Brainin's *vibrato* often sounds disturbing and a shade self-regarding, and the readings, particularly of the late quartets, no longer sound freshly experienced as they did when this ensemble was first before the public. There is some superb quartet playing in this cycle, but there are more searching accounts of the late quartets to be found (the Italians and the Hungarians to name only two).

String quartets Nos. 1–6 (complete).
> (M) ** (*) DGG Privilege 2733 002 (3 discs). Amadeus Quartet.

String quartets Nos. 1 in F major, Op. 18/1; 3 in D major, Op. 18/3.
> *** Philips 6500 181. Italian Quartet.

String quartets Nos. 1 in F major, Op. 18/1; 6 in B flat major, Op. 18/6.
> (M) *** Supraphon 111 1106. Vlach Quartet.

String quartets Nos. 1 in F major, Op. 18/1; 11 in F minor, Op. 95.
> (M) ** Supraphon SUAST 50478. Smetana Quartet.

String quartets Nos. 5 in A major, Op. 18/5; 6 in B flat major, Op. 18/6.
> *** Philips 6500 647. Italian Quartet.

String quartets Nos. 6 in B flat major, Op. 18/6; 16 in F major, Op. 135.
> (M) ** (*) Supraphon SUAST 50415. Janáček Quartet.

Undoubtedly this is the best part of the Amadeus cycle. The character of the playing is intimate if rather suave. Sometimes one might ideally ask for more bite even at the expense of polish, but certainly the technical perfection of the playing here yields its own pleasures, for Beethoven's music has its own natural spontaneity. The recording still sounds well.

The Italian performances are all in superlative style and are immaculately recorded. Without any doubt these are among the very best performances of these four quartets in the catalogue. Recommended with the strongest possible enthusiasm.

The performances of Op. 18 from the Vlach Quartet have been much and rightly admired. They combine strength and warmth in equal measure, and even in the slow movement of the *F major Quartet* they penetrate further than most of their rivals. Some readers may be slightly put out by the leader's *vibrato* but, this apart, the performances can be highly recommended. Indeed the sound is firmer and richer than that of the Smetana Quartet, also on Supraphon, now beginning to show its age, and in the *B flat* they are to be preferred to the Janáčeks on the same label, though their Op. 18/6 is coupled with a most impressive Op. 135, which deserves a very honourable mention.

Whether in part the fault of the recording or not, the Janáček Quartet does not sound as rich-toned as its Czech rivals, the Smetana and Vlach groups. But once the sourness of the violins is curbed there is everything to enjoy in these performances. Op. 18/6 is generally counted the weakest of the early quartets (and therefore put last in the group), but it has a joy and even a sense of irresponsibility which are hard to resist. The Janáček players give a forceful, committed performance, and the challenge of Op. 135, Beethoven's last quartet, draws from them even finer playing. As a sample it is worth trying the opening of the slow movement, where the simple melody has a rare romantic warmth combined with a sense of inner strength and with no obtrusive mannerism.

String quartets Nos. 7 in F major; 8 in E minor; 9 in C major (Rasumovsky Nos. 1–3), Op. 59/1–3; 10 in E flat major (Harp), Op. 74; 11 in F minor, Op. 95.

*** Telefunken SPA 25096 (1/3). Végh Quartet.

(M) ** DGG Privilege 2733 005 (3 discs). Amadeus Quartet.

String quartet No. 7 in F major (Rasumovsky No. 1), Op. 59/1.

(M) ** (*) HMV HQS 1159. Hungarian Quartet.

String quartet No. 8 in E minor (Rasumovsky No. 2), Op. 59/2.

(M) *** Supraphon SUAST 50616. Janáček Quartet.

String quartets Nos. 8 in E minor (Rasumovsky No. 2), Op. 59/2; 11 in F minor, Op. 95.

(M) ** (*) HMV HQS 1160. Hungarian Quartet.

String quartets Nos. 9 in C major (Rasumovsky No. 3), Op. 59/3; 10 in E flat major (Harp), Op. 74.

(M) *** HMV HQS 1161. Hungarian Quartet.

On balance, the Végh Quartet gives us by far the most searching and thoughtful account of the middle-period quartets, and for once it is possible to speak of one set being the best. These performances have genuine purity of style and feeling, and never indulge in any attempt to glamorize the music or admire their own warmth of tone. These are inward performances that remind one of the Busch and Pro Arte quartets, and they are matched by excellent engineering.

There is some splendid playing too in the Amadeus set, but just occasionally one has the nagging feeling that the tremendous self-assurance borders on complacency, for, in spite of the technical and musical polish, not all the music's secrets are uncovered.

The Hungarian performances, with their security of style and technique, avoid expressive gestures, letting the music speak for itself. Although initially the comparative reticence may seem disappointing, the impact is cumulative. With each of the Hungarians' records one is in the presence of sensitive, understanding musicians, rethinking the music with simple devotion. Such a movement as the *Allegretto ma non troppo* of Op. 95, taken rather slower than usual, has an inner concentration that puts it in the company of the late quartet slow movements. HQS 1161, coupling Op. 59/3 and Op. 74, *The Harp*, is an especially good sampler of the Hungarians' style. The recording quality, like the performances, is undistractingly faithful without achieving special brilliance.

Among single discs the Janáčeks' account of the *E minor Quartet* deserves special mention. They give a deeply satisfying performance and do not shy away from adopting a true *Adagio*, measured and intense, in the second movement. This is very fine playing, and the recording, too has admirable presence.

String quartets Nos. 9 in C major (Rasumovsky No. 3), Op. 59/3; 11 in F minor, Op. 95.
  (B) *** Classics for Pleasure CFP 40098. Drolc Quartet.
String quartet No. 10 in E flat major (Harp), Op. 74.
  (B) ** Oryx EXP 30. Arriaga Quartet
  – DVOŘÁK: *Quartet No. 6.***
String quartets Nos. 10 in E flat major (Harp), Op. 74; 11 in F minor, Op. 95.
  *** Philips 6500 180. Italian Quartet.
  (M) ** (*) Decca Ace of Diamonds SDD 309. Weller Quartet.

Recorded in 1960, the Classics for Pleasure coupling shows the Drolc Quar-

tet at their peak, magnificently precise in ensemble and intonation while giving middle-period Beethoven its full dramatic urgency. The slow movement of the *Third Rasumovsky* is wonderfully intense. With recording quality excellent for its age, this is an outstanding disc at CFP price, one suitable not only for the enthusiast but also for those wanting to experiment in chamber music.

The coupling of the *Harp quartet* and Op. 95 is a popular one. The Weller performances have polish and tonal beauty, unanimity of ensemble and attack; only in depth of insight are they outdone by the Italians, who are as eloquent as they are unmannered, and provide beautifully shaped readings, quite superlatively recorded, with splendidly clean and vividly defined detail.

A well characterized performance of the *Harp quartet* from the Arriaga Quartet, with conviction in the playing throughout and a pointed scherzo. The *Adagio* is taken fairly quickly, but is committed and therefore convincing. The finale is played without repeats. The sound is warm rather than especially vivid, but with an imaginative coupling this inexpensive disc makes a good recommendation, especially for newcomers to the chamber-music repertoire.

String quartets Nos. 12–16 (complete); Grosse Fuge, Op. 133.
  *** Telefunken SKA 25113 (4 discs). Végh Quartet.

Sandor Végh and his colleagues bring qualities of great insight and humanity to these masterpieces, and the set challenges the fine and perceptive readings by the Italian Quartet which are widely and rightly admired. There are some moments of discomfort as far as Végh's intonation is concerned but they are few and trivial in comparison with the wisdom and richness of experience that his playing communicates. These are deeply impressive readings and are finely recorded, though the Philips engineers produce a more transparent and detailed sound for the Italians. However, this is without doubt a most useful and distinguished alternative to the Italian set, and some readers may well prefer it.

String quartets Nos. 12 in E flat major, Op. 127; 16 in F major, Op. 135.
> *** Philips SAL 3703. Italian Quartet.
> (M) ** (*) HMV HQS 1177. Hungarian Quartet.

String quartet No. 12 in E flat major, Op. 127; Grosse Fuge, Op. 133.
> (M) ** Supraphon SUAST 50372. Smetana Quartet.

String quartet No. 13 in B flat major, Op. 130 (with Grosse Fuge, Op. 133, as a finale).
> (M) * (*) Supraphon SUAST 50604. Smetana Quartet.
> * (*) DGG 2530 351. LaSalle Quartet.

The Italians give a most searching account of the first movement of Op. 127, and their firmness of tone and accuracy of ensemble compel admiration. Indeed their account of the whole work goes far deeper than that of any of their full-priced rivals. Some may quarrel with their tempi in the inner movements of Op. 135 but on the whole this is a magnificent account which readers will find musically satisfying and marvellously recorded.

A strongly forceful performance of Op. 127 from the Smetana Quartet. The opening of the finale, for example, may at first seem a little clumsy, but overall the movement is given an unusual strength and size. The slow movement is treated romantically, but with no objectionable rhythmic distortions. The *Grosse Fuge* thrives on this group's characteristic treatment and the technical problems apparently hold no terrors for the players. The quartet's tone is rich and true, though the Supraphon recording gives a little too much edge unless it is curbed with the controls.

It is disappointing that the same quartet does not plumb the depths of Op. 130 as one might expect. The performance fails to convey the sort of inner intensity one has heard from the players in the flesh. Whether in the second subject of the first movement or the opening of the third movement *Andante* one really wants a greater sense of sublime joy. The LaSalle performance too, although finely played, fails to go to the heart of the work in quite the way that the Italian and the Végh quartets do. Another disadvantage that applies to both discs is the provision of the *Grosse Fuge* instead of the final *Allegro* for which Artaria had asked, whereas other ensembles give us Op. 130 with both finales.

A performance of Op. 127 by the Yale Quartet, recorded in a very dry acoustic (Vanguard VCS 10054), is distinctly uncompetitive.

String quartet No. 13 in B flat major, Op. 130; Grosse Fuge, Op. 133.
> *** Philips SAL 3780. Italian Quartet.
> (M) ** (*) HMV HQS 1178. Hungarian Quartet.

The Italians' disc coupling Op. 130 and the *Grosse Fuge* shows much the same qualities as the other recordings in the series, though it is perhaps less overwhelmingly successful than they. The *Grosse Fuge* sounds magnificent. As a set these performances have very strong all-round claims and no one investing in them need fear disappointment. Another disc, by the Yale Quartet (on Vanguard VCS 10096), offers a straightforward and unaffected performance, perhaps a little too detached for its own good. Even if the playing offered outstanding insight and penetration it would be difficult to recommend as the sound is unacceptably dry.

String quartet No. 14 in C sharp minor, Op. 131.
  *** Philips SAL 3790. Italian Quartet.
  (M) ** (*) HMV HQS 1179. Hungarian Quartet.
  (M) ** Supraphon SUAST 50365. Vlach Quartet.
  (B) ** Saga 5128. Fine Arts Quartet.

A magnificent reading from the Italian Quartet, sumptuously recorded and arguably the finest stereo version of this work. Of the full-price versions this is the one to have. Its nearest rival, that by the Végh Quartet, has no less depth and humanity, but it is not available separately. The Hungarian performance is also a fine one and in the opening fugue the players achieve spiritual power. The Vlach performance is more searching still, and it is probably more highly characterized than the Hungarians, but the recording is somewhat shallow, although this yields to appropriate use of the controls. At bargain price, the Fine Arts version is still amazingly good value. Their playing is restrained and subtle, and the recording, though not of recent vintage, is still eminently serviceable.

String quartet No. 15 in A minor, Op. 132.
  *** Philips SAL 3638. Italian Quartet.
  (M) *** HMV HQS 1180. Hungarian Quartet.
  *** BASF BAC 3071. Collegium Aureum Quartet (using original instruments).

The Italians offer the first account of Op. 132 worthy to be named alongside the famous pre-war set by the Busch

Quartet. It has greater technical security than the Busch though it does not in every detail match their warmth and humanity. Nonetheless it is the finest LP version of the work (although the Hungarians' account is outstanding too) and has moreover the advantage of the most impressive recorded sound. Strongly recommended.

The fascination of the Collegium Aureum record is the use of instruments producing a tone colour Beethoven would have known. Undoubtedly the warm acoustic enhances the effect of mellowness and the darker timbres of the gut strings. The performance itself is a fine one. The eloquence of the third movement is in no doubt and the players show an impressive grasp of its structure. How much the restraint in their playing is conditioned by the instruments used, listeners must judge for themselves, but the expressive feeling conveyed is not lessened by this gentleness of approach, and when emotional bite is needed it is readily forthcoming, yet in scale with the overall conception.

String quartet No. 16 in F major, Op. 135; Grosse Fuge, Op. 133.
  (M) * (*) Vanguard VCS 10097. Yale Quartet.

Like the other Yale performances discussed earlier this is not especially penetrating, and the recording is too dry for comfort.

String Trios

String trios Nos. 1 in E flat major, Op. 3; 3 in D major, Op. 9/2.
  *** Philips 6500 168. Grumiaux Trio.
String trios Nos. 2 in G major, Op. 9/1; 4 in C minor, Op. 9/3.
  *** Philips 6500 227. Grumiaux Trio.

When these versions first appeared they laboured under the handicap of having an equally superlative competitor in the DG set by the Italian String Trio. Somehow both sets drew attention from each other. The performances by the Grumiaux are supremely musical and marvellously effortless; the artists are content to let the music speak for itself and refrain from trying to score any interpretative points. In addition the recording is fresh and full-blooded in the best Philips chamber-music tradition. Strongly recommended.

Violin Sonatas

Violin sonatas Nos. 1–10 (complete).
  ** (*) HMV SLS 871 (5 discs). Pinchas Zukerman (violin), Daniel Barenboim (piano).
Violin sonatas Nos. 1–10 (complete); *Rondo in G major, G.155; 12 Variations on Mozart's Se vuol ballare, G.156.*
  ** (*) DGG 2735 001 (5 discs). Yehudi Menuhin (violin), Wilhelm Kempff (piano).
Violin sonatas Nos. 1 in D major, Op. 12/1; 8 in G major, Op. 30/3.
  ** Philips SAL 3416. David Oistrakh (violin), Lev Oborin (piano).
Violin sonatas Nos. 2 in A major, Op. 12/2; 10 in G major, Op. 96.
  ** Philips SAL 3417. David Oistrakh (violin), Lev Oborin (piano).
Violin sonatas Nos. 3 in E flat major, Op. 12/3; 7 in C minor, Op. 30/2.
  ** Philips SAL 3418. David Oistrakh (violin), Lev Oborin (piano).
Violin sonatas Nos. 4 in A minor, Op. 23; 9 in A major (Kreutzer), Op. 47.
  ** Philips SAL 3419. David Oistrakh (violin), Lev Oborin (piano).
Violin sonatas Nos. 5 in F major

(Spring), Op. 24; 6 in A major, Op. 30/1.
  ** Philips SAL 3420. David Oistrakh (violin), Lev Oborin (piano).

Zukerman and Barenboim, friends and colleagues, are both strong and positive artists, and in their collaborations on record they have consistently struck sparks of imagination off each other. They do so here, but there is a hint too that they may have been conscious of earlier criticism that their collaborations were too idiosyncratic. These are much more central performances than, say, those of the cycle of Beethoven *Trios* with du Pré. This set presents a safer recommendation than that of Menuhin and Kempff, if not always a more imaginative one. Good EMI recording.

Menuhin and Kempff, inspirational artists both, bring out the finest in each other, spontaneously seeing the music with matching imagination. The sessions were held one summer in London, and the happiness of the meeting is reflected all through. Though there are more precise, more brilliant, or even more dramatic readings on record, these have a unique place for their insight and feeling. Good recording.

The Oistrakh set is well recorded and flawlessly played. Certain movements – some of the finales especially – blaze into life; the minuet of the *C minor Sonata* is splendidly pointed, and the variations in the *Kreutzer* are often superb. Yet with all this perfection there are also moments when one feels the final spark of spontaneity does not ignite. One could certainly often return to these records with pleasure, and yet something is missing. Perhaps it is that, within the aura of the recording studio, the self-assurance that both these artists obviously possess tends sometimes to produce a feeling of detachment.

Besides the complete sets there is also available (on Supraphon SUAST 50905/7) a part-set containing Sonatas 2–7, played by Josef Suk and Jan Panenka. These performances are fresh and straightforward, but the balance of the instruments, with the violin brought markedly in front of the piano, precludes a very strong recommendation.

Violin sonata No. 5 in F major (Spring), Op. 24; Rondo in G major, G.155; 12 Variations on Mozart's Se vuol ballare, G.156.

> ** (*) DGG 2530 205. Yehudi Menuhin (violin), Wilhelm Kempff (piano).

Menuhin and Kempff's reading of the *Spring sonata* has the magic which characterizes their whole cycle, but unless you specially want the odd and none-too-generous coupling, it makes a less viable recommendation than several others in the catalogue.

Violin sonatas Nos. 5 in F major (Spring), Op. 24; 8 in G major, Op. 30/3; 9 in A major (Kreutzer), Op. 47.

> (M) ** RCA SER 5701/3. Henryk Szeryng (violin), Artur Rubinstein (piano) – BRAHMS: *Violin sonatas.* ** (*)

Violin sonatas No. 5 in F major (Spring), Op. 24; 9 in A major (Kreutzer), Op. 47.

> (M) *** HMV SXLP 30164. Yehudi Menuhin (violin), Hephzibah Menuhin (piano).

> (M) ** (*) DGG Privilege 135148. Wolfgang Schneiderhan (violin), Carl Seeman (piano).

RCA have put the Szeryng/Rubinstein set in a box, together with fine performances of the Brahms sonatas. It was a pity they did not instead restore the original coupling of No. 8 in G major alone with the three Brahms works, complete on two discs. The additional record weakens the set, for the performance of the *Kreutzer* is the least penetrating of the three and the *Spring sonata* (very well done) suffers from too high a modulation of cut and will offer some pick-ups tracking problems. The performance of No. 8 is, however, very successful.

The coupling by the Menuhin brother and sister of the *Spring* and *Kreutzer sonatas* is in an altogether different class. Menuhin's playing does not always offer absolutely immaculate technique. A slightly sharp note in a cadential phrase, perhaps, or a quick passage not perfectly controlled might catch the ear, but these are lost and forgotten in the nobility and warmth of the readings as a whole. The playing has great spontaneity – the wonderful flow of the opening pastoral melody of the *Spring sonata*, the sustained tension of the *Adagio* of the same work, or the beautiful closing pages of the variations in the *Kreutzer*: these are high spots in music-making which remains at a consistently high level. The recording is drier than the original full-priced issue, but is still of high quality. The balance is very good.

Schneiderhan and Seeman too provide an excellent coupling, beautifully played, with understanding from both artists and a characteristically pure, classical line from Schneiderhan. The variations in the *Kreutzer* are compelling and the bouncing finale of the Op. 47 contrasts with the lyrical first movement of the *Spring*. The forward projection of the recording seems to emphasize the intensity of the playing, besides putting a slight edge on the violin image. But in the last resort these performances lack the touch of magic that distinguishes the Menuhins' disc.

Violin sonatas Nos. 8 in G major, Op. 30/3; 9 in A major (Kreutzer), Op. 47.

> ** (*) DGG 2530 135. Yehudi Menuhin (violin), Wilhelm Kempff (piano).

Both Kempff and Menuhin have recorded the *Kreutzer* many times with different partners, but this version is unique. If in many ways it is not as immaculate as earlier accounts, the spontaneous imagination of the playing, the challenge between great artists on the same wavelength, is consistently present. Even on repetition the result is a live musical experience. Similarly with the little *G major Sonata*. Good recording.

Violoncello Sonatas

Violoncello sonatas Nos. 1 in F major, Op. 5/1; 2 in G minor, Op. 5/2; 3 in A major, Op. 69; 4 in C major, Op. 102/1; 5 in D major, Op. 102/2.
> *** Philips 6700 027 (2 discs). Mstislav Rostropovich (cello), Sviatoslav Richter (piano).
> *** HMV SLS 836 (2 discs). Paul Tortellier (cello), Eric Heidsieck (piano).

Violoncello sonatas Nos. 1–5; 7 Variations in E flat major on Bei Männern, G.158; 12 Variations in F major on Ein Mädchen, Op. 66; 12 Variations on See the conquering hero comes, G.157.
> (M) ** Supraphon MS 1091/3. Josef Chuchro (cello), Jan Panenka (piano).

The Philips is an excellent set, showing a true partnership between two giants among today's performing artists. There is a considerable difference in style between the music of Op. 5 and Op. 102, written some twenty years later, but the two players are fully equal to such subtleties. Above all these performances are spontaneous and committed. They are well recorded too.

On HMV distinguished performances that make a useful alternative to Rostropovich's set with Richter and are probably slightly better recorded than the Philips set, which dates from 1964. The

recorded sound rather lets down Chuchro and Panenka on Supraphon though their readings are every bit as perceptive and thoughtful.

Piano Sonatas

Piano sonatas Nos. 1–32 (complete).
> *** DGG 2721 060 (11 discs). Wilhelm Kempff (piano).
> (B) *** HMV SLS 794 (12 discs). Daniel Barenboim (piano).

Kempff's Beethoven has been providing a deeply spiritual experience for record-collectors since the twenties, and though there may be argument about his clear and refreshing style in Beethoven, there is no doubt whatever of the inner compulsion which holds all these performances together. Kempff more than any pianist has the power to make one appreciate and understand Beethoven in a new way, and that is so however many times one has heard him. It makes a fascinating study comparing the interpretations not only with those of other pianists but with his own previous ones. The new recording image the DGG engineers have chosen (and these discs are technically immaculate and very real in projection) is drier than the original pressings of the first mono LP set, but if anything this only serves to project the intellectual and spiritual power of the music-making, without in the least detracting from the poetry. Above all, these magnificent records never fail to reveal Kempff's own spontaneity in the studio, his ability to rethink the reading on each occasion.

The complete set of Barenboim's twelve discs of Beethoven sonatas is available on permanent special offer at a very reasonable price, making it a most attractive bargain, with good modern recording and unique interpretations. As the comments on the separate discs make plain, the readings are sometimes idiosyncratic, with unexpected tempi both fast and slow, but the spontaneous style is unfailingly compelling. This is a keenly thoughtful musician thinking through Beethoven's great piano cycle with an individuality that already puts him in the line of master pianists, however much one may disagree on detail.

Piano sonatas Nos. 1 in F minor, Op. 2/1; 2 in A major, Op. 2/2; 25 in G major, Op. 79.
    (B) ** (*) Turnabout TV 34120S. Alfred Brendel (piano).

From the very start of the little *F minor Sonata* which opens the greatest of all sonata cycles, Brendel makes clear the weight and seriousness of his approach. This is no mere Haydnesque reading, but a determined attempt to present the work as revolutionary in the way it must have struck the first listeners. A little more sparkle might have lightened the reading without any loss of weight, and in the longer Op. 2/2 Brendel does find a deeper imaginative vein. An excellent performance of the elusive *G major Sonata*, and more atmospheric recording than in most of the discs of this cycle.

Piano sonatas Nos. 1 in F minor, Op. 2/1; 17 in D minor (Tempest), Op. 31/2; 20 in G major, Op. 49/2.
    (M) ** (*) HMV HQS 1107. Daniel Barenboim (piano).

It seemed an astonishing decision by EMI to commission so youthful a pianist as Daniel Barenboim to do a complete cycle of the thirty-two Beethoven sonatas. One could hardly believe that a young man would be able to encompass all the facets of Beethoven's genius, when so many experienced pianists have fallen short of their own ideals in the recording studio. Yet here is Beethoven-playing that immediately shows a grasp of the music's essential style and, even after Kempff, can compel the listener's attention. The principal work here is the second of the set of three Op. 31 sonatas, and Barenboim rises to its powerfully emotional atmosphere. The shaping of the first movement, the pauses convincingly held, the poetry of the *Adagio*, and the rippling release from tension which the finale provides, are moulded here into a spontaneous and convincing whole. The playing in the other works is marginally less compelling, but the opening of No. 1 is well dramatized and the minuet has an enchanting fluid lyricism, while No. 20 in G major has all the necessary charm. Bright, crisp piano recording.

Piano sonatas Nos. 2 in A major, Op. 2/2; 24 in F sharp major, Op. 78; 30 in E major, Op. 109.
    (M) *** HMV HQS 1203. Daniel Barenboim (piano).

Barenboim's decision to mingle sonatas of all three periods on a single record (parallel to his practice in live cycles) brings rare rewards. This collection shows the full span of his achievement, the weight of utterance which, without any unwanted heaviness, links early Beethoven with late. As in the other records of the series it is the sense of spontaneity which compels attention. Op. 109 was in fact recorded at the very end of a long day's recording, and the single take has been left practically intact to give a performance of exceptional concentration.

Piano sonatas Nos. 3 in C major, Op. 2/3; 4 in E flat major, Op. 7.
    (B) ** (*) Turnabout TV 34121S. Alfred Brendel (piano).

A good coupling of two of Beethoven's most ambitious early sonatas. In both, Brendel's concentration underlines the strength, and in the orchestral textures of the first movement of Op. 7 his directness is particularly impressive. He is less persuasive in the slow movements.

131

Piano sonatas Nos. 3 in C major, Op. 2/3; 15 in D major (Pastoral), Op. 28.
(M) *** H M V HQS 1185. Daniel Barenboim (piano).

This marks another notable achievement in Daniel Barenboim's outstanding Beethoven sonata cycle. His tempi in both these early sonatas are controversially slow. His timing for Op. 2/3 (with all repeats) is over half an hour, and nearly as long for Op. 28, and those timings reflect an unusual weight of utterance that makes one rethink the aims and achievement of the young, revolutionary Beethoven. So far from being a mere reflection of his mentors, Haydn and Mozart, he was already a powerful creative personality in his own right, and this came out more clearly in his piano sonatas than in any other music. The scale of these works in relation to the time when they were written is colossal (neither Mozart nor Haydn had attempted piano sonatas anywhere near as expansive), and Barenboim's spacious, intense treatment makes one appreciate this more vividly than ever. Even if one disagrees with a tempo at the start of a movement, his concentration has one sympathizing, even thinking there is no alternative, by the end. At medium price this, like the other records in the series, is something not to miss.

Piano sonatas Nos. 4 in E flat major, Op. 7; 25 in G major, Op. 79; 28 in A major, Op. 101.
(M) *** H M V HQS 1205. Daniel Barenboim (piano).

Beethoven's Op. 7 is one of the most powerful of his first-period works, and characteristically Barenboim gives it big-scale treatment, though the first movement's orchestral textures could have sounded richer. The elusive Op. 101 sonata, the first genuinely last-period work, brings out Barenboim's spon-taneous lyricism and his fine sense of dramatic contrast.

Piano sonatas Nos. 4 in E flat major, Op. 7; 25 in G major, Op. 79; 31 in A flat major, Op. 110.
** Decca SXL 6300. Wilhelm Backhaus (piano).

Wilhelm Backhaus was one of the monumental figures of the gramophone, and one tends to listen to his more recent records, made in his eighties, with overtones of previous experiences in mind. Generally, the bigger the challenge for him was, the more impressive was his performance. His massive, rather gruff style naturally suited the later rather than the earlier sonatas, but even in Op. 110, where the challenge is greatest, the uninitiated will probably demand a more ingratiating style. These are personal documents, and it is fortunate that Backhaus rarely failed in the studio to convey the real feeling of his powerful presence, whatever one's detailed doubts.

Piano sonatas Nos. 5 in C minor, Op. 10/1; 6 in F major, Op. 10/2; 7 in D major, Op. 10/3.
(M) *** H M V HQS 1152. Daniel Barenboim (piano).

All three of the wonderful sonatas in Op. 10 are given superb performances by Barenboim, rhythmic, dramatic, intense. Where in early Beethoven he once used to ride roughshod over incidental markings (in live performance, not on record), the remarkable thing about these performances is the extra detail that is illuminated, quite apart from the overall conviction. It was daring of him to choose so intensely slow a tempo for the great D minor slow movement of Op. 10/3, *Largo molto e mesto*, but with a gravity of expression worthy of late Beethoven he controls and sustains the tension over the vastly expansive phrases. Good recording, as in the rest of the series.

Piano sonatas Nos. 5 in C minor, Op. 10/1; 6 in F major, Op. 10/2; 13 in E flat major, Op. 27/1.

(B) ** Turnabout TV 34117S. Alfred Brendel (piano).

Brendel's coupling spoils the usual arrangement of having all three Op. 10 sonatas together on a single disc. In these two shorter sonatas from the opus, his clear, direct style suits the pithiness of argument. For the first and less famous of the two Op. 27 'Fantasy' sonatas Brendel's concentration makes for satisfying results, though fantasy in a strict sense is not one of his strong suits.

Piano sonatas Nos. 6 in F major, Op. 10/2; 23 in F minor (Appassionata), Op. 57.

⊛ *** DGG 2530 406. Emil Gilels (piano).

Gilels is a supremely great pianist, and his record of the *Appassionata* must rank among the finest ever made. His art is so totally at the service of the composer and his playing is so subtle and poetic that these familiar sonatas emerge as fresh experiences. With artistry of this power and eloquence criticism is silenced. The DG recording is a fine one, with a genuine sense of presence.

Piano sonatas Nos. 7 in D major, Op. 10/3; 9 in E major, Op. 14/1; 10 in G major, Op. 14/2.

(B) ** (*) Turnabout TV 34118S. Alfred Brendel (piano).

Another attractive coupling of early sonatas from Brendel's complete cycle. Op. 10/3 is the most expansive of the early sonatas, with its orchestral textures in the first movement, its genuine depth in the D minor slow movement. It is well contrasted with the less ambitious but closely argued sonatas of Op. 14, both fine works despite their associations with

piano lessons. Except perhaps in the great D minor slow movement Brendel's strong, direct manner is consistently satisfying, and the recording is no more clattery than in most of the other discs of the series.

Piano sonatas Nos. 7 in D major, Op. 10/3; 23 in F minor (Appassionata), Op. 57.

*** Decca SXL 6603. Vladimir Ashkenazy (piano).

Ashkenazy's *Appassionata* is a superb one, and it is linked with a thoughtful and masterly account of the *D major Sonata*, Op. 10/3. However, those who feel strongly about matters of tempo may well find Ashkenazy a little too free in the first movement of the *Appassionata*. The sound is firm and well defined.

Piano sonatas Nos. 7 in D major, Op. 10/3; 14 in C sharp minor (Moonlight), Op. 27/2; 25 in G major, Op. 79.

** (*) Philips 6500 417. Alfred Brendel (piano).

The *D major Sonata*, one of the greatest and earliest of Beethoven's early works, inspires Brendel to his finest playing. It is surprising to find him in his own sleeve-note using the word 'exquisite' of a work which rightly he makes strong, notably in the visionary *Largo e mesto* slow movement. The *Moonlight* is indeed exquisite, lacking a little of the spontaneity of Brendel's Turnabout version (see below) but finely poised. The little Op. 79 sonata is a nicely varied makeweight. Good recording.

Piano sonatas Nos. 8 in C minor (Pathétique), Op. 13; 12 in A flat major, Op. 26; 14 in C sharp minor (Moonlight), Op. 27/2.

* (*) Turnabout TV 34122S. Alfred Brendel (piano).

This coupling of three favourite early sonatas is one of the less successful of Brendel's Beethoven cycle. Op. 26 prompts a comparatively pedestrian reading, and though the opening movement of the *Moonlight* is hushed and gentle in its cool stillness (a straight style helping), there is no mystery at all. The finale, at a relaxed tempo, is beautifully pointed but unexciting. The *Pathétique* has little sparkle in the allegros, and the slow movement is relatively inexpressive.

Piano sonata No. 8 in C minor (Pathétique), Op. 13.
** (*) Philips 6500 315. Stephen Bishop (piano) – *Piano concerto No. 3.****

Bishop's account of the *Pathétique* is totally unmannered and refreshing, though some will prefer more deliberate expressiveness in the lyrical slow movement. Recording to match that of the concerto with which the sonata is coupled.

Piano sonatas Nos. 8 in C minor (Pathétique), Op. 13; 14 in C sharp minor (Moonlight), Op. 27/2; 19 in G minor, Op. 49/1; 20 in G major, Op 49/2.
(M) **** HMV SXLP 30129. Walter Gieseking (piano).**

These recordings are not of recent provenance; they were made in the early days of stereo not long before Gieseking's death. Undoubtedly a great pianist, Gieseking will always interest students of the piano, and as an interpreter of French music he retains the undying allegiance of many collectors. These performances offer distinguished piano playing, of course, but they cannot be said to compete in interpretative insight with the very finest versions now before the public. There is something a little remote about his Beethoven. The piano

sound is admirably balanced but it lacks something of the presence of a modern recording.

Piano sonatas Nos. 8 in C minor (Pathétique), Op. 13; 14 in C sharp minor (Moonlight), Op. 27/2; 23 in F minor (Appassionata), Op. 57.
*** DGG SLPM 139300. Wilhelm Kempff (piano).
(M) **** (*) HMV HQS 1076. Daniel Barenboim (piano).**
** (*) CBS SBRG 72148. Rudolf Serkin (piano).
(M) **** (*) Philips 6599 308. Claudio Arrau (piano).**
(B) **** Decca SPA 69. Wilhelm Backhaus (piano).**
(B) **** Classics for Pleasure CFP 192. Daniel Chorzempa (piano).**

Kempff's disc shows so well his ability to rethink Beethoven's music within the recording studio. He coupled these three works together in a (no less successful) early stereo LP. Here the slow movement of the *Pathétique*, for example, is slower and more expressively romantic than before, but still restrained. The *Appassionata* is characteristically clear, and if anything more classically 'straight' than it was before (in the same way that the *Waldstein* – on another disc – is cooler and clearer, with a wonderful classical purity in the rippling quavers). The opening of the *Moonlight* is gently atmospheric, the scherzo poised, with admirable contrast in the finale. Everything Kempff does has his individual stamp, and above all he never fails to convey the deep intensity of a master in communion with Beethoven. The recording is a little shallow sometimes – one notices this more in a work like the *Pathétique* with a slow movement that makes special use of the piano's sustaining quality – but still faithful enough.

Barenboim's first popular coupling of

three named sonatas showed at once the sort of inspiration he can convey. The first movement of the *Pathétique*, for example, taken rather fast, has a natural wildness about it, but it is so compelling that one forgives minor blemishes. The second movement brings a tempo so slow that the result could have seemed too static had not Barenboim's control of line been so confident. The *Appassionata* too is rather wild and rhapsodic in the first movement, and again the slow speed for the central variations brings a simple, natural intensity, which contrasts well with the lightness and clarity of the finale.

Serkin has recorded remarkably few of the Beethoven sonatas, considering how eminent a Beethoven pianist he is. Instead he has concentrated on the popular named works and these three in particular, each recorded by him several times before. The result this time is as incisive and dramatic as before, and as with all master pianists one has dozens of points of new insight emerging as well as one or two points of personal mannerism that may or may not irritate. The piano tone is acceptable in a slightly hard American way.

Arrau's thoughtful and individual cycle of the Beethoven sonatas is well represented by a sampler disc of the three most popular sonatas. Plainly this is the playing of a master, sometimes wayward but deeply felt. The recording is good, but the extra alertness and spontaneity of Barenboim's similar coupling make that a better general choice in the middle price-range.

Decca issued this separate disc of favourite sonatas from Backhaus's stereo cycle as a cheap sampler to tempt buyers to the rest. It is amazing that an octogenarian could produce such positive, alert, imaginative playing, but by the standards of Barenboim, let alone Brendel, his style is wilful, with a touch of heaviness that is not always cancelled out by the electric concentration. All the same, at so cheap a price it is worth any

Beethovenian's while to sample the greatness of Backhaus.

It is remarkable that Daniel Chorzempa should be able to combine his work in the organ loft with continued devotion to piano virtuosity. His CFP coupling of Beethoven's three most popular sonatas is competitive in every sense, lacking a little in sparkle, the interpretations of a very serious young man who knows what he is doing. The clarity of his style is well caught.

Piano sonatas Nos. 8 in C minor (Pathétique), Op. 13; 14 in C sharp minor (Moonlight), Op. 27/2; 21 in C major (Waldstein), Op. 53.
** Decca SXL 6576. Radu Lupu (piano).

Radu Lupu has the gift of being able to create a spontaneous performance in the recording studio. Sometimes he is mannered, as in his rather deliberate approach to the famous slow movement of the *Pathétique sonata*, or at the opening of the *Moonlight*, but the playing carries conviction, and the performances of both these works are individual and enjoyable. But Lupu is less successful in holding the concentration of the *Waldstein* finale, after having prepared the opening beautifully, and it is this that lets down an otherwise impressive disc. Decca's recording is first-rate in every way, sonorous and clear, a real piano sound.

Piano sonatas Nos. 9 in E major, Op. 14/1; 10 in G major, Op. 14/2; 12 in A flat major, Op. 26.
(M) *** HMV HQS 1206. Daniel Barenboim (piano).

Barenboim gives true depth to the *Funeral march* of Op. 26 – hints of the *Eroica symphony* ahead – and in this sonata as well as in the two brief but attractive sonatas of Op. 14, his freshness and spontaneity are most convincing.

Piano sonatas Nos. 10 in G major, Op. 14/2; 11 in B flat major, Op. 22; 20 in G major, Op. 49/2.

(M) ** (*) Philips Universo 6580 095. Sviatoslav Richter (piano).

The performance of Op. 14/2 is rather detached, cool and poised, and the clear, somewhat dry recording adds to this impression; but the account of the *B flat major Sonata*, Op. 22, shows Richter at his most compelling. The strength and projection of the reading make one look askance at the early opus number. The power of the opening *Allegro* is counterpoised by the spontaneity and eloquence of the *Adagio*. The little work in G major, Op. 49/2, brings a glowing fluency and elegance: to use the description 'charm' would undervalue the stature Richter conveys. The recording of the two later works is crisp and clear.

Piano sonatas Nos. 11 in B flat major, Op. 22; 12 in A flat major, Op. 26; 13 in E flat major, Op. 27/1.

(B) ** Decca Eclipse ECS 724. Friedrich Gulda (piano).

In these early sonatas the range of recording is relatively restricted, but Gulda's direct, unmannered readings are consistently satisfying. An excellent bargain if this coupling suits you better than the Brendel Turnabout versions at the same price.

Piano sonatas Nos. 11 in B flat major, Op. 22; 13 in E flat major, Op. 27/1; 27 in E minor, Op. 90.

(M) *** HMV HQS 1202. Daniel Barenboim (piano).

The Op. 22 sonata is one of the most elusive in the whole cycle, starting gently as it does, and Barenboim's natural intensity makes it exceptionally compelling. The first of the two sonatas *quasi una fantasia* (the second being the *Moon-*

light) is similarly convincing, and the E minor sonata, Op. 90, product of the barren years before the last period took wing, conveys better balance than usual between the two strangely matched movements.

Piano sonatas Nos. 11 in B flat major, Op. 22; 15 in D major (Pastoral), Op. 28.

(B) ** Turnabout TV 34119S. Alfred Brendel (piano).

Brendel gives clean, concentrated performances of two of Beethoven's most imaginative 'in-between' sonatas, which give a clear foretaste of his middle-period strength. The nickname *Pastoral* has not brought Op. 28 the popularity it deserves, perhaps because it provides only a half-truth in describing the work's character. Brendel consistently holds the attention with his unforced straightforward manner, but by his very reticence misses some of the sparkle of the music, the element of charm which in his more idiosyncratic way a pianist like Barenboim uses to heighten the music's strength.

Piano sonatas Nos. 14 in C sharp minor (Moonlight), Op. 27/2; 15 in D major (Pastoral), Op. 28; 22 in F major, Op. 54.

(B) * (*) Decca Eclipse ECS 720. Friedrich Gulda (piano).

The series of Beethoven sonatas by Gulda on the Decca Eclipse label was recorded in the late fifties and early sixties – evidently not a complete cycle. The recording quality is variable, and this disc suffers more than most, but the directness of manner characteristic of this pianist still comes over.

Piano sonatas Nos. 15 in D major (Pastoral), Op. 28; 21 in C major (Waldstein), Op. 53; 24 in F sharp major, Op. 78; 25 in G major, Op. 79.

** (*) DGG slpm 139301. Wilhelm Kempff (piano).

Kempff's readings are individual and personal. In the *Waldstein*, for instance, although the opening movement is dramatic, Kempff's preparation for the great theme of the finale is gentle, and when it appears the effect is to give the melody a less joyous quality than we are used to. But there is a compensating spiritual depth, and with the suggestion of a more reserved forward momentum, the finale gains in grandeur what it loses in sheer vivacity. This reading certainly grows on one with repetition. The first movement of the *Pastoral* is imbued with the classical spirit, as if Kempff were anxious not to overplay the mood suggestion of the title, which was provided by the work's publisher, not its composer. The *Andante*, 'ticking' along with soft sombre colouring, is enchanting, and the opening of No. 24 with its almost immediate change of tempo is handled with typical Kempff subtlety. The atmosphere of No. 25 is more matter-of-fact: the performance is admirably fresh and spontaneous.

Piano sonatas Nos. 16 in G major, Op. 31/1; 17 in D minor (Tempest), Op. 31/2; 18 in E flat major, Op. 31/3.
 (B) ** Decca Eclipse ECS 725. Friedrich Gulda (piano).

It is an apt and generous coupling to have all three of the Op. 31 sonatas on a single disc and that at bargain price. Though the recording is limited, Gulda's readings are consistently refreshing in his satisfyingly direct way.

Piano sonatas Nos. 16 in G major, Op. 31/1; 18 in E flat major, Op. 31/3; 22 in F major, Op. 54.
 (M) *** HMV HQS 1201. Daniel Barenboim (piano).
 (B) ** (*) Turnabout TV 34114S. Alfred Brendel (piano).

Barenboim's disc provides a direct rivalry in its coupling with the equivalent Brendel issue, and the contrasts are instructive in characterizing the rival series. Brendel is unfailingly fresh, clean and stylistically straightforward; Barenboim is much more mercurial, with an element of fantasy, a degree of warmth and romanticism, a charm, lacking in the Brendel. Brendel provides the safer recommendation, with everything neatly in scale for comparatively early Beethoven, but the Barenboim interpretations are consistently more positive and characterful, running greater risks in choice of tempi and breadth of style, but communicating the more vividly for those prepared to accept Barenboim's guiding personality. Brendel is not helped by the comparatively thin recording.

Piano sonata No. 17 in D minor (Tempest), Op. 31/2.
 *** HMV ASD 450. Sviatoslav Richter (piano) – SCHUMANN: *Fantasia*.***

Dramatic contrasts in tempi establish Richter's account of the *Tempest sonata* as a characteristically powerful and individual interpretation. Richter observes the repeats in both opening and closing movements, and in the finale he takes the tempo indication literally: this is a genuine *Allegretto*, played with superb poise, the control never allowed to slip for a second. With a highly recommendable coupling, this well-recorded disc is a fine investment.

Piano sonatas Nos. 17 in D minor (Tempest), Op. 31/2; 18 in E flat major, Op. 31/3.
 *** Philips 6500 392. Stephen Bishop (piano).

Though Bishop's coupling of only two of the three Op. 31 sonatas is hardly generous, this is in fact an outstanding

137

disc, not only for the interpretations but for the superb recording quality, one of the most vividly life-like of any. Bishop plays with all his habitual concentration, pursuing the argument forcefully, never giving a Mendelssohnian tinge to the romanticism of the *D minor*. Yet the second and fourth movements of the *E flat* are superbly sprung.

Piano sonatas Nos. 17 in D minor (Tempest), Op. 31/2; 21 in C major (Waldstein), Op. 53.

(B) *** Turnabout TV 341151S. Alfred Brendel (piano).

Op. 31/2, with its romantic echoes of Beethoven's improvisation style, produces electrically sharp playing and spontaneity, as compelling in its way as Barenboim's version (differently coupled). In the *Waldstein* too, Brendel's fresh straightforward concentration produces a cleanly satisfying version, spontaneous-sounding but controlled. The finale, rippling and gentle, is less idiosyncratic than Barenboim's very slow reading, but very satisfying, and this is one of the very finest *Waldstein* performances ever recorded. Recording quality among the best of the series.

Piano sonatas Nos. 19 in G minor, Op. 49/1; 20 in G major, Op. 49/2; 28 in A major, Op. 101; 30 in E major, Op. 109.

(B) * (*) Turnabout TV 34111S. Alfred Brendel (piano).

Brendel's Op. 109 has not the same intensity as Barenboim's, and the first movement of Op. 101 is disappointingly underplayed. But the measure of music is very generous indeed for so cheap a record, and the recording is fair.

Piano sonatas Nos. 19 in G minor, Op. 49/1; 26 in E flat major (Les Adieux), Op. 81a; 32 in C minor, Op. 111.

⊛ (M) *** HMV HQS 1088. Daniel Barenboim (piano).

These performances are the work of a master pianist. In each sonata, early, middle and late, he compels the attention to a degree remarkable in any recorded version. The sonatina-like Op. 49/1 – early despite the opus number – is given unusual weight through rather slow speeds, yet Barenboim completely avoids any feeling of heaviness, but rather makes one rethink the music, just as he must have done himself. It is the same in *Les Adieux* – made to sound much stronger than usual – and in his account of the culminating sonata of all, Op. 111, Barenboim breasts the interpretative difficulties with a fearless confidence that has one weak with admiration. The result always has the spontaneity of a live performance – most of the takes were very long – yet it is amazing how closely Barenboim observes Beethoven's detailed markings. Admittedly in the final slow variations he has to speed up from his very slow adagio for the more dramatic variations, but his overall control is – to one's astonishment – even more complete than Schnabel's in his classic pre-war performance, not least in the way in which, after several pages of unresolved half-tone figuration (a mere whisper here), the final resolution on C major comes like an overwhelming wave of joy. Excellent recording; bargain price.

Piano sonatas Nos. 21 in C major (Waldstein), Op. 53; 23 in F minor (Appassionata), Op. 57.

** (*) Decca SXL 2241. Wilhelm Backhaus (piano).

These were two of the finest performances Backhaus recorded in his last years in the Decca studios. The *Appassionata* performance is available also on a bargain-priced SPA, coupled to the *Pathétique* and the *Moonlight* (see above), so the present issue would seem an expensive way to buy the *Waldstein*. But the performance has the characteristic Backhaus mixture of rugged spontaneity and wilfulness which can be remarkably compelling.

Piano sonatas Nos. 21 in C major (Waldstein), Op. 53; 28 in A major, Op. 101.

****** DGG** 2530 253. Emil Gilels (piano).

(B) ****** Decca Eclipse ECS 722. Friedrich Gulda (piano).

Gilels is at his most inspired in both sonatas, playing with the sort of rapt concentration that makes one forget that it is not a live performance. The elusive Op. 101 is given a superb reading, the first movement and the *Adagio* before the elaborate contrapuntal finale both deeply expressive. The *Waldstein* too has poetry in plenty, and the recording is first-rate.

Gulda's view of Op. 101 is thoughtful and unforced, and so in its way is the *Waldstein*, though there some may find too little weight. At the price, with very acceptable recording quality, the disc can be strongly recommended, though no one should neglect Brendel's Turnabout series.

Piano sonatas Nos. 21 in C major (Waldstein), Op. 53; 31 in A flat major, Op. 110.

(M) ****** HMV HQS 1181. Daniel Barenboim (piano).

Barenboim in his twenties already indulges in slow tempi that one normally associates with artists in their old age. Both these interpretations are remarkable for their expansiveness, and with such unconventional tempi as those in the outer movements of the *Waldstein* and the first movement of Op. 110, much will depend on individual taste or even on individual mood on a particular occasion. What makes this a worthy addition to Barenboim's unique Beethoven sonata cycle is

the clear concentration that is conveyed through the loudspeaker. Even when one most resists the choice of tempi, one is compelled to acknowledge the genuine point that Barenboim is making, whether it is the extra delicacy of the *Waldstein* finale (like lace embroidery) or the weight of the Op. 110 first movement, here less purely lyrical than usual.

Piano sonatas Nos. 23 in F minor (Appassionata), Op. 57; 24 in F sharp major, Op. 78; 25 in G major, Op. 79; 27 in E minor, Op. 90.

(B) ****** Decca Eclipse ECS 721. Friedrich Gulda (piano).

Beethoven's three brief 'in-between' sonatas make an interesting coupling for the *Appassionata*, and on this disc Gulda is better served by the engineers than in some of the others in his series. His view of the *Appassionata* is purposeful and direct, lacking something in fantasy but satisfying in its own terms.

Piano sonatas Nos. 23 in F minor (Appassionata), Op. 57; 26 in E flat major (Les Adieux), Op. 81a; 27 in E minor, Op. 90.

(B) ****** Turnabout TV 34116S. Alfred Brendel (piano).

Brendel's account of the *Appassionata* is one of the less imaginative readings in his earlier Beethoven cycle. The very opening is simply and directly done in a way that would have been satisfying enough in a lesser sonata but here gives little expectation of the great statements to come. The coda is clean and sharp to round the movement off consistently, but the variations sound a little heavy in their squareness. The slow movement of *Les Adieux* too lacks a hushed quality. The finale is strong and direct. There is much more *Innigkeit* in the wayward and elusive opening movement of Op. 90, and a smoothly flowing reading of the haunting second movement. From the sound of the

the recording, marginally less atmospheric than the best of them, this was one of the first discs of the set recorded.

Piano sonatas Nos. 23 in F minor (Appassionata), Op. 57; 32 in C minor, Op. 111.
- ** (*) Philips 6500 138. Alfred Brendel (piano).
- * RCA LRL 1 5016. Roger Woodward (piano).

Brendel's first disc in his new integral recording of the Beethoven sonatas for Philips was eagerly awaited, and when it arrived it proved a little disappointing. There is much eloquent and beautiful playing, of course, and the Philips engineers have obviously gone to some trouble to ensure an attractive piano image. Indeed the tone is almost too soft-centred. But it suits the new Brendel approach, which is less direct, more thoughtful than in the Turnabout series. This yields excellent results in the slow movement of Op. 57 which is beautifully relaxed, but the outer movements of the same work certainly have little suggestion of the passionate implications of the sonata's nickname. Such a reading – as Kempff has shown – can uncover hidden strengths in Beethoven's argument; but with Brendel the forward impulse tends to lose its spontaneity. There is a similar tendency in the *Adagio* of Op. 111, which is otherwise beautifully played and recorded. Different ears hear these performances differently, but the disc cannot be recommended unreservedly.

Woodward's performances of both works are rugged and individual to the point of being perverse. Recommended strongly to keen admirers of a very positive artist, but not otherwise. Good recording.

Piano sonatas Nos. 24 in F sharp major, Op. 78; 30 in E major, Op. 109; Rondo in G major, Op. 51/2.

* (**) BASF BAC 3063. Joerg Demus (Beethoven's 'last' piano, by Conrad Graf, Vienna, from the Beethovenhaus, Bonn).

As the slight waver on sustained chords readily confirms, 'Beethoven's piano' has not stayed perfectly in tune. One can adjust to the sound, the clattery treble and dry, forceful bass, and indeed familiarity brings affection, particularly as Demus's performances are so strongly characterized; but in the last resort one feels that for all the 'freshness' of effect here, the *E major Sonata* is best heard on a modern piano. Op. 78, however, suits the chunky sound of the older instrument rather well, and the *Rondo* best of all. In spite of everything, this is a fascinating disc (the playing really is first-rate) and one that grows on the listener, who may be very disconcerted indeed the first time round.

Piano sonatas Nos. 24 in F sharp major, Op. 78; 31 in A flat major, Op. 110; 32 in C minor, Op. 111.
- (B) * (*) Turnabout TV 34113S. Alfred Brendel (piano).

From the evidence of publication and of recording quality it seems that Brendel recorded the late sonatas first, probably a mistake, when his performances lack something of the depth and inner tension that distinguish the very best performances of the cycle. Neither of the last sonatas draws from him quite the *Innigkeit* one expects from such a master pianist (the variations of No. 32 are particularly disappointing), but it is a generous coupling and by most pianists' standards these are certainly distinguished performances.

Piano sonatas Nos. 29 in B flat major (Hammerklavier), Op. 106; 24 in F sharp major, Op. 78.
- ** Philips 6500 139. Alfred Brendel (piano).

Piano sonata No. 29 in B flat major (Hammerklavier), Op. 106.

   (M) *** HMV HQS 1207. Daniel Barenboim (piano).

   (B) ** Turnabout TV 34112S. Alfred Brendel (piano).

   ** Decca SXL 6355. Vladimir Ashkenazy (piano).

Piano sonatas Nos. 29 in B flat major (Hammerklavier), Op. 106; 30 in E major, Op. 109.

   ** (*) DGG SLPM 138944. Wilhelm Kempff (piano).

Piano sonatas Nos. 29 in B flat major (Hammerklavier), Op. 106; 30 in E major, Op. 109; 31 in A flat major, Op. 110; 32 in C minor, Op. 111.

   (M) *** DGG Privilege 2726 033 (2 discs). Wilhelm Kempff (piano).

Barenboim's approach to the first movement is surprisingly rhapsodic, with rallentandos underlined. Intense concentration holds the structure together, as it does even more impressively in the long slow movement, taken for once at a true expansive Adagio. Clarity and fire in the finale: spontaneity and thoughtfulness combined. An outstanding record, and a fitting climax to a fine series.

Kempff's Hammerklavier performance represents his interpretative approach to Beethoven at its most extreme and therefore controversial. Here his preference for measured allegros and fastish andantes gives a different weighting to the movements from usual, but in each the concentration of the playing is inescapable, and anyone prepared to hear the music with new ears will find profound enjoyment. The first two movements are far less hectic than usual, but the clarity of texture makes for a sharp, dramatic image, and though the slow movement flows quicker than is common, there is a thoughtfulness of utterance which gives it profundity and prevents it from sound-

ing lightweight. As for the finale, it provides the clearest justification for the approach. Where normally the complex contrapuntal writing gets muddled, Kempff's clarity of fingerwork brings a new freshness that lacks nothing in excitement. The reading of Op. 109 matches Kempff's other performances of the late sonatas, intense in its control of structure but with a feeling of rhapsodic freedom too, of new visions emerging.

A fine performance of Beethoven's most formidable sonata from Brendel on Turnabout. The concentration and sense of drama of the first movement are most striking, and only the comparatively unhushed view of the slow movement – taken on the fast side – mars the interpretation. Brendel's re-recordings for Philips of the Beethoven sonatas sometimes have not quite the fire and sense of spontaneity that marked his invigorating if variably recorded series for Turnabout. This Hammerklavier is more carefully considered than his earlier version and is superbly recorded, so that the great Adagio has a genuinely hushed tone, but otherwise there are few advantages. It remains a fine performance if not quite the supreme experience one hoped for from this pianist.

Ashkenazy's is a thoughtful reading of the Hammerklavier that yet misses greatness. One admires almost everything individually, but the total experience is less than monumental, and even for domestic performance one needs something stronger and more involving.

Piano sonatas Nos. 30 in E major, Op. 109; 31 in A flat major, Op. 110; 32 in C minor, Op. 111.

   (B) ** Decca Eclipse ECS 723. Friedrich Gulda (piano).

It makes a sensible and very generous coupling to have Beethoven's last three great sonatas on a single disc, particularly one in the cheapest price category. The recording, though limited, is more than acceptable, and the readings are consistently thoughtful, even if they rarely rise to the supreme heights of the greatest interpretations.

Piano sonatas Nos. 31 in A flat major, Op. 110; 32 in C minor, Op. 111.
> *** Decca SXL 6630. Vladimir Ashkenazy (piano).
> *** DGG SLPM 138945. Wilhelm Kempff (piano).

Ashkenazy plays Beethoven's last two sonatas with a depth and spontaneity which put the record among the very finest available. In the slow movement of Op. 111 Ashkenazy matches the concentration at the slowest possible speed which marks out the reading of his friend, Barenboim, but there is an extra detachment. If anything the interpretation of Op. 110 is even more remarkable, consistently revealing. The recording is a little clangorous, but the ear quickly adjusts.

Kempff gives intense readings of these sonatas, with characteristically light pedalling and sharp dynamic contrasts giving stature to the music in place of conventional 'big bow-wow' tactics. In both sonatas Kempff achieves a fine compromise between rhapsodic spontaneity and firm architectural control, always giving the impression of discovering the music afresh. The second movement of Op. 110 is not as fast as it might be, but the result is cleaner for that, and in typical Kempff style the great *Arietta* of Op. 111 is taken at a flowing tempo, not nearly as slowly as with many a recorded rival. Great performances both.

Piano sonata No. 32 in C minor, Op. 111.
> (M) ** HMV HQS 1331. Ronald Smith (piano) – SCHUBERT: *Wanderer fantasia.***

Ronald Smith gives a thoughtful interpretation of Beethoven's last sonata, but it lacks the sense of spontaneity, the span of inspiration, which mark his finest records.

Miscellaneous Piano Music

Albumblatt: Für Elise; Andante favori in F major; 6 Bagatelles, Op. 126; Ecossaises in E flat major; Rondo à capriccio in G major, Op. 129; 6 Variations on Paisiello's duet 'Nel cor più non mi sento' in G major; 2 Rondos, Op. 51/1 and 2.
> *** DGG SLPM 138934. Wilhelm Kempff (piano).

This is by no means all slight music, and the beautiful playing and wonderful sense of timing bring a memorable glow to a piece like *Für Elise*. Particularly delightful is the Scottish piece in E flat, where Kempff brings out the spontaneity of Beethoven's invention to perfection. The *Six Bagatelles*, Op. 126, are from the composer's late period, and their economy of expression adds rather than detracts from their simple eloquence. The recording is admirably clear and suits the pianist's firm and unsentimental approach to music which often displays unusual strength in its basic simplicity.

Allegretto in C minor; Rondo in G major, Op. 51/2; 7 variations on Winter's 'Kind, willst du ruhig schlafen' in F major; 12 variations on the Russian dance from Wranitzky's 'Das Waldmädchen' in A major; 24 variations on Righini's air 'Venni amore' in D major.
> (B) ** Turnabout TV 34252S. Alfred Brendel (piano).

Rondo in C major, Op. 51/1; 32 variations on an original theme in C minor; 6 variations on an original theme in F major, Op. 34; 6 variations on Paisiello's duet 'Nel cor più non mi sento' in G major; 8 variations on Süssmayr's

'Tändeln und scherzen' in F major; 13 variations on Dittersdorf's air 'Es war einmal' in A major.

(B) ** Turnabout TV 34253S. Alfred Brendel (piano).

15 variations and fugue on a theme from 'Prometheus' in E flat major ('Eroica' variations), Op. 35; 6 easy variations on a Swiss air in F major; 6 very easy variations on an original theme in G major; 8 variations on Grétry's air 'Une fièvre brûlante' in C major; 9 variations on Paisello's air 'Quant'è più bello' in A major; 10 variations on Salieri's air 'La stessa, la stessissima' in E flat major.

(B) ** Turnabout TV 34251S. Alfred Brendel (piano).

This is a splendid supplement to Brendel's set of the Beethoven sonatas on the same label. As in the sonatas his manner is strong and purposeful. Sometimes the toughness may seem too keen for what is trivial music, but his natural, spontaneous manner brings out many felicities and the playing is never merely matter-of-fact, even when, as in one of the longest sets of variations, on Righini's Venni amore, he takes a fast tempo and fails to observe the repeats. The well-known sets of variations on the Prometheus theme and the C minor set are done with directness and brilliance and muscular fingerwork, and the inclusion in the set (the discs are available separately) not only of variations but of incidental pieces like the two Rondos, Op. 51, makes it particularly valuable. Bright recording, a little light in the bass and clattery on top.

Andante favori in F major, G.170; 6 Ecossaises in E flat major; Für Elise; Klavierstück in B flat major; Polonaise in C major, Op. 89; Rondo à capriccio in G major, Op. 129 (Rage over a lost penny); 5 Variations on Rule Britannia, G.190; 6 Variations on the Turkish march from 'The Ruins of Athens', Op. 76; 7 Variations on God Save the King, G.189.

(B) ** (*) Turnabout TV 34162S. Alfred Brendel (piano).

The simplicity of Beethoven's Variations on God Save the King is disarming, and Rule Britannia is also without rhetoric. Brendel plays them eloquently but with the right, unforced manner, and he is equally at home in the attractive set using the Turkish march as their basis. Both Für Elise and the charming Andante favori have a gentle romanticism which Brendel matches exactly in his approach, and the Klavierstück is another pleasant example of mild Beethoven. The Rondo à capriccio is suitably impulsive, Brendel marginally less clean-fingered than usual here, but he throws off the Ecossaises splendidly and the Polonaise (not in the least characteristic) is given the proper rubato. The piano tone is variable, but always acceptable.

7 Bagatelles, Op. 33; 11 Bagatelles, Op. 119; 6 Bagatelles, Op. 126 (complete recording).

(B) ** (*) Turnabout TV 34077S. Alfred Brendel (piano).

Most of the familiar Bagatelles (including one or two that you and I have tried to play) are in the first set, Op. 33. These date from the very beginning of the new century, whereas Op. 119 spans the period between 1800 and 1825, when the third set was published. But if the listener expects the same kind of development in the writing that can be found in the composer's major output, he will be disappointed. These are chippings from the workshop, and the finish on some of the earlier pieces is as polished as in the later ones. Indeed the first four of Op. 119 (which close side one of the disc) are among the most attractive of all. Brendel treats them as miniatures, and he shapes

143

them with care and precision. His taste can never be faulted, and he is supported by mostly excellent recording. The treble is sometimes on the brittle side, but the focus is exact in all but the most complicated moments, when there is a slight excess of reverberation, not in the overall acoustic but in the piano's basic texture.

15 Variations and fugue on a theme from Prometheus in E flat major (Eroica variations), Op. 35.
   *** Decca SXL 6523. Clifford Curzon (piano) – SCHUBERT: *Moments musicaux.****

15 Variations and fugue on a theme from Prometheus in E flat major (Eroica variations), Op. 35; 32 Variations on an original theme in C minor, G.191; 6 Variations on an original theme in F major, Op. 34.
   *** DGG 2530 249. Wilhelm Kempff (piano).

Kempff is never less than interesting, and his account of the three major sets of variations Beethoven composed before the *Diabelli* is both powerful and eloquent. Indeed one would be hard put to it to choose between him and Curzon: perhaps the fill-up will be the decisive factor for most people. He plays the Op. 34 *Variations*, an under-rated and rewarding work, with great poetic feeling, and the *Eroica variations* are splendidly held together. The recording has admirable clarity and definition, and reproduces well at both ends of the dynamic range.

Now that Arrau's set on Philips has been deleted, Curzon's reading is the only full-price alternative to Kempff. His performance has commanding character and great pianistic strength: its coupling is also an attractive one, the *Moments musicaux* of Schubert, played with touching eloquence. (Only Brendel is his equal here.) The recording is a fine one too, though Decca surfaces can be variable and some copies have not reproduced as

smoothly as they might. However, there is a realistic piano balance and warm, well-focused sound. Of the bargain alternatives, Brendel is the only serious contender: see above.

33 Variations in C major on a waltz by Diabelli, Op. 120.
   *** Philips SAL 3676. Stephen Bishop (piano).
   (B) ** (*) Turnabout TV 34139S. Alfred Brendel (piano).

Bishop's marvellous interpretation of this most formidable of piano works does not make for easy listening. His manner is generally austere, but as he has repeatedly proved in the concert hall he has the firmest possible grasp of the massive structure, and the end result, less immediately exciting than some others as it may be, is ultimately the most satisfying of all. Unlike Brendel, for example, Bishop does not allow himself unmarked accelerandos in each half of the fast crescendo variations, but his use of sharp dynamic contrasts is fearless, and in the ultimate test of the concluding variations he surpasses even his earlier achievement – the simple gravity of No. 31 leading to an exultant release in the bravura of the fugue, the deepest *Innigkeit* on the repeated chords in diminuendo which conclude it and a further magical release into the final minuet. A beautiful performance, cleanly recorded.

As one would expect, Brendel gives a powerful, commanding performance of Beethoven's most taxing piano work. As in his live performances he builds up the variations unerringly, but it is surprising to find to what degree he indulges in little accelerandos in each half of those variations which involve crescendos. Broadly his approach is romantic, with the adagio variation, No. 29, made into a moving lament. Few, if any, performances of this work on record convey its continuity so convincingly. The recording is faithful enough, but not really soft enough in pianissimos.

VOCAL MUSIC

Ah perfido! (concert aria), *Op. 65.*
   (B) ** Decca Eclipse ECS 671. Birgit Nilsson (soprano), Royal Opera House, Covent Garden, Orchestra, Edward Downes – *Symphony No. 4.*** (*)

An unexpected and most welcome coupling for a fine performance of the *Fourth Symphony.*

An die ferne Geliebte (song cycle), *Op. 98; Sechs Lieder von Gellert, Op. 48.*
   * (*) Argo ZRG 664. John Shirley-Quirk (baritone), Martin Isepp (piano) – BRAHMS: *4 Serious songs; Lieder.* (*)

Like the Brahms songs on the reverse, this Beethoven offering is made to sound rather dull. The task of interpretation may not be nearly so challenging, and the result is enjoyable within limits, but for Lieder on the gramophone one needs imagination working at full stretch, and Shirley-Quirk's reading of *An die ferne Geliebte* – so much more inspired than most Beethoven commentators have allowed – has few moments of charm or insight.

Choral fantasia (for piano, chorus and orchestra), *Op. 80.*
   *** HMV ASD 2608. Daniel Barenboim (piano), New Philharmonia Orchestra, John Alldis Choir, Otto Klemperer – *Piano concerto No. 2.****
   (M) *** Decca Ace of Diamonds SDD 227. Julius Katchen (piano), London Symphony Orchestra and Chorus, Pierino Gamba – *Piano concerto No. 1.****

(B) * (*) Turnabout TV 34206S. Alfred Brendel (piano), Stuttgart Lehrergesangverein, Stuttgart Philharmonic Orchestra, Wilfried Boettcher – *Piano concerto No. 2.***

Beethoven's curious hybrid work for piano, chorus and orchestra, which so obviously anticipates the *Choral symphony,* has been extraordinarily lucky on records. Barenboim and Klemperer offer a magnificent account, the improvisatory nature of the writing producing a performance of exceptional life and spontaneity. The Katchen/Gamba performance too is highly compelling, and this is a generous coupling for a recommendable performance of the *First concerto* in the medium price-range. On the Turnabout disc the opening cadenza is exceedingly well done by Brendel, who makes up for the weakness of his partners. Boettcher is unimaginative in a work that is unusually difficult to hold together. The chorus sings well, but the brief vocal solos are poorly done.

Christus am Ölberge (Christ on the Mount of Olives) (oratorio), *Op. 85.*
   ** DGG 2530 228. Elizabeth Harwood (soprano), James King (tenor), Franz Crass (bass), Vienna Singverein, Vienna Symphony Orchestra, Bernhard Klee.

Beethoven's oratorio is an under-rated work, not sublime as you would hope from the composer of the *Missa solemnis* but compellingly dramatic for much of the time. James King as a Heldentenor soloist underlines the operatic quality, and the radiance of Elizabeth Harwood's voice is powerfully caught, while Franz Crass makes a comparably intense partner. Bernhard Klee draws lively playing from the Vienna Symphoniker, and the recording, one or two balances apart, is first-rate.

Egmont (incidental music), *Op. 84*: complete recording, with narration based on the text by Grillparzer, and melodrama from the play by Goethe.

** (*) Decca SXL 6465. Pilar Lorengar (soprano), Klausjuergen Wussow (speaker), Vienna Philharmonic Orchestra, George Szell.

Egmont: Overture and incidental music, Op. 84.

** DGG 2530 301. Gundula Janowitz (soprano), Erich Schellow (speaker), Berlin Philharmonic Orchestra, Herbert von Karajan.

(B) ** Turnabout TV 34262S. Friederike Sailer (soprano), Peter Mosbacher (speaker), South-West German Radio Orchestra, Eduard van Remoortel.

The problem of performing Beethoven's incidental music for Goethe's *Egmont* within the original dramatic context is at least partially solved by using a text by the Austrian poet Franz Grillparzer. The music is interspersed at the appropriate points, including dramatic drum-rolls in Egmont's final peroration, this last scene being from Goethe's original. The presentation here, with Klausjuergen Wussow the admirably committed speaker, is dramatic in the extreme. Szell's conducting is superb, the music marvellously characterized, the tension lightened in certain places with subtlety and the whole given a flowing dramatic impact. The snag is that whereas the experience of listening to the music is eminently renewable, one wonders if many will want to have the melodrama repeatedly. The songs are movingly sung by Pilar Lorengar.

Though the Berlin Philharmonic plays with all customary beauty of tone, the Karajan version cannot quite compare with George Szell's, whether in the intensity of the performance or in the brilliance of the recording quality.

The Turnabout recording is of excellent quality, vivid and immediate with atmosphere, a strong bass and an attractive overall bloom. Remoortel too finds drama in the music. The overture takes a little while to get under way, but the tension mounts to an exciting finish and the conductor re-creates this excitement when the closing music of the overture is used as the finale for the work itself. The narrator is not given much to do, but what he does, he does with style and conviction, and Friederike Sailer points her opening song, *The drum is sounding*, most attractively. In the slower music Szell finds expressive depths unrevealed here, but this performance is certainly alive, and with such good recording and an attractive price it has much to commend it.

Folk-song arrangements: *Behold, my love; Come, fill, fill, my good fellow; Duncan Gray; The elfin fairies; Faithful Johnnie; He promised me at parting; Highlander's lament; Highland watch; The Miller of Dee; Music, love and wine; Oh, had my fate been joined with thine; Oh, sweet were the hours; The pulse of an Irishman; Put around the bright wine.*

*** DGG 2530 262. Edith Mathis (soprano), Alexander Young (tenor), Dietrich Fischer-Dieskau (baritone), RIAS Chamber Choir, Andreas Röhn (violin), Georg Donderer (cello), Karl Engel (piano).

This delightful record comes from the bicentenary set of vocal music that DG issued in 1970. It need hardly be said that the singing is of the highest order, but for those who have not heard any of Beethoven's folk-song arrangements it is a must. Beethoven obviously lavished much attention on them and this present dics is as successful as the delightful compilation Fischer-Dieskau made in the mid sixties of folk-song settings by Haydn, Beethoven and Weber, surely one of the greatest records of its kind. This deserves a strong and unqualified recommendation.

King Stephen: Overture and incidental music, Op. 117; The Ruins of Athens: Overture and incidental music, Op. 113.
(B) ** Turnabout TV 34368S. N. Starling (soprano), V. de Kanell (baritone), Berlin Concert Chorus and Symphony Orchestra, Hans-Hubert Schönzeler.

These tend to be unsophisticated performances – although the conductor knows what he is about – but they are always alive, and above all the singers give the impression that they are enthusiastic about the music and are enjoying themselves. Little of these scores is well known, yet all the music is real Beethoven and enjoyably full of colour and strong melodic lines. The record is generously filled, and if the recording needs smoothing out in the treble, which is thin, it is not lustreless and it has plenty of weight.

Mass in C major, Op. 86.
*** HMV ASD 2661. Elly Ameling (soprano), Janet Baker (mezzo-soprano), Theo Altmeyer (tenor), Marius Rintzler (bass), New Philharmonia Chorus and Orchestra, Carlo Maria Giulini.
** (*) Argo ZRG 739. Felicity Palmer (soprano), Helen Watts (contralto), Robert Tear (tenor), Christopher Keyte (bass), St John's College, Cambridge, Choir, Academy of St Martin-in-the-Fields, George Guest.

Giulini directs the *C major Mass* without apology. After all it is only the dazzling splendour of the *Missa solemnis* that prevents this from being acclaimed

as a Beethoven masterpiece, and in a performance as inspired, polished and intense as Giulini's, with a fine quartet of soloists and a superb choir, the gramophone can make ample amends for the individual listener.

George Guest's reading is designedly more intimate than Giulini's. There is hardly a meeting point between them, for Guest continually reminds one that this work was specifically designed as a successor to the late great Haydn Masses, like them being commissioned for the Princess Esterhazy's name day. Naturally, with boys' voices in the choir and a smaller band of singers the results are not so dramatic as in the HMV version, but with superb recording quality this presents a very useful alternative.

Missa solemnis in D major, Op. 123.
*** Philips 6799 001 (2 discs). Agnes Giebel (soprano), Marga Höffgen (mezzo-soprano), Ernst Haefliger (tenor), Karl Ridderbusch (bass), Netherlands Radio Chorus, Concertgebouw Orchestra, Eugen Jochum.
(M) ** (*) CBS 77208 (2 discs). Eileen Farrell (soprano), Carol Smith (contralto), Richard Lewis (tenor), Kim Borg (bass), Westminster Choir, New York Philharmonic Orchestra, Leonard Bernstein.
** (*) HMV SLS 922 (2 discs). Elisabeth Søderstrøm (soprano), Marga Höffgen (contralto), Waldemar Kmentt (tenor), Martti Talvela (bass), New Philharmonia Chorus and Orchestra, Otto Klemperer.
** DGG 2707 030 (2 discs). Gundula Janowitz (soprano), Christa Ludwig (contralto), Fritz Wunderlich (tenor), Walter Berry (bass), Vienna Singverein, Berlin

Philharmonic Orchestra, Herbert von Karajan.

(M) ** RCA LRL 2 5045 (2 discs). Anna Tomova (soprano), Annelies Burmeister (contralto), Peter Schreier (tenor), Hermann Polster (bass), Leipzig Radio Choir, Leipzig Gewandhaus Orchestra, Kurt Masur.

Jochum's is the most inspired reading of the *Missa solemnis* yet issued, not so searingly intense as Toscanini's mono version, but with the spiritual intensity (which has eluded almost every rival) a consistent quality from beginning to end. The soloists make a satisfying team – particularly the two men – and though the choral recording is refined rather than brilliant the concentration of the performance comes over with the sort of glow one experiences only rarely even in concert performance. To cap a superb issue the solo violin playing of Hermann Krebbers is pure and beautiful beyond that of any rival.

Bernstein is at his most intense in his fine, dedicated account of Beethoven's supreme choral masterpiece. If anyone had thought that this conductor might dramatize the music too crudely, that is a danger Bernstein avoided, and more than Klemperer or Karajan he succeeds in creating a unity of the work, though he does not quite match Jochum in his spiritual intensity – only partly a question of the coarser recording quality. The recording has come up surprisingly well in this reissue, fresh and clear rather than rich and weighty, to suit the interpretation.

Klemperer's early LP account of the *Missa solemnis* was what more than anything alerted us to the approaching re-emergence of a master interpreter. His New Philharmonia account, recorded much later, gains above all in the superb choral singing of the New Philharmonia Chorus. It is not just their purity of tone

and their fine discipline but the real fervour with which they sing that make the choral passages so moving. The orchestra too is in fine form. The soloists are less happily chosen. Waldemar Kmennt seems unpleasantly hard, and Elisabeth Søderstrøm does not sound as firm as she can be.

Karajan's reading gains over Klemperer's in the quality of the soloists, and much more than Klemperer he concentrates on bringing out the most beautiful sound from singers and orchestra. But no matter how much Karajan scores on points of detail, the basic fact which cannot be ignored is that Klemperer much more than his rival finds spiritual strength in the work, which is easier to convey in a live performance than on record. Klemperer is also helped by the comparative immediacy of the EMI recording, where for all its beauty the DGG quality is not so clear or sharply defined.

The newer RCA set under Kurt Masur is reasonably priced and is generally well sung by the chorus. The soloists are good too, if not outstanding, but in the lower price-range Bernstein's account is more gripping altogether.

Fidelio (opera in 2 acts): complete recording.

⊛ *** HMV SLS 5006 (3 discs). Christa Ludwig (mezzo-soprano), Jon Vickers (tenor), Gottlob Frick, Walter Berry, Franz Crass (basses), Gerhard Unger (tenor), Philharmonia Chorus and Orchestra, Otto Klemperer.

*** HMV SLS 954 (3 discs). Helga Dernesch (soprano), Jon Vickers (tenor), Karl Ridderbusch (bass), Zoltan Kelemen (baritone), German State Opera Chorus, Berlin Philharmonic Orchestra, Herbert von Karajan.

(M) ** (*) DGG Privilege 2705 037 (2 discs). Leonie Rysanek, Irmgard Seefried (sopranos), Ernst Haefliger (tenor), Dietrich Fischer-Dieskau (baritone), Kieth Engen, Gottlob Frick (basses), Bavarian State Opera Chorus and Orchestra, Ferenc Fricsay.

* (*) Decca SET 272/3. Birgit Nilsson (soprano), James McCracken (tenor), Tom Krause (baritone), Kurt Bohme (bass), Graziella Sciutti (soprano), Vienna State Opera Chorus, Vienna Philharmonic Orchestra, Lorin Maazel.

Fidelio: highlights.

*** HMV ASD 2911 (from above recording cond. Karajan).

** Decca SXL 6276 (from above recording cond. Maazel).

Klemperer's great set of *Fidelio* has been remastered and reissued with improved sound. It is a massive performance but one with wonderful incandescence and spiritual strength, and with a final scene in which, more than in any other performance ever recorded, the parallel with the finale of the *Choral symphony* is underlined. Comparison between this and Karajan's measured and heroic reading is fascinating. Both have very similar merits, underlining the symphonic character of the work with their weight of utterance. Both may miss some of the sparkle of the opening scenes, but it is better that seriousness should enter too early than too late. When seriousness is the keynote, it is rather surprising to find Karajan using bass and baritone soloists lighter than usual. Both the Rocco (Karl Ridderbusch) and the Don Fernando (Jose van Damm) lack a true bass tone, which is disappointing, but their singing is intelligent, and there is the advantage that the Pizarro of Zoltan Kelemen sounds the more biting and powerful as a result – a fine performance. Vickers as Florestan is if anything even finer than he was for Klem-

perer, and though Helga Dernesch as Leonore does not have quite the clear-focused mastery that Christa Ludwig had for Klemperer, this is still a glorious, glowing performance, far outshining other rivals than Ludwig. The recording is rich and reverberant, and the orchestral playing superb.

Fricsay was at his finest in this Beethoven opera, and the singing of the strong cast is consistently satisfying, though Rysanek's Leonore, often beautiful in tone, is a little too soft-grained. The glory of the cast is, however, the Pizarro of Fischer-Dieskau, incisively evil-sounding and superbly characterized all through. This was one of DGG's earliest stereo recordings, and the balance puts the orchestra very much in the background, but for its period it is a refined sound. At medium price and with two discs instead of the usual three this is a remarkable bargain.

The Decca recording is outstandingly clear and vivid. It also shares the advantage of being on only two discs. But for the rest both the Fricsay and Karajan sets are easily preferable. Maazel's direction is erratic and sounds mannered or over-forced; and the vocal characterization is generally inferior to that in the alternative performances.

The Decca selection of highlights is exceedingly generous and the well-filled sides do not suffer any noticeable deterioration from the excellent standard of the original recording. If the alternative selection from the Karajan set is slightly less ample it remains a well-chosen, satisfying condensation from a finer overall performance. But Fricsay's complete version costs only about a pound more than either of these highlights discs.

COLLECTION

'*The world of Beethoven*': (i; ii; iii) *Piano concerto No. 5 in E flat major (Emperor), Op. 73*: finale. (ii; iv)

Egmont overture, Op. 84. (ii; v) *Symphony No. 5 in C minor, Op. 67:* 1st movement; *Symphony No. 6 in F major (Pastoral), Op. 68:* finale *(Shepherds' hymn); Symphony No. 9 in D minor (Choral), Op. 125:* finale (excerpt). (vi) *Piano sonata No. 8 in C minor (Pathétique), Op. 13:* 2nd movement; *Piano sonata No. 14 in C sharp minor (Moonlight), Op. 27/2:* 1st movement. (ii; vii) *Fidelio: Mir ist so wunderbar* (quartet).

> (B) * (*) Decca SPA 324. (i) Friedrich Gulda (piano); (ii) Vienna Philharmonic Orchestra, (iii) Horst Stein, (iv) George Szell, (v) Hans Schmidt-Isserstedt; (vi) Wilhelm Backhaus (piano); (vii) with soloists, cond. Lorin Maazel.

Such a collection indisputably shows the range of Beethoven's genius, but in itself does not make a very satisfactory concert. The performances are not even in quality. Szell's *Egmont overture* is a highlight, but the finale from Schmidt-Isserstedt's *Pastoral symphony* (which ends side one) lacks a feeling of spiritual repose, and the *Emperor* finale, which ends side two, is without the feeling of joyful exuberance which is the essence of the music.

Bellini, Vincenzo
(1801–35)

Oboe concerto in E flat major (for oboe and strings).

> ** EMI EMD 5505. Han de Vries (oboe), Amsterdam Philharmonic Orchestra, Anton Kersjes – HUMMEL: *Introduction, theme and variations*; KALLIWODA: *Concerto.***

An engaging performance of Bellini's charming miniature concerto is well if rather dryly recorded. The main interest of this record is the coupling by Kalliwoda. Those specially wanting the Bellini might do better with a delightful DGG anthology of four concertos played by Holliger (SLPM 139152), reviewed in our *Treasury* volume of collections.

Beatrice di Tenda (opera in 2 acts): complete recording.

> ** (*) Decca SET 320/2. Joan Sutherland (soprano), Josephine Veasey (mezzo-soprano), Luciano Pavarotti, Joseph Ward (tenors), Cornelius Opthof (baritone), Ambrosian Opera Chorus, London Symphony Orchestra, Richard Bonynge.

Beatrice di Tenda: highlights.

> ** (*) Decca SET 430 (from above recording).

Beatrice di Tenda was Bellini's last but one opera, coming after *Sonnambula* and *Norma* and before *I Puritani* (the latter written for Paris). It had an unfortunate birth, for the composer had to go to the law-courts to wring the libretto from his collaborator, Romani, and the result is not exactly compelling dramatically. The story involves a whole string of unrequited loves – X loves Y who loves Z who loves . . . and so on, and the culminating point comes when the heroine, Beatrice, wife of Filippo, Duke of Milan, is denounced falsely for alleged infidelity. There is an impressive trial scene – closely based on the trial scene of Donizetti's *Anna Bolena* – and the unfortunate Beatrice is condemned to death and executed despite the recantation of false witnesses. Bellini always intended to revise the score, but failed to do so before his death. As it is, the piece remains essentially a vehicle for an exceptional prima donna with a big enough voice and brilliant enough coloratura. Joan Sutherland has naturally made it her own, and though in this recorded version she indulges in some of the 'mooning' one hoped she had left behind, the many dazzling examples of her art on the six sides are a real delight. The other star of the set is Sutherland's husband, Richard Bonynge, whose powers as a Bellini conductor are most impressive. The supporting cast could hardly be better, with Pavarotti unusually responsive for a modern tenor. Outstanding recording.

The highlights are generous and well-chosen, and for those who find the complete work spoiled by the frustrating silliness of the plot, this single disc makes a satisfying condensation including the wronged heroine's great culminating aria.

Norma (opera in 2 acts): complete recording.
  *** Decca SET 424/6. Joan Sutherland (soprano), Marilyn Horne (mezzo-soprano), John Alexander (tenor), Richard Cross (bass), soloists, London Symphony Chorus and Orchestra, Richard Bonynge.

It is a measure of Joan Sutherland's concern for musical values that she deliberately surrounds herself with singers who match her own quality and not (as some divas have done) with singers who stand no chance of detracting from the star's glory. Sutherland is here joined by an Adalgisa in Marilyn Horne whose control of florid singing is just as remarkable as Sutherland's own, and who sometimes even outshines the heroine in musical imaginativeness. But fine as Horne's contribution is, Sutherland's marked a new level of achievement in her recording career. Accepting the need for a dramatic approach in very much the school of Callas she then ensures at the same time that something as near as possible to musical perfection is achieved. The old trouble of diction with the words

masked is occasionally present, and on the whole Sutherland's old account of *Casta diva* on her early recital disc, *The art of the prima donna*, is fresher than this. But basically this is a most compelling performance, musically and dramatically, and in this Sutherland is helped by the conducting of her husband, Richard Bonynge. On this showing there are few finer Bellini conductors before the public today, for in the many conventional accompaniment figures he manages to keep musical interest alive with sprung rhythm and with the subtlest attention to the vocal line. The other soloists are all very good indeed, John Alexander and Richard Cross both young, clear-voiced singers. The recording, made at Walthamstow, has the usual fine qualities of Decca opera recording.

Norma: slightly abridged recording.
  * (*) Decca SET 368/9. Elena Suliotis (soprano), Mario del Monaco (tenor), Fiorenza Cossotto (mezzo-soprano), Carlo Cava (bass), Chorus and Orchestra of St Cecilia Academy, Rome, Silvio Varviso.

Elena Suliotis, potentially one of the most exciting singers of the younger generation, has tended to rush the fences in her career. With her distinctive mezzo sound she produces some interesting and characterful results in the role of Bellini's Druid Priestess, but technically she is not nearly assured enough. Some of the results are vocally painful, and the adverse impact is not lessened by the coarse Pollione of Mario del Monaco. Good recording. With the Sutherland version available on the same label there is no point in considering this or the set of highlights taken from it (SET 458).

Duets from *Norma*: Act 1: *O rimembranza! ... O, non tremare*; Act 2:

*Deh! con te . . . Mira, o Norma . . . Sì,
fino all'ore estreme.*

** (*) Decca SET 456. Joan Sutherland (soprano), Marilyn Horne
(mezzo-soprano), London Symphony Orchestra, Richard Bonynge – ROSSINI: *Semiramide
duets.****

The collaboration of Joan Sutherland
and Marilyn Horne is a classic one, and it
was a good idea to collect the great duets
from *Semiramide* as well as from *Norma*,
a feast for vocal collectors. *Mira, o
Norma* is taken rather slowly, with a
degree more of mannerism than the
singers might currently allow themselves.

Il Pirata (opera in 2 acts): complete
recording.

** HMV SLS 953 (3 discs). Montserrat Caballé (soprano), Flora
Rafanelli (mezzo-soprano), Bernabé Martí (tenor), Piero Cappuccilli (baritone), Ruggero Raimondi (bass), Giuseppe Baratti
(tenor), Rome Radiotelevisione
Chorus and Orchestra, Gianandrea Gavazzeni.

Bellinians will welcome this first complete recording of *Il Pirata*, the composer's third opera, written for La Scala
to a libretto by Romani. It would be hard
to find another soprano today who better
fits the role of the heroine, though by
Caballé's standards there is some carelessness here – clumsy changes of register
and less than usual beauty of tonal
contrast. Nor is the conducting and presentation sparkling enough to mask the
comparative poverty of Bellini's invention
at this early stage of his career. Bellinians
will undoubtedly lap it up, but for others
there must be reservations about recommending an opera that is very long for
its material. Bernabé Martí, Caballé's
husband, makes a fair stab at the difficult

part of the Pirate himself: not many
current rivals could even manage the
range. The recording is full-blooded and
realistic.

I Puritani (opera in 3 acts): complete
recording.

** Decca SET 259/61. Joan Sutherland (soprano), Pierre Duval
(tenor), Renato Capecchi (baritone), Margreta Elkins (mezzo-
soprano), Ezio Flagello (bass),
Chorus and Orchestra of Maggio
Musicale Fiorentino, Richard
Bonynge.

I Puritani: highlights.

** Decca SXL 6154 (from above
recording).

There are many beautiful moments in
this set, and Bonynge displays his natural
feeling for Bellinian style, but not even he
and his wife, Joan Sutherland, can quite
prevent the work from showing its boring
side. Unlike the *Norma* set made later in
England, this Italian-made set is far from
perfect vocally. Quite apart from Sutherland – whose voice can hardly help
sounding beautiful even in her exaggerated swooning manner – the other
soloists are variable, and Renato Capecchi, a capable singer on his day, is miscast
as Riccardo. Pierre Duval, the tenor, is
horribly coarse as Arturo. The recording
quality as ever with Decca is very good
indeed, but even Decca cannot make
Sutherland's words clear. Only she should
do that. A comparison between *Qui la
voce* here and in the earlier recital disc
(*The art of the prima donna*) shows exactly
how the original fresh beauty of Sutherland's voice was here for a time larded
over with artificial masking of tone.

One tends to think far better of the
opera from a collection of highlights like
that on SXL 6154 than from the complete
set. The same comments apply to the performance, of course, but the concentration of Bellini's good ideas helps one to

forget shortcomings, even some of Pierre Duval's coarseness.

La Sonnambula (opera in 3 acts): complete recording.

** (*) Decca SET 239/41. Joan Sutherland (soprano), Nicola Monti (tenor), Margreta Elkins (mezzo-soprano), Sylvia Stahlman (soprano), Fernando Corena (bass), Chorus and Orchestra of Maggio Musicale Fiorentino, Richard Bonynge.

La Sonnambula: highlights.

** Decca SXL 6128 (from above recording).

The droopy style which came over Sutherland some time after she made the recital *The art of the prima donna* has not disappeared here. The contrast between the lovely Act 1 aria, *Come per me*, in this complete set and in the recital is very noticeable indeed. Simplicity and purity tend to be replaced by mannered phrasing, tolerable and even warming until Sutherland indulges in her swerves, languid equivalents of a Gigli sob. At such moments she spoils Bellini's clear vocal line, which she more than anyone today can sing like an angel if she likes. But the coloratura is if anything even more impressive than before, with a greater sense of ease and fuller tone. The final *Ah, non giunge* is fabulous. Richard Bonynge leads her into it at a speed one thinks initially is quite impossible, far faster even than Tetrazzini managed. But the result here is a complete success.

Bonynge's conducting is in fact one of the great merits of the set, for the playing and singing here, from a group not normally remarkable for alertness, has a crispness of discipline not heard in an opera set from Italy for a long time. The ensembles in particular are superb, and lighten the whole work. The Polonaise in Act 2 before Amina's entry has a won-

derful sparkle. Nicola Monti has a charming voice, and though he does not always use it with imagination he gives continual enjoyment – which is more than you can usually say for current Bellini tenors. Both Sylvia Stahlman as Lisa and Margreta Elkins as Teresa sing most beautifully and with keen accuracy. Even Fernando Corena's rather coarse, buffo-style Rodolfo has attractive vitality. It is a pity, however, that Bonynge could not persuade Monti and Corena to decorate their reprises, as Sutherland and Stahlman both do most beautifully. The recording has the pin-point clarity and immediacy of atmosphere that one has now come to expect from Decca.

The highlights disc is equally well recorded, but Sutherland's blemishes emerge more noticeably when items are taken from the complete performance and so highlighted. But as a sample of Sutherland's assumption of a role distinctively hers, this well-made selection is welcome, and not likely to be rivalled.

Arias: *Beatrice di Tenda*, Act 2: *Deh! se un'urna*. *Norma*, Act 1: *Casta diva* . . . *Ah! bello a me*. *I Puritani*, Act 1: *Son vergin vezzosa*; Act 2: *O rendetemi la speme* . . . *Qui la voce* . . . *Vien, diletto*. *La Sonnambula*, Act 3: *Ah, non credea mirarti* . . . *Ah, non giunge*.

** (*) Decca SXL 6192. Joan Sutherland (soprano), various orchestras and conductors.

Decca had the bright idea of collecting some of Sutherland's most spectacular performances of Bellini arias on to a single disc, and very impressive this concentration of jewels is. Even so it is a pity that the complete-set version of *Qui la voce* was used instead of the one from the recital *The art of the prima donna*, which was better enunciated than this. Recordings (from different sources) are all very good.

Benedict, Julius
(1804–85)

The Lily of Killarney (opera in 3 acts): highlights.
>   ** HMV CSD 3651. Veronica Dunne (soprano), Uel Deane (tenor), Eric Hinds (baritone), Orchestra, Havelock Nelson – BALFE: *Bohemian Girl*; WALLACE: *Maritana*.**

Benedict's music has a soft Irish lilt and also a strong rhythmic flavour of Sullivan. Its pastel shades make a pleasing contrast with the primary colours of Wallace's *Maritana* selection, which precedes it on the present LP. *The moon hath raised* is typical, but the other three numbers here are equally pleasant and they bring out the best in the soloists, who do not attempt to oversing them. Especially charming is Veronica Dunne's performance of *I'm alone*. The opera, which has a rustic plot with mistaken accusations of murder, has a happy ending. It was first produced at Covent Garden in 1862.

Benjamin, Arthur
(1893–1960)

Concertino for piano and orchestra; Concerto quasi una fantasia for piano and orchestra.
>   (M) ** Everest SDBR 3020. Lamar Crowson (piano), London Symphony Orchestra, the composer.

Benjamin's *Concertino* dates from 1928 and was directly inspired by Gershwin's *Rhapsody in blue*. The jazz influence is mostly rhythmic, and is felt at its strongest in the work's closing pages. The piece has an attractive spontaneity, the writing fluent, the style eclectic. In fact the atmosphere is not so very different from that of the *Concerto quasi una fantasia* of 1949, and the scherzando sections of both works have much in common. Lamar Crowson gives spirited accounts of them here and is well, if not impeccably, accompanied by the LSO under the composer's direction. The recording is crisp and clear, perhaps a little dry for the strong lyrical impulse which both pieces readily show. An entertaining if not distinctive disc.

Bennett, Richard Rodney
(born 1936)

(i) *Piano concerto*; (ii) *Jazz calendar.*
>   *** Philips 6500 301. (i) Stephen Bishop (piano), London Symphony Orchestra, Alexander Gibson; (ii) London Jazz Ensemble, John Lanchbery.

Richard Rodney Bennett wrote his *Piano concerto*, a work involving complex, endlessly fluttering figuration, specially with Stephen Bishop in mind. It is one of Bennett's most thoughtful works, music that repays the detailed study possible on record, particularly in a performance as dedicated as this. The coupling is unexpected but attractive, a representation of Bennett's other side. As a talented jazz pianist himself, he has here in the ballet score *Jazz calendar* managed to reconcile conflicting genres very convincingly. First-rate recording in the concerto.

Bentzon, Niels
(born 1919)

Chamber concerto for 11 instruments, Op. 52; Symphonic variations, Op. 92.
>   (B) *** Turnabout TV 34374S. Royal Danish Orchestra, Jerzy Semkow.

The Danish composer Niels Viggo Bentzon is now in his late fifties and has an enormous output behind him. His *Piano sonata No. 7* of 1969, for example, bears the opus number 243! The *Chamber concerto for 11 instruments*, three of them pianos, scored quite a success immediately after the war. It is highly inventive, entertaining and vital: there is a neo-classical, Hindemithian flavour to it, spiced with a Northern tang and some characteristic Danish humour. (On this record the composer is among the pianists taking part.) The *Symphonic variations* is the more powerful and impressive work, and anyone who enjoys Nielsen will find this work much to their taste. It is expertly wrought and full of strong ideas. The performances are good, and the recording is absolutely first-class in terms of both detail and presence.

Berg, Alban
(1885–1935)

Chamber concerto for piano, violin and 13 wind instruments.

(M) *** Supraphon SUAST 50679. Zdenek Kozina (piano), Ivan Straus (violin), Prague Chamber Harmony, Libor Pešek – STRAVINSKY: *Symphonies.***(*)

(i; iii) *Chamber concerto for piano, violin and 13 wind instruments; (iii) 3 Pieces for orchestra, Op. 6; (ii; iii) 5 Orchestral songs (Altenberg Lieder), Op. 4.*

** (*) CBS 72614. (i) Daniel Barenboim (piano), Saschko Gawriloff (violin); (ii) Halina Lukomska (soprano); (iii) BBC Symphony Orchestra, Pierre Boulez.

At any price the richly understanding Prague performance would be a bargain, and at Supraphon price it should not be missed, for the group of young musicians calling itself the Chamber Harmony has a really deep understanding of Berg's score. The basis of argument is much more intellectual than is common with Berg's music, in which, despite the application of Schoenbergian methods, emotion always seems to provide the driving force. In this score, on the other hand, emotion generally seems to be subordinated to pattern-making. What the Prague players do in an expressive but commendably accurate performance is to link the music more closely with Berg's other music by underlining an almost unsuspected emotional basis. Berg did in fact provide numerous markings in the score to suggest that he was thinking of expressive interpretation. Excellent recording.

Boulez's personality strongly dominates the CBS performances; even the *Altenberg Lieder* – with bright, clear-cut singing from Halina Lukomska – have the characteristic Boulez sharpness of projection. The CBS recording, very forward and sharp-edged, helps too, of course. In the *Concerto* Boulez is spikier and slightly stiffer than Pešek. The Czech performance is comparatively romantic, warmer with a real sense of direction conveyed (witness the preparation for the first violin entry at the beginning of the slow movement). But the Boulez finale has more bite and drama. Boulez's soloists too are on balance more assured, yet the team spirit of the Czechs is impressive, and if the result here is a more lightweight performance, the extra warmth unquestionably makes the music seem more approachable. Again in the *Orchestral pieces* the comparison with Dorati shows Boulez focusing the music more sharply; yet both accounts are completely valid.

Violin concerto.

*** Philips SAL 3650. Arthur Grumiaux (violin), Concertgebouw Orchestra, Igor Markevich – STRAVINSKY: *Violin concerto.****

*** HMV ASD 2449. Yehudi Menuhin (violin), BBC Symphony Orchestra, Pierre Boulez – BARTÓK: *Rhapsodies*.***

(M) *** Supraphon SUAST 50804. Josef Suk (violin), Czech Philharmonic Orchestra, Karel Ančerl – BACH: *Cantata No. 60*.* (*)

These are three outstanding versions of Berg's *Violin concerto*, and choice may be dictated by the coupling, or, in the case of Menuhin, by the strong, characteristic style of the playing. Grumiaux's performance could hardly be bettered, and Markevich gives him highly sympathetic support. There is a warmth and melancholy that make this splendidly recorded performance as convincing and moving as any ever committed to disc. Menuhin's is a warm, vibrant performance that is manifestly on the largest-scale expressive wavelength. One has no sense whatever of an intellectual serialist at work. Even more than usual Menuhin puts this among the great romantic violin concertos. The collaboration between the warm-hearted inspirational soloist and the clear-headed, micro-sensitive conductor works far better than one would have expected, for Boulez's insistence on orchestral precision gives Menuhin extra confidence, and though technically this is not so dashing or immaculate a performance as several others on record, it is one that compels admiration on its own terms of greatness. Good warm EMI recording.

Suk's moving account is aptly coupled with the Bach cantata from which Berg took the chorale theme for the culmination of his finale. The soloist's sweet unforced style brings out the work's lyrical side without ever exaggerating the romanticism. The arrival of the chorale is most delicately achieved, and the final coda has rarely if ever sounded so tender and hushed on record. A most beautiful performance, very well recorded.

Lyric suite: 3 Pieces; 3 Pieces for orchestra, Op. 6.

*** DGG 2711 014 (4 discs). Berlin Philharmonic Orchestra, Herbert von Karajan – SCHOENBERG and WEBERN: *Orchestral pieces*.***

Karajan's purification process gives wonderful clarity to these often complex pieces, with expressive confidence bringing out the romantic overtones. No more persuasive view could be taken, though next to Schoenberg and Webern Berg appears here as the figure who overloaded his music, rather than as the most approachable of the Second Viennese School. Beautiful, refined recording.

3 Pieces for orchestra, Op. 6.

*** Philips SAL 3539. London Symphony Orchestra, Antal Dorati – SCHOENBERG and WEBERN: *Pieces*.***

Schoenberg's *Five Pieces*, Op. 16, are the parent work on this disc, and it was a good idea to couple with them groups of pieces by his two famous pupils, Berg and Webern, showing what differing inspiration could be drawn from the same music. Berg has taken and developed the emotional basis of the Schoenberg, and treated it – at least by the standards of Schoenberg's school – expansively. There is brilliance, even a self-indulgence, which contrast strongly with Webern's spare, introspective thought, revealed at its purest in the *Five Pieces*, Op. 10. The LSO plays the Berg fluently and warmly.

3 Pieces for orchestra, Op. 6; Lulu: Symphonic suite; (i) 5 Orchestral songs (Altenberg Lieder), Op. 4.

** (*) DGG 2530 146. London Symphony Orchestra, Claudio Abbado, (i) with Margaret Price (soprano).

Price and Abbado produce beautiful sounds, something not always evident in performances of this music. Though some Bergians may prefer tougher, edgier performances than this, Margaret Price's glorious singing makes the items in which she appears a delight. The recording glows with beauty to match the performances.

4 Pieces for clarinet and piano, Op. 5.

(M) ** Oiseau-Lyre SOL 282. Gervase de Peyer (clarinet), Lamar Crowson (piano) – SCHOENBERG: Suite, Op. 29.**

Berg dedicated his clarinet pieces, written in 1913, to his master, Schoenberg, but particularly when heard in juxtaposition with the later Schoenberg piece on the reverse they sound very much the last products of nineteenth-century romanticism. De Peyer and Crowson play them stylishly.

Lyric suite for string quartet; String quartet, Op. 3.

*** DGG 2530 283. LaSalle Quartet.

** (*) Telefunken SAT 22549. Alban Berg Quartet.

(B) ** Turnabout TV 34021S. Ramor Quartet or Kohon Quartet.

This is an admirable coupling and an indispensable one for collectors interested in the Second Viennese School. The Lyric suite is both accessible and masterly, while the Op. 3 quartet is another of Berg's undoubted masterpieces. The LaSalle performances provide the most persuasive advocacy, with extremely fine playing. The recording is both natural and vivid, with good presence and firm detail. The performance by the Alban Berg Quartet is also excellent, the recording bright if perhaps not quite so refined as the DGG. On the Turnabout disc

the Ramor Quartet copes with the technical difficulties of the Lyric suite manfully and with spirit, and on the reverse the Kohon Quartet is similarly sympathetic in its performance of Berg's other work in the medium. Neither recording is ideal – the Kohon group obscured rather by reverberance – but at the very cheap price no one should complain.

String quartet, Op. 3.

*** Decca SXL 6196. Weller Quartet – SHOSTAKOVICH: Quartet No. 10.***

The Weller Quartet gives a polished and refined account of Berg's Op. 3. It is the last work of Berg's pupillage period with Schoenberg, and already shows his marked individuality within the group. As a coupling for Shostakovich's Tenth Quartet it may seem an odd choice, but a performance as assured as this and so well recorded is most welcome.

Lulu (opera): complete recording.

** (*) DGG 2709 029 (3 discs). Evelyn Lear (soprano), Patricia Johnson (mezzo-soprano), Dietrich Fischer-Dieskau (baritone), Donald Grobe (tenor), Berlin German Opera Orchestra, Karl Boehm.

Boehm's reading of Berg's incomplete opera reveals more beauties in the writing than one thought possible. This is not a tearingly bitter interpretation, but then Berg himself is quoted as saying that Lulu must be regarded as a female counterpart of Don Juan, and if that is so Boehm's leaning away from harshness is justified. Evelyn Lear – not the singer one would expect to be cast in this role – matches Boehm in his approach, and the keen intelligence of Fischer-Dieskau as Dr Schön confirms this as a performance without hysteria. If it fails to convey Berg's full message, it is in every way a worthy counterpart to Boehm's fine reading of *Wozzeck*. Aptly, after Act 2, Boehm includes the two movements from the *Lulu Symphony*, which use material from the incomplete Act 3. Fine recording.

Lulu: Symphonic suite.
> ** (*) Decca SXL 6657. Vienna Philharmonic Orchestra, Christoph von Dohnányi – R. STRAUSS: *Salome finale.* * (*)

With brilliant, atmospheric recording, Dohnányi secures a performance of Berg's complex score which reveals far more of the inner detail than is common. Though this record seems primarily to be aimed at admirers of Anja Silja – a vibrant but variable soprano – the strong, urgent reading of the Berg justifies a more general recommendation.

Wozzeck (opera): complete recording.
> ** (*) CBS SET 3003 (3 discs). Walter Berry (bass), Isabel Strauss (soprano), Fritz Uhl, R. van Vrooman, Albert Weikenmeier (tenors), Carl Doench (bass), Chorus and Orchestra of the Paris Opera, Pierre Boulez.
> ** DGG 2707 023 (2 discs). Dietrich Fischer-Dieskau (baritone), Evelyn Lear (soprano), Helmut Melchert, Gerhard Stolze, Fritz Wunderlich (tenors), Karl Kohn (bass), Schoenberger Sängerknaben, Chorus and Orchestra of German Opera, Berlin, Karl Boehm.

It is unfortunate for the hard-pressed record-collector that the Boulez and Boehm versions of *Wozzeck* are so exactly complementary. Walter Berry's view of the hero's character includes a strong element of brutishness. There is little that is noble here (compare Fischer-Dieskau), and Boulez's uncompromising, thrustful view of the whole score matches this conception, again a complete contrast with Boehm's lyrical search for orchestral beauty. Boulez is less concerned with pure atmosphere than with emotional drive, and undoubtedly he provides a more powerful experience. One is made to suffer. When the orchestral part has fine precision and clarity, it is a pity that Boulez allows his singers more latitude on pitch – whether on 'Sprechstimme' or occasionally on sung notes – than is desirable. Isabel Strauss makes a disappointingly shallow Marie, and the other supporting singing is variable too, but what matters is Boulez's and Walter Berry's sense of drama. The recording is immediate in the CBS manner. Given free in the album is an extra record containing a lecture of Berg on *Wozzeck* spoken (in translation) by Noel Goodwin.

Boehm finds more beauty in Berg's score than one ever thought possible, just as Fischer-Dieskau finds more nobility in the hero's character. Thanks largely to the timbre of Fischer-Dieskau's voice and to the intensity of projection in his words, one can hardly picture Wozzeck here as in any way moronic. His situation is much closer to conventional tragedy than one imagines Berg, or for that matter Büchner, original creator of the character, ever conceived. The result may be unconventional, unauthentic even, but it certainly makes one listen to the opera afresh, and on record there is a case for a performance which brings out clarity, precision and beauty, even in a work like this. Evelyn Lear is a far more convincing Marie than her CBS rival (still not ideal) and generally the supporting cast is vocally more assured than Boulez's Paris Singers. Even so, it is hard to recommend this in preference to the CBS, when in that the dramatic experience is undoubtedly more powerful. The DGG recording quality matches the refinement of the playing.

Bergsma, William
(born 1921)

Violin concerto.
(B) *** Turnabout TV 34428S. Edward Statkiewicz (violin), Polish Radio and TV Orchestra, Zdislav Szostak – EATON: *Concert piece***; SUBOTNIK: *Lamination.* (**)

The American musical scene is little explored on this side of the Atlantic. Apart from Ives, Copland and Gershwin and a smattering of Elliot Carter, we are not well served. Yet there are outstanding figures like Schuman, Piston and Sessions who deserve wider dissemination, and it goes without saying that Roy Harris and Samuel Barber should be represented more fully in the catalogue. William Bergsma is now in his middle fifties, and apart from his score *Gold and the Señor Commandante* which Hanson recorded for Mercury, he is a newcomer to our catalogue. The *Violin concerto* is extremely well wrought, and it is worth making its acquaintance. It is far from inaccessible, and given such persuasive advocacy and such good recording, it makes the disc an excellent investment.

Berio, Luciano
(born 1925)

(i) *Sinfonia*; (ii) *Visage for magnetic tape.*
(M) *** CBS Classics 61079. (i) Swingle Singers, New York Philharmonic Orchestra, the composer; (ii) based on the voice of Cathy Berberian and electronic sounds.

Berio's *Sinfonia* was commissioned by the New York Philharmonic Orchestra. It is a highly successful work that readily communicates to the listener. The longest movement is a musical collage using material from Mahler's *Second Symphony*, Ravel's *La valse*, Wagner's *Das Rheingold* and Strauss's *Der Rosenkavalier*, among other items. The Swingle Singers add their own comments (subconscious thoughts, perhaps?) to the proceedings, and the whole thing is highly spontaneous. The other movements are simple, more static, but contain the kernel of the work's musical thought. *Visage* is another fantasia on the sound of Cathy Berberian's voice and is even more successful than *Homage to Joyce* (see under Electronic Music). This disc is outstanding – just the record for the budding avantgarde enthusiast to start with.

(i) *Epifanie*; (ii) *Folk-song suite.*
*** RCA SB 6850. Cathy Berberian (soprano), with (i) BBC Symphony Orchestra, (ii) Juilliard Ensemble; the composer.

Epifanie, written in the early sixties, is one of the many works of Berio inspired by Cathy Berberian, and here as in the later and more ambitious *Recital I* he exploits her extraordinary versatility both as singer and as linguist. The very intensity of her performance makes it hard to decide how strong Berio's actual argument is, but it is worth giving him the benefit of the doubt, particularly when the reverse presents an enchanting collection of folk-songs arranged with twinkling ingenuity by Berio, again with Berberian very much in mind. First-rate recording.

Laborintus 2.
*** RCA SB 6848. Christiane Legrand, Janette Baucomont (sopranos), Claudine Meunier (contralto), Edoardo Sanguineti

159

(speaker), Ensemble Musique Vivante, the composer.

This elaborate, many-layered work is the composer's homage to Dante, using the words of T. S. Eliot and Ezra Pound as well as of Dante himself. The references at every level are exuberantly laid one upon the other – so much so that even those who question the musical logic will hardly fail to appreciate the dynamism. As any good Italian composer should, Berio works on the senses, and such passages as the final hushed sequence of lullaby have an immediate beauty rare in advanced music. Strong performance and good recording.

Recital I (for Cathy).
 *** RCA SER 5665. Cathy Berberian (soprano), London Sinfonietta, the composer.

Recital I is the most elaborate, colourful and intense work that Berio has written for Cathy Berberian, now his ex-wife but still a regular inspirer. Against fragmentary accompaniment from the instrumental band, the soloist in this semi-dramatic piece (presented in live performances as music-theatre) thinks back through her repertoire as a concert-singer from Monteverdi to the present day. The result is a sort of collage of musical ideas of a kind that Berio has always handled most skilfully, and with Berberian at her most intense the result is very compelling. As the music progresses, one realizes that the singer is in fact represented as a patient in a mental home, her mind unbalanced – the twilight world between past memory and living present very much the source of evocation here. It is not always a comfortable work, but more than most of the avant-garde it is a dramatic and eventful one. Excellent recording.

Berkeley, Lennox
(born 1903)

Violin concerto, Op. 59.
 *** HMV ASD 2759. Yehudi Menuhin (violin), Menuhin Festival Orchestra, Sir Adrian Boult – WILLIAMSON: *Violin concerto.****

The Berkeley *Concerto* dates from 1961 and was commissioned by the Bath Festival. It is scored for a small orchestra, horns, oboes and strings, and is slightly baroque in feeling. Its inspiration at times suggests something of Berkeley's keen admiration for Stravinsky, and its craftsmanship is as polished as one would expect from this composer. Although it is not one of his strongest works, it is well worth investigating and is beautifully played by Menuhin and the Menuhin Festival Orchestra under Boult and excellently recorded.

4 Ronsard sonnets (chamber orchestra version).
 ** (*) Decca Headline HEAD 3. Peter Pears (tenor), London Sinfonietta, the composer – BEDFORD: *Tentacles of the Dark Nebula;* LUTOSLAWSKI: *Paroles.*** (*)

Berkeley's settings of Ronsard, written for Peter Pears, date from 1963. Berkeley's sympathy with a French text is very evident in each song, with a finely drawn vocal line and well-shaped accompaniment. Like the other works on the disc, this one benefits from Pears's fine artistry and the understanding accompaniment of the composer. Excellent recording.

(i) *Sonatina for violin and piano*; (ii) *Sextet for clarinet, horn and string quartet, Op. 47.*

*** Argo ZRG 749. (i) Hugh Bean (violin), David Parkhouse (piano); (ii) Jack Brymer (clarinet), Alan Civil (horn), Hugh Bean, Frances Routh (violins), Christopher Wellington (viola), Eileen Croxford (cello) – BUSH: *Concert studies.*** (*)

Lennox Berkeley recorded his *Sonatina* with Frederick Grinke in the early days of LP, and this new version reinforces the pleasing impression it made. Like the *Sextet*, it is inventive, refined and polished, and it could hardly be more persuasively played than it is here. Berkeley's music is so civilized that it is all too readily assumed that it is wanting in substance. This is not the case, as these pieces amply demonstrate.

Berlioz, Hector
(1803–69)

La Damnation de Faust: Danse des sylphes.
** Decca Phase 4 PFS 4220. London Symphony Orchestra, Leopold Stokowski – DEBUSSY: *La Mer*; RAVEL: *Daphnis.****

This was recorded as a *bonne bouche* at the end of the *La Mer* sessions (part of the coupling). The performance is very slow and affectionate, more Stokowski than Berlioz, perhaps, but delicious of its kind. The sound is very good indeed.

Harold in Italy, Op. 16.
(M) ** (*) CBS 61091. William Lincer (viola), New York Philharmonic Orchestra, Leonard Bernstein.
** (*) HMV ASD 537. Yehudi

Menuhin (viola), Philharmonia Orchestra, Colin Davis.

Bernstein's account is most convincing and the finale is breathlessly exciting, helped by the extremely vivid CBS recording. Bernstein drives hard, but the dramatic tension is complete justification, and the reverberant stereo provides the sense of atmosphere. William Lincer – an excellent player – does not emerge as a strong personality, rather as the first among equals in the orchestra, but this prevents any conflict between soloist and conductor. Bernstein proves a much more forceful conductor in this elusive work than Colin Davis, who may perhaps have been overfaced by his viola soloist. The fact is that the HMV set openly treats the work as a concerto. The soloist often dictates the rhythm and the orchestra has to follow, where plainly Bernstein's less distinguished soloist is a less commanding personality. The HMV recording, besides giving the soloist a more prominent place than the CBS, makes the orchestra sound smaller and on the whole therefore less romantically ebullient.

Collections of Overtures etc.

Overtures: *Béatrice et Bénédict; Benvenuto Cellini, Op. 23; Le Carnaval romain, Op. 9; Le Corsaire, Op. 21. La Damnation de Faust: suite: Danse des sylphes; Marche hongroise; Menuet des follets.*
** Decca SXL 6165. Suisse Romande Orchestra, Ernest Ansermet.

Overtures: *Béatrice et Bénédict; Benvenuto Cellini, Op. 23; Le Carnaval romain, Op. 9; Le Corsaire, Op. 21. La Damnation de Faust: Marche hongroise.*
(M) ** Decca Ace of Diamonds SDD 217. Paris Conservatoire Orchestra, Jean Martinon.

Overture and entr'acte: *Béatrice et Bénédict*. Overture: *Le Carnaval romain, Op. 9. Les Troyens: Royal hunt and storm.*
 ** (*) CBS Quadraphonic MQ 31799; Stereo 73085. New York Philharmonic Orchestra, Pierre Boulez.

Overtures: *Béatrice et Bénédict; Benvenuto Cellini, Op. 23; Le Carnaval romain, Op. 9; Le Corsaire, Op. 21; Les Franc-juges, Op. 3; Waverley, Op. 2.*
 (B) ** Pye GSGC 15012. London Philharmonic Orchestra, Sir Adrian Boult.

Overtures: *Le Carnaval romain, Op. 9; Le Corsaire, Op. 21; Les Francs-juges, Op. 3; Le Roi Lear, Op. 4; Waverley, Op. 2.*
 ** (*) Philips SAL 3573. London Symphony Orchestra, Colin Davis.

Until recently, in considering recordings of the Berlioz overtures one had to bear in mind that the only way to make an integral collection without duplication was to invest in a pair of Boult Pye discs. Besides the best-known overtures, these bargain-price discs included not only *King Lear* and *Waverley*, but also the rarely heard *Rob Roy*, in which Berlioz used *Scots wah hae* as his principal theme. Although the Boult recordings were old and without the sonic brilliance which the Ansermet, Boulez and Martinon discs offer, they were not wanting in atmosphere, and they were certainly vivid. However, the rather backward woodwind balance was accentuated by the wide dynamic range of the recording. As this book was going to press, Pye withdrew these two records and reissued in their place a remastered disc containing six of the more popular overtures and omitting *Rob Roy* and *King Lear*. We are promised that these will reappear later within a collection of miscellanea. Meanwhile the present reissue can be welcomed at bargain price. Boult shows flair and perception throughout, with well-judged tempi and often masterly control of tension. The performance of *Le Carnaval romain* is especially exciting, and *Waverley* is finely done, whereas it sounds comparatively tame in the hands of Colin Davis. The orchestral playing has not the polish offered by Davis or by Boulez, but the enthusiasm of the orchestra is never in doubt.

The Colin Davis/Philips recording is good, if not outstandingly brilliant, although one has to allow for a not entirely happy balance of the brass section. The woodwind detail is, however, much better integrated than on the Pye discs, although the Philips acoustic is not so convincing in the matter of reverberation. The playing has fire and brilliance and the performance of *King Lear* is one of the finest available, challenging comparison with the famous Beecham disc.

Ansermet's selection overlaps only on two overtures but one would hesitate to recommend it alongside the Davis in spite of the excellence of the recording. However idiomatic Ansermet may be, the S R O do not quite command the requisite virtuosity and *élan* this music calls for.

Since going to New York Boulez's musical personality has become less severe. These performances of Berlioz overtures are far less clinical than his earlier Berlioz recordings made in England, but they still show toughness taking priority over flexible brilliance. Strongly recommended to Boulez admirers, with comparably aggressive New York recording. The quadraphonic disc adds a richness of tone and ambience less apparent in the stereo transfer, and the brass are notably effective.

Martinon's collection was one of the very first of Decca's stereo issues. In this mid-price reissue it comes up surprisingly well, and the performances, though blemished, have an authentic Parisian urgency.

Symphonie fantastique, Op. 14.

- *** HMV Quadraphonic Q4-ASD 2945; Stereo ASD 2945. ORTF National Orchestra, Jean Martinon.
- *** Philips 6500 774. Concertgebouw Orchestra, Colin Davis.
- (B) *** Contour 6870 575. Hague Philharmonic Orchestra, Willem von Otterloo.
- ** (*) Decca Phase 4 PFS 4160. New Philharmonia Orchestra, Leopold Stokowski.
- (B) ** (*) Pye GSGC 15010. Hallé Orchestra, Sir John Barbirolli.
- ** (*) CBS 72704. London Symphony Orchestra, Pierre Boulez.
- (M) ** (*) DGG Privilege 135 057. Lamoureux Orchestra, Igor Markevitch.
- ** (*) Philips SAL 3441. London Symphony Orchestra, Colin Davis.
- (B) ** (*) Decca SPA 222. Vienna Philharmonic Orchestra, Pierre Monteux.
- ** DGG 2530 358. Boston Symphony Orchestra, Seiji Ozawa.
- * (*) DGG SLPM 138964. Berlin Philharmonic Orchestra, Herbert von Karajan.
- * (*) Decca SXL 6571. Chicago Symphony Orchestra, Sir Georg Solti.

The *Symphonie fantastique* is a surprisingly elusive work to bring off on record, and, perhaps because of its quixotic character, opinions are likely to differ on the relative success of various interpretations. There is little doubt, however, that French musicians working under a French conductor show a unique seductiveness in Martinon's version. In its way this is as magically compelling as Beecham's ancient version with the same orchestra, now deleted. Martinon provides the extra brass parts normally omitted, and though the result is brilliant, he never presses on too frenetically. The *March to the scaffold* is aptly menacing, rather than merely jaunty. But most of all the reading is outstanding for its warm shaping of phrase, so that the slow movement – which so easily can fall apart in fragments – is here compellingly moulded from beginning to end. The quadraphonic version is richly atmospheric, although there is a reticence in the balance of the bass end of the strings that is difficult to understand in so full-blooded a recording.

Colin Davis chose the *Symphonie fantastique* for his first recording with the Amsterdam Concertgebouw Orchestra. The interpretation is very similar to his earlier account with the LSO (see below), only the performance has even more energy, life and colour. The slow movement too is more atmospheric than before if not quite as fine as Martinon's outstanding performance. It is not helped by Philips's crude side-break. In all other respects the engineering is outstandingly brilliant.

Otterloo's account is an outstanding bargain, a clear, almost classical reading which in the first movement at least lacks a little in frenetic excitement, but which yields to none in its sense of architecture. The recording, clean and undistracting, does not show its 1960 vintage at all. (This is a performance over which we are in marginal disagreement: R.L. finds Otterloo's view of the work compulsive and satisfying; E.G. and I.M. have some reservations about the spontaneity of the opening movement. But unquestionably this disc is splendid value at the price asked, so our third star cannot be withheld.)

One of the finest recordings is on Decca Phase 4, an idiosyncratic performance that by some Stokowskian magic manages to convey complete warm-hearted conviction. Stokowski's warmth of phrasing is aptly romantic, but generally the surprising thing is his meticulous concern for markings. The hairpin dynamic marks are even exaggerated, but unlike many less flamboyant conductors, he refuses to whip up codas into a frenzy, and some may be disappointed at his comparatively relaxed tempo for the finale.

Barbirolli provides a reading which not only is exciting but has a breadth missing in many other performances. He builds the first-movement climax with care, and the same thoughtfulness can be felt in the slow movement, which is most beautifully played. The thunder at the end, on the timpani, bursts into the room and anticipates the mood of the *March to the scaffold*. This is again spacious in style, rather than rhythmically pointed, and in the finale there is a strong feeling of atmosphere, helped by the fullest realization of Berlioz's orchestration. Fortunately the Pye stereo recording is good.

Boulez's account is intensely individual, crisp and intense, with clarity the essential all through, and with atmosphere taking little or no part. In many ways it makes the music sound even more modern than usual, underlining once again the amazing fact that this advanced score was written in the year after Beethoven's death. Sharp-edged recording to match the interpretation.

Markevitch's DGG recording was also technically among the best available, and in the reissue the sound is remarkably good, rich and clear and with plenty of bloom. The strings in the slow movement can be made to sound particularly fresh and pleasing. The performance is impulsive and if the reading falls just short of the standard set by Barbirolli's Pye disc, it is still very convincing and the orchestral playing is excellent. For some the extra clarity of the orchestral sound may commend the Privilege issue above Barbirolli's.

It was quite obvious from his earlier Philips disc that one day Colin Davis was going to give us a *Symphonie fan-tastique* to match all rivals. SAL 3441 was almost it but not quite. The first movement begins with a superb sense of atmosphere, but this tension is not always maintained throughout the movement, and the *Adagio*, although beautifully played, is a little detached. The two final movements are tremendous. In the *March to the scaffold*, Davis gives the rhythm exactly the right spring, and by doing the rarely-heard repeat he adds to our pleasure. The finale is exciting to the last bar, with really taut orchestral playing, and clear, vivid projection from the recording.

Monteux gives a vital reading, lacking just a little in spontaneity, though with a gracious waltz and fine excitement in the last two movements. A first-rate alternative to Otterloo and Barbirolli in the cheapest bargain category.

Ozawa's reading is characteristically flexible in expressiveness, but next to the finest versions it lacks something in sheer biting commitment. A comfortable performance with comfortably reverberant recording.

Although Karajan's version is superbly played and recorded, it is altogether too erratic to be entirely convincing. The first movement allegro, after the slow introduction, charges off at full speed in a most wilful and unspontaneous fashion, and throughout Karajan's tempo fluctuations are not only overtly personal but tend to break up the music's structure. The waltz is played with splendid panache, but Karajan's wilfulness is apparent at the end. This is another performance that different ears react to differently, but it cannot be recommended without considerable reservation.

Hardly a semiquaver is out of place in Solti's Chicago reading, but somehow for once the spirit has eluded him. The performance sounds over-rehearsed. Other accounts by Argenta (Decca Ace of Diamonds), Kempe (HMV), and Prêtre (RCA) seem uncompetitive in such a lively field.

Symphonie funèbre et triomphale, Op. 15; Marche funèbre pour la dernière scène de Hamlet, Op. 18/3; Les Troyens à Carthage: Prélude.

** Philips SAL 3788. John Alldis Choir, London Symphony Orchestra, Colin Davis.

The *Symphonie funèbre et triomphale* is a fascinating product of Berlioz's eccentric genius, designed as it was to be performed not just in the open air but on the march. The *Funeral march* itself provides the most haunting music, but it needs more persuasive handling than Colin Davis's if it is not to outstay its welcome. The *Apotheosis* too can be made to sound more effective than this. Despite this disappointment the disc is valuable both for the magnificent *Hamlet funeral march* and for the *Prélude* which Berlioz wrote for separate performances of the second half of *Les Troyens* – not a vitally original piece in itself, but a worthwhile supplement to the complete recording of the opera. The Philips recording is clear but not really bright enough for this extrovert music.

VOCAL MUSIC

Choral music: *Ballet des Ombres; Chanson à boire; Chant des Bretons; Chant guerrier; Chant sacré; Hymne à la France; La Menace des Francs; Prière du matin; Tantum ergo; Le Temple universel; Veni creator.*

** Argo ZRG 635. Heinrich Schütz Choir and Chorale, Roger Norrington, with Peter Smith (piano and harmonium), Ryland Davies (tenor), David Thomas (baritone).

An unusual record that shows Berlioz in an unfamiliar and often rewarding light. The performances and recordings are of high quality.

Chant de la Fête de Pâques; Irlande (Neuf mélodies), Op. 2; La Mort d'Ophélie, Op. 18/2; Le Trébuchet, Op. 13.

(M) ** Oiseau-Lyre SOL 305. April Cantelo (soprano), Helen Watts (contralto), Robert Tear (tenor), Richard Salter (baritone), Monteverdi Choir, John Eliot Gardiner; Viola Tunnard (piano).

Like the other Oiseau-Lyre disc of offbeat Berlioz pieces (SOL 304, conducted by Colin Davis; see below) this collection fills in some important gaps. In these songs one sees the composer's angularity, but his inspiration is always clear. The nine songs grouped together under the title *Irlande* were inspired by the words of Thomas Moore (set here in translation) and reflect early romantic ardour for the newly discovered ballad tradition. *Le Trébuchet* is a charming scherzo, and it is valuable to have *La Mort d'Ophélie* in the alternative solo version. Good performances and recording.

La Damnation de Faust, Op. 24: complete recording.

*** Philips 6703 042 (3 discs). Josephine Veasey (mezzo-soprano), Nicolai Gedda (tenor), Jules Bastin (bass), Ambrosian Singers, Wandsworth School Boys' Choir, LSO Chorus, London Symphony Orchestra, Colin Davis.

** (*) DGG 2709 048 (3 discs). Edith Mathis (soprano), Stuart Burrows (tenor), Donald McIntyre, Thomas Paul (basses), Tanglewood Festival Chorus, Boston Boys' Choir, Boston Symphony Orchestra, Seiji Ozawa.

** (*) HMV SLS 947 (2 discs). Janet Baker (mezzo-soprano), Nicolai Gedda (tenor), Gabriel Bacquier (baritone), Paris Opera Chorus, Orchestre de Paris, Georges Prêtre.

The current catalogue lists three full-price versions of *The Damnation of Faust*, and though one can rarely speak of a first choice where records are concerned (if only life were so simple), the Philips set is on balance the finest. Both Gedda as Faust and Bastin as Mephistopheles are impressive, and the response of the orchestra and chorus is never less than intelligent and in the quieter passages highly sensitive. The recording is altogether outstanding: its perspective is extraordinarily natural and realistic, every nuance truthfully reflected in relation to the aural picture, and the balance could not be improved on. The LSO play marvellously for Davis and the surfaces are particularly silent. All in all, this is a most satisfying and idiomatic account of the work.

Ozawa's performance provides an admirable alternative to Davis's, completely contrasted in a much more moulded style. The relative softness of focus is underlined by the reverberant, even over-reverberant, acoustic, but with superb playing and generally fine singing the results are seductively beautiful.

The best part of the HMV *Damnation* is Janet Baker's Marguerite. This affecting music is most beautifully sung and has fine focus of tone. Prêtre is less perceptive than Davis perhaps, though there are many dramatic touches in his reading of this inspired score. However, in general, this does not compete either with Colin Davis or Ozawa.

L'Enfance du Christ, Op. 25: complete recording.

> (M) *** Oiseau-Lyre SOL 60032/3.
> Elsie Morison (soprano), Peter Pears, Edgar Fleet (tenors), John Cameron (baritone), John Frost, Joseph Rouleau (basses), St An-

thony Singers, Goldsbrough Orchestra, Colin Davis.

L'Enfance du Christ, Op. 25: excerpts (Part 1: *Toujours ce rêve; O mon cher fils;* Part 2: *Shepherds' farewell*; Part 3: *Mystic chorus*).

> (M) *** Oiseau-Lyre SOL 322 (from above recording) – *Béatrice et Bénédict highlights*.***

This was the first recording to show Colin Davis at his full stature. It is not a sharp-edged, dramatic reading, but an easy, sweet-toned one to match Berlioz's blissfully wayward inspiration, so different from everything else he ever wrote. Davis and his singers revel in the sheer originality of the melody, and give it a childlike simplicity. Such moments as the angelic hosannas which end Part 2 are ravishingly beautiful, and wonderfully caught by the recording engineers. Peter Pears is as outstanding as ever, and Elsie Morison and John Cameron are perfectly cast as Mary and Joseph. It is good to hear Joseph Rouleau on record too as the Ishmaelite father. Not all the French pronunciations are immaculate. The recording on the whole is excellent, though in some of the very heavy passages there is a hint of distortion – perhaps introduced in the transfer from tape. There is an attractive album with excellent notes. Altogether an outstanding issue of a sacred drama that is uniquely moving.

SOL 322 provides a welcome selection from two outstanding examples of Colin Davis's Berlioz, each recorded early in his career but still sounding very well indeed. Both selections are cleverly made so that the listener who buys this generous double offering will surely be tempted to go on and acquire the complete sets.

(i) *Lélio (Le Retour à la vie), Op. 14b; Symphonie fantastique, Op. 14*.

> (M) ** (*) CBS SBRG 77226 (2 discs).
> London Symphony Orchestra,

Pierre Boulez, (i) with Jean-Louis Barrault (narrator), John Mitchinson (tenor), John Shirley-Quirk (baritone), LSO Chorus.
Lélio (Le Retour à la vie), Op. 14b.
** (*) CBS 72705 (from above recording).

Even by Berlioz's standards *Lélio* is a strange work. He intended it as a sequel to the *Fantastic symphony*, which made the original issue, coupling both in a two-disc album, very apt. As so often with a dotty work the gramophone tones down the oddity, allows one to appreciate genuine merits more clearly than a live performance. Though the spoken dialogue remains obtrusively long (even when spoken most beautifully by M. Barrault) the six musical numbers make a fascinating suite, ranging as they do from a Goethe Ballad with straight piano accompaniment through such pieces as a *Brigands' song* to an extended fantasy on Shakespeare's *The Tempest*. Coupled with a unique, individual reading of the *Fantastic* (clear-headed and intense rather than atmospheric) it makes a set that all Berlioz enthusiasts should investigate, for Boulez is never less than intensely convincing. Very good recording except for the difference of levels in *Lélio* between speech (loud and forward) and music.

La Mort de Cléopâtre (lyric scene for voice and orchestra).
*** HMV ASD 2516. Janet Baker (see *Les Troyens, Act 5*).
La Mort de Cléopâtre (lyric scene for voice and orchestra); *Méditation religieuse, Op. 18/1; La Mort d'Ophélie, Op. 18/2; Sara la baigneuse, Op. 11.*
(M) *** Oiseau-Lyre SOL 304. Anne Pashley (soprano), St Anthony Singers, English Chamber Orchestra, Colin Davis.

This is an invaluable collection of off-beat vocal works, with fine conducting from Colin Davis and splendid singing from Anne Pashley. She even manages to rival Janet Baker in her wonderfully intense account of the early scena (written for the Prix de Rome, to the embarrassment of the conservative judges) *La Mort de Cléopâtre*. If anything, in this most substantial of the pieces Miss Pashley is the more dramatic. A brief reference to a melody that Berlioz was later to use in *Benvenuto Cellini* and the *Roman Carnival overture* comes with charming point, and the end, where in her death throes Cleopatra can merely mutter disconnected phrases, is most affectingly done. The other three pieces are for chorus – the gentle *Méditation religieuse* is a setting of Thomas Moore in translation, *La Mort d'Ophélie* for women's chorus brings overtones of the choruses in *Romeo and Juliet*, and *Sara la baigneuse* is a strong, flowing setting of a Victor Hugo poem.

Les Nuits d'été (song cycle), *Op. 7.*
*** HMV ASD 2444. Janet Baker (mezzo-soprano), New Philharmonia Orchestra, Sir John Barbirolli – RAVEL: *Shéhérazade.***
*** Decca SXL 6081. Régine Crespin (mezzo-soprano), Suisse Romande Orchestra, Ernest Ansermet – RAVEL: *Shéhérazade.***

The collaboration of Janet Baker and Sir John Barbirolli in what is probably the most beautiful of all orchestral song cycles produces ravishing results. Admittedly the wide range demanded of the soloist puts some strain on Miss Baker, particularly in the first song, *Villanelle*, but she is so immersed in the mood of this and the other highly contrasted songs that it is always the musical line which holds attention, never any flaw. The half-tones in the middle songs are exquisitely controlled, and the elation of the final song, *L'île inconnue*, with its vision of an idyllic island has never been more rapturously captured on record. An outstandingly beautiful record, perfectly coupled.

The alternative version from Decca is also superb in a different, more direct way. Crespin's sheer richness of tone and a style which has an operatic basis do not prevent her from bringing out the subtlety of Berlioz's writing. *Le spectre de la rose* (a wonderful song) for instance has a bigness of style and colouring and an immediate sense of drama that immediately conjure up the opera-house. But this is not a criticism. With Ansermet brilliantly directing the accompaniment, this glowing performance is a tour de force. Decca's sound too is marvellous.

Les Nuits d'été (song cycle), *Op. 7; Songs: La Belle Voyageuse, Op. 2/4; La Captive, Op. 12; Le Chasseur danois, Op. 19/6; Le Jeune Pâtre breton, Op. 13/4; Zaïde, Op. 19/1.*
- * (*) Philips 6500 009, Sheila Armstrong (soprano), Josephine Veasey (contralto), Frank Patterson (tenor), John Shirley-Quirk (baritone), London Symphony Orchestra, Colin Davis.

It was an interesting and logical idea to present Berlioz's deeply expressive song cycle with different voices singing individual songs. The tessitura ranges so wide that it is hard for any one singer to compass them all. Once that is said, the success of the venture in this instance is limited. Davis's insight is not in doubt, but the unity of the work is undermined. It is a pity too that the weakest of the soloists, the tenor Frank Patterson, has two songs – the opening *Villanelle*, completely lacking in the necessary charm, and *Au cimetière*. Sheila Armstrong, the soprano soloist, is particularly successful in her two songs (including the final exhilarating *L'île inconnue*), as well as two of the five songs provided as fill-up.

Requiem mass (Grande messe des morts), Op. 5.
- ** (*) Philips 6700 019 (2 discs). Ronald Dowd (tenor), Wandsworth School Boys' Choir, London Symphony Orchestra and Chorus, Colin Davis.

It was perhaps expecting too much to look for a translation on record of the supreme dramatic experiences presented by Colin Davis in his live accounts of the Berlioz *Requiem* in St Paul's and the Royal Albert Hall. Philips went to Westminster Cathedral for the recording sessions, which should have been atmospheric enough, but then the engineers were allowed to produce a sound which minimizes the massiveness of forces in anything but the loudest fortissimos, thanks to the closeness of the microphones. In many passages one can hear individual voices in the choir. Once that is said, the performance itself is the finest yet recorded, though still not as full of mystery as it might be. The large-scale brass sound is formidably caught with not a trace of distortion, and the choral fortissimos are glorious, helped by the fresh cutting edge of the Wandsworth School Boys' Choir. It was Davis's idea not Berlioz's to have boys included, but it is entirely in character. Their brilliance rather shows up the adult singers. The London Symphony Orchestra provides finely incisive accompaniment.

Roméo et Juliette (dramatic symphony), *Op. 17.*
- *** Philips 6700 032 (2 discs). Patricia Kern (contralto), Robert Tear (tenor), John Shirley-Quirk (baritone), John Alldis Choir, LSO Chorus, London Symphony Orchestra, Colin Davis.
- *** Decca SET 570/1. Christa Ludwig (mezzo-soprano), Michel Senechal (tenor), Nicolai Ghiau-

rov (bass), Vienna State Opera Chorus, Les Solistes des Chœurs de l'ORTF, Vienna Philharmonic Orchestra, Lorin Maazel.

Roméo et Juliette, Op. 17: excerpts: *Introduction; Romeo alone; Melancholy; Concert and ball; Festivities at the Capulets; Queen Mab scherzo; Love scene; Romeo at the Capulets' tomb.*

(M) *** Philips Universo 6580 052 (from above recording cond. Davis).

Roméo et Juliette, Op. 17: orchestral music only.

*** HMV ASD 2606. Chicago Symphony Orchestra, Carlo Maria Giulini.

Roméo et Juliette, Op. 17: Love scene.

** DGG 2530 308. San Francisco Symphony Orchestra, Seiji Ozawa – PROKOFIEV: *Romeo and Juliet: ballet suite*; TCHAIKOVSKY: *Romeo and Juliet overture.***

Colin Davis has a rare sympathy with this score and secures playing of great vitality and atmosphere from the LSO. The recording is excellent; it is natural in tone and balance and has been recut to give added presence. The highlights disc drawn from it is exceptionally good value, and challenges Giulini's Chicago disc in terms of quality both of recording and of performance.

The Maazel performance on Decca is a fine one too, and the recording reproduces detail with superb clarity and definition. The Philips engineers get a more natural perspective, however, and also a greater sense of atmosphere and space. As there is little to choose between these two sets, readers can follow their own inclination; but one tends to prefer the Davis on balance.

The Chicago Orchestra responds to Giulini with predictably fine discipline and beauty of tone but also with tremendous conviction. Whether in the gossamer-like delicacy of the *Queen Mab scherzo* or the brilliance of the Capulets' festivities Giulini shapes each phrase with just the right degree of poetic feeling. This is a positively incandescent performance and the love music is most beautifully done. Excellent recording quality.

Ozawa with his 'other' orchestra presents an attractive coupling of three very contrasted views of Shakespeare's lovers. The Berlioz has all the warmth and glow required in this vision of the great love scene. Opulent recording.

Te Deum, Op. 22.

*** Philips SAL 3724. Franco Tagliavini (tenor), Wandsworth School Boys' Choir, LSO Chorus, London Symphony Orchestra, Nicolas Kynaston (organ), Colin Davis.

Davis's account of the *Te Deum* – a difficult work to balance in every sense – stands out even among his other Berlioz centenary recordings. He conveys the massiveness without pomposity, the drama without unwanted excesses of emotion, and his massed forces – not as numerous as the 950 reported to have taken part at the first performance in Paris in 1855 but still very large – respond superbly. The recording is aptly brilliant and atmospheric. It was a visit to London that persuaded the composer to add children's voices to the score, and the glorious fresh tone of the Wandsworth boys certainly confirms the wisdom of that decision. The only disappointment comes in the singing of Franco Tagliavini, reasonably restrained by the standards of most Italian tenors, but not really in style with the others or for that matter Berlioz.

OPERA

Béatrice et Bénédict (opera in 2 acts): complete recording.

(M) *** Oiseau-Lyre SOL 25/67. Josephine Veasey (mezzo-soprano), John Mitchinson (tenor), April Cantelo (soprano), Helen Watts (contralto), John Cameron, John Shirley-Quirk, Eric Shilling (baritones), St Anthony Singers, London Symphony Orchestra, Colin Davis.

Béatrice et Bénédict: highlights.

(M) *** Oiseau-Lyre SOL 322 (from above recording) – *L'Enfance du Christ* excerpts.***

Curious that this sparkling piece has not had greater success on the stage: it was Berlioz's last major work, a commission from Baden that he carried out enthusiastically knowing that – unlike *The Trojans* – there was certainty of a stage presentation. The adaptation from *Much Ado About Nothing* was drastic but straightforward. All Shakespeare's subplots are eliminated – and indeed the main one involving Hero's suspected infidelity – in the interests of the hate-to-love story between Beatrice and Benedict. It is a pity that on this set some sprinkling of the spoken dialogue was not included between numbers, but no doubt that would have involved the expense of a whole extra cast of French actors. As it is, the libretto given on the double-folder sleeve summarizes developments between numbers. What is really important is to have the music so scintillatingly performed. Above all it is a triumph for Colin Davis, who from the overture onwards shows his mastery as a Berlioz conductor. As always the inspiration is quirky in its unexpectedness, and Davis shows that delicacy is in the music as well as both humour and power. After his account of the opening of the overture (material used later in the final scherzo duet between Beatrice and Benedict) any other versions tend to sound clumsy.

The singing is equally fresh and vigorous. The action opens with a fear-

some aria for Hero, and April Cantelo in really top form copes splendidly, although even she does not always avoid some ungainliness on exposed entries. Josephine Veasey as Beatrice presents an appropriately formidable figure. It is a difficult part, for though officially written for a mezzo-soprano it requires dramatic soprano strength for full effect. Veasey sings with masterly precision and confidence. John Mitchinson as Benedict does not attempt a conventional tenor-hero approach, and rightly so. His distinctive voice matches an offbeat part. The other soloists and the chorus are excellent, and the recording is beautifully balanced and clear in detail. A splendid set which made a fittingly joyous memorial to the generous work of Mrs Dyer in promoting Oiseau-Lyre for so long.

Benvenuto Cellini (opera in 2 acts): complete recording.

⊕ *** Philips 6707 019 (4 discs). Nicolai Gedda (tenor), Christiane Eda-Pierre (soprano), Jules Bastin (bass), Robert Massard (baritone), Derek Blackwell (tenor), Jane Berbié (mezzo-soprano), Royal Opera House, Covent Garden, Chorus, BBC Symphony Orchestra, Colin Davis.

Benvenuto Cellini is just the sort of opera – almost impossibly ambitious in its vision for the stage, unconventionally structured – which comes superbly alive on record. Davis here achieves one of his most brilliantly incisive recorded performances ever, drawing electric playing and singing from his Covent Garden cast. The compelling success of the venture is crowned by the classic performance of Nicolai Gedda in the title role. Gedda has made dozens of superb records, but rarely has he sounded so confidently heroic as here, so deeply conscious of the overtones of characterization. The clarity and balance of the Philips recording can hardly be faulted in the slightest detail – a great achievement all round. For sample try the eavesdropping scene in Act 1, or the scene of the casting of Cellini's statue at the end.

Les Troyens (opera in 5 acts): complete recording.
⊕ *** Philips 6709 002 (5 discs). Josephine Veasey (mezzo-soprano), Jon Vickers (tenor), Berit Lindholm (soprano), Peter Glossop, Roger Soyer (baritones), Ian Partridge (tenor), Wandsworth School Boys' Choir, Royal Opera House, Covent Garden, Chorus and Orchestra, Colin Davis.
Les Troyens: highlights.
*** Philips 6500 161 (from above recording).

The complete recording of Berlioz's great epic opera was an achievement to outshine all other centenary offerings to this composer, indeed to outshine almost all other recording projects whatever. Davis had long preparation for the task, both in the concert performances he gave and in his direction of the Covent Garden production, on which this recording is firmly based. The result is that even more than in most of his other Berlioz recordings, he conveys the high dramatic tension of the music. Throughout this long and apparently disjointed score Davis compels the listener to concentrate, to appreciate its epic logic. His tempi are generally faster than in the theatre, and the result is exhilarating with no hint of rush. Only in the great love scene of *O nuit d'ivresse* would one have welcomed the more expansive hand of a Beecham. It is interesting too to find Davis pursuing his direct, dramatic line even in Dido's death scene at the end, where accompanying Janet Baker on HMV's single disc of the last scene Alexander Gibson was more warmly expressive.

Veasey on any count, even next to Baker, makes a splendid Dido, single-minded rather than seductive, singing always with fine heroic strength. Of the rest Berit Lindholm, the Cassandra, in the first half of the opera, is the only soloist who falls short – the voice is not quite steady – but otherwise one cannot imagine a more effective cast, with Vickers as a ringing Aeneas. The Covent Garden Chorus and Orchestra excel themselves in virtuoso singing and playing. The recording quality is outstandingly fine, brilliant, atmospheric and refined.

Choosing excerpts from so wide-ranging a work as *Les Troyens* is impossibly difficult. Any choice inevitably leaves out favourite items – the immolation of the women at the end of Act 1 or the great love duet *O nuit d'ivresse* are both omitted here – but what is included provides a superb sampler of the five-disc set, with the magnificent drama of the Trojan horse scene, the *Royal hunt and storm* with choral comment, Aeneas' magnificent Act 5 aria and Dido's death aria. There is the same superb quality of recording here as in the complete set.

(i) *Les Troyens, Act 5, Scenes 2 and 3.*
La Mort de Cléopâtre (lyric scene for voice and orchestra).
*** HMV ASD 2516. Janet Baker (soprano), (i) with Bernadette Greevy (contralto), Keith Erwen (tenor), Gwynne Howell (baritone), Ambrosian Opera Chorus; London Symphony Orchestra, Alexander Gibson.

Janet Baker's deeply moving rendering of the concluding scenes of Berlioz's epic opera makes an essential supplement to the complete opera recording for any devoted Berliozian and may conversely work towards persuading others to try the complete work. Baker, helped by the warm, sympathetic accompaniment under

171

Gibson's direction, allows herself a range of tone-colour and a depth of expressiveness not matched by Josephine Veasey, the Dido in the complete set. This is a more intimate, more personally agonized portrayal of Dido's tragedy, in many ways more moving. It is a pity that the reverse does not provide more music from *Les Troyens*, but Berlioz's early scena on the death of another classical heroine is a fine piece beautifully performed.

COLLECTION

(i) *Le Carnaval romain overture, Op. 9; Roméo et Juliette, Op. 17: Romeo alone; Melancholy; Concert and ball; Festivities at the Capulets; Symphonie fantastique, Op. 14:* 2nd and 5th movements; (ii) *Les Troyens: Royal hunt and storm.*

> (B) ** (*) Philips 6833 062. (i) London Symphony Orchestra; (ii) Royal Opera House, Covent Garden, Orchestra with Chorus; Colin Davis.

A generous and attractive sampler disc at bargain price which effectively represents Colin Davis's Berlioz cycle for Philips – even if the excerpt from *Romeo and Juliet* does not show Davis at his most inspired.

Bernstein, Leonard
(born 1918)

Candide: overture. Fancy Free (ballet): excerpts. *On the Town* (musical): Finale, Act 1: *Times Square*, 1944. *On the Waterfront* (film music): *Symphonic suite. West Side Story* (musical): *Symphonic dances.*

> * (*) Decca Phase 4 PFS 4211. Royal

Philharmonic Orchestra, Eric Rogers.

Eric Rogers directs these performances with gusto and obvious enjoyment, as his somewhat naïve sleeve-note confirms. The recording is really spectacular, stunningly vivid at times, but it is very close and this allows only a limited dynamic range. The overall effect is to combine with the conductor's relative lack of subtlety to present the music in an unsatisfactorily deadpan manner, although there is no lack of excitement.

Facsimile (choreographic essay from ballet score of same name).

> * (*) CBS 72374. New York Philharmonic Orchestra, the composer – *Chichester Psalms.***

This ballet score, written in 1946 for Jerome Robbins, tells of two boys and a girl and their balletic flirtations, culminating in their realization that 'they couldn't care less'. That unfortunate sentiment seems to have conveyed itself too readily to the composer. This is not one of Bernstein's vital scores, and it is a pity that something more inspired was not chosen as coupling for the attractive *Chichester Psalms.*

(i) *Symphony No. 1 (Jeremiah)*; (ii) *Symphony No. 2 (The Age of Anxiety)*; (iii) *Symphony No. 3 (Kaddish).*

> (M) ** (*) CBS 78228 (2 discs). (i) Jennie Tourel (mezzo-soprano); (ii) Philippe Entremont (piano); (iii) Felicia Montealegre (speaker), Camerata Singers, Columbus Boychoir; (i–iii) New York Philharmonic Orchestra, the composer.

Bernstein's musical inspiration may seem a fraction too easy to match the ambitiousness of his symphonic aim in all these works, but there is no denying the compelling confidence which makes all three warming and vivid experiences. The *Jeremiah symphony* dates from Bernstein's early twenties and ends with a moving setting of a passage from Lamentations, for the mezzo soloist. The *Second Symphony*, as its title suggests, was inspired by the poem of W. H. Auden, with the various movements directly reflecting dramatic passages in it. But oddly it remains a completely orchestral work, one notably less tough than the original poem. The *Third Symphony*, written in memory of President Kennedy, is marred by spoken dialogue, and not everyone will like the way that God is apostrophized on equal terms, but it still contains some of Bernstein's most impressive music. The composer inspires really committed performances in all these works.

On the Waterfront: Symphonic suite; West Side Story: Symphonic dances.

(M) ** CBS 61096. New York Philharmonic Orchestra, the composer.

The score from *On the Waterfront* is film music pure and simple and, expertly though it may underline the film's action, it does not bear too much repetition on its own. The *Symphonic dances* from *West Side Story* are misleadingly named: *Symphonic fragments* would be a better title, as this cleverly dovetailed piece contains much besides the dance sequences. The lyrical tunes have rightly already become 'standards', but the loud swing-dominated climaxes will not be to everyone's taste. The stereo is generally impressive on both sides of the disc.

West Side Story: Symphonic dances.

** (*) DGG 2530 309. San Francisco Symphony Orchestra, Seiji Ozawa – RUSSO: *3 Pieces for blues band*.**

Ozawa's performance, helped by DGG's rich, atmospheric recording, is more seductive than the composer's own. The result is vivid and attractive, and Bernstein's cunningly made selection emerges as a very successful concert piece in its own right, particularly with this approach, which innocently conceals any sentimentality. Incidentally the original cast recording of *West Side Story* is now available on CBS bargain label (Embassy EMB 31027) and is highly recommendable. Posterity may finally judge this score as Bernstein's finest overall achievement.

Chichester Psalms.

*** HMV ASD 3035. James Bowman (counter-tenor), King's College, Cambridge, Choir, James Lancelot (organ), David Corkhill (percussion), Osian Ellis (harp), Philip Ledger – BRITTEN: *Festival Te Deum; Jubilate Deo; Rejoice in the Lamb; Te Deum*.***

** CBS 72374. John Bogart (alto), Camerata Singers, New York Philharmonic Orchestra, the composer – *Facsimile*.* (*)

Bernstein wrote his *Chichester Psalms* in response to a commission from the Dean of Chichester, the Very Reverend Walter Hussey, who when he was at Northampton prompted notable works of art of all kinds. The occasion was the Southern Cathedrals Festival of July 1965, but Bernstein was not daunted from using the original Hebrew for the actual psalm texts instead of the Bible or Prayer-Book versions. It is the central setting of *Psalm 100* with jazz rhythms reminiscent of *West Side Story* that is the most obviously appealing section, but the *a cappella* setting of *Psalm 133* has a distinctive beauty, and whatever one's doubts about the music's ultimate value, it makes an attractive choral piece. Bernstein naturally secures a vivid performance from singers and players alike; but the version from the King's College Choir is even more distinctive, using the original accompaniment of organ, harp and percussion. The choir, under their new director, Philip Ledger, are wonderfully incisive and jaunty in the jazzy rhythms, but the palm goes to the counter-tenor, James Bowman, who revels in the blues overtones of the setting of *Psalm 23*. Splendid recording.

Mass (for the death of President Kennedy): complete recording.
*** CBS Quadraphonic M2Q 31008 (2 discs); Stereo 77256 (2 discs). Alan Titus (celebrant), Norman Scribner Choir, Berkshire Boy Choir, Rock Band and Orchestra, the composer.
Mass (for the death of President Kennedy): highlights.
*** CBS Quadraphonic MQ 31960 (from above recording).

Bernstein is nothing if not ambitious. Composed for the opening of the Kennedy Center for the Performing Arts in Washington, this is a full-length 'entertainment', outrageously eclectic in its borrowings from pop and the avantgarde, and with a scenario that boldly defies all sense of good taste, with the celebrant smashing the holy vessel before the altar. Its impact wanes demonstrably on repetition, but still it presents an extraordinary example of Bernstein's irresistible energy. To a remarkable degree he succeeds despite everything, and it is worth hearing these records – particularly in their quadraphonic form – to experience a unique, brave phenomenon.

For those wanting to sample the work's brilliance and variety of inspiration, the well-chosen highlights disc should serve admirably. Opening with the simple eloquence of the *Devotions before Mass* (its melody reminiscent of *West Side Story*), it includes the remarkable Confession Tropes, the *Gloria in excelsis, Credo, Sanctus*, and the work's climax,

the *Agnus Dei* with the celebration ending in turmoil. All this is admirably conveyed by the surround-sound of quadraphony, the percussion effects especially telling when heard from behind the listener. An excellent leaflet provides the words (which are very clear anyway) and details the 'action'.

'Greatest hits': (i) *Candide: overture. Fancy Free* (ballet): *suite. On the Town* (musical): *3 dance episodes. On the Waterfront* (film score): *Love theme. West Side Story* (musical): *Mambo;* (ii) *Somewhere; Maria; Tonight.*
(B) *** CBS Harmony 30043. (i) New York Philharmonic Orchestra, the composer; (ii) Orchestra, André Kostelanetz.

This is vintage Bernstein, brilliantly performed and recorded with the authentic transatlantic gloss. It is a pity that CBS did not choose to include vocal versions of the *West Side Story* items, but Kostelanetz knows how to play them, and with the rest of the programme under the composer's vivid baton this is a highly exhilarating disc and a very good bargain.

Berwald, Franz
(1796–1868)

Symphony No. 3 in C major (Singulière); Symphony No. 4 in E flat major.
*** Decca SXL 6374. London Symphony Orchestra, Sixten Ehrling.

Two of Berwald's symphonies conveniently coupled in fresh and alert performances under a Swedish conductor and expertly recorded make an attractive issue. The *Singulière* is arguably Berwald's most original work, and it seems unaccountable that it should have had to wait until the present century for its first performance. Written in 1845 both symphonies show considerable independence of thought as well as a quality of invention that places them well above their Scandinavian contemporaries. The LSO play admirably for Ehrling, whose reading of the *Singulière* is the best yet committed to disc. Even so he does not succeed in all respects, and the magical opening could be more imaginatively realized. However, this is still an outstanding record and no basic library should be without it.

Septet in B flat major (for clarinet, horn, bassoon, violin, viola, cello and double bass).
> *** Decca SXL 6462. Members of the Vienna Octet – KREUTZER: *Septet*.***

The *Septet* is an earlier work than any of Berwald's four symphonies. It dates from 1828, though how far it embodies material from an earlier work for the same combination is a matter for conjecture. Like the symphonies it has a freshness and grace that should earn wide appeal, and the Vienna Octet give a superlative account of it, sumptuous in tone and suave in phrasing. Decca provide an excellent recording.

Biber, Heinrich
(1644–1704)

Sonata St Polycarp à 9 (for 8 trumpets and bass); *In festo trium regium muttetum Natale* (Epiphany cantata); *Laetatus sum à 7* (cantata); *Requiem*.
> *** Telefunken SAWT 9537. Soloists, Vienna Boys' Choir, Chorus Viennensis, Vienna Concentus Musicus, Nikolaus Harnoncourt.

For many music-lovers Heinrich Biber will be unfamiliar. He was a well-known name in Europe in the latter part of the seventeenth century and an important figure in the development of the German school of violin performance and composition. On this beautifully recorded Telefunken disc we are given an opportunity to sample his talents over a wide field. The *Polycarp sonata*, using eight trumpets, makes a thrilling sound, and the two cantatas include music that is both beautiful and striking. The larger-scale *Requiem* (which occupies a side to itself) is perhaps the least convincing piece; it tends to lack consistency of musical purpose. But even this has fine moments, and the authenticity of the performance, here and in the smaller pieces, adds to the record's value. And the sound itself really is beautiful.

Birtwistle, Harrison
(born 1934)

Refrains and choruses (for wind quintet).
> *** Philips SAL 3669. Danzi Quintet – SCHOENBERG: *Wind quintet*.***

It is good that an impressive and uncompromising work of Harrison Birtwistle should be recorded outside Britain. Unmistakably he speaks with a distinctive, completely unparochial voice, and even in the company of a major work of Schoenberg his brief pithy *Refrains and choruses* sound impressive. A valuable fill-up.

(i) *Verses for ensembles;* (i; ii) *The Fields of Sorrow;* (ii; iii) *Nenia – The death of Orpheus*.
> *** Decca Headline HEAD 7. (i) London Sinfonietta, David Atherton; (ii) Jane Manning (soprano); (iii) The Matrix, Alan Hacker.

Of all British composers of the middle generation Harrison Birtwistle is the most sharply distinctive. You may not like his tough, often brutal style, but there is no denying the power which lies behind the inspiration in works like these. *Verses for ensembles*, dating from 1969, marks the end of what Birtwistle himself sees as a phase of his career, a phase when refrain-form supplied a ritualized structure in his extended works. The result is forceful in its chunky refusal to be budged, but it adds up in the end. *Nenia* tells of the death of Orpheus in a stylized vocal line, brilliantly sung by Jane Manning, while *The Fields of Sorrow*, another Orpheus inspiration, shows Birtwistle softening the lines of his ritualism, with evocative textures ever coagulating. Excellent performances and first-rate recording.

Bizet, Georges
(1838–75)

L'Arlésienne (incidental music): *Suites Nos. 1 and 2.*

   (M) ** (*) CBS Classics 61272. New York Philharmonic Orchestra, Leonard Bernstein – OFFENBACH: *Gaîté Parisienne.***

L'Arlésienne: Suite No. 1; Carmen: Suites Nos. 1 and 2.

   (M) ** (*) Philips Universo 6580 096. Lamoureux Orchestra, Igor Markevitch.

(i) *L'Arlésienne: Suites Nos. 1 and 2;* (ii) *Carmen: Suites Nos. 1 and 2.*

   (B) * (**) Decca SPA 220. Royal Opera House, Covent Garden, Orchestra, (i) Jean Morel, (ii) Alexander Gibson.

   (B) ** Decca Eclipse ECS 755. Suisse Romande Orchestra, Ernest Ansermet.

L'Arlésienne: Suites Nos. 1 and 2; Carmen: Suite No. 1.

   (M) *** HMV HQS 1108. Royal Philharmonic Orchestra or French National Radio Orchestra, Sir Thomas Beecham.

   *** DGG 2530 128. Berlin Philharmonic Orchestra, Herbert von Karajan.

L'Arlésienne: Suite No. 1 (complete); *Suite No. 2: Farandole* (only); *Carmen: Suites Nos. 1 and 2.*

   ** (*) Decca Phase 4 PFS 4127. New Philharmonia Orchestra, Charles Munch.

The very positive rhythmic opening of Bernstein's set immediately establishes the strong characterization, and this is balanced by an appealing lyricism. The orchestral playing is both brilliant and flexible, and if the American-style recording is not as rich in ambience as we expect in Europe, it is clear with plenty of sparkle. If the coupling, an exciting if somewhat brittle selection from *Gaîté Parisienne*, is wanted, this record is an attractive proposition.

Markevitch's record too is very well played. The modern recording is rich and colourful, although the warm reverberation does smooth out some of the edge on the orchestral playing in the *Carmen* excerpts. The sound in *L'Arlésienne* is brighter and more forward, often of demonstration quality, and the music is splendidly characterized. A very agreeable disc that can be cordially recommended.

It is a great pity that, at the time of going to press, the Decca SPA has a slight technical fault which appears to be common to all pressings, otherwise this would be virtually a 'best buy' among the bargain and medium-priced permutations of the *L'Arlésienne* and *Carmen* suites. (Decca are looking into this and it may be that corrected pressings are available by the time we are in print.) Gibson secures first-class orchestral playing with crisp rhythms and glowing woodwind colours. Decca have always had a special penchant for recording the *Carmen suites*, right from the FFRR 78 days, and the sound has a characteristic glowing brilliance, with only the upper string tone giving the slightest hint that this record was not made yesterday. Morel's performance of *L'Arlésienne* has a matching stylishness and breadth, and most of the recording is comparably vivid. But at the end of side one, where *L'Arlésienne Suite No. 1* opens, there is a curious patch of indistinct and insecure recording, as if something went wrong at the tape-to-disc transfer. This was definitely not present on the original full-priced issue.

Beecham's famous account of the *Carmen suite* was one of the highlights of HMV's *Legacy* series (mostly now deleted) in which many of his LP recordings were reissued at medium price. The new transfer is notably successful: whatever the engineers have done to the original, it sounds remarkably impressive here, with nicely judged reverberation and a fine bloom on everything. The characteristic Beecham swagger in the opening *Prélude* is unique; the conductor's use of the cymbals too is marvellously telling. The *L'Arlésienne suites* sounded poor in their original issue – one of EMI's first stereo records – but in the re-transfer the sound has much more glow, and the tapery treble has almost disappeared. ponically the disc cannot compare with She best of recent versions (the string tuttis are inclined to lack body), but the performances are in many ways incomparable: the wind solos are played with unique character.

The metallic clash of the cymbals for the opening *Carmen prélude* on Karajan's disc sets the seal of the brilliance of both orchestral playing and recording. Yet the acoustic is attractively resonant, allowing plenty of orchestral bloom. There is some marvellously crisp and stylish woodwind playing, and the characterization of the music is dramatic and vivid.

Munch's Phase 4 disc offers the best of this somewhat artificial system of recording balance, with few of the drawbacks. There is plenty of brilliance, and the many felicitous details of woodwind scoring, for which Bizet is justly famous, are projected without undue exaggeration. Generally the readings are stylish, and if the last ounce of sheer dash is missing, the Decca sound is often very good indeed.

Ansermet's selection is much more generous. The sound is brilliant, forward, and pithy, and the conductor's approach strong in personality. The *Carmen suites* are even more vivid, recorded with sparkling clarity; the only reservation is a slight glare to the upper string quality. Ansermet's percussion player (only too clearly reproduced) gets left behind once or twice.

L'Arlésienne: Suite No. 1; Carmen: Suite No. 1; Jeux d'enfants (Children's Games): Suite.
> *** HMV ASD 2915. Orchestre de Paris, Daniel Barenboim.

If this particular grouping of works appeals, Barenboim's disc can be cordially recommended. The performances are vivid and affectionate: the *Carmen suite* has notable gusto, and the orchestral playing is excellent. The recording is one of EMI's best, with a warm acoustic yet plenty of definition. Indeed the combination of richness and sparkle is of demonstration quality. However, the disc is not especially generous: side two contains only the first *L'Arlésienne suite,* leaving plenty of room for the second, or indeed more excerpts from *Carman.*

Carmen: Suites Nos. 1 and 2.
> (M) ** CBS Classics 61350. New York Philharmonic Orchestra, Leonard Bernstein – GRIEG: *Peer Gynt suites Nos. 1 and 2.***

Bernstein's opening *Prélude* may prove slower than some will expect, but these excerpts are vividly played and the recording highlights the music's primary colours. The use of the trumpet for the vocal line in the *Toreador song* is acceptable enough, and the intended hint of vulgarity in the playing is effective, coming after the beautifully stylish performance of the *Habañera*. If the very generous coupling is wanted, this could prove worthwhile.

Jeux d'enfants (Children's Games): Suite.
> (M) *** Ace of Diamonds SDD 144. Paris Conservatoire Orchestra, Jean Martinon – IBERT: *Divertissement*; SAINT-SAËNS: *Danse macabre*, etc.***
> (B) *** Classics for Pleasure CFP 40086. Scottish National Orchestra, Alexander Gibson – SAINT-SAËNS: *Carnival****; RAVEL: *Ma Mère l'Oye.*** (*)

Martinon's performance is colourful and vivid, and yet he retains a proper sense of proportion in this delicately scored music. This is among the best recorded performances of this charming suite, and the couplings are equally recommendable.

From Classics for Pleasure a fresh recording and lively orchestral playing. The lyrical movements, shaped with gentle affection, give much pleasure. and with good couplings this is an excellent bargain.

Roma (suite); *Symphony in C major.*
> *** HMV ASD 3039. City of Birmingham Orchestra, Louis Frémaux.

Roma was written over a period, some years after the *Symphony in C major*. Bizet originally called the work (first performed without the scherzo) a *Fantasie symphonique*, with its four movements labelled *Rome*, *Venice*, *Florence* and *Naples*. It has not the overall spontaneity of the *Symphony*, and it is uneven in its quality of invention, but it remains a piece easy to indulge, if like Sir Thomas Beecham you are a lover of Bizet's delicate feeling for the orchestral palette. The warmth of the lovely opening horn theme and the gaiety of the finale, with its striking secondary tune, are brought out affectionately here, and the orchestral playing is nearly always excellent. The performance of the *Symphony* is very good indeed, and the chosen acoustic, resonant but not as reverberant as Marriner's Argo disc, expands the orchestra without a sense of inflation. After a vivid opening movement the *Andante* is superbly done, its intense, lyrical flow making a perfect foil for the wit of the scherzo and finale; but in the last movement Frémaux is not quite so deliciously light and frothy as Marriner.

Symphony in C major.
> *** Argo ZRG 719. Academy of St Martin-in-the-Fields, Neville Marriner – PROKOFIEV: *Symphony No. 1.****
> (M) ** (*) CBS Classics 61071. New York Philharmonic Orchestra, Leonard Bernstein – DUKAS: *L'Apprenti sorcier*; PROKOFIEV: *Symphony No. 1.***

Symphony in C major; L'Arlésienne: Suite No. 1 (complete); Suite No. 2: Menuet; Farandole.
> ** Decca SXL 6350. Suisse Romande Orchestra, Alexander Gibson.

Symphony in C major; Jeux d'enfants (Children's Games): Suite; La Jolie Fille de Perth: suite.
> (M) ** (*) Decca Ace of Diamonds SDD 231. Suisse Romande Orchestra, Ernest Ansermet.

Marriner's performance is beautifully played and richly recorded, in a warm, resonant acoustic. Perhaps there is a trifle too much reverberation, but it is easy to adjust, and the wit of the finale is not blunted: this is irrepressibly gay and high-spirited. With an equally successful coupling this is a very desirable record. After this Bernstein seems somewhat glossy, but this is in part contributed by the rather glassy sound given to the upper strings by the CBS engineers. The performance is extremely brilliant and the ebullience of the orchestral playing is exhilarating, especially in the last two movements. The work is well characterized, the slow movement affectionately done, with a fine oboe solo, the contrast in the middle section heightened by the precision of the playing. Bernstein offers one more work than Marriner, and the disc, at middle price, is competitive if the CBS sound picture is to taste.

Gibson's performance is given a first-rate Decca recording, but in the last resort the music's presentation (like the generous coupling) is a little faceless. Ansermet's collection is a happy one, all the works included showing Bizet's orchestral genius at its most felicitous. The first movement of the symphony is characteristically neat and precise, the slow movement poised, and the two final movements elegant, if without Marriner's champagne-like gaiety. Both *Jeux d'enfants* and the *Fair Maid of Perth suite* are nicely done, with clean string playing and vivid wind colours, and the warm, clear Decca recording gives much pleasure.

Carmen (opera in 4 acts): complete recording.
   *** DGG 2740 101 (3 discs). Marilyn Horne (mezzo-soprano), James McCracken (tenor), Tom Krause (baritone), Adriana Maliponte (soprano), Manhattan Opera Chorus, Children's Chorus, Metro-

politan Opera Orchestra, Leonard Bernstein.
   *** HMV SLS 5021 (3 discs). Victoria de los Angeles (soprano), Nicolai Gedda (tenor), Janine Micheau (soprano), Ernest Blanc (baritone), Chorus and Orchestra of Radiodiffusion Française, Petits Chanteurs de Versailles, Sir Thomas Beecham.
   (M) *** RCA SER 5600/2. Leontyne Price (soprano), Franco Corelli (tenor), Robert Merrill (baritone), Mirella Freni (soprano), Vienna State Opera Chorus, Vienna Boys' Choir, Vienna Philharmonic Orchestra, Herbert von Karajan.
   ** HMV SLS 913 (3 discs). Maria Callas (soprano), Nicolai Gedda (tenor), Robert Massard (baritone), Andrea Guiot (soprano), Paris Opera Chorus and Orchestra, Georges Prêtre.
   ** HMV SLS 952 (3 discs). Grace Bumbry (mezzo-soprano), Jon Vickers (tenor), Mirella Freni (soprano), Kostas Paskalis (baritone), Paris Opera Chorus and Orchestra, Rafael Frühbeck de Burgos.
   * (*) Decca SET 256/8. Regina Resnik (mezzo-soprano), Mario del Monaco (tenor), Joan Sutherland (soprano), Tom Krause (baritone), Grand Theatre of Geneva Chorus, Suisse Romande Orchestra, Thomas Schippers.

Few operas have been more successful on record than *Carmen*. Choice between the first three sets listed will inevitably be one of personal preference, for each is different and each has special features to recommend it highly; and even the flawed Callas set has a special biting compulsion which may recommend it above all others to this diva's many admirers. It was bold of DGG to choose the USA for their sessions – the first major opera recording undertaken there for many years. It was based on the Metropolitan Opera's spectacular production of *Carmen* with Bernstein conducting the same cast as on record, and the sessions plainly gained from being interleaved with live performances. Bizet scholars may argue about details of the text used in the performances – Bernstein adopted the original version of 1875 with spoken dialogue but with variations designed to suit a stage production. Some of his slow tempi will be questioned too, but what really matters is the authentic tingle of dramatic tension which impregnates the whole entertainment. Never before, not even in Beecham's classic set, has the full theatrical flavour of Bizet's score been conveyed, and Marilyn Horne – occasionally coarse in expression – gives the most fully satisfying reading of the heroine's role yet heard on record, a great vivid characterization, warts and all. The rest of the cast similarly works to Bernstein's consistent overall plan. The singing is not all perfect, but it is always vigorous and colourful, and so (despite often poor French accents) is the spoken dialogue. A presentation hard to resist, with generally atmospheric recording.

Beecham's approach to Bizet's well-worn score is no less fresh and revealing. Like Bernstein, his speeds are not always conventional but they always *sound* right. And unlike so many strong-willed conductors in opera Beecham allows his singers room to breathe and to expand their characterizations. It seems he specially chose de los Angeles to be his Carmen although she had never sung the part on the stage before making the recording. He conceived the *femme fatale* not as the usual glad-eyed character, but as someone far more subtly seductive, winning her admirers not so much by direct assault and high voltage as by

genuine charm and real femininity. De los Angeles suits this conception perfectly: her characterization of Carmen is absolutely bewitching, and when in the Quintet scene she says *Je suis amoureuse* one believes her absolutely. Naturally the other singers are not nearly so dominant as this, but they make admirable foils; Gedda is pleasantly light-voiced as ever, Janine Micheau is a sweet Micaela, and Ernest Blanc makes an attractive Escamillo. The stereo recording does not add to things in the way that the best Decca opera recordings do, and there seems to have been little attempt at stage production, but in an excellent new transfer the sound is warm yet suitably brilliant, and the recording does not show its age.

With Karajan's version much depends on the listener's reaction to the conductor's tempi and to Leontyne Price's smoky-toned Carmen. Comparing records of the regular version with sung recitative, the Beecham set remains the most magical, but if you are looking for a heroine who is a sexual threat as well as a charmer, Price is the more convincing. Corelli has moments of coarseness, but his is still a heroic performance. Robert Merrill sings with gloriously firm tone, while Freni is, as ever, enchanting as Micaela. With more spectacular recording than is given to Beecham (still very good for its mid-sixties vintage), this set remains a keen competitor, with Karajan always inspired in his fresh look at a much-played score.

The Callas set is something of a disappointment. Fire is there in plenty, of course. Callas is Carmen, the advertisements said, but rather Callas is Callas, for the diva's interpretation gives only half the story, both dramatically and musically. Musically Callas has all her usual faults of sourness and wobbling, but what is more there are few of those individual touches in phrasing which make one catch the breath. This is a spiteful, malicious, even evil Carmen, not nearly as sexual as Price's. When Prêtre's conducting is relentless and the playing of the French orchestra less than brilliant, the issue is hardly in doubt. Gedda is a fair enough Don José, as he was in the Beecham set, but the voice has not the big heroic ring. All the other soloists are most disappointing.

Frühbeck uses the original 1875 version of Bizet's score without the cuts that were made after experience in the theatre, and with spoken dialogue instead of the recitatives which Guiraud composed after Bizet's early death. Quite apart from that, Grace Bumbry makes a disappointing, generally unimaginative Carmen, singing with good tone but with few of the individual touches that bring the words or musical phrases to life. Vickers makes a strong, heroic Don José, but he rarely sounds idiomatic; and surprisingly Frühbeck's conducting lacks sparkle. Paskalis makes a gloriously rich-toned Escamillo and Freni an exquisite Micaela. This is not nearly so compelling as Bernstein's version, the only rival with spoken dialogue.

The Decca set is very disappointing despite brilliant recording (by the same engineers as did the Karajan set a few months later). Resnik has a fruitier tone than her rivals, but her aim is wild, compared with Price and de los Angeles. Del Monaco sings coarsely, and though Sutherland sings as beautifully as ever, it sounds as though Lucia had strayed into the wrong opera. Schippers drives very hard indeed.

Carmen: highlights.

  *** HMV ASD 590 (from above recording with Los Angeles, Beecham).

  ** HMV ASD 2282 (from above recording with Callas, Prêtre).

  ** HMV ASD 2774 (from above recording with Bumbry, Frühbeck de Burgos).

  * (*) Decca SXL 6156 (from above recording with Resnik, Schippers).

Carmen: highlights: *Prelude; Habañera; Seguidilla and Duet; Gypsy song; Quintet; Card trio; Duet and Finale.*

  ** (*) Decca Phase 4 PFS 4204. Marilyn Horne (mezzo-soprano), Michele Molese (tenor), soloists, Royal Philharmonic Chorus and Orchestra, Henry Lewis.

ASD 590 offers a delightful collection of favourites, and anyone who, for whatever reason, decides to get another complete set instead of Beecham would do well to have this as a supplement. The transfer has been technically successful. But the most fascinating disc of *Carmen* excerpts is the Decca Phase 4 issue with Marilyn Horne, made some years before her complete New York recording. She it was who was the singing voice behind Dorothy Dandridge in the film *Carmen Jones*; and here, with a decade more of experience, she is even more searingly compelling as the fire-eating heroine. There is not only dramatic presence but musical control too, and the flair of the performance is well matched by the flamboyant spread of Phase 4 sound. The side-lengths are not generous, but the opulence of sound makes some amends, and Henry Lewis's conducting has no lack of sparkle.

Perhaps wisely, the selection from the Callas set is not so much designed to highlight the heroine as to provide as many 'pops' as possible from the opera. In isolation Callas's shortcomings – dramatic as well as vocal – are just as clear as in the complete set, and Prêtre is hardly a sensitive or understanding Bizet conductor. Only Gedda's *Flower Song* provides real enjoyment, though devotees will no doubt take comfort from the comparatively effortful examples of Callas's individual artistry.

With the selection from Bumbry's set the reservations remain. She is a less-than-compelling Carmen. The selection of highlights from the Beecham/de los Angeles set is far preferable.

When Sutherland's Micaela was one of the two memorable things about the complete Decca set (the other was the sound of Carmen's hob-nailed boots in the *Habañera*) it is disappointing of Decca to select only Micaela's Act 3 aria for inclusion in this selection. Otherwise del Monaco's Don José is predictably coarse, and Resnik has her vibrato brought out by the microphone.

Carmen: highlights (sung in English). Act 1: *Prelude; Habañera; Duet; Seguidilla.* Act 2: *Toreador Song; Quintet; Duet – Flower Song and Finale.* Act 3: *Card Trio; Micaela's Aria.*

** HMV CSD 1398. Patricia Johnson, Donald Smith, Raimund Herincx, Elizabeth Robson, Rita Hunter, Ann Robson, Leon Greene, John Stoddart, Julian Moyle, Sadler's Wells Orchestra, Colin Davis.

This was one of the most successful Sadler's Wells discs, thanks both to the forceful conducting of Colin Davis and to the rich-voiced, reliable singing of Patricia Johnson as Carmen. Nor is Johnson reliable and no more: time and again her phrasing is most imaginative and memorable. It is good that the microphone catches her voice so well. Donald Smith, the Don José, has been criticized in his stage performances for stiff acting, but on record he provides a wonderfully attractive, ringing tone. The selection is well made, and the ensemble work has the authentic enthusiasm of a live performance. The recording is very good.

Carmen: ballet from the music of the opera, arr. Rodion Shchedrin.

*** HMV ASD 2448. Bolshoi Theatre Orchestra, Gennady Rozhdestvensky.

Rodion Shchedrin's very free adaptation of Bizet's *Carmen* music has not generally been well received by the ears of professional critics. What he has done to create his ballet score is to take Bizet's tunes, complete with harmony, and rework them into a new orchestral tapestry, using only strings and a wide variety of percussion. To the listener very familiar with Bizet's note-for-note sequence the breaking up and rearrangement of many of the melodic ideas (some, of course, survive pretty well intact) are disconcerting to say the least. And the free use of percussive effects like the vibraphone involves the element of taste. Let it be said that the whole thing is brilliantly done, with a marvellous ear for the colour possibilities of the orchestral string section. The playing here is totally committed and exciting from the first bar to the last; the recording (once the treble is trimmed) is truly demonstration-worthy. If you like sparkling sound, and have not too strongly conceived notions about the 'sacredness' of accepted masterpieces, you may find this infectious champagne/vodka cocktail very much to your taste. But it is strictly not for purists.

Les Pêcheurs de perles (opera in 3 acts): complete recording.

** HMV SLS 877 (2 discs). Janine Micheau (soprano), Nicolai Gedda (tenor), Ernest Blanc (baritone), Jacques Mars (bass), Paris Opéra-Comique Chorus and Orchestra, Pierre Dervaux.

While the reissue of this only current version of *The Pearl Fishers* (at slightly more than medium price) is welcome, it remains rather a disappointing set. This is one of Bizet's most appealing works, not so much for the story (about pearl fishers and a priestess in medieval Ceylon) as for the relaxed charm of the score and in particular the soaring lyricism of five or six superb numbers. More than anything it needs affectionate treatment from the conductor and a fair degree of technical accomplishment in the singing. Dervaux is an efficient conductor, but one suspects it is largely his fault that the soloists do not acquit themselves better. Gedda in his romance *Je crois entendre encore* is rather lumpy and graceless; and it does not take comparison with Gigli and De Luca to realize that the great, thrilling duet *Au fond du temple saint* is below par. Ernest Blanc has an attractive voice, but there is comparatively little imagination here, and Janine Micheau is not so graceful as she has been on records in the past. The recording does not sound dated – it is acceptably warm and generally well-balanced.

COLLECTION

'Greatest hits': (i) *L'Arlésienne: Suite No. 1* (complete); *Suite No. 2: Farandole* (only). *Carmen:* highlights: (ii) *March of the Toreadors;* (i) *Habañera; Marche des Contrebandiers;* (ii) *Seguidilla;* (iii) *Flower song;* (i; iv) *Les voici;* (i) *Intermezzo; Les dragons d'Alcala;* (ii) *Micaëla's area;* (i) *Danse bohème.* (iii) *The Pearl Fishers: I hear as in a dream.*
  (B) ** CBS Harmony 30011. (i) Philadelphia Orchestra, Eugene Ormandy; (ii) New York Philharmonic Orchestra, Leonard Bernstein; (iii) Orchestra, André Kostelanetz; (iv) Mormon Tabernacle Choir.

The majority of Bizet's 'greatest hits', as chosen here, come from the world of opera, nearly all of them from *Carmen.* Only one contribution is vocal, and that a stirring one, from the Mormon Tabernacle Choir. But we are used to hearing *Carmen* in orchestral dress and some of the most attractive playing here is in the vocal numbers, Bernstein's *Seguidilla,*

for instance, or Kostelanetz's really beautiful *Flower song.* The opening *March of the Toreadors* (under Bernstein) is, surprisingly, rather lacking in brilliance, but generally the playing is excellent. This is good value for money, and the sound is generally bright and vivid without the surface brilliance being overdone.

Bliss, Arthur
(1891–1975)

Checkmate (ballet): *suite.*
  (M) *** HMV SXLP 30153. Sinfonia of London, the composer – BRITTEN: *Matinées and Soirées musicales;* LAMBERT: *Horoscope: Waltz.****

Bliss's pre-war ballet score has many admirers, and this recording, made during the early sixties, carries the authority of the composer's direction. The recording is extremely fine, and readers need have no qualms on that score. The music may strike some people as old-fashioned, but it has splendid vitality and fire to commend it.

Meditations on a theme of John Blow; Music for strings.
  ** Lyrita SRCS 33. City of Birmingham Symphony Orchestra, Hugo Rignold.
Music for strings.
  *** HMV ASD 3020. London Philharmonic Orchestra, Sir Adrian Boult – HOWELLS: *Concerto for string orchestra.****

Music for strings, which was written at the same time as another particularly memorable piece by Bliss, the music to the H. G. Wells film *Things to Come,* represents one in the long series of successful works for strings by British composers. It was first heard in Salzburg in 1935, with Boult conducting the Vienna Philharmonic, and here it receives a glowing performance under the same understanding interpreter. The LPO relishes the beautifully judged virtuoso writing, and the recording is first-rate.

The City of Birmingham Orchestra's playing is not of the same order as the LPO's, but Rignold's interpretation is an expressive one, with a tendency to slower tempi than usual. The result sounds convincing and committed. The *Meditations on a theme of John Blow* was written for the Birmingham Orchestra in 1955. It is a series of variations designed to illustrate the different verses of the 23rd Psalm. The result is an amiable but rather rambling piece lasting about 35 minutes.

Things to Come (incidental music for H. G. Wells film): suite *(Ballet for children; Attack; Pestilence; Reconstruction; Machines; March); Welcome the Queen:* march.

(M) ** Decca Ace of Diamonds SDD 255. London Symphony Orchestra, the composer – ELGAR: *Pomp and Circumstance marches.***

Things to Come (1935) was notable for producing the first serious film score to achieve popularity outside the cinema, and, in the famous *March*, what is perhaps the single most memorable musical idea to come from the pen of its composer. Apart from the *March*, the best number of the suite is the *Ballet for children* (appropriately reminiscent of Debussy's *Petite suite*, and, in the middle section, of Bizet's *Jeux d'enfants*), but the other music, which is more characteristic of its composer, is surprisingly successful divorced from the action, each piece catching the mood of its title. *Welcome the Queen* is an occasional piece written by the composer in his role of Master of the Queen's Musick, to celebrate the

return of the Queen from her Commonwealth tour in 1954. In the Elgar tradition of pageantry, the piece is of no particular distinction except for a very gracious middle tune. The performances could hardly be more authentic, and the recording is crisp and bright, although it has lost just a little of its original warmth.

(i) *Clarinet quintet;* (ii) *Oboe quintet.*

(M) *** HMV HQS 1299. Members of the Melos Ensemble, with (i) Gervase de Peyer (clarinet); (ii) Peter Graeme (oboe).

Both these works are given by pupils of the virtuosi for whom they were written, Gervase de Peyer being a pupil of Frederick Thurston and Peter Graeme of Leon Goossens. Furthermore the composer himself was present at the recording sessions, so we may be assured of authenticity. Both works are characteristic, the *Clarinet quintet* notably for a sparkling scherzo, while the *Oboe quintet* uses an Irish folk tune, *Connelly's jig*, to add an extra touch of colour to the finale. Performances are admirable, and the recordings are fresh and immediate with good balance.

Piano sonata.

*** Argo ZRG 786. Rhondda Gillespie (piano) – LAMBERT: *Elegiac blues; Piano sonata.***

The formidable *Piano sonata* was written in 1952 for Noel Mewton-Wood, who had given memorable performances of Bliss's other major work for piano, the *Piano concerto*. Despite some unexpected hints of neoclassicism – not too far distant from the Ravel of *Le Tombeau de Couperin* – this is a sweepingly passionate work, exuberant in its shower of notes. Rhondda Gillespie gives a strong, committed performance, well recorded.

(i; ii) *Hymn to Apollo;* (iii; iv) *A Prayer to the Infant Jesus;* (i; ii; v) *Rout;* (i;

vi; vii) *Serenade;* (iii; iv) *The World is Charged with the Grandeur of God.*

*** Lyrita SRCS 55. (i) London Symphony Orchestra; (ii) cond. the composer; (iii) Ambrosian Singers; (iv) cond. Philip Ledger; (v) Rae Woodland (soprano); (vi) John Shirley-Quirk (baritone); (vii) cond. Brian Priestman.

Although this is primarily a vocal collection – issued to celebrate the composer's eightieth birthday – it is in fact the orchestral writing that one remembers most vividly. Besides the short orchestral prelude, *Hymn to Apollo* (written in 1926) the major work here, the *Serenade* has two purely orchestral movements out of four. The second, *Idyll*, shows Bliss's lyrical impulse at its most eloquent. The orchestra is almost more important than the voice in *Rout.* One can see why Diaghilev admired this short cantata, for its music has a splendid vigour and spontaneity together with a certain *chic* quality characteristic of the period during which the great ballet impresario made his reputation. The solo vocal performances throughout the disc are of high quality, and John Shirley-Quirk's swashbuckling account of the gay finale of the *Serenade* must have pleased the composer greatly. In *The world is charged with the grandeur of God,* the invention is less memorable, and it is again the orchestration that shows the composer's imagination at work, notably the atmospheric scoring for the flutes in the second section. The recording is first-rate.

(i) *Pastoral (Lie strewn the white flocks);* (ii) *A Knot of Riddles.*

(M) ** (*) Pye Virtuoso TPLS 13036. (i) Sybil Michelow (mezzo-soprano), Bruckner-Mahler Choir of London; (ii) John Shirley-Quirk (baritone); both with London Chamber Orchestra, Wyn Morris.

Bliss's eightieth year produced a good crop of first recordings of his work. These are two attractive song cycles that show his art at its least demanding. He conceived the *Pastoral* as a classical fantasy, linking verse from widely different sources, and using mezzo-soprano, chorus, flute (beautifully played here by Norman Knight), timpani and strings. *A Knot of Riddles* is just as easy on the ear – arguably too easy – with English riddles translated from the Anglo-Saxon and provided with a solution by the soloist after each one. This is a much more recent work, written for the Cheltenham Festival in 1963. It is here sung with fine point by John Shirley-Quirk. Good recording.

Bloch, Ernest
(1880–1959)

Baal Shem (3 Pictures of Chassidic Life): No. 2, Nigun.

*** CBS 72942. Pinchas Zukerman (violin), Royal Philharmonic Orchestra, Lawrence Foster – KABALEVSKY: *Concerto;* WIENIAWSKI: *Concerto No. 2.*** (*)

The improvisatory second movement of Bloch's *Baal Shem* suite, with its dark colouring and dramatized mood changes, is well understood by Zukerman, who plays with intensity and a fine sense of atmosphere. With a sympathetic accompaniment and good recording this makes an attractive bonus for excellent performances of the Kabalevsky and Wieniawski concertos.

Violin concerto.

(M) *** HMV SXLP 30177. Yehudi Menuhin (violin), Philharmonia Orchestra, Paul Kletzki.

It is good to have Menuhin's splendid performance of the *Violin concerto* restored to the catalogue at medium price. Menuhin's account is passionate and committed from the first note, and any weaknessess in the score are quite lost when the playing is so compelling. Kletzki accompanies with equal distinction, and the Philharmonia playing is first-rate. The recording too sounds very well indeed. Highly recommended.

Schelomo: Hebrew rhapsody (for violoncello and orchestra).

(M) ** (*) RCA LSB 4101. Gregor Piatigorsky (cello), Boston Symphony Orchestra, Charles Munch – WALTON: *Violoncello concerto.***

(M) ** Supraphon SUAST 50581. André Navarra (cello), Czech Philharmonic Orchestra, Karel Ančerl – SCHUMANN: *Violoncello concerto.***

** Philips 6500 160. Christine Walevska (cello), Monte Carlo Opera Orchestra, Eliahu Inbal – SCHUMANN: *Violoncello concerto.***

Schelomo: Hebrew rhapsody (for violoncello and orchestra); *Voice in the Wilderness* (symphonic poem for orchestra with violoncello obbligato).

** (*) Decca SXL 6440. Janos Starker (cello), Israel Philharmonic Orchestra, Zubin Mehta.

These lush scores were previously coupled together by Nelsova with the LPO under Ansermet on an early Decca LP. *Voice in the Wilderness* is a rather diffuse piece which at times sounds for all the world like the sound track of a Hollywood Biblical epic, while at others its textures are so vivid and imaginative that such unworthy thoughts are promptly banished. *Schelomo* is the more disciplined work and is arguably Bloch's masterpiece. Feuermann's marvellously

full-blooded account on 78s, which should be transferred to LP, showed just how impressive this work can sound given a more tautly conceived reading. By its side Starker and Mehta seem a little lacking in intensity and fire though it is certainly well recorded. The Decca engineers have not succumbed to the temptation of making the soloist sound larger than life though the wind is fractionally forward.

The Piatigorsky performance is masterly – and the record is of particular interest since it was he who commissioned the Walton concerto – but the recorded sound is not as vivid or truthful as the Decca. However, the performance has greater personality than Walevska's with the Monte Carlo Opera Orchestra under Eliahu Inbal, though this is well recorded. For those wanting the coupling of Schumann's *Cello concerto*, the Supraphon disc has the price advantage. Navarra is less commanding than Piatigorsky, but his too is a fine reading and he is well supported by Ančerl.

Piano quintet No. 1.

(M) ** (*) Everest SDBR 4252. Frank Glazer (piano), Fine Arts Quartet.

Bloch's *Piano quintet* (first heard in 1923) was a work much prized among record connoisseurs in the days of 78 discs, but it has been badly neglected on LP. This splendid performance from one of America's finest chamber groups underlines the urgent energy of the writing, dramatic and outward-going unlike some of Bloch's later, self-important music. No one need feel frightened at this date of the occasional quarter-tone: it is one of the most richly communicative works that Bloch ever wrote. Clean recording.

Blomdahl, Karl-Birger
(1916–68)

Symphony No. 3 (Facetter).
(B) *** Turnabout TV 34318S. Stockholm Philharmonic Orchestra, Sixten Ehrling – ROSENBERG: *Symphony No. 6.****

Karl-Birger Blomdahl was perhaps the most influential post-war Swedish composer. His *Third Symphony* caused something of a stir when it was produced in 1950, and its dark, brooding intensity is impressive. Ehrling gives it a persuasive performance, and the recording, though made in the early 1960s, sounds remarkably fresh. The disc is of particular value in that it also includes a fine account of the *Sixth Symphony* of Hilding Rosenberg, with whom Blomdahl studied. Excellent recording of rewarding music.

Blow, John
(1649–1708)

Ode on the death of Mr Henry Purcell; Amphion Angelicus (songs): Cloë found Amintas lying all in tears; Why weeps Asteria; Loving above himself, Poor Celadon, he sighs; Shepherds, deck your crooks; Ah heav'n! What is't I hear; Epilogue: *Sing, sing, ye muses.*
*** Philips Seon 6575 016. René Jacobs, James Bowman (countertenors), and soloists, Leonhardt Consort, Gustav Leonhardt.

The *Ode on the death of Mr Henry Purcell* occupies one side and is a most welcome addition to the catalogue, particularly as it is so superbly performed here under Gustav Leonhardt. There are some striking chromaticisms and dissonances and some inventive and noble music. James Bowman is the only native singer (he is in good voice too) but the others are no less intelligent and stylish. Both the performance and the recording are up to the highest modern standards, and readers are strongly urged to investigate this rewarding disc.

Boccherini, Luigi
(1743–1805)

(i) *Violoncello concerto in B flat major* (revision and cadenzas by Gendron); (ii) *Violoncello concerto in G major* (revision and cadenzas by Gendron).
(M) ** (*) Philips Universo 6580 068. Maurice Gendron (cello); (i) Lamoureux Orchestra, Pablo Casals; (ii) London Symphony Orchestra, Raymond Leppard.

It is good to have Gendron's excellent performance of Boccherini's original version of the *B flat major Cello concerto* back at medium price, so that listeners can make up their own minds as to whether this or Grützmacher's reworking is the finer work. The coupling is another concerto of the same period, and both are given elegant performances with all opportunities for bravura taken with aplomb. Indeed one might question the profusion of cadenzas, which seem to go on rather a long time. The recording of both works is excellent, and one can forgive the forward balance of the soloist in works of this nature, which are primarily a vehicle for the cellist to show his mettle.

Violoncello concerto in B flat major (arr. Grützmacher).
*** HMV ASD 2331. Jacqueline du Pré (cello), English Chamber Orchestra, Daniel Barenboim – HAYDN: *Concerto in C major.****

(M) * (*) DGG Privilege 2538 259. Pierre Fournier (cello), Lucerne Festival Strings, Rudolf Baumgartner – HAYDN: *Concerto in D major.* (*)

(B) ** Oryx EXP 15. Jürgen Wolf (cello), Reutlingen Orchestra, Erich Reustlen – HAYDN: *Concerto in D major.***

It is surprising that Jacqueline du Pré chose to do the completely unauthentic Grützmacher version of this concerto, but, as she says herself, 'The slow movement is so beautiful', much more beautiful in fact than the one Boccherini provided. Working for the first time in the recording studio with her husband, Daniel Barenboim, du Pré was inspired to some really heart-warming playing, broadly romantic in style, but then that is what Grützmacher plainly asks for. Warm, atmospheric recording.

The first movement of Fournier's performance is not helped by a lustreless recording, but the performance of the slow movement is beautifully done, and the finale maintains the same level. Jürgen Wolf is not quite so imaginative an artist as Fournier, but he is obviously in good form here and his performance is certainly a good one. The accompaniment is spirited and the recording acceptable, so this very reasonably priced record is in many ways more competitive than the more expensive DGG Privilege coupling.

Violoncello concerto in D major; Violoncello concertos (for violoncello, strings and 2 horns) *Nos. 1 in C major; 2 in C major.*

(**) Telefunken SAWT 9473-A. Anner Bylsma (cello), Concerto Amsterdam, Jaap Schröder.

One does not know whether or not to be grateful to Telefunken for digging up these unknown cello concertos by Boccherini. No doubt they are admirable in showing us the features of the *galant* and classical styles of writing, which are readily juxtaposed in Boccherini's writing. But the music itself offers neither *galant* charm nor classical vitality. The quick finales are best; elsewhere one's attention falters. Anner Bylsma is a fine player, but his style, on the evidence of this record, is not a romantic one, and his playing does not mitigate the dryness of the music. The recording is excellent.

6 Symphonies, Op. 35: Nos. 1 in D major; 2 in E flat major; 3 in A major; 4 in F major; 5 in E flat major; 6 in B flat major.

** Telefunken SKH 24 (3 discs). I Filarmonici di Bologna, Angelo Ephrilian.

Boccherini's Op. 35 symphonies date from 1782. They are conventional in style and format, yet are not without their felicities of invention. The gracious cantilena of the slow movement of No. 3 and the *Andante* of No. 6 both show the composer at his most winning, and the buoyant outer movements have plenty of rhythmic life. They are not symphonies to listen to six at a time, and ideally they need rather stronger characterization than they receive here and a more consistently beguiling recording. The sound in the Telefunken set is variable, with some of the allegros sounding curiously dry and unresonant in the bass, almost as if the speakers were momentarily out of phase.

Guitar quintets (for guitar, 2 violins, viola and violoncello) *Nos 4 in D major, G.44; 7 in E minor, G.451; 9 in C major (La Ritirata di Madrid), G.453.*

** DGG 2530 069. Narciso Yepes (guitar), Melos Quartet of Stuttgart (with Lucero Tena (castanets) in Quintet No. 4).

The music on this record was arranged by Boccherini for his Spanish patron, the Marquis Benavente, even to the extent of adding a very fetching castanet part to the Fandango finale of the *D major Quintet*. The guitar part was obviously intended for the Marquis to perform, and so its contribution is sometimes limited to an accompanying role. But the music has considerable charm, though it is somewhat uneven, and the expert playing and good recording contribute to the listener's pleasure.

String quartet in E flat major, Op. 58/2.
(M) ** Supraphon 111 0573. Moravian Quartet – VERDI: *String quartet.***

Boccherini's output is almost as prodigal and inexhaustible as his charm. The *E flat major Quartet* is a smiling and appealing work of great warmth and impeccable craftsmanship. The Moravian Quartet, though not quite in the front rank, play with conviction: the record is of particular interest since it offers the Verdi *Quartet*, a charming piece not otherwise available save in an Eclipse reprocessed-mono version by the Italians, which has more sparkle than this one.

String quintet in E major, Op. 13/5; String quintet in A minor, Op. 47/1.
(B) ** Turnabout TV 34094S. Günter Kehr Quintet.

The *E major Quintet* is the source of the famous 'Boccherini Minuet'. It is beautifully played here, with delicacy and restraint, and one feels it deserves its fame. But the work as a whole is attractive, particularly the opening movement, which is harmonically rich, to remind the listener almost of Mozart. It is played here with warmth and gives much pleasure. Only in the finale does one feel that the players miscalculate, but it is partly Boccherini's fault for writing yet another *galant* movement instead of a rondo with

more fire to it. This tendency to blandness is felt throughout the A minor work, which is pleasant but less distinguished. But here the players could have helped with more bite to the outer movements. The recording is warm-toned but with the microphones very near the players, which exaggerates their reluctance to make contrasts of both style and dynamic.

Violoncello quintet, Op. 37/7 (Pleyel).
*** Argo ZRG 569. Academy of St Martin-in-the-Fields – MENDELSSOHN: *Octet.****

This is an inspired piece. It would be worth getting for its own sake, and the performance of the Mendelssohn *Octet* is a particularly fine one.

Boieldieu, François Adrien (1775–1834)

Harp concerto in C major.
*** DGG SLPM 138118. Nicanor Zabaleta (harp), Berlin Radio Symphony Orchestra, Ernst Märzendorfer – RODRIGO: *Concierto serenata.****

(i) *Harp concerto in C major;* (ii) *Piano concerto in F major.*
(B) ** Turnabout TV 34148S. (i) Marie-Claire Jamet (harp), Paul Kuentz Chamber Orchestra of Paris; (ii) Martin Galling (piano), Innsbruck Symphony Orchestra, Robert Wagner.

A portentous opening tutti shows that the *Harp concerto* is to be a battle between the meek and the powerful, but the composer's care not to overload the accompaniment to the solo passages, plus a number of very charming melodies, see that the gentle harp wins every battle. Nicanor Zabaleta plays with a remarkable sense of light and shade, and evokes a captivating delicacy of timbre in the quieter music. The balance leaves nothing to be desired, and Ernst Märzendorfer modulates his accompaniment with sensitivity, yet playing the tuttis with gusto. The recording is very fine indeed. Delightful!

Marie-Claire Jamet too plays with style and refinement, and she is especially good in the enchanting closing rondo. The balance is well managed and Paul Kuentz sees that the tuttis have plenty of life. As the DGG coupling, Rodrigo's *Concerto serenade*, is also available on a medium price-label coupled to Rodrigo's *Guitar concerto*, the Turnabout disc may well seem the better investment. It also includes Boieldieu's *Piano concerto*, a two-movement work with an attractive set of variations on a pastoral theme as its second section, which ends rather abruptly. It is played here with character and makes a good coupling, even if it is not as memorable as the work for harp.

La Dame blanche (opera in 3 acts): complete recording.

(M) ** Decca Ace of Diamonds GOSR 649/51. Michel Sénéchal (tenor), Françoise Louvay (soprano), Adrien Legros (bass), Aimé Doniat (baritone), Jane Berbié (soprano), Germaine Baudoz (mezzo-soprano), Pierre Héral (bass), Chorus and Orchestra Raymond Saint-Paul, Pierre Stoll.

This is just the sort of opera that should prove a gem. There is indeed much to enjoy in a light-hearted style that suggests a precursor of Gilbert and Sullivan. This recorded performance, though not polished, is still energetic enough to be enjoyable. The big snag lies in the spoken dialogue, which takes up far more time on these six sides than most opera-lovers will want to expend in frequent repetition.

Ma Tante Aurore (opera in 2 acts): abridged recording.

(B) ** (*) Turnabout TV 34222S. Françoise Ogeas, Berthe Kal, Jeanine Collard (sopranos), Jean Mollien, Bernard Plantey (tenors), Pierre Germain (baritone), ORTF Chamber Orchestra, Marcel Couraud.

If the complete recording of *La Dame blanche* proves a mixed delight, this well-chosen selection from another comic piece of Boieldieu provides on an excellent bargain-label disc exactly the sample one wants. With Marcel Couraud drawing a lively performance from his French Radio forces, this can be warmly recommended.

Boito, Arrigo
(1842–1918)

Mefistofele (opera in prologue, 3 acts and epilogue): complete recording.

(M) ** (*) Decca Ace of Diamonds GOS 591/3. Cesare Siepi (bass), Mario del Monaco (tenor), Renata Tebaldi (soprano), Chorus and Orchestra of St Cecilia Academy, Rome, Tullio Serafin.

** (*) HMV SLS 973 (3 discs). Norman Treigle (bass-baritone), Placido Domingo (tenor), Montserrat Caballé (soprano), Ambrosian Opera Chorus, Wandsworth School Boys' Choir, London Symphony Orchestra, Julius Rudel.

Boito's *Mefistofele* is a strange episodic work to come from the hand of the master-librettist of Verdi's *Otello* and *Falstaff*, but it has many fine moments, and in a bargain-label reissue with excellent sound it is very welcome. Serafin, the most persuasive of Italian opera conductors of his day, draws glorious sounds from his performers, even Mario del Monaco, who is here almost sensitive. Tebaldi is a rich-toned Margarita – almost too rich-toned for so frail a heroine – and Siepi makes an excellent Mefistofele.

Though Caballé misses some of the dark intensity that makes Tebaldi's Decca performance so moving, particularly in *L'altra notte*, Rudel's is a fine version of a fascinating opera. Certainly the contribution of Placido Domingo as Faust himself outshines that of Mario del Monaco on the Decca set, though Norman Treigle cannot compare with Siepi as Mefistofele himself, and the title role might well be counted the more important. Though HMV's recording is well over a decade more recent than Decca's the differences are not so great as seriously to unbalance other considerations.

Mefistofele: excerpts: Act 1: *Sediam sovra*; Act 2: *Il giardino*; Act 3: *Morte di Margherita; L'altra notte*; Epilogue: *Morte di Faust*.
** Decca SET 558. Cesare Siepi (bass), Giuseppe di Stefano (tenor), Renata Tebaldi (soprano), Lucia Danieli (contralto), Piero de Palma (tenor), Chorus and Orchestra of St Cecilia Academy, Rome, Tullio Serafin.

This disc of selections is a curiosity. The same record company at about the same time recorded this opera complete with the same forces except for the tenor. This represents the results of an unfinished project, and admirers of Giuseppe di Stefano – generally a subtler artist than his Decca rival, Mario del Monaco – will be pleased to have this unexpected sample of his work in the late fifties. Excellent recording for its period.

Mefistofele: excerpts: *Prologo in cielo: Ave, signor;* Act 1: *La Domenica di Pasqua: Olà! chi urla?;* Act 2: *La notte del Sabba: Su cammina; Epilogue*.
** Decca SXL 6305. Nicolai Ghiaurov (bass), Franco Tagliavini (tenor), Chorus and Orchestra of Rome Opera, Silvio Varviso.

It was a good idea to get Nicolai Ghiaurov to record one of his most famous parts, Mefistofele, in Boito's fascinating but unwieldy opera. It may on the face of it seem a rag-bag work, but when it is cut up into excerpts for a single disc, one seems more than ever to need the remaining pieces. No Margherita passages here at all, which leaves out a whole basic element in Boito's scheme. But Ghiaurov is the prime mover, and his singing here is firm and magnificent. Franco Tagliavini (not to be confused with the veteran Ferruccio) is an adequate Faust, but the choral singing could be more incisive. Splendid Decca recording.

Borodin, Alexander (1833–87)

Symphony No. 2 in B minor (see also below under *The world of Borodin*).
*** Decca SXL 6352. Suisse Romande Orchestra, Silvio Varviso – TCHAIKOVSKY: *Francesca da Rimini*.**
* (*) HMV ASD 2700. USSR Symphony Orchestra, Yevgeny Svetlanov – LIADOV: *Baba-Yaga etc.****

Symphony No. 2 in B minor; (i) *Polovtsian dances (Prince Igor)*.
(M) ** (*) Supraphon MS 1126. Czech Philharmonic Orchestra, Václav Smetáček, (i) with chorus.
Symphony No. 2 in B minor; Symphony

No. 3 in A minor (Unfinished); Prince Igor (opera): *Overture.*
(B) ** Decca ECS 576. Suisse Romande Orchestra, Ernest Ansermet.

Symphony No. 3 in A minor (Unfinished).
(M) *** Philips Universo 6580 053. London Philharmonic Orchestra, David Lloyd-Jones (with *Concert of Russian music***.)

In considering recordings of the *Second Symphony* one must not forget Martinon's immensely vivid account included complete in *The world of Borodin,* a remarkably successful anthology that for I.M. seems almost worthy of a rosette. Of the full-priced versions the palm must go to Varviso, whose performance is splendidly alive. He is given a truly magnificent recording, the best this symphony has ever received. The scherzo glistens with colour, and when the big tune comes back in full romantic sweep at the end of the slow movement the effect is superb. The Tchaikovsky coupling is less spontaneous as a performance, but this disc is still worth investigating.

Although the playing of the USSR Symphony Orchestra is both lively and expert and the HMV Melodiya recording is admirably vivid, this issue is not recommendable. Svetlanov pulls the work about in a way that is irritating on repeated hearing, if not on first acquaintance. This is a pity as the Liadov *Folksongs* with which the symphony is coupled are beautifully done.

Ansermet's performance of the *Second Symphony* is sturdy, and he shapes the overall symphonic structure convincingly. Other readings have found more incandescence in the scherzo, more blazing excitement in the first movement, but taken as a whole this is satisfying, and the climax of the slow movement is finely made. As always with this conductor, the sense of colour and inner orchestral balance makes a special effect. The unfinished *Third Symphony* is lighter in mood, and Ansermet's touch is attractively lyrical, with some delightful moments from the woodwind. The overture makes a fine bonus, and with excellent real stereo (the disc was previously available only in mono) this is a genuine bargain.

The Supraphon record is thoroughly recommendable, well played and excellently recorded. Only *The world of Borodin* offers this same music even more brilliantly recorded, plus two other pieces.

David Lloyd-Jones's Universo recording of the unfinished *Third Symphony* is also part of a highly recommendable anthology, including music by Balakirev, Mussorgsky, and Rimsky-Korsakov. This is discussed in our companion *Treasury* volume. The symphony is both pointedly and atmospherically done.

Piano quintet in C minor.
(M) *** Decca Ace of Diamonds SDD 410. Walter Panhoffer (piano), members of the Vienna Octet – MENDELSSOHN: *Piano sextet.***

The *Piano quintet* is an early work and reveals Borodin at a time when his musical equipment was not fully developed. But even if it is not as accomplished as his mature work and shows signs of technical caution it has an engaging freshness and charm that come across in this highly expert performance. The recording is altogether excellent, and those who have adventurous tastes will enjoy the disc.

String quartet No. 2 in D major.
*** Philips SAL 3708. Italian Quartet – DVOŘÁK: *Quartet No. 6.***
(M) *** Decca Ace of Diamonds SDD 156. Borodin Quartet – SHOSTAKOVICH: *Quartet No. 8.***

(B) *** Classics for Pleasure CFP 40041. Gabrieli Quartet – DVOŘÁK: *Quartet No. 6.****

** DGG SLPM 139425. Drolc Quartet – TCHAIKOVSKY: *Quartet No. 1.***

As themes were taken from this for *Kismet* it is surprising that Borodin's *Second Quartet* has been so long achieving wider popularity. Now with a good choice of attractive couplings, all collectors should find one of these discs to their taste.

Absolutely superlative playing from the Italian Quartet and no less excellent recording make a safe recommendation. There is a slight oversweetness about it though much of this resides in the music itself; in any event most readers will derive unalloyed pleasure from this record. The Borodin Quartet's performance is no less masterly and some might prefer the forward, rich-textured recording Decca provided. The imaginative coupling is equally desirable. Although not the equal of either the Philips or Decca versions the Gabrieli Quartet offers a finely wrought and thoroughly polished performance that makes a more than adequate substitute. At half the price of the Philips disc this is excellent value and the recording is first-class. A clear, direct performance from the Drolc Quartet, at its best in the outer movements. But the famous *Nocturne* is played with reserve, as if the players were afraid of sentimentalizing it. A laudable fear, no doubt, but the performance is rather too restrained, although enjoyable in its fresh, cool way.

Prince Igor (opera in 4 acts): complete recording.

(M) * (*) Decca Ace of Diamonds GOS 562/5. Dushan Popovich (baritone), Valeria Heybalova (soprano), Noni Zhunetz (tenor), Zharko Tzveych (bass), Melanie Bugarinovich (mezzo-soprano), Chorus and Orchestra of National Opera, Belgrade, Oscar Danon.

The great merit of Decca's complete opera recordings made in Yugoslavia in the mid-fifties was the quality of recording, unusually brilliant for its time. In transferring a set that previously took ten sides on to a mere eight – all very well filled – the engineers have had to reduce the recording level, but the sound is still very good, and with no rival version available this makes an acceptable stopgap. The performance is variable. The orchestra is not a virtuoso body, which makes the *Polovtsian dances* rather disappointing, and a high proportion of the cast display the sort of slavonic wobbles that trouble western ears – including Dushan Popovich as Igor, Valeria Heybalova as Yaroslavna, and Zharko Tzveych as Konchak. Melanie Bugarinovich as Konchakovna provides the best singing in the set, but with all its faults the performance sounds like a team enterprise, and can be recommended with reservations.

Prince Igor: Polovtsian dances.

(B) *** Decca SPA 127. London Symphony Chorus and Orchestra, Sir Georg Solti (with *Concert***).

(M) *** HMV SXLP 30171. Beecham Choral Society, Royal Philharmonic Orchestra, Sir Thomas Beecham – BALAKIREV: *Symphony No. 1.****

*** Decca Phase 4 PFS 4048. London Festival Chorus and Orchestra, Stanley Black – RAVEL: *Boléro.****

** (*) Decca Phase 4 PFS 4189. Welsh National Opera Chorus, Royal Philharmonic Orchestra, Leopold Stokowski – TCHAIKOVSKY: *1812*; STRAVINSKY: *Pastorale.***

** Decca SXL 2268. Chœur des Jeunes, Chœur de Radio Lausanne, Suisse Romande Orchestra, Ernest Ansermet – RIMSKY-KORSAKOV: *Scheherazade*.** (*)

The cheapest way to buy a really fine account of the *Polovtsian dances* is to invest in Decca's *George Solti conducts* anthology, a most attractive record on bargain label (discussed in detail in our *Treasury* volume), while Ansermet's account is also included in *The world of Borodin* (see below).

Beecham misses the percussion-led opening dance, but plays the remainder of the score with a charismatic mixture of lyricism and sparkle. He builds a splendid final climax and with remarkably good recording this record sounds only marginally dated. When one remembers the sound of those famous old Columbia 78s, one is glad that Beecham was persuaded to re-record the piece in stereo.

The performance under Stanley Black may not be a great one but it is excitingly directed, the solo orchestral playing is notably good, and the choral contribution is strikingly enthusiastic. The recording is quite superb, wonderfully warm and remarkably clear without resort to gimmickry of any kind. The total effect is to make the natural colour and sparkle of this immensely original and vivid writing come over very successfully in a commendably direct and exciting way.

Stokowski too misses out the percussion-led opening dance. His performance is a mannered one but there is no question about the sheer excitement he creates as the work reaches its final climax. The recording is superb, big and spectacular but encompassing the closing dance without any difficulty. A pity the *1812* coupling is not more directly recommendable: this is Stokoswki in eccentric mood.

Ansermet's performance is a reliably good one, although the tension tends to sag in the passages where the choir – which is not outstanding – is expected to carry the music with only slight support from the orchestra. The end goes well. The recording is bright and clear.

'The world of Borodin': (i) *In the Steppes of Central Asia;* (ii) *Symphony No. 2 in B minor;* (iii) *String quartet No. 2: Nocturne;* (i; iv) *Prince Igor,* Act 2: *Polovtsian dances.*

(B) *** Decca SPA 281. (i) Suisse Romande Orchestra, Ernest Ansermet, (iv) with chorus; (ii) London Symphony Orchestra, Jean Martinon; (iii) Borodin Quartet.

An extraordinarily successful disc that will provide for many collectors an inexpensive summation of the art of Borodin. There can be few collections of this kind that sum up a composer's achievement so succinctly or that make such a rewarding and enjoyable concert. Martinon's performance of the *Symphony* is notable for its fast tempo for the famous opening theme, but the strong rhythmic thrust suits the music admirably, and the slow movement, with a beautifully played horn solo, is most satisfying. The recording has remarkable presence and sparkle, and only in the massed violin tone (which is good) is there a suggestion that the recording dates from the early sixties. Side two opens with *In the Steppes of Central Asia*, a vivid rather than an atmospheric reading; then follows the *Nocturne*, so effectively that one might have thought it the composer's own plan. The disc ends generously with the complete set of *Polovtsian dances* reliably done, if not breathtakingly exciting, and very well recorded. A remarkable bargain indeed.

Bottesini, Giovanni
(1821–89)

Grand duo for violin, double bass, and orchestra.

- *** Unicorn RHS 304. Ruggiero Ricci (violin), Francesco Petracchi (double bass), Royal Philharmonic Orchestra, Piero Bellugi – PAGANINI: *Violin concerto No. 4.****
- ** Philips 6747 038 (2 discs). I Musici – ROSSINI: *String sonatas Nos. 1–6.***

Fun music for virtuosi. Bottesini's *Grand duo* makes an unusual but attractive fill-up for the rare Paganini work on the Unicorn disc. It is rather operatic in lay-out, often echoing the conventions of Donizetti or Bellini, and it provides a marvellous vehicle for Ruggiero Ricci and Francesco Petracchi. Excellent recording makes the Unicorn disc first-rate of its kind.

I Musici perform well, but the soloists do not play with quite enough of the magic that is essential if the work is not to outstay its welcome. But as a fill-up for the set of sure-fire Rossini *String sonatas*, this performance is acceptable.

Boulez, Pierre
(born 1926)

Constellation-Miroir; Piano sonata No. 1; Piano sonata No. 3 (Trope).

- *** CBS 72871. Charles Rosen (piano).

Charles Rosen, one of the most rigorously intellectual virtuosos today, a scholar and thinker as well as a performer, is the ideal pianist for Boulez's thorny piano writing. The *First Sonata*, written when Boulez was barely twenty, is already a very advanced work, requiring the subtlest control of rhythm if its serial argument is to sound anything but arid. The *Third Sonata* remains a work in progress – two movements (or *formants*) completed out of the five projected. This is music which defies even the devotion of the specialist, but with Rosen understanding it as deeply as anyone could, it is a tough challenge that many will find is worth taking up. Good bright recording.

(i) Le Marteau sans maître; (ii) Livre pour cordes.

- *** CBS Quadraphonic MQ 32160; Stereo 73213. (i) Yvonne Minton (mezzo-soprano), Ensemble Musique Vivante; (ii) New Philharmonia Orchestra Strings, both cond. the composer.

Le Marteau sans maître was the work with which Pierre Boulez as a composer first revealed a new world of sound. His method may have been rigorously serial, but the end result had an almost sensuous charm to it with its jingling, clinking percussion surrounding the stylized vocal line. It is still not an easy work, but with a fine performance under the composer's direction and with excellent, immediate recording (outstandingly effective in the quadraphonic version) it should be sampled by Boulez's admirers and all who want to venture into post-war serial developments. *Livre pour cordes*, adapted from an early string quartet, is a far less demanding piece, but one equally worth studying. Excellent performances of both works.

Pli selon pli.

- *** CBS SBRG 72770. Halina Lukomska (soprano), Maria Bergmann (piano), Paul Stingl (guitar),

Hugo d'Alton (mandolin), BBC Symphony Orchestra, the composer.

This is a grandly conceived work to refute the idea that serialists and their progeny are necessarily cramped in their inspiration. The title (literally 'fold upon fold') comes from the poet Mallarmé, and Boulez's layers of invention are used to illuminate as centrepieces three Mallarmé sonnets. Neither these craggy vocalizations nor the purely instrumental passages are at all easy to understand in a conventional sense, but the luminous texture of Boulez's writing is endlessly fascinating, and for the listener with an open mind there are few more rewarding records on which to widen experience of the avant-garde. Superb performance and recording under the composer's sharp-eared and electrifying direction.

Boyce, William
(1710–79)

6 Overtures (from Musica Britannica, Vol. XIII, ed. Gerald Finzi): Overture to the New Year's Ode, 1758; Overture to the Birthday Ode, 1768; Overture to His Majesty's Birthday Ode, 1769; Overture to the New Year's Ode, 1772; Overture to His Majesty's Birthday Ode, 1775; Overture Peleus and Thetis.
- (B) ** Oiseau-Lyre OLS 110. Lamoureux Orchestra, Anthony Lewis.

This reissue on Oiseau-Lyre's equivalent of the Turnabout label is most welcome, even if the composer's inspiration is somewhat variable. The performances are not ideal, but their French accent does give a certain piquancy to the colouring, although the trumpet playing is not as polished as we would expect here. The players sound as if they are enjoying

themselves, which is the main thing. The recording is a little fizzy in the treble but otherwise atmospheric and vivid.

Symphonies Nos. 1 in B flat major; 2 in A major; 3 in C major; 4 in F major; 5 in D major; 6 in F major; 7 in B flat major; 8 in D minor.
- (B) ** Turnabout TV 34133S. Württemberg Chamber Orchestra, Joerg Faerber.
- (M) ** HMV HQS 1302. Menuhin Festival Orchestra, Yehudi Menuhin.
- (M) ** Vanguard HM 23SD. I Solisti di Zagreb, Antonio Janigro.

The eight symphonies recorded here are wonderfully inventive and entertaining. The orchestration is nicely varied; No. 5, for instance, opens with trumpets in a most regal manner, and in the diversity of its melodic and rhythmic patterns evokes the spirit of Handel, as do the broad opening of No. 1, the jollier No. 4 and the slow movement of No. 6. One feels these Handelian associations are especially relished by Menuhin, whose gracious phrasing and elegant manner are supported by excellent orchestral playing and warm, clear recording. But Faerber is even more spirited, and where under Menuhin one sometimes thinks of the music in divertimento terms, the vigour and weight of the Württemberg approach are more in keeping with symphonic style. The Turnabout recording is lively and forward (a trifle thinner on side one than on side two, but always clean), but the HMV sound is obviously more modern if not always so clear in detail. Janigro's performances and recording fall somewhere between the two others, with resilient string playing and clear textures but a comparatively light bass and less weight in the impact of the music. Yet there is an attractive freshness about his presentation. In short each of these three records will give considerable pleasure and little cause for criticism.

Trio sonatas Nos. 2 in F major; 8 in E flat major; 9 in C major; 12 in G major.

    (B) ** (*) Oryx ORYX 1729. Malcolm Latchem, John Brown (violins), Jane Ryan (cello), David Lumsden (harpsichord).

These gracious and pleasing works date from 1747, when the trio sonata format had passed out of favour on the European continent but still flourished in England. The music is sympathetically played by a group who have a sense of inner balance to match secure technique and good phrasing. The blend of the two solo violins is especially pleasant and the recorded sound is beautiful, its only fault being a forward balance that reduces the dynamic range of the playing. But the spontaneity of the music-making and the lovely sound quality that reaches the ears still give a great deal of pleasure. The final sonata is a particularly inventive piece.

Brahms, Johannes
(1833–97)

Academic Festival overture, Op. 80; Tragic overture, Op. 81; Variations on a theme of Haydn (St Anthony chorale), Op. 56a; (i) Rhapsody for alto, male chorus and orchestra, Op. 53.

    (B) *** Classics for Pleasure CFP 40064. Hallé Orchestra, James Loughran, (i) with Bernadette Greevy (contralto), Hallé Choir.
    (B) * (*) Decca Eclipse ECS 701. Vienna Philharmonic Orchestra, Hans Knappertsbusch, (i) with Lucretia West (contralto), Vienna Academy Choir.

Apart from a rather limp start to the *Academic Festival overture*, the Classics for Pleasure disc offers excellent performances of the Brahms items normally provided as fill-ups to the symphonies. This was something of a trial run for Loughran's later cycle of the Brahms symphonies for the same company. Bernadette Greevy gives a strong forthright performance of the solo part in the *Alto Rhapsody*, not subtle but warmly enjoyable, and the *Tragic overture* is cuttingly dramatic. Good atmospheric recording. A first-rate bargain.

Hans Knappertsbusch was not a conductor who responded well to the recording studio, which often seemed to damp the spontaneity of his music-making. He is at his best here, however, in the *Tragic overture*, a performance in the German tradition but one with a fine sense of atmosphere and no lack of vitality. But the highlight of the disc is Lucretia West's rich performance of the *Alto rhapsody*, and here the conductor's restraint is not in the least deadening, but serves to give the performance genuine nobility and breadth. The recording is excellent in both these works, whereas on the first side it is rather plummy in the *Academic Festival overture*, while there is a fractional alteration of pitch at a tape join before the entry of the big tune at the close. The *Variations* too are not as spontaneous as the other performances, and the conductor has a tendency to plod.

Piano concertos Nos. 1 in D minor, Op. 15; 2 in B flat major, Op. 83.

    *** DGG 2707 064 (2 discs). Emil Gilels (piano), Berlin Philharmonic Orchestra, Eugen Jochum.
    *** HMV SLS 874 (2 discs). Daniel Barenboim (piano), New Philharmonia Orchestra, Sir John Barbirolli.
    (M) ** RCA DPS 2015 (2 discs). Artur Rubinstein (piano), Boston

Symphony Orchestra, Erich Leinsdorf; RCA Symphony Orchestra, Josef Krips.

** Philips 6700 018 (2 discs). Claudio Arrau (piano), Concertgebouw Orchestra, Bernard Haitink.

There are a number of boxes offering both the Brahms piano concertos together, and their attractions may to some extent depend on the price at which they are offered. Many will find the Gilels set the most artistically satisfying, although for both E.G. and I.M. the Barenboim/Barbirolli set has a glowing spontaneity, with a hushed degree of inspiration in the slow movements, that makes these performances uniquely rewarding. The recording too is superb. Choice rests between these two. The Rubinstein/Leinsdorf/Krips set is now beginning to show signs of age, though the playing, if sometimes lightweight, is unfailingly fresh and compulsive. Arrau is much better recorded, but his readings are not free from distractingly idiosyncratic touches.

(i) *Piano concerto No. 1 in D minor, Op. 15; Piano concerto No. 2 in B flat major, Op. 83;* (ii) *Violin concerto in D major, Op. 77;* (ii; iii) *Double concerto for violin, violoncello and orchestra in A minor, Op. 102.*

(M) ** CBS 77372 (3 discs). (i) Rudolf Serkin (piano); (ii) Isaac Stern (violin); (iii) Leonard Rose (cello); Philadelphia Orchestra, Eugene Ormandy.

Nearly all the performances here are distinguished. Serkin's earlier account of the *First piano concerto* is as impressive as his later recording with the Cleveland Orchestra under Szell. But the *Second concerto* is something of a disappointment. There is power in the first two movements, considerable poetry in the *Andante*, and poise and grace in the finale, yet the whole is not the sum of its parts and one feels the playing never really catches fire. Stern's account of the *Violin concerto* has both fire and nobility, and the finale sparkles. Ormandy's accompaniment, as always, is most understanding. With the *Double concerto* there are few reservations. The forward balance of the soloists means that there are no real pianissimos, but from the tone-colour one can tell when they are playing quietly. Whether in the strength of bravura, the detailed pointing of phrasing, or the rich expansiveness of the slow movement, this version is remarkably compelling throughout and has a wonderful unanimity of purpose.

Piano concerto No. 1 in D minor, Op. 15.

*** DGG 2530 258. Emil Gilels (piano), Berlin Philharmonic Orchestra, Eugen Jochum.

*** HMV ASD 2353. Daniel Barenboim (piano), New Philharmonia Orchestra, Sir John Barbirolli.

*** Decca SXL 6023. Clifford Curzon (piano), London Symphony Orchestra, George Szell.

** (*) Philips 6500 623. Alfred Brendel (piano), Concertgebouw Orchestra, Hans Schmidt-Isserstedt.

** (*) CBS 72718. Rudolf Serkin (piano), Cleveland Orchestra, George Szell.

(B) ** Decca SPA 385. Julius Katchen (piano), London Symphony Orchestra, Pierre Monteux (with *Ballade in B minor, Op. 10/3* ** (*)).

(B) ** Classics for Pleasure CFP 40028. Claudio Arrau (piano), Philharmonia Orchestra, Carlo Maria Giulini.

Curzon has a leonine power that fully matches Brahms's keyboard style and penetrates both the reflective inner world of the slow movement and the abundantly vital and massive opening movement. The recording, if sometimes a little fierce, has admirable detail, and there is an agreeable bloom on everything. This is still among the very best, though as a recording it has been superseded, notably by Barenboim on HMV. Yet among the most recent accounts, that of Gilels stands out as being to the 1970s what the Curzon was to the 1960s. It has a magisterial strength blended with a warmth, humanity and depth that are altogether inspiring. Jochum is a superb accompanist, and the only reservation is the recording, which though warm does not focus the piano and orchestra in truthful proportion. For all that, however, this remains an altogether outstanding performance artistically.

Barenboim and Barbirolli are superbly recorded, and their playing is heroic and marvellously spacious. Tempi are broad and measured, but the performance is sustained by its intensity of concentration. These three remain the finest in the top-price bracket. Serkin's finely wrought account with Szell has a somewhat constricted recording by comparison with these, while Weissenberg and Giulini (ASD 2992) give a fine enough account but one lacking in the last degree of sensitivity and poetry.

Brendel is such a powerful, positive pianist that it is a pity the engineers have thought to balance him so close – an unexpected fault from Philips. This was the last recording ever made by Schmidt-Isserstedt, and despite the orchestra's sonic disadvantage, he presents very positive direction – no mere accompaniment but a forceful symphonic partnership with the soloist. Though the central slow movement could be more hushed and intense, the outer movements, with fair freedom of tempo, are impressively dramatic.

In the mid-price and bargain fields, this concerto is not so well served: Gimpel with Kempe on HMV used to be a reliable fallback but neither Katchen nor Arrau on Classics for Pleasure is ideally served by the engineers. Katchen plays superbly, especially in the first movement and he is well partnered by Monteux. Arrau on his CFP disc gives a poetic but often wayward performance, the merits of which are not always enhanced by accompaniment which lacks something in bite and energy. This no longer sounds like the large-scale ambitious work of a young composer but the mature reflections of an old man. It is one way of looking at a masterpiece, and the disc is certainly well worth its reasonable price.

Piano concerto No. 2 in B flat major, Op. 83.

*** DGG 2530 259. Emil Gilels (piano), Berlin Philharmonic Orchestra, Eugen Jochum.

*** HMV ASD 2413. Daniel Barenboim (piano), New Philharmonia Orchestra, Sir John Barbirolli.

** (*) Decca SXL 6322. Wilhelm Backhaus (piano), Vienna Philharmonic Orchestra, Karl Boehm.

(B) ** RCA Victrola VICS 1563. Sviatoslav Richter (piano), Chicago Symphony Orchestra, Erich Leinsdorf.

(M) ** Decca Ace of Diamonds SDD 223. Julius Katchen (piano), London Symphony Orchestra, Janos Ferencsik.

** Philips 6500 767. Alfred Brendel (piano), Concertgebouw Orchestra, Bernard Haitink.

** Decca SXL 6309. Vladimir Ashkenazy (piano), London Symphony Orchestra, Zubin Mehta.

** HMV ASD 2554. Sviatoslav Richter (piano), Orchestre de Paris, Lorin Maazel.

* (*) RCA SB 6869. Artur Rubinstein (piano), Philadelphia Orchestra, Eugene Ormandy.

(B) * (*) Classics for Pleasure CFP 40034. Claudio Arrau (piano), Philharmonia Orchestra, Carlo Maria Giulini.

Brahms's *Second Piano concerto* remains much better served with recordings than the *First*. In many ways Gilels's DGG record is the most impressive. Indeed his partnership with Jochum produces music-making of rare magic, and it is only the want of sharp focus and more natural balance in the recording that prevents it sweeping the board altogether. Barenboim's account with Barbirolli is more controversial. It is a highly individual view, with slow tempi which enable Barbirolli to draw even more loving playing from the New Philharmonia than he had from the Vienna Philharmonic in the four *Symphonies*, which were recorded at the same time. If the first two movements are grandly heroic (with the lyrical passages merging naturally into the slow basic tempi) the slow movement has something of the awed intensity one finds in the middle movement of the *First Concerto*. A performance to love in its glowing spontaneity, with first-rate recording.

Backhaus in his eighties still managed to give a fabulous performance of what on any count is one of the most taxing of piano concertos. Some of the passagework is not as even as it might be, and the occasional rhythmic quirk has crept in, but always Backhaus compels attention. One may not like his rather gruff manner, and his very relaxed speed for the finale coupled with some odd underlining here and there will not please everyone, but no Backhaus enthusiast should fail to hear it. Excellent recording and first-rate accompaniment.

Richter recorded this most powerful of piano concertos in the earliest days of stereo for RCA. Richter's is a wayward account, mannered in places, but with an impressive weight and authority. The first movement is full of contrasts and the peaceful opening is set in greater relief than usual by the stormy allegro which follows. The powerful sweep of the second movement is matched by a poised and beautiful *Andante*, followed by a finale of great delicacy. The recording sounds somewhat shallow to today's ears, but this record remains a more satisfying achievement than Richter's later HMV version with Lorin Maazel. Maazel seems unable to match (as Leinsdorf did) the orchestral contribution to Richter's mercurial impetuosity. The HMV recording is obviously more modern and richer (though not necessarily clearer) than the Victrola version.

Katchen too is characteristically passionate and exciting, notably commanding in the outer movements, if slightly less spontaneous in the *Andante*. The orchestral contribution is not lacking in drive, but the recording balance places the soloist more backwardly than usual.

Brendel's is a finely recorded account, but the performance falls a little below expectations. He seems too judicious and adopts a deliberately restrained approach, so keen is he to eschew the grand manner. The results, though always commanding respect, are not wholly convincing; but the engineers produce first-rate sound.

Ashkenazy's version was recorded in conjunction with a live performance at the Royal Festival Hall, the sessions taking place (at Kingsway Hall) immediately after the concert. That being so, it is surprising to find that the chief shortcoming of the account, compared with the main rival versions, is a lack of tension. With much beautiful detail and some wonderfully poetic playing from Ashkenazy the performance still fails to come alive as it should. Naturally Ashkenazy is most successful in the lighter moments, but one is continually left uninvolved. The recording quality is outstandingly good, though the LSO strings are inclined to sound edgy.

The Rubinstein/Ormandy account has

many distinguished qualities – it could hardly be otherwise with artists of this stature – but the recording is less than ideal.

Of the bargain issues, Richter and Leinsdorf are more satisfying artistically than the Arrau/Giulini, though this has strong merits too. However, the piano tone is not always ideally focused, and though orchestral detail sounds natural and in good perspective, the performance suffers from one or two mannerisms which are unappealing, and there is some lack of overall spontaneity. Anda's account, which has been reissued on DGG Privilege (2538 256), is put out of court by its laboured and unconvincing account of the first movement.

Violin concerto in D major, Op. 77.

(M) *** Philips Universo 6580 087. Herman Krebbers (violin), Concertgebouw Orchestra, Bernard Haitink.

*** HMV ASD 2525. David Oistrakh (violin), Cleveland Orchestra, George Szell.

*** Philips 6500 299. Arthur Grumiaux (violin), New Philharmonia Orchestra, Colin Davis.

(M) *** HMV SXLP 30063. Leonid Kogan (violin), Philharmonia Orchestra, Kyril Kondrashin.

(M) * (**) RCA DPS 2002 (2 discs). Jascha Heifetz (violin), Chicago Symphony Orchestra, Fritz Reiner – MENDELSSOHN and TCHAIKOVSKY: *Concertos.* * (**)

** (*) DGG SLPM 138930. Christian Ferras (violin), Berlin Philharmonic Orchestra, Herbert von Karajan.

(M) ** (*) CBS Classics 61123. Zino Francescatti (violin), New York Philharmonic Orchestra, Leonard Bernstein.

Krebbers, concertmaster of the Concertgebouw but a master violinist of the first order in his own right, gives one of the most deeply satisfying readings of Brahms's *Violin concerto* ever recorded, strong and urgent yet tenderly poetic too, and always full of spontaneous imagination. The total commitment behind the performance is not only the work of the soloist but that of his colleagues and their conductor, who perform as at a live concert. The recording, with the violin slightly forward but not obtrusively so, is full and immediate.

In reissuing the Oistrakh disc from the two-record set in which it first appeared, HMV have taken the opportunity of improving the sound. Indeed, of the full-price versions currently available this must be numbered among the finest. The performance is full of controlled feeling and disciplined vitality, and even though the sound quality is not of the very first rank (it does not deserve a demonstration classification), playing of this order is rare enough to ensure a strong recommendation.

As a recording the Philips disc is, of course, much finer than the Oistrakh, which still suffers some slight coarseness at climaxes. The performance, it goes without saying, is full of insight and lyrical eloquence, and Colin Davis lends his soloist the most sympathetic support. Grumiaux is a wonderful player and this account might well be first choice for many readers, particularly in view of the excellence of the Philips sound, which is firm, detailed and refined without any loss of presence.

Kogan has long suffered from living rather in the shadow of David Oistrakh, but his strong, warm-hearted performance stands comparison with any on record, so that its reissue on bargain label is specially welcome. In the first movement, it is the bite and attack of Kogan's playing that is most striking (helped by rather forward balance in a pleasantly warm recording), and the slow movement brings a wonderful illustration of Kogan's spontaneously flexible *rubato*, occasionally overloaded with incipient *portamenti* but always natural-sounding. The finale by contrast is taken a little more rigidly than usual, so that – with the help of Kondrashin – the dance sounds as much Russian as Hungarian. Again the bite and attack are splendid. The recording quality does not in any way show its age.

Heifetz's 78 gramophone performances were always something of an occasion, and his early re-recording of the Brahms *Concerto* (not previously available in stereo) has something of this quality. By presenting it in a brochure sleeve with two other concertos RCA have solved with some delicacy the problem of issuing performances by an international celebrity of Heifetz's calibre on bargain label without loss of face. Technically the recording is not good, with rough patches in the louder orchestral moments and the violin spotlighted; the close microphoning gives a harsh quality to the strongly bowed passages. But there is a fine partnership here between Heifetz and Reiner. The interpretation is a satisfying one and it has some wonderful moments of lyrical strength and beauty. The close of the first movement is one such passage, where the melting beauty of tone shows the soloist's technique at its most moving; similarly the passionate climax of the slow movement (which Reiner too opens exceptionally well); and the bravura of the finale triumphs over the less than ideal quality of the recording.

Much depends on one's attitude to Ferras's tone-colour whether the Ferras/Karajan version is a good recommendation or not. Deutsche Grammophon have placed him close, so that the smallness of tone that in the concert hall is disappointing is certainly not evident. Moreover there is a jewelled accuracy about the playing that is most appealing, and Karajan conducts vividly. If Ferras is accepted, this can be recommended; if not look elsewhere.

The Francescatti/Bernstein account shows strongly those characteristics for which both artists are famous. Francescatti's tone is a very individual one, but this is passionate, warm-blooded playing, which Bernstein supports brilliantly. The CBS recording is bright and clear, with a strong forward placing for the soloist.

Violin concerto in D major, Op. 77; Double concerto for violin, violoncello and orchestra in A minor, Op. 102.

** (*) HMV SLS 786 (2 discs). David Oistrakh (violin), Mstislav Rostropovich (cello), Cleveland Orchestra, George Szell.

Double concerto for violin, violoncello and orchestra in A minor, Op. 102.

(M) ** (*) DGG Privilege 2726 008 (2 discs). Wolfgang Schneiderhan (violin), Janos Starker (cello), Berlin Radio Orchestra, Ferenc Fricsay – BACH and VIVALDI: *Double concertos*; BEETHOVEN: *Triple concerto*.** (*)

(B) ** (*) Classics for Pleasure CFP 40081. Christian Ferras (violin), Paul Tortelier (cello), Philharmonia Orchestra, Paul Kletzki – GLUCK: *Iphigénie overture*.***

* (*) Philips 6500 137. Henryk Szeryng (violin), Janos Starker (cello), Concertgebouw Orchestra, Bernard Haitink – BEETHOVEN: *Romances*.**

Double concerto for violin, violoncello and orchestra in A minor, Op. 102; Tragic overture, Op. 81.

(M) ** (*) Supraphon SUAST 50573. Josef Suk (violin), André Navarra (cello), Czech Philharmonic Orchestra, Karel Ančerl.

** DGG SLPM 139126. Schneiderhan, Starker, Fricsay (as above).

(i) *Double concerto for violin, violoncello and orchestra in A minor, Op. 102;*

(ii) *Alto rhapsody, Op. 53; Song of Destiny (Schicksalslied*; for chorus and orchestra), *Op. 54*.

(M) ** (*) CBS Classics 61428. (i) Zino Francescatti (violin), Pierre Fournier (cello); (ii) Mildred Miller (mezzo-soprano), Choir; Columbia Symphony Orchestra, Bruno Walter.

At the time of writing, the Oistrakh/ Rostropovich account is not available separately; were it to become so, it would have strong claims to be considered the most desirable of versions, even though the recording is not ideally smooth. This is perhaps the most powerful performance since the days of Heifetz and Feuermann or Thibaud and Casals, and it deserves the strongest recommendation.

Schneiderhan and Starker with Fricsay give a fine performance too, but it is perhaps overpriced now, considering its age: one must either pay full price for it or buy it in a two-record package with the Beethoven *Triple concerto*, which one may not want. In any event, it is a good, straightforward reading, very well shaped; the soloists are rather too forwardly balanced, although recorded very clearly.

The Szeryng/Starker version with Haitink and the Concertgebouw is impeccably played but ultimately disappointing. It remains obstinately unmemorable, and though it is not easy to fault any individual detail, the overall impact is not strong. The recording balances both Szeryng and Starker very closely, though the engineers produce truthful and musical results in every other respect.

At mid-price Francescatti and Fournier are competitive. Fournier is magnificent, and if one can adjust to Francescatti's rather nervous vibrato there is much to admire. Bruno Walter draws playing of great warmth from the Columbia Orchestra and the sound, though not first-class, is perfectly acceptable. Mildred Miller is

an accurate rather than an inspiring soloist in the *Alto rhapsody*; but the *Song of Destiny* is given a very satisfactory performance, displaying the capabilities of the chorus to good effect.

Navarra and Suk with Ančerl still remain excellent value, though the recording is not in the very first rank. Readers could do worse than try the Classics for Pleasure version with Christian Ferras, Tortelier and Kletzki, which has excellent sound to commend it. Honours are evenly divided between this and the CBS version with Walter; the recording is more natural in timbre and though the balance also places the two soloists a little forward, the CFP issue has the edge over the CBS in Ferras's contribution. The *Double concerto* is generally well served at all price ranges, and readers need not fear that they will be disappointed with any of the discs recommended here, save perhaps the Szeryng/Starker version.

Hungarian dances Nos. 1 in G minor; 3 in F major; 5 in G minor; 6 in D major.

(M) ** DGG Privilege 135031. Berlin Philharmonic Orchestra, Herbert von Karajan – LISZT: *Hungarian fantasia etc.*** (*)

The combination of Brahms *Hungarian dances* and Karajan would seem irresistible; but if these performances are not without the expected panache, they offer brilliance rather than affection, and there is not the warmth that some conductors find. The recording too is almost over-bright. But the selection offers four favourites, excellent orchestral playing and an unusual coupling, so most should be satisfied.

Hungarian dances Nos. 1 in G minor; 5 in G minor; 6 in D major; 7 in A major; 12 in D minor; 13 in D major; 19 in B minor; 21 in E minor.

(B) ** (*) Decca SPA 377. Vienna Philharmonic Orchestra, Fritz Reiner – DVOŘÁK: *Slavonic dances*.** (*)

Reiner's recording is in Decca's highest class, and the playing is lively and polished. Reiner treats the dances as conductor's display pieces, and he indulges in *rubato* and effects of his own (witness No. 12); but his affection is obvious and with such superb sound one can easily make allowances.

Serenade No. 1 in D major, Op. 11.
*** Decca SXL 6340. London Symphony Orchestra, Istvan Kertesz.

Kertesz gives a beautifully relaxed and warm-hearted account of this marvellous score, whose comparative neglect is unaccountable. The playing is as fresh as is the recorded sound. The Decca engineers provide an excellently balanced and vivid recording.

Serenade No. 2 in A major, Op. 16.
** (*) Decca SXL 6368. London Symphony Orchestra, Istvan Kertesz – DVOŘÁK: *Serenade*.***
* CBS 73197. New York Philharmonic Orchestra, Leonard Bernstein (with SCHUMANN: *Overtures Genoveva; Manfred* **).
Serenade No. 2 in A major, Op. 16; Academic Festival overture, Op. 80.
*** DGG SLPM 139371. Berlin Philharmonic Orchestra, Claudio Abbado.

'I was in a perfectly blissful mood. I have rarely written music with such delight,' wrote Brahms to Joachim when arranging this delectable *Serenade* for piano duet. The work has surprisingly autumnal colourings, and one would not be surprised to learn that it was a late rather than an early work. It was in fact begun before Brahms had finished work on the *D major Serenade* and thus dates from his mid-twenties. Kertesz gives an alert yet at the same time relaxed account of it, though the performance as a whole lacks the finish or sensitivity of Abbado's with the Berlin Philharmonic. The Berlin Philharmonic play superbly and are well recorded but collectors will probably find the Decca the more tempting issue. It offers better value in giving the Dvořák *Wind serenade* in an altogether admirable reading.

Bernstein, on his day a perceptive Brahmsian, gives an uncharacteristically dull performance. The Schumann-coupling is attractive, but this is not a recommendable disc overall.

SYMPHONIES

Symphonies Nos. 1–4 (complete recording).
*** DGG 2721 075 (4 discs). Berlin Philharmonic Orchestra, Herbert von Karajan.
Symphonies Nos. 1–4 (complete recording); *Academic Festival overture, Op. 80; Tragic overture, Op. 81.*
(M) *** HMV SLS 804 (4 discs). Philharmonia Orchestra, Otto Klemperer.
(M) ** CBS 77356 (3 discs). Cleveland Orchestra, George Szell.
Symphonies Nos. 1–4 (complete recording); *Variations on a theme of Haydn (St Anthony chorale), Op. 56a.*
** (*) Decca SXLH 6610/13. Vienna Philharmonic Orchestra, Istvan Kertesz.

The Karajan Brahms cycle is more than ten years old, but the sound is still fresh and warm, while the performances are no less vivid. As a box it is over-priced, but the orchestral playing is of such superlative quality that reservations are quickly eroded. The *First* and *Fourth Symphonies* are particularly powerful in these readings, although the *Second* is also impressive, a beautifully shaped reading, full of warmth and radiance. Perhaps there are one or two self-conscious moments, but in general this is playing of great mastery.

Klemperer's set is also highly competitive; the sound is refurbished and these classical readings have commanding strength and integrity to commend them. No. 2 is particularly fine, and although some collectors may have individual reservations (R.L. has never really enjoyed this *Fourth*), the box is a safe recommendation, particularly at the modest price now asked.

Kertesz gives eminently sane, straightforward performances, full of affectionate but not fussy detail, with splendid playing from the Vienna Philharmonic and admirably lucid recording from the Decca engineers. Ultimately the performances are less characterized than Karajan's or Walter's, but no one investing in them will be disappointed.

Szell's set of the Brahms symphonies is characterized by the keenest discipline and dramatic sense. Everything is tautly held together, but warmth and spontaneity are not Szell's strong suit and although the orchestral playing is superb, there is some want of humanity about these readings. The recording is not as wide in range or rich in sonority as its competitors. However, the box is cheap and it would be idle to deny its undoubted merits.

Symphony No. 1 in C minor, Op. 68.
  *** HMV ASD 2871. London Philharmonic Orchestra, Sir Adrian Boult.
  *** RCA SB 6873. Dresden State Orchestra, Kurt Sanderling.
  *** Philips 6500 519. Concertgebouw Orchestra, Bernard Haitink.
  *** DGG SLPM 138924. Berlin Philharmonic Orchestra, Herbert von Karajan.

  *** HMV ASD 2705. Philharmonia Orchestra, Otto Klemperer.
  (B) *** Classics for Pleasure CFP 40094. Hallé Orchestra, James Loughran.
  ** (*) Decca SXL 6675. Vienna Philharmonic Orchestra, Istvan Kertesz.
  ** (*) Decca Phase 4 PFS 4305. London Symphony Orchestra, Leopold Stokowski.
  (M) * (**) CBS Classics 61217. Columbia Symphony Orchestra, Bruno Walter.
  (B) * (*) Decca Eclipse ECS 643. Vienna Philharmonic Orchestra, Josef Krips.

Boult's is a noble and impressive record, arguably the finest account at present available. There is no attempt to score interpretative points; the reading is admirably classical and objective. Boult's tempi are not as flexible as Sanderling's and his performance reflects a lower emotional temperature. He observes the exposition repeat in the first movement and is true to every indication of Brahms's score. It is splendidly played, too, and to some extent, the soundest recommendation for the gramophone since, as one would expect from this of all conductors, it is wholly free of egocentric distortion. The recording is signally successful in terms of perspective and truthfulness of timbre as well as having splendid presence.

The magnificence of the Dresden Orchestra is seen to good advantage in their account of the *First Symphony*. Sanderling's reading has such natural warmth and is so strongly characterized that it has the keenest claims on the collector. It is less classical than Boult's eminently sound reading but evokes in some ways a warmer response. Although the recording is not quite so fine as the HMV, which has a marvellously natural string tone among other things, it is still extremely good and for some (R.L. among them) this will be the preferred reading in spite of some agogic distortions during its course. Everyone plays as if they meant every note, and this sense of conviction gives the performance a rare eloquence.

Haitink's performance with the Concertgebouw is far from being an also-ran. It is a strong, well-argued reading of considerable power and in some ways better played than the Boult version, though the latter receives the fresher and more detailed recording. Haitink does not observe the first-movement exposition repeat, but that apart, honours are very evenly divided, and the recording is spacious and well-balanced.

Turning to the older versions in the full-price range, Klemperer is a strong contender; so too is the Karajan, a noble and powerfully wrought performance that has as much grip as the Klemperer but more feeling. Both are fine recordings.

James Loughran provides an outstanding bargain version, the first to observe the exposition repeat in the first movement. The reading from first to last is as refreshing as Boult's superb account. The second and third movements both have a spring-like quality, the slow movement is less sweet than usual, while the 6/8 trio of the third movement is taken for once at a speed which allows the climax not to sound breathless. The introduction to the finale is unusually slow, weighty and concentrated, while the great string melody is not smoothed over at all. The entry of the chorale at the end finds Loughran characteristically refusing to slow down to half speed. Though some of the woodwind playing is not ideally responsive, the whole orchestra, particularly the strings, show a natural feeling for Brahms's style. The recording is a little light in bass but otherwise captures a ripe, clean Brahms sound.

Kertesz is beautifully recorded, and the orchestral playing is equally fine. But while anyone would be happy with this record, the reading is marginally undercharacterized. Even so the performance is both enjoyable and satisfying.

The Stokowski version is taken from live recordings of his sixtieth-anniversary concerts with the LSO. The Phase 4 engineers had to marry up recordings taken at two performances, one at the Royal Festival Hall, one at the Royal Albert Hall, which led to the sound being less expansive than it might be. The spontaneous sense of flow, the urgency of Stokowski's Brahms style are nonetheless well conveyed in an exciting performance. It may lack a degree of polish next to the finest studio-made versions, but it has its place. The sound is not ideal, not so much on account of the close balance on the wind (this is tastefully managed) but because of the lack of clarity at climaxes.

In the mid-price range Walter's performance is the most commanding, though the recording does it less than justice. It has a strident edge but this can be tamed by use of the controls. The Krips version with the Vienna Philharmonic on the Eclipse bargain label is a sound reading rather than an inspired one, and neither as a performance nor as a recording can it compare with Loughran's Classics for Pleasure disc.

Symphony No. 2 in D major, Op. 73.
   *** DGG 2530 125. Berlin Philharmonic Orchestra, Claudio Abbado.
   *** DGG SLPM 138925. Berlin Philharmonic Orchestra, Herbert von Karajan.
   *** Decca SXL 6676. Vienna Philharmonic Orchestra, Istvan Kertesz.
   (B) ** Decca Eclipse ECS 596. Vienna Philharmonic Orchestra, Pierre Monteux.

Symphony No. 2 in D major, Op. 73;
Academic Festival overture, Op. 80.

(M) ** Philips Universo 6580 054.
London Symphony Orchestra,
Pierre Monteux.

Symphony No. 2 in D major, Op. 73;
Tragic overture, Op. 81.

*** HMV ASD 2706. Philharmonia
Orchestra, Otto Klemperer.

(M) ** (*) CBS 61218. Columbia
Symphony Orchestra, Bruno Walter.

** RCA SB 6875. Dresden State
Orchestra, Kurt Sanderling.

Symphony No. 2 in D major, Op. 73;
(i) Alto rhapsody, Op. 53.

*** HMV ASD 2746. London Philharmonic Orchestra, Sir Adrian
Boult, (i) with Janet Baker
(mezzo-soprano), John Alldis
Choir.

The *Second Symphony* is well served at
present. Abbado's is a keenly lyrical and
sensitive account, by far the finest of his
cycle, and it is beautifully recorded too.
He observes the first-movement exposition repeat and has a firmer grip on the
structure than he shows in the other
symphonies. At the same time there is no
want of flexibility and imagination in the
shaping of the flow of the music. The
Berlin Philharmonic play with warmth
and finesse.

Karajan and the same orchestra give
perhaps a stronger performance. Karajan
has tremendous grip, tempered with
warmth and radiance, a capacity for
allowing the work's riches to take one by
surprise, beautifully shaped phrasing and
sumptuous orchestral tone.

Sanderling with the Dresden State
Orchestra is not at his best, and the reading strikes one as a shade too mannered
even though the orchestral playing is of
the highest quality. Like Klemperer,
Sanderling offers the *Tragic overture* as
fill-up, but both as performance and as

recording, the Klemperer is the stronger
contender. By the side of Boult or Walter,
Klemperer might seem a trifle severe and
uncompromising, but he underlines the
power of this symphony without diminish-
ing its lyrical eloquence in any way.

For some readers Boult's version will
occupy a special place of honour. It has
warmth, dignity and nobility and offers
playing of great expressive power which
scores over the Klemperer in having
slightly more sense of spontaneity. It is
superlatively recorded, and as the fill-up
is a memorable account of the *Alto
rhapsody* from Janet Baker, its claims are
indeed strong.

Kertesz's account of the symphony is
as direct and honest as it is attractive.
The playing of the Vienna Philharmonic
is absolutely first-class, and the Decca
recording has brilliance, clarity and
warmth. Kertesz, like Abbado and Monteux, observes the exposition repeat, and
the performance has a splendid freshness
and youthful vigour. At the same time,
it must be conceded that this is in no
sense a performance of commanding
stature. Much the same must regretfully
be said of the two readings by Pierre
Monteux, one with the Vienna Philharmonic on Eclipse, the other with the
LSO on Philips Universo. Both offer
relaxed, idiomatic playing and an eminently sound reading, but there is nothing
that makes these performances resound
in the memory in quite the way that the
Karajan or the Walter does. Kubelik's
recording with the Vienna Orchestra
(Decca Ace of Diamonds SDD 188) now
sounds its age, and the most impressive
account at less than full price remains
Bruno Walter's with the Columbia
Symphony Orchestra: not the finest of
recordings, perhaps, but a mellow, wise
and loving performance that will not
disappoint anyone who invests in it.

Symphony No. 3 in F major, Op. 90.
** DGG SLPM 138926. Berlin Phil-

harmonic Orchestra, Herbert von Karajan.

Symphony No. 3 in F major, Op. 90; Academic Festival overture, Op. 80.

*** HMV ASD 2707. Philharmonia Orchestra, Otto Klemperer.

Symphony No. 3 in F major, Op. 90; Tragic overture, Op. 81.

*** HMV ASD 2660. London Symphony Orchestra, Sir Adrian Boult.

*** Philips 6500 155. Concertgebouw Orchestra, Bernard Haitink.

(M) *** HMV SXLP 30100. Berlin Philharmonic Orchestra, Rudolf Kempe.

(M) ** Decca Ace of Diamonds SDD 284. Vienna Philharmonic Orchestra, Herbert von Karajan.

Symphony No. 3 in F major, Op. 90; Variations on a theme of Haydn (St Anthony chorale), Op. 56a.

*** RCA SB 6877. Dresden State Orchestra, Kurt Sanderling.

(M) ** (*) CBS 61219. Columbia Symphony Orchestra, Bruno Walter.

* (*) DGG 2530 452. Dresden State Orchestra, Claudio Abbado.

Sir Adrian's account of the *Third Symphony* has great dignity and spaciousness. He captures the autumnal feeling of the slow movement with great success and is only surpassed here by the old Reiner set made in the late fifties. The LSO play with great enthusiasm and fire and the recording has an impressive clarity and detail along with spaciousness. Sir Adrian's is a beautifully mellow performance, keenly lyrical in feeling, with a slightly sweeter and fuller flavour than Haitink's version with the Concertgebouw Orchestra which appeared at the same time. In the finale Haitink is to be preferred for his tauter, brisker approach and here Sir Adrian indulges in his only

eccentricity, a sudden spurt at bar 70 and at the corresponding passage later in the movement. (There is, too, a slight drop in pitch at bar 143 on the HMV record.) The orchestral playing of the Dutch orchestra is distinguished by unanimity of attack and chording, wonderfully true intonation and homogeneity of tone. The recording, however, is not as vivid or as sumptuous as the HMV, but Haitink's firmness of grip makes his a formidable reading. Honours are in fact fairly evenly divided between the two performances, but on balance we prefer Boult.

Though less impressively recorded than the Boult (and let down by the first pressings, which had an ill-focused side), Sanderling gives a marvellously rich performance, and his slow movement is particularly warm-hearted and generous in feeling. This is deeply experienced and yet spontaneous. Although in the top-price range Boult probably is the safest recommendation, collectors should hear this Sanderling for themselves. The Dresden Orchestra play with such eloquence that for some this will be the most rewarding version of all.

Klemperer's account of this symphony is even more individual than his other Brahms symphony performances. With slow speeds and all repeats taken his timing is much more extended than usual. But for all his expansiveness Klemperer does not make the music sound opulent. There is a severity about his approach which may at first seem unappealing, but which comes to underline the strength of the architecture.

Abbado with the Dresden Orchestra must, alas, be ruled out on account of the mannered tempo changes in which he indulges. The playing is beautiful, as it is for Sanderling, but whereas his expressive changes seem organic Abbado's do not.

The Karajan DGG account is very good but not quite so compelling as his No. 1 and No. 2. Here is a case where the Vienna version (for Decca) rivals the quality of the Berlin. In both he takes the opening expansively, which makes it surprising when he omits the exposition repeat and the movement is left rather short (by far the shortest of Brahms's orchestral first movements). The third movement too is very slow, and when the record gives such short measure, it is hardly a contender for first place. If Karajan is an essential, the Decca version has the *Tragic overture* as fill-up.

Kempe, however, is a clear first choice among the mid-priced versions. He gives a vividly characterized reading, with the Berlin Philharmonic Orchestra in excellent form, and he is fortunate in having fine recorded sound. Walter should not be passed over, and with a fine version of the *Variations* included this is excellent value, though the sound is by no means so rich or well detailed as Kempe.

Symphony No. 4 in E minor, Op. 98.
  *** RCA SB 6879. Dresden State Orchestra, Kurt Sanderling.
  (B) *** Classics for Pleasure CFP 40084. Hallé Orchestra, James Loughran.
  ** (*) HMV ASD 2708. Philharmonia Orchestra, Otto Klemperer.
  ** (*) DGG SLPM 138927. Berlin Philharmonic Orchestra, Herbert von Karajan.
  (B) ** (*) Pye GSGC 15014. Hallé Orchestra, Sir John Barbirolli.
  ** Philips 6500 389. Concertgebouw Orchestra, Bernard Haitink.
  ** HMV ASD 2650. Chicago Symphony Orchestra, Carlo Maria Giulini.

Symphony No. 4 in E minor, Op. 98; Academic Festival overture, Op. 80.
  (M) ** (*) CBS Classics 61211. Columbia Symphony Orchestra, Bruno Walter.

  ** (*) HMV ASD 2901. London Philharmonic Orchestra, Sir Adrian Boult.
  (M) * (*) Philips Universo 6580 024. Vienna Symphony Orchestra, Wolfgang Sawallisch.

Brahms's *Fourth Symphony* is not quite so well served as its companions. Boult's version with the LPO is magnificently recorded but it is sober almost to a fault. After the others it seems a little disappointing. It lacks the fire and eloquence that make Sanderling's version with the Dresden State Orchestra so striking. This is finely recorded, beautifully played and splendidly shaped, with some of the classical strength that distinguished this orchestra's account of the work under Karl Boehm in the days of 78s. However, it has a warmth and sense of enjoyment that make it an enormously rewarding performance. A fine recording too.

Loughran's account, like Barbirolli's before him with the same orchestra, is outstanding. At bargain price and with excellent sound it should not be missed. Loughran's approach is unobtrusively direct. He is rarely if ever concerned to underline interpretative points, yet as the concentration grows after the deceptively gentle start, so one more and more appreciates the satisfying assurance with which he solves every problem. His tempi – except perhaps for a relatively slow account of the scherzo – are unexceptionable, and like Barbirolli he believes in adopting expressive phrasing within a basically steady tempo. The Hallé strings are in excellent form, beautifully recorded, and so for that matter are all the sections of the orchestra.

Among the full-price versions the Klemperer has been much admired, and its sterling qualities have earned it an honoured place in the catalogue. It is a performance to admire rather than love, perhaps, and some may feel it a trifle earthbound in places. However, it has great integrity and offers some fine playing. The Karajan is also an impressive reading that was perhaps underrated in the earlier editions of the *Stereo Record Guide*. Certainly one of the finer versions of the work, Karajan's account will not command universal allegiance any more than Klemperer's does, but the Passacaglia has splendid grip in Karajan's hands, and so too does the eloquent slow movement.

It goes without saying that the Chicago Orchestra play with magnificent discipline and tonal refinement for Giulini and are well served by the HMV engineers. But as a whole the performance is not as commanding as one might have expected, though there are eloquent moments. The slow movement is most beautifully done, but elsewhere, both in the first movement and in the Passacaglia, Giulini does not resist the temptation to underline interpretative points. Haitink is not at his most penetrating in this symphony and though the performance is well played and recorded (and much more straightforward than Giulini), it is not as fine as his accounts of Nos. 1 and 3.

Turning to the mid-price range, Walter is to be preferred. His performance has much greater warmth and character than Sawallisch's eminently sound but slightly nondescript version on Universo. There is some fine playing in both accounts, and the Vienna Symphony respond more enthusiastically than is often the case. Walter, though not so well recorded, has a wisdom and authority that cannot fail to impress.

Barbirolli's Pye version makes another very good bargain recommendation. The playing lacks some brilliance – for example the brass in the last movement – but generally this is a most satisfying performance, with the first movement pressed ahead with just the right degree of urgency, and the second warm and romantic. The recording, though not outstanding, is still acceptable.

Variations on a theme of Haydn (St Anthony chorale), Op. 56a.
(B) *** Decca SPA 121. London Symphony Orchestra, Pierre Monteux – ELGAR: *Enigma variations.****

Monteux offers a fresh, enjoyable performance to match his *Enigma variations* on the reverse. The orchestral playing is excellent, and the vigorous style gives the music a splendid forward impulse. The bright recording still sounds well, and there are few better versions available at any price.

CHAMBER MUSIC

Clarinet quintet in B minor, Op. 115.
*** Philips 6500 453. Members of the Berlin Philharmonic Octet – DVOŘÁK: *Bagatelles.****
(M) ** (*) Decca Ace of Diamonds SDD 249. Alfred Boskovsky (clarinet), members of the Vienna Octet – WAGNER: *Adagio.****
** DGG SLPM 139354. Karl Leister (clarinet), Amadeus Quartet.
(B) ** Oiseau-Lyre OLS 146. Yona Ettlinger (clarinet), Tel-Aviv Quartet.
(B) * (*) Pye GSGC 15004. Jack Brymer (clarinet), Prometheus Ensemble.
(M) * (*) Philips Universo 6580 057. Oskar Michallik (clarinet), Egon Morbitzer, Wilhelm Martens (violins), Werner Buchholz (viola), Bernard Gunther (cello).

The Berlin version is exceptionally beautiful and faithful to Brahms's intentions, an outstanding version in every way. The delicacy with which the 'Hungarian' middle section of the great *Adagio* is interpreted gives some idea of the insight of these players. It is an autumnal reading, never overforced, and is recorded with comparable refinement. With an unusual and attractive coupling it makes an excellent recommendation.

The Decca performance too is most beautiful. Boskovsky has a warm, luscious tone, and it suits the relaxed atmosphere of the whole performance. Perhaps it is a shade too relaxed. The first movement could be tauter than this, and the slow movement is on the gentle side. But with its fascinating coupling (hardly a lost masterpiece) it is an excellent disc.

Karl Leister is the first clarinet of the Berlin Philharmonic, so that his playing is nothing if not accomplished. At times one feels that he could be a little more imaginative in matters of phrasing but his playing is admirably unmannered. The Amadeus give a lush, some might say overheated, account of their part, and the performance as a whole will not convince all listeners. It does not displace the Philips or Decca versions, both of which have fill-ups as well.

Yona Ettlinger gives an exceptionally smooth performance, liquidly expressive to contrast with rather sharp-edged strings. In its price-range this leisurely reading is well worth considering, and the recording is as clear as in most more expensive versions.

The Michallik version also offers no coupling, but it may be taken as reasonable compensation that it appears on the mid-price Universo label. Performance and recording are good, though the interpretation is not so firmly characterized as that of most rivals. Nor does Jack Brymer's account with the Prometheus Ensemble challenge the Berlin version or Boskovsky. His playing is often beautiful but the reading as a whole is a trifle wanting in real character and does not find these admirable artists at their best.

Clarinet sonatas Nos. 1 in F minor, Op. 120/1; 2 in E flat major, Op. 120/2.
   *** HMV ASD 2362. Gervase de Peyer (clarinet), Daniel Barenboim (piano).

Whatever reservations one may have about various details, these performances are eminently satisfying accounts of these two late sonatas, and any newcomer will have to be very good to beat them. The recordings are both particularly good as far as piano tone is concerned.

Clarinet trio in A minor (for clarinet, violoncello and piano), Op. 114.
   (B) * (*) Turnabout TV 34108S. David Glazer (clarinet), Frank Glazer (piano), David Soyer (cello) – BEETHOVEN: *Clarinet trio.***

This is less successful than its Beethoven coupling. It is well enough played but lacks warmth. This is partly caused by the dry recording acoustic, which seems to stop the music from expanding and may be why the cellist seems unable to broaden his tone in the *Adagio*. But there is generally not the spontaneity here that the same players find for the attractive Beethoven trio.

(i) *Clarinet trio in A minor (for clarinet, violoncello and piano), Op. 114;* (ii) *Horn trio in E flat major (for horn, violin and piano), Op. 40.*
   ** DGG SLPM 139398. Christoph Eschenbach (piano), with (i) Karl Leister (clarinet), Georg Donderer (cello); (ii) Gerd Seifert (horn), Eduard Drolc (violin).

A good performance of the *Clarinet trio*, well recorded, is coupled to an account of the *Horn trio* that improves as it goes along. The opening is romantic rather than purposeful, but the forward impulse gathers power as the music unfolds. Eschenbach emerges as the strongest personality; he dominates the scherzo, and obviously exerts a strong influence on the slow movement and finale. The horn player shows less individuality than his companions, but the well balanced recording compensates.

Horn trio in E flat major (for horn, violin and piano), *Op. 40*.
   *** Decca sxl 6408. Barry Tuckwell (horn), Itzhak Perlman (violin), Vladimir Ashkenazy (piano) – FRANCK: *Violin sonata*.***
   (M) ** Oiseau-Lyre sol 314. Neil Sanders (horn), Emanuel Hurwitz (violin), Lamar Crowson (piano) – SCHUBERT: *Auf der Strom****; SCHUMANN: *Adagio and allegro*.* (*)

A superb performance of Brahms's marvellous *Horn trio* from Barry Tuckwell, Itzhak Perlman and Vladimir Ashkenazy. They realize to the full the music's passionate impulse, and the performance moves forward from the gentle opening, through the sparkling scherzo (a typical Brahmsian inspiration, broad in manner as well as vivacious, with a heart-warming trio), the more introspective but still outgiving *Adagio* and the gay, spirited finale. The recording is worthy of the playing, although the engineers in their care not to out-balance the violin with the horn have placed the horn rather backwardly. They should have trusted Brahms: he knew what he was doing when he invented this unusual but highly effective combination.

This performance by Sanders, Hurwitz and Crowson is notable for its restraint. They treat the work as a classical masterpiece rather than a ripely romantic one. The reserve in the first movement means that the chosen tempo seems too slow, whereas in fact it is the lack of boisterousness in the playing that creates the lack of tension. The music wakes up in the scherzo and the finale, both of which are played with vivacity, and the subdued, musing quality at the opening of

the *Adagio* is effective. But taken as a whole this interpretation, although musical in its way, simply is not sufficiently emotionally extrovert for this particular Brahms work.

Piano quartet No. 1 in G minor, Op. 25.
   ** (*) DGG 2530 133. Emil Gilels (piano), Amadeus Quartet.
Piano quartets Nos. 1 in G minor, Op. 25; 2 in A major, Op. 26; 3 in C minor, Op. 60.
   (M) *** RCA ser 5628/30. Artur Rubinstein (piano), Guarneri Quartet – SCHUMANN: *Piano quintet*.***
Piano quartet No. 3 in C minor, Op. 60.
   (M) * (*) Oiseau-Lyre sol 320. Pro Arte Piano Quartet – SCHUMANN: *Piano quartet*.* (*)

For some reason the Brahms *Piano quartets* have never enjoyed the popularity that is their due among lovers of chamber music, but the splendid complete set by Rubinstein and the Guarneri Quartet should win the music many new friends. Although primarily famous for his Chopin performances, Rubinstein can be an equally persuasive Brahms advocate, and here he is at his most commanding, clearly inspiring the Guarneri players to match his power and emotional warmth. All three performances have tremendous spontaneity and conviction; moreover the recording is just right for the music, with rich, forward string textures, yet allowing the bold piano sound to dominate where Brahms and Rubinstein intend that it should. The Schumann coupling is of equal distinction, and this album is very highly recommendable.

As might be expected, the Gilels/Amadeus account of Op. 25 is also impressive, and many will like especially the withdrawn delicacy of the scherzo and the gypsy fire of the finale, where Gilels is at his most brilliant. But the Amadeus players do not match the Guarneri Quartet in romantic fire, and the slow movement lacks something in genuine warmth. Even so, with clear DGG recording there is a great deal to enjoy here. The Pro Arte account of Op. 60, although well played and recorded, is altogether less inspiring. The element of restraint in the overall conception does not do full justice to the spirit of the music, and although the performance has its moments, notably in the finale, this can only be recommended to those especially seeking this coupling.

Piano quintet in F minor, Op. 34.
> ** (*) HMV ASD 2873. André Previn (piano), Yale Quartet.
> ** DGG SLPM 139397. Christoph Eschenbach (piano), Amadeus Quartet.

Previn and his American colleagues recorded this at a few hours' notice, at the time when they were also giving the work in a South Bank Summer Music concert. The challenge of the occasion comes over strongly, particularly in the strongly rhythmic, infectiously pointed account of the piano part from Previn. There may be more polished versions, but this is the most spontaneous-sounding. The recording is good, though some will find it too reverberant.

Christoph Eschenbach gives a powerful – sometimes overprojected – account of his part. Now that Richter's memorable performance is no longer available we are not spoiled by the present catalogue. The DGG record offers good piano quality and tonally has the edge on its rival.

Piano trios Nos. 1 in B flat major, Op. 8; 2 in C major, Op. 87.
> ** Philips SAL 3627. Beaux Arts Trio.

Piano trios Nos. 1 in B flat major, Op. 8; 3 in C minor, Op. 101.

> *** Decca SXL 6387. Julius Katchen (piano), Josef Suk (violin), Janos Starker (cello).

Piano trio No. 2 in C major, Op. 87.
> (M) ** Pye Virtuoso TPLS 13018. Oromonte Trio – HAYDN: *Piano trio No. 28.***

Piano trio No. 2 in C major, Op. 87; Violoncello sonata No. 2 in F major, Op. 99.
> *** Decca SXL 6589. Julius Katchen (piano), Josef Suk (violin), Janos Starker (cello).

Piano trios Nos. 3 in C minor, Op. 101; 4 in A major, Op. posth.
> ** Philips SAL 3628. Beaux Arts Trio.

The Beaux Arts Trio, with brisk tempi in the allegros, are dramatic if somewhat matter-of-fact. But there is a good deal to be said for crispness, and with thoughtful, sensitive playing in the slow movements (if less individuality than in the Katchen set) this is recommendable enough if all four trios are wanted. The Philips image gives a natural impression of four players grouped together in a room, and in spite of the long sides the quality itself is excellent. But in the last resort the Philips performances are not as compelling as those on Decca. Katchen and his team judge the tempi admirably and resist the temptation to dwell too lovingly on detail. In addition they are given really excellent recording. SXL 6589 represents the results of Katchen's last recording sessions before his untimely death. They were held at Maltings, and the results have a warmth that did not always characterize Katchen's recordings of Brahms. The coupling may be unconventional, but both the tough *C major Trio* and the epic, thrustful *Cello sonata* are given strong and characterful performances.

The Oromonte performance of the *C major Trio* has exceptional life and spontaneity, the immediacy of the recording helping to give the impression of a live performance. The one snag is the lack of resonance of the cello line, so that at times it almost sounds like a viola. The part comes through, and the harmony always sounds complete, but when the cello leads one would ideally like a bigger image. In spite of this drawback of balance, the performance is very enjoyable.

String quartets Nos. 1 in C minor, Op. 51/1; 2 in A minor, Op. 51/2.
> (M) *** Decca Ace of Diamonds SDD 322. Weller Quartet.

String quartets Nos. 1 in C minor, Op. 51/1; 2 in A minor, Op. 51/2; 3 in B flat major, Op. 67.
> (M) * (*) RCA DPS 2050 (2 discs). Cleveland Quartet.

String quartets Nos. 1 in C minor, Op. 51/1; 3 in B flat major, Op. 67.
> *** DGG 2530 345. Melos Quartet of Stuttgart.

String quartet No. 2 in A minor, Op. 51/2.
> (B) ** (*) DGG Début 2555 005. Tokyo Quartet – HAYDN: *String quartet No. 75.** (*)*

The finest account of the *C minor Quartet* has recently been deleted: it is by the Italian Quartet on Philips. None of the present versions equals its insights or mastery. The Weller are fresh and spontaneous, and they are to be preferred for this coupling, particularly at the modest price asked. In addition they are superbly recorded. The Melos Quartet of Stuttgart on DG offer a different coupling, and their performances are eminently straightforward and unmannered. They are excellently recorded, with natural, open sound, and are much to be preferred to the RCA Cleveland set, which collects all three quartets but in highly polished and ruthlessly efficient performances that

hardly do justice to the stature of this music.

The Tokyo Quartet is an impressive group of young players whose ensemble is as immaculate in tone as in rhythm. The Brahms *A minor* is not an easy work for any quartet, and though you may feel that this reading lacks a sense of struggle, it is good to have the ear beguiled so consistently. Good firm recording: an excellent bargain.

String quintets Nos. 1 in F major, Op. 88; 2 in G major, Op. 111.
> *** Philips 6500 177. Members of the Berlin Philharmonic Octet.
> *** CBS 72588. Budapest Quartet with Walter Trampler (viola).
> ** DGG SLPM 139430. Amadeus Quartet with Cecil Aronowitz (viola).

The Amadeus version of these masterpieces was never altogether satisfactory. The playing was polished and the recording first-rate, but the style is too suave and lacking in depth. The performances by the Berlin Philharmonic group are much more searching and artistically satisfying. The recording does not reveal detail quite so effectively as one would wish, but in general there is little to cavil at here. Nor is the Budapest version with Walter Trampler an also-ran. CBS have made an excellent job of the transfer, which produces a smooth, rich sound, and the performances are nothing if not convinced.

String sextet No. 1 in B flat major, Op. 18.
> * (*) DGG SLPM 139353. Augmented Amadeus Quartet.

In purity of style this performance does not match that by the Berlin players on Philips (recently deleted), despite the excellence of the recording and the undoubted merits of this ensemble.

String sextet No. 2 in G major, Op. 36.
  *** Philips SAL 3763. Members of
  the Berlin Philharmonic Octet.
  * (*) DGG SLPM 139459. Augmented Amadeus Quartet.

The *G major Sextet* is one of the most
sublime of Brahms's chamber works, and
this Philips recording should be snapped
up by all admirers of the composer. The
playing has warmth and eloquence (it is
preferable to the deleted Menuhin
account and infinitely preferable to the
Amadeus version), while the recording
has admirable spaciousness and presence.

There is fine, polished playing from the
Amadeus ensemble, but also the mannered blandness of style which seems to
detract from the music's freshness.

*Violin sonatas Nos. 1 in G major, Op.
78; 2 in A major, Op. 100; 3 in D
minor, Op. 108.*
  (M) ** (*) RCA SER 5701/3. Henryk
  Szeryng (violin), Artur Rubinstein (piano) – BEETHOVEN: *Violin sonatas Nos. 5, 8, and 9.***
  ** (*) Decca SXL 6321. Josef Suk
  (violin), Julius Katchen (piano).
Violin sonata No. 3 in D minor, Op. 108.
  *** HMV ASD 2618. David Ois-
  trakh (violin), Sviatoslav Richter
  (piano) – FRANCK: *Violin sonata.****

Szeryng and Rubinstein are at their
finest in this triptych of Brahms sonatas.
This artistic partnership makes the best
of both worlds, for the players show
themselves as fine virtuosi and willing
partners, and are equally imbued with
the Brahmsian spirit. The performances
are sophisticated yet committed, strongly
felt yet careful in matters of detail and
balance. The recording is, however,
rather dry in acoustic; Brahms's chamber
music ideally needs a warmer acoustic
than this, and a richer piano sound. But
this remains a distinguished set.

Decca have squeezed all three sonatas
on a single disc with no loss in quality;
indeed the recording of the violin is
especially smooth and real and the
piano tone has both amplitude and clarity.
The balance is excellent. Suk's personal
blend of romanticism and the classical
tradition is warmly attractive but small
in scale. These are intimate performances,
with much less of the grand manner than
Szeryng and Rubinstein find in their
readings. But in their own way they are
most enjoyable. For R.L. they are first
choice.

The HMV record is taken from a live
concert given at the hall of the Moscow
Conservatory. The presence of an
audience (which is admirably silent)
seems to have fired these players to even
greater heights. One has all the electricity
and inner feeling of live music-making:
tremendous spontaneity blended with
virtuosity and personality of an outsize
order. This account of the Brahms is
totally compelling, and the sense of
occasion transmits itself to the listener.
The recording, though not quite the
equal of the finest studio recording, is
nonetheless of good quality. Even if
readers possess an account of all three
sonatas the risk of duplication is worth
taking for the sake of playing of this
order of imaginative and musical vitality.

*Violoncello sonatas Nos. 1 in E minor,
Op. 38; 2 in F major, Op. 99.*
  * (**) HMV ASD 2436. Jacqueline
  du Pré (cello), Daniel Barenboim
  (piano).

It is a highly subjective matter whether
the undeniable stylistic self-indulgence of
Jacqueline du Pré in these two rich works
will strike the listener as convincing or
not. At least the players tackle the second
and more taxing of the sonatas with the
sense of heroic size which the music
demands and which is usually missing in
recorded performances. This is on the

215

whole the more successful of the two performances. It is hard to accept the blatant change of tempo between first and second subjects in the earlier sonata, but here too there is warmth and flair. Not recommended for those who find themselves resisting the du Pré/Barenboim brand of romantic expressiveness. Well-balanced recording.

Collection: (i; ii) *Violin sonatas Nos. 1 in G major, Op. 78; 2 in A major, Op. 100; 3 in D minor, Op. 108; Scherzo in C minor.* (i) *4 Ballades, Op. 10; 7 Fantasias, Op. 116.* (i; iii) *21 Hungarian dances.* (i) *3 Intermezzi, Op. 117; 8 Pieces, Op. 76; 6 Pieces, Op. 118; 4 Pieces, Op. 119; Scherzo in E flat minor, Op. 4. Piano sonatas: in C major, Op. 1; in F sharp minor, Op. 2; in F minor, Op. 5; Variations and fugue on a theme by Handel, Op. 24; Variations on an original theme, Op. 21/1; Variations on a Hungarian song, Op. 21/2; Variations on a theme by Paganini, Op. 35; Variations on a theme by Schumann, Op. 9; 16 Waltzes, Op. 39.*

(M) *** Decca Ace of Diamonds SDDA 261/9. (i) Julius Katchen (piano); (ii) Josef Suk (violin); (iii) J.-P. Marty (piano).

The content of this album is discussed (above and below) with the original SXL issues. Only the *Scherzo in C minor* is a new addition. The album makes a fine investment at Ace of Diamonds price. Brahms brought out the best in Katchen; he is particularly good in the impulsive early music. If at times one could make small criticisms, the spontaneity and understanding are always there, and of course the excitement that comes when bravura is controlled by a sensitive and musical mind. The clear Decca sound is consistent throughout.

PIANO MUSIC

4 Ballades, Op. 10: Nos. 1 in D minor (Edward); 2 in D major; 3 in B minor; 4 in B major.

** (*) DGG 2530 321. Wilhelm Kempff (piano) – SCHUMANN: *Arabeske etc.****

4 Ballades, Op. 10. Intermezzi: Op. 116, No. 5 in E minor; Op. 117, No. 2 in B flat minor; Op. 118, No. 6 in E flat minor. Pieces, Op. 76, No. 2: Capriccio in B minor. Rhapsodies, Op. 79: Nos. 1 in B minor; 2 in G minor.

** RCA SB 6845. Artur Rubinstein (piano).

4 Ballades, Op. 10; 2 Rhapsodies, Op. 79; Waltzes, Op. 39.

** (*) Decca SXL 6160. Julius Katchen (piano).

4 Ballades, Op. 10; Variations on a theme by Paganini, Op. 35.

(M) ** (*) Vanguard VCS 10006. Earl Wild (piano) (with LISZT: *Paganini study No. 2 ***).

Fantasias, Op. 116 (complete); Pieces, Op. 76 (complete).

** Decca SXL 6118. Julius Katchen (piano).

Kempff more than any rival brings lightness and delicacy to the thick piano textures of Brahms. Here the four *Ballades* – the last three relatively neglected pieces – emerge very much as young man's music. Individual performances beautifully recorded.

Katchen's style in Brahms is distinctive. There is a hardness about it that suits some works better than others. In general the bigger, tougher pieces come off better than the gentle *Intermezzi* of Op. 116 and Op. 117, which lack the sort of inner tension that Curzon or Kempff can convey. But such pieces as the two *Rhapsodies*, Op. 79, are splendidly done and so are the *Ballades*. The *Waltzes*, brief trivial ideas but on the whole extrovert, come somewhere in between. Katchen misses some of the magic with his uncoaxing style, but the brightness is still attractive. The recording of the whole cycle can be recommended in Decca's bright, slightly percussive manner of the mid-sixties.

From Rubinstein a totally unsentimental approach – at times to the point of being almost matter-of-fact. Remarkably youthful in spirit and full of personality, this is playing to reckon with. The balance is a bit close and the acoustic cold, so that there are times when one feels it is a bit shorn of mystery. One misses the extremes of both tension and repose, and the record does not really match the poetry of Rubinstein's Brahms playing in the past.

The *Ballades* are not easy to bring off, but Earl Wild catches their colouring effectively, and a glittering performance of Liszt's *Second Paganini study* makes a suitable contrast to end the side. The performance of the *Variations* is exceptionally brilliant and spontaneous. The piano tone as recorded, although clear and truthful, is not especially sonorous, but this is the only possible reservation about an otherwise successful and enjoyable recital.

Fantasias, Op. 116; Pieces, Op. 119; Variations on an original theme, Op. 21/1.
  (M) *** Pye Virtuoso TPLS 13016. Balint Vazsonyi (piano).

Few of these pieces are among Brahms's best-known piano music and the very personal and introvert *Variations on an original theme* deserves to be better known. Vazsonyi plays this work with subtlety and understanding, the musing quality at the opening and close giving the listener the feeling that the pianist gets right inside the composer's mind. The *Fantasias*, Op. 116, and the four *Pieces*, Op. 119, again show the pianist's

thoughtful penetration below the music's surface. The tonal shading and control of mood are remarkably imaginative, witness the boldness of the *Capriccio in G minor* or the sensibility of the *Intermezzo*, Op. 119/1. The piano recording is absolutely natural, with both warmth of sonority and fine projection.

Hungarian dances Nos. 1–21 (for piano duet): complete recording.
  (B) *** Turnabout TV 34068S. Walter and Beatrice Klien (piano duet).
  *** Decca SXL 6217. Julius Katchen and J.-P. Marty (piano duet).
Hungarian dances Nos. 1–10 (for piano duet).
  * (*) Decca SXL 6389. Bracha Eden and Alexander Tamir (piano duet) – DVOŘÁK: *Slavonic dances.** (*)

The Klien disc makes a worthy companion to the fine Turnabout collection of the Dvořák *Slavonic dances*. The playing here is splendid, with plenty of rhythmic nuance and an excellent sense of style. However, it must be admitted that in some cases the Brahms pieces are not quite so effective on the piano as on the orchestra. But this is the way they were conceived (Brahms, in fact, only orchestrated three of them himself), and it is unlikely we shall have a jollier performance of them, nor indeed a better recording. An excellent bargain.

Katchen and Marty are also first-rate, offering playing with real sparkle, and the recording is suitably brilliant. But Katchen plays Book 1 in Brahms's later arrangement for piano solo, so this is an alternative choice rather than being competitive with the Turnabout disc.

Eden and Tamir are a skilled and brilliant husband-and-wife duo, but in this glowing music they are not really relaxed enough. The playing has a degree of stiffness alien to the dance, and the bargain version of the Kliens on Turnabout is far preferable.

Intermezzi: in A major; in A minor, Op. 76/6 and 7; in E major, Op. 116/4; in E flat major; in B flat minor; in C sharp minor, Op. 117/1–3; in A minor; in A major; in E flat minor, Op. 118/1, 2, and 6; in B minor, Op. 119/1.
> * CBS 73093. Glenn Gould (piano).

It was a good idea to collect Brahms pieces from various opus numbers labelled *Intermezzo*; but Gould's interpretations, characterful all right, are too wilful to recommend – except to this pianist's devoted admirers. Disagreeable piano tone.

3 Intermezzi, Op. 117; Pieces, Op. 118; Pieces, Op. 119.
> ** Decca SXL 6105. Julius Katchen (piano).

3 Intermezzi, Op. 117; Rhapsody in B minor, Op. 79/1.
> ** Decca SXL 6504. Radu Lupu (piano) – SCHUBERT: *Piano sonata No. 14.***(*)

3 Intermezzi, Op. 117; Pieces, Op. 119; Variations and fugue on a theme by Handel, Op. 24.
> *** Philips SAL 3758. Stephen Bishop (piano).

3 Intermezzi, Op. 117; 2 Rhapsodies, Op. 79; Variations and fugue on a theme by Handel, Op. 24.
> (M) *** Pye Virtuoso TPLS 13035. Balint Vazsonyi (piano).

Radu Lupu's Brahms is less than wholly convincing, though his mastery of keyboard colour is impressive. These are – with the exception of the *Rhapsody* – rather wayward readings. The *Rhapsody* has plenty of fire and colour, but the Op. 117 pieces lack the sense of mystery and the poetic discipline of Stephen Bishop's Philips recital. The latter is one of the

finest records of Brahms's piano music in the catalogue. Bishop's account of the *Handel variations* is impressive, but it is in the late piano pieces on the reverse side that he shows the most remarkable degree of poetic insight. Indeed his playing is quite magical here, and more searching and thoughtful performances would be hard to find. He has the benefit of excellent recording with plenty of range and firmness of tone.

Vazsonyi's recital too offers splendid Brahms playing. It is secure technically and the contrasts of mood of the three *Intermezzi* are nicely judged. There is a similar balance between the two *Rhapsodies*, but most rewarding of all is the superbly characterized set of *Handel variations*. The variety of style and colour within this work is masterly. The slightly dry, but admirably full, bold recording suits the playing, and at medium price this is a formidable bargain.

Piano sonatas Nos. 1 in C major, Op. 1; 2 in F sharp minor, Op. 2.
> ** Decca SXL 6129. Julius Katchen (piano).

Piano sonata No. 3 in F minor, Op. 5; Intermezzi: in E flat major, Op. 117/1; in C major, Op. 119/3.
> *** Decca SXL 6041. Clifford Curzon (piano).

Piano sonata No. 3 in F minor, Op. 5; Scherzo in E flat minor, Op. 4.
> ** Decca SXL 6228. Julius Katchen (piano).
> *(*) Philips 6500 377. Claudio Arrau (piano).

Katchen's playing of the first two Brahms sonatas hardly achieves the same compelling intensity as Clifford Curzon's of Op. 5, but the result is always exciting. The playing is extremely brilliant and assured, and a certain lack of resilience in the style hardly mars the performances, rather gives them a tough individuality.

The recording is excellent. Katchen's account of Op. 5 is similarly commanding. It is preferable to Arrau's Philips version. Although this is superbly engineered the performance is a highly idiosyncratic one and Arrau's mannerisms seem obtrusive. Curzon offers the more perceptive and humane approach, and one continues to prefer his greater intensity and freshness. Technically too this record is of the finest Decca vintage, and with Curzon at his very finest, powerful and sensitive and above all spontaneous-sounding, this is unbeatable.

Double piano sonata in F minor, Op. 34.
** (*) Decca SXL 6303. Bracha Eden and Alexander Tamir (2 pianos) –
SAINT-SAËNS: *Variations.***

Brahms's *Double piano sonata* began (in 1862) as a string quintet, then became the present work (in 1863) and found fulfilment in the familiar *Piano quintet.* But in its two-piano version it is highly compelling, especially in such a committed performance as this. Eden and Tamir catch all its youthful ardour and find obvious parallels with the Op. 2 solo sonata in the same key. The music really catches fire in the first movement, and the slow *Andante* is especially convincing. Only in the finale does the fervour abate a little. Splendid recording to match the clear articulation of the playing.

Theme and variations in D minor (without opus number); *Variations on a theme by Schumann, Op. 9; Variations and fugue on a theme by Handel, Op. 24.*
** (*) DGG 2530 335. Daniel Barenboim (piano).

The rarity on Barenboim's record is the set of variations transcribed from the *Sextet,* Op. 18 – not an important work but well coupled here with two better-known sets of variations. Barenboim as so often shows himself an inspirational pianist. Both sets have received more cohesive performances on record, but Barenboim has a magical way of making the listener's attention perk up at the start of each variation. He shares his own sense of discovery with you. Excellent recording quality.

Variations on a Hungarian song, Op. 21/2; Variations on an original theme, Op. 21/1; Variations on a theme by Schumann, Op. 9.
*** Decca SXL 6219. Julius Katchen (piano).

One of the most worthwhile of the complete Brahms cycle that Katchen recorded. The *Schumann* is a neglected work and so are the others, and they are played with the utmost persuasiveness and artistry by Katchen, who is also given the benefit of a vivid recording. This is a most compelling issue.

Variations and fugue on a theme by Handel, Op. 24; Variations on a theme by Paganini, Op. 35.
* (*) Decca SXL 6218. Julius Katchen (piano).

Brilliant though Katchen's performances are, they are not the finest of his impressive cycle. Oddly enough, for all their sheer pyrotechnical display, they remain curiously uncompelling. One admired the *Ballades* (on SXL 6160) and the *Schumann variations* much more; these sound comparatively unspontaneous by their side.

Variations on a theme by Paganini, Op. 35.
(M) ** Philips Universo 6580 049. Adam Harasiewicz (piano) –
LISZT: *Hungarian rhapsodies Nos. 6 and 11; Mephisto waltz.***

A fine, spontaneous account from Adam Harasiewicz, brilliantly recorded. The individual variations are strong in character and there is plenty of sparkle when called for. The piano tone itself is perhaps just a little lacking in weight in the bass, but is otherwise clear and truthful.

Collections

Ballade in G minor, Op. 118/3; Intermezzi: in E major, Op. 116/6; in E flat major, Op. 117/1; Rhapsody in G minor, Op. 79/2; Romance in F major, Op. 118/5; Variations and fugue on a theme by Handel, Op. 24; Waltzes, Op. 39, Nos. 1, 2, 4, 6, 9, 10, 11, 13, 14 and 15.

(B) ******* Turnabout TV 34165S. Walter Klien (piano).

This disc is cleverly planned, and superbly played. It has all the excitement and spontaneity of a live recital: there are few more enjoyable collections of Brahms's piano music at any price. The piano tone is a trifle hard – some machines will react to it more kindly than others – but it has plenty of brilliance, a wide dynamic range and a firm bass. This is very necessary to encompass Klien's range of dynamic and timbre, from the *sotto voce* of some of the *Handel variations* and *Waltzes* to the stormy passions of the *Rhapsody in G minor*, which begins side two superbly. After the extremely fine and varied reading of the *Variations*, side one closes with a melting performance of the *Intermezzo in E flat*, and side two ends equally memorably with the most famous of the Brahms *Waltzes*. Whether in the fully flowering lyricism of the *Romance in F*, the staccato forcefulness of the *G minor Ballade*, or the contrasting legato of the *Intermezzo in E major*, this is pianism of the very first rank.

Capriccio in B minor, Op. 76/2; Intermezzi: in E major, Op. 116/6; in E flat major, Op. 117/1; in E minor, Op. 119/2; in C major, Op. 119/3; Rhapsody in B minor, Op. 79/1; 6 Pieces, Op. 118.

(B) **** (*)** Decca Eclipse ECS 691. Wilhelm Backhaus (piano).

We underestimated this enjoyable recital on its first appearance: Backhaus plays with great character and spontaneity. His somewhat literal manner is surprisingly compelling in the *E flat major Intermezzo*, and in the more vigorous pieces he is always interesting rhythmically. The recording is surprisingly good, and although the recital is slightly uneven in quality the best performances are very good indeed.

ORGAN MUSIC

Organ chorale preludes, Op. 122: Nos. 1, Mein Jesu; 4, Herzlich tut mich erfreuen; 8, Es ist ein Ros' entsprungen; 10, Herzlich tut mich verlangen. (Vocal) *Geistliches Lied, Op. 30; 3 Motets, Op. 110; Motets: Es ist das Heil uns kommen; O Heiland, reiss; Warum ist das Licht gegeben.*

** Argo ZRG 571. Simon Preston (organ); New English Singers.

Like a similar recording of the Bach *Chorales* the choral items here alternate with the organ pieces. It is a good idea if you like both kinds of music. Not all of these works show Brahms at his very best. Some of the organ preludes are comparatively dull and some of the vocal music is not very individual. The organ playing is excellent; the choral singing is sympathetic but not always perfectly reliable in matters of intonation. The recording is up to Argo's usual high standard.

VOCAL AND CHORAL MUSIC

Choral music: *Abendständchen, Op. 42/1; Fahr wohl, Op. 93a/4; Fest- und Gedenksprüche, Op. 109; 4 Lieder aus dem Jungbrunnen, Op. 44/7–10; Nachtwache 1 and 2, Op. 104; Schaffe in mir, Gott, Op. 29; Vineta, Op. 42/2; Waldesnacht, Op. 62/3; Warum ist das Licht gegeben, Op. 74.*

(M) *** Telefunken SMT 1288. Hamburg Monteverdi Choir, Jürgen Jürgens.

Jürgen Jürgens captures beautifully the radiance, the gentle glow of this relatively little-known music of Brahms. In most of these motets Brahms seems centuries away from his contemporaries, bothering nothing about fashion, using archaic techniques, whether from the baroque school or earlier, to produce highly individual results. Even when in *Schaffe in mir* Brahms indulges in Bachian fugues one after the other, the result is achieved naturally, with seeming ease. First-rate recording.

Lieder (collection of songs suitable for male voice).

*** HMV SLS 5002 (7 discs). Dietrich Fischer-Dieskau (baritone); Gerald Moore, Wolfgang Sawallisch or Daniel Barenboim (piano).

The seven discs in this set contain some 150 songs of Brahms, roughly three quarters of the total and a very high proportion of those suitable for male voice. The first disc (originally made in 1964) has Moore accompanying and the last two have Barenboim, which means that the four in between with Sawallisch accompanying (on the whole the most strikingly imaginative of all) present the songs in illogical order. But that matters little, when consistently Fischer-Dieskau

and his accompanists make these endlessly tuneful songs blossom within the deliberate formal restrictions which Brahms – very much a successor of Schumann rather than of Schubert – imposed on himself. As Eric Sams has so perceptively said in his BBC Music Guide, 'his songs are always ready to turn into instrumental music'. They usually represent generalized emotions rather than a specific illumination of particular poems, but Fischer-Dieskau, as in Schubert, reveals what glowing inspiration is here, leading from guileless love songs to the profundity of the *Four serious songs*. Recording quality not quite consistent, but always acceptable.

Lieder and folk-songs: *Ach, Modr, ich well en Ding han; Ach, wende diesen Blick; Am Sonntag Morgen; Da unten im Tale; Es steht ein' Lind' in jenem Tal; Es träumte mir; Feinsliebchen, du sollst mir nicht barfuss geh'n; In stiller Nacht; Das Mädchen spricht; Mädchenlied; O kühler Wald; Schwesterlein; Ständchen; Unbewegte, laue Luft; Vergebliches Ständchen; Von ewiger Liebe; Während des Regens; Wenn du nur zuweilen lächelst.*

*** BASF BAC 3065. Elly Ameling (soprano), Norman Shetler (piano).

A delightful recital, but one that is not wide in expressive range. Its intimacy has obviously been determined by Miss Ameling's careful choice of songs, which nearly all suit her simple style and natural, unforced eloquence. The gentle, smiling quality of the opening *Wenn du nur zuweilen lächelst* immediately sets the mood of the recital, which is readily sustained by the lovely second song, *Es träumte mir* ('I had a dream'). The radiant stillness of *Unbewegte, laue Luft*, the lightness of touch in the folk-song *Ach, Modr* ('Oh, mother, there's a thing I want'), and the charming *Feinsliebchen* are matched by the gay lyricism of *Ständchen*, while *In stiller nacht* is meltingly lovely. If a song like *Vergebliches Ständchen* is rather under-characterized, the approach matches the overall atmosphere of the music-making, which is reflected in Norman Shetler's sensitive, gentle accompaniments. The recording itself too is warm and soft in outline rather than especially vivid.

A German requiem, Op. 45; Variations on a theme of Haydn (St Anthony chorale), Op. 56a.

** DGG 2707 018 (2 discs). Gundula Janowitz (soprano), Eberhard Waechter (baritone), Vienna Singverein, Berlin Philharmonic Orchestra, Herbert von Karajan.

(i) *A German requiem, Op. 45.* (ii) *Alto rhapsody, Op. 53. Tragic overture, Op. 81.*

*** HMV SLS 821 (2 discs). Philharmonia Chorus and Orchestra, Otto Klemperer, with (i) Elisabeth Schwarzkopf (soprano), Dietrich Fischer-Dieskau (baritone), (ii) Christa Ludwig (mezzo-soprano).

(i) *A German requiem, Op. 45.* (ii) *4 Serious songs, Op. 121.*

** (*) DGG 2707 066 (2 discs). (i) Edith Mathis (soprano), Dietrich Fischer-Dieskau (baritone), Edinburgh Festival Chorus, London Philharmonic Orchestra, Daniel Barenboim; (ii) Dietrich Fischer-Dieskau (baritone), Daniel Barenboim (piano).

Measured and monumental, Klemperer's performance would clearly have roused Bernard Shaw's Wagnerian derision, but, as so often, Klemperer's four-square honesty defies preconceived doubts. The speeds are consistently slow – too slow in the *vivace* of the sixth move-

ment, where Death has little sting – but with dynamic contrasts underlined, the result is uniquely powerful. The solo singing is superb, and though the chorus is backwardly placed, the Philharmonia singers were at the peak of their form. Excellent recording well-refurbished, providing the additional benefit of a fill-up.

Barenboim's interpretation, individual to the point of being idiosyncratic, is enormously persuasive. Though he cannot be said to copy Furtwängler, there is something about Barenboim's approach to Brahms here which recalls the older master. The solo and choral singing is beautiful, and the recording warmly captures the widest dynamic range. It is partly to the credit of the recording but also to Barenboim's cunning that the textures are clarified. Not a great performance, as Klemperer's is, but a highly enjoyable, persuasive one.

Karajan directs a restrained, refined performance of Brahms's big choral work, but though there are many beauties, it does not oust the magnificent Klemperer performance from first place. The solo singing is good, and some may prefer Gundula Janowitz's fresh style in *Ihr habt nun Traurigkeit* to Schwarzkopf's more coaxing, more deliberately beautiful manner. But generally both Schwarzkopf and Fischer-Dieskau are preferable, and the Columbia recording is more forward. The fourth side brings a magnificent performance of the Brahms *St Anthony variations*, but that hardly sways the balance.

Liebeslieder waltzes, Op. 52; Neue Liebeslieder waltzes, Op. 65.

(B) ** Turnabout TV 34277S. Gächinger Kantorei, Helmuth Rilling; Jurgen Uhde and Renate Werner (2 pianos).

These are rather hearty, jolly performances by a biggish vocal group. They sing with accuracy and enthusiasm, and although a more intimate and delicate approach to this music can yield even greater dividends, this is enjoyable, not least because the recording is atmospheric and the balance with the pianos is apt.

Rinaldo (cantata), *Op. 50; Song of Destiny (Schicksalslied;* for chorus and orchestra), *Op. 54.*
** Decca SXL 6386. James King (tenor), Ambrosian Chorus, New Philharmonia Orchestra, Claudio Abbado.

The cantata *Rinaldo* gives some idea of what a Brahms opera might have been like, but unfortunately for dramatic impact the text provides no music for the seducing Armida, and the work is limited vocally to the male voice. A pity when it contains some rich and enjoyable music. Unfortunately James King is far from ideal in the role of Rinaldo. His Wagnerian *Heldentenor* is really too coarse for music that is much more easily lyrical than Wagner, but in the absence of a rival version this well-recorded and strongly conducted account can be recommended. The *Schicksalslied* is also beautifully played, and like the cantata has refined contributions from the Ambrosian Chorus.

Die schöne Magelone (song cycle to words by Ludwig Tieck), *Op. 33.*
** (*) HMV SAN 291. Dietrich Fischer-Dieskau (baritone), Sviatoslav Richter (piano).

Fischer-Dieskau and Richter gave an intensely memorable performance of this rare and elusive song cycle at the Aldeburgh Festival, and a year or so later were persuaded to record it. With two such strong personalities the problems presented both by Brahms's often angular writing and by the unsatisfactory dramatic basis of the piece seem unimportant. The poems were taken from a novel by Tieck, simply illustrating a story, not

really linked at all. But even so the concentration of Fischer-Dieskau and Richter gives the illusion of a coordinated work. Good recording.

4 Serious songs, Op. 121; 5 Lieder, Op. 94.
* (*) Argo ZRG 664. John Shirley-Quirk (baritone), Martin Isepp (piano) – BEETHOVEN: *An die ferne Geliebte.** (*)

John Shirley-Quirk sounds overawed by these great songs of Brahms's last years. There is little of the natural tension that one needs if settings of Biblical words are not to sound out of place. It is surprising that so intelligent a singer is not inspired to turn phrases with more imagination, to give the sudden insights into words and music that are essential in a performance to be repeated on the gramophone. The feeling of an untroubled run-through rather than a searching performance is underlined by the uninspired accompaniment of Martin Isepp. A pity that this singer did not wait a little longer before attempting these most challenging songs.

COLLECTION

'*The world of Brahms*': (i) *Academic Festival overture, Op. 80;* (ii, iii) *Piano concerto No. 2 in B flat major, Op. 83:* finale; (ii; iv) *Hungarian dance No. 5 in G minor;* (ii; v) *Symphony No. 2 in D major, Op. 73:* 3rd movement; (ii; vi) *Symphony No. 3 in F major, Op. 90:* 3rd movement; (vii) *Clarinet quintet in B minor, Op. 115:* 3rd movement; (viii) *Intermezzo in B flat minor, Op. 117/2; Rhapsody No. 2 in G minor, Op. 79/2;* (ix) *Waltz No. 15 in A flat major, Op. 39;* (x; i) *A German requiem, Op. 45: How lovely are Thy dwellings* (in German); (xi) *Wiegenlied, Op. 49/4.*

223

(B) ** Decca SPA 315. (i) Suisse Romande Orchestra, Ernest Ansermet; (ii) Vienna Philharmonic Orchestra; (iii) cond. Karl Boehm, with Wilhelm Backhaus (piano); (iv) cond. Fritz Reiner; (v) cond. Istvan Kertesz; (vi) cond. Herbert von Karajan; (vii) Alfred Boskovsky (clarinet), members of Vienna Octet; (viii) Julius Katchen (piano); (ix) Bracha Eden and Alexander Tamir (piano duet); (x) Swiss Radio Choir and Lausanne Pro Arte Choir; (xi) Renata Tebaldi (soprano), New Philharmonia Orchestra, Anton Guadagno.

Although skilfully put together to make an agreeable overall concert, this collection does not gell as successfully as some in this series. It was a mistake to open with the *Hungarian dance*, certainly part of Brahms's world but surely not of prime importance. The *Academic Festival overture*, which begins side two, would have been a better choice. But the instrumental items here are notably successful, with Julius Katchen on top form, and the lovely *Andantino* from the *Clarinet quintet* should surely tempt many into investigating the complete work. It was a happy idea to include the finale from the Backhaus version of the Brahms *Second Concerto*, a movement for which he has always been famous since his early 78 recording. The recording is consistently good throughout.

Brian, Havergal
(1876–1972)

(i; ii) *English suite No. 5 (Rustic scenes);* (i; iii) *Symphony No. 22 (Symphonia brevis);* (i; iii; iv) *Psalm 23* (for tenor, chorus and orchestra).

(M) ** (*) CBS Classics 61612. (i) Leicestershire Schools Symphony Orchestra, cond. (ii) Eric Pinkett, (iii) Laszlo Heltay; (iv) with Paul Taylor (tenor) and Brighton Festival Chorus.

The *Symphonia brevis*, two brief but ambitious movements plus epilogue, represents Havergal Brian's later work at its most enjoyable, undisciplined in its way but with an unmistakable flavour. The Psalm setting of sixty years earlier is characteristically expansive, remarkable music to be written in the early years of the century. The *Suite* is a set of colourful, lightweight pieces, deliberately unambitious but more sharply memorable than most of Brian's music. Enjoyable performances for which very few allowances have to be made. Good recording.

(i) *Symphony No. 10 in C minor;* (ii) *Symphony No. 21 in E flat major.*
** Unicorn RHS 313. Leicestershire Schools Symphony Orchestra, (i) James Loughran, (ii) Eric Pinkett.

It is left to a small company and an amateur orchestra to make the first recording of a Brian symphony. Both are works of his old age: No. 10, a powerfully-wrought and original one-movement work, dates from 1953–4 and is the more immediately appealing of the two. No. 21 was composed when he was in his late eighties and is in four movements. There need be no serious reservations about the recording, and the performances are astonishingly accomplished.

Bridge, Frank
(1879–1941)

String quartet No. 3; String quartet No. 4.
*** Argo ZRG 714. Allegri Quartet.

Those who know Frank Bridge only as the composer of amiable songs will be surprised at the adventurousness of his idiom in these two works, products of his later years, when after the First World War his whole approach to his art grew tougher, less intent on pleasing. It was at exactly this period that Benjamin Britten as a boy became his pupil, and benefited enormously from his master's concentration on self-discipline. The *Third Quartet*, a powerful piece, even shows affinities with the second Viennese school, while the pithier, more rarefied *Fourth Quartet* equally reveals the questing spirit. Two fine works beautifully played and recorded: well worth investigating.

Violoncello sonata.
*** Decca SXL 6426. Mstislav Rostropovich (cello), Benjamin Britten (piano) – SCHUBERT: *Violoncello sonata (Arpeggione)*.**(*)

Frank Bridge wrote his *Cello sonata* during the First World War. At first sight it bears all the imprints of the English pastoral school with its pastel colourings and gentle discursive lines as well as a nod in the direction of Debussy. It has a sturdy independence of outlook nonetheless and a personality to which one increasingly warms. The craftsmanship is distinguished, the lines delicately traced, and the modulations are often personal. The playing is of an altogether rare order even by the exalted standards of Rostropovich and Britten, and the recording has immediacy, warmth and great presence.

Britten, Benjamin
(born 1913)

(i; iii) *Piano concerto, Op. 13;* (ii; iii) *Violin concerto, Op. 15.*
*** Decca SXL 6512. (i) Sviatoslav Richter (piano); (ii) Mark Lubotsky (violin); (iii) English Chamber Orchestra, the composer.
Violin concerto, Op. 15.
(M) *** Supraphon SUAST 50959. Nora Grumlikova (violin), Prague Symphony Orchestra, Peter Maag – VAUGHAN WILLIAMS: *Concerto accademico*.***

Both these works come from early in Britten's career, but as the Decca performances amply confirm there is nothing immature or superficial about them. Richter – a regular visitor to Aldeburgh but still awaiting a specially composed Britten work – is incomparable in interpreting the *Piano concerto*, not only the thoughtful introspective moments but the Liszt-like bravura passages (many of them surprising from this composer). The *Violin concerto* is constructed in three movements, but the manner and idiom are subtler. With its highly original violin sonorities it makes a splendid vehicle for another Soviet artist, the young violinist, Mark Lubotsky, whose Soviet-made recording (not available in the West) persuaded the composer that here was his ideal interpreter. Recorded in the Maltings, the playing of the ECO under the composer's direction matches the inspiration of the soloists.

Grumlikova's performance too is outstanding, and the work's final *Passacaglia* is played most movingly. The recording is one of Supraphon's best, and the coupling is equally desirable. Highly recommended, in spite of a grotesquely translated sleeve-note which tells us that 'usually slow movement is supplied here with vivace with a vivid stream of technique in double stopping and harmonics'.

Matinées musicales, Op. 24; Soirées musicales, Op. 9.
(M) *** HMV SXLP 30153. Philharmonia Orchestra, Robert Irv-

ing – BLISS: *Checkmate;* LAMBERT: *Horoscope: Waltz.****

Britten wrote his *Soirées musicales* for a GPO film score in the thirties. The *Matinées musicales* were intended as straight ballet music and written in 1941. Both suites, wittily (if rather sparsely) scored, use music by Rossini which is arranged as it stands, although the personality of the arranger often comes through. The music is pleasant, and if slight, is real light music in the best sense of the word. The performances here are nicely pointed and very well recorded indeed.

Prelude and fugue for eighteen-part string orchestra, Op. 29.
   *** Argo ZRG 754. Royal Philharmonic Orchestra, Norman Del Mar – LUTYENS: *Cantata: O saisons, O châteaux;* SCHOENBERG: *Suite.****

This was originally issued on the HMV label as one of the first two Gulbenkian Foundation records, coupling valuable modern works previously unrecorded. The *Prelude and fugue for strings* was written for birthday celebrations of the Boyd Neel Orchestra during the difficult wartime period: occasional music that in its vitality has outlived the original excuse for composition. Excellent performances and good recording.

The Prince of the Pagodas (complete ballet).
   (M) *** Decca Ace of Diamonds GOS 558/9. Royal Opera House Orchestra, Covent Garden, the composer.

Britten wrote his lovely ballet score immediately after a tour of the Far East, where he had encountered the enchantment of the Balinese Gamelan orchestra. That Eastern influence was finally to find expression in his *Parables for church per-*

formance, notably *Curlew River;* but immediately, in this lighter, fairy-tale context, he drew on its influence and devised an enchanting idea for the pagoda music. This recording was originally made after the first performances at Covent Garden in January 1957. The stereo version sounds astonishingly well, with Britten's many offbeat fanfares ringing out superbly. Highly recommended; Britten's music, more than that of most long ballets, is concentrated enough in its argument to stand gramophone repetition.

Simple symphony (for strings), Op. 4.
   *** Decca SXL 6405. English Chamber Orchestra, the composer (with *Concert****).
   (M) *** Philips Universo 6580 045. I Musici (with *Concert.*** (*)).
   ** Pye Ensayo NEL 2012. English Chamber Orchestra, Enrique Asensio – HINDEMITH: *5 Pieces for strings;* RESPIGHI: *Ancient airs and dances: suite 3.***

(i) *Simple symphony (for strings), Op. 4;* (ii) *The Young Person's Guide to the Orchestra (Variations and fugue on a theme of Purcell), Op. 34.*
   (M) ** HMV SXLP 30114. (i) Royal Philharmonic, (ii) BBC Symphony Orchestras, Sir Malcolm Sargent – WALTON: *Façade suites.***

From the composer an infectious and beautifully recorded performance of his little masterpiece based on juvenilia. For many of us this remains one of Britten's most spontaneous works; for all its simplicity the quality of the music itself is high, and the *Playful pizzicato* and *Frolicsome finale* are worthy of the young Mozart. The composer could have made no better personal contribution to his anthology of music by Bridge, Delius, Elgar and Purcell. This record, like the I

Musici concert of *Modern string music*, is discussed in our companion *Treasury* volume. The performance by the Italian group is distinguished. The slow movement is particularly memorable, played with considerable feeling and atmosphere. Both these accounts are generally preferable to Asensio's, which is well played but rather serious in tone. There is no hint of humour in the approach to Britten's youthful score, but no condescension either, and the finale is brilliantly done. If the couplings are attractive the recording is very lively. The surfaces, however, are not as silent as they should be.

Sargent gives his broad, authoritative reading of Britten's *Variations* and very enjoyable it is. The recording is faithful and reproduces extremely well on both big and modest equipment. In the *Simple symphony*, however, Sargent is rather bland. Surely the *Frolicsome finale* needs more of a feeling of irrepressible high spirits, and the bouncy trio of the *Playful pizzicato* could have a lighter touch.

Sinfonia da requiem, Op. 20.
   *** Decca SXL 6175. New Philharmonia Orchestra, the composer – *Cantata misericordium.****
(i) *Sinfonia da requiem, Op. 20*; (ii) *Symphony for cello and orchestra, Op. 68.*
   *** Decca SXL 6641. (i) New Philharmonia Orchestra, (ii) Mstislav Rostropovich (cello), English Chamber Orchestra, both cond. the composer.
Symphony for cello and orchestra, Op. 68.
   *** Decca SXL 6138 (performance as above) – HAYDN: *Cello concerto in C major.****

The *Sinfonia da requiem* was first issued coupled to the *Cantata misericordium*. The performance is a definitive one and the recording excellent. Many may prefer the new coupling of the *Cello symphony*, which is also available coupled to Haydn's *C major Concerto*. The performance of the *Cello symphony* is everything one could ask for, and with the help of the score it immediately dispelled any lingering doubts about the music. That initial impression of aridness was misleading. The style is not so immediately approachable perhaps as that of Britten's earlier works, but the same clarity of argument, the same magical use of sound is everywhere, and if at moments there is an echo of Shostakovich (deliberate compliment to the Russians?) or in the main theme of the finale a seemingly direct imitation of Copland's open-air style, the Britten characteristics are always uppermost. Though the work lasts a full thirty-five minutes, the recording is magnificent, and the English Chamber Orchestra fully justify the choice of players with splendid support for Rostropovich.

(i) *Sinfonia da requiem, Op. 20*; (ii) *The Young Person's Guide to the Orchestra (Variations and fugue on a theme of Purcell), Op. 34.*
   (M) ** CBS Classics 61427. (i) St Louis Symphony Orchestra, André Previn; (ii) Philadelphia Orchestra, Eugene Ormandy.

Previn's account of the *Sinfonia da requiem* is no match for the composer's own, which has the advantage of superb orchestral playing and a recording of wide range and splendid richness of sonority. Previn's orchestra plays with great spirit and his performance is obviously keenly felt; the recording, though it dates from the early 1960s, is well detailed. However, for all its merits, the composer's own performance is the one to have and well worth the extra money. Ormandy's account of the *Young Person's Guide* is brilliantly played and well recorded, though there is some congestion towards the end of the side.

Soirées musicales, Op. 9.

(M) ** CBS Classics 61365. Orchestra, André Kostelanetz – WALTON: *Capriccio burlesco; Façade suite No. 1; Johannesburg festival overture.*** (*)

Britten's arrangement of Rossini pieces represents light music at its best. Kostelanetz presents it with verve if not ideal delicacy.

Variations on a theme of Frank Bridge, Op. 10.

(M) *** HMV SXLP 30157. Bath Festival Orchestra, Yehudi Menuhin – TIPPETT: *Concerto for double string orchestra.***

(M) ** (*) Supraphon SUAST 50509. Czech Chamber Orchestra, Josef Vlach – STRAVINSKY: *Apollo.* (*)

(i) *Variations on a theme of Frank Bridge, Op. 10;* (ii) *The Young Person's Guide to the Orchestra (Variations and fugue on a theme of Purcell), Op. 34.*

*** Decca SXL 6450. (i) English Chamber Orchestra, (ii) London Symphony Orchestra, both cond. the composer.

Britten's set of *Variations on a theme of Frank Bridge* was conceived as a brilliant display piece for the Boyd Neel Orchestra, but there is no gainsaying the genuine depth Menuhin finds in the *Funeral march, Chant* and *Epilogue.* This is undoubtedly an outstandingly satisfying performance (with its equally fine Tippett coupling the disc is a bargain), and comparison with Britten's own account is fascinating. The latter is more restrained, helped by a rather less immediate but even clearer recording than the HMV one. This suits Menuhin's less fastidious approach, and bolder romantic contours.

Britten goes more for half-tones and he achieves an almost circumspect coolness in the waltz-parody of the *Romance.* In the Viennese waltz section later Britten is again subtly atmospheric, and in the *Funeral march* the composer is more solemn than Menuhin, showing here, as in the finale, that this is music to be taken seriously for all the lighthearted mood of the opening sections of the work. With its superb sound – a little under-recorded, but very natural – this is another example of Britten at his most convincing and spontaneous in the recording studio.

Vlach and his Czech players miss some of the light and shade which Britten himself found in these variations with their element of delicate tongue-in-cheek parody. But the incisiveness of the dotted rhythms in the *March* is thrilling, and always the Czech orchestra produces sonorous string tone in playing that is rarely less than passionate. Good recording.

The Young Person's Guide to the Orchestra (Variations and fugue on a theme of Purcell), Op. 34.

*** Decca SXL 6110 (without narration). London Symphony Orchestra, the composer – *Serenade.***

*** HMV ASD 2935. André Previn (narrator), London Symphony Orchestra, Previn – PROKOFIEV: *Peter and the Wolf.***

** (*) Decca Phase 4 PFS 4104. Sean Connery (narrator), Royal Philharmonic Orchestra, Antal Dorati – PROKOFIEV: *Peter and the Wolf.***(*)

(B) ** Classics for Pleasure CFP 185. Richard Baker (narrator), New Philharmonia Orchestra, Raymond Leppard – PROKOFIEV: *Peter and the Wolf.***

(M) ** Philips 6599 436 (without narration). Concertgebouw Orchestra, Bernard Haitink – PROKO-FIEV: *Peter and the Wolf.***

* (*) Columbia Studio 2 TWO 259. Eric Porter (narrator), Orchestre de Paris, Igor Markevitch – PROKOFIEV: *Peter and the Wolf** (*) (see p. 719).

Britten takes a very brisk view of his *Variations*, so brisk that even the LSO players cannot always quite match him. But every bar has a vigour which makes the music sound even more youthful than usual, and the headlong, uninhibited account of the final fugue (trombones as vulgar as you like) is an absolute joy. An unexpected coupling for the *Serenade* on the reverse, but a marvellous one for old and young alike. Outstanding recording, except that at one point the trumpet is pushed from one side to the other: only a very technically minded listener need worry about that.

Quite apart from the brilliance of the LSO's playing and the ripe realism of the recording, Previn's account of the *Young Person's Guide* is characterized by his own dry microphone manner in the narration. This is obviously directed at older children than those to whom Mia Farrow is talking in *Peter and the Wolf*, but it still makes a delightful coupling.

The Sean Connery/Dorati version is obviously aimed at the listener whose knowledge of the orchestra is minimal. Connery's easy style is attractive, and this version should go down well with young people, even if some of the points are heavily made. The orchestral playing is first-rate (although there is a momentary lack of perfection of ensemble by one of the percussion players at the beginning) and the Phase 4 techniques which can – and do – bring forward solo instruments and sections of the orchestra seem quite justifiable. The sound is abundantly clear, with a slight but consistent exaggeration of timbre contributing a certain pithiness to the variations for the various string sub-sections, but the overall effect is con-

vincing and exciting. This is perhaps not everyone's version, but many will like it very much, for it has an attractive spontaneous quality to which Connery contributes not a little.

The rather cosy narration by Richard Baker seems to hold up the flow of the music. The orchestral playing is lively and the recording vivid, but one feels that there are too many words here: this is not a version to stand constant repetition, although it would be admirable for school use or for a public library collection.

Haitink's is a comparatively straight-forward performance, with no special imaginative insight or sparkle. Partly because of the acoustic the climax of the fugue at the end lacks refinement, but taken as a whole the account, which is well played, is quite compelling.

Eric Porter as narrator certainly assumes the Soames mantle, for this is the kind of seriously-intentioned explanation of Britten's score which that most famous of the Forsytes might well have given. The continual interruptions hold up any possible forward flow in the music, and this is only really suitable for a school classroom, good though playing and recording are.

INSTRUMENTAL AND CHAMBER MUSIC

Suite: *The Courtly Dances from Gloriana (Marche; Corante; Pavan; Morris dance; Galliard; La Volta; March)* (arr. Bream).

*** RCA SB 6635. Julian Bream Consort – RODRIGO: *Concerto*; VIVALDI: *Lute concerto.*** (*)

Like all Britten's operas, *Gloriana*, with its moving portrayal of the ageing Queen and the fall of her ex-lover, Essex, is reliably gripping in the theatre. One of the highlights of the score is this group of Elizabethan dances, originally played by a small stage orchestra. The freshness of invention contains only a suggestion of pastiche, and although the emotional depth of the deceptively simple yet eloquent *Pavan* suggests a later century, somehow there is no feeling of anachronism. Julian Bream's arrangement for his six players is brilliantly done, and the music's wit emerges as strongly as its variety of melodic invention. The playing and recording here bring over all the spontaneity and warmth of a live performance.

Gemini variations (12 variations and fugue on a theme of Kodaly; for flute, violin and piano, four hands*), Op. 73.*
> *** Decca SXL 6264. Gabriel and Zoltan Jeney – *Psalm 150; Songs from Friday afternoons.****

The *Gemini variations* came in response to the insistent pleas of two young Hungarian boys, the Jeney twins, who perform the work here. Britten's ingenuity in switching the two young performers between one instrument and another (one plays violin, the other flute, and both the piano) is breathtaking, for the musical thread is never interrupted, and the final cadence brings a real coup, when all four instruments are somehow sounded together. A rare delight for youthful listeners of all ages.

Phantasy quartet for oboe, violin, viola and cello, Op. 2; Metamorphoses for solo oboe, Op. 49; String quartet No. 2 in C major, Op. 36.
> (M) ** (*) Supraphon SUAST 50960. Vítezslav Hánus (oboe), Janáček Quartet.

It is good to have superb Czech players taking up so convincingly some of Britten's most imaginative chamber works. The Janáček Quartet is one of the very finest groups in the world, and their

fervent playing helps to draw together the *Second string Quartet*, a strikingly original structure – a pithy sonata movement, a mysterious scherzo and an angular but imposing final chaconne as long as the first two movements put together. This is very nearly as fine as the Amadeus version on Argo (see below), and has a more suitable coupling of the two Britten works with oboe, the early *Phantasy Quartet*, with its unmistakable fingerprints, and the strange sequence of pieces for solo oboe. Hanus has a sharp, bright tone, caught well by the recording.

String quartets Nos. 1 in D major, Op. 25; 2 in C major, Op. 36.
> *** Decca SXL 6564. Allegri Quartet.
> (B) ** Pye GSGC 14025. Fidelio Quartet.

Britten's *Second Quartet* has been recorded a number of times, but never before with such rich sound as on this Decca issue, one of the finest recordings of a string quartet in the catalogue. The *First Quartet* makes a natural coupling, not so richly individual as the later piece but a striking youthful inspiration which the Allegri players interpret with a keen sense of drama.

Comparing the Pye group (unnamed individually on sleeve and label) in the *Second Quartet* with the Allegri on the fine Decca issue, one finds the music sounding quite different. It is not just that the Allegri playing has extra polish, but that the argument seems so much clearer and more compelling. But despite lack of polish, the Fidelio players have plenty of gusto, and when the works – both of them from early in Britten's career – are among the most interesting of modern quartets, that is the main thing. Indeed the *First Quartet* opens with one of those completely magical Britten sounds (a unique combination of notes and texture) that haunts the memory long after the record has been put away.

String quartet No. 2 in C major, Op. 36.
*** Argo ZRG 5372. Amadeus Quartet – FRICKER: *Quartet No. 2.****

The Amadeus Quartet plays the Britten No. 2 quartet immaculately. The first movement, in a kind of sonata form, is most memorable in its spare way; the scherzo is headlong and daemonic, with extraordinary banshee wails on muted instruments; and the final *Chacony* pays its direct tribute to Purcell, for whose 250th anniversary the work was written. The *Chacony* may seem disproportionately long, but Britten's ingenuity in variation form more than sustains interest, and the culmination is most powerful. The recording is excellent.

Suite for violin and piano, Op. 6.
(B) ** Pye GSGC 14111. Mary Nemet (violin), Roxanne Wruble (piano) – WALTON: *Violin sonata.** (*)
(M) ** Supraphon SUAST 50707. Ladislav Jašek (violin), Josef Hála (piano) – DALLAPICCOLA: *Tartiniana*; PROKOFIEV: *Sonata.***

Britten's *Suite for violin and piano* dates from 1935, but already shows much of that mastery which later works have proved time and time again. The five movements are beautifully contrasted, and they are played with great finesse and feeling by the excellent duo on Supraphon, Jašek and Hála.

The contrast between this Britten work, written when the composer was in his early twenties, and the rather overripe Walton work on the reverse of the Pye disc is astonishing. The Walton is expansive to the point of luxuriance, while from the very opening this *Suite* is sharp and commanding, and every idea is crisply and cleanly placed without fuss. Its style suits Nemet and Wruble very

well: the wit and brilliance are brought out as well as the deeper underlying emotions that even the youthful Britten could not conceal. First-rate recording.

Suite No. 1 for unaccompanied cello, Op. 72; Suite No. 2 for unaccompanied cello, Op. 80.
*** Decca SXL 6393. Mstislav Rostropovich (cello).

This is tough, gritty music in Britten's latter-day manner. It is characteristic of him that, not content with tackling the almost insoluble problem of writing for solo cello in a single work, he writes a sequel. The *First Suite*, with its clean-cut genre pieces, remains the more strikingly memorable of the two, but when Rostropovich gives an inspired account of the *Second Suite*, its even grittier manner reveals more and more with repetition on record. Fine recording; superlative performances.

Violoncello sonata in C major, Op. 65.
*** Decca SXL 2298. Mstislav Rostropovich (cello), Benjamin Britten (piano) – DEBUSSY: *Sonata*; SCHUMANN: *Fünf Stücke.***
(M) ** Supraphon SUAST 50559. Stanislav Apolin (cello), Radoslav Kvapil (piano) – KABALEVSKY: *Cello sonata.***

This strange, five-movement work was written specially for Rostropovich's appearance at the Aldeburgh Festival of 1961, and the recording was made soon after the first performance. It is unlike anything Britten had written previously. The idiom itself is unexpected, sometimes recalling Soviet models as in the spiky *March*, perhaps out of tribute to the dedicatee. Then although technically it demands fantastic feats from the cellist it is hardly a display piece. Each of the five movements is poised and concentrated. It is an excellent work to wrestle with on a record, particularly when the performance is never likely to be outshone. The recording is superb in every way.

It is always interesting to have a fresh view of a work specially associated with particular performers. The Czech players give an intense, thoughtful performance. But if you go back to the earlier record with Rostropovich accompanied by the composer, you will find – predictably enough – dozens of felicities and points of imagination missing here. The Czech issue is also very well recorded.

Two pieces for two pianos, Op. 23: Introduction and Rondo alla Burlesca; Mazurka elegiaca.

> (M) ** Supraphon SUAST 50694. Vera and Vlastimil Lejsek (pianos) – LUTOSLAWSKI: *Variations***; STRAVINSKY: *Concerto.** (*)

Britten's writing for piano is strangely angular, and such a piece as the *Rondo alla Burlesca* quickly runs into involvement that refuses to fit under the fingers. By contrast the preceding *Introduction* with its chains of fourths has the sort of illuminating simplicity one associates with the piano accompaniments to Britten's songs. The *Mazurka elegiaca* too runs a charmed course between the demands of an elegy and a vigorous dance. Both pieces were written during the dark days of the war, the *Mazurka* in memory of Paderewski. The Czech pianists here plainly enjoy the music, and with the Stravinsky and Lutoslawski works for coupling it makes an interesting and unusual two-piano disc, well recorded.

VOCAL AND CHORAL MUSIC

(i) *A Boy Was Born (Choral variations), Op. 3; Rejoice in the Lamb (Festival cantata), Op. 30.*

> (B) *** Decca Eclipse ECS 628. Purcell Singers with (i) boys' voices of the English Opera and Choir of All Saints, Margaret Street, the composer.

For this Eclipse reissue *A Boy Was Born* is presented in a good, genuine early stereo recording, whereas *Rejoice in the Lamb* is a stereo transcription of a mono master tape. But it would be a brave man who (without knowing) could tell which was which, for the recording of the latter work is very clear and immediate, with plenty of body and atmosphere. Both works represent early Britten at his freshest. *A Boy Was Born* was written just before Britten was twenty, but there is little hint of immaturity. *Rejoice in the Lamb* is a moving setting of words by the mad poet Christopher Smart – strikingly memorable. Both performances are splendid.

(i; ii) *Cantata academica;* (ii) *Hymn to St Cecilia, Op. 17; Hymn to the Virgin; Gloriana: Choral dances.*

> (M) *** Oiseau-Lyre SOL 60037. (i) Jennifer Vyvyan (soprano), Helen Watts (contralto), Peter Pears (tenor), Owen Brannigan (bass); (ii) LSO Chorus, London Symphony Orchestra, George Malcolm.

(i) *Cantata academica;* (ii) *Cantata misericordium, Op. 69;* (iii) *Rejoice in the Lamb (Festival cantata), Op. 30.*

> *** Decca SXL 6640. (i) as above recording; (ii) Peter Pears (tenor), Dietrich Fischer-Dieskau (baritone), LSO Chorus, London Symphony Orchestra, the composer; (iii) Robert Tear (tenor), Forbes Robinson (bass), St John's College Choir, George Guest.

Cantata misericordium, Op. 69.

> *** Decca SXL 6175 (as above

recording) – *Sinfonia da requiem.****

As with other Britten works Decca offer us a choice of couplings. More than anything the *Cantata Academica*, written for Basle University, is a work of joy. It is specially remarkable from a composer who was so soon to write the *War requiem* for Coventry. There is no cynicism here, only a reflection of the world in the most optimistic terms possible. But then the ultimate message of the *War requiem* too is optimistic, Britten no escapist. The final movements of each half of this work, a scherzo for part one and a Canon, Ostinato and Chorale for part two, have the exhilaration of the allelujahs which end *Belshazzar's feast*, and the idiom is surprisingly similar. Even Britten's tone-row (used not dodecaphonically but as a scheme of tonality for the thirteen movements), turns up as a meltingly beautiful melody in the seventh movement. Not least remarkable is the work's compression: it fits comfortably on to one side. The recording is beautifully clear and well-balanced. The *Hymn to the Virgin* is an early work, written in 1930, and the *Hymn to St Cecilia*, a much more ambitious piece, is also from the thirties, though later, just before the war, when Britten's technique was already prodigious. His setting exactly matches the imaginative, capricious words of Auden. The *Gloriana* dances confirm what riches there are in this seriously under-rated opera: dare one hope for a complete recording one day? The engineers have again done admirably, with clear, brilliant sound.

sxl 6175 happily couples an old work and a new one, and the coupling underlines the link both works have with Britten's *War requiem*. The reminder of the *War requiem* is the more striking in the *Cantata* in that the same soloists are used; but both here and in the earlier, purely orchestral *Sinfonia da requiem* the composer's theme is again the resolution of tremendous stress in a peace and tranquillity which come from within. At the end of the cantata the beautiful *Dormi nunc* ('*Sleep now*') in a gentle 9/8 rhythm is close in mood to the *Requiem aeternam* of the *Sinfonia* with its blissful tapestry of flutes and harp. Both performances are definitive, with the New Philharmonia in the *Sinfonia* and the smaller group from the LSO in the cantata playing with equal excellence. The solo singing too is memorable, and with superb Decca sound, this disc cannot be too highly recommended.

Canticles: My beloved is mine, Op. 40; Abraham and Isaac, Op. 51; Still falls the rain, Op. 55.
*** Argo zrg 5277. John Hahessy (alto), Peter Pears (tenor), Barry Tuckwell (horn), the composer (piano).

Abraham and Isaac, much the longest of the three *Canticles*, draws its text, as *Noyes Fludde* does, from the Chester Miracle Plays. Britten conveys the drama of the situation with extraordinary economy. Naturally much depends on the concentration of the tenor soloist as well as the pianist, for they both have passages that sound almost like extemporization. Hahessy takes the small part of Isaac. Much more concentrated is the third canticle, *Still falls the rain*, to words by Edith Sitwell. It was written in memory of the pianist Noel Mewton-Wood. Here the important horn obbligato is beautifully played by Barry Tuckwell to match the definitive performances of Pears and the composer.

A Ceremony of Carols, Op. 28.
(b) *** Argo spa 164. St John's College Choir, George Guest; Marisa Robles (harp) (with *Collection: 'The world of Christmas'****).
** BASF bac 3061. Vienna Boys' Choir, Anton Neyder; Elisabeth

Bayer (harp) – BRUCKNER: *Motets.***

A Ceremony of Carols, Op. 28. A Boy Was Born, Op. 3. Corpus Christi carol. Friday Afternoons: A New Year carol. Missa brevis in D major, Op. 63.

(M) ** Chapter One CMS 1007. Coventry Cathedral Boys' Choir, David Lepine; John Marson (harp) – DERING: *Motets.***

A Ceremony of Carols, Op. 28; Hymn to St Cecilia, Op. 17; Missa brevis in D major, Op. 63.

(M) ** (*) HMV HQS 1285. King's College Chapel Choir, David Willcocks; Osian Ellis (harp).

A Ceremony of Carols, Op. 28; Missa brevis in D major, Op. 63; Rejoice in the Lamb (Festival cantata), Op. 30.

*** Argo ZRG 5440. Robert Tear (tenor), Forbes Robinson (bass), St John's College Choir, George Guest; Marisa Robles (harp), Brian Runnett (organ).

Argo have provided us with a definitive recording of the *Ceremony of Carols*, one of Britten's freshest and more spontaneous works. The earlier Argo version was most disappointing in its lack of bite, partly the fault of the recording. This new version has an equal vitality, more spacious sound, and a superb contribution from Marisa Robles on the harp who plays with masterly sensitivity, especially in her solo *Interlude*. The performance of *Rejoice in the Lamb* is very similar to Britten's own but much better recorded, and the *Missa brevis* has the same striking excellence of style. As can be seen above, the *Ceremony of Carols* is also available on Argo's cheapest label coupled to a delectable selection of traditional carols and modern settings. This is one of the finest records of Christmas music in the catalogue.

Although not so polished and subtle as the superlative performance by the St John's Choir, the Coventry version of the *Ceremony of Carols* is attractively alert and direct in style. The recording producer does not make as much as he might of the opening and closing *Procession*, and *Deo gratias* lacks something in exuberance at its climax. This seems to damn the record with faint praise, but the fresh, positive style is enjoyable enough, and especially so in the *Missa brevis*. The choir's treble soloists, Jonathan Cooke and Paul Daniel, are both excellent and they manage the two Britten solo carols pleasingly. The Dering motets too are well done, and the recording throughout is of a high standard. John Marson, the harp soloist, plays capably if with no special imaginative touch.

It is good too to find a Viennese choir tackling Britten's masterpiece. They sing sturdily, if without a great deal of light and shade, and no attempt is made to create the processional effect of the choir approaching and departing at the beginning and end of the work. The recording is good rather than outstanding, not especially clear and without a compensating atmosphere. But the coupling is unusual and quite attractive.

There was a time when Britten's insistence on earthly boyish tone among trebles seemed at the farthest remove from the King's tradition. But towards the end of David Willcocks's stay at Cambridge, a happy accommodation was achieved not only in appearances of the choir at the Aldeburgh Festival but in this excellent record, conveniently coupling three of Britten's most appealing choral pieces. The King's trebles may still have less edge in the *Ceremony of Carols* than their rivals in Cambridge at St John's College, and the *Missa brevis* can certainly benefit from throatier sound, but the results here are dramatic as well as beautiful. Fine recording.

A Charm of Lullabies (song cycle), *Op. 41*. Folk-song arrangements: *The ash grove; The bonny Earl o' Moray; Come*

you not from Newcastle?; O can ye sew cushions?; Oliver Cromwell; O waly, waly; The sally gardens; Sweet Polly Oliver; There's none to soothe; The trees they grow so high.
** Decca SXL 6413. Bernadette Greevy (contralto), Paul Hamburger (piano).

Bernadette Greevy cannot match Pears or Ferrier in the folk-songs, but it is good to hear them again in the contralto register. Her voice is beautiful enough to make one forgive any slight shortcoming over control of dynamic or projection of word-meaning. In the cycle of lullabies Greevy is particularly impressive in the Scottish snapping of *The highland balou*. First-rate recording.

Children's Crusade; The Golden Vanity.
*** Decca SET 445. Wandsworth School Boys' Choir, Russell Burgess; the composer (piano).

Like most of Britten's output these two examples of his work for children were both written for specific occasions and performers. *The Golden Vanity* is a 'vaudeville' written for the members of the Vienna Boys' Choir, who asked for a piece which didn't involve their dressing up as girls (as most of their vaudevilles do). The tale of the cabin boy who sinks the threatening pirate ship and is then disowned by his wicked captain is simply and vividly told with the help of the well-known folk-song, and the recording does wonders in recapturing the fun of performance with its play ritual round the stage. The Wandsworth Boys are fresher and more idiomatic than the original Viennese. The other work, written for the fiftieth anniversary of the Save the Children Fund, is darker, a setting of a Brecht poem which in the most direct way, with vivid percussion effects, tells of the tragedy of children lost in Poland in 1939.

Festival Te Deum, Op. 32; Jubilate Deo; Rejoice in the Lamb (Festival cantata), Op. 30; Te Deum in C major.
*** HMV ASD 3035. James Bowman (counter-tenor), King's College Chapel Choir, Philip Ledger; James Lancelot (organ), David Corkhill (percussion) – BERNSTEIN: *Chichester Psalms.***

It was apt that Philip Ledger, for long active at the Aldeburgh Festival, should devote most of his first record as director of King's College Choir to the music of Britten. He scores a notable first in using here a new version of the cantata *Rejoice in the Lamb* with timpani and percussion added to the original organ part. The differences are minor, but they add to the weight and drama of this haunting setting of the words of the mad poet Christopher Smart. The biting climaxes are sung with passionate incisiveness, while the soloists make an attractive contrast one with another – James Bowman the counter-tenor in the delightful passage which tells you that 'the mouse is a creature of great personal valour'. The *Te Deum* settings and the *Jubilate* make an excellent coupling along with Bernstein's *Chichester Psalms*. First-rate recording.

(i) *The Holy Sonnets of John Donne, Op. 35;* (ii) *Songs and Proverbs of William Blake, Op. 74.*
*** Decca SXL 6391. (i) Peter Pears (tenor); (ii) Dietrich Fischer-Dieskau (baritone); both with the composer (piano).

It was high time that Peter Pears re-recorded in a modern LP version the *Donne sonnet* cycle, in some ways the deepest of the many sets of songs written for him by Benjamin Britten. This performance now sets a definitive standard, with Pears's voice still amazingly even,

235

coping beautifully with both the dramatic outbursts and the lyrical soaring which in fine contrast put this among the richest of modern song cycles. The *Blake* cycle, written much more recently with Fischer-Dieskau's voice in mind and here recorded by the dedicatee, makes an excellent coupling. It is an equally tough, intense setting of equally visionary words, but following Britten's latter-day pattern it presents fewer moments of sweetness or relaxation. The composer's bright eye and keen, original ear remain the same, however, compelling attention. Ideal performances, with the composer recreating his inspiration.

(i) *Les Illuminations* (song cycle), *Op. 18;* (ii) *Serenade for tenor, horn and strings, Op. 31.*

    *** Decca SXL 6449. Peter Pears (tenor), English Chamber Orchestra, the composer; (ii) with Barry Tuckwell (horn).

This superb interpretation of the *Serenade* by Peter Pears appeared first in coupling with Britten's *Young Person's Guide*, but this pairing with the earlier song cycle is clearly more logical. Pears's voice is so ideally suited to this music, his insight into word-meaning as well as into phrase-shaping so masterly, that for once one can use the word 'definitive'. With dedicated accompaniment under the composer's direction and superb recording this is a disc to recommend to all who have yet to discover the magic of Britten's music.

The Journey of the Magi, Op. 86; Tit for Tat (settings of Walter de la Mare); *Who are these children?* (cycle), *Op. 84.*

    *** Decca SXL 6608. Peter Pears (tenor), John Shirley-Quirk (baritone), James Bowman (countertenor), the composer (piano) – PURCELL: *Songs.****

This provides a convenient coupling of three Britten works previously unrecorded – the early songs, *Tit for Tat*, almost unbelievably assured juvenilia, sung here by John Shirley-Quirk; the settings of poems by the Scots poet William Soutar, *Who are these children?*; and the Fourth Canticle, *The Journey of the Magi*. The Soutar poems, cryptic and not quite as full of nursery innocence as they might seem to be, inspire a bald, direct style and are strongly sung by Pears. The Canticle, a setting of T. S. Eliot, has the three voices brilliantly matched and contrasted, a vivid, unforgettable piece. The recording, made in the Maltings, has warm but undistracting reverberation.

Nocturne (for tenor solo, 7 obbligato instruments and string orchestra), *Op. 60.*

    ** Argo ZRG 737. Robert Tear (tenor), Academy of St Martin-in-the-Fields, Neville Marriner – MAHLER: *Lieder.***

(i) *Nocturne, Op. 60;* (ii) *Peter Grimes: Four sea interludes and Passacaglia.*

    *** Decca SXL 2189. (i) Peter Pears (tenor), wind soloists, strings of the London Symphony Orchestra; (ii) soloists, Chorus and Orchestra of the Royal Opera House, Covent Garden; both cond. the composer.

In this wide-ranging cycle on the subject of night and sleep, Britten chooses from a diverse selection of poems – Coleridge, Tennyson, Wordsworth, Wilfred Owen and Keats, finishing with a Shakespeare sonnet. It is a work full – as so much of Britten's output is – of memorable moments. One thinks of the 'breathing' motif on the strings which links the different songs, the brilliant dialogue for flute and clarinet in the Keats setting, and above all the towering climax of the Wordsworth excerpt. Each song has a different obbligato instrument (with the ensemble unified for the final Shakespeare song), and each instrument gives the song it is associated with its own individual character. The Decca performance is as nearly definitive as anything could be. Pears as always is the ideal interpreter, the composer a most efficient conductor, and the fiendishly difficult obbligato parts are played superbly. The recording is brilliant and clear, with just the right degree of atmosphere. The *Four sea interludes* and *Passacaglia* are taken from the complete recording. This means that odd extracts from the vocal parts are included and the general effect is not so tidy as in the concert version. But that proviso apart these are wonderfully vital accounts of some superbly atmospheric music.

Robert Tear is a tenor very much of the school of Peter Pears, and it is disappointing to find him underlining the interpretative points in the *Nocturne* on the one hand and missing the finer overtones on the other. Even in sound – less clear than Pears's much earlier version – this is no improvement.

Noye's Fludde.
    *** Argo ZNF 1. Owen Brannigan (bass), Sheila Rex (contralto), Trevor Anthony (bass), East Suffolk Children's Chorus and Orchestra, English Opera Group Orchestra, Norman Del Mar.

Even when Britten has long been renowned as the supreme master of deceptive simplicity it is easy to be fooled into under-rating the musical value of this children's oratorio to words from the Chester Miracle Play. You can play through the piano score from beginning to end and wonder what the fuss was about, but the record brilliantly captures the flavour of a live performance together with the intense emotion hidden only just below the surface. There are a number of moments when the sheer

felicity is liable to strike home and overwhelm the listener – the entry of the animals into the Ark, the sound of *Eternal Father* rising above the storm, the atmospheric moments after the storm.

All the effects have been miraculously well captured, particularly the entry into the Ark. In a church the children dressed as animals rush down the centre aisle singing, shouting or squeaking their *Kyrie Eleisons* as they go to the Ark, while from the porch a bugle band blares out fanfares which finally turn into a rollicking march. All this has been caught in a way which makes this one of the finest examples of stereo yet heard. Another excellent passage to sample is the syncopated little song that Noah's children sing as the Ark is built. The recording was made during the 1961 Aldeburgh Festival and not only the professional soloists but the children too have the time of their lives to the greater glory of God. A wonderful record.

On this Island (song cycle to poems by W. H. Auden); *7 Sonnets of Michelangelo; Winter Words* (song cycle to poems by Thomas Hardy).
    (M) *** HMV HQS 1310. Robert Tear (tenor), Philip Ledger (piano).

Where in the *Nocturne* Tear gives a comparatively heavy, unconvincing interpretation of a Britten cycle, here he is back at his freshest and most communicative. It is a generous coupling to include not only the intensely atmospheric Hardy settings and the deeply expressive Michelangelo settings but also the rarer settings of Auden, which date from the beginning of Britten's career. These last may be less felicitous, a degree more effortful, than the later songs, but they are still strikingly individual. Excellent accompaniment by Philip Ledger, and good recording.

Parables for Church Performance

3 Parables for church performance:
Curlew River; The Burning Fiery Furnace; The Prodigal Son.
>   *** Decca 1 BB 101/3. Peter Pears
>   (tenor), John Shirley-Quirk (bari-
>   tone), Robert Tear (tenor), Eng-
>   lish Opera Group, Benjamin
>   Britten and Viola Tunnard.

Britten's conception of the church parable, so highly individual with its ritual elements (the audience turned into a medieval congregation), yet allows wide variety within these three works. Having them together in an album (with a substantial saving in price, incidentally) underlines both similarities and the profound contrasts – *Curlew River* the most visionary of the three; *The Burning Fiery Furnace* the most dramatic; *The Prodigal Son* the most consoling. Performances and recordings are immaculate.

Curlew River (1st parable for church performance).
>   *** Decca SET 301. Peter Pears
>   (tenor), John Shirley-Quirk (bari-
>   tone), Harold Blackburn (bass)
>   and others, instrumental ensemble
>   dir. the composer and Viola
>   Tunnard.

Few dramatic works have been based on a more unlikely idea than *Curlew River*. Whether you call it an opera or, as the composer does himself, a parable for church performance, the result is a dramatic entertainment that defies all convention. The work was initially inspired by Britten's recollections of a Noh-play which he saw in Japan, and in *Curlew River* he not only chose his story from a Noh-play (transferring it to a medieval monastery in East Anglia by the Curlew River) but deliberately adopted the slowest possible pace for the bald, uncomplicated drama. There are overtones too of Eastern music (Balinese rather than Japanese) in the highly original instrumentation and often free approach to rhythm, but mainly the work's ultimate success stems from the vividness of atmosphere within a monastery setting.

John Culshaw, the recording manager, with Britten's active help, succeeded wonderfully well in conveying the church atmosphere by stereo sound alone, and in some ways this presents a more intimate and vivid experience than even a live performance. Harold Blackburn plays the Abbot of the monastery, who introduces the drama, while John Shirley-Quirk plays the ferryman who takes people over the Curlew River, and Peter Pears sings the part of the madwoman who, distracted, searches fruitlessly for her abducted child. Following monastic as well as oriental practice, the woman's part goes to a male singer, but amazingly quickly one accepts the convention, for the stylization involved somehow adds to the impact of the emotions underlying the story. The recording is outstanding even by Decca standards, particularly when one remembers that each side lasts well over half an hour.

The Burning Fiery Furnace (2nd parable for church performance), *Op. 77.*
>   *** Decca SET 356. Peter Pears,
>   Robert Tear (tenors), John Shirley-
>   Quirk, Brian Drake (baritones),
>   original cast and members / of
>   Chorus and Orchestra of English
>   Opera Group, cond. Viola Tun-
>   nard and the composer.

The story of *Burning Fiery Furnace* is more obviously dramatic than *Curlew River* in the operatic sense, with vivid scenes like the Entrance of Nebuchadnezzar, the Raising of the Idol, and the putting of the three Israelites into the furnace. Britten is as imaginative as ever in his settings, and one must mention also the marvellous central interlude where the instrumentalists process round the church, which is stunningly well conveyed by the recording. The performers, both singers and players, are the same hand-picked cast that participated in the first performance at Orford Parish Church, where this record was made. This is another example of the way Decca have served Britten in providing definitive versions of his major scores for the guidance of all future performers as well as for our enjoyment at home.

The Prodigal Son (3rd parable for church performance), *Op. 81*.

> *** Decca SET 438. Peter Pears, Robert Tear (tenors), John Shirley-Quirk, Bryan Drake (baritones), English Opera Group Chorus and Orchestra, cond. the composer and Viola Tunnard.

The last of the set of parables is the sunniest and most heartwarming. Britten cleverly avoids the charge of oversweetness by introducing the Abbot, even before the play starts, in the role of Tempter, who confessedly represents evil and aims to destroy contentment in the family he describes: 'See how I break it up!' – a marvellous line for Peter Pears. Like the previous parables, *The Prodigal Son* receives an ideal performance with the composer supervising, and if anything the Decca recording is even more real and atmospheric: a fine demonstration disc as well as a moving experience.

The Poet's Echo (song cycle), *Op. 75*.

> ** Decca SXL 6428. Galina Vishnevskaya (soprano), Mstislav Rostropovich (piano) – TCHAIKOVSKY: *Songs*.**

Britten's setting of Pushkin poems in the original Russian were written, during a visit to Russia, as a personal tribute to Vishnevskaya and her versatile cellist/pianist husband. It was a happy chance that made Britten pick up a Penguin translation at the airport, for these miniatures (this is a less ambitious cycle than most he has written) have all his characteristic crispness of image. Vishnevskaya's voice, with its slavonic unevenness, is not the most suited in controlling the subtle line of such delicate songs, but with the help of Rostropovich the performance is warm and highly atmospheric.

Psalm 150 for voices and orchestra; songs from *Friday Afternoons* (song cycle), *Op. 7*.

> *** Decca SXL 6264. Downside School, Purley Boys' Choir and Orchestra; Viola Tunnard (piano), the composer – *Gemini variations*.***

Britten has called this record *School concert*, and with each contribution glowing in the uninhibited joy of the young artists involved, you might take it as a school concert from Elysium. Britten more than any composer of this century, perhaps ever, knows how to bring out youthful talents and youthful enjoyment in music to the full. The *Friday Afternoons* songs were written for a school where Britten's brother was headmaster; the Psalm 150 setting was done for the centenary of his own former preparatory school in Suffolk (the makeshift arrangements at the first performance involved a mouth-organ substituting for the trumpet).

Saint Nicolas (cantata), *Op. 42*.

> *** HMV ASD 2637. Robert Tear (tenor), Bruce Russell (treble), King's College Chapel Choir, Academy of St Martin-in-the-Fields, David Willcocks.

Britten's own recording of this charming cantata for children – precursor of the first church opera, *Noye's Fludde* – was made in mono only, and there was clearly room for a version in modern stereo. Though the balancing of the solo voices – St Nicolas respectively as a boy and as a man – is rather too close, the actual performance is vivid and dramatic, with particularly fine contributions from the boys of King's College Choir, belying the old idea that their style was too pure to be adapted to rugged modern works. A delightful issue. Try the scene of the child saint in the bathtub.

Serenade for tenor, horn and strings, Op. 31.
> *** Decca SXL 6110. Peter Pears (tenor), Barry Tuckwell (horn), English Chamber Orchestra, the composer – *Young Person's Guide.****

This performance is discussed above under its alternative coupling, *Les Illuminations.*

Spring symphony, Op. 44.
> *** Decca SXL 2264. Jennifer Vyvyan (soprano), Norma Proctor (contralto), Peter Pears (tenor), Chorus of boys from Emmanuel School, Wandsworth, with Chorus and Orchestra of the Royal Opera House, Covent Garden, the composer.

Decca took advantage of a BBC performance with the same forces to obtain a recording of unusual brilliance and strength. If the title 'Symphony' is misleading – the work is much more an anthology akin to the *Serenade* and the *Nocturne* – Britten again shows by the subtlest of balancing that unity and cohesion are not just a matter of formal patterns. The four parts do come to have the coherence of balanced movements. But it is the freshness of Britten's imagination in dozens of moments that makes this work as memorable as it is joyous. Who

but Britten would have dared use so unexpected an effect as boys whistling? Who but he would have introduced a triumphant C major *Sumer is icumen in* at the end, the boys' voices ringing out over everything else? Here of course a recording helps enormously. Thanks to the Decca engineers one hears more than is usually possible in a live performance. Jennifer Vyvyan and Peter Pears are both outstanding, and Britten shows that no conductor is more vital in his music than he himself.

War requiem, Op. 66.
> ⊛ *** Decca SET 252/3. Galina Vishnevskaya (soprano), Peter Pears (tenor), Dietrich Fischer-Dieskau (baritone), Bach Choir, LSO Chorus, Highgate School Choir, Melos Ensemble, London Symphony Orchestra, the composer.

This most successful project hardly needs a recommendation. With the composer's own choice of forces under his direction, and with all the technical care of the Decca engineers, it has deserved all its success, and it is worth noting that in an important respect the gramophone has been able to fulfil the composer's directions even more completely than any live performance. Britten pointed the contrast between the full choir and orchestra in the settings of the *Requiem* and the tenor, baritone and chamber orchestra in the intervening settings of the Wilfred Owen poems. But what a recording can do that is impossible in a cathedral or concert hall is to modify the acoustic for each, and this has been done most sensitively and effectively by the Decca engineers. The Owen settings strike one more sharply than the Latin settings, but gradually as the work progresses the process of integration is accomplished, and the way the soloists' cries of *Let us sleep now* fade into the final chorus is almost unbearably moving on record as in performance.

The recorded performance comes near to the ideal, but it is a pity that Britten insisted on Vishnevskaya for the soprano solos. Having a Russian singer was emotionally right, but musically Heather Harper would have been so much better still.

Collections

Choral songs: *The Ballad of Little Musgrave and Lady Barnard; 5 Flower songs; I lov'd a lass; Lift boy; Old Abram Brown; Oliver Cromwell; A shepherd's carol. Gloriana: Choral dances.*

*** Argo ZRG 5424. Elizabethan Singers, Louis Halsey; Wilfred Parry (piano).

This is a charming record of comparatively little-known Britten works, beautifully performed and recorded. The most substantial work is the *Ballad of Little Musgrave and Lady Barnard*, a curiously compelling setting of a highly-charged story of infidelity, written originally for performance in a prisoner-of-war camp. Only the rare combination of male voices and piano and perhaps the technical difficulties have prevented it from becoming better-known, and it is good that the record also salvages a little piece, *A shepherd's carol*, that Britten wrote for a radio programme by W. H. Auden. There is a magical resolution on to the tonic at the end of each stanza, a characteristic Britten touch, bringing each time a physical frisson when the singing is as beautiful as here. The *Gloriana Choral dances* have been recorded before, by the LSO Chorus, but that record had a very different coupling, and in any case the scale of the whole performance was quite different and much less intimate.

Folk-song arrangements: *The ash grove; Avenging and bright; La belle est au jardin d'amour; The bonny Earl o'Moray; A brisk young widow; Ca' the yowes; Come you not from Newcastle?; Early one morning; How sweet the answer; The last rose of summer; Minstrel boy; The miller of Dee; Oft in the stilly night; The plough boy; Le roi s'en va-t'en chasse; Sweet Polly Oliver; O waly, waly.*

** (*) Decca SXL 6007. Peter Pears (tenor), the composer (piano).

The sleeve quotes *Punch* in saying:

> There's no need for Pears
> To give himself airs:
> He has them written
> By Benjamin Britten.

We must be grateful for such bounty. *Earl o'Moray* has almost too much Britten, and the accompaniment for *Early one morning* is unnecessarily clever and almost distracting. But others are delightful, especially *The ash grove* and the French song about the king going hunting. The recording, while admirably faithful in timbre, is cut at a high level (with a hint of peaking on the vocal climaxes of some songs), and the acoustic lacks intimacy. Even so there is a great deal to enjoy here.

OPERA

Albert Herring (opera in 3 acts): complete recording.

** (*) Decca SET 274/6. Peter Pears (tenor), Sylvia Fisher (soprano), John Noble (baritone), Owen Brannigan (bass), April Cantelo (soprano), Joseph Ward (bass), English Chamber Orchestra, the composer.

Comic opera performances on record are curiously unpredictable, the absence of an audience often disturbing. This account of *Albert Herring* under the composer is as impressive musically as could be imagined, but somehow genuine gaiety is rather lacking. It is partly the fault of the libretto. In the theatre, with plenty of visual amusements to watch, one hardly notices the stiltedness of much of the language, but on record there are many lines that are just folksy and embarrassing. But with that reservation, there is everything to commend, and it is good to have Peter Pears's Albert so beautifully recorded before (may it be many years off) he is too old for the part. Sylvia Fisher makes a magnificent gorgon of a Lady Billows, and one welcomes the chance to hear so many excellent British singers on record who are normally neglected by the companies: Sheila Rex, for example, whose tiny portrait of Albert's mother is very funny indeed. Recording excellent.

Billy Budd (opera in prologue, 4 acts and epilogue): complete recording.
*** Decca SET 379/81. Peter Glossop (baritone), Peter Pears (tenor), Michael Langdon (bass), John Shirley-Quirk (baritone), Wandsworth School Boys' Chorus, Ambrosian Opera Chorus, London Symphony Orchestra, the composer.

This was the last opera-recording supervised for Decca by John Culshaw. By then he was already in his new BBC role, but with the keenest enjoyment he returned for this long-cherished project, and successfully capped his earlier outstanding achievements in Wagner as well as Britten. The opera itself, daring in its use of an all-male cast without any lack of variety of texture, emerges magnificently. The libretto by E. M. Forster and Eric Crozier is more skilled than those Britten has usually set, and the range of characterization – so apparently limited

in a tale of good and evil directly confronting one another – is masterly, with Peter Pears's part of Captain Vere presenting the moral issue at its most moving. Here as in the opera-house Britten's master-stroke of representing the confrontation of Vere and the condemned Billy in a sequence of 34 bare common chords is irresistible, and the many richly imaginative strokes – atmospheric as well as dramatic – are superbly managed. An ideal cast, with Glossop a bluff heroic Billy, and Langdon a sharply dark-toned Claggart, making these symbol-figures believable. Magnificent sound.

Billy Budd: highlights.
*** Decca SET 452 (from above recording).

With so closely knit an opera as *Billy Budd*, one which has an almost symphonic design in contrasting the keys of B flat and B minor (representing, respectively, good and evil) it was almost impossible to make a selection of satisfying excerpts, but this highlights disc contains a high proportion of the opera's finest music, including not only Claggart's great *Credo* of evil (comparable with Iago's) but the warmly atmospheric sea-shanties for the crew, Billy's '*Addio del passato*', and the strikingly imaginative interlude of 34 common chords that represents Billy's meeting with Captain Vere – this last naturally not quite so effective as when heard as part of the complete opera. Fine recording and performance as on the complete set.

Death in Venice (opera in 2 acts): complete recording.
*** Decca SET 581/3. Peter Pears (tenor), John Shirley-Quirk (baritone), James Bowman (countertenor), Kenneth Bowen (tenor), Peter Leeming (bass), English Opera Group Chorus, English

Chamber Orchestra, Steuart Bedford.

Even Britten has rarely chosen so offbeat an opera subject as Thomas Mann's novella which made an expansively atmospheric film far removed from the world of Mann, and here makes a surprisingly successful opera, totally original in its alternation of monologue for the central character, Aschenbach (on two levels, inner and external), and colourful set pieces showing off the world of Venice and the arrival of the plague.

Britten's inspiration, drawing together threads from all his earlier operas from *Peter Grimes* to the *Church parables*, is nothing less than exuberant, with the chamber orchestra producing the richest possible sounds. Pears's searching performance in the central role is set against the darkly sardonic singing of John Shirley-Quirk in a sequence of roles as the Dionysiac figure who draws Aschenbach on to his destruction. The recording is gloriously vivid, and though Steuart Bedford's assured conducting lacks some of the punch that Britten would have brought, the whole presentation (including a finely produced libretto) makes this a set to establish the work as the very culmination of Britten's cycle of operas.

A Midsummer Night's Dream (opera in 3 acts): complete recording.
*** Decca SET 338/40. Alfred Deller (counter-tenor), Elizabeth Harwood, Heather Harper (sopranos), Josephine Veasey (mezzo-soprano), Helen Watts (contralto), John Shirley-Quirk (baritone), Owen Brannigan (bass), Choirs of Downside and Emanuel Schools, London Symphony Orchestra, the composer.

Britten and Pears together prepared the libretto for this opera by careful compression and rearrangement of the Shakespeare words. What this recording confirms – with the aid of the score – more than any live performance is how compressed the music is, as well as the words. At first one may regret the comparative absence of rich, memorable tunes, but there is no thinness of argument, and the atmosphere of every scene is brilliantly re-created in the most evocative orchestral sounds. The beauty of instrumental writing comes out in this recording even more than in the opera-house, for John Culshaw, the recording manager, put an extra halo round the fairy-music. not to distort or confuse but to act as substitute for visual atmosphere. The problem of conveying the humour of the play-scene at the end with the 'rude mechanicals' cavorting about the stage proved more intractable. Humour is there all right, but the laughter of the stage audience is too ready for comfort.

Britten again proves himself an ideal interpreter of his own music, and draws virtuoso playing from the LSO (marvellous trumpet-sounds for Puck's music). Among the singers Peter Pears has shifted from his original role of Flute (the one who has the Donizetti mad-scene parody to sing) to the straight role of Lysander. The mechanicals are admirably led by Owen Brannigan as Bottom, and among the lovers Josephine Veasey (Hermia) is outstanding. Deller, with his magical male alto singing, is the eerily effective Oberon.

A Midsummer Night's Dream: highlights.
*** Decca SET 397 (from above recording).

Wisely Decca devoted the whole of the second side of this disc to the extraordinarily brilliant conclusion of the opera, with the 'rude mechanicals' doing their play and Britten's marvellous sequence of operatic parodies. The four excerpts on the first side consist of the lovely opening of the opera with its fairy music, the setting of *Over hill, over dale*, the mechanicals' first rehearsal for their play, and the passage where Oberon squeezes the juice into Demetrius's eyes and the lovers' quarrel which follows. Beautiful atmospheric recording and near-ideal performances.

Owen Wingrave (opera in 2 acts, for television): complete recording.

*** Decca SET 501/2. Peter Pears (tenor), Sylvia Fisher, Heather Harper, Jennifer Vyvyan (sopranos), Janet Baker (mezzo-soprano), Benjamin Luxon, John Shirley-Quirk (baritones), English Chamber Orchestra, the composer.

Britten's television opera had a bigger audience for its world-wide first performance than most opera composers receive for all the performances of all their operas put together. It marked a return after the *Church parables* to the mainstream Britten pattern of opera with a central character isolated from society. Each of the seven characters is strongly conceived, with the composer writing specially for the individual singers chosen for the television and gramophone presentations. This recording was made immediately after the trials of the television recording, and the result is even more concentrated and compelling. Strangely enough the drama, based on a short story by Henry James, seems less contrived when one has to imagine the setting instead of having it presented on the screen, particularly as the recording is so atmospheric and the production so sensitive. It is particularly good to hear Britten's highly original orchestral writing in high fidelity.

Peter Grimes (opera in 3 acts): complete recording.

⊛ *** Decca SXL 2150/2. Peter Pears (tenor), Claire Watson (soprano),

James Pease (baritone), Jean Watson (contralto), Raymond Nilsson (tenor), Owen Brannigan (bass), Geraint Evans (baritone), Chorus and Orchestra of Royal Opera House, Covent Garden, the composer.

The Decca recording of *Peter Grimes* was one of the first great achievements of the stereo era. Few opera recordings can claim to be so definitive, with Peter Pears, for whom it was written, in the name part, Owen Brannigan (another member of the original team) and a first-rate cast. One was a little apprehensive about Claire Watson as Ellen Orford, a part which Joan Cross made her own, but in the event Miss Watson gives a most sympathetic performance, and her voice records beautifully. Another member of the cast from across the Atlantic, James Pease, as the understanding Captain Balstrode, is brilliantly incisive musically and dramatically, but beyond that it becomes increasingly unfair to single out individual performances. Britten conducts brilliantly and secures splendidly incisive playing, with the whole orchestra on its toes throughout. The recording, superbly atmospheric, has so many felicities that it would be hard to enumerate them, and the Decca engineers have done wonders in making up aurally for the lack of visual effects.

Peter Grimes: highlights.

*** Decca SXL 2309 (from above recording).

It is disappointing that the exquisite quartet for Ellen, Auntie and the two Nieces is not included, but it would have been hard to decide what to sacrifice from the seven excerpts here. The whole of the first scene is given; the second excerpt has the carter's nagging little theme and the big ensemble which follows the hoisting of the storm cone; the third excerpt has

Peter's solo and the ensemble *Old Joe has gone fishing*; the fourth has the ensemble *The Borough keeps its standards up* and the march to Grimes's hut; the fifth is Grimes's extended scene with the boy in his hut; sixthly there is Ellen's little aria and finally the whole of the last scene with the search parties crying out through the fog and Grimes tragically unhinged. The selection has all the fine qualities of the complete set, which remains one of the most important opera sets ever made and one of the best recorded. Peter Pears almost certainly will never be surpassed as Grimes, and the composer's own direction is superbly dramatic.

Peter Grimes: Four sea interludes and Passacaglia (see also above under *Nocturne*).

(B) ** Pye GSGC 14059. London Philharmonic Orchestra, Sir Adrian Boult – ELGAR: *Falstaff*.**

The LPO's playing is capable rather than inspired in what is some of the most atmospheric music in all opera. Really to get the full salty flavour of Britten's pictures of the sea you need crisper, more biting playing than this, but with stereo to help and with the *Passacaglia* generously included as well as the four *Interludes*, it is recommendable enough.

The Rape of Lucretia (opera in 2 acts): complete recording.

*** Decca SET 492/3. Peter Pears (tenor), Heather Harper (soprano), John Shirley-Quirk (baritone), Janet Baker (contralto), Benjamin Luxon (baritone), English Chamber Orchestra, the composer.

This is outstanding even among the many fine opera recordings that Britten has made. In particular the performance of Janet Baker in the role of Lucretia underlines the depth of feeling behind a work which in its formal classical frame may on the face of it seem to hide emotion. The logical problems of the story remain – why *should* Lucretia feel so guilty? – but with Janet Baker the heart-rending tragedy of the heroine is conveyed with passionate conviction, her glorious range of tone-colours, her natural feeling for words and musical phrase used with supreme artistry. Benjamin Luxon too makes the selfish Tarquinius into a living, believable character. As the Male Chorus Peter Pears astonishingly matches his own achievement of a quarter-century earlier in an abbreviated recording, and Heather Harper's creamy tones as the Female Chorus are beautifully poised. The stylization of the drama with its frame of Christian comment comes over even more effectively when imagined rather than seen. The seductive beauty of the writing – Britten at his early peak – is gloriously caught, the melodies and tone-colours as ravishing as any that the composer has ever conceived. A lovely set.

COLLECTION

'The world of Britten': excerpts from *Simple symphony; Variations on a Theme of Frank Bridge; Young Person's Guide to the Orchestra; Burning Fiery Furnace; Nocturne; Serenade; War requiem; Billy Budd; Midsummer Night's Dream; Peter Grimes*. Folksong arr.: *Early one morning; The ploughboy*.

(B) *** Decca SPA 74. Various artists, dir. the composer.

This sampler disc, issued at the cheapest possible price, is not intended for the converted, but rather to whet appetites. Some of the snippets are unavoidably cut off, but this is a valuable and enjoyable collection suitable for enticing young listeners as well as old. The darker side of Britten is avoided, even in the excerpt from the *War requiem*, but that is understandable enough. Decca has consistently produced its most brilliant recording quality for Britten's music, and the sound here is excellent on very long sides. Perhaps the cleverest feature of this record is the way the items have been chosen to make attractive listening taken as a continuous programme. Highly recommended.

Bruch, Max
(1838–1920)

Violin concerto No. 1 in G minor, Op. 26.

*** HMV ASD 2926. Itzhak Perlman (violin), London Symphony Orchestra, André Previn – MENDELSSOHN: *Concerto.****

*** CBS 72612. Isaac Stern (violin), Philadelphia Orchestra, Eugene Ormandy – LALO: *Symphonie espagnole.****

*** HMV ASD 334. Yehudi Menuhin (violin), Philharmonia Orchestra, Walter Susskind – MENDELSSOHN: *Concerto.****

(B) *** Decca SPA 88. Ruggiero Ricci (violin), London Symphony Orchestra, Pierino Gamba – MENDELSSOHN: *Concerto.****

** (*) Philips 6500 708. Mayumi Fujikawa (violin), Rotterdam Philharmonic Orchestra, Edo de Waart – TCHAIKOVSKY: *Concerto.** (*)*

(M) ** Philips Universo 6580 022. Arthur Grumiaux (violin), Concertgebouw Orchestra, Bernard Haitink – MENDELSSOHN: *Concerto.** (*)*

(M) ** RCA LSB 4061. Jascha Heifetz (violin), New Symphony Orchestra of London, Sir Malcolm Sargent – GLAZOUNOV: *Concerto.****

(M) ** Supraphon SUAST 50546. Josef Suk (violin), Czech Philharmonic Orchestra, Karel Ančerl – MENDELSSOHN: *Concerto.***

(M) ** DGG Privilege 135039. Igor Oistrakh (violin), Royal Philharmonic Orchestra, David Oistrakh – BEETHOVEN: *Romances.****

(M) ** HMV SXLP 30137. Masuko Ushioda (violin), Japan Philharmonic Orchestra, Seiji Ozawa – SIBELIUS: *Concerto.***

Bruch's *First Violin concerto* is lucky in its recordings, and many of the above discs will satisfy in different ways. In discussing individual performances, that by Kyung-Wha Chung must be considered among the very finest – it is mentioned below coupled to the *Scottish fantasia*. Of the others perhaps the finest recorded is Perlman's. There is perhaps the faintest reservation about this reading, a glowing, powerful account that is almost too sure of itself. With Previn and the LSO backing him up richly, this is a strong, confident interpretation, forthrightly masculine – the contrast with Kyung-Wha Chung's inner qualities is very striking. The opulent, full recording suits the performance, and the Mendelssohn coupling is outstanding among many fine versions of that concerto.

Stern's warm-hearted and rich-toned account appeared originally in 1957, but the sound is still opulent, and the main flaw is that the soloist is – characteristically for CBS – recorded too close. The coupling is generous, the full five-movement version of Lalo's romantic work.

Menuhin's performance has long held an honoured place in the catalogue. The recording is beginning to show its age now, but Menuhin was in good form when he made the disc and his playing is much more technically secure than in his later version coupled to Bruch's *Second*

Concerto (see below). The performance has a fine spontaneity, the work's improvisatory quality skilfully caught, and there is no doubt about the poetry Menuhin finds in the slow movement, or the sparkle in the finale.

Ricci has an outstanding technique and he has also a very characteristic tone, which alongside Stern's velvety sound, for instance, is more open and uncovered. But the performance here has a fine intensity and there is a natural warmth which brings out the music's temperament without indulging it. The stereo recording matches the playing with well defined quality and plenty of depth.

Mayumi Fujikawa has a smallish tone, but his artistry and sensitivity is never in doubt. The performance of the slow movement is particularly beautiful, the concentration producing moments of considerable tension, even though the conception is gentle and unostentatious. With generally vivid recording and a good balance this is highly recommendable as the only record coupling the Bruch and Tchaikovsky concertos. The performance of the Tchaikovsky is more controversial with a notably slow, relaxed account of the first movement, but there is no question that this record marks the début of a gifted and imaginative artist.

Grumiaux's thoughtful approach, although tasteful and enjoyable in its way, is on the cool side for such a red-blooded work, but with clear, well-balanced recording this may well suit some, and the Mendelssohn coupling shows Grumiaux at his elegant best.

Heifetz's performance, originally rather inappropriately coupled to Mozart, is here joined with a marvellous performance of the Glazounov concerto. The account of the Bruch is not quite as fine. It takes a little while to warm up, but the slow movement shows Heifetz in top romantic form and the finale is brilliant – even to the point of hardness. Sargent accompanies sympathetically and the recording is good.

Suk's account is not as imaginative as some, but he provides rich tone and a sympathetic feeling for the music's melodic line, if less subtlety in the matter of light and shade. This could partly be the fault of the recording, which is reverberant (though for the most part pleasingly so). The finale, taken rather slowly, might be thought a shade heavy in impact, but better this than breathlessness.

On Privilege father and son make a convincing partnership, Igor shaping the solo line with sinuous intensity and bringing plenty of warmth to the slow movement and David attentive to his son's needs yet bringing passion to the tuttis. Both join to make the close of the *Adagio* swell up into a surge of feeling. The finale too has a splendid rhythmic verve. In many ways this is a three-star performance; the snag is the recording, which is very brilliant and slightly harsh. One would have willingly exchanged a little brightness for more opulence and colour in the overall sound.

Ushioda is one of the most talented of the many Japanese string players who have made a name in the West. This is a warm, beautifully poised performance but lacks the degree of imagination and commitment that would bring it fully to life. Fair recording. Another version by Yong Uck Kim on DGG fails to be competitive. It lacks the necessary intensity, in part the fault of a slack accompaniment.

Violin concertos Nos. 1 in G minor, Op. 26; 2 in D minor, Op. 44.

** (*) HMV ASD 2852. Yehudi Menuhin (violin), London Symphony Orchestra, Sir Adrian Boult.

Were not the Bruch *First Violin concerto* such a striking masterpiece the *Second* might be better known. Its melodies have less individuality but its romanticism is unforced and attractive and it is strong in atmosphere. Menuhin is persuasive in the warmth and obvious affection of his interpretation, but he tends to be somewhat sketchy in the detail of the solo part, and the intonation and focus of his playing are far from exact. Yet it says a great deal for the strength of his musical personality that, in spite of the technical lapses, the performance is so enjoyable. Boult's accompaniment is equally sympathetic and many will feel this a worthwhile addition to the catalogue. With the *G minor Concerto*, Menuhin is on familiar ground, but there is no sign of over-familiarity and the lovely slow movement is given a performance of great warmth and spiritual beauty. The orchestra accompanies admirably and the recording is excellent throughout the disc.

Violin concerto No. 1 in G minor, Op. 26; Scottish fantasia for violin and orchestra, Op. 46.

*** Decca SXL 6573. Kyung-Wha Chung (violin), Royal Philharmonic Orchestra, Rudolf Kempe.

The magic of Kyung-Wha Chung, a spontaneously inspired violinist if ever there was one, comes over beguilingly in this very desirable Bruch coupling. There may be more glossily perfect accounts of the famous *G minor Concerto*, but Kyung-Wha Chung goes straight to the heart, finding mystery and fantasy as well as more extrovert qualities. Just as strikingly in the *Scottish fantasia* she transcends the episodic nature of the writing to give the music a genuine depth and concentration, above all in the lovely slow movement. Kempe and the Royal Philharmonic, not always perfectly polished, give sympathetic accompaniment, well caught in a glowing recording.

Scottish fantasia for violin and orchestra, Op. 46.

*** Decca SXL 6035. David Oistrakh

(violin), Osian Ellis (harp), London Symphony Orchestra, Jascha Horenstein – HINDEMITH: *Violin concerto.****

(M) * (**) RCA LSB 4105. Jascha Heifetz (violin), New Symphony Orchestra, Sir Malcolm Sargent – KORNGOLD: *Violin concerto.***

(M) ** Decca Ace of Diamonds SDD 110. Alfredo Campoli (violin), London Symphony Orchestra, Sir Adrian Boult – MENDELSSOHN: *Violin concerto.***

The Oistrakh/Horenstein performance is very well recorded, and the reading owes nearly as much to the conductor as the soloist. The expansive dignity of the opening of the brass sets shows immediately how fine the orchestral contribution is going to be and Oistrakh's playing throughout is ravishing, raising the stature of the work immeasurably. The slow movement is especially memorable. This is a more extrovert account than that of Kyung-Wha Chung and satisfying in a quite different way.

Though the recording shows its age, and the balance favours the soloist to a distracting degree, Heifetz plays with such supreme assurance that all lovers of great violin-playing should hear the disc.

Campoli's performance is on an altogether smaller scale. But he plays with clean sweet tone (allowing for a certain wiriness in the Ace of Diamonds transfer) and Boult provides an accomplished account of the orchestral part of the score. The recording is good, although some of the woodwind detail is backwardly balanced.

Bruckner, Anton
(1824–96)

Symphony in F minor; Overture in G minor.

** HMV ASD 2803. London Symphony Orchestra, Elyakum Shapirra.

The F minor study symphony is naturally of interest and all Brucknerians will welcome the opportunity of hearing it. It was written in 1863, the same year as the *Overture in G minor* with which it is coupled, not long after Bruckner had completed his studies with Sechter. Although the work is not characteristic of the mature composer, there are some glimpses of the personality he was to develop, and both scherzo and trio have characteristic appeal. The performance is not particularly persuasive or distinguished, which is a pity, but in the absence of an alternative this will have to do.

Symphonies Nos. 0 in D minor; 1 in C minor; 2 in C minor; 3 in D minor; 4 in E flat major (Romantic); 5 in B flat major; 6 in A major; 7 in E major; 8 in C minor; 9 in D minor.

(M) ** (*) Philips 6717 002 (12 discs). Concertgebouw Orchestra, Bernard Haitink.

Whether as a box or taken individually Haitink's accounts of the ten Bruckner symphonies he has recorded have all the classical virtues. They are well-shaped, free from affectation and any kind of agogic distortion; Haitink's grasp of the architecture is strong and his feeling for beauty of detail refined. Perhaps he has a less developed sense of mystery and atmosphere than has Jochum, whose readings have a spiritual dimension at which Haitink only hints. However, Jochum recorded the Nowak editions, and Haitink's judgements on matters of text are more likely to please the scholar. As far as the recorded sound is concerned, the Philips is both cleaner and better defined; the balance is most musically judged in both but there

is a stronger sense of ambience in the Jochum recordings. (The Jochum boxed set is deleted as we go to press.)

Symphony No. 0 in D minor.

** (*) Philips SAL 3602. Concertgebouw Orchestra, Bernard Haitink.

Bruckner rightly took a middle course when faced with what to do with his early D minor symphony. He neither put it in the regular canon nor destroyed it but himself gave it the distinctive title *Symphony No. 0*. It was in fact written after the work we know as *Symphony No. 1*, but Bruckner may well have been influenced in his attitude to the D minor by its obvious similarities with the *Symphony No. 3* (also in D minor), with close connections in first movement, scherzo and finale. No. 0 remains a splendid piece that every Brucknerian should hear. Haitink is a dedicated and understanding interpreter of the composer, and if he hardly conveys the last degree of warmth and committedness, there is a good case for treating this comparatively modest symphony fairly gently.

Symphony No. 1 in C minor.

*** Philips 6500 439. Concertgebouw Orchestra, Bernard Haitink.

*** Decca SXL 6494. Vienna Philharmonic Orchestra, Claudio Abbado.

(M) * (*) Telefunken SMT 1326. Leipzig Gewandhaus Orchestra, Vaclav Neumann.

Haitink's account of the symphony is more recent than Abbado's and has the advantage of more vivid recorded quality. In some ways it is the safest all-round recommendation, though Abbado is hardly less fine. Perhaps the Haitink is the more opulent and deeply Brucknerian sound: the Amsterdam orchestra produce a more sumptuous quality, particularly in the wind department, than their illustrious Viennese colleagues. Yet Abbado's performance is beautifully proportioned: no detail is dwelt on at the expense of the whole; at the same time every nuance registers, and given a recording of such excellence and spaciousness it can hardly fail to satisfy.

Choice is clear-cut in the case of the Neumann account with the Leipzig Gewandhaus Orchestra. Neither performance nor recording is outstanding, and it in no way displaces Haitink or Abbado.

Symphony No. 2 in C minor (Haas edition).

> *** Philips SAL 3785. Concertgebouw Orchestra, Bernard Haitink.

Where Jochum used the Nowak edition embodying the cuts agreed to by the composer himself, Haitink uses the fuller version favoured by Haas. Characteristically Haas takes the view that Bruckner agreed to cuts with the thought that performance would be brought nearer and that left to himself he would not have favoured them. Most dedicated Brucknerians will probably agree, and this fine performance, clear-headed, direct, unmannered, presents the work in the freshest possible light. One sometimes misses Jochum's more persuasive manner (his record is deleted), and the extra length of the slow movement involves a break in the middle, but no one wanting Bruckner's fullest thoughts in this powerful and noble work need hold back. Clear Philips recording.

Symphony No. 3 in D minor.

> ** (*) Decca SXL 6505. Vienna Philharmonic Orchestra, Karl Boehm.
> ** (*) Philips SAL 3506. Concertgebouw Orchestra, Bernard Haitink.

Choice is not clear-cut with Bruckner's *Third Symphony*, as the two available performances use different editions of the score. Boehm's is the most recently recorded, with splendid detail and firm sonority, and the performance is admirably free from eccentricity. Now that Jochum's atmospheric and deeply-felt account has been deleted, Boehm's is the only recording using the Nowak edition, and with such lucid sound many will regard this as first choice.

Haitink uses the 1878 version, and his reading too is a safe if slightly sober recommendation. The text is far fuller than Nowak and its architecture is seen to good advantage here, while the recording has an impressive power and a wide dynamic range. With fine playing and effective stereo this disc has a great deal to offer.

Symphony No. 4 in E flat major (Romantic).

> (M) *** DGG Privilege 2535 111. Berlin Philharmonic Orchestra, Eugen Jochum.
> *** Decca 6BB 171/2. Vienna Philharmonic Orchestra, Karl Boehm.
> *** Decca SXL 6227. London Symphony Orchestra, Istvan Kertesz.
> (M) *** Philips 6599 729. Concertgebouw Orchestra, Bernard Haitink.
> (M) ** (*) HMV SXLP 30167. Philharmonia Orchestra, Otto Klemperer.
> (M) ** (*) CBS Classics 61137. Columbia Symphony Orchestra, Bruno Walter.
> * (*) DGG 2530 336. Chicago Symphony Orchestra, Daniel Barenboim.
> * (*) Decca SXL 6489. Los Angeles Philharmonic Orchestra, Zubin Mehta.

Symphonies Nos. 4 in E flat major (Romantic); 7 in E major.

*** HMV SLS 811 (3 discs). Berlin Philharmonic Orchestra, Herbert von Karajan.

Jochum's way with Bruckner is unique. So gentle is his hand that the opening of each movement or even the beginning of each theme emerges into the consciousness rather than starting normally. And when it is a matter of leading from one section to another over a difficult transition passage – as in the lead-in to the first-movement recapitulation – no one can match Jochum in his subtlety and persuasiveness. The purist may object that to do this Jochum reduces the speed far below what is marked, but Jochum is for the man who wants above all to love Bruckner; Klemperer and Kertesz are for those who want to find architectural strength. Originally issued on three sides, the new issue has been condensed to two and remains a fine recording.

Karajan is most impressive; his reading has all the simplicity and mystery of Jochum and the strength and power of Boehm. The playing of the Berlin Philharmonic is glorious and the recording is atmospheric and detailed. The discs are, however, only available in harness with an (equally noble) account of the *Seventh Symphony*, which will limit its appeal for those who already have one or other version of No. 7.

The advantages of Boehm's compulsive account on Decca are that it accommodates each movement on a side, is superbly recorded, it is splendidly free from eccentricity and it is beautifully shaped, though it does not match Karajan in its sense of mystery. It deserves a strong recommendation, and those who favour their Bruckner played in this way will find this the best version to have.

Kertesz shows himself the master of the long crescendo, so that with the widest dynamic range and beautifully controlled speeds, this is generally the most drama-tic account of No. 4. In the first two movements in particular he even outshines Klemperer in the feeling of architectural strength, and though he misses some of the boisterous humour that Klemperer finds in the last two movements, it is among the most generally recommendable single-disc versions.

Turning to other full-price accounts, Barenboim must regretfully be passed over. The Chicago Orchestra play magnificently and the recording is a fine one, but the reading is mannered and its insights confined to the surface. Nor can the Mehta lay claim to much depth of feeling. In the mid-price category, Haitink probably remains the best buy. His performance is noble and unmannered, the recording is excellent and the orchestral playing is eloquent. As far as the recorded sound is concerned, Klemperer's version with the Philharmonia is probably more vivid, particularly in the fine new HMV transfer; the reading is magisterial, and the finale has an impressive weight and cogency. Some ears find this performance wanting in atmosphere and too marmoreal, but there is no question about its strength. Walter's CBS account has no want of mystery or affection and some will prefer it to either of its medium-price rivals. It must, however, be given a qualified recommendation on account of the sound quality, which is not so natural or well balanced as either Haitink's or Klemperer's.

Symphony No. 5 in B flat major.

*** Philips 6700 055 (2 discs). Concertbegouw Orchestra, Bernard Haitink.

** (*) Decca SXL 6686/7. Vienna Philharmonic Orchestra, Lorin Maazel.

** (*) Columbia SAX 5288/9. New Philharmonia Orchestra, Otto Klemperer.

Among recent records of the *Fifth*, Haitink's takes pride of place. It lacks the last ounce of atmosphere and mystery, but it undoubtedly conveys the grandeur and sweep of this noble symphony. It is free from egocentric mannerisms – so for that matter is Maazel – but the orchestral playing has eloquence and the sound is rich and sonorous, even though the upper strings, as so often in the Concertgebouw's recordings, are a little wanting in bloom.

Maazel's performance has a great deal to commend it. It is beautifully played and recorded: it has greater detail and body than the Concertgebouw version. Maazel's control of tempo-changes is masterly, combining flexibility with firmness of grip. Yet ultimately the impression it leaves is curiously clinical. There is too little sense of atmosphere and of awareness of the spiritual dimensions of this composer.

Klemperer's account is expansive and some find it heavy-handed. Klemperer's conception is certainly massive; this results in wonderfully rich brass sonorities, with a cathedral-like breadth and spaciousness, but at other times there is a suspicion of bombast. In the beautiful slow movement the second C major theme makes a stirring impact as presented by Klemperer, where others are more lyrical; and taking the reading overall, one has the impression that lyricism is subordinate to architectural strength.

A further recording by Matačic on Supraphon has to be ruled out on textual grounds; and Jochum's later Philips recording is no match for his earlier DGG one (now deleted). Recorded at a live concert in the Concertgebouw, the newer discs offer string and brass tone without lustre and little internal clarity.

Symphony No. 6 in A major.
    *** Philips 6500 164. Concertgebouw Orchestra, Bernard Haitink.

** (*) Columbia SAX 2583. New Philharmonia Orchestra, Otto Klemperer.

Haitink's account of the *Sixth*, one of Bruckner's most seldom played symphonies, heads the list. It is not ideal (the opening could with advantage be slower) but it has breadth and a certain atmosphere. Klemperer's finely played Philharmonia version is excellently paced. The performance has dignity, adding a coherence (especially in the finale) which not all conductors are able to find in Bruckner. Some ears find this massive, architectural approach unimaginative, the terrain observed with the eye of a geographer or surveyor rather than that of a poet, but the strength of the reading is never in doubt. Klemperer is superbly served by the engineers, but the Concertgebouw version is well recorded too, and the greater imagination that Haitink brings to this noble symphony makes his the more desirable acquisition.

*Symphony No. 7 in E major (*see also under *Symphony No. 4).*
    (M) *** DGG Privilege 2726 054 (2 discs). Berlin Philharmonic Orchestra, Eugen Jochum – WAGNER: *Parsifal: Prelude and Good Friday music.*** (*)
    (B) ** (*) Turnabout TV 34083S. South-West German Radio Orchestra, Hans Rosbaud.
    ** Philips 6700 038 (2 discs). Concertgebouw Orchestra, Bernard Haitink – *Te Deum.****
    ** Decca SET 323/4. Vienna Philharmonic Orchestra, Sir Georg Solti – WAGNER: *Siegfried idyll.****
    * (*) Columbia SAX 2454/5. Philharmonia Orchestra, Otto Klemperer – WAGNER: *Siegfried idyll.*** (*)

Jochum's approach to the *Seventh Symphony* is entirely characteristic, with a relaxed manner and generally slow tempi in all four movements. But the concentration is never in doubt: such a passage as the transition into the second subject in the slow movement is characteristic of the magic that the conductor distils in this marvellous score. With no serious textual problems to worry about, this Privilege reissue stands high among the contrasted recorded performances of this symphony. The fill-up, originally coupled to the *Fifth Symphony*, is also recommendable.

Karajan has a superb feeling for atmosphere and no less firm a grip on the architecture. The playing of the Berlin Philharmonic is gorgeous, and the HMV engineers provide sound that is well-balanced, atmospheric and sonorous. Unfortunately it is at present coupled with the *Fourth Symphony* and so will be an uneconomic purchase for those who have already got No. 4 and are unwilling to duplicate.

R.L. admires the Solti account rather more than do E.G. or I.M., though he shares some of their reservations. Haitink's reading, coupled with the *Te Deum*, is an admirable alternative even if the slow movement could glow more. His performance is eminently committed and well recorded. Generally speaking, it is a safer recommendation than either Solti or Klemperer, on whose merits the three of us remain divided. The Turnabout version is amazing value, and many readers will warm to its atmosphere. A perceptive performance, well played by the South-West German Radio Orchestra, it is let down a little by the unnatural balance of the recording; but, given the price, and the quality of Rosbaud's insights, this reservation should not prove insurmountable.

Symphony No. 8 in C minor.
　** (*) Philips 6700 020 (2 discs).

Concertgebouw Orchestra, Bernard Haitink.
** (*) Decca SET 335/6. Vienna Philharmonic Orchestra, Sir Georg Solti.
** DGG 2707 017 (2 discs). Berlin Philharmonic Orchestra, Eugen Jochum.
* (*) Decca SXL 6671/2. Los Angeles Philharmonic Orchestra, Zubin Mehta.
* HMV SLS 872 (2 discs). New Philharmonia Orchestra, Otto Klemperer.

Haitink's is a fine, clear-headed version which also has the merit of using the full Haas edition, with its extended finale notionally put together as what the composer would have done had he been given the chance. Yet Haitink's tempi are generally fast, and many Brucknerians may find his approach not relaxed and spacious enough.

Jochum's account (using the Nowak edition) is poetic and intensely personal. The style of the reading sometimes seems to ramble, stopping and starting again at the conductor's whim. There is much beautiful playing, of course; the original recording rather lacked immediacy, although new pressings have improved on this.

Solti's performance with the Vienna Philharmonic is more controversial. He also uses the Nowak edition, and the Vienna orchestra respond to his direction with great fervour and incisiveness. Some may find the slow movement a little too mannered, though it is positively restrained by the side of Mehta in this music. Although the Los Angeles orchestra play well for Mehta, the Decca engineers do not match their colleagues in Vienna who recorded Solti. Technically impressive as the playing is, there is something too glossy, not searching enough, in the result, and the sublime slow movement tends to be vulgarized.

Klemperer's version is superbly re-corded, but the performance does little credit to his memory. It was one of his last records, and funereal tempi make it seem one of the longest. The performance suffers from untidiness here and there, and although many details inspire respect and admiration, the set must regretfully be passed over.

Symphony No. 9 in D minor.
- *** DGG SLPM 139011. Berlin Philharmonic Orchestra, Herbert von Karajan.
- (M) ** (*) CBS Classics 61194. Columbia Symphony Orchestra, Bruno Walter.
- ** (*) Philips SAL 3575. Concert-gebouw Orchestra, Bernard Hai-tink.
- ** (*) DGG 2707 024 (2 discs). Ber-lin Philharmonic Orchestra, Eugen Jochum – *Te Deum.*** (*)
- ** Decca SXL 6202. Vienna Phil-harmonic Orchestra, Zubin Meh-ta.
- * (*) HMV ASD 2719. New Phil-harmonia Orchestra, Otto Klem-perer.

Karajan's is a glorious performance of Bruckner's last, uncompleted symphony, moulded in a way that is characteristic of him, with a simple, direct nobility that is sometimes missing in his work. Here he seems not to feel it necessary to underline, but with glowing playing from the Berlin Philharmonic and superb recording he gives the illusion of letting the music speak for itself. Yet no one has a clearer idea of Bruckner's architecture, and as one appreciates the subtle gradation of climax in the concluding slow movement, one knows how firmly Karajan's sights have been set on this goal all along. Even in a competitive field this record stands out.

Although the CBS sound is not ideal

(the balance is not wholly natural among other things), Bruno Walter's version is a desirable one. It was a product of his Indian summer in the recording studio, with a hand-picked orchestra assembled near his California home. Its mellowness reflects his own love of life and humanity, his deep affection for the music and a keen awareness of its structure. At mid-price it is a formidable competitor, and with the deletion of Schuricht's version on Classics for Pleasure, there is no cheaper alternative.

Haitink's account is as powerful in conception and execution as any in the catalogue. It is a performance of real stature with tremendous grip and a vision that penetrates the sense of tragedy and dramatic power as do few others. Having said this, however, it must be admitted that Haitink achieves this at the cost of some of the atmosphere and mystery of the work. But even if one misses Walter's poetry and Jochum's deep love of this symphony, Haitink's mighty reading still shows the dramatic force of the work in a way that no other does. The recording is good, though cut at too low a level; and the orchestral playing from the Concert-gebouw Orchestra is predictably superb. A fine account, then, though one is not sure that one would always wish to turn to it first when wanting to hear the *Ninth*.

Jochum's recording, on the other hand, has greater mystery than almost any other, and the orchestral playing (at the individual level) reaches a degree of eloquence that disarms criticism. Unfor-tunately, however, Jochum does tend to phrase somewhat too affectionately at times, and the architecture of the work does not emerge unscathed as a result. The recording is fine, although (as is often the case from this source) it needs to be played at a high level if the necessary presence and impact are to be had.

There are moments of considerable power in Mehta's reading and orchestral playing of great splendour. In overall cogency and sense of mystery it does not match Walter's, and the somewhat febrile, oversweet *vibrato* on the strings at the opening of the finale is somewhat tiresome on repetition. Nonetheless this is not to be dismissed out of hand, and Decca's recording is up to the high standards of the house. Not a first recommendation, perhaps, but a much better performance than one had expected.

Klemperer's version is slow and deliberate but far from unimpressive; it is more effectively held together than his *Eighth* and it is excellently recorded. Devotees of Klemperer may feel this well worth pursuing, but for most collectors it will not seriously challenge Karajan, Walter, Haitink or Jochum.

CHAMBER MUSIC

String quartet in C minor; (i) *Intermezzo for string quintet.*
> (B) * (*) Oryx ORYX 1808. Keller Quartet; (i) with Georg Schmid (viola).

Bruckner's *String quartet* is a conventional early work (1862), but the last two movements have a lively momentum and the first two are pleasant enough. The performance is acceptable, but the very forward recording cuts down the dynamic range. The work would have fitted easily on one side but in fact spreads to the second, and thus only leaves room for the short *Intermezzo* as a filler. This is much more characteristic music and indeed is well worth having.

String quintet in F major.
> (B) * (*) Oryx ORYX 1807. Keller Quartet, Georg Schmid (viola).

The *String quintet* is a much more characteristic work than the *Quartet*. It dates from 1878–9, the period of the *Fifth* and *Sixth Symphonies*. Bruckner produced an alternative movement for the scherzo (which apparently gave the

work's first performers some difficulties), and this *Intermezzo* appears on the companion Oryx record; the performance here includes the original scherzo. It is sensitive and committed, but the close recorded balance rather reduces the dynamic range of the playing.

CHORAL MUSIC

Mass No. 1 in D minor.
> ** (*) DGG 2530 314. Edith Mathis (soprano), Marga Schiml (contralto), Wieslaw Ochman (tenor), Karl Ridderbusch (bass), Bavarian Radio Chorus and Orchestra, Eugen Jochum.

A noble and moving account of Bruckner's *D minor Mass*, the only version currently on the market. With Jochum in charge of the proceedings, the artistic success of the enterprise is assured; the D minor is an early work, dating from the same year as the *Symphony No. 0*, and it has not been recorded before. The recording is somewhat wanting in presence but although this qualifies the recommendation, it does not substantially weaken its strength, for the music and its performance are eminently worthwhile.

Mass No. 2 in E minor.
> *** Argo ZRG 710. Schütz Choir of London, Philip Jones Brass Ensemble, Roger Norrington.
> ** (*) Telefunken SAT 22545. Bergedorfer Chamber Choir, members of the Hamburg State Philharmonic Orchestra, Hellmut Wormsbächer – SCHUBERT: *Deutsche Messe.***

Norrington's performance of the *E minor Mass* is the best currently available. It is sung with great feeling and perception and is recorded in a flattering

255

acoustic which produces splendid depth and richness of sonority. Jochum's version, which briefly appeared as part of the complete sacred music, probably had greater spirituality and it is to be hoped that DGG will restore it to circulation.

Wormsbächer's account does not lag far behind the Norrington, though the brass tend on occasion to swamp the voices. The performance has obvious sincerity and a genuine feeling for Bruckner's style, and it is a pity that the balance is not ideally judged. The Schubert fill-up is an attraction, of course, though the work does not show that master at the height of his inspiration. Norrington offers no makeweight at all.

Mass No. 3 in F minor (Great).
* (*) HMV ASD 2836. Heather Harper (soprano), Anna Reynolds (contralto), Robert Tear (tenor), Marius Rintzler (bass), New Philharmonia Chorus and Orchestra, Daniel Barenboim.

The *F minor Mass* was completed in 1868, three or four years after the *D minor*, though Bruckner or Schalk made a number of later revisions. Committed Brucknerians will not find this version wholly satisfactory; Barenboim does not quite capture the right atmosphere, though his performance has no lack of character. Karl Forster's fine Berlin reading and the Jochum on DGG are no longer available, but readers might be better advised to await their return to circulation rather than invest in this thoroughly felt but far from idiomatic reading.

Motets

Afferentur regi Virgines; Ecce sacerdos magnus; Inveni David; Os justi; Pange lingua gloriosa.

*** Argo ZRG 760. St John's College Choir, George Guest – LISZT: *Missa choralis.****

Ave Maria; Christus factus est; Locus iste; Os justi; Virga Jesse floruit.
** BASF BAC 3061. Vienna Boys' Choir, Chorus Viennensis, Hans Gillesberger – BRITTEN: *Ceremony of Carols.***

Although on the Argo record the *Motets* are obviously not the main attraction, they make a welcome coupling for Liszt's *Missa choralis*. The performances are of the highest quality, and the recording is marvellously spacious and richly detailed. The combination of the Vienna Boys' Choir and the male voices of the Chorus Viennensis is a successful one, and the performances are effective in a straightforward way. But the acoustic is rather close and the overall effect lacks atmosphere.

Requiem in D minor; 4 Orchestral pieces.
(M) ** (*) Unicorn UNS 210. Barbara Yates (soprano), Sylvia Swan (contralto), John Steel (tenor), Colin Wheatley (bass), Alexandra Choir, London Philharmonic Orchestra, Hans-Hubert Schönzeler; Robert Muns (organ).

Bruckner's *Requiem* is an uncharacteristic early work, written when the composer was in his twenty-fifth year. It needs a strong, enthusiastic performance to make its effect, which is exactly what it receives here. The work is certainly spontaneous, with some fine pages, especially in the later sections. Bruckner places most of the burden on the chorus and less responsibility on his soloists, which suits the present team, for the soloists here are adequate rather than outstanding. The recording, however, is splendidly clear and atmospheric. The *Four Orchestral pieces* date from 1862 and are slight indeed, carrying little indication of the composer's later style.

Te Deum.

*** Philips 6700 038 (2 discs). Elly Ameling (soprano), Anna Reynolds (contralto), Horst Hoffmann (tenor), Guus Hoekman (bass), Netherlands Radio Chorus, Concertgebouw Orchestra, Bernard Haitink – *Symphony No. 7.***

** (*) DGG 2707 024 (2 discs). Maria Stader (soprano), Sieglinde Wagner (contralto), Ernst Haefliger (tenor), Peter Lagger (bass), Berlin Opera Chorus, Berlin Philharmonic Orchestra, Eugen Jochum – *Symphony No. 9.* ** (*)

** (*) HMV ASD 2533. Anne Pashley (soprano), Birgit Finnila (contralto), Robert Tear (tenor), Don Garrard (bass), New Philharmonia Chorus and Orchestra, Daniel Barenboim – BACH: *Magnificat.****

An eloquent performance with admirable breadth and humanity and some fine singing from Maria Stader and Ernst Haefliger as well as superbly loving orchestral support from the Berliners under Jochum. Nonetheless this must yield to Haitink's blazing performance on Philips coupled with a fine account of the *Seventh symphony*; the *Te Deum* is one of the best things Haitink has given us. The Philips recording is the more vivid.

Bruckner's *Te Deum* seems a strange coupling for the Bach *Magnificat*, but by the dynamism which Barenboim injects into both works there is an unexpected link of style. The Bruckner, like the Bach, receives a vivid, boisterous performance, relying not so much on massive choral effects (the recording was done with a comparatively small choir in a smallish church) as on rhythmic energy. Baren-

boim's approach to Bruckner will no doubt acquire more detail over the years, but this is already most warmly enjoyable. An excellent choice if the coupling suits.

Burgmüller, Friedrich (1804–74)

La Péri (ballet): complete recording (ed. Bonynge).

** Decca SXL 6407. London Symphony Orchestra, Richard Bonynge.

Burgmüller's *La Péri* is a contemporary of Adam's *Giselle*. Both works were originally danced by the famous ballerina Grisi, and the music was a key score in the development of ballet and what the composer was expected to provide for it. Burgmüller's writing is not as distinctive as Adam's, but it is tuneful in an obvious way and is both romantic and elegant in conception, while the orchestration has a certain colour and charm. The playing here is persuasive, and the recording is Decca's best.

Bush, Alan (born 1900)

Variations, Nocturne and Finale on an old English sea-song, Op. 60.

(B) ** Pye GSGC 14073. David Wilde (piano), Royal Philharmonic Orchestra, John Snashall – DELIUS: *Double concerto.***

Very little of Alan Bush's music is available on record, and this is a welcome issue, if only as a comparatively lightweight and palatable coupling for the magnificent Delius concerto on the reverse. The opening variations have the bright charm that wartime radio listeners will remember from Tommy Handley's *Itma* arrangements (many of them by very reputable composers), but the *Nocturne* and *Finale* both go on too long. Excellent playing by David Wilde, a pianist we should hear more of on record.

(i) *3 Concert studies for violin, cello and piano, Op. 31;* (ii) (piano) *2 Ballads of the Sea: The Cruel Sea Captain, Op. 50; Suite, Op. 54: Galliard; Air; Corentyne Kwee-Kwe.*

** (*) Argo ZRG 749. (i) Hugh Bean (violin), Eileen Croxford (cello), David Parkhouse (piano); (ii) the composer (piano) – BERKELEY: *Sonatina; Sextet.****

Alan Bush's *Concert studies* are perhaps not quite as successful as the Berkeley coupling: their content is not wholly in harmony with their dimensions, and the composer's own piano playing is not as completely assured as one would like. However, this composer is unfairly neglected; one wishes the *Dialectic for string quartet* would return to the catalogue.

Busoni, Ferruccio
(1866–1924)

(i) *Concertino for clarinet and small orchestra, Op. 48;* (ii) *Divertimento for flute and orchestra, Op. 52;* (iii) *Konzertstück for piano with orchestra, Op. 31a;* (iv) *Rondo arlecchinesco for orchestra with tenor, Op. 46.*

(M) ** (*) Vox STGBY 616. (i) Walter Triebskorn (clarinet); (ii) Herman Klemeyer (flute); (iii) Frank Glazer (piano); (iv) W. Moser (tenor);

all with Berlin Symphony Orchestra, C. A. Bünte.

This disc deserves three stars for enterprise, for the music it contains furthers the cause of Busoni as a brilliantly original composer more than some of his more ambitious works do. The short *Divertimento for flute and orchestra*, with its witty fanfare opening and quirky humour, is most fetching, and the cool *Clarinet concertino* is no less brilliantly inventive. The *Konzertstück* is a bravura, extrovert work with a very jolly scherzando section, and the *Rondo arlecchinesco* is modern-sounding (shades of Prokofiev and Shostakovich at the opening). It has a humorous finale, where the tenor voice comes in briefly. It must have been very avant-garde in its day. All the soloists are good; all the performances are committed; the recording has plenty of atmosphere even if it is not always tonally perfect. Highly recommended.

Piano concerto, Op. 39; Doktor Faust (opera): *Saraband* and *Cortège.*

** (*) HMV SLS 776 (2 discs). John Ogdon (piano), John Alldis Choir, Royal Philharmonic Orchestra, Daniell Revenaugh.

Busoni worked on his marathon *Piano concerto* from 1902 to 1904. As a concerto it is unique in running to 68 minutes, about the same time as Beethoven's *Choral symphony*, with which it has another parallel in its choral finale. Busoni sets words from Oehlenschlager, to be sung by a male chorus. With such an ambitious design it must be expected that the music's inspiration is uneven (or it would have managed a place in the repertory before now) but with John Ogdon's magisterial and enthusiastic advocacy to support it, the listener can be assured that its more effective sections are fully realized here. Even so, matters do not always rest in Ogdon's hands, for much of the most important material lies with the orchestra, the piano often tending to act more as a poetic obbligato to the work's main content. Unfortunately the opening, and the final *Cantico* (in which the contribution from the John Alldis Choir is first-rate) are among the work's weaker pages, and the *Tarantella* is somewhat relentless. Yet there are many fine moments too, not least the imaginative opening of the *Pezzo serioso*, the third movement.

John Ogdon's striking brilliance is well supported by Daniell Revenaugh, and he and the orchestra come into their own in the very attractive excerpts from *Doktor Faust* which fill up the fourth side of the set. These show the composer at his most imaginative. The recording throughout is first-rate.

Violin sonatas Nos. 1 in E minor, Op. 29; 2 in E minor, Op. 36a.

(M) * (*) Oiseau-Lyre SOL 296. Hyman Bress (violin), Bengt Johnsson (piano).

Although Hyman Bress shows plenty of temperament and his playing is always emotionally alive, he is also inclined to be slapdash in the music's more vigorous moments. But this is better than accurate playing without emotional impetus, and it does show us that both these sonatas are well constructed and that Busoni's melodic gift was considerable.

Ballet-scene No. 4; Elegies Nos. 1–7 (for piano).

*** Argo ZRG 741. Martin Jones (piano).

Busoni is better represented in the catalogue now than he has been for some time. Yet strangely enough his piano music is still neglected by recording artists. Martin Jones is to be congratulated for his enterprise and dedication in the *Elegies*, and neither the performance nor the recording can be seriously faulted. This is rewarding, thought-provoking music that should be in the library of every serious collector who cares about twentieth-century music.

Fantasia contrappuntistica (Preludio al corale 'Gloria al Signori nei Cieli' e fuga a quattro soggetti obligati sopra un frammento di Bach) (ed. Middelschulte).

(M) * (**) Pye Virtuoso TPLS 13024. Nicholas Danby (organ of the Royal Festival Hall, London).

Busoni's *Fantasia contrappuntistica* is based on Bach's Contrapunctus XVIII from the *Art of Fugue*. The work was inspired by the composer's wish to complete Bach's unfinished fugue. In order to do this he had to create the fourth subject, as Bach only revealed the first three, and Busoni decided to add a fifth contrasted idea to help cement the others. The resulting *Fantasia* is of formidable structural and emotional power. There are several versions, and the adaptation for organ was edited by the work's dedicatee, Wilhelm Middelschulte. Nicholas Danby plays it splendidly, building the final climax with a fine overall control of tension, so that the quieter music still retains the listener's emotional as well as intellectual ear. The work obviously suits the Festival Hall organ well, for the sombre colouring of the registration is highly effective, and it is a pity that Pye's recording, which, rightly, has a wide dynamic range, is over-modulated at the side-ends, so that few pick-ups will be able to cope without a degree of distortion.

Doktor Faust (opera in 2 prologues, intermezzo, 3 scenes and epilogue): complete recording.

*** DGG 2709 032 (3 discs). Dietrich Fischer-Dieskau (baritone), Karl Christian Kohn (bass), William Cochrane (tenor), Bavarian Opera Chorus, Bavarian Radio Orchestra, Ferdinand Leitner.

Busoni did not live to complete *Doktor Faust*, which crowns his creative career, and the task of finishing it was undertaken by his pupil Philipp Jarnach. It is a work of astonishing vision and originality whose fascination cannot be over-emphasized. This performance was recorded in conjunction with a broadcast mounted by the European Broadcasting Union, for the complexities of putting on a work of such importance are numerous. Fischer-Dieskau is, of course, a masterly Faust and dominates the proceedings (not that his is the only fine performance in the set), and the music is so deeply imaginative and richly rewarding that no one should lose the opportunity of investing in this recording. We are never likely to get another so that even the irritation one feels at the small but tiresome cuts made (presumably for the broadcast) and fury that these should all be applied to Busoni's text while Jarnach's completion is untouched, and the less than ideal casting for the Duchess of Parma, should not be allowed to qualify a recommendation. This is an enormously rewarding score, and DGG give us recording quality of their usual high standard, though the voices at times mask orchestral detail.

Butterworth, George
(1885–1916)

The Banks of Green Willow (Idyll); *A Shropshire Lad* (Rhapsody).

*** HMV CSD 3696. English Sinfonia, Neville Dilkes (with *Concert: 'English music'***).

English idylls Nos. 1 and 2.

*** HMV CSD 3705. English Sinfonia, Neville Dilkes (with *Concert: 'English music', Volume 2***).

Butterworth's *Shropshire Lad* represents the English folk-song school at its most captivatingly atmospheric, and the other works are in a similarly appealing pastoral vein. Whether Butterworth would have gone on, had he lived through the First World War, to develop as his friend Vaughan Williams did is an interesting point, but the delicate genius here is displayed at its most rewarding. The HMV performances are sensitive, and with fine, ripe recording both these discs are worth investigating. They are discussed more fully in our companion *Treasury* volume. There is also a performance available of *A Shropshire Lad* coupled to Bax's *Garden of Fand* and Vaughan Williams's *Eighth Symphony* (Pye GSGC 14061): here Barbirolli, with the benefit of very forward recording, good for its time (late fifties), gives an attractive performance, though without finding the last degree of hushed intensity.

Buxtehude, Dietrich
(1637–1707)

Ciacona in E minor; Passacaglia in D minor (Dorian); Prelude, fugue and chaconne in C major; Prelude and fugue in A minor; Prelude and fugue in F sharp minor; Prelude and fugue in G minor.

(B) ** Oryx ORYX 1732. Lionel Rogg (pedal harpsichord).

This is articulate playing, with tempi on the slow side but the clarity of the music realized to perfection. The recording too is excellent, and never oppressive. The disc does equal justice to the music of Buxtehude and to the image of the pedal harpsichord (the instrument is a Wittmayer).

Canzonettas in E minor and G minor;
Ciacona in E minor; Chorale fantasias:
Magnificat primi toni; Nun lob mein
Seel den Herren; Chorale prelude: Gott
der Vater, wohn uns bei; Preludes and
fugues in A minor and F major;
Toccata in D minor.

(M) *** Pye Virtuoso TPLS 13041.
Nicholas Danby (organ, or small
positive organ of the Marien-
kirche, Lemgo).

This admirable record, made on a perfectly chosen organ for the music, lets us
readily understand why Bach was prepared, as a youth, to walk some 200 miles
from Arnstadt to Lübeck to hear Buxtehude himself play. The music of Bach's
great North German precursor is strong
in personality, and its style, a curious
mixture of austerity and geniality, is
direct and appealing. Nicholas Danby
presents it here with great skill, and with
an unerring feeling for baroque colouring. Indeed the registration is a continual
source of pleasure and the relaxed playing
easily holds the listener's attention
whether the music is gentle, like the
charming Canzonetta in E minor, or
ambitious and forward-looking like the
large-scale Toccata in D minor, which
opens the concert so splendidly. The
recording is excellent and easy to reproduce once the upper register has been
smoothed.

Byrd, William
(1543–1623)

Cantiones sacrae: complete recording.
(M) *** Oiseau-Lyre SOL 311/3 (records available separately). Cantores in Ecclesia, Michael Howard
– TALLIS: Cantiones sacrae.***

This set of three records offers the
complete Cantiones sacrae that Byrd and

Tallis published jointly in 1575. The
Cantores in Ecclesia is a small body of
singers with extremely fine intonation
and clean, well-focused tone. Michael
Howard secures from them performances
of genuine fervour and does not shrink
from expressive dynamic shadings. These
are splendidly committed performances
and are beautifully recorded. Anyone
buying the first record will not fail to go
on to the others, and readers with special
interests in this period should not miss
this welcome issue.

Mass for three voices.
* (*) DGG Archive 2533 113. Pro
Cantione Antiqua, Bruno Turner
– TALLIS: Lamentations.* (*)

There are no complaints here about the
performance. It may be too overtly
expressive for some tastes, but it is
thoroughly convincing and superbly
executed. Unfortunately the recording
resorts to multi-mike techniques that
produce an unrealistic sound picture.
The voices tend to be close to us, and at
the same time the ambience is confused
and a little muddy. With this reservation
the disc can be recommended.

Mass for three voices; Mass for four
voices.
⊛ *** Argo ZRG 5362. King's College Chapel Choir, David Willcocks.

This is one of the very finest discs
among the many made by the King's
College Choir under David Willcocks.
The flowing lines of Byrd's two beautiful
settings of the Mass are sustained here
with an inevitability of phrasing and a
control of sonority and dynamic that
ravish the ear and at the same time soothe
the senses with a marvellous sense of
peace. The remarkable thing is that in
the Protestant England of the Elizabethan
period the music could only have been

written for private performance. But its dedication and inspiration pay eloquent testimony to the depth of the composer's own faith. The acoustic of the recording is admirably judged so that the music seems to float in space and yet retain its meaning and clarity.

Cage, John
(born 1912)

Concerto for prepared piano and orchestra.
(M) ** Nonesuch H 71202. Yuji Takahashi (piano), Buffalo Philharmonic Orchestra, Lukas Foss – FOSS: *Baroque variations.***

However hard John Cage presses his crusade for 'the depersonalization of music', a work like this (written in 1951, rather before his more extreme experiments) shows the deeply personal results of almost any musical self-expression. Wispy as the sound is, with the prepared piano contributing sounds of oriental delicacy, the result – taken from a live performance in Buffalo in 1958 – has a clear enough concentration to compare with more conventional music. Much is owed to the performance, by the work not only of Foss and the orchestra, but the fine Japanese pianist, Takahashi, best known for his interpretations of the music of Xenakis.

Campra, André
(1660–1744)

L'Europe galante (opera-ballet): suite.
(M) *** Oiseau-Lyre SOL 302. English Chamber Orchestra, Raymond Leppard – RAMEAU: *Le Temple de la gloire.***

Campra, who was a few years older than Couperin, possessed keen melodic instincts and a genuine freshness. His work seems to be gaining a wider following now, and this suite is marked by a characteristic lyrical grace. It is given a thoroughly idiomatic performance and an excellent recording. A most enjoyable disc.

Canteloube, Marie-Joseph
(1879–1957)

Chants d'Auvergne (arrangements): *Baïlèro; 3 Bourées; L'Aio dè rotso; Ound' onorèn gorda; Obal din lou Limouzi; La delaïssádo; Lo fiolaire; Passo pel prat; Brezairola* (Berceuse); *Chut chut.*
*** HMV ASD 2826. Victoria de los Angeles (soprano), Lamoureux Orchestra, Jean-Pierre Jacquillat – CHAUSSON: *Poème de l'amour et de la mer.***

Canteloube, pupil of Vincent d'Indy, made a collection of charming folk-songs from the Auvergne which he then presented with seductive opulence. Some might prefer an edgier, more French-sounding voice, but the warmth of Victoria de los Angeles's tone matches exactly the allure of the settings of this selection of ten songs. An irresistible disc, beautifully recorded.

Carissimi, Giacomo
(1605–74)

Jephtha (oratorio).
(M) * Philips Universo 6580 081. Rosemary Rönisch (soprano), Gertraud Prenzlow (contralto), Peter Schreier (tenor), Siegfried

Hausmann (bass), Berlin Radio Choir, Berlin Chamber Orchestra, Helmut Koch – HANDEL: *Armida abbandonata.**

Jephtha is arguably Carissimi's masterpiece. Until recently there was an eminently recommendable version on Turnabout, now deleted. The present version is too ornate and fussily realized to be more than a stopgap. Strings are added in this account, which robs the music of its purity of effect. Not really recommended.

Carter, Elliott
(born 1908)

(i) *Sonata for flute, oboe, cello and harpsichord;* (ii) *Violoncello sonata* (for cello and piano).
(M) ** (*) Nonesuch H 71234. (i) Harvey Sollbergerl (flute), Charles Kuskin (oboe), Fred Sherry (cello), Paul Jacobs (harpsichord); (ii) Joel Krosnick (cello), Paul Jacobs (piano).

Carter wrote his *Cello sonata* in the late 1940s, at a time when he had yet to develop his most uncompromising manner. The four movements, alternately lyrical and energetic, are immediately attractive yet also immediately reveal the seriousness of their argument. The *Sonata* for baroque ensemble gets away from neoclassic conventions in purposeful music, strongly argued in this performance. The balance in the *Cello sonata* is unkind to the piano, but the sound is more than faithful enough to let the music communicate.

String quartets Nos. 1 and 2.
(M) *** Nonesuch H 71249. Composers' Quartet.

Elliott Carter, tough and uncompromising, making severe demands on the concentration of even the most skilled and sympathetic listeners (let alone on performers) is well suited to the genre of the string quartet. These are works which naturally follow on where Bartók and Schoenberg left off, and though you may feel that Carter's personality is not so universally communicative as those two twentieth-century masters, his music never fails to present a challenge worth taking – and never more so than in these strong works, which are superbly performed here.

Castelnuovo-Tedesco, Mario
(1895–1968)

Double guitar concerto.
(M) * (*) CBS Classics 61469. Sergio and Eduardo Abreu (guitars), English Chamber Orchestra, Enrique Garcia Asensio – SANTÓRSOLA: *Double guitar concerto.****

The quality of invention of Castelnuovo-Tedesco's *Double concerto* is unimpressive to say the least, and all the brilliance of the excellent playing here fails to redeem its cheapness, except perhaps in the finale, where the 'Mexican' flavour adds a certain folksy spontaneity. But the coupling is well worth having, so guitar-lovers may feel inclined to be indulgent.

Catalani, Alfredo
(1854–93)

La Wally (opera in 4 acts): complete recording.

** Decca SET 394/6. Renata Tebaldi (soprano), Mario del Monaco (tenor), Piero Cappuccilli (baritone), Justino Diaz (bass), Turin Lyric Chorus, Monte Carlo National Opera Orchestra, Fausto Cleva.

Catalani's *La Wally* produced one well-known aria – the heroine's *Ebben? Ne andrò lontana* – and otherwise has languished outside Italy. Yet Verdi and Toscanini were among Catalani's enthusiastic admirers (Toscanini named his children after characters in this opera), and the neglect may in part be due to the composer's lamentably early death before the age of forty. It is good to have a lavishly presented performance of this, his most famous opera, but it does bring out clearly enough that the plot is curiously weak, with dramatic effects repeated in parallel, and that fundamentally, for all the romantic attractiveness of the idiom, Catalani was not a very distinctive melodist. Cleva directs a strong performance, in which Tebaldi sings with much of her old richness, power and feeling, and after an unpleasantly coarse start del Monaco provides some attractively ringing singing. Excellent recording.

La Wally: highlights.
** Decca SET 489 (from above recording).

Though the complete opera is well worth hearing, with its distinctive vein of lyrical high romanticism, it is a work which many record-collectors will prefer to sample rather than swallow complete. Decca's high standard of preparing highlights records is well maintained here. Needless to say, both of the heroine's two big scenes are included.

Cavalli, Francesco
(1602–76)

La Calisto (opera): complete recording (freely arranged performing version by Raymond Leppard).

⊛ *** Argo ZNF 11/12. Ileana Cotrubas (soprano), Janet Baker (mezzo-soprano), James Bowman (counter-tenor), Hugues Cuénod (tenor), Federico Davia (bass), Peter Gottlieb (baritone), Glyndebourne Festival Chorus, London Philharmonic Orchestra, Raymond Leppard.

No more perfect Glyndebourne entertainment has been devised than this freely adapted version of an opera written for Venice in the 1650s but never heard since. Even more than Leppard's other Cavalli confection, *L'Ormindo*, it exactly relates that permissive society of the seventeenth century to our own. It is the more delectable because of the brilliant part given to the goddess Diana, taken by Janet Baker. In Leppard's version she has a dual task: portraying the chaste goddess herself but then in the same costume switching immediately to the randy Jupiter disguised as Diana, quite a different character. Add to that a bad-tempered ageing nymph, hilariously portrayed by Hugues Cuénod, and parts for such singers as James Bowman that draw out their finest qualities, and the result is magic. No one should miss hearing Janet Baker's heart-breakingly intense singing of her tender aria *Amara servitù*. The recording, made at Glyndebourne, is gloriously atmospheric.

L'Ormindo (opera in 2 acts): complete recording (ed. Raymond Leppard).
*** Argo ZNF 8/10. John Wakefield (tenor), Peter-Christoph Runge

(baritone), Isabel Garcisanz, Hanneke van Bork (sopranos), Jean Allister (contralto), Hugues Cuénod (tenor), Anne Howells, Jane Berbié (mezzo-sopranos), Federico Davia, Richard von Allan (basses), London Philharmonic Orchestra, Raymond Leppard.

We owe it above all to Raymond Leppard that the name of Francesco Cavalli has become famous again. He discovered the long-forgotten score of this fascinating opera, and subjected it to his own magical Leppardization process to produce one of the most enchanting of Glyndebourne entertainments. The gaiety of Glyndebourne is superbly caught, for wisely Argo opted to record the work on the company's home ground in Sussex, using the Organ Room for studio instead of the excessively dry-sounding opera-house proper. The sounds are nothing short of luscious, often almost Straussian in their opulence, and Leppard's array of continuo instruments constantly charms the ear. Anne Howells makes a fine Erisbe, so pure-sounding one scarcely credits the blatant immorality of the story. Indeed the whole point is that one should not question it, but accept it as a product of the permissive society of 1750. Excellent contributions from the whole team, with special mention required for the veteran Hugues Cuénod in the 'drag' part of the maid Erice. Gloriously rich recording quality.

Chabrier, Emmanuel
(1841–94)

España (rhapsody).
(B) ** Classics for Pleasure CFP 169. London Philharmonic Orchestra, John Pritchard – RAVEL: *Rapsodie;* RIMSKY-KORSAKOV: *Capriccio espagnole.***(*)

A performance with *joie de vivre,* if without the humorous twinkle a Beecham could bring. Nevertheless the recording has sparkle and the overall effect of the piece is exhilarating and enjoyable.

España (rhapsody); *Marche joyeuse; Suite pastorale; Le Roi malgré lui* (opera): excerpts: *Danse slave; Fête polonaise.*
** (*) Decca SXL 6188. Suisse Romande Orchestra, Ernest Ansermet.

Extremely brilliant recording, typical of Decca's best in terms of amplitude (and percussion and bass drum) but with rather more edge to the treble than on some recordings from this source. The performances are all good, with a certain Gallic accent coming through in places, but *España* lacks the uninhibited exuberance that Beecham, for instance, brought to it. Those who like this touch of reserve will also like the *Suite pastorale,* which is rather contained, especially in the third movement, *Sous Bois.* However, by the second side the conductor seems to have warmed up. The *Marche joyeuse* certainly offers its measure of high spirits; the *Danse slave* has an agreeable panache, and the *Fête polonaise* goes splendidly. With all one's reservations, as a whole this disc offers an enjoyable selection of this composer's most attractive music.

Chappell, Herbert
(20th century)

Dead in Tune; George and the Dragonfly (stories for narrator and orchestra).
** Argo ZDA 134. Robin Ray, Susan Stranks, John Kershaw (narrators), Leicestershire Schools Symphony Orchestra, the composer.

These stories for narrator and orchestra are designed for children, which means that grown-ups should not groan too loud when they are faced with some of the most barefaced puns ever committed to record. *Dead in Tune*, first seen on television, is a detective story with the instruments of the orchestra as the main characters, and though the music of neither piece is particularly original or inspired, it is all good fun, and the performances, nicely recorded, are lively.

Charpentier, Marc-Antoine
(1634–1704)

Médée (opera): suite of ten movements.
> (M) *** Oiseau-Lyre SOL 300. English Chamber Orchestra, Raymond Leppard – COUPERIN: *Apothéose de Lully*.***

Marc-Antoine Charpentier is shown here as an attractive and inventive composer, and this suite arranged from his opera *Médée* by Raymond Leppard offers some pleasant, undemanding listening. The playing is immensely alert and undoubtedly stylish and the recording extremely fine.

Grand Magnificat; Te Deum (both trans. and realized Guy Lambert).
> (M) ** Vanguard HM 12SD. Martha Angelici, Jocelyne Chamonin (sopranos), André Mallabrera (counter-tenor), Rémy Corazza (tenor), George Abdoun (baritone), Jacques Mars (bass), Chorale des Jeunesses Musicales, France, Jean-François Paillard Orchestra, Louis Martini.

Charpentier was a pupil of Carissimi, and although inspiration does not run as freely as it does in the greatest Baroque masters, his music has undeniable appeal. These two works are well played and recorded, though the performances are not outstanding; but given the modest price, collectors need have no reservations about investigating what is attractive period music.

Midnight Mass for Christmas Eve.
> ** HMV ASD 2340. April Cantelo, Helen Gelmar (sopranos), Ian Partridge (tenor), James Bowman (alto), Christopher Keyte (bass), King's College Chapel Choir, David Willcocks – PURCELL: *Te Deum*.* (*)

There is a kinship here with the Czech settings of the Mass that incorporate folk material, and the combination of verse anthems and carol-like pieces is attractive, even the *Kyrie* having a jolly quality about it.

The performance is warm and musical (with a recording to match), but one feels a lack of bite and there is certainly no suggestion of any Gallic flavour. This is partly the fault of the acoustic, but remembering the fine – deleted – Argo recording by French artists one feels that the present HMV disc does not make an entirely satisfying alternative. The organist, Andrew Davis, intelligently uses realizations of the organ interludes – which the composer directs shall be based on the carol themes – by Nicolas Le Bègue.

Chausson, Ernest
(1855–99)

Poème for violin and orchestra, Op. 25.
> (M) *** HMV SXLP 30159. Nathan Milstein (violin), Philharmonia Orchestra, Anatole Fistoulari – SAINT-SAËNS: *Concerto No. 3; Introduction and rondo*.**(*)

Poème for violin and piano, Op. 25.
(M) * (*) DGG Privilege 2538 302.
Miriam Fried (violin), Gisele
Demoulin (piano) – SIBELIUS:
Concerto. * (*)

Chausson's *Poème* is a haunting piece full of delicate nostalgia. Older readers will recall Menuhin's wonderful account of it with Enesco on 78s, and more recently Grumiaux did a marvellously rapt stereo version. Unfortunately the work appears only as a fill-up so that recommendations are invariably hamstrung by extra-musical considerations. Milstein's account is probably the best on the market. Though not new, it sounds remarkably fresh and is excellently balanced. The brilliant young Israeli violinist, Miriam Fried, hardly competes: her version is recorded with piano, and the keyboard is a very monochrome substitute for Chausson's evocative scoring.

Symphony in B flat major, Op. 20.
** Decca SXL 6310. Suisse Romande Orchestra, Ernest Ansermet – FRANCK: *Les Eolides.***
(B) * (*) Decca Eclipse ECS 640. Paris Conservatoire Orchestra, Robert Denzler – HONEGGER: *Symphony No. 3.* * (*)

Ansermet's performance of Chausson's only symphony is warmly sympathetic, and those attracted by the unusual coupling will not be disappointed. The brilliant recording is an improvement on the Eclipse version with Denzler. This offers more music, and the performance of the Chausson is respectable, but for those wanting either this or the Honegger coupling, Denzler is not a first recommendation.

Poème de l'amour et de la mer (song cycle), *Op. 19.*
*** HMV ASD 2826. Victoria de

los Angeles (soprano), Lamoureux Orchestra, Jean-Pierre Jacquillat – CANTELOUBE: *Chants d'Auvergne.****

The voice of Victoria de los Angeles is ideally suited to Chausson's warm and evocative piece, a work unjustly neglected on record for not being the right length for LP. Coupled here with Canteloube's charming folk-song settings, it can be enthusiastically recommended. Good recording.

Cherubini, Luigi
(1760–1842)

Symphony in D major.
*** Philips 6500 154. New Philharmonia Orchestra, Wilfried Boettcher – WEBER: *Symphony No. 1.****

Since Toscanini's classic account, recordings of Cherubini's fine symphony have been few and far between. This is undoubtedly the best both in terms of performance, which is solid, lively and well thought-out, and recording, which is well balanced and truthful in timbre. Readers who do not know the symphony are strongly urged to investigate this admirable disc. Cherubini earned the admiration of no less a judge than Beethoven, and this work deserves more frequent hearings.

Chopin, Frédéric
(1810–49)

CONCERTANTE AND
ORCHESTRAL MUSIC

(i) *Andante spianato and Grande polonaise brillante in E flat major, Op. 22;*

(ii) *Piano concertos Nos. 1 in E minor, Op. 11;* (i) *2 in F minor, Op. 21.*

(M) ** (*) RCA DPS 2034 (2 discs). Artur Rubinstein (piano), (i) Symphony of the Air, Alfred Wallenstein, (ii) (London) New Symphony Orchestra, Stanislaw Skrowaczewski.

Andante spianato and Grande polonaise brillante, Op. 22; Fantasy on Polish airs, Op. 13; Krakowiak (Concert rondo), *Op. 14; Variations on 'Là ci darem' from Mozart's 'Don Giovanni,' Op. 2.*

** HMV ASD 2371. Alexis Weissenberg (piano), Paris Conservatoire Orchestra, Stanislaw Skrowaczewski.

* (*) Philips 6500 422 (without *Krakowiak*). Claudio Arrau (piano), London Philharmonic Orchestra, Eliahu Inbal.

Andante spianato and Grande polonaise brillante, Op. 22; Krakowiak (concert rondo), *Op. 14.*

(B) ** Turnabout TV 37015S. Peter Frankl (piano), Innsbruck Symphony Orchestra, Robert Wagner – LISZT: *Hungarian fantasia.***

Rubinstein's fine performances come from the mid sixties. In the *First Concerto* he does not quite rival Pollini (see below), whose fresh sensibility and impeccable technique are matchless, and in No. 2 there is much to be said in Vàsàry's favour: his is a beautifully controlled yet spontaneous version. However, Rubinstein's is an eminently desirable set, with all his keyboard distinction and personality to recommend it. Only the very last ounce of spontaneity is missing.

The HMV disc may be considered a useful compilation. Alexis Weissenberg plays musically, and the orchestral contribution is adequate. The recording is very pleasing indeed and compensates to a certain extent for a lack of panache in the performances. Arrau offers one work less and in any case the reservations that apply to his companion discs of the two concertos must, alas, also be noted here. If you are happy with the *Andante spianato* and *Krakowiak* (which has a couple of fetching tunes, one at the opening and one later on), then Frankl's sensitive performances have much to commend them, including economy. The Turnabout recording is good if a little reverberant.

Chopiniana (ballet; orchestrated and arranged by Glazounov and Keller): complete recording.

** HMV ASD 2925. Bolshoi Theatre Orchestra, Algis Zuraitis.

Chopiniana was the original of the Diaghilev ballet which was eventually to become *Les Sylphides.* The first score was based on Glazounov's *Chopiniana suite,* but as the ballet evolved so did the music, until dance and orchestration merged into the poetic imagery that is today one of the most beautiful of all abstract romantic ballets. The choreography of *Chopiniana* was a good deal more extrovert; instead of a moonlit opening scene, it began with the *Polonaise in A major,* danced in full Polish national regalia. This vivacious and intense account of the full *Chopiniana* is brilliantly recorded and is entertaining in its own right; but it has little of the unity or magic of *Sylphides* as we know it.

Piano concerto No. 1 in E minor, Op. 11.

⊛ (M) *** HMV SXLP 30160. Maurizio Pollini (piano), Philharmonia Orchestra, Paul Kletzki.

** (*) DGG SLPM 139383. Martha Argerich (piano), London Symphony Orchestra, Claudio Abbado – LISZT: *Concerto No. 1.*** (*)

* (*) Philips 6500 255. Claudio

Arrau (piano), London Philharmonic Orchestra, Eliahu Inbal.

Piano concerto No. 1 in E minor, Op. 11. Mazurkas Nos. 5 in B flat major, Op. 7/1; 46 in C major, Op. 67/3; 47 in A minor, Op. 68/2; 54 in D major, Op. posth.

** DGG SLPEM 136453. Tamàs Vàsàry (piano), Berlin Philharmonic Orchestra, Jerzy Semkow.

Piano concerto No. 1 in E minor, Op. 11. Piano sonata No. 2 in B flat minor (Funeral march), Op. 35.

* (*) Decca Phase 4 PFS 4311. Israela Margalit (piano), New Philharmonia Orchestra, Lorin Maazel.

Pollini's classic recording, made shortly after he won the Warsaw Prize in 1959 as a youth of eighteen, still remains the best, particularly now that the sound has been improved. One would not in fact guess the date of this recording, so fresh, well-defined and detailed is the sound picture. This is playing of such total spontaneity, poetic feeling and refined judgement that criticism is silenced. It is so marvellously sparkling and the *rubato* so superbly judged that one forgets about the performers and thinks only of Chopin.

The distinction of the Argerich/Abbado performance is immediately apparent in the opening orchestral ritornello with Abbado's flexible approach. Martha Argerich follows his lead and her affectionate phrasing provides some lovely playing, especially in the slow movement. Perhaps in the passage-work she is sometimes rather too intense, giving the music a toccata-like effect, but this is far preferable to the rambling style we are sometimes offered. With excellent recording this is, after Pollini, one of the most satisfactory versions available of this elusive concerto.

On SLPEM 136453, a big orchestral sound from DGG and an opening tutti full of personality with the second subject beautifully phrased by Semkow. After this Vàsàry sounds rather more ordinary. He seems marginally backwardly balanced, or perhaps it is a matter of his personality not coming through fully, rather than the dynamic. All in all, although very well recorded, for all its obvious freshness and intelligence, this just misses the top of the list.

On Philips the balance gives the soloist undue prominence, but the overall sound is beautifully fresh and truthful in timbre. Arrau's playing is immaculately aristocratic, but his *rubato* will not convince everyone. His expressive hesitations do not always grow naturally out of what has gone before, and for all its merits, this would not be a first choice.

On Decca Phase 4 husband and wife as conductor and soloist, Maazel and Margalit, produce a harmonious, enjoyable reading of the concerto; but with indifferent orchestral playing and idiosyncratic sound it is not one of the most recommendable versions. Nor can this version of the sonata quite compare with the finest available.

Piano concerto No. 2 in F minor, Op. 21.

*** Decca SXL 6174. Vladimir Ashkenazy (piano), London Symphony Orchestra, David Zinman – BACH: *Harpsichord concerto No. 1.***

** (*) Decca SXL 6528. Alicia de Larrocha (piano), Suisse Romande Orchestra, Sergiu Comissiona – FALLA: *Nights in the Gardens of Spain.****

Piano concerto No. 2 in F minor, Op. 21. Ballade No. 3 in A flat major, Op. 47; Barcarolle in F sharp major, Op. 60; Nocturne No. 17 in B major, Op. 62/1; Scherzo No. 3 in C sharp minor, Op. 39.

*** Decca SXL 6693. Vladimir

Ashkenazy (piano), London Symphony Orchestra, David Zinman.

Piano concerto No. 2 in F minor, Op. 21. Andante spianato and Grande polonaise brillante, Op. 22; Nocturne in C sharp minor, Op. posth.

   *** DGG SLPEM 136452. Tamàs Vàsàry (piano), Berlin Philharmonic Orchestra, Kulka.

Piano concerto No. 2 in F minor, Op. 21; Krakowiak (Concert rondo), Op. 14.

   * (*) Philips 6500 309. Claudio Arrau (piano), London Philharmonic Orchestra, Eliahu Inbal.

Vàsàry's performance is exceptionally well balanced and recorded. The direction of the orchestra is such as to give the tuttis much more stature and impact than usual, and the playing of the soloist is equally alive and spirited. Thus the passage-work never drags and the lyrical writing blossoms as it should. The slow movement is played most beautifully, and the sound throughout is first-rate. The fillers are generous and the *Andante spianato* is especially beguiling.

Ashkenazy's sympathy with the music is very obvious and his sophisticated use of light and shade in the opening movement, and the subtlety of phrasing and *rubato*, are a constant source of pleasure. The recitativo section in the *Larghetto*, which can often sound merely rhetorical, is here shaped with mastery, and there is a delicious lightness of touch in the finale. David Zinman and the players of the LSO are obviously in full contact with the soloist, and the recording is one of Decca's very best. The coupling of Bach seems inappropriate, and Decca made amends with a newer issue which supports the concerto with a fine recital selected from Ashkenazy's solo recordings.

Larrocha's account is attractive and poetic. It is less characterful than her excellent performance of the Falla coupling, but there is much to admire

here, including the fine Decca engineering. However, generally speaking this must yield to Vàsàry and Ashkenazy.

Arrau is forwardly balanced, and his *rubato* will at times seem mannered. The LPO under Inbal give loyal support, but the disc is not one to kindle universal enthusiasm. For Arrau specialists only.

Les Sylphides (ballet; orchestrated by Roy Douglas).

   *** DGG SLPEM 136257. Berlin Philharmonic Orchestra, Herbert von Karajan – DELIBES: *Coppélia*.***

   (M) ** (*) CBS Classics 61016. Philadelphia Orchestra, Eugene Ormandy – DELIBES: *Coppélia*; *Sylvia*.***

   (M) ** Decca Ace of Diamonds SDD 221. Paris Conservatoire Orchestra, Peter Maag – DELIBES: *La Source*.**

Karajan has the advantage of limpid and svelte playing from the Berlin Philharmonic Orchestra, and he evokes a delicacy of texture which consistently delights the ear. The woodwind solos are played gently and lovingly and one can feel the conductor's touch on the phrasing. The upper register of the strings is clearly focused, the recording is warm and atmospheric, and this is one of Karajan's finest discs. Ormandy's is a performance of strong contrasts. The lyrical music (for example, the opening *Prelude and Nocturne*) is gentle, but the lively sections are played with irrepressible brilliance. Some might feel that this extrovert approach is almost overdone in the first *Waltz*, where Ormandy gives the upper strings their head, but later the playing has that rich, expansive excitement for which this orchestra is famous. The orchestral playing is sensitive under the musical baton of Peter Maag, and even the French woodwind playing does not seem as nasal as usual, but the current transfer of the recording, although excellent in definition, has lost something in the way of warmth and bloom. This is fair value at Ace of Diamonds price.

CHAMBER AND INSTRUMENTAL MUSIC

Piano trio in G minor, Op. 8.
   *** Philips 6500 133. Beaux Arts Trio – SMETANA: *Piano trio in G minor.****

The *Piano trio* is an early work and not wholly characteristic of Chopin, but students of the composer will not fail to find it of interest. Moreover it is coupled with Smetana's excellent essay in the same medium, and the performance by the Beaux Arts Trio (particularly their admirable pianist, Menahem Pressler) could hardly be improved on; and the sound is amazingly life-like.

Violoncello sonata in G minor, Op. 65.
   ** (*) HMV ASD 2851. Jacqueline du Pré (cello), Daniel Barenboim (piano) – FRANCK: *Cello sonata.****
   * (*) HMV ASD 2587. Paul Tortelier (cello), Aldo Ciccolini (piano) – RACHMANINOV: *Cello sonata.** (*)

The easy lyrical romanticism of the *Cello sonata* is beautifully caught by Jacqueline du Pré and Daniel Barenboim. There is an autumnal quality in the writing which they present most persuasively. Though the cellist phrases with all her usual spontaneous-sounding imagination, this is one of her more reticent records, aptly so. Finely balanced recording. Tortelier's performance is obviously committed but rather lacks elegance and polish. Better vitality than perfumery, certainly, but Chopin's work needs grace as well as nervous tension. The recording is acceptable.

PIANO MUSIC

Andante spianato and Grande polonaise brillante, Op. 22; Ballades Nos. 1–4; Barcarolle, Op. 60; Berceuse, Op. 57; Boléro, Op. 19; Fantaisie, Op. 49; Impromptus Nos. 1–4; Fantasie-impromptu, Op. 66; Mazurkas Nos. 1–51; Nocturnes Nos. 1–19; 3 Nouvelles études; Polonaises Nos. 1–7; Scherzi Nos. 1–4; Sonatas Nos. 2 and 3; Tarantelle, Op. 43; Waltzes Nos. 1–14.
   (B) ** (*) RCA SER 5692 (12 discs). Artur Rubinstein (piano).

Although Rubinstein's playing in this anthology does not always equal the heights he scaled in the years before the war (witness his HMV mono set of *Mazurkas* and *Nocturnes*), there is marvellous treasure here. In so large an anthology both recording and performances are of course variable, but no collector could fail to derive pleasure from the set. All Chopin lovers will want this, especially at the very reasonable price RCA ask for it.

Andante spianato and Grande polonaise in E flat major, Op. 22; Impromptus Nos. 1 in A flat major, Op. 29; 2 in F sharp major, Op. 36; 3 in G flat major, Op. 51; Fantaisie-impromptu, Op. 66; Polonaise (Fantaisie) in A flat major, Op. 61.
   *** RCA SB 6649. Artur Rubinstein (piano).

In Chopin piano music generally Artur Rubinstein has no superior, and when it comes to polonaise rhythms he is in a class by himself. The great *Polonaise Fantaisie*, Op. 61, is given a stunning performance, and one has only to listen to the snap of dotted rhythms in the Rubinstein manner to realize what makes him so individual. The *Andante spianato and Grande polonaise* is a curious but memorable piece that again inspires Rubinstein, and his clear and relaxed accounts of the *Impromptus* make most other interpretations sound forced by comparison. The recording is not ideal, rather too hard for European taste, but with such playing it need not get in the way of enjoyment.

Ballades Nos. 1 in G minor, Op. 23; 2 in F major, Op. 38; 3 in A flat major, Op. 47; 4 in F minor, Op. 52.
  *** RCA SB 2082. Artur Rubinstein (piano).
Ballades Nos. 1–4; 3 Nouvelles études, Op. posth.
  *** Decca SXL 6143. Vladimir Ashkenazy (piano).
Ballades Nos. 1–4; Fantaisie in F minor, Op. 49.
  (B) ****** (*) Turnabout TV 34271S. Peter Frankl (piano).

Rubinstein's readings are unique, a miracle of creative imagination. From the hushed half-tones of the tiny coda of the *Second Ballade* to the romantic splendour of the great heroic theme of the *Ballade in G minor*, Rubinstein is at his most inspired. The recording is shallow by the best European standards, but with a reinforcement of bass it can be made to sound quite well.

There is no technical reservation about Ashkenazy's finely recorded Decca disc. Indeed the recording here is admirably natural and satisfying. The readings are thoughtful and essentially unflashy. The *rubato* arises naturally from Ashkenazy's personal approach to the music. The intimacy of the recording allows him to share this with the listener. The openings of the *First* and *Fourth Ballades* show this quality well; the music unfolds naturally and without emphasis. There is occasionally a touch of magic in the Rubinstein performances that Ashkenazy, with his seriousness, misses (the beginning of the *F major Ballade*, for instance) but on the whole this is a most satisfying disc, with

beautiful performances of the *Nouvelles études* thrown in for good measure.

Peter Frankl shows himself a Chopin player of remarkable sensitivity and flair. There is a most affecting intimacy in his gentle opening of the *F major* and *F minor Ballades* to show that his approach is not that of the barnstorming virtuoso yet there is romantic exuberance in plenty in the eloquent phrases of the *G minor* and *A flat major* works. The feeling of impetuosity which a youthful player can bring to this music is here tempered by the intelligence with which the mood and atmosphere of these contrasted pieces are so surely caught. The serious opening of the *Fantaisie* is particularly well managed. The recording is not outstanding; it is on the hard side, and some pressings have a tendency for the treble to splash a little at peaks. But with some attenuation it can be made to yield a more than acceptable sound.

Ballades Nos. 1–4; Études, Op. 10, Nos. 1–12; Op. 25, Nos. 1–12; Impromptus Nos. 1–3; Fantaisie-impromptu, Op. 66.
  (M) ****** (*) DGG Privilege 2726 014 (2 discs). Tamás Vàsàry (piano).

This is a generous and on the whole attractive coupling. Vàsàry is rather matter-of-fact in the *Impromptus*, but the *Ballades* are imaginatively played, and the performances, although personal, offer poetry as well as bravura. The G minor is outstanding with a fine romantic sweep but Nos. 2, 3 and 4 are each individual and rewarding. The reading of the *Études* is authoritative and commanding, with a wide emotional range. The piano recording is on the dry side but clear and never shallow.

Barcarolle in F sharp major, Op. 60; Berceuse in D flat major, Op. 57; Boléro in C major, Op. 19; 3 Nouvelles études, Op. posth.; Fantasy in F minor,

Op. 49; Tarantelle in A flat major, Op. 43.

*** RCA SB 6683. Artur Rubinstein (piano).

When regarded in relation to Chopin's complete works – so neatly docketed into *Nocturnes, Mazurkas, Waltzes* and so on – these pieces seem like the rag-bag elements, but in fact they contain some of Chopin's finest inspirations, notably the magnificent *Barcarolle* and *Berceuse*. The *Tarantelle* may be musically less interesting and not very characteristic, but in Rubinstein's hands it is a glorious piece, full of bravura. Rubinstein's way with Chopin is endlessly fascinating. Like almost all his other Chopin records, this collection is highly recommendable. Recording bright and a little clangy in the RCA manner.

Barcarolle in F sharp major, Op. 60; Berceuse in D flat major, Op. 57; Fantaisie in F minor, Op. 49; Polonaise (Fantaisie) in A flat major, Op. 61; Souvenir de Paganini in A major; Variations brillantes on a theme from Halévy's 'Ludovic', Op. 12.

*** HMV ASD 2963. Daniel Barenboim (piano).

Barenboim rarely if ever fails to convey a sense of new discovery. That is certainly so here in repertory with which he is not usually associated. He is imaginative and persuasive not only in the great mature works which make up the bulk of this collection but also in the two rarities the *Souvenir de Paganini* and the *Variations brillantes*, both sparklingly performed. First-rate recording.

'Rarities': Boléro in C major, Op. 19; 3 Ecossaises, Op. 72; Mazurka in F minor, Op. posth.; Nocturne in C sharp minor, 'Lento con gran espressione'; Polonaise (Fantaisie) in A flat major, *Op. 61; Rondo in E flat major, Op. 16; Tarantelle in A flat major, Op. 43; Variations brillantes on a theme from Halévy's 'Ludovic', Op. 12.*

(M) ***** HMV HQS 1290.** Ronald Smith (piano).

Ronald Smith is a great apostle of the unusual, the most persuasive of musical evangelists. Even devotees of Chopin who think they know the master's works from beginning to end could be surprised, and will certainly be charmed, by this imaginative selection of material off the main track. All the pieces have been recorded by others, but the sparkle and imagination of Smith's playing are irresistible. First-rate recording.

Études, Op. 10, Nos. 1–12; Op. 25, Nos. 1–12.

*** DGG 2530 291. Maurizio Pollini (piano).

(B) **** (*) Saga 5293.** Vladimir Ashkenazy (piano).

The *Études* are well-served on two price-levels. Pollini's electrifying account is masterly. He won the Warsaw Chopin Prize in 1959 when he was only eighteen and his playing of the Polish master has not declined in the meantime. These are without doubt the finest *Études* on record and must be given a strong recommendation in spite of the recording, which, though good, is not in the demonstration class.

Ashkenazy's set first appeared in the early sixties on the Chant du monde label. The playing is unfailingly rewarding, and given the remarkably low price it may well attract collectors who are daunted by full-price issues. The sound is perfectly acceptable, and the disc is excellent value.

Mazurkas Nos. 1–51: complete recording.

*** RCA SB 6702 (Nos. 1–17); SB

273

6703 (Nos. 18–33); SB 6704 (Nos. 34–51). Artur Rubinstein (piano).

(M) ** Pye TPLS 13038 (3 discs). Nina Milkina (piano).

(B) ** Decca Eclipse ECS 620 (Nos. 1–25); ECS 621 (Nos. 26–51). Nikita Magaloff (piano).

The *Mazurkas* contain some of Chopin's most characteristic music. That they are often ignored by virtuoso pianists simply reflects the fact that as a rule they are less tricky technically, and concert pianists prefer to show off. Yet, as Rubinstein continually demonstrates, they contain some wonderfully pianistic ideas, none the worse for being simply expressed. At the one end you have certain *Mazurkas* which are first cousins to Chopin's *Polonaises* and at the other end some that might almost be *Nocturnes*, while a lot in the middle could almost as readily have been included with the *Waltzes*. All are delightful, even if there is no need to linger very long over some of them. Rubinstein could never play in a dull way to save his life, and in his hands these fifty-one pieces are endlessly fascinating, though on occasion in such unpretentious music one would welcome a completely straight approach. By American standards of piano tone the recorded sound is very good.

Nina Milkina works her way through the *Mazurkas* sensitively and flexibly. She is at her best in the later, better-known pieces, where her *rubato* often has that gentle extra nuance which can make sensitive playing magical. Obviously she plays the earlier works less often and the *rubato* is more studied, although the playing is never prosaic. The piano tone throughout is convincing, although clear rather than luminous.

Choice between Nina Milkina's set and Nikita Magaloff's on Eclipse is not easy, except from the economic point of view. Decca have skilfully fitted all the *Mazurkas* on to two discs without loss of quality. The recording is quite pleasing if without

a great deal of projection. But this suits Magaloff's approach. The playing is consistent throughout and at its best in the gentle lyrical pieces, where the fine tonal shading is often beautiful. But the bolder *Mazurkas* are less effectively characterized, and because of this there is a lack of variety in the articulation and colouring when one listens to a whole group together. Yet the artist's sensibility is in no doubt and this pair of discs offers excellent value for money.

Mazurkas: Nos. 5 in B flat major, Op. 7/1; 7 in F minor, Op. 7/3; 15 in C major, Op. 24/2; 17 in B flat minor, Op. 24/4; 20 in D flat major, Op. 30/3; 21 in C sharp minor, Op. 30/4; 22 in G sharp minor, Op. 33/4; 27 in E minor, Op. 41/2; 32 in C sharp minor, Op. 50/3; 41 in C sharp minor, Op. 63/3; 45 in A minor, Op. 67/4; 47 in A minor, Op. 68/2; 49 in F minor, Op. 68/4.

(B) *** Classics for Pleasure CFP 40082. Witold Malcuzynski (piano).

This is an outstanding bargain. Malcuzynski's collection of *Mazurkas* is brilliantly successful – one of the best Chopin records in the catalogue at any price. The playing is immensely polished and stylish, yet finds an infinite range of mood and expression in this well-chosen programme. The personality of the player comes out as intensely as ever, yet the playing is always at the service of the composer. The recording too is remarkably good, clear and natural, perhaps the best sound Malcuzynski has ever had.

Nocturnes Nos. 1–19; 20 and 21, Op. posth.

⊛*** RCA SB 6731/2 (Nos. 1–19). Artur Rubinstein (piano).

(M) ** (*) Unicorn UNS 203/4 (Nos. 1–21). Peter Katin (piano).

** (*) DGG SLPEM 136486/7 (Nos. 1–20). Tamàs Vàsàry (piano).
** HMV SLS 838 (2 discs) (Nos. 1–21). Alexis Weissenberg (piano).
(B) ** Classics for Pleasure CFP 195 (Nos. 1–10). Moura Lympany (piano).

The Rubinstein set of *Nocturnes* makes a firm recommendation. The piano tone has a warm, rich quality and Rubinstein's magical sense of nuance and the fascinating inevitability of his *rubato* immediately capture the listener's imagination. Rubinstein is a magician in matters of colour, and again and again throughout these two discs (available separately) there are moments of sheer perfection, where the timing of a phrase exactly catches the mood and atmosphere of the composer's inspiration. The recording is excellent, much the best Rubinstein has ever had for his solo records.

Katin's approach is serene and civilized. Just occasionally he does not penetrate to the very core of the music, but for the most part the playing is highly sensitive, with subtle *rubato*, and exquisite shading in the gentle music; the *D flat Nocturne*, for instance, is beautifully managed. Excellent recording.

From Vàsàry, playing of character and insight by a pianist whose flexibility in moulding a Chopin phrase to find its kernel of poetry is always apparent. Why then the reservation? It is partly because sometimes the approach seems *too* positive, the relaxation within the melodic line *too* calculated. This impression is at least partly caused by the character of the recorded image the German engineers have provided. In technical terms this cannot be faulted; it is clear, bright, a little dry perhaps, but beautifully focused. But even in the softest music there is no conveyed sense of liquidity such as Askenase found in his mono set made a decade or so ago for the same company.

Alexis Weissenberg is a thoughtful, serious artist, who yet does not quite show his more searching qualities to best effect when working in the recording studio. There is much expressive playing here, but the expressiveness is often too heavily underlined. This is an enjoyable set of the *Nocturnes*, but the interpretations miss some of the more elusive, nocturnal qualities. Good recording.

Moura Lympany's record was originally part of a complete set. At first her interpretations may sound a little stiff, for she uses comparatively little *rubato*. But it is a fresh approach, with simplicity rather than sophistication the keynote, and in most of these night pieces these qualities produce most convincing readings. But sometimes one does miss the sheer musical imagination and poetry of a Rubinstein or an Askenase, and everything does flow a little too easily, with little of the concentrated intensity of those pianists at their best. But the recording is excellent and the disc is certainly good value.

Polonaises Nos. 1–16.
(B) *** Turnabout TV 34254/5S. Peter Frankl (piano).
Polonaises Nos. 1–16; Andante spianato and Grande polonaise brillante, Op. 22.
** (*) HMV SLS 843 (2 discs). Garrick Ohlsson (piano).
Polonaises Nos. 1 in C sharp minor, Op. 26/1; 2 in E flat minor, Op. 26/2; 3 in A major (Military), Op. 40/1; 4 in C minor, Op. 40/2; 5 in F sharp minor, Op. 44; 6 in A flat major (Heroic), Op. 53.
*** RCA SB 6640. Artur Rubinstein (piano).

The Turnabout set is in every way recommendable. Frankl approaches the music with a pleasing freshness. He eschews the grand manner and thus the two most famous pieces fit into the cycle naturally and dramatically, without being show-off warhorses. Elsewhere the pianist finds much that is reflective and poetic,

275

and reveals the complete set of *Polonaises* as much wider in musical range and less rhetorical, overall, than the better-known works suggest. The records are inexpensive, well recorded, and decently presented with good notes on each sleeve.

Artur Rubinstein has recorded these pieces more than once before, but his latest attempt – recorded in Carnegie Hall – is as freshly individual as ever. Master pianist that he is, he seems actually to be rethinking and re-creating each piece, even the hackneyed '*Military*' and *A flat* works, at the very moment of performance. Other performances may bring out different facets of the pieces, but none is likely to outshine Rubinstein's in easy majesty and natural sense of spontaneous phrasing. Despite Carnegie Hall the recording quality remains rather hard.

When still barely out of his teens Garrick Ohlsson won the 1970 Chopin Contest in Warsaw, and this début recording, a comprehensive collection of the *Polonaises* including the juvenilia and the *Grande polonaise brillante*, helps to explain why. He has a weighty style and technique very much of the modern American school, but with it all he is thoughtful. When he uses a flexible beat, it is only rarely that the result sounds wilful.

24 Preludes, Op. 28; Preludes: in C sharp minor, Op. 35; in A flat major, Op. posth.
   ** (*) DGG 2530 231. Christoph Eschenbach (piano).
   ** (*) CBS 72943 (Nos. 1–24 only). Nelson Freire (piano).
   (M) ** HMV HQS 1125. Rafael Orozco (piano).

Eschenbach is beautifully recorded. The tone is warm, clear and resonant, completely natural. His performances too are characteristically perceptive, thoughtful, with the bravura (which is never in doubt) always at the service of the music.

This is very enjoyable indeed, and, partly because of the sound, there are few records of this music that give more pleasure. Yet the playing is not always idiomatic and sometimes the Chopin flavour is not fully conveyed.

The performances of Nelson Freire display a formidable bravura and a fine grasp of the music's essentials. The touch can be melting when required (as in the best-known *Prelude in E major*), light and feathered, or immensely powerful. Perhaps in the last resort the performances display too much intellectual control and not enough charm, but as a display of the pianistic possibilities of the Op. 28 set they are impressive indeed. The piano tone is realistic but a trifle dry and unexpansive.

Rafael Orozco approaches the *Preludes* in a direct self-assured manner. The exciting *Prelude No. 16 in B flat minor*, a brilliant perpetuum mobile, is thrown off without a suspicion of breathlessness. Sometimes he might be more melting, as in the No. 4 in E minor, which is eloquent but not haunting, and the A major work associated with *Les Sylphides* is matter-of-fact. Yet there is some really beautiful playing in the trio of pieces which ends the first side, Nos. 13 to 15. Generally this is a rewarding set, given firm bold piano tone by EMI to match the mood of the playing.

Scherzi Nos. 1 in B minor, Op. 20; 2 in B flat minor, Op. 31; 3 in C sharp minor, Op. 39; 4 in E major, Op. 54.
   *** RCA SB 2095. Artur Rubinstein (piano).
   (B) (**) Turnabout TV 34460S. Abbey Simon (piano) – MENDELSSOHN: *Variations sérieuses.***

Scherzi Nos. 1–4; Barcarolle in F sharp major, Op. 60; Prelude in C sharp minor, Op. 45.
   *** Decca SXL 6334. Vladimir Ashkenazy (piano).

Scherzi Nos. 1–4; Fantaisie in F minor, Op. 49.
- (M) * (*) Unicorn UNS 244. Peter Katin (piano).
- (M) * (*) HMV HQS 1328. Garrick Ohlsson (piano).

Scherzi Nos. 1–4; Waltzes Nos. 1–17.
- (M) ** DGG Privilege 2726 029 (2 discs). Tamàs Vàsàry (piano).

Chopin's *Scherzi* are a long way from the original derivation of the genre as essentially light-hearted and humorous, and Rubinstein's immensely powerful readings play up the strength of the writing in a highly cogent way. The RCA recording is clear and reasonably faithful, though it needs plenty of bass boost to take off the dryness. This would be first choice were it not for the existence of the superb Ashkenazy disc offering dazzling playing of the highest order and first-rate Decca sound. Moreover the two substantial bonuses are played equally beautifully.

Abbey Simon's are worthwhile performances spoiled by the backward recording of the piano. The effect is to provide a rather lustreless basic tone quality and little brilliance in the treble.

Katin's are clear, purposeful accounts, well played if not glittering with bravura. The music's colours do not flash as iridescently as they might, but this is partly due to the recording, which is rather dry, without lustre in the upper register. There is no lack of sensibility; the gentle middle section of the first *Scherzo* is highly evocative.

Garrick Ohlsson's bravura is impressive, but he is inclined to rush his fences, as the opening of the *Scherzo in B minor* immediately demonstrates; and although he can also play thoughtfully he does not seem to sense the music's basic style. Chopin's *Scherzi* are notoriously difficult to bring off on record and they ideally need more poise than this. The recording is rather hard.

Vàsàry's set of *Waltzes* offers clean, stylish playing, but the performances lack charm, and the rather metallic piano image does not help. The *Scherzi* are another matter. They are played brilliantly and with much more flexibility. The recording too has more body without any loss of clarity.

Piano sonata No. 2 in B flat minor (Funeral march), Op. 35.
- (M) ** DGG Privilege 2538 260. Tamàs Vàsàry (piano) – LISZT: Sonata.* (*)

Piano sonatas Nos. 2 in B flat minor (Funeral march), Op. 35; 3 in B minor, Op. 58.
- *** RCA SB 2151. Artur Rubinstein (piano).
- *** CBS 76242. Murray Perahia (piano).
- (B) ** (*) Decca Eclipse ECS 770. Wilhelm Kempff (piano).
- (B) ** (*) Turnabout TV 34272S. Abbey Simon (piano).

Piano sonata No. 2 in B flat minor (Funeral march), Op. 35; Mazurka in A flat major, Op. 59/2; Nocturnes: in F major, Op. 15/1; in F sharp major, Op. 15/2; Grande valse brillante, Op. 18.
- *** Decca SXL 6575. Vladimir Ashkenazy (piano).

Piano sonata No. 2 in B flat minor (Funeral march), Op. 35; Études, Op. 10: Nos. 3 in E major; 4 in C sharp minor; 10 in A flat major; 11 in A minor; Polonaise No. 6 in A flat major, Op. 53.
- (B) ** Pye GSGC 14063. Mindru Katz (piano).

Piano sonata No. 3 in B minor, Op. 58; Ballade No. 4 in F minor, Op. 52; Mazurkas: in B flat major, Op. 7/1; in A minor, Op. 17/4; Nocturne No. 15 in F minor, Op. 55/1; Polonaise No. 3 in

A major (Military), Op. 40/1; Waltz No. 3 in A minor, Op. 34/2.

*** Decca Phase 4 PFS 4313. Ilana Vered (piano).

Ashkenazy's must rank as the finest among recorded performances of the *B flat minor Sonata*. It was made during a live recital at Essex University, and the concert was also filmed. Decca made sure that the sound suffered no loss from the circumstances; indeed the quality is outstandingly natural: the piano has splendid resonance and realism. The opening (and closing) applause is an irritant, but in all other respects this record earns the highest praise. The performance of the *Sonata* is of the highest distinction, of great power and eloquence, yet with the music's poetry fully realized – the playing of the middle section of the slow movement is exquisite. The rest of the programme has a comparable spontaneity, and if the final *Presto* of the *Sonata* is not absolutely immaculate, who will cavil, with music-making of this quality.

Vàsàry's performance is clear and dramatic and not without romantic flair. The recording is truthful but slightly dry, and this detracts slightly from the boldness of the pianist's approach. Thus in the first movement the second subject registers more effectively than the structure of the movement as a whole. The *Funeral march* is strong rather than tragic in feeling, but the reading as a whole is convincing. It is a pity that the recording has not slightly more resonance.

In the bargain field Mindru Katz's Pye record remains very competitive. The recording is excellent, and the performance of the *Sonata* is nicely judged. Katz shows a feeling for the grand manner and genuine lyrical flair. The *Études* have a proper variety of mood, if rather less flexibility, and the closing *Polonaise* displays a fine bravura.

Of the records coupling both *Sonatas*, Rubinstein's remains hard to surpass.

His strength is balanced by a poetic feeling that springs directly from the music, and the control of *rubato* brings many moments of magic, with wonderful examples in the second subject of the first movement and later in the central section of the *Funeral march*. The sound is richer and less brittle than some of Rubinstein's records.

Murray Perahia seems naturally attuned to working in the recording studio. Like his first record of Schumann this one shows a spontaneous imagination at work, questing onwards. The technique is remarkable even by today's standards, but it is so natural to the player that he never uses it for mere display, and always there is an underlying sense of structural purpose. The dry unrushed account of the finale of the *B flat minor Sonata* is typical of Perahia's freshness, and the only pity is that the recording of the piano is rather clattery and close.

The readings from Kempff are personal, but few can fail to respond to their sensitivity and spontaneity. Perhaps the final degree of technical brilliance – which we have come to take for granted in modern Chopin recordings – is lacking, But somehow the few technical smudges do not seem to matter: the very scale of the works seems to inspire Kempff to the sort of concentration that invariably marks his Beethoven performances. Only in the finale of the *Third Sonata* does Kempff sound a little less than happy; but, all told, these are wonderfully romantic readings, just such performances, one feels, as Clara Schumann might have given to her circle of intimate friends. Decca have improved the recording immeasurably in the transfer and it is clear, admirably full-blooded and firm in tone.

The Turnabout performances too are distinguished. Particularly convincing is Abbey Simon's account of the lesser-known *Third Sonata*. His nimble-fingered playing of the scherzo is delightful, and the slow movement has great eloquence. The performance has striking spontaneity and is such as to recommend the work alongside its more famous brother. This too is given a strong reading, the slightly dark tone of the piano giving the music extra colour in the first movement. The piano tone has excellent body and clarity, and this record can be recommended highly.

The recital from Ilana Vered featuring the *Third Sonata* within a well balanced programme is highly rewarding. The playing is unfailingly poetic, often inspirational, notably in the meltingly lovely performance of the *Largo* of the *B minor Sonata*. Equally distinctive are the accounts of the *Nocturne in F minor* and the deliciously rhythmic *Mazurka in B flat major*. The style is wayward (the *Ballade* is a deeply felt and very individual performance) but it is never less than compelling, and one often has the sensation of being at a live recital. The recording is excellent, with no Phase 4 exaggerations.

Waltzes Nos. 1–19.
  *** RCA SB 6600 (Nos. 1–14 only). Artur Rubinstein (piano).
  (B) *** DGG Heliodor 2548 146 (Nos. 1–14 only). Stefan Askenase (piano).
  (M) *** HMV SXLP 30130 (Nos. 1–14 only). Witold Malcuzynski (piano).
  (M) ** (*) HMV HQS 1208. Augustin Anievas (piano).
  (M) ** Philips Universo 6580 003. Adam Harasiewicz (piano).
  (M) ** Decca Ace of Diamonds SDD 353 (Nos. 1–15 and 19). Peter Katin (piano).
  (B) * (*) Classics for Pleasure CFP 40029 (Nos. 1–14 only). Samson François (piano).

Rubinstein's approach has a chiselled perfection that suggests finely cut and polished diamonds, and here the tonal quality of the recording, which is crystal-clear, hard and brilliant, emphasizes the metaphor. The *rubato* is subtle and the phrasing most beautiful, yet a fractional lack of warmth prevents the intimacy of approach from making absolute contact with the listener. In many ways this is a very fine record indeed, but it should be heard before purchase.

Reissued at bargain price and well recorded, Askenase's set is very attractive. It is interesting to compare this newer recording with his earlier mono set, once also available on Heliodor. The earlier performances were more withdrawn, with a magical inward glow, whereas the present interpretations are fresh and extrovert. If the quieter moments are less intimate, this is still a most satisfying record, with fuller sound than RCA provide for Rubinstein.

Malcuzynski's performances glitter in much the same way as Rubinstein's do. The playing is polished, crisp, and assured and has splendid style. The *Grande valse brillante* is thrown off with panache, and in the quieter, more reflective pieces Malcuzynski shows sensibility without seeking to find the gentlest nuances. The manner is unashamedly extrovert and there is no doubt that the readings taken as a whole show off this pianist's art to great advantage. The recording, forward and brilliant, a little light on bass sonority (but not shallow), suits the music-making admirably.

Anievas gives us all the *Waltzes*, including the five published posthumously, and HMV make room for them by not banding each piece individually, but instead dividing each side into three sections. The opening *Grande valse brillante* is somewhat lacking in flair, and generally Anievas is better in the reflective music than in providing glitter. His technique is absolutely secure, there is much to enjoy, and many will be glad to have the extra pieces.

279

Adam Harasiewicz also offers us the complete set of the *Waltzes*, and he is especially sympathetic in the posthumous ones. These are keenly musical performances, very well recorded, and should give satisfaction with such pleasing piano sound. However, in the last resort the musical characterization is not so strongly memorable as in some of the other sets.

Peter Katin plays the *Waltzes* not in numerical order, as is customary, but in chronological order, which seems more sensible. He is very well recorded. Having said this, one must confess to disappointment. The playing is thoughtful, even affectionate, and certainly assured. Yet there is a curious lack of life and spontaneity, and the vivid waltzes fail to sparkle as they might.

Samson François's disc cannot quite compete with the finest versions, but it is fair enough for a bargain version, with crisp, clean rhythms brightly recorded.

Miscellaneous Recitals

Allegro de concert in A major, Op. 46; Barcarolle in F sharp major, Op. 60; Mazurkas Nos. 42 in A minor (Notre temps); 43 in A minor (à Emile Gaillard), Op. posth.; 48 in C major; 49 in A minor; 50 in F major, Op. 68/1–3; 51 in D major; 52 in A flat major, Op. posth.; Polonaise No. 5 in F sharp minor, Op. 44.

(M) ** HMV HQS 1303. Roger Woodward (piano).

This is very positive and assured playing – the *Allegro de concert* is a *tour de force*, although rather Schumannesque in effect. The mood of the *Barcarolle* is very masculine, but Roger Woodward relaxes more for the *Mazurkas*, and the posthumous A minor work is very gentle and evocative. The bold piano tone, very

realistic and grand in scale, suits the performances.

Andante spianato and Grande polonaise brillante in E flat major, Op. 22; Ballade No. 3 in A flat major, Op. 47; Fantaisie in F minor, Op. 49; Polonaise (Fantaisie) in A flat major, Op. 61.

(B) ** Decca Eclipse ECS 768. Wilhelm Kempff (piano).

This was one of the three Kempff issues of Chopin in the earliest days of stereo. It then inspired markedly less enthusiasm than the other two records, and there is no doubt that the comparative absence of bravura in the *F minor Fantaisie* and even an occasional feeling of aimlessness give a one-sided idea of the music. But Kempff's individuality, above all in conveying real poetry, makes for fascinating listening none the less. Anyone wanting to hear Chopin with new ears should certainly try the record.

Andante spianato and Grande polonaise brillante in E flat major, Op. 22; Mazurkas Nos. 14 in G minor; 15 in C major, Op. 24/1 and 2; 24 in C major, Op. 33/3; 34 in C major; 35 in C minor, Op. 56/2 and 3; 36 in A minor, Op. 59/1; Rondo in C minor, Op. 1; Rondo à la mazurka in F major, Op. 5; Souvenir de Paganini in A major; Variations on a march from 'I Puritani'.

(M) ** Philips Universo 6580 062. Adam Harasiewicz (piano).

Opening with a fine performance of the *Andante spianato*, this recital covers a wide range including a good deal of unfamiliar music. The disc's title, ' *Virtuoso piano works*', is misleading in that there is a good deal of reflective music here to balance the bravura. Those interested in the programme will not be disappointed in the performances, which are assured and sympathetic, if lacking the final degree of individuality. The recording is good.

'The Chopin I love', Vol. 3: *Andante spianato and Grande polonaise brillante in E flat major, Op. 22; Mazurkas: in B minor, Op. 33/4; in A flat major, Op. 50/2; Nocturnes: in B major, Op. 32/1; in F minor, Op. 55/1; Scherzo No. 3 in C sharp minor, Op. 39; Waltzes: in A flat major; in A minor, Op. 34/1 and 2; in G flat major, Op 70/1 posth.*

** (*) RCA SB 6889. Artur Rubinstein (piano).

It is a pity that this recital was not planned to open with Rubinstein's exquisite performance of the *Andante spianato* (this in fact begins side two), for the *Waltz in A flat major*, which is chosen instead, comes from one of the shallower-sounding of Rubinstein's records. But there are some superb performances here, notably the delightful pair of *Nocturnes*, the *Mazurka in A flat major*, and the brilliant *Scherzo in C sharp minor*.

Andante spianato and Grande polonaise brillante in E flat major, Op. 22; Polonaises Nos. 4 in C minor, Op. 40/2; 5 in F sharp minor, Op. 44; 6 in A flat major, Op. 53; 7 (Fantaisie) in A flat major, Op. 61.

(M) * (*) Vanguard VCS 10058. Alfred Brendel (piano).

This is strong, intelligent playing, the *rubato* sensitive and the character of each piece well realized. Yet Brendel's style, for all its apparent flexibility, is essentially classical, and not very colloquial. At a concert these performances would be much enjoyed, but for repetition on the gramophone they are less satisfactory.

Ballade No. 1 in G minor, Op. 23; Barcarolle in F sharp major, Op. 60; Étude in E major, Op. 10/3; Fantaisie-impromptu in C sharp minor, Op. 66; Nocturne in D flat major, Op. 27/2; Scherzo No. 3 in C sharp minor, Op. 39; Waltzes: in D flat major (Minute), Op. 64/1; in C sharp minor, Op. 64/2.

** Decca Phase 4 PFS 4262. Ivan Davis (piano).

Despite unnaturally close recording (the effect is something like having one's ear inside the piano lid) this is an impressive recital, with Ivan Davis's mercurial imagination given full rein. It is a great pity the record was not made by Decca's standard techniques.

Ballade No. 1 in G minor, Op. 23; Études Nos. 3 in E major, Op. 10/3; 12 in C minor (Revolutionary), Op. 10/12; Fantaisie-impromptu in C sharp minor, Op. 66; Mazurkas Nos. 5 in B flat major, Op. 7/1; 23 in D major, Op. 33/2; Nocturnes Nos. 2 in E flat major, Op. 9/2; 5 in C sharp major, Op. 15/2; Polonaises Nos. 3 in A major, Op. 40/1; 6 in E flat major, Op. 53; Preludes Nos. 7 in A major, Op. 28/7; 15 in D flat major (Raindrop), Op. 28/15; Waltzes Nos. 6 in D flat major (Minute), Op. 64/1; 7 in C sharp minor, Op. 64/2.

(M) ** HMV HQS 1189. John Ogdon (piano).

This is playing of strong character, but it is a little uneven in penetrating the core of the music. Highlights include the two *Polonaises*, which open the disc boldly, and the *Ballade*, which provides a melting, romantic conclusion. The *Nocturnes* too are successful, the *rubato* personal but convincing. The *Mazurkas* seem less sure in style, and in the *Fantaisie-impromptu*, although the slow middle theme is beautiful, there is some flurry in the outer sections. But taken as a whole this recital is successful, even if the title of the disc – *Popular Chopin* – suggests a more out-and-out popular selection than Ogdon provides.

'Favourite Chopin': Ballade No. 1 in G minor, Op. 23; Études: in E major, Op. 10/3; in C minor (Revolutionary), Op. 10/12; in G flat major, Op. 25/9; Fantaisie-impromptu in C sharp minor, Op. 66; Nocturnes Nos. 2 in E flat major, Op. 9/2; 5 in F sharp minor, Op. 15/2; Polonaise No. 6 in A flat major, Op. 53; Scherzo No. 1 in B minor, Op. 20; Waltzes: Nos. 1 in E flat major, Op. 18 (Grande valse brillante); 6 in D flat major (Minute), Op. 64/1; 7 in C sharp minor, Op. 64/2.

   (M) * (*) DGG Privilege 2538 096. Tamàs Vàsàry (piano).

Vàsàry's collection is disappointing. The recording is rather dry, and although many of the performances are not lacking in poetic feeling the effect of the sound is not to convey enough warmth to advocate such an essentially popular programme.

'The Chopin I love', Vol. 1: Ballade No. 1 in G minor, Op. 23; Fantaisie-impromptu in C sharp minor, Op. 66; Mazurka in D major, Op. 33/2; Nocturnes: in E flat major, Op. 9/2; in F sharp minor, Op. 15/2; in D flat major, Op. 27/2; Polonaises: in A major, Op. 40/1; in A flat major, Op. 53; Waltzes: in A flat major, Op. 34/1; in D flat major, Op. 64/1; in C sharp minor, Op. 64/2.

   *** RCA SB 6874. Artur Rubinstein (piano).

Rubinstein opens with the *Polonaise in A flat major*, and the rather dry recorded quality is a shade disconcerting in so bold a work. But one soon adjusts and the quality is a little richer in the *Waltz*

in C sharp minor, which follows. In fact the transfers here are all well managed, clear with plenty of sparkle when required. The performances are incomparable and gain from the care with which the selection has been made and arranged into a highly rewarding recital. This series deserves to be popular.

Ballade No. 1 in G minor, Op. 23; Mazurkas Nos. 19 in B minor; 20 in D flat major, Op. 30/2 and 3; 22 in G sharp minor; 25 in B minor, Op. 33/1 and 4; 34 in C major, Op. 56/2; 43 in G minor, Op. 67/2; 45 in A minor, Op. 67/4; 46 in C major; 47 in A minor; 49 in F minor, Op. 68/1, 2 and 4; Prelude No. 25 in C sharp minor, Op. 45; Scherzo No. 2 in B flat minor, Op. 31.

   ** (*) DGG 2530 236. Arturo Benedetti Michelangeli (piano).

Although this recital does not seem to quite add up as a whole, the performances are highly distinguished. Michelangeli's individuality comes out especially in the *Ballade*, a very free rhapsodic performance, which nevertheless holds together by the very compulsion of the playing. Michelangeli's special brand of poetry is again felt in the Mazurkas, which show a wide range of mood and dynamic; and the *Scherzo* is extremely brilliant yet without any suggestion whatsoever of superficiality. The piano tone is real and life-like.

Ballade No. 1 in G minor, Op. 23; Nocturnes Nos. 4 in F major; 5 in F sharp major, Op. 15/1 and 2; 7 in C sharp minor, 8 in D flat major, Op. 27/1 and 2; Polonaises Nos. 5 in F sharp minor, Op. 44; 6 in A flat major (Heroic), Op. 53.

   *** HMV ASD 2577. Maurizio Pollini (piano).

This highly distinguished recital offers playing of great contrasts. The romantic boldness of the *Polonaise in F sharp minor* commands the listener's attention like a thunderclap, yet the bravura is disciplined by the innate poise of the playing. The two *Nocturnes*, in C sharp minor and D flat, which follow are exquisitely played, the delicate tonal shading in Op. 27/2 transporting the listener by its effortless poetry. Side two opens with a stirring *Ballade in G minor*, its full romantic flow shaped with a natural spontaneity. Again two magical *Nocturnes* follow, and the recital ends with the passionate *A flat Polonaise*. The disc is as well planned as it is superbly played, and HMV's recording is first-rate, splendidly brilliant and full-blooded, with luminous sustained tone in the gentler music.

'*The world of Chopin*': *Ballade No. 3 in A flat major, Op. 47; Barcarolle in F sharp major, Op. 60; Berceuse in D flat major, Op. 57; Fantaisie-impromptu in C sharp minor, Op. 66; Impromptu No. 1 in A flat major, Op. 29; Scherzo No. 3 in C sharp minor, Op. 39; Piano sonata No. 2 in B flat minor (Funeral march), Op. 35.*

(B) ** (*) Decca SPA 280. Wilhelm Kempff (piano).

This exceedingly generous sampler of Kempff's individuality in 'the world of Chopin' makes a fine bargain. Kempff is not at his best in music that calls for striking bravura, like the *Scherzo*, or the finale of the *Sonata*, but his special quality of poetry infuses the overall performance of Op. 35 with great romantic warmth. Kempff's shading of phrases, even if the *rubato* is slightly mannered, also illuminates pieces like the *Barcarolle* and *Berceuse*, while the *Ballade* and *Fantaisie-impromptu* are full of personality. The recording is bold and clear, perhaps a little too dry.

'*The Chopin I love*', *Vol. 2: Ballade No. 3 in A flat major, Op. 47; Berceuse in D flat major, Op. 57; Mazurkas in B flat major, Op. 7/1; in A flat major, Op 59/2; Nocturne in A flat major, Op. 32/2; Scherzo No. 2 in B flat minor, Op. 31; Waltzes in E flat major, Op. 18 (Grande valse brillante); in A flat major, Op. 42; in A flat major, Op. 69/1; in E minor, Op. posth.*

** (*) RCA SB 6885. Artur Rubinstein (piano).

Volume 2 of *The Chopin I love* shows equal distinction in performance and the recording is clear and immediate. Perhaps the recital as arranged is marginally less successful than the first, although side two, with the *Ballade in A flat major* and the *Berceuse*, shows Rubinstein at his very best.

'*Favourites*': *Ballade No. 3 in A flat major, Op. 47; Études: in G flat major, Op. 10/5; in A flat major, Op. 25/1; in G flat major, Op. 25/9; Nocturnes Nos. 10 in A flat major, Op. 32/2; 15 in F minor, Op. 55/1; Polonaise No. 6 in A flat major, Op. 53; Preludes, Op. 28, Nos. 6 in B minor; 20 in C minor; Scherzo No. 3 in C sharp minor, Op. 39; Waltzes Nos. 1 in E flat major, Op. 18 (Grande valse brillante); 11 in G flat major, Op. 70/1.*

(M) *** HMV HQS 1251. Daniel Adni (piano).

A brilliant début by an outstandingly talented young artist (only nineteen at the date of the recording). His sensibility in this repertoire is remarkable, and his musicianship is matched by the kind of effortless technique that is essential to give Chopin's music its essential line and flow. From the glitter and brilliance of the opening *Grande valse brillante* to the evocative yet expansive reading of the famous '*Sylphides*' *Nocturne in A flat major*, the tonal shading is matched by the spontaneity of the *rubato*. The whole of the first side of the disc is beautifully balanced to make a miniature recital, working towards a superb account of the *Scherzo in C sharp minor*. This is one of the most enjoyable Chopin collections available at any price, and it is given beautiful recorded sound, with sparkle and sonority in equal measure.

Ballade No. 3 in A flat major, Op. 47; Fantaisie-impromptu in C sharp minor, Op. 66; Impromptus Nos. 1 in A flat major, Op. 29; 2 in F sharp major, Op. 36; 3 in G flat major, Op. 51; Mazurkas, Op. 41: Nos. 1 in C sharp minor; 2 in E minor; 3 in B major; 4 in A flat major; Scherzo No. 3 in C sharp minor, Op. 39.

(M) *** DGG Privilege 2538 078. Stefan Askenase (piano).

This is marvellously positive playing, full of personality and character. The recording too is remarkably bold and full, better than many of DGG's more recent (and more expensive) piano records. Askenase always compels the attention, and his vigorous romantic style here makes a very attractive recital.

Ballades Nos. 3 in A flat major, Op. 47; 4 in F minor, Op. 52; Fantaisie-impromptu in C sharp minor, Op. 66; Nocturnes Nos. 12 in G major, Op. 37/2; 18 in E major, Op. 62/2; Scherzi Nos. 2 in B flat minor, Op. 31; 4 in E major, Op. 54.

(M) ** HMV SXLP 30075. Benno Moiseiwitsch (piano).

Moiseiwitsch's way with Chopin may offend modern taste in many respects. For a recording he uses the pedal too freely, he plays fast and loose with the marked dynamics and even with the text, and there is the occasional slip to suggest that the pianist was past his best. Yet Moisei-

witsch was still a compelling, individual player, and this provides an excellent reminder of his singing, freely rhapsodic style. It is not a record to compare with other Chopin discs, but to cherish for the personality revealed by the performer. Fair recording of late fifties vintage.

(i) Ballade No. 4 in F minor, Op. 52; (ii) Barcarolle in F sharp major, Op. 60; (iii) Boléro in C major, Op. 19; (i) Étude in C minor (Revolutionary), Op. 10/12; (iv) Mazurkas Nos. 5 in B flat major, Op. 7/1; 47 in A minor, Op. 68/2; Polonaise No. 6 in A flat major, Op. 53; (v) Preludes, Op. 28, Nos. 3 in G major; 5 in D major; (vi) Waltzes Nos. 1 in E flat major, Op. 18 (Grande valse brillante); 7 in C sharp minor, Op. 64/2.

(M) ** (*) DGG Privilege 135013. (i) Sviatoslav Richter; (ii) Martha Argerich; (iii) Julian von Karolyi; (iv) Tamàs Vàsàry; (v) Géza Anda; (vi) Stefan Askenase (piano).

This collection is titled 'Brilliant interpretations' and with such a glittering array of talent the content does not belie the description. Even the least interesting player here, Julian von Karolyi, is at his best in the little-known *Boléro*, not one of Chopin's most revealing essays. But many of the others are favourites, and the excitement of Richter's impetuous *Revolutionary study* and the more controlled heroism of Vàsàry's *Polonaise in A flat major* contrast well with the sheer style of Askenase's *Waltzes* (superb playing this), and the effortless brilliance of Anda's *Études*. Richter's *Ballade No. 4* is a personal reading but always interesting; Vàsàry's *Mazurkas* are in the best tradition of Chopin playing. All are well recorded.

Barcarolle in F sharp major, Op. 60; Berceuse in D flat major, Op. 57; Im-

promptus Nos. 1 in A flat major, Op. 29; 2 in F sharp major, Op. 36; 3 in G flat major, Op. 51; 4 in C sharp minor (Fantaisie-impromptu), Op. 66; Nocturne No. 3 in B major, Op. 9/3; Scherzo No. 3 in C sharp minor, Op. 39.

(B) ** (*) Decca Eclipse ECS 769. Wilhelm Kempff (piano).

In the pieces included in this recital – the *Fantaisie-impromptu* apart – it is the poetry which matters above all. Kempff shows a natural feeling for the shading of a phrase so that it sounds not like an 'interpretation' in inverted commas but an inevitable part of the music. For that reason the performances are refreshing, even if the *rubato* is personal – as in the *Berceuse* – and different from the kind of graduations Rubinstein, for instance, would manage.

Barcarolle in F sharp major, Op. 60; Impromptu No. 3 in G flat major, Op. 51; Mazurkas Nos. 39 in B major; 40 in F minor; 41 in C sharp minor, Op. 63/1–3; Nocturnes Nos. 17 in B major; 18 in E major, Op. 62/1 and 2; Polonaise (Fantaisie) No. 7 in A flat major, Op. 61.

*** Philips 6500 393. Stephen Bishop (piano).

Chopin is not the composer with whom one would normally associate Stephen Bishop, but the nicely varied selection of pieces from the composer's last years shows very effectively how a more thoughtful, less showy Chopin style than is common can bring unusual rewards. Not that Bishop is at all stiff or inflexible; far from it. Just that he naturally relates the depth of feeling of the composer to that which we naturally associate with, say, the great slow movements of Beethoven or Schubert. Fine, forward recording.

Étude No. 5 in G flat major, Op. 10/5; Introduction and rondo, Op. 16; Mazurka No. 13 in A minor, Op. 17/4; Polonaises Nos. 6 in A flat major, Op. 53; 7 (Fantaisie) in A flat major, Op. 61; Waltz No. 3 in A minor, Op. 34/2.

*** CBS 72969. Vladimir Horowitz (piano).

A stunning recital by any standards. It also contains a rarity in the *Introduction and rondo*, Op. 16. The playing is dazzling; its virtuosity is enormously refreshing and illumined by the sense of poetry and fine musical judgement that Horowitz so abundantly commands. The *Polonaise Fantasy* was recorded at a public concert, the remainder in a studio. Reservations about the thin quality of the sound must be made and then firmly set aside, given artistry of this rarity. What a pity that Horowitz has never been accorded really first-rate piano sound of the kind that much lesser artists have been blessed with.

Cilea, Francesco
(1866–1950)

Adriana Lecouvreur (opera in 4 acts): complete recording.

** Decca SET 221/3. Renata Tebaldi (soprano), Giulietta Simionato (mezzo-soprano), Mario del Monaco (tenor), Giulio Fioravanti (baritone), Chorus and Orchestra of St Cecilia Academy, Rome, Franco Capuana.

This is a curious but attractive opera with one pervading Grand Tune that should alone ensure its survival. It is the story of a great actress caught up in international intrigue, and in the manner of the veristic school we are given a chance to observe her for a moment or

285

two in her roles before she deals with her own life-drama. Tebaldi, of course, is a little stiff as an actress to make much of those effects. One really wants a Callas, and if one goes to the account of the two big arias that Callas gave in a recital record some years ago one finds far more intense and convincing vocal acting. With Tebaldi both *Io sono l'umile ancella* and *Poveri fiori* are rich and beautiful but little more. But then this is an opera which relies very largely on its vocal line for its effect. I only wish del Monaco was as reliable as Tebaldi, but as always we have some coarse moments amid the fine plangent top notes. Simionato is a little more variable than usual, but a tower of strength nonetheless. The recording is outstanding in every way, rich, brilliant and atmospheric, and the album contains excellent notes and translation by Peggie Cochrane.

Cimarosa, Domenico
(1749–1801)

Oboe concerto in C minor (arr. Benjamin).
(B) *** Pye GSGC 15011. Evelyn Rothwell (oboe), Pro Arte Orchestra, Sir John Barbirolli – ALBINONI and MARCELLO: *Concertos.****

This enchanting concerto, arranged by Arthur Benjamin from four single-movement keyboard sonatas, was given a quite ideal performance and recording by Evelyn Rothwell and her late husband. The pastoral opening theme is phrased exquisitely, and after the gentle allegro which follows, the beautiful flowing Siciliana is played with a wonderful combination of affection and style. The gently rollicking finale is again caught to perfection, with Sir John sensitive to his wife's mood in every bar. The recording

is excellently judged in matters of balance and tone. This is perhaps the most successful of all the six oboe concertos recorded by this memorable partnership.

Clementi, Muzio
(1752–1832)

Piano concerto in C major.
(B) ** (*) Turnabout TV 34375S. Felicja Blumenthal (piano), Prague New Chamber Orchestra, Alberto Zedda – KUHLAU: *Concerto.** (*)

Collectors of unfamiliar classical concertos should not miss this one by Clementi, for its invention is full of vitality, and it is played most stylishly. The crisp classicism of the first movement is balanced by an *Adagio* which sounds almost like early Beethoven in its simple eloquence. The finale has wit and sparkle. The performance is most enjoyable and the rather dry acoustic suits the music well. A most welcome disc.

Sonatas for piano duet: in C major, Op. 3/1; in E flat major, Op. 3/2; in C major, Op. 14/2; in E flat major, Op. 14/3.
** (*) Telefunken SAWT 9599. Gina Gorino and Sergio Lorenzi (piano duet).

Clementi wrote seven sonatas for piano duet, and here we are offered four of them. The Op. 14 works are noticeably more mature and adventurous than the Op. 3, but all the music is attractive. The performances are accomplished and lively and the recording good, although there is a hint of end-of-side deterioration in the quality.

Piano sonatas: in G minor, Op. 7/3; in B flat major, Op. 24/2; in A major, Op. 25/4; in B minor, Op. 40/2.

(M) *** Oiseau-Lyre SOL 307. Lamar Crowson (piano).

Piano sonatas: in F sharp minor, Op. 25/5; in A major, Op. 33/1; in C major, Op. 33/3; in G minor (Didone abbandonata), Op. 50/3.

(M) *** Oiseau-Lyre SOL 306. Lamar Crowson (piano).

There used to be an HMV recital by Horowitz devoted to three Clementi sonatas, a high-powered and impressive disc. For Horowitz these sonatas were full of Beethovenian fire, and he exercised on them a splendid rhythmic grip. Lamar Crowson is much more flexible in his handling of rhythm and makes no attempt to project on to this music a sensibility that lies beyond the range of the period. In the *B minor Sonata, Op. 40/2*, he embodies much of the intensity of expression that one finds in Cherubini without ever suggesting the cosmic vision or emotional range of Beethoven. Crowson plays a Bösendorfer which has an appropriate lightness of colour, and his *rubati* are well judged. In an indifferent performance this music can sound shallow but given playing as stylish as this, the sonatas emerge in their true light: they are not invested with false depths but are seen in the right historical perspective. Both records are worth having but if you cannot afford both, try the one with the remarkable *B minor Sonata* (SOL 307).

Clérambault, Louis-Nicolas
(1676–1749)

(Organ) Suite du premier ton; Suite du deuxième ton.

(B) ** Oryx ORYX 1737. Kenneth Gilbert (organ of St Joseph's, Montreal).

This disc is persuasively recorded and very well played. The organ at St Joseph's Oratory, Montreal, is particularly well suited to French organ music, and the special reedy colouring adds character to the presentation. The music is variable in appeal but nearly always inventive, and it does not have the fault of so much organ music in being too static to appeal to the non-specialist listener.

Coates, Eric
(1886–1958)

By the Sleepy Lagoon. The Dambusters: march. From Meadow to Mayfair: suite (complete). London suite: Knightsbridge march. Music Everywhere: (i) Saxo-rhapsody. Summer Days suite: At the dance. The Three Elizabeths suite: Elizabeth of Glamis. Wood nymphs.

** Columbia Studio 2 TWO 226. Royal Liverpool Philharmonic Orchestra, Sir Charles Groves, (i) with Jack Brymer (alto-sax).

One had looked forward to the first stereo LP of Eric Coates's music but in the event it proved slightly disappointing. The Studio Two brashness takes some of the geniality out of the *Knightsbridge march* (which opens the disc), and the choice of the complete *From Meadow to Mayfair* is curious: it is not one of the composer's strongest suites. The most striking work here is the *Saxo-rhapsody*. It is played with considerable subtlety by Jack Brymer and Groves accompanies skilfully. The piece is thematically repetitive but has both character and atmosphere. *Elizabeth of Glamis*, the central movement of the *Three Elizabeths suite*, does not expand as it might (the composer is much more beguiling on his Eclipse stereo transcription, ECS 2088). It is surprising that the first movement was not included too, as this is familiar as the introductory music for the BBC TV *Forsyte Saga*. On the whole Groves proves – with his obvious affection – a good conductor of this music, and although the collection is valuable one laments that it was not recorded in ordinary EMI sound.

Calling all Workers march; The Jester at the Wedding: suite; The Merrymakers: overture; Miniature suite; The Three Elizabeths: suite.
*** EMI Studio 2 Quadraphonic Q4-TWO 361; Stereo TWO 361. City of Birmingham Orchestra, Reginald Kilbey.

This is much the finest of the Studio 2 Eric Coates anthologies, and the quadraphonic version is very impressive, with an effective ambience and some marvellously regal brass sounds. Reginald Kilbey unexpectedly proves himself the ideal Coates conductor, with a real flair for catching the sparkle of Coates's leaping allegro figurations. His shaping of the secondary theme of the lovely slow movement of the *Three Elizabeths suite* has an affectionate grace. Equally the *Scène de bal*, with its delightful evocation of porcelain china dancing figures, is done with superb point and style. The marches are splendidly alive and vigorous, and the first movement of the *Three Elizabeths* is sustained with a consistent throbbing forward momentum, in spite of the fact that the lack of middle frequencies, caused by the Studio 2 brightening effect (which even quadraphonic sound cannot cure), gives less internal support than intended by the composer. Otherwise the sound is good, in the ordinary stereo version a trifle overbright, but with plenty of colour and impact from the brass.

Cinderella (fantasy). London suite: Covent Garden; Westminster; Knights-
bridge march. London Again suite: Oxford Street; Langham Place; Mayfair. The Three Bears (fantasy).*
** Columbia Studio 2 TWO 321. Royal Liverpool Philharmonic Orchestra, Sir Charles Groves.

Like its companion disc this second Eric Coates anthology from Groves has been tarted up by the Studio 2 transfer. Eric Coates's music is bright and breezy in its own right and, especially when given lively and idiomatic performances, does not need the violin line artificially brightening – particularly when this seems to have been achieved by adding an unsubtle top lift, so that the middle frequencies lack richness. Thus when the opening impetus of *Covent Garden*, the first movement of the *London suite*, softens a little to introduce *Cherry ripe*, the cherries are given a very unripe sound by the middle strings. Needless to say, this marvellously spontaneous music triumphs over the sharp-edged sound, especially *The Three Bears* fantasy. Here Groves catches the pastiche element of the dance rhythms of the twenties splendidly. *Cinderella* is a marginally less inspired piece, but Groves makes the very most of it, and throughout the verve and musicality of the writing come over with such enthusiastic and polished orchestral playing. One can only wish the same EMI producers who have given us the marvellous records of Elgar's light music had had artistic control of the present issue.

London suite.
(B) ** RCA Victrola VICS 1530. Orchestra, Morton Gould – VAUGHAN WILLIAMS: *Collection.***

This is a very lively performance of Eric Coates's best-known orchestral suite, including the famous *Knightsbridge march*. The recording is bright, and the coupling completes a surprisingly successful concert of English music from a conductor who has made his reputation in the fringe area between American serious and popular music.

Coleridge-Taylor, Samuel
(1875–1912)

Hiawatha's wedding feast.
*** HMV ASD 467. Richard Lewis (tenor), Royal Choral Society, Philharmonia Orchestra, Sir Malcolm Sargent.

In its day *Hiawatha's wedding feast* blew a fresh breeze through a turgid British Victorian choral tradition, and freshness is exactly the quality of this splendid performance from Sir Malcolm. The music throughout is delightfully melodious and extremely well written for the voices. The somewhat over-heavy orchestration which one notices at a live performance is happily toned down by the recording balance, which is nigh perfect. Indeed this is a most spectacular record from a technical point of view and a wonderful demonstration of how much a fine choir benefits from the ambience around it. Everything about this disc is a success, including of course Richard Lewis's stylish performance of *Onaway! Awake, Beloved!*

Connolly, Justin
(born 1933)

(i) *Cinquepaces;* (ii) *Triad III;* (iii) *Poems of Wallace Stevens;* (iv) *Verse for 8 solo voices I and II.*
*** Argo ZRG 747. (i) Philip Jones Brass Ensemble; (ii) Vesuvius Ensemble; (iii) Jane Manning (soprano), Nash Ensemble, the composer; (iv) John Alldis Choir.

This British Council record gives an excellent idea of the achievement to date of Justin Connolly, a composer who till his mid-twenties insisted that he was going to be a lawyer, but who finally gave in. His music has its wildness, and it is almost always challenging to the performers as well as to listeners. Obvious energy compensates for any difficulties, and these excellent performances provide the most persuasive advocacy. Jane Manning is particularly impressive in the Stevens settings, but *Cinquepaces*, the most striking of the pieces, is the one for new listeners to sample first. Excellent recording.

Copland, Aaron
(born 1900)

Appalachian Spring (ballet).
(M) ** Everest SDBR 3002. London Symphony Orchestra, Walter Susskind – GOULD: *Spirituals.***
Appalachian Spring (ballet); *Billy the Kid* (ballet): *suite.*
(M) *** RCA LSB 4018. Philadelphia Orchestra, Eugene Ormandy.
Appalachian Spring (ballet); *El Salón México; Music for the Theatre: Dance.*
*** CBS 72074. New York Philharmonic Orchestra, Leonard Bernstein.
Appalachian Spring (ballet); *Fanfare for the Common Man;* (i) *Lincoln Portrait* (for speaker and orchestra).
** (*) CBS 72872. (i) Henry Fonda (narrator); London Symphony Orchestra, the composer.
Appalachian Spring (ballet); *The Tender Land* (opera): *orchestral suite.*

(B) *** RCA Victrola VICS 1488. Boston Symphony Orchestra, the composer.

All these records are of high quality, and choice must to some extent be dictated by coupling (and price). Susskind on Everest gives a dramatic and sympathetic reading and the recording still sounds extremely vivid. Although it is an English performance the American-style engineering, with wide dynamics, gives a touch of brashness to the sound, but not at the expense of amplitude. Susskind conducts the piece in a completely spontaneous way; the string ostinatos have the proper rhythmic bite and the unfolding of the Shaker variations is managed with a simplicity of great charm. With its apt coupling – no less well done – this is an excellent issue.

On RCA too splendid performances very well recorded. For most, Ormandy's coupling will be preferred to the composer's own on Victrola (see below), even though that disc perhaps contains marginally the more understanding account of *Appalachian Spring*. But Ormandy is very sympathetic too and the atmospheric RCA stereo adds a great deal to the polished Philadelphia playing. In *Billy the Kid* the quality of the sound does not give the kind of edge to the pistol shots that we are used to from Bernstein, for instance, but there is no lack of bite in the playing itself.

Bernstein's reading of *Appalachian Spring* is extremely brilliant and thus – especially in the taut opening pages – very exciting; yet one feels a little of the humanity of the music has eluded the conductor. One can have almost no reservations about *El Salón México*. The music glitters and although there is a fractional tendency to be mannered in the basic rhythm of the main theme, this is only an excess of style, and there is no lack of spontaneity. The *Dance* is a slight, rather grotesque piece, attractive in an unpretentious way.

There is an innocence, a fresh purity about Copland's London reading of *Appalachian Spring* which is most appealing. His earlier version with the Boston Symphony Orchestra has moments of greater resonance, but with cleaner recording quality and beautiful hushed string playing this is preferable. The coupling does not help. The *Fanfare for the Common Man* is the more effective for being slightly underplayed, but with narration that sounds too stagey the *Lincoln Portrait* is unconvincing. For non-Americans Copland ought to devise a version without narration.

The Tender Land suite is from an opera dating from 1954. We are given the *Love duet* virtually complete, the *Party music* from Act 2, and the quintet *The promise of living*, which forms the first act finale. This is again very typical Copland and attractive enough, if not as memorable melodically as its coupling. One can imagine how effective the chorale-like quintet would be in its original version with voices. One also is reminded how near the American 'musical' is in style to Copland's conception of American opera.

Billy the Kid (ballet); *Fanfare for the Common Man; Rodeo* (ballet): *4 Dance episodes.*

(B) ** Turnabout TV 34169S. Dallas Symphony Orchestra, Donald Johanos.

Billy the Kid (ballet); *Rodeo* (ballet): *4 Dance episodes.*

*** CBS 72888. London Symphony Orchestra, the composer.

*** CBS 72411. New York Philharmonic Orchestra, Leonard Bernstein.

Copland and the LSO have, over the years of their recording sessions together, built up a splendid rapport, and it would be hard to find any rival version that nudged Copland's dance rhythms so seductively. In these same two pieces

Bernstein may be more thrustfully extrovert – it is arguable that the intense, extended structure of *Billy the Kid* hangs together better with him – but Copland himself is unrivalled in implying emotion even in apparently light-hearted genre dances, tears and laughter often very close. The playing and recording are outstanding. A coupling to recommend warmly to anyone wanting to sample this composer at his most approachable.

Both these scores are right up Bernstein's street and he makes the most of Copland's tart rhythmic pulse; everything glitters and glows spontaneously in his hands. Bernstein finds a depth of beauty too in the quiet lyrical music; he is clearly revelling in every bar and this inevitably affects the listener. The orchestral playing itself is splendid. The recording is forward and precise, with a slight ambience.

The Turnabout record is highly enjoyable and a very real bargain. The Dallas Orchestra does not provide the incisive discipline of, say, the New York Philharmonic under Bernstein, but – being Texans – they know what cowboy music is about and the playing is both colloquial and spontaneous. The barn-dance rhythmic style also comes naturally, and the gun battles are done with the percussive effectiveness of familiarity. The recording is strongly atmospheric.

Clarinet concerto.
　** (*) Unicorn RHS 314. Gervase de Peyer (clarinet), London Mozart Players, Bernard Jacob – CRUSELL: *Clarinet concerto No. 2.*** (*)

The Copland *Clarinet concerto* was written for Benny Goodman. It is in a single continuous movement and is one of the composer's most approachable and delightful pieces. Although the performance here is not quite as idiomatic as that directed by the composer on CBS (Goodman and he respond in the manner born to the jazz elements in the work) there is

no doubt about its merits, and with the CBS version for the moment out of the catalogue, the London recording is well worth investigating. In any case the interest of the coupling makes this a worthwhile issue.

Piano concerto.
　(M) ** (*) Vanguard VSD 2094. Earl Wild (piano), Symphony of the Air, the composer – MENOTTI: *Piano concerto.***

Copland has recorded his *Piano concerto* at least twice, once for CBS as soloist (with Leonard Bernstein conducting), and here for Vanguard in the role of conductor. In the absence from the catalogue of the CBS version – in which the composer is freer and more persuasive in the passages influenced by jazz – this one with Earl Wild a powerful soloist is very recommendable, and the recording is first-rate, hardly showing its age.

Lincoln Portrait (for speaker and orchestra).
　** (*) Decca SXL 6388. Los Angeles Philharmonic Orchestra, Zubin Mehta, with Gregory Peck (narrator) – KRAFT: *Concerto for percussion.*** (*)

The *Lincoln Portrait* does not show Copland at his most inventive or consistently inspired. This performance is well recorded, as one would expect from this source, but the coupling does not make this issue a particularly attractive proposition. There are finer works with which to represent Copland than this example of wartime patriotism.

Orchestral variations; Preamble for a solemn occasion; Symphonic ode.
　** (*) CBS SBRG 73116. London Symphony Orchestra, the composer.

The *Orchestral variations*, though strictly an orchestral version of the *Piano variations* of 1930, make a unique and impressive contribution to Copland's *œuvre*. It was twenty-seven years after their first composition that the composer decided to present them in this new form, but the instrumentation is so ingenious and imaginative that you would never suspect their history. The result is epigrammatic and tough, yet unmistakably the work of Copland. The *Symphonic ode*, a one-movement symphony in all but name, is another major piece, strong and memorable, while the *Preamble* is occasional music in the best sense. The *Variations* are superbly played; the others really require a little more flamboyance. Big-scale, rather aggressive recording quality – an essential disc for all devotees of Copland's music.

Corelli, Arcangelo
(1653–1713)

Concerti grossi, Op. 6, Nos. 1–12: complete recording.
> *** Argo ZRG 773/5. Academy of St Martin-in-the-Fields, Neville Marriner.

Corelli has never enjoyed a boom comparable with that of Vivaldi in the 1950s, and this is currently the only complete set of the masterly Op. 6 concertos. They are rich in melodic invention and harmonic resource, and one wonders why they have been neglected for so long at a time when much lesser music of this period has been duplicated on record. The set has been prepared with evident thought and care, and if one must cavil it is only at two small points: some fussy continuo playing here and there, and a certain want of breadth and nobility of feeling in some of the slow movements. These are small points, however, when weighed alongside

the vitality and intelligence of these performances, expertly played as ever by the Academy, and beautifully recorded.

Concerti grossi, Op. 6, Nos. 1 in D major; 2 in F major; 3 in C minor; 4 in D major.
> (M) *** Philips Universo 6580 074. I Musici.

Concerti grossi, Op. 6, Nos. 1 in D major; 8 in C minor (Christmas); 9 in F major; 12 in F major.
> *** DGG Archive 2533 124. Naples Scarlatti Orchestra, Ettore Gracis.

The artists on the Archive set have the measure of the Corelli style, and their readings have the breadth and majesty that are required, along with imaginative phrasing and rhythmic liveliness. The recordings too are secure and immediate in impact, with good stereo separation. Were the set from which this is taken generally available it would be preferred to the Academy on Argo.

The performances on Universo are also eloquent and commanding, and the recording is musically balanced, with fine presence and sonority. The playing is immaculate and it also has more life and breadth than many from this source. There is not quite the imagination and nobility of the Gracis set, but the music is unfailingly inventive, and this record only duplicates one concerto on the DGG issue. Given the attractiveness of the price, this too is highly recommendable.

Oboe concerto (arr. Barbirolli).
> (B) *** Pye GSGC 14065. Evelyn Rothwell, Hallé Orchestra, Sir John Barbirolli – HAYDN and PERGOLESI: *Concertos*.***

Barbirolli's concerto is cunningly arranged from a trio sonata, and in its new form it makes one of the most enchanting works in the whole oboe repertoire. The performance here is treasurable. The opening, with its beautiful Handelian theme, is shaped with perfect dignity, and the gracious, stately allegro that follows has the touch of gossamer from the soloist. The perky finale is no less delectable, and the clean, clear recording projects the music admirably. A few clicks marred our pressing.

Violin sonatas, Op. 5, Nos. 1–12: complete recording.

> (M) ** (*) Pye Virtuoso TPLS 13058 (2 discs). Ruggiero Ricci (violin), Ivor Keyes (harpsichord), Dennis Nesbitt (viola da gamba).

Corelli's brilliant variations on the tune *La Folia* (the last of these twelve sonatas) are well enough known but otherwise this set is seriously neglected. The first six, described as being 'for use in church', are a degree more weighty than the rest, including as they do a quota of fugal movements; but all twelve show the trio sonata genre at its most invigorating. Though a modern virtuoso violinist with his bright, forward tone inevitably overbalances a gamba player, these are first-rate performances well recorded.

Corrette, Michel
(1709–95)

Organ concerto in D minor, Op. 26/6.

> (B) ** Turnabout TV 34135S. Helmuth Rilling (organ), Württemberg Chamber Orchestra, Joerg Faerber – ALBINONI: *Adagio*: HANDEL: *Organ concerto*; MOZART: *Sonata di chiesa No. 4.***

Michel Corrette's *Concerto* is charmingly slight, and the performance and recording here are particularly successful

in catching the gentle baroque miniaturism.

Couperin, François
(1668–1733)

Apothéose de Lully (Concert instrumental sous le titre d'Apothéose, composé à la mémoire immortelle de l'incomparable Monsieur De Lully): complete (includes *La Paix du Parnasse*: Italian sonata da chiesa).

> (M) *** Oiseau-Lyre SOL 300. English Chamber Orchestra, Raymond Leppard – CHARPENTIER: *Médée suite.****

This is a piece of pure programme music, and it contains some remarkably inventive writing. The orchestration is the work of Raymond Leppard, who directs some alert and stylish playing from the keyboard; the English Chamber Orchestra respond excellently, and the recording is quite superlative in its range and clarity of definition.

Les Nations: Premier ordre: *La Françoise*; Deuxième ordre: *L'Espagnole*; Troisième ordre: *L'Impériale*; Quatrième ordre: *La Piémontoise.*

> ** (*) Telefunken TK 11550 (1/2). Amsterdam Quartet.
> (B) ** (*) Oiseau-Lyre OLS 137/8. Jacobean Ensemble, Thurston Dart.

Expert and stylish performances of Couperin's splendid *Les Nations*. The Amsterdam Quartet offer a useful if more expensive alternative to the distinguished account by the Jacobean Ensemble and Thurston Dart on Oiseau-Lyre. Admirers of the late Thurston Dart will no doubt incline to the latter, for he had a special flair in this repertoire, but the Amsterdam

Quartet are also thoroughly idiomatic, and their recording is marginally richer. These are, of course, not available separately, while Dart's are, and cost much less.

Harpsichord suites, Volume 1.
> (M) *** RCA LSB 4067 (Premier ordre); LSB 4077 (Deuxième ordre); LSB 4087 (Troisième ordre; Quatrième ordre); LSB 4098 (Cinquième ordre). Kenneth Gilbert (harpsichord).

Harpsichord suites, Volume 2.
> (M) *** RCA LHL 1 5048 (Sixième ordre; Septième ordre); LHL 1 5049 (Huitième ordre; also *L'Art de toucher le clavecin: Preludes Nos. 1–8; Allemande in D minor*); LHL 1 5050 (Neuvième ordre; Dixième ordre); LHL 1 5051 (Onzième ordre; Douzième ordre). Kenneth Gilbert (harpsichord).

Harpsichord suites, Volume 2: Huitième ordre; Onzième ordre. *Volume 3:* Treizième ordre; Quinzième ordre. *L'Art de toucher le clavecin: Prelude No. 6.*
> ** Philips 6700 035 (2 discs). Rafael Puyana (harpsichord), with Christopher Hogwood (second harpsichord).

Harpsichord suites, Volume 3 (complete); (i) *Troisième Concert royal; Deuxième Concert royal: Echos.*
> (M) *** RCA SER 5720/23. Kenneth Gilbert (harpsichord), (i) with Gian Lyman-Silbiger (viola da gamba).

The Canadian scholar Kenneth Gilbert has edited the complete keyboard works of Couperin, and his recording of them is made on an exact copy of an instrument by Henry Hemsch (1750) made by Hubbard in Boston. It is slightly below modern pitch and tuned to unequal temperament, which Couperin is known to have preferred. Kenneth Gilbert's performances are scrupulous in matters of registration: Couperin following what is known of eighteenth-century practice in France. Changes of registration within a piece are rare, but it must be not be thought that his playing is in any way cautious or austere. There is no want of expressive range throughout the series and it must at once be said that Professor Gilbert plays with authority and taste – and, more to the point, artistry. He is also well served by the engineers. In the later records, Books 2, 3 and 4, a different recording venue is used: the first Book (Ordres 1–5) was recorded in Montreal and the others in the Abbey of St-Benoît-du-Lac, which produces a slightly richer sonority. Readers should note that the sound throughout the series is of excellent quality and altogether on a par with the performances. It is impossible to dwell on the individual felicities of each Ordre. As with the *48*, there is little to be gained in making recommendations to start with any particular disc; the important thing is to start somewhere. (Perhaps the *Huitième Ordre*, containing the famous *Pasacaille*, might make a good beginning, though Professor Gilbert does not play it with the panache of the late Thurston Dart.) Once started, the listener will want to explore this rewarding world more fully, and there is no doubt that Kenneth Gilbert is an eminently authoritative guide. It is a pity that the set is disfigured by pop-art sleeves that have nothing to recommend them and may well serve to put some collectors off. Volume 3, however, is handsomely packaged – the four discs together in a stylishly printed box with good notes. Volume 4 is still not released as we go to press.

By comparison with Kenneth Gilbert, Rafael Puyana seems larger than life, thanks mainly to the close balance of the recording. There is no want of panache or excitement here, and Mr Puyana has obviously thought deeply about what he is doing. However, Professor Gilbert's series is the one to have: it is complete, thoroughly scholarly and in superb style. Some of the registration in Puyana's set will not be to all tastes, and there are some inconsistencies of interpretation too.

La Reine des cœurs: Ordres 8; 14; 21: complete recording.
   *** Argo ZRG 632. George Malcolm (harpsichord).

Couperin has, fancifully perhaps, been described as the Chopin of the eighteenth century. Certainly his keyboard miniatures enshrine a wealth of poetic feeling and musical imagination as well as a subtle harmonic language. However, he is not so immediate in impact as the Polish master. This excellent anthology, comprising three *Ordres* or suites of keyboard pieces, serves as an admirable introduction to Couperin's art. George Malcolm is seen at his very finest and plays with great elegance and flair. The recording will strike some as being slightly more closely balanced than is desirable, but the sound is clear and vivid. A fine record.

Messe propre pour les couvents des religieux et religieuses; Messe solomnelle à l'usage des paroisses.
   (M) *** Argo 4BBA 1011/12. Gillian Weir (organ).
   (M) ** HMV SLS 820 (2 discs). Lionel Rogg (organ).

Rarely has the sound of the baroque organ (Miss Weir has chosen a modern tracker-action instrument) been captured on disc so vividly yet so engagingly on the ear. The works themselves, far more than conventional commentaries on the theme of the Mass, are among the finest of all Couperin's inspirations. The *Mass for parishes* is the grander work, but the *Mass for convents*, basically simpler, has its contrapuntal complexities, which Miss

Weir interprets not only with clarity but with an ability to lead the ear on. Few records of baroque organ music can be recommended so enthusiastically as this.

Lionel Rogg is a keenly perceptive interpreter of baroque organ music, but his readings of these two Couperin masterpieces are altogether cooler, ultimately less imaginative than those of Gillian Weir. He is not helped by heavier organ tone and more aggressive recording quality.

Couperin, Louis
(1626–61)

Pavane; Suites: in C major; in D major (La Piémontaise); in F major.
   *** Telefunken SAWT 9605. Blandine Verlet (harpsichord).

Louis Couperin is much less well represented in the catalogue than his nephew François, so this recital is doubly welcome. The playing is accomplished and alive, cleanly articulated; the ornamentation is stylish and the music well characterized. The harpsichord used has a richness of timbre which is a welcome relief from the clatter we are sometimes offered. The only drawback to the disc is the poor sleeve-notes, which tell us too little about the music.

Croft, William
(1678–1727)

Violin sonatas: in B minor; in G minor. Harpsichord suites: in C minor; in C minor; in E flat major; in E minor. By Purling Streams (cantata); A Hymn on divine musick.
   (B) ** (*) Oryx ORYX 1730. Marjorie Lavers (violin), Michael

Dobson (oboe), Robert Elliott (harpsichord), Jane Ryan (viola da gamba), Honor Sheppard (Soprano).

William Croft, who succeeded John Blow as organist of Westminster Abbey (and Master to the Children and Composer to the Chapel Royal), was born about twenty years after Purcell. His music has a fairly strong individuality; its invention is attractively fresh. This anthology seems an admirable way of presenting him to the modern listener. The blend of keyboard, instrumental and vocal music is nicely balanced and the performances are skilful and eloquent. The recording too, in a fairly reverberant acoustic, is warm and pleasing, and this enjoyable concert is of a good deal more than purely historical interest.

Crosse, Gordon
(born 1937)

Changes: complete recording.
*** Argo ZRG 656. Jennifer Vyvyan (soprano), John Shirley-Quirk (baritone), Orpington Junior Singers, Highgate School Boys' Choir, London Symphony Orchestra and Chorus, Norman Del Mar.

The title *Changes* is a pun, referring not merely to the transience of nature but to the tolling of bells. Crosse wrote this large-scale work on a commission for the Three Choirs Festival of 1966, and with striking confidence managed – as the title itself does – to achieve a balance between conflicting needs and ideas. This is consequently a work which can be appreciated at many different levels, whether by children or more sophisticated listeners. The choice of words, ranging from prayers to a poem of Blake, is simple and satisfying, and

Crosse's use of serial techniques (*not* twelve-note) does not distract from the general approachability of the music, with its occasional echoes of Britten. A good piece to have on record, particularly when it is so well performed and recorded.

Cruft, Adrian
(born 1921)

Divertimento for string orchestra, Op. 43.
(M) *** Pye Virtuoso TPLS 13005. London Philharmonic Orchestra, John Snashall – MCCABE: *Symphony;* LEIGHTON: *Concerto.****

Adrian Cruft is especially good at creating atmosphere from texture, and it is this rather than the thematic content that sets the delicate mood of the opening of his *Divertimento* and sustains the intensity which begins the finale. This appears to be a lightweight work, but it has more substance than a first impression might suggest. It has an individual melodic charm (especially in the spiritual-flavoured slow movement) and a craftsmanship that only just falls short, in terms of personality, of the Dag Wiren *Serenade*. This very spontaneous performance catches the music's flavour fully, and the recording is excellent.

Crumb, George
(born 1926)

Ancient voices of children (song cycle).
(M) ** Nonesuch H 71255. Jan De Gaetani (mezzo-soprano), Michael Dash (treble), Contemporary Chamber Ensemble, Arthur Weisberg.

Crumb, like many other composers today, whether in America or in Europe, uses weird effects on conventional instruments ('preparing' piano, harp and mandolin in various unexpected ways) as well as using unconventional percussion instruments such as a toy piano. The wonder is that this setting of extracts from Lorca's poems shows genuine imagination. Whatever the means, the words are enhanced, and this brilliant performance gives one all the dynamism needed if one is to surmount the difficulties of such music.

Crusell, Bernhard
(1775–1838)

Clarinet concerto No. 2 in F minor, Op. 5.
> ** (*) Unicorn RHS 314. Gervase de Peyer (clarinet), London Mozart Players, Bernard Jacob – COPLAND: *Clarinet concerto.*** (*)

Bernhard Crusell was a Finnish composer who lived for some time in Sweden. He was himself a fine clarinettist and he composed three concertos for the instrument. The *Second*, recorded elegantly here by Gervase de Peyer, is a sunny, smiling work, not dissimilar from Mozart and Weber, though it has a distinct individuality. Although the recording is not in the first flight, the interest of the music outweighs this consideration.

Clarinet quartet No. 2 in C minor, Op. 4.
> *** Oiseau-Lyre DSLO 501. The Music Party (with Alan Hacker, clarinet) – HUMMEL: *Clarinet quartet.****

Bernhard Crusell's work enjoyed a good deal of popularity in its day and its influence was felt as far as Russia, where Glinka was one of his admirers. His

Clarinet quartet No. 2 is a piece of much charm, and in such hands as these its attractions are highly persuasive. The Music Party play on contemporary instruments, and their performances are as revealing as they are masterly. The balance of the recording is eminently musical, and the vividness of the sound could not be improved upon. The Hummel coupling is equally fine.

Dallapiccola, Luigi
(1904–75)

Tartiniana (for violin and piano).
> (M) ** Supraphon SUAST 50707. Ladislav Jašek (violin), Josef Hála (piano) – BRITTEN: *Suite;* PROKOFIEV: *Sonata.* **

Dallapiccola's pastiche is tastefully done and the recording is good. This makes an attractive bonus for the Britten and Prokofiev works.

Danzi, Franz
(1763–1826)

Violoncello concerto in E minor.
> (B) ** (*) Turnabout TV 34306S. Thomas Blees (cello), Berlin Symphony Orchestra, C. A. Bünte – WEBER: *Grand pot-pourri.***

Franz Danzi was an almost exact contemporary of Beethoven, but unlike that master he stayed happily within the proper court circles of the lesser German princes during his whole working career. He wrote an opera based on Gozzi's *Turandot*, but generally he is dismissed as a rather insignificant follower of the late Mannheim school of symphonists. The *Cello concerto*, vividly played by Thomas Blees (a fine artist of whom we should hear more), suggests that there is more to discover. Danzi himself was a cellist, leaving the Mannheim Orchestra to become a conductor and court composer, and this work exploits the potentiality of the instrument far more than was common at the time. A valuable novelty, well recorded.

Davy, Richard
(15th–16th century)

St Matthew Passion.
*** Argo ZRG 558. Ian Partridge (tenor), Christopher Keyte (bass), Boys of All Saints, Margaret Street, Purcell Consort, Grayston Burgess.

This is one of the earliest settings of the Passion in England to have come down to us. The manuscript is to be found in the Eton College Choir Book, which dates from about 1500. In 1491, Davy was the choirmaster of Magdalen College, Oxford, and it is probable that the first performance of the *Passion* took place there. It is an austere but moving work – almost as austere as the Schütz *Passions* of two centuries later. It would be difficult to imagine a finer performance of the work than this and the recording makes telling use of special effects. Strongly recommended.

Debussy, Claude
(1862–1918)

Berceuse héroïque; La Boîte à joujoux; Children's Corner suite; (i) *Danse sacrée et danse profane;* (ii) *Fantasy for piano and orchestra; Images; Jeux; Khamma; Marche écossaise; La Mer; Nocturnes; Petite suite; Prélude à*

l'après-midi d'un faune; Printemps; (iii) *Rhapsody for clarinet;* (iv) *Rhapsody for saxophone; Le Roi Lear; Tarantelle styrienne.*
(M) *** HMV SLS 893 (5 discs). Orchestre National de l'ORTF, Jean Martinon, with (i) Marie-Claire Jamet (harp), (ii) Aldo Ciccolini (piano), (iii) Guy Dangain (clarinet), (iv) Jean-Marie Londeix (saxophone).

Debussy's orchestral output can be comfortably fitted on to four records: the present set fills out the ten sides with the *Fantasy* for piano and orchestra, *La Boîte à joujoux*, which is scored by André Caplet, *Khamma*, which is scored by Koechlin, Caplet's scoring of *Children's Corner* and Henri Büsser's of the *Petite suite*. Even so, the orchestral interludes to *Le Martyre de Saint Sébastien*, in whose scoring Caplet also had a hand, are omitted. We do get the rarely heard music to *Le Roi Lear* and the *Rhapsodies*. Martinon gets some extremely fine playing from the ORTF Orchestra, and these performances can in general hold their own with almost any in the catalogue. The *Nuages* is perhaps too slow and could be more atmospheric. *Jeux* could, one feels, breathe a little more freely, though in some ways it is to be preferred to Boulez's almost clinical account. Certainly this *La Mer* is highly competitive: only Karajan and Ormandy are better. *La Boîte à joujoux* is not so delicately articulated or quite as atmospheric as Ansermet's, though there is no doubt that this is the better orchestral playing. The recording throughout is quite superb, with great atmosphere and space though without any loss of presence or detail. This set will give great pleasure, and at its permanent bargain price is highly competitive.

La Boîte à joujoux (children's ballet): complete recording.

(M) *** Decca Ace of Diamonds SDD 293. Suisse Romande Orchestra, Ernest Ansermet – DUKAS: *La Péri*.** (*)

Debussy's enchanting score about adventures in a children's box of toys has an entirely miniature flavour. Although the work was completed by the composer in 1913, five years before his death, he only sketched the orchestration, which was completed later by André Caplet. The music shows Ansermet at his most imaginative, and the performance was one of his finest. The recording too is first-rate and has both the clarity and the bloom characteristic of this conductor's best discs.

Fantasy for piano and orchestra.
*** Decca SXL 6435. Jean-Rodolphe Kars (piano), London Symphony Orchestra, Alexander Gibson – DELIUS: *Piano concerto*.***

A Debussy rarity, written between 1889 and 1890 but withdrawn by the composer just as its first performance, under Vincent d'Indy, was about to take place. If it does not find Debussy's language fully formed it is still well worth investigating, and though this is by no means its first appearance on LP, it is undoubtedly the most successful. Kars plays with great sympathy and is well accompanied. Coupled as it is with the Delius *Piano concerto*, this is a most valuable disc, beautifully recorded.

(i) *Fantasy for piano and orchestra;* (ii) *Rhapsody for clarinet and orchestra;* (iii) *Rhapsody for saxophone and orchestra.*
(M) ** (*) Vox STGBY 679. (i) Marylene Dosse (piano); (ii) Serge Dangain (clarinet); (iii) Jean-Marie Londeix (saxophone); all with Radio Luxembourg Orchestra, Louis de Froment.

If without quite the refinement of Kars on Decca, this is still an excellent performance of the *Fantasy*, showing considerable poetic feeling in the slow middle section. The accounts of the two *Rhapsodies* are even finer, outstandingly vivid and spontaneous. The clarinettist produces a lovely dreamy quality at the opening of his piece, while Jean-Marie Londeix shows that in skilful hands the saxophone can provide a much greater sophistication of mood and colour than one would expect. The orchestral support is good and the recording more spacious and atmospheric than on some other discs from this source.

Images; Marche écossaise; La Mer; Nocturnes; Petite suite; Prélude à l'après-midi d'un faune; Printemps; (i) *Rhapsody for clarinet and orchestra; Suite bergamasque: Clair de lune; Tarantelle styrienne.*
(M) ** Decca Ace of Diamonds SDDK 396/8. Suisse Romande Orchestra, Ernest Ansermet, (i) with Robert Gugholz (clarinet).

This compilation which includes Ansermet's *La Mer, Nocturnes* and *Images* is an attractive one, for although the SRO is not the finest of orchestras, Ansermet has undoubted feeling for Debussy and his readings will not fail to give pleasure to the listener. The only possible reservation here concerns the *Petite suite*, which for some ears is unsatisfactory (see below), mainly on account of less than perfect intonation; otherwise this set will give general satisfaction and can be recommended, for its sound quality is well up to the high standard that Decca set themselves in Geneva.

Images pour orchestre (Ibéria; Gigues; Rondes de printemps); (i) *Danse sacrée et danse profane.*

** (*) CBS 72725. Cleveland Orchestra, Pierre Boulez, (i) with Alice Chalifonx (harp).

Images pour orchestre; Prélude à l'après-midi d'un faune.

** (*) DGG 2530 145. Boston Symphony Orchestra, Michael Tilson Thomas.

Images pour orchestre; Printemps (suite symphonique).

(M) ** Decca Ace of Diamonds SDD 373. Suisse Romande Orchestra, Ernest Ansermet.

Boulez's versions have rather more atmosphere than his account of *La Mer*, which, in spite of the acclaim with which it was greeted, must yield to the claims of its rivals. The performance of *Images* is carefully shaped and performed: *Gigues* has genuine atmosphere. The CBS balance is closer than ideal but by no means unacceptable, except in the *Danse sacrée et danse profane*, where an absurdly vast harp assumes an importance equal to that of the strings. String tone, too, is a bit overnourished in the American manner.

Michael Tilson Thomas's set of *Images* is recorded with exceptional vividness: this version offers the finest sound outside Martinon's five-disc anthology. The performance too is alive, not without atmosphere, and the orchestral playing is admirable. The approach is youthfully impulsive, and this creates a strong forward momentum in the *Prélude à l'après-midi d'un faune*. Here perhaps a greater feeling of repose is desirable in the outer sections; but taken as a whole this is an attractive disc.

Ansermet's readings are eminently serviceable without being really distinguished. His earlier account of the *Images*, an early mono disc now transferred to Eclipse (ECS 565), is infinitely more subtle and atmospheric. This is better recorded and is still worth considering, particularly in this price bracket. There is some poor wind intonation in *Rondes de printemps*, but in general readers will find more to admire than to cavil at in this performance. Ansermet's account of *Printemps* is straightforward and unmannered, and again the recording is eminently clean and well-detailed.

Jeux; Nocturnes (Nuages; Fêtes; (i) Sirènes); Tarantelle styrienne.

(M) ** Decca Ace of Diamonds SDD 375. Suisse Romande Orchestra, Ernest Ansermet, (i) with female chorus.

Ansermet's account of *Jeux* has plenty of atmosphere: it is in fact one of his finest Debussy records. The *Nocturnes*, though perfectly acceptable, is not the most distinguished account of the work in the catalogue; *Sirènes* is a bit lacklustre. However, at mid-price this disc is well worth considering and the recording is admirably clear and detailed in spite of its age (it comes from the late 50s–early 60s).

Jeux; La Mer; Prélude à l'après-midi d'un faune.

** CBS 73533. New Philharmonia Orchestra, Pierre Boulez.

La Mer.

*** Decca Phase 4 PFS 4220. London Symphony Orchestra, Leopold Stokowski – BERLIOZ: *Danse des sylphes*; RAVEL: *Daphnis.****

(M) ** CBS 61075. Cleveland Orchestra, George Szell – RAVEL: *Daphnis; Pavane.***

(B) ** Pye GSGC 15013. Hallé Orchestra, Sir John Barbirolli – RAVEL: *Daphnis; La Valse.***

La Mer; Nocturnes (Nuages; Fêtes; (i) Sirènes).

(M) ** (*) HMV SXLP 30146. Philharmonia Orchestra, Carlo Maria Giulini, (i) with chorus.

** HMV ASD 2442. Orchestre de Paris, Sir John Barbirolli, (i) with chorus.

(M) * (*) Supraphon SUAST 50575. Czech Philharmonic Orchestra, Jean Fournet, (i) with chorus.

La Mer; Prélude à l'après-midi d'un faune.

*** DGG SLPM 138923. Berlin Philharmonic Orchestra, Herbert von Karajan – RAVEL: *Daphnis.****

*** RCA Quadradisc ARD 1 0029; Stereo ARL 1 0029. Philadelphia Orchestra, Eugene Ormandy – RAVEL: *Daphnis.****

La Mer; (i) Danse sacrée et danse profane.

(M) * (*) DGG Privilege 2538 080. Lamoureux Orchestra of Paris, Igor Markevitch, (i) with Suzanne Cotelle (harp) – ROUSSEL: *Bacchus et Ariane.*(*)

As far as *La Mer* is concerned, Karajan's ten-year-old recording with the Berlin Philharmonic still remains first choice. It has total commitment and a fastidious care for detail, and it evokes the spirit of the work as effectively as it observes the letter. The performance of the *Prélude à l'après-midi d'un faune* is no less outstanding, the cool perfection of the opening flute solo matched by ravishing string playing in the central section. The sound remains fresh and well-detailed.

Ormandy, who offers the same coupling exactly, is every bit as good. The sheer physical excitement generated by this performance of *La Mer*, as well as its feeling for sensitive detail, is matched by an exquisite account of the *Prélude* with superb atmosphere and impeccable polish. The RCA recording is admirable: the balance is natural and the sound quality truthful in both timbre and perspective. A most realistic sound impression of superb performances, and those

who recall Ormandy's marvellous 78s of the Ravel *Daphnis et Chloé* fragments may rest assured that the coupling here is every bit as magical.

Boulez has won critical accolades for his concert performances of *La Mer* and *Jeux*, but there seems little to excite undue enthusiasm here. True, he secures some first-class playing from the New Philharmonia Orchestra, and no one would deny that *Jeux* is persuasively given. However, the playing lacks atmosphere and the last degree of poetry, and were Boulez's name left off the record label, one doubts whether the performances would have aroused anything like the enthusiasm they did in the press. *La Mer* is not remotely comparable with the best, the Karajan on DGG, and is not superior to most rival accounts listed. Much the same applies to the *Prélude à l'après-midi d'un faune*, which is a good deal better than some accounts but by no means the equal of the best. It is in *Jeux*, a work of seminal importance in Boulez's development, that this record is far more competitive.

Giulini's account of *La Mer* is very distinguished indeed, and it is given the benefit of excellent EMI recording. It would be difficult to fault this reading, and at its new and highly competitive price, this disc should come near to the top of the recommended list. The Philharmonia are in splendid form. Under Giulini the *Nocturnes* are played with great delicacy of feeling and refinement of detail. *Nuages* is perhaps a little too dreamy but nonetheless full of atmosphere. *Sirènes* is all too wanting in a sense of movement: it is slow to the point of sluggishness. However, it is beautifully recorded and preferable in some ways to many of its rivals. (Abbado has the same refinement but better-judged tempi; Ansermet and Boulez have better-judged tempi but less well-shaped detail and atmosphere.)

Barbirolli's HMV direction of both scores is sympathetic, and he shows a strong feeling for atmosphere. His performances are to be preferred to Boulez's on CBS, but they do not figure high on the list all the same. There is a lack of inner tension about the playing, and the recordings, though they have plenty of body, need just a little more clarity of detail.

Stokowski's performance of *La Mer* has surprisingly slow basic tempi, even for Stokowski. But the playing has a wonderful intensity, with marvellously moulded sound. Like Ansermet and Karajan, Stokowski adds the extra brass parts in the last movement, which are authentic although excised from the printed score, and with the most brilliant Phase 4 recording the effect is breathtaking in its brilliance and impact. This is among the finest performances of *La Mer* available on disc, and with a rich version of the *Second suite* from *Daphnis et Chloé* as the main coupling, it is highly recommendable.

Szell's zest for detail as well as brilliance gives the Cleveland performance some splendid moments. The tension is held tautly throughout and the excitement of the closing pages is supported by superb orchestral playing. There is a certain lack of atmosphere caused by the immediacy of the microphones, and the brightness of the sound has a tendency to glare, but this is a distinguished coupling.

Fournet's *La Mer* is carefully prepared but there is relatively little atmospheric magic, and the overall temperature of the performance is low. The three *Nocturnes* are rather more successful. *Nuages* is rather precise, but the processional in *Fêtes* is extremely effective, partly because the tempo chosen is exactly right. The stereo here is vivid.

Markevitch provides a good routine account of *La Mer* without special claims on one's purse. It is well recorded, but the merits of the disc lie in the attractions of the couplings, an enjoyable performance of the *Danse sacrée et danse profane*, and a serviceable one of

Roussel's *Second suite* from *Bacchus et Ariane*.

In the bargain basement Barbirolli's early recording of *La Mer* for Pye must not be forgotten. It is an atmospheric performance, which becomes especially exciting in its closing section, but Ansermet's version (see below) is probably the better buy (his later, full-priced disc, coupled to *Khamma*, is by no means as successful or competitive).

La Mer; Petite suite; Prélude à l'après-midi d'une faune; Suite bergamasque: Clair de lune; Tarantelle styrienne.
  (B) ** (*) Decca SPA 231. Suisse Romande Orchestra, Ernest Ansermet.

This anthology, issued on Decca's cheapest label, is an excellent way of sampling Ansermet's individual and often rewarding approach to the music of Debussy. It includes the second of Ansermet's three LP versions of *La Mer*, which was made in 1957. Yet the sound is not in the least dated, and the performance is direct and unmannered. The *Petite suite*, heard in Büsser's charming orchestration, is more controversial: some ears find the phrasing charmless and the weakness of intonation distracting. The other fill-ups are attractively played, and given the low price tag, the record makes an eminently worthwhile bargain.

Nocturnes (Nuages; Fêtes; (i) Sirènes).
  *** DGG 2530 038. Boston Symphony Orchestra, Claudio Abbado, (i) with New England Conservatory Chorus – RAVEL: *Daphnis; Pavane.****

Nocturnes (Nuages; Fêtes; (i) Sirènes); (ii) Rhapsody for clarinet and orchestra; Printemps.
  ** CBS SBRG 72785. New Philharmonia Orchestra, Pierre Boulez,

with (i) John Alldis Choir, (ii) Gervase de Peyer (clarinet).

Nocturnes (Nuages; Fêtes only); Prélude à l'après-midi d'un faune.

(M) ** (*) Decca Ace of Diamonds SDD 425. London Symphony Orchestra, Pierre Monteux – RAVEL: *Pavane; Rapsodie espagnole.****

Abbado's account of the *Nocturnes* is one of the finest now in the catalogue. He shows fastidious care for detail without ever succumbing to preciosity and has a keen feeling for atmosphere without ever losing sight of the music's structure. The playing of the Boston Orchestra is immensely polished but not glossy, and there is a naturalness about this performance that also distinguishes the recording. Here the balance is good, dynamics are allowed to register without artificial boosting, and the tone quality is firm. The acoustic may be a little too reverberant for some tastes but most people will find this a rewarding issue in every way.

In *Nuages* Boulez sets a brisk tempo only to abandon it a few bars later; apart from that inconsistency this performance has atmosphere. *Fêtes* is relatively matter-of-fact and lacking in electricity, while *Sirènes* is too languid and lush. A pity, as the coupling comes off well. Boulez often lacks atmosphere even in some of his Debussy, but both *Printemps* and the *Clarinet rhapsody* are given convincing performances and are well recorded on the whole.

Monteux was not able, unfortunately, to complete his set of *Nocturnes*: *Sirènes*, with its need of a chorus, is omitted. Even so this disc is highly competitive, with its excellent couplings. The *Nuages* drift by gently and the *Fêtes* has a luminous quality that is highly attractive. The *Prélude à l'après-midi d'un faune* is cool, clearly focused and perhaps a shade wanting in atmosphere. (Karajan and Ormandy are more magical.) The recording has plenty of detail and presence and a natural aural perspective.

Petite suite.

(M) * (*) Decca Ace of Diamonds SDD 388. Suisse Romande Orchestra, Ernest Ansermet – FAURÉ: *Masques et Bergamasques; Pelléas et Mélisande; Pénélope Prélude.****

This is currently the only available recording of the *Petite suite* (apart from Martinon's in his five-disc HMV anthology), and it is also available differently coupled (see above under *Images*). We have praised it in earlier editions of the SRG, but reservations must now be made about the orchestral playing, even though some ears unrepentantly find the performance characterful and spontaneous. Certainly there is no disagreement about the coupling of this Ace of Diamonds issue, a unique and desirable collection of Fauré's orchestral music which alone is worth the price of the disc.

CHAMBER AND INSTRUMENTAL MUSIC

String quartet in G minor.

⊛ *** Philips SAL 3643. Italian Quartet – RAVEL: *Quartet.****

*** DGG 2530 235. LaSalle Quartet – RAVEL: *Quartet.****

** (*) CBS 72998. Juilliard Quartet – RAVEL: *Quartet.** (*)

(M) * (*) HMV HQS 1231. Parrenin Quartet – RAVEL: *Quartet.***

What does one say about playing like that provided by the Italian Quartet except that it is so superlative that it cannot fail to win over any listener to Debussy's quartet; not that that would be difficult anyway. Perfectly judged ensemble, weight of tone and balance make this a most satisfying performance,

303

and the recording engineers have produced a vivid and truthful sound picture with plenty of impact. One of the finest chamber-music records made in recent years.

Expert playing too, on DGG, by the fine LaSalle Quartet. They are splendidly recorded, and their reading takes a place of honour alongside the fine account by the Italian Quartet, though the latter would remain a first buy.

The Juilliards give a polished account that will also give great pleasure. In spontaneity, however, and sheer beauty of tone it must yield to the Italians and the LaSalle Quartet. The recording, too, does not produce such satisfying results as the others: it is less wide in range and truthful in timbre. But in a less competitive field, it might have been a strong contender.

The HMV disc has the advantage of economy, but the Parrenin Quartet's performance is rather less successful than the Ravel coupling. The recording is clear and immediate.

Sonata (Trio) for harp, flute and viola.
* (*) Argo ZRG 574. Robles Trio –
BAX: *Elegiac trio;* RAVEL: *Introduction and allegro.***

This performance of Debussy's ethereal *Trio* has the advantage of superb recording; everything is beautifully focused and clear. Unfortunately the viola intonation is too vulnerable for the performance to give unalloyed pleasure. Marisa Robles plays beautifully, but the reading as a whole cannot match the atmosphere and magic of the Melos Ensemble's recording in their marvellous concert of French music on Oiseau-Lyre SOL 60048 (discussed in our *Treasury* volume).

Violoncello sonata in D minor.
*** Decca SXL 2298. Mstislav Rostropovich (cello), Benjamin Brit-

ten (piano) – BRITTEN: *Sonata;*
SCHUMANN: *Fünf Stücke.****

This *Cello sonata* is one of the handful of pieces that Debussy wrote during the First World War, when he was already suffering from the disease which finally killed him. It was the first of a planned cycle of six sonatas for different instruments, written, so Debussy emphasized, by a 'musicien français'. Yet there is nothing of war or even patriotism in this flowing, elusive work. The writing for the instruments is brilliant, yet, as in the Britten *Sonata* on the reverse, there is little display. Britten and Rostropovich bring a clarity and point which suit it perfectly. The recording is excellent.

PIANO MUSIC

Ballade; Cortège et airs de danse; En Blanc et noir; 6 Épigraphes antiques; Marche écossaise; Petite suite; Lindaraja; Prélude à l'après-midi d'un faune; Symphonie en si mineur.
** DGG 2707 072 (2 discs). Alfons and Aloys Kontarsky (two pianos) – RAVEL: *Piano duet music.***
En Blanc et noir; 6 Épigraphes antiques; Petite suite.
(B) ** Turnabout TV 37032S. Walter and Beatrice Klien (two pianos) (with BIZET: *Jeux d'enfants***).

The DGG set provides a useful anthology since it presents a number of rarities, including the keyboard arrangement of *Prélude à l'après-midi d'un faune* as well as *Lindaraja* and the little *Symphony*. The playing is eminently stylish and cool, possibly a little wanting in magic. The value of the set is diminished by the dry acoustic and the somewhat unbeguiling, lacklustre sound.

The Turnabout collection is much less complete than that offered by the Kontarsky's, but their two-record set is more than four times the price of this, and now that Noël Lee and Werner Haas are no longer available on Philips, the Turnabout disc is welcome. *En Blanc et noir* is of course a masterpiece and its neglect is unaccountable. The playing here is sensitive, and the recording, if not ideal, is clear and fully acceptable at the modest price asked.

Berceuse héroïque; La Boîte à joujoux; Children's Corner; Études, Books 1 and 2; Hommage à Haydn; Images; Préludes, Book 2; La plus que lente.
  * (**) Telefunken SMA 25110 (1/3). Noël Lee (piano).
Berceuse héroïque; Children's Corner; Hommage à Haydn; Le Petit Nègre; Pour le piano; Suite bergamasque; Valse romantique.
  (B) ** (*) Turnabout TV 37024S. Peter Frankl (piano).
La Boîte à joujoux; Images, Set 2; Nocturne; La plus que lente.
  (B) ** (*) Turnabout TV 37026S. Peter Frankl (piano).
Children's Corner; Images, Sets 1 & 2.
  ⊛ *** DGG 2530 196. Arturo Benedetti Michelangeli (piano).
Études, Books 1 and 2; L'Isle joyeuse.
  (B) ** (*) Turnabout TV 37025S. Peter Frankl (piano).
Danse bohémienne; D'un cahier d'esquisses; Estampes; Images, Set 1; Masques; Mazurka; Tarantelle styrienne.
  (B) ** (*) Turnabout TV 37023S. Peter Frankl (piano).
Images, Sets 1 and 2.
  (M) *** HMV HQS 1284. Michel Béroff (piano) – PROKOFIEV: *Visions fugitives.****

Michelangeli's record is outstanding here. It is a magical and beautifully recorded disc. Michelangeli has made few records, but this is one of his best. It is

also perhaps the most distinguished Debussy playing in the catalogue.

From Noël Lee on Telefunken good and even distinguished playing that reveals his Debussian instincts as highly developed. Unfortunately this anthology is let down by less than ideal recording. Were it available at bargain price and, like Peter Frankl's set on Turnabout, separately, it would carry a strong recommendation. There is some discomfort at ends of sides and a little twanginess, which prevent this being the strong contender Mr Lee's splendid playing should make it.

Peter Frankl is an eminently stylish Debussy player and readers need feel no hesitation in investing in this set. It has the advantage of economy, and moreover as each record is available separately, readers can pick and choose. Béroff's set of the *Préludes* is preferable, but in the *Études*, for example, Frankl is without serious rival. Likewise his *La Boîte à joujoux* is a delight. The recordings date from the early 1960s and are not first-class, but they are still very acceptable. With the Béroff set, Michelangeli's superb recital and perhaps Daniel Adni's fine disc (see below), one could safely fill in the rest of Debussy's piano *œuvre* from these Turnabout discs.

Béroff's set of *Images*, Books 1 and 2, can certainly be cordially welcomed. The playing is beautifully clean and the lines finely drawn. Lucid though it is, there is no lack of atmosphere. The textures glisten, and every detail is in place. The recording is beautifully realistic and deserves the highest praise: the faintest trace of flutter is discernible but this should not inhibit a full three-star recommendation.

Estampes; Pour le piano; Préludes, Books 1 and 2.
  (M) *** HMV SLS 803 (2 discs). Michel Béroff (piano).
Préludes, Books 1 and 2.
  (M) ** Decca 3BB 107/8. Jean-Rodolphe Kars (piano).

** DGG 2530 304/5. Dino Ciani (piano).

Préludes, Book 1.

(B) ** (*) Turnabout TV 37027S. Peter Frankl (piano).

2 Arabesques; Ballade; Préludes, Book 2; Rêverie.

(B) ** (*) Turnabout TV 37028S. Peter Frankl (piano).

Préludes, Book 2.

(B) ** (*) Turnabout TV 34360S. Sviatoslav Richter (piano).

The young French pianist Michel Béroff gives most accomplished performances of both books of *Préludes*. His technique is formidable, and he has an enviable sureness of style as well as impeccable control and a wide range of keyboard colour. The HMV recording reproduces great clarity of detail and firm tone. All in all this is the most impressive set now on the market.

Jean-Rodolphe Kars is a pianist of undoubted sensibility and impeccable keyboard control. Ideally suited to Debussy though he is, his account of the two books of *Préludes* is a little disappointing. His performance is a little wanting in colour and atmospheric tension; there is much beautiful pianism, but keener characterization is called for. By the side of Michel Béroff's excellently recorded HMV account this sounds a little monochrome.

Unlike the Kars or Béroff versions, Dino Ciani's set of the Debussy *Préludes* can be bought as two separate discs, though the cost is somewhat greater. They are impeccably recorded, but the performances are not as well shaped or their character so keenly in focus as they are in Béroff's hands; moreover, the HMV set is the more vividly recorded too. Ciani has a fine technique and plays with intelligence and taste, but ultimately the greater electricity and enthusiasm of Béroff tells.

Peter Frankl's set is, like Ciani's,

available separately, but unlike that, it is by far the cheapest. Frankl plays with impeccable style and his complete survey of the Debussy piano music is an undoubted bargain, particularly as the recording, while not perhaps as distinguished as the one HMV provide for Béroff, is really very good. Moreover his recording of Book 2 offers some fill-ups in the form of the *Ballade* and the *Deux Arabesques*.

Richter's recording was made at a public recital, and the soft outlines of the piano image seem ideal for spinning the magic of most of these *Préludes*, creating a mood and texture exactly like a French impressionist painting. Perhaps in *General Lavine – eccentric* one would ideally ask for more bite, but the superb virtuosity of *Les tierces alternées* comes over unscathed, and the fiery cascades and splutters of *Feux d'artifice* are projected by the sheer bravura of the pianism. Elsewhere the gentle haze over the piano (the articulation itself is clear enough) suits Richter's musing, introvert style, and *Brouillards* (*Mists*), *Feuilles mortes* (*Dead leaves*), and especially *Bruyères* are wonderfully atmospheric. The audience for the most part listen in silence, in spite of an intrusive neighbouring church bell at the opening.

Collections

Arabesques; Ballade; Images (Book 1: Reflets dans l'eau; Mouvement. Book 2: Poissons d'or); L'Isle joyeuse; Préludes, Book 2: Feux d'artifice. Suite bergamasque.

(M) *** HMV HQS 1262. Daniel Adni (piano).

An outstanding collection in every way: this young Israeli pianist proves himself a Debussian of no mean order. His recital is well planned and offers playing that is as poetic in feeling as it is accomplished in technique. The HMV engineers have provided piano tone of outstanding realism, and readers wanting this particular compilation need not hesitate.

2 Arabesques; Children's Corner; Estampes: No. 3, Jardins sous la pluie; L'Isle joyeuse; La plus que lente; Suite bergamasque: Clair de lune.

> (B) ** (*) Turnabout TV 34166S. Peter Frankl (piano).

This attractive recital, if it has not quite the distinction of Daniel Adni's outstanding disc, is a good sampler of the quality of Peter Frankl's Debussy playing. The recording is good.

2 Arabesques; L'Isle joyeuse; Masques; La plus que lente; Pour le piano; Suite bergamasque; Tarantelle styrienne.

> ** (*) DGG SLPM 139458. Tamàs Vàsàry (piano).

This is distinguished playing, and the disc is well planned so that side one includes the earlier works written between 1888 and 1890 and side two shows the composer's developing style, although it is a pity that the most mature item, *La plus que lente* (1910), receives the least convincing performance. Here Vàsàry's *rubato* sounds slightly unspontaneous. He is at his very best, however, in the opening *Suite bergamasque*, and *Clair de lune* is beautifully played, as is the more famous of the *Arabesques*. In all, this is a satisfying recital and DGG's clear, slightly dry piano image suits it well.

La plus que lente; Préludes, Book 1: *La Cathédrale engloutie;* Book 2: *General Lavine – eccentric; Feux d'artifice.*

> (M) ** (*) RCA LSB 4113. Joaquin Achucarro (piano) – RAVEL: *Gaspard de la nuit.****

Good, sparkling performances. *La Cathédrale engloutie* needs more space,

perhaps; Achucarro hurries it along. However, he is generally sensitive and carefully observes dynamic markings. He is given first-rate recording.

VOCAL MUSIC

Chansons de Bilitis: complete recording.

> (M) ** Vox STGBY 645. Marie-Thérèse Escribano (soprano), Die Reihe Ensemble, Friedrich Cerha – SATIE: *Socrate.***

Debussy's *Chansons de Bilitis* are spoken here by Marie-Thérèse Escribano against a delightfully limpid instrumental setting provided by the Die Reihe Ensemble. The presentation is appealingly atmospheric and the work highly enjoyable.

Le Martyre de Saint Sébastien (incidental music to a mystery play by Gabriele d'Annunzio): music virtually complete but without narration.

> (M) ** (*) Decca Ace of Diamonds SDD 314. Suzanne Danco (soprano), Nancy Waugh, Marie-Lise de Montmellin (contraltos), Union Chorale de la Tour-de-Peilz, Suisse Romande Orchestra, Ernest Ansermet.

Debussy's marvellous score to d'Annunzio's *Le Martyre de Saint Sébastien* has not been well served by the gramophone. Ormandy's finely played and beautifully shaped account on CBS was spoilt by the histrionics of Vera Zorina. The orchestral fragments have been done superbly by both Cantelli on HMV and Monteux on Philips, but both, alas, are deleted. Ansermet's is the only current version, and it is beautifully played and sung. The recording belies its age (it first appeared in 1955 in mono) and sounds amazingly vivid. There is an occasional patch of less-than-perfect intonation but this should not bother most listeners, for in other respects the production is excellent.

OPERA

Pelléas et Mélisande (opera in 5 acts): complete recording.

   ** (*) CBS 77324 (3 discs). George Shirley (tenor), Elisabeth Söderström (soprano), Donald McIntyre (baritone), David Ward (bass), Yvonne Minton (mezzo-soprano), Royal Opera House, Covent Garden, Chorus and Orchestra, Pierre Boulez.

   ** Decca SET 277/9. Camille Maurane (tenor), Erna Spoorenberg (soprano), George London (bass-baritone), Guus Hoekman (bass), Josephine Veasey (mezzo-soprano), Chorus of the Grand Theatre, Geneva, Suisse Romande Orchestra, Ernest Ansermet.

Boulez's sharply dramatic view of Debussy's atmospheric score made a strong impact at Covent Garden, and this complete recording vividly recaptures the intense excitement of that experience. This is a performance which will probably not please the dedicated Francophile – for one thing there is not a single French-born singer in the cast – but it rescues Debussy from the languid half-tone approach which for too long has been accepted as authentic. Boulez's approach may initially stem from a searching analysis of the musical structure – Debussy anticipating today's avant-garde in so many ways – but the dramatic element has become sharper-focused too, for he sees the characters as flesh and blood, no mere wayward shadows. He is loyally supported by a strong cast. The singing is not always very idiomatic, but it has the musical and dramatic momentum which stems from sustained experience on the stage. In almost every way this has the tension of a live performance: as much a tribute to standards at the Royal Opera House as Colin Davis's recording of *Les Troyens*. The recording – made in EMI's Abbey Road studio – does not allow a true pianissimo, but is still aptly vivid although the balance is not very natural.

Debussy's great opera is nothing if not atmospheric, and the gain from having superlative stereo recording is enormous. But Ansermet as in so many of his Debussy recordings is curiously literal, and rarely does the beauty of sound bring with it that evocative frisson that the composer surely intended. It is largely a question of tension, and Ansermet's direction tends to be in a low key. One can imagine Ansermet going through everything with civil-service reliability but rarely the sort of urgency that makes for great music-making. Maurane's Pelléas is excellent, and Spoorenberg has a simple charm without ever seeming quite at home in the part. George London's Golaud is coarse and ill-defined, but that is perhaps right with so unpleasant a character.

Pelléas et Melisande: highlights.

   ** Decca SET 475 (from above recording cond. Ansermet).

Pelléas et Mélisande is not an opera from which extracts can be selected with any fairness to the composer, but these 'highlights' – Mélisande letting down her tresses, Golaud and Yniold spying, Golaud's outburst, Pelléas and Mélisande admitting their love, and the heroine's death scene – make a good sample. Nothing is included from the first two acts, and the omission of the scene by the well is serious. These performances are characteristic of Ansermet's Debussy, meticulous and precise with convincing musical flow but no great expression of emotion. Excellent recording.

Delibes, Léo
(1836–91)

Coppélia (ballet): complete recording.
   ** (*) Decca SET 473/4. Suisse Romande Orchestra, Richard Bonynge.
   (M) ** (*) Decca Ace of Diamonds SDD 371/2. Suisse Romande Orchestra, Ernest Ansermet.

Delibes's masterpiece makes admirable gramophone listening. The impression of *Coppélia* in the theatre is of an unending succession of colour and memorable tunes. Tchaikovsky admired the score, and rightly so, for it has not a dull bar. Ansermet's classic recording emerges with astonishing freshness in the very successful Ace of Diamonds re-transfer. There is a hint of congestion when the bass drum adds weight to the climaxes on side one, but for the most part the recording remains of a uniformly high standard and is of demonstration quality in the long *Divertissement* that makes up most of the last act. The orchestral playing is always good and sometimes very good, but one must accept the French quality of the woodwind: the oboe and clarinet soloists sound a little reedy. Ansermet's authoritative hand is always apparent and his power of evocation in the opening scenes of Act 2 (especially) produces some delightful effects. The *Dance of the Automatons* sparkles like a musical-box and, as might be expected, the passage (at the beginning of side three) where Swanhilda pretends to be Coppélia coming to life and dances her stiff little waltz is pointed with loving care. The whole of the *Divertissement* is brilliantly played. The good things easily outbalance the reservations, and this set will give a lot of pleasure.

The newer Decca recording under Bonynge also uses the Suisse Romande Orchestra, with its reedy wind colouring (appropriate in a French score, but not as attractive as the best British woodwind playing). The recording is up to the highest standards of the house, with sparkling string and wind textures and sonority and bite from the brass. Bonynge achieves a high degree of polish in the playing itself, and sets a higher standard than Ansermet in this respect, yet the older set has a special character of its own and is not entirely superseded.

Coppélia (ballet): highlights; *Sylvia* (ballet): suite.
   (B) *** Decca SPA 314. Suisse Romande Orchestra, Ernest Ansermet.
Coppélia (ballet): suite.
   *** DGG SLPM 136257. Berlin Philharmonic Orchestra, Herbert von Karajan – CHOPIN: *Les Sylphides.****
Coppélia (ballet): suite; *Sylvia* (ballet): suite.
   (M) *** CBS 61016. Philadelphia Orchestra, Eugene Ormandy – CHOPIN: *Les Sylphides.** (*)
   ** (*) HMV ASD 439. Yehudi Menuhin (violin), Philharmonia Orchestra, Robert Irving.

An excellent selection from Ansermet's *Coppélia* is balanced by an equally vivacious suite from *Sylvia* (originally part of a concert disc that did not stay in the catalogue very long). With sound that seldom even hints at the age of the originals, this is a first-rate bargain. There are just a couple of moments where an over-effusive bass drum seems to muddy the texture slightly in tutti, but these are not serious.

Karajan secures some wonderfully elegant playing from the Berlin Philharmonic Orchestra, and his lightness of touch is delightful. The *Valse de la Poupée* is beautifully pointed and the variations which follow have a suave panache which is captivating. The *Czárdás* is played very slowly and heavily, and its curiously studied tempo may spoil the disc for some. The recording is even better than on the reverse and can be made to sound very impressive.

Ormandy and the Philadelphia Orchestra are on top form. The playing is committed with a fine sense of panache. *Sylvia* is particularly successful. The earthy gusto of the opening and closing sections is most enjoyable, with its simple life-assertive geniality; and the more delicate numbers, including the *Pizzicato*, are played with affection and style. The recording is notably full and brilliant. The selection of items from *Coppélia* is generous, each strongly characterized. Again, full, bright recording, the focus marginally less sharp.

Irving's disc (which includes a bonus of *La Prière* from Act 3 of *Coppélia*) is well played, and the recording, although perhaps a little dated, still sounds well. *Sylvia* is a fraction more lively than *Coppélia*, but the quality is generally agreeable. Menuhin's contributions are minimal but beautifully played, although the solo violin seems balanced slightly too near the microphone and may require a little smoothing on some reproducers.

Sylvia (ballet): complete recording.
*** Decca SXL 6635/6. New Philharmonia Orchestra, Richard Bonynge.

The ballet *Sylvia* appeared five years after *Coppélia* and was first produced at the Paris Opera in 1875. While confirming the success of the earlier work, *Sylvia* has never displaced it in the affections of the public, and understandably so. It is an attractive score with some memorable tunes, but to be honest nearly all of these are contained in the suite, and in the full score we hear them more than once. But if the work is not as consistently inspired as *Coppélia*, it contains some delightful music and characteristically felicitous scoring. It is played here with wonderful polish and affection under Bonynge, and the recording is superb, demonstration-worthy in every sense of the word.

La Source (ballet): excerpts.
(M) ** Decca Ace of Diamonds SDD 221. Paris Conservatoire Orchestra, Peter Maag – CHOPIN: *Les Sylphides*.**

La Source (1866) was the earliest of the Delibes ballets. It was written in collaboration with Leon Minkus (each wrote half the music), and the success of the Delibes music (Act 2 and the first part of Act 3) did much to establish his reputation as a composer. Delibes used his own sections again (with more music added) for a later ballet called *Natla*. Maag's account is characterful and stylish – the pointed string tunes are particularly well done. There is some excellent wind playing too and both the solo flautist and the first horn are given opportunities to distinguish themselves. The recording is clear and vivid rather than rich.

Lakmé (opera in 3 acts): complete recording.
*** Decca SET 387/9. Joan Sutherland (soprano), Jane Berbié (contralto), Alain Vanzo (tenor), Gabriel Bacquier (baritone), Monte Carlo Opera Chorus and Orchestra, Richard Bonynge.
Lakmé: highlights.
*** Decca SET 488 (from above recording).

Lakmé is a strange work, not at all the piece one would expect, knowing simply the famous *Bell song* with its clattering coloratura at the end. Predictably enough it has its measure, at the beginning, of orientalism, but quickly we have comedy introduced in the shape of Britons abroad, and Delibes presents it with wit and charm. This performance (with Monica Sinclair a gloriously outrageous Governess) seizes its opportunities with both hands, while the more serious passages are sung with a regard for beautiful vocal line that should convert anyone. Of course, as so often, Sutherland swallows her consonants, but the beauty of the singing with its ravishing ease and purity up to the highest register is what matters, and she has opposite her one of the most pleasing and intelligent of French tenors, Alain Vanzo. Excellent contributions from the others too, spirited conducting and brilliant, atmospheric recording. Highly recommended.

Those wanting a shorter selection will find the highlights disc reflects the qualities of the set admirably and is generously filled.

Delius, Frederick
(1862–1934)

*Brigg Fair (*see also under *Appalachia). Brigg Fair; Dance rhapsody No. 2; On Hearing the First Cuckoo in Spring; In a Summer Garden.*

(M) ** CBS Classics 61426. Philadelphia Orchestra, Eugene Ormandy.

Brigg Fair; Fennimore and Gerda: Intermezzo; A Song before Sunrise; Marche-caprice; On Hearing the First Cuckoo in Spring; Summer Night on the River; Sleigh Ride.

⊛ *** HMV ASD 357. Royal Philharmonic Orchestra, Sir Thomas Beecham.

Beecham's collection is a unique and treasurable memorial of his art. His finespun magic with Delius's orchestral textures is apparent from the delicate opening bars of *Brigg Fair*, and the string playing in *On Hearing the First Cuckoo*

and more especially *Summer Night on the River* is ravishing yet never too indulgent. The recording was one of the finest Beecham was given in stereo and still sounds beautiful.

Ormandy (or maybe his recording engineers) miss the fragility, the evanescence of Delius's visions, but there is much to enjoy in warm, stirring performances of these favourite works. There is no danger here of Delius sounding faded. In its way this is a very successful disc.

Piano concerto in C minor.

*** Decca SXL 6435. Jean-Rodolphe Kars (piano), London Symphony Orchestra, Alexander Gibson – DEBUSSY: *Fantasy.****

Delius's *Piano concerto* has been neglected by the gramophone and this is its first recording since Sir Thomas Beecham's account of it with Betty Humby Beecham as soloist, made for HMV as long ago as 1946. Jean-Rodolphe Kars proves a superb and eloquent advocate of what, it must be conceded, is one of Delius's weaker pieces. He plays with great refinement of touch and sensitivity and brings great artistry and imagination to his part. The Grieg-like middle section is beautifully done, and his playing throughout has great taste. The LSO under Gibson provide admirable support, and the recording preserves an excellent balance between the two. The piano is extremely well captured by the engineers and the recording is in the best traditions of Decca.

Violoncello concerto.

*** HMV ASD 2764. Jacqueline du Pré (cello), Royal Philharmonic Orchestra, Sir Malcolm Sargent – ELGAR: *Cello concerto.****

It was an excellent idea to recouple this recording of the Delius *Cello con-*

certo with a famous recording of the Elgar. No cellist could play it more persuasively than Jacqueline du Pré, whose first major recording this was. It was Delius's own favourite among his four concertos, because, as he said, of the 'melodic invention'. It is certainly lyrical, and du Pré makes up for the waywardness of the form with a purposeful grasp of the seamless melody. The recording quality is warm to match the music.

Double concerto for violin, violoncello and orchestra.

(B) ** Pye GSGC 14073. Raymond Cohen (violin), Gerald Warburg (cello), Royal Philharmonic Orchestra, Norman Del Mar – BUSH: Variations.**

Delius's Double concerto has long been neglected (even Peter Warlock was somewhat scathing about it), but it proves to be one of the most cogently argued of Delius's longer works, using – like the Violin concerto written about the same time during the First World War – an extended one-movement form with confidence and real sense of logic. This performance was made possible by the generosity of Gerald Warburg, a member of an American banking family as well as a talented player, and though the playing is far from immaculate it has a red-blooded committedness that is far more important in such music. Norman Del Mar draws playing from the Royal Philharmonic of which Beecham himself might have been proud. Recording rather forward, but vivid enough.

Dance rhapsody No. 1; Eventyr; Paris – the song of a great city.

** (*) HMV ASD 2804. Royal Liverpool Philharmonic Orchestra, Charles Groves.

For any conductor attempting to interpret Delius today the first thing is

to try to forget the ghost of Sir Thomas Beecham and to produce spontaneous-sounding performances that may or may not correspond to his. Groves does just this in the magnificent picture in sound Paris, as well as the two shorter works. The tempi are less extreme than Beecham's, but refreshingly persuasive. The recording is excellent.

Dance rhapsody No. 2; Florida suite; Over the Hills and Far Away.

(M) *** HMV HQS 1126. Royal Philharmonic Orchestra, Sir Thomas Beecham.

The Florida suite, Delius's first orchestral work, is lightweight, but strong in melodic appeal and orchestral colour. The tune we know as La Calinda appears in the first movement. Elsewhere the composer's absorbed Negro influences even suggest a Dvořákian flavour. The writing is untypical of the mature Delius rather in the same way as the Karelia suite of Sibelius. With the Second Dance rhapsody and the somewhat episodic Over the Hills this makes a fine medium-priced anthology, and the recording is clear and immediate with plenty of sparkle in the Florida suite.

Fennimore and Gerda; Intermezzo; Irmelin: Prelude; On Hearing the First Cuckoo in Spring; The Walk to the Paradise Garden (A Village Romeo and Juliet).

(B) ** Pye GSGC 14075. Hallé Orchestra, Sir John Barbirolli – Idyll.* (*)

Barbirolli offers here four of Delius's most characteristically beautiful pieces of orchestral tone-painting. They are lovingly played, the Hallé responding well. The recording is good throughout, except at the loudest climaxes, which tend to become a little messy; but these are among the most evocative Delius performances in the catalogue, and the disc is excellent value at the price asked.

In a Summer Garden; Koanga: La Calinda (dance); *Late Swallows* (arr. Fenby); *On Hearing the First Cuckoo in Spring; A Song before Sunrise; Summer Night on the River; Hassan* (incidental music): *Intermezzo;* (i) *Serenade.*
*** HMV ASD 2477. Hallé orchestra, Sir John Barbirolli, (i) with Robert Tear (tenor).

Atmospheric and loving performances of these colourful scores. Sir John shows an admirable feeling for the sense of light Delius conjures up and for the luxuriance of texture his music possesses. At times he dwells a little too affectionately over details and one wishes for the music to move on, but for the most part reservations on this score are few. The recording is admirably rich and detailed, but there are times when one could wish for a slightly more backward woodwind balance.

Irmelin: Prelude; A Song of Summer; The Walk to the Paradise Garden (A Village Romeo and Juliet).
** (*) HMV ASD 2305. London Symphony Orchestra, Sir John Barbirolli – BAX: *Tintagel;* IRELAND: *London overture.****

These are richly romantic rather than delicately subtle performances. Sir John does not provide here the limpid evanescent textures for which Beecham was famous (and which he does achieve on his Pye Hallé collection). The music is not most persuasive when it is in repose, but rather when Barbirolli can bring his almost Italianate romanticism to Delius's passionate arching string phrases. Lovely playing throughout, and again first-rate sound.

CHAMBER AND INSTRUMENTAL MUSIC

String quartet (Late Swallows).
(B) ** Pye GSGC 14130. Fidelio Quartet – TIPPETT: *String quartet No. 2.**

Delius's *Quartet* was composed at the height of the First World War and is his only essay in this medium. The slow movement in its transcription for string orchestra is, of course, included on Barbirolli's HMV anthology. It is not the composer's strongest work, though it has distinguished admirers. The performance is a trifle cautious and leaves an overall impression of pallor, but the recording is acceptable and in the absence of an alternative Delians will no doubt want this.

Violin sonatas Nos. 1–3.
*** Unicorn RHS 310. Ralph Holmes (violin), Eric Fenby (piano).

Eric Fenby with the help of Ralph Holmes has often given deeply illuminating as well as witty lectures on his years as Delius's amanuensis. These sonatas, particularly the last, which we owe entirely to Fenby's ability to transcribe the blind and paralysed composer's inspirations, form an important part of his theme. Here we have a historic and moving set of all three sonatas – among the finest of all Delius's chamber works – which amply confirms the high claims made by Fenby for their cogency of argument. Though Fenby as pianist may not be a virtuoso, the persuasiveness of his playing and that of Ralph Holmes makes this one of the most treasurable of Delius records. Fenby himself contributes a spoken introduction. Good recording.

Violoncello sonata; 5 Piano pieces; 3 Preludes.
** Argo ZRG 727. George Isaac

313

(cello), Martin Jones (piano) – PROKOFIEV: *Cello sonata.*** (*)

As one might expect, Delius's *Cello sonata*, written in 1916, is a flowing, endlessly lyrical work. It is good to have it restored to the catalogue in this version, even though George Isaac and Martin Jones interpret it not so much with love as with a literal freshness. Similarly with Jones in the piano pieces. The recording, not so clean as for the Prokofiev on the reverse, has the cello rather too close.

VOCAL AND CHORAL MUSIC

(i) *Appalachia; Brigg Fair.*
  *** HMV ASD 2635. Hallé Orchestra, Sir John Barbirolli, (i) with Alun Jenkins (baritone), Ambrosian Singers.

A good stereo recording of *Appalachia* was a long-felt want, and Barbirolli's account could hardly be more welcome. Beecham's famous LP was marred by an unconvincing soloist but in every other respect was totally magical. Barbirolli dwells a little too lovingly on detail to suit all tastes, but for the most part he gives an admirably atmospheric reading that conveys, with the help of a richly detailed recording, the exotic and vivid colouring of Delius's score.

(i; ii; iv) *An Arabesque;* (i; iv) *Cynara;* (i; ii; iii; iv) *Songs of Sunset.*
  *** HMV ASD 2437. (i) John Shirley-Quirk (baritone); (ii) Liverpool Philharmonic Choir; (iii) Janet Baker (mezzo-soprano); (iv) Royal Liverpool Philharmonic Orchestra, Sir Charles Groves.

We have long needed a good modern recording of Delius's *Songs of Sunset*, settings of Arthur Symons that date from 1906–7. This fine record also gives us

Cynara (1907), a setting of Dowson, and *An Arabesque*, a setting of Jacobsen done during the First World War. John Shirley-Quirk does the solo part impressively (it was the poor solo singing that so badly let down Beecham's mono LP of this work) and the performances of these works are all very fine, falling not far short of Beecham's standard though they lack his sense of magic.

Idyll (Once I passed through a populous city) (see also under *Requiem*).
  (B) * (*) Pye GSGC 14075. Sylvia Fisher (soprano), Jess Walters (baritone), Hallé Orchestra, Sir John Barbirolli – *Orchestral collection.***

For his *Idyll*, completed in 1932, Delius drew on music from an opera, *Margot-la-Rouge*, written at the turn of the century. To introduce the work the gently rapturous prelude is transplanted complete. The words which follow are from Walt Whitman and they form a duologue between baritone and soprano. The work is rather patchy – the setting of the opening words is not very imaginative – but as the passion of the lovers reaches its climax, the quality of the music deepens. Sir John makes a fine climax and it is a pity that Sylvia Fisher's voice is inclined to become squally when pressed. Jess Walters is rather more reliable, and both singers are thoroughly professional, but although there is considerable poignancy in the blissful closing pages, neither voice is in essence tonally beautiful enough for such limpid music.

A Mass of Life.
  *** HMV SLS 958 (2 discs). Heather Harper (soprano), Helen Watts (contralto), Robert Tear (tenor), Benjamin Luxon (bass), London Philharmonic Choir, London Philharmonic Orchestra, Sir Charles Groves.

There are few moments in Delius quite so exhilarating as the opening of his *Mass of Life*, and though the inspiration does not remain on quite the same level of white heat throughout the work, it still stands as one of his masterpieces. That passionate invocation to the Will (to words of Nietzsche taken from *Also sprach Zarathustra*) is followed by a sequence of poetic visions, superbly illustrated by Delius. Groves inspires his performers to a magnificent account, fully worthy of the work. It is good to have this music in such fine modern stereo, though curiously the very mistiness of some passages in Beecham's old mono set made the results more evocative still.

Part songs: *Midsummer Song; On Craig Dhu; The Splendour Falls on Castle Walls; To Be Sung of a Summer Night on the Water.*
> *** Argo ZRG 607. Louis Halsey Singers, Louis Halsey – ELGAR: *Part songs.****

These are charming part songs exquisitely performed. The two wordless songs *To be Sung of a Summer Night on the Water* were later orchestrated by Eric Fenby as the two *Aquarelles*, but they are even more delicate in this original vocal form.

(i) *Requiem; Idyll (Once I passed through a populous city).*
> *** HMV ASD 2397. Heather Harper (soprano), John Shirley-Quirk (baritone), Royal Philharmonic Orchestra, Meredith Davies, (i) with Royal Choral Society.

This disc is particularly welcome since it couples two Delius rarities. Barbirolli has given us the *Idyll* on a Pye record, but the *Requiem* is not only new to records but until recently has remained unperformed since the 1920s. It was written during the First World War and Delius's well-known atheism as well as his disillusion with life did not find a responsive echo at the first performance: indeed the work was written off. Though it is not an austere work, it is far sparer than most other Delius works of the period and much of it is rewarding, particularly in so fine a performance as this. The *Idyll* is much earlier, or at least its material is. The music, though uneven in inspiration, is often extremely impressive, and readers need have no reservations about either performance or recording.

(i) *Sea Drift; Song of the High Hills.*
> ** HMV ASD 2958. (i) John Noble (baritone), Liverpool Philharmonic Chorus, Royal Liverpool Philharmonic Orchestra, Sir Charles Groves.

A modern stereo version of one of Delius's most moving works, *Sea Drift*, was badly needed, but Groves is disappointingly matter-of-fact. No conductor today can exactly match the persuasiveness of Beecham, but this fails seriously to convey the surge of inspiration which so exactly matches the evocative colours of Walt Whitman's poem about the seagull, 'a solitary guest from Alabama'. The *Song of the High Hills*, another great and neglected Delius work with its wordless chorus, is more perceptively interpreted, but even here Groves understates the case. The recording is first-rate.

OPERA

Koanga (opera in 3 acts): complete recording.
> *** HMV SLS 974 (2 discs). Eugene Holmes (baritone), Claudia Lindsey (soprano), Raimund Herincx (baritone), Keith Erwen (tenor), Jean Allister (contralto), Simon

315

Estes (bass), John Alldis Choir, London Symphony Orchestra, Sir Charles Groves.

With big Verdian ensembles and Puccinian ariosos (the style still unmistakably Delian) *Koanga* is a big, red-blooded opera which makes a striking impact on record. Koanga is a proud African prince brought as a slave to a Mississippi plantation. He falls in love with a mulatto girl who is then abducted. Told in flashback this simple story gives Delius the excuse to write a marvellous sequence of evocative passages, not least the Negro choruses. This recording uses a revised libretto, much more effective than the original, and Groves's red-blooded reading plus excellent singing from the whole cast suggests that this is a work which could readily be taken into regular repertory in the opera house. A recording not just for Delians but for potential converts too. Superb recording.

A Village Romeo and Juliet (opera in 6 scenes): complete recording.
** HMV SLS 966 (3 discs). Benjamin Luxon (baritone), Noel Mangin (bass), Robert Tear (tenor), Elizabeth Harwood (soprano), John Shirley-Quirk (baritone), John Alldis Choir, Royal Philharmonic Orchestra, Meredith Davies.

There are some wonderfully sensuous moments in this highly characteristic opera of Delius written at the turn of the century. The famous *Walk to the Paradise Garden* with its passionate orchestral climax (superbly performed here) is the most memorable passage, but the music of the Dark Fiddler and much of the music for the two ill-starred lovers is intensely expressive. Unfortunately there is too little mystery in Meredith Davies's performance. He fails to persuade one to listen on when Delius's inspiration lets

him run on dangerously long. Some excellent singing and playing, and first-rate recording.

Dering, Richard
(1580–1630)

Gaudent in coelis; O bone Jesu.
(M) ** Chapter One CMS 1007. Coventry Cathedral Boys' Choir, David Lepine – BRITTEN: *Ceremony of Carols etc.***
Gaudent in coelis; Contristatus est rex David; O bone Jesu; Ave verum Corpus; Duo seraphin; Factum est silentium.
(B) ** Argo Eclipse ECS 681. Peterborough Cathedral Choir, Richard Latham (organ), Stanley Vann – BATTEN: *Anthems.** (*)

Dering was a contemporary of Batten, but had a Roman Catholic musical training in Italy. His musical style is in consequence more colourful and florid than that of Batten, and one feels that the Peterborough choir have been fired by this often dramatic music. The solo singing here is rather better than on the reverse side. Well recorded as it is, the Argo disc certainly makes an interesting and often enjoyable sampler of church music at the beginning of the seventeenth century.

The performances in Coventry are also well done, and this makes an imaginative coupling for an attractive medium-priced collection of Britten's choral music.

Destouches, André
(1672–1749)

Issé (opera): orchestral suite.
(M) *** Oiseau-Lyre SOL 303. English Chamber Orchestra, Ray-

mond Leppard – LECLAIR: *Scylla et Glaucus suite.****

The music for André Destouches's *Issé* pre-dates the coupling by about fifty years, and perhaps this suite has rather less variety of colour and less striking melodic characterization than that by Leclair. But it certainly has charm when presented so stylishly; the slow movements are most appealing in their gentle evocation, and the dances crisp and spirited. Excellent recording.

Diabelli, Anton
(1781–1858)

Variations on a waltz (including Beethoven's *33 Variations* and variations by many other composers, including Czerny; Hoffman; Hummel; Kreutzer; Moscheles; Schubert).
** Telefunken SMA 25081 (1/3). Rudolf Buchbinder (piano).

An ingenious idea to collect all the 'other' Diabelli variations, although they only go to confirm Beethoven's original doubts about being coupled with his less talented contemporaries. Rudolf Buchbinder is an intelligent, perceptive interpreter.

Dodgson, Stephen
(born 1924)

Guitar concerto (for guitar and chamber orchestra).
*** CBS 72661. John Williams (guitar), English Chamber Orchestra, Sir Charles Groves – RODRIGO: *Fantasia para un gentilhombre.****

Stephen Dodgson has written a quantity of music for the guitar, much of it inspired by John Williams's artistry. This concerto is an inventive and civilized work, deftly scored and well constructed. An attractive piece, then, and superbly played by these artists. John Williams is in his usual excellent form, and the CBS recording is good.

Dohnányi, Ernst von
(1877–1960)

Piano concerto No. 1 in E minor, Op. 3.
(M) ** (*) Pye Virtuoso TPLS 13052. Balint Vazsonyi (piano), New Philharmonia Orchestra, John Pritchard.

A committed and fiery account by Balint Vazsonyi of an early and very Brahmsian concerto by Dohnányi. Vazsonyi is a Dohnányi pupil as well as his biographer, and he commands a very considerable technique. Both the orchestral accompaniment and the Pye recording are of excellent standard, and those interested in this underrated Hungarian master's output will find this disc useful. It is unashamedly derivative but no worse for that.

Variations on a nursery tune (for piano and orchestra), *Op. 25.*
(M) *** Decca Ace of Diamonds SDD 428. Julius Katchen (piano), London Philharmonic Orchestra, Sir Adrian Boult – RACHMANINOV: *Rhapsody on a theme of Paganini.****

In the early days of LP a distinguished Decca mono record of this coupling by these same artists held the field for many years. In due course this was reissued on Ace of Clubs and more recently in an admirable stereo transcription on Eclipse

(ECS 668), where it still holds its own in the bargain price-range. However, the stereo remake is a fully worthy successor to it. The account of Dohnányi's attractive variations is perceptive and spontaneous, and the recording is first-rate in every way.

Donizetti, Gaetano
(1797–1848)

String quartet in D major (arr. for string orchestra).
> *** Argo ZRG 603. Academy of St Martin-in-the-Fields, Neville Marriner – ROSSINI: *String sonatas Nos. 2 and 4.****

This delightful 'prentice work has a sunny lyricism and a melodic freshness that speaks of youthful genius. The composer's craftsmanship is obvious and the writing is such that (unlike Verdi's *String quartet*) it lends itself readily to performance by a string orchestra, especially when the playing is as warm-hearted and polished as on this immaculately recorded Argo disc. Most enjoyable.

Anna Bolena (opera in 2 acts): complete recording.
> ** (*) Decca SET 446/9. Elena Suliotis (soprano), Marilyn Horne (mezzo-soprano), John Alexander (tenor), Nicolai Ghiaurov (bass), Vienna State Opera Chorus, Vienna Opera Orchestra, Silvio Varviso.
> ** (*) HMV SLS 878 (4 discs). Beverly Sills (soprano), Shirley Verrett (mezzo-soprano), Stuart Burrows (tenor), John Alldis Choir, London Symphony Orchestra, Julius Rudel.

Anna Bolena: highlights.
> ** (*) Decca SET 522 (from above recording cond. Varviso).

It really is a sign of the times when one of the longer Donizetti operas which was totally neglected until recently should appear in more than one recording, each stretching to eight full sides. Both these recordings are far more complete than any stage performance is likely to be, and each gives a fine idea of an opera which represents the composer in his most exuberant early flight (date 1830). The choice between the Sills version conducted by Rudel and the Suliotis account conducted by Varviso is difficult. Much will depend on your response to the two divas in the name part. Sills is by far the more reliable, though her characterization is not so memorable. Suliotis, a formidable heroine, often produces Callas-like overtones. But with such dramatic command it is sad to report vocal carelessness that sometimes verges on the painful. The rest of the cast is more evenly matched, Marilyn Horne notable as Giovanni Seymour in the Decca set and Ghiaurov a rich-toned if rather unimaginative Henry VIII. Both recordings are excellent – the EMI warmer, the Decca brighter, and the Decca highlights disc, with a well-made selection, obviously serves a useful purpose.

Don Pasquale (opera in 3 acts): complete recording.
> ** (*) Decca SET 280/1. Fernando Corena (bass), Graziella Sciutti (soprano), Juan Oncina (tenor), Tom Krause (baritone), Vienna State Opera Chorus and Orchestra, Istvan Kertesz.
> (M) ** DGG Privilege 2705 039 (2 discs). Alfredo Mariotti (bass), Anna Maccianti (soprano), Ugo Benelli (tenor), Mario Basiola (baritone), Maggio Musicale Fiorentino, Ettore Gracis.

Choice between Kertesz's sparkling Decca set and the more restrained DGG one will depend largely on preference over studio 'production'. The Decca set is very much presented with built-in humour, where the D G G recording managers just let the music speak for itself. That would probably be the better course, had Gracis been as sparkling a conductor as Kertesz, and the singers as characterful. As it is, the D G G cast often has the edge vocally over opposite numbers (notably the tenor, Ugo Benelli, as Ernesto over Juan Oncina) but the result is rarely as vivid dramatically. So Sciutti proves a more vivacious Norina than Anna Maccianti, Corena is a more commanding Pasquale than Alfredo Mariotti, and Krause a more incisive Malatesta than Mario Basiola. Some may still feel the incidental laughter included on the Decca set too much to take, in which case the DGG is a good alternative. In keeping with the approach to production, the DGG recording is faithful but much less atmospheric than the Decca.

Don Pasquale: highlights.
*** Decca SET 337 (from above recording cond. Kertesz).

Rightly this selection from the splendid complete Decca set concentrates on the great comic ensembles. Only three of the arias are included (both of Ernesto's – Com'è gentil attractively off-stage – and Norina's essential Quel guardo) but very full versions are given of such concerted numbers as the Pasquale-Ernesto duet and Norina-Malatesta duet from Act 1; the Act 2 trio and the finale from Act 2; the Norina-Pasquale duet and the Pasquale-Malatesta duet and final ensemble from Act 3. Such a selection is very generous, and gives an admirable idea of the piece's dramatic lay-out, particularly when the complete words and translation are included with the sleeve. Outstandingly good recording.

L'Elisir d'amore (opera in 2 acts): complete recording.

*** Decca SET 503/5. Joan Sutherland (soprano), Luciano Pavarotti (tenor), Dominic Cossa (baritone), Spiro Malas (bass), Ambrosian Singers, English Chamber Orchestra, Richard Bonynge.
(M) ** (*) Decca Ace of Diamonds GOS 566/7. Giuseppe di Stefano (tenor), Hilde Gueden (soprano), Fernando Corena (bass), Renato Capecchi (baritone), Maggio Musicale Fiorentino, Francesco Molinari-Pradelli.

L'Elisir d'amore: highlights.
*** Decca SET 564 (from above recording cond. Bonynge).

Joan Sutherland's comic talents in a Donizetti role came out delectably in her performances on stage and on record of La Fille du régiment. Here she repeats that success in the less rumbustious, more delicate part of Adina. Malibran, the first interpreter of the role, was furious that the part was not bigger, and got her husband to write an extra aria. Richard Bonynge found a copy of the piano score, had it orchestrated, and included it here. Quite apart from that the text of this frothy piece is unusually complete, and in the key role of Nemorino Luciano Pavarotti proves ideal, vividly portraying the wounded innocent. Spiro Malas is a superb Dulcamara, while Dominic Cossa is a younger-sounding Belcore, more of a genuine lover than usual. Bonynge points the skipping rhythms delectably, and the recording is sparkling to match. The highlights disc reflects the complete set's qualities admirably, but for not very much more money one can buy Decca's earlier set under Molinari-Pradelli, which still sounds well, even though this charming version of Donizetti's irresistible score was made in the mid-fifties. Giuseppe di Stefano was at his most headily sweet-toned, and Hilde Gueden at her most seductive, and the performance conveys the sparkle of

Donizetti's inspiration admirably. Capecchi as Belcore and Corena as Dulcamara are both splendidly comic. A fine bargain, if without the sophistication of Decca's full-priced set.

La Favorita (opera in 4 acts): complete recording.

(M) ** Decca Ace of Diamonds GOS 525/7 Giulietta Simionato (mezzosoprano), Gianni Poggi (tenor), Ettore Bastianini (baritone), Jerome Hines (bass), Maggio Musicale Fiorentino, Alberto Erede.

La Favorita has at least three outstandingly memorable numbers – *Spirto gentil*, *O mio Fernando* and *Per tanto amore* – as well as some characteristically brisk ensembles, but on the whole it falls well short of the most famous Donizetti operas. The story of the young man who falls in love with his father's mistress has its dramatic point, but this was the sort of situation that Verdi was to develop much further. Nor is this performance ingratiating enough to make one forget the weaknesses, for Poggi is a coarse tenor and neither Simionato nor Bastianini (duettists once in *Anything you can do . . .* in a *Fledermaus* gala concert) is in top form, for one detects the stiffness of new learning. Nor is Erede's conducting very dramatic, but with good stereo (considering the date of recording, 1955) and at bargain price, any Donizettian could readily find the set worthwhile.

La Fille du régiment (opera in 2 acts): complete recording.

*** Decca SET 372/3. Joan Sutherland (soprano), Luciano Pavarotti (tenor), Monica Sinclair (mezzosoprano), Spiro Malas (bass), Edith Coates (contralto), Royal Opera House, Covent Garden, Chorus and Orchestra, Richard Bonynge.

This is a fizzing performance of a delightful Donizetti romp that can be confidently recommended for both comedy and fine singing. It was with this cast that the piece was revived at Covent Garden, and Sutherland immediately showed how naturally she takes to the role of tomboy. Marie is a *vivandière* in the army of Napoleon, and the jolly, almost Gilbertian, plot involves her translation back to a noble background from which as an infant she was lost. This original French version favoured by Richard Bonynge is fuller than the Italian revision, and with a cast that at the time of the recording sessions was also appearing in the theatre the performance could hardly achieve higher spirits with keener assurance. Sutherland is in turn brilliantly comic and pathetically affecting, and no better sampler of the whole set need be suggested than part of the last side, where Marie is reunited with her army friends (including the hero). Pavarotti makes an engaging hero, Monica Sinclair a formidable Countess, and even if the French accents are often suspect it is a small price to pay for such a brilliant, happy opera set.

La Fille du régiment: highlights.

*** Decca SET 491 (from above recording).

A generous helping from one of the most infectiously enjoyable opera sets that Decca has issued. Sutherland, aided by a Covent Garden cast that had worked with her in stage performances, is at the very peak of her form, and the recording quality is superb. The only doubt is that for just twice the price you can buy the whole opera, and that is even more enjoyable.

Linda di Chamounix, Act 1: *Ah! tardai troppo . . . O luce di quest'anima. Lucia di Lammermoor,* Act 1: *Ancor non giunse! . . . Regnava nel silenzio;* Act 2: Mad scene (complete).

⊛ (M) *** Decca Ace of Diamonds sDD 146. Joan Sutherland (soprano), Paris Conservatoire Orchestra, Nello Santi – VERDI: *Arias*.***

No rave notice could really exaggerate the quality of this singing, and in many ways this first recording made by Joan Sutherland of the *Lucia* Mad scene has not been surpassed by either of her complete recordings of the opera (1961 and 1971). In fact this disc must be set on a pedestal as one of the finest and most dramatically thrilling displays of coloratura ever recorded. It is not just that Sutherland shows here a Tetrazzini-like perfection, but that she makes these stylized tunes and florid passages into something intensely moving. The youthful freshness of the voice is extremely appealing, and the tonal beauty is often quite magical. With an excellent stereo recording this disc remains one of the gramophone's great recital discs.

Lucia di Lammermoor (opera in 3 acts): complete recording.

 *** Decca SET 528/30. Joan Sutherland (soprano), Luciano Pavarotti (tenor), Sherrill Milnes (baritone), Nicolai Ghiaurov (bass), Ryland Davies (tenor), Huguette Tourangeau (mezzo-soprano), Royal Opera House, Covent Garden, Chorus and Orchestra, Richard Bonynge.

 ** (*) HMV SLS 797 (3 discs). Beverly Sills (soprano), Carlo Bergonzi (tenor), Piero Cappuccilli (baritone), Justino Diaz (bass), Ambrosian Opera Chorus, London Symphony Orchestra, Thomas Schippers.

It was hardly surprising that after ten years Decca should want to re-record Sutherland in the role with which she is inseparably associated. Though some of the girlish freshness of voice which marked the 1961 recording has disappeared, the detailed understanding has been intensified, and the mooning manner which in 1961 was just emerging has been counteracted. Really there is no one today to outshine Sutherland in this opera; and rightly for this recording she insisted on doing the whole of the Mad scene in a single session, making sure it was consistent from beginning to end. Power is there as well as delicacy, and the rest of the cast is first-rate. Pavarotti, not so sensitive as he can be through much of the opera, proves magnificent in his final scene. The recording quality is superb, though choral interjections are not always forward enough. This time, unlike last, the text is absolutely complete. (At the time of going to press the earlier set, conducted by Pritchard, is still available on SET 212/4.)

The giving personality of Beverly Sills has never been so warmly conveyed on record as in this formidable performance. The Mad scene in particular is deeply moving. The initial 'takes' were recorded at the very end of a taxing six hours of sessions, in which, like the heroine, Miss Sills was literally at the end of her tether. That tension has been retained in the finished recording, and with glass harmonica adding an authentic – if hideously out-of-tune – dimension to the score, any Sills devotee need not hesitate. Her coloratura is as effortlessly fluent as ever, and though the decorations to the cabaletta of the first-act aria are uncomfortably elaborate, the technical assurance is never in doubt. But as in the opera house the voice has an uneven register towards the top of the stave, and when it comes to sheer beauty of tone, Miss Sills cannot compare with the singer who since 1959 has made the part her own, Joan Sutherland. Miss Sills's supporting cast is first-rate, and so is the vigorous direction of Thomas Schippers. The recording balance is not always consistent, but the sound is warm and faithful.

Lucia di Lammermoor: highlights.
*** Decca SET 559 (from above recording cond. Bonynge).

Those who already have Joan Sutherland's 1961 version of this opera may not wish to invest in another complete performance by her, even one as tempting as the 1971 recording. For them this selection of items should be ideal, containing as it does the Fountain scene, the sextet, the Mad scene and the great tenor aria in the last scene. Superb recording quality. (Incidentally the earlier highlights disc – SXL 2315 – is still available as we go to press.)

Maria Stuarda (opera in 3 acts): complete recording.
** (*) HMV SLS 848 (3 discs). Beverly Sills (soprano), Eileen Farrell (soprano), Stuart Burrows (tenor), John Alldis Choir, London Philharmonic Orchestra, Aldo Ceccato.

It is a great pity that HMV did not wait to record Janet Baker's superlative assumption of the role of Mary Queen of Scots in the English National Opera's stage production of a fine, dramatic work. Unlike that production, which used the original score, this one has Mary as a high soprano and Queen Elizabeth as a dramatic soprano. It remains effective (if more conventional), for the apocryphal story of Mary meeting Elizabeth, insulting her and consequently being sent to the scaffold inspired Donizetti to produce some of his most striking ideas. Though not everyone will warm to Sills's voice, it is a memorable performance, and the rest of the cast is comparably strong, set against an urgent reading from Aldo Ceccato. Good if rather reverberant recording.

Dufay, Guillaume
(*c.* 1400–1474)

Audi benigne (hymn): *Ave maris stella* (hymn); *Gloria ad modum tubae; Kyrie (HS. Cambrai); Kyrie paschale; Lux et origo; Magnificat VI toni; Salve regina; Sanctus papale.*
** Telefunken SAWT 9439. Munich Capell Antiqua, Konrad Ruhland.

These performances have excellent recording to commend them, and they have been prepared with great regard to historical accuracy and use authentic instruments. But there is a lack of sparkle and one or two lapses of intonation that detract from the value of this record.

Mass: *Se la face ay pale.*
⊛ *** HMV CSD 3751. Early Music Consort of London, David Munrow.
(M) ** Vanguard HM 2SD. Vienna Chamber Choir, Musica Antiqua of Vienna, Hans Gillesberger – OBRECHT: Mass: *Sub tuum praesidium.***

The quincentenary of Dufay's death passed relatively quietly in 1974, but appreciation of his genius will be enhanced by the HMV disc, which was issued to mark the occasion. David Munrow's Early Music Consort has won many friends for this repertoire without making any attempts at dressing up the music or pretending that it is anything other than it is. Their performance of the austere yet moving Mass *Se la face ay pale* is superb in every way. They preface the Mass itself with the chanson on which it is based, first in its original three-part version, then in two keyboard versions from the *Buxheimer* Organ Book, and finally in a four-part instrumental version attributed to the great Burgundian master himself. The performance is accompanied by instruments, tenor and bass viols in the solo sections of the Gloria and Credo, cornetts and sackbutts in the full sections. The soloists are all distinguished (they include James Bowman), and Mr Munrow himself plays the alto shawm. The recording is superb. This is an indispensable issue. It calls for and rewards concentrated and repeated listening.

Gillesberger's version is also scholarly and rewarding, though it sounds dated by comparison with the newer HMV issue. Its value is enhanced by its excellent coupling, the Obrecht Mass *Sub tuum praesidium*, not otherwise available.

Collection: *'Music from the Court of Burgundy': Adieu ces bons vins de Lannoys* (rondeau); *La belle se siet au piet de la tour; Bon jour, bon mois* (chansons); *Mon cuer me fait tous dis penser; Par droit je puis bien complaindre et gemir; Pour l'amour de ma doulce amye* (rondeaux); *Resvelliés vous et faites chiere lye* (ballade); *Se la face ay pale* (ballade – 3 versions); *Vergine bella, che di sol vestita* (stropha).* ANON.: *La bassa Castiglya; La Spagna; Collinetto* (basses danses). MORTON, Robert: *Le souvenir de vous* (rondeau).

** (*) Philips 6500 085. Musica Reservata, John Beckett.

This is a finely recorded anthology with many good things in it. Some of the singing is more sensitive and expressive than Musica Reservata often permit themselves, and although there are some less appealing items – the anonymous basses danses – the merits of this disc outweigh shortcomings. Even those who normally feel somewhat unenthusiastic about this ensemble will find pleasure here.

Dukas, Paul
(1865–1935)

L'Apprenti sorcier (The Sorcerer's apprentice).

(B) *** Decca SPA 175. Suisse Romande Orchestra, Ernest Ansermet (with Concert: 'Danse macabre'***).

*** Decca SXL 6065. Suisse Romande Orchestra, Ernest Ansermet – HONEGGER: *Pacific 231;* RAVEL: *Boléro; La Valse.****

** (*) HMV Quadraphonic Q4-ASD 3008; Stereo ASD 3008. City of Birmingham Orchestra, Louis Frémaux (with *Concert** (*)).

(B) ** Decca SPA 376. Israel Philharmonic Orchestra, Sir Georg Solti – ROSSINI: *La Boutique fantasque.***

(B) ** Decca Eclipse ECS 703. Israel Philharmonic Orchestra, Sir Georg Solti – TCHAIKOVSKY: *Symphony No. 2.***

(M) ** CBS Classics 61071. New York Philharmonic Orchestra, Leonard Bernstein – BIZET and PROKOFIEV: *Symphonies.** (*)

(B) ** Music for Pleasure MFP 57012. Scottish National Orchestra, Alexander Gibson – ROSSINI: *La Boutique fantasque;* SAINT-SAËNS: *Danse macabre.** (*)

It is perhaps strange that the current catalogue does not contain an outstanding modern recording of *L'Apprenti sorcier* to provide for the seventies the equivalent of Stokowski's memorable 78 set. Ansermet's account is easily the best recommendation. The recording perhaps lacks the last degree of brilliance, but it is still a fine one. The performance too is slightly relaxed, yet it has a cumulative

323

effect: one has the feeling of real calamity before the magician hurriedly returns at the end to put right the mischief his apprentice has wrought. This performance is available as part of two collections (both discussed fully in our *Treasury* volume): the first is an especially good bargain as *L'Apprenti sorcier* acts as a bonus for a collection by the New Symphony Orchestra under Gibson entitled *Danse macabre*.

The Frémaux version (a vividly atmospheric one, lacking something in sheer élan) is also part of an enjoyable if not distinctive concert of French music which includes also Chabrier's *España*, Debussy's *Prélude à l'après-midi d'un faune*, Ravel's *Bolero* and Saint-Saëns's *Danse macabre*. Recorded in the Great Hall of Birmingham University this disc is also available in quadraphonic form, where it achieves even greater vividness.

Solti's natural intensity suits the music and his tempi are very well chosen: the first entry of the main tune is immediately right. The recording is spacious, and the strings swirl nicely in their watery descriptive passages. A choice of couplings is offered.

Bernstein's performance is a brilliant one and the recording has plenty of glitter if less warmth. The bright lighting the CBS engineers favour does not uncover all the inner detail and one feels that other performances tell the famous story with more affection for the apprentice's bungling. However, if you want the coupling, there is no lack of excitement.

A crisp, straightforward account from Gibson, dramatic enough but not especially atmospheric. Clean, bright recording. This disc is notable for a fine performance of the suite from Rossini-Respighi's *La Boutique fantasque*.

Fanfare pour précéder La Péri; La Péri (poème dansé).

  (M) ** (*) Decca Ace of Diamonds SDD 293. Suisse Romande Orchestra, Ernest Ansermet – DEBUSSY: *La Boîte à joujoux*.***

Dukas's *La Péri* was written for Diaghilev in 1912. It is based on a tale from ancient Persian mythology. The King Iskander discovers the Péri asleep and steals her lotus blossom with its power of immortal youth. The Péri awakens and stimulates the King's desire with an erotic dance (hints of *Salome* in the music). The King succumbs and returns the flower, whereupon the object of his passion promptly vanishes, leaving him to reflect that he has been caught out by the oldest trick of all. The opening fanfare is reminiscent of the brass writing of Gabrieli, but the rest of the score, while imaginatively orchestrated, contains relatively unmemorable thematic material. Ansermet is clearly a sympathetic conductor of this music and he moulds the picturesque writing with his characteristically sure touch. The Decca recording is admirably clear and handles the climaxes vividly. Ideally the sound quality itself could be a trifle more alluring, although the closing pages are beautiful.

Symphony in C major; Pastorale d'été; Ariane et Barbe-bleue (opera): *Introduction to Act 3.*

  ** HMV ASD 2953. French National Radio Orchestra, Jean Martinon.

Dukas was born in the same year as Sibelius and Nielsen and came rather late to music; indeed he did not learn to read music until he was fifteen. He attracted attention in 1892 with the overture *Polyeucte*, and four years or so after wrote this *Symphony*. Its invention is not as original as *La Péri* or *L'Apprenti sorcier*, and it is no surprise that it has failed to establish itself in the repertory. It is rather thickly scored and the ideas are not quite distinguished enough to sustain the demands placed on them. However, it is good to see it represented in the catalogue, particularly in so persuasive a performance and recording as this. Yet in many respects it is an academic work. The prelude to Act 3 of *Ariane et Barbe-blue* of 1907 shows the strides Dukas made in the intervening years: it is high time we had the complete opera on record.

Variations, interlude and finale on a theme by Rameau.

(M) ** (*) VOX STGBY 671. Grant Johannesen (piano) – ROUSSEL: *3 Pieces*; SÉVERAC: *Pieces*.** (*)

As well as a composer Dukas was a scholar who edited a series of Rameau's most important works. Here with obvious affection he takes a theme of Rameau (from a keyboard piece) and uses it to fantasize in his own clear-headed but sensitive way. A welcome item in a fascinating recital superbly played. The recording clangs a little.

Dunstable, John
(died 1453)

Alma redemptoris mater; Ave Maris stella; O Rosa bella; Sancta Maria succurre miseris; Veni sancte spiritus – Veni creator spiritus.

*** Argo ZRG 681. Purcell Consort of Voices, Elizabeth Consort of Viols, Grayston Burgess – JOSQUIN DES PRÉS: *Collection*.***

John Dunstable was one of the great figures of the English Renaissance. In his day he was an internationally famous composer, and his music has strong individuality as well as striking emotional depth. His most famous (and justly so) piece is the isorhythmic motet *Veni sancte spiritus*, in which a comparatively complex formal structure becomes completely dwarfed by the music's expressive

beauty. It is most eloquently performed here and the solo singing elsewhere is of a very high standard indeed. With discreet accompaniments and immaculate recording this superb collection (with an equally recommendable coupling) shows how well Dunstable deserved his fame. Highly recommended. Incidentally several of these pieces are included in an outstanding Turnabout collection of Renaissance music (TV 34058S) by the same group, but even if you already have that the superb Argo disc is well worth having too.

Duparc, Henri
(1848–1933)

Mélodies: *Chanson triste; Élégie; Extase; L'Invitation au voyage; Lamento; Le Manoir de Rosemonde; Phidylé; Sérénade Florentine; Soupir; Testament; La Vague et la cloche; La Vie antérieure.*

(M) *** HMV HQS 1258. Gérard Souzay (baritone), Dalton Baldwin (piano) – FAURÉ: *Songs*.***

A pity that Duparc's output for the voice can be accommodated on one record. One would give a lot for some more. As it is the songs could find no more eloquent interpreter than Gérard Souzay, who also recorded them some years ago for Philips. These performances are equally fine, and every bit as well recorded. A superlative record in every way.

Duphly, Jacques
(1715–89)

Pièces de clavecin: *Allemande – Courante; La de belombre; Chaconne; La damazy (1 and 2); La felix; La forqueray; Les grâces; Menuets; La pothoüin.*

*** Philips SEON 6575 017. Gustav Leonhardt (harpsichord).

Duphly started life as an organist before going to Paris, where he gained an enviable reputation as a harpsichord player. His pieces were described as 'douces et aimables', and so they are in this admirable recital by Gustav Leonhardt. Those interested in keyboard music after Couperin and before the harpsichord gave way to the fortepiano will find much to reward them here. Gustav Leonhardt calls him 'delicate Duphly', and although the debt to Couperin and, of course, Rameau is strong, there is a gentleness about some of this music that is most attractive. The recording could hardly be improved upon.

Dupré, Marcel
(1886–1971)

Annonciation: 2 Méditations, Op. 56: Nos. 1 in E minor; 2 in G minor; 2 Esquisses, Op. 41: Nos. 1 in E minor; 2 in B flat minor; 3 Preludes and fugues, Op. 7: Nos. 1 in B major; 2 in F minor; 3 in G minor; Variations sur un Noël, Op. 20.

(B) *** RCA Victrola LVL 1 5018. Graham Steed (organ of Coventry Cathedral).

Graham Steed continues to be Dupré's most persuasive advocate, and this finely recorded album will not fail to give pleasure to his admirers. The sound is rich and has splendid presence, and even though the music lacks the strong individuality of a Messiaen, it too deserves some place in the sun.

Organ symphonies Nos. 1, Op. 23 (Symphonie-Passion); 2, Op. 26.

(B) ** (*) RCA Victrola VICS 1573. Graham Steed (organ of Westminster Cathedral).

Dupré's organ works have an improvisatory quality that is not easy to capture. Graham Steed does not entirely catch this rhapsodical manner, but he gives strong, intelligent performances. English cathedral organs are never ideal for French music, but this one is certainly well recorded and the sound is not too muffled for detail to emerge.

Poème symphonique: Évocation, Op. 37; Poème symphonique: Psaume XVIII: Caeli enarrant gloriam Dei, Op. 47.

(B) ** RCA Victrola VICS 1661. Graham Steed (organ of St Edmundsbury Cathedral).

Although not as impressive as the two symphonies Graham Steed recorded at Westminster Cathedral – the sound is more diffuse, some may think atmospheric – this disc gives us a deeper insight into Dupré's powers as a composer. His personality is not a powerful one, but his music is cultivated and often brings surprises. At this modest price, readers should be encouraged to investigate this unfashionable but eminently fine musician.

Durante, Francesco
(1684–1755)

Concertos for strings and continuo: in C major; in E minor; in F minor; in G minor.

*** BASF BAC 3060. Collegium Aureum (using original instruments).

The Collegium Aureum have acquired an enviable reputation for the authenticity of spirit and the sheer musicality that inform their performances. Durante, who was a contemporary of Bach and Handel, is much under-rated nowadays, though readers who have heard the odd concerto that I Musici have recorded will know him to be a considerable figure, full of originality and power. Some movements from these concertos are the equal of anything from the great Baroque masters, and the recording matches the beauty of the sound this ensemble produces from their fine instruments. It can be strongly recommended to all collectors irrespective of height of brow.

Dussek (Dusik), Jan
(1760–1812)

Piano concerto in B flat major.
(B) ** Turnabout TV 34362S. Rena Kyriakou (piano), Berlin Symphony Orchestra, C. A. Bünte – STAMITZ: *Cello concerto.***

Dussek's *Piano concerto* does not display quite the quality of invention of his *Double concerto* (see below) but it has a delightful, short slow movement and a gay finale. Rena Kyriakou plays the *Larghetto* affectionately and stylishly, and the outer movements are spirited. The recording is over-bright but yields to the controls.

Double piano concerto in B flat major.
(B) *** Turnabout TV 34204S. Toni and Rosi Grünschlag (pianos), Vienna Volksoper Orchestra, Paul Angerer – SCHUMANN: *Andante and variations.****

It is something of a tradition for double piano concertos to be genial works, and Dussek's is no exception. Above all such a piece needs spontaneity and conveyed enjoyment from the performers, and here the Grünschlag duo offers this quality in abundance. They are experts both as a partnership and in matters of technique and they play with such *brio* that a relatively slight work is made very en-

joyable indeed. The lyricism of the slow movement and the gay chatter of the finale are especially enjoyable, and the first-rate recording balances the personalities of the solo team against a lively orchestral accompaniment. This is highly infectious. A good coupling too.

Trio in F major, Op. 65 (for flute, cello and piano).
(B) ** Turnabout TV 34329S. Bernard Goldberg (flute), Theo Salzman (cello), Harry Franklin (piano) – WEBER: *Trio.****

A pleasant lightweight work, with an eloquent slow movement (rather more substantial in invention than one might expect) and a gently evoked yet gay finale. The performance is skilful and spontaneous (Bernard Goldberg a pleasing and stylish flautist); the recording is acceptable, though it is somewhat reverberant, with a certain amount of buzz from the cellist picked up by the microphones.

Dvořák, Antonín
(1841–1904)

Overtures: *Carnaval, Op. 92; In Nature's Realm, Op. 91; My Home, Op. 62; Othello, Op. 93.*
(M) ** Supraphon SUAST 50432. Czech Philharmonic Orchestra, Karel Ančerl.
Overtures: *Carnaval, Op. 92; In Nature's Realm, Op. 91; Othello, Op. 93; Scherzo capriccioso, Op. 66.*
*** Decca SXL 6348. London Symphony Orchestra, Istvan Kertesz.
The Golden Spinning Wheel, Op. 109; Symphonic variations, Op. 78.
*** Decca SXL 6510. London Symphony Orchestra, Istvan Kertesz.

*The Golden Spinning Wheel, Op. 109;
The Wild Dove, Op. 110.*

(M) ** (*) Supraphon SUAST 50435.
Czech Philharmonic Orchestra,
Zdenek Chalabala.

*Hussite overture, Op. 67; My Home
overture, Op. 62; The Noonday Witch,
Op. 108; The Water Goblin, Op. 107.*

*** Decca SXL 6543. London Sym-
phony Orchestra, Istvan Kertesz.

*Hussite overture, Op. 67; The Noonday
Witch, Op. 108; The Water Goblin,
Op. 107.*

(M) *** Supraphon SUAST 50455.
Czech Philharmonic Orchestra,
Ančerl or Chalabala.

Dvořák has a cheerfully extrovert way
of looking at the morbid national legends
on which he bases his symphonic poems.
It would be difficult to guess from hearing
the music, without pre-knowledge of the
programmes, the amount of unpleasant
sudden death that goes on within. The
heroine of the charming *Golden Spinning
Wheel* (a just favourite of Sir Thomas
Beecham's) is killed and mutilated by her
stepmother; *The Wild Dove* begins with
a beautiful young widow just burying the
husband she has poisoned; *The Noonday
Witch* is the traditional ogre threatened
to erring children by distraught mothers
and here she gets her prey; *The Water
Goblin*, having ensnared his maiden
dashes their green-haired child, decapi-
tated, at her feet when she escapes back
to mother. The music is colourful, with
attractive invention and characteristically
imaginative orchestration. The watery
scene of the *Goblin* provides the most
evocative and atmospheric writing, while
the elegy for the repenting widow in *The
Wild Dove* is touching. Both the Kertesz
discs are outstanding. The coupling of
The Golden Spinning Wheel, with its
magical horn calls, and a fine performance of the *Symphonic variations* makes a
highly desirable issue, with playing and

recording well up to the high standard
Kertesz and the LSO consistently
achieved in their Dvořák series. Yet the
collection on SXL 6543 seems even more
attractive: the performance of the *Water
Goblin* is wonderfully atmospheric, the
rest of the programme extremely vivid
and given Decca's richest recording, with
superb brass sounds in the *My Home
overture*. This was written as an expression of patriotic Czech sentiment at a
time when, under the thumb of the
Austrians, the Czechs were turning to
music as an important safety-valve. The
themes are taken from Czech folk music,
and one of them in fact will be recognized
from being used in the Czech national
anthem.

The *Hussite overture* is also patriotic in
inspiration, if rather less successful than
My Home. The musical material includes
themes based on the Hussite hymn and
St Wenceslas plain chant. The overtures
Othello and *In Nature's Realm* together
with the famous *Carnaval* originally
formed a triptych, linked by a recurring
main theme. Dvořák wrote them immediately before his first visit to America in
1892. The Supraphon disc (which is well
played, with a particularly brilliant
account of *Carnaval*, but only moderately
well recorded) conveniently re-creates the
original format. But the Kertesz versions
are in almost every way superior. While
it is obvious enough why *Carnaval* is the
only piece to have entered the repertoire,
Othello has colourful opening and closing
sections, and if the development does not
show itself as one of Dvořák's most
inspiring arguments, Kertesz makes the
very most of it and he gives an equally
bright and delightful account of *In
Nature's Realm*. The recordings are first-
rate.

The two Supraphon discs containing
the symphonic poems are eminently
recommendable in the medium-price
range. The orchestral playing is good, the
presentation vivid and the recording
bright and not lacking in atmosphere.

Piano concerto in G minor, Op. 33.

(B) ** Turnabout TV 34539S. Michael Ponti (piano), Prague Symphony Orchestra, Jindrich Rohan.

Dvořák's *Piano concerto* was written in 1876 (after the *Fifth Symphony*, but before the *Slavonic dances*). It is hardly one of his most compelling works but it has an agreeable strain of lyricism running through it, and the second movement is attractive. Michael Ponti's performance is well supported by the Prague Orchestra under Rohan, and the first movement is dramatic, while the *Andante* has a simple eloquence in keeping with its inspiration. The finale is perhaps the weakest movement but it is brought off quite well. The recording is full and vivid, with better piano tone than is usual from this source.

Violin concerto in A minor, Op. 53.

(M) ** (*) HMV SXLP 30170. Herman Krebbers (violin), Amsterdam Philharmonic Orchestra, Anton Kersjes – TCHAIKOVSKY: *Trois Souvenirs d'un lieu cher.****

(M) ** Decca Ace of Diamonds SDD 126. Ruggiero Ricci (violin), London Symphony Orchestra, Sir Malcolm Sargent – TCHAIKOVSKY: *Violin concerto.***

Violin concerto in A minor, Op. 53; Romance for violin and orchestra, Op. 11.

(M) ** (*) Supraphon SUAST 50181. Josef Suk (violin), Czech Philharmonic Orchestra, Karel Ančerl.

** CBS 72457. Isaac Stern (violin), Philadelphia Orchestra, Eugene Ormandy.

Suk's performance – once issued on Music for Pleasure, but now back on Supraphon again at mid-price – is lyrical in the simplest possible way, and its eloquence is endearing, in spite of the somewhat dated Supraphon sound. The bonus is the charming *Romance* which Dvořák adopted from the slow movement of his *F minor String quartet*. This is played to perfection by Suk, who realizes its simple charm with skill and affection. The glowing orchestral part is equally enjoyable.

Krebbers too is a fine player and he has the advantage of a vivid, comparatively modern recording. The soloist's image is bigger, with more body of tone than Suk's; on the other hand some might feel the forward balance is less natural. This is a bold reading, with a strongly felt *Adagio* and an irresistibly gay finale. If the first two movements show marginally less individuality than Suk's reading, the sound is unquestionably superior, and the Tchaikovsky coupling is played with affection and panache.

Ricci's is a plainspun performance, well made and not without style. But Ricci does not seem temperamentally suited to the work and the performance has no special idiomatic character. The recording is good, and the coupling attractive. Stern offers the same coupling as Suk. His performance is not lacking in power or eloquence, but it is less natural in feeling than Suk's, and the recording is not so convincing tonally as the HMV issue.

Violoncello concerto in B minor, Op. 104.

*** DGG SLPM 139044. Mstislav Rostropovich (cello), Berlin Philharmonic Orchestra, Herbert von Karajan – TCHAIKOVSKY: *Variations on a rococo theme.****

(M) *** HMV SXLP 30018. Paul Tortelier (cello), Philharmonia Orchestra, Sir Malcolm Sargent.

(M) *** DGG Privilege 2535 106. Pierre Fournier (cello), Berlin Philharmonic Orchestra, George Szell.

(M) *** H M V SXLP 30176. Mstislav
Rostropovich (cello), Royal Phil-
harmonic Orchestra, Sir Adrian
Boult.

(B) ** Classics for Pleasure CFP
40070. Janos Starker (cello),
Philharmonia Orchestra, Walter
Susskind – FAURÉ: *Élégie.***

*Violoncello concerto in B minor, Op.
104; Rondo in G major* (for cello and
orchestra), *Op. 94; Waldesruhe* (for
cello and orchestra), *Op. 68.*

*** Philips SAL 3675. Maurice Gen-
dron (cello), London Philharmonic Orchestra, Bernard Haitink.

*Violoncello concerto in B minor, Op.
104; Silent Woods* (for cello and
orchestra) (arr. of No. 5 of *From the
Bohemian Woods* for piano duet).

** (*) H M V ASD 2751. Jacqueline
du Pré (cello), Chicago Symphony
Orchestra, Daniel Barenboim.

The collaboration of Rostropovich and
Karajan makes for superb results, warm
as well as refined in reflection of the finest
qualities in each of the two principals.
If Rostropovich can sometimes sound
self-indulgent in this most romantic of
cello concertos, the degree of control
provided by the conductor gives a firm
yet supple base, and there have been
few recorded accounts so deeply satisfying. The result is unashamedly romantic, with many moments of dalliance, but
the concentration is never in doubt.
Superb playing by the Berliners, beautifully refined recording, and a bonus (not
to be taken for granted with this concerto) in the shape of Tchaikovsky's
glorious variations.

The Tortelier performance on Concert
Classics has all the rich, romantic concentration one expects from this great
cellist. There are minor technical blemishes in the finale (so there always were
with Casals), but this is a performance

that hangs together and reveals new
facets in the work every time one hears it.
With the genuine tension of a live performance (in the first two movements at
least) it is one of the most enjoyable and
warm-hearted performances ever recorded. The stereo gives an excellent
sense of atmosphere but does not always
provide absolute inner clarity. Otherwise
the recording is excellent for its age, and
the disc has a considerable price-advan-
tage if the additional items offered by
Rostropovich and Gendron are not
required.

Fournier's reading has a sweep of conception and richness of tone and phrasing
which carry along the melodic lines with
exactly the mixture of nobility and tension that the work demands. Fournier
can relax and beguile the ear in the lyrical
passages, and yet catch up the listener in
his exuberance in the exciting finale. The
phrasing in the slow movement is ravishing, and the interpretation as a whole
balances beautifully. D G G's recording
is rich, forward and vivid, with a broad,
warm tone for the soloist. This is yet
another highly recommendable disc, and
for those who prefer a straightforwardly
romantic reading of this concerto it
could prove first choice, irrespective of
price.

If Gendron's performance is a little
less larger than life than Rostropovich's
it is nonetheless well worth considering
as an alternative. It is unidiosyncratic,
marvellously fresh and lyrical, and has
the advantage of impeccable orchestral
support from the LPO under Haitink.
There is a real spontaneity about this
playing, and its warmth is splendidly
captured by the Philips engineers, who
produce magnificent sound. There are
two engaging fill-ups.

Rostropovich's earlier version of the
Dvořák concerto (also now on Concert
Classics) was recorded with Boult in the
late 1950s and still sounds amazingly
fresh and vital. No one would guess its
age. The balance is superbly judged and

the timbre truthful; the texture sounds open and vivid, so there need be no reservations in recommending this classic account, particularly at its new price. It competes very strongly with any of the available alternatives and will be preferred by many to them all. Jacqueline du Pré's reading conveys the spontaneous passion which marks her playing in public. There are more immaculate readings available, but for du Pré's admirers this performance will be impossible to resist. The pity is that the recording is badly balanced. The trumpet is ridiculously backward at the end of the first movement, and the cello is too forwardly balanced. Nonetheless it is a performance which captures very vividly the urgent interpretative flair of both husband and wife, soloist and conductor.

Though Starker's was one of the very first versions of the Dvořák concerto to appear in stereo, its reissue is welcome: the sound is still vivid and the performance is tough and virile, though Starker misses the hushed introspection of the slow movement.

Czech suite, Op. 39.
   ** Philips 6500 203. English Chamber Orchestra, Charles Mackerras – VOŘIŠEK: *Symphony in D major.***
Czech suite, Op. 39; Slavonic dances Nos. 1–16, Op. 46/1–8; Op. 72/1–8 (complete recording); Slavonic rhapsodies, Op. 45: Nos. 1 in D major; 2 in G minor; 3 in A flat major; The Wood Dove, Op. 110.
   ** (*) Telefunken SAT 22523/5. Czech Philharmonic Orchestra, Václav Neumann.

An excellent set from Telefunken, gathering together some useful lesser-known works of Dvořák with what is unquestionably the best current complete recording of the *Slavonic dances*. These are spread over three sides, and the sound

is consequently much more expansive than in the issues that squeeze all the music on to two. The dances are vivaciously played with convincingly flexible *rubato*, and the same idiomatic quality illuminates the two *Rhapsodies*, which are melodically appealing and full of character. The *Czech suite* and the melodramatic tone poem are almost equally convincing. The sound quality throughout is vivid in Telefunken's characteristic bright-eyed manner.

Mackerras gives a fresh, lively performance of the *Czech suite*, and some may prefer the Philips recording for its greater naturalness of recorded sound. The Telefunken account has rather more brilliance and impact, but the upper strings seem almost excessively bright after the Philips version.

Legends, Op. 59 (complete recording).
   *** Philips 6500 188. London Philharmonic Orchestra, Raymond Leppard.

Delightful and warm-hearted performances of these glorious pieces. Raymond Leppard and the LPO are well served by the engineers: the sound is beautifully natural and fresh. For Dvořákians this will be an indispensable disc and at present there is no alternative on record.

Scherzo capriccioso, Op. 66.
   (M) ** (*) Philips Universo 6580 014. Concertgebouw Orchestra, Bernard Haitink – TCHAIKOVSKY: *Capriccio italien; Romeo and Juliet.** (*)
   (M) ** HMV SXLP 30125. Royal Philharmonic Orchestra, Rudolf Kempe – SMETANA: *Bartered Bride: Overture and suite;* WEINBERGER: *Schwanda: Polka and fugue.***

Kertesz's vivacious performance, available coupled to either the *Eighth Sym-*

phony or the set of *Overtures Opp. 91/3*, is an obvious first choice, with notably brilliant Decca recording. Haitink's account has come up well in this reissue. It has an attractive lyrical character and is not without charm, yet there is no affectation. The recording is well-balanced, the woodwind detail telling as it should, and there is more sparkle than in the original issue. Kempe's account too has a nice lyrical feeling, but it is lacking in exuberance. However, if the couplings are suitable this HMV disc makes quite an enjoyable concert.

Serenade for strings in E major, Op. 22.
  (M) *** DGG Privilege 2538 313. English Chamber Orchestra, Rafael Kubelik – SMETANA: *Vltava; From Bohemia's Woods and Fields.***(*)
  ** (*) Argo ZRG 670. Academy of St Martin-in-the-Fields, Neville Marriner – GRIEG: *Holberg suite.****
  ** (*) Pye Ensayo NEL 2002. English Chamber Orchestra, Enrique Garcia Asensio – TCHAIKOVSKY: *String serenade.***
  ** (*) HMV ASD 3036. English Chamber Orchestra, Daniel Barenboim – TCHAIKOVSKY: *String serenade.** (*)
  (B) ** Decca SPA 375. Israel Philharmonic Orchestra, Rafael Kubelik – TCHAIKOVSKY: *String serenade.***

Serenade for strings in E major, Op. 22;
Symphonic variations, Op. 78.
  *** Philips SAL 3706. London Symphony Orchestra, Colin Davis.

The English Chamber Orchestra seem to have made a speciality of recording Dvořák's delightful *Serenade*, for they are shown here in three recordings, each substantially different in character.

On Kubelik's Privilege disc they are particularly successful, creating a performance that is beautifully lyrical, yet strong in impulse. The recording is brightly lit but of very good quality. With its attractive coupling this is a genuine bargain at medium-price. Asensio's performance too is very enjoyable. His touch is marginally lighter, and there is a splendid lyrical grace about this reading. The recording too is first-rate, if a little less fine-grained than Kubelik's. With Barenboim directing the eloquence of the playing is in no doubt, though one or two details are underlined with rather more expressive emphasis than necessary. The sound is open and fresh, though the upper strings have a slight edge to them which is less than attractive.

The finest sound of all, perhaps, comes from the fine Argo disc. Some ears might find this almost too rich-textured for the innocent simplicity of Dvořák's invention. Even so this is splendidly played and recorded, and the coupling, Grieg's *Holberg suite*, is superbly done.

Although it opens persuasively, Kubelik's earlier performance on Decca relies on virility rather than charm to make its appeal. It is certainly splendidly alive and the finale gains from such treatment. But the third movement is very fast indeed. Kubelik's recording is wide in range, with a very bright treble, and on SPA this coupling is certainly good value.

The *Symphonic variations* is one of Dvořák's greatest orchestral works and we have long needed a good version of it. Colin Davis's account with the LSO is a fine one; he has genuine feeling for the work and keeps a firm grip on the structure. The *Serenade*, too, comes off well and although the recording is not quite so immediate as some Philips issues, the sound is musical and well-balanced. A recommendable coupling.

Serenade in D minor (for 10 wind instruments, violoncello and double-bass), *Op. 44.*

*** Philips 6500 163. Netherlands Wind Ensemble, Edo de Waart – GOUNOD: *Petite symphonie;* SCHUBERT: *Octet* (excerpts).***
*** Decca SXL 6368. Members of the London Symphony Orchestra, Istvan Kertesz – BRAHMS: *Serenade No. 2.*** (*)
(B) ** Pye GSGC 14082. A section of the Hallé Orchestra, Sir John Barbirolli – GOUNOD: *Petite symphonie.***

The playing of the Netherlands Wind Ensemble under Edo de Waart blends spontaneity and discipline in just the right proportions. It is not easy to imagine a more refreshing and delightful performance, and given such musically balanced and vividly recorded sound (as well as attractive couplings) the claims of this issue will be seen to be pressing.

Kertesz too gives a delightfully idiomatic account of the enchanting *Wind serenade* and he is accorded splendid treatment by the Decca engineers. Choice between this and Edo de Waart's record will doubtless hinge on couplings.

Sir John Barbirolli directs a performance of persuasive charm, and his affection is answered with good playing. Originally this issue suffered from pre-echo and other cutting faults, but recent pressings seem to have cured these defects. A good bargain recommendation.

Slavonic dances Nos. 1–16, Op. 46/1–8 Op. 72/1–8 (complete recording).
  (M) ** (*) Supraphon MS 0105. Czech Philharmonic Orchestra, Karel Sejna.
  (M) ** (*) CBS Classics 61089. Cleveland Orchestra, George Szell.

Dvořák's sixteen *Slavonic dances* are not easy to fit on two LP sides (with dividing bands) without some loss of amplitude in the recording. The finest complete set is under Neumann, which is spread onto three sides, with obvious gain in the richness and resonance of the sound. But this is only available as part of a (desirable) three-disc collection (see above under *Czech suite*). Of the other complete sets the Supraphon disc seems marginally the better buy. The recording focus lacks something in precision: there is a lack of bite in the cymbals (for instance), but the overall sound is pleasing and the performances are idiomatic and enjoyable. However, many may prefer the alternative CBS disc under Szell. Even though the recording is harder in outline and not ideally transparent, with careful use of the controls it can be made to sound well. And Szell provides a really first-rate set, with brilliant and often virtuoso playing, witness the confidence of the strings, and the superbly moulded *rubato* of the reprise of the main theme in Op. 72/2. This is an orchestra glorying in its own virtuosity in the most musical way, and Dvořák's texture glows with life. Szell's *rubato*, here as throughout, is most skilfully managed, and the bright Cleveland sound suits his extrovert approach. Perhaps in some of the gentler moments a touch more of intimacy would have added an extra degree of charm, but for the most part these performances are very satisfying.

Slavonic dances Nos. 1–8, Op. 46/1–8; 15, Op. 72/7.
  (B) ** Decca Eclipse ECS 632. London Symphony Orchestra, Jean Martinon (with BARTÓK: *Roumanian folk dances;* WEINBERGER: *Schwanda: polka and fugue* * (*)).
Slavonic dances Nos. 1, 3, 8, Op. 46/1, 3, 8; 9, 10, Op. 72/1 and 2.
  (B) *** Decca SPA 202. Israel Philharmonic Orchestra, Istvan Kertesz – SMETANA: *Vltava; Bartered Bride: Overture; Polka; Furiant.****

(B) ** (*) Decca SPA 377. Vienna Philharmonic Orchestra, Fritz Reiner – BRAHMS: *Hungarian dances.*** (*)

Slavonic dances Nos. 1, 3, 8, Op. 46/1, 3, 8; 10, Op. 72/2.

** Decca Phase 4 PFS 4245. London Philharmonic Orchestra, Stanley Black – SMETANA: *Vltava; Bartered Bride: Polka; Dance of the comedians.***

Of the shorter collections, Martinon's Eclipse disc seems a particular bargain, with imaginative couplings (the Weinberger not in real stereo). Those who like plenty of brilliance in the *Slavonic dances* will be well pleased with Martinon's approach. The orchestral playing is nicely turned but the prevailing mood is an uninhibited one. The recording is early stereo but is brightly lit and does not sound its age.

Kertesz's disc too is a first-rate bargain. The Israel Orchestra is not one of the world's finest, but here the playing is irresistible in its gaiety and vivacious colouring. The furiants go with the wind, but Kertesz maintains the underlying lyricism of the music. The recording is marginally over-reverberant and may need a slight treble control, but is otherwise first-rate.

Reiner's disc is given a fine lustre by the engineers. His readings are polished and enjoyable, if not penetrating too far below the surface in the lyrical music, where he is inclined to be mannered. But the overall effect has plenty of sparkle, and one's reservations are soon forgotten in the pleasure of listening to such colourful music so vivaciously presented.

But those seeking the very finest sound might well turn to Stanley Black's issue on Phase 4. By including only four dances to the side, the engineers can provide spacious sound of the highest quality, and the performances, if not highly idiomatic,

are flexible and musicianly as well as brilliant.

SYMPHONIES

Symphonies Nos. 1–9 (complete recording).
⊛ *** Decca SXLD 6515/21. London Symphony Orchestra, Istvan Kertesz.

Kertesz's idiomatic and exciting performances of the symphonies are here coupled economically together in an album of seven records, a magnificent memorial to a conductor who died sadly young.

Symphony No. 1 in C minor (The Bells of Zlonice) Op. 3.
*** Decca SXL 6288. London Symphony Orchestra, Istvan Kertesz.

This symphony, written early in 1865, was lost for over half a century, and even when the score turned up in Germany in the possession of a namesake of the composer (no relation) it had to wait years for performance, and was not published until 1961. Even so Dvořák remembered it when on the fly-leaf of the score of the *New World* he made a complete list of his symphonies. Clearly, had he kept hold of the score he would have made revisions. Though the piece took him only five weeks to write, it is the longest of all his symphonies – over 54 minutes in this performance – and the fluency is not always matched by the memorability of the material. But it still has much attractive writing in it, and no one should miss it who has enjoyed the other early Dvořák symphonies. Zlonice was the place where Dvořák served his musical (and butcher's) apprenticeship, but the music is not intended to convey a programme. The LSO under Kertesz play excellently and give us the complete score without any of the cuts introduced into the earlier LP on Supraphon under Václav Neumann. The Decca recording has splendid detail and presence.

Symphony No. 2 in B flat major, Op. 4.
*** Decca SXL 6289. London Symphony Orchestra, Istvan Kertesz.

Dvořák wrote his *Second Symphony* in 1865 within months of his *First*, but then he left it on the shelf for a full fifteen years before submitting it to a thorough revision. The original 260 pages of score were contracted to 212, and though this left the finale in an oddly unbalanced state, it is surprising that Dvořák's publisher, Simrock, refused to take the work when it was submitted to him along with Symphonies Nos. 3 and 4. Admittedly the ideas are not so strongly Dvořákian as they might be, and some movements tend to outstay their welcome, but anyone who has ever been charmed by Dvořák's wide-eyed genius will find much to enjoy notably in the highly engaging ideas of the first movement. One oddity – and weakness – is that each movement has a slow introduction, a case of the composer 'clearing his throat' before launching out. As in his other Dvořák performances, Kertesz takes a crisp, fresh, straightforward approach to the music, and the recording is first-rate. Thus this symphony is admirably served in every way and the scherzo has all the authentic, idiomatic flavour one could possibly want. The recording has the finest qualities of the Decca set.

Symphony No. 3 in E flat major, Op. 10; Hussite overture, Op. 67.
*** Decca SXL 6290. London Symphony Orchestra, Istvan Kertesz.

This was the first of Dvořák's symphonies to show the full exuberance of his genius. When he wrote it in 1873 – eight years after the first two – he was very much under the influence of Wagner, but nowhere do the Wagnerian ideas really

conceal the essential Dvořák. Even the unashamed crib from *Lohengrin* in the middle section (D flat major) of the slow movement has a Dvořákian freshness, particularly when, as here, Kertesz adopts a fastish speed – faster than the score would strictly allow – and deliberately lightens the texture. This very long slow movement is in any case the weakest of the three, but the outer movements are both delightful and need no apology whatever. The very opening of the symphony with its 6/8 rhythm and rising-scale motifs can hardly miss, and the dotted rhythms of the second subject are equally engaging. Fresh, bright playing from the LSO; fresh, bright recording from Decca.

Symphony No. 4 in D minor, Op. 13; In Nature's Realm overture, Op. 91.
*** Decca SXL 6257. London Symphony Orchestra, Istvan Kertesz.

Compared with the exuberant symphonies which flank it on either side in the Dvořák canon, this is a disappointment. The opening theme – a fanfare-like idea – is not so characterful as one expects, but then the second subject soars aloft in triple time. The slow movement begins with so close a crib from the *Pilgrims' Music* in *Tannhäuser* one wonders how Dvořák had the face to write it, but the variations which follow are attractive, and the scherzo has a delightful lolloping theme, which unfortunately gives way to a horribly blatant march trio with far too many cymbal crashes in it. The finale, despite rhythmic monotony, has at least one highly characteristic and attractive episode. And whatever the shortcomings of the work, there is much that is memorable. Kertesz gives a good dramatic performance, and receives excellent recording quality.

Symphony No. 5 in F major (originally Op. 24 (1875); published as Op. 76); *My Home overture, Op. 62.*

*** Decca SXL 6273. London Symphony Orchestra, Istvan Kertesz.

Even more than most Dvořák, this is a work to make one share, if only for a moment, in the happy emotions of a saint, and what could be more welcome in modern nerve-racked life? The feeling of joy is here expressed so intensely that it provokes tears rather than laughter, and it is hard to understand why this marvellous work has been neglected for so long. It used to be called the *Pastoral*, but although it shares Beethoven's key and uses the flute a great deal (a Dvořákian characteristic) the nickname is not specially apt. What initially strikes one are the echoes of Wagner – forest murmurs (Bohemian ones) in the opening pages, a direct lift from *Siegfried's Rhine Journey* in the second theme and so on – but by the time he wrote the work, 1875, Dvořák's individuality as a musician was well established, and the composer's signature is in effect written on every bar. The slow movement is as beautiful as any in the symphonies, the scherzo is a gloriously bouncing piece with themes squandered generously, and the finale, though long, is intensely original in structure and argument. Kertesz's performance is straight and dramatic, with tempi very well chosen to allow for infectious rhythmic pointing. Excellent recording.

Symphony No. 6 in D major, Op. 60.
    *** DGG 2530 425. Berlin Philharmonic Orchestra, Rafael Kubelik.
Symphony No. 6 in D major, Op. 60; Carnaval overture, Op. 92.
    *** Decca SXL 6253. London Symphony Orchestra, Istvan Kertesz.

If the three immediately preceding Dvořák symphonies reflect the influence of Wagner, this one just as clearly reflects that of Brahms, and particularly of the Brahms *Second Symphony*. Not only the

shape of themes but the actual lay-out in the first movement have strong affinities with the Brahmsian model, but Kertesz's performance effectively underlines the individuality of the writing as well. This is a marvellous work that with the *Fifth* and *Seventh* forms the backbone of the Dvořák cycle, and that is hardly an idea we should have been likely to advance before Kertesz gave us fresh insight into these vividly inspired works. Kertesz's reading is fresh, literal and dramatic in his characteristic Dvořák manner, and his tempi are eminently well chosen. The recording too is excellent.

Kubelik's account comes from the DGG Symphony edition box that appeared in 1973. The performance is a glowing and radiant one; the Berlin Philharmonic play with great eloquence and conviction and although the recording is not quite as open and vivid as the Decca, the sound is unfailingly smooth and well-blended. Kertesz gives an unmannered reading, of course, and the greater brightness and immediacy of the Decca recording might encourage some readers to prefer him, but the Kubelik performance has greater inner feeling; it is more deeply experienced and commanding. Kertesz, however, offers an exceedingly brilliant account of the *Carnaval overture* as a considerable bonus.

Symphony No. 7 in D minor, Op. 70.
    *** DGG 2530 127. Berlin Philharmonic Orchestra, Rafael Kubelik.
    (M) *** Decca Ace of Diamonds SDD 260. London Symphony Orchestra, Pierre Monteux.
    (B) ** (*) Classics for Pleasure CFP 40088. London Philharmonic Orchestra, Arthur Davison.
    ** Decca SXL 6115. London Symphony Orchestra, Istvan Kertesz.
    * Decca SXL 6381. Israel Philharmonic Orchestra, Zubin Mehta.

Symphony No. 7 in D minor, Op. 70; Legends, Op. 59, Nos. 4, 6 and 7.
(B) * (*) Pye GSGC 14068. Hallé Orchestra, Sir John Barbirolli.
Symphony No. 7 in D minor, Op. 70; My Home overture, Op. 62.
** Philips 6500 287. London Symphony Orchestra, Witold Rowicki.

Kubelik gives a glowing performance of one of Dvořák's richest inspirations. His approach is deliberately expressive, but his romanticism never obscures the overall structural plan, and the playing of the Berlin orchestra is radiant set against opulent but refined DG recording.

Monteux's disc is a strong contender at medium-price. His performance has always been a favourite: it is exciting, idiomatic, and pleasingly tinged with geniality. The orchestral playing is first-rate and the Decca recording has withstood the test of time. The beautiful opening and closing pages of the *Poco adagio*, and the brilliant finale are highlights of a reading which, if it has a slightly mannered effect here and there, is satisfying overall.

Davison chooses fast tempi for the first three movements, but with warmly committed playing from the LPO the result is never rigid or unfeeling. The finale, though less incisive, erupts infectiously, and with vivid forward recording this makes a good bargain recommendation, even if it lacks the persuasive subtlety of Monteux's superb mid-price version.

Kertesz offers a relaxed reading, beautifully recorded. There is much to give pleasure here, especially the warm orchestral playing. There is no lack of tension, yet somehow the excitement of the climaxes does not always completely catch fire and the last degree of spontaneity is missing, although the finale is especially successful.

Rowicki's version is fresh and direct, with very little pointing. Cool and detached, he fails to illuminate Dvořák's individual vein of melancholy in this work, though the playing of the LSO is excellent, and the recording first-rate.

Barbirolli offers a fair recommendation in the bargain range. The first movement has a fine lyrical exhilaration; the slow movement has stature and warmth, and the scherzo individuality. The finale gathers momentum to become highly exciting. The snag is the recording, which tends to be gritty in the treble, with not enough weight for the upper strings, and rather light and dead in the bass. However, with flexible controls an acceptable sound can be obtained. The *Legends* are better recorded and make an attractive bonus.

Mehta's performance has relatively little to commend it. His reading is inclined to be brash, and though it is very well recorded it is concerned to make effects rather than penetrate Dvořák's depths. Not recommended

Symphony No. 8 in G major, Op. 88.
*** DGG SLPM 139181. Berlin Philharmonic Orchestra, Rafael Kubelik.
(M) ** (*) Decca Ace of Diamonds SDD 440. Vienna Philharmonic Orchestra, Herbert von Karajan.
(M) * (**) Nonesuch H 71262. Hamburg Philharmonic Orchestra, Charles Mackerras.
** Philips SAL 3761. London Symphony Orchestra, Witold Rowicki.
Symphony No. 8 in G major, Op. 88; Carnaval overture, Op. 92.
(B) ** Classics for Pleasure CFP 40075. London Philharmonic Orchestra, Constantin Silvestri.
Symphony No. 8 in G major, Op. 88; Scherzo capriccioso, Op. 66.

*** Decca SXL 6044. London Symphony Orchestra, Istvan Kertesz.

(B) ** Pye GSGC 14069. Hallé Orchestra, Sir John Barbirolli.

Symphony No. 8 in G major, Op. 88; Slavonic dances Nos. 3, Op. 46/3; 10, Op. 72/2.

** HMV ASD 2653. Cleveland Orchestra, George Szell.

Kertesz's coupling is a happy choice and it helps to place his performance of the symphony at the top of the list. The reading is fresh, spontaneous and exciting. The slow movement is affectionate and captures well the pastoral quality of the writing, and the tempo for the *Allegretto grazioso* is particularly well judged. The Decca recording is extremely brilliant but is notable also for warmth in the middle and lower strings.

Kubelik's recording is hardly less brilliant than Kertesz's Decca, yet the DGG engineers manage to avoid the impression that the strings are very close to the microphones. Indeed the stereo lay-out here is highly convincing. The performance is very fine. Without personal idiosyncrasy (except for a slight touch of schmaltz for the string theme in the trio of the scherzo) this is a vibrant reading, very faithful to the composer's intention, and with the personality of the orchestra coming through strongly. It is possible to prefer it to the Decca disc on the grounds of a marginal greater warmth from the middle strings. There is little to choose between the performances, but of course the Decca issue offers a formidable and attractive bonus in the *Scherzo capriccioso*.

Karajan's is a rich, expansive performance in the front rank. It gets off to a very good start with an especially warm treatment of the lovely opening theme, and it is only later, when an occasional mannerism tends to hold up the music's flow in the slow movement or add a little extra unnecessary schmaltz to the string

tune in the third movement, that one's preference veers firmly back to the fresh spontaneity of Kertesz. The present disc is extremely well engineered, but so is Kertesz's.

Mackerras's account on Nonesuch is outstandingly vital and spontaneous. Its freshness and the conviction it generates would place it at the very top of the list were it not for certain deficiencies in the recording. This has an obvious studio ambience, but is not unnaturally dry. The sound is clear and vivid and not without atmosphere, but in the climaxes of the outer movements there is a hint of congestion and there are some severe examples of pre-echo in the quieter passages of the slow movement. These are presumably cutting faults and may not apply to every pressing. The performance has such vigour and warmth, however, that it remains enjoyable in spite of the technical blemishes.

Silvestri's reading, reissued on Classics for Pleasure, makes a good bargain recommendation. The performance is bold and dramatic, but not wilful, and not eccentric in matters of rhythm and tempo as this conductor sometimes was. The London Philharmonic Orchestra respond with excellent playing and the recording is vivid if slightly dry in acoustic. It seems slightly more expansive and atmospheric in the *Carnaval overture*, which is outstandingly well done.

Barbirolli's performance of this symphony was one of his best Pye records. The reading has immense vitality and forward impetus, the kind of spontaneous excitement that is rare in the recording studio, and yet the whole performance is imbued with a delightful, unforced lyricism. Only in the third movement does Sir John miscalculate. When the strings take over the main tune of the trio he indulges in a heavy vibrato and fruity portamento which the Philadelphia Orchestra's strings might have brought off but the Hallé cannot. But this is a small blot on an otherwise remarkably good performance. The recording can be made to sound well, and the *Scherzo capriccioso*, if not on the level of the symphony, is exciting.

Szell recorded the symphony at least twice before his Cleveland EMI version. His earlier Decca account is available in a stereo transcription on Eclipse (ECS 690) and, with allowances made for the early date of the recording, is still recommendable. The new EMI reading is strong and committed, consistent from first to last, and obviously gains from the spread of modern stereo. It is not, however, quite so electrifying as the earlier performance.

Symphony No. 9 in E minor (From the New World), Op. 95.

   *** DGG 2530 415. Berlin Philharmonic Orchestra, Rafael Kubelik.

   *** DGG SLPM 138922. Berlin Philharmonic Orchestra, Herbert von Karajan.

   *** Decca Phase 4 PFS 4128. New Philharmonia Orchestra, Antal Dorati.

   (B) *** Decca SPA 87. Vienna Philharmonic Orchestra, Istvan Kertesz.

   (M) ** (*) DGG Privilege 135053. Berlin Philharmonic Orchestra, Ferenc Fricsay.

   (M) ** (*) CBS Classics 61053. London Symphony Orchestra, Eugene Ormandy.

   ** (*) RCA ARL 2 0334 (2 discs). Philadelphia Orchestra (1927 recording); New Philharmonia Orchestra (1973 recording), Leopold Stokowski.

   ** (*) HMV ASD 2863. Berlin Philharmonic Orchestra, Herbert von Karajan – SMETANA: *Vltava*.** (*)

   (B) ** Pye GSGC 14070. Hallé Orchestra, Sir John Barbirolli.

   (B) ** Contour 2870 118. Berlin Philharmonic Orchestra, Otto Gerdes.

Symphony No. 9 in E minor (From the New World), Op. 95; Carnaval overture, Op. 95.

   (M) ** (*) HMV SXLP 30163. Philharmonia Orchestra, Carlo Maria Giulini.

   (B) ** Music for Pleasure MFP 57001. London Philharmonic Orchestra, Alexander Gibson.

   (B) ** Classics for Pleasure CFP 104. Philharmonia Orchestra, Wolfgang Sawallisch.

Symphony No. 9 in E minor (From the New World), Op. 95; Othello overture, Op. 93.

   *** Decca SXL 6291. London Symphony Orchestra, Istvan Kertesz.

There are some two dozen recordings of the *New World* listed in the current catalogue, nearly all of them serviceable, and many of outstanding merit. This symphony has fared exceptionally well on LP. Each generation of new recordings has provided one that is really memorable, and there are at least half a dozen which are outstanding enough to make a positive first recommendation very difficult. Certainly Kubelik's marvellously fresh account with the Berlin Philharmonic is one of the finest of these. The hushed opening immediately creates a tension which is to be sustained throughout, and the approach to the gentle second subject of the first movement underlines the refinement which is the hallmark of the reading. The slow movement has a compelling lyrical beauty, with playing of great radiance from the orchestra. With a scherzo of striking character and a finale of great urgency – the forward impulse magically slackened as the composer is allowed to dreamily recall his earlier themes – the playing is throughout of the first rank.

The recording is well up to the standard of Kubelik's DGG series, firm, smoothly blended and clear, if lacking something in resonance in the bass.

Karajan too reveals a freshness that will surely remind the listener of the first time he was bowled over by the melodic spontaneity of Dvořák's inspiration. The accent here is on lyricism, and in spite of the exciting build-up of power in the first movement it is the lovingly phrased second subject group that remains in the memory. In the great *Largo*, Karajan achieves a kind of detached repose which lets the music speak for itself, and in the scherzo the rustic qualities in the second strain of the first section as well as the trio are evoked gently to captivating effect. The finale begins boldly and conveys a feeling of sheer high spirits; then in the marvellous lyrical reflective passage (just before the music sweeps away tremendously in its final burst of passion) the conductor relaxes and invites the listener to revel with him in the sheer beauty of the writing. DGG's recording still sounds extremely well, although it is about ten years old.

Kertesz made his earlier recording of the *New World* with the Vienna Philharmonic, but to make his cycle of the symphonies really uniform, Decca sponsored an entirely new version with the London Symphony Orchestra. In the seven years which separated the two, Kertesz had matured enormously, so that the later version is one of the finest ever committed to record and on many counts the most completely recommendable of all. Above all Kertesz has learnt to cover his interpretative tracks, so that the tempo changes in the first movement – almost inevitable and certainly desirable – are achieved with utmost subtlety. This time, too, Kertesz takes the exposition repeat, so giving the first movement – otherwise very short – its proper stature. But it is in the slow movement that Kertesz's sensitivity emerges most vividly. In essence his approach is as simple and straightforward

as could be, yet the hushed intensity of the playing conveys a depth of feeling that makes one hear the music with new ears. Tempi in the last two movements are also perfectly judged – not too fast in the finale – and the recording quality is outstanding, the best this symphony has ever had. The Dorati performance makes a perfect foil to Kertesz. Contrasting with Kertesz's simple lyricism Dorati is immediate and direct, with bold primary colours heightening the drama throughout. Rarely have the Decca Phase 4 techniques been used to better artistic effect, and the recording is extremely vivid, without loss of warmth. This is a most exciting disc.

Decca have also reissued Kertesz's earlier Vienna performance in their *World of . . .* series. One might cavil at the unnaturally forward balance of the timpani in the introduction, but in all other respects, the full-blooded sound eclipses other bargain competitors. The performance is enjoyable and agreeably fresh, not without its occasional idiosyncrasy – the gentle treatment of the first movement's second subject is less convincingly prepared than in Kertesz's later LSO disc, and there is a sudden quickening of tempo after its reprise at the end. There is plenty of excitement, and the Vienna Philharmonic play the *Largo* most beautifully.

Fricsay's reading is more controversial, but remains a favourite of I.M.'s. The style is somewhat oldfashioned, unashamedly romantic, including an affectionate and considerable ritardando at the entry of the first movement's secondary theme. The orchestra are on top form, especially in the *Largo*, and the finale is splendid, with a very exciting coda. The recording has been given greater projection in the Privilege reissue: there is a hint of stridency in the last movement, but generally the sound is brilliant in the best sense.

Giulini recorded the *New World* when the old Philharmonia was at its peak.

The result has a refinement, coupled with a degree of detachment, which for some will make it an ideal reading. This is emotion observed from outside rather than experienced direct, and the result, with its beautiful moulding of phrase, is very refreshing. For a general recommendation this may well be too cool a reading, but with vivid recording quality, excellent for its period, this clearly has its place in the catalogue.

Ormandy's performance, recorded in London, besides offering plenty of excitement shows unusual care in preparation. The orchestral playing has life and spontaneity, and the rhythmic freshness of the scherzo (achieved by unforced precision) is matched by the lyrical beauty of the *Largo* and the breadth and vigour of the finale. Perhaps the reading has not the individuality of the very finest versions, and the sound, although full, with a firm bass, becomes somewhat fierce in the treble under pressure. The climaxes of the outer movements and the big surges of tone which come at the centre of both the slow movement and the scherzo are rather explosive. Such a sense of artificial brilliance is unfortunate in a record which should have combined the best of both the old and new worlds.

It was a fascinating idea of RCA to record the veteran Stokowski in Dvořák's *New World symphony* and couple it with the LP transfer of his 1927 version. Certainly as an interpretation as well as technically the new version is the one to admire. In 1927 Stokowski was surprisingly fast, even perfunctory, in each movement. In every way the new one reveals more intensely the maestro's genius for moulding phrases and tempi, for pointing the drama of such music as this. There are one or two Stokowskian idiosyncrasies – trumpet trills at the end of the first movement, for example – and almost every repeat is omitted, but as a historic document of a great musician in his nineties it provides a warming experience. Sharp stereo separation and

particularly vivid reproduction of timpani and brass.

Karajan's HMV Berlin Philharmonic record (coupled with *Vltava*) dates from the earliest days of stereo. The recording still sounds amazingly vivid. It is somewhat dry in acoustic, although admirably clear and not without warmth or lustre. The interpretation is expressively romantic and not so different from Karajan's later DGG account; it is certainly distinctive as well as fresh and exciting. If the coupling appeals this might well be considered, although the later disc is to be preferred on interpretative grounds as well as recording quality.

Barbirolli achieves his memorable performance by the utmost simplicity of approach. Apart from an effective broadening at the ends of both the first and last movements there are no mannerisms of tempo. The first movement begins with great warmth, and the allegro unfolds dramatically with a well contrasted, gentle second subject and an electrifying tightening of the tension towards the end of the movement (an effect which is repeated with equal success in the finale). The *Largo* is sustained with unaffected beauty and the scherzo is notable for its woodwind colour and especially the delightful trills in the trio. At the beginning of the finale the strings sing out splendidly, and throughout, the orchestra – in spite of one or two moments of less than perfect ensemble – are obviously on their toes. The stereo recording is generally good, with only marginal touches of stridency at the loudest moments.

Alexander Gibson's account is fresh and immediate. It has a genuine spontaneity even if the playing itself – one thinks particularly of the cor anglais solo in the *Largo*, which is a trifle deadpan – has no special memorability. The recording is a modern one and, apart from an occasional grunt, is very good indeed. The attractive thing about this disc is the inclusion of the *Carnaval overture* in a vivacious and compelling performance, even better than the symphony.

Otto Gerdes is DGG's chief recording producer and has presided over many a Karajan session. Here he shows his considerable skill on the rostrum, and although the reading has no striking individuality the Berlin Philharmonic play beautifully for him. The *Largo* is especially fine, memorable for the warm orchestral playing, and the modern recording is excellent.

Sawallisch's approach is straightforward and without mannerisms. There is more poetry in the slow movement than he finds, but overall the orchestral playing is sensitive, and the conductor's conception consistent and well integrated. The stereo recording is excellent, and with a brilliant and idiomatic performance of *Carnaval* thrown in, this record is among the best buys in the lowest price-range.

CHAMBER AND INSTRUMENTAL MUSIC

Bagatelles (for 2 violins, cello and harmonium), *Op. 46* (see also under *String quartet No. 3*).
*** Philips 6500 453. Members of the Berlin Philharmonic Octet – BRAHMS: *Clarinet quintet.****

Dvořák wrote his *Bagatelles* for two violins, cello and harmonium for performance at the house of a critic who possessed no other keyboard instrument. They present a charming solution to a technical problem which Dvořák seems to solve with characteristic artlessness. They are not great music, but have enough haunting moments to make an unusual attractive coupling for a fine account of Brahms's *Clarinet quintet*.

Ballad in D minor, Op. 15; Humoresque in G major, Op. 101/7; Mazurek in E minor, Op. 49; Nocturne in B major, Op. 40; Romantic pieces, Op. 75;

Slavonic dance No. 2 Op. 46/2 (all for violin and piano); *Violin sonata in F major, Op. 57; Violin sonatina in G major, Op. 100*.
(M) ** Supraphon 1111 311/12. Josef Suk (violin), Alfred Holeček (piano).

Idiomatic performances, as one would expect from the composer's grandson and his accomplished partner. The *Sonata* and the *Sonatina* are both delightful pieces, and these artists have recorded them before. The sound quality stands in the way of an unqualified recommendation, but the music will more than reward perseverance.

Piano quartets Nos. 1 in D major, Op. 23; 2 in E flat major, Op. 87.
*** Philips 6500 452. Beaux Arts Trio with Walter Trampler (viola).
Piano quartet No. 2 in E flat major, Op. 87.
* (*) RCA SB 6884. Artur Rubinstein (piano), Guarneri Quartet.

These are delightfully inventive works and will give enormous pleasure to all music lovers. The playing on Philips is as fresh and spontaneous as the music itself, and given superlative engineering, with smooth, well-defined and admirably blended tone quality, the record is self-recommending. Rubinstein and the Guarneri Quartet are not so well recorded; the sound appears glaring, and although they observe the repeat, it is at the cost of giving us another work. The Beaux Arts sound far more relaxed than their glossier colleagues, and their disc is to be preferred on artistic as well as economic and technical grounds.

Piano quintet in A major, Op. 81.
(M) *** Decca Ace of Diamonds SDD 270. Clifford Curzon (piano), Vienna Philharmonic Quartet – SCHUBERT: *Quartettsatz.***

This wonderfully warm and lyrical performance of Dvořák's *Piano quintet* is among the most beautiful and satisfying of all chamber-music records. At Ace of Diamonds price it is an obvious bargain and the new transfer has lost none of the richness and glow of the original recording, which was one of Decca's very finest. Highly recommended.

(i) *Piano quintet in A major, Op. 81;*
(ii) *Piano trio No. 4 in E minor (Dumky), Op. 90.*
> (B) ** Turnabout TV 34075S. (i) György Sándor (piano), Berkshire Quartet; (ii) Dumka Trio.

The Turnabout performance is extracted from a (now deleted) Vox Box. It receives a fresh but not especially subtle reading. The recording is clear with a tendency for the top end of the audio spectrum to be stronger than the bottom. But with a brilliant and enjoyable *Dumky trio* as a coupling, this is a formidable bargain.

Piano trios Nos. 1 in B flat major, Op. 21; 2 in G minor, Op. 26.
> *** Philips LY 802 916. Beaux Arts Trio.

This was the last of the Philips set of Dvořák's *Piano trios* to be issued, and it is no less recommendable than its companions. The *G minor Trio* is a particularly fine one, with an eloquent and beautiful slow movement, but both are played here in the most compulsive way and the Philips recording is clear, full-toned and immediate.

Piano trio No. 3 in F minor, Op. 65.
> (M) ** Supraphon SUAST 50817. Suk Trio.

A committed and idiomatic performance of the *F minor Trio*, a work of great interest and quality written not long before the great *D minor Symphony*. The

sound is not as full in range or well defined as that on the Beaux Arts disc (now deleted) but the price difference is considerable.

Piano trio No. 4 in E minor (Dumky), Op. 90.
> (M) *** Supraphon 111 1089. Czech Trio, with Josef Páleníček (piano) – NOVÁK: *Trio*.***
> *** Philips LY 802 918. Beaux Arts Trio.

The Beaux Arts Trio play the *Dumky* with superb spirit, and their recording is remarkably realistic and truthful. Its imminent deletion, however, makes the Supraphon disc a strong contender for a first recommendation. The Czechs play with enormous commitment and find a little more in the music than do the Beaux Arts. Moreover, they are well recorded and offer an interesting fill-up in the shape of Novák's *Trio quasi una ballata*.

String quartet No. 2 in D minor, Op. 34.
> (M) ** (*) Supraphon SUAST 50529. Smetana Quartet – MARTINŮ: *String quartet No. 4*.**
String quartets Nos. 2 in D minor, Op. 34; 6 in F major (American), Op. 96.
> (M) *** Decca Ace of Diamonds SDD 250. Janáček Quartet.

The *D minor* is one of Dvořák's most inspired quartets, particularly the eloquent slow movement. The Smetana Quartet play superbly, and there is little to choose between their performance and that of the Janáčeks on Ace of Diamonds. However, the Decca recording has greater depth and definition than the Supraphon, and given the small price difference it is to be preferred unless the Martinu quartet is a strong attraction. The Janáček performance of the *American quartet* is equally fresh, the superb playing and fine ensemble ensuring that

343

the fast tempi chosen for the outer movements are exciting without the music sounding rushed. This is virtuosity of a high order put completely at the service of the composer.

String quartet No. 3 in E flat major, Op. 51; (i) Bagatelles for two violins, violoncello and harmonium, Op. 47.

(M) *** Supraphon SUAST 50463. Vlach Quartet, (i) with Miroslav Kampelsheimer (harmonium).

A warm and idiomatic account of one of Dvořák's most appealing quartets and an equally endearing performance of the delightful *Bagatelles*. No Dvořák-lover should overlook this issue; the recording is good.

String quartet No. 5 in E major, Op. 80; 2 Waltzes, Op. 54: Nos. 1 in A major; 4 in D major.

(M) ** Supraphon SUAST 50528. Dvořák Quartet.

Dvořák's *E major Quartet*, in spite of the misleading opus number, is a middle-period work, displaying a typical melodic lyricism and a firm grasp of formal design. If this is in no way a memorable work, like most of Dvořák's chamber music it is easily enjoyable. The two *Waltzes* are part of a cycle of piano pieces written in 1879–80. They are lightweight but attractive, if not so individually striking as the *Slavonic dances*. The performances are accomplished and spontaneous; the recording good if a little sharply focused (in both senses of the word) on the leader.

String quartet No. 6 in F major (American), Op. 96.

*** Philips SAL 3708. Italian Quartet – BORODIN: *Quartet No. 2.****

(B) *** Classics for Pleasure CFP 40041. Gabrieli Quartet – BORODIN: *Quartet No. 2.****

(B) ** Oryx EXP 30. Arriaga Quartet – BEETHOVEN: *Quartet No. 10.***

A predictably fine account of the *American quartet* from the Italians, splendidly recorded by the Philips engineers. Although the Gabrieli performance on Classics for Pleasure is not quite its equal, it is still a satisfying account, with an equally good coupling. At bargain price this is an outstanding issue. An attractive if restrained performance on Oryx, with emphasis on lyricism rather than excitement. But the quartet plays as a team, and the inner balance is good. The recording is warm to match the playing, and with a good coupling this disc is certainly value for money.

String quintet in G major, Op. 77.

(M) ** (*) Decca Ace of Diamonds SDD 423. Members of the Vienna Octet – SPOHR: *Piano and wind quintet.*** (*)

Despite its late opus number this is an early work: it is sometimes billed as Op. 18. Its inspiration is uneven but there is plenty to be found in the beautiful slow movement and in the vital finale. The Viennese players are especially sympathetic to the lyrical elements in the music. The first movement is warmly played, drama giving way to the music's expressive quality; the *Poco andante* is most beautiful, its drooping principal melodic phrase reminding one of Tchaikovsky. The scherzo lacks something in sparkle. It is not an easy movement to bring off, for although it has a dance-like quality it is by no means a furiant. The Viennese group catch the gaiety of the finale more readily, and with first-rate Decca sound this is enjoyable enough, even if one sometimes misses the authentic Czech lilt.

String quintet in E flat major, Op. 97; The Cypresses, Nos. 1, 2, 8, 9 and 11.

(M) ** Supraphon SUAST 50684. Augmented Dvořák Quartet.

String quintet in E flat major, Op. 97; String sextet in A major, Op. 48.

(M) ** (*) Decca Ace of Diamonds SDD 315. Members of the Vienna Octet.

(i) *String sextet in A major, Op. 48; Miniatures, Op. 75.*

(M) ** Supraphon SUAST 50824. Dvořák Quartet, (i) with members of the Vlach Quartet.

The Dvořák Quartet's performance of the splendid *E flat Quintet*, one of the greatest works of Dvořák's American period, is of high quality: the scherzo has notable character, while there is some fine solo playing in the *Largo*. The recording is basically warm and realistic, but there is a certain edge to the upper string tone. The coupling here is a hand-picked selection of some of the finest of Dvořák's *Cypresses*. Originally written as songs, the composer's literal transcriptions show the source of the material fairly obviously, but the music is attractively melodic, if with a touch of 'salon' style here and there. The last two pieces, the very quiet and pensive *Thou only dear one* and the quicksilver mood-changes of *Nature lies dreaming*, are charming miniatures.

The *Sextet*, Op. 48, was one of the works that served to establish Dvořák's name in England in the 1880s, and it is undoubtedly one of the Czech master's most spontaneous and flowing works. Of the two versions now available, the Decca has the stronger claims since it also offers one of his late masterpieces, the *E flat Quintet*. The Supraphon disc gives shorter measure and in any event is fairly elusive. The members of the Vienna Octet give eloquent performances and the recording, though not outstanding by Decca's high standards – the string tone could be more firmly focused – is still very good indeed.

PIANO MUSIC

3 Album leaves; Eclogues; Impromptu in G major; Pieces, Op. 52.

(M) ** (*) Supraphon 111 1395. Radoslav Kvapil (piano).

Dumka, Op. 35; 2 Furiants, Op. 42; 2 Minuets, Op. 28; Scottish dances, Op. 41; Theme and variations, Op. 36.

(M) ** (*) Supraphon 111 0862. Radoslav Kvapil (piano).

Humoresques Nos. 1–8, Op. 101; Mazurkas Nos. 1–6, Op. 57; No. 7 (from Supplement).

(M) ** Vox STGBY 674. Rudolf Firkusny (piano).

Humoresques Nos. 1–8, Op. 101; Suite in A major, Op. 98.

(M) ** (*) Supraphon 111 0865. Radoslav Kvapil (piano).

Poetic pictures, Op. 85, Nos. 1–13.

(M) ** (*) Supraphon 111 0566. Radoslav Kvapil (piano).

Poetic Pictures, Op. 85, Nos. 3, In the Old Castle; 6, Sorrowful Reverie; 9, Serenade; Silhouettes, Op. 8, Nos. 1–12; Theme and variations, Op. 36.

(M) ** Vox STGBY 672. Rudolf Firkusny (piano).

Silhouettes, Op. 8; Waltzes Op. 54.

(M) ** (*) Supraphon 111 0820. Radoslav Kvapil (piano).

Dvořák's piano music is not as widely known as his chamber music; nor is it as good. The composer was a formidable sight-reader and a highly musical but not a great pianist. Many of the works recorded in Kvapil's survey are pleasing rather than memorable. The *Silhouettes* will give pleasure to those who know the first two symphonies, for they use some of the same thematic material. Even though the recording could be richer, it is still to be preferred to the series on which Firkusny has embarked for Vox, although Kvapil is not quite the artist that Firkusny is.

Kvapil's account of the *Silhouettes* is in any event the one to have, and it is coupled with the delightful *Waltzes*, Op. 54. This is the record with which to start, for it can hardly fail to delight the true Dvořákian. The *A major Suite* is delightful too and readers not intending to collect the whole series will probably find that 1110 820 and 1110 865 will give them a fair taste of Dvořák's output in this medium at a very reasonable cost. Others of course will want the lot; Dvořák is rarely less than endearing though the inspiration in some of the shorter pieces is distinctly variable. Kvapil is a faithful guide through this terrain and although the recordings are not the last word in brilliance, they are eminently acceptable.

Of the two Firkusny collections, the first is worth investigating for the *Silhouettes* and for the admirable set of *Variations*, Op. 36. Firkusny slightly overpedals at times but in all other respects his playing is characteristically distinguished. The second collection (STGBY 674) is rather more successful. The pieces are all worth getting to know and are far from wanting in variety of feeling or quality of invention. The great Czech pianist is in good form though some may find that he again overpedals at times (this may well be accentuated by the recording balance). The sound quality is far from first-class, but the disc is to be recommended for the sake of the repertoire.

Slavonic dances Nos. 1–8, Op. 46.
　* (*) Decca SXL 6389. Bracha Eden and Alexander Tamir (piano duet) – BRAHMS: *Hungarian dances.** (*)
Slavonic dances, Nos. 1–16, Op. 46/1–8, Op. 72/1–8.
　(B) *** Turnabout TV 34060S. Alfred Brendel and Walter Klien (piano duet).*

On Turnabout polished and affectionate playing. Both pianists show a real feeling for the style of the music and there will be many who find that the music sounds fresher on the piano than it does on the orchestra. The acoustic here is a little over-reverberant but the sound itself is good and the Decca pressings are a vast improvement on the original. Not to be played all at once, but taken in sections this is very enjoyable indeed.

As with the Brahms coupling, the playing of Eden and Tamir is brilliant but inflexible. There is not enough relaxed warmth or sparkle, and the players do not convey their own enjoyment, an essential in this music.

VOCAL AND CHORAL MUSIC

Biblical songs, Op. 99 (complete recording); *I Dreamed Last Night; Songs My Mother Taught Me.*
　(M) ** Supraphon SUAST 50898. Vera Soukupová (contralto), Ivan Moravec (piano).

These are committed performances of the *Biblical songs* – there is no other complete recording currently in the catalogue – and although not all of them are masterpieces, they could not be more eloquently sung than they are here. The recording is a little resonant, perhaps, but by no means unserviceable.

Biblical songs, Op. 99 Nos. 1–5; Mass in D major, Op. 86; Psalm 149, Op. 79; Te Deum, Op. 103.
　(M) ** Supraphon MS 0981/2. Soloists, Czech Philharmonic Chorus, Prague Symphony Orchestra, Václav Smetáček.

A useful compilation. The *Te Deum*, a delightful work (not otherwise available), is full of a Haydnesque joy in life and a charming rusticity. This is music that glows from the page. The *D major Mass* is of course available in its original form (chorus and organ) on Preston's admirable Argo record: it is here recorded in the orchestral version on which Dvořák's publishers insisted. There are no alternative versions of this or *Psalm 149*, and although the acoustic is a little over-resonant, the set must be recommended. It also includes the first five of the *Biblical songs*, which Soukupová has recorded complete.

Mass in D major, Op. 86.
*** Argo ZRG 781. Christ Church Cathedral Choir, Oxford, Simon Preston.

Dvořák's *D major Mass* is also available in the two-disc Supraphon set (see above), and on an Abbey record (ABM 18), which offers a bigger, more robust choir and style of performance. This is quite good, but does not match the fine performance and recording that we have here from Oxford. The *Mass* was originally scored for small forces, and this version presents it in its original form. It was finished in 1887, a year or two before the *G major Symphony*, and though not a major work by any means, it has many delights to offer. In such a beautifully shaped reading, and given such impeccable recording, the disc is self-recommending.

Requiem, Op. 89 (complete recording).
*** Decca SET 416/7. Pilar Lorengar (soprano), Erszébet Komlóssy (contralto), Robert Ilosfalvy (tenor), Tom Krause (baritone), Ambrosian Singers, London Symphony Orchestra, Istvan Kertesz.

The *Requiem* reflects the impact of the English musical world of the day on Dvořák and has a good deal of relatively conventional writing in it. However, no Dvořák work is wholly conventional, and given such fervent advocacy the work cannot fail to make its maximum effect. Kertesz conducts with a total commitment to the score and secures from both singers and orchestra an alert and sensitive response. Pilar Lorengar's vibrato is at times a trifle disturbing but it is the only solo performance that is likely to occasion any reserve. The recording matches the performance: it has a splendid weight and sonority and a life-like balance. The recording certainly outclasses the DGG which was available at one time, and readers who are attracted by the work can rest assured that any new version will have to be very good indeed to equal this.

The Spectre's Bride (cantata), Op. 69.
(M) ** Supraphon SUAST 50381/2. Drahomira Tikalová (soprano), Beno Blachut (tenor), Ladislav Mráz (bass-baritone), Czech Singers Chorus, Czech Philharmonic Orchestra, Jaroslav Krombholc.

For *The Spectre's Bride*, a cantata commissioned for the Birmingham Festival, Dvořák chose a typical nineteenth-century subject, a folk legend of a man risen from the grave to claim his promised bride. Dvořák was not really the composer to write horror music on a large scale, but with a red-blooded performance in Czech (so avoiding the Victorian infelicities of the English text) there is much to enjoy. Blachut at the time of the recording was at his peak, but it is a pity that a more youthful voice was not chosen for the heroine: Tikalová is heavy and wobbly. Variable recording.

COLLECTION

'*Greatest hits*': (i) *Carnaval overture, Op. 92*. (ii) *Humoresque* (arr. Harris). (iii) *Serenade for strings in E major,*

Op. 22: Waltz. (iv) Slavonic dances Nos. 1 in C major, Op. 46/1; 8 in G minor, Op. 46/8. (iii) Songs My Mother Taught Me. (iv) Symphony No. 7 in D minor, Op. 70: Scherzo. (ii) Symphony No. 9 in E minor (New World), Op. 95: Largo.

(B) ** CBS Harmony 30012. (i) New York Philharmonic Orchestra, Leonard Bernstein; (ii) Philadelphia Orchestra, Eugene Ormandy; (iii) Orchestra, André Kostelanetz; (iv) Cleveland Orchestra, George Szell.

We are offered the brilliant, extrovert Dvořák of the Slavonic dances and Carnaval overture on side one, with Szell and Bernstein in good form, and on side two the lyrical aspect of the composer. This makes quite a good anthology, and the disc ends cleverly with the attractive scherzo from the Seventh Symphony, given the right rhythmic pointing by Szell. The recording throughout is bright, with only a tendency to hardness in the dances and the overture.

Eaton, John
(born 1935)

Concert piece for synket and orchestra.
(B) ** Turnabout TV 34428S. Dallas Symphony Orchestra, Donald Johanos – BERGSMA: Violin concerto***; SUBOTNIK: Lamination.(**)

The synket is an electronic instrument and this work sets its sound patterns against a conventional orchestra. The result is in no way memorable, but the disc is worth having for the fine Bergsma Violin concerto which is the main coupling.

Electronic music

BERIO, Luciano: (i) Thema Omaggio a Joyce (Homage to Joyce). DRUCKMAN, Jacob: (ii) Animus 1. MIMAROGLU, Ilhan: (iii) Piano music for performer and composer; (iv) Preludes for magnetic tape.

(B) * (*) Turnabout TV 34177S. Includes: (i) the voice of Cathy Berberian; (ii) André Smith (trombone); (iii) George Flynn (piano); (iv) in Prelude XII the voice of Güngor Bozkurt.

Berio's electronic fantasy, developed from taped sounds of Cathy Berberian reading, is one of the most genuinely imaginative examples of the genre, but the other works here – all of them substantially longer – are more doubtful quantities. The first Mimaroglu piece involves extemporization by a pianist which in turn is developed electronically, and the interaction of direct and electronic sound is a vital element in his preludes too.

BERIO, Luciano: Visage (for magnetic tape, based on the voice of Cathy Berberian and electronic sounds). CAGE, John: Fontana Mix (a realization of the version for magnetic tape alone). MIMAROGLU, Ilhan: Agony (visual study No. 4, after Arshile Gorky).

(B) ** Turnabout TV 34046S.

Cornelius Cardew, our own British avant-gardiste, is quoted on the sleeve as saying that there seems to be a sense of logic and cohesion in Cage's indeterminate music. 'The logic', Cage replied, 'was not put there by me.' He can say that again. Even so, a record like this of highly experimental music does give the average listener an excellent chance to work hard at this apparently impossible music. Whether in fact with indeterminate music there is any purpose in having an utterly fixed performance on record is a question that the avant-gardistes will have to sort out, but that philosophical point need hardly worry anyone else. The Cage is the most interesting of the pieces here, a sort of musical equivalent of a *collage*, with voices, whistling, dog-barking superimposed in wild array. What it all means is anyone's guess, but perhaps one should not take it too seriously.

WILSON, Olly: *Cetus*. HELLERMANN: *Ariel*. RUDNIK, Eugeniusz: *Dixi*. SMILEY, Pril: *Eclipse*. MAZUREK, Bodham: *Bozzetti*. MALOVEC, Josef: *Orthogenesis*.

(B) * (*) Turnabout TV 34301S.

These are student works chosen from over a hundred entries for an electronic music competition held in 1968 at Hanover, New Hampshire. Most of the items show promise and a striking command of the medium, but no great potential electronic composer seems revealed here.

Elgar, Edward
(1857–1934)

Collection: *3 Bavarian dances, Op. 27; Chanson de Matin; Chanson de Nuit, Op. 15/1 and 2; The Wand of Youth suites Nos. 1 and 2, Op. 1a and b* (complete recording).

*** HMV ASD 2356. London Philharmonic Orchestra, Sir Adrian Boult.

Sir Adrian's performances of the *Wand of Youth* music catch both the innocence and the intimacy of this very personal music. The fragile charm of the delicate scoring is well realized and there is plenty

of schoolboy gusto for the rollicking *Wild Bear* (only playfully wild, of course). The orchestral playing is first-rate and carries through the conductor's obvious affection to the listener. The excellent recording is only just short of EMI's highest standard; occasionally there might have been more inner transparency, and the reverberation has not been perfectly calculated to prevent the roisterous scoring for *Wild Bear* becoming a fraction noisy. The string tone, however, is very beautiful. It is a pity that, instead of the admittedly attractive salon pieces, we were not given a full version of the *Bavarian dances*, with chorus.

Collection: *'The miniature Elgar': Bavarian dance No. 2; Beau Brummel: Minuet; Chanson de Matin; Dream Children, Op. 43/1 and 2; Nursery suite; The Serious Doll; The Starlight Express* (incidental music): (i) *Organ Grinder's songs: My Old Tunes; To the Children; The Wand of Youth suites* excerpts: *Serenade; Sun dance; The Tame Bear.*

*** HMV CSD 1555. Royal Philharmonic Orchestra, Lawrance Collingwood, (i) with Frederick Harvey (baritone).

Inspired by the *Monitor* film on Elgar's life, this wholly delightful anthology collects together some of the composer's most attractive contributions in the lighter field, including several of those fragile and nostalgic little portraits which give the *Nursery* and *Wand of Youth* suites their special character. Frederick Harvey joins the orchestra for two *Organ Grinder's songs* written as incidental music for *The Starlight Express*. These are splendidly alive, with as much interest in the orchestra as in the stirringly melodic vocal line. Throughout this very well recorded collection the orchestral playing under Lawrance Collingwood is especially sympathetic, and the programme as a whole has been cleverly planned to make a highly enjoyable concert in itself.

Collection: *Caractacus, Op. 35: Introduction; Woodland interlude;* (i) *Triumphal march;* (i) *Coronation march, Op. 65* (1911); *Crown of India suite, Op. 66; Imperial march, Op. 32;* (i) *The Light of Life, Op. 29: Meditation.*

*** HMV ASD 2672. Royal Liverpool Philharmonic Orchestra, Sir Charles Groves, (i) with Noel Rawsthorne (organ).

This is a feast for Elgarians. It is a fascinating piece of information (provided by Michael Kennedy on the sleeve) that a theme from the *Coronation march* of 1911 had its source in a projected Rabelais cantata: and other themes have been tracked down to equally surprising places in Elgar's sketchbooks. What matters is that the results give enormous musical pleasure, expanding not in mere jingoism but in genuinely ripe splendour. One does not have to be an imperialist to enjoy any of these occasional pieces, and it is interesting to find the patriotic music coming up fresher than the little interlude from *The Light of Life*, beautiful as that is. The *Triumphal march* from *Caractacus* makes one hope for a complete recording of this major cantata before long. Fine rich recording, and superb swagger from Groves and the Liverpool Orchestra.

Collection: *Caractacus, Op. 34: Triumphal march; Carillon, Op. 75; Dream Children, Op. 43/1 and 2; Elegy for strings, Op. 58; Grania and Diarmid, Op. 42; Funeral march; The Light of Life, Op. 29: Meditation; Polonia, Op. 76; Funeral march* (Chopin, orch. Elgar).

** (*) HMV ASD 3050. London

Philharmonic Orchestra, Sir Adrian Boult.

The main interest here is provided by two pieces Elgar wrote at the beginning of the First World War as a gesture to help refugees from Belgium and Poland. The *Carillon*, written for 'gallant little Belgium', is rather effective and one can imagine its success at the time; the *Polonia* has character too, and both show the composer's flair for flag-waving orchestral sounds. The rest of the programme, although it displays a good sprinkling of Elgarian fingerprints, is uneven in quality and does not seem to fire Sir Adrian to his more persuasive advocacy. Even the *Dream Children* seem on the cool side, although some will undoubtedly like the restraint which Boult provides. The orchestration of Chopin's *Funeral march* is moderately effective. Excellent recording throughout.

Collection: *'The lighter Elgar': Carissima; Contrasts (The gavotte, A.D. 1700 and 1900); May song; Mazurka, Op. 10/1; Mina; Minuet, Op. 21;* (i) *Romance for bassoon and orchestra; Rosemary (That's for remembrance); Sérénade lyrique; Sérénade mauresque, Op. 10/2; Sevillana, Op. 7.*

*** HMV ASD 2638. Northern Sinfonia Orchestra, Neville Marriner, (i) with Michael Chapman (bassoon).

The best of Elgar's light music has a gentle delicacy of texture, and as often as not a touch of melancholy, which is irresistible to nearly all Elgarians. Not everything here is on the very highest level of invention, but all the music is pleasing and a good deal of it is delightful for its tender moods and restrained scoring, favouring flute, bassoon, and the clarinet in middle or lower register. A boisterous piece like *Sevillana* may be rather conventional, but it has Elgar's characteristic exuberance, which represents the other side of the coin. The most distinguished item here is the rhapsodic *Romance for bassoon and orchestra*, but the whole programme offers quiet enjoyment and is just the thing for the late evening. It is played with style and affection by the Northern Sinfonia under Neville Marriner, and HMV have provided that warm, glowing orchestral sound that is their special province for Elgar's music.

'Favourites': Chanson de Matin; Chanson de Nuit, Op. 15/1 and 2; Cockaigne overture, Op. 40; Imperial march, Op. 32; Pomp and Circumstance marches Nos. 1 and 4, Op. 39; Salut d'Amour, Op. 12.

** Polydor 2383 155. Bournemouth Symphony Orchestra, George Hurst.

George Hurst creates vigorous, strong performances, and *Cockaigne* is played with notable gusto. The salon pieces are used to provide contrast, but essentially it is the pomp and circumstance one remembers at the close of this collection. The recording has a fine impact and is brilliant to suit Hurst's forcefulness, but the acoustic is rather dry and there is a lack of resonance in the deep bass, even when Elgar adds an organ to the orchestra.

Cockaigne overture, Op. 40; Falstaff (symphonic study), *Op. 40.*

*** CBS 76284. London Philharmonic Orchestra, Daniel Barenboim.

Cockaigne overture, Op. 40; Froissart (concert overture), *Op. 19; In the South (Alassio), Op. 50; Overture in D minor* (Handel, arr. Elgar).

** (*) HMV ASD 2822. London Philharmonic Orchestra, Sir Adrian Boult.

Cockaigne overture, Op. 40; Variations on an original theme (Enigma), Op. 36.

*** HMV ASD 548. Philharmonia Orchestra, Sir John Barbirolli.

** Philips SAL 3516. London Symphony Orchestra, Colin Davis.

Elgar's picture of London in *Cockaigne* is of course an Edwardian one, but little of the scenery has changed; the military bands and the Salvation Army are still there, and if the lovers in the park today are more uninhibited, they should not be disappointed with Barbirolli's warmth in their music. Indeed, Barbirolli, himself a Londoner, paints an extremely vivid picture and HMV's splendid recording does Elgar's richly painted canvas real justice. The climaxes are exciting, and the whole piece moves forward with a sweep worthy of the greatest city in the world. Barbirolli's reading of the *Enigma variations* is no less satisfying. It has great richness and warmth, and is superbly played and recorded, and especially in the variations where the strings are given their head, the music could have no more eloquent advocate. This is one of Barbirolli's very finest discs.

Boult's unique insight into the problems of Elgar interpretation is characteristically illustrated in his record of overtures. Though other Elgarians may be more ripely romantic, Boult with his incisiveness is both dramatic and noble. The recording – not quite consistent between items – is rich and atmospheric. It is good to have the Handel arrangement included as a makeweight.

Barenboim's view of *Falstaff* could hardly provide a stronger contrast to Boult's (see below). Rarely even under the composer has the story-telling element in the music been so captivatingly presented. Barenboim's habit in Elgar of moulding the music in flexible tempi, of underlining romantic expressiveness, has never on record been so convincing as here, where the big contrasts of texture, dynamic and mood are played for all they are worth. The Gadshill episode with its ambush is so vivid one can see the picture in one's mind's eye. *Cockaigne* also is given a colourful reading and though the recording is not ideally balanced, this is certainly the finest of the Barenboim Elgar series.

Davis's reading of the *Enigma variations* is in the main a traditional one, with each variation carefully shaped, and really first-rate playing from the LSO throughout. In *Cockaigne*, however, the conductor is more wilful in his choice of tempi, and this is less evocative than it can be. The Philips recording is good but only good. The snag is that this record comes into competition with Barbirolli's superb disc for HMV, which features the same coupling but with readings that are altogether riper.

Violin concerto in B minor, Op. 61.
> ** (*) HMV ASD 2259. Yehudi Menuhin (violin), New Philharmonia Orchestra, Sir Adrian Boult.
> ** HMV ASD 2883. Hugh Bean (violin), Royal Liverpool Philharmonic Orchestra, Sir Charles Groves.

It was an invidious task for Menuhin to try to remake what is one of the most famous gramophone recordings ever. It was in 1932 that young Master Menuhin played the solo part in this work with the composer himself conducting, and it took over thirty years for Menuhin to be persuaded back to do it again. In the event one has to admit that in the first two movements at least much of the magic is less than it was. The poise of the violin's first entry and the sweetness of tone in the elegiac slow movement are not quite as they were, but the finale – longer than the other two movements and the most difficult to keep together – is stronger and more confident than it was. The long-breathed musings of the violin in the

accompanied cadenza have a wonderful intensity, and throughout the work, Boult conducts with the warmest Elgarian understanding. Warm atmospheric recording to match.

Those for whom Menuhin's lapses in technique provide too many uncomfortable moments may find a satisfactory alternative in the performance by Hugh Bean, authoritatively conducted by Sir Charles Groves and superbly recorded. There is no question about Bean's technical assurance or his sympathy for the work; equally there is no doubt that he is much less successful than Menuhin in sustaining the tension of his performance. One's initial disappointment comes with the first movement's second subject, which is beautifully played but sounds somehow too slight and insubstantial. The full beauty of the slow movement is only patchily conveyed, but the finale is rather more successful, with some fine moments.

Violoncello concerto in E minor, Op. 85.
> ⊛*** HMV ASD 655. Jacqueline du Pré (cello), London Symphony Orchestra, Sir John Barbirolli – *Sea Pictures.****
> *** HMV ASD 2764. Jacqueline du Pré (cello), London Symphony Orchestra, Sir John Barbirolli – DELIUS: *Cello concerto.****

(i) *Violoncello concerto in E minor, Op. 85; Introduction and allegro for strings, Op. 47; Serenade for strings in E minor, Op. 20.*
> *** HMV ASD 2906. (i) Paul Tortelier (cello); London Philharmonic Orchestra, Sir Adrian Boult.

(i) *Violoncello concerto in E minor, Op. 85; Variations on an original theme (Enigma), Op. 36.*
> (B) ** Pye GSGC 15005. (i) André Navarra (cello); Hallé Orchestra, Sir John Barbirolli.

It was in the Elgar *Cello concerto* that Jacqueline du Pré first won world recognition, and this record gives a wonderful idea of how so young a girl captured such attention and even persuaded the Americans to listen enraptured to Elgar. Du Pré is essentially a spontaneous artist. No two performances by her are exactly alike, and wisely Barbirolli at the recording sessions encouraged her above all to express emotion through the notes. The style is freely rhapsodic. The tempi, long-breathed in first and third movements, are allowed still more elbow-room when du Pré's expressiveness requires it, and in the slow movement, brief and concentrated, her 'inner' intensity conveys a depth of expressiveness rarely achieved by any cellist on record. Brilliant virtuoso playing too in scherzo and finale. The original apt coupling with the *Sea Pictures* has now been joined by an alternative choice: a unique version of the Delius *Cello concerto*, written at very much the same period and performed by Jacqueline du Pré in her first major recording session.

Tortelier gives a noble and restrained performance of the Elgar which will appeal to those who feel that Jacqueline du Pré wears her heart a little too much on her sleeve in this work, marvellous though her playing is. Boult accompanies with splendid tact and on the reverse side gives committed and finely recorded accounts of the *Introduction and allegro* and the *Serenade for strings*. The recording has splendid breadth and range, detail is well defined and vivid, and the balance admirably judged.

Navarra's is a strong and firm view, and with his control of phrasing and his wide range of tone-colour, the performance culminates in a most moving account of the Epilogue. Only the scherzo falls short – slower than usual and not completely assured – but Navarra manages the virtuoso passages of the finale with reliable intonation. Barbirolli's view of *Enigma* as ever is rich and red-blooded,

not as polished as his later HMV, but enjoyable.

Crown of India suite, Op. 66; Imperial march, Op. 32; Pomp and Circumstance marches, Op. 39, Nos. 1 in D major; 2 in A minor; 3 in C minor; 4 in G major; 5 in C major.

** CBS 77248. London Philharmonic Orchestra, Daniel Barenboim.

Barenboim is never less than interesting in these readings of Elgar's ceremonial music, well coupled, but his judgement is not infallible. His tempi are surprisingly fast (though Elgar's own tended to be fast too), and not all Elgarians will approve his updating of Edwardian majesty. If only the recording were richer, the interpretations would emerge more convincingly than they do.

(i) *Elegy for strings, Op. 58; Froissart overture, Op. 19; Pomp and Circumstance marches, Op. 39, Nos.* (ii) *1 in D major;* (i) *2 in A minor; 3 in C minor;* (ii) *4 in G major;* (i) *5 in C major;* (i) *Sospiri, Op. 70.*

*** HMV ASD 2292. (i) New Philharmonia; (ii) Philharmonia Orchestra; Sir John Barbirolli.

The HMV disc puts the five marches complete on one side, and a very good suite they make, with plenty of contrast in Nos. 2 and 3 to offset the Edwardian bombast of 1 and 4. The splendid *nobilmente* of No. 5 closes the disc in rousing fashion. Barbirolli is obviously determined not to overdo the patriotism, and the crisp studio recording suits this fresh approach. The sound is brilliant, but on side two one notices that the recording of the string pieces offers more warmth in the middle range. The *Elegy* shows Barbirolli at his gentle best; *Sospiri* is contrastingly passionate, and the side concludes with the early concert overture

353

Froissart. Here the orchestral links with Brahms are strong, but the fingerprints of the Elgar to emerge later are everywhere, and if the piece is loose in structure it has a striking main theme.

Elegy for strings, Op. 58; Introduction and allegro for strings, Op. 47; Serenade for strings in E minor, Op. 20; Sospiri, Op. 70; The Spanish Lady: suite (ed. Young).

** (*) Argo ZRG 573. Academy of St Martin-in-the-Fields, Neville Marriner.

At first hearing Marriner's interpretations of these Elgar works sound strangely unidiomatic. They grow on one – even the somewhat stiff manner of the *Introduction and allegro* – and the subtlety and strength of Marriner's unique band of string players are never in doubt. The disc is valuable for Elgarians in including the brief snippets arranged by Percy Young from Elgar's unfinished opera *The Spanish Lady*, but musically they have little substance. But what musical riches in all the rest – reflection of the composer's lifelong understanding of string tone.

Falstaff (symphonic study), *Op. 68* (see also under *Cockaigne*).

(B) ****** Pye GSGC 14059. London Philharmonic Orchestra, Sir Adrian Boult – BRITTEN: *Peter Grimes: 4 sea interludes and Passacaglia.***

(i) *Falstaff* (symphonic study), *Op. 68;* (ii) *Froissart overture, Op. 19;* (iii) *Introduction and allegro for strings, Op. 47.*

*** HMV ASD 2762. (i) Hallé Orchestra; (ii) New Philharmonia Orchestra; (iii) Sinfonia of London, Allegri String Quartet; Sir John Barbirolli.

Falstaff (symphonic study), *Op. 68; The Sanguine Fan* (ballet), *Op. 81.*

Fantasia and fugue in C minor (Bach, trans. Elgar), *Op. 86.*

*** HMV ASD 2970. London Philharmonic Orchestra, Boult.

Boult treats *Falstaff* essentially as a symphonic structure. As far as one can, one tends to forget that this is programme music, and the result is musically invigorating, for this is one of Elgar's most masterly scores. It follows that some of the mystery, some of the delicate sense of atmosphere that impregnates the interludes for example, is under-characterized. But the crispness of the playing and Boult's unfailing alertness amply compensate for that. Outstandingly good recording. The Bach transcription and the little-known score written for a ballet during the First World War make unexpected and richly enjoyable fill-ups.

Ripe and expansive, Barbirolli's view of *Falstaff* is wonderfully colourful and convincing. It appeared originally as a fill-up to the *Second Symphony* in its two-disc version, but here is obviously better coupled. Though the recordings are of different vintage, they are all impressive even by today's standards.

Boult's Pye recording dates from the earliest days of stereo, when it originally appeared on two sides of a 10-inch LP. The later transfer to one side of a 12-inch was managed successfully, and the sound if not of the most modern is well-balanced. Boult's literal account of the score makes obviously less impact here than in his HMV version which has much richer recording.

In making a choice for *Falstaff*, Barenboim's account for CBS (see under *Cockaigne*) should also be considered, for its programmatic approach is fascinatingly different from that of either Barbirolli or Boult.

In the South (Alassio) (concert overture), *Op. 50.*

*** HMV ASD 2370. Bournemouth Symphony Orchestra, Constantin

Silvestri – VAUGHAN WILLIAMS: *Tallis fantasia etc.****

A really stunning performance of *In the South*, given one of EMI's most spectacular and satisfying recordings, from the first groove to the last. Silvestri knits the work's structure together more convincingly than one would have believed possible, and the strong forward momentum does not prevent the Italian sunshine (seen through English eyes) bringing a Mediterranean glow to the gentler, atmospheric pages of the score. But it is the virile opening and closing sections which Silvestri makes especially compelling, and at the same time he shows the music's parallel with the style of Richard Strauss. It was not a coincidence that the composer of *Don Juan* found an affinity with the bursting melodic fervour which was a dominant part of Elgar's musical personality, and which is so exhilarating here. The Bournemouth Orchestra offers playing of a virtuoso order and the same absolute commitment which distinguishes Silvestri's direction.

Introduction and allegro for strings, Op. 47 (see also under *Violoncello concerto; Elegy; Falstaff*).

** (*) Decca SXL 6405. English Chamber Orchestra, Benjamin Britten (with *Concert* ***).
** RCA Victrola VICS 1540. Boston Symphony Orchestra, Charles Munch – BARBER: *Adagio;* TCHAIKOVSKY: *Serenade.***
Introduction and allegro for strings, Op. 47; Serenade for strings in E minor, Op. 20.

⊛ *** HMV ASD 521. Sinfonia of London, Allegri String Quartet, Sir John Barbirolli – VAUGHAN WILLIAMS: *Tallis fantasia etc.****
Introduction and allegro for strings, Op. 47; Variations on an original theme (Enigma), Op. 36.

(B) ** Classics for Pleasure CFP 40022. London Philharmonic Orchestra, Sir Adrian Boult.

Barbirolli's passionate lyricism plus exceptionally fine string playing from the London Sinfonia provide here quite outstanding and definitive performances of two of Elgar's masterpieces. The EMI stereo is fully worthy of the playing, and this is a record not to be missed. On really first-rate reproducing equipment this disc offers remarkable realism and tonal beauty in the matter of string timbre.

Like Neville Marriner's account of the *Introduction and allegro* on Argo, Britten's is not idiomatic, but then as a fellow creator he provides a slant that is interesting for its own sake, and in any case secures the richest, most committed playing from the ECO strings. Characteristically Britten marks out the geography of the work more clearly than usual, but departs from his generally brisk manner for a gloriously romantic interpretation of the 'Welsh' tune. One would like to hear him conducting one of the symphonies. A valuable item in an outstanding disc superbly recorded.

Boult's earliest stereo account of the *Enigma variations* is enjoyable enough if seeming a little undercharacterized. This is partly caused by the recording, which is vivid and clear but lacking in richness and atmosphere. Even so, if the coupling is suitable this is quite a good bargain, for the performance of the *Introduction and allegro*, athletic and strong rather than indulgent, is very successful.

From Munch a fine performance on a worthwhile bargain disc. The reading has character and is surprisingly idiomatic.

King Arthur (incidental music): *suite;* (i) *The Starlight Express, Op. 78: suite.*

** (*) Polydor 2383 224. Bournemouth Sinfonietta, George Hurst,

(i) with Cynthia Glover (soprano), John Lawrenson (baritone).

The *King Arthur suite* is put together from incidental music that Elgar wrote in 1923 – well after his creative urge had fallen away – for a pageant-like play by Laurence Binyon. Though not great at all, it is full of surging, enjoyable ideas and makes an interesting novelty on record. *The Starlight Express suite* is similarly taken from music Elgar wrote in the First World War for a children's play, very much from the same world as the *Wand of Youth suites*, with a song or two included. Though the singers here are not ideal interpreters, the enthusiasm of Hurst and the Sinfonietta is well caught, particularly in the *King Arthur suite*. The recording is atmospheric if rather over-reverberant.

Nursery suite; Grania and Diarmid, Op. 42: Funeral march; Severn suite, Op. 87 (orchestral version).

*** HMV ASD 2502. Royal Liverpool Philharmonic Orchestra, Sir Charles Groves.

It is good to have Charles Groves on record conducting his own orchestra in music that he understands warmly. Both the *Nursery suite* (written for the Princesses Elizabeth and Margaret Rose) and the *Severn suite* (originally written for a brass-band contest and later orchestrated for full symphony orchestra) come from Elgar's very last period, when his inspiration came in flashes rather than as a sustained searchlight. The completely neglected *Funeral march* was written in 1901 for a play by W. B. Yeats and George Moore and provides more substantial fare: a splendid piece. Good recording, fine performances.

Pomp and Circumstance marches, Op. 39, Nos. 1 in D major; 2 in A minor; 3 in C minor; 4 in G major; 5 in C major (see also under *Elegy*).

(M) ** Decca Ace of Diamonds SDD 255. London Symphony Orchestra, Sir Arthur Bliss – BLISS: *Things to Come.***

Sir Arthur Bliss shows himself an admirable conductor for this music. He plays the marches with rumbustious vigour, yet preserves a sense of style so that the *nobilmente* is never cheapened. The recording is bright and crisp, with rather less sonority than the original.

Pomp and Circumstance marches, Op. 39, Nos. 1–5 (complete)*; Variations on an original theme (Enigma), Op. 36.*

(B) *** Contour 2870 440. Royal Philharmonic Orchestra, Norman Del Mar.

In the *Enigma variations* Del Mar comes closer than any other conductor to the responsive rubato style of Elgar himself, who directed an unforgettable performance on record in 1926. Like the composer, Del Mar uses the fluctuations to point the emotional message of the work with wonderful power and spontaneity, and the RPO play superbly. Recorded in Guildford Cathedral with plentiful reverberation, this version has the advantage of a splendid contribution from the organ at the end. The five *Pomp and Circumstance marches* on the reverse are given Prom-style performances full of flair and urgency. At bargain price this is a record not to be missed.

Serenade for strings in E minor, Op. 20 (see also under *Violoncello concerto; Elegy; Introduction and allegro*).

*** HMV ASD 2830. Sinfonia of London, Sir John Barbirolli – ARENSKY: *Variations on a theme of Tchaikovsky*; R. STRAUSS: *Metamorphosen.****

(M) ** HMV SXLP 30126. Philharmonia Orchestra, Sir Malcolm Sargent – HOLST: *Beni Mora; St*

Paul's suite; WARLOCK: *Capriol suite.***

Barbirolli's fine performance is beautifully recorded, and if the couplings are attractive this record is unreservedly recommended. Sargent's couplings are equally enterprising and his is a characteristically well-made reading, without the individuality of Barbirolli's (or Marriner's – which is also available complete on an excellent bargain sampler disc, *The World of the Academy, Volume 2*, Argo SPA/A 163) but well recorded.

Symphony No. 1 in A flat major, Op. 55.

⊛ *** Decca SXL 6569. London Philharmonic Orchestra, Sir Georg Solti.

** (*) Lyrita SRCS 39. London Philharmonic Orchestra, Sir Adrian Boult.

** (*) HMV ASD 2748. Philharmonia Orchestra, Sir John Barbirolli.

** (*) CBS 76247. London Philharmonic Orchestra, Daniel Barenboim.

(B) ** Pye GSGC 15022. Hallé Orchestra, Sir John Barbirolli.

No work of Elgar's more completely captures the atmosphere of uninhibited opulence which his generation of composers was the last to enjoy. Elgar, unlike composers after him, did not have to apologize for writing a symphony nearly an hour long, nor for writing tunes of a warmth and memorability that are strikingly his.

Before Solti recorded the Elgar *First* he made a searching study of the composer's own 78 recording, and the modifications of detailed markings implicit in that are reproduced here, not with a sense of calculation but with very much the same rich, committed qualities that mark out the Elgar performance. Solti even more

than in Mahler seems freed from emotional inhibition, with every climax superbly thrust home and the hushed intensity of the glorious slow movement captured on record as never before. The recording is of demonstration quality, rich but refined too, and rightly Decca ensured that the important link between the second and third movements comes in mid-side, even though that makes for a very long second side. A superlative disc in every way.

The enterprise of Lyrita must be welcomed in presenting Boult's unique interpretations of the Elgar symphonies in modern recordings. The sad thing is that at the time the LPO was not in the form it went on to achieve within a few months, and Sir Adrian was persuaded by the recording manager to have all the violins on the left – previously unheard-of in a Boult performance. The sessions in consequence were not the most carefree and enjoyable, and that is reflected in this gloriously warmhearted music in a degree of reserve.

Barbirolli's HMV disc too has the advantage of modern recording; the Philharmonia playing is more polished than the Hallé's on the old Pye issue, and it is a pity about the very slow tempo for the first movement. The main allegro after the slow march introduction should surge along, and instead there is a hint of heaviness.

Barenboim like Solti studied Elgar's own recording before interpreting the *First Symphony*, and the results are certainly idiomatic, though in the long first movement Barenboim overdoes the fluctuations, so losing momentum. The other three movements are beautifully performed, with the slow movement almost as tender as in Solti's reading with the same players. Recording not as opulent or well-balanced as Elgar's orchestration really demands.

Compared with Barbirolli's Philharmonia version the Hallé account has its moments of roughness in the playing (the strings by no means so smooth), but the first movement is far more vigorous. Barbirolli's faster tempo means that the expansively unfolding argument carries through more convincingly, whereas on HMV he does not avoid a feeling of dragging. The slow movement too is more affectionately done in this earlier version. The snag is that the recording quality is far less vivid.

Symphony No. 2 in E flat major, Op. 63.
  *** Decca SXL 6723. London Philharmonic Orchestra, Sir Georg Solti.
  ** (*) Lyrita SRCS 40. London Philharmonic Orchestra, Sir Adrian Boult.
  (B) ** (*) Pye GSGC 15008. London Philharmonic Orchestra, Boult.
  ** (*) CBS Quadraphonic MQ 31997; Stereo 73094. London Philharmonic Orchestra, Daniel Barenboim.
  ** HMV ASD 2749. Hallé Orchestra, Sir John Barbirolli.

Solti's is the most incandescent performance of Elgar's *Second Symphony* ever recorded, modelled closely on the composer's own surprisingly clipped and urgent reading, but benefiting from virtuoso playing by the LPO and superbly balanced sound. Fast tempi bring searing concentration and an account of the finale that for once presents a true climax. This is a fitting companion to Solti's magnificent account of No. 1.

The reservations mentioned in relation to Boult's Lyrita recording of Elgar's *First Symphony* apply here too, but in this work the authority of Boult is even more unassailable, with a noble approach that puts even Barbirolli in the shade. Boult's bargain version on Pye, recorded much earlier than the Lyrita, presents an even nobler, more dedicated performance, and the sound, though dated, has come up surprisingly well in the latest dubbing.

The performance is glorious, and at the price many Elgarians will accept the less than ideal recording.

Barenboim, having conducted this symphony all over the world, made it his first exercise in Elgar recording. It seems as though his individual reading grew more, rather than less, idiosyncratic after that sustained preparation. Following very much in the path set by Barbirolli, Barenboim underlines and exaggerates the contrasts of tempi, pulling the music out to the expansive limit. But given a willingness to accept an alternative viewpoint, this is still a red-blooded, passionate performance, capable of convincing for the moment at least. The LPO violins sound disappointingly thin, and even in the quadraphonic version the sound is starved of middle frequencies. Obviously (and perhaps not surprisingly) the CBS engineers do not understand the aesthetic of the 'Elgar sound', but this is still a record that Elgarians who want to hear the music from a new standpoint should sample.

Barbirolli's version was originally issued as a two-disc set coupled to *Falstaff*. This reissue fits the performance on to two sides, in spite of Barbirolli's slow tempi. The performance is richly recorded but the interpretation is a very personal one, the pace of the music often excessively varied, coarsening effects which Elgar's score specifies very precisely, and weakening the structure of the finale.

Variations on an original theme (Enigma), Op. 36 (see also under *Cockaigne; Cello concerto; Introduction and allegro; Pomp and Circumstance marches*).
  *** HMV ASD 2750. London Symphony Orchestra, Sir Adrian Boult – VAUGHAN WILLIAMS: *English folksongs suite etc.*** (*)
  (B) *** Decca SPA 121. London Symphony Orchestra, Pierre Monteux – BRAHMS: *Variations on a theme of Haydn.****

** (*) Decca SXL 6592. Los Angeles Philharmonic Orchestra, Zubin Mehta – IVES: *Symphony No. 1*.** (*)

** (*) CBS 72982. Philadelphia Orchestra, Eugene Ormandy – VAUGHAN WILLIAMS: *Tallis fantasia*.** (*)

(M) ** HMV SXLP 20007. Philharmonia Orchestra, Sir Malcolm Sargent – VAUGHAN WILLIAMS: *Tallis fantasia*.**

The nobility of Boult's reading of *Enigma* is marvellously captured in his latest version with the help of opulent recording. *Nimrod* in particular glows in beauty, superbly sustained. Though the finale lacks the final fire that Barbirolli gives it, the richness of texture, detailed but beautifully moulded, has rarely if ever been so magnificently captured on disc.

There is a marvellous freshness about Monteux's approach – what a remarkably versatile musician he was – and the music is obviously deeply felt. He secures a real *pianissimo* at the beginning of *Nimrod*, the playing hardly above a whisper, yet the tension electric. Slowly the great tune is built up in elegiac fashion, and the superb climax is the more effective in consequence. Differences from traditional tempi elsewhere are marginal, and add to rather than detract from one's enjoyment. The stereo recording is outstanding: this is a splendid record.

Mehta, born and brought up in India, has evidently not rejected all sympathy for the British Raj and its associations. (He even claims that cricket is his favourite sport.) Certainly he is a strong and sensitive interpreter of Elgar if this highly enjoyable account is anything to go by. There are no special revelations, but with spectacular recording quality and fine playing it can be warmly recommended to those who fancy the Ives coupling.

Ormandy's view of *Enigma* is charac-teristically forthright, lacking some Elgarian nuance but, with the help of superb Philadelphia string playing, urgently convincing all the same. The recording similarly is not subtle, but it helps the overall sense of conviction.

Sargent's recording is impressive in sonority (if not always in clarity) and the closing pages with their organ bass are very exciting. Sargent's performance is a traditional one and makes much of the *nobilmente* character of the score. With its well-chosen coupling this is a good bargain.

CHAMBER MUSIC

(i) *Piano quintet in A minor, Op. 84.* Piano pieces: *Adieu; Concert allegro, Op. 41; Serenade.*

** (*) HMV ASD 2501. John Ogdon (piano), (i) with Allegri String Quartet.

Elgar turned to chamber music towards the end of the First World War at a time of personal disillusion which also produced the elegiac *Cello concerto*. The *Piano quintet* is the most ambitious of the three chamber works, and though there are moments when Elgar's instrumentation brings unwanted Palm Court associations, the slow movement is among the composer's greatest, and every bar is distinctive and memorable. John Ogdon and the Allegri Quartet give a strong performance which misses some of the deeper, warmer emotions in the music but which is unlikely to be bettered unless the Cassini/Aeolian performance (not nearly so well recorded) is reissued. The *Concert allegro* is a valuable oddity newly resurrected by Ogdon and splendidly played (the music was long thought to be lost), and the shorter pieces too bring some charming ideas, even if they reveal Elgar's obvious limitations when writing for the keyboard.

String quartet in E minor, Op. 83.
> (M) ** (*) Nonesuch H 71140. Clare-
> mont Quartet – SIBELIUS: *Quar-
> tet*.** (*)

Of the three chamber works which
Elgar wrote at the end of his career the
String quartet shows the clearest mastery.
On the face of it the mood is one of
restraint. Elgar makes no grand gestures,
gives no echo of late Beethoven, yet the
intimacy of expression brings intensity of
its own. On the surface some of the ideas
may have kinship with Elgar's salon
pieces, yet their refinement belongs to an
utterly different world, and even Elgar
rarely wrote a slow movement so beautiful as the middle movement here. English
performances, when one hears them, tend
to underline the gentleness, yet an American group coming to Elgar fresh takes
an entirely different view, and though the
result may upset the Elgarian traditionalists there is no denying that, in the outer
movements at least, the inner strength of
the work is reinforced. The slow movement unfortunately is not hushed enough:
like so many American players the
Claremont Quartet is reluctant to give
anything less than a *mezzo piano*. Unless
the Sibelius coupling is particularly
wanted, the HMV disc (see below) is
preferable.

(i) *String quartet in E minor, Op. 83;*
(ii) *Violin sonata in E minor, Op. 82.*
> (M) *** HMV HQS 1252. (i) Music
> Group of London Quartet; (ii)
> Hugh Bean (violin), David Park-
> house (piano).

This is a delightful record, superbly
recorded. There is an autumnal quality
about the music, but it responds to ripe
treatment such as Hugh Bean and David
Parkhouse provide for the *Sonata*. The
Quartet is well done too, but not so
understandingly as by the Aeolian Quartet in a much less well-recorded disc

earlier available. The work is a masterpiece, using the medium of the string
quartet with tender originality.

VOCAL AND CHORAL MUSIC

(i) *Organ suite, Op. 14:* excerpts (*Introduction; Andante; Allegretto piacevole;
Intermezzo; Poco Lento*). (ii) Choral
music: *Angelus, Op. 56/1; Ave Maria,
Op. 2/2; Ave maris stella, Op. 2/3; Ave
verum, Op. 2/1; Give unto the Lord,
Op. 74; O hearken Thou, Op. 64.*
> ** HMV CSD 3660. (i) Harry
> Bramma (organ); (ii) Worcester
> Cathedral Choir, Christopher Ro-
> binson.

Elgar was one of the few Roman
Catholics among our major English com-
posers (Byrd was another). Like Byrd he
wrote much of his early sacred music
within a Protestant tradition, so that it
was suitable for presentation at the Three
Choirs Festivals (the *Te Deum*) and even
St Paul's Cathedral (*Give unto the Lord*).
O hearken Thou is a coronation anthem,
written in Elgar's official capacity for the
coronation of George V. The genuinely
Catholic works were written during
Elgar's apprenticeship as organist at St
George's Church, Worcester. Both the
Ave verum and the *Ave Maria* have a
gentle romantic colouring, but most
memorable is the *Angelus*, with its repeated figure like an echoing bell. This
was written in Italy in 1909 and has a
touch of Mediterranean sunshine in its
mood. There is little on this record to
anticipate the Elgar of *Gerontius*, although
much to show an emerging musical
individuality. Performances are sympathetic and alive and the recording is
excellent. The relatively slight organ
pieces are successfully used to provide
variety within the concert.

The Apostles, Op. 49 (oratorio): complete recording. Talk: *The Apostles and the Kingdom* (written by Michael Kennedy; read by Sir Adrian Boult).
>   *** HMV SLS 976 (3 discs). Sheila Armstrong (soprano), Helen Watts (contralto), Robert Tear (tenor), Benjamin Luxon (baritone), Clifford Grant, John Carol Case (basses), Downe House School Choir, London Philharmonic Orchestra and Choir, Sir Adrian Boult.

Sir Adrian Boult at eighty-five directed one of his most inspired recordings, an account of Elgar's long-neglected oratorio (the first of a projected trilogy of which *The Kingdom* was the second) which must warm the heart of any Elgarian. That the work failed earlier to make the impact it deserves stands as a condemnation of fashion. It may not have quite such memorable melodies as *Gerontius* or *The Kingdom*, but many of the set numbers, like the setting of the Beatitudes, *By the Wayside*, show Elgar at his most inspired, and the characters of Mary Magdalene and Judas are unexpectedly rounded and sympathetic. Generally fine singing – notably from Sheila Armstrong and Helen Watts – and a recording as rich and faithful as anyone could want.

Part songs: *As Torrents in Summer; Deep in my Soul; The Fountain; Go, Song of Mine; Love's Tempest; My Love Dwelt in a Northern Land; O Wild West Wind; Owls; The Shower; There is Sweet Music.*
>   *** Argo ZRG 607. Louis Halsey Singers, Louis Halsey – DELIUS: *Part songs.****

My Love Dwelt in a Northern Land is reasonably well-known, but most of the other part songs here are even more attractive, and all credit to Louis Halsey

and his splendid choir for showing that as a writer for chorus Elgar did not need massive expanses. *Owls*, for example, is a strange song intended to evoke the atmosphere of a wood at night with the help of evocative words. An attractive disc, beautifully recorded.

The Dream of Gerontius, Op. 38 (oratorio): complete recording.
>   ** (*) Decca SET 525/6. Yvonne Minton (mezzo-soprano), Peter Pears (tenor), John Shirley-Quirk (bass), LSO Chorus, King's College Chapel Choir, London Symphony Orchestra, Benjamin Britten.
>   ** (*) HMV SLS 770 (2 discs). Janet Baker (contralto), Richard Lewis (tenor), Kim Borg (bass), Hallé and Sheffield Philharmonic Choirs, Ambrosian Singers, Hallé Orchestra, Sir John Barbirolli.

Britten may seem an unlikely interpreter of Elgar, and he was persuaded to interpret *The Dream of Gerontius* as a result of hearing Peter Pears singing in it under Sir Adrian Boult. He first conducted the work at the Aldeburgh Festival, later recording it (also in the Maltings), and the pity is that a different chorus was imported. For whatever reason, the LSO Chorus is well below its finest form, the sound not nearly so powerful as it can and should be. Nonetheless the dedication of Britten's reading, the sense of fresh creation, is most moving. Pears (not always in his finest voice) is an involving Gerontius, while John Shirley-Quirk and Yvonne Minton are both excellent too, even if Minton can hardly match Janet Baker in spiritual concentration. Atmospheric recording, generally helped by the lively Maltings acoustic.

Those who do not look for a spiritual experience from *Gerontius* will not be disappointed with Sir John's red-blooded and dramatic reading. Janet Baker, especially, sings superbly – even if her style is purposely operative, following Sir John's conception – and Richard Lewis is also good. Kim Borg makes a disappointing priest. His rather colourless account of the music is not helped by his lack of command of the diction of the English language, and the blurred consonants prevent forthright delivery. The *Go forth* chorus is splendid, however, and so is the music of the demons, helped by the modern stereo recording. Elsewhere, and especially in the dialogue between the soul of Gerontius and the angel, and in the closing pages, Sir Malcolm Sargent in his earlier (mono only) recording evoked a much greater feeling of spirituality and repose.

(i) *From the Bavarian Highlands* (suite), *Op. 27* (complete recording). (ii) *Ecce sacerdos magnus. The Light of Life, Op. 29: Doubt not thy Father's care. Light of the World. O salutaris hostia, Nos. 1–3. Tantum ergo.*
** (*) Polydor 2460 239. Worcester Cathedral Choir, Christopher Robinson, with (i) Frank Wibaut (piano), (ii) Harry Bramma (organ).

Welcome as is this fine performance of *From the Bavarian Highlands*, the use of the piano accompaniment is a disappointment. It is undoubtedly authentic, but to ears used to the orchestral suite it sounds bare, and in the big final number, *The Marksman*, with its characteristic rising melody, there is simply not enough weight. Having made this point one must emphasize how enjoyable the disc is as it stands. The singing is assured and sensitive, often very beautiful, and the recording – made in an ideal acoustic – is first-class. All Elgarians will enjoy the choral items on side two, from the simple eloquence of the settings of *O salutaris hostia* to the striking *Ecce sacerdos magnus*.

The Kingdom, Op. 51 (oratorio): complete recording.
*** HMV SLS 939 (2 discs). Margaret Price (soprano), Yvonne Minton (contralto), Alexander Young (tenor), John Shirley-Quirk (bass), London Philharmonic Choir and Orchestra, Sir Adrian Boult.

Boult has long been devoted to this noble oratorio, openly preferring it even to *Gerontius*, and his dedication emerges clearly throughout a glorious performance which should help to establish a splendid work at last in the repertory. It has often been suggested that it is too static, but the Pentecost scene is intensely dramatic, and the richness of musical inspiration in the rest prevents any feeling of stagnation, certainly in a performance as inspired as this. The melody which Elgar wrote to represent the Holy Spirit is one of the noblest that even he created, and the soprano aria *The sun goeth down* (beautifully sung by Margaret Price) leads to a deeply affecting climax. The other soloists too sing splendidly, and the only reservation concerns the chorus, which is not quite so disciplined as it might be and sounds a little too backward to some of the massive effects which cap the power of the work. Excellent recording otherwise.

The Music Makers, Op. 69 (cantata): complete recording.
** (*) HMV ASD 2311. Janet Baker (contralto), London Philharmonic Choir and Orchestra, Sir Adrian Boult – PARRY: *Blest pair of sirens.***

Elgar's long-neglected cantata sets the Shaughnessy poem of the same name. It was a mature work, written soon after the *Symphonies* and *Violin concerto*, and is full of warm, attractive writing for both the voices and the orchestra. But it is some measure of the musical material that the passages which stand out are those in which Elgar used themes from his earlier works. If only the whole piece lived up to the uninhibited choral setting of the *Nimrod variation* from *Enigma*, it would be another Elgar masterpiece. As it is there are enough moments of rich expansiveness to make it essential for any Elgarian to hear, particularly in so understanding a performance as this. Janet Baker sings with committed mastery, though unfortunately her example is not always matched by the comparatively dull-sounding choir.

Sea Pictures, Op. 37 (song cycle): complete recording.
  ⊛*** HMV ASD 655. Janet Baker (mezzo-soprano), London Symphony Orchestra, Sir John Barbirolli – *Cello concerto.***
  *** HMV ASD 2721. Janet Baker (mezzo-soprano), London Symphony Orchestra, Sir John Barbirolli – MAHLER: *Rückert Lieder.***

The song cycle *Sea Pictures* hardly matches the mature inspiration of the *Cello concerto*, with which it is coupled, but it is heartwarming here nonetheless. Like du Pré, Janet Baker is an artist who has the power even on record to convey the vividness of a live performance. With the help of Barbirolli she makes the cycle far more convincing than it usually seems, with words that are often trite clothed in music that seems to transform them. Warm recording.

Although the original coupling with the *Cello concerto* was particularly apt, the alternative realignment will especially please Janet Baker's admirers for some of her finest recorded art is here.

Eloy, Jean-Claude
(born 1938)

Equivalences for 18 instruments.
  (M) ** Everest SDBR 3170. Strasbourg Percussion Group, Domaine Ensemble, Pierre Boulez – SCHOENBERG: *Verklaerte Nacht*; POUSSEUR: *Madrigal III.***

Eloy favours the kind of exotic percussion sounds which were the trademark of Boulez in his earlier creative years. Whether this Boulez pupil has the intellectual toughness to prevent the jingling from becoming self-indulgent is another matter. This work at least is compressed and the performance brilliant enough to have one convinced.

Enesco, Georges
(1881–1955)

Violin sonata No. 3 in A minor (In the popular Rumanian style), Op. 25.
  ** HMV ASD 2294. Yehudi Menuhin (violin), Hephzibah Menuhin (piano) – SHANKAR: *Swarq – Kakali.***

It is difficult to be enamoured of the current fashion for marrying east and west, and this disc, which offers a post-romantic sonata based on Balkan folk material together with some Ravi Shankar, seems a bizarre coupling. The Enesco is a fine work, with a rapt, thoughtful slow movement which Menuhin plays with a sense of commitment, though Gertler had more of the withdrawn, poetic quality on his older Supraphon disc (SUAST 50483), which is still available.

363

Erb, Donald
(born 1927)

(i) *Concerto for solo percussionist and orchestra. The Seventh Trumpet. Symphony of overtures (The Blacks; Endgame; The Maids; Rhinoceros).*

(B) ** (*) Turnabout TV 34433S. Dallas Symphony Orchestra, Donald Johanos, (i) with Marvin Dahlgren (percussion).

The music of Donald Erb reflects something of his experience as a jazz trumpeter. Highly professional, he presents attractive, inventive music full of colour and drama. The *Symphony of overtures* is based on different plays of Genet, Beckett and Ionesco, while the *Percussion concerto* presents the most noisily dramatic music of all. Well worth sampling at the price. Bright recording quality.

Falla, Manuel de
(1876–1946)

El amor brujo (Love, the Magician) (ballet).

(M) *** CBS Classics 61288. Shirley Verrett (mezzo-soprano), Philadelphia Orchestra, Leopold Stokowski – WAGNER: *Tristan: Love music.** (*)

*** Decca SXL 6287. Nati Mistral (mezzo-soprano), New Philharmonia Orchestra, Rafael Frühbeck de Burgos – GRANADOS; RAVEL: *Pieces.***

(M) ** Decca Ace of Diamonds SDD 134. Maria de Gabarain (mezzo-soprano), Suisse Romande Orchestra, Ernest Ansermet – *Master Peter's puppet show.***

(i) *El amor brujo (Love, the Magician); The Three-cornered Hat (El sombrero de tres picos): ballet suites 1 and 2.*

(M) *** HMV SXLP 30140. (i) Victoria de los Angeles (soprano); Philharmonia Orchestra, Carlo Maria Giulini.

Fierce and sumptuous by turns, Stokowski's interpretation of *El amor brujo* is unique. It was he who introduced the ballet to America, and rarely if ever on record has its drama been so vividly presented. The orchestra, reunited with their one-time principal, play with passionate conviction, and Shirley Verrett, matching their variety of tone-colour, ranges between rich *vibrato* and raucous flamenco-like tone. Purists may object, but this is music which communicates the more powerfully for such treatment. Opulent Philadelphia recording to match the interpretation.

Frühbeck de Burgos also provides us with a completely recommendable version of *El amor brujo*. His superbly graduated crescendo after the spiky opening is immediately compelling, and the control of atmosphere in the quieter music is masterly. Equally the *Ritual fire dance* is blazingly brilliant. Nati Mistral has the vibrant open-throated production of the real flamenco singer. She is less polished than Los Angeles, but if anything the music sounds more authentic this way. Brilliant sound, a trifle light in the bass, but offering luminous textures in the quieter sections.

Ansermet's meticulous reading is certainly colourful if sometimes a little emotionally reticent. This is partly caused by a lack of tonal warmth in some of the woodwind solos. The soloist sings admirably, but the Decca recording has less than usual of the incandescence of texture associated with this conductor.

Beautifully civilized and atmospheric accounts of both scores from Giulini with extremely fine recorded sound into the bargain. Thoroughly enjoyable, even if the performance of *El amor brujo* is not as vivid and red-blooded as Stokowski's.

Nights in the Gardens of Spain.
*** Decca SXL 6528. Alicia de Larrocha (piano), Suisse Romande Orchestra, Sergiu Comissiona – CHOPIN: *Concerto No. 2.***(*)
** (*) Decca SXL 2091. Gonzalo Soriano (piano), National Orchestra of Spain, Ataulfo Argenta – RODRIGO: *Concierto de Aranjuez.***(*)
** RCA SB 6841. Artur Rubinstein (piano), Philadelphia Orchestra, Eugene Ormandy – SAINT-SAËNS: *Piano concerto No. 2.***

Nights in the Gardens of Spain; El amor brujo: Ritual fire dance. La vida breve: Spanish dance No. 1.
(M) *** HMV SXLP 30152. Gonzalo Soriano (piano), Paris Conservatoire Orchestra, Rafael Frühbeck de Burgos – TURINA: *Danzas fantásticas.***(*)

Miss de Larrocha is in even better form in the Falla than in the Chopin with which it is coupled. She brings plenty of poetry and vitality to this evocative score, and she receives admirable support from Comissiona and the engineers. All in all, hers is one of the finest versions of the work now available.

Gonzalo Soriano has recorded the work twice. His earlier Decca version might seem due for reissue on Ace of Diamonds, particularly as its coupling, the Rodrigo *Guitar concerto*, has also been made available in the Decca SPA *World of . . .* series. The late Ataulfo Argenta was justly famous for his perceptive concerto accompaniments, and he gives a colloquial reading. The Spanish National Orchestra is a body which is stronger in ensemble than as a vehicle for star wind soloists, yet the orchestral colours are vivid and convincing. However, the accompaniment under Frühbeck de Burgos is more sophisticated and shows splendid feeling for Falla's subtleties of scoring. Soriano gives fine performances on both discs, but the later account on HMV seems marginally more penetrating and the recording of the piano slightly more modern-sounding – although the Decca is still very competitive. The two bonuses on the HMV disc are well done.

Rubinstein's latest recording of *Nights in the Gardens of Spain* is bold and rather straightforward. Ormandy's accompaniment and the clear RCA sound matches the playing, which, though not lacking brilliance or subtlety in musical matters, misses some of the evocative quality and Spanish atmosphere of the score.

The Three-cornered Hat (El sombrero de tres picos) (ballet): complete recording; *La vida breve: Interlude and Dance.*
(M) *** Decca Ace of Diamonds SDD 321. Teresa Berganza (mezzo-soprano), Suisse Romande Orchestra, Ernest Ansermet.

The only complete account of *The Three-cornered Hat* currently in the catalogue, and at a very competitive price considering its excellence. The playing has great vigour and spirit; even the occasional roughness of detail seems appropriate. Berganza is in good voice, and the Decca engineers have produced bright, well-detailed sound with plenty of impact.

Cuatro piezas españolas (Aragonesa; Cubana; Montanesa; Andaluza); Fantasia Baetica; El amor brujo (Love, the Magician): ballet suite; El sombrero de tres picos (The Three-cornered Hat): 3 dances.
*** Decca SXL 6683. Alicia de Larrocha (piano).

There is no current alternative for the fine *Fantasia Baetica*, and this present issue fills an admirable place in the catalogue. It assembles all the piano music of Falla on two sides in exemplary performances and good recordings.

Master Peter's Puppet Show (El Retablo de Maese Pedro).

(M) *** Decca Ace of Diamonds SDD 134. Julita Bermajo (soprano), Carlos Munguia (tenor), Raimunde Torres (baritone), National Orchestra of Spain, Ataulfo Argenta – *El amor brujo.***

This captivating piece was commissioned by the Princesse de Polignac for her puppet theatre. The work was finished and first performed in 1923, and the instrumental writing, not inappropriately, carries a little influence from Stravinsky's *Petrushka*. The work is not really an opera but a play within a play, both audience and performers being puppets. A series of tableaux is presented with The Boy as M.C. He describes the action (which is illustrated instrumentally) in a fascinating quick recitative style. At the climax of the story Don Quixote, who is in the 'audience', can contain himself no longer and rushes to save the escaping lovers.

It would be difficult to imagine the part of The Boy being better done than it is here by Julita Bermajo, and both Master Peter (Carlos Munguia) and Don Quixote (Raimunde Torres) are excellent, the latter especially so in his expressive closing address to his fellow members of the 'audience'. The orchestra in the hands of Argenta is suitably descriptive and the recording outstandingly real and atmospheric.

Fauré, Gabriel
(1845–1924)

Ballade for piano and orchestra, Op. 19.
** HMV ASD 2753. John Ogdon

(piano), City of Birmingham Orchestra, Louis Frémaux – LITOLFF: *Scherzo*; SAINT-SAËNS: *Carnival of the Animals.***

The elusive and delicate essence of Fauré's *Ballade* is not easy to capture, but Ogdon's warmly affectionate approach is enjoyable and is notably sensitive in the central and closing sections of the work. The recording is rich and ample in texture to match the style of the playing.

Élégie in C minor (for cello and orchestra), Op. 24.

(B) ** Classics for Pleasure CFP 40070. Janos Starker (cello), Philharmonia Orchestra, Walter Susskind – DVOŘÁK: *Cello concerto.***

* (*) Philips 6500 045. Maurice Gendron (cello), Monte Carlo Opera Orchestra, Roberto Benzi – LALO: *Cello concerto*; SAINT-SAËNS: *Cello concerto No. 1.***

Starker plays Fauré's charming, lyrical piece with beautiful tone and firm line but too little sense of poetry. An acceptable fill-up nonetheless to a good bargain version of the Dvořák *Concerto*. Gendron's performance is an eloquent one but it is disfigured by an undistinguished accompaniment, notably some poor woodwind intonation.

Fantaisie for piano and orchestra. Op. 111.

*** Decca SXL 6680. Alicia de Larrocha (piano), London Philharmonic Orchestra, Rafael Frühbeck de Burgos – RAVEL: *Piano concertos.****

The Fauré *Fantaisie* is a late work which has been neglected by the gramophone. Grant Johannesen recorded it some years ago, but this is at present deleted. Alicia de Larrocha's fine recording is the only current version and its presence as a fill-up makes her Ravel *Concertos*, the main items on the record, well worth considering. An aristocratic work of great distinction, the *Fantaisie* is to late Fauré what the *Ballade* is to his earlier period.

Masques et Bergamasques, Op. 112; Pelléas et Mélisande (incidental music), *Op. 80; Pénélope: Prélude.*
> (M) *** Decca Ace of Diamonds SDD 388. Suisse Romande Orchestra, Ernest Ansermet – DE-BUSSY: *Petite suite.** (*)

An admirable introduction to Fauré's orchestral music, this record offers sympathetic and stylish accounts of *Masques et Bergamasques* and *Pelléas et Mélisande*, both written for the theatre. The *Prélude* to *Pelléas* must be among the most eloquent and moving pieces written by any French composer, and it is affectingly played here by the Suisse Romande Orchestra under Ansermet. Though the wind is not as sensitive as in Baudo's (recently deleted) HMV disc, the playing has conviction. There are no current recommendable alternatives of either suite, and the disc also has the advantage of a Fauré rarity in the form of the *Prélude* to *Pénélope*, a noble and impressive piece that is worth the price of the record alone.

CHAMBER AND INSTRUMENTAL MUSIC

(i; ii; iii; iv) *Piano quartet No. 1 in C minor, Op. 15;* (i; iv) *Andante in B flat major, Op. 75; Berceuse in D major, Op. 16* (both for violin and piano); (iii; iv) *Papillon, Op. 77; Romance in A major, Op. 69* (both for violoncello and piano).
> (M) *** HMV HQS 1245. (i) Yehudi Menuhin (violin); (ii) Ernst Wallfisch (viola); (iii) Maurice Gen-

dron (cello); (iv) Jeremy Menuhin (piano).

Piano quartets Nos. 1 in C minor, Op. 15; 2 in G minor, Op. 45.
> (B) ** Turnabout TV 37037S. Jacqueline Eymar (piano), Günter Kehr (violin), Erich Sichermann (viola), Bernhard Braunholz (cello).

Piano quartet No. 1 in C minor, Op. 15; Piano trio in D minor, Op. 120.
> (M) *** Oiseau-Lyre SOL 289. Pro Arte Piano Quartet.

A warmly enjoyable performance of Fauré's attractive *Piano quartet* from the Menuhin group, notable for the effective contrast of a vivaciously light-textured scherzo and an eloquent *Adagio*. The 'encores' too are well worth having, especially the lovely *Berceuse*, which is given a memorable and devoted account by Menuhin senior, and the fetching *Papillon*, in which Maurice Gendron shines. The sound is rich and clear, the textures very well judged indeed to suit the music.

On Oiseau-Lyre fluent and sensitive performances of two of Fauré's finest chamber works. The *C minor Piano quartet* is one of his most lyrical works and justly popular. The *Trio* is more recondite, but like the *String quartet* that succeeded it, it is immensely rewarding and wonderfully rich in invention. Unfortunately an editing error deprived the *C minor Quartet* of four bars but apart from the copies on which this fault has not been rectified, it would be difficult to better these fine performances. The recording is excellent.

On Turnabout, not the most subtle interpretations of this subtle music, but their very vigour is engaging, and at the price, with fair recording quality, the disc is well worth considering. A good sampler disc for those not normally attracted to Fauré.

Piano quintets Nos. 1 in D minor, Op. 89; 2 in C minor, Op. 115.

(B) ** Turnabout TV 37038S. Jacqueline Eymar (piano), Günter Kehr, Werner Neuhaus (violins), Erich Sichermann (viola), Bernhard Braunholz (cello).

Curiously, Fauré's two *Piano quintets* are rarities – whether in concert or on record – compared with the *Piano quartets* but, as these dedicated performances show, the richer-textured ensemble inspired him to some characteristically subtle ideas. The ensemble is not always immaculate, and the recording is variable, though well weighted in bass. At the price, like the two companion discs, this makes an excellent recommendation.

(i) *Piano trio in D minor, Op. 120;* (ii) *String quartet in E minor, Op. 121.*

(B) ** Turnabout TV 37039S. (i) Jacqueline Eymar (piano), Günter Kehr (violin), Bernhard Braunholz (cello); (ii) Loewenguth Quartet.

This apt coupling of Fauré's last two chamber works completes a set of three bargain records which presents consistently urgent and persuasive readings. These late works may benefit from gentler handling (the leader of the quartet has rather an edgy tone), but these readings, with their passionate undertones, are never less than convincing. Recording quality that copes well with the spare lines of the writing.

PIANO MUSIC

Barcarolles Nos. 1–11; Thème et variations in C sharp minor, Op. 73.

(B) * (*) Turnabout TV 37070S. Evelyne Crochet (piano).

Barcarolles Nos. 1 and 6; Impromptu No. 3 in A flat major, Op. 34; Nocturnes Nos. 1 in E flat minor, Op. 33/1; 3 in A flat major, Op. 33/3; 4 in E flat major, Op. 36; 6 in D flat major, Op. 63; 13 in B minor, Op. 119; Romance sans paroles, Op. 17/3.

(B) *** Saga 5385. Albert Ferber (piano).

Barcarolles Nos. 12 and 13; Pièces brèves, Op. 84/1–7; Préludes Nos. 1–3, Op. 103/1–3; Valses-caprices Nos. 1–3.

(B) * (*) Turnabout TV 37041S. Evelyne Crochet (piano).

Impromptus Nos. 1–5; Mazurka in B flat major, Op. 32; Nocturnes Nos. 1–3, Op. 33/1–3; 4, Op. 36; Préludes, Op. 103, Nos. 4–9.

(B) * (*) Turnabout TV 37042S. Evelyne Crochet (piano).

Nocturnes Nos. 5–13; 3 Romances sans paroles, Op. 17/1–3.

(B) * (*) Turnabout TV 37043S. Evelyne Crochet (piano).

Miss Crochet is talented, and her playing is informed with sensibility as well as an excellent basic technique. Although she has now settled in America, her Paris training should have helped to provide a background suitable to the undertaking of a recording of all Fauré's piano music; but in the event she has not the experience to bring much of this music completely to life. Her approach is rigid and positive where it should be flexible and imaginative. Thus the *Thème et variations* and the collections of short pieces come off better than the *Barcarolles*, where the rhythmic style is too severe. The recording is good. However, Albert Ferber, a grossly under-rated English artist, has recorded a selection of pieces here on a cheap Saga disc that will prove invaluable to the impecunious collector. Not only is it artistically worthwhile, it also happens to be technically good. This is a real find.

VOCAL AND CHORAL MUSIC

Les Berceaux; Lydia: Poème d'un jour (Rencontre; Toujours; Adieu), Op. 21.

(M) *** HMV HQS 1258. Gérard Souzay (baritone), Dalton Baldwin (piano) – DUPARC: *Mélodies.****

Although these songs serve as a fill-up to the Duparc, they still deserve special mention, such is the artistry with which they are performed. Splendid recording makes this an added inducement, albeit where none is needed.

La Bonne Chanson, Op. 61; Deux mélodies, Op. 76 (Le Parfum impérissable; Arpège); Trois mélodies, Op. 85 (Dans la Forêt de septembre; La Fleur qui va sur l'eau; Accompagnement); Mirages, Op. 113.
** (*) Telefunken SAT 22546. Bernard Kruysen (baritone), Noël Lee (piano).

We are not so well served that we can afford to pass over any Fauré song recital on record. Now that Souzay's wonderful performance on Philips (ABL 3373) is deleted, we have no alternative version of the masterly *Bonne Chanson*, and though Bernard Kruysen's account does not match the ardour and poetry of Souzay's, it is more than just a stop-gap. Not an inspired version by any means, but with many musicianly virtues and goodish recording to commend it.

Requiem, Op. 48.
** (*) HMV Angel SAN 107. Victoria de los Angeles (soprano), Dietrich Fischer-Dieskau (baritone), Elisabeth Brasseur Choir, Paris Conservatoire Orchestra, André Cluytens.
(M) * (*) Decca Ace of Diamonds SDD 144. Suzanne Danco (soprano), Gérard Souzay (baritone), L'Union Chorale de la Tour de Peilz, Suisse Romande Orchestra, Ernest Ansermet.

(i) *Requiem, Op. 48;* (ii) *Pavane, Op. 50.*
*** HMV Quadraphonic Q4-ASD 3065. (i) Sheila Armstrong (soprano), Dietrich Fischer-Dieskau (baritone); (i; ii) Edinburgh Festival Chorus, Orchestre de Paris, Daniel Barenboim.
** (*) HMV ASD 2358. New Philharmonia Orchestra, David Willcocks, with (i) Robert Chilcott (treble), John Carol Case (baritone), King's College Chapel Choir, John Wells (organ), (ii) Gareth Morris (flute).

Both the performances recorded by EMI in Paris underline the music's expressive beauty. Barenboim tends to choose tempi rather faster and more flowing than those adopted by Cluytens. That is particularly important in the *Agnus Dei*, where Cluytens sounds relatively heavy next to Barenboim, whose approach brings out what to British listeners must always seem an Elgarian flavour. Barenboim also has the advantage of excellent quadraphonic sound, a fresher, more responsive choir, and purer soprano singing from Sheila Armstrong. Fischer-Dieskau is more dramatic under Barenboim, if not always quite so mellifluous as with Cluytens. Barenboim provides an attractive fill-up in a version of the beautiful *Pavane* with chorus. The pity is that Cluytens' version was recorded when Victoria de los Angeles was not in her very best voice; the high tessitura of *Pie Jesu* strains her uncomfortably.

The King's style is very much in the English cathedral tradition. The solo soprano role is taken by a boy, as was the case in Louis Frémaux's record in the mid-1960s. The performance is certainly an eloquent one, but collectors should sample it for themselves, as many admirers of the composer will undoubtedly feel its Anglican accents unidiomatic. The recording is extremely fine and the performance a moving one. The *Pavane*

369

makes an attractive bonus. Nonetheless the Barenboim version is a safer recommendation.

The Ace of Diamonds transfer of Ansermet's version is technically immaculate, but its clarity serves only to emphasize the rather thin-toned contribution of the chorus. But the solo singing is still good (even if Danco is no match for los Angeles in sheer spiritual beauty), and this may be considered fair value for money at its price.

Field, John
(1782–1837)

Piano concerto No. 1 in E flat major.
(M) ** Unicorn UNS 227. Felicja Blumenthal (piano), Vienna Chamber Orchestra, Hellmuth Froschauer – HUMMEL: *Rondo brillant.**

John Field was born in Dublin (some thirty years before Chopin) and led the life of an itinerant musician in Europe before finally settling in Russia, where he died. Among his surviving works are concertos and sonatas for the piano as well as chamber music, but he is best known as the inventor of the *Nocturne,* a style of composition which Chopin brought to perfection. Field gave his *First Concerto* its début in London before he was seventeen, and it is a surprisingly well-made piece. The first movement has one memorable theme (reminiscent of Mozart) and the second uses a pretty Scottish air, *Within a mile of Edinburgh Town,* which Field manages to invest with a Celtic charm distinctly Irish in flavour. The finale is jolly but, like much of the first movement, contains a good deal of rhetoric. The performance here is sympathetic and the recording acceptable if not outstanding.

(i) *Piano concerto No. 2 in A flat major; Nocturnes Nos. 1 in E flat major; 2 in C minor; 3 in A flat major; 4 in A major; 7 in C major; 10 in E minor; 11 in E flat major.*
(M) * (*) VOX STGBY 625. Rena Kyriakou (piano), (i) with Berlin Symphony Orchestra, C. A. Bünte.

This concerto dates from 1808, yet its evocation – in the *Poco adagio* – of the spirit of the then unborn Chopin is uncanny. The main theme of this delightful 'lollipop' of a movement has not quite the distinction of Chopin, but its Irish charm is irresistible, and the filigree decoration anticipates the Polish composer in no uncertain manner. Unfortunately the rest of the concerto is not on this level. Rena Kyriakou shows her sensitivity to Field in the slow movement, which she plays deliciously well, but in the solo *Nocturnes* she is less happy. Her *rubato* – as instanced in the first piece – is curiously awkward, and the flow of the music is interrupted.

Piano concerto No. 3 in E flat major. (Also includes: CZERNY: *Piano concerto in A minor, Op. 214.*)
(B) Turnabout TV 34389S. Felicja Blumenthal (piano), Vienna Chamber Orchestra, Hellmuth Froschauer.

The *Third Concerto* is such a thin, uninspired work that it seems unlikely that the finest performance could make a great deal of it. But the performance here is of poor quality anyway, and the same applies to the coupling.

Nocturnes Nos. 1–19 (complete recording).
(B) * (*) Turnabout TV 34349/50S. Mary Louise Boehm (piano).

Now that the Gemini set by Rucky van Mill has been deleted, we are left with Mary Boehm's recording. She is classically exact in style rather than flexible and gently romantic, and her approach does not serve the music ideally. The piano tone is clear rather than luminous. There is also another set available on the imported Irish label, Claddagh. This is very well recorded (although the surfaces are not always silent) but the pianist, Veronica McSwiney, is deliberate and stiff in manner. She shows little feeling for the delicacy of Field's inspiration, and the Turnabout version is to be preferred on most counts, including that of economy.

Finzi, Gerald
(1901–56)

Dies Natalis.
(M) *** HMV HQS 1260. Wilfred Brown (tenor), English Chamber Orchestra, Christopher Finzi – HOLST: *Choral fantasia.****

Finzi's sensitive setting of words by the seventeenth-century poet Thomas Traherne was recorded by Joan Cross in the days of 78, and though as an interpreter even Wilfred Brown does not quite match Miss Cross at her most sensitive, it is very welcome to have a modern version, beautifully recorded. With an equally interesting coupling, this record must be strongly recommended to all interested in modern English song-setting: in a way you can look at this as a preparation for Britten's achievement in his orchestral cycles, the *Serenade* and the *Nocturne.*

(i) *Before and After Summer* (ten songs for baritone and piano) (words by Hardy); *I Said to Love* (six songs for baritone and piano) (words by Hardy); (ii) *Till Earth Outwears* (seven songs for tenor and piano) (words by Hardy).

** Lyrita SRCS 38. (i) John Carol Case (baritone); (ii) Robert Tear (tenor); both with Howard Ferguson (piano).

Generally this is the more attractive of the two Lyrita records of Finzi's Hardy settings. Finzi had a fine feeling for words, and if the music itself is not very forward-looking it matches the Hardy melancholia and pastoral imagery well. Both singers appear to find the songs rewarding, and the accompaniments are dedicated and obviously searching. The recording is generally good, with an occasional trace of peakiness.

(i) *Earth and Air and Rain* (ten songs for baritone and piano) (words by Hardy); (ii) *A Young Man's Exhortation* (ten songs for tenor and piano) (words by Hardy).
** Lyrita SRCS 51. (i) John Carol Case (baritone); (ii) Neil Jenkins (tenor); both with Howard Ferguson (piano).

Finzi's Hardy settings are shared by John Carol Case and Neil Jenkins, the former singer being the stronger of the two. The songs are sensitive and characteristically fastidious. The composer's personality is slight but distinctive, although there is sometimes a flavour of Vaughan Williams in the music. The recording is good of the voices, but gives less body to the piano.

Foss, Lukas
(born 1922)

Baroque variations (1, On a Handel Larghetto; 2, On a Scarlatti Sonata; 3, On a Bach Prelude, Phorion).
(M) ** Nonesuch H 71202. Buffalo Philharmonic Orchestra, the composer – CAGE: *Concerto.***

The Webernization of three baroque models: Lukas Foss describes the three sections as not so much variations as 'dreams', and with the original pieces providing virtually all the notes, in however skeletal a form, the results are nothing less than charming. The specialist can delve into the detailed musical logic, the non-specialist can simply enjoy the dreamlike experience of tuning to music as though from another room, or even another world.

Françaix, Jean
(born 1912)

Concertino for piano and orchestra.
> *** Philips SAL 3637. Claude Françaix (piano), London Symphony Orchestra, Antal Dorati – AURIC: *Overture*; MILHAUD: *Le Bœuf*; SATIE: *Parade*.***

At last we have a recommendable stereo recording of Françaix's delectable little four-movement concerto. The conductor's touch is deliciously light in the outer movements and the pianist is neat and accomplished. The scherzo is colourful too, but the gentle slow movement is the final test and this is taken a fraction too fast. Kathleen Long in her outstanding Decca mono (Ace of Clubs) disc was preferable here, but undoubtedly the stereo adds a great deal to the delicate orchestral effects, especially in the winsome finale, which is particularly successful.

Divertissement for oboe, clarinet and bassoon; Divertissement for bassoon and string quintet.
> *** HMV ASD 2506. Melos Ensemble – POULENC: *Trio*; RAVEL: *Introduction and allegro*.***

Jean Françaix is a composer of great charm and wit who is under-represented in the current catalogue. Works like *La Dame dans la lune* have an enormous fund of high spirits and melodic fertility to commend them and an infectious zest for life. Unfortunately neither of the two *Divertissements* on this record shows him at his most inventive, though both pieces are pleasant. Recordings and performances are of high quality.

Franck, César
(1822–90)

Le Chasseur maudit (The Accursed Huntsman); (i) *Les Djinns; Les Eolides; Rédemption* (symphonic poems).
> (M) ** Supraphon SUAST 50800. Czech Philharmonic Orchestra, Jean Fournet, (i) with Frantisek Maxian (piano).

Jean Fournet is one of the most direct and convincing conductors of French music on record, and here with Czech forces he gives dramatic and forceful performances of four of César Franck's neglected symphonic poems. *Le Chasseur maudit* comes off best, with the galloping rhythms of the accursed huntsman's horse pushed on relentlessly. The interlude from the oratorio *Rédemption* is done in the original version, not the later concert arrangement, but this and the other performances are marred by thin string tone. Even so, *Les Eolides* comes to a climax of tremendous surge and power, while *Les Djinns*, based on Hugo's poem, has an understanding piano soloist in Frantisek Maxian. It is Franck's fault if this fails to convey the mounting excitement of the original poem. Recording good, except for the thinness of string tone.

Les Eolides (symphonic poem).
> ** Decca SXL 6310. Suisse Romande Orchestra, Ernest Ansermet – CHAUSSON: *Symphony.***

Ansermet's performance of *Les Eolides* is well played and recorded, and it makes a good fill-up for an enjoyable performance of the Chausson *Symphony.*

Symphonic variations for piano and orchestra.
> *** Decca SXL 2173. Clifford Curzon (piano), London Symphony Orchestra, Sir Adrian Boult – GRIEG: *Piano concerto*; LITOLFF: *Scherzo.****
> ** (*) HMV ASD 2872. Alexis Weissenberg (piano), Berlin Philharmonic Orchestra, Herbert von Karajan – RACHMANINOV: *Piano concerto No. 2.***
> ** (*) Decca SXL 6599. Alicia de Larrocha (piano), London Philharmonic Orchestra, Rafael Frühbeck de Burgos – KHACHATURIAN: *Piano concerto.***
> * HMV ASD 542. John Ogdon (piano), Philharmonia Orchestra, Sir John Barbirolli – TCHAIKOVSKY: *Piano concerto No. 1.***

Curzon's Decca performance has stood the test of time. It is a deliciously fresh reading without idiosyncrasy. It can be recommended without reservation, particularly with the coupling equally brilliantly done. The recording is beautifully clean and clear.

With its hushed beginning, Weissenberg's essentially gentle reading is sensitive to the poetry of the opening and to the work's lyrical sections. Karajan ensures that the orchestral contribution is a strong one (the balance favours the orchestra more than usual, although the piano is never buried). There are more sparkling accounts of the closing pages,

but taken as a whole this is a spontaneous and enjoyable reading. The coupling, however, is not a first choice among the many versions of Rachmaninov's *Second Concerto.*

The Spanish interpreters, Alicia de Larrocha and Frühbeck de Burgos, give a reading that more than usual brings out the French delicacy of the variations. Good recording quality: an unexpected coupling for a variable account of the Khachaturian *Concerto.*

Ogdon's performance is disappointingly dull and unspontaneous-sounding: the best section is the finale, where a certain rhythmic spring catches the listener's previously flagging interest.

Symphony in D minor; (i) *Symphonic variations for piano and orchestra.*
> (M) ** CBS Classics 61356. Philadelphia Orchestra, Eugene Ormandy, (i) with Robert Casadesus (piano).

It is curious that this coupling has not been more often used, for its attractions are obvious. Here Casadesus gives an agreeable performance of the *Symphonic variations* but is let down somewhat by the piano recording, which is rather shallow. Ormandy's account of the *Symphony* is bold and powerful, and the recording has plenty of impact without being glossy. Nevertheless some ears find that this music-making has a certain streamlined quality, although it has plenty of character too. The record is quite a good bargain.

Symphony in D minor; Le Chasseur maudit (The Accursed Huntsman).
> (M) ** Decca Ace of Diamonds SDD 320. Suisse Romande Orchestra, Ernest Ansermet.

Symphony in D minor.
> ** (*) HMV ASD 2552. Orchestre de Paris, Herbert von Karajan.

(B) ** (*) Classics for Pleasure CFP 40090. Philharmonia Orchestra, Constantin Silvestri.

* (*) Decca Phase 4 PFS 4218. Hilversum Radio Philharmonic Orchestra, Leopold Stokowski – RAVEL: *Fanfare*.**

The Franck *Symphony* has not been very fortunate in its recordings and the best ones seem too readily to get deleted. Currently we are without Munch and Monteux (both RCA) and we must hope they return in bargain reissues before too long. Ansermet's disc is attractive for its inclusion of *Le Chasseur maudit*, a simplistic but vivid symphonic poem. The reading of the *Symphony* is dramatic, but Ansermet is inclined to let the tension subside between climaxes (something which can easily happen in this work). The recording is first-rate, but the orchestral playing is not always polished.

Silvestri's version, first issued in the early sixties, makes an excellent bargain choice, with vintage Philharmonia string and brass tone ringing out sonorously. The performance is vivid and exciting with relatively few mannerisms, so that the outer movements are wonderfully buoyant.

On the whole, the best recommendation, irrespective of price, would seem to be Karajan, whose account is opulent and expansive without falling into the obvious vulgarity which mars such an interpretation as Stokowski's. Helped by the big, beefy recording quality provided by the Paris engineers, he draws richly warm and expressive playing from the musicians of France's premier orchestra. This marked Karajan's return to EMI after years devoted mainly to DGG, and that return seemed to restore the large-scale quality of the earlier Karajan, somehow different from the ultra-refined conductor we know in so many DGG recordings. In the Franck Karajan's tempi are all on the slow side, but his control of rhythm prevents any feeling of sluggishness or heaviness. There is always energy underlying the performance, and by facing the obvious problems squarely Karajan avoids the perils.

The conviction with which Stokowski moulds a romantic symphony like this is very striking. Though not such a virtuoso band as the LSO, with which Stokowski has made many of his Phase 4 recordings, the Hilversum Orchestra plays with tremendous energy and warmth. The problem remains of Stokowski's reading, which underlines vulgarities in the score that most conductors seek to conceal. In Tchaikovsky any Stokowskian approach usually makes for highly enjoyable results, thanks to the strength of the music. With César Franck the cliff edge is closer, and intending purchasers should sample first. The recording is very good, but not so brilliant as most in this series.

CHAMBER MUSIC

Piano quintet in F minor.

(M) ** (*) Decca Ace of Diamonds SDD 277. Clifford Curzon (piano), Vienna Philharmonic Quartet.

Not as seductive a performance as some will want in a work that can sound very luscious indeed. But for repeated playing there is a strong case for not letting the emotion spill over, and both Curzon and the Vienna Philharmonic Quartet are sensitive and firm at the same time. Curzon's playing is particularly fine. The recording sounds appropriately full-blooded. It has a rather ample bass, which wants cutting back a little for an ideal balance. One might criticize the lack of inner clarity, but the rich, homogeneous texture happens to suit the music rather well.

Violin sonata in A major.

*** Decca SXL 6408. Itzhak Perlman (violin), Vladimir Ashkenazy (piano) – BRAHMS: *Horn trio*.***

*** HMV ASD 2618. David Oistrakh (violin), Sviatoslav Richter (piano) – BRAHMS: *Violin sonata No. 3.****

A superb account from Perlman and Ashkenazy. The first movement catches the listener by the ears with its tremendous forward impulse, and the whole performance has the kind of spontaneity which is too rare on record. The passionate commitment of the playing in no way swamps the work's lyrical flow, and it is difficult to imagine the music being more convincingly presented. The coupling is not less desirable, and with sound of Decca's very highest quality, this disc is among the very few really great records of instrumental music.

The Oistrakh/Richter performance comes from a live recital given at the Grand Hall of the Moscow Conservatory and has an electricity and excitement that few studio accounts can match. There is an impressive spontaneity allied with a virtuosity and musical feeling of an altogether outstanding order. This is playing of outsize personality and of an imaginative and musical vitality that is unsurpassed on records. The sound is not quite as good as one would expect from a studio recording, but it is more than adequate. Choice between this and the no less fine (and better recorded) Decca will obviously depend on coupling.

Violoncello sonata in A major (transcription of the *Violin sonata*).
    *** HMV ASD 2851. Jacqueline du Pré (cello), Daniel Barenboim (piano) – CHOPIN: *Cello sonata.** (*)

Franck's *Violin sonata* in its original form emerges as a strikingly brilliant work. Inevitably, when translated to the cello it is mellower, less extrovert, but its originality of structure based on strikingly memorable material is underlined all the more. Here is a fine, mature,

deeply expressive reading of a richly satisfying work, beautifully recorded.

ORGAN MUSIC

Andantino in G minor; Choral No. 3 in A minor; Prélude, fugue et variation, Op. 18. (Also includes: BOELLMANN: *Suite Gothique, Op. 25.*)
    (M) * Decca Ace of Diamonds SDD 365. Ralph Davier (organ of the Royal Albert Hall, London).

Marvellous recording, but the performances are almost completely static.

Cantabile; Choral No. 1 in E major; Fantaisie in A major; Pièce héroïque.
    (M) (**) Decca Ace of Diamonds SDD 202. Jeanne Demessieux (organ).
Choral No. 2 in B minor; Fantaisie in C major, Op. 16; Grande pièce symphonique, Op. 17.
    (M) * (*) Decca Ace of Diamonds SDD 203. Jeanne Demessieux (organ).
Choral No. 3 in A minor; Final in B flat major, Op. 21; Pastorale, Op. 19; Prélude, fugue et variation, Op. 18; Prière, Op. 20.
    (M) * (*) Decca Ace of Diamonds SDD 204. Jeanne Demessieux (organ).

These are distinguished performances, offering excitement, where appropriate, as well as obvious authority, but there are two snags. The first is that César Franck's organ music is extremely uneven. The *Choral No. 1* for instance seems to go on a long time without anything very important happening. For most of us the most striking works are the *Pièce héroïque*, the *Grande pièce symphonique*, and the *Choral No. 3*, which are cunningly spread across the three discs. But the worst snag here is the quality of the recording. The organ of the Church of the Madeleine, Paris, where these records were made, must be very difficult to record. The reverberation on the first disc is almost totally uncontrolled and the overall sound is muddy, and oppressive in the louder climaxes. Very little detail emerges at all. The second disc begins badly, but the *Grande pièce symphonique* is very successful. Here the organ writing is emphatic but relatively uncomplicated and the sound mostly good. The performance is outstanding. The third disc too is also generally effective. The *Choral No. 3* is superbly played, and the *Prière* has only one moment of blurring.

Cantabile; Choral No. 2 in B minor; Fantaisie in A major; Pièce héroïque.
(M) * (*) Philips Universo 6581 004. Pierre Cochereau (organ of Notre Dame, Paris).

Like the discs listed above, this issue does not convey the inner detail of Franck's writing ideally. The recording is highly spectacular and there is a slight sense of strain in the loudest moments. The style of the playing is impulsive, with bravura and weight to the fore, so that the *Cantabile* which closes the recital makes a restful contrast.

Cantabile; Pièce héroïque.
(B) * (*) Turnabout TV 34238S. René Saorgin (organ of St Sernin, Toulouse) – SAINT-SAËNS and WIDOR: *Pieces.* (*)

These are acceptable performances but the recording of the organ is on the harsh side.

Choral No. 2 in B minor; Pièce héroïque.
** (*) Argo ZRG 5339. Simon Preston (organ) – MESSIAEN: *L'Ascension.****

These performances are well made, but the rich resonance of English organ tone is too mellifluous for Franck and there is no French accent. In all other respects the recording is excellent.

Grande pièce symphonique, Op. 17.
(B) ** (*) DGG Début 2555 012. David Sanger (organ of Hercules Hall, Munich) – BACH: *Prelude and fugue in G minor; Trio sonata No. 5.****

The organ recording here is superbly managed so that David Sanger has a vast dynamic range at his disposal and the listener is made to catch his breath when the tone swells out almost to engulf him. The organ is obviously suited to the music, and except for one moment soon after the beginning of the second section, when Sanger plays just too fast for complete clarity of articulation, this performance is very impressive indeed. The disc is a real bargain.

CHORAL MUSIC

Psyché (symphonic poem for orchestra and chorus): complete recording.
(M) ** Supraphon SUAST 50674. Czech Philharmonic Chorus, Prague Symphony Orchestra, Jean Fournet.

Franck wrote the massive symphonic poem *Psyché* – his longest orchestral work – when he was in his early sixties, but as a whole it has never established its place in the repertory. When Franck was still in vogue the subject was considered rather too daring (or so Mme Franck thought, for she objected to the sensuality), and when the idea of carnal pleasures being illustrated in music no longer excited opposition, the music itself seemed out-of-date. A complete performance like this shows that though it has not the memorability of the *Symphony*, written about the same period, much of the writing has a distinct kinship. The choral passages bring unexpected echoes of Delius in the sliding, chromatic harmonies. Fournet, always a strong and convincing conductor in French music, makes the most of the work in a ripe, romantic style. Good recording quality.

Fricker, Peter Racine
(born 1920)

Violin concerto.
   *** Argo ZRG 715. Yfrah Neaman (violin), Royal Philharmonic Orchestra, Norman Del Mar – BANKS: *Violin concerto.****

Peter Racine Fricker's *Violin concerto* is a strongly lyrical work, looking back to the Walton *Concerto* in its atmosphere and style. The performance here is firstrate and the recording excellent. With its coupling of the Don Banks *Concerto*, this is one of the most rewarding of British Council sponsored issues.

String quartet No. 2, Op. 20.
   *** Argo ZRG 5372. Amadeus Quartet – BRITTEN: *Quartet No. 2.****

Peter Racine Fricker, after becoming for a time the best-known British composer of his generation, has tended to fade out of the public eye a little. All the more reason to welcome this thoughtful and well-argued quartet, splendidly played by the Amadeus Quartet. It may not quite match the Britten on the reverse in sheer memorability, but it is good to have such music available.

Froberger, Johann
(1616–67)

Capriccio; Fantasia; Lamentation for Ferdinand III; Lamentation for Ferdinand IV; Suites Nos. 3 in G major; 7 in E minor; 10 in A minor; 14 in G minor; 19 in C minor; Allemandes from Suites Nos. 20 and 30, Le Tombeau de M. Blanceroche.
   (M) ** Oiseau-Lyre SOL 60038. Thurston Dart (clavichord).

Johann Jacob Froberger was organist at the Imperial Viennese Court. He studied under Frescobaldi, but his style of composition retains an essentially French flavour (French keyboard music has had a strong atmosphere of its own throughout its history). The cool intimacy of the writing suits the clavichord; and Dart, whose playing is never dry, makes much of the music, although a more varied effect might have been obtained if a harpsichord had been put into service for some of the pieces. The recording is excellent, but the volume needs turning well down to re-create the original effect.

Fux, Johann
(1660–1741)

Concentus musico instrumentalis, 1701: Serenada à 8; Rondeau à 7; Sonata à 4.
   *** Telefunken SAWT 9619. Vienna Concentus Musicus, Nikolaus Harnoncourt.

The *Serenada à 8* takes its time – it spreads over to the second side – but it is amazingly inventive. It was written for the Hapsburg Emperor's son in 1701 as an outdoor entertainment. There is some highly original writing for the high trumpets and a most beautiful minuet.

Indeed by the time one has heard this record through, one is tempted to dismiss the common view of Fux as a dull academic. There is nothing academic about this music, and for that matter nothing dull about the performances. Excellent recording.

Gabrieli, Giovanni
(1557–1612)

Canzon per sonar primi toni; Canzona à 7; Canzonas II, VII and X; Sonata con tre violini; Sonata pian' e forte alla quarta bassa; Sonata XIII.

** Decca sxl 6441. Stuttgart Chamber Orchestra, Karl Münchinger, with Brian Runnett (harpsichord).

A pleasant enough record, but it does seem odd to give us the *Sonata pian' e forte* served up for strings. Odd too that the admirable continuo player should be 'featured'. The playing is good and the recording has warmth, but when authentic Gabrieli is available it would be perverse to recommend these arrangements.

'Venetian festival music': Canzon septimi toni à 8 (for brass); Angelus ad pastores; Buccinate in Neomenia tuba; Hodie Christus natus est; Hodie completi sunt; O domine Jesu Christe; O magnum mysterium; Omnes gentes, plaudite manibus.

*** HMV Quadraphonic Q4-CSD 3755; Stereo csd 3755. King's College Chapel Choir, Cambridge University Musical Society, Bach Choir, Wilbraham Brass Soloists, David Willcocks – SCHEIDT: *In dulci jubilo*; SCHÜTZ: *Psalm 150*.***

This is impressive in ordinary stereo, but the quadraphonic disc is even more

exciting, with the richness of brass and choral sounds echoing all around one. Gabrieli expected it to sound like this: his music is impossible to realize on disc without quadraphony. The performances are splendid, of great power and dignity. The focus of the sound is a little blurred by the acoustic, but at a high volume level one can shut one's eyes and imagine oneself wafted away to St Mark's, Venice.

'Processional and ceremonial music': Concerti (1587): Angelus ad pastores; Inclina domine; O magnum mysterium. Sacrae symphoniae (1597): Canzona quarti toni; Exaudi Deus; Nunc dimittis; O domine Jesu Christe; Sancta et immaculata Virginitas. Sacrae symphoniae (1615): O Jesu mi dulcissime; Hodie completi sunt.

(M) ** Vanguard HM 8SD. Gabrieli Festival Choir and Orchestra, Edmund Appia.

Although neither the focus of the singing itself nor the recording is exact, this is a very enjoyable concert, with plenty of atmosphere. The conductor shows genuine sympathy for Gabrieli's style, and the balance between instruments and voices is well managed.

Gade, Niels
(1817–90)

String quartet in D major, Op. 63.

(B) ** Turnabout TV 34187S. Copenhagen String Quartet – NIELSEN: *Quartet No. 1*.**

Gade was the leading Danish composer of the nineteenth century and a keen champion of Mendelssohn, whose work much influenced him. He wrote eight symphonies and a large quantity of other music, but his *First Quartet* is a late work, composed when he was seventy-one. Even so it is still firmly in the tradition of Mendelssohn, though the ideas have genuine freshness and charm. It is extremely well played by the Copenhagen Quartet and well recorded. It is not great music but it is pleasant, well-written and civilized.

The Fairy Spell (opera-ballet), *Op. 30*.
(B) ** Turnabout TV 34381S. Kirsten Hermansen (soprano), Gurli Plesner (contralto), Ib Hansen (baritone), Royal Danish Opera Chorus, Royal Danish Orchestra, Johan Hye-Knudsen.

Gade's delightful opera-ballet *The Fairy Spell* comes from the mid-1850s. Like so much of his music, it is strongly Mendelssohnian in feeling, but there are a number of passages that are distinctly Danish in character. It is probably Gade's most successful work, and it is surely well performed and recorded on this excellently cast disc. At its modest price, it should be snapped up by all who like Weber, Mendelssohn and Berwald.

Geminiani, Francesco
(1687–1762)

The Enchanted Forest (La Foresta incantata) (ballet).
(M) ** (*) Nonesuch H 71151. Milan Angelicum Orchestra, Newell Jenkins, with Frederick Hammond (harpsichord) – LOCATELLI: *Pianto d'Arianna*.** (*)

The Enchanted Forest was first given in Paris in 1754, and charmingly reflects the taste of what was musically a transitional period. The performance is well pointed and the recording well focused.

Gerhard, Roberto
(1896–1970)

Concerto for orchestra.
*** Argo ZRG 553. BBC Symphony Orchestra, Norman Del Mar – RAWSTHORNE: *Symphony No. 3.****

This is one of the most impressive records of modern British music yet sponsored by the British Council. Gerhard's *Concerto for orchestra* – used by the BBC Orchestra as a showpiece on its American tour in 1965 – is the more adventurous piece, an astonishing feat of imagination for a septuagenarian and intensely rewarding in its avant-garde 'difficulty', but the Rawsthorne too is most satisfying. Both works receive superb performances and outstanding recording.

(i) *Violin concerto; Symphony No. 4.*
*** Argo ZRG 701. BBC Symphony Orchestra, Colin Davis, (i) with Yfrah Neaman (violin).

The *Fourth Symphony*, written in Gerhard's seventieth year, shows him at his most imaginatively adventurous. The work, bearing the subtitle *New York* and written for that city's Philharmonic Orchestra, is brilliant and colourful. Even more than in the *Concerto for orchestra* Gerhard resorts to crypto-electronic sounds which delight the ear rather than baffling it. It is superbly played by the BBC Orchestra under Davis. The *Violin concerto* dates from Gerhard's early years in Cambridge and, rather like the violin concerto of a fellow pupil of Schoenberg, Alban Berg, it successfully combines a lyrical style with serial method, though the virtuoso writing has one thinking of the violin pyrotechnics of another Spaniard, Sarasate. A brilliant performance from Yfrah Neaman.

Symphony No. 1; Don Quixote (ballet): *Dances.*

*** Argo ZRG 752. BBC Symphony Orchestra, Antal Dorati.

Before this Gulbenkian Foundation record appeared there was next to no music of Roberto Gerhard available on record. The choice of these two works is ideal, the suite representing Gerhard at his most colourful and immediately attractive, and the symphony at his toughest and most ambitious. Though the symphony is difficult in its idiom, there is never any doubt about Gerhard's ability to argue strongly, and unlike many atonalists he does not make the mistake of avoiding strong rhythmic movements. Dorati brings out not only the strength but the Spanish warmth of the music. Originally issued by EMI, this reissue has retained the excellence of the original recording.

The Plague.

** (*) Decca Headline HEAD 6. Alec McCowen (narrator), Washington National Symphony Orchestra and Chorus, Antal Dorati.

Gerhard, whose originality blossomed with the years, was inspired by a sinister passage from Camus which he fashioned into this melodrama – 'melodrama' in the strict sense of a work for speaker and orchestra. The impact is immediate if hardly ingratiating in any way, but closer acquaintance allows one to appreciate the purely musical strength of argument. Dorati's performance with Washington forces is strong and committed if not ideally atmospheric. The discrepancy between McCowen's English accent and the American accents of the chorus may be distracting for some. A powerful work, well recorded.

German, Edward
(1862–1936)

Welsh rhapsody.

*** HMV ASD 2400. Scottish National Orchestra, Alexander Gibson – HARTY: *With the Wild Geese*; MACCUNN: *Land of Mountain and Flood*; SMYTH: *The Wreckers overture.****

Edward German's *Welsh rhapsody,* written for the Cardiff Festival of 1904, makes a colourful and exciting finale for this enterprising collection of genre British tone pictures. German is content not to interfere with the traditional melodies he uses, and he relies on his orchestral skill to retain the listener's interest, in which he is very successful. The closing pages, based on *Men of Harlech*, are prepared in an almost Tchaikovskian manner to provide a rousing conclusion. This is a good example of a tune with an inbuilt eloquence that cannot be improved upon.

Gershwin, George
(1898–1937)

An American in Paris (rev. F. Campbell-Watson); *Cuban overture; Porgy and Bess: Symphonic picture* (arr. Robert Russell Bennett).

*** Philips 6500 290. Monte Carlo National Opera Orchestra, Edo de Waart.

An American in Paris; Piano concerto in F major; Rhapsody in Blue.

** (*) HMV ASD 2754. André Previn (piano and cond.), London Symphony Orchestra.

An American in Paris; Rhapsody in Blue.

*** CBS 72080. Leonard Bernstein (piano and cond.), New York Philharmonic Orchestra.

** Decca Phase 4 PFS 4098. Stanley Black (piano and cond.), London Symphony Orchestra.

Piano concerto in F major.

*** DGG 2530 055. Roberto Szidon (piano), London Philharmonic Orchestra, Edward Downes — MACDOWELL: *Piano concerto No. 2.****

Piano concerto in F major; Rhapsody in Blue.

(B) ** (*) Classics for Pleasure CFP 40005. Malcolm Binns (piano), Sinfonia of London, Kenneth Alwyn.

(B) ** Music for Pleasure MFP 2107. Reid Nibley (piano), Utah Symphony Orchestra, Maurice Abravanel.

(B) ** CBS Embassy EMB 3011. André Previn (piano), Orchestra, André Kostelanetz.

(M) CBS Classics 61240. Philippe Entremont (piano), Philadelphia Orchestra, Eugene Ormandy.

Piano concerto in F major; Rhapsody in Blue (original version); *3 Preludes for piano.*

(B) ** Turnabout TV 34457S. Eugene List (piano), Berlin Symphony Orchestra, Samuel Adler.

Rhapsody in Blue.

** (*) Decca SXL 6411. Julius Katchen (piano), London Symphony Orchestra, Istvan Kertesz — RAVEL: *Left-hand concerto*; PROKOFIEV: *Piano concerto No. 3.****

All performances of *An American in Paris* and the *Rhapsody in Blue* stand to be judged by Bernstein's outstanding disc, which dates from 1960 but still sounds

astonishingly well, the *Rhapsody* in particular being of demonstration quality, with better piano tone than CBS often give us in the seventies. Bernstein's approach is exceptionally flexible but completely spontaneous. It is a masterly account in every way, quixotic in mood, rhythmically subtle and creating a great surge of human warmth at the entry of the big central tune. The performance of *American in Paris* is vividly characterized, brash and episodic, an unashamed American view, with the great blues tune marvellously phrased as only an American orchestra can do it. The recording here is not so rich but certainly brilliant.

Edo de Waart's Monte Carlo performance of *American in Paris* misses Bernstein's idiomatic quality, but it is better recorded than the CBS disc. The *Cuban overture* is played boisterously, which is the only possible way to approach it, for it is a comparatively empty piece. But the performance of the *Porgy and Bess Symphonic picture* is quite superb and makes this one of the most desirable Gershwin collections. Robert Russell Bennett's cleverly dovetailed selection has long been a gramophone demonstration piece but never more effectively than here, where the sound is rich and sparkling. The performance is more 'symphonic' than usual, with an imaginatively atmospheric opening section, very effective characterization of the individual tunes, and a blaze of splendour at the finale.

Previn's HMV disc would seem an obvious investment for those wanting Gershwin's three key orchestral and concertante works, but is in the last resort disappointing. The HMV recording, although warm and atmospheric, lacks sparkle, notably in the *Rhapsody* and *American in Paris*, which have been squeezed on to one side. The sound is, of course. very pleasing and it suits the mellow Previn approach. This is essentially a European one, with an overlay of smooth sophistication. Listen to the way the famous tune in the *Rhapsody* comes over, and compare it with any of the other versions to see the way the character of the melody has lost its transatlantic feeling. Previn's sophistication is more effective in the *Concerto*, a fine performance by any standards, and here the recording has more bite. In some ways Previn's earlier disc, recorded with Kostelanetz for CBS, is more telling stylistically, but the piano tone is shallow. The recording otherwise sounds unexpectedly vivid, and has much more impact than the HMV disc, especially in the brilliant finale of the *Concerto*. Kostelanetz and his Orchestra play a major part in the interpretation. The main lyrical theme in the first movement of the *Concerto* has a wonderful lyrical warmth yet is not overindulged, and the slow movement has urgency of feeling, conveyed in the opening trumpet solo and especially at the passionate close of the movement. Previn's impetuosity in the *Rhapsody* produces some rushed playing in places, but the pungent comments from the orchestral wind soloists are particularly compelling.

Stanley Black's Phase 4 disc might be considered for the brilliance of its recording. In the *Rhapsody* the effect is rather brash, but these performances show a real feeling for the music's style, although *American in Paris* is not held together with any special skill.

Roberto Szidon on DGG treats the work as he would any other romantic concerto, and with rhythm superbly lithe and tonal colouring enchantingly subtle in its range, the result gives new stature to the music. The jazz idiom is seen – as it regularly and naturally is for example in the Ravel *Concertos* – as an essential but not overwhelmingly dominant element. Downes and the LPO match the soloist in understanding and virtuosity, while the recording is of demonstration standard from the vivid timpani at the beginning onwards.

There are some excellent performances too at the bargain end of the market. On

Classics for Pleasure the Binns/Alwyn performance of the *Rhapsody* has a thoughtful contribution from Binns and a more exuberant one from Alwyn (a much under-rated British conductor). The performance of the *Concerto* has fine vitality and plenty of bravura in the outer movements, though not at the expense of lyrical warmth. In the slow movement, however, the opening trumpet solo (played unmuted) is not very idiomatic in style.

The Music for Pleasure disc is a real bargain, even though the recording is not outstandingly brilliant. The performances of both works have the colloquial quality that only an American recording can bring, and there is an attractive rhythmic quirkiness in the *Concerto*, with a fine trumpet solo in the slow movement. The *Rhapsody* has both warmth and power.

Eugene List's Turnabout account is much admired in some quarters. In the *Rhapsody* it uses the original scoring made to suite Paul Whiteman's particular orchestral combination. This has an undoubted historical interest, but the effect is shallow compared with Ferde Grofé's fuller version, which had the composer's directing influence. The rather thin Turnabout recording creates a very brash effect at the first brass entry, with a hard edge to it. In spite of the crisp precision of the solo playing one cannot recommend this without some reservation. The *Concerto* fares better, although the quality is never really rich. But what redeems the disc is the distinguished solo performance, always brilliant but never hard. The three piano *Preludes* make a fine bonus.

The CBS sound for Entremont and Ormandy is even less agreeable. These are bright, attractive performances, but the exaggerated, brittle treble makes the piano sound thin and the upper strings screechy and gritty.

Julius Katchen made an early stereo record, coupling the *Concerto* and the *Rhapsody*, with Mantovani, and this is available now on Eclipse (ECS 2146), but the partnership was not a particularly fruitful one. Katchen re-recorded the *Rhapsody* with Kertesz not long before he died, and listening to this vivid and exciting playing no one would suspect that his health was anything other than robust. The Ravel and Prokofiev couplings are both splendid, but the *Rhapsody* lacks that elusive idiomatic quality it needs to spring fully to life.

'Greatest hits': (i) *An American in Paris;* (ii) *Piano concerto in F major:* finale. (i) *Porgy and Bess: Symphonic picture* (arr. Robert Russell Bennett): excerpts; (iii) *Rhapsody in Blue;* (iv) *3 Preludes for piano.*

(B) *** CBS Harmony 30022. (i) Philadelphia Orchestra, Eugene Ormandy; (ii) André Previn (piano), Orchestra, André Kostelanetz; (iii) Leonard Bernstein (piano), New York Philharmonic Orchestra; (iv) Oscar Levant (piano).

The highlight here is undoubtedly Bernstein's distinguished and exciting performance of *Rhapsody in Blue*, one of the very finest accounts available of this masterpiece. Ormandy's *American in Paris* too is brilliant and colloquial, but both this and the selection from Russell Bennett's *Porgy and Bess Symphonic picture* are given super-brilliant sound, with a tendency to harshness. The *Preludes* are welcome and very well characterized, although they are hardly among the composer's most familiar music.

Gesualdo, Carlo
(*c.* 1560–1613)

Madrigals from Book V: *Correte amanti; Dolcissima mia vita; Itene, O,* *miei sospiri; Mercè, grido piangendo; O dolorosa gioia; O tenebroso giorno; O voi, troppo felice.* Motets and Responsories: *Ave dulcissima Maria; O vos omnes; Tribulationem et dolorem; Three Responsories for Good Friday.*

(M) ** Pye Virtuoso TPLS 13012. Accademia Monteverdiana, Denis Stevens.

Don Carlo Gesualdo was Prince of Venosa for a period of two decades from 1591. He must have been among the most talented of all royal composers, for much of this music is not only beautiful but shows a strong individual musical personality, a supremacy in what Robert Craft has called the ability 'to choose correctly the intensifying step in a harmonic progression'. This is immediately apparent in the sombre beauty of the opening *O vos omnes,* a particularly striking start for a well performed and recorded collection. As presented here the sustained music is particularly expressive, so that, on the whole, the sacred music emerges as the more memorable of the two collections.

Collection: *Responsoria et alia ad Officium Sabbati Sancti: Sicut ovis ad occisionem ductus est; Jerusalem, surge; Plange quasi virgo; Recessit pastor noster; O vos omnes; Ecce quomodo moritur justus; Astiterunt reges terrae; Aestimatus sum cum descentibus in lacum; Sepulto Domino; Miserere; Benedictus.*

*** Telefunken SAWT 9613. Prague Madrigal Singers, Miroslav Venhoda.

These are marvellously expressive pieces, and the Prague Madrigal Singers and Venhoda give them performances of great power. Gesualdo's strange and overheated sensibility is not for all tastes, but those who admire this extraordinarily

383

intense and visionary figure will find this a satisfying experience. (His wife and her lover no doubt took a different view!) The recording is admirably vivid and clearly-defined, if just a shade too forwardly balanced.

Motets: *Ave dulcissima Maria; Dolcissima mia vita; Ecco morirò dunque; Hei mihi Domine; Moro lasso al mio duolo; O vos omnes.*

 ** Argo ZRG 645. Monteverdi Choir (with instrumental accompaniment), John Eliot Gardiner – MONTEVERDI: *Motets.***

Here are convincing and fluent performances of six Gesualdo pieces, music that is full of character even when it is not wholly convincing. The singers have excellent ensemble and intonation and are well recorded, though they tend to leave nothing to the listener's imagination. An interesting recital nonetheless.

Gibbons, Orlando
(1583–1625)

Song 1; Second preces; Psalm 145; Voluntary; Te Deum; Voluntary; Jubilate; This is the record of John; See, see, the word is incarnate; Glorious and powerful God.

 ** Argo ZRG 5151. King's College Chapel Choir, Jacobean Consort of Viols, Simon Preston (organ), David Willcocks.

This is an early Argo stereo record. and the attempt to simulate antiphonal alternation in the *Psalm* is not wholly clear. But generally the sound is very good, although not perhaps ideally intimate for the verse-anthems. The programme is imaginatively chosen and the music all of high quality. The consort of viols is

not too well balanced, however, and makes less than its full effect.

Ginastera, Alberto
(born 1916)

Estancia; Panambi (choreographic legend).

 (M) ** Everest SDBR 3041. London Symphony Orchestra, Sir Eugene Goossens – VILLA-LOBOS: *Little train.***

These characteristic ballet scores by the Argentinian composer Ginastera are notable for their exotic orchestral colouring. The music is alive if not especially substantial, and it is well presented by Goossens with the immediacy of Everest sound.

Giordano, Umberto
(1867–1948)

Andrea Chénier (opera in 4 acts): complete recording.

 (M) *** Decca Ace of Diamonds GOS 600/1. Renata Tebaldi (soprano), Mario del Monaco (tenor), Ettore Bastianini (baritone), Chorus and Orchestra of St Cecilia Academy, Rome, Gianandrea Gavazzeni.

Apart perhaps from *La Forza del destino*, this is the most desirable of the Tebaldi/del Monaco sets. The blood and thunder of the story, with the threat of the guillotine hanging over, suits both singers admirably, and Gavazzeni is at his best. It is a work that thrives on 'give-it-all-you've-got' technique, and Tebaldi and Monaco certainly oblige. Sample the final duet if you have any doubts. But finer still than the soprano and tenor is Bastianini as Gérard. His finely focused voice is beautifully caught and he conveys vividly the conflicts in the man's character. The full-priced stereo version was originally issued on six sides, against four in mono. Now the stereo version is also accommodated on four sides in this reissue, without loss of vividness or atmosphere.

Fedora (opera in 3 acts): complete recording.
>> ** (*) Decca SET 435/6. Magda Olivero (soprano), Mario del Monaco (tenor), Tito Gobbi (baritone), Monte Carlo Opera Chorus, Monte Carlo National Opera Orchestra, Lamberto Gardelli.

Puccini was unique among his Italian contemporaries in sustaining his operatic reputation over a long series of works. Giordano, like Leoncavallo, Mascagni and others, failed to live up to early success, and with Giordano it is significant that this opera, like his most famous one, *Andrea Chénier*, dates from his earliest career. He went on to marry the rich daughter of an hotelier, and prosperity was no doubt the bogey of invention. *Fedora* will always be remembered for one brief aria, the hero's *Amor ti vieta*, but, as this highly enjoyable recording confirms, there is much that is memorable in the score even if nothing else quite approaches that. The piece is adapted from a Sardou melodrama designed for Sarah Bernhardt (parallel with *Tosca*), with an absurd plot involving a passionate volte-face when the heroine's hate of the hero (her wicked brother's murderer) suddenly turns to love. Meaty stuff which brings some splendid singing from Magda Olivero and (more intermittently) from Mario del Monaco and Gobbi in a light comedy part. Fine atmospheric recording. Well worth trying by anyone with a hankering after *verismo*.

Fedora: highlights.
>> ** (*) Decca SET 494 (from above recording).

Those not wanting to buy the complete opera will find this set of highlights generous in including long excerpts from each of the three acts, together with the *Intermezzo* (and of course the famous *Amor ti vieta*). The recording maintains the vivid quality of the original.

Giuliani, Mauro
(1781–1828)

Guitar concerto in A major, Op. 30.
>> *** RCA SB 6826. Julian Bream (guitar), Melos Ensemble – ARNOLD: *Concerto.****
>> *** CBS 72798. John Williams (guitar), English Chamber Orchestra – VIVALDI: *Concertos.** (*)
>> ** (*) HMV ASD 2363. Alirio Diaz (guitar), Professors of Spanish National Orchestra, Rafael Frühbeck de Burgos – RODRIGO: *Concierto de Aranjuez.** (*)

Some years ago Malcolm Arnold told me personally (I.M. writing) that this Giuliani *Concerto* is in fact a pastiche written by himself. If so the assumption of the *galant* style is uncannily accurate, for the main theme of the first movement and the jolly finale certainly sound like early nineteenth-century music. The melodies have a genuine Italian lyric flavour and the concerto's structure is equally convincing. The piece is uncommonly well played by Julian Bream on the RCA disc. Bream's record dates from 1961, but the sound is extremely fine and it has the attraction of Malcolm Arnold's *Guitar concerto* as a coupling, one of the composer's best and certainly his wittiest work. John Williams's account too is elegantly turned, and choice will rest with

385

coupling. The HMV disc is notable for particularly graceful orchestral ritornelli directed by Frühbeck de Burgos, who also communicates a spirit of gaiety in the outer movements. The soloist is more circumspect but plays sensitively enough. A warm, expansive recording completes the listener's pleasure.

Glazounov, Alexander (1865–1936)

Violin concerto in A minor, Op. 82.
> (M) *** RCA LSB 4061. Jascha Heifetz (violin), RCA Symphony Orchestra, Walter Hendl – BRUCH: *Concerto No. 1.***
> * (*) Decca SXL 6532. Josef Sivó (violin), Suisse Romande Orchestra, Horst Stein – PROKOFIEV: *Concerto No. 1.***
> (M) * (*) Supraphon SUAST 50687. Ida Haendel (violin), Prague Symphony Orchestra, Václav Smetáček – WIENIAWSKI: *Concerto No. 2.** (*)

Heifetz is incomparable here; his account is the strongest and most passionate (as well as the most perfectly played) in the catalogue. In his hands the *Concerto*'s sweetness is tempered with strength. It is altogether a captivating performance that completely absolves the work from any charge of synthetic sweetness. The RCA Orchestra under Hendl gives splendid support, and although the recording is not beyond reproach, the disc is a must.

Sivó is a fine artist, but the Glazounov does not really find him at his best. There is some less than ideal intonation, and the performance, though unfailingly conscientious and extremely well recorded, does not present a challenge to the Heifetz account.

Miss Haendel shows herself happiest in the lyrical music. In the fireworks her playing is hardly breathtaking, although she competently skates over the difficult bits. The recording projects a rather rough upper register to her violin but is otherwise atmospheric.

Raymonda (ballet), *Op. 57*: complete recording.
> (M) *** HMV SLS 826 (3 discs). Bolshoi Theatre Orchestra, Yevgeny Svetlanov.

Glazounov's *Raymonda* follows very much in the tradition of Tchaikovsky's *Nutcracker*, a Russian fairy tale set to sweet, sumptuously scored music. Svetlanov's direction points the story very vividly. For the general, non-balletomane listener this is an attractive set which will provide a whole stream of colourful and undemanding music ideal for background listening. Recording far richer than is common from Russian Melodiya engineers.

Scènes de ballet (suite), *Op. 52.*
> *** HMV ASD 2974. Moscow Radio Symphony Orchestra, Gennady Rozhdestvensky – RIMSKY-KOR-SAKOV: *Antar.** (*)

Glazounov's *Scènes de ballet* is a charming, lightweight score which shows the composer's orchestral palette at its prettiest. The invention of the earlier movements is the more striking: the opening fanfare section almost sounds like modern film music, while the delightful *Marionettes*, without being a crib, pays obvious homage to Delibes's automatons' music in *Coppélia*. But the whole suite is attractive, especially when played and recorded as vividly as it is here.

The Seasons (ballet), *Op. 67.*
> (B) ** (*) Decca Eclipse ECS 642. Paris Conservatoire Orchestra,

Albert Wolff – BALAKIREV: *Thamar*.**

The Seasons, Op. 67; Concert waltzes Nos. 1 in D major, Op. 47; 2 in F major, Op. 51.

** (*) Decca SXL 6269. Suisse Romande Orchestra, Ernest Ansermet.

(i) *The Seasons, Op. 67;* (ii) *Finnish fantasy, Op. 88;* (iii) *Wedding Procession, Op. 21.*

** (*) HMV ASD 2522. Moscow Radio Symphony Orchestra, (i) Boris Khaikin; (ii) Yevgeny Svetlanov; (iii) Alexander Gauk.

Apart from the charming *Violin concerto, The Seasons* would seem to be Glazounov's strongest claim to the attention of posterity. It is an early work, first performed at St Petersburg in 1900, the choreography being by the famous Petipa. With colourful orchestration, a generous sprinkling of distinctive melody, and, at the opening of *Autumn*, one of the most virile and memorable tunes the composer ever penned, the ballet surely deserves to return to the repertoire.

The Moscow account is brilliantly played, with that special flair and temperament which the Russians bring to performances of their own ballet music. But the recording, although sophisticated in matters of atmosphere and colour, has a very bright treble, and the upper strings show a tendency to glassiness.

Ansermet's is the finest recording and his reading is characteristically meticulous. It takes a little while to warm up – in that respect some may prefer the extra warmth of the Russian performance – but it is satisfying overall. Of the two *Concert waltzes* the first is by far the more attractive, but both are played with affection and beautifully recorded. But in most ways the best buy, in spite of dated recording, is the Eclipse issue. Wolff's performance is admirable, obviously affectionate and stylish, and the orchestral

playing is good. The recording produces a rather feathery string tone (but Ansermet's disc is not entirely free from this criticism, in its quieter moments), especially when muted on side one. But the strings are joyously firm in the big tune in the finale, and the wind and brass have a characteristic Decca bloom throughout.

Stenka Razin (symphonic poem), *Op. 13.*

(B) ** Decca Eclipse ECS 641. Suisse Romande Orchestra, Ernest Ansermet – KHACHATURIAN: *Violin concerto*.** (*)

Stenka Razin, if not a masterpiece, is an effective descriptive piece which uses the *Volga Boat song* at the opening and again at its Lisztian climax. The performance here is effective, if lacking something in romantic thrust. The recording sounds astonishingly vivid when one considers it dates from 1955.

Symphony No. 3 in D major, Op. 33.

*** HMV ASD 2900. Moscow Radio Symphony Orchestra, Boris Khaikin.

Glazounov's *Third* (like his other symphonies) is delightful: it is inventive, full of attractive ideas, and distinguished by fine craftsmanship and warmth of feeling. Khaikin gives an alert and vivid performance, even if the playing of the Moscow Orchestra could be more refined and sensitive at times. The scherzo is a very strong movement, as is so often the case in Glazounov (take the *Fifth*, for example), but the work as a whole is unfailingly engaging. The recording becomes a little blowzy at climaxes, but on the whole there need be no reservation about quality.

387

Glière, Reinhold
(1875–1956)

The Red Poppy (ballet): *Russian sailors' dance.*
  (M) ** Vanguard VCS 10060. Utah Symphony Orchestra, Maurice Abravanel – IPPOLITOV-IVANOV: *Caucasian sketches*; RIMSKY-KORSAKOV: *Antar.***

The well-known *Russian sailors' dance* is the only really memorable number in Glière's *Red Poppy* ballet music. Abravanel's lively account makes a pleasant bonus to this generously filled disc. Both the couplings are worthwhile.

Symphony No. 3 (Ilya Murometz), Op. 42.
  *** RCA SB 6859. Philadelphia Orchestra, Eugene Ormandy.

To fit this sumptuous fairy-tale symphony – fairly closely related to Rimsky-Korsakov's *Scheherazade* – on to a single disc Ormandy, like most interpreters before him, has sanctioned a number of cuts in a work that would last *in extenso* some eighty minutes. None of the losses is serious, and the resulting jigsaw of rich ideas is thoroughly enjoyable, particularly in a performance as superbly played as this. The recording is one of the most atmospheric from Philadelphia. This can be warmly recommended, especially to anyone who likes spotting influences.

Glinka, Michail
(1804–57)

Kamarinskaya (fantasy on two Russian folk-songs).

** HMV ASD 2617. USSR Symphony Orchestra, Yevgeny Svetlanov – TCHAIKOVSKY: *Symphony No. 6.** (*)

This makes a colourful fill-up for Tchaikovsky's *Pathétique symphony*. The performance is idiomatic and enjoyable, if a little mannered, and the recording is good.

Russlan and Ludmilla: Oriental dances; Chernomor's march.
  *** HMV ASD 2520. USSR Symphony Orchestra, Yevgeny Svetlanov – RIMSKY-KORSAKOV: *Scheherazade.****

These are exceptionally attractive bonuses for a fine performance of *Scheherazade*. The *Oriental dances* are highly exciting in the most red-blooded Russian way, and *Chernomor's march* is exotic and delightfully coloured. Its strong orchestral character reminds one of Liadov or Tchaikovsky. Both performances here are first-rate, and so is the recording.

Ivan Susanin (or *A Life for the Tsar*) (opera in 4 acts and epilogue): complete recording.
  (M) * (*) Decca Ace of Diamonds GOS 646/8. Miro Changalovich (bass), Militza Mladinovich (mezzo-soprano), Drago Startz (tenor), Maria Glavachevich (soprano), Yugoslav Army Chorus, Orchestra of the National Opera, Belgrade, Oscar Danon.

Glinka's long historical opera may be historic musically too, but in a performance as flawed as this one from Belgrade, its delights are somewhat submerged. The soloists are the main problem with their range of Slavonic wobbles, but there is

still enough life and colour in the music –
well recorded for its period – to make this
a useful stopgap.

Gluck, Christoph
(1714–87)

Don Juan (ballet): complete recording.
  *** Decca SXL 6339. Academy of
  St Martin-in-the-Fields, Neville
  Marriner, with Simon Preston
  (harpsichord continuo).

Although some of the music is known
from the French version of *Orfeo*, and
three numbers turn up in *Iphigénie en
Aulide*, *Don Juan* never preserved the
popularity it enjoyed during the 1760s
and 1770s. (Even Boccherini paraphrased
some of it in his *La Casa del Diavolo*
symphony.) The lack of tonal variety may
worry some listeners but for the most part
the sheer delight at the quality and
imaginative vitality of Gluck's invention
will reward those who persevere. The
playing is altogether excellent and captures the lightness of touch and the
dramatic intensity of the score. The
Decca engineers produce vivid yet well-
focused sound quality, and there is an
informative sleeve-note by Erik Smith.
An outstanding record.

Iphigénie en Aulide: overture.
  (B) *** Classics for Pleasure CFP
  40081. Royal Philharmonic Orchestra, Paul Kletzki – BRAHMS:
  Double concerto.** (*)

A first-class performance of Gluck's
little-known *Iphigénie en Aulide* overture.
It is a strong piece, both dramatic and
atmospheric, and Kletzki makes the very
most of its possibilities.

Alceste (opera in 3 acts): complete recording.

  (M) ** Decca Ace of Diamonds GOS
  574/6. Kirsten Flagstad (soprano),
  Raoul Jobin, Alexander Young
  (tenors), Thomas Hemsley (baritone), Geraint Jones Singers and
  Orchestra, Geraint Jones.

This originally appeared in 1957 on four
mono LPs, but the stereo is genuine and
considering its age remarkably good.
Alceste is a magnificent work, and this
performance is notable for Kirsten Flagstad's noble queen. She is not always in
perfect sympathy with the style, and her
intonation is a trifle suspect at times, but
this is of small account given her star
quality. The rest of the cast is perfectly
acceptable, even if Raoul Jobin's Ad-
metus is not absolutely ideal. Geraint
Jones directs the chorus and orchestra to
good effect: tempi are well judged and
though the performance is not a thrilling
one (it wants the last ounce of polish) it is
still worth having. Jones does the Italian
version of the work, and even though the
quality of recorded sound is not in the
first flight, the set is valuable when
Gluck's representation in the catalogue is
so meagre.

Orfeo ed Euridice (opera in 3 acts):
complete recording.
  ** (*) Decca SET 443/4. Marilyn
  Horne (mezzo-soprano), Pilar Lo-
  rengar, Helen Donath (sopranos),
  Chorus and Orchestra of Royal
  Opera House, Covent Garden, Sir
  Georg Solti.
  (M) ** (*) RCA SER 5539/41. Shir-
  ley Verrett (mezzo-soprano), Anna
  Moffo, Judith Raskin (sopranos),
  Polyphonic Chorus of Rome,
  Virtuosi di Roma, Collegium Mu-
  sicum Italicum Ensemble, Renato
  Fasano.

The surprise of the Decca set is the
conducting of Georg Solti, which com-

bines his characteristic brilliance and dramatic bite with a feeling for eighteenth-century idiom which is most impressive. Where often in this opera the progress of the drama can be forgotten, here the experience is riveting, the more so when Solti and Horne opt to conclude Act 1, not as the Gluck score prescribes, but with a brilliant display aria, *Addio, o miei sospiri*, taken from the contemporary opera *Tancredi* by Ferdinando Bertoni. That may sound like cavalier treatment for Gluck, but stylistically in every way Solti justifies not only that course but his whole interpretation, which combines drama with delicacy. Marilyn Horne makes a formidably strong Orfeo, not so deeply imaginative as Shirley Verrett on RCA, but wonderfully strong and secure with fine control of tone. Pilar Lorengar sings sweetly, but is not always steady, while Helen Donath is charming in the role of Amor. Recording quality is outstandingly fine.

Clearly if you have a mezzo as firm and sensitive as Shirley Verrett there is everything in favour of using the original Italian version rather than the later Paris version with tenor. Quite apart from making the right decision over text, Fasano uses the right-sized orchestra and adopts an appropriately classical style. Anna Moffo and Judith Raskin match Verrett in clean, strong singing, and the Rome Polyphonic Chorus is far more incisive than most Italian choirs. The recording is vivid and atmospheric, but the closeness of the voices tends to bring out the music's dramatic qualities rather than its tenderness.

Orfeo ed Euridice: highlights.
** (*) Decca SET 495 (from above recording cond. Solti).

Solti's vigorous account of Gluck's *Orfeo* with Marilyn Horne a vibrant Orfeo may have its controversial passages, but this selection has been well made to include not only the predictable numbers but even the superb display aria inserted here at the end of Act 1 (see above).

Goehr, Alexander
(born 1932)

Violin concerto, Op. 13.
*** HMV ASD 2810. Manoug Parikian (violin), Royal Philharmonic Orchestra, Norman Del Mar – HAMILTON: *Concerto.****

Goehr's *Violin concerto*, commissioned by the soloist here who is the most persuasive of advocates, is characteristically thorny, yielding little to the temptation to make the solo instrument sing. The first movement is pure and cool; the second, longer and more complex, culminates in a cadenza which draws all the threads together – a satisfying shape, though the structure may well baffle even the skilled listener. His greatest hope lies in the playing of soloist and orchestra, which by its commitment leads the ear on to investigate and identify. Excellent recording.

(i) *Piano trio, Op. 20;* (ii) *String quartet No. 2, Op. 23.*
*** Argo ZRG 748. (i) Orion Piano Trio; (ii) Allegri String Quartet.

Thanks to the British Council these two powerful and individual works are made available in recorded performances which should readily communicate their distinction to any open-minded listener. The *Quartet*, written for Lord Dynevor in 1967, is the tougher and more challenging work but not necessarily the more difficult to comprehend. The very uncompromising quality of its arguments has one concentrated, and the serene finale has its obvious links with late

Beethoven. The *Trio*, written for the Menuhins at Bath in 1966, is rather less introspective, with dance rhythms and bell effects prominent. First-rate recording.

Four songs from the Japanese: Things have never changed; Do torrents spare the fresh bloom flower; I love and I love; The truth is.

> (B) ** Pye GSGC 14105. Marni Nixon (soprano), John McCabe (piano) – IVES and SCHÜRMANN: *Songs.***

We know Marni Nixon from an entirely different field, for she has ghost-voiced in American film musicals including the Deborah Kerr part in *The King and I*. Here she shows her mettle in a difficult modern idiom that could so easily disintegrate into apparently unconnected phrases. With a firm sense of line and arching curves of simple yet well sustained tone she wrings every drop of lyricism out of these four songs. They were originally written to be sung with orchestra, but John McCabe brings a composer's understanding to the piano transcription and makes the most of the sometimes thick piano texture. The best song is the last and this is beautifully sung. The recording is basically good, the voice well balanced with the piano in a spacious acoustic.

Goldmark, Carl
(1830–1915)

Rustic Wedding symphony, Op. 26.

> (B) ** Turnabout TV 34410S. Westphalian Symphony Orchestra, Hubert Reichert.

This charming and colourful suite of movements – it is hardly a genuine symphony – is given a bright performance by the Westphalian Orchestra, if hardly one which magicks the music in the way that a great conductor like Beecham or Bernstein can. But their versions are, alas, no longer available. At bargain price with fair recording this is well worth investigating.

Gottschalk, Louis
(1829–69)

(i; ii) *Grande Fantaisie triomphale sur l'Hymne Nationale Brésilien, Op. 69* (arr. Adler); (i; iii) *Grande tarantelle* (arr. Kay); *'The Union': Concert paraphrase on national airs, Op. 48* (arr. Adler); *Variations on the Portuguese national hymn* (ed. List); (i; iv or i; v) *5 pieces for piano, four hands.*

> (B) *** Turnabout TV 37034S. (i) Eugene List (piano); (ii) Berlin Symphony Orchestra, Samuel Adler; (iii) Vienna State Opera Orchestra, Igor Buketoff; (iv) Cary Lewis (piano); (v) Brady Millican (piano).

(i) *Grande tarantelle; Symphony No. 1 (A Night in the Tropics);* (ii) Piano pieces: *Bamboula; Danse des nègres, Op. 2; The Banjo, Op. 15; The Dying Poet; Ojos Criolos (Danse Cubaine), Op. 37; Souvenir de Porto Rico; Marche des Gibaros.*

> (B) ** (*) Vanguard SRV 275SD. (i) Reid Nibley (piano), Utah Symphony Orchestra, Maurice Abravanel; (ii) Eugene List (piano).

(i) *Symphony No. 1 (A Night in the Tropics)* (ed. Buketoff); *Symphony No. 2 (A Montevideo);* (ii) *Escenas campestres (Cuban country scenes);* (iii) *Marche solennelle* (for orchestra and bands); *March triunfal y final de opera* (for orchestra and band).

(B) *** Turnabout TV 37035S. (i) Vienna State Opera Orchestra, Igor Buketoff; (ii) Trinidad Paniagua (soprano), José Esteves (tenor), Pablo Garcia (baritone), Vienna State Opera Orchestra, Igor Buketoff; (iii) Berlin Symphony Orchestra and Band, Samuel Adler.

Louis Gottschalk was born in New Orleans of mixed German and French parentage. He studied music in Paris under Charles Hallé and then launched himself on a hugely successful career as composer/conductor/virtuoso pianist. He travelled widely (constantly moving throughout Europe and the USA), appealing to a society whose musical taste was without pretensions. As a touring star (perhaps comparable in many ways to the pop stars of today) he was to some extent an isolated figure, cut off from serious musical influences. His subservience to public taste led to a continual infusion of national and patriotic airs into his scores, and his music retained a refreshing naïvety to the last.

The two Turnabout discs offer a distinguished anthology with obvious dedication from editors and executants alike. Fortunately the recording is of high quality, not rich, perhaps, but always vivid and sparkling. Eugene List (as we know from his Gershwin recordings) was just the man to choose as soloist: he is marvellously deadpan. Whether tongue-in-cheek or not he manages to sound stylish throughout and in *The Union concert paraphrase*, which is outrageous, he is superb. There is no space here to dwell on the felicities of Gottschalk's elegant vulgarity. If you want Lisztian bravura try the first disc; if you fancy romanticism mixed with popular national dance rhythms sample the two symphonies. The second collection includes some attractive vocal music (the *Escenas campestres*), which is vividly

sung, and also an imitation of Tchaikovsky's *Marche slave* which does not quite come off. The solo piano pieces are more variable: *La Gallina* is particularly likable.

The Vanguard collection offers a cross-section of the other two discs: the performance of the *Symphony 'A Night in the Tropics'* is rather more atmospheric here, and Eugene List is again on hand for the solo piano items. As a musical personality Gottschalk has not quite the individuality of Scott Joplin, but his range was far wider and if someone were to use one or more of his pieces in a film we might well have a comparable cult figure emerging.

Gould, Morton
(born 1913)

Spirituals for string choir and orchestra.
(M) ** Everest SDBR 3002. London Symphony Orchestra, Walter Susskind – COPLAND: *Appalachian Spring.***

It is unexpected to find an English performance of this essentially American piece, but the Everest engineers add a gloss of transatlantic brilliance to the recording, so that it almost sounds like an American product – except perhaps that the performance has an extra degree of depth which springs from the European tradition. The music has never sounded more rewarding on disc, and the slow movement is really moving here, while the wide-ranging recording looks after the dramatic needs of *Protest* and the ambivalent exuberance of *Jubilee* with panache. A fine disc whose only technical fault is a high degree of background tape hiss, common to many issues on this label.

Gounod, Charles
(1818–93)

Petite symphonie in B flat major (for wind).

*** Philips 6500 163. Netherlands Wind Ensemble, Edo de Waart – DVOŘÁK: *Serenade*; SCHUBERT: *Octet* (excerpts).***

(B) ** Pye GSGC 14082. A section of the Hallé Orchestra, Sir John Barbirolli – DVOŘÁK: *Serenade*.**

An astonishingly fresh and youthful work, the *Petite symphonie* is in fact a work of Gounod's later years: he was nearly seventy when he wrote it for one of the celebrated Parisian wind ensembles of the day. The work has impeccable craftsmanship and is witty and civilized. It makes ideal listening at the end of the day, and its charm is irresistible, particularly in so crisp and vital a performance. The Philips recording is altogether excellent, and the couplings further enhance the attraction of the disc. Barbirolli's performance too has plenty of character yet a suitably light touch. His affection is obvious, and this is enjoyable and good value in the bargain range.

Faust (opera in 5 acts): complete recording.

(M) ** (*) HMV SLS 816 (4 discs). Victoria de los Angeles (soprano), Nicolai Gedda (tenor), Ernest Blanc (baritone), Boris Christoff (bass), Paris National Opera Chorus and Orchestra, André Cluytens.

** Decca SET 327/30. Joan Sutherland (soprano), Franco Corelli (tenor), Nicolai Ghiaurov (bass), Margreta Elkins (mezzo-soprano), Robert Massard (baritone), Ambrosian Singers, Highgate School Choir, London Symphony Orchestra, Richard Bonynge.

Originally appearing at about the same time as the HMV *Carmen*, this was in fact a re-make of an earlier mono set, and the contributions of de los Angeles, Gedda and Christoff have all, if anything, improved. The seductiveness of de los Angeles's singing is a dream and, as she has twice shown before on record, the agility required in the *Jewel song* holds no terrors for her. It is a pity that the recording hardens the natural tone-colour slightly. Christoff is magnificently Mephistophelian. The dark rich bass voice with all its many subtle facets of tone-colour is a superb vehicle for the part, at once musical and dramatic. Gedda, though showing some signs of strain, sings intelligently, and among the other soloists Ernest Blanc has a pleasing, firm voice which he uses to make Valentine into a sympathetic character. Cluytens's approach is competent but somewhat workaday. He rarely offers that extra spring which adds so much to Gounod's score in sheer charm, and he shows a tendency to over-drive in the more dramatic passages. The recording is good but not exceptional, atmospheric in choral and offstage passages, and on the whole well balanced, although at times some of the soloists are oddly placed on the stereo stage.

Decca provide a performance of *Faust* with only one Frenchman in the cast (Robert Massard as Valentine). In the event it is not surprising if the flavour is only intermittently authentic. Richard Bonynge's conducting is fresh and stylish – the most consistently successful contribution – but much of the singing, including Sutherland's, falls short. It goes without saying that the heroine produces some exquisite sounds, but too often she indulges in her 'mooning' style, so that *Le Roi de Thule* provokes unclean attack all through, and ends with a really disagreeable last phrase on *Et doucement*.

Corelli's faults are more than those of style, and his French is excruciating. Ghiaurov too hardly sounds at home in the music. But when Gounod's aim is clear, then all the singers' efforts click into place, and the final trio is wonderfully rousing. A memorable contribution from Monica Sinclair as Martha. The text is more complete than that of any previous recording, and the recording quality is outstanding.

Faust: highlights.
> ** (*) HMV ASD 421 (from above recording cond. Cluytens).
> ** Decca SET 431 (from above recording cond. Bonynge).

The one important snag in the HMV complete set was Cluytens's rather ungracious conducting. The effect of that was cumulative, and in these well-chosen highlights his crisp efficiency is more than acceptable. The singing is more of a delight than ever, particularly that of de los Angeles and Christoff. The recording is warm and easy to reproduce.

In the Decca disc Bonynge's achievement is beyond question. If not exactly in the Beecham class in his handling of this lovely score, he at least treats it with rare delicacy and sympathy, and arguably provides the strongest constituent in a set that contains irritating disappointments. Excellent recording.

Faust: Ballet suite (Act 5); *Waltz* (Act 1).
> ** DGG 2530 199. Berlin Philharmonic Orchestra, Herbert von Karajan – OFFENBACH: *Gaîté Parisienne.***

Brilliant orchestral playing from Karajan and vivid recording. But the music is too streamlined here, the waltz hard-driven, and the charm is missing. An excellent Decca collection, *The world of ballet, Volume 2* (SPA 97), includes a

stylish account of the suite conducted by Alexander Gibson, and this is in Decca's cheapest price-range.

Gowers, Patrick
(20th century)

Chamber concerto for guitar.
> ** (*) CBS 72979. John Williams (guitar), Chamber Ensemble, with the composer (organ) – SCARLATTI: *Keyboard sonatas.** (*)

As long as you do not take it too seriously, Patrick Gowers's *Chamber concerto* is crisp, enjoyable music complete with parts for alto saxophone, bass guitar and electric organ and drums as well as string trio. It is made far more persuasive by the artistry of John Williams, a superb advocate. Close recording.

Rhapsody for guitar, electric guitars and electric organ.
> ** (*) CBS 73350. John Williams (guitar and electric guitars), Patrick Gowers (electric organ) – VILLA-LOBOS: *Preludes.** (*)

Patrick Gowers is a highly intelligent and resourceful musician but this *Rhapsody* will not automatically enjoy universal appeal. It does, however, have many imaginative effects and the musician will find it a rewarding piece to hear and rehear. Unfortunately, the recording is rather closely balanced, but that apart, the disc can be recommended.

Grainger, Percy
(1882–1961)

Air from County Derry (Londonderry air); Country Gardens; Handel in the

Strand; Mock Morris; Molly on the Shore; Shepherd's Hey.

*** Columbia Studio 2 TWO 295. Light Music Society Orchestra, Sir Vivian Dunn (with *Concert*** (*)).

These settings have an admirably pithy directness of appeal, especially when played so effectively as they are here. The performances are particularly spontaneous, and as this attractive and well-planned disc also includes Roger Quilter's *Children's overture* and the charming *Haunted Ballroom* waltz by Geoffrey Toye, it deserves to be popular. The recording is bright and vivid without the exaggerated treble that almost spoils the two Eric Coates collections. Only the *Londonderry air* could do with a more expansive treatment, but better this approach than swoopy over-sentimentalization.

Duke of Marlborough fanfare; Lisbon; My Robin is to Greenwood Gone; Shepherd's Hey; Piano duet: *Let's Dance Gay in Green Meadow;* Vocal and choral: *Bold William Taylor; I'm Seventeen come Sunday; Lord Maxwell's Goodnight; The Lost Lady Found; The Pretty Maid Milkin' her Cow; Scotch strathspey and reel; Shallow Brown; The Sprig of Thyme; There Was a Pig Went out to Dig; Willow Willow.*

*** Decca SXL 6410. Peter Pears (tenor), John Shirley-Quirk (baritone), Ambrosian Singers, English Chamber Orchestra, Benjamin Britten; Britten and Viola Tunnard (pianos).

This is an altogether delightful anthology, beautifully played and recorded by these distinguished artists. Grainger's talent was a smaller one than his more fervent advocates would have us believe, but his imagination in the art of arranging folk-song was prodigious. The *Willow song* is a touching and indeed haunting piece and shows the quality of Grainger's harmonic resource. The opening fanfare too is strikingly original and so is *Shallow Brown.* Indeed each of the items here with one or two exceptions is obstinately memorable, and the recording is an extremely good one.

Granados, Enrique
(1867–1916)

Goyescas: Intermezzo.

*** Decca SXL 6287. New Philharmonia Orchestra, Rafael Frühbeck de Burgos – FALLA: *El amor brujo;* RAVEL: *Alborado etc.****

A lusciously brilliant performance of the *Goyescas intermezzo,* superbly recorded by Decca.

Goyescas: complete recording.

(B) ** SAGA 5343/4. Mario Miranda (piano) – SOLER: *6 Piano sonatas.***

Goyescas: complete recording; *Escenas poeticas; Libro de horas.*

** CRD CRD 1001/2. Thomas Rajna (piano).

Goyescas, Part 1: *Los majos enamorados, Nos. 1–4;* Part 2: *Nos. 5 and 6.*

(B) * (*) Turnabout TV 34247S. Rena Kyriakou (piano).

Once one gets used to the off-centre balance of the piano, Thomas Rajna's interpretations of Granados are clear and persuasive. In his hands the music is made to sound greater than one expects. The fill-ups, more immediately charming, less ambitious, are valuable too.

Maria Miranda's performances are also accomplished and idiomatic, and the recording is good. These records cost very much less than the C R D set.

Rena Kyriakou's Turnabout collection is nearly complete. The performances are well made but not very flexible. The famous *Maiden and the Nightingale* is not as poetic as it should be. The piano tone is clear but without much lustre.

Gregorian chant

Music for Christmas: *Introits for the 1st, 3rd and 4th Sundays in Advent; Communions for: the 3rd Sunday in Advent; the Feast of St Stephen; 2nd Sunday after Epiphany; Offertories for: 4th Sunday in Advent; 2nd Sunday after Epiphany; Hymn for Christmas Vespers; Introit for the 3rd Christmas Mass; Alleluia of the 3rd Christmas Mass; Gradual for the Feast of the Holy Confessor.*
  (B) *** Turnabout TV 34181S. Vienna Hofburgkapelle Choir, Josef Schabasser.

Music for Lent and Easter: Sexagesima Sunday: *Introit* (Mode 1); *Tract* (Mode 8). 2nd Sunday in Lent: *Communion* (Mode 5). Palm Sunday: *Offertory* (Mode 8). Maundy Thursday: *Gradual* (Mode 5); *Offertory* (Mode 2). Easter Sunday: *Introit* (Mode 4); *Gradual* (Mode 2); *Alleluia* (Mode 7); *Sequence* (Mode 1). Easter Sunday: *Offertory* (Mode 4); *Communion* (Mode 6); *Antiphon* (Mode 6). Ascension: *Introit* (Mode 7); *Offertory* (Mode 1). Pentecost Sunday: *Introit* (Mode 8); *Sequence* (Mode 1). Corpus Christi Day: *Communion* (Mode 7).
  (B) *** Turnabout TV 34070S. Vienna Hofburgkapelle Choir, Josef Schabasser.

The singing of this Viennese choir is strikingly beautiful. The mellifluous lines and positive phrasing afford the ear constant pleasure, especially when the style chosen discreetly varies the rhythmic flow and does not insist on an unending stream of even notes. The recording is very good indeed, and selections from the liturgy surrounding Christmas and Holy Week are a sensible idea for single-disc collections. At their very reasonable price these discs are no less recommendable than those costing nearly three times as much, and make an excellent introduction to Gregorian music for the small collection.

Einsiedeln Codex: First Mass for Christmas; Mass for Epiphany; Mass for Easter Sunday; Mass for Ascension Day.
  *** DGG Archive 2533 131. Choir of Maria Einsiedeln Monastery, Father Roman Bannwart.
Responses for Matins at Christmas.
  *** DGG Archive 2533 158. Choir of Montserrat Benedictine Monastery, Pater Gregori Estrada.

These two discs offer a fascinating glimpse into other traditions of performing the Roman liturgy. Their production is well up to the high standards of the DGG Archive series, but at the price asked, they are of interest to the specialist rather than the ordinary collector.

OTHER COLLECTIONS

Ancient Spanish chants: *Dominus regnavit; Vide domine; Laudate dominum; Ecclesiam sanctam catholicam; Nomina offerentium; Pacem meam; Introibo ad altare; Sanctus; Vere sanctus; Credo; Pater noster; Gustate et videte; Kyrie; Gloria; Offerte domino; Sanctus; Agnus*

Dei; Statuit Dominus; Lamentatio Jeremiae.
> *** DGG Archive 2533 163. Santo Domingo de Silos Abbey Choir, Dom Ismael de la Cuesta.

Like the companion Archive anthologies centred on Christmas and Easter, this record is of the highest quality, imaginatively extending our knowledge of Gregorian tradition in different parts of Europe.

Antiphons; Gospel tone; Hymns; Responsories; Laudes seu Acclamationes; Gradual: Flores apparuerunt; Alleluia; Communions; Antiphon: Montes Gilboe; Ave verum; Antiphonal Psalmody; Mariam antiphons.
> (M) *** Oiseau-Lyre SOL 60040. Carmelite Priory Choir, London, dir. John McCarthy.

Planned by Alec Robertson, who also provides a fascinating sleeve-note describing the music's ecclesiastic and spiritual background, this beautifully sung and excellently recorded anthology is the finest possible introduction to plainsong. Extra variety of tone is provided by the use of female voices as well as male. But care is taken to see that the ladies do not introduce an unwanted romantic element, and their vibrato-less vocal line is admirably pure in character. Edgar Fleet acts as cantor, and John McCarthy directs the singing with dedication and authority.

Hymns; Sequences; Responses: Ad coegam agni providi; Aeterne rerum conditur; Conditor alme siderum; Cum natus esset Jesus; Kyrie fons bonitatis; Lumen ad revelationem and Nunc dimittis; Mittit ad Virginem; Nato canunt omnia; O Redemptor sume carmen; Surrexit dominus vere; Te deum; Veni sancte spiritus.

> *** Telefunken SAWT 9493-A. Munich Capella Antiqua, Konrad Ruhland.

Only about half of the music on this disc remains in liturgical use; the rest was removed when the Liturgy was extensively revised after the Council of Trent. Thus this disc has an historical interest in showing us the *Tropes*, or inserted sections of words and music, by which medieval musicians cunningly extended the musical possibilities of liturgical setting. One can see the Papal point of view, but one can also understand how for the composer the interpolation of text could add variety and contrast. There is some beautiful music here – well worth preserving in recorded form – and this scholarly octet present it with plenty of vitality, using the style of unequal notes which is the antithesis of the Solesmes presentation. It is a pity that the sleeve includes only a small section printed in English. Otherwise this is a fine disc.

Grétry, André
(1741–1813)

Ballet suite (L'Épreuve villageoise: Overture; La Caravane de Caire: Chaconne; Minuet; Tambourin; Céphale et Procris: Ballet des Nymphes de Diane; Tambourin).
> (M) *** Oiseau-Lyre SOL 297. English Chamber Orchestra, Raymond Leppard – RAMEAU: *Le Temple de la gloire.****

This suite of ballet music from Grétry's operas was presumably chosen and arranged by the conductor, Raymond Leppard. He has Sir Thomas Beecham's skill in picking lollipops, but adds to his performances a feeling for the style of the period, about which Sir Thomas would not have been quite so scrupulous. The result is most enjoyable, and if the music itself is not quite so memorable as the Rameau suite on the other side of the disc, the two familiar final pieces, *Ballet des Nymphes de Diane* and *Tambourin,* are particularly delectable. Beautiful playing and equally lovely sound.

Grieg, Edvard
(1843–1907)

Piano concerto in A minor, Op. 16.
> *** Philips 6500 166. Stephen Bishop (piano), BBC Symphony Orchestra, Colin Davis – SCHUMANN: *Piano concerto.****
> *** Decca SXL 2173. Clifford Curzon (piano), London Philharmonic Orchestra, Øivin Fjeldstad – FRANCK: *Symphonic variations*; LITOLFF: *Scherzo.****
> (B) *** Music for Pleasure MFP 57002. Shura Cherkassky (piano), London Philharmonic Orchestra, Sir Adrian Boult – SCHUMANN: *Piano concerto.****
> (M) ** (*) Decca Ace of Diamonds SDD 422. Julius Katchen (piano), Israel Philharmonic Orchestra, Istvan Kertesz – SCHUMANN: *Piano concerto.** (*)*
> ** (*) Decca SXL 6624. Radu Lupu (piano), London Symphony Orchestra, André Previn – SCHUMANN: *Piano concerto.***
> (B) ** (*) Contour 6870 581. Hans Richter-Haaser (piano), Vienna Symphony Orchestra, Rudolf Moralt – SCHUMANN: *Piano concerto.** (*)*
> (M) ** (*) CBS Classics 61040. Philippe Entremont (piano), Philadelphia Orchestra, Eugene Or-

mandy – RACHMANINOV: *Rhapsody on a theme of Paganini.** (*)*
> ** HMV ASD 272. Solomon (piano), Philharmonia Orchestra, Herbert Menges – SCHUMANN: *Piano concerto.**(*)*
> * HMV ASD 2802. John Ogdon (piano), New Philharmonia Orchestra, Paavo Berglund – SCHUMANN: *Piano concerto.**

Stephen Bishop and Colin Davis have already proved how fruitful is their recording collaboration in the music of Beethoven. Turning now to two of the great romantic concertos they show an equal freshness and imagination. Whether in the clarity of virtuoso fingerwork or the shading of half-tone, Bishop is among the most illuminating of the many great pianists who have recorded the Grieg *Concerto.* This is Grieg presented with bravura and refinement, the spontaneity of the music-making bringing a sparkle throughout. With excellent recording this is highly recommendable among many discs of this particular coupling.

The sensitivity of Curzon in the recording studio is never in doubt, and his has been a favourite disc over a long period. The recording does not show its age, and the coupling provides the finest available account of Franck's *Symphonic variations.* Curzon's approach to the Grieg is not as individual as Bishop's – there is a suggestion of self-effacement – but the performance has strength and power as well as freshness.

On Music for Pleasure Cherkassky's performance with Boult makes an astonishing bargain. It is coupled to a wonderfully poetic account of the Schumann *Concerto* – one of the very finest performances of this elusive work, at any price. Cherkassky's reading of the Grieg is bold and extrovert: he is particularly commanding in the slow movement, which also has considerable depth. The current EMI transfer offers first-class sound, clear and bright yet never shallow. This would be recommendable at full price.

Katchen's reading is also a strong one, a hint of wilfulness tempered by a natural flexibility and a feeling for the work's poetry. Kertesz provides plenty of life in the accompaniment, and the recording is vivid and powerful in Decca's more spectacular manner. This performance has its own kind of spontaneity and is very attractive in its way. Some ears find the sound here has a reverberant twang but others find it vivid.

Radu Lupu too is given a bold, brightly lit recording (one of Decca's very best, in fact) and his performance is enjoyable. There is both warmth and poetry in the slow movement – the hushed opening particularly telling. There is a hint of calculation at the coda of the first movement, but the performance – if without quite the individuality of Katchen's – does not lack spontaneity, and the orchestral contribution under Previn is a strong one. The Schumann coupling, however, is rather less attractive.

Richter-Haaser's account has been praised by us in the earlier editions of the *SRG*, when the competition was not so strong. It is a fine performance, blending sensibility with brilliance, and above all it sounds really alive. This in spite of a recording which is not well-balanced. Even though the piano tone is satisfying, the orchestra is less well defined. In the lowest price-range this is still excellent value, but while Cherkassky's disc remains available, the Contour issue must take second place.

Entremont's is a fresh, vital performance, but CBS also offer this as part of their *Greatest hits* anthology, which costs much less and is generously filled. However, if the Rachmaninov coupling is wanted, readers will find this performance too is a fine one, with Ormandy as well as Entremont on top form.

HMV have successfully re-cut their Solomon record, and although the piano tone still sounds somewhat shallow in the first movement, the clear and well-balanced all-over quality is now maintained right through the disc. This is not as fine a performance as that of the Schumann on the reverse but it is fresh and enjoyable, featuring beautifully pearly passage-work. The orchestral accompaniment is sound rather than inspired, although there is some sensitive string playing in the *Adagio*.

Ogdon's version is not recommended. It is disappointingly dull, with indifferent accompaniment.

(i) *Piano concerto in A minor, Op. 16;* (ii) *Peer Gynt* (incidental music): *Suite No. 1, Op. 46* (complete).

(B) ** Decca SPA 170. (i) Peter Katin (piano), London Philharmonic Orchestra, Colin Davis; (ii) London Symphony Orchestra, Øivin Fjeldstad – LITOLFF: *Scherzo.***

Peter Katin's earlier Decca performance (issued here for the first time in stereo) is fresh and completely unhackneyed. Katin seems to have reacted deliberately against the frequently made criticism that his performances are lightweight. There is no question of the comment applying here. If anything he seems loath to colour his playing with halftones. The outer movements are the most successful, with Davis's brisk and masterly conducting adding to the feeling of a new work. The slow movement does not relax quite enough, but there is the compensation that this is utterly unsentimental. With Fjeldstad's fine account of the *Peer Gynt suite* (extracted from his Ace of Diamonds disc) added, besides the original mono coupling of the Litolff *Scherzo*, this is a hot competitor for its very positive qualities. The recording is excellent.

(i) *Piano concerto in A minor, Op. 16; Peer Gynt* (incidental music), *Op. 23:*

Morning; Anitra's dance; In the Hall of the Mountain King; Arab dance; Solveig's song.

(B) * (*) Classics for Pleasure CFP 160. (i) Peter Katin (piano); London Philharmonic Orchestra, John Pritchard.

This is a modern recording, but it is clear rather than lustrous. Katin's approach to the *Concerto* is fresh, but the performance is somehow unmemorable, and the *Peer Gynt* music seems equally matter-of-fact.

Cowkeeper's tune and Country dance, Op. 63/2; 2 Elegiac melodies, Op. 34; Wedding Day at Troldhaugen, Op. 65/6.

(B) *** Decca SPA 91. London Proms Orchestra, Charles Mackerras – SIBELIUS: *Collection.****

Mackerras offers here a most pleasant selection of Grieg miniatures played with sympathy and taste. The *Cowkeeper's tune and Country dance* (which end one side of the disc) are particularly enjoyable, the gentle eloquence of the opening delightfully offset by the rustic pizzicatos of the dance. The *Elegiac melodies* too are played most beautifully, although the recording here is bright and clear rather than especially rich. Mackerras has arranged the programme to intersperse the Grieg items with some little-known but attractive music of Sibelius. This enjoyable lightweight disc is a good deal more than the sum of its component parts. Highly recommended.

2 Elegiac melodies, Op. 34; Holberg suite, Op. 40.

*** HMV ASD 2954. Northern Sinfonia Orchestra, Paul Tortelier – TCHAIKOVSKY: *Pezzo capriccioso; Variations on a rococo theme.****

Affecting performances of these perennially fresh pieces, admirably recorded and arguably the best version in the catalogue. The sound is really first-class.

2 Elegiac melodies, Op. 34; Lyric suite, Op. 54: Norwegian rustic march; Norwegian dance, Op. 35/2; Peer Gynt suite No. 1, Op. 46; Sigurd Jorsalfar, Op. 56: Homage march.

(M) ** (*) CBS Classics 61286. Philadelphia Orchestra, Eugene Ormandy – SIBELIUS: *Valse triste; Finlandia.***(*)*

This is a most attractive collection, showing most facets of Grieg's orchestral personality, and as it includes the complete *First Peer Gynt suite* it will be a useful disc for smaller collections. The orchestral playing is very good indeed, and Ormandy's warmth is obvious. The recording is not always as rich as would be ideal but it is always vivid and with a slight treble reduction can be made to sound very well indeed. The two Sibelius couplings are also recommendable.

Holberg suite, Op. 40.

*** Argo ZRG 670. Academy of St Martin-in-the-Fields, Neville Marriner – DVOŘÁK: *Serenade.** (*)*

If perhaps not quite as fresh as Tortelier's (see above), this richly lyrical account of the *Holberg suite* is still very enjoyable. The *Air* has a pleasing graciousness and the final *Rigaudon* plenty of sparkle, and with first-class sound and a good coupling this can be recommended.

Lyric suite, Op. 54; Norwegian dances, Op. 35; Peer Gynt (incidental music), Op. 23: Overture; Dance of the Mountain King's Daughter; Norwegian bridal procession; Sigurd Jorsalfar, Op. 56: Homage march.

** HMV ASD 2773. Hallé Orchestra, Sir John Barbirolli.

There are characteristic touches in Barbirolli's Grieg anthology, notably in the *Lyric suite* and in the *Homage march* from *Sigurd Jorsalfar*. But the performances, like the recording, are a little variable (the sound in the *Lyric suite* is not always crystal clear). However, many will find this valuable for the latter work and the complete set of *Norwegian dances*, neither of which are generously represented in the catalogue.

Lyric suite, Op. 54; Norwegian dance No. 2, Op. 35; Peer Gynt (incidental music), *Op. 23: Morning; Death of Aase; Anitra's dance; Ingrid's lament; In the Hall of the Mountain King.*
    ** Decca Phase 4 PFS 4206. London Symphony Orchestra, Stanley Black.

Stanley Black's performance of the *Peer Gynt* incidental music is generally lithe and pleasing. He sets a too careful tempo for *Morning* and does not quite solve the *accelerando* problems of *In the Hall of the Mountain King* with complete spontaneity; on the other hand the *Death of Aase* is shaped eloquently and *Ingrid's lament* has a fine passionate lyricism. The *Lyric suite* too is successful. The conductor shows a feeling for the music's line and colour, and again the listener has a feeling of the music's spring-like freshness. The best-known *Norwegian dance* makes an attractive bonus. The sound is rich and vivid, with sparkle as well as atmosphere. The climax of the *Death of Aase* is quite clear and generally the stereo is of Decca's superior quality.

Peer Gynt (incidental music), *Op. 23:* complete recording.
    *** Columbia Studio 2 TWO 269. Sheila Armstrong (soprano), Ambrosian Singers, Hallé Orchestra, Sir John Barbirolli.

(B) *** Music for Pleasure MFP 57010. April Cantelo (soprano), Royal Philharmonic Orchestra, Alexander Gibson.
(M) ** Philips Universo 6580 056. Adele Stolte (soprano), Leipzig Gewandhaus Orchestra, Václav Neumann (without *Overture* and *Dance of the Mountain King's Daughter*.)

Warm, committed performances from Barbirolli of some of the most colourful incidental music ever written. Beecham may have achieved a subtler panache in some of this music, but with fine, ripe recording in Studio Two Barbirolli is at least equally impressive, and has fine vocal contributions from his soprano soloist, Sheila Armstrong, and the Ambrosian Chorus. He also has the advantage of including two extra movements.

Gibson's selection is complete, and although he does not have the advantage of a chorus, April Cantelo's contribution is a striking one. In the new Music for Pleasure transfer the recording is of demonstration quality. Its clear, vivid qualities really make one sit up, yet the string tone is natural and there is plenty of atmosphere. The performances show Gibson at his very best. They are bright-eyed and spontaneous and full of character. This would be a very desirable issue even if it were not in the cheapest possible price-range; as such it is irresistible.

The Leipzig performances are warm and attractive, with a good soloist in Adele Stolte. The recording is over-reverberant but pleasantly so. However, this offers two items fewer than Gibson.

Peer Gynt (incidental music): *Suite No. 1, Op. 46; Suite No. 2, Op. 55; Cradle song; Wedding march.*
    *** HMV ASD 258. Ilse Hollweg (soprano), Royal Philharmonic Orchestra, Sir Thomas Beecham.

Peer Gynt (incidental music): *Suite No. 1, Op. 46; Suite No. 2, Op. 55; Prelude; Dance of the Mountain King's Daughter.*

(M) ** (*) Decca Ace of Diamonds SDD 111. London Symphony Orchestra, Øivin Fjeldstad.

Peer Gynt (incidental music): *Suite No. 1, Op. 46; Ingrid's lament; Solveig's song.*

*** Decca SXL 2308. Vienna Philharmonic Orchestra, Herbert von Karajan – TCHAIKOVSKY: *Nutcracker suite.****

Beecham uses a chorus, and Ilse Hollweg as a soprano soloist both in the *Lullaby* and *Solveig's song*. She sings very beautifully. The recording itself is not so wide in range as the Decca. But the inimitable Sir Thomas adds many touches of his own and in the two lesser-known pieces especially, there is much that is magical – the beautiful string playing at the opening of the *Cradle song*, for instance, H M V, too, have recut their recording and although the choral interpolations are still not entirely convincing, at least they are not fierce, which is a great improvement. In all other respects the silky recording can be commended. The attractive *Wedding march* deserved its place on the E M I Stereo Demonstration Disc, and now the *Arab dance* with a superb bass drum deserves a place alongside it. The acoustic inevitably still has a studio flavour, but for those wanting a full selection this disc is now a preferable choice to Fjeldstad's.

In its original form Fjeldstad's record was one of the really outstanding early Decca stereo LPs, and its reissue on Ace of Diamonds makes an attractive purchase in spite of some over-modulation at the side ends and a general tightening up of the treble and thus a sharpening of the upper string image. The LSO are very sensitive, and the tender string playing in *Solveig's song* is quite lovely. The

conductor begins *In the Hall of the Mountain King* rather slowly but builds up a blaze of excitement at the end and quite justifies his conception. It is a pity that where on the original issue the recording contained the wide dynamic of the final crescendo at a demonstration quality, here the over-modulation produces a less satisfying and noisier effect. But even so this is a recommendable issue.

Karajan's more limited selection offers the best sound of any of these three discs. There is occasionally a faint buzz in the upper string tone, but otherwise the rich, clear recording is outstanding. The readings are broader in style than either Fjeldstad's or Beecham's, less individual perhaps, but they do not lack freshness. *Solveig's song* is particularly beautiful.

Peer Gynt (incidental music): *Suite No. 1, Op. 46; Suite No. 2, Op. 55.*

** H M V ASD 2952. Bournemouth Symphony Orchestra, Paavo Berglund – ALFVÉN: *Elegy; Swedish rhapsody;* JÄRNEFELT: *Praeludium.***

(M) ** CBS Classics 61350. New York Philharmonic Orchestra, Leonard Bernstein – BIZET: *Carmen suites Nos. 1 and 2.***

Berglund's performances are strongly characterized – *Ingrid's lament* is notably sombre – and well played. But there is some lack of charm here, and the recording has the artificial brilliance one normally associates with Studio Two techniques, so that the upper string sound is clear and vivid rather than rich-textured.

The slightly mannered performance of *Anitra's dance* and the touch of melodrama in the *Second Suite* add individuality to Bernstein's performances, which are well played and brilliantly recorded. The string tone in *Morning* is a little unyielding, but the *Arab dance* is splendidly exotic. Good value if the coupling is attractive.

Peer Gynt (incidental music): *Suite No. 1, Op. 46; Suite No. 2, Op. 55; Sigurd Jorsalfar* (suite), *Op. 56.*

⊛ *** DGG 2530 243. Berlin Philharmonic Orchestra, Herbert von Karajan.

Highly expressive performances played with superlative skill and polish. Some may even feel that they are a little too expressive and that the simplicity and freshness of Grieg are somewhat lost to view. However, most people will merely be lost in admiration for the superb playing. The recording is extremely fine.

Peer Gynt (incidental music): *Suite No. 1, Op. 46; Suite No. 2, Op. 55; 4 Symphonic dances, Op. 64.*

(M) *** HMV SXLP 30105. Philharmonia Orchestra, Walter Susskind.

Susskind's performances of the *Peer Gynt suites* are beautifully played and richly and spaciously recorded. Both *Morning* and *Solveig's song* offer lovely strings and melting playing. At the very beginning of the *Arab dance* the bass drum is only just audible, but this is the only miscalculation in an outstanding set of performances. The recording is somewhat less full in the *Symphonic dances* but still vivid, and Susskind's performances are very well characterized. He finds plenty of colour in Nos. 2 and 3 and the contrasts in No. 4 are made with the subtlety only possible with an orchestra of the calibre of the Philharmonia.

INSTRUMENTAL MUSIC

Violin sonatas Nos. 1 in F major, Op. 8; 2 in G major, Op. 13; 3 in C minor, Op. 45.

(B) ** (*) Saga 5296. Alan Loveday (violin), Leonard Cassini (piano).

This Saga record, very sensibly, presents the *Third Sonata* first. This is a fine work, easily deserving a place among the 'top ten' of violin sonatas. The first movement has a strong main theme and a very characteristic second subject; the melodic content of the *Allegretto* is no less appealing, and the finale is splendid, with a stirring dominating tune that might have come from César Franck. Loveday manages it perfectly and his blend of passion and restraint is ideal in catching the romantic ardour without recourse to melodrama. The other two works were written in 1865 and 1867, when Grieg was in his early twenties. The first is particularly spontaneous and surprisingly characteristic. Saga's recording is a good deal better than some we have had from this source. The piano tone is spread by the reverberation, but the balance is good and the slight rawness on the forward violin image can be smoothed out. The only snag is the disc's surfaces, which are rather clicky. Otherwise a fine issue.

Ballade, Op. 24; Holberg suite, Op. 40; Lyric pieces, Op. 43.

(B) ** (*) Turnabout TV 34365S. Walter Klien (piano).

For those who do not want to invest in Daniel Adni's four-record set of the *Lyric pieces* but do want to represent Grieg's piano music in their collection, this is obviously an excellent buy. True, the *Ballade* is a bit discursive at times, but Walter Klien plays most sensitively and the recording, although not by any means outstanding, can be made to produce very pleasing results. Moreover the record has the advantage of cheapness.

Lyric pieces (complete): *Book 1, Op. 12; Book 2, Op. 38; Book 3, Op. 43; Book 4, Op. 47; Book 5, Op. 54; Book 6, Op. 57; Book 7, Op. 62; Book 8, Op. 65; Book 9, Op. 68; Book 10, Op. 71.*

(M) *** HMV SLS 898 (4 discs).
Daniel Adni (piano).

Grieg is almost a neglected composer nowadays: the songs have dropped from their pre-war position of pre-eminence, and while the *Concerto* and *Peer Gynt* form the tip, the bulk of his music consitutes the unseen mass of the iceberg. It is good to find Daniel Adni espousing the cause of the *Lyric pieces*, which are not otherwise available complete. He plays them with genuine feeling for their character and a strong sense of atmosphere, though few will want to play more than a handful at a sitting. The E M I recording is very good indeed: the piano is firmly in focus and well balanced; there is plenty of presence and the studio has agreeable ambience.

Lyric pieces: Op. 12/1; Op. 38/1; Op. 43/1 and 2; Op. 47/2–4; Op. 54/4 and 5; Op. 57/6; Op. 62/4 and 6; Op. 65/5; Op. 68/2, 3 and 5; Op. 71/1, 3, 6, and 7.
⊛ *** DGG 2530 476. Emil Gilels (piano).

A generous selection of Grieg's *Lyric pieces*, from the well-known *Papillon*, Op. 43/1, to the less often heard and highly poetic set Op. 71, written at the turn of the century. This excellently recorded survey is an admirable alternative to Daniel Adni's complete box, but the playing is of a wholly different order. Good though Mr Adni is, with Gilels we are in the presence of a great keyboard master whose characterization and control of colour and articulation are wholly remarkable. An altogether outstanding record in every way.

Nocturne in C major, Op. 54/4; Piano sonata in E minor, Op. 7.
* (*) Decca SXL 6466. Alicia de Larrocha (piano) – MENDELSSOHN: *Capriccio; Variations.** (*)

The *Nocturne* is a familiar one, and the *Sonata* is an early work on which many young pianists have cut their teeth. It offers the outward impression of virtuosity without actually demanding it. At a time when Grieg's piano music is so neglected it is a pity that Miss Larrocha preferred this to better works. We badly need good accounts of the *Slåtter*. The playing is sadly let down by an unappealing recorded sound: it is slightly clangorous and reverberant.

COLLECTION

'Greatest hits': (i; ii) Piano concerto in A minor, Op. 16; (iii) Ich liebe dich (arr. Harris); (ii) Lyric suite, Op. 54: March of the Dwarfs; (iv) Norwegian dance, Op. 35/2; (v) Peer Gynt suite No. 1, Op. 46; (ii) Sigurd Jorsalfar, Op. 56: Homage march.
(B) *** CBS Harmony 30004. (i) Philippe Entremont (piano); (ii) Philadelphia Orchestra, Eugene Ormandy; (iii) Columbia Symphony Orchestra, André Kostelanetz; (iv) New York Philharmonic Orchestra, Leonard Bernstein; (v) Cleveland Orchestra, George Szell.

There are not many records offering both the *Piano concerto* and the famous *First Peer Gynt suite*, and certainly not one with performances better than these. Entremont's account of the *Concerto* was one of the best early stereo versions, and the recording stills sounds well. The performance is fresh and vital, with an especially vivid finale. Ormandy too is on top form, as he shows in the sensitive opening to the slow movement. Szell's *Peer Gynt suite* is on an equally high level, the music sympathetically characterized and very well recorded. Of the bonus items the *Norwegian dance No. 2* (Bernstein) is particularly fetching, but the

March of the Dwarfs suffers from shrill recording. But taken as a whole this collection makes a splendid bargain.

other current recommendation for this work, as the Decca Phase 4 version is too over-modulated for comfort.

Grigny, Nicolas de
(1672–1703)

Organ Mass: excerpts; *Pange lingua; Veni creator.*
  (B) ** Turnabout TV 34054S. René Saorgin (organ).

Only a small amount of de Grigny's music has survived, in a single *Livre d'orgue,* and this disc contains a third of it. The craftsmanship is impressive throughout and suggests a kind of French Buxtehude without the melodic individuality. The composer, as was the practice at that time, left details of the intended registration. René Saorgin understands the music's style, and as the organ presents the characteristic French reedy tone colour, this may be regarded as a representative and authentic disc. Music by an important, if minor talent. Apart from a little unsteadiness at the beginning the recording is good, if not outstanding.

Grofé, Ferde
(1892–1972)

Grand Canyon suite.
  (M) * (*) CBS Classics 61266. Philadelphia Orchestra, Eugene Ormandy – ALFVÉN: *Swedish rhapsody.*(**)

Grofé's technicolour picture of the *Grand Canyon* is painted with relish by the Philadelphia Orchestra. They manage the storm with the utmost sense of spectacle, and play *On the trail* with idiomatic wit. The recording is on a big scale but is unfortunately rather harsh. There is no

Halévy, Jacques
(1799–1862)

La Juive (opera in 5 acts): *excerpts* (Act 1: *Si la rigueur;* Act 2: *O Dieu de nos pères; Lorsqu'à toi;* Act 3: *Mon doux seigneur et maître; Vous qui du Dieu vivant;* Act 4: *Ah, que ma voix plaintive; Va prononcer ma mort; Rachel, quand du Seigneur;* Act 5: *Il est temps).*
  ** RCA ARL 1 0447. Martina Arroyo, Anna Moffo (sopranos), Richard Tucker, Juan Sabaté (tenors), Bonaldo Giaiotti (bass), Leslie Fyson (baritone), Ambrosian Opera Chorus, New Philharmonia Orchestra, Antonio de Almeida.

Halévy's *La Juive,* a fascinating historical document of a transitional period between Rossini and Meyerbeer, is even today too long to command a complete recording. This selection of vital items is invaluable but as a performance disappointing, with less than inspired conducting and playing, and with solo singing which suffers as a consequence. But as a stopgap no one need complain. Reverberant recording.

Halffter, Ernesto
(born 1905)

Guitar concerto.
  ** DGG 2530 326. Narciso Yepes (guitar), Spanish Radio and TV Orchestra, Odón Alonso – BACARISSE: *Concertino.** (*)

Halffter, the favourite pupil of Manuel de Falla, echoes some of his master's later music, developing on the spareness of, for example, the Falla *Harpsichord concerto*. It is not what one thinks of as typical Spanish music, but the Spanish flavour is still there behind a gritty façade. Superb playing from Yepes.

Hamilton, Iain
(born 1922)

Violin concerto, Op. 15.
> *** HMV ASD 2810. Manoug Parikian (violin), Scottish National Orchestra, Alexander Gibson – GOEHR: *Concerto.****

Hamilton wrote his *Violin concerto* in 1952 at the beginning of his career, before his music took on the craggy quality of his serial works. It is lyrical, with overtones from Sibelius and Walton, brooding melancholy alternating with red-blooded passion – very much young man's music, here persuasively presented.

Violoncello sonata: 3 Pieces for piano, Op. 30.
> *** Argo ZRG 5425. Joan Dickson (cello), Margaret Kitchin (piano), Katharina Wolpe (piano) – LUTYENS: *Quintet etc.****

Hamilton's *Cello sonata* is a curiously spiky, unlyrical work with solo cadenzas tending to give the impression of disjointedness. The most immediately understandable passage is a slow section near the end. The *Three Pieces for piano* bring something readily appreciable, light colourful ideas very well written within a deliberately limited technical range. A British Council issue, beautifully recorded, and with all the pieces very well played.

Handel, George Frederick
(1685–1759)

Ballet music from *Alcina* (including *Overture* and *Dream music*); *Ariodante* (including *Overture*); *Il Pastor Fido:* Hunting scene.
> *** Argo ZRG 686. Academy of St Martin-in-the-Fields, Neville Marriner.

One of Sir Thomas Beecham's hobbies was exploring the lesser-known music of Handel to find items for his ballet suites. Here we have a generous selection using Handel's original scoring. The music from *Alcina* is particularly diverse in invention, and all is played with grace and marvellous rhythmic point by Marriner and his splendid orchestral group. The recording is of superlative quality, except that some pick-ups may have trouble tracking the last few bars of the hunting music from *Il Pastor Fido*, in which the horns are suitably exuberant.

Concerti grossi, Op. 3, Nos. 1–6.
> *** Argo ZRG 5400. Academy of St Martin-in-the-Fields, Neville Marriner.
> (B) ** Turnabout TV 34103S. Mainz Chamber Orchestra, Günter Kehr.
> * (*) DGG Archive 2533 116. Munich Bach Orchestra, Karl Richter.

Concerti grossi, Op. 3, Nos. 1–4; 4b (from first edition); *5–6; Concerto grosso (Alexander's Feast).*
> ** BASF BAC 3026/7. Collegium Aureum (using original instruments).

Concerti grossi, Op. 3, Nos. 1–6; Concerto grosso (Alexander's Feast); Hornpipe in D major; Overtures in B flat major and D major.
> *** Philips 6700 050. English Chamber Orchestra, Raymond Leppard.

Argo's fine recording is of outstanding quality both for musical scholarship and, what is even more to the point, for musical expressiveness and spontaneity. Kehr too provides admirably stylish performances, with appropriate ornamentation, not overdone, and excellent wind playing to match the contribution from the strings. The recording is fresh and immediate and if this is not quite of the quality of the Argo set, it makes a fine bargain. Both these performances fit on to a single disc. The Collegium Aureum set needs two, though it offers extra concertos. The BASF recording is of the highest quality, warm, clear and spacious, and the performances are lively and attractive. The oboes here sound more like cor anglais, with their deeper timbre. The playing is excellent, with only occasionally a suspicion of less than perfect tuning. There is no doubt that the use of original instruments enhances the music's character, yet in spite of its authenticity the performers do not appear to use a double continuo, and the harpsichord is often virtually inaudible.

Lively, fresh performances in the Philips set, beautifully recorded. At times one wonders whether Leppard isn't just a shade too elegant, as if he were playing Arne, but these are fleeting thoughts, and in general this set ranks among the very best versions of Op. 3, and can be recommended alongside Marriner.

Concerti grossi, Op. 3, Nos. 1–6; Concerti grossi, Op. 6, Nos. 1–12.
　⊛ (M) *** Decca SDDB 294/7. Academy of St Martin-in-the-Fields, Neville Marriner; Thurston Dart (harpsichord), Andrew Davis (organ).

Like the fine set of Bach orchestral suites this integral recording of the Handel *Concerti grossi* makes a permanent memorial of the partnership formed by the inspired scholarship of Thurston Dart

and the interpretative skill and musicianship of Neville Marriner and his superb ensemble. Great care went into preparing the scores which are the basis of these recordings. A double continuo of both organ and harpsichord is judiciously used to vary textural colour and weight. Flutes and oboes are employed as Handel intended in Op. 3, and in Op. 6 the optional oboe parts indicated by the composer are used in concertos 1, 2, 5 and 6. The final concerto of Op. 3 features the organ as a solo instrument, which very much conjures up the composer's spirit hovering in the background. Incidentally Thurston Dart makes the point that the warm and beautiful acoustic used in the recording is different from the dry theatre ambience Handel would have expected. The recording engineers show they have understood the tonal subtleties involved in this change by their careful balance of the chamber organ. With the greater degree of reverberation (and indeed the richer sound possible from the techniques of modern string playing) there is less need to add tonal body to the main orchestral group. 'Marvellous music', comments Dart in his notes, and how right he is! With such superlative playing Op. 3 emerges as gloriously extrovert, enjoyable music, and Op. 6 as one of the great masterpieces of the Baroque period. (Incidentally the Op. 6 set is also available on separate records at full price on Decca SXL 6369/71.)

Concerti grossi, Op. 6, Nos. 1–12.
　** (*) Philips 6703 003 (3 discs). English Chamber Orchestra, Raymond Leppard.

All great works of art from the Baroque period offer an essential dichotomy of structural grandeur and decorative splendour. At different periods and in different places one of these two features gains the ascendancy over the other, but Handel's great set of *Concerti grossi*, Op. 6, is a marvellous example of a musical work in which the balance between structure and façade is perfectly integrated so that while the ear is able to delight itself in the detail, the senses and spirit are consciously affected by the underlying nobility of the whole. Raymond Leppard's conception, although it offers many incidental pleasures (brightness of presentation, well sprung, dotted rhythms, and a nice feeling for line in the slow melodies), misses much of the grandeur, and the listener is sometimes reminded of Lully rather than Handel. Both playing and recording are first-rate, but compare Leppard's No. 5 with Marriner's to find how much more there is in the music than is revealed on the Philips version, for all its stylishness.

(i) *Concerto grosso in D major, Op. 6/5;* (i; ii) *Harp concerto in B flat major, Op. 4/6;* (iii) *The Harmonious Blacksmith* (air and variations); (iv) *Trio No. 2, Quel Fior che all'alba;* (i; v) *Funeral anthem:* Choral sinfonia and fugue.
  (B) ** Oryx EXP 4. (i) Heidelberg Chamber Orchestra; (ii) Giselle Herber (harp); (iii) Nicholas Jackson (harpsichord); (iv) H. Sheppard, Sally Le Sage, M. Bevan; (v) Mannheim Youth Choir.

This anthology is obviously designed to tempt purchasers to explore the records in the Oryx catalogue from which the items are taken. This it should certainly do, but it makes a very enjoyable collection in its own right. The recording of the *Concerto grosso,* Op. 6/5 (one of the very finest of the set), has a touch of edginess but is otherwise good, and the performance is of the right scale. The *Harp concerto* too is nicely done, and the Kirkman harpsichord of 1788 on which Nicholas Jackson plays the famous *Harmonious Blacksmith variations* emerges with strong personality. Its action obviously prevents swirling cascades of virtuosity but the timbre has been skilfully

caught. It has substance and not too much clang. Of the vocal items the two verses from the noble *Funeral anthem* make one want to hear the complete work, and if the solo singing in the *Trio* is not absolutely secure it is fresh and stylishly conceived.

Concerto grosso in G minor, Op. 6/6; (i) *Organ concertos in F major, Op. 4/4; in A major, Op. 7/2.*
  ** (*) Telefunken SAWT 9437. Amsterdam Chamber Orchestra, Anthon van der Horst, (i) with Albert de Klerk (organ).

Undoubtedly the star of this excellent record is the Flenthrop organ on which Albert de Klerk plays. The flute pipes have a most delectable sound and the overall texture has the right degree of weight for this music. Albert de Klerk plays stylishly and fills out the written music convincingly. He is especially successful in the *F major Concerto* with its characteristic opening *Allegro.* The Amsterdam Chamber Orchestra accompany with style and spirit and they bring plenty of warmth to their performance of the *Concerto grosso.* Perhaps the last degree of imagination is missing in the slower movements, but the splendidly clear and sonorous recording (throughout the disc) more than compensates, and this record is most enjoyable.

Harp concerto in B flat major, Op. 4/5; Concerto for lute and harp in B flat major, Op. 4/6; Concerto grosso (Alexander's Feast).
  (M) *** Oiseau-Lyre SOL 60013. Osian Ellis (harp), Desmond Dupré (lute), Philomusica Orchestra, Granville Jones; Thurston Dart (organ continuo).
Harp concerto in B flat major, Op. 4/5.
  (M) ** DGG Privilege 135093. Nicanor Zabaleta (harp), Paul Kuentz

Chamber Orchestra – MOZART: *Flute and harp concerto*; WAGEN-SEIL: *Harp concerto.****

The Oiseau-Lyre collection comes from the early days of stereo, but the sound is not dated. The performances are fresh and attractive, and the recording is beautifully balanced. A delightful disc.

The Privilege recording is clear and immediate, but Zabaleta's approach is rather cool and detached. The crystalline stream of sound is attractive and the performance appeals in its own way. The couplings are well done.

(i) *Oboe concertos Nos. 1 in B flat major; 2 in B flat major; Variant of No. 2 in B flat major; 3 in G minor. Solomon* (oratorio): *Arrival of the Queen of Sheba; Berenice* (opera): *Overture.*
   ** (*) Argo ZRG 5442. Academy of St Martin-in-the-Fields, Neville Marriner, (i) with Roger Lord (oboe).

This is an attractively planned disc, beautifully played, and recorded with the richness of timbre Argo characteristically provide for music of this period. If the overall style could have had a touch more vivacity (the famous *Arrival of the Queen of Sheba*, for instance, lacks bite in the tuttis) this collection would have been really memorable. The Overture *Berenice* is best-known for its famous minuet tune, but it is all attractive, and the *Oboe concertos* have a similar immediate appeal, their style predominantly lyrical.

Oboe concertos Nos. 1 in B flat major; 2 in B flat major; 3 in G minor; Concerto grosso in G major, Op. 3/3; (i) *Sonata a cinque in B flat major* (for violin, oboe and strings).
   ** Philips 6500 240. Heinz Holliger (oboe); (i) Kenneth Sillito (violin);

English Chamber Orchestra, Raymond Leppard.

Holliger, being a creative artist as well as a masterly interpreter, does not hesitate to embellish repeats, and his ornamentation may overstep the boundaries some listeners are prepared to accept. His playing and that of the other artists in this recording is exquisite, and the Philips engineers produce a smooth and well-detailed recording. With the Philips box of Op. 3 etc. (6700 050), this record comprises all the music printed in Chrysander's Handel Society Volume reproduced inexpensively in the Kalmus series (No. 778). However, for the *Oboe concertos* many readers may prefer Roger Lord (see above), who eschews the exaggerated ornamentation in which Holliger indulges.

Oboe concerto No. 1 in B flat major; Organ concerto No. 13 in B flat major, Op. 7/1; Rodrigo: suite; *Xerxes:* suite (including *Ombra mai fù*).
   (B) ** Pye GSGC 14086. Richard Lewis (tenor), Evelyn Rothwell (oboe), Eric Chadwick (organ), Hallé Orchestra, Sir John Barbirolli.

This collection is decently recorded, and Barbirolli's directing hand ensures that all the music is alive. The trouble is the question of style, over which Barbirolli seems not to have managed a happy compromise. He uses a fairly large modern orchestral group, and includes a harpsichord to be on the safe side. Yet he cannot resist indulging himself with affectionate nudges to the phrasing. *Ombra mai fù* therefore opens gorgeously, with a richly phrased orchestral ritornello, and when Richard Lewis begins to sing, his purity of style is a little disconcerting. But Sir John plays the two orchestral suites with vigour and some of this music is of the kind that needs enthusiasm rather more than scholarship. Lady Barbirolli's playing is, as ever, delightful, and if the effect of the *Organ concerto* is somewhat stolid, the grandeur of the piece comes over too.

Organ concertos Nos. 1 in G minor; 2 in B flat major; 3 in G minor; 4 and 5 in F major; 6 in B flat major, Op. 4/1–6; 7 in F major (The Cuckoo and the Nightingale); 8 in A major; 9 (from Concerto grosso, Op. 6/10); 10 (from Concerto grosso, Op. 6/1); 11 (from Concerto grosso, Op. 6/5); 12 (from Concerto grosso, Op. 6/6) (all Set 2); 13 in B flat major; 14 in A major; 15 in B flat major; 16 in D minor; 17 in G minor; 18 in B flat major, Op. 7/1–6; 19 in D minor; 20 in F major (miscellaneous): Organ concertos Nos. 1–10; 13–18.

  (M) ** (*) HMV SLS 824 (4 discs). Simon Preston (organ), Menuhin Festival Orchestra, Yehudi Menuhin.

Organ concertos Nos. 1–8; 13–20.

  (M) ** (*) CBS 77358 (3 discs). E. Power Biggs (organ of Great Packington Church), London Philharmonic Orchestra, Sir Adrian Boult.

Organ concertos Nos. 1–3; 7; 8; 15; 17–19.

  ** BASF BAC 3024/5. Rudolf Ewerhardt (organ), Collegium Aureum (using original instruments).

Organ concertos Nos. 4–6; 13; 14; 16; 20.

  ** BASF BAC 3022/3. Rudolf Ewerhardt (organ), Collegium Aureum (using original instruments).

Organ concertos Nos. 1–6; 13–18.

  (M) ** (*) Decca Ace of Diamonds SDD 470; SDD 471; SDD 472. Karl Richter (organ), with Chamber Orchestra

Organ concertos Nos. 2; 4; 7; Il trionfo del tempo e del disinganno: Sonata.

(B) ** Classics for Pleasure CFP 40044. Nicolas Kynaston (Royal Festival Hall organ), Virtuosi of England, Arthur Davison.

Preston uses four different organs, including those recently built at the Queen Elizabeth Hall and St Paul's School, Hammersmith, as well as the famous instrument at Great Packington Church also favoured by Biggs. He uses a new edition prepared by Neville Boyling. There are criticisms to be made of tempi and phrasing, but on the whole the orchestral playing is very fine. Simon Preston's playing is somewhat variable. He is especially good in the Great Packington recordings (Op. 4/2 and 3, Op. 7/3 among them) but here the organ is obviously just right for the music. Taken as a whole this is a recommendable set, and the support given by the HMV engineers is excellent.

Biggs uses the Aylesford organ at Great Packington throughout his set, and his performances gain immeasurably from a genuine eighteenth-century tone colour. Boult's support too is impeccable, with crisp buoyant rhythms in the allegros (try Op. 7/⅓ or Op. 7/6) and beautifully judged tempi throughout. The slow movements have nobility and poise, and throughout Boult shows a feeling for colour and texture. Although Biggs is no great Handelian stylist, he has clearly been inspired here by Boult to give of his very best. His crisp, clear playing frequently brings delightful results, and he is never stolid (as he sometimes is on his solo records). The recording is outstandingly well balanced and sounds extraordinarily modern. There is just the occasional roughness of orchestral focus, but for the most part the sound is clean as well as lively and it has no lack of depth. This is a genuine bargain in the medium price-range.

The Decca set, by Karl Richter, has just been reclassified in the Ace of Diamonds series. It has the merits of the right kind of organ (at St Mark's, Munich) and a small, flexible orchestral group which Richter directs from the keyboard. The recording is of high quality. The first disc of the three (SDD 470) is the weakest, but if the performances there are somewhat unimaginative, the other two records offer satisfactory playing from all points of view, including that of cadential extemporization. With such lively baroque sounds they can be readily recommended.

The BASF set spreads its sixteen concertos over four full-priced discs, against Biggs's three medium-priced LPs. The advantages of original orchestral instruments are obvious, and Rudolf Ewerhardt uses different organs, some of which are more attractive than others. The recording is generally lively, but sometimes too thick-textured. Tempi are generally rather sedate and leisurely. Frankly, for all its claims to scholarship, this music-making does not come to life in the vivid way the Biggs/Boult set does. But individual performances are enjoyable, and the recording is likable for its atmospheric qualities and the generally clear projection of the soloist. (Incidentally there is a patch of 'wow' at the opening of Op. 4/1.)

The Classics for Pleasure disc offers spirited performances of three favourite concertos. The registration in The Cuckoo and the Nightingale is piquant, and to end the performance of Op. 4/4 Davison uses the choral finale (Alleluia) of the original version, which comes as a pleasant surprise. The Sonata from Il trionfo is short and sweet. Good, atmospheric recording.

Organ concerto No. 7 in F major (The Cuckoo and the Nightingale).
(B) ** Turnabout TV 34135S. Helmuth Rilling (organ), Württemberg Chamber Orchestra, Joerg Faerber – ALBINONI: Adagio;

CORRETTE: Concerto; MOZART: Sonata.**

It is useful to have a separate version on bargain label of The Cuckoo and the Nightingale, although the bird effects are played rather literally and without any special charm. The performance throughout is accurate and musical rather than imaginative.

Love in Bath (ballet: arr. and ed. Beecham from various sources).
(M) ** (*) HMV SXLP 30156. Royal Philharmonic Orchestra, Sir Thomas Beecham.

Unless you are an out-and-out purist this is an irresistible record. The title Love in Bath in fact conceals the identity of Beecham's ballet, first performed just before the end of the war, called The Great Elopement. Beecham recorded a suite from this on 78, but the present disc contains much more music – nineteen numbers, plus a rondeau purloined from yet another Handel/Beecham suite. In these days of authentic Handel Beecham's arrangements are no longer fashionable, but when played like this – the sound is ripe, with a mellow bloom on brass and strings – they make delightful entertainment.

Overtures: Admeto; Alcina; Esther; Lotario; Orlando; Ottone; Partenope; Poro.
(M) *** Philips Universo 6599 053. English Chamber Orchestra, Raymond Leppard.

Characteristically elegant performances from Leppard, richly recorded. The orchestral playing is gracious and polished, and the acoustic adds the necessary weight to Leppard's conceptions. There is some fine music here and at middle price this disc is worth exploring by everyone.

411

Overtures: *Agrippina; Alcina; Belshazzar; Deidamia; Jephtha; Radamisto; Rinaldo; Rodelinda; Susanna.*
** (*) DGG 2530 342. London Philharmonic Orchestra, Karl Richter.

Richter is weighty, but his heaviness of style is tempered by some brilliant orchestral playing, with allegros taken exhilaratingly fast. With superb DGG sound, this is very enjoyable, and those who admire the German tradition in Handel will find this partnership with a British orchestra highly successful.

Overtures and sinfonias (ed. Bonynge): *Ariodante: Overture; Berenice: Overture; Esther: Overture; Jephtha, Act 3: Sinfonia; Rinaldo: Overture; Act 3: March and Battle; Solomon: Overture; Act 3: Sinfonia: Arrival of the Queen of Sheba; Sosarme: Overture; Teseo: Overture.*
*** Decca SXL 6360. English Chamber Orchestra, Richard Bonynge.

The Arrival of the Queen of Sheba is as popular as it always was, but almost all the rest of this splendid collection has been left in neglect, and all credit to Richard Bonynge for resurrecting it with such vigour. Handel's cosmopolitan qualities give such music the benefit of all traditions of the time – French finesse, Italian elaboration, English plainspokenness and so on. The specialists may argue about Bonynge's style of ornamentation – it often trespasses into post-Handelian territory – but the result here could hardly be more enjoyable. Fine recording.

Overtures (ed. Bonynge): *Arminio; Belshazzar (Sinfonia); Deidamia; Faramondo; Judas Maccabaeus; Julius Caesar (Overture and Minuet, Act 1); Radamisto; Scipio; Semele (Sinfonia, Act 2).*

*** Decca SXL 6496. English Chamber Orchestra, Richard Bonynge.

This is a delightful record in every way. Bonynge uses his scholarship to produce results that are the very opposite of dry-as-dust. He may use double-dotting, notes inégales and added appoggiaturas beyond what other scholars would allow, but the baroque elaboration is justified in the exuberance of the end result. The rarities included here are all delightful, and the recording is superbly vivid.

Overtures: (i) *Brockes Passion;* (ii) *Judas Maccabaeus;* (iii) *Giulio Cesare; Messiah;* (iv) *Royal Fireworks music;* (iii) *Samson;* (i) *Saul; Water music.*
(M) * (*) DGG Privilege 2538 164. (i) Schola Cantorum Basiliensis, August Wenzinger; (ii) Berlin Radio Orchestra, Helmut Koch; (iii) Munich Bach Orchestra, Karl Richter; (iv) Archive Wind Ensemble, August Wenzinger.

A mixed bag of performances, all well recorded and nearly all demonstrating that the German style of playing Handel is weightier and rhythmically less resilient than the home product. But Wenzinger shows an attractive buoyancy in his spirited wind version of the prelude to the *Royal Fireworks music.*

Music for the Royal Fireworks; Concerti grossi, Op. 3, Nos. 2 in B flat major; 5 in D major.
(B) * (*) Classics for Pleasure CFP 105. Virtuosi of London, Arthur Davison.
Music for the Royal Fireworks; Concerto in D major; 2 Concertos in F major.
** (*) Philips 6500 369. English Chamber Orchestra, Raymond Leppard.

Music for the Royal Fireworks; Concerto a due cori No. 1 in B flat major.
> * CBS 73172. La Grande Écurie et La Chambre du Roy, Jean-Claude Malgoire.

Music for the Royal Fireworks (original wind scoring); *Concerto a due cori No. 2 in F major.*
> (B) *** Pye GSGC 15009. Pro Arte Orchestra, Charles Mackerras.

Music for the Royal Fireworks; Concerti a due cori Nos. 2 and 3 in F major.
> ** DGG Archive 2533 151. English Chamber Orchestra, Karl Richter.

Music for the Royal Fireworks; Water music: suite (original versions).
> (M) ** (*) DGG Privilege 2538 100. Schola Cantorum Basiliensis, August Wenzinger.

Music for the Royal Fireworks; Water music (complete); *Concerti a due cori Nos. 2 and 3 in F major.*
> (M) ** (*) DGG Privilege 2726 026 (2 discs). Schola Cantorum Basiliensis, August Wenzinger.

Music for the Royal Fireworks; Water music: suites Nos. 1–3 (complete recording).
> *** Argo ZRG 697. Academy of St Martin-in-the-Fields, Neville Marriner.

Music for the Royal Fireworks (original wind scoring); *Water music: extended suite.*
> (M) ** Vanguard VSD 71176. English Chamber Orchestra, Johannes Somary.

Music for the Royal Fireworks; Water music: extended suite.
> (B) ** Contour 6870 579. Berlin Radio Orchestra, Lorin Maazel.

Royal Fireworks music: suite; Water music: suite (both arr. Harty).
> (M) ** HMV SXLP 20033. Royal Philharmonic Orchestra, George Weldon.

Royal Fireworks music: suite; Water music: suite (arr. Harty and Szell); *The Faithful Shepherd* (suite, arr. and ed. Beecham): *Minuet; Xerxes: Largo* (arr. Reinhardt).
> (B) *** Decca SPA 120. London Symphony Orchestra, George Szell.

Water music: suites Nos. 1–3 (complete recording).
> *** Philips 6500 047. English Chamber Orchestra, Raymond Leppard.
> *** HMV ASD 577. Bath Festival Chamber Orchestra, Yehudi Menuhin.
> (M) ** Oiseau-Lyre SOL 60010. Philomusica Orchestra, Thurston Dart.
> (B) * Turnabout TV 34323S. Chicago Chamber Orchestra, Dieter Kober.

Water music: suite (arr. Harty).
> (M) ** HMV SXLP 30161. Berlin Philharmonic Orchestra, Herbert von Karajan – LEOPOLD MOZART: *Toy symphony*; MOZART: *Ave verum; Serenade No. 13; German dance, K.605/3.***

Among the many fine records of the *Royal Fireworks* and *Water music*, there are three that stand out from the others. For those wanting a first-class disc combining both scores complete, the Argo issue by the Academy of St Martin-in-the-Fields is an obvious choice. Marriner directs the most sparkling account of the complete *Water music* yet to appear on record. All the well-loved movements we knew in the Harty suite come out even more refreshed than usual, and the rest is similarly stylish. Scholars may argue about some textual points, but even before the Leppard/ECO version this account

413

by the Academy must stand at the head of the list. It is a substantial advantage that the disc – unlike its rivals – also includes the complete *Fireworks music*. There Marriner's interpretation is more obviously controversial, for he deliberately avoids a weighty manner, even in the magisterial opening of the overture. In this Leppard, who manages to combine point with a sense of ceremony, is preferable. But with superb, resonant recording Marriner's generous coupling makes very sound sense.

Having purchased this admirable disc, one can make a worthwhile supplement to it with the outstanding bargain disc of the original wind scoring of the *Fireworks music* which Charles Mackerras made on the night of the 200th anniversary of Handel's death during the hours when virtually all of London's oboists and a sufficient number of brass players would be free. Here is the original as Handel scored it for twenty-four oboes, twelve bassoons and contra-bassoons, nine horns, nine trumpets, side-drums and three pairs of kettle-drums. The result is a *tour de force*, and the recording sounds as fresh now as on the night when it was made. The spontaneity of the playing is exhilarating and the sonorities rich and exciting. It is coupled to an attractive *Double concerto*, where strings are added.

The third special recommendation is a highly enjoyable account of the two Handel–Harty suites under George Szell, with Handel's *Largo* and the *Minuet* from Beecham's *Faithful Shepherd suite* thrown in for good measure. The orchestral playing throughout this disc is quite outstanding, and the strings are wonderfully expressive in the slower pieces. The horns too excel, and the crisp new Decca re-transfer makes for a remarkable bargain on this company's low-priced label.

Of the other discs, Davison's Classics for Pleasure coupling is crisply immediate, but rather lacks resonance in the bass. The playing is fresh and stylish but lacks weight in the *Fireworks music*. Leppard's

account of the *Fireworks music*, on the other hand, is very resonant, the interpretation broad and spectacular. The couplings are three orchestral *Concertos* which feature themes used in the *Water* and *Fireworks music*. Handel was adept at borrowing from himself, and these are attractive small-scale examples, elegantly played and very well recorded. Some might feel they are lightweight, but they do not lack charm. The CBS disc has lots of character, but the quality of the wind timbres as recorded (the *Fireworks music* is in the original score) is nasal, and the intonation leaves much to be desired.

Richter's Archive coupling features strong contrasts of light and shade in the *Fireworks music*, and the performance is not sufficiently robust to be fully in character. The *Concerti a due cori* suit Richter's approach readily. The playing of the Schola Cantorum Basiliensis, however, has a splendid feeling for the open-air style of the music, with crisp buoyant rhythms. The use of original instruments in the *Fireworks music* gives a suitably robust effect, while a fuller orchestra is used in the *Water music*.

The Vanguard coupling under Somary offers the same scoring as Mackerras and a similarly spectacular effect in the *Royal Fireworks music*. The *Water music*, however, is played orchestrally in chamber style, and makes less impact. On the Contour disc Maazel's tempi in the *Fireworks music* are very brisk, the main allegro surely too fast, but otherwise this is an enjoyable performance. The *Water music* suite is very successful, and here the superbly sprung rhythms are infectious. With good stereo recording this is a bargain, provided you do not find the tempi too unrelaxed.

Weldon's approach is traditional and the RPO play well for him. With good sound this is reasonably competitive, but the Decca SPA disc is cheaper and preferable.

Of the other discs including the complete *Water music* score, Menuhin uses a new edition prepared by Neville Boyling; Leppard, presumably, has edited his own version. Both reveal Handel's score as containing a wealth of invention of the highest quality. Leppard offers elegant, beautifully-turned and stylish performances, with well-judged and truthful recording. This has the edge over the Menuhin record, which is not so recent but still sounds well. Menuhin's approach is genial and warm-hearted and with excellent playing and a quality of lively spontaneity throughout this disc remains competitive.

Thurston Dart's Oiseau-Lyre disc is a good one too, stylishly played and with an excellent recording. Spontaneity and scholarship make a very happy partnership here. The Chicago Chamber Orchestra is thinly recorded and not really very congenial.

Karajan favours a big-orchestra sound, and originally the recording was rich but slightly woolly. The face-lift has made the strings sound rather out of focus in the loudest moments, but the performance is good of its kind and should suit those who want the concert as a whole.

INSTRUMENTAL MUSIC

Sonatas, Op. 1: Nos. 1b in E minor for flute; 2 in G minor for recorder; 4 in A minor for recorder; 5 in G major for flute; 7 in C major for recorder; 8 in C minor for oboe; 11 in F major for recorder; Flute sonata in B minor; Oboe sonata in B flat major; Recorder sonatas in B flat major; in D minor; Allegro in F major for oboe; Andante in B minor for flute; Minuet in E minor for flute; Movement in D minor for recorder.

(M) ** (*) Philips 6747 096 (3 discs). Frans Brüggen (recorder and flute), Bruce Haynes (oboe), Hans Jürg Lange (bassoon), Anner Bylsma (cello), Bob van Asperen (harpsichord and organ).

These performances are enormously accomplished – indeed that is an understatement: Brüggen plays with characteristic mastery and so do his companions on this set. There are some mannerisms: he swells all-too-predictably on sustained notes and is generous with stress accents. However, Handelians will want the set for its scholarship and expertise even though the flute is balanced rather close, which will not be to all tastes.

Flute sonatas (complete recording): *in E minor, Op. 1/1a; in E minor, Op. 1/1b; in G major, Op. 1/5; in B minor, Op. 1/9; in A minor; B minor; D major; E minor.*

(B) *** Oryx ORYX 1712/13. Peter-Lucas Graf (flute), Manfred Sax (bassoon), Jörg Ewald Dähler (harpsichord).

The idea of using a bassoon to support the continuo in these sonatas was a happy one. With excellent, clear recording the textures are delightfully fresh, especially when both flautist and bassoonist are such excellent players. The harpsichord is balanced less clearly, and produces a small-scale sound. But the overall effect is very pleasing and the whole set is refreshing to listen to.

Recorder sonatas in G minor, Op. 1/2; in A minor, Op. 1/4; in C major, Op. 1/7; in F major, Op. 1/11; in B major; in D minor.

*** Telefunken SAWT 9421. Frans Brüggen (recorder), Gustav Leonhardt (harpsichord), Anner Bylsma (cello).

The four sonatas from Op. 1 are those the composer intended for recorder; the other two can be found in the Fitzwilliam collection. All the works offer delightfully

415

inventive music and these performances are outstandingly successful. The spontaneity of the playing is no less striking than the way the scholarship and artistry underpin the style of the music-making. Both the harpsichordist and the cellist make an equal contribution to this excellent partnership.

Trio sonatas in C minor, Op. 2/1; in G minor, Op. 2/2; in B flat major, Op. 2/4; in F major, Op. 2/5; in G minor, Op. 2/7; in G minor, Op. 2/8; in E major, Op. 2/9; in D minor, in A major, Op. 5/1; in D major, Op. 5/2; in G major, Op. 5/4; in G minor, Op. 5/5; in F major, Op. 5/6.

(M) ** Supraphon 111 1251/3. Ars Rediviva Ensemble, Milan Munclinger.

The catalogue lists no alternative version of these sonatas, which is surprising, considering their quality. The six sonatas of Op. 2 were published in 1733, and Chrysander added three further sonatas he found in Dresden when he published his complete edition. The Op. 5 come from 1739, and are six in number. The set falls short of completeness (the fine Op. 2/3 is missing), and Handelians will not need to be reminded that the Op. 5 set includes some borrowings. (Op. 2/4 draws on the overture to *Esther*.) The performances are vital and stylish, though some reviewers have complained that there are not enough trills. Given the moderate price and good recording the set can be recommended *faute de mieux*.

Aylesford pieces (Overture; Entrée; Gavotte; Toccata; Fugue; Impertinence; Concerto; Prelude; Minuets 1 and 2; Allegro minuet; Air; Minuets 1 and 2 (Trio); Air with variations; Allemande; Passepied; Minuet (Trio); Sonatine); Chaconne in G major; Sarabande and Gigue.

(B) ** Turnabout TV 34448S. Janos Sebestyen (harpsichord).

Janos Sebestyen is not always as imaginative as he might be, and the manner of his playing includes rather too much rhythmic emphasis. However, the programme is an adventurous one and the harpsichord is recorded agreeably. The performances are certainly not without personality; they have plenty of light and shade, and the anthology seems good value at the price asked.

VOCAL AND CHORAL MUSIC

Cantatas: Ah, che troppo inegali; Look down, harmonious Saint; Nel dolce dell'oblio; Pensieri notturni di Filli; Praise of harmony; Silete venti. Joseph (oratorio): Overture.

** BASF BAC 3058/9. Elly Ameling, Halina Lukomska (sopranos), Theo Altmeyer (tenor), Collegium Aureum (using original instruments).

The *Pensieri notturni di Filli* are superb; the music is exquisite, and so too are the performances; both Elly Ameling and Hans-Martin Linde, who plays the recorder obbligato, are on top form. *Look down, harmonious Saint* on the second side was probably intended for inclusion in *Alexander's Feast*, and this too is admirably done, even if the side offers short measure – as does the second record for that matter. *Silete venti* fares less well in this version than it did in Ameling's Philips account (6500 008, now deleted) and is recorded in a somewhat reverberant acoustic. A not wholly successful coupling.

Cantatas: Ah! crudel, nel pianto mio; Armida abbandonata.

*** HMV ASD 2468. Janet Baker

(mezzo-soprano), English Chamber Orchestra, Raymond Leppard (harpsichord), Bernard Richards (cello).

Cantata: *Armida abbandonata.*

(M) * Philips Universo 6580 081. Stefania Woytowicz (soprano), Berlin Chamber Orchestra, Kurt Masur – CARISSIMI: *Jephtha.**

A lovely record. Handel's cantatas, like so much of his enormous output, are seriously neglected, and all credit to Janet Baker and the effervescent Raymond Leppard for giving us a splendid coupling of two of the finest. For the modern listener it is a positive advantage that Miss Baker adopts a strongly impassioned style for music which, though formal in layout, expresses far-from-formal emotions. Her singing is magnificent, even though the tessitura is a little high for her mezzo; a display of virtuosity as well as of incomparable tone-colour. Leppard provides spirited accompaniments with his characteristically elaborate continuo support at the harpsichord. Fine recording. Stefania Woytowicz faces stiff competition in this cantata from Janet Baker, and although this is a cheaper disc with considerable merits (Masur is generally stylish, though tempi can be sluggish) the rival account is undeniably the one to have.

Cantatas: *Carco sempre di gloria; Splenda l'alba in oriente; Tu fedel? Tu costante?*

(M) ** Oiseau-Lyre SOL 60046. Helen Watts (contralto), English Chamber Orchestra, Raymond Leppard.

These performances by Helen Watts are sympathetic and enjoyable, direct in manner rather than especially subtle in the use of vocal colouring. But there is some fine music here, and Raymond Leppard ensures that the background for the voice is always well in the picture, at once alive and stylish. The recording is excellent.

L'Allegro ed il penseroso (ode in the dramatic style).

(M) * (*) Oiseau-Lyre SOL 60025/6. Elsie Morison, Jacqueline Delman, Elizabeth Harwood (sopranos), Helen Watts (contralto), Peter Pears (tenor), Hervey Alan (bass), St Anthony Singers, Philomusica of London, David Willcocks; Thurston Dart (harpsichord and organ).

Somehow this performance does not quite come to life, perhaps because it tries too hard. Pace is all-important in Handel, and at times the impression is too leisurely, at others too hurried for comfort. Pears sings intelligently as ever, but the other soloists are uneven in quality and seem unable to offer sufficient variety of tone-colour and phrasing. Nevertheless, Handel lovers will find much to admire in the elegance and appeal of the words and music.

Belshazzar (oratorio): complete recording.

(B) ** Turnabout TV 37019/21S. Sylvia Stahlman (soprano), Helen Raab, Heidrun Ankersen (contraltos), Wilfrid Jochims (tenor), Helge Birkeland (bass), Stuttgart Memorial Church Choir, Stuttgart Kirchenmusiktage Orchestra, Helmuth Rilling.

Though some of the German singers seem a little uncomfortable singing in English, and the long recitatives are made to sound heavy in the German manner, this is a well-sung, enjoyable account of what is probably Handel's most dramatic oratorio, with the three nations in the story – Jews, Persians and Babylonians – neatly characterized in the choruses. To

417

fit the work on to three records the score has to be drastically cut; but this is a fair recommendation at bargain price.

Chandos anthems: As Pants the Hart; The Lord is my Light.

> *** Argo ZRG 541. April Cantelo (soprano), Ian Partridge (tenor), King's College Chapel Choir, Academy of St Martin-in-the-Fields, David Willcocks; Andrew Davis (organ continuo).

Handel wrote eleven anthems for his patron the Duke of Chandos, to be performed at his country house, Canons, near Edgware. Reflecting the period, they have grandeur but a direct unpretentiousness as well, and the elements of Italianate elaboration and German fugal complexity are married in them with an assurance that only Handel could achieve. These two, Nos. 6 and 10, provide an attractive disc with all Teutonic pomposity avoided and the freshness of inspiration underlined. No. 6 includes a lovely *Adagio* chorus and a beautiful soprano aria, while No. 10 is remarkable for some magnificent fugal writing. Excellent recording.

Chandos anthems: In the Lord Put I my Trust; I Will Magnify Thee.

> *** Argo ZRG 766. Caroline Friend (soprano), Philip Langridge (tenor), King's College Chapel Choir, Academy of St Martin-in-the-Fields, David Willcocks.

Here are two more of Handel's anthems (these are Nos. 2 and 5) written for the Duke of Chandos, attractive for their freshness of inspiration, their economical vocal writing for small forces producing agreeably resilient textures. The choral singing here is well up to standard, and the solo contributions have plenty of character, Philip Langridge notable for his eloquence and simplicity

of approach. With characteristically fine Argo recording, in the best King's tradition, this can be enthusiastically recommended beside the others of this series.

Chandos anthems: Let God Arise; O Praise the Lord with One Consent.

> *** Argo ZRG 5490. Elizabeth Vaughan (soprano), Alexander Young (tenor), Forbes Robinson (bass), King's College Chapel Choir, Academy of St Martin-in-the-Fields, David Willcocks.

The instrumentation here is simple, including only oboe and bassoon besides strings and continuo, and the choral writing effectively uses a small group of singers. The freshness of the idiom is delightful. The opening line of *O Praise the Lord with One Consent* fits very nicely to the hymn tune we know as *O God our Help in Ages Past*, but Handel only helps himself to this first line of the hymn and weaves his own music therefrom. This is an especially pleasing cantata with more than one reminder of *Messiah* (only the idiom less grandiose), and in this and in its companion, *Let God Arise*, the writing for the soloists is rewarding too. This latter work is marginally more conventional in style but redeems itself with a wonderfully imaginative chorus to the words *Praised be the Lord*. Excellent singing and recording from soloists and chorus alike and a stylish accompaniment, all beautifully recorded, make this a most desirable disc for all Handelians.

Coronation anthems (for the coronation of King George II and Queen Caroline): 1, *Zadok the Priest;* 2, *The King shall Rejoice;* 3, *My Heart is Inditing;* 4, *Let Thy Hand be Strengthened.*

> ** Argo ZRG 5369. King's College Chapel Choir, English Chamber Orchestra, David Willcocks; Thurston Dart (harpsichord).

These are fine performances, brilliantly recorded, except in the matter of balance, and that is a problem inherent in the choral singing itself. This is stylish enough but the kind of sound the choir makes is rather too light-textured for these large-scale ceremonial pieces. The result is that the orchestra tends to overwhelm the vocal sound, even though the engineering minimizes this as much as possible. However, with any reservations this is a sensible collection, extremely well recorded, and there is a great deal to enjoy.

Israel in Egypt (oratorio): complete recording.

** DGG Archive 2708 020 (2 discs). Heather Harper, Patricia Clark (sopranos), Paul Esswood (counter-tenor), Alexander Young (tenor), Michael Rippon, Christopher Keyte (basses), Leeds Festival Chorus, English Chamber Orchestra, Charles Mackerras.

(B) * (*) Turnabout TV 37013/4S. Miriam Burton (soprano), Betty Allen (contralto), Leslie Chaby (tenor), Dessoff Choirs, Symphony of the Air, Paul Boepple.

Although it has many merits Mackerras's performance is in some ways disappointing. It represents a curious dichotomy of styles in using the English Chamber Orchestra, sounding crisp, stylish and lightweight in the opening overture (borrowed from *Solomon*), and the thick textures of the fairly large amateur choir, competent enough but almost entirely lacking in incisive quality. Thus the work makes its effect by weight and grandiloquence rather than athletic vigour. The recording balance too reflects the problems of the basic set-up, with the chorus sometimes virtually drowning the orchestra in the epic pieces, and then suddenly coming forward for the lighter moments of the score. The solo singing is

distinguished but its style is refined rather than earthy and so again makes a contrast with the choral manner (although this contrast is not unfamiliar in the English tradition of live performance). The performance here has integrity and purpose but the music does not come alive in quite the same way as it does in the much less sophisticated Turnabout set, even though Mackerras demonstrates a feeling for the style and period.

It is the choruses which are the glory of *Israel in Egypt* and Handel uses them to make all the dramatic points of his story. The Dessoff choristers rise to their words with vigour and conviction rather than any special sophistication, but they are directed with spirit by Boepple, who shows in the accompaniments that he has a feeling for the period style. The stereo recording, although dated, has been greatly improved in the new transfer and generally can be made to sound effective. The soloists' contribution is less distinguished. The tenor is best; the ladies are prone to squalliness and when they get together in their duet at the end of side two (*The Lord is my strength*) their wobbles do not quite match. However, this is a comparatively unimportant criticism in a bargain-priced set where such a small proportion of the music is given to the solo voices.

Judas Maccabaeus (oratorio): complete recording.

(M) ** (*) Vanguard VCS 10105/7. Heather Harper (soprano), Helen Watts (contralto), Alexander Young (tenor), John Shirley-Quirk (baritone), Amor Artis Chorale, Wandsworth School Boys' Choir, English Chamber Orchestra, Johannes Somary; Harold Lester (harpsichord and organ).

Judas Maccabaeus, though its popularity has been eclipsed, contains much fine and noble music, as Johannes Somary's vital performance underlines. The choruses of lamentation for the Israelites in Act 1 and strong, heroic solos and choruses all through – the tenor's *Sound an alarm* typical of them – make for a work which may be long but which has much to hold the attention. The solo singing is excellent, with Alexander Young a ringing tenor, and Helen Watts singing the opening aria in Act 3 exquisitely. Good recording – not ideally clear in the choruses – and a sense of commitment throughout from all departments.

Lucrezia (cantata); Arias: *Ariodante: Dopo notte; Atalanta: Care selve; Hercules: Where shall I fly?; Joshua: O had I Jubal's lyre; Rodelinda: Dove sei, amato bene?; Xerxes: Ombra mai fù (Largo)*.

*** Philips 6500 523. Janet Baker (mezzo-soprano), English Chamber Orchestra, Raymond Leppard.

Even among Janet Baker's records this Handel recital marks a special contribution, ranging as it does from the pure gravity of *Ombra mai fù* to the passionate commitment and supreme coloratura virtuosity in *Dopo notte* from *Ariodante*. Leppard gives sparkling support, and the whole is recorded with natural and refined balance. An outstanding disc.

Messiah (oratorio): complete recording.

*** Philips 6703 001 (3 discs). Heather Harper (soprano), Helen Watts (contralto), John Wakefield (tenor), John Shirley-Quirk (baritone), LSO Chorus, London Symphony Orchestra, Colin Davis.

(M) *** HMV SLS 845 (3 discs). James Bowman (counter-tenor), Robert Tear (tenor), Benjamin Luxon (bass), King's College Chapel Choir, Academy of St Martin-in-the-Fields, David Willcocks.

(M) ** (*) HMV SLS 774 (3 discs). Elizabeth Harwood (soprano), Janet Baker (contralto), Paul Esswood (counter-tenor), Robert Tear (tenor), Raimund Herincx (baritone), Ambrosian Singers, English Chamber Orchestra, Charles Mackerras.

(M) ** (*) RCA SER 5631/4. Jennifer Vyvyan (soprano), Monica Sinclair (contralto), Jon Vickers (tenor), Giorgio Tozzi (bass), Royal Philharmonic Chorus and Orchestra, Sir Thomas Beecham.

(M) ** (*) Vanguard VCS 10090/2. Margaret Price (soprano), Yvonne Minton (contralto), Alexander Young (tenor), Justino Diaz (bass), Amor Artis Chorale, English Chamber Orchestra, Johannes Somary.

** (*) Decca SET 465/7. Joan Sutherland (soprano), Huguette Tourangeau (contralto), Werner Krenn (tenor), Tom Krause (bass), Dermot Coleman (boy soprano), Ambrosian Singers, English Chamber Orchestra, Richard Bonynge.

** Decca SET 218/20. Joan Sutherland (soprano), Grace Bumbry (contralto), Kenneth McKellar (tenor), Joseph Ward (bass), LSO Chorus, London Symphony Orchestra, Sir Adrian Boult.

* (*) HMV SLS 915 (3 discs). Elisabeth Schwarzkopf (soprano), Grace Hoffman (contralto), Nicolai Gedda (tenor), Jerome Hines (bass), Philharmonia Chorus and Orchestra, Otto Klemperer.

* (*) DGG 2720 069 (3 discs). Helen

Donath (soprano), Anna Reynolds (contralto), Stuart Burrows (tenor), Donald McIntyre (bass), John Alldis Choir, London Philharmonic Orchestra, Karl Richter.
(B) * (*) Saga 5111/3. Heather Harper (soprano), Helen Watts (contralto), Duncan Robertson (tenor), Roger Stalman (bass), LPO Choir, London Philharmonic Orchestra, Frederic Jackson.

Few recordings of much-repeated works have made such an impact as Colin Davis's account of *Messiah*. With the help of the recording manager, Harold Lawrence, he took a completely new look at the score, attempted to give an authentic reading, and as a result made everyone hear the music with new ears. Initially the traditionalist may be worried by the very fast speeds Davis tends to adopt for choruses, but a fine professional body (unnamed) copes with every technical difficulty with ease. The chorus is always fresh, the texture beautifully clear and, thanks to Davis, the rhythmic bounce of such choruses as *For unto us* is really infectious. Even *Hallelujah* loses little and gains much from being performed by an authentic-sized chorus, and the bite of the recorded sound more than makes amends at every point for lack of 'Huddersfield-style' massiveness. Excellent singing from all four soloists, particularly Helen Watts, who following early precedent is given *For He is like a refiner's fire* to sing instead of the bass, and produces a glorious chest register. With Davis's briskness there is everything to be said for the inclusion of all the numbers traditionally omitted.

Often as Handel's *Messiah* has been recorded on LP, there seems plenty of room in the market for new versions, particularly ones which show a new and illuminating view of the work. Willcocks's recording has been described as the 'all-male *Messiah*', for a counter-tenor takes over the contralto solos, and the full complement of the trebles of King's College Choir sing the soprano solos, even the florid ones like *Rejoice greatly*, and the result is enchanting. The whole approach is light and airy, with some delightful continuo playing and splendid contributions from the St Martin's Academy as well as the famous choir. Vivid atmospheric recording against the King's acoustic. A gimmick version, perhaps, but one that few will resist.

Mackerras on his set has the misfortune to come into direct competition with Davis's performance, which was issued a month or so earlier. The choruses in particular have nothing like the same vitality. Even so there is much to commend the set, not least the modest price. One could well argue that Basil Lam's edition of the score goes deeper than Davis's in pursuing the authentic approach, but for the layman the main difference will be that, more than Davis, Mackerras adopts Handel's generally forgotten alternative versions. So the soprano aria *Rejoice greatly* is given in its optional 12/8 version, with compound time adding a skip to the rhythm. A male alto is also included among the soloists, and he is given some of the bass arias as well as some of the regular alto passages. Among the soloists Janet Baker is outstanding. Her intensely slow account of *He was despised* – with decorations on the reprise – is sung with profound feeling. Good recording, rather warmer and less bright than the rival Philips. Like Davis, Mackerras includes all the numbers traditionally omitted.

Sir Thomas Beecham presents Handel's masterpiece in something like modern dress, for he uses a version of the score prepared by Sir Eugene Goossens which includes parts not only for heavyweight brass but for elaborate percussion including cymbals and anvil, and a full complement of strings. Surprisingly his chorus is not large, for he was one of the first on record to insist on a relatively small chorus being drilled to professional standards, and the results are exhilarating. One can disapprove in principle, but Beecham's genius shines through everything, making this an unforgettable experience. For its age the recording is amply brilliant, and the solo singing is consistently good.

Somary directs a crisp, small-scale performance that features sparkling orchestral playing and first-rate singing from soloists and chorus alike. His direction is not always consistent, but it is never dull, and those in particular who have special fondness for all or any of the soloists will be well pleased with this version. Clean if sometimes overbright recording.

On his Decca set, much of the electricity which marked Bonynge's live accounts of the oratorio at the Festival Hall and Albert Hall is captured on disc. This is an exuberant *Messiah*, more remarkable for brilliance and colour than for any more meditative qualities. As in Colin Davis's account the tempi for the choruses are often very fast, and the overall result is most refreshing. But as a whole the performance does not quite add up as Davis's so clearly did. The one serious blot is the choice of Huguette Tourangeau as contralto soloist. Hers is a remarkable voice for opera but not suited here. Werner Krenn and Tom Krause sing neatly and enjoyably, matching the performance as a whole, while the treble's piping tone adds point to a number of passages. When one expects the voice of Sutherland to enter for the very first time on *There were shepherds*, you have instead this very different voice. Sutherland here is far fresher-toned than she was in 1961, and *I know that my Redeemer*, rather surprisingly, is done with no trills at all — very different from last time. First-rate recording.

The earlier Decca set also featured Joan Sutherland but in doing so created problems. She alone pays any attention to the question of whether or not to use ornamentation in the repeats of *da capo* arias.

What she does is mostly in good taste, and her sense of style usually saves the situation when there is any doubt; but none of the other singers does anything apart from give us the notes as they stand in the score. Grace Bumbry has a pleasant but somewhat invariable timbre, not always too secure in intonation. McKellar's tenor contribution lacks the dramatic vitality of Vickers in the Beecham set, and the same may be said for Ward (who is a better singer than McKellar). The recording is excellent. Chorus and orchestra play well under Boult's distinguished baton; but *Messiah*, for all the importance of its choruses, ultimately stands or falls by its soloists.

The glory of Klemperer's *Messiah* is the singing of the chorus. There is a freshness, clarity and edge to it that shows up nearly all rival performances on record. Nor is Klemperer's direction dull despite his characteristic determination to underline the solidity of the music and to pay no heed to scholarly ideas on the text. So far so good, but the soloists' contribution is far more questionable. Schwarzkopf sings very beautifully, and in the recitatives she is most imaginative, with expressive enunciation of the words (the link with opera is as delightful as it is unexpected), but in the arias her line is not always impeccable. Even so she is unfailingly interesting, which is more than one can say for Grace Hoffman. *O thou that tellest* is badly sung, though *He was despised* is far better. Gedda is interesting but not always comfortable in the part; Jerome Hines, despite a big, dark voice, seems out of his element too and is hardly imaginative. But the chorus is always wonderful, and the recording captures its sound gloriously. In any case Klemperer's magisterial touch is unique all through.

Where for its Archive recording of *Messiah* D G G chose a British conductor to direct a German-speaking cast, the parent company chose one of Germany's favourite conductors to direct this version recorded in England. Maybe it is a comment on national preferences in Handel performance, but to English ears at least Richter's direction is unrelievedly dull, and the fine singing of choir and soloists hardly has a chance to make its point.

The Saga set is good value for money. Its style is more traditional than most of the other current versions. At times the orchestra seems a little thick-textured, and the chorus lacks something in agility and crispness. Of the soloists the ladies show more subtlety in the matter of vocal colour, but the tenor and bass both have fine voices and sing eloquently. The recording is variable. The focus of the loudest climaxes is not perfect, but for the arias the sound and background ambience combine to produce a pleasing atmosphere.

Messiah (arr. Mozart; sung in German).
*** (*) DGG Archive 2723 019 (3 discs). Edith Mathis (soprano), Birgit Finnilä (contralto), Peter Schreier (tenor), Theo Adam (bass), Austrian Radio Chorus and Orchestra, Charles Mackerras.

It is a sign of our scholarly times that DGG's Archive label, dedicated to authenticity in performance above all, can devote so much care to reproducing the Mozart arrangement of Handel's *Messiah* (or *Messias*, as it becomes in German). It is not simply a question of trombones being added but of elaborate woodwind parts too – fascinating ones in such a number as *All we like sheep*. *Rejoice greatly* is given to the tenor (even Peter Schreier sounding too heavy), and *The trumpet shall sound* is considerably modified to avoid the need to use a baroque trumpet. Charles Mackerras, an outstanding Handelian, leads his fine team through a performance that is vital, not academic in the wrong sense, and the

recording is excellent. Not an alternative one would always want to hear, but a valuable offering in the catalogue.

Messiah: Christmas music (Part 1): from *Comfort ye* to *His yoke is easy.*
** HMV CSD 3669. Gloria Jennings (contralto), Robert Tear (tenor), John Carol Case (bass), King's College Chapel Choir, Academy of St Martin-in-the-Fields, David Willcocks.

This is a pleasant selection of the Christmas music from *Messiah*, with the trebles of the choir taking the place of the soprano soloist. The record contains nearly all the music of Part 1. The solo singing is good, Gloria Jennings's somewhat reserved but nevertheless sensitive manner being particularly attractive. The chorus offers the beauty of line for which King's is famous, and the effect is fresh rather than weighty. Excellent recording.

Messiah: highlights.
(B) *** Philips 6833 050 (from above complete recording cond. Davis).
(M) ** (*) HMV HQS 1183 (from above recording cond. Mackerras).
(B) ** (*) Vanguard SRV 96SD (from above recording cond. Somary).
** (*) Decca SXL 6540 (from above recording cond. Bonynge).
** Decca SXL 2316 (from above recording cond. Boult).
(B) * (*) SAGA 5150 (from above recording cond. Jackson).

Messiah: excerpts.
(B) * (*) Classics for Pleasure CFP 40020. Elsie Morison (soprano), Marjorie Thomas (contralto), Richard Lewis (tenor), Huddersfield Choral Society, Royal Liverpool Philharmonic Orchestra, Sir Malcolm Sargent.

(M) * (*) CBS Classics 61418. Adele Addison (soprano), David Lloyd (tenor), Russell Oberlin (counter-tenor), William Warfield (bass), Westminster Choir, New York Philharmonic Orchestra, Leonard Bernstein.

(B) * (*) Music for Pleasure MFP 2108. Annon Lee Silver (soprano), Patricia Payne (contralto), Wynford Evans (tenor), Alan Opie (bass), London Chorus and Little Symphony, Arthur Davison.

(B) * (*) Decca SPA 284. Sheila Armstrong (soprano), Norma Procter (contralto), Kenneth Bowen (tenor), John Cameron (bass), LSO Chorus, London Symphony Orchestra, Leopold Stokowski.

Messiah: choruses.

(M) ** (*) HMV HQS 1244. Ambrosian Singers, English Chamber Orchestra, Charles Mackerras.

(M) ** (*) CBS Classics 61582. Mormon Tabernacle Choir, Royal Philharmonic Orchestra, Richard Condie.

* (*) Decca SXL 6009. LSO Chorus, London Symphony Orchestra, Sir Adrian Boult.

The obvious choice for a highlights disc from *Messiah* is that of the Colin Davis performance. There is a touch of fizz on the upper strings but in every other way the recording is demonstration-worthy. At the price this is an outstanding bargain, and even traditionalists should be tempted to sample this. The other discs reflect the qualities of the complete sets from which they are taken, and each gives a fairly generous selection.

Of the other collections many will undoubtedly want a sampler of Sir Malcolm Sargent's traditional account of *Messiah*. This contains some fine solo singing, notably from Elsie Morison and Richard Lewis, but the choruses are disappointing, heavy in style and recorded in a curiously muffled way which cannot entirely be the fault of the singing itself.

The Bernstein collection sounds much fresher than this, although the choral singing is not of the standard we expect today. There is some excellent solo singing on this record, notably a fine counter-tenor contribution from Russell Oberlin.

The version specially recorded for Music for Pleasure is well conducted by Arthur Davison, and with very vivid sound and excellent choral singing, it has many enjoyable moments. The selection favours the end of the work, so that *Hallelujah* comes at the end of the first side, and the third and shortest part of the oratorio is well represented on side two. Wynford Evans has a sensitive tenor, but one needs more power for *Comfort ye*. Alan Opie, a most promising young singer with a potentially fine voice, sings too much under the note in crooning style, and both the women singers similarly leave one wishing for more stylish assurance. At the price, with excellent stereo, it is still worth considering.

Stokowski can hardly be taken seriously as a Handel interpreter, for plainly all he is after is dramatic sound. As always with him there is a musical personality to admire, and the performers are all first-rate artists, but they must have had their tongues in their cheeks over some of the things Stokowski asked them to do.

One wonders what Handel would have thought of the idea of listening to his *Messiah* choruses without the contrasting arias in between. The effect is certainly invigorating in the Mackerras performances, but there is little feeling of repose. On the other hand the recording is splendid, and there is no doubt about the vitality and impact of the closing *Worthy is the Lamb* and *Amen*.

The Mormon Tabernacle Choir offer an excellent selection, and their performances have clarity and bite as well as characteristic fervour. This record was made during the Choir's European tour in the summer of 1973. The recording – made in the Kingsway Hall – is splendid, and this spontaneous disc will give much pleasure. Try *Worthy is the Lamb* as a sampler of the vigour and conviction of the singing. But the *Hallelujah chorus* is allowed to get faster as it progresses, and the result becomes uncontrolled rather than exuberant.

Hearing them separated from their context one notices how reverberant the choruses from the Boult recording sound. The quality certainly has plenty of bloom, but less clarity for the fugal entries. The performances themselves, however, are excellent.

Ode for St Cecilia's Day.
   * (*) Argo ZRG 563. April Cantelo (soprano), Ian Partridge (tenor), King's College Chapel Choir, Academy of St Martin-in-the-Fields, David Willcocks.

Argo seldom disappoint with their choral records, but this must have been a King's off-day. The recording is very fine (although the disc is cut at rather a low level, especially on side one), but somehow the performance never seems to spring fully to life. It is not the fault of the Academy of St Martin-in-the-Fields, for the *Overture* is one of the highlights of the disc, and there is superb solo playing throughout, and a notably warm contribution from the cellos. April Cantelo phrases sensitively and accurately, if with rather a white tone, but her singing never beguiles, and it is the tenor who brings the disc momentarily to life with *The trumpet's loud clangour.*

Saul (oratorio): complete recording.
   *** DGG Archive 2722 008 (3 discs). Sheila Armstrong, Margaret Price (sopranos), James Bowman (counter-tenor), Ryland Davies, Gerald English (tenors),

Stafford Dean, Donald McIntyre (basses), Leeds Festival Chorus, English Chamber Orchestra, Charles Mackerras.

Few Handel choral works have been recorded with such consistent imagination as this fine performance conducted by Mackerras. With an excellent complement of soloists he steers an exhilarating course that naturally needs to be presented with authenticity but equally needs to have dramatic edge. His scholarship is worn lightly, and the result is powerful on one hand, moving on another, sparkling on yet another. The contrast of timbre between Armstrong and Price, for example, is beautifully exploited, and Donald McIntyre as Saul, Ryland Davies as Jonathan, and James Bowman as a counter-tenor David are all outstanding, while the chorus willingly contributes to the drama. An outstanding set, beautifully recorded.

Sing unto God (anthem).
   ** (*) H M V CSD 3741. London Bach Society and Players, Paul Steinitz – BACH: *Cantata No. 131.*** (*)

A strong, intense performance of Handel's anthem, if lacking something in refinement of mood, makes an attractive coupling with Bach.

Theodora (dramatic oratorio): complete recording.
   (M) ** (*) Vanguard VCS 10050/2. Heather Harper (soprano), Maureen Forrester, Maureen Lehane (contraltos), Alexander Young, Edgar Fleet (tenors), John Lawrenson (baritone), Amor Artis Chorale, English Chamber Orchestra, Johannes Somary.

Theodora was a Christian martyr, and Handel broke his normal rule in dramatic oratorios of keeping to Old Testament subjects to set this rather diffuse story involving five characters – Theodora, a princess of Antioch, and her friends on one hand; Valens, the Roman commander, on the other. There is much fine music in Handel's score – it is said to have been his own favourite among his oratorios – and it is good to have a complete recording (or at least more complete than any live performance would be today) directed by an understanding and intelligent Handelian. Johannes Somary may not rise to great heights of inspiration, but with his care and the fresh, sympathetic singing from the soloists, the result is most enjoyable. Maureen Forrester in particular sings superbly, but all the singing is at least reliable and the recording is good.

OPERA

Alcina (opera in 3 acts): complete recording.

(M) ** Decca Ace of Diamonds GOS 509/11. Joan Sutherland (soprano), Teresa Berganza (mezzo-soprano), Graziella Sciutti (soprano), Monica Sinclair (contralto), Luigi Alva (tenor), Mirella Freni (soprano), Ezio Flagello (bass), London Symphony Orchestra, Richard Bonynge; George Malcolm (harpsichord).

This represents the extreme point of what can be described as Sutherland's dreamy, droopy period. The fast arias are stupendous. The conductor, Sutherland's husband Richard Bonynge, does not spare her at all, and in the brilliant Act 1 finale he really does rush her too fast, the result dazzling rather than musically satisfying. But anything slow and reflective, whether in recitative or aria, has Sutherland mooning about the notes, with no consonants audible at all and practically every vowel reduced to

'aw'. It is all most beautiful, of course, but she could have done so much better. Of the others, Berganza is completely charming in the castrato part of Ruggiero, even if she does not manage trills very well. Monica Sinclair shows everyone up with the strength and forthrightness of all her singing. Both Graziella Sciutti and Mirella Freni are delicate and clear in the two smaller parts of Morgana and Oberto. Richard Bonynge is very good indeed, drawing crisp, vigorous playing from the London Symphony Orchestra. Only in those rushed showpiece arias for his wife does he sound too inflexible. The recording is well up to Decca's incomparably brilliant standard, and at Ace of Diamonds price this is an excellent bargain, for all one's reservations.

Giulio Cesare (Julius Caesar) (opera in 3 acts): abridged version.

** RCA SER 5561/3. Norman Treigle (bass-baritone), Beverly Sills (soprano), Maureen Forrester, Beverly Wolff (contraltos), Spiro Malas (bass), New York City Opera Chorus and Orchestra, Julius Redel.

This RCA recording of *Julius Caesar* is fairly complete and based on a New York stage production. While not all the problems are solved it has the life of a performance that has existed in its own right (rather than being created in the studio). The conductor's approach is intelligent and tries to pay homage to scholarship, but one is not sure that the solution to the *da capo* arias, having a bare initial statement and reserving all the decoration to the reprise, is entirely successful. Nor does the singing of the name part by a baritone (while effective on the stage) mean that the music lies exactly right for the voice. But with all reservations, the overall effect is accomplished, and the atmospheric recording gives considerable enjoyment.

Giulio Cesare: highlights.

Act 1: *Tu la mia stella; Va tacito e nascosto; Priva son d'ogni conforto;* Act 2: *Si, spietata il tuo rigore; V'adoro pupille; Venere bella; Se pietà di me non senti;* Act 3: *Da tempeste; Aure, deh, per pietà; Sperai nè m'ingannai; Piangerò la sorte mia.*

(M) *** Decca Ace of Diamonds SDD 213. Joan Sutherland (soprano), Margreta Elkins, Marilyn Horne (mezzo-sopranos), Monica Sinclair (contralto), Richard Conrad (tenor), London New Symphony Orchestra, Richard Bonynge.

This has some marvellous singing, not only from Sutherland but from Marilyn Horne and Monica Sinclair too. But it is mainly Sutherland's record, and her florid elaborations of melodies turn *da capos* into things of delight and wonder and not of boredom. Richard Bonynge, too, conducts with a splendid sense of style, and anyone wanting to extend his knowledge of Handel could not do better than hear this. As a sample try the slow aria *V'adoro pupille* – believe it or not, Cleopatra's seduction aria. The recording is excellent.

Giulio Cesare: arias (sung in German): *V'adoro pupille; Tu la mia stella; Che sento; Piangerò la sorte mia; Da tempeste.*

(M) ** Decca Ace of Diamonds SDD 288. Lisa della Casa (soprano), Vienna Philharmonic Orchestra, Heinrich Hollreiser – MOZART: *Arias.** (*)

This recording dates from 1957 when Lisa della Casa's voice possessed a delightful freshness. Her singing has both grace and tonal beauty. The style is cool and classical but because of the purity of line and articulation, the singer's reserve

if anything heightens the music's emotional point by her subtlety of tonal shading. There are some lovely sounds here (in spite of the singing being in German, the music's character is not lost) and it is a pity that the sound is dated with a thin orchestral image. This would have been a better bargain at Eclipse price, but even so Miss della Casa's admirers will welcome this example of her art recorded when the voice was at its best. The accompaniments are much less praiseworthy.

Opera excerpts: (i) *Alcina: Tornami a vagheggiar; Ombre pallide. Esther:* (ii) *Tune not your harps;* (iii) *Turn not, O queen. Jephtha: Sinfonia and Symphony. Rodrigo: Suite (Overture, gigue, sarabande, air, 2 minuets, matelot, bourrée).*

(M) ** Oiseau-Lyre SOL 60001. (i) Joan Sutherland (soprano); (ii) William Herbert (tenor); (iii) Hervey Alan (bass); Philomusica Orchestra, Anthony Lewis.

This is an attractive anthology. The stereo gives the small orchestra an attractive sonority and projects the voices realistically within a convincing acoustic. The music is divided so that one side consists of vocal music, including some of Joan Sutherland's earliest recordings, when the voice was at its freshest, and the diction clearer than it sometimes has been more recently. The contributions of William Herbert and Hervey Alan too are sensitive and in good style. On the other side the orchestral music from *Jephtha* and *Rodrigo* is played with spirit and colour by the Philomusica group under Anthony Lewis.

Vocal Collections

Arias: *Acis and Galatea: I rage, I melt, I burn ... O ruddier than the cherry·*

Alcina: Pensa a chi geme. Alexander's Feast: Revenge, Timotheus cries. Berenice: Si, tra i ceppi. Ezio: Se un bell'ardire. Hercules: The god of battle. Judas Maccabaeus: I feel the Deity within . . . Arm, arm, ye brave. Samson: Honour and arms. Semele: Leave me, loathsome light. Susanna: Peace crown'd with roses. Theodora: Wide spread his mane.

(B) ** Argo Eclipse ECS 738. Forbes Robinson (bass), Academy of St Martin-in-the-Fields, dir. Philip Ledger (harpsichord).

Forbes Robinson built up a formidable reputation in the Covent Garden company – not least as Moses in Schoenberg's *Moses and Aaron* – and here he shows his versatility in eleven taxing arias. If he fails to give them the variety one would ideally like, that should not weigh too heavily when he has such a firm, strong tone. These are all arias that were favourites during the last century, and with singing like this they could quickly return to favour. First-rate recording.

Arias: *Alcina: Tiranna gelosia . . . Tornami a vagheggiar; Ah! mio cor! schernito sei! Giulio Cesare: Da tempeste; V'adoro pupille; Piangerò la sorte mia. Samson: Let the bright Seraphim; With plaintive note. Messiah: Rejoice greatly; How beautiful; I know that my Redeemer liveth.*

** (*) Decca SXL 6191. Joan Sutherland (soprano), with various orchestras.

Like the collections of Sutherland in Verdi and Bellini, this record is made up of excerpts from earlier recordings. It is no less impressive for that, though it is noticeable how the voice changes a little in timbre from the comparatively early days of *Let the bright Seraphim* onwards. The first *Alcina* aria is taken at what with

any other singer would be an impossible speed, and though occasionally the style in slow arias might be questioned, the fast coloratura is unfailingly brilliant.

Arias: Cantata à 3: *La Rondinella. Admeto: Cangio d'aspetto. Alcina: Verdi prati. Alexander Balus: Convey me. Atalanta: Care selve. Ottone: Vieni, O figlio; La Speranza. Partenope: Voglio dire. Rinaldo: Lascia ch'io pianga. Rodelinda: Dove sei.*

** Argo ZRG 501. Bernadette Greevy (contralto), Academy of St Martin-in-the-Fields, Raymond Leppard.

Bernadette Greevy is shown here as the possessor of a fine, rich, if sometimes unwieldy contralto, and the expansive phrases of these magnificent arias and songs display it at its best. One is treated to a glorious stream of sound, but the interpretation could be more imaginative. When Raymond Leppard's accompaniment is so stylish, it is surprising Miss Greevy was reluctant to decorate the reprises of the *da capo* arias. Excellent recording quality.

Arias: *Jephtha: Waft her, angels. Judas Maccabaeus: How vain is man; Sound an alarm. Messiah: Comfort ye; Ev'ry valley.* Opera arias: *Acis and Galatea: Love in her eyes sits playing. Ptolemy: Silent worship (Did you not hear my lady?). Semele: Where'er you walk. Xerxes: Ombra mai fù (Largo).*

** Decca SKL 4121. Kenneth McKellar (tenor), Royal Opera House, Covent Garden, Orchestra, Sir Adrian Boult.

Kenneth McKellar sings in fair style, his words are clear, and Boult's accompaniment is most sympathetic and, like the voice, beautifully recorded. Handel's melisma needs a perfectly managed breath control if it is to fall into its natural shape, and here and there one senses that McKellar has not calculated the music's line perceptively. There is a suggestion, if not of strain, that the voice is being taxed to its limit at the end of a long phrase. However, one can exaggerate this: there is a great deal to enjoy here and much beautiful tone.

Arias: *Judas Maccabaeus: Father of Heaven. Messiah: He was despised; O thou that tellest. Samson: Return, O God of hosts.*

> (M) *** Decca Ace of Diamonds SDD 286. Kathleen Ferrier (contralto), London Philharmonic Orchestra, Sir Adrian Boult – BACH: *Arias.****

The reissue of Kathleen Ferrier's outstanding recital of Bach and Handel arias, where the new stereo-recorded accompaniment was lovingly superimposed over the old mono orchestral contribution, is most welcome.

'Great choruses': *Coronation anthem: Zadok the Priest. Israel in Egypt: He spake the word; He gave them hailstones. Jephtha: When his loud voice. Judas Maccabaeus: See the conqu'ring hero comes. Messiah: Hallelujah; For unto us a child is born; Worthy is the Lamb; Amen. Saul: Gird on thy sword. Solomon: May no rash intruder.*

> ** (*) Decca Phase 4 PFS 4295. Handel Opera Society Chorus and Orchestra, Charles Farncombe.

A most enjoyable concert, freshly sung and vividly recorded. The disc opens with an attractively buoyant account of *Hallelujah*, and there is an unexpected refinement in *For unto us a Child is born*. Of the lesser-known choruses, *May no rash intruder* from *Solomon* with its evocative pastoral scene is particularly

successful. The small orchestral group and indeed the excellent amateur choral singing readily make up in spontaneity for any lack of polish. The recording is forward but has depth as well as impact.

COLLECTION

'Greatest hits': (i) *Organ concerto No. 13 in F major (The Cuckoo and the Nightingale)*: excerpt. (ii) *Water music: suite* (arr. Ormandy). *Xerxes: Largo.* (iii) *The Harmonious Blacksmith* (air with variations). (ii; iv) *Judas Maccabaeus: See the conqu'ring hero comes; Hallelujah, Amen. Messiah: Hallelujah chorus; For unto us a Child is born.* (v) *Ode for St Cecilia's Day: Awake the trumpets' lofty sound.* (vi) *Semele: Wher'er you walk.*

> (B) ** CBS Harmony 30009. (i) E. Power Biggs (organ), London Philharmonic Orchestra, Sir Adrian Boult; (ii) Philadelphia Orchestra, Eugene Ormandy; (iii) Igor Kipnis (harpsichord); (iv) Mormon Tabernacle Choir; (v) E. Power Biggs (organ), New England Brass Ensemble; (vi) Biggs (organ), Royal Philharmonic Orchestra, Sir Charles Groves.

This is an old-fashioned Handel collection. The Mormon Tabernacle Choir, as everybody knows, is no chamber group, and Ormandy uses the full Philadelphia Orchestra for the *Water music*. But it is difficult for any but the purist to complain, for the orchestral playing itself is well pointed, with some stylish solo work from the wind section. The chorus too sing with conviction, and in *See the conqu'ring hero* there is some marvellously restrained horn playing. (This solo is notorious among horn players for it goes up to high G in alt – a note above the normal horn compass.) Biggs manages his bird effects in the *Organ concerto* nicely, and surely only the most satiated listener will fail to be taken by the rich playing in the famous *Largo*. The full measure of Handelian grandeur is here, and the concert ends resoundingly with the *Hallelujah chorus*. Recording good throughout and sometimes excellent.

Hartmann, Karl Amadeus (1905–63)

Concerto funèbre for violin and orchestra.

> (M) ** (*) Supraphon 110 0508. André Gertler (violin), Czech Philharmonic Orchestra, Karel Ančerl – HINDEMITH: *Violin concerto*.** (*)

Hartmann, born in Denmark, settled in Germany, where in 1939 he wrote this dark, elegiac work, which no doubt reflects the political clouds which were gathering. Ironically it includes fragments of the Hussite chorale, *Ye who are warriors of God*. Gertler's performance is most sensitive, helped by responsive accompaniment. The recording is rather too close but acceptable.

Harty, Hamilton (1897–1941)

With the Wild Geese (symphonic poem).

> *** HMV ASD 2400. Scottish National Orchestra, Alexander Gibson – GERMAN: *Welsh rhapsody*; MACCUNN: *Land of Mountain and Flood*; SMYTH: *The Wreckers overture*.***

With the Wild Geese, written in 1910 for the Cardiff Festival, is a melodramatic piece about the Irish soldiers fighting on the French side in the Battle of Fontenoy. The ingredients – a gay Irish theme and a call to arms among them – are effectively deployed, and although the music does not reveal a strong individual personality, it is carried by a romantic sweep which is well exploited here.

Haydn, Josef (1732–1809)

Harpsichord concerto in D major; Overture in D major.

> *** Decca SXL 6385. George Malcolm (harpsichord), Academy of St Martin-in-the-Fields, Neville Marriner – J. C. BACH: *Harpsichord concerto*.***

An excellent record. The Haydn *Concerto* is well known and is expertly played here by George Malcolm and the Academy of St Martin-in-the-Fields, while the recording is exemplary both in tone quality and balance. The *Overture* is an alternative finale (version B) to the *Symphony No. 53 in D major* (*L'Impériale*), and is a light-hearted piece dating from the mid-1770s. The coupling, a concerto attributed to J. C. Bach, is a happy one, and whatever the doubts may be about its authorship, it will give musical satisfaction particularly given such persuasive advocacy as it is here by these artists.

Harpsichord concerto in D major (see also below under *Piano concerto in D major*).

> * (*) CBS Quadraphonic MQ 32300. Anthony Newman (harpsichord), Instrumental Ensemble, Edward Brewer (continuo) – BACH: *Concerto, BWV 1052*.* (*)

The acoustic here is dry, but the orchestral group is small and, with care, one can achieve a fairly intimate balance. The bright CBS sound is rather lacking in bloom, but the performance is keen and intelligent and quite enjoyable in its way.

Horn concerto No. 1 in D major.
**** BASF BAC 3005.** Erich Penzel (hand horn), Collegium Aureum (using original instruments) – HOFFMANN: *Flute concerto.** (*) (i) *Horn concertos Nos. 1 in D major; 2 in D major. Acide e Galatea* (opera): *Overture. 6 German dances.*
***** Argo ZRG 5498.** Academy of St Martin-in-the-Fields, Neville Marriner, (i) with Barry Tuckwell (horn).

Haydn's *Horn concerto No. 1* is a fine work, worthy to stand alongside the four Mozart concertos. It is technically more difficult than any of these, especially as played by Barry Tuckwell with a profusion of ornaments and trills. These help to lighten the basically rather square main theme of the opening movement, the soloist adding asides, witty or decorative. The finale is in the 'hunting' style of the period. But the highlight of the work is the *Adagio*, a beautifully shaped cantilena for the soloist. Tuckwell plays it superbly; indeed his playing throughout the Argo disc is of the very highest order, worthy of Dennis Brain. The *Second Concerto* is less memorable. It has an attractive first movement with a basic dotted rhythm; the slow movement, not unlike that of the *First Concerto* in style, has a touch of melancholy to its mood, but seems a trifle over-long. The authorship of this work is not proved. Marriner's accompaniment throughout is deliciously pointed, and the playing in the *Dances* and *Overture* is a wonderful example of sheer style, yet at the same time readily conveying the players' joy in this simple but rewarding music. Outstanding recording to match.

The interest of Penzel's account is the use of the original hand horn (without valves), which Penzel plays with great skill and commanding eloquence in the *Adagio*. The evenness of tone and intonation is remarkable. But when all is said and done this is altogether more square as a performance and does not match Tuckwell, musically speaking, although the warm, resonant recording is attractive.

(i) *Horn concerto No. 2 in D major;* (ii) *Oboe concerto in C major;* (iii) *Trumpet concerto in E flat major.*
(B) **** Turnabout TV 34031S.** (i) Karl Arnold (horn); (ii) Friedrich Milde (oboe); (iii) Walter Gleisle (trumpet); all with Stuttgart Pro Musica, Rolf Reinhardt.

The soloists here are uneven, but in a generously full disc two of the three performances can be recommended. Friedrich Milde is an excellent oboe player; he has an agreeable tone and assured technique. His phrasing is no less a source of pleasure, especially in the minuet finale, where the soloist's arabesques around the charming main theme are shaped stylishly. Gleisle too plays impressively, with bold tone and flexible technique. This is a forthright account of the *Trumpet concerto*, but one with plenty of character. The hornist, Karl Arnold, is a much less effective soloist, and he fails to bring the *D major Horn concerto* fully to life. Reinhardt's accompaniments are of a good standard, and the recordings are acceptable, although the upper strings have the characteristic Turnabout thinness through being too closely balanced.

Lira concertos (for lira organizzata and chamber orchestra) *Nos. 1 in C major; 3 in G major; 5 in F major.*
(B) ***** Turnabout TV 34055S.** Hugo Ruf (lira), with chamber ensemble.

Haydn's *Lira concertos*, commissioned by King Ferdinand IV of Naples, were written for a curious obsolete instrument

431

which was a cross between a hurdy-gurdy and a mechanical violoncello. How the problems of intonation were solved, for the pitch of the string notes was achieved mechanically, is difficult to imagine, but the instrument was a favourite of its time. The music Haydn composed for this instrument (or rather two of them, for it was played in duet with a chamber group) is most attractive and worth reviving. Turnabout employ a modern electronic 'lira' constructed by Johannes Koch. This enables one musician to play both of the duet parts (for originally each player had also to turn a handle with one hand to work the mechanism). The sound is piquant. It would appear that the drone-like string notes (which were a feature of the original instrument) are played by the orchestra, so the listener has the best of both worlds. Thus this record is very entertaining, taken a concerto at a time, not least because the orchestral tuttis are so alive and the recording balance so expertly managed. Listeners will be surprised to find that the second movement of the *Third Concerto* is almost identical with the slow movement of the *Military symphony*. Incidentally the concertos missing here (Nos. 2 and 4) are available coupled to the *Sinfonia concertante* (see below).

Oboe concerto in C major.

> (B) ** (*) Pye GSGC 14065. Evelyn Rothwell (oboe), Hallé Orchestra, Sir John Barbirolli – CORELLI and PERGOLESI: *Concertos.****

Of the three concertos on this delectable disc the Haydn, because of its very positive classicism, suits Miss Rothwell's style marginally less well than the other two. But Sir John's strong opening has all the classical verve anyone could want, and in the first movement his wife's delicacy makes a delicious foil for the masculine orchestral sound; in particular the phrasing of the second subject is enchanting. The slow movement too is

well brought off, and it is only in the finale that, for all the pleasure of the feminine tessitura, others have shown that a stronger style is even more effective. But the rest of this collection is treasurable and, taken as it is, the performance offers much pleasure in its own way.

> (i) *Organ concerto No. 1 in C major;*
> (ii) *Violin concerto No. 2 in G major.*
> (B) ** Oryx EXP 24. (i) Rolf Schweizer (organ); (ii) György Terebesi (violin); both with South-West German Chamber Orchestra.

These are sound, musical performances, if without that touch of individuality in the solo playing that one would expect from more famous artists. But both are able technically, and the violinist, György Terebesi, produces a pleasing if small tone. The accompaniments are well made and the stereo is satisfactory, if a trifle dry, in timbre rather than acoustic.

Organ concerto No. 2 in C major.

> ** (*) Argo ZRG 631. Simon Preston (organ), Academy of St Martin-in-the-Fields, Neville Marriner – M. HAYDN: *Duo concertante.** (*)

This is the first of the set of three Haydn *Organ concertos*. It is not one of Haydn's most memorable concertos, but the performance here is persuasive, with vivid registration and a spirited accompaniment. The recording is of fine Argo quality, although sometimes the reverberation means that the organ's bass line seems a little heavy-footed.

Piano concerto in D major.

> (B) ** Turnabout TV 34073S. Alfred Brendel (piano), Vienna Chamber Orchestra, Paul Angerer – HUMMEL: *Piano concerto in B minor.**

Brendel's performance (which was originally coupled with Mozart's K.482 concerto) is a neat small-scale reading, with crisp enunciation from the pianist and an attentive accompaniment. The recording is bright and fresh.

Trumpet concerto in E flat major.

(B) ** Classics for Pleasure CFP 40046. Elgar Howarth (trumpet), Orchestra of St James, Steuart Bedford – MOZART: *Clarinet concerto.*** (*)

(i) *Trumpet concerto in E flat major; 6 Allemandes* (for small orchestra).

** Argo ZRG 543. (i) Alan Stringer (trumpet); Academy of St Martin-in-the-Fields, Neville Marriner – M. HAYDN: *Horn concerto etc.***

Both Alan Stringer and Elgar Howarth favour a forthright open tone, and no doubt there is a conscious attempt in each case to simulate the primitive instrument Haydn would have been used to. On the Classics for Pleasure disc the orchestral playing seems to match the soloist's no-nonsense approach (and the recording too is not especially smooth), and this account has plenty of character. On Argo, with beautiful recorded sound, the orchestral playing has more finesse and reminds us that the famous 78 recording by George Eskdale brought a graciousness to the slow movement and an elegant virtuosity to the finale which in no way detracted from the robustness of Haydn's conception. Argo offer a delectable bonus of six dances, beautifully played.

Violin concerto No. 2 in G major.

** Philips SAL 3660. Arthur Grumiaux (violin), New Philharmonia Orchestra, Raymond Leppard – MOZART: *Adagio*; *Rondo*; SCHUBERT: *Rondo.***

A direct, well-judged performance of an early work, notable for its eloquent slow movement. Grumiaux shows a natural sympathy for the music's simple lines and he is admirably supported by Leppard. With interesting couplings this is a good disc, and it is well recorded.

Double concerto in F major for violin, fortepiano and string orchestra.

(M) ** (*) Unicorn UNS 251. Sidney Weiss (violin), Jeanne Weiss (fortepiano), London Mozart Players, Harry Blech – R. STRAUSS: *Violin sonata.*** (*)

Haydn's *Double concerto* is a delightful work and it is given a charming performance here. The recording helps by the intimacy it gives to the sound of the fortepiano, which has a most attractive timbre. The playing of the soloists is excellent; the accompaniment is good, though perhaps the string tone is not as sweetsounding as it might be. But this is a most enjoyable record, with an unexpected but successful coupling, and it can be cordially recommended.

Violoncello concerto in C major.

*** Decca SXL 6138. Mstislav Rostropovich (cello), English Chamber Orchestra, Benjamin Britten – BRITTEN: *Cello symphony.****

*** HMV ASD 2331. Jacqueline du Pré (cello), English Chamber Orchestra, Daniel Barenboim – BOCCHERINI: *Concerto in B flat major.****

(i) *Violoncello concerto in C major;* (ii) *Violoncello concerto in D major.*

(M) *** Philips Universo 6580 040. Maurice Gendron (cello), (i) London Symphony Orchestra, Raymond Leppard; (ii) Lamoureux Orchestra, Pablo Casals.

Violoncello concerto in D major.

(M) * (*) DGG Privilege 2538 259. Pierre Fournier (cello), Lucerne Festival Orchestra, Rudolf Baumgartner – BOCCHERINI: *Concerto in B flat major.** (*)

(B) ** Oryx EXP 15. Jürgen Wolf (cello), Reutlingen Orchestra, Erich Reustlen – BOCCHERINI: *Concerto in B flat major.***

The discovery of Haydn's early *C major Cello concerto* in Prague in the early 1960s provided a marvellous addition to the limited cello repertory. For some this concerto is even more attractive than the well-known D major work that for a time was fathered on Anton Kraft instead of Haydn. As a fill-up to Britten's fierce and moody masterpiece this is unexpected but still most welcome. Rostropovich's view of the concerto is markedly more romantic than that of Maurice Gendron. Some may think he takes too many liberties in the slow movement, but with marvellously sympathetic conducting from Britten, Rostropovich's expressiveness and beauty of tone-colour are bewitching. Recording of Decca's finest quality.

The HMV issue was Jacqueline du Pré's first record with her husband, Daniel Barenboim, and she gives a performance of characteristic warmth and intensity. Her style is sometimes romantic in a way that strictly is inappropriate in such music, yet when the very power of her personality is vividly conveyed, even through rhythmic distortions, and Barenboim ensures that the orchestra follows every nuance, one can but marvel. This is the sort of performance that defies cold analysis. Good, atmospheric recording.

If Gendron's account has less panache, it is nonetheless highly musical and is sensitively accompanied. In the *D major Concerto* he is right on form, and the stylishness of his phrasing, coupled to complete security of intonation make for an admirable performance of this attractive concerto, which can be recommended very highly, especially when one bears in mind the coupling. Pablo Casals's sympathetic handling of the orchestral contribution plays no little part in making this record the success it undoubtedly is.

As with the Boccherini coupling, DGG's Privilege recording is rather lustreless and lacking in bloom. Fournier plays with style and polish, but Baumgartner's accompaniment is relatively unimaginative.

The inexpensive Oryx record offers a pair of excellent performances by a good soloist, who, if not as strong in personality as some more famous names, serves the composer's musical demands eloquently. The recording is good.

Katherinentänze (12 Minuets).

(B) * (*) Turnabout TV 34011S. Innsbruck Symphony Orchestra, Robert Wagner – MOZART: *12 German dances.***

See under the coupling.

Sinfonia concertante in B flat major (for oboe, bassoon, violin, cello and orchestra).

*** HMV ASD 2462. English Chamber Orchestra, Daniel Barenboim – MOZART: *Sinfonia concertante.****

(i) *Sinfonia concertante in B flat major;*
(ii) *Lira concertos Nos. 2 in G major; 4 in F major.*

(B) ** (*) Turnabout TV 34418S. (i) Württemberg Chamber Orchestra, Joerg Faerber; (ii) Hugo Ruf (lira), with chamber ensemble.

Sinfonia concertante in B flat major; Symphony No. 90 in C major.

** (*) DGG 2530 398. Vienna Philharmonic Orchestra, Karl Boehm.

The *Sinfonia concertante* is a splendid, imaginative work, an ideal companion piece for the Mozart work for wind quartet and orchestra on the reverse of the HMV disc. It is much more compressed than the Mozart, and has some wonderful unexpected touches, with, for example, side-slipping chromatics in the first movement cadenza (with the four soloists' parts written out), and there is a romantic side too – exaggerated perhaps in Barenboim's slow tempo – to the 6/8 *Andante* middle movement. Splendid solo playing and lively direction.

On Turnabout, an attractive collection of concertante works that for practical reasons rarely get performed in the concert hall. Though this version of the *Sinfonia concertante* does not quite compare with the best available at full price, it is freshly enjoyable, and the unusual coupling is charming. The soloist uses a modern adaptation of the lira – a development of the hurdy-gurdy – and the sounds are as a result sweet to the demanding modern ear, which is more than the original instrument might be. The music is charming. Clean recording. (For Haydn's other *Lira concertos*, see above.)

Boehm is a genial Haydn interpreter, more relaxed in these works than Dorati (see below under *Symphonies Nos. 82–92*), but sometimes – as in the *Andante* of No. 90 – sounding a little bland. Beautiful polished playing – not least from the violinist, Rainer Küchl, in the *Sinfonia concertante* – and mellow, well-focused recording.

SYMPHONIES

Symphonies Nos. 1 in D major; 2 in C major; 3 in G major; 4 in D major; 5 in A major; 6 in D major (Le Matin); 7 in C major (Le Midi); 8 in G major (Le Soir); 9 in C major; 10 in D major; 11 in E flat major; 12 in E major; 13 in D major; 14 in A major; 15 in D major; 16 in B flat major; 17 in F major; 18 in G major; 19 in D major.

⊛ (for the entire Philharmonia Hungarica series) (M) *** Decca HDNA 1/6. Philharmonia Hungarica, Antal Dorati.

Dorati's complete set of Haydn symphonies is one of the gramophone's

finest achievements, in many ways an achievement for the seventies that can be justly compared to the first complete stereo recording of Wagner's *Ring* cycle made by the same record company a decade earlier. Our rosette is awarded to the complete series.

Though Haydn's earliest symphonies make such a long list, there is not an immature one among them. By his own calculation he did not start writing symphonies until he was twenty-five. The urgent crescendo which opens *Symphony No. 1* at once establishes the voltage of inspiration, and from then on there is no suspicion of a power failure. These works – antedated by one or two works that are later in the Breitkopf numbering – come from the early Esterhazy period, 1759–63, and show the young, formidably gifted composer working at full stretch, above all in the relatively well-known trilogy of symphonies, *Le Matin, Le Midi* and *Le Soir*, with their marvellous solos for members of the Esterhazy orchestra. Dorati left these symphonies until well on in his great recording project, and the combination of exhilaration and stylishness is irresistible. Excellent recording.

Symphonies Nos. 3 in G major; 39 in G minor; 73 in D major (La Chasse).

(B) ** Pye GSGC 14021. Little Orchestra of London, Leslie Jones.

The early symphony is attractive in its simplicity, with a pleasing slow movement. No. 39 is a highly individual work with a particularly strong first movement. *La Chasse* brings in some striking brass parts in the finale but is otherwise slightly less successful than the other occupants of this disc. Recording and performance up to the usual excellent standard of this bargain series, with the harpsichord just about audible in the early music.

Symphonies Nos. 6 in D major (Le Matin); 7 in C major (Le Midi); 8 in G major (Le Soir).

435

(B) ** Turnabout TV 34150S. Vienna Festival Chamber Orchestra, Wilfried Boettcher.

Haydn was twenty-nine when his first contract with Prince Esterhazy began in May 1761, and these works were the first he composed for the new Esterhazy orchestra. The writing is always buzzing with ideas and the scoring abounds in instrumental solos. The performances here are lively, the solo playing nearly always worthy of the music. The wind players are perhaps better than the string soloists in this respect. Boettcher is at his best in the fast movements, which are gay and light-hearted, but the expressive playing too is good and the recording throughout is one of Turnabout's best.

Symphonies Nos. 6 in D major (Le Matin); 13 in D major; 64 in A major.
(B) ** Pye GSGC 14045. Little Orchestra of London, Leslie Jones.

Excellent performances, graceful and stylish, with well-played obbligato passages. The harpsichord is used discreetly. Of special interest is Haydn's use, in the finale of No. 13 in D, of the four-note idea that Mozart also uses in the last movement of the *Jupiter symphony.*

Symphonies Nos. 12 in E major; 26 in D minor (Lamentatione); 83 in G minor (La Poule).
(B) ** Pye GSGC 14014. Little Orchestra of London, Leslie Jones.

The direction here is crisp and well-shaped if not outstandingly imaginative, and the bright recording allows the harpsichord to come through in No. 26 (which has a genuine baroque texture and flavour). Jones is a little stiff in No. 83, but the good playing makes amends, and the finale is especially spirited.

Symphonies Nos. 15 in D major; 16 in B flat major; 17 in F major.

(B) * (*) Turnabout TV 34092S. Vienna Festival Chamber Orchestra, Wilfried Boettcher.

No. 15 opens most winningly to show a master is at work. This symphony, given a side to itself, is the most interesting of the three and its first movement the most immediately attractive. The other two are more conventional, but have hints every now and then of a genius in embryo breaking free of the formal straitjacket of the French and Italian overtures. Friendly playing, the conductor not trying to make the music seem mature Haydn, which it is not. Good recording too.

Symphonies Nos. 19 in D major; 31 in D major (Hornsignal); 45 in F sharp minor (Farewell).
(B) ** (*) Pye GSGC 14001. Little Orchestra of London, Leslie Jones.

This beautifully recorded disc can be cordially recommended. The horn-playing in the famous *Hornsignal symphony* is not absolutely immaculate but it is still good, and the performance as a whole goes with a fine swing. The little D major symphony which fills up the rest of the side is given a splendidly vigorous reading, and the charming slow movement anticipates the *Adagio* of No. 45 in its poised string writing. This is also well played but in a more relaxed fashion. The highlight is the finale, where each player executes his final solo most affectionately before departing. The sound, especially the strings, is excellent; the reverberation all but obscures the continuo part.

Symphonies Nos. 20 in C major; 21 in A major; 22 in E flat major (Philosopher) (1st version); 23 in G major; 24 in D major; 25 in C major; 26 in D minor (Lamentatione); 27 in G major; 28 in A major; 29 in E major; 30 in C major (Alleluja); 31 in D major (Horn-

signal); 32 in A major; 33 in C major; 34 in D minor; 35 in B flat major.

(M) *** Decca HDNB 7/12. Philharmonia Hungarica, Antal Dorati.

Because of the idiosyncrasies of the Breitkopf numbering, this sequence of symphonies includes one work later than the rest, *Lamentatione*, a transitional work leading into the dark, intense manner of Haydn's middle period. It gives marvellous perspective to the rest, all of them fascinating and many of them masterly. What an amazing sound Haydn creates, for instance, by using two cor anglais in the opening chorale of the *Philosopher*, almost like an anticipation of *Zauberflöte*. But even the early festive symphonies, like Nos. 32 and 33, both in C major with trumpets and timpani, have their individual marks of inspiration, for example in the C minor slow movement of No. 33. As in the rest of the cycle, Dorati's performances, helped by vivid recording, have you listening on from one symphony to another, compulsively following the composer's career.

Symphonies Nos. 22 in E flat major (Philosopher); 39 in G minor; 47 in G major.

** Philips SAL 3776. English Chamber Orchestra, Raymond Leppard.

These are warm, gracious performances, notable for their elegant playing rather than for any special degree of sparkle. Raymond Leppard seems taken with Haydn's 'walking style', which he emphasizes in each of these works by crisp playing and even, rhythmic accents. So we find this characteristic in the opening *Adagio* of No. 22 (Leppard bringing out the unusual colouring featuring cor anglais), in the *Andante* second movement of No. 39, and in the minuet of No. 47. The playing is excellent throughout and the recording pleasant if with no striking brilliance.

Symphonies Nos. 26 in D minor (Lamentatione); 34 in D minor; 77 in B flat major.

*** Philips 6500 084. English Chamber Orchestra, cond. from harpsichord Raymond Leppard.

Leppard's performance of No. 77 is effervescent and full of life; it is arguably the best in the catalogue, though Dorati does this symphony well too. The ECO play with great poise and sense of style, and the Philips recording is flawless. The two D minor symphonies, the *Lamentatione* and No. 34, are beautifully done, and no one wanting this particular coupling need really hesitate.

Symphonies Nos. 31 in D major (Horn-signal); 59 in A major (Fire).

(B) * (*) Turnabout TV 34104S. Stuttgart Bach Collegium, Helmuth Rilling.

These performances have plenty of character, so important with early Haydn. The horn-playing in the virtuoso *Horn-signal symphony* is excellent. Perhaps the conductor does not make enough differentiation in tempo between the last two movements but generally this reading is well conceived and carried out with spirit. After this the performance of No. 59 (which in spite of its number belongs to the same period) is rather ordinary. The most striking movement is the finale, in which the horns are again in the limelight. The recording is basically excellent but with the strings rather close to the microphones.

Symphonies Nos. 34 in D minor; 54 in G major; 75 in D major.

(B) * (*) Pye GSGC 14047. Little Orchestra of London, Leslie Jones.

These performances are well rehearsed and crisply played and recorded, but Leslie Jones shows no special feeling for the structures of the allegros; he is content to play the notes, in spirited fashion, but without any subtlety in dovetailing theme to theme and in dynamic contrast. Equally, the slow movements are phrased with no special warmth or nobility of phrase.

Symphonies Nos. 35 in B flat major; 43 in E flat major (Mercury); 80 in D minor.

(B) ** Pye GSGC 14046. Little Orchestra of London, Leslie Jones.

With this record Leslie Jones and his orchestra move into the realms of Haydn's late-middle period. The 35th and 43rd symphonies, dating from 1767 and 1772 respectively, are both scored for the usual early Haydn orchestra of two oboes, two horns and strings, but No. 80 (1784) is more sophisticated, adding a flute and a pair of bassoons. It is a fine work and brings out the best in the orchestra, and this well-recorded disc is one of the most attractive in the series.

Symphonies Nos. 36 in E flat major; 37 in C major; 38 in C major (Echo); 39 in G minor; 40 in F major; 41 in C major; 42 in D major; 43 in E flat major (Mercury); 44 in E minor (Trauersymphonie); 45 in F sharp minor (Farewell); 46 in B major; 47 in G major; 48 in C major (Maria Theresia).

(M) *** Decca HDNC 13/18. Philharmonia Hungarica, Antal Dorati.

Despite the numbering this set of symphonies arguably includes the very first work of all, No. 37 in C, revealing – as H. C. Robbins Landon points out in his absorbing commentary – 'impeccable craftsmanship and enormous energy'. The 3/8 finale is exhilarating, but then all of these works as played by Dorati and the Philharmonia Hungarica reflect the composer's unquenchable genius. This

particular sequence brings the frontier in Dorati's interpretations between using and not using harpsichord continuo. He switches over in the middle of No. 40 – not illogically when the finale is a fugue in which continuo would only be muddling. The last three named symphonies make a superb trio of works, leading into the searing intensity of Haydn's so-called *Sturm und Drang* period. Unfailingly lively performances and first-rate recording.

Symphonies Nos. 42 in D major; 45 in F sharp minor (Farewell).

(M) *** Decca Ace of Diamonds SDD 414. Philharmonia Hungarica, Antal Dorati.

Two first-rate samples of Dorati's complete cycle. While facing the tragic quality of the *Farewell*, with its extraordinary key-colours, Dorati gives it resilient rhythms. No. 42 is another superb work, 'witty, bright and marvellously written', as Robbins Landon says. Fine recording.

Symphonies Nos. 44 in E minor (Trauersymphonie); 45 in F sharp minor (Farewell).

(B) ** (*) Classics for Pleasure CFP 40021. London Philharmonic Orchestra, John Pritchard.

A good bargain coupling of two of Haydn's magnificent middle symphonies, dark and intense in *Sturm und Drang*. Pritchard underlines the ambitious scale by observing second-half as well as first-half repeats in the outer movements. In the *Farewell symphony* that is all to the good; but No. 44 is played a degree less pointedly. Pritchard's manner in slow movements is cool. The recording is full and atmospheric.

Symphonies Nos. 44 in E minor (Trauersymphonie); 49 in F minor (La Passione); Overture Armida.

(B) * (*) Pye GSGC 14006. Little Orchestra of London, Leslie Jones.

One of Leslie Jones's less successful couplings: the performances are rather under-characterized. The recording is warm and resonant.

Symphonies Nos. 46 in B major; 52 in C minor.
(B) ** Oiseau-Lyre OLS 135. Haydn Orchestra, Harry Newstone.

A distinguished early stereo coupling which Oiseau-Lyre have reissued on their cheapest label. The playing has plenty of sparkle and the sound – if slightly over-bright – is good.

Symphonies Nos. 48 in C major (Maria Theresia); 70 in D major.
** (*) Philips 6500 194. English Chamber Orchestra, Raymond Leppard.

In the *Maria Theresia symphony* Leppard uses trumpets rather than alto horns, so that those familiar with the Goberman or Dorati performances will register surprise. However, in every musical respect these are both fine performances and readers wanting this particular coupling need have no hesitation. The slow movement of No. 70 is grave and haunting, and though David Blum and the Esterhazy Orchestra (now deleted) gave it more poignancy, this is a beautifully judged and eminently stylish reading too. Good, well-focused recording.

Symphonies Nos. 49 in F minor (La Passione); 50 in C major; 51 in B flat major; 52 in C minor; 53 in D major (L'Impériale); 54 in G major; 55 in E flat major (Der Schulmeister); 56 in C major.
(M) *** Decca HDND 19/22. Philharmonia Hungarica, Antal Dorati.

These eight symphonies show Haydn in the full flight of his *Sturm und Drang* period – tense, exhilarating works full of anguished minor-key arguments that belie the old idea of jolly 'Papa' Haydn working patiently for his princely master. The emotional basis of these works points forward very clearly to the romantic movement which within decades was to overtake music. Indeed the literary movement which gives the appellation *Sturm und Drang* itself marks the stirring of romanticism. To hear a sequence of eight such works as this is to experience their historical impact in the way that Prince Esterhazy and his court must have done. The impact is the more powerful because of the splendid notes written by Professor Robbins Landon, whose comments are fascinating at every level, whether for the specialist or for the beginner. Such works as *La Passione* are already reasonably well-known, but the others are no less compelling, and in vigorous, committed performances by Dorati and his orchestra of Hungarian exiles it is impossible to be bored for a moment. The recording is outstandingly vivid.

Symphonies Nos. 52 in C minor; 53 in D major (L'Impériale).
** (*) Philips 6500 114. Academy of St Martin-in-the-Fields, Neville Marriner.

This disc originally appeared in the Philips *Rise of the Symphony* album. The performances are alert and well pointed in the true Academy fashion. Marriner plays the second of the three finales that Landon prints for *L'Impériale*. (As the side is not long it is a pity that the other alternatives were not included.) Although the playing is spirited there are one or two moments where one would have welcomed greater polish (for example, some of the passage-work in the end of the exposition of the first movement of No. 53). However, these are of small account

439

given the warmth of the readings and the excellence of the recordings.

Symphonies Nos. 52 in C minor; 60 in C major (Il Distratto).

(M) ** (*) Vanguard HM 27SD. Esterhazy Orchestra, David Blum.

David Blum's performance of the attractive six-movement *Il Distratto symphony* is first-rate, stylish and bringing out all the humour. He is slightly less successful with the companion work, but this is still a good disc, and the recording is excellent.

Symphonies Nos. 57 in D major; 58 in F major; 59 in A major (Fire); 60 in C major (Il Distratto); 61 in D major; 62 in D major; 63 in C major (La Roxolane); 64 in A major.

(M) *** Decca HDNE 23/6. Philharmonica Hungarica, Antal Dorati.

It may help that three of these middle-period symphonies have nicknames. All in major keys, they represent the comparatively extrovert period immediately after Haydn had worked out the bitterest tensions of the *Sturm und Drang* period. As in the other albums, Professor Robbins Landon's notes provide an ideal preparation for listening with a historical ear, and even his tendency to underestimate the merits of the lesser-known works makes one enjoy them the more out of defiance for his authority. Even if these are not quite so interesting as the surrounding works, they maintain an amazing standard of invention, with such movements as the *Adagio* and 6/8 finale of No. 61 endlessly fascinating. The only serious flaw in Dorati's interpretations – and it is something to note in a few of the symphonies in other albums too – is his tendency to take minuets rather slowly. In many of them Haydn had already moved halfway towards a scherzo. With

amazing consistency the Philharmonia Hungarica maintains its alertness, never giving the suspicion of merely running through the music. Excellent recording to match the rest of this outstanding series.

Symphonies Nos. 60 in C major (Il Distratto); 67 in F major.

(M) *** Decca Ace of Diamonds SDD 358. Philharmonia Hungarica, Antal Dorati.

Fresh and affectionate examples of the work of Dorati and the Philharmonia Hungarica in their complete Haydn cycle. The works themselves are both fascinating, No. 60 living up to its nickname with a brief comic last movement which features the tuning-up of violins.

Symphonies Nos. 65 in A major; 66 in B flat major; 67 in F major; 68 in B flat major; 69 in C major (Laudon); 70 in D major; 71 in B flat major; 72 in D major.

(M) *** Decca HDNF 27/30. Philharmonia Hungarica, Antal Dorati.

This was the first album of symphonies to be issued in Decca's integral series, and with works that had previously been not just neglected but absurdly underrated, the dynamic tone of the whole project was at once brought home. This was not the first time that a complete series of Haydn symphonies was planned – the late Max Goberman in New York had started one – but with superb notes by Professor Robbins Landon the attractions of the Dorati cycle at once set a new standard. One was forced to take one's bearings in a comparatively uncharted sector of the Haydn globe, and the result was exhilarating. Even Robbins Landon underestimates the mastery of these symphonies from the period after Haydn had worked *Sturm und Drang* tensions out of his system but before he expanded into the international world of music-making with the *Paris* and *London symphonies*. With the exception of an occasional movement (No. 69/II or No. 70/III) this music is riveting, and even where the actual material is conventional, as in the theatrical first movement of No. 69 (nicknamed '*Laudon*' after a field-marshal), the treatment is sparkling, with many surprising turns. The recording matches the vividness of the playing.

Symphonies Nos. 73 in D major (La Chasse); 74 in E flat major; 75 in D major; 76 in E flat major; 77 in B flat major; 78 in C minor; 79 in F major; 80 in D minor; 81 in G major.

(M) *** Decca HDNG 31/4. Philharmonia Hungarica, Antal Dorati.

This collection, unlike the previous albums in Dorati's series, contains nine works written more or less consecutively over a compact period of just over four years. Professor Robbins Landon emphasizes that these are much more courtly works than their *Sturm und Drang* predecessors, and that Haydn was regarding the symphony at this time as a side concern, being mainly concerned with opera. Even so, what will strike the non-specialist listener is that whatever the courtly manners of the expositions (and even there moods vary, particularly in the two minor-key symphonies) the development sections give a flashing reminder of Haydn's tensest manner. Kaleidoscopic sequences of minor keys whirl the argument in unexpected directions. On this showing, even when he was not really trying, Haydn was incapable of being boring, and some of these works are in every way remarkable in their forward-looking reminders, often of Mozart's most visionary works. At the time Haydn had just made contact with Mozart, and though the direct similarities can only be accidental on chronological evidence, the influence is already clear. The performances achieve an amazing degree of intensity, with alertness maintained throughout.

Symphonies Nos. 73 in D major (La Chasse); 74 in E flat major.

(M) *** Decca Ace of Diamonds SDD 413. Philharmonia Hungarica, Antal Dorati.

Two excellent performances from Dorati's complete cycle – useful for those who have not been tempted to buy the full set. No. 74, with its poised slow movement and snapping minuet, proves just as compelling as the more famous work on the reverse.

Symphonies Nos. 82 in C major (The Bear); 83 in G minor (La Poule); 84 in E flat major; 85 in B flat major (La Reine): 86 in D major; 87 in A major (Paris symphonies); 88 in G major; 89 in F major; 90 in C major; 91 in E flat major; 92 in G major (Oxford). Sinfonia concertante in B flat major.

⊛ (M) *** Decca HDNH 35/40. Philharmonia Hungarica, Antal Dorati.

We award a token rosette again here to remind readers of the outstanding excellence of this set, which confirms the quality of Dorati's direction of Haydn: these versions almost always outshine their direct rivals in sparkling performances, vividly recorded. Not just the set of six *Paris symphonies* (Nos. 82–7), with which this album begins, but the other Paris-based works too are given fresh, stylish performances by Dorati and his indefatigable band of Hungarian exiles. Even the least-known of the Paris set, No. 84, has a first movement of the most delicate fantasy, and No. 89 is rounded off with an extraordinarily witty movement that looks straight forward to the fun of Johann Strauss's polkas with a delicious *portamento* in each reprise down to the main theme.

The performance of the *Sinfonia concertante* is also issued on Ace of Diamonds (SDD 445), coupled to Mozart's *Sinfonia concertante for violin, viola and orchestra, K.364.*

Symphonies Nos. 82 in C major (The Bear); 86 in D major (Paris symphonies).
> (M) ** Ace of Diamonds SDD 182. Suisse Romande Orchestra, Ernest Ansermet.

There is a certain stiffness here (more apparent in the performance of No. 82) but also the kind of strong characterization that shows the hand of a major conductor. Thus the opening movement of No. 82 has a striking vigour, and the last two movements of No. 86 are particularly successful. While not without a certain rigidity, this coupling offers a great deal to enjoy, not least the good sound.

Symphonies Nos. 83 in G minor (La Poule); 87 in A major (Paris symphonies).
> (M) ** Ace of Diamonds SDD 183. Suisse Romande Orchestra, Ernest Ansermet.

SDD 183 is better than the earlier Ansermet coupling. The Swiss conductor is still rigid (witness the second subject of the first movement of *La Poule*), but he displays more affection in No. 87, and there is some charming woodwind playing in the *Adagio* of this work and a nicely played oboe solo in the trio of the third movement. The recording is excellent.

Symphony No. 84 in E flat major.
> (M) ** Oiseau-Lyre SOL 60030. English Chamber Orchestra, Colin Davis – MOZART: *Concertone.** (*)

No. 84 (1786) is an attractive work with a genial first movement, a set of variations for its *Andante*, and besides a typical sprightly finale a specially enjoyable minuet and trio which is very well done on this disc. The playing is good throughout and it is helped by a lively recording, in a dry but not too dry acoustic just right for the music. Colin Davis is perhaps a little humourless but otherwise this straightforward reading is very acceptable.

Symphonies Nos. 84 in E flat major; 85 in B flat major (La Reine) (Paris symphonies).
> (M) ** Ace of Diamonds SDD 184. Suisse Romande Orchestra, Ernest Ansermet.

Again these are relatively straightforward accounts, but Ansermet's plainness pays off and the music comes alive in quite a stylish way. The Decca sound has both clarity and presence, and anyone collecting the set of Ansermet's *Paris symphonies* should not be disappointed here on either technical or musical grounds.

Symphonies Nos. 85 in B flat major (La Reine); 87 in A major (Paris symphonies).
> *** BASF BAC 3006. Collegium Aureum (using original instruments).

These two fine symphonies serve the 'original instruments' cause particularly well. The warm and resilient string tone on this disc is matched by wind sounds of strong character, while the 'hand horns' have a more open resonance. The playing here is really first-class so that differences in sound are subtle. It is perhaps in the slow movement of No. 87 that the wind playing serves to suggest a special feeling of the period. The actual readings have plenty of personality, and with clear, full recording this is a highly recommendable coupling.

Symphonies Nos. 88 in G major; 89 in F major.

(M) *** Decca Ace of Diamonds SDD 431. Philharmonia Hungarica, Antal Dorati.

** DGG 2530 343. Vienna Philharmonic Orchestra, Karl Boehm.

These are both among the most exhilarating symphonies in the whole Haydn cycle, and Dorati's performances have all the spontaneous joy you could ask for. Boehm's are beautifully cultured and expertly recorded. In No. 88 he is more deliberate and measured than Dorati and lacks the lightness and sparkle of his reading. Likewise in No. 89 Dorati has greater lightness of touch; his players have more delicacy and sensitivity and they appear to delight in the music. Of course the Vienna Philharmonic play with great polish and tonal refinement, but after listening to Dorati (No. 89 is one of the finest performances in his *Paris* to *Oxford* box), Boehm seems a little dour.

Symphonies Nos. 88 in G major; 98 in B flat major.

*** DGG SLPM 138823. Berlin Philharmonic Orchestra, Eugen Jochum.

This is an outstanding coupling and the recording does not sound in the least dated. Jochum has recorded No. 98 again for Philips with the Dresden State Orchestra and the two performances are discussed together below under No. 95.

Symphony No. 90 in C major.

** Abbey ABY 733. London Mozart Players, Harry Blech – MOZART: *Symphony No. 35.***

Blech and the London Mozart Players made a breakthrough in performance of Mozart and Haydn in the fifties, and though they have not quite kept up with their younger rivals, it is good to have them represented once again on record in this repertory. The woodwind players are specially impressive. The recording is acceptable but not ideally clear.

Symphonies Nos. 90 in C major; 92 in G major (Oxford).

(M) *** Decca Ace of Diamonds SDD 412. Philharmonia Hungarica, Antal Dorati.

Urgent, vigorous readings of these 'in-between' works. The symphonies come from the period between the *Paris* and the *London symphonies*, fine inspirations both. A first-rate coupling, especially as neither work is over-represented in the catalogue.

Symphonies Nos. 92 in G major (Oxford); 95 in C minor.

** HMV ASD 2818. New Philharmonia Orchestra, Otto Klemperer.

Klemperer's readings of Haydn are relatively heavyweight, but except in the first movement of No. 95, where the tempo is very slow indeed, the results are spirited and even charming. First-rate recording.

Symphonies Nos. 93 in D major; 94 in G major (Surprise).

(M) *** CBS Classics 61052. Cleveland Orchestra, George Szell.

** (*) CBS Quadraphonic MQ 32101. New York Philharmonic Orchestra, Leonard Bernstein.

Szell's performances are outstandingly brilliant. The perfection of detail, the buoyancy of the playing (Szell's minuets have a greater rhythmic spring than Bernstein's), the precision all add up to music-making of striking character and memorability. And this is not cold playing: there are many little touches from Szell to show that his perfectionist

443

approach is a dedicated and affectionate one. But the recording is very brightly lit, the violin tone in the tuttis conveys a hint of aggressiveness, and the slightly dry, close CBS sound emphasizes this.

Bernstein's is one of the best of CBS's quadraphonic issues, with a most attractive bloom on the orchestral sound and a convincing ambient effect. The performances are among the finest Bernstein has given us of Haydn, warmly affectionate, with gracious opening movements (the second subject of No. 93 attractively relaxed) and equally striking accounts of the slow movements. Bernstein is inclined to be too rhythmically forceful in the minuets, and in No. 94 this heaviness of articulation extends to the finale. But taken as a whole this is a most enjoyable disc, and apart from a touch of fierceness in the strings in No. 94 the quadraphonic sound is of high quality.

Symphonies Nos. 93 in D major; 94 in G major (Surprise); 95 in C minor; 96 in D major (Miracle); 97 in C major; 98 in B flat major; 99 in E flat major; 100 in G major (Military); 101 in D major (Clock); 102 in B flat major; 103 in E flat major (Drum Roll); 104 in D major (London).
(M) *** Decca HDNJ 41/6. Philharmonia Hungarica, Antal Dorati.

Dorati and the Philharmonia Hungarica, working in comparative isolation in Marl in West Germany, carried through their monumental project of recording the complete Haydn symphonies with not a suspicion of routine. These final masterpieces are performed with a glowing sense of commitment, and Dorati, no doubt taking his cue from the editor, H. C. Robbins Landon, generally chooses rather relaxed tempi for the first movements – as in No. 93, which is just as deliciously lilting as in Szell's masterly version. In slow movements his tempi are on the fast side, but only in No. 94,

the *Surprise*, is the result really controversial. Though an extra desk of strings has been added to each section, the results are authentically in scale, with individual solos emerging unforcedly against the glowing acoustic, and with intimacy comes extra dramatic force in sforzandos. A magnificent conclusion to a magnificent project.

Symphonies Nos. 94 in G major (Surprise); 99 in E flat major.
(M) *** Decca Ace of Diamonds SDD 174. Vienna Philharmonic Orchestra, Josef Krips.

Those who enjoy Viennese performances of Haydn will find this exceptionally well recorded disc very much to their taste. Krips is on top form and the playing has that extra relaxation and flexibility that bring out Haydn's essential geniality and humanity. The extrovert quality of the *Surprise* performance is matched by the depth Krips and the Vienna players find in the eloquent slow movement of the *E flat Symphony*.

Symphonies Nos. 94 in G major (Surprise); 101 in D major (Clock).
(B) *** Decca Eclipse ECS 574. Vienna Philharmonic Orchestra, Pierre Monteux.

A captivating pair of performances from Monteux. He turns a genial eye on a genial composer, and secures very polished playing throughout, with many a turn of phrase to delight the ear. Highlights are the delicious *Andante* of the *Surprise* and the contrasting finale of the same work, bustling with vigour and high spirits. In the *Clock* the conductor sets a perky mood in the second movement, and a very pointed tick-tock emphasizes Haydn's gentle humour. The recordings are excellent, warm-toned to suit the conductor's approach. This was a highly recommended three-star disc at full price; it is even more desirable now, one of the finest bargains in the symphonic catalogue.

Symphonies Nos. 95 in C minor; 96 in D major (Miracle).

*** DGG 2530 420. London Philharmonic Orchestra, Eugen Jochum.

Jochum recorded the twelve *London symphonies* as part of DGG's 75th-birthday symphony project. Linking the recording sessions with four concerts spaced over a year, he secured fine stylish playing from the LPO, challenging them with often very fast tempi in outer movements. Those fast tempi sometimes prevent the music from having quite the lilt it has with Beecham or Dorati, but the athletic exuberance of Jochum in Haydn, and his ability to mould slow movements with tenderness that never spills over into unstylish mannerism, make these wonderfully satisfying readings of Haydn's greatest symphonies. The recording, rather reverberant, presents the works on a somewhat bigger scale than Dorati does on Decca, but many will prefer that. The complete set is now deleted and the performances are issued separately.

Symphonies Nos. 95 in C minor; 96 in D major (Miracle).

(M) *** CBS 61246. Cleveland Orchestra, George Szell.

An outstanding companion record for Szell's brilliant coupling of Nos. 93 and 94. With superb polish in the playing and precise phrasing it would be easy for such performances to sound superficial, but Haydn's music obviously struck a deep chord in Szell's musical sensibility, and there is humanity underlying the technical perfection. There is also the most delectable pointing and a fine judgement of the inner balance of woodwind colouring which compares favourably even with Beecham's (mono)

recording of No. 96, with Szell having the additional advantage of using modern editions of both scores. The recording acoustic suits the music-making admirably with clarity of texture as well as bloom.

Symphonies Nos. 96 in D major (Miracle); 97 in C major.

(M) ** Unicorn UNS 232. Rome Haydn Foundation Orchestra, Antonio de Almeida.

These are as attractive a pair of Haydn symphonies as one can find for spontaneity of invention and colour of orchestration, and the conductor here realizes this. If the strings were as rich as the solo wind contributions this would be a top recommendation. Even as it is, these performances are enjoyable for their infectious sense of style, but the strings as recorded sound rather dry in timbre, although the playing itself is good. The ear adjusts to this studio-ish quality and there is no question as to the vigour and life of the playing. The Landon edition is used.

Symphonies Nos. 96 in D major (Miracle); 102 in B flat major.

(B) ** Classics for Pleasure CFP 40073. Royal Philharmonic Orchestra, Hans-Hubert Schönzeler.

Though in the lovely slow movement of No. 102 – one of the most beautiful melodies that Haydn ever composed – the violins of the RPO are not as pure in tone as they might be, this is a highly enjoyable bargain coupling of two of the *London symphonies* that are linked by the nickname *Miracle*. It was during a performance of No. 102 that a chandelier fell and miraculously did not injure anyone, but it was No. 96 which unfairly acquired the resulting nickname. Both works, given spirited performances here, particularly No. 96, are miraculous musically, of course. Good recording.

445

Symphonies Nos. 97 in C major; 98 in B flat major.

(M) ** (*) CBS 61291. Cleveland Orchestra, George Szell.

Influenced by the rather aggressive recording quality, these performances underline the forcefulness of Haydn's writing rather than its joy. But like Szell's other Haydn records this is a mid-price issue that presents superlative playing as well as searching direction.

Symphonies Nos. 99 in E flat major; 100 in G major (Military).

*** DGG 2530 459. London Philharmonic Orchestra, Eugen Jochum.

Fast as Jochum is in outer movements, the rhythm is superbly controlled, above all in the final *Presto* of No. 100, where the triplets are miraculously well defined. In the spacious *Adagio* of No. 99 Jochum inspires radiant playing in the reprise. Excellent recording.

Symphonies Nos. 100 in G major (Military); 101 in D major (Clock).

(M) ** DGG Privilege 135037. Berlin Radio Symphony Orchestra, Rolf Kleinert.

These are warm, musical performances, especially notable for wind-playing which brings out the full colour of Haydn's scoring. The recording is atmospheric and reverberant. It produces an ample texture but this seems to suit the warm approach of the conductor, although it does not give ideal transparency to the middle of the orchestra. The upper strings are smooth rather than sparkling, while the percussion in the *Military symphony* lacks bite. But this coupling of two justly favourite symphonies is certainly enjoyable and fairly priced.

Symphonies Nos. 100 in G major (Military); 102 in B flat major.

* (*) Columbia SAX 5266. New Philharmonia Orchestra, Otto Klemperer.

Good playing from the New Philharmonia, but there is little of the magic or poetry that marked the old Beecham set or the warmth and humanity that endeared Walter to us. These are correct, grave and unsmiling performances with little that could be called spontaneous. Other Klemperer Haydn issues have been favourably received but no amount of repetition has modified the impression of joyless rectitude that these performances communicate. The stereo recording is faithful and well balanced: the sound has plenty of body.

Symphony No. 103 in E flat major (Drum Roll).

(M) ** Decca Ace of Diamonds SDD 312. Vienna Philharmonic Orchestra, Herbert von Karajan – MOZART: *Symphony No. 41.** (*)

Symphonies Nos. 103 in E flat major (Drum Roll); 104 in D major (London).

(M) ** (*) Decca Ace of Diamonds SDD 362. Vienna Philharmonic Orchestra, Herbert von Karajan.

Symphony No. 104 in D major (London).

(M) *** Decca Ace of Diamonds SDD 233. Vienna Philharmonic Orchestra, Herbert von Karajan – MOZART: *Symphony No. 40.** (*)

The two Decca-Karajan Haydn/Mozart discs have been with us since the early sixties. Now Decca have sensibly coupled the Haydn symphonies together. No. 103 is a polished, well-made account, but there is some lack of warmth and humanity in the reading, although the tempi are sensible and the recording balance is good. The reading of No. 104 is more direct, with plenty of earthy vigour in the outer movements and a beautifully shaped slow movement. If the Mozart couplings are chosen, No. 41 is more successful than No. 40. The recordings are excellent and do not show their age.

Symphonies Nos. A in B flat major; B in B flat major; 22 in E flat major (Philosopher) (second version); *53 in D major (L'Impériale)*: 3 finales; *63 in C major (La Roxolane)* (second version); *103 in E flat major (Drum Roll)*: original finale.

    (M) *** Decca HDNK 47/8. Philharmonia Hungarica, Antal Dorati.

It is a measure of Dorati's dedication to Haydn scholarship – helped by the editor of the scores and commentator for the series, H. C. Robbins Landon – that he included this supplementary album of alternative movements in his complete Haydn series. So far from proving a merely academic exercise, the result might almost be regarded as a sampler for the series, with examples of Haydn's work at every period, culminating in the magnificent, somewhat more expanded version of the finale of the *Drum Roll*. Symphonies Nos. A and B were not included in the original numerical list, simply because they were originally thought not to be symphonies at all, while the other alternative movements – some of them probably not by Haydn at all – come from different editions of his work published through Europe. It gives a vivid idea of the working conditions of the music world in Haydn's time. Exhilarating performances, superb recording.

CHAMBER MUSIC

Cassation in C major (for lute, violin and cello) (arr. of *String quartet, Op. 1/6*); *Quartet in D major* (for lute, violin, viola and cello) (arr. of *String quartet, Op. 2/2*); *Trio in F major* (for lute, violin and cello).

    (B) ** Turnabout TV 34227S. Michael Schaeffer (lute), Eva Nagora (violin), Franz Beyer (viola), Thomas Blees (cello).

Another Turnabout disc (TV 34171S) gives us the alternative arrangement of the *Cassation*, using a guitar instead of a lute, but the present performance has an attractive intimacy. The snag to this disc is the limitations of tone-colour possible. Michael Schaeffer, although musical, seems a rather self-effacing player. But if you fancy the combination the music is pleasant enough, if hardly characteristic of the mature Haydn.

Flute quartets, Op. 5, Nos. 1 in D major; 2 in G major; 3 in D major; 4 in G major.

    (B) ** Turnabout TV 34007S. Camillo Wanausek (flute), members of the Europa Quartet, Joseph Nebois (harpsichord).

These are delightful works and receive felicitous performances from this group. Wanausek's tone is beautiful and he is well supported by strings and harpsichord. The recording is good.

Guitar quartet in E major, Op. 2/2.

    *** CBS SBRG 72678. John Williams (guitar), Alan Loveday (violin), Cecil Aronowitz (viola), Amaryllis Fleming (cello) – PAGANINI: *Terzetto.****

This is the usual arrangement (of an early string quartet) from the Op. 2 set. An attractive performance from John Williams of this slight but very agreeable work that makes ideal late-evening listening. With its lightweight coupling this is a most attractive disc, closely but realistically recorded.

Piano trios Nos. 18 in A major; 19 in G minor; 22 in E flat major.

 ☮ (for the entire Beaux Arts series) *** Philips 6500 521. Beaux Arts Trio.

Piano trios Nos. 20 in B flat major; 24 in D major; 32 in G major.

 *** Philips 6500 522. Beaux Arts Trio.

Piano trios Nos. 21 in C major; 23 in D minor; 28 in E major.

 *** Philips 6500 401. Beaux Arts Trio.

Piano trio No. 25 in G major.

 (B) * (*) Decca Eclipse ECS 658. Valda Aveling (piano), Donald Weekes (violin), Dennis Nesbitt (cello) – MENDELSSOHN: *Piano trio No. 1.* * (*)

Piano trios Nos. 25 in G major; 26 in F sharp minor; 27 in C major.

 *** Philips 6500 023. Beaux Arts Trio.

Piano trio No. 28 in E major.

 (M) ** Pye Virtuoso TPLS 13018. Oromonte Trio – BRAHMS: *Piano trio No. 2.***

Piano trios Nos. 29 in E flat major; 30 in D major; 31 in E flat minor.

 *** Philips 6500 400. Beaux Arts Trio.

Although Haydn's symphonies and quartets have made enormous headway in the catalogue over the past decade or so, the piano trios have remained grievously neglected. Now that amends are being made, they are being made handsomely; the Beaux Arts Trio have so far produced five discs and will, one hopes, go on to record Haydn's complete output in this medium. They could scarcely be improved upon from the point of view of style or recording. Menahem Pressler's piano-playing is marvellously crisp, beautifully articulated and always alive and sensitive, while his two companions are no less intelligent and accomplished. The Philips engineers have produced a recording which is not only fresh and vivid in every way but also balanced with complete naturalness and marvellous musicianship. It is not easy to flaw this set; it is distinguished throughout, and all five discs are absolutely outstanding musically and technically. They can all be cordially recommended and do not call for detailed comment. Readers should perhaps start by trying No. 26, in F sharp minor, which calls on the *Symphony No. 102 in B flat* for its slow movement. Thus launched, most readers will want to go on and collect the remainder, for the series is one of the most rewarding (and least trumpeted) achievements of the gramophone in recent years.

The Oromonte performance is spontaneous and enjoyable with an almost Brahmsian richness of texture in the two final movements. The clear recording is not quite so full here as in the Brahms coupling, with a touch of hardness given to the violin's upper notes.

The Trio offered separately by the Aveling group is popular because of its Hungarian 'gipsy' finale, a gay, extrovert movement performed with spirit here. The playing has less polish than it has life, but this is serviceable and clearly recorded.

String quartets: in E flat major, Op. 0; Nos. 1 in B flat major; 2 in E flat major; 3 in D major; 4 in G major; 6 in C major, Op. 1/1–4 and 6; 7 in A major; 8 in E major; 10 in F major; 12 in B flat major, Op. 2/1–2, 4 and 6.

 (M) ** (*) Argo HDNM 52/6. Aeolian Quartet.

The early quartets of Haydn have not quite the unquenchable flow of original ideas that the early symphonies have, but they make easy and enjoyable listening, even if some of them outstay their welcome. Even the Aeolians cannot quite sustain our interest, when the quartets of Opp. 1 and 2 all have five movements with two minuets and trios in each. It is not always an advantage that the Aeolians are wedded to observing repeats. Nonetheless, on their own relatively unpretentious level these are charming works, and Emanuel Hurwitz, the leader of the quartet, readily takes his chances in such a quartet as Op. 2/1, which includes stylish cadenzas. Good, atmospheric recording, with none of the disadvantages of the sound quality in the set of quartets Opp. 71 and 74.

String quartets Nos. 17 in F major (Serenade), Op. 3/5; 38 in E flat major (Joke), Op. 33/2; 76 in D minor (Fifths), Op. 76/2.
(M) *** Decca Ace of Diamonds SDD 285. Janáček Quartet.

The performances here are superlative, strong and dedicated, and careful to sense that the style of Haydn is not that of either Beethoven or Mozart. The music itself is highly agreeable; whether or not Haydn did write that delicious tune which forms the slow movement of the *Serenade quartet* seems irrelevant; it is an attractive little work and makes a good foil for the really splendid music of its companions. The recording is outstanding, even by Decca's standards, and it is quite possible to imagine that the Janáček Quartet are recessed in a small concert chamber at the end of one's living room. Very highly recommended.

String quartets Nos. 17 in F major (Serenade), Op. 3/5; 67 in D major (Lark), Op. 64/5; 76 in D minor (Fifths), Op. 76/2.
*** Philips SAL 3591. Italian Quartet.

At first hearing these strike one as prosaic performances, but on closer acquaintance they reveal qualities of insight that at first escape one. The first movement of the *Lark* is a bit too measured in feeling and could do with more sparkle, but the *Serenade quartet* (for so long attributed to Haydn and now shown to be the work of Hofstetter; an inspired work nevertheless) is as fine as one has heard. The *D minor Quartet* is admirably poised and classical in feeling. It rivals, if not outclasses, the performance by the Janáček Quartet on Decca. The recording is most musically balanced.

String quartets Nos. 19 in C major; 20 in E flat major; 21 in G major; 22 in D minor; 23 in B flat major; 24 in A major, Op. 9/1–6; 25 in E major; 26 in F major; 27 in E flat major; 28 in C minor; 29 in G major; 30 in D major, Op. 17/1–6.
(M) *** Decca HDNQ 61/6. Aeolian Quartet.

Though few of these early works are consistently inspired from beginning to end (the G major, No. 29, is a marvellous exception), they all contain their moments of magic and every one of them has a superb finale, showing the young Haydn at full stretch. At this period in his career at the Palace of Esterhaz Haydn was experimenting in every direction, and though the first movements here are not all as inventive as one might hope, they generally match the equivalent symphonies of the period in sharpness of inspiration. Even at this period Haydn had developed his quartet-writing beyond the stage of giving all the interesting writing to the first violin. The Aeolian Quartet, having settled into their task of recording the complete cycle, play with consistent freshness and imagination, and are well recorded.

String quartets Nos. 34 in D major, Op. 20/4; 78 in B flat major, Op. 76/4.
(M) * (*) Supraphon SUAST 50668. Prague City Quartet.

This coupling by the Prague City Quartet is disappointing. The music is well rehearsed, the ensemble is accurate and the recording is excellent. Yet the whole approach is so deadly serious that all charm flies out of the window. This pays certain dividends in the *Adagio* of Op. 76/4, where no one could accuse the group of superficiality, but it is far too rigid for the *Theme and variations* which make the slow movement of Op. 20/4.

String quartets Nos. 37 in B minor; 38 in E flat major (Joke); 39 in C major (Bird), Op. 33/1–3.
  (M) ** (*) Decca Ace of Diamonds SDD 278. Weller Quartet.
String quartets Nos. 40 in B flat major; 41 in G major; 42 in D major (How do you do?), Op. 33/4–6.
  (M) *** Decca Ace of Diamonds SDD 279. Weller Quartet.

This is exceptionally polished and lively playing, beautifully recorded. If the performances are not as penetrating as the very finest, they are sunny and civilized and always enjoyable. There is a genial touch too, and certain movements – the trio of the scherzo in the *Joke quartet*, the first movement of Op. 33/3 – are memorable, while the delightful *spiccato* playing in the latter work's *Allegretto* shows the character of the music-making. The slow movements are sophisticated in approach yet not inexpressive; however, perhaps there is a lack of depth. Tempi are generally well considered, even if the finale of the *Joke* is perhaps rather too fast; on the other hand the last movement of Op. 33/4 is beautifully judged.

String quartets Nos. 38 in E flat major (Joke); 39 in C major (Bird), Op. 33/2–3.
  (B) ** Saga 5271. Alberni Quartet.
  (B) * (*) Turnabout TV 34062S.

Dekány Quartet – *Quartet No. 67.***

Two excellent performances on Saga, with warmth rather than vitality the dominating factor, but the sound is excellent. The Turnabout disc is notable for the Hungarian Quartet's coupling of the *Lark quartet*. These two Dekány performances are less interesting; they are discussed under the coupling.

String quartets Nos. 44 in B flat major; 45 in C major, Op. 50/1–2 (Prussian quartets).
  ⊛ *** DGG 2530 440. Tokyo Quartet.

Not since the Schneider Quartet in the 1950s, or perhaps even the pre-war 78s of the Pro Arte, have these two quartets of Op. 50 been better served on record. The Tokyo Quartet plays with impeccable style and a refreshing and invigorating vitality. They are admirably unaffected but phrase with real imagination. DGG give them well defined and excellently balanced recording and the usual impeccable surfaces. This is an outstanding Haydn disc, strongly recommended.

The Seven Last Words of Christ (version for string quartet): *String quartets Nos. 50–56, Op. 51/1–7.*
  (B) ** Saga 5245. Aeolian Quartet.
  * (*) DGG 2530 213. Amadeus Quartet.

Haydn's *Seven Last Words* were originally written for performance in Cadiz Cathedral, as orchestral interludes to separate the bishop's seven sermons. Haydn made a quartet version of the work, and later added choral parts to his original. Here is the quartet version. The Aeolian Quartet play it with fine expressive feeling and supple lines. Their restraint does not lead to dullness, and this can be recommended in spite of the rather dry recording acoustic. The Amadeus Quartet, immaculate as ever, smooth over the darker side of Haydn, and the result is disappointingly superficial.

String quartets Nos. 57 in G major; 58 in C major, Op. 54/1–2.
> ** (*) D G G 2530 302. Amadeus Quartet.

The Amadeus are at their best here, though that is not to say that these performances are wholly free from the over-expressive style which this ensemble seems to favour. Brainin's *vibrato* is in evidence, but much less disturbing than in, say, their Schubert *C major Quintet.* This disc undoubtedly deserves a qualified recommendation, and the sound is eminently satisfactory.

String quartets Nos. 57 in G major; 58 in C major; 59 in E major, Op. 54/1–3.
> (M) ** (*) CBS 61549. Juilliard Quartet.

The Juilliard players respond strongly and positively to the vividly imaginative writing of Haydn in these quartets dedicated to Johann Tost. Their tempi tend to be relatively extreme, fast movements dashingly exciting (notably the finale of the G major) and slow movements measured and intense. Exposition repeats have been omitted to get three quartets on a single disc, very generous measure. The recording, matching the performances, is tough, immediate, and a little edgy.

String quartets Nos. 57–68 (Tost quartets): Nos. 57 in G major; 58 in C major; 59 in E major, Op. 54/1–3; 60 in A major; 61 in F minor (Razor); 62 in B flat major, Op. 55/1–3; 63 in C major; 64 in B minor; 65 in B flat major; 66 in G major; 67 in D major (Lark); 68 in E flat major, Op. 64/1–6.

> ** (*) D G G 2740 107 (3 discs). Amadeus Quartet.

These twelve quartets were dedicated to a rich self-made patron, Johann Tost, who was also a violinist, and they include a number of masterpieces. Op. 55/2 acquired its nickname *The Razor* from a curious story. 'My best quartet for a decent razor,' Haydn said one day, and an enterprising publisher successfully took up the challenge. Though the Amadeus Quartet does not always play with the fullest intensity in some of the great slow movements, the ensemble is superb, and the results are always gentle on the ear. A fine set, though it may be worth waiting to find out how the Aeolian Quartet succeeds in these works when it reaches them in its complete cycle. Immaculate D G G recording.

String quartet No. 67 in D major (Lark), Op. 64/5.
> (B) ** Turnabout TV 34062S. Hungarian Quartet – *Quartets Nos. 38 and 39.* (*)

The Hungarian performance of the *Lark* has not gained in quality in its present transfer. The recording is clearer but slightly less warm, and the leader's tone sounds not quite as sweet. However, this is still a sensitive performance and the brilliance of the sound focuses the vivacious *moto perpetuo* finale with precision. The other two performances on this disc, by the Dekány Quartet, are of an altogether lower voltage. They are accurate but bland in style. The recording is very pleasing but there is no subtlety in the playing. But as a whole this is fair enough value for money.

String quartets Nos. 69 in B flat major; 70 in D major; 71 in E flat major, Op. 71/1–3; 72 in C major; 73 in F major; 74 in G minor (Rider), Op. 74/1–3.
> (M) ** Argo HDNL 49/51. Aeolian Quartet.

451

This was the first album to be issued of the complete quartet cycle by the Aeolians, using a new edition prepared by H. C. Robbins Landon and Reginald Barrett-Ayres. Though the performances of these works, which have been unjustifiably neglected on record, are vigorously enjoyable, the recording quality masks their merit. In this first album – but not in the succeeding ones – the engineers gave the four players a degree of 'helpful' reverberation which made them sound like a string orchestra. It is perhaps a marginal shortcoming, but it does get in the way of more intimate expression. No. 69 has a magnificent slow movement, surprisingly romantic, and No. 70 is intensely original from first to last.

String quartets Nos. 74 in G minor (Rider), Op. 74/3; 77 in C major (Emperor), Op. 76/3.

⊛ *** Telefunken SAT 22550. Alban Berg Quartet, Vienna.

A quite superb disc in every way, with playing of wonderful resilience and sparkle. The famous slow movement of the *Emperor quartet* has never before been played on record with such warmth and eloquence, and the slow movement of No. 74 is even more beautiful. Indeed the performance of this quartet is masterly. The bright, clear sound matches the resilience of the playing, and this is one of the most rewarding of all Haydn quartet couplings.

String quartet No. 75 in G major, Op 76/1.

(B) ** (*) DGG Début 2555 005. Tokyo Quartet – BRAHMS: *Quartet No. 2.** (*)*

The refinement of the Tokyo Quartet is admirably demonstrated in their record of the first of Haydn's great Op. 76 quartets. At times they may betray their relative inexperience on details, and even in Haydn one would welcome a little

more sense of struggle, but the sheer command is marvellous. The recording is firm and life-like. A very impressive first disc.

String quartets Nos. 75 in G major; 76 in D minor (Fifths); 77 in C major (Emperor); 78 in B flat major; 79 in D major; 80 in E flat major, Op. 76/1–6; 81 in G major; 82 in F major, Op. 77/1–2; 83 in B flat major, Op. 103.

(M) *** Argo HDNP 57/60. Aeolian Quartet.

String quartets Nos. 75 in G major; 76 in D minor (Fifths); 77 in C major (Emperor); 78 in B flat major; 79 in D major; 80 in E flat major, Op. 76/1–6; 81 in G major; 82 in F major, Op. 77/1–2.

** (*) DGG 2734 001 (4 discs). Amadeus Quartet.

String quartets Nos. 75 in G major; 76 in D minor (Fifths); 77 in C major (Emperor); 78 in B flat major; 79 in D major; 80 in E flat major, Op. 76/1–6.

(M) ** (*) Hungaroton SLPX 1205/7. Tátrai Quartet.

Continuing their series of the complete quartets the Aeolians give eminently straightforward and unmannered accounts of Opp. 76 and 77 and the two-movement Op. 103 quartet. This is by far the most successful of their albums so far, and the excellence of the annotations enhances the value of the box.

The Amadeus performances of Opp. 76 and 77 are in some ways more polished and certainly more mannered than those of the Aeolian. Brainin's *vibrato* is a little tiresome on occasion, but generally speaking those who invest in the set will find much to reward them; the recordings are vivid and have plenty of body. But the Aeolians remain preferable on balance; their box provides an extra quartet, better annotation (the DGG notes are scanty), and their unaffected approach should prove more rewarding in the long run.

The Tátrai Op. 76 is also a desirable set, beautifully played with remarkably good stereo for a Hungarian import label. The playing is serious but dedicated; the *Adagios* are played as real adagios and most expressively sustained, and the finales are notable for their high spirits as well as the virtuosity of the playing. Only sometimes in the opening movements does the playing seem too lightweight, and in the *Emperor* the variations on the famous tune are not very imaginatively done.

String quartets Nos. 76 in D minor (Fifths); 79 in D major, Op. 76/2 and 5.
(B) ** Turnabout TV 34012S. Hungarian Quartet.

Clean performances here, with excellent playing and clear recording. The Hungarians' style may lack something in expressive qualities, but it is always alive and commanding.

String quartet No. 77 in C major (Emperor), Op. 76/3.
*** DGG SLPM 138886. Amadeus Quartet – MOZART: *Quartet No. 17 (Hunt).****
(B) ** Oryx EXP 6. Salzburg Mozarteum Quartet – MOZART: *Quartet No. 17 (Hunt).***

Like the Mozart on the reverse this performance shows the Amadeus Quartet in the finest possible light. The playing is sensitive and alive, and the famous variations, which need some subtlety of treatment to avoid sounding repetitive, are memorable. Excellent sound too. The Oryx performance is most enjoyable, not highly polished but alive; and with a warm yet transparent sound the stereo too is convincing. The slow movement is carefully done, but does not become torpid. Technically the disc is good value at the price.

String quartets Nos. 79 in D major; 80 in E flat major, Op. 76/5–6.
* (*) DGG 2530 072. Amadeus Quartet.

This is incredibly deadpan playing. It is immaculate technically, of course, but the Amadeus players convey little of the sunny warmth of Haydn's inspiration in two of his very finest late quartets. On the face of it the approach is musical enough, with care in dynamic shading and phrasing, but there is absolutely no conveyed sense of enjoyment and a total absence of humour. In the trio of the minuet of Op. 76/6 (which Haydn entitles *Alternativo*) the players answer each other with simple ascending and descending scales. This can be deliciously witty when played with a twinkle, but here the players miss the point altogether. The recording is clear but rather resiny and not especially congenial.

String quartets Nos. 81 in G major; 82 in F major, Op. 77/1–2.
** DGG SLPM 138980. Amadeus Quartet.

These two masterpieces of Haydn's last years are rather better served by the Amadeus than are Mozart and Schubert. Even so one must confess to finding their performances tinged with a note of instant rapture that sounds so characteristically mannered. The recording has admirable quality.

String trios, Op. 53, Nos. 1 in G major; 2 in B flat major; 3 in D major.
*** Philips SAL 3782. Grumiaux Trio – SCHUBERT: *String trios.****

The *String trios* are arrangements of keyboard pieces and none of them is of more than slight musical interest. They are, however, so persuasively played here that no one could fail to be delighted. The recording too is excellent and has no lack of body or colour.

453

PIANO MUSIC

Andante with variations in F minor; Fantasia in C major; Piano sonatas Nos. 34 in E minor; 48 in C major; 52 in E flat major.

(B) ** (*) Decca Eclipse ECS 692. Wilhelm Backhaus (piano).

On Decca's cheapest label it is good to have so illuminating and even unexpected an example of Backhaus's art. His manner can sometimes be rather heavyweight, even charmless, for Haydn, but generally the spontaneous imagination behind this playing bubbles out and silences any reservations on minor stylistic points. Including as it does some of Haydn's greatest keyboard music, this is a valuable disc. Excellent recording for its age.

Piano sonatas Nos. 6 in G major; 13 in E major; 52 in E flat major.

(M) *** HMV HQS 1301. John McCabe (piano).

Elegantly turned performances that will give pleasure to all lovers of Haydn's keyboard sonatas. The success of this disc, which includes the great *E flat Sonata*, has prompted Decca to invite Mr McCabe to record the whole œuvre. HMV have evidently missed a trick here. Excellent piano sound makes this moderately priced disc eminently desirable.

Piano sonatas Nos. 18 in B flat major; 22 in E major; 28 in E flat major; 46 in A flat major.

(B) *** Oiseau-Lyre OLS 136. Artur Balsam (piano).

Artur Balsam has made some fine records in the past – notably a Mozart sonata series, also for Oiseau-Lyre – but none as fine as this. There is a joyful sense of alertness in every bar which infectiously captures the mood of Haydn's own exuberant music-making. If ever these works have been used for grinding lessons in the classroom, they now emerge as the most exciting series of piano sonatas written before Beethoven, with Haydn working his way towards accepted sonata form. So delightful is each sonata and each performance that it is impossible to single out any particular one. The recording is excellent. Balsam uses Päsler's edition and numbering.

Piano sonata No. 34 in E minor; 12 Pieces for a Musical Clock (1792).

(M) ** Pye Virtuoso TPLS 13021. Nina Milkina (piano) – MOZART: *Piano sonata No. 8.***

This sonata, the only one Haydn wrote in the key of E minor, is a characteristic work, serenely confident and not suggesting hidden musical depths. Nina Milkina plays it well, the finale especially so, but she is in her element in the twelve charming pieces Haydn wrote in 1792 for his patron's musical clock. The source of the material varies from vocal music to the trio of the *La Reine symphony*, and each of the twelve miniatures is quite delightful in Miss Milkina's hands. The recording is excellent.

VOCAL AND CHORAL MUSIC

Cantilena pro adventu: Ein' Magd, Ein' Dienerin.

(B) ** Turnabout TV 34180S. Gertraut Stoklassa (soprano), Mainz Chamber Orchestra, Günter Kehr – PURCELL: *Behold, I bring you glad tidings;* A. SCARLATTI: *Cantata pastorale.***

This cantilena, which H. C. Robbins Landon has dated within Haydn's Eisenstadt period, between 1766 and 1769, is a *da capo* aria in praise of the Virgin. Its romantic eloquence has a Mozartian richness, and this strong performance by

Gertraut Stoklassa is most enjoyable. The recording too is rich and full, and the couplings are valuable.

The Creation (Die Schöpfung) (oratorio): complete recording.

> *** DGG 2707 044 (2 discs). Gundula Janowitz (soprano), Christa Ludwig (mezzo-soprano), Fritz Wunderlich, Werner Krenn (tenors), Dietrich Fischer-Dieskau (baritone), Walter Berry (bass), Vienna Singverein, Berlin Philharmonic Orchestra, Herbert von Karajan.

> *** Decca SET 362/3. Elly Ameling, Erna Spoorenberg (sopranos), Werner Krenn (tenor), Tom Krause, Robin Fairhurst (basses), Vienna State Opera Chorus, Vienna Philharmonic Orchestra, Karl Münchinger.

> (B) * (*) Turnabout TV 34184/5S. Mimi Coertse (soprano), Julius Patzak (tenor), Dezso Ernster (bass), Vienna Singverein and Volksoper Orchestra, Jascha Horenstein.

The Creation is a lucky work on record, and Karajan produces one of his most rapt choral performances. His concentration on refinement and polish might in principle seem out of place in a work which tells of religious faith in the directest terms. In fact the result is outstanding. The combination of the Berlin Philharmonic at its most intense and the great Viennese choir makes for a performance that is not only polished but warm and dramatically strong too. The soloists are an extraordinarily fine team, more consistent in quality than those on any rival version. This was one of the last recordings made by the incomparable Fritz Wunderlich, and fortunately his magnificent contribution extended to all the arias, leaving Werner Krenn to fill in

the gaps of recitative left unrecorded. The recording quality has a warm glow of atmosphere round it. Though Münchinger's set has more cleanly brilliant recording, Karajan's is clearly the safest recommendation.

A fine performance from Münchinger that stands well even in competition with Karajan. Münchinger has rarely conducted with such electric tension on record, and some no doubt will prefer his more direct, squarer style in comparison with the highly polished Karajan. His soloists nearly match those of the Karajan set (the sopranos not quite so beautiful as Janowitz). Fine vivid recording in Decca's finest Vienna tradition.

Horenstein's is a fresh and enjoyable performance, given a lively recording. There is not the utmost degree of sophistication; the soloists' runs, for instance, leave something to be desired, especially in the florid music in Part 2. But Mimi Coertse makes an appealing Eve: her *With verdure clad* has real charm. The bass too is good, and both these singers project strong vocal personalities. The choral singing is spirited, and Horenstein directs with spontaneity. It is surprising that such a distinguished conductor is responsible for the one blot on the performance, his slow and unbuoyant account of *The heavens are telling*, which means that Part 1 ends without the kind of thrill one takes for granted at a live performance.

The Creation: complete recording (in English).

> ** (*) HMV SLS 971 (2 discs). Heather Harper (soprano), Robert Tear (tenor), John Shirley-Quirk (baritone), King's College Chapel Choir, Academy of St Martin-in-the-Fields, David Willcocks.

There are special reasons for breaking the general rule of the recording world today and presenting this oratorio in an

English version. Quite apart from the fact that it is based on Milton, the idea was first presented to Haydn in the form of an English libretto provided by the impresario Salomon. Baron Gottfried van Swieten prepared not only a German version but an English one too, which was later modified in the score published in England. David Willcocks captures something of the spirit which made the King's version of *Messiah* so captivating, and it is good to have 'the flexible tiger' and 'the nimble stag' so vividly portrayed. Though Heather Harper is not always quite so steady or sweet-toned as usual, this is a first-rate team of soloists, and the choral singing and the playing of the Academy could hardly be more stylish. Warm reverberant recording in the King's manner.

Mass in G major (Rorate coeli desuper): Missa brevis alla cappella.
(B) * (*) Turnabout TV 34501S. Zurich Singkreis and Kammerchoir, Willi Gohl – MOZART: *Mass No. 7.**

The *Rorate coeli desuper* is a short work, though a pleasing one. Incidentally a recording of it in liturgical context has been issued on the continent and would be welcome here. There is no alternative version currently in the catalogue, so that this will have to do. It is not ideal: the playing is acceptable enough but the recording is somewhat coarse-grained and wanting in detail.

Mass No. 5 in B flat major (Little organ Mass): Missa brevis St Johannis de Deo.
(B) ** Turnabout TV 34132S. Eiko Katonosaka (soprano), Hans Haselböck (organ), Vienna Chamber Choir and Volksoper Orchestra, Hans Gillesberger – MOZART: *Mass No. 13.**

This is a small-scale work relying for its effect on a partnership between the soprano soloist and the organist, whose important part in the proceedings has given the work its nickname. Eiko Katonosaka and Hans Haselböck meet this joint demand here admirably, with fluency and musicianship, and Gillesberger sees that overall texture is properly shaped and balanced. The recording of the chorus is only fair, but otherwise this is an enjoyable disc.

Mass No. 7 in C major (Missa in tempore belli; Paukenmesse).
*** Argo ZRG 634. April Cantelo (soprano), Helen Watts (contralto), Robert Tear (tenor), Barry McDaniel (bass), St John's College, Cambridge, Choir, Academy of St Martin-in-the-Fields, George Guest – M HAYDN: *Salve regina.****
* CBS Quadraphonic MQ 32196; Stereo 73147. Patricia Wells (soprano), Gwendolyn Killebrew (contralto), Alan Titus (tenor), Michael Devlin (bass), Norman Scribner Choir, Leonard Bernstein.

The final offering in Argo's series of Haydn's magnificent late Masses is well up to the standard set previously. With the St John's College Choir George Guest provides a clean, brightly recorded account with good soloists, although Heather Harper (in the earlier HMV recording from King's College, now deleted) was markedly sweeter-toned than April Cantelo here. That said, the Argo disc is every bit the equal of the earlier one, and it offers a splendid fill-up in the beautiful *Salve regina* by Haydn's brother Michael.

Bernstein recorded this masterpiece of Haydn's last years in conjunction with a peace demonstration in Washington. The result has emotional intensity but not of a kind that adds to an appreciation of Haydn. Neither in execution, style nor recording quality can this compare with the finest versions, even though the quadraphonic version obviously adds something in atmosphere.

Mass No. 8 in B flat major (Heiligmesse): Missa Sancti Bernardi von Offida.

*** Argo ZRG 542. April Cantelo (soprano), Shirley Minty (contralto), Ian Partridge (tenor), Christopher Keyte (bass), St John's College Chapel Choir, Academy of St Martin-in-the-Fields, George Guest.

The *Heiligmesse* is one of the most human and direct in its appeal of all Haydn's Masses. Its combination of symphonic means and simple vocal style underlines its effectiveness. Haydn started writing this Mass in the first year after his return from London at about the time he wrote the *Paukenmesse*, but it was not completed until later, and was finally dedicated to the memory of St Bernard of Offida, newly canonized by Pope Pius VI barely a century after his death. The name *Heiligmesse* derives from the church song on which Haydn based the *Sanctus*. Among the special points of interest in the work are the slow introduction to the *Kyrie*, very like the introductions to Haydn's late symphonies, and the subdued *Agnus Dei* in the (for the time) extraordinary key of B flat minor. Like the other records in this series this is superlatively engineered and splendidly performed. The solo singing is good if not always equally distinguished and the choral response is excellent. Along with the *Harmoniemesse*, this is among the most successful of the Argo series.

Mass No. 9 in D minor (Nelson Mass): Missa in angustiis.

*** Argo ZRG 5325. Sylvia Stahlman (soprano), Helen Watts (contralto), Wilfred Brown (tenor), Tom Krause (baritone), King's College Chapel Choir, London Symphony Orchestra, David Willcocks.

Haydn's *Nelson Mass* is a tremendous work and clearly among his greatest music. Its impact in this splendid performance and recording is breathtaking. The solo singing is uniformly good, Sylvia Stahlman negotiating her florid music with great skill, and David Willcocks maintains quite remarkable tension throughout. The recording manages the many exciting and very loud climaxes without any difficulty and transfers the King's acoustic with complete success.

Mass No. 10 in B flat major (Theresienmesse).

*** Argo ZRG 5500. Erna Spoorenberg (soprano), Bernadette Greevy (contralto), John Mitchinson (tenor), Tom Krause (baritone), St John's College, Cambridge, Choir, Academy of St Martin-in-the Fields, George Guest.

The *Theresa Mass* followed on a year after the *Nelson Mass*, the best known of the six magnificent settings of the Mass which Haydn wrote for his patron, Prince Esterhazy, after his return from London. It may be less famous, but the inspiration is hardly less memorable, and Haydn's balancing of chorus against soloists, contrapuntal writing set against chordal passages, was never more masterly than here. George Guest injects tremendous vigour into the music (as in the *Harmoniemesse* there is a 'military' conclusion in the *Dona nobis pacem*), and the St John's Choir shows itself a ready match for the more famous choir at King's College. Good solo singing and brilliant, vivid recording.

Mass No. 11 in B flat major (Schöpfungsmesse).

*** Argo ZRG 598. April Cantelo (soprano), Helen Watts (contralto), Robert Tear (tenor), Forbes Robinson (bass), St John's College, Cambridge, Choir, Academy of St Martin-in-the-Fields, George Guest.

(B) * (*) Turnabout TV 34289S. Elisabeth Thomann (soprano), Christa Zottl-Holmstaed (mezzo-soprano), Rudolf Resch (tenor), Alois Buchbauer (bass), Vienna Chamber Choir and Volksoper Orchestra, Hans Gillesberger.

The *Schöpfungsmesse* or *Creation Mass* was the last but one of the magnificent series that Haydn wrote yearly in his retirement for his patron, Prince Esterhazy. George Guest draws from his own St John's College Choir and an excellent band of professionals a fresh, direct performance to match the others of his highly successful series. Argo started recording these masses with the other great Cambridge choir, at King's College, but after the *Nelson Mass* Argo moved down the road to St John's. Excellent solo singing, notably from Robert Tear in the lovely *Incarnatus est.* Clear, forward recording. As a bargain version the Turnabout issue is recommendable, though Gillesberger's performance, vital but unsubtle, cannot match George Guest's. Fair recording.

Mass No. 12 in B flat major (Harmoniemesse).

*** Argo ZRG 515. Erna Spoorenberg (soprano), Helen Watts (contralto), Alexander Young (tenor), Joseph Rouleau (bass), St John's College, Cambridge, Choir, Academy of St Martin-in-the-Fields, Brian Runnett (organ), George Guest.

The *Harmoniemesse* was the last of the six Masses, all of them masterpieces, that Haydn wrote after his return from London. In 1802 when he wrote it, the Esterhazy orchestra was at its most expansive, and Haydn typically took advantage of the extra wind instruments available. He was already over seventy when he started writing it, but the freshness and originality of the writing are as striking as anything in the earlier works. In particular the last section of the Mass brings a wonderfully memorable passage, when from a gentle setting of the *Agnus Dei*, Haydn bursts out with fanfares into a vigorous, even aggressive *Dona nobis pacem*. The performance matches the fine quality of George Guest's other recordings with the St John's Choir and Academy of St Martin's. The quartet of soloists is strong, with Helen Watts in particular singing magnificently. The recording is brilliantly real even by Argo standards.

The Seasons (Die Jahreszeiten) (oratorio): complete recording.

*** DGG 2709 026 (3 discs). Gundula Janowitz (soprano), Peter Schreier (tenor), Martti Talvela (bass), Vienna Symphony Orchestra, Karl Boehm.

** (*) HMV SLS 969 (3 discs). Gundula Janowitz (soprano), Werner Hollweg (tenor), Walter Berry (bass), German Opera Chorus, Berlin Philharmonic Orchestra, Herbert von Karajan.

The Seasons shows Haydn in the innocent pictorial vein of the Adam and Eve music of *The Creation*, and the imagery is brilliantly realized. The atmospheric orchestral writing describing the character of the seasons; the pictures of birds and animals; the storm; the hunt; the chorus in praise of the pleasures of the cup: all these are among the many imaginative delights. Haydn shows here, as often in the works of his maturity, that his eye sees with the freshness of youth, while his genius can record with the skill and experience that can only come from many years of apprenticeship to a beloved art. The work, essentially genial, ends with the composer looking towards heaven and after-life. It is an expression of a simple faith and of a human being to whom life on the whole has been kind, and who was duly grateful to record the many earthly pleasures he had enjoyed. Boehm's performance fully enters into the spirit of the music. The soloists are excellent and characterize the music fully; the chorus sing enthusiastically and are well recorded. But it is Boehm's set. He secures fine orchestral playing throughout, an excellent overall musical balance and a real spontaneity to music that needs this above all else.

Karajan draws from his Berlin performers a fine, polished performance, atmospherically recorded. If it were the only version available it would be very welcome, but both Boehm and Colin Davis give performances that are at once fresher and more in style. Warm, reverberant recording.

The Seasons: complete recording (in English).
  *** Philips 6703 023 (3 discs). Heather Harper (soprano), Ryland Davies (tenor), John Shirley-Quirk (baritone), BBC Chorus, BBC Choral Society, BBC Symphony Orchestra, Colin Davis.

Like Karl Boehm on DGG, Colin Davis directs a tinglingly fresh performance of Haydn's mellow last oratorio, and choice between them can safely be left to a preference for the original German text or an excellent English translation. In this work – based with flamboyant freedom on a German translation of James Thomson's English poem – there is more than usual reason for using a translation, and the excellent soloists and chorus attempt with fair success to get the words over clearly.

The Seasons: highlights (in English).
  (M) *** Philips Universo 6580 015 (from above recording cond. Davis).

There are many attractive things here, from the warm-hearted opening chorus, *Come gentle spring,* and the infectious song of the whistling ploughman, superbly sung by John Shirley-Quirk, to the glorious music of autumn and the chorus of gratitude for the fruits of the vineyard. The recording is warm and atmospheric but not as clear as the selection from Davis's recording of *Messiah.*

VOCAL COLLECTIONS

Arias: *Acide e Galatea: Tergi i vezzosi rai. Il Disertore: Un cor si tenero. La scuola di gelosi: Dice benissimo. La vera constanza: Spann' deine lange Ohren.*
  ** (*) Decca SXL 6490. Dietrich Fischer-Dieskau (baritone), Vienna Haydn Orchestra, Rheinhold Peters – MOZART: *Arias.*** (*)

'Haydn and Mozart rarities', the disc says, and very delightful they prove, even if Haydn gets much less attention, with comparatively lightweight and simple pieces. Fischer-Dieskau is as thoughtfully stylish as ever, though it is a pity that he did not take more advice about the inclusion of appoggiaturas. Excellent recording.

Scena di Berenice (Concert aria); *St Cecilia Mass: Laudamus te; Quoniam.*
  (B) *** Decca Eclipse ECS 635. Jennifer Vyvvan (soprano), Haydn Orchestra, Harry Newstone – MOZART: *Arias.****

This is a brilliant piece of singing which everyone should hear. It is astonishing that Jennifer Vyvyan could manage such agility with so rich a voice. One is occasionally worried by her tendency to sing deliberately under the note (intending to soften the tone-colour, presumably), but on any count the *Scena di Berenice* is given a wonderful performance, and what a gloriously dramatic piece this isolated aria is. It makes one regret more than ever that Haydn did not really test himself as an opera composer. Good recording.

Haydn, Michael
(1737–1806)

Double concerto for harpsichord, viola and strings.
(B) ** Turnabout TV 34079S. Lory Wallfisch (harpsichord), Ernst Wallfisch (viola), Württemberg Chamber Orchestra, Joerg Faerber – HUMMEL: *Fantasy.***

This concerto by Michael Haydn, Josef's brother, was only recently unearthed. It shows a musical craftsman of considerable competence, although not a specially individual musical imagination. The first movement is rather square and its themes obvious, but the slow movement has an almost Handelian melodic breadth, particularly well presented by the spacious acoustic here, and the finale is vivacious and colourful. Not an uncovered missing masterpiece, but interesting enough. The only snag to the otherwise first-rate recorded quality is the somewhat metallic quality of the harpsichord.

(i) *Horn concerto in D major; 6 Minuets* (for small orchestra).
** Argo ZRG 543. (i) Barry Tuckwell (horn); Academy of St Martin-in-the-Fields, Neville Marriner – J. HAYDN: *Trumpet concerto etc.***

Another interesting but not memorable addition to the virtuoso horn repertory serves to show what masterpieces were the four Mozart concertos (and indeed the one by Josef Haydn, to a lesser extent). The writing here is clumsier, but this impression is not helped by the performance, which is vigorous but slightly square. The *Minuets*, a most attractive bonus, are beautifully played, and are almost worthy of Josef!

Duo concertante for viola and organ.
** (*) Argo ZRG 631. Simon Preston (organ), Stephen Shingles (viola), Academy of St Martin-in-the-Fields, Neville Marriner – J. HAYDN: *Organ concerto.** (*)

An unusual and attractive combination is here more effective in terms of colour and balance than one might have expected. The work's outer movements are well made and spirited, but it is the gracious and elegant *Adagio* that makes the strongest impression. It has a most imaginative middle section where the organ is delicately florid and the viola sustains the melodic interest. The performance is in the main excellent and the recording solves the balance problems skilfully.

(i) *Violin concerto in A major; Symphony in G major, P.16; Symphony in A major, P.33.*
(B) ** Pye GSGC 14131. Little Orchestra of London, Leslie Jones, (i) with William Armon (violin).

The style of the symphonies reminds one of Mozart of the period of, say, the twenty-eighth and twenty-ninth symphonies. The music is fresh, vital and inventive, if without the distinguishing strength of individuality that marks out the music of a great composer. Yet even so the *G major Symphony* was originally mistaken for Mozart (and published as this composer's Symphony No. 37); Mozart borrowed it for a concert at Linz in 1783, and wrote a twenty-bar introduction for it himself. This is included on the record, separately banded. The *Concerto* is attractive but rather less memorable. Performances here are bright and stylish, with a vivid recording acoustic to match.

String quintet in G major; String quintet in F major.

(M) *** Decca Ace of Diamonds SDD 340. Vienna Philharmonic Quintet.

The only example of Michael Haydn's chamber music currently in the catalogue. He wrote seven quintets in all, though four of them must be numbered among the divertimenti since they have seven or so movements. (The F major here has six.) Both works recorded here are for two violas and were composed in 1773. Neither of them offers music that is wildly memorable but it is always charming, urbane and civilized; and so too are the performances by the Vienna Philharmonic Quintet, expertly recorded on this reasonably priced disc. An admirable and worthwhile issue that all lovers of eighteenth-century music should pursue.

Salve regina.

*** Argo ZRG 634. St John's College, Cambridge, Choir, George Guest – J. HAYDN: *Mass No. 7.****

This lovely unaccompanied motet makes an unexpected and welcome fill-up for the fine Argo version of the *Paukenmesse.*

Henze, Hans Werner
(born 1926)

(i) *Compases para preguntas ensimismadas* (music for viola and 22 players); (ii) *Violin concerto No. 2* (for solo violin, tape voices and 33 instrumentalists, using Hans Magnus Enzensberger's poem: *Homage à Gödel*).

*** Decca Headline HEAD 5. (i) Hirofumi Fukai (viola); (ii) Brenton Langbein (violin); both with London Sinfonietta, the composer.

Compases is a gentle work with the solo instrument supported by a shimmering orchestral texture, a piece that can easily seem flat and uneventful until you have a chance to hear it repeatedly on record. Of the *Violin concerto No. 2* Henze has said that it is 'very nearly a stage piece but not quite', and with a poem by Enzensberger sung and recited during its course, the drama of the music is strongly presented, with the violin as the prime actor. Excellent performances and vivid recording.

Hérold, Ferdinand
(1791–1833)

La Fille mal gardée (ballet, arr. John Lanchbery): extended excerpts.

*** Decca SXL 2313. Orchestra of the Royal Opera House, Covent Garden, John Lanchbery.

The ballet *La Fille mal gardée* dates originally from 1789 and has had a long and chequered history. The tale is a simple one of thwarted rustic love which comes right in the end, and the original score was made up from folk melodies and 'pop' songs of the time. Since 1789 it has been revised and rewritten by Hérold

(1828), Hertel (1864) and Feldt (1937). The present score, commissioned by Frederick Ashton for a Royal Ballet revival, was prepared and exceedingly skilfully scored by John Lanchbery, who drew in the main on Hérold's version. However, Lanchbery also interpolates a single Hertel number, a gorgeously vulgar *Clog Dance* for Simone (who as a character is one of the ancestors of our pantomime Dame). Hérold's score also included tunes from Rossini's *Barber of Seville* and *Cenerentola*, together with a Donizetti selection (mainly from *L'Elisir d'amore*). That the ballet is therefore a complete hotch-potch does not prevent it from being marvellously entertaining. The music is popular in appeal but, being French, is witty too and of course it is tuneful from beginning to end. The performance here is brilliantly played, displaying both affection and sparkle in ample quantity. The recording quality is a fraction dry, with a splendid bloom on everything; a perfect recipe for such music. Recommended.

Herrmann, Bernard
(born 1911)

Echoes (for string quartet).
> (B) *** Pye GSGC 14101. Amici Quartet – RUBBRA: *Quartet No. 2.****

Echoes is an elegiac work of immediate melodic appeal. Its romantic style might be slightly eclectic but its lack of aggressive 'modernity' produces at least an extended twentieth-century piece of expressive writing which has one theme to haunt the memory afterwards. The structure is kept together by this most memorable phrase, which serves as an interlude between the eight sub-sections. Not all the music is slow; there is, for instance, a highly effective *Scherzo macabre*. The playing is warm but restrained, and with

excellent recording and a good coupling this can be cordially recommended.

The Devil and Daniel Webster: suite; *Welles raises Kane:* suite.
> (M) ** (*) Unicorn UNS 237 London Philharmonic Orchestra, the composer

The Devil and Daniel Webster suite is a reworking of music from a film-score. The style is attractive but predictable; the musical material is not always distinguished enough and one or two of the movements outlast their welcome. *Welles raises Kane* is another matter. Beecham himself gave one of its first performances in New York during the war. The source of the music is again film-scores, this time Orson Welles's *Citizen Kane* and *The Magnificent Ambersons*, but the music itself (unlike the atmosphere of those films) is snappily and evocatively extrovert, showing a brilliant flair for orchestral colour. This is very attractive indeed, and it is superbly played and very well recorded.

Moby Dick (cantata).
> (M) *** Unicorn UNS 255. John Amis, Robert Bowman (tenors), David Kelly, Michael Rippon (basses), Aeolian Singers, London Philharmonic Orchestra, the composer.

Bernard Herrmann's *Moby Dick* is written in an immediately approachable idiom, and like Gilbert Vinter's *The Trumpets* this is a work deserving the attention of choral societies, because it makes a maximum impact at first hearing. The present extremely dramatic and spontaneous performance should recommend it to any listener who can enjoy a setting of the English language by a composer who shows a real feeling for words. The soloists, notably John Amis as Ishmael, and David Kelly as Ahab, are first-rate, and the chorus and orchestra convey their enthusiasm and excitement in such effective and rewarding music. Outstandingly good recording, to match the vigour of the performance.

Wuthering Heights (opera): complete recording.

> (M) ** (*) Unicorn UNB 400 (4 discs). Elizabeth Bainbridge (mezzo-soprano), David Kelly, Donald Bell (baritones), Morag Beaton (soprano), John Kitchiner (baritone), Michael Rippon (bass), Joseph Ward (tenor), Pamela Bowden (mezzo-soprano), Elizabethan Singers, Pro Arte Orchestra, the composer.

Bernard Herrmann, best known for his film music and as a conductor, spent many years working on his operatic adaptation of Emily Brontë's novel, and though it inevitably gives an oversimplified idea of the tensions in the original story, the result is confident and professional. Much of the writing is fittingly atmospheric, though it is a pity that Herrmann detracts from his final effect by going on too long (3½ hours in all) and keeps the pace of the music consistently slow. Though the writing is purely illustrative rather than musically original, this performance, strongly conducted by the composer, makes for a colourful telling of the story. The solo singing is consistently good, and the recording beautifully clear. The Elizabethan Singers come in rather incongruously as the highly civilized 'carolers from Gimmerton'. Perhaps the whole opera is too civilized to represent stark Brontë emotions, but it is good to have a complete recording of an ambitious modern opera, as yet unstaged.

Hindemith, Paul
(1895–1963)

Concert music for strings and brass, Op. 50; Mathis der Maler (Symphony).

> *** DGG 2530 246. Boston Symphony Orchestra, William Steinberg.

The *Concert music for brass and strings* is one of Hindemith's most deeply characteristic utterances. Steinberg gives it a thoroughly committed performance and it is beautifully recorded. He also gives a well-controlled and spacious account of the *Mathis symphony*, and he has the advantage of excellently balanced DGG recording. Some may find the balance a little distant but there is a spaciousness about the perspective and a consistency that is rewarding. Climaxes open out beautifully and the overall effect is unfailingly musical. The performance is on the sober side, which is not inappropriate in this music; it falls short perhaps of the inspired quality that Hindemith himself brought to it in his very first recording.

Horn concerto.

> (M) *** HMV HLS 7001. Dennis Brain (horn), Philharmonia Orchestra, the composer – R. STRAUSS: *Horn concertos.****

The Hindemith *Concerto* was the only recording Dennis Brain made in stereo. The work is rather spare in atmosphere, and its melodic appeal is no less dry, but Dennis's natural exuberance puts as much red blood into the music's veins as it will take. With the composer conducting this is a classic performance.

Violin concerto, Op. 14.

> *** Decca SXL 6035. David Oistrakh (violin), London Symphony

Orchestra, the composer – BRUCH: *Scottish fantasia.****

(M) ** (*) Supraphon 110 0508. André Gertler (violin), Czech Philharmonic Orchestra, Karel Ančerl – HARTMANN: *Concerto funèbre.*** (*)

(M) ** Everest SDBR 3040. Joseph Fuchs (violin), London Symphony Orchestra, Sir Eugene Goossens – MOZART: *Violin concerto No. 3.***

(B) * (*) Turnabout TV 34276S. Ivry Gitlis (violin), Westphalian Symphony Orchestra, Hubert Reichert (with STRAVINSKY: *Violin concerto* * (*)).

Oistrakh's performance here is a revelation. Hindemith's concerto can never before have blossomed into such rewarding lyricism. Even the orchestral contribution, under the composer himself, is strikingly passionate, and with the soloist providing many moments when the ear is ravished by the beauty of phrasing and inflection, the listener has much to enjoy. The recording is one of the very finest ever made of the combination of solo violin and orchestra.

Even set against this, which must be counted as the definitive reading on record of this attractive work, the Supraphon Czech version proves itself a formidable rival. A mid-price issue so well played, well recorded and well coupled is very welcome.

On Everest, a bright, somewhat aggressive performance which accentuates the dry, sinewy quality of Hindemith's lyricism rather than bringing out its romantic warmth (as does Oistrakh's full-priced Decca performance). It is nothing if not compelling, and it is very well played, with a brilliant, dry recording to match the music-making.

The Turnabout recording of the Hindemith *Concerto* is genuine stereo but the Stravinsky on the reverse side is not. Ivry Gitlis's account is among the most convinced and convincing on record and it is a pity that the quality of the recorded sound is not better. Detail is not well defined, and there is a certain coarseness in tutti passages which diminishes the appeal of what is in many respects a most desirable issue, particularly at the price.

(i) *Der Dämon* (concert suite from the ballet pantomime), *Op. 28;* (ii) *Nusch-Nuschi Tänze* (dance suite), *Op. 20;* (iii) *Hin und Zurück* (sketch with music), *Op. 45a.*

(M) ** Vox STGBY 662. (i) Stuttgart Soloists; (ii) Berlin Symphony Orchestra, with (iii) Claus Bock (tenor), Barbara Miller (soprano), Ulrich Schaible (baritone), Helmut Kühnle (bass); all cond. Arthur Grüber.

A useful anthology of Hindemith's music from the 1920s. *The Demon* is a dance pantomime, *Nusch-Nuschi* a one-act marionette play, and *Hin und Zurück* a one-act opera sketch in which the action and in part the music go into reverse. Thus all the music reflects Hindemith's activities for the stage at this period. The recording tends to favour the voices somewhat, and the sound quality is a little lacking in warmth, but the music has great interest and will add a new perspective for those who think of Hindemith as dry and academic, so that reservations should be put aside.

Die Harmonie der Welt (Symphony).

** (*) HMV ASD 2912. Leningrad Philharmonic Orchestra, Yevgeny Mravinsky.

Hindemith compiled this symphony from his opera, *Die Harmonie der Welt,* much in the same way as he had done in the case of *Mathis der Maler.* His own recording of it on DGG has long been deleted and remains unsurpassed. (The later recording on Everest, SDBR 3226, is less satisfactory from the standpoint of sound quality.) This powerful version from Leningrad was made at a public concert, and one is occasionally aware of the presence of the audience. The playing is of the highest order, although the brass tend to bray a little and the recording does not always negotiate climaxes without slight (though very slight) discomfort. However, any performance conducted by Mravinsky is inevitably distinguished and the symphony itself has some noble music in it. Strongly recommended.

(i) *Kammermusik No. 2: Concerto for piano and 12 solo instruments, Op. 36/1;* (ii) *Kammermusik No. 7: Organ concerto (for organ and chamber orchestra), Op. 46/2.*

*** Telefunken SAT 22539. (i) Gerhard Van Blerk (piano); (ii) Albert De Klerk (organ); both with Concerto Amsterdam.

After the success of the first set of *Kammermusik*, Hindemith embarked on a set of six, two of which are coupled on this record. The first, for piano and twelve instruments, may well remind some listeners of Bartók; the piano writing tends to favour two-part polyphony, but the score is unfailingly inventive. The *Organ concerto*, the last of the six (*Kammermusik No. 7*), was written to inaugurate a new instrument at Frankfurt Radio and is distinguished by a canon at the seventh – and indeed many other canons – during the slow movement. Alert, intelligent performances and good, well balanced recording make this a desirable acquisition.

Mathis der Maler (Symphony).

** (*) Decca SXL 6445. Suisse Romande Orchestra, Paul Kletzki – LUTOSLAWSKI: *Concerto.*** (*)

** (*) Unicorn RHS 312. London

Symphony Orchestra, Jascha Horenstein – R. STRAUSS: *Death and Transfiguration.***

(M) ** CBS Classics 61347. Philadelphia Orchestra, Eugene Ormandy – RACHMANINOV: *Symphonic dances.***

Ormandy's earlier set of *Mathis der Maler* was the only alternative to Hindemith's own much-coveted 78s. This latest account, which has been available in America for some years, is better-recorded but has formidable competition to contend with. Kletzki on Decca offers a well-prepared account (though the Suisse Romande is not the virtuoso body that Ormandy has at his fingertips), which has the advantage of superbly balanced and truthful recording. Ormandy's is a fine performance and his coupling an attractive one, but it is not at the top of the league, given present-day standards of recorded sound. Horenstein's account of the *Symphony* was the last record he made and has the merit of breadth and weight. Although the coupling is not a welcome one (there are at least two stunning accounts of *Death and Transfiguration*, namely Karajan and Reiner, that eclipse the present version), Horenstein's admirers will probably want this issue nonetheless. But a reader wanting to add a representative Hindemith disc to his library should find the Steinberg disc on DGG (see above under *Concert music*) the more satisfactory proposition.

5 Pieces for strings (Fünf Stücke), Op. 44/4.

*** Argo ZRG 763. Academy of St Martin-in-the-Fields, Neville Marriner – SCHOENBERG: *Verklaerte Nacht*; WEBERN: *5 movements.****

** Pye Ensayo NEL 2012. English Chamber Orchestra, Enrique Asensio – BRITTEN: *Simple sym-*

465

phony; RESPIGHI: *Ancient airs and dances: Suite No. 3.***

With finely etched playing in precise ensemble Marriner and the Academy transform the Hindemith *Pieces* from exercises to works of genuine imagination. This is an unexpected but worthwhile coupling for Schoenberg and Webern, with excellent recording. Asensio gives a straight-faced account, with no attempt to charm. But Hindemith would surely have approved; the effect is very like a German performance, and the individual movements are effectively characterized. The recording is good, the surfaces less so.

Symphonic metamorphoses of themes of Carl Maria von Weber.
*** Decca SXL 6398. London Symphony Orchestra, Claudio Abbado – JANÁČEK: *Sinfonietta.****
(M) ** (*) CBS Classics 61367. Cleveland Orchestra, George Szell – JANÁČEK: *Sinfonietta.** (*)

Good though Szell's account of this work is, it must yield pride of place to Abbado's version. It is a relief to find a conductor content to follow the composer's own dynamic markings and who does not succumb to the temptation to score interpretative points at the music's expense. The stopped notes on the horns at the beginning of the finale, for example, are marked *piano* and are played here so that they add a barely perceptible touch of colour to the texture. The Decca engineers balance this so musically that this effect is preserved. This admittedly unimportant touch is symptomatic of the subtlety of the conductor's approach in a performance that in every respect is of the highest quality.

Szell is less subtle and the recording less refined both in its handling of detail and in its dynamic range than Decca's account. The latter is worth the extra money, particularly if you have strong feelings about the recording of the woodwind, which is beautifully natural in the Decca version. Szell gives a reading of dazzling precision and much greater warmth than is his wont, and the record is undoubtedly good value in the medium price-range.

CHAMBER AND INSTRUMENTAL MUSIC

(i) *Kleine Kammermusik, Op. 24/2* (for wind quintet); (ii) *Harp Sonata;* (iii) *Organ sonata No. 2;* (iv) *Trumpet sonata* (for trumpet and piano).
(M) ** Supraphon SUAST 50431. (i) Czech Philharmonic Wind Quintet; (ii) Karel Patras (harp); (iii) Jiří Ropek (organ); (iv) Vaclav Junek (trumpet), Zorka Lochmanova (piano).

A useful anthology, as it gives us the excellent *Kleine Kammermusik* for wind quintet, a superb piece full of lively invention, warmth and wit. The recording is rather closely balanced, but the performance has character. The *Trumpet sonata* is something of an acquired taste, but both the succinct and attractive *Organ sonata* and the *Harp sonata* are fine works. They are given goodish performances but less than ideal recording.

Ludus tonalis: Fugues Nos. 1–12; Interludes Nos. 1–11.
(B) * (*) Pye GSGC 14150. Peter Roggenkamp (piano).

The playing is accomplished enough, and much of Hindemith's writing, which is more rewarding for the pianist than the listener, is effectively encompassed. Some of the slow interludes are beautiful, but there is on the other hand a fair amount of *Gebrauchsmusik* as well. Unfortunately the recording is somewhat shallow and wanting in sonority.

Organ sonatas Nos. 1–3.
- (B) *** Oryx ORYX 1923. Lionel Rogg (Metzler organ of Grossmunster, Zurich).
- ** Argo ZRG 663. Simon Preston (organ of St John the Evangelist, Islington).

Simon Preston's account of three Hindemith *Organ sonatas* is disappointing, and does not match the exciting Oryx record by Lionel Rogg. Preston's registration makes the reflective music sound 'churchy', and he does not approach Rogg in his presentation of the marvellous finale to the *Third Sonata*, based on the chorale *So wünsch ich ihr.* The Argo recording is technically superb, but the Oryx disc too is surprisingly good. Here Hindemith's voice speaks with far greater urgency.

Violin sonata No. 1.
- (M) ** Supraphon SUAST 50693. Petr Messiereur (violin), Jarmila Kozderková (piano) – SCHOENBERG; STRAVINSKY; WEBERN: *Pieces.***

A strong, sensitive performance to match the other three works on this well-planned disc of twentieth-century music for violin and piano duo.

Violoncello sonata (for cello and piano).
- ** (*) Argo ZRG 762. George Isaac (cello), Martin Jones (piano) – KODÁLY: *Sonata.****

The Hindemith *Sonata,* written in 1948, is a tough but attractive work, with a strong, extended passacaglia and fugato for finale. It is this last movement which George Isaac and Martin Jones play most effectively. The first two movements are not given quite the positive, sharp edge that Hindemith requires, enjoyable as the results are. Excellent recording.

Hoddinott, Alun
(born 1929)

(i) *Harp concerto, Op. 11;* (ii) *Clarinet concerto, Op. 3.*
- *** Decca SXL 6513. (i) Osian Ellis (harp); (ii) Gervase de Peyer (clarinet); both with London Symphony Orchestra, David Atherton – MATHIAS: *Piano concerto No. 3.****

The *Clarinet concerto* is an early work which Gervase de Peyer and Barbirolli gave at the 1954 Cheltenham Festival and which served to put Hoddinott on the map. Fluent as it is, it does not match the *Harp concerto* in the quality of its invention or the intensity of its atmosphere. The *Harp concerto,* written for Osian Ellis in 1957, is a most beautiful work, strongly individual in feeling and quite haunting. The textures are splendidly lucid and transparent, and the recording is a model of its kind. The soloist is given just the right degree of prominence without falsifying the perspective in any way, and every strand of the texture is clear and yet well placed in relation to the overall sound picture. A distinguished record.

(i) *Horn concerto, Op. 65;* (ii) *Piano concerto No. 2, Op. 21; Symphony No. 5, Op. 81.*
- *** Decca SXL 6606. Royal Philharmonic Orchestra, Andrew Davis, with (i) Barry Tuckwell (horn); (ii) Martin Jones (piano).

The *Fifth Symphony* is a more abrasive work than the *Third* and less immediately approachable. It is, however, splendidly powerful, and along with the early *Piano concerto No. 2* and the *Horn concerto* it reinforces Hoddinott's growing representation in the catalogue. The recording is spectacularly vivid and has tremendous range and definition.

Symphony No. 2, Op. 29; Variants for orchestra.
>   (M) ** Pye Virtuoso TPLS 13013. London Symphony Orchestra, Norman Del Mar.

Alun Hoddinott is a serialist who refuses to be channelled into formalism, and uses twelve-note technique as a spur rather than a crutch. This symphony dates from 1962 and still retains an allegiance to tonal centres; *Variants*, dating from four years later, is more ingenious in formal layout (in modern terms just as much a symphony), with six movements that are 'a double set of variants running out of parallel'. The orchestration too is here more individual, and the main point that brings a reservation is that too high a proportion of the music in both works is slow and solemn. Hoddinott should let his vivid sense of humour have freer reign, even in his most serious utterances. Fine direction from Del Mar, good recording.

Symphony No. 3, Op. 61; Sinfonietta No. 3, Op. 71; Music for orchestra: The Sun, the Great Luminary of the Universe, Op. 76.
>   *** Decca SXL 6570. London Symphony Orchestra, David Atherton.

A stunningly impressive recording of Hoddinott's *Third Symphony* which offers sound of remarkable presence, range and definition. The music too is powerfully wrought, dark in colouring and deeply imaginative. It is well laid out for the orchestra and thoroughly effective. *The Sun, the Great Luminary of the Universe* is another imposing work that strengthens this composer's claims to be among the most substantial figures on the post-war musical scene in this country. Atherton's performances with the LSO sound wholly

convincing and the disc serves, along with the *Harp concerto*, as an admirable introduction to Hoddinott's work.

Symphony No. 5: see under *Horn concerto.*

Welsh dances, Op. 15.
>   *** HMV ASD 2739. Royal Philharmonic Orchestra, Sir Charles Groves – JONES: *The Country beyond the Stars*; WILLIAMS: *Penillion.****

Hoddinott's *Welsh dances* are the equivalent of Malcolm Arnold's sets of orchestral dances, just as colourful and unpretentious – surprising pieces, perhaps, from a serialist composer but welcome ones. An attractive supplement to a nicely planned disc, featuring excellent performances and recording.

(i) String quartet No. 1, Op. 43; (ii) Clarinet sonata, Op. 50.
>   (B) ** Pye GSGC 14107. (i) Cardiff University Ensemble; (ii) Gervase de Peyer (clarinet), Eric Harrison (piano) – RAWSTHORNE: *Piano quintet; Cello sonata.***

Hoddinott's *Quartet* and *Clarinet sonata* are both recent works in his tautest, most cogent vein. The playing of the *Quartet* by an ensemble formed under the guidance of the composer (Professor of Music at Cardiff University) is strongly committed, and predictably Gervase de Peyer plays the brilliant outer movements of the *Sonata* with incomparable virtuosity and the central slow movement with lyrical intensity.

(i; ii) Violin sonata No. 3, Op. 78/1; (ii) Piano sonata No. 6.
>   *** Argo ZRG 761. (i) James Barton (violin); (ii) Martin Jones (piano) – MCCABE: *String trio.****

Hoddinott is gaining increasing representation on records. The *Third Violin sonata* was written in response to a BBC commission in 1971; the *Sixth Piano sonata* is an impressively argued and often intense piece, well worth the trouble of investigating. Those who, say, have come to enjoy the *Harp concerto* and the *Third Symphony* can safely go on to these examples of Hoddinott's instrumental music, particularly in view of the excellent advocacy he receives from these artists and the quality of the Argo recording.

(i) *Roman Dream; Trio for violin, cello and piano.*
   ** (*) Argo ZRG 691. Cardiff Festival Players, (i) with Margaret Price (soprano) – TATE: *Apparitions.****

The *Roman Dream* is a scena for soprano, piano, harp and percussion, a setting of a somewhat macabre poem by Emrys Humphreys which tells how the favourite of some Roman emperor has killed an unknown prisoner at his master's behest and is now being hunted to death in his turn. The setting is effective and atmospheric without being strongly compelling. Nor is the *Piano trio* one of Hoddinott's strongest works, though much of its invention is distinguished and the music is always craftsmanlike and intelligent. The performances are expert and the recording admirable.

Hoffmann, Johann
(1776–1822)

Mandolin concerto in D major.
   (B) ** Turnabout TV 34003S. Elfriede Kunschak (mandolin), Vienna Pro Musica Orchestra, Vinzenz Hladky – HUMMEL: *Mandolin concerto.***

This work is of considerably less musical interest than the Hummel concerto on the other side, but the playing of Elfriede Kunschak is lively enough. By no means a masterpiece, but of interest to mandolin enthusiasts.

Hoffmann, Leopold
(1730–93)

Flute concerto in D major.
   * (*) BASF BAC 3005. Hans-Martin Linde (flute), Collegium Aureum (using original instruments) – HAYDN: *Horn concerto No. 1.***

Leopold Hoffmann, a musician greatly respected in his day, was organist at St Stephen's Cathedral, Vienna, where Mozart joined him as assistant in 1791. His *Flute concerto* shows no special individuality. It is well made, but its invention is undistinguished. And the point of creating original sounds in this performance seems to some extent nullified by the microphone placing and acoustic. This produces a warm, resonant sound, but blows up the flute's image to unnatural proportions.

Holmboe, Vagn
(born 1909)

Symphony No. 8 (Sinfonia Boreale), Op. 56.
   (B) ** Turnabout TV 34168S. Royal Danish Orchestra, Jerzy Semkow – NØRGÅRD: *Constellations.* (*)

This is unquestionably a work of power and integrity. From the first note to the last the composer (a leading figure in contemporary Scandinavian music) knows where he is going, and his control of the orchestra is impressive. The opening movement is compellingly atmospheric, the second bold and strong, and the *Andante* imaginative. Most important, the finale has a strong life-assertive force which makes an immediately gripping impression. The performance is obviously a good one and the recording excellent.

Holst, Gustav
(1874–1934)

(i) *Beni Mora (oriental suite), Op. 29/1;* (ii) *St Paul's suite, Op. 29/2.*

(M) ** HMV SXLP 30126. (i) BBC Symphony Orchestra; (ii) Royal Philharmonic Orchestra; both cond. Sir Malcolm Sargent – ELGAR: *Serenade;* WARLOCK: *Capriol suite.***

Beni Mora (oriental suite), Op. 29/1; Hammersmith: Prelude and scherzo for orchestra, Op. 52; Scherzo; A Somerset rhapsody, Op. 21.

*** Lyrita SRCS 56. London Philharmonic Orchestra, Sir Adrian Boult.

Beni Mora, an attractively exotic piece that shows Holst's flair for orchestration vividly, is well played on both these discs. Sir Malcolm Sargent's account of the *St Paul's suite* is splendid, full of verve and character with very good recording. The Elgar *Serenade* is well done too, but the *Capriol* coupling is rather more controversial. The Lyrita collection is consistently successful, with outstanding performances and recording throughout. The most ambitious work here is *Hammersmith,* far more than a conventional tone picture, intensely poetic. The *Scherzo,* from a projected symphony that was never completed, is strong, confident music. The *Somerset rhapsody* similarly exploits Holst's mastery over the orchestra, and is unpretentious but very enjoyable.

Brook Green suite for strings; Nocturne for strings; St Paul's suite, Op. 29/2; (i) *Fugal concerto for flute, oboe and strings, Op. 40/2;* (ii) *Lyric movement for viola and small orchestra.*

** (*) Lyrita SRCS 34. English Chamber Orchestra, Imogen Holst, with (i) William Bennett (flute), Peter Graeme (oboe), (ii) Cecil Aronowitz (viola).

An enterprising Holst anthology, excellently played and recorded. The familiar *St Paul's suite* ought to be as popular as any work in the string repertoire, and apart from this splendid work, the record offers the pensive and searching *Lyric movement for viola and small orchestra,* one of the most beautiful of Holst's later pieces. Its addition to the catalogue is most welcome and Cecil Aronowitz gives the most convincing and persuasive account of it. The *Fugal concerto* is much less taking. It seems little more than an academic study with none of the character or inspiration of the *Lyric movement.* But the latter is so outstanding that the record is worth getting for its sake.

Capriccio for orchestra; (i) *Double concerto for 2 violins and orchestra, Op. 49; The Golden Goose (ballet music), Op. 45/1; 2 Songs without words (Country song; Marching song), Op. 22.*

*** Lyrita SRCS 44. English Chamber Orchestra, Imogen Holst, (i) with Emmanuel Hurwitz and Kenneth Sillito (violins).

There are some delightful rarities here. The *Capriccio* was originally written on an American commission for 'jazz band', but never performed because it lacked the essential folk-theme. Rescued by Imogen Holst, who has arranged it for more conventional orchestra (if with some unexpected brass and percussion), it proves an exuberant piece, with some passages not at all capriccio-like. The ballet music *The Golden Goose* was written for St Paul's Girls' School; the snippets were put together by Imogen Holst to make this attractive piece – reflecting the sharpness of an imagination that was often inspired by the needs of an occasion. The *Double concerto* is grittier but a good example of late Holst. The two *Songs without words* – much better-known than the rest – are early works, tuneful and colourful. Superb playing and recording.

Egdon Heath, Op. 47; The Perfect Fool (opera): *ballet suite, Op. 39.*
  *** Decca SXL 6006. London Philharmonic Orchestra, Sir Adrian Boult – *Hymn of Jesus.****

These excellent performances are discussed under their coupling.

A fugal overture, Op. 40/1.
  ** (*) Lyrita SRCS 37. London Philharmonic Orchestra, Sir Adrian Boult – BAX: *November Woods;* MOERAN: *Sinfonietta.****

Not one of Holst's most inspired compositions, but no one is likely to complain at its representation on record, particularly in so admirable a performance and recording. The main interest of the disc lies in the couplings.

The Planets (suite), *Op. 32.*
  *** HMV Quadraphonic Q4-ASD 3002; Stereo ASD 3002. London Symphony Orchestra, Ambrosian Singers, André Previn.
  (M) *** Decca Ace of Diamonds SDD 400. Vienna Philharmonic Orchestra, Vienna State Opera Chorus, Herbert von Karajan.
  *** HMV ASD 2301. New Philharmonia Orchestra, Ambrosian Singers, Sir Adrian Boult.
  (B) ** (*) Contour 2870 367. Bourne-mouth Symphony Orchestra and Municipal Choir, George Hurst.
  ** (*) Decca SXL 6529. Los Angeles Philharmonic Orchestra and Chorus, Zubin Mehta.
  (B) ** (*) Classics for Pleasure CFP 175. BBC Symphony Orchestra and Chorus, Sir Malcolm Sargent.
  ** DGG 2530 102. Boston Symphony Orchestra and Chorus, William Steinberg.
  ** Philips 6500 072. London Philharmonic Orchestra, John Alldis Choir, Bernard Haitink.
  ** CBS Quadraphonic MQ 31125; Stereo 73001. New York Philharmonic Orchestra with chorus, Leonard Bernstein.
  * Decca Phase 4 PFS 4184. London Philharmonic Orchestra and Chorus, Bernard Herrmann.

Previn's is an outstandingly attractive version in both its quadraphonic and its ordinary stereo formats. The recording is of demonstration quality, exceptionally clear and vivid, with many of Holst's subtleties of orchestral detail telling with greater point than on any other disc. The performance is basically traditional, yet has an appealing freshness, and it is marginally more imaginative than Boult's. The recording acoustic, however, is a trifle dry, and both the Decca records and even the Contour disc have slightly more resonance and the extra feeling of atmosphere which this creates.

Heard through quadraphonic equipment (as well as ordinary stereo) the richly atmospheric Karajan set remains very impressive indeed, and for I.M. this recording is still a marginal first choice, particularly as the Ace of Diamonds reissue has, if anything, improved on the quality of the full-priced original.

But it is the performance itself which is so fascinating. Here we have a conductor of world reputation turning his attention to a work which one has tended to think of as essentially English and transforming it into an international score. Karajan's reading is a revelation. The terrifying impact of *Mars* with those whining Wagnerian tubas we have never heard before like this. Boult finds a purity of texture in *Venus* that Karajan transmutes into a more sensuous sheen – this is the Venus of ardour rather than mysticism – but in *Mercury* the gossamer textures at the end of the piece are as striking as the impact of the central climax. *Jupiter* is bucolic and breezy, the Vienna strings bringing their own characteristic tone-colour to the big central tune, and *Saturn* and *Uranus* are outstanding. Here the Vienna Philharmonic brass comes completely into its own: the slow, sad march of *Saturn* is wonderfully cumulative in its emotional effect. The wordless chorus too at the end of *Neptune* is more atmospheric than ever before.

Boult's performance is brilliantly literal and it is given an equally clear and brilliant HMV recording. Those who find Karajan too wayward in style should be well satisfied. Boult's *Venus* is without the sensual undertones of Karajan's reading, and the beginning of the big string tune in *Jupiter* is a splendid moment of truly British orchestral tone. Yet as a whole this reading seems less imaginative than Karajan's or Previn's.

At Contour price George Hurst's Bournemouth performance is very competitive. The recording is superbly done; the rich brass sounds here often more thrilling even than with Previn. But the music's characterization is less positive and individual, and the big tune in *Jupiter* seems rather too leisurely. But if in this respect the performance is less imaginative than Sargent's Classics for Pleasure reissue, the recording is much finer and this makes a very attractive bargain.

The Los Angeles Decca recording set a new standard of sonic splendour for a work which has, since the 78 days, put recording engineers on their mettle. The power and impact of *Mars* are impressive indeed; the strings in *Venus* are richly sensuous; and the brass and timpani in *Uranus* have superb body, colour and bite. One has a few reservations about the performance, which has not the individuality of those of Karajan, Previn or Boult. Mehta's approach is literal, but not without character and impulse. As sheer sound (and Holst's score depends a good deal on the orchestral sound itself) this is very exciting indeed.

The Classics for Pleasure engineers have freshened the quality of Sargent's early stereo recording, especially on side two, where *Uranus* has splendid clarity and bite, and the organ pedals come through well in *Saturn*. Sargent's performance is full of character, with a sombre *Saturn* and the central tune in *Jupiter* given special dignity.

In the DGG American performance Steinberg draws sumptuous playing from the Boston Symphony, and he is helped by reverberant recording that makes this a feast of sound. Anyone who wants to wallow in the opulence and colour of this extrovert work will certainly be delighted, the more so, one suspects, when Steinberg departs in certain respects from British convention. *Mars* in particular is intensely exciting. At his fast tempo he may get to his fortissimos a little early, but rarely has the piece sounded so menacing on record. The testing point for most will no doubt be *Jupiter*, and there Steinberg the excellent Elgarian comes to the fore, giving a wonderful *nobilmente* swagger. It is sad that bad tape-editing – at least one presumes that that is the explanation – has snipped a bar or two out.

Haitink starts off *Mars* at a very slow tempo, and dissects the texture almost as though he were putting it under a musical microscope. The hairpin dynamic marks, for example, are very precise, but the result hardly sweeps one away. *Venus* here is certainly the bringer of peace but not of love. *Mercury* brings reminders of

Strauss and Rimsky-Korsakov. *Jupiter* sounds the more noble for restrained treatment. And so on. It is all very different from usual, and with fine playing and unobtrusively clean recording it will please many. But it is plainly not for those who want excitement from this colourful work.

Bernstein's account is brilliantly played but curiously literal, and the CBS sound is clear but lacking richness in the bass to balance the bright treble. The performance is never less than interesting, but not nearly as compelling as Hurst's record, which costs far less. We have been unable to obtain the quadraphonic version.

Unconventionally slow tempi from Bernard Herrmann go with surprisingly slack playing. It was a good idea to record *The Planets* in Phase 4, but such an account fails to exploit the possibilities.

VOCAL AND CHORAL MUSIC

(i) *Choral fantasia, Op. 51;* (ii) *Psalm 86.*

    (M) *** HMV HQS 1260. (i) Janet Baker (mezzo-soprano); (ii) Ian Partridge (tenor); both with Purcell Singers, English Chamber Orchestra, Ralph Downes (organ), Imogen Holst – FINZI: *Dies Natalis.****

Holst's *Choral fantasia* – a setting of words written by Robert Bridges in commemoration of Purcell – was one of his later works, and probably the unusual combination of performers has prevented more frequent performances. It is not an easy work to grasp, and Holst's extremes of dynamic tend to hinder rather than help. But it is well worth getting to know, and so is the setting of Psalm 86 with its expressive tenor part, sung beautifully by Ian Partridge. In the *Fantasia* Janet Baker once again shows her supreme quality as

a recording artist. The recording is outstanding, and the success of both performances owes much to the inspired direction of the composer's daughter, Imogen Holst.

Choral symphony, Op. 41.

    *** HMV SAN 354. Felicity Palmer (soprano), London Philharmonic Choir and Orchestra, Sir Adrian Boult.

Though the Keats poems give a faded air to this ambitious work, Boult and his performers demonstrate the beauty and imagination of the writing. Holst even manages to set the *Ode on a Grecian Urn* without being overfaced; and until the finale the writing is always taut and intensely individual. The finale is altogether looser-limbed, but Boult in this totally unsentimental performance manages to draw it together. As samplers try the strange *Prelude* with its monotone mutterings or the seven-in-a-bar energy of the *Bacchanal*. A fine and unjustly neglected work superbly performed and recorded.

6 Choruses with medieval lyrics (Drinking song; Love song; How mighty are the Sabbaths; Intercession; Good Friday; Before sleep); 7 Part-songs, Op. 44 (Say, who is this?; O love, I complain; Angel spirits of sleep; When first we met; Sorrow and joy; Love on my heart from heaven fell; Assemble, all ye maidens).

    *** Argo ZRG 5495. Purcell Singers, English Chamber Orchestra, Imogen Holst.

As the *Hymn of Jesus* bears witness, Holst had a rare gift for writing freely and flexibly for chorus, and these less ambitious choruses and part-songs show the subtlety of his feelings for English words. He would never be bound by arbitrary limits, and so with the utmost naturalness his writing here breaks free from rhythmic norms (his use of five-beat and seven-beat measures is always effective), and more important he ranges through some bitonal and polytonal effects that are far more adventurous musically than they actually sound. Under the direction of the composer's daughter, a magical interpreter of her father's works, the Purcell Singers make light of the technical difficulties, and the recording is first-rate.

Hymn of Jesus, Op. 37.
> *** Decca SXL 6006. BBC Symphony Orchestra and Chorus, Sir Adrian Boult – *Egdon Heath; Perfect Fool.****

Fine performances of *Hymn of Jesus* and *Egdon Heath* are suitable leavened here with a brilliant and flashingly colourful account of *The Perfect Fool* ballet suite. The mysical element of *The Planets* (with phrases borrowed from *Neptune*) is very apparent in the *Hymn*, which has many pages of beauty and some splendidly stirring climaxes – such is the dynamic range of the recording here. The music is ideal for gramophone listening, especially in such a superb performance as is given by Sir Adrian. Those willing to explore and who like the Holst idiom will find this work becomes more attractive with each hearing. The bleak sombre music for *Egdon Heath* is hauntingly evocative and provides yet another contrast. The recording of all three works is of Decca's highest quality.

(i) *12 Songs, Op. 48* (to words by Humbert Wolfe); (ii) *Ave Maria, Op. 9; Of one that is so bright and fair; Bring us in good ale; Pastorale; The Swallow; The Song of the Blacksmith; 3 Welsh folksongs.*
> ** Argo ZRG 512. (i) Peter Pears (tenor), Benjamin Britten (piano); (ii) Purcell Singers, Imogen Holst.

This is essentially a record for the Holst specialist rather than the general listener. Holst's earlier songs dating from 1900 are not always very individual, and some of them are frankly very ordinary indeed. Even the 1929 settings of Humbert Wolfe are rather uneven in appeal and the composer himself did not seem to arrive at a unifying style. Some seem deliberately bare, while others are much richer, and the words do not always provide the obvious clue to the composer's choice. Peter Pears and Benjamin Britten bring a characteristic creative quality to the performances, but this only serves to highlight the difference between the less interesting songs and the one or two masterpieces. The choral singing is excellent.

Collection: *6 Canons for equal voices (If you love songs; Lovely Venus; The Fields of Sorrow; David's Lament for Jonathan; Evening on the Moselle; If 'twere the time of lilies); 2 Carols with oboe and viola (A Welcome Song; Terly, terlow); Evening Watch* (motet), *Op. 43/1; Jesus, Thou the Virgin-born* (carol), *Op. 20b; 4 Songs, Op. 35, for voice and violin (Jesu sweet, now will I sing; My soul has nought but fire and ice; I sing of a maiden; My leman is so true); Terzetto for flute, oboe, and viola; This have I done for my true love, Op. 34/1.*
> *** Argo ZRG 5497. Peter Pears (tenor), Richard Adeney (flute), Cecil Aronowitz (viola), Norbert Brainin (violin), Peter Graeme (oboe), Viola Tunnard (piano), Purcell Singers, Imogen Holst.

This collection of vocal and instrumental music, the third of Argo's Holst records made under the direction of the composer's daughter, brings together an illuminating group of works, easy and difficult, simple and highly experimental.

Technically the most interesting is the *Terzetto*. Holst wrote it right at the end of his career as an experiment in polytonality, with each of the three instruments using a different key signature. At the time he was not even sure whether he liked it himself, but as Imogen Holst pointed out – and the record bears witness – to ears thirty years later it sounds delightfully pointed and even charming, not least because of the endlessly fascinating rhythms. The choral pieces range from simple and imaginative carol-settings (plus a very long unaccompanied one, *This have I done*) to crisp canons which, like the *Terzetto*, experiment in lines following contrasted key signatures. The *Four Songs*, sung beautifully by Peter Pears, are also examples of Holst's austere style, but were written at roughly the same apparently expansive period of *The Planets*. Sensitive, committed performances and outstandingly clear recording.

OPERA

(i) *Savitri* (chamber opera in 1 act), *Op. 25* (complete recording); (ii) *Choral Hymns from the Rig Veda (3rd group)*, *Op. 26/3*.
*** Argo ZNF 6. (i) Janet Baker (mezzo-soprano), Robert Tear (tenor), Thomas Hemsley (bass), Purcell Singers, English Chamber Orchestra, Imogen Holst; (ii) Purcell Singers (sopranos and altos), Osian Ellis (harp).

There are few chamber operas so beautifully scaled as Holst's *Savitri*. The simple story is taken from a Sanskrit source – Savriti, a woodcutter's wife, cleverly outwits Death who has come to take her husband – and Holst with beautiful feeling for atmosphere sets it in the most restrained way. With light texture and many slow tempi, it is a work which

can fall apart in an uncommitted performance, but the interpreters here could hardly be more imaginative, and Janet Baker in particular produces some of her most intense and expressive singing. There is no mistaking that the piece is one of Holst's most perfectly conceived works. Aptly the *Rig Veda Hymns* which make the fill-up are also from a Sanskrit source, and the composer himself suggested that the last of them could, if necessary, be used as a prelude to *Savitri*. The opening *Hymn to the Dawn* brings echoes of *Neptune* from *The Planets*, and the fast and rhythmically fascinating *Hymn to the Waters* is even more attractive. Beautifully atmospheric recording to match intense and sensitive performances.

Honegger, Arthur (1892–1955)

Concertino for piano and orchestra.
(B) ** Turnabout TV 34130S. Walter Klien (piano), Vienna Pro Musica Orchestra, Heinrich Hollreiser – BARTÓK: *Rhapsody;* JANÁČEK: *Concertino;* STRAVINSKY: *Capriccio.***

This lightweight Honegger work makes a welcome contribution to a well-chosen anthology of short twentieth-century works for piano and orchestra. The recording quality is not very brilliant, but acceptable at the price.

Violoncello concerto (in one movement).
(M) ** Supraphon 110 0604. Milos Sádlo (cello), Czech Philharmonic Orchestra, Václav Neumann – SHOSTAKOVICH: *Concerto No. 1.***

Honegger's *Cello concerto* is attractively lyrical, a work with the occasional exotic overtone, and in its unpretentious way well worth knowing. It makes a charming coupling for the magnificent Shostakovich *Concerto*. Good recording.

Pacific 231.
> *** Decca SXL 6065. Suisse Romande Orchestra, Ernest Ansermet – DUKAS: *L'Apprenti sorcier;* RAVEL: *Boléro; La Valse* ***
> ** HMV Quadraphonic Q4-ASD 2989; Stereo ASD 2989. City of Birmingham Orchestra, Louis Frémaux – IBERT: *Divertissement;* POULENC: *Les Biches;* SATIE: *Gymnopédies.*** (*)

The polyphonic climax of Honegger's orchestral portrayal of a railway locomotive needs reasonable clarity of recording to achieve its maximum impact. The reverberation is perhaps not quite perfectly judged on Ansermet's disc, but the power of the mighty engine is marvellously conveyed and its surging lyricism too, while the grinding tension of the final braking gives this mechanical monster an almost human personality. This is much preferable to the HMV version, which is almost oppressively reverberant. Some might like the almost overwhelming effect of the quadraphonic ambience, but there is no doubt that the Decca engineering creates more bite.

Symphony No. 2 (for strings and trumpet); (i) *A Christmas cantata.*
> (M) ** Decca Ace of Diamonds SDD 189. Suisse Romande Orchestra, Ernest Ansermet, (i) with Pierre Mollet (baritone), Radio Lausanne Choir and Children's Chorus.

Ansermet's performance is vigorous and spirited, and it is well recorded. The Suisse Romande strings, however, are no match for those of the Orchestre de Paris in their now-deleted Münch version on HMV, nor for the Czech Philharmonic strings in Serge Baudo's Supraphon

account which is sporadically available. The Berlin version under Karajan (see below) is, of course, in a class of its own. The *Christmas cantata* dates from 1953, and much of it was written in hospital during a painful illness which brought the composer's early death a couple of years later. It is an effective and often moving work which is enjoying increasing popularity. The performance is committed, and though problems of intonation crop up from time to time, they do not detract from the overall pleasure this disc gives.

Symphony No. 2 (for strings and trumpet); *Symphony No. 3 (Liturgique).*
> ⊛ *** DGG 2530 068. Berlin Philharmonic Orchestra, Herbert von Karajan.

An altogether marvellous record. The playing of the Berlin strings in the wartime *Second Symphony* is superb, sumptuous in tone and refined in texture. The performance is quite masterly and the recording is splendidly balanced and richly sonorous. This is a first recommendation not only for this coupling but for both works irrespective of coupling. Karajan's sensitive feeling for texture can be seen at its finest in the coda of the *Liturgique,* which is quite magical here.

Symphony No. 3 (Liturgique).
> ** (*) HMV ASD 2964. Leningrad Philharmonic Orchestra, Yevgeny Mravinsky – BARTÓK: *Music for strings, percussion and celesta.** (*)
> (B) * (*) Decca Eclipse ECS 640. Paris Conservatoire Orchestra, Robert Denzler – CHAUSSON: *Symphony.** (*)

Honegger's symphonies are currently neglected in the concert hall, though the wartime *Second Symphony* for strings is occasionally performed. Here the *Third* is given an urgent, electrifying performance by the Leningrad Orchestra, recorded live at a concert. The impact of the opening *Dies irae* is overwhelming, with the sound very close, less analytical than in some rival versions. But with the violence of the war music (*Dona nobis pacem*) committedly conveyed, this is a performance to make converts. After Karajan or Mravinsky, the Denzler is a less attractive proposition. The performance is nowhere near as polished as Karajan's or Mravinsky's, and the sound, though acceptable at this price level, is not comparable with any of the full-price versions.

Symphony No. 3 (Liturgique); Symphony No. 4 (Deliciae Basiliensis).
> ** Decca SXL 6394. Suisse Romande Orchestra, Ernest Ansermet.

The *Fourth Symphony*, written for Paul Sacher and the Basle Chamber Orchestra (hence its title), is new to the domestic catalogue. It is a charming work, full of character and invention, and probably the most relaxed, unpretentious and successful of the cycle. Quite frankly the playing here does not do full justice to its lightness and wit; the orchestra is neither as alert nor as sensitive in its phrasing as one could wish. However, the recording is extremely fine.

Collection of piano music: *Le Cahier romand; Deux Esquisses; Hommage à Albert Roussel; Trois pièces; Sept pièces brèves; Prélude, arioso, fuguette sur le nom de Bach; Sarabande; Souvenir de Chopin; Toccata et variations.*
> (B) ** (*) Turnabout TV 34377S. Jürg von Vintschger (piano).

This useful disc presents a survey of a neglected aspect of Honegger's output, his piano music. Some of it is highly attractive: *Hommage à Ravel* from the *Trois pièces* is beautifully wrought, and Jürg von Vintschger plays with total commitment. The sound is fully accept-able, and readers who want to investigate this side of Honegger's musical personality can do so at little cost and with remarkably rich rewards.

Le Roi David (oratorio).
> (M) ** (*) Decca Ace of Diamonds GOS 602/3. Suzanne Danco (soprano), Marie-Lise de Montmollin, Pauline Martin (mezzo-sopranos), Michel Hamel (tenor), Stéphane Audel (narrator), Suisse Romande Orchestra, Ernest Ansermet – RAVEL: *Shéhérazade.****
> (M) ** Vanguard VSD 2117/8. Netania Davrath (soprano), Jean Preston (mezzo-soprano), Marvin Sorenson (tenor), Martial Singher (narrator), Utah Symphony Orchestra, Maurice Abravanel – MILHAUD: *La Création du monde.***

Le Roi David is full of atmospheric pageant and was for years Honegger's best-known work (apart from *Pacific 231*). Of these two performances Ansermet's is the more idiomatic and is better sung. The recording comes from the 1950s but is remarkably good for the period, albeit cut at a slightly lower level than its competitor. The fill-up is Danco's memorable *Shéhérazade*, which despite a certain pallor – this too is cut at a low level – is a magical performance.

Hovhaness, Alan
(born 1911)

Fra Angelico, Op. 220; Symphony No. 11, Op. 186.
> (M) ** Unicorn UNS 243. Royal Philharmonic Orchestra, the composer.

Hovhaness is enormously prolific, as a glance at the opus numbers he has so far reached will show. There are at least twenty-two symphonies now. These scores have more colour than substance and suggest the cinema rather than the concert hall. The performances under the composer may be assumed to be authoritative, and the recordings are satisfactory though somewhat wanting in weight of string sonority.

Saint Vartan symphony, Op. 80.
** (*) Unicorn RHS 317. National Philharmonic Orchestra, the composer.

Hovhaness's *St Vartan symphony* comes from 1951 and celebrates the stand made by Vartan Marmikonian in A.D. 451 against the Persian invaders who imposed Zoroastrianism on an unwilling Armenia. Hovhaness himself has Armenian blood in his cosmopolitan veins. This extraordinary work is in twenty-four movements and has more colour and exoticism than genuine musical substance. It tends to sprawl somewhat and concentrates on atmosphere rather than argument. The performance is presumably authoritative and the recording has plenty of presence and clarity. Some may be tempted on hearing this work to feel that perhaps the Persians had a point.

Howells, Herbert
(born 1892)

Concerto for string orchestra.
*** HMV ASD 3020. London Philharmonic Orchestra, Sir Adrian Boult – BLISS: *Music for strings.********

The Howells *Concerto for strings*, dedicated to Sir Adrian, makes an excellent companion piece to the Bliss *Music for strings*, another virtuoso string work which stands at the heart of the English tradition. A vigorous and attractive opening movement leads to an elegiac slow movement written in memory of Howells's son as well as of Elgar. The finale is a little long for its material but hardly detracts from a finely written work, here given an understanding and vigorous performance. Fine recording.

Organ: (i) *Psalm prelude, Op. 32/1;* Choral: (ii) *2 Carol-Anthems (Here is the little door; Sing lullaby); Collegium Regale (Jubilate; Magnificat; Nunc dimittis; Te Deum); Motet on the Death of President Kennedy: Take him, earth, for cherishing; St Paul's Service: Magnificat; Nunc dimittis.*
*** Argo ZRG 507. (i) Andrew Davis (organ); (ii) King's College Chapel Choir, David Willcocks.

The outstanding item in this valuable collection of Howells's music is the setting of Anglican morning and evening services he wrote for this very choir of King's College, Cambridge (hence the subtitle *Collegium Regale*). Few settings of Matins and Evensong rival it in the sensitivity and aptness of word treatment, and the *Gloria* is almost unequalled in Anglican church music for the exuberance and intensity of joy it conveys. Not that the King's Choir quite launches into the music as one knows from live performances in the past they can do. Even so it is good to have this music so well performed, and the St Paul's setting of Evensong (more obviously influenced by the French impressionists) is welcome on record too, not to mention the other less well-known items. Excellent recording quality.

Hymnus Paradisi.
*** HMV ASD 2600. Heather Harper (soprano), Robert Tear (tenor), Bach Choir, King's College Chapel Choir, New Philharmonia Orchestra, David Willcocks.

Howells is one of the most respected English composers of the older generation, though his music has made little real headway in the concert hall. *Hymnus Paradisi* is a dignified and beautifully wrought work but, more important, it is both moving and powerful. Howells is not the most original of English composers but on the strength of this he is surely among the most civilized and disciplined. The performance is an eloquent one and the recording exemplary. All who care about English music should investigate this issue.

Hsien Hsing-hai (and others)
(20th century)

Piano concerto (Yellow River) (communally adapted from cantata by Central Philharmonic Society).
* * (*) Decca Phase 4 PFS 4299. Ilana Vered (piano), National Philharmonic Orchestra, Elgar Howarth – MOZART: *Piano concerto No. 21.**

The *Yellow River concerto*, written by a committee of Chinese musicians rather than by a single composer, is as crude a piece as you would expect from such a source. Echoes of Tchaikovsky, Rachmaninov, Dvořák and Hollywood film scores, not to mention Negro spirituals and *The Sound of Music*, make an extraordinary mixture, which just conceivably might acquire unthinking popularity with a Royal Albert Hall audience. Coarse recording to match.

Hummel, Johann
(1778–1837)

(i) *Bassoon concerto in F major;* (ii) *Concertino in G major for piano and orchestra, Op. 73* (arr. of *Mandolin concerto); 'La Galante' Rondeau for piano, Op. 120.*
* (B) *** Turnabout TV 34348S. (i) George Zukerman (bassoon), Württemberg Chamber Orchestra, Joerg Faerber; (ii) Martin Galling (piano), Berlin Symphony Orchestra, C. A. Bünte.

Hummel's *Bassoon concerto* is a winner, with all the charm, if perhaps not quite the depth, of the famous work by Mozart. It is played with real appreciation of its genial humour by George Zukerman, who shows himself also an uncommonly good musician in matters of technique and phrasing. The *Concertino* with its immediately catchy dotted melody in the first movement has an equally *galant* quality and its amiable chatter is never empty. Again good playing, and an excellent recording for both works: the clicks you hear on side two, incidentally, are not pressing faults but the bassoonist's busy keys.

Mandolin concerto in G major.
* (B) ** Turnabout TV 34003S. Edith Bauer-Slais (mandolin), Vienna Pro Musica Orchestra, Vinzenz Hladky – HOFFMANN: *Mandolin concerto.***

Mandolin enthusiasts will be glad to have this coupling; others might find the limitation of tone-colour a drawback, although Hummel exploits the instrument's possibilities skilfully. The invention is attractive if not memorable. The soloist here makes the most of the work, and the accompaniment is sound.

(i) *Piano concerto in A minor, Op. 85*‡
(i; ii) *Double concerto in G major for piano and violin (and orchestra), Op.17.*
* (B) * (*) Turnabout TV 34028S. (i) Martin Galling (piano); (ii) Susanne Lautenbacher (violin); both

479

with Stuttgart Philharmonic Orchestra, Alexander Paulmüller.

Hummel's *A minor Piano concerto* is conventional structurally but uses attractive melodic material, operatic in style. The work is well played and recorded here, and lovers of the early-nineteenth-century piano concerto will find this an agreeable addition to the repertory. The *Double concerto* is less interesting as a work and not improved by a highly modulated recording which places the soloists rather on top of the listener.

Piano concerto in B minor, Op. 89.
> (B) ** Turnabout TV 34073S. Martin Galling (piano), Innsbruck Symphony Orchestra, Robert Wagner – HAYDN: *Piano concerto.***

Hummel's *B minor Concerto* is not so attractive as its better-known companion in A minor, Op. 85, but it has some good tunes and is well made. There is some adventurous writing for the horns in the slow movement, but the playing here (as of the orchestra generally) is not refined enough to do it full justice. The soloist, however, is excellent, and the stereo recording is good.

Fantasy ('Potpourri') in G minor for viola and orchestra (based on *Il mio tesoro* from Mozart's *Don Giovanni*, Act 2).
> (B) ** Turnabout TV 34079S. Ernst Wallfisch (viola), Württemberg Chamber Orchestra, Joerg Faerber – M. HAYDN: *Double concerto.***

Hummel's *Fantasy on 'Il mio tesoro'* is quite an entertaining piece, showing how the *potpourri* of the period served as the Radio One of its day, keeping the 'pop' tunes of the eighteenth and nineteenth century alive outside the opera house. It is quite well played, the viola rather forward in the recording balance.

Introduction, theme and variations in F minor for oboe and orchestra, Op. 102.
> ** EMI EMD 5505. Han de Vries (oboe), Amsterdam Philharmonic Orchestra, Anton Kersjes – BELLINI and KALLIWODA: *Concertos.***

This is rather a conventional Hummel display piece, but it is given a sprightly performance, and for those wanting the Kalliwoda it should be acceptable.

Rondo brillant on a Russian theme (for piano and orchestra).
> (M) * Unicorn UNS 227. Felicja Blumenthal (piano), Vienna Chamber Orchestra, Hellmuth Froschauer – FIELD: *Piano concerto No. 1.***

This is an overlong piece based on a Russian folk-song in praise of raspberries. Miss Blumenthal does her best with it, but the basic melody is rather banal and Hummel's treatment of it vapid.

Septet in D minor (for flute, oboe, horn, viola, violoncello, double bass and piano), *Op. 74; Piano quintet in E flat major* (for violin, viola, violoncello, double bass and piano), *Op. 87.*
> (M) *** Oiseau-Lyre SOL 290. Melos Ensemble, Lamar Crowson (piano).

These two most engaging works show the composer at his most melodically fecund and his musical craftsmanship at its most apt. One can see here how Hummel charmed nineteenth-century audiences into regarding him as a greater composer than he was, for his facility and skill at shaping and balancing a movement can be impressive. It is the ideas themselves (as in all music) that make or break the structure, and here they are entirely appropriate to music designed in the first instance to entertain. This these works certainly do in such spontaneous and polished performances, and this is the best Hummel record in the catalogue.

Clarinet quartet in E flat.

*** Oiseau-Lyre DSLO 501. The Music Party (with Alan Hacker, clarinet) – CRUSELL: *Quartet.****

A delectable work, played as beautifully as the Crusell coupling. This is an altogether outstanding disc.

Humperdinck, Engelbert
(1854–1921)

Hänsel und Gretel (opera in 3 acts): complete recording.

** (*) RCA ARL 2 0637 (2 discs). Anna Moffo, Helen Donath, Lucia Popp, Arleen Auger (sopranos), Christa Ludwig (mezzosoprano), Dietrich Fischer-Dieskau (baritone), Bavarian Radio Chorus and Orchestra, Kurt Eichhorn.

** Telefunken SAT 22521/2. Renate Holm (soprano), Ingeborg Springer (mezzo-soprano), Peter Schreier (tenor), Gisela Schröter (contralto), Theo Adam (bass), Dresden Choir and State Orchestra, Otmar Suitner.

There are some fine solo performances on the RCA set, notably from Helen Donath as Gretel and Christa Ludwig as the witch, and Kurt Eichhorn's direction is vigorous, with excellent orchestral playing and full, atmospheric recording. It is a pity that a more boyish-sounding singer than Anna Moffo could not have been chosen for the role of Hänsel, but all told this is a colourful and enjoyable account of a unique, eternally fresh opera.

The fascinating difference between the Telefunken set and the RCA (and indeed previous LP recordings) is the casting of the witch, pantomime-fashion, for a male singer. Peter Schreier makes a splendid characterization, with singing of striking bravura, and fully justifies the experiment. Hänsel (Ingeborg Springer) and Gretel (Renate Holm) have voices slightly more contrasted than usual, and Theo Adam, Gisela Schröter and Renate Krahmer (a charming Sandman) complete a strong cast. This is very enjoyable and the recording has plenty of atmosphere. It is, however, somewhat lacking in brilliance, and the resonance seems to damp down the sparkle of the performance in places.

Ibert, Jacques
(1890–1962)

Divertissement for chamber orchestra.

(M) *** Decca Ace of Diamonds SDD 144. Paris Conservatoire Orchestra, Jean Martinon – BIZET: *Jeux d'enfants*; SAINT-SAËNS: *Danse macabre; Le rouet.****

** HMV Quadraphonic Q4-ASD 2989; Stereo ASD 2989. City of Birmingham Orchestra, Louis Frémaux – HONEGGER: *Pacific 231*; POULENC: *Les Biches*; SATIE: *Gymnopédies.*** (*)

The recording throughout the Ace of Diamonds collection is in Decca's highest class. The *Divertissement* is played with wit and superb aplomb and is alone worth the price of the disc. The couplings are almost equally desirable.

The reverberant acoustic (exaggerated by the quadraphonic effect) of the HMV recording is less than ideal for Ibert's witty piece, and while the performance is vigorous and warm-hearted it is not in the same class as Martinon's version.

Ippolitov-Ivanov, Mikhail
(1859–1935)

Caucasian sketches: suite.

(M) ** Vanguard VCS 10060. Utah Symphony Orchestra, Maurice Abravanel – GLIÈRE: *Russian sailors' dance;* RIMSKY-KORSAKOV: *Antar.***

Ippolitov-Ivanov's *Caucasian sketches* have long been known only for the final number, the *Procession of the Sardar,* but the rest of the suite, with its reminders of Rimsky-Korsakov, is worth exploring. The Utah recording is clearer than the only alternative version (on Turnabout) and its coupling of *Antar* is worthwhile. Abravanel treats the music in a sophisticated manner, and he is helped by the wide dynamic range of the recording and some excellent solo wind playing from the orchestra. Some might feel that a little more flair and gusto would be appropriate in this picture-postcard imagery, and in that respect the Turnabout record (TV 34218S) is superior. As a bonus Abravanel offers a lively performance of Glière's *Russian sailors' dance.*

Ireland, John
(1879–1962)

Concertino pastorale; Downland suite: Minuet and Elegy (only)*; Epic march; The Holy Boy: Prelude; A London overture.*

*** Lyrita SRCS 31. London Philharmonic Orchestra, Sir Adrian Boult.

The *Concertino pastorale* has a really beautiful *Threnody* for its slow movement, and the first movement is attractive too.

The *Epic march,* with its patriotism tempered by the composer's essential distaste for bombast, deserves to be more popular. The pieces from the *Downland suite* are readily enjoyable, but clearly Ireland's best orchestral work was the *London overture.* The recording here gives even more bite to the music than the HMV version listed below, and this is very enjoyable indeed.

Piano concerto in E flat major.

** (*) Lyrita SRCS 36. Eric Parkin (piano), London Philharmonic Orchestra, Sir Adrian Boult – *These Things Shall Be.** (*)

John Ireland's only *Piano concerto* is worthy to rank with the finest twentieth-century works in this form. It has distinctive melodic inspiration throughout all three movements, and its poetic lyricism, if not forward-looking, is in the ageless tradition of the greatest English music. The work's potentialities are fully realized in this sensitive performance by Eric Parkin, and there is some obviously dedicated playing by the LPO under Boult. The recording is outstanding technically, and it is a great pity that the reverberant acoustic rather blows up the textures of the music – piano and orchestra alike – detracting from the intimacy of the presentation.

The Forgotten Rite: prelude; (i) *Legend for piano and orchestra; Mai Dun* (symphonic rhapsody)*; Satyricon overture.*

** (*) Lyrita SRCS 32. London Philharmonic Orchestra, Sir Adrian Boult, (i) with Eric Parkin (piano).

It seems churlish to welcome this enterprising collection with anything but open arms, but glad as one is to have the music on disc, it is impossible to give the record an unqualified recommendation – not because of the performances, which are beautifully made and most sensitively conducted, but because the music itself is disappointingly uneven. There is an attractive pervading lyricism throughout, of course, but much of the writing simply is not positive enough to command the attention on repeated hearings. The *Legend for piano and orchestra* is a good example. This has much of the atmosphere of the *Concerto*, yet the music itself is rhapsodically aimless. The *Satyricon overture* has a well characterized principal theme, reminiscent of the *London overture*, but as a whole lacks conciseness of thought. *The Forgotten Rite* has a haunting opening harmonic figure, but the big rhapsodic climax, although skilfully scored, is not memorable. *Mai Dun*, symbolizing the life of the inhabitants of a prehistoric fort and earthworks near Dorchester (the pseudonym was Thomas Hardy's), is in the last resort melodramatic.

A London overture.
> *** HMV ASD 2305. London Symphony Orchestra, Sir John Barbirolli – BAX: *Tintagel*; DELIUS: *Collection.*** (*)

Barbirolli's performance of the *London overture* is a great success. The pithy main theme has character, and the warm romanticism of the middle section is not allowed to overwhelm the work's conciseness (as in other Ireland pieces). Ripe, rich recording.

The Overlanders (suite) (arr. Charles Mackerras); *Scherzo and Cortege on themes from 'Julius Caesar'* (arr. Geoffrey Bush); *2 Symphonic studies* (arr. Geoffrey Bush); *Tritons* (symphonic prelude).
> ** Lyrita SRCS 45. London Philharmonic Orchestra, Sir Adrian Boult.

This disc obviously scrapes the bottom of the barrel of Ireland's existent orchestral music by including the very early *Tritons prelude*. Both the suite arranged by Charles Mackerras and the *Symphonic studies* come from the incidental music Ireland wrote for the film *The Overlanders*. The *Symphonic studies* were arranged by Geoffrey Bush, who also turned a series of musical fragments into the *Julius Caesar* pieces. As can be seen, then, there are other hands besides Ireland's in the finished products, but admirers of his music will be glad to have this sympathetically played and well recorded selection available.

(i) *Sextet for clarinet, horn, and string quartet;* (ii; iii) *Fantasy-Sonata for clarinet and piano in E flat major;* (iv; iii) *Violoncello sonata in G minor.*
> ** (*) Lyrita SRCS 59. (i) Melos Ensemble; (ii) Gervase de Peyer (clarinet); (iii) Eric Parkin (piano); (iv) André Navarra (cello).

The *Sextet* is an early work (1898), inspired by a performance of the Brahms *Clarinet quintet*. Its Brahmsian flavour is unmistakable, and the music has an attractive autumnal mood. The *Cello sonata* is both passionate and rhapsodic in feeling, and the performance here catches its romantic flair, even though the cello tone does not display much variety of colour, partly because of the close balance against a reverberant background. The performance of the *Fantasy-Sonata* is marvellously persuasive, and this emerges as the most memorable of the three works recorded here.

Violin sonatas Nos. 1 in D minor; 2 in A minor.
> *** Lyrita SRCS 64. Yfrah Neaman (violin), Eric Parkin (piano).

John Ireland's *First Violin sonata* is an early work, dating from 1909. It is an attractive, spontaneous piece, with a fine slow movement and a characteristically gay, dance-like finale. The *Second Sonata* was composed during the First World War, and made a great success at its first performance, by Albert Sammons and William Murdoch in 1917. It is a splendid work, and admirers of Ireland's *Piano concerto* are urged to discover its qualities in this very fine performance, which catches so well the atmosphere of the first movement. This is genuinely inspired and shows the composer at his most imaginative. After the gentle eloquence of the song-like main theme of the slow movement, the lightweight finale may seem insubstantial, but its invention is attractive and the work as a whole is very rewarding. With dedicated performances and excellent recording this disc is highly recommendable.

These Things Shall Be (for baritone solo, chorus and orchestra).
** (*) Lyrita SRCS 36. John Carol Case (baritone), London Philharmonic Choir and Orchestra, Sir Adrian Boult – *Piano concerto.*** (*)

John Ireland chose exactly the right moment to write *These Things Shall Be* (1936–7). The words, taken from *A Vista* by John Addington Symonds, are optimistic in an almost unbelievably naïve way, but during the war when things were not going well, this direct life-assertive faith in a possible Utopian state of human relationships suited the need of public mood and morale exactly. One can remember Prom performances of great power and eloquence, and certainly the music, with its mixture of Elgarian *nobilmente* and Waltonian declamation (without the dissonant bite of *Belshazzar's Feast*), is very effective and easy to enjoy. This recorded performance has less thrust and conviction than those far-off wartime accounts, but it is well sung and played, and if you turn up the volume – for the recording is very good indeed – a

good deal of the impact of the writing comes over. The music itself is melodic, spacious in phrase and very readily enjoyable at its face value.

Ishii, Maki
(20th century)

So-Gu II (for gagaku and symphony orchestra).
*** EMI Quadraphonic Q4-EMD 5508. Gagaku ensemble, Japan Philharmonic Orchestra, Seiji Ozawa – TAKEMITSU: *Cassiopeia.****

So-Gu II is a combination of two works performed simultaneously, symbolic of the meeting of Eastern and Western cultures. The Gagaku ensemble is a mixture of wind instruments (mostly reed) and percussion. Traditionally the choice of flow and tempi is spontaneous in performance, although here there is a written score. The Western orchestral group also has written music to play. The two different scores (called *Gu* and *So* respectively) are combined quite spontaneously in performance, and the conductor decides how to make them fit. There is a broad pattern, and here Ozawa begins with *So* for orchestra, and introduces the Gagaku contribution after the first tutti. In the centre of the work the orchestra pauses to allow for a solo section for the Gagaku group, then they play together again and after a climax of considerable power the orchestra is left to finish softly. With quadraphonic sound to spread the image widely the sounds here are certainly exotic, fascinating and sometimes even alarming. However, a recording can only fix this single performance in time: on the next occasion everything might be very different!

Ives, Charles
(1874–1954)

*Holidays symphony (*also called *New England holidays) (Washington's birthday; Decoration day; The Fourth of July; Thanksgiving).*

(B) ** Turnabout TV 34146S. Dallas Symphony Orchestra, Donald Johanos.

The so-called *Holidays symphony* is made up of four fine Ives pieces normally heard separately. The first three are well enough known, but the fourth – full title: *Thanksgiving and/or Forefathers' Day* – is a rarity, bringing in a full choir to sing a single verse of a hymn. The performances here are enthusiastic but a little rough. The recording is first-rate if not perfectly balanced.

Orchestral set No. 2.

*** Decca Phase 4 PFS 4203. London Symphony Orchestra, Leopold Stokowski – MESSIAEN: *L'Ascension.****

The *Second Orchestral set* consists of three highly evocative pieces crammed with the sort of wild devices that make Ives's music so distinctive. Most memorable is the third of the pieces called (extravagantly) *From Hanover Square North at the End of a Tragic Day (1915) the Voice of the People Again Rose.* It depicts an incident on the elevated railway on the day when the *Lusitania* was sunk, when the crowd spontaneously started to sing *In the sweet bye and bye.* In such atmospheric music Stokowski's wonderful sense of dramatic development is perfectly exploited. The multi-channel recording is well suited to the music, and the LSO obviously enjoys the experience, not least in the ragtime of the second piece.

*Symphonies Nos. (*i) *1 in D minor; (*ii) *2; 3 (The camp meeting); (*iii) *4; (*ii) *Holidays symphony; (*ii) *Central Park in the Dark; (*i) *Three Places in New England; (*ii) *The Unanswered Question; (*i) *Variations on 'America'.*

(M) ** (*) CBS 77424 (4 discs). (i) Philadelphia Orchestra, Eugene Ormandy; (ii) New York Philharmonic Orchestra, Leonard Bernstein; (iii) American Symphony Orchestra, Leopold Stokowski.

CBS had the idea at the time of the Ives centenary of issuing a collection of the symphonies and important orchestral pieces in various versions directed by Ormandy, Bernstein and Stokowski. The recording, not always improved by the change of format, is variable, but the performances are all red-bloodedly convincing, an extraordinary phantasmagoria of ideas jostling and overlaying one another. Of the symphonies No. 3, *The Camp Meeting,* is the most readily approachable and yet typical of Ives. Of the separate pieces the gentle *Central Park in the Dark* and *The Unanswered Question* may well surprise with their poetry those who think of Ives's music as inevitably rowdy.

Symphony No. 1 in D minor.

** (*) Decca SXL 6592. Los Angeles Philharmonic Orchestra, Zubin Mehta – ELGAR: *Enigma variations.** (*)

Ives's charming *First Symphony,* a student work much influenced by Dvořák and Tchaikovsky but still with touches of individuality, is given a superb performance by Mehta, beautifully recorded. The pity is that he makes a substantial cut in the finale, to make it 'more compact and convincing'. One is inevitably suspicious of such claims, though there is the practical advantage that the symphony can be squeezed on to a single side.

Symphony No. 2.

** (*) Decca Phase 4 PFS 4251. London Symphony Orchestra, Bernard Herrmann.

Herrmann treats this wild score a shade more carefully than Bernstein in his New York version (see above), but it is music, many-layered, that benefits not only from care in execution but from the multi-channel techniques of Phase 4. This may not be so exciting as Bernstein's more extrovert reading, but under the direction of a conductor long associated with Ives it has tremendous conviction and authority. For anyone not wanting to invest in the full Ives cycle this could provide an excellent introduction.

Symphony No. 4.

** (*) RCA ARL 1 0589. John Alldis Choir, London Philharmonic Orchestra, José Serebrier.

José Serebrier acted as subsidiary conductor for Stokowski when he conducted the world premiere of this wild and complex work in New York. In this English performance he somehow manages to find his way through multilayered textures which have deliberately conflicting rhythms. The players respond loyally, and the movement representing Chaos is particularly colourful and dramatic in its sharp contrasts of dynamic, brutal but somehow poetic. Order is represented by a fugue, and the finale brings an apotheosis, a vivid, gripping work, but maybe not so great as some American commentators originally thought. For the record collector at least it provides a store-house of fantastic orchestral sound, particularly in a recording as vivid as this.

Three Places in New England (The St Gaudens in Boston Common; Putnam's

Camp; The Housatonic at Stockbridge).
*** DGG 2530 048. Boston Symphony Orchestra, Michael Tilson Thomas – RUGGLES: Sun-treader.***

Tilson Thomas gives eloquent and poetic accounts of Ives's pioneering and imaginative score. The performances are beautifully polished and recorded, and all in all this is probably the best version of the work now in the catalogue, provided that the coupling is acceptable.

String quartet No. 1.

(B) ** Pye GSGC 14104. Amici Quartet – SHOSTAKOVICH: Quartet No. 10.**

String quartets Nos. 1 and 2.

(B) ** Turnabout TV 34157S. Kohon Quartet.

When Ives's First Quartet was given its first public performance in 1957 – more than sixty years after its composition – the American critic, Harold Schonberg, complained that it contained 'too many white notes', for Ives at twenty-one had yet to taste the thrill of biting dissonance. Even so there are quirks of argument unmistakably his, and when you come to the Second Quartet, written between 1907 and 1913, there is no restraining him from his thorniest manner. He himself described the piece on the title page as 'S Q for four men – who converse, discuss, argue (in re "politics"), fight, shake hands, shut up – then walk up the mountainside to view the firmament.' Fair comment from a master of the offbeat. There was a far more impressive version of these two quartets on CBS (by the Juilliard Quartet), but this is now deleted. The Turnabout coupling makes a fair recommendation on bargain label. The playing could be more incisive, but with wide stereo separation, the recording is faithful enough. A good performance from the Amici, also lacking the virtuosity of the Juilliard group, but enjoyable enough. Recording well balanced and truthful.

Piano sonata No. 2 ('Concord, Mass, 1840–60').

** CBS SBRG 72763. John Kirkpatrick (piano).

Ives's *Second Sonata* is a demanding work that will appeal more to serious collectors than the general music-lover. Fine though much of it is, the absence of real concentration diminishes its impact. John Kirkpatrick plays authoritatively and with considerable virtuosity. The recording does not offer first-class piano tone but those with inquiring minds and tastes should acquire this disc before it disappears.

Songs: *Ann Street; At the River; The Cage; Charlie Rutlage; A Christmas Carol; Evening; A Farewell to Land; From 'The Swimmers'; General William Booth Enters Heaven; The Greatest Man; The Side Show; Soliloquy; West London.*

(B) *** Pye GSGC 14105. Marni Nixon (soprano), John McCabe (piano) – GOEHR and SCHÜRMANN: *Songs.*** (*)

The fascinating Ives discography has tended to show a brilliant imagination, plus a remarkably original mind, but not always enough musical consistency to back the originality. Here is a disc that completely validates the eccentricity and not only proclaims the composer's individuality but lays his claim to being considered one of the most spontaneous of twentieth-century song writers. The opening song, *Ann Street*, with its entirely individual melodic and harmonic path; the breathtaking descriptive accompaniment for *From 'The Swimmers'* – which needs a real virtuoso at the keyboard: both these songs are worthy of Schubert.

Equally appealing is the naïve charm of the songs based on the revivalist tradition, *At the River* or the delightfully simple *Christmas Carol* (sentimentality crystallized into art!). Ives's introspective, lyrical vein is shown by the haunting *Soliloquy* and the lovely nocturne, *Evening*. Then there is the 'folk' quality of the cowboy song *Charlie Rutlage* and the rumbustious panache of *General William Booth* entering heaven. Marni Nixon sings them superbly with the right simplicity of approach. John McCabe accompanies splendidly and the spacious stereo helps to create the fullest possible atmosphere.

Songs: *At the River; The Circus Band; The Greatest Man.*

(M) ** (*) RCA LRL 1 5058. Cleo Laine, Anthony Hymas (piano) – SCHOENBERG: *Pierrot Lunaire.*** (*)

Ives's memorable little songs should be far better known. They make a charming makeweight for Cleo Laine's highly individual account of *Pierrot Lunaire.*

Janáček, Leoš
(1854–1928)

Idyla.

(M) ** RCA LHL 1 5086. Prague Chamber Orchestra, Hans-Hubert Schönzeler – MARTINŮ: *Concerto for double string orchestra, piano and timpani.****

Janáček's *Idyla* is an early work, written in 1878, only a year after the *Suite for strings*, and when he was still in his early twenties. It is played with impeccable precision and liveliness, though one would welcome a little more charm, particularly in the slow fourth movement. It does not show Janáček at his most dis-

487

tinguished or characteristic, but the disc is well worth considering for the sake of the Martinů with which it is coupled.

Lachian dances; Taras Bulba (rhapsody for orchestra).
> ** (*) Decca SXL 6507. London Philharmonic Orchestra, François Huybrechts.

François Huybrechts is a young Belgian conductor, winner of several major awards, who has trained alongside Bernstein and Szell. Here he shows flair as well as expertise in an excellent performance of *Taras Bulba*. He is helped by splendid playing from the LPO and top-quality Decca sound. The sophistication with which the engineers have balanced the important organ part is an additional aid to the effect of the scoring, which is highly imaginative. Huybrechts does not overplay his hand in the first two sections of the work, which can easily sound melodramatic, and in the closing part, *The Prophecy and Death of Taras Bulba*, his restrained eloquence in the visionary section representing the liberation of the Cossacks is genuinely moving. The music of the *Lachian dances*, while vividly scored, is on a rather lower level of inspiration, but the performance here is highly idiomatic and effective.

Sinfonietta.
> *** Decca SXL 6398. London Symphony Orchestra, Claudio Abbado – HINDEMITH: *Symphonic metamorphoses.****
> (M) ** (*) CBS Classics 61367. Cleveland Orchestra, George Szell – HINDEMITH: *Symphonic metamorphoses.** (*)

Sinfonietta; Preludes: The House of the Dead; Jenůfa; Kátya Kabanová; The Makropoulos Affair.
> (B) ** (*) Pye GSGC 14004. Pro Arte Orchestra, Charles Mackerras.

Sinfonietta; Taras Bulba (rhapsody for orchestra).
> ** (*) DGG 2530 075. Bavarian Radio Symphony Orchestra, Rafael Kubelik.
> (M) ** Supraphon SUAST 50380. Czech Philharmonic Orchestra, Karel Ančerl.

Abbado gives a splendid account of the *Sinfonietta* and evokes a first-class response from the LSO. One of the strengths of this young conductor is his acute sensitivity to dynamic nuances and his care for detail, which never seems to degenerate into pedantry or excessive fastidiousness. This is thoroughly alive and fresh playing, and the Decca engineers have given him a superb balance in which the subtlest of colours is allowed to register without artificial boosting. The coupling too is first-class.

The Cleveland Orchestra under Szell play with immense zest and excitement, and it is a pity that the close balance of the recording – much less natural than that afforded to Abbado – while adding plenty of impact and presence, particularly to the wind section, robs the sound picture of refinement. Even so, with its vivid coupling this record is worth considering in the medium price-range for its vitality and robustness of spirit.

Mackerras's disc makes a fine companion to his version of the original score of Handel's *Fireworks music*, which was recorded about the same time. The sound here has the same spacious sonority for the brass (the *Sinfonietta* uses twelve trumpets) and the performance is vivid and sympathetic, lacking only the last degree of refinement. Both in sound balance and playing this version is superior to its Supraphon competitor. This is not without character but there is far more detail and colour in the Pye stereo. The couplings are, of course, a consideration, but the four operatic preludes were an imaginative choice and they are well realized here. If *Taras Bulba* is preferred, Ančerl's account has no lack of vitality, although the recording has less impact than the Decca or DGG versions.

The Bavarian Orchestra is in virtuoso form and there is some splendid bravura, particularly in the committed and exciting playing in the last two sections of *Taras Bulba*. The DGG recording is both brilliant and atmospheric, if rather less sophisticated in the matter of inner balance. But many may prefer Kubelik's coupling of the *Sinfonietta*, where the acoustic is especially well judged to suit the massed brass effects at the opening and close of the work. The performance is strong and direct rather than especially subtle.

Suite for string orchestra.
*** Argo ZRG 792. Los Angeles Chamber Orchestra, Neville Marriner – R. STRAUSS: *Capriccio: Introduction;* SUK: *Serenade.* ***

Marriner's first record with his new Los Angeles group was made in England during the orchestra's 1974 tour. The recording site was St John's, Smith Square (where many successful Argo discs have been made), and the recording is characteristically ripe. The *Suite for strings* is an early and not entirely mature piece, but when played as committedly as it is here, its attractions are readily perceived, and it does not want character.

CHAMBER MUSIC

Concertino for piano and chamber ensemble.
(B) ** Turnabout TV 34130S. Walter Klien (piano) with Chamber Ensemble – BARTÓK: *Rhapsody;* HONEGGER: *Concertino;* STRAVINSKY: *Capriccio.* **

This *Concertino* is a difficult work to hold together, and Walter Klien manages it very well, helped by excellent accompaniment from an instrumental septet. If none of the performances or recordings on this record is quite of the top flight, the four works together make an attractive sample of concertante piano works of this century.

String quartets Nos. 1 (Kreutzer); 2 (Intimate Pages).
(M) *** Supraphon SUAST 50556. Janáček Quartet.
(B) ** Turnabout TV 34471S. Austrian Quartet.

Good performances from the Austrian Quartet, thoroughly committed in every way, but falling short of the Janáček Quartet on Supraphon (formerly on Classics for Pleasure) in panache and authenticity of feeling. The latter is better recorded and has a wider dynamic range.

VOCAL AND CHORAL MUSIC

Male choruses: *Ach vojna (The Soldier's Lot); Ceská legie (Czech Legion); Coz ta nase bríza (Our Birch Tree); Kantor Halfar (Schoolmaster Halfar); Klekánica (The Evening Witch); Marycka Magdonova; Potulý silenec (The Wandering Madman); Rozlouceni (Leave-taking); Sedmesát tisíc (Seventy-thousand).*
(M) ** (*) Supraphon 112 0878. Moravian Teachers' Choir, Antonín Tucapský.

This is marvellous stuff. Janáček was a master of this medium and the Moravian Teachers' Choir was closely associated with him throughout his mature life. *The Evening Witch* was especially written for them after he first heard them in 1904. The singing has great eloquence and the music has both passion and inspiration to commend it. Strongly recommended, even though the recording is not ideally refined.

The Diary of One Who Disappeared (English version by Bernard Keeffe).

** (*) Argo ZRG 692. Robert Tear (tenor), Elizabeth Bainbridge (mezzo-soprano), with Elizabeth Gale (soprano), Rosanne Creffield (mezzo-soprano), Marjorie Biggar (contralto), Philip Ledger (piano).

Bernard Keeffe, who prepared the English edition, comments in his sleeve-note on the differences in stress between the English and Czech languages. No doubt his solution is essentially a compromise between the demands of vocal delivery and the music itself, but certainly a performance in English ensures that the meaning of the words communicates very directly to the listener. Robert Tear's well-projected tenor tone suits the music beautifully. As a narrative cycle this stands alone, and with finely atmospheric recording, this is a most moving performance. (N.B. The only Czech-language version is available in a mono recording.)

Choral cantatas: *The Eternal Gospel; Lord Have Mercy; Our Father; There upon the Mountain.*

(M) * (*) Supraphon SUAST 50680. Jadwiga Wysoczanská (soprano), Marie Mrázová (contralto), Beno Blachut, Miroslav Svejda (tenors), Dalibor Jedlicka (bass), Czech Philharmonic Chorus, Prague Symphony Orchestra, Jiří Pinkas or Josef Veselka.

These are not major Janáček compositions but they are more than welcome as additions to the catalogue. *The Eternal Gospel* and *Our Father* are the major pieces here; the other two are short.

Some of the inspiration is noble and ardent, but readers should not expect any of these works to be the equal of the Janáček of the *Glagolitic Mass*. The performances are well-shaped and spirited, but the recordings are satisfactory rather than excellent. There is a certain pallor about the sound quality that suggests they originate from the early 1960s.

Glagolitic Mass.

*** Decca SXL 6600. Teresa Kubiac (soprano), Anne Collins (contralto), Robert Tear (tenor), Wolfgang Schone (bass), Brighton Festival Chorus, Royal Philharmonic Orchestra, Rudolf Kempe.

(M) ** (*) Supraphon SUAST 50519. Libuse Domaninská (soprano), Vera Soukupová (mezzo-soprano), Beno Blachut (tenor), Eduard Haken (baritone), Czech Philharmonic Chorus and Orchestra, Karel Ančerl.

Written when Janáček was over seventy, this is one of his most important and most exciting works, full of those strikingly fresh uses of sound that make his music so distinctive. The opening instrumental movement has much in common with the opening fanfare of the *Sinfonietta*, and all the other movements reveal an original approach to the church service. The text is taken from native Croatian variations of the Latin text, and Janáček himself said that he had village services in mind when he wrote the work. Not that this complex and often advanced music could be performed in any ordinary village church, but its vitality bespeaks a folk inspiration. Though Kempe's interpretation and the singing of the Brighton Festival Chorus do not always have the snapping authenticity of the Supraphon performance, it is an important advantage having recording of such realism and brilliance, and the playing of the Royal Philharmonic is wonderfully committed and vivid. First-rate solo singing, with Teresa Kubiak particularly impressive.

The Czech performance remains a classic account and the recording is atmospheric, if not as clear and vivid as the Decca.

OPERA

The Cunning Little Vixen (opera in 3 acts): complete recording.
(M) *** Supraphon MS 1181/2. Zdenek Kroupa (baritone), Jaroslava Procházková (contralto), Jan Hlavsa, Rudolf Vonásek (tenors), Dalibor Jedlicka, Jozef Heriban (basses), Helena Tattermuschová, Jaroslav Dobrá (sopranos), Prague National Theatre Chorus and Orchestra, Bohumil Gregor.

On the face of it Janáček's choice of a story of wild life in the countryside (a gnat, a rooster and a grasshopper are among the cast) sounds softly sentimental. In fact with his characteristically sharp and direct expression the result is just the opposite. It is a fascinating, totally original opera, given here with slavonic warmth by the composer's compatriots. Some might prefer a more detached reading, but this shows very clearly the red-blooded nature of Janáček's inspiration even in a stylized subject. The part of the little vixen herself is charmingly sung by Helena Tattermuschová. Good recording.

The Excursions of Mr Brouček (two one-act operas): complete recording.
(M) ** (*) Supraphon SUAST 50531/3. Bohumir Vich, Ivo Zídek (tenors), Premysl Kočí (bass-baritone), Libuse Domaninská, Helena Tattermuschová (sopranos), Karel Berman (bass), Prague Smetana Theatre Chorus, Prague

National Theatre Orchestra, Václav Neumann.

The sardonic side of Janáček was at work when he chose the strange libretto for this work. Mr Brouček, dreaming, has two excursions, one back to medieval Bohemia at the time of the Hussites, the other to the moon. The situations give him plenty of opportunity to poke gentle fun at the more absurd aspects of pattriotism and at the pretentiousness of artists. It is an attractive score, if more uneven than most of Janáček's operas. Well worth getting to know in this authentic and colourful performance from Prague. Fair recording.

From the House of the Dead (opera in 3 acts): complete recording.
(M) *** Supraphon SUAST 50705/6. Helena Tattermuschová (soprano), Ivo Zídek, Milan Karpísek, Beno Blachut (tenors), Premysl Kočí, Václav Bednár (baritones), Prague National Theatre Chorus and Orchestra, Bohumil Gregor.

From the House of the Dead is the toughest of Janáček's operas, taking Dostoyevsky's novel as its unlikely subject and presenting a sequence of episodic scenes exposing the life of the brutal Siberian prison camp, and – more important – giving a series of sharply defined character studies, which with operatic gesture reduced to the minimum have a cumulative emotional impact. The part of the boy Aljeja, befriended by the central character, is taken by a soprano, but otherwise it is almost entirely a male-voice opera. But that restriction of vocal colour heightens the impact of Janáček's cutting textures, his brutally clipped style of utterance. On record it is a particularly moving work, when every word can readily be followed, and in this strong, authentic performance, beautifully recorded, it certainly makes its full impact, with fine playing and a fine singing cast.

Jenůfa (opera in 3 acts): complete recording.

(M) ** (*) Supraphon 112 0711/2. Libuse Domaninská, Nadézda Kniplová (sopranos), Ivo Zídek, Vilém Pribyl (tenors), Prague National Theatre Chorus and Orchestra, Bohumil Gregor.

Jenůfa: highlights.

(M) ** (*) Supraphon 112 0791 (from above recording).

It was with *Jenůfa* that Janáček scored his first real success in the opera house: the work has a striking and immediate sense of identity, a powerful atmosphere and a strong dramatic argument. The main strength of this version lies in the fine characterization of the mother, the Kostelnička, the most complex and dominant figure in the action. Though none of the singers may be absolutely first-class, and they are not free from Slav *vibrato*, the company has fine team-work and Bohumil Gregor directs the performance with genuine imaginative vitality and succeeds in conveying the compelling atmosphere of the score. Unfortunately the acoustic of the recording is too reverberant and detail is inevitably smudged. For those wanting a disc of highlights the single disc provides a well-chosen selection from what is undoubtedly a strong and colourful set.

Kátya Kabanová (opera in 3 acts): complete recording.

(M) ** (*) Supraphon SUAST 50781/2. Drahomira Tikalová (soprano), Ivana Mixová (mezzosoprano), Beno Blachut (tenor), Zdeněk Kroupa (bass), Prague National Theatre Chorus and Orchestra, Jaroslav Krombholc.

This was one of the first complete recordings of a Janáček opera made by Supraphon, but the stereo sound remains very acceptable, and the performance has the loving authenticity one expects from this company. Something of the authentic sharpness of sound is lost – in part because of the recording, in part because Vaclav Talich's reorchestration is used – a point that may well be noted by those who have enjoyed this opera at Sadler's Wells under Charles Mackerras. The cast is strong, with a superlative performance from the tenor Beno Blachut, then at the peak of his career.

The Makropoulos Affair (opera in 3 acts): complete recording.

(M) ** (*) Supraphon SUAST 50811/2. Libuse Prylová (soprano), Ivo Zídek, Rudolf Vonásek (tenors), Helena Tattermuschová (mezzo-soprano), Premysl Kočí (baritone), Victor Kočí, Milan Karpísek (tenors), Prague National Theatre Chorus and Orchestra, Bohumil Gregor.

In this strange opera Janáček's heroine was a 400-year-old opera singer, possessor of the secret of prolonging her life. Total disillusion is the ultimate result, and the inevitable denouement, when time catches up with her, takes us far above the chill, unemotional world of the rest of the opera. Opera-lovers in Britain will remember the unforgettable performance in the central role of the late Marie Collier; Libuse Prylová cannot match that superb characterization, but it is a strong, enjoyable performance of a fine, distinctive piece. Good, undistracting recording.

Järnefelt, Armas
(1869–1958)

Praeludium.

** HMV ASD 2952. Bournemouth Symphony Orchestra, Paavo Berglund – ALFVÉN: *Elegy; Swedish* *rhapsody*; GRIEG: *Peer Gynt suites.***

Järnefelt's charming miniature has been absent from the catalogues too long (it used to be very familiar because it fitted easily on to a 78 side). Here it is nicely played and the recording is clear and immediate.

Jones, Daniel
(born 1912)

The Country beyond the Stars.
*** HMV ASD 2739. Chorus, Royal Philharmonic Orchestra, Sir Charles Groves – HODDINOTT: *Welsh dances*; WILLIAMS: *Penillion.****

Daniel Jones's cantata is designed to suit the traditional qualities of Welsh choirs, warm, relaxed writing, easy on the ear. The five choral movements are settings of the Breconshire poet Henry Vaughan, and are divided by a purely orchestral third movement, *Joyful Visitors.* Fine performance and recording.

Symphony No. 4 (In memory of Dylan Thomas); Symphony No. 7.
*** HMV ASD 2855. Royal Philharmonic Orchestra, Sir Charles Groves.

There is no doubt listening to these two symphonies that Daniel Jones is a genuine symphonic thinker, capable of arguing in long, coherently related paragraphs. The *Fourth Symphony*, written in memory of Dylan Thomas, is powerful in atmosphere and the *Seventh* too is strong in feeling and organically conceived. Unfortunately here there is a want of real musical personality: one does not immediately feel that the composer has created a world that is instantly recognizable as his

own and his own alone! All the same, these are well worth hearing and, given such fine playing and recording, can be strongly recommended.

Symphony No. 6.
(M) *** Pye Virtuoso TPLS 13023. Royal Philharmonic Orchestra, Sir Charles Groves – MATHIAS: *Symphony No. 1.** (*)

The *Sixth Symphony* is eclectic in style, but strong in personality, and the cogency of the argument (all six movements use the same basic material) is matched by an ability to communicate emotional experience. The main 'first movement' *Agitato*, the following *Sostenuto*, and the scherzo, if somewhat conventional in material, are striking in their projection of the composer's personality. The symphony is splendidly played, and both conductor and orchestra show their commitment. The recording too has plenty of body and colour.

Joplin, Scott
(1868–1917)

Orchestral Collections

Bethena; A Breeze from Alabama; The Favourite; Gladiolus rag; Palm Leaf rag; Pineapple rag; Pleasant Moments; Solace (A Mexican serenade); Stop-time rag; Wall Street rag.
** EMI EMD 5517. Southland Stingers, George Sponhaltz; Ralph Grierson (piano).
Bethena; Elite syncopations; Euphonic sounds; Gladiolus rag; Magnetic rag; Original rags; Palm Leaf rags; Peacherine rag; Pineapple rag; Scott Joplin's new rag; Solace (A Mexican serenade); Wall Street rag.

** (*) London HSU 5009. New England Conservatory Ragtime Ensemble, Gunther Schuller.

Bink's waltz; Elite syncopations; Eugenia; Heliotrope bouquet; Lily Queen; Magnetic rag; The Nonpareil; Something Doing; The Strenuous Life; The Sycamore.

** EMI EMD 5522. Southland Stingers, George Sponhaltz; Ralph Grierson (piano).

The Cascades; The Chrysanthemum; The Easy Winners; The Entertainer (2 versions); Maple Leaf rag; Rag-time dance; Sugar Cane; Sunflower slow drag (2 versions).

** (*) EMI EMD 5503. New England Conservatory Ragtime Ensemble, Gunther Schuller; Myron Romanul (piano).

Scott Joplin wrote fifty-one piano rags (some in conjunction with other composers) and it is not clear how much hand he had in the orchestrations: probably little, the arrangements being fitted to the instrumentation available. Joplin's talent was narrow in range but strong in personality, so that almost any of his compositions is instantly recognizable, not only by the fairly rigid rhythmic straitjacket, but also by its melodic and harmonic individuality. The orchestral versions, however, with their unsophisticated scoring, add little to the music's impact, and purists will undoubtedly prefer the piano anthologies. Of the two ensembles here, Gunther Schuller's New England Group has marginally the more striking projection. There is plenty of atmosphere and spontaneity, and the playing is rhythmically convincing. The second disc issued (HSU 5009) seems to have a crisper rhythmic point, helped by the brighter focus of the London recording. The sound image provided by the Southland Stingers is fatter, with the tuba part coming through well at the bottom. There

are some nice wind solos here, and the effect is slightly more sophisticated, with something of a bland parlour atmosphere. Both orchestras fall back on the solo piano every now and then, and EMD 5503 offers alternative piano and orchestral versions of two favourite items.

Piano Collections

Bethena; Elite syncopations; Eugenia; Leola; Paragon rag; Pineapple rag; Rose leaf rag; Solace (A Mexican serenade).

(M) ** (*) Nonesuch H 71264. Joshua Rifkin (piano).

Bethena; Harmony Club waltz; Magnetic rag; Maple Leaf rag; Paragon rag; Pineapple rag; Scott Joplin's new rag; Solace (A Mexican serenade); Swipesy cake walk.

* (*) Decca Phase 4 PFS 4292. Eric Rogers (piano).

Bink's waltz; Cleopha; Easy Winners; Elite syncopations; Maple Leaf rag; Original rags; Peacherine rag; Pineapple rag; The Strenuous Life; Sunflower slow drag.

(M) ** (*) CBS Classics 61478. E. Power Biggs (pedal harpsichord).

The Cascades; The Chrysanthemum; Country Club; The Nonpareil; Original rags; Stoptime rag; Sugar Cane; Weeping Willow.

(M) ** (*) Nonesuch H 71305. Joshua Rifkin (piano).

Cleopha; Easy Winners; Elite syncopations; The Entertainer; Gladiolus rag; Maple Leaf rag; Original rags; Pineapple rag; Rag-time dance; Scott Joplin's new rag; Solace (A Mexican serenade); Sunflower slow drag.

(B) ** (*) CBS Embassy EMB 31043. Ronnie Price (piano), with rhythm.

The Entertainer; Euphonic sounds; Fig

Leaf rag; Gladiolus rag; Magnetic rag; Maple Leaf rag; Ragtime dance; Scott Joplin's new rag.

(M) *** Nonesuch H 71248. Joshua Rifkin (piano).

Joshua Rifkin is the pianist whose name has been indelibly associated with the current Scott Joplin cult, stimulated here by the soundtrack background music of the very successful film *The Sting.* There is no question that, of the pianists represented here, his contribution is the most distinguished. His relaxed, cool style, rhythms not too exact, and more than a hint of monochrome in the tone-colour, is distinctive. Perhaps the playing is a trifle too studied – a little more obvious joy in the music would be attractive – but there is no doubt that this playing has style. However, taken a whole record at a time (and one assumes that Mr Rifkin will eventually work his way through all fifty-one pieces) the danger of monotony is real, when the basic approach is comparatively rigid. The recording is excellent, slightly more mellow on the first album (H 71248), to match the playing itself.

For conveyed enthusiasm E. Power Biggs undoubtedly takes the cake. The unlikely combination of Biggs and a pedal harpsichord provides irresistibly jolly performances, the rhythms crisply articulate (and undoubtedly square), the music coming across with splendid spontaneity. The sleeve-note suggests that the harpsichord was the true instrument of the saloon, which seems unlikely, and certainly this Challis two-manual pedal instrument is a long way from the authentic sound. The recording is resonantly vivid, very forward in the CBS manner. Most enjoyable, but not too much at once!

Eric Rogers plays his opening number, *Maple Leaf rag,* on a very old upright Bechstein, slightly twangy in the treble and not quite in tune. It sounds marvellous. He appears to use several pianos on his record, including a Steinway grand for one item, but unfortunately we are not given more details. This record has plenty of personality but the playing itself is not really distinctive.

For those wanting an inexpensive disc including both *The Entertainer* (of *The Sting* fame) and *Maple Leaf rag,* Ronnie Price's CBS Embassy disc should serve admirably. The recording is bold and forward, the rhythm group unostentatious but not unstylish; the playing is alive and spontaneous, and the selection generous.

Arrangements

The Prodigal Son (ballet, orch. and arr. Grant Hossack).

** CBS 73363. London Festival Ballet Orchestra, Grant Hossack.

Grant Hossack's ballet compiled from the music of Joplin follows an honourable tradition which includes *Pineapple Poll* and Lanchbery's *Tales of Beatrix Potter.* The arranger has tried to use the instrumental traditions of both symphonic and popular idioms, and his score is considerably more vivid than the original orchestrations used in Joplin's own time. But in the last resort Joplin's music is not varied enough for this kind of treatment, although one can imagine that when the eye is absorbed with the stage action it would be effective enough. Good performance and recording.

Josquin des Prés
(*c.* 1450–1521)

Collection: *Ave Maria; Baises Moy; La Bernadina; Coeurs desolez; La déploration sur la mort de Johan Okeghem; Fortuna desperata; El Grillo; Petite Camusette; Vive le roy.*

*** Argo ZRG 681. Purcell Consort of Voices, Elizabethan Consort of Viols, Grayston Burgess – DUNSTABLE: *Collection.****

Josquin des Prés's music shows an advance in colour, variety and style over that of John Dunstable, the English composer featured on the reverse of this disc, and whereas Dunstable's output appears to have been mainly ecclesiastical, Josquin had moved with the times to produce secular material of high quality, instrumental as well as vocal. Notable here is the charming *El Grillo*, with its humorous allusions to his employer, Cardinal Sforza, who was not the most likable of patrons. This and the gay instrumental fanfare *Vive le roy* (played with the exotic colouring of shawm, sackbuts and organ) are demonstration items of the colour and immediacy of appeal of Josquin's art, but the other songs too are highly rewarding, with their beauty of line and form. The performances here, like the recording, are admirable.

Missa de Beata Virgine. Motets: *Ave Christe immolate; Tulerunt dominum meum. Dominus regnavit (Psalm 92)*.
   (B) * Turnabout TV 34437S. Dessoff Choir, Paul Boepple.

Rather indifferent singing and recording make it difficult to generate enthusiasm for what should have been an interesting anthology.

Mass: *L'Homme armé* (a sexti toni). Motets: *Absalom fili mi; Illibata Dei Virgo nutrix; Regina coeli laetare*.
   (M) *** Vanguard HM 3SD. Josquin Choir, Jeremy Noble.

The Mass *L'Homme armé*, on the sixth mode (there is another Mass of the same name in which Josquin transposes the same theme through all the modes), was written during his time in Rome during

the late 1480s and early 1490s. Jeremy Noble, well-known as a broadcaster and contributor to the *Gramophone*, has done a great deal of research on Josquin during the past decade but his gifts are more than those of the scholar and critic; these performances have strong musical instinct and refinement of feeling. The Mass and motets are given in performances that he has himself edited and are excellently recorded. Apart from its artistic excellence, the record is admirably cheap and readers wanting to start a collection of great Renaissance music could well begin with these scholarly and above all musical performances.

Missa pange lingua.
   (B) ** Turnabout TV 34431S. Spandauer Kantorei, Martin Behrmann – RUE, PIERRE DE LA: *Requiem.***

Missa pange lingua. Motets: *Alma redemptoris mater – Ave regina coelorum; O virgo virginium; Planxit autem David*.
   * (*) Telefunken SAWT 9595. Prague Madrigal Singers, Miroslav Venhoda.

The *Missa pange lingua* is one of Josquin's late masterpieces and on Turnabout it is given a thoroughly unaffected, straightforward performance that will commend itself to the discriminating listener. It is perhaps less imaginatively phrased than the singing Jeremy Noble secures on his record of the *L'Homme armé* Mass, but it is nonetheless welcome, particularly at its price. The sound image could be more clearly focused with advantage, though it must be conceded that the acoustic is agreeably warm.

The Telefunken disc is beautifully recorded and offers a genuine alternative in that instrumental support is added. However, the blend of this choir and the tone it produces will not please all tastes, and even though the Spandauer Kantorei are somewhat wanting in fervour and expressive power, theirs is the version to have. This mass and the *Missa de Beata Virgine* together with some motets and psalms are available inexpensively in score (Kalmus, Edition No. 702).

Motets: *Ave Maria ... virgo serena; Benedicta es coelorum regina; Dominus regnavit; Inviolata, integra et casta es, Maria; Miserere mei; Tu solus qui facis mirabilia.*

*** BASF BAC 3039. Soloists of the Tolz Boys' Choir, Pro Cantione Antiqua Ensemble, Collegium Aureum, Bruno Turner.

The 450th anniversary of Josquin's death in 1971 brought a renewed impetus to Josquin studies, and in its wake followed a number of recordings. This is among the most successful of them. The selection recorded here includes two of the most familiar of his motets (*Tu solus*, which includes a quotation from Okeghem, and the *Ave Maria*) as well as the *Miserere mei, Deus*, which is a little-known piece, a setting of one of the penitential psalms written for the Holy Week observances at Ferrara. Bruno Turner conducts this repertoire with great authority and feeling; his is undeniably one of the best male-voice ensembles in the country, and although some small reservations must be made (the Tolz Boys' Choir is less than sensitive at times, and the use of instruments tends to thicken the texture without adding anything distinctive), the record must be cordially welcomed. It is recorded in a warm acoustic and reproduces smoothly.

Kabalevsky, Dmitri
(born 1904)

The Comedians (incidental music): *suite.*

(B) *** Vanguard SRV 207 SD. Vienna State Opera Orchestra, Vladimir Golschmann – KHACHATURIAN: *Gayaneh suite.***

The second item in this suite (the *Galop*) is well-known, but the rest of the music is almost equally rewarding. It is gay, colourful and tuneful, and bright as fresh paint. It is presented vivaciously here and the recording is vivid.

Violin concerto, Op. 48.
** (*) CBS 72942. Pinchas Zukerman (violin), Royal Philharmonic Orchestra, Lawrence Foster – BLOCH: *Baal Shem*; WIENIAWSKI: *Concerto No. 2.*** (*)

Kabalevsky's gay, extrovert concerto dates from 1948. If its style is essentially old-fashioned, the work is spontaneous and tuneful and has a fine slow movement, which Zukerman plays tenderly. Indeed the panache of Zukerman's playing, together with a sensitive accompaniment and good recording, makes for very enjoyable listening.

Kalliwoda, Johannes
(1801–66)

Oboe concerto in F major, Op. 110.
** EMI EMD 5505. Han de Vries (oboe), Amsterdam Philharmonic Orchestra, Anton Kersjes – BELLINI: *Concerto*; HUMMEL: *Introduction, theme and variations.***

Johannes Kalliwoda was a Czech musician whose main career was spent as maestro at the court of the obscure Prince of Fürstenburg, at Donaueschingen. It is therefore not surprising that his name is now almost forgotten, although on the evidence of this concerto he was a composer of considerable skill. As the opus number suggests, his output was comparatively large, including an opera, seven symphonies and a corpus of religious music. His musical style owes a lot to Hummel but something also to Rossini. This *Oboe concerto* plays for a little over a quarter of an hour (which means that EMI give short value in allotting it a whole LP side). It has a very fetching opening theme with a Hummel-like dotted rhythmic impulse, and the main ideas of the finale are also spirited and attractive. The slow movement is not ambitious but has more depth than one might expect, and if some of the passagework in the outer movements is rather conventional, one would not be surprised if the piece caught the favour of the public rather like Hummel's *Trumpet concerto*. The performance here is accomplished, bringing out the music's character fully, and the studio recording is pleasing.

Kálmán, Emmerich
(1882–1953)

Gräfin Mariza (Countess Maritza) (operetta in 2 acts): highlights.
(B) *** Decca Eclipse ECS 2154. Herbert Prikopa, Marika Németh, Sonja Draksler, Vienna Volksoper Chorus and Orchestra, Anton Paulik.

Enchanting : much good singing and the whole production in excellent style, even to the inclusion of an authentic gipsy band. You will be surprised how many familiar melodies there are. The recording is bright and lively.

Karg-Elert, Sigfrid
(1879–1933)

Kaleidoscope, Op. 144; 7 Pastels from Lake Constance: The reed-grown waters,

Op. 96/4; Sonatina No. 1 in A minor, Op. 74; Triptych for organ: No. 1, Legend, Op. 141/1.
** (*) Polydor 2460 231. Michael Austin (organ of Birmingham Town Hall).

Sigfrid Karg-Elert was Max Reger's successor as Professor of Composition at Leipzig Conservatoire. He seems to have inherited from his predecessor the device of strong dynamic contrasts in his writing for the organ. The quality of the invention itself is seldom very memorable, in spite of the eloquence of Michael Austin's advocacy. The recording is outstandingly realistic, although the reverberation prevents absolute clarity in the bravura passages.

Kay, Norman
(born 1929)

Miniature quartet.
(B) ** Pye GSGC 14040. London Baroque Ensemble, Karl Haas – ARNELL: *Serenade*; R. STRAUSS: *Suite.*(*)

Kay's *Miniature quartet* is written with great charm, the opening movement showing the composer's feeling for colour, and the *Andante* expressive in a genuinely lyrical way. The miniaturism is retained in the finale, which has a touch of melancholy underlying its chatter. This is better recorded than the Strauss on the reverse.

Ketèlbey, Albert
(1875–1959)

'Appy 'Ampstead; Bells across the Meadows; In a Chinese Temple Garden; In a Monastery Garden; In a Persian Market; In the Mystic Land of Egypt; The

Phantom Melody; The Sanctuary of the Heart; Wedgwood Blue.

*** Decca Phase 4 PFS 4170. Royal Philharmonic Orchestra and Chorus, Eric Rogers.

(B) * (*) Decca SPA 187. New Symphony Orchestra of London, Robert Sharples.

In a somewhat gushing sleeve-note Eric Rogers tells how at the recording sessions the RPO musicians, rather than 'turning up their noses' at this picture-postcard music, instead welcomed it, the leader confessing to owning a full 78 collection of the Ketèlbey canon given to him by his father. The orchestra certainly present these pieces with both warmth and a sense of style: *Wedgwood Blue* is so much the epitome of a salon piece that it becomes a caricature of itself. But in its way it is fetching enough, and throughout the tunes come tumbling out, vulgar, but irresistible when played so elegantly. The birds twittering in the monastery garden make perfect 'camp' but the playing is straight and committed, and marvellously recorded.

The earlier Decca record is well played and recorded but lacks flair. The chorus is rather unimpressive; the bell across the meadow is obviously the same one that calls the monks in from their garden and it is too loud and too near anyway. There is no imagination here and no feeling of good humour either.

Bells across the Meadows; By the Blue Hawaiian Waters; In a Chinese Temple Garden; In a Monastery Garden; In a Persian Market; In the Mystic Land of Egypt.

(B) ** Contour 6870 576. Stuttgart Philharmonic Chorus and Orchestra, Marczek.

In spite of critical sneers Ketèlbey's music, for all its lack of 'taste', has an inherent vitality that makes it refuse to lie down and die. Early gramophone catalogues showed these novelties as the staple popular diet of past generations, and this record – from Stuttgart of all places – is evidence that the music's continuing popularity is not just a British phenomenon. The Stuttgart orchestra play with enthusiasm, and who could resist a smile at the gusto of the vocal contribution in the opening *In a Persian Market*. The sinuous pseudo-Eastern lyrical tunes (and they are real tunes) are phrased with affection; and throughout, the sheer liveliness of the performances carries the music and the listener, who may surely enjoy it with a clear conscience in the best 'camp' tradition. There is no refinement here, but the atmospheric stereo does its job admirably.

Khachaturian, Aram
(born 1903)

Piano concerto in D flat major.

(B) *** Pye GSGC 14013. Mindru Katz (piano), London Philharmonic Orchestra, Sir Adrian Boult – PROKOFIEV: *Piano concerto No. 1.****

** (*) CBS Quadraphonic MQ 31075. Philippe Entremont (piano), New Philharmonia Orchestra, Seiji Ozawa – LISZT: *Hungarian fantasia.***

** Decca SXL 6599. Alicia de Larrocha (piano), London Philharmonic Orchestra, Rafael Frühbeck de Burgos – FRANCK: *Symphonic variations.*** (*)

Mindru Katz gives a really gripping performance of this colourful work. It is the breadth of his playing that is so impressive, the bravura (and there is plenty of opportunity for it in the outer movements) not turning the work into a mere display of pianistic fireworks, but used to add strength and shape to the overall structure. Yet there is plenty of sparkle too, and the slow movement – complete with the original flexotone, played perhaps somewhat hesitantly – is highly expressive. The recording of both piano and orchestra is really first-class, one of the best Pye have given us. An excellent bargain.

The CBS disc is an example where the improvement in the sound of the quadraphonic version over the ordinary stereo (now deleted) is very marked. There is a slight excess of brilliance in the sound picture (and of course the balance is unnaturally close) but there is a compensating weight to give real substance to Entremont and Ozawa's rhapsodical approach to the first movement (with a marked *rallentando* for the lyrical secondary material). The flexotone too is much more effectively balanced in the slow movement within the greater atmosphere of the quadraphony, and the finale, brilliantly played, is especially enjoyable.

On Decca the slow movement as interpreted by a Spanish pianist and a Spanish conductor sounds evocatively like Falla, and the finale too is infectiously jaunty. Not so in the first movement, which is disappointingly slack in rhythm at a dangerously slow tempo. First-rate recording.

Violin concerto in D minor.
- (B) ** (*) Decca Eclipse ECS 641. Ruggiero Ricci (violin), London Philharmonic Orchestra, Anatole Fistoulari – GLAZOUNOV: *Stenka Razin.***

The writer was present at the London premiere of Khachaturian's *Violin concerto* during the war, when, with its obvious melodic spontaneity, it was enthusiastically received. It had a considerable vogue at the time, complete with an imported Decca recording, made from a Russian film soundtrack, by

David Oistrakh. Since then it seems to have lapsed in public favour and the catalogue does not hold a modern recording. However, Ricci's account, which dates from 1957, is a good deal more than serviceable. He does not quite supply the daemonic energy which the outer movements ideally call for, but his lyrical approach has its own attractions, and the closing pages of the slow movement are wonderfully atmospheric. The recording does not have the projection we would expect today, but it is pleasing to listen to and Ricci's fine playing is well focused. A most enjoyable disc and a real bargain.

Gayaneh (ballet): *suites Nos. 1 and 2: excerpts.*
- (M) *** Everest SDBR 3052. London Symphony Orchestra, Anatole Fistoulari.

Gayaneh (ballet): *suite.*
- (M) *** DGG Privilege 2538 345. Leningrad Philharmonic Orchestra, Gennady Rozhdestvensky – TCHAIKOVSKY: *Francesca da Rimini.****
- (B) ** Vanguard SRV 207SD. Vienna State Opera Orchestra, Vladimir Golschmann – KABALEVSKY: *The Comedians suite.****

The Everest disc provides the most extensive selection from *Gayaneh* available in stereo, and Fistoulari imparts his usual magical touch, especially in the quieter music, where there is some melting orchestral playing. This is not to suggest that the exciting moments are not equally well handled: the *Russian dance* which begins side two and the exciting *Fire* sequence are both splendidly colloquial. The recording is well balanced and realistic. This is an outstanding issue.

No one does the *Sabre dance* quite like the Russians themselves, and with Rozhdestvensky it makes a sensational opening to a suite which includes most of the well-known items. The recording is reverberant, but it suits the music-making, which has panache as well as excitement.

Golschmann's suite too is vividly done, and his record, in the bargain range, has an attractive coupling. The resonance of the acoustic produces a somewhat un-refined effect in the loudest moments but the recording is otherwise well focused and colourful.

Gayaneh (ballet): excerpts; *Spartacus* (ballet): excerpts.
*** Decca SXL 6000. Vienna Phil-harmonic Orchestra, the compo-ser.

The reader's interest in the composer's record will be dictated solely by whether he thinks the *Spartacus* music will be to his taste. The ballet is immensely spec-tacular and produced on Hollywood lines. The music itself is colourful, passionate, melodically attractive if not distinctive in any sophisticated sense, and capable of making a considerable impact. There is no doubt whatsoever of the composer's brilliant talent or his capacity for writing popular tunes and scoring them in tech-nicolor. The orchestral playing here is marvellous – both in *Gayaneh* and *Sparta-cus* – and the luscious and sumptuous Decca sound is almost overwhelming, but highly appropriate.

Spartacus (ballet): excerpts *(Dance of the shields; Adagio of Spartacus and Phrygia)*.
(M) ** Philips Universo 6585 012. Monte Carlo Opera Orchestra, Eduard van Remoortel – SHOS-TAKOVICH: *Execution of Stepan Razin.***

This will obviously attract those whose interest in *Spartacus* is primarily drawn to the tune used for the BBC TV series *The Onedin Line*. The coupling is a curious but enterprising one.

Symphony No. 2 in C minor.
(***) Decca SXL 6001. Vienna Phil-harmonic Orchestra, the compo-ser.

This was a propaganda piece written during the war when the composer was evacuated from Moscow. Khachaturian lays the Armenian colour on very thickly, but unlike the splendid *Violin concerto* of two years earlier this does not develop into a coherent argument, let alone a genuinely symphonic one. Roughly the musical value is in inverse proportion to the noise made, and it is a very loud score indeed. The performance is very fine and the magnificent quality of the recording deserves better material.

Symphony No. 3.
(***) RCA SB 6804. Chicago Sym-phony Orchestra, Leopold Sto-kowski – RIMSKY-KORSAKOV: *Russian Easter Festival overture;* RACHMANINOV: *Vocalise.****

Khachaturian's *Third Symphony* might almost have been designed to demonstrate how not to write symphonically. The composer's chronic tendency to repeat a phrase ad nauseam, his refusal to appre-ciate that enough is enough – there is a truly terrible organ passage in mad triplets early in this symphony – are the antithesis of true development. Even so Stokowski's richly expressive direction and the virtuoso playing of the Chicago Orchestra almost make the results toler-able, particularly when the recording is super-brilliant.

Klemperer, Otto
(1885–1973)

(i) *Symphony No. 2;* (ii) *String quartet No. 7.*
** HMV ASD 2575. (i) New Phil-

harmonia Orchestra, the composer; (ii) Philharmonia Quartet.

It is good to have a memento of Klemperer relaxing his magisterial image to let us know what inner emotions have been moving him in music. Unlike his master, Mahler, he was not a great composer, and he obviously found difficulty in resolving his stylistic discrepancies between grittily chattering fast music (sometimes with a touch of Bartók in the *Quartet*) and slow romantic music. The *Quartet* is the more vital work, though even there the concluding sweet slow movement does not quite belong, and the best movement is the charming, unpretentious scherzo, which relaxes in a very Mahlerian way into a contrasting waltz theme. The *Symphony* too has a passage – clarinet over pizzicato strings – which recalls Viennese operetta, but there the influence is unassimilated. For all the reservations it is fascinating to find what lies behind the interpretative façade of a great musician. The *Symphony* could have done with an extra rehearsal, but the *Quartet* is splendidly played.

Kodály, Zoltán
(1882–1967)

Ballet music; Concerto for orchestra; Dances of Galánta; Dances of Marosszék; Háry János: suite; Hungarian rondo; Minuetto serio; Summer Evening; Symphony in C major; Theatre overture; Variations on an Hungarian folk-song (The Peacock).
*** Decca SXLM 6665/7. Philharmonia Hungarica, Antal Dorati.

When Dorati and the Philharmonia Hungarica finished their monumental task of recording Haydn's symphonies complete, they turned to the music of their compatriot Kodály. Though of

course the string section is augmented, there is the same sense of commitment here as in the performances of Haydn. That is all to the good in music which, though it is always beautifully written and often colourful, is not always as cogent as it might be. The more ambitious orchestral works like the *Concerto for orchestra* and the *Symphony in C* are highly enjoyable, but they lack the sharpness of inspiration that pervades the music of Kodály's friend Bartók. The *Peacock variations*, luxuriantly extended, should be much better-known, and it is good to have a novelty in the snatch of *Ballet music* originally intended for *Háry János*. The recording is outstandingly vivid.

Háry János (play with music): complete recording of music, with narration by Peter Ustinov.
** (*) Decca SET 399/400. Olga Szönyi, Márgit László (sopranos), Erszébet Komlössy (mezzo-soprano), György Melis, Zsolte Bende (baritones), Laszló Palócz (bass-baritone), Wandsworth School Boys' Chorus, Edinburgh Festival Chorus, London Symphony Orchestra, Istvan Kertesz.

Here we have an attempt to re-create in gramophone terms for English-speaking listeners the curious humour of the original Hungarian play. All of Kodály's music is included, and the links are provided by Peter Ustinov in many guises. Whether the comedy stands the test of repetition is another matter, but it is good to have Kodály's full score, including a number of pieces as attractive as those in the well-known suite, and vocal versions of some that we know already. Superb recording.

Háry János (play with music): highlights.

*** Decca SXL 6631 (from above recording).

This extensive selection from the complete *Háry János* provides the ideal answer for those who want to explore further than the popular suite but who resist the idea of the complete work, a full two discs with the narration by Peter Ustinov. Superb performance and recording.

Háry János: orchestral suite.
(M) *** CBS 61193. Cleveland Orchestra, George Szell – PROKOFIEV: *Lieutenant Kijé.****
** (*) Philips 6500 015. Concertgebouw Orchestra, Bernard Haitink – BARTÓK: *Music for strings, percussion and celesta.*** (*)

Szell – Budapest-born – is in his element. Superb Cleveland polish matches the vitality of the playing, with a humorous sparkle in Kodály's first two movements, and the mock pomposity of the Napoleon episode wittily dramatized. The full romantic sweep of the *Song* and *Intermezzo* comes over too, with deliciously pointed woodwind in the trio of the latter. The recording is CBS sound at its most glittering. Some might feel that its excess in the upper register verges on crudeness, but the recording itself is dramatically right; the engineers certainly capture the exhilaration of the playing in this way, and with a little tonal control a sparkling, reasonably lustrous sound emerges, if you don't mind the too-forward cimbalom.

An eminently satisfactory account too from Haitink, beautifully played by the Concertgebouw Orchestra and well recorded. The string tone could sound a little more expansive but on the whole there are no quarrels with this recording, which reproduces detail with admirable clarity while at the same time preserving a good musical perspective.

Háry János: suite and two arias: *Poor I am still; Once I had a brood of chicks; Dances of Galánta.*
*** Decca SXL 6136. Olga Szönyi (soprano), London Symphony Orchestra, Istvan Kertesz.

Háry János is superbly played and recorded. This has always been something of a demonstration piece, even in mono days, and once again *The battle and defeat of Napoleon* proves an example of how much modern recording can offer in realism and clarity. There is a complete absence of pre-echo here in a passage notorious for this fault. In the *Viennese musical clock*, the percussion balance might ideally have achieved a crisper effect, especially from the side-drum, but some will be glad not to have the kitchen department exaggerated as it sometimes is. One certainly could not fault the balance of the cimbalom, which emerges as soloist in the *Intermezzo* without drowning everything. Throughout, the orchestral playing has great élan, something which the *Dances of Galánta* share; indeed they are so well played they almost rise to the stature of *János*. The two arias are short but attractive, and Miss Szönyi sings with such character that her Slavonic wobbles can be quite forgiven.

Violoncello sonata (for cello and piano), *Op. 4*.
*** Argo ZRG 762. George Isaac (cello), Martin Jones (piano) – HINDEMITH: *Sonata.*** (*)

The *Cello sonata*, an early work, contains some of Kodály's most vital and immediate inspiration. The first movement, labelled *Fantasia*, is a searching *adagio*, which George Isaac and Martin Jones tackle with keen intensity. The other movement is an extended *Allegro con spirito*, clearly influenced by Kodály's friend Bartók, but still distinctive in its use of Hungarian folk material. A fine, incisive performance. Excellent recording.

(Unaccompanied) *Violoncello sonata, Op. 8;* (i) *Duo for violin and violoncello, Op. 7.*
  (B) *** Saga 5386. Janos Starker (cello), (i) with Arnold Eidus (violin).

The *Duo* is a fine work and it is marvellously played by Eidus and Starker. The recording is not new but is genuine and well-defined stereo. The coupling is Starker's first recording of the *Solo cello sonata*; no one has ever surpassed it on record and its virtuosity and intensity are as striking as ever. It is not in genuine stereo but that is of small account, for this is one of the classics of the gramophone.

(i) *The Peacock* (folk-song for unaccompanied chorus); (i; ii; iii) *Psalmus Hungaricus, Op. 13;* (iii) *Variations on a Hungarian folk-song (The Peacock).*
  *** Decca SXL 6497. (i) LSO Chorus; (ii) Lajos Kozma (tenor), Brighton Festival Chorus, Wandsworth School Choir; (iii) London Symphony Orchestra; all cond. Istvan Kertesz.

There was a crying need for a good modern version of the *Psalmus Hungaricus*, Kodály's most vital choral work, and this version comes as close to the ideal as one is likely to get. Kertesz's energy takes one compellingly through all the straight homophonic writing, which in a lesser performance can diminish the work's stature. Here, with a chorus trained by another Hungarian musician, the results are electrifying, and the recording is outstandingly brilliant to match. The light tenor tone of Lajos Kozma is not ideal for the solo part, but again the authentic Hungarian touch helps. The *Peacock variations* make a

marvellous display piece. No attempt here to build an intellectual structure: orchestral resource provides the mainspring, and the LSO revels in the virtuoso challenge.

Settings of folk-songs: *A csitári hegyek alatt; Akkor szép az erdö; Este rozsám ne jöjj hozzám; Ifj úság mint sólyommadár; Kocsi szekér Magas köszik-lának; Törik már a réteket; Virágos kenderem.* (Also includes: Negro Spirituals: *Ain't got time to die; Chere mo lemme toi; City called heaven.* NILES: *Go 'way from my window. Hush li'l baby; Jesus lay your head in de winder; Mr Banjo; My good Lord done been here.*)
  *** Decca SXL 6245. Felicia Weathers (soprano), Georg Fischer (piano), Karl Scheidt (guitar).

Miss Weathers is a Negro singer of great accomplishment and her powers are seen to excellent advantage both in the Negro spirituals and in the colourful Kodály folk-songs. Readers will find this a highly attractive and pleasurable recital, well worth investigating.

Kokkonen, Joonas
(born 1921)

Symphony No. 3.
  ** (*) Decca SXL 6432. Finnish Radio Symphony Orchestra, Paavo Berglund – SIBELIUS: *Tapiola.***

Kokkonen's *Third Symphony* is undoubtedly the finest Finnish symphony to have appeared in the past few years. It has a genuine sense of forward flow and an arresting musical argument. The texture is clear and the musical language thoroughly approachable even though it has uncompromising integrity. It is unusual for a Scandinavian symphony to be accorded the compliment of two recordings but Kokkonen's *Third* was twice recorded within a short time of its first appearance, once during the 1968 Nordic Music Days at Stockholm, and on a second occasion in the Finnish Radio's studios. Good though not outstanding recording.

Korngold, Erich
(1897–1957)

Violin concerto in D major, Op. 35.
   (M) ** RCA LSB 4105. Jascha Heifetz (violin), Los Angeles Philharmonic Orchestra, Alfred Wallenstein – BRUCH: *Scottish fantasia.** (**)

Korngold's concerto (see also below) is an agreeable confection made up of ideas taken from his Hollywood film music. In Heifetz's hands the result is richly enjoyable, though even he cannot quite convince you that it is great music. Wiry recording.

(i) *Violin concerto in D major, Op. 35; Much Ado About Nothing* (incidental music): *suite No. 11; Theme and variations, Op. 42.*
   ** (*) EMI EMD 5515. South German Radio Symphony Orchestra, Willy Mattes, (i) with Ulf Hoelscher (violin).

Korngold's *Violin concerto* was written for Huberman but the great violinist died shortly after its completion. Hoelscher plays it with great sympathy and warmth though not quite the panache and virtuosity of Heifetz. The music has touches of kitsch that justify the tired but true quip about more Korn than gold, but there is much that is endearing about the concerto. The *Much Ado About Nothing*

music is much earlier, dating from the end of the First World War. It is indebted to the Strauss of *Till* and *Le Bourgeois Gentilhomme* but there is still much to admire in the sheer musicality of invention, even if the idiom might seem outmoded. The music benefits from the committed playing of the South German Radio Orchestra and the warm and pleasing acoustic of the recording.

Symphony in F sharp major, Op. 40.
   *** RCA ARL 1 0043. Munich Philharmonic Orchestra, Rudolf Kempe.

This is a work of Korngold's last years, overtly and unashamedly romantic in idiom. Written in 1950 it was admired by Mitropoulos, who planned to conduct its first performance, but death intervened and its premiere, under Kempe, did not take place until 1972. Some of its ideas are freshly imagined, and the work is laid out with great expertise and impeccable craftsmanship. Whether its appeal can sustain its time-scale will inevitably be a matter for individual judgement (there are many post-romantic symphonies with stronger claims on the repertoire) but it is undoubtedly worth hearing, and Kempe's advocacy and the fine if reverberant recording could hardly be more persuasive.

Kozeluch, Jan
(1738–1814)

Piano concerto in D major.
   (B) ** Turnabout TV 34279S. Felicja Blumenthal (piano), Prague New Chamber Orchestra, Alberto Zedda – KROMMER: *Clarinet concerto.***

Jan (Leopold) Kozeluch was a Czech émigré who made his reputation in

Vienna. The piano concerto recorded here (he wrote over a dozen) is conventional in form but elegant in style and quite attractive, if without any really memorable themes. It is given a neat, small-scale performance and is well recorded.

Kraft, William
(born 1923)

Concerto for four percussion soloists and orchestra; Contextures: Riots-Decade '60.
** (*) Decca SXL 6388. Los Angeles Philharmonic Orchestra, Zubin Mehta, with William Kraft, W. Goodwin, C. Delancey, F. Clark (percussion) – COPLAND: *Lincoln Portrait.*** (*)

William Kraft's *Contextures* was inspired by the various themes that so disturbed America during the 1960s, the racial turmoil in the cities and the war in Vietnam. The musical invention hardly measures up to the seriousness of these themes, and although it is magnificently recorded it is not a work of great substance. The *Concerto for four percussion soloists and orchestra* produces some telling effects, and the performance is splendidly efficient. Exemplary recording.

Kreutzer, Conradin
(1780–1849)

Grand septet in E flat major (for clarinet, horn, bassoon, violin, viola, violoncello and double-bass).
*** Decca SXL 6462. Members of the Vienna Octet – BERWALD: *Septet.****

Kreutzer's *Septet* is a delightful work, and this is the second time the members of the Vienna Octet have recorded it. Their playing is splendidly elegant and their tone sumptuous, as is the Decca recording. It makes an excellent makeweight to Berwald's *Septet* and gives unalloyed pleasure.

Krommer, Franz
(1759–1831)

Clarinet concerto in E flat major.
(B) ** Turnabout TV 34279S. David Glazer (clarinet), Württemberg Chamber Orchestra, Joerg Faerber – KOZELUCH: *Piano concerto.***

Krommer's *Clarinet concerto* has been available before. It is an attractive work with a particularly fetching closing *Rondo*. It is well played here and the recording is generally good. The coupling, by another émigré composer, Kozeluch, is well chosen.

Kuhlau, Friedrich
(1786–1832)

Piano concerto in C major, Op. 7.
(B) ** (*) Turnabout TV 34375S. Felicja Blumenthal (piano), Salzburg Symphony Orchestra, Theodor Guschlbauer – CLEMENTI: *Piano concerto.*** (*)

Although Kuhlau and Clementi (the composer of the coupling) both died in 1832, Kuhlau's career began about three decades after Clementi's and the style of their music is remarkably different. Whereas Clementi's work is brittly classical (though delightful withal) Kuhlau has much in common with Beethoven: it is surprising how often one is reminded of that master when listening to the present work. Its melodies are not in themselves memorable but the writing is fluent and attractive. The performance here is most persuasive, both committed and stylish, and the recording – appropriately warmer than for the coupling – is good.

Elf Hill (incidental music), *Op. 100: suite*.

(B) * (*) Turnabout TV 34230S. Royal Danish Orchestra, Johan Hye-Knudsen – LANGE-MÜLLER: *Once Upon a Time*.**

This mild and rather conventional incidental music was commissioned for a play written to celebrate a royal Danish wedding in 1828. It is based on folk-tunes, none of which seems particularly strong in character (perhaps the more pungent ones were not considered suitable for a royal occasion). The music is quite nicely played and the recording is atmospheric.

Lalo, Édouard
(1823–92)

Piano concerto in C minor.

(B) * Turnabout TV 34423S. Orazio Frugoni (piano), Vienna Volksoper Orchestra, Michael Gielen – SAINT-SAËNS: *Piano concerto No. 5*.* (*)

Lalo, sparkling with inspiration when he wrote for violin and orchestra in the *Symphonie espagnole*, failed completely in this piano concerto, with thin ideas stretched out interminably. The recording, dating from the late fifties, is dim, with bad balance.

Violoncello concerto in D minor.

** Philips 6500 045. Maurice Gendron (cello), Monte Carlo Opera Orchestra, Roberto Benzi – SAINT-SAËNS: *Cello concerto No. 1*; FAURÉ: *Élégie*.* (*)

Lalo's *Cello concerto* is an uninspired work: if it were written for an instrument better served with concertos it would never be played. Maurice Gendron, like Starker before him, plays it eloquently, but manages to bring the score to life only patchily.

Divertissement for orchestra: Andantino (originally from *Fiesque* (opera) ballet); *Namouna* (ballet): excerpts; *Rapsodie norvégienne pour orchestre: Andantino; Presto*.

*** Decca SXL 6302. Suisse Romande Orchestra, Ernest Ansermet.

This is an outstanding collection. The conductor shows his affection in every note and phrase, and the recording quality is superb. Not least in contributing to the listener's pleasure is the cunning order in which the pieces have been arranged on the disc, not as listed above, but rather to give maximum variety and enjoyment. On side two the charming *Divertissement Andantino* is placed between two of the *Namouna* movements, and the concert ends with the jolly and colourful *Rapsodie*, itself very like Lalo's ballet music, but more positive in style. The opening *Prélude* of *Namouna* is both glowing and spectacular. Wagnerian in contour, it is like the *Rainbow bridge* sequence from *Das Rheingold*, and very effective too. But for the most part the content of this record is true French ballet music, gently and prettily scored, occasionally repetitive (as in the *Fête foraine* from *Namouna*), but always entertaining.

Scherzo for orchestra.

** Decca SXL 6395. Suisse Romande Orchestra, Ernest Ansermet – MAGNARD: *Symphony No. 3*.**

An attractive piece that enhances the value of this issue. The Magnard *Symphony* is something of a rarity and the recording is first-class, even though the performance is somewhat lacking in polish.

Symphonie espagnole (for violin and orchestra), *Op. 21*.

　*** CBS 72612. Isaac Stern (violin), Philadelphia Orchestra, Eugene Ormandy – BRUCH: *Violin concerto No. 1*.***

　(B) ** (*) Classics for Pleasure CFP 40040. Leonid Kogan (violin), Philharmonia Orchestra, Kyril Kondrashin – TCHAIKOVSKY: *Méditation; Sérénade mélancolique*.***

　(B) ** Decca Eclipse ECS 670. Ruggiero Ricci (violin), Suisse Romande Orchestra, Ernest Ansermet RAVEL: *Tzigane*.**

The full five-movement version of Lalo's colourful concertante work coupled with the Bruch *Concerto* provides generous measure on LP, and the performances have the rich, red-blooded quality of Stern at his best. He is recorded very close in relation to the orchestra, but in this music that is not a great disadvantage and for its age (late fifties) the sound is still commendably opulent.

The Classics for Pleasure recording dates from 1960 but is of very good quality, brilliant but with plenty of body and a realistic portrayal of the soloist. Kogan's assurance and sensibility throughout are impressive, and the finale has a fine sparkle. But the music's Spanish quality – the French composer's vivid response to local colour and atmosphere – eludes the performers here. Even so, with a very attractive coupling this disc is competitive in such a narrow field.

Ricci's account has no lack of sparkle, but the nervous intensity of his playing and the characteristic close *vibrato* of his tone production do not always catch the music's atmosphere. The second subject of the first movement, for instance, needs to blossom in a more relaxed way. Like Stern, Ricci is balanced close, but Ansermet sees that the orchestral detail comes through. The recording does not sound its age, and the disc is good value.

Lambert, Constant (1905–51)

Horoscope (ballet): *Valse for the Gemini*.

　(M) *** HMV SXLP 30153. Royal Opera House, Covent Garden Orchestra, Robert Irving – BLISS: *Checkmate*; BRITTEN: *Matinées and Soirées musicales*.***

This performance of the delightful *Gemini waltz* serves only to whet one's appetite for the ballet suite itself. This is available in an excellent stereo transcription (Decca Eclipse ECS 657), also conducted by Irving and coupled with Holst's *Perfect Fool ballet suite* and the Bach/Walton *Wise Virgins ballet music*.

Elegiac blues; Piano sonata.

　*** Argo ZRG 786. Rhondda Gillespie (piano) – BLISS: *Sonata*.***

Lambert's was a very positive creative genius but he more than most showed up the limitations of a jazz-based style. Anyone who knows the vividly colourful *Rio Grande* will recognize here the same exciting blend of snapping, Cuban rhythms and blues-based lyricism. The *Sonata* is a magnificent work, taking this distinctive style to what in effect proved its culmination, for after this Lambert turned in slightly different stylistic directions, and never again quite recovered his youthful urgency. The three massive movements are powerfully presented by Rhondda Gillespie, who must be congratulated too on including the little *Elegiac blues*, hauntingly melancholy, written in memory of the blues singer Florence Mills. First-rate, if reverberant, recording.

The Rio Grande.
> ** (*) HMV ASD 2990. Cristina Ortiz (piano), Jean Temperley (mezzo-soprano), London Madrigal Singers, London Symphony Orchestra, André Previn – WALTON: *Symphony No. 2 etc.****

The Rio Grande is one of the most evocative works of the twenties, with its colourful and genial jazz references in a setting of Sacheverell Sitwell's exotic poem. Though Cristina Ortiz is not quite idiomatic in her playing of the central piano solo, Previn directs a strong and enjoyable performance, superbly recorded. Lambert, one of the great characters of British music, may not have been a great composer, but this is his masterpiece.

Lanchbery, John
(born 1923)

Tales of Beatrix Potter (ballet arranged from popular tunes of the Victorian era).
> *** HMV CSD 3690. Royal Opera House, Covent Garden, Orchestra, John Lanchbery.

Here is a companion score for John Lanchbery's arrangement of *La Fille mal gardée*. The music is not as distinguished melodically as the compilation of Hérold tunes, but the colourful and witty orchestration is a source of delight and this is really top-drawer EMI sound, as the

opening bars readily show. The composer-arranger used Victorian tunes (including some by Sullivan) of the period of the Beatrix Potter stories and they are so skilfully linked that one would think the score was 'composed' as original music. The film of the ballet was a great success and this record deserves to be too. The sleeve-presentation is very attractive.

Lange-Müller, Peter
(1850–1926)

Once Upon a Time (incidental music), Op. 25: suite.
> (B) ** Turnabout TV 34230S. Willy Hartmann (tenor), Royal Danish Opera Chorus, Royal Danish Orchestra, Johan Hye-Knudsen – KUHLAU: *Elf Hill.** (*)

In the summer of 1884 the Danish author Holger Drachmann wrote to Lange-Müller: 'Here you have two thirds of a fairy-tale comedy entitled *Once Upon a Time*. The lacking third arrives in a fortnight. So you can get busy!' Lange-Müller did and the result is delightful. The genial overture is followed by some operetta-style *Gipsy music*, then after a *Serenade* there is the jolly *Hunters' music*, a boisterous *Peasant dance*, and numbers for *Twilight*, the *Kitchen* and a *Wedding*. The closing *Midsummer song* lacks the final distinction to create a new national song as the author intended, but it remains deservedly popular in Denmark. The invention throughout is spontaneous, and if the composer's orchestral sense has not the individuality of a Sullivan or an Offenbach it is felicitous enough. The basic atmosphere is rather naïve, as befits a fairy-story setting, but the whole score is enjoyable. It is played and sung here enthusiastically and idiomatically, and the recording is atmospheric.

Lassus, Orlandus
(c. 1530–1594)

Missa pro defunctis (Requiem); O bone Jesu (motet).

** BASF BAC 3040. Pro Cantione Antiqua Ensemble, Bruno Turner.

Bruno Turner makes dramatic use of dynamic contrast in these performances. Perhaps he is in conflict with authentic practice, but he does provide a surging forward impulse in music that can sometimes sound rather static. Another contrary feature of the performance is the singing of the plainsong intonations by a tenor instead of a bass. The higher register is certainly effective but it is not quite what the composer would have expected. But with rich sound the singing here makes a strong effect, and it is easy for stylistic reservations to be swept aside.

Missa super Bell' Amfitrit' altera; Psalmus poenitentalis VII.

⊛ *** Argo ZRG 735. Christ Church Cathedral Choir, Oxford, Simon Preston.

Lassus is scantily represented in the current catalogue and what there is can often be faulted on either stylistic or technical grounds. This splendid record is doubly welcome for, along with Bruno Turner's fine version of the five-part Mass of 1580, it can be recommended wholeheartedly. The trebles are firm in line, strong in tone, and the choir produces marvellously blended tone-quality. The acoustic is warm and atmospheric (the performances were recorded in Merton College, Oxford) and the texture is thus heard to best advantage. The performances have an admirable vitality and plenty of expressive range, though there is not the slightest trace of self-indulgence or excessive fervour. The *Mass* comes

from about 1585 and is Venetian in style, scored for double choir each comprising SATB. Simon Preston secures magical results, and the recording is one of the finest choral records of recent years, rich in detail and firmly focused in sound.

Lawes, William
(1602–45)

Consort music: *Six-part Consort suite No. 1 in C minor; Five-part Consort suite No. 1 in G minor* (both for viols and organ). *Consort No. 8 in G major* (for violin, division viol, theorbo, harp and organ continuo). *Sonatas Nos. 1 in G minor* (for 2 violins, bass viol, organ); *8 in D major* (for violin, bass viol, harp, organ).

*** Argo ZRG 555. Elizabethan Consort, Thurston Dart.

William Lawes was born in Salisbury in 1602. His elder brother, Henry, was also a musician and both eventually found employment with Charles I. William was killed at the Siege of Chester, and his music was forgotten when Purcell appeared. The present disc reveals a distinct musical personality, not as strong as Purcell perhaps, but with an individual, lyrical gift and the skill of a musical craftsman. In a fascinating note about the preparation for these performances Margaret Bent explains the problems of balance which modern players find in these scores, the five-part voicing being easier to manage than the six-part. One feels that in the items including the triple-harp, which tends to dominate, these problems have not been completely solved, but the result is so colourful and pleasing that one cannot possibly complain. The organ is used discreetly (again because of balance problems) but effectively. The music itself is highly rewarding, only the *G minor Suite* relatively austere. The rest has a 'madrigal' flavour with the distinct melodic appeal of vocal music, yet is instrumentally conceived in construction. The playing here is so expressive and the intonation so sure that it was some time before one realized that the players were not using a vibrato. One cannot pay a higher compliment. The recording is most beautiful.

Leclair, Jean-Marie
(1697–1765)

Scylla et Glaucus (opera): orchestral suite.

> (M) *** Oiseau-Lyre SOL 303. English Chamber Orchestra, Raymond Leppard – DESTOUCHES: *Issé suite.****

Raymond Leppard has found an attractive suite in Leclair's only known opera, and with his usual flair brings some very fetching music back to life. The style of the writing is as much Italian as French, and Leppard's light touch reveals melodic charm and graciousness of phrase and form. This is most entertaining when the playing and recording are so good.

Lecocq, Alexandre
(1832–1918)

Mam'zelle Angot (ballet): suite (arr. Gordon Jacob).

> (B) *** Decca Eclipse ECS 586. Royal Opera House, Covent Garden, Orchestra, Anatole Fistoulari – WALTON: *Façade suites Nos. 1 and 2.****

La Fille de Madame Angot was a highly successful operetta of the 1870s. The ballet, which dates from 1943, follows the story of the operetta but includes also music from other sources, all by Lecocq. The score is wittily arranged by Gordon Jacob in the manner of Constant Lambert's *Les Patineurs* (Meyerbeer). A strong flavour of Adam's style pervades some of the pieces (the *Adagio*, for instance), and the spirit of Offenbach peeps in too, particularly in the final carnival scene. One could hardly imagine a better recipe for pure enjoyment, and Fistoulari's vivacious performance is well supported by excellent recording.

Lehár, Franz
(1870–1948)

Giuditta (operetta): complete recording.

> (M) ** Decca Ace of Diamonds GOS 583/4. Hilde Gueden (soprano), Waldemar Kmentt (tenor), Emmy Loose (soprano), Murray Dickie (tenor), Walter Berry (baritone), Oskar Czerwenka (bass), Vienna State Opera Chorus and Orchestra, Rudolf Moralt.

Decca celebrated the Lehár centenary in 1970 with a reissue in stereo of this late and comparatively ambitious operetta. The performance is affectionately idiomatic, well-sung, and for its period (1958) beautifully recorded. But the music only goes to prove once more that even the most lyrical composer tends to lose his gift of melody as he grows older. This score of 1934 shows all the old technical skill but is nowhere near so haunting.

(i) *Das Land des Lächelns* (operetta): excerpts; (ii) *Der Zarewitsch* (operetta): excerpts.

> (M) *** Telefunken NT 113. Anneliese Rothenberger (soprano), Sonja Schoner (mezzo-soprano),

Heinz Hoppe (tenor), (i) North German Radio Orchestra, Hamburg, Richard Müller-Lampertz, (ii) Berlin State Opera Chorus and Orchestra, Hansgeorg Otto.

Both selections here are done potpourri style and are splendidly sung, Anneliese Rothenberger and Heinz Hoppe being especially well matched in the *Land of Smiles* selection. Herr Hoppe sings *You are my heart's delight* stirringly. The selection on side two is equally enjoyable, and starts with a most atmospheric choral item in which the stereo effect is superb.

The Merry Widow (Die lustige Witwe) (operetta): complete recording.

⊕ (M) *** HMV SLS 823 (2 discs). Elisabeth Schwarzkopf (soprano), Nicolai Gedda (tenor), Eberhard Waechter (baritone), Hanny Steffek (soprano), Josef Knapp (baritone), Kurt Equiluz (tenor), Philharmonia Chorus and Orchestra, Lovro von Matačić.

** DGG 2707 070 (2 discs). Elizabeth Harwood (soprano), René Kollo (tenor), Zoltan Kelemen (baritone), Teresa Stratas (mezzo-soprano), Werner Hollweg, Donald Grobe (tenors), Chorus of German Opera, Berlin, Berlin Philharmonic Orchestra, Herbert von Karajan.

(M) ** Decca Ace of Diamonds SDD 113/4. Hilde Gueden (soprano), Waldemar Kmentt (tenor), Per Grunden (baritone), Emmy Loose (soprano), Karl Donch (baritone), Peter Klein (tenor), Vienna State Opera Chorus and Orchestra, Robert Stolz.

HMV provides a magical set, guaranteed to send shivers of delight through any listener with its vivid sense of atmo-

sphere and superb musicianship. It is one of Walter Legge's masterpieces as a recording manager. He had directed the earlier *Merry Widow* set, also with his wife Elisabeth Schwarzkopf as Hanna, and realized how difficult it would be to outshine it. But outshine it he did, creating a sense of theatre that is almost without rival in gramophone literature. If the Decca approach to opera has always been to conceive it in terms of a new medium, Legge went to the opposite view and produced something that is almost more theatrical than the theatre itself. No other opera record more vividly conveys the feeling of expectancy before the curtain rises than the preludes to each act here.

The performances retain this sense of heady Viennese gaiety, and above all the singing of Elisabeth Schwarzkopf has intense beauty. The famous *Viljalied* is a shade faster and less mannered than before but with even deeper undertones, and the emotional climax of the act when her ruse has worked and she knows that Danilo still loves her has the intensity of a *Rosenkavalier* climax. Eberhard Waechter may be thought a little gruff in tone for Danilo, but the standard of singing is generally beyond criticism, and how worthy the music is of such treatment. The recording is one of EMI's most spectacular, dazzling in the climaxes but even more remarkable for distant off-stage effects that make one catch the breath. An irresistible set, now offered at mid-price. The purists may like to note that the text has been cut to make the action smoother and more convincing.

'Brahms's *Requiem* performed to the tunes of Lehár' was how one wit described the Karajan version, with its carefully measured tempi and absence of sparkle. Though Harwood is an appealing widow, she is colourless beside Schwarzkopf. The recording has religious reverberation.

In the original pressings the Decca recording was notable for its liveliness and strongly atmospheric background effect. The Ace of Diamonds transfer seems curiously dry, and while the sound is crisp, much of the stereo ambience seems to have disappeared. Gueden makes a vivacious Widow; the rest of the cast certainly capture the style of the music admirably, but the whole effect is altogether less magical than in the alternative EMI set. Stolz conducts well, but the inflated overture he provides to open the performance is no particular asset. This is an enjoyable bargain but for vocal richness does not match the HMV version.

The Merry Widow: highlights.
*** HMV ASD 2252 (from above recording cond. Matačić).

This selection manages to include most of the essential numbers, but in an operetta so crammed with good things. there are inevitable casualties. The only real answer is to get the complete set, but if makeshift is essential, this is a marvellous reminder of an unmatchable performance and recording.

The Merry Widow (in an English version by Christopher Hassall): concise recording.
** HMV CSD 1259. Sadler's Wells Opera Company and Orchestra, Reid.

This performance does not always have an *echt-Viennese* flavour; nevertheless it says much for the achievement of the Sadler's Wells production that their concise version is so successful – even in comparison with the Decca Viennese set. For many, the deciding factor will be the English words, sung in an admirable translation, but one is not sure that this is so important on a gramophone record. The Sadler's Wells cast is strongly characterized; only in Howell Glynne's approach is there a suspicion of Gilbert

and Sullivan. Thomas Round is an appropriately raffish Danilo, though it is a pity the recording tends to exaggerate the unevenness in his voice. William McAlpine as the second tenor, Camille de Rosillon, comes over much better, and his *Red as the rose* is exquisitely sung. The chorus is outstandingly good (especially the men) in the big scenes, and HMV have recorded the orchestra with a fine tonal bloom.

The Merry Widow (in Christopher Hassall's English version): highlights.
** Columbia Studio 2 TWO 234. June Bronhill, Jeremy Brett, David Hughes, Ann Howard, John McCarthy Singers and Orchestra, Vilem Tausky.

The Studio 2 recording here is brilliant to the point of shrillness in the orchestral introduction, but settles down when the voices enter, although there are patches of roughness, especially at the side ends. When sung in English the *Merry Widow* tends to sound more like a musical comedy than operetta; however, Christopher Hassall's translation is a great improvement on what we usually get, and at least the words do not sound gauche. The singing here has a nice light touch. June Bronhill's *Vilja* is delightful (much preferable to Anneliese Rothenberger's account in her recital) and her duet with Jeremy Brett, *Jogging in a one-horse gig*, is no less fetching. The two lovers close the disc with equal charm in a warm, stylish account of *the* waltz, *Love unspoken*. It is this lyrical quality rather than any Viennese insouciance that makes this selection a little out of the ordinary.

Arias from: *Eva; Friederike; Giuditta; Der Graf von Luxembourg; Das Land des Lächelns; Die lustige Witwe; Paganini; Schön ist die Welt; Der Zarewitsch; Zigeunerliebe.*

** HMV CSD 3695. Anneliese Rothenberger (soprano), various orchestras and conductors.

This is a bright, idiomatic selection sung with style but little magic. Even the famous *Vilja* sounds comparatively straightforward, with no melting quality. The recording has plenty of sparkle and with so many good tunes this is attractive enough. It is certainly preferable to Gedda's selection (see below).

Arias from: *Frasquita; Friederike; Giuditta; Der Graf von Luxembourg; Das Land des Lächelns; Die lustige Witwe; Paganini; Schön ist die Welt; Der Zarewitsch.*
  * (*) HMV CSD 3676. Nicolai Gedda (tenor), Graunke Orchestra, Willy Mattes.

This is disappointing. Gedda's voice does not sound its freshest; a good deal of his singing is not ideally flexible and it is seldom melting. An exception is *Von Apfelbluten einen Kranz* from the *Land of Smiles*, which has a really beautiful closing cadence. But the disc opens with *You are my heart's delight* from the same operetta and this is curiously stiff, as if the singer had to be careful about letting his voice really go.

Leighton, Kenneth
(born 1929)

Concerto for string orchestra, Op. 39.
  (M) *** Pye Virtuoso TPLS 13005. London Philharmonic Orchestra, John Snashall – CRUFT: *Divertimento;* MCCABE: *Symphony.****

Kenneth Leighton's *Concerto* has touches of eclecticism (the finale almost quotes from Shostakovich) but the writing is never dry, and indeed the inter-

nal passion of the opening *Lento sostenuto* requires very strong playing, yet precise discipline. It does not quite receive this here, but the spontaneity of the performance (as throughout this excellent collection) more than compensates. The wit of the pizzicato second movement is conveyed with evident pleasure. The recording is very good indeed. The string textures are clear and sonorous, the overall sense of atmosphere not preventing inner clarity, yet there is a complete absence of grittiness. Most recommendable to all those interested in twentieth-century music.

Leoncavallo, Ruggiero
(1858–1919)

I Pagliacci (opera in 2 acts): complete recording.
  *** DGG 2709 020 (3 discs). Joan Carlyle (soprano), Carlo Bergonzi, Ugo Benelli (tenors), Giuseppe Taddei, Rolando Panerai (baritones), Chorus and Orchestra of La Scala, Milan, Herbert von Karajan – MASCAGNI: *Cavalleria Rusticana.****
  (M) ** Decca Ace of Diamonds GOS 588/90. Gabriella Tucci (soprano), Mario del Monaco (tenor), Cornell MacNeil (baritone), Chorus and Orchestra of St Cecilia Academy, Rome, Francesco Molinari-Pradelli – MASCAGNI: *Cavalleria Rusticana.***

I Pagliacci: complete recording. Arias: *La Bohème: Ed ora, conoscetela; Musette svarie sulla bocca; Non parlate così; Io non ho; Scuoti o vento. Zazà: Mamma, io non l'ho avuta mai; Zazà, picco la zingara. Chatterton: Non saria meglio.*

*** RCA SER 5635/6. Montserrat Caballé (soprano), Placido Domingo (tenor), Sherrill Milnes (baritone), John Alldis Choir, London Symphony Orchestra, Nello Santi.
I Pagliacci: complete recording. (Also includes Italian song recital by Del Monaco: CINQUE: *Trobadorica.* CIOFFI: *'Na sera.* DI CAPUA: *O sole mio.* DE CURTIS: *Tu ca'nun chiagne.* MAINARDI: *Varca d'o primo.* LARA: *Granada.*)

(M) * (*) Decca Ace of Diamonds GOS 658/9 (same performance as above cond. Molinari-Pradelli).
I Pagliacci: complete recording. (Also includes recital by McCracken: arias from GIORDANO: *Andrea Chénier;* MASCAGNI: *Cavalleria Rusticana*; PUCCINI: *Tosca; Turandot.*)

* (*) Decca SET 403/4. Pilar Lorengar (soprano), James McCracken (tenor), Robert Merrill, Tom Krause (baritones), Chorus and Orchestra of St Cecilia Academy, Rome, Lamberto Gardelli.

The Italian opera traditionalists may jib at Karajan's treatment of Leoncavallo's melodrama – and for that matter its companion piece. He does nothing less than refine them, with long-breathed, expansive tempi and the minimum exaggeration. One would expect such a process to take the guts out of the drama, but with Karajan – as in *Carmen, Tosca, Aida,* etc. – the result is superb. One is made to hear the beauty of the music first and foremost, and that somehow makes one understand the drama more. Passions are no longer torn to tatters, Italian-style – and Karajan's choice of soloists was clearly aimed to help that – but the passions are still there, and rarely if ever on record has the Scala Orchestra played with such beautiful feeling for tone-colour. Bergonzi is among the most sensitive of Italian tenors of heroic

quality, and it is good to have Joan Carlyle doing a major operatic role on record, touching if often rather cool. Taddei is magnificently strong and Benelli and Panerai could hardly be bettered in the roles of Beppe and Silvio. The recording is good but needs to be reproduced at a high volume level if it is to have full immediacy.

For those who do not want the obvious coupling with *Cavalleria Rusticana,* the RCA set is a first-rate recommendation, with fine singing from all three principals, vivid playing and recording, and one or two extra passages not normally performed – as in the Nedda–Silvio duet. Milnes is superb in the Prologue, and though Caballé does not always suggest a young girl this is technically the most beautiful account of the role of Nedda available on record. The fill-up of six rare Leoncavallo arias sung by the three principals is particularly attractive.

The Ace of Diamonds reissue offers a lively performance, extremely well and dramatically recorded, so that with a genuine opera-house atmosphere and sense of realism one is prepared to accept singing that would otherwise seem undistinguished. Yet Cornell MacNeil is a splendid Tonio, and Gabriella Tucci a sweet-voiced Nedda, if without much imagination. This is available coupled either to *Cavalleria Rusticana* or to a lusty Italian song recital by Mario del Monaco. The coarse-grained style here is not altogether out-of-keeping, but what one misses is a sense of charm.

The newer, more expensive Decca set centres round the Canio of James McCracken, intentionally a big scale heroic performance with Othello-like overtones. But the execution is too rough to be tolerable. *Vesti la giubba* may begin promisingly, but later on the voice is made to crack at every bar, and conviction as well as musical interest wanes. Whatever the effect on stage, this sounds crude on record, and though the rest of

515

the cast is good – Merrill at his finest, Benelli sweet-toned as ever and Lorengar tenderly expressive if fluttery in vibrato – this cannot match the finest rival versions. The tenor recital on the fourth side shows McCracken again in uningratiating form.

I Pagliacci: highlights.
* ***DGG SLPEM 136281 (from above recording cond. Karajan).
* (M) ** Decca Ace of Diamonds SDD 418 (from above recording cond. Molinari-Pradelli).
* * (*) Decca SET 490 (from above recording cond. Gardelli).

These three selections are all coupled to highlights from the companion *Cavalleria Rusticana* recordings (the Gardelli to Varviso's recording on SET 343/4). Karajan's, with all the advantages of his complete set, is easily the finest. The Ace of Diamonds coupling is good value, but on the more expensive Decca issue McCracken is disappointingly coarse, although Lorengar and Krause sing well in the Nedda–Silvio duet.

Liadov, Anatol
(1855–1914)

Baba-Yaga, Op. 56; The Enchanted Lake, Op. 62.
* ***HMV ASD 2499. USSR Symphony Orchestra, Konstantin Ivanov – TCHAIKOVSKY: *Symphony No. 3.*** (*)
Baba-Yaga, Op. 56; The Enchanted Lake, Op. 62; Polonaise, Op. 49.
* (B) ***HMV SLS 881 (7 discs). USSR Symphony Orchestra, Konstantin Ivanov – TCHAIKOVSKY: *Symphonies Nos. 1–6 ** (*)* ; RIMSKY-KORSAKOV: *Overtures.***

Baba-Yaga, Op. 56; Kikimora, Op. 63.
* (B) ** Decca Eclipse ECS 735. Suisse Romande Orchestra, Ernest Ansermet – RIMSKY-KORSAKOV: *Scheherazade.***
Baba-Yaga, Op. 56; 8 Russian folksongs, Op. 58.
* ***HMV ASD 2700. USSR Symphony Orchestra, Yevgeny Svetlanov – BORODIN: *Symphony No. 2.* (*)
8 Russian folksongs, Op. 58.
* (B) ***Decca Eclipse ECS 742. Suisse Romande Orchestra, Ernest Ansermet – TCHAIKOVSKY: *Symphony No. 4.*(*)

Although Liadov was a miniaturist and was not prolific, his art is endearing, atmospheric and highly attractive. Of all the post-nationalist Russian composers he was the least flamboyant. The *Russian folksongs*, *Baba-Yaga*, *Kikimora* and *The Enchanted Lake* are all well-known miniatures. Both Ivanov and Svetlanov secure performances of great sensitivity and brilliance, and they are well served by the HMV Melodiya engineers. Ansermet too is a perceptive conductor in this music: *Kikimora* has characteristic detail and atmosphere, and his set of *Russian folksongs* is quite delightful, beautifully played and recorded. It is a pity that in each case the Eclipse couplings are not among the first recommendations of the works for which the Liadov pieces act as fillers, but this also applies to Svetlanov's Borodin coupling.

Liszt, Franz
(1811–86)

Symphonic poems: *Ce qu'on entend sur la montagne, G.95; Hunnenschlacht, G.105; Von der Wiege bis zum Grabe, G.107.*

** (*) Philips 6500 189. London Philharmonic Orchestra, Bernard Haitink.

Though undeniably they contain their longueurs, Liszt's symphonic poems have a wider range of imagination than most listeners will realize. The relatively popular works have by no means the monopoly of Liszt's inspiration, and the final work, *From the Cradle to the Grave*, has a visionary quality which shows Liszt thinking far ahead of his time. *Ce qu'on entend sur la montagne* was inspired by Victor Hugo, sketched in 1847 and completed in full score, with the help of Joachim Raff, three years later. Liszt then made a number of revisions; the fourth and last in 1857 is recorded here. For all its historical importance the work is less compelling than some of its companions. The performances here are fresh and direct, if lacking in the strain of vulgarity which makes such a piece as *Hunnenschlacht* (*The Battle of the Huns*) more ear-catching. Haitink draws fine playing from the LPO and the recording is excellent, but in a way the devotion is too complete.

Piano concerto No. 1 in E flat major, G.124.
 ** (*) DGG SLPM 139383. Martha Argerich (piano), London Symphony Orchestra, Claudio Abbado – CHOPIN: *Concerto No. 1.* ** (*)
Piano concertos Nos. 1 in E flat major, G.124; 2 in A major, G.125.
 ⊛ (M) *** Philips Universo 6580 071. Sviatoslav Richter (piano), London Symphony Orchestra, Kyril Kondrashin.
 (M) ** (*) Philips Universo 6582 003. Byron Janis (piano), Moscow Philharmonic Orchestra, Kyril Kondrashin, or Moscow Radio Orchestra, Gennady Rozhdestvensky.

** (*) Decca Phase 4 PFS 4252. Ivan Davis (piano), Royal Philharmonic Orchestra, Edward Downes.
 (B) ** Turnabout TV 34215S. Alfred Brendel (piano), Vienna Pro Musica Orchestra, Michael Gielen.
 (B) * (*) Classics for Pleasure CFP 40057. Samson François (piano), Philharmonia Orchestra, Constantin Silvestri.

Piano concertos Nos. 1 in E flat major, G.124; 2 in A major, G.125; Totentanz (for piano and orchestra), G.126.
 ⊛ *** Philips 6500 374. Alfred Brendel (piano), London Philharmonic Orchestra, Bernard Haitink.

Piano concertos Nos. 1 in E flat major, G.124; 2 in A major, G.125. Hungarian rhapsody No. 12 in C sharp minor, G.244; Mephisto waltz No. 1, G.514.
 (B) ** (*) Decca SPA 318. Julius Katchen (piano), London Symphony Orchestra, Ataulfo Argenta.

Piano concertos Nos. 1 in E flat major, G.124; 2 in A major, G.125. Études d'exécution transcendante d'après Paganini, G.140: No. 2 in E flat major; Legend: St Francis of Paola walking on the waves, G.175/2.
 (M) ** (*) DGG Privilege 2538 255. Tamàs Vàsàry (piano), Bamberg Symphony Orchestra, Felix Prohaska.

Among many fine records coupling the Liszt concertos, two stand out even above the high standards set by the others. Richter's record, now reissued at medium price, tends to sweep the board for those wanting just the concertos. It is particularly distinguished, not only by the power and feeling of Richter's own playing and the obvious rapport between conductor and soloist, but also because of a similar and striking communication between Richter and the orchestra. The orchestral playing throughout is of the very highest order and achieves a remarkable poetic feeling when orchestral soloists are called on to share a melody with the piano. The recording is vivid, with bold piano tone, but perhaps slightly below the finest modern standard. We are to some extent divided over the award of a (clearly deserved) rosette to either this record or Brendel's Philips issue.

This offers an extra work and well-nigh flawless recording; the sound is beautifully balanced and produces the most truthful and well-detailed quality throughout the spectrum. The performances are as poetic as they are brilliant and those who doubt the musical substance of No. 2 will find their reservations melt away. Richter's accounts are most brilliant and perceptive, but his disc is by no means so well balanced as a recording, and taking this into account it will be a long time before the Philips Brendel issue is challenged, let alone surpassed.

The other Universo disc is also a distinguished one, and brilliantly recorded too, even if the balance is somewhat less natural than on Brendel's issue. Again in both works the partnership between soloist and conductor (Kondrashin in No. 1, Rozhdestvensky in No. 2) is unusually close. In the slow movement of No. 1 Byron Janis offers most poetic playing, and the scherzo is deliciously light, while the clipped martial rhythms of the finale are almost over-characterized. The reflective opening of the *Second Concerto* is another superb moment and Rozhdestvensky's contribution throughout has an appealing lyrical feeling. The finale, as in the *First Concerto*, has an unashamed touch of melodrama about it and there is an exhilarating dash in the pianism at the closing pages.

Ivan Davis's performances too are vividly characterized and are not without poetic feeling. Those to whom the vivid spotlighting of Phase 4 techniques

appeals will not be disappointed with this record on musical grounds, and certainly the recording is demonstration-worthy, in its way.

Katchen is superb in the *E flat Concerto*, slightly less successful with the changes of mood of the *Second*. But by any standards these are commanding performances, showing this pianist in his best light. They are well recorded too, and many will feel that at the price, with characteristically strong accounts of the *Twelfth Hungarian rhapsody* and the *Mephisto waltz* thrown in for good measure, this record is very competitive in the bargain range.

Vàsàry also offers two worthwhile bonuses, and his recording still sounds well. The performance of the *First Concerto* is distinguished by considerable subtlety and little barn-storming. It is not the most exciting version available, but it shows characteristic sensibility, and the approach to the *A major* is also thoughtful and sensitive. The accompaniments under Prohaska are sympathetic.

Brendel's earlier performances for Turnabout are perhaps not entirely superseded by the newer Philips issue. The orchestral support, particularly in No. 2, is not very polished, and the balance, with a tendency to spotlight orchestral solos, is rather artificial against the reverberant acoustic chosen. But the playing has a striking freshness and spontaneity. Brendel brings a musing, improvisatory quality to the *A major* work and his control of bravura in both concertos is illuminating as well as exciting.

Against this François and Silvestri on Classics for Pleasure are not especially competitive. The extrovert brilliance of No. 1 is well caught, but, with somewhat deliberate tempi, the account of No. 2 is less spontaneous. But in any case Katchen would seem a first choice in the bargain price-range.

A clear, direct, sometimes even fastidious approach to the *First Concerto*, coupled to Chopin, from Martha Argerich. She plays the *Larghetto* meltingly and makes the crisp 'Triangle' scherzo very much her own. There is an excellent partnership between pianist and conductor, and both are agreed to minimize the work's flamboyance without reducing the voltage. This is very much a performance to live with and many should find it exactly to their taste, even if Liszt himself might have found it a trifle too sophisticated.

A Faust symphony, G.108.

(M) ** Vox STGBY 614. Ferdinand Koch (tenor), Chorus and Symphony Orchestra of South-West German Radio, Baden-Baden, Jascha Horenstein.

(i) *A Faust symphony, G.108; 2 Episodes from Lenau's 'Faust' (Nocturnal procession; Dance in the village inn: 1st Mephisto waltz), G.110.*

** Decca SET 370/1. Suisse Romande Orchestra, Ernest Ansermet, (i) with Werner Krenn (tenor), Le Chœur Pro Arte de Lausanne.

Ansermet's account of the *Faust symphony* is superbly recorded and the *Nocturnal procession* from Lenau's *Faust* with which it is coupled is a highly interesting and compelling piece, recorded with exceptional clarity and depth. By the side of the Beecham account, not available at the time of writing but surely a set that will reappear in due course, the playing is simply not good enough to warrant an unqualified recommendation. However, the Ansermet is to be preferred on technical grounds to Horenstein's one-record version, which has less refined sound, though the performance has the greater intensity.

Symphonic poems: *Festklänge, G.101; Die Ideale, G.106.*

** Philips 6500 191. London Philharmonic Orchestra, Bernard Haitink.

Neither of these works is among Liszt's finest symphonic poems although they both have imaginative moments. *Festklänge (Festive Sounds)*, written in 1883, was associated with the composer's hopes of marriage with the Princess Wittgenstein. The music mixes polonaise dance rhythms with more romantic sections, perhaps reflecting Liszt's thoughts about the Princess. *Die Ideale* is based on Schiller's poem and has a musing rhapsodic feeling, imbued with melancholy, until the self-assurance of the closing pages. It is not an easy work to bring off, and Haitink's literal, dedicated manner does not always catch its changing moods. The performance of *Festklänge* is more successful, but lacks the extrovert bravura that brings Liszt's orchestral music fully to life. The recording is refined, to suit Haitink's approach.

Symphonic poems: *Hamlet, G.104; Mazeppa, G.100.*

(B) * Decca Eclipse ECS 702. Paris Conservatoire Orchestra, Karl Münchinger – RACHMANINOV: *Isle of the Dead.**

Symphonic poems: *Hamlet, G.104; Hungaria, G.103; Mazeppa, G.100.*

** Philips 6500 046. London Philharmonic Orchestra, Bernard Haitink.

The London Philharmonic Orchestra under Haitink catch the spirit and flamboyance of the idiom without self-consciousness and play throughout with polish and conviction. *Hamlet* and *Hungaria* do not contain Liszt's greatest music: the latter piece is the more successful. *Mazeppa* is a masterpiece, as anyone who has heard Karajan's marvellous Berlin Philharmonic performance well knows. (This is currently out of the

British catalogue.) Haitink's account is well made rather than especially revealing.

Münchinger is ponderous and unimaginative. His rhythmic articulation of the main theme of *Mazeppa* is heavily Teutonic, and *Hamlet* is almost totally without atmosphere. The effect in both works is far too literal and the recording is clinical too.

Symphonic poems: *Héroïde funèbre, G.102; Mephisto waltz No. 1, G.110/2; Prometheus, G.99.*

** (*) Philips 6500 190. London Philharmonic Orchestra, Bernard Haitink.

Liszt's *Héroïde funèbre* is nobly conceived and although it is rather extended it shows the composer at his most eloquent. This must be a very difficult work to perform in public, for it has a solemnly repeated cadence in the middle which would tempt an audience unfamiliar with the piece to clap halfway through. However, on a record this is not a problem and there is no doubt that Haitink's restrained yet powerful performance does the work full justice. *Prometheus* – a less memorable work – is successful too, although in the familiar *Mephisto waltz* there is a hint of reserve not entirely in the spirit of a Bacchanalian dance. The orchestral playing is first-rate and the recording extremely vivid, with splendid brass sounds in the *Funeral march*.

Hungarian fantasia for piano and orchestra, G.123.

** CBS Quadraphonic MQ 31075. Philippe Entremont (piano), New Philharmonia Orchestra, Seiji Ozawa – KHACHATURIAN: *Piano concerto.***(*)

(B) ** Turnabout TV 37015S. Peter Frankl (piano), Innsbruck Symphony Orchestra, Robert Wagner

– CHOPIN: *Andante spianato; Krakowiak.***

(i) *Hungarian fantasia for piano and orchestra, G.123; Hungarian rhapsodies* (for orchestra) *Nos. 4 in E flat major; 5 in E minor, G.359.*

(M) ** (*) DGG Privilege 135031. Berlin Philharmonic Orchestra, Herbert von Karajan, (i) with Shura Cherkassky (piano) – BRAHMS: *Hungarian dances.***

Hungarian fantasia for piano and orchestra, G.123; Totentanz (for piano and orchestra), *G.126.*

** Philips 6500 095. Michele Campanella (piano), Monte Carlo Opera Orchestra, Aldo Ceccato – SAINT-SAËNS: *Piano concerto No. 4.***

Ozawa opens his performance rather heavily, but later Entremont's whimsical *rubato* is attractive, and the account is given a rousing finale. The recording is full-blooded, the quadraphonic effect adding spaciousness to CBS's rather close balance.

Peter Frankl is less concerned with bravura than some other interpreters are, but he is spontaneous and thoroughly musical. The sound is good and this makes an acceptable coupling for the two Chopin works.

Campanella is an imaginative pianist born in Naples in 1947, who uses bravura writing not so much to display a very formidable technique as for genuinely expressive ends. Though the Monte Carlo strings are not ideally refined, these are enjoyable performances that can be recommended to anyone who fancies the coupling. First-rate recording.

Cherkassky plays the *Hungarian fantasia* affectionately, with glittering fingerwork, and there are some delightful touches from the orchestra; a little more panache from the soloist would have made the performance irresistible. The recording throughout is first-rate and this is now probably the best available version of this piece. Of the two *Rhapsodies*, No. 5 is less known. It is a fine work, not in the least superficial, and Karajan's memorable performance, passionate yet with a touch of restraint, raises its deep melancholy to the level of grand tragedy. This is most moving. No. 4 is more quixotic in style but its flashes of orchestral colour and changes of mood are well managed. Again the recording is excellent.

Hungarian rhapsody (for orchestra), *No. 2, G.359; Les Préludes* (symphonic poem), *G.97.*

> ** DGG SLPM 139037. Berlin Philharmonic Orchestra, Herbert von Karajan – SMETANA: *Vltava etc.** (*)

Karajan certainly plays *Les Préludes* with plenty of gusto, but his approach is also bombastic in the outer sections and he does not find the redeeming dignity in the music that Furtwängler (for instance) did. This is certainly exciting; the contrast in the pastoral section is well made, and the orchestral playing is first-rate, but something is missing in this reading. Karajan tends to over-sophisticize the *Hungarian rhapsody*, but this is enjoyable – it can hardly fail to be when so well played. The recording has sonority in the *Rhapsody* but in *Les Préludes* it is top-heavy as if, following Karajan's lead, the engineers sought surface brilliance above all else.

Symphonic poems: Hunnenschlacht, G.105; Mazeppa, G.100; Orpheus, G.98.

> *** Decca SXL 6535. Los Angeles Philharmonic Orchestra, Zubin Mehta.

These performances of *Hunnenschlacht* and *Mazeppa* are the complete reverse of the coin from those offered by Haitink (see above). The strain of vulgarity which is an essential part of certain of Liszt's symphonic poems is not subdued here and the performances are red-blooded and exciting in the most extrovert manner. With superbly ripe recording, of spectacular demonstration quality, *Hunnenschlacht* is immensely vivid and *Mazeppa* irresistible. *Orpheus* too is finely played, although it is perhaps less suited to Mehta's directness.

(i) *Malédiction* (for piano and string orchestra), *G.121. Mephisto waltz No. 1, G.514; Die Traurige Gondel No. 2, G.200; Unstern, G.208.*

> (B) * (*) Turnabout TV 34269S. Alfred Brendel (piano), (i) with Vienna Symphony Orchestra, Michael Gielen.

Malédiction is a characteristic piece, much more lyrical than the title might suggest. Brendel is on top form and plays with sympathy and power. The recording acoustic is over-resonant, but this is a rare work and well worth having in so committed a performance. This is real stereo, but the solo piano items on the disc are transcriptions of old mono recordings and sound it. The playing however is characteristically intelligent, and the *Mephisto waltz* is played with some subtlety.

Mephisto waltz No. 1, G.110/2; Tasso, lamento e trionfo (symphonic poem), *G.96; Von der Wiege bis zum Grabe* (symphonic poem), *G.107.*

> *** Decca SXL 6709. Orchestre de Paris, Sir Georg Solti.

Solti secures playing of the finest quality from the Orchestre de Paris, and the refinement of the closing section of *From the Cradle to the Grave* is used to create an electrifying diminuendo. The recording is superb to match the playing, and it expands marvellously in *Tasso*, where Solti provides a reading of great power and atmosphere; the lightening of mood in the work's central section is marvellously done. The *Mephisto waltz* has never been more vividly played on record.

Symphonic poems: *Orpheus, G.98; Les Préludes, G.97; Tasso, lamento e trionfo, G.96.*
** Philips SAL 3750. London Philharmonic Orchestra, Bernard Haitink.

The music of *Les Préludes* and *Tasso* creates its scenic backgrounds and unfolds its narrative with bold strokes of the brush. To realize the composer's intentions a full-blooded, committed approach from the conductor and players needs to be married to spectacular recording. Here Haitink is successful only with gentler, poetic moments, and although the orchestral playing is in itself beautiful and the recording smooth, the music's emotional and literal essence is not projected here as it should be. The result is rather pale. *Orpheus*, however, is much more successful.

Les Préludes (symphonic poem), *G.97.*
** Decca SXL 6298. Vienna Philharmonic Orchestra, Zubin Mehta –
WAGNER: *Orchestral preludes.***

Mehta's account has plenty of gusto, but the recording balance (the sound itself is spectacular) emphasizes the heavy brass and percussion in a blatant way, and the listener might reasonably suspect that neither conductor nor engineers quite take the piece seriously. As Furtwängler has shown us, with a degree of dignity as well as zest in the playing *Les Préludes* shows itself as one of the finest of Liszt's orchestral works. Probably the most satisfying version current in stereo is Ančerl's (part of a concert with the Czech Philharmonic Orchestra on Supra-

phon SUAST 50625). Ančerl provides a thrilling finale and, though he is perhaps too restrained in the romantic middle section, obviously he takes the music seriously.

Rapsodie espagnole, G.254 (transcribed for piano and orchestra by Busoni).
(B) ** Turnabout TV 34372S. Felicja Blumenthal (piano), Prague Chamber Orchestra, Vienna Wind Ensemble, Hellmuth Froschauer –
ALBÉNIZ: *Piano concerto No. 1.***

Liszt's *Rapsodie espagnole* is based on two well-known tunes. The first is a stately Portuguese *Folia*, which Corelli made famous in a set of variations in his *Violin sonata in D minor*. The second is a *Jota aragonesa* which Glinka used as a basis for his exotic orchestral work of the same name. Liszt skilfully contrasts the two, with dark, sombre colouring for the first and characteristically sparkling figurations for the second. Busoni's arrangement adds more colour and variety of effect, and it is surprising that this extrovert but rewarding piece is not heard more often in the concert hall. The performance here has both flair and glitter and is very enjoyable. The recording too is good, although the orchestral strings are clear rather than rich.

(i) *Totentanz* (for piano and orchestra), *G.126. Csárdás macabre, G.224.* (i)
SCHUBERT-LISZT: *Wanderer fantasia* (for piano and orchestra).
(B) ** (*) Turnabout TV 34265S. Alfred Brendel (piano), (i) with Vienna Volksoper Orchestra, Michael Gielen.

As Brendel suggests in his sleeve-note, Liszt's transcription for piano and orchestra of Schubert's *Wanderer fantasia* must be thought of not as an attempt to improve on Schubert but rather as an interesting example of stylistic contrast.

Certainly Liszt's flamboyant opening gets the piece off to a good start, and so convincing is the orchestration that – without preconceptions – it does not sound any more like a transcription than, say, Liszt's *Hungarian fantasia*. The present performance is characteristically spontaneous, and if neither the orchestral playing nor the recording is refined, the reverberant acoustic suits the ambience of the music. The *Totentanz* is another vivid Brendel performance, and the *Csárdás macabre* an interesting bonus. A most enjoyable collection.

INSTRUMENTAL MUSIC

Violin sonata, G.127 (ed. Serly).
(M) ** Pye Virtuoso TPLS 13017. Alfredo Campoli (violin), Valerie Tryon (piano) – R. STRAUSS: *Violin sonata*.**

All four movements of Liszt's *Violin sonata* use Chopin's *Mazurka in C sharp minor*, Op. 6/2, as a thematic basis. The result, whilst giving the work a structural unity, has the effect for the listener of sounding like a continuous set of variations on a given theme. The violin writing is seldom very grateful, and indeed Tibor Serly, who prepared the performing edition, adjusted some of the more awkward passages for the violin. The music itself has a certain characteristic flair, but it must be admitted that almost all the most striking music is to be found in the piano part. This Valerie Tryon plays splendidly. Campoli does his best with the sometimes clumsy violin pyrotechnics, although his intonation is not always absolutely secure. The recording clearly separates the artists to left and right, is very good in its picture of the piano, but gives a somewhat bare, wiry violin image. As the work progresses, Campoli covers his tone rather more, and in any case if the treble is pared a successful image emerges.

Piano Music

Années de pèlerinage, 2nd year, G.161: Sposalizio; Il penseroso; Canzonetta del Salvator Rosa; Sonetto del Petrarca Nos. 47, 104, 123; Après une lecture du Dante.
⊛ *** Philips 6500 420. Alfred Brendel (piano).

Superlative playing and recording. This is one of the finest Liszt recitals to have appeared in recent years; not only is the playing highly poetic and brilliant, but the recording presents some of the most realistic piano quality.

Années de pèlerinage, 2nd Year, G.161; Sonetto del Petrarca Nos. 47, 104, 123; Tarantella. Études d'exécution transcendante d'après Paganini, G.140, Nos. 1–6.
(B) ** (*) Turnabout TV 34353S. Alfred Brendel (piano).

Brendel is on top form in the *Paganini studies*. Characteristically there is little extrovert flamboyance. But the mixture of delicacy and brilliance which informs the playing still captures the Lisztian spirit, and Brendel's subtlety adds an extra dimension. The recording is excellent, better than most of Brendel's Turnabout discs. The *Années de pèlerinage* are thoughtfully played, evoking the classical spirit of their inspiration.

L'Arbre de Noël, G.186; Ballades Nos. 1 in D flat major, G. 170; 2 in B minor, G.171; Berceuse, G. 174; Consolations, G.172; Harmonies poétiques et religieuses, G.173; 3 Nocturnes, G.541.
(M) * (*) Decca 8BB 132/5. France Clidat (piano).

France Clidat enjoys a considerable reputation as a Lisztian in her own country, and this volume of four records proves her a talented and often thoughtful artist. However, though many of these performances are more than acceptable, none is really outstanding measured by the cruel standards of the gramophone. Given such pianists as Brendel, Earl Wild, Roberto Szidon, to mention only the most recent keyboard lions to enter the lists, there is little incentive to follow Madame Clidat through the complete canon. Good recording.

Concert paraphrases on Verdi's operas (complete): *Aïda: Danza sacra e duetto finale, G. 436; Don Carlos: Transcriptions, Coro di feste e marcia funebre, G.435; Ernani, G.432; I Lombardi: Salve Maria, G.431; Rigoletto, G.434; Réminiscences de Boccanegra, G.438; Miserere du Trovatore, G.433.*
** (*) Philips 6500 368. Claudio Arrau (piano).

Arrau characteristically refuses to indulge in display for its own sake, even in these deliberate showpieces. His technique remains effortlessly superb, and if there is inevitably a certain lack of sheer excitement, he shows what inner intensity some of this music contains in deeply expressive playing.

Concert paraphrases: *Bénédiction et serment, deux motifs de Benvenuto Cellini (Berlioz), G.396; Isoldens Liebestod from Tristan und Isolde (Wagner), G.447; Miserere du Trovatore (Verdi), G.433; Oberon overture (Weber), G.574; Pilgrims' chorus from Tannhäuser (Wagner), G.443; Réminiscences de Lucia di Lammermoor (Donizetti), G.397; Réminiscences de Norma (Bellini), G.394.*
(B) * (*) Turnabout TV 34352S. Alfred Brendel (piano).

On the evidence of this disc, operatic style (especially Donizetti, Bellini and early Verdi) is not Alfred Brendel's special métier. He plays strongly and emotionally but does not easily catch the spirit of the music. The most enjoyable performance here is the transcription of the *Oberon overture* of Weber, which is played with appealing delicacy and lightness of touch. Elsewhere the reverberant and rather clangy piano tone does not help with the louder climaxes.

Concert paraphrases: *Faust* (Gounod): *Waltz, G.407; Der fliegende Holländer* (Wagner): *Spinning song, G.440; A Midsummer Night's Dream* (Mendelssohn): *Wedding March; Dance of the elves, G.410; Réminiscences de Don Juan* (Mozart), *G.418.*
(B) * Turnabout TV 34163S. Louis Kentner (piano).

These are strong, authoritative performances, and it is a pity that the recording is so unconvincing. The quieter music is effective enough, but the big moments do not give a great deal of pleasure because the sound is bony yet curiously flabby in tone.

Concert paraphrases: *Réminiscences de Lucia di Lammermoor* (Donizetti), *G.397; Der fliegende Holländer* (Wagner): *Spinning song, G.440; Rigoletto* (Verdi), *G.434; Lieder: Chants polonais, Op. 74* (Chopin): *Mädchens Wunsch, G.480/1; Meine Freuden, G.480/5; Ständchen: Horch, horch, die Lerch, G.558/9; Die Forelle, G.563/6* (Schubert); *Widmung, G.566; Frühlingsnacht, G.568* (Schumann).
* (*) Pye Ensayo NEL 2013. Jorge Bolet (piano).

It is interesting to have on disc some of Liszt's paraphrases of Lieder, which are comparatively straightforward except for the characteristic elaboration of the piano accompaniments. But Jorge Bolet is not a persuasive advocate. In *Die Forelle*, which opens the recital, he breaks up the line of the music with unnecessary *rubato*, and elsewhere he is inclined to be heavy-handed. The operatic transcriptions suit him best, but the playing, although very assured, reveals no imaginative insights. The recording is basically quite good, but the quality has a tendency to break up a little under extreme pressure, especially at the side ends.

Concerto pathétique in E minor, G.258 (for 2 pianos).

* (*) Argo ZRG 721. John Ogdon, Brenda Lucas (pianos) – SCHU-MANN: *Andante and variations; Canonic studies.* * (*)

(i) *Concerto pathétique in E minor, G.258. Rapsodie espagnole, G.254; Rhapsody on Hungarian songs in A minor, G.242; Rumanian rhapsody, G.242.*

(B) * (*) Turnabout TV 34444S. Louis Kentner (piano), (i) with Joan Havill (piano).

Neither of these performances of the *Concerto pathétique* is ideal. It is a difficult work to bring off: it needs a partnership in virtuosity, yet both participants must retain overall control. The husband-and-wife team of Ogdon and Lucas are not helped by their recording acoustic, which is too reverberant and makes the textures of the music sound muddled. The approach to the music's lyrical element is thoughtful, but as a whole the account lacks panache.

Louis Kentner and Joan Havill are rather more successful with the rhapsodic flow, and, with Kentner clearly dominating, they make a good team. But the Turnabout recording is also inclined to smudge with resonance. The rest of Kentner's programme is an attractive one, but the playing, if sometimes powerful in manner, lacks incandescence. Again the recording with its reverberant sound does

not help the music-making to sound fresh.

Études d'exécution transcendante, G.139: Nos. 1, Prélude; 2 in A minor; 3, Paysage; 4, Mazeppa; 5, Feux follets; 6, Vision; 7, Eroica; 8,Wilde Jagd; 9, Ricordanza.

(B) * (**) Turnabout TV 34224S. Louis Kentner (piano).

Liszt's *Transcendental studies* are among his most difficult works to bring off, from an interpretative as well as a technical point of view. Louis Kentner solves most of the interpretative problems and nearly all the technical ones. Just occasionally his playing is inclined to be splashy, but his filigree decoration, as in *Feux follets,* for instance, can be breathtaking. This same kind of virtuosity married to a perfect understanding of romantic line can be heard in the attractive *Ricordanza*. Kentner's style sometimes sounds a little old-fashioned. He can create the grand manner without overdoing it, but sometimes his impulsiveness and *rubato* can seem too personal. On the other hand in a tempestuous descriptive piece like *Mazeppa* it can be just right. The disappointing thing here is not the playing, but the recording, which has a rather dim treble and no sense of immediacy.

Études d'exécution transcendante, G.139: Nos. 10 in F minor; 11, Harmonies du soir; 12, Chasse-neige; Ballade No. 2 in B minor, G.171; Elegy No. 2, G.197; La lugubre gondola (1st version), G.200; Nuages gris, G.199.

(B) ** (*) Turnabout TV 34225S. Louis Kentner (piano).

The opening *Allegro agitato* is a very strong performance indeed, and the recording seems clearer than before. It recedes again somewhat for *Harmonies du soir*, but once again the playing is most powerful, and the swirls of snow in *Chasse-neige* are a blizzard. The additional pieces are extremely successful and again the recording seems clearer. The *Ballade* is marvellously imaginative – this is an outstandingly poetic conception – and after the restrained beauty of the *Elegy*, the two late works sound remarkably stark and modern.

Harmonies poétiques et religieuses, G.173: Nos. 1, Invocation; 3, Bénédiction de Dieu dans la solitude; 4, Pensées des morts; 7, Funérailles; 10, Cantique d'amour.
(B) ** Turnabout TV 34246S. Alfred Brendel (piano).

This is most imaginative playing, thoughtful and beautiful. Brendel's feeling for the music's atmosphere triumphs over the rather bare-sounding recording, especially in the middle section of *Pensées des morts* and *Funérailles*.

Hungarian rhapsodies, G.244, Nos. 1–19: complete recording.
(B) ** (*) Turnabout TV 34266S (Nos. 1–7); TV 34267S (8–13); TV 34268S (14–21). Louis Kentner (piano).
Hungarian rhapsodies, G.244, Nos. 2 in C sharp minor; 3 in B flat major; 8 in F sharp minor; 13 in A minor; 15 in A minor (Rakóczy march); 17 in D minor; Csárdás obstiné, G.225/2.
(M) ** (*) Vanguard VCS 10035. Alfred Brendel (piano).
Hungarian rhapsodies, G.244, Nos. 2 in C sharp minor; 5 in E minor (Héroïde élégiaque); 9 in E flat major (Carnival in Pest); 14 in F minor; 15 in A minor (Rakóczy march); 19 in D minor.
*** DGG 2530 441. Roberto Szidon (piano).
Hungarian rhapsodies, G.244, Nos. 6 in

D flat major; 11 in A minor; Mephisto waltz No. 1, G. 514.
(M) ** Philips Universo 6580 049. Adam Harasiewicz (piano) –
BRAHMS: *Paganini variations.***

The Turnabout set is not so well recorded, nor are Kentner's performances so youthfully robust, as Szidon's recently deleted box, but it represents outstandingly good value both musically and economically. If occasionally Kentner falls slightly short of the extreme bravura Liszt asks for, he compensates with his sincerity of approach and obvious feeling for the idiom. Whether or not the performances were recorded in numerical order, there is a feeling that he has not warmed up on the first side of TV 34266S, for the famous *C sharp minor Rhapsody* seems a trifle mannered. But when one turns the disc over, No. 4 shows Kentner on top form, with beautifully light staccato playing. No. 6 too is most expressively played, and No. 7 finishes the disc boldly. The performances of the second record are at a consistently high temperature, and TV 34268S opens with a memorably full-blooded version of the other rhapsody well-known in orchestral (and concertante) form, the one in F minor.

Roberto Szidon offers Liszt playing of the highest order, comparable with that of Brendel, and recording quality to match. Szidon won acclaim some years ago with a debut record (Prokofiev *Sixth Sonata*, Scriabin No. 4 and Rachmaninov No. 2), and his set of the complete *Hungarian rhapsodies*, from which this disc is drawn, more than fulfilled the promise shown in his very first record. He has flair and panache, genuine keyboard command and, when required, great delicacy of tone.

Although the Vanguard recording is not a recent one, it sounds very good; and the playing is very distinguished indeed. The Philips engineers provide Brendel elsewhere with much finer piano tone and an enormously wide dynamic range, whereas on this disc, quality is distinctly thinner. However, there should be no doubts about the brilliance of the playing or the quality of the musical thinking that informs it.

Harasiewicz's performances of the *Hungarian rhapsodies* are slightly less penetrating, but the playing is brilliant and assured in style and the recording is good. Taken as a whole (with the spontaneous account of the Brahms *Variations*), this is an enjoyable recital; there are few finer accounts available of the *Mephisto waltz*.

Piano sonata in B minor, G.178 (see also below).
>   ****** DGG 2530 193. Martha Argerich (piano) – SCHUMANN: *Piano sonata No. 2.* (*)*
>   (M) * (*) DGG Privilege 2538 260. Tamàs Vàsàry (piano) – CHOPIN: *Piano sonata No. 2.***

Argerich's account of the Liszt *Sonata* has tremendous assurance and vigour. Indeed the bravura is breathtaking. There is no lack of spontaneity, but the work's lyrical feeling and indeed its breadth are to some extent sacrificed to the insistent forward impulse of the playing. By contrast Vàsàry gives a contained performance, not without romantic feeling, but in the last resort thoughtful rather than flamboyant. Liszt's inspiration needs a performance somewhere between these two extremes, and in both cases the recording is clear rather than richly resonant.

Piano sonata in B minor, G.178; Années de pèlerinage, 1st Year, G.160: Vallée d'Obermann; Études d'exécution transcendante, G.139: No. 4, Mazeppa; Liebestraum No. 3, G.541.
>   ******* Decca SXL 6485. Pascal Rogé (piano).

This record by the talented young Frenchman was made when he was only eighteen. The *Sonata* is given a brilliant and commanding performance, and he is as well recorded as anyone now in the catalogue. Rogé won the second prize in a French piano competition in 1971 and is obviously an artist to watch. He has no lack of poetry and has first-class technical equipment. Decca have given him a sonorous and truthful recording, so that readers wanting this particular collection of pieces need not hesitate.

Piano sonata in B minor, G.178; Années de pèlerinage, 2nd Year, G.161: Dante sonata; Bagatelle without tonality (1885); Hungarian rhapsody No. 11, G.244.
>   (B) * (*) Turnabout TV 34232S. Alfred Brendel (piano).

A powerful reading of the *Sonata*, as emotionally strong as it is structurally convincing, is rather spoilt by the hard piano tone, which tends to tire the ear in the loudest moments. The other pieces suffer too from this defect, although the playing itself is fine.

Piano sonata in B minor, G.178; Années de pèlerinage, 2nd Year, G.161: Sonetto del Petrarca Nos. 104, 123; Consolation No. 3, G.172.
>   (B) ** (*) Classics for Pleasure CFP 40051. Craig Sheppard (piano).

Craig Sheppard was the second prizewinner in the Leeds Piano Competition of 1972, a formidable challenger for the eventual winner, Murray Perahia. Though he lacks Perahia's individuality and sparkle, his playing of Liszt on record is a marvellous tribute to his technique. He does not quite sustain full intensity over the span of the great *Sonata*, but this is a first-rate bargain offering of some of Liszt's greatest piano music. Good if rather clangy recording.

Piano sonata in B minor, G.178; Berceuse, G.174; Concert study No. 2 (Gnomenreigen), G.145/2; Liebestraum No. 3, G.541.

*** Decca SXL 6076. Clifford Curzon (piano).

Curzon shows an innate understanding of the *Sonata*'s cyclic form, so that the significance of the principal theme is brought out subtly in relation to the music's structural development. There are few performances to compare with this and none superior, and Decca's recording matches the playing in its excellence. The shorter pieces too are imaginatively played.

Piano sonata in B minor, G.178; Concert studies, G.145, Nos. 1 (Waldesrauschen); 2 (Gnomenreigen); Harmonies poétiques et religieuses: Bénédiction de Dieu dans la solitude, G.173/3.

** (*) Philips 6500 043. Claudio Arrau (piano).

Arrau's performance of the *Sonata* has a characteristic eloquence and power. Its style, however, is somewhat deliberate, even pontifical, but admirers of this pianist should not be disappointed. About the rest of the recital there are no reservations whatsoever: the *Bénédiction* is exceptionally imaginative and rewarding, and the bravura in *Gnomenreigen* is riveting. The recording is resonant and full-blooded and makes a considerable impact.

Piano sonata in B minor, G.178; Études d'exécution transcendante d'après Paganini, G.140 (complete).

(B) ** Pye GSGC 14098. Bela Siki (piano).

Liszt without flamboyance is what Bela Siki offers us, and if this means an essential facet is missing, the conception presented here is impressive. The overall

control of the work's shape is compelling, with the closing pages showing the culmination of a thoughtful rather than an extrovert personality. The lack of conscious bravura is not entirely absent from the *Paganini studies*, and although the opening and closing pieces suffer marginally from Siki's avoidance of outward show, the refinement carries its own rewards. The recording is warm rather than brilliant.

Miscellaneous Collections

Années de pèlerinage, 1st Year, G.160: Vallée d'Obermann; 2nd Year, G.161: Sonetto del Petrarca Nos. 104, 123; 3rd Year, G.163: Les jeux d'eaux à la Villa d'Este; Ballade No. 2 in B minor, G.171; Valse oubliée No. 1, G.21.

*** Philips SAL 3783. Claudio Arrau (piano).

This is one of the very finest of all Liszt recitals. Claudio Arrau is extremely well recorded, the piano tone has depth as well as brilliance, and the effect is highly satisfying. The performances have remarkable eloquence and power. There is superb bravura in the *Ballade*, while the *Petrarch sonnets* (like the other items from *Années de pèlerinage*) have a finely calculated atmosphere and most subtle colouring. Sometimes on records Arrau's intellectual powers have been apparent at the expense of musical spontaneity but that is not the case here, for the playing throughout is remarkably alive and gripping. A most distinguished issue.

Années de pèlerinage, 2nd Year, G.161: Sonetto del Petrarca Nos. 104, 123; Ballade No. 2 in B minor, G.171; Études d'exécution transcendante, G.139: Nos. 5, Feux follets; 9, La Ricordanza; Études d'exécution transcendante d'après Paganini, G.140: No.3, La Campanella; Tarantella de La Muette *de Portici* (Auber), *G.386; Valse oubliée No. 1, G.21.*

(M) ** (*) H M V HQS 1332. Earl Wild (piano).

Although the piano sound is not ideal (there is some brittleness on top and a certain dryness about the sound) this disc should not be overlooked. In any event the recording is more than just tolerable: it is life-like and truthful in timbre. And the playing is quite stunning; no Lisztian should fail to acquire this disc. Its interest is enhanced by the presence of a *Tarantella* rarely heard in the recital room, a piece of some virtuosity which Mr Wild dispatches with characteristic aplomb.

Apparitions No. 1, G.155; Harmonies poétiques et religieuses, G.154; Harmonies poétiques et religieuses, G.173: Bénédiction de Dieu dans la solitude; 5 Hungarian folk-songs, G.245; 4 Little pieces, G.192; En rêve, G.207; Valse à capriccio sur deux motifs de Lucia et Parisina, G.401.

(B) *** Turnabout TV 34310S. Louis Kentner (piano).

Among Kentner's Liszt series this collection stands out. The performance of the early fantasy version of the *Harmonies poétiques et religieuses* has real power, and the same combination of strength and poetry infuses the *Bénédiction de Dieu dans la solitude*, one of Liszt's most atmospheric tone paintings. Equally the restrained romanticism in *Apparitions* is just right. The recording is good.

Concert study No. 2 (Gnomenreigen), G.145/2; Faust waltzes, G.407; Mephisto polka, G.217; Mephisto waltz No. 1, G.514; Réminiscences de Don Juan, G.148; Réminiscences de Robert le diable: Valse infernal, G.413.

(M) ** Vanguard VCS 10041. Earl Wild (piano).

To fit the disc's title, *The daemonic Liszt*, the first three works depend on sheer bravura to make their effect, and, though Earl Wild's technique is prodigious, a little more variety in the music itself would have been welcome. As it is, the rather dry piano tone becomes slightly oppressive. On side two the pianist is often beguiling in his operatic selections, and there is some glittering tessitura in the *Don Juan fantasia.* As a display of brilliant playing this is first-rate, and it is a pity that the programme is not arranged on the disc in such a way as to provide more contrast on each side.

Consolation No. 3, G.172; Concert study No. 3 (Un sospiro), G.144; Études d'exécution transcendante d'après Paganini, G.140 (complete); Hungarian rhapsody No. 12 in C sharp minor, G.244; Mephisto waltz No. 1, G.514.

(M) ** H M V HQS 1307. Agustin Anievas (piano).

The piano here is extremely well recorded – it is a pleasure to listen to – and the playing has character. Whether Anievas shows a special perception in the music of Liszt is another matter. He is at his very best in the fourth of the *Paganini studies*, which is deliciously pointed, and in the *Hungarian rhapsody*. But his phrasing of the famous D flat major melodies of the *Consolation* and the *Concert study* is rather cool; it is possible to provide a greater degree of romanticism here without swooning. Although the playing is generally accomplished there is the occasional technical 'fluff' (runs not quite clearly articulated, for instance). Better spontaneity than rigid precision, but this is music where bravura and absolute accuracy are important.

Études d'exécution transcendante,
G.139: Nos. 1, Prélude; 2 in A minor;
3, Paysage; 5, Feux follets; 8, Wilde
Jagd; 10 in F minor; 11, Harmonies du
soir. Gortschakoff-Impromptu. Meph-
isto waltz No. 3, G.216.

**(*) Decca SXL 6508. Vladimir
Ashkenazy (piano).

This is playing of outstanding brilliance and eloquence. The sheer bravura
is almost shattering in its impact, but
there is an underlying vein of poetry
throughout. *Harmonies du soir* is a marvellous penetrating performance, and
even the much-recorded *Mephisto waltz*
sounds strikingly fresh. The recording is
almost excessively bright and immediate,
especially on side one, which contains
five of the studies, and this metallic
quality in the treble means a qualified
recommendation; about the playing there
are no reservations whatsoever.

Organ Music

Évocation à la Chapelle Sixtine, G.658;
Trauerode, G.268/2; Prelude and fugue
on the name BACH, G.260; Tu es
Petrus, G.664.

*** Philips 6500 376. Daniel Chorzempa (organ).

This is a later recording than the
coupling discussed below and the performances, while no less distinguished, are
more considered. Indeed some might find
the style in the *Évocation* rather deliberate. The recording is superb, wide in
dynamic range and with great impact and
atmosphere, yet easy to reproduce. Chorzempa's registration finds some lovely
sounds in the more restrained sections,
notably in the *Trauerode*, which is finely
judged, and Allegri's *Miserere* which
forms the first half of the *Évocation* (the
latter part being based on Mozart's *Ave
verum*).

Fantasia and fugue on 'Ad nos, ad
salutarem undam', G.259; Variations
on Bach's 'Weinen, Klagen, Sorgen,
Zagen', G.673.

*** Philips 6500 215. Daniel Chorzempa (organ of De Doelen Concert Hall, Rotterdam).

Fantasia and fugue on 'Ad nos, ad
salutarem undam', G.259; Prelude and
fugue on the name BACH, G.260.

** (*) Argo ZRG 503. Simon Preston
(organ of Hull City Hall).

The character of Chorzempa's interpretations is one of vivid contrasts
rather than subtlety in overall shaping.
The central and final climaxes of the *Ad
nos, ad salutarem* are quite shattering in
their sudden surge of power, and there is
beautifully sustained quiet playing in the
Bach variations, the tension really coming
through, which is something few
organists manage. Chorzempa is rather
too emphatic in the heavy repeated
chords near the beginning of the latter
work, and the opening of *Ad nos* does not
grip the listener immediately. But these
are slight miscalculations only; this is an
outstanding disc and the recording accommodates the big climaxes splendidly. For
maximum effect a high volume level of
reproduction is necessary, as this gives
the organ texture more bite.

Simon Preson gives eloquent performances, and his recording too is both
spectacular and easy to reproduce.
Preston's approach is more considered
and, to be frank, not so exciting as Chorzempa's, although it could fairly be
argued that Preston's overall control of
each work is better disciplined.

Variations on Bach's 'Weinen, Klagen,
Sorgen, Zagen', G.673.

(B) *** Saga 5340. Peter Le Huray
(organ of Salisbury Cathedral) –
REUBKE: *Sonata on the 94th
Psalm.****

An excellent and imaginative performance of Liszt's variations, very well recorded. The review copy has excellent surfaces too, and the only technical fault was a slight rumble, which was mainly noticeable during the Liszt piece.

VOCAL AND CHORAL MUSIC

Missa choralis, G.10.
> *** Argo ZRG 760. St John's College, Cambridge, Choir, soloists, George Guest; Stephen Cleobury (organ) – BRUCKNER: *Motets.****
> (B) ** Saga 5105. BBC Northern Singers, Gordon Thorne; Francis Jackson (organ).

(i) *Missa choralis, G.10;* (ii) (Organ) *Évocation à la Chapelle Sixtine, G.658.*
> (B) ** Turnabout TV 34201S. (i) Elisabeth Thomann (soprano), Gertrude Jahn (mezzo-soprano), Stafford Wing (tenor), Eishi Kawamura (baritone), Harald Buchsbaum (bass), Vienna Chamber Choir, Hans Gillesberger; Josef Nebois (organ); (ii) Xavier Darasse (organ).

Liszt's *Missa choralis* comes from the mid-1860s after he received the tonsure. It is written for mixed choir and organ, and is an impressive and often moving work. Argo provide a beautifully sung version with well-blended tone, and it has the benefit of spacious and richly detailed recording. It would be difficult to flaw this important issue, which is far more successful than the other two versions currently available.

The Turnabout performance is forthright, but not unsubtle. The organ accompaniment is rather subdued, but in all other respects the record is successful. The short bonus from the organ is interesting, with its quotations from Mozart's *Ave verum,* and it is well played and recorded. This is probably a better buy in the bargain range than the Saga version, which has no coupling. But the Saga sound is good, and the crisp attack of the BBC Northern Singers adds enormously to one's enjoyment of the music.

Via Crucis (The 14 Stations of the Cross) (for soloists, mixed choir and organ).
> (B) ** (*) Saga 5079. BBC Northern Singers, Gordon Thorne; Francis Jackson (organ).

This rarely heard work was written late in Liszt's career, and shows how his style was developing from lush romanticism towards much balder, austere lines. Short, dramatic choruses are punctuated by most imaginative organ solos to make this an extraordinarily compelling account of the Crucifixion story, unelaborated as it is. The performance is splendid, Francis Jackson's organ-playing outstanding, and the recording generally good. There is an occasional patch of roughness in the organ recording, and the chorus at the beginning of side two is somewhat fierce.

Litolff, Henri
(1818–91)

Concerto symphonique No. 4 in D minor, Op. 102.
> * Genesis GS 1035. Gerald Robbins (piano), Monte Carlo Opera Orchestra, Eduard van Remoortel.

This is the source of the famous *Scherzo* and what a disappointment it proves. The first movement is rhetorical, the slow movement (not helped here by some unstylish horn-playing) uninspired and the finale empty. Gerald Robbins's performance is strong and dedicated, but the orchestral support is not very polished, and the rather coarse, resonant recording is not helped by cutting-fault rasps on side one.

Concerto symphonique No. 4 in D minor, Op. 102: Scherzo (only).

*** Decca SXL 2173. Clifford Curzon (piano), London Philharmonic Orchestra, Sir Adrian Boult – GRIEG: *Piano concerto;* FRANCK: *Symphonic variations.****

(B) *** Classics for Pleasure CFP 115. Peter Katin (piano), London Philharmonic Orchestra, John Pritchard – TCHAIKOVSKY: *Piano concerto No. 1.* (*)

(B) ** Decca SPA 170. Peter Katin (piano), London Philharmonic Orchestra, Colin Davis – GRIEG: *Piano concerto; Peer Gynt suite No. 1.***

** HMV ASD 2753. John Ogdon (piano), City of Birmingham Orchestra, Louis Frémaux – FAURÉ: *Ballade;* SAINT-SAËNS: *Carnival of the Animals.***

Curzon provides all the sparkle Litolff's infectious *Scherzo* requires, and this is a delightful makeweight to excellent performances of the Grieg and the Franck. The recording has the same fine qualities as the rest of the issue.

On Classics for Pleasure too a scintillating performance, brilliantly recorded; if only the concerto which forms the coupling had the same kind of panache this disc would be a world-beater.

On Decca SPA the *Scherzo* is rattled off at hair-raising speed. One might prefer something more infectiously gay, but Katin and Davis still manage something of a skipping lilt, and as a fill-up for an excellent Grieg coupling, it is welcome enough. Like the coupling it is very well recorded.

Ogdon's performance is also vividly recorded, with a forward balance. The style is rather too determinedly brilliant: a lighter, more graceful approach would have been more exhilarating.

Locatelli, Pietro
(1695–1764)

Violin concertos, Op. 3: Nos. 1 in D major; 8 in E minor; 9 in G major.

(M) *** Philips Universo 6580 035. Roberto Michelucci (violin), I Musici.

Locatelli was a pupil of Corelli and the three concertos recorded here come from the set of concertos and caprices called *The art of the violin.* The caprices are an integral part of the concertos, taking the place of the normal cadenza. These are attractive pieces and are beautifully played; although the recording is not of recent provenance, they sound remarkably fresh and well detailed. What a splendid soloist Michelucci is!

Il Pianto d'Arianna, Op. 7/6.

(M) ** (*) Nonesuch H 71151. Renata Biffoli (violin), Milan Angelicum Orchestra, Newell Jenkins – GEMINIANI: *The Enchanted Forest.** (*)

Locatelli's concertante piece for violin and orchestra makes an attractive fill-up for the unusual Geminiani ballet. It is in the form of an operatic *scena* with recitative leading to elegiac slow movements and a brilliant allegro before a final slow movement resolving the tension. Well performed and recorded.

Loewe, Karl
(1796–1869)

Erlkönig; Goldschmieds Töchterlein; Heinrich der Vogler; Der Nöck; Prinz

Eugen; Süsses Begräbnis; Tom der Reimer; Die Uhr; Der Wirtin Töchter- lein.

(M) ** Telefunken SMT 1289. Theo Adam (bass), Rudolf Dunckel (piano).

Loewe's songs are more imaginative than their status as 'interesting historical documents' suggests, and records of them are so rare that Theo Adam's collection should not be ignored. It includes the rival setting to Schubert's of the *Erlkönig* (which Wagner perversely claimed to prefer) and a magnificent song, *Die Uhr*. Though Adam's dark voice is not ideally suited to the microphone this is most welcome on Telefunken's mid-price label.

Lübeck, Vincenz
(1654–1740)

Fantasia on 'Ich ruf zu dir, Herr Jesu Christ'; Preludes and fugues: in C major; C minor; D minor; E major; F major; G minor.

** Telefunken SAWT 9616. Michel Chapuis (organ of St Nicholas Church, Altenbruch, Niedersachsen).

Although some of his highly idiomatic organ music has reached the gramophone in miscellaneous recitals, this is the first disc to be wholly devoted to Lübeck, who with Bruhns and Buxtehude was a forma- tive influence on Bach. His music has been described as rather more austere than Buxtehude and less exuberant, but it is always ingeniously conceived in key- board terms. Lübeck had a long and fruitful career; he was active as an organist for some sixty years. Michel Chapuis is a distinguished artist, and though he delights in rather more fre- quent changes of registration than some listeners will care for, his performances are never less than commanding. Unfor-

tunately the recording is closely balanced and cut at a rather high level, so that everything is consistently loud.

Lully, Jean-Baptiste
(1632–87)

Pièces de symphonie (suite of music from operas: *Acis et Galathée; Amadis; Atys; Béllérophon; Persée; Phaeton; Thésée*).

(M) *** Oiseau-Lyre SOL 301. Eng- lish Chamber Orchestra, Ray- mond Leppard.

Here is another of Raymond Leppard's enjoyably stylish selections from the high noon of classical French opera. The playing is first-rate, and the excellent recording presents the music in the best possible light.

Lutoslawski, Witold
(born 1913)

Concerto for orchestra.

** (*) Decca SXL 6445. Suisse Ro- mande Orchestra, Paul Kletzki – HINDEMITH: *Mathis*.** (*)

The Lutoslawski *Concerto* is (or ought to be) to the mid-1950s what Bartók's *Concerto* is to the mid-40s. It is a bril- liant, highly attractive and inventively scored work with great potential appeal. Its idiom is accessible and the ideas have character. It plumbs no great depths, it is true, but then neither do Lutoslawski's later and less accessible works. The Swiss orchestra play here much better than they have done on records in recent years and they are superbly recorded; but Kletzki's performance makes a small cut in the second move- ment, though with the composer's per- mission.

Variations on a theme of Paganini (for 2 pianos).

> (M) ** Supraphon SUAST 50694. Vera and Vlastimil Lejsek (pianos) – BRITTEN: *Pieces* **; STRAVINSKY: *Concerto.** (*)

One would have thought that Paganini's fragment of a theme (just as much a 'cobbler's patch' as Beethoven's Diabelli one) would have yielded its last inspiration, what with Brahms and Rachmaninov, not to mention Paganini himself. Lutoslawski here shows what charm and entertainment the unlikely material can still provoke. This set of *Variations* has been recorded several times in recent years, for it is completely engaging two-piano music, and makes a welcome contrast after the comparative grimness of Stravinsky and Britten.

Paroles tissées.

> ** (*) Decca Headline HEAD 3. Peter Pears (tenor), London Sinfonietta, the composer – BEDFORD: *Tentacles of the Dark Nebula*; BERKELEY: *4 Ronsard sonnets.** (*)

Lutoslawski, like the other two composers represented on the disc, has written with fine understanding of Peter Pears's special qualities. The texts are from poems of Jean François Chabrun, with haunting imagery recurring in a manner mirrored exactly by Lutoslawski's finely textured, sharply conceived writing. Performance and recording are ideal.

Lutyens, Elisabeth
(born 1906)

Wind quintet, Op. 45; String quartet No. 6, Op. 25; 5 Bagatelles for piano, Op. 48.

> *** Argo ZRG 5425. Leonardo Wind Quintet; Dartington String Quartet; Katharina Wolpe (piano) – HAMILTON: *Cello sonata etc.***

Elisabeth Lutyens's *Sixth String quartet* was written at a single sitting, and the intensity of the inspiration comes across, even if the argument is initially difficult. The *Five Bagatelles* too were each written on a single day, a conscious exercise, and their angular lines are even more uncompromising, though the listener is greatly helped by Katharina Wolpe's expressive playing. The *Wind quintet* takes one still further into Miss Lutyens's private territory (surrounded by barbed wire), and one at least lives in hope that gramophone repetition will bring understanding.

And suddenly it's evening.

> ** Argo ZRG 638. Herbert Handt (tenor), members of the BBC Symphony Orchestra, Herbert Handt – BEDFORD: *Music for Albion Moonlight.***

It is good to have so thoughtful a composer as Elisabeth Lutyens being properly represented on record, though unfortunately this is not so immediately understandable or attractive a piece as *O saisons, O châteaux* (see below). There are the same qualities of concentration as in the shorter work, but unfortunately the impact of this setting of words by the poet Quasimodo (translated by Jack Bevan) is blunted when the music is so unrelievedly slow. There are some striking moments of *parlando* and fine effects for brass and timpani. Superbly recorded.

Cantata: *O saisons, O châteaux, Op. 13.*

> *** Argo ZRG 754. Marilyn Tyler (soprano), Royal Philharmonic Orchestra, Norman Del Mar – BRITTEN: *Prelude and fugue;* SCHOENBERG: *Suite.***

This short cantata may at first seem a curious work; more than half of it is taken up with a purely instrumental introduction, and the Rimbaud poem is illustrated with wispy twelve-note sounds. But the underlying passion of the music is clear even at a first hearing, and it certainly repays study. Both performance and recording are excellent, and one is grateful to Argo for reissuing this collection, originally a Gulbenkian Foundation HMV record.

Quincunx.
  *** Argo ZRG 622. Josephine Nendick (mezzo-soprano), John Shirley-Quirk (baritone), BBC Symphony Orchestra, Norman Del Mar – MAW: *Scenes and Arias.****

Quincunx is a hauntingly original work, well coupled with Maw's equally memorable and equally euphonious work. The setting of lines by Sir Thomas Browne forms only a central vocal oasis (unaccompanied) in the middle of a complex series of instrumental pieces, until the music grows slower and stiller at the end, and one is reminded in the brass solos of the more direct Stravinsky. Generally, with twelve-note serialism thoroughly absorbed, Miss Lutyens's idiom comes closer to that of Berg in its flavour, though any parallel is misleading with a work that is original in its own right. Excellent recording.

McCabe, John
(born 1939)

Symphony (Elegy), Op. 40.
  (M) *** Pye Virtuoso TPLS 13005. London Philharmonic Orchestra, John Snashall – CRUFT: *Divertimento*; LEIGHTON: *Concerto.****

John McCabe's *Symphony (Elegy)*, written in 1965, has a strong instrumental personality, apparent from the opening bars, and this prevents the Stravinskian influences from giving the piece an eclectic flavour. The concise construction (on the basis of a tritone) shows McCabe's economy of thought and material. The melodic style sometimes suggests an austere Malcolm Arnold, and there is an orchestral power and a controlled use of dissonance which promise well. The recording is immediate, yet atmospheric. Without the last degree of clarity, it has plenty of colour, and timbres are most naturally conveyed.

Symphony No. 2; (i) Notturni ed Alba.
  *** HMV ASD 2904. City of Birmingham Orchestra, Louis Frémaux, (i) with Jill Gomez (soprano).

John McCabe is a composer who refuses to worry too much about fashion. These are warm, approachable and atmospheric works, which should communicate immediately to most music-lovers, if only because McCabe in his chosen idiom is often intent on charming the listener's ear, even when his argument is far from simple. The *Symphony*, in contrasted sections, fast and slow, within a single-movement framework, has an underlying bitterness to it, an expression of tension not entirely resolved. *Notturni ed Alba*, with its lovely writing for the soprano, is a setting of Latin words, which yet inspire often passionate music, exciting sounds, a joy in sonorities. Fine committed performances, richly recorded.

String trio, Op. 37.
  *** Argo ZRG 761. Cardiff Festival Ensemble – HODDINOTT: *Violin sonata No. 3; Piano sonata No. 6.*

McCabe is intelligent and often highly imaginative, and his craftsmanship is unfaltering even when his invention is

535

less than inspired. In this *String trio*, however, his inspiration is generous and the work is lively and diverting. Splendid playing and excellent recording make this disc a worthwhile acquisition for all who care about new British music.

MacCunn, Hamish
(1868–1916)

Overture: Land of the Mountain and the Flood.

   *** HMV ASD 2400. Scottish National Orchestra, Alexander Gibson – HARTY: *With the Wild Geese;* GERMAN: *Welsh rhapsody;* SMYTH: *The Wreckers overture.****

Hamish MacCunn's descriptive overture is no masterpiece, but it is attractively atmospheric and effectively constructed. It makes a more than agreeable Scottish contribution to this anthology of music from the four countries that make up the United Kingdom. Performance and recording are both excellent.

MacDowell, Edward
(1861–1908)

Piano concerto No. 2 in D minor, Op. 23.

   *** DGG 2530 055. Roberto Szidon (piano), London Philharmonic Orchestra, Edward Downes – GERSHWIN: *Concerto.****

MacDowell's best-known concerto makes an unexpected but attractive coupling for the Gershwin offering. Szidon's sparkling, alert qualities are here just as remarkable. The Mendelssohnian central movement, marked *Giocoso*, gives a physical thrill with its delicacy. Some years ago Van Cliburn made a recording

which seemed as though it would never be surpassed; but Szidon has achieved that. The recording is outstanding.

(i) *Piano concerto No. 2 in D minor, Op. 23; Suite No. 2 (Indian), Op. 48.*

   (B) ** Turnabout TV 34535S. Westphalian Symphony Orchestra, Siegfried Landau, (i) with Eugene List (piano).

Although List plays brilliantly, the performance of the *Concerto*, with its shallow recording, lacks the refinement of the DGG account (see above), after which it comes a long way second choice. But the *Indian suite* is another matter. It is based on genuine folk melodies of the Iroquois, Chippewa, Iowa and Kiowa tribes, and what memorable tunes they are. MacDowell gives them a civilized gloss, but their vitality remains unimpaired. The performance is sympathetic and the recording is better on this side of the disc. At the price this is well worth investigating.

Machaut, Guillaume de
(*c.* 1300–1377)

La Messe de Notre Dame.

   (M) * (*) Vanguard HM 1SD. Deller Consort with Medieval Chamber Ensemble, Alfred Deller – PEROTINUS: *Graduales.** (*)

La Messe de Notre Dame; Amours me fait desirer (ballade); *Douce dame jolie; Foy porter* (virelais); *Nuls ne doit avoir merveille* (lai); *Quant ma dame; Tant doucement* (rondeaux); *Tres douce dame* (ballade).

   (M) *** Oiseau-Lyre SOL 310. Ian Partridge, John Buttrey, Nigel Rogers (tenors), Grayston Burgess (counter-tenor), Geoffrey Shaw (baritone), Purcell Choir, Instrumental Ensemble, Grayston Burgess.

On Oiseau-Lyre the *Mass* is not done with instruments but it is beautifully sung, and as the recording was supervised by so distinguished a medievalist as Frank Harrison its authenticity must be regarded as unimpeachable. Instead of the plainsong interludes we are given organ pieces, not incidentally by Machaut himself but from a contemporary manuscript. The performance is thoroughly convincing nonetheless and so are the secular pieces on the other side. The balance is often a bit too close to be ideal, but for all that, the charm and freshness of the music and the excellence of the quality are likely to ensure a far wider appeal than is normally the case with this kind of repertoire.

Deller's version has admirable vigour though there are certain dubious features that will puzzle some listeners. The recording is not of recent provenance and does not offer a real challenge to the Oiseau-Lyre disc.

Collection: *Amours me fait desirer* (ballade); *Aucune gent – Qui plus aimme* (motet); *Biaute qui toutes autres pere* (ballade); *Comment puet on mieus* (rondeau); *Comment qu'a moy lonteinne* (virelai); *Dame, je suis cilz – Fins cuers doulz; He! Mors; Fine amour; J'ay tant mon cuer – Lasse! je sui en aventure* (motets); *Ma fin est mon commencement* (rondeau); *Quant en moy – Amour et biaute* (motet); *Quant je sui mis au retour* (virelai); *Quant Theseus – Ne quier veoir* (ballade).
  (M) * (*) Philips Universo 6580 026. Capella Lipsiensis, Dietrich Knothe.

While enlarging our knowledge of Machaut's music, this collection is rather

disappointing in execution. The singing is technically secure and the voices pleasing enough, but the style is unimaginative, with little variety of light and shade. This curious stiffness of manner is not helped by the instrumental accompaniments. The recording balance mixes instruments in with voices, and the nasal-sounding crumhorn is particularly penetrating at times. The recording is otherwise clear and truthful, but the lack of atmosphere and a convincing overall perspective is less satisfactory.

Maconchy, Elizabeth
(born 1907)

String quartet No. 5 (1948).
  *** Argo ZRG 5329. Allegri Quartet – WALTON: *Quartet in A minor.***

This quartet was written just after the war at exactly the same period as the Walton work on the reverse. In tone it is more bitter, more reflective of the period, and it makes an excellent coupling for the Walton with its mellifluous beauty and professional assurance. The British Council is to be congratulated on sponsoring the issue. The Allegri players are very good indeed, and the Argo recording as ever is excellent.

Ariadne (dramatic monologue).
  (M) ** (*) Oiseau-Lyre SOL 331. Heather Harper (soprano), English Chamber Orchestra, Raymond Leppard – WALTON: *A Song for the Lord Mayor's Table etc.** (*)

Ariadne is a thoughtful setting of a poem by Cecil Day Lewis. Partly because of the rapid changes of mood in the words, it rather lacks a sustained climax to crown the progress of the dramatic monologue, but it is good to welcome

537

music to the catalogue which shows Elizabeth Maconchy's purposeful and highly professional powers to advantage. Fluent performance and good recording.

Magnard, Albéric
(1865–1914)

Symphony No. 3 in B flat major, Op. 11.
** Decca SXL 6395. Suisse Romande Orchestra, Ernest Ansermet – LALO: *Scherzo.***

Albéric Magnard was born in the same year as Glazounov and Nielsen and has never made much headway outside France. He was killed by the Germans during the First World War. The *Third Symphony* has less character than other Franckist symphonies (like Chausson's and d'Indy's), though it has relatively few longueurs. Much of the writing is of interest and the craftsmanship is eminently sound. Magnard's inspiration was not always even, however, and the overall impression is a trifle academic. Nonetheless there is an integrity of mind that one immediately recognizes and a genuine creative impulse. The performance, though not distinguished, is adequate and the recording is extremely fine.

Mahler, Gustav
(1860–1911)

Symphonies Nos. 1–9.
(M) ** (*) Decca 7BB 173/7 (Nos. 1–3); 7BB 178/82 (Nos. 5–7); 7BB 183/7 (Nos. 4, 8, 9). London Symphony Orchestra, Concertgebouw Orchestra, or Chicago Symphony Orchestra, with Chorus and Soloists, Sir Georg Solti.

Though at various times and at various prices the companies have issued complete Mahler cycles in collected sets, Solti's set has kept a consistent place in the catalogue. Now it is reissued in three albums each of five records at medium price, and on the whole, crowned as it is by a transcendent version of the *Eighth* and a fine one of the *Ninth*, this composite issue will stand almost any current competition. The only seriously marred performance is of the *Third Symphony*, not as well disciplined as the rest and coarse in the final movement, while the *Fourth* (the earliest recording, dating from 1961) does not show the overall grip which distinguishes the later issues. The *Fifth* too is rather self-conscious. But with consistently bright Decca recording, each of these albums is not easily surpassed when one considers the overall achievement.

Symphony No. 1 in D major (Titan).
*** Decca SXL 6113. London Symphony Orchestra, Sir Georg Solti.
*** DGG SLPM 139331. Bavarian Radio Orchestra, Rafael Kubelik.
*** Unicorn RHS 301. London Symphony Orchestra, Jascha Horenstein.
*** HMV ASD 2722. Chicago Symphony Orchestra, Carlo Maria Giulini.
** (*) Philips 6500 342. Concertgebouw Orchestra, Bernard Haitink.
(M) ** (*) CBS Classics 61116. Columbia Symphony Orchestra, Bruno Walter.
** (*) Decca Phase 4 PFS 4232. Royal Philharmonic Orchestra, Erich Leinsdorf.
(M) ** Supraphon SUAST 50675. Czech Philharmonic Orchestra, Karel Ančerl.

Symphony No. 1 in D major (Titan) (original 1893 version including *Blumine*).

(M) ** (*) Pye Virtuoso TPLS 13037. New Philharmonia Orchestra, Wyn Morris.

Among the top three or four discs listed it is very difficult to suggest a clear first recommendation. Each represents conductor, orchestra, and engineers on top form, and the final choice will be personal and subjective. The London Symphony Orchestra play Mahler's *First* like no other orchestra. They catch the magical writing at the opening with a singular evocative quality, at least partly related to the peculiarly characteristic blend of wind timbres. Solti gives the orchestra its full head and coaxes some magnificent playing from the brass in the finale and throughout wonderfully warm string tone. His tendency to drive hard is only felt in the second movement, which is pressed a little too much, although he relaxes beautifully in the central section. Specially memorable is the poignancy of the introduction of the *Frère Jacques* theme in the slow movement, and the exultant brilliance of the closing pages.

Kubelik gives an intensively poetic reading. He is here at his finest in Mahler, and though as in later symphonies he is sometimes tempted to choose a tempo on the fast side, the result here could hardly be more glowing. The *rubato* in the slow funeral march is most subtly handled.

Unicorn had the laudable aim of securing a modern recording of Horenstein in Malher's *First*, and the result has a freshness and concentration which put it in a special category among the many rival accounts. Solti and Kubelik both provide a sharper experience, more immediately exciting in virtuosity; but with measured tempi and a manner which conceals much art, Horenstein links the work more clearly with later Mahler symphonies. Fine recording, though the timpani is balanced rather too close.

With superbly resonant playing and rich recording quality Giulini's too is an outstanding version. The conductor's transparent honesty prevents any feeling of excessive sophistication, and he never whips up excitement synthetically, for his tempi are generally on the slow side, like those of Horenstein.

When Philips gathered together Haitink's recordings of Mahler symphonies, they took the trouble to make a new version of No. 1; and not only is it far more refined as a recording, the reading is if anything even more thoughtfully idiomatic than before in Haitink's unexaggerated Mahler style.

To have a modern stereo recording of a characteristic Bruno Walter Mahler performance on medium-priced label will seem to most a bargain too good to miss. The sound is good, and the opening movement, with especially fine horn-playing, has rarely been performed on disc with more atmosphere. The finale is less successful; here Walter's broad treatment lets the tension sag, and the closing pages of the work have not the apotheosis-like concentration that the music needs.

Leinsdorf's is a strong and colourful version, finely controlled and built with sustained concentration. The recording, with brass well forward, is one of the best from Phase 4.

Ančerl's control of tension during the atmospheric opening pages is unconventional, and one's first impression is that he has failed to grasp the overall shape of the movement. But this reading grows on one, and it is helped throughout by one of the most atmospheric recordings we have had from Supraphon.

Wyn Morris, like Ormandy on his RCA disc (now deleted), adds to the usual four movements of Mahler's *First Symphony* the recently unveiled movement *Blumine* that came second in the composer's original scheme. Morris goes further than Ormandy in adopting in the other four movements the original scoring instead of Mahler's revision. The result is a curiosity well worth investigating, if with less polished playing than in the best rival versions. Fair recording.

Symphony No. 2 in C minor (Resurrection).

*** HMV SLS 806 (2 discs). Elisabeth Schwarzkopf (soprano), Hilde Rössl-Majdan (mezzo-soprano), Philharmonia Chorus and Orchestra, Otto Klemperer.

*** Decca SET 325/6. Heather Harper (soprano), Helen Watts (contralto), LSO Chorus, London Symphony Orchestra, Sir Georg Solti.

(M) *** CBS Classics 61282/3. Emelia Cundari (soprano), Maureen Forrester (contralto), Westminster Choir, New York Philharmonic Orchestra, Bruno Walter.

(M) ** (*) RCA LSB 4003/4. Evelyn Mandac (soprano), Birgit Finnila (contralto), Singing City Choirs, Philadelphia Orchestra, Eugene Ormandy.

* (**) CBS 78249 (2 discs). Sheila Armstrong (soprano), Janet Baker (mezzo-soprano), Edinburgh Festival Chorus, London Symphony Orchestra, Leonard Bernstein.

This is one of Klemperer's most compelling performances on record, bringing out the music's ruggedness. The first movement, taken at a fairly fast tempo, is intense and earth-shaking, and that is surely as it should be in a work which culminates in a representation of Judgement Day itself. Though in the last movement some of Klemperer's speeds are designedly slow he conveys supremely well the mood of transcendent heavenly happiness in the culminating passage, with chorus and soloists themselves singing like angels. The Last Trump brings a shudder of excitement to make one forget any prejudice against such literal representation. The less grand middle movements too have their simple charm under Klemperer and the recording is among EMI's best.

Solti's account too is one of his most impressive Mahler performances, superbly tense in the first movement to match and even outshine the heroic model of Klemperer. In the slow *Ländler* of the second movement Solti brings superb refinement of detail and a precise control of dynamic, and again in the third movement he concentrates with hushed intensity on precise control of dynamic and atmosphere. In the fourth movement, the setting of *Urlicht* from *Des Knaben Wunderhorn*, Solti's contralto, Helen Watts, is even more expressive than her recorded rivals, with real 'inner' feeling conveyed in the chorale. On the first four movements Solti's is on balance the most completely satisfying performance, but when he comes to the massive finale with its expansive picture of Judgement Day, he falls a little short of the spiritual nobility that Klemperer for one brings to the music. Superlative Decca recording.

Like Walter's other Mahler recordings the CBS reissue will remain a classic of the gramophone. In the first movement there is a restraint and in the second a gracefulness which provide a strong contrast with a conductor like Klemperer. The recording, one of the last Walter made in New York, is remarkably good, and for those who warm to Walter's Mahler this will be an indispensable set.

Ormandy was the first conductor to record this symphony, way back in the early thirties when he was still at Minneapolis forging his career. The freshness remains. Though in some music he may add an excessive layer of emotionalism, he takes a direct approach to Mahler which underlines the music's strength and confidence, minimizes the neurosis. The first movement is commanding, and the final vision of Judgement Day has the impact of a live performance. On mid-price label with first-rate recording, this is an excellent recommendation, though Klemperer's performance is even finer.

Bernstein made a memorable television film concurrently with recording this symphony in Ely Cathedral. The CBS set with the LSO is valuable in recalling that idiosyncratic performance with its superb contributions from the two soloists, not to mention the chorus and orchestra, but the recording is far too badly balanced for the discs to be recommended generally. Much better recorded sets are also available under Haitink (Philips) and Kubelik (DGG), but these versions do not really compete with the finest of those listed above.

Symphony No. 3 in D minor.

  *** Unicorn RHS 302/3. Norma Procter (contralto), Wandsworth School Boys' Choir, Ambrosian Singers, London Symphony Orchestra, Jascha Horenstein.
  *** Philips 6700 037 (2 discs). Maureen Forrester (contralto), Netherlands Radio Choir, St Willibrord Boys' Choir, Concertgebouw Orchestra, Bernard Haitink.
  (M) ** (*) CBS 77206 (2 discs). Martha Lipton (mezzo-soprano), Schola Cantorum Women's Chorus, Boys' Choir of Church of Transfiguration, New York Philharmonic Orchestra, Leonard Bernstein.
  ** DGG 2707 036 (2 discs). Marjorie Thomas (contralto), Bavarian Radio Chorus, Tolzer Boys' Choir, Bavarian Radio Orchestra, Rafael Kubelik.
  * (*) Decca SET 385/6. Helen Watts (contralto), Wandsworth School Boys' Choir, Ambrosian Chorus, London Symphony Orchestra, Sir Georg Solti.

More than the earlier issues of Mahler, Nielsen and Simpson in Unicorn's excellent series of records with Horenstein, this account of the Mahler *Third* shows the conductor at his most intensely com-

mitted. The manner is still very consistent in its simple dedication to the authority of the score, its rejection of romantic indulgence, but with an extra intensity the result has the sort of frisson-making quality one knew from live Horenstein performances. Above all the restraint of the finale is intensely compelling. Though the strings are rather backwardly balanced and the timpani are too prominent, the recording quality is both beautiful and brilliant. Fine vocal contributions from Norma Procter, the Ambrosian Singers and the Wandsworth School Boys' Choir.

In a work that can seem over-inflated Haitink's straightforwardness as a Mahlerian makes for a deeply satisfying performance. Though in the first movement his rather fast speed allows for less lift in the rhythm than, say, Bernstein's, he captures to perfection the fresh, wide-eyed simplicity of the second movement and the carol-like quality of the fifth movement *Bell song*. Best of all is the wonderfully simple and intense reading of the long concluding slow movement, which here is given an inner intensity that puts it very close to the comparable movement of Mahler's *Ninth*. Haitink's soloists are excellent, the playing of the Concertgebouw is refined and dedicated, and the recording is clean and natural even in the heaviest passages.

Bernstein's reading of the *Third*, one of the first to be recorded in his Mahler cycle, remains one of the most satisfying, strong and passionate with few of the stylistic exaggerations that sometimes overlay his interpretations. His style in the final slow movement is more heavily expressive than Haitink's, but some will prefer a more extrovert way. The recording copes well with the heavy textures, though next to the finest versions it is somewhat coarse. At mid-price this makes an excellent recommendation.

There is a practical advantage in Kubelik's version: the first movement is squeezed without a break on to the first side, but this is bought at the expense of tempo. As in the later Mahler symphonies Kubelik is tempted to lighten the music with rushed speeds, and when there are such fine rival versions, his can only be commended to those who want his cycle complete.

Solti's is a disappointing reading, with not even the merit of good discipline. To compare these same players under Solti and under Horenstein is most illuminating, particularly in the finale, where for Solti there is no half tone.

Symphony No. 4 in G major.

⊛ (M) *** CBS Classics 61056. Judith Raskin (soprano), Cleveland Orchestra, George Szell.

(M) ** (*) H M V S X L P 30054. Emmy Loose (soprano), Philharmonia Orchestra, Paul Kletzki.

(M) ** (*) D G G Privilege 2535 119. Elsie Morison (soprano), Bavarian Radio Symphony Orchestra, Rafael Kubelik.

** H M V A S D 2799. Elisabeth Schwarzkopf (soprano), Philharmonia Orchestra, Otto Klemperer.

** Decca S X L 2276. Sylvia Stahlman (soprano), Concertgebouw Orchestra, Sir Georg Solti.

(B) * Classics for Pleasure C F P 159. Margaret Price (soprano), London Philharmonic Orchestra, Jascha Horenstein.

Szell's is one of the greatest performances of a Mahler symphony on record. His approach throughout the work is cool but never detached: he seems to let the music blossom itself, such moments of beauty growing naturally and spontaneously out of the texture. The exquisitely gentle, yet pointed contour of the opening theme, with its comma perfectly judged, catches one's imagination, and as the work unfolds, initial expectancy is not disappointed. Indeed the

radiant playing at the close of the movement has never been excelled on record. The scherzo is crisp, almost pert, with splendid wind-playing, and the opening of the *Poco Adagio* shows Szell's restraint at its most magical. The texture is luminous and the music moves with a wonderful inner tension to its central climax and falls back, so that the 'heavenly gates' sequence bursts on the listener with splendid exuberance. In the finale Szell found the ideal soprano to match his conception; Judith Raskin sings without artifice, and her voice has an open colouring, like a child's. The recording is one of the finest ever from Cleveland.

Kletzki's performance too is beautifully recorded. The orchestral playing is radiant in the slow movement and Emmy Loose's simplicity in the finale is most affecting. One's reservations principally concern the opening movement, which Kletzki treats episodically, so that it tends to become a series of separate events rather than a carefully planned symphonic pattern. Yet the reading as a whole has a spontaneous individuality which is easy to enjoy.

The Bavarian Orchestra phrase beautifully, and their playing has great vitality. With generally faster tempi than is common the effect is light and luminous, with a charming, boyish account of the final song from Elsie Morison. Recommended to those collecting Kubelik in Mahler, but it is not so generally recommendable as Szell or Kletzki.

Klemperer is slow in the first movement and, strangely, fractionally too fast in the slow movement. Yet the Philharmonia make some ravishing sounds, and one can easily come under Klemperer's spell, especially with such rich and spacious recording. The two highlights of the reading are the marvellously beautiful *Ländler*, which forms the central section of the second movement, and the simplicity of Elisabeth Schwarzkopf's singing in the finale. This is a record to enjoy, but perhaps not the one to buy as a single representation of Mahler's *Fourth* in a collection.

Solti's performance is disappointing. It is extremely well balanced as a recording but the conductor is not altogether happy in the first movement, and besides a wilfulness of style there are dull patches which he is unable to sustain with any richness of emotional expression. He does the finale best, and here Sylvia Stahlman sings charmingly.

Horenstein's characteristic simplicity of approach seems too deliberate, and even the great slow movement seems didactic and relatively uncommitted. Margaret Price's singing in the finale is beautiful but cool, in line with the rest of the interpretation; the sound is clear but unatmospheric.

Symphony No. 5 in C sharp minor.
  ⊛ *** HMV SLS 785 (2 discs). New Philharmonia Orchestra, Sir John Barbirolli – *5 Rückert Lieder*.***
  ** (*) Decca SET 471/2. Chicago Symphony Orchestra, Sir Georg Solti – *Des Knaben Wunderhorn*.** (*)
  ** CBS 72182/3. New York Philharmonic Orchestra, Leonard Bernstein – *Kindertotenlieder*.**
  * (*) DGG 2707 056 (2 discs). Bavarian Radio Symphony Orchestra, Rafael Kubelik – *Lieder eines fahrenden Gesellen*.***

Symphony No. 5 in C sharp minor; Symphony No. 10 in F sharp major (Unfinished).
  ** (*) Philips 6700 048 (2 discs). Concertgebouw Orchestra, Bernard Haitink.

Barbirolli's recording of Mahler's *Fifth* provides a unique experience. On any count it is one of the greatest, most warmly affecting performances he ever committed to record, and it brings on the fourth side a performance of the *5 Rückert Lieder* with Janet Baker as soloist that achieves a degree of poetic intensity rarely heard on record even from these superlative artists. The *Fifth* saw Barbirolli as ever an expansive Mahlerian, yet far more than in his recording of the *Sixth* (made a year earlier) his concentration convinces one that his tempi are right. Though the very opening may lose something in sheer dramatic bite there is always a sense of power in reserve, and when the main funeral march emerges there is a frisson such as one would experience in the concert hall but rarely on record. A classic performance, given a gloriously ripe recording.

Those who resist Barbirolli's expansiveness will probably find the ideal alternative in Haitink's fresh and direct reading, with finely judged tempi, unexaggerated observance of Mahler's markings, and refined playing from the Concertgebouw. The famous *Adagietto* is relatively cool, but its beauty is as intense as ever. Good, well-balanced Philips recording.

The opening Funeral march sets the tone of Solti's reading. At a tempo faster than usual, it is wistful rather than deeply tragic, even though the dynamic contrasts are superbly pointed, and the string tone could hardly be more resonant. In the pivotal *Adagietto* too Solti secures intensely beautiful playing, but the result lacks the 'inner' quality one finds so abundantly in Barbirolli's interpretation. Gloriously rich if slightly over-reverberant recording.

The highlight of Bernstein's performance is in the *Adagietto* for strings and harp, which has a heavenly beauty so delicate one holds one's breath. Elsewhere Bernstein's care for detail means that he never seems quite to plumb the depth of Mahler's inspiration. The first movement, for example, seems too careful, for all the virtuosity of the playing.

Kubelik in the opening funeral march is gentle rather than tragic, and his relative lightness of manner coupled with refined textures misses the epic quality of the work. Nor does he succeed in disguising the patchwork structure of the last movement.

Symphony No. 6 in A minor.
   *** Decca SET 469/70. Chicago Symphony Orchestra, Sir Georg Solti – *Lieder eines fahrenden Gesellen.****
Symphony No. 6 in A minor (revised by Erwin Ratz); *Gustav Mahler remembered:* reminiscences by Mahler's daughter, Anna Mahler, associates and musicians who played under his baton.
   (M) *** CBS 77215 (2 discs). New York Philharmonic Orchestra, Leonard Bernstein.
(i) *Symphony No. 6 in A minor;* (ii) *Symphony No. 9 in D major.*
   ** (*) HMV SLS 851 (3 discs). (i) New Philharmonia Orchestra; (ii) Berlin Philharmonic Orchestra; both cond. Sir John Barbirolli.

Solti draws stunning playing from the Chicago Orchestra. This was his first recording with them after he took up his new post as principal conductor, and, as he said himself, it represented a love-affair at first sight. The electric excitement of the playing confirms this, and with brilliant, immediate but atmospheric recording, Solti's rather extrovert approach to Mahler is here at its most convincing. His fast tempi may mean that he misses some of the deeper emotions, but with an outstandingly successful performance of the *Wayfaring Lad* cycle on the fourth side (Yvonne Minton a splendid soloist) this is a very convincing and attractive set.

Leonard Bernstein's account of the *Sixth* stands out even among the other fine Mahler recordings he has made. One can argue that his tempi are inclined to be too fast – particularly in the first movement, which no longer sounds like a funeral march – but here, even more than usual, the searing intensity of a live Bernstein performance comes over, and the experience puts any rival version in the shade. The recording is one of CBS's finest, despite the usual close-up sound. The fourth side includes an interesting collection of personal reminiscences of the composer.

The HMV set couples two highly individual readings of Mahler by Barbirolli. He gives a characteristically expansive account of No. 6, but in places – particularly in the long first movement, where the exposition repeat is faithfully observed – tension is allowed to sag a little. Nonetheless with fine recording it makes a worthwhile coupling for what is one of the finest accounts of Mahler's *Ninth* ever recorded. Barbirolli greatly impressed the Berliners with his Mahler performances live, and this recording reflects the players' warmth of response. He opted to record the slow and intense finale before the rest, and the beauty of the playing makes it a fitting culmination. The other movements are strong and alert too, and though the recording is not of the most modern it is warm and atmospheric.

Symphony No. 7 in E minor.
   *** Decca SET 518/9. Chicago Symphony Orchestra, Sir Georg Solti.
   *** Philips 6700 036 (2 discs). Concertgebouw Orchestra, Bernard Haitink.
   ** DGG 2707 061 (2 discs). Bavarian Radio Symphony Orchestra, Rafael Kubelik.
   * (*) HMV SLS 781 (2 discs). New Philharmonia Orchestra, Otto Klemperer.

The sound of Solti's Decca issue is glorious, even riper and more brilliant than that of his two previous Chicago recordings of Mahler and much clearer. In interpretation this is as successful as Solti's fine account of No. 6, extrovert in display but full of dark implications. The tempi tend to be challengingly fast – at the very opening, for example, and in the scherzo (where Solti is mercurial) and the finale (where his energy carries shock-waves in its trail). The second *Nachtmusik* is enchantingly seductive, and throughout the orchestra plays super-latively well. On balance this is even finer than the Haitink version.

Haitink gives a finely wrought, inten-sely convincing reading. It is less idiosyn-cratic than the versions of his more flam-boyant rivals, but for many this will prove more satisfying for repeated listening, when the drama is clear-headed rather than darkly intense. With Haitink one can see forward more clearly to the sublimities of the *Ninth Symphony*, where his approach to Mahler is so completely at home. The tempo for the most delect-able movement of this work, the second *Nachtmusik*, is on the fast side, but Haitink's pointing is still persuasive. The recording is one of Philips' finest.

Kubelik is at his most impressive in what can be described as the composer's *Knaben Wunderhorn* manner. The start of the second movement has an open-air innocence, but conversely Kubelik pro-duces no sense of nocturnal mystery in the second *Nachtmusik*. The outer move-ments are characteristically refined and resilient, but something of Mahler's strength is missing. Fine recording.

Klemperer's is not one of his most convincing Mahler performances. The recording session caught him and the orchestra at less than their best, and one misses the concentrated sense of flow which normally ran through any of his performances, however magisterially slow. There is, however, a magically sen-sitive account of the second *Nachtmusik*.

Symphony No. 8 in E flat major (Sym-phony of 1000).

⊛ *** Decca SET 534/5. Heather Harper, Lucia Popp (sopranos), Yvonne Minton, Helen Watts (contraltos), René Kollo (tenor), John Shirley-Quirk, Martti Tal-vela (basses), Vienna Boys' Choir, Vienna State Opera Chorus and Singverein, Chicago Symphony Orchestra, Sir Georg Solti.

(M) ** (*) Independent World Re-leases SYM 1/2. Josie Barker, Elizabeth Simon (sopranos), Joyce Blackham, Alfreda Hodgson (con-traltos), John Mitchinson (tenor), Raymond Myers, Gwynne Howell (baritones), Choruses and Sym-phonica of London, Wyn Morris.

* (**) CBS SET 2112 (2 discs). Erna Spoorenberg, Gwyneth Jones (so-pranos), Anna Reynolds, Norma Procter (contraltos), John Mitch-inson (tenor), Vladimir Ruzdjak (baritone), Donald McIntyre (bass), Leeds Festival Chorus, Orpington Junior Singers, High-gate School Boys' Choir, Finchley Children's Music Group, London Symphony Orchestra, Leonard Bernstein.

** DGG 2707 062 (2 discs). Martina Arroyo, Erna Spoorenberg, Julia Hamari (sopranos), Norma Proc-ter (contralto), Donald Grobe (tenor), Dietrich Fischer-Dieskau (baritone), Franz Crass (bass), Bavarian Radio, North and West German Radio Choirs, Regens-burg Cathedral Choir, Bavarian Radio Symphony Orchestra, Raf-ael Kubelik.

** Philips 6700 049 (2 discs). Ileana Cotrubas, Heather Harper, Han-neke van Bork (sopranos), Birgit Finnila, Marianne Dieleman (con-traltos), William Cochran (tenor),

Hermann Prey (baritone), Hans Sotin (bass), Amsterdam Choirs and Concertgebouw Orchestra, Bernard Haitink.

Solti's is a classic recording. Challenged by the tightest possible recording schedule, the American orchestra and European singers responded to Solti at his most inspired with a performance that vividly captures the atmosphere of a great occasion – essential in this of all works. There is nothing cautious about the surging dynamism of the first movement, the electrifying hymn, *Veni Creator spiritus*; and the long second movement setting the final scene of Goethe's *Faust* proceeds through its contrasted sections with unrelenting intensity. The hushed prelude in Solti's hands is sharp-edged in *pianissimo*, not at all comforting, while the magnificent recording copes superbly with every strand of texture and the fullest range of dynamic – spectacularly so in the great final crescendo to the words *Alles vergängliche*. A triumph for everyone concerned.

Wyn Morris's version, recorded like Solti's and Bernstein's in conjunction with a live performance, has its flaws of detail but triumphantly conveys a sense of occasion against a warm atmospheric acoustic. Morris's approach to Mahler is consciously expressive, more like Walter's than Solti's. At medium price, with first-rate playing from the pick-up orchestra and dedicated singing from soloists and choirs, this is a valuable alternative even to Solti's incandescent performance. (However, readers are warned that this set is not easily obtainable – and they will have to search to find a retailer who regularly stocks it.)

Bernstein recorded Mahler's epic *Symphony of a Thousand* at Walthamstow Town Hall in the days immediately following a hazard-ridden live performance at the Royal Albert Hall, in which emergency measures had to be taken to reinforce the choral strength. You would

hardly know that from this fine recorded performance, though the hazards still left their mark. One of them was entirely to the good, the last-minute inclusion of John Mitchinson among the soloists following his predecessor's indisposition. The Orpington Junior Singers too did valiant work in taking on more than their share of the children's choir music. In the final recorded account the Leeds Festival Chorus is strongly stiffened with professional choristers, and the result is splendidly incisive. The unfortunate point, undermining much of the superb achievement in the performance, is the closeness of sound and resulting lack of atmosphere in the recording quality. This of all symphonies requires spacious, reverberant sound, and here one seems to be among the very performers.

Even in this massive symphony Kubelik concentrates on refinement, and the recording engineers faithfully match him. The result is crisp and clear but largely unexciting, giving little idea of a live occasion. Generally good solo singing.

Haitink's reading, characteristically thoughtful, lacks the electricity needed in this work, and the solo singing is very variable, while the recording lacks the expansive atmosphere one wants in such massive music. A disappointment compared with the rest of Haitink's cycle.

Symphony No. 9 in D major.

⊛ *** Philips 6700 021 (2 discs). Concertgebouw Orchestra, Bernard Haitink.

(M) *** CBS Classics 61369/70. Columbia Symphony Orchestra, Bruno Walter – *Lieder eines fahrenden Gesellen.***

** (*) Decca SET 360/1. London Symphony Orchestra, Sir Georg Solti.

** (*) DGG 2707 038 (2 discs). Bavarian Radio Symphony Orchestra, Rafael Kubelik.

Haitink is at his very finest in Mahler's *Ninth,* and the last movement, with its slow expanses of melody, reveals a unique concentration. Unlike almost all other conductors he maintains his intensely slow tempo from beginning to end. This is a great performance, beautifully recorded, and with the earlier movements superbly performed – the first movement a little restrained, the second pointed at exactly the right speed, and the third gloriously extrovert and brilliant – this will be for most Mahlerians a first recommendation.

Walter's performance – recorded during his Indian summer in retirement in California – lacks mystery at the very start, but through the long first movement Walter unerringly builds up a consistent structure, controlling tempo more closely than most rivals, preferring a steady approach. The middle two movements similarly are sharply focused rather than genial, and the finale, lacking hushed pianissimos, is tough and stoically strong. A fine performance, not at all the reading one would have predicted from Walter. Mildred Miller's somewhat unimaginative reading of the *Wayfaring Lad* cycle makes a worthwhile fill-up on this mid-price reissue.

Solti's is a brilliant, dramatic performance, but one which finally falls just a little short of being a great performance in its extrovert approach to the spiritual beauty of the finale. In the middle two movements it would be hard to match Solti for the point and precision of the playing. The tempo for the second movement *Ländler* may be slow, but with such pointing the slowness is amply justified – quite apart from following Mahler's marking. The third movement is given the most brilliant account ever; but in the outer movements one feels that Solti is not penetrating deeply enough. He allows Mahler's passionate utterances to emerge too readily. He makes Mahler wear his heart on his sleeve, and although there may be justifications for that, it leaves

something out we have come to expect. The recording quality is superb, with a fantastic range of dynamic, confidently handled by the engineers.

A fine performance too from Kubelik, but one which in the last resort has to yield before its direct rivals in simple, dedicated intensity. The playing and recording are most beautiful, and the version can be safely recommended to those who follow Kubelik through his Mahler cycle.

Symphony No. 10 in F sharp major (Unfinished): completed Deryck Cooke.

   (M) ** (*) CBS Classics 61447. Philadelphia Orchestra, Eugene Ormandy.

Symphony No. 10 in F sharp major (final performing version, completed Deryck Cooke).

   *** Philips 6700 067 (2 discs). New Philharmonia Orchestra, Wyn Morris.

Deryck Cooke describes the score he has prepared of Mahler's *Tenth Symphony* as a 'performing version', for the composer sketched the outline of all five movements to the last bar. The precise proportions were clear, and the harmony and much of the instrumentation could be inferred, while the first movement and the central *Purgatorio* movement were complete. In the earlier version recorded by Ormandy, Cooke left the last two movements relatively bald in their scoring, and the finale in particular did not sound quite authentically Mahlerian. With sensitive rescoring the last two movements are transformed in the newer Philips set, and with dedicated if not always immaculate playing the result is a revelation one had never dared to expect, as near a true completion of the composer's vision as one could ever hope to hear. First-rate recording.

Ormandy's tempi, particularly for the fateful slow finale with its hammer blows, are substantially faster than Wyn Morris's, which has allowed CBS to squeeze the whole symphony on to two sides with reasonable recording – excellent value at mid-price. Even so this earlier version of Cooke's score lacks the finer Mahlerian colouring of the rival account, and though the Philadelphia strings are more polished than those of the New Philharmonia, the finale in particular is relatively lacking in sense of tragic weight.

LIEDER AND SONG CYCLES

Kindertotenlieder.
** CBS 72182/3. Jennie Tourel (mezzo-soprano), New York Philharmonic Orchestra, Leonard Bernstein – *Symphony No. 5.***
* (*) Decca SXL 6446. Marilyn Horne (soprano), Royal Philharmonic Orchestra, Henry Lewis – WAGNER: *Wesendonk Lieder.* (*)

There is a statuesque quality about Marilyn Horne's singing here that does not suit Mahler's intensely personal inspiration. There is much to admire, and the voice is always beautiful, but tenderness is completely missing. A disappointment, despite excellent recording quality. Jennie Tourel is in excellent voice, and her performance makes a good coupling for the *Fifth Symphony*.

Kindertotenlieder; Lieder eines fahrenden Gesellen.
** Philips 6500 100. Hermann Prey (baritone), Concertgebouw Orchestra, Bernard Haitink.
(M) ** Decca Ace of Diamonds SDD 215. Kirsten Flagstad (soprano), Vienna Philharmonic Orchestra, Sir Adrian Boult.

Hermann Prey's performances are fresh and intelligent, and the colour of the baritone voice sometimes brings a darkness of timbre which is especially poignant, as in the third song of the *Wayfaring Lad* cycle. Haitink's accompaniments too are understanding, yet create urgency with the briskness of the chosen tempi. But in the last essence Prey cannot match Fischer-Dieskau or indeed Janet Baker (see below) in intensity of expression or imagination. Fischer-Dieskau's coupling of these two song cycles is available in mono only (although very good mono and on bargain label), while here the Philips sound quality offers all the advantages of first-rate modern stereo.

Flagstad sings masterfully in these two most appealing of Mahler's orchestral cycles, but she was unable to relax into the deeper, more intimate expressiveness that they really require. The voice is magnificent, the approach always firmly musical (helped by Sir Adrian's splendid accompaniment), but this record is recommendable for the singer rather than for the way the music is presented. Excellent recording for its late-fifties period.

Kindertotenlieder: Lieder eines fahrenden Gesellen; 5 Rückert Lieder: No. 4.
** (*) HMV ASD 2338. Janet Baker (contralto), Hallé Orchestra, Sir John Barbirolli.

Like Janet Baker's collaboration with Barbirolli on the complete *Rückert Lieder* (the fourth-side fill-up for the *Fifth Symphony*) this represents the affectionate approach to Mahler at its warmest. The Hallé strings are not quite of the sweetest and the recording is not ideally clear, but the result is still intensely beautiful, full of breathtaking moments. The spontaneous feeling of soloist and conductor for this music comes over as in a live performance, and though a baritone like Fischer-Dieskau can give a stronger idea of these most appealing of Mahler's orchestral cycles, this brings out the tenderness to a unique degree.

Kindertotenlieder; 5 Rückert Lieder: Nos. 1 and 3–5.
> *** DGG SLPM 138879. Dietrich Fischer-Dieskau (baritone), Berlin Philharmonic Orchestra, Karl Boehm.

This disc includes superb performances of the *Kindertotenlieder* and four (why not five?) of the *Rückert songs*. The missing one is *Liebst du um Schönheit*. The recording is atmospheric, with the singer placed backwardly, but as there is much to enjoy in the orchestra, this balance is highly effective. Karl Boehm's accompaniment is a model in its loving care of detail and shading of orchestral timbre to match and blend with the vocal line.

Das klagende Lied (published version): complete recording.
> (M) *** Decca Ace of Diamonds SDDR 327. Teresa Zylis-Gara (soprano), Anna Reynolds (mezzo-soprano), Andor Kaposy (tenor), Ambrosian Singers, New Philharmonia Orchestra, Wyn Morris.
> ** (*) CBS 72773. Evelyn Lear (soprano), Grace Hoffman (mezzo-soprano), Stuart Burrows (tenor), LSO Chorus, London Symphony Orchestra, Pierre Boulez.
> ** Philips 6500 587. Heather Harper (soprano), Norma Procter (contralto), Werner Hollweg (tenor), Netherlands Radio Choir, Concertgebouw Orchestra, Bernard Haitink.

Das klagende Lied was written when Mahler was only seventeen. Though now the second of its three sections, *Waldmärchen*, has been rescued from oblivion and recorded by Boulez (see below), the

work with its gruesome story of the days of chivalry and knights in armour was originally presented as here in two parts merely, the first and third of the original scheme. They present strong and colourful music, not at all immature. With fine recording, Wyn Morris and his team present committed and idiomatic performances that are consistently enjoyable. The off-stage band at the wedding celebrations is vividly caught.

Boulez is a distinctive Mahlerian. His clear ear concentrates on precision of texture rather than warmth of overall effect, and some will find that there is an unexpected chill in the heart of this high romantic music as Boulez presents it. But with its macabre subject that is in its way very apt. And since with the same orchestra (though not the same team of soloists) Boulez has recorded the previously buried second part of the work, there is a strong case for preferring his version in the interests of linking up a complete performance under the same conductor. Fine singing and recording.

Bernard Haitink's reading does not quite compare in imagination or urgency with the rival versions, but the recording is wonderfully refined, making this a demonstration disc worth considering for extra-musical reasons.

(i) *Das klagende Lied: Part 2, Waldmärchen. Symphony No. 10: Adagio.*
> ** CBS SBRG 72865. London Symphony Orchestra, Pierre Boulez, (i) with Elisabeth Soederstroem (soprano), Grace Hoffman (mezzo-soprano), Ernst Haefliger (tenor), Gerd Nienstedt (bass).

This part of the early cantata *Das klagende Lied* was left on one side by the composer when he revised the work for performance, but it is arguable that he did not want the piece completely neglected. He gave the score to a relation, and it has only recently been brought out for regular public performance. It proves a splendid example of early Mahler (he destroyed ruthlessly most of the products of that period), and with its thematic links with the two other parts of the cantata, it adds to our appreciation of those too. With this separate Boulez recording of the piece added to his existing recording of the rest, we can now choose for ourselves, on record at least, the form of presentation. Good singing from the chorus, less good from the soloists. Fine playing and fair recording. The version of the first movement of the *Tenth Symphony*, however, cannot be recommended; a corrupt edition is used, and the performance itself is variable.

Des Knaben Wunderhorn.
> *** HMV SAN 218. Elisabeth Schwarzkopf (soprano), Dietrich Fischer-Dieskau (baritone), London Symphony Orchestra, George Szell.
> (M) ** Decca Ace of Diamonds SDDR 326. Janet Baker (contralto), Geraint Evans (baritone), London Philharmonic Orchestra, Wyn Morris.

In his last years Szell on his visits to Europe made a number of records which reflect a warmth and tenderness in his nature not often revealed in his work in Cleveland. This is one of that superlative group of records, with the most refined control of *pianissimo* in the orchestra matching the tonal subtleties of the two incomparable soloists. Wit and dramatic point as well as delicacy mark these widely contrasted songs, and the device of using two voices in some of them is apt and effective. There is more polish and style here than in the earlier version with Janet Baker and Geraint Evans, though in some songs that is not surpassed, and the EMI recording quality here is no finer.

The Decca reissue was Wyn Morris's first major essay in the recording studio,

and though he secures crisp playing from the LPO, there is far too little affection in the phrasing, and the rhythm consistently sounds too metrical in charming songs that need some coaxing. Janet Baker in particular shows him up when she turns a phrase with real imagination and then has it echoed stiffly by the orchestra. Baker could hardly be more ideally cast, but Geraint Evans is more variable. He points the humour of the song about the cuckoo and the donkey with characteristic charm, but sometimes the voice does not sound perfectly focused. Otherwise the recording is bright and clear.

Des Knaben Wunderhorn: excerpts *(Das irdische Leben; Verlor'ne Müh; Wo die schönen Trompeten blasen; Rheinlegendchen).*
> ** (*) Decca SET 471/2. Yvonne Minton (contralto), Chicago Symphony Orchestra, Sir Georg Solti – *Symphony No. 5.*** (*)

Yvonne Minton, a singer whom Solti encouraged enormously in her career at Covent Garden, makes a splendid soloist in these colourful songs from *Des Knaben Wunderhorn*. A pity that as a fill-up they make rather short measure. Fine recording, as in the symphony.

Das Lied von der Erde.
> *** Decca SET 555. Yvonne Minton (contralto), René Kollo (tenor), Chicago Symphony Orchestra, Sir Georg Solti.
> *** HMV SAN 179. Christa Ludwig (mezzo-soprano), Fritz Wunderlich (tenor), New Philharmonia and Philharmonia Orchestras, Otto Klemperer.
> *** Decca SET 331. James King (tenor), Dietrich Fischer-Dieskau (baritone), Vienna Philharmonic Orchestra, Leonard Bernstein.

(M) ** (*) CBS Classics 61261. Mildred Miller (mezzo-soprano), Ernst Haefliger (tenor), New York Philharmonic Orchestra, Bruno Walter.

(M) ** (*) HMV SXLP 30165. Murray Dickie (tenor), Dietrich Fischer-Dieskau (baritone), Philharmonia Orchestra, Paul Kletzki.

* (*) CBS 76105. Christa Ludwig (mezzo-soprano), René Kollo (tenor), Israel Philharmonic Orchestra, Leonard Bernstein.

(B) * (*) Turnabout TV 34220S. Grace Hoffman (contralto), Helmut Melchert (tenor), South West German Radio Orchestra, Hans Rosbaud.

In sheer beauty of sound and precision of texture no version has matched Solti's with the Chicago Orchestra, helped by brilliant but refined recording. As an interpretation it may lose something in mystery from this very precision, but the concentration of Solti in a consciously less romantic style than Walter or Bernstein adopt has never been surpassed, above all in the final *Abschied*, slower than usual and bringing in the final section an unusually close observance of Mahler's *pianissimo* markings. Minton exactly matches Solti's style, consistently at her most perceptive and sensitive, while Kollo presents Heldentenor strength combined with sensitivity. The recording (unlike that on rival discs) has no need to give the tenor an unnaturally close balance, and the result is the more exciting. On most counts a clear first choice.

It is a pity that the great merits of the Bernstein and Klemperer sets of this greatest of orchestral song cycles cannot be married together. The Decca engineers gave Bernstein a ravishing recording aura in which the sound of the Vienna Philharmonic is magically beautiful, and all through his tempi are less wilful than Klemperer's, suiting the music more naturally. So the tenor songs sparkle as they should, and though the final *Abschied*, taken at a very slow tempo indeed, puts extra strain on everyone, Bernstein's intensity carries the performance through. Doubts do arise over the soloists. James King is a strong-voiced tenor, but compared with Wunderlich his phrasing and word-pointing sound comparatively stiff. Fischer-Dieskau is as sensitive as ever, but it is doubtful whether even he can match the finest contralto in the role, for one needs a lightening of tone in the even-numbered songs rather than – as here – a darkening. Nor can a baritone voice give quite such precision to the notes, which Mahler's rounded melodies clearly need.

Klemperer's way with Mahler is at its most individual in *Das Lied von der Erde*, and that will enthral some as it must infuriate others. True, there is less case for Klemperer nobility in so evocative, oriental-inspired a piece as *Das Lied* than there is in the symphonies, but if the ear is open, Klemperer's preference for slow tempi and his refusal to languish reveal qualities far removed from the heaviness his detractors criticize. With slower speeds the three tenor songs seem initially to lose some of their sparkle and humour, but thanks to superb, expressive singing by the late Fritz Wunderlich – one of the most memorable examples of his artistry on record – and thanks to pointing of rhythm by Klemperer himself, subtle but always clear, the comparative slowness will hardly worry anyone intent on hearing the music afresh as Klemperer intends. As for the mezzo songs, Christa Ludwig sings them with a remarkable depth of expressiveness. In particular the final *Abschied* has the intensity of a great occasion. Excellent recording apart from forward woodwind balance.

Though Walter's New York version does not have the tear-laden quality in the final *Abschied* that made his earlier Vienna account (in mono) with Kathleen Ferrier unique, that is its only serious shortcoming. Haefliger sparkles with imagination, Miller is a warm and appealing mezzo soloist, lacking only the last depth of feeling you find in a Ferrier, and the maestro himself has rarely sounded so happy on record, even in Mahler. Recording slightly coarse, but on this mid-price reissue very acceptable.

Kletzki's version makes a welcome reappearance on two sides instead of three and on a mid-price label. It is chiefly valuable for the singing of Fischer-Dieskau, a thoughtful and imaginative interpretation to justify this alternative use of the male voice, though Bernstein on Decca drew even more intense singing from him. Murray Dickie does not have the Heldentenor quality required, but the recording balance helps him, and Kletzki's reading with the Philharmonia at its peak has colour and imagination in plenty. Fine vintage recording to match the vintage playing.

Bernstein, Ludwig and Kollo had all earlier appeared in other versions of *Das Lied von der Erde*, but the conjunction of the three in Israel did not produce extra illumination; rather the reverse. The recording, idiosyncratically balanced and put together from a series of live performances, hardly rivals the best available.

Rosbaud's is a performance with much to commend it – he plainly understands Mahler's varying heartbeats, and the phrasing is nicely affectionate – but he misses the music's greatness. Melchert has a dry Germanic tenor quality that rings out well on powerful top notes, but there is a sense of tension and strain. Grace Hoffman has a beautiful contralto, but the feeling of commitment is limited. One wants something more deeply expressive. Even so, with good stereo at such a reasonable price this version is worth considering.

Lieder und Gesänge aus der Jugendzeit, Nos. 1–3, 5–7, 9, 12, 13.
  (M) ** Oiseau-Lyre SOL 327. Anna Reynolds (mezzo-soprano), Geoffrey Parsons (piano) – SCHUMANN: *Liederkreis.***

Anna Reynolds was the excellent mezzo soloist on Wyn Morris's record of *Das klagende Lied*, and this recital reinforces one's good opinion. She does not characterize each song as sharply as more famous Lieder singers, but in an entirely fresh and musical way they emerge tastefully and effectively. After all the records of Mahler songs with orchestral accompaniment it is good to have nine of this set of fourteen Lieder with piano. The recording of the piano is not entirely successful, but the voice comes over well.

Lieder eines fahrenden Gesellen.
  *** Decca SET 469/70. Yvonne Minton (contralto), Chicago Symphony Orchestra, Sir Georg Solti – *Symphony No. 6.****
  *** DGG 2770 056 (2 discs). Dietrich Fischer-Dieskau (baritone), Bavarian Radio Symphony Orchestra, Rafael Kubelik – *Symphony No. 5.* * (*)
  (M) ** CBS Classics 61369/70. Mildred Miller (mezzo-soprano), Columbia Symphony Orchestra, Bruno Walter – *Symphony No. 9.****
  ** Argo ZRG 737. Robert Tear (tenor), Academy of St Martin-in-the-Fields, Neville Marriner – BRITTEN: *Nocturne.***

Minton's performance of Mahler's *Wayfaring Lad* cycle is outstandingly successful. Fischer-Dieskau's set too is a fine one, the use of the baritone voice bringing its own special colouring. Mildred Miller's account is less imaginative, but has the advantage of medium price and an outstanding coupling. Having a tenor soloist subtly changes the character of Mahler's colourful music; and though Tear's dramatic approach has its effective moments, there is too little feeling for details of word meaning – a disappointing performance from fine musicians.

5 Rückert Lieder (Blicke mir nicht in die Lieder; Ich atmet' einen linden Duft; Um Mitternacht; Liebst du um Schönheit; Ich bin der Welt abhanden gekommen).
⊛ *** HMV SLS 785 (2 discs). Janet Baker (mezzo-soprano), New Philharmonia Orchestra, Sir John Barbirolli – Symphony No. 5.***
*** HMV ASD 2721 (same recording as above) – ELGAR: Sea Pictures.***

Few more lovely Mahler records have ever been made than this collection of the Five Rückert Lieder used as a fill-up for Barbirolli's ripe and expansive account of the Fifth Symphony. The range of tone-colour used by Janet Baker in these subtly contrasted songs is ravishing, and it is matched by dedicated playing from the New Philharmonia. No Mahlerian should miss hearing this. The recording is one of the finest ever produced by EMI. For those who, for whatever reason, do not want the symphony, the alternative coupling with Elgar's Sea Pictures is equally recommendable.

COLLECTION

'The world of Mahler': Symphonies Nos. (i) 1 in D major: 2nd movement; (ii) 4 in G major: 1st movement; (iii) 5 in C sharp minor: Adagietto; (iii; iv) 8 in E flat major: finale. (iii; v) Lieder eines fahrenden Gesellen: Ging heut' morgen uber's Feld.
(B) ** Decca SPA 362. (i) London Symphony Orchestra; (ii) Concertgebouw Orchestra; (iii) Chicago Symphony Orchestra; (iv) René Kollo (tenor), and choruses; (v) Yvonne Minton (contralto); all cond. Sir Georg Solti.

It is not certain that a collection of odd movements of this kind serves Mahler's cause. The Adagietto from the Fifth Symphony, which opens side two, stands well on its own (as we remember from 78 days), but in general this is a sampler for public libraries rather than a rewarding disc for regular use in even the small private collection. It is a pity that the record opens with the first movement of the Fourth which (attractive though it is) is not one of Solti's most convincing Mahler performances. The transfers are of good quality.

Malcolm, George
(born 1917)

Variations on a theme by Mozart (for 4 harpsichords).
(M) ** Decca Ace of Diamonds SDD 451. George Malcolm, Valda Aveling, Geoffrey Parsons, Simon Preston (harpsichords) – C. P. E. BACH and J. S. BACH: Harpsichord concertos.***

An excellent performance of a pleasingly facile work by George Malcolm which makes full use of the possibilities of modern harpsichord technique.

Malipiero, Gian
(1882–1973)

Violin concerto.
(M) *** Supraphon 110 1120. André Gertler (violin), Prague Symphony

553

Orchestra, Václav Smetáček –
MILHAUD: *Violin concerto No.
2.****

Malipiero died in 1973 at the ripe old
age of ninety-one. To most English
music lovers he is little more than a name,
though record collectors will recall that
his *Sixth Symphony* and some of his
chamber music have been available.
Apart from his creative output, his
reputation rests on his pioneering Monteverdi edition and his tireless work on
behalf of contemporary Italian music.
The *Violin concerto* (1932) is a rewarding
piece that improves greatly on acquaintance. Its scoring is inventive and expert.
The slow movement is pastoral in feeling
and its tranquillity of spirit recalls
Vaughan Williams, though the idiom is
by no means modal. André Gertler is a
persuasive soloist, and although the
recording is not outstanding, it is
eminently serviceable. The issue is so
enterprising that the unremarkable
recording quality should not detract
from the recommendation: this is well
worth acquiring.

Marais, Marin
(1656–1728)

*Sonnerie de Sainte Geneviève du Mont
de Paris. Suites Nos. 1 in C major; 4
in D major.*
> (B) ** (*) Oryx Musical Heritage
> MHS 964. Alice Harnoncourt
> (violin), Leopold Stastny (flute),
> Nikolaus Harnoncourt (viola da
> gamba; dessus de viole), Herbert
> Tachezi (harpsichord).

Marin Marais was a contemporary
of Couperin, and on this showing he had
a charming lyrical gift. Some of the
movements in these dance suites are
merely conventional, but the two *Sara-*

bandes and a magnificent *Plainte* show
how slow tempi could inspire him.
Delightful, stylish performances and fine
if rather distant recording.

Marcello, Alessandro
(1684–1750)

Oboe concerto in C minor (arr. Bonelli).
> (B) *** Pye GSGC 15011. Evelyn
> Rothwell (oboe), Pro Arte Orch-
> estra, Sir John Barbirolli – ALBI-
> NONI and CIMAROSA: *Con-
> certos.****

Sir John's subtlety in matters of light
and shade within an orchestral phrase
brings the music immediately alive and at
the same time prevents the rather jolly
opening tune from sounding square.
There is a beautiful *Adagio* and a gay
finale, both showing the soloist on top
form, and the well-balanced recording
adds to one's pleasure.

Marcello, Benedetto
(1686–1739)

12 Concerti a cinque, Op. 1.
> *** Telefunken SAWT 9601/2. I
> Solisti di Milano, Angelo Ephri-
> kian.

Marcello's set of concertos are much
in the standard pattern of those by
Corelli, but they are not without individuality, and their special feature is the
use of a violin (and sometimes a cello)
soloist. The solo line is often imaginative
and the concertos have many felicities of
invention to appeal to the lover of this
period. The performances are generally
excellent, and the sound and balance are
first-rate.

Martin, Frank
(1890–1974)

(i) *Ballade for piano and orchestra;* (ii) *Ballade for trombone and orchestra;* (iii) *Harpsichord concerto* (for harpsichord and small orchestra).

> (M) *** Vox STGBY 669. (i) Sebastian Benda (piano); (ii) Armin Rosin (trombone); (iii) Christiane Jaccottet (harpsichord); all with Lausanne Chamber Orchestra, the composer.

Like so much of Martin's best work, the *Harpsichord concerto* (1952) is a work of strong presence and personality with a distinctive atmosphere. The first movement is built on a sequence of six notes inspired by the steady rocking of the waves on the North Sea. The orchestral forces are small so as to lend transparency to the texture and help the soloist. An imaginative and rewarding score, the work makes a valuable contribution to the repertoire, and the performance, admirably recorded here, has the additional authority of the composer's direction to recommend it. On the reverse the two *Ballades*, earlier works dating from the period 1939–40, are no less thoughtful and poetic. All in all, this is a most worthwhile disc and a valuable addition to the representation of the Swiss master on disc.

(i) *Piano concerto No. 2;* (ii) *Violin concerto.*

> (M) ** (*) Vox STGBY 661. (i) Paul Badura-Skoda (piano); (ii) Wolfgang Schneiderhan (violin); both with Radio Luxembourg Orchestra, the composer.

Martin's *Violin concerto* is one of the most rewarding post-war essays in this form, and anyone who likes, say, the Bartók or Shostakovich concertos will warm to it. Written in 1951, it shows Martin at his very best: it is consistently lyrical and its textures are marvellously limpid and luminous, its colours muted but highly distinctive. Some music lovers complain of the limited range of expressive devices he employs, but here his highly personal habits of mind seem totally attuned to his imaginative purposes. It is a misfortune that it has not attracted advocates other than Schneiderhan; not that he is unpersuasive, but it deserves the widest representation in the concert hall and on record. The recording is a good one, though the violin tends to sound a trifle hard and steely. The *Piano concerto No. 2* is a less impressive work, but it is nonetheless a welcome addition to the catalogue.

Petite symphonie concertante.

> (M) *** Unicorn UNS 233. London Chamber Orchestra, Paul Tortelier (with *Concert* ** (*)).

Martin's *Petite symphonie concertante* is a masterpiece and ought to be in the standard repertoire. We had to wait a long time for a modern stereo recording, and fortunately this performance is a fine one. The recording acoustic is a little dry and the internal balance is not ideally clear, but the playing itself has a finely judged atmosphere, bringing out the work's fascinating colouring and sense of mystery. The originality of the writing comes over vividly, particularly the unusual use of the harpsichord within the texture of the music. Highly recommended. This is part of a concert of French music discussed in our *Treasury* volume.

555

Martinů, Bohuslav
(1890–1959)

Harpsichord concerto (for harpsichord and small orchestra).

> (M) ** Supraphon SUAST 50926. Zuzana Růžičková (harpsichord), Prague Chamber Soloists, Kurt Sanderling – POULENC: *Concerto.* (*)

The *Harpsichord concerto* dates from 1935. It is a characteristically vital work, with a strong underlying vein of lyricism to balance the abounding energy. The performance by Růžičková is spirited, and she is fortunate in having her instrument recorded with notable presence and clarity.

Oboe concerto.

> (M) *** Supraphon SUAST 50486. František Hanták (oboe), Brno State Philharmonic Orchestra, Martin Turnovsky – R. STRAUSS: *Oboe concerto.***

Martinů's *Concerto* is a splendid addition to the modern repertory for the oboe. While the writing is not so florid as that in the Richard Strauss *Concerto* on the reverse, it still needs considerable flexibility of technique on the part of the soloist if the work's essential lyricism is to flow through the decoration. The basic quality of the work is high-spirited and confident. The recording is somewhat close, but otherwise good. Recommended.

(i) *Piano concerto No. 3;* (ii) *Violin concerto.*

> (M) ** Supraphon SUAST 50386. (i) Josef Páleníček (piano), Czech Philharmonic Orchestra, Karel Ančerl; (ii) Bruno Bělčík (violin), Prague Symphony Orchestra, Václav Neumann.

Both these somewhat eclectic works were commissioned by American artists, the *Piano concerto* (1948) by Firkusny, and the *Violin concerto* (1943) by Elman. The *Piano concerto* displays an infectious and lively facility, but (in the slow movement especially) is rather too long for its content. The *Violin concerto* is more lyrical, with a charming carillon effect at the beginning of the *Andante*, but again rather tends to outstay its welcome. Both works, one feels, would go down well at a live performance by their very vitality. Here Páleníček is impressive, but Bělčík offers adequate rather than outstanding playing. The recording is good, crisper in the *Violin concerto*.

(i) *Piano concerto No. 4 (Incantation);* (ii) *Sinfonietta giocosa.*

> (M) *** Supraphon SUAST 58591. (i) Josef Páleníček (piano), Brno State Philharmonic Orchestra, Jiri Pinkas; (ii) Stanislav Knor (piano), Prague Symphony Orchestra, Václav Smetáček.

The *Sinfonietta giocosa* is a masterpiece, full of life and brimming over with first-rate ideas. It is strongly neo-classical in feeling and redolent in spirit of the concerto grosso. One splendid idea follows another and the music seems to be light-hearted and carefree, although Martinů, a refugee from the Gestapo in Vichy France, must have felt anything but free from anxiety during the months when this was written. The musicians play with appropriate liveliness and affection, and are well recorded. The fill-up brings us the *Fourth Piano concerto*, written in the mid-1950s for Firkusny, a highly imaginative and original score. A most valuable and rewarding issue that cannot be too strongly recommended.

(i) *Double piano concerto;* (ii) *Concertino for piano and orchestra.*

> (M) * (*) Supraphon SUAST 50909.

Brno State Philharmonic Orchestra, cond. (i) Jiři Waldhans, with Vera and Vlastimil Lejsek (pianos); (ii) Jiři Pinkas, with Eva Bernáthová (piano).

Of these two works the *Concertino* is the more attractive, although neither shows the composer at his most inventive. The music bustles along without anything very distinctive happening. The *Concertino* is the better recorded; the *Double concerto* is rather reverberant. This is of interest to the Martinů specialist rather than the average music-lover, though both performances are good.

(i) *Violoncello concerto No. 1;* (ii) *Double concerto for violin, piano and orchestra.*
  (M) *** Supraphon 110 1348. (i) Josef Chuchro (cello); (ii) Nora Grumliková (violin), Jaroslav Kolar (piano); both with Czech Philharmonic Orchestra, Zdeněk Košler.

A welcome coupling of two works that have much in common. In each the outer movements have strong elements of concerto-grosso style, and in fact the *First Cello concerto* (an early work dating from 1930) was originally planned as a concerto grosso using a small wind group and strings. The composer had second thoughts about it and rescored it twice more to produce the final version recorded here. Like the *Double concerto* the work has an eloquent and highly rewarding slow movement. If anything the *Concerto for violin and piano* is an even finer piece. Of the same vintage as the *Sixth Symphony* (1953), it shows the composer at his most engaging. The first movement is fresh and vital and the slow movement is very beautiful indeed. The performances are spirited, and although the recording is reverberant it does not detract from the great pleasure to be had from this disc.

Violoncello concerto No. 2.
  (M) * (*) Supraphon SUAST 50883. Sasa Večtomov (cello), Prague Symphony Orchestra, Zdeněk Košler.

This is an ambitious work and has a fine opening sweep that the rest of the first movement fails to live up to. The slow movement also begins more promisingly than it continues, and the toccata-like finale is empty. The soloist makes the most of the material and plays with enthusiasm but the orchestral contribution seems less spontaneous. Typical reverberant Supraphon sound.

Concerto for double string orchestra, piano and timpani.
  (M) *** RCA LHL 1 5086. Prague Chamber Orchestra, Hans-Hubert Schönzeler – JANÁČEK: *Idyla.***
(i) *Concerto for double string orchestra, piano and timpani;* (ii) *3 Frescoes (Les Fresques de Piero della Francesca).*
  (M) ** (*) Supraphon SUAST 50109. Czech Philharmonic Orchestra, cond. (i) Karel Sejna; (ii) Karel Ančerl.

The Supraphon recording dates from the early sixties, though this new pressing is cut at a slightly lower level than the original. The *Double concerto*, written for Paul Sacher and the Basle Chamber Orchestra in 1938, at about the same time as Bartók wrote his *Music for strings, percussion and celesta* for the same artists, is arguably Martinů's masterpiece and this performance has an enormous sweep and energy. But more vivid is the Prague Chamber Orchestra's account under Schönzeler, which has splendid ensemble and attack to commend it as well as clean well-articulated phrasing. The RCA recording has much greater presence; it is recorded in a smaller acoustic and obviously benefits from the Dolby process, since both background noise and surfaces are totally silent. It all boils down to a matter of couplings: the Schönzeler offers a relatively uninteresting early work of Janáček while the Supraphon disc has the *Frescoes of Piero della Francesca*, glowingly played and recorded. These are much later than the *Concerto* but have a strong appeal; the slow movement is marvellously atmospheric.

(i; ii) *Jazz suite;* (iii) *La Revue de cuisine;* (ii) *Who is the most powerful in the world – Shimmy foxtrot;* (iv) *Sextet for piano and wind;* (i) (Piano) *Trois Esquisses;* (v; ii) (Choral) *Le Jazz.*
  (M) ** (*) Supraphon 110 1014. (i) Zdenek Jílek (piano); (ii) Prague Symphony Orchestra, Zbynek Vostrák; (iii) Instrumental Ensemble; (iv) Jan Panenka (piano), Prague Wind Quintet; (v) Lubomir Pánek Singers.

This record presents a useful compilation of Martinů's jazz-inspired compositions from the 1920s. They are moderately entertaining, and readers interested in the development of the great Czech composer will want to investigate this aspect of his personality. On the whole, however, the disc will enjoy limited appeal and none of the music, even if it offers amusing moments as in *La Revue de cuisine*, is in any way substantial.

Spalícek (ballet): *suites Nos. 1 and 2.*
  (M) ** Supraphon 110 1129. Brno State Philharmonic Orchestra, Jiři Waldhans.

A lively inventive score that will delight admirers of this composer. It was written in the early thirties but revised and expanded in Paris in 1940. No one listening to it would guess that it was finally put into shape during a period of anxiety and uncertainty, for it is relentlessly extrovert and cheerful in mood. *The Dance of the Maids of Honour* from the second suite is highly memorable and is difficult to dislodge from one's mind. There are other attractive ideas too; but at the same time it must be conceded that there is also a good deal of routine Martinů optimism. The performance is a fine one, though it is recorded in a somewhat reverberant studio.

Symphony No. 4; Tre ricercari.
  (M) *** Supraphon SUAST 50669. Czech Philharmonic Orchestra, Martin Turnovsky.

Martinů's *Fourth Symphony* dates from 1945. It is written in the more popular style which marks the composer's later works. The dichotomy of the first movement, with its swinging (lyrical) harmonic theme on the strings in contrast with the florid counter-subject on the wind, is particularly successful, and throughout the work one feels a strong thematic unity. The scherzo is exhilarating, with an attractive middle section, and the *Lento* has a genuine depth of expression (again the characteristic spacious harmony making its effect). The *Three Ricercari* are less substantial works, but attractive enough; the outer movements rattle along with characteristic toccata-like brilliance. The performances here, especially that of the symphony, are first-rate and the recording one of Supraphon's best.

Symphony No. 6 (Fantaisies symphoniques).
  * Unicorn RHS 309. New Philharmonia Orchestra, Michael Bialoguski – VOŘIŠEK: *Symphony.**

Martinů's *Fantaisies symphoniques* is one of his most imaginative and evocative scores and one must salute Dr Bialoguski's judgement as well as his courage in choosing to record it. He is not a professional conductor; he committed his savings and hired an orchestra to prove himself in this capacity. Unfortunately this performance sounds too wanting in authority and the phrasing is anaemic, and it is not, alas, possible to recommend it with any conviction. Munch recorded this work for RCA in the 1950s and the Supraphon catalogue boasts a version under Ančerl, and readers are advised to await their return.

Piano trio No. 3 in C major; Bergerettes.
> (M) ** (*) Supraphon SUAST 50698. Foerster Trio.

Martinů's five *Bergerettes* for piano trio make enchanting listening. They have the melodic and rhythmic spontaneity of Dvořák's *Slavonic dances* and the scoring for piano trio gives them an even greater bite and freshness than if they were conceived for orchestra. The spirited performances here are ideal and the recording quality matches the vivacious playing. The *Third Piano trio* is slightly less successful. Its kernel is in the pungent *Andante*. The outer movements follow Martinů's moto perpetuo manner, the strong rhythmic impetus not covering the underlying lyricism. Here the playing is alive but the recording not quite so clear as in the *Bergerettes*. But this remains a valuable disc and one not to be missed by those who have already discovered the immediacy of the composer's style.

String quartet No. 4.
> (M) ** Supraphon SUAST 50529. Smetana Quartet – DVOŘÁK: *Quartet No. 2.** (*)

The *Fourth Quartet* is a lively and inventive work but not one of Martinů's most searching compositions. The performance here is masterly but those wanting to build a basic library of Martinů could well turn to the *Fifth* and *Sixth Quartets* rather than this work.

String quartets Nos. (i) *5;* (ii) *7.*
> (M) *** Supraphon SUAST 50424. (i)

Janáček Quartet; (ii) Vlach Quartet.

The autograph of the *Fifth Quartet* was lost during the war and only came to light in 1955. Written for the famous Pro Arte Quartet in 1938, it is one of Martinů's strongest chamber works. Finest is the slow movement, which has genuine vision; elsewhere there is at times the suspicion that craftsmanship outstrips inspiration. The *Seventh Quartet* is a post-war work, written immediately after the *Fifth Symphony*: it is subtitled *Concerto da camera* and is very much in Martinů's concerto-grosso style, fluent and lyrical with plenty of bustling activity. A representative disc, then, and both performance and recording are of a high standard.

String quartet No. 6.
> (M) *** Supraphon SUAST 50950. Novák Quartet – ROUSSEL: *String quartet.***

If the *Fifth* and *Seventh* between them offer a representative sample of Martinů's chamber music, the *Sixth Quartet*, written in 1946, is arguably the most impressive of the series. Its invention is strong and distinguished, its character well defined. Readers who want only the smallest handful of Martinů's works in their library (pieces like the *Concerto for double string orchestra*, the *Sinfonietta giocosa* and the *Fourth Symphony*, all of them masterpieces) can safely include this quartet. The Nováks give it a thoroughly well-prepared and intensely felt reading and are well served by the engineers.

Borová: Czech dances Nos. 1–7; Etudes and polkas, Books 1–3 (complete).
> (M) * (*) Supraphon 111 1104. Josef Hála (piano).

These are lively and engaging pieces. Martinů composed the *Etudes and Polkas* in America during the war years; many of them are delightful and all of them are short. They are not particularly varied in style or mood and one only wants to hear one book at a time, but they are inventive and highly characteristic pieces. The *Czech dances* are much earlier but no less rewarding. Josef Hála plays intelligently but he is not well served by the engineers and the disc must be given a qualified recommendation on that account. The piano tone is not well focused: it is fuzzy and glassy, and the acoustic is reverberant. This does seriously impair pleasure and calls for some tolerance.

The Prophecy of Isaiah (cantata for soloists, male chorus and chamber ensemble).

> (M) * (*) Supraphon SUAST 50778. Helena Tattermuschová (soprano), Marie Mrázová (contralto), Karel Berman (bass), Czech Philharmonic Chorus and Orchestra, Karel Ančerl – STRAVINSKY: *Symphony of Psalms*.* (*)

This cantata, a setting of words from Isaiah, was the last work that Martinů completed, and perhaps in anticipation of approaching death, the style is sparer and darker than we expect of this composer. The choral writing is powerful, and though some of the soloists have troublesome Slavonic wobbles, the performance is vivid and dramatic. This is not immediately attractive music, despite the easiness of the idiom, but it is an important extension of our knowledge of a composer not yet given his due. Excellent recording quality.

Julietta (opera): complete recording.

> (M) *** Supraphon SUAST 50611/3. Maria Tauberová (soprano), Ivo Zídek (tenor) and cast of Prague National Theatre production, Prague National Theatre Chorus

and Orchestra, Jaroslav Krombholc.

Julietta is a key work in Martinů's output and highly esteemed by all the authorities on the composer. It dates from the 1930s and is based on Georges Neveux's play *La Clé des songes*. The opera has no plot in the proper sense of the word, for the play balances on the fine edge of reality and illusion, so that all reality seems to be fiction, and fiction assumes the guise of reality. Suffice it to say that the opera drew from Martinů inspiration of the highest quality: the score is full of variety, both of texture and colour, the music is unfailingly inventive and imaginative, with a strong and at times luminous atmosphere. This magical work will more than repay study, particularly in so idiomatic and beautifully recorded a performance.

Mascagni, Pietro
(1863–1945)

Cavalleria Rusticana (opera in 1 act): complete recording.

> *** DGG 2709 020 (3 discs). Fiorenza Cossotto (mezzo-soprano), Carlo Bergonzi (tenor), Giangiacomo Guelfi (baritone), Chorus and Orchestra of La Scala, Milan, Herbert von Karajan – LEONCAVALLO: *I Pagliacci*.***

> (M) ** Decca Ace of Diamonds GOS 588/90. Giulietta Simionato (mezzo-soprano), Mario del Monaco (tenor), Cornell MacNeil (baritone), Chorus and Orchestra of St Cecilia Academy, Rome, Tullio Serafin – LEONCAVALLO: *I Pagliacci*.**

Cavalleria Rusticana: complete recording. (Also includes recital by Bjoerling:

arias from CILEA: *L'Arlesiana*; GIOR-
DANO: *Fedora*; PONCHIELLI: *La
Gioconda*; PUCCINI: *La Fanciulla del
West*; VERDI: *Un Ballo in maschera*.)

(M) ** (*) Decca Ace of Diamonds
GOS 634/5. Renata Tebaldi (sop-
rano), Jussi Bjoerling (tenor),
Ettore Bastianini (baritone), Cho-
rus and Orchestra of Maggio
Musicale Fiorentino, Alberto
Erede.

Cavalleria Rusticana: complete recording.

** Decca SET 343/4. Elena Suliotis
(soprano), Mario del Monaco
(tenor), Tito Gobbi (baritone),
Rome Opera Chorus and Orchestra, Silvio Varviso – VERDI:
Arias from *Un Ballo in maschera*
and *La Forza del destino**(*) (also
PONCHIELLI: Aria from *La
Gioconda*).

Karajan's direction of the other half of
the inevitable partnership matches that of
Pagliacci. He pays Mascagni the tribute
of taking his markings literally, so that
well-worn melodies come out with new
purity and freshness, and the singers have
been chosen to match that. Cossotto
quite as much as Bergonzi keeps a pure,
firm line that is all too rare in this much-
abused music. Together they show that
much of the vulgarity lies in interpretations rather than in Mascagni's inspiration. Not that there is any lack of
dramatic bite (except marginally, because
of the recording balance in some of the
chorus work). Good recording but at
rather a low level.

The early Decca set with Tebaldi offers
a forthright, lusty account of Mascagni's
piece of blood and thunder and has the
distinction of three excellent soloists.
Tebaldi is most moving in *Voi lo sapete*,
and the firm richness of Bastianini's
baritone is beautifully caught. As always
Bjoerling shows himself the most intelli-

gent of tenors and it is only the chorus
that gives serious room for disappointment. They are enthusiastic and accurate
enough when accompanying Bjoerling's
superb account of the drinking scene (in
Italy no doubt the directions for wine
were taken literally), but at other times
they are very undisciplined. On the fourth
side Bjoerling rides the group of war-
horse arias almost as though he were
twenty years younger; only occasionally
does a trace of hardness creep in. A fine
recital.

The full-priced Decca set under Varviso is also coupled to a recital of arias
(not as rewarding as Bjoerling's collection, but showing well the power and
colour of Suliotis's voice) and it is plain
enough that the recording company saw
this as primarily a vehicle for Suliotis.
Hers can be an exciting voice, and she
gives a dramatic performance, but in
many details it seems unfinished, and
though the voice is characterful it is not
always under complete control. If Suliotis
was caught too early as Santuzza, Gobbi
was caught just in time as Alfio, and for
that many thanks. He turns the conventional figure of the carter into a real three-
dimensional character. Mario del Monaco is not at his best, but neither is he at
his coarsest – a fair enough big-voiced
performance that had best not be compared with the artistically assured Bergonzi. Nor does Varviso's conducting
emerge with any special individuality, but
with magnificent sound from the Decca
engineers the result is undeniably dramatic.

The tone of the other Decca performance is set by Serafin. It is comparatively
restrained. Simionato is not ideal as
Santuzza: her *Easter hymn* should be
steadier than this. Cornell MacNeil is an
efficient but not terribly imaginative
Alfio. Again the redeeming feature is the
splendid recording.

Cavalleria Rusticana: highlights.

*** DGG SLPEM 136281 (from
above recording cond. Karajan).

561

(M) ** Decca Ace of Diamonds SDD
418 (from above recording cond.
Serafin).

** Decca SET 490 (from above
recording cond. Varviso).

These three selections are all coupled
to highlights from the companion *Pagliacci* recordings (the Varviso to Gardelli's
recording on SET 403/4). Karajan's disc,
with its refinement of direction as well
as the fresh sophistication of the solo
singing, is easily preferable to either of
the Decca issues. Suliotis's contribution
is not always fully controlled vocally, and
del Monaco is not at his best either. Of
the two Decca discs the cheaper Ace of
Diamonds issue seems much the better
buy.

Massenet, Jules
(1842–1912)

Scènes pittoresques (suite); *Le Cid:
ballet music* (from Act 2 of the opera);
La Vierge: The last sleep of the Virgin.
*** Columbia Quadraphonic Q4-
TWO 350; Stereo TWO 350. City
of Birmingham Orchestra, Louis
Frémaux.

Le Cid: ballet music.
(M) ** Decca Ace of Diamonds SDD
139. Israel Philharmonic Orchestra, Jean Martinon – MEYER-
BEER: *Les Patineurs.****

The action of Massenet's opera *Le Cid*
takes place in Spain during the twelfth
century. The ballet music, with its
abundance of local colour and rhythms,
is another example of the peculiar talent
of French composers for capturing the
Spanish idiom. Martinon gives a sparkling performance and the orchestra
displays the utmost virtuosity. Unfortunately the Decca recording acoustic
does not quite suit the music, and its

rather open reverberation exaggerates the
brashness of Martinon's basic approach.

Fine though it sounds in ordinary
stereo, this EMI quadraphonic disc is a
superb demonstration of the potential of
the SQ quadraphonic system. For the
best effect the volume needs to be well
up, then the illusion of being in the Great
Hall of Birmingham University, where
the recording was made, is remarkable.
The sound is superbly vivid and rich,
and the performances of these attractive
lightweight scores are wonderfully affectionate and colourful. A quadraphonic
feast, to convince the doubters that those
two extra speakers *can* add to the realism
without any gimmicks whatsoever.

Manon (opera in 5 acts, original version): complete recording.
** (*) HMV SLS 800 (4 discs).
Beverly Sills (soprano), Nicolai
Gedda (tenor), Gabriel Bacquier,
Gérard Souzay (baritones), Ambrosian Opera Chorus, New Philharmonia Orchestra, Julius Rudel.

Beverly Sills scored an enormous success at the New York City Opera with
this enchanting opera, and she brings to
the recording the benefits of intensive
stage experience of the role. Her voice
too is more naturally suited to the character of the flirtatious Manon than it is to
some of her bigger roles, and there is
much to charm and delight the ear in a
long opera which yet sustains its length
with range of dramatic experience. The
other soloists too are well cast, though
neither Gedda nor Souzay is in his sweetest voice. Julius Rudel of the New York
City Opera makes a strong and understanding conductor, and the only reservation – which for some will be serious – is
that the old mono version with Victoria
de los Angeles at her most golden-toned
and magical and Monteux at his most
mellow made for an altogether more
intense experience. But we are not likely

to get a more compelling *Manon* than this in stereo for a long time. Good recording.

Manon: highlights.
** (*) HMV ASD 2877 (from above recording).

Not everyone will want so long an opera as *Manon* on record: well-chosen excerpts from an enjoyable set should be the answer. Good recording.

Thaïs (opera in 3 acts): complete recording.
(M) ** Decca Ace of Diamonds GOS 639/42. Renée Doria (soprano), Janine Collard (mezzo-soprano), Robert Massard (baritone), Michel Sénéchal (tenor), Chorus and Orchestra, Jésus Etcheverry.

Thaïs is an exotic period piece, set in Egypt in the early Christian era, the story of a monk who seeks to save a beautiful courtesan and is himself destroyed. Sentimental as the plot is, it inspired Massenet to some of his characteristically mellifluous writing, with atmospheric choruses and sumptuous orchestration. This French version is not helped by the rather dated recording, but the authenticity of the performance is not in doubt; in many ways it is more sympathetic than one with more star names. Renée Doria as the courtesan Thaïs has a thin, very French-sounding voice but rises well to the big moments, and Robert Massard as Athanaël is excellent.

Thérèse (opera in 2 acts): complete recording.
*** Decca SET 572. Huguette Tourangeau (mezzo-soprano), Ryland Davies (tenor), Louis Quilico (baritone), Linden Singers, New Philharmonia Orchestra, Richard Bonynge.

This story of the French Revolution, showing a conflict of love and loyalty, has so many parallels with Puccini's *Tosca* and Giordano's *Andrea Chénier* of the previous decade that it is surprising Massenet chose it. He was then (1905) at the end of his career, and was freshly inspired by the charms of a young mezzo-soprano, Lucy Arbell, who by all accounts was (vocally at least) unworthy of his attentions. The result was this passionate score, compressed and intense, lacking only the last degree of memorability in the melodies that makes Massenet's finest operas so gripping. Bonynge is a splendid advocate, amply proving how taut and atmospheric the writing is. There is some first-rate singing from the three principals, and the format on a single disc complete with notes (but not libretto) is attractively neat. Excellent recording.

Mathias, William
(born 1934)

Piano concerto No. 3, Op. 40.
*** Decca SXL 6513. Peter Katin (piano), London Symphony Orchestra, David Atherton – HODDINOTT: *Harp concerto; Clarinet concerto.***

Mathias is a composer of genuine talent, and his *Piano concerto* is both fluent and well-argued even if its invention is not as memorable or its atmosphere as haunting as in the Hoddinott concertos on the reverse. Impeccable performance and recording.

Dance overture, Op. 16. (i) *Harp concerto, Op. 50. Invocation and dance, Op. 17.* (ii) *Ave Rex – A carol sequence, Op. 45.*
⊛ *** Decca SXL 6607. London

563

Symphony Orchestra, David Atherton, with (i) Osian Ellis (harp); (ii) Welsh National Opera Chorale.

Even by Decca's high standards this record is stunningly well recorded (it sounds splendid through quadraphonic speakers). Of the current records of Mathias's music, this is obviously the one to start with. The music has genuine spontaneity of invention. The *Dance overture* is vividly scored in the manner of Malcolm Arnold, and the delightful carol sequence has the robust inspiration of Britten's *Ceremony*, with which it has much in common. The *Harp concerto*, although mainly gentle in texture, is a substantial work. The scoring is deliciously imaginative, using other percussion instruments to add to the galaxy of twinkling sound which the harp itself can create. The character of the piece is at once tranquil and robust. An admirable collection for those who have despaired of finding any mid-twentieth-century music with melodic appeal and staying power.

Symphony No. 1, Op. 31.

(M) ** (*) Pye Virtuoso TPLS 13023. Royal Philharmonic Orchestra, Sir Charles Groves – JONES: *Symphony No. 6.****

William Mathias is of a different generation from his compatriot Daniel Jones, whose *Sixth Symphony* forms the coupling on this valuable record of contemporary Welsh music. Mathias's *First Symphony* was commissioned for the 1966 Llandaff Festival. The music is more aggressive, less comfortable than Jones's idiom. The work has a tonal basis, but relies a good deal on rhythmical elements (in the scherzo with a Stravinskian flavour) and colouristic devices. The writing in the outer movements has plenty of energy and forward momentum, but for all its driving force does not stay

in the memory in the same way as the more conventional structure by Daniel Jones on the reverse. Nevertheless with such a committed and well played performance this is valuable.

Maw, Nicholas
(born 1935)

(i) *Sonata for strings and two horns. Sinfonia.*

*** Argo ZRG 676. English Chamber Orchestra, Norman Del Mar, (i) with Alan Civil and Ian Harper (horns).

Nicholas Maw is well served by the gramophone, and that is hardly surprising when his writing is so rich in texture and warmly emotional in mood. That is not to say that either of these works is simply a bath of self-indulgence. In some ways both works are very tough, and the arguments are certainly closely wrought. But an unprejudiced listener should find immediate as well as lasting enjoyment. It is rare that a young composer these days can write with such energy and keen love of sound. Both works, written at very much the same period, in the mid-sixties, have echoes of Britten and late Strauss, but still present an individual idiom, each in extended three-movement structures. Superb committed performances and excellent recording.

String quartet.

*** Argo ZRG 565. Aeolian Quartet – WOOD: *Quartet No. 1.****

Nicholas Maw's *String quartet* is a massive and strongly argued piece that has the courage to talk in terms not so far removed from late Beethoven. Maw is a very serious-minded composer (despite having two *comic* operas to his credit) and this richly conceived work, spreading over nearly forty minutes, is well worth serious study, particularly in this excellent performance by the Aeolian Quartet recorded in the presence of the composer. First-rate recording.

Scenes and Arias.
> *** Argo ZRG 622. Jane Manning, Anne Howells (mezzo-sopranos), Norma Procter (contralto), BBC Symphony Orchestra, Norman Del Mar – LUTYENS: *Quincunx.****

Scenes and Arias is a setting of medieval love-letters that unexpectedly explodes into soaring passionate music of a richness such as you would expect in a Richard Strauss opera. The parallel with Strauss is inevitable when Maw uses women's voices with an intertwining mellifluousness one associates above all with the great Trio from *Rosenkavalier*, and though it may be argued that such rich texture extended to a full half-hour of music inclines to the self-indulgent, it is good to find a post-war composer who is ready to create sounds pleasing to the ear. Maw has a habit of setting elaborately decorated figures to long-sustained chords, but he avoids the charge of writing in too static a way with vigorous allegros full of jagged syncopations. First-rate recording considering the great length of side. Lovely singing from the soloists, and passionately committed conducting by Norman Del Mar.

Maxwell Davies, Peter
(born 1934)

(i) *Antechrist;* (i; ii) *From Stone to Thorn;* (i; iii) *L'Homme armé;* (iv) *Hymnos.*
> *** Oiseau-Lyre DSLO 2. (i) Fires of London, the composer; (ii) Mary

Thomas (soprano); (iii) Vanessa Redgrave (speaker); (iv) Alan Hacker (clarinet), Stephen Pruslin (piano).

Much of Maxwell Davies's creative energy has been projected towards writing works for the two overlapping groups which he formed and directs, first the Pierrot Players and later the Fires of London. These are four characteristic works regularly given at their concerts starting with *Antechrist*, a sort of exuberant overture. *L'Homme armé*, a more extended but comparable work, similarly working on a medieval motif, is also most approachable, while the other two works, thornier in argument, directly display the formidable talents of – among others – the soprano Mary Thomas and the clarinettist Alan Hacker. A valuable disc, well recorded.

(i) *Second Fantasia on John Taverner's In nomine;* (ii) *Taverner* (opera): *Points and dances.*
> ** (*) Argo ZRG 712. (i) New Philharmonia Orchestra, Sir Charles Groves; (ii) Fires of London, the composer.

In an age of crabbed inspiration on the one hand, uncharted wildness on the other, it is remarkable that a composer making no concessions should argue strongly, satisfyingly and movingly over a span of forty minutes, using the conventional symphony orchestra but producing something totally original and new. At its first public performance the *Second Fantasia* required an introductory lecture from the conductor (John Pritchard), but now the logic in its thirteen sections seems plain enough. Some of the music was later used in *Taverner*, the opera about the composer whose *In nomine* forms the basis of this work. Groves's performance is not ideally incisive or polished, but anyone willing to accept a challenge will find this record very rewarding. The *Points and dances* make an attractive, undemanding fill-up. Excellent recording.

Fantasia on O magnum mysterium (for organ); *O magnum mysterium.*
> *** Argo ZRG 5327. Simon Preston (organ); Choir and Orchestra of Cirencester Grammar School, the composer.

Both these brilliantly imaginative works are based on the same theme, which we hear as a solo at the opening of the cantata. This was written for the children of Cirencester Grammar School, where Peter Maxwell Davies once taught, and his pupils sing it with skill and enthusiasm, while the school orchestra provides the exotic accompanimental texture. The organ work, like the vocal one, is exploratory in matters of timbre and effect, and with Argo's excellent recording there is no doubt of the originality of the writing.

Eight songs for a mad king.
> ** Unicorn RHS 308. Julius Eastman (reciter), Fires of London, the composer.

There are many levels of imagination at work in this extraordinary, unforgettable piece, probably the most successful example of music-theatre that Davies has written. It is at once a recreation of George III's madness, the reciter/singer taking the role of the king with nerve-jangling realism; at once an extraordinary example of new expression in sing-speech with vocal harmonics and double-notes produced as part of the king's raving; at once a dramatic fantasy with flute, clarinet, violin and cello representing birds in cages, the birds the king tried to teach; at once a musical fantasy on tunes played by a mechanical organ that the king actually possessed and which survives today. It is harrowing

in its surrealism, its playing on the hidden nerve, but the power of inspiration, superbly interpreted here, and splendidly recorded, is undeniable.

Vesalii Icones.
> *** Unicorn RHS 307. Jennifer Ward Clarke (cello), Fires of London, the composer.

Maxwell Davies has the great quality of presenting strikingly memorable visions, and this is certainly one, an extraordinary cello solo with comment from a chamber group. It was originally written to accompany a solo dancer in a fourteen-fold sequence, each dance based on one of the horrifying anatomical drawings of Vesalius (1543) and each representing one of the stations of the Cross. Characteristically Davies has moments not only of biting pain and tender compassion but of deliberate shock-tactics – notably when the risen Christ turns out to be Antichrist and is represented in a final jaunty fox-trot. This is difficult music, but the emotional landmarks are plain from the start, and that is a good sign of enduring quality. Jennifer Ward Clarke plays superbly, and so do the Fires of London conducted by the composer. Excellent recording.

Mayr, Johann Simon (1763–1845)

Piano concerto No. 1 in C major.
> ⊛ (B) *** Turnabout TV 34526S. Maria Littauer (piano), Hamburg Symphony Orchestra, Alois Springer – RIES: *Concerto No. 3.***

This enchanting concerto by Johann Mayr is a real find. Play the crisply classical opening of the first movement or the graceful cantilena of the *Andantino* to almost anyone and the assured verdict is: 'Mozart'. The work is certainly worthy of that master, full of flowing melody and felicitous control of phrase and harmonic structure. The performance here is elegant and spontaneous and this is very enjoyable indeed. The rosette is awarded in appreciation of the enterprise of the Vox catalogue (of which Turnabout is a part) in unearthing and recording so many unknown concertos, of which this is one of the very finest.

Medea in Corinto (opera in 2 acts): complete recording.
> (M) ** (*) Vanguard vcs 10087/9. Marisa Galvany, Joan Patenaude, Molly Stark (sopranos), Allen Cathcart, Robert White (tenors), Thomas Palmer (baritone), Clarion Concerts Chorus and Orchestra, Newell Jenkins.

Mayr was the teacher of Donizetti and the acclaimed progenitor of nineteenth-century opera. Until the young Rossini burst on the scene he was Italy's most famous composer of the early years of the century, and certainly an opera like this, with its pointers towards dramatic developments to come, shows why his work held the stage. The sad thing is that one can also appreciate exactly why it failed to compete with Rossini and later with Donizetti. The story of Medea's vengeance on Jason and his intended bride Creusa is slow-moving, and Mayr's melodies, engaging in their way, are not quite memorable enough to have one riveted. Nonetheless, a generally vigorous and reasonably well sung recording of an important historical document is well worth while. Mayr's revised score, with a soprano as Medea, is used here. Good recording.

Medtner, Nikolai
(1880–1951)

Improvisation, Op. 31/1.
> *** RCA sb 6815. Earl Wild (piano) – BALAKIREV: *Reminiscences;* D'ALBERT: *Scherzo;* SCHARWENKA: *Piano concerto No. 1.****

Medtner is one of the most neglected of Russian composers, and even though he made his home in this country his music is rarely heard here nowadays. This *Improvisation* is a haunting piece whose individuality is slow to assert itself. But it has personality nonetheless and subtlety as well as brilliance. One wishes that Earl Wild, whose keyboard virtuosity and natural musicianship are second to none, would give us some more music by this composer, for his performance here is quite masterly.

Mendelssohn, Felix
(1809–47)

(i) *Piano concerto in A minor* (for piano and strings); (ii) *Rondo brillante in E flat major, Op. 29;* (ii) *Serenade and Allegro giocoso, Op. 43.*
> (B) * (*) Turnabout tv 34170S. Rena Kyriakou (piano), (i) Vienna Symphony Strings, Matthieu Lange; (ii) Vienna Pro Musica Orchestra, Hans Swarowsky.

There is a good deal of Mendelssohnian chatter in these pieces, and it takes inspired playing and super recording to bring them fully to life. Rena Kyriakou shows a genuine feeling for the Mendelssohn phrase in the *Serenade*, and there is no heavy-handed playing. But the feeling of chatter remains throughout the disc. The recording is good of the piano but renders a very thin image for the strings. It may well be faithful in this respect, for the orchestral playing is not especially distinguished.

Piano concerto No. 1 in G minor, Op. 25.
(B) * (*) Turnabout TV 34468S. Rudolf Firkusny (piano), Radio Luxembourg Orchestra, Louis de Froment – SCHUMANN: *Piano concerto in A minor.** (*)

Piano concertos Nos. 1 in G minor, Op. 25; 2 in D minor, Op. 40; Rondo brillante in E flat major, Op. 29.
*** HMV ASD 2546. John Ogdon (piano), London Symphony Orchestra, Aldo Ceccato.

Piano concertos Nos. 1 in G minor, Op. 25; 2 in D minor, Op. 40.
(B) ** Decca Eclipse ECS 627. Peter Katin (piano), London Symphony Orchestra, Anthony Collins.

The HMV issue is one of John Ogdon's very best records. These are well-made works, elegant and tuneful. If neither is quite on the level of the *Violin concerto*, both have attractive slow movements, and the *G minor Concerto* has distinctive themes throughout. The *Rondo brillante* is essentially a dazzling showpiece, but here, as in the outer movements of the concertos, the bravura must have lightness and sparkle, for Mendelssohn's fairies peep in, as they do in the early string quartets. Ogdon meets the needs of the music admirably; he produces a scintillating lightness of touch in the allegros and the *Andante* of the *First Concerto* is given a direct eloquence worthy of Beethoven. With excellent, clear HMV sound, a little dry, this is highly recommended.

Katin too has the measure of these remarkably similar works. His crisp, sympathetic playing prevents the passage-work of the opening movements from becoming lifeless, and he offers a pleasingly light touch in the finales. But in each performance the slow movement is the most memorable, Katin's style sensitive without sentimentality. The warmth of the recording – very early, but real stereo – adds to the listener's pleasure, although the upper strings sound rather thin and feathery in the *First Concerto*.

Firkusny couples the *First Concerto* with the Schumann. His playing has plenty of character, and the slow movement is finely done. But the conductor drives the outer movements in such a way as to minimize the charm in favour of dramatic effect, and with a rather hard recording the result is somewhat aggressive.

(i) *Double piano concerto in E flat major. Piano concerto in A minor* (for piano and strings).
*** Argo ZRG 605. John Ogdon (piano), (i) Brenda Lucas (piano); Academy of St Martin-in-the-Fields, Neville Marriner.

Two delightful Mendelssohn rarities played with great verve and spirit by John Ogdon and his wife. The orchestral playing is equally lively and fresh and given such vivid recording, the disc can be confidently recommended. Both concertos have engaging ideas and though neither can be ranked among Mendelssohn's finest work, they have genuine charm.

Violin concerto in D minor, Op. posth.; Violin concerto in E minor, Op. 64.
** (*) HMV ASD 2809. Yehudi Menuhin (violin), London Symphony Orchestra, Rafael Frühbeck de Burgos.
** (*) Philips 6500 465. Arthur Grumiaux (violin), New Philharmonia Orchestra, Jan Krenz.

Mendelssohn's early *D minor Violin concerto* was completed when the composer was thirteen, after he had written the first five *Symphonies for strings*. As a structure it is amazingly accomplished, but only the finale has memorable themes. It is difficult to choose between these two discs. Grumiaux's is undoubtedly the more polished, and he is probably first choice for the earlier work, although Menuhin plays it with obvious devotion. But in the famous *E minor Concerto* Menuhin is to be preferred. His performance has its moments of roughness but it has a magic too – at the appearance of the first movement's second subject and in the slow movement, where Grumiaux, although he plays beautifully, is very slightly bland. With Menuhin the freshness is never in doubt. The Philips recording is richer than the HMV, but the latter has plenty of life.

Violin concerto in E minor, Op. 64.
*** HMV ASD 2926. Itzhak Perlman (violin), London Symphony Orchestra, André Previn – BRUCH: *Concerto No. 1.****
*** DGG 2530 359. Nathan Milstein (violin), Vienna Philharmonic Orchestra, Claudio Abbado – TCHAIKOVSKY: *Concerto.****
*** HMV ASD 334. Yehudi Menuhin (violin), Philharmonia Orchestra, Efrem Kurtz – BRUCH: *Concerto No. 1.****
(M) (***) RCA DPS 2002 (2 discs). Jascha Heifetz (violin), Boston Symphony Orchestra, Charles Munch – BRAHMS * (**) and TCHAIKOVSKY: *Concertos.(**)*
(B) *** Decca SPA 88. Ruggiero Ricci (violin), London Symphony Orchestra, Pierino Gamba – BRUCH: *Concerto No. 1.****
** (*) CBS 72768. Pinchas Zukerman (violin), New York Philharmonic Orchestra, Leonard Bernstein – TCHAIKOVSKY: *Concerto.** (*)*
(M) ** (*) Philips Universo 6580 022. Arthur Grumiaux (violin), Concertgebouw Orchestra, Bernard Haitink – BRUCH: *Concerto No. 1.***
(M) ** CBS Classics 61029. Isaac Stern (violin), Philadelphia Orchestra, Eugene Ormandy – TCHAIKOVSKY: *Concerto.***
(M) ** Supraphon SUAST 50546. Josef Suk (violin), Czech Philharmonic Orchestra, Karel Ančerl – BRUCH: *Concerto No. 1.***
(M) ** Decca Ace of Diamonds SDD 110. Alfredo Campoli (violin), London Philharmonic Orchestra, Sir Adrian Boult – BRUCH: *Scottish fantasia.***

Perlman gives a performance of the Mendelssohn as full of flair as any available, and he is superbly matched by the LSO under Previn, always an illuminating interpreter of this composer. With ripe recording quality, this stands as one of the first recommendations for a deservedly much-recorded work.

A highly distinguished account too from Milstein, particularly if the Tchaikovsky coupling is desired. With first-rate recording and balance, this is worthy to rank with the best and it is greatly enhanced by the sensitivity of Abbado's accompaniment.

Menuhin's recording is not new, but it has withstood the test of time. The restrained warmth of his phrasing of the famous principal melody of the slow movement has long been a hallmark of Menuhin's reading, and the finale has plenty of sparkle. Kurtz accompanies ably.

As one might expect, Heifetz gives a fabulous performance, but one which will probably infuriate almost as many listeners as it enthrals. His speeds are consistently fast. Some will consider that the slow movement, for example, is rattled through, but when Heifetz's flexible phrasing sounds so inevitable and easy it is hard not to be convinced. The finale is taken at a fantastic lick; and the temperature rises consistently until the coda achieves an intensity and excitement that even Heifetz has rarely conveyed on record. The stereo recording is clean enough but on the hard side, with comparatively little feeling of atmosphere.

Ricci's performance is clean and sympathetic, and technically brilliant. Some soloists find greater repose and depth of feeling in the slow movement, but Ricci is far from being one of the virtuosi who ride roughshod over a work. Gamba too conducts with vigour and sympathy. For those who need a bargain stereo recording, and who particularly want the very fine Bruch coupling, this is a good buy.

Zukerman gives a sweet-toned but never cloying account. His playing is impeccable from the technical point of view and the support he receives from Bernstein and the New York Orchestra is thoroughly sympathetic. An extremely fine performance, and one which would be more than a match for Grumiaux's were it not for the recording, which is not as naturally balanced or as rich in tone as one would like.

Grumiaux's performance is characteristically assured and graceful. There is a suggestion of reticence in the slow movement which some will like more than others, but the finale has a compensating brilliance. Haitink accompanies convincingly, and the balance and recorded sound are both good.

Stern's performance with the Philadelphia Orchestra has great bravura, culminating in a marvellously surging account of the finale, but when pianissimos are non-existent – partly, but only partly, the fault of the recording – some of the poetry of Mendelssohn is missing.

A sympathetic account from Suk, whose tone and intonation are always congenial. There is plenty of sparkle in the finale, which gains from not being rushed off its feet. The slow movement is straightforwardly lyrical, and the warm, reverberant recording is effectively balanced. Good value.

Campoli gives a characteristically assured performance, notable for the easy brilliance of the finale, and the simple song-like eloquence of his presentation of the lovely slow movement. But the performance has not the distinction of his earlier mono account with Van Beinum. This has been very successfully transferred to Eclipse (ECS 505) and remains one of the most beautiful and satisfying accounts of the concerto ever recorded. Campoli's tone is much richer here, whereas the stereo remake seems to harden the violin image by its forward brilliance.

There is also available on DGG an account by Yong Uck Kim (2530 224) coupled to the Bruch, but this is uncompetitive. Intensity is lacking here – in great measure the fault of the accompanists.

Overtures: *The Hebrides (Fingal's Cave), Op. 26; A Midsummer Night's Dream, Op. 21.*
  (B) ** Decca SPA 92. London Symphony Orchestra, Peter Maag – ROSSINI: *Overtures.***

Overtures: *The Hebrides (Fingal's Cave), Op. 26; Ruy Blas, Op. 95; Die schöne Melusine (Fair Melusina), Op. 32.*
  ** Decca SXL 6166. Suisse Romande Orchestra, Ernest Ansermet – *Symphony No. 4.***

Overture: *A Midsummer Night's Dream, Op. 21.*
  (B) ** Decca SPA 178. Vienna Philharmonic Orchestra, Pierre Monteux – MOZART: *Serenade No. 13;* SCHUBERT: *Symphony No. 8.***

(B) ** Decca Eclipse ECS 760. London Symphony Orchestra, Rafael Frühbeck de Burgos – SCHUMANN: *Symphony No. 3*.**

The two Maag performances are well-known from other records (see below) where the couplings are different. They are both first-rate; *Fingal's Cave* is especially exciting and colourful, and vividly recorded

Ansermet is affectionate without being slack. This warmth is helped by one of Decca's best recordings, and if *Fingal's Cave* is a little circumspect in its detail, *Ruy Blas* is striking, with rich brass chords, while *Fair Melusina* is presented with the proper fragile charm.

From Monteux, a most musical account, as might be expected, of the *Midsummer Night's Dream* overture. His opening really suggests the gentle grace of dancing fairies, and he is wonderfully warm and affectionate in the lovely closing pages. The Vienna Philharmonic play well for him but the recording is not very vivid, with a comparatively limited dynamic range. The couplings make this record excellent value for money.

Frühbeck de Burgos is rather detached, but well recorded, and at the new bargain price this is quite acceptable, if the coupling is suitable.

Symphonies for string orchestra Nos. 1 in C major; 2 in D major; 3 in E minor; 4 in C minor; 5 in B flat major; 6 in E flat major; 7 in D minor; 8 in D major (2 versions); 9 in C major; 10 in B minor; 11 in F minor; 12 in G minor; Symphony movement in C minor.

*** DGG 2722 006 (5 discs). Leipzig Gewandhaus Orchestra, Kurt Masur.

Hans Keller has argued that Mendelssohn wrote more finished masterpieces as a boy than even Mozart, and this magnificent set of the string symphonies that he wrote for family concerts in Berlin from the age of eleven shows just what a naturally fertile imagination the child had. Though the influences – from J. S. Bach, C.P.E. Bach, Mozart, and even Beethoven – are obvious enough, the genuine individuality is what makes most of the works a consistent delight, particularly in performances as refreshing as these. The ambitious No. 9 is relatively well-known, but the others too, even the early ones, with their oddly adventurous use of chromatic writing, are well worth investigating. No. 8, another large-scale work, given here in alternative scoring with and without woodwind, is a major discovery, a work that should be in the regular repertory. Excellent recording.

Symphonies for string orchestra Nos. 9 in C major; 10 in B minor; 12 in G minor.

*** Argo ZRG 5467. Academy of St Martin-in-the-Fields, Neville Marriner.

The opening of No. 9 (the most extended piece here) hints at the later oratorio style until its seriousness dissolves into an attractive walking pizzicato that might remind one of the second movement of the *Italian symphony*. The writing throughout is masterly, with some fine individual movements, especially the *Poco Adagio* of No. 9 and the flowing tranquillity of the *Andante* of No. 12. All the music is splendidly brought to life here by committed, vivacious playing and excellent recording.

Symphonies Nos. 1 in C minor, Op. 11; (i) 2 in B flat major (Hymn of Praise), Op. 52.

** RCA SER 5683/4. Leipzig Gewandhaus Orchestra, Kurt Masur, (i) with Celestina Casapietra, Adele Stolte (sopranos), Peter Schreier (tenor), Leipzig Radio Choir.

Though it may fall short of the ideal, Kurt Masur makes out a good case for the *Hymn of Praise*. The work, which contains some pretty thin stuff, was once much beloved of Victorian choral societies. The *First Symphony*, written when Mendelssohn was a mere youth of fifteen, is very well played, and as the set is excellently recorded into the bargain, it has strong claims on the allegiance of collectors.

When D G G reissue Karajan's account of these two works, that will be the first recommendation. Those investing in Masur will still find much to enjoy, however, for his is undoubtedly a musical and warm-hearted reading.

Symphony No. 3 in A minor (Scottish), Op. 56.
    ** RCA LRL 1 5005. Leipzig Gewandhaus Orchestra, Kurt Masur.
Symphony No. 3 in A minor (Scottish), Op. 56; Overture: The Hebrides (Fingal's Cave), Op. 26.
    *** DGG 2530 126. Berlin Philharmonic Orchestra, Herbert von Karajan.
    (M) *** Decca Ace of Diamonds SDD 145. London Symphony Orchestra, Peter Maag.
Symphonies Nos. 3 in A minor (Scottish), Op. 56; 4 in A major (Italian), Op. 90.
    *** Decca SXL 6363. London Symphony Orchestra, Claudio Abbado.

Peter Maag's Decca record of this coupling has virtually had the field to itself. Now comes a splendid challenge from Karajan, and this new D G G disc is very fine indeed. There are some slight eccentricities of tempo: the opening of the *Symphony* is rather measured under Karajan, while the closing pages of the finale are taken with exuberant brilliance. But the orchestral playing is superb, the

conductor's warmth comes over readily, and the direct eloquence of the reading, with no fussiness, is irresistible. The scherzo is marvellously done and becomes a real highlight of the performance, while there is no doubt that Karajan's final coda has a splendid buoyancy and power. With bright, clear recording, and a characterful account of *Fingal's Cave*, this disc is highly recommendable.

Under Maag the *Symphony* is played most beautifully, and its pastoral character, occasioned by Mendelssohn's considerable use of the strings throughout, is amplified by a recording of great warmth. The opening string cantilena is poised and very gracious and thus sets the mood for what is to follow. The stereo is excellent. One small complaint: the conductor is too ponderous in the final *Maestoso*, and here the Decca recording – hitherto first-class – is slightly overmodulated.

While Karajan's is undoubtedly the finest performance in the current catalogue, Abbado has the advantage of a highly competitive coupling. His *Scottish* is beautifully played, each phrase sensitively moulded, and the LSO respond to his direction with the greatest lightness of tone and delicacy of feeling. The Decca engineers also provide first-rate recording, notwithstanding the length of the sides.

Masur's reading, though it has many virtues, does not eclipse Karajan. The Leipzig orchestra plays well and there is some fine detail; but neither the performance nor the recording has the distinction of Abbado's record, which also offers an extra symphony.

Symphony No. 4 in A major (Italian), Op. 90.
    (M) *** HMV SXLP 30178. Philharmonia Orchestra, Otto Klemperer – SCHUMANN: *Symphony No. 4.****
    (M) ** Decca Ace of Diamonds SDD

121. Israel Philharmonic Orchestra, Sir Georg Solti – SCHUBERT: *Symphony No. 5.***

** Decca SXL 6166. Suisse Romande Orchestra, Ernest Ansermet – *Overtures.***

Symphony No. 4 in A major (Italian), Op. 90; Ruy Blas overture, Op. 5.

*** RCA SB 6847. London Symphony Orchestra, André Previn – PROKOFIEV: *Symphony No. 1.****

(i) *Symphony No. 4 in A major (Italian), Op. 90;* (ii) *A Midsummer Night's Dream: Overture, Op. 21; Incidental music: Scherzo; Nocturne; Wedding march, Op. 61.*

(M) ** Philips Universo 6580 027. Concertgebouw Orchestra, cond. (i) Bernard Haitink; (ii) George Szell.

Klemperer takes the first movement substantially slower than we are used to, but this is no heavily monumental and humourless reading. The playing sparkles and has an incandescence which tends to outshine all other stereo versions. There is again a slowish speed for the second movement, but the way Klemperer moulds and floats the main theme over the moving bass defeats all preconceptions in its sustained beauty. A fast tempo in the minuet, but still with wonderful phrasing; and it is the beautiful shaping of a phrase that makes the finale so fresh and memorable. There is no lack of exhilaration yet none of that feeling of being rushed off one's feet that Solti gives. The recording is rich and atmospheric, yet admirably clear.

A delightful performance from Previn, every bit as fresh yet as disciplined as Abbado's with the same orchestra (see under *Symphony No. 3*). Detail is beautifully articulated and the proceedings have a spontaneous yet well-controlled vitality. Previn makes no egocentric interpretative points: his view of the work is admirably unfussy and straightforward, and the recording is a good one with plenty of stereo information and firm well-focused tone.

Solti sets off at and maintains a really sparkling pace in the first movement, and although one may feel this is over-driven there is no doubt that the orchestra can play the music at this speed. The first violins are agile, there is never the slightest feeling of flurry, and a clear recording brightens every detail. In the *Andante* the staccato lower strings immediately achieve a gentle forward movement which has the right degree of insistence throughout, and the woodwind phrase the melancholy little march-theme above. The third movement is gracious, and the scintillating final *Saltarello* is again played at breathless speed. The recording is bright and clear.

The Ansermet version of the *Italian* comes in one of his series of composer-recital records. The coupling of three Mendelssohn overtures – *Die schöne Melusine* rare and welcome – may be a reasonable attraction for some, but the performance of the symphony is hardly distinguished enough to stand out among the current rivals. The interpretation is fresh and unexaggeratedly straightforward, but the playing of the Suisse Romande Orchestra does not convey enough of Mendelssohn's *élan*. This performance of the symphony is also available on bargain label (SPA 153) but here it is coupled to an uncharacteristically dull account of the *Overture* and suite from *A Midsummer Night's Dream*. This is not recommended.

Haitink's account of the symphony offers generally fast tempi in the opening two movements, but the third movement has something of the poise which Mendelssohn in his civilized way requires, and the orchestral playing is superb throughout. In the transfer the recording sounds well, with a fine, open acoustic. Szell's performances of the items from *A Midsummer Night's Dream* also have plenty of character, although they have not the magnetism of his CBS set with the Cleveland Orchestra (now deleted). Again the sound is open and bright, although not as pleasingly full as the symphony. The orchestral playing is first-rate, especially the violins in the overture.

Symphonies Nos. 4 in A major (Italian), Op. 90; 5 in D major (Reformation), Op. 107.

- (M) ******* DGG Privilege 2538 329. Berlin Philharmonic Orchestra, Lorin Maazel.
- ****** (*) DGG 2530 416. Berlin Philharmonic Orchestra, Herbert von Karajan.
- ****** (*) Philips SAL 3727. New Philharmonia Orchestra, Wolfgang Sawallisch.
- ****** RCA LRL 1 5006. Leipzig Gewandhaus Orchestra, Kurt Masur.

Each of the discs coupling these two symphonies has distinctive features, but Maazel's is first choice and not only because of its competitive price. The account of the *Italian symphony* offers a fast, hard-driven, but joyous and beautifully articulated performance of the first movement and equal clarity and point in the vivacious finale. The central movements are well sustained, and altogether this is highly enjoyable. The *Reformation symphony* too springs grippingly to life in Maazel's hand. The Berlin Philharmonic brass makes an immediate impact in the commanding introduction and the orchestral playing throughout continues on this level of high tension. The finale is splendidly vigorous, the choral *Ein' feste Burg ist unser Gott* ringing out resplendently. The recording of both works is spacious with a fine bloom.

It goes without saying that the playing of the Berlin Philharmonic for Karajan is outstandingly fine, but good though the performances are, they are just a shade wanting in spontaneity and sparkle.

The *Reformation symphony* is most beautifully shaped and finely phrased, though rhythms in the first movement are perhaps a little too heavily accented, with the result that there is a certain lack of forward movement.

Sawallisch's comparatively reticent Mendelssohnian style suits these two fine works very well. A fast tempo in the first movement of the *Italian* for once does not sound breathless, and it is particularly welcome that Sawallisch observes the exposition repeat and so lets us hear a score of bars in the first-time lead-back, normally neglected. The *Reformation symphony* is a work that gains from not being over-inflated. The opening slow introduction with its quotation of the *Dresden Amen* later used by Wagner in *Parsifal* may suggest Mendelssohn in ponderous mood, but this is belied by the rest of the symphony. Good clear recording.

As is the case with his account of the *Scottish symphony* Masur secures good, well-shaped performances – in no way dull or pedestrian – decently recorded by the engineers. However, the playing is not as distinguished and the readings not as highly characterized as Karajan's on DGG. In the *Reformation symphony* Masur is less portentous than Karajan, perhaps, for some readers may find Karajan slightly mannered here, but in any case Maazel's Privilege disc remains the first recommendation.

CHAMBER AND INSTRUMENTAL MUSIC

Octet (for strings) *in E flat major, Op. 20.*

- ******* Argo ZRG 569. Academy of St Martin-in-the-Fields – BOCCHERINI: *Quintet, Op. 37/7.********
- ******* Philips SAL 3640. I Musici – WOLF: *Italian serenade********; ROSSINI: *Sonata.*******

(M) *** Decca Ace of Diamonds SDD 389. Members of the Vienna Octet — RIMSKY-KORSAKOV: *Piano and wind quintet.****

(M) ** (*) Supraphon 111 0426. Combined Janáček and Smetana Quartets.

The performance by the Academy of St Martin-in-the-Fields is exceptionally fresh and buoyant, and the superb recording offers that perfect judgement in matters of clarity and sonority for which the Argo engineers are famous. Choice between this and the no less desirable Philips disc is most difficult. This is also a most satisfying account, smoother in contours than the well-pointed Argo version. Preference will no doubt be determined by couplings. The Boccherini *Quintet* offered by the St Martins group is delightful, but then so is the Wolf *Italian serenade.* Those investing in either of these discs of Mendelssohn's glorious and youthful masterpiece will be amply repaid.

The Vienna version of the *Octet* is also highly competitive and is happily accommodated on one side without any loss of quality. Its coupling, Rimsky-Korsakov's entertaining *Piano and wind quintet*, is an added inducement to choose it.

The Decca recording is finer than that given by Supraphon to the combination of the Janáček and Smetana Quartets. But this is an intense and well-integrated performance, with a quietly beautiful account of the *Andante*, a splendidly vivacious scherzo and a busy, crisp finale.

Piano sextet in D major, Op. 110.

(M) *** Decca Ace of Diamonds SDD 410. Walter Panhoffer (piano), members of the Vienna Octet — BORODIN: *Piano quintet.****

Despite its high opus number the *Piano sextet* is a work of the composer's youth,

written when he was only fifteen. Like much of his music of that time, it has an engaging immediacy and remarkable sureness of technique. The performance here is of a very high standard, with a recording to match.

Piano trio No. 1 in D minor, Op. 49.

(B) * (*) Decca Eclipse ECS 658. Valda Aveling (piano), Donald Weekes (violin), Dennis Nesbitt (cello) — HAYDN: *Piano trio No. 25.* (*)*

Piano trios Nos. 1 in D minor, Op. 49; 2 in C minor Op. 66.

*** Philips SAL 3646. Beaux Arts Trio.

This is a sensible coupling, and the present record is one of the best the Beaux Arts have given us. Their playing is always splendidly alive and musical and they are extremely vividly recorded. Neither of the trios is great music but it is all excellently fashioned, warm-hearted and attractive. The playing of the *D minor* is not in the same category as that of its first recording by the Cortot, Thibaud, Casals Trio, who shed greater light and warmth, but nonetheless it is extremely acceptable, and as the *C minor* work is not otherwise available, this record is a valuable one.

The Aveling group's performance of Op. 49 is serviceable, not really polished enough to bring out the elegance of the slow movement, but very spirited in the scherzo and not lacking in spontaneity throughout. The recording is clear without being outstanding.

String quartet No. 4 in E minor, Op. 44/2; 4 Pieces for string quartet (Andante; Scherzo; Capriccio; Fugue), Op. 81.

(M) *** Decca Ace of Diamonds SDD 469. Gabrieli Quartet.

575

These are first-class performances in every way, warm, elegant, yet in no way superficial. The *Quartet*, dating from 1837, is rewarding but not more so than the *Four pieces*, which were written independently, at different times. The *Andante* is a set of variations with a particularly beguiling melody – Mendelssohn at his most gracious – and the *Scherzo* is one of the composer's very best. The recording is quite outstanding, wonderfully rich and natural.

Violoncello sonatas Nos. 1 in B flat major, Op. 45; 2 in D major, Op. 58; Variations concertantes, Op. 17; Song without words in D major, Op. 109.

(M) ** Vox STGBY 605. Joseph Schuster (cello), Artur Balsam (piano).

Mendelssohn's *Second Cello sonata* is one of the most exhilarating pieces of music ever written for the cello, and here, very well played, it is coupled with all Mendelssohn's other cello music. The *Second Sonata*, a comparatively late work, counters any idea that Mendelssohn lost his gift for tunefulness as he grew older. The melodies in each movement are as memorable as any he ever conceived. The *First Sonata* does not achieve the same level of inspiration, but it is still attractive, and so are the rather facile *Variations* and *Songs without words*, the latter an original work, not an arrangement from the piano series. Schuster is a formidable virtuoso, possibly too formidable for Mendelssohn. His tempi are sometimes hectic, but his concentration never fails to convince. The recording is rather dry, with the cello balanced too far forward, but so generous a record at this price can be warmly recommended.

Piano Music

Capriccio, Op. 33/1; Variations sérieuses, Op. 54.

* (*) Decca SXL 6466. Alicia de Larrocha (piano) – GRIEG: *Pieces.** (*)

Alicia de Larrocha gives an accomplished account of the *Variations sérieuses* but some of her *rubati* are a shade unconvincing. The piano tone is not as faithful in quality as most records from this source.

Piano sonata in E major, Op. 6.

(B) ** Oryx ORYX 1805. Karl Ulrich Schnabel (piano) – SCHUBERT: *German dances etc.***

This early piano sonata was written when Mendelssohn was seventeen, in the year when he also wrote the *Octet* and the *Midsummer Night's Dream overture.* The piano work does not have the magic of either of these masterpieces, but the second movement is attractively characteristic. Karl Ulrich (the son of Artur Schnabel) plays the music with sympathy. He is eloquent in the slow movement, which has breadth. The piano recording is good, and with an attractive coupling this is worth exploring.

Songs without words Nos. 1–48 (complete); Albumblatt in E minor, Op. 117; Gondola song in A major; Variations sérieuses, Op. 54; 2 Klavierstücke.

(M) ** HMV SLS 862 (3 discs). Daniel Adni (piano).

Songs without words Nos. 1–48 (complete); Albumblatt in E minor, Op. 117; Kinderstücke, Op. 72; 2 Klavierstücke.

*** DGG 2740 104 (3 discs). Daniel Barenboim (piano).

Barenboim is the ideal pianist for what have come to be regarded (for the most part wrongly) as faded Victorian trifles. Whether in the earlier, technically more difficult pieces or in the later simple inspirations, Barenboim conveys perfectly the sense of a composer relaxing. He himself seems to be discovering the music afresh, regularly turning phrases with the imagination of a great artist, relishing the jewelled passage-work of many of the pieces in superb, easy virtuosity. With fine recording quality this is a set to charm any listener.

Adni's reading of Mendelssohn's charming pieces is much more straight-faced than Barenboim's, rather too serious to convey their full, gentle flavour. But it is agile pianism nonetheless, well recorded.

Variations sérieuses, Op. 54.
> (B) ** Turnabout TV 34460S. Abbey Simon (piano) – CHOPIN: *Scherzi.* (**)

The mellow tone of the recorded piano rather suits Mendelssohn's *Variations sérieuses*, whereas it is too lacking in brilliance for the Chopin coupling. Simon's account of the *Variations* is characteristically sensitive and this is distinctly enjoyable.

Organ Music

Prelude and fugue in C minor, Op. 37/1; Organ sonatas Nos. 1 in F minor; 3 in A major; 6 in D minor, Op. 65.
> (B) ** (*) Oryx BRL 53. David Sanger (organ of Brompton Oratory, London).

Organ sonatas Nos. 1 in F minor; 2 in C minor; 3 in A major; 4 in B flat major; 5 in D major; 6 in D minor, Op. 65/1–6.
> (B) ** Oryx ORYX 1813 (Sonatas 1–3); ORYX 1814 (Nos. 4–6). Wolfgang Dallmann (Overmann organ in the Unteröwisheim, near Heidelberg).

Now that Philip Dore's splendid Victrola set (which combined all the six

Sonatas plus the three *Preludes and fugues* within the space of two discs) has been deleted, we are left with a serviceable complete set of the *Sonatas* from Wolfgang Dallmann, or a more easily recommendable single-disc selection from David Sanger. Both are well, if not outstandingly well recorded – there were cutting faults at the end of the *Second Sonata* on ORYX 1813, and Sanger's disc had more clicks than desirable. Dallmann is a capable player but he is too solemn in the reflective music, and his registration in the closing *Andante* of *Sonata No. 6* is far too conventional. David Sanger is altogether more exciting; his playing is clearly articulated and always holds the attention. The bravura in the brilliant sections of No. 6 (a masterpiece) is most impressive. Both organs, as recorded, seem light in the bass, and Dallmann's has very much the character of a baroque instrument, which would surely not have been what the composer had in mind.

VOCAL AND CHORAL MUSIC

Lieder: Allnächtlich im Traume; Altdeutsches Lied; And'res Maienlied; An die Entfernte; Auf der Wanderschaft; Auf Flügeln des Gesanges (On wings of song); Bei der Wiege; Der Blumenkranz; Da lieg' ich unter den Bäumen; Erntelied; Erster Verlust; Das erste Veilchen; Es lauschte das Laub; Frühlingslied (3 versions: Lenau, Lichtenstein and Klingemann settings); Grüss; Hirtenlied; Jagdlied; Minnelied (Deutsches Volkslied); Minnelied (Tieck); Der Mond; Morgengruss; Nachtlied; Neue Liebe; O Jugend; Pagenlied; Reiselied (2 settings: Heine and Ebert); Scheindend; Schiflied; Schlafloser Augen Leuchte; Tröstung; Venetianisches Gondellied; Volkslied (Feuchtersleben);

Das Waldschloss; Wanderlied; Warnung vor dem Rhein; Wenn sich zwei Herzen scheiden; Winterlied.
> (M) ** (*) HMV SLS 805 (2 discs). Dietrich Fischer-Dieskau (baritone), Wolfgang Sawallisch (piano).

Though Mendelssohn generally reserved for the *Songs without words* his finest song-like inspirations, the lyrical directness of these settings of Heine, Eichendorff, Lenau and others assures him of a niche of his own among composers of Lieder. Dieskau conveys his joy in fresh discovery, but in some of the well-known songs – *Grüss* or *On wings of song* – he tends to overlay his singing with heavy expressiveness. Lightness should be the keynote, and that happily is wonderfully represented in the superb accompaniments of Sawallisch. First-rate recording.

Ave Maria; Beati mortui (motet); *Hör mein Bitten (Hear my prayer); Psalm 22; Sechs Sprüche (6 Aphorisms); Veni domine* (motet).
> *** Argo ZRG 716. Felicity Palmer (soprano), Heinrich Schütz Choir and Chorale, Gillian Weir (organ), Roger Norrington.

A beautiful record. None of this music is familiar except *Hear my prayer*, and that only in an Anglican performance with treble solo. Inspired though Ernest Lough's account was, it is stimulating to hear the piece performed more dramatically, with Felicity Palmer's voice having the darker, richer colouring almost of a mezzo, in complete contrast to the piping treble sounds that are so familiar. The other music here is rewarding too, notably the motet *Veni domine* written in 1837 after the composer's visit to Rome. The *Ave Maria* setting was done while Mendelssohn was still in Rome in 1830. It is more ambitious than other more famous settings and not in the least sentimental. The restrained eloquence of the performances here is extremely well judged; the singing has marvellous freshness and spontaneity. The recording too is superb, the stereo giving a wonderfully natural reproduction of the voices, yet everything is clear. Highly recommended.

Elijah (oratorio), *Op. 70:* complete recording.
> *** HMV SLS 935 (3 discs). Gwyneth Jones (soprano), Janet Baker (contralto), Nicolai Gedda (tenor), Dietrich Fischer-Dieskau (baritone), Simon Woolf (treble), Wandsworth School Boys' Choir, New Philharmonia Chorus and Orchestra, Rafael Frühbeck de Burgos.

It is some years since Mendelssohn's *Elijah* was the public's firm second favourite among choral works in Britain after Handel's *Messiah*. The time has now come when we can appreciate once more its fine dramatic directness which, with the Baal Choruses as centre-piece, makes this oratorio far more vivid in its story-telling than many an opera. Frühbeck proves an excellent Mendelssohnian, neither a callous driver nor a romantic meanderer. The choice of Fischer-Dieskau to take the part of the prophet is more controversial. His pointing of English words is not always idiomatic, but his sense of drama is infallible and goes well with a Mendelssohnian new look. Gwyneth Jones and Nicolai Gedda similarly provide mixed enjoyment, but the splendid work of the chorus and above all the gorgeous singing of Janet Baker, dominant whether in hushed intensity or commanding *fortissimo*, make this a memorable and enjoyable set.

Elijah: highlights.
> *** HMV ASD 2609 (from above recording).

The complete set of *Elijah* from which this selection is taken may have disturbed the traditionalists, but in its simple direct honesty, its refusal to indulge in sentimental tricks to build up a vital, dramatic structure, it could hardly be rivalled. This is a fair sample from those three discs, and no one, not even the traditionalists, will be disappointed by Janet Baker's deeply felt account of *O rest in the Lord*, immaculate in style, gloriously free in tone.

(i) *Die erste Walpurgisnacht (The First Walpurgis Night)* (cantata), *Op. 60;* (ii) *Infelice* (concert aria), *Op. 94.*

** (*) HMV ASD 3009. Leipzig Gewandhaus Orchestra, Kurt Masur, with (i) Annelies Burmeister (contralto), Eberhard Büchner (tenor), Siegfried Lorenz (baritone), Leipzig Radio Choir; (ii) Edda Moser (soprano).

As a boy Mendelssohn became a favourite visitor of the poet Goethe, and later he repaid the affection in this setting of an early and rather odd Goethe poem about Druids and their conflict with early Christians, seen – perhaps unexpectedly – from the point of view of the Druids. It is not great music, but especially in the big tarantella-like chorus for the Druids it is lively and enjoyable, particularly as played and sung here by Leipzig forces. The concert aria is more conventional but a worthwhile fill-up. Good atmospheric recording.

A Midsummer Night's Dream: Overture, Op. 21; Incidental music, Op. 61 (1, Scherzo; 2, Melodrama; 2a, Fairy march; 3, You spotted snakes; 4, Melodrama; 5, Intermezzo; 6, Melodrama; 7, Nocturne; 8, Melodrama; 9, Wedding march; 10, Melodrama; 10a, Funeral march; 11, Dance of the clowns; 12, Melodrama; 13, Finale).

*** DGG SLPM 138959 (omitting Nos. 2, 4, 6, 8, 10, 12). Edith Mathis (soprano), Ursula Boese (contralto), Bavarian Radio Chorus and Orchestra, Rafael Kubelik.

*** Philips SAL 3548 (omitting Nos. 2, 4, 6, 8, 10, 12). Rae Woodland (soprano), Helen Watts (contralto), Chorus, Concertgebouw Orchestra, Bernard Haitink.

** (*) Decca SXL 6404 (complete). Hanneke van Bork (soprano), Alfreda Hodgson (contralto), Ambrosian Singers, New Philharmonia Orchestra, Rafael Frühbeck de Burgos.

(M) ** Decca Ace of Diamonds SDD 159 (omitting Nos. 2, 2a, 4, 6, 8, 10, 10a, 12). Jennifer Vyvyan (soprano), Marion Lowe (mezzo-soprano), Female Chorus, Royal Opera House, Covent Garden, London Symphony Orchestra, Peter Maag.

The Bavarian Radio Orchestra are on top form and they play magically. Kubelik's direction of the *Overture* is fresh but straightforward. The *Nocturne* is not outstanding but the beautiful recorded quality is the compensating factor. The fascinating choral section in the finale which is so like Sullivan that it might have been written for *Iolanthe* is well worth having. Altogether a good disc.

In their earlier stereo recordings the Philips engineers had trouble with the acoustic of the Concertgebouw, and here they have not avoided a certain muddiness in the tuttis of the overture. Yet the *Wedding march*, played with superb dignity and panache, is highly successful. Audiophiles might prefer the Kubelik disc, which is given excellent DGG sound; but the delight of the Dutch performance is the individuality of the orchestral playing. The violins in the *Overture* really sound like fairies, and everywhere the woodwind solos offer the listener continual pleasure. The *Scherzo* is delicious and the little *Funeral march* is memorable. The grace of the ensemble in the *Intermezzo* gives this less-inspired piece an unusual delicacy, and the horn-playing in the *Nocturne* is excellent. The finale could have had rather more clarity (again the recording) but for the most part this disc is highly enjoyable, although Kubelik is not entirely displaced.

The Decca recording is complete almost to the point of pedantry, including one or two melodramas that have very limited musical interest. But the orchestral playing is fine and most of the content of this LP comes over freshly. The performance of the *Overture*, however, although the fairies dance in the violins with exquisite daintiness, misses the last touch of magic, and the Decca recording is not as clear-cut and transparent as it might be. In general the Philips and DGG selections, although they contain less music, are more enjoyable.

Maag's disc dates from the early days of stereo, and although his selection is less complete than the others, at Ace of Diamonds price it makes a very serviceable collection. The fairy string music is beautifully played. Maag's treatment of the *Overture*'s forthright second subject strikes the ear as curiously mannered, and the recording includes a strong contribution from a fruity bass wind instrument that might possibly be Mendelssohn's ophicleide, but is probably a well-played tuba. The horn soloist in the *Nocturne* is perhaps over-careful, but the tranquil mood is nicely contrasted with the short *agitato* middle section. The vocal contributions are excellent. The recording is clean and well projected but in the recut some of the luminous quality one remembers in the original has been usurped by the greater clarity.

Menotti, Gian-Carlo
(born 1911)

Piano concerto in F major.

(M) ** Vanguard VSD 2094. Earl Wild (piano), Symphony of the Air, Jorge Mester – COPLAND: *Piano concerto.*** (*)

Menotti's *Piano concerto*, like most of his music, is easy and fluent, never hard on the ear. As a coupling for the Copland *Concerto* it is very attractive, even if it is unlikely to stand repeated listening. The recording is marred by the balance favouring the piano.

Amahl and the Night Visitors (opera for television): complete recording.

(M) ** (*) RCA LSB 4075. Kurt Yaghjian, Martha King, John McCollum, Richard Cross, Willis Paterson, Orchestra and Chorus, Herbert Grossman.

Menotti's television opera for Christmas may not stand the test of time as comparable Britten works for children do. Its musical inspiration is altogether more ephemeral, but with a sure-fire – if blatantly sentimental – plot, it certainly has a magic of its own, and a stereo version which brings out the highly atmospheric qualities – the arrival of the Wise Men and so on – is most welcome. This performance was based on the NBC presentation in 1963, and is attractively direct, with few of the distracting exaggerations of characterization that marred the earlier mono version. The voices may sometimes sound a little pale, but the atmosphere of a home entertainment (preferable to something sophisticatedly professional) is attractively maintained.

Messiaen, Olivier
(born 1908)

L'Ascension (orchestral version).
> *** Decca Phase 4 PFS 4203. London Symphony Orchestra, Leopold Stokowski – IVES: *Orchestral set No. 2.****

L'Ascension is an early work, written first for organ but then in 1935 orchestrated with a different third movement. Stokowski is characteristically persuasive in developing the smooth flow of the music, though some will object to the opulence of sound he (and the engineers) favour in the final sweet meditation for strings alone, *Prayer of Christ ascending to the Father*.

(i) *Les Couleurs de la cité céleste (The Colours of the Celestial City)* (for solo piano, wind and percussion); *Et exspecto resurrectionem mortuorum* (for woodwind, brass and metallic percussion).
> ** (*) CBS 72471. Strasbourg instrumental and percussion group, Orchestre du Domaine Musical, Pierre Boulez, (i) with Yvonne Loriod (piano).

These are two of Messiaen's most ambitious later works, and with vivid performances under Pierre Boulez the record gives an excellent idea of the strange, wilful directions in which this massively inspired composer is working. His genius is French in the sense that Berlioz's was, rather than Debussy's. Not for him any sparing of notes or even much restraint. *Et exspecto resurrectionem mortuorum* lasts roughly half an hour, during which time Messiaen devotes most of his attention to drawing strange sonorities from his large orchestra of wind, brass and percussion alone. Listening conventionally, one cannot help feeling that the musical interest is spread rather thin, with too meandering a tempo predominating – pregnant pauses repeated overmuch lose their pregnancy. The other work, written a year earlier than *Et exspecto* in 1963, is on a smaller scale, but gives a much crisper idea of Messiaen's curious genius. As he says himself, the piece 'turns on itself like a rose-window', and brings together with astonishing assurance elements from plainsong, Greek music, Hindu music, not to mention the persistent birdsong that runs through so much of Messiaen's writing.

7 Haikai.
> (M) * (*) Everest SDBR 3192. Yvonne Loriod (piano), Strasbourg Percussion Ensemble, Orchestre du Domaine Musical, Pierre Boulez – SCHOENBERG: *Chamber symphony etc.** (*)

In spite of the dry, close Everest recording, which does not provide an ideally atmospheric setting, one must welcome this obviously authentic performance, even though it does not tell the whole story. The work was written in 1962 following the composer's trip to Japan, and the seven pieces are short and descriptive, their format suggesting the Japanese poems (the meaning of the title) in its conciseness. The scoring uses a variety of metallic percussive effects and is often preoccupied with Messiaen's bird evocations.

Réveil des oiseaux (The Awakening of the Birds); Oiseaux exotiques (Exotic Birds); La Bouscarle (from *Catalogue d'oiseaux*).
> (M) *** Supraphon SUAST 50749. Yvonne Loriod (piano), Czech Philharmonic Orchestra, Václav Neumann.

All three scores here are associated with Messiaen's beloved birdsong. There is no question of Messiaen's imaginative flair, and the music is vivid, varied and colourful to match the plumage of the creatures which provided the composer's inspiration. With the dedicated Yvonne Loriod as soloist and the composer himself supervising the recording sessions, this is an authentic and important issue.

Quatuor pour la fin du temps (Quartet for the End of Time); (i) *Le Merle noir (The Blackbird)* (for flute and piano).
(M) ** (*) Vox STGBY 670. New York Philomusica Chamber Ensemble, (i) with Paige Brook (flute).

Messiaen's inspired and visionary quartet was written during the war when he was in a Silesian prison-camp. Among his fellow-prisoners were a violinist, a clarinet-player, and a cellist, so with the composer at the piano an actual performance was possible. Messiaen tells us that the lack of food gave him semi-nightmares and colouristic visions. Certainly instrumental colouring plays a large part in the *Quatuor*, and besides the visions of 'the Angel who announces the end of Time', there are also the composer's birdsongs. Generally the New York performance is a fine one, if somewhat uneven. Many of the individual solos have considerable intensity and atmosphere, and the resonant acoustic of the recording is well judged.

Cantéyodjayâ; Île de feu 1 and 2; Neumes rythmiques.
** (*) Argo ZRG 694. Robert Sherlaw Johnson (piano) – SHERLAW JOHNSON: *Sonata; Pieces.*(***)

These pieces, written in 1949 and 1950, are not easy to come to grips with, in spite of Robert Sherlaw Johnson's eloquent advocacy. There are serial

influences in *Cantéyodjayâ*, but the most striking association here is with the piano music of Debussy. The opening of this work immediately introduces a striking idea which is used as a kind of refrain against a collage of other ideas. The argument is easier to follow here than in the other pieces, which have a greater degree of fragmentation. Excellent recording.

Catalogue d'oiseaux Books 1–7 (complete).
(M) *** Argo 2BBA 1005/7. Robert Sherlaw Johnson (piano).

The basic raw material of this set of piano pieces is birdsong as heard and remembered by the composer in his homeland. But the substance of the music is refined by a brilliantly imaginative mind, and what we hear is far removed from an imitative set of bird calls. The performance by Robert Sherlaw Johnson is highly distinguished, poetic in feeling, and with a natural understanding of the music's atmosphere. The Argo recording is outstandingly fine.

Catalogue d'oiseaux: La Bouscarle. Préludes Nos. 5, Les sons impalpables du rêve; 6, Cloches d'angoisse et larmes d'adieu. Rondeau. Vingt regards sur l'Enfant-Jésus: Regard de l'Esprit de Joie; Première communion de la Vierge; Noël; Regard du silence.
*** Oiseau-Lyre DSLO 6. Paul Crossley (piano).

These are impressively communicative performances – and not all of this music is easy listening. But Paul Crossley shows himself a distinguished interpreter of Messiaen's kaleidoscopic pianism: the veiled tone at the very opening of *Les sons impalpables du rêve* immediately shows his subtlety of manner, and the bravura is in no doubt in the brilliant *Regard de l'Esprit de Joie*, with its strong links with Debussy. The tone of the Bösendorfer piano seems well suited to this programme. The disc provides an admirable insert sleeve-note, quoting extensively the composer's comments on the music.

Vingt regards sur l'Enfant-Jésus.
  (B) ** (*) Saga 5351/3. Thomas Rajna (piano).
  ** Argo ZRG 650/1. John Ogdon (piano).

John Ogdon is unfailingly thoughtful and conscientious, but Thomas Rajna on Saga provides a more satisfying alternative. Both in their way reveal many individual beauties in these twenty varied miniatures, but Rajna is the more spontaneous and perceptive artist. His recording is not so fine as the Argo but it is perfectly acceptable, and although this version spreads over six sides, it is still considerably cheaper.

Visions de l'Amen (for two pianos).
  *** RCA ARL 1 0363. Peter Serkin and Yuji Takahashi (pianos).
  *** Argo ZRG 665. John Ogdon and Brenda Lucas (pianos).

Messiaen's *Visions de l'Amen*, written in 1943, is a suite of seven movements inspired by the act of creation. Its mysticism is characteristically wide in range. Choice resides between the RCA with Serkin *fils* and the Japanese composer-pianist Yuji Takahashi, and Ogdon and Brenda Lucas on Argo. The work's considerable demands are triumphantly met by both, and the recording engineers produce beautifully detailed and clearly defined tone throughout the RCA disc, save perhaps in the bass register, which tends to be unnatural. (One hears too much of the action.) In any event readers can follow their own inclination with some confidence: both records of this remarkable score are successful.

L'Ascension (Four symphonic meditations).
  *** Argo ZRG 5339. Simon Preston (organ) – FRANCK: *Choral No. 2; Pièce héroïque.** (*)

The almost chocolate-box sweetness of Messiaen's sonorities suits the sound of an English organ better than the César Franck pieces which form the coupling. Messiaen's original, indeed unique work is very well played here, and the recording is excellent.

Collection: *L'Ascension*, Part 3: *Transports de joie d'une âme devant la gloire du Christ. Les Corps glorieux*, Book 1, No. 2: *Les eaux de la Grâce*; Book 1, No. 3: *L'ange aux parfums. Messe de la Pentecôte: Les oiseaux et les sources; Le vent de l'Esprit. La Nativité du Seigneur*: Book 1, No. 2: *Desseins éternels*; Book 4, No. 9: *Dieu parmi nous.*
  (M) ** VOX STGBY 657. Jean-Claude Raynaud (Cavaillé-Coll organ at the Basilica of St Sernin, Toulouse).

This recital provides an excellent introduction to the varying styles of Messiaen's organ works, from the blazingly inspirational *Transports de joie d'une âme devant la gloire du Christ*, which opens the recital, to the mysticism of *L'ange aux parfums*, and the fascinating *Desseins éternels*, which closes the disc in a mood which is visionary in a gently evocative way. Jean-Claude Raynaud, who plays impressively throughout, is to be complimented on the high degree of tension with which he sustains this latter piece, which reminds one of the *Turangalila symphony*. The disc would be given an unqualified three-star recommendation were it not for the slight harshness which appears in the recording's loudest moments. But better this degree of brightness than a muffled, reverberant effect and the quieter music is certainly atmospheric.

Le Banquet celeste; Les Corps glorieux.
*** Argo ZRG 633. Simon Preston
(organ of St Alban's Abbey).

A most impressive record of some of Messiaen's most atmospheric and imaginative music. Both the playing and the recording are exemplary. Strongly recommended.

La Nativité du Seigneur (9 meditations).
*** Argo ZRG 5447. Simon Preston
(organ of Westminster Abbey).
(B) ** Saga 5339. Allan Wicks
(organ of St Paul's Cathedral).

Simon Preston is a convinced advocate of this score and conveys its hypnotic power most successfully. The recording reproduces with great fidelity. Allan Wicks too is most successfully recorded (the notorious St Paul's reverberation is remarkably well controlled here) but the performance itself is less imaginative, the registration showing much less feeling for Messiaen's mysticism.

Chants de terre et de ciel (song cycle);
Poèmes pour Mi (song cycle).
** (*) Argo ZRG 699. Noelle Barker
(soprano), Robert Sherlaw Johnson (piano).

Noelle Barker is a useful singer of modern music, but her tone is not really seductive enough for Messiaen's song cycles inspired by the sacrament of marriage. The two cycles, written in the mid-thirties, are linked; each was inspired by his marriage to the violinist Claire Delbos, expressions of a tender and searching love. Thoughtful performances and good recording.

Harawi (song cycle).
** (*) Argo ZRG 606. Noelle Barker
(soprano), Robert Sherlaw Johnson (piano).

It is good to have *Harawi* on record if only because it completes the cycle of three Messiaen works inspired by the Tristan and Isolde legend. They are vastly different from each other. This one is a plain song cycle, the *Cinq rechants* (recorded on Argo ZRG 523) are for unaccompanied chorus, while the third is the expansive *Turangalîla symphony* for a very large orchestra. (This has unaccountably been deleted, but should be back in the catalogue before long.)
Though Noelle Barker's voice is not ideal, she is enormously helped by having as her pianist a pupil of the composer, and those who respond to Messiaen's curious brand of evocation will not be disappointed.

Poèmes pour Mi (song cycle).
*** Argo ZRG 703. Felicity Palmer
(soprano), BBC Symphony Orchestra, Pierre Boulez – TIPPETT:
*Songs for Dov.****

This orchestrated version of the cycle *Poèmes pour Mi* makes a fascinating comparison with the balder original version with simple piano accompaniment. The seductive beauty of the writing is enormously enhanced, and the voice of Felicity Palmer, vibrant and characterful, is wonderful suited to these reflections on the meaning of marriage. An unexpected coupling for Tippett, but an attractive and important one. Outstandingly good recording.

La Transfiguration de Notre Seigneur Jésus-Christ.
*** Decca Headline HEAD 1/2.
Michael Sylvester (tenor), Paul Aquino (baritone), Westminster Symphonic Choir, Yvonne Loriod (piano) and instrumental soloists,

Washington National Symphony Orchestra, Antal Dorati.

This massive work of fourteen movements – divided into two parallel septenaries – seems to sum up the whole achievement of Messiaen. It was written for the Gulbenkian Festival in 1969 (having taken nearly four years to complete), and though the unconverted may feel it has its longueurs, no one can doubt the dedication of the composer, his ability beyond almost any contemporary to convey through music his personal religious exaltation. Dorati magnificently holds together the unwieldy structures, and though such an evocative work ideally ought to be heard against a more reverberant acoustic, the brilliance and immediacy of the recording are most impressive.

Meyerbeer, Giacomo
(1791–1864)

Les Patineurs – ballet suite (orch. Lambert).

(M) *** Decca Ace of Diamonds SDD 139. Israel Philharmonic Orchestra, Jean Martinon – MASSENET: *Le Cid*.**

Les Patineurs was arranged by Constant Lambert using excerpts from two of Meyerbeer's operas, *Le Prophète* and *L'Étoile du Nord*. The vivacious music is played with great enthusiasm and panache under Martinon, and – unlike the coupling – the brashness of the acoustic suits the music exactly. There is an exuberant bass drum in the opening number

Les Huguenots (opera in 5 acts): complete recording.

** (*) Decca SET 460/3. Joan Suth-

erland (soprano), Huguette Tourangeau (mezzo-soprano), Anastasios Vrenios (tenor), Nicola Ghiuselev (bass), Gabriel Bacquier (baritone), Martina Arroyo (soprano), Dominic Cossa (baritone), Ambrosian Opera Chorus, New Philharmonia Orchestra, Richard Bonynge.

The revival of Meyerbeer's once-popular opera of epic length provided an exceptional challenge for Richard Bonynge. He prepared for this recording with a concert performance in the Royal Albert Hall, and in both instances his own passionate belief in the music was amply evident. It is good too to have Sutherland augmenting the enticing sample of the role of the Queen which she gave in *The art of the prima donna*. The result is predictably impressive, though once or twice there are signs of a 'beat' in the voice, previously unheard on Sutherland records. But the rest of the cast is uneven, and in an unusually episodic opera with passages that are musically less than inspired (Meyerbeer's melodic inspiration was often very square) that brings disappointments. Gabriel Bacquier and Nicola Ghiuselev are fine in their roles, and though Martina Arroyo is below her best as Valentine the star quality is unmistakable. The tenor Anastasios Vrenios can easily be criticized in the role of Raoul in that this is too small a voice for a heroic part, but very few other tenors and certainly not those who have been applauded in stage performances can cope with the extraordinarily high tessitura and florid divisions. Vrenios sings the notes, which is more than almost any rival could. Fine recording to make this ambitious project well worth investigating by lovers of French opera.

Les Huguenots: highlights.

*** Decca SET 513 (from above recording).

The Decca highlight selection is generous and for many will be the ideal way of sampling this long and somewhat uneven work. The recording has the same qualities as the original.

Miaskovsky, Nikolai
(1881–1950)

Violoncello concerto.
(M) *** HMV SXLP 30155. Mstislav Rostropovich (cello), Philharmonia Orchestra, Sir Malcolm Sargent – PROKOFIEV: *Violin concerto No. 2.*⊕ ***

The *Cello concerto* is one of Miaskovsky's finest works; its opening is dignified and elegiac, and its gentle melancholy and rich melodic flow will ensure its appeal to readers who enjoy, say, Elgar's *Cello concerto*. Its atmosphere of nostalgia is well conveyed in this masterly performance by Rostropovich and Sargent, who have the full measure of its nobility. The recording comes from the early days of stereo, though one would scarcely suspect this; the sound is beautifully balanced and well detailed. The upper strings would sound slightly richer if the recording had been made more recently, but in every other respect, spaciousness and firmness of definition, this is a first-class recording.

Symphony No. 22 in B minor.
** HMV ASD 3062. USSR Symphony Orchestra, Yevgeny Svetlanov – SVETLANOV: *Festive poem.** (*)

Like the *Leningrad symphony* of Shostakovich (though it is not as long) Miaskovsky's *Twenty-second Symphony* was written in response to the Nazi invasion of Russia in the autumn of 1941. It is a one-movement work, though it falls clearly into three sections. Its thematic substance is endearingly old-fashioned (there is nothing that would have surprised Glazounov), and yet its slow section sounds a note of nostalgia and keen lyrical feeling. (Miaskovsky is really at his best in slow movements, musing gently on past happiness and its transience.) The performance is totally committed but the recording, though equally full-blooded, does not handle climaxes smoothly enough, and in the slow movement the strings are too close, with the consequent tendency almost to overload. However, an interesting work. There is an unimportant fill-up by the conductor.

Symphony No. 23 in A minor, Op. 56.
*** HMV ASD 2927. Moscow Radio Symphony Orchestra, Alexei Kovlyov – SHCHEDRIN: *Symphony No. 1.***

Miaskovsky's musical language is not exploratory though it is nonetheless distinctive. He was a prolific symphonist though his reputation has so far rested on the *Symphony No. 21*, which won a Stalin Prize in 1940. The present work was written not long after the Nazi invasion of Russia and was first performed in 1942. Like Prokofiev's *Second String quartet* it makes use of folk material from the Caucasus; indeed the work is subtitled *Symphonic suite on Caucasian themes*. The music is full of nostalgia, and although Prokofiev uses the same themes with greater resource and mastery, Miaskovsky's symphony, is well worth hearing. The weakest movement is the finale; the other two movements have some imaginative strokes. The performance and recording are not of recent provenance but are nonetheless of good quality.

Milhaud, Darius
(1892–1974)

Le Bœuf sur le toit.
*** Philips SAL 3637. London Symphony Orchestra, Antal Dorati – AURIC: *Overture*; FRANÇAIX: *Concertino*; SATIE: *Parade*.***

Philips have given Dorati a perfectly judged recording, the touch of dryness in the acoustic exactly right to give the music its proper edge. The sound itself too is brilliant without being aggressive. Dorati's reading catches the idiom splendidly; there is a touch of rhythmic rigidity but nothing serious. Perhaps the piece is a trifle long for its content, but its audacious mood still entertains.

(i) *Le Carnaval d'Aix;* (ii) *Concerto for percussion and small orchestra;* (iii) *Concerto for viola and orchestra of soloists.*
(M) * (*) Vox STGBY 640. (i) Carl Seeman (piano); (ii) Fauré Daniel (percussion); (iii) Ulrich Koch (viola); all with Radio Luxembourg Orchestra, the composer.

These performances are obviously authentic and they are also spirited. The account of *Le Carnaval d'Aix*, an attractive, spontaneous piece written in Paris in 1926 for the composer's forthcoming visit to the USA, is particularly vivid. Unfortunately the Vox recording is very close up, with little or no dynamic range, and it becomes wearing to listen to before the music has run its course.

(i; iii) *Piano concerto No. 2;* (ii; iii) *Suite cisalpine sur les airs populaires Piémontais* (for cello and orchestra); (i) *La Muse ménagère* (suite).
(B) ** Turnabout TV 34496S. (i)

Grant Johannesen (piano); (ii) Thomas Blees (cello); (iii) Radio Luxembourg Orchestra, Bernard Kontarsky.

The *Second Piano concerto* (1941) is a jazzy work with obvious associations with the Ravel concertos. Grant Johannesen plays it brilliantly, but the accompaniment is undistinguished and the recording shallow: the finale sounds very much of a scramble here. Thomas Blees is a first-class cellist and he is persuasive in the rather jolly *Suite cisalpine*, in spite of a much too forward balance. But what makes the disc worthwhile is *La Muse ménagère*, which takes up the whole of the second side. This paints a series of fifteen simple domestic scenes from *Getting up* to *Reading at night*, which produce surprisingly sensitive and poetic miniatures. They are played with great affection by Johannesen and the recording of his solo piano is excellent.

Violin concerto No. 2.
(M) *** Supraphon 110 1120. André Gertler (violin), Prague Symphony Orchestra, Václav Smetáček – MALIPIERO: *Violin concerto*.***

Milhaud's *Second Violin concerto* comes from 1946 and is not new to the gramophone: Louis Kaufmann recorded it with the French Radio Orchestra under Milhaud himself in the early days of LP. The work strikes a more serious note than pieces like *Carnaval d'Aix* or *Le Bœuf sur le toit*. At no time is the texture anywhere as thick as in some of the symphonies, and except in the finale, there is little of the easy-going Mediterranean charm that you find in the *First Cello concerto* or the *Suite provençale*. It is an inventive piece, and in the slow movement it is both powerful in feeling and dark in colouring. This is a most impressive movement and will surprise those who think of Milhaud as being always light of heart. The performance is thoroughly committed and well-prepared, with fine playing from Gertler. The recording is very good, though the strings have something of the pallor characteristic of Supraphon in the 1960s.

(i) *Violoncello concertos Nos. 1 and 2;*
(ii) *Elegy for cello and piano.*
　(M) ** Supraphon SUAST 50864.
　　Stanislav Apolín (cello), with (i) Brno State Philharmonic Orchestra, Jiří Waldhans; (ii) Josef Hála (piano).

An, enterprising and welcome release. The *First Concerto* dates from 1934 and is an easy-going work full of attractive ideas in Milhaud's sunniest and most Mediterranean mood. Only the slow movement permits a cloud to cross the horizon. The *Second Concerto* is worth hearing too, and in the absence of any alternative (Starker's record of No. 1, coupled with the Prokofiev *Concerto* in its original form, albeit slightly cut, is deleted) this performance and recordng must perforce be recommended.

La Création du monde (ballet).
　(M) ** Vanguard VSD 2117/8. Utah Symphony Orchestra, Maurice Abravanel – HONEGGER: *Le Roi David.***

La Création du monde dates from the jazz era of 1923 and was written by Milhaud after a visit to the United States. It is colourful 'avant-garde' music of its period, sinuously and rhythmically attractive. Abravanel gives an understanding and vivid account of it and he is well recorded.

Suadades do Brazil (suite of dances).
　* Decca Phase 4 PFS 4286. London Festival Players, Bernard Herrmann – SATIE: *Les Aventures de Mercure etc.**

The *Suadades do Brazil* are piano pieces that Milhaud orchestrated when he returned to Europe after his years as secretary to Claudel in the French Embassy in Rio. They are delightful and full of character, but the performances here are wanting in finesse and lightness of touch, and matters are not improved by singularly crude recording.

Symphonies pour petit orchestre Nos. 1–5; (i) *No. 6* (with soloists). *L'Homme et son désir* (ballet).
　(M) ** (*) Vox STGBY 626. Radio Luxembourg Orchestra, the composer, (i) with Josette Doemer (soprano), Marie-Jeanne Klein (contralto), Venent Arend (tenor), Raymond Koster (bass).

The best of the six symphonies is the *Third*, subtitled *Serenade*, that will probably be remembered by some collectors from Walter Goehr's ten-inch 78. None of these symphonies is longer than about four minutes and all are highly agreeable. *L'Homme et son désir* comes from 1918 and is an evocative score inspired by Milhaud's contact with the sounds of the Brazilian jungle. Perhaps the most effective part is the very opening. The performances under the composer must be regarded as authoritative, and the only drawback about this issue is the recording, which is closely balanced and does not allow a real *pianissimo* to register.

Milner, Anthony
(born 1925)

(i) *Roman Spring;* (ii) *Salutatio angelicus* (cantata).
　*** Decca SXL 6699. (i) Felicity Palmer (soprano), Robert Tear (tenor); (ii) Alfreda Hodgson

(mezzo-soprano); both with London Sinfonietta Chorus, London Sinfonietta, David Atherton.

Milner, an academic and lecturer as well as a composer, writes civilized, well-constructed music that deserves a place in the catalogue. *Salutatio angelicus*, his opus 1, uses the text of the *Angelus*, with each of the three settings of the *Ave Maria* given to the mezzo soloist (most beautifully sung by Alfreda Hodgson). The other cantata, written twenty-one years later, is more ambitious and more lively, a setting of five well-contrasted Latin poems, grouped in three separate movements. The writing is generously lyrical and often vigorously rhythmic – no suspicion here that Latin is a dead language. Excellent performance and recording.

Minkus, Ludwig
(1827–90)

Don Quixote (ballet; score arranged by John Lanchbery).
 ** (*) H M V CSD 3749. Elizabethan Trust Melbourne Orchestra, John Lanchbery.

Minkus's *Don Quixote* ballet dates back to 1869, when it was first performed in Russia. But this version is a modernized score, deftly arranged by John Lanchbery for the Australian Ballet. The recording comes from the soundtrack of a film version, but it is bright and colourful and readers need have no qualms on technical grounds. The music is pretty enough, but for all Lanchbery's skill he has been unable to disguise the comparatively thin inspiration of the score itself.

Moeran, Ernest J.
(1894–1950)

(i) *Violoncello concerto. Overture for a masque; Rhapsody No. 2 in E major.*
 ** Lyrita SRCS 43. London Philharmonic Orchestra, Sir Adrian Boult, (i) with Peers Coetmore (cello).

Peers Coetmore, widow of E. J. Moeran, is the dedicatee of the *Cello concerto*, a fine lyrical work written as a wedding present in 1945, the year of their marriage. One cannot miss the intensity of feeling in her playing. This is a deeply felt offering to a long-neglected composer, but the solo playing falls short of the virtuoso standard that one demands on record. One has to listen with a sympathetic ear. No such reservations about the colourful *Rhapsody* (an early work dating from 1924) and the jolly *Overture*, written in wartime to lighten the blackout. Boult is an intensely sympathetic conductor, and the recording quality matches Lyrita's excellent standards.

Sinfonietta.
 *** Lyrita SRCS 37. London Philharmonic Orchestra, Sir Adrian Boult – BAX: *November Woods*; HOLST: *Fugal overture.*** (*)

Moeran's music has fallen out of favour in recent years. His invention is fresh and original in the English pastoral vein but here he lacks the capacity to think in long paragraphs. The *Sinfonietta* is nonetheless an attractive work despite this shortcoming, and given such eloquent advocacy and good recording it should make many friends for the composer.

Symphony in G minor.
 ⊛ *** Lyrita SRCS 70. New Philharmonia Orchestra, Sir Adrian Boult.

*** HMV ASD 2913. English Sinfonia Orchestra, Neville Dilkes.

Moeran's superb *Symphony in G minor* was written between 1934 and 1937. It is in the best English tradition of symphonic writing and worthy to rank with the symphonies of Vaughan Williams and Walton, with which it has much in common. But for all the echoes of these composers (and Holst and Butterworth too) it has a strongly individual voice. There is no question of the quality of the invention throughout the lyrical sweep of the first two movements, and in the rhythmically extrovert and genial scherzo. If the structure and atmosphere of the finale are unmistakably Sibelian – there is a striking passage very like the climax in *Tapiola* – it makes a cogent and satisfying close to a very rewarding work.

Sir Adrian Boult directs a radiant performance, more spacious and more opulent in sound than Dilkes's on HMV. Characteristically he refuses to push too hard too soon, but the ebb and flow of tension are superbly controlled to build the most powerful possible climaxes. Rarely, even in Vaughan Williams, has Boult adopted so overtly expressive a style, and the recording quality, more refined than on HMV, allows the widest dynamic range down to the gentlest pianissimo for the hushed intense opening of the slow movement.

Dilkes's fine, lusty performance is in many ways complementary to Boult's, setting out more urgently if without quite the subtlety of rubato that the veteran conductor draws from his bigger orchestra. With a smaller string band recorded relatively close, the sound is vivid and immediate, if lacking a little in atmosphere compared to the Lyrita disc.

Violoncello sonata in A minor; Prelude for cello and piano. Piano pieces: *Bank Holiday; 2 Legends (A Folk Story; Rune); Prelude and Berceuse; Stalham River; Toccata; The White Mountain.*

** (*) Lyrita SRCS 42. Peers Coetmore (cello), Eric Parkin (piano).

Peers Coetmore brings a dedicated intensity to the *Cello sonata*, which her husband wrote for her in 1948, not long before he died. It is thoughtful introspective music, well worth getting to know. The piano pieces, which date from the twenties, are less distinctive but fresh and enjoyable in their English adaptation of Debussian trends. Excellent recording.

Mondonville, Jean-Joseph de (1711–72)

Violin sonatas Nos. 1 in G minor; 2 in F major; 3 in B major; 4 in C major; 5 in G major; 6 in A major.
** Telefunken SAWT 9497. Lars Fryden (baroque violin), Gustav Leonhardt (harpsichord).

Mondonville's *Violin sonatas* are important in that they helped the development of this form as we know it today, away from the violin plus continuo style. Thus both instruments are given proper 'solo' parts to play, and they are often very florid parts. One might be forgiven for thinking on occasion that the composer had forgotten himself and allotted two accompaniment parts instead! But generally the music is inventive enough and the disc has a real historical interest in demonstrating the duet sonata when ideas for the marriage of two instruments were very much in the melting pot. The recording is good – the harpsichord a little sharp-toned but generally well balanced – and the players seem pretty sure of themselves.

Monteverdi, Claudio
(1567–1643)

MADRIGALS

Madrigals, Books 3 and 4 (for 5 voices): complete recording.

** (*) Philips 6703 035 (3 discs). Sheila Armstrong, Wendy Eathorne, Lillian Watson (sopranos), Alfreda Hodgson (mezzo-soprano), Anne Collins, Helen Watts (contraltos), Bernard Dickerson, Gerald English, Ian Partridge, Robert Tear (tenors), Stafford Dean, Christopher Keyte (basses), Glyndebourne Opera Chorus, Raymond Leppard.

This was the second album issued in Leppard's projected complete recording. With choral madrigals limited here to a handful in Book 4 there is not quite the same variety in this as in Leppard's album of Books 8–10. Though the style and direction are as lively and captivating as ever, at least one of the soloists is fallible in ensembles of five voices, which need meticulous tuning. These earlier madrigals (Book 3 was published in 1592, Book 4 in 1603) show the transition from Monteverdi's early mastery in the accepted genre to the full flowering of his individual originality in Book 4, where he chooses to set poems much more overtly emotional. Excellent recording.

Madrigals, Books 8–10 and *Supplement*: complete recording.

⊛ *** Philips 6799 006 (5 discs). Sheila Armstrong, Angela Bostock, Yvonne Fuller, Heather Harper, Anne Howells, Lillian Watson (sopranos), Alfreda Hodgson (mezzo-soprano), Anne Collins, Helen Watts (contraltos), Luigi Alva, Ryland Davies, Bernard Dickerson, Alexander Oliver, Robert Tear, John Wakefield (tenors), Stafford Dean, Christopher Keyte (basses), Ambrosian Singers, Glyndebourne Chorus, English Chamber Orchestra, Raymond Leppard.

This set provided the richly enjoyable start to a magnificent project, nothing less than the complete recording by Leppard and varied forces of Monteverdi's enormous total output of madrigals. This album contains virtually all those that Monteverdi wrote during his last years, not only the massive Book 8, with its songs of love and war, but the 'musical jokes' and other madrigals of Books 9 and 10. Leppard ensures that there is nothing earnest or pedestrian about the results. Some may criticize the warmth and richness, starting with the two magnificent six-part choruses which open the set, but here as elsewhere Leppard is demonstrating the enormous variety of expression in Monteverdi's work, and string accompaniments sound very much in place. Book 8 also includes the longer pieces – almost short operas – *Il Combattimento di Tancredi e Clorinda* and *Il Ballo delle ingrate*, both vividly done. Stylish singing and playing – a delight from beginning to end, helped by excellent, atmospheric recording.

Madrigali guerrieri: Sinfonia. Altri canti d'amor; Ardo, avvampo; Armato il cor; Il ballo per l'imperatore Ferdinando; Gira il nemico; Hor che'l ciel e la terra; Ogni amante è guerrier; Se vittorie sì belle.

*** Philips 6500 663 (from above recording).

This sample disc from the madrigals in Monteverdi's Volume 8 makes an admirable introduction to an endlessly rewarding world. The *Altri canti d'amor* are particularly captivating.

Il Ballo delle ingrate; Il Combattimento di Tancredi e Clorinda.
> *** Philips 6500 457 (from above recording).

To have the two longer pieces from Volume 8 coupled as here makes an outstanding disc. Fine singing and lively direction, helped by excellent recording.

Other Collections of Madrigals

Ah dolente partita; Al lume delle stelle; Amor, che deggio far; Chiome d'oro; Damigella tutta bella; Dolci miei sospiri; Eccomi pronta ai baci; La piaga ch'ho nel core; Lamento della ninfa; Non vedro mai le stelle; O come sei gentile; Sfogava con le stelle; Si ch'io vorrei.
> *** Argo ZRG 668. Purcell Consort, Grayston Burgess.

Ever since Nadia Boulanger made her historic 78 collection of Monteverdi madrigals in the late thirties, the Nymph's Lament, *Lamento della ninfa*, has been a favourite madrigal, and here again it stands at the centre of the collection. With Eileen Poulter as soloist, this is a less personal reading than Boulanger's, but at a slower tempo and with a purertoned soprano this is if anything even more beautiful. *Chiome d'oro* is another which coincides with the original Boulanger collection, here more authentically allotted to two sopranos instead of Boulanger's tenors (one of them the incomparable Hugues Cuénod) and not nearly so witty. But the wonder is that these performances stand comparison so well with that classic example. This is cleaner and straighter in style than Raymond Leppard's Oiseau-Lyre collection (see below), and on the whole it is

preferable. A wonderful record for anyone simply wanting to sample the irresistible glories of this great musical revolutionary. It is beautifully recorded.

A Dio, Florida bella; Altri canti d'amor; Amor che deggio far; Hor che'l ciel e la terra; Presso un fiume tranquillo; Questi vaghi concenti; Qui rise, o Tirsi.
> *** Telefunken SAWT 9438-A. Hamburg Monteverdi Choir, Jürgen Jürgens.

This is a splendid ensemble and their performances are as stylish as they are sensible. The quality of the recorded sound and the balance conform to the high standard of this company.

Ahi com'a un vago sol; Augellin; Dell'usate mie corde; Introduction and Ballo; Mentre vaga Angioletta; Ninfa che scalza il piede/Qui deh meco; Non voglio amare; O mio bene; Se vittorie sì belle; Vaga su spina ascosa; Zefiro torna e di soavi accenti; Zefiro torna e'l bel tempo riemena.
> * DGG Archive 2533 087. Soloists, Hamburg Monteverdi Choir, Jürgen Jürgens.

This is not a wholly successful disc. Tempi tend to be a shade too fast and there is little sense of poetic feeling. The recording is rather forward, which does not help. *Zefiro torna* is absurdly fast.

Madrigals: Altri canti di Marte; Ardo, avvampo; Hor che'l ciel e la terra; Ballo: Movete al mio bel suon; O ciecchi, ciecchi; Questi vaghi concenti.
> *** Argo ZRG 698. Heinrich Schütz Choir, Roger Norrington.

These fine madrigals, also recorded by Raymond Leppard in his complete collection of Book 8, are given crisp, well-drilled performances by Norrington, not so relaxedly expressive as Leppard's but most refreshing. The ample acoustic of St John's, Smith Square, adds agreeable atmosphere.

Madrigali amorosi: Altri canti di Marte; Chi vol haver felice; Dolcissimo uscignolo; Mentre vaga Angioletta; Ninfa che scalza il piede; Non havea Febo ancora; Non partir ritrosetta; Perchè t'en fuggi; Su, su, su pastorelli vezzosi; Vago augelletto.

(M) ** Vanguard HM 10SD. Deller Consort with Baroque String Ensemble.

Highly expressive singing of music that is often expressive enough in its own right not to need more. But apart from a tendency to emote, the singing is beautiful, and the music is of such interest and eloquence that it carries all before it. The recording is a little dated but fully acceptable.

Scherzi musicali: Amorosa pupilletta; Clori amorosa; Damigella tutta bella; Della bellezza le dovute lodi; Dolci miei sospiri; Ecco di dolci raggi/Io ch'amato; Fugge il verno; I bei legami; Lidia spina del mio core; Maledetto sia l'aspetto; La mia turca; Non così; O Rosetta; La pastorella; Quando l'alba; La violetta.

(B) ** Turnabout TV 34388S. Boston Camerata, Joel Cohen.

This is pleasingly performed and acceptably recorded. It is not the most ideally planned issue (for that one must look to the many anthologies of Monteverdi's music) but it offers all the light-hearted and gay *Scherzi musicali* included in Raymond Leppard's set. It is a disc that it is best to sample rather than play all the way through, but given the modest price asked, this is a useful addition to the now impressive Monteverdi discography.

Bel pastor; Della bellezza le dovute lodi; Dolci miei sospiri; Fugge il verno dei dolori; Gira il nemico insidioso; Lamento della ninfa; Lidia spina del mio core; Non così tosto io miro; Ohimè ch'io cado; O Rosetta; La pastorella mia spietata; Si dolce è il tormento.

(M) *** Oiseau-Lyre SOL 299. Ilse Wolf (soprano), Robert Tear, Gerald English (tenors), Christopher Keyte (bass), English Chamber Orchestra, Raymond Leppard.

This was the first of Raymond Leppard's madrigal anthologies, dating from the mid-sixties, and at medium price it still makes a splendid introduction to this wonderful repertoire. Not since Nadia Boulanger made her first, historic recording of Monteverdi madrigals in Paris in the thirties (imagine it, a piano continuo!) had the most sensuously beautiful of the works in this form, *Il lamento della ninfa*, been recorded with such feeling. For that item alone the record would be worth it, for with wonderfully clear recording and imaginative direction by Raymond Leppard, its beauty is irresistible. Some who know the Boulanger version may feel it is taken too slowly, but that only prolongs the ecstasy. Not only this but all the other items on the disc are most welcome. The singing is fresh – if not always as sweet-toned as on the later Philips or Argo anthologies.

CHURCH MUSIC

Sacred concertos: Audi caelum; Beatus vir; Exsulta filia; Gloria in excelsis Deo; Laudate Dominum omnes gentes.

** DGG Archive 2533 137. Dorothy Dorow, Birgit Nordin (sopranos), Nigel Rogers, Ian Partridge (tenors), Christopher Keyte, Friedhelm Hessenbruch (basses), Hamburg Monteverdi Choir, Instrumental Ensemble, Jürgen Jürgens.

A finely recorded and well performed set of sacred concertos from the *Selva morale e spirituale*. Perhaps there is some evidence of fussiness in the continuo support, and the instrumental accompaniment is editorial. However, given such good singing and recording, the disc can be recommended.

Beatus vir; Confitebor tibi Domine (1st setting); *Gloria à 7 voci concertata; Laudate dominum in sanctis ejus; Salve Regina. Salve O Regina* (motet).

(M) * (*) Pye Virtuoso TPLS 13003. Nigel Rogers, Ian Partridge (tenors), Thames Chamber Choir, London Trombone Quartet, Instrumental Ensemble, Louis Halsey.

This is an attractive programme, but the conductor is not always sensitive in matters of style and, especially, tempi. The solo pieces are much more satisfactory and the recording is good.

Laudate pueri; Messa à 4 voci (1640); *Messa à 4 voci* (1651).

** (*) Argo ZRG 494. Michael Turner, Benjamin Odom (trebles), Peter Birts, Robert Bishop (tenors), Gareth Keene (bass), St John's College Choir, Cambridge, Academy of St Martin-in-the-Fields, George Guest.

Magnificat à 6 voci; Messa à 4 voci (1640).

(M) *** Oiseau-Lyre SOL 263. Carmelite Priory Choir, London, George Malcolm; Colin Mawby (organ).

The four-part *Mass* of 1640 is common to both discs, and of the two performances George Malcolm's has the greater character. But the other items on the Argo disc, which is generally well sung, contain some fine music and are well worth having. The *Magnificat* is part of the collection of pieces more familiar as the *Vespers*. Like the *Mass* it shows Monteverdi's genius at its most spontaneous. The recording of both discs is excellent.

Vespro della Beata Vergine (Vespers).

*** Decca SET 593/4. Jill Gomez, Felicity Palmer (sopranos), James Bowman (counter-tenor), Robert Tear, Philip Langridge (tenors), John Shirley-Quirk (baritone), Michael Rippon (bass), Monteverdi Choir and Orchestra, Salisbury Cathedral Boys' Choir, Jones Brass Ensemble, Munrow Recorder Consort, John Eliot Gardiner.

** (*) Telefunken SAWT 9501/2. Rotraud Hansmann, Irmgard Jacobeit (sopranos), Nigel Rogers, Bert van t'Hoff (tenors), Max van Egmond (baritone), Jacques Villisech (bass), Vienna Boys' Choir soloists, Hamburg Monteverdi Choir, Vienna Concentus Musicus, Plainsong Schola of Munich Capella Antiqua, Jürgen Jürgens.

'The grand quasi-theatrical design of this spectacular work has always seemed compelling to me,' says John Eliot Gardiner, and this fine set presents the music very much in that light. Modern instruments are used and women's voices, but Gardiner's rhythms are so resilient the result is more exhilarating as well as grander. The whole span of the thirteen movements sweeps you forward with a sense of complete unity. Singing and playing are exemplary, and the recording is one of Decca's most vividly atmospheric.

The Jürgens set of the *Vespers* is scholarly yet not without warmth. The liturgical sequence is respected and authentic instruments are used. The continuo tends to be somewhat lightweight, but there is a sure sense of style. Some might feel that the approach could be less smooth, more dramatic, but the beautifully judged aural perspective of the Telefunken recording helps to give atmosphere and a feeling of space. This is a good deal more than a routine performance, but the Decca version more satisfactorily combines authenticity with a strong dramatic impulse.

COURT AND CHURCH MUSIC

Adoramus te; Cantate Domino; Domine ne in furore; Era l'anima mia; Ohime se tanto amate; Zefiro torna.

** Argo ZRG 645. Monteverdi Choir, John Eliot Gardiner – GESUALDO: *Motets.* **

Another addition to the growing representation of Monteverdi on records. These performances are marked by excellent singing, with firm tone and intonation, but there is an element of interpretative exaggeration that is not wholly in style. Dynamics and tempi are rather extreme, but still there is no lack of life here, and the excellent recording will undoubtedly tempt many collectors.

OPERA

L'Incoronazione di Poppea (opera in Prologue and 3 acts): complete recording.

** (*) Telefunken HD 6 35247 (5 discs). Helen Donath, Elisabeth Söderström (sopranos), Cathy Berberian (mezzo-soprano), Paul Esswood (counter-tenor), Giancarlo Luccardi (bass), Rotraud Hansmann (soprano), Philip Langridge (tenor), Vienna Concentus Musicus, Nikolaus Harnoncourt.

Harnoncourt's new recording of *L'Incoronazione di Poppea* has the dual advantages of being both complete and authentic. There are features of any performance of this great work which are bound to be conjectural, and here scholars may argue about the instrumentation used or the ornamentation (which matches it in elaboration). But there is no question that the dramatic power of the music comes across. Helen Donath is commanding as Poppea, and she is extremely well supported by Paul Esswood as Ottone and Cathy Berberian, whose characterization of Ottavia is an imaginative one. Donath's singing has not the richness and dignity that Janet Baker gives to this role, but she brings the character fully to life. Elisabeth Söderström has the almost impossible task of creating a heroic image in the role of Nero, written for a high castrato, but her performance is excellent, even if she fails wholly to submerge her feminity. Harnoncourt brings plenty of vitality to the performance as a whole, and his instrumental group provides beautiful if arguably over-decorative accompaniments.

L'Incoronazione di Poppea, Act 1: *Disprezzata Regina* (Ottavia's lament); Act 3: *Addio Roma* (Ottavia's farewell). *L'Arianna: Lasciatemi morire* (Ariadne's lament).

*** HMV ASD 2615. Janet Baker (contralto), English Chamber Orchestra, Raymond Leppard – A. and D. SCARLATTI: *Cantatas.* ***

In the operatic field Leppard's approach to Monteverdi and his school sometimes raises scholarly temperatures, but the general listener can revel in the richness and elaboration. In any case, in these extended Monteverdi offerings the artistry of Janet Baker provides the cornerstone, and the flowing *arioso* of these classically inspired scenas inspires her to bring out the living, human intensity of each situation. There is not quite the variety of expression one finds in the madrigals – inevitably so with operatic *arioso* – but the range of emotion is if anything greater. Highly recommended. Fine recording.

Orfeo (opera in Prologue and 5 acts): complete recording.

   *** DGG Archive 2723 018 (3 discs). Nigel Rogers (tenor), Emilia Petrescu (soprano), Anna Reynolds (mezzo-soprano), James Bowman (counter-tenor), John Elwes, Ian Partridge (tenors), Stafford Dean, Alexander Malta (basses), Hamburg Monteverdi Choir, Instrumental Ensemble, Jürgen Jürgens.

   ** Telefunken SKH 21 (3 discs). Lajos Kozma (tenor), Rotraud Hansmann (soprano), Cathy Berberian (mezzo-soprano), Nigel Rogers, Kurt Equiluz (tenors), Max van Egmond (baritone), Jacques Villisech (bass), Munich Capella Antiqua, Vienna Concentus Musicus, Nikolaus Harnoncourt.

In a lively, atmospheric performance like Jürgens's, Monteverdi's score emerges as amazingly modern, an innovatory work that reveals its total originality still. In the massive aria in which Orfeo pleads with Charon, Nigel Rogers treats the florid writing not as a technical obstacle race but as a test of expressiveness, giving the character extra depth. His fine virtuoso performance is matched by the singing of such artists as James Bowman and Ian Partridge. Alexander Malta as Charon and Stafford Dean as Pluto are wonderfully dark and firm in bass tone, while Emilia Petrescu as Euridice and Anna Reynolds as Silvia

equally combine stylishness with expressive strength. The chorus and orchestra are outstanding. The recording – in total contrast with the Telefunken version – has an ample acoustic, simulating a performance in a nobleman's hall. The sound of the plucked instruments is specially beguiling.

Harnoncourt's speciality in the endless search for authenticity is the use of ancient instruments, and the Ritornello of the Prologue here might almost be by Stravinsky, so sharply do the sounds cut. Otherwise Harnoncourt is an altogether more severe Monteverdian than Jürgens. In compensation the simple, straightforward dedication of this performance is most affecting, and the solo singing, if not generally very characterful, is clean and stylish. One exception to the general rule on characterfulness comes in the singing of Cathy Berberian as the Messenger. She is strikingly successful, and though slightly different in style from the others, she sings as part of the team. Excellent restrained recording.

Orfeo: highlights.

   (M) ****** Telefunken SMT 1319 (from above recording cond. Harnoncourt).

If a single-disc selection is required, this medium-priced disc should serve. Harnoncourt provides a genuine alternative to Jürgens, a plainer, less elaborately ornamented version set in a dry acoustic and using sharper instrumentation. Lajos Kozma may not have quite the ease or sweetness of Nigel Rogers (who here sings the role of Second Shepherd), but it is a strong, stylish cast with Cathy Berberian outstanding. Excellent recording.

Il Ritorno d'Ulisse in patria (opera in Prologue and 5 acts): complete recording.

   (B) ****** Turnabout TV 37016/8S. Maureen Lehane (mezzo-soprano), Gerald English (tenor), Antonia Fahberg (soprano), Margarethe Bence (contralto), Bernhard Michaelis (tenor), Eduard Wollitz (bass), Santini Chamber Orchestra, Rudolf Ewerhart.

This is the third and least-known of the Monteverdi operas that have survived (if only, by some magic, more could be unearthed!), and it is good to have a conscientiously authentic performance at so cheap a price. It would be silly to deny that *Ulisse* has its longueurs, but there is so much to delight anyone who has ever fallen under Monteverdi's spell. The performance is sound rather than sparkling, but one welcomes two such excellent British singers in the principal roles as Maureen Lehane (Penelope) and Gerald English (Ulisse). The sober authenticity of Ewerhart's direction allows one to enjoy the music without distraction. The recording quality is good, though some of the directional separations between voice and continuo are excessive. The performance, as recorded, has minor cuts.

Morley, Thomas
(1557–1603)

The first Booke of Ayres: A painted tale; Thyrsis and Milla; She straight her light green silken coats; With my love; I saw my lady weeping; It was a lover; Who is it that this dark night; Mistress mine; Can I forget; Love winged my hopes; What if my mistress; Come, sorrow, come; Fair in a morn; Absence, hear thou; Will you buy a fine dog; Sleep, slumb'ring eyes.

** Telefunken SAWT 9568. Nigel Rogers (tenor), Nikolaus Harnon-

court (viola da gamba), Eugen Dombois (lute).

This integral recording is welcome in a catalogue not notably generous to Morley's music. The settings heard together show the scope of the composer's imagination in his sensitivity to the words themselves, in the variety of style and metre, and in the diversity of manner of the accompaniments. The performances are fresh and direct and scholarly in the use of decoration. The vocal personality is slight but pleasant. There is a small technical fault in *With my love*, where the pitch varies between verses; otherwise the recording is excellent.

Madrigals: April is in my mistress' face; Arise, get up, my dear; Besides a fountain; Fire! fire! my heart!; Good morrow, fair ladies; Hard by a crystal fountain; Hark, alleluia cheerly; I follow, lo, the footing; I go before, my darling; In dew of roses; Leave this tormenting; Miraculous love's wounding; Now is the month of maying; O grief; Say, gentle nymphs; Shoot, false love, I care not; Though Philomela lost her love; When, lo, by break of morning; Whither away so fast.

(M) ** Vanguard HM 4SD. Deller Consort, Alfred Deller.

This disc will give undoubted pleasure. When it first appeared, the madrigals on the first side were coupled with some Wilbye, but now we get a more comprehensive picture of Morley's output. The singing is splendidly expressive, words are clearly audible, and there is a predictably fine sense of style. The sopranos, however, suffer from a wide *vibrato*, and the recording is not of the most distinguished. However, the disc is recommendable.

Moscheles, Ignaz
(1794–1870)

(i) *Piano concerto in G minor, Op. 58.*
Characteristic études, Op. 95, Nos. 2,
4, 6, 9; Études, Op. 70, Nos. 5, 9, 12,
13, 14, 24.

> (M) ** Vox STGBY 636. Michael
> Ponti (piano), (i) with Philhar-
> monia Hungarica, Othmar Maga.

Moscheles, a friend and contemporary
of Beethoven, was born in Prague, but
spent part of his later career in London.
He was a well-liked man, and the simplicity and geniality of his character
come over in his *Piano concerto*, which
has a pleasing lyrical strain in the first
movement and an attractive finale. The
studies are purposeful and well made if
not really memorable as music to be
listened to frequently. They are boldly
played here by Michael Ponti, and the
performance of the *Concerto* is sympathetic with an atmospheric recording
to match.

Moszkowski, Moritz
(1854–1925)

(i) *Piano concerto in E major, Op. 59.*
Caprice espagnole, Op. 37; 8 Charac-
teristic pieces, Op. 36/6: Étincelles;
Danse bohème (after Bizet's Carmen);
Étude in F major, Op. 72; Venusberg
bacchanale (Paraphrase for piano after
music by Wagner).

> (M) ** (*) Vox STGBY 647. Michael
> Ponti (piano), (i) with Philhar-
> monia Hungarica, Hans Stracke.

Moszkowski's *Piano concerto* is undeniably fetching, even if the amiable
quality of its invention hovers dangerously near the Palm Court. It is good

to welcome an unfamiliar concerto with
tunes in all four of its movements,
although the first is the weakest from the
melodic point of view. The slow movement has genuine charm, and the scherzo
nearly (but not quite) manages the
memorability of the famous movement
by Litolff, with which it has a good deal
in common. The finale is sprightly and,
like the scherzo, gives Michael Ponti a
chance to demonstrate his bravura. He is
an excellent artist, just the man to make
the very most of this Vox series of 'near-
miss' romantic concertos, and he obviously enjoys himself in the characterful
genre pieces which are offered as an
encore on side two. Of these the three
original items are very attractive but the
two paraphrases are disappointing, being
little more than transcriptions. On the
whole a most enjoyable disc, and well
recorded too.

Mozart, Leopold
(1719–87)

Musical Sleighride (Schlittenfahrt);
Toy symphony (attrib. Haydn).

> (B) ** Turnabout TV 34134S. Würt-
> temberg Chamber Orchestra,
> Joerg Faerber – MOZART: *Musi-*
> *cal Joke.***

Quite whether the *Toy symphony* and
Musical Sleighride fit the title on this
disc, *Humour in music*, one is not sure,
but both pieces are brightly played here
and well recorded. The record is cheap,
and whether or not one agrees with the
title, the collection is convenient enough.

Toy symphony (attrib. Haydn).

> (B) ** Music for Pleasure MFP 2126.
> Little Symphony of London,
> Arthur Davison – MOZART:
> *German dance, K.605/3; PROKO-*
> *FIEV: Peter and the Wolf.****

(M) * (*) HMV SXLP 30161. Philharmonia Orchestra, Herbert von Karajan – HANDEL: *Water music;* MOZART: *Ave verum; Serenade No. 13; German dance, K.605/3.***

An excellent performance on Music for Pleasure, vividly recorded; it makes a good coupling for *Peter and the Wolf.* Karajan is gracious, but plodding and totally devoid of humour. However, the rest of his concert is quite attractive.

Mozart, Wolfgang
(1756–91)

Adagio in E major, K.261; Rondo in C major, K.373 (both for violin and orchestra).

** Philips SAL 3660. Arthur Grumiaux (violin), New Philharmonia Orchestra, Raymond Leppard – HAYDN: *Violin concerto No. 2;* SCHUBERT: *Rondo.***

These two Mozart movements are far from slight; the *Adagio* is really lovely, and the *Rondo*'s sparkle shows its composer on top form. Both are very sympathetically played by Grumiaux, and the disc altogether makes an attractive anthology.

There are also performances of the *Adagio* by Szeryng, Schneiderhan and David Oistrakh; see under *Violin concertos.*

Adagio and fugue in C minor, K.546; Divertimento in D major for strings, K.136; Serenades Nos. 6 in D major (Serenata notturna), K.239; 13 in G major (Eine kleine Nachtmusik), K.525.

(M) ** Philips Universo 6580 030. I Musici.

The Universo disc is a reissue of a very early stereo LP with the addition of the

Adagio and fugue. Little or no attempt has been made to brighten the recording, which is ample in texture rather than especially clear. In the *Nachtmusik* some may prefer a crisper sound. The performances are very relaxed (the central movements of K.525 especially so) but the breadth of the sound and warmth of the playing generally carry the day. The *Adagio and fugue* lacks cumulative tension, and the *Serenata notturna* is played steadily; but if one accepts the approach, there is much to enjoy. I Musici have re-recorded the *Adagio and fugue*, and the new performance, given a rich, refined recording, has much greater impulse; see under *Violin concerto No. 5.*

(i) *Andante for flute and orchestra in C major, K.315* (see also below under *Flute concertos*); (ii) *Bassoon concerto in B flat major, K.191* (see also below); (iii) *Clarinet concerto in A major, K.622* (see also below).

*** Philips 6500 378. (i) Claude Monteux (flute); (ii) Michael Chapman (bassoon); (iii) Jack Brymer (clarinet); all with Academy of St Martin-in-the-Fields, Neville Marriner.

This recording of the *Clarinet concerto* is the third that Jack Brymer has made. In some ways it is the best, for he plays with deepened insight and feeling. Only in the balance of the recording must we enter a reservation: Brymer plays a jumbo clarinet and is thus out of proportion to the excellent Academy. However, the recording is otherwise realistic and eminently truthful in timbre, and the performance is altogether outstanding. Although Michael Chapman too is rather prominently positioned in relation to the orchestra, his record of the *Bassoon concerto* is eminently recommendable. He plays with great spirit and verve, and is stylishly supported. Indeed in some respects this is to be preferred to almost any of its rivals, though Zeman and Boehm are better balanced, and Gwydian Brooke on HMV has special claims to consideration.

Cassations Nos. 1 in G major, K.63; 2 in B flat major, K.99.

(B) ** Turnabout TV 34373S. Zürich Collegium Musicum, Paul Sacher.

The delightful *First Cassation* has two enchanting slow movements. The first is a delicate *Andante* (nicely atmospheric here), which is reminiscent of *Così fan tutte* in its mood and colour; the second introduces a cantilena for solo violin. K.99 is almost equally attractive, and both works are sympathetically played by a small orchestra of the right size and balance. The recording is not brilliantly clear, but its warmth and resonance do not destroy the music's intimacy and the result is most enjoyable.

Cassation No. 2 in B flat major, K.99; Divertimento in G major, K.63.

*** Decca SXL 6500. Vienna Mozart Ensemble, Willi Boskovsky.

These are excellent performances, flawlessly recorded. The *Divertimento in G* is a comparatively slight work, but so alive and stylish is the playing here that it is invested with considerable stature.

Cassation No. 2 in B flat major, K.99; Divertimento No. 7 in D major, K.205; March in D major, K.290.

(M) *** Decca Ace of Diamonds SDD 325. Members of the Vienna Octet.

An outstanding medium-priced coupling. Both the *Cassation* and the *Divertimento* are given peerless performances, and the quality of Mozart's invention in the latter work shows the composer at his most gracious and smiling. The recording is first-rate and this is a fine bargain.

Bassoon concerto in B flat major, K.191; Clarinet concerto in A major, K.622; Flute concerto No. 1 in G major, K.313; Flute and harp concerto in C major, K.299; Oboe concerto in C major, K.314b; Sinfonia concertante for oboe, clarinet, horn, bassoon and orchestra in E flat major, K.297b.

** HMV SLS 817 (3 discs). Soloists, Berlin Philharmonic Orchestra, Herbert von Karajan.

Solo wind players who spend most of their musical lives working in orchestras develop an aptitude for blending their musical personalities to work within a team. This often means that if they take on a solo role in a concerto the listener is aware of a lack of individual strength of character in the player's image. So it is in this otherwise beautifully played series of performances, and Karajan's rather bland manner with the accompaniments does not help to give them individuality. The recording is warm and pleasing.

Bassoon concerto in B flat major, K.191.

(B) ** Turnabout TV 34039S. George Zukerman (bassoon), Württemberg Chamber Orchestra, Joerg Faerber – WEBER: *Bassoon concerto etc.***

George Zukerman is the principal bassoonist of the CBC Radio Orchestra, and he is a soloist of the very front rank. His flexible phrasing and sweetness of tone are a constant source of pleasure, and if he emphasizes the lyrical side of the bassoon's character rather at the expense of its secondary humorous role, there is no lack of high spirits in the finale. The only reservation about this otherwise admirable performance is Mr Zukerman's decision to add fairly long cadenzas to each movement, which would be more sensible in a concert performance than for repeated gramophone listening. The recording is excellent.

(i) *Bassoon concerto in B flat major, K.191;* (ii) *Clarinet concerto in A major, K.622* (see also above).

*** DGG 2530 411. (i) Dietmar Zeman (bassoon); (ii) Alfred Prinz (clarinet); both with Vienna Philharmonic Orchestra, Karl Boehm.

*** HMV ASD 644. (i) Gwydian Brooke (bassoon); (ii) Jack Brymer (clarinet); Royal Philharmonic Orchestra, Sir Thomas Beecham.

** HMV ASD 2916. (i) Günter Piesk (bassoon); (ii) Karl Leister (clarinet); Berlin Philharmonic Orchestra, Herbert von Karajan.

The early HMV coupling of the *Bassoon* and *Clarinet concertos* is one of Beecham's most beguiling records. Both his soloists play with great character and beauty, and the affectionate accompaniment is wonderfully gracious. Some listeners, however, might resist these blandishments, and find the approach too richly indulgent, lacking momentum and vitality. For them Karl Boehm's disc provides an admirable alternative, even if Boehm's cultured approach seems slightly dour after Beecham's warmth. Dietmar Zeman, the bassoonist, gives a highly competitive account, and this is a distinguished performance by any standards. Prinz's account of the *Clarinet concerto* too is beautifully turned and both deserve a position of honour in the field. The recording is truthful and well balanced.

Günter Piesk gives a predictably fine account of the *Bassoon concerto,* but there is a certain want of sparkle and spontaneity here. The recording will appeal to those who like a warm, homogeneous orchestral blend rather than those who respond to a bright, well-lit sound picture with analytical detail. The Berlin Philharmonic play marvellously but the overall

effect is a trifle bland. Leister is by no means as individual in approach as he was in his earlier DGG performance with the same orchestra under Kubelik (now deleted). The tone is beautifully mellow but the contours are a little too smooth, and, as in the *Bassoon concerto,* the overall effect is a little suave.

Clarinet concerto in A major, K.622.

(B) ** (*) Classics for Pleasure CFP 40046. Keith Puddy (clarinet), Orchestra of St James, Stuart Bedford – HAYDN: *Trumpet concerto.***

(M) ** (*) Unicorn UNS 239. John McCaw (clarinet), New Philharmonia Orchestra, Raymond Leppard – NIELSEN: *Concerto.*** (*)

As we know from his recording of the Brahms *Clarinet quintet* (now deleted) Keith Puddy is a first-rate artist, and his performance here is warm and beautifully phrased. The approach is straightforward, not as romantic as some, but never inflexible, and there is no lack of spontaneity. With a good accompaniment this is an excellent bargain, if missing the eloquence of the very finest versions.

John McCaw's tone production is well suited to Mozart and his playing gives pleasure. The accompaniment under Leppard is beautifully made and the recording is clear and immediate. McCaw's approach is comparatively leisurely and the performance as a whole has no special individuality, but if the imaginative coupling is attractive, this is certainly recommendable.

(i) *Clarinet concerto in A major, K.622;* (ii) *Flute and harp concerto in C major, K.299.*

(M) *** Decca Ace of Diamonds SDD 155. (i) Alfred Prinz (clarinet); (ii) Werner Tripp (flute), Hubert Jellinek (harp), both with Vienna

Philharmonic Orchestra, Karl Münchinger.

*** Philips SAL 3535. (i) Jack Brymer (clarinet); (ii) Hubert Barwahser (flute), Osian Ellis (harp); London Symphony Orchestra, Colin Davis.

The Decca recording, smooth, rich and well judged in reverberation, is very good indeed. The balance between soloists and orchestra is finely calculated and the performances are admirable. Refinement and beauty of tone and phrase form a hallmark throughout, and Münchinger provides most sensitive accompaniments. Highly recommended.

On Philips Jack Brymer plays his concerto beautifully, conveying a most eloquent, autumnal serenity. The reading has a soft lyricism that is especially appealing in the slow movement. Barwahser, the first flute of the Concertgebouw, and Osian Ellis give a sparkling account of the *Flute and harp concerto*, and Colin Davis accompanies both with the greatest sprightliness and sympathy. The recording is smooth to match and this is unquestionably a fine coupling. However, it comes into competition with the equally recommendable and much cheaper Ace of Diamonds disc which is even better recorded.

(i) *Clarinet concerto in A major, K.622;*
(ii) *Oboe concerto in C major, K.314b.*
(B) ** Oryx BRL 21. (i) Thea King (clarinet); (ii) Derek Wickens (oboe); both with Little Orchestra of London, Leslie Jones.

Thea King gives an altogether first-rate performance of the *Clarinet concerto* to match her fine account of the *Clarinet quintet* on Saga. Her articulation and phrasing are a constant joy, and the unforced eloquence of the slow movement, shaped most beautifully, is matched by the sparkle and point of the finale. It

is a pity the orchestral accompaniment is not more polished and the recording of the strings sweeter. Derek Wickens's tone is piquant and characterful, and this is a fresh account of the *Oboe concerto*, again coloured by the somewhat coarse-grained sound the recording provides for the orchestra. But the disc is well worth having in spite of reservations and it is modestly priced.

(i) *Clarinet concerto in A major, K.622;*
(ii) *Horn concerto No. 3 in E flat major, K.447.*
** BASF BAC 3001. (i) Hans Deinzer (original clarinet); (ii) Hubert Crüts (hand-horn); both with Collegium Aureum (using original instruments).

The instrument for which Mozart wrote his *Clarinet concerto* had an extra four semitones in its lower register, and in order that the work could be played on the modern instrument certain sections of the solo part had to be revised. This is the first recording of the concerto exactly as Mozart conceived it (and Mozart was rather taken with the dark, honeyed tone of those lower notes). Of course the differences are not fundamental to the work's essential character, but every now and then the ear is caught by an operatic-styled descent to the lowest range, which, needless to say, Hans Deinzer makes tell, without crude exaggeration. His performance is a good one, although there are more sensuous accounts of the slow movement elsewhere. The coupling is the *Third Horn concerto* played on a hand-horn without valves. The player provides the extra notes by a device called hand-stopping, which, as we can hear for ourselves, is capable of producing a very serviceable chromatic scale. The sound of the instrument is rather open and uncovered, and the performance of the beautiful slow movement is careful rather than lyrical. The finale comes off best. Both recordings are good and the accompaniments well made. A fascinating disc, but on purely musical terms these performances do not compete with the finest available.

(i) *Clarinet concerto in A major, K.622.*
Symphony No. 38 in D major (Prague),
K.504.

> (M) *** Decca Ace of Diamonds SDD 331. London Symphony Orchestra, Peter Maag, (i) with Gervase de Peyer (clarinet).

Gervase de Peyer's admirable performance was originally issued coupled to the first and third *Horn concertos* and that disc (SXL 2238) is still available. However, as the *Horn concertos* have now been reissued all together on Ace of Diamonds, the present coupling makes a good alternative. The performance of the *Clarinet concerto* is as fine as any available, fluent and lively, with masterly phrasing in the slow movement and a vivacious finale. The coupling, Maag's superb account of the *Prague symphony*, is one of the best in the catalogue, and with excellent recording this is a wholly desirable disc.

(i) *Clarinet concerto in A major, K.622;*
(ii) *Sinfonia concertante for violin and viola in E flat major, K.364.*

> (M) *** CBS 61195. (i) Robert Marcellus (clarinet); (ii) Rafael Druian (violin), Abraham Skernick (viola); both with Cleveland Orchestra, George Szell.

These concertante performances with soloists from Szell's own orchestra show the level of artistry he gathered in that unique band. There is no stronger performance of the *Sinfonia concertante* available on record, and though in the first movement some may wish that Szell allowed more rhythmic latitude to his soloists (as most other versions do) the

result is cleaner and ultimately more consistent for it. Plenty of rich expressiveness in the slow movement, and a superb finale, brisk and brilliant but never rushed. Marcellus's excellent performance of the *Clarinet concerto* makes a splendid match in every way, with clean, classical style and tight-lipped tone married to tender expressiveness where appropriate. An outstanding and generous bargain in every way.

Flute concertos Nos. 1 in G major,
K.313; 2 in D major, K.314; Andante in
C major for flute and orchestra, K.315.

> ** (*) DGG 2530 344. Karlheinz Zöller (flute), English Chamber Orchestra, Bernhard Klee.
> (B) ** (*) Classics for Pleasure CFP 40072. Richard Adeney (flute), English Chamber Orchestra, Raymond Leppard.
> (M) ** HMV SXLP 30150. Elaine Shaffer (flute), Philharmonia Orchestra, Efrem Kurtz.

Karlheinz Zöller is a superb flautist. K.313 is a little cool, but is played most elegantly, with pure tone and unmannered phrasing. The charming minuet finale is poised and graceful. The performance of K.314 is more relaxed and smiling, and the *Andante*, K.315, is admirably flexible. Bernhard Klee provides adept accompaniments. Herr Zöller does favour the use of comparatively extended cadenzas whenever Mozart has provided space for them, and one wonders whether they will not seem too much of a good thing on repetition. However, the recording is good and for this reason the disc is preferable to the Classics for Pleasure issue.

Richard Adeney's are fine performances too, matched by Leppard's crisply turned accompaniments. The only snag is the recording, which, although admirably clear, is lacking in inner warmth and bloom: the orchestral strings are not very attractively caught by the microphones. But this disc is excellent value. Shaffer's performances are not strong in personality and can only be given a qualified recommendation. The recording of the HMV disc is acceptable rather than distinguished.

(i) *Flute concerto No. 1 in G major, K.313;* (ii) *Flute and harp concerto in C major, K.299.*

** HMV ASD 2993. (i) Andreas Blau (flute); (ii) James Galway (flute), Fritz Helmis (harp); both with Berlin Philharmonic Orchestra, Herbert von Karajan.

Despite the superb artistry of James Galway and Fritz Helmis and the refined and highly polished response of the Berlin Philharmonic, this well recorded performance does not wholly escape the blandness that afflicts Karajan's set of the wind concertos. Of course there are many details to enjoy and admire, and the HMV engineers produce a warm, well-detailed sound picture. Andreas Blau's account of the *Flute concerto* too is impeccably played and superbly accompanied, but it has less freshness and sparkle than its competitors.

(i) *Flute concerto No. 1 in G major, K.313;* (ii) *Oboe concerto in C major, K.314b.*

*** Philips 6500 379. (i) Claude Monteux (flute); (ii) Neil Black (oboe); both with Academy of St Martin-in-the-Fields, Neville Marriner.

Exquisite playing in both works from soloists and orchestra alike. The only reservation that must be made concerns the excessive prominence of the soloists, which detracts from the realism of the overall sound. In every other respect the disc is highly recommendable.

Readers might also like to be reminded

that Claude Monteux's delightfully sunny performance of the *Second Flute concerto* (another version of the *Oboe concerto* above) is available on Decca Ace of Diamonds SDD 427. This is part of a concert, including music of Bach and Gluck, and the disc is discussed in our *Treasury* volume (under its original full-priced SXL catalogue number).

Flute and harp concerto in C major, K.299.

(M) ***** DGG** Privilege 135093. Nicanor Zabaleta (harp), Karlheinz Zöller (flute), Berlin Philharmonic Orchestra, Ernst Märzendorfer – HANDEL and WAGENSEIL: *Harp concertos.***

*** DGG SLPM 138853 (same recording as above) – REINECKE: *Harp concerto.****

The outer movements of this performance have an attractive rhythmic buoyancy. The flautist is a most sensitive player and his phrasing is a constant pleasure, while Zabaleta's poise and sense of line knits the overall texture of the solo-duet together most convincingly. Märzendorfer conducts with warmth yet with a firm overall control. In short, with most pleasing recorded sound, this is highly successful.

(i) *Flute and harp concerto in C major, K.299;* (ii) *Adagio in C major for glass harmonica, K. 617a;* (iii) *Fantasia for mechanical organ in F minor, K.608.*

(B) **** (*) Turnabout** TV 34087S. (i) Jean Patéro (flute), Helga Storck (harp), Württemberg Chamber Orchestra, Joerg Faerber; (ii) Bruno Hoffman (glass harmonica); (iii) Helmuth Rilling (organ).

Here is another attractive performance and recording of the *Flute and hard concerto*, achieving a gossamer delicacy of texture. The quality of the Turnabout recording is not quite as substantial as some more recent recordings, but it is still excellent, and the couplings here are imaginative. First we have the *Fantasia* Mozart wrote for a mechanical organ, played on an instrument able to produce convincing registrations for such a piquant work. The last piece is really played on the glass harmonica, which has a unique and memorable delicacy of timbre.

(i) *Flute and harp concerto in C major, K.299. Sinfonia concertante for oboe, clarinet, horn and bassoon in E flat major, K.297b.*
    *** Philips 6500 380. Academy of St Martin-in-the-Fields, Neville Marriner, (i) with Claude Monteux (flute), Osian Ellis (harp).

Delightful performances, but Osian Ellis and Claude Monteux play on jumbo-sized instruments and the flautist's intake of breath is all too audible. Karlheinz Zöller and Nicanor Zabaleta (see above) are much better balanced, and their performance is also a distinguished one; however, they use Reinecke's cadenza, which may not be to all tastes, and the splendid wind *Sinfonia concertante* gives this disc a strong advantage. Marriner's account of this latter work is also handicapped by larger-than-life soloists but the performance is so songful and elegant that it carries all before it.

Harpsichord concertos, K.107, Nos. 1 in D major; 2 in G major; 3 in E flat major.
    (B) * (*) Turnabout TV 34312S. Martin Galling (harpsichord), Stuttgart Soloists.

The three concertos recorded here are transcriptions by the young Mozart of J. C. Bach's Op. 5 *Piano sonatas*. The only music here composed by Mozart himself is the cadenzas for the *D major*

Concerto, but the young musician shows himself a dab hand at organizing the simple orchestrations. The music itself is extrovert and jolly, and one can see how it would appeal to the child composer. The playing here is spontaneous enough and the recording acceptable, though the upper register shows the age of the original.

Horn concertos Nos. 1 in D major, K.412; 2 in E flat major, K.417; 3 in E flat major, K.447; 4 in E flat major, K.495:

Horn concertos Nos. 1–4.
    *** DGG SLPM 139038. Gerd Seifert (horn), Berlin Philharmonic Orchestra, Herbert von Karajan.
    *** Telefunken SAWT 9627. Hermann Baumann (natural handhorn), Vienna Concentus Musicus, Nikolaus Harnoncourt.
    (B) *** Classics for Pleasure CFP 148. James Brown (horn), Virtuosi of London, Arthur Davison.

Horn concertos Nos. 1–4; Fragment of Horn concerto No. 5 in E major, K.App.98a.
    (M) *** Decca Ace of Diamonds SDD 364. Barry Tuckwell (horn), London Symphony Orchestra, Peter Maag.

Horn concertos Nos. 1–4; Concert rondo for horn and orchestra in E flat major, K.371 (ed. Civil).
    *** Philips 6500 325. Alan Civil (horn), Academy of St Martin-in-the-Fields, Neville Marriner.

Horn concertos Nos. 1–4; Fragment of Horn concerto No. 5 in E major, K.App.98a; Concert rondo in E flat major, K.371.
    *** HMV ASD 2780. Barry Tuckwell (horn), Academy of St Martin-in-the Fields, Neville Marriner.

All recordings of the Mozart *Horn concertos* stand to be judged by the set recorded by Dennis Brain in mono and now available in a highly successful stereo transcription (ASD 1140). Boyd Neel once said that Brain, besides being a superb horn player, was also the finest Mozartian of his generation. Certainly his accounts of these marvellous concertos have a unique combination of poetry and exuberance of spirit. Barry Tuckwell was the first 'natural successor' to the Brain mantle. His easy technique, smooth, warm tone and obvious musicianship command attention and give immediate pleasure. His actual tone is broader than that of Brain and he spreads his phrases widely. His HMV disc conveniently collects together all Mozart's concertante music for horn and orchestra. The *Fragment in E major* ends where Mozart left it at bar 91. It provides a rather inconclusive close to side one, rather after the manner of some performances of Bach's *Art of fugue*. Throughout the playing is vigorous, rich in phrase, with beautifully managed accompaniments. The recording too is warm and the quality does not appear to suffer from cramming a good deal of music on to each side. This is a very enjoyable disc, but the approach is straightforward, rather than providing special moments of magic or new illumination of the three more famous concertos. Indeed Tuckwell's robust style here seems to suit No. 1 best of all.

On the whole Tuckwell's earlier collection on Decca is to be preferred. Here Peter Maag's accompaniments are admirably crisp as well as elegant, giving an attractive buoyancy to the orchestra. With first-rate Decca sound, admirably fresh and detailed, this is highly enjoyable.

The Philips disc is Alan Civil's third recording of the Mozart concertos. His previous records (with Klemperer on Columbia and Kempe on World Record Club) are deleted. This new set is highly

enjoyable, but the balance has the effect of making the horn sound somewhat larger than life, and on most counts (in spite of Marriner's elegant accompaniment) the earlier World Records disc was to be preferred.

Gerd Seifert has been principal horn of the Berlin Philharmonic since 1964, and his warm, rich tone is familiar on many records. His approach to the Mozart concertos has an attractive, simple eloquence based on the absolute technical mastery of his difficult instrument. His phrasing and control of light and shade give particular pleasure and he shows here a special feeling for Mozart's lyrical flow, so that the slow movement of the *Second Concerto* and the first movement of the *Third* are memorable. His nimbleness brings an effective lightness to the gay rondos of all three works, the agility of his tongue giving the production of the notes themselves a Mozartian delicacy. Yet there is no lack of robust quality to the music-making, as is shown in the rondo of the *First Concerto*. As a soloist Seifert has slightly less personality than some players, but the strong directing force of Karajan's beautifully polished accompaniments compensates. A most enjoyable disc.

On Classics for Pleasure James Brown's performances have plenty of life and spirit and are enjoyably spontaneous. Arthur Davison's contribution is a major one. Using a small group of genuine Mozartian dimensions, he achieves crisply sprung accompaniments and he is always attentive to the soloist's style. This is straightforward and musical.

Like Hubert Crüts, who plays No. 3 with the Collegium Aureum (coupled to the *Clarinet concerto*), Hermann Baumann, on Telefunken uses the original hand-horn, without valves, for which the concertos were written. This implies at least some alteration in timbre, as certain notes have to be 'stopped', with the hand in the bell of the instrument, if they are to be in tune. But Herr Baumann is not in

the least intimidated by this problem: he
plays throughout with consummate tonal
smoothness and a totally relaxed manner.
He only lets the listener hear the stopped
effect when he decides that the tonal
change can be put to good artistic effect,
as for instance in the rondo of No. 2 or
his own cadenza for No. 3. Here also he
uses horn chords (where several notes are
produced simultaneously by resonating
the instrument's harmonics) but as a
complement to the music rather than as a
gimmick. The slow movement of No. 3
has one of Mozart's richest melodies and
its touch of chromaticism is managed
with superb flexibility and smoothness, so
that one can only wonder at Baumann's
artistry and skill. In short these are
remarkably satisfying performances, by
any standards. Baumann's execution in
the gay rondos is a delight and his tone is
particularly characterful. It is splendid to
have such a successful representation of
the horn sound that Mozart would have
recognized, and which indeed all nineteenth-century composers would have
expected.

Oboe concerto in C major, K.314b.
  *** Philips 6500 174. Heinz Holliger
  (oboe), New Philharmonia Orchestra, Edo de Waart – R.STRAUSS:
  Oboe concerto.** (*)

Holliger's reputation goes from
strength to strength. This is his second
version of Mozart's charming *Oboe concerto*, and it is even more masterly, more
refined than the DGG one made in
Munich and now deleted. The coupling
is imaginative, the most delectable of
twentieth-century oboe concertos.

Piano Concertos

Piano concertos Nos. 1–27 (complete
recording).
  (B) *** DGG 2720 030 (12 discs).

Géza Anda (piano), Camerata
Academica of the Salzburg Mozarteum.

At its current price this is an outstanding bargain. Anda's performances are
beautifully poised and have excellent
feeling for style. The recordings do not
quite match those of Barenboim in
clarity or definition but they are well
balanced, and given the rough-and-ready
justice involved in preferring one complete set to another, readers could not do
better than this set even if there are
individual instances where newer versions
might be preferred.

*Piano concertos Nos. 1 in F major,
K.37; 2 in B flat major, K.39; 3 in D
major, K.40; 4 in G major, K.41.*
  (M) *** DGG Privilege 2538 261.
  Géza Anda (piano), Camerata
  Academica of the Salzburg Moz-
  arteum.
  (B) ** Turnabout TV 34260S. Martin
  Galling (piano), Stuttgart Soloists,
  Günter Wich.

Mozart composed these concertos in
Salzburg at the tender age of eleven. He
apparently borrowed much of the music
from three minor contemporaries, Johan
Schobert, Leontzi Honnauer, and Hermann Raupach (the originals were discovered in 1908). Even so, if none of the
works is a masterpiece, Mozart somehow put an overriding stamp of personality on the music which is not
without interest. One of the more striking
movements is the *Andante* of K.37
(probably based on Schobert), with its
'Scottish snap' rhythmic feature, which
obviously caught the young composer's
fancy. Galling's performances have not
quite the authority and style of Anda's,
taken from his complete set, but they are
done with plenty of rhythmic point and
they are certainly not dull. The recording
of the orchestra glares too brightly but

607

MOZART

responds to the controls. However, Anda's very well recorded disc is the one to have.

Piano concertos Nos. 5 in D major, K.175; 9 in E flat major, K.271.
  *** HMV ASD 2484. Daniel Barenboim (piano), English Chamber Orchestra.
  (B) *** Turnabout TV 34135S. Peter Frankl (piano), Vienna Volksoper Orchestra, Georg Fischer.

Barenboim's record of K.175 is delightful and played with great spirit. Some may find that his version of K.271 displays too great an awareness of refinements of tone and dynamics that are strictly speaking anachronistic. Faced with such masterly pianism, however, and such alert and musical direction few are likely to grumble. The most serious reservation concerns the minuet of the last movement, which is far too measured. On balance Ashkenazy's sparkling account on Decca (see below) remains the finest in the current catalogue and it is better recorded; but those who want the Barenboim coupling can rest assured that this is a distinguished record.

Peter Frankl has given us fine Mozart-playing on Turnabout before, but this splendid account of K.271 is outstanding among all bargain Mozart concerto performances. As a work K.175 is less remarkable, but again the life and style of the playing give immense pleasure, particularly in the finale. The recording, generally excellent in K.271, is slightly drier here.

Piano concertos Nos. 6 in B flat major, K.238; 8 in C major, K.246.
  (B) ** Turnabout TV 34326S. Martin Galling (piano), Philharmonia Hungarica, Othmar Maga.

These two concertos have much in common. It is very likely that they were written for the harpsichord. They are precise in manner, small in scale. Martin Galling plays them freshly, but in a formal way, and he catches their ingenuous classicism rather well. In the slow movements the playing is not stiff, but Galling is careful not to over-romanticize the texture. The finales are sprightly but not too fast. With bright recording this is an agreeable coupling.

Piano concertos Nos. 6 in B flat major, K.238; 20 in D minor, K.466.
  ** (*) Decca SXL 6353. Vladimir Ashkenazy (piano), London Symphony Orchestra, Hans Schmidt-Isserstedt.

An eloquent performance of a charming work, beautifully accompanied, and an altogether worthy companion to Ashkenazy's other disc of early Mozart concertos. Unfortunately the great *D minor Concerto* is too well regulated in emotional temperature and is a little lacking in spontaneity and sparkle. The recording is excellent.

Piano concertos Nos. 6 in B flat major, K.238; 22 in E flat major, K.482.
  ** (*) DGG SLPM 138824. Géza Anda (piano), Camerata Academica of the Salzburg Mozarteum.

These are characteristically rewarding Anda performances, outstandingly well recorded. There is perhaps a certain rhythmic stiffness in the outer movements of K.482 (one does not need to feel the beat quite so firmly), but the elegant classicism of the slow movement is balanced by a finale of captivating spontaneity. K.382 is hardly less stylish, and the readings, if a trifle unsmiling, are both well up to the high standard of this series.

Piano concertos Nos. 6 in B flat major, K.238; 26 in D major (Coronation), K.537.

*** HMV ASD 3032. Daniel Barenboim (piano), English Chamber Orchestra.

Excellent playing from Barenboim, particularly in the *Coronation concerto*, makes this a most desirable issue. Along with Casadesus this must be accounted one of the most successful versions of K.537.

Piano concertos Nos. 8 in C major, K.246; 9 in E flat major, K.271; Rondo No. 1 in A major (for piano and orchestra), *K.386.*
  ⊛ *** Decca SXL 6259. Vladimir Ashkenazy (piano), London Symphony Orchestra, Istvan Kertesz.

Magnificent performances and recording. Ashkenazy has the requisite sparkle, humanity and command of keyboard tone, and his readings can only be called inspired. Both concertos are underrepresented in the catalogue, but with playing of this order further duplication is rendered unnecessary. Ashkenazy is well supported by the LSO under Kertesz, and the recording is superb.

Piano concertos Nos. 8 in C major, K.246; 25 in C major, K.503.
  *** HMV ASD 3033. Daniel Barenboim (piano), English Chamber Orchestra.
  ** DGG SLPM 139384. Géza Anda (piano), Camerata Academica of the Salzburg Mozarteum.

Barenboim's account of K.503 is far less Beethovenian than the rather heavyhanded reading he recorded earlier with Klemperer. This has more inner life and vitality even though it is not wholly free from the expressive underlining in which this artist occasionally indulges. The recording is first-class; it has radiance, clarity of texture and well-defined detail. Anda's tempi in the outer movements

of K.503 are brisker than Brendel's and detail registers less impressively. Indeed in the finale Anda sounds a trifle rushed, whereas Brendel's more leisurely approach enables him to pay greater attention to refinement of phrasing. Anda's piano tends to spread between the two speakers (RH from far right and LH from the opposite channel), but reservations notwithstanding, his is a good performance. Brendel on Turnabout remains amazingly good in the bargain category; Barenboim and Stephen Bishop are to be preferred at full price.

Piano concertos Nos. 8 in C major, K.246; 26 in D major (Coronation), K.537.
  * (**) BASF BAC 3003. Joerg Demus (Hammerflügel fortepiano, made by Schantz, Vienna, 1790), Collegium Aureum (using original instruments).

This is a remarkable disc, but one to be approached with caution. The fortepiano Joerg Demus uses is in excellent mechanical shape, and in tune, and it undoubtedly gives a true picture of the instrument Mozart would have known. Its tone is clearly etched but twangy, and it takes at least one playing of both sides of this record to adjust to it. In many ways it suits a work like K.246, for Demus plays it with understanding and his approach to the music is never rigid. However, in a concerto like K.537, which can be so richly expressive on a modern concert grand, it is very difficult to adjust to this sound with its faint hints of the barrel-organ. The orchestra, recorded in a flatteringly warm acoustic, sounds very beautiful, and this serves to contrast the image of the fortepiano the more strikingly. Certainly there is no doubt about the perception of Demus's playing nor its authenticity.

Piano concertos Nos. 9 in E flat major, K.271; 14 in E flat major, K.449.

(M) *** Vanguard HM 30 SD. Alfred Brendel (piano), I Solisti di Zagreb, Antonio Janigro.

Brendel's performance of No. 9 is quite outstanding, elegant and beautifully precise. The classical-sized orchestra is just right, and the neat, stylish string playing matches the soloist. Both soloist and conductor are sensitive to the gentle melancholy of the slow movement, and in the contrasting middle section of the finale Brendel's tonal nuance is beautifully shaded. The recording is good. The performance of K.449 is also first-rate, with a memorably vivacious finale. Altogether this is an outstanding issue.

Piano concertos Nos. 11 in F major, K.413; 15 in B flat major, K.450.
   *** DGG SLPM 139393. Géza Anda (piano), Camerata Academica of the Salzburg Mozarteum.
   (B) ** Turnabout TV 34027S. Peter Frankl (piano), Württemberg Chamber Orchestra, Joerg Faerber.

Anda gives an exemplary account of both concertos, the great K.450 and the lesser-known K.413. The latter has a ravishing slow movement, and Anda gives a most poetic account of it. DGG provide excellent quality and collectors of the series need have no fears. Peter Frankl too gives sensitive and assured accounts of both works, and he plays the slow movement of the *F major Concerto* beautifully. The Württemberg Orchestra provide excellent accompaniments, and the recording of both piano and orchestra is pleasingly full.

Piano concertos Nos. 11 in F major, K.413; 16 in D major, K.451.
   *** HMV ASD 2999. Daniel Barenboim (piano), English Chamber Orchestra.

Barenboim's performances are even more persuasive than those in Géza Anda's cycle of the concertos, not averse to idiosyncrasy, full of charm and sparkle. K.451 is particularly enjoyable, with a brisk, jaunty account of the first movement, a flowing, expressive slow movement and an exuberant finale. Good recording.

Piano concertos Nos. 11 in F major, K.413; 24 in C minor, K.491.
   (M) ** Philips Universo 6580 069. Ingrid Haebler (piano), London Symphony Orchestra, Colin Davis.

Within her well-demarcated limits Miss Haebler plays with great pianistic delicacy, but she does take a distinctly non-dramatic, non-operatic view of Mozart. She excludes perhaps too much, but within the chosen boundaries of sensibility she explores with the utmost skill. Her account of K.413 is beautifully alert, although the slow movement is a little sluggish: it first impresses with its poetry but eventually the lack of forward movement produces a slightly wilting effect. In the *C minor Concerto* Miss Haebler plays with the clarity of articulation and sense of poise that one has come to take for granted from her, but she tends to scale down the dark sense of passion in this work, though Colin Davis's strong and virile accompaniment prevents prettification. The recording, as in all these Philips Mozart concertos, is admirably balanced and clearly detailed. At the price, the record offers good value, but there are finer accounts of K.491 to be had: Casadesus on CBS Classics is one, and at full price Kempff, Anda and Curzon are not to be passed over lightly.

Piano concertos Nos. 12 in A major, K.414; 17 in G major, K.453.
   ** (*) Philips 6500 140. Alfred Brendel (piano), Academy of St Martin-in-the-Fields, Neville Marriner.

Brendel is a thoughtful Mozartian, and this coupling will not disappoint his admirers. Even so, in K.453 he fails to match the high spirits of André Previn in the outer movements or his hushed intensity in the slow movement; and in the little A major, K.414, Brendel sounds a little sober in comparison with, say, Barenboim. Good recording.

Piano concertos Nos. 12 in A major, K.414; 19 in F major, K.459.
*** HMV ASD 2956. Daniel Barenboim (piano), English Chamber Orchestra.

There is something a little wild in Barenboim's recordings of Mozart piano concertos, but the urgency of communication is hard to resist. K.414 is presented with all his usual character and flair, but it is K.459 with its *Figaro* overtones which prompts the more remarkable performance, brisk in its march rhythms in the first movement, tender in the Susanna-like sweetness of the *Andante*, and strong and resilient in the finale with its great fugal tutti. Good recording.

Piano concertos Nos. 12 in A major, K.414; 21 in C major, K.467.
** Decca SXL 6698. Radu Lupu (piano), English Chamber Orchestra, Uri Segal.

There is much that is beautiful here, including really lovely sounds from the orchestra, and hushed playing from Radu Lupu in the slow movements of both concertos. The music-making is not without life and sensibility, yet with all these advantages, in the last resort the performances lack style.

Piano concertos Nos. 12 in A major, K.414; 26 in D major (Coronation), K.537.

** DGG SLPM 139113. Géza Anda (piano), Camerata Academica of the Salzburg Mozarteum.

Having the greatest admiration for Géza Anda as a Mozartian of the first order, one must confess a slight sense of disappointment at this account of the *Coronation*, an under-rated masterpiece among the canon. Anda's performance lacks the magisterial quality that Casadesus brings to it on his CBS record. There is a slightly routine feeling about the accompaniment in both concertos, and although the playing is accomplished one did not find oneself enjoying it as much as expected. The recording is good.

Piano concertos Nos. 12 in A major, K.414; 27 in B flat major, K.595.
*** BASF BAC 3066. Joerg Demus (fortepiano), Collegium Aureum (using original instruments).

Hearing this performance underlines the inappropriateness of readings such as Barenboim's K.595, beautiful though it is in its way, for the sensibility is at variance with the period. Demus plays a fortepiano of about 1785, and the Collegium Aureum, using period instruments and small forces, accompany. The sound takes a little getting used to but the expressive power of the instrument is quite remarkable. One wonders whether the fortepiano will oust the modern grand from performances of Mozart in much the same way as the harpsichord has ousted it from Bach in the last two or three decades! (Let us hope not.) In any event these performances fall into a special category, and all libraries should have them as a means of correcting the view of Mozart so often taken for granted by pianists.

(i) *Piano concerto No. 13 in C major K.415. Piano sonata No. 2 in F major,*

611

K.280; 12 Variations on 'Ah, vous dirai-je, maman', K.265.

(M) ** DGG Privilege 2538 139. Clara Haskil (piano), (i) with Lucerne Festival Strings, Rudolf Baumgartner.

Baumgartner provides an accompaniment without wind, but Clara Haskil gives a performance of considerable charm. Some might feel that the couplings are relatively unsubstantial, but they are done stylishly and the *Variations* are delightful. Good but not outstanding recording.

Piano concertos Nos. 13 in C major, K.415; 17 in G major, K.453.

** (*) HMV ASD 2357. Daniel Barenboim (piano), English Chamber Orchestra.

The *C major Concerto* is given one of the finest performances of Barenboim's series. It is full of life, imaginatively phrased, sparkling, thoroughly musical and beautifully shaped. The orchestral playing is of the highest order and the recording excellent. The *G major Concerto* has similar virtues, but will be spoiled for some by the unusually brisk tempo Barenboim adopts for the first movement. In some ways he recalls the pre-war Fischer Mozart concerto recordings, but comparison here is not to Barenboim's advantage, for Fischer succeeds in maintaining forward movement without loss of poise or adopting too fast a tempo. Nonetheless, this is a fine record and worth acquiring for the sake of the *C major Concerto* alone.

Piano concertos Nos. 13 in C major, K.415; 19 in F major, K.459.

** (*) DGG SLPM 139319. Géza Anda (piano), Camerata Academica of the Salzburg Mozarteum.

As always, Géza Anda gives deft and sparkling accounts of these concertos and secures vital and affectionate phrasing from the Salzburg Mozarteum orchestra. But the piano sound is not always clearly focused, and in any event, good though these readings are, they must yield to Brendel in K.459 and Barenboim and Clara Haskil in K.415. However, those investing in this coupling will still find much to admire.

Piano concerto No. 14 in E flat major, K.449.

(M) * (*) Philips Universo 6580 086. Veronica Jochum von Moltke (piano), Bamberg Symphony Orchestra, Eugen Jochum – BEETHOVEN: *Piano concerto No. 1.***

Veronica Jochum von Moltke, daughter of the conductor, is rather a rugged Mozartian, but her fresh and urgent performance makes an unexpected and agreeable coupling for the Beethoven *First Concerto*. Good recording and excellent accompaniment.

Piano concertos Nos. 14 in E flat major, K.449; 15 in E flat major, K.450.

*** HMV ASD 2434. Daniel Barenboim (piano), English Chamber Orchestra.

This is one of the most successful records in Barenboim's cycle. The playing is spontaneous and smiling, while the orchestra respond with genuine vitality and sparkle. Both concertos are well recorded, and readers wanting this coupling can invest in this issue with confidence.

Piano concertos (i) *No. 14 in E flat major, K.449;* (ii) *No. 18 in B flat major, K.456.*

(B) ** Turnabout TV 34503S. Walter Klien (piano), with (i) Vienna Pro

Musica Orchestra, Paul Angerer, (ii) Mainz Chamber Orchestra, Günter Kehr.

What a good Mozartian Walter Klien is! The orchestral playing is good, and the sound, though not distinguished, is perfectly acceptable, particularly at so modest a price. Both these readings can be recommended, for Klien is a superb stylist, even if the dated sound quality must perforce marginally diminish the strength of the recommendation.

Piano concertos Nos. 14 in E flat major, K.449; 24 in C minor, K.491.
   ** (*) DGG SLPM 139196. Géza Anda (piano), Camerata Academica of the Salzburg Mozarteum.

Anda's Mozart is as sparkling and polished as one could wish for, and yet there is no sense that the tragic or prophetic overtones in the *C minor* are lost sight of. Perhaps the final touch of individuality and depth that marks a great interpretation are missing, but the recording has warmth and clarity and this is a most enjoyable disc. A fairly high volume setting is called for to achieve a properly vivid effect.

Piano concerto No. 15 in B flat major, K.450.
   * (**) Decca SET 332. Leonard Bernstein (piano), Vienna Philharmonic Orchestra – *Symphony No. 36.* (**)

Even more than in the symphony with which it is coupled, the concerto conveys the feeling of a conductor enjoying himself on holiday. Bernstein's piano playing may not in every detail be as poised as that of full-time virtuoso pianists, but every note communicates vividly. So much so that in the slow movement he even manages to make his dual tempo convincing – faster for the tuttis than for the more romantic solos. The finale is

taken surprisingly slowly, but with such individuality, Bernstein brings it off. Even so, for some ears the romantic overtones and *rubato* will sound unacceptably out of key with Mozartian sensibility, and in spite of alert orchestral playing and good recording this disc will not be to all tastes.

Piano concertos Nos. 15 in B flat major, K.450; 17 in G major, K.453.
   (M) *** CBS Classics 61348. Robert Casadesus (piano), Cleveland Orchestra, George Szell.

The combination of Casadesus and Szell – a meeting of sympathetic opposites, it has often seemed – makes for fascinating results in Mozart. Both these interpretations, cool but dramatic, and not without sparkle and charm, are strongly recommendable on CBS's midprice label. Sharp recording.

Piano concertos (i) No. 16 in D major, K.451; (ii) No. 23 in A major, K.488.
   ** DGG SLPM 138870. Géza Anda (piano), Camerata Academica of Salzburg Mozarteum.
   (B) ** Turnabout TV 34286S. Walter Klien (piano), Vienna Volksoper Orchestra, (i) Paul Angerer, (ii) Peter Maag.

Characteristically well-made performances from Anda, who is impressive in K.451 but rather unsmiling in the lovely *A major Concerto*. The DGG sound is excellent, but there are several finer versions of K.488. That concerto has always been poorly represented on bargain labels, so Klien's very sympathetic performance is doubly welcome. The approach is essentially simple, but the lyrical flow is well sustained by both soloist and orchestra, and the beauty of the slow movement gives much pleasure. The sound too is excellent. The coupling is rather less successful. The recording of the orchestra here is very forward and communicates a touch of aggressiveness. Angerer is not so stylish a Mozartian as Maag, but both he and Klien are not helped by the recording, which also spreads the piano image unrealistically. Yet one's ear adjusts, and the disc is worth having for K.488 alone.

Piano concertos (i) *No. 17 in G major, K.453;* (ii) *No. 19 in F major, K.459.*

(B) ** Turnabout TV 34080S. Alfred Brendel (piano), Vienna Volksoper Orchestra, (i) Paul Angerer, (ii) Wilfried Boettcher.

Brendel is a reliable Mozartian, and this coupling is helped by a vivacious orchestral contribution. In No. 17 the recording is on the thin side in the orchestra, but at Brendel's entry one forgets this slight fault. His phrasing of the second subject of the first movement and throughout the *Andante* is a constant source of pleasure, whereas both soloist and orchestra share in the high spirits of the finale. In No. 19 the sound is immediately fuller and richer, generally very satisfying, with excellent quality and a good balance for the soloist. Again the genial touch which soloist and orchestra show in the shaping of the melodic line is immediately felt from the opening.

Piano concertos Nos. (i) *17 in G major, K.453; 20 in D minor, K.466; 21 in C major, K.467; 23 in A major, K.488;* (ii) *24 in C minor, K.491. Rondo in A minor (piano solo), K.511.*

(M) ** (*) RCA SER 5716/8. Artur Rubinstein (piano), RCA Victor Symphony Orchestra, cond. (i) Alfred Wallenstein, (ii) Josef Krips.

Rubinstein's performances of these favourite concertos, reissued in a box at medium price, should find a ready welcome from most Mozartians. Their style

could not be further removed from the current trend to classicism, using the fortepiano. Here the orchestra is rich, even plushy, and some might feel an occasional lack of sparkle in the outer movements in consequence. But RCA were right not to try and artificially brighten the sound. Rubinstein has seldom been caught so sympathetically by the microphones. In each concerto the slow movement is the kernel of the interpretation, and Rubinstein's playing is meltingly lovely, notably in the three middle concertos (which are the finest accounts of the set), where the hushed orchestral playing catches the intensity of the pianist's inspiration. The opening of the first movement of No. 20 is less than ideally clear (which reduces the dramatic impact), but generally one adjusts to the silky smoothness of the sound, and much of the music-making here is richly rewarding.

Piano concertos Nos. 17 in G major, K.453; 21 in C major, K.467.

** DGG SLPM 138783. Géza Anda (piano), Camerata Academica of the Salzburg Mozarteum.

In the *G major* Anda, who is soloist and conductor, errs a little on the side of heaviness of style. But the Salzburg performance has strength and poetry, while the DGG recording is excellent both in balance and clarity. Anda continues with a successful performance of K.467, notable for a beautifully poised orchestral introduction to the slow movement. One notices a certain rhythmic rigidity, and a lighter touch in the finale would have been acceptable, but on the whole this is a satisfying reading, very well recorded.

Piano concertos Nos. 17 in G major, K.453; 24 in C minor, K.491.

*** HMV ASD 2951. André Previn (piano), London Symphony Orchestra, Sir Adrian Boult.

André Previn is a stylish Mozartian at the keyboard, presenting a sparkling and resilient account of K.453 and a somewhat cooler one of the great *C minor*. In K.491 Boult seems to discipline the performance a degree too much (one suspects that Previn alone would have produced more sparkle), but K.453 is as fine a version as has yet been put on disc, beautifully recorded.

Piano concertos Nos. 17 in G major, K.453; 26 in D major (Coronation), K.537.
> (M) ** Philips Universo 6580 043. Ingrid Haebler (piano), London Symphony Orchestra, Witold Rowicki.

In the *G major Concerto*, it is difficult not to admire Ingrid Haebler's elegant cool style and her meticulously clean articulation, even if one regrets a certain want of temperament and intensity. One can do better at full price (Barenboim or Brendel), and at mid-price Casadesus is a strong competitor; all three artists encompass a greater range of feeling and colour than Ingrid Haebler. Rowicki and the LSO give excellent support and the engineers produce a warm, spacious sound in which detail tells without any loss of natural perspective. Whatever reservations one may have, there is no denying that Miss Haebler plays lovingly and with great poetry. This coupling of the *Coronation concerto* is not to be confused with the earlier version she made with Colin Davis and the same orchestra (SGL 5813). Her account of the first movement is straightforward and dignified but in the main theme of the slow movement she exaggerates staccato markings and even plays the top A of the theme staccato, which seems to trivialize it. (Her earlier version is more judiciously pedalled.) Casadesus pedals it throughout and underlines its shape, lending it an almost legato character, while Anda steers a middle course. Despite the excellent balance, with admirably clean detail, this version is not to be preferred to the less well-recorded Casadesus/Szell reading, also at mid-price, let alone to Anda or Barenboim.

Piano concertos Nos. 18 in B flat major, K.456; 20 in D minor, K.466.
> ** (*) DGG SLPM 138917. Géza Anda (piano), Camerata Academica of the Salzburg Mozarteum.

The K.456 concerto admirably suits this chamber style of performance, the soloist directing from the keyboard, but in the first movement of K.466 a conductor is clearly needed. Here the special timbre for which this work is famous simply becomes *sotto voce* playing rather than a subtle emotional colouring of the music. But judged as a chamber performance, which is what it is, this is highly enjoyable. In the slow movement, if the phrasing of the famous main theme is not as expressive as one might ideally ask, the episodes are full of character (both in the orchestra and in the solo part) and the contrasts are strikingly made. In the finale too there is the same buoyancy from the strings which makes the *B flat Concerto* so memorable, and the woodwind solos are delectable. The recording is well up to DGG standard.

Piano concertos Nos. 18 in B flat major, K.456; 24 in C minor, K.491.
> ** (*) HMV ASD 2887. Daniel Barenboim (piano), English Chamber Orchestra.

Barenboim's account of K.456 is among the most sparkling of his cycle, full of imaginative touches which have one chuckling with delight. K.491 brings a more controversial performance; the very first entry of the piano shows to what degree Barenboim wants to make it a romantic work. His conviction is unfail-

615

ing, but some may find the first two movements too heavy for their taste, while the finale is compensatingly fast and hectic. Good recording.

Piano concertos Nos. 19 in F major, K.459; 20 in D minor, K.466.

(M) *** CBS Classics 61136. Rudolf Serkin (piano), Columbia Symphony Orchestra, George Szell.

A superb coupling of two of Mozart's greatest concertos in performances that match the music's greatness. There is no charm in Serkin's approach to Mozart, and in his essential seriousness he is supported by Szell. But the subtle refinement of the orchestra goes hand in hand with the natural spontaneous mastery of Serkin, who for all his failure to ingratiate himself with the listener grips the attention infallibly. In the searchingly romantic *D minor Concerto* Serkin aptly uses the Beethoven cadenzas (no Mozart ones surviving). The *F major Concerto*, equally strong in the contrapuntal complexities of the finale, has Mozart's own cadenzas. Among Mozart concerto records there is no finer bargain in the catalogue.

Piano concertos Nos. 19 in F major, K.459; 23 in A major, K.488.

*** Philips 6500 283. Alfred Brendel (piano), Academy of St Martin-in-the-Fields, Neville Marriner.

Brendel's reputation as a Mozart interpreter of the first order is more than vindicated by this disc, his first Mozart concerto record for Philips. The first movement of K.459 is played at a slightly quicker tempo than usual, but the performance sparkles throughout, and the playing of the Academy of St Martin-in-the-Fields could hardly be improved upon. The slow movement is quite magical, and the finale again has great zest and brilliance. Brendel's account of K.488 is arguably among the best in the catalogue. It is more spontaneous in feel-

ing than Curzon's (masterly though that is), in better taste than Barenboim's (he indulges in some marvellously sensuous but out-of-style phrasing and rushes the finale), and is impeccably played. The decoration of the solo part in the slow movement is never obtrusive, always in style, and the playing exhibits throughout a sensibility that is at one with the composer's world. The recording is a fine one, with truthful balance and wide range. A self-recommending disc.

Piano concertos Nos. 20 in D minor, K.466; 21 in C major, K.467.

** RCA LRL 1 5020. Géza Anda (piano), Vienna Symphony Orchestra.

There seems little real sense in this issue, good though it is, since Anda has already recorded a complete Mozart cycle for DGG. There is not all that much difference between the two recordings – at least not enough to justify the exercise – and these two performances do not add greatly to what he has said before.

Piano concertos Nos. 20 in D minor, K.466; 23 in A major, K.488.

(B) *** Philips 6833 119. Alfred Brendel (piano), Academy of St Martin-in-the-Fields, Neville Marriner.

*** HMV ASD 2318. Daniel Barenboim (piano), English Chamber Orchestra.

(M) ** HMV SXLP 30148. Annie Fischer (piano), Philharmonia Orchestra, Sir Adrian Boult.

(M) ** Philips Universo 6580 008. Ingrid Haebler (piano), London Symphony Orchestra, Alceo Galliera (K.466) or Witold Rowicki (K.488).

As a sampler disc for Brendel's projected cycle this could hardly be more enticing, coupling what always used to be regarded as the two most popular Mozart concertos – that is before K.467 was elevated by the inescapable film *Elvira Madigan*. Brendel here sounds more spontaneous than on some of his other Mozart records, notably in K.488, which is given a performance both strong and lyrical, with the F sharp minor slow movement intensely beautiful.

An enchanting record from Barenboim. This was the first of his Mozart concerto series with the ECO, and his playing has all the sparkle and sensitivity one could ask for. There are times when his delicacy of fingerwork comes close to preciosity, as at the end of the opening of the theme in the slow movement of the *A major*, but it never goes over the edge. The orchestral accompaniment is admirably alive, and one's only serious reservation concerns the somewhat fast tempi he adopts in the finales. The stereo sound is spacious and truthful and the whole production is a distinguished one.

Annie Fischer's record is over fifteen years old yet sounds remarkably fresh. It was obviously made in a lively and clean acoustic, and the piano tone is immediate and realistic; the instrument does not loom too large in the aural picture and the balance is most musically judged. In the *D minor Concerto* Miss Fischer has spontaneity and her phrasing is invariably alive and imaginative. Tempi are sensible and the orchestral playing is felicitous, particularly from the wind. It misses perhaps the ultimate in breadth and dramatic fire but it is a good performance all the same. In K.488 she plays with liveliness of feeling and refinement of touch, and much of the passage-work is deft. The slow movement is in less than perfect style perhaps (but then so is Barenboim's), with the main theme given a quasi-Chopinesque dressing. In any event this is a thoroughly enjoyable and often perceptive performance.

Haebler is a fine Mozartian with an impressive command of keyboard colour. Her tempi in the *D minor Concerto* are relaxed and leisurely: she takes 34'35" over it, which many listeners might feel was too much of a good thing. One would welcome greater tautness in the outer movements and more sense of momentum throughout. The recording is well balanced but in general the performance, for all its merits (by no means inconsiderable), must yield to rival versions. In the *A major Concerto* Miss Haebler gives a characteristically poised and beautifully controlled account of the solo part and coaxes tone of great beauty from the keyboard. She is well supported by Rowicki and the LSO. A stylish performance in every way, though the familiar reservations that must be applied to her art still stand.

Piano concertos Nos. 20 in D minor, K.466 (cadenzas by Beethoven); *25 in C major, K.503* (cadenzas by Katchen).
** Decca SXL 6297. Julius Katchen (piano), Stuttgart Chamber Orchestra, Karl Münchinger.

One does not think of Katchen as primarily a Mozartian, and perhaps, in partnership with Münchinger, the manner of these performances is sometimes a little stiff. Yet they have character too, and in the *D minor Concerto* there is strength as well as plenty of life and spirit. In both works the finales are vivacious. The recording, however, is not one of Decca's best. It is very close and immediate, with luminous woodwind, but a tendency for the strings to sound edgy.

Piano concerto No. 21 in C major, K.467.
(M) ****** Philips Universo 6580 083. Ingrid Haebler (piano), London Symphony Orchestra, Witold Rowicki – *Double piano concerto, K.365.*******

* Decca Phase 4 PFS 4299. Ilana Vered (piano), Royal Philharmonic Orchestra, Lawrence Foster – HSIEN HSING-HAI: *Yellow River concerto*.* (*)

The first movement of Haebler's K.467 is a little straitlaced and prim, without the breadth and dignity that some artists have brought it or the urgency that one has from others. Neither soloist nor conductor can wholly escape the charge of prettifying the music. Haebler plays her own cadenzas – and very good they are – but in the heavenly slow movement she is not as imaginative as either Casadesus or Annie Fischer. (Alas, Miss Fischer uses Busoni's somewhat inappropriate cadenzas.) Rowicki's direction is on the whole excellent and the sound beautifully clean.

Ilana Vered, an imaginative pianist in romantic music, gives a sticky account of the *C major Concerto*, coarsely recorded – an unappealing coupling for the strange *Yellow River concerto*.

Piano concertos Nos. 21 in C major, K.467; 22 in E flat major, K.482.

(M) ** (*) HMV SXLP 30124. Annie Fischer (piano), Philharmonia Orchestra, Wolfgang Sawallisch.

This coupling was very highly regarded when it first appeared in 1959 (mono only) on CX 1630. The general style of performance of Mozart concertos in recent years has tended to become more robust, but even so Miss Fischer's gentle, limpid touch with its frequent use of half tones gives a great deal of pleasure. The slow movements of both concertos are beautifully done, and the pianist's intimate manner is often shared by the Philharmonia's wind soloists, who offer playing of polish and delicacy. Sawallisch's contribution too is considerable, and his firm directing hand ensures that neither performance becomes effete. These are essentially small-scale readings, and the refined approach does reduce the opportunities for displaying sparkle and wit. But the coupling is convenient and Miss Fischer's silken touch is highly persuasive. The recording is nicely balanced, full in tone, and does not sound dated.

Piano concertos Nos. 21 in C major, K.467; 24 in C minor, K.491.

(M) ** (*) CBS Classics 61578. Robert Casadesus (piano), members of the Cleveland Orchestra, George Szell.

Casadesus has made an earlier version of K.467 with Münch, and its ravishing slow movement has never sounded more magical. As in the earlier version he takes the finale at a tremendous speed here, but for the most part this is exquisite Mozart playing, beautifully paced and articulated. The recording is not of the finest but it is more than acceptable at the price. Casadesus's pre-war account of K.491 with Eugene Bigot was one of the glories of the Columbia catalogue, and his post-war LP was no less fine. Perhaps memory deceives, for the present account does not seem to scale quite those heights, but it is still pretty marvellous, and for all the shortcomings of the recording and the slightly overdriven precision of Szell, this is not a record to overlook. The disc should belong in any Mozartian's library.

Piano concertos Nos. 21 in C major, K.467; 25 in C major, K.503.

⊕ *** Philips 6500 431. Stephen Bishop (piano), London Symphony Orchestra, Colin Davis.

This is among the most searching and satisfying records of Mozart piano concertos available. The partnership of Bishop and Davis almost invariably produces inspired performances, and here their equal dedication to Mozart, their balancing of strength and charm, drama and tenderness, make for performances which retain their sense of spontaneity but which plainly result from deep thought. Never has the famous slow movement of K.467 sounded so ethereally beautiful on record as here, with superb LSO string tone, and the weight of both these great C major works is formidably conveyed. The recording is beautifully balanced and refined.

Piano concertos Nos. 21 in C major, K.467; 27 in B flat major, K.595.
  ** (*) HMV ASD 2465. Daniel Barenboim (piano), English Chamber Orchestra.

There need be no reservations about Barenboim's account of K.467, which is accomplished in every way. His version of K.595 will be more controversial. He indulges in great refinements of touch, and his reading of the slow movement in particular is overtly romantic. Anda (now deleted) was more successful in obtaining the right perspective and holding the balance between detail and structure.

(i) *Piano concerto No. 21 in C major, K.467. Piano sonata No. 11 in A major, K.331; 12 Variations on 'Ah, vous dirai-je, maman', K.265.*
  (B) ** Turnabout TV 34504S. Walter Klien (piano), (i) with Mainz Chamber Orchestra, Günter Kehr.

More fine performances here from Klien, whose expressive playing and stylishness give constant pleasure, particularly as the piano is well recorded throughout. The Mainz Chamber Orchestra under Kehr accompanies with character, and if the strings in their poetic cantilena in the concerto's famous *Andante* are not as richly immaculate as in some full-priced versions, the finale is marvellously vivacious, with some spirited playing from the orchestra's wind soloists.

The accounts of the *Sonata* (the *Rondo alla turca* infectiously done) and the charming *Variations* greatly add to the attractions of this issue.

(i) *Piano concerto No. 21 in C major, K.467. Serenade No. 13 in G major (Eine kleine Nachtmusik), K.525.*
  (B) ** (*) Classics for Pleasure CFP 40009. Virtuosi of London, Arthur Davison, (i) with Moura Lympany (piano).

Although this issue is obviously inspired by the *Elvira Madigan* film, the performance is in no way over-romanticized. It is of authentic Mozartian proportions, neat, small in scale, but with plenty of character. The account of *Eine kleine Nachtmusik* is first-rate. It is robust yet elegant, not polished to the final degree but crisply articulated, with a beautifully judged *Romanze*, spontaneous and graceful. The recording is clear and vivid to suit the performances.

(i) *Piano concerto No. 22 in E flat major, K.482.* (ii) *Concert rondos* (for piano and orchestra) *Nos. 1 in D major, K.382; 2 in A major, K.386.*
  (M) ** DGG Privilege 2538 258. (i) Joerg Demus (piano), Berlin Radio Symphony Orchestra, Franz Paul Decker; (ii) Annie Fischer (piano), Bavarian State Orchestra, Ferenc Fricsay.

Joerg Demus's performance seems a little dry in the first two movements of the concerto, but the playing is stylish. Those who like small-scale Mozart playing should find this to their taste, particularly as, when the record turns over, Demus gives a sparkling account of the finale which is delightful in every way. The recording is a little lack-lustre but perfectly acceptable. The performances of the *Concert rondos* by Annie Fischer are attractive, especially the lesser-known

A major work, which is most gracefully done.

Piano concerto No. 22 in E flat major, K.482; Concert rondo (for piano and orchestra) No. 1 in D major, K.382.
   *** HMV ASD 2838. Daniel Barenboim (piano), English Chamber Orchestra.
   (B) * (*) Turnabout TV 34233S. Alfred Brendel (piano), Vienna Chamber or Pro Musica Orchestras, Paul Angerer.

Barenboim gives a persuasive, at times even wilful, account of K.482, relishing its expansiveness with dozens of spontaneous-sounding inflections. For listening on record some may prefer a firmer, less idiosyncratic version, but with the *D major Rondo* (written at the same time as *Entführung* and showing signs of that) this is another highly enjoyable offering in the Barenboim cycle, well played and recorded.

On Turnabout the orchestra plays with plenty of character and there is some excellent wind-playing in the slow movement and finale. The snag is the string tone, which is thin and whiskery. If, however, your machine is flexible in this matter, the recording is basically well balanced. Brendel plays the first movement with authority, the *Andante* very beautifully, and the finale quite enchantingly. His limpid, silken tone contrasts with the pithy orchestra at his first entry in the opening movement, and his gentle sound for the opening of the closing *Allegro* is most beautiful, as is the contrasting middle section. The attractive *Rondo*, K.382, is given a scaled-down performance that suits its intimate atmosphere perfectly.

Piano concertos Nos. 23 in A major, K.488; 24 in C minor, K.491.
   ⊛ *** DGG SLPM 138645. Wilhelm Kempff (piano), Bamberg Symphony Orchestra, Ferdinand Leitner.
   ** (*) Decca SXL 6354. Clifford Curzon (piano), London Symphony Orchestra, Istvan Kertesz.

Kempff's is a quite outstanding coupling of two of Mozart's greatest concertos. The sunny mood of the outer movements of the *A major Concerto* is perfectly contrasted here with the darker colouring of the *Adagio* (a wonderfully expressive performance), and the sombre yet dramatic atmosphere of the opening of the C minor work is perceptively caught by Leitner, who provides distinguished accompaniments to both works. The poetry of Kempff's playing is a constant joy, and with excellent recording this remains very highly recommendable.

Curzon's account of these two concertos is immaculate and no connoisseur of the piano will fail to derive pleasure and instruction from them. Curzon has the advantage of sensitive support both from Kertesz and the Decca engineers, and only the absence of the last ounce of sparkle and spontaneity prevents this from being strongly recommended. Kempff's DGG record remains preferable.

(i) *Piano concerto No. 24 in C minor, K.491. Piano sonata No. 14 in C minor, K.457; Fantasia in C minor, K.475.*
   (B) ** (*) Turnabout TV 34178S. Walter Klien, (i) with Vienna Volksoper Orchestra, Peter Maag.

In the concerto Maag's strong opening tutti has plenty of character, and at his first entry Klien's piano image seeks to contrast the meek with the powerful. But although the possibilities of contrast are fully exploited, during the movement the soloist's contribution expands to match that of the orchestra. The slow movement again shows the felicity of the partnership and the finale is particularly successful.

All in all this is a satisfying performance and if the string playing is not immaculate, Maag's direction is distinguished and the wind playing in the *Larghetto* is nicely pointed. What puts this disc into the three-star class are the outstandingly fine performances of the *C minor Sonata* and *Fantasia* which make the coupling. This is most sensitive Mozart playing, and beautifully recorded.

Piano concertos (i) *No. 25 in C major, K.503;* (ii) *No. 27 in B flat major, K.595.*
(B) ** (*) Turnabout TV 34129S. Alfred Brendel (piano), (i) Vienna Pro Musica, (ii) Vienna Volksoper Orchestra, both cond. Paul Angerer.

This transfer of Brendel's K.503, in squeezing about half an hour's music on to one side, loses a little of the original amplitude and throws into bold relief the orchestral upper strings. Such emphasis of playing which is not altogether immaculate is not entirely desirable, but Brendel's contribution is eminently stylish: his phrasing of the lyrical secondary themes of the outer movements gives much pleasure. The recording of No. 27 is different again, with the soloist recorded backwardly in a curiously reverberant acoustic and the orchestra brightly forward. But the ear adjusts to a balance in antithesis to concert-hall procedure, and the ear is soon taken with Brendel's sure phrasing and natural feeling for nuance and tempo. With any reservations the disc remains an outstanding bargain, offering as it does a full hour of Mozart.

Piano concertos Nos. 26 in D major (Coronation), K.537; 27 in B flat major, K.595.
(M) *** CBS Classics 61597. Robert Casadesus (piano), Cleveland Symphony Orchestra, George Szell.

Mozart's last piano concertos inspire Casadesus and Szell to two intensely memorable performances, each of them underlining the dramatic contrast of soloist and orchestra, almost as a meeting of heroine and hero. Casadesus's Mozart may at first seem understated, but the imagination behind his readings is apparent in every phrase, and though the balance favours the soloist, the accompaniment too could hardly be more stylish. Strongly recommended at medium price.

(i) *Piano concerto No. 26 in D major (Coronation), K.537. Fantasy in D minor, K.397; Piano sonata No. 17 in D major, K.576.*
(B) * (*) Turnabout TV 34194S. Walter Klien (piano), (i) with Vienna Volksoper Orchestra, Peter Maag.

The orchestral tone here is rather thin and papery and the bass is not strong. But the recording has plenty of middle and on some machines it can be made to sound acceptable. The textures are fresh (Peter Maag usually manages a nice Mozartian balance, even when his orchestra is not of the top flight), and they suit Walter Klien's cool classical approach. The slow movement is phrased nicely and the finale is gay. When playing alone Klien tends to be rhythmically impulsive, and this shows up even more in his solo performances, which are splendidly alive. The piano tone is dry but quite pleasant.

(i) *Piano concerto No. 27 in B flat major, K.595. Piano sonatas Nos. 10 in C major, K.330; 11 in A major, K.331.*
(B) ** Decca Eclipse ECS 749. Wilhelm Backhaus (piano), (i) with Vienna Philharmonic Orchestra, Karl Boehm.

Backhaus is magisterial, but rhythmically rather uneven, and the performance of the concerto does not always flow as smoothly as one might wish. Even so, with quite enjoyable performances of two of Mozart's most attractive piano sonatas as a filler, this is quite a fair bargain. The piano tone, good, for the most part, in the concerto, is rather more wooden in the sonatas.

Piano concerto No. 27 in B flat major, K.595; (i) *Double piano concerto in E flat major, K.365.*

⊛ *** DGG 2530 456. Emil Gilels (piano), Vienna Philharmonic Orchestra, Karl Boehm, (i) with Elena Gilels (piano).

Gilels playing Mozart is in a class of his own. His is supremely lyrical playing that evinces all the classical virtues. No detail is allowed to detract from the picture as a whole; the pace is totally unhurried and superbly controlled. There is no point-making by means of agogic distortion or sudden rapt *pianissimo*; all the points are made by means of articulation and tone and each phrase is marvellously alive. The slow movement theme, for example, is played with a simplicity that is not arch as is the case with some performances; nor is it over-refined in tone, and the result gives added depth and spirituality. This is playing of the highest order of artistic integrity and poetic insight, while Boehm and the Vienna Philharmonic provide excellent support. The recording is very fine, though it falls short of being really outstanding. But this is a marvellous disc, certainly one of the very finest Mozart piano concerto records in the catalogue.

Double piano concerto in E flat major, K.365.

(B) *** Turnabout TV 34064S. Alfred Brendel, Walter Klien (pianos), Vienna Volksoper Orchestra, Paul Angerer – *Sonata; Fugue for 2 pianos.****

(M) ** HMV SXLP 30175. Clara Haskil, Géza Anda (pianos), Philharmonia Orchestra, Alceo Galliera – BACH: *Double clavier concerto, BWV 1061.***

(M) ** Philips Universo 6580 083. Ingrid Haebler, Ludwig Hoffmann (pianos), London Symphony Orchestra, Alceo Galliera – *Piano concerto No. 21.***

The Turnabout collection is very successful indeed. Brendel and Klien give an entirely delightful performance of the concerto, and if the orchestral contribution is not especially polished it is lively and spirited. The stereo separates the two pianos to perfect effect, and one's enjoyment is enhanced by the *rapport* between the two soloists, who readily convey their pleasure in Mozart's skilful antiphonal writing. The opening tutti is light in bass and there is a slight tendency for the left channel to be stronger than the right, but the overall stereo effect remains convincing. Both couplings are attractive, again displaying Mozart's genial preoccupation with the antiphonal possibilities of his medium. The piano tone is forward and very faithful in timbre. A splendid bargain.

Impeccable playing from Clara Haskil and Géza Anda makes theirs too a memorable disc. It was recorded as long ago as 1957 but has striking range and fidelity. The piano tone is clean and firm, while the strings of the Philharmonia Orchestra sound rich and warm even if the conducting of Alceo Galliera is not particularly distinguished on this occasion. However, this has greater personality than the Haebler/Hoffmann version and is welcome as a mid-price alternative to the Gilels. Haebler and Hoffmann play splendidly, though the Klien/Brendel partnership on Turnabout has more vitality and inner life. However, this is a fresh and unaffected reading, very well recorded, and though it is overshadowed by Gilels *père et fille* on DGG at full price (and worth every penny), those who buy it will not be disappointed.

(i) *Double piano concerto in E flat major, K.365;* (ii) *Triple piano concerto in F major, K.242.*

** HMV ASD 2280. (i) Fou Ts'ong, Hephzibah Menuhin (pianos), Bath Festival Orchestra; (ii) Hephzibah, Yaltah and Jeremy Menuhin (pianos), London Philharmonic Orchestra; both cond. Yehudi Menuhin.

This was obviously a family occasion and it is surprising there is not more of a conveyed sense of enjoyment and high spirits. The *E flat major Concerto* is given a more polished performance than that on Turnabout, but also a more careful one, lacking spontaneity. The *Triple concerto,* not one of Mozart's best works, also lacks sparkle.

Violin Concertos

Adagio in E major (for violin and orchestra), *K.261; Violin concertos Nos. 1 in B flat major, K.207; 2 in D major, K.211; 3 in G major, K.216; 4 in D major, K.218; 5 in A major (Turkish), K.219.* (i) *Concertone in C major, K.190. Rondos* (for violin and orchestra) *in B flat major, K.269; in C major, K.373.* (i) *Sinfonia concertante in E flat major, K.364.*

(M) ** HMV SLS 828 (4 discs). David Oistrakh (violin), Berlin Philharmonic Orchestra, (i) with Igor Oistrakh (violin).

Oistrakh is predictably strong and positive as a Mozartian, and he is well accompanied by the Berlin Philharmonic; but there are too many touches of unwanted heaviness to make this an ideal

cycle of the Mozart. Other versions are preferable (see below).

Adagio in E major, K.261; Violin concerto No. 1 in B flat major, K.207; Rondos in B flat major, K.269; in C major, K.373.

** (*) DGG SLPM 139464. Wolfgang Schneiderhan (violin), Berlin Philharmonic Orchestra.

Schneiderhan's performances are light, classical in scale, and very musical and polished. It is clearly easier to direct a violin concerto as soloist than a piano concerto, and Schneiderhan is obviously in full command of the orchestra, which shows personality and discipline. The recorded sound is crisp and bright, light in the bass, and this matches the silvery, elegant violin image. The playing has authority and integrity and is sensitive and appealing in a characteristically non-romantic manner. Schneiderhan is at his very best in the *Adagio in E major* and the two *Rondos,* which are by no means trivial Mozart, even though they are independent movements.

Violin concertos Nos. 1 in B flat major, K.207; 2 in D major, K.211.

*** RCA LRL 1 5084. Josef Suk (violin), Prague Chamber Orchestra.

Josef Suk's performances are highly distinguished. The playing has character and warmth, and its unaffected manner is admirably suited to these two concertos. The accompaniment, however, has less personality and impact; these performances are dominated by the soloist throughout, although the balance is not unnatural. For this reason and also for its inclusion of two extra works the Szeryng disc (see below) is first recommendation, but admirers of Suk should in no way be disappointed with this coupling. The recording is good.

623

Violin concertos Nos. 1 in B flat major, K.207; 2 in D major, K.211; Rondos in B flat major, K.269; in C major, K.373.
*** Philips 6500 035. Henryk Szeryng (violin), New Philharmonia Orchestra, Alexander Gibson.

In 1970 Philips released a set comprising all Mozart's concertos and concerted pieces for violin and orchestra played by Szeryng and the New Philharmonia under Gibson. The discs are now available separately, and they can be recommended without reservation. Szeryng plays with great purity of style and musical insight, and the orchestral support is beautifully shaped and responsive. Recordings, too, are musically balanced and truthful in tone-quality.

Violin concertos Nos. 1 in B flat major, K.207; 4 in D major, K.218.
(M) *** Philips Universo 6580 009. Arthur Grumiaux (violin), London Symphony Orchestra, Colin Davis.

Grumiaux's accounts of the Mozart concertos come from the early 1960s and are among the most beautifully played in the catalogue at any price. The orchestral accompaniment has sparkle and vitality, and Grumiaux's playing has splendid poise and purity of tone. The recording sounds amazingly good, with fresh, clean string tone and well defined bass. These are humane performances, second to none.

Violin concerto No. 2 in D major, K.211.
*** Philips SAL 3492. Arthur Grumiaux (violin), London Symphony Orchestra, Colin Davis – *Sinfonia concertante, K.364.****

This *Second Concerto* – even more neglected than K.207 – provides an excellent fill-up for the great *Sinfonia concertante*. Truth to tell it is not quite so interesting as the others in the Salzburg group, but in Grumiaux's hands it has many delights, providing relaxation after the major masterpiece.

Violin concerto No. 3 in G major, K.216.
(M) *** HMV SXLP 30086. David Oistrakh (violin), Philharmonia Orchestra – BEETHOVEN: *Piano concerto No. 4.****
(M) ** Everest SDBR 3040. Joseph Fuchs (violin), London Symphony Orchestra, Sir Eugene Goossens – HINDEMITH: *Violin concerto.***

David Oistrakh is at his finest in this beautiful performance of Mozart's *G major Concerto*. His supple, richly toned yet essentially classical style suits the melodic line of this youthful work and gives it the stature of maturity. The orchestral contribution is directed by the soloist himself and is surprisingly polished. EMI contribute a smooth, vivid sound and with its unexpected but highly successful coupling this disc is certainly a fine bargain.

Fuchs's style is much less polished and warm than Oistrakh's. But this performance is spontaneous-sounding throughout, and the playing committed (in the slow movement especially), so that one can enjoy it in a quite different way. The recording is bright and lively to suit the comparatively unsubtle approach.

Adagio in E major, K.261; Violin concertos Nos. 3 in G major, K.216; 4 in D major, K.218.
*** Philips 6500 036. Henryk Szeryng (violin), New Philharmonia Orchestra, Alexander Gibson.

Besides these first-rate performances of two favourite concertos, Szeryng includes the *Adagio, K.261*, a short but most expressive piece.

Violin concertos Nos. 3 in G major, K.216; 4 in D major, K.218.

*** RCA LRL 1 5046. Josef Suk (violin), Prague Chamber Orchestra.

Suk's playing is distinguished by warmth and humanity and he is well supported by the Prague Chamber Orchestra. He plays Henri Marteau's cadenza in the G major, which will not be to all tastes. The earlier of Oistrakh's two accounts of this concerto (on Concert Classics; see above) is still a strong favourite, but those requiring this coupling need not hesitate in this instance. The recording has less refinement than the balance Philips provide for Szeryng but Suk's performance has the greater spontaneity.

(i) Violin concerto No. 3 in G major, K.216; (ii) Concertone in C major (for 2 violins and orchestra), K.190.

** (*) Argo ZRG 729. (i) Alan Loveday, (ii) Iona Brown, Carmel Kaine (violins); both with Academy of St Martin-in-the-Fields, Neville Marriner.

With the ample acoustic of St John's, Smith Square, to help, this account of the early *Concertone* is amiable and charming, with a fastish tempo for the central *Andantino grazioso*. The playing of the soloists is very capable, though when it comes to Mozartian styli:..ness they are both outshone by Alan Loveday, the soloist on the reverse in an intimate reading of the most popular of the Mozart violin concertos. A special mention is also required for the oboist in the *Concertone*, Tess Miller, whose playing is exquisite.

Violin concertos Nos. 3 in G major, K.216; 5 in A major (Turkish), K.219.

** HMV ASD 2988. David Oistrakh (violin), Berlin Philharmonic Orchestra.

Distinguished performances from Oistrakh, taken from his complete set of the *Violin concertos*. Partly as a result of close recording there is a heaviness in the slow movements and a lack of sparkle elsewhere, which prevents these from competing with the best available.

(i) Violin concerto No. 3 in G major, K.216; (ii) Sinfonia concertante for violin and viola in E flat major, K.364.

(M) ** DGG Privilege 2538 262. (i) Wolfgang Schneiderhan (violin), Berlin Philharmonic Orchestra; (ii) Thomas Brandis (violin), Giusto Cappone (viola), Berlin Philharmonic Orchestra, Karl Boehm.

The Schneiderhan account of the *G major Concerto* comes from the complete set he made with the Berlin Philharmonic in the late 1960s; it is a finely-wrought performance, strongly classical in feeling and beautifully recorded. Schneiderhan plays his own cadenzas, and although there is a slight want of sparkle and (by comparison with Oistrakh) warmth, the reading is thoroughly enjoyable.

The *Sinfonia concertante* is let down ultimately by the slow movement, which is just a shade too brisk and prosaic; the finale is also a little unyielding. The soloists have excellent style and are perfect in all matters of phrasing, intonation and so on, but the reading is just a shade lacking in personality by comparison with the most formidable accounts in the catalogue.

Violin concertos Nos. 3 in G major, K.216; 7 in E flat major, K.268 (attrib. Mozart).

(B) * (*) Decca Eclipse ECS 697. Christian Ferras (violin), Stuttgart Chamber Orchestra, Karl Münchinger.

Ferras made this record as long ago as

625

1955 and it sounds astonishingly vivid for its age. The performance is not as serenely classical as Schneiderhan's G major nor as perfectly moulded as Oistrakh's Concert Classics version (to take two inexpensive comparisons) and for all Ferras's elegance and feeling, the somewhat faceless accompaniment by Münchinger and the Stuttgart Chamber Orchestra renders this version a good deal less competitive than it would otherwise be. The *E flat major Concerto* is given similar treatment.

Violin concertos Nos. 4 in D major, K.218; 5 in A major (Turkish), K.219.

(M) ** (*) RCA LSB 4063. Jascha Heifetz (violin), New Symphony Orchestra of London, Sir Malcolm Sargent.

** CBS 72859. Pinchas Zukerman (violin), English Chamber Orchestra, Daniel Barenboim.

(M) ** DGG Privilege 2538 094. Wolfgang Schneiderhan (violin), (i) Berlin Philharmonic Orchestra; (ii) NDR Symphony Orchestra; both cond. Hans Schmidt-Isserstedt.

(B) * (*) Turnabout TV 34186S. György Pauk (violin), Württemberg Chamber Orchestra, Joerg Faerber.

Marvellously exhilarating performances from Heifetz. K.218 is perhaps the less successful of the two: Heifetz's briskness of manner provides crystalline clarity in the outer movements and this is a distinct advantage in the vivacious finale, but some of the slow movement's lyricism evaporates. The opening of K.219, however, is marvellously spirited, with superb tone and absolute accuracy of intonation married to a complete mastery of style. The slow movement is shaped with grace and subtlety, and the finale (its *Turkish* interludes brought off

with *élan*) is wonderfully buoyant. Sargent's accompaniments are highly professional, and the brightly lit, rather dry recording can be softened up with flexible controls.

The opening of Zukerman's account of K.218 with its warm, plushy sound is not in the least like the usual CBS recording, although there is some spotlight on the soloist. This is in essence a very romantic conception for although Barenboim's direction of the first movement is literal, the slow movement is played with an almost cloying warmth, and the finale, also taken slowly, is affectionate to the point of self-indulgence. The character of the *Turkish concerto* is markedly brighter and more extrovert, and this performance can be recommended readily enough. Throughout Zukerman's tone is rich and his phrasing affectionate but stylish, the violin image much broader than Schneiderhan's.

Schneiderhan's accounts of these concertos should not be confused with the set he made in the late 1960s with the Berlin Philharmonic. The performances are not wholly free from pedantry, and although they are alive and thoughtful, readers will find better value elsewhere. The recordings are, however, admirably balanced and reproduce smoothly.

The recorded tone on Turnabout is very thin in the treble and needs paring down, but when this is done the orchestra has enough body and the soloist's gleaming timbre and sure classical line are acceptable. These are neat, stylish performances accurate in intonation and with unindulgent sensitivity in the slow movements. If your reproducer can filter out too much high treble without making the middle plummy this is a fair bargain.

Violin concertos Nos. 5 in A major (Turkish), K.219; 6 in D major, K.271a.

*** Philips SAL 3588. Henryk Szeryng (violin), New Philharmonia Orchestra, Alexander Gibson.

Marvellous performances by Szeryng of the well-known *A major Concerto* and the lesser-known *D major*, on whose authenticity some doubts have been cast. An autograph does not survive but there seems no evidence to support these doubts and every reason from the musical point of view to suppose it to be by Mozart. Gibson accompanies as sensitively as Szeryng plays, and the recording does justice to them both. An outstanding record.

(i) *Violin concerto No. 5 in A major (Turkish), K.219. Adagio and fugue in C minor* (for strings), *K.546; Serenade No. 13 in G major (Eine kleine Nachtmusik), K.525.*
   *** Philips 6500 537. I Musici, (i) with Roberto Michelucci (violin).

Michelucci is a distinguished player and his reading of the concerto has great fluency and poise to commend it. He plays his own cadenzas, which are stylish, and he is admirably accompanied by I Musici, whose ensemble and beauty of tone remain unfailingly reliable. The Philips engineers offer recording quality of the first order. The two pieces on the reverse of the disc, *Eine kleine Nachtmusik* and the superb *Adagio and fugue in C minor*, receive performances of genuine personality. This disc is recommended on all counts.

Concertone in C major (for 2 violins and orchestra), *K.190.*
   ** (*) CBS 76310. Isaac Stern, Pinchas Zukerman (violins), English Chamber Orchestra, Daniel Barenboim – PLEYEL: *Sinfonia concertante.** (*)
   (M) *(*) Oiseau-Lyre SOL 60030. Emanuel Hurwitz, Eli Goren (violins), Peter Graeme (oboe), Terence Weil (cello), English

Chamber Group, Colin Davis – HAYDN: *Symphony No. 84.* **

Mozart's *Concertone* was written in 1773 when the composer was only seventeen. The format is clearly derived from that of the concerto grosso but its weightier style betrays the late eighteenth century. The work is attractive, if not one of Mozart's most inspired pieces. On CBS the dryness of acoustic rather detracts from the charm of a work that on any count goes on too long for its material. Stern, Zukerman and Barenboim pay the central *Andantino grazioso* the compliment of a really slow tempo, and though this makes a very long movement, the concentration is superb. And whatever the shortcomings of the recording, the artistry of the soloists readily outshines that of rival versions. On Oiseau-Lyre Colin Davis sees that everything is well balanced and the accompaniment in good order, but his somewhat rigid approach lacks that touch of flexibility that such music needs to beguile the listener. The recording is lively but the basically attractive sound has a tendency to smudge in the treble.

Dances and Marches

Collection of Contredanses; German dances; Marches; Minuets; Les Petits Riens (ballet), *K.299b* (from records listed below).
   (M) *** Decca Ace of Diamonds SDDH 347/51. Vienna Mozart Ensemble, Willi Boskovsky.
La Chasse, K.320f; 2 Contredanses for Graf Czernin, K.270a; 3 Contredanses, K.535a; Contredanse ('Das Donnerwetter'), K.534; 6 German dances, K.536; March in D major, K.290; 2 Minuets, K.61g, K.94; Minuet in E flat major, K.122; 8 Minuets, K.315a; 3 Minuets, K.363; Minuet in C, K.409.

*** Decca SXL 6248. Vienna Mozart Ensemble, Willi Boskovsky.

4 Contredanses, K.101; 3 German dances, K.605; 6 Ländler, K.606; March in D major, K.335/2; March in F major, K.248; 6 Minuets, K.61h; 6 Minuets, K.104; 2 Minuets, K.604.

  *** Decca SXL 6247. Vienna Mozart Ensemble, Willi Boskovsky.

Contredanse in B flat major, K.123; Contredanse 'Les filles malicieuses', K.610; Gavotte in B flat major, K.300; 6 German dances, K.571; March in D major, K.189; 6 Minuets, K.105; 6 Minuets, K.599; Overture and 3 contredanses, K.106.

  *** Decca SXL 6198. Vienna Mozart Ensemble, Willi Boskovsky.

4 Contredanses, K.267; 6 Contredanses, K.462; 6 German dances, K.509; 6 German dances, K.567; March in C major, K.408/1; March in D major, K.215.

  *** Decca SXL 6131. Vienna Mozart Ensemble, Willi Boskovsky.

Contredanse 'La Bataille', K.535; Contredanse 'Il trionfo delle donne', K.607; 5 Contredanses ('Non più andrai'), K.609; March in D major, K.455; 19 Minuets, K.103.

  *** Decca SXL 6197. Vienna Mozart Ensemble, Willi Boskovsky.

2 Contredanses, K.603; 4 German dances, K.602; March in D major, K.237; 15 Minuets, K.176; 4 Minuets, K.601.

  *** Decca SXL 6199. Vienna Mozart Ensemble, Willi Boskovsky.

6 German dances, K.600; March in D major, K.249; March in D major, K.335/1; 12 Minuets, K.568.

  ** (*) Decca SXL 6133. Vienna Mozart Ensemble, Willi Boskovsky.

Idomeneo: ballet music, K.367; March,

K.206; Les Petits Riens (ballet), K.299b.

  *** Decca SXL 6275. Vienna Mozart Ensemble, Willi Boskovsky.

This series that encompasses Mozart's complete marches and dances is one of the triumphs of the modern gramophone. Much of the credit for it should go to its expert producer, Erik Smith, who provides some of the most informative and economically written sleeve-notes that have ever graced a record. On its completion H. C. Robbins Landon cabled his praises and hailed 'the most beautiful Mozart playing and most sophisticated sound I know'; and one cannot imagine that anyone would dissent from this view. But one also sympathizes with the dilemma of the record buyer faced with such an *embarras de richesse* that he doesn't know where to start. The important thing is, however, to start somewhere. since each record offers a generous sample of delightful and most often inspired music: the fifth disc (SXL 6197), for example, with the sparkling *La Bataille*, and SXL 6199 with the poignant hurdy-gurdy colouring in the *Minuets* and *Dances*, K.601, K.602. But even to select these seems invidious, since there are equally inspired pieces elsewhere. The last disc, the ballet music to *Les Petits Riens* and *Idomeneo*, is an absolute must, and SXL 6131 is outstanding too. SXL 6133 has a rather less interesting selection.

Since the original issue of the individual discs, Decca have made a five-disc selection in album form at medium price. The discs are generously full with no loss in recording quality, and the collector who invests in this set can dip into it at will.

Collection: *'Mozart in Chelsea'* (arr. and orch. Erik Smith): *3 Contredanses in F major; 2 Contredanses in G major; 6 Divertimenti: in C major; G minor; D major; F major; B flat major; E flat major* (from 2nd London Notebook), *K.15.*

*** Philips 6500 367. Academy of St Martin-in-the-Fields, Neville Marriner.

This is a delightful disc. Erik Smith, scholar as well as recording manager, has taken the innocent little piano pieces to be found in the child Mozart's London Notebook (written while his father was ill) and orchestrated them, on the theory that they are not really suited to the keyboard, and that the child would have performed the same task had he been given the chance. The results may not be important, but they charm the ear at least as much as Mozart's early symphonies, with many unexpected touches. Marriner and the Academy are ideal performers, and the recording is beautifully refined.

12 German dances, K.586.

(B) ** Turnabout TV 34011S. Innsbruck Symphony Orchestra, Robert Wagner – HAYDN: *Katherinentänze.* (*)*

This selection is performed with spirit. The music is much more inventive than the Haydn coupling.

6 German dances, K.600; Marches in C major and D major, K.408/1 and 2; 2 Minuets, K.604; Les Petits Riens (ballet), *K.299b; Divertimento No. 1 in E flat major, K.113.*

(B) *** Pye GSGC 14033. Pro Arte Orchestra, Charles Mackerras.

This is a highly agreeable collection, well recorded. The playing is gracious and spirited, and both the attractive little *Divertimento*, K.113 and the colourful *Les Petits Riens* ballet music are most enjoyable. This is an excellent bargain in every way.

German dance, K.605/3: Sleighride.

(B) *** Music for Pleasure MFP 2126. Little Symphony of London, Arthur Davison – LEOPOLD MOZART: *Toy symphony*; PROKOFIEV: *Peter and the Wolf.****

A vivid, strongly characterized account of Mozart's famous *Sleighride*, the sleighbells section given a splendid lilt, and the recording extremely lively.

Divertimenti

3 Divertimenti for strings (Nos. 1 in D major; 2 in B flat major; 3 in F major), K.136–8; Serenade No. 6 in D major (Serenata notturna), K.239.

*** Argo ZRG 554. Academy of St Martin-in-the-Fields, Neville Marriner.

*** Philips 6500 536. I Musici.

(M) * (*) DGG Privilege 2538 234. Lucerne Festival Strings, Rudolf Baumgartner.

3 Divertimenti for strings, K.136–8; Serenade No. 13 in G major (Eine kleine Nachtmusik), K.525.

* Pye Ensayo NEL 2009. Orchestra da Camera di Padova, Claudio Scimone.

These early string divertimenti need really committed and stylish playing to make their full effect, and they certainly receive this on the superb Argo disc. The playing is marvellous, so much so that one finds that K.137 and 138 are as memorable here as the more often played K.136. The same warm stylishness shows itself in the *Serenata notturna*, where timpani are added to the strings. Not least of the pleasures on this disc is the feeling Neville Marriner shows for choosing exactly the right tempo for each movement, and the Argo recording is rich in texture and detail.

The playing of I Musici is spirited and beautifully stylish, as is that of the Academy. The Philips recording is very fine indeed, though perhaps marginally less warm and realistic than the Argo. No one investing in either will be disappointed. By comparison Baumgartner directs charmless though efficient performances; the music needs more persuasive handling than this. The Ensayo performances are not polished and stylish enough to command a recommendation.

3 Divertimenti for strings, K.136–8; Divertimenti Nos. 10 in F major, K.247; 11 in D major, K.251; Serenade No. 6 in D major (Serenata notturna), K.239.

(M) ** DGG Privilege 2726 031 (2 discs). Berlin Philharmonic Orchestra, Herbert von Karajan.

Needless to say these are beautifully played performances and as such prompt the liveliest admiration. At the same time there is a predictably suave elegance that seems to militate against spontaneity. Cultured and effortless readings, beautifully recorded and well balanced, they somehow leave one untouched. There is too much legato and too little sparkle.

Divertimento for strings No. 1 in D major, K.136; A Musical Joke (Ein Musikalischer Spass), K.522; Serenade No. 13 in G major (Eine kleine Nachtmusik), K.525.

(B) ** Decca Eclipse ECS 686. Stuttgart Chamber Orchestra, Karl Münchinger.

Münchinger's hand is rather heavy in the matter of Mozartian humour, yet the last two movements of the *Musical Joke* are played spontaneously enough and the *Divertimento for strings* too has plenty of spirit. There are more gracious accounts of Mozart's *Nachtmusik* available, but this one is not unattractive in its straight-

forward way. The recording is good throughout.

Divertimento for strings No. 1 in D major, K.136; Serenade No. 13 in G major (Eine kleine Nachtmusik), K.525; Church sonata, K.245: Allegro in D major.

(B) ** Oryx EXP 16. Heidelberg Chamber Orchestra.

This is a good collection, competently played. The recording is reverberant, but this does not disguise a certain thinness in the upper string image. Even so the overall sound is most satisfactory for an inexpensive record. No conductor is named on the record sleeve.

Divertimenti Nos. 1 in E flat major, K.113; 2 in D major, K.131.

*** Decca SXL 6366. Vienna Mozart Ensemble, Willi Boskovsky.

Beecham's performance (mono only) of the *Divertimento in D major* remains firmly in the memory, but even by Beecham's standards these are fine performances, offering grace as well as sparkle. The playing itself is of the highest standard, as is the recording.

Divertimenti Nos. 7 in D major, K.205; 11 in D major, K.251.

*** Decca SXL 6670. Vienna Mozart Ensemble, Willi Boskovsky.

This record, the eighth in the series of Mozart serenades from this source, is as sparkling and enjoyable as the others. Indeed, like the Beaux Arts Trio's accounts of Haydn's *Piano trios*, or these same artists' set of Mozart's *Dances* and *Marches*, the series is one of the great achievements of the gramophone in the 1970s. The playing is so totally idiomatic and masterly that one scarcely thinks of the artists at all, only of the music. Decca provide a recording that is as delightfully fresh as the music itself; detail is excellently captured and yet the aural perspective remains consistent and truthful.

Divertimento No. 7 in D major, K.205; 2 Marches in D major, K.335; Serenade No. 13 in G major (Eine kleine Nachtmusik), K.525.
> *** H M V ASD 2610. English Chamber Orchestra, Daniel Barenboim.

Barenboim is splendidly recorded, with rich sound in a glowing acoustic. The *Divertimento* responds well to his affectionate treatment (its *Adagio* is particularly memorable), while the two *Marches* are attractively jaunty and colourful. The performance of *Eine kleine Nachtmusik* is warm and gracious yet never merely suave, and altogether this beautifully played collection makes highly congenial listening, more indulgent perhaps than Boskovsky's approach, but still first-class.

Divertimenti Nos. 10 in F major, K.247; 15 in B flat major, K.287.
> (M) ** (*) Decca Ace of Diamonds SDD 290. Members of the Vienna Octet.

This is a generous re-coupling of two major divertimenti in smooth, pleasing recordings. The performance of No. 10 is not especially vivid and the playing is rather unsmiling until towards the end, when it enlivens itself for a very spirited finale. K.287, written in 1777 for the countess Lodron of Salzburg, produces playing of stronger projection and personality. This is a beautifully made work, in six well contrasted movements, including an expressive *Adagio* and an attractive set of variations. Considerable demands are made on the sensibility and skill of the first violinist, and here Anton Fietz rises to the occasion. In short this is an expert performance and ideal music for late-evening listening.

Divertimenti Nos. 10 in F major, K.247; 11 in D major, K.331.
> (M) ** Oiseau-Lyre SOL 60029. English Chamber Orchestra, Colin Davis.

Divertimenti Nos. 10 in F major, K.247; 11 in D major, K.251; March in F major, K.248.
> *** Philips 6500 538. I Musici.

The I Musici performances are first-rate in every way. They are not small-scale readings, i.e. one instrument to each part, but orchestral in nature, and they are superbly played and recorded. The *March* properly belongs to the *Divertimento K.247* but here is heard before K.331, where it fits very well. An excellent record in every way.

On Oiseau-Lyre Davis shows a light hand with these works so that they sparkle, yet the body of string tone helps to add to the momentum. The recording matches the performances, not so rich and full as the admirable Philips, but clean and athletic.

Divertimento No. 11 in D major, K.251; Les Petits Riens (Overture and ballet music), K.Anh.10.
> (B) ** Decca Eclipse ECS 687. Stuttgart Chamber Orchestra, Karl Münchinger – SCHUBERT: *5 German dances; 5 Minuets.****

An enjoyable record, particularly at its modest price. Admittedly one could at times do with more sparkle and a greater sense of enjoyment, but although they fall short of distinction, the performances are stylish. The sound is clean, though the rather close balance robs the string tone of the bloom it needs. In K.251 Münchinger does not make enough of the dynamic contrasts; repeats are observed in the first minuet but not in the *Andantino* or the rondo.

(i) *Divertimento No. 11 in D major,*

K.251; (ii) *Sinfonia concertante for oboe, clarinet, horn and bassoon in E flat major, K.297b.*

(B) * (*) Turnabout TV 34416S. (i) Hungarian Chamber Orchestra, Vilmos Tátrai; (ii) Württemberg Chamber Orchestra, Joerg Faerber.

Faerber and his Württemberg players produce a characteristically warm and spontaneous performance of the *Sinfonia concertante.* The acoustic is slightly reverberant, with the wind soloists rather backward, but the effect is pleasing. Unfortunately the Hungarian account of the *Divertimento* is comparatively graceless.

Divertimenti Nos. 15 in B flat major, K.287; 17 in D major, K.334; Serenade No. 13 in G major (Eine kleine Nachtmusik), K.525.

(M) ** DGG Privilege 2726 032 (2 discs). Berlin Philharmonic Orchestra, Herbert von Karajan.

Beautiful and sometimes marvellously precise playing from the Berlin Philharmonic Orchestra (especially in the slow movement and finale of K.287). But the divertimentos suffer from excessive smoothness of the orchestral texture. Each phrase is exquisitely moulded, perfumed and powdered, and the result, although beguiling in its way, is just too much of a good thing. The recording is well balanced, but somewhat lacking in impact. The performance of *Eine kleine Nachtmusik* is, however, first-rate, among the best available. Lithe playing in the first movement, the second theme given an attractive, spongy rhythmic spring; the *Romanze* not dragged yet not over-indulged. The last two movements, although a little lacking in bite, fit well into this spacious reading to match the largish body of strings used. The recording is excellent.

Divertimento No. 15 in B flat major, K.287; Divertimento for strings No. 3 in F major, K.138.

(M) ** Vanguard VCS 10082. English Chamber Orchestra, David Blum.

David Blum uses a larger group than the Vienna Octet (see under *Divertimento No. 10*) and the orchestra has less bite and intimacy. But these are warm, smiling performances with an attractively gracious quality in the orchestral playing. The recording too is good, if not so refined as the Decca.

Divertimento No. 17 in D major, K.334; Divertimento for strings No. 1 in D major, K.136.

(M) *** Decca Ace of Diamonds SDD 251. Members of the Vienna Octet.

The K.334 *Divertimento* is a captivating piece scored for string quintet (including double bass) and two horns (used sparingly but effectively). It has a famous minuet which everyone knows, but the whole work offers Mozartian melody at its most attractive. The coupling is the best known of the *Divertimenti* for strings alone. Both are given here with fine verve, and the style of the leader (Anton Fietz) in his many solo passages is exactly right for this kind of music-making. This is in fact just how to play Mozart, with no stiffness anywhere. The recording is smooth, immediate and has striking presence.

Divertimento No. 17 in D major, K.334; Notturno (Serenade) in D major for 4 orchestras, K.286.

*** Argo ZRG 705. Academy of St Martin-in-the-Fields, Neville Marriner.

One day soon no doubt a quadraphonic version of Mozart's innocently tricky *Notturno for four orchestras* will be appearing, but until it does, this superbly stylish and beautifully recorded account will hold a necessary place. The *Divertimento* equally finds the Academy at its peak, relishing the technical problems of co-ordinating music which is often performed by solo strings. Opulent recording.

Wind Divertimenti

2 Divertimenti in B flat major for 3 basset horns, K.439b/2 and 4.

(B) * (*) Turnabout TV 34417S. Hans-Rudolf Stalder, Rolf Kubli, Hansjurg Leuthold (basset horns) – *6 Notturni for voices and wind.***

The rather dry sound conjured up by this Turnabout recording is not particularly beguiling. The performance of the *Divertimento*, K.439b, No. 2, which is on side one, is rather matter-of-fact and unspontaneous. Side two opens with the charming *Nocturnes* and these are followed by K.439b, No. 4, which has much more life and impact. But it is the *Nocturnes* that provide the main interest of this disc.

Divertimento for wind in B flat major, K.196f.

(B) ** DGG Heliodor 2548 122. Detmold Wind Sextet – SCHUBERT: *Trout quintet.***

This attractive *Divertimento* is given a lively performance and is well recorded. It makes an agreeable makeweight for a good bargain version of Schubert's *Trout quintet.*

Wind divertimenti and serenades as listed below; plus *Serenade No. 10 in E flat major, K.361* (as available separately on SXL 6049/53).

(M) *** Decca Ace of Diamonds SDD 405/9. London Wind Soloists, Jack Brymer.

Wind divertimenti Nos. 3 in E flat major, K.213; Serenade No. 11 in E flat major, K.375.

*** Decca SXL 6050. London Wind Soloists, Jack Brymer.

Wind divertimenti Nos. 4 in B flat major, K.186; 13 in F major, K.253; Serenade No. 12 in C minor, K.388.

*** Decca SXL 6051. London Wind Soloists, Jack Brymer.

Wind divertimenti Nos. 9 in B flat major, K.240; 12 in E flat major, K.252; Divertimento in E flat major, K.196e; Adagio in F major, K.410.

*** Decca SXL 6052. London Wind Soloists, Jack Brymer.

Wind divertimenti Nos. 14 in B flat major, K.270; 16 in E flat major, K.289; Divertimento in B flat major, K.196f; Adagio in B flat major, K.411.

*** Decca SXL 6053. London Wind Soloists, Jack Brymer.

As we go to press the set of recordings of this repertoire by the Netherlands Wind Ensemble has been deleted, so Brymer and his London Wind Soloists have the field to themselves until the Philips recordings are reissued, perhaps in an album. Certainly the Decca Ace of Diamonds album reissue makes a splendid bargain. But while factory stocks last the Decca records remain available separately. There is some gorgeous music here and much superb music-making. The bubbling spontaneity of the performances is matched by first-rate Decca sound, sweet, smooth and clear. A fine achievement.

Wind Divertimenti Arranged from Operas

Don Giovanni: excerpts (arr. for wind octet by Johann Triebensee); *Die*

Entführung aus dem Serail: excerpts (arr. for wind octet by Johann Wendt).
>> ** (*) Philips 6500 783. Netherlands Wind Ensemble.

Le Nozze di Figaro: excerpts (arr. for wind by Johann Wendt).
>> (M) *** Decca Ace of Diamonds SDD 280. London Wind Soloists, Jack Brymer.

These charming arrangements keep to the spirit if not always the letter of the music. The *Figaro* selection is notably high-spirited, and with polished and witty playing, marvellously recorded, this is most entertaining. The quality Philips provide for the Netherlands group is particularly rich. The warm, spacious acoustic adds nobility to the sound, so that the music-making in *Don Giovanni* – a particularly attractive selection – is so gracious and satisfying that one almost forgets about the missing voices. The items from *Die Entführung* seem rather less suitable for transcription, or perhaps Johann Wendt was not quite so skilful here as in *Figaro*, and the effect of the music-making is sometimes rather bland.

A Musical Joke (Ein Musikalischer Spass), K.522.
>> (B) ** Turnabout TV 34134S. Württemberg Chamber Orchestra, Joerg Faerber – LEOPOLD MOZART: *Musical Sleighride.***

The best way to bring off the *Musical Joke* on a disc is to do what the ensemble does here and play it absolutely deadpan. The outrageously wrong notes for the horns in the minuet sound grotesque, and the ridiculous coda lets the piece grind effectively to its close. The music is well played and recorded.

Notturno (Serenade) in D major for 4 orchestras, K.286; Lucio Silla: overture, K.135; Serenade No. 6 in D major

(Serenata notturna), K.239; Symphony No. 32 in G major, K.318; Thamos, King of Egypt (incidental music): *4 Interludes* (Nos. 2–5 of cpte edition), K.345.
>> (B) *** Decca Eclipse ECS 740. London Symphony Orchestra, Peter Maag.

An outstanding collection. Decca have not only reissued this on their cheapest label but have thrown in for good measure Maag's excellent performance of the little *G major Symphony*. The recording here is marginally less rich than the rest, but as the sound generally is of demonstration quality, this issue can certainly be recommended on technical as well as musical grounds. The *Notturno* really needs quadraphonic sound, but what the engineers have done is to combine, most artistically, stereo and distance effects so that the left-right alternation is helped out by a forward-backward placement to suggest Mozart's four groups. Using an SQ quadraphonic reproducer with the back speakers at a lower volume than the front, one can simulate Mozart's intentions with remarkable accuracy, and on an ordinary stereo set-up the illusion is pretty good. Of the other items the *Lucio Silla overture* and the *Thamos incidental music* are delightful and played with the crisply pointed style at which this conductor is so adept. There is perhaps marginally less sparkle in the *Serenata notturna*, but taken as a whole this is most rewarding.

Serenades

Serenade No. 1 in D major, K.100; A Musical Joke (Ein Musikalischer Spass), K.522.
>> *** Decca SXL 6499. Vienna Mozart Ensemble, Willi Boskovsky.

Serenades Nos. 3 in D major, K.185;

13 in G major (Eine kleine Nacht-musik), K.525.

> *** Decca SXL 6420. Vienna Mozart Ensemble, Willi Boskovsky.

After their success with the Mozart *Dances* and *Marches*, Boskovsky and the Vienna Mozart Ensemble turned their attention to the *Serenades* and the *Divertimenti.* Given playing of such elegance and sparkle and recording quality of the highest Decca standard, it is unlikely that confidence in the series will be misplaced. They even succeed with a piece like the *Musical Joke* (SXL 6499) in making it appear as an almost unqualified masterpiece.

Serenade No. 4 in D major (Colloredo), K.203; (i) *Concerto rondo in E flat major for horn and orchestra, K.371* (arr. Smith).

> *** Decca SXL 6330. Vienna Mozart Ensemble, Willi Boskovsky, (i) with Roland Berger (horn).

This *Serenade* dates in all probability from the year 1774, when Mozart was eighteen, and the suggestion by Mozart's first biographer that it was written for the name-day of Archbishop Colloredo has resulted in it being called the *Colloredo serenade.* The work embraces a violin concerto, as do many other of the serenades (preceding the independent concertos by several months), the solo part being played by Alfred Staar with great distinction. The music – in particular the Night Music for muted strings – is altogether delightful. The *Rondo,* K.371, is the earliest of Mozart's horn pieces. It survives in a fragmentary condition, and the arrangement here is by the producer of the Decca Mozart series, Erik Smith.

Serenade No. 4 in D major (Colloredo), K.203; Divertimento for strings No. 3 in

F major, K.138; March in D major, K.237.

> ** (*) HMV ASD 2309. Bath Festival Chamber Orchestra, Yehudi Menuhin.

Menuhin is not so well recorded as Boskovsky; the sound, although full and wide in range, has a touch, if marginal, of astringency. Menuhin's contribution as soloist in the *Serenade* is stylish, and the crisp vitality displayed by the orchestra in the outer movements matches the charm of the solo oboist in the sixth movement *Andante.*

Serenades Nos. 6 in D major (Serenata notturna), K.239; 9 in D major (Posthorn), K.320.

> ** (*) DGG 2530 082. Berlin Philharmonic Orchestra, Karl Boehm.

These are characteristic Boehm performances. A large orchestra is used in the *Posthorn serenade* and the playing is sophisticated (including the posthorn solos), warm, and civilized. There is a hint of suavity, although there is plenty of spirit in the allegros. The *Serenata notturna* gives a slightly more intimate impression, and the orchestra, as in the larger work, cannot be faulted. Excellent DGG sound, full yet lithe.

Serenades Nos. 6 in D major (Serenata notturna), K.239; 13 in G major (Eine kleine Nachtmusik), K.525; Minuet in C major, K.409; Minuet in D major (from *Divertimento No. 17 in D major, K.334).*

> (M) *** HMV SXLP 20019. Philharmonia Orchestra, Colin Davis.

An admirable collection of mainly night-music is played with stylish skill by Davis and the Philharmonia, whose soloists in the *Serenata notturna* are of a very high order indeed. The well-known

Nachtmusik is relaxed yet entirely convincing, and the string tone comes through with splendid clarity. The stereo perfectly adds an extra dimension, with striking directional effects, plus a congenial warmth. A fine bargain.

Serenade No. 7 in D major (Haffner), *K.250.*

*** Decca SXL 6614. Vienna Mozart Ensemble, Willi Boskovsky.

*** HMV ASD 2884. English Chamber Orchestra, Pinchas Zukerman.

** DGG 2530 290. Berlin Philharmonic Orchestra, Karl Boehm.

(M) * (*) Decca Ace of Diamonds SDD 198. Vienna Philharmonic Orchestra, Karl Münchinger.

* (*) BASF BAC 3015. Collegium Aureum (using original instruments).

We are well served as far as the *Haffner serenade* is concerned, for the first three performances will all give satisfaction in their different ways. The Berlin Philharmonic play with such polish and refinement of tone and their recording is so perfectly balanced that one is inclined to overlook a certain dourness on the part of Boehm. In the last analysis he is a shade wanting in sparkle and a sense of enjoyment.

Zukerman gives a beautifully turned and sparklingly recorded account of the work with the admirable ECO, not as impeccable in terms of sheer orchestral beauty of tone – or rather homogeneity of tone – but more spirited and eminently stylish. Perhaps Zukerman will be a little too sweet for some tastes in the solo violin sections; here Thomas Brandis on the DGG issue may have greater appeal. (The latter plays his own cadenzas in the second and fourth movements.)

However, the safest recommendation is undoubtedly the Decca version with Boskovsky conducting the Vienna Moz-

art Ensemble. It is marvellously alive, full of sparkle and elegance, with admirable phrasing and feeling for detail. The recording too is outstanding, more fresh and vivid than the DGG and as detailed and warm as the HMV.

Münchinger is surely a bit stiff for such a joyous occasion – the music, after all, was written to be played at a wedding – and, especially on side one, the direction is unnecessarily rigid and formal. The recording is good, but much less spacious than Boskovsky's disc, which is worth the extra cost. The Collegium Aureum account is outstandingly well recorded in a clear spacious acoustic. They play the opening movement with splendid point, Mozart's delicious arpeggio figure sounding particularly graceful. But after this the performance seems to lose its fire and spontaneity, and for all its instrumental authenticity is disappointing.

Serenade No. 9 in D major (Posthorn), *K.320.*

*** Decca SXL 6615. Adolf Holler (posthorn), Vienna Mozart Ensemble, Willi Boskovsky.

*** Philips 6500 627. Dresden State Orchestra, Edo de Waart.

The Decca disc upholds the fine tradition set by this series. None of its competitors matches its natural musicality and sense of sparkle. We have had some fine accounts in the past; Max Rudolf and the Cincinatti Orchestra was a much underrated and thoroughly idiomatic version, and both Boehm at full price and Szell at mid-price have much to recommend them, though the latter is a little too perfectly disciplined for all tastes. However, Boskovsky's version of this marvellous work is without question the best. It also has the advantage of superb Decca recording.

The version on Philips under Edo de Waart is, however, a very strong competitor, in some ways preferable even to

Boskovsky, though the recorded sound is not as fresh or rich. The Dresden Orchestra plays with superb musicianship and affection, and the result reminds one a little of some of Bruno Walter's pre-war Mozart records. With sparkling playing and very well disciplined, the reading also uses the marches Christa Landon includes in her edition of the score, which preface and round off the performance. Well worth considering alongside the Boskovsky.

Serenades Nos. 9 in D major (Posthorn), K.320; 13 in G major (Eine kleine Nachtmusik), K.525.

> (M) ** CBS Classics 61585. Cleveland Orchestra, George Szell.

Szell was not a man for charm in Mozart, and though the toughness of these performances of relatively lightweight works has its attractions, there are more sympathetic versions available. Bright-edged recording.

Serenade No. 10 in B flat major for 13 wind instruments, K.361.

> *** Philips LY 839734. Netherlands Wind Ensemble, Edo de Waart.
> *** Decca SXL 6049. London Wind Soloists, Jack Brymer.
> ** DGG 2530 136. Members of the Berlin Philharmonic Orchestra, Karl Boehm.
> (M) ** Vanguard VSD 71158. Wind Group of American Symphony Orchestra, Leopold Stokowski.

The Dutch players offer a marvellously fresh and alive performance. They are admirably sensitive both in feeling for line and phrasing but never linger lovingly over detail. This is both refreshing and satisfying and apart from the sheer quality of the playing, the impact of the disc is enhanced by the presence and sonority of the recording, which is beautifully balanced and marvellously crisp.

Brymer's group too give a strong, stylish performance with plenty of imagination in matters of phrasing. The Decca recording is rather close, which gives excellent inner clarity but sometimes means that the overall blend is not perfectly balanced. But this remains an outstanding alternative to the Netherlands disc. The playing of the Berlin Philharmonic wind under Karl Boehm shows impeccable refinement, but the recording quality is not the equal of the Philips either in presence or detail.

Stokowski's expressive exaggerations – inevitable even in Mozart – are never extreme, so that they do not seriously get in the way of enjoyment. The solo work in the lovely *Adagio* third movement is exceptionally sensitive in its flexibility, and the sprung rhythms of the fast movements are infectiously controlled. With no current bargain rival, this characterful performance is most recommendable. The recording can be made to sound very well.

Serenades Nos. 11 in E flat major, K.375; 12 in C minor, K.388.

> *** Philips LY 802907. Netherlands Wind Ensemble, Edo de Waart.
> (B) *** Classics for Pleasure CFP 40211. New London Wind Ensemble.
> ** (*) DGG 2530 369. Vienna Philharmonic Orchestra Wind Ensemble.
> (B) ** Pye GSGC 14062. London Baroque Ensemble, Karl Haas.

The Netherlands record easily leads the field of performances of this coupling. Like the rest of this set the performances here are remarkably fresh and clean, and the recording is first-rate.

The Classics for Pleasure disc, however, is a very strong contender, even making no allowance for its bargain price. The New London Wind Ensemble is made up of some of the finest soloists from the London orchestras. Their approach to these intense masterpieces – among Mozart's most compelling chamber works – is fresh and direct but full of spontaneous artistry to have one listening afresh. These enjoyable performances are even more stylish than the relatively mannered readings of Jack Brymer's London Wind Soloists (see under Wind divertimenti above). Good firm recording.

The Vienna Philharmonic wind will not satisfy some listeners. By comparison with the Berlin Philharmonic it is not by any means as perfectly blended; the Viennese oboe is thinner and reedier than one would like, though the clarinet is particularly silky and rich in tone. Both of these well recorded performances will give pleasure but it must be admitted that this ensemble is not what it was when it recorded the *K.361 Serenade* with Furtwängler: the tone is by no means as homogeneous. The Netherlands Wind Ensemble are crisper and more alert in this repertoire.

The recording quality of the Pye disc is not new, but wind instruments sound well enough even without the latest hi-fi, and Karl Haas's interpretations, rather hard-driven as they are, still allow plenty of stylish pointing by individual players. The phrasing of the oboe is specially ingratiating, even at high speed. Above all these are strong performances. As a worthwhile bonus the record includes alternative versions of the second *Minuet* and two *Trios* for the *Serenade, K.375.*

Serenade No. 13 in G major (Eine kleine Nachtmusik), K.525.
(B) ** Decca SPA 178. Vienna Philharmonic Orchestra, Karl Münchinger – MENDELSSOHN: *Midsummer Night's Dream overture;* SCHUBERT: *Symphony No. 8.***
Serenade No. 13 in G major (Eine kleine Nachtmusik), K.525; German dance, K.605/3: Sleighride.

(M) ** HMV SXLP 30161. Berlin Philharmonic Orchestra, Herbert von Karajan – *Ave verum;* LEOPOLD MOZART: *Toy symphony;* HANDEL: *Water music.***

There are many other excellent versions of Mozart's famous *Night music* coupled in various ways, notably Boskovsky's (with *Serenade No. 3*), Davison's on bargain label (with *Piano concerto No. 21*), Davis's (with *Serenade No. 6*) and Marriner's (see below). Karajan's later DGG recording is now only available in a two-disc set (see *Divertimento No. 15*), but this earlier EMI performance, characteristically smooth, but not without spirit, is attractive enough if the couplings are suitable. The favourite *German dance* is well done too.

Münchinger's approach is characteristically deadpan. But such a straightforward account can have its advantages when both playing and recording are so good. This performance is also available differently coupled – see under *Divertimento for strings No. 1.*

Serenade No. 13 in G major (Eine kleine Nachtmusik), K.525; (i) Sinfonia concertante for violin and viola in E flat major, K.364; Symphony No. 32 in G major, K.318.
** (*) Argo ZRG 679. Academy of St Martin-in-the-Fields, Neville Marriner, (i) with Ian Loveday (violin), Stephen Shingles (viola).

An attractive Mozart coupling stylishly played by the St Martin's Academy with refined atmospheric recording. The performance of the *Sinfonia concertante* with two regular members of the Academy as soloists goes for elegance rather than any stronger Mozartian qualities. Rival versions may make the outer movement sound more searingly inspired, and the slow movement here is wistfully refined rather than tragic, but there is a clear case for this approach. Both the brief exuberant *Symphony* and *Eine kleine Nachtmusik* are delightfully played. Versions of this most popular serenade which have such fresh, unaffected refinement are rare.

Sinfonia concertante in E flat major, K.297b (see also under *Flute and harp concerto*).

> *** HMV ASD 2462. English Chamber Orchestra, Daniel Barenboim – HAYDN: *Sinfonia concertante.****

Mozart's less famous and less great *Sinfonia concertante* has had a chequered career. The score was lost before its first Paris performance (for which it was written), and ever since it was recovered in the middle of the nineteenth century doubts have been expressed on its authenticity. One suspicious point is that the central slow movement fails to alter the basic tonality from E flat. But whatever the source there is much delightful music here, and with four fine wind soloists from the ECO and fullblooded direction by Barenboim this is a most attractive version, particularly when it is coupled with Haydn's wind *Sinfonia concertante*, a crisper, less expansive work.

Sinfonia concertante for violin and viola in E flat major K.364 (see also under *Clarinet concerto*).

> *** Philips SAL 3492. Arthur Grumiaux (violin), Arrigo Pelliccia (viola), London Symphony Orchestra, Colin Davis – *Violin concerto No. 2.****
>
> *** CBS Quadraphonic MQ 31369; Stereo 73030. Isaac Stern (violin), Pinchas Zukerman (viola), English Chamber Orchestra, Daniel Barenboim – STAMITZ: *Sinfonia concertante.****

Sinfonia concertante for violin and viola

in E flat major, K.364; Duo for violin and viola in G major, K.423.

> ** (*) Decca SXL 6088. Igor Oistrakh (violin), David Oistrakh (viola), Moscow Philharmonic Orchestra, Kyril Kondrashin.

Each of these records offers distinguished soloists and each offers in its own way a rewarding musical experience. But first choice goes to Philips. With crisp direction from Colin Davis, Grumiaux and Pelliccia give a most expressive performance, but one completely free from any thought of over-romanticizing Mozart. The phrasing in the slow movement is wonderfully flexible and as a whole the playing is very enjoyable indeed. The coupling is more appropriate than on rival versions and the recording follows the good qualities of Davis's Mozart series.

Stern recorded the great *Sinfonia concertante* for CBS at least twice before this version, which stands among the finest available, presenting as it does two soloists of equally strong musical personality. The central slow movement is taken at a very expansive *Andante*, but the concentration intensifies the beauty and the finale is sparkling and resilient – more so than on Stern's previous version in which he conducted himself. Fair if somewhat aggressive recording in stereo. The quadraphonic version mellows the first movement, marginally, but adds considerable ambient richness to the *Andante* and also in the finale, although here the sharply etched quality for the soloists is not entirely smoothed. Indeed the close balance of the soloists (who are larger than life) really makes nonsense of claims of a completely realistic quadraphonic image.

The performance by the Oistrakh duo is notable for its relaxed manner. Everything is shaped most musically, but sometimes the listener might feel that the performers in their care for detail and balance are less involved in the music itself. But the Decca recording is first-rate. As we go to press this performance has been reissued on Ace of Diamonds appropriately coupled to Haydn's *Sinfonia concertante* (under Dorati): SDD 445.

(i) *Sinfonia concertante for violin and viola in E flat major, K.364. Symphony No. 29 in A major, K.201.*

    (M) ** HMV SXLP 20112. Netherlands Chamber Orchestra, David Zinman, (i) with Norbert Brainin (violin), Peter Schidlof (viola).

A fine performance of the *Sinfonia concertante* with members of the Amadeus Quartet as soloists and lively, sympathetic accompaniment from the Dutch players under David Zinman. They cannot of course match Szell and the Cleveland Orchestra (discussed under the *Clarinet concerto* coupling) in purity of phrasing and subtlety of tone, but it is an apt enough accompaniment for a more relaxed approach from the two soloists, with greater rhythmic freedom used to good effect. Unfortunately Brainin's *vibrato* strikes the microphone unhappily at times. The glorious *A major Symphony* is given a delightful, youthfully fresh performance. First-rate recording.

(i) *Sinfonia concertante for violin and viola in E flat major, K.364;* (ii) *Concertone in C major for 2 violins, oboe, violoncello and orchestra, K.190.*

    (B) * (*) Turnabout TV 34098S. Susanne Lautenbacher (violin), Stuttgart Bach Collegium, Helmuth Rilling, with (i) Ulrich Koch (viola), (ii) Werner Keltsch (violin), Alfred Sous (oboe), Horst Beckedorf (cello).

The chief attraction of this Turnabout issue is the suitability of the coupling,

the rare *C major Concertone* with its unexpected collection of solo instruments. It is not the most vivid of early Mozart works, but it is interesting to hear. Otherwise the *Sinfonia concertante* is given a less polished account than one would normally ask for, with intonation by the soloists that is not always very sweet.

Organ sonata No. 4 in D major (for organ and chamber orchestra), *K.144.*

    (B) * (*) Turnabout TV 34135S. Helmuth Rilling (organ), Württemberg Chamber Orchestra, Joerg Faerber – ALBINONI: *Adagio;* HANDEL: *Cuckoo and the Nightingale concerto.***

Helmuth Rilling gives a sturdy if unsubtle account of K.144, but the disc is not likely to be chosen for this piece among its varied contents.

Symphonies

Symphonies Nos. 1–41 (complete recording).

    (M) ** (*) DGG 2740 109 (Nos. 1–24); 2740 110 (Nos. 25–41). Berlin Philharmonic Orchestra, Karl Boehm.

Symphonies Nos. 1 in E flat major, K.16; 4 in D major, K.19; 5 in B flat major, K.22; 6 in F major, K.43; 7a in G major, K.45a; 8 in D major, K.48; 9 in C major, K.73; 10 in G major, K.74; 11 in D major, K.84; 12 in G major, K.110; 13 in F major, K.112; 14 in A major, K.114; 15 in G major, K.124; 16 in C major, K.128; 17 in G major, K.129; 18 in F major, K.130; 19 in E flat major, K.132; and 1st version of *Andantino; 20 in D major, K.133; 42 in F major, K.75; 43 in F major, K.76; 44 in D major, K.81; 45 in D major, K.95; 46 in C major, K.96; 47 in D major,*

K.97; 55 in B flat major, K.45b; in C major, K.208/102; in D major, K.45; in D major, K.111/120; in D major, K.141a; in D major, K.196/121; in G major.

(M) *** Philips 6747 099 (8 discs). Academy of St Martin-in-the-Fields, Neville Marriner.

The two DGG boxes of Mozart symphonies under Boehm are ultimately let down by a certain dourness and want of sparkle. Of course, the orchestral playing from the Berlin Philharmonic is a joy in itself; phrasing is immaculate and en-semble beautifully disciplined. Yet in a sense, Günter Kehr's earlier Vox set, some of which are still in circulation, had a more Mozartian spirit, and they were far from second-rate recordings. (Indeed they stand up well to competition from 1970 sound.) Marriner's survey has a splendid Mozartian vitality and seems to combine the best qualities of both its predecessors. The Academy play with great style, warmth and polish, while the Philips engineers respond with alive and vivid recording. These are altogether delightful records and can be strongly recommended.

Symphonies Nos. 13 in F major, K.112; 14 in A major, K.114; 15 in F major, K.124; 16 in C major, K.128.

** (*) Argo ZRG 594. Academy of St Martin-in-the-Fields, Neville Marriner.

Brisk, fresh performances of four early Mozart symphonies to extend the high reputation of this fine group. These sym-phonies come from the period after Mozart's initial essays when he was beginning to imitate rather than to express his own untrammelled if im-mature genius. They are smoother than the very first symphonies but not more interesting. Marriner's directness refuses to compromise – Boehm in his complete

set is gentler, more persuasive – and with bright, clean recording they give much pleasure.

Symphonies Nos. 13 in F major, K.112; 16 in C major, K.128; 42 in F major, K.75; 44 in D major, K.81.

** (*) Philips 6500 535. I Musici.

The earliest of the symphonies re-corded here is the D major, K.81 (No. 44), written in Rome during Mozart's first visit to Italy in 1770. K.75 was probably written in Salzburg the follow-ing summer, K.112 (No. 13) in Milan in the same year (1771), and No. 16, K.128, dates from 1772. I Musici give eminently enjoyable performances and readers who for some reason do not want to invest in Marriner's disc of early symphonies or a complete box (see above) may well find this record a useful acquisition. It is cer-tainly an attractive one, and only the fact that the recording, though good, is not distinguished prevents a whole-hearted recommendation.

Symphonies Nos. 18 in F major, K.130; 19 in E flat major, K.132; 24 in B flat major, K.182 (EK.166e).

(B) ** Turnabout TV 34038S. Mainz Chamber Orchestra, Günter Kehr.

Symphonies Nos. 20 in D major, K.133; 23 in D major, K.181; 25 in G minor, K.183.

(B) ** Turnabout TV 34002S. Mainz Chamber Orchestra, Günter Kehr.

An eminently serviceable pair of discs for those interested in exploring the early Mozart symphonies if the expense be not too great. The playing is crisp and clean and not without warmth; the acoustic is agreeable and the recording good.

Symphonies Nos. 23 in D major, K.181; 24 in B flat major, K.182; 26 in E flat major, K.184; 27 in G major, K.199.

*** Argo ZRG 653. Academy of St Martin-in-the-Fields, Neville Marriner.

These were the last symphonies that Mozart wrote before the sequence of really great works starts with the little *G minor*, No. 25, and the *A major*, No. 29, and Marriner secures effervescent performances, more detailed in their lightness and understanding than those on the earlier Mozart symphony disc from this group. Any interpretative freedoms are positive additions to enjoyment, and with an aptly-sized group superbly recorded this is highly recommended.

Symphonies Nos. 25 in G minor, K.183; 26 in E flat major, K.184; 27 in G major, K.199.
   ** (*) DGG 2530 120. Berlin Philharmonic Orchestra, Karl Boehm.

These three symphonies come from the complete box that Boehm recorded in the late 1960s (see above). The playing of the Berlin Philharmonic is quite superlative, but enjoyment is marred somewhat by the want of spontaneity that distinguishes Boehm's direction. Marriner is far more spirited in No. 25 than Boehm, though the orchestral playing is less cultured. The finale rules the present reading 'out of court', for it is positively funereal. A pity, because the Berlin wind phrase exquisitely and the DGG recording is beautifully balanced.

Symphonies Nos. 25 in G minor, K.183; 29 in A major, K.201.
   ** (*) Argo ZRG 706. Academy of St Martin-in-the-Fields, Neville Marriner.

These performances have splendid life and polish. The pointing of the phrases of the 'little G minor' is done with a superb sense of style, and the scale of No. 29 is broad and forward-looking. The

recording may be too reverberant for some tastes, but the disc can be warmly recommended to all Morzartians.

Symphonies Nos. 25 in G minor, K.183; 40 in G minor, K.550.
   ** (*) Decca SXL 6617. Vienna Philharmonic Orchestra, Istvan Kertesz.

Mozart's two G minor symphonies make an apt coupling – Mozart in tragic mood commemorating a conductor much missed. In No. 40 Kertesz underlines the richness of the music, tempi on the slow side (except in the finale) with dramatic underlining of dynamic contrasts. The reading of No. 25 is the more remarkable, giving this relatively early work a comparable weight and strength – arguably too much so. But with superb playing and rich recording quality this makes a first-rate coupling.

Symphonies Nos. 28 in C major, K.200; 38 in D major (Prague), K.504; 4 Minuets, K.601.
   (M) *** Oiseau-Lyre SOL 266. English Chamber Orchestra, Colin Davis.

Colin Davis is at his most infectiously inspired in the early *C major Symphony*, and despite the use of a comparatively small-scale band, he captures the strength of the *Prague symphony*, with its obvious links with *Don Giovanni*, written about the same time. His treatment of the slow movement steers an admirable course between severity and affectionate treatment, and the English Chamber Orchestra responds wonderfully well. The recording is outstanding, and there are few more attractive Mozart symphony records in the catalogue.

Symphonies Nos. 29 in A major, K.201; 30 in D major, K.202; 34 in C major, K.338.

*** H M V ASD 2806. English Chamber Orchestra, Daniel Barenboim.

With fine rhythmic pointing and consistently imaginative phrasing Barenboim can be strongly recommended in all three of these symphonies – Nos. 29 and 34 among the most exhilarating of the Mozart symphonies with their heaven-scaling finales. No. 30 is among the less inspired of the cycle but worth hearing in a performance like this. Fine, vivid recording.

Symphonies Nos. 29 in A major, K.201; 33 in B flat major, K.319.
   ** (*) DGG SLPM 139002. Berlin Philharmonic Orchestra, Herbert von Karajan.

A very sparkling account of the *A major Symphony* from Karajan but one which may be a trifle too smooth for some tastes. The orchestral playing is, of course, superlative, and the DGG sound is warm and velvety. Much the same comments apply to the *B flat Symphony.*

Symphonies Nos. 29 in A major, K.201; 35 in D major (Haffner), K.385.
   ** Decca SXL 6616. Vienna Philharmonic Orchestra, Istvan Kertesz.

Kertesz secures good playing from the Vienna Philharmonic and is well served by the engineers, but though these are eminently serviceable accounts, they are somewhat faceless. There are other performances of greater character currently available which will give more satisfaction.

Symphonies Nos. 29 in A major, K.201; 41 in C major (Jupiter), K.551.
   (B) * (*) Pye GSGC 14060. Hallé Orchestra, Sir John Barbirolli.

A warm but rather slack performance of No. 29 from Barbirolli, given a matching, pleasant-sounding recording with not a great deal of bite, even in the finale. The minuet is the weakest movement. Here Barbirolli's affection cannot compensate for a lack of rhythmic vigour. The *Jupiter* too is exceedingly mellow, and the first movement is almost gentle. There is a curiously Italianate flavour to the textures, especially in the *Andante cantabile*, which is done with considerable warmth in spite of the very relaxed playing; and the minuet's main theme floats gracefully over its accompanying chords at exactly the right tempo. The whole effect is amplified by the bland recorded quality (which has only a minimal stereo effect).

Symphonies Nos. 31 in D major (Paris), K.297; 41 in C major (Jupiter), K.551.
   *** H M V ASD 2379. English Chamber Orchestra, Daniel Barenboim.

In Mozart's last and longest symphony Barenboim rightly focuses attention on the grand sweep of the finale. He observes the second-half repeat as well as the first to give Mozart's complex fugal design a majesty comparable only with Beethoven, and that at a brisk, swashbuckling tempo. The rest of the symphony is interpreted with equal compulsion, and the *Paris* is also given an outstanding performance, the contrasts of mood in the first movement underlined and the finale taken at a hectic tempo that would have sounded breathless with players any less brilliant than the modest-sized ECO. Though Barenboim insists on an authentically-sized orchestra so that balance between sections is accurate, the sound caught by the EMI engineers is forward and full-blooded. A good first record to sample in the Barenboim series.

Symphonies Nos. 32 in G major, K.318; 35 in D major (Haffner), K.385; 38 in D major (Prague), K.504.

** HMV ASD 2327. English Chamber Orchestra, Daniel Barenboim.

Barenboim offers a spirited, straightforward account of Mozart's 'Italian overture' symphony, and the finale is especially successful. Playing and recording are both excellent. He is again strongly vigorous in the first movement of the *Haffner*, bold almost to the point of brusqueness, the polish of the orchestral playing itself contributing a modicum of poise. The slow movement is nicely done, but this is an enjoyable rather than a memorable performance. In the *Prague* Barenboim obviously intends the full weight of the imposing introduction to the first movement to be felt, and to tell the truth he miscalculates a trifle, and the listener is impatient for the allegro to begin. When it does it is gracious yet alive and the scale of impetus of the music is right. The finale too is beautifully turned, with a spirit of light-hearted gaiety throughout. The *Andante*, however, although nicely shaped, is rather serious-minded. But taken together these performances are certainly enjoyable.

Symphonies Nos. 33 in B flat major, K.319; 36 in C major (Linz), K.425.

(M) ** (*) Oiseau-Lyre SOL 60049. English Chamber Orchestra, Colin Davis.

Davis gave us the first stereo recording of No. 33, and it still sounds well. The crisp strings and clean-sounding woodwind of the English Chamber Orchestra respond immediately to Davis's lively direction, and the performance has wit as well as breadth. The *Linz* is equally successful. There is no forcing of the issue here, but a direct, forthright account of the quick movements and a decorous shaping of the slow movement's incomparable contours. The woodwind are very occasionally prominent in a way that would never happen in a concert hall, but otherwise the balance is admirable.

Symphonies Nos. 33 in B flat major, K.319; 39 in E flat major, K.543.

** Decca SXL 6056. Vienna Philharmonic Orchestra, Istvan Kertesz.

Beautiful orchestral playing, warm recording and a gracious feeling for eighteenth-century style characterize this enjoyable, but not outstanding disc. The earlier symphony, played in a simple and relaxed way, comes off very well but the great *E flat Symphony* does not display its full character as it does under, say, Davis or Barenboim.

Symphony No. 35 in D major (Haffner), K.385.

** Abbey ABY 733. London Mozart Players, Harry Blech – HAYDN: *Symphony No. 90.***

Compare this Mozart sound with one of the early LPs (mono) that Blech made with his then pioneering chamber orchestra, and it is amazing, allowing for the development of recording technique, that the sound is so consistent. This is not as polished a performance as the best in the catalogue, but it will please the many devotees of Blech and the L M P.

Symphonies Nos. 35 in D major (Haffner), K.385; 36 in C major (Linz), K.425; 38 in D major (Prague), K.504; 39 in E flat major, K.543; 40 in G minor, K.550; 41 in C major (Jupiter), K.551.

(B) ** (*) CBS 77308 (3 discs). Columbia Symphony Orchestra, Bruno Walter.

(M) ** (*) HMV SLS 809 (4 discs, including rehearsal record). Berlin Philharmonic Orchestra, Herbert von Karajan.

Bruno Walter in his time was among the most persuasive Mozartians, and it is fascinating to have this substantial sample of his interpretations recorded during his retirement in California. Maybe over the years he modified his view to suit contemporary taste, but there are relatively few of the romantic exaggerations one might expect from a conductor who learnt his Mozart from Mahler. Warmth and expressiveness are the touchstones, still very appealing for the sympathetic listener. Very good recording.

Karajan's set has a rehearsal record thrown in at no extra charge. However, as the conductor's comments are spoken in German, the non-linguist will need the translation in the booklet which goes with the records. This is large-orchestra Mozart, the fairly reverberant acoustic giving considerable breadth and impact to the orchestra. The interpretations too have plenty of weight, notably so the *Jupiter*, although Karajan shows poise and grace: the opening of No. 36 is especially fine. Yet in the last resort this music-making is wanting in the final touch of spontaneity and fire, and for all the magnificent orchestral playing the listener is sometimes left vaguely unsatisfied.

Symphonies Nos. 35 in D major (Haffner), K.385; 39 in E flat major, K.453.
   *** HMV ASD 3016. Berlin Philharmonic Orchestra, Herbert von Karajan.

Karajan's account of the *E flat Symphony* is the best of the six he recorded for EMI. The playing of the Berlin Orchestra has superb polish and refinement of tone, and few readers will find much to quarrel with in Karajan's interpretation. Ultimately the same strictures that apply to the companion discs apply also to this, but the performance has great power for all that. Admirers of these artists need have no occasion to hesitate.

Symphonies Nos. 35 in D major (Haffner), K.385; 40 in G minor, K.550; March in D major, K.385a.

   *** Philips 6500 162. Academy of St Martin-in-the-Fields, Neville Marriner.

Marriner's stylish coupling uses original scorings of both works – minus flutes and clarinets in the *Haffner*, minus clarinets in No. 40. The *March* is included as makeweight, since (having the same K. number) it has long been associated with the *Haffner symphony*. Marriner's readings are finely detailed but dynamic too, nicely scaled against refined recording.

Symphonies Nos. 35 in D major (Haffner), K.385; 41 in C major (Jupiter), K.551.
   ** Philips 6500 429. Concertgebouw Orchestra, Josef Krips.
   (B) * (*) Decca SPA 336. Israel Philharmonic Orchestra, Josef Krips.

We still hope to see Jochum's outstanding record of this coupling return on Philips's Universo label. The reissue of Krips's earlier disc on Decca's cheapest label may attract some, for his performance of the *Haffner* is bright and alive, with zest in the outer movements, a pert yet gracious *Andante*, and a notably elegant minuet. The recording too is good, forwardly projected, well balanced and natural. The sound has noticeably less body and impact in the *Jupiter*, and here Krips holds the tension much more slackly. Generally the newer Philips disc is finer, notably so in the *Jupiter*, with good recording and good playing. But ultimately these readings disappoint. There is something unmemorable and wanting in character here that does not do full honour to the fine Mozartian that Krips was.

Symphony No. 36 in C major (Linz), K.425.
   * (**) Decca SET 332. Vienna Philharmonic Orchestra, Leonard

645

Bernstein – *Piano concerto No. 15.* (**)

Such a record as this claims Leonard Bernstein as a European at heart. In the performance of the *Linz symphony* one may keep recognizing the characteristic Bernstein touches that we know from his New York performances – the glowing violin lyricism in the slow introduction, the bristling manner of the *Allegro* – but somehow a carefree quality is there too, such as one finds only rarely in his American records. In addition the recording quality provided by the Decca engineers, not to mention the comparatively small forces used, give a transparency to the sound of a kind one may hear from Bernstein in the concert-hall but rarely on record. Yet some ears find Bernstein's music-making here too individually mannered, emphasizing detail in an overtly personal way.

Symphonies Nos. 36 in C major (Linz), K.425; 38 in D major (Prague), K.504.
- (M) *** Philips Universo 6580 023. Concertgebouw Orchestra, Eugen Jochum.
- (B) *** Classics for Pleasure CFP 40079. London Philharmonic Orchestra, Charles Mackerras, with Mauritz Sillem (harpsichord).
- ** (*) HMV ASD 2918. Berlin Philharmonic Orchestra, Herbert von Karajan.

Jochum's earlier account of the *Linz* with the Bavarian Radio Orchestra was one of his finest records. This version is a worthy successor to it: these are performances with genuine inner vitality, an abundant warmth and plenty of power. There is a classical poise and humanity about Jochum's Mozart which never fail to impress. The Concertgebouw Orchestra is at its finest and the recording quality is very truthful.

Though the inclusion of harpsichord continuo will not please everyone, Mackerras's are fine, stylish performances of both works, splendidly played and recorded. An outstanding bargain.

Marvellous playing from the Berlin Philharmonic and excellent HMV recording. There is superb polish and the most refined musicianship here and this alone cannot fail to give pleasure. Yet for all Karajan's authority and musical insight, there is a want of sparkle and inner vitality – perhaps spontaneity is the best word – that slightly diminishes the impact of these performances. Yet too much should not be made of this, for by any standards this is most distinguished music-making.

Symphonies Nos. 36 in C major (Linz), K.425; 39 in E flat major, K.543.
- *** DGG SLPM 139160. Berlin Philharmonic Orchestra, Karl Boehm.

Boehm can be an unsmiling Mozart conductor, but at his best he is as sparkling as he is humane and poetic. This record is altogether one of his best, with effortlessly alert orchestral playing of great tonal beauty. It is difficult to choose between Boehm's *Linz* and Jochum's; perhaps there is a marginal difference in favour of Boehm as far as the quality of the orchestral tone is concerned, but doubtless questions of coupling will decide. The recording is one of the best from this source.

Symphony No. 38 in D major (Prague), K.504.
- *** Decca SXL 6539. English Chamber Orchestra, Benjamin Britten – SCHUBERT: *Symphony No. 8.****

Here as in his unique record of Mozart's *40th Symphony* Britten conveys a real sense of occasion, from the weighty introduction through a glowing and resilient account of the *Allegro* to a full flowing reading of the *Andante*. The *Giovanni* overtones are very clear indeed, with fine resonant Maltings recording.

Symphonies Nos. 39 in E flat major, K.543; 40 in G minor, K.550.
- *** H M V A S D 2424. English Chamber Orchestra, Daniel Barenboim.
- (M) *** Philips Universo 6580 029. London Symphony Orchestra, Colin Davis.
- ** Philips 6500 430. Concertgebouw Orchestra, Josef Krips.

Strong, straightforward performances from Davis, refreshingly stylish and alive. The vivacious finale of No. 39 and the slow movement of the *G minor Symphony* have special character. The recording is very good. Yet with all the undoubted excellence of the Davis coupling there is an extra warmth and luminosity about Barenboim's approach. Imaginative phrasing from the strings is matched by wind playing in which the colour is well brought out. The performances are thoughtful, yet spacious, alive and exciting too. The scale is right and the warm, smooth recording, perhaps a little lacking in sparkle, but very well balanced, is satisfying.

Krips offers well-shaped readings and good recording, but in the last resort these performances do not kindle one's enthusiasm like those of Barenboim or Davis.

Symphony No. 40 in G minor, K.550.
- (B) *** Philips 6833 102. London Symphony Orchestra, Colin Davis – BEETHOVEN: *Symphony No. 5.***
- (M) ** (*) Decca Ace of Diamonds SDD 233. Vienna Philharmonic Orchestra, Herbert von Karajan – HAYDN: *Symphony No. 104.****

Whether coupled with Mozart's *Symphony No. 39* (as it is in the Universo

issue) or with George Szell's impressive account of Beethoven's *Fifth*, Davis's version of No. 40 is one of the most recommendable versions ever issued, with its direct, alert interpretation, stylish from first bar to last. Karajan's account is also available coupled to the *Jupiter symphony* and is discussed below.

Symphony No. 40 in G minor, K.550; Serenade No. 6 in D major (Serenata notturna), K.239.
- ** (*) Decca SXL 6372. English Chamber Orchestra, Benjamin Britten.

Britten takes *all* repeats (the slow movement here is longer than that of the *Eroica*) but is almost totally convincing, with the rich Maltings sound to give added weight. The filler is enchanting.

Symphonies Nos. 40 in G minor, K.550; 41 in C major (Jupiter), K.551.
- (M) ** (*) Decca Ace of Diamonds SDD 361. Vienna Philharmonic Orchestra, Herbert von Karajan.
- ** H M V A S D 2732. Berlin Philharmonic Orchestra, Herbert von Karajan.
- (B) ** Classics for Pleasure CFP 127. Sinfonia of London, Anthony Collins.

The Ace of Diamonds coupling is excellent value. In the *G minor* every detail is beautifully in place, each phrase nicely shaped and in perspective. The exposition repeat in the first movement is observed, though the chords linking it to the development are prominent at a slightly higher level and the balance thereafter appears to be closer. Beautifully articulate and suave, this performance has a genuine dramatic power, even though one feels that it all moves within carefully regulated emotional limits. Karajan does tend to beautify detail without adding corresponding stature. The reading of the *Jupiter* is a strong one, one of the best things Karajan did in his short period in the Decca studios. The performance is direct and has breadth as well as warmth. The orchestral playing is excellent, and with first-rate sound this is a certainly enjoyable.

In the last resort, however, though one cannot fail to admire these performances, there is some want of spontaneity here. But the same must also be said of the readings Karajan gives with the Berlin Philharmonic, though the recorded sound is slightly richer and more detailed. The playing of this orchestra is a joy in itself and the interpretations on HMV are purposeful and considered, even if they do not have the sparkle and naturalness of the very finest recorded performances of these works.

Clear, direct accounts of both symphonies from Collins, with good orchestral playing, and crisp if rather dry recording. Some might feel that the first movement of the *G minor Symphony* is slightly under-characterized, but although Collins's manner is comparatively robust, the overall shaping is sensitive and alive. The allegros in both works are pleasingly spirited, while the conductor gets a little carried away at the very end of the *Jupiter symphony* and suddenly presses his tempo forward in the concluding few bars. But this is a rewarding coupling and an excellent bargain.

Symphony No. 41 in C major (Jupiter), K.551.

   *** DGG 2530 357. Boston Symphony Orchestra, Eugen Jochum – SCHUBERT: *Symphony No. 8.****

   (M) ** (*) Decca Ace of Diamonds SDD 312. Vienna Philharmonic Orchestra, Herbert von Karajan – HAYDN: *Symphony No. 103.***

Jochum's strong, classical reading of

the *Jupiter* is superbly backed by splendid playing from the Boston Orchestra and fine, atmospheric recording. With one of the most beautiful performances available of the *Unfinished symphony* for coupling, it makes an outstanding recommendation. Karajan's account is discussed above under its alternative coupling, the *Symphony No. 40.*

CHAMBER AND INSTRUMENTAL MUSIC

(i) *Clarinet quintet in A major, K.581;* *Divertimento in D major, K.136* (quartet version).

   (B) *** Saga 5291. Aeolian String Quartet, (i) with Thea King (clarinet).

Thea King is a fine Mozartian. She plays the work in a classical manner, but with great refinement in matters of tonal shading, and her phrasing is most beautiful. There is, it is true, a touch of coolness in the first two movements, but the music still glows, and Miss King's articulation in the third-movement solos and in the delightfully pointed finale is a joy to hear. The closing pages of the work are especially beautiful. This is all helped by excellent support from the Aeolian Quartet and one of the best recordings we have had from Saga. The filler is bright and breezy, with very fast tempi for the outer movements and a graceful, if matter-of-fact account of the *Andante.*

(i) *Clarinet quintet in A major, K.581;* (ii) *Clarinet trio in E flat major, K.498.*

   *** HMV ASD 605. Gervase de Peyer (clarinet), members of the Melos Ensemble.

   ** Philips 6500 073. Jack Brymer (clarinet), (i) Allegri Quartet; (ii) Stephen Bishop (piano), Patrick Ireland (viola).

The lovely H M V disc is among the finest of Mozart chamber music records. These two warm, limpid yet vital performances make a very happy coupling and are supported by first-class recording. An outstandingly beautiful issue.

Brymer's interpretation of the *Quintet* is warm and leisurely. In some ways Brymer follows the famous Bavier recording from Decca's early mono LP days in choosing slow tempi throughout. He is nearly as successful as Bavier in sustaining them, although in the finale the forward flow of the music is reduced to a near-crawl. In the *Trio* the piano is backwardly balanced and Stephen Bishop's contribution makes less than its proper effect. But otherwise the recorded sound is beautiful.

(i) *Clarinet quintet in A major, K.581;*
(ii) *Oboe quartet in F major, K.370.*
    ** DGG SLPM 138996. (i) Karl Leister (clarinet); (ii) Lother Koch (oboe); both with members of the Berlin Philharmonic Orchestra.
    (B) ** Classics for Pleasure CFP 121. (i) Keith Puddy (clarinet); (ii) Ian Wilson (oboe); both with Gabrieli Quartet.

The DGG coupling of the *Clarinet quintet* and *Oboe quartet* offers fine playing and suave recording. Of the two soloists, Karl Leister the clarinettist does not emerge as a strong individual personality, but his colleague, Lothar Koch, shows a sweetly pointed timbre and an exact feeling for the style of the work featuring the oboe. Those wanting this coupling should not be disappointed here on musical or technical grounds; but there are more glowing accounts of the *Clarinet quintet* available.

Keith Puddy and the Gabrieli Quartet give a fine straightforward reading of the *Quintet*, not quite so deeply understanding as Thea King's on Saga, but better recorded and with a coupling which

could hardly be more apt. Ian Wilson misses some of the charm of the delectable *Oboe quartet*, but the freshness in so buoyantly open a work is hard to resist, and the recording quality is good.

Clarinet quintet in A major, K.581; (i) *Piano and wind quintet in E flat major, K.452.*
    (M) ** Decca Ace of Diamonds SDD 289. Members of the Vienna Octet, (i) with Walter Panhoffer (piano).

Boskovsky's account of the *Clarinet quintet* is gracious and intimate, a little lacking in individuality, but enjoyable in its unforced way. The closing pages of the work are given a real Viennese lilt. The recording is warm and sympathetic. The account of the *Piano and wind quintet* might best be described as sturdy. Not all the subtleties of Mozart's part-writing are fully revealed, and the playing is rather earthbound. The recording is a fairly old one but sounds remarkably well, although the stereo has not a great deal of inner separation when the group are all playing together.

Clarinet trio in E flat major, K.498.
    (M) ** Oiseau-Lyre SOL 60020. Melos Ensemble – WEBER: *Quintet.***

A fine performance of the *Clarinet trio* clearly recorded. The coupling with the Weber *Quintet* is a valuable one, and this disc can be confidently recommended. The players here are Gervase de Peyer (clarinet), Cecil Aronowitz (viola) and Lamar Crowson (piano).

(i) *Clarinet trio in E flat major, K.498;*
(ii) *Horn quintet in E flat major, K.407.*
    (B) ** Oryx EXP 43. Consortium Classicum, with (i) Dieter Klocker (clarinet); (ii) Erich Penzel (horn).

The clearly separated realistic sound picture offered by the Oryx stereo contributes a great deal to the success of this coupling. Both soloists are excellent players and they are well supported by the string players. The readings have character and are musical in a pleasurable way, if perhaps lacking that extra degree of personality that Dennis Brain, for instance, could bring to the *Horn quintet*. Most enjoyable just the same.

Divertimento in E flat major for string trio (violin, viola, and violoncello), *K.563.*
> *** Philips SAL 3664. Arthur Grumiaux (violin), Georges Janzer (viola), Eva Szabo (cello).
> ** (*) DGG SLPM 139150. Trio Italiano d'Archi.

Grumiaux has long been remarkable even among the most outstanding virtuosi of the day for his purity of intonation, and here he is joined by two players with a similarly refined and classical style. They may only be an ad hoc group, but their unanimity is most striking, and Grumiaux's individual artistry gives the interpretation an extra point over the rival Italian Trio's. The hushed opening of the first-movement development – a visionary passage – is played with a magically intense half-tone, and the lilt of the finale is infectious from the very first bar. The title *Divertimento* is of course a monumental misnomer, for this is one of the richest of Mozart's last-period chamber works, far too rarely heard in the concert-hall. The recording is one of the most vivid that Philips has ever produced.

Like the Grumiaux version, the DGG performance is remarkable for its accuracy of intonation. The Italian String Trio is a wonderfully polished group, in a way too polished, for their trim, fast speeds reveal rather too little 'temperament'. This is not quite so communica-

tive or characterful a performance as Grumiaux's. Were the rival version to disappear, this one would be highly acceptable as an alternative, for the recording is superbly engineered.

Flute quartets Nos. 1 in D major, K.285; 2 in G major, K.285a; 3 in C major, K.285b; 4 in A major, K.298.
> *** Philips 6500 034. William Bennett (flute), Grumiaux Trio.
> *** DGG SLPM 138997. Karlheinz Zöller (flute), members of the Berlin Philharmonic Orchestra.

There seems general agreement about the merits of the William Bennett-Grumiaux Trio account of the Mozart quartets. They are, to put it in a nutshell, exquisitely played and recorded and are in every way finer than their rivals. The freshness both of playing and recording makes them preferable to the DGG recording, although this too is a fine disc. Karlheinz Zöller is a first-class artist and he is supported with affection and style by his fellow-musicians from the Berlin Philharmonic. The balance is excellent and DGG's recording of high quality.

Flute quartets Nos. 1 in D major, K.285; 4 in A major, K.298; Horn quintet in E flat major, K.407; Oboe quartet in F major, K.370.
> (B) ** Saga 5127. Augmented Fine Arts Quartet.

(i) *Horn quintet in E flat major, K.407;* (ii) *Oboe quartet in F major, K.370;* (iii) *Clarinet trio in E flat major, K.498.*
> (B) ** Turnabout TV 34035S. (i) Sebastian Huber (horn); (ii) Alfred Sous (oboe); (iii) Walter Triebskorn (clarinet); all with members of the Endres Quartet.

The performances on Turnabout are all characterful and they are well recorded.

But the Saga coupling is a strong competitor. Here the horn-player, John Barrows, and the oboist, Ray Still, have individual personalities, and both are fine executants; the flautist has less personal presence, but produces a beautiful tone. Both discs are well recorded; on balance the Turnabout is slightly preferable, and pressings are rather more reliable in the matter of quiet surfaces.

Flute sonatas (for flute and harpsichord) *Nos. 1 in B flat major; 2 in G major; 3 in A major; 4 in F major; 5 in C major; 6 in B flat major, K.10–15.*
- (B) ** (*) Turnabout TV 34314S. Gottfried Hechtl (flute), Beatrice Klien (harpsichord).
- (M) * (*) Decca Ace of Diamonds SDD 449. Wolfgang Schulz (flute), Heinz Medjimorec (piano).

Mozart composed these sonatas at the age of eight. They were probably written in London and they are dedicated to Queen Charlotte. Much of the music is primitive by Mozartian standards, with plenty of Alberti basses in the keyboard part. But odd movements show the individuality of genius emerging, and the last three sonatas (K.15 in particular) have many points of interest. There is no problem of choice between the two discs, which were issued at the same time. The Ace of Diamonds is recorded in an unsuitably reverberant acoustic, and besides lacking inner clarity, the piano sound is all wrong, much too rich and romantic for works clearly designated for the harpsichord. The Turnabout disc has its faults of balance; the flautist is too close (his image is large and one can hear him taking breaths), but the harpsichord is not out of the picture and is given an attractive sound. These are sprightly performances, stylish, with no lack of sparkle, and a spontaneous impulse that is hard to resist; but this is not a record to be played all at once.

(i) *Horn quintet in E flat major, K.407;* (ii) *String quintet No. 4 in G minor, K.516.*
- ** (*) DGG 2530 012. Amadeus Quartet, with (i) Gerd Seifert (horn); (ii) Cecil Aronowitz (viola).

This disc combines the well-known Amadeus interpretation of the *G minor String quintet* with an equally assured performance of the *Horn quintet*. Gerd Seifert is an accomplished hornist, and sensitive in matters of phrasing and dynamics. Thus both performances are eloquently played, without either having that extra degree of magic (and in the case of the *Horn quintet* irrepressible high spirits) that makes a truly memorable effect on the listener. However, at the moment the Amadeus performance of the *String quintet* is the finest the catalogue has to offer and it is perhaps easy to underestimate its very real merits. Recordings of both works are immaculate in matters of tone and balance.

Piano quartets Nos. 1 in G minor, K.478; 2 in E flat major, K.493.
- (M) ** Oiseau-Lyre SOL 285. Pro Arte Piano Quartet.
- (M) * (*) Philips Universo 6500 098. Ingrid Haebler (piano), Michel Schwalbe (violin), Giusto Cappone (viola), Ottomar Borwitzky (cello).

The Pro Arte Quartet performances are both spirited and stylish and they are very well recorded. Ingrid Haebler too plays with elegance and grace, but this account has rather less substance, although the recording is first-class. Readers are reminded that Clifford Curzon's set with the Amadeus Quartet (dating from 1953) is available on Decca Eclipse (ECS 523). The performances have a unique sparkle, but the recording, in spite of the stereo transcription, is without the lustre of the more modern issues.

Piano and wind quintet in E flat major, K.452.

> *** Decca SXL 6252. Vladimir Ashkenazy (piano), London Wind Soloists – BEETHOVEN: *Quintet.****
>
> * (*) Philips 6500 326. Ingrid Haebler (piano), Bamberg Wind Quartet – BEETHOVEN: *Quintet.** (*)

Ashkenazy's performance is in a class of its own, polished, urbane, yet marvellously spirited. The balance and sound-quality are of the highest rank. Ingrid Haebler is characteristically stylish, but the wind-playing in Bamberg does not take flight, and the performance as a whole is straightforward rather than imaginative. There is also a version by Brendel on Turnabout (TV 34095S), coupled to a recommendable account of the *Piano concerto No. 20 in D minor, K.466.* Brendel himself is on top form, but is let down by unpolished wind playing, with individual solos out of tune.

Piano trios Nos. 1 in B flat major, K.254; 2 in G major, K.496; 5 in C major, K.548.

> ** (*) Philips SAL 3682. Beaux Arts Trio.

Piano trios Nos. 3 in E flat major, K.502; 4 in E major, K.542; 6 in G major, K.564.

> ** (*) Philips SAL 3681. Beaux Arts Trio.

Mozart's *Piano trios* are somewhat uneven in quality and substance, and Philips have divided their layout so that each disc contains at least one masterpiece. The playing is generally fresh and alive, the piano dominating as Mozart obviously intended. The recording too is excellent: this is a field in which the smooth, clear Philips sound suits the music very well indeed.

String Quartets and Quintets

String quartets Nos. 1–23; Adagio and fugue in C minor, K.546; Divertimenti for strings Nos. 1 in D major, K.136; 2 in B flat major, K.137; 3 in F major, K.138.

> ⊛ (M) *** Philips 6747 097 (9 discs). Italian Quartet.

String quartets Nos. 1 in G major, K.80; 2 in D major, K.155; 3 in G major, K.156; 4 in C major, K.157; Adagio (originally intended for Quartet No. 3, K.156).

> *** Philips 6500 142. Italian Quartet.

This playing is absolutely first-class, everything perfectly matched, with beautifully homogeneous tone, spontaneous yet polished phrasing in a recording of great naturalness and realism. The album containing the complete set makes an outstanding investment – unlikely to be bettered in the immediate future.

String quartets Nos. 5 in F major, K.158; 6 in B flat major, K.159; 7 in E flat major, K.160; 8 in F major, K.161.

> *** Philips 6500 172. Italian Quartet.

The Italian Quartet play these early Mozart works with the poise and perfection of ensemble that distinguish their set as a whole. The only special point to note here is that these are not otherwise available separately at present. Given the sumptuous recording and the superb performances, there is no need for alternatives.

String quartets Nos. 9 in A major, K.169; 10 in C major, K.170; 11 in E flat major, K.171; 12 in B flat major, K.172.

> *** Philips 6500 644. Italian Quartet.

String quartet No. 13 in D major, K.173; Adagio and fugue in C minor, K.546; Divertimenti for strings Nos. 1 in D major, K.136; 2 in B flat major, K.137; 3 in F major, K.138.

   *** Philips 6500 645. Italian Quartet.

String quartets Nos. 14 in G major, K.387; 15 in D minor, K.421; 16 in E flat major, K.428; 17 in B flat major (Hunt), K.458; 18 in A major, K.464; 19 in C major (Dissonance), K.465.

   *** Philips SAL 3632 (Quartets 14 and 15); SAL 3633 (16 and 17); SAL 3634 (18 and 19). Italian Quartet.

The Italian Quartet continue their series in impeccable style, including also outstanding performances of the *Adagio and fugue* and the sparkling string *Divertimenti*. Their set of the six *Haydn quartets* is the finest available. The playing is always stylish, unfailingly perceptive, and most musical. Moreover, the recordings are excellent and truthful.

String quartets Nos. 14 in G major, K.387; 15 in D minor, K.421; 16 in E flat major, K.428; 17 in B flat major (Hunt), K.458; 18 in A major, K.464; 19 in C major (Dissonance), K.465; 20 in D major (Hoffmeister), K.499; 21 in D major (Prussian No. 1), K.575; 22 in B flat major (Prussian No. 2), K.589; 23 in F major (Prussian No. 3), K.590.

   (M) ** DGG 2720 055 (5 discs). Amadeus Quartet.

The DGG album offers us the 'Ten Celebrated Quartets', as opposed to the complete *œuvre* on Philips. The Amadeus play with great polish and fluency, though their style in Mozart is not to everyone's taste. They have a devoted following, however, and the set can be warmly recommended to their admirers. However, the Italians offer the more musically satisfying readings, plainer in some ways, more classically poised and perfectly blended in tone, and much better recorded.

String quartets Nos. 14 in G major, K.387; 18 in A major, K.464.

   ** DGG SLPM 138909. Amadeus Quartet.

The performance of the *G major Quartet* is the finer of the two here. The phrasing in the slow movement shows the Amadeus at their most perceptive, and the concentration in the finale is remarkable. In the account of K.464, the blandness that at times pervades Amadeus performances mars the playing here to some extent. The curious mannerism of sometimes swelling out on individual notes is noticeable, and there is generally not the tension that is found in the performance of K.387. The recording is excellent.

String quartets Nos. 15 in D minor, K.421; 19 in C major (Dissonance), K.465.

   ** DGG SLPM 139190. Amadeus Quartet.

The playing here is wonderfully poised and stylish, but there are a number of interpretative points to question, notably on the choice of speeds. The choice of an exceptionally slow speed for the first movement of the *D minor* is presumably intended to give it tragic depth, but if that is so, why did the Amadeus omit the exposition repeat, which one would think essential to balance the weight of argument with an appropriate time-scale? Curiously in the *C major Quartet*, after a wonderfully tense account of the famous dissonance passage, the main allegro is very much on the fast side, and in both quartets the slow movements are too fast to relax properly. Admittedly in the *C major* Mozart himself changed the *Adagio* marking to *Andante*, but the Amadeus seem to go too far. Even so, despite the points of dispute, this is exceptionally refined quartet-playing, well recorded.

String quartet No. 17 in B flat major (Hunt), K.458.

    *** DGG SLPM 138886. Amadeus Quartet – HAYDN: *Quartet No. 77.****

    (B) ** Oryx EXP 6. Salzburg Mozarteum Quartet – HAYDN: *Quartet No. 77.***

This is one of the Amadeus Quartet's very best records. The outer movements are crisp and vital, and the slow movement has warmth without blandness. With excellent sound, clearly separated yet offering a convincing overall blend, this record, with its attractive coupling, can be highly recommended.

The Oryx performance is marginally less good than the Haydn coupling. The leader's intonation is just that bit less true, and the minuet is a trifle slow, although its trio is gracious and nicely poised. But the *Adagio* is played expressively, and if in the finale the sound lacks something in bite, the accomplished and genial playing is attractive. At the price this is an undoubted bargain.

String quartets Nos. 19 in C major (Dissonance), K.465; 22 in B flat major (Prussian No. 2), K.589.

    *** DGG 2530 468. Tokyo Quartet.

The fine playing of the youthful Tokyo Quartet offers here a real challenge to the refinement and experience of the Italians. This playing is both expressive and spirited, and the finales have splendid vivacity. The recording is of DGG's best quality, and if in the last resort it is not as natural as the Philips sound, it has

fine detail and presence. This coupling is, of course, not otherwise available, and anyone wanting these two quartets need not hesitate.

String quartets Nos. 20 in D major (Hoffmeister), K.499; 21 in D major (Prussian No. 1), K.575.

    *** Philips 6500 241. Italian Quartet.

It is not often that one can speak of one record as the best in any field, but one can say of the Italian Quartet's coupling of the *Hoffmeister* and K.575 that there is no finer version either as a performance or recording on the market. The playing is altogether superb, beautifully lyrical in feeling and yet classically disciplined too. The recording is wide in range, firmly defined and rich; it brings the artists into one's very room. In K.499 the Vienna Quartet seem too sweet by comparision while in K.575, the Italians seem more inside the music than either the Weller Quartet, who give a very fine performance indeed, or the Amadeus. Highly recommended.

String quartets Nos. 20 in D major (Hoffmeister), K.499; 22 in B flat major (Prussian No. 2), K.589.

    *** DGG SLPM 139355. Amadeus Quartet.

    (M) *** Decca Ace of Diamonds SDD 291. Vienna Philharmonic Quartet.

String quartets Nos. 21 in D major (Prussian No. 1), K.575; 23 in F major (Prussian No. 3), K.590.

    *** DGG SLPM 139437. Amadeus Quartet.

    (M) *** Decca Ace of Diamonds SDD 330. Weller Quartet.

The Amadeus Quartet are at their finest in these late products of Mozart's genius – the three *Prussian quartets*, written for the cello-playing King of Prussia. These are works which after the density and tensions of the six *Haydn quartets*, are comparatively relaxed and the Amadeus brand of stylishness and refinement is entirely apt for the music. Such playing is a delight, particularly when recorded so beautifully, but some will still prefer the rather more robust treatment of the Weller and Vienna Philharmonic Quartets on Decca. These accounts have splendid inner vitality and warmth. The slow movements are beautifully moulded and there is virtuosity when the music calls for it. The recording is excellent and at medium price this pair of discs makes a splendid investment.

String quartets Nos. 22 in B flat major (Prussian No. 2), K.589; 23 in F major (Prussian No. 3), K.590.
   *** Philips 6500 225. Italian Quartet.

In terms of sheer musical distinction, these superbly shaped and balanced performances are unlikely to be surpassed for a very long time. They are among the very best Mozart performances on disc. These readings of Mozart's last two quartets are free from any mannerisms, but apart from this, they have a warmth of tone, purity of intonation and blend, and a sense of classical proportion that mark them off from their rivals, good though some of them are. The Philips recording is remarkably realistic, firm in tone and wide in range.

String quintets Nos. 2 in C minor, K.406; 3 in C major, K.515.
   ** (*) DGG SLPM 139356. Amadeus Quartet with Cecil Aronowitz (viola).

This is one of the more impressive of the Amadeus Mozart records. The playing is both searching and spontaneous, and obviously thought and skill have gone into the matter of internal balance as well as the interpretations. The recording too is excellent, clear in detail as well as truthful in timbre.

String quintets Nos. 4 in G minor, K.516; 5 in D major, K.593.
   ** (*) DGG SLPM 138057. Amadeus Quartet with Cecil Aronowitz (viola).

The Amadeus performance of the *G minor Quintet* with its elysian slow movement has long been admired. The current catalogue offers no competition except an alternative coupling with the *Horn quintet* which is in many ways more attractive than the present disc, as the performance of K.593 has a lower level of tension. But there is no question about the suave immaculacy of the Amadeus playing, beautifully refined and polished, in both works. The recording dates from 1962, but still sounds well.

Violin Sonatas

Violin sonatas Nos. 17 in C major, K.296; 21 in E minor, K.304; 34 in A major, K.526.
   *** Philips 6500 053. Henryk Szeryng (violin), Ingrid Haebler (piano).

Violin sonatas Nos. 17 in C major, K.296; 22 in A major, K.305 (293d); 32 in B flat major, K.454.
   (B) ** Oiseau-Lyre OLS 173. William Kroll (violin), Artur Balsam (piano).

Violin sonatas Nos. 18 in G major, K.301; 22 in A major, K.305; 24 in F major, K.376; 27 in G major, K.379.
   *** Philips 6500 143. Henryk Szeryng (violin), Ingrid Haebler (piano).

Violin sonatas Nos. 19 in E flat major, K.302; 20 in C major, K.303; 35 in F major, K.547; 12 Variations in G major on 'La bergère Célimène', K.359.

*** Philips 6500 145. Henryk Szeryng (violin), Ingrid Haebler (piano).

Violin sonatas Nos. 21 in E minor, K.304 (300c); 27 in G major, K.379; 33 in E flat major, K.481.

(B) ** Oiseau-Lyre OLS 172. William Kroll (violin), Artur Balsam (piano).

Violin sonatas Nos. 23 in D major, K.306; 25 in F major, K.377; 32 in B flat major, K.454; 33 in E flat major, K.481.

** RCA SER 5681/2. David Oistrakh (violin), Paul Badura-Skoda (piano).

Violin sonatas Nos. 23 in D major, K.306; 28 in E flat major, K.380; 6 Variations in G minor on 'Au bord d'une fontaine', K.360.

*** Philips 6500 144. Henryk Szeryng (violin), Ingrid Haebler (piano).

Violin sonatas Nos. 25 in F major, K.377; 26 in B flat major, K.378.

*** Philips 6500 054. Henryk Szeryng (violin), Ingrid Haebler (piano).

Violin sonatas Nos. 32 in B flat major, K.454; 33 in E flat major, K.481.

*** Philips 6500 055. Henryk Szeryng (violin), Ingrid Haebler (piano).

Ingrid Haebler's Mozart has sometimes in the past been disfigured by a certain primness and rectitude that qualified admiration for her purely pianistic skill. However, there is no hint of Dresden china in her playing of these sonatas: she brings an admirable vitality and robustness to her part: her playing has sparkle and great spontaneity. Szeryng's contribution is altogether masterly, and all these

performances find both partners in complete rapport. Philips provide recordings of outstanding realism and truthfulness. These are the finest versions of the Mozart sonatas to appear on LP, and the *Variations* also included in the set are managed with charm.

On bargain label the performances by Kroll and Balsam cannot really be faulted. They are sensitive and stylish, without the individuality and refinement of Szeryng and Haebler, perhaps, but not lacking in personality. The recording is faithful and pleasing, although just occasionally one senses that Kroll is rather too close to the microphone.

Oistrakh and Badura-Skoda give taut, efficient performances of works which really require a degree more affection if their full power is to be realized. The recording is on the cold side, so that even Oistrakh's tone is not given its full bloom.

Piano Duet

Fantasia in F minor (for mechanical clock), *K.457; Piano duet sonata in F major, K.497; 5 Variations on an Andante in G major K.501.*

*** DGG 2530 363. Christoph Eschenbach, Justus Frantz (piano, 4 hands).

This is a superb record of Mozart piano duet music, even finer than the earlier one recorded by this excellent team (see below). The *F major Sonata* is a magnificent work, here presented in all its expansive strength, while the *Variations* and the little *Fantasia for mechanical clock* (more suited to the organ than in this arrangement) show equally the artists' sensitive care for detail and balance. Fine recording.

Fugue in C minor for 2 pianos, K.426; Double piano sonata in D major, K.448.

(B) *** Turnabout TV 34064S. Alfred Brendel, Walter Klien (pianos) – *Double concerto.****

Double piano sonata in D major, K.448.
** Decca SXL 6130. Vladimir Ashkenazy, Malcolm Frager (pianos) –SCHUMANN: *Andante and variations; Étude in the form of a canon.***

No musician composed more naturally for the stereo medium than Mozart. The way he dovetails the writing for the two players so that the musical argument is deftly handed to and fro commands wonder as well as pleasure. The music is cogently and gracefully presented by Ashkenazy and Frager, but the playing, although fluent, lacks something in the matter of tension. In spite of first-rate recording this performance is too smooth. Brendel and Klien are much to be preferred (although they are not so beautifully recorded): theirs is a quite outstanding bargain coupling.

Double piano sonata in D major, K.448; Piano duet sonata in C major, K.521.
** (*) DGG 2530 285. Christoph Eschenbach, Justus Frantz (pianos; piano, 4 hands).

These magnificent works – neglected like so much piano-duet and two-piano music – receive scrupulous and stylish performances from a sensitive pair of artists. They miss some of the strength, but with fine recording this can be strongly recommended.

Solo Piano Music

Adagio in B minor, K.540; Andante for mechanical organ in F major, K.616; Fantasy and fugue in C major, K.394; Rondo in A minor, K.511; 6 Variations on an Allegretto, K.54; 9 Variations on a Minuet by Duport, K.573.

(B) *** Turnabout TV 37011S. Walter Klien (piano).

Adagio for glass harmonica in C major, K.356; Allegros: in B flat major, K.3; in C major, K.9a; Allegro and Rondo (Allegretto) in F major, K.Anh.135; Kleiner Trauermarsch in C minor, K.453a; 3 Minuets in F major, K.2, 4, and 5; Minuet and Trio in G major, K.1; 8 Variations on Sarti's 'Come un'agnello' from 'Fra i due litiganti il terzo gode', K.460; 8 Variations on Schack's 'Ein Weib ist das herrlichste Ding' from 'Der dumme Gärtner', K.613.

(B) *** Turnabout TV 37012S. Walter Klien (piano).

Allegro of a sonata in G minor, K.312; Capriccio in C major, K.395; 6 Pieces from the London Notebook (1764): Rondeau; Andantino; Contredanse 1 and 2; Andante; Final movement of a Sonata; 6 Variations on Salieri's 'Mio caro Adone' from 'La Fiera di Venezia', K.180; 12 Variations on 'Ah, vous dirai-je, maman', K.265; 12 Variations on Beaumarchais's 'Je suis Lindor' from 'Le Barbier de Séville', K.354.

(B) *** Turnabout TV 37008S. Walter Klien (piano).

Allegro and Minuet of a Sonata in B flat major, K.Anh.136; Fantasy in C minor, K.396; 8 Variations on the March from Grétry's 'Les Mariages samnites', K.352; 9 Variations on Dezède's 'Lison dormait' from 'Julie', K.264; 12 Variations on 'La Belle Françoise', K.353.

(B) *** Turnabout TV 37009S. Walter Klien (piano).

Eine kleine Gigue in G major, K.574; Fantasy in D minor, K.397; Minuet in D major, K.355; Rondo in D major, K.485; 6 Variations on Paisiello's 'Salve tu' from 'I filosofi immaginarii',

K.398; 10 Variations on Gluck's 'Unser dummer Pöbel meint' from 'Pilgrimme von Mecca', K.455; 12 Variations on an Allegretto, K.500.

(B) *** Turnabout TV 37010S. Walter Klien (piano).

Fugue in G minor, K.401; Sonata movement in B flat major, K.400; Suite in the style of Handel in G major, K.399; 7 Variations on 'Willem van Nassau', K.25; 8 Variations on a Dutch song by Graaf, K.Anh.208; 12 Variations on a Minuet by Fischer, K.179.

(B) *** Turnabout TV 37007S. Walter Klien (piano).

Some of Mozart's earliest piano pieces, like the *Variations on a Dutch song by Graaf*, written when he was in Amsterdam and barely ten years old, are of relatively slight musical interest, but the *Suite in the style of Handel* (ideal, incidentally, for quiz sessions) or the *G minor Fugue*, the product of his intense interest in Bach, are works of substance. The merit of these Turnabout reissues is that they skilfully plan each record so that it contains reasonable variety and contrast. The juvenilia from the London sketchbook (on the eighth record in the set) rub shoulders with the striking *C major Capriccio*, K. 395, while on the next record in the series the remarkable *C minor Fantasy* and the charming *La Belle Françoise* variations are alone worth the price of the record. Mozart's variations were often intended for pupils' use, but the finest of them went into his own repertoire.

Walter Klien's playing can only be described as in exemplary taste: there is nothing self-conscious about it, his phrasing is unfailingly musical and every detail is beautifully placed without there being the slightest suggestion of precocity. Indeed as a Mozartian he is in the very first rank. The recorded sound is not first-class: the piano tone sometimes lacks the freshness and naturalness of a modern recording, but despite some artificiality in the sound, it is perfectly acceptable and is a good deal rounder and more full-bodied than, say, the Brendel Beethoven *Sonatas* on the same label. The whole series can be recommended and if one starts with, say, Vol. 7 as a sampler or perhaps better still Vol. 11, which has the incomparable *A minor Rondo* as well as the *Andante for mechnical organ in F*, K.616, the temptation to collect the rest of the series can be assessed.

10 Variations on Gluck's 'Unser dummer Pöbel meint' from 'Pilgrimme von Mecca', K.455.

(B) * (*) Pye GSGC 14085. Peter Cooper (piano) – BAX: *Sonata;* TIPPETT: *Sonata.* * (*)

Peter Cooper is an accomplished pianist, but he is not well served by the engineers, who do not produce a particularly pleasant sound. The coupling as a whole is of some interest, but both the Bax and Tippett sonatas have been excellently recorded on alternative labels, the Bax by Iris Loveridge (mono only) and the Tippett coupled with Ogdon's indispensable account of the *Piano concerto*.

Piano sonatas Nos. 1 in C major; 2 in F major; 3 in B flat major; 4 in E flat major; 5 in G major; 6 in D major, K.279/284; 7 in C major; 8 in A minor; 9 in D major, K.309/311; 10 in C major; 11 in A major; 12 in F major; 13 in B flat major, K.330/333; 14 in C minor, K.457; 15 in C major, K.545; 16 in B flat major, K.570; 17 in D major, K.576; Allegro and Andante, K.533; Rondo in D major, K.485.

(B) ** Oiseau-Lyre OLS 177/181. Artur Balsam (piano).

Balsam has chosen a piano which is tonally gentle and mellow, and his small-scale playing is perfectly judged. There is musicianship and continual sensitivity of phrasing to delight the ear, and besides this, a readily communicated feeling of affection for the music. However, the performances show less penetration than Klien's (see below). Furthermore, on occasion, Balsam is too ready to solve the problems of a comparatively straightforward movement by adopting a brisk tempo, and although this is generally successful, Klien's more imaginative approach can often yield greater dividends for the listener. Even so the Mozartian will find a wealth of pleasure in the Oiseau-Lyre set, which is consistent in maintaining its artistic and technical standards throughout. The records are currently available in album form only, but by omitting all but a few of the miscellaneous items, this set fits on five discs, one less than Klien's recording, with consequent saving in cost.

Piano sonatas Nos. 1 in C major, K.279; 2 in F major, K.280; 3 in B flat major, K.281; 4 in E flat major, K.282.

(B) *** Turnabout TV 37001S. Walter Klien (piano).

Piano sonatas Nos. 5 in G major, K.283; 6 in D major, K.284; 7 in C major, K.309.

(B) *** Turnabout TV 37002S. Walter Klien (piano).

Piano sonatas Nos. 8 in A minor, K.310; 9 in D major, K.311; 10 in C major, K.330.

(B) *** Turnabout TV 37003S. Walter Klien (piano).

Piano sonatas Nos. 11 in A major, K.331; 12 in F major, K.332; 13 in B flat major, K.333.

(B) *** Turnabout TV 37004S. Walter Klien (piano).

Piano sonata No. 14 in C minor, K.457; Allegro and Andante, K.533; Fantasy in C minor, K.475; Rondo, K.494.

(B) *** Turnabout TV 37005S. Walter Klien (piano).

Piano sonatas Nos. 15 in C major, K.545; 16 in B flat major, K.570; 17 in D major, K.576.

(B) *** Turnabout TV 37006S. Walter Klien (piano).

Walter Klien's set of Mozart sonatas were originally issued in Vox Boxes (three discs at a time) but now they are issued separately on Turnabout to form part of his integral recording of all Mozart's piano music. Surely no better choice of pianist could have been made, for Klien's playing is fresh, strongly characterized and determined to show that there are no favourites, just a succession of masterpieces. With this degree of spontaneity and intellectual conviction many of the slighter early works emerge anew, for the strength of the playing is as marked in the earlier sonatas as in the later ones. The recording here is crisp and clear, with slightly more body than in the recordings of piano miscellanea discussed above.

Piano sonatas Nos. 3 in B flat major, K.281; 8 in A minor, K.310; Fantasia in D minor, K.397; 6 Variations on Paisiello's 'Salve tu' from 'I filosofi immaginarii', K.398.

** (*) DGG 2530 061. Emil Gilels (piano).

This was recorded at a public recital, but instead of imparting an extra degree of life and spontaneity to the playing, one is given the feeling of a studied care by the pianist, to ensure technical accuracy. The result conveys strong intellectual control but little lightness or sparkle. The most successful piece here is the *Fantasia in D minor*, but the two sonatas are extremely serious-minded and not everyone will enjoy them. The recording is clear, if not rich, and the audience noises are minimal.

Piano sonatas Nos. 4 in E flat major, K.282; 5 in G major, K.283; 10 in C major, K.330; 12 in F major, K.332; Rondo in A minor, K.511.

* (**) Decca SXL 6301. Wilhelm Backhaus (piano).

Backhaus was always magisterial and here his playing, if heavy in style, commands the listener's interest throughout. The rhythmic control is not exact but this slight fluctuation gives the melodic flow a certain rugged individuality. The whole effect is far removed from the scented periwig style of Mozart pianism, and if the sonatas are taken one at a time the spontaneous quality of the playing is enjoyable for its sheer strength of personality. However, listening to the LP as a whole one is conscious that rather more lightening of the textures is needed in the slow movements and some ears find the phrasing too mechanical and detached to give more than sporadic pleasure.

Piano sonata No. 8 in A minor, K.310.

(M) ** Pye Virtuoso TPLS 13012. Nina Milkina (piano) – HAYDN: Sonata No. 34 etc.**

This is small-scale 'eighteenth-century' Mozart played with the grace of a feminine touch (using the description in the best sense). There may be deeper feeling underlying the music of the *Andante cantabile* than Nina Milkina reveals, but Mozart would surely have enjoyed the pianist's naturally expressive, flowing style. The recording is excellent.

Piano sonata No. 8 in A minor, K.310; Fantasy in C minor, K.396; Rondo in A minor, K.511; 9 Variations on a Minuet by Duport, K.573.

(M) ** Vanguard VCS 10043. Alfred Brendel (piano).

Strong, rather serious performances from Brendel, with a particularly good

set of *Variations*, K.573. Brendel's shaping and care with individual variations raise the stature of this work to put it at least on a par with the sonatas. The recording is good but seems rather forward. Tonally it is acceptable.

Piano sonatas Nos. 8 in A minor, K.310; 14 in C minor, K.457; 15 in C major, K.545.

** (*) DGG 2530 234. Christoph Eschenbach (piano).

Cool, classical readings notable for their poise and clarity of thought. The playing is not without strength of personality, but it is rather short on charm. The recording is admirable.

Piano sonatas Nos. 8 in A minor, K.310; 17 in D major, K.576; Rondo in A minor, K.511.

*** Decca SXL 6439. Vladimir Ashkenazy (piano).

Immaculate playing. Ashkenazy shows his usual impeccable judgement and taste, and this Mozart recital must be numbered among the finest records he has ever made. The recording is first-class. No serious collector should overlook this release.

Piano sonatas Nos. 10 in C major, K.330; 11 in A major, K.331; Rondo in A minor, K.511; Rondo in D major, K.485.

** DGG SLPM 139318. Christoph Eschenbach (piano).

Eschenbach's recital calls for little detailed comment. He gives well-turned, cool and elegant performances without affectation and mannerism. Eschenbach finds greater depth in the *A minor Rondo*. The recording is a little lacking in vividness but it is perfectly agreeable, and given such tasteful playing the disc is very acceptable.

Organ Music

Fantasia in F minor, K.594; Fantasia in F minor, K.608.

* Argo ZRG 5419. Simon Preston (organ) – BACH: *Schübler chorales.* *

Fantasia in F minor, K.608.

(B) *** Turnabout TV 34087S. Helmuth Rilling (organ) – *Flute and harp concerto; Adagio for glass harmonica.** (*)

Mozart wrote these *Fantasias* for a mechanical organ, attached to a clock. He had no opinion of the mechanism for which his music was commissioned and may well have had an eye on a more ambitious instrument in conceiving the music; nevertheless this simple, direct writing sounds grotesque when blown up as it is on the Argo disc by the ambience of Westminster Abbey. However, Helmuth Rilling's performance is of exactly the right scale and uses the right kind of instrument.

VOCAL AND CHORAL MUSIC (see also 'Miscellaneous Vocal Recitals' section below)

Music for Masonic occasions: *Adagio and fugue in C minor, K.546; Adagio and Rondo in C major, K.617; Ave verum corpus (Motet), K.618; Die ihr des unermesslichen Weltalls Schöpfer ehrt (Cantata), K.619; Ihr unsere neuen Leiter (Song), K.484; Lasst uns mit geschlungnen Händen, K.623a; Laut verkünde unsere Freude, K.623; Zerfliesset Heut', geliebte Brüder, K.483.*

(B) ** Turnabout TV 34214S. Kurt Equiluz (tenor), Vienna Volksoper Chorus and Orchestra, Peter Maag; Kurt Rapf (piano; organ); Chamber Ensemble.

Music for Masonic occasions: *Masonic funeral music (Maurerische Trauermusik), K.477; Adagio in B flat major for 2 clarinets and 3 basset horns, K.411; Canonic adagio in F major for 2 basset horns and bassoon, K.410; De Profundis (Psalm 129), K.93; Dir, Seele des Weltalls (Cantata), K.429; Die ihr einen neuem Grade, K.468; Die Maurerfreude (Cantata), K.471; O heiliges Band (Song), K.148; Sancta Maria, Mater Dei (Gradual), K.273.*

(B) ** Turnabout TV 34213S. Kurt Equiluz (tenor), Vienna Volksoper Chorus and Orchestra, Peter Maag; Kurt Rapf (piano; organ); Wind Ensemble.

This may be thought an ingenious way of collecting some of Mozart's shorter works together, but in fact, whether or not all this music was intended for masonic purposes by its composer (*De profundis*, for instance, was written when Mozart was only fifteen), it is now used by the Viennese Lodge, of which the conductor (an excellent Mozartian) is himself a member. If the best-known music comes off least well, much of the rest is attractive, and each disc has its fair share of interesting items. The recording is excellent, and the performers make up in vigour and enthusiasm for what they lack in polish.

Masonic music: *Masonic funeral music (Maurerische Trauermusik), K.477; Die ihr des unermesslichen Weltalls Schöpfer ehrt (Cantata), K.619; Die ihr einen neuem Grade, K.468; Dir, Seele des Weltalls (Cantata), K.429; Ihr unsere neuen Leiter (Song), K.484; Lasst uns mit geschlungnen Händen, K.623a; Laut verkünde unsere Freude, K.623; O heiliges Band (Song), K.148; Sehen, wie dem starren Forscherange,*

K.471; Zerfliesset heut', geliebte Brüder, K.483.

> *** Decca SXL 6409. Werner Krenn (tenor), Tom Krause (bass), Edinburgh Festival Chorus, London Symphony Orchestra, Istvan Kertesz.

This Decca issue contains the more important of Mozart's Masonic music. A fuller selection is available on two Turnabout discs (see above), and those two records together cost less than this one. However, the Decca recording is very beautiful and the performances here are more polished and sophisticated. The highlights are Kertesz's strongly dramatic account of the *Masonic funeral music* and the two lovely songs for chorus which begin side two, *Zerfliesset heut'* and *Ihr unsere neuen Leiter*, which are sung with warm humanity. Indeed the choral contribution is most distinguished throughout; the tenor, Werner Krenn, who dominates much of the other music, is lyrical rather than especially direct in manner. Occasionally one feels a sturdier approach would have been more effective.

Lieder: *Abendempfindung; An Chloe; An die Freundschaft; Die betrogene Welt; Geheime Liebe; Gesellenreise; Die grossmütige Gelassenheit; Ich würd' auf meinen Pfad; Die ihr des unermesslichen Weltalls; Lied der Freiheit; Das Lied der Trennung; Das Traumbild; Das Veilchen; Wie unglücklich bin ich; Die Zufriedenheit; Die Zufriedenheit im niedrigen Stande.*

> *** HMV ASD 2824. Dietrich Fischer-Dieskau (baritone), Daniel Barenboim (piano).

Characteristically Fischer-Dieskau and Barenboim refuse to take even these seemingly simple songs for granted. Though some may prefer a more direct manner (such as Edith Mathis brings)

there are ample reasons for registering many of these songs as forerunners of the German *Lied*, not least *Abendempfindung* and some of the Masonic songs. Regularly Fischer-Dieskau and Barenboim in perfect, seemingly spontaneous understanding have the art of concealing art in deeply satisfying performances. Fine recording.

Lieder: *Abendempfindung; Ah! Spiegarti, O Dio; Als Luise; Die Alte; Der Frühling; Das Kinderspiel; Des kleinen Friedrichs Geburtstag; Die kleine Spinnerin; Oiseaux, si tous les ans; Ridente la calma; Sehnsucht nach dem Frühling; Sei du mein Trost; Un moto di gioia; Das Veilchen; Die Verschweigung; Die Zauberer; Die Zufriedenheit.*

> *** DGG 2530 319. Edith Mathis (soprano), Bernard Klee (piano), Takashi Ochi (mandolin).

Mozart's forty songs usually seem among his most innocent inspirations, and the fresh, unmannered singing of Edith Mathis bears that out in this selection, even while she succeeds in intensifying her manner for such obviously deeper songs as *Abendempfindung*. Klee accompanies on all but one of the songs. Good recording.

Concert arias: *Ah, lo previdi . . . Ah, t'invola agl'occhi miei, K.272; Ch'io mi scordi di te ?, K.505.*

> (B) *** Decca Eclipse ECS 635. Jennifer Vyvyan (soprano), Haydn Orchestra, Harry Newstone – HAYDN: *Scena di Berenice.****

Mozart wrote K.272 in 1776 deliberately as a concert aria, but the words were taken direct from a libretto already used by Paisiello on the Andromeda story, and so have the same kind of dramatic context as Haydn's *Scena di Berenice* on the reverse. The original version of K.505 was written for an amateur production of *Idomeneo* and then Mozart elaborated it and added a piano obbligato which he himself played. Vyvyan's performance has both power and flexibility. She was an artist that it is too easy to underestimate, and here she shows her range, technique and artistry fully stretched; she copes with the fiendish difficulties of Mozart's *fioriture* with assurance.

Concert arias: *Alma grande e nobil core*, K.578. (i) *Ch'io mi scordi di te?*, K.505. *Nehmt meinen Dank!*, K.383; *Vado, ma dove?*, K.583.
> *** HMV ASD 2493. Elisabeth Schwarzkopf (soprano), London Symphony Orchestra, George Szell, (i) with Alfred Brendel (piano) – R. STRAUSS: *Lieder*.***

To have an artist as potent as Alfred Brendel doing the piano obbligato in *Ch'io mi scordi di te* may give some idea of the sumptuousness of the presentation of this disc, and it is reflected by superb performances from Schwarzkopf and Szell. Their finesse and refinement are a joy to the ear, and even if some of the florid singing finds Schwarzkopf taxed rather hard (a pity she did not record them at the time when she sang Fiordiligi in *Così fan tutte* so commandingly), the Mozartian stylishness is still as compelling as ever. Fine recording – a lovely coupling for the lusciously beautiful Strauss songs on the reverse.

Concert arias: *A questo seno . . . Or che il cielo*, K.374; *Basta; vincesti . . . Ah, non lasciarmi, no*, K.486a; *Voi avete*, K.217. *Exsultate jubilate* (Motet), K.165. *Litaniae de venerabili altaris sacramento*, K.243: *Dulcissimum convivium. Vesperae de Dominica*, K.321: *Laudate Dominum*.

> *** Philips 6500 006. Elly Ameling (soprano), English Chamber Orchestra, Raymond Leppard.

Miss Ameling's natural reserve can sometimes bring a coolness to her presentation, but here the singing, besides being marvellously secure technically, has a simple radiance in the phrasing that is often very beautiful indeed. The opening phrase of *Voi avete* (which opens side two) is particularly memorable, as indeed is the beautiful closing section of *Ah, non lasciarmi*. But perhaps the most flexible control of line comes in the final rondo, *A questo seno . . . Or che il cielo*, which offers some of the most melting Mozart singing on disc. On the first side of the disc Miss Ameling's style for the arias with an ecclesiastical context is suitably less operatic. With splendidly balanced accompaniments and natural recording this collection is highly recommendable.

Ave verum corpus, K.618 (see also under *Mass No. 16*).
> (M) ** HMV SXLP 30161. Vienna Singverein, Philharmonia Orchestra, Herbert von Karajan – *Serenade No. 13; German dance*, K.605/3; LEOPOLD MOZART: *Toy symphony;* HANDEL: *Water music*.**

This is part of a quite attractive anthology, and if Karajan's account of the *Ave verum* is rather suave, it is well sung and smoothly recorded.

Church music: *Ave verum corpus*, K.618; *Exsultate jubilate*, K.165; *Kyrie in D minor*, K.341; *Vesperae solennes de confessore in C major*, K.339.
> *** Philips 6500 271. Kiri Te Kanawa (soprano), Elizabeth Bainbridge (contralto), Ryland Davies (tenor), Gwynne Howell (bass),

LSO Chorus, London Symphony Orchestra, Colin Davis.

This disc could hardly present a more delightful collection of Mozart choral music, ranging from the early soprano cantata *Exsultate jubilate*, with its famous setting of *Alleluia*, to the equally popular *Ave verum*. Kiri Te Kanawa is the brilliant soloist in the cantata, and her radiant account of the lovely *Laudate Dominum* is one of the highspots of the *Solemn vespers*. That work, with its dramatic choruses, is among Mozart's most inspired of his Salzburg period, and here it is given a fine responsive performance. Good, reverberant recording.

Litaniae Lauretanae in D major, K.195; Mass No. 16 in C major (Coronation), K.317.
*** Argo ZRG 677. Ileana Cotrubas (soprano), Helen Watts (contralto), Robert Tear (tenor), John Shirley-Quirk (baritone), Schola Cantorum of Oxford, Academy of St Martin-in-the-Fields, Neville Marriner.

This fine coupling of two of Mozart's most appealing early choral works can be strongly recommended. The solo work is outstandingly good (notably the singing of the soprano, Ileana Cotrubas), and the Academy provides the most sensitive, stylish accompaniment, beautifully recorded.

Mass No. 7 in C major (Missa Trinitatis), K.167.
(B) * Turnabout TV 34501S. Soloists, Akademie Kammerchor, Vienna Volksoper Orchestra, Ferdinand Grossman – HAYDN: *Mass in G major.* (*)

The current catalogue lists no alternative version of Mozart's early *Trinity Mass*, so that this will have to do. However, given the undistinguished singing here, this is no more than a stop-gap recommendation.

Mass No. 11 in C major (Credo), K.257; Mass No. 16 in C major (Coronation), K.317.
*** Philips 6500 234. Helen Donath (soprano), Gillian Knight (contralto), Ryland Davies (tenor), Clifford Grant, Stafford Dean (basses), John Alldis Choir, London Symphony Orchestra, Colin Davis.

Colin Davis relishes the youthful high spirits of the *Coronation Mass*, here given a vital performance with a strong team of soloists. The *Credo Mass*, a much rarer work, is equally spirited in performance – a disc to get new listeners discovering this dramatic, often secular-sounding music. Good, reverberant recording.

Mass No. 13 in C major (Organ solo), K.259.
(B) ** Turnabout TV 34132S. Eiko Katonosaka (soprano), Gertrude Jahn (contralto), Kurt Equiluz (tenor), Leo Heppe (bass), Hans Haselböck (organ), Vienna Chamber Choir, Vienna Volksoper Orchestra, Hans Gillesberger – HAYDN: *Mass No. 5.**

Gillesberger directs an excellent performance with good soloists, including the organist, Hans Haselböck. The work pairs naturally with Haydn's *Little organ Mass*, and with good recording this is a most enjoyable coupling.

(i) *Mass No. 16 in C major (Coronation), K.317;* (ii) *Missa brevis in C major (Spatzenmesse), K.220; Ave verum corpus, K.618.*
** (*) DGG 2530 356. (i) Edith

Mathis (soprano), Norma Procter (contralto), Donald Grobe (tenor), John Shirley-Quirk (bass); (ii) Edith Mathis (soprano), Tatiana Troyanos (contralto), Horst Laubenthal (tenor), Kieth Engen (bass); Regensburg Domchor; Bavarian Radio Chorus and Orchestra, Rafael Kubelik.

Kubelik draws a fine, mellow-toned performance of the *Coronation Mass* from his Bavarian forces, but he misses some of the youthful exuberance which Davis finds in his version. Nonetheless those who prefer this coupling, with the lovely *Ave verum* as well as another early *Mass*, will be well pleased.

Mass No. 16 in C major (Coronation), K.317; Vesperae solennes de confessore in C major, K.339.

(B) * (*) Turnabout TV 34063S. Wilma Lipp (soprano), Christa Ludwig (mezzo-soprano), Murray Dickie (tenor), Walter Berry (bass), Vienna Oratorio Choir, Vienna Pro Musica Orchestra, Jascha Horenstein.

The striking thing about the Turnabout performance of the *Coronation Mass* is the good teamwork of the soloists. Each is rather less effective on his or her own, but the composite singing is most enjoyable. Horenstein's account of the *Solemn vespers* is a broad one, yet there is no lack of bite in the orchestra and the immediacy of the recording helps to give an impression of liveliness. Wilma Lipp sings her famous aria here very nicely. The recording is well focused, open and clear.

Mass No. 18 in C minor (Great), K.427.

*** HMV ASD 2959. Ileana Cotrubas, Kiri Te Kanawa (sopranos), Werner Krenn (tenor), Hans Sotin (bass), John Alldis Choir, New Philharmonia Orchestra, Raymond Leppard.

*** Philips 6500 235. Helen Donath, Heather Harper (sopranos), Ryland Davies (tenor), Stafford Dean (bass), LSO Chorus, London Symphony Orchestra, Colin Davis.

(B) ** Turnabout TV 34174S. Wilma Lipp (soprano), Christa Ludwig (mezzo-soprano), Murray Dickie (tenor), Walter Berry (bass), Vienna Oratorio Choir, Vienna Pro Musica Orchestra, Ferdinand Grossman.

Colin Davis follows the trend today by rejecting the accretions which were formerly used to turn this incomplete torso of a work into a full setting of the liturgy. Robbins Landon's edition prompts him to a strong and intense performance which brings out the darkness of tragedy behind Mozart's use of the minor key, helped by fine soprano singing from Helen Donath and Heather Harper. Excellent recording too.

Like Davis, Raymond Leppard uses the Robbins Landon edition and a choir of comparable proportions. His manner is a degree more affectionate than Davis's, which many will prefer, even in this dark work. The sopranos are the light-givers here, and the partnership of Ileana Cotrubas and Kiri Te Kanawa is if anything even more radiantly beautiful than that of Harper and Donath. Fine, atmospheric recording.

An enjoyable rather than an outstanding performance on Turnabout, with Wilma Lipp tending to let the side down with her lack of poise at times. Her part in the proceedings is a dominant one, so the good contribution from the other soloists does not entirely compensate, particularly as the recording balance is only fair. However, the life and spontaneity of the performance make considerable amends.

Requiem Mass (No. 19) in D minor, K.626.

*** **HMV ASD 2788.** Sheila Armstrong (soprano), Janet Baker (mezzo-soprano), Nicolai Gedda (tenor), Dietrich Fischer-Dieskau (baritone), John Alldis Choir, English Chamber Orchestra, Daniel Barenboim.

** (*) **HMV SAN 193.** Edith Mathis (soprano), Grace Bumbry (contralto), George Shirley (tenor), Marius Rintzler (bass), New Philharmonia Chorus, New Philharmonia Orchestra, Rafael Frühbeck de Burgos.

** (*) **Decca SET 302.** Elly Ameling (soprano), Marilyn Horne (mezzo-soprano), Ugo Benelli (tenor), Tugomir Franc (bass), Vienna State Opera Chorus, Vienna Philharmonic Orchestra, Istvan Kertesz.

** **Philips SAL 3649.** Helen Donath (soprano), Yvonne Minton (contralto), Ryland Davies (tenor), Gerd Nienstedt (bass), John Alldis Choir, BBC Symphony Orchestra, Colin Davis.

(M) ** **Decca Ace of Diamonds SDDR 380.** Maria Stader (soprano), Hertha Töpper (contralto), John van Kesteren (tenor), Karl Christian Kohn (bass), Munich Bach Choir and Orchestra, Karl Richter.

** **DGG 2530 143.** Edith Mathis (soprano), Julia Hamari (contralto), Wieslaw Ochman (tenor), Karl Ridderbusch (bass), Vienna State Opera Chorus, Vienna Philharmonic Orchestra, Karl Boehm.

** **DGG SLPM 138767.** Wilma Lipp (soprano), Hilde Rössl-Majdan (contralto), Anton Dermota (tenor), Walter Berry (bass), Vienna Choral Society, Berlin Philharmonic Orchestra, Herbert von Karajan.

As in his recording of Bach's *Magnificat*, Barenboim's exuberance may raise a few eyebrows. Mozart's *Dies irae*, for instance, has such zest that one senses the chorus galloping towards the Day of Judgement with enthusiasm. Yet the underlying drama and musicality of the performance as a whole disarm criticism. The intensity of Barenboim's feeling comes over from the opening bar, and the *Kyrie eleison* is stirring indeed. The lyricism of the score is beautifully calculated; the operatic-styled quartet which closes the *Tuba mirum* is particularly lovely. So too is the closing section of *Confutatis maledictis*, which creates a gentle mood for the opening of the *Lacrimosa*. Here Barenboim's emotional contrasts dramatize the words superbly. The *Sanctus* is gloriously forthright. With a good solo team, excellent choral singing and fine orchestral playing (the opening of the *Lacrimosa* is beautifully managed), this is a splendidly alive performance, and HMV's sound is first-rate.

The glory of Frühbeck's HMV Angel set is the singing of the New Philharmonia Chorus, and with the choral music very much the centre of interest, that gives it an edge over the direct rivals, Davis on Philips and Kertesz on Decca. This is unashamedly big-scale Mozart, and that is perhaps apt for a work that has less need for apology than was once thought. Latest researches suggest that Süssmayr's contribution to the composition (after Mozart's death) is less than used to be thought, and certainly the aesthetic test is clear: that very little indeed falls below what one would expect of a Mozart masterpiece and much is of supreme greatness. Frühbeck does not have a very subtle Mozart style, and on detail Davis outshines him, with Davis's *Recordare* much more relaxed and refined. But as an interpretation it stands well in the middle of the road, not too romantic, not too frigidly classic, and quite apart from the choral singing – recorded with beautiful balance and richness – the soloists are all first-rate, on balance as good as Davis's and rather better than Kertesz's.

Dutch, American, Italian, and Yugoslav soloists join with a Hungarian conductor to produce the Viennese performance and the result is generally a success, both musically and from the recording viewpoint. In few other works are the voices called upon to exhibit such a wide range of technical virtuosity. At one moment the texture demands that they must blend; at another they are required to exhibit the maximum of individuality and independence. Kertesz, like Frühbeck de Burgos, takes a large-scale view of Mozart's last work, but unlike him he cannot rely on a really first-rate chorus. Much of the choral singing here is rather wild and smudgy, enthusiastic but not stylish enough for Mozart, and the impression is made worse by the forward balance of the singers against the orchestra. Kertesz goes further than Frühbeck towards a romantic view of the work, and though the recording has the usual Decca brilliance, it does not quite match that of the H M V Angel.

Davis with a smaller choir gives a more intimate performance than is common, and with his natural sense of style he finds much beauty of detail. In principle the performance should have given the sort of 'new look' to the Mozart *Requiem* that was such a striking success in Handel's *Messiah*, but Davis does not provide the same sort of 'bite' that in performances on this scale should compensate for sheer massiveness of tone. The BBC Symphony Orchestra is in good form, and the soloists – although varying in quality – keep up a laudably high

standard. Anyone wanting a version on this authentic scale need not hesitate, but this is plainly not the definitive version. The recording is good but neither as sweet nor as crystal-clear as it might be.

At medium price Karl Richter's account can be recommended. This is a powerful reading with a strong forward impulse throughout. The soloists make an excellent contribution; Maria Stader and John van Kesteren are the more distinguished but the bass, Karl Christian Kohn, is impressively dramatic, even operatic in style. The choral singing is firm and the orchestral support of high quality. The recording was originally issued on Telefunken, but this Ace of Diamonds reissue if anything improves the sonority and impact of a recording that was always good and certainly wears its years lightly.

Boehm's is a spacious and solemn view of the work with good solo singing and fine choral and orchestral response. It is not as dramatic a reading as Davis's with more modest forces nor quite as lively in expressive detail as the Frühbeck de Burgos on Angel. An immensely polished performance in every way, though not as fully satisfying as the H M V, Angel or Philips issues.

Karajan's is a typical suave view. The only objection to it is that some may find detail sacrificed in favour of warmth and atmosphere. The solo quartet are wonderfully blended, so rare an occurrence in this work above all, and although the chorus lack firmness of line they are helped out by the spirited playing of the Berlin Philharmonic.

6 Notturni for 3 voices and 3 basset horns, K.436–9; K.439a; K.549.

(B) ** Turnabout TV 34417S. Elisabeth Speiser (soprano), Verena Gohl (mezzo-soprano), Kurt Widmer (baritone), Hans-Rudolf Stalder, Rolf Kubli, Hansjurg Leuthold (basset horns) – *2 Divertimenti for basset horns*.* (*)

These are charming works, simple in form and inspiration, yet given the Mozartian genius for blending woodwind and voices the result is delightful. The voices and instruments are nicely balanced here and although the couplings are less attractive, this is worth investigating for the *Notturni* alone.

OPERA

La Clemenza di Tito (opera in 2 acts): complete recording.
** Decca SET 357/9. Maria Casula, Lucia Popp (sopranos), Werner Krenn (tenor), Teresa Berganza, Brigitte Fassbaender (mezzo-sopranos), Tugomir Franc (bass), Vienna State Opera Chorus and Orchestra, Istvan Kertesz.

La Clemenza di Tito is Mozart's last opera, a static, formal *opera seria* written to a classical text by Metastasio. Even Mozart's genius could not revive what by that time was a dead medium. Metastasio's libretto, written sixty years earlier, was altogether too stiff, and though the score contains much marvellous music, it has never been outstandingly effective on the stage, as is his other great *opera seria*, *Idomeneo*. Just how much fine music is hidden in this dramatically dead opera comes out in such a recording as this, and maybe this provides the answer – to have a recording available to give life to Mozart's music without being troubled by a stage production that adds comparatively little. Inevitably most of the best music is purely formal, and Kertesz attacks it with fine, dramatic directness, but over so long a span one cannot help missing a more individual interpretative hand. What would Beecham have done? What Klemperer? In any case

Kertesz seems to have no idea about the grammar of the *appoggiatura*, for the endings of phrases requiring them are regularly left blunt. The recitative too is taken ponderously – surprisingly a regular thing in Vienna – and one longs to have more pace and contrast in the story-telling. But with superb recording and production, generally excellent singing – particularly from Teresa Berganza as Sextus – and strong playing, this will fill the bill for the dedicated Mozartian.

La Clemenza di Tito: highlights.
** Decca SET 432 (from above recording).

Kertesz is not an affectionate Mozartian, and though a straight, crisp approach has much to commend it and here brings some cleanly attractive playing and singing, the length of the piece, the comparative absence of flights of inspiration of the highest Mozartian order, become apparent at the end of six long sides in the complete set. But a highlights disc is ideal, particularly when so well chosen and with text provided. Of the soloists the most appealing is Teresa Berganza. Excellent recording.

Così fan tutte (opera in 2 acts): complete recording.
*** Philips 6707 025 (4 discs). Montserrat Caballé (soprano), Janet Baker (mezzo-soprano), Ileana Cotrubas (soprano), Nicolai Gedda (tenor), Wladimiro Ganzarolli (baritone), Richard van Allan (bass), Chorus and Orchestra of Royal Opera House, Covent Garden, Colin Davis.
*** HMV SLS 5028 (3 discs). Elisabeth Schwarzkopf (soprano), Christa Ludwig (mezzo-soprano), Hanny Steffek (soprano), Alfredo Kraus (tenor), Giuseppe Taddei (baritone), Walter Berry (bass),

Philharmonia Chorus and Orchestra, Karl Boehm.

(M) ** (*) Decca Ace of Diamonds GOS 543/5. Lisa della Casa (soprano), Christa Ludwig (mezzo-soprano), Emmy Loose (soprano), Anton Dermota (tenor), Erich Kunz, Paul Schoeffler (baritones), Vienna State Opera Chorus, Vienna Philharmonic Orchestra, Karl Boehm.

** (*) HMV SLS 961 (4 discs). Margaret Price (soprano), Yvonne Minton (mezzo-soprano), Lucia Popp (soprano), Luigi Alva (tenor), Geraint Evans (baritone), Hans Sotin (bass), John Alldis Choir, New Philharmonia Orchestra, Otto Klemperer.

** Decca SET 575/8. Pilar Lorengar (soprano), Teresa Berganza (mezzo-soprano), Jane Berbié (soprano), Ryland Davies (tenor), Tom Krause, Gabriel Bacquier (baritones), Royal Opera House, Covent Garden, Chorus, London Philharmonic Orchestra, Sir Georg Solti.

Colin Davis has rarely if ever made a more captivating record than this magical set of *Così fan tutte*. His energy and sparkle are here set against inspired and characterful singing from the three women soloists, with Montserrat Caballé and Janet Baker proving a winning partnership, each one challenging and abetting the other all the time. Cotrubas equally is a vivid Despina, never merely arch. The men too make a strong team. Though Gedda has moments of rough tone, his account of *Un aura amorosa* is honeyed and delicate, and though Ganzarolli falls short in one of his prominent arias, it is a spirited, incisive performance, while Richard van Allan here naturally assumes the status of an international recording artist with flair and imagination. Sparkling recitative (complete) and recording which has you riveted by the play of the action.

Karl Boehm's HMV set was one of the first Angel issues, and in opulence of sound and charm of manner it is not likely to be surpassed for a long time. The cast unites the best elements in most of the earlier versions – Schwarzkopf, who dominated the previous Columbia issue under Karajan, Christa Ludwig and the conductor, Karl Boehm, who shone in the Decca set, and Walter Berry, who sang Guglielmo in the Philips mono set once available on bargain label. The whole performance is wonderfully relaxed in just the right way, with the humour of each situation bubbling up naturally and the beauty of the music presented without affectation against an atmospheric but intimate background. Those who knew the Karajan set may find this a little too relaxed, but there is no doubt that Schwarzkopf gives an even more accomplished performance under Boehm, beautifully controlled in *Come scoglio* and dramatically most convincing. Touching too at the climax, which is after all not so very far off tragedy. The other soloists are excellent, and the recording, recently refurbished, is one of EMI's most impressive.

Boehm's Ace of Diamonds set is not as polished a performance as the later one on Angel, and the persistent cutting of brief passages from the ends of arias is irritating, but anyone who at bargain price wants a thoroughly likeable and convincing account of the frothiest of Mozart's comedies can have this warmly recommended. It is a strong vocal cast with Lisa della Casa less characterful than Schwarzkopf but strong and sweet-toned, and the rest often sparklingly good. Paul Schoeffler was nearing the end of his career when the record was made in 1956, but in the role of Don Alfonso his singing is most appealing. This was one of Decca's early stereo experiments in opera, and there is little attempt at stage production, but the result is still surprisingly vivid and atmospheric. It is a very enjoyable set.

Klemperer's last opera set was predictably idiosyncratic. When the record company jibbed at his suggestion to record this sparkling comedy, he is alleged to have protested (aged eighty-six at the time) 'What do you want? A posthumous interpretation?' The result proved by no means as funereal as was predicted, with fine rhythmic pointing to lighten the slow tempi. There is fine singing too from the whole cast (Alva alone at times disappointing) to make the whole a satisfying entertainment, a different view of Mozart to be heard at least once. It is a pity the recitatives are not more imaginatively done. First-rate recording.

Solti's set will please those who want high voltage at all costs even in this most genial of Mozartian comedies. There is little relaxation and little charm, which underlines the shortcomings of the singing cast, notably of Pilar Lorengar, whose grainy voice is not well treated by the microphone, and who here in places conveys uncertainty. It is a pity that the crackling wit of Solti's Covent Garden performances was not more magically captured on record. Brilliant recording.

Così fan tutte: highlights.
(M) ** (*) Decca Ace of Diamonds SDD 208 (from above Decca recording cond. Boehm).

This collection of highlights is very well chosen to show the best of the earlier Boehm set, and for those who do not want a complete Così this selection is delectable. The stereo is sometimes remarkably clear for its age, as in the cross-rhythms of the delicious Terzetto for the three men, E voi ridente, but the sound of this Ace of Diamonds transfer is not as smooth as the original, and there is a

degree of edge in the recording of the voices.

(i) *Don Giovanni* (complete); (ii) *Le Nozze di Figaro* (complete); (iii) *Die Zauberflöte* (complete).
(M) ** (*) DGG 2740 108 (11 discs). (i) Peter Schreier, Birgit Nilsson, Martina Arroyo; (ii) Edith Mathis, Gundula Janowitz, Hermann Prey; (iii) Evelyn Lear, Fritz Wunderlich, Franz Crass; all with Dietrich Fischer-Dieskau, cond. Karl Boehm.

To package three Mozart operatic masterpieces into a single box with hard-covered libretto to match may seem cumbersome, but the result is undeniably enticing. Though this version of *Zauberflöte* has claims to be the finest ever, the other two performances here are flawed, notably *Don Giovanni*, in which the orchestra as well as the complement of singers is very variable. Nonetheless, with the three operas together the magic of Boehm compensates for everything – a package to get you returning to Mozart for refreshment.

Don Giovanni (opera in 2 acts): complete recording.
*** Philips 6707 022 (4 discs). Ingvar Wixell (baritone), Martina Arroyo, Kiri Te Kanawa, Mirella Freni (sopranos), Stuart Burrows (tenor), Wladimiro Ganzarolli (baritone), Royal Opera House, Covent Garden, Chorus and Orchestra, Colin Davis.
(M) *** Decca Ace of Diamonds GOS 604/6. Cesare Siepi (bass), Hilde Gueden, Lisa della Casa, Suzanne Danco (sopranos), Anton Dermota (tenor), Fernando Corena (baritone), Vienna State

Opera Chorus, Vienna Philharmonic Orchestra, Josef Krips.

** (*) HMV SLS 923 (4 discs). Nicolai Ghiaurov (bass), Claire Watson, Mirella Freni (sopranos), Christa Ludwig (mezzo-soprano), Nicolai Gedda (tenor), Walter Berry (bass), New Philharmonia Chorus and Orchestra, Otto Klemperer.

(M) ** DGG Privilege 2728 003 (3 discs). Dietrich Fischer-Dieskau (baritone), Sena Jurinac, Maria Stader, Irmgard Seefried (sopranos), Ernst Haefliger (tenor), Karl Christian Kohn (bass), Berlin RIAS Chamber Choir, Berlin Radio Orchestra, Ferenc Fricsay.

** Decca SET 412/5. Gabriel Bacquier (baritone), Joan Sutherland, Pilar Lorengar (sopranos), Marilyn Horne (mezzo-soprano), Werner Krenn (tenor), Donald Gramm (bass), Ambrosian Singers, English Chamber Orchestra, Richard Bonynge.

* (*) HMV SLS 978 (4 discs), Roger Soyer (baritone), Antigone Sgourda, Heather Harper, Helen Donath (sopranos), Luigi Alva (tenor), Geraint Evans (baritone), Scottish Opera Chorus, English Chamber Orchestra, Daniel Barenboim.

The final test is whether a recording of this most searching of operas adds up to more than the sum of its parts. Colin Davis's certainly does, with a singing cast that has fewer shortcomings than any other on record and much of positive strength. For once one can listen untroubled by vocal blemishes. Martina Arroyo controls her massive dramatic voice more completely than one would think possible, and she is strongly and imaginatively contrasted with the sweetly expressive Elvira of Kiri Te Kanawa and the sparkling Zerlina of Freni. As in the Davis *Figaro* Ingvar Wixell and Wladimiro Ganzarolli make a formidable master/servant team with excellent vocal acting, while Stuart Burrows sings gloriously as Don Ottavio and Richard van Allan is a characterful Masetto. Colin Davis draws a fresh and immediate performance from his team, riveting from beginning to end, and the recording, though not as clear as it might be, is refined in the recognizable Philips manner.

Krips's version of this most challenging of operas has kept its place as a version which is consistently satisfying, with a cast of all-round quality headed by the dark-toned Don of Cesare Siepi. The women are not ideal, but they form an excellent team, never overfaced by the music, generally characterful, and with timbres well contrasted. To balance Siepi's darkness, the Leporello of Corena is even more saturnine, and their dramatic teamwork is brought to a superb climax in the final scene – quite the finest spine-tingling performance of that scene yet recorded. The 1955 recording – genuine stereo – still sounds remarkably well, despite being squeezed on to six instead of eight sides. A most compelling set.

The lumbering tempo of Leporello's opening music will alert the listener to the predictable Klemperer approach, and some may at that point dismiss his performance as 'too heavy'; but the issue is far more complex than that. Most of these slow tempi which Klemperer regularly adopts, far from flagging, add a welcome spaciousness to the music, for they must be set against the unusually brisk and dramatic interpretation of the recitatives between numbers. Added to that, Ghiaurov as the Don and Berry as Leporello make a marvellously characterful pair. If the glory of Giulini's Philharmonia performance (currently unobtainable) was the dominance of the female cast – originally planned for

Klemperer to conduct – this one restores the balance to the men, and with Klemperer's help they make the dramatic experience a strong masculine one. Nor is the ironic humour forgotten, for with Berry and Ghiaurov about, the Klemperer spaciousness allows them extra time for pointing. Among the women Ludwig is a strong and convincing Elvira, Freni a sweet-toned but rather unsmiling Zerlina; only Claire Watson seriously disappoints, with obvious nervousness marring the big climax of *Non mi dir*. It is a serious blemish, but with the usual reservations, for those not allergic to the Klemperer approach, this stands as a good recommendation – at the very least a commanding experience.

Fischer-Dieskau's youthfully resilient singing as the Don has much in its favour, even if he ogles his women too lasciviously. This strong, urgent performance, with enjoyable contributions from the women, is worth investigating, though on almost every count the Krips set is preferable as a bargain choice.

Bonynge's is a curious *Giovanni*, in some ways the very antithesis of Klemperer's because, with a lightweight manner and the maximum permissible elaboration, it underplays the symphonic strength of this most formidable of Mozart's operas. Only a partial idea of the opera's greatness is given, though the incidental delights of fine singing have plenty of play, with Joan Sutherland showing even more assurance in the role of Donna Anna than she did when she recorded the role (with Giulini on Columbia) soon after her first international success at Covent Garden. But then her singing was matched superbly by the dominant Elvira of Schwarzkopf, and here Lorengar is by no means so strong. Marilyn Horne sings with richness, but it is a strange voice for Zerlina. The men are reliable rather than inspired. At least the performance is never less than interesting, and it is beautifully recorded.

Barenboim's recording is directly based on the stage production heard at the 1974 Edinburgh Festival, but the often slack and unsparkling performance recorded here can hardly reflect the live account. Barenboim, surprisingly, seems to be echoing Klemperer in his steady approach and exaggeratedly slow tempi. With Klemperer himself there was a granite-like solidity, where with Barenboim, uncharacteristically, the rhythms sag. Roger Soyer's performance as the Don is refreshingly youthful in feeling, and it is good to have Geraint Evans's Leporello on disc, but Luigi Alva's Ottavio is distressingly unsure. Heather Harper as Elvira and Helen Donath as Zerlina battle well against the tempi, but Antigone Sgourda as Anna uses her big, floppy voice in hit-or-miss fashion.

Don Giovanni: highlights.

(M) ** (*) Decca Ace of Diamonds SDD 382 (from above recording cond. Krips).

** Decca SET 496 (from above recording cond. Bonynge).

Krips's version made for the Mozart bicentenary stands the test of time remarkably well, with an intense, dramatic account of the Don's disappearance to Hell which has still not been outshone on record. As a bass Don, Siepi is marvellously convincing. Recorded quickly at a time when stereo was very much an experiment, this is not a perfect set, and the sound begins to show its age, but with a team of singers used to working together on the stage it remains a colourful and engaging performance, an admirable recommendation on a mid-price label.

What matters about the other Decca highlights disc is that it includes as much as possible of Joan Sutherland's contribution as Donna Anna. As a whole Bonynge's is a lightweight account of a towering masterpiece, which will prove acceptable on occasion but will hardly satisfy a Mozartian who has no other version in his collection. Maybe these highlights are the answer to supplement a rival complete set. First-rate Decca recording.

Die Entführung aus dem Serail (opera in 3 acts): complete recording.

> *** DGG 2740 112 (3 discs). Arleen Auger, Reri Grist (sopranos), Peter Schreier, Harald Neukirch (tenors), Kurt Moll (bass), Leipzig Radio Choir, Dresden State Orchestra, Karl Boehm – *Der Schauspieldirektor.****

Boehm's is a delectable performance, superbly cast and warmly recorded, providing at last an adequate successor to the inspired but flawed Beecham version (now deleted). Arleen Auger proves the most accomplished singer on record of the role of Constanze, girlish and fresh, yet rich, tender and dramatic by turns with brilliant, almost flawless coloratura. The others too are outstandingly good, notably Kurt Moll, whose powerful, finely focused bass makes him a superb Osmin, one who relishes the comedy too. Boehm with East German forces finds a natural, unforced Mozartian expression which carries the listener along in glowing ease. Good if rather reverberant recording.

Die Entführung aus dem Serail: excerpts.

> (B) ** Classics for Pleasure CFP 40032. Margaret Price, Daniele Perriers (sopranos), Ryland Davies, Kimmo Lappaleinen (tenors), Noel Mangin (bass), London Philharmonic Orchestra, John Pritchard.

Margaret Price, so accomplished a Constanze, is rather disappointing here, with her hooting tone too often catching the microphone, while the rest of the cast also fails to capture the lighthearted sparkle of the Glyndebourne production on which the recording is based. Nonetheless, on a bargain label it is a sampler worth having.

La finta giardiniera (Die Gärtnerin aus Liebe; opera in 3 acts): complete recording (sung in German).

> ** (*) Philips 6703 039 (3 discs). Gerhard Unger, Werner Hollweg (tenors), Helen Donath, Jessye Norman, Ileana Cotrubas (sopranos), Tatiana Troyanos (mezzosoprano), Hermann Prey (baritone), North German Radio Chorus and Orchestra, Hans Schmidt-Isserstedt.

This is the only *opera buffa* that Mozart wrote in his youth that can be regarded as a preparation for *Figaro*. Particularly in the extended finales you find Mozart at nineteen confidently using techniques which he was to perfect in the Da Ponte masterpiece. The story is unconvincing. In the manner of the time every possible excuse (including bouts of madness for both hero and heroine) is used to prevent true love from being fulfilled until the end of Act 3, yet with Mozart the more improbable the story the more inspired the music. German is used here (with spoken dialogue), since the Italian text and recitatives have been lost for Act 1. Though this performance is slow in getting off the ground, it readily makes up later, with particularly delightful performances from Ileana Cotrubas and Hermann Prey in the two servant roles. Good sound except for thin violin tone.

Idomeneo (opera in 3 acts): complete recording.

> ** (*) HMV SLS 965 (3 discs). Anneliese Rothenberger, Edda Moser (sopranos), Nicolai Gedda, Adolf

Dallapozza, Peter Schreier (tenors), Theo Adam (bass), Leipzig Radio Chorus, Dresden State Orchestra, Hans Schmidt-Isserstedt.

** (*) Philips 6703 024 (3 discs). Margherita Rinaldi, Pauline Tinsley (sopranos), George Shirley, Ryland Davies, Robert Tear (tenors), Stafford Dean (bass), BBC Chorus, BBC Symphony Orchestra, Colin Davis.

Schmidt-Isserstedt's version of Mozart's great essay in *opera seria* was issued as a timely memorial soon after his death. Though not perfect, it is the most stylishly performed as well as the most complete recording yet made. The only cuts here are of recitative, and those relatively minor. It is a pity that the role of Idamante is given to a tenor, when sopranos today are so accomplished at presenting castrato roles effectively, and here the textures are made so much cleaner with the higher voice. The decision to have a tenor is the more irritating when Adolf Dallapozza is by far the least accomplished soloist. Otherwise the cast is good, with Gedda strongly heroic as Idomeneo, Rothenberger an appealing Ilia, and Edda Moser a richly characterful Elektra. Though Davis's very variably sung version on Philips may be more urgent, this one is more commanding, with finer concern for detail. Good recording.

It is the greatest pity that Colin Davis was not allowed a more impressive singing cast for this his first complete Mozart opera recording. His direction is never less than fresh and stylish, and the orchestra responds with vitality, but the singers when taxed with their important arias lack the polish and refinement one needs in recorded Mozart. It is good to welcome Pauline Tinsley on to record, but even for the part of Elektra the voice has an uncomfortable edge. George

Shirley as Idomeneo and Ryland Davies as Idamante are well contrasted in timbre, but in John Pritchard's Glyndebourne version (now deleted) Richard Lewis and Leopold Simoneau were far finer, and in any case Britten's solution (a recording one day perhaps?) of having a woman in the castrato role of Idamante is preferable for reasons of vocal texture. Margherita Rinaldi makes a sweet-voiced Ilia. The Philips recording is acceptable but not outstanding.

Le Nozze di Figaro (opera in 4 acts): complete recording.

*** Philips 6707 014 (4 discs). Mirella Freni, Jessye Norman (sopranos), Yvonne Minton (mezzo-soprano), Wladimiro Ganzarolli (baritone), Ingvar Wixell (baritone), Clifford Grant (bass), Robert Tear (tenor), BBC Chorus, BBC Symphony Orchestra, Colin Davis.

*** DGG 2711 007 (4 discs). Gundula Janowitz, Edith Mathis, Tatiana Troyanos (sopranos), Dietrich Fischer-Dieskau, Hermann Prey (baritones), Erwin Wohlfahrt (bass), German Opera Chorus and Orchestra, Berlin, Karl Boehm.

(M) *** Decca Ace of Diamonds GOS 585/7. Hilde Gueden, Suzanne Danco, Lisa della Casa (sopranos), Murray Dickie (tenor), Alfred Poell, Fernando Corena (baritones), Cesare Siepi (bass), Vienna State Opera Chorus, Vienna Philharmonic Orchestra, Erich Kleiber.

** (*) HMV SLS 955 (4 discs). Reri Grist, Elisabeth Söderström (sopranos), Teresa Berganza (mezzo-soprano), Geraint Evans, Gabriel Bacquier (baritones), John Alldis

Choir, New Philharmonia Orchestra, Otto Klemperer.

(B) ** (*) Decca Eclipse ECS 743/5. Lisa della Casa, Roberta Peters (sopranos), Rosalind Elias (mezzo-soprano), George London (baritone), Giorgio Tozzi, Gabor Carelli (basses), Vienna State Opera Chorus, Vienna Philharmonic Orchestra, Erich Leinsdorf.

(M) * (*) DGG Privilege 2728 004 (3 discs). Maria Stader, Irmgard Seefried (sopranos), Hertha Töpper (mezzo-soprano), Dietrich Fischer-Dieskau, Renato Capecchi (baritones), Berlin RIAS Chamber Choir, Berlin Radio Symphony Orchestra, Ferenc Fricsay.

Colin Davis welds together a cast which includes surprisingly few star names, and produces generally the most enjoyable of all modern versions of this much recorded opera. In particular his pacing of the recitatives has a sparkle that directly reflects experience in the opera house, and his tempi generally are beautifully chosen to make their dramatic points. Vocally the cast is exceptionally consistent, and arguably the most famous name, Mirella Freni (Susanna), is the least satisfying. These are all steady voices which take to recording well, and it is good to have so ravishingly beautiful a voice for the Countess. Jessye Norman, a striking young negro singer, makes a fine impression, and the Figaro of Wladimiro Ganzarolli and the Count of Ingvar Wixell project with exceptional clarity and vigour. Fine singing too from Yvonne Minton as Cherubino, Clifford Grant as Bartolo and Robert Tear as Basilio. The recording, though not so clean as EMI's for Klemperer (it has more reverberation than many will like for this opera), is commendably atmospheric.

Boehm's earlier version of *Figaro* was, until comparatively recently, available on the cheap Fontana Special label, but unlike that sprightly performance this one gives a complete text, with Marcellina's and Basilio's Act 4 arias included. In that completeness only Kleiber (in Decca's Grand Opera Series) provides direct rivalry, even if his Susanna has to sing the Barbarina number. In many ways this is the most consistently assured performance available. The women all sing most beautifully, with Janowitz's Countess, Mathis's Susanna and Troyanos's Cherubino all ravishing the ear in contrasted ways. Prey is an intelligent if not very jolly-sounding Figaro, and Fischer-Dieskau gives his dark, sharply defined reading of the Count's role. All told, a great success with fine playing and recording, though at about half the price Kleiber presents a version with at least as many merits.

Kleiber's is an attractive, strong performance, with much fine singing and with recording that is remarkably fine for its age (it was one of Decca's bicentenary recordings of the mid-1950s). The recitatives are rather slow and unsparkling, but few if any rival sets have since matched the consistent stylishness of the singing. Gueden's Susanna might be criticized, but her golden tones are certainly characterful, and Danco and Della Casa are both at their finest. A dark-toned Figaro in Siepi, and with fine conducting from Kleiber this remains a unique set.

Klemperer may seem the most solemn of conductors, but he had a great sense of humour. Here he shows very clearly how his humour fits in with the sterling characteristics we all recognize. Though the tempi are often slow, the pointing and shading are most delicate, and the result, though hardly sparkling, is full of high spirits. A clue to the Klemperer approach comes near the beginning with Figaro's aria *Se vuol ballare*, which is not merely a servant's complaint about an individual master, but a revolutionary call, with horns and pizzicato strings strongly defined, to apply to the whole world: *'I'll play the tune, sir!'* Geraint Evans is masterly in matching Klemperer, for though his normal interpretation of the role of Figaro is more effervescent than this, he is superb here, singing and acting with great power. Reri Grist makes a charming Susanna – her finest achievement yet on record – and Teresa Berganza is a rich-toned Cherubino. Gabriel Bacquier's Count is darker-toned and more formidable than usual, while Elisabeth Söderström's Countess, though it has its moments of strain, gives ample evidence of this artist's thoughtful intensity. Though this is not a version one would regularly laugh over, it represents a unique experience. The recording is first-rate, wonderfully rich, smooth and clean.

The reissue of the Leinsdorf set in a bright recording at the cheapest possible price (unusually complete and on three discs, but without a libretto) will certainly be tempting for those with limited resources. Although not as satisfying, overall, as the Kleiber Decca set, and not as warmly recorded, this performance has a great many points in its favour. It is perhaps the women that stand out in a generally good cast, Roberta Peters a sparkling Susanna, and Lisa della Casa characteristically fine as the Countess. Rosalind Elias is a magnificent Cherubino, one of the most memorable characterizations on disc. Leinsdorf's manner is fresh and straightforward, not especially imaginative, but keeping the music flowing. The stereo is notable for good directional placing in the recitatives.

Fischer-Dieskau's commanding assumption of the role of the Count is the outstanding point of Fricsay's set. The conductor's urgent manner ensures fine team work, but the level of singing generally falls well below that on the rival Decca mid-price set.

Le Nozze di Figaro: highlights.
> *** Philips 6500 434 (from above recording cond. Davis).
> (M) ** (*) Decca Ace of Diamonds SDD 237 (from above recording cond. Kleiber).

The Davis selection is attractive – though what disc could possibly contain every favourite item from such an opera? The Kleiber disc is marginally less successful: these excerpts do not show Kleiber's compulsive overall shaping, which is a distinctive feature of the complete recording.

Der Schauspieldirektor (The Impresario; opera in 1 act): complete recording.
> *** DGG 2740 112 (3 discs). Reri Grist, Arleen Auger (sopranos), Peter Schreier (tenor), Kurt Moll (bass), Dresden State Orchestra, Karl Boehm – *Die Entführung.****

The performance here is without dialogue, so it fits on to a single side. Grist's bravura as Madame Herz is impressive and Arleen Auger – the attractive Constanze in the *Entführing* coupling – is again pleasingly fresh and stylish here. The tenor and bass make only minor contributions, but Boehm's guiding hand keeps the music alive from the first bar to the last.

Die Zauberflöte (The Magic Flute; opera in 2 acts): complete recording.
> *** DGG 2709 017 (3 discs). Evelyn Lear, Roberta Peters, Lisa Otto (sopranos), Fritz Wunderlich (tenor), Dietrich Fischer-Dieskau (baritone), Hans Hotter, Franz Crass (basses), Berlin RIAS Chamber Choir, Berlin Philharmonic Orchestra, Karl Boehm.
> *** HMV SLS 912 (3 discs) (without dialogue). Gundula Janowitz,

Ruth Margret Putz, Lucia Popp (sopranos), Nicolai Gedda (tenor), Walter Berry, Gottlob Frick (basses), Elisabeth Schwarzkopf (soprano), Christa Ludwig (mezzo-soprano), Marga Höffgen (contralto) (3 Ladies), Philharmonia Chorus and Orchestra, Otto Klemperer.

** (*) Decca SET 479/81. Pilar Lorengar, Cristina Deutekom (sopranos), Stuart Burrows (tenor), Dietrich Fischer-Dieskau, Hermann Prey (baritones), Martti Talvela (bass), Vienna State Opera Chorus, Vienna Philharmonic Orchestra, Sir Georg Solti.

(M) ** Decca Ace of Diamonds GOS 501/3. Wilma Lipp, Hilde Gueden, Emmy Loose (sopranos), Leopold Simoneau (tenor), Walter Berry (baritone), Kurt Boehme (bass), Vienna State Opera Chorus, Vienna Philharmonic Orchestra, Karl Boehm.

One of the glories of Boehm's DGG set is the singing of Fritz Wunderlich as Tamino, a wonderful memorial to a singer much missed. Passages that normally seem merely incidental come alive thanks to his beautiful intense singing. Fischer-Dieskau, with characteristic word-pointing, makes a sparkling Papageno on record (he is too big of frame, he says, to do the role on stage) and Franz Crass is a satisfyingly straightforward Sarastro. The team of women is well below this standard – Lear taxed cruelly in *Ach, ich fühl's*, Peters shrill in the upper register (although the effect is exciting), and the Three Ladies do not blend well – but the direction of Boehm is superb, light and lyrical, but weighty where necessary to make a glowing, compelling experience. Fine recording.

Klemperer's conducting of *The Magic Flute* at Covent Garden was disappoint-ing, but here he is inspired, making the dramatic music sound more like Beethoven in its monumental strength. But he does not miss the humour and point of the Papageno passages, and to a surprising degree he gets the best of both worlds. The cast is outstanding – look at the distinction of the Three Ladies alone – and curiously it is the most generally reliable of all the singers, Gottlob Frick as Sarastro, who comes nearest to letting the side down. Lucia Popp is an exciting discovery, and Gundula Janowitz sings Pamina's part with a creamy beauty that is just breathtaking. Nicolai Gedda too is most tasteful as Tamino and Walter Berry is a firm-voiced Papageno. The recording was made in the summer of 1964 at a time when Philharmonia fortunes were not at their happiest, but from the results you would never know that. It is a pity the dialogue is not included, but on that point Klemperer was insistent, and the set is after all his triumph.

If one is looking for Mozartian charm in this most monumental of Mozart's operas, then plainly Solti's reading must be rejected. It is tough, strong and brilliant, and it is arguable that in this opera those are the required qualities above all; but even so the absence of charm has a cumulative effect. The drama may be consistently vital, but ultimately the full variety of Mozart's inspiration is not achieved. On the male side the cast is very strong indeed, with Stuart Burrows assuming his international mantle easily with stylish and rich-toned singing. Martti Talvela and Fischer-Dieskau as Sarastro and the Speaker respectively provide a stronger contrast than usual, each superb in his way, and Hermann Prey rounds out the character of Papageno with intelligent pointing of words. The cast of women is less consistent. Pilar Lorengar's Pamina is sweetly attractive as long as your ear is not worried by her obtrusive vibrato, while Cristina Deutekom's Queen of the Night is technically impressive, though marred by a curious warbling quality in the coloratua. almost like an intrusive 'w' where you sometimes have the intrusive 'h'. The Three Ladies make a strong team (Yvonne Minton in the middle), and it was a good idea to give the parts of the Three Boys to genuine trebles. Superb recording quality, and sumptuously illustrated libretto.

The principal attraction of the Ace of Diamonds *Zauberflöte* is the conducting of Karl Boehm; and on bargain label with surprisingly good recording quality, that might well be counted enough recommendation, particularly when the Tamino of Leopold Simoneau and the Papageno of Walter Berry are strongly and sensitively sung. But the rest of the singing is rather variable, with Hilde Gueden a pert characterful Pamina unhappy in the florid divisions, Wilma Lipp an impressive Queen of the Night but Kurt Boehme a gritty, ungracious Sarastro. Another snag is the complete absence of dialogue, but after all Klemperer was equally insistent that the work is better for repeated listening on the gramophone without it. Certainly with such remarkably atmospheric recording this is most enjoyable as it stands.

Die Zauberflöte: highlights.
** DGG SLPEM 136440 (from above DGG recording cond. Boehm).
** Decca SET 527 (from above recording cond. Solti).
(M) ** Decca Ace of Diamonds SDD 218 (from above Decca recording cond. Boehm).

The selection from the DGG *Zauberflöte* is a generous one but obviously not directed towards bringing out the special qualities of Boehm's performance. Much of the least impressive singing with the Three Ladies, Pamina and the Queen of Night gets chosen; conversely one would like more of Wunderlich's Tamino,

the great glory of the set. Including the *Overture* in such a disc seems a waste. The Solti highlights disc makes a fair sampler for those who want to try his strong Mozartian approach but not to invest in the complete set. It is Boehm's strong directing hand rather than the rather uneven singing that commends the Ace of Diamonds selection.

'Opera festival': excerpts from *Così fan tutte; Don Giovanni; Die Entführung aus dem Serail; Idomeneo; Le Nozze di Figaro; Il Re pastore; Zaïde; Die Zauberflöte.*
** Decca SET 548/9. Lucia Popp (soprano), Brigitte Fassbaender (mezzo-soprano), Werner Krenn (tenor), Tom Krause (baritone), Manfred Jungwirth (bass), Vienna Haydn Orchestra, Istvan Kertesz.

These are essentially concert performances. There are plenty of favourites here, including the overtures to *Così*, *Figaro* and *Zauberflöte*, and the performances are enjoyable. Kertesz shows no special feeling for Mozartian opera, and some of his tempi are not too well judged. Most of the singing is fresh-sounding, though not always stylish, and there is little attempt at characterization; Brigitte Fassbaender's *Voi che sapete*, for instance, is not very convincing. But for those wanting a set of concentrated highlights of this kind, this well recorded collection should serve.

MISCELLANEOUS VOCAL RECITALS (INCLUDING OPERA)

Concert arias: *Ch'io mi scordi di te?, K.505; Chi sà, chi sà qual sia, K.582; Misera dove son!, K.369; Vado, ma dove?, K.583.* Opera arias: *Così fan tutte: Temerari! ... Come scoglio. Don*

*Giovanni: Batti, batti, o bel Masetto;
Vedrai carino. Le Nozze di Figaro: Non
so più; Giunse alfin . . . Deh vieni, non
tardar; Voi che sapete.*

** (*) Philips 6500 544. Elly Ame-
ling (soprano), English Chamber
Orchestra, Edo de Waart; Dalton
Baldwin (piano).

Performances of great charm and
vocal freshness. The operatic excerpts
are perhaps a shade under-characterized,
with no great differences made in the
arias for Susanna, Zerlina and Cherubino, but they are delightfully sung. The
scene from *Così fan tutte* is, however,
much more dramatic; this matches and
almost surpasses Berganza's fine account
on her Ace of Diamonds recital. Miss
Ameling is very much at home in the concert arias. Her performances have not
quite the distinction of Schwarzkopf
(who includes two of them in her recital
with Szell – see above) but the singing is
so assured, sensitive and accurate that it
cannot fail to give pleasure. *Misera dove
son!* is especially telling. Excellent
recording.

Arias: (i) *Ch'io mi scordi di te?, K.505.
Le Nozze di Figaro: Non so più; Voi che
sapete. La Clemenza di Tito: Parto,
parto. Così fan tutte: Come scoglio;
È Amore un ladroncello; Per pietà.*

(M) *** Decca Ace of Diamonds SDD
176. Teresa Berganza (soprano),
London Symphony Orchestra,
John Pritchard, (i) with Geoffrey
Parsons (piano).

This is marvellous Mozart singing that
must be enthusiastically recommended.
Berganza is if anything more impressive
on record than in person, and her technical virtuosity in these difficult arias is
breathtaking. What is more the tone-
colour is unfailingly beautiful, and the
sense of style immaculate. If one has to
mark any failing at all it is that the last

degree of dramatic urgency is lacking,
but when separate arias are involved that
is the smallest drawback. The recording
is excellent.

Arias: *Così dunque tradisci . . . Aspri
rimorsi atroci, K.432; Un bacio di
mano, K.541; Mentre ti lascio, K.513;
Ein deutsches Kriegslied, K.539: Ich
möchte wohl der Kaiser sein. La finta
giardiniera: Nach der welschen Art. Le
Nozze di Figaro: Hai già vinta la
causa; Vedrò mentr'io sospiro. Warnung, K.433; Männer suchen stehts zu
naschen.*

** (*) Decca SXL 6490. Dietrich
Fischer-Dieskau (baritone), Vien-
na Haydn Orchestra, Rheinhold
Peters – HAYDN: *Arias.*** (*)

The Mozart rarities on this disc are
more numerous and more interesting
than the Haydn items, and it is particularly fascinating to hear the Count's
aria from *Figaro* in a version with a
high vocal line which the composer
arranged for performances in 1789. There
is also a beautiful aria from two years
earlier, *Mentre ti lascio*, which reveals
Mozart's inspiration at its keenest. The
other items too bring their delights.
Fischer-Dieskau sings most intelligently,
if with some pointing of word and phrase
that is not quite in character with the
music.

Arias: *Exsultate, jubilate, K.165. Mass
in C minor, K.427: Et incarnatus est.
Idomeneo: Padre germani addio; Se il
padre. Il Re pastore: L'amerò.*

(M) ** (*) Argo Ace of Diamonds
SDD 335. Erna Spoorenberg (soprano), Academy of St Martin-in-
the-Fields, Neville Marriner; Philip Ledger (organ and harpsichord).

The natural quality of Erna Spoorenberg's voice is exceptionally creamy-

toned, and though an edge occasionally appears nowadays in the upper register, the singing here is more than enough to make one welcome this Mozart recital. As a collection of beautiful soprano arias it could hardly be bettered, with the *Alleluia* from *Exsultate, jubilate* sounding really joyous, and *Et incarnatus est* from the *C minor Mass* (Schmidt's version) soaring heavenward as it should. Perhaps the most impressive item of all is the first of Ilia's arias from *Idomeneo*, *Padre germani addio*. All through, the accompaniment of Neville Marriner's Academy of St Martin's is most stylish. Excellent recording quality.

Arias: *La Clemenza di Tito: Parto, parto. Don Giovanni: In quali eccessi ... Mi tradì quell'alma ingrata; Crudele? Ah no! mio bene ... Non mi dir. Die Entführung aus dem Serail: Martern aller arten. Idomeneo: Parto, e l'unico oggetto. Il Re pastore: L'amerò. Le Nozze di Figaro: Giunse alfin ... Deh vieni, non tardar; E Susanna non vien ... Dove sono; Voi che sapete.*

   *** R C A SER 5675. Margaret Price (soprano), English Chamber Orchestra, James Lockhart.

An impressive disc of display arias. Margaret Price shows her versatility by singing arias from all three soprano roles in *Figaro*, but her most impressive performances remain those which demand coloratura brilliance combined with dramatic power. Strong accompaniment and good recording.

Arias: *Così fan tutte: Per pietà. Don Giovanni: Ah! fuggi il traditor; In quali eccessi. Le Nozze di Figaro: Dove sono.*

   (M) * (*) Decca Ace of Diamonds SDD 288. Lisa della Casa (soprano), Vienna Philharmonic Orchestra, Boehm, Krips, Hollreiser,

Kleiber – HANDEL: *Giulio Cesare arias.***

These arias are beautifully sung, but Lisa della Casa's classical restraint does not always bring out the full drama when the music is heard out of context. This is not as attractive as the Handel coupling, and the recording is dated, with thin orchestral sound, the focus of the voice sometimes involving too much emphasis on certain consonants.

COLLECTION

'The world of Mozart': (i) *Clarinet concerto in A major, K.622:* 2nd movement. (ii) *Horn concerto No. 4 in E flat major, K.495:* finale. (iii) *Piano concerto No. 20 in D minor, K.466:* 2nd movement. (iv) *German dance, K.605/3 (Sleighride); Serenade No. 13 in G major (Eine kleine Nachtmusik), K.525:* 1st movement. (v) *Symphony No. 40 in G minor, K.550:* 1st movement. (vi) *Piano sonata No. 11 in A major, K.331: Rondo alla Turca.* (Vocal) (vii) *Ave verum corpus, K.618.* (viii) *Exsultate jubilate, K.165: Alleluia.* (ix) *Così fan tutte: Soave sia il vento* (trio). (x) *Don Giovanni: Deh vieni alla finestra* (serenade). (xi) *Le Nozze di Figaro: Voi che sapete.* (xii) *Die Zauberflöte: Der Vogelfanger.*

   (B) *** Decca SPA 251. (i) Gervase de Peyer (clarinet), (ii) Barry Tuckwell (horn), both with London Symphony Orchestra, Peter Maag; (iii) Julius Katchen (piano), Stuttgart Chamber Orchestra, Karl Münchinger; (iv) Vienna Mozart Ensemble, Willi Boskovsky; (v) New Philharmonia Orchestra, Carlo Maria Giulini; (vi) Wilhelm Backhaus (piano); (vii)

Choir of St John's College, Cambridge; (viii) Erna Spoorenberg (soprano); (ix) Lucia Popp (soprano), Brigitte Fassbaender (contralto), Tom Krause (bass), Vienna Opera Orchestra, Istvan Kertesz; (x) Gabriel Bacquier (baritone); (xi) Teresa Berganza (mezzosoprano); (xii) Geraint Evans (baritone) (with orch.).

A really outstanding collection, brilliantly compiled so that each excerpt makes the right kind of contrast with what has gone before. The performances are all of high quality and this should tempt many to explore further, while for the confirmed Mozartian it makes a glorious concert of favourites. Highly recommended.

Musgrave, Thea
(born 1928)

(i; ii) *Horn concerto;* (iii) *Concerto for orchestra.*
   *** Decca Headline HEAD 8. (i) Barry Tuckwell (horn); Scottish National Orchestra, cond. (ii) the composer; (iii) Alexander Gibson.

Thea Musgrave's *Horn concerto* has a spatial concept as part of its construction. The orchestral brass form a concertante group within the orchestra, with the percussion spread round the back. At one stage the trumpets take up antiphonal positions on either side of the orchestra, while the orchestral horns move out into the hall, strategically placed so as to surround the soloists. All this is vividly captured by the recording engineers. This and the *Concerto for orchestra* (its five sections impressively inter-linked) are among Thea Musgrave's most vital and original works, and both are superbly performed and recorded.

Night music for chamber orchestra.
   *** Argo ZRG 702. London Sinfonietta, Frederick Prausnitz –
   RIEGGER: *Dichotomy;* SESSIONS: *Rhapsody; Symphony No. 8.****

Night music, sensitive and intense, like some of this composer's concertos presents peripatetic soloists, in this instance two horn-players variously positioned in relation to the orchestra. The effect is not simply gimmicky but genuinely expressive in a performance as fine as this. Excellent recording.

Mussorgsky, Modest
(1839–81)

Night on the Bare Mountain.
   *** Decca SXL 6399. Suisse Romande Orchestra, Paul Kletzki –
   RACHMANINOV: *Symphony No. 3.** (*)

Night on the Bare Mountain; Khovantschina: Prelude to Act 1; Dance of the Persian slaves.
   (B) *** Decca SPA 257. Berlin Philharmonic Orchestra, Sir Georg Solti (with *Concert ***).

Night on the Bare Mountain appears in a great many concert discs (including a splendid Universo disc conducted by David Lloyd-Jones – 6580 053 – which uses Mussorgsky's original score). The performance (and recording) by Solti is among the very best, and the performance of the beautiful *Khovantschina* prelude is the finest in the present catalogue. This disc is called *The world of Russia* and is discussed in more detail, along with the Lloyd-Jones issue, in our *Treasury* volume. Kletzki's version is brilliantly done, and the Decca recording is first-class. The coupling, however, is not the primary recommendation for Rachmaninov's *Third Symphony.*

Night on the Bare Mountain; Pictures at an Exhibition (orch. Ravel).

  (M) ** CBS Classics 61050. Philadelphia Orchestra, Eugene Ormandy.

On Ormandy's disc the opening trumpet of *Pictures at an Exhibition* is very forward and almost aggressively brilliant, but one can adjust to the glassiness of the CBS sound, which has plenty of weight to support it. The performance has a characteristic Ormandy warmth which shows more and more as the work proceeds. The orchestral playing is superb. With such a loud score one ideally wants a more spacious acoustic instead of everything searchlighted and up close like this, but both *Pictures* and *Night on the Bare Mountain* are certainly compulsive as performances.

Pictures at an Exhibition (orch. Ravel).

  *** DGG SLPM 139010. Berlin Philharmonic Orchestra, Herbert von Karajan – RAVEL: *Boléro.****

  ** (*) Decca Phase 4 PFS 4255. New Philharmonia Orchestra, Lorin Maazel – PROKOFIEV: *Piano concerto No. 3.** (*)

  ** (*) Decca SXL 6328. Los Angeles Philharmonic Orchestra, Zubin Mehta – *Pictures* (piano version). ** (*)

  (B) ** (*) Classics for Pleasure CFP 106. London Philharmonic Orchestra, John Pritchard – TCHAIKOVSKY: *Romeo and Juliet.***

  (M) ** (*) Philips Universo 6580 059. Concertgebouw Orchestra, Bernard Haitink (with *Concert* ** (*)).

  (B) * (*) Decca SPA 229. Suisse Romande Orchestra, Ernest Ansermet – PROKOFIEV: *Lieutenant Kijé; Love of 3 Oranges excerpts.* (*)

Pictures at an Exhibition (orch. Ravel); *Khovantschina: Prelude to Act 1.*

  (M) ** (*) Vanguard VSD 71188. New Philharmonia Orchestra, Charles Mackerras.

The superb DGG record under Karajan is easily the most distinguished *Pictures at an Exhibition* we have had in stereo. As with many of Karajan's best issues one has the feeling that he has rethought the score. One fascinating feature of this reading is that the *Promenades* are often slower than usual, suggesting that the 'visitor to the exhibition' is taking a more leisurely stroll between the exhibits. It is the remarkable sophistication of the orchestral playing that makes this issue so distinctive. The brass in particular are superb, and especially so in the famous *Catacombs* sequence, where the aural sonority has a majesty found in no other recording. The lightly pointed tuba playing in the *Hut on fowl's legs* is a delicious example of the subtlety of this performance, which is again shown in the restraint of *The old castle*. A splendid disc in every way.

Though the characterization is less subtle than Karajan's, Maazel's is an immensely vivid reading, brilliantly recorded. Indeed, considering that the work is given the most spectacular Phase 4 treatment, it is remarkable that it has fitted on to a single side (with only a touch of brashness at the very end) to make room for an unexpected and attractive coupling.

The other Decca disc, under Mehta, offers the most intelligent coupling of all and thus becomes more than the sum on its parts, even though it is not as imaginative as Karajan nor as vivid as Maazel. The recording is warm and atmospheric, without lack of impact, and this issue certainly is remarkable value.

A superbly brilliant account under Pritchard, in which the personality of the orchestra comes over strongly, the players obviously enjoying themslves and their own virtuosity. The very clear recording (not especially atmospheric) makes every detail of the orchestration glitter, and the conductor's characterization of each picutre is equally positive. The building of the *Great Gate of Kiev* finale is nearly as exciting as Karajan's performance.

Haitink's account is part of a collection discussed in our *Treasury* volume. This is not perhaps the most electric performance of the *Pictures*, but the orchestral playing is marvellous and the rich, detailed recording suits Haitink's relaxed yet never dull approach. The atmosphere of each picture is caught with considerable skill; for instance, *Cum mortuis in lingua mortua*, which comes immediately before the side break, is wonderfully serene.

Mackerras paints a characteristically vivid set of pictures. The orchestral playing does not show Haitink's refinement but has verve and colour, and the recording has plenty of life and impact. At the side-turn *Limoges* shows Mackerras at his most excitingly imaginative, the teeming market scene excitingly drawn; and the three remaining pictures produce some very dramatic brass playing. With modern recording and an attractive, resonant acoustic this is good value at medium price, although in the *Khovantschina Prelude* Mackerras is not as evocative as Solti (see above).

There is a cool circumspection about Ansermet's reading which is not quite compensated for by the meticulous detail and clarity with which he displays Ravel's orchestration. In short, this lacks atmosphere and excitement.

'Greatest hits': (i; ii) *Night on the Bare Mountain.* (i; iii) *Pictures at an Exhibition* (orch. Ravel). *Khovantschina:* (iv) *Prelude;* (v) *Dance of the Persian slaves.* (vi) (Piano) *Intermezzo.*

(B) ** CBS Harmony 30050. (i) New York Philharmonic Orchestra, cond. (ii) Leonard Bernstein, (iii) Thomas Schippers; (iv) Cleveland Orchestra, George Szell; (v) Orchestra, André Kostelanetz; (vi) André Previn (piano).

This is an exceptionally generous disc. Schippers's account of *Pictures at an Exhibition* is brilliantly recorded. The performance is a little under-characterized, but it has more life than Ansermet's; and Szell's account of the lovely *Khovantschina Prelude* is not wanting in poetic feeling. Bernstein's *Night on the Bare Mountain* is good, if not outstanding, but Previn's sturdy performance of the *Intermezzo* makes an unusual bonus. Certainly this collection is excellent value.

Pictures at an Exhibition (original piano version).

** (*) Decca SXL 6328. Vladimir Ashkenazy (piano) – *Pictures* (orchestral version).** (*)

(M) ** (*) Unicorn UNS 206. Ronald Smith (piano) – ALKAN: *Symphony for piano.* (*)

We badly need a modern recording of this by Richter. Anyone who has heard him play it in the concert-hall will remember the experience as more memorable than any orchestral performance. Ashkenazy's account is distinguished by the poetic feeling that is characteristic of all his records. The performance is undoubtedly compelling, but it does not have the extrovert flair which is needed for the finale to make its full effect. But for those interested in a comparison between the original and Ravel's inspired transcription this disc is very worthwhile.

A committed and convincing performance from Ronald Smith, with the individual pictures strongly projected and the finale well prepared and excitingly brought off. The playing perhaps lacks bravura of the calibre for which Richter is justly famous, but it has plenty of spontaneity, with the pianist nearly always in firm technical control. Clear recording, with a close balance.

The Nursery (song cycle); *Sunless* (song cycle). Songs: *Gathering mushrooms; Gopak: The magpie; The Orphan; Where art thou, little star?*
> (B) ** (*) Saga 5357. Oda Slobodskaya (soprano), Ivor Newton (piano).

It is sad that so positive an artist as Oda Slobodskaya did not record much more. This is a welcome sample, even though the voice is not caught at its best, and the recording is limited. But her interpretations of Mussorgsky are unique and characterful, and on a bargain label they are well worth investigating.

Songs and Dances of Death (song cycle); *Sunless* (song cycle). Songs: *Classic; The flea; Where are you, little star?*
> ** (*) Argo ZRG 708. Benjamin Luxon (baritone), David Williamson (piano).

This is a valuable record of sensitive performances. A certain grittiness in Luxon's voice may catch the recording microphone, but that is appropriate enough in songs which are essentially dark. A Russian timbre is obviously more suited, but Luxon's concern for word meaning, and his powers of vocal acting – particularly in the *Songs and Dances of Death* – are impressive. Sympathetic accompaniment and good recording.

Boris Godunov (opera in Prologue and 4 acts): complete recording.
> ** (*) Decca SET 514/7. Nicolai Ghiaurov (baritone), Galina Vishnevskaya (soprano), Aleksei Maslennikov, Ludovico Spiess (tenors) Martti Talvela, Zoltan Kelemen (basses), Vienna Boys' Choir,

Sofia Radio Chorus, Vienna State Opera Chorus, Philharmonia Orchestra, Herbert von Karajan.

This Decca set comes nearer than previous versions to conveying the rugged greatness of Mussorgsky's masterpiece, partly because of the superb control of Karajan, partly because of the recording quality, more vivid than that of earlier versions. If Ghiaurov in the title role lacks some of the dramatic intensity of Christoff on the two HMV sets (both now deleted) he is more accurate in singing the notes rather than indulging in evocative sing-speech. Not everyone will like the baritonal tinge which results, but ultimately this is exceedingly satisfying for repeated hearings. Karajan – as in his Salzburg performances, on which this is based – has opted for the Rimsky-Korsakov version, which will disappoint those who have been waiting to hear the darker, earthier original version on record, but which matches Karajan's qualities. Only the Coronation scene lacks something of the weight and momentum one ideally wants. For the rest the chorus is finely intense. The only serious disappointment vocally is the Marina of Vishnevskaya, too squally for Western ears.

Boris Godunov: highlights.
> ** (*) Decca SET 557 (from above recording).

A useful selection from Karajan's superbly recorded version. Do not be put off by the relatively low-powered account of the Coronation scene: it is not representative of the whole performance.

Boris Godunov (arr. Shostakovich): excerpts (sung in German).
> ** Telefunken SAT 22526. Theo Adam (bass), Hanne-Lore Kuhse, Roswitha Trexier (sopranos), Peter Schreier, Martin Ritzmann (tenors), Siegfried Vogel (bass),

Dresden Philharmonic Children's Choir, Leipzig Radio Choir, Dresden State Orchestra, Herbert Kegel.

There seems little point in having a record of Mussorgsky in German, though in this East German performance the Shostakovich arrangement is heard on record for the first time. Theo Adam makes an impressive, intense Boris, lacking a little in weight of tone, while Schreier is excellent as the Simpleton in his scene with the Tsar. Good recording.

Khovantschina (opera in 4 acts): complete recording.

(M) * (*) Decca Ace of Diamonds GOS 619/21. Nicholas Tzveych (bass), Alexander Marinkovich, Drago Startz (tenors), Dushan Popovich (baritone), Melanie Bugarinovich (mezzo-soprano), Anita Mezetova (soprano), Miro Changalovich (bass), Chorus and Orchestra of Belgrade National Opera, Kreshimir Baranovich.

It is important that so powerful an opera as *Khovantschina* should be available on record, but this Yugoslav performance of the mid-fifties gives only a partial idea of the work's epic strength, its vivid representation of medieval Russia and its religious movements. At mid-price it makes a fair stopgap, and for its age the recording is good, though the singing is very variable indeed.

Nenna, Pomponio
(*c.* 1555–*c.* 1615)

Ricercare à 2. Madrigals and motets: *Ahi, dispietata e cruda; L'amoroso veleno; Asciugate i begli occhi; Deh! scoprite il ben seno; Ecco, O dolce; Ecco, O mia dolce; In monte Olivetti; La mia doglia s'avanza; Lasso, ch'io moro; Mercè, grido piangendo; Signora, io penso; S'io taccio; Tenebrae factae sunt; Tristis est anima mea.*

(M) ** Nonesuch H 71277. Accademia Monteverdiana, Croydon Trinity Boys' Choir, Jaye Consort of Viols, Denis Stevens.

Very little is known about Pomponio Nenna except that he spent a period of his life at Prince Carlo Gesualdo's court at Venosa. He wrote eight books of madrigals for five voices and a single book for four. Here we have a selection, plus three responsories for Holy Week, and an instrumental *Ricercare*. The collection is completed with a *Gagliarda à 4* by Gesualdo which makes a suitable break between the madrigals and the liturgical settings on side two. The performances are scholarly and quite pleasing, although the music's impulse seems slightly pale alongside the masterpieces of Monteverdi.

Nielsen, Carl
(1865–1931)

Clarinet concerto, Op. 57.

(M) ** (*) Unicorn UNS 239. John McCaw (clarinet), New Philharmonia Orchestra, Raymond Leppard – MOZART: *Clarinet concerto.** (*)

A fine performance from John McCaw, direct, but not lacking atmosphere. Perhaps the element of mystery and the musing improvisatory quality of the music are not entirely caught here, but the excellent accompaniment and clear recording certainly offer a very positive reproduction of Nielsen's score.

(i) *Clarinet concerto, Op. 57;* (ii) *Flute concerto.*
> (B) ** Turnabout TV 34261S. (i) Josef Deak (clarinet); (ii) Paul Pázmándi (flute); both with Philharmonia Hungarica, Othmar Maga.

Both the *Clarinet* and *Flute concertos* are late works, which form a logical coupling. They were written for members of the Danish Wind Quintet and it is to be regretted that Nielsen did not live to complete the remaining concertos he had planned for each of the players. The *Clarinet concerto* is of course one of his most searching and profound works, and although Josef Deak's performance is not quite so impressive as Ib Eriksson's on an early Decca LP, it is still an eloquent one. The flautist, Paul Pázmándi, is also a good player, if not outstanding. The orchestral playing, however, is pedestrian, and although there are some details to admire, the disc cannot be recommended without some reservation.

(i) *Flute concerto. Symphony No. 2 (The Four Temperaments), Op. 16.*
> ** CBS 73299. New York Philharmonic Orchestra, Leonard Bernstein, (i) with Julius Baker (flute).

The *Four Temperaments* has not been so well served on records. Best is the marvellous Jensen version made after the war, but among modern sets Garaguly and the Tivoli Orchestra (see below), though not of recent provenance, give the soundest interpretation. Bernstein has plenty of fire in the first movement but the inner movements are too slow and expressive detail too heavily underlined to be wholly satisfactory. There is a ruinous agogic change in the coda of the finale. The recording is bright and shallow but with some adjustment of the controls can be made to yield acceptable results. Among modern versions Ole Schmidt's

account with the LSO is by far the best, but it is not available separately. Julius Baker gives a fine performance of the *Flute concerto,* even if Bernstein gives a heavyweight and rather over-emphatic account of the accompaniment.

Little suite for string orchestra, Op. 1.
> (B) ** Turnabout TV 34049S. Tivoli Concert Symphony Orchestra, Carl Garaguly – *Symphony No. 2; Serenata.***

The *Little suite* is an enchanting piece and an incredibly assured work for so young a composer. The recording is good though a little lacking in warmth. Garaguly, a Hungarian, has a distinct feeling for this music – sympathies no doubt fostered by his long residence in Scandinavia.

Symphonies Nos. 1 in G minor, Op. 7; 2 (The Four Temperaments), Op. 16; (i) 3 (Espansiva), Op. 27; 4 (Inextinguishable), Op. 29; 5, Op. 50; 6 (Sinfonia semplice).
> *** Unicorn RHS 324/30. London Symphony Orchestra, Ole Schmidt, (i) with Jill Gomez (soprano), Brian Raynor Cook (baritone).

In general this is a very fine set though it has the handicap of being a package and not available separately. (The bonus record, an illuminating series of talks by Robert Simpson, is an attraction, though it has been poorly produced.) The performances are highly idiomatic and full of good things: Ole Schmidt's account of the *Fifth Symphony* is as good as any we have heard; his *Second* is as fresh and vital as Jensen's pioneering discs on HMV 78s; the *Sixth* is most revealing and thoughtful and in many ways outdistances Jensen's noble account (issued here on World Records). More controversial are No. 1, which is disfigured by a number of agogic distortions, and the *Espansiva*, whose outer movements are also handicapped in this respect. But for the most part this is altogether an admirable enterprise and can be recommended. The recording is detailed and strikes an excellent balance between wind and strings. Some ears find the wind a little recessed and the brass sound untamed and out of perspective, but other ears find the sound wonderfully ripe and compulsive, indeed of demonstration quality. Certainly this set, even though it is not inexpensive, makes a splendid investment for the reader wanting to explore this marvellous set of symphonies.

Symphony No. 2 (The Four Temperaments), Op. 16.

(B) ** Turnabout TV 34049S. Tivoli Concert Symphony Orchestra, Carl Garaguly – *Little suite; Serenata.***

The *Second Symphony* is one of Nielsen's most attractive works; compact in layout, direct in utterance, it is an admirable example of his early style at its very best. It first made its appearance on record in the late forties on Danish 78s conducted by the late Thomas Jensen, and this has never been surpassed since. The Garaguly performance is brisk but has plenty of fire and attack. It has not the breadth or majesty of Jensen's 78s and the second movement is too fast. The recording is not ideal, rather dry in the bass and with a tendency to shrillness in the treble, but for all that the disc is enjoyable and the reading as a whole has a certain dignity.

Symphony No. 3 (Espansiva), Op. 27.

** (*) CBS 72369. Ruth Guldback (soprano), Niels Moller (tenor), Danish Royal Orchestra, Leonard Bernstein.

* (**) Decca SXL 6695. Felicity Palmer (soprano), Thomas Allen (baritone), London Symphony Orchestra, François Huybrechts.

Bernstein's performance of the genial *Espansiva* won golden opinions in Denmark when he conducted it in Copenhagen with the present forces. Rarely can the Danish Royal Orchestra have sounded so superlatively full-bodied in tone and so disciplined in attack. And yet for all the excellence of the orchestral playing this performance misses something of the innocence and rapture of the Tuxen LP that introduced this symphony to the catalogues in the early fifties. The difference is to be seen at its greatest in the slow movement, where Bernstein favours great intensity of string tone and Tuxen had much greater intimacy, lyricism and poetry. Bernstein tends to over-accent details in the scherzo, and many readers may well take exception to the rather sluggish tempo for the finale. Nielsen's own tempo was broad, but the effect here (the bass line slightly trailing the main tune) is a trifle overdone. It would, however, be churlish to concentrate on the defects in this performance: it has many merits, liveliness, enthusiasm and admirable orchestral playing, and moreover Bernstein communicates a genuine love of the music for all the overstatement in which he occasionally indulges. The recording is eminently satisfactory, and there is no lack of stereo detail.

François Huybrechts is a young Belgian conductor who made a favourable impression with his début record of Janáček's *Taras Bulba*. He has obvious talents and it is a pity that he has not waited longer before embarking on this present disc. In his concern to convey the breadth of Nielsen's structure and to do justice to its geniality of spirit, he has chosen measured tempi. Unfortunately they are far too measured and add more than six minutes on to Tuxen's timings. (It does not eclipse that performance but at the risk of an appalling pun let us hope that Decca do.) The result sounds unidiomatic, and although Huybrechts's reading, which is admirably recorded, has integrity – at no point does one feel that this conductor is using the music as the vehicle for his own ego – it conveys too little of the character of Nielsen's score to be acceptable.

Symphony No. 4 (Inextinguishable), Op. 29.

  (B) ** Pye GSGC 15025. Hallé Orchestra, Sir John Barbirolli.

  ** Decca SXL 6633. Los Angeles Philharmonic Orchestra, Zubin Mehta.

  * (*) CBS 72890. New York Philharmonic Orchestra, Leonard Bernstein.

Three American orchestras have recorded this symphony. Martinon has done a chromium-plated, gleamingly efficient and brilliant account of the work with the Chicago Orchestra. Bernstein's with the New York Philharmonic has less ruthless forward drive, but Nielsen's finely-drawn lines often quiver with an expressive emphasis that strikes a jarring note. Moreover Bernstein does not hesitate to distort the rhythmic flow of the music to underline an expressive point. The recording is coarse-grained, and there is a disturbing leap in level in the finale which does not appear to have been corrected since the disc was first issued.

Mehta's version is extremely well played but scarcely penetrates below the surface of this powerful symphony. There is no want of surface activity but little feeling of the primeval energy of nature. Things come to life in the finale, but for the most part the reading is efficient, detached and slick, though the recording is admirably detailed and well-lit.

Schmidt's version (see above) is the best since Grøndahl's fine record from the early 1950s but it is not available

separately. Blomstedt's account will shortly be appearing on HMV and we have high hopes of it; but at the time of writing Sir John Barbirolli's version remins the safest recommendation despite the less-than-distinguished recording.

Symphony No. 5, Op. 50.

  *** HMV ASD 3063. Bournemouth Symphony Orchestra, Paavo Berglund.

  ** (*) Decca SXL 6491. Suisse Romande Orchestra, Paul Kletzki.

Symphony No. 5, Op. 50; En Sagadrøm (tone poem), Op. 39.

  ** (*) Unicorn RHS 300. New Philharmonia Orchestra, Jascha Horenstein.

Berglund's disc, which arrived just as we were going to press, is probably the best buy both in terms of performance and recording. Berglund is sometimes unimaginative on disc, but here he gives of his very best. The recording has wide range and atmosphere, and is of demonstration quality.

Horenstein gives a dignified but slightly detached account of the symphony. His feeling for the overall structure of the work is strong, but poetic detail is not savoured to the same extent as it was in Tuxen's old set or as it is in Jensen's LP now transferred to Eclipse. There is considerable interest in that Horenstein restores Nielsen's original and omits some of the accretions to be found in Tuxen's edition. The string-playing of the New Philharmonia is extremely fine, though they do not have quite the lyrical fervour of the Danes or even of the Suisse Romande. Horenstein's record has the advantage of an interesting fill-up, the tone poem *En Sagadrøm*, which is poetically done and beautifully recorded. In the symphony the balance gives far too great a prominence to the percussion, and not quite enough weight to the strings.

Kletzki offers no fill-up and thirty-odd minutes seems rather short value these days. However, the recording is so superlative that many collectors might be inclined to prefer the issue on that count alone. Kletzki also secures playing of great freshness from the SRO. Admittedly the second movement places some strain on the strings, and the woodwind tone is not always beyond reproach. But there is an enthusiasm and directness about this performance that make its imperfections seem of small account.

Symphony No. 6 (Sinfonia semplice).
  (B) * (*) Turnabout TV 34182S.Westchester Symphony Orchestra, Siegfried Landau – SIBELIUS: *6 Humoresques.****

Nielsen's *Sinfonia semplice* is anything but simple – one of this rarefied composer's most subtle and original utterances, a work unusually difficult to keep together in performance. Landau with the Westchester Orchestra copes competently enough, with well-chosen speeds, but the performance suffers seriously from lack of finesse in the playing. Landau finds little mystery in the music, and that is to miss much of its point. The coupling is most welcome, a rare Sibelius offering very well played. The recording of the symphony (1967 vintage) is bright and forward-sounding. The strings sound thin, but that need not be the engineers' fault.

Serenata in vano.
  (B) ** Turnabout TV 34049S. Nielsen Quintet – *Symphony No. 2; Little suite.***

The *Serenata in vano* is a slight work, not the best Nielsen by any means, but enjoyable nonetheless. It receives a thoroughly idiomatic reading, and although the original Danish pressings had rather more impact and warmth, this transfer is still very good and the collection is a bargain at the price.

String quartet No. 1 in G minor, Op. 13.
  (B) ** Turnabout TV 34187S. Copenhagen Quartet – GADE: *Quartet.***

This is a very early work which shows Nielsen still in the process of digesting the influences of Svendsen and Dvořák. There are many distinctive and personal touches, though his language is not at this stage fully formed. The Copenhagen Quartet play with conviction and are well recorded.

String quartets Nos. 2 in F minor, Op. 5; 3 in E flat major, Op. 14.
  (B) ** Turnabout TV 34109S. Copenhagen Quartet.

Nielsen's four published quartets are all comparatively early works. The third, published as Op. 14, was written between the first and second symphonies, while the *F minor* is very early indeed. There is, however, no lack of character, and admirers of the great Danish composer need not hesitate to acquire them. The scherzo of the third is curiously anticipated in the Berwald *A minor Quartet* of 1849, and the work as a whole is full of splendid ideas. The *F minor* was briefly available in an inadequate account in the early days of LP, but the *E flat Quartet* has not been recorded since the days of 78s. Its appearance on so economical a label is to be welcomed, and the performance by the Copenhagen Quartet is characterized by warmth and vitality. The recording, even if it lacks some of the presence and range of the Fona originals, is still very good indeed.

Commotio, Op. 58; Préludes, Op. 51, Nos. 2–6, 8–13, 15–16, 18, 21–3, 26–8.
  (B) *** Turnabout TV 34193S. Jørgen Ernst Hansen (organ).

689

Nielsen turned to the organ relatively late in his career, but in *Commotio* we have a masterpiece, which is here reproduced with admirable fidelity. The score provides no indications as to timbre, and although the composer had in mind the classical organ he occasionally writes the kind of gradual *crescendo* that is only possible on more modern instruments. This recording was made on the Frobenius organ in St Andreas Church, Copenhagen, and in order to achieve the *crescendo* effect, two assistants operated the stops, leaving the organist, Jørgen Hansen, free to concentrate on the music. The result is a magnificent and moving performance. The smaller preludes are also rewarding for the listener, and they too receive a sympathetic touch.

Nitzsche, Jack
(20th century)

St Giles Cripplegate: 6 pieces, Nos. 6, 4, 2, 3, 1, 5.
> *** WEA Reprise K 44211. London Symphony Orchestra, David Measham.

Having made his name scoring for pop records, Jack Nitzsche turned back in part to his classical training, and produced such outpourings as these pieces, full of spectacular orchestral effects. In style they range from imitation Ligeti (the Space odyssey, *2001*, no doubt the influence) to sweet melodic ideas not too far from the world of *Carousel*. Maybe you could regard it as music for hi-fi maniacs, but in any case it is superbly done by the L S O under David Measham, a talented young conductor who at the time was still earning his living in the violin section of the orchestra.

Nono, Luigi
(born 1924)

(i) *Como una ola de fuerza y luz* (music for soprano, piano, orchestra and tape); (ii) *Y entonces comprendio* (music for 6 female voices, chorus and tape).
> *** DGG 2530 436. (i) Clavka Taskova (soprano), Maurizio Pollini (piano), Bavarian Radio Orchestra, Claudio Abbado; (ii) Soloists, Coro da Camera of R A I, Rome, Nico Antonellini.

Like Henze, Nono has been much influenced by the Cuban revolution, and these two large-scale works involving sumptuous sound are among the direct inspirations. Both involve electronic devices, the first with blocks of sound and a hammering piano soloist (what a waste to use Pollini!) subjected to electronic treatment, the second using interweaving sopranos. It may not be music at all in the conventional sense, but with superb recording it is well worth investigating.

Nørgård, Per
(born 1932)

Constellations, Op. 22.
> (B) * (*) Turnabout TV 34168S. Royal Danish Orchestra, Jerzy Semkow – HOLMBOE: *Symphony No. 8.***

This is a kind of twentieth-century concerto grosso, and characteristically it lacks the genial life-assertive force which characterized the great works of the eighteenth century. Its basic harmonic style is astringent. The sleeve-note tells us that throughout the work, and especially in the finale, the composer had in mind the spirit of the dance. Well certainly there are some light-textured dance rhythms, but the pungency of the idiom does not exactly compel one to leave one's chair The most imaginative section of the work is the *Andante* (*Contrasts*), which has a haunting atmospheric quality, and some affinity with Bartók. The performance and recording here are both excellent.

Novák, Vítézslav
(1870–1949)

About the Eternal Longing (tone poem), *Op. 33*; *In the Tatras* (tone poem), *Op. 26*.
  (M) ** Supraphon SUAST 50747. Czech Philharmonic Orchestra, Karel Sejna.

Novák was a pupil of Dvořák, and his best work, *The Storm*, is warm-hearted, richly generous music which shows perhaps the influence of Strauss, Debussy and Janáček. *In the Tatras* is an opulent Straussian tone poem, though Novák speaks with distinctive accents. Both works here are persuasively played, though the recordings are reverberant and a little pale.

De profundis (tone poem), *Op. 67*.
  (M) ** (*) Supraphon SUAST 50476. Brno State Philharmonic Orchestra, Jaroslav Vogel – SUK: *War triptych*.** (*)

De profundis is a wartime work, written in 1941 during the last decade of the composer's life. It is noble and dignified, well argued and obviously deeply felt. This fine performance should win many friends for the piece; it also has the merit of excellent recording.

Marysa overture; Slovak suite.
  (M) *** Supraphon 110 0648. Brno State Philharmonic Orchestra, Karel Sejna.

What a heavenly score the *Slovak suite* is! *Two in love*, its fourth movement could well become as widely popular as any piece of music you care to think of. Much of the score is as appealing as Dvořák; and although the *Marysa overture* is not quite as delightfully inventive it is still a welcome bonus. Sejna does not play with quite the open-hearted geniality that marked Talich's LP of the 1950s, but he is better recorded and there need be no reservations on grounds of quality.

Trio quaso una ballata, Op. 27.
  (M) *** Supraphon 111 1089. Czech Trio with Josef Páleníček (piano) – DVOŘÁK: *Piano trio No. 4*.***

Novák's finest music has a nobility that recalls his master, Dvořák, as well as his freshness, with something too of the richness and the dignity of Elgar and Strauss. The *Trio quasi una ballata* is an intense, rather emotional piece, and here is given an impassioned performance.

Obrecht, Jacob
(*c*. 1453–1505)

Massa super Maria Zart.
  (M) *** Supraphon 112 0464. Prague Madrigal Singers, Miroslav Venhoda.

An urgent, well-sung performance of a fascinating work by a fifteenth-century Dutch composer, who like his compatriots wove his music ingeniously. The *cantus firmus* here is a German song, which Obrecht uses brilliantly and inventively in many ways. Good recording.

Mass: *Sub tuum praesidium.*

> (M) ** Vanguard HM 2SD. Vienna Chamber Choir, Musica Antiqua of Vienna, Clemencic – DUFAY: *Se la face ay pale.***

The recording is not new – it dates from the early 1960s – but Obrecht is so scantily represented in the catalogue that no disc can be overlooked. Nor is there any need to do so in this case. The performance is thoroughly scholarly and conscientious, and the sound, though wanting the last ounce of range, is eminently satisfactory. The Mass itself is an interesting one: it begins with a three-part texture and gradually adds voices based on plainsong melodies, all in honour of the Virgin Mary, until we end up with a seven-part texture. This is a fascinating and original score that can be strongly recommended even though it may involve duplicating the Dufay Mass, *Se la face ay pale.*

Ockeghem, Johannes
(c. 1430–1495)

Ecce ancilla Domini (Mass for four voices); *Intemerata dei Mater* (motet for five voices).

> ** (*) BASF BAC 3038. Pro Cantione Antiqua, Collegium Aureum Soloists, Hamburg Old Music Wind Ensemble, Bruno Turner.

Johannes Ockeghem had an enviable reputation in his day, the late fifteenth century, and became an establishment figure as director of the French Chapel Royal. His is not music which readily makes an impact on the listener, but the rehearings possible with the gramophone soon reveal Ockeghem's imaginative power. The performances here are refined and scholarly; sometimes one feels the need of a stronger forward

impulse, but the atmosphere of the music is readily communicated. Instrumental doubling is used in the Mass only. The recording is not too dry, but the internal balance is not always ideal. A worthwhile issue just the same.

Offenbach, Jacques
(1819–80)

Gaîté Parisienne (ballet music, arr. Rosenthal).

> (M) *** HMV SXLP 30111. Philharmonia Orchestra, Charles Mackerras – J. STRAUSS: *Graduation Ball.****

> ** DGG 2530 199. Berlin Philharmonic Orchestra, Herbert von Karajan – GOUNOD: *Faust ballet.***

> (M) ** CBS Classics 61272. New York Philharmonic Orchestra, Leonard Bernstein – BIZET: *L'Arlésienne suites.*** (*)

> * (*) Decca Phase 4 PFS 4096. New Philharmonia Orchestra, Charles Munch.

The HMV record is the one to go for. It is generously coupled, and the playing sparkles without being aggressive. It is not absolutely complete, but will contain enough music for most people. The playing is infectious, with the care given to detail not interfering with the bounce. In the new transfer (for the reissue) the brass come over marvellously, but there is a certain edge on the string tone: in seeking brilliance the engineers have lost a little of the lustre of the original. But the recording still sounds attractively bright and fresh, and few will complain.

Karajan's selection is brilliantly played and vividly recorded. It lacks something in charm, but nothing in boisterousness. Bernstein's suite includes a good deal of the raciest part of the score and then closes with the *Barcarolle*. The playing is characteristically exciting, but the rather hard light of the CBS sound emphasizes the brittleness of Bernstein's approach (not inappropriate in such frothy music).

The Decca Phase 4 sound is predictably spectacular, and it is the performance that is the disappointment here. Side two is much better than side one, but the first part of the ballet is often sadly lacking in wit and vivacity. The electronic sparkle given by the engineers cannot make up for the absence of charm, and with so much loud music the gaiety soon evaporates. This is a good deal better, however, than another Decca complete account, conducted by Solti (SXL 2280). Solti drives hard and misses the music's geniality altogether. The orchestra gives a virtuoso performance, but the recording is ridiculously overhung with reverberation, which confuses the loud passages to the point almost of distortion and is tiring to listen to. There is a cheap Saga disc too (SAGA 5244), conducted by Leibowitz, but the conductor displays a distinctly un-Gallic touch, and his somewhat heavy-handed approach is not helped by the Saga stereo, which emphasizes the bass end of the orchestra. There are some curiously slow tempi too. Not recommended.

Overtures: *Barbe-Bleue; La Belle Hélène; La Grande-Duchesse de Gérolstein; Orpheus in the underworld; La Vie Parisienne.*
** Columbia Studio 2 TWO 388. City of Birmingham Symphony Orchestra, Louis Frémaux.

Vividly recorded, these performances are enjoyable enough, with good orchestral playing throughout. But the wit and sparkle and indeed the subtlety which Martinon provided in his Decca mono collection of overtures are absent. One only has to compare the introduction of

the waltz tune in *La Belle Hélène* to realize how much more imaginative the earlier performances were. They have been transferred on to Eclipse with some success (ECS 547), but the upper string sound (never refined) of the stereo transcription is difficult to accept on modern equipment. As it happens, the best performance under Frémaux, which has a certain flair, is *La Vie Parisienne*, which was not included on the Martinon disc.

Le Papillon (ballet-pantomime in 2 acts); complete recording.
*** Decca SXL 6588. London Symphony Orchestra, Richard Bonynge.

Le Papillon is Offenbach's only full-length ballet and it dates from 1860. The quality of the invention is high, the music sparkles from beginning to end, and in such a sympathetic performance, vividly recorded, it cannot fail to give pleasure. Highly recommended to all lovers of ballet and Offenbach.

Les Contes d'Hoffmann (The Tales of Hoffmann; opera in Prologue, 3 acts and Epilogue): complete recording.
⊛ *** Decca SET 545/7. Joan Sutherland (soprano), Placido Domingo (tenor), Huguette Tourangeau (mezzo-soprano), Gabriel Bacquier (baritone), Radio Suisse Romande and Lausanne Pro Arte Choruses, Suisse Romande Orchestra, Richard Bonynge.
Les Contes d'Hoffmann: highlights.
*** Decca SET 569 (from above recording.

Joan Sutherland gives a virtuoso performance in four heroine roles here, not only as Olympia, Giulietta and Antonia but as Stella in the Epilogue, which in this version – very close to that prepared

by Tom Hammond for the English
National Opera – is given greater weight
by the inclusion of the ensemble previously inserted into the Venice scene as a
septet, a magnificent climax. Bonynge
opts for spoken dialogue, and puts the
Antonia scene last, as being the more
substantial. His direction is unfailingly
sympathetic, while Sutherland is impressive in each role, notably as the doll
Olympia and in the pathos of the Antonia
scene. As Giulietta she hardly sounds like
a *femme fatale*, but still produces beautiful singing. Domingo gives one of his
finest performances on record, and so
does Gabriel Bacquier. Superb atmospheric recording quality.

The highlights disc gives a generous
helping of favourites.

Orpheus in the Underworld (operetta in
2 acts): abridged version (in English).
** (*) HMV CSD 1316. June Bron-
hill (soprano), Eric Shilling (bari-
tone), Kevin Miller, Jon Weav-
ing, Susanne Steele, Margaret
Nisbett, Deidree Thurlow, Alan
Crofoot, Sadler's Wells Opera
Chorus and Orchestra, Alexander
Faris.

With a single reservation only this is
an enchanting disc. Without visual help
the recording manages to convey the
high spirits and genuine gaiety of the
piece, plus – and this is an achievement
for a non-Parisian company – the sense
of French poise and precision. June
Bronhill in the *Concerto duet* is infectiously provocative about her poor suitor's
music. One's only complaint is that Alan
Crofoot's King of the Boetians is need-
lessly cruel vocally. The sound is full and
brilliant, with plenty of atmosphere, and
there is no doubt that this issue is very
successful.

Ogdon, John
(born 1937)

Piano concerto No. 1.
** (*) HMV ASD 2709. John Ogdon
(piano), Royal Philharmonic Orchestra, Lawrence Foster – SHOS-
TAKOVICH: *Piano concerto No.
2.* ***

John Ogdon's *Theme and variations*
(recorded with Ronald Stevenson's *Passacaglia* and now deleted) made a
favourable impression which is confirmed
by this *Piano concerto*. Ogdon has the
capacity to sustain a musical argument,
and although the musical material is not
always highly individual or memorable,
his craftsmanship is equal to so ambitious
a canvas. The *concerto* is often inventive
and certainly has the advantage of first-
class advocacy. Ogdon plays the Shostakovich on the reverse side with an altogether admirable sense of character, and
both the orchestral support and the
HMV recording are of the highest quality.

Orff, Carl
(born 1895)

Carmina Burana (cantiones profanae).
*** HMV SAN 162. Lucia Popp
(soprano), Gerhard Unger (tenor),
Raymond Wolansky, John Noble
(baritones), New Philharmonia
Chorus, Section of the Wands-
worth School Boys' Choir, New
Philharmonia Orchestra, Rafael
Frühbeck de Burgos.
*** DGG SLPM 139362. Gundula
Janowitz (soprano), Gerhard
Stolze (tenor), Dietrich Fischer-
Dieskau (baritone), Schöneberger
Boys' Choir, German Opera,

Berlin, Chorus and Orchestra, Eugen Jochum.

(M) ** (*) RCA LSB 4006. Evelyn Mandac (soprano), Stanley Kolk (tenor), Sherrill Milnes (baritone), New England Conservatory Chorus and Children's Chorus, Boston Symphony Orchestra, Seiji Ozawa.

(M) ** (*) Supraphon SUAST 50409. Milada Šubrtová (soprano), Jaroslav Tomanek (tenor), Teodor Šrubar (baritone), Czech Philharmonic Chorus and Orchestra, Václav Smetáček.

Burgos gives the kind of performance of *Carmina Burana* which is ideal for gramophone listening. Where Ozawa favours a straightforward approach, with plenty of impact in the climaxes, it is in the more lyrical pages that Burgos scores with his much greater imagination and obvious affection. This is not to suggest that the Philharmonia account has any lack of vitality. Indeed the sheer gusto of the singing is the more remarkable when one considers the precision from both singers and orchestra alike. The brass too bring out the rhythmic pungency, which is such a dominating feature of the work, with splendid life and point. Lucia Popp's soprano solo *Amor volat* is really ravishing, and Gerhard Unger the tenor brings a Lieder-like sensitivity to his lovely singing of the tessitura in his solo in the Tavern scene. To complete the picture the HMV stereo is wide in dynamic range; while being as vivid as anyone could want in the climaxes, it also brings out the gentler colourings that Burgos coaxes so luminously from singers and orchestra alike. An outstanding disc.

The DGG production under Jochum too is highly distinguished, and some might well acquire it for Fischer-Dieskau's contribution. His singing is refined but not too much so, and his first solo, *Omnia Sol temperat*, and later *Dies,* non et omnia are both very beautiful, with the kind of tonal shading that a great Lieder singer can bring. Perhaps *Estuans interius* needs a heavier voice, but Fischer-Dieskau is suitably gruff in the Abbot's song – so much so that for the moment the voice is unrecognizable. Gerhard Stolze too is very stylish in his falsetto *Song of the roasted swan*. The soprano, Gundula Janowitz, finds a quiet dignity for her contribution and this is finely done. But she is no match for Lucia Popp in *Amor volat*, where her upper register is less creamy. The chorus are best when the music blazes, and the closing scene is moulded by Jochum with a wonderful control, almost Klemperian in its restrained power. The snag is that in the quieter music the choral contribution is less immediate. The recording is wide in dynamic range, and the spacious acoustic (with plenty of detail coming through nonetheless) means that when the singing is quiet it is in danger of losing impact, and there is not a compensating increase of tension in the performance.

A strong, incisive performance from Seiji Ozawa. The clarity of the recording emphasizes the bold simplicity of the score, rather than dwelling on its subtlety of colour. The solo singers too are characterful rather than showing great beauty of tone, although there is no lack of understanding of the music's line. But of its kind this is an effective account, and the blaze of inspiration of Orff's masterpiece comes over with spontaneity.

The Supraphon performance is if anything even more exhilarating than Ozawa's, and Orff's primitive rhythms come over with splendid impact. This is all superbly colourful and exciting. But the soloists are uneven. Milada Šubrotvá is the most striking, but of the men Teodor Šrubar has a very wide *vibrato* which may not appeal to all ears. Even so the power and exuberance of this account are in no doubt, and the recording is both atmospheric and vivid.

Catulli Carmina (cantata).

** (*) D G G 2530 074. Arleen Auger (soprano), Wieslaw Ochman (tenor), German Opera, Berlin, Chorus, 4 pianos and percussion, Eugen Jochum.

(M) ** Supraphon SUAST 50627. Helena Tattermuschová (soprano), Ivo Zídek (tenor), Czech Philharmonic Chorus, 4 pianos, members of Prague Symphony Orchestra, Václav Smetáček.

Orff's successor to *Carmina Burana* uses four pianists and percussion instead of an orchestra, but the result is vivid enough, and those who have a soft spot for the earlier work surely will not be disappointed here. The D G G recording is admirably brilliant and clear but also rather dry, and although the performance is well projected it has not a great deal of atmosphere. This is a work that needs vocal precision (which it receives here) but also enthusiasm and high spirits, which are less evident in this rather circumspect account. But both soloists are very good, and the soprano is notably pure in intonation and vocal line, and undoubtedly this is the most polished account available, while there is no lack of vigour. But D G G's presentation without notes or translation leaves much to be desired.

Smetáček has distinguished Czech soloists, and his recording has plenty of atmosphere. But it is less immediate than the D G G and makes that much less impact in consequence. In any case Smetáček's performance is rather relaxed for a work using persistent rhythmic ostinatos that must have plenty of attack and bite to make their full effect.

De temporum fine comoedia.

(***) D G G 2530 432. Christa Ludwig (mezzo-soprano), Peter Schreier (tenor), Josef Greindl (bass), Rolf Boysen (speaker), Cologne Radio Chorus, R I A S Chamber Chorus, Tölz Boys' Choir, Cologne Radio Symphony Orchestra, Herbert von Karajan.

There must be some merit in this tiresome, meretricious stuff. Musical invention is not its strong suit; the simplicity and melodic spontaneity that one encounters in *Carmina Burana* or *Catulli Carmina* are not to be found here. Performance and recording are of the highest standards, but this is musically a very thin brew, whatever impact it may have made as theatre.

Trionfo di Afrodite (cantata).

(M) ** (*) Supraphon 112 0877. Helena Tattermuschová (soprano), Ivo Zídek (tenor), soloists, Czech Philharmonic Chorus, Prague Symphony Orchestra, Václav Smetáček.

Supraphon are good with Orff, and this is one of their best issues of his music. The recording has the usual reverberation but is also vivid. This wedding cantata uses a large orchestra, with various percussion, including pianos and harps. The music itself is characteristically rhythmic in style and has plenty of vitality. Both soloists are on top form, Tattermuschová sweet-voiced and Zídek superbly confident in tenor tessitura which often lies high up in the register, notably in the bridal duet. The chorus and orchestra have plenty of verve and impact, and if the account lacks the last degree of refinement it makes enjoyable listening.

Pachelbel, Johann
(1653–1706)

Hexachordum apollinis (6 arias with variations).
- (B) *** Oryx ORYX 1701. Marga Scheurich (harpsichord).

The *Hexachordum Apollinis* consists of six arias each with about half-a-dozen variations and provides an admirable example of the variation technique of the period. Pachelbel's *Hexachordum* was published in 1699. Marga Scheurich uses a modern Neupert and employs considerable freedom of registration, always to good effect. The playing is full of life, rhythmic vitality and clarity of articulation, and the recording is extremely fine. At its modest price this is an obvious bargain.

Organ music: *Chaconne in F minor; Chorales: Allein Gott in der Hoh' sei Ehr'* (2 versions); *Allein zu dir, Herr Jesu Christ* (2 versions); *Da Jesus an dem Kreuze stund; Jesus Christus, unser Heiland. Fantasy in G minor; 3 Magnificat fugues; Partita: Ach, was soll ich Sünder Machen; Prelude in D minor; Toccata in C minor.*
- ** (*) Telefunken SAWT 9614. Jörgen Hansen (organ of Our Lady's Church, Skänninge, Sweden).

The organ, a Marcussen, at Skänninge is a fine one and Jörgen Hansen an admirable player. Pachelbel, like many of Bach's precursors, was a composer of much interest, though hardly comparable with the greatest baroque masters. However, enthusiasts for this period and its lesser masters will find much to reward them here, and there is no serious hindrance in the way of a recommendation.

Paderewski, Ignacy
(1860–1941)

Piano concerto in A minor, Op. 17.
- (B) ** Turnabout TV 34387S. Felicja Blumenthal (piano), Vienna Symphony Orchestra, Hellmuth Froschauer – RUBINSTEIN: *Konzertstück.***

Paderewski's *Piano concerto* opens with strong thematic promise, and the secondary lyrical material is attractive too. The invention has vitality throughout, and even though some of the passage writing is relatively conventional the work is well worth having back in the gramophone repertoire. Felicja Blumenthal's performance is well made and alive, and the accompaniment has plenty of spirit too. The artists are given a somewhat hard recording, but it can be softened with the controls and made to sound enjoyable.

Paganini, Niccolò
(1782–1840)

Violin concerto No. 1 in D major, Op. 6.
- ⊛ *** HMV ASD 2782. Itzhak Perlman (violin), Royal Philharmonic Orchestra, Lawrence Foster – SARASATE: *Carmen fantasy.****

(i) *Violin concerto No. 1 in D major, Op. 6. Caprices, Op. 1, Nos. 1–24.*
- (M) *** HMV SLS 832 (2 discs). Itzhak Perlman (violin), (i) with Royal Philharmonic Orchestra, Lawrence Foster – SARASATE: *Carmen fantasy.****

This is exactly the way to play and record Paganini. Itzhak Perlman demonstrates a fabulously clean and assured technique. His execution of the fiendish upper harmonics in which Paganini delighted is almost uniquely smooth, and with the help of the EMI engineers, who have placed the microphone in exactly the right place, he produces a gleamingly rich tone, free from all scratchiness. The orchestra is splendidly recorded and balanced too, and Lawrence Foster matches the soloist's warmth with an alive and buoyant orchestral accompaniment. There has been no better record of the *D major Concerto*, and when it is played with this kind of panache the effect is most entertaining. The *Caprices* are done with equal virtuosity, and the Sarasate *Carmen fantasy* offered as a bonus is quite stunning. The alternative issue (without the *Caprices*) will for most collectors be irresistible – the finest of all available discs of Paganini's music.

Violin concerto No. 1 in E flat major (arr. Kreisler).

(B) ** Decca SPA 183. Alfredo Campoli (violin), London Symphony Orchestra, Pierino Gamba – TCHAIKOVSKY: *Violin concerto*.***

Kreisler's condensation of the *Concerto* into one-movement form is quite effective, and Campoli's performance is a good one. However, the early stereo recording has no special lustre, and this must be regarded as merely a filler for a very fine performance of the Tchaikovsky *Concerto*.

Violin concertos Nos. 1 in D major, Op. 6; 2 in B minor (La Campanella), Op. 7.

*** DGG SLPM 139424. Shmuel Ashkenasi (violin), Vienna Symphony Orchestra, Heribert Esser.

** (*) HMV ASD 440. Yehudi Menuhin (violin), Royal Philharmonic Orchestra, Alberto Erede.

(B) ** Decca Eclipse ECS 654. Ruggiero Ricci (violin), London Symphony Orchestra, Anthony Collins.

With Shmuel Ashkenasi the many technical difficulties are surmounted in an easy, confident style which gives the playing a distinctly twentieth-century ethos. The accompaniment too is nicely made, and the slightly dry recording focuses everything exactly, with the soloist spotlighted in the foreground. Some might feel a lack of nineteenth-century flamboyance, but most will sense Ashkenasi's natural sympathy. The close microphone produces a little tonal scratchiness in some of the more fiendish tessitura, but this appears to be almost unavoidable with brilliant modern recording techniques. Certainly the breathtaking aplomb displayed by the soloist in the *La Campanella* finale of No. 2 shows how completely he is in control, and this is one of the highlights of a remarkable coupling.

Menuhin's performances have plenty of attack, although the accompaniments have rather less life and fire. But characterful though these readings are – and Menuhin can be very rewarding in the lyrical music – one feels that fiery bravura is not really Menuhin's *métier*. It is Ricci's speciality, however, and his performances have characteristic flair and assurance, notably in the *fioratura* of the finales. The recording, however, is very dated, and while the soloist is quite effectively projected, the orchestra is dim.

Violin concertos Nos. 1 in D major, Op. 6; 4 in D minor.

*** Philips 6500 411. Arthur Grumiaux (violin), Monte Carlo National Opera Orchestra, Piero Bellugi.

If you want this particular coupling, rest assured that Grumiaux's performances, while deeply musical, have no want of bravura; indeed in the first movement of No. 1 the brilliance is very impressive indeed. It is perhaps in the slow movements that Grumiaux comes especially into his own, with playing of real tenderness, and in the finales there is delicacy to enhance the sparkle. The recording is excellent. But Perlman remains uniquely compelling in No. 1, and Ricci's extrovert bravura is very exhilarating in No. 4.

Violin concerto No. 3 in E major.
** (*) Philips 6500 175. Henryk Szeryng (violin), London Symphony Orchestra, Alexander Gibson.

Paganini kept for himself the prerogative of performing his own violin concertos, and took strict security precautions to ensure that the orchestral parts could not fall into other hands. His two best-known works were not published until after his death, and the secrets of his *Fourth Concerto* were successfully kept until 1954 when the lost score came to light and the work was recorded by Grumiaux. Now the Paganini family have made available the orchestral parts of the *Third Concerto*, and with a good deal of publicity Henryk Szeryng has given its first posthumous performances and made the present record. The performance is dazzling technically. The first movement, however, is not of great musical interest and even Szeryng's expertise cannot bring it fully to life. The best movement is undoubtedly the *Adagio*, a brief aria-like movement, eloquent in shape and marked by the composer *Cantabile spianato*. The work would have fitted comfortably on to a single LP side, so is rather expensive in its present form, in spite of the elegant brochure-sleeve.

Violin concerto No. 4 in D minor; Le Streghe (Witches' dance), Op. 8.
*** Unicorn RHS 304. Ruggiero

Ricci (violin), Royal Philharmonic Orchestra, Piero Bellugi – BOTTESINI: *Grand duo.****

Paganini's *Fourth Concerto*, not nearly so well known as the first two, has some attractive music in it, once the boring tutti at the beginning is over. The simple melodies over ticking pizzicato accompaniments are most attractive; the slow movement (F sharp minor contrasting interestingly with D minor) is not too heavily tragic, and the finale brings a bolero complete with tambourine. The *Witches' dance* is not so diabolical as the composer may have intended, a piece full of jolly fireworks and one ludicrous passage involving left-hand pizzicato. Superb playing from Ricci and good recording.

Violin concerto No. 6 in E minor, Op. posth.
** (*) DGG 2530 467. Salvatore Accardo (violin), London Philharmonic Orchestra, Charles Dutoit.

This further newly discovered concerto (one wonders how many more will be unearthed) is entirely characteristic, tuneful and bristling with bravura. If not quite on the level of Perlman's account of No. 1, Salvatore Accardo gives a fine performance with warmly romantic phrasing in the slow movement and much brilliance in the finale. However, this seems short measure for two sides of an LP.

Violin and guitar: *Cantabile; Cantone di sonate Nos. 1 in A major; 3 in C major; 4 in A major; 6 in A major; Sonatas in A major, Op. 2/6; in A minor, Op. 3/4; Sonata concertata in A major.*
** Telefunken SAT 22548. György Terebesi (violin), Sonja Prunnbauer (guitar).

This record contains works that only came to light in 1910, when Paganini's effects were auctioned. There are a number of works for violin and guitar, all highly accomplished but light and undemanding. Most of them are very short; the most substantial item here is the *Sonata concertata*, which takes about twelve minutes. Good performances and recording make this an attractive though not important disc.

Caprices, Op. 1, Nos. 1–24 (for solo violin).
  (M) ** Vanguard VCS 10093/4. Paul Zukofsky (violin).

Paul Zukovsky's set is brilliantly played but it does not yield to the fine set by Perlman (see above under *Violin concerto No. 1*) or indeed Ricci's recording, which was complete on a single Decca disc (this is currently out of the catalogue but will no doubt return in due course on Eclipse).

Guitar quartet No. 7 in E major (for guitar, violin, viola and violoncello); *Terzetto concertante in D major* (for guitar, viola and violoncello).
  (B) ** Turnabout TV 34322S. Luise Walker (guitar), Paul Roczek (violin), Jürgen Geise (viola), Wilfred Tachezi (cello).

This is attractive music, slight but inventive, and the *Quartet*, with its fetching pizzicato second movement, has something of the quality of a Mozart divertimento. The playing here is intimate and quite stylish; the violinist, who has a demanding role, fulfils it capably. The recording too is good.

Terzetto in D major for violin, violoncello and guitar.
  *** CBS SBRG 72678. John Williams (guitar), Alan Loveday (violin), Amaryllis Fleming (cello) – HAYDN: *Guitar quartet*.***

This *Terzetto* is a small-scale but very charming work and it is beautifully played on this CBS disc. An ideal record for late-evening listening.

Paisiello, Giovanni
(1741–1816)

Piano concerto in C major.
  (B) ** Turnabout TV 34001S. Felicja Blumenthal (piano), Württemberg Chamber Orchestra, Joerg Faerber – STAMITZ: *Piano concerto*.**

This is a pleasant, sunny little concerto, with no great individuality but persuasively played and well accompanied. The recording too is good.

Palestrina, Giovanni da
(*c*. 1525–1594)

Antiphon – Assumpta est Maria; Missa – Assumpta est Maria; Missa brevis.
  *** Argo ZRG 690. Thomas Hunt (treble), John Tudhope (tenor), St John's College, Cambridge, Choir, George Guest.

The *Assumpta est Maria* Mass is one of Palestrina's most sublime works, and its return to the catalogue, coupled with the four-part *Missa brevis*, is more than welcome, particularly when the performances are as persuasive as here. Some may find them a little lacking in Latin fervour: the trebles sound distinctly Anglican, but this reservation apart, this is fine singing by any standards and is splendidly recorded. It was a good idea to include the Antiphon on which this Mass is based.

Ave Regina (antiphon); *Magnificat primi toni (Anima mea); Surge illuminare* (motet); *Veni sancte spiritus.*

(M) *** Oiseau-Lyre SOL 283. Carmelite Priory Choir, London, John McCarthy – VICTORIA: *Ave Maria etc.****

John McCarthy's collection of music by Palestrina and Victoria provides one of the outstanding records in the catalogue of liturgical Renaissance music. The recording has splendid atmosphere and the performances are restrained, yet have an underlying depth of feeling. We have the opportunity of comparing a setting of the *Magnificat primi toni* by each composer (the only small snag being an organ continuo which is occasionally marginally out of pitch with the singers). The whole programme has been chosen with care to make a balanced whole, and at medium price this is a splendid investment.

Exsultate Deo; Hymnus in adventu Dei; Jesu Rex admirabilis (hymn); *Magnificat VI toni; Tua Jesu dilectio; Veni sponsa Christi* (antiphon; mass and motet).

*** Argo ZRG 578. St John's College, Cambridge, Choir, George Guest, with Michael Turner (treble).

Dignified performances, well recorded, of some fine Palestrina works. Although these performances are firmly in the Anglican tradition and lack some of the fervour one would find on the Continent, they have great purity of tone and beauty of phrasing.

Missa – Aeterna Christi munera (with ANON.: *Music for the Common of the Apostles*).

** Argo ZRG 5186. Renaissance Singers, Michael Howard.

This is an early Argo stereo record made in the Church of St Philip Neri, in Arundel, Sussex, and the recording is very successful. The performance of the Mass is a good one if not absolutely pure in style. The record includes also the plainsong hymn on which the Mass is based, together with other extracts from the *Common of the Apostles.*

Missa Papae Marcelli; Missa brevis.

(M) ** H M V HQS 1237. King's College, Cambridge, Choir, David Willcocks.

These are smooth, limpid performances, well recorded. The singing style is straightforward, and although the control of dynamic is impressive, the inner mystery of the music is not readily conveyed. It is surprising that, at the time of writing, the catalogue does not contain another satisfactory performance of Palestrina's most famous mass, so this issue is welcome enough.

Masses: *Sine nomine; Ecce ego Joannes.*

(M) *** Oiseau-Lyre SOL 269. Mary Thomas (soprano), Jean Allister (contralto), Edgar Fleet (tenor), Christopher Keyte (bass), Carmelite Priory Choir, London, John McCarthy.

The two works offered here make a good foil for each other, for they are contrasted in style and texture. The Mass 'without name' is a small-scale work, whereas *Ecce ego Joannes* is more ambitious and dramatic. Both are beautifully sung and very well recorded. With the availability of this record at medium price one hopes that more music-lovers will be tempted to sample this wonderfully expressive and rewarding music.

The Song of Songs (cycle of motets): complete recording.

(M) ** (*) Oiseau-Lyre SOL 338/9.

701

Cantores in Ecclesia, Michael Howard.

The Song of Songs: 21 motets.

(M) * (*) Vanguard HM 9SD. Prague Madrigal Choir, Miroslav Venhoda.

Palestrina's twenty-nine motets setting words from the *Song of Songs* were published in 1584 and are regarded as among his supreme achievements. (During his lifetime no fewer than nine editions were published in about as many years.) The performances by the Cantores in Ecclesia derive from a series of broadcasts which Michael Howard introduced, and although not everyone will agree with the interpretation placed on the texts by the conductor, few will fail to respond to these highly expressive and beautifully phrased performances with marvellous intonation. The recordings do not always produce smoothly at climaxes, but generally speaking they are of the highest quality and readers should not hesitate in investing in this rewarding (and very reasonably priced) album.

Venhoda does not present all twenty-nine motets from Palestrina's Fourth Book, and the singing of the Prague Madrigal Choir, good though it is, is perhaps a little too austere and wanting in expressive range. The recording is eminently acceptable, but in spite of its modest cost, Michael Howard's collection is really worth the extra outlay involved and will give more lasting satisfaction.

Stabat Mater; Hodie Beata Virgo; Senex puerum portabat; Magnificat in eight parts; Litaniae de Beata Virgine Maria in eight parts.

*** Argo ZRG 5398. King's College, Cambridge, Choir, David Willcocks.

This is an exceptionally fine collection. The flowing melodic lines and serene beauty which are the unique features of

Palestrina's music are apparent throughout this programme, and there is no question about the dedication and accomplishment of the performance. Argo's recording is no less successful and this record may be highly recommended.

Panufnik, Andrzej
(born 1914)

(i) *Autumn music. Heroic overture.* (i) *Nocturne. Tragic overture.*

*** Unicorn RHS 306. London Symphony Orchestra, Jascha Horenstein, (i) with Anthony Peebles (piano).

A collection of four works by the Polish composer Panufnik who fled from Warsaw in the early 1950s and settled in this country. The two overtures are early pieces and of relatively little musical interest, but the other works are worth hearing though they may strike some listeners as musically uneventful. Indeed they are static mood pieces that perhaps too readily fall back on repetition and ostinati, but the opening of the *Nocturne* is really very beautiful indeed and there is a refined feeling for texture and a sensitive imagination at work here. The LSO under Horenstein play with conviction and they are beautifully recorded; in fact this is one of the finest recordings as such that Unicorn have so far put on the market. If Panufnik employed a wider range of musical devices and had a more robust inventive resource, he would be a very considerable composer indeed.

Sinfonia rustica (Symphony No. 1); Sinfonia sacra (Symphony No. 3).

** (*) Unicorn RHS 315. Monte Carlo Opera Orchestra, the composer.

The *Sinfonia rustica* was the work which first attracted attention to Panufnik shortly after the war. It is the more individual of the two works recorded here and has plenty of character, though its invention is less symphonic than in the style of a sinfonietta. The performances of both works under the composer's baton are alert and spirited, though the Monte Carlo orchestra is not in the first flight. The recording, made by EMI, is excellent: the stereo is very much in the demonstration class.

Universal prayer.
*** Unicorn RHS 305. April Cantelo (soprano), Helen Watts (contralto), John Mitchinson (tenor), Roger Stalman (bass), David Watkins, Maria Korchinska, Tina Bonifacio (harps), Nicolas Kynaston (organ), Louis Halsey Singers, Leopold Stokowski.

Panufnik's music has been scandalously neglected even in Britain, his adopted country. Stokowski's urgent advocacy has now allowed us to hear on record this ambitious and ingenious setting of words by Alexander Pope, 'a prayer to the God of all religions'. Panufnik takes the thirteen stanzas of the poem and frames them in twenty-seven sections laid out with the symmetry of an Italian garden. There is an elaborate diagram on the sleeve explaining the elaborate contrasts and relationships, but once the basic approach has been grasped it is not all that difficult. Soloists (alone or in various combinations), chorus (singing the note B in more ranges of tone and expression than one would have thought possible) and instrumentalists are introduced in varying patterns. The cumulative experience is certainly impressive, even though the sectionalizing tends to hold up the flow. With superb recording and the sort of intensity one always expects in a Stokowski performance (he later

recorded it for television too) this is well worth hearing.

Parish-Alvars, Elias
(1809–1849)

Harp concerto in G minor, Op. 81.
** HMV ASD 3034. Nicanor Zabaleta (harp), Spanish National Orchestra, Rafael Frühbeck de Burgos – RODRIGO: *Concierto de Aranjuez.***

Elias Parish-Alvars was an English harpist and composer who travelled extensively in Europe and eventually settled in Vienna. He was considered a remarkable virtuoso on the harp of his day by no less an authority than Berlioz. His concerto, however, is very slight, with invention of some charm, but very little substance. It is played here with affection and suitable delicacy.

Parry, Hubert
(1848–1918)

An English suite; Lady Radnor's suite; Overture to an unwritten tragedy; Symphonic variations.
*** Lyrita SRCS 48. London Symphony Orchestra, Sir Adrian Boult.

Sir Hubert Parry has for too long been known as the composer of *Jerusalem* and nothing else. His achievement, like that of Stanford and MacKenzie, was easily outshone by that of Elgar immediately after him. One day no doubt some of his choral music will be recorded – it is far finer than is suggested by Shaw's famous remark that 'Parry is sickening for another oratorio'. The orchestral works here are not among his most ambitious, but they

703

are intensely attractive, and should delight any Elgarian wanting to venture into the late Victorian hinterland. The two *Suites* have some charming genre music and the *Overture* is very strongly constructed. But best of all is the set of variations, with its echoes of Brahms's *St Anthony* set and its foretastes of *Enigma*. Shorter than either, it does not waste a note: a big work in a small compass. Boult's advocacy is irresistible, and the recording is excellent.

Blest Pair of Sirens.
> ** H M V ASD 2311. London Philharmonic Choir and Orchestra, Sir Adrian Boult – ELGAR: *The Music Makers.*** (*)

As a fill-up to Elgar's rarely heard cantata it is good to welcome so enjoyably professional a motet as Parry's *Blest Pair of Sirens.* Much of the once-popular music by Parry and his contemporaries is unacceptably inflated, but certainly not this. The performance by the London Philharmonic Choir should be more incisive, but it still conveys much of the right atmosphere.

Penderecki, Krzysztof
(born 1933)

(i) *Capriccio for violin and orchestra.* (ii) *Cello concerto. De Natura sonoris No. 2; Emanations; Fonogrammi; Kanon.* (iii) *Partita for harpsichord and orchestra.*
> (M) *** H M V SLS 850 (2 discs). Polish Radio Symphony Orchestra, the composer, with (i) Wanda Wilkomirska (violin); (ii) Siegfried Palm (cello); (iii) Felicja Blumenthal (harpsichord).

For those who admire this athematic

music, this anthology of Penderecki's works in authoritative performances under the composer's own direction will have much to commend it. Wilkomirska is a superb player and so is Palm in the *Cello concerto.* Penderecki's music relies for its appeal on its resourceful use of sonorities and his sound world is undoubtedly imaginative, albeit limited. Superb recording will enhance the value of this disc for those who want a representative collection of Penderecki's music.

De Natura sonoris (for orchestra); *Polymorphia for 48 string instruments;* (i) *Dies Irae* (oratorio).
> *** Philips SAL 3680. Cracow Philharmonia Orchestra, Henryk Czyz, (i) with Stefania Woytowicz (soprano), Wieslaw Ochman (tenor), Bernard Ladysz (bass) and Chorus.

Penderecki's setting of the *Dies Irae* was written in 1967 to commemorate those killed in Auschwitz, and its spectacular sonic effects will not disappoint those who were moved by the *St Luke Passion.* In the opening *Lamentatio* the cloud-like dissonances, overlapping and merging, establish the composer's individual style, and the second section, *Apocalypsis*, ends most strikingly with the wailing of a siren, echo of the siren in the concentration camp. Whether or not the musical material proves to be of lasting vitality, this is a sincere and original attempt to set words of universal appeal, not just Biblical but from Aeschylus and a whole range of modern writers. *Polymorphia for 48 strings* is interesting in its use of conventional instruments to imitate electronic sounds (why bother, one might ask?), and *De Natura sonoris* is another work showing Penderecki's preoccupation with sonic effects, one striking passage bringing a surrealistic jazz-inspired intrusion. Excellent performances and fine recording engineered by Polskie Nagrania.

Symphony; Anaklasis for strings and percussion.

> *** EMI Quadraphonic Q4-EMD 5507; Stereo EMD 5507. London Symphony Orchestra, the composer.

The *Symphony*, Penderecki's most ambitious orchestral work so far, was commissioned by a British engineering firm and first heard in Peterborough Cathedral. That setting has influenced the range of sumptuous orchestral colours devised by the composer. You may regard this as merely a sequence of brilliant effects rather than a logically argued symphony, but in this committed performance, helped by wide-ranging stereo, it is certainly striking and memorable. There is no question but that the quadraphonic version, which is superbly atmospheric, increases the listener's awareness of the tension in the performances still further.

Utrenja (oratorio).

> *** Philips 6700 065 (2 discs). Delfina Ambroziak, Stefania Woytowicz (sopranos), Krystyna Szczepánska (mezzo-soprano), Kazimierz Pustelak (tenor), Wlodzimierz Denysenko, Bernard Ladysz (basses), Boris Carmeli, Peter Lagger (bassi profondi), Pioneer Choir, Warsaw National Philharmonic Chorus and Orchestra, Andrzej Markowski.

Utrenja, inspired by Eastern church music, is a massive piece in two ritually balanced halves, entitled *The Entombment of Christ* and *The Resurrection*. This first complete recording of both halves brilliantly conveys the splendour of Penderecki's concept with its highly original use of voices. Like the Ormandy version of the first half it makes a striking and immediate impact, though the effect-making hardly stands frequent repetition.

The sound here is spacious and atmospheric. Ormandy's account of the first half of the work is available on RCA SB 6857; although the performance is vivid it seems perverse to list an incomplete version when a more idiomatic account of the full score is available.

Pergolesi, Giovanni (1710–36)

Concerti armonici for strings Nos. 1 in G major; 2 in G major; 3 in A major; 4 in F minor.

> (M) ** (*) Decca Ace of Diamonds SDD 318. Stuttgart Chamber Orchestra, Karl Münchinger.

Concerti armonici Nos. 5 in E flat major; 6 in B flat major; (i) Flute concertos Nos. 1 in G major; 2 in D major.

> (M) *** Decca Ace of Diamonds SDD 319. Stuttgart Chamber Orchestra, Karl Münchinger, (i) with Jean-Pierre Rampal (flute).

Scholars tell us that this set of concertos is not by Pergolesi, but they are works of definite character, if perhaps without the individuality of the best concerti grossi of the period. The writing, although elegant and gracious, is somewhat static, although this impression is increased by Münchinger's rather literal approach. But perhaps the conductor is right: his degree of expressiveness keeps the phrasing supple, and there is no hint of sentimentality. The string-playing itself is very fine and the beautiful quality of the recordings adds much to the listener's pleasure. Of the two discs the second is the more attractive, for the *Flute concertos* offer invention of a high order and they are played delightfully by Jean-Pierre Rampal. Again the recording is very fine.

Oboe concerto (arr. Barbirolli).

> (B) *** Pye GSGC 14065. Evelyn Rothwell, Hallé Orchestra, Sir John Barbirolli – HAYDN and CORELLI: *Concertos.****

Miss Rothwell's neat, feminine style suits this work to perfection. This is a Barbirolli arrangement using tunes from sonatas, a song and the *Stabat Mater*; but the whole is so felicitously put together that no one could guess it was not conceived in this form. The predominant mood is pastoral, with a slow opening leading to a gracious *Allegro* with an *Andantino* intervening before the gentle finale. The performance characterizes the music perfectly.

Violin concerto in B flat major; Salve regina.

> (B) ** Pye GSGC 14041. Carlos Villa (violin), Austin Miskell (tenor), Anglian Ensemble, John Snashall – VIVALDI: *Concertos.***

Austin Miskell is a tenor of no mean sensibility, and he manages the extremely florid writing in Pergolesi's solo cantata with skill. Carlos Villa's solo playing is perhaps less polished, but he is a capable player and this little *Violin concerto* is a pleasing work. An enterprising if not an outstanding disc, worth exploring by reason of its modest price.

Magnificat.

> ** (*) Argo ZRG 505. Elizabeth Vaughan (soprano), Janet Baker (contralto), Ian Partridge (tenor), Christopher Keyte (bass), King's College, Cambridge, Choir, Academy of St Martin-in-the-Fields, David Willcocks – VIVALDI: *Gloria.*** (*)

This Pergolesi *Magnificat* – doubtfully attributed like so much that goes under

this composer's name – is a comparatively pale piece to go with the great Vivaldi *Gloria*. But King's Choir gives a beautiful performance, and the recording matches it in intensity of atmosphere.

Stabat Mater (revision and organ part by M. Zanon).

> (M) ** Decca Ace of Diamonds SDD 385. Judith Raskin (soprano), Maureen Lehane (contralto), Rossini Orchestra of Naples, Franco Caracciolo; M. Zanon (organ).

Pergolesi's *Stabat Mater* is modest in its demands, requiring originally two castrati plus strings and continuo. In this performance the voices of the two soloists blend nicely, yet have enough difference in timbre (without the contralto sounding plummy) for the listener to separate them. The delightful opening tonal suspensions make this immediately apparent. The orchestral accompaniment is spirited, and a warm acoustic adds richness to a fairly small body of strings. There is a discreet organ continuo. The overall effect is fresh and enjoyable.

La Serva padrona (opera in 2 scenes): complete recording.

> ** (*) Pye Ensayo NEL 2014. Carmen Bustamante (soprano), Renato Capecchi (baritone), English Chamber Orchestra, Antonio Ros-Marbá.

> (B) * (*) Saga 5360. Virginia Zeani (soprano), Nicola Rossi-Lemeni (bass), members of Hamburg Radio Symphony Orchestra, George Singer.

The Spanish conductor directs the ECO in a lively, attractive account of this charming one-act comedy, with light bright singing from Carmen Bustamente as the servant and characterful *buffo* blustering from Capecchi, vocally past his prime but dramatically very effective. The result is marred by square unimaginative continuo playing in the extended *secco* recitatives. Good, bright recording.

The Saga performance, originally issued on Vox, is essentially a concert version, stylish, lively and pleasing, with an especially good finale. The characterization is less vivid than on the Pye Ensayo disc; Zeani is somewhat stiff and not coquettish enough, but this is quite enjoyable and very reasonably priced.

Peri, Jacopo
(1561–1633)

Euridice (opera in Prologue and 1 act): complete recording.
> ** Telefunken SAWT 9603/4. Nerina Santini (soprano), Adele Bonay (contralto), Rodolfo Farfolfi (tenor), Gastone Sarti (baritone), Coro Polifonico di Milano, Solisti di Milano, Angelo Ephrikian.

Peri's *Euridice* antedates Monteverdi's *Orfeo* by seven years or so, and as this set shows, it is more than a historical curiosity. The score gives only the voice parts and the bass-line, of course, but the edition recorded here is sensible; there is no excess of elaboration or interference with the effectiveness and simplicity of the vocal line. The singers are not outstanding vocally, but they do appear to be inside the music, and most readers will be impressed by the quality of this performance, which never draws attention away from the opera. The recording is eminently satisfactory without being spectacularly good.

Perotinus Magnus
(12th century)

Sederunt principes (Graduale for the Feast of St Stephen); Viderunt omnes (Graduale for the Feast of the Circumcision).
> (M) * (*) Vanguard HM 1SD. Deller Consort with Medieval Chamber Ensemble, Alfred Deller – MACHAUT: *Notre Dame Mass.** (*)

These are both impressive works. The approach is highly conjectural, but the performances have plenty of impulse and the recording is atmospheric. But the appeal of the disc will undoubtedly hinge on interest in the Machaut *Mass* on the reverse side, which is not a first recommendation.

Pettersson, Allan
(born 1911)

Symphony No. 7.
> *** Decca SXL 6538. Stockholm Philharmonic Orchestra, Antal Dorati.

Allan Pettersson is a Swedish composer who was a pupil of Honegger and Leibowitz and has followed an independent path in modern Swedish music. His musical language is diatonic and direct in utterance, though some of his gestures are strongly Mahlerian in character and not wholly free from self-pity. It is the kind of music that excites strong allegiance in some people and impatience in others. Perhaps, given its dimensions, the quality of the material is not varied enough to sustain the one-movement structure. Dorati, who is the dedicatee, conducts a committed performance and is excellently recorded.

Pfitzner, Hans
(1869–1949)

Palestrina (opera in 3 acts): complete recording.

> *** DGG 2711 013 (4 discs). Nicolai Gedda (tenor), Helen Donath (soprano), Brigitte Fassbaender (contralto), Dietrich Fischer-Dieskau (baritone), Karl Ridderbusch (bass), John van Kesteren, Herbert Steinbach (tenors), Hermann Prey (baritone), Tölz Boys' Choir, Bavarian Radio Chorus and Symphony Orchestra, Rafael Kubelik.

Many in Germany have for years been telling us of the mastery of this unique opera, and this rich and glowing performance goes a long way to explain why. Though Pfitzner's melodic invention hardly matches that of his contemporary Richard Strauss, his control of structure and his drawing of character through music (using his own patiently written libretto) make an unforgettable impact in all their expansiveness. The central act is a massive and colourful tableau representing the Council of Trent and the discussion of the role of music in the church; the outer acts – more personal and more compelling – show the dilemma of the composer Palestrina at this crisis, and the inspiration which led him to write *Missa Papae Marcelli*, which resolved the crisis. At every point Pfitzner's response is illuminating, and this glorious performance, superbly sung, played and recorded, should at last ensure that the whole world appreciates a rare and individual creation.

Platti, Giovanni
(1690–1763)

Piano concerto No. 1 in G major

> (B) ** Turnabout TV 34284S. Felicja Blumenthal (piano), Salzburg Symphony Orchestra, Theodor Guschlbauer – VIOTTI: *Piano concerto.***

Giovanni Platti was born in Venice but spent his musical life as part of the establishment of the court at Würzburg. This is a pleasant little concerto, but its style is more that of a string concerto grosso with a harpsichord concertante part. The piano sounds out of place in the same way as it does when used for Bach's keyboard concertos. Having said that, it can be added that this is an enjoyable makeweight for the fairly large-scale Viotti concerto which takes up most of the disc. It is well played and recorded.

Pleyel, Ignaz
(1757–1831)

Sinfonia concertante in E flat major for violin, viola and orchestra, Op. 29.

> ** (*) CBS 76310. Isaac Stern (violin), Pinchas Zukerman (viola), English Chamber Orchestra, Daniel Barenboim – MOZART: *Concertone.*** (*)

This work, recently unearthed in Paris by the oboist James Brown, is in two extended movements – an ambitious *Maestoso* followed by a gently playful rondo. Though it goes on rather too long for its material, it provides splendid opportunities for Stern and Zukerman to display their artistry. Dry recording quality.

Ponce, Manuel
(1882–1948)

Concierto del Sur (for guitar and orchestra).
> *** CBS Quadraphonic MQ 31963; Stereo 73060. John Williams (guitar), London Symphony Orchestra, André Previn – PREVIN: *Guitar concerto*.***

So close are the echoes of Falla at the start of this concerto that it might be called 'Nights in the gardens of Mexico'. Like most guitar concertos it is not a specially memorable work, but it prompts John Williams, Previn and the orchestra to deft and delightful performances. Good atmospheric recording: the quadraphonic version adds extra warmth and naturalness to the sound (although the larger-than-life guitar image remains).

Ponchielli, Amilcare
(1834–86)

La Gioconda (opera in 4 acts): complete recording.
> *** Decca SET 364/6. Renata Tebaldi (soprano), Marilyn Horne (mezzo-soprano), Carlo Bergonzi (tenor), Robert Merrill (baritone), Chorus and Orchestra of St Cecilia Academy, Rome, Lamberto Gardelli.
> (M) ** Decca Ace of Diamonds GOS 609/11. Anita Cerquetti (soprano), Giuletta Simionato (mezzo-soprano), Mario del Monaco (tenor), Ettore Bastianini (baritone), Franca Sacchi (contralto), Cesare Siepi (bass), Maggio Musicale Fiorentino Chorus and Orchestra, Gianandrea Gavazzeni.

Tebaldi's complete *Gioconda*, made when many were mourning the end of her recording career, is one of her most impressive performances ever put on record. She had never taken the role on the stage, and asked for advice beforehand on what other singers to study. Tactfully her adviser suggested the Milanov version, but when later he visited her, he found her absorbed studying with rapt attention the Callas version (now deleted). 'Why didn't you tell me Maria's was the best?' she asked. It is doubtful now whether Maria's does remain the best, for Tebaldi conveys an astonishing depth of dramatic feeling and though the actual voice quality is not so even as it used to be, the actual musical interest of the performance is far more intense than one would have expected from earlier Tebaldi performances. Though Callas does of course remain unique, no one who has ever been won over by Tebaldi should miss hearing this set, which if anything has a better supporting cast – Bergonzi, Horne and Merrill all very good, if a little too comfortable-sounding – and has superlative recording quality.

Reissued on Ace of Diamonds the early Decca set has much to commend it. The cast is generally distinguished, Cerquetti very powerful in the name part, and although Gavazzeni is not always the most dramatic of conductors, the performance has many fine moments and is satisfying as a whole. The recording, though clean enough, is not one of Decca's very best and is no match for the newer Tebaldi set.

La Gioconda: highlights.
> *** Decca SET 450 (from above recording cond. Gardelli).

It is difficult to make selections from so wide-ranging an opera as this, with no

709

fewer than six star parts in it, but once again the Decca selection is apt and generous, with Tebaldi's fine assumption of the title role well represented. Excellent recording.

Poulenc, Francis
(1889–1963)

Les Biches (ballet): suite.
>** (*) HMV Quadraphonic Q4-ASD 2989: Stereo ASD 2989. City of Birmingham Orchestra, Louis Frémaux – IBERT: *Divertissement*; HONEGGER: *Pacific 231*; SATIE: *Gymnopédies Nos. 1 and 3.*** (*)

The reverberation of the Great Hall of Birmingham University, where this record was made, does not have such an adverse effect on Poulenc's *Les Biches* as it does on the Ibert and Honegger scores. The performance is a jolly one, even if the tempo for the opening trumpet tune seems too fast. It does not have quite the distinction of Desormière's early Decca mono account (now on ACL 189) and if that was successfully transferred to Eclipse it could remain highly competitive.

Concerto champêtre for harpsichord and orchestra.
>(M) * (*) Supraphon SUAST 50926. Zuzana Růžičková (harpsichord), Czech Philharmonic Orchestra, Kurt Sanderling – MARTINŮ: *Harpsichord concerto.***

Although not as fine as the HMV performance (see below), this Supraphon account is a lively one and it is a pity that the heavily reverberant recording damps down some of the wit and charming point of Poulenc's elegant score.

(i) *Concerto in G minor for organ, strings and timpani;* (ii) *Gloria in G major.*
>*** HMV ASD 2835. ORTF Orchestra, Georges Prêtre, with (i) Maurice Duruflé (organ) (ii) Rosanna Carteri (soprano), and Chorus.

The *Gloria*, one of Poulenc's last works, has an arresting theatrical quality as well as many touching moments. Poulenc could move from Stravinskian high spirits to a much deeper vein of feeling with astonishing sureness of touch. Carteri is a rather glacial soloist but the performance in every other respect is exemplary and – since it was recorded in the presence of the composer – presumably authoritative. The *Organ concerto* is a splendid piece and receives a spirited performance from Duruflé and the ORTF Orchestra. The recording has admirable presence and definition. Strongly recommended.

(i) *Double concerto in D minor for two pianos and orchestra;* (ii) *Concerto champêtre for harpsichord and orchestra.*
>** (*) HMV ASD 517. Francis Poulenc, Jacques Février (pianos); (ii) Aimée van de Wiele (harpsichord); both with Paris Conservatoire Orchestra, Georges Prêtre.

Poulenc himself was a pianist of limited accomplishment, but his interpretation (with partner) of his own skittish concerto is infectiously jolly. One could never mistake the tone of voice intended. In the imitation pastoral concerto on the reverse Prêtre's inflexibility as a conductor comes out more, but the finale at least has the right high spirits.

Trio for oboe, bassoon and piano; Sonata for clarinet and bassoon.

*** HMV ASD 2506. Melos Ensemble – RAVEL: *Introduction and allegro;* FRANÇAIX: *Divertissement.****

Both these Poulenc pieces are delightful, particularly the delicious *Trio for oboe, bassoon and piano*, which has an admirably dry wit and unfailing inventiveness. The record is worth having for this alone, and the playing is above reproach. Excellent recording.

Sonata for 2 pianos.
* (*) Decca SXL 6357. Bracha Eden, Alexander Tamir (pianos) – BARTÓK: *Sonata for 2 pianos and percussion.**

This relatively late work (1953) should not be confused with the more popular two-piano sonata of 1918, which Eden and Tamir have also recorded (within a recital disc). Here again they bring their formidable technique to bear on tricky music, but the result rather lacks the lighter, more sparkling qualities that one wants in Poulenc. Good recording.

Christmas motets (O magnum mysterium; Quam vidistis pastores dicite; Videntes stellam; Hodie Christus natus est); Easter motets (Timor et tremor; Vinea mea electa; Tenebrae factae sunt; Tristis est anima).
*** Argo ZRG 720. Christ Church Cathedral Choir, Oxford, London Sinfonietta, Simon Preston – STRAVINSKY: *Mass.****

These motets are of great beauty and simplicity. Simon Preston's account of them with the Christ Church Cathedral Choir could hardly be improved on, and the Argo engineers produce mellifluous and rich quality.

Pousseur, Henri
(born 1929)

Madrigal III.
(M) ** Everest SDBR 3170. Domaine Ensemble, Pierre Boulez – SCHOENBERG: *Verklaerte Nacht;* ELOY: *Equivalences.***

This Pousseur work follows the exotic percussion-based piece of a fellow pupil of Boulez, Jean-Claude Eloy. The contrast is marked. Pousseur is far more spare in his textures, more precise in his thought, and though this does not make for easy listening, the result compels attention, invites rehearing.

Praetorius, Michael
(1571–1621)

Dances from Terpsichore (Suite de ballets; Suite de voltes). (i) Motets: *Eulogodia Sionia: Resonet in laudibus; Musicae Sioniae: Allein Gott in der Höh sei Ehr; Aus tiefer Not schrei ich zu dir; Christus der uns selig macht; Gott der Vater wohn uns bei; Polyhymnia Caduceatrix: Erhalt uns, Herr, bei deinem Wort.*
*** HMV CSD 3761. Early Music Consort of London, David Munrow, (i) with Boys of the Cathedral and Abbey Church of St Alban.

The early stereo catalogue contained a famous selection from Praetorius's arranged *Terpsichore dances* (appropriately played by a group called the Collegium Terpsichore), and these performances were famous not only for their scholarly preparation but for the marvellous freshness and spontaneity of their execution. *Terpsichore* is a collection of

711

folk music, compiled from some 300 dances used by the French court dance bands of Henry IV. Any suite is arbitrary in choice of items and conjectural in the matter of their presentation and orchestration (although Praetorius left plenty of information and advice and would not have expected any set instrumentation for any given piece). The instrumentation here is certainly imaginatively done (the third item, a *Bourrée* played by four racketts – a cross between a shawm and comb and paper in sound – is fascinating), but the playing itself sometimes seems too refined in manner. The Archive selection was rather more robust and certainly more exhilarating. But one must not exaggerate this. This collection is still a delightful one and the motets on side two remind one very much of Giovanni Gabrieli. The record is splendidly documented (with an eight-page insert leaflet, record-sleeve size) and most atmospherically recorded. The internal balance suggests that a quadraphonic version may be even more effective if it appears later.

Previn, André
(born 1929)

Guitar concerto.
*** CBS Quadraphonic MQ 31963; Stereo 73060. John Williams (guitar), London Symphony Orchestra, the composer – PONCE: *Concierto del Sur.****

André Previn as a composer is nothing if not inventive, and though this is not great music, it uses a sequence of colourful ideas and instrumental effects easily and seductively. The opening is hauntingly effective, and so is the reprise of the main theme in the central *Adagio*, though that movement is a shade too long. The finale introduces electronic interruptions from a jazz group, but peace, order and good orchestral values win in the end. A fine confident performance from the composer with the soloist for whom the work was written. The stereo recording is good, but the quadraphonic version adds an extra dimension. Not only has it greater naturalness and warmth; it adds considerable point to the 'battle' music of the finale.

Prokofiev, Serge
(1891–1953)

Chout (The Buffoon; ballet): *Suite, Op. 21; Romeo and Juliet* (ballet): *Suite, Op. 64.*
** (*) Decca SXL 6286. London Symphony Orchestra, Claudio Abbado.

It is difficult to see why a well-selected suite from *Chout* should not be as popular as any of Prokofiev's other ballet scores. It is marvellously inventive music which shows Prokofiev's harmonic resource at its most delicious. Abbado's version with the LSO offers a generous part of the score, including some of the loosely-written connecting tissue, and Abbado reveals a sensitive ear for balance of texture. The excerpts from *Romeo and Juliet* are well chosen: they include some of the most delightful numbers that are normally omitted from the suites such as the *Dance with mandolins,* the *Aubade* and so on. The *Dance of the girls* is very sensuous but too slow, far slower than Prokofiev's own 78s. But despite a slight want of intensity and fire, there is an admirable delicacy and lightness of touch that are most captivating. The recording is a model of its kind, with a beautifully balanced perspective and no lack of stereo presence.

Cinderella (ballet): *Suites Nos. 1, Op. 107; 2, Op. 108.*

(B) ** Decca Eclipse ECS 597. Royal Opera House, Covent Garden, Orchestra, Hugo Rignold.

Rignold's selection is generous and the Decca re-cut (this was originally issued by RCA) is rich and beautiful as sound. But some might find a lack of pungency in Rignold's approach, which is almost excessively lyrical. He plays down the explosive climax when the clock strikes midnight. However, while this scene can certainly sound much more dramatic, there is no denying that Rignold's overall conception goes along well with the fairy-tale atmosphere of the story. Certainly the Decca sound is sweeter than the original RCA full-price issue.

Cinderella (ballet), *Op. 87:* excerpts.

(M) ** Everest SDBR 3016. New York Stadium Orchestra, Leopold Stokowski – VILLA-LOBOS: *Bachianas Brasileiras no. 1.***

Stokowski made up his own suite from the Prokofiev ballet to follow the story sequentially, where the composer's own suites both depart radically from the ballet sequence. It is well played and brilliantly recorded.

Cinderella (ballet), *Op. 87*: excerpts; *Romeo and Juliet* (ballet), *Op. 64:* excerpts.

(B) * (*) Decca SPA 226. Suisse Romande Orchestra, Ernest Ansermet.

These excerpts are taken from a two-disc album, providing extended selections from both ballets, which Ansermet recorded in 1962. The one-disc condensed version is fair value for money, as Ansermet's Prokofiev is nearly always characterful. But the orchestral playing is less than distinguished, and Ansermet's

directing hand seems less assured than usual in matters of style. The recording is vivid but at the loudest moments it is not as open and free from congestion as are the best recordings from this source. A useful disc for low-budget collections, but there are much better selections from both scores available.

(i; ii) *Piano concertos Nos. 1 in D flat major, Op. 10; 2 in G minor, Op. 16; 3 in C major, Op. 26; 4 in B flat major (for left hand), Op. 53; 5 in G major, Op. 55;* (i; iii) *Overture on Hebrew themes for clarinet, string quartet and piano, Op. 34.*

(M) *** HMV SLS 882 (3 discs). (i) Michel Beroff (piano), (ii) Leipzig Gewandhaus Orchestra, Kurt Masur; (iii) Michel Portal (clarinet) and Parrenin Quartet.

Michel Beroff is an enormously gifted player, and his set of the Prokofiev concertos can be welcomed most warmly. There are tiny reservations: in No. 4, for instance, one feels that though Beroff is playing sensitively and expressively there is also a hint that he has not fully absorbed the work into his bloodstream. Here Browning on the older, deleted RCA set sounded more thoroughly at home. But Beroff is given a fresher and more truthful overall sound than the RCA, besides which he has a feeling for Prokofiev: the way in which he handles the cryptic figure in the second group of the finale of the *Third Concerto* could hardly be more idiomatic. Indeed it reminds one almost of the composer's own reading with Piero Coppola, made in the 1930s. The performance of the *Second Concerto*, however, shows some want of dash and verve: Browning sounded more completely at ease here. But Nos. 1 and 5 could hardly be bettered, and Masur and the Leipzig Orchestra provide first-rate accompaniment. Strongly recommended.

Piano concerto No. 1 in D flat major, Op. 10.

(B) *** Pye GSGC 14013. Mindru Katz (piano), London Philharmonic Orchestra, Sir Adrian Boult – KHACHATURIAN: *Piano concerto.****

A sparkling performance from Katz, the bravura very apparent. The piano tone is bold and clear, but the balance is excellent. The orchestral playing is good if not as polished as that of the soloist. Overall the effect is of sophisticated brilliance, which is very effective in making the most of the music without introducing artificiality. This is most enjoyable, and as the coupling is outstanding this makes a highly recommendable bargain disc, particularly as the recording is so good.

Piano concerto No. 2 in G minor, Op. 16.

(M) * (*) Supraphon SUAST 50551. Dagmar Baloghová (piano), Czech Philharmonic Orchestra, Karel Ančerl.

Slowish tempi and rather pale recorded quality limit the appeal of this issue. Dagmar Baloghová is a sensitive player, but since most recordings of this fine concerto have managed to accommodate a fill-up, this version is not outstandingly good value.

Piano concertos Nos. 2 in G minor, Op. 16; 3 in C major, Op. 26.

(M) * (*) Vox STGBY 675. Gabriel Tacchino (piano), Radio Luxembourg Orchestra, Louis de Froment.

Gabriel Tacchino is a stylish and intelligent artist, but his playing on this record is rather let down by the quality of his orchestral support. Louis de Froment does not succeed in getting playing of much refinement or sensitivity from the Radio Luxembourg Orchestra. However, the overall performance does not lack spontaneity, and although the recording is not particularly distinguished, this is better value than the Supraphon disc above.

Piano concerto No. 3 in C major, Op. 26.

(M) *** Philips Universo 6582 008. Byron Janis (piano), Moscow Philharmonic Orchestra, Kyril Kondrashin – RACHMANINOV: *Piano concerto No. 1.****

*** DGG SLPM 139349. Martha Argerich (piano), Berlin Philharmonic Orchestra, Claudio Abbado – RAVEL: *Concerto in G major.****

** (*) Decca SXL 6411. Julius Katchen (piano), London Symphony Orchestra, Istvan Kertesz – GERSHWIN: *Rhapsody in Blue*; RAVEL: *Concerto in D major.****

** (*) Decca Phase 4 PFS 4255. Israela Margalit (piano), New Philharmonia Orchestra, Lorin Maazel – MUSSORGSKY: *Pictures at an Exhibition.*** (*)

Recorded in Moscow by a Mercury recording team from America, the Janis version is outstanding in every way, soloist and orchestra plainly challenging each other in a performance full of wit, drama and warmth. The recording still sounds amazingly clean and faithful.

Martha Argerich is one of the most vital and positive women pianists in the world today. There is nothing ladylike about her playing, but it displays countless indications of feminine perception and subtlety. This concerto, once regarded as tough music, is here given a sensuous performance, and Abbado's direction underlines that from the very first with a warmly romantic account of the ethereal opening phrases on the high violins. When it comes to the second subject Argerich makes one smile with pleasure at the lightness of her pointing, and surprisingly a likeness emerges with the Ravel concerto (given on the reverse), which was written more than a decade later. This is a more individual performance of the Prokofiev than any other, but more revealing too.

Katchen gives a first-class performance of the solo part and is well accompanied by the LSO under Kertesz. It is difficult to fault it on any particular detail, and yet the overall impression it leaves is of having less character than Katchen's earlier mono version with Ansermet. It goes without saying that the recording is of fine quality.

The performance by Israela Margalit and Maazel is not the most poised available, but it has a splendid feeling of spontaneity and enjoyment. The recording balance is far from natural, the resonance of the acoustic competing with the microphone spotlighting, but the end result is unfailingly vivid. It is not unlikely that those who buy this disc for the Mussorgsky coupling may find themselves turning just as readily to the concerto, for the personality and colour of the score emerge strongly here.

Piano concerto No. 5 in G major, Op. 55.
> * (*) HMV ASD 2744. Sviatoslav Richter (piano), London Symphony Orchestra, Lorin Maazel – BARTÓK: *Piano concerto No. 2.* (*)

Richter is his own keenest rival in this last of the Prokofiev concertos. His much earlier version for DGG was presented in sharper focus – not just a question of recording acoustic. This is now deleted, and the newer account is not its match; but anyone who wants the coupling will enjoy this account of one of Prokofiev's more elusive works. The recording balance favours the soloist.

Violin concerto No. 1 in D major, Op. 19.
> ** Decca SXL 6532. Josef Sivó (violin), Suisse Romande Orchestra, Horst Stein – GLAZOUNOV: *Violin concerto.* (*)

Sivó is better in the Prokofiev concerto than in the Glazounov coupling. His is a lyrical reading in good taste, and he is generally well supported both by the orchestra and by the Decca team of engineers, though the record is not a winner.

Violin concertos Nos. 1 in D major, Op. 19; 2 in G minor, Op. 63.
> *** CBS 72269. Isaac Stern (violin), Philadelphia Orchestra, Eugene Ormandy.
> (B) * (*) Decca Eclipse ECS 746. Ruggiero Ricci (violin), Suisse Romande Orchestra, Ernest Ansermet.

Stern's are superb, deeply perceptive performances, revelling in and bringing out the lyricism of these fine concertos. Ormandy as usual is a first-rate accompanist, providing an immaculate orchestral texture faithfully matched to the needs of the soloist, but having a strong personality in its own right. The recording, not of the most modern now, was one of CBS's best.

Ricci's is the only bargain record to couple these concertos. He is forwardly balanced (but so is Stern), and his intonation is not always impeccable. The orchestral playing is somewhat lacklustre, but the performances are not without merit, and there are glimpses of magic in the outer movements of the *D major Concerto.* It must be conceded that these are not among the most distinguished accounts in the catalogue, and in the case of the *G minor Concerto,* Oistrakh's superb account with Galliera, at middle price, is the one to have.

Violin concerto No. 2 in G minor, Op. 63.

⊕ (M) *** HMV SXLP 30155. David Oistrakh (violin), Philharmonia Orchestra, Alceo Galliera – MIASKOVSKY: *Violoncello concerto.****

(M) *** RCA LSB 4048. Jascha Heifetz (violin), Boston Symphony Orchestra, Charles Munch – SIBELIUS: *Violin concerto.****

Oistrakh's account of Prokofiev's *G minor Concerto*, made in the early 1960s, occupies a place of honour in the catalogue. In some respects it has never been surpassed, though Heifetz's recordings with Koussevitzky and Munch fall into a special category. Oistrakh's is a beautifully balanced reading which lays stress on the lyricism of the concerto, and the orchestral support he receives could hardly be improved upon. The recording is admirably spacious and atmospheric, with splendidly focused detail and great warmth. An altogether marvellous record, whose value is enhanced by the interest of the coupling, Rostropovich's masterly account of the Miaskovsky *Cello concerto.*

Heifetz made the first recording of this work in the thirties under Koussevitzky. His newer recording uses the same Boston orchestra, and Munch proves a worthy successor to the Russian conductor. It is interesting to compare Heifetz's approach with Oistrakh's. Oistrakh is altogether more lush and romantic, and this pays wonderful dividends in the *arioso*-like slow movement. But just because Heifetz chooses a much faster speed for this movement it would be wrong to think of his performance as cold and unemotional, even in comparison with Oistrakh's, for his expressive *rubato* has an unfailing inevitability. In the spiky finale Heifetz is superb, and indeed throughout his playing is glorious. The recording is serviceable merely, but no one is going to be prevented from enjoying this ethereal

performance because of indifferent recording.

(i) *Concertino for violoncello and orchestra* (unfinished), *Op. posth.;* (ii) *Ballad of the Boy who Remained Unknown* (cantata), *Op. 93.*

(**) HMV ASD 2947. (i) Lev Yevgrafov (cello); (ii) vocal soloists and Moscow Radio Chorus; Moscow Radio Symphony Orchestra, cond. (i) Algis Zuraitis, (ii) Gennady Rozhdestvensky.

Prokofiev left his *Cello concertino* incomplete; the score was finished by Rostropovich. It is not one of his strongest pieces, and the wartime ballad about a youthful hero, with which it is coupled, does not find the Soviet master in his most inventive or compelling vein. Both the performances and recording are satisfactory.

Lieutenant Kijé (incidental music for a film): *Suite, Op. 60.*

*** HMV ASD 3029. London Symphony Orchestra, André Previn – SHOSTAKOVICH: *Symphony No. 6.****

(M) *** CBS Classics 61193. Cleveland Orchestra, George Szell – KODÁLY: *Háry János suite.****

(M) ** Everest SDBR 3054. London Symphony Orchestra, Sir Malcolm Sargent – SHOSTAKOVICH: *Symphony No. 9.***

(B) * (*) Vanguard SRV 174 SD. Vienna State Opera Orchestra, Mario Rossi – *Peter and the Wolf.***

Lieutenant Kijé is given a colourful, swaggering performance by Previn and the LSO, an excellent fill-up for their fine account of Shostakovich's *Sixth Symphony.* Szell, even more than in the *Háry János* coupling, is on his highest form. Seldom on record has the *Lieutenant Kijé* music been projected with such drama and substance, and Szell is wonderfully warm in the *Romance* without a suggestion of sentimentality. The recording, like the coupling, is aggressively close but it can be tamed, and there is no doubt about the projection of the music.

Bright recording and sharp, reasonably idiomatic playing from Sargent. Prokofiev's ironic music originally written for a Soviet film can hardly fail in such circumstances, and as a fill-up to a very good version of the light-hearted Shostakovich *Ninth* it can be welcomed. Mario Rossi is less incisive here than in the coupling of *Peter and the Wolf*; the reading is straightforward and colourful. Reverberant recording, betraying its late-fifties vintage.

Lieutenant Kijé: Suite, Op. 60; The Love of Three Oranges (opera)*: orchestral suite; Symphony No. 1 in D major (Classical), Op. 25.*
> ** (*) CBS 72185. Philadelphia Orchestra, Eugene Ormandy.

This collection was one of the great early successes of the CBS stereo catalogue. The recording now sounds just a little tart in the *Classical symphony* (which is played with great brilliance and *élan*) but elsewhere it is outstanding, and this is one of Ormandy's very best discs, with his orchestra on top form. The atmospheric performance of the *Lieutenant Kijé suite* is one of the finest available, but bargain-hunters will notice that this is also available on the CBS *Greatest hits* disc (see below).

(i) *Lieutenant Kijé: Suite, Op. 60;* (ii) *The Love of Three Oranges: March; Scherzo.*
> (B) * (*) Decca SPA 229. (i) Paris Conservatoire Orchestra, Sir Adrian Boult; (ii) Suisse Romande

Orchestra, Ernest Ansermet – MUSSORGSKY: *Pictures at an Exhibition.** (*)

These recordings are very early examples of Decca stereo, Boult's dating from 1956, and the reverberant acoustic takes away some of the sparkle and wit from the music. Ansermet suffers less than Boult in this respect, and his two items are quite vivid; but the *Lieutenant Kijé* excerpts are not very refined.

(i) *Overture on Hebrew themes, Op. 34;* (ii) *Symphony No. 1 in D major (Classical), Op. 25.*
> (M) ** (*) DGG Privilege 2538 232. (i) Monte Carlo National Opera Orchestra, Louis Frémaux; (ii) Dresden Philharmonic Orchestra, Kurt Masur – TCHAIKOVSKY: *String serenade.****

A sparkling account of the *Classical symphony*, one of the best in the catalogue, and a serviceable one of the *Overture on Hebrew themes*. Good recording.

Overture russe, Op. 72.
> (B) ** Decca Eclipse ECS 619. Paris Conservatoire Orchestra, Jean Martinon – *Symphony No. 7.***

The rumbustious *Overture russe* is a noisy piece, not one of Prokofiev's best works. Martinon's account is lively but brash.

Peter and the Wolf, Op. 67.
> (B) *** Music for Pleasure MFP 2126. Paul Daneman (narrator), Little Symphony of London, Arthur Davison – LEOPOLD MOZART: *Toy symphony;* MOZART: *German dance, K.605/3.****
> *** HMV ASD 2935. Mia Farrow (narrator), London Symphony

Orchestra, André Previn – BRIT-TEN: *Young person's guide to the orchestra.****

** (*) Decca Phase 4 PFS 4104. Sean Connery (narrator), Royal Philharmonic Orchestra, Antal Dorati – BRITTEN: *Young person's guide to the orchestra.*** (*)

** (*) HMV ASD 299. Michael Flanders (narrator), Philharmonia Orchestra, Efrem Kurtz – SAINT-SAËNS: *Carnival of the Animals.*** (*)

(B) ** Classics for Pleasure CFP 185. Richard Baker (narrator), New Philharmonia Orchestra, Raymond Leppard – BRITTEN: *Young person's guide to the orchestra.***

(M) ** Philips 6599 436. Alec McCowen (narrator), Concertgebouw Orchestra, Bernard Haitink – BRITTEN: *Young person's guide to the orchestra.***

(B) ** Vanguard SRV 174SD. Boris Karloff (narrator), Vienna State Opera Orchestra, Mario Rossi – *Lieutenant Kijé.** (*)

There are a great many recordings of *Peter and the Wolf* and we have listed the outstanding ones. Finest of all – to which we award a rosette – is Sir Ralph Richardson's incomparable account (see below) but other than this, first choice seems to go to the Music for Pleasure disc. The stereo reveals the orchestra in a fairly reverberant acoustic, the voice forward and in a drier one. At first this is slightly disconcerting, but the ear adjusts almost immediately, so vivid is the orchestral commentary right from the start. In the introduction the horns immediately create a very greedy-sounding wolf and the drums provide highly enthusiastic gunshots (indeed they sound almost like cannon, but that was Prokofiev's miscalculation!). Paul Daneman's easy

colloquial style is most pleasing, and he enters fully into the spirit of the tale as the excitement mounts.

It is a change to have a woman narrator for *Peter and the Wolf*, and Mia Farrow treats it as a bed-time story, admirably unmannered and direct. Almost certainly the best version for younger children, and the recording quality is the finest yet given to this colourful fable. It is an advantage too having the narrator in the same acoustic as the orchestra, which under Previn's direction produces playing both rich and jaunty, with some superb solo work.

Sean Connery uses a modern revision of the narrative by Gabrielle Hilton. This exchanges economy of words for a certain colloquial friendliness and invites the narrator to participate more than usual in the narrative. Sean Connery does this very well. His relaxed style, the vocal colour like brown sugar, is certainly attractive from the very beginning (if you can accept such extensions as a 'dumb duck' and a pussy-cat who is 'smooth, but greedy and vain') and when the tale reaches its climax he joins in the fray most enthusiastically. Dorati supports him well and the pace of the orchestral contribution quickens appropriately (in tension rather than tempo). The recording is clear, brilliant and colourful, the Phase 4 spotlighting well used. Children of all ages – who have no preconceived notions about the words of the narrative – will enjoy this. Both sides of the disc start attractively with the orchestra tuning-up noise, and here the introductory matter is entirely fresh and informal.

Michael Flanders adds a touch or two of his own to the introduction (which may irritate some) but includes relatively few embellishments to the main text of the story. This is a version which stands repetition, and HMV's recording is first-class. The coupling too is an imaginative one.

Richard Baker, balanced well forward in a different acoustic from the orchestra, provides an extra introductory paragraph which might become tedious on repetition. But he enters into the spirit of the story well enough and is only occasionally too coy. Leppard provides an excellent account of the orchestral score and the recording is vivid. But in the last resort one's reaction to this record depends on how one takes to the narration, and there will be mixed views on this. The disc is excellent value.

Alec McCowen uses a new text by Erik Smith which is intelligently prepared to give a fresh look at the story. However, the addition of bird imitations, including the duck quacking in the wolf's stomach at the end, is rather twee and seems designed to appeal to the youngest of listeners. McCowen is recorded closely, in a different acoustic from the orchestra, and as the story reaches its climax some over-modulation produces some ugly vocal reproduction. But taken as a whole the presentation is vivid and undoubtedly children will enjoy its liveliness.

Karloff is a benign grandfather figure telling the musical fairy story, though his sinister inflections make the most of the dramatic climaxes. Mario Rossi directs the orchestra colourfully without slackness. Other versions that might be mentioned are Ustinov's with Karajan (Ustinov perhaps too dramatic but offering a delightful impersonation of 'grandpa'; Karajan on the other hand tending to plod – Columbia SAX 2375) and a disappointing account from Eric Porter with Markevitch (EMI Studio 2 TWO 259 – Porter pitches his account in too low an emotional key and the conductor seems to follow his lead). Bernstein (CBS Classics 61057) opens his narration with a kind of quiz. The effect is mildly patronizing. The narration itself is curiously lacking in charm, although the orchestral playing is brilliant. This performance (slightly abridged) is also available *without narration*, as a 'do-it-yourself' version – see *Prokofiev's greatest hits* below.

(i) *Peter and the Wolf, Op. 67. Symphony No. 1 in D major (Classical), Op. 25.*

⊕ (B) *** Decca SPA 90. (i) Sir Ralph Richardson (narrator); London Symphony Orchestra, Sir Malcolm Sargent.

Sir Ralph Richardson's account is superbly recorded in the very best Decca manner, sumptuous and colourful. Sir Malcolm's direction of the orchestral contribution shows his professionalism at its very best, with very finely prepared orchestral playing, and many imaginative little touches of detail brought to one's attention, yet with the forward momentum of the action perfectly sustained. Sir Ralph brings an actor's feeling for words to the narrative. He dwells lovingly on their sound as well as their meaning, and this preoccupation with the manner in which the story is told matches Sargent's feeling exactly. There are some delicious moments when that sonorous voice delights in its own coloration, none more taking than Grandfather's very reasonable moral: 'and if Peter had not caught the wolf . . . what then?' But of course he did, and in this account it was surely inevitable. The *Symphony* too is superbly played and recorded. All the tempi, except perhaps the finale, are slow, but Sir Malcolm's self-assurance carries its own spontaneity, and this is one of the richest gramophone offerings he gave us.

The Prodigal Son (symphonic suite), *Op. 46 bis* (complete recording).

** Decca SXL 6308. Suisse Romande Orchestra, Ernest Ansermet – *Scythian suite.***

This attractive score bears much the same relationship to the *Fourth Symphony* as *The Fiery Angel* bears to the *Third*. Prokofiev thought so highly of it that he made from the complete ballet the suite recorded here, refashioned the material for use in the *Fourth Symphony*

719

and used the third movement of the present suite as a piano piece. He was right to do so, for this lyrical and inventive work must rank among his finest ballets. Ansermet gives it a sympathetic reading, though his orchestra has neither the polish nor the opulence of tone to do it full justice. Nonetheless this is – in the absence of any alternative – a thoroughly acceptable and welcome record and the stereo information is both detailed and realistic.

Romeo and Juliet (ballet), *Op. 64:* complete recording.
> *** HMV SLS 864 (3 discs). London Symphony Orchestra, André Previn.
> *** Decca SXL 6620/2. Cleveland Orchestra, Lorin Maazel.

Almost simultaneously two outstanding versions appeared of Prokofiev's complete *Romeo and Juliet* ballet, strongly contrasted to provide a clear choice on grounds of interpretation and recording. Previn and the LSO made their recording in conjunction with live performances at the Royal Festival Hall, and the result reflects the humour and warmth which went with those live occasions. Previn's pointing of rhythm is consciously seductive, whether in fast jaunty numbers or the soaring lyricism of the love music. The recording quality is warm and immediate to match.

Maazel by contrast will please those who believe that this score should above all be bitingly incisive. The rhythms are more consciously metrical, the tempi generally faster, and the precision of ensemble of the Cleveland Orchestra is little short of miraculous. The recording is one of Decca's most spectacular, searingly detailed but atmospheric too.

Romeo and Juliet, Op. 64: excerpts.
> *** Decca SXL 6668. Cleveland Orchestra, Lorin Maazel.

> *** HMV ASD 3054. London Symphony Orchestra, André Previn.
> ** (*) Philips 6500 640. Rotterdam Philharmonic Orchestra, Edo de Waart.

The Decca and HMV discs predictably reflect the qualities of the complete sets from which they come. Previn's selection is entitled *Scenes and dances* and seems chosen fairly arbitrarily on the 'highlights' basis. The Decca selection has been chosen to follow through the action of each of the three acts, and besides giving a bird's-eye picture of the complete work, it shows marvellously the diversity of Prokofiev's inspiration.

Edo de Waart, principal conductor of the Rotterdam Philharmonic, was here intent on demonstrating the international achievement of his orchestra, and the result is impressive, with fine playing and recording. Even so it is a pity that the two suites could not have been included complete on the disc. Here we are given only eleven numbers.

Romeo and Juliet, Op. 64: Suite No. 1: excerpts.
> ** DGG 2530 308. San Francisco Symphony Orchestra, Seiji Ozawa – BERLIOZ: *Roméo et Juliette: Love scene;* TCHAIKOVSKY: *Romeo and Juliet.***

The Prokofiev items make an attractive contrast to the other two very romantic evocations of Shakespeare on the same theme. Ozawa draws from his 'other' orchestra warmly committed playing, helped by rich recording quality.

Scythian suite (Ala and Lolly), Op. 20.
> ** Decca SXL 6308. Suisse Romande Orchestra, Ernest Ansermet – *Prodigal Son.***

The *Scythian suite* is one of Prokofiev's most powerful and imaginative scores.

Grossly underrated because of the parallels its savagery suggests with *The Rite of Spring*, it has a genuine sense of forward propulsion, a harmonic subtlety that is as striking as it is satisfying. In terms of sheer virtuosity the SRO would not win any prizes, but they have the benefit of first-class recording. This captures with admirable clarity the fantastic complexity of Prokofiev's score. If only these performances had more fire and panache as well as greater opulence of tone, this would have been truly competitive. The strings in the middle of the first movement sound emaciated (this might be the fault of the balance) and the third movement hasn't the atmosphere or sensuousness that it must have.

(i) *Scythian suite, Op. 20;* (ii) *Seven, they are seven* (cantata).

*** HMV ASD 3060. (i) Moscow Philharmonic Orchestra, Kyril Kondrashin; (ii) Yuri Elnikov (tenor), Chorus, Moscow Radio Orchestra, Gennady Rozhdestvensky – SHOSTAKOVICH: *Symphony No. 2.****

The Russian performance of the *Scythian suite* is excitingly played and very vividly recorded. The cantata, one of Prokofiev's most adventurous scores, is a welcome bonus. With its imaginative coupling this can be recommended.

The Stone Flower (ballet): extended excerpts.

** Decca SXL 6203. Suisse Romande Orchestra, Silvio Varviso.

The Stone Flower is not one of Prokofiev's strongest works. A full-length ballet, written after the war, it marks a distinct falling off in his inventive powers. But it is not without some striking episodes and many of the most attractive numbers are collected on this record.

Silvio Varviso secures some good playing from the Suisse Romande Orchestra, who seem to respond enthusiastically to some guest conductors, and the recording is one of Decca's most faithful and vivid. *The Stone Flower* would not rank high on one's short list of Prokofiev works (*Chout* and the *Scythian suite* and many other works that are lesser known should be sampled first), but no confirmed Prokofievian need fear to invest in this.

Symphonies Nos. 1 in D major (Classical), Op. 25; 2 in D minor, Op. 40; 3 in C minor, Op. 44; 4, Op. 47/112; 5 in B flat major, Op. 100; 6 in E flat minor, Op. 111; 7 in C sharp minor, Op. 131; Andante for strings, Op. 50a; In Autumn, Op. 8; Le Pas d'acier, Op. 41; Overture russe, Op. 72.

(M) ** (*) HMV SLS 844 (6 discs). Moscow Radio Symphony Orchestra, Gennady Rozhdestvensky – SHCHEDRIN: *Merry ditties.***

With the exception of Nos. 1 and 7 (see below), these discs are now not available except in a package format. They are good performances, at best (as in Nos. 3 and 6) quite distinguished and never less than vital and well-characterized. The album is also valuable in containing the only current accounts of *In Autumn*, *Le Pas d'acier* and the *Andante for strings*. As it is moderately priced it makes an admirable alternative to the Martinon set on Turnabout, though the raw-sounding Russian brass may not appeal to all collectors. The recordings are extremely fine, and are wide in range. Rozhdestvensky plays the revised edition of the *Fourth Symphony*, a longer and somewhat less satisfactory version than the 1930 original.

Symphony No. 1 in D major (Classical), Op. 25.

*** Argo ZRG 719. Academy of St

Martin-in-the-Fields, Neville Marriner – BIZET: *Symphony*.***

*** RCA SB 6847. London Symphony Orchestra, André Previn – MENDELSSOHN: *Symphony No. 4 etc.****

(M) ** CBS Classics 61071. New York Philharmonic Orchestra, Leonard Bernstein – BIZET: *Symphony*; DUKAS: *L'Apprenti sorcier*.** (*)

(M) * (*) Vanguard VCS 10099. English Chamber Orchestra, Johannes Somary – ARENSKY: *Variations on a theme of Tchaikovsky*; TCHAIKOVSKY: *String serenade*.**

It is very sad that Kurtz's delightful and marvellously played account recently reissued on Classics for Pleasure should again have disappeared. It seems wrong that some means cannot be found of retaining a record as good as this one in the catalogue. However, fortunately this symphony is well served by the gramophone. Marriner is beautifully recorded, in a warm, resonant acoustic. The sound has a quite splendid bloom, but, perhaps partly because of the resonance, Marriner's tempi are comparatively leisurely. The detail is deliciously pointed (the bassoon solo in the first movement is a joy), and the finale, if not as irrepressible as with Kurtz, has no lack of vivacity.

A neatly turned account of this delightful symphony from Previn and the LSO, and well recorded into the bargain. The performance is not quite as distinguished as that of the Mendelssohn *Italian symphony* on the reverse side but it is still highly competitive.

In the first two movements Bernstein's homage to the symphony's eighteenth-century ancestry produces a slight stiffness of manner, but even so the basoon manages a gentle smile in his solo, and the poise of the strings in the slow move-

ment's upper cantilena is superb. The finale is exhilarating, yet played with admirable precision. The recording is very brilliant in the CBS manner without being hard.

Somary's version is only recommended if the couplings are especially wanted. The performance is competent but unmemorable: it is at its best in the high-spirited finale.

Symphonies Nos. 1 in D major (Classical), Op. 25; 2 in D minor, Op. 40.

(B) *** Turnabout TV 37050S. National Orchestra of the ORTF, Jean Martinon.

This is the first of a complete set, with records available separately, and its appearance on so cheap a label is doubtless due to the presence of the low hum which equipment of wide range will bring to light. But taken as a whole the set represents excellent value and the first record is very fine indeed. Martinon shapes the *Second Symphony* most imaginatively and gives as good an account of the slow movement as either Rozhdestvensky (now not available separately) or Leinsdorf (deleted).

Symphonies Nos. 1 in D major (Classical), Op. 25; 3 in C minor, Op. 44.

** (*) Decca SXL 6469. London Symphony Orchestra, Claudio Abbado.

Abbado's account of the *Classical symphony* is fresh and beautifully played. It is (alongside Sargent's) the best recorded version of all, but the reading has not quite the sparkle offered by Kurtz. In the *Third Symphony* Abbado penetrates the amosphere and mystery of the highly imaginative inner movements more successfully than Martinon. These inner movements exert quite a powerful spell and their impact is all the greater on account of Abbado's total lack of exaggeration. The other movements are not quite as impressive: Rozhdestvensky has slightly more bite and momentum. The Abbado issue scores in the opulence and presence of the recording, which is in the demonstration class. It has great range, clarity of detail, and body of sound.

Symphonies Nos. 1 in D major (Classical), Op. 25; 5 in B flat major, Op. 100.

  (M) ** (*) Decca Ace of Diamonds SDD 399. Suisse Romande Orchestra, Ernest Ansermet.

The Fifth was one of Ansermet's finest performances, straight and unaffected, and the playing of the Suisse Romande Orchestra, though not the last word in virtuosity, is eminently spirited. The recording still sounds amazingly vivid and has presence as well as splendid range. The performance of the *Classical*, now added as a fill-up, has not diminished its detail or impact and many will be pleased to have this account, which if not refined in the matter of orchestral playing (and with a rather slow first movement) has considerable character and spontaneity. In any case the *Fifth* is well worth the price of the disc.

Symphonies Nos. 1 in D major (Classical), Op. 25; 7 in C sharp minor, Op. 131.

  *** HMV ASD 2410. Moscow Radio Symphony Orchestra, Gennady Rozhdestvensky.

  *** Decca SXL 6702. London Symphony Orchestra, Walter Weller.

The coupling of the brilliant Moscow performance (among the best available) of the *Classical symphony* with the *Seventh* was a happy idea. The *Seventh* is generally regarded as a lightweight piece of little consequence by the side of its illustrious predecessor. True, its inven-

tion is less vital than that of the best Prokofiev, but it is still full of delightful touches. Its somewhat balletic second movement or the fairy-tale overtones in the second group of the first are both charming, and even if the inspiration is not fully representative, Prokofiev at second best is a good deal better than most of his contemporaries at their very best. Rozhdestvensky gives a thoroughly convincing account of the work, more idiomatic in flavour and expert in execution than Martinon's cheap-label versions and well worth the extra money. The recording is a vivid one, though the acoustic is a bit reverberant, and is up to the usual high standard of HMV Melodiya.

The Decca recording has even greater presence and range: it is one of their very finest orchestral discs, truthfully balanced and with splendid impact. Weller's performances are excellent ones, without quite the imagination of Rozhdestvensky's, and perhaps a shade earthbound. But those for whom recorded quality is of paramount importance will find the music-making here satisfying enough and the sound of a demonstration standard.

Symphony No. 3 in C minor, Op. 44; Overture on Hebrew themes, Op. 34.

  (B) **(*) Turnabout TV 37051S. National Orchestra of the ORTF, Jean Martinon.

Prokofiev's *Third Symphony* is largely based on material from his opera *The Fiery Angel*, though the composer indignantly refused to give the symphony a subtitle and wanted it regarded as absolute music. Provided one does not take its symphonic claims too seriously it is an attractive work. The performance under Martinon does not quite show Abbado's degree of insight with the inner movements, but taken as a whole the interpretation has considerable power and impact, and the recording copes well with the work's big and complex climaxes.

Symphony No. 4, Op. 47; Overture russe, Op. 72.

(B) ** (*) Turnabout TV 37052S. National Orchestra of the ORTF, Jean Martinon.

Martinon plays the more compact original version of the *Fourth* (whose material derives from *The Prodigal Son* ballet). This is welcome, and its attractions are enhanced by persuasive and idiomatic playing.

Symphony No. 5 in B flat major, Op. 100.

⊛ *** DGG SLPM 139040. Berlin Philharmonic Orchestra, Herbert von Karajan.

(B) ** Turnabout TV 37053S. National Orchestra of the ORTF, Jean Martinon.

Karajan's is undoubtedly the finest currently available version of the *Fifth*. It is admirably unaffected, beautifully played, with the Berlin Philharmonic at the height of its form, and the DGG engineers at their best. The recording is a model, allowing all the subtleties of the orchestral colouring to register without any distortion of perspective. It has splendid range and fidelity and is wholly free from the kind of artificial balance favoured by American engineers.

A good account from Martinon (who also recorded the work earlier for Decca with the Paris Conservatoire Orchestra – a version marred by uncharacteristic harshness of sound) but it is one that faces far stiffer competition. Now that Kletzki's CFP account is deleted, this is good value in the bargain range, but the playing of the ORTF Orchestra is not quite as distinguished as that of the Philharmonia for Kletzki and the reading will give less satisfaction than Karajan or Ansermet (see under *Symphony No. 1*).

Symphony No. 6 in E flat minor, Op. 111.

(B) ** Turnabout TV 37054S. National Orchestra of the ORTF, Jean Martinon.

There is at present no alternative separate version of Prokofiev's *Sixth Symphony*, arguably his finest work, and Martinon's usefully fills a gap. The recording, though not distinguished, is perfectly acceptable, and at its bargain price the disc offers excellent value.

Symphony No. 7 in C sharp minor, Op. 131.

(B) ** Decca Eclipse ECS 619. Paris Conservatoire Orchestra, Jean Martinon – *Overture russe.***

(B) * (*) Turnabout TV 37055S. National Orchestra of the ORTF, Jean Martinon.

The *Seventh Symphony* is less successful in Martinon's newer Turnabout version than in his earlier disc with the Paris Conservatoire. The agogic distortions are generous and the playing is less distinguished than in Nos. 2 or 6. The Eclipse issue offers a clear-headed but somewhat rough and ready account. Again the orchestral playing is less than distinguished but the recording is quite a good one. While Rozhdestvensky is still available separately (see above under *Symphony No. 1*) that is the record to have, well worth the extra money.

Symphony-Concerto for violoncello and orchestra, Op. 125.

(M) ** Supraphon SUAST 50689. André Navarra (cello), Czech Philharmonic Orchestra, Karel Ančerl – RESPIGHI: *Adagio.***

The *Symphony-Concerto* is a reworking of the *First Violoncello concerto* (1938) and there are grounds for believing that the new version (provided at the instigation of Rostropovich) was a step backwards rather than forwards. Some of the most imaginative passages seem to have been omitted from the new work and padding substituted. Prokofiev admirers will find Navarra's performance strong and committed, and the recording atmospheric in Supraphon's reverberant manner (the soloist well forward).

Visions fugitives, Op. 22 (arr. Barshai).
*** Argo ZRG 711. Academy of St Martin-in-the-Fields, Neville Marriner – WALTON: *Sonata for strings.****

Rudolf Barshai made these brilliant string arrangements of Prokofiev's piano pieces for his Moscow Chamber Orchestra, but the St Martin's Academy equally relish the ingenuity of the transcription, which makes this sound like original string music. Fine atmospheric recording. An unexpected coupling for the fine Walton work, but an attractive one.

'Greatest hits': (i) *Lieutenant Kijé* (incidental music): *Suite, Op. 60; The Love of Three Oranges* (opera): *March.* (ii) *Peter and the Wolf, Op. 67:* orchestral music only (slightly abridged); *Symphony No. 1 in D major (Classical), Op. 25.*
(B) *** CBS 30032. (i) Philadelphia Orchestra, Eugene Ormandy; (ii) New York Philharmonic Orchestra, Leonard Bernstein.

This is an exceptionally successful and generous anthology. Besides a complete and brilliant account of the *Classical symphony* under Bernstein it includes Ormandy's distinguished account of the *Lieutenant Kijé* incidental music and the famous *March* from *The Love of Three Oranges*, vividly recorded. But the most fascinating item is *Peter and the Wolf* without the narration. Many will like to have the music alone for repeated listening; and its availability means that, with a score, you can do your own version. Transferred on to cassette it is relatively easy to stop the orchestra at the required moments (remembering that much of the story is spoken over the music). There are a few small cuts, but for regular listening (without the narrative) these are nearly always advantageous. A most recommendable bargain issue.

CHAMBER MUSIC

Quintet in G minor, Op. 39.
(M) ** Oiseau-Lyre SOL 267. Melos Ensemble – SHOSTAKOVICH: *Piano quintet.** (*)

Prokofiev's *Quintet* for oboe, clarinet, violin, viola and double-bass is a product of his Parisian exile in the twenties, and in its quirky style and odd layout of five movements it is characteristic. The composer himself said it started life as music commissioned for a ballet, and there are certainly some passages you could very well dance to. But in its fairly light-hearted way mixed with the usual measure of bitterness it is an agreeable work, and very well played here. The recording is excellent.

String quartet No. 2 in F major (Kabardin), Op. 92.
(M) *** Supraphon 111 0698. Prague Quartet – TCHAIKOVSKY: *Quartet No. 1.** (**)
(B) ** Decca Eclipse ECS 696. Carmirelli Quartet – RAVEL: *String quartet.***

The *Second Quartet* was written in 1942 when Prokofiev was evacuated to the Caucasus along with other Soviet composers. It incorporates folk elements, many of the same themes that Miaskovsky uses in his *Symphony No. 23*, though Prokofiev employs them with infinitely greater resource and imagination. This is a marvellous work, and it is good to have a choice of performance and couplings. It is uncommonly well played by the Prague Quartet and the recording is excellent; the acoustic and sharpness of outline suit the music admirably. The Eclipse recording dates from the 1950s but is genuine stereo, and with some filtering produces excellent results. The playing by the Italian ensemble is excellent.

Solo violin sonata, Op. 115.

(M) ** Supraphon SUAST 50707. Ladislav Jašek (violin) – BRITTEN: *Suite*; DALLAPICCOLA: *Tartiniana.***

Although clearly inspired by Bach's examples, Prokofiev here strikes out on his own as regards form and technique. The result is a truly original work of considerable power. This performance is faultless.

Violin sonatas Nos. 1 in F minor, Op. 80; 2 in D major, Op. 94a.

(M) *** RCA LSB 4084. Itzhak Perlman (violin), Vladimir Ashkenazy (piano).

Both of the *Violin sonatas* date from the years immediately after Prokofiev returned to the Soviet Union. The *F minor Sonata* is one of his very finest works and the *D major*, originally written for the flute and sometimes heard in that form, has a winning charm and melodiousness. Both works are masterly and rewarding, and Perlman and Ashkenazy play them superbly. The recording is well balanced, but the sound is not always as rich and truthful in tone as one would ideally like, though it is fully acceptable. Perhaps

some machines will respond more warmly to it than others, and reservations on this score should not deter anyone from investing in this record.

Violoncello sonata, Op. 119.

** (*) Argo ZRG 727. George Isaac (cello), Martin Jones (piano) – DELIUS: *Cello sonata; Piano pieces.***

Evidently George Isaac and Martin Jones have more affection for Prokofiev than for Delius. From the very first bar this is an intense and gripping performance of one of Prokofiev's most lyrical chamber works. Bright, vivid recording.

PIANO MUSIC

Chose en soi, Op. 45a and 45b; Music for children, Op. 65; 3 Pieces, Op. 59; Sonatine in E minor, Op. 54/1; Sonatine in G major, Op. 54/2.

(B) ** Turnabout TV 37068S. György Sándor (piano).

10 Episodes, Op. 12; 4 Etudes, Op. 2 (Nos. 1 in D minor; 2 in E minor; 3 in C minor; 4 in C minor); 4 Pieces, Op. 3; 4 Pieces, Op. 4; Piano sonata No. 1 in F minor, Op. 1; Toccata, Op. 11.

(B) ** Turnabout TV 37065S. György Sándor (piano).

Piano sonatas Nos. 2 in D minor, Op. 14; 3 in A minor, Op. 28; Five Sarcasms, Op. 17; Visions fugitives, Op. 22.

(B) ** Turnabout TV 37066S. György Sándor (piano).

Piano sonatas Nos. 4 in C minor ('from old notebooks'), Op. 29; 5 in C major, Op. 135 (38); 4 Pieces, Op. 32; Tales of an Old Grandmother, Op. 31.

(B) ** Turnabout TV 37067S. György Sándor (piano).

Piano sonatas Nos. 6 in A major, Op.

82; 7 in B flat major, Op. 83; Pensées, Op. 62.

    (B) ** Turnabout TV 37069S. György Sándor (piano).

Piano sonatas Nos. 8 in B flat major, Op. 84; 9 in C major, Op. 103.

    (B) ** Turnabout TV 37070S. György Sándor (piano).

There need be no qualms about György Sándor's prowess or keyboard personality, and he shows here a genuine feeling for Prokofiev's style. His performance of the *Second Sonata* has tremendous dash and brilliance and in the *Sixth* and *Seventh* he shows himself completely in command of both detail and structure. Nearly all of the records have the additional advantage of offering some of the lesser-known piano music of the Soviet master, much of it rewarding and played with enviable mastery. Unfortunately the recordings call for some degree of tolerance: the sound is lacking in depth; the piano is very closely balanced but has a very resonant acoustic and a slightly metallic tone. There is not really enough dynamic range and the result is that the ear tires very rapidly. Some works are better recorded than others and may respond to some machines better than others. But the recordings do detract somewhat from the undoubted value of this series.

Piano sonata No. 7 in B flat major, Op. 83.

    ⊛ *** DGG 2530 225. Maurizio Pollini (piano) – STRAVINSKY: *Three movements from Petrushka.****

This is a great performance, one of the finest Prokofiev performances committed to disc, well in the Horowitz or Richter category. So too is the coupling, the three movements from *Petrushka*. Good recording.

Piano sonatas Nos. 7 in B flat major, Op. 83; 8 in B flat major, Op. 84; Romeo and Juliet (ballet), *Op. 75: Romeo and Juliet before parting; Masks.*

    *** Decca SXL 6346. Vladimir Ashkenazy (piano).

Ashkenazy gives commanding readings of these two Prokofiev sonatas. He plays with such authority and conviction that one hopes Decca may one day persuade him to record the complete cycle. The piano tone is altogether excellent and the recording has a wide dynamic range and fidelity. This is a most distinguished record.

Piano sonata No. 9 in C major, Op. 103.

    (M) ** Vanguard VCS 10048. Joseph Kalichstein (piano) – BARTÓK: *Allegro barbaro; Sonata etc.***

Prokofiev's late sonata makes a happy coupling for the dramatic Bartók works on the reverse. The *Ninth Sonata* is a more sober, classically conceived work than some earlier sonatas in Prokofiev's magnificent series, but Kalichstein's performance brings out its full power and intensity. Good recording.

Visions fugitives Nos. 1–20, Op. 22 (complete).

    (M) *** HMV HQS 1284. Michel Béroff (piano) – DEBUSSY: *Images.****

Béroff is every bit as much in sympathy with Prokofiev as he is with the Debussy on the other side. Firmly etched lines, evocative atmosphere and keen rhythmic drive make these *Visions fugitives* eminently desirable. The recording is admirable and only the slightest trace of flutter disturbs the effect of total realism.

727

VOCAL AND CHORAL MUSIC

Alexander Nevsky (cantata), *Op. 78*.
  *** HMV ASD 2800. Anna Reynolds (mezzo-soprano), L S O Chorus, London Symphony Orchestra, André Previn.
  (B) **** (*) RCA Victrola VICS 1652.** Rosalind Elias (mezzo-soprano), Chicago Symphony Chorus and Orchestra, Fritz Reiner.

One great merit of Previn's version of Prokofiev's vivid cantata is the recording quality. All the weight, bite and colour of the score are captured here, and though the timbre of the singers' voices may not suggest Russians, they cope very confidently with the Russian text, and Previn's direct and dynamic manner ensures that the great *Battle on the ice* scene is powerfully effective. Anna Reynolds sings the lovely *Lament* for the dead most affectingly.

Reiner's performance too is of high quality, gripping from the first bar to the last. The music for the Teutonic invaders is as sinister as the *Battle on the ice* is thrilling. No less effective is the scherzando-like middle section of the battle music, which Reiner points in the most sparkling manner. The fervour of the choral singing is matched by the eloquence of Rosalind Elias's *Lament*. The performance is in English, of course, with an American accent, and quite a lot of the words come over clearly. The recording has not quite the richness and weight of Previn's disc, and is somewhat lacking in refinement in the loudest moments, but has splendid range and impact.

(i) *Ivan the Terrible, Op. 116* (film scores arranged in oratorio form by Stasevich); (ii) *On Guard for Peace* (oratorio), *Op. 124*.

** (*) HMV SLS 860 (2 discs). (i) Valentina Levko (mezzo-soprano), Anatoly Mokrenko (baritone), Aleksander Estrin (narrator), Moscow State Chorus, USSR Symphony Orchestra, Abram Stasevich; (ii) Irina Arkhipova (mezzo-soprano), Taimuraz Mironov (boy soprano), Ludmila Maksakova, Yuri Mishkin (speakers), Moscow Radio Symphony Chorus and Orchestra, Boys' Chorus of the Moscow Choral School, Gennady Rozhdestvensky.

It is good to have Prokofiev's powerfully atmospheric scores to the Eisenstein films on disc, for the music stands up well on its own account even when divorced from the gripping and intense films it so effectively accompanied. *On Guard for Peace* is far less interesting but still has strong moments. In any event this box is a must for all lovers of Prokofiev and serious aficionados of the cinema.

The Fiery Angel (*L'Ange de feu*; opera in 5 acts): complete recording (in French).

  (M) **** Decca Ace of Diamonds GOSR 652/4.** Jane Rhodes (soprano), Xavier Depraz (bass), Irma Kolassi (soprano), Jean Giraudeau (baritone), ORTF Choir, Paris Opera Orchestra, Charles Bruck.

Despite ageing recording (1957) and variable singing, the intense originality of Prokofiev's opera, with its painful study of religious mania, comes over strongly here, if without the light and shade which make such a score more appealing on record. The dramatic weight is shouldered by two characters merely, Jane Rhodes as the possessed nun, Renata, Xavier Depraz as the soldier, Ruprecht – flawed performances but convincing ones.

War and Peace (opera in 13 scenes): abridged recording.

(M) *** HMV SLS 837 (4 discs). Yevgeny Kibkalo (baritone), Galina Vishnevskaya (soprano), Alexei Krivchenya (bass), Vladimir Petrov (tenor), Pavel Lisitsian (baritone), Bolshoi Theatre Chorus and Orchestra, Alexander Melik-Pashayev.

As the English National Opera Company's production demonstrated very clearly, this late opera of Prokofiev, which tragically was never produced in the composer's lifetime, is a masterpiece. Prokofiev responded superbly to the almost impossible challenge of writing an epic work which yet communicated to the simplest listener. The result can be appreciated on every level, for the scenes of peace in the first half have sumptuous love music as well as vivid dance music in the ball scenes, while the second half has not only its patriotic choruses and the death scene of Andrei, hauntingly moving, but a truly splendid character-study of the Russian general Kutuzov, culminating in a monologue that is a masterpiece of lyrical fervour. The Bolshoi text is not so complete as the one we know in London, and there are incidental shortcomings in the performance, but this is still a magnificent representation of an epic opera, unique in twentieth-century music. The coarse recording balances rarely get in the way of enjoyment.

Puccini, Giacomo
(1858–1924)

La Bohème (opera in 4 acts): complete recording.

⊛ *** HMV SLS 896 (2 discs). Victoria de los Angeles (soprano), Jussi Bjoerling (tenor), Robert Merrill, John Reardon (baritones), Giorgio Tozzi (bass), Lucine Amara (soprano), RCA Victor Chorus and Orchestra, Columbia Boychoir, Sir Thomas Beecham.

*** Decca SET 565/6. Mirella Freni (soprano), Luciano Pavarotti (tenor), Rolando Panerai (baritone), Nicolai Ghiaurov (bass), Elizabeth Harwood (soprano), German Opera Chorus, Berlin, Berlin Philharmonic Orchestra, Herbert von Karajan.

** (*) HMV SLS 907 (2 discs). Mirella Freni (soprano), Nicolai Gedda (tenor), Mario Sereni, Mario Basiola (baritones), Ferruccio Mazzoli (bass), Mariella Adani (soprano), Chorus and Orchestra of Rome Opera, Thomas Schippers.

** (*) RCA ARL 2 0371 (2 discs). Montserrat Caballé (soprano), Placido Domingo (tenor), Sherrill Milnes, Vincenzo Sardinero (baritones), Ruggero Raimondi (bass), Judith Blegen (soprano), John Alldis Choir, Wandsworth School Boys' Choir, London Philharmonic Orchestra, Sir Georg Solti.

** Decca SXL 2170/1. Renata Tebaldi (soprano), Carlo Bergonzi (tenor), Ettore Bastianini (baritone), Cesare Siepi, Fernando Corena (basses), Gianna d'Angelo (soprano), St Cecilia Academy, Rome, Chorus and Orchestra, Tullio Serafin.

(M) * DGG Privilege 2705 038 (2 discs). Renata Scotto (soprano), Gianni Poggi (tenor), Tito Gobbi, Giorgio Giorgietti (baritones), Jolanda Meneguzzer (soprano),

Chorus and Orchestra of Maggio Musicale Fiorentino, Antonio Votto.

Beecham recorded his classic interpretation of *Bohème* in 1956 in sessions in New York that were arranged at the last minute. It was a gamble getting it completed, but the result was incandescent, a unique performance with two favourite singers, Victoria de los Angeles and Jussi Bjoerling, challenged to their utmost in loving, expansive singing. It was always rumoured that three of the four acts had been recorded in stereo, and though this reissue claims only that this is 'transcription stereo' it sounds remarkably like the real thing, with the voices made more vivid. With such a performance one hardly notices the recording, but those who want the very finest modern stereo can turn readily to Karajan.

Karajan too takes a characteristically spacious view of *Bohème*, but there is an electric intensity which holds the whole score together as in a live performance – a reflection no doubt of the speed with which the recording was made, long takes the rule. Karajan unerringly points the climaxes with full force, highlighting them against prevailing pianissimos. Pavarotti is an inspired Rodolfo, with comic flair and expressive passion, while Freni is just as seductive a Mimi as she was in the Schippers set ten years earlier. Elizabeth Harwood is a charming Musetta, even if her voice is not so sharply contrasted with Freni's as it might be. Fine singing throughout the set. The reverberant Berlin acoustic is glowing and brilliant in superb Decca recording.

Mirella Freni's characterization of Mimi on HMV is so enchanting that it is worth ignoring some of the less perfect elements in this set. The engineers placed Freni rather close to the microphone, which makes it rather hard for her to sound tentative in her first scene, but the beauty of the voice is what one remembers, and from there to the end her performance is conceived as a whole, leading to a supremely moving account of the death scene. Nicolai Gedda's Rodolfo is not rounded in the traditional Italian way but there is never any doubt about his ability to project a really grand manner of his own. Thomas Schippers's conducting starts as though this is going to be a hard-driven, unrelenting performance, but quickly after the horse-play he shows his genuinely Italianate sense of pause, giving the singers plenty of time to breathe and allowing the music to expand as it should.

The glory of Solti's set of *Bohème* is the singing of Montserrat Caballé as Mimi, an intensely characterful and imaginative reading which makes you listen with new intensity to every phrase, the voice at its most radiant. Domingo is unfortunately not at his most inspired. *Che gelida manina* is relatively coarse, though here as elsewhere he produces glorious heroic tone, and never falls into vulgarity. The rest of the team is strong, but Solti's tense interpretation of a work he had never conducted in the opera-house does not quite let the full sparkle of the music have its place or the full warmth of romanticism. Good recording, not quite as detailed as Decca's for Karajan.

The earlier Decca set with Tebaldi and Bergonzi was technically an outstanding recording in its day. Vocally the performance achieves a consistently high standard, Tebaldi as Mimi the most affecting: she offers some superbly controlled singing, but the individuality of the heroine is not so indelibly conveyed as with Los Angeles, Freni or Caballé. Carlo Bergonzi is a fine Rodolfo; Bastianini and Siepi are both superb as Marcello and Colline, and even the small parts of Benoit and Alcindoro (as usual taken by a single artist) have the benefit of Corena's magnificent voice. The veteran Serafin was more vital than on some of his recordings.

When one remembers that the Beecham set costs only slightly more than medium price, the DGG set, even at Privilege price, seems completely uncompetitive. Even Gobbi is less than a success as Marcello: do we really want to hear a Bohemian snarling? Scotto's voice is not at all well caught and as for Poggi, he makes the most frightful noises.

La Bohème: highlights.

 *** Decca SET 579 (from above recording cond. Karajan).
 ** (*) HMV ASD 2271 (from above recording cond. Schippers).
 ** Decca SXL 2248 (from above recording cond. Serafin).

It is a pity to cut anything from so taut a score as *Bohème,* but those who need a single disc instead of two will find the selection from the Karajan set ideal. The HMV disc shows a marked concentration on the Act 3 music. The Act 3 extract goes from the Mimi/Marcello duet to the final curtain, with a side-break where there is none in the complete set. It is a pity that Mimi's Act 4 entry is omitted, but even reducing *Bohème* by a mere half makes it impossible to include all the highlights. Good atmospheric recording, marred at the very end by Musetta's whispered commands somehow blasting. Those wanting a reminder of Tebaldi with Bergonzi in *Bohème* will find the Decca SXL selection well chosen, the recording reflecting the excellence of the complete set.

Edgar (Act 2) – see under *Le Villi.*

La Fanciulla del West (The Girl of the Golden West; opera in 3 acts): complete recording.

 (M) *** Decca Ace of Diamonds GOS 594/6. Renata Tebaldi (soprano), Mario del Monaco (tenor), Cornell MacNeil (baritone), Gior-

gio Tozzi (bass), Chorus and Orchestra of St Cecilia Academy, Rome, Franco Capuana.

Like *Madama Butterfly,* 'The girl,' as Puccini called it in his correspondence, was based on a play by the American, David Belasco. The composer wrote the work with all his usual care for detailed planning, both of libretto and of music. In idiom the music marks the halfway stage between *Butterfly* and *Turandot,* and the first audience must have been astonished at the opening of an Italian opera dependent on the whole-tone scale in a way Debussy would have recognized as akin to his own practice. Nevertheless it produces an effect wildly un-Debussian and entirely Puccinian.

This admirable Decca recording offers a most sympathetic account of the work. Tebaldi gives one of her most warm-hearted and understanding performances on record, and Mario del Monaco displays the wonderfully heroic quality of his voice to great – if sometimes tiring – effect. Cornell MacNeil as the villain, Sheriff Rance, sings with great precision and attack, but unfortunately has not a villainous-sounding voice to convey the character fully. Jake Wallace's entry and the song *Che faranno i viecchi miei* is one of the highspots of the recording, with Tozzi singing beautifully and the Decca engineers providing brilliant stereo atmosphere.

La Fanciulla del West: highlights.

 (M) *** Decca Ace of Diamonds SDD 333 (from above recording).

This is an excellent selection from the set. Capuana is warm and lyrical, Tebaldi is at her best, Monaco far from worst, Cornell MacNeil not villainous enough but superb musically and Tozzi makes the most of Jake Wallace's minstrel song – still an excellent passage for stereo demonstration. Besides that this selection has Jack Rance's powerful little *arioso* followed immediately by Tebaldi's answering aria; the Act 1 duet between Minnie and Johnson (not strictly a love duet – that comes much later); the climax of their duet in Act 2 before Johnson goes out into the snow; the Card Scene and the great aria *Ch'ella mi creda*. It is a pity that the final farewell scene was not included too – Act 3 is probably the finest last act Puccini ever wrote – but this is a fair sample beautifully recorded.

Gianni Schicchi (opera in 1 act): complete recording.

> * (*) Decca SXL 6124. Renata Tebaldi (soprano), Fernando Corena (bass), Lucia Danieli (mezzo-soprano), Agostino Lazzari (tenor), Chorus and Orchestra of Maggio Musicale Fiorentino, Lamberto Gardelli.

On recording there is no question that the new Decca version wins comfortably from the old HMV with Gobbi in the name part. But that said, there is not all that much to recommend it. Above all, Fernando Corena's Schicchi is too coarse-grained both vocally and dramatically. This is buffo-bass style with too much parlando 'acting', and Gobbi was to be preferred every time. Neither is Tebaldi entirely at home in the open-eyed part of the young Lauretta, though she sings *O mio babbino caro* very sweetly.

Madama Butterfly (opera in 3 acts): complete recording.

> ⊛ *** Decca SET 584/6. Mirella Freni (soprano), Luciano Pavarotti (tenor), Christa Ludwig (mezzo-soprano), Robert Kerns (baritone), Vienna State Opera Chorus, Vienna Philharmonic Orchestra, Herbert von Karajan.
>
> *** HMV SLS 927 (3 discs). Renata Scotto (soprano), Carlo Bergonzi (tenor), Anna di Stasio (mezzo-soprano), Rolando Panerai (baritone), Rome Opera Chorus and Orchestra, Sir John Barbirolli.
>
> ** (*) Decca SXL 2054/6. Renata Tebaldi (soprano), Carlo Bergonzi (tenor), Fiorenza Cossotto (mezzo-soprano), Enzo Sordello (bass), St Cecilia Academy, Rome, Chorus and Orchestra, Tullio Serafin.

Karajan inspires singers and orchestra to a radiant performance, which brings out all the beauty and intensity of Puccini's score, sweet but not sentimental, powerfully dramatic but not vulgar. He pays the composer the compliment of presenting each climax with precise dynamics, fortissimos surprisingly rare but those few presented with cracking impact. Freni is an enchanting Butterfly, consistently growing in stature from the young girl to the victim of tragedy, sweeter of voice than any rival on record. Pavarotti is an intensely imaginative Pinkerton, actually inspiring understanding for this thoughtless character, while Christa Ludwig is a splendid Suzuki. The recording is one of Decca's most resplendent, with the Vienna strings producing glowing tone.

Sir John Barbirolli had some apprehensions before going to Rome to make his first major recording of a complete opera, but at the very first session he established his mastery. The result is a performance in which against all the rules the conductor emerges as the central hero not through ruthlessness but sheer love. Players and singers perform consistently with a dedication and intensity rare in opera recordings made in Italy, and the whole score – orchestrated with masterly finesse – glows more freshly than ever. One has only to hear such a passage as the nostalgic duet between Pinkerton and Sharpless in the first scene to realize how Barbirolli reinforces the work of the singers, draws them out to their finest. There is hardly a weak link in the cast.

Bergonzi's Pinkerton and Panerai's Sharpless are both much more sensitively and beautifully sung than one expects these days; Anna di Stasio's Suzuki is more than adequate, and Renata Scotto's Butterfly has a subtlety and perceptiveness in its characterization that more than make up for any shortcoming in the basic beauty of tone-colour. It is on any count a highly individual voice, used here with great intelligence to point the drama up to its tragic climax. Gloriously rich orchestral sound.

This is Tebaldi's second recording of *Butterfly* and it is rather surprising to find that the part was not a regular one in her stage repertory. That may well account for a certain clumsiness in the dramatic handling. But Tebaldi does sing beautifully all through, and it is only because other sopranos today have read so much into the part that one feels any lack. Few sopranos can float a soft high note with such apparent ease as Tebaldi, and her rich creamy tone – which she uses here for example in the lovely passage when she tells Pinkerton she has changed her religion – is all-enveloping in its beauty. The conducting by Serafin accounts partly for the comparatively restrained effect the performance has. His speeds for much of the time are strangely slow. With such fine sound the result is most impressive, but in the last resort it lacks the full dramatic impact a Puccini opera should have.

Madama Butterfly: highlights.
*** HMV ASD 2453 (from above recording cond. Barbirolli).
** Decca SXL 2202 (from above recording cond. Serafin).

It is a pity that the selection from Barbirolli's set does not include any of the music before Butterfly's entrance (outstandingly done), but the items here amply demonstrate the glories, vocal and orchestral, of the performance, and those investing in the Karajan complete set

will find this an unusually satisfying supplement. Barbirolli shares in the enjoyment with great groans of pleasure in places. First-rate recording. There are many beautiful moments too in Tebaldi's performance, even if here she rarely shows the creative insight of characterization that Freni brings to the part. Serafin's conducting is restrained but the recording reflects the excellence of the complete set.

Madam Butterfly: abridged version (in English): *Opening and duet; Love duet; One fine day; Telescope duet; Flower duet; Trio and Pinkerton's farewell; Death scene.*
(B) ** Music for Pleasure MFP 6036. Marie Collier (soprano), Charles Craig (tenor), Ann Robson (mezzo-soprano), Gwyn Griffiths (bass), Sadler's Wells Chorus and Orchestra, Bryan Balkwill.

This highly successful disc was the first of a series of Sadler's Wells highlights discs of opera in English. There are few better examples, for the clear recording lets the listener hear almost every word and this is achieved without balancing things excessively in favour of the voices. Marie Collier got inside the part very well, and she had a big, full voice. Some may be troubled by her pronounced vibrato; others may find the vibrato nothing more than a natural colouring of the voice. As to the choice of extracts, the one omission which is at all serious is the entry of Butterfly. As it is the duet of Pinkerton and Sharpless cuts off just as she is about to come in. But Craig is a splendid Pinkerton and he was in particularly fresh voice when this record was made.

Manon Lescaut (opera in 4 acts): complete recording.
** (*) HMV SLS 962 (2 discs). Montserrat Caballé (soprano),

Placido Domingo (tenor), Vincenzo Sardinero (baritone), Noel Mangin (bass), Robert Tear (tenor), Ambrosian Opera Chorus, New Philharmonia Orchestra, Bruno Bartoletti.

(M) ** (*) Decca Ace of Diamonds GOS 607/8. Renata Tebaldi (soprano), Mario del Monaco (tenor), Fernando Corena (bass), Chorus and Orchestra of St Cecilia Academy, Rome, Francesco Molinari-Pradelli.

Manon Lescaut, Puccini's first great success, has latterly been neglected unjustly in the opera-house. Fortunately on record its great merits come out vividly, whether in the richly inspired first act, with its intricate interweaving of music and drama into a kind of massive rondo form, whether in the superb scene at the end of Act 3, where Manon and the prostitutes board the ship for America, whether in the heroine's agonized death scene, which on the stage is too static to be effective, but which on record can be most affecting.

Caballé makes a sympathetic Manon, particularly in that last scene, where her translation from flirtatious girl to tragic heroine is complete. Placido Domingo sings strongly and sensitively, and the rest of the cast is consistently good. Bartoletti is not quite as understanding a conductor as he might be, overforcing in places, and the recording is not always ideally clear. But in general this makes a good first choice.

The Decca set with Tebaldi, dating from the mid-fifties, is by no means outclassed by the more recent version. The recording still sounds very well, with good detail, and the direction of Molinari-Pradelli is warm and intense. While Tebaldi is not quite the little woman of Puccini's dreams, she still produces a flow of gorgeous, rich tone. Only the coarseness of Mario del Monaco as Des

Grieux mars the set, but this is exciting, red-blooded singing and he does not overwhelm Tebaldi in the duet sequences.

La Rondine (opera in 3 acts): complete recording.

(M) ** (*) RCA DPS 2055 (2 discs). Anna Moffo, Graziella Sciutti (sopranos), Daniele Barioni, Piero de Palma (tenors), Mario Sereni (baritone), RCA Italiana Chorus and Orchestra, Francesco Molinari-Pradelli.

La Rondine was a product of the First World War, and though in subject nothing could be less grim than this frothy tale told in Viennese operetta-style, the background to its composition and production may have had their effect. It has never caught on, and a recording like this will almost certainly surprise anyone at the mastery of the piece, with a captivating string of catchy numbers. The story is based on a watered-down *Traviata* situation culminating not in tragedy but a sad-sweet in-between ending such as the Viennese (for whom it was written) loved. It is not just a question of Puccini taking Viennese waltzes as model but all kinds of other suitable dances such as tangos, foxtrots and two-steps. Not aggressively at all, for as with so much that this most eclectic of composers 'cribbed', he commandeered them completely, to make the result utterly Puccinian.

If there is a fault, it lies in the inability of the story to move the listener with any depth of feeling, but a recording does at least allow one to appreciate each tiny development with greater ease than in the theatre. The performance, though not ideal, is still highly enjoyable, with understanding direction from Molinari-Pradelli and excellent recording quality from RCA.

Suor Angelica (opera in 1 act): complete recording.

***RCA SER 5673. Katia Ricciarelli (soprano), Fiorenza Cossotto, Maria Grazia Allegri (mezzo-sopranos), Anna di Stasio (soprano), Coro Polifonico di Roma, St Cecilia Academy Orchestra, Bruno Bartoletti.

** Decca SXL 6123. Renata Tebaldi (soprano), Giulietta Simionato, Lucia Danieli (mezzo-sopranos), Chorus and Orchestra of Maggio Musicale Fiorentino, Lamberto Gardelli.

Ricciarelli here shows on record something of the star quality which has brought her such acclaim in Italy. The legato is sometimes marred by mannered nudging, but the voice is expressive and beautiful. The big aria *Senza mamma* is delicately done, a touching portrait of the tragic nun who has just learnt of the death of her child. The singing of Cossotto as the grim Zia Principessa is formidably impressive, while the direction of Bartoletti is finely detailed, never sentimental. This is a work which on acquaintance reveals its underlying tautness, far more than a sentimental story of a convent. Good, atmospheric recording.

Tebaldi makes a rich-voiced and affecting Sister Angelica, and seems only slightly troubled by the top notes at the end. Simionato makes a fine, firm Zia Principessa; one can really believe in her relentlessness, and the bright Decca recording captures the atmosphere of the convent very clearly. Gardelli keeps the performance moving gently but firmly, and in a somewhat static piece, that is most important; but this is generally not as fine as the RCA version.

Il Tabarro (opera in 1 act): complete recording.

** (*) RCA SER 5619. Leontyne Price (soprano), Placido Domingo (tenor), Sherrill Milnes (baritone), John Alldis Choir, New Philharmonia Orchestra, Erich Leinsdorf.

** Decca SXL 6122. Renata Tebaldi (soprano), Mario del Monaco (tenor), Robert Merrill (baritone), Chorus and Orchestra of Maggio Musicale Fiorentino, Lamberto Gardelli.

The unforgettably atmospheric colouring in Puccini's essay in Grand Guignol is beautifully caught by the RCA recording made in Walthamstow Assembly Hall, and the refinement of the New Philharmonia playing puts this clearly ahead of the Decca rival. Leontyne Price may not be ideally cast as the bargemaster's wife, but she is more in character than her direct rival, Tebaldi, even though she does not point word-meaning in enough detail. Sherrill Milnes is rather young-sounding for the bargemaster, but he sings memorably in the climactic aria *Nulla, silenzio*, sustaining an unusually slow tempo. It is good to have a supplement (as in the Decca version) in the original aria, later replaced, *Scorri, fiume eterno*. Placido Domingo makes a fresh-voiced young bargee, again more in character than his Decca rival, while Leinsdorf is at his most sympathetic.

The scene of the opera is set on a barge on the banks of the Seine, in Paris, and though the Decca recording captures all of Puccini's background effects – the hooters of ships and taxis, bells, off-stage singers – the result has not so much a Parisian flavour as the acoustic of an empty opera-house. Merrill sings very strongly as the cuckolded bargemaster and Tebaldi and del Monaco are good in a conventional whole-hogging Italian way. But the RCA disc is the one to have.

Tosca (opera in 3 acts): complete recording.

(M) *** Decca 5BB 123/4. Leontyne

735

Price (soprano), Giuseppe di Stefano (tenor), Giuseppe Taddei (baritone), Vienna State Opera Chorus, Vienna Philharmonic Orchestra, Herbert von Karajan.

*** RCA ARL 2 0105 (2 discs). Leontyne Price (soprano), Placido Domingo (tenor), Sherrill Milnes (baritone), John Alldis Choir, Wandsworth School Boys' Choir, New Philharmonic Orchestra, Zubin Mehta.

* (**) HMV Angel SLS 917 (2 discs), Maria Callas (soprano), Carlo Bergonzi (tenor), Tito Gobbi (baritone), Paris Opera Chorus, Paris Conservatoire Orchestra, Georges Prêtre.

(M) * (*) Decca Ace of Diamonds GOS 612/3. Renata Tebaldi (soprano), Mario del Monaco (tenor), George London (baritone), Chorus and Orchestra of St Cecilia Academy, Rome, Francesco Molinari-Pradelli.

* Decca SET 341/2. Birgit Nilsson (soprano), Franco Corelli (tenor), Dietrich Fischer-Dieskau (baritone), Chorus and Orchestra of St Cecilia Academy, Rome, Lorin Maazel.

Karajan deserves equal credit with the principal singers for the vital, imaginative performance here. Some idea of its quality may be gained from the passage at the end of Act 1, just before Scarpia's *Te Deum*. Karajan takes a speed far slower than usual, but there is an intensity which both takes one vividly to the Church of San Andrea and builds the necessary tension for depicting Scarpia's villainy. Taddei himself has a marvellously wide range of tone-colour, and though he cannot quite match the Gobbi snarl, he has almost every other weapon in his armoury. Leontyne Price is at the

peak of her form and di Stefano sings most sensitively. The sound of the Vienna Orchestra is enthralling – both more refined and richer than usual in a Puccini opera – and the recording is splendidly vivid in this new transfer.

Price made her second complete recording of *Tosca* ten years after the first, and the interpretation remained remarkably consistent, a shade tougher in the chest register – the great entry in Act 3 a magnificent moment – a little more clipped of phrase. That last modification may reflect the relative manners of the two conductors – Karajan more individual in his refined expansiveness, Mehta more thrustful. On balance, taking Price alone, the preference is for the earlier set, but Mehta's with fine modern recording (no more refined than the earlier one) also boasts a fine cast, with the team of Domingo and Milnes at its most impressive.

EMI chose a tigress for their Tosca. This Callas set is exciting and disappointing in roughly predictable proportions. There are very few points of improvement on the old mono set with Callas in the title role and de Sabata conducting far more imaginatively than Prêtre here. And when it comes to vocal reliability the comparison with the old is just as damaging as an impartial observer might predict. Gobbi is magnificent still, but no more effective than he was in that old Columbia set, and Bergonzi's Cavaradossi, intelligent and attractive, is belittled by the recording balance in his disfavour. Fortunately EMI have reissued the older set in a stereo transcription and this rosette-worthy performance is a fine investment on SLS 825, even if the sound, although good, does not match either of the two versions with Leontyne Price.

In the Ace of Diamonds set, well recorded, Tebaldi is splendidly dramatic and it is a great pity that the other two principals do not match her. The cast of the other Decca *Tosca*, conducted by

Maazel, is impressive on paper, but the result is intensely disappointing. Not only is it a question of both Nilsson and Fischer-Dieskau sounding so completely un-Italianate that Puccini's phrases stiffen and die, but the conducting of Maazel seems to have little sympathy for the passion and warmth of Puccini's writing.

Tosca: highlights.

    ** HMV ASD 2300 (from above recording cond. Prêtre).

    (M) * (*) Decca Ace of Diamonds SDD 334 (from above recording cond. Molinari-Pradelli).

    * Decca SET 451 (from above recording cond. Maazel).

Even to Callas-admirers her remake of *Tosca* must be a disappointment when it fails so obviously to match the dramatic intensity of the first version under de Sabata. In the Ace of Diamonds disc, Tebaldi's contributions are enjoyable but not much else, and it seems perverse to recommend the other Decca highlights disc, even though the selection is well made, when the excerpts come from such an unidiomatic and generally unpassionate performance.

Il Trittico: Il Tabarro; Suor Angelica; Gianni Schicchi.

    ** Decca SET 236/8. Renata Tebaldi (soprano), Giulietta Simionato (mezzo-soprano), Mario del Monaco (tenor), Robert Merrill (baritone), Fernando Corena (bass), Chorus and Orchestra of Maggio Musicale Fiorentino, Lamberto Gardelli.

Puccini's three one-act operas show him musically and dramatically at the peak of his achievement. They are balanced like the movements of a concerto: *Il Tabarro*, sombre in its portrait

of the cuckolded bargemaster, but made attractive by the vividness of the atmosphere and the sweetness of the love music; *Suor Angelica*, a lyrical slow movement with its picture of a nunnery, verging on the syrupy but never quite falling; *Gianni Schicchi*, easily the most brilliant and witty one-act comedy in the whole field of opera. This careful balance does in a way justify Decca's decision to put this out as a set although the separate discs are now available (and are reviewed above as such). There is also an album with complete libretto and notes by Peggy Cochrane.

Turandot (opera in 3 acts): complete recording.

    *** Decca SET 561/3. Joan Sutherland (soprano), Luciano Pavarotti (tenor), Montserrat Caballé (soprano), Peter Pears (tenor), Nicolai Ghiaurov (bass), John Alldis Choir, Wandsworth School Boys' Choir, London Philharmonic Orchestra, Zubin Mehta.

    *** HMV SLS 921 (3 discs). Birgit Nilsson (soprano), Franco Corelli (tenor), Renata Scotto (soprano), Angelo Mercuriali (tenor), Rome Opera Chorus and Orchestra, Francesco Molinari-Pradelli.

    (M) ** RCA SER 5643/5. Birgit Nilsson (soprano), Jussi Bjoerling (tenor), Renata Tebaldi (soprano), Giorgio Tozzi (bass), Rome Opera Chorus and Orchestra, Erich Leinsdorf.

    (M) * (*) Decca GOS 622/4. Inge Borkh (soprano), Mario del Monaco (tenor), Renata Tebaldi (soprano), Chorus and Orchestra of St Cecilia Academy, Rome, Alberto Erede.

The role of Turandot, the icy princess, is not one that you would expect to be in

Joan Sutherland's repertory, but here on record she gives an intensely revealing and appealing interpretation, making the character far more human and sympathetic than ever before. This is a character, armoured and unyielding in *In questa reggia*, whose final capitulation to love is a natural development, not an incomprehensible switch. Sutherland's singing is strong and beautiful, while Pavarotti gives a performance equally imaginative, beautiful in sound, strong on detail. To set Caballé against Sutherland was a daring idea, and it works superbly well; Pears as the Emperor is another imaginative choice. Mehta directs a gloriously rich and dramatic performance, superlatively recorded.

The HMV set brings Nilsson's second assumption on record of the role of Puccini's formidable princess. As an interpretation it is very similar to the earlier RCA performance, but its impact is far more immediate thanks to the conducting of Molinari-Pradelli – far warmer than Leinsdorf's for RCA – and thanks to the more forward if less refined recording quality. The climax of *In questa reggia* is far more telling when the conductor pushes forward beforehand with a natural – if unexaggerated – *stringendo*. There are many similar effects to make. Corelli may not be the most sensitive prince in the world – Bjoerling is far better on detail – but the voice is in glorious condition. Scotto's Liù is very beautiful, more in character than Tebaldi's on RCA.

On RCA Nilsson is certainly an icy princess. She has power and attack, even if some of her top notes are too hard to be acceptable even from the Princess Turandot. Tebaldi as Liù is warmer and more sympathetic than she was in the earlier Decca set and Bjoerling is a splendid Calaf. This was one of his last recordings, but he was as clear-voiced and youthful-sounding as ever. The rest of the cast matches this standard, but Leinsdorf's conducting is chilly. The

recording is brilliant but, like the performance, rather lacking in warmth.

The early Decca recording still has glitter and brilliance. Yet the performance lacks atmosphere and sheer vitality; nor does the singing match that on the other sets.

(i) *Le Villi* (opera in 2 acts): complete recording; (ii) *Edgar* (opera in 3 acts): Act 2 (complete).
(M) ** (*) RCA DPS 2052 (2 discs). (i) Adriana Maliponte (soprano), Matteo Manuguerra (baritone), G. de Monaco (narrator); (ii) Nancy Stokes (soprano), Walker Wyatt (baritone); (i; ii) Barry Morell (tenor), Vienna Academy Chamber Chorus, Vienna Volksoper Orchestra, Anton Guadagno.

Though this is a flawed set, it is very welcome to have a stereo version of Puccini's first opera, coupled with the central act of his second opera. Both works have failed to establish themselves in the Puccini canon, but they are far from being the featureless products of an unskilled beginner. There are many foretastes of the later Puccini, though inevitably the melodies have not quite the same distinctiveness, and the librettos – *Le Villi* based on a similar story to that of *Giselle*, *Edgar* a tale of high melodrama in medieval times – are relatively inept and uninvolving. These are not polished performances, but they carry red-blooded conviction. Fair recording.

COLLECTIONS

'Heroines'; La Bohème, Act 1: *Sì, m chiamano Mimì*; Act 2: *Quando me'n vo'*; Act 3: *Donde lieta uscì*. Edgar, Act 3: *Addio, mio dolce amor. La*

Fanciulla del West, Act 1: *Laggiù nel Soledad. Madama Butterfly*, Act 2: *Un bel dì. Manon Lescaut*, Act 2: *In quelle trine morbide;* Act 4: *Sola, perduta, abbandonata. La Rondine*, Act 1: *Ore dolci e divine. Tosca*, Act 2: *Vissi d'arte. Le Villi*, Act 1: *Se come voi piccina.*

*** RCA SER 5674. Leontyne Price (soprano), New Philharmonia Orchestra, Edward Downes.

A formidable collection of Puccini arias with Price at the peak of her career, still marvellously subtle in control (the end of Tosca's *Vissi d'arte*, for example), powerfully dramatic, yet able to point the *Rondine* aria with delicacy and charm. Good recording.

Arias: *La Bohème*, Act 1: *Sì, mi chiamano Mimì;* Act 3: *Donde lieta uscì. Gianni Schicchi: O mio babbino caro. Madama Butterfly*, Act 2: *Un bel dì;* Act 3: *Tu, tu piccolo Iddio. Manon Lescaut*, Act 2: *In quelle trine morbide;* Act 4: *Sola, perduta, abbandonata. La Rondine: Chi il bel sogno di Doretta. Tosca*, Act 2: *Vissi d'arte. Turandot*, Act 1: *Signore, ascolta!;* Act 3: *Tu che di gel sei cinta. Le Villi*, Act 1: *Se come voi piccina.*

*** HMV ASD 2632. Montserrat Caballé (soprano), London Symphony Orchestra, Charles Mackerras.

Montserrat Caballé uses her rich, beautiful voice to glide over these great Puccinian melodies. The effect is ravishing, with lovely recorded sound to match the approach. This is one of the loveliest of all operatic recital discs and the comparative lack of sparkle is compensated by the sheer beauty of the voice.

'*The world of Puccini*': (i; ii; iii) *La Bohème*, Act 1: *Che gelida manina; Sì,*

mi chiamano Mimì; O soave fanciulla; Act 4: *In un coupé . . . O Mimì, tu più non torni.* (i; ii; iv) *Tosca*, Act 1: *Te Deum;* Act 2: *Vissi d'arte;* Act 3: *E lucevan le stelle.* (i; ii) *Madama Butterfly*, Act 1: *Love duet;* Act 2: *Un bel dì; Humming chorus.* (i; v) *Turandot*, Act 1: *Signore, ascolta!; Non piangere, Liù!; Ah! per l'ultima volta!;* (vi) *Nessun dorma.*

(B) *** Decca SPA 365. (i) Renata Tebaldi (soprano); (ii) Carlo Bergonzi (tenor); (iii) Ettore Bastianini (baritone); (iv) George London (baritone); (v) Mario del Monaco (tenor); (vi) Giuseppe di Stefano (tenor); various orchestras and conductors.

This is a splendid anthology and is immensely valuable in reminding collectors of the many fine things the Decca Puccini series of complete opera recordings contained, not least the contributions of Tebaldi and Bergonzi. The collection has been arranged with great skill so that we do not get a string of purple passages yet many favourites are included. The scene from Act 1 of *La Bohème* has Tebaldi and Bergonzi on top form and also shows the fine atmospheric sound for which these recordings have been justly famous. After the *Love duet* and *Un bel dì* from *Butterfly* we are given the magical *Humming chorus*, and side two includes a scene from the early *Turandot* to show Tebaldi in ravishing voice as Liù. To finish the concert, Giuseppe di Stefano sings *Nessun dorma*. This is taken from a recital disc: a cunning idea, as Mario del Monaco's version from the complete set is considerably less stylish. Sometimes the age of the originals shows in the string tone, but for the most part the sound is as vivid as the performances. Highly recommended and very generous too.

Purcell, Henry
(1658–95)

Chaconne in G minor for 3 violins and continuo. Anthems: *Blow up the trumpet in Zion; My heart is inditing; O God, Thou art my God; O God, Thou hast cast us out; Remember not, Lord, our offences; Rejoice in the Lord.*
> *** Telefunken SAWT 9558. King's College, Cambridge, Choir, David Willcocks, Leonhardt Consort, Gustav Leonhardt.

An attractive concert which happily blends scholarship and spontaneity. The instrumental ensemble uses period instruments and playing style, and the character of the sound is very distinctive. Not all the anthems have instrumental accompaniments but they are all well sung with the characteristic King's penchant for tonal breadth and beauty. Excellent sound.

Chaconne in G minor. Trumpet sonata. Dioclesian: What shall I do? The Tempest: Arise, ye subterranean winds; Aeolus you must appear; Your awful voice I hear; Halcyon days; See, see, the heavens smile. The Virtuous Wife: suite.
> (M) *** Oiseau-Lyre SOL 60002. Jennifer Vyvyan (soprano), William Herbert (tenor), Hervey Alan (bass), Philomusica of London, Anthony Lewis.

This is one of several attractive single-disc anthologies (others are devoted to Handel and Bach) issued by Oiseau Lyre in the earliest days of stereo. The recording was notably good for its time and now wears its years easily. The programme here, as in the other issues, is very well planned. Side one is devoted

to a selection from Purcell's music for *The Tempest*, with good solo singing and plenty of life and spirit in the presentation. The other side includes an attractive *Trumpet sonata*, and, of course, the *Chaconne*, which brings out the very best from the orchestra.

Harpsichord suites Nos. 1 in G major; 2 in G minor; 3 in G major; 4 in A minor; 5 in C major; 6 in D major; 7 in D minor; 8 in F major.
> (B) ** Oiseau-Lyre OLS 149. Isabelle Nef (harpsichord).

Although Isabelle Nef does not give readings of exceptional insight or imagination, her performances are eminently spirited. The recording sounds good for its age, and given the price bracket and the absence of any alternative, the disc is both useful and welcome.

MISCELLANEOUS VOCAL MUSIC

Behold, I bring you glad tidings (Christmas verse anthem).
> (B) ** Turnabout TV 34180S. Linda Karen-Smith (contralto), Hanns-Friedrich Kunz (baritone), Laerte Malaguti (bass), Mainz Chamber Chorus and Orchestra, Günter Kehr – HAYDN: *Cantilena pro adventu;* A. SCARLATTI: *Cantata pastorale.***

Although the soloists are not individually outstanding, they make a fair team, and this performance of Purcell's Christmas verse anthem has a Handelian nobility of phrase. The choir is serviceable and the recording pleasingly rich and full. With enterprising couplings this is a valuable minor contribution to the vocal catalogue.

Funeral music for Queen Mary; Jubilate Deo in D major; Te Deum.

** (*) Argo ZRG 724. James Bowman, Charles Brett (counter-tenors), Ian Partridge (tenor), Forbes Robinson (bass), St John's College, Cambridge, Choir, English Chamber Orchestra, George Guest.

The *Funeral music for Queen Mary* consists of far more than the unforgettable march for timpani and trumpets, which still sounds so modern to our ears. In the event the march brings the least effective performance here, not so bitingly tragic as it might be. The rest is beautifully done, and so are the grand ceremonial settings of the *Te Deum* and *Jubilate*. Excellent recording.

Anthems: *Jehova, quam multi sunt hostes mei: Lord, how long wilt Thou be angry; My beloved spake; O sing unto the Lord a new song; They that go down to the sea in ships; Who hath believed our report.*

*** Argo ZRG 5444. Soloists, St John's College, Cambridge, Choir, Academy of St Martin-in-the-Fields, George Guest.

This anthology, entitled *Music for the Chapel Royal*, is very successful; the content is varied and nicely balanced. The late Inia te Wiata shows his sense of style as well as bravura in *They that go down to the sea in ships*. The recording is first-rate.

Ode for Mr Louis Maidwell's School ('Celestial music'); Ode for Queen Mary's birthday ('Now does the glorious day appear')

(M) ** (*) Pye Virtuoso TPLS 13011. Patricia Clark (soprano), Tom Sutcliffe (counter-tenor), Edgar

Fleet (tenor), Roger Stalman, John Frost (basses), Chorus and Orchestra of Accademia Monteverdiana, Denis Stevens.

It is good to welcome two fine examples of Purcell's occasional music into the catalogue. 'Occasional music' one says, but in fact in this *Birthday Ode* – the first of a whole series Purcell wrote – the writing has an intensity that completely belies the comparative triviality of the commission. There is not a weak number in it, and the counter-tenor solo *By beauteous softness* is outstanding even by Purcell's standards. The other ode was written in the same year (1689) as *Dido and Aeneas*, another commission from an academic establishment. One of the scholars of Mr Maidwell's school provided the words (full of classical allusions) and Purcell managed to be completely undeterred by their poverty of inspiration. Two recorders provide an enchanting descant for the loveliest of the songs, *Her charming strains*. Denis Stevens draws some excellent singing from soloists and chorus of the Accademia Monteverdiana. The orchestral accompaniment is not always quite so polished and the recording balance is not ideal, but the greatness of the music comes over with full force.

Ode on St Cecilia's Day.

*** DGG Archive 2533 042. Simon Woolf (treble), Paul Esswood, Roland Tatell (counter-tenors), Alexander Young (tenor), Michael Rippon, John Shirley-Quirk (basses), Tiffin Choir, Ambrosian Singers, English Chamber Orchestra, Charles Mackerras.

(M) ** (*) Vanguard HM 33SD. April Cantelo (soprano), Alfred Deller, Peter Salmon (counter-tenors), Wilfred Brown (tenor), Maurice Bevan (baritone), John Frost

741

(bass), Ambrosian Singers, Kalmar Chamber Orchestra, Sir Michael Tippett.

A splendid all-male performance of Purcell's joyous masterpiece with an exceptionally incisive and vigorous choral contribution matched by fine solo singing. Simon Woolf has made a recital record to show his amazing technical and musical range, and he is ideally cast here. The recording is excellent, although the balance between soloists and tutti does not make much distinction in volume between the smaller and larger groups. The rival version on Vanguard is well worth its modest cost, but this newer disc is even finer.

On Vanguard the magnificent principal male alto part is superbly sung by Alfred Deller. The composer originally designed it for himself and did in fact sing it – as they said at the time – 'with incredible graces'. The rest of the performance matches Deller's contribution, with Sir Michael Tippett (editor as well as conductor) obviously relishing his task, and the Kalmar Chamber Orchestra (later to form the nucleus of the English Chamber Orchestra) giving stylish support with the Ambrosian Singers in excellent form. The recording, made originally in the midfifties, may not be of the smoothest, but it is not likely to distract anyone from the glories of the music and its performance.

Sweeter than roses (realized Britten); *When the cock begins to crow.*
> *** Decca SXL 6608. Peter Pears (tenor), John Shirley-Quirk (baritone), James Bowman (countertenor), Benjamin Britten (piano) – BRITTEN: *Journey of the Magi etc.****

To hear the counter-tenor, James Bowman, whooping the Purcellian cry 'Cock-a-doodle-doo' is delightful. These two brief Purcell items make an unexpected but charming fill-up to the Britten items.

Te Deum.
> * (*) HMV ASD 2340. April Cantelo, Helen Gelmar (sopranos), Ian Partridge (tenor), James Bowman (alto), Christopher Keyte (bass), King's College, Cambridge, Choir, David Willcocks – CHARPENTIER: *Mass.***

It was a bright idea to couple Purcell's *Te Deum* setting with the Charpentier *Christmas Eve Mass*, for these composers were contemporaries, although their styles have marked differences. The Purcell work is one of those brilliant, fullblooded scores which have contributed to the English oratorio tradition over the centuries, and the orchestration is replete with most effective trumpet parts. The performance is a good one, but the recording lacks bite and takes the edge off the dramatic effect of the music.

STAGE WORKS

Dido and Aeneas (opera in 3 acts): complete recording.
> ⊛ (M) *** Oiseau-Lyre SOL 60047. Janet Baker, Patricia Clark (sopranos), Monica Sinclair (mezzo-soprano), Raimund Herincx (baritone), St Anthony Singers, English Chamber Orchestra, Anthony Lewis.
> ** (*) DGG Archive 198424. Tatiana Troyanos, Sheila Armstrong (sopranos), Patricia Johnson (mezzo-soprano), Barry McDaniel (baritone), Hamburg Monteverdi Choir, NDR Chamber Orchestra, Charles Mackerras.
> ** Philips 6500 131. Josephine Vea-

sey, Helen Donath (sopranos), Elizabeth Bainbridge (mezzo-soprano), John Shirley-Quirk (baritone), John Alldis Choir, Academy of St Martin-in-the-Fields, Colin Davis.

** HMV SAN 169. Victoria de los Angeles, Heather Harper (sopranos), Patricia Johnson (contralto), Peter Glossop (baritone), Ambrosian Singers, English Chamber Orchestra, Sir John Barbirolli.

(B) * (*) Vanguard SRV 279 SD. Mary Thomas, Honor Shepherd (sopranos), Helen Watts (contralto), Maurice Bevan (bass), Oriana Concert Choir and Orchestra, Alfred Deller.

Janet Baker's is a truly great performance as Dido. The radiant beauty of her voice is obvious enough, but here she goes beyond that to show what stylishness and insight she can command. The emotion is implied, as it should be in this music, not injected in great uncontrolled gusts. Listen to the contrast between the angry, majestic words to Aeneas, *Away, away!*, and the dark grief of the following *But death alas I cannot shun*, and note how Baker contrasts dramatic soprano tone-colour with darkened contralto tone. Even subtler is the contrast between the opening phrase of *When I am laid in earth* and its repeat a few bars later: it is a model of graduated *mezza voce*. Then with the words *Remember me!* in a monotone she subdues the natural vibrato to produce a white tone of hushed, aching intensity. It will be surprising if a more deeply satisfying interpretation is recorded within the foreseeable future, and the rest of this production heightens the effect of Janet Baker's work. Anthony Lewis chooses fast speeds, but they challenge the English Chamber Orchestra (Thurston Dart a model continuo player)

to produce the crispest, lightest playing, which never sounds rushed. The soloists and chorus give very good support. Herincx is a rather gruff Aeneas, and the only serious blemish is Monica Sinclair's Sorceress. She overcharacterizes in a way which is quite out of keeping with the rest of the production. Generally by concentrating on musical values, Lewis and his singers and instrumentalists make the clear, simple dramatic point of the opera all the more telling: it provides a most moving experience. Like most Oiseau-Lyre discs the record is beautifully engineered.

The other different versions of Purcell's compressed operatic masterpiece make for tantalizing comparisons. Charles Mackerras gives perhaps the most satisfying direction, for as well as being scholarly it is very vital, with tempi varied more widely and – as he himself suggests – more authentically than usual. There is also the question of ornamentation, and as a whole Mackerras manages more skilfully than any of his rivals, with shakes, backfalls, forefalls, springers and so on, all placed authentically. Even so, his ideas for ornamenting Dido's two big arias are marginally less convincing than Anthony Lewis's on the Oiseau-Lyre disc, with many appoggiaturas and comparatively few turns and trills. He has the edge over Lewis in using Neville Boyling's edition based on the Tatton Park manuscript, and he adds brief extra items from suitable Purcellian sources to fill in the unset passages of the printed libretto. As to the singing, Tatiana Troyanos makes an imposing, gorgeous-toned Dido, and Sheila Armstrong as Belinda, Barry McDaniel as Aeneas, and Patricia Johnson all outshine the rival performances, but ultimately the Dido of Janet Baker on Oiseau-Lyre is so moving it more than compensates for any relative shortcomings, particularly when Thurston Dart's continuo-playing is much more imaginative than the Hamburg harpsichordist's.

Davis's version is fresh and enjoyable but hardly inspired. It was a fascinating idea to have the same Dido here in Purcell as Davis chose for Berlioz's great opera on the same subject, and Veasey sings most reliably. But next to Baker and Troyanos she sounds a little stiff and unsympathetic. Good recording.

Barbirolli – not the most likely conductor in this opera – takes some trouble with his text, using the Neville Boyling edition that Mackerras also prefers. But on questions of authenticity Mackerras – and for that matter Anthony Lewis – have every advantage, and Barbirolli finds fewer moments of high emotional intensity such as would justify a 'personality' reading than one would expect. The tempi are generally perverse, with slow speeds predominating – sometimes grotesquely slow – but with Dido's *When I am laid in earth* taken equivalently fast. Victoria de los Angeles makes an appeal-Dido, but she does not have anything like the dramatic weight of Janet Baker or Tatiana Troyanos, and the tone sometimes loses its bloom on top. The other singers are good, but with keen competition this version commands only a qualified recommendation.

Deller is a masterly Purcellian, but here with a cast that often falls short of the standards set on rival versions he does not do himself justice. Helen Watts's Sorceress is superb, but Mary Thomas as Dido is very variable, rarely achieving the necessary emotional weight.

The Fairy Queen: complete recording.
  *** Decca SET 499/500. Jennifer Vyvyan (soprano), James Bowman (counter-tenor), Peter Pears (tenor), Mary Wells (soprano), Ian Partridge (tenor), John Shirley-Quirk (baritone), Owen Brannigan (bass), Norma Burrowes (contralto), Ambrosian Opera Chorus, English Chamber Orchestra, Benjamin Britten.

The Fairy Queen: highlights.
  *** Decca SET 560 (from above recording).

This is a sumptuous offering of some of Purcell's most inspired dramatic music, presented in a newly reshaped version by Benjamin Britten, Imogen Holst and Peter Pears. The original cumbersome collection of pieces is here grouped into four satisfying sections: *Oberon's Birthday*; *Night and Silence*; the *Sweet Passion*; and *Epithalamium*. This version was first heard at the Aldeburgh Festival in 1967, and here the authentic glow of a Maltings performance (1971 vintage) is beautifully conveyed in the playing, the singing and the recording. Philip Ledger's imaginative harpsichord continuo is placed too far to one side, but otherwise the sound can hardly be faulted. The cast is consistently satisfying, with Peter Pears and Jennifer Vyvyan surviving from the much earlier 'complete' version of Anthony Lewis on Oiseau-Lyre, now reissued in a stereo transcription on OLS 121/3.

The Indian Queen (incidental music): complete recording.
  (M) *** Oiseau-Lyre SOL 294. April Cantelo (soprano), Wilfred Brown, Robert Tear (tenors), Christopher Keyte (bass), St Anthony Singers, English Chamber Orchestra, Charles Mackerras; Raymond Leppard (harpsichord).

It is one of the tragedies of British music that so much of Purcell's most inspired music lies locked up in outmoded forms. This incidental music to a play that has long since disappeared from the stage is a mine of riches, and the modern LP record makes an ideal medium for restoring the music to currency. Not all of it shows Purcell at his most inspired – some of the earlier numbers are frankly disappointing – but with stylish singing and superb direction and accompaniment

(Raymond Leppard's continuo-playing must be singled out) this is an invaluable issue. Charles Mackerras once again shows himself a strong, vivid as well as scholarly Purcellian. First-rate recording.

King Arthur (opera): complete recording.

⊛ (M) *** Oiseau-Lyre SOL 60008/9. Elsie Morison, Heather Harper, Mary Thomas (sopranos), John Whitworth (counter-tenor), Wilfred Brown, David Galliver (tenors), John Cameron (baritone), Trevor Anthony, Hervey Alan (basses), Philomusica of London, St Anthony Singers, Anthony Lewis.

This splendid performance and recording of King Arthur is fully worthy to stand alongside the Oiseau-Lyre set of Dido and Aeneas, although here the success of the interpretation does not centre on the contribution of one inspired artist, but rather on team work between a number of excellent singers and the stylish and sensitive overall direction of Anthony Lewis. Oiseau-Lyre's excellent stereo too plays a big part. This was an early set but one would never guess it from the warmth of the sound and indeed the sophistication with which the stereo is used for special effects. A very happy example is the chorus This way, this way, when the opposing spirits (good and wicked) make a joint effort to entice the King. Purcell's music is marvellously spontaneous and full of imaginative touches, like the famous freezing aria, which will surely send a shiver through the most warm-blooded listener. The story is easy to follow, for the libretto gives details of the action between the songs. The spoken dialogue is, sensibly, not included in the recording.

The Masque in Dioclesian; Dioclesian (incidental music): suite.

(M) ** Vanguard HM 13SD. Alfred Deller (counter-tenor), Honor Sheppard, Sally le Sage (sopranos), Max Worthley, Philip Todd (tenors), Maurice Bevan (baritone), Vienna Concentus Musicus (dir. Nikolaus Harnoncourt), Alfred Deller.

The History of Dioclesian enjoyed great success in Purcell's lifetime. It appeared between Dido and Aeneas and King Arthur and contains music of characteristic dignity and nobility, notably the Masque which occupies the bulk of this record. It goes without saying that there is excellent singing in the course of this performance, and Harnoncourt's Vienna Concentus Musicus give a good account of themselves. Perhaps the great Chaconne itself could be more successful: it is a trifle pedestrian here. Although the performance is a good one, it falls short of the last ounce of imagination. The recording yields good results and at the price offers excellent value. Despite the reservations made, this disc can be recommended, particularly to admirers of the artistry of Alfred Deller.

Quilter, Roger (1877–1953)

A Children's overture.

** Columbia Studio 2 TWO 295. Light Music Society Orchestra, Sir Vivian Dunn – GRAINGER: Pieces *** (also Concert).

This charming overture, skilfully constructed from familiar nursery-rhyme tunes, has hitherto not been available in stereo, or even in a decent mono LP recording. It was a pity George Weldon did not remake his 78 version. As it is, Sir Vivian Dunn shapes the piece carefully, but there is no incandescence in the playing. The recorded quality has plenty of colour and is softer in outline than the sound on the rest of the disc, and with all one's reservations, this is such a delightful and spontaneous work that it cannot fail to be enjoyable when the recording is so warm and sparkling. (The concert from which this comes is reviewed in our *Treasury* volume.)

Rachmaninov, Sergei
(1873–1943)

Caprice bohémien, Op. 12; Symphonic dances, Op. 45.

** (*) Philips 6500 362. London Philharmonic Orchestra, Edo de Waart.

If the quality of recorded sound were the only consideration, this version of the *Symphonic dances* by the LPO under Edo de Waart would surely sweep the board. The Philips engineers produce sound of the utmost clarity of detail. The orchestral textures are beautifully luminous; each strand can be clearly heard by the discerning ear yet is carefully balanced to produce a consistently rich and homogeneous body of sound. The recording has splendid range and a most musically judged perspective. The performance under de Waart is a very fine one and will undeniably give pleasure, even though it falls short of being totally idiomatic. Mr de Waart (sympathetically but unwisely) confessed that he had not taken the work into his repertoire before recording it and his reading does not sound so full-blooded as those of Ormandy or Kondrashin (see below), who have this work in their blood. The *Caprice bohémien* is not otherwise available and makes an added attraction.

Piano concertos Nos. 1 in F sharp minor, Op. 1; 2 in C minor, Op. 18; 3 in D minor, Op. 30; 4 in G minor, Op. 40; Rhapsody on a theme of Paganini, Op. 43.

*** Decca SXLF 6565/7. Vladimir Ashkenazy (piano), London Symphony Orchestra, André Previn.

(M) ** (*) HMV SLS 855 (3 discs). Agustin Anievas (piano), New Philharmonia Orchestra, cond. Rafael Frühbeck de Burgos (Nos. 1 and 4); Moshe Atzmon (2 and *Rhapsody*); Aldo Ceccato (3).

Ashkenazy's recording of the Rachmaninov concertos and the *Rhapsody on a theme of Paganini* stands out as a major achievement. The individuality and imagination of the playing, and its poetic feeling, provide special rewards, and if sometimes one might ask for a more commanding style, Previn's accompaniments are sympathetic and perceptive to match Ashkenazy's sometimes withdrawn manner. The *Second Concerto* is an outstanding success, notable for perhaps the most beautiful performance of the slow movement currently on disc; the *Third* is more controversial in its waywardness, but undoubtedly has inspired moments, while the *Rhapsody* has received more brilliant, more boldly romantic performances from other hands (notably Katchen's). Michelangeli's account of the *Fourth Concerto* is uniquely magical, but Ashkenazy is very fine too and more richly recorded. The Decca sound casts a warm glow over the music-making. Sometimes it is not ideally clear and sometimes one misses an element of glitter, but generally it matches the rhapsodic, musing lyricism of the performances admirably.

Anievas cannot match Ashkenazy as a searching and individual interpreter of Rachmaninov, but his youthful freshness makes all these concerto performances intensely enjoyable. With three Mediterranean conductors to help him and with fruity EMI recording, the result has red-blooded romanticism which never lets go, even if it rarely produces the moments of magical illumination that mark the most inspired interpretations. Anievas, like Ashkenazy, gives the *Third Concerto* absolutely uncut, and uses the longer and more difficult version of the first-movement cadenza. It is a strong, direct interpretation, though at the very end of the finale the big melody comes perilously near the vulgar associations of Hollywood. A good set at permanent bargain price.

Piano concerto No. 1 in F sharp minor, Op. 1.

(M) *** Philips Universo 6582 008. Byron Janis (piano), Moscow Philharmonic Orchestra, Kyril Kondrashin – PROKOFIEV: *Piano concerto No. 3.****

As in the Prokofiev on the reverse, soloist and orchestra plainly challenged each other to the limit, and the American recording team brilliantly captured the red-blooded interpretation which resulted. Even now the recording is impressive for clarity of texture within a warm acoustic. An outstanding mid-price disc.

Piano concertos Nos. 1 in F sharp minor, Op. 1; 2 in C minor, Op. 18.

*** Decca SXL 6554. Vladimir Ashkenazy (piano), London Symphony Orchestra, André Previn.

(B) * (*) Decca SPA 169. Peter Katin (piano), London Philharmonic Orchestra, Sir Adrian Boult, or New Symphony Orchestra, Colin Davis.

In the opening movement of the *First Concerto* Ashkenazy's light, rhapsodic approach minimizes the drama: other accounts have provided more pointed music-making here, but the poetry of the slow movement and the sparkling lilt of of the finale (the secondary lyrical theme

played with just the right touch of restraint) are irresistible. Again in the *Second Concerto* it is the warm lyricism of the playing which is so compulsive. The opening tempo, like Richter's, is slow, but the tension is finely graduated towards the great climax, and the gentle, introspective mood of the *Adagio* is very beautiful indeed. The finale is broad and spacious rather than electrically exciting, but the scintillating, unforced bravura provides all the sparkle necessary. The recording is richly spacious, the piano tone slightly brighter in the *First Concerto.*

Boult brings a sympathetic freshness to the *First Concerto*, and his conducting is matched by Katin's spirited playing. The pianist does not attempt a conventional bravura style, and some may be disappointed on this account, but in this shortest of Rachmaninov's concertos the added clarity and point given to so many passages more than make amends (if indeed amends need to be made). The orchestra responds well but does not always play with perfect precision. The stereo is excellent, with good definition and balance. Unfortunately the performance of the *Second Concerto* is underpowered. Katin takes the opening chords in a brisk, matter-of-fact way, and although the lyricism of the first movement is nicely managed, the performance as a whole is dull. The recording in No. 2 needs a reduction of bass and an increase of top, an unusual recipe for a Decca issue. Many will feel this good value at the price for the *First Concerto* alone, but there are more vital bargain accounts of the *Second.*

Piano concertos Nos. 1 in F sharp minor, Op. 1; 4 in G minor, Op. 40.

(M) ** CBS Classics 61310. Philippe Entremont (piano), Philadelphia Orchestra, Eugene Ormandy.

Entremont gives a marvellously dashing account of both early and late concertos, rivalling the composer himself in the sheer effrontery of his bravura. By rights no ten fingers could possibly play like this, and as with Rachmaninov himself the speeds have one on the edge of one's seat. Where Entremont falls short – and he is not helped by the American recording, which boosts pianissimos – is in the gentler music, where he could be more affectionate. The recording quality could be sweeter too, and the piano tone is rather clattery; but it is still a recommendable version of a most sensible coupling.

Piano concerto No. 2 in C minor, Op. 18.

*** DGG slpm 138076. Sviatoslav Richter (piano), Warsaw Philharmonic Orchestra, Stanislav Wislocki – *Preludes.****

(M) ** (*) Decca Ace of Diamonds SDD 181. Julius Katchen (piano), London Symphony Orchestra, Sir Georg Solti – BALAKIREV: *Islamey.****

** (*) Decca Phase 4 PFS 4214. Ivan Davis (piano), Royal Philharmonic Orchestra, Henry Lewis.

(B) ** (*) Classics for Pleasure CFP 167. Moura Lympany (piano), Royal Philharmonic Orchestra, Sir Malcolm Sargent – *Preludes.***

** Decca SXL 6099. Vladimir Ashkenazy (piano), Moscow Philharmonic Orchestra, Kyril Kondrashin – *Études-tableaux.****

** HMV ASD 2872. Alexis Weissenberg (piano), Berlin Philharmonic Orchestra, Herbert von Karajan – FRANCK: *Symphonic variations.*** (*)

* (*) HMV ASD 492. John Ogdon (piano), Philharmonia Orchestra, John Pritchard – *Preludes.****

Richter has strong, even controversial ideas about speeds in this concerto. The long opening melody of the first movement is taken abnormally slowly, and it is only the sense of mastery which Richter conveys in every note which prevents one from complaining. One ends by admitting how convincing that speed can be in Richter's hands, but away from the magic one realizes that this is not quite the way Rachmaninov himself intended it. The slow movement too is spacious – with complete justification this time – and the opening of the finale lets the floodgates open the other way, for Richter chooses a hair-raisingly fast allegro, which has the Polish players scampering after him as fast as they are able. Richter does not, however, let himself be rushed in the great secondary melody, so this is a reading of vivid contrasts. Good recording of the piano, less firm of the orchestra, but an atmospheric acoustic adds bloom overall.

Katchen gives a dramatic and exciting account, such as we would expect from this pianist. He had a fabulous technique and was always at pains to demonstrate it at its most spectacular. Generally in this recording this leads to the highest pitch of excitement, but there are a number of passages – notably the big climax as well as the coda of the first movement – where he plays almost too fast. Miraculously he gets round the notes somehow but the result inevitably seems breathless, however exciting it is. The stereo recording is in Decca's best manner and manages to be brilliant and well co-ordinated at the same time.

Though the names of the participants on the Phase 4 disc are less imposing, this is a splendid record, given a full-blooded, rich recording, the piano image large and forward, but not distractingly so. The interpretation is spaciously conceived, the tempo and control of tension in the first movement broad: not as slow as Richter, nor as exuberant as Katchen's. Thus the style of the interpretation falls somewhere between these two alternative recommendations, and the recording is the finest of the three. At slightly less than full price this is very competitive.

The Classics for Pleasure performance has not quite the temperament of Moura Lympany's earlier, mono account, in which she was partnered by Malko; but this is a good, straightforward reading, helped by superb recording, with full, rich piano tone and excellent balance. There are many little touches of phrasing and dynamic shading to distinguish the orchestral playing, and the slow movement is notably beautiful. Just occasionally there is the feeling that the tension is *too much* under control, but this is only momentary, for clearly both conductor and soloist are in great sympathy with Rachmaninov's melodic inspiration. The three *Preludes* are admirably chosen and are very effective indeed.

Ashkenazy's earlier recording is disappointing. It is a relaxed, lyrical reading which rises to the climaxes, but it is seldom as compelling as the best versions. The *Études-tableaux* are attractive and very well played. With a sleeve-note by Ashkenazy himself and an excellent Decca recording (although not very convincing massed string sound), this will appeal to Ashkenazy's admirers rather than as a high general recommendation.

The partnership of Alexis Weissenberg and Karajan produces a reading which rises splendidly to the climaxes, notably in the first movement and the finale, but which elsewhere sustains the tension less readily. Weissenberg's thoughtful manner often seems too deliberate, although the slow movement produces some hushed playing which has undoubted magnetism. Taken as a whole this is not entirely satisfying, although the recording is vivid.

John Ogdon's sound is good, and the receded balance gives a very convincing illusion. He plays sensitively, introspectively, but there is none of the impulsive romantic virility which this work demands and which one would expect from a

younger player. Strangely enough, exactly this quality is paramount in the fine performances of the *Preludes* which act as a filler. These are a *tour de force*.

There is also an account by Entremont and Bernstein on CBS Classics (61026) but this has not the individuality and fire of this pianist's coupling of Nos. 1 and 4: in the last resort it is emotionally underpowered, although not wanting in technical brilliance.

Piano concerto No. 2 in C minor, Op. 18; Rhapsody on a theme of Paganini, Op. 43.
** (*) HMV ASD 2361. Agustin Anievas (piano), New Philharmonia Orchestra, Moshe Atzmon.

With splendidly rich recording this is an obviously attractive coupling, and certainly these are rewarding performances. The first movement of the concerto is the least convincing part of the performance, which is otherwise full-blooded and romantic; the *Rhapsody* is presented straightforwardly, and here the recording is particularly vivid to match the extrovert nature of the music-making. The famous eighteenth variation is passionately done, yet without creating a sense of anti-climax afterwards.

(i) *Piano concerto No. 2 in C minor, Op. 18;* (ii) *Rhapsody on a theme of Paganini, Op. 43.* (Piano) *Prelude in C sharp minor, Op. 3/2.*
* (*) Decca Phase 4 PFS 4327. Ilana Vered (piano), (i) New Philharmonia Orchestra, Andrew Davis (ii) London Symphony Orchestra, Hans Vonk.

Ilana Vered is a naturally expressive interpreter of Rachmaninov, but these performances are put out of court by absurd balance, with the orchestra heard faintly behind elephantine piano tone. In interpretation the *Variations* are more sharply pointed than the *Concerto*, where Miss Vered's style comes to sound mannered.

Piano concerto No. 3 in D minor, Op. 30.

- ** (*) Decca SXL 6555. Vladimir Ashkenazy (piano), London Symphony Orchestra, André Previn.
- (M) ** (*) Philips Universo 6582 006. Byron Janis (piano), London Symphony Orchestra, Antal Dorati.
- ** (*) Decca SXL 6057. Vladimir Ashkenazy (piano), London Symphony Orchestra, Anatole Fistoulari.
- ** Philips 6500 540. Rafael Orozco (piano), Royal Philharmonic Orchestra, Edo de Waart.

Ashkenazy's reading with Previn of the *Third Concerto*, played absolutely complete, is the controversial performance in his new complete set. In some ways his earlier account with Fistoulari is fresher, and the recording, if not so rich, is certainly clearer, but it showed a certain lack of spontaneity and emotional thrust. It is not so much the lack of spontaneity as an unevenness of approach that detracts from the new version. The recording too seems at times enveloped in a kind of romantic resonance, although at other moments (the opening of the finale, for instance) there is no lack of projection and brilliance. The performance has moments of great poetry – the *Adagio* shows a strongly passionate feeling – but also at times one senses (as in the climax of the first movement) some lack of coherence in the overall shaping, and certainly the slightly mannered statement of the work's exciting final section has the effect of broadening the music's forward impulse in a not altogether spontaneous way. The reading has moments of imaginative insight and touches of

sheer magic, but in the last resort remains not quite satisfying.

The Byron Janis/Dorati disc is unquestionably a most distinguished account of this lovely concerto, and one can only lament that the splendid (originally Mercury) recording, made on 35 mm. film, has been damped down in this new Philips transfer. The original was notable for its clarity, lustre and range. No doubt the upper strings needed taming by today's standards of smoothness, but this should have been left to the listener. As it is, although the piano tone remains excellent, the upper orchestral sound is now limited in range, even muffled in places, especially at the opening and close of the work. Even so the record gives rare pleasure. The surging romanticism from both pianist and conductor communicates readily, and in the great closing climax of the finale the passion is built up – not too hurriedly – to the greatest possible tension. Equally the romantic glow at the introduction of the second subject of the first movement is no less moving, and throughout the style of the solo playing and Janis's natural response to Rachmaninov's winding melodic lines is a constant source of delight.

Ashkenazy's earlier performance was obviously carefully thought out. The delightful principal opening subject sets off with a pleasing freshness, but in between bursts of strong romanticism, the tension relaxes a shade too much: one feels that the pianist miscalculates the emotional pressure required, and there is just not enough forward surge. One must emphasize that the playing itself is never dull and that the climaxes rise splendidly, with one of Decca's best recordings to contain them.

Rafael Orozco provides an essentially youthful approach, extrovert in manner, with bravura well to the fore. The recording is very bold and the piano tone is inclined to be slightly hard. The first movement lacks subtlety and atmosphere, and while the finale is undoubtedly exciting it is also somewhat aggressive; this is partly the fault of the recording balance, which is lacking in natural resonance and depth.

Piano concerto No. 4 in G minor, Op. 40.

⊛ (M) *** H M V SXLP 30169. Arturo Benedetti Michelangeli (piano), Philharmonia Orchestra, Ettore Gracis – RAVEL: *Piano concerto in G.****

As a performance this is one of the most brilliant piano records ever made. It puts the composer's own recorded performance quite in the shade and makes one wonder why the work has failed to achieve anything like the popularity of earlier concertos. The fact that the slow movement has a theme which is a cross between *Three blind mice* and *Two lovely black eyes* – one reason given for its poor impact on the general public – in no way justifies neglect, for it is a very beautiful movement, set between two outer movements which have a brilliance that even Rachmaninov rarely achieved. Michelangeli's performance of the climax of the first movement has an agility coupled with sheer power which has one on the edge of one's seat. The recording does not quite match the superlative quality of the playing, but in the new transfer it has been made to sound amazingly well, the piano tone clear and not hard.

Piano concerto No. 4 in G minor, Op. 40; Rhapsody on a theme of Paganini, Op. 43.

*** Decca SXL 6556. Vladimir Ashkenazy (piano), London Symphony Orchestra, André Previn.

Ashkenazy's special quality of poetry, searchingly individual, is at its most illuminating in this coupling. The performance of the *Fourth Concerto* is the finest on disc since Michelangeli's, and in the first movement the richness of the

recording and its detail (the tuba making a striking contribution to the first movement) score points over the outstanding HMV record. The *Largo* is played with a disarming, simple eloquence and the finale is characteristically assured. The *Rhapsody* is completely different in atmosphere from other current recordings, poetic and reflective in mood. Some might feel that the sound itself is wanting in sparkle: certainly the excellent Katchen performance – outstanding in its own way – has more crystalline clarity, the approach more robust and red-blooded. With Ashkenazy even the famous eighteenth variation is comparatively restrained, although its climax is not without ripeness. But the imagination of the playing is never in doubt, and this is a reading to become increasingly satisfying with repetition.

The Crag (fantasia for orchestra), *Op. 7.*

(M) *** RCA LSB 4090. London Symphony Orchestra, André Previn – *Symphony No. 3.****

Rachmaninov's *The Crag* (sometimes known as *The Rock*), written when he was barely twenty, is not fully characteristic, but it is worth hearing. Of the two recordings currently available, Svetlanov's is marginally the finer, but that is only obtainable in the box with the symphonies. Previn's account is also an eloquent one, finely played, and it has the advantage of a rather more refined recording.

5 Études-tableaux (orch. Respighi) *(La Foire, Op. 33/7; La Mer et les mouettes, Op. 39/2; Marche funèbre, Op. 39/7; La Chaperon Rouge et le Loup, Op. 39/6; Marche, Op. 39/9).*

** HMV ASD 3013. New Philharmonia Orchestra, Yuri Krasnapolsky – TCHAIKOVSKY: *The Storm; The Voyevode.** (*)

Rachmaninov himself authorized these orchestral transcriptions by Respighi, and at the same time provided Respighi with programmatic descriptions. The performances here are acceptable without inspiring great enthusiasm, and the recording, though good, is not particulary distinguished.

The Isle of the Dead (symphonic poem), *Op. 29.*
(B) * Decca Eclipse ECS 702. Paris Conservatoire Orchestra, Ernest Ansermet – LISZT: *Hamlet; Mazeppa.* *

Ansermet's account of *The Isle of the Dead* is not without atmosphere and intensity – the closing pages are notably well managed – but the pale recording does not help and the coupling is undistinguished. The finest performance of this work on disc is the composer's own (again available in the final album of RCA's integral Rachmaninov series), but Svetlanov's modern version has the advantage of excellent stereo and is beautifully played with plenty of atmosphere (this is now available only in the box with the symphonies).

Prince Rostislav (symphonic poem); *Scherzo for orchestra; Aleko* (opera): *orchestral suite.*
** (*) HMV ASD 3019. USSR Symphony Orchestra, Yevgeny Svetlanov.

The *Scherzo* is a very youthful work (Rachmaninov wrote it at the age of fourteen); the excerpts from *Aleko* date from 1892, when he was twenty, and the symphonic poem *Prince Rostislav* is also from this period. None of the music is as distinctive as the *First Symphony* of only three years later, but it makes an interesting addition to the catalogue and is well played and recorded here.

Rhapsody on a theme of Paganini, Op. 43.
(M) *** Decca Ace of Diamonds SDD 428. Julius Katchen (piano), London Philharmonic Orchestra, Sir Adrian Boult – DOHNÁNYI: *Nursery variations.****
(M) ** (*) CBS Classics 61040. Philippe Entremont (piano), Philadelphia Orchestra, Eugene Ormandy – GRIEG: *Piano concerto.* ** (*)

Rachmaninov's *Rhapsody* dates from 1934 and thus belongs to the same period as the *Third Symphony*. In many ways it is the most satisfying work the composer wrote for piano and orchestra, its invention consistently inspired. By virtue of the famous eighteenth variation, which turns Paganini's tune upside-down and imbues it with a lyrical intensity seldom surpassed in the composer's music, the work has remained high in public favour. The impact of this famous section tends to separate the rest of the music into two parts on either side of it, and this factor can sometimes throw a performance out of balance. But the Katchen performance with Boult is superbly shaped and is notable not only for its romantic flair and excitement but for the diversity and wit displayed in the earlier variations. There is no question of anti-climax after the eighteenth, for the forward impetus of the playing has tremendous power and excitement. Decca have, of course, merely repeated an earlier success, for a 1954 mono issue offered the same artists and coupling, with no less merit; that version is still available in an amazingly fresh-sounding Eclipse stereo transfer, ECS 668.

A strongly directed performance from Ormandy, with Entremont rising excitingly to the challenge. Ormandy is one of the finest of all concerto conductors, and this work suits him admirably. The forward momentum becomes increasingly compulsive but does not prevent a full romantic blossoming and the closing section of the work, after the eighteenth variation, is a blaze of excitement. The recording is not as naturally balanced as the Decca, but is of good quality, and if the Grieg coupling is suitable this is certainly recommendable.

Symphonic dances, Op. 45.
   (M) ** CBS Classics 61347. Philadelphia Orchestra, Eugene Ormandy – HINDEMITH: *Mathis der Maler.***

The *Symphonic dances* were written for the Philadelphia Orchestra and Ormandy, so their performance has some authority. It is superbly and idiomatically played, but the recording is a little congested in climaxes and does not do full justice to the sumptuous tone that this orchestra commands. Kondrashin's masterly performance on HMV Melodiya is the one to have, but it is available only in the five-record box including the three symphonies. Edo de Waart's version (see under *Caprice bohémien*) is quite marvellously recorded but is bloodless by comparison with either of these, though detail is carefully observed and phrasing meticulously studied; one feels that the LPO and in particular their strings need lots of vodka. Though the recording is less than ideal, the Ormandy/Philadelphia probably remains the better buy at present, and as the dedicatees their version has undoubted interest and authenticity.

Symphonic dances, Op. 45; Vocalise (for orchestra), *Op. 34/14.*
   (B) ** Turnabout TV 34145S. Dallas Symphony Orchestra, Donald Johanos.

These are pleasant, mellow performances recorded in a reverberant acoustic without much bite.

Symphonies Nos. (i; ii) *1 in D minor, Op. 13;* (iii; ii) *2 in E minor, Op. 27;* (iv; ii) *3 in A minor, Op. 44;* (iv; v) *The Crag* (fantasia), *Op. 7;* (i; ii) *The Isle of the Dead* (symphonic poem), *Op. 29;* (vi; vii) *Symphonic dances, Op. 45;* (viii; vi; vii) *The Bells* (cantata), *Op. 35;* (ix; iii; ii) *3 Russian folksongs* (for chorus and orchestra), *Op. 41.*
   (M) *** HMV SLS 847 (5 discs). (i) USSR Symphony Orchestra; (ii) Yevgeny Svetlanov; (iii) Bolshoi Theatre Orchestra; (iv) Moscow Radio Symphony Orchestra; (v) Gennady Rozhdestvensky; (vi) Moscow Philharmonic Orchestra; (vii) Kyril Kondrashin; (viii) Y. Shumskaya (soprano), M. Dovenman (tenor), A. Bolshakov (baritone), RSFSR Chorus; (ix) Bolshoi Theatre Chorus.

At the time of writing, the *First Symphony* is the only one of these discs available separately. All three performances of the symphonies are distinguished by their Slavonic intensity. The eloquence and power of the playing are deeply satisfying; the performance of No. 2 rivals Previn's, and the surge of rich Russian romanticism at the opening of the *Third*, together with great virtuosity in the finale, puts a seal also on this performance. The only serious reservation, which will concern some collectors, is the slightly raw quality of the Russian brass and woodwind, but the voluptuous string sound more than makes amends. With excellent performances of a number of important shorter works included, this is an indispensable set for Rachmaninovians.

Symphonies Nos. 1 in D minor, Op. 13; 2 in E minor, Op. 27; 3 in A minor, Op. 44; Vocalise (for orchestra), *Op. 34/14.*
   (M) ** (*) CBS 77345 (3 discs). Phil-

adelphia Orchestra, Eugene Ormandy.

Ormandy's set is also distinguished, and the performance of No. 1 is particularly commanding. But in the last resort the American manner of recording prevents unqualified recommendation; it is characteristically forward, sometimes with a touch of aggressiveness to mar the romantic warmth of the playing. Even so, at medium price this is a worthwhile set.

Symphony No. 1 in D minor, Op. 13.
  ** (*) HMV ASD 2471. USSR Symphony Orchestra, Yevgeny Svetlanov.
  ** (*) CBS 72571. Philadelphia Orchestra, Eugene Ormandy.
  ** (*) Decca SXL 6583. Suisse Romande Orchestra, Walter Weller.

The *First Symphony* was a failure when it first appeared, and the composer suffered so keenly that he suppressed the work, which only came to light after his death. Its merits are now well-known, and high among them must be the sheer originality and lyrical power of the eloquent slow movement. Svetlanov's is a sonorously recorded and well played account. The reservation made about the complete HMV set (see above) applies here, but this is a useful alternative to Ormandy's disc, which is a smoother and more voluptuous performance, with the CBS recording lending a slightly strident edge. Ormandy shows his affection in the luminous phrasing of the lyrical tunes, and the committed intensity of his reading, supported by superb orchestral playing, is compulsive throughout.

Weller's accounts of the three Rachmaninov symphonies are distinguished. But his fine performance of No. 1 suffers from the fact that the Suisse Romande Orchestra is unable to produce the body

and richness of tone that the slow movement ideally demands. The performance has subtlety and power and a fine feeling for the music's atmosphere (both inner movements show this readily). The recording is quite splendid, the finest available; its range and impact tell in the outer movements and never more vividly than in the work's dramatic closing pages.

Symphony No. 2 in E minor, Op. 27.
  ⊛ *** HMV ASD 2889. London Symphony Orchestra, André Previn.
  *** Decca SXL 6623. London Philharmonic Orchestra, Walter Weller.
  (B) ** (*) Classics for Pleasure CFP 40065. Hallé Orchestra, James Loughran.
  (B) ** (*) RCA LSB 4089. London Symphony Orchestra, André Previn.
  * (*) Decca SXL 6342. Suisse Romande Orchestra, Paul Kletzki.

Previn's newer HMV record sweeps the board; it is one of the outstanding Rachmaninov records in the catalogue. The passionate intensity of this reading, with rich sweeps of string tone, is immensely satisfying, and although the performance is richly romantic, the underlying feeling of melancholy is not glossed over. With splendid orchestral playing and vivid recording this is very highly recommended.

Weller's performance too is a fine one, more restrained, but genuinely symphonic in stature, with a dreamy poetic quality in the slow movement. Here the LPO strings do not match the eloquence of the LSO playing under Previn, but the slight reserve of the reading is not unattractive for repeated hearings, and Decca's recording is superb, finer even than the HMV, with greater inner detail achieved without loss of body and weight.

In the bargain range, Loughran's account makes an excellent recommendation. Although the performance takes a little while to warm up, this is a more intense reading than Weller's, with a fine slow movement, and the orchestral playing is excellent. The recording too is vivid and refined in detail. Loughran, like Previn and Weller, plays the work uncut and this gives his record the edge over Previn's earlier RCA disc, although that is slightly richer in sound. Recorded in the Kingsway Hall it has a fine glow, but the reading, although gloriously affectionate, is not as fine as Previn's later one and is disfigured by the cuts.

Kletzki shows more of a feeling for this score than his orchestra. When vigour and forward drive can make an effect, as in the scherzo or the climax of the slow movement, the music blossoms fully. But unfortunately the orchestral playing lacks refinement, and the second subject of the first movement has little charm. The clarinet solo in the slow movement is the very opposite of luscious, and Decca's close, vivid recording seems to emphasize the orchestra's faults instead of covering them in a warm glow of kindly reverberation.

There is also a recording by Boult with the LPO (ECS 594), but this sounds pale beside the other versions. The strings are thin, and this comparative lack of romantic substance in the orchestral tissue affects the music adversely, although Boult's reading has plenty of character and impulse.

Symphony No. 3 in A minor, Op. 44.
- (M) *** RCA LSB 4090. London Symphony Orchestra, André Previn – *The Crag.****
- ** (*) Decca SXL 6399. Suisse Romande Orchestra, Paul Kletzki – MUSSORGSKY: *Night on the Bare Mountain.****
- (B) ** Decca Eclipse ECS 573. London Philharmonic Orchestra, Sir

Adrian Boult – RIMSKY-KORSA-KOV: *Russian Easter Festival overture.***

Previn's account was made at the same time as his earlier version of the *Second Symphony*. It does not show quite the firm grasp on overall shape that distinguishes his HMV record of the *Second*, but the reading is very sympathetic and brilliantly played. The shaping of the second subject of the first movement is matched by the eloquence of the slow movement, and the bravura in the finale almost manages to make it sound completely convincing. The recording is first-class, with sparkle as well as richness, and with its useful coupling this is highly recommended at medium price.

Kletzki secures some fine playing from the Suisse Romande Orchestra and they are handsomely served by the Decca engineers. However, it must be admitted that in terms of orchestral polish and opulence of tone this orchestra is no match for its competitors, and the Moscow performance under Svetlanov (in the boxed set) or the LSO under Previn are the ones to have.

Sir Adrian secures the kind of sympathetic performance we have come to expect of him. He does not allow his own personality to intrude, but he captures the idiom with plenty of conviction. The LPO play well for him, although – as in his version of the *Second Symphony* – a greater breadth of tone from the higher strings would have been welcome. But the stereo is effective enough, warm-toned and colourful. The scherzo section of the second movement is particularly successful.

Piano trio No. 2 in D minor (Trio élégiaque), Op. 9.
- *** HMV ASD 3061. Yevgeny Svetlanov (piano), Leonid Kogan (violin), Fedor Luzanov (cello).

Svetlanov, forsaking the rostrum temporarily for the keyboard, is joined by Kogan and Luzanov to give a persuasive reading of Rachmaninov's magnificent *Trio élégiaque*. Though the brief finale of this elegy for Tchaikovsky fails to maintain the grand design of the first two movements, much of the score compares with the masterly *Cello sonata*, particularly in the restless ostinatos of the first movement.

Violoncello sonata in G minor, Op. 19.
　　(*) HMV ASD 2587. Paul Tortelier (cello), Aldo Ciccolini (piano) – CHOPIN: Cello sonata.* (*)

This work suits Tortelier better than its Chopin coupling; its passionate melodic lines are shaped with the right degree of nervous tension. Ciccolini sounds here rather more like an accompanist than a full participant, although his playing is technically secure.

Études-tableaux, Op. 33, Nos. 1 in F minor; 2 in C major; 3 in E flat minor; 4 in E flat major; 5 in G minor; 6 in C sharp minor; Op. 39, Nos. 1 in C minor; 2 in A minor; 3 in F sharp minor; 4 in B minor; 5 in E flat minor; 6 in A minor; 7 in C minor; 8 in D minor; 9 in D major.
　　(M) * (*) HMV HQS 1329. John Ogdon (piano).

The *Études-tableaux* find John Ogdon in less than his top form. The recording is of excellent quality, but readers will find Ashkenazy's readings (see below) more commanding and of higher voltage.

Études-tableaux, Op. 39, Nos. 1–9; Preludes Nos. 1 in C sharp minor, Op. 3/2; 21 in B minor, Op. 32/10.
　　** CRD CRD 1003. Janos Solyom (piano).

The Hungarian pianist Janos Solyom is now resident in Sweden, where he

recorded this recital. The playing is good, though not as impressive as Ashkenazy's or as imaginative. He is well but not outstandingly recorded; the acoustic does not give the sound much room to expand.

Études-tableaux, Op. 39, Nos. 1–9; Variations on a theme of Corelli, Op. 42.
　　*** Decca SXL 6604. Vladimir Ashkenazy (piano).

Superb performances from Ashkenazy make this the most desirable of Rachmaninov issues. The *Corelli variations* is a rarity and a very fine work which is not otherwise available. The recording is first-class.

Nos. 1, 2, and 5 of the Op. 39 *Études-tableaux* are also available coupled to the *Second Concerto* on SXL 6099.

Fantaisie, Op. 5 (Barcarolle; La nuit, l'amour; Les larmes; Pâques); 6 Pieces, Op. 11 (Barcarolle; Scherzo; Russian theme; Waltz; Romance; Slava); Prelude in C sharp minor, Op. 3/2 (arr. for piano duet by composer).
　　** Decca SXL 6618. Bracha Eden, Alexander Tamir (pianos).

A thoroughly worthwhile coupling of little-known but highly rewarding Rachmaninov piano duets. The *Fantaisie* dates from 1893 and was written during a summer spent in the country. It is an imaginative work with four titled movements, *Les larmes* being particularly memorable. The *Six Pieces* (written for four hands, one piano, but played here using two instruments) are immensely varied and sparkling with vivid ideas. They suit Eden and Tamir rather better than the *Fantaisie*, for the comparatively direct performance reveals much of the music's charm, whereas the approach to the *Fantaisie*, although conscientious and not without feeling, lacks something in spontaneity, notably in the final piece, *Pâques*, which needs more flair than this. Even so, with good recording this disc is well worth investigating.

24 Preludes (complete).
(M) ** (*) Unicorn UNS 230/1. Peter Katin (piano).

Katin is splendidly recorded, and the bold, clear piano image itself lends a certain romantic splendour to the pianist's conceptions. He has the measure of the lyrical music, and it is only in the pieces that make their full effect with sheer bravura that he is less than completely convincing. Anyone who has been swept off his seat in the concert hall hearing Sviatoslav Richter play, for instance, No. 3 in B flat major with unforgettable flamboyance will realize that Katin does not paint the full picture. But this comment applies to a few preludes only: for the most part Katin reveals with artistry what fine music there is to be found in this set of pieces.

Preludes Nos. 3 in B flat major, Op. 23/2; 5 in D major, Op. 23/4; 6 in G minor, Op. 23/5; 8 in C minor, Op. 23/7; 12 in C major, Op. 32/1; 13 in B flat minor, Op. 32/2.
*** DGG SLPM 138076. Sviatoslav Richter (piano) – *Piano concerto No. 2.****

Preludes Nos. 5 in D major, Op. 23/4; 16 in G major, Op. 32/5; 23 in G sharp minor, Op. 32/12.
(B) ** Classics for Pleasure CFP 167. Moura Lympany (piano) – *Piano concerto No. 2.** (*)

Preludes Nos. 6 in G minor, Op. 23/5; 16 in G major, Op. 32/5; 23 in G sharp minor, Op. 32/12.
*** HMV ASD 492. John Ogdon (piano) – *Piano concerto No. 2.* (*)

Richter's marvellous performances

make one hope that his complete recording, available in Europe, will soon appear in the British catalogue. The Lympany and Ogdon recordings are discussed under their coupling.

Piano sonata No. 2 in B flat minor, Op. 36; Études-tableaux, Op. 33, Nos. 2 in C major; 3 in E flat minor; Op. 39, No. 9 in D major; Moment musical in B minor, Op. 16; Prelude No. 1 in C sharp minor, Op. 3/2.
*** CBS SBRG 72940. Vladimir Horowitz (piano).

Horowitz has recorded a conflation of Rachmaninov's original and the revision he subsequently made of his *B flat minor Sonata*, and the result is predictably dazzling. Now that Ogdon's recording on RCA is deleted, this is the only version currently in the catalogue and it is unlikely to be surpassed. The miscellaneous *Études-tableaux* and other pieces on the reverse side, all recorded at public performances, are no less breathtaking, and even though there is the odd cough and the recording quality is not absolutely first-class, this is a record that no one should overlook. The playing beggars description and the music itself is thoroughly rewarding.

Suites for 2 pianos Nos. 1 (Fantasy), Op. 5; 2, Op. 17.
*** Decca SXL 6697. Vladimir Ashkenazy, André Previn (pianos).
(M) ** HMV HQS 1340. John Ogdon, Brenda Lucas (pianos).

A delectable coupling of the two fine *Piano suites* on Decca, beautifully recorded. The colour and flair of Rachmaninov's writing are captured with wonderful imagination – reflection of a live performance by Ashkenazy and Previn at London's South Bank Summer Music in the summer of 1974. John Ogdon and Brenda Lucas on HMV mid-price label are enjoyable too, but altogether straighter and less evocative.

Suite No. 2 for 2 pianos, Op. 17.
>*** Decca SXL 6158. Bracha Eden, Alexander Tamir (pianos) (with *Recital* ***).

This is an excellent performance, and it is part of one of the finest piano-duet collections in the catalogue, with music by Milhaud, Poulenc, and Lutoslawski. It is fully discussed in our *Treasury* volume.

Songs: *Again I am alone; Beside a new grave; Do not believe, my dearest; Do not sing, beautiful maiden; The fountain; Halloo; I am no prophet; I pray for mercy; The islet; Let us leave, dear one; The muse; The night is sorrowful; The Pied Piper – The ratcatcher; They answered; This day I remember; To her; To the children.*
>** (*) Argo ZRG 730. Robert Tear (tenor), Philip Ledger (piano).

Rachmaninov's songs are not so generously represented on record that we can afford to look askance at any addition to the catalogue. Christoff's fine anthology (HMV ALP 1830) enjoyed only a short life and was soon deleted. Robert Tear's collection duplicates Gedda in one or two instances but that is of little account. He is always sensitive and musical, shows a good understanding of the poetry, and only occasionally seems to suffer strain on top notes. Ledger's accompanying and the Argo recording are both of high standard; the artists are not too closely balanced and there is a pleasing ambience.

Songs: *The answer; Arion; Before my window; Christ is risen; Day to night comparing; The harvest of sorrow; How fair this spot; In the silent night; The lilacs; Loneliness; The morn of life; Oh, do not grieve; Oh, never sing to me again; Spring waters; The storm; To the children; Vocalise.*
>*** HMV ASD 2928. Nicolai Gedda (tenor), Alexis Weissenberg (piano).

Both Gedda and Weissenberg are searchingly illuminating interpreters of Rachmaninov here. If Rachmaninov's status as a symphonist is now increasingly recognized, his individual genius as a song composer – no mere imitator of Tchaikovsky – is almost equally striking. An outstanding selection here, well recorded.

(i) *The Bells* (cantata), *Op. 35. 3 Russian folksongs, Op. 41.*
>** (*) RCA ARL 1 0193. Temple University Choirs, Philadelphia Orchestra, Eugene Ormandy, (i) with Phyllis Curtin (soprano), George Shirley (tenor), Michael Devlin (baritone).

Thoroughly idiomatic performances of *The Bells* and the *Three Russian folksongs* by the distinguished soloists, the choir and the orchestra with which Rachmaninov was so closely associated. Both works are sung in English, and those who recall Kondrashin's Melodiya recording of the *Russian folksongs* will feel that something is lost. The Russian artists bring just that much more intensity, nostalgia and dark, rich sonority to this powerful music. However, the present disc is well recorded, and the Russian performances are only available as part of the boxed set of the symphonies (see above), so this will have a strong appeal for those who want these works only.

Vespers, Op. 37.
>*** HMV ASD 2973. RSFSR Academic Russian Choir with soloists, Alexander Sveshnikov.

Rachmaninov's *Vespers* (1915) must be counted among his most profound and fascinating works. The fifteen movements are superbly written and are as dark, deeply affecting and richly sonorous as any Orthodox Church music. The performances can only be called superlative, and it will be a long time before they are superseded. The basses in particular have incredible richness (at one point they sing a low B flat) and the recording is in an appropriately resonant acoustic. The recording is lively and has plenty of atmosphere, sometimes at the expense of detail, but no reservation should be put in the way of what is an outstanding record.

Vocalise, Op. 34.

** RCA SB 6804. Anna Moffo (soprano), American Symphony Orchestra, Leopold Stokowski – KHACHATURIAN: *Symphony No. 3* (***); RIMSKY-KORSAKOV: *Russian Easter Festival overture.****

A charming fill-up for an offbeat record, presented in Stokowski's characteristically sweet manner.

The Covetous Knight (opera): complete recording.

*** HMV ASD 2890. Lev Kuznetsov, Alexei Usmanov (tenors), Ivan Budrin, Sergei Yakovenko (baritones), Boris Dobrin (bass), Moscow Radio Symphony Orchestra, Gennady Rozhdestvensky.

This is a strong and powerful one-act opera, which comes over most effectively on record in a performance as idiomatic as this. The role of the miserly knight ('covetous' is really a mistranslation) was originally intended for Chaliapin, and though he never sang it, it presents a powerful character, surrounded as he is

in this ironic story (based on a Pushkin play) by a grasping son and a corrupt money-lender. In Soviet terms it presents an indictment of capitalism, but we can readily see it as a fine compact opera, almost as tautly organized as a symphony. Good, colourful recording.

'The world of Rachmaninov': (i; ii) *Piano concerto No. 2 in C minor, Op. 18:* 1st movement; 3rd movement (abridged). (i; iii) *Piano concerto No. 3 in D minor, Op. 30:* 3rd movement. (iv; v) *Rhapsody on a theme of Paganini, Op. 43:* Variations 16–18. (vi) *Symphony No. 1 in D minor, Op. 13:* 4th movement (excerpt). (v) *Symphony No. 2 in E minor, Op. 27:* 3rd movement. *Preludes:* (vii) *No. 1 in C sharp minor, Op. 3/2;* (viii) *No. 6 in G minor, Op. 23/5.*

(B) ***** Decca SPA 310.** (i) Vladimir Ashkenazy (piano); (ii) Moscow Philharmonic Orchestra, Kyril Kondrashin; (iii) London Symphony Orchestra, Anatole Fistoulari; (iv) Julius Katchen (piano); (v) London Philharmonic Orchestra, Sir Adrian Boult; (vi) Suisse Romande Orchestra, Walter Weller; (vii) Bracha Eden, Alexander Tamir (pianos); (viii) Moura Lympany (piano).

This is another of those Decca anthologies that succeed by clever arrangement of items. All the performances are first-rate, although the surprise is how well this transfer of the slow movement of Boult's performance of the *Second Symphony* sounds. Boult conducts the *Rhapsody on a theme of Paganini* too, and it was a happy idea to prepare for the famous eighteenth variation by including the two that come immediately before it. This is followed by (only) part of the finale of the *Second Concerto,* but the transition is painless. We have already had the first movement on side one. With generally excellent sound this makes enjoyable listening for any Rachmaninov-lover and avoids being just a selection of purple patches. Moura Lympany's performance of the *G minor Prelude* is a stereo transcription, but it sounds well.

Raff, Joachim
(1822–82)

Piano concerto in C minor, Op. 185. (Also includes HILLER: *Piano concerto*.)

> (M) Vox STGBY 666. Michael Ponti (piano), Hamburg Symphony Orchestra, Richard Kapp.

Raff's *Concerto* with its strong Mendelssohnian flavour is attractive enough, but the recording here precludes recommendation; it is shallow, with clattery piano tone. The Hiller coupling is no better. This disc is only of interest to dedicated Raffians: the performance itself is acceptable.

(i) *Ode to Spring for piano and orchestra, Op. 76;* (ii) *Symphony No. 3 (Im Walde), Op. 153.*

> (M) ** Vox STGBY 667. (i) Michael Ponti (piano), Hamburg Symphony Orchestra; (ii) Westphalian Symphony Orchestra; both cond. Richard Kapp.

Raff, now best remembered for one or two trivial pieces, was a prodigious symphonist. His writing in the *Third Symphony* is charmingly inventive, with many echoes of Mendelssohn and with consistently skilful use of the orchestra; it is a programme work of woodland scenes through day and night. The *Ode to Spring* makes an agreeable fill-up. The performances are warm and sympathetic,

though the recording could be more refined.

Symphony No. 5 (Lenore).

> (M) *** Unicorn UNS 209. London Philharmonic Orchestra, Bernard Herrmann.

The eleven symphonies of Joachim Raff have long been left in neglect, but Bernard Herrmann is an enthusiastic propagandist, and here thanks to the enterprise of Unicorn we have the chance to appreciate the colourful programmatic writing of what the surviving Raff enthusiasts often count the finest of the cycle. In some ways it is a very naïve work, based as it is on a high romantic ballad by the poet Bürger. A dead soldier lover calls for the girl he has left behind, and on a devil's ride he turns disconcertingly into a skeleton. The first two movements merely provide preparation for that dramatic development, and the third depicts the lovers' parting, with the main march heard first in crescendo and then diminuendo to represent the arrival and departure of a troop of the lover's regiment – a piece much beloved by the Victorians. A thoroughly enjoyable Mendelssohnian symphony, colourfully performed with clean and vivid recording and forward percussion.

Rainier, Priaulx
(born 1903)

String trio; Quanta.

> *** Argo ZRG 660. London Oboe Quartet – RAWSTHORNE: *Clarinet quartet.****

Quanta, a work for oboe quartet, is one of the toughest and most impressive pieces that Priaulx Rainier has composed. Here, writing in 1966, she develops on the technique of coagulating fragments (the scientific term of the title refers to that) which is seen at an earlier stage of development in the *String trio* of 1962. This is not easy music, and it is a pity the whole record was not devoted to Miss Rainier, but when the performances are first-rate (Janet Craxton an outstanding oboe soloist in *Quanta*) and the Rawsthorne work on the reverse is lyrically attractive in his off-centre manner, it is a disc worth investigating. First-rate recording.

Rameau, Jean Philippe (1683–1764)

Gavotte with six variations (orch. Klemperer).
** HMV ASD 2537. New Philharmonia Orchestra, Otto Klemperer (with BEETHOVEN: *Symphony No. 7* * (*)).

Though Klemperer is no baroque stylist, it is good to have his individual comments on Rameau in a piece he himself thought highly of. Loyal playing, beautifully recorded, though it is a doubtful purchase on a disc mainly devoted to a disappointing account of Beethoven's *Seventh* (see p. 113).

Suite from *Les Indes Galantes*; *Suite of dances* from *Platée*; *Dardanus*; *Zais*; *Zéphyre*.
(M) * (*) Oiseau-Lyre SOL 60024. Lamoureux Orchestra, Louis de Froment.

In 1730 Le Riche de la Pouplinière, a generous benefactor of the arts in Paris at that time, became Rameau's patron and took the composer into his service. It was La Pouplinière's contacts and backing that helped Rameau to make a name at the Paris Opéra. In return

Rameau organized frequent musical entertainments at his patron's home and it was no doubt for these occasions that the present suites of dances were selected. This highly elegant and very French music makes pleasant lightweight listening. It is nicely played here, although the recording tends a little to peakiness, especially on the first side.

Le Temple de la gloire: suite.
(M) *** Oiseau-Lyre SOL 297. English Chamber Orchestra, Raymond Leppard – GRÉTRY: *Ballet suite*.***

This is an enchanting record, and the demonstration-standard recording is fully worthy of the attractive music and the spirited, stylish playing. Rameau's score has much character, and the *Air for the Demons* is especially evocative. Raymond Leppard too gives us here an object lesson on how to perform music of this period. His springy rhythms and, especially, his use of the continuo to colour the texture are most imaginative. This is a record not to be missed.

Pièces de clavecin en concert: Premier concert: La Coulicam; La Livri; Le Vézinet. Deuxième concert: La Laborde; La Boucon; L'Agaçante; Menuet 1 and 2. Troisième concert: La Polpinière; La Timide, rondeau 1 and 2; Tambourin 1 and 2. Quatrième concert: La Pantomime; L'Indiscrète; La Rameau. Cinquième concert: La Forqueray; La Cupis; La Marais.
(M) * (*) Vanguard HM 36. Gustav Leonhardt (harpsichord), Nikolaus Harnoncourt (viola da gamba), Lars Fryden (baroque violin).

Good playing from these fine artists. However, the harpsichord should dominate proceedings and unfortunately it does not; Lars Fryden is balanced too close to the microphone, and his baroque violin sounds less than opulent in any event. There are more appealing Rameau discs than this in the catalogue.

Pièces de clavecin en concert: Nos. 1 in C minor; 2 in G major; 3 in A major; 4 in E flat major; 5 in D minor.
> *** Telefunken SAWT 9578. Frans Brüggen (transverse flute), Sigiswald Kuijken (baroque violin), Wieland Kuijken (viola da gamba), Gustav Leonhardt (harpsichord).

These pieces, published in 1741, have not been wholly successful on disc up to the present (though the two versions made with Rampal, one on Nonesuch with Robert Veyron-Lacroix, and the other on Fontana with Ruggiero Gerlin, had undoubted merits). This newcomer, however, has a surer sense of style and deeper understanding of the niceties of the period than any of its predecessors. It is recorded on period instruments but, rest assured, this is no dull, pedantic performance full of musicological rectitude and little musical life; on the contrary, it is scholarly but has genuine liveliness and authenticity of feeling. The music is, of course, utterly delightful and the recorded sound exemplary.

Pièces de clavecin: Suite (No. 1) in A minor (complete); Pièces de clavecin avec une méthode; Suite in E minor; Suite in D minor (both complete); Nouvelles Suites de pièces de clavecin; Suite (No. 2) in A minor; Suite in G major (both complete); La Dauphine (in G minor).
> ** (*) Argo ZRG 5491/2. George Malcolm (harpsichord).

Rameau's output for keyboard is neglected by the gramophone and its stature undervalued by even knowledgeable musicians. It is as fine in many respects as that of his great countryman and contemporary Couperin, and its inspiration rises at times to considerable heights. George Malcolm gives secure and brilliant performances, but purists – and even the general listener – should approach them with some caution. His ornamentation departs from the original in places, and the handling of *notes inégales* does not always carry conviction.

Harpsichord suites: in A minor (1728); in E minor (1724).
> ** CRD CRD 1010. Trevor Pinnock (harpsichord).

Excellent performances. Trevor Pinnock is more restrained in the matter of ornamentation than Malcolm, but his direct manner is both eloquent and stylish. The harpsichord is of the French type and is well recorded.

Castor et Pollux (opera in 5 acts): complete recording.
> *** Telefunken SAWT 9584/7. Jeanette Scovotti, Marta Schèle (sopranos), Zeger Vandersteene (tenor), Rolf Leanderson, Gérard Souzay (baritones), Norma Leren (mezzo-soprano), Jacques Villisech (bass), Stockholm Chamber Choir, Vienna Concentus Musicus, Nikolaus Harnoncourt.

Harnoncourt and his Viennese colleagues went to Stockholm to record this richly varied score, the second of Rameau's *tragédies lyriques*, telling the mythological story of Castor and Pollux, the heavenly twins, with many interludes for choral and balletic divertissements. Harnoncourt is a direct rather than a persuasive interpreter of old music. He brings edge rather than elegance to the music, underlining detail and contrasts of colour, with his refusal to smooth over lines in expressive legato. The result is fresh and immediate, helped by a strong singing cast. An invaluable recording of a masterpiece long neglected. Excellent clean recording.

Hippolyte et Aricie (opera in 5 acts): complete recording.

> (M) ** (*) Oiseau-Lyre SOL 286/8. John Shirley-Quirk (baritone), Janet Baker (contralto), Robert Tear (tenor), Angela Hickey (soprano), St Anthony Singers, English Chamber Orchestra, Anthony Lewis.

Rameau's operas are unjustly neglected, as readers who have heard *Dardanus* or the present work will know. Although his operas have their longueurs, they reveal a vein of melodic invention of the highest order and a harmonic sophistication that more than compensate for them. Readers will find the quality of inspiration strikingly well sustained in this opera, which is a work whose impact deepens on closer acquaintance. Few scholars have greater authority in this area than Professor Lewis, though scholarship is not always a guarantee of an inspired performance. On this occasion, however, he secures playing of genuine liveliness and feeling, and the St Anthony Singers too show a more than adequate response. Of the soloists, both Janet Baker and John Shirley-Quirk give pleasure, though the rest of the cast is uneven and their French is not uniformly good. Angela Hickey does not always seem to be secure, but it is only fair to say that such reservations as one has are more than outweighed by gratitude at having the opera available at last. The recording has admirable clarity and detail.

Hippolyte et Aricie: highlights.

> (M) *** Oiseau-Lyre SOL 321 (from above recording).

A generous selection from Rameau's splendid opera, moderately priced and excellently recorded. Readers who don't want to buy the complete opera should certainly invest in this well-chosen anthology of highlights.

Les Indes galantes (opera-ballet in Prologue and 4 acts): complete recording.

> *** CBS 77365 (3 discs). Anne-Marie Rodde, Rachael Yakar, Sonia Nigoghossian, Jeanine Micheau (sopranos), Bruce Brewer (tenor), Jean-Christoph Benoît (baritone), Christian Tréguier, Pierre-Yves Le Maigat (basses), La Grande Écurie et la Chambre du Roy, Jean-Claude Malgoire.

Jean-Claude Malgoire is a persuasively energetic scholar who brushes away the cobwebs from a ceremonial work so expansive that its richness can be masked in a dull performance. Rival scholars may argue about the text and instrumentation that Malgoire uses, and the recording is not ideally refined. But this vivid performance leaves no doubts of the continued vitality of Rameau's score, with its series of stylized tales of chivalry and love in the Indies. The spectacle of the opera-ballet as conceived in eighteenth-century France may be impossible for us to re-create today, but on record here, with some fine singing and enthusiastic playing, you get a far clearer idea than usual of its charms.

Zoroastre (opera-ballet): abridged recording.

> (B) ** Turnabout TV 34435S. Lou Ann Wyckoff (soprano), Nancy Deering (mezzo-soprano), Bruce Brewer (tenor), William Workman (baritone), Hamburg Chamber Orchestra, Richard Kapp.

Rameau's *Zoroastre* was written in 1749 and is set in Persia. The fairly generous selection here includes eight vocal numbers and an extended suite of ballet music. The invention is characteristically appealing and colourful, and with expressive singing of some charm from Lou Ann Wyckoff and an impressively flexible performance from Bruce Brewer (whose part is florid and lies high up in the tenor range) this is very much a worthwhile disc. Richard Kapp's direction is spirited and stylish, and the recording is good.

Ravel, Maurice
(1875–1937)

Collection: *Alborado del gracioso; Boléro; Daphnis et Chloé: Suite No. 2; Ma Mère l'Oye (Mother Goose): suite; Pavane pour une infante défunte; Rapsodie espagnole; Le Tombeau de Couperin;* (i) *Tzigane* (for violin and orchestra); *La Valse; Valses nobles et sentimentales;* (ii) *Shéhérazade* (song cycle).

(M) ** Decca SDDF 337/9. Suisse Romande Orchestra, Ernest Ansermet, with (i) Ruggiero Ricci (violin); (ii) Régine Crespin (soprano).

This compilation is variable in quality: the *Daphnis* fragments are a little lacklustre and *Le Tombeau de Couperin* could do with more polish. *La Valse*, on the other hand, is excellent, and Régine Crespin's account of *Shéhérazade* was highly acclaimed on its first appearance, though some readers will retain a preference for Danco's earlier recording with Ansermet. Ricci's version of the *Tzigane* is not among the anthology's successes. The recordings throughout are of the usual high Decca standard.

Alborado del gracioso; Boléro; Pavane pour une infante défunte; La Valse.

** (*) Columbia Studio 2 TWO 409. New Philharmonia Orchestra, Lorin Maazel.

(B) ** (*) Classics for Pleasure CFP 40036. Paris Conservatoire Orchestra, André Cluytens.

Maazel's are brilliant, extrovert performances of characteristic flair and intensity. The orchestral playing is first-class, the recording is spectacular, if slightly artificial in balance, but its sharp-edged glitter is especially effective in the *Alborado del gracioso*. The *Pavane* is played very beautifully. Maazel is rhythmically mannered at the climaxes of both *La Valse* and *Boléro*. The former lacks something in refinement but the latter has plenty of panache and excitement. This is a successful issue of its kind; however, the competition from Cluytens's excellent Classics for Pleasure issue is considerable, with its more natural sound balance.

Cluytens too gives a brilliant account of the *Alborado*, although his orchestral playing lacks something in precision; the *Pavane*, however, with its French french horn is slightly less appealing. In *Boléro* Cluytens maintains a consistent tempo: this is vivid and unaffected but in the last resort not as exciting as Maazel. *La Valse*, on the other hand, is most successful, rising to a climax of considerable intensity. The recording does not date; it is atmospheric with no lack of body or sparkle, and this certainly makes a very good bargain at the price asked.

Alborado del gracioso; Daphnis et Chloé: Suite No. 2; Pavane pour une infante défunte; Rapsodie espagnole.

*** CBS SBRG 72975. Cleveland Orchestra Chorus, Cleveland Orchestra, Pierre Boulez.

A distinguished record, among the best

things Boulez has done for the gramophone so far. Detail is sensitively shaped and the orchestra respond with splendid virtuosity to Boulez's direction. His *Rapsodie espagnole* is beautifully shaped and atmospheric in an entirely different way from Karajan's; the latter is heavy with exotic scents and sultry half-lights, whereas Boulez's Spain is brilliant, dry and well-lit. The recording is discreetly balanced and the woodwind, though slightly forward in the CBS manner, are kept in reasonable perspective. Detail is clear and although one could wish for a more expansive sound on climaxes, where there is a tendency toward shrillness, the quality is really very good. The range is wide, though not sensationally so as is the case with the Karajan. Boulez's *Daphnis* is beautifully done though it does not equal in magic or sense of poetry the Karajan DGG account. The *Alborado* is quite brilliant.

Alborado del gracioso; Daphnis et Chloé: Suite No. 2; Pavane pour une infante défunte; Rapsodie espagnole; La Valse.
> (B) ** (*) Decca SPA 230. Suisse Romande Orchestra, Ernest Ansermet.

Decca's collection, issued as part of 'The world of great classics' series, is exceedingly generous value at the price asked. The *Daphnis* suite is not as well played nor as sensuous as one might ideally ask (the latter being partly the fault of the clinical sound balance of the recording). The *Alborado* is less vivid than with Boulez. But Ansermet's coolness suits the *Pavane*, and the *Rapsodie* is quite effective. *La Valse*, always a piece Ansermet did well, is spectacular and atmospheric.

Alborado del gracioso; Pavane pour une infante défunte.
> *** Decca SXL 6287. New Philhar-

monia Orchestra, Rafael Frühbeck de Burgos—FALLA: *El amor brujo*; GRANADOS: *Goyescas*.***

Frühbeck de Burgos's *Alborado* is glitteringly brilliant, helped by one of Decca's best and most transparent recordings. The lovely *Pavane* is hardly less attractive, but this piece almost always seems to come off well on disc.

Alborado del gracioso; Rapsodie espagnole; Le Tombeau de Couperin; La Valse.
> *** HMV ASD 2766. Orchestre de Paris, Herbert von Karajan.

These are superb performances. The Orchestre de Paris respond splendidly to Karajan's sensuous approach to these scores, and only the saxophone-like quality of the French horns gives cause for complaint. The dynamic range is extremely wide and the acoustic somewhat too resonant. The atmospheric quality of these performances is not wholly free from a trace of self-consciousness, as if Karajan were admiring his own enormously subtle control of texture and colour. Still there is no doubt about the mastery of *La Valse*, which is extremely fine, or the *Rapsodie espagnole*, the best performance since Reiner's. The *Alborado* is a bit too slow (doubtless the reverberant acoustic prompted this).

Une Barque sur l'océan (from Miroirs); Le Tombeau de Couperin; Valses nobles et sentimentales.
> *** CBS Quadraphonic MQ 32159; Stereo 73212. New York Philharmonic Orchestra, Pierre Boulez.

Boulez has often struck us as being a little prosaic in Debussy; his well-defined detail somehow robs the score of its mystery. In this Ravel disc, however, he allows the music ample time to breathe; the texture has all the translucence and clarity for which Boulez is admired, and there is – in the *Valses nobles et sentimentales* and *Une Barque sur l'océan* – a genuine sense of magic. *Le Tombeau* is perhaps less successful. The CBS engineers provide an atmospheric recording, with plenty of space for the sound to expand and fine string quality. With recording and playing of this refinement, Ravel is well served, and the only reservation collectors may have is that the disc is not generously filled. As usual with CBS, the quadraphonic version adds extra glow and atmosphere.

Boléro.

> *** DGG SLPM 139010. Berlin Philharmonic Orchestra, Herbert von Karajan – MUSSORGSKY: *Pictures*.***
> *** Decca Phase 4 PFS 4048. London Festival Orchestra, Stanley Black – BORODIN: *Polovtsian dances*.***

Karajan's version is contained, but one feels the forward pulse and the impression is of quickening, yet a check reveals the tempo at the end has hardly varied from the opening bars (as the composer intended). The orchestral playing is very sophisticated; the trombone *glissandi* in the famous solo are thrown off without a wink and the overall crescendo is beautifully balanced. The DGG sound is still excellent, even at the end of a long side. Stanley Black achieves an exciting yet musical reading, with good solo playing and a convincing increase of tension, secured without increasing the tempo. The recording is superb, and its colour, impact and tremendous dynamic range put this among the very best versions.

Boléro; Ma Mère l'Oye (ballet): complete recording; La Valse.

> (M) *** Philips Universo 6580 106. London Symphony Orchestra, Pierre Monteux.

Monteux's complete version of *Ma Mère l'Oye* is a poetic, unforced reading, given a naturally balanced sound, though the recording is not quite so vivid as that given to Boulez by CBS or as translucent as Haitink's full-priced Philips account. But at medium price this can be strongly recommended, even though Monteux's reading of *Boléro* offers a quickening of tempo in the closing pages.

Boléro; Pavane pour une infante défunte; La Valse.

> ** Decca Phase 4 PFS 4226. Royal Philharmonic Orchestra, Claude Monteux.

Excellent performances from Monteux, but the Phase 4 recording, vivid though it is, with solo spotlighting, will not be to all tastes. The orchestral balance is basically good and so is the sound, but the perspective here is essentially for the audiophile.

(i) Boléro; (ii) Rapsodie espagnole; (iii) Tzigane (for violin and orchestra); (iv) La Valse.

> (M) ** Philips Universo 6580 031. (i) Spanish Radio and TV Orchestra, Igor Markevitch; (ii) Concertgebouw Orchestra, Bernard Haitink; (iii) Arthur Grumiaux (violin), Lamoureux Orchestra, Manuel Rosenthal; (iv) London Symphony Orchestra, Pierre Monteux.

This is certainly a mixed bag, but it is on the whole enjoyable. The highlight is the *Tzigane*; Grumiaux is a wonderfully pure player whose flawless intonation cannot be too highly praised. His performance of the *Tzigane* is very persuasive, although the recording is rich rather than sparkling. It is the lack of sparkle which tends to let down Haitink's otherwise very musical account of the *Rapsodie espagnole*. The recording for Monteux's

La Valse, although rather more immediate than the original SAL from which it is taken, is atmospheric rather than clearly defined. Markevitch's *Boléro*, an excellent, straightforward performance, is well caught by the engineers.

Boléro; Rapsodie espagnole; La Valse.
- (M) ** (*) CBS Classics 61027. New York Philharmonic Orchestra, Leonard Bernstein.
- * (*) DGG 2530 475. Boston Symphony Orchestra, Seiji Ozawa.

Characteristically brilliant playing from Bernstein – the American conductor at his most electric. There are few more compulsive versions of *Boléro* on disc, and the final cataclysm of *La Valse* is equally spectacular, with virtuoso orchestral playing to match. The reading of the *Rapsodie espagnole* is wilful and certainly not subtle, but there is no question about the sparkle, and one capitulates easily to Bernstein's magnetism. The recording lacks refinement and is raw in the treble. This has to be accepted in an early stereo recording from this source; the overall sound has plenty of breadth.

Ozawa's recording is of the most modern and is predictably refined and sumptuous. On grounds of recording quality the DGG disc wins hands down. But the performances are of a much lower voltage. *Boléro* lacks a compulsive forward thrust and *La Valse* exuberance. The *Rapsodie* too is rather undercharacterized, although the exciting moments are superb as sheer sound.

Boléro; La Valse.
- *** Decca SXL 6065. Suisse Romande Orchestra, Ernest Ansermet – DUKAS: *L'Apprenti sorcier*; HONEGGER: *Pacific 231.****

Outstanding performances, very well recorded. Both are also available on *The world of Ravel* (see p. 776).

Piano concerto in G major.
- ⊛ (M) *** HMV SXLP 30169. Arturo Benedetti Michelangeli (piano), Philharmonia Orchestra, Ettore Gracis – RACHMANINOV: *Piano concerto No. 4.****
- *** DGG SLPM 139349. Martha Argerich (piano), Berlin Philharmonic Orchestra, Claudio Abbado – PROKOFIEV: *Piano concerto No. 3.****
- *** Decca SXL 6209. Julius Katchen (piano), London Symphony Orchestra, Istvan Kertesz – BARTÓK: *Piano concerto No. 3.****
- *** CBS 72170. Leonard Bernstein (piano), New York Philharmonic Orchestra – SHOSTAKOVICH: *Piano concerto No. 2.****
- (B) * (*) Turnabout TV 34405S. Maria Littauer (piano), Hamburg Symphony Orchestra, Alois Springer – ROUSSEL: *Piano concerto.* (*)

There are some exceptionally distinguished accounts of Ravel's *Concerto* on record, but the first choice is clear. It was daring of Michelangeli to couple this neo-classical, jazz-influenced work with the sunset-glow of Rachmaninov's No. 4. In the event he plays both with superlative brilliance which yet has great sympathy for the tender moments. He achieves exactly the right compromise between inflating the Ravel work and preventing it from seeming 'little'. The opening whipcrack could have been more biting, but the orchestra generally plays with great vigour. The recording shows the same characteristics as that of the Rachmaninov but is if anything warmer. The exquisite playing in the slow movement (surely one of the most melting of all recordings of piano and orchestra) makes up for any deficiencies of dimensional balance.

Argerich's half-tones and clear finger-work give the piece unusual delicacy, but its urgent virility comes over more strongly by contrast. In the finale Katchen may catch the uninhibited brilliance more fearlessly, but in the first movements it would be hard to match Argerich's playing. The compromise between coolness and expressiveness in the slow minuet of the middle movement is tantalizingly sensual. Fine recording.

Katchen makes no apology for this as an allegedly light-weight work. He plays it forcefully and strongly, with a brilliance in the finale that would be hard to match, but there is real poetry in the central slow minuet – here made the work's emotional core – and the clarity of texture in the sound of both piano and orchestra gives the necessary Gallic point. The LSO under Kertesz is just as sparkling as the soloist, and the recording quality – with the piano balanced less forwardly than usual – is superb. With its excellent coupling, this is one of Katchen's most impressive records.

While not as brilliant pianistically as Michelangeli's incomparable interpretation, Bernstein's is a most beautiful performance, and with its equally enchanting coupling makes one of the most desirable of all records of twentieth-century concertos. It is astounding how in a modern concerto Bernstein performs the classical feat of conducting as well as playing the solo. One would never know from any lack of precision. As on the reverse the recording is well-defined. It is not new but was one of CBS's best.

A good performance by Maria Littauer is let down by undistinguished recording. There is a good rapport between soloist and orchestra, but the overall sound is dry, close and unexpansive.

Piano concerto in G major; Piano concerto for the left hand in D major.

*** Decca SXL 6680. Alicia de Larrocha (piano), London Philhar-

monic Orchestra, Lawrence Foster – FAURÉ: *Fantaisie for piano and orchestra.****

(M) ** DGG Privilege 2538 320. Monique Haas (piano), Orchestre National de Paris, Paul Paray.

(B) * (*) Classics for Pleasure CFP 40071. Samson François (piano), Paris Conservatoire Orchestra, André Cluytens.

* (*) CBS 73070. Philippe Entremont (piano), Philadelphia Orchestra, Eugene Ormandy or Cleveland Orchestra, Pierre Boulez.

Alicia de Larrocha's account of this popular coupling is the only one to find room (without loss of recording quality) for a substantial bonus, Fauré's *Fantaisie*, not otherwise in circulation. The performances of the two concertos are fine ones, and given Decca's first-class sound, this would seem a good investment, although the *G major Concerto* does not have the incandescence of Michelangeli's account (see above).

Monique Haas's accounts of the concertos are serviceable and welcome. They are more refined than Samson François's, have the advantage of good recording and their merits cannot be denied.

Samson François has full-blooded recording in his favour and good playing from the Paris Conservatoire Orchestra under André Cluytens. His spirited account of the *Left-hand Concerto* is really very competitive, given this price bracket, for although the piano is closely balanced, this is not at the expense of orchestral detail, which is splendidly vivid. He was not a particularly sensitive player, however, and there is little to recommend in his efficient account of the *G major*.

Entremont's account of the *G major Concerto* is insensitive and is crudely recorded. The *Left-hand Concerto* is, however, another matter. This is among the most highly characterized readings of the work currently before the public and can be confidently recommended. The recording here, too, is more satisfactory than the Philadelphia one.

Piano concerto for the left hand in D major.
>   *** Decca SXL 6411. Julius Katchen (piano), London Symphony Orchestra, Istvan Kertesz – PROKO-FIEV: *Piano concerto No. 3;* GERSHWIN: *Rhapsody in Blue.*** (*)

Katchen gives a brilliant account of the concerto and is most expertly accompanied by the LSO, under Kertesz and no less brilliantly served by the Decca engineers. This was his last recording, alas, and a splendid achievement. It is without doubt among the best versions of the work currently available.

Daphnis et Chloé (ballet): complete recording.
>   ✸ (M) *** Decca Ace of Diamonds SDD 170. Chorus of Royal Opera House, Covent Garden, London Symphony Orchestra, Pierre Monteux.
>   ** (*) Decca SXL 6703. Cleveland Chorus, Cleveland Orchestra, Lorin Maazel.
>   ** Decca SXL 6204. Lausanne Radio Choir, Suisse Romande Orchestra, Ernest Ansermet.

Monteux conducted the first performance of *Daphnis et Chloé* in 1912, and it is a matter for gratitude that his poetic and subtly shaded reading should have been made available in such an outstanding recording. The performance was one of the finest things Monteux did for the gramophone, and the richly sensuous and atmospheric orchestral and choral sheen Decca have provided is fully worthy of such distinguished and memorable music-making.

Maazel directs a finely moulded performance of Ravel's most magic score. His tempi in the brilliant numbers are fast, the precision of ensemble phenomenal, but elsewhere he indulges in a far more flexible style than is common with him. The result, helped by brilliant recording more atmospheric than CBS used to produce with this orchestra, is most impressive, though Monteux with the LSO is clearer, fresher and more idiomatic.

Ansermet is magnificently served by the Decca engineers but his account misses the rapture and magic that one recalls from his earlier Ravel records, and the Suisse Romande do not always play with the virtuosity or sensitivity this score must have. The recording, however, is quite superb and deserves a high rating.

Daphnis et Chloé: Suites Nos. 1 and 2; Ma Mère l'Oye (*Mother Goose*; ballet): complete recording.
>   *** Philips 6500 311. Concertgebouw Orchestra, Bernard Haitink.

Luminous recording, with beautifully focused detail, makes this an attractive proposition. The *Daphnis suites*, however, are just a shade wanting in atmosphere and sparkle. But the performance of *Ma Mère l'Oye* is very beautiful, with wonderfully refined orchestral playing.

Daphnis et Chloé: Suite No. 2.
>   *** DGG SLPM 138923. Berlin Philharmonic Orchestra, Herbert von Karajan – DEBUSSY: *La Mer; Prélude à l'après-midi d'un faune.****
>   *** RCA Quadradisc ARD 1 0029; Stereo ARL 1 0029. Mendelssohn Club Chorus, Philadelphia Orchestra, Eugene Ormandy – DEBUSSY: *La Mer; Prélude à l'après-midi d'un faune.****

*** Decca Phase 4 PFS 4220. LSO Chorus, London Symphony Orchestra, Leopold Stokowski – DEBUSSY: *La Mer*; BERLIOZ: *Danse des sylphes.****

Karajan's performance is outstanding among all others. It is one of the very best things he has ever done for the gramophone. He has the advantage of the Berlin Philharmonic Orchestra on top form and it would be difficult to imagine better or more atmospheric playing, which is coupled to a superb DGG recording.

Ormandy's account too is among the most magical currently available on disc. It rivals his wonderful account on 78s with the Philadelphia Orchestra, and along with Karajan it must be recommended as the best now before the public. The playing is impeccable, totally committed in every way, and the RCA recording is admirably balanced. The praises of this disc cannot be too highly sung.

The Phase 4 disc is first-class too – one of the finest issues yet put out on this label. Not only does Stokowski secure a glowing performance with sumptuous playing from the LSO, but the Phase 4 multi-channel technique is used to produce exactly the right disembodied, ethereal effect from the off-stage chorus. It is true that Phase 4 highlights some of the woodwind bird noises excessively, but with the chorus the pervading presence is richly satisfying. Stokowski takes the choral parts from the complete ballet version of *Daphnis*, rather than the usual *Suite No. 2*. He adds a *fortissimo* chord at the very end, but after such an involving performance few will grudge him that.

Daphnis et Chloé: Suite No. 2; Pavane pour une infante défunte.

*** DGG 2530 038. New England Conservatory Chorus, Boston Symphony Orchestra, Claudio Abbado – DEBUSSY: *Nocturnes.****

(M) ** CBS 61075. Cleveland Orchestra, George Szell – DEBUSSY: *La Mer.***

Abbado's performance of the suite is characteristically refined. His feeling for the music's atmosphere is matched by care for detail. The recording is natural yet vivid, and although the acoustic is resonant, there is no resulting inflation of tone and texture. This is a splendid coupling, and the disc is comparable with Karajan's (see above).

Szell controls the tension of the opening superbly, and Ravel's great tune unfolds in a magical arch, some curious points of detail being highlighted by the close microphones without the overall picture being spoiled. The playing throughout is extremely vivid, and while the performance misses the final degree of sensuous essence and mystery, it is very good of its kind.

Daphnis et Chloé: Suite No. 2; La Valse.

(B) ** Pye GSGC 15013. Hallé Orchestra and Chorus, Sir John Barbirolli – DEBUSSY: *La Mer.***

The Pye recording here is much more immediate than on the reverse. In *Daphnis et Chloé* Sir John uses a choir as well as orchestra, and his shaping of the great yearning string tune is characteristically sensuous. Perhaps the *Danse générale* has sometimes exploded with greater abandon in a live performance, but this is still very exciting. All in all, this disc represents a most successful and genuine bargain.

Fanfare for 'L'Éventail de Jeanne'.

** Decca Phase 4 PFS 4218. Hilversum Radio Philharmonic Orchestra, Leopold Stokowski – FRANCK: *Symphony.** (*)

Ravel's tiny fanfare makes a charming if irrelevant fill-up to the Franck *Symphony*. It was written in the late twenties for a children's play to which a number of French composers contributed pieces. It is good to have this one salvaged.

Ma Mère l'Oye (*Mother Goose*; ballet): complete recording; *Menuet antique; La Valse*.
    *** CBS 76306. New York Philharmonic Orchestra, Pierre Boulez.

Like Boulez's other recent CBS anthology (see above under *Une Barque*), this is extremely well recorded. The vivid detail in *Ma Mère l'Oye* reminds one almost of Ansermet's Suisse Romande records, although of course the orchestral playing in New York is of a very high order indeed. Boulez is at his very best in *Ma Mère l'Oye*, and this is now the finest account of Ravel's miraculous score before the public. The luminous textures of the gentle music are matched by the glitter and impact of the more dramatic moments of the score. *La Valse* is perhaps a less subtle performance, somewhat high-powered, but the *Menuet antique* has a pleasing directness of manner.

Ma Mère l'Oye: suite; Le Tombeau de Couperin; Valses nobles et sentimentales.
    (M) ** Decca Ace of Diamonds SDD 374. Suisse Romande Orchestra, Ernest Ansermet.

Eminently serviceable accounts, with the usual distinguished recording from the Decca engineers. The playing lacks the last ounce of polish and refinement, but at its price level the disc is well worth considering if this coupling is required.

Ma Mère l'Oye: suite.
    (B) ** (*) Classics for Pleasure CFP

40086. Scottish National Orchestra, Alexander Gibson – SAINT-SAËNS: *Carnival*; BIZET: *Jeux d'enfants*.***

Gibson is highly persuasive, shaping the music with obvious affection and a feeling for both the spirit and the texture of Ravel's beautiful score. The orchestral playing is excellent, the recording very good but wanting a little in atmosphere. But with its excellent couplings this is a fine bargain.

Pavane pour une infante défunte; Rapsodie espagnole.
    (M) *** Decca Ace of Diamonds SDD 425. London Symphony Orchestra, Pierre Monteux – DEBUSSY: *Nocturnes; Prélude à l'après-midi d'un faune.*** (*)

The LSO plays superbly for Monteux and he achieves a balance and a contrast between a mood of quiet introspection for the opening of the *Rapsodie* and a vivid, flashing brilliance for the *Feria*. The *Pavane* is wonderfully poised and played most beautifully. The recording expands and glows excitingly in Decca's demonstration manner.

Rapsodie espagnole.
    (B) ** (*) Classics for Pleasure CFP 169. London Philharmonic Orchestra, John Pritchard – CHABRIER: *España*; RIMSKY-KORSAKOV: *Capriccio espagnole*.**

Pritchard's account is a good one, poised, with a sense of atmosphere and very well played. The Classics for Pleasure recording is rich rather than crystal-clear in detail in the Ansermet manner, but it has an attractive sparkle, the castanets coming over exotically.

Le Tombeau de Couperin.
    (M) *** Unicorn UNS 253. London

771

Mozart Players, Yuval Zaliouk – STRAVINSKY: *Pulcinella suite.*** (*)

A delicately pointed chamber version of a charming score, perhaps the finest in the present catalogue. Zaliouk, a talented newcomer, draws from LMP a delightfully relaxed and smiling performance, especially in the haunting rhythms of the *Forlane*. Very good recording.

Tzigane (for violin and orchestra).
(B) ** Decca Eclipse ECS 670. Ruggiero Ricci (violin), Suisse Romande Orchestra, Ernest Ansermet – LALO: *Symphonie espagnole.***

A glittering, extrovert performance from Ricci, treating the music as a bravura display piece. This is certainly one aspect of the score, but there is an underlying refinement and an atmosphere which are passed by in this approach. The overall sound is clear but without a great deal of lustre. The finest available account of this piece is by Grumiaux (see above under *Boléro*), but that is comparatively indifferently coupled.

CHAMBER MUSIC

Introduction and allegro for harp, flute, clarinet and string quartet.
⊕ (M) *** Oiseau-Lyre SOL 60048. Melos Ensemble – ROUSSEL: *Serenade; etc.***
*** HMV ASD 2506. Melos Ensemble – POULENC: *Trio*; FRANÇAIX: *Divertissement.***
** Argo ZRG 574. Robles Trio, Delme Quartet – BAX: *Elegiac trio* **; DEBUSSY: *Sonata.* * (*)
(B) * (*) Turnabout TV 34161S. Helga Storck (harp), Gerd Starke (clarinet), Conrad Hampe (flute),

Endres Quartet – DEBUSSY: *Sonata*; ROUSSEL: *Serenade.* * (*)

The beauty and subtlety of Ravel's sublime *Septet* are marvellously realized by the earlier Melos account on Oiseau-Lyre, coupled to Roussel's almost equally delightful *Serenade* and music by Guy-Ropartz. The interpretation has great delicacy of feeling and is finely recorded. This is one of the most rewarding concerts of French music in the catalogue. The later HMV account is also first-class, and the couplings are equally attractive.

Although the Argo disc has the advantage of Marisa Robles as the eloquent harpist this is not as masterly a performance, or as well integrated, as the Melos Ensemble's. The recording, however, is excellent.

Bargain issues of this kind of repertoire are more than welcome. However, it must be admitted that the performance on Turnabout comes under the category of sound but undistinguished, and the recording is unappealingly balanced.

Piano trio in A minor.
(M) *** HMV HQS 1330. André Previn (piano), Yong Uck Kim (violin), Ralph Kirshbaum (cello) – SHOSTAKOVICH: *Piano trio No. 2.*** (*)

Previn and his young colleagues made this recording of one of the finest piano trios of this century as a by-product of their appearance at South Bank Summer Music, and the stylish zest of the playing reflects the flair of a live performance. Good recording.

String quartet in G major, Op. 10.
⊕*** Philips SAL 3643. Italian Quartet – DEBUSSY: *Quartet.***
*** DGG 2530 235. LaSalle Quartet – DEBUSSY: *Quartet.***
** (*) CBS 72998. Juilliard Quartet – DEBUSSY: *Quartet.*** (*)

(M) ** HMV HQS 1231. Parrenin Quartet – DEBUSSY: *Quartet.* (*)

(B) ** Decca Eclipse ECS 696. Carmirelli Quartet – PROKOFIEV: *String quartet No. 2.***

A gorgeous performance of the Ravel quartet from the Italian group, no less sumptuously recorded than the Debussy. The playing is perfect in ensemble, attack and beauty of tone. One of the most satisfying chamber-music records in the catalogue; this cannot be too strongly recommended.

But really there is little to choose between the DGG, LaSalle performance and the Italian Quartet on Philips, though perhaps the latter have the greater immediacy and sense of vitality. The LaSalle are beautifully recorded (as indeed are the Italians) and bring great freshness and delicacy of feeling to the score. This record can be safely recommended alongside the fine account by the Italians, though the latter remains a first buy.

The Juilliard Quartet offer a good but not particularly fresh performance. Oddly enough there is some less than perfect intonation (octaves slightly out of true) and a drop in pitch (obviously a different take) during the first-movement exposition. These are not serious flaws, but when finer and more perfect alternatives are on the market, both of them better recorded, the CBS disc seems naturally less competitive.

Without penetrating its mystical atmosphere to the full, the Parrenin Quartet give a committed account of Ravel's elusive work. The playing is sensitive to the delicate instrumental colouring, and, if not absolutely immaculate, the performance has spontaneity and conviction. The recording is clear and well defined.

With such superb accounts of the Ravel quartet in the catalogue as those by the Italians and the LaSalle it is tempting to pass over the Carmirelli. But this would be unjust, for their playing, if not

as distinguished as the Italians', is still very good, and the recording is perfectly acceptable even though it dates from the mid-1950s.

PIANO MUSIC

À la manière de Borodine; À la manière de Chabrier; Gaspard de la nuit; Habanera; Jeux d'eau; Menuet antique; Menuet sur le nom de Haydn; Miroirs; Pavane pour une infante défunte; Prélude; Sonatine; Le Tombeau de Couperin; Valses nobles et sentimentales; (i) *Ma Mère l'Oye.*

* (*) CBS 77380 (3 discs). Philippe Entremont (piano), (i) with Dennis Lee (piano).

CBS have deleted the Casadesus survey of Ravel's piano music, presumably to ease the path of this newcomer. Casadesus's recordings were made in the 1950s but still sound better than this, and the performances were infinitely more sensitive and distinguished. Entremont sets greater store by clarity of detail than atmosphere, and he is encumbered by a very close balance in a reverberant and unsympathetic acoustic. The opening of *Ondine* sounds brutally prosaic in his hands, and the set as a whole has very little to recommend it.

À la manière de Borodine; À la manière de Chabrier; Gaspard de la nuit; Menuet antique; Menuet sur le nom de Haydn; Pavane pour une infante défunte; Prélude.

** Decca SXL 6700. Pascal Rogé (piano).

This is the second of a series of records intended to cover Ravel's complete piano music. The playing continues to be sensitive but showing no special feeling for Ravel's keyboard nuance. The manner is unfailingly clear, but in the last resort the characterization has not the imaginative essence of the very finest interpretations. The recording is good.

Collection of piano duets: *Frontispiece; Ma Mère l'Oye; Rapsodie espagnole; Sites auriculaires: Entre cloches.*
> ** DGG 2707 072. Alfons and Aloys Kontarsky (piano duo) – – DEBUSSY: *Collection.***

As with the Debussy on the reverse side, the set is valuable in that it offers a number of rarities not otherwise available, including the *Sites auriculaires* and the *Frontispiece.* Unfortunately the dry acoustic and generally lacklustre sound diminish the appeal of this set.

Gaspard de la nuit.
> *** Decca SXL 6215. Vladimir Ashkenazy (piano) (with *Recital* ***).
> (M) *** RCA LSB 4113. Joaquín Achucarro (piano) – DEBUSSY: *Collection.*** (*)

A finely-shaped and sensitive account from Achucarro, not so magical perhaps as Ashkenazy on Decca but very fine indeed, and incomparably more musical than Entremont in the CBS box. An evocative *Le gibet* with its tolling bells, and good sound make this a useful issue at its medium price.

Ashkenazy's account, the finest since Gieseking's 78s, is available as part of a recital which includes music by Chopin and Debussy. This is discussed in our *Treasury* volume.

Gaspard de la nuit; Sonatine; Le Tombeau de Couperin.
> (M) *** RCA LSB 4096. John Browning (piano).

John Browning's fine Ravel recital is a welcome reinstatement: its life on the full-price label was all too short. His is playing of great refinement and elegance.

His *Gaspard de la nuit* is second only to Ashkenazy in sensitivity and brilliance, while his readings of both *Le Tombeau* and the *Sonatine* are totally idiomatic. The recording, too, is excellent.

Gaspard de la nuit; Valses nobles et sentimentales.
> (B) *** Turnabout TV 34397S. Abbey Simon (piano).

A fine bargain coupling. The piano tone, with only a touch of hardness in *Gaspard de la nuit*, is unusually good for this label, and it enables Abbey Simon to provide luminous tonal shading, both in the *Valses*, which are imaginatively done with impressive rhythmic flexibility, and in the eloquent and atmospheric performance of *Le gibet. Ondine* too is fresh and appealing, and *Scarbo* vivid, with striking bravura. An outstanding issue in its price range.

Jeux d'eau; Miroirs (Noctuelles; Oiseaux tristes; Une Barque sur l'océan; Alborado del gracioso; La Vallée des cloches); Pavane pour une infante défunte; Sonatine.
> (M) ** HMV HQS 1336. Daniel Adni (piano).

Daniel Adni's playing here is unexceptionable and thoroughly musical, and the recording is excellent. But the performances are undercharacterized, and this recital has not the distinction of Adni's companion disc of Debussy's piano music.

Sonatine; Le Tombeau de Couperin; Valses nobles et sentimentales.
> ** Decca SXL 6674. Pascal Rogé (piano).

A widely praised anthology of Ravel's music by this gifted young French artist. However, we have heard more imaginative and sensitive accounts of *Le Tombeau* and finer piano recording too. Good but not remarkable playing; the *Forlane* is not keenly delineated and characterized. The Decca engineers have not produced the most natural piano sound, and given these reservations, the disc is not among the finest anthologies of Ravel's piano music.

VOCAL MUSIC AND OPERA

Deux Mélodies hébraïques; Shéhérazade (song cycle).

> (M) *** Decca Ace of Diamonds GOS 602/3. Suzanne Danco (soprano), Suisse Romande Orchestra: Ernest Ansermet – HONEGGER: *Le Roi David.*** (*)

Suzanne Danco was one of the most intelligent, sensitive French singers of the post-war period, and her account of Ravel's exotic and elusive *Shéhérazade* is freshly authentic, the voice at its sweetest and brightest. This is a work that gains enormously from stereo, and even though the sound has an unnatural glitter to it, it is good to have it as a highly attractive fill-up to Honegger's oratorio. Generous to include the *Two Hebrew melodies* as well.

Shéhérazade (song cycle).

> *** HMV ASD 2444. Janet Baker (mezzo-soprano), New Philharmonia Orchestra, Sir John Barbirolli – BERLIOZ: *Nuits d'été.****
> *** Decca SXL 6081. Régine Crespin (mezzo-soprano), Suisse Romande Orchestra, Ernest Ansermet – BERLIOZ: *Nuits d'été.****

Janet Baker inspired Barbirolli to one of his most glowing performances in this atmospherically scored music. As in the Berlioz cycle on the reverse – given a peerless performance – Baker's range of tone and her natural sympathy for the French language make for heartwarming singing. Few records convey such natural intensity as this, and the recording is warm to match.

Crespin too finds a special sympathy for Ravel's magically sensuous writing, and she is superbly supported by Ansermet. As in the Berlioz coupling her style has distinct echoes of the opera-house, but the sheer richness of the singer's tone does not prevent this fine artist from being able to achieve the delicate languor demanded by an exquisite song like *The enchanted flute.* Indeed her operatic sense of drama brings almost a sense of self-identification to the listener as the slave-girl sings to the distant sound of her lover's flute (while her master sleeps). This is ravishing. The warm sheen of the glorious Decca recording spins a tonal web around the listener which is quite irresistible.

L'Enfant et les sortilèges (opera in 1 act): complete recording.

> (M) ** (*) Decca Ace of Diamonds SDD 168. Flore Wend, Suzanne Danco (sopranos), Hugues Cuénod (tenor), Pierre Mollet (bass), Motet Choir of Geneva, Suisse Romande Orchestra, Ernest Ansermet.

This is generally a performance of high quality with Hugues Cuénod, Pierre Mollet and Suzanne Danco all making distinguished contributions. The performance of Flore Wend in the central character of the Child is not ideally characterized, but Ansermet's direction shows this conductor at his most imaginative, achieving glittering colouristic effects from the orchestra and a wonderful relaxed tension over the performance as a whole. The recording is not always too well balanced, but this is partly the conductor's fault: the biting comments of the orchestra are sometimes over-enthusiastic to the detriment of the singers. However, admirers of Ansermet will still find this one of his most vivid discs: the *Cats' duet* on side two is memorable.

COLLECTION

'*The world of Ravel*': (i) *Boléro;* (ii; iii; iv) *Piano concerto in G major:* Finale; (iii; iv; v) *Daphnis et Chloé: Daybreak;* (iii; iv) *Pavane pour une infante défunte; Rapsodie espagnole: Habanera;* (i) *La Valse;* (vi) *Introduction and allegro for harp, flute, clarinet and string quartet;* (vii; i) *Shéhérazade: La flûte enchantée.*

(B) ** (*) Decca SPA 392. (i) Suisse Romande Orchestra, Ernest Ansermet; (ii) Julius Katchen (piano); (iii) London Symphony Orchestra; (iv) Pierre Monteux; (v) Chorus of the Royal Opera House, Covent Garden; (vi) Osian Ellis (harp), Melos Ensemble; (vii) Régine Crespin (soprano).

This ingenious Ravel anthology, cunningly assembled by Ray Crick of Decca, has two small drawbacks. It begins, understandably, with Monteux's gorgeous opening to *Daphnis et Chloé,* but because this is taken from a complete set and not a suite, it has to be faded. Also there is a slight miscalculation in including Katchen's brilliant account of the *Piano concerto* finale at the end of side one, immediately following the wonderful sense of stillness of the closing bars of the *Introduction and allegro.* Although the idea of complete contrast is good in theory, in practice this jars on the listener's sensibility. Having said that, one must add that the collection is a marvellous bargain including as it does Ansermet's two best Ravel performances, *Boléro* and *La Valse,* Monteux's beautiful *Pavane,* the incomparable Melos account of the *Introduction and allegro,* and a reminder of Crespin's dramatic account

of the song cycle *Shéhérazade.* The sound is of the highest class, although the end of *Boléro* (which comes at the close of a long side) is perhaps not quite as clean here as on some other discs (it is used on several).

Rawsthorne, Alan
(1905–71)

Symphony No. 3.
*** Argo ZRG 553. BBC Symphony Orchestra, Norman Del Mar – GERHARD: *Concerto for orchestra.****

This is one of the most impressive records of modern British music sponsored by the British Council. Gerhard's *Concerto for orchestra* is the more adventurous piece, an astonishing feat of imagination for a septuagenarian and intensely rewarding in its avant-garde 'difficulty', but the Rawsthorne too is most satisfying. Though the actual thematic material is sometimes hard to identify (it is possibly too consistent in style and cut for conventional ideas of sonata-form) the formal layout of the work is never in doubt. Even a newcomer to the work will find his way around very easily. The first movement culminates in a calm recapitulation that resolves earlier tensions most satisfyingly, and the separate variations of the *Sarabande* slow movement build up into one of the most passionate climaxes that Rawsthorne ever wrote. A scherzo with nebulous, rather Waltonian motifs flying around is followed by a finale that daringly keeps changing gear between fast and slow. It is questionable whether Rawsthorne keeps the flow of argument going with sufficient momentum in this movement, but there is no doubt whatever of the beauty and effectiveness of the hushed epilogue. Both works receive superb performances and outstanding recording.

Clarinet quartet.

    *** Argo ZRG 660. Thea King (clarinet), members of the Aeolian Quartet – RAINIER: *String trio; Quanta.****

The clarinet quintet medium has produced a series of masterpieces; but Rawsthorne dispenses with the second violin and opts for the more compressed form of the clarinet quartet. This balances the ensemble clearly in favour of the wind instrument, but here Thea King, one of the most sensitive of clarinettists, responds to that position of prominence with intensely imaginative playing, drawing out the lyricism which reveals Rawsthorne's deep understanding of the instrument. Excellent recording.

(i) *Concertante for piano and violin; Trio for piano, violin and cello;* (ii) *4 Romantic pieces; Sonatina; Theme and four studies.*

    *** Argo ZRG 743. (i) Cardiff Festival Ensemble; (ii) Martin Jones (piano).

This is a valuable and readily approachable sample of Rawsthorne's chamber and piano music, spanning the years 1935 to 1962. The most ambitious piece is the last, the *Piano trio*, strongly constructed from sharply alternating sections and beautifully written for the instruments. Even the earliest work, the *Concertante for piano and violin*, is distinctively Rawsthornian, and the piano works, alertly played by Martin Jones, fill in a good composite portrait. Good recording.

(i) *Piano quintet;* (ii) *Violoncello sonata* (for cello and piano).

    (B) ** Pye GSGC 14107. (i) Cardiff University Ensemble; (ii) George Isaac (cello), Eric Harrison (piano)
    HODDINOTT: *Quartet No. 1; Clarinet sonata.***

Rawsthorne's *Piano quintet* is one of his last works, a strong piece specially commissioned for the Cardiff University Ensemble. Its clean, refined textures make a significant contrast with the example of Rawsthorne's earlier style in the *Cello sonata*, written in 1949. In keeping with the character of the solo instrument it is a passionate, warm-hearted work, well played and recorded here.

String quartets Nos. 1 (Theme and variations); 2; 3.

    ** Argo ZRG 5489. Alberni Quartet.

The three string quartets of Alan Rawsthorne span his whole creative career, and it says much for his stylistic consistency that they stand together here in harness so well. The *First*, written in 1939, is a set of six variations, with contrasts used to parallel the natural dichotomy of sonata-form. The *Second Quartet* of 1954 was the culmination of a period when Rawsthorne had come to write more happily in large-scale sonata-form, with his most lyrical vein running freely in the middle movements. The *Third Quartet* of 1965, the longest and most ambitious of the three, is in four movements played without a break, with the opening six bars providing the germ-material for the whole work. Every bar of all three works is finely wrought, and it is a pity the playing of the Alberni Quartet does not quite come up to expectations. This is a promising, vigorous young group (named after the town in Canada where the leader was born) but for recording purposes they have their rough side, which the superbly clear Argo recording tends to show up.

Reger, Max
(1873–1916)

Ballet suite, Op. 130; (i) *Concerto in the old style, Op. 123.*

** (*) RCA SB 6878. Berlin State Orchestra, Otmar Suitner, (i) with Karl Suske, Heinz Schunk (violins).

The Reger centenary celebrations were relatively muted in this country though they were extensive and exhaustive in Germany. Those who think of Reger's scoring as thick and unimaginative and his musical processes as Teutonic and laboured should listen to the *Ballet suite*. True, it is let down by its last two movements, but the remainder (in particular the *Pierrot et Pierrette*, the fourth of the six movements) is of so high an order of inspiration and evinces such delicacy of feeling that one regrets the subsequent decline even more acutely. The playing is thoroughly committed, and the *Concerto in the old style* is also persuasively done under Otmar Suitner. The RCA recording, which stems from the Ariola catalogue, is extremely good, though it falls short of being distinguished.

Ballet suite, Op. 130; Variations and fugue on a theme of Hiller, Op. 100; Variations and fugue on a theme of Mozart, Op. 132.

(M) ** Telefunken TK 11520 (2 discs). Bamberg Symphony or Hamburg Philharmonic Orchestras, Joseph Keilberth.

Both the *Mozart* and the *Hiller variations* are masterpieces, and the *Ballet suite* has many delightful things to commend it. Keilberth's performances are serviceable rather than inspired, and much the same can be said of the recordings, which are not of recent provenance.

However, the set is not expensive and yields very acceptable results. Neither set of variations is otherwise available.

(i) *3 Canons and fugues in the old style, for 2 violins, Op. 13b, Nos. 1 in E minor; 2 in D minor; 3 in A major;* (ii) *Serenades for flute, violin and viola Nos. 1 in D major, Op. 77a; 2 in G major, Op. 141a.*

(B) ** Turnabout TV 37056S. Susanne Lautenbacher (violin), with (i) Georg Egger (violin), (ii) Aurèle Nicolet (flute), Ulrich Koch (viola).

Clarinet quintet in A major, Op. 146.

(B) ** Oryx ORYX 1832. Rudolf Gall (clarinet), Keller Quartet.

Clarinet quintet in A major, Op. 146; Allegro for 2 violins in A major, Op. posth.

(B) ** Turnabout TV 37058S. Bell' Arte Ensemble (with Susanne Lautenbacher, Georg Egger, violins).

String trios Nos. 1 in A minor, Op. 77b; 2 in D minor, Op. 141b.

(B) ** Turnabout TV 37057S. Bell' Arte String Trio.

The first three discs in this admirable Turnabout survey of Reger chamber music give us the *Serenades, Op. 77a* and *Op. 141a*, as well as their companion trios. The third disc offers a bargain version of the *Clarinet Quintet, Op. 146*. Those who imagine Reger's writing is as laboured and congested as legend has it will be agreeably surprised by the translucence and warmth of these pieces. The *String trios* are delightful pieces, fresh and engaging on the surface with moments of genuine depth, and anyone who enjoys the nineteenth-century classical repertoire from Schumann, Brahms, Dvořák onwards will not feel in the least out of his depth.

The performances are all first-class and although the recording is not quite as distinguished as the players deserve, it can be made to yield acceptable results by judicious use of the controls. The overall sound is a little dry.

With the *Clarinet quintet*, a reflective, thoughtful work which will reward study, one comes up against competition from the Oryx version, Rudolf Gall's old recording made with the Keller Quartet in the early 1960s. This is good, and the recording is rather smoother than the Turnabout and nicely balanced, if less well detailed.

String quartets Nos. 1 in G minor, Op. 54; 4 in E flat major, Op. 109.
    (B) ** Turnabout TV 37059S. Reger Quartet.
String quartets Nos. 2 in A major, Op. 54; 5 in F sharp minor, Op. 121.
    (B) ** Turnabout TV 37060S. Reger Quartet.
String quartet No. 3 in D minor, Op. 74.
    (B) ** Turnabout TV 37061S. Reger Quartet.

The last three Turnabout discs present all five Reger quartets, fine works fashioned with superb musical craftsmanship and discipline. The same strictures apply to the recordings as to the first three issues, but the playing is eminently satisfactory and the music, particularly in No. 5 in F sharp minor, and the delightful E flat quartet that precedes it – it is richly melodious and resourceful – should not be passed over. The last quartet, Op. 74, is the longest – and some say the finest – of Reger's quartets, and the excellence of the performance by the eponymous group on Turnabout is not in question.

Toccata and fugue, Op. 59/5 and 6; Fantasia on the chorale 'Straf mich nicht in deinem Zorn', Op. 40/2.

** (*) Argo ZRG 5420. Simon Preston (organ) – REUBKE: *Sonata on the 94th Psalm.*** (*)

This is not particularly inspired music, relying for its main effect on strong, dramatic dynamic contrasts. Here Argo's recording certainly accommodates Simon Preston's spectacular dynamics without a shudder.

Reinecke, Carl
(1824–1910)

Harp concerto in E minor, Op. 182.
    *** DGG SLPM 138853. Nicanor Zabaleta (harp), Berlin Philharmonic Orchestra, Ernst Märzendorfer – MOZART: *Concerto for flute and harp.****

Zabaleta's performance is an outstanding one and it is beautifully recorded here. If the coupling is attractive this is a highly recommendable disc.

Respighi, Ottorino
(1879–1936)

Adagio con variazioni (for cello and orchestra).
    (M) ** Supraphon SUAST 50689. André Navarra (cello), Czech Philharmonic Orchestra, Karel Ančerl – PROKOFIEV: *Symphony-Concerto.***

This short but charming set of variations shows Respighi in top form. It is an Italianate equivalent of Tchaikovsky's *Rococo variations* and has a burst of almost Russian romantic expressiveness to make a sunset-like ending. It is well played here and the recording, if not especially immediate, is good.

Ancient airs and dances (for lute – arr. for orchestra): *Suite No. 3.*

** Pye Ensayo NEL 2012. English Chamber Orchestra, Enrique Asensio – BRITTEN: *Simple symphony*; HINDEMITH: *5 Pieces.***

This is perhaps the most striking of the three performances on this quite attractive Pye disc. The conductor's approach is rather literal in manner, but the playing is vivid and the slightly pungent sound projects the music well.

The Birds (suite); *Church Windows* (symphonic impressions).

(M) ** CBS Classics 61082. Philadelphia Orchestra, Eugene Ormandy.

This disc offers a suitable contrast of simplicity and flamboyance. The four-movement suite *Church Windows* is not a masterpiece of the order of the *Pines* or *Fountains*, but it shows the same brilliant feeling for orchestral colour. The picture of the baby Jesus in *The flight into Egypt* has a Latin intensity of feeling, and in the second movement the conception of *St Michael*, flaming sword in hand, is indulgent. The finale, a papal blessing scene, is on the largest scale. Ormandy rises to the occasion and the spectacular – if slightly harsh – recording is a match for the Philadelphia big guns. *The Birds* is slighter but charming, especially in the *Cuckoo* evocation. Again brilliant sound.

The Birds (suite); *The Fountains of Rome* (symphonic poem); *The Pines of Rome* (symphonic poem).

*** Decca SXL 6401. London Symphony Orchestra, Istvan Kertesz.

Those who tend to undervalue Respighi's two pictorial masterpieces drawn from Roman scenes as 'picture postcard music' will surely think again when they hear Kertesz's deeply musical approach

to these two scores. He is helped, admittedly, by one of the finest recordings to come from Decca, and the warm, almost plushy beauty of the orchestral textures can burst into iridescent brilliance at the turning on of the Triton fountain, for instance. Equally the engineers contain the great climax of the Trevi fountain (the 'difficult' underlying sustained drum roll beautifully balanced) with sumptuous ease. There are few grander moments in programme music than this picture of the triumphal procession across the heavens of Neptune's chariot. Kertesz creates a magical sense of atmosphere in the central sections of *The Pines*; seldom before has the entry of the nightingale's song been so beautifully prepared, and if the tension is held a little slackly in the finale, one can look elsewhere for extrovert brilliance. *The Birds* had been absent from the catalogues for too long, and again the rich, smooth – almost plushy – recording helps the warmth of Kertesz's approach. Altogether an outstanding collection.

Feste romane.

(M) *** RCA LSB 4109. Los Angeles Philharmonic Orchestra, Zubin Mehta – R. STRAUSS: *Don Juan.****

This was one of Mehta's first recordings with the orchestra of which he became principal conductor in his twenties. Its flair for display is irresistible in one of Respighi's most brilliant – if musically empty – showpieces. Bright recording to match.

The Fountains of Rome (symphonic poem).

(B) *** Classics for Pleasure CFP 40204. Philharmonia Orchestra, Sir Eugene Goossens – ROSSINI: *La Boutique fantasque.* (*)

This is a distinguished performance, beautifully played, atmospheric and with an impressive central climax, spaciously conceived. The recording has body and lustre and is naturally balanced, far superior to that of the coupling.

The Fountains of Rome (symphonic poem); *The Pines of Rome* (symphonic poem).

(B) *** RCA Victrola VICS 1565. Chicago Symphony Orchestra, Fritz Reiner.

This is a truly marvellous disc. Reiner gives memorable performances of both works, sensitive and evocative in the quieter music and exciting and spectacular in the big climaxes. The recording is wonderfully atmospheric, and the slightly recessed orchestral picture adds to the magic of the playing. The climax of *The pines of the Appian way* is prepared with subtlety, the tension carefully controlled, and when the big moment comes it is emotionally overwhelming. Yet the recording reproduces with ease. Equally in the companion work, the iridescent brilliance of the turning on of the Triton fountain is matched by the moment of splendour of the passing of Neptune's chariot. An outstanding bargain.

There are also records by Munch (Decca Phase 4 PFS 4131) and Ansermet (Decca SPA 227), but vivid though they are, they cannot compare with the Reiner disc, which also has the advantage of economy.

Rossiniana (suite arr. from piano pieces by Rossini: *Quelques riens pour album*).

* (*) Decca SXL 6312. Suisse Romande Orchestra, Ernest Ansermet – TCHAIKOVSKY: *Suite No. 4.***

This suite is seldom played, whereas *La Boutique fantasque* is almost over-familiar. The reason is not hard to find. Respighi displays a similar subtlety and skill in his orchestrations, but the music itself (taken from late Rossini piano music) is rather slight. Of the four pieces which make up *Rossiniana* only the final *Tarantella* has the panache of *La Boutique*. Ansermet's performance is at its best in the central movement, but the orchestral playing is not especially polished; the coupling is ingenious, but the recording tends to over-brilliance in the finale.

Reubke, Julius
(1834–58)

Sonata on the 94th Psalm.

(B) *** Saga 5340. Peter le Huray (organ of Salisbury Cathedral) – LISZT: *Variations on 'Weinen, Klagen'.****

** (*) Argo ZRG 5420. Simon Preston (organ) – REGER: *Toccata and fugue etc.** (*)

Psalm 94 (which opens 'O Lord God, to whom vengeance belongeth' and closes 'But the Lord is my refuge . . . the Lord shall destroy them' [the ungodly]), seems admirably suited as the basis for a large-scale piece of nineteenth-century keyboard rhetoric. Reubke's *Sonata* is far from being great music, but in the hands of an imaginative player like Peter le Huray – whose feeling for atmosphere is as impressive as his technical control – it can be quite a *tour de force*. Certainly the Saga recording is splendidly managed and the surfaces on our review copy were good. An exciting disc. Simon Preston's account is also recommendable and marvellously recorded, but it is less compulsive than the Saga, which also has a considerable price advantage.

Rheinberger, Josef
(1839–1901)

Organ concertos in F major, Op. 137; in G minor, Op. 177.

> (M) ** (*) CBS Classics 61574. E. Power Biggs (organ), Columbia Symphony Orchestra, Maurice Peress.

Although uneven in inspiration, and with a quality of invention that is not always too sophisticated, these two organ concertos of Rheinberger are certainly enjoyable when played with such gusto and aplomb, as is provided here by Mr Biggs. The CBS balance is not very natural, with the organ very forward, but the orchestral writing is attractively flamboyant, and Maurice Peress often matches the exuberance of his soloist. The writing itself reminds one somewhat of Saint-Saëns, although neither the melodic flow nor the construction shows that composer's easy mastery of style. But if the music has a few laboured patches, this is certainly a disc for organ-lovers to investigate.

Fugues, Op. 123, Nos. 1–3; Meditation, Op. 167/10; Monologue in B minor, Op. 162; Passacaglia in E minor; Organ sonata No. 11 in D minor, Op. 148: Cantilene in F major; Organ sonata No. 17 in B major, Op. 181 (complete); Trios, Op. 49/1 and 2.

> (B) * (*) Oryx ORYX 1815. Martin Weyer (Josef Rheinberger organ, Vaduz, Liechtenstein).

Martin Weyer is not the most imaginative of organists, and his somewhat plodding manner in the fugues (including the one which comes at the end of the *Sonata*) is characteristic of his studied approach to this essentially romantic music. He is at his best in the bright *Cantilene* which opens side two, a somewhat trivial but not unattractive voluntary. Elsewhere his registration sometimes suggests the atmosphere of a church before the minister has arrived to begin the service. The *Sonata No. 17 in B major*, which takes up a whole side, is a comparatively ambitious piece that would no doubt readily flower in more persuasive hands. The recording is excellent, and this disc does at least enlarge our knowledge of a far from insignificant organ composer.

Riegger, Wallingford
(1885–1961)

Dichotomy for chamber orchestra, Op. 12.

> *** Argo ZRG 702. London Sinfonietta, Frederick Prausnitz – MUSGRAVE: *Night music;* SESSIONS: *Rhapsody; Symphony No. 8.****

Wallingford Riegger, an American who away from the Viennese stream adopted and developed a form of serialism of his own, is an interesting figure. *Dichotomy* was the first of his serial works; it is strong, dramatic and involving, and is well played and recorded here.

Ries, Ferdinand
(1784–1838)

Piano concerto No. 3 in C sharp minor, Op. 55.

> (B) ** Turnabout TV 34526S. Maria Littauer (piano), Hamburg Symphony Orchestra, Alois Springer – MAYR: *Piano concerto No. 1.*⊛ ***

Ferdinand Ries had a varied and fascinatingly successful career, beginning as Beethoven's protégé (he was eventually to write an admired set of *Biographical Notices*) and going on to found a successful career as composer/pianist in England before returning to his homeland, where he continued to prosper as musical director of a series of music festivals on the Lower Rhine. He wrote nine piano concertos; the *Third* is rather a square work, with a comparatively gruff first movement, a short, intermezzo-like *Larghetto*, but an eloquent finale with a strikingly florid principal theme. One of the more original features, which comes towards the end of the first movement, is an unusual declamatory passage for the solo piano over *tremolando* strings. The performance here is a good one and the recording bright and not without depth. An interesting coupling for the outstanding Mayr concerto.

Rimsky-Korsakov, Nikolas
(1844–1908)

Antar (symphonic suite), *Op. 9* (also called *Symphony No. 2*).

   (M) ** Vanguard VCS 10060. Utah Symphony Orchestra, Maurice Abravanel – IPPOLITOV-IVANOV: *Caucasian sketches;* GLIÈRE: *Russian sailors' dance.***

   * (*) HMV ASD 2974. Moscow Radio Symphony Orchestra, Konstantin Ivanov – GLAZOUNOV: *Scènes de ballet.****

Antar dates from 1869, some twenty years before *Scheherazade*, yet although its composer first called it a symphony (he had second thoughts later) it obviously anticipates the more famous work in

style and shape, to say nothing of its similarly exotic atmosphere and sinuous melodic contours. Indeed the melodic content is strong in character. The motto theme is memorable, and the third-movement scherzo contains some of Rimsky-Korsakov's most attractive invention. The scoring too is full of felicitous touches. Now that Morton Gould's superb RCA disc has been deleted, apart from an old but serviceable Ansermet Eclipse version (a stereo transcription of a mono recording), we are left with Abravanel's Utah disc and a newer Russian one. Abravanel's is a characteristically direct account, well played and recorded. The conductor concentrates on atmosphere rather than drama in the outer movements, and makes a strong contrast with the central ones. The fairly wide dynamic range rather accentuates this effect, but with generous couplings this is quite an attractive issue.

Comrade Ivanov's view of *Antar* is not altogether convincing. With red-blooded Russian orchestral playing it has some striking moments, but structurally the interpretation does not make a convincing whole.

Capriccio espagnole, Op. 34.

   (M) *** DGG Privilege 135011. Berlin Philharmonic Orchestra, Lorin Maazel (with *Russian music concert* ** (*)).

   (B) *** Decca SPA 182. London Symphony Orchestra, Jean Martinon (with *Concert ***).

   (B) ** Classics for Pleasure CFP 169. London Philharmonic Orchestra, John Pritchard – CHABRIER: *España **;* RAVEL: *Rapsodie espagnole.** (*)

The two finest recorded performances of Rimsky's glittering *Capriccio* are both within concerts discussed more fully in our *Treasury* volume. Maazel's performance comes from an early Berlin Philharmonic Orchestra collection, long ago deleted. Now it is reissued in a concert of Russian music featuring various orchestras and conductors. The playing of the Berlin Philharmonic Orchestra is unforgettable, with some gorgeous string and horn playing and breathtaking virtuosity in the closing pages, yet every note in its place. The Decca S P A disc (which includes Spanish-inspired music by Glinka, Moszkowski and Ravel) is actually called *Capriccio espagnole*. With outstanding recording quality throughout and an undoubtedly brilliant performance of the *Capriccio* this is an excellent bargain. There is also a good Supraphon version by the Czech Philharmonic Orchestra under Ančerl (SU A S T 50625), coupled with, amongst other things, a recommendable performance of Liszt's *Les Préludes*, but the account of the Rimsky-Korsakov piece has not the panache of Maazel or Martinon.

The recording balance at the opening tutti of Pritchard's performance is rather thick in texture, and this detracts a little from the sparkle. The performance is a good one, and the recording presents the orchestral strings and various instrumental solos warmly. But the account lacks the kind of compulsive excitement in the closing pages that illuminates Maazel's illustrious performance.

Capriccio espagnole, Op. 34; Le Coq d'or (opera): orchestral suite; Russian Easter Festival overture, Op. 36.

(M) ** CBS Classics 61586. Philadelphia Orchestra, Eugene Ormandy.

This disc is worth having for the glittering account of the suite from *Le Coq d'or*, highly attractive and characteristic music which is not otherwise available, save in a stereo transcription of an early Ansermet record. The recording is not without lustre, if not ideally sumptuous, but the Philadelphia playing is superbly assured. The *Russian Easter Festival overture* is well done too, but the *Capriccio* lacks something in sparkle and spontaneity. The recording of these two pieces is rather more shallow.

Christmas Eve (opera): suite; Dubinushka, Op. 62; May Night (opera): overture; Sadko (opera): Musical picture, Op. 5; Tsar Saltan (opera): Flight of the bumble bee; Russian Easter Festival overture, Op. 36.

(M) *** Decca Ace of Diamonds SDD 281. Suisse Romande Orchestra, Ernest Ansermet.

This record is generously filled. It opens with our old friend the bumble bee, who takes a rather leisurely flight, but perhaps we are too used to this piece being used as a virtuoso show-off. Then comes *Dubinushka*, a piece with a revolutionary connection (all the composer's music was banned for a while in consequence of his writing it). It has some typical brass fanfare writing, and Ansermet is richly served here by the engineers. *Sadko* is an exotic fairy tale with a colourful storm for its climax. Side one ends with a characteristic performance of the *Russian Easter Festival overture*, warmly coloured rather than specially vital. *May Night* opens side two attractively, and the collection closes with the *Christmas Eve suite*, with its imagery of a broomstick ride in the snow, a ballet of stars and comets (delightful idea!), and a snowstorm of falling stars. Thence to a witches' sabbath, and on to the Imperial Palace and a grand polonaise. Finally, as we draw near home Christmas day is dawning and we hear the church bell and the horns softly intoning a Christmas hymn. This is most enjoyable music and it is played with affection. Throughout the disc, the sound is warm and richly coloured. Recommended.

(i) *Piano concerto in C sharp minor, Op. 30. Symphony No. 3 in C major, Op. 32.*

** HMV ASD 2846. Moscow Radio Symphony Orchestra, Gennady Rozhdestvensky, (i) with Igor Zhukov (piano).

Neither of these works shows Rimsky-Korsakov at his most inspired. The *Concerto* is short, though not always effective, while the *Symphony* is a somewhat manufactured piece. There are good things in it, but in general there is little sense of freshness about it. However, the performances and recordings are satisfactory. There is an alternative performance of the *Concerto* by Michael Ponti on Vox STGBY 659, but the coupling, Tchaikovsky's *Third Concerto*, is much less attractively played.

Ivan the Terrible: Overture; May Night: Overture.
** HMV ASD 2490. Bolshoi Theatre Orchestra, Yevgeny Svetlanov – TCHAIKOVSKY: *Symphony No. 2.** (*)
(B) ** HMV SLS 881 (7 discs; same performances as above) – TCHAIKOVSKY: *Symphonies Nos. 1– 6 ** (*); LIADOV: *Baba-Yaga etc.****

Brilliant, colloquial performances, brightly recorded. While the Russian orchestral playing is rather more polished than we sometimes experience with Ansermet's Suisse Romande records, Decca have accustomed us to a richness and sheen for their Rimsky-Korsakov recordings which make the Russian sound seem dry and matter-of-fact. The acoustic too and the style of the Russian brass playing mean that the scoring of *Ivan the Terrible* tends to become noisy at its loudest moments.

Russian Easter Festival overture, Op. 36.
*** RCA SB 6804. Chicago Symphony Orchestra, Leopold Stokowski – KHACHATURIAN: *Symphony No. 3* (***); RACHMANINOV: *Vocalise.***

(B) ** Decca Eclipse ECS 573. London Philharmonic Orchestra, Sir Adrian Boult – RACHMANINOV: *Symphony No. 3.***

Stokowski's performance of this work has been famous since the days of his black-label 78 discs, when he substituted a human voice for the trombone solo. The present performance is not eccentric but broad and sympathetic, with plenty of colour and excitement. The recording is rich, but lacks something in sparkle in the upper register. Boult offers a small-scale performance, bringing out the colour of the score, with typically good LPO woodwind playing and stylish trumpets (apart from a single momentary lapse of intonation). The strings, however, rather lack weight, and the trombone soloist is not as bold as he should be.

Scheherazade (symphonic suite), *Op. 35.*
*** Philips 6500 410. London Philharmonic Orchestra, Bernard Haitink.
(M) *** HMV SXLP 20026. Philharmonia Orchestra, Paul Kletzki.
(B) *** Decca SPA 89. London Symphony Orchestra, Pierre Monteux.
(B) *** RCA Camden CCV 5010. Chicago Symphony Orchestra, Fritz Reiner.
*** HMV ASD 2520. USSR Symphony Orchestra, Yevgeny Svetlanov – GLINKA: *Russlan excerpts.***
** (*) HMV Quadraphonic Q4-ASD 3047; Stereo ASD 3047. Orchestre de Paris, Mstislav Rostropovich.

** (*) HMV ASD 251. Royal Philharmonic Orchestra, Sir Thomas Beecham.

** (*) Decca SXL 2268. Suisse Romande Orchestra, Ernest Ansermet – BORODIN: *Polovtsian dances.***

** (*) DGG SLPM 139022. Berlin Philharmonic Orchestra, Herbert von Karajan.

(B) ** Decca Eclipse ECS 735. Paris Conservatoire Orchestra, Ernest Ansermet – LIADOV: *Baba-Yaga; Kikimora.***

(B) * (*) Classics for Pleasure CFP 174. Royal Philharmonic Orchestra, Rudolf Kempe.

Haitink's Philips record is the finest account of *Scheherazade* to appear for more than a decade. Even those who, understandably, have one of its competitors might feel that duplication is worthwhile for such a very fine performance, outstandingly well recorded. The playing of the LPO is both sensitive and alert, the interpretation wholly unaffected and totally fresh in impact. The pleasure it affords is greatly enhanced by the quality of the sound, which is exceptionally truthful in both timbre and perspective. It is a relief to hear a solo violin sounding its natural size in relation to the orchestra as a whole. Yet Rodney Friend, who plays the solos subtly, dominates the performance with his richly sinuous picture of Scheherazade herself as narrator of each episode. Highly recommended.

But the competition from the three bargain alternatives, Kletzki, Monteux and Reiner, is very strong indeed. Kletzki's recording has a warm, natural acoustic, and heard through quadraphonic equipment the illusion of an extra perspective is very striking in places. The Philharmonia solo playing is superb, and Hugh Bean's violin solos are distinguished. Kletzki's reading is broad in the first

movement (the wide spaciousness of the acoustic is just right for the style), and he makes the second glow and sparkle (the famous brass interchanges having the most vivid projection). The richness of the string playing in the third movement is matched by the exhilaration of the finale.

Monteux is, if anything, even more vivid. The recording is at once brilliant and sparkling and full-blooded, the performance sensuous and exciting. The orchestral playing is perhaps not quite as polished as the Philharmonia, but it has tremendous zest and spontaneity. This is a good bargain alternative to Kletzki for those who put dramatic bite before tonal sumptuousness. In the finale Monteux holds back the climax until the last minute and then unleashes the storm with devastating effect.

Reiner's account is a dramatic one, the first movement having a strong forward impulse, and the finale equally brilliant and exciting. The two central movements are beguilingly played, but the readings are individual, and some may not care for the conductor's romantic nudgings here and there. However, Reiner always sounds spontaneous: there are many delightful touches and the third movement is wonderfully languorous. The recording is vivid, with the strong character of Chicago Hall adding its own atmosphere, but the sound itself has not quite the inner clarity and luminous wind colouring which are notable in both the Kletzki and the Monteux versions. As we go to press this reissue is still priced below a pound and as such is remarkable value for money.

With Svetlanov one is less conscious of balletic associations: here the power and drama, the symphonic quality of the work come over. This is not to say that this marvellous score's colouring is in any way dimmed or its exotic qualities undercharacterized, but merely that the music emerges with enhanced stature. The first movement has a monolithic boldness, the enunciation of the dominating main theme strikingly Russian (in the Mussorgskian rather than the Tchaikovskian sense); the rich slow movement melody is phrased with a languorous grace, and the finale has a symphonic culminating force. The whole reading is immensely satisfying and the performance, like the really outstanding Russian recording, has a superb sense of atmosphere. The sound itself is different from the characteristically more sumptuous British recordings: the strings have more edge and the trombones are buzzy, but this is the authentic Russian quality that Rimsky himself would have known.

Rostropovich's account offers alluringly rich sound, particularly the quadraphonic version, which warmly cocoons the listener in its ambience. This is very impressive indeed, and the brass interchanges in the second movement have never sounded so vivid and three-dimensional on record. The performance of the first movement, superbly opulent, is extremely convincing, but in the second the conductor's flexibility in the matter of *rubato* is not entirely matched by precision in the orchestral playing itself. It is perhaps a small matter and in the performance as a whole there is much infectious rhythmic pointing, while the finale is splendidly exciting. The stereo disc is marginally brighter, sharper in outline than the quadraphonic, which, with no loss of inner detail, has the warmer, more natural sound.

Beecham's *Scheherazade* was originally issued at the same time as Monteux's (in the earliest days of stereo) and now seems expensive. It is a superlative account, more sensuous than Monteux's, and originally it had sumptuous recording to match. But the record has been remastered, and the recut is not entirely a success. It is clearer, certainly, but the upper strings are harder, and some of the warmth and voluptuousness have evaporated. In the finale the general lightness at the bass end means that the

bass drum does not tell as effectively as it does with Kletzki.

Ansermet's Suisse Romande account was famous as a recording for its crystal clarity and sparkle when first issued. However, the string tone lacks something in body and richness, and in the slow movement this is a drawback. The outer movements are the finest; the first is dramatic and in the last the final climax is overwhelming. The *Polovtsian dances* bonus is a considerable one, but the performance is not outstanding. Ansermet's earlier recording with the Paris Conservatoire Orchestra is a respectable enough disc and the new transfer is technically successful. Some might be attracted by the delightful Liadov couplings, but generally speaking this cannot compare with Monteux in the same price range.

On DGG the smooth rich expertise of the Berlin Philharmonic solo playing is immediately apparent from the opening violin solo, which is superbly sumptuous. But this is not a quality one could apply to the recording itself, which although vivid is somewhat light in the bass. The first movement is hard-driven and has plenty of excitement, as has the finale (a resounding success), but the inner movements have not the glow of the Kletzki disc.

Scheherazade is not a score that easily yields to the German romantic tradition, and the music does not really suit Kempe. He is broad in the first movement, at his best in the slow movement, but elsewhere the performance, although beautifully played and warmly recorded, lacks vitality.

There are as many more records of this popular work in the current catalogue but none that really compete with the best of those discussed above. Among them are two versions by Ormandy, a brilliant record made by Silvestri in Bournemouth (TWO 167), a rather undercharacterized account by Ozawa on HMV, and a more than acceptable Universo disc by Markevitch (6580 025),

787

which throws in the *Capriccio espagnole* at medium price.

Piano and wind quintet in B flat major.
(M) *** Decca Ace of Diamonds SDD 389. Walter Panhoffer (piano), members of the Vienna Octet – MENDELSSOHN: *Octet.****

The Rimsky-Korsakov *Quintet* is no masterpiece, but it is thoroughly diverting. Some of its ideas outstay their welcome, but even this does not seriously detract from the pleasure it gives. The piece is like a garrulous but endearing friend whose loquacity is easily borne for the sake of the accompanying charm and good nature. Sparkling performance and excellent recording.

The Snow Maiden (opera in 4 acts): complete recording.
(M) ** Decca GOS 642/5. Sofiya Jankovich, Valeria Heybalova (sopranos), Militza Miladinovich (mezzo-soprano), Stepan Andrashevich (tenor), Dushan Popovich (baritone), Miro Changalovich (bass), Chorus and Orchestra of Belgrade National Opera, Kreshimir Baranovich.

The Snow Maiden is a delightful fairytale opera, but unless it is very well performed it can seem terribly long. This Yugoslav performance from the midfifties falls rather below the necessary level of inspiration, though for its age the recording is good, and there are many incidental delights in a rich, colourful and varied score.

(i) *The Snow Maiden: suite; Tsar Saltan: suite.*
(M) *** Decca Ace of Diamonds SDD 282. Suisse Romande Orchestra, Ernest Ansermet, (i) with chorus (with *Concert* ** (*)).

These two suites are among the highlights of a generously-filled concert LP reviewed in our *Treasury* volume. *Tsar Saltan* shows Ansermet and the Decca engineers in glittering form, and if the best item from the *Snow Maiden* suite proves to be our old friend the *Dance of the Tumblers*, the choral *Dance of the Birds* is also an attractive trifle.

The Tsar's Bride (opera in 4 acts): complete recording.
(M) *** HMV SLS 885 (3 discs). Galina Vishnevskaya (soprano), Irina Arkhipova (mezzo-soprano), Vladimir Atlantov (tenor), Yevgeny Nesterenko (bass), Bolshoi Theatre Chorus and Orchestra, Fuat Mansurov.

Anyone curious to know about Rimsky-Korsakov's exotic collection of operas should certainly investigate this vigorous and delightful set, featuring two of Russia's most impressive women singers, Vishnevskaya as the girl whose love is fated to be destroyed by the Tsar's wooing, Arkhipova as the jealous figure in the story. It is a strange piece, inconsequential at times in the Russian manner, but full of marvellous musical ideas which somehow manage to flower despite the oddities of the story. The recording is one of the most vivid yet to have come from Russia.

Roberday, François (1624–80)

Fugues et caprices pour orgue Nos. 1–12.
** (*) Argo ZRG 744. Gillian Weir (organ of St Leonhardkirche, Basel).

François Roberday will be little more than a name – if that – to most readers.

He is a *petit maître* who occasionally figures in recitals but has so far eluded the gramophone. This recording is made on a modern instrument in Basel which produces very authentic-sounding quality. Gillian Weir plays with enormous style and aplomb, but it would be idle to maintain that this is music of more than passing interest. For specialists rather than the general collector. The Argo recording has splendid range and presence.

Rodrigo, Joaquín
(born 1902)

(i) *Concierto Andaluz* (for 4 guitars and orchestra); (ii) *Concierto de Aranjuez* (for guitar and orchestra).
*** Philips SAL 3677. (i) The Romeros (guitars); (ii) Angel Romero (guitar); both with San Antonio Symphony Orchestra, Alessandro.

The only snag about this highly enjoyable LP is that anyone who has discovered what an attractive composer Rodrigo is will already have the *Concierto de Aranjuez*. Those who have not will find the performance here as satisfying as any available, with a strong Spanish flavour and the musing poetry of the slow movement beautifully caught. The recording is bright and free. But the real find here is the *Concierto Andaluz*. The movements tend to be monothematic, and some might feel that each is too long. But the invention is fresh and full of character. The catchy opening tune on the strings is only rivalled by that which dominates the finale, while the *Adagio* is wonderfully atmospheric from the first bar. The strong Andalusian flavour is caught to perfection by the performers, and the crisp, slightly pithy recording is exactly right. Perhaps surprisingly, there are not vast lengths of guitar roulades; much of the interest is in the witty

orchestration (and the woodwind of the San Antonio orchestra excel themselves).

Concierto de Aranjuez (for guitar and orchestra).
*** CBS 76369. John Williams (guitar), English Chamber Orchestra, Daniel Barenboim – VILLA-LOBOS: *Guitar concerto*.***
** (*) RCA SB 6635. Julian Bream (guitar), Melos Ensemble, Colin Davis – BRITTEN: *Courtly dances***; VIVALDI: *Lute concerto*.**
** (*) Decca SXL 2091. Narciso Yepes (guitar), National Symphony Orchestra of Spain, Ataulfo Argenta – FALLA: *Nights in the Gardens of Spain*.** (*)
(B) ** Classics for Pleasure CFP 40012. John Zaradin (guitar), Philomusica of London, Guy Barbier (with *Recital* **).

John Williams's newest recording of the delectable *Concierto de Aranjuez* with Barenboim is superior to his earlier version with Ormandy. The playing has marvellous point and spontaneity, and the famous *Adagio* has rarely been played with this degree of poetic spontaneity. There is a hint of rhythmic over-emphasis in the articulation of the finale, but in general this performance is outstanding above nearly all its competitors (although on middle-price and bargain labels respectively, Behrend and Yepes also give first-class accounts, attractively coupled; see below). The balance is characteristically forward, but in all other respects the bright, detailed recording is highly attractive.

Bream's version predictably has an intimate, chamber flavour, with the individual personalities of the wind players emerging colourfully near the very opening of the first movement. There is too a degree of introspection both in the *Adagio* and in the finale, and it is a pity that Colin Davis's overall direction has a few moments of slackness, particularly compared with the CBS performance. The recording is a typical, bright RCA product, slightly inclined to brashness. Most enjoyable in its way, if you need this particular coupling.

The older Decca version now seems over-priced in its present coupling with Falla. It is also available on SPA (see below). It is a most attractive performance: the first movement is deliciously pointed, the wind entries made doubly effective by the attractively warm recording acoustic; the *Adagio* has a thoughtful improvisatory quality, and the finale a lively spontaneity. With a Spanish orchestra the effect is, not surprisingly, more idiomatic than most versions. The recording is a little tight in the upper strings, but the soloist is beautifully recorded and the balance is excellent.

Zaradin's performance is bright-eyed and straightforward, with a crisp, immediate recording. The orchestral outline is clear-cut in the somewhat dry manner favoured by John Boyden, who produced many of the Classics for Pleasure original recordings. This is coupled with a recital of solo guitar pieces, mentioned in our companion *Treasury* volume.

Concierto de Aranjuez (arr. for harp by the composer).
> ** HMV ASD 3034. Nicanor Zabaleta (harp), Spanish National Orchestra, Rafael Frühbeck de Burgos – PARISH-ALVARS: *Harp concerto.***

Nicanor Zabaleta plays the famous concerto with characteristic delicacy and achieves a musing poetic feeling in the slow movement which is very pleasing. However, the outer movements are less effective, although Frühbeck de Burgos's gentle accompaniments are nicely matched to the mood of his soloist.

Concierto de Aranjuez; Fantasia para un gentilhombre (both for guitar and orchestra).
> (B) *** Decca SPA 233. Narciso Yepes (guitar), National Orchestra of Spain, Argenta or Frühbeck de Burgos.
> ** Philips 6500 454. Alexandre Lagoya (guitar), Monte Carlo Opera Orchestra, Antonio de Almeida.
> * (*) DGG SLPM 139440. Narciso Yepes (guitar), Spanish Radio and TV Orchestra, Odon Alonso.

The choice here is clear. The Decca disc is brightly recorded; Yepes's early performance of the *Concierto de Aranjuez* is one of the finest available (see above) and the coupling has comparable personality and style. This is a splendid bargain. Neither of its competitors, both of which are at full price, are as distinctive. Alexandre Lagoya is a good player but does not emerge with a very strong personality, except perhaps in the slow movement of the *Concierto*, which he plays with considerable feeling. The outer movements lack the sprightly momentum which distinguishes the best versions. Yepes's DGG coupling is disappointing, for the playing is almost entirely without sparkle. The artists have been recorded in a studio with a dry acoustic which seems to have damped the spontaneity out of the performances, except in the slow movement of the *Concierto*, which seems indestructible.

(i) *Concierto de Aranjuez* (for guitar and orchestra); (ii) *Concierto serenata* (for harp and orchestra).
> ⊛ (M) *** DGG Privilege 135117. (i) Siegfried Behrend (guitar), Berlin Philharmonic Orchestra, Rheinhold Peters; (ii) Nicanor Zabaleta (harp), Berlin Radio Orchestra, Ernst Märzendorfer.

This is an outstanding coupling. Rodrigo's charming *Concierto de Aranjuez* receives here a first-rate modern recording, projected well, bright as a button, and with an excellent balance between soloist and orchestra. Behrend's approach is alive and strong in personality, and the effect is to make this fine work sound less insubstantial than it sometimes does. Most enjoyable, with the player's pleasure in such rewarding music readily conveyed. The delicious *Harp concerto* displays a similar piquancy and charm of melody. In the outer movements, especially, the delicate yet colourful orchestration tickles the ear in delightful contrast to the beautifully focused timbre of the harp. Both performance and recording are immaculate, and this enjoyable disc cannot be too highly recommended.

Concierto serenata (for harp and orchestra).
*** DGG SLPM 138118 (same performance as above) – BOIELDIEU: *Harp concerto*.***

The performance as above is here coupled to another attractive harp concerto, by Boieldieu.

Fantasia para un gentilhombre (for guitar and orchestra) (ed. Segovia).
*** CBS 72661. John Williams (guitar), English Chamber Orchestra, Sir Charles Groves – DODGSON: *Guitar concerto*.***

An innocuous and pleasant work, if not quite as imaginative or inventive as the famous concerto. The performance is impeccable and the recording warm and lively.

Rosenberg, Hilding
(born 1892)

Symphony No. 6 (Sinfonia semplice).
(B) *** Turnabout TV 34318S. Stockholm Philharmonic Orchestra, Stig Westerberg – BLOMDAHL: *Symphony No. 3*.***

Hilding Rosenberg, now in his eighties, is the doyen of Swedish composers. The sixth of his eight symphonies dates from 1951 and is a powerfully-wrought, highly imaginative score with a strong feeling for nature. It will greatly appeal to readers who admire Nielsen and Hindemith, both of them potent influences on his earlier musical language. The recording comes from the early sixties but is vivid and well detailed, and the performance is authoritative. The excellence of this issue is enhanced by the interest of the coupling, Blomdahl's *Facetter*, and given the modest price asked, this disc is astonishingly good value.

Rosetti, Francesco
(né Rössler, Franz)
(1746–92)

Horn concerto in D major.
(B) ** Turnabout TV 34078S. Erich Penzel (horn), Württemberg Chamber Orchestra, Joerg Faerber – TELEMANN: *Suite* ***; VIVALDI: *Double concerto*.**

Francesco Rosetti provided here a quite characterful little concerto, with a well laid out first movement, requiring spurts of virtuosity and receiving it here from the soloist, Erich Penzel. The slow movement has a romantic flair, and the finale is jolly. Quite a useful addition to the repertoire.

Rossini, Gioacchino
(1792–1868)

La Boutique fantasque (ballet music; arr. Respighi).
- (B) ** (*) Music for Pleasure MFP 57012. Scottish National Orchestra, Alexander Gibson – DUKAS: *L'Apprenti sorcier*; SAINT-SAËNS: *Danse macabre*.**
- (B) ** Decca SPA 376. Israel Philharmonic Orchestra, Sir Georg Solti – DUKAS: *L'Apprenti sorcier*.**
- (B) * (*) Classics for Pleasure CFP 40204. Royal Philharmonic Orchestra, Sir Eugene Goossens – RESPIGHI: *Fountains of Rome*.***

Ansermet's glowing account of Respighi's ballet score based on Rossini's late piano music has never been superseded. Dating from the earliest days of mono LP, this record is now available in an excellent stereo transcription (ECS 529).

Alexander Gibson's performance sounds for all the world as if the conductor has been listening to Ansermet's famous record. Tempi are similar, and the opening is cunningly slow with much of the magic that Ansermet found. The selection on Music for Pleasure is generous, if not as extended as on the Eclipse disc, but the recording is excellent.

Solti begins much faster than Ansermet or Gibson and plays the opening more precisely and with less magic. But as the music continues the listener is caught up in the intensity of this quite different conception, and the mood of the opening drops into place. The vitality of the playing, particularly of the Israeli strings, is notable, and as the recording is crisp and spacious, this is attractive at its reissue price.

Goossens is inclined to drive the fast passages hard and let the tension sag in the lyrical quieter music. This is especially noticeable in the more relaxed second part of the ballet. The recording is good, if not distinguished: it is somewhat lacking in lustre and the upper strings are thin and insubstantial. However, the coupling is outstanding.

String sonatas (Sonatas a quattro) Nos. 1 in G major; 2 in A major; 3 in C major; 4 in B flat major; 5 in E flat major; 6 in D major.
- ⊛ *** Argo ZRG 506 (Sonatas 1, 3, 5, 6). Academy of St Martin-in-the-Fields, Neville Marriner.
- *** Argo ZRG 603 (Sonatas 2 and 4). Academy of St Martin-in-the-Fields, Neville Marriner – DONIZETTI: *String quartet*.***
- ** Philips 6747 038 (2 discs; Sonatas 1–6). I Musici – BOTTESINI: *Grand duo*.**
- ** Philips SAL 3640 (Sonata 3). I Musici – MENDELSSOHN: *Octet*; WOLF: *Italian serenade*.***

Argo's ZRG 506 has long been a demonstration record of superb string quality in music which is wonderfully entertaining and witty. Unbelievably, the sonatas were written when the composer was only twelve, yet their invention is consistently on the highest level, bubbling over with humour and infectious spontaneity. The playing of the St Martins group under Marriner is marvellously fresh and polished, the youthful high spirits of the writing presented with glowing affection and sparkle. The performances by I Musici are enjoyable too, although they hardly achieve the delectable wit and point which make the Argo set so enchanting. The Philips recording is excellent and the playing both refined and alert.

Overtures

Overtures: *Il Barbiere di Siviglia; La Cenerentola; La Gazza ladra; L'Italiana in Algeri; La Scala di seta; Il Signor Bruschino.*
> ** Pye Ensayo NEL 2005. English Chamber Orchestra, Enrique Garcia Asensio.

These performances appear to use a comparatively small ensemble, and the chamber quality is especially attractive in *La Scala di seta*, where the neat string playing gives pleasure. However, elsewhere the absence of a robust quality is a drawback: the side-drum at the opening of *La Gazza ladra* is far too reticent. With generally good recording, these are performances of character but they are not among the finest available.

Overtures: *Il Barbiere di Siviglia; La Cenerentola; La Gazza ladra; Guillaume Tell; L'Italiana in Algeri; La Scala di seta.*
> (B) *** Contour 6870 585. Lamoureux Orchestra, Roberto Benzi.

Benzi's collection is the very antithesis of the Toscanini-style presentation, where the orchestra – supremely disciplined – reacts as one man to every subtlety of phrase and shading, as dictated by the maestro's whim. Here instead – although the orchestral discipline is still good, helped by a fairly small body of first violins – one is conscious of the orchestra's joint personality and how much they are enjoying themselves. The playing has tremendous spirit and gusto, and if the polish in the violins (as at the opening of *La Scala di seta*) or the poise of the wind soloists (as in the oboe solo in the *Italian Girl*) is marginally below the very best, the infectious playing is a source of great enjoyment. It is helped by a lively and reverberant recording with a wide dynamic range and natural yet vivid colouring. And Benzi's control of

dynamic is notable. His conception of the allegro of *La Scala di seta* is particularly stylish. For sheer personality this collection is hard to beat.

Overtures: *Il Barbiere di Siviglia; La Cenerentola; La Gazza ladra; Guillaume Tell; Il Signor Bruschino; La Scala di seta.*
> (B) *** RCA Camden CCV 5020. Chicago Symphony Orchestra, Fritz Reiner.

Reiner offers sparkling, vivacious performances. One would have liked the opening bars of *La Scala di seta* neater – they are too lavishly presented here – and there is a hint of coolness at the opening of *William Tell*. But generally this is a very fine set of performances, and *La Cenerentola* offers superb orchestral bravura. The recording has a very wide dynamic range, and the reverberation of Chicago's Symphony Hall is well controlled by the recording. The blaze of brass tone at the beginning of the *William Tell* galop reminds us that the Chicago orchestra was always famous in this department.

Overtures: *Il Barbiere di Siviglia; La Gazza ladra; Guillaume Tell; L'Italiana in Algeri; La Scala di seta; Semiramide.*
> *** DGG 2530 144. Berlin Philharmonic Orchestra, Herbert von Karajan.

Superbly made performances offering polish and sheer bravura rather than any special individuality. Karajan takes the main allegro of *La Scala di seta* very fast indeed, but the playing is beautifully light and assured, the oboist managing felicitous control of the phrasing without any suggestion of breathlessness. The oboe solo in *L'Italiana in Algeri* is played with similar poise and assurance. Of their kind these performances are beautifully shaped and the recording is first-class.

Overtures: *Il Barbiere di Siviglia; La Gazza ladra; Guillaume Tell; La Scala di seta; Semiramide.*

*** Decca SXL 2266. London Symphony Orchestra, Pierino Gamba.

(M) ** DGG Privilege 2538.045. Rome Opera House Orchestra, Tullio Serafin.

The Gamba Decca collection is a good one. The performances are taut and exciting and the orchestral playing splendidly alive and polished, even at the very fast speeds sometimes chosen for the allegros. A strong disciplining force – not unlike Toscanini's style – is felt in every piece, and care in phrasing is noticeable at every turn. Particularly captivating is the string cantilena at the introduction of *The Barber of Seville*, which is phrased with a wonderful sense of line. Decca's recording is quite superlative. The only quality perhaps missing is a touch of geniality.

Serafin's disc includes also the *Storm music* from *William Tell*, but this is the only advantage it has, apart from price. The performances are affectionate and relaxed, sometimes to the point of slackness of style. We are given extra measure in *La Gazza ladra*, where for some reason there is an extra repeat of the second subject.

Overtures: *Il Barbiere di Siviglia; La Gazza ladra; Guillaume Tell; La Scala di seta; Le Siège de Corinthe; Il Signor Bruschino.*

(M) * Decca Ace of Diamonds SDD 392. New Philharmonia Orchestra, Lamberto Gardelli.

A disappointingly mundane set of performances, surprising from such an experienced conductor. *La Scala di seta* offers curious tempo changes that sound almost like unmatched tape-joins. Even the recording is below Decca's usual sparkling standard in this kind of music.

Overtures: *Il Barbiere di Siviglia; L'Italiana in Algeri; La Scala di seta; Il Signor Bruschino.*

(M) *** HMV SXLP 30094. Philharmonia Orchestra, Carlo Maria Giulini – VERDI: *Overtures.****

Anyone fancying a mixture of Rossini and Verdi will be well satisfied with this generous collection, for the inclusion of four overtures on one side hardly affects the quality of the last, *La Scala di seta*, which incidentally has a very fast introduction that sacrifices poise for bravura. The performances are generally brilliant, with first-class orchestral playing. The recording quality is bright and a trifle dry.

Overtures: *La Cenerentola; La Gazza ladra; Guillaume Tell; Semiramide; Tancredi.*

(M) *** HMV SXLP 30143. Philharmonia Orchestra, Carlo Maria Giulini.

Like the collection above, coupled with Verdi, these performances offer characteristically refined Philharmonia playing, of impressive brilliance matched by a bold resonant recording of wide dynamic range. Giulini's careful attention to detail is balanced by a strong sense of drama, and although these are not the most genial performances on disc, they are strong in personality. The account of *William Tell* is quite outstanding for the warmth of the opening and the affectionate detail of the pastoral section. A highly enjoyable disc.

Overtures: *La Gazza ladra; L'Italiana in Algeri; La Scala di seta; Il Turco in Italia; Il Viaggio a Reims.*

(M) ** (*) CBS Classics 61215. Cleveland Orchestra, George Szell.

Here the orchestral playing is superbly disciplined, and the spirit of Toscanini hovers in the background. There is wit here, certainly, and *La Scala di seta* (not taken too fast) is played with appealing delicacy, while *L'Italiana in Algeri* is infectiously pointed. But for sheer excitement try *La Gazza ladra*, where the forwardly placed side-drum adds a military precision and a flavour of battle itself to the climax. The recording is not as rich as one would ideally like, but the extreme brilliance suits the performances.

Overtures: *La Gazza ladra; Guillaume Tell; L'Italiana in Algeri; Semiramide; Il Signor Bruschino.*
  (B) *** Classics for Pleasure CFP 40077. Royal Philharmonic Orchestra, Colin Davis.

A splendid bargain collection from Colin Davis. He is rather more relaxed than Gamba on Decca, but these performances are admirably stylish, with an excellent sense of nuance. The orchestral playing is splendid, and the new Classics for Pleasure pressing of a very good EMI recording is admirably natural and full-blooded, though there seems marginally more sparkle on side two than side one, which contains *William Tell* and *La Gazza ladra. Semiramide*, which opens side two, is a superb performance, wonderfully crisp and vivid. In *Il Signor Bruschino*, which comes next, it sounds, as if the bow-tapping device is done by the leader only, in the interest of precision; but this is not what Rossini indicated, and the effect is somehow too refined.

Overtures: *La Gazza ladra; Guillaume Tell.*
  (B) ** Decca SPA 92. Paris Conservatoire Orchestra, Peter Maag – MENDELSSOHN: *Overtures.***

Peter Maag brings a classical restraint to these performances, and perhaps the opening of *William Tell*, given a comparatively dry acoustic, lacks something in romantic flair. But there is plenty of colour in the final gallop, and the excitement, if controlled, is real enough. The sense of discipline is even more effective in *La Gazza ladra*, where the crisp pointing gives much pleasure. The recording is clear and clean in Decca's best manner.

VOCAL AND CHORAL MUSIC

Messa di gloria.
  *** Philips 6500 612. Margherita Rinaldi (soprano), Ameral Gunson (contralto), Ugo Benelli, John Mitchinson (tenors), Jules Bastin (bass), BBC Chorus, English Chamber Orchestra, Herbert Handt.

This fascinating and invigorating work was rescued from oblivion by the conductor of this record, himself a singer. It consists of appropriately ambitious but never heavy settings of the *Kyrie* and *Gloria*, products of Rossini's first full maturity at a time (1820) when he was otherwise totally occupied with writing operas. There are links between the tenor duet which starts the *Christe* and Mathilde's aria in *Guillaume Tell*, but the delight is that so much unknown Rossini contains so much new to charm us. The performance here is lively and well sung. Good atmospheric recording too.

Petite Messe solennelle.
  *** RCA SER 5693/4. Kari Lovaas (soprano), Brigitte Fassbaender (contralto), Peter Schreier (tenor), Dietrich Fischer-Dieskau (baritone), Münchner Vokalisten, Hans Ludwig Hirsch, Wolfgang Sawallisch (pianos), Reinhardt Raffalt (harmonium), Wolfgang Sawallisch.

Rossini's *Petite Messe solennelle* must be the most genial contribution to the church liturgy in the history of music. The description *Petite* does not refer to size, for the piece is comparable in length to Verdi's *Requiem*; rather it is the composer's modest evaluation of the work's 'significance'. But what a spontaneous and infectious piece of writing it is, bubbling over with characteristic melodic, harmonic and rhythmic invention. The composer never overreaches himself. 'I was born for *opera buffa*, as well Thou knowest,' Rossini writes touchingly on the score. 'Little skill, a little heart, and that is all. So be Thou blessed and admit me to paradise.' The performance here would surely merit the granting of the composer's wish. The soloists are first-rate, the contralto outstanding in the lovely *O salutaris* and *Agnus Dei*. Good choral singing, and fine imaginative playing from the two pianists. The Ariola recording (issued here by RCA) is very good indeed.

Stabat Mater.
　** (*) Decca SXL 6534. Pilar Lorengar (soprano), Yvonne Minton (mezzo-soprano), Luciano Pavarotti (tenor), Hans Sotin (bass), LSO Chorus, London Symphony Orchestra, Istvan Kertesz.

Rossini loses nothing of his natural jauntiness in setting a religious text, and generally conductors treat this music simply as an offshoot of Rossini opera. But Kertesz, a refined and thoughtful musician, seems intent on avoiding any charges of vulgarity. This brings out an unexpected degree of beauty, notably in the fine choral singing, and even *Cujus anima* is given extra delicacy, with Pavarotti singing most beautifully and linking back to the main theme with a subtle half-tone. Some may understandably complain that Kertesz underplays the music in removing the open-hearted vulgarity, but he certainly makes

one enjoy the music afresh. Soprano, mezzo and bass may not have all the idiomatic Italian qualities, but their singing matches the conductor's interpretation. Excellent recording quality.

OPERA

Il Barbiere di Siviglia (opera in 2 acts): complete recording.
　*** HMV SLS 853 (3 discs). Maria Callas (soprano), Tito Gobbi (baritone), Luigi Alva (tenor), Fritz Ollendorff (bass), Philharmonia Chorus and Orchestra, Alceo Galliera.
　** (*) DGG 2709 041 (3 discs). Teresa Berganza (mezzo-soprano), Hermann Prey (baritone), Luigi Alva (tenor), Paolo Montarsolo (baritone), Ambrosian Chorus, London Symphony Orchestra, Claudio Abbado.
　** (*) Decca SET 285/7. Teresa Berganza (mezzo-soprano), Manuel Ausensi (baritone), Ugo Benelli (tenor), Fernando Corena, Nicolai Ghiaurov (basses), Rossini Chorus and Orchestra of Naples, Silvio Varviso.
　(M) * (*) DGG Privilege 2728 005 (3 discs). Gianna d'Angelo (soprano), Renato Capecchi (baritone), Nicola Monti (tenor), Carlo Cava, Giorgio Tadeo (basses), Bavarian Radio Chorus and Orchestra, Bruno Bartoletti.

Gobbi and Callas were here at their most inspired, and with the recording quality nicely refurbished the HMV set is an outstanding version, not absolutely complete in its text, but so crisp and sparkling it can be confidently recommended as the most enjoyable version of all. Callas remains supreme as a minx-like Rosina, summing up the character superbly in *Una voce poco fa*. Rightly in the final ensemble, despite the usual reading of the score, Rosina's verse is given premier place at the very end.

Abbado directs a clean and satisfying performance that lacks the last degree of sparkle. Berganza's interpretation of the role of Rosina remains very consistent with her earlier performance on Decca, but the Figaro here, Hermann Prey, is more reliable, and the playing and recording have an extra degree of polish. The text is not so complete as the Decca (omitting the tenor's Act 2 aria, for example).

Vocally the Decca set of the *Barber*, with Teresa Berganza as an agile Rosina, is most reliable. It is also very well recorded, and Silvio Varviso secures electrifying effects in many of Rossini's high-spirited ensembles. There remain important reservations. Manuel Ausensi as Figaro himself is rather gruff both vocally and dramatically, though he was chosen specifically because of the authenticity of having a darker-toned voice than is usual in the part. Ugo Benelli is charming as the Count, a free-voiced 'tenorino', though he sounds nervous in his first aria. Corena's fine Dr Bartolo is already well-known from two earlier sets, and Ghiaurov sings with characteristic richness as Basilio. This version is textually not quite complete, but it contains much more than usual and it includes the often omitted Act 2 tenor aria which uses the *Non più mesta* theme from *La Cenerentola*.

The Privilege set is not a very serious contender. Gianna d'Angelo is a sweet enough Rosina, but not especially individual. Capecchi gives an over-respectable portrait of the barber himself, sometimes a little like a pompous politician. The recording, as with many of the earlier DGG opera sets, favours the voices unduly.

Il Barbiere di Siviglia: highlights.
   ** (*) DGG 2536 029 (from above recording cond. Abbado).

** (*) Decca SXL 6271 (from above recording cond. Varviso).

These are both good selections reflecting the best features of the sets from which they come.

Il Barbiere di Siviglia: highlights; *La Cenerentola:* highlights.
   (M) *** DGG Privilege 2538 324 (from complete sets, as above and below, with Berganza, cond. Abbado).

On a mid-price label a collection of excerpts from the two Rossini comedies strongly featuring Berganza's contribution is attractive and welcome. First-rate recording.

La Cenerentola (opera in 2 acts): complete recording.
   ** DGG 2709 039 (3 discs). Teresa Berganza (soprano), Luigi Alva (tenor), Paolo Montarsolo, Renato Capecchi (baritones), Scottish Opera Chorus, London Symphony Orchestra, Claudio Abbado.
   (M) * (*) Decca Ace of Diamonds GOS 631/3. Giulietta Simionato (mezzo-soprano), Ugo Benelli (tenor), Paolo Montarsolo, Sesto Bruscantini (baritones), Chorus and Orchestra of Maggio Musicale Fiorentino, Olivero de Fabritiis.

La Cenerentola has not been lucky on records, and the DGG set, although enjoyable, lacks the extrovert bravura and sparkle of an ideal performance. The atmosphere in places is almost of a concert version, with excellent balance between the participants, helped by the fine recording. The recitative in general has plenty of life, particularly when Dandini (Renato Capecchi) is involved. Berganza, agile in the coloratura, seems too mature, even matronly, for the fairy-tale role of Cinderella. Alva sings well enough but is somewhat self-conscious in the florid writing. Abbado, though hardly witty in his direction, inspires delicate playing throughout.

On Decca, with never very refined singing from any of his soloists, Fabritiis makes the piece sound longer and less interesting than it is. Simionato is well below her best vocally, wobbling far more than she used to, and it is small consolation that the Decca recording is as brilliant as could be.

Guillaume Tell (opera in 4 acts): complete recording.
> *** HMV SLS 970 (5 discs). Montserrat Caballé (soprano), Gabriel Bacquier (baritone), Nicolai Gedda (tenor), Mady Mesplé (soprano), Louis Hendrikx (bass) Ambrosian Opera Chorus, Royal Philharmonic Orchestra, Lamberto Gardelli.

Famous as the overture is, few will know the full opera – fuller here than ever before, with an extra aria for Tell's son (the role taken by a high soprano) that was probably discarded before performance. There are some magnificent numbers, but these ten sides include a number of less inspired passages too. It is fortunatate that Gardelli is such an imaginative Rossini interpreter, rallying his formidable team to vigorous and sensitive performances. Bacquier makes an impressive Tell, developing the character as the story progresses; Gedda is a model of taste, and Montserrat Caballé copes with the coloratura problems of Mathilde's role ravishingly. Excellent recording quality. The choral passages, incisively sung, are among the most impressive.

L'Italiana in Algeri (opera in 2 acts): complete recording.

> *** Decca SET 262/4. Teresa Berganza (mezzo-soprano), Fernando Corena (bass), Luigi Alva (tenor), Rolando Panerai (baritone), Chorus and Orchestra of Maggio Musicale Fiorentino, Silvio Varviso.

This set appeared at about the same time as Decca's *Cenerentola*, also with the chorus and orchestra of the Maggio Musicale Fiorentino. But there the similarities end, for where *Cenerentola* lacked the right Rossinian sparkle, this performance has it in abundance, and the music blossoms readily. Teresa Berganza makes an enchanting Italian girl, and the three principal men are all better – and certainly more characterful – than one has any right to expect in these days when florid singing is no longer cultivated (by men at least) in the way it should be. The recording is outstanding, and adds enormously to the sparkle of the whole presentation.

L'Italiana in Algeri (opera in 2 acts): highlights.
> *** Decca SXL 6210 (from above recording).

This is a first-rate selection from a highly enjoyable set. Berganza is at her most beguiling, and though Alva like almost all tenors today is occasionally tripped by the *fioriture*, it is a charming, sweet-toned performance. The numbers have been well selected to provide a potted version of the opera, and an excellent text and translation of the words give all the necessary help. Recording among the most brilliant from this source.

Semiramide (opera in 2 acts): complete recording.
> *** Decca SET 317/9. Joan Sutherland (soprano), Marilyn Horne (mezzo-soprano), John Serge (ten-

or), Joseph Rouleau (bass), Ambrosian Opera Chorus, London Symphony Orchestra, Richard Bonynge.

Wagner once said of this opera that 'it exhibits all the faults by which Italian opera can be distinguished': but, taking the modern view, that is rather to its credit. The story is admittedly improbable, involving the love which almost all the male characters bear for the Princess Azema, a lady who rather curiously appears very little in the opera. Instead Rossini concentrates on the love of Queen Semiramide for the Prince Arsace (a mezzo-soprano role), and musically the result is a series of fine duets, superbly performed here by Sutherland and Horne. There are other numbers too – notably the big soprano aria, *Bel raggio* – that have survived the general neglect, but what a complete account brings out is the consistency of the drama, the music involving the listener even where the story falls short. Semiramide in Sutherland's interpretation is not so much a Lady Macbeth figure as a passionate, sympathetic woman, and with dramatic music predominating over languorous cantilena, one has her best, bright manner rather than her 'mooning' style. Horne is well contrasted, direct and masculine in style, and Spiro Malas makes a firm, clear contribution in a minor role. Rouleau and Serge are variable but more than adequate, and Bonynge once again confirms the high opinions of his alert, rhythmic control in opera recordings. Brilliant recording.

Semiramide: highlights.
*** Decca SET 391 (from above recording).

The complete set of *Semiramide* brings some of Joan Sutherland's most impressive ever singing on record, notably in the duets with Marilyn Horne. But it remains a very long opera, and this well-chosen collection of excerpts gathers together very conveniently some of the most wonderful highspots. Sample the duet *Serbami ognor*: it is irresistible. First-rate recording quality.

Duets from *Semiramide*, Act 1: *Mitrane! ... Serbami ognor si fido;* Act 2: *No non ti lascio ... Eben ... a te ferisci ... Giorno d'orrore!*
*** Decca SET 456. Joan Sutherland (soprano), Marilyn Horne (mezzo-soprano), London Symphony Orchestra, Richard Bonynge – BELLINI: *Duets from Norma.*** (*)

Serbami ognor from the complete set of *Semiramide* provides one of the finest examples of duet-singing ever recorded. Even Sutherland and Horne have never surpassed this in their many collaborations. With a second *Semiramide* duet and two duets from *Norma* the disc is most attractive.

COLLECTION

Stabat Mater: Fac ut portem. Il Barbiere di Siviglia, Act 1: Una voce poco fa; Act 2: Contro un cor. La Cenerentola, Act 2: Nacqui all'affano ... Non più mesta. L'Italiana in Algeri, Act 1: Cruda sorte; Amor tiranno; Act 2: Per lui che adoro; Amici in ogni ... Pensa alla patria'. Semiramide, Act 1: Bel raggio lusinghier.
(M) *** Decca Ace of Diamonds SDD 224. Teresa Berganza (mezzo-soprano), London Symphony Orchestra, Alexander Gibson.

A most exciting reissue in every way. In this early recital, made before her complete opera sets, Berganza displays a voice of great richness which she controlled with the sort of vocal perfection one associates with her compatriot,

Victoria de los Angeles. She seems rarely to provide a true staccato, but that may be entirely a question of choice and in any case it is the most minor of criticisms of a singer who can here stand comparison with the very greatest mezzos of the past. For a sample try the second of three arias from the *Italian Girl in Algiers*, in which Berganza's phrasing is quite irresistible. The recording is brilliantly clear.

Roussel, Albert
(1869–1937)

Bacchus et Ariane (ballet): *Suite No. 2.*
(M) * (*) DGG Privilege 2538 080. Lamoureux Orchestra, Igor Markevitch – DEBUSSY: *La Mer; Danses.* (*)

Markevitch's version of the *Second Suite* from *Bacchus et Ariane* is worth considering, though the performance is not so distinguished or poetic as to obliterate memories of some of the earlier versions of the suite from Cluytens and Munch, which may of course reappear during the lifetime of this book.

Bacchus et Ariane: Suite No. 2; Symphony No. 3 in G minor, Op. 42.
(M) ** Supraphon SUAST 50482. Brno State Philharmonic Orchestra, Václav Neumann.

A useful coupling of Roussel's tautly written *Third Symphony* and parts of his imaginative score to *Bacchus et Ariane.* The performances are lively and spirited, and the recording has good presence and a spacious acoustic. A competitive issue at present, particularly when Roussel's representation in the catalogue is not as strong as it was three or four years ago.

Piano concerto, Op. 36.
(B) * (*) Turnabout TV 34405S. Maria Littauer (piano), Hamburg Symphony Orchestra, Alois Springer – RAVEL: *Piano concerto in G major.* (*)

Roussel's vivid and vital *Piano concerto* is well enough served by these artists, but unfortunately the dry and closely balanced recording inhibits a recommendation. This is a pity since the catalogue lists no current alternative.

Symphonies Nos. 3 in G minor, Op. 42; 4 in A major, Op. 53.
(B) ** Decca Eclipse ECS 673. Suisse Romande Orchestra, Ernest Ansermet.

The recording is genuine but early stereo and remarkably good for its date. The performances are suitably abrasive, with the odd scruffy edges, but currently there is no alternative coupling to be had. Munch's version was much more alert and the Cluytens on EMI was admirably atmospheric. At the price these performances represent good value but it would be idle to pretend that they are representative of Ansermet at his best.

Serenade for flute, violin, viola, violoncello and harp, Op. 30.
(M) *** Oiseau-Lyre SOL 60048. Melos Ensemble – RAVEL: *Introduction and allegro; etc.*⊛ ***
(B) * (*) Turnabout TV 34161S. Wilhelm Schwegler (flute), Helga Storck (harp), members of the Endres Quartet–RAVEL: *Introduction and allegro;* DEBUSSY: *Sonata.* (*)

The Turnabout version is a good, workmanlike performance, well if not very subtly recorded, but it cannot compare with the inspired Melos version, which is beautifully engineered. This is part of a concert which includes an equally memorable account of Ravel's *Introduction and allegro.*

String quartet in D major, Op. 45.
(M) ** Supraphon SUAST 50950. Novák Quartet – MARTINŮ: *Quartet No. 6.****

Roussel's only quartet, a work of his late maturity, is otherwise available in an inadequate version by the Loewenguth Quartet and on an imported Erato disc at full price. This fluent account by the Novák Quartet has solid merits to commend it and the advantage of a highly interesting coupling, Martinu's *Sixth Quartet.* On balance, and given its moderate price, this is the version to have.

3 Pieces for piano, Op. 49; Suite pour piano, Op. 14: Bourrée (only).
(M) ** (*) Vox STGBY 671. Grant Johannesen (piano) – DUKAS: *Variations*; SÉVERAC: *Pieces.** (*)

As well as being a formidable composer of symphonies, all of them intensely refreshing, Roussel was a strong and imaginative writer for the piano. The *Three Pieces* were written for Robert Casadesus, and their nobility and their teeming energy reflect that. The *Bourrée* is much earlier, but for its period, 1909, it is surprisingly original. Johannesen, as in the rest of an imaginatively chosen programme, plays with purposeful conviction. Clattery recording.

Suite pour piano, Op. 14; Sonatine, Op. 16; 3 Pieces, Op. 49.
(M) * (*) Oiseau-Lyre SOL 60052. Françoise Petit (piano).

A useful collection, offering terse, clean, sensitive playing. The recording, however, is less than distinguished: it is full-blooded but lacks brilliance and bite.

Rubbra, Edmund
(born 1901)

Symphony No. 7 in C major, Op. 88.
*** Lyrita SRCS 41. London Philharmonic Orchestra, Sir Adrian Boult – VAUGHAN WILLIAMS: *Tallis fantasia.****

Rubbra has been neglected on record, and this record of a comparatively late symphony (1956) helps to right the balance, particularly in an outstanding performance. The longest and most ambitious movement of the three – maybe the most enigmatic too – is the finale, an extended *Passacaglia and fugue* displaying the composer's naturally contrapuntal mode of thought at its most typical. The first movement brings a cogent argument based on a simple four-note motif, and the second a rhythmic scherzo that leads to a more lyrical, noble climax. A thoughtful work well worth investigation, particularly when it is coupled with Boult's fine interpretation of the *Tallis fantasia.* First-rate recording.

String quartet No. 2 in E flat major, Op. 73.
(B) *** Pye GSGC 14101. Amici Quartet – HERRMANN: *Echoes.****

Rubbra's *Second Quartet* is one of his most thoughtful works, arguably the finest of his three quartets. Its inspiration is consistently eloquent. Excellent, committed playing and a very good recording make this a worthwhile bargain.

Rubinstein, Anton
(1829–94)

(i) *Piano concerto No. 4 in D minor, Op. 70. Great étude in C major, Op. 23/2;*

Melody in F major, Op. 3/1; Polka bohème, Op. 82/7; Rêve angélique, Op. 10/22; Romance in E flat major, Op. 44/1; Valse in F major, Op. 82/6; Valse-caprice in E flat major.

(M) * (*) Vox STGBY 642. Michael Ponti (piano), (i) with Philharmonic Hungarica, Othmar Maga.

The *Concerto* is slight, even though it has a pleasant *Andante* and a vigorous finale. Rubinstein's métier is clearly shown by his salon pieces, of which the *Melody in F* is the most famous and most characteristic. Performances good, recording more than acceptable.

Konzertstück for piano and orchestra, Op. 113.

(B) ** Turnabout TV 34387S. Felicja Blumenthal (piano), Vienna Symphony Orchestra, Hellmuth Froschauer – PADEREWSKI: *Piano concerto.***

Although not without its melodic interest, Rubinstein's *Konzertstück* tends to rather outstay its welcome. But Felicja Blumenthal gives a strong performance, and her advocacy is persuasive. Recording clear rather than rich.

Symphony No. 2 in C major (Ocean), Op. 42.

(M) ** Vox STGBY 665. Westphalian Symphony Orchestra, Richard Kapp.

In its full expanse the *Ocean symphony* of Rubinstein contains no fewer than seven movements – covering the world's seven seas, commentators used to explain. This flawed but enjoyable recording includes only five movements on two well-crammed sides, and the textual confusion is the more complicated since Rubinstein replaced movements with new ones, as well as adding to the list. This recording was made on the basis of choosing the five best movements out of all that are available, some in the first version, others in the revised version. The results go a long way to explain Rubinstein's nineteenth-century fame as a symphonist, in colourful and attractive writing inclined to be verbose. Well worth investigating at medium price. Fair recording.

Rue, Pierre de La
(died 1518)

Requiem: Missa pro defunctis.

(B) ** Turnabout TV 34431S. Spandauer Kantorei, Martin Behrmann – JOSQUIN DES PRÉS: *Missa pange lingua.***

Although the recording as such is not distinguished, the Spandauer Kantorei give eminently acceptable value in this noble work. It is a more spirited account than the full-price alternative on Telefunken, within a recital by the Munich Capella Antiqua (SAWT 9471), though that enjoys more refined recording.

Ruggles, Carl
(1876–1972)

Sun-treader.

*** DGG 2530 048. Boston Symphony Orchestra, Michael Tilson Thomas – IVES: *Three Places.****

Ruggles had an independence of outlook that commands admiration, and he was a more accomplished craftsman than Ives, his work showing a more finished surface. *Sun-treader*, written in the 1930s but not performed until the 1960s, deserves a hearing, and such sympathetic advocacy as Thomas's should stimulate further interest in this worthwhile composer.

Russo, William
(20th century)

3 Pieces for blues band and symphony orchestra, Op. 50.
>** DGG 2530 309. Siegel-Schwall Band, Boston Symphony Orchestra, Seiji Ozawa – BERNSTEIN: *West Side Story: Symphonic dances.*** (*)

As a coupling for Bernstein's colourful suite from *West Side Story*, the Russo confection is interesting in choice if not in content. The piece represents a vigorous attempt at barrier-leaping, and will appeal to those who like such mixtures. To others it is likely to seem both over-sweet and over-aggressive. Recording both rich and aggressive.

Saint-Saëns, Camille
(1835–1921)

Carnival of the Animals.
>(B) *** Classics for Pleasure CFP 40086. Peter Katin, Philip Fowke (pianos), Scottish National Orchestra, Alexander Gibson – RAVEL: *Ma Mère l'Oye*; BIZET: *Jeux d'enfants.*** (*)
>** (*) HMV ASD 299. Hephzibah Menuhin, Abbey Simon (pianos), Philharmonia Orchestra, Efrem Kurtz – PROKOFIEV: *Peter and the Wolf.*** (*)
>** HMV ASD 2753. John Ogdon, Brenda Lucas (pianos), City of Birmingham Orchestra, Louis Frémaux – FAURÉ: *Ballade*; LITOLFF: *Scherzo.***

Apart from an excess of resonance at the opening, the Classics for Pleasure recording is freshly immediate, and Gibson's performance has both character and spontaneity. There is affection, and the humour is not overdone. With good couplings this is a most attractive disc. Kurtz's record is very well played and with one exception well recorded. The exception is *Tortoises* where the double-basses are recorded with very poor definition. But with such alert orchestral detail and a firm, well-balanced stereo image this can otherwise be recommended alongside the Philips Universo disc below. The Ogdon duo give a characteristically sturdy performance with competent support from Frémaux. The recording is vivid but the poker-faced approach offers neither humour nor a gracious touch. Even *The Swan* seems comparatively stoic.

(i) Carnival of the Animals. (Also includes: (ii) VIVALDI: *Flute concerto in D major (The Goldfinch), Op. 10/3, P.155.* RAMEAU: *La Poule (The Hen).* MUSSORGSKY: *Pictures at an Exhibition: Ballet of the unhatched chicks.* RIMSKY-KORSAKOV: *Flight of the bumble bee.* TCHAIKOVSKY: *Swan Lake: Dance of the queen of the swans; Dance of the cygnets.*)
>(M) *** Philips Universo 6580 085. (i) Soloists, Lamoureux Orchestra, Roberto Benzi; (ii) various artists.

This is an imaginative and attractive way of filling up a medium-priced disc which includes a very good performance of Saint-Saëns's famous miniature zoo. Benzi gives a characteristically fresh reading and his unnamed pianists are excellent players who obviously enjoy poking fun at themselves in their own portrait. The recording is bright and vivid, and the couplings are no less well played and recorded. Vivaldi's *Flute concerto* is enchanting as presented here by Severino Gazzelloni and I Musici. An excellent idea, well realized.

(i) *Piano concertos Nos. 1–5.* (ii) *Septet for trumpet, strings and piano, Op. 65.*
*** HMV SLS 802 (3 discs). (i) Aldo Ciccolini (piano), Orchestre de Paris, Serge Baudo; (ii) Groupe Instrumental de Paris.

This makes an immensely enjoyable collection. There may be little development of style between the first concerto, written when the composer was twenty-three, and the fifth, *The Egyptian,* written at Luxor when he was in his fifties, but this is first-rate gramophone material. Beethoven, Bach and Mendelssohn all get their due in the *First Concerto.* The *Second* and *Fourth* are already well known, but No. 5 is unexpectedly attractive, with oriental atmosphere tinging the music rather than overwhelming it. The finale, in which Egyptian ideas are punctuated in turn by early honky-tonk and a big Tchaikovskian melody, is delightful. Only No. 3 falls short in its comparatively banal ideas, and even in that there is a hilarious finale which sounds like a Viennese operetta turned into a concerto. Spirited performances from Ciccolini and his colleagues. The *Septet* too shows the composer at his most vivid.

Piano concertos Nos. 1 in D major, Op. 17; 3 in E flat major, Op. 29.
*** HMV CSD 3734. Aldo Ciccolini (piano), Orchestre de Paris, Serge Baudo.

The *First Concerto* is a notably spontaneous work, and if the invention in No. 3 is below the level of the rest, this is still a most attractive coupling.

Piano concerto No. 2 in G minor, Op. 22.
** RCA SB 6841. Artur Rubinstein (piano), Philadelphia Orchestra, Eugene Ormandy – FALLA: *Nights in the Gardens of Spain.***

Rubinstein's distinctive, neo-classical approach to Saint-Saëns's most popular concerto is familiar from an earlier RCA stereo LP differently coupled. This new recording is much more satisfactory, technically speaking, but the earlier performance had more sparkle than this.

Piano concertos Nos. 2 in G minor, Op. 22; 4 in C minor, Op. 44.
*** HMV CSD 3750. Aldo Ciccolini (piano), Orchestre de Paris, Serge Baudo.

A highly recommendable coupling of the two most popular Saint-Saëns concertos.

Piano concerto No. 4 in C minor, Op. 44.
** Philips 6500 095. Michele Campanella (piano), Monte Carlo Opera Orchestra, Aldo Ceccato – LISZT: *Hungarian fantasia; Totentanz.***

Campanella's thoughtful artistry gives this Saint-Saëns concerto an extra dimension, even if some of the sparkle is lost. Well recorded, this is an excellent version for those who fancy the unexpected coupling.

Piano concerto No. 5 in F major (Egyptian), Op. 103.
(B) * (*) Turnabout TV 34423S. Orazio Frugoni (piano), Vienna Symphony Orchestra, Hans Swarowsky – LALO: *Piano concerto.**

The last of Saint-Saëns's piano concertos is a delightful work with its Egyptian overtones, but it deserves better performance and recording than this dated reissue.

Violin concerto No. 3 in B minor, Op. 61.

(B) ** Decca Eclipse ECS 663. Alfredo Campoli (violin), London Philharmonic Orchestra, Pierino Gamba – SARASATE: *Zigeunerweisen* ***; WIENIAWSKI: *Legende*.**

Campoli's performance, dating from the mid-fifties, is highly enjoyable, and the orchestral detail is surprisingly vivid for such early stereo. There is some lack of swagger at the opening of the first movement, but with the romantic flair of the second subject Campoli comes fully into his own. The *Siciliano* is very beautifully played, and the finale is superbly vigorous and stylish. Gamba provides a fine partnership, and the orchestral contribution is telling throughout: the brass chorale in the finale has a fine thrust.

Violin concerto No. 3 in B minor, Op. 61; Havanaise (for violin and orchestra), *Op. 86; Introduction and rondo capriccioso* (for violin and orchestra), *Op. 28.*

(M) ** Philips Universo 6580 016. Henryk Szeryng (violin), Monte Carlo Opera Orchestra, Eduard van Remoortel.

Clean, immaculate performances from Szeryng, whose approach is aristocratic rather than indulgent. The orchestral contribution is adequate but is not helped by the recording balance, which spotlights the violin and tends to dim the colour in the important woodwind solos. In the finale of the *Concerto* the brass chorale lacks resonance, but there is no doubt that Szeryng's solo playing gives this collection a distinct character: in the *Havanaise* and *Introduction and rondo capriccioso* the bravura and sense of style make for impressive results.

(i) *Violin concerto No. 3 in B minor, Op. 61;* (ii) *Introduction and rondo capriccioso, Op. 28.*

(M) ** (*) HMV SXLP 30159. Nathan Milstein (violin), with (i) Philharmonia Orchestra, Anatole Fistoulari, (ii) Concert Arts Orchestra, Walter Susskind – CHAUSSON: *Poème*.***

Milstein's strong, imperious style adds stature to the first movement of the *Concerto*, and Fistoulari provides a matching strong accompaniment throughout. His presentation of the brass chorale in the finale creates an effect of considerable power. The solo playing is both beautiful and assured, although it does not perhaps have quite the gentle charm that Campoli finds. Milstein is glitteringly assured in the *Introduction and rondo capriccioso*, and his effortless bravura is easy to enjoy. His tone is fractionally hardened here by the brightly lit recording, whereas in the *Concerto* the sound is natural. But in both works the overall quality is good.

Violoncello concerto No. 1 in A minor, Op. 33.

*** HMV ASD 2498. Jacqueline du Pré (cello), New Philharmonia Orchestra, Daniel Barenboim – SCHUMANN: *Cello concerto*.***

** Philips 6500 045. Maurice Gendron (cello), Monte Carlo Opera Orchestra, Roberto Benzi – LALO: *Concerto*; FAURÉ: *Élégie*.* (*)

Jacqueline du Pré was seen launching into this virtuoso concerto with unparalleled passion in a television film about her, which alternated shots of her in a railway carriage playing a 'pop' number. The contrast between the great virtuoso and the fun-loving girl was irresistible, and it is illuminating that so young an artist can find a great depth, a more heroic quality, in a work which is generally dismissed as

805

merely elegant (Tovey used the diminutive term 'opusculum'). One is convinced by du Pré that it is greater music than one ever suspected, and that is some achievement. The charming minuet movement is done with great delicacy. Coupled with a fine performance of the Schumann, well recorded, it makes an excellent disc.

A good performance from Maurice Gendron with an adequate accompaniment. But the recording is not especially distinguished, with the soloist balanced too far forward.

Danse macabre, Op. 40.
  (B) ** Music for Pleasure MFP 57012. Scottish National Orchestra, Alexander Gibson – DUKAS: *L'Apprenti sorcier*; ROSSINI: *La Boutique fantasque.*** (*)

A clear, straightforward account from Gibson, but perhaps not quite as attractive as the performance he gave in an earlier recording for Decca with the New Symphony Orchestra, now included in a very attractive collection called *Danse macabre* (Decca SPA 175), which is discussed in our *Treasury* volume.

Danse macabre, Op. 40; Le Rouet d'Omphale, Op. 31.
  (M) *** Decca Ace of Diamonds SDD 144. Paris Conservatoire Orchestra, Jean Martinon – BIZET: *Jeux d'enfants*; IBERT: *Divertissement.****

These two performances are well characterized, and the excellent orchestral playing, coupled to Martinon's real sense of style, is supported by a recording which is tonally excellent if with a touch of hardness in the treble, and which sounds even more immediate in its Ace of Diamonds transfer.

Tone-poems: Danse macabre, Op. 40; La Jeunesse d'Hercule, Op. 50; Phaëton, Op. 39; Le Rouet d'Omphale, Op. 31.

  *** HMV CSD 3729. Orchestre de Paris, Pierre Dervaux.

Excellent performances of two familiar tone-poems coupled with two rarities. Both *Phaëton*, a familiar piece at one time, and *La Jeunesse d'Hercule* are well-wrought pieces, fashioned with Saint-Saëns's usual skill and with lively invention. Good recording too.

Symphonies Nos. 1 in E flat major, Op. 2; 2 in A minor, Op. 55.
  *** HMV ASD 2946. French National Radio Orchestra, Jean Martinon.

The *First Symphony* is a youthful work, written when Saint-Saëns was eighteen. It is a well-fashioned and genial piece, much indebted to Mendelssohn and Schumann but with some delightfully fresh invention. The *Second Symphony* was a later work, written in 1878, and is more familiar, for although it rarely features in the concert hall it does occasionally appear in broadcast programmes. This is full of excellent ideas and makes a welcome change from the familiar *Third*. The French Radio Orchestra play splendidly for Martinon, and the engineers have produced agreeably balanced and well-detailed sound.

Symphony No. 3 in C minor, Op. 78.
  *** EMI Quadraphonic Q4-TWO 404; Stereo TWO 404. City of Birmingham Orchestra, Louis Frémaux.
  *** Decca SXL 6482. Los Angeles Philharmonic Orchestra, Zubin Mehta.
  (M) ** Philips Universo 6580 070. Hague Philharmonic Orchestra, Roberto Benzi.
  (B) ** Classics for Pleasure CFP 40053. Paris Conservatoire Orchestra, Georges Prêtre.

(B) ** RCA Victrola VICS 1508. Boston Symphony Orchestra, Charles Munch.

This once neglected but now popular symphony is well served by the gramophone. At all price levels there is a good version to be had. There need be no reservations about the Mehta. The playing of the Los Angeles Orchestra is first-class and Mehta draws a well-disciplined and exuberant response from all departments. The recording too is extremely fine, with good detail and a well-lit texture. Frémaux's account with the CBSO is superbly played, and it too is given the benefit of excellent recording, which effectively reveals detail without any obtrusive effects and which has plenty of impact. There is really little to choose between the two in stereo, but the quadraphonic version of the Birmingham recording is in a class of its own. The richness of the slow movement is impressive enough, but the finale is breathtaking in its overwhelming impact.

In the mid-price bracket the Hague version under Roberto Benzi is eminently serviceable and has excellent recording to commend it, but the performance is good rather than outstanding and will not generate unlimited enthusiasm.

At its bargain price Prêtre's reading on Classics for Pleasure has much to commend it. The recording is open to the charge of being over-reverberant, but although some detail is not firmly in focus, the overall sound is musical and the performance, even if it falls short of distinction, has vigour and commitment. Not a first choice by any means but a record that will do good service. Munch conveys a true sense of strength in the outer sections and is not tempted to sentimentalize the slow section. The finale is extraordinarily exciting, with fine organ tone. This is another excellent bargain alternative, although the recording is not as fine as Ansermet's on Decca (see below).

(i) *Symphony No. 3 in C minor, Op. 78;* (ii) *Le Rouet d'Omphale, Op. 31.*
(B) **(*) Decca SPA 228. (i) Suisse Romande Orchestra, Ernest Ansermet; (ii) Paris Conservatoire Orchestra, Jean Martinon.

The Ansermet account is an excellent bargain. Unlike the Prêtre on Classics for Pleasure the recording has plenty of detail and a well-focused sound picture. The orchestral playing has spirit though it is perhaps wanting in finesse. In any event it is thoroughly recommendable (as in its different way is the Prêtre).

Variations on a theme of Beethoven (for 2 pianos), *Op. 35.*
** Decca SXL 6303. Bracha Eden, Alexander Tamir (pianos) – BRAHMS: *Double sonata.** (*)

One feels that Eden and Tamir forget that these are Saint-Saëns's variations rather than Beethoven's and their approach is just that bit too serious. Certainly Beethoven's own style spills over into the French composer's music, yet a fine early stereo recording by Kurt Bauer and Heidi Bung, which is now deleted, showed us that a light touch is rewarding here. But this is a strong, classical reading, crisply recorded and enjoyable as such.

(Organ) *Preludes and fugues Nos. 1 in E major; 2 in B major; 3 in E flat major, Op. 99/1–3; 4 in D minor; 5 in G major; 6 in C major, Op. 109/1–3.*
(B) * (*) RCA LVL 1 5024. Odile Pierre (organ of La Madeleine, Paris).
Preludes and fugues Nos. 4 in D minor; 5 in G major, Op. 109/1 and 2.
(B) * (*) Turnabout TV 34238S. Jean-Claude Raynaud (organ of St Sernin, Toulouse) – FRANCK and WIDOR: *Organ pieces.** (*)

Saint-Saëns's *Preludes and fugues* are written in diverse styles, sometimes piquant, sometimes expansive, sometimes even quirky, but the quality of the invention is below the composer's very best. The performances by Odile Pierre are adequate, but the organ is recorded with a touch of harshness and the tone is to some extent lacking in body. Better this than the more muffled effect of an English cathedral organ, but a happier compromise between substance and clarity has been found on other records of French organ music. The Turnabout performances are not very compulsive either.

Requiem Mass, Op. 54.
> *** RCA SB 6864. Danielle Galland (soprano), Jeannine Collard (contralto), Francis Bardot (tenor), Jacques Villisech (bass), Contrepoint Choral Ensemble, ORTF Orchestra Lyrique, Jean-Gabriel Gaussens; Micheline Lagache (organ).

This is an affecting and well-wrought work with a distinct nobility and depth to it. It comes from the late 1870s and was written in memory of a friend who had died. It is a restrained work and is given a performance of dignity and quiet eloquence here. The recording is not outstanding but it is more than satisfactory, having warmth and clarity. This is an issue that could easily pass collectors by, but it well repays investigation.

Samson et Dalila (opera in 3 acts): complete recording.
> * (*) RCA LRL 3 5017 (3 discs). Christa Ludwig (mezzo-soprano), James King (tenor), Bernd Weikl (baritone), Alexander Malta (bass), Bavarian Radio Chorus, Munich Radio Orchestra, Giuseppe Patané.

Whenever a French version of this dated but memorable score is in the catalogue, the Munich performance could hardly be recommended with any enthusiasm, so unidiomatic is it in style. The Prêtre version on HMV outshone this one at every point, including solo singing and recording quality, but until the HMV set returns this will have to do.

Sallinen, Aulis
(born 1935)

Mauermusik.
> ** (*) Decca SXL 6431. Swedish Radio Orchestra, Paavo Berglund – SIBELIUS: *Symphony No. 4.*** (*)

The 'Mauer' in question is the Berlin wall. Aulis Sallinen's piece is by no means without atmosphere: he is obviously a gifted composer with a refined aural palette. At the same time the score does not rise much above the level of general-purpose modernity and there is little that is either memorable or highly individual. Good performance and recording.

Santórsola, Guido
(born 1904)

Double guitar concerto.
> (M) *** CBS Classics 61469. Sergio and Eduardo Abreu (guitars), English Chamber Orchestra, Enrique Garcia Asensio – CASTELNUOVO-TEDESCO: *Double concerto.** (*)

Guido Santórsola's *Double concerto* is a serial composition of remarkable spontaneity and popular appeal. Its material is in no way trite, and it has a striking atmosphere throughout. It is splendidly played here and is a work to reward the listener, with its happy combination of traditional forms (the first movement an energetic toccata) and exploratory melodic and harmonic techniques. The recording is vivid; the soloists are spotlighted but not at the expense of the telling orchestral contribution. Recommended.

Sarasate, Pablo
(1844–1908)

Carmen fantasy (for violin and orchestra), *Op. 25.*
> *** HMV SLS 832 (2 discs). Itzhak Perlman (violin), Royal Philharmonic Orchestra, Lawrence Foster – PAGANINI: *Violin concerto No. 1; Caprices.****
> ⊛ *** HMV ASD 2782 (same performance as above) – PAGANINI: *Violin concerto No. 1.****

This is the filler for side two of Paganini's *First Violin concerto*, but what a gorgeous filler. Sarasate's *Fantasy* is a selection of the most popular tunes from *Carmen*, with little attempt made to stitch the seams between them. But played like this, with superb panache, luscious tone, and glorious recording, the piece almost upstages the concerto with which it is coupled.

Zigeunerweisen (Gypsy airs), Op. 20/1.
> (B) *** Decca Eclipse ECS 663. Alfredo Campoli (violin), London Philharmonic Orchestra, Pierino Gamba – SAINT-SAËNS: *Violin concerto No. 3;* WIENIAWSKI: *Légende.***

A characteristically brilliant and stylistically assured performance from Campoli, who is completely at home in this music and knows just how to shape the famous lyrical centrepiece and provide plenty of fireworks for the finale. The soloist is recorded closely and faithfully.

Satie, Erik
(1866–1925)

Les Aventures de Mercure (ballet); *La Belle Excentrique; Jack in the Box* (orch. Milhaud).
> * Decca Phase 4 PFS 4286. London Festival Players, Bernard Herrmann – MILHAUD: *Suadades do Brazil.**

Rather heavy-handed performances and a crudely balanced recording limit the appeal of this disc.

Les Aventures de Mercure: ballet suite; *La Belle Excentrique: Grande ritournelle; Cinq grimaces pour 'Un Songe d'une nuit d'été'; Parade:* ballet suite; *Relâche:* ballet suite; *Deux Préludes posthumes et une Gnossienne* (orch. Poulenc); *En habit de cheval; Le Fils des Étoiles* (orch. Manuel); *Gymnopédies Nos. 1 and 3* (orch. Debussy); *Jack in the Box* (orch Milhaud); *Trois Morceaux en forme de poire* (orch. Desormière).
> (M) ** (*) Vanguard VCS 11037/8. Utah Symphony Orchestra, Maurice Abravanel.

A collection of Satie's orchestral music including various orchestrations made by friends and disciples is very welcome. Abravanel, an inveterate searcher after new material on record, fails to throw off some of the more pointed pieces, such as *Jack in the Box*, with quite the lightness required, but these are enjoyable performances, well recorded.

(i) *La Belle Excentrique;* (i; ii) *Embryons desséchés;* (i) *Les Pantins dansent;* (iii) *Parade;* (i; ii) *Piège de Méduse;* (i) *Relâche* (ballet): *Entr'acte cinématographique;* (i; ii) *Trois petites pièces montées.*

> (M) ** Vox STGBY 646. (i) Die Reihe Ensemble, Friedrich Cerha; (ii) Marie-Thérèse Escribano (speaker); (iii) Radio Luxembourg Orchestra, Louis de Froment.

This is an excellent and enjoyable anthology, very well recorded, and it might have earned three stars had the producer been more enterprising in the matter of sound effects for *Parade.* As it is, they all appear to be simulated, except the pistol shots. The typewriter is ingeniously imitated by the percussion department and the siren is achieved electronically – an organ perhaps? However, the performance itself has an attractive impulse and atmosphere, and all the other music here is very successful. *Trois petites pièces montées* and *Les Pantins dansent* are played with pleasing delicacy. The *Entr'acte cinématographique* has some outrageously repetitive sections which originally served as background music for a film of the composer's antics crawling on the façade of Notre Dame Cathedral. But the piece is played with such aplomb and humour that the listener readily forgives an initial impression that his pick-up has stuck in a repeating groove!

En habit de cheval; Parade; Trois petites pièces montées; Socrate, Part 3: (i) *La Mort de Socrate.*

> (M) * (*) Everest SDBR 3234. ORTF Orchestra, Manuel Rosenthal, (i) with Denise Monteil (soprano).

The performances here have a certain style, but *Parade* is rather slow. Certainly the special-effects department is on top form, and the clarity of the Everest recording helps. The highlight of the disc is the excerpt from the cantata *Socrate,* which is sung very well by Denise Monteil.

Gymnopédies Nos. 1 and 3 (orch. Debussy).

> *** HMV Quadraphonic Q4-ASD 2989; Stereo ASD 2989. City of Birmingham Orchestra, Louis Frémaux – IBERT: *Divertissement;* HONEGGER: *Pacific 231;* POULENC: *Les Biches.*** (*)

Beautiful orchestral playing and rich resonant recording suit Debussy's indulgent scoring perfectly. The quality of Satie's inspiration is in no doubt in this beautiful music.

Parade.

> *** Philips SAL 3637. London Symphony Orchestra, Antal Dorati – AURIC: *Overture;* FRANÇAIX: *Concertino;* MILHAUD: *Le Bœuf.****

Satie's *Parade* is the most audacious piece in an excellent collection of entertaining twentieth-century French music. The bright recording joins Dorati's approach in presenting the music vividly, and the necessary atmosphere is given to the more restrained sections of the score. Of all the music on this disc only Françaix's economical *Concertino* effectively avoids sounding a trifle inflated for its musical substance, but it is a real pleasure to listen to music of our own century that sets out to please the ear, for all its extravagances.

(i; ii) *Choses vues à droit et à gauche (sans lunette)* (for violin and piano). Piano duo: (i; iii) *Aperçus désagréables; En habit de cheval; Trois Morceaux en forme de poire.* Songs: (iv; i) *La diva de L'Empire; Je te veux; Ludions* (5 songs); *Quatre petits mélodies; Tendrement; Trois Mélodies; Trois Poèmes d'amour.*

(M) ** Vox STGBY 656. (i) Frank Glazer (piano); (ii) Millard Taylor (violin); (iii) Richard Deas (piano); (iv) Elaine Bonazzi (mezzo-soprano).

An attractive anthology of chamber music and songs. The little violin duo is played with unpretentious charm by Millard Taylor, and the piano duet pieces are no less successful, with unusually warm and pleasing piano tone for this label. Elaine Bonazzi gives robust, colourful performances of these sets of miniature songs, not revealing all their charm and humour, but enjoyable in their directness.

Avant-dernières Pensées; La Belle Excentrique (4 hands); *Descriptions automatiques; Embryons desséchés; Trois Gnossiennes; Trois Gymnopédies; Trois Morceaux en forme de poire; Passacaille; Préludes flasques (pour un chien); Le Piège de Méduse; Véritables préludes flasques (pour un chien).*

*** HMV ASD 2389. Aldo Ciccolini (piano).

Although Satie's music is often overrated by his admirers, there is a desperate melancholy and a rich poetic feeling about much of this music which are altogether unique. The *Gymnopédies* or the famous *Morceaux en forme de poire* show such flashes of innocence and purity of inspiration that criticism is disarmed. Aldo Ciccolini is widely praised as a Satie interpreter, and he plays here with unaffected sympathy. The recording is first-rate.

Avant-dernières Pensées; Croquis et agaceries d'un gros bonhomme en bois; Embryons desséchés; Passacaille; Prélude en tapisserie; Premier menuet;

Rêverie; Sonatine bureaucratique; Trois Gnossiennes; Trois Gymnopédies; Les trois valses du précieux dégoûté; Vieux sequins; Véritables préludes flasques.

(M) *** Vox STGBY 633. Frank Glazer (piano).

Chapitres tournés en tous sens; Descriptions automatiques; Heures séculaires et instantanées; Nocturnes; Pièces froides: 1, Airs à faire fuir; 2, Danses de travers; Trois Sarabandes; Sports et Divertissements.

(M) ** (*) Vox STGBY 634. Frank Glazer (piano).

Danses gothiques; Enfantillages pittoresques; Menus propos enfantins; Les Pantins dansent; Peccadilles importunes; Prélude de la Porte Héroïque du Ciel; Quatre Préludes; Quatre Ogives.

(M) ** (*) Vox STGBY 635. Frank Glazer (piano).

Vox offer Satie's piano music on three discs in excellent performances by Frank Glazer. This artist seems to penetrate the character of each of these aphoristic and haunting miniatures with genuine flair and insight. In some ways these are more searching and sympathetic performances than those of Aldo Ciccolini, and the recording, although rather reverberant, is full-blooded and faithful. There is much attractive music here, but Satie's output was uneven and some of the pieces are insubstantial. From the point of view of musical substance the first disc, STGBY 633, which includes the *Gnossiennes* and *Gymnopédies*, is the most rewarding and fully earns the three stars allotted. But those who are attracted to the idiom of the music can safely go on to explore the other two.

Chapitres tournés en tous sens: 1, Celle qui parle trop; Croquis et agaceries: 3, Espanana; Embryons desséchés; Trois Gnossiennes; Trois Gymnopédies; Noc-

turne No. 3; Le Piège de Méduse; Premier menuet; Sports et divertissements; Véritables préludes flasques; Vieux sequins: 2, Danse cuirassée.

(M) *** RCA LSB 4097. William Masselos (piano).

Masselos, best known for his interpretations of Ives's piano music, proves equally at home with another musical eccentric. An outstanding and well-chosen selection of the Satie piano music, beautifully played and well recorded.

Passacaille; Prélude en tapisserie; Sports et divertissements; Trois Gymnopédies; Trois Sarabandes; Trois Valses distinguées; Les trois valses du précieux dégoûté.

* (*) Pye Ensayo NEL 2003. Laurence Allix (piano).

Although this is well recorded, Laurence Allix's deliberate presentation often fails to create a convincing atmosphere. Even the Gymnopédies show less than their usual incandescence.

Socrate (symphonic drama with voice in 3 parts): complete recording.

(M) ** Vox STGBY 645. Marie-Thérèse Escribano (soprano), soloists, Die Reihe Ensemble, Friedrich Cerha – DEBUSSY: Chansons de Bilitis.**

(M) * Everest SDBR 3246. Violette Journeaux (soprano), soloists, Paris Philharmonic Orchestra, René Leibowitz.

The Vox performance of the complete Socrate is an eloquent one. Marie-Thérèse Escribano always sings expressively, but she rises to the challenge of the inspired third section of the work most evocatively. The supporting cast and sensitive direction by Friedrich Cerha are matched by good recording.

The Everest disc has no coupling, but in any case the performance is unattractive, with shrill singing from the principal soprano soloist.

Scarlatti, Alessandro
(1660–1725)

Cantata pastorale per la Natività di Nostro Signore Gesù Cristo.

*** HMV ASD 2615. Janet Baker (contralto), English Chamber Orchestra, Raymond Leppard – MONTEVERDI: L'Incoronazione di Poppea excerpts; D. SCARLATTI: Salve Regina.***

(B) ** Turnabout TV 34180S. Gertraut Stoklassa (soprano), Mainz Chamber Orchestra, Günter Kehr – HAYDN: Cantilena pro adventu; PURCELL: Behold, I bring you glad tidings.**

The cooler enchantments of Alessandro Scarlatti make an admirable foil for the intense Monteverdi offerings on the HMV disc. Janet Baker's depth of expression brings vividness to this Cantata pastorale written in Christmas celebration. Gertraut Stoklassa is no match for Janet Baker, but she sings with moving eloquence, and Kehr's accompaniment provides excellent support. With rich, pleasing recording and excellent couplings, this is certainly a recommendable disc in the bargain range.

Domine, refugium factus es nobis; O magnum mysterium.

** (*) Argo ZRG 768. Schütz Choir of London, Roger Norrington – D. SCARLATTI: Stabat Mater.** (*)

These two motets are fine pieces that show how enduring the Palestrina tradition was in seventeenth-century Italy.

They are noble in conception and are beautifully performed here, making an excellent fill-up to the Domenico Scarlatti *Stabat Mater*.

Scarlatti, Domenico
(1685–1757)

Keyboard sonatas (arr. for guitar) *in E major, L.23; in D major* (originally C major), *L.104; in D minor, L.108; in A major, L.238; in A minor, L.429; in A major, L.485.*

** (*) CBS 72979. John Williams (guitar) – GOWERS: *Chamber concerto.*** (*)

Guitar arrangements of Scarlatti sonatas have their charms when played by an artist as imaginative as John Williams. They make a strange coupling for the Gowers *Concerto*, but guitar enthusiasts will not object. Close recording.

Keyboard sonatas in E major, L.21; in E minor, L.22; in F minor, L.118; in D major, L.146; in F minor, L.187; in F major, L.188; in E flat major, L.203; in A minor, L.241; in G major, L.349; in A major, L.391; in D major, L.424; in D major, L.465.

*** CBS SBRG 72274. Vladimir Horowitz (piano).

This is a marvellous disc, which sweeps away any purist notions about Scarlatti being played on the harpsichord, and has one marvelling at the richness not merely of the musical argument but of the often orchestral-sounding texture. As Horowitz himself says in an interesting sleeve-note, quoting Ralph Kirkpatrick, Scarlatti often had string or brass tone in mind. The twelve sonatas are mostly unavailable otherwise (on whatever instrument) and Horowitz selected them after he had recorded twice as many. The two slow F minor sonatas are particularly beautiful in a way not normally expected of Scarlatti.

Keyboard sonatas in E major, L.23; in G major, L.37; in G minor, L.126; in A major, L.135; in D major, L.162; in D major, L.165; in F minor, L.173; in C major, L.274; in F major, L.280; in D minor/major, L.420; in E major, L.430; in C major, L.439; in G major, L.445; in C major, L.Suppl.4; in D major, L.Suppl.15; in B flat major, L.Suppl.36.

(B) * (*) Turnabout TV 34434S. Joseph Payne (harpsichord).

The heavy resonance of the modern harpsichord on which Joseph Payne gives his recital sometimes seems at odds with Scarlatti's delicacy of feeling. But those who favour a robust approach to this composer's keyboard writing will find Payne a nimble and not unimaginative player, if sometimes prone to over-accentuation. The recording is faithful but close and sounds best with the volume set at a relatively low level.

Keyboard sonatas in E flat major, L.113; in F minor, L.187; in B flat major, L.250; in G major, L.286; in E major, L.375; in F major, L.384; in G minor, L.422; in B major, L.446; in B minor, L.449; in D major, L.463; in F major, L.474; in G major, L.487.

(M) *** Pye Virtuoso TPLS 13057. Nina Milkina (piano).

This is fresh, intelligent playing of high quality. Nina Milkina's choice of sonatas is nicely balanced and the character of her playing shows a fine sensibility in this repertoire. For those who enjoy Scarlatti on the piano this can be strongly recommended at medium price; the recording, made in the Wigmore Hall, in a lively acoustic, is natural and well judged.

Keyboard sonatas in D minor, Kk.213; in D major, Kk.214; in F sharp major, Kk.318, 319; in G minor, Kk.347; in G major, Kk.348; in C major, Kk.356, 357; in E major, Kk.380, 381; in G major, Kk.454, 455; in D major, Kk.478, 479; in F major, Kk.524, 525; in C minor, Kk.526; in C major, Kk.527.
 *** DGG 2533 072. Ralph Kirkpatrick (harpsichord).

Kirkpatrick's monumental study of Domenico Scarlatti still remains the standard work on the subject and is an enormously readable and erudite book. These performances, paired according to his theory, have all the panache and scholarship one would expect from this artist, in addition to a welcome degree of freedom and poetry. Having found some of his Bach playing pedantic, it is a pleasure to welcome this well-recorded set without reservation.

Salve Regina (arr. Leppard).
 *** HMV ASD 2615. Janet Baker (contralto) English Chamber Orchestra, Raymond Leppard – MONTEVERDI: *L'Incoronazione di Poppea excerpts*; A. SCARLATTI: *Cantata pastorale.****

The *Salve Regina* by Alessandro's brilliant son has conventional passages, but Janet Baker and Leppard together hardly let you appreciate any weakness, so intense is the performance.

Stabat Mater.
 ** (*) Argo ZRG 768. Schütz Choir of London, Roger Norrington – A. SCARLATTI: *Motets.*** (*)

The *Stabat Mater* is an early work, written during Scarlatti's sojourn in Rome (1714–19) when he was maestro di capella at S. Giulia, and it shows him to be a considerable master of polyphony. It is extended in scale and taxing to the performers. The performance here is admirable, though not always impeccable in matters of tonal balance, and the recording is good, even if it suffers from a certain want of focus at the top.

Scharwenka, Xaver (1850–1924)

Piano concerto No. 1 in B flat minor, Op. 32.
 *** RCA SB 6815. Earl Wild (piano), Boston Symphony Orchestra, Erich Leinsdorf – BALAKIREV: *Reminiscences*; MEDTNER: *Improvisation*; D'ALBERT: *Scherzo.****

Scharwenka's *Concerto No. 1* is no doubt thoroughly empty but it is no less thoroughly entertaining. It is full of vitality, and given a performance as stunning as this it is totally compelling. Earl Wild's virtuosity should be heard to be believed, and both he and the orchestra play this music as if their lives depended on it. A dazzling and astonishing performance which should on no account be missed. The recording is a bit shallow but don't let this put you off. The playing of the Balakirev and Medtner pieces on the reverse side is better recorded and no less remarkable artistically.

(i) *Piano concerto No. 2 in C minor, Op. 56. Erzählung am Klavier, Op. 5/2: Sehr schnell bewegt; Novelette, Op. 22/1; Polonaise, Op. 42; Scherzo, Op. 4.*
 (M) * (*) Vox STGBY 651. Michael Ponti (piano), (i) with Hamburg Symphony Orchestra, Richard Kapp.

The *Adagio* and finale of Scharwenka's *Second Piano concerto* are not short of ideas and the performance here is a strong one. Michael Ponti plays the finale with splendid dash and point and he is well supported by the orchestra. The recording too is warm and atmospheric, with good piano tone. But unfortunately the work's first movement is singularly unmemorable, and the short pieces which fill up the rest of side two are not very interesting either. The piano tone is less attractive here; it becomes hard and unresilient.

Scheidt, Samuel
(1587–1654)

Cantiones sacrae a 8: In dulci jubilo.
*** HMV Quadraphonic Q4–CSD 3755; Stereo CSD 3755. King's College Choir, Cambridge, Cambridge University Musical Society, Bach Choir, Wilbraham Brass Soloists, David Willcocks – GABRIELI: *Collection*; SCHÜTZ: *Psalm 150.****

Scheidt's attractive setting of *In dulci jubilo* is a favourite demonstration item from this superb simulation of choral antiphony as practised at St Mark's, Venice, in the sixteenth and seventeenth centuries. The recording seems particularly successful in this short piece, which is strong in personality and superbly sung and played. Whether in stereo or quad, this is an outstanding issue.

Schmidt, Franz
(1874–1939)

Symphony No. 4 in C major.
*** Decca SXL 6544. Vienna Philharmonic Orchestra, Zubin Mehta.

The Schoenberg centenary overshadowed that of Franz Schmidt, whose noble *Fourth Symphony* is much loved in Vienna, as this performance so readily testifies. The work has the intensity of Mahler, without the hint of hysteria, and the breadth and spaciousness of Bruckner, though it is very different from either. It has the true breath of the symphonist (as Schoenberg said of Sibelius and Shostakovich) and a dignity that reminds one a little of Elgar. This is a deeply rewarding work, beautifully played and recorded.

Schmitt, Florent
(1870–1958)

(i) *Psalm 47. La Tragédie de Salomé (tone poem).*
*** HMV ASD 2892. ORTF Orchestra, Jean Martinon, (i) with Andrea Guiot (soprano), Gaston Litaize (organ), Maîtrise (Choir).

Schmitt's *La Tragédie de Salomé* dates from 1907, when Oscar Wilde's play and Strauss's opera were much in the air. The score has a certain hothouse exoticism, and like the *Psalm 47* with which it is coupled, it belongs firmly in the *art nouveau* ethos. Even if it lacks the imaginative vitality of Debussy and Ravel, it is a colourful score and well worth hearing. The performance by the excellent ORTF Orchestra under Martinon is authoritative and idiomatic, while the recording is beautifully detailed, spacious and atmospheric. The *Psalm* is less evocative but has a strong, direct appeal: it dates from the composer's stay in Rome some years before. Anyone who likes French music of this period will find the disc rewarding; the incisive clarity of the choral singing, the sheer splendour of the orchestral sound, the impact of the percussion all make a quite overwhelming impact.

Schoenberg, Arnold
(1874–1951)

(i) *Piano concerto in C major, Op. 42;*
(ii) *Violin concerto, Op. 36.*
> ** (*) DGG 2530 257. (i) Alfred
> Brendel (piano); (ii) Zvi Zeitlin
> (violin), both with Bavarian Radio
> Symphony Orchestra, Rafael
> Kubelik.

Schoenberg devotees tend to suggest
that both these works, consciously echoing the world of the romantic concerto in
twelve-note serial terms, present the most
approachable road to appreciating the
master. For some that may be so, particularly in performances as sympathetic
as these, but more than usual in these
relatively late works the thick textures
favoured by Schoenberg obscure the
focus of the argument rather than making
it sweeter on the ear. Brendel – who made
a recording for Vox very early in his
career – remains a committed Schoenbergian, and Zeitlin is impressive too.
Though even the DGG engineers do not
manage to clarify the thorny textures
completely, the sound is good.

Violin concerto, Op. 36.
> (M) ** Supraphon SUAST 50878.
> Hyman Bress (violin), Prague
> Symphony Orchestra, Jindrich
> Rohan – STRAVINSKY: *Violin
> concerto.*(*)

Bress gives a wild, red-bloodedly emotional performance of the Schoenberg
Violin concerto, and though his wildness
leads him at times into error, the point of
the music is convincingly conveyed. One
can even detect echoes of Jewish music
fluttering round what with many artists
is still a comparatively desiccated work.
This is plainly not a performance for the
Schoenberg specialist who must have

every marked *Hauptstimme* (leading
voice) meticulously observed, but with
good, warm recording (favouring the
violin) it will win converts. The coupling
is well chosen, but unfortunately Bress
is there not so convincing.

*Pelleas und Melisande, Op. 5; Varia-
tions for orchestra, Op. 31; Verklaerte
Nacht (orchestral version), Op. 4.*
> *** DGG 2711 014 (4 discs). Berlin
> Philharmonic Orchestra, Herbert
> von Karajan – BERG: *Lyric suite;
> 3 Pieces;* WEBERN: *Collection.****

It is a pity that Karajan in his superb
four-disc collection of the orchestral
music of the Second Viennese School
omitted the key work of Schoenberg, the
Five Pieces, Op. 16. Once that is said,
these are superb performances, which
present the emotional element at full
power but give unequalled precision and
refinement. *Pelleas und Melisande,* written at the same time as the Debussy opera
but in ignorance of the rival project, is in
its way a Strauss-like masterpiece, while
the Op. 31 *Variations,* the most challenging of Schoenberg's orchestral works,
here receives a reading which vividly
conveys the ebb and flow of tension within the phrase and over the whole plan.
Superb recording.

5 Pieces for orchestra, Op. 16.
> *** Philips SAL 3539. London Sym-
> phony Orchestra, Antal Dorati –
> BERG and WEBERN: *Pieces.****

Schoenberg put evocative titles on his
Five Pieces, but it would be misleading
to think of them as programmatic pieces.
His titles were prompted by his publisher,
and the arguments – colourful as they
may be – had been established without
them. Here for the first time he was
writing 'abstract' instrumental music in
his new role as atonalist, and even today
it is amazing that such forward-looking

music could have been written in 1909. When at a Prom in 1912 Sir Henry Wood gave the first performance, the music was hissed, but already two years later in London the composer himself was able to command fair appreciation for his own interpretation. Nowadays it is the combination of clarity and colour, with an enormous orchestra used in chamber style, that still seems intensely original and new. Dorati here uses the version the composer made in 1949 with a slightly reduced orchestra. The performance is strong and vivid, and the coupling of works written at the same period by Schoenberg's emergent pupils could hardly have been better devised.

Suite for string orchestra.
> *** Argo ZRG 754. Royal Philharmonic Orchestra, Norman Del Mar – BRITTEN: *Prelude and fugue*; LUTYENS: *O saisons, O châteaux.****

Schoenberg's *Suite for strings* was written in an unexpectedly diatonic style, but shows the same uncompromising strength as the composer's other works written after his exile to America in the thirties. Excellent, full-blooded performance and recording.

Variations for orchestra, Op. 31; Chamber symphony No. 1, Op. 9.
> *** Decca SXL 6390. Los Angeles Philharmonic Orchestra, Zubin Mehta.

It is good to have two Schoenberg masterpieces, one from early in his career, one from the very peak, arguably his finest instrumental work, coupled in brilliant performances from a virtuoso orchestra. It was, after all, to Los Angeles that Schoenberg went to settle in his last years, and it would have gladdened him that his local Philharmonic Orchestra had achieved a degree of brilliance to match

that of any other orchestra in America. The Op. 31 *Variations*, among the most taxing works Schoenberg ever wrote, somehow reveal their secrets, their unmistakable greatness, more clearly when the performances have such sense of drive, born of long and patient rehearsal under a clear-headed conductor. The *First Chamber symphony* is also given a rich performance, arguably too fast at times, but full of understanding for the romantic emotions which underlie much of the writing. Brilliant recording quality.

Verklaerte Nacht (orchestral version), *Op. 4.*
> *** Decca SXL 6325. Los Angeles Philharmonic Orchestra, Zubin Mehta – SCRIABIN: *Poème de l'extase.****
> *** Argo ZRG 763. Academy of St Martin-in-the-Fields, Neville Marriner – HINDEMITH: *5 pieces*; WEBERN: *5 Movements.****

Even if Zubin Mehta is not a conductor of uniform accomplishment, his version of *Verklaerte Nacht* could hardly be bettered. It has warmth, feeling and yet is free of *schmalz*: it is sympathetically recorded and the strings play with great virtuosity and opulence of tone.

Marriner manages to have the best of both worlds with the richness of orchestral texture and the clarity of the string sextet version. His interpretation is relatively reticent until the culminating climaxes, when the final thrust is more powerful than with any rival. In a performance such as this *Verklaerte Nacht* is sensuously beautiful. Superb atmospheric recording.

Chamber symphony No. 1, Op. 9; 3 Pieces for chamber orchestra; Die eiserne Brigade (march for string quartet and piano); (i) *Phantasy for violin with piano accompaniment, Op. 47;*

Ein Stelldichein (for oboe, clarinet, violin, cello and piano); *Suite, Op. 29* (for wind, strings and piano); *Verklaerte Nacht* (for string sextet), *Op. 4*; *Weihnachtsmusik* (for 2 violins, cello, harmonium and piano); *Wind quintet*. (Choral) *Der neue Klassizismus, Op. 28/3* (for mixed chorus, viola, cello and piano); *Der Wunsch des Liebhabers, Op. 27/4* (for mixed chorus, mandolin, clarinet, violin and cello). (Vocal) (ii) *Herzgewächse, Op. 20* (for soprano, celeste, harmonium and harp); (iii) *Lied der Waldtaube* (for mezzo-soprano and chamber ensemble); (iv) *Nachtwandler* (for soprano, piccolo, trumpet, side-drum and piano); (v) *Ode to Napoleon, Op. 41* (for reciter, string quartet and piano; (iv) *Pierrot Lunaire, Op. 21*; (vi) *Serenade, Op. 24* (for clarinet, bass clarinet, mandolin, guitar, violin, viola, cello and bass voice).

> *** Decca SXLK 6660/4. Members of the London Sinfonietta, David Atherton; (i) Nona Liddell (violin), John Constable (piano); (ii) June Barton (soprano); (iii) Anna Reynolds (mezzo-soprano); (iv) Mary Thomas (soprano and reciter); (v) Gerald English (reciter); (vi) John Shirley-Quirk (bass-baritone).

Collections as wide-ranging as this of all Schoenberg's chamber music outside the string quartets and the solo piano music carry the threat that the results will be earnest rather than invigorating. In fact these recordings by the London Sinfonietta were made in conjunction with a series of centenary concerts at the Queen Elizabeth Hall. Happily the studio used was not on the South Bank but at a church with a lively acoustic. Even the most uncompromising of these works (such as the massive *Wind quintet*) prove

richly rewarding, and though not even these players can make the humour of the *Suite* and the *Serenade* anything but Germanic and heavy, the whole collection has you wanting to search further, including as it does such oddities as a piece written by Schoenberg in the army for an officer's mess celebration. *Verklaerte Nacht* in its sextet form has never sounded so radiant as here, and this version of *Pierrot Lunaire* is among the most incisive and dramatic yet recorded. Strongly recommended.

Chamber symphony No. 1, Op. 9; 3 pieces for orchestra (1910).

> (M) * (*) Everest SDBR 3192. Domaine Musical Orchestra, Pierre Boulez – MESSIAEN: *7 Haikai*.* (*)

Boulez's performance of the *Chamber symphony* characteristically uncovers the inner detail, and the close, dry Everest recording completes the process, so that one has the experience of not altogether comprehending the wood for the trees, and the emotional core of the work is not vividly projected because of this. The orchestral playing is competent rather than outstanding.

Chamber symphony No. 1, Op. 9 (arr. Webern); (i) *Pierrot Lunaire* (song cycle), *Op. 21*.

> ** (*) Unicorn RHS 319. The Fires of London, (i) with Mary Thomas (reciter), Peter Maxwell Davies.

The *Chamber symphony* is performed here in the arrangement made by Webern for the same quintet of instruments used in *Pierrot Lunaire*. It is not nearly so rich in texture and is liable to sound congested, but Stephen Pruslin's playing is most invigorating, making it a generous and attractive coupling for Mary Thomas's strong and colourful reading of *Pierrot Lunaire*, more inspirational here than in the sharper-focused version she made with the London Sinfonietta for Decca's Schoenberg album (see above). Good recording.

Fantasy for violin and piano, Op. 47.

(M) ** Supraphon SUAST 50693. Petr Messiereur (violin), Jarmila Kozderková (piano) – HINDEMITH: *Sonata*; STRAVINSKY: *Duo concertante*; WEBERN: *4 Pieces.***

The *Fantasy for violin and piano* is the last work that Schoenberg completed. In a way one can compare it with the Bartók solo *Violin sonata*, which similarly came at the end of his career (involving exile in America) and similarly represented the composer's style not in its mellowed later state but with uncompromising firmness. Schoenberg even conceived this piece as a work for solo violin alone, but there the parallel breaks down, for the finished work conveys little of the emotional soul-searching that readily emerges from the Bartók. Maybe we shall learn to find an emotional core, just as we have in other seemingly difficult Schoenberg works, but it is hard to detect. This performance is first-rate and comes on an excellent recital disc of four outstandingly important modern violin works.

Serenade for septet and bass voice, Op. 24.

(M) ** Oiseau-Lyre SOL 250. John Carol Case (bass-baritone), Melos Ensemble.

This is one of the most accessible of the works Schoenberg wrote after adopting serial technique. Not that his application of serialism is strict here, except in the rather angular-sounding setting of a Petrarch sonnet, which is perhaps the least attractive of the movements. Conversely the most immediately attractive is a *Song without words* that seems to have very little relationship with serialism at all. It would be unfair to draw generalizations from this, for above all the work shows that twelve-note music can express far more than gloomy neurotic self-torture. The performance by fine British musicians is on the cool side, not nearly so vital as a muzzily recorded old one with Mitropoulos. But the dazzling recording here does help one to accept the argument, and the playing is crisp and polished. John Carol Case does wonders with the cruel vocal line.

(i) *Serenade for septet and bass voice, Op. 24;* (ii) *Pierrot Lunaire* (song cycle), *Op. 21.*

(M) ** (*) Everest SDBR 3171. (i) Louis-Jacques Rondeleux (bass); (ii) Helga Pilarczyk (reciter), both with Domaine Musical Ensemble, Pierre Boulez.

Boulez directs strong and convincing interpretations of both *Pierrot Lunaire* and the strange craggy *Serenade*, but the playing is not as polished as in the finest rival versions. In *Pierrot Lunaire* the soloist – impressively dramatic – is balanced far too close, obscuring the delicate detail.

(i) *String quartet No. 2 in F sharp minor, Op. 10;* (ii) *Verklaerte Nacht* (for string sextet), *Op. 4.*

(B) * (*) Turnabout TV 34032S. Ramor String Quartet, with (i) Marie-Thérèse Escribano (soprano), (ii) Edith Lorincz (viola), Zsolt Deaky (cello).

The performance of the *Second Quartet* is undistinguished, though it is probably more persuasive than its coupling. The work is well worth exploring and a good account of it is sorely needed, but this does not fill the gap very adequately. *Verklaerte Nacht* is heard here in its original form for string sextet and it has a greater intimacy and delicacy of feeling in this version. There is the additional advantage of greater textural clarity as well, but having said this and in spite of the economical form in which it is offered here, one must add that the performance is not particularly distinguished. It is certainly nowhere near as persuasive as are Mehta or Marriner in the recordings for full strings, and intonation is by no means always perfect. The recorded sound is inclined to be rough, and though there is plenty of spread, the overall impression left by this side is not wholly favourable.

Suite (for E flat clarinet, clarinet, bass clarinet, violin, viola, violoncello and piano), *Op. 29.*

> (M) ** Oiseau-Lyre SOL 282. Melos Ensemble – BERG: *4 Pieces.***
>
> (M) * (*) Supraphon SUAST 50819. Musica Viva Pragensis, Zbynek Vostrák – WEBERN: *Quartet*; *Trio.***

In his *Suite*, Op. 29, Schoenberg deliberately found inspiration in Viennese dance rhythms, and modelled the structure on the serenades and divertimentos of the Mozart/Haydn period. But those associations are misleading, for Schoenberg was virtually incapable of producing genuinely light music, and this piece only nags at one, if one tries to treat it trivially. It is as formidable as most of the composer's other work of the mid-twenties, and deserves close study. The Melos performance is more relaxed than the composer's own metronome markings would strictly allow, but with superb playing from de Peyer and Crowson the conviction of the writing should be apparent even to a listener who has not yet fathomed its logic. Good recording.

The Supraphon performance is rather less successful. It is not helped by the balance, which fails to integrate the piano well into the texture. The composer's metronome markings are followed, and

the fast tempi mean that the music's expressive content loses against the desire for technical accuracy. Yet the playing itself is often excellent.

Verklaerte Nacht (for string sextet), *Op. 4.*

> (M) ** Everest SDBR 3170. Domaine Ensemble, Pierre Boulez – ELOY: *Equivalences*; POUSSEUR: *Madrigal III.***

Both the use of the original chamber version of *Verklaerte Nacht* and the direction of Pierre Boulez make for clarity rather than the opulent textures one normally associates with this earliest, highly romantic demonstration of Schoenberg's genius. The commitment and warmth of style of the players counterbalance this, though the recording is rather dry.

3 Piano pieces, Op. 11; 6 Small piano pieces, Op. 19; 5 Piano pieces, Op. 23; 2 Piano pieces, Op. 33a and 33b; Suite for piano, Op. 25.

> (B) ** Turnabout TV 34378S. Jürg von Vintschger (piano).

Schoenberg's piano music has eluded many interpreters and it has never managed to secure a broad-based public acceptance. Jürg von Vintschger is a scrupulously conscientious artist and has prepared these performances with the utmost care. The playing is cleanly recorded, though some readers might prefer a slightly warmer acoustic. Nonetheless these are sound and at times eloquent performances, and at the modest price asked they constitute a useful addition to the catalogue.

Gurre-Lieder (for soloists, chorus and orchestra).

> *** CBS 78264 (2 discs). Jess Thomas (tenor), Marita Napier (soprano), Yvonne Minton (con-

tralto), Siegmund Nimsgern (bass), Kenneth Bowen (tenor), BBC Singers, BBC Choral Society, Goldsmith's Choral Union, Men's voices of LPO Choir, BBC Symphony Orchestra, Pierre Boulez.

** (*) HMV SLS 884 (2 discs). Alexander Young (tenor), Martina Arroyo (soprano), Janet Baker (mezzo-soprano), Odd Wolstad (bass), Niels Meller (tenor), Danish State Radio Chorus, Symphony and Concert Orchestras, Janos Ferencsik.

(M) ** (*) DGG Privilege 2727 046 (2 discs). Herbert Schachtschneider (tenor), Inge Borkh (soprano), Hertha Töpper (contralto), Kieth Engen (bass), Lorenz Fehenberger (tenor), Bavarian Radio Chorus and Orchestra, Rafael Kubelik.

Boulez's warm, expressive style, using slow, luxuriant tempi, brings out the operatic quality behind Schoenberg's massive score. With Boulez the Wagnerian overtones are richly expressive, and though Marita Napier and Jess Thomas are not especially sweet on the ear, they show the big, heroic qualities which this score ideally demands, while Yvonne Minton is magnificent in the *Song of the Wood Dove*. Boulez builds that beautiful section to an ominous climax, which far outshines previous versions. In most ways this recording, with attractively vivid and atmospheric sound, combines the best features of both the earlier sets.

Though the HMV recording of a live performance given in Copenhagen is noticeably less precise of ensemble than Kubelik's Munich version on DGG, it is far more dynamic musically, the forward movement of the writing far more

effectively presented, whether in lyrical or dramatic passages of this extraordinarily rich and evocative score. Janet Baker in the *Song of the Wood Dove* gives expressive weight to every word, and though Alexander Young may seem too light a tenor for a Heldentenor role, the result as heard on record is the more beautiful. Martina Arroyo as Tove is also impressive, and it is good to hear the veteran Patzak in the non-singing role of the narrator. Vividly atmospheric recording.

The DGG set under Kubelik has won golden opinions (and rightly so) for the eloquence of the performance and the excellence of the recording. The balance is most musically done, and Kubelik's approach shows both sympathy and insight, while the team of artists he has assembled work well together. But in the last resort Kubelik's coolness of manner misses the music's red-blooded dramatic qualities, and this performance will suit best those for whom refinement is more important than dynamism.

Pierrot Lunaire (song cycle), *Op. 21* (see also above under *Chamber symphony No. 1* and *Serenade*)

(M) *** Nonesuch H 71251. Jan DeGaetani (soprano), Contemporary Chamber Ensemble, Arthur Weisberg.

(M) ** (*) RCA LRL 1 5058. Cleo Laine, Nash Ensemble, Elgar Howarth – IVES: *Songs.* ** (*)

(B) ** (*) Turnabout TV 34315S. Marie-Thérèse Escribano (soprano), Ivan Eröd (piano), Instrumental soloists, Friedrich Cerha.

The New York performance on the Nonesuch mid-price label steers a splendidly confident course between all the many problematic points of interpretation. Jan DeGaetani is a superbly precise soloist, but there is no feeling whatever of pedantry in this performance, which more than most allows a welcome degree of expressiveness while keeping a sharp focus.

Those Schoenberg devotees who wince at the idea of Cleo Laine presenting his masterpiece in English should remember the element of cabaret parody in this extraordinary cycle of twenty-one songs in sing-speech. Cleo Laine may not be as accurate as other interpreters in matching the notes in the score (the composer deliberately notating the *Sprechstimme*) but her personality comes over compellingly to underline the eerily atmospheric variety of mood. That her voice is balanced too far forward helps to make the words clear, but the excellent playing of the Nash Ensemble is not so well served.

The Turnabout presents on a very cheap label a fine intelligent performance, exceptionally clear but lacking only a degree of dramatic tension.

Moses und Aron (opera in 3 acts): complete recording.
** (*) Philips 6700 084 (2 discs). Günter Reich (speaker), Louis Devos (tenor), Eva Csapo (soprano), Elfriede Obrowsky (contralto), Roger Lucas (tenor), Richard Salter, Ladislav Illavský (baritones), Werner Mann (bass), Chorus and Orchestra of Austrian Radio, Michael Gielen.

Introducing the Covent Garden production of *Moses und Aron*, Peter Hall described it as 'the grandest opera of them all', but you would hardly know that from Gielen's performance, impressive as it is. With rather close recorded sound and a relatively small chorus, it makes up in immediacy and precision for the grandeur that should be part of a stage presentation. The opening scene of the Burning Bush is underpowered, but after that soloists, chorus and orches-

tra all sing confidently and incisively, to demonstrate this as a viable and enjoyable opera even taken in conventional terms. Though Boulez's version may well prove finer than this, Gielen provides a contrasted alternative.

Schubert, Franz
(1797–1828)

Overtures: *Fierrabras, D. 796; in the Italian style in C major, D. 591; Des Teufels Lustschloss, D.84.*
*** Decca SXL 6090. Vienna Philharmonic Orchestra, Istvan Kertesz – *Symphony No. 8.****

These overtures provide an enterprising coupling for a first-rate account of the *Unfinished symphony. Des Teufels Lustschloss* is a juvenile work, and its bright-eyed freshness shows much in common with the music of the young Mendelssohn. *Fierrabras* is more melodramatic but lively in invention; and Schubert's Rossini-imitation nearly comes off here with such neat, sparkling playing. Excellent recording too.

5 German dances, D.90; 5 Minuets, D.89.
(B) *** Decca Eclipse ECS 687. Stuttgart Chamber Orchestra, Karl Münchinger – MOZART: *Divertimento No. 11; Les Petits Riens.***

These *Minuets* and *German dances* are absolutely delightful and are well worth the price of the record alone. There is some poetic playing from the solo violin in the trio of the *D minor Minuet*, and the acoustic is slightly warmer and more ample than on the reverse side. One or two harmonic touches in these Schubert pieces are remarkably prophetic. The sound is really very good for its age (the first years of stereo), and though enthusiasm is not unqualified for the Mozart, this fill-up is really a find.

(i) *Marche militaire in D major, D.733/1;* (ii) *Rosamunde: Overture (Die Zauberharfe, D.644);* incidental music: *Entr'acte in B flat major; Ballet music Nos. 1 and 2, D.797;* (iii) *Symphony No. 8 in B minor (Unfinished), D.759.*

(B) ** Decca SPA 225. Vienna Philharmonic Orchestra, (i) Hans Knappertsbusch, (ii) Pierre Monteux, (iii) Carl Schuricht.

Schuricht's performance of the *Unfinished* dates from 1957 and was admired in its day. It is an affectionate reading, warmly played, with a strong forward impulse but some lack of drama. This latter aspect is emphasized by the stereo, which, while glowing and natural, has a very limited dynamic range, with pianissimos and fortissimos levelled out. The *Marche militaire* is played with lots of character by Knappertsbusch and vividly recorded. Monteux's *Rosamunde* excerpts (another early stereo recording, and a good one on all counts) are distinctive, with striking characterization and good playing. In spite of the reduced dynamics in the *Unfinished*, this makes an excellent anthology at the modest price asked.

Rondo in A major (for violin and orchestra), *D.438.*

** Philips SAL 3660. Arthur Grumiaux (violin), New Philharmonia Orchestra, Raymond Leppard – HAYDN: *Violin concerto No. 2;* MOZART: *Adagio; Rondo.***

This is the nearest Schubert got to writing a violin concerto. It is a small-scale piece, characteristically well-made, and Grumiaux plays it with warmth and style. This is an attractive anthology that

will be even more attractive if Philips later reissue it at Universo price.

Symphonies Nos. 1–6 and 8–9; Overtures: *Alfonso and Estrella, D.732; in the Italian style in D major, D.590, in C major, D.591; Die Zwillingsbrüder, D.647.*

(B) ** (*) HMV SLS 5007 (5 discs). Bath Festival or Menuhin Festival Orchestra, Yehudi Menuhin.

Supplied in a box at a fraction more than bargain price, Menuhin's set has much to commend it. Youthful ardour burns in most of these performances. Some will find them too thrustful, not gentle enough. Beecham made No. 3 sparkle far more than Menuhin does, but at least the Menuhin approach shows the music's underlying strength, and although the gaiety in the early symphonies sometimes becomes a little relentless the energy is never in doubt. The approach to Nos. 4 and 5 is unsentimental and direct, altough the finale of No. 5 is comparatively leisurely; a greater degree of expressiveness in slow movements would have been welcome. No. 6 is a delicious performance, of the kind that Beecham used to give, and the affectionate touch in the slow movement brings a glow of warmth. The *Unfinished* returns to the mood of Nos. 4 and 5, and here a little more relaxation would have been ideal. But, as in the overtures which are offered as a sizeable bonus, the playing is unmannered and fresh. With No. 9, the forward, clear recorded quality characteristic of the set as a whole means that there is no feeling of a large orchestra in the concert hall. Menuhin has preferred to retain the smaller (and authentic) scale. The performance is brisk, lightweight and refreshing, very enjoyable in its way even though it leaves one remembering more searching interpretations.

Symphonies Nos. 1–6 and 8–9; Overtures: *Fierrabras, D.796; in the Italian style in C major, D.591; Des Teufels Lustschloss, D.84.*

** (*) Decca SXLJ 6644/8. Vienna Philharmonic Orchestra, Istvan Kertesz.

Nos. 8 and 9 are the best in this compilation. Now that the Boehm set has been withdrawn this is probably the one to have. It is well recorded and the Vienna Philharmonic, though they do not always play with sparkle, give eminently acceptable accounts of the early works. However, Menuhin's set has much to recommend it and is very economically priced. The Dresden set with Sawallisch (see below) is very fine too and those who have it need feel no regrets.

Symphonies Nos. 1–6 and 8–9; Overtures in the Italian style in D major, D.590, in C major, D.591.

** (*) Philips 6729 001 (5 discs). Dresden State Orchestra, Wolfgang Sawallisch.

Sawallisch's complete cycle of the Schubert symphonies may not be as colourful and extrovert as some would wish, but the refinement of the playing and the quiet, unhurried stylishness of the interpretations make for a set which quickly wins one by its calculated understatement.

Symphonies Nos. 1 in D major, D.82; 2 in B flat major, D.125.

*** DGG 2530 216. Berlin Philharmonic Orchestra, Karl Boehm.

** (*) Decca SXL 6552. Vienna Philharmonic Orchestra, Istvan Kertesz.

Characteristically strong performances from Boehm, classical in spirit and beautifully played. The music-making is a little lacking in charm, although there is plenty of warmth and spirit. With clear, vivid sound this should please those for whom this coupling is convenient. Kertesz's performances are good but not inspired. They are well recorded but fail to sparkle. Boehm's accounts would also benefit from greater lightness of touch, but his are more affectionate and animated. The Decca sound is first-class.

Symphonies Nos. 2 in B flat major, D.125; 3 in D major, D.200.

(M) ** DGG Privilege 2538 166. Berlin Philharmonic Orchestra, Lorin Maazel.

Maazel's performance of No. 2 is harddriven, and some ears find it seriously lacking in charm and poise. However, its energy and vitality are not entirely unsuited to a youthful work. No. 3 is much more poised and, if somewhat lacking in glow, compensates with its sense of dramatic purpose. The orchestral playing is first-rate and the recording good.

Symphonies Nos. 2 in B flat major, D.215; 8 in B minor (Unfinished), D.759.

(B) ** Decca Eclipse ECS 761. Vienna Philharmonic Orchestra, Karl Münchinger.

Münchinger's is a serviceable if not outstanding coupling. The performance of the youthful *B flat major Symphony* is appropriately brisk and energetic, with clean lines. But it misses the golden touch which Beecham, for instance, brought to early Schubert. Münchinger is rather too dead-pan to capture the naïve felicities which even in his teens Schubert just could not help creating. The recording of both this symphony and the *Unfinished* has an exceptionally wide dynamic range. At the beginning of No. 8 Münchinger achieves a degree of pianissimo rare on disc – cellos and basses barely audible – and the exposition is slow, steady and rather withdrawn. Then in the development Münchinger suddenly comes out into the open. The orchestral sound is brighter and freer: it is as though the climax is the real argument of the work, and the business of the first and second subjects before and after is no more than a setting, for at the recapitulation we return to the withdrawn mood of the opening. The second movement is less idiosyncratic, thoughtful and again withdrawn. (This performance is also available on SPA 178; see pp. 826–7.)

Symphonies Nos. 3 in D major, D.200; 6 in C major, D.589.
>   ** (*) Decca SXL 6553. Vienna Philharmonic Orchestra, Istvan Kertesz.
>   (B) * (*) Decca Eclipse ECS 763. Vienna Philharmonic Orchestra, Karl Münchinger.

Good performances from Kertesz, but without the last ounce of character and distinction. In No. 3, Boehm's performance (in his complete survey, recently deleted but due for release separately) is more smiling, and Maazel's account with the same orchestra is also highly competitive. Of course the ideal version was Beecham's, and one hopes that EMI will restore this in the lifetime of this book. Kertesz's account of No. 6 is likewise serviceable without being distinguished.

Münchinger is not at his most inspired in Schubert. The music needs more magic than he finds here, and though the playing of the Vienna Philharmonic is stylish enough, one needs more care for detail if Schubert's joyful inspiration is to be appreciated. Second subjects often give a clue to a conductor's understanding of Schubert, and Münchinger's treatment of that in the first movement of No. 6 leaves one completely cold.

Symphonies No. 4 in C minor (Tragic), D.417; 5 in B flat major, D.485.
>   ** (*) Decca SXL 6483. Vienna

Philharmonic Orchestra, Istvan Kertesz.
>   (B) ** Decca Eclipse ECS 762. Vienna Philharmonic Orchestra, Karl Münchinger.

Apart from a few extreme tempi – a fast minuet in No. 4, a fast first movement and a slow start to the second in No. 5 – the Kertesz coupling offers attractive, stylish Schubert playing. Kertesz does not always find the smile in Schubert's writing, but the playing of the Vienna Philharmonic is beyond reproach and the recording exemplary. Münchinger is not the most exciting or flexible of conductors in Schubert (nor does he produce a compensatory glow on his orchestral textures), but these accounts are musical enough and well recorded. Quite a fair bargain at the price asked.

Symphony No. 5 in B flat major, D.485.
>   (M) ** Decca Ace of Diamonds SDD 121. Israel Philharmonic Orchestra, Sir Georg Solti – MENDELSSOHN: *Symphony No. 4.***

Solti's pleasantly cool opening catches the spirit of the music; there is neat string-playing and not too big a sound generally. The *Andante* is gracious, and there is plenty of movement without a sense of hurry. A fast minuet but a relaxed trio is followed by a brisk finale, which loses nothing of the music's elegance. The performance has not the bloom of Beecham's famous version, but the recording in the present transfer is excellent.

Symphonies Nos. 5 in B flat major, D.485; 8 in B minor (Unfinished), D.759.
>   *** DGG SLPM 139162. Berlin Philharmonic Orchestra, Karl Boehm.

825

*** H M V ASD 2942. New Philharmonia Orchestra, Dietrich Fischer-Dieskau.

(M) ** Philips Universo 6580 010. Dresden State Orchestra, Wolfgang Sawallisch.

Boehm's version of No. 5 makes a perfect coupling for an unusually successful account of the *Unfinished*; the first movement is wonderfully light and relaxed, the slow movement, though relaxed too, never seems to outstay its welcome, and in the last two movements the polish of the Berlin playing makes for power as well as lightness. Superb recording. The *Unfinished* with the Berlin Philharmonic, like No. 5, combines deep sensitivity and great refinement. For this coupling at least there is no better recommendation, and the points of detail as well as the overall warmth put this *Unfinished* among the very finest. The opening of the development – always a key point – is magically done, and throughout the superb recording quality gives unusual clarity while allowing the Berlin Philharmonic ensemble its natural opulence.

Beautifully lyrical playing from the New Philharmonia under their eminently lyrical conductor. Both performances are of the highest quality, and there are times when one imagines one can hear the strings or wind phrase as Fischer-Dieskau would were he singing. (No doubt he did during his rehearsals.) Sometimes the feeling may seem a little too overtly expressed – some of the phrasing in the slow movement of the *Unfinished* seems slightly exaggerated – but both in No. 5 and No. 8 the playing is full of vitality and intelligence. The recording is very good, though the last degree of transparency is missing, so that the textures are not always fully revealed.

Sawallisch offers a fresh, nicely judged performance of No. 5, lacking the final degree of distinction in the matter of colour. His slow tempi in the *Unfinished* are supported by eloquent orchestral playing and natural phrasing. Of its kind this is very rewarding, although the recording is clear and slightly dry rather than lustrous and rich.

Symphony No. 6 in C major, D.589; Rosamunde: Overture (Die Zauberharfe, D.644); incidental music: Ballet music Nos. 1 and 2, D.797.

*** D G G 2530 422. Berlin Philharmonic Orchestra, Karl Boehm.

Boehm gives a glowing performance of one of Schubert's most genial works. Characteristically he takes an easy-going view, with relaxed tempi that never grow heavy. Natural, utterly sympathetic performances too of the *Rosamunde* music. Ripe recording quality.

Symphony No. 8 in B minor (Unfinished), D.759.

*** D G G 2530 357. Boston Symphony Orchestra, Eugen Jochum – MOZART: *Symphony No. 41.****

*** D G G SLPM 139001. Berlin Philharmonic Orchestra, Herbert von Karajan – BEETHOVEN: *Overtures.*** (*)

*** Decca SXL 6539. English Chamber Orchestra, Benjamin Britten – MOZART: *Symphony No. 38.****

*** Decca SXL 6090. Vienna Philharmonic Orchestra, Istvan Kertesz – *Overtures.****

** (*) Decca SXL 6549. Vienna Philharmonic Orchestra, Josef Krips – BEETHOVEN: *Symphony No. 8.*** (*)

(B) ** Decca SPA 178. Vienna Philharmonic Orchestra, Karl Münchinger – MENDELSSOHN: *Midsummer Night's Dream overture*; MOZART: *Serenade No. 13.***

(M) ** DGG Privilege 135089. Berlin Philharmonic Orchestra, Lorin Maazel – BEETHOVEN: *Symphony No. 5.***

* (*) Decca Phase 4 PFS 4197. London Philharmonic Orchestra, Leopold Stokowski – BEETHOVEN: *Symphony No. 5.***

After his incisively classical reading of the *Jupiter symphony* on the reverse, Jochum turns to Schubert with the glow of romantic warmth. Not that this is an over-romantic reading, but with its high dynamic contrasts from whispered string pianissimo to dramatic fortissimo in tuttis it reminds one directly of Jochum's long love of Bruckner. No more beautiful version of a much-recorded symphony is available. Beautiful recording to match.

Karajan characteristically gives extraordinary polish to the *Unfinished*, lighting up much that is often obscured. Some may feel that in the first movement he lacks warmth, but on any count it is extremely compelling, and the slow movement too brings tingling precise attack and a wonderful sense of drama. Particularly with a coupling of Beethoven overtures, it may not be the best general recommendation, but it is certainly a remarkable individual one. First-rate recording.

Britten also takes an individual view of the *Unfinished*, setting off at a fastish tempo for the first movement, refusing to inflate the cello theme, but underlining the symphonic tensions with crisp rhythms in the development. The second movement too is strongly rhythmic – an individual and refreshing interpretation, beautifully recorded.

Kertesz's reading is one of the finest of his Schubert cycle, spacious and unaffected and supported by fine orchestral playing. The recording is of the highest quality, with a wide dynamic range so that the woodwind solos in the second movement tend to sound a little distant. The pianissimo at the opening, however, immediately creates a degree of tension that is to be sustained throughout the performance.

Krips recorded the *Unfinished* in the very early days of LP in a gentle, glowing performance, and here again he directs an unforced, wonderfully satisfying account, helped by excellent playing and recording. It may lack some of the bite which even this symphony should have, but anyone wanting this coupling will not be disappointed.

Münchinger's account is also available coupled to the *Second Symphony*; it is discussed above (pp. 824–5).

A fresh approach is always acceptable with the *Unfinished*, but Maazel's first movement is relatively uneventful and the second is without the sustained sense of lyricism and tension that a Beecham can bring. Nevertheless, the playing is for the most part excellent and the recording good. This is an acceptable coupling for a brilliant reading of Beethoven's *Fifth*.

Stokowski's approach to the *Unfinished* is heavyweight. His tempi are slow, and he makes little attempt to draw a pianissimo or anything like it from his players. Even the great second subject lacks delicacy. This can hardly be recommended on its own, but anyone particularly fancying Stokowski's dramatic account of Beethoven's *Fifth* might well tolerate this *Unfinished*, when as ever Stokowski grips the ear with his persuasive moulding of the music. Well-spread Phase 4 sound.

Symphony No. 8 in B minor (Unfinished), D.759; Rosamunde: Overture (Die Zauberharfe, D.644); incidental music: Entr'acte in B flat major; Ballet music No. 2, D.797.

(M) ** HMV SXLP 20029. Royal Philharmonic Orchestra, Sir Malcolm Sargent.

Sargent provides an excellent middle-priced coupling. The performance of the

827

symphony is most satisfying, with a fine sense of architecture and exactly the right approach to details of phrasing – neither too stiff nor too romantic. The reading of the *Rosamunde* music is unpretentious but attractive, and with good playing and recording throughout this can be recommended.

Symphony No. 9 in C major (Great), D.944.

*** HMV ASD 2251. Hallé Orchestra, Sir John Barbirolli.

*** DGG SLPM 138877. Berlin Philharmonic Orchestra, Karl Boehm.

*** HMV ASD 2856. London Philharmonic Orchestra, Sir Adrian Boult.

*** Decca SXL 6089. Vienna Philharmonic Orchestra, Istvan Kertesz.

(M) *** Decca Ace of Diamonds SDD 153. London Symphony Orchestra, Josef Krips.

** (*) Decca SXL 6427. Klassische Philharmonic Stuttgart, Karl Münchinger.

* (*) DGG SLPM 139043. Berlin Philharmonic Orchestra, Herbert von Karajan.

Barbirolli gives a warm, lyrical reading, with the speeds perfectly chosen to solve all the notorious interpretative traps with the minimum fuss. The Hallé playing may not be quite so polished as that of, say, the Berlin Philharmonic on the Boehm version, but it is far more important that the Barbirollian magic is conveyed at its most intense. Barbirolli is completely consistent, and though characteristically he may always indulge in affectionate phrasing in detail, he is unusually steady in maintaining tempi broadly through each movement. The second subject of the first movement, for example, brings no 'gear-change', but

equally no sense of the music being forced, and again with the tempo changes at the end of the movement, his solution is probably more satisfying than that of any rival. Recording is rich and warm.

Boehm's is a good first choice alongside Barbirolli, among the many good accounts of the *Great C major*. It stands in the lyrical Furtwängler tradition rather than the forceful dramatic Toscanini stream, but it is the balance between the conflicting interests in this symphony which distinguishes Boehm's reading. His modification of tempo in the various sections of the first movement is masterly in its finesse, often so subtle that it requires close attention to be spotted. In the slow movement the rhythmic spring to the repeated quavers is delectable, with the Berlin players really on their toes. Nor is there any lack of drama in the performance, for the playing is marvellous throughout. Only in the finale, taken rather fast, is the playing slightly less gripping, and even there one has excitement in plenty. The recording is very good.

A splendidly wise and magisterial account from the doyen of British conductors. There is none of the overstatement that some find in Barbirolli's account; indeed Sir Adrian's tendency to understate is evident in the slow movement, just as his feeling for the overall design is undiminished. The LPO respond with playing of high quality, and the EMI engineers have produced excellent results too. An eminently sound recommendation.

Kertesz's disc is also in its way outstanding. It is remarkably well recorded, with a splendid overall bloom, yet plenty of bite and clarity. One is made conscious that the symphony is scored for trombones as well as horns, something that does not emerge clearly in many recordings. The performance is fresh, dramatic and often very exciting. Those who – like I.M. – always have doubts about the symphony's 'heavenly length' may find that Kertesz's springlike approach counteracts the feeling that each movement is just a shade too long. A most enjoyable disc.

The Krips version on Ace of Diamonds makes an outstanding mid-priced recommendation, with good recording, polished playing, and an interpretation of the last two movements that has yet to be equalled on record. In these two movements Krips finds an airy exhilaration which makes one wonder how ever other conductors can keep the music earthbound as they do. The pointing of the trio in the scherzo is delectable, and the feathery lightness of the triplets in the finale makes one positively welcome every single one of its many repetitions. The first two movements show Krips's natural feeling for Schubertian lyricism at its most engaging, and even making no allowance for price this is one of the finest versions available.

Münchinger, who in baroque music has often seemed a little too rigid in his approach, here shows an unexpected suppleness. With fine recording quality his is an attractive version that brings out the pastoral qualities of the music, sunny and glowing, even if it misses some of the greatness.

Karajan's account is an intense disappointment, with the ruggedness of the writing smoothed over to a degree surprising even from this conductor. The tempi are fast, but, as Menuhin has shown, that does not necessarily mean the work need be weakened. Karajan skates over the endless beauties. There is no impression of glowing expansiveness: this is a tour of a chromium heaven.

CHAMBER MUSIC

Adagio and rondo concertante in F major, D.487.
    ** HMV ASD 2328. Lamar Crowson (piano), Melos Ensemble – *Trout quintet.***

Schubert wrote this unexpected piece in 1816 when he was still in his teens. The piano part has a concertante bravura, so that the result is more like a concerto for piano and solo strings than a conventional quintet. In fact this version adds a double-bass to the piano and string quartet originally prescribed, a perfectly justifiable course. This may not be one of Schubert's masterpieces, but it makes a welcome fill-up for the *Trout quintet.*

Fantasia in C major (for violin and piano), *D.934; Violin sonata in A major, D.574.*
    (M) ** Vox STGBY 611. György Pauk (violin), Peter Frankl (piano).

Neither of these works is generously represented in the catalogue at present, and both have moments of charm and indeed sublimity. Both performances are persuasive and intelligent and the recording reasonably well balanced. (The violin is a bit forward, but this is not a serious matter.)

Collection: (i) *Notturno in E flat major* (for piano trio), *D.897;* (ii) *Octet in F major, D.803;* (i) *Piano quintet in A major (Trout), D.667;* (iii) *String quintet in C major, D.956.*
    (M) ** DGG 2733 003 (3 discs). (i) Christoph Eschenbach (piano), members of the Koeckert Quartet; (ii) Berlin Philharmonic Octet; (iii) Amadeus Quartet (augmented).

The best thing here is the Eschenbach Koeckert *Trout*, which is fresh and unmannered. Eschenbach's playing, if not the last word in poetry, is invariably sensitive and intelligent. The Berlin version of the *Octet* is not as winning as either the Melos or the Viennese account, though it is well recorded. The other versions convey greater natural charm and sense of enjoyment. The Amadeus account of the *Quintet* has little to recommend it. Their mono version was infinitely superior and free from the mannerisms that afflict this.

Octet in F major (for clarinet, horn, bassoon and strings), *D.803*.
*** HMV ASD 2417. Melos Ensemble.
(M) *** Decca Ace of Diamonds SDD 230. Vienna Octet.
** (*) Philips 6500 269. Berlin Philharmonic Octet.
** DGG SLPM 139102. Berlin Philharmonic Octet.

A very fine performance indeed from the Melos group. This is arguably the best version now before the public, and even if readers dissent from this view they are unlikely to feel this is inferior to either the Viennese or the Berlin performances. The playing is fresh and spontaneous yet polished, with excellent ensemble. The recording is splendidly detailed and truthful. Strongly recommended.

The Decca version wears its years remarkably well, for the stereo with its clean separation was always impressive. As to the performance it has the glow of the Vienna Octet at its peak under the leadership of Willi Boskovsky. The horn has a Viennese fruitiness, but that only makes the performance more authentic. This is good value at mid-price, but a disc of this vintage (1957) might reasonably have been made even cheaper.

The Philips performance by the Berlin Philharmonic Octet is warm and mellifluous. The playing is a little sober in the opening two movements, but the scherzo has splendid life, and the last three movements have a stronger forward impulse, with a sparkling finale. The recording is rich, quite clearly defined, but rather heavily weighted at the bass end, and this imparts a touch of blandness to the music-making.

The earlier Berlin Philharmonic performance on DGG is often spirited, but it does not display quite the lightness of touch of the Viennese one, and the Vienna Octet capture the full character of Schubert's muse more naturally.

Octet for wind, D.72: Minuet and finale in F major.
*** Philips 6500 163. Netherlands Wind Ensemble, Edo de Waart – DVOŘÁK: *Serenade*; GOUNOD: *Petite symphonie*.***

Two charming little miniatures from Schubert's youth, crisply and attractively played. An admirable fill-up to the delightful Gounod piece.

Piano quintet in A major (Trout), D.667.
(M) *** Decca Ace of Diamonds SDD 185. Clifford Curzon (piano), members of the Vienna Octet.
** (*) Philips SAL 3621. Ingrid Haebler (piano), Arthur Grumiaux (violin), Georges Janzer (viola), Eva Czako (cello), Jacques Cazauran (double-bass).
(B) ** (*) Classics for Pleasure CFP 40085. Moura Lympany (piano), principals of the LSO.
(B) ** DGG Heliodor 2548 122. Joerg Demus (piano), Schubert Quartet – MOZART: *Divertimento for wind, K.196f.***
** HMV ASD 2328. Lamar Crowson (piano), Melos Ensemble – *Adagio and rondo*.**
(B) ** Oryx EXP 10. Richard Laugs Piano Quintet.
(B) * (*) Vanguard SRV 151SD. Denis Matthews (piano), Vienna Konzerthaus Quartet.
(B) * (*) Turnabout TV 34140S. Louis Kentner (piano), Hungarian Quartet.

The Decca Ace of Diamonds record offers a classic performance, with a distinguished account of the piano part from Clifford Curzon and splendidly stylish support from the Vienna players. Schubert's warm lyricism is caught with remarkable freshness, and the stereo is of first-class quality. Some might find the brilliant scherzo a little too fierce to match the rest of the performance, but such vigorous playing introduces an element of contrast at the centre of the interpretation.

From Haebler a small-scale performance, in some ways not comparable to the Curzon/Vienna set but nonetheless enormously enjoyable. There is some admirably unassertive and deeply musical playing from Miss Haebler and from the incomparable Grumiaux, and it is this freshness and joy in music-making that render this disc memorable. These artists do not try to make 'interpretative points' but are content to allow the music to speak for itself. The balance is not altogether perfect, but the quality of the recorded sound is good and the separation and spread more than adequate. One of the most natural performances, and enjoyable.

Moura Lympany's performance sets off with a brisk manner, the playing lively and fresh. In the second movement the interpretation relaxes, and the variations are attractively done. The matter-of-fact approach is balanced by the overall spontaneity of the music-making. The balance favours the piano and the first violin seems backwards – in his decorations of the 'Trout' theme he is too distant, with less body to his tone, as recorded, than the lower strings. But in most respects this is a lively and enjoyable account, not wanting in perception.

An excellent performance on Heliodor, with Demus dominating, partly because the piano recording and balance are bold and forward and the string tone is thinner. There is – as befits the name of the string group – a real feeling for Schubert, and the performance has spontaneity and style. The first movement is especially arresting, and the *Theme and variations* are well shaped. The sound is good. Excellent value.

The Melos Ensemble's performance brings a stunning account of the third movement, very fast, clear and energetic; but having breasted that challenge, they let one down too much in the other movements. Generally, although the interpretation as such is sound and enjoyable, the discipline has not quite the pinpoint precision one needs in a recording. The rare fill-up might sway some buyers in the version's favour. Good recording.

The Oryx issue offers a warm, relaxed reading which gives much pleasure. The players not only catch the full Schubert flavour but seem to be enjoying themselves. The pianist is especially good, and he is helped by the spacious recording acoustic, which gives the piano a nicely resonant tone. The leader's violin is a trifle thin as recorded. The string playing is not impeccable but perfectly acceptable.

The Vienna Konzerthaus/Denis Matthews version chooses brisk tempi and gives an attractive airy grace and lightness of texture which offer charm if not quite revealing the full stature of Schubert's masterpiece. Here the balance accentuates the treble of the piano, and the bass is rather shallow. However, the strings can be made to sound quite well, and the playing is fairly sensitive if not really distinguished.

Although Kentner plays with distinction, this particular *Trout* is let down by indifferent recording, thin and lacking in body. The string playing too has an unsmiling approach, and all in all this issue is not especially competitive.

Piano quintet in A major (Trout), D.667; Notturno in E flat major (for piano trio), *D.897.*
** (*) BASF BAC 3004. Joerg

Demus (Hammerflügel piano), Franzjosef Maier (violin), Heinz-Otto Graf (viola), Rudolf Mandalka (cello), Paul Breuer (double-bass) (original instruments).

** DGG 2536 020. Christoph Eschenbach (piano), Koeckert Quartet.

The great interest of the BASF issue is the use of a fortepiano made by Conrad Graf of Vienna in 1830. As we know from his record of the Beethoven *Fourth Concerto*, Demus is completely at home on an instrument which suits Schubert's textures here remarkably well. The clarity and sparkle of the piano part are increased, although in the variations the decorative writing sounds a shade clattery. The string players, presumably using gut strings, make a blend of sound which in this kindly acoustic has an almost orchestral breadth. This does tend to rob the performance of some of its freshness, but the playing itself has no lack of bite, and the scherzo shows splendid energy and attack. But for all its merits this has not quite the distinction of the Curzon account, and the thickness of texture will not be to all tastes (although the recording is very natural). The account of the *Notturno* is really outstanding, with a compulsive tension to catch the listener at the very first bar.

Eschenbach is a fluent enough pianist, but neither he nor the Koeckert Quartet are helped by the somewhat unsympathetic acoustic in which this recording was made and the performance, although admirably lacking in mannerisms, is not to be numbered alongside the best. The Grumiaux/Haebler version on Philips is greatly to be preferred. The *Notturno* is given the advantage of a warmer acoustic, though it is not superior to the BASF version.

Piano trios Nos. 1 in B flat major, D.898; 2 in E flat major, D.929; Notturno in E flat major (for piano trio), D.897; *Sonata in B flat major* (for piano trio), *D.28*.

** Philips 6700 014 (2 discs). Beaux Arts Trio.

The Beaux Arts Trio have the advantage of a first-class pianist in Menahem Pressler, whose contributions to the proceedings are always imaginative and intelligent. The violinist, Daniel Guilet, on the other hand, is somewhat ungenerous in tone and though capable of fine artistry occasionally lets the proceedings down. There seems no sensible reason why these discs were not issued separately, as each contains a complete trio plus one of the shorter works. Perhaps Philips were conscious that the first record is rather more desirable than the second, and decided that putting the two together evens things out. They may have a case, for although the performance of the *Second Trio* is good rather than memorable, the bonus on this record is the attractive early *Sonata in B flat*. Written during Schubert's student days this work has the same kind of fluency as Beethoven's first piano trio, although the lyrical flow of the writing is unmistakably Schubert. The recording is first-class throughout.

Piano trio No. 1 in B flat major, D.898.

(B) ** (*) Classics for Pleasure CFP 40037. David Oistrakh (violin), Sviatoslav Knushevitzky (cello), Lev Oborin (piano).

Alas, all three artists have died during the lifetime of this record. The performance has great spirit and warmth and has the merit of being unfussy and straightforward. It is all beautifully phrased and musical through and through. The recording still sounds fresh, and readers, whatever their means, need look no further than this version.

Piano trio No. 1 in B flat major, D.898; Sonata in B flat major (for piano trio), *D.28*.

(M) ** (*) DGG Privilege 2538 213.
Trio di Trieste.

The Trio di Trieste give an eminently
lively and sensitive account of the *Trio*,
and they are well recorded. This is a
useful alternative to the above versions,
and will give pleasure on all counts.

*String quartets Nos. 1 in C major, D.18;
2 in C major, D.32; 3 in B flat major,
D.36.*

*** DGG 2530 322. Melos Quartet
of Stuttgart.

Admirable, unfussy, straightforward
accounts of these juvenile quartets, all
written before Schubert was sixteen:
indeed the first was written when he was
only thirteen. Well recorded performances of music that has a touching
charm all its own.

*String quartets Nos. 9 in G minor,
D.173; 13 in A minor, D.804.*

* (*) DGG SLPM 139194. Amadeus
Quartet.

The *G minor* is an attractive quartet
that deserves more eloquent presentation
than the Amadeus performance. These
players have developed a distressing
tendency over the past few years to make
all music sound much the same. There
is little tenderness or insight here but a
good deal of instant rapture and ersatz
warmth, as if Schubert was merely an
amiable composer. Norbert Brainin's
playing is mannered.

*String quartets Nos. 10 in E flat major,
D.87; 14 in D minor (Death and the
maiden), D.810.*

(M) *** Decca Ace of Diamonds
SDD 254. Vienna Philharmonic
Quartet.

The Vienna Philharmonic Quartet are
in top form in this excellent coupling of a
famous masterpiece with an apprentice

work written when the composer was
only sixteen. But Schubert was no mean
apprentice, even at that early age, and
the *E flat major Quartet* has no lack of
inventive quality. The Vienna performance treats the music with affection and
brings out the youthful vitality of the
outer movements. In the *Death and the
maiden quartet* the playing is peerless,
Boskovsky, the leader, showing all his
skill and musicianship in the variations.
The team give a genuine Viennese quality
to the scherzo, which is most fetching.
The Decca recording is first-rate.

*String quartet No. 12 in C minor
(Quartettsatz), D.703.*

(M) ** Decca Ace of Diamonds
SDD 270. Vienna Philharmonic
Quartet – DVOŘÁK: *Piano quin-
tet.****

This is a rather mannered performance,
but it has a natural warmth to compensate
for a certain lack of consistency in internal
balance.

*String quartet No. 14 in D minor (Death
and the maiden), D.810.*

(B) * (*) Turnabout TV 34472S. Hungarian Quartet.

This account does not offer a strong
challenge to the Italians (see below) or
the Vienna Quartet. The Hungarians are
of course a distinguished body but they
are not at their most inspired here, and
the quality of the recorded sound is not
particularly distinguished. There is also
an account by the Cleveland Quartet on
RCA. The playing is far superior to that
of the Hungarians, but expression seems
imposed rather than felt, and the music-
making never really penetrates far
beneath the surface. The recording too is
shallow and glossy.

*String quartets Nos. 14 in D minor
(Death and the maiden), D.810; 12 in
C minor (Quartettsatz), D.703.*

** (*) DGG SLPM 138048. Amadeus Quartet.

The Amadeus performances give a wonderful impression of unity as regards the finer points of phrasing, for example at the very beginning of the variations. The quality of the DGG stereo is commendable. This is a fine disc, even if the account of the *Death and the maiden quartet* has not the depth of the very finest versions.

String quartet No. 15 in G major D.887.
* (*) DGG SLPM 139013. Amadeus Quartet.

As in the case of their Schubert *C major Quintet*, the tonal accomplishments of this ensemble are not matched by comparable insight into the music itself. Their earlier account of the work for DGG was not ideal but it went deeper than this. The surface gloss which this Quartet superimposes on the music seems quite out of place.

String quintet in C major, D.956; String quartet No. 12 in C minor (Quartettsatz), D.703.
** Decca SXL 6481. Weller Quartet (augmented in *Quintet*).

Very fine playing though a trifle sweet and suave. The unpretentious account given by the Aeolian Quartet on Saga is somehow more searching. The performance is excellently recorded, and the *Quartettsatz* is an attractive fill-up.

String quintet in C major, D.956.
(B) ** (*) Saga 5266. Aeolian Quartet with Bruno Schrecker (2nd cello).
* DGG SLPM 139105. Amadeus Quartet with William Pleeth (2nd cello).

The Aeolian Quartet gives a strong,

virile performance of what is arguably Schubert's greatest chamber work. Their style is direct, with no mannerism whatever. It might seem bald were it not for the depth of concentration that the players convey in every bar. The finale for example is fresh and rustic-sounding, not because of pointing of the rhythm, but because of the very simplicity of utterance. In the slow movement the Aeolians daringly adopt the slowest possible *Adagio*, and the result might have seemed static but for the 'inner' tension which holds one breathless through hushed pianissimos of the most intense beauty. Never before on record, not even in Casals' old Prades version (mono), has the profundity of this music been so compellingly conveyed. The recording is not of the clearest, but quite acceptable, and at super-bargain price no one is likely to complain. A superb issue to make one clamour for more recordings from the Aeolians.

Many find the playing of the Amadeus so refined and perfect in technique that this outweighs any reservations they harbour on points of interpretation. But not here. This performance of the *C major Quintet*, Schubert's sublimest utterance, is perfumed, mannered and superficial. The less technically accomplished Aeolians give a much more honest account that goes right to the heart of Schubert's masterpiece, but those who find the Saga recording too unsophisticated would do better with the excellent Decca disc listed above. The other alternative performance, by the Juilliard Quartet on CBS, must be passed over on account of the shallow and somewhat shrill recorded sound.

(i) *String quintet in C major, D.956. String trio in B flat major, D.471.*
(M) ** Decca Ace of Diamonds SDD 376. Vienna Philharmonic Quartet, (i) with Roger Harand (2nd cello).

If only the performance of the *String quintet* were as good as that of the *Trio*, which is attractively fresh, this record would be a top recommendation, for the recording is first-class, clear yet with a natural warmth. But the performance of the *Quintet* is patchy. It has its good moments: the scherzo is superbly played, and the mood of the opening and closing sections of the *Adagio* is well caught. But this elusive movement is not sustained with the tension that the Aeolian players find, and the outer movements do not seem completely spontaneous. The playing is thoughtful and polished but no more than that.

String trios: in B flat major, D.471; in B flat major, D.581.
*** Philips SAL 3782. Grumiaux Trio – HAYDN: *String trios.****

These are slight pieces, but given such persuasive advocacy they cannot fail to make a good impression. The performances are deeply musical, unforced and well shaped, while the recording has vividness and presence as well as a natural, lifelike sound quality.

Violoncello sonata in A minor (originally for Arpeggione), D.821.
** (*) Decca SXL 6426. Mstislav Rostropovich (cello), Benjamin Britten (piano) – BRIDGE: *Cello sonata.****
(M) * (*) Supraphon SUAST 50610. Saša Večtomov (cello), Vladimir Topinka (piano) – STRAVINSKY: *Italian Suite.* (*)

Rostropovich gives a curiously self-indulgent interpretation of Schubert's slight but amiable *Arpeggione sonata.* The playing of both artists is eloquent and it is beautifully recorded, but it will not be to all tastes. However, the record is particularly valuable for the sake of the Frank Bridge *Sonata* on the other

side. The two Czech artists also give an unashamedly romantic reading of the difficult sonata that Schubert originally wrote for the arpeggione – a curious combination of cello and guitar. The style allows plenty of rubato, a portamento or two, and classicists had perhaps better be warned away, but as a rule the players' conviction carries sympathy with it, and the result is warm-hearted and enjoyable. Reasonable recording.

PIANO MUSIC

Allegretto in C minor, D.915; Impromptus, D.946, Nos. 1 in E flat minor; 2 in E flat major; 3 in C major; Klavierstück in A major, D.604; 13 Variations on a theme by Anselm Hüttenbrunner in A minor, D.576.
*** DGG 2530 090. Wilhelm Kempff (piano).

Kempff injects all his habitual magic into these often deceptively simple pieces. The three *Impromptus* were written in the last year of Schubert's life, easy, happy inspirations that wear greatness easily. Such items as the *Hüttenbrunner variations* (echoes there of the *Allegretto* of Beethoven's *Seventh Symphony*) are more decoratively trivial, but whatever the tone of Schubert's voice Kempff's crystal touch and natural intensity make for pure delight. First-rate recording.

Collection: *Allemande in E flat major, D.366; Cotillon in E flat major, D.976; 11 Ecossaises, D.781; 4 German dances, D.783; 12 German dances (Ländler), D.790; German dance, D.973; Kuppelwieser Waltzer in G flat major, 3 Ländler, D.734; Minuet in C sharp minor, D.600; 2 Scherzi, D.593: Nos. 1 in B flat major; 2 in D flat major; 2 Trios (in A flat major and B major),*

835

D.146; Trio in E major, D.610; Variations on a waltz by Diabelli, D.718; 6 Waltzes, D.145; 2 Waltzes, D.146; 12 Waltzes, D.365; 2 Waltzes, D.779.

(M) *** DGG Privilege 2538 237. Joerg Demus (piano).

Readers need have no hesitation in investigating this delightful collection of Schubert's warm-hearted and exhilarating piano music. Demus plays it with excellent judgement and musicianship, and the recording is fully acceptable.

Fantasia in C major (The Wanderer), D.760.

*** Philips 6500 285. Alfred Brendel (piano) – *Piano sonata No. 21.****

(M) ** HMV HQS 1331. Ronald Smith (piano) – BEETHOVEN: *Piano sonata No. 32.***

Brendel's playing is of a high order, and he is superbly recorded. This is coupled with a sonata that is sometimes given a record to itself or provided with only a small filler, so it is excellent value. Ronald Smith, an inspired and dedicated pianist, gives a precise, strongly shaped reading of Schubert's one-movement sonata, not so full of fantasy as some but very satisfying. The recording is excellent.

Fantasia in C major (The Wanderer), D.760; Moments musicaux, D.780, Nos. 1–6.

*** DGG SLPM 139372. Wilhelm Kempff (piano).

A charming coupling of one of the most original of Schubert's solo piano pieces with the six trifles which under the title *Moments musicaux* range so much farther than one expects from their scale. Kempff characteristically gives intimate performances. His allegros are never very fast, and the results sing in the most relaxed way. In the *Wanderer fantasia* the

high drama which such a pianist as Sviatoslav Richter finds is missing, but the result is equally compelling, with a moulding of the structure which gives the illusion of spontaneity.

Fantasia in C major (The Wanderer), D.760; Piano sonata No. 16 in A minor, D.845.

*** DGG 2530 473. Maurizio Pollini (piano).

This is piano-playing of an altogether exceptional order. Pollini's account of the *A minor Sonata* is searching and profound. He is almost without rival in terms of sheer keyboard control, and his musical insight is of the same order. The piano sound as such could do with slightly more presence, but this apart, the recording is musically balanced and full of warmth.

Piano duets: *Fantasia in F minor, D.940; ' Grand duo' Sonata, D.812.*

(B) *** Turnabout TV 34144DS. Alfred Brendel, Evelyne Crochet (piano duo).

This record generously couples what are arguably the two greatest works ever written for piano duet. The *F minor Fantasy*, with its haunting recurrent main theme, is certainly the greatest, an inspired masterpiece in every respect, and here it receives a performance that for the first time on record conveys its full spiritual depth. Brendel and Crochet play with rare *Innigkeit* that makes one forget the comparatively limited range of recording. In the *Grand duo* too, heroically expansive in structure if not quite so distinguished in its material, Brendel and Crochet are ideal interpreters, conveying the urgency of the writing as well as its lyricism. At the extremely cheap Turnabout price this is one of the outstanding bargains in the current catalogue.

German dances, D.783; Valses nobles, D.969; Waltzes, D.365.

(B) ** Turnabout TV 34006S. Walter Hautzig (piano).

This is essentially not a disc to play all at once, but when dipped into, it offers many delights and overwhelming proof of Schubert's amazing fecundity. Most of these pieces in triple time are very short indeed, but their perfection is that their triviality is exactly calculated, and the length of each piece is judged to make a miniature gem of the germinal musical idea it contains. And every now and then there is one of those typical Schubertian flashes of melodic and harmonic genius that is over all too quickly. Walter Hautzig plays these miniatures with obvious affection and real sympathy; they could so easily be ruined by ham-fisted virtuosity. The recording too is good.

20 German dances, Ländler and Waltzes.

(B) ** Oryx ORYX 1805. Karl Ulrich Schnabel (piano) – MENDELS-SOHN: *Piano sonata.***

This is an arbitrary selection from various groups, but the pieces make a most enjoyable recital, especially when they are played so sympathetically. The recording too is good but the record-side is only about half full, so this disc is not as cheap as it looks.

Impromptus Nos. 1–4, D.899; Nos. 5–8, D.935.

*** Philips 6500 415 (Nos. 1–4). Alfred Brendel (piano) – *Piano sonata No. 19.***

** (*) DGG SLPM 139149 (Nos. 1–8). Wilhelm Kempff (piano).

(B) ** (*) Turnabout TV 34141S (Nos. 1–8). Alfred Brendel (piano).

Predictably fine playing from Kempff, although here the magic comes more unevenly than usual. The D.899 set is

beautifully done, and all the pieces are well characterized. DGG's recording is faithful but a little dry in acoustic, so that the piano's middle register does not glow as perhaps it might. Brendel's newer Philips set of the D.899 *Impromptus* is delightful and very well recorded indeed. But there are some reservations about the performance of the sonata which forms the coupling. On the earlier Turnabout disc his approach is more matter-of-fact, often classical in manner rather than romantic. But the unaffected eloquence of the playing carries its own rewards, and the recording is surprisingly good.

Moments musicaux Nos. 1–6, D.780.

*** Philips 6500 418. Alfred Brendel (piano) – *Piano sonata No. 14.***

*** Decca SXL 6523. Clifford Curzon (piano) – BEETHOVEN: *Eroica variations.***

Moments musicaux Nos. 1–6, D.780; Impromptus (Klavierstücke), D.946, Nos. 1–3.

(B) *** Turnabout TV 34142S. Alfred Brendel (piano).

Both Curzon and Brendel (on Philips) give superb performances of the *Moments musicaux*. These readings are the most poetic now in the catalogue, and the recording in both cases is exemplary. The Turnabout record too is no less highly recommendable in its price-range. The performances have a simple, direct eloquence that is quite disarming, and the sound is astonishingly good, if not as fine as the later recording. The three *Klavierstücke* are an acceptable bonus.

Piano sonatas Nos. 2 in C major, D.279; 20 in A major, D.959.

** DGG 2530 327. Wilhelm Kempff (piano).

This coupling of an early and a late

sonata is an attractive one, even if the piano recording is somewhat lacking in lustre. Kempff is less mannered in the *A major Sonata* than Brendel, but there is no doubt that Brendel has the finer recording. However, first choice remains with Eschenbach (see below), even though he offers no coupling.

Piano sonatas Nos. 13 in A major, D.664; 14 in A minor, D.784; Ungarische Melodie, D.817; 12 Waltzes, D.145.
　⊛*** Decca SXL 6260. Vladimir Ashkenazy (piano).

A magnificent record in every respect. Ashkenazy is a great Schubertian who can realize the touching humanity of this giant's vision as well as his strength. There is an astonishing directness about these performances and a virility tempered by tenderness. This surpasses Ashkenazy's own high standards, and Decca have risen admirably to the occasion. The recording has splendid range and fidelity.

Piano sonata No. 14 in A minor, D.784.
　*** Philips 6500 418. Alfred Brendel (piano) – *Moments musicaux.****
　** (*) Decca SXL 6504. Radu Lupu (piano) – BRAHMS: *Intermezzi.***

Brendel's disc couples a fine account of the *Sonata* with an altogether superlative one of the *Moments musicaux.* The playing has such marvellous eloquence that one almost feels one hears the music speak. The piano tone is most subtly captured. This cannot be too strongly recommended.

But Radu Lupu's performance, full of poetry, is highly competitive, and it is well recorded.

Piano sonatas Nos. 15 in C major, D.840; 18 in G major, D.894.
　*** Philips 6500 416. Alfred Brendel (piano).

Brendel is a safer recommendation in the *G major Sonata* than Ashkenazy. His tempi are less leisurely, yet he manages to convey within a tauter framework much of the poetic feeling that we see in Ashkenazy. He has room for a performance of the *C major Sonata* whose eloquence and poetry leave nothing to be desired. Philips's recording is among the best piano sound we have on disc today.

Piano sonata No. 17 in D major, D.850; Impromptus in G flat major, D.899/3; in A flat major, D.899/4.
　*** Decca SXL 6135. Clifford Curzon (piano).

The passage to try first in the *Sonata* is the beginning of the last movement, an example of the Curzon magic at its most intense, for with a comparatively slow speed he gives the rhythm a gentle 'lift' which is most captivating. Some who know more forceful interpretations (Richter did a marvellous one) may find this too wayward, but Schubert surely thrives on some degree of coaxing. Curzon could hardly be more convincing – the spontaneous feeling of a live performance better captured than in many earlier discs – and the *Impromptus* make an attractive fill-up. Superb recording.

Piano sonata No. 18 in G major, D.894.
　** (*) Decca SXL 6602. Vladimir Ashkenazy (piano).

Ashkenazy's record of the *G major Sonata* is likely to be one of his most controversial. The first movement should be very leisurely indeed if it is to convey the self-communing as well as the sense of peace that lie at its heart. On first hearing Ashkenazy seems too slow by any standards: he robs it of its normal sense of movement. Further hearings prove much more convincing, largely because his reading is so totally felt and equally perceptive. He succeeds in making the piano sound exceptionally expressive and is given a recording that is unfailingly flattering. A most searching and poetic account, even if Brendel (see above) remains a safer general recommendation.

Piano sonata No. 19 in C minor, D.958.
  ** Philips 6500 415. Alfred Brendel (piano) – *Impromptus.****
Piano sonata No. 20 in A major, D.959.
  *** DGG 2530 372. Christoph Eschenbach (piano).
Piano soñata No. 20 in A major, D.959; 12 German dances, D.790.
  ** Philips 6500 284. Alfred Brendel (piano).
Piano sonata No. 21 in B flat major, D.960.
  *** DGG 2530 477. Christoph Eschenbach (piano).
  *** Philips 6500 285. Alfred Brendel (piano) – *Wanderer fantasia.****

Brendel's late Schubert records are among his finest, but the *A major* suffers from rather more agogic change than is desirable. Some listeners will find these interferences with the flow of the musical argument a little too much of a good thing. The *C minor Sonata* is not free from this charge, and in both sonatas Kempff remains the safer choice (see above), though it must be conceded that he is by no means so well recorded. In both cases Brendel's couplings are delightful, and particularly beautifully played.

Better than either in the *A major*, though he too pulls the finale about a little, is Eschenbach, who gives a most impressive account of this great sonata. Again, alas, the DGG recording has a slight pallor, but with that small reservation the disc deserves a strong recommendation.

Brendel's account of the *B flat major Sonata* is as impressive and full of insight as one would expect. He is not unduly wayward, for his recording has

room for the *Wanderer fantasy* as well, and he is supported by quite outstanding Philips sound. Eschenbach takes the whole of two sides, but his playing is of the highest order and he observes the first exposition repeat, which Brendel omits. If anything, his account of this sonata is even finer than his *A major*, and it is a pity that his recording, though good, is a little pale by the side of the Philips. In the slow movement Eschenbach attains genuine spirituality, as does Kempff, but in assessing recordings of this masterpiece one must also not forget Curzon's outstanding version (see below).

Piano sonata No. 21 in B flat major, D.960; Impromptu in A flat major, D.935/2.
  *** Decca SXL 6580. Clifford Curzon (piano).

This is one of the finest accounts of the *B flat Sonata* in the catalogue. Tempi are beautifully judged, and everything is in fastidious taste. Detail is finely drawn but never emphasized at the expense of the architecture as a whole. It is beautifully recorded, and the piano sounds marvellously truthful in timbre.

Piano sonata No. 21 in B flat major, D.960; Scherzo in B flat major, D.593.
  ⊛ *** DGG SLPM 139323. Wilhelm Kempff (piano).

It is a tribute to Kempff's artistry that with the most relaxed tempi he conveys such consistent, compulsive intensity. Hearing the opening, one might feel that this is going to be a lightweight account of Schubert's greatest sonata, but in fact the long-breathed expansiveness is hypnotic, so that here quite as much as in the *Great C major Symphony* one is bound by the spell of heavenly length. Rightly Kempff repeats the first-movement exposition with the important nine bars of lead-back, and though the overall manner is less obviously dramatic than is common, the range of tone-colour is magical, with sharp terracing of dynamics to plot the geography of each movement. Though very much a personal utterance this interpretation is no less great for that. It belongs to a tradition of pianism that has almost disappeared, and we must be eternally grateful that its expression has been so glowingly captured on this disc.

VOCAL AND CHORAL MUSIC

Vocal trios: *Die Advokaten; Cantata zum Geburtstag des Sängers Johann Michael Vogl; Cantata zur fünfzig-jährigen Jubelfeier Salieris; Der Hoch-zeitsbraten; Punschlied; Trinklied; Ver-schwunden sind die Schmerzen.*

   *** D G G 2530 361. Elly Ameling (soprano), Peter Schreier (tenor), Horst Lanbenthal (tenor), Diet-rich Fischer-Dieskau (baritone), Gerald Moore (piano).

Domestic music in the best sense. Schubert wrote these trios at various periods of his career for his friends and colleagues to perform. Specially delight-ful are the two contrasted drinking songs. Superb performances and recording.

Vocal quartets: *An die Sonne; Begräb-nislied; Gebet; Gott der Weltschöpfer; Gott im Ungewitter; Hymne an den Unendlichen; Lebenslust; Des Tages Weihe; Der Tanz.*

   *** D G G 2530 409. Elly Ameling (soprano), Janet Baker (mezzo-soprano), Peter Schreier (tenor), Dietrich Fischer-Dieskau (bari-tone), Gerald Moore (piano).

These vocal quartets, like Schubert's vocal trios, were written for various domestic occasions through his career,

but the idea of four voices seems to have led him regularly to serious or religious subjects. These are sweet and gentle rather than intense inspirations, but you could hardly want more polished or inspired performances than these. Fine recording.

Duets: *Antigone und Oedip; Cronnan; Hektors Abschied; Hermann und Thus-nelda; Licht und Liebe; Mignon und der Harfner; Selma und Selmar; Sing-übungen; Szene aus Goethes Faust.*

   *** D G G 2530 328. Janet Baker (mezzo-soprano), Dietrich Fisch-er-Dieskau (baritone), Gerald Moore (piano).

Not all these duets are vintage Schu-bert – some of the narrative pieces go on too long – but the artistry of Baker and Fischer-Dieskau makes for magical results, above all in a fascinating wordless melisma written as an exercise. Moore relishes the magic too. Excellent record-ing.

Part songs: *Christ ist erstanden; Gebet; Der Gondelfahrer; Gott im Ungewitter; Gott in der Natur; Gott meine Zuver-sicht; Junglingswonne; Nachthelle; Ständchen.*

   (M) *** Argo Ace of Diamonds SDD 377. April Cantelo (soprano), Helen Watts (contralto), Robert Tear (tenor), Elizabethan Singers, Louis Halsey; Viola Tunnard (piano).

Schubert's part songs are unaccount-ably neglected, and yet they contain some of his most characteristic and beguiling invention. The selection recorded here contains some of his finest, and it is difficult to imagine the musical listener not responding to it with the warmth of feeling that this open-hearted music inspires. The performances could hardly be bettered, and Argo record them with the utmost clarity and sonority. Helen Watts sounds a trifle matronly at times, but all in all this is an issue of such high quality that one feels it should be a part of every serious collector's library. It is a record that will give pleasure out of all proportion to its cost.

Abendstern; Am See; Auflösung; Der blinde Knabe; Grablied; Herrn Joseph Spaun; Im Haine; Der Jüngling auf dem Hügel; Der Jüngling und der Tod; Der Knabe in der Wiege; Leiden der Trennung; Der Strom; Totengräbers Heimweh; Der Vater mit dem Kind; Wehmut; Der zürnende Barde; Der Zwerg.

*** D G G 2530 347. Dietrich Fischer-Dieskau (baritone), Gerald Moore (piano).

A rich and varied selection of miscellaneous Lieder, taken from the big collection recorded by Fischer-Dieskau and Moore. Superb performances and recording.

Am Bach im Frühling; An die Nachtigall; Auf der Donau; Ave Maria; 4 Frühlingsglaube; Gretchen am Spinnrade; Im Abendrot; Die junge Nonne; Der König in Thule; Lachen und Weinen; Des Mädchens Klage; Mignon Romanze; Der Tod und das Mädchen.

** D G G 2530 404. Christa Ludwig (mezzo-soprano), Irwin Gage (piano).

A somewhat uneven recital. Christa Ludwig is at her best in the dramatic songs. *Auf der Donau* and *Der Tod und das Mädchen* are both strikingly done, while the *Mignon Romanze* is beautiful. But the simpler songs are somewhat lacking in sheer charm, while *Ave Maria* is not relaxed enough. Irwin Gage accompanies sympathetically, and the recording is good.

An die Laute; Auf der Riesenkoppe; Dass sie hier gewesen; Du bist die Ruh; Des Fischers Liebesglück; Fischerweise; Die Forelle; Heidenröslein; Der Jüngling an der Quelle; Lachen und Weinen; Sei mir gegrüsst!; Seligkeit; Ständchen; Waldesnacht.

*** H M V ASD 2263. Dietrich Fischer-Dieskau (baritone), Gerald Moore (piano).

Alec Robertson chose this recital for inclusion in *The Great Records* as a 'friendly, treasurable disc, very well recorded'. He chose well, for the selection, besides including many favourites, also shows these artists on peak form. The opening songs on each side, *Lachen und Weinen* and *Seligkeit*, are – in the writer's view – best suited to the female voice, but that is a matter of opinion. Certainly *Du bist die Ruh, Heidenröslein*, the *Serenade, Der Jüngling an der Quelle*, the delicious *To my lute*, offer some of the most marvellous singing ever committed to disc.

An die Musik; Ave Maria; Erlafsee; Die Forelle; Frühlingslaube; Ganymed; Gretchen am Spinnrade; (i) Der Hirt auf dem Felsen; Im Frühling; Der Jüngling und der Tod; Liebe schwärmt; Ständchen.

(M) ** H M V HQS 1261. Elly Ameling (soprano), Joerg Demus or Irwin Gage (piano), (i) with George Pieterson (clarinet).

This is in fact two recitals in one, as the songs were recorded in two groups (in 1970 and 1972). Quite apart from the fact that the recording is warmer and more kindly to the voice in the later recordings, the singing too shows greater maturity. The earlier songs are sung freshly and straightforwardly and give pleasure from their simple eloquence, but the later recordings, notably *Die*

841

Forelle, Der Jüngling und der Tod and *Im Frühling*, are of a different calibre, showing much greater imagination, yet the voice as lovely as ever. *Der Hirt auf dem Felsen* is finely done; the contribution of the clarinettist, George Pieterson, is sensitive if without any special magic. At medium price this seems excellent value.

'*A Schubert evening*': *An die Nachtigall; An die untergehende Sonne; Berthas Lied in der Nacht; Delphine; Ellen's songs* from *The Lady of the Lake (Raste Krieger!; Jäger, ruhe von der Jagd; Ave Maria); Epistel an Herrn Josef von Spaun; Gretchen am Spinnrade; Hin und wieder; Iphigenia; Die junge Nonne; Liebe schwärmt; Das Mädchen; Das Mädchens Klage; Die Männer sind mechant; Mignon's songs* from *Wilhelm Meister, Nos. 1–3 (Heiss mich nicht reden; So lasst mich scheinen; Nur wer die Sehnsucht kennt); Mignons Gesang: Kennst du das Land?; Schlummerlied; Schwestergruss; Suleika songs 1 and 2 (Was bedeutet die Bewegung?; Ach, um deine feuchten Schwingen); Wiegenlied; Wiegenlied (Schlafe, schlafe!).*

> (M) *** HMV sls 812 (2 discs). Janet Baker (mezzo-soprano), Gerald Moore (piano).

Janet Baker ranges wide in an imaginative *Liederabend* of Schubert songs that includes a number of rarities. They range from the delectably comic *Epistel* to the ominous darkness of *Die junge Nonne*. The two cradle songs are irresistible, the Seidl setting even more haunting than the more famous one; and throughout the four sides Baker consistently displays the breadth of her emotional mastery and of her range of tone-colour. With Gerald Moore (returning to the studio out of retirement) still at his finest, this is a rarely satisfying album. Only *Gretchen*

842

am Spinnrade brings a performance which one feels Baker could have intensified on repetition. First-rate recording.

Schiller Lieder: *An den Frühling; An die Freude; Die Bürgschaft; Das Geheimnis; Die Götter Griechenlands; Gruppe aus dem Tartarus; Der Jüngling am Bache; Das Mädchen aus der Fremde; Der Pilgrim; Sehnsucht.*

> *** DGG 2530 306. Dietrich Fischer-Dieskau (baritone), Gerald Moore (piano).

Unlike his Goethe settings, Schubert's settings of Schiller here include relatively few which are well-known – the magnificent *Gruppe aus dem Tartarus*, most advanced for its time, an obvious exception. It is not generally realized that Schubert like Beethoven made a setting of the *Ode to Joy* (hardly inspired); but ranging from the lilting *An den Frühling* to the extended ballad, *Die Bürgschaft*, this makes an intensely enjoyable collection, superbly performed and recorded.

Goethe Lieder: *An der Mond I and II; Erlkönig; Der Fischer; Gesäng des Harfners I, II and III; Heidenröslein; Meeres Stille; Nachtgesang; Nähe des Geliebten; Rastlöse Liebe; Der Sänger; Shäfers Klagelied; Wanderers Nachtlied.*

> *** DGG 2530 229. Dietrich Fischer-Dieskau (baritone), Gerald Moore (piano).

These fifteen settings of Goethe poems date from Schubert's earliest creative period up to the age of twenty, magically fresh inspirations ranging wide in mood and expression, and here performed with charm as well as deep insight. The *Songs of the Harper* are among the finest Schubert performances that even Fischer-Dieskau and Moore have given us. Fine recording.

Goethe Lieder: (i) *An die Türen will ich schleichen; Erlkönig; Ganymed;* (ii) *Heidenröslein; Heiss mich nicht reden; Kennst du das Land; Die Liebende schreibt; Liebhaber in allen Gestalten; Nähe des Geliebten; Nur wer die Sehnsucht kennt;* (i) *Der Sänger;* (ii) *So lasst mich scheinen;* (i) *Wer nie sein Brot; Wer sich der Einsamkeit ergibt.*
** (*) Philips 6500 515. (i) Hermann Prey (baritone), Karl Engel (piano); (ii) Elly Ameling (soprano), Dalton Baldwin (piano).

An attractive collection of Goethe settings, with the soloists well contrasted. Though Prey cannot quite match the imagination of Fischer-Dieskau, his singing is strong and satisfying, and Ameling makes a persuasive interpreter, gently pointing each verse of the strophic songs. This early setting of Mignon's *Kennst du das Land* is charmingly simple in contrast to the great Wolf setting. Good recording.

Auf der Strom (for tenor, horn and piano), *D.943.*
(M) *** Oiseau-Lyre SOL 314. Robert Tear (tenor), Neil Sanders (horn), Lamar Crowson (piano) – BRAHMS: *Horn trio* **; SCHUMANN: *Adagio and allegro.** (*)

Schubert's ballad *Auf der Strom* is an extended duet for tenor and horn, with a florid yet essentially lyrical horn part which needs real virtuosity if it is to be realized in the proper relaxed way. The song tells of a lover departing on a voyage whose consolation is found in the radiance of the stars shining down on him. The horn echoes the vocal line and provides beautiful solo bridge-passages between each verse. The performance here is first-rate in every way, Robert Tear singing with sensitivity and understanding, while the horn part has exactly

the right degree of eloquence without overwhelming the voice. The pianist too plays a major part in sustaining the mood, and the recording balance is most convincing.

'*Schubertiade*': (Piano) *12 Ländler, D.970.* (Vocal) *Gretchen am Spinnrade; Heimliches Lieben;* (i) *Der Hirt auf dem Felsen; Im Frühling; Der Jüngling an der Quelle; Du liebst mich nicht; Der Musensohn; Seligkeit; Die Vögel.*
* (*) BASF BAC 3088. Elly Ameling (soprano), Joerg Demus (Rausch piano, Vienna, 1835), (i) with Hans Deinzer (clarinet).

This is a delightful mixture of items in the manner of one of Schubert's own private concerts, but the lack of charm in the performances is a serious drawback. Hollow recording.

Deutsche Messe, D.872.
** Telefunken SAT 22545. Bergedorfer Chamber Choir, members of the Hamburg State Philharmonic Orchestra, Hellmut Wormsbächer – BRUCKNER: *Mass No. 2.** (*)

The *Deutsche Messe* is not great music, but rather simple, unaffected homophonic settings of a text by J. P. Neumann, accompanied by wind. Few are likely to buy the disc for this particular work but those wanting the Bruckner *Mass* may regard this charming makeweight as a deciding factor.

Mass No. 3 in B flat major, D.324; Deutsche Messe, D.872.
(B) ** Turnabout TV 34282S. Elisabeth Thomann (soprano), Gertrude Jahn (contralto), Stafford Wing (tenor), Kunizaku Ohashi (bass), Vienna Chamber Choir,

Vienna Pro Musica Orchestra, Hans Gillesberger.

These are lively enjoyable performances of lesser-known, frankly less inspired Schubert. But even in his routine moments Schubert cannot help sounding fresh and alert, particularly in the folk-like inspirations of the *Deutsche Messe*. Well worth investigating at bargain price.

Rosamunde: Overture (Die Zauberharfe, D.644); incidental music (complete), *D.797.*

   *** Philips SAL 3534. Aafje Heynis (contralto), Netherlands Radio Chorus, Concertgebouw Orchestra, Bernard Haitink.

   ** Turnabout TV 34330S. Oksana Sowiak (contralto), Philharmonia Vocal Ensemble, Philharmonia Hungarica, Peter Maag.

Haitink shows here the simple eloquence and musical sensitivity that he found also for his companion disc of the incidental music for Mendelssohn's *A Midsummer Night's Dream*. This record is an equal success. It is beautifully played and smoothly recorded. It is perhaps a pity that room was not found for the real *Rosamunde overture*, but as that actually used at the first performance was in fact written for *Alfonso and Estrella*, one cannot really grumble. What we do have here, besides the familiar ballet music and entr'acte (played with a deliciously light touch), are the vocal numbers with Aafje Heynis in fine voice as soloist in the lovely *Romance (The full moon shines on mountain peaks)* and lively contributions from the chorus in the music from Spirits, Shepherds (a touch of Sullivan here), and Weberian Huntsmen. The Amsterdam acoustic is perhaps a trifle thick for scoring expressly (and skilfully) designed for the less reverberant theatre-pit, but with that

one reservation this is a fine record indeed.

Maag's account offers neat, musical playing and a good contribution from the chorus. Oksana Sowiak is an acceptable soloist, if no match for Aafje Heynis. The recording is clear, a little lacking in glow, but well balanced. This is excellent value at the modest price asked, but Haitink's account has much more magic.

Die schöne Müllerin (song cycle), *D.795.*

   *** HMV ASD 481. Dietrich Fischer-Dieskau (baritone), Gerald Moore (piano).

   *** Decca SXL 2200. Peter Pears (tenor), Benjamin Britten (piano).

   (B) *** Classics for Pleasure CFP 40043. Ian Partridge (tenor), Jennifer Partridge (piano).

   ** (*) DGG 2530 362. Peter Schreier (tenor), Walter Olbertz (piano).

   (M) * (*) DGG Privilege 2538 001 Ernst Haefliger (tenor), Jacqueline Bonneau (piano).

Fischer-Dieskau may find more drama in the poems, and Gerald Moore matches his subtlety of inflection at every point; but Pears is imaginative too, if for once in rather gritty voice, and Britten brings a composer's insight to the accompaniments, which are even finer than Moore's. Both are well recorded, the HMV acoustic more intimate than the Decca and the piano tone slightly more sonorous. The spontaneity of the HMV account is striking and on balance Fischer-Dieskau provides more charm in this most sunny of song cycles.

Partridge's is an exceptionally fresh and urgent account. Rarely if ever on record has the dynamic quality of the cycle been so effectively conveyed, rising to an emotional climax at the end of the first half (complete on side one, unlike some other versions), with the song *Mein!*, expressing the poet's ill-founded joy, welling up infectiously. Partridge's subtle and beautiful range of tone is a constant delight, and he is most imaginatively accompanied by his sister Jennifer. An outstanding bargain disc that should win many new friends for Lieder.

Schreier is a thoughtful and sensitive interpreter of Schubert, and though his account of *Die Schöne Müllerin* is less intense than some of his finest performances on record, it will certainly please his admirers. The tone, well caught by the recording, sometimes loses its natural freshness.

Haefliger's sweet tenor brings out the charm of these songs, the phrasing finely shaded. This is enjoyable, if not comparable with an account like Fischer-Dieskau's, and the accompanist, Jacqueline Bonneau, is unimaginative.

Song cycles: *Die schöne Müllerin, D.795; Schwanengesang, D.957; Winterreise, D.911.*

(M) *** DGG 2720 059 (4 discs). Dietrich Fischer-Dieskau (baritone), Gerald Moore (piano).

Fischer-Dieskau and Moore had each recorded these great cycles of Schubert several times already before they embarked on this set as part of DGG's Schubert song series. It was no mere repeat of earlier triumphs. If anything these performances – notably that of the greatest and darkest of the cycles, *Winterreise* – are even more searching than before, with Moore matching the hushed concentration of the singer in some of the most remarkable playing that even he has put on record.

Schwanengesang (song collection), *D.957.*

** (*) Decca SXL 6590. Tom Krause (baritone), Irwin Gage (piano).

Schwanengesang, containing some of Schubert's last and most memorable songs, presents the interpreter with an insuperable problem in that no single voice is suited to every one of them. Krause, with his dark, even aggressive tone, is most effective in such songs as *Aufenthalt,* though he turns the famous *Serenade* very charmingly. Fine accompaniment and first-rate recording.

Winterreise (song cycle), *D.911.*

⊛ *** Decca SET 270/1. Peter Pears (tenor), Benjamin Britten (piano) – SCHUMANN: *Dichterliebe.****

*** HMV ASDS 551/ASD 552. Dietrich Fischer-Dieskau (baritone), Gerald Moore (piano).

(M) ** DGG Privilege 2726 030 (2 discs). Hans Hotter (baritone), Erik Werba (piano).

Schubert's darkest song cycle was in fact originally written for high not low voice, and quite apart from the intensity and subtlety of the Pears/Britten version it gains enormously from being at the right pitch throughout. When the message of these poems is so gloomy, a dark voice tends to underline the sombre aspect too oppressively, where the lightness of a tenor is even more affecting. That is particularly so in those songs where the wandering poet in his despair observes triviality – as in the picture of the hurdy-gurdy man in the last song of all. What is so striking about the Pears performance is its intensity. One continually has the sense of a live performance, and next to it even Fischer-Dieskau's beautifully wrought singing sounds too easy. As for Britten he re-creates the music, sometimes with a fair freedom from Schubert's markings but always with scrupulous concern for the overall musical shaping and sense of atmosphere. The sprung rhythm of *Gefror'ne Tränen* is magical in creating the impression of frozen drops falling, and almost every song brings similar magic.

After Britten even Gerald Moore sounds comparatively stiff, but the combination of Dieskau and Moore still provides a deeply satisfying performance, darker but more extrovert than its rival. Dieskau's underlining of German words remains unrivalled, and when all is said and done his pronunciation is to be preferred to Pears!

Hotter has recorded *Winterreise* before, but with age his voice has become gritty and less well focused. The darkness of a bass has something to be said for it in bringing out the work's bleakness, but gloom that is unrelieved can in the end be less moving. Nor is Werba so sensitive an accompanist as his rivals. Recommended to Hotter admirers.

Schuller, Gunther
(born 1925)

(i) *Symphony;* (ii) *Quartet for double-basses.*

> (B) *** Turnabout TV 34412S. (i) Dallas Symphony Orchestra, Donald Johanos; (ii) Sam Hollingsworth, Clifford Spohr, James Carroll, Arnold Craven (double-basses).

Schuller is an imaginative composer, and these two works reveal considerable inventive resource. His *Symphony* is highly stimulating, and although there is a certain general-purpose modernity about it it is unfailingly compelling. The *Quartet* too is an ingenious piece, and given the excellence of both performance and recording and the modest price asked, the disc will be welcomed by those wanting to investigate more deeply a composer who has perhaps suffered unnecessarily by his Third Stream image.

Schumann, Clara
(1819–96)

(i) *Piano concerto in A minor, Op. 7. Four fugitive pieces; Scherzi Nos. 1 in D minor, Op. 10; 2 in C minor, Op. 14; Variations on a theme of Robert Schumann, Op. 20.*

> (M) ** (*) Vox STGBY 649. Michael Ponti (piano), (i) with Berlin Symphony Orchestra, Schmidt-Gertenbach.

The music of Clara Schumann, Robert's wife, had hitherto been virtually unknown, so this fine Vox collection was especially welcome. As might be expected Clara's inspiration is redolent of her husband's style, and the Schumann-esque atmosphere is strong. Taken as whole the *Concerto* is not really a success, but the writing has character throughout and is never just empty. Some of the solo pieces are very striking, however, and the *Second Scherzo* is genuinely memorable. Michael Ponti is a splendid advocate. He plays with conviction and assurance. The recording too is good throughout and no Schumann-lover will want to be without this disc. It would be a brave man who would say with assurance, on aural evidence alone, that the best music here was not by Robert himself.

(i) *Piano trio in G major, Op. 17;* (ii) *(Piano) Prelude and fugue in G minor, Op. 16/1; Souvenir de Vienne – Impromptu, Op. 9; Variations on a theme of Robert Schumann, Op. 20.*

> (B) ** Oryx ORYX 1819. (i) Clara-Wieck Trio; (ii) Monica von Saalfeld (piano).

Clara Schumann's *Piano trio* is a slight but attractive work, Chopinesque in manner as well as showing Robert's influence. The *Variations* are also agreeably spontaneous, and this well played and recorded disc reinforces Clara's modest claims to being remembered as composer as well as performer.

Schumann, Robert
(1810–56)

Piano concerto in A minor, Op. 54.

*** Philips 6500 166. Stephen Bishop (piano), BBC Symphony Orchestra, Colin Davis – GRIEG: *Piano concerto.****

(B) *** Music for Pleasure MFP 57002. Shura Cherkassky (piano), London Philharmonic Orchestra, Sir Adrian Boult – GRIEG: *Piano concerto.****

(B) ** (*) Contour 6870 581. Hans Richter-Haaser (piano), Vienna Symphony Orchestra, Rudolf Moralt – GRIEG: *Piano concerto.** (*)*

** (*) HMV ASD 272. Solomon (piano), Philharmonia Orchestra, Herbert Menges – GRIEG: *Piano concerto.***

(M) ** (*) Decca Ace of Diamonds SDD 422. Julius Katchen (piano), Israel Philharmonic Orchestra, Istvan Kertesz – GRIEG: *Piano concerto.** (*)*

** Decca SXL 6624. Radu Lupu (piano), London Symphony Orchestra, André Previn – GRIEG: *Piano concerto.** (*)*

(B) * (*) Turnabout TV 34468S. Rudolf Firkusny (piano), Radio Luxembourg Orchestra, Louis de Froment – MENDELSSOHN: *Piano concerto No. 1.* (*)*

* HMV ASD 2802. John Ogdon (piano), New Philharmonia Orchestra, Paavo Berglund – GRIEG: *Piano concerto.**

As in Grieg so with Schumann, Bishop and Davis give an interpretration which is both fresh and poetic, unexaggerated but powerful in its directness and clarity. Bishop more than most shows the link between the central introspective slow movement and the comparable movement of Beethoven's *Fourth Concerto*, and the spring-like element of the outer movements is finely presented by orchestra and soloist alike. Excellent recording.

With a fine, modern recording the partnership between Cherkassky and Boult produces one of the most satisfying accounts of this elusive concerto available at any price. The reading strikes a near-perfect balance between romantic boldness – the masculine element – and feminine waywardness and charm. The pastel shades of the opening pages are realized with delicacy and when the first tutti arrives there is strength of the right kind, helped by the excellent balance between piano and orchestra and the ringing, sonorous tone of the piano itself. The dialogues between the soloist and the woodwind are managed with sensitivity, and later the interplay with the strings in the *Andante* has an appealing simplicity. Boult's affection can be felt here in the gracious string-playing, and he shows his control of the overall structure in the finale, which moves forward with a splendid impetus and never rambles.

The engineers seem to have left the sound of Richter-Haaser's reissue virtually untampered with, and they are surely right, for the warmth of the recording was one of the disc's prime virtues. The performance remains deeply musical, and the balance between soloist and orchestra is well managed. The spontaneous quality of this reading outweighs any reservations, and this most enjoyable coupling is a splendid bargain at its new price, for all but those who seek the most brilliant modern sound.

HMV have successfully recut the Solomon recording, and although the piano and string tone is on the shallow side the overall effect is crisp and fresh. Solomon often plays very beautifully, with most delicate fingerwork in the quieter moments, and both he and the principal clarinet caress lovingly their famous duet passage in the central section of the first movement. There is some fine oboe-playing also. It is the conductor who lets the performance down slightly, for his slow movement seems perfunctory and there is also a dull section in the middle of the last movement.

Katchen is given a beautiful clear, brilliant recording. This is essentially a virtuoso reading, but Katchen's wilfulness does not eschew romantic charm and there is a pervading freshness. The opening movement has a number of tempo changes and sounds more rhapsodical than usual. In the finale, which is basically very spirited, the fast main tempo hardly relaxes for the bumpy little second subject.

Radu Lupu's performance with André Previn is not as successful as the Grieg coupling. The clean boldness of approach is enjoyable enough, but the elusive poetry of this most romantic of concertos is not always fully revealed. The end of the slow movement is not as magical as it might be, and the finale, although brilliantly played, lacks the forward surge of the very finest accounts. The recording is vivid, the orchestral detail remarkably clear.

Firkusny's performance has a characteristic freshness, but the orchestra shows less flexibility, and it is the accompaniment which prevents this performance from receiving a stronger recommendation. Even so, the reading does not want character, and although the recording is rather too brightly lit, those wanting this unusual coupling with the Mendelssohn will find much to admire in Firkusny's contribution.

Ogdon, as in the Grieg, is unexpectedly below form in what should be one of the most poetic of piano concertos.

Piano concerto in A minor, Op. 54; Introduction and Allegro appassionato in G major (Konzertstück) for piano and orchestra, Op. 92.

> *** DGG 2530 484. Wilhelm Kempff (piano), Bavarian Radio Symphony Orchestra, Rafael Kubelik.
>
> ** HMV ASD 3053. Daniel Barenboim (piano), London Philharmonic Orchestra, Dietrich Fischer-Dieskau.
>
> * (*) DGG SLPM 138077. Sviatoslav Richter (piano), Warsaw National Philharmonic Orchestra, Rowicki or Wislocki.

Kempff, after a very solid account of the opening chords of the *Concerto*, proceeds characteristically to produce an unending stream of poetry. His tempi are generally leisurely and he is richly supported by Kubelik and the Bavarian Radio Orchestra. The *Konzertstück* too, not one of Schumann's most inspired pieces, is most persuasively played, with Kempff's magic leading the ear on.

Barenboim is altogether brisker and less poetic than Kempff. His interpretation is often imaginative, but with the NPO below its best under Fischer-Dieskau (a good but not an outstanding conductor), this performance lacks what Barenboim usually achieves on record, a sense of spontaneity, a simulation of a live performance. That lack is more serious in the *Konzertstück* than in the *Concerto*. Good recording.

Richter's performance of the *Concerto* is discussed below, where it is differently coupled on a cheaper label. The performance of the *Konzertstück* is not sufficiently interesting to make the present record really competitive, although for good measure Richter also includes performances of the *Novellette in F major, Op. 21/1* and the *Toccata in C major, Op. 7*. These are fabulous performances, full of hair-raising virtuosity, but shaped with an unerring sense of style and musical as well as technical control. The piano tone is excellent.

(i) *Piano concerto in A minor, Op. 54;*
(ii) *Violoncello concerto in A minor, Op. 129.*
   (M) ** (*) DGG Privilege 2538 025. (i) Sviatoslav Richter (piano), Warsaw Philharmonic Orchestra, Witold Rowicki; (ii) Mstislav Rostropovich (cello), Leningrad Philharmonic Orchestra, Gennady Rozhdestvensky.

Richter's performance of the *Piano concerto* is not so interesting as one would expect. Its opening speed is fast and the interpretation is in the main without idiosyncrasy, but only in the finale does one feel that vibrant quality in his playing which marks Richter out among even the greatest virtuosos. One suspects that the orchestra was partly to blame, and that its comparative sluggishness affected Richter's concentration. Not that the performance lacks style, but the intensity could be greater. Rostropovich's account of the *Cello concerto* is another matter. This is a superbly made performance, introspective yet at the same time outgoing, with a peerless technique at the command of a rare artistic imagination. Taken as a whole this disc is worth the price asked for it.

(i) *Piano concerto in A minor, Op. 54. Waldscenen, Op. 82.*
   (M) * (*) Decca Ace of Diamonds SDD 201. Wilhelm Backhaus, (i) with Vienna Philharmonic Orchestra, Wand.

Backhaus's performance of the *Concerto* has appeared before, uncoupled, on a cheap 10-inch Decca disc. It was a well regarded performance, weighty and essentially masculine, but fresh too and notable for Wand's vivid account of the orchestral contribution. In the transfer the sound is more transparent and brighter, but one notices that the romanticism of the slow movement still sounds rich rather than delicate. This is enjoyably valid in its own right and the only snag is the coupling. This is one of those literal, circumspect readings typical of Backhaus's later solo recordings.

Violoncello concerto in A minor, Op. 129.
   *** HMV ASD 2498. Jacqueline du Pré (cello), New Philharmonia Orchestra, Daniel Barenboim – SAINT-SAËNS: *Cello concerto No. 1.***
   (M) ** Supraphon SUAST 50581. André Navarra (cello), Czech Philharmonic Orchestra, Karel Ančerl – BLOCH: *Schelomo.***
   ** Philips 6500 160. Christine Walevska (cello), Monte Carlo Opera Orchestra, Eliahu Inbal – BLOCH: *Schelomo.***

It takes all of Jacqueline du Pré's youthful ardour to project this most difficult of cello concertos with the momentum needed, and she is ably assisted by Daniel Barenboim. Some will find this a wild performance, but anyone who has ever thrilled to du Pré's essentially spontaneous style will probably prefer this to more staid readings. The slow movement is particularly beautiful. The coupling is unexpected, but well worth having. Good recording.

André Navarra too, on his day, is one of the most commanding of cellists, even in an age when we are exceptionally well served for cello virtuosi. More brilliant recording might have made this fine

849

account even more compelling, but even as it is, the performance rivals those on dearer labels. By comparison the account by Walevska and Inbal has less personality and impact.

Konzertstück in F major for 4 horns and orchestra, Op. 86 (arr. for 5 horns).

*** BASF BAC 3037. Hermann Baumann and soloists, Vienna Symphony Orchestra, Dietfried Bernet (with *Concert ***).

Schumann's horn writing often shows a limited knowledge of what the horn can and can't do in reasonable comfort. The problem applies in particular to this very difficult concerto, which is why it is seldom heard in public. But by subdividing the four parts to engage five players it is more easily possible to sustain the continual high-flown bravura of the melodic line. The result here is to provide a confident, soaringly romantic performance of irresistible impetus, and the work emerges as about the most exciting concerto in the horn repertoire. Its invention is not of the quality of Mozart's solo horn concertos but at least comparable with those of Richard Strauss. This is part of a concert of horn music discussed in our *Treasury* volume.

Symphony in G minor (rev. and ed. Andreae); *Overture, Scherzo and Finale, Op. 52.*

* (*) BASF BAC 3041. Munich Philharmonic Orchestra, Marc Andreae.

It is difficult to work up a great deal of enthusiasm for Schumann's early *G minor Symphony*, which appeared in 1833. Schumann completed two movements and sketched out a finale, and performance requires some touching-up of the score. The hints of the mature style are undoubtedly there, but the account here does not make a very persuasive case for the music itself. The performance of the *Overture, Scherzo and Finale* might be described as sturdy. The recording is good.

Symphonies Nos. 1–4; Manfred overture, Op. 115; Overture, Scherzo and Finale, Op. 52.

(M) ** (*) HMV SLS 867 (3 discs). Dresden State Orchestra, Wolfgang Sawallisch.

Symphonies Nos. 1–4. (i) *Piano concerto in A minor, Op. 54. Manfred overture, Op. 115.*

(M) ** CBS 77344 (3 discs). Cleveland Orchestra, George Szell, (i) with Leon Fleischer (piano).

The excellence of the Dresden State Orchestra can be taken for granted nowadays: it is surely second to none at the present time, and this set of Schumann's symphonies under Sawallisch will be eagerly sought out by discriminating collectors. The performances are as deeply musical as they are carefully considered, and the orchestral playing combines superb discipline with refreshing naturalness and spontaneity. Sawallisch catches all the varying moods of Schumann, and his direction has splendid vigour. Unfortunately the sound is less than ideal: the acoustic is reverberant and the upper strings have an unappealing edge. Yet Schumann's scoring does not suffer as much as it would from too analytical or detailed a recording. His symphonic argument is not conceived in terms of primary colours or clearly-etched lines, and the sound picture has the warmth so essential.

Szell too is a conductor of strong Schumannesque instinct. His readings have precision, momentum and vigour, tempered by a warmth not always present in this conductor. His set has the additional advantage of including the *Piano concerto.* There is little price difference between the two sets, though honours must finally go to Sawallisch, who has the greater humanity and the more spontaneous orchestral response. Karajan's set in the D G G Symphony Edition was undoubtedly the best, and even in the more expensive form of three separate discs, some readers may feel that it has stronger claims on their allegiance.

Symphonies Nos. 1 in B flat major (Spring), Op. 38; 2 in C major, Op. 61; 3 in E flat major (Rhenish), Op. 97; 4 in D minor, Op. 120.
- (B) ** (*) Philips 6870 015 (2 discs). Leipzig Gewandhaus Orchestra, Franz Konwitschny.
- (B) * (*) Pye GGCD 302 (2 discs). London Philharmonic Orchestra, Sir Adrian Boult.

Both the Philips and the Pye issues are priced under £3, and the Konwitschny set makes a splendid bargain. The recording is not of the most brilliant, but with careful use of the controls – a little brightening of the treble and reduction of bass – a most satisfying and natural sound can be achieved. The performances show a natural feeling for Schumann; they are eloquent and persuasive. The allegros have a natural spring, and the slow movements are warmly done, while the finales are fittingly incisive. The performances of Nos. 2 and 4 are notably successful.

By comparison the Pye performances – made at a time when the LPO strings were undernourished and the orchestra far from its present form – are distinctly rough and ready. But if the playing is totally lacking in polish, the readings have a full-blooded quality and a vigour that may compensate to some extent for the rough edges and the lack of real beauty of tone. However, Konwitschny's set is altogether more rewarding.

Symphony No. 1 in B flat major (Spring), Op. 38; Overture, Scherzo and Finale, Op. 52.
- ** (*) Decca SXL 6486. Vienna Philharmonic Orchestra, Sir Georg Solti.

Though Solti's performance of Schumann's *Spring symphony* does not quite match the glowing inspiration of the companion performances it provides a very welcome completion to the cycle, particularly when the unjustly neglected *Overture, Scherzo and Finale* is provided as an ideal coupling. Solti's fine springing of rhythm is always a delight, and he shows conclusively how many imaginative points of orchestration Schumann devised for this work, whatever may have been said over the years. Excellent recording.

Symphonies Nos. 1 in B flat major (Spring), Op. 38; 3 in E flat major (Rhenish), Op. 97.
- (M) *** CBS Classics 61595. Cleveland Symphony Orchestra, George Szell.

Szell and the Cleveland Orchestra are at their most incisive but also their warmest in the *Spring symphony*, and the account of the *Rhenish* is even finer, marvellously full of life. The playing is breathtaking, with horns gloriously full-blooded. The recording is brightly lit in the Cleveland manner. A first-class coupling.

Symphonies Nos. 1 in B flat major (Spring), Op. 38; 4 in D minor, Op. 120.
- *** DGG 2530 169. Berlin Philharmonic Orchestra, Herbert von Karajan.
- (M) ** (*) DGG Privilege 2535 116. Berlin Philharmonic Orchestra, Rafael Kubelik.

(B) ** Decca Eclipse ECS 758. London Symphony Orchestra, Josef Krips.

Karajan provides beautifully shaped performances, with orchestral playing of the highest distinction. The sound is sumptuous. In the *Fourth Symphony* Karajan is totally attuned to Schumann's sensibility: one is reminded of the pre-war Bruno Walter LSO set. Although Krips is competitive at bargain price, this is well worth the extra outlay involved.

Kubelik's accounts are beautifully played and well recorded. They have not the drive of Karajan's, and this is especially noticeable in No. 4, but they are direct in manner and certainly enjoyable.

Krips offers lightweight performances, and there is certainly a case for regarding these works as he does. If one tends to prefer something bigger and more dramatic, Krips is wonderfully persuasive. particularly in the *Spring symphony*. The playing is a good deal more accomplished than the Boult, yet has less drive and enthusiasm. These are nonetheless balanced readings and they are freshly recorded, so this coupling must be counted good value at the price asked.

Symphony No. 2 in C major, Op. 61; Genoveva overture.

(M) ** (*) DGG Privilege 2535 117. Berlin Philharmonic Orchestra, Rafael Kubelik.

This is one of the finest performances in the Kubelik set. It is beautifully played, eloquently shaped, and warmly recorded in a spacious acoustic. If the performance has less individuality than Solti's, it remains very enjoyable, and the *Genoveva overture* is a welcome novelty.

Symphony No. 2 in C major, Op. 61; Julius Caesar overture.

*** Decca SXL 6487. Vienna Philharmonic Orchestra, Sir Georg Solti.

Anyone who has ever doubted whether Solti could convey genuine *Innigkeit*, with unwanted tensions removed and a feeling of spontaneous lyricism paramount, should hear the slow movement in this magnificent performance of Schumann's least popular symphony. Both there and in the other movement Solti's performance glows with Viennese warmth, a masterly culmination of his excellent cycle of Schumann symphonies. The *Julius Caesar overture* is no masterpiece, but it makes an enjoyable fill-up. Excellent recording.

Symphony No. 2 in C major, Op. 61; Manfred overture, Op. 115.

(B) ** Decca Eclipse ECS 759. Suisse Romande Orchestra, Ernest Ansermet.

The Suisse Romande Orchestra is not the subtlest of instruments and neither in beauty of tone nor purity of intonation can it match the leading continental orchestras. Nor is Ansermet noted as a Schumann interpreter of distinction. Yet allowing for the comparatively unpolished orchestral performance, there is something to be said for the plainness and honesty of his approach, and the result is to be preferred to an excess of affection. The clarity of the recording is excellent, and the general coolness that greeted this issue on its first appearance is undeserved.

Symphony No. 3 in E flat major (Rhenish), Op. 97.

*** DGG 2530 447. Berlin Philharmonic Orchestra, Herbert von Karajan.

(B) ** Decca Eclipse ECS 760. London Symphony Orchestra, Rafael Frühbeck de Burgos –

MENDELSSOHN: *Midsummer Night's Dream overture.***

Karajan's account of the *Rhenish* is one of the most impressive versions committed to disc and certainly the finest currently available in what is a highly competitive field. The playing of the Berlin Philharmonic is beyond praise, and the recording has rich ambience and pleasing tone. A marvellous disc.

Frühbeck de Burgos secures clean and alert playing from the LSO, and the Decca recording does a great deal to render Schumann's textures as clear as possible. Having said this it is only fair to add that this is not a performance that matches Karajan's in terms of warmth. Perhaps it lacks fervour and the last ounce of character, for it is not a record to which one instinctively returns for greater illumination of Schumann's fine score.

Symphony No. 3 in E flat major (Rhenish), Op. 97; Manfred overture, Op. 115.

(M) ** (*) DGG Privilege 2535 118. Berlin Philharmonic Orchestra, Rafael Kubelik.

In the *Rhenish symphony*, again Kubelik's straightforward, unmannered approach, coupled to a natural warmth, provides a musical and thoroughly enjoyable account. The coupling too is apt and very well played, and the recording is up to the high standard of this series.

Symphonies Nos. 3 in E flat major (Rhenish), Op. 97; 4 in D minor, Op. 120.

*** Decca SXL 6356. Vienna Philharmonic Orchestra, Sir Georg Solti.

This is a generous coupling of two symphonies which in Solti's hands glow with exuberance. Maybe it takes a great conductor to present this music with the intensity it deserves, making light of the problems of balance in the orchestration. Solti's sense of rhythm in Schumann is strikingly alert, so that the first movement of the *Rhenish* hoists one aloft on its soaring melodies, and the drama of the *Fourth Symphony* is given full force without ever falling into excessive tautness. There is still room to breathe. Though in some ways Szell's performances with the Cleveland Orchestra are even finer, these provide an admirable alternative at what in effect is a very reasonable price. First-rate recording quality, despite the very long sides.

Symphony No. 4 in D minor, Op. 120.

(M) *** HMV SXLP 30178. Philharmonia Orchestra, Otto Klemperer – MENDELSSOHN: *Symphony No. 4.****

Klemperer's is a masterly performance. His slow introduction has a weight and consequence that command attention, and the slow tempo for the allegro is equally weighty and compelling, even if initially one disagrees with it. The scherzo with its striking main theme packs enormous punch, and the brief slow movement is exquisitely played. For the finale Klemperer's speed is faster than many, and he makes the conclusion most exciting. Plainly the Philharmonia players were on their toes throughout the recording session: the intensity of Klemperer's conviction comes over in shaping of phrases that is often quite breathtaking. The recording is full and rounded in EMI's best manner.

CHAMBER MUSIC

Adagio and allegro in E flat major for horn and piano, Op. 70.

(M) * (*) Oiseau-Lyre SOL 314. Neil

Sanders (horn), Lamar Crowson (piano) – BRAHMS: *Horn trio* **; SCHUBERT: *Auf der Strom.* ***

Schumann's *Adagio and allegro* is an elusive work. It tries the virtuosity of its performer to the utmost limits, for although Schumann appreciated the range of the horn, he did not entirely understand the instrument's technique and its relative flexibility in different registers. The tessitura of the *Allegro* holds no terrors for Neil Sanders, who throws it off with tremendous bravura. His vivacity, however, does not always fully realize the music's lyrical element, and in the opening *Adagio* he is wont to sound somewhat lugubrious in the low notes at which Schumann sometimes – not very sensitively – pitches his melodic line. The accompaniment is well managed and the recording is good.

Andante and variations in B flat major for 2 pianos, 2 violoncellos and horn.
(B) *** Turnabout TV 34204S. Toni and Rosi Grünschlag (pianos), Walther Tomböck (horn), Richard Harand, Gunther Weiss (cellos) – DUSSEK: *Double concerto.* ***
** Decca SXL 6130. Vladimir Ashkenazy, Malcolm Frager (pianos), Barry Tuckwell (horn), Amaryllis Fleming, Terence Weil (cellos) – MOZART: *Double piano sonata.* **

This broadly romantic and not ineffective work is something of a musical curiosity. Presumably it was written for the composer's circle of intimate friends, for the subsidiary instrumental parts are not very demanding, except for the main horn variation, which demands a repeated leap, a cello acting in the place of 'second horn'. Before the music was published the composer deleted these mainly instrumental (as distinct from pianistic) sections and the work has become known for two pianos alone (for that version, see under

Piano music below). However, the original scheme can be very effective and the spontaneous playing on the Turnabout disc catches the style and brings the music's lyricism fully to life enjoyably.

The Decca performance is beautifully played too and the balance of the admirably truthful recording takes into account the subsidiary nature of the horn and cellos. The account here is certainly persuasive, but has not quite the life and spontaneity of the Turnabout version, which is to be preferred, even though it is not quite so richly recorded. The Decca disc includes as a bonus the *Canonic study*, Op. 56/4, for two pianos.

Piano quartet in E flat major, Op. 47.
(M) * (*) Oiseau-Lyre SOL 320. Pro Arte Piano Quartet – BRAHMS: *Piano quartet No. 3.* * (*)

A clear, direct account of a work that needs less restraint and more romantic fire, this gives a certain pleasure because of the unaffected manner and the good recording.

Piano quintet in E flat major, Op. 44.
(M) *** RCA SER 5628/30. Artur Rubinstein (piano), Guarneri Quartet – BRAHMS: *Piano quartets.* ***

With good recording, warm and clear, this is very enjoyable. Rubinstein dominates the performance, but the Guarneri players help to provide a richly lyrical account of the slow movement. The finale is rather lightweight, but this is obviously planned to make a contrast with the broadly conceived opening movement. An excellent partner for a distinguished set of Brahms *Piano quartets.*

Piano trio No. 2 in F major, Op. 80.
(M) ** Supraphon SUAST 50639. Prague Trio – BEETHOVEN: *Piano trio No. 1.* ***

Schumann's piano trios are not well known. The present one, the second, was written in 1847. Imbued with the German classic/romantic spirit, it tends to fall between the two styles. It is not melodically memorable. The best movement is the third, in which the romanticism is given full head. Persuasively played and recorded here, the work is recommendable to the Schumann enthusiast rather than the general music-lover.

Fünf Stücke im Volkston for violoncello and piano, Op. 132.
> *** Decca SXL 2298. Mstislav Rostropovich (cello), Benjamin Britten (piano) – BRITTEN and DEBUSSY: *Sonatas.****

Though simpler than either the Britten or Debussy sonatas with which it is coupled this is just as elusive a work. Rostropovich and Britten show that the simplicity is not so square and solid as it might seem at first, and that in the hands of masters these *Five Pieces in folk style* have a rare charm, particularly the last, with its irregular rhythm. Excellent recording.

Violin sonata No. 1 in A minor, Op. 105.
> (M) ** Decca Ace of Diamonds SDD 401. Josef Sivó (violin), Rudolf Buchbinder (piano) – R. STRAUSS: *Violin sonata.*** (*)

Though Sivó and Buchbinder miss much of the romantic passion of this fine sonata, it stands as a useful stopgap while there is no other version in the catalogue. Good recording on a mid-price label.

PIANO MUSIC

'Abegg' variations, Op. 1; 6 Intermezzi, Op. 4; Kinderscenen (Scenes from Childhood), Op. 15; Waldscenen, Op.

82, excerpts (Introduction; Lonely flowers; The prophet bird; Farewell).
> ** (*) DGG SLPM 139183. Christoph Eschenbach (piano).

Christoph Eschenbach shows himself here a talented and sensitive interpreter of Schumann. The *Scenes from childhood* are played with great charm, the miniaturism evoked without the music seeming small in stature. The *Abegg variations* are brilliant, Eschenbach displaying a glittering right-hand technique; but he is just a little inclined to lose the music's colour in the piano's middle range. The four excerpts from *Waldscenen* are splendidly characterized, showing again the pianist's feeling for Schumann's textures. The *Intermezzi* are less interesting, and one feels that Eschenbach devoted less time to their preparation. DGG have provided excellent piano image, and with all reservations taken into account this is a fine disc.

'Abegg' variations, Op. 1; Études symphoniques, Op. 13.
> ** (*) Philips 6500 130. Claudio Arrau (piano).

A commanding if not always ideally relaxed account of the *Études symphoniques* from Arrau, very well recorded. The serious manner of the performance means that there is little if any charm here, but the intellectual grip is never in doubt and the bravura in the *Abegg variations* is matched by playing of considerable character. But in the last resort, like so many of Arrau's other discs, this lacks the incandescence of his live performances.

Allegro, Op. 8; Kreisleriana, Op. 16; Novelette, Op. 21/8; Romance, Op. 28/2.
> ** (*) Decca SXL 6546. Alicia de Larrocha (piano).

Alicia de Larrocha shows herself here

855

an accomplished and searchingly reflective artist in this repertoire. Her performance of *Kreisleriana* is notable for its blend of thoughtfulness and romanticism, the control of *rubato* wayward but unaffected. The style in the shorter pieces is bolder to match their character. The disc makes quite a satisfying recital, and the slightly reverberant piano image is very truthful.

Two pianos: *Andante and variations, Op. 46* (see also p. 854); *6 Canonic studies, for pedal piano, Op. 56.*
  * (*) Argo ZRG 721. John Ogdon, Brenda Lucas (pianos) – LISZT: *Concerto pathétique.** (*)

The playing here is rather studied. Some of the variations are strikingly characterized, but on the whole the performances do not catch fire and they are not helped by the rather too resonant recording acoustic.

Arabeske in C major, Op. 18; Bunte Blätter, Op. 39: No. 9, Novellette; 3 Romances, Op. 28; Waldscenen, Op. 82: The prophet bird.
  *** DGG 2530 321. Wilhelm Kempff (piano) – BRAHMS: *4 Ballades.** (*)

Kempff is in his element in these attractively chosen Schumann pieces, an excellent coupling for the early Brahms pieces on the reverse. He inspires an element of fantasy, of spontaneous re-creation, which brings Schumann to life, not only in the well-known pieces but in such music as the relatively little-known first and third *Romances* and the *Novellette* (not to be confused with the *Novelletten*), which is otherwise unavailable on record. Good recording.

Arabeske in C major, Op. 18; Études symphoniques, Op. 13; Kinderscenen (Scenes from Childhood), Op. 15.

(M) *** Pye Virtuoso TPLS 13026. Balint Vazsonyi (piano).

Balint Vazsonyi shows here that his sympathy with the elusive Schumann idiom is no less sure than his command of the Brahms piano repertoire. The *Scenes from Childhood* are most beautifully played, with a gentle yet never patronizing lyricism; the feeling of repose in quieter evocations, such as *Träumerei*, is especially rewarding. The shaping of the *Symphonic studies* is masterly, and the steady build-up of tension from the relaxed opening gives the work a splendid flowing momentum. There is no better performance in the catalogue, and it is only in the *Arabeske* that one feels that Vazsonyi's romantic musing loses some of the lightness of texture the composer intended. But in general this is very distinguished playing, with that remarkable feeling of a live performance that illuminates all this pianist's records. The sound too is excellent, sonorous and realistic.

Arabeske in C major, Op. 18; Faschingsschwank aus Wien, Op. 26; Humoreske in B flat major, Op. 20.
  ** (*) Philips SAL 3690. Claudio Arrau (piano).

Schumann is a composer who inspires Arrau to some of his most deeply perceptive playing. You might argue that he is too thoughtful at times, seems unwilling to throw off the scherzando passages with a shrug of flippancy, but these are still wonderful performances. The *Humoreske* is the most ambitious of the pieces, lasting a full side. It is deeper music than the title might suggest, for as Schumann himself said when telling Clara about his new composition, he laughed and cried at the same time as he wrote it. Its massive structure is impressively held together. Fine, discreet recording quality.

Arabeske in C major, Op. 18; Faschingsschwank aus Wien, Op. 26; Kinderscenen (Scenes from Childhood), Op. 15; Papillons, Op. 2.
> (B) * (*) Turnabout TV 34438S. Walter Klien (piano).

Klien, always a thoughtful artist, is at his best in the *Arabeske* and especially the *Kinderscenen*, which he plays very beautifully. But the impulsive manner in the *Faschingsschwank aus Wien* is not helped by a very hard and uncongenial recorded quality, and the same is true for *Papillons*, where the recording is only marginally better.

Carnaval, Op. 9; Fantasia in C major, Op. 17.
> ** (*) DGG 2530 185. Wilhelm Kempff (piano).
> (B) Turnabout TV 34432S. Abbey Simon (piano).

The comparatively extrovert style of *Carnaval* does not seem to suit Kempff too well. There is no special degree of illumination, such as we expect from this artist, in his performance, which even seems to lack absolute technical assurance. But the *Fantasia* is a different matter. The reading is wayward and personal, but the poetry of the playing is never in doubt. The recording too is good here; in *Carnaval* it is clear but a little lacking in richness of sonority.

Abbey Simon's performance of *Carnaval* is an unattractive one, curiously unidiomatic, and it is not helped by the undistinguished recording. However, Simon – usually a most sensitive artist – is obviously more at home in the *Fantasia*, which he plays with a fair degree of imagination and thoughtfulness. The recording too is much better on this side.

Carnaval, Op. 9; Kinderscenen (Scenes from Childhood), Op. 15; Papillons, Op. 2.

* Turnabout TV 34164S. Guiomar Novaes (piano).

The recording provided here for Guiomar Novaes is rather woody and mellow, and the performances do not seek brilliance either. There is some less than immaculate playing in the more florid passages of *Carnaval*, which is otherwise a pleasing account. *Papillons* too is enjoyable in its undemonstrative manner, if lacking in drama, but the *Kinderscenen* is the finest performance here, played with real poetic feeling.

Davidsbundlertänze, Op. 6; Fantasiestücke, Op. 12.
> *** CBS SBRG 73202. Murray Perahia (piano).

Perahia, winner of the Leeds Piano Competition in 1972, has a magic touch, and his electric spontaneity is naturally caught in the studio. In works of Schumann which can splinter apart this quality of concentration is enormously valuable, and the results could hardly be more powerfully convincing, despite rather coarse recording quality.

Davidsbundlertänze, Op. 6; Nachtstücke, Op. 23.
> ** (*) Philips 6500 178. Claudio Arrau (piano).

Wayward but consistently imaginative playing by Arrau: here in elusive Schumann he seems almost to be thinking aloud to himself. A record for the devotee rather than the uninitiated. Good recording.

Davidsbündlertänze, Op. 6; 3 Romances, Op. 28.
> (B) * (*) Turnabout TV 34379S. Walter Klien (piano).

The strong impulse of Walter Klien's playing, coupled to a rather hard, bold piano image, misses some of the lyrical flow of the *Davidsbündlertänze*. Klien is at his best in the work's more thoughtful moments, and here the piano tone is fully acceptable. The *Romances* are well done; the second, *Einfach*, shows Klien at his most poetic.

Études symphoniques, Op. 13; Fantasia in C major, Op. 17.
> ** (*) Decca SXL 6214. Vladimir Ashkenazy (piano).
> (M) ** (*) Vanguard VCS 10020. Alfred Brendel (piano).

Ashkenazy's playing is extremely fine: technically he is superb, and intellectually he obviously dominates the music. There are flashes of poetry and one or two really commanding moments where the sheer power of the pianism is most gripping. Ashkenazy includes all the studies, the original twelve and the five discovered later, which he inserts three-quarters of the way through the set. The recording is first-rate.

Brendel's opening phrase of the *Symphonic studies* is immediately individual, and yet in essence these are not wayward readings, even though they are strongly personalized. Brendel's reputation is as a player in the mainstream of the classical tradition, and it is the strength of that tradition that gives these performances their character and power. There are other ways of approaching Schumann (Kempff's, for instance), but in Brendel's hands the music's structure emerges anew and has the emotional grip one associates with Beethoven. Excellent recording to match the playing.

Études symphoniques, Op. 13; Kreisleriana, Op. 16.
> ** (*) DGG 2530 317. Wilhelm Kempff (piano).

If Kempff's thoughtful intimate readings of two of Schumann's most ambitious piano works miss some of the

heroism of the music, they are still marvellously persuasive, giving a clear illusion of live performances, spontaneously caught. Good recording.

Fantasia in C major, Op. 17.
> *** HMV ASD 450. Sviatoslav Richter (piano) – BEETHOVEN: *Sonata No. 17.****

A wonderfully poetical performance of a great masterpiece of the piano repertoire. Richter's phrasing, his magnificent control of dynamics (especially in those typically Schumannesque accompanimental arpeggios), his gift of seeing a large-scale work as a whole – all these contribute towards the impression of unmatchable strength and vision which make this record one of the finest he has yet made. The tonal balance of the piano is first-rate, and we really seem to be in the same room.

Fantasia in C major, Op. 17; Piano sonata No. 1 in F sharp minor, Op. 11.
> *** DGG 2530 379. Maurizio Pollini (piano).

Pollini's accounts of the *C major Fantasia* and the *Op. 11 Sonata* are among the most distinguished Schumann records in the catalogue. The *Fantasia* is as fine as Richter's, and the playing throughout has a command and authority on the one hand and deep poetic feeling on the other that instantly capture the listener spellbound. The recording is good but not outstanding.

Fantasiestücke, Op. 12; Piano sonata No. 4 in G minor, Op. 22.
> (B) ** Oiseau-Lyre OLS 175. Annie D'Arco (piano).

These are good performances which do justice to Schumann without ever rising to the heights commanded by such players as Richter or Pollini in this repertoire. The recording is acceptable, though the piano tone is not always free from metallic clangour. However, at the price it is well worth considering.

Fantasiestücke, Op. 111; Piano sonata No. 1 in F sharp minor, Op. 11.
> ** (*) Philips SAL 3663. Claudio Arrau (piano).

Schumann wrote this massive early sonata for his beloved Clara. This is a dedicated poetic interpretation, not always content to let the music speak for itself but subtly shaded in the way one recognizes with Arrau in Schumann. Not surprisingly it is in the charming, simple slow movement that Schumann is most at home and his lyrical genius blossoms most freely, but the outer movements still make one regret that he did not pursue sonata form more consistently in his later career. The three late *Fantasiestücke* make a fine coupling, with Arrau again at his finest. Good recording.

Humoreske in B flat major, Op. 20; Kreisleriana, Op. 16.
> * (*) Decca SXL 6642. Vladimir Ashkenazy (piano).

One of Ashkenazy's least successful records. Not that his playing is a source of reproach; indeed its eloquence can be taken for granted. Unfortunately, though, the recording is too clangorous to give real pleasure: it is very reverberant and lacking in focus, though the ear can adjust to some extent.

Humoreske in B flat major, Op. 20; Piano sonata No. 3 in F minor (Concerto without orchestra), Op. 14.
> (B) ** Turnabout TV 34533S. Jerome Rose (piano).

A young man's approach to Schumann can often be refreshing, as is readily shown in these attractively impulsive performances. They have not the poise and thoughtfulness of an Arrau, but they are not without imagination either, as the third movement of the sonata (a set of variations on a theme by Clara Wieck) shows. The bravura comes easily to Mr Rose's nimble fingers, and occasionally he is carried away, as in the finale of the *Sonata*, but this at least keeps all the music tingling with life (not something one could say of all Schumann performances). The recording is good if not distinguished.

Humoreske in B flat major, Op. 20; Waldscenen, Op. 82.
> *** DGG 2530 410. Wilhelm Kempff (piano).

Personal, individual performances from Kempff, guaranteed to charm the ear. If the sharper contrasts of the *Humoreske* are toned down in charm and geniality, the *Waldscenen* are glowingly relaxed and persuasive. Fine recording.

Kinderscenen (Scenes from Childhood), Op. 15; Piano sonata No. 2 in G minor, Op. 22.
> ** DGG 2530 348. Wilhelm Kempff (piano).

Neither of these is among Kempff's more compelling Schumann performances, although both are enjoyable. But Walter Klien in each case provides a more poetic account, and although his recording on Turnabout is less than ideal, this one for Kempff is not really distinguished either.

Kreisleriana, Op. 16; Romanze II, Op. 28; Piano sonata No. 2 in G minor, Op. 22.
> (B) (**) Turnabout TV 34317S. Walter Klien (piano).

Walter Klien's impulsive way with Schumann is rather effective in the *Sonata*, a work that can easily lose the listener's interest if the playing is in the

859

least unspontaneous. It is very lively indeed here, and the slow movement is particularly beautiful, finer than Kempff's. *Kreisleriana* is successful too, although Klien is a little inclined to rush his fences. The piano tone is bold and clear, not ideal but not bad at all. The snag to current pressings of this disc are three tiny passages of wow on side two, one towards the end of *Kreisleriana*, another towards the end of the *Sonata*, and then again in the *Romanze*, which is played with both feeling and taste.

Kriesleriana, Op. 16; Variations on a theme by Clara Wieck (Sonata No. 3 in F minor, Op. 14; 3rd movement: Andantino).
    *** CBS SBRG 72841. Vladimir Horowitz (piano).

Playing of such dazzling brilliance and authority that criticism is silenced. This is quite breathtaking in its poetry and mastery; the recording is unfortunately not first-class, but it is fully acceptable.

Piano sonatas Nos. 1 in F sharp minor, Op. 11; 2 in G minor, Op. 22 (also Presto passionato in G minor, Op. posth.); 3 in F minor (Concerto without orchestra), Op. 14; Scherzi in F minor and B flat major, Op. posth; 3 Sonatas for the young, Op. 118; Album for the young, Op. 68.
    * Telefunken SKA 25112 (1/4). Karl Engel (piano).

In a catalogue that can boast outstanding Schumann piano records from Richter and Pollini, this set has few attractions. Karl Engel's playing is not particularly distinguished or authoritative, and his insights are far from searching or profound. There is little that need detain the discriminating collector here.

Piano sonata No. 2 in G minor, Op. 22.
    * (*) DGG 2530 193. Martha Ar-

gerich (piano) – LISZT: *Piano sonata.***

Argerich's impetuosity of approach is less suitable in Schumann than in the Liszt coupling. Certainly here she keeps the music alive – something not all pianists are able to do in Schumann's piano repertoire – but the wide dynamic contrasts are sometimes inappropriate. There is no lack of impulse, but this degree of urgency (in the central section of the slow movement, for instance) seems out of style.

VOCAL AND CHORAL MUSIC

Dichterliebe (song cycle), *Op. 48.*
    *** Decca SET 270/1. Peter Pears (tenor), Benjamin Britten (piano) – SCHUBERT: *Winterreise.*⊛***

Schumann's greatest song cycle coupled with Schubert's greatest: the combination is irresistible. On this fill-up Pears is not in quite such perfect voice, the vibrato occasionally gritty and obtrusive, but the imaginativeness of the whole interpretation is so compelling that that is merely a minor detail. In *Dichterliebe*, with its long piano postludes to many of the songs, the role of the accompanist is specially important, and Britten brings to the piano part an intense creative understanding unrivalled on any other version. Recording excellent.

Dichterliebe (song cycle), *Op. 48; Liederkreis* (song cycle), *Op. 24.*
    *** DGG SLPM 130109. Dietrich Fischer-Dieskau (baritone), Joerg Demus (piano).
    *** DGG 2530 353. Peter Schreier (tenor), Norman Shetler (piano).

A pity that DGG fail – as they did with Fischer-Dieskau's earlier (mono) version of *Dichterliebe* – to get the whole cycle on a single side. It is perhaps the most concentrated of all song cycles, and any interruption is distracting. Otherwise this performance is every bit as intense and expressive as before, with an even more tragic account of *Ich grolle nicht*. The voice is if anything in even better condition. Demus is most sympathetic, though, in the manner of the solo artist, his rubato is more marked than one would normally expect of an accompanist. The *Liederkreis* of 1840 makes an excellent coupling, for as in *Dichterliebe* the poems are by Heine. Again Fischer-Dieskau conveys vividly the range of emotion from the anguish of the spurned lover to the delight of the traveller.

The contrasts of emotion behind the sequence of songs in *Dichterliebe* are strongly brought out by Schreier, underlying tensions made painful. Schreier similarly treats the Heine *Liederkreis* as a unified whole by giving it emotional shape. This is tenor Lieder-singing that reflects the baritone art and technique of Fischer-Dieskau. Fine recording.

Dichterliebe (song cycle), *Op. 48; Liederkreis* (song cycle), *Op. 39*.
(B) *** Classics for Pleasure CFP 40099. Ian Partridge (tenor), Jennifer Partridge (piano).

Ian Partridge, as in his earlier CFP record of Schubert's *Schöne Müllerin*, shows himself a deeply sensitive Lieder singer, blessed with a radiantly beautiful light voice. Both in *Dichterliebe* and in the Eichendorff *Liederkreis* Partridge's thoughtfulness illuminates every line, helped by superbly matched accompaniment from his sister. Good recording.

Frauenliebe und Leben (song cycle), *Op. 42*.
(B) *** Saga 5277, Janet Baker (contralto), Martin Isepp (piano) (with *Recital* ** (*)).

(M) ** Oiseau-Lyre SOL 293. Helen Watts (contralto), Geoffrey Parsons (piano) – WOLF: *Lieder*.**

As in the Wolf songs on the reverse, Helen Watts sings *Frauenliebe und Leben* most beautifully. but she puts up a curious emotional barrier that does not suit Schumann's concept of the devoted wife. The element of tenderness is too often missing, and the range of tone-colour has nothing like the ravishing beauty that so marks out Janet Baker's singing of the cycle on Saga. Few Lieder records – let alone one by an English singer – are more satisfying than this. Janet Baker's range of expression in the Schumann cycle runs the whole gamut from a joyful golden tone-colour in the exhilaration of *Ich kann's nicht fassen* through an ecstatic half-tone in *Süsser Freund* (the fulfilment of the line *Du geliebter Mann* wonderfully conveyed) to the dead, vibratoless tone of agony at the bereavement in the final song. The Saga recording is not perfect. The balance favours the piano, and in the stereo version the piano and voice tend to be separated to left and right, although newer pressings are better in this respect. (This is part of a Lieder recital discussed in our *Treasury* volume.)

Frauenliebe und Leben (song cycle), *Op. 42; Liederkreis* (song cycle), *Op. 24*.
*** HMV ASD 3037. Elisabeth Schwarzkopf (soprano), Geoffrey Parsons (piano).

The art of Schwarzkopf remains irresistible, even here where, with the voice no longer young, she has to spin the notes out more cunningly than before. The range of mood in *Frauenliebe* has rarely been more subtly expressed – no mere conventional emotions, however conventional the words – and the Heine *Liederkreis* brings even warmer and more searching interpretations, not least in the tantalizing *Lorelei* song. Anyone who

861

has relished Schwarzkopf's live Lieder recitals in her later career should hear this re-creation on record. Fine recording.

Liederkreis (song cycle), *Op. 24;* *Liederkreis* (song cycle), *Op. 39.*
** Argo ZRG 718. Robert Tear (tenor), Philip Ledger (piano).

A useful coupling of Schumann's two contrasted cycles labelled *Liederkreis.* Tear and Ledger are imaginative interpreters, though Tear's voice is at times harshly caught by the microphone in what sounds like a very faithful recording.

Liederkreis (song cycle), *Op. 39.*
(M) ** Oiseau-Lyre SOL 327. Anna Reynolds (mezzo-soprano), Geoffrey Parsons (piano) – MAHLER: *Lieder und Gesänge aus der Jugendzeit.***

A restrained account of Schumann's Op. 39 *Liederkreis,* tastefully effective like the Mahler on the reverse. Anna Reynolds is a singer who ought to be heard more often on record. Good recording of the voice.

Scenes from Goethe's Faust: Overture; Scene in the garden; Scene in the cathedral; Ariel sunrise; Death of Faust; Transfiguration of Faust.
⊛ *** Decca SET 567/8. Elisabeth Harwood (soprano), Peter Pears (tenor), John Shirley-Quirk, Dietrich Fischer-Dieskau (baritones), Aldeburgh Festival Singers, Wandsworth School Choir, English Chamber Orchestra, Benjamin Britten.

Britten made this superb recording of a major Schumann work long neglected soon after a live performance at the Aldeburgh Festival. Though the reasons for neglect remain apparent – this episodic sequence of scenes is neither opera nor cantata – the power and imagination of much of the music, not least the delightful garden scene and the energetic setting of the final scene, are immensely satisfying. Britten inspires his orchestra and his fine cast of singers to vivid performances, which are here superlatively recorded against the warm Maltings acoustic.

Schürmann, Gerard
(born 1928)

Chuench'i (song cycle from the Chinese: *New corn; Plucking the rushes; Shang ya!; Flowers and moonlight on the Spring river; Look at that little bay of the Chi'i; Self-abandonment; At the end of spring).*
(B) *** Pye GSGC 14105. Marni Nixon (soprano), John McCabe (piano) – IVES and GOEHR: *Songs.****

Gerard Schürmann is a Dutchman who has spent most of his life in England. His song cycle *Chuench'i* tells of the feelings of a woman at different stages of her life, symbolized by her memories of spring, from childhood to maturity. The work is bound together by the opening and closing songs about the nature of spring itself, and its coming and departing. The piano introduction is Debussian and the work as a whole is immediately approachable, but the middle four songs, from the impulsive *Shang ya!* (adolescence) through to *Self-abandonment* (maturity) – which is the climax of the cycle – are really outstanding. *Flowers and moonlight* is strikingly atmospheric, and the brilliant toccata-like *Look at that little bay of the Chi'i* is memorable.

The work was commissioned by Marni Nixon, who obviously completely identifies herself with the music, negotiating the leaps not only with skill but with obvious ease, and in such a way as to emphasize the basic lyricism of the idiom. She makes the cycle a highly compelling experience, and she is helped by John McCabe's sensitive accompaniment and a suitably spacious acoustic.

Schütz, Heinrich
(1585–1672)

Motets: *Ach Herr, straf mich nicht* (Psalm 6); *Cantate Domino* (Psalm 96); *Deutsches Magnificat; Herr unser Herrscher* (Psalm 8); *Ich freu mich des* (Psalm 122); *Unser Herr Jesus; Wie lieblich* (Psalm 84).

*** Argo ZRG 666. Heinrich Schütz Choir, Symphoniae Sacrae Ensemble and continuo, Roger Norrington.

This is a most valuable issue and one of the most successful these artists have given us. The choral singing is impressively firm, and the recording does justice to the antiphonal effects. The *Deutsches Magnificat* is given with admirable authority and this splendid example of Schütz's last years (he was eighty-five when he wrote it) is one of the best things on the disc. The instrumental playing is fully worthy of the singing, and given the richly sonorous recording Argo provide there need be no qualification in recommending this to all who have discovered this remarkable composer. The *Cantate Domino*, by the way, may well be by Giovanni Gabrieli, with whom Schütz studied in Venice in the early years of the seventeenth century.

Cantiones sacrae (1625).
*** Telefunken SAWT 9468/70. Dresden Kreuzchor, Rudolf

Mauersberger; Hans Otto (Schleiflade organ from the Kunsthandwerk Museum, Dresden).

A complete recording of Schütz's *Cantiones sacrae* is no mean undertaking, and this well-packaged set of three discs (with notes, Latin texts, and translations into German) leaves no page unturned. Local atmosphere is secured by using the Dresden Kreuzchor throughout, and their clear enunciation and purity of tone make most of the performances a vital and enjoyable experience. The organ support is beautifully balanced, yet contributes much to the tonal picture. The finely woven threads of Schütz's polyphony emerge with exceptional clarity thanks to a spacious stereo picture, which allows the choir to appear in a natural, spread-out position with boys at the outside and men in the centre. Warmly recommended for all Schütz lovers.

Christmas oratorio (Historia der Geburt Jesu Christe).
** (*) Argo ZRG 671. Ian Partridge (tenor), soloists, Heinrich Schütz Choir, Instrumental Ensemble, Philip Jones Brass Ensemble, Roger Norrington.
(B) ** Turnabout TV 34088S. Adele Stolte (soprano), Hans Mielsch (tenor), August Messthaler (bass), Swabian Choir and Symphony Orchestra, Hans Grischkat.

The Argo version is more richly and vividly recorded than the alternative set on Turnabout though whether readers will think it worth twice as much is another matter. There is some extremely fine singing from Ian Partridge as the Evangelist, and the Heinrich Schütz Choir phrase with great feeling and subtlety. Indeed some may feel that their singing is a little too self-consciously beautiful for music that is so pure in style. The instrumental accompaniment on modern instruments may also strike some listeners as too much of a good thing: the brass has more than a suspicion of heaviness at times. However, for all that, this version offers much to admire and the recording has great detail and sonority.

Grischkat has good if not outstanding soloists who work well together, and the choral singing is good. The recording is not brilliant, but it is not lacking in atmosphere, and there is a simple eloquence to this account which is appealing, in spite of its comparative lack of sophistication.

Easter oratorio: The Resurrection of our Lord Jesus Christ.

> *** Argo ZRG 639. Peter Pears, Robert Tear (tenors), John Shirley-Quirk (baritone), Heinrich Schütz Choir, Elizabethan Consort, London Cornett and Sackbut Ensemble, Roger Norrington.

> (B) ** Turnabout TV 34231S. Herrad Wehrung, Edith Schodt (sopranos), Margarete Witte-Waldbauer (mezzo-soprano), Hans Mielsch, Reinhold Bartel (tenors), Erich Wenk, Ulrich Schaible (basses), Swabian Chorus and Instrumental Ensemble, Hans Grischkat.

Schütz's masterly setting of the Resurrection story will not appeal to all tastes. It will seem too uneventful and austere for some, but its rewards are rich. Part of its musical success depends on the artistry of the Evangelist, sung here by Peter Pears, who has impressive authority and insight and is given admirable support by the soloists and instrumentalists. The recording is rather more sonorous and detailed than that of the Turnabout disc (though twice as expensive), and this is to be preferred on artistic grounds too.

The Turnabout performance matches

and even improves on the companion Turnabout disc of the *Christmas oratorio*. The solo singing is of good quality; Hans Mielsch stands out as the Evangelist – an eloquent performance. The choral singing too is of an excellent standard, and the internal balance is convincing. The use of stereo within the choral grouping is skilfully managed, and with the instrumental accompaniment nicely judged (the continuo is good) this performance – if without the last degree of refinement – is distinctly rewarding.

Musikalische Exequien.

> (M) *** Philips Universo 6580 039. Dresden Kreuzchor, Rudolf Mauersberger.

Schütz's *Mass for the dead* is one of his most austere and serious masterpieces. All too often it is performed with elaborate scoring and rich sonority. Here no attempt is made to dilute its character, and the performance cannot be too strongly praised for its penetration and depth. The recording too is eminently truthful both in timbre and in balance.

Psalm 150.

> *** HMV Quadraphonic Q4–CSD 3755; Stereo CSD 3755. King's College Choir, Cambridge, Cambridge University Musical Society, Bach Choir, Wilbraham Brass Soloists, David Willcocks – GABRIELI: *Collection*; SCHEIDT: *In dulci jubilo etc.****

Schütz's setting of Psalm 150 is for double choirs and soloists, each used in juxtaposition against the others, with built-in antiphony an essential part of the composer's conception. The majesty of Schütz's inspiration comes over vividly here, the closing *Alleluja* having remarkable weight and richness. The performance sounds well in stereo but even more resplendent with the quadraphonic sound echoing round the listener's head in the most realistic manner. The choral focus is not as clean as on the Argo King's records, but in all other respects this is superb.

St Matthew Passion.

*** Argo ZRG 689. Peter Pears (tenor), John Shirley-Quirk (baritone), Benjamin Luxon (bass), Heinrich Schütz Choir, Roger Norrington.

Schütz's setting of the St Matthew Passion is an austere one. The story is told for the most part in a series of unaccompanied recitatives, eloquent but restrained in style. The drama is suddenly heightened at the choral entries, but these are comparatively few, and the work relies on the artistry of the soloists to project itself on the listener. The solo singing here is of a high order and the choral contribution fine enough to make one wish there was more of it. The closing chorus, Glory be to Thee, is more familiar than the rest of the work for it is sometimes extracted to be sung on its own. The recording is excellent, and it is understandable that the original language is used. Even so, one feels the work would communicate more readily when sung in English.

Scriabin, Alexander (1872–1915)

(i) Piano concerto in F sharp minor, Op. 20; (ii) Poème de l'extase, Op. 54; (iii) Rêverie, Op. 24; (ii; iv) Symphony No. 1 in E major, Op. 26; (ii) Symphony No. 2 in C minor, Op. 29; (ii) Symphony No. 3 in C minor (Divine poem), Op. 43.

(M) *** HMV SLS 835 (4 discs). (i) Stanislav Neuhaus (piano), USSR Symphony Orchestra, Vic-

tor Dubrovsky; (ii) USSR Symphony Orchestra, Yevgeny Svetlanov; (iii) Moscow Radio Orchestra, Gennady Rozhdestvensky; (iv) soloists, chorus.

The First Symphony has recently been deleted and so has the Divine poem. The Second Symphony on the other hand has never been available separately and its only rival, Semkow conducting the LPO on CBS, has also succumbed to the deletions axe. So this moderately-priced album is now the only means of representing Scriabin's early orchestral works in one's collection. HMV Melodiya have not chosen to include Prometheus or the Fifth Symphony, but provide the early Piano concerto as a fill-up. The merits of these performances are well known, and the recordings have warmth and opulence to commend them, although climaxes in Poème de l'extase and the Divine poem do not always reproduce smoothly. However, the set is indispensable for lovers of this composer.

Piano concerto in F sharp minor, Op. 20; Prometheus – The poem of fire, Op. 60.

*** Decca SXL 6527. Vladimir Ashkenazy (piano), London Philharmonic Orchestra, Lorin Maazel.

This is an admirable introduction to Scriabin's art and a very distinguished record in every respect. Ashkenazy plays the Piano concerto with great feeling and authority, and though it would be an oversimplification to suggest that it completely outclasses Neuhaus's interpretation on HMV Melodiya, the greater clarity and luminosity of the Decca recording ensure this pride of place in the catalogue. Moreover Maazel accompanies most sympathetically throughout. Prometheus too is given a thoroughly poetic and committed reading by Maazel and the LPO, Ashkenazy coping with the virtuoso obbligato part with predictable distinction. Powerfully atmospheric and curiously hypnotic, the score reeks of Madame Blavatsky and Scriabin's wild mysticism, while abounding in the fanciful lines of *art nouveau*. Given such outstanding recording and, one might add, performance, this makes a splendid starting point for any Scriabin collection. It was issued on 6 January, 1972, the centenary of the composer's birth.

Poème de l'extase (Poem of ecstasy), Op. 54.
   *** Decca SXL 6325. Los Angeles Philharmonic Orchestra, Zubin Mehta – SCHOENBERG: *Verklaerte Nacht.****
   *** DGG 2530 137. Boston Symphony Orchestra, Claudio Abbado – TCHAIKOVSKY: *Romeo and Juliet.* (*)

The *Poème de l'extase* is one of Scriabin's most successful scores, and its reappearance in a good stereo recording is long overdue. The engineers do ample justice to the complexity and opulence of this lavish, self-intoxicated and orgasmic score with its overtones of *art nouveau* and theosophy! Its opening comes close to suggesting perfume, and its originality is beyond all question. The sound is superbly analytical without being in any way clinical, and the tone of the strings is extremely rich. Mehta and the Los Angeles Orchestra give an admirable account of the work and it is difficult to imagine it being surpassed for a very long time.

A superbly controlled performance, too, from Abbado, the conductor's refinement acting as a brake on the blatancy of the score without destroying its impulse. The recording is splendidly atmospheric in the quiet opening pages, but has a touch of shrillness in the loudest moments. In all other respects it is first-rate. Here also the orchestra's principal trumpet uses a very striking vibrato in

his dominating solos, which some may not care for, but this certainly fits the character of the music. It is a pity that the coupling is not more successful.

Poème de l'extase (Poem of ecstasy), Op. 54; (i) *Prometheus – The poem of Fire, Op. 60.*
   ** RCA SB 6854. Philadelphia Orchestra, Eugene Ormandy, (i) Mendelssohn Club Choir, Vladimir Sokoloff (piano).

This was the coupling pioneered by Mitropoulos and the New York Orchestra in the early days of LP, though CBS never issued that disc here. Ormandy shapes everything with care and has a genuine feel for this lush, sensuous music. Accomplished though the performance of *Prometheus* is, it must yield pride of place to Maazel's more poetic and imaginative account (see above), which is helped by the presence of Ashkenazy and an outstanding Decca recording. Here the pianist, Vladimir Sokoloff, appears to be in a different acoustic and the piano quality is not good. Nor do the RCA engineers rest content with a concert-hall balance and their resultant sound picture is as artificial as it is unconvincing. Ormandy does the *Poème de l'extase* beautifully, but again Mehta or Abbado are better served by the engineers. This is a record that contains much to admire and it is a pity that it falls short of the ideal on quality grounds.

(i) *Piano concerto in F sharp minor, Op. 20.* (Piano) *Nocturne, Op. 9/2; Poème satanique, Op. 36; Prelude, Op. 9/1; Piano sonata No. 5 in F sharp major, Op. 53; Waltz, Op. 38.*
   (M) * (*) VOX STGBY 655. Michael Ponti (piano), (i) with Hamburg Symphony Orchestra, Hans Drewanz.

Although this offers no competition to Ashkenazy's beautifully recorded account (see above), it is serviceable, and the *Sonata* and piano pieces are worth hearing. Ponti is a gifted player but the quality of the orchestral sound and the relatively undistinguished orchestral playing count against the success of this issue.

PIANO MUSIC

Études, Op. 42/1–8; Fantasy in B minor, Op. 28; Poèmes, Op. 32/1 and 2; Preludes, Op. 11/1–24.
(M) ** HMV HQS 1296. John Ogdon (piano).

John Ogdon has put us in his debt with his pioneering work for Scriabin, Busoni, Stevenson and a host of other composers. There is no alternative recording of the Op. 11 *Preludes* at the moment, so that this disc is both timely and welcome. It is well recorded and though there are times when one feels that Ogdon is not playing from within and that his interpretations are slightly wanting in authority, he is nonetheless an artist who rarely fails to illuminate what he plays.

Études Nos. 2 in F major; 8 in A flat major; 10 in D flat major; 11 in B flat minor, Op. 8/2, 8, 10 and 11; 15 in F sharp minor; 16 in F sharp major; 17 in C sharp minor, Op. 42/3, 4 and 5; Feuillet d'album, Op. 45/1; 2 Poèmes, Op. 69; Piano sonata No. 10 in C major, Op. 70; Vers la flamme, Op. 72.
*** CBS SBRG 73072. Vladimir Horowitz (piano).

Horowitz has a special affinity with Scriabin, so we are told, and there is no lack of evidence here to substantiate this claim. These are performances of total and complete mastery, and it is difficult to imagine them being improved upon

even by the composer himself. It would, however, be easy to improve on the recording, which (characteristically from this source) is shallow and starved of timbre. Too much should not be made of this, for the playing is electrifying and has great authority, but it is one of the great misfortunes of the gramophone that this great artist has never found a recording team that could do real justice to his instrument.

Piano sonatas Nos. 1 in F minor, Op. 6; 2 (Sonata-fantasy) in G sharp minor, Op. 19; 4 in F sharp major, Op. 30; 5 in F sharp major, Op. 53.
(B) ** Turnabout TV 37029S. Michael Ponti (piano).
Piano sonatas Nos. 3 in F sharp minor, Op. 23; 6 in G major, Op. 62; 7 in F sharp major (White Mass), Op. 64; Sonata-fantasy in G sharp minor, Op. posth.
(B) ** Turnabout TV 37030S. Michael Ponti (piano).
Piano sonatas Nos. 8 in A major, Op. 66; 9 in F major (Black Mass), Op. 68; 10 in C major, Op. 70; Piano sonata in E flat minor, Op. posth.
(B) ** Turnabout TV 37031S. Michael Ponti (piano).

Ponti's three discs on Turnabout present all the ten sonatas, plus the two additional pieces that Roberto Szidon also included on his now deleted set. Ponti's playing is not wanting in feeling but it does not compare with Szidon, let alone Horowitz, for it lacks the last ounce of polish. The recordings too are a little shallow. Ogdon's set was the best recorded, but that too has now suffered the deletions axe, so that Ponti's are the only performances in the current catalogue.

Searle, Humphrey
(born 1915)

(i) *Symphony No. 1, Op. 23;* (ii) *Symphony No. 2, Op. 33.*
*** Lyrita SRCS 72. London Philharmonic Orchestra, (i) Sir Adrian Boult, (ii) Josef Krips.

Josef Krips in one of his last recording sessions conducted a superbly expressive performance of Searle's *Second Symphony.* Like its predecessor it follows the composer's characteristic brand of twelve-note serialism, but even more than the earlier work it shows Searle following the central English tradition. If Walton had ever written a serial symphony, it might sound very like this. The Boult performance of No. 1, also sponsored by the British Council, dates from the early 1960s, but still sounds excellent – a worthy match for the fine new recording of No. 2.

Sessions, Roger
(born 1896)

Rhapsody for orchestra; Symphony No. 8.
*** Argo ZRG 702. New Philharmonia Orchestra, Frederick Prausnitz – MUSGRAVE: *Night music;* RIEGGER: *Dichotomy.****

Roger Sessions is on any count one of the toughest and most impressive musical arguers among American composers. His *Eighth Symphony,* first heard in 1968, is a forceful work in two movements, the first *Adagio e mesto,* the second *Allegro con fuoco,* a 'study in flexibility', as it has been called. The *Rhapsody* of 1970, more readily approachable, makes a good companion work on this Gulbenkian-sponsored record, though more Sessions music would have been welcome for coupling. First-rate recording.

Séverac, Déodat de
(1873–1921)

Pippermint-Get (Valse brillante de concert); Sous les lauriers roses (Under the Oleanders).
(M) ** (*) Vox STGBY 671. Grant Johannesen (piano) – DUKAS: *Variations;* ROUSSEL: *3 Pieces.* ** (*)

The relatively lighthearted contributions of Déodat de Séverac, a talented but short-lived contemporary of Dukas and Roussel, prove totally enchanting in Johannesen's excellent French recital. The brilliant waltz, *Pippermint-Get,* is as delightful as its title.

Shankar, Ravi
(born 1920)

Sitar concerto.
** (*) HMV ASD 2752. Ravi Shankar (sitar), London Symphony Orchestra, André Previn.

This record is an oddity. It would be easy to dismiss this concerto, since fairly evidently it is neither good Western music nor good Indian music. The idiom is sweet, arguably too sweet and unproblematic, but at least this is an attractive and painless conducted tour over the geographical layout of the Raga. It also prompts some brilliant music-making from Previn and the LSO, not to mention the composer himself, who launches into solos which he makes sound spontaneous in the authentic manner, however prepared they may actually be. In fact his playing has stiffened up compared with the original concert performance in January 1971. Provided one is not worried at having a forty-minute work with comparatively little meat in the way of good material, this provides a charming experience – ideal atmospheric background music. The recording is superb.

(i; ii) *Prabhati* (based on the raga *Gunkali*); (iii) Raga; *Puriya Klayan*; (i; iii) *Swarq-Kakali* (based on the raga *Tilang*).
   ** HMV ASD 2294. (i) Yehudi Menuhin (violin); (ii) Alla Rakha (tabla); (iii) Ravi Shankar (sitar) – ENESCO: *Violin sonata.***

This record marrying the very different arts of Asia and Eastern Europe savours just a little too much of the gimmick to arouse enthusiasm in all quarters, and it is difficult to imagine the same listener responding warmly to both sides. But undoubtedly there will be some, and admirers of Ravi Shankar and Menuhin will wish to hear them together; the violin after all has been absorbed into Indian music for many decades. It is interesting to note that this issue, titled *East meets West*, caught the public fancy; it has been a best-seller in Britain, and in America actually made the top-twenty LP chart – something an Enesco violin sonata was highly unlikely to manage on its own!

Shchedrin, Rodion
(born 1932)

Anna Karenina (ballet): complete recording.
   *** HMV SLS 887 (2 discs). Bolshoi Theatre Orchestra, Yuri Simonov.

Shchedrin's score is unfailingly imaginative, atmospheric and rewarding, though it is musically insubstantial. None of it lingers obstinately in the memory; no doubt the work makes a greater impact in the theatre than it does when divorced from the action. However, Shchedrin's marvellously inventive scoring and imaginative textures are a source of pleasure, and both playing and recording (particularly the latter) are expert. Indeed the recording is impressively wide in range and detail and is almost in the demonstration class. Those who have (understandably) enjoyed Shchedrin's rearrangement and rescoring of Bizet's music for the *Carmen ballet* (see under Bizet) will have a field-day here.

Concerto for orchestra (Merry ditties).
   (M) ** HMV SLS 844 (6 discs). Moscow Philharmonic Orchestra, Kyril Kondrashin – PROKOFIEV: *Symphonies etc.* ** (*)

The title *Merry ditties* is enough to put anyone off, but as long as you do not take Shchedrin seriously, his music is attractively companionable. Good recording.

Symphony No. 1 in E flat minor.
   *** HMV ASD 2927. Moscow Philharmonic Orchestra, Nikolai Anosov – MIASKOVSKY: *Symphony No. 23.***

Shchedrin is nothing if not a superb orchestrator, and this early symphony, written when he was in his mid-twenties, shows him to be an astonishingly assured craftsman. The work has the genuine feel of a symphony about it, as well as a remarkably refined mastery of colour. There are moments of bombast, it is true, and some may feel that the work takes itself a little too seriously given the hollowness of some of its gestures; but even though its facility at times runs away with it, the work is resourceful, intelligent and immensely approachable. Not a great work, then, but thoroughly enjoyable at its own (highly accomplished) level. A brilliant performance and good recording.

Sherlaw Johnson, Robert
(born 1932)

7 Short piano pieces; Piano sonata No. 1.

(***) Argo ZRG 694. The composer (piano) – MESSIAEN: *Cantéyodjayâ etc.*** (*)

The *Sonata* was written in 1963, and the *Seven Pieces*, commissioned by the BBC, were first performed in 1969. This music is of the thorniest kind, and while repeated hearings may provide a greater degree of enlightenment, it is difficult to take seriously some of the twangs, plonks and rumbles that appear towards the end of the set of *Pieces*.

Shostakovich, Dmitri
(1906-75)

The Age of Gold (ballet)*: suite, Op. 22.*

(B) *** Decca Eclipse ECS 580. London Symphony Orchestra, Jean Martinon – *Symphony No. 1.***

This Eclipse reissue offers not only real stereo, but very good stereo. The original RCA pressings seemed somewhat dry and cramped, but now the Decca engineers have opened out the sound very successfully, and the *Age of Gold* suite is demonstration-worthy. The orchestral playing is first-class and brings out all the wit and colour in the music.

Piano concertos Nos. (i) *1* (for piano, trumpet and strings), *Op. 35*; (ii) *2, Op. 101.*

*** CBS 73400. (i) André Previn (piano), William Vacchiano (trumpet); (ii) Leonard Bernstein (piano); both with New York Philharmonic Orchestra, Leonard Bernstein.

Piano concertos Nos. (i) *1, Op. 35; 2, Op. 101; 3 Fantastic dances.*

*** HMV ASD 3081. Cristina Ortiz (piano), Bournemouth Symphony Orchestra, Paavo Berglund, (i) with Rodney Senior (trumpet).

CBS and HMV simultaneously appreciated the need for a good coupling of the two Shostakovich *Piano concertos*. CBS have shrewdly recoupled Bernstein's radiant account of No. 2 with Previn's equally striking reading of No. 1. Though these New York performances bring somewhat dated recording, both pianists have a way of turning a phrase to catch the imagination, and a fine balance is struck between Shostakovich's warmth and his rhythmic alertness.

Cristina Ortiz gives fresh and attractive performances of both concertos, a degree undercharacterized, but beautifully recorded and with a fine accompaniment from the Bournemouth orchestra. This music-making is not so individual as that on the CBS disc, but many will find more than enough compensation in the superb EMI sound, and this disc offers a small bonus in the *3 Fantastic dances*.

Piano concerto No. 1 (for piano, trumpet and strings), *Op. 35.*

*** Argo ZRG 674. John Ogdon (piano), Academy of St Martin-in-the-Fields, Neville Marriner – STRAVINSKY: *Capriccio.****

As in the Stravinsky *Capriccio* Ogdon gives a clean, stylish performance of the *First Concerto*, which compasses both the humour and the hints of romanticism. He keeps a little more detached than his accompanists in the tender slow movement, and the trumpet-playing of John Wilbraham is masterly. In addition the recording quality is most vivid. The comparatively backward balance of the strings gives the work a chamber quality to match that of the work on the reverse, an unexpected but attractive coupling.

Piano concerto No. 2, Op. 101.
  *** CBS 72170. Leonard Bernstein (piano), New York Philharmonic Orchestra – RAVEL: *Piano concerto in G major.****
  *** HMV ASD 2709. John Ogdon (piano), Royal Philharmonic Orchestra, Lawrence Foster – OGDON: *Piano concerto No. 1.** (*)

This is a delightful concerto in every way, an unpretentious work which has all the qualities to become widely popular. Shostakovich had a wonderful deadpan way of making the most outrageously simple idea into vitally interesting music. Everything here is so memorable – the bright-eyed first subject, the sinuous second subject, the memorable tune of the slow movement, Rachmaninov distilled down to a single line of piano melody, and the captivating 7/8 rhythms of the finale. Bernstein's performance is first-rate in every way, finer even than the composer's own recording (in the Russian catalogue). Where Shostakovich himself, in apparent impatience, rushes the speeds, Bernstein sounds more sympathetic and just as alive. Few piano-concerto records of any period outshine this in attractiveness (one is thinking of the Ravel as well); and the recording, although an early one, still sounds full-blooded and reasonably atmospheric.

Ogdon too gives a splendidly idiomatic account of this concerto, written originally for the composer's son Maxim. The playing is full of character and humour. Bernstein's version in which he both plays and conducts has no less dash, but

the HMV version is the more recent recording and the sound is richer and the balance more natural. However, it must be admitted that Ogdon's coupling is no match for Ravel's illustrious concerto.

Violin concerto No. 1 in A minor, Op. 99.
  ** (*) HMV ASD 2936. David Oistrakh (violin), New Philharmonia Orchestra, Maxim Shostakovich.

Oistrakh made three records of this concerto, which was written for him. The first, with Mitropoulos, had the most powerful atmosphere, and this new account does not dim memories of it. This is not so keenly characterized or as deeply experienced (in the mid-1950s when the work was fresh), but having said that, it is only fair to add that it is a fine performance for all that. It also benefits from well-balanced and finely detailed EMI recording. Maxim Shostakovich does not display so firm a grip on proceedings as did Mitropoulos or Mravinsky, but the New Philharmonia play with no want of commitment. This version, it goes without saying, is still highly recommendable.

(i) *Violin concerto No. 2 in C sharp minor, Op. 129; Symphony No. 6 in B minor, Op. 54.*
  ** (*) HMV ASD 2447. Moscow Philharmonic Orchestra, Kyril Kondrashin, (i) with David Oistrakh (violin).

Oistrakh's performance of the *Second Violin concerto* has characteristic assurance, and the coupling is a generous one. The performance of the *Sixth Symphony* is less compelling, however, as Kondrashin misses the stark, visionary quality of the slow, intense first movement. But this is the only available version of the *Concerto*, which is splendidly played.

Violoncello concerto No. 1 in E flat major, Op. 107.

   *** HMV ASD 2924. Paul Tortelier (cello), Bournemouth Symphony Orchestra, Paavo Berglund – WALTON: *Cello concerto.****

   (M) ** Supraphon 110 0604. Milos Sádlo (cello), Czech Philharmonic Orchestra, Karel Ančerl – HONEGGER: *Cello concerto.***

(i) *Violoncello concerto No. 1 in E flat major, Op. 107; Symphony No. 1 in F minor, Op. 10.*

   *** CBS 72081. Philadelphia Orchestra, Eugene Ormandy, (i) with Mstislav Rostropovich (cello).

Tortelier's reading of the first of Shostakovich's two cello concertos is both tough and passionate. In sheer precision of bravura passages it does not always quite match the example of the dedicatee and first performer, Rostropovich, but in the urgency and attack of his playing Tortelier even outshines the Russian master, who made his recording at the time of the first American performance, before his interpretation really matured. Berglund and the Bournemouth Orchestra provide colourful and committed accompaniment, and the recording is rich and vivid.

Within a few months of the first performance in Russia and within days of the first Western performance, Shostakovich himself attended the recording session in Philadelphia and gave his approval to the performance here recorded by Rostropovich and Ormandy. Rostropovich gives a uniquely authoritative reading, Ormandy and the Philadelphia Orchestra accompanying superbly with a precision and warmth rare with new scores. The recording is clear and spacious but the balance is far from natural. The soloist is far too prominent, and incongruously, so is the glockenspiel at the end of the first movement. The coupling is a stunning performance of the

First Symphony with Ormandy and his orchestra in glowing form.

To have so strong a performance as the Supraphon is welcome on bargain label. Sádlo is a fine artist for whom the technical difficulties of the solo part hold no terrors. One might almost feel that he copes with them too easily, but in every way this is a satisfying performance, well recorded and interestingly coupled.

Symphony No. 1 in F major, Op. 10.

   (B) ** Decca Eclipse ECS 580. London Symphony Orchestra, Jean Martinon – *Age of Gold.****

Symphony No. 1 in F minor, Op. 10; Festival overture, Op. 96.

   (M) ** Supraphon SUAST 50576. Czech Philharmonic Orchestra, Karel Ančerl.

Martinon's performance is quite a good one. The recording is dry, and its slight touch of astringency adds a certain point to the account of the first movement and the scherzo. The finale is the least successful part of the performance, and here there is a touch of harshness in the recording too. But with a good coupling this is more than acceptable in the bargain range. Ančerl's account is more vivid and is better engineered too – this is one of Supraphon's brighter recordings. The *Festival overture*, written to celebrate an anniversary of the Russian Revolution, is an attractively boisterous piece and makes a good filler. This is a fair recommendation in the middle price-range. But Ormandy's performance (see above under *Cello concerto No. 1*) is far superior to either of these discs.

Symphonies Nos. 1 in F minor, Op. 10; 3 in E flat major (May Day), Op. 20.

   ** HMV ASD 3045. Moscow Philharmonic Orchestra, Kyril Kondrashin.

Kondrashin's account of No. 1 has expert playing and good recording to commend it. The poetry of the slow movement, however, seems to elude him and matters are not helped by somewhat insensitive oboe-playing in the opening theme and some less than perfect intonation. (Weller and the Suisse Romande have to be ruled out of court for much the same reason.) This is no challenge to Ormandy (see above), and its main claim on the attention of readers is the *Third Symphony*, which is not otherwise available. Written in 1927, it still remains something of a rarity. It is not difficult to see why, for it is probably the least substantial of the fifteen and is marred by banal ideas and empty rhetorical gestures. The recording is excellent.

Symphonies Nos. 1 in F minor, Op. 10; 9 in E flat major, Op. 70.
    ** Decca sxl 6563. Suisse Romande Orchestra, Walter Weller.
    * (*) CBS 73050. New York Philharmonic Orchestra, Leonard Bernstein.

Walter Weller and the Suisse Romande are given the benefit of exceptionally fine recording. The playing is good without being distinguished, but it is let down by poor oboe intonation in the slow movement of No. 1. It is not easy to summon up much enthusiasm for this coupling, although it is preferable to Bernstein's disc. Bernstein's readings lack the delicacy of touch essential in works which depend to a great degree on musical wit. The recording similarly is coarse.

Symphony No. 2 (October), Op. 14.
    *** HMV asd 3060. RSFSR Academic Russian Choir, Moscow Philharmonic Orchestra, Kyril Kondrashin – PROKOFIEV: *Scythian suite; Seven, they are seven.****
    (M) ** (*) Supraphon suast 50958.

Slovák Chorus, Slovák Philharmonic Orchestra, Ladislav Slovák – *Execution of Stepan Razin.*** (*)

Shostakovich's *Second Symphony* may not have quite the same precocious brilliance as his *First*, but it is a remarkable piece to have been written by a twenty-one-year-old. Like the *Third Symphony* it is a one-movement work with a choral conclusion showing a political purpose. The Russian performance has splendid fire and strength to overcome any of the work's structural weaknesses. The recording too is extremely vivid. With a generous coupling, this is certainly a recommendable issue.

The Slovák view of the work is a lively one and does not suffer from comparison with the Russian performance. The Supraphon recording is vivid and the coupling equally recommendable at medium price, even if neither is of the highest distinction.

Symphony No. 5 in D minor, Op. 47.
    *** HMV asd 2668. USSR Symphony Orchestra, Maxim Shostakovich.
    *** RCA sb 6651. London Symphony Orchestra, André Previn.
    (M) ** (*) Everest sdbr 3010. New York Stadium Orchestra, Leopold Stokowski.
    (M) ** (*) CBS 61643. Philadelphia Orchestra, Eugene Ormandy.
    (M) ** (*) Supraphon suast 50423. Czech Philharmonic Orchestra, Karel Ančerl.
    (B) ** Decca Eclipse ecs 767. Suisse Romande Orchestra, Istvan Kertesz.
    (B) * Classics for Pleasure cfp 40080. Royal Philharmonic Orchestra, Massimo Freccia.

It does not take long in the fine interpretation of Shostakovich's *Fifth Sym-*

873

phony by his son for the young man to establish his insight. The crucial transition between the bald, dramatic close to the first subject and the first throbbing rhythms of the second subject has a poise which conveys a frisson of expectation with a delectable easing of tempo. Not even Previn on RCA (in most ways at least as recommendable as this) quite achieves that. In the *Largo* third movement Previn's very slow tempo conveys a depth of concentration that the young Shostakovich does not quite achieve, but the faster tempo does allow a warmth of expressiveness that is most compelling. In the *Allegretto* second movement the Russian finds an almost Prokofiev-like wit, and in the finale his extreme contrast of tempi allows more tenderly romantic expressiveness than usual. Fine recording too.

From Previn an altogether superlative account. The recording too is outstanding, and in all departments of the orchestra and in fidelity of recorded sound it scores heavily. Freshness and vitality, genuine musicianship, and a basic approach uncluttered with academic shibboleths combine to produce really first-class playing from the LSO, and an interpretative quality that is literal without lacking spontaneity. The kind of radiance that the strings achieve at the opening of the great slow movement of Shostakovich's finest symphony clearly has its technical source in the new world rather than the old, but Previn's conception of the work is extrovert and optimistic, and he clearly sees the piece as a whole, not a succession of four movements. Because of this the buoyancy and verve of the scherzo and the *élan* of the finale are doubly exhilarating.

Stokowski gave us the first recording of this symphony in the 78 era, and it was one of the very finest of his many outstanding achievements with the Philadelphia Orchestra. The Stadium Symphony Orchestra of New York is neither as flexible nor as virtuoso an ensemble as the superb instrument Stokowski created in Philadelphia during the first decade of electric recording, but the Stokowski electricity is here as intensely as ever and it makes his stereo LP an unforgettable experience. There is less subtlety in the individual wind solos than in the old 78 set, but the strings again create that intense 'drenched' radiance of texture in the upper register that Stokowski has made his own, and which makes the lyrical climaxes of the first and third movements so memorable. This is a thrilling performance and the sound is nearly always worthy of it, although there is a fairly high background hiss.

A good straightforward performance from Ormandy, with predictably distinguished orchestral playing and acceptable recording quality. This makes a good mid-priced alternative to Stokowski's Everest disc. The performance has less electricity, but the recording, if shallower, is more consistent.

Inevitably Ančerl's account has not the vivid and distinctive individuality of Stokowski's interpretation and some may like it the more because of this. The kernel of this eloquent symphony is undoubtedly the *Largo*, and any conductor who fails to sustain this extremely beautiful movement must have his performance discounted. Ančerl comes through this test well. He gives a supply-shaped reading, which is especially moving in the closing pages. The first movement too is well-balanced and the *Allegro* takes its place in the structure of the movement, instead of sounding like a rather vulgar episode, as it sometimes does. Ančerl takes the *Allegretto* fairly slowly, but vivid solo playing, especially from the horns, supports this account well. The finale too is broad, rather than frenetic, and if it loses a little out-and-out excitement, it gains in dignity. The Supraphon recording is one of this company's best, vivid as well as atmospheric.

Kertesz's reading is thoroughly musical but somewhat circumspect. Yet it is not uncommitted; and the clear yet vivid Decca sound adds much to the impact of the performance. Kertesz is especially good at the close of movements, and both the first and third end in a mood of radiant simplicity, although Previn and Stokowski both find much more tension and colour in the climax of the *Largo*. The finale is taken steadily, but Kertesz provides a splendid burst of controlled exuberance for the coda. This is excellent value at bargain price.

Freccia shows little understanding for the subtler points in a symphony more difficult to interpret than it seems. The performance lacks tension and the violin tone is often thin.

Symphony No. 6 in B minor, Op. 54.
 *** HMV ASD 3029. London Symphony Orchestra, André Previn – PROKOFIEV: *Lieutenant Kijé.****
 *** HMV ASD 2805. Leningrad Philharmonic Orchestra, Yevgeny Mravinsky – SIBELIUS: *Symphony No. 7 etc.** (**)
 (M) ** Philips Universo 6580 042. Berlin Radio Orchestra, Rolf Kleinert – STRAVINSKY: *4 Norwegian moods.***
 (M) ** Everest SDBR 3007. London Philharmonic Orchestra, Sir Adrian Boult.

The opening slow movement of the *Sixth Symphony* is parallel to those of the *Fifth* and the *Eighth*, each among the composer's finest inspirations. Here Previn shows his deep understanding of Shostakovich in a powerfully drawn, unrelenting account of that massive structure, his slow tempo adding to the overall impact. After that the offhand wit of the central scherzo comes over the more delicately at a slower tempo than usual, leaving the hectic finale to hammer home the deceptively joyful conclusion to the argument. Even at the end Previn

effectively avoids bombast in the exuberance of joy. Excellent recording.

Although not so impressively recorded as the Previn/LSO account, Mravinsky's performance is electrifyingly intense. Mravinsky, it will be remembered, conducted the premiere of the symphony in 1939, and his account has enormous authority. The playing of the Leningrad Philharmonic is superb, but the recording derives from a concert performance and is thus less detailed and vivid. Given playing of this quality and vision, however, qualifications about recording seem of small account, and do not justify a less than whole-hearted recommendation.

Kleinert is at his best in the finale, where his refinement counteracts the Soviet rabble-rousing quality, but in the first movement there is a lack of intensity. The playing is good and the recording warm and atmospheric. The sound here is more modern than Boult's alternative mid-price version on Everest, and this disc has the advantage of a slight but attractive filler.

Though Boult secures very good playing from the LPO, and the recording is excellent, he is not as intense as he might be, and this inevitably detracts from the sense of symphonic architecture.

Symphony No. 7 in C major, Op. 60.
 ** (*) HMV SLS 897 (2 discs). Bournemouth Symphony Orchestra, Paavo Berglund.

Berglund directs a doggedly powerful performance of a symphony of Shostakovich that has long been underestimated. It was unfortunate that the work in all its massiveness was first presented to the Western public during the war in terms which labelled it as essentially a propagandist piece. Initially that brought success, but reaction soon hit back. Now we can see that the long unrelenting ostinato of the first movement, representing the Nazi invasion (a passage that

Bartók parodied in his *Concerto for orchestra*), has more than a programmatic purpose. Though Berglund is not always sensitive to the finer points of expressiveness, it is good to have a fine performance of what is often a noisy symphony recorded with such rich, vivid sound.

Symphony No. 8 in C minor, Op. 64.
*** HMV ASD 2917. London Symphony Orchestra, André Previn.

** (*) HMV ASD 2474. Moscow Philharmonic Orchestra, Kyril Kondrashin.

The *Eighth Symphony*, written in response to the sufferings of the Russian people during the Second World War, is one of Shostakovich's most powerful and intense creations, starting with a slow movement almost half an hour long, which in such a performance as Previn's emerges as not only emotionally involving but cogent in symphonic terms too. The sharp unpredictability of the remaining movements, alternately cajoling and battering the listener, shows Shostakovich at his most inspired. The London Symphony Orchestra is prompted by Previn to playing that is both intense and brilliant, while the recording is outstandingly rich and vivid, even making no allowance for the very long sides.

Though Kondrashin's version is strong and full-blooded, it does not convey the full range of expression implied in the massive opening slow movement. Previn is far more successful in evoking the ominous hushed intensity, while the Melodiya recording, acceptable enough, cannot compare with the British one in range and refinement.

Symphony No. 9 in E flat major, Op. 70.
*** HMV ASD 2409. Moscow Philharmonic Orchestra, Kyril Kondrashin – *Execution of Stepan Razin*.***

(M) ** Everest SDBR 3054. London Symphony Orchestra, Sir Malcolm Sargent – PROKOFIEV: *Lieutenant Kijé*.**

Kondrashin's is the best account of the delightful *Ninth Symphony* to appear in this country. It even challenges memories of Koussevitzky's legendary account on RCA. The playing is sparkling and vital, and Kondrashin has the full measure of the score, conveying both its wit and its poetry. There is a departure from the tempo indications in the printed score in the finale, but this apart the performance could hardly be bettered. The recording too is first-rate and the issue is strongly recommended. Sargent's account is lyrical and attractive, relaxed and lightweight. The recording is excellent, and with a recommendable coupling this is good value, if without the distinction of the Russian issue.

Symphony No. 10 in E minor, Op. 93.
*** DGG SLPM 1390 20. Berlin Philharmonic Orchestra, Herbert von Karajan.

*** HMV ASD 2420. USSR State Symphony Orchestra, Yevgeny Svetlanov.

(B) *** Classics for Pleasure CFP 40216. London Philharmonic Orchestra, Andrew Davis.

Shostakovich's finest symphony has been well served on record. Mitropoulos, Ančerl, Efrem Kurtz have all given first-class accounts of it on mono LP, the finest of all, by Mravinsky, who conducted its premiere, being let down by dim recording. Karajan gives a superbly moulded reading that does not smooth over the contours too much and which has the advantage of magnificent orchestral playing from the Berlin Philharmonic. Both the playing and recording have a refinement that eludes the USSR Symphony Orchestra. Choice between the two full-price versions is difficult: the Svetlanov has the greater rawness and idiomatic flavour, yet Karajan matches this with genuine tragic feeling and authenticity. Neither version will fail to satisfy.

Svetlanov secures playing of great sensitiveness and breadth from this fine orchestra and he is excellently served by the engineers. Perhaps the balance favours the first violins at one or two points in the first movement, but this is a small detail, and most listeners will not be put off. Svetlanov is slower than his predecessors in the first movement, and there is a gain in breadth. On the other hand there is a certain loss of forward momentum in the big, sustained climax in the first movement. But apart from small reservations, this fine performance can be thoroughly recommended and the recording quality is of a high standard, with plenty of spread and no lack of detail.

Andrew Davis draws a fresh and direct reading from the LPO, not so powerfully individual as Karajan's or Svetlanov's, but consistently compelling both in the long paragraphs of the first and third movements and in the pointedly rhythmic second and fourth. Excellent recording quality. A first-rate bargain.

Symphony No. 11 in G minor (1905), Op. 103.
   ** (*) HMV ASD 3010. Moscow Philharmonic Orchestra, Kyril Kondrashin.

As in the *Eighth Symphony* Kondrashin refuses to let Shostakovich's ampler inspirations linger. His performance of this uninhibited programme symphony is far less expansive than earlier versions on record. He misses some of the atmospheric subtlety, but the commitment of the playing is never in doubt. Kondrashin like his predecessors shows that though this may not match the finest of Shostakovich's symphonic inspirations, it is

still an intensely imaginative work, worth studying not just as an evocation of the abortive 1905 revolution but as a distinctive musical structure in its own right. Good, immediate recording quality.

Symphony No. 12 in D minor (The year 1917), Op. 112.
   (M) *** Philips Universo 6580 012. Leipzig Gewandhaus Orchestra, Ogan Durjan.

More than in his other mature symphonies Shostakovich gave way in this evocation of the Revolution year to overtly propagandist aims. It is easy to dismiss it on that account, and during performance the dangers of falling over the cliff-edge into banality are enormous. Durjan avoids them most effectively, fearless in attack on even the apparently bombastic passages, for the precision of the playing and the control of texture reveal a far wider range of emotion than usual. In such a performance the work can take its place as a worthy companion to the other symphonies in the cycle. The recording is clean, bright and atmospheric.

Symphony No. 13 (Babi-Yar), Op. 113.
   *** HMV ASD 2893. Arthur Eisen (bass), RSFSR Academic Russian Choir, Moscow Philharmonic Orchestra, Kyril Kondrashin.
   *** RCA SB 6830. Tom Krause (baritone), Mendelssohn Club Choir, Philadelphia Male Chorus, Philadelphia Orchestra, Eugene Ormandy.

This was the symphony, setting words by the young poet Yevtushenko, which for a time at least was frowned on by the Soviet authorities, and which by implication presents a direct criticism of the regime. In every one of these vivid if often disorganized poems, the composer has intensified the original images. The sequence is sharply memorable: the relentless plod of *Babi-Yar*, the poem about antisemitism; the dark irony of the scherzo, *Humour*; the chilling flatness of *At the store*, where women queue hopelessly in the snow and the clanking of cans measures out wasted time; the even stiller opening of *Fears*, leading to a ghostly march and a haunted reference to 'the fear of judgement without trial'; the final magic resolution (much more convincing in its hope for the future than any patriotic jollification) with gentle flutings and talk of Galileo and Shakespeare.

Kondrashin directs a vivid committed performance that has all the ring of authenticity with vocal tone (chorus and soloist alike) that could only come from Russian singers. The recording is forward and colourful to underline the urgency of the conductor's reading.

Ormandy's performance may not be so idiomatic as the Russian one, but it has many compensating qualities, which may make some turn to it in preference. The playing, particularly of the strings, is more refined, and so is the recording, which is superbly atmospheric. That allows the chilling picture of the women outside the store to come out the more subtly, the colours more delicate. Tom Krause is a magnificently steady soloist.

Symphony No. 14, Op. 135.

(M) *** RCA LSB 5002. Phyllis Curtin (soprano), Simon Estes (bass), Philadelphia Orchestra, Eugene Ormandy.

Shostakovich's *Fourteenth Symphony* has much in common with Mahler's *Das Lied von der Erde*. The work's dominating theme is death, and it consists of a cycle of eleven songs for soprano and bass soloists, string orchestra and a wide range of percussion instruments. The songs are separate in that there is little attempt to connect them thematically, but the choice of poetry and the music itself provide a strange but convincing

cohesion of parts. The settings are immensely varied and imaginative and make compelling listening, the atmosphere sometimes Mussorgskian (this effect amplified on the RCA disc by the dark colouring of Simon Estes's bass voice), but the overall effect of the work, in spite of its sombre theme, is essentially life-assertive. The ninth and tenth songs are especially moving, and the closing short hymn to Death itself has a touch of the grotesque about it that somehow conveys a refusal to be intimidated. The performance here is splendid, with excellent soloists, and Ormandy at his most persuasive. The RCA recording is of demonstration quality, clearly projected yet very atmospheric.

Symphony No. 15 in A major, Op. 141.

*** HMV ASD 2857. Moscow Radio Symphony Orchestra, Maxim Shostakovich – *String quartet No. 11.***

*** RCA Quadradisc ARD 1 0014; Stereo ARL 1 0014. Philadelphia Orchestra, Eugene Ormandy.

Shostakovich's *Fifteenth Symphony* dates from 1972, and despite the quotations from Rossini and Wagner it strikes serious resonances. Like its predecessor it ruminates on the subject of death, though with very different artistic results. The HMV Melodiya performance has the authority of the composer's presence and his son's baton. The orchestral playing is spirited and alert, and the recording is naturally balanced and wide-ranging. It seems to have an extra octave at the top compared with the RCA, though the latter is richer in sonority. The HMV disc has the additional attraction of the *Eleventh Quartet* expertly played by the Borodins.

The RCA Ormandy version is quadraphonic, though a stereo version will be on the market by the time this book appears in print. The performance is also very fine, though perhaps the Russians have the more refined pianissimo tone. The RCA quadraphonic recording is one of the most successful yet made of the Philadelphia Orchestra. Their tone has outstanding depth and definition, and the detail is separated out with great clarity. The overall balance is most musically judged and there is exceptional presence. Only at the very top does one feel a certain loss of detail. Both versions are strongly recommended and the choice can be left to individual taste.

CHAMBER AND PIANO MUSIC

Piano quintet, Op. 57.
  *** HMV ASD 3072. Lyubov Yedlina (piano), Borodin Quartet – STRAVINSKY: *Pieces.****
  (M) * (*) Oiseau-Lyre SOL 267. Melos Ensemble – PROKOFIEV: *Quintet.***

Shostakovich's *Piano quintet*, written in 1940, is one of his most deeply moving works. It includes two intensely serious movements, a slow opening prelude and fugue and a slow Intermezzo, alternating with characteristically offbeat movements – a rumbustious scherzo and a wayward finale. It has long needed a first-rate recording, and the Borodin Quartet with Lyubov Yedlina come near the ideal. The rock-like slow prelude and fugue and the lovely Intermezzo are played with pure dedication, and this is altogether superior to the Melos account. The Melos players seem to skate over the prelude and fugue and later the slow movement too, and in spite of good sound their disc cannot command much enthusiasm.

Piano trio No. 2 in E minor, Op. 67.
  (M) ** (*) HMV HQS 1330. André Previn (piano), Yong Uck Kim (violin), Ralph Kirshbaum (cello) – RAVEL: *Piano trio.****

Though not quite so alert as the performance of the Ravel on the reverse (for one thing Previn has far less to do, with a relatively bald piano part), this is a fine performance, well recorded. Not so consistently inspired as the *Piano quintet* (written at about the same period during the Second World War) this trio is still unforgettable.

Piano trio No. 2 in E minor, Op. 67; (i) *7 Romances on words of Alexander Blok* (for soprano, violin, violoncello and piano), *Op. 127.*
  (B) * (*) Turnabout TV 34280S. New Amsterdam Trio, (i) with Mary Ellen Pracht (soprano).

The Turnabout performance of the *Piano trio* is serviceable, well played and alive. The snag is that the solo violinist's tone appears to catch the microphone and is very thin and wiry. It is difficult to tame this without blanketing the sound, which is otherwise good. For many the main interest of this disc will be the *Seven Romances on words of Alexander Blok*, written in 1967. These are characteristically imaginative settings, but the effect is somewhat spoiled here by the open and sometimes squally quality of the soloist. It might be suggested that her style is suitably Slavic, but it is not always too comfortable, although she sings with obvious eloquence and feeling.

String quartets Nos. 1 in C major, Op. 49; 2 in A major, Op. 68; 3 in F major, Op. 73; 4 in D major, Op. 83; 5 in B flat major, Op. 92; 6 in G major, Op. 101; 7 in F sharp minor, Op. 108; 8 in C minor, Op. 110; 9 in E flat major, Op. 117; 10 in A flat major, Op. 118; 11 in F minor, Op. 122; 12 in D flat major, Op. 133; 13 in B flat minor, Op. 138.

✿ (M) *** HMV SLS 879 (6 discs). Borodin Quartet.

An indispensable set. The Shostakovich quartets are to the post-war years what the Bartók were to the first three decades of the century. They are far more even in inspiration than the symphonies, and their rewards are rich. This set is not quite complete: it appeared before No. 14 had seen the light of day, but the performances and recordings could hardly be improved on. The set is modestly priced and not only is it important, it is immensely pleasurable.

String quartet No. 8 in C minor, Op. 110.

(M) *** Decca Ace of Diamonds SDD 156. Borodin Quartet – BORODIN: *Quartet No. 2.****

As the central motif of this fine quartet Shostakovich used a group of four notes derived, cipher-like, from his own name, and somewhat unpatriotically the cipher has a decided German bias. He takes his initial D, plus (in German notation) the first three notes of his surname (in German spelling) – E flat (or Es, as it is in German), C and B (or H, as it is in German). Hence the motif spells DSCH. All very involved, but in fact the motif is at least as fruitful as the famous one in the name BACH, and the argument throughout this impressive work is most intense. The fourth movement was inspired by memories of a German air-raid, with a high-pitched whine interrupted by crackling gunfire, but one does not have to know that fragment of programme to appreciate the immediacy of the music. The work concludes with a fine slow fugue on the DSCH motif. This performance is outstanding and the recording superb. With so attractive a coupling there are few more desirable string quartet records available.

String quartet No. 10 in A flat major, Op. 118.

*** Decca SXL 6196. Weller Quartet – BERG: *Quartet, Op. 3.* ***

(B) ** Pye GSGC 14104. Amici Quartet – IVES: *Quartet No. 1.***

The *Tenth* is one of Shostakovich's most fully realized and perfect quartets. It has a sense of mastery rare in post-war music, and by concentrating on content rather than expressive means it succeeds in saying more than most contemporary works put together. The Weller Quartet play with great suavity and fervour and the recording could not be bettered.

Conscientious though the Amici playing is, it must yield to the more polished and accomplished Viennese ensemble on Decca. Pye provide a goodish recording, a little too closely balanced perhaps but with plenty of body, but again not as mellow or truthful as the Decca. But those who want the Ives coupling will find this quite satisfactory in its own right.

String quartet No. 11 in F minor, Op. 122.

*** HMV ASD 2857. Borodin Quartet – *Symphony No. 15.****

This outstanding performance, taken from the complete set listed above, makes a generous coupling for the symphony.

Preludes and fugues for piano from Op. 87, Nos. 4 in E minor; 12 in G sharp minor; 14 in E flat minor; 15 in D flat major; 23 in F major.

(M) ** (*) Philips Universo 6580 084. Sviatoslav Richter (piano).

Shostakovich wrote twenty-four *Preludes and fugues*, one in each key. They are thus a modern equivalent of the Bach *48*, but they are far from cerebral pieces and are often dramatic and emotional. Their form too is by no means conventional. No. 15, for instance, has an ABA structure, with the most winning middle section, which Richter points beautifully. The present selection in fact has no unifying factor; these are presumably Richter's own favourites. He plays them superbly and even though the recording tends to be rather hard, this reissue is very worthwhile.

VOCAL AND CHORAL MUSIC

The Execution of Stepan Razin, Op. 119.
*** HMV ASD 2409. Vitaly Gromadsky (bass), RSFSR Chorus, Moscow Philharmonic Orchestra, Kyril Kondrashin – *Symphony No. 9.****
(M) ** (*) Supraphon SUAST 50958. Bohus Hanak (bass), Slovák Chorus, Slovák Philharmonic Orchestra, Ladislav Slovák – *Symphony No. 2.** (*)
(M) ** Philips Universo 6585 012. Siegfried Vogel (bass), Leipzig Radio Chorus and Symphony Orchestra, Herbert Kegel – KHACHATURIAN: *Spartacus excerpts.***

The Execution of Stepan Razin, which like the *Thirteenth Symphony* is based on a Yevtushenko poem, is a vigorous and full-blooded cantata with some highly characteristic Shostakovich in it. It was first heard in London in 1964 at a Prom given by the Mosow Philharmonic. Vitaly Gromadsky is a splendidly larger-than-life bass with ringing resonant tones, and the Moscow Chorus has superb ensemble and bite. The HMV performance all in all is highly successful and is most vividly recorded. Though the cantata is not one of Shostakovich's most inspired compositions, it is thoroughly enjoyable, particularly when it is so marvellously played and recorded as it is here.

The Supraphon soloist has not quite the outsize personality of Gromadsky on the HMV Melodiya recording, nor has the performance quite the same zest and brilliance. Still, having said this, it must be confessed that the performance is very fine indeed and many may be tempted by the price and the interest of the coupling to consider it as a useful alternative to Kondrashin's. The latter is coupled, however, with an absolutely first-rate account of Shostakovich's delightful *Ninth Symphony*. The Supraphon recording is well-focused and intelligently balanced but is slightly lacking in impact and body by the side of the Russian disc.

The Universo performance too is a dramatic one, with an impressive contribution from the bass soloist, Siegfried Vogel. The recording is reverberant but vivid. However, this would not be first choice among the available versions, as the coupling is not very generous.

Song of the Forests, Op. 81.
(**) HMV ASD 2875. Vladimir Ivanovsky (tenor), Ivan Petrov (bass), Moscow State Choral Singing School Boys' Choir. RSFSR Academic Russian Choir, Moscow Philharmonic Orchestra, Alexander Yurlov – SVIRIDOV: *Kursk songs.****

The Song of the Forests, inspired by the reafforestation of Soviet Turkestan, was the outcome of the spirit of pale caution that afflicted Soviet music after the 1948 Congress presided over by Zhdanov. Never has the exploration of C major been more thorough or the composer's inspiration so insipid and characterless. Good performance and recording cannot redeem this conventional work, the musical equivalent of officialese.

Sibelius, Jean
(1865–1957)

The Bard (tone poem), *Op. 64; Karelia (incidental music): Overture, Op. 10; King Christian II suite, Op. 27; Scènes historiques, Op. 25: Festivo* (only).

   (M) ** (*) HMV HQS 1070. Scottish National Orchestra, Alexander Gibson.

This is an enterprising anthology and as it is Alexander Gibson's finest Sibelius disc to date, it is well worth exploring. There is no great music here but plenty that is colourful and attractive. The extrovert pieces come off best, particularly the *Karelia overture*, with its tantalizing reminders of the suite, and the vivid *Festivo* movement from the *Scènes historiques. The Bard* is a short concentrated piece. Gibson's feeling for the idiom here is very impressive, but more intensity is needed and the performance hasn't quite enough atmosphere. Greater weight of string tone would have enhanced the *King Christian suite*. This is warm-hearted music and delightfully fresh, with the individual flavour of the composer's style coming across most of the time. Generally the recording is excellent, although the upper register of the strings sounds thin in tutti, and it may well not be the players' fault. Otherwise the orchestra shows considerable competence and quite a degree of flair too. The stereo is fine, and the overall image spreads admirably and has plenty of warmth. Greater definition of the inner parts would have made it superlative.

Violin concerto in D minor, Op. 47.

   (M) *** RCA LSB 4048. Jascha Heifetz (violin), Chicago Symphony Orchestra, Walter Hendl – PROKOFIEV: *Violin concerto No. 2.****

   *** Decca SXL 6493. Kyung-Wha Chung (violin), London Symphony Orchestra, André Previn – TCHAIKOVSKY: *Violin concerto.****

   (M) ** (*) Decca Ace of Diamonds SDD 276. Ruggiero Ricci (violin), London Symphony Orchestra Øivin Fjeldstad – TCHAIKOVSKY: *Sérénade; Souvenir.****

   (M) ** HMV SXLP 30137. Masuko Ushioda (violin), Japan Philharmonic Orchestra, Seiji Ozawa – BRUCH: *Violin concerto No. 1.***

   (M) * (*) RCA LSB 4066. Itzhak Perlman (violin), Boston Symphony Orchestra, Erich Leinsdorf – TCHAIKOVSKY: *Violin concerto.* (*)

   (M) * (*) DGG Privilege 2538 302. Miriam Fried (violin), Belgian Radio and TV Symphony Orchestra, René Defossez – CHAUSSON: *Poème.* (*)

Originally issued on two full sides, this is one of Heifetz's finest gramophone performances. The purity and luminous beauty of the violin tone at the opening set the seal on this as an interpretation of unusual depth, consummate technique and supreme artistry. With its new coupling, at medium price, this is one of the outstanding bargains of the current catalogue.

The alternative recommendation on Decca is a most beautiful account of the work, poetic, brilliant and thoroughly idiomatic. Kyung-Wha Chung has impeccable style and an astonishing technique, and her feeling for the Sibelius *Concerto* is second-to-none. André Previn's accompanying cannot be too highly praised: it is poetic when required, restrained, full of controlled vitality and well-defined detail. The recording is superbly balanced and produces an unforced truthful sound. This must be numbered among the finest versions of the work now available and takes its place alongside the Heifetz and Oistrakh accounts (see below).

Ricci has the clean, clear-cut, and effortless kind of technique that is a prime necessity for the Sibelius *Concerto*, and he makes light of its many difficulties. The reading is straightforward, with no lack of dash and intensity. A great contribution to the success of the performance is made by Fjeldstad and the orchestra. Fortunately the recording is very good indeed. The soloist, although well forward, is sufficiently detached from the orchestra to give an impression of depth. As we go to press, this performance has also been reissued on SPA 398, coupled to the Dvořák *Concerto*.

Masuko Ushioda could hardly play with greater assurance, but the result seems almost too easy, lacking the sort of idiosyncrasy that brings a performance to life. Satisfying but a little bland.

In the mid-price bracket Perlman is more competitive than he was on the original Red Seal. However, it must be confessed that Perlman's reading hasn't the character and personality of the Heifetz, finely played though it is. Nor is the recording particularly outstanding.

Miriam Fried is a young Israeli violinist who won first prizes at the Genoa Paganini Competition in 1968 and the Concours Reine Elisabeth in Brussels in 1971. The Sibelius was recorded on the latter occasion. The reading is a highly romantic, self-indulgent affair and will appeal to those who like their Sibelius played with the last ounce of emotion. The Chausson coupling would be more acceptable if it were not recorded with piano accompaniment. Not a distinguished issue.

Violin concerto in D minor, Op. 47; Finlandia, Op. 26.
** (*) DGG SLPM 138961. Chris-

tian Ferras (violin), Berlin Philharmonic Orchestra, Herbert von Karajan.

Ferras's performance is a very good one. It has the advantage of being much better recorded than Heifetz's RCA version (which sounds harsh by comparison) but although Ferras begins the work with a winningly golden tone, when under stress at the end of the first movement and in the finale, his intonation and general security are no match for the superbly accurate Heifetz performance. But there is still much to enjoy and Ferras develops a rich, romantic tone for the main tune of the slow movement. The coupling is an extremely expansive reading of *Finlandia* in which Karajan broadens the grand tune almost as far as it will go to accentuate its patriotic dignity. Only Karajan could bring this off, and he does, with superb Berlin Philharmonic brass playing to support him.

Violin concerto in D minor, Op. 47; 2 Humoresques, Op. 87b; Belshazzar's Feast (suite), Op. 5; Kuolema (incidental music)*: Valse triste, Op. 44; Romance in C major for strings, Op. 42.*
** (*) HMV ASD 2407. David Oistrakh (violin), Moscow Radio Symphony and Leningrad Philharmonic Orchestra, Gennady Rozhdestvensky.

Oistrakh gives a warm-hearted and in general well-recorded account of the Sibelius *Concerto*. His approach is of course well known and is sweet-toned, lyrical and romantic. He generates none of the electricity of Heifetz but, make no mistake, this is still a powerfully conceived reading and ranks among the best. It is all the more competitive on account of the backing: the two glorious *Humoresques*, touching but brilliant pieces, and the rarely recorded *Belshazzar's Feast*, which in a performance like Kajanus's on 78s emerges as one of Sibelius's most delicately wrought and poetic compositions. The Rozhdestvensky account isn't quite as good as that, but it is more than acceptable, save in the *Khadra's dance*, where the raw, coarse-grained Leningrad oboe spoils the chaste, fragrant quality of this piece. The *Romance* is well played but, like everything on this disc, too closely balanced, with the result that the upper strings have a certain edginess. Otherwise, however, this well-filled disc is to be welcomed for a fine account of the *Concerto* and the interest of the two rarities. The stereo spreads very well and the pressing is extremely smooth.

Violin concerto in D minor, Op. 47; Legends, Op. 22/2: The Swan of Tuonela.
> (M) ** CBS Classics 61041. David Oistrakh (violin), Philadelphia Orchestra, Eugene Ormandy.

A predictably good performance from Oistrakh, but it fails to be fully competitive on grounds of recording quality. Oistrakh's account of the work for HMV Melodiya (see above) has much richer sonority and more lifelike sound as well as far more interesting fill-ups.

Symphonic poems: En Saga, Op. 9; Finlandia, Op. 26. Karelia suite, Op. 11; Legends, Op. 22/2: The Swan of Tuonela.
> ** (*) HMV ASD 541. Vienna Philharmonic Orchestra, Sir Malcolm Sargent.

Sargent's collection is highly successful. Without being especially idiomatic, each performance has conviction and character, and the four pieces complement each other to make a thoroughly enjoyable LP programme. The Vienna Philharmonic Orchestra bring a distinct freshness to their playing of music which must have

been fairly unfamiliar to them, and Sir Malcolm imparts his usual confidence. The brass is especially full-blooded in *En Saga*, and even *Finlandia* sounds unhackneyed. Perhaps Sir Malcolm's tempi for *Karelia* are on the brisk side, but the music projects vividly and the orchestral playing is distinctly superior to a rather similar HMV collection by Barbirolli and the Hallé (see below).

Symphonic poems: En Saga, Op. 9; Finlandia, Op. 26; Night Ride and Sunrise, Op. 55; Pohjola's Daughter, Op. 49.
> *** Decca SXL 6542. Suisse Romande Orchestra, Horst Stein.

These are distinguished and finely calculated performances offering some of the finest playing we have had from the Suisse Romande Orchestra in recent years. It is a great pity the disc had to include *Finlandia*. The performance here is exciting and sonorously recorded, but the achievement of the rest of the programmes makes one wish that something less ubiquitous had been included. Stein shows a gift for the special atmosphere of Sibelius. The highlight of the disc is an outstandingly exciting account of *En Saga*, with quite superb recording from Decca including the flamboyant use of the bass drum, though there is a low-pitched hum on one side. *Night Ride and Sunrise* and *Pohjola's Daughter* too are highly successful, although the broadening of the climax of the latter work does let the tension slip momentarily. But taken as a whole this is a fine disc in every way.

Symphonic poems: En Saga, Op. 9; Night Ride and Sunrise, Op. 55; The Oceanides, Op. 73.
> ** (*) HMV ASD 2486. London Symphony Orchestra, Antal Dorati – *Luonnotar*.***

This record is of exceptional interest for *Luonnotar*, one of Sibelius's most magical and imaginative scores. Both *Night Ride and Sunrise* and *The Oceanides* are given fine performances though not inspired ones and only *En Saga* lacks the last ounce of poetry. The recordings are beautifully transparent and rich in sonority. Strongly recommended.

Finlandia, Op. 26. Karelia suite, Op. 11: Intermezzo. King Christian II suite: Nocturne; Élégie; Musette. Kuolema: Valse triste, Op. 44. Legends: The Swan of Tuonela, Op. 22/2; Lemminkäinen's Return, Op. 22/4.

** Columbia Studio 2 Quadraphonic Q4–TWO 380; Stereo TWO 380. Bournemouth Symphony Orchestra, Paavo Berglund.

The sound is glamorized in the Studio 2/Phase 4 manner, but not unacceptably so. The performances are straightforward, and the excellence of the sound ensures that this popular Sibelius programme will enjoy wide success. The Bournemouth Orchestra play with enthusiasm for their Finnish conductor, and those requiring this anthology will find little to quarrel with. The sound flatters small machines: the quadraphonic version, however, does not offer the degree of improvement in realism experienced with certain other EMI issues. It adds some atmosphere to the items on side two (notably the *Karelia Intermezzo*), but *Finlandia* sounds slightly brash and artificially bright. Other straight stereo accounts of *The Swan of Tuonela* have produced a more magical ambience.

Finlandia, Op. 26. Karelia suite, Op. 11. Kuolema: Valse triste, Op. 44. Legends: Lemminkäinen's Return, Op. 22/4; Pohjola's Daughter, Op. 49.

** (*) HMV ASD 2272. Hallé Orchestra, Sir John Barbirolli.

Although the orchestral playing is not as polished as that of a virtuoso orchestra it is enthusiastic and has the advantage of superlative recording. *Pohjola's Daughter* is extremely impressive, spacious but no less exciting for all the slower tempi. A desirable introduction to Sibelius's smaller orchestral pieces, with admirable stereo definition.

Finlandia, Op. 26. King Christian II suite, Op. 27: Élégie; Musette. Kuolema: Valse triste, Op. 44. Pelléas et Mélisande, Op. 46; No. 7, Entr'acte.

(B) *** Decca SPA 91. London Proms Orchestra, Charles Mackerras – GRIEG: *Collection.****

The performance of *Finlandia* is brashly exciting, but other versions make a greater impact with a more sonorous sound balance. In the rest of the pieces the sound is first-rate and the programme is sheer joy. The *Musette* from the *King Christian II suite* is enchanting, and the *Entr'acte* from *Pelléas* is almost equally delightful: both have the kind of vivid colouring which has made the *Karelia* suite so famous. The *Elegy* too is beautiful, and this attractive collection is well worth its modest cost in this clear new transfer.

(i) *Finlandia, Op. 26. Kuolema: Valse triste, Op. 44.*

(M) ** (*) CBS 61286. Philadelphia Orchestra, Eugene Ormandy, (i) with Mormon Tabernacle Choir – GRIEG: *Collection.** (*)

On Ormandy's disc the two Sibelius items are a makeweight for an attractive anthology of Grieg's music. *Valse triste* is presented with characteristic Philadelphia panache, and the atmospheric recording matches up well: the *Finlandia* performance is the version with the Mormon Tabernacle Choir providing a thrilling vocal setting of the chorale

885

theme. This is demonstration-worthy and most exhilarating, although it is not for purists.

Finlandia, Op. 26. Kuolema: Valse triste, Op. 44. Legends: The Swan of Tuonela, Op. 22/2; Tapiola (symphonic poem), Op. 112.
> ** (*) DGG SLPM 139016. Berlin Philharmonic Orchestra, Herbert von Karajan.

All these, save *Valse triste*, are familiar: they are coupled with the *Violin concerto* and the *Fourth* and *Fifth Symphonies* respectively. The newcomer, *Valse triste*, is played very slowly and in a somewhat mannered fashion. *Finlandia* is one of the finest performances available (tremendous orchestral tone from the Berliners), and the *Tapiola* is also impressive. Readers who recall Kajanus or Beecham will not need to be reminded that Karajan does not present the whole picture, but it is a performance of great intensity and offers superlative playing. The recording, too, is excellent, but the disc offers short value for a full-priced record.

6 Humoresques for violin and orchestra, Op. 87b and 89.
> (B) *** Turnabout TV 34182S. Aaron Rosand (violin), South-West German Radio Orchestra, Tibor Szöke – NIELSEN: *Symphony No. 6.* (*)

These *Humoresques* date from the same period as the *Fifth Symphony*, that is to say the First World War. They are altogether delightful miniatures, with a dazzlingly virtuosic solo part. Like the *Violin concerto*, they betray the composer's familiarity with all the tricks of violinistic bravura. Some of them have great poetry and a certain wistful melancholy, while the fifth of the set has an irresistibly memorable tune. Rosand

plays superlatively, and the recording, though it is far from new, is fully acceptable. A great pity that these rarities which are wholly captivating should be coupled with an indifferent recording of Nielsen's *Sixth Symphony*.

Karelia suite, Op. 11.
> *** Decca SXL 6084. Vienna Philharmonic Orchestra, Maazel – *Symphony No. 1.****
> (M) *** HMV SXLP 30149. Sinfonia of London, Tauno Hannikäinen – *Symphony No. 5.***
> (B) * (*) Decca SPA 122. London Symphony Orchestra, Alexander Gibson – *Symphony No. 5.* (*)

Fine performances by both Maazel and Hannikäinen. The latter conductor's feeling for Sibelian orchestral colouring can be especially felt in his sensitive account of the *Intermezzo*. Gibson's performance is disappointing; the approach to the delightful *Ballade* is unimaginative and half-hearted, and the *Alla marcia* too never really catches fire.

Legends: The Swan of Tuonela, Op. 22/2.
> ** (*) DGG SLPM 138974. Berlin Philharmonic Orchestra, Herbert von Karajan – *Symphony No. 4.** (*)
> ** (*) HMV ASD 2308. Hallé Orchestra, Sir John Barbirolli – *Symphony No. 2.**(*)

Smooth, beautiful playing under Karajan and excellent recording. The reading lacks perhaps the final touch of idiomatic character. Barbirolli's unique account is discussed with the symphony.

Legends: The Swan of Tuonela, Op. 22/2. Pelléas et Mélisande (incidental music), Op. 40: 1, At the castle gate; 2, Melisande; 7, Melisande at the

spinning wheel; 9, Death of Melisande.
Scènes historiques: All'overtura, Op.
25/1; The Chase, Op. 66/1; Scena, Op.
25/1. Rakastava (suite), Op. 14.

> (M) ** HMV SXLP 30162. Hallé
> Orchestra, Sir John Barbirolli.

This record will undoubtedly be popular, for it includes At the castle gate,
famous as the signature-tune of the
BBC TV series The Stars at Night. But
as an anthology it is not especially satisfying. The transfers seem to produce a
rather dry quality and the musical layout
does not provide a great deal of variety.
But it is useful to have the Rakastava
suite and the selection from Pelléas et
Mélisande available separately, for those
who do not want Sir John's accounts of
the symphonies with which they were
originally coupled.

Pelléas et Mélisande (incidental music),
Op. 40: 1, At the castle gate; 2, Melisande; 9, Death of Melisande.

> ** HMV ASD 2366 Hallé Orchestra,
> Sir John Barbirolli – Symphony
> No. 1.**

These three movements are poetically
done though it must be admitted that
there is not sufficient contrast in mood
between Melisande and the Death of
Melisande to justify their being played
in sequence. The playing itself is rather
beautiful and Barbirolli generates an
intensity of atmosphere, even if the pale
colours of the Northern latitudes are less
in evidence than one might expect. This
evokes sultrier climes! The recording has
warmth and spaciousness and the stereo
definition is admirably clear.

Symphonies Nos. 1–7.

> ** (*) Decca SXLE 6558/61. Vienna
> Philharmonic Orchestra, Lorin
> Maazel.

Maazel's set with the Vienna Philharmonic is still the best all-round version

of the complete Sibelius cycle, even
though there are individual weaknesses:
No. 6 is not particularly successful or
idiomatic, and the slow movement of
No. 3 also misses the point. In the first
two and in Nos. 4 and 7 Maazel remains
superb; it is strange that the mystery and
breadth of No. 5 should elude him since
he has done it admirably in the concert
hall. The Decca engineers have succeeded
in improving the already excellent sound
in these transfers, which reduce the
original five records to four.

Symphony No. 1 in E minor, Op. 39.

> *** Decca SXL 6084. Vienna Phil-
> harmonic Orchestra, Lorin Maazel
> – Karelia suite.***
> ** HMV ASD 2366. Hallé Orches-
> tra, Sir John Barbirolli – Pelléas et
> Mélisande.**
> (B) * (*) Classics for Pleasure CFP
> 40055. Scottish National Orches-
> tra, Alexander Gibson.

Symphony No. 1 in E minor, Op. 39;
The Bard (symphonic poem), Op. 64.

> ** DGG 2530 455. Helsinki Radio
> Orchestra, Okko Kamu.

Even after more than a decade Maazel's
version of the First Symphony still leads
the field. It has freshness of vision to
commend it, along with careful attention
both to the letter and to the spirit of the
score. The Vienna Philharmonic respond
with enthusiasm and brilliance and the
Decca engineers produce splendid detail
(except for the important timpani part in
the first movement, echoing the main
theme in canon, which is clearer in the
earlier Collins recording). This is a very
satisfying disc.

On HMV a good, straightforward
account of the symphony from Barbirolli
and the Hallé Orchestra, but after the
enthusiastic account these artists gave of
the Second, this is just a little lacking in
panache and colour. Whatever its merits,
and the record will undoubtedly give

pleasure, the Maazel performance or the Collins (in stereo transcription) have orchestral playing that is distinguished by greater weight of tone and virtuosity in attack. The stereo recording here is very good; it has warmth and spaciousness though the woodwind are balanced fairly far forward. But there is no doubt that the performance, free from mannerisms though it is, is less successful than Sir John's accounts of Nos. 2 and 5.

Okko Kamu with the Helsinki Radio Orchestra gives an account that rarely rises much above the routine. But his record contains an exceptionally fine account of *The Bard* as a fill-up, and it is beautifully recorded.

Turning to cheap recordings, Classics for Pleasure have now deleted Sargent's account of the work with the BBC Symphony Orchestra for Gibson's less well-played reading with the Scottish National. Although the recording is a good one, there is little to kindle much enthusiasm here, and readers who do not want to buy a full-price account should consider Collins's full-blooded version with the LSO, which has tremendous electricity (ECS 581), or Kajanus's pre-war version (WRC SH 191/2), which sounds amazingly fresh and enjoyed the *imprimatur* of the composer.

Symphony No. 2 in D major, Op. 43.
- (M) *** Philips Universo 6580 051. Concertgebouw Orchestra, George Szell.
- *** Decca SXL 6125. Vienna Philharmonic Orchestra, Lorin Maazel.
- ** (*) HMV ASD 2308. Hallé Orchestra, Sir John Barbirolli – *Legends: The Swan of Tuonela.** (*)
- ** (*) DGG 2530 021. Berlin Philharmonic Orchestra, Okko Kamu.
- (M) ** (*) Decca Ace of Diamonds SDD 234. London Symphony Orchestra, Pierre Monteux.

- ** RCA Quadradisc ARD 1 0018. Philadelphia Orchestra, Eugene Ormandy.
- (B) ** Classics for Pleasure CFP 40047. Scottish National Orchestra, Alexander Gibson.
- (i) *Symphony No. 2 in D major, Op. 43;*
- (ii) *Kuolema: Valse triste, Op. 44.*
- (B) * Decca SPA 282. (i) Suisse Romande Orchestra, Ernest Ansermet; (ii) London Proms Orchestra, Charles Mackerras.

The *Second Symphony* is exceptionally well served on records. One cannot go far wrong with any version currently on the market, with the possible exception of Ansermet's scruffily played account, which does scant justice to the memory of the great Swiss conductor. The best value is Szell and the Concertgebouw Orchestra on Philips's mid-price label: classically conceived, tautly held together, and superbly played and recorded. One need really look no further.

Maazel's account is more traditionally lush: it is sumptuously recorded and beautifully played by the Vienna Philharmonic, but his reading leans more to the romantic view of the work favoured by some virtuoso conductors. The Tchaikovskian inheritance is stressed, rather than the classical forebears. Barbirolli's reading with the Hallé Orchestra is also superbly recorded and stresses the Slav ancestry and Italianate warmth of the work. Its fill-up is an additional attraction for the singing *Swan of Tuonela*; Barbirolli's vocalizations are clearly audible.

Among the remaining full-price versions, Ormandy's account is marvellously played but the reading rarely sheds new light on this wonderful score. Best recorded is Okko Kamu, who secures highly polished and superbly refined playing from the Berlin Philharmonic; he indulges in some impulsive touches – the odd attention-seeking speed-up or slow-down – but these are not destructive.

In the mid-price range, Monteux and the LSO give a thoroughly acceptable and agreeably unmannered account of the work and Decca accord them excellent sound. Collins's famous account (ECS 582) is well worth considering though it is not genuine stereo; it has greater electricity and attack than the Scottish National Orchestra's account on Classics for Pleasure, which is extremely well recorded.

Decca provide excellent recording for the Suisse Romande, and Ansermet's view of this great symphony is refreshingly unmannered; but the playing really will not do.

Symphony No. 3 in C major, Op. 52; En Saga (symphonic poem), Op. 9.
   *** DGG 2530 426. Helsinki Radio Orchestra, Okko Kamu.

Among modern accounts of the *Third Symphony*, Okko Kamu's has strong claims to be considered the best. Tempi are well judged and the atmosphere is thoroughly authentic, particularly in the slow movement, whose character seems to have eluded so many distinguished conductors since Kajanus's pioneering account with the LSO, fortunately available once again on World Record Club (SH 191/2). The recording is excellent and most musically balanced. Readers requiring this bracing and rewarding symphony should turn to this in preference to any of its competitors. The performance of *En Saga* is also admirable and justifies Kamu's growing reputation.

Symphonies Nos. 3 in C major, Op. 52; 6 in D minor, Op. 104.
   * (**) Decca SXL 6364. Vienna Philharmonic Orchestra, Lorin Maazel.
   * (*) HMV ASD 2648. Hallé Orchestra, Sir John Barbirolli.

In the *Third Symphony* Maazel keeps a firm grip on the proceedings. He moulds phrases naturally and without affectation, and his build-up in the finale is most impressive. The slow movement is not quite poetic or reflective enough; he has little success in achieving the tranquillity and rapture (at fig. 6) that made Kajanus's pre-war set so memorable an experience. The *Sixth* is much less successful than the *Third*; Maazel does not penetrate beneath the surface and seems to have little sympathy for this most elusive and refined of Sibelius's scores. The recording is first-class, and it is a pity that this issue is only partly successful.

Sir John's tempi in the *Third Symphony* are well-judged, but the inner tension is not maintained. His *Sixth* is better in some respects, though ensemble is not perfect and the orchestral playing not quite up to the standards of the best of the cycle. The recording is very fine indeed, but these performances can only be recommended with qualification to collectors of the whole cycle.

Symphony No. 4 in A minor, Op. 63.
   *** Decca SXL 6365. Vienna Philharmonic Orchestra, Lorin Maazel – *Tapiola*.***
   ** (*) DGG SLPM 138974. Berlin Philharmonic Orchestra, Herbert von Karajan – *Legends: The Swan of Tuonela*.** (*)
   ** (*) Decca SXL 6431. Finnish Radio Orchestra, Paavo Berglund – SALLINEN: *Mauermusik*.** (*).

This is perhaps the most impressive of the Maazel Sibelius cycle. The orchestral tone is less richly upholstered than that of the Berlin Philharmonic in Karajan's account, and the players seem to make much closer contact with the music. Maazel brings to the music great concentration and power: the first movement is as cold and unremitting as one could wish, and throughout the work Maazel comes closer to the atmosphere and mystery of this music than anyone since Beecham. Apart from the slow movement, which could be a little more poetic, and one or two small points, there are no real reservations to be made. The recording is superbly opulent and vivid and the performance stands as the finest at present in the catalogue.

Karajan secures, as always, playing of astonishing tonal beauty and virtuosity from the Berlin Philharmonic. On a first hearing one felt the tone seemed too plush for this stark, severe work. It is as if one were observing the iciness of a Finnish winter landscape from the comfort of a smooth-running, well-heated limousine. Repeated hearings, however, have revealed the strength and power of this performance (sumptuously recorded) and suggest that Karajan has penetrated much closer to the heart of the work than first seemed the case. There is tremendous power and intensity here, yet in the last resort Maazel's account is the more searching.

Berglund's version is highly competitive, well recorded and bleak in atmosphere. Ultimately Maazel has the greater imaginative intensity and the finer orchestral playing, but this account is by no means to be ignored.

Symphony No. 5 in E flat major, Op. 82.
 ** DGG SLPM 138973. Berlin Philharmonic Orchestra, Herbert von Karajan – *Tapiola.***
 (M) ** HMV SXLP 30149. Sinfonia of London, Tauno Hannikäinen – *Karelia suite.****
 (B) * (*) Decca SPA 122. London Symphony Orchestra, Alexander Gibson – *Karelia suite.* (*)

Karajan's account is superbly played, but the richness of orchestral texture and the sophistication of Karajan's approach do not fully reveal the atmosphere of the early sections of the work. The best movement is the finale, where the Berlin Philharmonic brass carry the day superbly in Sibelius's surging chorale theme.

Hannikäinen's performance is sound enough without being in any way outstanding. It is well recorded, though it could do with more atmosphere. Given its price level, it is undoubtedly serviceable.

The fine Decca recording has come up splendidly in the new transfer: the climax of the first movement is especially exciting, and a good deal of the effect comes from the projection and colour of the sound. Gibson's reading is capable, and rises to the climaxes, but does not control the overall tension convincingly. There is a lack of tautness.

Symphony No. 5 in E flat major, Op. 82; En Saga (symphonic poem), *Op. 9.*
 ** (*) HMV ASD 3038. Bournemouth Symphony Orchestra, Paavo Berglund.

Berglund's account of the *Fifth* with the Bournemouth Orchestra has been widely praised. It is certainly recorded with great fidelity, presence and atmosphere, and the orchestral playing is of a uniformly high standard. Berglund's tempi are admirably judged and there is no lack of breadth in this unmannered and conscientious account. At the same time there is a want of mystery and magic that we have often noticed with this conductor. The reading of *En Saga* is likewise straightforward and unmannered.

Symphonies No. 5 in E flat major, Op. 82; 6 in D minor, Op. 104.
 ** (*) CBS 73162. New York Philharmonic Orchestra, Leonard Bernstein.

Bernstein's account of the *Fifth* is admirably straightforward and unmannered. It falls short of being a first recommendation on account of the quality of the recording, which is less well-defined and rich in sonority than its competitors. His *Sixth* is much more competitive, though it is let down by the failure of American orchestras to give real pianissimo tone when required. However, although it does not quite challenge Karajan's *Sixth*, it is a desirable disc.

Symphonies Nos. 5 in E flat major, Op. 82; 7 in C major, Op. 105.
** (*) Decca SXL 6236. Vienna Philharmonic Orchestra, Lorin Maazel.
** (*) HMV ASD 2326. Hallé Orchestra, Sir John Barbirolli.

Maazel's *Fifth Symphony* is terribly fast, though it sets out at the same tempo as do Karajan's and Barbirolli's. His second movement is twice as fast as either of them; hence there is little sense of space or breadth – or for that matter mystery – in this performance. The *Seventh*, on the other hand, is marvellous: this is the greatest account of the work since Koussevitzky's and has a rugged, epic power that is truly thrilling. Indeed the closing pages are as fine as Koussevitzky's, and no praise could be higher. The recording is superlative.

In No. 5 Sir John draws playing of high quality from the Hallé Orchestra. Here they are obviously on top form and play with evident enthusiasm and conviction. Sir John takes an unhurried view of the first movement and one feels a certain lack of the requisite tension and mystery. In the first two movements he is altogether less powerful than, say, Karajan, but the latter's beautifully suave lines and textures do strike an alien chord, and the sparer, less opulent tone of the Hallé has a more authentic Nordic sound to commend it. Sir John's finale is admirably broad and extremely imposing. He takes 32'55" overall, whereas Maazel

rushes through in a mere 27'05". A good performance, not as compelling as Karajan's but much more idiomatic than Maazel's. However, his *Seventh* does not match Maazel's in breadth and majesty.

Symphonies No. 6 in D minor, Op. 104; 7 in C major, Op. 105.
** DGG SLPM 139000. Berlin Philharmonic Orchestra, Herbert von Karajan.

We are badly in need of a new account of the *Sixth*. This present issue was the first in stereo. Karajan had coupled these two works together when he recorded them for EMI with the Philharmonia in the mid 1950s, and in body of sound and tonal range, his earlier recording was superior. This sounds pale and hollow in tone even when the volume is increased (as is sometimes their practice, DGG have cut this at a somewhat low level). The performance has some impressive things to commend it and generates much power, even if the finale is taken at slightly too fast a tempo for comfort. The playing is always magnificent, though Karajan tends to smooth the contours a little too much for this music. His *Seventh* is at times most impressive (it is better recorded than the *Sixth*) but it is ruined by some unacceptable bassoon intonation at one point which really brings one up with a jolt. All in all it does not displace the Maazel; the latter's recording has much more impact too.

Symphony No. 7 in C major, Op. 105; Legends: The Swan of Tuonela, Op. 22/2.
* (**) HMV ASD 2805. Leningrad Philharmonic Orchestra, Yeveny Mravinsky – SHOSTAKOVICH: *Symphony No. 6.****

Mravinsky's is arguably the finest version of the *Seventh* to appear since Koussevitzky. It is more intense and more tautly held together even than Maazel's and has all the electricity of a live performance. It suffers only from the wide vibrato of the Leningrad brass, which robs the majestic trombone theme of some of its nobility. Audience noises are also obtrusive. However, this remains a most worthwhile record. (*The Swan of Tuonela* must be ruled out of court: audience coughs are a constant irritant and prove in the end ruinous.)

Symphony No. 7 in C major, Op. 105 (rev. Berglund); *The Oceanides* (symphonic poem), *Op. 73.*

** HMV ASD 2874. Bournemouth Symphony Orchestra, Paavo Berglund – *Tapiola*.**

Berglund corrects a number of small mistakes that have crept into the Hansen score, mostly dynamic and expressive indications that affect tonal balance. His reading is smoother in contour as a result. The warm, spacious acoustic serves to Latinize this starkest and most powerful of Sibelius symphonies. The effect is more suited to *The Oceanides*.

Tapiola (symphonic poem), *Op. 112.*

*** Decca SXL 6365. Vienna Philharmonic Orchestra, Lorin Maazel – *Symphony No. 4.****

** DGG SLPM 138973. Berlin Philharmonic Orchestra, Herbert von Karajan – *Symphony No. 5.***

** Decca SXL 6432. Finnish Radio Symphony Orchestra, Paavo Berglund – KOKKONEN: *Symphony No. 3.** (*)

** HMV ASD 2874. Bournemouth Symphony Orchestra, Paavo Berglund – *Symphony No. 7 etc.***

As with the *Fourth Symphony* on the reverse, Maazel gives a most impressive account of this score. It is not so atmos-

pheric as Karajan's at the outset but grows in power and impact as it proceeds. Maazel takes the famous storm section far more slowly than any of his colleagues (not excepting Hannikäinen) and it gains immeasurably by his so doing. (Kajanus in his famous old set for the Sibelius Society (SH 191/2) did the same.) All in all this is one of the best *Tapiolas* of the post-war recording scene.

Karajan's performance has splendid atmosphere at the opening, but it tends to light up detail instead of creating a compulsive forward impulse. Of Berglund's two recordings neither has the full measure of the power and sense of desolation this music encompasses, though both are in many ways impressive performances. Neither orchestra is in the luxury class; the Bournemouth has the more flattering acoustic. Maazel or Karajan are the ones to have.

The Tempest (incidental music), *Op. 109; Suites Nos. 1 and 2; In memoriam* (funeral march), *Op. 59.*

** (*) HMV ASD 2961. Royal Liverpool Philharmonic Orchestra, Charles Groves.

The Tempest, Op. 109: Suites Nos. 1 and 2; Scaramouche.

(M) ** Decca Ace of Diamonds SDD 467. Hungarian State Symphony Orchestra, Jussi Jalas.

The EMI version of *The Tempest* music is the finer recording by far. It is naturally balanced and well detailed. In the *Oak-tree* and *The Chorus of the Winds* Groves does not distil the magic that distinguished Beecham's famous mono set, but the playing is eminently satisfactory. There is no alternative account of Sibelius's noble *In memoriam*.

The version by Jussi Jalas also offers a rarity, the music to the dance-pantomime *Scaramouche*, composed during the First World War. It is well worth having on record even if it does not rank with the finest Sibelius. Jussi Jalas is Sibelius's son-in-law and a noted conductor in Finland. His performance of *The Tempest* is every bit as idiomatic as Groves's, though again the last ounce of poetry and mystery eludes him. The balance is not a natural one and the sound badly needs room to expand, but the overall effect that the engineers achieve is far from unmusical.

String quartet in D minor (Voces intimae), Op. 56.

> (M) ** (*) Nonesuch H 71140. Claremont Quartet – ELGAR: *String quartet.** (*)

Voces intimae is Sibelius's only mature quartet; it dates from 1909, just two years before the *Fourth Symphony*. It was the only occasion in later life when he returned to chamber music; his early output includes more than two dozen chamber pieces and there is an early but uncharacteristic quartet, Op. 4. The Claremont Quartet give a finely poised account of the work, the opening breathes naturally, and the inwardness and poetry in the slow movement are matched by a *Lemminkäinen*-like dash in the finale.

Songs: *Arioso; Demanten på Marssnön; Den Första Kyssen; Flickan kom ifrån sin älsklings möte; Höstkväll; Kom nu hit; Men min Fågel märks dock icke; Om Kvällen; På Verandan vid Havet; Säf, säf, susa; Se'n har jag ej frågat mera; Svarta Rosor; Var det en dröm; Våren flyktar hastigt.*

> (M) *** Decca Ace of Diamonds SDD 249. Kirsten Flagstad (soprano), London Symphony Orchestra, Øivin Fjeldstad.

The songs of Sibelius command a much smaller audience than his symphonies, but they are not less reflective of his genius for melody. Some of the songs were orchestrated by the composer, but seven of them remained in their original form (voice and piano) until transformed, usually with great skill, by such arrangers as Jalas, Pingoud, Fougsted, and Hellman. One does not think usually of Flagstad as a performer of art songs, but here her voice of many colours is ideally suited to the music, and she is sympathetically accompanied by Fjeldstad and the LSO. No lover of Sibelius should miss this collection.

(i) *Kullervo symphony, Op. 7. Kuolema* (incidental music), *Op. 44: Scene with cranes. Swanwhite: suite, Op. 54.*

> *** HMV SLS 807 (2 discs). Bournemouth Symphony Orchestra, Paavo Berglund, (i) with Raili Kostia (mezzo-soprano), Usko Viitanen (baritone). Helsinki University Male Voice Choir.

The *Kullervo symphony* is an ambitious five-movement work for two soloists, male-voice choir and orchestra, some seventy or so minutes in length, that Sibelius wrote at the outset of his career in 1892. It brought him national fame and a commission from Kajanus that resulted in *En Saga*. After its first performance Sibelius withdrew the score and it was never performed in its entirety until 1958, a year after his death. It is revealed here as an impressive work, full of original touches, particularly in its thoroughly characteristic opening. Naturally there are immaturities: the slow movement is overlong and overtly Tchaikovskian. What impresses, however, is the powerful vocal writing, and the astonishing purity and dark, black tone of the Finnish choir. There are many exciting facets of Sibelius's early style to be found in this rewarding score, which is spectacularly well recorded. The fourth side offers some attractive rarities that enhance the value of this impressive set.

893

Luonnotar (for soprano and orchestra), *Op. 70.*

> *** HMV ASD 2486. Gwyneth Jones (soprano), London Symphony Orchestra, Antal Dorati – *En Saga etc.*** (*)

Luonnotar, one of Sibelius's most deeply original and totally inspired compositions, is a short tone poem for soprano and orchestra on a text from the *Kalevala* telling of the creation of the universe. The taxing soprano role is splendidly sung by Gwyneth Jones and Dorati accompanies most idiomatically.

Simpson, Robert
(born 1921)

Symphony No. 3.

> (M) *** Unicorn UNS 225. London Symphony Orchestra, Jascha Horenstein.

All credit to Unicorn for recording a fine powerful British symphony in an excellent performance under a great conductor. Robert Simpson, himself an authority on Nielsen and Bruckner and a purposeful propagandist on behalf of Havergal Brian, has sometimes had his own music related to these favourite composers of his, but in fact this symphony, written in 1962, is striking in its own right. It is in two long movements, the first hammering home in a developed sonata structure the contrast of adjacent tonal centres, B flat against C; the second combining the functions of slow movement, scherzo and finale in a gradually accelerating tempo. There is something Sibelian in the way that in the first movement Simpson gradually brings together fragments of musical ideas, but generally this is a work which within its frankly tonal idiom asks to be considered in Simpson's own individual terms. The sound is first-rate.

Skalkottas, Nikos
(1904–49)

(i) *Octet;* (ii) *String quartet No. 3;* (iii) *8 Variations on a Greek folk tune* (for piano trio).

> *** Argo ZRG 753. (i) Melos Ensemble; (ii) Dartington Quartet; (iii) Marcel Gazelle (piano), Robert Masters (violin), Derek Simpson (cello).

This disc forms an admirable introduction to the music of the Greek composer Nikos Skalkottas. He was for some time a pupil of Schoenberg, but his musical language has a greater luxuriance of texture than his master's. In a sense it would have been better to introduce some of his orchestral music to the catalogue, as that seems more likely to arouse public interest than his chamber works. He was a prolific composer and was cruelly neglected in Athens. The finest of the three works on the present disc is probably the *Third Quartet*, which has an integrity that is commanding. The *Octet* is a relaxed piece by comparison, though one is left with the feeling that it would like to be even more relaxed than it is. This reissue is well worth investigating and the performances are as dedicated as the recording is faithful.

Smetana, Bedřich
(1824–84)

Symphonic poems: *Carnival in Prague; Hakon Jarl, Op. 16; Richard III, Op. 11; Wallenstein's Camp, Op. 14.*

> *** DGG 2530 248. Bavarian Radio Symphonic Orchestra, Rafael Kubelik.

These symphonic poems can be recommended to those who are attracted to the *Má Vlast* cycle. *Carnival in Prague* was written in 1883; the other three are much earlier works, dating from around 1860. The music is melodramatic, with a flavour of Dvořák if without that master's imaginative flair. The most spectacular is *Wallenstein's Camp* with its opportunities for offstage brass fanfares, very well managed here. This is very enjoyable in its ingenuous way, but perhaps the most distinguished piece here is *Hakon Jarl*, which has a strong vein of full-blooded romanticism. The playing is first-class throughout, the conductor's approach is fresh and committed, and the recording has excellent body and atmosphere,

Czech dances: *Furiant; The Little Hen; The Lancer; Obkročak; Skočná. Polkas: Louisa; Dahlia; From the Student's Life; The Country Woman; Bettina; To our Girls.*

   (M) ** Supraphon 110 1225. Brno State Philharmonic Orchestra, František Jilek.

The Czech dances were originally piano pieces and they have been orchestrated by other hands. This is all sparkling music, vividly played; the recording is clear but lacking something in bloom and atmosphere.

Festive symphony in E major.

   (M) * (*) Supraphon SUAST 50875. Czech Philharmonic Orchestra, Karel Sejna.

Smetana's *Festive symphony* quotes from the Austrian National anthem (the tune by Haydn), and like many occasional pieces (it was composed for, but never played at, the wedding of the Emperor) it is not very distinguished music, apart from an attractive scherzo. The performance makes the most of it, but the recording is not one of Supraphon's best.

Má Vlast (Vyšehrad; Vltava (Moldau); Sárka; From Bohemia's Woods and Fields; Tábor; Blanik).

   ** (*) DGG 2707 054 (2 discs). Boston Symphony Orchestra, Rafael Kubelik.

   (M) ** (*) Telefunken KT 11043(1/2). Leipzig Gewandhaus Orchestra, Václav Neumann.

   (M) ** HMV SXLP 20064 *(Vyšehrad; Vltava; Sárka; From Bohemia's Woods and Fields)*. Royal Philharmonic Orchestra, Sir Malcolm Sargent.

   (M) * HMV SXLP 20065 *(Tábor; Blaník)*. Royal Philharmonic Orchestra, Sargent (with DVOŘÁK: *Symphonic variations**).

   (M) ** Supraphon 50521/2. Czech Philharmonic Orchestra, Karel Ančerl.

   (M) * Decca Ace of Diamonds SDD 161/2. Vienna Philharmonic Orchestra, Rafael Kubelik.

Kubelik's DGG performance is much more perceptive and penetrating than his earlier Decca set. He is careful to temper the bombast which too readily comes to the surface in this music (in *Tábor* and *Blaník* especially), and his skill with the inner balance of the orchestration brings much felicitous detail. The performances of the two unquestioned masterpieces of the cycle, *Vltava* and *From Bohemia's Woods and Fields*, are very well made, and throughout the orchestral playing is first-class. Just occasionally a touch more flair would have brought the orchestral colours out more vividly, but this lack of colour is partly caused by the DGG sound, which, although admirably brilliant and clear, rather lacks sumptuousness and warmth of texture. However, this has the advantage that the louder, brassy passages are not allowed to degenerate into noise.

Many may consider the medium-priced

Telefunken set a viable alternative. The characterization is considerably less vivid than Kubelik's, but the recording is well projected if not especially refined. The orchestral playing is good.

Sir Malcolm Sargent's performances are not so individual and imaginative as those under Kubelik but they are warmly recorded. The disc containing four of the works (SXLP 20064), including the two most famous, is an attractive proposition at the price, but the companion disc is less recommendable. Sargent is unable to temper the bombast and rhetoric of *Tábor* and *Blaník*, and the Dvořák coupling is not especially winning.

Ančerl's performances have more character than Sargent's (although not so much more) but he is let down by the Supraphon recording, which sounds artificially brightened, for it is hardedged and not quite natural. It has more body, however, than the Ace of Diamonds set. This must be discounted on grounds of recording. The strings are thin and papery, the high treble peaky, and there is a feeling of congestion at climaxes. The Vienna Philharmonic are on good form, but Kubelik's readings here are somewhat lacking in purpose and colour.

Má Vlast: Vltava; From Bohemia's Woods and Fields.

(M) ** (*) DGG Privilege 2538 313. Boston Symphony Orchestra, Rafael Kubelik – DVOŘÁK: *String serenade.****

It was a happy idea to couple the two favourites from *Má Vlast* with Dvořák's *String serenade*. Hearing them out of context, however, one is more conscious that the recordings, while admirably clear and well-balanced, are slightly dry and lacking in atmosphere.

Má Vlast: Vltava.

** (*) HMV ASD 2863. Berlin Philharmonic Orchestra, Herbert von Karajan – DVOŘÁK: *Symphony No. 9.** (*)*

Má Vlast: Vyšehrad; Vltava.

** (*) DGG SLPM 139037. Berlin Philharmonic Orchestra, Herbert von Karajan – LISZT: *Hungarian rhapsody No. 2; Les Préludes.***

Vltava is such a well made piece that it cannot but suit the virtuoso conductor, who has only to conjure first-rate playing, following the score, and the music makes its own points. Karajan brings the music fully alive and he is also most persuasive in the beautiful opening and closing pages of *Vyšehrad*, dominated by the bard-like harp. The central section is less convincing, but perhaps this is partly the composer's fault. Brilliant recording.

Karajan's earlier performance of *Vltava* was a good one, and it still sounds well. It makes a generous filler for his excellent early account of the *New World.*

Má Vlast: Vltava; The Bartered Bride: Overture; Polka; Furiant.

(B) *** Decca SPA 202. Israel Philharmonic Orchestra, Istvan Kertestz – DVOŘÁK: *Slavonic dances.****

With Kertesz these pieces are exceptionally vivid. The separate entries in the overture are beautifully positioned by the stereo, and the ambience makes the background rustle of all the strings weaving away at their fugato theme sound quite captivating. *Vltava* too is very brilliant, with fast tempi, yet not losing its picturesque qualities. The recording is perhaps over-bright, but it glows in Decca's best fashion. It is a shade over-reverberant but not seriously so. With its excellent coupling this is a fine bargain.

Má Vlast: Vltava; The Bartered Bride: Polka; Dance of the Comedians.

** Decca Phase 4 PFS 4245. London Philharmonic Orchestra, Stanley

Black – DVOŘÁK: *Slavonic dances*.**

Stanley Black's performances with the LPO are outstandingly well recorded, with spacious, sparkling sound. *Vltava* is affectionately done, the individual incidents in the progress of the river portrayed with character, if a little at the expense of the forward impulse of the work as a whole. The dances are lively, but lack something in idiomatic rhythmic lift. But with such good sound and obvious commitment from the orchestra, this is easy to enjoy and will suit those for whom brilliance of recording is of prime importance.

Piano trio in G minor, Op. 15.
   *** Philips 6500 133. Beaux Arts Trio – CHOPIN: *Piano trio*.***

Smetana's *Piano trio* is a fine work, and given such powerful advocacy as that of the Beaux Arts Trio (and in particular their fine pianist, Menahem Pressler) and the superbly vivid and truthful Philips recording, there is nothing in the way of a strong recommendation. The Chopin is not a mature work but the coupling is still an attractive and logical one.

Choruses: *The Dedication; Festive chorus; My Star; Our Song; The Peasant; The Prayer; The Renegade I and II; Song of the Sea; The Sunset; The Swallows Arrived; The Three Riders; Two Slogans.*
   (M) ** Supraphon 112 1143. Czech Philharmonic Chorus, Josef Veselka.

Apart from three short items, all the choruses here are for male voices. The writing has plenty of vigour, and the singing here makes up in enthusiasm for what it lacks in refinement. The idiomatic quality of the Czech language brings a special colour to the music, and with translations provided this is an enjoyably spontaneous concert.

The Bartered Bride (opera in 3 acts): complete recording.
   (M) ** (*) Supraphon SUAST 50397/9. Drahomira Tikalová (soprano), Oldrich Kovár, Ivo Zídek (tenors), Eduard Haken (bass), Prague National Theatre Chorus and Orchestra, Zdenek Chalabala.

Though the Supraphon recording – particularly of the chorus – is limited in range and atmosphere, Chalabala directs an authentic and enjoyable account of this irrepressible comic opera. The principal soloists, though not always ideally sweet on the ear, give distinctive and idiomatic performances that plainly stem from long experience in the opera-house.

The Bartered Bride: Overture; Polka; Furiant; Dance of the Comedians.
   (M) ** HMV SXLP 30125. Royal Philharmonic Orchestra, Rudolf Kempe – DVOŘÁK: *Scherzo capriccioso***; WEINBERGER: *Schwanda the Bagpiper*.* (*)

The new transfer of this reissue loses none of the original warmth, but by adding slightly more edge to the sound, it increases the brilliance. The performances are attractive if without the last degree of sparkle.

Dalibor (opera in 3 Acts): complete recording.
   (M) ** Supraphon 112 0241/3. Vilém Přibyl (tenor), Jindrich Jinrák, Antonin Svorc (baritones), Jaroslav Horácek (bass), Naděžda Kniplová (soprano), Prague National Theatre Chorus and Orchestra, Jaroslav Krombholc.

Smetana's *Dalibor*, with its plot of the imprisoned hero's lover disguised as the gaoler's assistant, readily evokes associations with *Fidelio*, and if the music is not on the level of Beethoven's masterpiece, its invention is often vivid and the work has considerable interest. Here Vilém Přibyl is excellent in the name part, and his eloquence is matched by Naděžda Kniplová as Milada. The rest of the cast are reliable, and with an idiomatic contribution from chorus and orchestra and an atmospheric if not very refined recording, this is worth investigating.

Libuse (opera in 3 acts): complete recording.

(M) * (*) Supraphon SUAST 507014 (4 discs). Milada Subrtová, Naděžda Kniplová (sopranos), Václav Bednář (baritone), Zdeněk Kroupa (bass), Ivo Zídek (tenor), Prague National Theatre Chorus and Orchestra, Jaroslav Krombholc.

Written for the opening of the National Theatre of Prague in 1881, this strongly nationalist piece (the plot is concerned with the Czech royal dynasty) has a limited appeal for the non-Czech listener. The characters are two-dimensional and the opera itself has little real dramatic development. The cast here is strong by Czech standards, but the recording is only fair. For the specialist rather than the ordinary opera-lover.

Smyth, Ethel
(1858–1944)

The Wreckers: overture.

*** HMV ASD 2400. Scottish National Orchestra, Alexander Gibson – HARTY: *Wild Geese:* MACCUNN; *Land of Mountain and Flood;* GERMAN: *Welsh rhapsody.****

Ethel Smyth, one of the first emancipated English feminists, almost unbelievably managed to get all six of her operas produced during the time when the suffragette movement was gathering momentum. The best-known is *The Wreckers* (first performed in England in 1909), and we must hope that one day the piece will be revived. Meanwhile the *Overture* is a strong meaty piece, which shows the calibre of this remarkable woman's personality, for while the material itself is not memorable it is put together most compellingly and orchestrated with real flair. The story concerns the wrecking of ships by false signal lights on the Cornish coast.

Soler, Antonio
(1729–83)

Concertos for 2 (solo) *keyboard instruments: Nos. 1 in G minor* (a); *2 in A minor* (b); *3 in G major* (a); *4 in F major* (c); *5 in A major* (c); *6 in D major* (b).

(B) *** Turnabout TV 34136S. Anthony Newman and Joseph Payne ((a) organ and harpsichord; (b) 2 harpsichords; (c) 2 organs).

Soler is an individual composer who has a quantity of keyboard music much influenced by Domenico Scarlatti to his credit. He has less character than his illustrious model and is in many respects more conventional, but he still has the capacity to offer surprising and original touches.

This is perhaps the most imaginatively planned of the available Soler recordings, since the artists have sought to vary the tonal resources by playing these double concertos on a variety of instrumental combinations. The listening ear is thus provided with plenty of tonal contrast and change of timbre, which (in the course of six works by the same composer) is surely a necessity. This is not to imply that Soler's music is repetitive or cut to a pattern: on the contrary it is full of novel ideas, piquant harmonies, and enchanting melodies. There is much to be said for the skilful engineering whereby the different placing of the instruments allows true echo effects, as well as stereo separation, to be accomplished. The recordings were made in the Passionist Monastery Church of St Gabriel in Boston, Mass. Newman and Payne both exhibit musical sense and taste, in addition to virtuosity.

Piano sonatas in D major; F sharp major; C minor; G major; C minor; F major.
> (B) ** Saga 5343/4. Mario Miranda (piano) – GRANADOS: *Goyescas.***

A useful addition to our knowledge of Soler is provided by these accomplished performances of six of his keyboard sonatas. The recording is good, and this makes an imaginative filler for the *Goyescas* recording.

Sor, Fernando
(1778–1839)

24 Studies for guitar.
> *** DGG SLPM 139364. Narciso Yepes (guitar).

This is not a set of studies but a selection from various sets made by Narciso Yepes. The music is on the whole slight, like most guitar pieces, but its ingenuous facility, given such brilliant and imaginative playing, has certain rewards, although this is a specialist record rather than

one to recommend generally. The recording is immaculate.

Sousa, John Philip
(1854–1932)

Marches: *Beau Ideal; The Corcoran Cadets; The Directorate; El Capitan; Fairest of the Fair; The Freelance March; King Cotton; Nation Fencibles; Our Flirtations; Occidental march; The Picadore; Semper Sousa.*
> ** Columbia Studio 2 TWO 385. Men o'Brass: combined Fairey's, Foden's, and City of Coventry bands, Harry Mortimer.

It is a pity that EMI have gone for brilliance here above all else. Their recording team have made such magnificent brass and military band records in the past, the rich middle sonorities superbly caught; but here the cymbals, recorded with a slightly exaggerated metallic clamour, seem to dominate and there is not a compensating weight in the bass. The performances have plenty of vigour and spirit, and at times a certain sophistication too.

Marches: *Belle of Chicago; The Crusader; The Gladiator; The Gridiron Club; Hands across the Sea; High School Cadets; Invincible Eagle; The Liberty Bell; Manhattan Beach; Semper fidelis; Stars and Stripes Forever; The Thunderer; Washington Post.*
> ** Columbia Studio 2 TWO 113. Massed (brass) bands of BMC, Fairey's, Foden's, Harry Mortimer.

Sousa sounds his best on a military rather than a brass band, but these performances, although essentially English rather than American in style, are breezy

899

and attractive. The Studio 2 sound again emphasizes brilliance at the expense of middle, and there are some spectacular two-speaker side-drum effects used as introductions.

Marches: *Belle of Chicago; Daughters of Texas; The Diplomat; El Capitan; The Gladiator; The Gridiron Club; Hail to the Spirit of Liberty; Kansas Wildcats; King Cotton; National Game; New York Hippodrome; Solid Men to the Front; Sound Off; The Thunderer.*
> ** (*) Columbia Studio 2 TWO 235. HM Royal Marines Band, Lt-Col. Vivian Dunn.

These are vigorous, essentially British performances, with self-assured aplomb in the place of transatlantic exuberance. The band is on top form and plays superbly. The recording too is brilliant, matching clarity with sonority, and it is a pity it is so forward, so that dynamic range is reduced. But the playing itself has plenty of sparkle.

Marches: *El Capitan; Hands across the Sea; High School Cadets; The Invincible Eagle; King Cotton; Liberty Bell; Manhattan Beach; The Picadore; Semper fidelis; Stars and Stripes Forever; The Thunderer; Washington Post.*
> *** Decca Phase 4 PFS 4134. Grenadier Guards Band, Major Rodney Bashford.

The buoyant breeziness of the presentation here is admirable and the piccolo solo in *Stars and Stripes* floats out beautifully. If only Decca could add to the presence and bite the kind of middle range EMI can achieve with their incomparable military-band recordings this would be even more recommendable. But this is still a three-star disc and includes a highly enjoyable programme

of some of Sousa's best and most famous pieces.

Spohr, Ludwig
(1784–1859)

Clarinet concerto No. 1 in C minor, Op. 26.
> (M) ** Oiseau-Lyre SOL 60035. Gervase de Peyer (clarinet), London Symphony Orchestra, Colin Davis – WEBER: *Clarinet concerto No. 2.***

Clearly modelled on Mozart's masterpiece, Spohr's *Concerto* primarily exploits the lyrical side of the clarinet. The main theme of the first movement, besides being the kind that stays in the memory, is perfectly conceived for the instrument, and the *Adagio* – very much Mozart-patterned – is charming too. The finale is a captivating Spanish rondo. It chuckles its way along in sparkling fashion and then surprises the listener by ending gently. Gervase de Peyer is just the man for these suave melodic lines, and he is ably supported by Davis and the LSO. The stereo is well detailed and the recording convincing, except for a suspicion of stridency in the tuttis.

Clarinet concerto No. 2 in E flat major, Op. 57.
> (B) ** Oryx ORYX 1828. John Denman (clarinet), Sadler's Wells Opera Orchestra, Hazel Vivienne – STAMITZ: *Clarinet concerto No. 3.* (*)

A fine, strong performance of a first-rate concerto. John Denman's tone is not as melting as it could be, but his playing does not want character, and he is especially good in the work's infectiously brilliant finale. The recording is clear rather than rich, but the orchestral accompaniment has plenty of life.

Violin concertos Nos. 8 in A minor (Gesangszene), Op. 47; 9 in D minor, Op. 55.

(M) ** Oiseau-Lyre SOL 278. Hyman Bress (violin), Symphony Orchestra, Beck.

These are two quite striking concertos, No. 8 in the fairly free form 'of a vocal scena', but well handled to make the most of contrast rather than cohesion, and No. 9 more conventional but with a gay finale. In both concertos Spohr favours a characteristic device of writing a lyrical passage above a pizzicato bass. In No. 8 this makes for a very successful episode in the finale, and in No. 9 he uses it in the *Adagio* with equal effect. Hyman Bress shows a good grasp of the music's basic style, and if the recording in its clarity emphasizes his rather thin tone and tendency to scratchiness in the very florid writing, on the whole he is convincing. Good recording.

Nonet in F major, Op. 31; Double quartet in E minor, Op. 87.

(M) ** Decca Ace of Diamonds SDD 416. Members of the Vienna Octet.

The playing of the *Nonet* is immaculate, but the atmosphere of the music-making is less friendly and spontaneous. The scherzo comes off well, but the *Adagio*, taken very slowly, never smiles. However, the Decca recording fits the work on one side and makes room for the *Double Quartet* on the other. This is what might well be described as a well-wrought piece, but although it begins with some imaginative antiphony the music itself is unmemorable. The recording, suave in texture, very sensibly makes the most of the interplay between the various melodic lines without exaggerated separation.

Octet in E major, Op. 32 (for violin, two violas, cello, clarinet, two horns and double-bass).

(M) *** Decca Ace of Diamonds SDD 256. Members of the Vienna Octet – BEETHOVEN: *Piano and wind quintet.****

Spohr's *Octet* is a work of great charm, and the variations on Handel's *Harmonious Blacksmith* which form one of the central movements offer that kind of naïveté which (when stylishly played) makes for delicious listening. The playing is expert here, the five strings blending perfectly with the two horns and clarinet, and altogether this is a most winning performance. The recording is fresh and open, rich in tone with the right kind of resonance, and leaves little to be desired. This is a most attractive record in every way.

Piano and wind quintet in C minor, Op. 52.

(M) ** (*) Decca Ace of Diamonds SDD 423. Members of the Vienna Octet – DVOŘÁK: *String quintet.*** (*)

The piano dominates Spohr's Op. 52 *Quintet* throughout and the music has a suave fluency, with rippling perpetuum mobile figurations which in the end outwear their welcome. Melodically this is not one of Spohr's most appealing works. Performance and recording alike do their best to project music which is essentially vapid.

Stainer, John
(1840–1901)

The Crucifixion.

(B) *** Argo SPA 267. Richard Lewis (tenor), Owen Brannigan (bass), St John's College Choir, Cambridge, George Guest; Brian Runnett (organ).

(B) *** Classics for Pleasure CFP 40067. David Hughes (tenor), John Lawrenson (bass), Guildford Cathedral Choir, Barry Rose; Gavin Williams (organ).

(B) ** (*) EMI Starline SRS 5154. Alexander Young (tenor), Donald Bell (bass), Leeds Philharmonic Choir, Herbert Bargett; Eric Chadwick (organ).

The music of Stainer's famous *Crucifixion* (written in 1887) is central to the tradition of nineteenth-century English oratorio and owes not a little to the Mendelssohn of *Elijah*. It is not melodically distinguished and includes such harmonic clichés as the cadence at the climax of *Fling wide the gates, the Saviour waits* (but one cannot be surprised at that, since the couplet is not the happiest choice of rhyme). There are five hymns in which the congregation is invited to join: the Classics for Pleasure version omits one of these but the Argo version is complete. All three recordings here are of fine quality, the Argo and Classics for Pleasure forward with clear projection of the words (the CFP version – which is perhaps the best judged recording of all – is exceptionally clear). The HMV sound is more recessed, with a 'churchier' ambient effect. Owen Brannigan is splendidly dramatic and his voice makes a good foil for the tenor in the duets, but on the other hand the lyrical manner of Alexander Young is very pleasing. The choral singing is more polished in Cambridge than in Leeds, but is very professional at Guildford too. John Lawrenson makes a movingly eloquent contribution to this performance, and it is very difficult to choose between this and the Argo record.

Stamitz, Karl
(1745–1801)

(i) *Bassoon concerto in F major;* (ii) *Clarinet concerto No. 3 in B flat major;* (iii) *Flute concerto in G major.*

(B) ** Turnabout TV 34093S. (i) George Zukerman (bassoon), Württemberg Chamber Orchestra, Joerg Faerber; (ii) David Glazer (clarinet), Innsbruck Symphony Orchestra, Robert Wagner; (iii) Camillo Wanausek (flute), Vienna Musikgesellschaft, Anton Heiller.

Of these three concertos by Karl Stamitz, the *Clarinet concerto* is the most individual, showing a touch of humour in its passage-work for the soloist. The other concertos are typical of their period but pleasant rather than memorable. All three performances are good ones, and the Vox recording is vivid, if not refined.

Clarinet concerto No. 3 in B flat major.

(B) * (*) Oryx ORYX 1828. John Denman (clarinet), Sadler's Wells Opera Orchestra, Hazel Vivienne – SPOHR: *Clarinet concerto No. 2.***

Denman's performance is not as attractive as Glazer's (see above) but the accompaniment is a lively one, and if the coupling (the Spohr *Concerto* is a fine one) is wanted this performance is not wanting in character. The recording is clear but the clarinet tone is rather hard.

Piano concerto in F major.

(B) ** Turnabout TV 34001S. Felicja Blumenthal (piano), Württemberg Chamber Orchestra, Joerg Faerber – PAISIELLO: *Piano concerto.***

This is a concerto of almost Mozartian

charm, and the performance here is very pleasing. Both soloist and conductor are obviously taken with the felicity of the writing and they give a persuasive account of it, well recorded.

(i) *Viola concerto in D major, Op. 1;* (ii) *Sinfonia concertante in D major for violin, viola with orchestra.*

> (B) *** Turnabout TV 34221S. Ernst Wallfisch (viola), (i) Württemberg Chamber Orchestra, Joerg Faerber; (ii) Susanne Lautenbacher (violin), Stuttgart Soloists

Two charming examples of Stamitz's virile music-making. He may not match his great contemporary, Mozart, but he is a personality in his own right, and such a work as the *Viola concerto*, with its magnificently expansive first movement, its deeply felt D minor slow movement, and its exhilarating finale, is music that should clearly be in the repertory. As for the *Sinfonia concertante*, nearly if not quite so interesting in its material, its historic link with Mozart's work for the same combination makes it fascinating listening. The performances have the keen vigour one expects of these two chamber groups, and though the solo instruments are balanced too closely, the playing is warmly committed as well as stylish.

Violoncello concerto in A major.

> (B) ** Turnabout TV 34362S. Thomas Blees (cello), Württemberg Chamber Orchestra, Joerg Faerber – DUSSEK: *Piano concerto.***

Thomas Blees is an uncommonly good cellist and he gives a highly eloquent account of the fine slow movement of Stamitz's *Cello concerto* and a beautifully turned performance of the delightfully gay finale. The recording balances him far too near the microphone, and while some improvement can be effected with the controls, in the first movement

the buzziness of the cello tone (in no way the soloist's fault) tends to interfere with the music's appeal. But this is a three-star performance and in spite of the technical drawback the work is very much worth investigating.

Sinfonia concertante in D major for violin, viola with orchestra.

> *** CBS Quadraphonic MQ 31369; Stereo 73030. Isaac Stern (violin), Pinchas Zukerman (viola), English Chamber Orchestra, Daniel Barenboim – MOZART: *Sinfonia concertante.****

A relatively lightweight but enjoyable fill-up to a superb account of Mozart's great *Sinfonia concertante* – again giving these vital artists an opportunity to strike musical sparks off each other. The quadraphonic version adds marginal extra warmth and atmosphere to the recording but does not affect the unnaturally forward balance of the soloists.

Stanley, John
(1713–86)

Concertos, Op. 2: Nos. 1 in D major; 2 in B minor; 3 in G major; 5 in A major; 6 in E flat major.

> (M) *** Oiseau-Lyre SOL 315. Hurwitz Chamber Orchestra, Emanuel Hurwitz; Charles Spinks (harpsichord).

Concertos, Op. 2: Nos. 1 in D major (for strings); *2 in B minor* (for organ and strings); *3 in G major* (for organ and strings); *4 in D minor* (for strings); *5 in A major; 6 in E flat major* (both for harpsichord and strings).

> (B) ** Oryx ORYX 1742. Harold Lester (organ or harpsichord), Little Orchestra of London, Leslie Jones.

John Stanley was a blind musician who seems to have inspired much affection among his contemporaries. Certainly these concertos show him to have been a composer of genuine talent who need not fear comparison with some of his lesser contemporaries on the Continent. There is a genuine lyrical gift, even though the influence of Handel is dominant. Of the two recordings the Hurwitz offers the better performances and sound-quality but includes only five of the concertos. The Oryx record offers all six, but with organ or harpsichord featured as a solo instrument, and the performances, though well prepared. are not as elegantly engineered.

Organ voluntaries: in D minor, Op. 5/6; in D minor, Op. 5/8; in G minor, Op. 6/2; in D major, Op. 6/6; in A minor, Op. 6/8; in D major, Op. 7/5; in F major, Op. 7/6; in E minor, Op. 7/7.
> *** Argo ZRG 745. Richard Elfyn Jones (Walker organ of University College, Cardiff).

Stanley's so-called *Voluntaries* vary richly from the simple slow-fast form of movement to three-movement and four-movement works, and even a prelude and fugue. Often echoing the great Mr Handel, Stanley produces a colourful and invigorating sequence of ideas, well played and recorded here on a new instrument which produces fine, ringing trumpet tone.

Still, Robert
(1910–70)

(i) *Symphony No. 3;* (ii) *Symphony No. 4.*
> ** Lyrita SRCS 46. (i) London Symphony Orchestra, Sir Eugene

Goossens; (ii) Royal Philharmonic Orchestra, Myer Fredman.

Robert Still was a gifted composer and a very considerable musician. His *Third Symphony* is an expertly written piece (the opening sounds a bit Prokofievian and is undeniably attractive), though the slow movement is lacking in depth. It is extremely well played and recorded. Not a work perhaps that one would wish to hear often but not by any means a negligible piece. The *Fourth Symphony* is inspired by a psychological case-history and reflects the composer's interest and specialized knowledge of psychiatry. The RPO respond well for Myer Fredman and are well recorded. A useful disc.

Stockhausen, Karlheinz
(born 1928)

Gesang der Jünglinge; Kontakte.
> ** (*) DGG 138811. Realization under the direction of the composer.

This was the first of the DGG series under the direction of the composer. *Gesang der Jünglinge* was originally conceived in terms of five channels (quintophony?), while *Kontakte* is quadraphonic. No doubt one day we shall be offered quadraphonic versions of both, but meanwhile it can be assumed that the use of a mere two channels gives some idea of the composer's original intentions. *Gesang* uses words as its raw material for electronic improvisation (with allusions to the fiery furnace from the Book of Daniel). *Kontakte* is electronic music in its own right. (The work exists in two versions, and the other is also available; see below.) The effect of all the music here depends partly on spatial imagery, and this, of course, the present disc can only partially realize.

Gruppen (for 3 orchestras); (i) *Carré* (for 4 orchestras and 4 choirs).

(M) *** DGG 137002. Cologne Radio Symphony Orchestra, (i) North German Radio Symphony Orchestra and Chorus; cond. the composer; Maderna; Gielen; Kagel; Markowski.

Gruppen has made a powerful impact even among those listeners who do nót normally count themselves Stockhausen admirers. With the three orchestras spread around the arena of the Royal Albert Hall in a Prom performance, it was enormously impressive, and though a two-channel recorded version cannot convey anything like the same atmosphere, this attempt is effective enough with the three separate bands brilliantly conducted by Bruno Maderna, Michael Gielen and Stockhausen himself. *Carré* in the spread of forces used goes even further, with four orchestras and four choirs, and the recording here is even more impressive, very vivid indeed. What comes out of both these works is that ultimately they are not going to be judged by any sonic tricks, but whether they convey emotion not just once but on repeated hearings. There is little doubt that, given a receptive listener, both *Gruppen* and *Carré* can make an impact comparable with that of the musical masterpieces which follow more recognizable rules. What matters is the composer's imagination, aural and emotional, and in these two works it is at its clearest.

Kontakte for electronic sounds, piano and percussion; Refrain for three instrumentalists.

(M) *** Vox STGBY 638. Aloys Kontarsky, Christoph Caskel (piano and percussion), the composer (celesta, cymbales antiques), musical supervision by the composer.

At a modest price this is an excellent disc for anyone looking for a sample of Stockhausen's later electronic music. Like other more expensive Stockhausen discs, this offers authoritative performances under the direction of the composer himself, with his most dedicated henchman, Aloys Kontarsky. When chance rules so much in scores such as this, the composer's collaboration is more than usually desirable. The mixture in *Kontakte* of electronic and natural sounds is splendidly caught. This is the alternative version of this work: the other version, which is purely electronic, is also available (see above).

Mantra.

*** DGG 2530 208. Alfons and Aloys Kontarsky (piano), the composer (ring modulator).

Written in 1970, *Mantra* represents a welcome return by Stockhausen from his wilder electronic inspirations. Though a ring modulator is used to modify the timbre of the piano tone in places during this massive sixty-five-minute structure, purely musical procedures, cogently employed, are what holds it together, along with the intense, committed playing of the Kontarsky brothers, for whom the piece was written. Excellent recording.

(i) *Mixtur for orchestra, sine-wave generators and ring modulators* (version for small orchestra); (ii) *Telemusik.*

(M) ** (*) DGG 137012. (i) Hudba Dneska Ensemble, Bratislava, Ladislav Kupkovic; directed by the composer; (ii) NKH Studios, Tokyo.

Telemusik stems from a visit Stockhausen made to Japan. Rather in the manner of *Hymnen* it is a musical collage of varying sources of experience, not the crude sort of collage that John Cage developed but one in which electronic

905

developments of each element fuse the texture together more subtly, more effectively. *Mixtur* is based on orchestral sounds electronically distorted, a common enough practice, and made individual here only by the aural imagination of Stockhausen. One has to take it largely on trust that the formal beauties of Stockhausen's massive, or at least very long, structures are as cogently put together as his adoring admirers tell us. If you want examples of Stockhausen's electronic music that recognizably show his individual imagination, then this is an excellent disc to get.

Prozession (for tamtam, viola, elektronium, piano, filters, and potentiometers).

(M) *** Vox STGBY 615. Alfred Alings (tamtam), Rolf Gehlhaar (tamtam), Johannes Fritsch (viola), Harald Bojè (elektronium), Aloys Kontarsky (piano), the composer (filters and potentiometers).

The title refers to the concept of the work as a procession of ideas and excerpts from Stockhausen's earlier works. That may sound intolerably narcissistic but in fact the composer is asking his players to delve back in their experience of his music and form an 'aural tradition' for the performance. This was one of the first important scores in which Stockhausen developed aleatory techniques, with the performer required to react to material which he and his colleagues had already presented. In addition electronic devices are used to modify and distort the sounds. All this has now become common practice, and one might well object that the recording of any particular performance is defeating the composer's aim of freedom for the performers. What matters here is that Stockhausen – whether as composer or merely as electronic wizard on filters

and potentiometers – conveys an undoubted cohesion in the procession of sound. On a mid-price disc it is well worth investigating, even by those not normally drawn to the avant-garde. Impressive recording quality.

Stimmung (Tuning) (for 6 vocalists).

** (*) DGG 2543 003. Collegium Vocale Cologne at the Rheinische Musikschüle, directed by the composer.

There are those who have claimed this as the most beautiful music of the twentieth century, and certainly it is unforgettable, because the six vocalists perform in what approximates to a transcendental trance, never rising above the softest dynamics, and using a range of gentle vocal effects that might provide material for the psychiatrist's consulting room, both for analysis and for use in soothing the patient. It is a remarkable *tour de force*, but the experience it provides is not one to repeat too often, unless it is merely required for background. The six singers under the composer's direction, all of them young, are obviously dedicated in their sensitive singing.

'Greatest hits': excerpts from: *Aufwärts (Upwards): Carré: Es-It; Gruppen* (for 3 orchestras); *Hymnen, 4. Region; Kontakte; Kurzwellen (Short waves); Mantra for 2 pianos; Opus 1970; Song of the youths; Stimmung (Tuning); Telemusik.*

(M) *** DGG 2612 023 (2 discs). Directed by the composer.

Anyone wanting to see what the fuss over Stockhausen has been about will find this an ideal sampler. Where the original works tend to expand uninhibitedly, these crisp five-minute snippets, well chosen, show you what musical imagination lies behind each work without letting you get bored. Generally spectacular recording.

Straus, Oscar
(1870–1954)

Ein Walzertraum (A Waltz Dream;
operetta): abridged version.
> (M) ** Telefunken NT 779. Else
> Liebesberg, Eva Kasper, Elisabeth Sobota, Peter Minich, Herbert Prikopá, Hans Strohbauer,
> Roland Neumann, Vienna Volksoper Chorus and Orchestra, Franz
> Bauer-Theussl.

The sense of style and original language give the Vienna recording an authentic flavour, and with excellent singing from the principals all is thoroughly enjoyable, although the recording lacks opulence.

Strauss, Franz
(1822–1905)

Horn concerto in C minor, Op. 8.
> * (*) Decca SXL 6285. Barry Tuckwell (horn), London Symphony
> Orchestra, Istvan Kertesz – R.
> STRAUSS: *Horn concertos.***

This concerto by Franz Strauss, Richard's father, has its moments, but it has a distressing tendency to fall into the style of the cornet air with variations. There are some bright ideas in the work too, of course, but nothing to stop the score being put back in the attic where it rightly belongs.

Strauss, Johann, Snr
(1804–49)
Strauss, Johann, Jnr
(1825–99)
Strauss, Josef
(1827–70)
Strauss, Eduard
(1835–1916)

(All music listed is by Johann Strauss Jnr unless otherwise stated)

Graduation ball (ballet, arr. Dorati).
> (M) *** HMV SXLP 30111. Philharmonia Orchestra, Charles Mackerras – OFFENBACH: *Gaîté Parisienne.****

This delightful score is one of my favourite ballets – I.M. writing – both musically and choreographically. Here the music is given a performance where the music is treated as a whole and not just a series of Strauss tit-bits. The gay music is vivacious as anyone could wish and the brass has a splendid lustre and sonority. The strings, however, have suffered in the new transfer and the quality lacks the grace and transparency of the original. Thus the wistful romantic interlude (between the gauche cadet and the young lady from the girls' finishing school) has not the fragile, gauze-like texture that was so appealing on the CSD issue. However, when *Perpetuum mobile* appears near the end it sounds particularly fresh. This remains a very good disc, though not as sweet as it was.

COLLECTIONS OF WALTZES, POLKAS, etc.

(Listed in alphabetical order under the name of the conductor and then in numerical order using the manufacturers' catalogue numbers, which often produces a date-of-issue sequence)

Annen polka, Op. 117; An der schönen blauen Donau (Blue Danube) waltz, Op. 314; Geschichten aus dem Wiener Wald (Tales from the Vienna Woods) waltz, Op. 325; Overtures: *Die Fledermaus; Der Zigeunerbaron; Pizzicato polka* (written with Josef Strauss). STRAUSS, Johann, Snr: *Radetzky march, Op. 228.*

(B) ** (*) Pye GSGC 14078. Hallé Orchestra, Sir John Barbirolli.

This collection overlaps somewhat with Henry Krips's HMV medium-priced collection (see below), but the two discs could hardly be more different in character. Where the HMV stereo is brash and bright, Sir John's is mellow with especially warm middle strings, and it is somewhat less crisp in definition. The performances have a genuine Viennese lilt and are full of the warmth that comes from affectionate familiarity. Those who enjoyed Sir John's Manchester Viennese concerts will find that he managed to capture much of the spontaneity of those occasions in this well planned concert. Each side begins with an overture, presented with great panache and vivacity, and after the march or polkas comes one of the two greatest waltzes. And the performance of the *Blue Danube* is stunning – there is no better on record. Highly recommended, in spite of dated recording.

Perpetuum mobile, Op. 257. Polkas: *Annen, Op. 117; Unter Donner und Blitz (Thunder and Lightning), Op. 324; Tritsch-Tratsch, Op. 214; Pizzicato* (with Josef). Waltzes: *An der schönen blauen Donau, Op. 314; Kaiser (Emperor), Op. 437; Rosen aus dem Süden (Roses from the South), Op. 388.*

** DGG 2530 316. Vienna Philharmonic Orchestra, Karl Boehm.

Boehm's affection is obvious throughout this concert and he is especially warm in shaping the lovely preludes and postludes to the waltzes. But the rhythmic life which makes the dance rhythms sparkle tends to elude him, although both the *Blue Danube* and *Roses from the South* are not without lilt. The polkas, however, are just a little too heavy in style to be thoroughly exhilarating: they are German rather than Austrian in their ambience. The recording is rich and atmospheric.

'Invitation to a Strauss festival': Marches: *Napoleon, Op. 156; Persian, Op. 289. Perpetuum mobile, Op. 257.* Polkas: *Auf der Jagd* (galop), *Op. 373; Banditen (galop), Op. 378; Champagne, Op. 211; Eljen a Magyar, Op. 332; Explosionen, Op. 43; Neue Pizzicato (Fürstin Ninetta), Op. 449; Pizzicato* (with Josef); *Unter Donner und Blitz, Op. 324.* Waltzes: *An der schönen blauen Donau, Op. 314; Frühlingsstimmen (Voices of Spring), Op. 410; Geschichten aus dem Wienerwald, Op. 325; Kaiser, Op. 437; Künstlerleben (Artist's Life), Op. 316; Morgenblätter (Morning Papers), Op. 279; Rosen aus dem Süden, 388; Wiener Blut (Vienna Blood), Op. 354; Wiener Bonbons, Op. 307; Wo die Zitronen blühn (Where the Lemon Trees Bloom), Op. 364.* STRAUSS, Eduard: *Bahn frei (polka), Op. 45.* STRAUSS, Josef: Polkas: *Eingesendet, Op. 240; Feuerfest, Op. 269; Jockey, Op. 278; Plappermaulchen, Op. 245.* Waltzes: *Mein Lebenslauf ist Lieb' und Lust, Op. 263; Sphärenklänge (Music of the spheres), Op. 235.* STRAUSS, Johann, Snr: *Radetzky march, Op. 228.*

(M) *** Decca Ace of Diamonds SDDC 298/300. Vienna Philharmonic Orchestra, Willi Boskovsky.

Following a tradition begun in the days of mono LPs with Clemens Krauss, Decca have over the years issued a series of incomparable stereo issues of the music of the Strauss family conducted with almost unfailing sparkle by Willi Boskovsky. The VPO have a tradition of New Year Strauss concerts, and it has become a happy idea at Decca to link the new issues with the year's turn. The above anthology has been skilfully compiled from the earlier records in the series, which are slowly being withdrawn from the catalogue and their content reissued either as above or in the SPA series *The world of Strauss*. The early recordings are perhaps not so uniformly natural and rich as current ones, but from the beginning Decca set a high technical standard, and if the sound of the strings sometimes dates the source of individual items the overall ambient glow is consistent throughout. The playing is reliably idiomatic and usually has fine spontaneity and life, but one or two of the more famous waltzes, the *Blue Danube* and the *Emperor*, for instance, have been recorded elsewhere with greater distinction. But reservations about a few individual items are forgotten in the excellence of the set as a whole.

'The world of Strauss', Vol. 1: An der schönen blauen Donau waltz, Op. 314; Auf der Jagd (galop), Op. 373; Egyptian march, Op. 335; Frühlingsstimmen waltz, Op. 410; Geschichten aus dem Wiener Wald waltz, Op. 325; Perpetuum mobile, Op. 257; Pizzicato polka (with Josef); Rosen aus dem Süden waltz, Op. 388; Tausend und Eine Nacht (1001 Nights) waltz, Op. 346; Wiener Blut waltz, Op. 354.

(B) *** Decca SPA 10. Vienna Philharmonic Orchestra, Willi Boskovsky.

Decca have been unbelievably generous to offer so much, and although the disc is crammed full of good things, the recording quality does not suffer. Indeed in the *Pizzicato polka*, *Auf der Jagd* (watch out for the explosions – they will make you jump), and several other items, this is top Decca sound. Of the waltzes the *Blue Danube* is not so fetching as Barbirolli's, but *Tales from the Vienna Woods* is excellent, and both *Roses from the South* and *1001 Nights* are superb. An exhilarating collection – to be played through at one go, and one still could take more! This LP got into the 'Top twenty' when it was first issued and deservedly so.

'The World of Strauss', Vol. 2: Accelerationen (Accelerations) waltz, Op. 234; Annen polka, Op. 117; Kaiser waltz, Op. 437; Künstlerleben waltz, Op. 316; Leichtes Blut polka, Op. 319; Neue Pizzicato polka, Op. 449; Tritsch-Tratsch, Op. 214; Der Zigeunerbaron overture. STRAUSS, Johann, Snr: Radetzky march, Op. 228.

(B) ** Decca SPA 73. Vienna Philharmonic Orchestra, Willi Boskovsky or Hans Knappertsbusch.

Knappertsbusch has earned a gramophone reputation for rather slow and sometimes lethargic tempi. But these performances (he conducts the *March* and all the polkas except the *New pizzicato*, plus the *Accelerations waltz*) are lively and committed. Boskovsky conducts the rest of the programme, and the recording for his items adds an extra richness. The playing throughout has the authentic Viennese lilt and this is an enjoyable disc, if not as fine as the first volume of this series.

'The World of Strauss,' Vol. 3: Persian march, Op. 289; Die Fledermaus over-

ture; Polkas: *Eljen a Magyar, Op. 332; Explosionen, Op. 43; Unter Donner und Blitz, Op. 324;* Waltzes: *(Die Fledermaus): Du und du, Op. 367; Liebeslieder; Morgenblätter, Op. 279; Wein, Weib und Gesang (Wine, Women and Song), Op. 33; Wiener Bonbons, Op. 307.*

(B) ** (*) Decca SPA 312. Vienna Philharmonic Orchestra, Willi Boskovsky.

Most of these recordings date from the end of the fifties, but the warm resonance of the recording provides a pleasing bloom, characteristic of this series, and only the string tone hints at the age of the originals. The *Fledermaus waltz* with its massed upper strings sounds a little spiky but yields to the controls. Boskovsky and his orchestra are on top form throughout, playing the waltzes with affection but without slackness. The overture opens the concert, and the march and polkas are interspersed to make a most attractive selection. The measure is generous and this is excellent value.

Waltzes: *An der schönen blauen Donau, Op. 314; Kaiser, Op. 437; Tausend und Eine Nacht, Op. 346; Wiener Blut, Op. 354.* STRAUSS, Josef: *Sphärenklänge, Op. 235; Transaktionen, Op. 184.*

** (*) Decca SXL 6029. Vienna Philharmonic Orchestra, Willi Boskovsky.

Boskovsky's *Blue Danube* is a little mannered, and the *Emperor* lacks regality (although it has a very beautiful coda). The programme is well chosen and the transfers are if anything even better than the originals, but unless a selection of favourite waltzes together on one disc is essential there are more economical ways of buying most of these recordings (see above).

Demolirer polka, Op. 269; Waltzes: *Du und du, Op. 367; Rosen aus dem Süden, Op. 388; Geschichten aus dem Wiener Wald, Op. 325; Spanish march, Op. 433.* STRAUSS, Josef: *Brennende Liebe, Op. 129; Eingesendet, Op. 240.* STRAUSS, E.: *Bahn frei galop, Op. 45.* STRAUSS, Johann, Snr: *Radetzky march, Op. 228.*

** (*) Decca SXL 6040. Vienna Philharmonic Orchestra, Willi Boskovsky.

These transfers, taken from earlier issues, tend to be spikier than usual, and although this provides the marches and polkas with a suitably lively acoustic, the waltzes are not so smooth as on some of the Boskovsky discs. The performances and programme are well up to standard.

Der Zigeunerbaron: Overture and Entrance march; Polkas: *Im Krapfenwald'l, Op. 336; Tritsch-Tratsch, Op. 214; Vergnügungszug (Train), Op. 281;* Waltzes: *Seid umschlungen Millionen, Op. 443; Wein, Weib umschlungen.* STRAUSS, Josef: *Aquarellen waltz.*

** (*) Decca SXL 6256. Vienna Philharmonic Orchestra, Willi Boskovsky.

From the first bars of the delectable performance of the *Gipsy Baron* overture the listener's ears prick up, not only at the superb style of the playing but also at the superlative recorded quality. The polkas go especially well, and it is only in the waltzes that one feels the direction is a little too affectionate and relaxed. But *Seid umschlungen Millionen* is not an especially memorable waltz anyway, although it has an attractive opening, and quite a pleasant main theme.

Cagliostro in Wien: Overture; Karnivalsbotschafter waltz, Op. 270; Leichtes Blut polka, Op. 319; Ritter Pásmán:

Csárdás, Op. 44; Das Spitzentuch der Königin: Overture. STRAUSS, Josef: Dorfschwalben aus Osterreich waltz, Op. 164; Dynamiden waltz, Op. 173; Die Libelle polka, Op. 204; Moulinet polka, Op. 57.

** (*) Decca SXL 6332. Vienna Philharmonic Orchestra, Willi Boskovsky.

Delicious playing here and glorious recording. Some of the music is less than first-rate, in the sense that the tunes are not always worthy of the dressing. Best are the gay overture, the splendid Ritter Pásmán csárdás and the two polkas.

'Vienna imperial': Franz Josef I, Jubel march, Op. 126; Lagunen waltz, Op. 411; Orpheus quadrille, Op. 236 (formal and concert versions); Schneeglöckchen waltz, Op. 143; S'Gibt nur a Kaiserstadt polka, Op. 291; So ängstlich sind wir nicht polka, Op. 413; Waldmeister overture.

*** Decca SXL 6419. Vienna Philharmonic Orchestra, Willi Boskovsky.

This disc is interesting in including two versions of the Orpheus quadrille, a gay Offenbach pot-pourri. We hear it through first comparatively slowly, in Viennese strict tempo! But the Viennese equivalent of Come Dancing has a good deal more grace and colour than the British product, to add to its formal elegance. Then on side two we are offered the concert version, and the music's irresistible high spirits come bubbling to the surface. There are other good things here too; the Waldmeister overture is full of striking tunes, and the two waltzes (especially Lagunen) are most fetching. With Decca's usual fine recording this is highly recommendable.

'Happy New Year': Die Fledermaus: Czárdás; Bei uns z'Haus waltz, Op.

361; Indigo und die vierzig Räuber: Overture. STRAUSS, Johann, Jnr, Josef, and Eduard: Schützenquadrille. STRAUSS, Josef: Die Schwätzerin, Op. 144; Im Fluge, Op. 230; Die Emancipierte, Op. 282; Extempórere, Op. 240; Auf Ferienreisen, Op. 133. STRAUSS, E.: Fesche Geister; Mit Extrapost.

*** Decca SXL 6495. Vienna Philharmonic Orchestra, Willi Boskovsky.

It would be difficult to discover a disc with a gayer atmosphere. The programme is full of the most delicious Straussian confectionery, played with the lightest possible touch and beautifully recorded. The very Austrian Bei uns z'Haus waltz has one of Johann's most beguiling openings: it is a little-known piece that deserves to be more familiar. This and the Indigo overture offer a touch of extra substance among the sweetmeats, but the infectious quality of the playing ensures there is no danger that the ear is sated. There is not a dull moment here. Marvellous recording too.

'Welcome the New Year': Accelerationen waltz, Op. 234; Annen polka, Op. 117; Bitte schön polka, Op. 373; Freikugeln polka, Op. 326; Freut euch des Lebens waltz, Op. 340; Mephistos Höllenrufe waltz, Op. 101; Nordseebilder waltz, Op. 390; Russischer Marsch, Op. 426; Stürmisch in Lieb' polka, Op. 393. STRAUSS, Josef: Frauenherz polka, Op. 166.

*** Decca SXL 6526. Vienna Philharmonic Orchestra, Willi Boskovsky.

Welcome the New Year is one of Boskovsky's happiest discs. Apart from the first two items listed, most of the music is completely unfamiliar and Boskovsky is a persuasive advocate. The music is played

911

in a relaxed, completely assured manner, and the rich, spacious recording adds to the conductor's natural warmth. Side one closes with the *Russischer Marsch*, a characterful little piece that ends in the manner of a patrol, with the orchestration being gently reduced so that the music fades into the distance. This is done with simplicity and great charm and it alone is a strong enough recommendation for adding the disc to any collection.

'*New Year concert 1973/4*': *An der schönen blauen Donau waltz, Op. 314; Auf's Korn march, Op. 478; Carnaval in Rom: overture; Erinnerung an Covent-Garden waltz, Op. 329; Musikalischer Scherz, Op. 257; Perpetuum mobile, Op. 257; Sängerslust polka, Op. 328; Tik-Tak polka, Op. 365.* STRAUSS, Johann, Snr: *Wettrennen-Galopp, Op. 29.* STRAUSS, Josef: *Rudolfscheimer polka; Sphärenklänge waltz, Op. 325.*

> *** Decca SXL 6692. Vienna State Opera Chorus, Vienna Philharmonic Orchestra, Willi Boskovsky.

The novelty here is the inclusion of the Vienna State Opera Chorus in the original choral version of the *Blue Danube*. These are not the original words (which caused a political storm at the time). The use of the male chorus gives the piece an unexpectedly robust quality, attractive in its way but without the grace of the version for orchestra alone. The chorus also contributes with entirely fruitful effect to the *Sängerslust polka* and the *Auf's Korn march*; but perhaps the highlights of this collection are a beguiling performance of Josef's *Music of the Spheres waltz* and the attractive pot-pourri of English musical-hall airs. This is titled *Erinnerung an Covent Garden, Walzer nach englischen Volksmelodien* (because Strauss conducted a series of Promenade concerts there during the summer and autumn of 1867). The piece is dominated by the tune *Champagne Charlie*, which sounds exotic in the context of a Strauss waltz. Excellent playing and recording throughout, and Boskovsky's final comment (in English) at the end of *Perpetuum mobile* is most apt.

Waltzes: *An der schönen blauen Donau, Op. 314; Frühlingsstimmen, Op. 410; Geschichten aus dem Wiener Wald, Op. 325; Künstlerleben, Op. 316; Wein, Weib und Gesang, Op. 333.*

> ** Decca Phase 4 PFS 4117. London Philharmonic Orchestra, Antal Dorati.

These are highly invigorating performances rather than romantic ones, supported by an extremely brilliant recording, with pithy strings. Of its kind this is a good record, and those for whom the Viennese style is too droopy will not find a hint of slackness here. *Tales from the Vienna Woods* uses a zither, and the recording is never gimmicky.

Waltzes: *An der schönen blauen Donau, Op. 314; Kaiser, Op. 437; Künstlerleben, Op. 316; Wein, Weib und Gesang, Op. 333.*

> (B) ** (*) Classics for Pleasure CFP 165, London Philharmonic Orchestra, Theodor Guschlbauer.

Theodor Guschlbauer readily conveys his affection in these Viennese-style performances, and he makes the London Philharmonic play almost as if they were Vienna-born. The shaping of the opening of each waltz is very nicely done, and the orchestra are obviously enjoying themselves, even though the tension is held on comparatively slack reins. The recording, made in a reverberant acoustic, has warmth and bloom, and the percussion comes over well.

Polkas: *Annen, Op. 117; Champagne, Op. 211; Eljen a Magyar, Op. 332; Leichtes Blut, Op. 319; Tritsch-Tratsch, Op. 214; Unter Donner und Blitz, Op. 324. Perpetuum mobile, Op. 257. Persian march, Op. 289.* Overtures: *Die Fledermaus; Der Zigeunerbaron.*

(B) *** Classics for Pleasure CFP 40048. London Philharmonic Orchestra, Theodor Guschlbauer.

Even finer than his first disc, Guschlbauer's collection of overtures and polkas sparkles from beginning to end. The playing is remarkably idiomatic and stylish, and the music-making is a constant joy. With the acoustic even better judged than on the first issue in terms of atmosphere, warmth and brilliance, the reproduction here is of demonstration quality.

Annen polka, Op. 117; Auf der Jagd galop, Op. 373; Geschichten aus dem Wiener Wald waltz, Op. 325. Overtures: *Die Fledermaus: Der Zigeunerbaron.* STRAUSS, Joseph: *Delirien waltz, Op. 212.*

(M) *** Decca Ace of Diamonds SDD 259. Vienna Philharmonic Orchestra, Herbert von Karajan.

Warmly recorded, presumably in the same hall where the Boskovsky records are made, this early stereo collection is distinguished. Karajan's touch with the *Gypsy Baron overture* is irresistible, and *Tales from the Vienna Woods* is really beautiful, the finest recorded performance of this piece, with a perfectly judged zither solo. The polkas have that panache for which this conductor at his best is famous. Highly recommended: this is among the best popular Strauss collections available.

Overtures: *Die Fledermaus; Der Zigeunerbaron. Perpetuum mobile, Op. 257;* Polkas: *Annen, Op. 117; Tritsch-*

Tratsch, Op. 214. Waltzes: *An der schönen blauen Donau, Op. 314; Kaiser, Op. 437.* STRAUSS, Johann, Snr: *Radetzky march, Op. 228.* STRAUSS, Josef: *Delirien waltz, Op. 212.*

** DGG SLPM 139014. Berlin Philharmonic Orchestra, Herbert von Karajan.

DGG have chosen an unusually reverberant acoustic for this record, to suggest the ballroom, no doubt; but as a concert this is less memorable than Karajan's earlier Decca disc (see above). The playing is warmly idiomatic but has a touch of blandness too in the waltzes, although the polkas are lively enough.

Auf der Jagd polka, Op. 373; Egyptian march, Op. 335; Geschichten aus dem Wiener Wald waltz, Op. 325; Morgenblätter waltz, Op. 279; Persian march, Op. 289; Pizzicato polka (with Josef); *Unter Donner und Blitz polka, Op. 324; Wiener Blut waltz, Op. 354.*

** DGG 2530 027. Berlin Philharmonic Orchestra, Herbert von Karajan.

Karajan is a persuasive conductor of Strauss waltzes, but here he is not helped by a recording which has brilliance but less warmth or bloom. Thus, although beautifully played, *Tales from the Vienna Woods,* which opens the disc, has much less magic here than on Karajan's Ace of Diamonds collection, which is preferable in every way. On DGG the polkas are lively enough (the *Pizzicato polka* played very gently as a foil to the others) and the bright-edged recording projects them well. It is a curiosity indeed to hear the Berlin orchestral players making a robust vocal contribution to the middle section of the *Egyptian march,* which is made to sound like Ketèlbey.

Overtures: *Die Fledermaus; Der Zigeunerbaron. Perpetuum mobile, Op. 257.*

913

Polkas: *Tritsch-Tratsch, Op. 214; Unter Donner und Blitz, Op. 324. Quadrille, Op. 272, on themes from Verdi's 'Un Ballo in maschera'*. Waltzes: *Kaiser, Op. 437; Künstlerleben, Op. 316*.

(M) *** HMV SXLP 30173. Philharmonia Promenade Orchestra, Henry Krips.

This is another excellent mediumpriced collection. Its style is rather more alert than the traditional Viennese manner. These are immensely lively readings full of affection, very well and never stodgily played, and always sparkling with vitality. Only in the *Die Fledermaus overture* will some readers find the conductor's slow accelerandos at the beginning of the 2/4 and waltz sections a trifle mannered. The *Quadrille* on themes from *Un Ballo in maschera* is highly diverting. The recording (not a new one) still sounds spacious and brilliant.

Waltzes: *Accelerationen, Op. 234; An der schönen blauen Donau, Op. 314; Kaiser, Op. 437; Rosen aus dem Süden, Op. 388. Pizzicato polka* (with Josef).

(M) ** Decca SDD 133. Vienna Philharmonic Orchestra, Josef Krips.

Krips gives affectionate if rather bland performances. His style is inclined to rhythmic emphasis but is otherwise without eccentricity, and with the VPO in good form the result is bound to be enjoyable. The recording wants just a little taming but is otherwise good, and the pizzicato strings in the famous polka are exceptionally lifelike.

'*Greatest hits*'. Polkas: *Tritsch-Tratsch, Op. 214; Pizzicato* (with Josef Strauss, arr. Ormandy). Waltzes: *An der schönen blauen Donau, Op. 314; Frühlingsstimmen, Op. 410; Kaiser, Op. 437*.

(B) *** CBS 30002. Philadelphia Orchestra, Eugene Ormandy.

This is one of the very best of the *Greatest hits* series. The performances are first-rate, brilliant yet genial, and given bright, full-blooded recording to match. Three great favourite waltzes are here, and Ormandy conveys his own affection for them in his typically extrovert way. The orchestra responds well and the rhythmic flexibility of the direction has the kind of spontaneity that suggests an audience is present, when of course it is not.

'*Greatest hits*', *Vol. 2*: Polkas: (i) *Explosionen, Op. 43; Neue Pizzicato, Op. 449; Unter Donner und Blitz, Op. 324*. Waltzes: (ii) *Kaiser, Op. 437; Künstlerleben, Op. 316*; (i) *Rosen aus dem Süden, 388; Wein, Weib und Gesang, Op. 333*; (ii) *Wiener Blut, Op. 354*.

(B) ** CBS 30040. (i) Philadelphia Orchestra, Eugene Ormandy; (ii) New York Philharmonic Orchestra, Leonard Bernstein.

This is not quite as successful as the first volume. Bernstein's account of the *Emperor waltz* is rather slack, although he gives a most distinguished account of *Vienna Blood*, which is beautifully recorded too. The polkas are all on side two, and Ormandy gives a ripe reading of the *New pizzicato polka*, with mannered rubato throughout, but totally compulsive, as at a live performance. On side two there are a few cutting-fault rasps (and our pressing was a normal shop copy – not one supplied for review).

'*Greatest hits*', *Vol. 3*: Polkas: (i) *Annen, Op. 117; Auf der Jagd, Op. 373; Liechtes Blut, Op. 319*. (ii) *Perpetuum mobile, Op. 257*. Waltzes: (i) *Tausend und Eine Nacht, Op. 346*; (iii) *Die Fledermaus; Der Zigeunerbaron*.

(B) ** CBS 30049. (i) Philadelphia Orchestra, Eugene Ormandy; (ii) Cleveland Orchestra, George Szell; (iii) Orchestra, André Kostelanetz.

A bright, pleasing collection, without overall distinction but entertaining enough and well recorded. Kostelanetz's *Zigeunerbaron waltz* has an element of *kitsch* about it but is none the worse for that, within the context of this programme.

Perpetuum mobile, Op. 257; Polkas: *Auf der Jagd, Op. 373; Neue Pizzicato, Op. 449; Tik-Tak, Op. 365; Tritsch-Tratsch, Op. 214; Unter Donner und Blitz, Op. 324.* Waltzes: *Accelerationen, Op. 234; An der schönen blauen Donau, Op. 314; Frühlingsstimmen, Op. 410; Kaiser, Op. 437; Künstlerleben, Op. 316; Morgenblätter, Op. 279; Rosen aus dem Süden, Op. 388; Wein, Weib und Gesang, Op. 333; Wiener Bonbons, Op. 307; Wo die Zitronen blühn, Op. 364.*

(B) ** Philips Fontana 6747 051 (2 discs). Vienna Symphony Orchestra, Wolfgang Sawallisch.

A recommendable bargain collection, attractively presented in a double sleeve. The performances are not as distinctive as Boskovsky's, but they are rhythmically alive without being in any way rigid, and the polkas come off especially well. Sawallisch's solution for the way to end *Perpetuum mobile*, a gentle fade-out, seems preferable to the various gruff announcements that the piece can continue by conductors on some discs. The recording is quite fresh, but shows its age by the string tone, which has not the bloom of the best modern discs. But the quality is generally very acceptable and this is certainly enjoyable.

'In St Petersburg': *Fest-Polonaise, Op. 352; Fantasie: Im russischen Dorfe (In a Russian village), Op. 355.* Marches: *Grossfürsten-Marsch, Op. 107; Krönungs-Marsch, Op. 183; Russischer Marsch, Op. 426;* Polkas: *An der Wolga Op. 425; Auf dem Tanze, Op. 436; Newa-Polka, Op. 288; Vergnügungszug, Op. 281.* Quadrilles: *Alexander, Op. 33; Hofball, Op. 116; Nikolai, Op. 65; St Petersburg, Op. 255.* Waltzes: *Abschied von St Petersburg, Op. 210; Grossfürstin Alexandra, Op. 181; Krönungslieder, Op. 184.*

** (*) BASF BAC 3045/6. Berlin Symphony Orchestra, Robert Stolz.

This collection (issued in a well-documented and attractively decorated double sleeve) is of considerable historical interest, commemorating as it does Strauss's visits to the Vauxhall Pavilion in Pavlovsk, near St Petersburg, over a ten-year period from 1855 to 1865. The entertainment complex at Pavlovsk was based on the similar pleasure gardens in London (hence the name), and one reason for Strauss's contract was to improve business on the railway line that connected Pavlovsk with the city. Strauss's seasons were enormously successful and, of course, produced some music with an eye to this new Russian market. In fact many of the pieces here had no direct connection with the St Petersburg seasons, but were no doubt put to good use there. The snag with this double album, which is brightly played and recorded, is the music itself. Of the seventeen pieces included – all very gay and lively – there are only a few vintage items, and this set is best used as background music or taken a side at a time.

Marches: *Austria, Op. 20; Brünn National Guard, Op. 58; Deutschmeister-Jubiläumsmarsch, Op. 470; Verbrüderungsmarsch, Op. 287.* Polkas: *Aus der Heimat, Op. 347; Blumenfest,*

Op. 111; Heiligenstadt Rendezvous, Op. 78; Im Krapfenwaldl, Op. 336; Neuhauser, Op. 137; Pizzicato (with Josef); *'S gibt nur a Kaiserstadt, 's gibt nur a Wien, Op. 291; Tik-tak, Op. 365; Vöslau, Op. 100.* Waltzes: *Bei uns z'Haus, Op. 361; Frühlingsstimmen, Op. 140; Geschichten aus dem Wiener Wald, Op. 325; Wiener Bonbons, Op. 307; Wiener Grauen, Op. 423.*

** BASF BAꞌC 3069/70. Berlin Symphony Orchestra, Robert Stolz.

This collection opens with *Tales from the Vienna Woods* (which forms the title for the album). It is a rather mannered performance, affectionate but bland, and this same rather slack rhythmic style gives a similar easy-going atmosphere to the concert as a whole. The set includes several attractive novelties, and some of the polkas have a jaunty quality that is infectious. The acoustic is reverberant, giving fine atmosphere in certain numbers, but sometimes marginally coarsening the orchestral focus. This is more noticeable on the second disc.

Banditen-Galop, Op. 378; Cagliastro waltz, Op. 370; Elektropher polka, Op. 297; Gross Wien polka, Op. 440; Lagerlust polka, Op. 431; Mephistos Höllenrufe waltz, Op. 101; Nordseebilder waltz, Op. 380; Pariser polka, Op. 282; Das Spitzentuch der Königin: overture; I Tipferl polka, Op. 377.

(B) ** Turnabout TV 34328S. Philharmonia Hungarica, Eduard Strauss.

The playing is idiomatic and the recording atmospheric. There are no hidden masterpieces here, but the polkas are jolly, and one or two of the waltzes are catchy enough. The overture offers a snippet of one really familiar tune, but its source is elusive.

OPERA

Die Fledermaus (opera in 3 acts): complete recording.

*** HMV SLS 964 (2 discs). Anneliese Rothenberger, Renate Holm (sopranos), Nicolai Gedda (tenor), Dietrich Fischer-Dieskau (baritone), Brigitte Fassbaender (mezzo-soprano), Vienna State Opera Chorus, Vienna Symphony Orchestra, Willi Boskovsky.

** (*) Decca SXL 6015/6. Hilde Gueden, Erika Köth (sopranos), Waldemar Kmentt (tenor), Eberhard Waechter (baritone), Walter Berry (bass), Giuseppe Zampieri (tenor), Regina Resnik (contralto), Vienna State Opera Chorus, Vienna Philharmonic Orchestra, Herbert von Karajan.

** Decca SET 540/1. Gundula Janowitz, Renate Holm (sopranos), Waldemar Kmentt (tenor), Eberhard Waechter, Heinz Holecek, Erich Kunz (baritones), Wolfgang Windgassen (tenor), Vienna State Opera Chorus, Vienna Philharmonic Orchestra, Karl Boehm.

If the LP catalogue has never been infested with Fledermice, that is a recognition of the quality of earlier sets, first in mono, and then notably Karajan's Decca version of 1960. The Boskovsky version, recorded with the Vienna *Symphoniker* instead of the Philharmonic, is more intimate than its predecessor, to provide a clear alternative. Though Boskovsky sometimes fails to lean into the seductive rhythms as much as he might, his is a refreshing account of a magic score. Rothenberger is a sweet, domestic-sounding Rosalinde, relaxed and sparkling, while among an excellent supporting cast the Orlofsky of Brigitte Fassbaender must be singled out as quite the finest on record, tough and firm. The entertainment has been excellently produced for records, with German dialogue inserted, though the ripe recording sometimes makes the voices jump between singing and speaking.

Karajan's set was originally issued – with much blazing of publicity trumpets – as a so-called 'Gala performance', with various artists from the Decca roster appearing to do their turn at the 'cabaret' included in the Orlofsky ball sequence. This was a famous tradition of performances of *Die Fledermaus* at the New York Met. in the early years of this century. In due course Decca issued the set without the gala, and now the three-disc gala album has been withdrawn. The performance itself has all the sparkle one could ask for. If anything, Karajan is even more brilliant than he was on the old Columbia mono issue, and the Decca recording is scintillating in its clarity. Where it does fall short, alas, is in the singing. Hilde Gueden is deliciously vivacious as Rosalinde, a beautifully projected interpretation, but vocally she is not perfect, and even her confidence has a drawback in showing how tentative Erika Köth is as Adèle, with her wavering vibrato. Indeed *Mein Herr Marquis* is well below the standard of the best recorded performances. Waldemar Kmentt has a tight, German-sounding tenor, and Giuseppe Zampieri as Alfred (a bright idea to have a genuine Italian for the part) is no more than adequate. The rest of the cast are very good, but even these few vocal shortcomings are enough to take some of the gilt off the gingerbread. It all depends on what you ask from *Fledermaus*; if it is gaiety and sparkle above everything, then with Karajan in control this is an excellent recommendation, and it certainly cannot be faulted on grounds of recording, which leaves nothing to be desired.

Boehm conducts with great warmth and affection, if without the sparkle of Karajan. The recording is made without dialogue (and many will prefer it for this) and with one or two traditional cuts. Also the ballet music is replaced with the *Thunder and Lightning polka*. The stars of the performance are undoubtedly Gundula Janowitz, in rich voice as Rosalinde, and Renate Holm as Adèle, which of course she also sings on the HMV set. The male principals are less impressive. The use of a male Orlofsky has less dramatic point on record than it would on stage, and Windgassen is vocally here much inferior to Brigitte Fassbaender, who is so good in the HMV set.

Die Fledermaus: highlights.

⊛ *** HMV Quadraphonic Q4–ASD 2891 (from above set cond. Boskovsky).

*** Decca SXL 6155 (from above set cond. Karajan).

The generous selection from the superbly recorded Decca set is highly attractive, but the HMV quadraphonic disc has a quality all its own and provides an exciting foretaste of what quadraphonic sound is going to do for opera recordings. Just as in the early days of stereo one felt the sound slipping free of the loudspeakers, here is a further extension of the illusion of being in an ideal theatre seat, with three-dimensional sound on the 'stage' at the end of one's room. The ripe glow of the stereo recording (and this disc sounds remarkably well on ordinary stereo equipment) is further enhanced by the background ambience, and the ensembles especially have marvellous presence and freshness. The famous *Trinke Liebchen, trinke schnell* from Act 1 is matched by the ball scene, where all sing in praise of champagne and its delicious effects. Indeed this sequence (*Im Feuerstrom der Reben . . . Bruderlein und Schwesterlein*) has some of the magic of the irreplaceable old Krauss mono set. All the solo performances seem to acquire extra sparkle, and Orlofsky's *Chacun à son goût* is quite superb. It is a pity there is a cutting fault on side two which momentarily breaks the illusion, but it is to be hoped that later pressings will be free of these rasps.

Die Fledermaus: highlights (in English).
  ** HMV CSD 1266. Victoria Elliot, Marion Studholme (sopranos), Alexander Young (tenor), John Heddle Nash (baritone), Sadler's Wells Opera, Vilem Tausky.

The Sadler's Wells Company often showed in the theatre that it was second to none in capturing Viennese gaiety, and on this record the whole production moves with great vigour. The chorus in particular has an incisiveness which will disappoint no one, but it must be admitted that the soloists, while always reliable, are not particularly memorable in their singing. Marion Studholme, for example, as Adèle sings with great flexibility, but there is a 'tweety' quality to her voice, as caught by the microphone, which prevents the final degree of enjoyment. Anna Pollak is the one serious disappointment. In the theatre this highly intelligent singer rarely failed to give dramatic as well as understanding performances, but here as Prince Orlofsky she sounds too old-womanly by far, and her attempts at vocal acting – effective in the theatre – sound over-mannered and only add to the womanliness. The recording is brilliant, with a clarity of definition and numerous directional effects which are most realistic. There are one or two patches of faint tape-hiss.

Der Zigeunerbaron (operetta): abridged version.
  (M) ** Telefunken NT 729. Erika Köth, Rita Bartos, Reinhold Bartel, Kurt Böhme, Willy Schneider, Rudolf Lamy Choir, Bavarian Radio Orchestra, Carl Michalski.

This is done pot-pourri style with linking dialogue, the voices well forward, and the whole production rather lacking in atmosphere. The singing itself is idiomatic and dramatically effective, if without a great deal of charm. But there are some good tunes in *Der Zigeunerbaron* (if fewer than in *Die Fledermaus*), and this is an adequate presentation of them.

Strauss, Richard
(1864–1949)

Alpine symphony, Op. 64; Also sprach Zarathustra (symphonic poem), *Op. 30; Le Bourgeois Gentilhomme: suite; Don Juan* (symphonic poem), *Op. 20; Macbeth* (symphonic poem), *Op. 23; Metamorphosen for 23 solo strings; Schlagobers* (ballet), *Op. 70: Waltz.*
  *** HMV SLS 861 (4 discs). Dresden State Orchestra, Rudolf Kempe.

This was the first of Kempe's three boxes comprising Strauss's symphonic poems as well as some miscellaneous orchestral pieces. He has recorded the *Alpine symphony* before, with the RPO, and there is little to choose between the two as far as interpretation is concerned. The *Zarathustra* is a convincing and well-paced performance, and so too is *Macbeth*, something of a rarity in the concert hall nowadays. *Don Juan* is perhaps the least electrifying of these performances, which in every other respect are as distinguished as Kempe's reputation as a Straussian would lead one to expect. The Dresden Orchestra is a magnificent body and their strings produce sumptuous tone, which is strikingly in evidence in *Metamorphosen*. The engineers produce a clean, well-balanced and most musical sound.

Also sprach Zarathustra, Op. 30; Death and Transfiguration, Op. 24; Don Juan, Op. 20; Don Quixote, Op. 35; Ein Heldenleben, Op. 40; Metamorphosen for 23 solo strings; Till Eulenspiegels lustige Streiche, Op. 28; Salome: Dance of the Seven Veils.

*** DGG 2740 111 (5 discs). Berlin Philharmonic Orchestra, Herbert von Karajan.

A fabulous collection. All these performances are of superlative quality and sumptuously recorded. *Ein Heldenleben* was recorded as long ago as 1959, but no one would suspect it was not made in the seventies. Fournier's reading of the solo part in *Don Quixote* is arguably the finest on the market, and Karajan's *Metamorphosen* is without question the best version. (He made the very first records of that work for Columbia 78s.) Excellent though the Kempe sets are, this is in a class of its own.

Also sprach Zarathustra, Op. 30; Don Juan, Op. 20; Festival prelude, Op. 61; Till Eulenspiegels lustige Streiche, Op. 28; Der Rosenkavalier: Waltzes; Salome: Dance of the Seven Veils.

(M) ** (*) DGG Privilege 2726 028 (2 discs). Berlin Philharmonic Orchestra, Karl Boehm.

Boehm is a fine Straussian, and this double album might be considered good value at medium price. But *Also sprach Zarathustra* is a very early stereo recording (also available separately; see below), and nearly all the other performances are gathered together on an outstanding single (full-priced) LP (see below under *Don Juan*).

Also sprach Zarathustra, Op. 30.

⊛ *** DGG 2530 402. Berlin Phil-

harmonic Orchestra, Herbert von Karajan.

*** Philips 6500 624. Concertgebouw Orchestra, Bernard Haitink.

(M) ** (*) Decca Ace of Diamonds SDD 174. Vienna Philharmonic Orchestra, Herbert von Karajan.

** (*) DGG SLPEM 136001. Berlin Philharmonic Orchestra, Karl Boehm.

** Decca SXL 6379. Los Angeles Philharmonic Orchestra, Zubin Mehta.

** CBS Quadraphonic MQ 30443; Stereo 72941. New York Philharmonic Orchestra, Leonard Bernstein.

Sumptuous tone and virtuosity of the highest order make the DGG Karajan an electrifying *Zarathustra*. It is arguably the best on the market. The engineers produce recorded sound of the greatest realism and warmth, wholly natural in its aural perspective and free from gimmickry. Karajan's earlier account, with the Vienna Philharmonic Orchestra, was also a fine one, famous for its spectacular recording of almost too wide a dynamic range. The playing was first-class and had considerable tonal opulence, but the new DGG version eclipses it in almost every way, although it remains a good recommendation in the medium price-range.

Haitink's account with the Concertgebouw Orchestra is no less impressively recorded than Karajan's on DGG, though the strings of the Berlin Philharmonic have greater rapture and lyrical intensity. This record was issued very much in the shadow of the Karajan and its merits did not perhaps receive full recognition. The recording is extremely fine and admirably detailed, and although Karajan remains the first choice, this is a good second.

Boehm's performance is characteristically broad, with splendid orchestral playing to support the conductor's spacious conception. However, the recording is now an old one and the upper strings do not have the richness we would expect today. To reissue this at full price is ungenerous when Decca's early Karajan recording (which does not sound dated) is available on Ace of Diamonds.

In the never-to-be-forgotten opening of *Also sprach Zarathustra* Mehta has the distinction of stretching those famous first pages longer than any rival. For many readers another point in favour will be the hi-fi brilliance of the recording quality. From the start this is plainly intended as a demonstration record, and as such it succeeds well, but there are other versions more understanding interpretatively. Mehta is a good Straussian, but he is a forceful rather than an affectionate one.

The CBS stereo issue is super-glossy, with little bloom on strings and brass and a harsh upper register. The quadraphonic version is, however, immensely superior, with fresh textures and plenty of weight and clarity. The famous opening section is handled without any sign of strain and it is not surprising that CBS often use this to open their public quadraphonic demonstrations. However, it must be admitted that even with the advantages of quadraphony the American recording does not produce the body of string tone that distinguishes the DGG Karajan disc, which sounds marvellous through four speakers. And Bernstein's performance, though exciting, has not the romantic impetus of the finest versions.

Also sprach Zarathustra, Op. 30; Till Eulenspiegels lustige Streiche, Op. 28.

(M) *** HMV SXLP 30133. Philharmonia Orchestra, Lorin Maazel.

This excellent disc adds yet another outstanding *Also sprach Zarathustra* to the catalogues. The performance is very fine, and the richness of the Kingsway Hall

acoustic gives the orchestra glowing textures to match the ardour of Maazel's reading. A strong, impetuous *Till* is recorded with equal brilliance, and for those who want the coupling this can be recommended at mid-price alongside Karajan. The sound is perhaps not quite so stunning as the Decca version, but it is very good indeed and makes up in warmth for what it lacks in inner clarity.

Aus Italien (symphonic fantasy), *Op. 16; Josephslegende* (symphonic fragment) (1947); *Symphonia domestica, Op. 53; Till Eulenspiegels lustige Streiche, Op. 28; Salome: Dance of the Seven Veils.*

*** HMV SLS 894 (3 discs). Dresden State Orchestra, Rudolf Kempe.

Another outstanding boxed set. Kempe's version of the *Symphonia domestica* is no less desirable than Karajan's (see below): the latter is brilliant and virtuosic with marvellously luxurious tone; Kempe is a little more relaxed, without being in any way less masterly. His control of rubato is as wholly idiomatic as that of Clemens Krauss (and no praise could be higher). Karajan's was the most persuasive *Domestica* since Krauss, yielding to him only in delicacy of feeling and humanity. Kempe's is as fine. Certainly the *Aus Italien* is more convincing than in any previous version: the more luminous and transparent quality of the sound, with its finely judged perspective and excellent body and range, is a decisive factor here. Kempe's *Till Eulenspiegel* is also magnificent, but *Josephslegende* will call for tolerance even in this committed version. Strauss's inspiration is thin here and his craftsmanship runs away with him. This work apart, the set is most strongly recommended.

Aus Italien (symphonic fantasy), *Op. 16.*

(M) ** Supraphon 110 1127. Ostrava State Philharmonic Orchestra, Otakar Trhlík.

Strauss wrote *Aus Italien* in his early twenties, just after he had taken up his first post as conductor in Meiningen. In it he exuberantly uses the full orchestra to convey his fairly conventional impressions of a visit to Italy. The musical material does not approach that of Strauss's later orchestral works in memorability, but the very enthusiasm (one senses a young man finding his feet for the first time) can be compelling in a really imaginative performance. This one is fairly straightforward, though a good deal more than serviceable. It does not match Krauss's account on Eclipse (ECS 610), a stereo transcription which still sounds remarkably fresh, but there is no doubt that Supraphon's stereo provides a far richer sound picture, with a wide dynamic range.

Le Bourgeois Gentilhomme (suite of incidental music for Molière's play), *Op. 60; Der Rosenkavalier: 1st Waltz sequence.*
   * (*) Decca SXL 6304. Vienna Philharmonic Orchestra, Lorin Maazel, with Friedrich Gulda (piano), Willi Boskovsky (violin), Emanuel Brabec (cello).

Perhaps memories of the old Beecham 78s of *Le Bourgeois Gentilhomme* are too rosy, but they are not effaced by this issue. Maazel is not helped by a balance that focuses too much attention on the pianist and for all the merits of the performance, this score misses the last ounce of charm and grace to enable it really to shine.

Capriccio (opera): *Introduction* (arr. for string orchestra).
   ** (*) Argo ZRG 792. Los Angeles Chamber Orchestra, Neville Mar-

riner – JANÁČEK: *Suite*; SUK: *Serenade.****
   ** Decca SXL 6533. Stuttgart Chamber Orchestra, Karl Münchinger – SUK: *Serenade*; WOLF: *Italian serenade.***

A pity that on both discs the opening sextet to *Capriccio* is given to full strings, for it completely alters the intimate quality of this beautiful piece. Having said that, however, one must admit that it is easy to succumb to the eloquence of Marriner's account, which is superbly played and recorded. Münchinger's performance is well played too, but the phrasing is stiffer and the effect is less imaginative.

Horn concertos Nos. 1 in E flat major, Op. 11; 2 in E flat major.
   (M) *** HMV HLS 7001. Dennis Brain (horn), Philharmonia Orchestra, Wolfgang Sawallisch – HINDEMITH: *Horn concerto.****
   ** Decca SXL 6285. Barry Tuckwell (horn), London Symphony Orchestra, Istvan Kertesz – Franz STRAUSS: *Horn concerto.** (*)

Stereo transcriptions are not normally included in our survey, but here the exception must be made. Dennis Brain's wonderfully ripe performances were not recorded in real stereo like the Hindemith coupling, but the sound is good, and Brain's superb tone is truthfully caught. These are unique performances, catching the music's character with a perception to match the flawless bravura of the playing itself.

Tuckwell does not usually disappoint, but here he does not get the style right. One can play the *First Concerto* as a successor to Mozart and it can be effective that way; but better to bring out the *Don Juan* boldness that is also inherent in the music, as Dennis Brain demonstrates readily. Tuckwell falls between the

921

two, and his manner and line are unconvincing. He is at his best in the finale of the otherwise less memorable *Second Concerto*. The Decca recording is sumptuous, and on recording grounds alone is far superior to the H M V issue.

(i) *Horn concerto No. 2 in E flat major;*
(ii) *Oboe concerto in D major.*
** (*) DGG 2530 439. (i) Norbert Hauptmann (horn); (ii) Lothar Koch (oboe); both with Berlin Philharmonic Orchestra, Herbert von Karajan.

Distinguished playing from both soloists here and a superb contribution from the Berlin Philharmonic. There is perhaps a slight want of spontaneity, and some ears may find a certain lack of individuality too, but this record as a whole is a useful addition to the Strauss discography. The soloists are rather forwardly balanced, but otherwise the recording is impeccable.

Oboe concerto in D major.
** (*) Philips 6500 174. Heinz Holliger (oboe), New Philharmonia Orchestra, Edo de Waart — MOZART: *Oboe concerto.****
(M) ** Supraphon SUAST 50486. František Hanták (oboe), Brno State Philharmonic Orchestra, Jaroslav Vogel — MARTINŮ: *Oboe concerto.****

Holliger is never less than masterly, and few oboists today could begin to match the assurance of this performance of one of Strauss's most glowing 'Indian summer' works. But there is a hint of efficiency at the expense of ripeness, an absence of sheer love for the music in its most absolute sense, which prevents this from being quite the ideal version one hoped for. The lack is comparatively small, and with a delightful coupling the disc can still be warmly recommended.

In the Supraphon recording Hanták is placed right on top of the microphone, which gives a certain 'squawkiness' to the tone. The orchestra too is on the fierce side, although both these defects of balance are reasonably tameable on a flexible reproducer. The performance is vivid and forthright, not quite relaxed enough but by no means insensitive.

Dance suite (from Couperin harpsichord pieces); *Death and Transfiguration (Tod und Verklärung), Op. 24; Don Quixote, Op. 35; Ein Heldenleben, Op. 40; Der Rosenkavalier: Waltzes.*
*** HMV SLS 880 (3 discs). Dresden State Orchestra, Rudolf Kempe.

This second box from Kempe and the Dresden Orchestra is no less successful than the first. Perhaps one could quarrel with the balance in *Don Quixote*, which gives Tortelier exaggerated prominence and obscures some detail. The performance, however, is another matter and must rank with the best available. Kempe gives a most musical account of the delightful *Dance suite* based on Couperin keyboard pieces, which is not otherwise available. A distinguished set.

Death and Transfiguration (Tod und Verklärung), Op. 24.
*** Decca Phase 4 PFS 4227. New Philharmonia Orchestra, Lorin Maazel — TCHAIKOVSKY: *Francesca da Rimini.****
** Unicorn RHS 321. London Symphony Orchestra, Jascha Horenstein — HINDEMITH: *Mathis der Maler.***(*)

One of the most impressive interpretations of *Death and Transfiguration* ever put on record was Toscanini's, searingly intense. Maazel similarly shows that clearheaded purposefulness can replace romantic warmth as the driving force in a work which in some hands can seem glutinous. With fine Phase 4 sound and an attractive if unexpected coupling, this is very recommendable. Horenstein's account is spacious, and the recorded sound is vivid and has presence. However, competition is stiff and Horenstein would not displace Karajan or Reiner as first recommendations.

Death and Transfiguration, Op. 24; Don Juan, Op. 20.
*** Decca sxl 6134. Vienna Philharmonic Orchestra, Lorin Maazel.

Lorin Maazel has recorded *Death and Transfiguration* twice. This Viennese account dates from 1964, seven years before his Phase 4 disc. Both the performances here have great vitality and youthful ardour and they are splendidly recorded. The huge final climax of *Death and Transfiguration* is spectacularly caught by the engineers, but Maazel invests it with breadth and dignity; and he makes the strings glow with romantic warmth in the love music of *Don Juan*. Neither performance is perhaps the most distinguished available, but if you want this particular coupling, you cannot go far wrong with this.

Death and Transfiguration, Op. 24; Don Juan, Op. 20; Till Eulenspiegels lustige Streiche, Op. 28.
(M) ** (*) CBS Classics 61216. Cleveland Orchestra, George Szell.

This is an exhilarating record, superbly played and, on the whole, well recorded. *Death and Transfiguration* is tremendously exciting; the closing pages are the more satisfying for Szell's complete lack of indulgence. *Till* is irrepressibly cheeky (this characterization created from the most polished orchestral playing, and here the recording acoustic is impressive, with a fine glow, yet every detail (and Szell makes sure one can hear every

detail) crystal-clear. Then *Don Juan,* sounding really impetuous yet never rushed, delights ear and senses by its forward surge of passionate lyricism. Again marvellous playing, the whole interpretation founded on a bedrock of virtuosity from this remarkable orchestra. The recording here is brilliant but rather dry.

Death and Transfiguration, Op. 24; Till Eulenspiegels lustige Streiche, Op. 28.
(B) *** Decca Eclipse ecs 674. Vienna Philharmonic Orchestra, Fritz Reiner.

These recordings were – unbelievably – made as long ago as 1957. Yet in terms of presence and sonority they compare favourably with the most modern recordings. *Death and Transfiguration* is in some ways more vivid here than in Karajan's DGG recording, though its detail is neither so refined nor so clean. The performances are quite superb, and the Vienna orchestra respond to this great Straussian in the manner born. It is astonishingly good value at its absurdly low price.

Death and Transfiguration, Op. 24; Till Eulenspiegels lustige Streiche, Op. 28; Salome: Dance of the Seven Veils.
(M) *** Decca Ace of Diamonds sdd 211. Vienna Philharmonic Orchestra, Herbert von Karajan.

Karajan's earlier recording for Decca of *Death and Transfiguration* is a powerful and convincing one, and he draws a piquant, witty portrait of *Till*. The *Dance of the Seven Veils* is a richly sensuous performance, and the recording throughout, if not as refined in matters of texture and internal clarity as the newer DGG versions, was outstanding in its day (1961). This record remains excellent value in this mid-price reissue.

923

Death and Transfiguration, Op. 24; (i) *Vier letzte Lieder (Four Last Songs).*

** (*) DGG 2530 368. Berlin Philharmonic Orchestra, Herbert von Karajan, (i) with Gundula Janowitz (soprano).

As in the opera *Capriccio*, Janowitz comes into direct rivalry with the incomparable Schwarzkopf (see below), and on that level she simply produces a beautiful flow of creamy soprano tone while leaving the music's deeper and subtler emotions underexpressed. But coupled with a superlative version of *Death and Transfiguration*, which can be regarded as a showpiece even among Karajan's Berlin recordings, this is an attractive record.

Don Juan, Op. 20.

(B) *** Decca SPA 119. Vienna Philharmonic Orchestra, Herbert von Karajan – TCHAIKOVSKY: *Romeo and Juliet.****

(M) *** RCA LSB 4109. Los Angeles Philharmonic Orchestra, Zubin Mehta – RESPIGHI: *Feste romane.****

Karajan's SPA, like Reiner's coupling of *Death and Transfiguration* and *Till* on Eclipse, is one of the great bargains of the Richard Strauss discography. The price is absurdly low, for the performance is superbly played, Karajan as beguiling in the love music of *Don Juan* as he is exhilarating in the chase. The recording is excellent. Karajan's Tchaikovsky coupling is equally exciting, but if this is not suitable, Mehta's disc might well be considered an alternative.

Though extrovert brilliance is very much the principal quality of Mehta's version (one of the first records he ever made with the Los Angeles Philharmonic), he relaxes expansively in the rich music of the love scene, drawing hushed and intense string playing from the orchestra. Bright, atmospheric recording.

Don Juan, Op. 20; Festival prelude, Op. 61; Till Eulenspiegels lustige Streiche, Op. 28; Salome: Dance of the Seven Veils.

*** DGG SLPM 138866. Berlin Philharmonic Orchestra, Karl Boehm.

Strongly characterized, essentially German performances, marvellously well played and brilliantly and sonorously recorded. This was always one of Boehm's very best discs. Besides the vivid *Don Juan* (glorious leaping strings and rich thrusting horns), the peasant-flavoured picture of Till, and the highly sensuous *Salome Dance*, the disc offers a fascinating bonus, the *Prelude* Strauss wrote for the opening of a concert hall in Vienna in 1913. It is characteristically inflated; using the organ as well as a huge orchestra, the composer piles sequence upon sequence to produce a climax of shattering sonority. Boehm's account produces a dignity not really inherent in the music, and he is splendidly supported by the engineers.

Don Juan, Op. 20; Till Eulenspiegels lustige Streiche, Op. 28.

(B) ** Classics for Pleasure CFP 40042. London Philharmonic Orchestra, Charles Mackerras.

Good, serviceable accounts of these two popular symphonic poems, recorded with admirable detail and perspective. They are good value at the price, but it would be idle to pretend that there are not more distinguished versions in the catalogue.

Don Juan, Op. 20; Till Eulenspiegels lustige Streiche, Op. 28; Salome: Dance of the Seven Veils.

*** DGG 2530 349. Berlin Philharmonic Orchestra, Herbert von Karajan.

Vividly characterized performances of both symphonic poems, as well as a highly seductive *Dance of the Seven Veils* played with stunning virtuosity and recorded with great fidelity by the DGG engineers. These are among the finest performances of these works in current circulation.

Don Juan, Op. 20; Festival prelude, Op. 61; Till Eulenspiegels lustige Streiche, Op. 28; Salome: Dance of the Seven Veils.

(M) ** Everest SDBR 3023. New York Stadium Orchestra, Leopold Stokowski.

Not surprisingly with the old magician Stokowski in charge, Salome is made to languish more unashamedly than ever before, and even Till in his posthumous epilogue has a languishing mood on him. Surprisingly, on the great unison horn call of *Don Juan* Stokowski holds back a little, with less than spacious phrasing. But as ever Stokowski is nothing if not convincing, and those looking for really ripe versions of these pieces need not hesitate. The recording is not of the most modern, basically spacious and atmospheric but with a little fuzz on the sound at climaxes.

Don Quixote, Op. 35.

*** DGG SLPM 139009. Pierre Fournier (cello), Berlin Philharmonic Orchestra, Herbert von Karajan.

*** Decca SXL 6367. Emanuel Brabec (cello), Vienna Philharmonic Orchestra, Lorin Maazel.

* (*) Decca SXL 6634. Kurt Reher (cello), Los Angeles Philharmonic Orchestra, Zubin Mehta.

A superbly eloquent account by Fournier and Karajan. It supersedes Fournier's earlier performance under Szell and in fact rivals his first LP account for Decca with Krauss. The orchestral play-

ing is, as one would expect from the Berlin Philharmonic, of the very highest order, and Karajan is at his finest too. A noble reading of the solo part is backed by a virtuoso account from the orchestra. There is no finer version of Strauss's masterpiece. The DGG recording is very good, and played at a suitable volume-setting produces plenty of impact.

A brilliant performance from Emanuel Brabec and the Vienna orchestra, who play eloquently for Maazel. The recording is rather brightly lit and some of the wind are slightly too forward, but there is no doubting the clarity and detail that are brought to light. However, the performance, fine though it is, has not the depth and nobility of Fournier's with Karajan and the Berlin Philharmonic, which is undoubtedly the one to have.

Kurt Reher is somewhat backwardly balanced in his account with Mehta and the Los Angeles orchestra. Decca provide a well-lit, finely detailed recording with no want of colour and vividness, but the soloists are swamped at times (though given the viola intonation this is no bad thing). Mehta's reading has none of the refinement or perception that distinguish Karajan's, and it cannot be recommended.

Don Quixote, Op. 35; Der Rosenkavalier: Waltz sequence.

*** HMV ASD 3074. Paul Tortelier (cello), Dresden State Orchestra, Rudolf Kempe.

(B) *** RCA Victrola VICS 1561. Antonio Janigro (cello), Chicago Symphony Orchestra, Fritz Reiner.

Kempe's performance of *Don Quixote* is one of the very finest available and comes from his box album (above). The balance gives the cellist an exaggerated forward projection, but the overall effect remains impressive.

Even at full price Reiner's performance

of *Don Quixote* was a top recommendation. This was one of the very best of RCA's Chicago Hall recordings, offering a widespread and rich tapestry of sound. The quality is not so clear-cut and vivid as Maazel's Decca disc but it is more atmospheric, with a fine bloom on the orchestra. Antonio Janigro plays stylishly and with assurance; if he brings less intensity than Fournier to the ecstatic solo cadenza in variation V, his contribution to the close of the work is distinguished. With a warm and not unsubtle performance of the *Waltzes* from *Der Rosenkavalier* as a bonus this record at Victrola price is a bargain.

Ein Heldenleben, Op. 40.
    *** Philips 6500 048. Concertgebouw Orchestra, Bernard Haitink.
    ** (*) DGG SLPM 138025. Berlin Philharmonic Orchestra, Herbert von Karajan.
    ** Decca SXL 6382. Los Angeles Philharmonic Orchestra, Zubin Mehta.

Haitink is a remarkably fine Straussian. One day no doubt he will start devoting himself to the operas, but here with his own orchestra he gives just the sort of performance, brilliant and swaggering but utterly without bombast, which will delight those who normally resist this rich and expansive work. With a direct and fresh manner which yet conveys consistent urgency, he gives a performance which makes even such fine rival versions as Mehta's or Karajan's sound a little superficial. In the culminating fulfilment theme, a gentle, lyrical 6/8, Haitink finds a raptness in restraint, a hint of agony within joy, that links the passage directly with the great *Trio* from *Rosenkavalier*. The Philips sound is exceptionally faithful, refined but rich and brilliant too.

Karajan's is also a performance of great power and distinction, and radiant

playing from the orchestra ensures that the sensuous love music and the serene closing section of the work are realized with memorable beauty. The recording was originally not too clear, especially in the 'battle music', but it has been successfully refurbished, and current pressings hardly betray the age of the original (1959).

Mehta's is a hi-fi performance to impress the Straussian weaned on the opening bars of *Also sprach Zarathustra*. It is very exciting, but misses some of the subtler qualities of a richly varied score. Haitink is much more recommendable. Brilliant Decca recording.

Metamorphosen for 23 solo strings.
    *** HMV ASD 2830. New Philharmonia Orchestra, Sir John Barbirolli – ARENSKY: *Variations on a theme of Tchaikovsky;* ELGAR: *Serenade.* ***
    *** Argo ZRG 604. Academy of St Martin-in-the-Fields, Neville Marriner – WAGNER: *Siegfried idyll etc.* ** (*)

Both versions of *Metamorphosen* are fine ones, though Barbirolli seems to have the warmer glow and more intense valedictory feeling. His recording has weight and opulence, and the playing of the NPO strings is most eloquent. This performance has a remarkably powerful ambience. The Academy of St Martin-in-the-Fields also give a good account of this, but it is not as strongly characterized or as deeply felt as Sir John's. The recording is predictably excellent.

Der Rosenkavalier: suite.
    ** Decca Phase 4 PFS 4187. London Symphony Orchestra, Erich Leinsdorf – WAGNER: *Tannhäuser overture and Venusberg music.* **

Leinsdorf gives an extrovert reading of music which in its original operatic setting transcends predictable limits. One cannot say the same here – particularly not in the arrangement of the great *Trio* – but with fine playing from the LSO and a typically well-spread, if inflated, sound from the Phase 4 engineers this serves its purpose well.

Symphonia domestica, Op. 53.
>   *** HMV ASD 2955. Berlin Philharmonic Orchestra, Herbert von Karajan.
>   ** Decca SXL 6442. Los Angeles Philharmonic Orchestra, Zubin Mehta.

Symphonia domestica, Op. 53; (i) Horn concerto No. 1 in E flat major, Op. 11.
>   (M) * (*) CBS Classics 61355. Cleveland Orchestra, George Szell, (i) with Myron Bloom (horn).

Not since Krauss's unforgettable performance on Decca, currently available on Eclipse (ECS 606) and not to be missed even though it is not genuine stereo, had Strauss's much maligned *Symphonia domestica* been so well served as it is by Karajan. The playing is stunningly good, and the sumptuous Berlin strings produce tone of great magnificence. EMI provide a recording of wide range, superbly focused detail and warm ambience, and it was difficult to imagine that this version would be surpassed for many years to come; but Kempe's performance (see under *Aus Italien*) now presents a formidable challenge.

Mehta's account is eminently well-recorded too, and the Los Angeles Philharmonic respond with virtuosity to the demands of this score. But the overall impression is very streamlined. It is as if Mehta had relegated Strauss's domestic household to a well-lit penthouse in downtown Manhattan, far from the ethos of Wilhelmine Germany that this work celebrates. Nor does the Szell version, played with great virtuosity,

prove much more satisfying. It is not as well recorded as its full-priced rivals, though of course it has the advantage of a fill-up.

'Greatest hits': (i) Also sprach Zarathustra, Op. 30; opening sequence; *(ii) Don Juan, Op. 20; (i) Till Eulenspiegels lustige Streiche, Op. 28; (iii) Der Rosenkavalier: suite; Salome: Dance of the Seven Veils.*
>   (B) ** CBS 30047. (i) New York Philharmonic Orchestra, Leonard Bernstein; (ii) Cleveland Orchestra, George Szell; (iii) Philadelphia Orchestra, Eugene Ormandy.

This is a generous selection and excellent value, but it is a pity that CBS chose to include Bernstein's *Till Eulenspiegel* instead of the superb Szell version. Szell's *Don Juan* is included, but (like *Till*) it is a little lacking in weight in the bass, presumably because of the long side. Otherwise the quality is good, and it is even better on side one for Ormandy's affectionate *Rosenkavalier suite*, which includes a waltz sequence presented with characteristic panache and some most beautifully refined orchestral playing throughout. Curiously, the *Dance of the Seven Veils* is lacking in the last degree of sensuous impact, something one would not have expected from this orchestra and conductor.

CHAMBER MUSIC

Serenade for wind instruments, Op. 7; Symphony for wind instruments (The Happy Workshop) (1945).
>   *** Philips 6500 097. Netherlands Wind Ensemble, Edo de Waart.

A marvellously crisp and alert performance of Strauss's *Wind symphony*, the only stereo version in the catalogue at the moment. The Netherlanders produce a beautifully homogeneous tone and their phrasing is splendidly alive. The recording is bright and truthful, and the disc is on no account to be missed by lovers of this composer's music.

Sonatina No. 1 in F major for wind instruments; Suite in B flat major for 13 wind instruments, Op. 4.
> *** Philips 6500 297. Netherlands Wind Ensemble, Edo de Waart.

The *Sonatina* is a late work, written while Strauss was recovering from an illness, and indeed subtitled 'From an invalid's workshop'. It is a richly scored piece, as thoroughly effective as one would expect from this master of wind writing. (The scoring is for double wind, a C clarinet, a corno di bassetto, bass clarinet and double bassoon, and marvellously sonorous it is.) The *B flat Suite* was written in 1884 but not published until 1911. Both these delightful pieces are given beautifully characterized accounts here, and they are crisply and cleanly recorded.

Suite in B flat major for 13 wind instruments, Op. 4.
> (B) * (*) Pye GSGC 14040. London Baroque Ensemble, Karl Haas – ARNELL: *Serenade;* KAY: *Quartet.***

Although the *Suite* is an early work, it already shows Strauss's command of sonority and texture as well as a developing melodic gift. The first movement is busy and youthfully passionate; the *Romance* has a most attractive opening horn theme, the *Gavotte* is scored with delightful wit, and the finale, after beginning romantically, ends in rumbustious high spirits. Dennis Brain's thrusting horn is most effective here, and his playing is distinct in personality in the first two movements. It is a pity that the dry, rather grainy recording cannot quite

cope with the amplitude of the loudest moments, for the performance is first-rate.

Violin sonata in E flat major, Op. 18.
> (M) ** (*) Decca Ace of Diamonds SDD 401. Josef Sivó (violin), Rudolf Buchbinder (piano) – SCHUMANN: *Violin sonata No. 1.***
> (M) ** (*) Unicorn UNS 251. Sidney Weiss (violin), Jeanne Weiss (piano) – HAYDN: *Double concerto.** (*)
> (M) ** Pye Virtuoso TPLS 13017. Alfredo Campoli (violin), Valerie Tryon (piano) – LISZT: *Violin sonata.***

This early work of Strauss inspires Sivó and Buchbinder to a passionate performance, markedly more convincing than the Schumann on the reverse. Good recording. Choice between this and the account by the Weiss Duo is not straightforward. While Sivó and Buchbinder show a more passionate impulse, the Unicorn disc has a more attractive coupling; and perhaps Campoli's coupling is the most interesting of all.

Sidney Weiss plays with a sweet tone and a disarming eloquence, and his technique is admirably secure. The balance ensures that the piano is given a genuine partnership with the violin, and Mrs Weiss makes an understanding contribution. The effect of the performance is lyrical rather than dramatically commanding, but the music-making is highly enjoyable. The recording is on the reverberant side but never muddy.

Campoli takes a little while to warm up, but as the performance gathers momentum one feels the music's impulse flowering, rather as at a live concert. There are one or two moments of poor intonation uncharacteristic of this artist, which should have been edited out, but the playing has spontaneity, and Valerie

Tryon makes a committed partner, playing with flair as well as accuracy. As in the coupling the close microphone placing tends to make the violin sound uncovered and sometimes wiry, but this effect diminishes as the performance catches fire, which it certainly does in the finale.

VOCAL MUSIC AND OPERA

Lieder: *Das Bächlein; Das Rosenband; Meinem Kinde; Morgen; Ruhe, meine Seele; Wiegenlied; Winterweihe.*

> *** HMV ASD 2493. Elisabeth Schwarzkopf (soprano), London Symphony Orchestra, George Szell – MOZART: *Concert arias.****

These orchestrations by the composer of some of his best-loved Lieder are ravishing when sung by the greatest Strauss singer of recent years and accompanied by a master conductor who on his visits to Europe loved to relax. No one who has heard the earlier record of orchestrated songs (the coupling to the *Four Last Songs*; see below) will doubt that this collaboration is a magical one, even if some of the velvet quality of that Berlin-made disc is missing here. The recording is beautifully refined to match the performances.

Vier letzte Lieder (Four Last Songs); Lieder: *Freundliche Vision; Die Heiligen drei Könige; Muttertändelei; Waldseligkeit; Zueignung.*

> ⊛ *** HMV ASD 2888. Elisabeth Schwarzkopf (soprano), Berlin Radio Symphony Orchestra, George Szell.

Even Elisabeth Schwarzkopf rarely if ever made a more radiantly beautiful record than this, and it is not surprising that it became one of EMI's classical best-sellers. Schwarzkopf's interpretation

of the *Four Last Songs* had long been known and loved in her old mono version, but if anything this is even more ravishingly expressive, with an 'inner' intensity adding to the depth of feeling as well as the beauty. Anyone who has ever fallen for Schwarzkopf must certainly hear this, and the Strauss Lieder with orchestral accompaniment on the reverse (all the orchestrations except *Zueignung* by Strauss himself) are just as captivating, ranging as they do from the playful song of the mother talking about her child to *Freundliche Vision* (somehow made more intimate by having orchestra instead of piano) and the lovely song, the most extended of the group, that Strauss wrote for his mother, telling of the Three Kings. George Szell conducts and the Berlin Radio Orchestra plays with the deepest sympathy and understanding for both the music and the singer. This is a desert-island record if ever there was one.

Die aegyptische Helena (The Egyptian Helen): Act 2: *Awakening scene (Zweite Brautnacht!); Salome: Dance of the Seven Veils; Interlude;* Final Scene: *Ah! Du wolltest.*

> (M) ** RCA LSB 4083. Leontyne Price (soprano), Boston Symphony Orchestra, Erich Leinsdorf.

The awakening scene from the beginning of Act 2 of Strauss's rarely heard *Die aegyptische Helena* is welcome as a comparatively brief fill-up to the other items on this record. The opera, first heard in Dresden in 1928, is the least known of the Strauss/Hofmannsthal collaborations, and this appetite-whetting excerpt makes one anxious to hear more. It shows Strauss in his sunset ripeness. Helen, restored to the favour of King Menelaus, sings a hymn of rapture after her second bridal night. Beautifully sung and played, though Miss Price's voice does not sound quite so well on this American recording as it does in most

European studios. Price makes an impressive Salome, not so bitingly dramatic as Birgit Nilsson, not so coolly beautiful as Montserrat Caballé, but with plenty to contribute on both sides of that comparison ledger. It is always hard to sing this scene straight without having prepared for it with the first part of the opera, and though Miss Price misses the last degree of venom at the end in the climax (the absence of Herod does not help the listener) her singing is undeniably powerful. The voice does not sound quite so rich and fresh here as it can do on record.

Arabella (opera in 3 acts): complete recording.

(M) *** Decca GOS 571/3. Lisa della Casa, Hilde Gueden (sopranos), George London (baritone), Otto Edelmann (bass), Anton Dermota (tenor), Vienna State Opera Chorus, Vienna Philharmonic Orchestra, Sir Georg Solti.

This Decca performance is most brilliant and persuasive. Solti produces some glittering sounds from the Vienna Philharmonic, faithfully captured in stereo. Della Casa soars above the stave with the creamiest, most beautiful sounds, and constantly charms one with her swiftly alternating moods of seriousness and gaiety. One moment one thinks of in particular is where in Act 1 she sees the stranger through her window, *der Richtige* ('Mr Right'), later to appear as Mandryka. Della Casa conveys wonderfully the pain and disappointment of frustrated young love as the man turns away and passes on. Perhaps Solti does not linger as he might over the waltz rhythms, and it may be Solti too who prevents Edelmann from making his first scene with Mandryka as genuinely humorous as it can be, with the Count's *Teschek, bedien'dich* as he goggles at Mandryka's generosity. Edelmann other-

wise is superb, as fine a Count as he was an Ochs in the Karajan *Rosenkavalier*. Gueden too is ideally cast as Zdenka and if anything in Act 1 manages to steal our sympathies from Arabella, as a good Zdenka can. George London is on the ungainly side, but then Mandryka is a boorish fellow anyway. Dermota is a fine Matteo, and Mimi Coertse makes as much sense as anyone could of the ridiculously difficult part of Fiakermilli, the female yodeller. The stereo is most brilliant; one wishes that some of the effects could have been more realistic, such as the bells of Elemer's sleigh outside the hotel, but that is a tiny complaint. Altogether this outstanding set is fully worthy of the opera.

Ariadne auf Naxos (opera in Prologue and 1 act): complete recording.

** (*) HMV SLS 936 (3 discs). Gundula Janowitz, Teresa Zylis-Gara, Sylvia Geszty (sopranos), James King, Peter Schreier (tenors), Hermann Prey (baritone), Dresden State Opera Orchestra, Rudolf Kempe.

(M) * (*) Decca 2BB 112/4. Leonie Rysanek, Roberta Peters, Sena Jurinac (sopranos), Jan Peerce (tenor), Walter Berry (baritone), Vienna Philharmonic Orchestra, Erich Leinsdorf.

Kempe's relaxed, languishing performance of this most atmospheric of Richard Strauss's operas is matched by opulent EMI recording. Janowitz sings with heavenly tone-colour (marred only when hard-pressed at the climax of the Lament), and Zylis-Gara makes an ardent and understanding Composer. Sylvia Geszty's voice is a little heavy for the fantastic coloratura of Zerbinetta's part, but she sings with charm and assurance. James King sings the part of Bacchus with forthright tone and more taste than most tenors. Those who remember Karajan's mono set with Schwarzkopf will not find this ideal, but there is warmth and atmosphere here in plenty.

Although one has reservations about Leinsdorf's contribution to the proceedings (compared with Karajan's great mono set the lack of sparkle is too readily obvious), it is good to see a well produced medium-priced version of so enchanting an opera. Rysanek's rather fruity voice is not ideally cast in the part of Ariadne. Sena Jurinac, as the Composer, in the Prologue is very effective; her singing has character, and there is good support from the rest of the cast, but the set is not strong on charm. Fair value at the price asked. The recording sounds well in this Decca transfer (the set was originally issued here at full price by RCA).

Capriccio (opera in 1 act): complete recording.
> *** DGG 2709 038 (3 discs). Gundula Janowitz (soprano), Dietrich Fischer-Dieskau (baritone), Peter Schreier (tenor), Hermann Prey (baritone), Karl Ridderbusch (bass), Tatiana Troyanos (mezzosoprano), Bavarian Radio Symphony Orchestra, Karl Boehm.

No recorded performance of this last and most elusive of Strauss's operas – who else would so seductively have presented a dialogue like this on the rival demands of words and music in dramatic form? – can hope to avoid comparison with the classic mono version with Schwarzkopf and Fischer-Dieskau. Janowitz is not so characterful and pointful a Countess as one really needs (and no match for Schwarzkopf), but this is a most beautiful performance of a radiant score, well sung, finely recorded and lovingly conducted.

Elektra (opera in 1 act): complete recording.
> *** Decca SET 354/5. Birgit Nilsson, Marie Collier (sopranos), Regina Resnik (mezzo-soprano), Gerhard Stolze (tenor), Tom Krause (bass), Vienna State Opera Chorus, Vienna Philharmonic Orchestra, Sir Georg Solti.

The Decca set of *Elektra* was a *tour de force* of John Culshaw and his engineering team. Not everyone will approve of the superimposed sound-effects, but as in Wagner every one of them has justification in the score, and the end result is a magnificently vivid operatic experience created without the help of vision. Nilsson is nowadays incomparable in the part, with the hard side of Elektra's character brutally dominant. Only when – as in the recognition scene with Oreste – she tries to soften the naturally bright tone does she let out a suspect flat note or two. As a rule she is searingly accurate in approaching even the most formidable exposed top notes. One might draw a parallel with Solti's direction – sharply focused and brilliant in the savage music which predominates, but lacking the languorous warmth one really needs in the recognition scene if only for contrast. Those who remember Beecham's old 78 set of the final scene may not be completely won over by Solti, but we are not likely to get a finer complete *Elektra* for a long time.

Elektra: highlights.
> *** Decca SET 459 (from above recording).

It is almost impossible to choose excerpts from so tautly conceived a one-act piece as *Elektra*, but these selections are well made, including as they do the meltingly affecting duet between Elektra and her long-lost brother. Solti may lack something in magic, but his dramatic power is irresistible. Fine recording.

Die Frau ohne Schatten (opera in 3 acts): complete recording.

(M) ** Ace of Diamonds GOS 554/7. Leonie Rysanek, Emmy Loose (sopranos), Hans Hopf, Karl Terkal (tenors), Elizabeth Höngen (mezzo-soprano), Kurt Böhme (bass), Vienna State Opera Chorus, Vienna Philharmonic Orchestra, Karl Boehm.

It was a labour of love on the part of the Decca recording manager, Christopher Raeburn, that rescued this early stereo version of an opera – some would suggest Strauss's greatest – which is unlikely to be recorded again in the near future. For its mid-fifties period the sound is remarkably good, while Boehm's direction is masterly. Once one accepts the strange symbolism of Hofmannsthal's libretto, one can go on to appreciate the richness of Strauss's inspiration, a score utterly different, in many ways more ambitious, than anything else he ever did. On any count this is a work that deserves the closest study, not just by Straussians but by those not normally attracted. The singing is variable, with a high proportion of wobblers among the soloists and Hans Hopf often producing coarse tone as the Emperor. But with stereo to help, the singing is still more than acceptable, and at mid-price on only four discs (the original mono took five) this is good value together with an excellently produced libretto.

Der Rosenkavalier (opera in 3 acts): complete recording.

⊛ (M) *** HMV SLS 810 (4 discs). Elisabeth Schwarzkopf (soprano), Christa Ludwig (mezzo-soprano), Otto Edelmann (bass), Eberhard Waechter (baritone), Teresa Stich-Randall (soprano), Philharmonia Chorus and Orchestra, Herbert von Karajan.

*** Decca SET 418/21. Régine Crespin (soprano), Yvonne Minton (mezzo-soprano), Otto Wiener (bass-baritone), Manfred Jungwirth (bass), Helen Donath (soprano), Vienna State Opera Chorus, Vienna Philharmonic Orchestra, Sir Georg Solti.

** (*) CBS 77416 (4 discs). Christa Ludwig (mezzo-soprano), Gwyneth Jones (soprano), Walter Berry (bass), Ernst Gutstein (baritone), Lucia Popp (soprano), Vienna State Opera Chorus, Vienna Philharmonic Orchestra, Leonard Bernstein.

From Karajan one of the greatest opera sets that Walter Legge ever produced, a classic performance with sound improved beyond recognition in the new transfer. Schwarzkopf points her phrases, underlining the meaning of the words after the manner of a Lieder-singer, bringing out a character at once human and emotional yet at the same time restrained and an object for admiration. She makes of the Marschallin more of a lover figure than a mother figure, and that is something which adds to the reality of the situation. Instead of the buxom prima donna we have a mature woman, still attractive, whom it would be quite understandable and sympathetic for the young Octavian to love. The moment in Act 1 when she tells Octavian how sometimes in the middle of the night she comes downstairs and stops all the clocks, so disturbed is she about the passage of time and the approach of old age, is particularly moving. With Schwarzkopf one feels that the singer is still young and attractive enough to feel this emotion as a pressing thing. She is matched by an Octavian in Christa Ludwig who has a rich mezzo but one which is neither fruity nor womanly, but steady and youthful-sounding. Teresa Stich-Randall too is wonderfully steady but her light soprano is exquisitely sweet, so that when in the presentation of the silver rose she sings the soaring phrase *Wie himmlische* one wants to use this same phrase ('How heavenly!') to describe her singing.

In the final trio three such beautifully contrasted yet steady voices make a perfect match. Karajan here, as in the other emotional climaxes, chooses a speed rather slower than is customary. Some have objected, but when the result is vocally so secure and the playing of the Philharmonia Orchestra is so full-blooded the music can certainly take this treatment, and the emotional peak seems even higher than usual. These emotional climaxes are places where – as in Puccini – Strauss seems to intend his audience to weep, and Karajan plays up to this. Otto Edelmann's Ochs is rather coarser than the characterizations of some previous singers in the part, and he exaggerates the Viennese accent on such words as *Polizei*, *gut* and *herzel*; but vocally it is most commendable, for Edelmann really does sing on the notes and does not merely give the impression in sing-speech. The discs have been reprocessed from the original tapes to produce a sound of superb quality, even by the latest standards.

On two counts Solti scores over any other rival in this much-recorded opera. He opens out all the tiny cuts which over the years have been sanctioned in opera-house performances (often with the composer's blessing). In the second place the sound is sumptuously fine even by Decca standards, far finer than that of the later CBS set with Bernstein, also recorded in the Sofiensaal, with Decca engineers attending. Curiously enough the Karajan set, beautifully refurbished for its HMV reissue, is a nearer rival in sound-quality, and the big question for most lovers of this opera will be the contrasting merits of the two Marschallins. Crespin is here at her finest on record, with tone well-focused; the slightly maternal maturity of her approach will for many appear

ideal, but the range of expression, verbal and musical, in Schwarzkopf's interpretation stands unrivalled, one of the great performances of the gramophone. Manfred Jungwirth makes a firm, virile if not always imaginative Ochs, Yvonne Minton a finely projected Octavian and Helen Donath a sweet-toned Sophie. Solti's direction is fittingly honeyed, with tempi even slower than Karajan's in the climactic moments. The one serious disappointment is that the great concluding Trio does not quite lift one to the tear-laden height one ideally wants.

Bernstein's account, though not so polished in orchestral playing or so consistently well sung as the rival versions of Karajan and Solti, has its place in commemorating a great theatrical occasion. The Viennese were swept off their feet – much to their surprise – by the magic of the American conductor. His direction of this opera at the Vienna State Opera was an almost unparalleled success, and this recorded version captures much of the ripeness, notably in the fine, mature Marschallin of Christa Ludwig, which plainly owes much to the example of Schwarzkopf (for whom, on the Karajan, Ludwig was the Octavian). Lucia Popp (as at Covent Garden) makes a charming Sophie, and Walter Berry a strong and expressive Ochs, less limited in the lower register than one might expect. But Gwyneth Jones's Octavian, despite the occasional half-tone of exquisite beauty, has too many passages of raw tone to be very appealing, a bad blot on the set. Bernstein follows traditional cuts, where Solti records the score absolutely complete. Surprisingly when Decca engineers were responsible, the sound here is much more variable than on the Decca set, with a vulgarly close horn balance.

Der Rosenkavalier: highlights.
*** Decca SET 487 (from above recording cond. Solti).

A good, generous selection from a superb set. This one-disc potted version reproduces the magnificent recording quality of the original.

Salome (opera in 1 act): complete recording.
> *** Decca SET 228/9. Birgit Nilsson (soprano), Grace Hoffman (mezzo-soprano), Gerhard Stolze, Waldemar Kmentt (tenors), Eberhard Waechter (baritone), Vienna Philharmonic Orchestra, Sir Georg Solti.

This was the first Decca 'Sonicstage' production (strange jargon), with its remarkable combination of clarity and opulence: so often with Strauss recordings we have had to choose between brilliance, with details so clear they sound fussy, and rich, fruity sound that swallows up most of the inner parts. Here the orchestral balance brings out details never heard in the opera-house, yet never getting the proportions wrong so that, say, a flute swamps the violins. The balance between voices and orchestra is just as precisely calculated. Some may complain that in the big climaxes the orchestra is too dominant, but what is remarkable is that even then the voice is clearly separated, an ideal solution. The technical trickery is on the whole discreet, and when it is not – as in the close-up effect at the end when Salome in delighted horror whispers 'I have kissed thy mouth, Jokanaan!' – it is very much in the interests of the drama, the sort of effect that any stage producer would include were it possible in the theatre.

Nilsson is splendid. She is hard-edged as usual but on that account-more convincingly wicked: the determination and depravity are latent in the girl's character from the start. In the final scene she rises to new heights, compelling one to accept and even enjoy the horror of it, while the uncleanness is conveyed more vividly than I can ever remember. One's spine tingles even as one squirms.

Of this score Solti is a master. He has rarely sounded so abandoned in a recorded performance. The emotion swells up naturally even while the calculation of impact is most precise. Waechter makes a clear, young-sounding Jokanaan. Gerhard Stolze portrays the unbalance of Herod with frightening conviction, and Grace Hoffman does all she can in the comparatively ungrateful part of Herodias.

Salome: highlights.
> *** Decca SET 457 (from above recording).

A sense of compelling evil such as has rarely been conveyed on record pervades the final scene in the magnificent collaboration of Solti and Birgit Nilsson. What matters in this one-disc 'potted' version is that a more than usually generous measure of the final scene is included. Outstanding recording.

Salome: Final scene: *Es ist kein Laut zu vernehmen.*
> * (*) Decca SXL 6657. Anja Silja (soprano), Vienna Philharmonic Orchestra, Christoph von Dohnányi – BERG: *Lulu: suite.*** (*)

Anja Silja is a vibrant singer with a strong vocal personality, but the technical flaws in her singing of Strauss will damp down the enthusiasm of all but her keenest admirers.

Stravinsky, Igor
(1882–1971)

Apollo (*Apollon Musagète*; ballet): complete recording.
> ** (*) DGG 2530 065. Berlin Philharmonic Orchestra, Herbert von Karajan – BARTÓK: *Music for strings, percussion and celesta.*** (*)

(M) * (*) Supraphon SUAST 50509. Czech Chamber Orchestra, Josef Vlach – BRITTEN: *Variations on a theme of Frank Bridge*.** (*)

Though Stravinsky tended to disparage Karajan's approach to his music as not being rugged enough, here is a performance where Karajan's moulding of his phrase, his care for richness of string texture, make for wonderful results. This neoclassical ballet score is strong enough to stand individual treatment, and the writing is consistently enhanced by the magnificent playing of the Berlin Orchestra. Excellent recording.

After their committed performance of the Britten *Variations*, it is disappointing that the Czechs give a relatively coarse performance of Stravinsky's classically pure ballet score. The sound is rich, but the rhythms are not always delicately pointed enough.

Apollo: complete recording; *Pulcinella* (ballet): *suite*.

*** Argo ZRG 575. Academy of St Martin-in-the-Fields, Neville Marriner.

This was one of the first records on which the St Martin's Academy, known for many years as an outstanding recording team in baroque music, spread its wings in the music of the twentieth century. The results are superb. In every way this is a demonstration disc, particularly the *Pulcinella* side, where the sharp separation of instruments (e.g. double-basses against trombones in the *Vivo*) makes for wonderful stereo. The Academy may at root be a democratic organization, with discussion of interpretation always encouraged, but here, with Marriner conducting rather than leading from the violin in *Pulcinella*, the precision outshines that of rival performances. The ethereal string-tones of *Apollo* (Stravinsky finally came to prefer the English to the

French title) make an ideal and well-contrasted coupling.

Capriccio for piano and orchestra.

*** Argo ZRG 674. John Ogdon (piano), Academy of St Martin-in-the-Fields, Neville Marriner – SHOSTAKOVICH: *Piano concerto No. 1*.***

(B) ** Turnabout TV 34130S. Charlotte Zelka (piano), South-West German Radio Orchestra, Harold Byrns – BARTÓK: *Rhapsody*; HONEGGER: *Concertino*; JANÁČEK: *Concertino*.**

Thanks to the fine recording and the pointed playing of the St Martin's Academy the neoclassical quality of this charming work is beautifully underlined, while the soloist provides the contrasting element of sinewy toughness. The Turnabout performance is warm and understanding, but not always as light and stylish as one would want. Charlotte Zelka is better at giving punch to the jazz rhythms than stylishness to the Bach echoes. The recording is fair only, but this is still an attractive collection of twentieth-century concertante works too rarely heard.

Capriccio for piano and orchestra; Concerto for piano and wind instruments.

(M) ** Decca Ace of Diamonds SDD 242. Nikita Magaloff (piano), Suisse Romande Orchestra, Ernest Ansermet.

Stravinsky's two piano concertos from the twenties (both written for himself to play) make an ideal coupling, and though under Ansermet's direction the performances lack some of the bite and sharp wit that this neoclassical music needs, they follow an authentic tradition from Parisian music-making between the wars. Nikita Magaloff was in fine form, and the recording sounds remarkably well for its mid-fifties vintage.

Circus polka; Concerto for strings in D major; Symphony in C major.
* (*) DGG 2530 267. Berlin Philharmonic Orchestra, Herbert von Karajan.

These are extreme examples of Karajan's refined Stravinsky style. Though undeniably he brings elegance to these examples of Stravinsky's late neoclassicism, they lose their characteristic acerbity with lines smoothed over and rhythms weakened. Smooth, refined recording to match.

(i; ii) *Ebony concerto;* (ii) *Ragtime for eleven instruments;* (iii) *The Soldier's Tale (L'Histoire du soldat): suite;* (iv) *Piano rag music.*
(M) ** (*) Supraphon SUAST 50698. (i) Karel Krautgartner (clarinet); (ii) Chamber Orchestra, Karel Krautgartner; (iii) Chamber Harmony, Libor Pešek; (iv) Jan Novotný (piano).

An appropriate coupling of Stravinsky's jazz-based works, from his first flurry of enthusiasm for the new ragtime flavour through to the *Ebony concerto* written for Woody Herman in 1945. These sharp and pointed performances, well recorded, can be warmly recommended.

(i) *Ebony concerto;* (ii) *Symphony in 3 movements.*
(M) * (*) Everest SDBR 3009. (i) Woody Herman and his Orchestra; (ii) London Symphony Orchestra, Sir Eugene Goossens.

This record gives very poor value for the *Symphony*, only 24 minutes long, spreads on to the second side, and the brief *Ebony concerto* is only an apology for a coupling. Nor is Goossens's performance as strong as some others in the catalogue, for the playing of the LSO is less than brilliant, and the recording masks much of the detail.

Concerto for piano and wind instruments (see also under *Capriccio*).
(B) ** Turnabout TV 34065S. Walter Klien (piano), Vienna Pro Musica Orchestra, Heinrich Hollreiser – BARTÓK: *Piano concerto No. 1.***

Walter Klien has been making impressive records for Vox for some years, and his live appearances in London have confirmed what a major artist he is. His performance of the *Concerto* has a fittingly bright clarity in the playing, but the result is seriously marred by the muddily reverberant acoustic. The result is still highly enjoyable, provided one's ears have had a modicum of training in the Royal Albert Hall. With the Bartók coupling this is well worth the very reasonable price.

Violin concerto in D major.
*** Decca SXL 6601. Kyung-Wha Chung (violin), London Symphony Orchestra, André Previn – WALTON: *Violin concerto.*⊛***
*** Philips SAL 3650. Arthur Grumiaux (violin), Concertgebouw Orchestra, Ernest Bour – BERG: *Violin concerto.****
(M) * (*) Supraphon SUAST 50878. Hyman Bress (violin), Prague Symphony Orchestra, Jindrich Rohan – SCHOENBERG: *Violin concerto.***

Kyung-Wha Chung is at her most incisive for the spikily swaggering outer movements, which with Previn's help are presented here in all their distinctiveness, tough and humorous at the same time. In the two movements labelled *Aria* Chung brings fantasy as well as lyricism, less overtly expressive than direct rivals but conveying instead an inner brooding quality. Excellent recording.

A lithe and beautifully refined account from Grumiaux and the Concertgebouw Orchestra. In some respects this is the most thoroughly enjoyable version on record. It is enormously vital, but its energy is controlled and the tone never becomes unduly aggressive or spiky. The recording is faithful and reproduces smoothly; it preserves an excellent balance between soloist and orchestra. Grumiaux's performance of the Berg *Concerto* on the reverse side is also particularly moving and makes the record a most desirable acquisition.

Bress's overtly romantic style suits the sharp-edged Stravinsky less well than the Schoenberg *Concerto* on the reverse. Possibly to compensate, he takes the outer movements so fast as to trip himself up. He is not helped by the reverberant recording, but as a sensible coupling for the warmly enjoyable performance of the Schoenberg this is still worth considering.

Besides Oistrakh's superb version (below), there is also a fine account of the work by Ivry Gitlis on Turnabout (TV 34276S). But this is only in simulated stereo, although its coupling, the Hindemith *Concerto* (reviewed earlier), is genuine stereo.

(i) *Violin concerto in D major;* (ii) *The Song of the Nightingale* (*Le Chant du rossignol*; symphonic poem).

(M) ** (*) Philips Universo 6585 003. (i) David Oistrakh (violin), Lamoureux Orchestra, Bernard Haitink; (ii) London Symphony Orchestra, Antal Dorati.

Oistrakh's is a stunning performance of the Stravinsky *Concerto*, even stronger and more penetrating than Isaac Stern's under the composer (temporarily out of the catalogue). Both violinists scotch the old idea of this work as something cold and arid, bringing out unexpectedly Russian qualities behind the neoclassical façade. It is almost as though Oistrakh first studied his friend's record and then refined and enriched the interpretation – which he could well have done. The only drawback is the recording – absurdly reverberant for so crisply conceived a work (although warm and pleasing as sound). Dorati's performance of *The Song of the Nightingale*, on the other hand, is given a marvellous recording, rich and detailed, with sparkle in the upper register and a superbly managed bass drum. Without losing the music's attractive exotic qualities Dorati's reading is urgent and finely pointed. This is very enjoyable indeed.

Concerto in D major for string orchestra; Danses concertantes; Dumbarton Oaks concerto in E flat major.

(M) *** Oiseau Lyre SOL 60050. English Chamber Orchestra, Colin Davis.

The *Danses concertantes* date from early in Stravinsky's Hollywood period. Despite the name the work was not planned as a ballet, but the dancing quality of much of the music has since attracted choreographers. Like the other two works on the disc it is one of Stravinsky's most light-hearted pieces, and the highly original scoring is a constant delight, particularly when recorded as brilliantly as here. The *Concerto in D for strings* was written in 1946, and the *Dumbarton Oaks concerto* in 1938, the year Stravinsky settled in America. Their neoclassicism need not deter anyone who has ever enjoyed Bach's Brandenburgs. Indeed Stravinsky himself has admitted that the Brandenburgs were his starting-point for the earlier work. Colin Davis brings enormous vitality as well as the right degree of humour. A splendid disc in every way.

Dumbarton Oaks concerto in E flat major; Octet for wind; The Soldier's Tale (L'Histoire du soldat): suite.
(B) * (*) Classics for Pleasure CFP 40098. Nash Ensemble, Elgar Howarth.

The performance of the *Octet* is most enjoyable, witty and spontaneous. The *Dumbarton Oaks concerto* has rather less impact, though the *Allegretto* is nicely done, with both warmth and charm. There is some lack of bite in the outer movements, and this lack of a strongly incisive quality means that the suite from the *Soldier's Tale* sounds less vivid than it should. The recording is natural, with an attractively judged acoustic, and the balance is good.

4 Études; Suites for orchestra Nos. 1 and 2; Symphony in C major; Symphonies for wind instruments.
(M) ** (*) Decca SDD 239. Suisse Romande Orchestra, Ernest Ansermet.

This happily-chosen collection shows Ansermet only just short of top form. The *Symphony* is strongly played, often incisive, and here, as in the fine performance of the haunting *Symphonies for wind instruments*, Ansermet's warmth more than compensates for any lack of tautness. The *bonnes bouches*, very well recorded indeed, show the lighter side of Stravinsky. The *Quatre études* have considerable subtlety, the little *Suites* are enjoyable in a spontaneous, extrovert way, and Ansermet plays them with spirit and style.

Complete ballets: *The Fairy's Kiss (Le Baiser de la fée); The Firebird (L'Oiseau de feu); Petrushka* (1911 score);

The Rite of Spring (Le Sacre du printemps).
(M) ** Decca Ace of Diamonds GOS 540/2. Suisse Romande Orchestra, Ernest Ansermet.

In their day these were admired performances, and only *The Fairy's Kiss*, a record of comparatively recent origin, was accorded a cool reception, deservedly so since the orchestral playing is disfigured by shoddy ensemble and poor intonation. At this distance of time the shortcomings of the SRO, which in the late fifties was not the fine body it had been in the immediate post-war period, are evident, and the transfers (cut at a lower level) tend to highlight the weakness of tone in the upper strings. On balance one is prepared to put up with the defects of the orchestra for the sake of Ansermet's view of *The Rite of Spring*, which has integrity; but his earlier *Petrushka* (now on Eclipse) has more guts. Dorati's *Firebird* is more imaginatively done and better played by the LSO. This is not one of Decca's most successful reissues.

The Fairy's Kiss (Le Baiser de la fée; ballet after Tchaikovsky): complete recording.
(M) * (*) Decca Ace of Diamonds SDD 244. Suisse Romande Orchestra, Ernest Ansermet.

One remembers Ansermet's early Decca disc of the *Divertimento* taken from *The Fairy's Kiss* as being crisper and rhythmically more taut, but if this performance of the complete score has moments of slackness and under-par orchestral playing, it also has an agreeable warmth. Ansermet's affection certainly projects the music vividly, helped by Decca's superb recording.

The Fairy's Kiss: Divertimento; The Soldier's Tale: suite.

(M) ** Decca Ace of Diamonds SDD 247. Suisse Romande Orchestra, Ernest Ansermet.

This is a different, later, performance of the *Fairy's Kiss Divertimento* from the one reproduced in electronic stereo on the Eclipse label. The sound is excellent, noticeably better than in the *Soldier's Tale* music on the reverse. Ansermet may not be so sharp or electrifying an interpreter of Stravinsky as the composer himself, but these clean, stylish performances have much to commend them.

Complete ballets: *The Firebird (L'Oiseau de feu)*; *Petrushka* (original score); *The Rite of Spring (Le Sacre du printemps)*.

*** Philips 6747 094 (3 discs). London Philharmonic Orchestra, Bernard Haitink.

As recordings these are in the demonstration category. Every strand in the orchestral texture is there, transparent, perfectly in proportion, giving a vivid illusion of depth and space, while the dynamic range from the gentlest string whisper to the most explosive tutti is truthfully represented. If Haitink's readings of these three great ballets of Stravinsky's early career seem rather understated, their sharp focus and rhythmic point make them increasingly satisfying on repetition. Haitink leaves the music to speak for itself; he is unhurried yet never sluggish and there is a marvellous freshness about all three readings. The result is always musical, never brilliant for its own sake – as in the evocative music at the start of *Firebird*. In *Le Sacre* he makes no gestures to the groundlings; indeed some may find him too cautious in the *Danse sacrale* and not atmospheric enough at the opening of the second part. In general, however, the performances must be counted among the very best in the catalogue, and the recordings are superbly refined.

The Firebird (L'Oiseau de feu; ballet): complete recording.

*** Decca SET 468 A/B (includes rehearsal). New Philharmonia Orchestra, Ernest Ansermet.

(B) *** Contour 6870 574. London Symphony Orchestra, Antal Dorati.

(M) *** Decca Ace of Diamonds SDD 246. Suisse Romande Orchestra, Ernest Ansermet.

** (*) HMV Quadraphonic Q4–ASD 2845; Stereo ASD 2845. Orchestre de Paris, Seiji Ozawa.

** (*) CBS 72046. Columbia Symphony Orchestra, the composer.

Ansermet came to London to record the complete *Firebird* only a few months before he died. He was in great spirits, fiery and not easily pleased, a fact which comes out in the rehearsal disc, which is included here without extra cost. It is not one of the most illuminating rehearsal records we have had, being far too closely concerned with details of the score (almost essential to have a copy before the references are plain), but overall the character of the man comes out vividly, and there are one or two moments which are inimitable, as when he recognizes one of the NPO percussion players and warmly says 'I'm glad to see you since long time', only to resume his manner of irritation at once: 'Then do it as you did it in the old times!'

This NPO version has more polished playing than that which Ansermet recorded earlier with his own Suisse Romande Orchestra, but generally the interpretations are amazingly consistent. At times one suspects that the new version is a degree slower, but on checking you find that the difference lies in the extra flexibility and polish of the London players. The recording is of demonstration quality.

Dorati's dramatic and compulsive reading of Stravinsky's complete *Firebird*

939

score makes an outstanding bargain, and this reissue of the originally Mercury disc still sounds extraordinarily rich and vivid. In fact the stereo is so good the sound hardly dates at all, although the upper string partials are thinner than we expect today. The exciting performance is as fresh and spontaneous as ever, and this record is quite ridiculously cheap. It is well worth having even if you already possess a record of the suite.

Ansermet's Ace of Diamonds disc was one of his finest early records, and although the recording has not quite the body of the newer one the disc remains a fine demonstration of the high standard this conductor achieved in his earlier Suisse Romande recordings. The Swiss conductor shows a sensibility to the atmosphere of the quieter pages of the score which Dorati sometimes misses, and he fills in the detail like delicate embroidery on the finest gauze, helped by the translucence of Decca's recording. He takes the finale slower than Dorati and is generally less dramatic.

Ozawa treats *Firebird* as an evocative, impressionistic work. His approach is markedly different from that of Ansermet and others, who consistently demonstrate the distinctiveness of even this early work, where with Ozawa it might easily be by Rimsky-Korsakov. The result is sumptuous and seductive, if not ideally clear – partly the result of the ample recording acoustic. The quadraphonic pressing is sharper in detail than the stereo version, and indeed also has a touch of brightness in the treble that seems not wholly natural. But, good though the sound is, one would not prefer this to the best of the ordinary stereo versions (Dorati or Ansermet, for instance), where the conductor's touch is more positive.

The composer's version reveals much detail of his intentions regarding balance, and as such it will be much in demand by students. As a reading it falls between Ansermet and Dorati: not so dramatic as

Dorati, not so crystalline in texture as Ansermet. The overall effect has some want of tension, and the recording, although good, is no match for Ansermet or Dorati. On the sleeve there are some fascinating reminiscences by the composer of the period of his life when the *Firebird* score was composed.

The Firebird: suite (1945 score); *Petrushka: suite* (abridged 1947 version); *Pulcinella: suite; The Rite of Spring* (complete); (i) *Symphony of Psalms; Symphony in C major.*
  (M) *** CBS 77333 (3 discs). Columbia or CBC Symphony Orchestra, the composer, (i) with Toronto Festival Singers.

These are first-rate performances dating from the 1960s. This compilation at a cheap price may attract collectors who haven't purchased the individual items previously, and it will no doubt be welcomed by those starting a Stravinsky library.

The Firebird: suite (1911 score).
  *** CBS 72652. BBC Symphony Orchestra, Pierre Boulez – BAR-TÓK: *Music for strings, percussion and celesta.*** (*)

An atmospheric and highly colourful performance from Boulez; the BBC Symphony Orchestra play with genuine responsiveness, and the performance, like that of the Bartók with which it is coupled, places this among Boulez's more successful discs. The recording is a little overlit and glamorous: the perspective is not that of a normal concert hall, but the tonal quality is satisfactory, and most readers will not find the spotlighting of wind instruments close enough to be offensive. Boulez uses a rare early selection from the ballet, ending with *Kaschei's dance* and omitting the lovely final scene.

The Firebird: suite (1919 score); Jeu de cartes (ballet): complete recording.

⊛ *** DGG 2530 537. London Symphony Orchestra, Claudio Abbado.

Stunning performances of great vitality and sensitivity. The LSO plays with superb virtuosity and spirit, and Abbado's feeling for atmosphere and colour is everywhere in evidence. Moreover the DGG recording is of demonstration standard; it has plenty of detail, presence and impact, as well as an excellently judged musical perspective. This is one of the finest Stravinsky records in the catalogue.

The Firebird: suite (1919 score); Petrushka: complete recording (1911 score).

(B) *** Decca SPA 152. Paris Conservatoire Orchestra, Pierre Monteux.

This record restores to the catalogue a coupling originally issued on RCA in the earliest days of stereo. The actual recording was made by Decca and this has now been greatly enhanced. The closing pages of Petrushka are of demonstration quality, and throughout the sound has richness and lustre, and the natural bloom more than compensates for a certain lack of refinement in the orchestral playing. Julius Katchen, no less, was recruited for the piano part in Petrushka. The style of the French wind-playing is noticeable in The Firebird, where the Paris brass bring a characteristic bray to the finale. But with any reservations these are still fine, idiomatic performances, vividly recorded, even if Monteux's view of Petrushka is more conscious of the dance, its rhythms and colours, and less emotionally involved with the dramatic events of the story.

The Firebird: suite (1919 score); Petrushka: complete recording (1947 score).

(M) *** CBS Classics 61122. New York Philharmonic Orchestra, Leonard Bernstein.

Bernstein's performance of Petrushka is one of the most involved and warm-hearted ever recorded. Even more than the composer himself, or Ansermet (whose sense of humour was pointedly stirred in this of all Stravinsky's music), Bernstein goes to the emotional heart of the score, without violating Stravinsky's expressed markings except in a couple of minor instances. The panoply of the fair music, the inbred hysteria of the puppet's rage, and above all the tragedy of his death are here conveyed with unrivalled intensity; and it adds to the compulsion of the performance to have it complete on one side (35 minutes), with splendidly vivid recording. Firebird is warmly done too, if without quite the same superb precision. An outstanding disc at the price.

The Firebird: suite (1945 score); Petrushka: suite (abridged 1947 version).

** (*) HMV ASD 2614. Chicago Symphony Orchestra, Carlo Maria Giulini.

Giulini's version of Petrushka begins with the Russian dance and stops short of the moving end. This is a very great pity, as it is one of the very best performances of the work on record; the playing of the Chicago Symphony Orchestra is absolutely magnificent, and the engineers give a finely detailed aural picture without in any way distorting the perspective. And what a fresh and vital account of the piece this is. In The Firebird, on the other hand, though this is highly sensitive and beautifully played, Giulini lingers in the already slowly paced Dance of the princesses, and some readers may find him too slow here. But there is tremendous atmosphere and in some ways this is to be preferred to many others in the catalogue on that very count.

941

The Firebird: suite (1919 score); *Petrushka: suite* (arr. Stokowski).

(B) ** Classics for Pleasure CFP 134. Berlin Philharmonic Orchestra, Leopold Stokowski.

Stokowski's account of the *Firebird suite* is predictably sumptuous; the recording is rich rather than detailed. The suite from *Petrushka* rearranges the music completely. It opens with the *Russian dance*, includes most of the ballet's highlights, and closes with Stravinsky's concert ending. Again the sound is rich rather than offering the kind of bite we are used to from Decca and Ansermet.

(i) *The Firebird: suite* (1919 score); *Petrushka: suite* (1947 score); (ii) *The Rite of Spring*.

(M) ** RCA DPS 2039 (2 discs). (i) Boston Symphony Orchestra; (ii) Chicago Symphony Orchestra; both cond. Seiji Ozawa.

Ozawa's accounts of *Petrushka* and the *Firebird suite* are lightweight interpretations in the best sense, with Ozawa's feeling for the balletic quality of the music coming over, sometimes at the expense of dramatic emphasis. Ozawa is at times too dainty. In *Petrushka* the underlying tension suggesting the strong feeling of the puppet characters is not always apparent, and there are certainly more earthy accounts of the *Rite of Spring* available. The recordings are modern and of high quality, although the acoustic is a little reverberant for the pungent rhythms of *Petrushka*.

The Firebird: suite (1919 score); *The Song of the Nightingale*.

(B) *** DGG Heliodor 2548 145. Berlin Philharmonic Orchestra, Lorin Maazel.

This attractive Heliodor disc restores to the catalogue a much-praised coupling dating from the earliest days of LP. *Le Rossignol* is an underrated Stravinsky opera, its derivative opening, with overtones of *Nuages*, and its Rimskian flavour have led to its virtues being undervalued. Among them is its extraordinarily rich fantasy and vividness of colouring; and the symphonic poem that Stravinsky made from the material of this work deserves a more established place in the concert repertoire. The exotic effects and glittering colours are superbly caught here; the Berlin Philharmonic offers the utmost refinement. Maazel's reading of the *Firebird suite* too has an enjoyable *éclat*, and he has the advantage of the most beautiful woodwind playing, notably the oboe in the *Princesses' dance* and the bassoon in the *Berceuse*. The recording of both works was notable for its splendid atmosphere, and only the massed upper strings hint at its early date. A first-rate record and a fantastic bargain!

The Firebird: suite (1919 score); *Symphony in C major*.

** Decca SXL 6582. Suisse Romande Orchestra, Uri Segal.

Segal draws a vigorous, enjoyable performance of the *Symphony* from the Suisse Romande Orchestra. It is not ideally polished, but its rhythmic resilience holds the attention keenly, and the brilliant recording reinforces the impact. The account of the *Firebird suite*, though not among the most refined, is rich and amiable and equally well recorded. Recommended to those who fancy the unexpected coupling.

4 Norwegian moods.

(M) ** Philips Universo 6580 042. London Symphony Orchestra, Igor Markevitch – SHOSTAKOVICH: *Symphony No. 6*.**

Stravinsky composed his *Four Norwegian moods* in Hollywood in 1942. The music is comparatively slight, but attractive. It is well played here, and the atmospheric recording suits it well.

Orpheus (ballet): complete recording; *Pulcinella: suite.*

(M) ** (*) Supraphon 110 1135. Czech Philharmonic Orchestra, Oskar Danon.

In a useful and attractive mid-price coupling Danon presents two of Stravinsky's neoclassic ballets that make a marked and characterful contrast. This performance of the popular *Pulcinella suite* shows Danon and the orchestra as refined and pointed interpreters, classical in the best sense. The later *Orpheus ballet*, a beautiful work but not so distinctive as most Stravinsky, is given a comparably polished performance, cooler than the composer's own. Good recording.

Pastorale.

** Decca Phase 4 PFS 4189. Royal Philharmonic Orchestra, Leopold Stokowski – BORODIN: *Polovtsian dances*** (*); TCHAIKOVSKY: *1812.***

Stravinsky's *Pastorale*, a 'song without words' written in 1908, makes a pleasant if unusual bonus for Stokowski's coupling of the *Polovtsian dances* and *1812*. It is warmly played, and Stokowski's eloquence is matched by rich recording.

Petrushka (ballet): complete recording (1911 score) (see also under *Firebird*).

⊛ *** CBS Quadraphonic MQ 31076; Stereo 73056. New York Philharmonic Orchestra, Pierre Boulez.

** Decca Phase 4 PFS 4207. New Philharmonia Orchestra, Erich Leinsdorf.

(M) * (*) Vanguard VSD 71177. London Symphony Orchestra, Charles Mackerras.

(M) * (*) Decca Ace of Diamonds SDD 240. Suisse Romande Orchestra, Ernest Ansermet – *Les Noces.** (*)

There is a controlled intensity about Boulez's interpretation which in this original version puts *Petrushka* closer than usual to the barbaric ballet which followed. In this process of clarification and intensification – often using tempi rather slower than usual – Boulez may miss some of the wit, but it is undeniably a thrilling performance. The quadraphonic recording is of outstanding quality, perhaps the finest of the CBS quad issues so far. The increase in intensity of atmosphere is remarkable, and one special feature is the way the simple drum-rolls in between the Tableaux are made fully part of the music: the effect of tension they create here is most compelling.

Leinsdorf's version is disappointing, for the NPO was below form, and even this fine orchestral trainer was unable to enforce the required precision of ensemble. The interpretation is always interesting, sympathetic and never forced. Technically this disc is of demonstration quality, with something of the vividness of Ansermet's famous early mono LP.

Mackerras's performance suffers from an unnaturally balanced recording, with the strings backward and lacking in bite. The performance is confident in manner, but the playing lacks the final degree of precision and drama, and the turnover is badly placed, in the middle of the Third Tableau.

Ansermet's performance on Ace of Diamonds does not match his earlier mono disc (still available on Eclipse ECS 508) but the reading is still a vivid one. Unfortunately the transfer is not completely successful. The First Tableau is included after *Les Noces* at the end of side one, and the original fine, brilliant stereo is transformed into something rather undernourished. Side two sounds better, but there are far better recommendations for *Petrushka* than this.

Petrushka: complete recording (1947 score).

*** CBS 72055. Columbia Symphony Orchestra, the composer.

Stravinsky offers us a genial, lightweight performance, mellow and colourful, always rhythmic and alive, but not often especially dramatic. A listener used to recordings of the more vivid 1911 score may find the composer's own conception lacking in bite. This effect is accentuated by a recording quality which spreads smoothly, but seldom focuses sharply. Yet Stravinsky evokes an incandescent quality in the orchestration which makes it sound fresh to the ear, and there are frequent touches of humour – for instance the bassoon chords in the Third Tableau, before the trumpet and drum duet – which other conductors have missed. Against such a mood the poignant final scene of the death of Petrushka is highlighted – the contrast is striking and especially moving.

Petrushka: complete recording (1947 score); *Circus polka.*

* (*) Decca SXL 6324. Los Angeles Philharmonic Orchestra, Zubin Mehta.

This reproduces the sound of the orchestra with superlative clarity and impact. In a sense the balance is a little too close: one feels as if one is in among the members of the orchestra or suspended a few feet above them; but allowing for this, few will have anything but praise for the sound produced and the quality of the playing. As an interpretation, however, Mehta's reading is a nonstarter. There is no electricity about the performance at all, no sense of excitement or of occasion. There is undoubted brilliance of execution, but little of the spirit of this immortal music comes across.

Pulcinella (ballet after Pergolesi): complete recording.

(M) * (*) Decca Ace of Diamonds SDD 245. Marilyn Tyler (soprano), Carlo Franzini (tenor), Boris Carmeli (bass), Suisse Romande Orchestra, Ernest Ansermet.

It was Diaghilev who suggested to Stravinsky that he might orchestrate some of Pergolesi's music, rather as Tommasini had orchestrated Scarlatti in *The Good-humoured Ladies*. Stravinsky took up the idea, but did not stick at mere orchestrations, turning the fragile Pergolesi fragments into something much tougher than was expected, if still very charming. Diaghilev did not approve, and, as Stravinsky said later, 'went about for a long time with a look that suggested The Offended Eighteenth Century'. Some may still resist, but most of us have capitulated long ago to the bright blandishments of the orchestral suite from the complete ballet. Ansermet here records the whole ballet; its vocal numbers add enormously to the variety of the piece. The performance is acceptable, but regularly sounds underpowered and does not match the same conductor's highly successful account of the orchestral suite (see below). In the *Serenata* of the full version Ansermet's slow speed and the romanticizing of the oboe solo are stylistically quite wrong. Good, bright Decca recording.

Pulcinella: suite.

(M) ** (*) Unicorn UNS 253. London Mozart Players, Yuval Zaliouk – RAVEL: *Le Tombeau de Couperin.****

Though Zaliouk's mid-price version cannot quite compare in polish and precision with the finest available, it is still intensely enjoyable in its bouncing vigour. Do not judge this by the slack opening of the *Sinfonia*. The rasping bravura of the trombone solo in the *Vivo* movement is much more typical. Good recording.

Pulcinella: suite; The Song of the Nightingale (Le Chant du rossignol).
> (B) *** Decca Eclipse ECS 776. Suisse Romande Orchestra, Ernest Ansermet.

This is interpretatively one of the very best of Ansermet's Stravinsky discs, and both sides provide recording quality of demonstration standard. *The Song of the Nightingale* shows how clearly and beautifully early Decca stereo could cope with a really big orchestra, and *Pulcinella* demonstrates even more impressively how a small chamber group of instruments can be caught with uncanny presence, especially the double-basses in the *Vivo* movement towards the end. Each has just the edge and rasp one hears in the flesh, without exaggeration, and the brilliance of the recording is the more remarkable considering its age (1957).

The Rite of Spring (Le Sacre du printemps; ballet*)*: complete recording; *Apropos of Le Sacre* – a recorded commentary by Igor Stravinsky about the history of a musical landmark.
> ⊛ *** CBS 72054. Columbia Symphony Orchestra, the composer.

In his invaluable introductory talk the composer tells us much of the historical background of *Le Sacre* and his own attitude to its composition. This alone gives a remarkable documentary value to this issue. But it is a mere bonus to a performance which in its vivid drama, its care for detail, and its sheer excitement leads all other versions. Time and again the composer shows the balance he intended in a complex piece of orchestration and he is able to achieve an effect only hinted at in most earlier performances. A good example is near the beginning of Part Two, where those heavy accented chords have never before sounded so sinister. But it is perhaps in the lyrical passages that the richness of colour brings the greatest gain. The recording is atmospheric, not always analytically clear, but with solo instruments mostly well projected.

The Rite of Spring: complete recording.
> *** CBS 72807. Cleveland Orchestra, Pierre Boulez.
> *** Decca SXL 6691. Chicago Symphony Orchestra, Sir Georg Solti.
> ** (*) CBS Quadraphonic MQ 31520; Stereo 73104. London Symphony Orchestra, Leonard Bernstein.
> (B) *** Classics for Pleasure CFP 129. Philharmonia Orchestra, Igor Markevitch.
> ** (*) DGG SLPM 138920. Berlin Philharmonic Orchestra, Herbert von Karajan.
> (M) ** (*) Philips 6580 013. London Symphony Orchestra, Colin Davis.
> (B) ** (*) Decca Eclipse ECS 750. Paris Conservatoire Orchestra, Pierre Monteux.
> (M) ** CBS Classics 61104. New York Philharmonic Orchestra, Leonard Bernstein.

The CBS engineers have served Boulez and the Cleveland Orchestra particularly well. The massive vividness of the sound matches the monolithic quality of the Boulez interpretation. Boulez developed his reading over the years, so that finally he came to this recorded view that tempi should be generally measured, approaching those of Stravinsky himself in his final recorded version. Boulez is less lyrical than the composer, but compensates with a relentless rhythmic urgency. After Stravinsky's own version, which is not only uniquely authoritative but uniquely compelling too, this is the most completely recommendable account, and the sound is thrilling, particularly in such moments as the brass contrasts in the *Jeux des cités rivales*.

Solti's is a powerful, unrelenting account of Stravinsky's revolutionary score, with virtuoso playing from the Chicago Orchestra and recording that demonstrates with breathtaking clarity the precision of inner detail. Some of the gentler half-tones of the score are presented rather glaringly, but this view of the work is magnificently consistent, showing Solti at his most tautly dramatic.

Bernstein's reading was recorded with quadraphonic 'surround sound' specifically in mind, the players actually situated at all points of the compass, not just placed there by the acoustic engineers. Though the performance has not quite the same pinpoint precision of more conventional versions, the electric intensity with which Bernstein approaches the score is never in doubt. More consciously romantic in expressiveness than is common, Bernstein conveys more than usual the illusion of a live performance, with the drama of the piece unfolding. The quadraphonic version is, as might be expected, immensely spectacular, and has the usual effect of tightening up the tension, while the beginning of Part 2 is more atmospheric than in ordinary stereo. But it seems that in order to put the directional information in the grooves, the resonance and weight at the bass end have been diluted a little and there is a certain harshness in the sound, which, though overwhelming in its impact, also tires the listener easily. This will be more readily apparent on some reproducers than others.

On its original issue the Markevitch version became rather submerged, partly because there were several other outstanding records available. But now at its new price, and with the stereo recording sounding remarkably vivid and modern, it is very highly recommendable indeed. The Philharmonia playing is superbly exciting (one of the highlights

of this performance is the spectacular use of the tam-tam) and at all times equal to the conductor's vitality and ruthless forward momentum.

Davis's and Karajan's accounts of the *Rite of Spring* could hardly be more contrasted. Davis is characteristically straightforward and thrusting; Karajan is smooth and civilized, yet not lacking in excitement. In this work the odds are heavily weighted in favour of the Davis approach, and whatever the incidental shortcomings – sometimes Davis misses out on detail – his full-bloodedness is to be preferred. Even so, the splendid Berlin playing for Karajan matches the conductor's approach, and it is certainly interesting to hear so sophisticated a performance, even though the absence of elemental strength is striking. The DGG recording is technically outstanding, and its very vivid projection counteracts a high degree of reverberation. The Philips recording for Davis is not super-brilliant but still very good.

Monteux conducted the first performance of *Sacre* and it is valuable to have his account returned to the catalogue in an excellent new Eclipse transfer sounding fresh and vivid. But the French orchestral playing is not ideally assured, and in the bargain range Markevitch is a much stronger competitor.

Bernstein's New York account is a wilful reading that, even more than his later version with the LSO, romanticizes Stravinsky's barbaric masterpiece. It is never less than convincing, but it has not the compulsive electricity of the London version and is not nearly so well recorded.

The Rite of Spring: complete recording; *8 Instrumental miniatures for 15 players*.
   ** (*) Decca SXL 6444. Los Angeles Philharmonic Orchestra or Chamber Ensemble, Zubin Mehta.

Mehta, in contrast with Boulez – whose Cleveland version appeared in the same month as this – favours very fast tempi in such passages as the *Spring augurs* and the final *Danse sacrale*. By contrast some of the contemplative passages, such as the *Rondes printanières*, are unusually expansive. It is an individual and interesting reading, and the playing, while not achieving Cleveland polish, is extremely brilliant. The *Eight Miniatures* are a comparatively recent orchestration of some of the easy piano pieces Stravinsky labelled *Cinq doigts*, *Five-finger exercises:* an attractive fill-up but not so important that it affects the list of preference in the *Rite*. Fine Decca recording.

The Rite of Spring: complete recording; (i) *The King of the Stars (Le Roi des étoiles*; cantata).
> ** (*) DGG 2530 252. Boston Symphony Orchestra, Michael Tilson Thomas, (i) with New England Male Conservatory Chorus.

Michael Tilson Thomas's version of *The Rite of Spring* has an important if brief makeweight in the rare motet of the same period – unperformed for several decades but here shown as an intensely imaginative, evocative choral work. The major offering is presented in a warmly expressive reading that misses some of the music's bite. The amply reverberant recording matches that approach.

Symphony in C major; (i) *Symphony of Psalms.*
> *** CBS 72181. Columbia Symphony Orchestra, the composer, (i) with Toronto Festival Singers.

Stravinsky has never quite equalled the intensity of the pre-war 78 performance of the *Symphony of Psalms* he conducted with the Walter Straram Chorus and Orchestra. That had many more technical faults than this, and it is only fair to say that this later account still outshines any other by conductors like Ansermet. It is just that with so vivid a work it is a shade

disappointing to find Stravinsky as interpreter at less than maximum voltage. The *Symphony in C*, with its extraordinary bleak ending, is splendidly done, and this is a valuable coupling of high quality.

Symphony in 3 movements; The Song of the Nightingale (Le Chant du rossignol).
> (B) ** Classics for Pleasure CFP 40094. Philharmonia Orchestra, Constantin Silvestri.

Silvestri was a romantic, and his performances carry great conviction in his effort to give these works a new warmth. This record may in fact win converts to Stravinsky, but one is less sure that it would have converted Stravinsky himself to such interpretations. The composer has shown in the *Symphony* how a sharper-edged performance not only has more vitality but conveys the implicit emotion. But with very good orchestral playing and plenty of bite to the recorded sound, the *Symphony* is certainly enjoyable here, and *The Song of the Nightingale*, if not as fine as Ansermet's or Maazel's (see above), makes a vivid coupling.

Symphony in 3 movements; (i) *Symphony of Psalms.*
> (M) * (*) Decca SDD 238. Suisse Romande Orchestra, Ernest Ansermet, (i) with Le Chœur des Jeunes de Lausanne, Le Chœur de Radio-Lausanne.

There is something curiously heavy and lethargic about Ansermet's approach to the *Symphony of Psalms*. But this performance is better than his earlier one, originally issued on 78s, and the well-projected recording adds sharpness to the performance, which might otherwise have seemed flat. The *Symphony in 3 movements* similarly lacks a feeling of strong rhythmic vitality. The work is full of Stravinsky subtleties of mood and balance, and

Ansermet's reading is obviously authoritative in detail, but it lacks essential impetus.

CHAMBER AND PIANO MUSIC

(i) *Concertino for 12 instruments; Symphonies for wind instruments;* (ii) *3 Pieces for string quartet;* (iii) *3 Pieces for clarinet;* (i; iv) *Renard.*

(M) * (*) Everest SDBR 3184. (i) Domaine Musical Ensemble, Pierre Boulez; (ii) Parrenin Quartet; (iii) Guy Deplus (clarinet); (iv) soloists.

This is a useful collection of some of Stravinsky's shorter works. The best performance is of the farmyard tableau *Renard*, which under Boulez's direction has humour in plenty. It is also good to have the very rare clarinet pieces, though the soloist, Guy Deplus, has not quite the assurance to carry them off as he should. Boulez's direction of the *Concertino* in its twelve-instrument version (arranged from the original string quartet) is not biting enough, and that criticism, surprising for Boulez, also applies to the most searching work on the disc, the *Wind symphonies*, written in memory of Debussy, which contains some of Stravinsky's most bitingly compressed thoughts. Even so, anyone who wants this rare collection may find the shortcomings tolerable.

Duo concertante for violin and piano.

(M) ** Supraphon SUAST 50693. Petr Messiereur (violin), Jarmila Kozderková (piano) – HINDEMITH: *Sonata*; SCHOENBERG: *Fantasy*; WEBERN: *4 Pieces.***

Stravinsky's *Duo concertante* was written at the period in the early thirties when with the help of Samuel Dushkin, the violinist, he was interesting himself in the technical problems of the violin. The two principal works that emerged, the *Violin concerto* and this *Duo concertante*, have both taken a long time to penetrate into the regular repertory, but at last the *Violin concerto* has been accepted as a work far more weighty than its apparently trivial outlines would suggest, and the *Duo concertante* similarly emerges as more than a neoclassical trifle. The first movement may start rather like a Bach prelude, but the slow concluding *Dithyramb* has a characteristically cool beauty which haunts one. The performances – like those of the other important works on the disc – are first-rate.

Italian suite (for violoncello and piano).

(M) * (*) Supraphon SUAST 50610. Saša Večtomov (cello), Vladimir Topinka (piano) – SCHUBERT: *Sonata in A minor.** (*)

Večtomov and Topinka carry over their expressive style from Schubert, where arguably it is very apt, to Stravinsky, where on any reckoning it is less so. The music is taken from Stravinsky's *Pulcinella* adaptations of Pergolesi, which provides a reason of its own for romanticism being avoided. But despite purist doubts, the playing is very convincing and as a coupling for the Schubert work it is a reasonable enough recommendation.

2 Pieces for string octet, Op. 11; 3 Pieces for string quartet.

*** HMV ASD 3072. Augmented Borodin Quartet – SHOSTAKOVICH: *Piano quintet.****

An odd but attractive coupling for an outstanding version of Shostakovich's *Piano quintet*. Excellent playing and recording.

Symphonies for wind instruments.

(M) ** (*) Supraphon SUAST 50679.

Prague Chamber Harmony Wind Ensemble, Libor Pešek – BERG: *Chamber concerto.****

Written as a tribute to Debussy on his death, this is elegiac, in that grief and tragedy are uppermost. But the emotion is savage, the colours are stark and bare, and everything is expressed with telegraphic compression, so that in under nine minutes one has the sense of experiencing a far longer work. It is almost as though *The Rite of Spring* had been reduced to its barest essentials in texture as well as musical argument. This was the work whose notorious first performance in London under Koussevitzky set off a serious quarrel between conductor and composer. The composer argued that music could not express anything *per se*, but ever after he has been misquoted as saying that his music could not evoke emotions. Among twentieth-century works this has a specially deep store of implicit emotion. As in the Berg *Concerto* which takes up most of the disc, the style of the Prague players is consciously expressive. The result tends to soften the original sharp edges.

Collection: *Circus polka; 4 Études, Op. 7; Piano rag music; Ragtime; Serenade in A major; Piano sonata; Tango.*
　(M) ** Nonesuch H 71212. Noël Lee (piano).

Noël Lee misses the full range of tone needed in this angular piano music. He has nothing like the sharpness that the composer himself brought to the opening of the *Serenade*, and in gentler passages his touch is a degree too heavy. But there is still real spirit and understanding throughout the whole collection (which gathers together all of Stravinsky's music originally written for piano solo) and with good bright recording, it is a valuable record, even making no allowance for price.

Concerto for 2 (solo) *pianos.*
　(M) * (*) Supraphon SUAST 50694. Vera and Vlastimil Lejsek (pianos) – BRITTEN: *Pieces*; LUTOSLAWSKI: *Paganini variations.***

Stravinsky wrote his *Concerto for two pianos* (without orchestra) for himself to play with his son Soulima. Many Stravinskians praise its boldness, for the writing is as uncompromising as anything Stravinsky produced in that pre-war period. He intended the first piano to stand out as a concertante instrument against the other, and that is where above all this Czech performance falls down, for the separation is poor, and the listener is faced with a veritable jungle of counterpoint in first and last movements, 'bold' only in the sense of being aggressively hard on the ear. Plainly the work should be represented in the catalogue, but one hopes for a more searching account than this. The performance has not the same sensitivity that marks out the Britten and Lutoslawski pieces on the record.

Three movements from Petrushka.
　*** DGG 2530 225. Maurizio Pollini (piano) – PROKOFIEV: *Piano sonata No. 7.*⊛ ***

Staggering, electrifying playing of the highest degree of excitement. Good recording.

The Rite of Spring (piano duet version); *3 Easy pieces; 5 Easy pieces.*
　** Decca SXL 6403. Bracha Eden, Alexander Tamir (piano, four hands).

It is the greatest pity that the incomparable performance of the *Rite of Spring* in its duet version which Daniel Barenboim and Vladimir Ashkenazy gave in South Bank Summer Music was never committed to disc. There the interplay of two imaginative personalities and their

949

exuberance in rhythmic pointing made up for the obvious lack of orchestral colour. Here Eden and Tamir are just not creative enough in their interpretation. Particularly for repetition on the gramophone you need a more striking performance of a piano-duet arrangement. The *Easy pieces* make an excellent fill-up, but there should be more wit conveyed.

VOCAL MUSIC AND OPERA

Cantata for soprano, tenor, female voices and instrumental ensemble; Mass.

(M) *** Oiseau-Lyre SOL 265. Doreen Murray (soprano), Patricia Kern (mezzo-soprano), Jean Allister (contralto), Alexander Young, Edgar Fleet (tenors), Christopher Keyte (bass), St Anthony Singers, section of the English Chamber Orchestra, Colin Davis.

Stravinsky had a way of setting words already set by Benjamin Britten (with what effect on communications between Aldeburgh and Beverly Hills we do not know), and one of the most striking examples is Stravinsky's setting of the Lyke-Wake Dirge in the *Cantata* of 1952. Where Britten in his setting in the *Serenade* harrows one by the sheer atmospheric intensity of the slow crescendo, Stravinsky chills one by harshness and cruelty. After the Britten, one is at first alienated, almost revolted. But then, as so often with Stravinsky, the sharp originality of the concept forces itself through the initial barrier, and the grinding relentlessness makes its inspiration felt. The *Cantata* is an interesting work in the other movements too, and the mastery of the quickest ever setting of the *Mass* is never in doubt, though Davis is not so successful as Stravinsky himself in conveying the essential starkness. Excellent recording.

Mass.

*** Argo ZRG 720. Christ Church Cathedral Choir, Oxford, London Sinfonietta, Simon Preston – POULENC: *Christmas motets etc.****

A finely classical reading of Stravinsky's austerely beautiful *Mass* for voices and instruments. Excellent recording.

Les Noces (ballet-cantata).

(M) * (*) Decca Ace of Diamonds SDD 240. Basia Retchitzka (soprano), Lucienne Devallier (contralto), Hugues Cuénod (tenor), Heinz Rehfuss (bass), Motet Choir of Geneva, Suisse Romande Orchestra, Ernest Ansermet – *Petrushka.* (*)

Ansermet fails to capture the essential bite in Stravinsky's sharply-etched portrayal of a peasant wedding. The hammering rhythms must sound ruthless, and here they are merely tame.

Symphony of Psalms (see also under *The Firebird; Symphony in C; Symphony in 3 movements*).

(M) * (*) Supraphon SUAST 50778. Czech Philharmonic Chorus and Orchestra, Karel Ančerl – MARTINŮ: *Prophecy of Isaiah.* (*)

Ančerl's account of the *Symphony of Psalms* suffers from rhythmic heaviness in all three movements, for he fails to sustain his rather slow tempi, notably in the finale. The phrasing is not as flexible as it might be, but with more vivid and immediate choral recording than is usual from Supraphon the result still makes a fair coupling for the rare Martinů work on the reverse.

(i) *Mavra* (opera in 1 act; sung in English); (ii) *Renard* (burlesque; sung in English); *Scherzo à la Russe.*

(M) *** Decca Ace of Diamonds SDD 241. (i) Joan Carlyle (soprano), Kenneth MacDonald (tenor), Helen Watts, Monica Sinclair (contraltos); (ii) Gerald English, John Mitchinson (tenors), Peter Glossop, Joseph Rouleau (basses); all with Suisse Romande Orchestra, Ernest Ansermet.

A fascinating Stravinsky collection, vividly performed and brilliantly recorded. The one-act comic opera *Mavra*, with its impossible story of the hussar-lover who dresses up as a servant-girl in pursuit of his beloved, is an attractive addition to the medium-price catalogue and it is convincingly sung here by a British cast. It is well coupled with the curious burlesque fable *Renard*, with its striking rhythmic ideas. The use of English will for most listeners be an obvious advantage. Here more than usual Ansermet caught the sort of toughness that one recognizes in the composer's own performances of his music. The haunting yet light-hearted *Scherzo à la Russe*, with its bouncing main theme, is a splendid makeweight.

Oedipus Rex (opera-oratorio): complete recording.

(M) * (**) Supraphon SUAST 50678. Jean Desailly (narrator), Ivo Zídek (tenor), Vera Soukupová (mezzo-soprano), Karel Bermann, Eduard Haken, Zdenek Kroupa (basses), Czech Philharmonic Chorus and Orchestra, Karel Ančerl.

Surprisingly the Czech performers give a far more convincing and moving account of Stravinsky's intensely compressed operatic masterpiece than the composer did himself in his stereo version. There is a degree of expressiveness in the phrasing that might not please the composer himself, but when instead of an American amateur chorus (such as

Stravinsky had) you have a group of virtuoso singers, the result is sharp and committed. Though the chorus is larger here, the precision of discipline is much more acute. The Czech soloists bring a slavonic timbre which is not at all inappropriate in this work with its lingering traces of Russian influence, and the recording quality is very good indeed. There remains one maddening technical flaw. The final two pizzicato notes at the very end of the opera have been snipped off the tape, and the piece is made to end with the gradual diminuendo on repeated triplets. The price may help to smooth any wound caused by that inadequacy.

The Rake's Progress (opera): complete recording.

*** CBS 77304 (3 discs). Alexander Young (tenor), Judith Raskin (soprano), Regina Sarfaty (mezzo-soprano), John Reardon (baritone), Don Garrard (bass), Sadler's Wells Chorus, Royal Philharmonic Orchestra, the composer.

It was a splendid idea to get Stravinsky to come to London to record *The Rake's Progress* in what has many elements of the Sadler's Wells production – which incidentally Stravinsky attended some time earlier. In particular the Rake of Alexander Young is a marvellous achievement, sweet-toned and accurate and well characterized. In the choice of the other principals too it is noticeable what store Stravinsky set by vocal precision; generally he seemed to like voices with little vibrato. Judith Raskin makes an appealing Anne Trulove, sweetly sung if not specially well projected dramatically. John Reardon too is remarkable more for vocal accuracy than striking characterization, but Regina Sarfaty's Baba is marvellous on both counts, and her anger at being spurned just before the 'squelching' makes a superb moment. The

951

Sadler's Wells Chorus sings with even greater drive under the composer than in the theatre, and the Royal Philharmonic (the only element from the earlier Glyndebourne production) plays with warmth and a fittingly Mozartian sense of style, to match Stravinsky's surprisingly lyrical approach to his own scores. The recording is excellent, and few modern opera sets can be recommended more warmly: it is a work that grows in strength on the one hand and charm on the other with every hearing.

Subotnik, Morton
(born 1933)

Lamination.

(B) (**) Turnabout TV 34428S. Buffalo Philharmonic Orchestra, Lukas Foss – BERGSMA: *Violin concerto***; EATON: *Concert piece.***

This work represents a curious reversal, for here the orchestra makes sound patterns to simulate an electronic instrument itself designed to simulate: i.e. a synthesizer. A fascinating exercise, no doubt, but the end result does not provide a piece suitable for repeated listening.

Suk, Josef
(1874–1935)

(i) *Fantasy in G minor for violin and orchestra, Op. 24;* (ii) *Ballad for violin and piano, Op. 30; 4 Pieces for violin and piano, Op. 17.*

(M) ** Supraphon SUAST 50777. Josef Suk (violin), (i) Czech Philharmonic Orchestra, Karel Ančerl; (ii) Jan Panenka (piano).

We sorely need a first-class account of Suk's masterpiece, the *Asrael symphony,* a work of great depth and originality. Readers will get little idea of Suk's imaginative power from the three works collected on this disc, even if they make more than acceptable listening. The *Fantasy* is a brilliant piece full of virtuosity that relates to the traditional essays in violin wizardry as well as to the Czech national tradition. The work has music of characteristic fantasy, though the rhetorical brilliance tends to dominate. The orchestral accompaniment under Ančerl is no less staggering than Suk's playing, and most listeners will find the results refreshing and enjoyable even if they convey an inadequate picture of the composer's stature. The *Four Pieces,* Op. 17, are better known and very attractive, and the early *Ballad,* if unmemorable, is by no means without interest. The recording of the orchestral side is a trifle reverberant and very bright, but the other side is altogether excellent.

Serenade for strings in E flat major, Op. 6.

*** Argo ZRG 792. Los Angeles Chamber Orchestra, Neville Marriner – JANÁČEK: *Suite***; R. STRAUSS: *Capriccio: Introduction.** (*)

** Decca SXL 6533. Stuttgart Chamber Orchestra, Karl Münchinger – R. STRAUSS: *Capriccio: Introduction*; WOLF: *Italian serenade.***

Suk's attractive *Serenade* ought to be better known. It is a work of considerable charm, but it has an underlying power and eloquence, as this superb account by Marriner and his Los Angeles Orchestra fully reveals. The recorded sound is more brilliantly lit than we are used to in Marriner's Academy of St Martin-in-the-Fields discs, but it is of the highest quality and naturally balanced. The

Stuttgart account is beautifully recorded too, with fresh and lively string tone, and the only drawback is a certain unsmiling quality that detracts from the charm and spontaneity of the score. Marriner's is the version to have; moreover it is coupled with Janáček's haunting *Suite*, an early work of considerable substance.

War triptych, Op. 35.
> (M) ** (*) Supraphon SUAST 50476. Czech Philharmonic Orchestra, Alois Klima – NOVÁK: *De profundis.* ** (*)

Like the Novák *De profundis*, this is a noble and eloquent work, though it dates of course from the First rather than the Second World War. The performance has great conviction and is well recorded. Suk's music may have less personality than Janáček or Martinů, let alone his father-in-law Dvořák, but it has rich rewards for those who will take the trouble to investigate it.

String quartet No. 2, Op. 31; Meditation on the Czech chorale 'St Wenceslas', Op. 35.
> (M) ** (*) Supraphon SUAST 50818. Vlach Quartet.

The *Quartet* is altogether more intense in feeling than its predecessor, which used to be available on Supraphon, and it reflects something of the melancholy of spirit of the *Asrael symphony*, written only a few years before. Its expressive opening, which runs through the whole work, was originally intended for a piece called *Mysterium*. It is a single-movement work lasting about a half-an-hour; its thematic material is curiously haunting and in some respects its boldness and integrity suggest that Janáček's quartets are just round the corner. Though not wholly convincing formally, this is music of genuine personality and eloquence. Good though not outstanding recording for a fine performance, full of spirit and distinguished by excellent intonation. The *Meditation* is a more familiar work and is equally well played.

Sullivan, Arthur
(1842–1900)

Symphony in E minor (Irish); Overture Di Ballo.
> *** HMV ASD 2435. Royal Liverpool Philharmonic Orchestra, Sir Charles Groves.

The *Symphony* is a delightful work, once the overweening self-importance of the opening slow introduction (understandable in a composer of twenty-one) is left behind. Sullivan, already at twenty-one the golden boy of English music, went to Ireland and there, with echoes almost as much of Schumann as of the predictable Mendelssohn and Schubert, he was inspired to conceive this lyrical symphony. It is not great music, but it rarely if ever loses the attention, and the jaunty *Allegretto* of the third movement with its 'Irish' tune on the oboe is nothing less than haunting. Groves and the Royal Liverpool Philharmonic give an affectionate performance, and provide an ideal fill-up in the well-known *Overture Di Ballo*. First-rate, colourful recording.

Overtures: (i; ii) *Di Ballo;* (i; iii) *The Gondoliers;* (iv; v) *HMS Pinafore;* (i; iii) *Iolanthe; The Mikado;* (iv; iii) *The Pirates of Penzance;* (iv; vi) *The Yeomen of the Guard.*
> (B) *** Decca SPA 259. (i) New Symphony Orchestra of London; (ii) Anthony Collins; (iii) Isidore Godfrey; (iv) Royal Philharmonic Orchestra; (v) James Walker; (vi) Sir Malcolm Sargent.

The opera overtures are taken from the Decca complete sets. They readily reflect the unfailing sparkle and spontaneity Godfrey brought to his performances and the remarkably consistent quality of the Decca recording. The acoustic is slightly dry but gives an authentic flavour of the theatre. *HMS Pinafore* is directed by James Walker and represents the best part of an otherwise disappointing set, while *The Yeomen of the Guard* reflects the extra spaciousness Sir Malcolm Sargent brought to this score. As a bonus Decca have discovered a vivacious recording of the *Di Ballo overture* conducted by Anthony Collins which must date from the mid-fifties yet still provides stereo of excellent quality. This is much the best available disc of Sullivan overtures and makes a splendid bargain.

Overtures: *The Gondoliers; HMS Pinafore; Iolanthe; The Mikado; Patience; The Yeomen of the Guard*.
   ** Columbia Studio 2 TWO 403. Royal Liverpool Philharmonic Orchestra, Sir Charles Groves.

Broadly spacious performances here, essentially those of the concert hall rather than the opera-house. The big, fat bass drum at the opening of *The Mikado overture* epitomizes the breadth of approach, and this is one of the items which gains most from the resonance of the acoustic and the lyrical richness of the string sounds. But there is much less sparkle than on the Decca disc, which in its own way is just as impressively recorded.

Overtures: *The Gondoliers; HMS Pinafore; Iolanthe; The Mikado; The Pirates of Penzance; The Yeomen of the Guard*.
   (M) * HMV SXLP 30172. Pro Arte Orchestra, Sir Malcolm Sargent.

In spite of the warm, vivid recording one cannot praise Sir Malcolm's selec-

tion of overtures. The playing and tempi are unbelievably limp: there is an almost total absence of vivacity and sparkle. The Decca disc is the one to have.

Pineapple Poll (ballet music, arr. Mackerras).
   *** HMV CSD 1399. Royal Philharmonic Orchestra, Charles Mackerras.
   (B) ** Pye GSGC 15023. Pro Arte Orchestra, John Hollingsworth.

If ever there was a definitive record, here is one from Mackerras of his own brilliantly witty score. The orchestral playing is immaculate; among the fine wind-playing the solo oboe is especially delightful. HMV have provided a quite outstanding recording, colourful, wide in range, with a splendid bloom and ambience, which will surely be hard to beat. Highly recommended.

Hollingsworth offers a lively reading supported on the whole by good orchestral playing, and the slightly brash recorded quality quite suits the ebullience of the score. The upper register is a trifle unclean but is easily smoothed out.

OPERAS

Cox and Box: complete recording.
   *** Decca SKL 4138/40. Alan Styler, Joseph Riordan, Donald Adams, New Symphony Orchestra of London, Isidore Godfrey – *The Gondoliers*.***

Cox and Box is a superb performance in every way. It is given a recording which without sacrificing clarity conveys with perfect balance the stage atmosphere. Those who feel that Sullivan's genius could operate solely with the catalyst of Gilbert's words will be surprised to find here that the music is almost as delightful as any written for Gilbert. *Cox and Box* has in fact words by F. C. Burnand and is based very closely on Maddison Morton's farce *Box and Cox*. It was written in 1867 and thus pre-dates the first Gilbert and Sullivan success, *Trial by Jury*, by eight years. One must notice the lively military song *Rataplan*, splendidly sung by Donald Adams, an ideal Bouncer – which was to set the style for many similar and later pieces with words by Gilbert – and also the captivating *Bacon 'Lullaby'*, so ravishingly sung by Joseph Riordan. Later on in Box's recitative telling how he 'committed suicide' Sullivan makes one of his first and most impressive parodies of grand opera, which succeeds also in being effective in its own right.

(i) *The Gondoliers; The Mikado;* (ii) *The Yeomen of the Guard*: complete recordings.

(M) *** Decca 9 BB 162/7. John Reed or Peter Pratt, Donald Adams, Kenneth Sandford, Thomas Round, Alan Styler, Gillian Knight, Jean Hindmarsh, Joyce Wright, D'Oyly Carte Opera Company, Royal Philharmonic Orchestra or New Symphony Orchestra of London, cond. (i) Isidore Godfrey, (ii) Sir Malcolm Sargent.

This album is one of two that collect together at reduced price the stereo recordings of the popular Savoy operas made under Godfrey's inimitable baton (although here Sargent conducts *The Yeomen of the Guard*). *The Mikado* is the only performance about which one could have any serious reservations (see below).

The Gondoliers: complete recording with dialogue.

*** Decca SKL 4138/40. John Reed, Jeffrey Skitch, Kenneth Sandford, Thomas Round, Alan Styler, Gil-lian Knight, Jennifer Toye, Mary Sansom, Joyce Wright, D'Oyly Carte Opera Chorus, New Symphony Orchestra of London, Isidore Godfrey – *Cox and Box*.***

Even on musical grounds one would prefer the D'Oyly Carte *Gondoliers* to the alternative HMV performance under Sir Malcolm Sargent (currently out of the catalogue). Certainly in that set there is some very fine singing, both solo and ensemble, but this is offset by Sir Malcolm's often unaccountably slow tempi (especially in the *Cachucha*). Isidore Godfrey's conducting here is vividly alive and this is perhaps the best Gilbert and Sullivan he has given us on record, better even than the splendid *HMS Pinafore*. Decca generously provided a large and first-class orchestra and a superbly spacious recording (far, far better than the HMV sound). Perhaps during the opening scene one has the feeling of almost too much orchestra, the solo singers being a shade backward, but this is largely a question of getting the volume setting just right. The solo singing throughout is consistently good. Jeffrey Skitch and Jennifer Toye are a well-matched pair of lovers, and the two Gondoliers and their wives are no less effective. Thomas Round sings *Take a pair of sparkling eyes* very well indeed. The ensemble singing is superbly balanced and always both lively and musical. The *Cachucha* is captivating and goes at a sparkling pace. Everywhere one can feel the conductor's guiding hand – an instance is the splendidly managed broadening of the orchestral ritornello which forms the closing bars of Act 1.

The dialogue is for the most part well spoken, and Kenneth Sandford, who is a rather light-voiced Don Alhambra, makes much of his spoken part as well as singing his songs with fine style. The fact that he is no match for Owen Brannigan on HMV is more a question of vocal timbre than poor singing or acting. John Reed is a suitably dry Duke of Plaza-Toro: he is not perhaps as funny as Martyn Green was in the earlier Decca set, but he makes the part his own and is well partnered by Gillian Knight. All in all a considerable achievement.

The Grand Duke: complete recording.
Pearl SHE 516/7. John Gilbert, Paul Simmonds, John Sowden, Richard Doran, Don Powell, Pat Thom, Joan Edwards, Elsie Broadbent, Cheam Operatic Society Chorus, Southern Festival Orchestra, David Harding.

Dedicated Savoyards will be glad to know that this recording of an amateur performance is available. But the records cannot possibly be recommended for general use. The principals no doubt are effective enough on stage, and John Gilbert has the right style in the title role. But the recording offers no projection whatsoever, and these singers are not experienced enough to project themselves. The choral singing is sometimes enthusiastic but always undisciplined, the orchestral playing is often appalling, and the whole production fails to have the compensating gusto which can make amateur performances (in the North of England at least) a rewarding experience in spite of the lack of polish. The quality of the recording itself, made at a low level, is poor, with a sprinkling of cutting faults on the discs themselves to distract the listener further.

HMS Pinafore; The Pirates of Penzance; Iolanthe: complete recordings.
(M) *** Decca 9BB 156/61. John Reed, Donald Adams, Valerie Masterson, Owen Brannigan, Kenneth Sandford, Thomas Round, Jeffrey Skitch, Gillian Knight, Joyce Wright, Alan Styler, D'Oyly Carte Opera Company, Royal Philharmonic Orchestra or New Symphony Orchestra of London, Isidore Godfrey.

No reservations here. *HMS Pinafore* (along with *The Gondoliers*) marked the high-water mark of Godfrey's achievement on disc (along with the marvellous old mono *Mikado*, still available on Ace of Clubs), and *The Pirates* was not far behind. *Iolanthe* has been re-recorded, but the new set is different from, rather than superior to, the old. Excellent value.

HMS Pinafore: complete recording with dialogue.
⊛ *** Decca SKL 4081/2. John Reed, Jeffrey Skitch, Thomas Round, Donald Adams, Jean Hindmarsh, Joyce Wright, Gillian Knight, D'Oyly Carte Opera Chorus, New Symphony Orchestra of London, Isidore Godfrey.
Decca Phase 4 OPFS 1/2. John Reed, Thomas Lawlor, John Ayldon, Valerie Masterson, Ralph Mason, Christine Palmer, D'Oyly Carte Opera Chorus, Royal Philharmonic Orchestra, James Walker.

Everyone has their own G. and S. favourite and *HMS Pinafore* is mine (I.M. writing). There is a marvellous spontaneity about the invention, and somehow the music has a genuine briney quality. *Pinafore* also contains Dick Deadeye, the strangest character in all the Savoy operas, who seems to have popped suddenly to the surface – in Freudian fashion – from Gilbert's subconscious, a more powerful figure than any of the matronly ladies at whom Gilbert liked to poke fun. It would be difficult to imagine a better recorded performance of *Pinafore* than the earlier Decca. It is complete with dialogue, and while there is controversy about this (I personally find that I never tire of the best lines), here the dialogue is vital in establishing the character of Deadeye, as much of his part is spoken rather than sung. The dialogue is spoken extremely well here. Donald Adams is a totally memorable Deadeye and his larger-than-life personality underpins the whole piece. Among the others Jeffrey Skitch is a first-class Captain; Jean Hindmarsh is absolutely convincing as Josephine (it was a pity she stayed with the company for so short a time), and she sings with great charm. Thomas Round is equally good as Ralph Rackstraw. Little Buttercup could be slightly more colourful, but this is a small blemish, and among the minor parts George Cook is a most personable Bill Bobstay. The choral singing is excellent, the orchestral playing good and Godfrey conducts with marvellous spirit and lift. The recording has splendid atmosphere.

Apart from a very distinguished portrayal of Sir Joseph Porter K.C.B. by John Reed (which deserves to be preserved in an excerpts disc) and a fresh account of Josephine's songs from Valerie Masterson, the Phase 4 set is an artistic disaster. The recording is technically brilliant, but at the same time is a perfect demonstration of how not to present Gilbert and Sullivan on disc. There is no suggestion of an overall stage acoustic; often the voices are unrealistically close and dry (although the words are made crystal-clear in this way). Extra background noises, including seagulls and lapping water, are added ad lib to no effect whatsoever. The result is a total lack of real atmosphere. The performance itself is little better. James Walker directs the jaunty numbers with a curiously clipped rhythm and an absence of lightness, and there is little spontaneity anywhere; even the famous *Wedding bells trio* in Act 2 is dull. The dialogue is poorly directed and sounds very self-conscious.

HMS Pinafore: complete recording without dialogue.

(M) *** H M V SXLP 30088/9. George Baker, John Cameron, Richard Lewis, Owen Brannigan, Elsie Morison, Monica Sinclair, Glyndebourne Festival Chorus, Pro Arte Orchestra, Sir Malcolm Sargent – *Trial by Jury*.***

It is to Owen Brannigan's great credit that, little as he has to do here, without the dialogue, he conveys the force of Deadeye's personality so strongly. For those who find the dialogue tedious in repetition this is a very happy set, offering some good solo singing and consistently lovely ensemble singing and chorus work. The whole of the final scene is musically quite ravishing, and throughout if Sir Malcolm fails to find quite all the wit in the music (which Isidore Godfrey points so successfully in his Decca set) he is never less than lively. George Baker is of course splendid as Sir Joseph, and John Cameron, Richard Lewis and (especially) Monica Sinclair, as Buttercup, make much of their songs. Elsie Morison I found disappointing; she spoils the end of her lovely song in Act 1 by singing sharp. However, she brings plenty of drama to her Scena in Act 2. The male trio near the end of Act 1 is quite outstandingly well sung – full of brio and personality. H M V's recording is bright and easy to reproduce, and this coupling with *Trial by Jury* makes a fine bargain.

Iolanthe: complete recording with dialogue.
*** Decca SKL 4119/20. John Reed, Mary Sansom, Yvonne Newmann, Gillian Knight, Alan Styler, Kenneth Sandford, Donald Adams, Thomas Round, D'Oyly Carte Opera Chorus, New Symphony Orchestra of London, Grenadier Guards Band, Isidore Godfrey.
** (*) Decca SKL 5188/9. John Reed, Pamela Field, Judi Merri,

Lyndsie Holland, Malcolm Williams, Kenneth Sandford, Michael Rayner, John Ayldon, D'Oyly Carte Opera Chorus, Royal Philharmonic Orchestra, Royston Nash.

On two counts only does the new Decca *Iolanthe* improve on the old. John Reed's portrayal of the Lord Chancellor has understandably matured, and in the new set the character has a real vintage quality. The vocal inflections, squeaks and other speech mannerisms are a delight. Only in the *Nightmare song* does one feel that familiarity has bred too easy a manner, and with hardly any feeling of bravura (so fluently do the words trip out) some of the tension goes. The recording too offers a marginal gain in quality; notably the spoken words have remarkable naturalness and realism, though there are a few moments when some emphasized sibilants are irritating. But as a whole the account has less charm and sparkle, and Nash's refined manner, immediately apparent in the overture, is not a good exchange for Godfrey's more robust high spirits. The over-pointing of the fairies' chorus is matched by a lack of spontaneity in the first-act finale, which contains some of the most felicitous word-setting in all the operas. The spoken dialogue is rather prim in Act 1, and especially in the fairies' scene which opens the opera (but it was not ideal in the earlier recording either). The new Queen of the Fairies has a splendidly ripe speaking voice, yet when she sings the tone is much less attractive. Pamela Field as Phyllis is comparable with Mary Sansom, and she manages her spoken dialogue with the two Earls in the second act very well indeed. John Ayldon's singing voice is rather throaty, and Michael Rayner as Strephon is very dark-toned. He is no match for Alan Styler, whose vocal personality makes for an ideal characterization. Kenneth Sand-

ford shows a disappointing lack of resonance and authority in the *Sentry song*. On the earlier set he was in much better form, and Donald Adams and Thomas Round made a superb pair of Earls. Decca's first producer chose to use the Grenadier Guards Band to add spectacle to the *Entry of the peers*; however, the new version suffers no loss from their absence, for the choral singing is first-rate.

Iolanthe: complete recording without dialogue.

(M) ** (*) HMV sxlp 30112/3.
George Baker, Ian Wallace, John Cameron, Alexander Young, Owen Brannigan, Monica Sinclair, Elsie Morison, Glyndebourne Festival Chorus, Pro Arte Orchestra, Sir Malcolm Sargent.

There is much to praise in the HMV set, and EMI have refurbished the recording very successfully; while it is not as spacious and atmospheric as either of the Decca sets, it suits the studio-based performance and projects the music brightly without loss of inner warmth. The climax of Act 1, the scene of the Queen of the Fairies' curse on members of both Houses of Parliament, shows most excitingly what can be achieved with the 'full operatic treatment': this is a dramatic moment indeed. George Baker too is very good as the Lord Chancellor, although his entry song in Act 1 is disappointing. He tries too hard, and some of his vocal business sounds forced. One finds oneself longing for the dry monotone of John Reed. But if there is room for personal taste to hold sway here, surely John Cameron's dark timbre certainly does not evoke an Arcadian Shepherd. The Peers' famous chorus is a poor thing: they really do sound like old dodderers. This is surely carrying musical characterization too far. Nevertheless there is much to enjoy. The two Earls and

Private Willis are excellent, the famous *Nightmare song* is very well and clearly sung, and all of the second act (except perhaps Iolanthe's recitative and ballad near the end) goes very well. The famous *Trio* with the Lord Chancellor and the two Earls is a joy.

Iolanthe: highlights (without dialogue).
*** HMV CSD 1434. Patricia Kern, Elizabeth Harwood, Heather Begg, Julian Moyle, Eric Shilling, Denis Dowling, Stanley Beavan, Leon Greene, Elizabeth Robson, Cynthia Morey, Sadler's Wells Chorus and Orchestra, Band of the Irish Guards, Alexander Faris.

The Sadler's Wells *Iolanthe* is stylistically superior to the HMV complete recording and often musically superior to the Decca D'Oyly Carte versions. If you do not mind a rather piecemeal selection, but want a one-disc *Iolanthe*, you will not do better than this. Alexander Faris often chooses untraditional tempi. *When I went to the bar* is very much faster than usual, has less dignity, but a compensating lightness of touch. Eric Shilling is excellent here, as also in the *Nightmare song*, which is really *sung*, much being made of the ham operatic recitative at the beginning. The words too are admirably clear (as they are everywhere, even in the choruses). Gilbert would have been delighted. The Peers are splendid. Their opening chorus is thrilling and their reaction to the Fairy Queen's curse is delightfully and emphatically horrified. All the solo singing is of a high standard; both lovers are excellent and Leon Greene sings the *Sentry song* well. But I reserve my greatest praise for Patricia Kern's really lovely singing of Iolanthe's final aria. This beautiful tune has never before been properly sung on a record and it is one of Sullivan's highest inspirations. This whole scene is very moving indeed and rounds off a very enjoyable record. The

recording is superb, less stagey than the Decca manner, but rich and with the voices finely focused.

The Mikado: complete recording without dialogue.
*** Decca SKL 5158/9. John Ayldon, Colin Wright, John Reed, Kenneth Sandford, Valerie Masterson, Lyndsie Holland, D'Oyly Carte Opera Chorus, Royal Philharmonic Orchestra, Royston Nash.
(M) *** World Records SOC 244/5. John Wakefield, John Holmes, Clive Revill, Denis Dowling, Marion Studholme, Jean Allister, Sadler's Wells Chorus and Orchestra, Alexander Faris.
** (*) Decca SKL 4006/7. Donald Adams, Thomas Round, Peter Pratt, Kenneth Sandford, Alan Styler, Ann Drummond-Grant, Jean Hindmarsh, D'Oyly Carte Opera Chorus, New Symphony Orchestra of London, Isidore Godfrey.

The new D'Oyly Carte *Mikado* is a complete success in every way and (apart from individual performances like Donald Adams's famous portrayal of the Mikado himself) it eclipses the earlier Decca set in almost every way. The Sadler's Wells recording, however, remains very competitive, and while traditionalists will undoubtedly go for Nash's account, others may find that the new look taken by Alexander Faris and his excellent cast is very rewarding. Not that there is any lack of freshness in the new Decca recording. Indeed its effect is like a coat of bright new paint and the G. and S. masterpiece emerges with a pristine sparkle. Musically this by is far the finest version the D'Oyly Carte Company have ever put on disc. The choral singing is first-rate, with much refinement of detail. The glees, *Brightly dawns* and *See how the fates*, are robust in the D'Oyly Carte manner but more polished than usual. The words are exceptionally clear throughout without sizzling sibilants. This applies to an important early song in Act 1, *Our great Mikado*, which contains the seeds of the plot and is sometimes delivered in a throaty indistinct way. Not so here: every word is crystal-clear.

Of the principals, John Reed is a delicious Ko-Ko, a refined and individual characterization, and his famous *Little list* song has an enjoyable lightness of touch. Kenneth Sandford gives his customary vintage projection of Pooh Bah – a pity none of his dialogue has been included. Valerie Masterson is a charming Yum-Yum; *The sun whose rays* has rarely been sung with more feeling and charm, and it is followed with a virtuoso account of *Here's a how-de-do* which one longs to encore but cannot, because there is no dividing band. Colin Wright's vocal production has a slightly nasal quality, but one soon adjusts to it and his voice has the proper bright freshness of timbre for Nanki-Poo. John Ayldon's Mikado has not quite the satanic glitter of Donald Adams's version, but he provides a laugh of terrifying bravura. Katisha (Lyndsie Holland) is commanding, and her attempts to interrupt the chorus in the finale of Act 1 are superbly believable and dramatic. With excellent sound throughout (heard through quadraphonic equipment the presence and realism are remarkable at times) this is very enjoyable indeed.

But so is the Sadler's Wells set. It is traditional in the best sense, bringing also a humorous sparkle to the proceedings which gives a great delight. Clive Revill is a splendid Ko-Ko; his performance draws something from the Martyn Green stylization but adds colour to it, so that *Tit willow* and his verse of *The flowers that bloom in the spring* (aided by a momentary touch of stereo gimmickry) have a charming individuality. John Heddle Nash is perhaps the best Pish-Tush we have ever had on record, and it is partly because of him that the *Chippy chopper* trio is so effective. The madrigal, *Brightly dawns*, is beautifully sung (more refined than in the D'Oyly Carte version), and in contrast the tale of the mythical execution of Nanki-Poo (*The criminal cried*) is a revelation, so humorously is the story told by each of the three 'guilty' parties. Denis Dowling is a superb Pooh Bah, and Marion Studholme a charming Yum-Yum. She sings *The sun whose rays* with a delectable lightness of style. Katisha is first-rate in every way. Her two lyrical numbers are sung with delicate feeling and are most affecting. The part is not hammed at all and she is often very dramatic. Listen to the venom she puts into the word 'bravado' in the Act 1 finale. Even the chorus scores a new point by their stylized singing of *Mi-ya-sa-ma*, which sounds superbly mock-Japanese. The one disappointment is John Holmes in the name part. He sings well but conveys little of the satanic quality. But this is a small point in an otherwise magnificent set, excellently recorded, and available now in a medium-priced reissue. It has a new overture arranged by Charles Mackerras.

The earlier Decca set is enjoyable enough and well cast. Donald Adams is outstanding, and Thomas Round is a very good Nanki-Poo; some will prefer his voice to that of Colin Wright on the new version. Peter Pratt is a good Ko-Ko, but this performance has not the memorability of either John Reed's or Clive Revill's characterizations. Jean Hindmarsh is a petite Yum-Yum and Ann Drummond-Grant is a compelling Katisha, with both her lyrical arias movingly sung. Isidore Godfrey conducts with characteristic point and sparkle, but generally speaking this performance is not as strong as the newer D'Oyly

Carte recording nor as exhilarating as the EMI set.

Patience: complete recording with dialogue.

** (*) Decca SKL 4146/7. Mary Sansom, Donald Adams, John Cartier, Philip Potter, John Reed, Kenneth Sandford, Jennifer Toye, Gillian Knight, D'Oyly Carte Company, Isidore Godfrey.

It always seems to me that the D'Oyly Carte *Patience* only really wakes up when the Dragoons come on stage, and this effect is accentuated in the Decca recording by the low volume level of the ladies' opening dialogue (compared to the music). *Patience* has some charming music, to be sure, but the first-act finale is poor, and throughout one is led to feel that Sullivan is better with primary colours than pastel shades. Certainly *When I first put this uniform on* and *The soldiers of the Queen* are among the very best of all Sullivan's military numbers. Donald Adams is a worthy successor to Darrell Fancourt in these. Patience herself is well characterized by Mary Sansom, but her singing is less impressive. She is thoroughly professional, and excellent in the dialogue, but her songs lack style, although they are not without moments of charm. All the dialogue is here, and very important it is to the action. Unfortunately the poems are somewhat spoilt by both 'poets'. They are spoken with too much intensity, whereas they need throwing off if the barbs of the satire are to be lightly pointed as Gilbert intended. In all other respects both Bunthorne and Grosvenor are well played. Both chorus and orchestra have never sounded better, and Isidore Godfrey displays his usual skill with the accompaniments, which have a splendid bounce. The wide dynamic range of the recording (which is resplendent in the loud music) means that the quieter moments are prone to any surface noises there are about.

The Pirates of Penzance: complete recording with dialogue.

*** Decca SKL 4925/6. John Reed, Donald Adams, Philip Potter, Valerie Masterson, Christine Palmer, Owen Brannigan, D'Oyly Carte Opera Chorus, Royal Philharmonic Orchestra, Isidore Godfrey.

Isidore Godfrey is helped by a more uniformly excellent cast than was present on the earlier Decca stereo recording, and now for the first time we are given all the dialogue too. The theatrical spontaneity is well maintained, and the spoken scenes with the Pirate King are particularly effective. Donald Adams has a great gift for Gilbertian inflection and some of his lines give as much pleasure as his splendidly characterized singing. Christine Palmer's Ruth is not quite so poised, but her singing is first-rate – her opening aria has never been better done. John Reed does not show the Martyn Green poise in the patter songs (Green always seems to take a fiendish delight in the profusion of tongue-twisting consonants, where others just manage to negotiate them), but this is a real characterization of the part and it grows on one. Valerie Masterson is an excellent Mabel, and if her voice is not creamy throughout its range, she controls it with great skill to delight us often. Her duet with Frederick, *Leave me not to pine alone*, is enchanting, sung very gently. Godfrey has prepared us for it in the overture, and it is one of the highlights of the set. Godfrey's conducting is as affectionate as ever, more lyrical here, without losing the rhythmic buoyancy, and one can hear him revelling in the many touches of colour in the orchestration, which the Royal Philharmonic Orchestra present with great sophistication. But perhaps the greatest new joy of the set is Owen Brannigan's Sergeant of Police, a part this artist was surely born to play. It is a marvellously humorous performance, yet the humour is never clumsy, and the famous *Policeman's song* is so fresh that it is almost like hearing it for the first time. The recording is superbly spacious and clear throughout, with a fine sense of atmosphere.

The Pirates of Penzance: complete recording without dialogue.

> (M) *** H M V s x L P 30131/2. George Baker, James Milligan, John Cameron, Richard Lewis, Owen Brannigan, Elsie Morison, Glyndebourne Festival Chorus, Pro Arte Orchestra, Sir Malcolm Sargent.

This was one of the finest of Sir Malcolm Sargent's Gilbert and Sullivan sets. Besides a performance which is both stylish and lively, conveying both the fun of the words and the charm of the music, the H M V recording has more atmosphere than usual in this series. Undoubtedly the star of the piece is George Baker. He is a splendid Major-General. Here is an excellent example of a fresh approach yielding real dividends, and Sargent's slower than usual tempo for his famous patter song means that the singer can relax and add both wit and polish to the words. Owen Brannigan, as in the Decca set, gives a rich portrayal of the Sergeant of the Police. The performance takes a little while to warm up: Sargent's accompaniment to the Pirate King's song is altogether too flaccid. Elsie Morison is a less than ideal Mabel. Her opening cadenza of *Poor wandering one* is angular and over-dramatic and she is not relaxed enough throughout. However, elsewhere she is much more convincing, especially in the famous duet, *Leave me not to pine alone*. The choral contributions (the opening of Act 2, for instance) are pleasingly refined, yet have no lack of vigour. *Hail poetry* is resplendent, while

the choral finale is managed with poise and a balance which allows the inner parts to emerge pleasingly. The whole performance is in fact more than the sum of its parts.

Princess Ida: complete recording without dialogue.

> ** Decca s k L 4708/9. Elizabeth Harwood, Kenneth Sandford, Donald Adams, Jeffrey Skitch, John Reed, D'Oyly Carte Opera Chorus, Royal Philharmonic Orchestra, Sir Malcolm Sargent.

This is well sung and played and very well recorded, but Sir Malcolm's hand is a restraining influence. One would have thought that this 'grandest' of the Savoy operas, with three acts instead of the usual two, would have suited Sir Malcolm's broad lyrical approach. But often throughout the set one remembers the sprightliness of Isidore Godfrey's conducting in the earlier set (an excellent mono recording, and one of the last of the first Decca series). Even the patter songs here are over-dramatic and seem forced instead of genially humorous.

Princess Ida: highlights.

> ** Decca s k L 4845 (from above recording).

For most Gilbert and Sullivan fans a highlights disc is all that will be required of *Princess Ida*, and this one seems to include all the lollipops. It begins well with *Now hearken to my strict command*, but this (if always interesting) is not Sullivan's most memorable score, and that fact shows more strikingly in a selection. Also John Reed's contributions are rather heavily characterized; a degree more lightness would have brought more humour too. Sir Malcolm's touch has not the sprightly aplomb of Godfrey.

Ruddigore: complete recording without dialogue.

** (*) Decca SKL 4504/5. John Reed, Thomas Round, Kenneth Sandford, Stanley Riley, Donald Adams, Jean Hindmarsh, Gillian Knight, Mary Sansom, Jean Allister, D'Oyly Carte Opera Chorus, Orchestra of Royal Opera House, Covent Garden, Isidore Godfrey.

After *The Sorcerer*, this is the least successful of all the D'Oyly Carte/Godfrey recordings. There are several instances of tempi that are fractionally too brisk (a fatal sign that a conductor is trying to brighten things up), and altogether a degree of charm is missing throughout. Savoyards will not be disappointed; here is the production they are used to, very well recorded, but in the deliciously subtle Act 2 duet for the reformed Mad Margaret and Sir Despard the point is missed and this becomes another standard song. The omission of the dialogue is a mistake; the scene mentioned above is incomplete without the delightful spoken interchange about Basingstoke! Instead of the dialogue we have the original overture complete with the music for the original finale to whet our appetitites. The performance also includes the attractive duet *The battle's roar is over*, which is now (for whatever reason) traditionally omitted. There is much to enjoy here. The principals are good (especially Gillian Knight and Donald Adams, whose *Ghosts' High Noon* is a marvellous highlight), and the chorus and orchestra (the company have been promoted to Covent Garden level!) are excellent.

The Sorcerer: complete recording without dialogue.
** (*) Decca SKL 4825/6. John Reed, Donald Adams, David Palmer, Valerie Masterson, D'Oyly Carte Opera Chorus, Royal Philharmonic Orchestra, Isidore Godfrey.

John Reed's portrayal of the wizard himself is one of the finest of all his characterizations. It has matured even more since this recording was made, and in the current D'Oyly Carte production is an absolute delight. Godfrey, with his robust, sparkling manner, seems at less than his usual inspired best in this recording, dating from 1967. The plot, with a love potion administered to the whole village by mistake, has considerable potential, but it drew from Sullivan a great deal of music in his fey pastoral vein, and not all of it comes fully to life here. The performance wakes up marvellously at the entrance of John Wellington Wells, and his famous introductory aria is given a virtuoso performance here, while the spell-casting scene is equally enchanting. The performance retains its buoyancy till the end of the act but is variable again in Act 2 until the final sequence of numbers which go splendidly. An uneven performance, but with some good things and notably fine singing from the chorus.

Trial by Jury: complete recording.
(M) *** HMV SXLP 30088/9. George Baker, John Cameron, Richard Lewis, Owen Brannigan, Elsie Morison, Monica Sinclair, Glyndebourne Festival Chorus, Pro Arte Orchestra, Sir Malcolm Sargent – *HMS Pinafore*.***

An enjoyable, thoroughly musical account, with a shade more 'production' than usual in the HMV series. The casting is excellent, and George Baker makes a good judge. The recording is quite the best HMV have given us so far for G. and S.: it is clear, spacious and bright, and has some good but unexaggerated stereo effects.

(i) *Trial by Jury*: complete recording. *Overture Macbeth; Henry VIII* (incidental music): *March; Graceful dance*.

963

** (*) Decca TXS 113. (i) John Reed, Michael Rayner, Colin Wright, Julia Goss, Kenneth Sandford, John Ayldon, D'Oyly Carte Opera Chorus; Royal Philharmonic Orchestra, Royston Nash.

The fillers here are inconsequential; the *Macbeth overture* is brightly coloured, but not really inspired, and the orchestration is without the felicity Sullivan showed in the opera pit: it sometimes sounds curiously thin. The performance of *Trial by Jury* is thoroughly professional and alive, with first-class individual contributions from the small cast, notably John Reed. But the forward balance, all the voices projected out, does not help to create atmosphere and one has the impression of everyone trying too hard. Every bit of choral 'business' is put over emphatically, and while the impact is never in doubt the whole effect is unsubtle. The earlier Decca version is the one to go for (or indeed the HMV set if the coupling is right), and the excerpts from *Utopia Ltd* are far more valuable than these puny orchestral items.

Trial by Jury: complete recording; *Utopia Ltd*: excerpts.
*** Decca SKL 4579. John Reed, Anne Hood, Thomas Round, Kenneth Sandford, Donald Adams, Anthony Raffell, Jean Allister, D'Oyly Carte Opera Chorus, Orchestra of the Royal Opera House, Covent Garden, Isidore Godfrey.

Trial by Jury is lovingly conducted by Godfrey, and this immaculate and very well recorded disc gives an illusion of an ideal performance from a perfectly placed seat. The balance and dynamic range are both judged to perfection, and the orchestral score tells without ever being too loud. Perhaps George Baker

on the HMV disc gets a little more wicked geniality into his characterization of the judge, but John Reed does the part worthily, if sometimes sounding a little youthful in voice. But in any case the Decca issue offers a splendid bonus in five numbers from *Utopia Ltd*. *Oh, make way for the Wise Men* has the same swing as the *Cachucha* from *The Gondoliers*. *Oh, maiden rich* has a splendid military chorus and ends with a characteristic Sullivan ensemble. *Oh, Zara* is unusual in being a semi-comic tenor aria with a cracked top note (the style is that of the music for Jack Point in *Yeomen*); *Words of love* is a charming duet (chorus *Sweet and Low*) with a demanding introduction for the soprano. The unaccompanied chorus *Eagle high* (written in Sullivan's best Chapel Royal style) is splendidly sung and makes a stirring conclusion to a fine set of excerpts.

The Yeomen of the Guard: complete recording without dialogue.
*** Decca SKL 4624/5. Anne Hood, Elizabeth Harwood, John Reed, Philip Potter, Kenneth Sandford, Donald Adams, Gillian Knight, D'Oyly Carte Opera Chorus, Royal Philharmonic Orchestra, Sir Malcolm Sargent.

Sir Malcolm's breadth of approach is at once apparent in the overture. The spinning number which follows also begins deliberately; it has a striking lyricism, with much play with echo effects, but has not quite the lightness of touch that Godfrey would manage. This is not to imply that Sargent's result is less effective, only that it is not quite what one expects from a traditional D'Oyly Carte reading on Decca. As soon as the chorus enter (*Tower warders*), the degree of Sargent's 'grand operatic' approach makes a remarkable impact; indeed one has seldom heard the choruses in *Yeomen* expand with such power, nor indeed has the orchestra (especially the brass) produced such a regal sound. As the work proceeds the essential lyricism of Sargent's reading begins to emerge more and more, and the ensemble singing is especially lovely. There is no lack of drama either, and indeed the only aspect of the work to be played down somewhat is the humorous side. The interjections of Jack and Wilfred in the Act 1 finale are obviously seen as part of the whole rather than a suggestion of the humour that somehow seems to intrude into the most serious of human situations. The pathos of the famous Jester's song in the second act is played up, and the only moment to raise a real smile is the duet which follows, *Tell a tale of cock and bull*. But with consistently fine singing throughout from all the principals (and especially Elizabeth Harwood as Elsie), supported by perfectly balanced recording, this *Yeomen* is unreservedly a success. Apart from the brilliant and atmospheric Decca recording, the style of this performance is not so very different from Sargent's earlier one on HMV (currently unobtainable).

The Yeomen of the Guard: highlights.
    *** Decca SKL 4809 (from above recording).

This is a delightful record, a fine memento to Sir Malcolm's Gilbert and Sullivan conducting at its best. The playing down of the humour to bring out the lyricism is appropriate in *Yeomen* but in any case the comic description of the escape of Fairfax is well done. It is the breadth of conception for which Sargent's *Yeomen of the Guard* is admired and this is never better shown than in the rich, expansive treatment he gives to the opening of Act 2. The singing throughout is of the highest D'Oyly Carte standard (except for one rather grey contribution from a member of the chorus near the beginning), and the glowing recording gives great pleasure in itself.

COLLECTIONS

'Gilbert and Sullivan spectacular': excerpts from: *HMS Pinafore; The Mikado; The Pirates of Penzance; Ruddigore*.
    ** Decca Phase 4 PFS 4097. John Reed, Donald Adams, Kenneth Sandford, Valerie Masterson, soloists, D'Oyly Carte Opera Chorus, Royal Philharmonic Orchestra, Sir Malcolm Sargent.

Basically the recording is certainly spectacular, with a rich overall ambience and the soloists spotlighted well forward. The choral sound, however, is somewhat grainy and the very loudest moments have a touch of discoloration. The conducting is musical and solid, without the wit of Godfrey but genial in its way. The memorable items are *A wandering minstrel* very nicely turned by Philip Potter, and Donald Adams's superb versions of the Mikado's famous song (that laugh sounds even more horrifying than usual in Phase 4) and the *Policeman's song* from *Pirates* (which he does not usually sing). John Reed's contributions are very closely microphoned indeed and reveal a break in the voice occasionally.

Choruses from: *The Gondoliers; HMS Pinafore; Iolanthe; The Mikado; Patience; The Pirates of Penzance; Princess Ida; Ruddigore; The Sorcerer; Trial by Jury; The Yeomen of the Guard*.
    * (*) Decca Deram SML 722. John Reed, John Webley, Clifford Parkes, D'Oyly Carte Opera Chorus, Royal Philharmonic Orchestra, James Walker.

This is disappointing both technically and musically. The recording acoustic is not entirely happy and the overall balance not convincing. The orchestral trumpets emerge strongly, but the chorus has not

965

the sonority one would like. The performances are all lively but only occasionally spark into real excitement, as in the *Trial by Jury* and *Patience* items. An anthology of this kind has to be chosen, and the order arranged, with a care almost verging on inspiration, but here the order of the items is not always happy, and the jumping from one mood or opera to another is not well managed.

'*Songs and snatches*' from: *The Gondoliers; Iolanthe; Ruddigore; The Yeomen of the Guard.*
> *** Decca SKL 5044. Soloists, D'Oyly Carte Opera Company, James Walker.

This happily-titled collection offers a highly recommendable anthology, notable not so much for the choice of items as for the charm and style of the performances. James Walker was for a long time the supervisor of the Decca recordings of G. and S. conducted by Godfrey, and when Godfrey retired he took over for a short time as the D'Oyly Carte company's musical director. As those who have heard him conduct in the theatre realize, his special contribution to the Savoy operas was to bring out the lyricism rather than the sparkle of the scores (although his style is by no means lacking in high spirits). This shows especially well here; the solos and ensembles have a delightfully light touch and the conductor's delicacy is shared by the performers. *There grew a little flower* from *Ruddigore* is a good example; it is gently touching, and John Reed's performances of the patter songs are cleverly used to make effective contrast. His vocal inflections have a sophistication and spontaneity that put him in the class of Martyn Green and Lytton. The stereo-conscious recording (try the very opening of *The Gondoliers* selection) is splendid.

'*The world of Gilbert and Sullivan*': excerpts from: *The Gondoliers; HMS Pinafore; The Mikado; Patience; Princess Ida.*
> (B) *** Decca SPA 28. D'Oyly Carte Opera Company, Isidore Godfrey or Sir Malcolm Sargent.

This is a brilliant anthology which is successful in picking not only some of the outstanding highlights from these operas but also from the records of them. With perhaps the single exception of the *Princess Ida* item, *For a month to dwell* (not showing Sir Malcolm Sargent in top form), everything is infectious and highly enjoyable. The other *Princess Ida* excerpt, *If you give me your attention*, is a favourite patter song, and John Reed does it well. The performances here are all from the Decca G. and S. complete sets, which are excellent technically, and indeed the disc opens with a stunning piece of atmospheric business before *I am the monarch of the seas* begins a trio of songs from *Pinafore*. The *Mikado* songs too (and this was not one of the best of the series) are cleverly chosen to show the cast at their most sparkling. *A wandering minstrel* (Thomas Round), *Three little maids*, and *Tit willow* (Peter Pratt) are all excellent. *The Gondoliers* was perhaps the best thing Godfrey did, and all five excerpts are winners. Perhaps most striking of all are the *Patience* songs with Donald Adams in splendid form in his *Catalogue song* and *When I first put this uniform on*. This is now the best G. and S. anthology available at any price.

'*The world of Gilbert and Sullivan*', *Vol. 2*: excerpts from: *Iolanthe; The Pirates of Penzance; Ruddigore; The Yeomen of the Guard.*
> (B) *** Decca SPA 29. D'Oyly Carte Opera Company, Isidore Godfrey or Sir Malcolm Sargent.

This second disc is worth having for Donald Adams's classic performance of *When the night wind howls* from *Ruddigore*, which is superbly done. The record also includes *I know a youth*, with its Schubertian charm, and the patter trio *My eyes are fully open*, which is very successful. There is a nice selection from *Iolanthe*, ending with the vivacious final trio, and the *Pirates* excerpts are most enjoyable too. In the *Yeomen* section the chorus *Tower warders* comes before *When maiden loves*, but this seems sensible enough in this context. Good sound throughout.

'The world of Gilbert and Sullivan', Vol. 3: excerpts from: *The Gondoliers; Iolanthe; The Mikado; Patience; Ruddigore; The Sorcerer; Trial by Jury.*

   (B) ** Decca SPA 147. D'Oyly Carte Opera Company, Isidore Godfrey.

The third selection in this series is notable for a marvellous performance by John Reed of *My name is John Wellington Wells*, from *The Sorcerer*. This is one of Gilbert's very finest inspirations and the music points the words to perfection, but it comes from an otherwise comparatively unmemorable performance, as the companion duet, *Oh, I have wrought much evil with my spells*, readily shows. There are some good excerpts from *The Gondoliers* and *Patience*, and the selection is generous enough to merit recommendation even though one or two items have to be very quickly faded out at the end. In a selection of this kind, and with the whole range of operas to choose from, it ought to be possible to manage by only including pieces that extract easily from the master tape.

Suppé, Franz von
(1819–95)

Overtures: *Beautiful Galathea; The Jolly Robbers; Light Cavalry; Morning, Noon and Night in Vienna; Pique Dame; Poet and Peasant.*

   *** DGG 2530 051. Berlin Philharmonic Orchestra, Herbert von Karajan.

   (B) ** Pye GSGC 14094. Hallé Orchestra, Sir John Barbirolli.

Karajan's record is irresistible, a swaggering display disc with superlatively fine recording that quite sweeps the board. Sir John's collection is lively and the orchestral playing alert. The recording has a good immediacy but is somewhat dry, uncovering a curiously mannered vibrato in the strings, which are not immaculate when exposed. There is plenty of excitement, of course, and the conductor's sense of style (in the shaping of the *Galathea waltz*, for instance) compensates for a certain overall brashness.

Overtures: *Light Cavalry; Morning, Noon and Night in Vienna; Pique Dame; Poet and Peasant.*

   (B) ** (*) Decca SPA 374. Vienna Philharmonic Orchestra, Sir Georg Solti.

   * (*) Decca Phase 4 PFS 4236. London Festival Orchestra, Robert Sharples.

With only four items included (admittedly the most popular four) Solti's record, even at bargain price, would be difficult to recommend were not both performances and recordings so brilliant. The recording has a wide dynamic range, perhaps too wide for the cello solos in *Morning, Noon and Night* and *Poet and Peasant*, where the instrument is backwardly balanced and sounds not unlike a viola. But if you like the old-fashioned, rather mellow type of Suppé performance, be warned, this is not the shop for that.

For Robert Sharples's collection Decca have placed their Phase 4 microphones to achieve brilliance above all, so the brightly lit first violins dominate. Sharples directs fast (except for the opening of *Poet and Peasant*, which must be the slowest on record), deadpan performances, but they are well played, if without any special sparkle or affection. If these four overtures are needed Solti's disc has far more character.

Svetlanov, Yevgeny
(born 1928)

Festive Poem, Op. 9.
> * (*) HMV ASD 3062. USSR Symphony Orchestra, the composer – MIASKOVSKY: *Symphony No. 22.***

This is a conventional piece, of no great interest, but it is well played and recorded.

Sviridov, Georgy
(born 1915)

Kursk songs: The green oak; Sing lark!; The town bells ring; Oh! sadness!; Vanka has bought a scythe; My confused nightingale; Beyond the fast flowing river.
> *** HMV ASD 2875. Narina Valkovskaya (mezzo-soprano), Anatol Legutin (tenor), M. Zlatopolsky (bass), RSFSR Academic Russian Choir, Moscow Philharmonic Orchestra, Kyril Kondrashin – SHOSTAKOVICH: *Song of the Forests.*(**)

Sviridov is a Shostakovich pupil and his music enjoys high repute in the USSR. These *Kursk songs* are fresh and attractive, inventively scored and often imaginative. They are given persuasive advocacy here but are encumbered by an unwelcome coupling; the Shostakovich work hardly repays repeated listening.

Szymanowski, Karol
(1882–1937)

Violin concerto No. 2, Op. 61.
> *** Philips 6500 421. Henryk Szeryng (violin), Bamberg Symphony Orchestra, Jan Krenz – WIENIAWSKI: *Violin concerto No. 2.****

It is surprising that a composer as deeply individual and rewarding as Szymanowski has received so little attention in this country. This concerto is not the equal of his *First*, but it has a nostalgia and power all its own. Szeryng's performance is both more commanding and more magical than the earlier version by Charles Trebor, and the orchestral playing under Jan Krenz glows with that ecstatic, luminous radiance that Szymanowski made so much his own. The delicacy and refinement of the colouring are sensitively captured, and the climaxes have the appropriate fervour and intensity, enveloping the listener far more completely than in the earlier version. Szeryng is forwardly balanced, but relatively little of the complex texture is masked, and the recording is vivid and detailed without ever being unnatural or larger than life.

Mythes (3 poems for violin and piano), *Op. 30.*
> (M) ** Supraphon SUAST 50580. Karel Sroubek (violin), Josef Hála (piano) – YSAŸE: *Au rouet etc.**

The *Mythes* include one of Szymanowski's best-known pieces, *The Fountain of Arethusa*, which Grumiaux recorded at the very outset of his gramophone career in the days of 78s. It is one of Szymanowski's most luminous pieces, with typically ecstatic violin writing soaring away above the stave. It is by far the most memorable of the three pieces and the Czech violinist Karel Sroubek captures its rapture as well as that of its companion pieces on this slightly too reverberant disc. Unfortunately it is coupled with some of Ysaÿe's least interesting characteristic music. Perhaps Grumiaux will re-record the Szymanowski pieces; until he does, these performances have the field to themselves.

Études, Op. 4; Fantasia in F minor, Op. 14; Masques, Op. 34; Métopes, Op. 29.
*** Argo ZRG 713. Martin Jones (piano).

A most valuable and enterprising issue which does great credit to all concerned. The early pieces suggest Chopin or more accurately early Scriabin, though their melancholia seems, with the benefit of hindsight, particularly individual. The later pieces, *Masques* and *Métopes*, written at about the time of the *First Violin concerto*, show Szymanowski responding to Gallic influences, early Stravinsky, and evolving a sophisticated exoticism all his own. They are demanding pieces and Martin Jones plays them splendidly. Argo provides a fine wide-ranging recording.

Takemitsu, Toru
(born 1930)

Cassiopeia (for percussionist and orchestra).
*** EMI Quadraphonic Q4-EMD 5508. Stomu Yamash'ta (percussion), Japan Philharmonic Orchestra, Seiji Ozawa – ISHII: *So-Gu II.***

'What I want to do is not to put sounds in motion towards a goal by controlling them; I would rather prefer to let them free, if possible without controlling them'; so Takemitsu in 1968 summed up his approach to composition. But this is not an aleatory work. The percussion soloist is given a lot of freedom within a framework fixed by the demands of the orchestral score. Of course to give a creative artist of the calibre of Stomu Yamash'ta such freedom can only be a gain, and there is no doubt about the spontaneity of effect here. With quadraphonic sound essential to give the music the space it needs, this four-part work (subdivided *Entrance*; *Scene*; *Solo*; *Scene*) makes a strong assault on the senses, even if its actual argument is less readily perceived.

Corona (London version – for pianos, organ and harpsichord); *Far away; Piano distance; Undisturbed rest.*
*** Decca Headline HEAD 4. Roger Woodward (piano, organ, harpsichord); multiple recording techniques.

Roger Woodward sympathetically draws out a seductive range of keyboard colours in *Corona*, a work which seems to be more the performer's improvisation than a true creative product of the composer. The other music, in spite of its too easy reliance on texture, is still undeniably attractive if you are looking for music which doodles between Scriabin and the avant-garde. Excellent recording.

Tallis, Thomas
(*c.* 1505–1585)

Organ pieces: *Clarifica me, Pater; Fantasy*. Motets: *Audivi vocem; In jejunio et fletu. Te Deum for 5 voices.*

(B) ** Argo Eclipse ECS 683. Choir of St John's College, Cambridge, George Guest; Peter White (organ) – WEELKES: *Collection.***

Tallis is best-known to many of us by the theme which Vaughan Williams used in his famous *Fantasia*. Here is a chance to get to know him better and confirm that the curiously dark melodic colouring of the tune in the variations is typical. The Choir of St John's College under George Guest give an adequate performance of the *Te Deum* but sound happiest in the two motets. The organ pieces are not especially distinguished but they are well played.

Cantiones sacrae: complete recording.
(M) *** Oiseau-Lyre SOL 311/3 (records available separately). Cantores in Ecclesia, Michael Howard – BYRD: *Cantiones sacrae.****

Tallis published his settings of the *Cantiones sacrae* jointly with Byrd in 1575. The performances are unlikely to be improved upon (see under the Byrd coupling).

Derelinquat impius; Ecce tempus idoneum; In jejunio et fletu; In manus tuas; O nata lux; Salvator mundi; Spem in alium (40-part motet); *Te lucis ante terminum* (settings 1 and 2); *Veni Redemptor gentium.*
*** Argo ZRG 5436. King's College, Cambridge, Choir, Cambridge University Musical Society Chorus, David Willcocks.

An outstanding collection. The King's College Choir are in their element for this music, written for Waltham Abbey and the Chapel Royal. The highlight of the programme is the magnificent forty-part motet *Spem in alium*, in which the Cambridge University Musical Society joins forces with King's. But the simpler hymn-settings are no less impressive, with performances and recording equally distinguished.

Ecce tempus idoneum; Gaude gloriosa Dei Mater; Hear the voice and prayer; If ye love me; Lamentations I; Loquebantur variis linguis; O nata lux; Spem in alium.
(B) ** Classics for Pleasure CFP 40069. Clerkes of Oxenford, David Wulstan.

A useful issue, since it gives us a bargain-label alternative to the King's version of *Spem in alium*. At the same time its value is diminished by the somewhat brisk tempi Dr Wulstan chooses, which leave the music wanting in its proper dignity. There is also some sense of strain among the women, though their tone is clean and well-focused. Reservations notwithstanding there are fine things on this disc and it can be recommended.

Gaude gloriosa Dei Mater.
(M) *** Pye Virtuoso TPLS 13019. BBC Chorus, Alan G. Melville – VAUGHAN WILLIAMS: *Mass.***

Writing before the Elizabethan age really began, Tallis achieved astonishing feats of sustained inspiration. His polyphonic church music speaks in more consistently spacious paragraphs than that of almost all his contemporaries throughout Christendom, and this six-part setting of *Gaude gloriosa Dei Mater*, intended as a magnificent Antiphon before Vespers, is an outstanding example. The spaciousness of the *Amen* is characteristic. Under Alan G. Melville the BBC Chorus sings at its very finest: a pity that this excellent choir has not made more records. Splendid recording quality.

The Lamentations of Jeremiah the Prophet.

* (*) DGG Archive 2533 113. Pro Cantione Antiqua, Bruno Turner – BYRD: *Mass for 3 voices*.* (*)

The Lamentations of Jeremiah the Prophet. Motets: *Sancte Deus; Videte miraculum. Organ lesson.*

** (*) Argo ZRG 5479. Choir of King's College, Cambridge, David Willcocks; Andrew Davis (organ).

The Argo disc is the one to have. It is authentically performed, using men's voices only, and the singing, without being inexpressive, has the right element of restraint. The two motets are for full choir, and here the balance is less than ideal, giving over-prominence to the trebles. Andrew Davis provides an excellent performance of the *Lesson* for organ, and the recording itself is natural and atmospheric.

Bruno Turner's account is perhaps a little too expressive and with too wide a dynamic range for some tastes. The voices are closely balanced and the ambience confused and muddy. Still this performance is worth investigating for those wanting the coupling.

Tartini, Giuseppe
(1692–1770)

Violin concertos in G major, D.78; in A major, D.96; in B flat major, D.117.

** (*) Philips 6500 784. Salvatore Accardo (violin), I Musici.

Tartini is most famous as an innovator of violin technique, but as these three violin concertos (chosen from a complete collection of 125 works) show, the quality of his invention was often considerable. The slow movements are melodically gracious, and the allegros have plenty of vitality. If they are sometimes repetitive, so were Vivaldi's, and these concertos,

strong in baroque atmosphere, are often reminiscent of that master. Salvatore Accardo is an excellent soloist, and the accompaniments have plenty of life. The recording is clear and fresh and well balanced, though perhaps a little lacking in body. A pleasant disc for undemanding late-evening listening.

Sonatas Nos. 1–12 for violin and violoncello.

** Telefunken SAWT 9592/3. Giovanni Guglielmo (violin), Antonio Pocaterra (cello).

The combination of violin and cello here proves a somewhat incomplete instrumentation for an extended series of sonatas; sometimes the ear is given the feeling that the music is all top and bottom and no middle, in spite of the violinist's double-stopping. But Giovanni Guglielmo is a first-class player, and his performances are persuasive as well as brilliant. His partner, Antonio Pocaterra, has a much less interesting part to play in the proceedings, but the recording balances him well in the picture. Some of the music shows considerable imagination, not only in its invention but in solving, or partly solving, the problems of part-writing for an awkward combination. In the last resort, however, this is of specialist rather than general interest.

Violin sonata in G minor (The Devil's Trill) (arr. Kreisler).

(B) *** RCA Camden CCV 5015. Henryk Szeryng (violin), Charles Reiner (piano) – TCHAIKOVSKY: *Violin concerto*.***

This is a generous fill-up for an outstanding bargain performance of the Tchaikovsky *Violin concerto*. Szeryng's style is not so romantic that he is hampered in his treatment of a classical work.

Tate, Phyllis
(born 1911)

Apparitions (The wife of Usher's Well; The Suffolk miracle; The unquiet grave; Unfortunate Miss Bailey); Celtic ballads (The Lake of Coolfin; Hark! the soft bugle; Hush).

> *** Argo ZRG 691. Margaret Price (soprano), Gerald English (tenor), James Lockhart (piano), Cardiff Festival Players – HODDINOTT: *Roman Dream; Trio.*** (*)

Phyllis Tate is a resourceful and fluent composer who is not well represented in the current catalogues. Of these two works, the more immediately impressive is the *Apparitions for tenor, harmonica, string quartet and piano*, a work that is delicate in feeling and imaginative in every way. This disc is well worth investigating, and the performances and recording are of the highest standard.

Tavener, John
(born 1944)

(i–v; vii) Celtic Requiem; (i; ii; vii) Coplas; (i; ii; vi; viii) Nomine Jesu.

> *** Apple SAPCOR 20. (i) London Sinfonietta; (ii) London Sinfonietta Chorus; (iii) children from Little Missenden Village School; (iv) June Barton (soprano); (v) the composer (organ); (vi) Margaret Lensky (soprano); cond. (vii) David Atherton; (viii) the composer.

Where Britten intensified the Requiem liturgy with Wilfred Owen's war poems, Tavener devised a comparable intensification from children's games. With healthy abandon during the *Dies Irae*, the child performers on the record cry out *Die, Pussy, die*, relaxing only for a moment in seeming wide-eyed innocence before they launch into their next bout of brutality: *Doctor, doctor, shall I die? Yes, my dear, and so shall I.* The sharpness of focus is striking, for Tavener has a multi-layered texture, with not only a setting of liturgical words and children playing their games in front of the choir but a soprano singing Irish medieval lyrics (hence the title). The musical argument itself is what the composer calls 'a gigantic decoration on the chord of E flat major', which may sound limiting. In fact that is not apparent when the dramatic points are made with an emotional force worthy of opera, as when in the cut-off coda a single child's voice sings without the slightest sentimentality *I am the ghost of Jenny Jones.* David Atherton conducts the London Sinfonietta in a fine, fresh performance, and on the reverse come two shorter Tavener choral works that have a comparably simple intensity, *Nomine Jesu* (a multilingual fantasia on the name Jesus) and *Coplas*, a beautiful slow setting of lines from St John of the Cross, which come to mingle mystically with the *Crucifixus* from Bach's *B minor Mass*. Both these shorter motets are designed to provide material for a much bigger work, *Last rites*, that is still being conceived. Fine recording.

The Whale.

> *** Apple SAPCOR 15. Anna Reynolds (mezzo-soprano), Raimund Herincx (baritone), Alvar Lidell (speaker), London Sinfonietta and Chorus, David Atherton; the composer (organ and Hammond organ).

The first performance of John Tavener's *The Whale* at Queen Elizabeth Hall was one of the great occasions in London music-making of recent years, with the arrival not only of a brilliant new work but a composer barely known till then, a conductor who was plainly destined to achieve brilliance in many fields, and a new chamber group that had a unique freshness. The same performers as on that début occasion convey the urgency of Tavener's extraordinary music, with its strange admixtures of unexpected textures. To say that it begins with Alvar Lidell reciting the entry on whales from the *Encyclopaedia Britannica* may give the impression that it is lightweight. In fact the often zany originality of *The Whale* has a purely musical strength which seems to grow with repeated hearings. There are not many pieces by young British composers as impressive as this, the more so when its methods and techniques can readily provide a bridge between pop and the avant-garde. Tavener writes music which is positively attractive to listen to, however difficult it may sometimes seem to the classical-trained listener. It is greatly to the credit of the Apple label that this extremely fine performance, beautifully recorded, should be made available.

Taverner, John
(*c.* 1495–1545)

Collection: *Christe Jesu pastor; Dum transisset sabbatum; Kyrie Le roy; Mater Christi; The Western Wind* (Mass).
*** Argo ZRG 5316. Choir of King's College, Cambridge, David Willcocks.

John Taverner's remarkable individuality is admirably shown by this excellent collection of early Tudor music. The *Western Wind Mass* (so called because of its use of this secular tune as a constantly recurring ground) is a masterpiece of the highest order. It is hauntingly memorable.

All the music here shows the composer's wide range of expressive power: the motets are also works of great beauty. With first-class performances from King's and one of Argo's most evocative recordings, this is a record that could easily be missed by the ordinary music-lover, but should certainly not be.

Dum transisset sabbatum; Missa corona spinea.
(B) ** (*) Saga 5369. Oxford Schola Cantorum, John Byrt.

The *Missa corona spinea* is a magnificent example of John Taverner's extraordinary choral music, which unlike most church music of the polyphonic period betrays something of the tensions of the composer – tensions which we can recognize in his equally untypical life story. This musical genius ended up by condemning his own creativity along with the church which he had rejected – a process intensely portrayed in the opera *Taverner* by Peter Maxwell Davies. This Mass is one of Taverner's most expansive works, and though John Byrt does not always let it unfold at its own pace, this is a refreshing and sensitive reading which, on a bargain label, reasonably well recorded, can be strongly recommended.

Tchaikovsky, Peter
(1840–93)

Capriccio italien, Op. 45; 1812 overture, Op. 49; Nutcracker suite, Op. 71a; Serenade for strings in C major, Op. 48; Sleeping Beauty, Op. 66: suite; Swan Lake, Op. 20: suite; Eugene Onegin: Act 2: *Waltz;* Act 3: *Polonaise.*
(M) ** CBS 77343 (3 discs). Philadelphia Orchestra, Eugene Ormandy.

This collection offers some of Tchaikovsky's most immediately attractive music. The performances are polished and brilliant, often exciting, with characteristic Philadelphia panache. The recordings, while generally good, are not always as rich as European ones and sometimes show a touch of transatlantic gloss.

(i) *Capriccio italien, Op. 45; Marche slave, Op. 31;* (ii) *Francesca da Rimini, Op. 32;* (iii; iv) *Romeo and Juliet* (fantasy overture); (iii; v) *Serenade for strings in C major, Op. 48.*
> (M) *** D G G Privilege 2726 011 (2 discs). (i) Berlin Philharmonic Orchestra, Ferdinand Leitner; (ii) Leningrad Philharmonic Orchestra, Gennady Rozhdestvensky; (iii) Dresden State Orchestra, cond. (iv) Kurt Sanderling, (v) Otmar Suitner.

A first-class anthology. All these performances are distinctive, and the recording throughout is of high quality. The individual performances are discussed below, but for the reader wanting all this music, the set can be cordially recommended as first-class value at medium price.

Capriccio italien, Op. 45.
> ** (*) D G G SLPM 139028. Berlin Philharmonic Orchestra, Herbert von Karajan – *Violin concerto.*** (*)
> (B) ** Classics for Pleasure CFP 40083. Philharmonia Orchestra, Paul Kletzki – *Violin concerto.****

Karajan's is a brilliant account, the Berlin Philharmonic brass telling especially well. The combination of sophistication and panache (without any special affection tellingly conveyed) makes for a very professional kind of excitement, and on big machines this record should

sound very well indeed, as the recording is bright and vivid. Kletzki's performance is enjoyable if not outstanding. It is well recorded.

Capriccio italien, Op. 45. (i) *1812 overture, Op. 49. Marche slave, Op. 31.*
> (B) *** Decca SPA 108. London Symphony Orchestra, Kenneth Alwyn, (i) with Band of Grenadier Guards.

This was Kenneth Alwyn's gramophone début. He shows a flair for Tchaikovsky rare in English conductors, and all three performances generate a real intensity and excitement while at the same time showing the conductor's fine sense of style and care for detail. The stereo is as demonstration-worthy as it ever was, with the climax to *1812* really spectacular. This is a remarkable bargain at its new price.
There is a similar coupling by Silvestri on EMI Studio 2 (TWO 139), but the Decca disc is preferable on both performance and recording grounds.

(i) *Capriccio italien, Op. 45; Marche slave, Op. 31.* (ii) *Serenade for strings in C major, Op. 48.*
> (M) *** D G G Privilege 135109. (i) Berlin Philharmonic Orchestra, Ferdinand Leitner; (ii) Dresden State Orchestra, Otmar Suitner.

This record is a delightful surprise, one of the best discs in the Privilege range. Leitner's *Capriccio* is not especially Italianate. When the 'echo' tune returns at the end, amply scored, the atmosphere has the plump enthusiasm of Munich beer cellars, rather than Italian piazzas, but the playing throughout is superb, and in its own way this is most enjoyable. The *Marche slave* is even better, dignified yet exciting and marvellously recorded, the sound unbelievably better than the original full-price LP (differently coupled). The *Serenade* too is an imaginative and very well played account. The recording is excellent, and this performance can compete with the very best.

Capriccio italien, Op. 45; Romeo and Juliet (fantasy overture).
(M) ** (*) Philips Universo 6580 014. Concertgebouw Orchestra, Bernard Haitink – DVOŘÁK: *Scherzo capriccioso*.** (*)

Haitink's *Capriccio italien* is warm-blooded, with the string-playing elegantly turned. The restatement of the main theme at the end is given tremendous weight, and to be honest it sounds too phlegmatic played like this: it also means that the coda gets under way too slowly. But this is distinctly enjoyable and the Concertgebouw acoustic, warm and spacious, matches the reading. One has very few reservations about *Romeo and Juliet*, a fine, passionate account, with superb string-playing in the love theme. The recording has much more impact here than in the original full-priced issue.

Piano concertos Nos. 1 in B flat minor, Op. 23; 2 in G major, Op. 44 (arr. Siloti); *3 in E flat major, Op. 75.*
** HMV SLS 865 (2 discs). Emil Gilels (piano), New Philharmonia Orchestra, Lorin Maazel.

It is a pity that Gilels elects to play the truncated Siloti edition of the *Second Piano concerto*, for it effectively diminishes the claim that this set has as a whole on the collector's allegiance. His playing is of the highest order of mastery, and has the virtue of presenting the works with the freshness of new discovery. It is well recorded, and the New Philharmonia under Maazel provide admirable support. However, the set is worth having primarily for the sake of Nos. 1 and 3, and these are now available separately.

Piano concertos Nos. (i) *1 in B flat minor, Op. 23;* (ii) *2 in G major, Op. 44* (arr. Siloti); *3 in E flat major, Op. 73;* (iii) *Violin concerto in D major, Op. 35;* (iv) *Variations on a rococo theme* (for violoncello and orchestra), *Op. 33.*
(B) * CBS 77357 (3 discs). (i) Eugene Istomin, (ii) Gary Graffman (piano); (iii) David Oistrakh (violin); (iv) Leonard Rose (cello); all with Philadelphia Orchestra, Eugene Ormandy.

The CBS set has the merit of cheapness but in other respects it is not particularly competitive. Istomin is not the most sensitive of pianists and, like Gilels, he plays the Siloti truncation of No. 2. The Oistrakh account of the *Violin concerto* is worth having, and Rose's account of the *Rococo variations* is not inconsiderable; but the recording, which is not particularly distinguished, makes this album an also-ran, rather than a strong recommendation.

Piano concerto No. 1 in B flat minor, Op. 23.
(M) *** CBS Classics 61174, Gary Graffman (piano), Cleveland Orchestra, George Szell.
*** DGG 2530 112. Martha Argerich (piano), Royal Philharmonic Orchestra, Charles Dutoit.
*** Decca SXL 6058. Vladimir Ashkenazy (piano), London Symphony Orchestra, Lorin Maazel.
** (*) Decca Phase 4 PFS 4196. Ivan Davis (piano), Royal Philharmonic Orchestra, Henry Lewis.
(B) ** RCA Camden CCV 5016. Emil Gilels (piano), Chicago Symphony Orchestra, Fritz Reiner.
(M) ** Decca Ace of Diamonds SDD 191. Clifford Curzon (piano), Vienna Philharmonic Orchestra, Sir Georg Solti.

** HMV ASD 542. John Ogdon (piano), Philharmonia Orchestra, Sir John Barbirolli – FRANCK: *Symphonic variations.**

(B) * (*) Classics for Pleasure CFP 115. Peter Katin (piano), London Philharmonic Orchestra, John Pritchard – LITOLFF: *Scherzo.****

(**) DGG SLPM 138822. Sviatoslav Richter (piano), Vienna Symphony Orchestra, Herbert von Karajan.

The Tchaikovsky *Piano concerto No. 1* has always been lucky on gramophone records, and there is an excellent current choice. Readers must not forget the outstanding version by Entremont and Bernstein, which is hidden away on a bargain-priced CBS disc called *Tchaikovsky's greatest hits, Volume 3* (reviewed at the very end of the Tchaikovsky listings). One could be readily satisfied with this, or indeed any of the top three or four versions listed above. Both the Decca and the DGG discs spread the work over two full-priced LP sides; but the advantage – on the DGG disc especially – is particularly full-blooded sound. Of the single-sided versions (see below) Peter Katin's Decca SPA issue is remarkably successful, with no lack of body to the reproduction, and the medium-priced LSB RCA disc combining the *Piano* and *Violin concertos* also sounds well, if not so rich as the Decca.

Szell opens with a splendid, bold romanticism, the strings singing out the great opening tune with a weight surprisingly rare on record. Graffman is clean and direct, cool in the lyrical music, obviously feeling this a contrast to the bravura, to which he rises excitingly. One senses Szell's personality strongly, and the results of this partnership, if too tense for some Tchaikovskians, are so direct they have a unique impact. The slow movement has a slightly detached freshness and the central section has an inimitable airy grace in the wispy orchestral tune which is often lost in the pyrotechnics of the solo piano. The finale, taken at a fantastic tempo, screws up the tension so that at the close one is reminded of the famous Horowitz/Toscanini 78s. This is matched by excellent CBS close-up sound.

On DGG the sheer weight of the opening horn figure creates the mood of the big, broad performance from Martha Argerich and Charles Dutoit. The recording too is quite splendid, full-bodied, wide in dynamic range, and yet with a surprisingly natural balance. Martha Argerich's conception encompasses the widest possible range of tonal shading. In the finale she often produces a scherzando-like effect; then the orchestra thunders in with the Russian dance theme to create a real contrast. The tempo of the first movement is measured, seeking power rather than tingling surface excitement, and again when the build-up begins for the final statement of the great lyrical tune of the finale, the conductor creates his climax in deliberate, measured fashion. The slow movement is strikingly atmospheric, yet delicate, its romanticism lighthearted. As a reading this could not be more different from the Szell/Graffman disc, but it has plenty of life and impulse, and, apart from the uneconomical presentation, it is highly recommendable.

Ashkenazy's essentially lyrical performance offers a genuine alternative to those of Graffman and Argerich. While these remain more obvious first recommendations, there are many who will enjoy Ashkenazy's thoughtfulness and his refusal to be stampeded by Tchaikovsky's passionate rhetoric. The biggest climaxes of the first movement are made to grow out of the music, instead of being part of a sweeping forward momentum, and the lyrical side of the writing associated with the beautiful second subject is distilled with obvious affection. In the *Andantino* too, Ashkenazy refuses to play flashily and thus uses the middle section as a contrasting episode to set in the boldest relief the return of the opening tune, which is played very beautifully. The finale is very fast and brilliant, yet the big tune is broadened at the end in a most convincing way. The recording, although now fairly old, was one of Decca's best.

The partnership of Ivan Davis and Henry Lewis is successful in providing a fresh look at Tchaikovsky's masterpiece. In spite of the strong opening, with plenty of weight from the strings, the first movement is without a thrustful forward momentum, but is spacious, pianist and conductor both relaxing to take in the movement's lyrical detail. The *Andantino* is played simply, and as in the first movement the element of contrast is strong. The restatement of the main theme is played very slowly and gently, the performers' affection clearly shown. The finale is comparatively lightweight but has genuine sparkle, and the closing pages have plenty of impact. The Decca sound is brilliant, clear and immediate, without any special Phase 4 exaggerations, and the result is distinctly enjoyable.

Gilels's early RCA recording is somewhat over-reverberant, with a hint of coarseness. However, this is a very exciting, full-blooded version, including a beautifully gentle account of the outer sections of the slow movement.

Curzon, as always, plays thoughtfully and intelligently, and this disc will obviously give a great deal of pleasure even if there is neither the world-shaking bravura of a powerful virtuoso nor any specially fresh insight. The recording is good, but the orchestral balance is not always wholly natural.

Katin's Classics for Pleasure version is given a brilliant, modern recording (paid for by Wills' cigarettes, whose masthead is on the sleeve), and this is basically quite a strong, musical reading. But somehow there is a lack of drama, and the lack of extrovert bravura from the soloist (es-

pecially in the middle section of the slow movement) produces an impression of facelessness. But no one could fault this disc on grounds of taste, and it has an excellent filler.

One of the reasons why Ogdon's reading as a whole does not appear entirely consistent is that the personalities of the soloist and the conductor do not seem to complement each other as they might. Where Barbirolli is clearly at the helm, as in the broad-spanned, majestic opening and the vivacious full-blooded finale, the music has a strong forward emotional thrust, which Ogdon follows well; but as the solo piano part takes over the style of the performance alters, and in the quieter, lyrical music the tension sags. One has the feeling of emotional inconsistency in what is essentially a work that represents an intense and consistent struggle between pianist and orchestra. Under no circumstances must the soloist seem to give up the struggle and go his own way. Fortunately in the *Andantino* both Ogdon and the conductor see eye to eye, and the result is an appealing natural simplicity. The recording is clear and spacious.

This element of struggle is only too clear in the Richter/Karajan performance on DGG. Richter and Karajan, not surprisingly, do not always agree. Each chooses a different tempo for the second subject of the finale and maintains it in spite of the other. However, in both the dramatic opening and the closing pages of the work they are agreed in a hugely mannered, bland stylization which is not easy to enjoy. Elsewhere in the first movement both conductor and pianist play havoc with any sense of forward tempo (although they both produce some real bursts of excitement here and there), and Richter's excessive rubato in the lyrical second-subject group is unspontaneous. Clearly two major artists are at work, but it is difficult to praise the end product as a convincing reading. The recording is full-blooded, with a firm piano image.

Piano concertos Nos. 1 in B flat minor, Op. 23; 3 in E flat major, Op. 75.

> ** (*) HMV ASD 3067. Emil Gilels (piano), New Philharmonia Orchestra, Lorin Maazel.
>
> ** Philips 6500 196. Werner Haas (piano), Monte Carlo Opera Orchestra, Eliahu Inbal.

This HMV disc is a much more attractive proposition than Gilels's boxed set of the three concertos (see above), which includes the Siloti version of No. 2. The performances here are distinguished and have an undoubted freshness. No. 3 in particular has a poetic quality which is highly rewarding, in spite of some lack of robustness. The account of No. 1, however, is lightweight. It has a very fast opening, exhilarating in its way, but for some ears Tchaikovsky's famous melody needs a broader treatment. The balance places the piano well forward, and the orchestral recording, although good, is not as refined and lustrous as it might be.

Werner Haas is an intelligent and masterly player whose accounts of these two concertos, particularly given the finely recorded sound, is highly competitive. Unfortunately the Monte Carlo Opera Orchestra is not his equal, and their playing under Inbal cannot be described as distinguished.

(i) *Piano concerto No. 1 in B flat minor, Op. 23;* (ii) *Concert fantasia* (for piano and orchestra) *in G major, Op. 56.*

> (B) *** Decca SPA 168. Peter Katin (piano), (i) London Symphony Orchestra, Kundall; (ii) London Philharmonic Orchestra, Sir Adrian Boult.

The Decca recording of the *First Piano concerto* is quite splendid, bold and vivid, clear and immediate, and excellently balanced. After this there seems no reason why the work should not always be presented complete on one side. The performance is equally alive and direct, the opening big tune taken fairly fast but with a fine sweep, the *Andantino* played very stylishly and the finale with plenty of bravura. Katin's Kempff-like clarity perfectly suits the *Concert fantasia*, with its *Nutcracker* overtones in the first movement. This two-movement piece is much less ambitious than the well-known concerto. Boult as well as Katin obviously relishes the delicacy of much of this music, and he induces his players to give a rhythmic spring which compensates completely for the occasional fault of ensemble. There is an overall freshness about the playing – in the full emotional passages as well as the rest – which should help to bring the piece the attention and popularity it deserves. The stereo is clear, the piano tone firm and bright. Altogether this is a most enjoyable record and a very happily planned coupling.

(i) *Piano concerto No. 1 in B flat minor, Op. 23;* (ii) *Violin concerto in D major, Op. 35.*

> (M) *** RCA LSB 4016. (i) John Browning (piano); (ii) Erik Friedman (violin); both with London Symphony Orchestra, Seiji Ozawa.

An attractive and generous coupling, with fresh, youthful performances of both works surprisingly well recorded for the length of sides. The opening of the *Piano concerto* may not convey quite enough power, but that is the result of the orchestral balance, and Browning's interpretation of the solo role is remarkable not only for power and bravura but for wit and point in the many scherzando passages. His slow movement, like Graffman's on the CBS version, is attractively cool, and in the finale he adopts an even faster and more furious tempo. Erik Friedman, Heifetz's pupil, is a thoughtful violinist who gives a keenly intelligent, completely unvulgar performance, with a particularly poetic and beautiful account of the slow movement. Two performances to match those of almost any rival.

Piano concerto No. 2 in G major, Op. 44 (complete recording of original score).
*** HMV ASD 2825. Sylvia Kersenbaum (piano), ORTF National Orchestra, Jean Martinon.

This is far and away the most vivid and enjoyable account of this uneven concerto to have appeared on LP. It is absolutely complete, and one's only reservation concerns the slow movement, which is finely played by the violin and cello soloists as well as the pianist: the recording acoustic is not ideally glowing here. One feels the balance has been managed to give maximum brilliance to the first movement, where the massed violin tone is somewhat pithy too. But these criticisms are insignificant compared to the success of the enterprise as a whole. The chosen tempo for the opening movement is perfect, and the opening has a sweep to compare with that of the *B flat minor concerto*. The finale too has much more lyrical power than usual. A little of the wit is sacrificed in consequence, but the basic sparkle is in no doubt, and the overall effect is highly exuberant.

Violin concerto in D major, Op. 35.
*** Decca SXL 6493. Kyung-Wha Chung (violin), London Symphony Orchestra, André Previn – SIBELIUS: *Concerto*.***
*** DGG 2530 359. Nathan Milstein (violin), Vienna Philharmonic Orchestra, Claudio Abbado – MENDELSSOHN: *Concerto*.***
(B) *** Classics for Pleasure CFP 40083. Leonid Kogan (violin), Paris Conservatoire Orchestra,

Constantin Silvestri – *Capriccio italien*.**
(B) *** RCA Camden CCV 5015. Henryk Szeryng (violin), Boston Symphony Orchestra, Charles Munch – TARTINI: *Devil's Trill sonata*.***
(B) *** Decca SPA 183. Alfredo Campoli (violin), London Symphony Orchestra, Ataulfo Argenta – PAGANINI: *Concerto No. 1* (arr. Kreisler).**
** (*) Philips 6500 708. Mayumi Fujikawa (violin), Rotterdam Philharmonic Orchestra, Edo de Waart – BRUCH: *Concerto No. 1*.** (*)
** (*) CBS 72768. Pinchas Zukerman (violin), London Symphony Orchestra, Antal Dorati – MENDELSSOHN: *Concerto*.** (*)
** (*) DGG SLPM 139028. Christian Ferras (violin), Berlin Philharmonic Orchestra, Herbert von Karajan – *Capriccio italien*.** (*)
(M) ** CBS Classics 61029. Isaac Stern (violin), Philadelphia Orchestra, Eugene Ormandy – MENDELSSOHN: *Concerto*.**
(M) (**) RCA DPS 2002 (2 discs). Jascha Heifetz (violin), Chicago Symphony Orchestra, Fritz Reiner – BRAHMS: *Concerto* * (**); MENDELSSOHN: *Concerto*.(***)
(M) ** Decca Ace of Diamonds SDD 126. Ruggiero Ricci (violin), London Symphony Orchestra, Sir Malcolm Sargent – DVOŘÁK: *Concerto*.**
(M) * (*) RCA LSB 4066. Itzhak Perlman (violin), Boston Symphony Orchestra, Erich Leinsdorf – SIBELIUS: *Concerto*.* (*)

Like the Sibelius with which it is coupled, Kyung-Wha Chung's performance of the Tchaikovsky *Violin concerto* is among the finest in the catalogue. Her technique is impeccable and her musicianship of the highest order, and Previn's accompanying is highly sympathetic and responsive. This has warmth, spontaneity and discipline; every detail is beautifully shaped and turned without a trace of sentimentality. The recording is well balanced and detail is clean, though the acoustic is warm. This is a very distinguished account.

Milstein's performance too is a highly impressive one and is the finest available of this particular coupling. Abbado secures playing of genuine sensitivity and scale from the Vienna Philharmonic, and the D G G recording is first-class.

Kogan's disc is not in this class as a recording; the solo violin is well caught but the orchestra is not quite as rich in the tuttis as in the full-priced versions. Kogan plainly enjoys this concerto enormously. His build-up of tension when the main theme is developed in the first movement is most exciting through his very refusal to slacken the basic speed. His tone is gloriously rich, and only occasionally does he mar a phrase with a rather soupy swerve. He rarely achieves a true pianissimo, but that may be the fault of the recording.

When it first appeared at full-price (without a coupling), Szeryng's performance was widely accounted to provide the ideal combination of brilliance, warmth and subtlety. In the bargain Camden reissue that enthusiasm must be reinforced. The purity of Szeryng's playing is remarkable, when the technical problems are so demanding, and quite apart from his effortless sense of bravura, he is able to bring all the lyrical sweetness and slavonic yearning needed for Tchaikovsky's big melodies. First-rate playing by the Boston Orchestra and a wide stereo spread.

Campoli's fine performance has been highly praised for its technical brilliance and sense of style. The soloist's judicious editing of his part does not interfere with the music's impulse and line, and although this is a rather personal reading, its natural warmth and spontaneity are appealing. Argenta accompanies with sensitivity and shows his feeling for Tchaikovsky's orchestral colouring as well as creating plenty of excitement and contrast in the tuttis. The recording needs cutting well back in the treble, but is basically rich and glowing. The coupling, Kreisler's one-movement arrangement of Paganini's *First Concerto*, shows less flair from both Campoli and the recording engineers, but makes an acceptable filler.

Mayumi Fujikawa's performance is controversial in its choice of slow tempi and a generally relaxed feeling throughout the work. But there is no question of the spontaneity of the music-making, and it is clear that the conductor shares the soloist's warm feeling for the music. The tenderness of the solo playing, in the beauty of the first movement's second subject, in the *Andante*, and notably in the finale, which is far more lyrical than usual, is echoed by the orchestral wind. The recording is absolutely first-class, which is the more remarkable considering the length of the side.

Zukerman's record isn't in the same class as a recording but the performance is undoubtedly very fine, Zukerman's tone being clean and sweet. Perhaps his taste is not as refined as Kyung-Wha Chung's, but were this as well engineered as the Decca, competition would be much closer than it is.

Consideration of the Ferras/Karajan performance must be affected by personal reactions to Ferras's characteristic tone, with its rather close vibrato in lyrical passages and tendency to emphasize the schmalz on the G string. One finds too that Ferras's playing tends to lack charm, but some may react differently, and this is a well-conceived reading, with Karajan shaping the work as a whole very convincingly. The recording is excellent, the brilliance emphasizing the style of the soloist.

A strong performance from Stern, but like the Mendelssohn on the reverse it lacks poetry when pianissimos consistently become mezzo fortes. Close balance for the soloist, with typical CBS Philadelphia sound.

Heifetz is recorded near the microphone and this emphasizes the powerful tension of his reading, but also provides the listener with some uncomfortable sounds as bow meets string in the many florid moments which this concerto offers. At the same time there is some gorgeous lyrical playing, and the slow movement marries passion and tenderness in ideal proportions. There is no question about the excitement of this performance or its technical assurance, but the snag is the orchestral recording, which is never more than fair, and distinctly rough in the louder tuttis.

Ricci made an outstanding record of the concerto in the early days of mono LP. This is not its equal, although there is no lack of brilliance. The slow movement is without the warmth of lyrical feeling that Kogan, for instance, brings to it, but the performance has a sparkling finale. Sargent accompanies sympathetically, and the recording balance is good, although the sound has a rather sharply focused treble.

Perlman too provides a good performance in the mid-price bracket, though in a field as competitive as this, his version does not figure high in the recommended lists. The recording is far from distinguished.

1812 overture, Op. 49.
  (M) *** RCA LSB 4031. Philadelphia Orchestra, Temple University Chorus, Brass Band, electronic cannon, Eugene Ormandy – BEETHOVEN: *Wellington's victory*.***
  (M) ** (*) DGG Privilege 2538 142.

Don Cossack Choir, Berlin Philharmonic Orchestra, Herbert von Karajan – BEETHOVEN: *Wellington's victory*.**
** Decca Phase 4 PFS 4189. Royal Philharmonic Orchestra and Chorus, Grenadier Guards Band, Leopold Stokowski – BORODIN: *Polovtsian dances* ** (*); STRAVINSKY: *Pastorale*.**

Ormandy's is a highly enjoyable *1812*, among the best available, using a chorus besides all the usual effects of cannon and so on. The performance is musical and exciting, enthusiastic and dignified, with a grand broadening of tempo for the final peroration. Here, however, the balance engineers don't manage their unenviable task with absolute perfection, for the chorus is all but drowned. But it is all highly exhilarating. This is generally preferable to Karajan's account, and the engineering has more flair.

Karajan's recording is discussed below in its different coupling.

Stokowski's *1812* opens with strings not chorus, and his performance is curiously slow and mannered. It only really catches fire in the closing pages, where there are no cannon and quite eccentrically the chorus appears out of nowhere to sing the Russian hymn. The recording is highly spectacular, but the reverberation at the very end prevents absolute clarity.

(i) *1812 overture, Op. 49. Francesca da Rimini* (fantasy), *Op. 32; Marche slave, Op. 31.*
  ** (*) Philips 6500 643. Concertgebouw Orchestra, Bernard Haitink, (i) with members of the Royal Military Band.

The recording of *1812* is purposefully brilliant, almost aggressively so: one feels that this music is not really in Haitink's special province and he and the engineers are trying very hard. *Francesca da Rimini* too, although finely played, lacks the kind of compulsive excitement in the closing pages that Rozhdestvensky, for one, provides. *Marche slave* is the most successful item here (although all are enjoyable), and Haitink conveys his affection readily. The performance itself is not unlike Kenneth Alwyn's on Decca (see above), with a fast coda. Excellent sound throughout, but not quite as natural-sounding as the finest that Philips are currently giving us.

(i) *1812 overture, Op. 49. Marche slave, Op. 31; Romeo and Juliet* (fantasy overture).

*** HMV Quadraphonic Q4-ASD 2894; Stereo ASD 2894. London Symphony Orchestra, André Previn.

** (*) DGG SLPM 139029. Berlin Philharmonic Orchestra, Herbert von Karajan, (i) with Don Cossack Choir.

(B) * (*) Contour 2870 419. New Philharmonia Orchestra, Norman Del Mar.

Previn takes a clear-headed, totally unsentimental view of three of Tchaikovsky's most popular orchestral works. As a result the music emerges stronger in design (even *1812*) and no less exciting than usual. The recording quality is a little dry, concentrating on fidelity of sound and balance, but there is a hint of the studio rather than the concert hall in the overall ambience, and even the quadraphonic version does not add a great deal of extra atmosphere. But of its kind this is satisfying.

Karajan's *1812* is also available on a mid-price disc (see above), coupled, like Ormandy's, to Beethoven's *Wellington's victory*. The performance is very professional and quite exciting, with fine orchestral playing, but the chorus used to open the piece is not very sonorously

recorded, and the closing pages have the cannon added in a calculated fashion rather than showing a touch of engineering flair. Karajan's interpretation of *Romeo and Juliet* is very effective here, with passion and dignity nicely blended. *Marche slave* too is presented with its full solemn character. It is a work that the Berlin Orchestra do especially well, and the recording is splendid.

Del Mar's disc is very well recorded indeed and the engineers handle the end of *1812* with spectacular yet thoroughly musical results. The orchestral playing too is excellent, but the performances, although offering plenty of detail, are lacking in a compulsive emotional thrust. *Marche slave* comes off the most effectively, its colourful orchestration well realized by performers and recording alike.

1812 overture, Op. 49; Marche slave, Op. 31; Romeo and Juliet (fantasy overture); *Sleeping Beauty: Waltz.*

(M) ** HMV SXLP 20023. Royal Philharmonic Orchestra, Sir Malcolm Sargent.

Sargent's performances are good ones, *Marche slave* the most exciting, *Romeo and Juliet* too restrained in the love music. The recording is excellent, with plenty of weight at the lower end (bass drum and tuba really come through). At medium price this is excellent value.

(i) *1812 overture, Op. 49. Romeo and Juliet* (fantasy overture).

⊛ *** CBS Quadraphonic MQ 31276. Philadelphia Orchestra, Eugene Ormandy, (i) with Mormon Tabernacle Choir, Valley Forge Military Academy Band, cannon and bells.

*** Decca SXL 6448. Los Angeles Philharmonic Orchestra, Zubin Mehta.

Ormandy's CBS quadraphonic record of *1812* is quite stunning. It is made unashamedly in 'surround sound', and the illusion of being in a large hall with the performers is uncannily real. The opening Russian hymn, sung by the Mormon Choir, begins very quietly but then rises to a climax where the tension is quite electric. Ormandy's spacious reading is matched by the wide, reverberant acoustic, and the work's closing pages are quite overwhelmingly exciting. The sound has superb richness and cocoons the listener in the most thrilling orgy of blazing brass, spitting cannon, and resonant bells. At the very end, as the last orchestral chord dies away, the bells are left momentarily 'hanging in the air'. This is a demonstration record *par excellence*. The performance of *Romeo and Juliet* is characteristically assured, lacking something in individuality, but with a tremendous romantic climax at the final statement of the love theme. The recording here is equally resplendent, but the reverberation seems too opulent and there is a bass drum recorded with such resonance that it becomes too insistent. But this disc is worth having for *1812* alone.

For the owner of ordinary stereo equipment not contemplating the addition of quadraphony, Maazel's *1812* is also extremely spectacular and vivid. Moreover it is easy to reproduce, and while it will sound splendid on a really big machine it also makes a very striking effect on a small one. The performance itself, like that of *Romeo and Juliet*, is straightforward and exciting. Certain other accounts of *Romeo* are more individual, but this one, which lets the music speak for itself, is very effective.

(i) *1812 overture, Op. 49. Serenade for strings in C major, Op. 48.*

> (M) ** CBS Classics 61441. Philadelphia Orchestra, Eugene Ormandy, (i) with Mormon Tabernacle Choir, Valley Forge Military Academy Band.

The opening of *1812* is very beautiful here, with the Mormon Choir creating a frisson of tension in their quiet singing of the Russian hymn. The performance is a spacious one, and the end is spectacular, with really explosive cannon and bells joining in the general mêlée. But the sounds are shallow here compared to the quadraphonic version (coupled to *Romeo and Juliet*), which is one of the most thrilling of all Tchaikovsky recordings (see above). The *Serenade* is marvellously assured and the orchestral playing splendid. This performance has a lot of character, yet there remains a streamlined effect, in the main contributed by the brilliant but glossy recording. But there is no doubt about the strength of Ormandy's reading.

Fatum (symphonic poem), *Op. 77; Romeo and Juliet* (fantasy overture); *The Tempest* (fantasy), *Op. 18.*

> ** (*) Decca SXL 6694. National Symphony Orchestra of Washington, Antal Dorati.

Fatum, though published as Op. 77, is one of Tchaikovsky's earliest works, dating from 1868. Its invention is not of high quality; the second half of the work (which here is split between the two sides) is rather more spontaneous than the first. But many of Tchaikovsky's orchestral fingerprints are already apparent. *The Tempest* is another matter. If not as straightforward in construction as *Romeo and Juliet*, it has a haunting opening section evocative of the sea and a rapturous love theme that is distinctly memorable, if not as fine as *Romeo and Juliet* (which dates from only a year after *Fatum*). With vivid performances of the two early works this is a worthwhile disc, although the performance of *Romeo and Juliet* takes a little while to warm up. When it does so Dorati gives the love theme a distinctive sweep, and the closing pages are very convincing. With good orchestral playing and an excellent recording, wide in range and with a natural perspective, this can be recommended.

Francesca da Rimini (fantasy), Op. 32.
(M) *** DGG Privilege 2538 345. Leningrad Philharmonic Orchestra, Gennady Rozhdestvensky – KHACHATURIAN: Gayaneh suite.***
*** Decca Phase 4 PFS 4227. New Philharmonia Orchestra, Lorin Maazel – R. STRAUSS: Death and Transfiguration.***
** Decca SXL 6352. Suisse Romande Orchestra, Silvio Varviso – BORODIN: Symphony No. 2.***
* CBS 73047. New York Philharmonic Orchestra, Leonard Bernstein – Symphony No. 2.*

Rozhdestvensky's Francesca da Rimini is a tour de force. The inferno music is breathtakingly done, and the music for the lovers' passion is conveyed with great intensity. Yet the idyllic central section is relaxed, Tchaikovsky's imaginative writing for the woodwind nicely pointed. The recording is reverberant and the brass-playing somewhat blatant in the climaxes, but such is the excitement and spontaneity of the performance that one is swept along uncomplaining.

Maazel's Tchaikovsky interpretations stand the test of gramophone repetition remarkably well. His account of Francesca da Rimini, unexpectedly appearing on the Phase 4 label, may not have all the romantic flair of Stokowski's, but in brilliance and excitement as well as structural control it can hardly be bettered. A good coupling, presented with Phase 4's multi-channel brilliance.

Although stunningly recorded, Varviso's performance is not as memorable

as the coupling. In particular the glowing colours of the middle section of the work are not fully revealed, and Varviso favours a rather brisk tempo for Francesca's theme. But the inferno music is superbly managed by the recording, and its subtlety is revealed by the clever way the tam-tam is balanced, so that it adds its sombrely sinister warnings, as Tchaikovsky intended, and then at the end does not drown the orchestra in the final chords of the coda.

Bernstein's account is exciting, but the shallow, artificial recording precludes a recommendation.

Francesca da Rimini (fantasy), Op. 32; Hamlet (fantasy overture), Op. 67a.
⊛ (M) *** Everest SDBR 3011. New York Stadium Orchestra, Leopold Stokowski.

One had always tended to think of Hamlet as one of Tchaikovsky's near-misses, but here it emerges as a superb piece of writing, and Stokowski plays the central string tune so convincingly that, if it has not quite the romantic panache of Romeo and Juliet, it has instead the proper sombre passion suitable to the altogether different atmosphere of Shakespeare's Hamlet. It is the dignity of the music and its close identification with the play that comes over so strikingly. And, fascinatingly, Stokowski shows us how intensely Russian the music is: this is Shakespeare played in the vernacular of that great country, with its national feeling for epic drama; the funeral march at the end is extremely moving. Francesca is hardly less exciting. Surely the opening whirlwinds have seldom roared at such tornado speeds before, and the skilful way Stokowski builds up the climax out of the fragmentation of Tchaikovsky's score is thrilling indeed. The central section is played with the beguiling care for detail and balance for which this conductor is famous. When the great polyphonic climax comes, and the themes for the lovers' passion intertwine with music to suggest they are discovered, the tension is tremendous. The recording throughout is astonishingly vivid when one considers that it was made about two decades ago: this is an outstanding bargain in every way.

Francesca da Rimini (fantasy), *Op. 32;* *Hamlet* (fantasy overture), *Op. 67a;* *The Voyevode* (symphonic ballad), *Op. 78.*
  ** (*) Decca SXL 6627. National Symphony Orchestra of Washington, Antal Dorati.

Dorati's accounts of *Francesca da Rimini* and *Hamlet* are rather under-powered compared with Stokowski (and, in the case of the former, Rozhdestvensky), but they are spacious readings of some distinction, and the central section of *Francesca* is poetically done, with sensitive wind-playing. However, the main interest of this disc lies in *The Voyevode*, a melodramatic work dating from 1890–91. It is hardly one of the composer's more inspired pieces but has a strong ending to compare with *Francesca da Rimini* in its explosive power, which is not surprising as the plot is almost identical, husband returning to slay wife's lover; only here it is the husband (the Voyevode) who gets the bullet by error. The recordings are excellent throughout.

Francesca da Rimini (fantasy), *Op. 32;* *Romeo and Juliet* (fantasy overture).
  (M) ** (*) HMV SXLP 30183. USSR Symphony Orchestra, Yevgeny Svetlanov.

This record is issued in a handsome folder-sleeve and is obviously designed to attract listeners to Svetlanov's other Russian recordings, which are listed in detail on the back. But in its own right this is excellent value at medium price, with a powerful, modern recording, not

over-refined, but extremely vivid. The acoustic is a little dry but not unnaturally so; the brass sounds a little blatant at times, but not out of place in these intensely Russian performances. *Romeo and Juliet* has a splendidly red-blooded romanticism, and the middle section of *Francesca da Rimini* has a unique lyrical fervour.

Hamlet (fantasy overture), *Op. 67a;* *Romeo and Juliet* (fantasy overture).
  * (*) Decca SXL 6206. Vienna Philharmonic Orchestra, Lorin Maazel.

Maazel offers hard-driven, exciting readings, which are well supported by extremely brilliant recording. However, the reading of *Hamlet* is rather literal; a little more affectionate bending of the score would have been welcome.

Manfred symphony, Op. 58.
  *** HMV ASD 2558. USSR Symphony Orchestra, Yevgeny Svetlanov.
  ** Decca SXL 6562. Vienna Philharmonic Orchestra, Lorin Maazel.
  * (*) HMV ASD 3018. London Symphony Orchestra, André Previn.

Manfred is an uneven work, but its moments of inspiration offer some of the finest pages Tchaikovsky ever wrote. One thinks especially of the broad statement of the main theme which comes at the end of both the first and last movements, heard against a background of hammering brass chords; the delicious orchestration of the scherzo and the fine tune which forms its centrepiece, and the pastoral simplicity of the slow movement. The finale is melodramatic, but its orchestral dress is characteristically brilliant, and the closing pages with organ offer a bold final stroke, in keeping with Byronic romantic flair. The work needs a strong, uninhibited performance and it receives this from Svetlanov, while the orchestral playing has splendid colour and urgency. The full-blooded Russian recording is entirely appropriate, and while the work's weaker moments are not entirely disguised this is a very satisfying record that no Tchaikovskian should miss.

Maazel's is a fresh, straightforward account, characteristic of his Tchaikovsky series but not really a distinctive part of it. The performance is enjoyable but has nothing like the power and impulse of Svetlanov's reading. The recording is first-class.

Previn's disc is outstandingly well recorded, the finest of the three listed, with vivid sound recorded in the most natural way. But the performance is disappointing. The best movement is the scherzo, which is charmingly done, but the outer movements, spaciously conceived, are unconvincing, without the forward impulse that this score must have if it is to succeed.

(i) *Méditation in D minor, Op. 42;* (ii) *Sérénade mélancolique, Op. 42* (both for violin and orchestra).

> (B) *** Classics for Pleasure CFP 40040. Leonid Kogan (violin), with (i) Paris Conservatoire Orchestra, Constantin Silvestri; (ii) Philharmonia Orchestra, Kyril Kondrashin – LALO: *Symphonie espagnole.*** (*)

Kogan is completely at home in both these works, and the performances are first-class, with excellent accompaniments and good recording. If the coupling is attractive, this disc is splendid value, for the music here is delightful.

The Nutcracker, Op. 71 (ballet): complete recording.

> ⊛ (M) *** Decca Ace of Diamonds SDD 378/9. Suisse Romande Orchestra (with chorus), Ernest Ansermet.

> (M) *** HMV SLS 834 (2 discs). London Symphony Orchestra (with the Ambrosian Singers), André Previn.

The HMV set is affectionately and sumptuously played by Previn and the LSO. The recording is warm and pleasing on side one, but immediately becomes more vivid and dramatic on side two when, after the end of the children's party, the magic begins to work. The transformation scene is richly done, and the famous dances of Act 2 are played with much sophistication: indeed the orchestral playing throughout is of very high quality. This set can be recommended most warmly, but even so (for I.M.) it has nothing like the magic of Ansermet's Decca set, one of the very finest things he did for the gramophone. The Decca recording too, which dates from the earliest days of LP, is astonishingly rich and vivid, with a freshness and sparkle to match Ansermet's approach. The whole of the opening scene has a point and bright-eyed quality which is not so readily conveyed by the Previn set: the famous *March* comes here, and how deliciously crisp it sounds. The transformation scene and the *Waltz of the snowflakes* have a frisson-making quality, with radiant freshness in the waltz – one of Tchaikovsky's totally magical inspirations, with its wordless chorus. In the dances of Act 2 Previn may be able to offer more polished playing (and greater body of string sound), but the piquancy of colouring that Ansermet finds gives unending delight: the short characteristic dances, many of which Tchaikovsky included in the famous suite, have never sounded more characterful. A superb set, worthy of a desert-island collection.

The Nutcracker, Op. 71: highlights.

> (B) *** Decca SPA 357 (from above recording cond. Ansermet).

> *** HMV ASD 3051 (from above recording cond. Previn).

Both these excellent records reflect the splendid qualities of the sets from which they come. But Ansermet's selection is not only rather more generous (it includes the transformation scene, with Tchaikovsky's marvellously memorable climbing scale, invested with great richness and tension by Ansermet), it is also on Decca's cheapest label. In spite of the long side, the loss in richness is marginal, but the transfer seems slightly crisper in outline than the complete set.

Nutcracker suite, Op. 71a.
  *** Decca SXL 2308. Vienna Philharmonic Orchestra, Herbert von Karajan – GRIEG: *Peer Gynt.****

Anyone who wants this coupling should be well satisfied with Karajan's disc. The readings are characteristically broad: the *Overture* is less miniature in effect than usual; the *Chinese dance* could be more piquant, and the *Waltz* could have a lighter touch, but these are mere carping criticisms. This is typical Karajan conducting, with its usual panache, and the fine orchestral playing is matched by vivid recording of Decca's best quality. The upper strings have a suggestion of fizz, but it is easily tidied, and this is generally preferable to Karajan's Berlin Philharmonic version (see above under *Serenade for strings*).

There is also available a Bernstein performance (CBS Classics 61057) coupled to a less than ideal version of *Peter and the Wolf*. This has characteristic brilliance but also a tendency to glossiness, with edginess in the upper string tone.

Nutcracker suite, Op. 71a; Sleeping Beauty suite, Op. 66a.
  * (*) Philips 6500 851. Orchestre de Paris, Seiji Ozawa.

This is the only current record offering this particular coupling. The recording is vivid and the orchestral playing good, but Ozawa's readings are curiously lacking in character and charm.

Nutcracker suite, Op. 71a; Swan Lake, Op. 20: suite.
  (B) * Classics for Pleasure CFP 40002. Philharmonia Orchestra, Wolfgang Sawallisch.

This coupling dates from the earliest days of stereo. The playing is brilliant, but the recording tends to be glossy and too brightly lit. Also in *Swan Lake* the internal balance is not good, so that in the *Scene* from Act 4 (No. 28), when Tchaikovsky gives his big, romantic tune to the four horns in unison, they are lost in the distance. The best part of this performance is the *Dance of the Queen of the Swans*, where the violin and cello duet is beautifully done.

The Nutcracker, Op. 71: extended excerpts; *The Sleeping Beauty, Op. 66*: extended excerpts; *Swan Lake, Op. 20*: extended excerpts.
  (M) ** (*) HMV SLS 859 (3 discs). Philharmonia Orchestra, Efrem Kurtz (violin solos played by Yehudi Menuhin).
  (M) ** (*) RCA LRL 3 7519 (3 discs). Philadelphia Orchestra, Eugene Ormandy.
  (M) ** CBS 77373 (3 discs). Philadelphia Orchestra, Eugene Ormandy.

Each of these albums offers a generous selection from the three major ballets. They are not identical; they duplicate the more popular items and then each makes an individual choice from the remaining riches of each score. Kurtz's selection offers the advantage of beautiful Philharmonia wind-playing and a star violin soloist, although Menuhin has not a great deal to do until it comes to *Swan Lake*, where he is featured quite a bit. These are

987

all nicely turned performances, and they are well recorded. The *Nutcracker* disc is generally less attractive than the other two, both as recording (which is not so rich) and performance, and *Swan Lake* the finest of the three, with really full-blooded sound. But the difference is less apparent in these excellent new pressings.

Ormandy's RCA set has the advantage of a more modern recording and a splendidly judged acoustic, resonant and spacious. The performances have more life and sparkle than his earlier CBS set, and the recording certainly helps, with its extra atmosphere. It is not perfect; the strings have not the firmness of focus of the finest European recordings – this is also noticeable in the violin and cello duet of the *Swan Queen's dance* – but the balance is natural. There is much judicious playing, and if the Snowflakes in the *Nutcracker* are without a chorus, the Sugar Plum Fairy's celesta sounds beautifully translucent. Ormandy's manner is broader than Kurtz's, and the finale of *Swan Lake* is certainly resplendent here. The music is done fairly continuously without individual bands between items.

The earlier CBS set is less recommendable than the others, as the sound is more variable. It is least attractive in the *Nutcracker* selection, where there is the streamlined effect characteristic of some CBS issues. The orchestral playing is marvellously assured, but it lacks daintiness, and Tchaikovsky's gentler inspirations are less individual than they should be. The acoustic for *Sleeping Beauty* is more reverberant, and it is even more sumptuous for *Swan Lake*, which approaches the quality of the RCA set. The *Nutcracker* and *Swan Lake* discs are individually banded, but *Sleeping Beauty* is done as a continuous performance, with a very generous measure. Ormandy is sometimes a shade rhythmically square (as he is, though less often, in the RCA set), but this is a feature of his broad, spacious manner.

Pezzo capriccioso, Op. 62; Variations on a rococo theme, Op. 33 (both for violoncello and orchestra).

*** HMV ASD 2954. Paul Tortelier (cello), Northern Sinfonia Orchestra, Yan Tortelier – GRIEG: *Elegiac melodies; Holberg suite.****

A finely-wrought account from Tortelier *père*, accompanied by the Northern Sinfonia under Tortelier *fils*, though it must perhaps yield to Rostropovich (see below). The *Pezzo capriccioso* is not otherwise available.

Romeo and Juliet (fantasy overture).

(B) *** Decca SPA 119. Vienna Philharmonic Orchestra, Herbert von Karajan – R. STRAUSS: *Don Juan.****

(M) ** (*) DGG Privilege 2538 233. Dresden State Orchestra, Kurt Sanderling – *Symphony No. 2.** (*)*

** DGG 2530 308. San Francisco Symphony Orchestra, Seiji Ozawa – BERLIOZ: *Roméo et Juliette: Love scene*; PROKOFIEV: *Romeo and Juliet: excerpts.***

(B) ** Classics for Pleasure CFP 106. London Philharmonic Orchestra, John Pritchard – MUSSORGSKY: *Pictures.** (*)*

*(*) DGG 2530 137. Boston Symphony Orchestra, Claudio Abbado –SCRIABIN: *Poème de l'extase.****

Karajan's *Romeo* is both dramatic and exciting. The tension relaxes in the quieter music, but if the reading is carefully drawn there is no lack of passion. The recording is splendid except perhaps for a slight over-balance of percussion against the massed strings in the climaxes. The illusion of the concert hall is well conveyed.

Sanderling's performance too is distinguished. It has more romantic flair than Karajan's, and is played with exciting spontaneity. The recording is not a new one but emerges here with remarkable freshness.

In a collection of three musical evocations of Romeo and Juliet it was inevitable that the Tchaikovsky fantasy overture should be included. Ozawa draws from the San Francisco Orchestra warmly committed playing, well recorded. This should not disappoint anyone who likes the idea of having three Romeos contrasted.

Pritchard's account, brilliant and exciting, is emotionally rather reserved and lacking romantic flair. The clear, immediate but comparatively unatmospheric Classics for Pleasure recording underlines Pritchard's conception.

Abbado attempts a broad, spacious reading, which, in spite of fine orchestral playing, is too refined by half. The recording is excellent but this is disappointing.

(i) *Romeo and Juliet* (fantasy overture); (ii) *Nutcracker suite, Op. 71a.*

(M) ** (*) DGG Privilege 2538 346. (i) Dresden State Orchestra, Kurt Sanderling; (ii) Berlin Philharmonic Orchestra, Ferdinand Leitner.

(B) ** Contour 6870 584. Vienna Symphony Orchestra, Karel Ančerl.

Sanderling's first-class performance of *Romeo and Juliet* is discussed above, where it is differently coupled. Leitner's account of the *Nutcracker suite* sounds fresh, and the early recording is astonishingly vivid. The Berlin Philharmonic playing here is petite and very polished. The *Waltz* lacks something in panache, but taken as a whole this version is among the best available.

Ančerl's coupling on one of the cheapest bargain labels offers a noble and dignified account of *Romeo and Juliet,*

bringing out the intensity rather than the drama, and a vivid, spontaneous *Nutcracker suite.* The recording is pleasing rather than especially brilliant, but *Romeo* has plenty of weight. Good value.

Serenade for strings in C major, Op. 48 (see also under *1812*).

(M) *** DGG Privilege 2538 232. Dresden State Orchestra, Otmar Suitner – PROKOFIEV: *Symphony No. 1; Overture on Hebrew themes.*** (*)

** (*) HMV ASD 3036. English Chamber Orchestra, Daniel Barenboim – DVOŘÁK: *Serenade.*** (*)

(B) ** RCA Victrola VICS 1540. Boston Symphony Orchestra, Charles Munch – BARBER: *Adagio*; ELGAR: *Introduction and allegro.***

(B) ** Decca SPA 375. Israel Philharmonic Orchestra, Sir Georg Solti – DVOŘÁK: *Serenade.***

** Pye Ensayo NEL 2002. English Chamber Orchestra, Enrique Garcia Asensio – DVOŘÁK: *Serenade.*** (*)

(M) ** Vanguard VCS 10099. English Chamber Orchestra, Johannes Somary – ARENSKY: *Variations on a theme of Tchaikovsky*; PROKOFIEV: *Symphony No. 1.***

Suitner's account of the *Serenade for strings* is very competitive, and the strings of the Dresden Staatskapelle have splendid bloom and warmth. At its mid-price level, this disc is highly recommendable.

Barenboim must yield to his competitors, in particular Marriner (see below). The ECO strings are not always reproduced with comfort on this HMV disc, not one of their very best, though it is far from unacceptable. There is some expressive underlining here and there which might possibly prove tiresome after a number of hearings. A good but not the finest version.

A strong, full-blooded reading from Munch, with an elegant waltz and an especially well prepared finale. The conductor does not overplay his hand in the *Elegy*, and the only relative disappointment is the lack of Mozartian pointing in the second subject of the first movement. The recording has a touch of the characteristic Boston harshness, but has plenty of colour and atmosphere.

Solti's disc is an early stereo recording but technically it is impressive. The engineers have cut the disc at a very high level, and this tends to emphasize the glossiness of the playing of the Israel strings as well as their undoubted brilliance. The performance is certainly gripping, yet Solti overplays the work; it wants more elegance and repose, and the *Waltz* has insufficient lustre. Solti brings considerable intensity to the *Elegy* and he catches the evocative atmosphere of the opening of the finale especially well.

Asensio's is a strongly musical performance, well played and recorded. The allegros of the two outer movements are robust but lack something in exuberance. The *Waltz* is gracious and the *Elegy* expressive, but the performance as a whole has no really memorable features.

Somary's performance seems rather cool, but this is partly the fault of the dry acoustic. The *Waltz* lacks charm, but the slow movement comes off rather well. Acceptable value if the coupling is desired.

Serenade for strings in C major, Op. 48; Nutcracker suite, Op. 71a.
   ** DGG SLPM 139030. Berlin Philharmonic Orchestra, Herbert von Karajan.
   * (*) Decca Phase 4 PFS 4126. Royal Philharmonic Orchestra, Stanley Black.

Karajan's reading of the *Serenade* is brilliantly played but lacks charm. The *Waltz* is suavely done, and the main points of the slow movement are made without expressive underlining, but Karajan seems uninvolved. This impression may partly be caused by the unexpansive recorded sound, which is neither sumptuous nor revealing of detail. The *Nutcracker suite* is similarly presented with bright clear sound but a lack of colour. The *Miniature overture* and *Waltz of the flowers* are well projected, but the characteristic dances lack piquancy.

Stanley Black's recording is much more vivid, but the spotlighting of the wind solos in the *Nutcracker suite* will not appeal to everyone. The *Serenade* is played very conscientiously, but there is a lack of individuality here.

Serenade for strings in C major, Op. 48; Souvenir de Florence, Op. 70.
   *** Argo ZRG 584. Academy of St Martin-in-the-Fields, Neville Marriner.

Though Tchaikovsky asked for as big a body of strings as possible in his delectable *Serenade*, there is much to be said, in these days of increased string resonance and clever microphone placing, for having a modest band like the Academy of St Martin's. The insight of Marriner's performance, its glowing sense of joy combined with the finest pointing and precision of ensemble, put it in a class of its own. The unanimity of phrasing of the Academy's violins in the intense slow movement is breathtaking in its expressiveness, although here one does notice the lack of the sheer tonal weight that a bigger body of strings would afford. The coupling could hardly be more delightful, with the Academy tackling a work normally played by six solo strings and producing delectable results. The haunting second subject of the opening movement should certainly be sampled. The one snag is that to fit it on one side, the work has been subjected to some tactful cutting. Excellent, vividly atmospheric recording quality.

Sérénade mélancolique, Op. 26; Souvenir d'un lieu cher: Scherzo, Op. 42/2 (orch. Glazounov).

(M) *** Decca Ace of Diamonds SDD 276. Ruggiero Ricci (violin), London Symphony Orchestra, Øivin Fjeldstad – SIBELIUS: *Violin concerto.*** (*)

Here are two delightful movements that might well be part of an early Tchaikovsky violin concerto. The *Sérénade* was written in 1875, three years before the well-known concerto. It is slighter than the slow movement for the actual concerto, but it has similar wistful sweetness, entirely characteristic of the composer. It is most appealing melodically. The *Scherzo*, arranged from a group of pieces written for violin and piano, is short, genial, pithy and very attractive. Ricci plays both works admirably, and the accompaniment is very well managed, as is the recording.

The Sleeping Beauty, Op. 66 (ballet): complete recording.

(M) ** (*) Decca Ace of Diamonds SDDD 301/3. Suisse Romande Orchestra, Ernest Ansermet.

(M) ** (*) HMV SLS 5001 (3 discs). London Symphony Orchestra, André Previn.

Ansermet's recording has been remastered with great success. The stereo conveys the attractive hall ambience splendidly, and the climaxes are highly spectacular. The strings have a clean outline and no lack of body. If the solo wind-playing sometimes lacks individual distinction and bloom, the overall effect is alive and colourful. The ballet's opening scenes contain much that is very dramatic, but the composer's inspiration here is

thinner than in Acts 2 and 3, and neither Ansermet or Previn are successful in bringing Act 1 fully to life, although the Decca recording is much more vivid than the HMV. Ansermet is at his best in the many characteristic dances, showing Tchaikovsky at his most felicitous, which fill out the latter parts of the score, and here the sparkle of the Decca recording tells again and again.

Previn's HMV set is altogether more plushy as sound. It is rich and pleasing, but however one manipulates the controls it is difficult to achieve any sense of glitter or real brilliance. The orchestral playing is of course more polished than Ansermet's and the string tone has more substance. Previn conveys his affection throughout, but too often there is a lack of vitality, and in the *Entr'acte* (No. 18), with its violin solo by John Brown, the atmosphere is so cosy that the style hovers perilously near that of the salon. On the other hand the *Panorama* which comes immediately before shows Previn and his orchestra at their very best, the tune floating over its rocking bass in the most magical way.

The Sleeping Beauty, Op. 66: highlights.

*** Philips SAL 3415. London Symphony Orchestra, Anatole Fistoulari.

(B) ** (*) Decca SPA 358 (from above recording cond. Ansermet).

(B) ** Decca Eclipse ECS 575. London Symphony Orchestra, Pierre Monteux.

(B) ** Classics for Pleasure CFP 133. Philharmonia Orchestra, George Weldon.

The Philips is an issue to set beside Fistoulari's fine single-disc selection from *Swan Lake*. It is extremely well recorded, nearly as good as the superlative Decca, which is saying a lot, and the phrasing has that masterly warmth which sets Fistoulari without peer among European ballet conductors. Listen to the richness and breadth he imparts to the famous *Rose adagio*, dispelling any frenetic sense of hysteria, and above all the wonderful relaxed shaping of the beautiful *Panorama* tune – one of Tchaikovsky's greatest melodic inspirations. The collection mixes familiar with unfamiliar as it should and is highly satisfying.

Ansermet's selection faithfully reflects the character of the complete set. The Prologue and Act 1 excerpts are dramatic but rather cool. With the opening of side two and Act 2 the music comes over more vividly, although the playing has not the warmth of the outstanding *Nutcracker* recording.

Monteux's selection is generous, and mixes a good deal of unfamiliar music with some of the best-known items. The recording is brilliant and does not offer very rich string tone, but Monteux conducts with great zest and obvious enjoyment. If the famous *Panorama* is taken rather too quickly, the grand finale is really vivid.

Weldon's selection follows the same basic lines as Monteux's, but omits the *Farandole* and *Panorama* from Act 2 and extends the Act 3 selection to include one or two more of the characteristic dances. The orchestral playing is excellent, and Weldon's personality emerged here more strongly than was usual on his records. The music-making has not quite the character of Monteux's selection but it is vivid and easy to enjoy. Originally the E M I sound was notably opulent, but in this new transfer some richness in the bass has been sacrificed to achieve more brilliance. The result is that the upper register sounds shrill, although it is clean and yields to a reduction of treble.

The Sleeping Beauty, Op. 66: excerpts; *Swan Lake, Op. 20*: excerpts.
- ** (*) Decca Phase 4 PFS 4083. New

Philharmonia Orchestra, Leopold Stokowski.

This is among the most distinguished sets of excerpts from the Tchaikovsky ballets, and it is a pity that the Phase 4 techniques have contributed a gloss of added brilliance to reduce the naturalness of the sound. The orchestral playing is very fine, and no one knows better than Stokowski how to shape a Tchaikovsky melody, or indeed (and here he uses the possibilities of artificial balancing unashamedly) how to reveal a felicitous detail of scoring. But there is a great deal of loud music here, and with the excess of treble not all machines will be able to cope with it. For those that can this is a generous and superbly presented selection.

The Sleeping Beauty, Op. 66: suite; Swan Lake, Op. 20: suite.
- *** D G G 2530 195. Berlin Philharmonic Orchestra, Herbert von Karajan.
- ** (*) Decca SXL 6187. Vienna Philharmonic Orchestra, Herbert von Karajan.

Karajan has recorded this coupling three times in stereo. The first, on Columbia, was resplendent in sound and one of the very best discs in E M I's early stereo catalogue. It remains a good disc by any standards, but is currently out of the catalogue. The second recording, for Decca, is comparatively disappointing, the sound clear and brilliant, but, like the performances, curiously unexpansive. Then Karajan completed his hat-trick with an exciting D G G disc that is the best of the three. The level of the tension (immediately created at the beginning of the *Sleeping Beauty* selection) is consistently high, and with first-rate orchestral playing throughout this is very attractive. The D G G sound aims for brilliance rather than richness, but it is well balanced and suits Karajan's extrovert approach. There are few more sheerly exciting Tchaikovsky ballet records than this.

The Sleeping Beauty, Op. 66: suite; Swan Lake, Op. 20: suite; Eugene Onegin: Polonaise.
> (B) ** DGG Heliodor 2548 125. Warsaw National Philharmonic Symphony Orchestra, Witold Rowicki.

Rowicki is sometimes mannered and he chooses some curious tempi; the opening oboe theme of *Swan Lake*, for instance, is surprisingly slow. But this is mostly excellent playing with plenty of life in it, and the Polish woodwind soloists have strong individual personalities. The recording is bright, with a tendency for the brass to blare a little, but at the price this is a reasonable coupling, in spite of dated string tone.

Trois Souvenirs d'un lieu cher, Op. 42 (orch. Glazounov).
> (M) *** HMV SXLP 30170. Herman Krebbers (violin), Amsterdam Philharmonic Orchestra, Anton Kersjes – DVOŘÁK: *Violin concerto.* ** (*)

Krebbers's performances here make an excellent coupling for the Dvořák. They are played with style and warmth and are vividly recorded.

The Storm (overture), Op. 76; The Voyevode (symphonic ballad), Op. 78.
> * (*) HMV ASD 3013. New Philharmonia Orchestra, Yuri Krasnapolsky – RACHMANINOV: *5 Études-Tableaux.* **

Although the recording here is first-class the performances are not distinguished. For *The Voyevode* it is best to stay with the Dorati set on Decca, which accommodates all the tone poems of Tchaikovsky on two discs (see above).

Suite No. 1 in D minor, Op. 43.
> ** (*) Philips SAL 3734. New Philharmonia Orchestra, Antal Dorati.

Suite No. 3 in G major, Op. 55: Theme and variations (only).
> (B) * (*) Decca Eclipse ECS 636. London Philharmonic Orchestra, Sir Adrian Boult – *Symphony No. 3.* * (*)

Tchaikovsky's four orchestral suites are a nineteenth-century descendant of the dance suites which were popular in the seventeenth and early eighteenth centuries and which made the original foundation for the symphony. Each of the Tchaikovsky works (except No. 4) is quite as long as the average symphony and it might be reasonably felt – unless one thinks of them as ballets without choreography – that their content is rather slight for the size of their structure. As a complete work the first is by far the most rewarding, with a generally well argued first movement, the fughetta not petering out as so often with this composer. The *Divertimento* second movement and the gentle melancholy of the *Andantino* which follows are both attractive, the composer's craftsmanship always giving pleasure, but when one turns over for the masterly piquancy of the *Marche miniature* (with all the orchestral brilliance of the *Nutcracker suite*, and deliciously short) one realizes that the rest was on a distinctly more workaday level of inspiration. The scherzo is pretty and the finale, a *Gavotte*, again has a really characteristic main theme, although it loses some of its poise when it breaks into a rather brash final tutti.

Dorati's recording is a comparatively modern one, balanced very musically, if without quite the sparkle and colour one would ideally like. The Decca sound for Boult does not approach this. This is a very early stereo recording, and with Boult and the LPO below their best form this cannot be more than a stopgap until a better version is restored to the catalogue. The *Theme and variations* as music shows Tchaikovsky at his most inspired.

Suite No. 4 (Mozartiana), Op. 61.
   ** Decca SXL 6312. Suisse Romande Orchestra, Ernest Ansermet – RESPIGHI: *Rossiniana.** (*)

Tchaikovsky's *Mozartiana suite* (a tribute from one great composer to another) is hardly one of his masterpieces, but as finale it has an attractive set of variations (based closely on Mozart's *Variations on a theme of Gluck*, K.455 – for piano). Above all this music needs elegance and a sense of style, and also really polished orchestral playing. The playing here is competent, and Ansermet is reasonably affectionate, but this performance has not the character of Fistoulari's on a (now deleted) HMV disc, and Ricci was not the ideal choice for soloist in the concertante section of the variations. The recording, however, is excellent.

Swan Lake, Op. 20 (ballet): complete recording of original score.
   (M) *** Decca 10BB 168/70. Ruggiero Ricci (violin), Netherlands Radio Philharmonic Orchestra, Anatole Fistoulari.
   (M) ** HMV SLS 795 (3 discs). Moscow Radio Symphony Orchestra, Gennady Rozhdestvensky.
Swan Lake, Op. 20: fairly complete recording of European score.
   (M) ** (*) Decca Ace of Diamonds SDD 354/5. Suisse Romande Orchestra, Ernest Ansermet.

Tchaikovsky's score for *Swan Lake* is among his supreme masterpieces. It has a lyrical flow of inspired musical invention which runs uninterrupted for about two and a half hours. There is not a dull bar, and everywhere the felicity of the orchestration matches the quality of the invention. This is not surprising, for the composer told us that his ideas came to him (sometimes in the middle of the night, when he was forced to get up to write them down, so persistently did they demand his attention) complete with their harmony and orchestral dress. The Decca set was made in the unnatural balance of Phase 4, and for all its vivid qualities the romantic sweep of the music is hampered by the comparatively dry acoustic and the occasional (fortunately not too exaggerated) spotlighting of wind soloists. Having said that, there is nothing but praise for this splendid performance. It is at once dramatic and expressive; the orchestral playing is marvellously alert and there is plenty of sparkle. The wind-playing is beautifully pointed where necessary, and the piquant piccolo is matched by a particularly expressive contribution from the principal oboe. There is much music here that is unfamiliar (some sixteen hundred bars of music have been absent from the European edition of the score until comparatively recently) but none that is uninspired, and one is struck again and again how each item follows on with a spontaneous flow, rather like a Schubertian song cycle. Fistoulari's performance helps a great deal here, for spontaneity is one of its strongest features, and the conductor rises splendidly to the big emotional climaxes, producing orchestral playing of splendid body and power, in spite of the unexpansive acoustic.

The Moscow performance is obviously sympathetic and idiomatic, and this recording is available at a permanent special-offer price from HMV. But there is a certain edge to the sound in the louder moments which makes listening for long stretches somewhat tiring, whereas with Fistoulari one is tempted to go on and play more and more.

For those wanting a shorter selection,

Ansermet's two-disc Ace of Diamonds set is excellent value. Ansermet is comparatively restrained after Fistoulari's vivid sense of drama, and is at his best in the characteristic dances in Act 3, where the colouring of Tchaikovsky's scoring is perceptively shown. The acoustic is on the cool side, compared to Ansermet's *Nutcracker* set, but the actual quality is excellent, and there is much pleasure to be had from this pair of discs, although Fistoulari is well worth the extra outlay.

Swan Lake, Op. 20: highlights.
　　*** Decca sxl 2285. Concertgebouw Orchestra, Anatole Fistoulari.
　　(m) ** (*) Philips Universo 6580 020. London Symphony Orchestra, Pierre Monteux.
　　(b) ** (*) Decca spa 224. Royal Opera House, Covent Garden, Orchestra, Jean Morel.
　　(m) ** (*) Decca Ace of Diamonds sdd 257 (from above recording cond. Ansermet).
　　** (*) HMV asd 2757 (from above recording cond. Rozhdestvensky).
　　(m) ** HMV sxlp 20101. Vienna Symphony Orchestra, John Lanchbery.
　　(m) * (*) CBS Classics 61205. New York Philharmonic Orchestra, Leonard Bernstein.

Fistoulari is gracious, his rhythms flexible (sometimes they err a fraction to slackness); this is real ballet conducting, making this the finest *Swan Lake* selection in the catalogue, particularly as the Decca recording is in this company's highest class of both richness and transparency. The Concertgebouw playing is good although their solo violin and cello are not as polished as one might expect.

Philips have greatly improved the sound in their new transfer. The recording lacks the last degree of brilliance but is warm and realistic. The expansive acoustic suits Monteux's approach, which is affectionate rather than especially exciting. The LSO playing is beautifully turned (more polished than Ansermet's); only perhaps in the finale, which Monteux plays slowly and grandly, does the slight lack of bite and concentration in the music-making affect the directness of Tchaikovsky's inspiration. And even here the spacious sound, with rich-toned brass, makes an excellent effect.

The selection by Morel and the Covent Garden Orchestra was originally issued in the earliest days of stereo on RCA. Now reverting to the Decca label (which company originally provided the recording team), it emerges as a vividly enjoyable disc, with excellent sound that does not date in the least. The acoustic is very slightly dry but it matches the keen, alert playing. The scale of the performance is essentially of the orchestral pit rather than the concert hall, but the intimacy of the *Waltz*, for instance, brings an added freshness. There is some very sensitive woodwind-playing, especially by the oboe, who is splendid. With such vitality throughout this is a fine bargain, although there is a moment in the finale when the recording loses its clarity of focus in the opulence of Tchaikovsky's scoring.

The Ansermet selection comes from the complete recording, and taken out of their context some of the items on side one seem less spontaneous in effect than in the complete set. But this is a well-chosen selection, and the recording is of Decca's very best, rich and wide in range, with a particularly sonorous bass. It sounds especially well on the second side, which offers some of the most enjoyable music from Act 3.

The generous selection from the complete Russian set includes some music which is little known in this country. Most of the favourite numbers are here too; the playing is red-blooded and idiomatic, and the recording is colourful. Generally the sound is smoother here than in the complete set, and it is often really vivid, if not

995

so fresh as, for instance, the Ansermet selection, or as warm as Monteux's.

John Lanchbery's collection is not a predictable one; it misses out some of the purple patches and includes unfamiliar material. The selection is generous and the sides are full without loss of quality, which is fresh and pleasing, well detailed, if a trifle dry in the bass. Those who have seen the Royal Ballet film will find this a worthy memento (the recording was obviously made for, rather than from, the soundtrack). The tempi are sensible – for they have to be danced to – but if the conductor is thus unable to whip up the excitement as he might at a concert performance, he maintains a consistent level of tension.

Bernstein's selection is also generous and the playing is superbly pointed, the New York Philharmonic obviously a finer orchestra than the Swiss one Ansermet uses. The performances have typical Bernstein zest and extreme brilliance, with a recording to match. In fact the treble of the CBS disc is aggressively bright. But one can adjust the controls, and basically the recording is excellent, if not of the richness of the Decca.

Symphonies Nos. 1–6; Manfred Symphony, Op. 58.
- (B) ** (*) HMV SLS 881 (7 discs). USSR Symphony Orchestra, Yevgeny Svetlanov – LIADOV: *Baba-Yaga etc*.***; RIMSKY-KORSAKOV: *Overtures*.**
- ** (*) Decca SXLC 6476/80 (without *Manfred*). Vienna Philharmonic Orchestra, Lorin Maazel.

Svetlanov's set, unlike Maazel's, has the inestimable advantage of offering a superb account of *Manfred*, quite the best on the market, as well as a host of other fill-ups. These are performances of much temperament and fire, though the orchestral playing is a little variable: ensemble in No. 3 is not absolutely perfect. The

recordings are all of high standard, and as the price is extremely reasonable this is probably to be preferred to the Maazel set, excellent though that is.

Maazel's performances are well-judged and clearly thought out. There is a coolness about them, a certain detachment, which might appeal to some readers. The recording has clearly defined detail and much presence; it is well-lit in the Decca manner but never at the expense of musical perspective, nor does it ever produce glare.

Symphony No. 1 in G minor (Winter Day-dreams), Op. 13.
- ** (*) Decca SXL 6159. Vienna Philharmonic Orchestra, Lorin Maazel.
- ** (*) DGG 2530 078. Boston Symphony Orchestra, Michael Tilson Thomas.

Maazel's recording is highly enjoyable. If the opening movement is driven hard and the Mendelssohnian quality is played down, there is also evidence of the care with which the conductor has studied the score. Much felicitous detail emerges afresh, and the delightful scherzo comes to life splendidly, with a real feeling displayed for the line of the waltz which forms its centrepiece. The finale too is very successful; even Tchaikovsky's somewhat academic fugato section is made to come off, with short stabbing emphases of each entry of the theme. The slow movement is not as dreamy as one might ideally ask, but the style of the playing, with strong, thrusting horn-playing for the final statement of the main tune, is convincing enough in the context of the other movements.

There is no doubt that Michael Tilson Thomas's approach matches Tchaikovsky's subtitle. The freshness of the opening, played much more gently than with Maazel, is matched by the poetic feeling of the slow movement, the opening superbly atmospheric. As shaped by Thomas the main tune shows a haunting Russian melancholy which catches the music's spirit to great effect. The snag is the recording, which, though pleasant, is far too reverberant. This dulls the conductor's pointing in the first movement and, especially, the scherzo. The finale too loses its full bite and impact, although it is splendidly played. But this record, with its affectionate sympathy, is easy to enjoy in spite of its lack of clarity.

Symphony No. 2 in C minor (Little Russian), Op. 17.

   ** (*) HMV ASD 2490. USSR Symphony Orchestra, Yevgeny Svetlanov – RIMSKY-KORSAKOV: *Overtures.***

   (M) ** (*) DGG Privilege 2538 233. Dresden Philharmonic Orchestra, Kurt Masur – *Romeo and Juliet.*** (*)

   ** DGG SLPM 139381. New Philharmonia Orchestra, Claudio Abbado.

   (B) ** Decca Eclipse ECS 703. Paris Conservatoire Orchestra, Sir Georg Solti – DUKAS: *L'Apprenti sorcier.***

   * (*) Decca SXL 6162. Vienna Philharmonic Orchestra, Lorin Maazel.

   * CBS 73047. New York Philharmonic Orchestra, Leonard Bernstein – *Francesca da Rimini.**

Svetlanov's account of the *Little Russian* has plenty of character: the playing is crisp, and the clear, immediate recording suits the almost 'classical' style. Svetlanov takes the *Andantino* very slowly, and this brings out the charm of the orchestration, but his somewhat matter-of-fact approach to the finale lacks the kind of affectionate geniality that can make these simple variations really glow. And at the close the rhetoric is kept firmly under control

instead of letting the music have its full head of steam. But the whole reading is consistent, and in its way enjoyable. This is the most satisfying account of the work currently available.

The Dresden recording is reverberant, but not excessively so. The performance of the first movement has some want of bite, but the slow movement has both character and charm, Tchaikovsky's little march tune beautifully pointed. The scherzo is splendid, with a real sparkle, and the finale, if without the panache that Beecham brought to it on an old mono disc, has plenty of life and colour. With a good coupling (only given half a side here and not apparently suffering to any great degree) this is a worthwhile medium-priced recommendation.

Abbado's recording is fresh and immediate and his approach direct. He uncovers no new subtleties in the score and shows no special affection for it to tempt the listener. But the reading is well made; the slow movement is nicely done, and the performance wakes up fully in the variations which make the finale. We know this is by far the best movement, but Abbado makes it specially obvious and his enthusiasm lets rip with a splendid gong near the end.

Solti's account (previously not available in stereo) makes an acceptable bargain version. After a commanding opening he is slightly gruff in the first movement, but there is no lack of vitality, and the delightful slow movement is affectionately shaped. The scherzo and finale lack something in elegance and charm, but this is partly caused by the rather dry recording. The Dukas coupling is well done.

Maazel's hard, driving brio does not always suit this work. However, the effect of his reading is not helped by the rather reverberant recording, which although spectacular (and brilliantly engineered) tends to stop the music from ever smiling. Thus the scherzo is vivid but not gay, and the finale has little geniality.

Bernstein provides the symphony complete on one side, but the recording is too shallow and uncongenial for this to be recommended with any confidence.

Symphony No. 3 in D major (Polish), Op. 29.
- ** (*) HMV ASD 2499. USSR Symphony Orchestra, Yevgeny Svetlanov – LIADOV: *Baba-Yaga; Enchanted Lake.******
- ** (*) Decca SXL 6163. Vienna Philharmonic Orchestra, Lorin Maazel.
- ** DGG 2530 401. Vienna Symphony Orchestra, Moshe Atzmon.
- (B) * (*) Decca Eclipse ECS 636. London Philharmonic Orchestra, Sir Adrian Boult – *Suite No. 3: Theme and variations.* (*)

Until Markevitch's outstanding record is reissued (on Universo?) Svetlanov's performance is the best recommendation. It is a strong, colloquial account, making vivid contrasts between the outer and inner movements. The rhetoric of the finale is well handled, and except for the repetitive closing bars the work is made to end convincingly. The scherzo is deliciously pointed, and the slow movement has a splendid climax. The opening of the *Alla tedesca* ('In the German style') is almost too German in its ponderous way, but everywhere else the music's characterization is apt. Altogether this is most enjoyable, with a brilliant recording, which sounds well when the edge on the treble is slightly cut back.

Maazel's approach is relatively straightforward and admirably fresh, and he uncovers plenty of orchestral detail to delight the ear along with the tunes. The recording too is excellent. Anyone collecting the complete Maazel set of Tchaikovsky symphonies can invest in this disc with confidence.

The DGG performance directed by Moshe Atzmon is warmly affectionate and easy to enjoy. Atzmon brings out the ballet-music associations of the score, but he misses much of its vigour and brilliance. The reverberant recording is kindly but has less impact than is ideal. This is not really distinctive enough to earn a full recommendation on a top-priced label.

Neither of the performances on Boult's disc has been available before in stereo; indeed the stereo effect is primitive, the recording acceptable but not vivid. Boult's reading is well made and musical, but tends to sound colourless; the rhetoric is underpowered, although the central movements come off quite well. The disc is reasonably priced, however, and many may find the coupling attractive on that account.

Symphonies Nos. 4 in F minor, Op. 36; 5 in E minor, Op. 64; 6 in B minor (Pathétique), Op. 74.
- (M) ** (*) HMV SLS 833 (3 discs). Berlin Philharmonic Orchestra, Herbert von Karajan.

In many ways this album is a satisfying achievement, with fine orchestral playing and recording of splendid richness and body. However, the recording does produce a certain edgy fierceness at moments of extreme pressure, and this detracts from the set as a whole. Karajan's readings are in many ways similar to his earlier ones for DGG, but both No. 5 and No. 6 have moments where the music-making is less than completely spontaneous. A fine set nevertheless.

Symphony No. 4 in F minor, Op. 36.
- (B) *** Decca SPA 206. London Symphony Orchestra, George Szell.
- *** Decca SXL 6157. Vienna Philharmonic Orchestra, Lorin Maazel.
- (M) *** DGG Privilege 2538 178. Leningrad Philharmonic Orchestra, Yevgeny Mravinsky.

** (*) HMV ASD 2814. Berlin Philharmonic Orchestra, Herbert von Karajan.

** (*) CBS 72926. New York Philharmonic Orchestra, Daniel Barenboim.

** (*) Decca SXL 6323. Los Angeles Philharmonic Orchestra, Zubin Mehta.

** (*) DGG SLPM 139017. Berlin Philharmonic Orchestra, Herbert von Karajan.

(B) ** (*) Pye GSGC 14028. Hallé Orchestra, Sir John Barbirolli.

(B) ** (*) Classics for Pleasure CFP 161. National Youth Orchestra of Great Britain, Øivin Fjeldstad.

** Philips 6500 012. Concertgebouw Orchestra, Bernard Haitink.

(B) * (*) Decca Eclipse ECS 742. Suisse Romande Orchestra, Ataulfo Argenta – LIADOV: *8 Russian folksongs*.***

Szell's recording (not previously available here) dates from a short but particularly successful Decca recording period, when he also made a record of Handel's *Fireworks* and *Water music suites*. Like that disc his performance of Tchaikovsky's *Fourth Symphony* is highly recommendable; indeed at the modest price asked it is currently the best buy for this much-recorded symphony. The approach is straightforward (without the individuality of Mravinsky), the first movement taking a little while to generate full tension. But the finely rehearsed orchestral playing and Szell's consistency add up to a reading which yields great satisfaction on repeated hearings. The characterization of the central movements is strong, and the finale is superbly exciting. Decca have placed the second movement on the first side, leaving plenty of groove space to expand the finale, and this is arguably the most effective sonic presentation of the symphony's closing pages on record. On side one, the sound is a little drier, and some might feel this adds to a certain lack of conveyed warmth, yet listening to the delicious way Szell focuses the gentle woodwind decorations at the reprise of the main theme in the *Andantino*, one can have no doubt of the conductor's dedication to the spirit as well as the letter of Tchaikovsky's score.

The very strength of Maazel's reading is its basic simplicity and lack of personal mannerism. The dramatic and emotional power of the writing emerges in consequence with tremendous effect, and in the first movement for once the appearance of the relatively gentle second subject is not over-romanticized, and the contrast Tchaikovsky intended is underlined by this lack of emphasis. The movement moves towards its central climax with growing tension and the emotional architecture reveals a remarkable intellectual spontaneity. The slow movement is played most beautifully and the scherzo for once is not too fast. The finale explodes just as it should and is superbly recorded. Indeed, the sound throughout, except for one moment verging on overmodulation in the first movement, is tremendous.

Mravinsky's reading has a striking tension, and the first and second movements are very well done indeed. The interpretation has a very special sympathy for the mood of Russian melancholy which lies behind the music: the opening of the first-movement allegro (after the fanfare) is exceptionally perceptive, and the slow movement has a similar distinction. The centrepiece of the scherzo is full of personality, and it is only the finale that is relatively disappointing: Mravinsky's manner is so brisk that some of the character of the music is lost, although he provides a culminating climax (after a splendidly broad return of the motto theme) of great power. The DGG engineers have re-transferred the recording skilfully. It is not without a hint of congestion in the outer movements, but has a splendid lively quality to match the vivid music-making. Though this is not made a first choice, any Tchaikovskian will be greatly satisfied with it as an alternative.

Karajan's most recent Berlin Philharmonic account, for HMV, is in some ways preferable to his earlier one for DGG, although that too is a fine performance. But here Karajan's reading has more individuality: the swaying string tune in the first movement is played with compelling sensuous grace; and the climax of the slow movement has striking body and power. There is occasionally a hint of aloofness, but taken as a whole this is satisfying. The recording is spacious and spectacular, but a certain edgy coarseness is apparent at the louder climaxes.

Barenboim offers a characteristically committed reading but one which does not offer all-out brilliance. The first movement begins slowly, and the tension is built up slowly. Indeed the conductor is especially good with the end of movements; the close of the *Andantino* is gentle and moving and the end of the symphony itself, after a finale which lacks the sheer boisterousness of some accounts, is thrilling. The scherzo is wittily played to contrast with the simple warmth of the slow movement. With a good recording this is a fairly competitive account, but it has not the urgency of Szell or Maazel or the individuality of Mravinsky.

Mehta's is a straightforward account rather like Maazel's, but rather less compulsive. It is superbly recorded, showing that Decca are never content to rest on their laurels. The climax of the first movement is prepared with skill and blazes with colour, and the rocking *ben sostenuto* is properly beguiling. Yet the second subject proper does not glow as it might, and the interpretation as a whole is a shade faceless.

After a riveting opening fanfare, the first-movement allegro of Karajan's

DGG performance takes a little while to generate its full tension. The slow movement makes amends and the central climax really takes wing, to be followed by a beautifully shaped closing section, Karajan here at his most effective. The scherzo goes well, but the central wind interlude is rather slow and heavy. The finale is superb, taken at a fantastic pace, and tremendously exciting in a purely physical way. The orchestral playing is unbelievably accurate at this tempo.

Barbirolli's disc leads the remaining bargain versions. The recording is acceptable rather than outstanding, with a touch of coarseness here and there, and the strings, as recorded, are lacking in glow; but the reading is a spontaneous and thoroughly exciting one, with a well-shaped slow movement and a rousing finale. The few personal touches do nothing to detract from the conviction of the reading as a whole, and with adjustments a good tonal balance can be achieved.

The exciting performance on Classics for Pleasure was recorded at a live concert in the splendid acoustic of the Colston Hall, Bristol. At no time during the record need one apologize for the playing. It is technically expert, it has flair, and above all it is committed. The wind solos just occasionally are not dovetailed into the texture perfectly (the second subject of the first movement), but this is lack of experience rather than of musicianship. The phrasing in the slow movement is exemplary, and the scherzo is quite marvellous: the balalaika effect is perfectly captured by the murmuring waves of flowing pizzicatos from the strings, and the wind in the centrepiece is colourful and witty.

Haitink's performance is well made and in its way satisfying. It is beautifully played, and the recording is sonorous and clear. The scherzo is particularly well characterized and the crisp wind and brass playing at the centrepiece has wit and sparkle. The finale too is satisfying, if lacking the last degree of brilliance. But the first two movements have not quite the intensity and excitement that are needed if they are to flare up; Haitink's civilized manner rather damps down the strongly Russian quality of the work.

Argenta's record dates from the earliest stereo days. This new transfer is an improvement on the original; the recording has more lustre now, in spite of a dry acoustic. Argenta's account is serviceable, missing the restless intensity of the first movement, but quite characterful elsewhere. The orchestral playing lacks body and refinement. This might be considered in the bargain range for its very attractive coupling, but it has not the character of Barbirolli's Pye disc.

There is also a comparatively new account (among many others) by Dorati and the National Symphony Orchestra of Washington on Decca (SXL 6574), but this is neither especially individual nor strikingly spontaneous, and Ormandy's newest RCA disc (ARL 1 0666) is a disappointingly routine account.

Symphony No. 5 in E minor, Op. 64.
- (M) *** CBS Classics 61289. Cleveland Orchestra, George Szell.
- (M) *** DGG Privilege 2538 179. Leningrad Philharmonic Orchestra, Yevgeny Mravinsky.
- (B) *** RCA Victrola VICS 1422. Boston Symphony Orchestra, Pierre Monteux.
- ** (*) Decca Phase 4 PFS 4129. New Philharmonia Orchestra, Leopold Stokowski.
- ** (*) HMV Quadraphonic Q4-ASD 2815; Stereo ASD 2815. Berlin Philharmonic Orchestra, Herbert von Karajan.
- ** (*) DGG 2530 198. London Symphony Orchestra, Claudio Abbado.
- ** (*) DGG SLPM 139018. Berlin

Philharmonic Orchestra, Herbert von Karajan.
- ** (*) Columbia SAX 2497. Philharmonia Orchestra, Otto Klemperer.
- ** Decca SXL 6085. Vienna Philharmonic Orchestra, Lorin Maazel.
- (B) * (*) Decca SPA 223. Paris Conservatoire Orchestra, Sir Georg Solti.

Of the many recorded performances of this symphony, none is ideal in combining first-class recorded quality (and this symphony must have rich sound, with a proper weight in the bass, if its impact is to come across) with a performance of matching perception and spontaneity. Of those listed above Szell's disc makes the best compromise. His recording has a fine, resonant bass, and with a treble cut-back, the string tone, if not ideal in the matter of body and richness, can be made to produce satisfactory results. The performance is even finer than Szell's *Fourth* for Decca. Its sense of romantic urgency is finely judged, with a splendid surge and momentum in the outer movements. The style of the horn soloist in the *Andante* may not suit every taste, but in all other respects the orchestral playing is first-rate. The third movement is beautifully done and the finale is most satisfying.

In the Privilege transfer DGG have greatly improved the immediacy and impact of Mravinsky's version, and the sound now has both body and presence. The performance is full of vitality, and the lyrical movements have an intensity characteristic of Mravinsky's Tchaikovsky readings. There are occasional mannerisms, rhythmic in the first movement and dynamic in the reprise of the second subject of the *Andante cantabile*. The great drawback for some ears is the horn solo in the slow movement with its undeniable wobble. Otherwise the orchestra plays splendidly and is equal to the fantastic speed at which Mravinsky takes the finale. One has to adjust to this, and there is no doubt that it provides breath-taking excitement.

Monteux's RCA recording, although vivid, lacks something in richness, and the Boston acoustic as captured (at the end of the fifties) by the engineers is here without a really expansive bass. How-ever, recent comparisons using a current pressing, tried on various equipment, have produced surprisingly good results, and at bargain price this issue has some claims to be at the very top of the list. Monteux's reading is straightforward and exciting, among the best available. There are a few personal eccentricities of tempo (he is rather mannered in the finale), but the conductor convinces the listener in what he does and there is no doubt that this is fresh, spontaneous and exciting.

Stokowski's disc offers, besides a fine performance, the most spectacular of currently available recordings. But his concern with tonal grandeur (and cer-tainly the richness of texture on this record is as much due to Stokowski's skill as the, admittedly brilliant, efforts of the recording engineers) has its drawbacks. He tends to languish rather than press forward, and although the tension is well maintained the speeds for the main allegros of the first and last movements are considered rather than breathless, and there is some sacrifice of vitality in con-sequence. Yet with a flick of the wrist, as it were, Stokowski can create some fine blazes of excitement, as in the coda of the opening movement, or the climax of the *Andante cantabile*, or the closing moments of the symphony. The vivid impact of every department of the orchestra too makes each point of Tchaikovsky's imaginative orchestration. There are a few small cuts (four bars, twice, in the first movement, two bars in the introduc-tion to the finale, and a longer cut later), but the most noticeable effect, for anyone without a score, is that Stokowski dis-penses with the pause before the final coda.

Karajan's newest HMV version is superbly played, and the performance carries a very considerable feeling of weight and power. The body of tone at the opening of the last movement is glorious, and the final statement of the big tune before the coda is suitably res-plendent. The excitement here and at the climax of the slow movement is con-siderable, and the impact of the sound, particularly in the quadraphonic version, is overwhelming. But the reading of the first two movements is not entirely con-vincing, and there is sometimes a lack of spontaneity, notably in the slow tempi for the presentation of the first move-ment's second subject, and the opening section of the *Andante cantabile*. The recording too has an element of coarse-ness in the loudest climaxes, which some reproducers (and ears) will notice more than others.

A sound, musical account from Abbado, very well recorded. The per-formance gives pleasure by its freshness and the sophistication of the sound, which is weighty and sonorous yet brilliant at the same time. Certainly Tchaikovsky's score tells splendidly here, and it is a pity that Abbado's view of the work is not more extrovert. As it is, he tends to play down the music's most passionate moments. But of its kind this account is very enjoyable, and DGG certainly pro-ject it vividly.

Karajan's earlier Berlin Philharmonic performance is finely played and well conceived. The horn solo in the slow movement is beautiful. But in the last analysis, though Karajan's conception has both weight and power there is a sense of restraint which prevents a feeling of exhilaration. Even the finale, which is excitingly played, lacks the kind of exuberance that both Mravinsky and Stokowski bring in their different ways.

Klemperer's performance is surpris-ingly successful in a way one would not perhaps expect. There is an expanding emotional warmth in the treatment of the opening movement, with the second subject blossoming in a ripely romantic way. The slow movement too, if not completely uninhibited, is played richly, with a fine horn solo from Alan Civil. The *Waltz* is perhaps marginally disappointing, but the finale has splendid dignity, and as the recording is a very good one, this is preferable to Maazel's brasher brilliance which shows less understanding.

Maazel's Decca recording is magnificent, but his is rather a cool reading. In the *Andante* he brings in the motto theme pungently enough, but the movement as a whole has no broad emotional sweep, although the horn solo is beautifully phrased. The finale too begins and closes without a great deal of conviction, although the string-playing at the opening of the *Allegro vivace* is taut.

Solti's is a passionate and often very exciting reading which some find very enjoyable, in spite of the less than polished orchestral playing. The snag is the horn solo in the slow movement, played with the traditional French vibrato. The recording is very vivid.

Symphony No. 6 in B minor (Pathétique), Op. 74.

    *** DGG SLPM 138921. Berlin Philharmonic Orchestra, Herbert von Karajan.

    (M) *** DGG Privilege 2538 180. Leningrad Philharmonic Orchestra, Yevgeny Mravinsky.

    *** Philips 6500 081. Concertgebouw Orchestra, Bernard Haitink.

    (M) *** HMV SXLP 20027. Philharmonia Orchestra, Paul Kletzki.

    *** HMV Quadraphonic Q4-ASD 2816; Stereo ASD 2816. Berlin Philharmonic Orchestra, Herbert von Karajan.

    (M) ** (*) CBS Classics 61077. Philadelphia Orchestra, Eugene Ormandy.

    ** (*) DGG 2530 350. Vienna Philharmonic Orchestra, Claudio Abbado.

    ** (*) HMV ASD 2617. USSR Symphony Orchestra, Yevgeny Svetlanov–GLINKA: *Kamarinskaya*.**

    ** Decca SXL 6163. Vienna Philharmonic Orchestra, Lorin Maazel.

    (B) ** Music for Pleasure MFP 57017. London Symphony Orchestra, Jascha Horenstein.

    (M) ** Decca Ace of Diamonds SDD 138. Vienna Philharmonic Orchestra, Jean Martinon.

    (B) ** Pye GSGC 14030. Hallé Orchestra, Sir John Barbirolli.

As with the *Fifth*, it is very difficult to recommend a clear first choice for the *Pathétique*. Karajan's new version with the Berlin Philharmonic Orchestra is in some ways finer than his earlier account for DGG. The more modern recording (and particularly the quadraphonic disc) produces sound of splendid body and power in the third movement, but unfortunately it also has an edgy rough quality in the treble, which is noticeable only in moments of extreme fortissimo but coarsens the climax of the first movement. Also the phrasing of the famous secondary theme of the first movement seems less spontaneous, more consciously shaped, than in the earlier performance. The earlier DGG performance was also given a first-class recording which does not noticeably date. This is a very satisfying record, the interpretation having an element of restraint, Karajan standing back slightly from the music. But the listener can sense how the orchestral players have been moved by the first movement's climax, and there is great depth of feeling in the culminating coda. In the *Allegro con grazia* Karajan uses the repeats most imaginatively, and his graciousness prevents the movement from sounding like an intermezzo, as it sometimes can. After a breathlessly played scherzo (superb brass), Karajan's restraint achieves a moving performance of the finale, as again in his later version. Here Mravinsky shows a more direct passion, which has an even stronger emotional tug, and for many this will give the Russian performance (together with its medium price-tag) pride of place. But Haitink should also be seriously considered, a less spectacular but very satisfying performance to live with. Kletzki's Concert Classics disc too is splendid value at middle price; for some ears this s the most vivid and satisfying account oif all, and it loses no points on recording quality.

DGG have completely transformed the recording of Mravinsky's performance. The sound-quality is not sumptuous but has splendid bite and no lack of body. This is a powerful, intense performance, deeply felt. The last two movements are very fine indeed; the scherzo/march is brilliantly pointed, yet has plenty of weight, and the finale is deeply moving without ever letting the control slip. The first movement is not as richly recorded as either of Karajan's discs, but its eloquence and power are never in doubt.

Haitink's performance has less obvious excitement than Karajan's, and it is less brilliantly recorded, but it is not less satisfying. Indeed it could be said that the comparative sobriety of Haitink's approach is ideal for this work, especially for repeated listening via the gramophone. The great second theme of the first movement is shaped with moving restraint: no other performance offers quite this quality of gentle dignity, and after the fiery development section, the slow, stately coda makes a fitting culmination. Equally in the second movement the pathos of the throbbing middle section is perfectly judged. Haitink's third movement has a true scherzando lightness, and the broadening for the final statement of the march is expertly managed. Here the

recording has less glitter and sparkle than the DGG, but it has a fine sonority, which is again effective in giving depth and weight to the climax of the finale, just before the coda. A satisfying record in every way.

Kletzki's medium-price version continues to hold its place at the top of the list. There is a feeling of impetuosity (rather than dignity) in the first movement and the conductor broadens the reprise of the March considerably; but on the whole this is a fine, passionate reading, with a deeply-felt closing movement. The HMV stereo is extraordinarily good, with rich, lustrous strings.

Ormandy's professionalism is extremely effective in this work. Although the passion is not worn on the sleeve, the superbly fine Philadelphia orchestral playing makes much of the first-movement climax. In the finale, Ormandy's restraint does not prevent the music from having a powerful emotional feeling. The recording is excellent, one of the very best in this CBS series, and its weight and sparkle help the scherzo (the march theme emerges as a real march) to have a strong impact. The second movement too is gracious, the repeats effectively taken. In short this is an excellent disc, and its total lack of hysteria makes it one to live with.

Abbado's account, like his performance of the Fifth, is relatively lightweight. He provides a strong impulse throughout, and the second subject of the first movement sounds remarkably fresh, with radiant sounds from the strings. The climax, however, is slightly underpowered, and the finale too is restrained. The third movement is essentially a scherzo, the march-rhythms never becoming weighty and pontifical. This has many attractions for those who prefer a reading that is not too intense, and the slightly dry recording matches Abbado's conception, clean and clear in sound, rather than ripe.

Svetlanov offers a well-made and emotionally convincing first movement, exciting and with natural contours for the second subject. The second movement goes well too, the pathos brought out rather more than the music's elegance. The scherzo/march is vivid but lacks an overall compulsive grip from the conductor; the finale is eloquent and controlled, and undoubtedly moving. A distinctive account but perhaps not one of the very finest. The recording shows a touch of glassiness in the upper strings, but is otherwise of excellent quality. Some will understandably be attracted to the bonus, Glinka's *Kamarinskaya*, which is well worth having.

Maazel's is a good straightforward account, most impressive in the first and third movements, with a somewhat deadpan account of the second and a restrained finale, lacking in emotional depth. But this clean, unmannered playing offers its own rewards, and the recording is brilliant with plenty of resonance, as in the rest of Maazel's series.

Horenstein's account makes a fine bargain recommendation for those who can enjoy his coolness of manner. His sober restraint in the outer movements has an undoubted compulsive quality, and while he misses the charm in the second movement, his reading is a rewarding one. His performance of the third movement is at the opposite pole from Abbado, who sees the music as a march/scherzo rather than the other way round. The preparation for the emergence of the march tune in the full brass is superbly managed, but the broadening which follows will not be to all tastes, although with resplendent recording the tune emerges with striking weight and impact. The recording is wide in range but dry in acoustic; but this suits the meticulous manner of the playing. At the price this is well worth investigating, for the reading unquestionably shows Tchaikovsky's masterpiece in a fresh light.

When first issued, Martinon's Decca was the best-recorded *Pathétique*, with a first-rate Vienna sound, transparent and

sonorous, and especially exciting brass. However, the disc has been recut, and while the brass is still exciting, the overall sound is tighter and sharper-edged, less, in fact, like an orchestra in actuality. The effect is now to project the reading rather brashly in places, and the current disc is less competitive. Kletzki has more humanity.

The strength of Barbirolli's reading lies in the noble performance of the finale, which is deeply moving. The first movement begins rather coolly, but the slight restraint adds to the dignity of the climax. The second movement is gracious, and the third is a genuine scherzo, with Sir John holding back the big guns until the final peroration. A convincing reading, with the recording well balanced if not as sumptuous as Kletzki's.

Neither of the more recent versions, by Stokowski (R C A A R L 1 0426) and Ozawa (Philips 6500 850), competes with the finest discs listed above.

Symphony No. 7 in E flat major (reconstructed by Bogatyrev).

** (*) C B S 72042. Philadelphia Orchestra, Eugene Ormandy.

In 1892 Tchaikovsky began a new symphony, but he was not too satisfied with the way his ideas were working out and he decided instead that the material was more suitable for a piano concerto. If one listens to the one-movement *Third Piano concerto* one can easily feel that the composer was right, for several of the tunes are very pianistic. Tchaikovsky discarded the rest of his material, but the sketches for the originally planned symphony were not destroyed, and it was to these that the Soviet musicologist Bogatyrev turned. As there were no sketches for a scherzo one was provided from a set of piano pieces written in 1893. This is so skilfully orchestrated that it might well have been done by the composer himself. It is reminiscent of the scherzo from *Manfred*, and the central section, introduced by oboe and harp and then taken up by the strings, is ravishing in the best Tchaikovsky manner. The finale is rumbustious, blatant, even vulgar, and the reprise of the main theme against a sidedrum reminds one more of Glière than Tchaikovsky. Still, it is not as bad as all that, and anyway if it offends you you can always take up the pick-up after the scherzo. Given a tighter focus of performance with less opulence and more pointing than here, it might come off quite well.

Variations on a rococo theme (for violoncello and orchestra), *Op. 33* (see also under *Pezzo capriccioso*).
> *** DGG SLPM 139044. Mstislav Rostropovich (cello), Berlin Philharmonic Orchestra, Herbert von Karajan – DVOŘÁK: *Cello concerto.****

No grumbles here. Rostropovich plays this as if it were one of the greatest works for the cello, and he receives glowing support from Karajan and the Berlin Philharmonic. The *Rococo variations* is a delightful work, and it has never sounded finer than it does here.

CHAMBER MUSIC

Piano trio in A minor, Op. 50.
> ** (*) Philips 6500 132. Beaux Arts Trio.
> (M) ** Unicorn UNS 240. London Czech Trio.

Tchaikovsky's *Piano trio*, with its huge set of variations acting as slow movement and finale combined, is not an easy work to bring off on record. It ideally needs the sense of bravura and flair that characterizes the playing of Russian virtuosi. Critical opinion seems generally agreed that the Beaux Arts performance is the finer of the two versions currently available. It is certainly given a most natural (if not especially vivid) recording, and the playing is polished and eloquent, offering much pleasure in its care for detail. The performance cuts Variation VIII (Fugue) in the second movement.

The Czech performance is eloquent enough, if on a rather small scale. The players make a good team, if individually they are accomplished musicians rather than virtuosi. This is a well-made performance and as such enjoyable. It would have been even more so if the recording acoustic had been less dry, which would have helped Tchaikovsky's 'orchestral' climaxes to expand more. But each instrument is faithfully caught, and the clear stereo separation does not prevent a good tonal blend.

Souvenir de Florence (string sextet), *Op. 70.*
> (B) * Turnabout TV 34370S. Augmented Copenhagen String Quartet – VOLKMANN: *Serenade.**

The lack of refinement in the performances here is emphasized by the close balance of the recording, which has a flattened dynamic and a rather aggressive tone-quality. The playing is not without impulse, and the coupling is an imaginative one, but this cannot be recommended with any confidence.

String quartets Nos. 1 in D major, Op. 11; 2 in F major, Op. 22; 3 in E flat minor, Op. 30; in one movement in B flat major; (i) *Souvenir de Florence* (string sextet), *Op. 70.*
> (M) *** HMV SLS 889 (3 discs). Borodin String Quartet, (i) with Genrikh Talalyan (viola), Mstislav Rostropovich (cello).

This set assembles all three Tchaikovsky quartets together with an early movement and the glorious *Souvenir de Florence*. Given performances of this distinction and music of this quality of inspiration, the set is self-recommending. The recording is not perhaps quite so outstanding as the performances, but there is no reason to qualify the strength and warmth of our recommendation.

String quartet No. 1 in D major, Op. 11.
** DGG SLPM 139425. Drolc Quartet – BORODIN: *Quartet No. 2.***
(M) * (**) Supraphon 111 0698. Prague Quartet – PROKOFIEV: *Quartet No. 2.****

The Drolc performance is well planned and expertly played. The *Andante cantabile* is a little dry but comes off quite well, and the cogency of Tchaikovsky's writing in the outer movements is successfully conveyed. With just a little more communicated warmth this would have been outstanding, for the clear, clean recording is very satisfactory.

From Prague a fine performance overall, strong and spontaneous, the *Andante cantabile* most beautiful, played with a simple, direct eloquence. The finale too is very successful, and the only snag is that the sharp-edged recording verges on harshness, which does not suit the music too well.

PIANO MUSIC

Capriccio, Op. 8; Dumka, Op. 59; Humoreske, Op. 10/2; Impromptu in E flat minor, Op. 1/2; Nocturne, Op. 10/1; 3 Pieces, Op. 9; Romanze, Op. 5; Scherzo à la Russe, Op. 1/1; Souvenir de Hapsal, Op. 2; Valse caprice, Op. 5.
(B) ** Turnabout TV 37044S. Michael Ponti (piano).
Children's album, Op. 39; 5 Pieces without opus nos. (Impromptu; Impromptu-Caprice; Valse-Scherzo; Impromptu; Aveu passionné); Piano sonata, Op. 80 (posth.).

(B) ** Turnabout TV 37047S. Michael Ponti (piano).
12 Études, Op. 40; 6 Pieces on one theme, Op. 21.
(B) ** Turnabout TV 37046S. Michael Ponti (piano).
6 Pieces, Op. 19; Piano sonata in G major, Op. 37; Valse scherzo, Op. 7.
(B) ** Turnabout TV 37045S. Michael Ponti (piano).
18 Pieces, Op. 72.
(B) ** Turnabout TV 37049S. Michael Ponti (piano).
The Seasons, Op. 37a; 6 Pieces, Op. 51.
(B) ** Turnabout TV 37048S. Michael Ponti (piano).

Michael Ponti, a dedicated interpreter of rare romantic piano music, plays crisply and efficiently through the collected piano music of Tchaikovsky, but too often he fails to realize that the simpler inspirations need not just strong fingers but subtler qualities too. In short, he lacks charm. In the bigger pieces like the two sonatas, or even the collection of pieces, *The Seasons*, he is more successful, and it is good that the different discs are available separately. Bright, rather brittle recording.

VOCAL MUSIC AND OPERA

Songs: *Again, as before; As over hot embers; Cradle song; Disappointment; Don Juan's serenade; Do not believe me; Do not leave me; Great deeds; In the clamour of the ballroom; Is it not so?; Mignon's song; My genius, my angel, my friend; My little minx; No answer, no word, no greeting; O stay!; Reconcilement; They kept on saying 'You fool'; Through the window; To forget so soon.*
** (*) Argo ZRG 707. Robert Tear (tenor), Philip Ledger (piano).

Though Robert Tear's voice is not ideally sweet for these generally lyrical offerings, he sings sensitively and intelligently, helped by the crisp and perceptive accompaniment of Philip Ledger. Good atmospheric recording.

Songs: *Mid the noisy stir of the ball; Night; O child, beneath thy window; Over the golden cornfields; Why?* (2 versions).

** Decca SXL 6428. Galina Vishnevskaya (soprano), Mstislav Rostropovich (piano) – BRITTEN: *The Poet's Echo.***

Vishnevskaya sounds rather happier in these Tchaikovsky songs than in the Britten cycle on the reverse, but it is still a massive instrument for chamber music, not controlled quite precisely enough. One could think of more apt couplings for the Britten (some Shostakovich, for example), but it is good to hear songs that are inexplicably neglected. Excellent recording.

Eugene Onegin (opera in 3 acts): complete recording.

*** Decca SET 596/8. Teresa Kubiak (soprano), Bernd Weikl (baritone), Stuart Burrows (tenor), Anna Reynolds (mezzo-soprano), Nicolai Ghiaurov (bass), Julia Hamari (mezzo-soprano), Michel Sénéchal (tenor), John Alldis Choir, Orchestra of Royal Opera House, Covent Garden, Sir Georg Solti.

** HMV SLS 951 (3 discs). Galina Vishnevskaya (soprano), Yuri Mazurov (baritone), Vladimir Atlantov (tenor), Tamara Sinyavskaya (mezzo-soprano), Bolshoi Opera Chorus and Orchestra, Mstislav Rostropovich.

(M) * (*) Decca Ace of Diamonds GOS 551/3. Valeria Heybalova (soprano), Dushal Popovich (baritone), Drago Startz (tenor), Miro Changalovich (bass), Belgrade National Opera, Oscar Danon.

In terms of recorded sound, the Decca/Solti version has tremendous transparency and detail. In addition to the superb sound, the orchestral playing is a delight. This set satisfies an important need. Solti, characteristically crisp in attack, has warmed to the score, allowing his singers full rein in rallentando and rubato to a degree one might not have expected of him. The Tatiana of Teresa Kubiak is most moving – rather mature-sounding for the *ingénue* of Act 1, but with her golden, vibrant voice rising to the final confrontation of Act 3 most impressively. The Onegin of Bernd Weikl may have too little variety of tone, but again this is firm singing that yet has authentic slavonic tinges. Onegin becomes something like a first-person story-teller. The rest of the cast is excellent, with Stuart Burrows as Lensky giving one of his finest performances on record yet. Here for the first time the full range of musical expression in this most atmospheric of operas is superbly caught, with the Decca recording capturing every subtlety of sound – including the wonderful offstage effects – with richness as well as brilliance.

EMI cunningly arranged to record this opera while the Bolshoi Company was in Paris. There was an obvious advantage in having the same cast as in live performances, and these discs certainly serve as a fine memento of the company's historic visit to the West, but Rostropovich's contribution is so wilful that many will resist. In his cello-playing the natural romanticism of his style brings few drawbacks, but here his preference for slow tempi and a rallentando style is questionable. True, the Russian performers have this music in their blood, and this is certainly preferable to a 'safe' performance, but without the thrill of a live occasion the romantic style quickly sounds mannered.

Galina Vishnevskaya, Rostropovich's wife, may be the most celebrated Tatiana of the day, but her tones, with their characteristic slavonic vibrato, are no longer girlish enough to give great pleasure on record. Good recording.

The quality of sound in Decca's Yugoslav opera recordings of the mid-fifties is amazing. The big reservation must be that this performance lacks the finesse which so beguilingly sophisticated an opera really needs. As in a less-than-perfect performance heard in the opera-house, one quickly adjusts to the roughness of ensemble in chorus and orchestra, for example – the subtle atmospheric effects are often made coarse – but the magic of the music still, comes over through the straight honesty of the approach. None of the singing is outstanding.

Eugene Onegin: highlights.
** HMV ASD 2771 (from above recording cond. Rostropovich).

Rostropovich's interpretation of the complete opera is idiosyncratic, but the selection is sensible, and the recording has the same qualities as the Paris-made complete set.

The Maid of Orleans (opera in 4 acts): complete recording.
(M) *** HMV SLS 852 (4 discs). Irina Arkhipova (mezzo-soprano), Klavdiya Radchenko (soprano), Vladimir Vlaitis (baritone), soloists, Chorus and Orchestra of Moscow Radio, Gennady Rozhdestvensky.

This long opera on the theme of Joan of Arc may lack the sheer melodic memorability of Tchaikovsky's immediately preceding opera, *Eugene Onegin*, and in typical Russian manner the story is told episodically; but even so the writing is more than rich enough to provide a fine dramatic sequence that in a performance as idiomatic as this makes for attractive and even powerful listening. Arkhipova as Saint Joan is particularly impressive, and the recording is richer and more vivid than many from this source. Rozhdestvensky proves a strong and incisive guide.

Queen of Spades (opera in 3 acts): complete recording.
(M) ** Decca GOS 568/70. Alexander Marinkovich (tenor), Valeria Heybalova (soprano), Melanie Bugarinovich (mezzo-soprano), Yugoslav Army Chorus, Radio Belgrade Children's Chorus, Belgrade National Opera Orchestra, Kreshimir Baranovich.

Many of the same remarks apply to this performance of *Queen of Spades* as are made on the Belgrade *Onegin.* It is extremely well recorded for its period, but the performance lacks the sort of polish one expects in recorded opera. Even so, in the absence of any rival version it is a set to cherish, a fine, vividly atmospheric work with a performance from Melanie Bugarinovich as the old Countess which with its slavonic timbre has the right sense of command.

COLLECTIONS

'*Biggest hits*': (i) *Capriccio italien, Op. 45;* (ii) *1812 overture, Op. 49;* (iii; iv) *Marche slave, Op. 31;* (iii; v) *Sleeping Beauty, Op. 66: Waltz; Swan Lake, Op. 20: Waltz.*
(B) ** RCA Victrola VICS 1676. (i) RCA Symphony Orchestra, Kyril Kondrashin; (ii) Orchestra and Band, Morton Gould; (iii) Chicago Symphony Orchestra, (iv) Fritz Reiner; (v) Morton Gould.

Kondrashin's account of *Capriccio italien*, currently available only in this anthology, is one of the finest, spectacularly recorded (the acoustic perhaps a trifle too full at the opening fanfare) and played with great flair and excitement. Gould's *1812* was also admired on its original issue, but the recording seems rather unrefined here, particularly in the peroration. However, with Fritz Reiner's vivid *Marche slave* also included besides two favourite waltzes, this is a generous and serviceable disc for the smaller collection.

'Favourites': (i; ii) *Capriccio italien, Op. 45;* (i; iii) *1812 overture, Op. 49;* (iv) *Marche slave, Op. 31;* (v; vi) *Nutcracker suite, Op. 71a; Sleeping Beauty, Op. 66: Waltz; Rose adagio; Panorama; Serenade for strings, Op. 48: Waltz;* (vii) *Sérénade mélancolique, Op. 26;* (v; viii) *Swan Lake, Op. 20: Waltz; Dance of Cygnets; Dance of Swans;* (v; ix) *Mazeppa: Gopak.*

(B) ** Philips Fontana 6747 056 (2 discs). (i) Concertgebouw Orchestra; (ii) Bernard Haitink; (iii) Igor Markevitch; (iv) Vienna Symphony Orchestra, Karel Ančerl; (v) London Symphony Orchestra; (vi) Anatole Fistoulari; (vii) Arthur Grumiaux (violin), New Philharmonia Orchestra, Edo de Waart; (viii) Pierre Monteux; (ix) Charles Mackerras.

This two-disc set is an extension of the fairly successful Philips *World of Tchaikovsky* LP discussed below. The additions are Fistoulari's *Nutcracker suite*, winningly (if not brilliantly) played but suffering from a recording that lacks something in sparkle, the *Swan Lake* and *Sleeping Beauty* excerpts, which are of good quality, and Grumiaux's characteristically fresh account of the *Sérénade mélancolique*. The attractive *Gopak* from

Mazeppa (common to both issues), which brings back nostalgic memories of 78 days, is splendidly done.

'Greatest hits, Vol. 1': (i) *1812 overture, Op. 49; Nutcracker, Op. 71: Trepak; Waltz of the Flowers;* (ii) *Serenade for strings, Op. 48: Waltz; Symphony No. 5 in E minor, Op. 64: Andante cantabile.*

(B) * (*) CBS Harmony 30003. (i) New York Philharmonic Orchestra, Leonard Bernstein; (ii) Philadelphia Orchestra, Eugene Ormandy.

Perhaps surprisingly, this is one of the least successful of the *Greatest hits* series. The performances are brilliant enough, but the dance movements lack charm, and the recording needs more glow and richness instead of the glassy brightness offered here. *1812* goes well, and the end is effective, with particularly clear cannon, on the beat with a rhythmic precision that is possible electronically but impossible in real life. But again the overall sound sacrifices depth to surface brilliance.

'Greatest hits, Vol. 2': (i) *Andante cantabile (from String quartet No. 1);* (ii) *Capriccio italien, Op. 45;* (i) *Eugene Onegin: Waltz; The Months: June* (Barcarolle)*; None but the lonely heart; Sleeping Beauty, Op. 66: Waltz; Swan Lake, Op. 20: Waltz.*

(B) ** CBS Harmony 30027. (i) Philadelphia Orchestra, Eugene Ormandy; (ii) New York Philharmonic Orchestra, Leonard Bernstein.

This is an agreeable collection of lightweight Tchaikovsky. Bernstein's *Capriccio italien* is exciting and brilliantly played, the recording not as rich as some but certainly vivid. The shorter pieces, all played with considerable panache, have been arranged with the *Capriccio* to make a well balanced programme of its kind. *None but the lonely heart* in its orchestral dress sounds effective with string-playing as good as this.

'*Greatest hits, Vol. 3*': (i; ii) *Piano concerto No. 1 in B flat minor, Op. 23;* (ii) *Marche slave, Op. 31;* (iii) *Nutcracker, Op. 71: Dance of the Sugar Plum Fairy; Final waltz and apotheosis; Eugene Onegin: Polonaise;* (i) (Piano) *Song without words, Op. 2/3.*

  (B) ** (*) CBS Harmony 30041. (i) Philippe Entremont (piano); (ii) New York Philharmonic Orchestra, Leonard Bernstein; (iii) Philadelphia Orchestra, Eugene Ormandy.

The performance of the *First Piano concerto* is one of the most satisfying available. It is a broad, romantic account, slightly old-fashioned, but after listening to the splendid opening pages one realizes what Gilels loses on his HMV version by taking this section too fast. Curiously this CBS record reminds one very much of the kind of performance we had, of necessity, in the 78 days, when the first movement was broken into four sections. Bernstein and Entremont seem almost to do the same, but the reading has a compensating spaciousness. The slow movement is sensitive and the finale brilliant, with a nice rhythmic buoyancy, yet never sounding uncontrolled. The work fits on one side, yet the sound is remarkably good, with bold piano tone and plenty of orchestral body. The sound on side two, which opens with the *Polonaise* from *Eugene Onegin*, is altogether brasher, if not beyond control. But Bernstein's *Marche slave* is splendidly exciting, especially at the end, and this coupled to the *Piano concerto* makes the disc well worth while.

'*The world of Tchaikovsky*': (i; ii) *Capriccio italien, Op. 45;* (i; iii) *1812 overture, Op. 49;* (iv) *Marche slave, Op.*

31; (v; vi) *Mazeppa: Gopak;* (v; vii) *Nutcracker, Op. 71: Waltz of the Flowers.*

  (B) ** Philips 6833 032. (i) Concertgebouw Orchestra; (ii) Bernard Haitink; (iii) Igor Markevitch; (iv) Vienna Symphony Orchestra, Karel Ančerl; (v) London Symphony Orchestra; (vi) Charles Mackerras; (vii) Anatole Fistoulari.

The attraction of this record is that it takes its title seriously and provides a fascinating brochure-sleeve, illustrated with many photographs, fitting the music and events of Tchaikovsky's life into the context of what else was happening in the world during this period. The performances are without the distinction that attended a similar Philips record of Bach's music, but they are all well-made, and at least the recorded sound is natural and does not seek artificial brilliance. Perhaps one needs a more spectacular *1812* than this, but the recording has body and atmosphere. Elsewhere the sound is obviously not modern, but taken as a whole this collection is enjoyably musical.

'*The world of Tchaikovsky*': (i) *Piano concerto No. 1 in B flat minor, Op. 23:* 2nd movement; (ii) *1812 overture, Op. 49:* Finale; (iii) *Romeo and Juliet* (fantasy overture); (iv) *Swan Lake, Op. 20:* Act 3: *Pas de deux;* (v) *Symphony No. 6 in B minor, Op. 74:* 4th movement; (vi) *Eugene Onegin: Tatiana's letter scene.*

  (B) * (*) Decca SPA 142. Various orchestras, (i) cond. Henry Lewis, Ivan Davis (piano); (ii) Kenneth Alwyn; (iii) Leopold Stokowski; (iv) Ernest Ansermet; (v) Henry Lewis; (vi) Valeria Heybalova (soprano).

This is designed to attract the filmgoer who has seen *The Music Lovers*. The selection is arbitrary, and the only complete work is *Romeo and Juliet*, curiously given in Stokowski's truncated version with the ending cut off so that the piece closes quietly. The excerpt from *Tatiana's letter scene* is not ideally secure vocally. The disc is highly modulated and the closing pages of *1812*, at the end of side one, will surely defeat most commercial pick-ups to reproduce it without distortion at this level.

Tcherepnin, Alexander
(born 1899)

(i; ii) *Duo for violin and cello, Op. 49;* (iii; iv) *Piano quintet, Op. 44;* (i; ii; iii) *Piano trio, Op. 34;* (iv) *String quartet No. 2, Op. 40;* (ii) *Suite for solo cello, Op. 76.*

> *** HMV CSD 3725. (i) Yan Pascal (violin); (ii) Paul Tortelier (cello); (iii) the composer (piano); (iv) Groupe Instrumental de Paris.

This disc provides a fascinating cross-section of the chamber music of Alexander Tcherepnin, representative of the middle generation of a family of composers. His whole creative career has developed since he left Russia after the Revolution, and his visits to the Far East have added to his distinctive concept of tonality, but at heart he remains a true Russian. These works are all crisp and incisive, each one making its points neatly and attractively in writing that is consistently stylish. The advocacy of Paul Tortelier as well as the composer himself is powerful and passionate. Good recording.

Telemann, Georg Philipp
(1681–1767)

Concerto in E major for flute, oboe d'amore, violin and strings; Concerto in G major for two violas and strings; (i) *Suite in A minor for flute and strings.*

> (M) * (*) Vanguard HM 17SD. I Solisti di Zagreb, Antonio Janigro, (i) with Julius Baker (flute).

This is a fair disc but not really a distinguished one. The recording, once the treble is cut back a little, can be made to sound well and the solo playing is good. But Janigro's direction lacks something in poise and style. His rhythms in the *Overture* of the splendid *Suite in A minor* lack crispness, and elsewhere one feels a similar lack of rhythmic firmness and bite.

(i) *Concerto in G major for oboe d'amore and strings;* (ii) *Viola concerto in G major.*

> (B) * (*) Pye GSGC 14149. (i) Kurt Hausmann (oboe d'amore); (ii) Karl Bender (viola), both with Wurzburg Camerata Accademica, Hans Reinartz.

Both soloists provide expressive performances of high quality, and the recording is warm and pleasing. The balance, however, projects each of the solo instruments so far forward that the dynamics between soloists and orchestra are levelled out. This especially applies to the *Viola concerto*, where the viola is cello-sized. Even so this inexpensive disc is most enjoyable.

Double concerto in F major for 2 horns; Concerto in B flat major for 3 oboes and 3 violins; Double concerto in F major for recorder, bassoon and strings; Concerto in G major for 4 violins.

*** Telefunken SAWT 9483. Vienna Concentus Musicus, Nikolaus Harnoncourt.

One of the best Telemann discs currently available. The *Concerto for two horns* shows the composer at his most characteristic (natural horns are used), and the performances are most persuasive. The oboes also sound splendidly in tune, which is not always the case with the baroque instrument, and phrasing is alive and sensitive. Indeed these performances are extremely fine, and only the *Concerto for recorder and bassoon* lets the disc down a little; it is also not as well played as the others. The quality is good and the disc deserves a strong recommendation.

(i) *Concerto in B flat major for three oboes, three violins and continuo;* (ii) *Triple violin concerto in F major;* (iii) *Oboe concerto in C minor;* (iv) *Trumpet concerto in D major.*

(M) *** DGG Privilege 135080. (i) Emil Seiler Chamber Group; (ii) Schola Cantorum Basiliensis, August Wenzinger; (iii) Lothar Koch (oboe), Hamburg Telemann Society, Wilfried Boettcher; (iv) Adolf Scherbaum (trumpet), Hamburg Bach Orchestra, Stehli.

An excellent anthology, stylishly played and offering a nice variety of colour in the solo instruments used. The recording is excellent and this is one of those collections that offers more than the sum of its individual components. Most enjoyable.

Viola concerto in G major; Suite 'La Lyra' in E flat major; Suite in F major for violin and orchestra.

*** Telefunken SAWT 9541. Jaap Schröder (violin), Paul Doktor (viola), Concerto Amsterdam, Franz Brüggen.

A most distinguished and enjoyable collection. The performance of the *Viola concerto* has splendid life and impulse and confirms the work as a masterpiece, its distinct flavour of J. S. Bach not obscuring the composer's own personality. The *Lyra suite* too is highly inventive and colourful, with a marvellously apt imitation of a hurdy-gurdy. The *Suite in F major* features the solo violin as a concertante instrument rather than a dominating soloist. The scoring with its use of woodwind and horns is felicitous. Brüggen directs throughout with plenty of spirit, though he is inclined to overdo the accents in the *Minuet* which closes the *F major Suite*. The recording is excellent.

(i–iii) *Double concerto in G major for 2 violas and strings;* (i; iii) *Viola concerto in G major; Suite in D major for viola da gamba and string orchestra;* (iv) *Triple violin concerto in F major.*

(B) * (*) Turnabout TV 34288S. (i) Ernst Wallfisch (viola or viola da gamba); (ii) Ulrich Koch (viola); (iii) Württemberg Chamber Orchestra, Joerg Faerber; (iv) Georg Egger, Susanne Lautenbacher, Adelhaid Schaeffer (violins), Stuttgart Soloists.

The *Viola concerto in G major* is well-known as one of Telemann's most striking works, and the *Concerto in F major for three violins* has a similar attractive affinity with Bach. The expressive slow movement is notable. The playing here is alive and musicianly, the slight snag being the recording, which has a rather fizzy upper register.

The Constant Music-master: excerpts: *Scenes from Old Hamburg (Love in the Goose Market; Promenade in the Virgins' Walk; Two pastors inspect and leave the tavern; Rendezvous on the*

Alster; The sailor and the shy maiden;
The Johannisfest).

⊕ (M) *** DGG Privilege 2538 263.
Soloists, Instrumental Ensemble
of Archive Production, Josef Ul-
samer.

This is a delightful record. The music
is constantly diverse (no pun intended)
in invention and instrumental colour.
The listener may read the programmatic
titles into the pieces or not, according to
taste, but the music stands up admirably
without them. Each of the ingenuous
titles provides a suite of miniature pieces
(sometimes as many as six or seven) of
great felicity and charm. The playing is
first-rate, always showing both warmth
and a pleasing lightness of touch, and the
recording is immaculate. Highly recommended.

Suite in A minor; Suite in F minor.
** (*) Telefunken SAWT 9507. Franz
Brüggen (recorder), Vienna Concentus Musicus, Nikolaus Harnoncourt.

Of these two suites the recorder features prominently only in the A minor,
which is Telemann's equivalent to Bach's
Orchestral suite No. 2 in B minor. It
is a fine work, varied in invention and
offering the flautist plenty of latitude to
show his ability in the matter of decoration and phrasing. Franz Brüggen is
noted for his sense of style in music of
this period, and he turns here many an
elegant phrase, but the overall direction
is just a little on the stiff side. In the F
minor suite too Nikolaus Harnoncourt
favours very brisk allegros, which are
brilliantly managed by his small group,
projected as they are by a typically forward, crisp Telefunken recording, but
one wonders if the composer would have
expected such tempi. Even so the playing
is exhilarating and enjoyable in its own
right.

Suite in F major for 4 horns, 2 oboes
and string orchestra.

(B) *** Turnabout TV 34078S. Mainz
Chamber Orchestra, Günter Kehr
– ROSETTI and VIVALDI: Con-
certos.**

The Suite in F is one of Telemann's
most striking and original works. Interestingly enough it uses the key that was not
to settle down as the natural 'home' key
of the french horn until the end of the
nineteenth century (D or E flat being
favoured before then). It is a good key for
the instrument, bright as well as flexible,
and Telemann's writing, although it
demands virtuosity, is very sympathetic
as well as imaginative. The work's programme conjures up Greek mythology,
but transferred to the Alster riverside in
Hamburg, Telemann's home town. There
are echoes, of course, and shepherds and
nymphs, but the most striking and original
item is a concert by frogs and crows. The
music is not strictly speaking imitative,
but the writing for the horns is surprisingly modern. The recording is
atmospheric; there is a suggestion of
overloading from the horns but nothing
serious, and generally this is most
unusual and enjoyable.

Tafelmusik: Production 2 (complete
recording).

(M) ** (*) Telefunken TK 11548(1/2).
Concerto Amsterdam, Franz
Brüggen; Gustav Leonhardt
(harpsichord).

Part 2 contains some of the best music
from the Tafelmusik, and now that the
Wenzinger version is deleted, this remains
the only account. The set contains a concerto for three violins framed by a suite,
a lively finale for oboe, trumpet and
strings, and two chamber works. Good
performances and recording make this a
worthwhile acquisition.

CHAMBER MUSIC

Der getreue Musikmeister: Trio sonatas in F major; F minor; B flat major; C major. Essercizii Musici: Trio sonatas in C major; D minor.
   *** Telefunken SAWT 9435. Franz Brüggen (recorder), Anner Bylsma (violoncello), Gustav Leonhardt (harpsichord).

This anthology is most welcome. Brüggen plays with his usual mastery and as one would expect from Gustav Leonhardt's ensemble the performances have polish and authority, and they are excellently recorded.

Paris Quartets Nos. 1 in D minor; 2 in A minor; 3 in G major; 4 in B minor; 5 in A major; 6 in E minor.
   ⊛ (M) *** Telefunken TK 11565 (1/2). Amsterdam Quartet.

This really is altogether delightful. These are most inventive works and the level of inspiration is extraordinarily even. The performances are of such an order of virtuosity that they silence criticism, and Franz Brüggen in particular dazzles the listener. The recording is in the very first class, beautifully balanced and tremendously alive (like the performances themselves). A wonderful set that will convert the most doubtful to Telemann's cause.

VOCAL MUSIC AND OPERA

Cantata oder Trauer-Music eines kunsterfahrenen Canarien-Vogels (Funeral music for a sweet-singing canary); Der Schulmeister (The Schoolmaster; cantata); Die Landlust (The Joys of Country Life; cantata).
   *** Philips 6500 116. Hermann Prey (baritone), Salzburg Boys' Choir,

German Bach Soloists, Helmut Winschermann.

An attractive record that will appeal to collectors with a taste for baroque music. Fischer-Dieskau recorded the *Canary cantata*, but his version is long since deleted. There is no autograph of the *Schoolmaster* and Winschermann has indulged in some arranging, but this is tastefully done, and given the accomplishment of both the performances and the recording engineers this is in general a highly recommendable disc.

Der Tag des Gerichts (The Day of Judgement; oratorio): complete recording.
   ** Telefunken SAWT 9484/5. Gertraud Landwehr-Herrmann (soprano), Cora Canne-Meijer (contralto), Kurt Equiluz (tenor), Max van Egmond (bass), soprano and contralto soloists from Vienna Boys' Choir, Hamburg Monteverdi Choir, Vienna Concentus Musicus, Nikolaus Harnoncourt.

Although there are moments of considerable inspiration here, one feels that Telemann was far too urbane a master to measure himself fully against so cosmic a theme as *The Day of Judgement*. But the work is well worth sampling, particularly as the performers give it so persuasive and musical an advocacy and are, moreover, given the advantage of beautifully balanced recording. Nonetheless this is not a work that would figure high on the list of priorities for most Telemann admirers.

Pimpinone (opera in 1 act, 3 intermezzi): complete recording.
   (B) ** Turnabout TV 34124S. Yvonne Ciannella (soprano), Erich Wenk (bass), Stuttgart Bach Collegium, Helmuth Rilling.

This charming chamber opera anticipates *La Serva padrona* and offers music of great tunefulness and vivacity. The opera has only two characters, no chorus whatever, and a small orchestra. Yet its music is as witty as its libretto, and from the very opening one can sense that Telemann is enjoying every moment of this absurd comedy about a serving maid (Vespetta) who battens on a wealthy but stupid gentleman (Pimpinone), eventually persuading him not only to marry her, but to give her the freedom of his purse and at the same time to do her bidding. Yvonne Ciannella and Erich Wenk carry off the honours with spirited and flexible voices, well supported by the Stuttgart Bach Collegium under Rilling, and the performance has plenty of life.

Theodorakis, Mikis
(born 1925)

7 Songs of Lorca (arr. for voice and guitar by Stephen Dodgson); *I Pandermi; 3 Songs: To Yelasto Pedi (Theme from Z); Silva; Irtham I Anthropoi* (arr. Dodgson). *4 Epitafios for solo guitar* (arr. Myers).

> *** CBS SBRG 72947. Maria Farandouri (folk singer), John Williams (guitar).

Theodorakis's talent is a limited one, and his bigger pieces are brash and often banal. But the music on this disc is unpretentious and often appealing and should find a response among collectors of all heights of brow. It goes without saying that John Williams's playing is as expert as ever, and the record should prove popular among those without prejudices and even among those who have!

Tippett, Michael
(born 1905)

Concerto for double string orchestra.

> (M) *** HMV SXLP 30157. Moscow Chamber and Bath Festival Orchestras, Rudolf Barshai – BRITTEN: *Variations on a theme of Frank Bridge.****

> (B) *** Classics for Pleasure CFP 40068. London Philharmonic Orchestra, Vernon Handley – VAUGHAN WILLIAMS: *Fantasia on a theme of Tallis.****

Tippett's eloquent concerto is well served in each price category: Marriner's version (below) at full price is three-star and this HMV disc is hardly less fine. The recording sounds amazingly vivid and the coupling is attractive. Barshai's account has a slight edge over Vernon Handley's, but the CFP disc is a first-rate bargain, well recorded and coupling two of the warmest and most memorable string works of the present century in strong, committed performances. No one could here miss the passion behind both the sharp rhythmic inspirations of the outer movement and the glorious lyricism of the central slow movement.

Concerto for double string orchestra; Fantasia concertante on a theme of Corelli; Little music for string orchestra.

> *** Argo ZRG 680. Academy of St Martin-in-the-Fields, Neville Marriner.

The *Concerto for double string orchestra*, on any count one of the most beautiful of twentieth-century works for strings, here receives a performance more sumptuous and warm-hearted than any on record. With utter commitment Marriner and his colleagues allow the jazz inflections of the outer movements to have their lightening effect on the rhythm, and in the heavenly slow movement the slowish tempo and hushed manner display the full romanticism of the music without ever slipping over the edge into sentimentality. The *Corelli fantasia*, a similarly sumptuous work but without quite the same lyrical felicity, and the *Little music* provide an ideal coupling. The recording is outstanding.

(i) *Concerto for orchestra;* (ii) *The Midsummer Marriage: Ritual dances* (vocal version).
> (M) *** Philips Universo 6580 093. (i) London Symphony Orchestra; (ii) Joan Carlyle, Elizabeth Bainbridge (sopranos), Alberto Remedios (tenor), Stafford Dean (bass), Chorus and Orchestra of Royal Opera House, Covent Garden; both cond. Colin Davis.

The *Concerto for orchestra* was a by-product of the opera *King Priam*, and even more successfully than the opera it exploits a new thorny style, tough and sinewy, hardly at all lyrical in the manner of Tippett's earlier music. To study such a piece on record is immensely rewarding, and here it is well coupled with some of the most immediately attractive music from Tippett's first opera, one of his most warmly appealing scores. Fine recording and excellent performances; highly recommendable as a mid-price issue.

(i) *Piano concerto. Piano sonata No. 2.*
> *** HMV ASD 621. John Ogdon (piano), (i) with Philharmonia Orchestra, Colin Davis.

The *Concerto* represents Tippett's complex-textured earlier style, but it is a lyrical and often deeply inspired piece. In both works it is a pity that the recording is not clearer, but the *Concerto* performance is a fine one, and although in the

Sonata Ogdon is made to sound less incisive than he should be in such starkly conceived music, this remains a welcome coupling. Particularly after the waywardness of the *Concerto*, the compression of the *Sonata* is emphasized. The argument proceeds by way of kaleidoscopic re-shuffling of tiny motifs rather than by any conventional development, and although a more uninhibited reading would bring out the point of Tippett's scheme better, Ogdon's performance is powerfully wrought and there is no question about its bravura.

(i) *Fantasia on a theme of Handel;* (i; ii) *The Vision of St Augustine.*
> *** RCA SER 5620. (i) Margaret Kitchin (piano); (ii) John Shirley-Quirk (baritone), LSO Chorus; both with London Symphony Orchestra, the composer.

The Vision of St Augustine is a masterpiece of Tippett's later, thorniest period to set beside the *Midsummer Marriage*, culmination of his euphonious years. It is nothing short of an attempt to convey the impossible – a momentary glimpse of heaven itself, taking the narrative of St Augustine. Where most composers would kneel humbly and purify their style in the face of heaven, Tippett carries in his thorny, complex textures the fanaticism of a mystic. The result is not easy music, but in this magnificent performance and recording, burning with intensity from beginning to end, few will miss the excitement of the work even at a first hearing, and this is amply confirmed by repetition. The *Fantasia* is essentially a much easier piece to come to grips with, similarly complex, but less jagged. It makes a generous coupling for an imaginatively conceived project. Again the performance and recording quality are first-class.

(i) *Symphony No. 2;* (ii) *Sonata for 4 horns;* (iii) *The Weeping Babe.*

*** Argo ZRG 535. (i) London Symphony Orchestra, Colin Davis; (ii) Barry Tuckwell Horn Quartet; (iii) John Alldis Choir.

The *Second Symphony* is a superb work: it bears constant repetition and like Tippett's *Piano concerto* offers a wealth of interesting ideas to the listener. The composer began work on it in the mid-1950s and completed it in response to a commission from the BBC to mark the tenth anniversary of the Third Programme. When first one encounters it, the proliferation of ideas seems almost to undermine the sense of forward direction, and the detail attracts attention to itself before dissolving into another idea of almost equal interest. But closer acquaintance shows this to be misleading: the parts fit into an integrated and logical whole. The slow movement in particular has an atmosphere of striking imaginative quality: it explores the 'magical side' of Tippett's personality and deserves a place among his finest inspirations. The first movement opens with pounding C's, suggested to the composer when listening to some Vivaldi, and the music that flows from this has enormous vitality and complexity. The LSO under Colin Davis rise to the occasion and give a performance of great confidence and brilliance, and the sound-quality is quite superlative. Like the *Concerto for double string orchestra* and the *Piano concerto*, this is a must for all who care deeply about English music in general and Tippett in particular. *The Weeping Babe*, a setting of Edith Sitwell, is a wartime piece, of lyrical simplicity, and is excellently sung by the Alldis Choir. The *Sonata for four horns* is a brilliant virtuoso piece, whose hurdles the Barry Tuckwell Horn Quartet take in their stride. They complete an altogether outstanding disc.

Symphony No. 3.
   *** Philips 6500 662. Heather Harper (soprano), London Symphony Orchestra, Colin Davis.

Tippett himself describes this ambitious work as a hybrid symphony, and consciously follows the example of Beethoven's *Ninth Symphony* in the transition to the final vocal sections, in which the soprano sings three blues numbers and a dramatic scena to words by the composer. The first half consists of a powerful first section in Tippett's brand of sonata form and a deeply intense second section which exploits total stillness in a fascinating variety of textures. Before the blues conclusion the second half is introduced by a busy scherzo. The pity is that the first half is far more cogent than the second, and the two halves do not really match up with each other. In this fine performance Colin Davis is as persuasive as any conductor could be, while Heather Harper almost manages to mute the crudities of Tippett's text. It is good to find a composer in his late sixties writing at full stretch with no compromise. Excellent recording.

String quartets Nos. 1 and 3.
   (B) ** Pye GSGC 14079. Fidelio Quartet.

It is good to have a coupling of these quartets, both of them fine examples of Tippett's most thoughtful style. The *First* was originally written in 1935 – it is the first work Tippett continues to acknowledge – but was drastically revised in 1943, when he replaced the first two movements with the clear and direct piece which now stands first. The *Third Quartet* followed quickly in 1946, and showed the new trend in Tippett's writing towards contrapuntal complexity. Its idiom may not initially sound very startling, but in fact it is a difficult piece to come fully to terms with, and a record is invaluable for one's understanding of these five closely wrought movements. It would have been even more valuable had the performance by the Fidelio Quartet been a degree more polished. The intonation is by no means flawless, and the recording tends to add to the acidity. But at bargain price this unique coupling obviously merits a recommendation.

String quartet No. 2 in F sharp major.
> (B) ** Pye GSGC 14130. Fidelio Quartet – DELIUS: *Quartet.***

Tippett's *Second Quartet* has not fared too well on record since the advent of stereo. This performance, although serviceable, is somewhat lacking in intensity and tautness. However, with its useful coupling, it makes a welcome stopgap until something more eloquent comes along.

Piano sonatas Nos. 1 (Fantasy), 2, and 3.
> *** Philips 6500 534. Paul Crossley (piano).

These sonatas range over three decades and afford an interesting glimpse into Tippett's musical development. The *Fantasy sonata* is a pre-war work, dating from 1938; the *Second*, a parergon to the opera *King Priam*, appeared in 1962, and the *Third*, which shows how potent Beethoven's influence still is, comes from 1973. The *Second* is the most haunting, but all are deeply impressive. Crossley is the dedicatee of No. 3, and his playing could hardly be more persuasive or committed. The quality of the recording is stunningly real and totally natural. It is one of the finest of its kind yet to appear.

Piano sonata No. 2.
> (B) * (*) Pye GSGC 14085. Peter Cooper (piano) – BAX: *Sonata No. 2*; MOZART: *Variations.* (*)

Not a performance that rivals Ogdon's or Crossley's in sheer panache or briliance, but those who are attracted to the coupling or to the price need not worry

unduly; Peter Cooper's playing is highly competent and the recording is acceptable.

A Child of our Time (oratorio); *The Midsummer Marriage: Ritual dances.*
> ** Argo ZDA 19/20. Elsie Morison (soprano), Pamela Bowden (contralto), Richard Lewis (tenor), Richard Standen (bass), Royal Liverpool Philharmonic Choir and Orchestra, John Pritchard.

This recording of Tippett's oratorio was first available in mono only on the Pye label, but in taking over responsibility for its issue Argo provided a stereo alternative. The recording quality is not of the most modern, but it is still perfectly acceptable and the lower price may compensate a little for any deficiency. The work itself wears well. Tippett was inspired by a story of Nazi persecution, and his somewhat illogical use of Negro spirituals where in Bach Passion music you would get chorales is most moving, with the setting of *Deep river* providing an overwhelming emotional climax. Not everything is as easily understood as that, and Pritchard's performance is not as full-blooded as it might be, but these records are invaluable in letting us hear repeatedly one of the great masterpieces of the modern English choral tradition. The fill-up provides a sampler of Tippett's first opera – not the most characteristic passage, but one that represents Tippett's earlier style at its most developed.

Songs for Dov.
> *** Argo ZRG 703. Robert Tear (tenor), London Sinfonietta, David Atherton – MESSIAEN: *Poèmes pour Mi.***

These strange songs, with their words by Tippett himself full of dated expressions like 'Oh boy!' and 'Sure, baby!', are an offshoot of the opera *The Knot Garden*, with its composer character

Dov. Though the poems are often embarrassing, the music is characteristically imaginative, with sparks flying in all directions. Well worth having on record with fine singing from the original interpreter and meticulous accompaniment. Fine recording.

The Knot Garden (opera in 3 acts): complete recording.

> *** Philips 6700 063 (2 discs). Raimund Herincx (baritone), Yvonne Minton (mezzo-soprano), Jill Gomez, Josephine Barstow (sopranos), Thomas Carey (baritone), Robert Tear (tenor), Thomas Hemsley (baritone), Royal Opera House, Covent Garden, Orchestra, Colin Davis.

As Tippett has grown older, so his music has grown wilder. Those who enjoy the ripe qualities of *The Midsummer Marriage* may be disconcerted by the relative astringency of this later opera, a garden conversation piece to a libretto by the composer very much in the style of a T. S. Eliot play. The result characteristically is a mixture, with the mandarin occasionally putting on a funny hat, as in the jazz and blues passages for the male lovers Dov and Mel. The brief central act, called *Labyrinth*, has characters thrown together two at a time in a revolving maze, a stylized effect which contributes effectively to Tippett's process of psychiatric nerve-prodding. The style of the music is tough and astringent, quite unlike *The Midsummer Marriage*. Colin Davis draws a superb performance from his Covent Garden cast, and the recording, a little dry, is vivid.

The Midsummer Marriage (opera in 3 acts): complete recording.

> ✹ *** Philips 6703 027 (3 discs). Alberto Remedios, Stuart Burrows (tenors), Joan Carlyle, Elizabeth Harwood (sopranos), Raimund Herincx (baritone), Helen Watts (contralto), Chorus and Orchestra of Royal Opera House, Covent Garden, Colin Davis.

By almost every known rule of opera Tippett's great visionary work, created over a long period of self-searching, should not be an artistic success. That it does succeed triumphantly – if anything with even greater intensity on record than in the opera-house – is a tribute above all to the exuberance of Tippett's inspiration, his determination to translate the glowing beauty of his vision into musical and dramatic terms. Any one moment from this 154-minute score should be enough to demonstrate the unquenchable urgency of his writing, his love of rich sounds. There are few operas of any period which use the chorus to such glorious effect, often in haunting off-stage passages, and with Colin Davis a burningly committed advocate and a cast that was inspired by live performances in the opera-house, this is a set hard to resist even for those not normally fond of modern opera. The so-called 'difficulties' of the libretto, with its mystic philosophical references, fade when the sounds are so honeyed in texture and so consistently lyrical, while the story – for all its complications – preserves a clear sense of emotional involvement throughout. The singing is consistently fine, the playing magnificent, the recording outstandingly atmospheric.

Tomkins, Thomas
(1572–1656)

Consort music: *Fantasia à 3; Pavan in A minor. Organ voluntaries in A major ; D major.* Vocal music: *Above the stars; The Heavens declare* (anthem)*; How great delight; Jubilate* (Fifth Service)*; Music divine; O let me live for true* love; O let me die for true love; Sure there is no God of love; When I observe.

(B) * (*) Oryx EXP 63. Ambrosian Singers, In Nomine Players, Denis Stevens; Martindale Sidwell (organ).

The instrumental performances here are played expressively and recorded well, but the vocal items are let down by rough recording, and the internal balance is not good. This is a pity, for the performances themselves are good.

Organ Fancy (for two to play); Organ voluntary. Vocal music: Above the stars; Hear my prayer; Holy, holy, holy; My shepherd is the living Lord (anthems); Psalm XV; Responses; Te Deum and Benedictus (First Service); Turn unto the Lord; When David heard.

(B) ** Argo Eclipse ECS 682. Magdalen College, Oxford, Chapel Choir, Bernard Rose; Christopher Gower (organ).

Although this is not one of Argo's most distinguished issues it remains a serviceable collection of the music of one of the great Elizabethan composers for the new Anglican liturgy. The performances are eloquent and devoted in style, but it is a pity that the recording, although otherwise good, does not take advantage of the antiphonal possibilities inherent in the Psalm and Te Deum.

Turina, Joaquín
(1882–1949)

Danzas fantásticas, Op. 22.

(M) ** (*) HMV SXLP 30152. Paris Conservatoire Orchestra, Rafael Frühbeck de Burgos – FALLA:

Nights in the Gardens of Spain; Dances.***

(M) ** (*) Decca Ace of Diamonds SDD 180. Suisse Romande Orchestra, Ernest Ansermet – ALBÉNIZ: Iberia.** (*)

The performances under Frühbeck de Burgos have a Mediterranean sensuousness that only a Spanish conductor could evoke. The recording has a fine atmosphere but shows its age in a certain lack of body to the string tone. But this is not too serious, and the woodwind is nicely balanced within an acoustic suitable to the music's more spectacular and gaudy moments. The playing has plenty of impulse and a proper degree of subtlety too.

Ansermet's approach is more refined, less sensuous, but he draws constantly vivid sounds from his orchestra and there is no want of atmosphere. The Decca recording still sounds brilliant and sophisticated in matters of detail.

La oración del torero, Op. 34.

(M) ** Unicorn UNS 241. Gabrieli Quartet – ALWYN: String quartet; String trio.**

This short piece makes an attractive filler for the Alwyn works, and it is both persuasively played and effectively recorded.

Tye, Christopher
(born c. 1500)

Euge Bone Mass; Western Wind Mass.

*** Argo ZRG 740. King's College, Cambridge, Choir, David Willcocks.

Tye was born five years before Tallis, and his style is a good deal less personal than Fayrfax, Tallis or Taverner. Both these works are beautifully sung and recorded, and collectors with special interests in this period should not fail to investigate what is by any standards an invaluable disc.

Varèse, Edgar
(1885–1965)

Arcana; Intégrales; Ionisation.
   *** Decca SXL 6550. Los Angeles Philharmonic Orchestra, Los Angeles Percussion Ensemble, Zubin Mehta.

Sumptuous presentation of three of Varèse's most characteristic works, an ideal disc for converting the unconvinced. Each work exploits unusual timbres and textures with a directness and freedom that suggest the work of the post-war avant-garde; yet the latest of these works, *Ionisation* for thirteen percussionists, dates from as long ago as 1931. The performances here have the easy expressiveness that comes from close and warm acquaintance by the players. The recording is brilliant to match.

Density for flute; Hyperprism; Intégrales; Ionisation; Octandre; Offrandes.
   (M) ** Vox STGBY 643. Die Reihe Ensemble, Friedrich Cerha.

That Varèse was an inspired revolutionary, thinking and writing well ahead of his time, has become clearer over the last few years, when many of his wild ideas have found favour with today's avant-garde. Percy Scholes chose him to represent the last word in zany modernity in his Columbia History of Music in the thirties, but mockery backfired. The value of *Octandre* (one movement then recorded) became evident by gramophone repetition, and here we have a valuable collection of vivid works of the twenties

and early thirties. *Ionisation* in particular stands as a historic pointer towards developments in percussion writing. When little of Varèse is currently available, there is special value in this disc, though ideally there ought to be more barbaric bite in the performances.

Intégrales; Octandre; (i) *Ecuatorial;* (ii) *Offrandes.*
   (M) *** Nonesuch H 71269. Contemporary Chamber Ensemble, Arthur Weisberg, with (i) Thomas Paul (bass), (ii) Jan DeGaetani (mezzo-soprano).

This useful collection of attractive and sharply distinctive works duplicates other Varèse discs, but it can be strongly recommended for the only available recording of *Ecuatorial*, a setting in Spanish with bass soloist of a Maya prayer, brightly colourful and sharp with heavy brass and percussion, organ, piano and ondes martenot. One is never in doubt that Varèse as a revolutionary had a mind of his own, and was as a rule decades ahead of his time. Good clear recording.

Vaughan Williams, Ralph
(1872–1958)

Concerto accademico (for violin and orchestra) *in D minor.*
   *** RCA SB 6801. James Buswell (violin), London Symphony Orchestra, André Previn – *Symphony No. 4.** (*)
   (M) *** Supraphon SUAST 50959. Nora Grumlikova (violin), Prague Symphony Orchestra, Peter Maag – BRITTEN: *Violin concerto.***

Vaughan Williams's *Concerto accademico* is a delightful work, written in his most attractive pastoral vein. It dates from 1925, and the finale quotes from his opera *Hugh the Drover*. The performance on RCA is highly sensitive: the slow movement is played with great feeling for its reticence and poetry. The disc is cut at a rather low level and the soloist is placed a little too far forward, but in all other respects the recording is excellent.

The Supraphon recording too is of high quality and the performance is first-rate, Maag ensuring a sympathetic accompaniment. This is an imaginative coupling and the disc is well worth investigating at the modest price asked.

(i) *Concerto accademico for violin and orchestra in D minor*. (ii) *Tuba concerto in F minor. The England of Elizabeth: suite; The Wasps: Overture.*
   *** RCA SB 6868. London Symphony Orchestra, André Previn, with (i) James Buswell (violin), (ii) John Fletcher (tuba).

When Previn's cycle of Vaughan Williams symphonies appeared in a collected edition, it was useful for the couplings to be issued separately on this disc. The two concertos are particularly valuable in these fine performances, splendidly recorded.

Double piano concerto in C major.
   *** HMV ASD 2469. Vitya Vronsky, Victor Babin (pianos), London Philharmonic Orchestra, Sir Adrian Boult – *Symphony No. 8*.***

(i) *Double piano concerto in C major. The Wasps: Overture and suite.*
   *** HMV ASD 2914. London Philharmonic Orchestra, Sir Adrian Boult, (i) as above.

This arrangement for two pianos was made when Vaughan Williams realized that his solo piano concerto – originally written for Harriet Cohen – would be

more effective in a new form. The new version, prepared with the help of Joseph Cooper, was first performed by Cyril Smith and Phyllis Sellick in 1946. It remains one of RVW's less tractable works, with its characteristic first-movement *Toccata*, but Vronsky and Babin are marvellously persuasive with the help of Boult's authority. The thick texture is well handled by the engineers. Of the alternative couplings, the performance of *The Wasps* incidental music is highly attractive for those not requiring the symphony.

Tuba concerto in F minor.
   *** RCA SB 6861. John Fletcher (tuba), London Symphony Orchestra, André Previn – *Symphony No. 3*.***

A first-class performance of an attractive and imaginatively conceived work. John Fletcher's nimble and sensitive playing fully justifies the composer's choice of this apparently unwieldy instrument for a concertante piece.

The England of Elizabeth (incidental music for film): *suite* (arr. Muir Mathieson).
   *** RCA SB 6842. London Symphony Orchestra, André Previn – *Symphony No. 9*.***

A film score of no great musical interest but undoubtedly pleasant to listen to. Both performance and recording are first-class.

English folksongs suite (arr. Gordon Jacob); *Fantasia on Greensleeves.*
   ** (*) HMV ASD 2750. London Symphony Orchestra, Sir Adrian Boult – ELGAR: *Enigma variations*.***

The *Folksongs suite* is not a very appropriate coupling for Boult's splendid account of *Enigma*, but this is delightful, unpretentious music, beautifully played and recorded.

English folksongs suite (arr. Jacob); *Fantasia on Greensleeves; Fantasia on a theme of Thomas Tallis.*

(B) ** RCA Victrola VICS 1530. Orchestra, Morton Gould — COATES: *London suite.***

The Americans always play our *Greensleeves* tune with an extra degree of stateliness, and it is effective here. So too is the *English folksongs suite*; Gould's brashness effectively reminds us that the work was originally written for military band. Most surprising is the success of the *Tallis* work. The reading has not the subtlety and depth of the very finest versions, but it is obviously strongly felt by conductor and players alike, and by keeping the music moving Gould ensures that the piece does not sag in the middle as it does in some home-spun performances. Rich atmospheric recording completes a good bargain.

Fantasia on Greensleeves; Fantasia on a theme of Thomas Tallis.

⊛ *** HMV ASD 521. Sinfonia of London, Allegri Quartet, Sir John Barbirolli — ELGAR: *Introduction and allegro; Serenade.****

Fantasia on a theme of Thomas Tallis.

*** HMV ASD 2698 (same performance as above) — *Symphony No. 5.***

*** Lyrita SRCS 41. London Philharmonic Orchestra, Sir Adrian Boult — RUBBRA: *Symphony No. 7.***

(B) *** Classics for Pleasure CFP 40068. London Philharmonic Orchestra, Vernon Handley — TIPPETT: *Concerto for double string orchestra.***

** (*) CBS 72982. Philadelphia Orchestra, Eugene Ormandy — ELGAR: *Enigma variations.** (*)

(M) ** HMV SXLP 20007. Philharmonia Orchestra, Sir Malcolm Sargent — ELGAR: *Enigma variations.***

The rich projection of the theme when it first appears in full, after the pizzicato introduction, sets the seal on Barbirolli's quite outstanding performance of the *Tallis fantasia*, one of the great masterpieces of all music. The wonderfully ethereal and magically quiet playing of the second orchestra is another very moving feature of this remarkable performance. HMV should be very proud both of the excellence of their stereo effect and of the warm realism of the string textures. The delightful *Greensleeves fantasia* makes a pleasing bonus on ASD 521.

It is a pity that Boult's authoritative reading was not presented on a record representing VW alone, but for those who fancy the thoughtfulness of Rubbra's *Symphony* it makes a splendid bonus, beautifully played and atmospherically recorded, with good separation between the different sections of players.

Vernon Handley proves a passionately persuasive interpreter of this masterpiece, aptly coupled with another great string work. Good playing and good sound; a first-rate bargain.

Ormandy characteristically underlines the drama of a work that is generally regarded as delicate and atmospheric. Devotees may object to the lustiness of the first great climax, but it is undeniably convincing in richness. An excellent coupling to a comparable performance of Elgar's *Enigma*. Full-blooded Philadelphia recording, with the different sections well separated if not ideally balanced.

One could hardly fail to be moved by the tonal quality HMV provide in the Philharmonia recording, but Sir Malcolm's performance is disappointing. He is content simply to play the notes and there is little spiritual quality.

Fantasia on Greensleeves; Fantasia on a theme of Thomas Tallis; Five Variants of Dives and Lazarus; (i) *The Lark ascending.*
*** Argo ZRG 696. Academy of St Martin-in-the-Fields, Neville Marriner, (i) with Iona Brown (violin).

Superbly balanced and refined performances of four favourite Vaughan Williams works which with the help of sumptuous recorded sound here have great power and intensity. A richly rewarding record.

Fantasia on a theme of Thomas Tallis; The Wasps: overture.
*** HMV ASD 2370. Bournemouth Symphony Orchestra, Constantin Silvestri – ELGAR: *In the South.****

Those wanting Silvestri's exhilaratingly memorable account of Elgar's *In the South* need not be deterred if they already have Barbirolli's account of the *Tallis fantasia.* This reading is quite different, more brilliant, less expansive, with remarkable tension in the opening and closing pages, and a touch of restraint in the handling of the second orchestra. But the central climax of the work is tremendously passionate, in a tighter, more direct way than Barbirolli. The playing is excellent, the recording only marginally less good. Silvestri's account of the *Wasps overture* makes the most of the brio, with crisp, fast tempi and the expansiveness of the great tune in the middle not allowed to interfere with the forward momentum. The vivacity of the playing and the vivid recording (only a trifle less good than *In the South*) make this very enjoyable indeed.

In the Fen Country (symphonic impression).

*** HMV ASD 2393. New Philharmonia Orchestra, Sir Adrian Boult – *Symphony No. 3.***

In the Fen Country follows on so naturally after the *Pastoral symphony* that it might be an extra movement. The middle section of the piece is perhaps on the whole less interesting, but the gentle rapture of the closing pages – beautifully sustained here – shows the composer weaving his most imaginative textures.

In the Fen Country. (i) *The Lark ascending. Norfolk rhapsody No. 1.* (ii) *Serenade to Music.*
*** HMV ASD 2847. London Philharmonic Orchestra, Sir Adrian Boult, with (i) Hugh Bean (violin) (ii) 16 vocal soloists.

An attractive coupling of four works that originally appeared as fill-ups to Boult versions of the symphonies, all beautifully performed and recorded.

Job (masque for dancing).
*** HMV ASD 2673. London Symphony Orchestra, Sir Adrian Boult.

Job is undeniably one of Vaughan Williams's very greatest compositions. It shows his inspiration at its most deeply characteristic and at its most consistently noble. Boult is its dedicatee and this is his fourth recording of it. It is probably his most successful, and the LSO give of their very best throughout. The recording has exceptional range and truthfulness; indeed it is one of the finest of any modern orchestral recordings. This is an altogether outstanding record and should be in the library of all collectors who care about twentieth-century music.

There is also an earlier Boult performance on Everest (SDBR 3019), but the recording cannot compare with this.

The Lark ascending (for violin and orchestra).

*** HMV ASD 2329. Hugh Bean (violin), New Philharmonia Orchestra, Sir Adrian Boult – *Symphony No. 6.*** (*)

(M) * (*) Vox STGBY 658. Oscar Chauson (violin), Utah Symphony Orchestra, Maurice Abravanel – WALTON: *Belshazzar's Feast.***

If one has some reservations about the performance of the symphony with which Boult's performance is coupled, one can find nothing but praise for this most beautiful account of *The Lark ascending*. Hugh Bean understands the spirit of the music perfectly; the lyricism of his tone and style is never over-indulgent, and the accompaniment is perfectly managed. The recording is fully worthy of the playing.

Abravanel directs a sympathetic performance, but it is rather marred by the heavy-handed contribution of the soloist.

Norfolk rhapsody No. 1 in E minor.

*** HMV ASD 2375. New Philharmonia Orchestra, Sir Adrian Boult – *Symphony No. 4.*** (*)

The *Norfolk rhapsody* is a lovely work and this, its first stereo recording, could not be bettered. It dates from the years immediately preceding the First World War, and despite its obvious indebtedness to the English folk-music tradition, it has great freshness and individuality and in its pensive moments a genuine delicacy of feeling. Boult evokes the most eloquent playing from the New Philharmonia and the HMV engineers give us a well-focused, musically balanced and full-blooded sound.

Symphonies Nos. 1–9.

(B) *** RCA SER 5649/55. Soloists, LSO Chorus, London Symphony Orchestra, André Previn.

Previn's cycle of the nine symphonies minus the couplings has been neatly compressed on to seven discs. The most striking performances are those which were recorded last, Nos. 2, 3 and 5, for there Previn achieves an extra depth of understanding, an extra intensity whether in the purity of pianissimo or the outpouring of emotional resolution. For the rest there is only one performance that can be counted at all disappointing, and that of the symphony one might have expected Previn to interpret best, the taut and dramatic *Fourth*. Even that is an impressive performance, if less intense than the rest. Otherwise the great landscape of the whole cycle is presented with richness and detail in totally refreshing interpretations brilliantly recorded.

Symphonies Nos. 1–9; Fantasia on the 'Old 104th'; In the Fen Country; The Lark ascending; Norfolk rhapsody No. 1; Serenade to Music.

(M) *** HMV SLS 822 (9 discs). Soloists, London Philharmonic Choir and Orchestra, Sir Adrian Boult.

By including the couplings which accompanied the original issues the EMI set is stretched to nine records instead of RCA's seven for Previn. Boult's performances of the symphonies are wonderfully satisfying too, and many lovers of Vaughan Williams will prefer their superbly consistent view, patiently studied and broadly presented. If at times the playing is not so electrically urgent as with Previn, the maturity of Vaughan Williams's vision has never been more convincingly presented. The recording throughout is of the highest quality.

A Sea symphony (No. 1).

*** RCA SER 5585. Heather Harper (soprano), John Shirley-Quirk (baritone), LSO Chorus, London

Symphony Orchestra, André Previn.

Previn's is a fresh, youthful reading of a young composer's symphony. If his interpretation lacks some of the honeyed sweetness that Boult brings to music that he has known and loved for half a century and more, Previn's view provides a clearer focus. His nervous energy is obvious from the very start. He does not always relax as Boult does, even where, as in the slow movement, he takes a more measured tempo than the older conductor. In the scherzo Boult concentrates on urgency, the emotional surge of the music, even at the expense of precision of ensemble, where Previn is lighter and cleaner, holding more in reserve. The finale similarly is built up over a longer span, with less deliberate expressiveness. The culminating climax with Previn is not allowed to be swamped with choral tone, but has the brass and timpani still prominent. The Epilogue may not be so deliberately expressive but it is purer in its tenderness and exact control of dynamics. Even if Vaughan Williams devotees will disagree over the the relative merits of the interpretations, Previn has clear advantages in his baritone soloist and his choir and in the fact that the whole symphony, with fine recording quality, is fitted on a single disc.

(i) *A Sea symphony (No. 1). The Wasps: Overture and suite.*
  ** (*) HMV SLS 780 (2 discs). London Philharmonic Orchestra, Sir Adrian Boult, (i) with Sheila Armstrong (soprano), John Carol Case (baritone), London Philharmonic Choir.

Boult's is a warm, relaxed reading of Vaughan Williams's expansive choral symphony. If the ensemble is sometimes less perfect than one would like, the flow of the music consistently holds the lis-

tener, and this is matched by warm, rounded recorded sound. Boult, often thought of as a 'straight' interpreter, here demonstrates his affectionate style, drawing consistently expressive but never sentimental phrasing from his singers and players. John Carol Case's baritone does not sound well on disc with its rather plaintive tone-colour, but his style is right, and Sheila Armstrong sings most beautifully. This will certainly not disappoint collectors of Boult's HMV Vaughan Williams cycle, and the fill-up (the same as on his earlier mono Decca version on its first issue) is colourfully played and well recorded. The early Boult version of the symphony has been most successfully condensed on to two sides on Eclipse (ECS 583), where it remains a formidable competitor. Even though the stereo transcription cannot, of course, match the recording quality of the newer issue, it still sounds astonishingly well.

A London symphony (No. 2).
  ⊛ *** RCA SB 6860. London Symphony Orchestra, André Previn.
  *** HMV ASD 2740. London Philharmonic Orchestra, Sir Adrian Boult.
  (M) ** (*) HMV SXLP 30180. Hallé Orchestra, Sir John Barbirolli.
  (B) ** (*) Pye GSGC 14012. Hallé Orchestra, Sir John Barbirolli.

Previn underlines the greatness of this work as a symphony, not just a sequence of programmatic impressions. Though the actual sonorities are even more subtly and beautifully realized here than in rival versions, the architecture is equally convincingly presented, with the great climaxes of the first and last movements powerful and incisive. Most remarkable of all are the pianissimos, which here have new intensity, a quality of frisson as in a live performance. The LSO plays superbly and the recording, made in Kingsway Hall, is beautifully balanced and refined, coping perfectly with the widest possible dynamic range.

Boult's newer record of the *London symphony* is also given a superbly rich and spacious recording. The orchestral playing too is outstandingly fine. The reading itself is basically the same as on Boult's earlier Decca record (now available on ECS 616 in a good stereo transcription), although the outer movements in the newer performance are more expansive, rather less taut. The central *tranquillo* episode of the first movement, for instance, is very relaxed, Boult indulging himself in the mood of nostalgic reverie. But here, as in the slow movement, the orchestra produces such lovely sounds, the playing obviously deeply committed, that criticism is disarmed. The scherzo is as light as thistledown, and the gentle melancholy which underlies the solemn pageantry of the finale is coloured with great subtlety.

Barbirolli's newer HMV recording is more expansive than his earlier Pye version, with a considerable broadening of style and tempi. In many places this yields greater authority to the interpretation. Towards the end of the first movement the threads are drawn together with striking majesty and breadth, and the slow movement gains in spaciousness and atmosphere. The scherzo is more controversial. It is played gracefully, but the lack of boisterousness in the 'street dance' sequence seems wilful, even though it fits in with the overall interpretation. The powerful finale and finely graduated closing pages of the Epilogue make considerable amends, and the rich yet finely detailed HMV recording adds much to the success of this record, even if the earlier Pye version is not entirely eclipsed.

Barbirolli's first recording of the symphony for Pye still sounds surprisingly well and continues to make a good bargain investment. Barbirolli's reading is a warm, romantic one, less expansive than his HMV remake, where the scherzo is

taken too slowly. In many ways the Pye disc is very attractive. The recording has a wide dynamic range, and the quieter music – especially at the opening and close of the work – is cut at a very low level. This is prone to surface imperfections and not all the pressings are good in this respect.

A Pastoral symphony (No. 3).
*** RCA SB 6861. Heather Harper (soprano), London Symphony Orchestra, André Previn – *Tuba concerto.****
*** HMV ASD 2393. Margaret Price (soprano), New Philharmonia Orchestra, Sir Adrian Boult – *In the Fen Country.****

One tends to think Vaughan Williams's pastoral music is essentially synonymous with the English countryside, and it is something of a shock to discover that in fact the *Pastoral symphony* was sketched in Northern France while the composer was on active service in 1916, and the initial inspiration was a Corot-like landscape in the sunset. But the music remains English in essence, and its gentle rapture is not easily evoked.

Previn draws an outstandingly beautiful and refined performance from the LSO, the bare textures sounding austere but never thin, the few climaxes emerging at full force with purity undiminished. In the third movement the final coda – the only really fast music in the whole work – brings a magic tracery of pianissimo in this performance, lighter, faster and even clearer than in Boult's version. The recording adds to the beauty in its atmospheric distancing, not least in the trumpet cadenza of the second movement and the lovely melismas for the soprano soloist in the last movement.

Boult here is not entirely successful in controlling the tension of the short but elusive first movement, although it is beautifully played. The opening of the

Lento moderato, however, is very fine, and its close is sustained with a perfect blend of restraint and intensity. After the jovial third movement, the orchestra is joined by Margaret Price, whose wordless contribution is blended into the texture most skilfully. The recording throughout is superb. For the most part this performance is successful and enjoyable.

Symphony No. 4 in F minor.

** (*) HMV ASD 2375. New Philharmonia Orchestra, Sir Adrian Boult – *Norfolk rhapsody.****

** (*) RCA SB 6801. London Symphony Orchestra, André Previn – *Concerto accademico.****

Boult's was the first stereo recording of the *Fourth*, and although it would be possible to imagine a performance of greater fire and tenacity few will find much to disappoint them in this persuasive account. Sir Adrian procures orchestral playing of the highest quality from the NPO, and the slow movement, one of the composer's finest inspirations, is particularly successful. The recording, too, falls into the superlative category: it has body, clarity of detail and spaciousness. The performance does not obliterate memories of the composer's own recording, which Sir Adrian helped to prepare, and whose intensity and anguish had an immediacy that this does not quite capture. But it is very fine.

Previn secures a first-rate performance; only the somewhat ponderous tempo he adopts for the first movement lets this down. But still on the whole this is a powerful reading and it is vividly recorded. A good alternative to the Boult, though not superior to it.

The composer's own version, made with the BBC Symphony Orchestra in the 1930s, is at the moment available in a first-class transfer (World Record Club SH 128), and it outstrips any of the stereo versions in sheer fire and guts.

Symphony No. 5 in D major.

*** HMV ASD 2538. London Philharmonic Orchestra, Sir Adrian Boult – *Serenade to Music.*** (*)

*** HMV ASD 2698. Philharmonia Orchestra, Sir John Barbirolli – *Fantasia on a theme of Tallis.****

Boult gives a loving performance of the *Fifth Symphony*, one which links it directly with the great opera *The Pilgrim's Progress*, from which (in its unfinished state) the composer drew much of the material. It is a gentler performance, easier, more flowing than Previn's, and some may prefer it for that reason, but the emotional involvement is a degree less intense, particularly in the slow movement.

The reissue of Barbirolli's performance is highly successful, and the recording sounds fresh and modern without loss of warmth. Barbirolli's reading shows rather more temperament than Boult's and there are many wonderfully glowing moments. The string-playing is distinguished. With the generous coupling of the *Tallis fantasia*, one of the finest things Barbirolli did for the gramophone, this disc remains very competitive.

Symphony No. 5 in D major; The Wasps: Overture.

*** RCA SB 6856. London Symphony Orchestra, André Previn.

If anyone has ever doubted the dedication of Previn as an interpreter of Vaughan Williams, this glowing disc will provide the clearest proof. In this most characteristic – and many would say greatest – of the Vaughan Williams symphonies Previn refuses to be lured into pastoral byways. His tempi may – rather surprisingly – be consistently on the slow side, but the purity of tone he draws from the LSO, the precise shading of dynamic and phrasing, and the sustaining of tension through the longest, most hushed passages produce results that will persuade many not normally convinced of the greatness of this music. In the first movement Previn builds the great climaxes of the second subject with great warmth, but he reserves for the climax of the slow movement his culminating thrust of emotion, a moment of visionary sublimity, after which the gentle urgency of the *Passacaglia* finale and the stillness of the Epilogue seem a perfect happy conclusion. It is some tribute to Previn's intensity that he can draw out the diminuendi at the ends of movements with such refinement and no sense of exaggeration. The fill-up may not be generous, and not so apt as those provided by Boult and Barbirolli, but with such an outstanding performance, superbly recorded, few will worry about that.

Symphony No. 6 in E minor.
** (*) HMV ASD 2329. New Philharmonia Orchestra, Sir Adrian Boult – *The Lark ascending.****

There is an element of disappointment in discussing Boult's re-recording of the powerful *Sixth Symphony*, and perhaps one expected too much. The performance is without the tension of the earlier mono recording Boult made for Decca, with the composer present, which is still available on Eclipse (ECS 602). The sound of that record cannot of course compare with that of the newer version, but Boult's comparative mellowness here means that the reading is not as searching as the score demands. The strange finale is beautifully played, with a finely sustained pianissimo from wind and strings alike, but the atmosphere, if not without a sense of mystery, is somehow too complacent.

Symphonies Nos. 6 in E minor; 8 in D minor.
** (*) RCA SB 6767. London Symphony Orchestra, André Previn.

Previn's is a sensible and generous coupling. The *Sixth Symphony*, with its moments of darkness and brutality contrasted against the warmth of the second subject or the hushed intensity of the final other-worldly slow movement, is a work for which Previn has a natural affinity. In the first three movements his performance is superbly dramatic, clearheaded and direct with natural understanding. His account of the mystic final movement with its endless pianissimo is not, however, on the same level, for – whether or not the fault of the recording – the playing is not quite hushed enough, and the tempo is a little too fast. In its closely wrought contrapuntal texture this is a movement which may seem difficult to interpret, but which should be allowed to flow along on its own intensity. Boult here achieves a more vital sense of mystery, even though his account is not ideal. Previn's account of the *Eighth* brings no such reservations, with finely pointed playing, the most precise control of dynamic shading, and a delightfully Stravinskian account of the bouncing scherzo for woodwind alone. Excellent recording considering the length of sides, although the string tone is not always ideally expansive.

Sinfonia Antartica (No. 7).
*** HMV ASD 2631. Norma Burrows (soprano), London Philharmonic Choir and Orchestra, Sir Adrian Boult.
** (*) RCA SB 6736. Heather Harper (soprano), Ambrosian Singers, London Symphony Orchestra, André Previn; Ralph Richardson (narrator).

The *Antartica* may be episodic but it is still a vital and dramatic symphony, deriving as it does from the score to *Scott of the Antarctic*. Sir Adrian gives a stirring account of it and is quite superlatively served by the EMI engineers.

There is not really a great deal to choose between this and Previn's version as performances: both are convincing. Perhaps the EMI recording has slightly greater range and a more natural balance. The RCA recording, in its relatively distant balance, as well as Previn's interpretation concentrate on atmosphere rather than drama. The performance is sensitive and literal. Because of the recessed effect of the sound the picture of the ice fall (represented by an almost startling entry of the organ) has a good deal less impact here than on Boult's old Decca disc (ECS 577), which still sounds astonishingly fine.

Symphony No. 8 in D minor.
   *** HMV ASD 2469. London Philharmonic Orchestra, Sir Adrian Boult – *Double piano concerto.****
   (B) * (*) Pye GSGC 15017. Hallé Orchestra, Sir John Barbirolli (with BAX: *Garden of Fand*; BUTTERWORTH: *A Shropshire Lad*).
Symphony No. 8 in D minor; Partita for orchestra.
   (B) ** (*) Decca Eclipse ECS 644. London Philharmonic Orchestra, Sir Adrian Boult.

Sir Adrian's HMV performance of the *Eighth* is a fine one, spacious and measured, with an excellent recording. Boult shows all the genial good humour one would expect. This may not be so sharply pointed as Previn's account (see above), but some will prefer the extra warmth of the Boult interpretation, its rather more lyrical approach. The coupling will also plainly affect choice, for this is an important first recording of a work which for many years was seriously underestimated. The HMV disc produces a somewhat fresher and more naturally balanced quality.

This was the only Vaughan Williams symphony that Boult recorded for Decca in real stereo, and its quality in the

Eclipse reissue is excellent, vivid and fresh, if not so rich as the newer HMV disc. The *Partita for orchestra* is not one of the composer's most inspired works (it was originally a double string trio), but it serves as makeweight for what is in essence an excellent bargain.

Barbirolli must yield, both for performance and recording, to Boult. Barbirolli was of course the dedicatee; his account is bluff in manner. He is at his best in the genial scherzo.

Symphony No. 9 in E minor.
   *** RCA SB 6842. London Symphony Orchestra, André Previn – *England of Elizabeth suite.****
   (M) ** Everest SDBR 3006. London Philharmonic Orchestra, Sir Adrian Boult.
Symphony No. 9 in E minor; (i) Fantasia (quasi variazione) on the 'Old 104th' Psalm tune (for piano, chorus and orchestra).
   *** HMV ASD 2581. (i) Peter Katin (piano), London Philharmonic Choir and Orchestra, Sir Adrian Boult.

The *Ninth*, Vaughan Williams's last symphony, is one of his most consistently under-rated works. It contains much noble and arresting invention and given a performance and recording as fine as on the HMV disc it should enjoy its proper due. Sir Adrian gets most committed playing from the LPO, and the recording is splendidly firm in tone. The *Fantasia on the 'Old 104th'* is unlikely to sway prospective purchasers one way or the other; it is not a particularly successful work, but these artists do their best for it in an eloquent performance.

Although in many of the Vaughan Williams symphonies there is not very much to choose between Boult and Previn, the *Ninth* is a case where Previn's freshness and sense of poetry prove particularly thought-provoking and rewarding. He secures smoother contours in the first movement, and as a result also of some refined string playing he produces the more transparent texture. The RCA recording too is highly successful and the string tone is expansive, well balanced in relation to the rest of the orchestra and free from the slight hint of hardness that sometimes disturbs this cycle. Listening to this reading reinforces the view that the critics of the day were unfairly harsh to this fine score. Both Boult and Previn can be recommended, but if in doubt choose the Previn.

Boult's earlier Everest disc makes quite a good mid-price alternative to the HMV one. The recording was very good for its day, with a wide dynamic range. The actual tonal quality has not the warmth and lustre of the newer HMV but remains very acceptable. Boult's interpretation has changed only a little over the years, and the more relaxed, more spacious feeling of the newer disc is contributed partly by the recording, although the orchestral playing is finer too.

CHAMBER MUSIC

(i) *Phantasy quintet* (for 2 violins, 2 violas and cello); (ii; iii) *6 Studies in English folk song for cello and piano*; (iii; iv) *Violin sonata in A minor*.
> (M) ** (*) HMV HQS 1327. (i) Music Group of London; (ii) Eileen Croxford (cello); (iii) David Parkhouse (piano); (iv) Hugh Bean (violin).

This collection of relatively little-known chamber works, well recorded and well performed, can be strongly recommended to devotees of Vaughan Williams. The *Phantasy quintet* dates from the composer's full maturity in 1912, written, as the title suggests, in the compressed one-movement form advocated by W. W.

Cobbett. The *Violin sonata* (1954) is a relatively gawky work, but one which, like much later Vaughan Williams, has a tangily distinctive flavour, especially in a performance as fine as this. First-rate recording.

String quartets Nos. 1 in G minor; 2 in A minor.
> (M) *** HMV HQS 1292. Music Group of London Quartet.

The two string quartets of Vaughan Williams present a striking contrast – the one written soon after his period of study with Ravel and strongly reflecting that, the other a product of his last period, an ostensibly amiable work written as a birthday present for a viola player, Jean Stewart. In both works the Music Group of London reveals deeper qualities than these associations might suggest. The *Second Quartet* in particular contains some strikingly original ideas. First-rate recording.

VOCAL AND CHORAL MUSIC

(i) *10 Blake songs. Songs of Travel.* Songs: *Linden Lea; Orpheus with his Lute; The Water Mill.*
> *** Argo ZRG 732. Robert Tear (tenor), Philip Ledger (piano), (i) with Neil Black (oboe).

Robert Tear cannot match the sheer beauty of Ian Partridge in his wonderfully sensitive account of the *Blake songs* (see under *On Wenlock Edge*), but his rougher-grained voice brings out a different kind of expressiveness, helped by Neil Black's fine oboe-playing. The *Songs of Travel*, here presented complete with the five extra songs published later, make an excellent coupling, with Ledger a most perceptive accompanist. Excellent recording.

Sacred music: *3 Choral hymns (Easter hymn; Christmas hymn; Whitsunday hymn); Come down, O love divine; For all the Saints; O taste and see; Prayer to the Father; Te Deum in G major; Valiant for truth; We've been awhile a-wandering; Wither's Rocking hymn.*
** Polydor 2383 219. Worcester Cathedral Choir, Christopher Robinson; Harry Bramma (organ).

A useful collection of Vaughan Williams' shorter choral settings and arrangements, let down only by poor sleeve documentation: there are no notes about the music whatsoever. Besides the short *Te Deum*, among the more striking settings is *Valiant for truth*, a much subtler piece than its Salvation Army-like title would suggest. The three *Choral hymns* are spaciously conceived, but would have benefited from a recording with more bite. As it is, the sound is atmospheric but not very clear in detail. The performances generally are of a good standard.

(i) *Dona nobis pacem;* (ii) *Flos campi.*
(M) ** (*) Vanguard VSD 71159. (i) Blanche Christensen (soprano), William Metcalf (baritone), Utah University Civic Chorale; (ii) Sally Peck Lentz (viola), Utah University Chamber Choir; both with Utah Symphony Orchestra, Maurice Abravanel.

Though more refined performances have been recorded of both these elusive works, this is a highly enjoyable coupling on a mid-price label, well recorded. *Dona nobis pacem* presents a passionate cry for peace in its settings of Whitman and the Bible, while the evocation of the Song of Solomon contained in *Flos campi* shows Vaughan Williams at his most rarefied and imaginative.

(i) *Dona nobis pacem. Towards the Unknown Region.*

*** HMV ASD 2962. London Philharmonic Choir and Orchestra, Sir Adrian Boult, (i) with Sheila Armstrong (soprano), John Carol Case (baritone).

Dona nobis pacem appeared in 1936 as a direct response to the dark uneasy peace of the thirties, a work which was obviously relevant but still elusive. The central setting of a Whitman poem, *Dirge for two veterans*, may not be stylistically quite consistent with the rest, but in a performance as sensitive and understanding as this, the whole scheme emerges powerfully. In its simplicity, the Dirge presents a powerful and sustained climax, while the more austere settings of Biblical texts have a dark simplicity that is most compelling. Fine performances of this and of the early setting of Whitman, *Towards the Unknown Region*. Excellent recording.

Five Variants of Dives and Lazarus; (i; ii) *Flos campi;* (i; iii) *An Oxford elegy.*
*** HMV ASD 2487. Jacques Orchestra, David Willcocks, with (i) King's College, Cambridge, Choir; (ii) Cecil Aronowitz (viola), (iii) John Westbrook (speaker).

Flos campi is one of Vaughan Williams's most sensuously beautiful works, with its deeply expressive solo for the viola – here beautifully played by Cecil Aronowitz. It needs persuasive interpretation, and that it receives in Willcocks's hands. The *Five Variants*, described as 'the dreams and memories of a folk-song collector', is an easy, unpretentious work in the composer's most characteristic vein, while the *Oxford elegy* (1949) is one of those occasional works which rises well above its original commission, mellifluous music characteristic of the composer's ripe Indian summer. The spoken quotations from Matthew Arnold are effectively presented by John Westbrook, while the Cambridge choir is admirable in its words of tribute to Oxford. A valuable record.

Fantasia (quasi variazione) on the 'Old 104th' Psalm tune.
>** HMV ASD 2581. Peter Katin (piano), London Philharmonic Choir and Orchestra, Sir Adrian Boult – *Symphony No. 9.****

This is discussed under its coupling.

4 Hymns (Lord, come away!; Who is this fair one; Come love, come Lord; Evening hymn); Merciless beauty; 3 Rondels.
>(M) *** HMV HQS 1325. Ian Partridge (tenor), Music Group of London – WARLOCK: *The Curlew.****

These rare songs of Vaughan Williams make an attractive coupling for the fine version of Warlock's *The Curlew*. The *Four Hymns* are distinctively accompanied by viola and piano, beautifully balanced on this well recorded disc.

(i) Magnificat; (i; ii) Riders to the Sea (opera in 1 act): complete recording.
>*** HMV ASD 2699. (i) Helen Watts (contralto), Ambrosian Singers; (ii) Norma Burrowes, Margaret Price (sopranos), Benjamin Luxon (tenor), Pauline Stevens (mezzo-soprano); both with Orchestra Nova of London, Meredith Davies.

The *Magnificat* shows Vaughan Williams in his most Holstian vein. It dates from the early thirties and has strong suggestions of *Flos campi*. Its inspiration is of high quality and it is performed with sympathy and imagination on this excellent record. *Riders to the Sea* is a moving one-act opera, probably Vaughan Williams's most dramatically effective piece,

with a consistently high level of inspiration. It is beautifully performed and recorded, though there is a bit too much of the wind machine. All who care about the composer should investigate this little-known but compelling work.

Mass in G minor.
>(M) *** Pye Virtuoso TPLS 13019. BBC Chorus, Alan G. Melville – TALLIS: *Gaude gloriosa.****

Some may feel it a drawback that this fine performance of Vaughan Williams's *Mass* uses women's voices in the upper parts, but the purity of tone is still striking and is made the more beautiful by the size of the choir – not too large to be ungainly but big enough for tonal fullness. The interpretation is most searching and expressive, with a rhythmic flexibility that prevents Vaughan Williams's flowing polyphony from ever stagnating or sounding monotonous. As sung here this is one of the most intensely beautiful works he ever wrote. Excellent recording.

(i) Mass in G minor; (i; ii; iii) 5 Mystical songs (Rise, heart; I got me flowers; Love bade me welcome; The call; Antiphon); (i; ii) O clap your hands (motet).
>*** HMV ASD 2458. (i) King's College Choir, Cambridge; (ii) English Chamber Orchestra; (iii) John Shirley-Quirk (baritone); all cond. David Willcocks.

Vaughan Williams's beautiful setting of the *Mass* has proved an elusive work on record, but here with the finest band of trebles in the country David Wil'cocks captures its beauty more completely than any rival, helped by fine, atmospheric recording quality. This is a work which can on the one hand easily seem too tense and lose its magic, or on the other fall apart in a meandering style, and Willcocks admirably finds the middle course. In the *Five Mystical songs* to words by George Herbert, John Shirley-Quirk sings admirably. Considering the problems of balance the recording is first-class.

On Wenlock Edge (song cycle from Housman's *A Shropshire Lad*); *10 Blake songs; The New Ghost; The Water Mill.*

⊛ (M) *** HMV HQS 1236. Ian Partridge (tenor), Music Group of London, Janet Craxton (oboe), Jennifer Partridge (piano).

This is an outstandingly beautiful record, with Ian Partridge's intense artistry and lovely individual tone-colour used with compelling success in Vaughan Williams songs both early and late. The Housman cycle has an accompaniment for piano and string quartet which can sound ungainly, but here, with playing from the Music Group of London which matches the soloist's sensitivity, the result is atmospheric and moving. The *Ten Blake songs* come from just before the composer's death, bald, direct settings that with the artistry of Partridge and Craxton are darkly moving. The tenor's sister accompanies with fine understanding in two favourite songs as a welcome extra. Warm, rounded recording.

(i) *Sancta Civitas (The Holy City;* oratorio). *Benedicite* (for soprano, chorus and orchestra).

*** HMV ASD 2422. Heather Harper (soprano), Bach Choir, London Symphony Orchestra, David Willcocks, (i) with Ian Partridge (tenor), John Shirley-Quirk (baritone), boys of King's College Choir.

This is the most valuable of the series of Vaughan Williams choral works recorded by David Willcocks, for *Sancta civitas*, a product of the composer's visionary years in the early twenties, is a masterpiece,

elusive in its apparent meandering but in fact as sharply focused as another important and still under-appreciated work of the period, the *Pastoral symphony*. The words, mostly from the Revelation, are set to wonderful, shifting choral textures (a main chorus set against semi-chorus and boys' chorus off-stage), and the whole has been beautifully captured on this record. The *Benedicite* is another strong work, compressed in its intensity, too brief to be accepted easily into the choral repertory, but a fine addition to RVW's discography.

Serenade to Music.

** (*) HMV ASD 2538. Vocal soloists, London Philharmonic Orchestra, Sir Adrian Boult – *Symphony No. 5.****

The *Serenade to Music*, written in honour of Sir Henry Wood, makes an ideal coupling for the *Fifth Symphony*, and it is good to have a performance which, following the original idea, uses solo singers, though these cannot, except in one or two instances, match the quality of the originals whose initials were placed in the score. The violin soloist disappointingly uses too sweet a style in his important part in the introduction. The recording matches the rest of the Boult cycle of the symphonies in its atmospheric warmth.

5 Tudor portraits (The tunning of Elinor Rumming; My pretty Bess; Epitaph on John Jayberd of Diss; Jane Scroop – her lament for Philip Sparrow; Jolly Rutterkin).

** (*) HMV ASD 2489. Elizabeth Bainbridge (contralto), John Carol Case (baritone), Bach Choir, New Philharmonia Orchestra, David Willcocks.

Ursula Vaughan Williams reports in her biography of the composer that the first performance of the *Five Tudor portraits* – in Norwich in 1936 – was remarkable for shocking many of the audience. ('The elderly Countess of Albemarle sat in the front row getting pinker and pinker in the face', says Mrs Vaughan Williams, and after the old lady had departed, the composer complimented the chorus on its diction.) The composer deliberately chose bawdy words by the early Tudor poet, John Skelton, and set them in his most rumbustious style. This is a good, strong performance, but the soloists are not earthy enough for such music. It is a pity that the humour was not more strongly underlined, but the musical invention is still more than strong enough to sustain compelling interest. Excellent recording.

Arrangements of folk songs: *An acre of land; Bushes and briars; Ca' the Yowes; Early in the spring; Five English folksongs (The dark-eyed sailor; The spring time of the year; Just as the tide was flowing; The lover's ghost; Wassail song); Greensleeves; John Dory; Loch Lomond; The seeds of love; The turtle dove; The unquiet grave; Ward the pirate.*
> (M) *** HMV HQS 1215. London Madrigal Singers, Christopher Bishop.

As recording manager Christopher Bishop has supervised many fine records of Vaughan Williams's music (as well as much else), and here with a choir of hand-picked singers he shows that in his own right he is a first-rate interpreter of the composer. This is a delightful collection of part songs, far more varied than one might expect. There is nothing whatever pretentious about the settings, and each one shows subtly the distinction of RVW's mind, never falling into mere routine. The singing of the London Madrigal Singers is admirably lithe and sensitive, and this is altogether a lovely record, beautifully engineered.

OPERA

The Pilgrim's Progress (opera in prologue, 4 acts and epilogue): complete recording.
> (M) *** HMV SLS 959 (3 discs). John Noble, Raimund Herincx, John Carol Case, John Shirley-Quirk (baritones), Norma Burrowes, Sheila Armstrong (sopranos), Christopher Keyte (bass), London Philharmonic Choir and Orchestra, Sir Adrian Boult.

This glowing performance under Boult should effectively ensure that this inspired opera, one of the composer's culminating life-works, is at last given its due. Though Vaughan Williams was right in insisting that it is not an oratorio (his word was 'a morality'), the choral writing frames it, sung here with heartfelt warmth by the London Philharmonic Choir. What comes out in a recorded performance is that, so far from being slow and undramatic, the score is crammed full of delectable ideas one after the other, and the drama of the mind – as in the book – supplements more conventional dramatic incident. John Noble gives a dedicated performance in the central role of Pilgrim, and the large supporting cast is consistently strong. Much of the material of Act 1 was also used in the *Fifth Symphony*, and like that masterpiece this opera stands at the heart of the composer's achievement. Vanity Fair may not sound evil here, but Vaughan Williams's own recoil is vividly expressed, and the jaunty passage of Mr and Mrs By-Ends brings the most delightful light relief. Boult underlines the virility of his performance with a fascinatingly revealing collection of rehearsal excerpts. Outstanding recording quality.

COLLECTION

'*R.V.W.*' (sampler): (i) *Concerto grosso: March and Reprise;* (ii) *Greensleeves fantasia;* (iii) *Job: A vision of Satan;* (iv) *Rhosymede: Prelude;* (v) *A Sea symphony: Scherzo* (vi) *The Wasps: March-past of the kitchen utensils;* (vii) *Linden Lea;* (viii) *Mass in G minor: Gloria;* (viii; ix) *5 Mystical songs: Rise, heart;* (x) *On Wenlock Edge: From far, from eve and morning. The Water Mill.* (xi) Folk songs: *Wassail song; An acre of land.* (xii) *The Pilgrim's Progress: Act 4, Scene 3 and Epilogue.*

(B) ** HMV SEOM 12. (i) Bournemouth Symphony Orchestra, Norman Del Mar; (ii) London Symphony Orchestra, André Previn; (iii) London Symphony Orchestra, Sir Adrian Boult; (iv) Academy of St Martin-in-the-Fields, Neville Marriner; (v) Soloists, London Philharmonic Orchestra and Choir, Boult; (vi) London Philharmonic Orchestra, Boult (vii) Janet Baker (mezzo-soprano), Gerald Moore (piano); (viii) King's College, Cambridge, Choir, David Willcocks; (ix) John Shirley-Quirk (baritone); (x) Ian Partridge (tenor); (xi) London Madrigal Singers, Christopher Bishop; (xii) K. Woolam, J. Temperley, D. Price, London Philharmonic Orchestra and Choir, Boult.

Opening with the piquant *March-past of the kitchen utensils* from *The Wasps* and following it with *Greensleeves,* warmly played under Previn, this 'sampler' gets off to a good start. But after that the selection is less effective, and it might have been better for the producer to have concentrated on fewer and longer excerpts. However, the song from *On Wenlock Edge* should catch anyone by the ears and the *Epilogue* from *The Pilgrim's Progress* makes a ravishing final item. The recording is virtually of demonstration quality throughout, but as an anthology this is not really very satisfying.

Verdi, Giuseppe (1813–1901)

Ballet music from: (i) *Don Carlo (Il ballo della regina);* *I Lombardi (Jérusalem);* (ii) *Macbeth; Otello;* (i) *Il Trovatore; I Vespri siciliani.*

** (*) Philips 6747 093 (2 discs). (i) Monte Carlo National Opera Orchestra; (ii) London Symphony Orchestra; all cond. Antonio de Almeida.

Strong, colourful performances of undemanding music that for practical reasons no longer gets performed in the opera-house. Two-steps, waltzes fast and slow, galops and lyrical adagios, all have their place here, all unmistakably the work of the master, and well worth hearing if not with any solemnity. The *Macbeth* and *Otello* items, in which the LSO appears, are markedly more spirited in performance. Good recording.

Aïda: Prelude; La Forza del destino: Overture; Giovanna d'Arco: Overture; Luisa Miller: Overture; Macbeth: Ballet music; La Traviata: Preludes to Acts 1 and 3; I Vespri siciliani: Overture.

(M) ** (*) Philips Universo 6580 073. New Philharmonia Orchestra, Igor Markevitch.

A generous collection, with four items to a side and strongly dramatic performances; *Giovanna d'Arco* and *I Vespri siciliani* are especially vivid. The *Aīda prelude* is beautifully played, and the *Traviata preludes* are well done too. The only reservation is about the recording balance. Verdi's brass writing is powerful enough without any help from the microphone balance, and here the strings tend to be overwhelmed at times. The middle strings in particular seem unable always to expand their tone, although when the whole section is playing together alone, the sound has plenty of lustre.

La Forza del destino: Overture; La Traviata: Preludes to Acts 1 and 3; I Vespri siciliani: Overture.
> (M) *** HMV SXLP 30094. Philharmonia Orchestra, Carlo Maria Giulini – ROSSINI: *Overtures.****

Giulini's collection is first-class and very clearly if slightly drily recorded. The playing is excellent and the performances full of tension, the two *Traviata preludes* being especially well contrasted. The *Sicilian vespers overture* makes an exciting end to the concert.

String quartet in E minor.
> (M) ** Supraphon 111 0573. Moravian Quartet – BOCCHERINI: *Quartet in E flat major.***

Verdi's *String quartet* was written in 1873 while the composer was in Naples supervising rehearsals for *Aīda*. His principal soprano fell ill, so Verdi amused himself with the present work in his hotel. It is a charming piece, and is played here with plenty of spirit. The recording is good if not outstanding.

Requiem Mass.
> ⊛ *** HMV SLS 909 (2 discs). Elisabeth Schwarzkopf (soprano), Christa Ludwig (mezzo-soprano), Nicolai Gedda (tenor), Nicolai Ghiaurov (bass), Philharmonia Chorus and Orchestra, Carlo Maria Giulini.
> *** Decca SET 374/5. Joan Sutherland (soprano), Marilyn Horne (mezzo-soprano), Luciano Pavarotti (tenor), Martti Talvela (bass), Vienna Symphony Orchestra Chorus, Vienna Philharmonic Orchestra, Sir Georg Solti.
> ** (*) CBS 77231 (2 discs). Martina Arroyo (soprano), Josephine Veasey (mezzo-soprano), Placido Domingo (tenor), Ruggero Raimondi (bass), LSO Chorus, London Symphony Orchestra, Leonard Bernstein.
> (M) ** Decca GOS 617/8. Leontyne Price (soprano), Rosalind Elias (mezzo-soprano), Jussi Bjoerling (tenor), Giorgio Tozzi (bass), Society of Friends of Music, Vienna, Vienna Philharmonic Orchestra, Fritz Reiner.
> ** DGG 2707 065 (2 discs). Mirella Freni (soprano), Christa Ludwig (mezzo-soprano), Carlo Cossuta (tenor), Nicolai Ghiaurov (bass), Vienna Singverein, Berlin Philharmonic Orchestra, Herbert von Karajan.

Over the years Giulini's interpretation of the Verdi *Requiem* with the Philharmonia Chorus and Orchestra became world-renowned – even Italy asked to hear it – and this recording is a worthy representation. It is the refinement quite as much as the elemental strength which comes across under Giulini. Such passages as the *Dies Irae* are overwhelmingly exciting (though never merely frenetic) but the hushed tension of the chorus's whispers in the same movement and the warm lyricism of the solo singing are equally impressive. What Giulini proves is that refinement added to power can provide an even more intense experience than the traditional Italian approach. In this concept a fine English chorus and orchestra prove exactly right: better disciplined than their Italian counterparts, less severe than the Germans. The array of soloists could hardly be bettered. Schwarzkopf caresses each phrase, and the exactness of her voice matches the firm mezzo of Christa Ludwig in their difficult octave passages. Again with Ludwig you have to throw aside conventional Italian ideas of performance, but the result is undeniably more musical. Gedda is at his most reliable, and Ghiaurov with his really dark bass actually manages to sing the almost impossible *Mors stupebit* in tune without a suspicion of wobble. Excellent recording, recently reprocessed, to become clearer and more vivid than the original.

Solti's performance is not really a direct rival to any other, for with the whole-hearted co-operation of the Decca engineers he has played up the dramatic side of the work at the expense of the spiritual. There is little or nothing reflective about this account, and those who criticize the work for being too operatic will find plenty of ammunition here. The team of soloists is a very strong one, though the matching of voices is not always ideal. It is a pity that the chorus is not nearly so incisive as the Philharmonia on the HMV set – a performance which conveys far more of the work's profundity than this. But if you want an extrovert performance with superlative recording you could hardly do better.

CBS opted to record the *Requiem* in the Royal Albert Hall. By rights the daring of that decision should have paid off, but with close-balancing of microphones and later processing of the tapes that did not allow a full, free atmosphere, the result is disappointing compared with other recent versions. Bernstein's interpretation remains marvellously persuasive in its drama, exaggerated at times maybe, but red-blooded in a way that is hard to resist. The quartet of soloists is particularly strong, which makes it all the more disappointing that the sound does not match the quality of performance.

Reiner's opening is strangely slow and mannered. He takes the music at something like half the speed of Toscanini and his very careful shaping of phrases loses the music's forward impulse. But as the work proceeds the performance quickly comes alive, and there is some superb singing from a distinguished quartet of soloists. The new transfer of the recording (originally made by Decca for RCA) shows its brilliance, although the dynamic range is almost too wide. A fine bargain at medium price.

Karajan smoothes over the lines of Verdi's masterpiece with the help of a mellow Berlin acoustic. The result is undeniably beautiful, but it loses most of its dramatic bite.

Four Sacred pieces (Ave Maria; Stabat Mater; Laudi alla Vergine; Te Deum).
*** HMV SAN 120. Janet Baker (contralto), Philharmonia Chorus and Orchestra, Carlo Maria Giulini.
** Decca SET 464. Yvonne Minton (contralto), Los Angeles Master Chorale, Los Angeles Philharmonic Orchestra, Zubin Mehta.
(M) * (*) DGG Privilege 2538 343. Choir and Orchestra of Maggio Musicale Fiorento, Ettore Gracis.

Verdi's *Four Sacred pieces* form his very last work – or, to be precise, group of works. There are echoes of the great *Requiem*, and many of the ideas have a genuine Verdian originality, but in general they mark a falling-off after the supreme achievement of the last two Shakespeare operas, *Otello* and *Falstaff*. All the same, in a performance as polished and dramatic as the superlative one by Giulini and the Philharmonia Orchestra and Chorus, the element of greatness is magnified, and any Verdi lover should certainly make a point of hearing the disc.

The Mehta version has more brilliant, sharper-focused recording than Giulini's, but in every other way the earlier disc provides a deeper, more searching experience. At least as strikingly as in the *Requiem*, Verdi was seeking here to convey spiritual meaning, and Mehta remains too much on the surface, where Giulini has true intensity. Fine as Yvonne Minton's singing is here, Janet Baker's is even more moving.

The DGG Privilege version from Florence may have the advantage of Italian performers, but in every way the Philharmonia performance is preferable.

OPERA

Aïda (opera in 4 acts): complete recording.

*** Decca SXL 2167/9. Renata Tebaldi (soprano), Carlo Bergonzi (tenor), Giulietta Simionato (mezzo-soprano), Cornell MacNeil (baritone), Arnold van Mill, Fernando Corena (basses), Vienna Singverein, Vienna Philharmonic Orchestra, Herbert von Karajan.

*** Decca SET 427/9. Leontyne Price (soprano), Jon Vickers (tenor), Rita Gorr (mezzo-soprano), Robert Merrill (baritone), Giorgio Tozzi (bass), Rome Opera Chorus and Orchestra, Sir Georg Solti.

** (*) HMV SLS 977 (3 discs). Montserrat Caballé (soprano), Placido Domingo (tenor), Fiorenza Cossotto (mezzo-soprano), Nicolai Ghiaurov (bass), Royal Opera House, Covent Garden, Chorus, New Philharmonia Orchestra, Riccardo Muti.

(M) ** (*) RCA SER 5609/11. Leontyne Price (soprano), Placido

Domingo (tenor), Grace Bumbry (mezzo-soprano), Sherrill Milnes (baritone), Ruggero Raimondi (bass), John Alldis Choir, London Symphony Orchestra, Erich Leinsdorf.

The spectacular Decca set with Karajan and the Vienna Philharmonic has long stood unrivalled as a stereo version of this most stereophonic of operas. This is one of those almost ideal gramophone performances: the more you hear it the more satisfying it becomes, largely because it lays stress all the time on the musical values, if necessary at the expense of the dramatic ones. In this Karajan is of course helped by having a Viennese orchestra rather than an Italian one determined to do things in the 'traditional' manner. The chorus too is a very different thing from a normal Italian opera-house chorus, and the inner beauty of Verdi's choral writing at last manages to come out. But most important of all is the musicianship and musical teamwork of the soloists.

Bergonzi in particular emerges here as a model among tenors, with a rare feeling for the shaping of phrases and attention to detail. Cornell MacNeil too is splendid. Tebaldi's interpretation of the part of Aïda is well-known and much loved. Her creamy tone-colour rides beautifully over the phrases (what a wonderful vehicle for sheer singing this opera is), and she too acquires a new depth of imagination. Too dominant a characterization would not have fitted Karajan's total conception, but at times Tebaldi is too selfless. Vocally there are flaws too; notably at the end of *O patria mia*, where Tebaldi finds the cruelly exposed top notes too taxing. Among the other soloists Arnold van Mill and Fernando Corena are both superb, and Simionato provides one of the very finest portrayals of Amneris we have ever had in a complete *Aïda*. The recording has long been famous for its technical bravura and flair.

The control of atmosphere is phenomenal, changing as the scene changes, and some of the off-stage effects are strikingly effective in their microscopic clarity at a distance. Helped by Karajan, the recording team have, at the other end of the dynamic scale, managed to bring an altogether new clarity to the big ensembles, never achieved at the expense of tonal opulence. But – and it is an important but – the dynamic range between loud and soft is almost too great, and for the quiet passages not to sound too distant, giving a 'back of the gallery' effect, the big climaxes must be played at a very high level, perhaps too high a level for small rooms. But this is a comparatively small niggle when the technical achievement is so outstanding.

The earlier Price version, recorded by Decca in Rome for RCA, has been refurbished to fine effect, for it actually outshines the later Price version recorded at Walthamstow ten years later, in sound as in performance. Price is an outstandingly assured Aïda, rich, accurate and imaginative, while Solti's direction is superbly dramatic, notably in the Nile Scene. Anyone wanting a more expansive, contemplative view still has the option of Karajan, but this second Decca set is more clearly red-blooded in its Verdian commitment. Merrill is a richly secure Amonasro, Rita Gorr a characterful Amneris, and Jon Vickers is splendidly heroic as Radames. First-rate sound even by today's standards, although not as richly atmospheric as the outstanding Karajan/Culshaw set.

Caballé's portrait of the heroine is superb, full of detailed insight into the character and with countless examples of superlative singing. The set is worth having for her alone, and Cossotto makes a fine Amneris. Domingo produces glorious sound, but this is not one of his most imaginative recordings, while the Amonasro of Piero Cappuccilli is prosaic. So is much of Muti's direction – no swagger in the Triumphal Scene, unfeel-ing metrical rhythms in the Death Scene – and the recording, not quite boldly expansive enough, is a shade disappointing, not so vivid as the Decca sets of a decade and more earlier.

There is much to commend in Leontyne Price's 1971 recording of Aïda, and with a fine cast at less than full price it is a set worth considering. But it comes inevitably into direct comparison with Price's earlier set (still issued at full price) and by that standard it is a little disappointing. Price's voice is not so glowing as it was, and though there are moments where she shows added insight, it is the earlier performance which generates more electricity, has more dramatic urgency. Domingo makes a warm and stylish Radames, Milnes a strong if hardly electrifying Amonasro and Bumbry a superb imaginative Amneris. It is a pity that the recording, by the latest standards, does not capture the glamour of the score. Many of the earlier sets are more impressive in sound.

Aïda: highlights.
  *** Decca SXL 2242 (from above recording cond. Karajan).

For anyone choosing one of the other complete versions of *Aïda* this will be a splendid reminder of the musical and technical excellence of Karajan's set although not all its magnetism can be fully revealed in a set of excerpts, however generous and well managed.

Attila (opera in 3 acts): complete recording.
  *** Philips 6700 056 (2 discs). Ruggero Raimondi (bass), Cristina Deutekom (soprano), Carlo Bergonzi (tenor), Sherrill Milnes (baritone), Ambrosian Singers, Finchley Children's Music Group, Royal Philharmonic Orchestra, Lamberto Gardelli.

It is easy to criticize the music Verdi wrote during his 'years in the galleys', but a youthfully urgent work like this makes you marvel not at its musical unevenness but at the way Verdi consistently entertains you. The dramatic anticipations of *Macbeth*, with Attila himself far more than a simple villain, the musical anticipations of *Rigoletto*, the compression which on record if not on the stage becomes a positive merit – all these qualities, helped by a fine performance under Gardelli, make this an intensely enjoyable set. Deutekom, not the most sweet-toned of sopranos, has never sung better on record, and the rest of the cast is outstandingly good. First-rate recording.

Un Ballo in maschera (opera in 3 acts): complete recording.

(M) *** RCA Victor SER 5710/12. Leontyne Price, Reri Grist (sopranos), Shirley Verrett (mezzosoprano), Carlo Bergonzi (tenor), Robert Merrill (baritone), RCA Italiana Opera Chorus and Orchestra, Erich Leinsdorf.

** Decca SET 484/6. Renata Tebaldi, Helen Donath (sopranos), Regina Resnik (mezzo-soprano), Luciano Pavarotti (tenor), Sherrill Milnes (baritone), Chorus and Orchestra of St Cecilia Academy, Rome, Bruno Bartoletti.

On RCA an outstanding set not likely to be outshone for some time. All the principals are in splendid voice, and Leinsdorf's direction – too often inflexible in Italian opera – here has resilience as well as brilliance and urgency. Verdi peppers the score with the marking *con eleganza*, and that is exactly what Leinsdorf observes, giving elegance even to the obviously vulgar dance numbers of the final scene. Price is a natural for the part of Amelia, and with one notable reservation hers comes near to being a model

interpretation – exact in its observance of Verdi's detailed markings but spontaneous-sounding and full of dramatic temperament. Only in the two big arias does Price for a moment grow self-conscious, and there are one or two mannered phrases, overloaded with the wrong sort of expressiveness. Robert Merrill, sometimes thought of as an inexpressive singer, here seems to have acquired all sorts of dramatic Gobbi-like overtones to add to the flow of firm, satisfying tone. Bergonzi is a model of sensitivity, and the climax of the Act 2 love duet is one of the most satisfying moments in the whole opera. Reri Grist makes a light, bright Oscar, and the Ulrica of Shirley Verrett has a range of power, richness and delicacy coupled with unparalleled firmness that makes this one of her most memorable recorded performances. Excellent recording with the voices rather forward.

It is hard to assess Decca's latest set of *Ballo* dispassionately, if only because Tebaldi in her full maturity is a singer one so desperately wants to like. She radiates good will, and much of her singing is very fine indeed, but there is no mistaking that her voice is nowhere near as even as it once was. For the command of her performance this is a version well worth hearing, and the supporting cast is strong, but while the superb RCA version with Leontyne Price is available, this one can hardly be given first preference. The Decca recording quality is outstandingly vivid.

Un Ballo in maschera: highlights.

** Decca SET 538 (from above recording cond. Bartoletti).

The complete set from which these well-chosen excerpts are taken is seriously flawed. This disc can be recommended to those who want to sample the singing of Tebaldi, obviously past her prime but still strong and distinctive. Good recording.

Don Carlo (opera in 5 acts): complete recording.

(M) *** HMV SLS 956 (4 discs). Montserrat Caballé (soprano), Shirley Verrett (mezzo-soprano), Placido Domingo (tenor), Sherrill Milnes (baritone), Ruggero Raimondi (bass), Ambrosian Opera Chorus, Royal Opera House, Covent Garden, Orchestra, Carlo Maria Giulini.

*** Decca SET 305/8. Renata Tebaldi (soprano), Grace Bumbry (mezzo-soprano), Carlo Bergonzi (tenor), Dietrich Fischer-Dieskau (baritone), Nicolai Ghiaurov (bass), Chorus and Orchestra of Royal Opera House, Covent Garden, Sir Georg Solti.

Giulini was the conductor who in the Covent Garden production of 1958 demonstrated in the opera-house the supreme mastery of Verdi's score. Here he is conducting the same orchestra as Solti directed in the Decca version five years earlier, and predictably he is more flowing, more affectionate in his phrasing while conveying the quiet dramatic intensity which made his direction so irresistible in the opera-house. There is extra joy for example in the *Auto da fe* scene as it is pointed by Giulini, and even when his singer is less effective than his Decca rival (as with the King Philip, Raimondi against Ghiaurov) the direction of Giulini amply compensates. Generally the new cast is a little stronger than the old, but each is admirably consistent. The only major vocal disappointment among the principals lies in Caballé's account of the big aria *Tu che la vanità* in the final act. Like the Decca set this one uses the full five-act text. The recording, not quite so pinpointed in brilliance, is even more warmly atmospheric.

Unlike earlier 'complete' recordings, which used the four-act revision, the Decca version includes the important passages excised, notably the Fontainebleau scene, and that may underline the one major deficiency of the set, that the dramatic temperature fails to rise as it should until the duet between Philip and Rodrigo at the end of Act 2 (Act 1 in the four-act version). Till then Solti tends to be somewhat rigid, but once the right mood is established he does marvellously with his own Covent Garden forces, and the result in the *Auto da fe* scene is very fine. Tebaldi too in this most exacting Verdian role warms up well, and gives a magnificent account of *Tu che la vanità*. Bumbry and Bergonzi both sing splendidly, and after some rather gritty singing early on, Fischer-Dieskau rises fittingly to Rodrigo's great death scene, sounding almost (but not quite) as moving as Gobbi in the old HMV set (mono). Ghiaurov as Philip is obviously not so dramatic as Christoff was in both HMV and DGG sets, but the straighter approach brings a nobility, a sense of stoic pride, that is most compelling. The recording is of Decca's usual high standard, and though with such a marvellous array of talent one might feel the result should be still more overwhelming, there is no doubt that this version has a great deal to commend it.

Don Carlo: highlights.

** (*) HMV ASD 2823 (from above recording cond. Giulini).

** (*) Decca SET 353 (from above recording cond. Solti).

From so wide-ranging a score it is impossible to choose an entirely satisfactory sequence of excerpts. The HMV disc has the advantage over the Decca that Posa's death is included, though otherwise a direct comparison underlines the extra urgency of the singing in the Solti set.

Falstaff (opera in 4 acts): complete recording.

(M) *** Decca 2BB 104/6. Geraint Evans, Robert Merrill (baritones), Ilva Ligabue, Mirella Freni (sopranos), Rosalind Elias, Giulietta Simionato (mezzo-sopranos), Alfredo Kraus (tenor), RCA Italiana Opera Chorus and Orchestra, Sir Georg Solti.

*** CBS SET 3002 (3 discs). Dietrich Fischer-Dieskau, Rolando Panerai (baritones), Ilva Ligabue, Graziella Sciutti, Hilde Rössl-Majdan (sopranos), Regina Resnik (mezzo-soprano), Juan Oncina (tenor), Vienna State Opera Chorus, Vienna Philharmonic Orchestra, Leonard Bernstein.

The combination of Solti and Geraint Evans is irresistible. Their set, originally issued by RCA, comes up as sparkling as ever in this Decca reissue at a very modest price, and is arguably the best version on any count. Certainly there is an energy, a sense of fun, a sparkle that outshines rival versions, outstanding as they may be. Evans has never sounded better on record, and the rest of the cast admirably lives up to his example. Solti drives hard, and almost any comparison with the ancient Toscanini set will show his shortcomings, but it is still an exciting and well-pointed performance, the rest of the cast well contrasted.

The CBS set is based on a production at the Vienna State Opera, and the fleetness of execution in hair-raisingly fast speeds suggests that Bernstein was intent on out-Toscanini-ing Toscanini. The allegros may be consistently faster than Toscanini's, but they never sound rushed, and always Bernstein conveys a sense of fun, while in relaxed passages, helped by warm Viennese sensitivity, he allows a full rotundity of phrasing, at least as much so as any rival. It does not really matter, any more than it did in the Toscanini set, that the conductor is the

hero rather than Falstaff himself. Fischer-Dieskau does wonders in pointing the humour. In his scene with Mistress Quickly arranging an assignation with Alice, he can inflect a simple 'Ebben?' to make it intensely funny, but he finally suffers from having a voice one inevitably associates with baritonal solemnity, whether heroic or villainous. Just how noble Falstaff should seem is a matter for discussion. The others are first-rate – Rolando Panerai singing superbly as Ford, Ilva Ligabue (also the Alice of the Solti set), Regina Resnik as Mistress Quickly, and Graziella Sciutti and Juan Oncina as the young lovers. Excellent engineering by Decca.

Falstaff: highlights.

(M) ** Decca Ace of Diamonds SDD 429. Fernando Corena (bass), Regina Resnik (mezzo-soprano), Ilva Ligabue (soprano), Luigi Alva (tenor), New Symphony Orchestra of London, Edward Downes.

Compared with the complete recordings, this is an undistinguished offering, designed to show off Corena's assumption of the central role, which proves disappointing. Resnik and Alva sing well, and the playing and recording are first-rate.

La Forza del destino (opera in 4 acts): complete recording.

(M) ** (*) HMV SLS 948 (4 discs). Martina Arroyo (soprano), Carlo Bergonzi (tenor), Piero Cappuccilli, Geraint Evans (baritones), Ruggero Raimondi (bass), Ambrosian Opera Chorus, Royal Philharmonic Orchestra, Lamberto Gardelli.

(M) ** (*) Decca Ace of Diamonds GOS 597/9. Renata Tebaldi (soprano), Mario del Monaco (tenor), Fernando Corena, Ettore Bastianini (baritones), Cesare Siepi (bass), Chorus and Orchestra of St Cecilia Academy, Rome, Francesco Molinari-Pradelli.

Gardelli, normally a reliable recording conductor in Italian opera, here gives a disappointing account of a vividly dramatic score. The cast is vocally strong, and each member of it lives up to expectations, but it is vital in so long and episodic a work that overall dramatic control should be firm. Gardelli's contribution prevents this from being a definitive version, but in the absence from the catalogue – temporarily one hopes – of the Schippers set with Price, Tucker, Verrett and Merrill this is marginally the most recommendable version, partly because the recording quality is so much more modern than that of its current rival.

The Ace of Diamonds set, however, with Tebaldi on top form, offers formidable competition at its modest price, complete, yet now on three discs instead of the original four, with no loss in sound-quality; and the recording was outstanding for its time. Tebaldi, as always, makes some lovely sounds, and the *mezza voce* in the soaring theme (first heard in the overture) in *Madre, madre, pietosa Vergine* is exquisite. Mario del Monaco never really matches this. He sings straight through his part – often with the most heroic-sounding noises – with little attention to the finer points of shading that Verdi expects. That the whole performance does not add up to the sum of its parts, is largely the fault of the conductor, Molinari-Pradelli. He is exciting enough in the proper places but his control of ensemble is a marked weakness. Fortunately this deficiency in the conducting is not nearly enough to mar enjoyment of the performance. The brilliance and atmosphere of the recording add much to the listener's pleasure.

La Forza del destino: highlights.
(M) ** (*) Decca Ace of Diamonds SDD 292 (from above recording cond. Molinari-Pradelli).

Decca's early set seems indestructible. The mid-fifties stereo comes up remarkably well, and the performance – headed by Tebaldi at her most richly satisfying – still stands up well in its rich-toned directness. There may be comparatively few interpretative subtleties, but the dynamism of the score is conveyed. At this stage such highlights as this ought really to be appearing on a full bargain label rather than at mid-price.

Un Giorno di regno (King for a Day; opera in 2 acts): complete recording.
*** Philips 6703 055 (3 discs). Fiorenza Cossotto, Jessye Norman (sopranos), José Carreras (tenor), Ingvar Wixell, Vincenzo Sardinero, Wladimiro Ganzarolli (baritones), Ambrosian Singers, Royal Philharmonic Orchestra, Lamberto Gardelli.

This comic opera was Verdi's second work for the stage, and for almost 150 years it has been written off as a failure; but this superb, scintillating performance under Gardelli gives us a chance to make a complete reappraisal. It may not be the greatest comic opera of the period, but it clearly reveals the young Verdi as a potent rival even in this field to his immediate predecessors, Rossini and Donizetti. The Rossinian echoes are particularly infectious, though every number reveals that the young Verdi is more than an imitator, and there are striking passages which clearly give a foretaste of such numbers as the duet *Si vendetta* from *Rigoletto*. Despite the absurd plot (no sillier than is common) this is as light and frothy an entertainment as anyone could want. Excellent singing from a fine team, with Jessye Norman and José Carreras outstanding. Superb recording.

Giovanna d'Arco (opera in 3 acts): complete recording.

** (*) HMV SLS 967 (3 discs). Montserrat Caballé (soprano), Placido Domingo (tenor), Sherrill Milnes (baritone), Ambrosian Opera Chorus, London Symphony Orchestra, James Levine.

This seventh of Verdi's operas, based very loosely indeed on Schiller's drama, is an archetype of the works which the master was writing during his 'years in the galleys'. 'Melodic generosity and youthful resilience' are the qualities singled out by Charles Osborne in his study of Verdi operas, and the score certainly confirms that. The pity is that James Levine, a youthful whirlwind, does not understand the resilience more effectively. Though the ensemble is superb, he consistently presses too hard in fast music, with the rum-ti-tum hammered home. He is far more sympathetic in passages of 'melodic generosity', particularly when Caballé is singing. What has become a standard trio of principals for the seventies gives far more than a routine performance. With fine recording there is much to enjoy, even when the plot – whittled down to Joan, her father (who betrays her) and the King – is so naïve.

I Lombardi (opera in 4 acts): complete recording.

** (*) Philips 6703 032 (3 discs). Cristina Deutekom (soprano), Placido Domingo (tenor), Ruggero Raimondi (baritone), Ambrosian Singers, Royal Philharmonic Orchestra, Lamberto Gardelli.

I Lombardi, first produced in 1843, followed *Nabucco*, which had appeared

the year before, and it is good to welcome the first stereo recording of so virile an early opera. If you are looking for sophisticated perfection this is not the opera to sample, but the directness of Verdi's inspiration is in no doubt. The many choruses bring an expected quota of rum-ti-tum, but they also look to the future in the most fascinating way, foreshadowing *Ballo in maschera* and *Macbeth*. In the arias *Otello* is anticipated, with Pagano's evil Credo and the heroine Giselda's *Salve Maria*. The work reaches its apotheosis in the famous *Trio*, well-known from the days of 78 recordings. By those standards Cristina Deutekom is not an ideal Verdi singer. Her tone is sometimes hard and the voice is not always perfectly in control, yet there are some glorious moments too, and the phrasing is often impressive. Placido Domingo as Oronte is in superb voice, and the villain Pagano is well characterized by Raimondi. Among the supporting cast Stafford Dean and Clifford Grant must be mentioned, and Gardelli conducts dramatically. The recording is excellent, with plenty of atmosphere.

Luisa Miller (opera in 3 acts): complete recording.

(M) ** (*) RCA SER 5713/5. Anna Moffo (soprano), Shirley Verrett (mezzo-soprano), Carlo Bergonzi (tenor), Cornell MacNeil (baritone), Giorgio Tozzi (bass), RCA Italiana Opera Chorus and Orchestra, Fausto Cleva.

The Met. in New York had one of its most striking successes with this improbable opera (Montserrat Caballé in the name part), and though Verdi jogs along for much of the time, the big emotional moments prod him to characteristic heights of inspiration. For those alone the opera is worth hearing, and here – under one of the Met.'s regular conductors – it is strongly performed. Moffo makes a very sweet-toned Luisa, Bergonzi is most sensitive as the hero, and Shirley Verrett is magnificent as the Amneris-like rival. MacNeil and Tozzi are both in excellent voice, and the recording is well up to the best Rome standards.

Macbeth (opera in 4 acts): complete recording.

> ** (*) Decca SETB 510/2. Dietrich Fischer-Dieskau (baritone), Elena Suliotis (soprano), Luciano Pavarotti (tenor), Nicolai Ghiaurov (bass), Ambrosian Opera Chorus, London Philharmonic Orchestra, Lamberto Gardelli.

> (B) ** (*) RCA Victrola VICS 6121 (3 discs). Leonard Warren (baritone), Leonie Rysanek (soprano), Carlo Bergonzi (tenor), Jerome Hines (bass), Metropolitan Opera Chorus and Orchestra, Erich Leinsdorf.

Macbeth: abridged recording.

> * (*) Decca SET 282/4. Giuseppe Taddei (baritone), Birgit Nilsson (soprano), Bruno Prevedi (tenor), Giovanni Doiani (bass), Chorus and Orchestra of St Cecilia Academy, Rome, Thomas Schippers.

It is now a matter of history that when, at the very last minute, Gobbi was prevented from attending the London recording sessions of _Macbeth_, Decca had the great good fortune to persuade Fischer-Dieskau to take part instead. The German baritone does not give a traditional performance in this great tragic role, for characteristically he points the words in full Lieder-style. Nor is he in his freshest voice growing gritty in some climaxes; but it is still a marvellous, compelling performance which stands repeated hearing. Suliotis is – to put it kindly – a variable Lady Macbeth. There is none

of the security of Nilsson's singing on Decca's other set. In the first aria there are moments where Suliotis's voice runs completely out of control, but she still has imagination, and her 'voice of a she-devil' (Verdi's words) is arguably the precise sound needed. Certainly she settles down into giving a striking and individual performance, while Ghiaurov as Banquo and Pavarotti as Macduff sing with admirable poise. What makes this indispensable as a first choice for this opera is that the text is performed absolutely complete with all the very necessary rum-ti-tum choruses which Verdi wrote for the first version. Gardelli and the LPO are treated to spectacularly vivid recording.

Birgit Nilsson makes a fearsomely impressive Lady Macbeth, sounding like the devil of Verdi's imaginings but with glorious tone and spot on the note. It is her success and that of Taddei as Macbeth himself that make it all the more infuriating that Schippers was allowed to cut the score to shreds. With the bewildering variation between editions, it is always a difficult opera to get right textually, but there is no defending the absurd solution of whittling down the parts of the witches and the murderers until they virtually disappear. Their rum-ti-tum choruses may not be the greatest Verdi, but without that music the opera loses its balance, and the central tragedy is weakened by not being set in relief.

In any case Schippers's direction is on the whole less effective than that of Leinsdorf in the RCA Metropolitan set, which, with recording less brilliant than this but still splendidly atmospheric, has been reissued on Victrola and makes a fine bargain alternative to the Suliotis set. With a minimum of Italian singers in the cast, this is a fittingly large-scale performance, recorded within a large-scale acoustic, which is striking from the first bar of the Introduction. Rysanek, sometimes unpredictable, is here in fine voice, with powerful, rich, creamy sound soaring over the orchestra in the sleepwalking scene. She does of course find it rather hard to cope with the important coloratura passages, and in moments of extreme difficulty she lets out a few parrot-squawks, but these are comparatively small blemishes in so fittingly dramatic a performance. Leonard Warren, before his untimely death, was one of the pillars of any Met. production, and this recording shows him at his best. It is an intelligent performance and intelligence – a rare quality in tenors – also marks the performance of Carlo Bergonzi as Macduff, while the American bass, Jerome Hines, makes a fine Banquo. Leinsdorf has some moments of slackness – notably just before the sleepwalking scene – but generally he directs his performers with crisp, unmannered vitality.

Macbeth: highlights.
  *** Decca SET 539 (from above recording cond. Gardelli).
  ** Decca SET 409 (from above recording cond. Schippers).

Decca SET 539 offers a generous selection from a finely dramatic set, superbly recorded and flawed only by the variable singing of Suliotis. This is arguably Fischer-Dieskau's finest Verdi performance on récord. The alternative set is more uneven, but some will want a sample of the searingly intense singing of Birgit Nilsson in the role of Lady Macbeth, not a great performance, because Nilsson's deepest emotions rarely seem to be engaged, but certainly a formidable one. It is a joy to have her hitting each note so firmly and truly, and Giuseppe Taddei matches her with powerful singing in the role of Macbeth. Good recording.

Nabucco (opera in 4 acts): complete recording.
  ** (*) Decca SET 298/300. Tito Gobbi (baritone), Elena Suliotis (soprano), Carlo Cava (bass), Bruno Prevedi (tenor), Vienna State Opera Chorus and Orchestra, Lamberto Gardelli.

Nabucco was the first opera to show Verdi at full stretch and the one which set the seal on his popular success. Though the Viennese chorus here does not quite sing with the commitment one wants in this magnificently chorus-based work, the result is still dramatic, and it is especially welcome to have Gobbi as dramatic as ever in the title role of the Babylonian king. Elena Suliotis, a little wild still, is formidably impressive as the fire-eating Abigail – a most memorable performance – and Carlo Cava is adequate as the high priest Zaccaria, though one regrets that a bass with a richer, firmer voice was not chosen. This is still not the overwhelming experience that it could be, but with brilliant recording, no one – except perhaps the Welsh choral enthusiast – need hold back.

Nabucco: highlights.
  ** (*) Decca SET 367 (from above recording cond. Gardelli).

Suliotis's impressive contribution is well represented on this highlights disc, and that alone will be enough to attract those who simply want a sampler of this first of Verdi's successes. Fine contributions too – if not quite so firm as of old – by Tito Gobbi. Needless to say the great chorus *Va pensiero* is given its place of honour. First-rate recording.

Otello (opera in 4 acts): complete recording.
  ** (*) HMV SLS 975 (3 discs). Jon Vickers (tenor), Mirella Freni (soprano), Peter Glossop (baritone), Chorus of German Opera, Berlin, Berlin Philharmonic Orchestra, Herbert von Karajan.
  (M) ** (*) RCA SER 5646/8. Jon Vickers (tenor), Leonie Rysanek

(soprano), Tito Gobbi (baritone), Rome Opera Chorus and Orchestra, Tullio Serafin.

** (*) Decca SET 209/11. Mario del Monaco (tenor), Renata Tebaldi (soprano), Aldo Protti (baritone), Vienna State Opera Chorus, Vienna Grisstadtkinderchor, Vienna Philharmonic Orchestra, Herbert von Karajan.

(B) * (*) Decca Eclipse ECS 732/4. Mario del Monaco (tenor), Renata Tebaldi (soprano), Aldo Protti (baritone), Chorus and Orchestra of St Cecilia Academy, Rome, Alberto Erede.

A clear first recommendation for *Otello* is not easy to make, now that the superb Barbirolli set has been deleted. Both the Karajan sets are fine, of course, and the early Decca scores with its clear, vivid recording. But the RCA, reissued at medium price, is a strong competitor, with Gobbi superb as Iago and Leonie Rysanek extremely sympathetic as Desdemona. On the newest HMV set Karajan directs a big, bold and brilliant account, for the most part splendidly sung, and with all the dramatic contrasts (above all those in the orchestra) confidently underlined. There are occasional unimportant flaws in ensemble, uncharacteristic of Karajan (he was making a film version as well), but more seriously he makes several minor but irritating cuts. Freni's Desdemona is delightful, a delicate voice beautifully used. Both Vickers and Glossop give characterful performances, vocally uneven. Vickers sometimes forces his tone and Glossop too sounds ill-focused at times, though the bravura of both is hard to resist. Good resonant recording.

If only the two casts on the Decca and RCA set could have been combined. If Vickers and Gobbi had been in the Karajan Decca recording it could have

stood unchallenged for ever, or even if just Gobbi replaced the inadequate Protti. As it is, both sets are flawed. Karajan is much more dramatic in his conducting than Serafin. Often he even rivals Toscanini. This is a different Karajan from the one who directed the Decca *Aïda*. Restraint is no longer the keynote: drama rather. Once again, clarity of texture, helped by the recording and the precision of players and singers, will tell the discerning listener that this is not an Italian group, but it is still completely idiomatic. Tebaldi and Monaco give one of their finest gramophone performances, but Vickers, potentially at least the finest Otello in the world today, is excellent too and on many points of style he shows up Monaco. Protti is admittedly not nearly so inadequate as Iago as one expected. His performance on the older Decca set (now reissued on Eclipse) was not far short of pathetic, in the wrong sense, but here he is always reliable, if never imaginative and never sinister – and that is a drawback in an opera whose plot hinges on Iago's machinations. Gobbi on RCA is far superior, as dramatically imaginative as one would expect. But what may clinch things in favour of the Decca for some is the quality of the recording. The RCA is excellent (and the deleted Barbirolli set was finest of all) but the Decca is remarkable from the opening storm onwards (the pedal bass reinforced as Verdi asked by an organ note, this one brought all the way from Liverpool Cathedral!). The placing of the singers is astonishingly exact and a deliberate attempt has been made to vary the stage perspective between scenes.

Though Tebaldi's touching portrait of Desdemona is always worth hearing, and this is Mario del Monaco's most successful role, it is false economy to choose the Erede version on Decca Eclipse. While the Serafin set is offered at what in effect is mid-price, that is clearly the version for bargain-hunters to choose.

The mid-fifties Decca recording betrays its age.

Otello: highlights.

    ** (*) Decca SXL 2314 (from above Decca recording cond. Karajan).

A well-chosen collection from Decca's fine complete set. The recording remains outstanding in the new transfers.

Rigoletto (opera in 3 acts): complete recording.

    *** Decca SET 542/4. Joan Sutherland (soprano), Sherrill Milnes (baritone), Luciano Pavarotti (tenor), Martti Talvela (bass), Huguette Tourangeau (mezzo-soprano), Ambrosian Opera Chorus, London Symphony Orchestra, Richard Bonynge.

    (M) ** (*) Decca Ace of Diamonds GOS 655/7. Joan Sutherland (soprano), Cornell MacNeil (baritone), Renato Cioni (tenor), Cesare Siepi (bass), Chorus and Orchestra of St Cecilia Academy, Rome, Nino Sanzogno.

    * (*) DGG 2709 014 (3 discs). Renata Scotto (soprano), Dietrich Fischer-Dieskau (baritone), Carlo Bergonzi (tenor), Ivo Vinco (bass), Fiorenza Cossotto (mezzo-soprano), Chorus and Orchestra of La Scala, Milan, Rafael Kubelik.

    * (*) HMV SLS 933 (3 discs). Reri Grist (soprano), Cornell MacNeil (baritone), Nicolai Gedda (tenor), Agostino Ferrin (bass), Anna di Stasio (mezzo-soprano), Rome Opera Chorus and Orchestra, Francesco Molinari-Pradelli.

Just over ten years after her first recording of this opera Sutherland appeared in it again, and the set was far more than a dutiful remake. Richard Bonynge from the very start shows his feeling for resilient rhythms, and the result is fresh and dramatic, underlining the revolutionary qualities in the score which nowadays we tend to ignore. Pavarotti too is an intensely characterful Duke: an unmistakable rogue but an unmistakable charmer too. Thanks to him and to Bonynge above all, the *Quartet* for once on a complete set becomes a genuine musical climax. Sutherland's voice has acquired a hint of a beat, but there is little of the mooning manner which disfigured her earlier assumption, and the result is glowingly beautiful as well as supremely assured technically. Milnes is a strong Rigoletto, vocally masterful and with good if hardly searching presentation of character. Urgently enjoyable, with good atmospheric recording.

The earlier Sutherland recording, now available on Ace of Diamonds as an alternative, represents her soft grained style at its most extreme. The result is often intensely beautiful, particularly in *Caro nome*, but as a dramatic experience it is not so vivid as the later set. Nino Sanzogno jogs through everything very neatly, but it is the technical quality of the recording and the reliability of the singing that engage the attention, rather than the drama. Excellent value nevertheless.

Reaction to the DGG set will depend very much on reaction to Fischer-Dieskau's singing of the name part. There is no denying the care and sensitivity with which he approaches the music, and almost every phrase has the nicety of Lieder-singing, but the end result is oddly unconvincing and mannered. It is partly that Fischer-Dieskau's voice is just too young-sounding here for the old jester: you cannot quite believe in him as a grief-stricken father. Bergonzi's Duke is beautifully sung, but the Gilda of Renata Scotto is disappointing. On this showing the engineers seem to find it impossible to capture the special tangy quality which has made her stage appearances so attractive: instead the sound has the throaty 'little-girl' quality one associates with some pre-electric records of sopranos. Kubelik's conducting is frankly dull and the set can only be recommended to those who must hear Fischer-Dieskau as Rigoletto.

There is very little to praise in the newest HMV set. The recording is vivid, it is true, but that only serves to show up the poorly-disciplined orchestral playing. Gedda has some good moments, even if his voice is not always shown at its sweetest, but he gives a strong dramatic lead, and because of this the *Quartet* is one of the few highlights. MacNeil is not a very dominant Rigoletto, and here he has no Sutherland to compensate; Reri Grist's Gilda is lightweight, without any real charm. What this set lacks is 'star quality', which is surely an essential in the earlier Verdi masterpieces.

Rigoletto: highlights.
   *** Decca SET 580 (from above recording cond. Bonynge).

An excellent selection from an outstanding set.

Simon Boccanegra (opera in Prologue and 3 acts): complete recording.
   ** RCA SER 5696/8. Piero Cappuccilli (baritone), Ruggero Raimondi (bass), Gian Piero Mastromei (baritone), Maurizio Mazzieri (bass), Katia Ricciarelli (soprano), Placido Domingo (tenor), RCA Italiana Opera Chorus and Orchestra, Gianandrea Gavazzeni.

Except for the singing of Placido Domingo as the hero – almost an incidental role in this strangely constructed plot – this first stereo recording of *Simon Boccanegra* is disappointing. As stage productions have repeatedly demonstrated, this opera can make a formidable dramatic effect, but the production here

gives the impression of singers lined up in front of a microphone, and Gavazzeni's often rushed direction is unimaginative. But beside Domingo – the ripeness of the middle voice gloriously caught – there are firm performances from Cappuccilli and Raimondi (paling of course in comparison with Gobbi and Christoff on an ancient mono set) and an appealing performance from Katia Ricciarelli, marred by ugly portamenti. As a stopgap this is fair enough, but a masterpiece like this, containing in the Council Chamber Scene one of Verdi's supreme inspirations, deserves more. Unatmospheric recording.

La Traviata (opera in 3 acts): complete recording.
   ** (*) Decca SET 249/51. Joan Sutherland (soprano), Carlo Bergonzi (tenor), Robert Merrill (baritone), Chorus and Orchestra of Maggio Musicale Fiorentino, John Pritchard.
   (M) ** (*) RCA SER 5564/6. Montserrat Caballé (soprano), Carlo Bergonzi (tenor), Sherrill Milnes (baritone), RCA Italiana Opera Chorus and Orchestra, Georges Prêtre.
   (B) ** (*) RCA Victrola VICS 6111 (3 discs). Anna Moffo (soprano), Richard Tucker (tenor), Robert Merrill (baritone), Rome Opera Chorus and Orchestra, Fernando Previtali.
   (M) ** (*) HMV SLS 960 (3 discs). Beverly Sills (soprano), Nicolai Gedda (tenor), Rolando Panerai (baritone), John Alldis Choir, Royal Philharmonic Orchestra, Aldo Ceccato.
   ** Decca SET 401/2. Pilar Lorengar (soprano), Giacomo Aragall (tenor), Dietrich Fischer-Dieskau

(baritone), German Opera, Berlin, Chorus and Orchestra, Lorin Maazel.

(B) * (*) Decca Eclipse ECS 726/8. Renata Tebaldi (soprano), Gianni Poggi (tenor), Aldo Protti (baritone), Chorus and Orchestra of St Cecilia Academy, Rome, Francesco Molinari-Pradelli.

Opinions on Sutherland's Violetta are sharply divided, and this characteristic performance from her will not win over her determined critics. It is true that her diction is poor, but it is also true that she has rarely sung with such deep feeling on record as in the final scene. The *Addio del passato* (both stanzas included and sung with an unexpected lilt) merely provides a beginning, for the duet with Bergonzi is most winning and the final death scene, *Se una pudica vergine*, is overwhelmingly beautiful. This is not a sparkling Violetta, true, but it is more perfect vocally than almost any other in a complete set. Bergonzi is an attractive Alfredo and Merrill an efficient Germont. Pritchard sometimes tends to hustle things along, with too little regard for shaping Verdian phrases, but the recording quality is outstandingly good.

Caballé too gives a wonderfully poised and pure account of Violetta's music, but this was one of her earlier complete opera sets, and she still had to learn how to project depth of emotion. Vocally, with such fine technicians as Bergonzi and Milnes as her colleagues, this set is consistently satisfying, but it does not add up as a dramatic experience. One is rarely moved, and that is partly the fault too of the conductor, Georges Prêtre, a degree too detached for Verdi. Good recording and an absolutely complete text (as also in the Sutherland version).

Anna Moffo makes a most beautiful Violetta in a performance that is never less than sympathetic. She is not as assured as she might be in the coloratura of Act 1,

but everywhere else her unaffected manner and care for phrasing and tonal nuances make for a performance to match any in the catalogue at whatever price. Richard Tucker too makes a strong and on the whole not coarse Alfredo, and though Merrill is not so understanding a Germont here as he was in the Sutherland set, the casting is more consistent than in most full-priced versions. The conducting of Previtali could be more colourful, and the usual performing cuts are made, but at Victrola price this is highly recommendable.

Beverly Sills makes an affecting Violetta, tenderly beautiful, with poised legato in *Dite alla giovine*, and producing much lovely singing elsewhere too. But when the voice is pressed, it grows shrill and unfocused. The character of an older woman knowing what suffering is to come remains firm, however, and with a fine Alfredo in Gedda, managing a genuine half-tone of delight at the start of *De' miei bollenti spiriti*, this is a serious contender among current *Traviata* sets. Ceccato proves an alert and colourful director, and the Royal Philharmonic plays well for him, though the recording is almost too vividly realistic. Its reverberation brings home far too clearly the recording venue in a South London church. Panerai is a strong-voiced Germont, showing less imagination than one expects from him. Like the Sutherland and Caballé sets, this is complete down to the repetitions of cabalettas normally omitted entirely.

The Maazel set, though squeezed on to only four sides, is more complete in its text than such three-disc versions as Previtali's on Victrola. Though second verses of arias are excluded (always the practice in the opera-house), Alfredo's cabaletta after *De' miei bollenti spiriti* and Germont's after *Di Provenza* are both included at least once round, which is rare enough. As to the performance, much will depend on the listener's reaction to Lorengar's voice. Her interpretation is most affecting, deeply felt and expressively presented, but the vibrato is often instrusive to the point where the tone-colour is seriously marred. That will not worry all ears, and in any case with Fischer-Dieskau a searchingly intense Germont (if hardly an elderly-sounding one) and Aragall making impressive trumpet-sounds as Alfredo, this is a strong cast. Maazel's conducting is characteristically forceful. At first he may seem over-forceful, as though attempting to out-Toscanini Toscanini, but once he settles down after the first party music, his reading is both intelligent and sensitive. The recording quality is excellent, unaffected by the very long sides.

On Eclipse, with a clumsy Alfredo in Poggi and a boring Germont in Protti, one is left simply with the often affecting Violetta of Tebaldi – clumsy too in the coloratura of Act 1 but warmly imaginative later. Good recording considering its early experimental stereo origins.

La Traviata: highlights.
   *** Decca SXL 6127 (from above recording cond. Pritchard).
   ** (*) RCA SB 6779 (from above recording cond. Prêtre).
   ** Decca SET 483 (from above recording cond. Maazel).

A good selection from the Sutherland set, but by some sleight of hand only one stanza is given in the *Addio del passato*.

The RCA highlights disc from a complete set that is satisfying vocally but dramatically variable may prove the answer for those who simply want to sample the wizardry of Caballé. A fair selection and good recording.

Just as the complete Maazel set is squeezed on to a mere four sides, so Decca have squeezed more than is common in *Traviata* highlights records on to two. Excellent recording.

Il Trovatore (opera in 4 acts): complete recording.

(M) ⊕ *** RCA SER 5586/8. Leontyne Price (soprano), Placido Domingo (tenor), Sherrill Milnes (baritone), Fiorenza Cossotto (mezzo-soprano), Ambrosian Opera Chorus, New Philharmonia Orchestra, Zubin Mehta.

Caruso once said of *Il Trovatore* that all it needs are 'the four greatest singers in the world'. Abounding as the opera does in great and memorable tunes, the orchestration is comparatively primitive (which is why it is so effective in such a blood-and-thunder narrative), often like a kind of orchestral guitar. The support for the voices is a framework only, a dramatic framework, to be sure, but it covers up nothing. The singers alone have to create the necessary breadth and beauty of tone, and the proper dramatic projection. That is not to say the conductor is not important: red-blooded conducting is vital; but he can do nothing unless his singers have a true feeling for the Verdi melodic contour. This is why *Trovatore* is difficult to bring off in the opera-house, and even more so on record. Of the earlier sets only the Callas/Karajan can match the RCA set in overall excellence. The soaring curve of Price's rich vocal line (almost too ample for some ears) is immediately thrilling in her famous first-act aria, and it sets the style of the performance, full-blooded, the tension consistently held at the highest levels. The choral contribution is superb; the famous *Soldiers'* and *Anvil choruses* are marvellously fresh and dramatic, and this is more than a little due to the conductor's obvious commitment. When *Di quella pira* comes, the orchestra opens with tremendous gusto and Domingo sings with a ringing, heroic quality worthy of Caruso himself (if not Tamagno). There are many dramatic felicities, and Sherrill Milnes is in fine voice throughout, but perhaps the highlight of the set is the opening section of Act 3 when Azucena finds her way to Conte di Luna's camp.

1053

The ensuing scene, with Fiorenza Cossotto vocally and dramatically quite electrifying, is one of the most thrilling in all recorded Verdi. For I.M. this is favourite among Verdi opera recordings (although Barbirolli's *Otello*, alas deleted, and Karajan's *Aïda* run it close). The recording is rich and atmospheric.

Il Trovatore: highlights.
** HMV ASD 2395. Gabriella Tucci (soprano), Franco Corelli (tenor), Robert Merrill (baritone), Giulietta Simionato (mezzo-soprano), Rome Opera Chorus and Orchestra, Thomas Schippers.

With a text and translation included, a good selection of numbers and first-rate stereo, this potted version of *Trovatore* makes a fair enough introduction to the opera for anyone not too exacting in his vocal demands. But hearing the big arias 'cold' without the preparation of the complete performance does underline the shortcomings, and Merrill's Conte di Luna, firmly sung, is made to seem rather ungainly. Nor is Simionato's *Stride la vampa* as effective as one would expect from that fine singer. Schippers's conducting, inclined to be rigid, rather prevents the temperature from rising, and one is almost grateful for the crude histrionics of Corelli in *Di quella pira*. Tucci sings very beautifully, if with a hint of flutter, but hers is still not a very positive performance. Excellent, vivid recording quality.

I Vespri siciliani (opera in 5 acts): complete recording.
** (*) RCA ARL 4 0370 (4 discs). Martina Arroyo (soprano), Placido Domingo (tenor), Sherrill Milnes (baritone), Ruggero Raimondi (bass), John Alldis Choir, New Philharmonia Orchestra, James Levine.

This opera, epic in scale to please the Parisian audiences for whom it was written, is a transitional piece, following the firmly confident middle-period Verdi of *Rigoletto*, *Trovatore* and *Traviata*, but not quite achieving the dramatic intensity and musical richness of later operas. The work's great merit is not so much its grandeur as its searching portrayal of the father–son relationship between Monforte, the tyrannical governor of Sicily, and Arrigo, the son he has never known. Their Act 2 duet, using a melody well known from the overture, is nothing short of magnificent, with Domingo and Milnes at their very peak. The rest of the singing is good if rarely inspired, and though Levine's direction is colourful and urgent, such a score needs more persuasiveness. Good recording.

COLLECTIONS

Choruses: *Aïda: Triumphal march and ballet music. Attila: Urli rapine. La Battaglia di Legnano: Giuriam d'Italia. I Lombardi: O Signore dal tetto natio. Nabucco: Gli arredi festivi; Va pensiero. Otello: Fuoco di gloria. Il Trovatore: Vedi! le fosche; Squilli, echeggi.*
*** Decca SXL 6139. Chorus and Orchestra of St Cecilia Academy, Rome, Carlo Franci.

This is an extraordinarily brilliant disc, and one wonders if the engineers have artificially brightened the sound. Both choral and orchestral sound have a bite in the treble which, for some ears, needs taming. But in other respects the sound is resplendent. The performances are vivid, with a willingness to sing softly and indeed sometimes a degree of refinement in the approach surprising in an Italian chorus. The *I Lombardi* excerpts at the end of side one are especially appealing, but all the little-known items come up freshly. The trumpets in the *Aïda*

Triumphal Scene get the full stereo treatment.

'Heroines': Arias: *Aïda: Ritorna vincitor; O patria mia. Un Ballo in maschera: Ecco l'orrido campo; Ma dall'arido stelo divulsa; Morrò, ma prima in grazia. Ernani: Surta è la notte; Ernani, involami. La Forza del destino: Me pellegrina ed orfana; Son giunta!; Madre, pietosa Vergine; Il santo nome di Dio; La Vergine degli angeli; Pace, pace, mio Dio. Macbeth:* Sleepwalking scene. *Otello: Era più calmo; Willow song; Ave Maria. La Traviata: Teneste la promessa; Addio del passato. Il Trovatore: Che più t'arresti; Tacea la notte placida; D'amor sull'ali rosee.*

(M) *** RCA DPS 2001 A/B (2 discs). Leontyne Price (soprano), various artists.

This two-disc recital, offered at less than full price, provides a fine survey of the achievement of one of the really great Verdi sopranos of today, maybe the greatest. The items are taken from various sources, complete operas as well as earlier recitals. Not all of Miss Price's characterizations are equally vivid (Lady Macbeth is plainly not one of her best parts) but vocally the performances are amazingly consistent. The recording quality varies with the source, but not too distractingly.

Arias: *Aïda: Ritorna vincitor; Qui Radames verrà . . . O patria mia. La Forza del destino: La Vergine degli angeli; Pace, pace, mio Dio. Macbeth:* Sleepwalking scene. *Otello: Willow song; Ave Maria.*

* (**) HMV ASD 2787. Montserrat Caballé (soprano), Royal Philharmonic Orchestra, Anton Guadagno.

Caballé's Verdi recital offers singing of great tonal beauty. Indeed her control of line and phrase is often ravishing, and the voice has a breadth and boldness to satisfy the most demanding Verdian. Yet the singing in the last resort is strangely unmoving. One feels no personal commitment to the roles: the drama all lies on the surface of the music. In *O patria mia*, for instance, she conveys no poignancy, no sense of Aïda's longing for her homeland; in the *Willow song* and *Ave Maria*, she places every note exquisitely, yet one has no feeling of Desdemona's trepidation. Here, as in *La Vergine degli angeli* from *Forza*, there is a surprising lack of emotional intensity in her pleas to the Virgin Mary. In the latter piece she is not helped by the conductor, Anton Guadagno, who soups up the choral backing with exaggerated dynamics. Throughout his accompaniments are beautifully made (and the RPO playing is often gorgeous) but his care for perfection of detail misses the essentially red-blooded quality of the underlying drama. One must emphasize again how much there is to admire in this recital, but Verdi's music cannot fully communicate on vocal beauty alone.

Arias: *Aïda: Ritorna vincitor. La Forza del destino: Madre, pietosa Vergine. Giovanna d'Arco: O fatidica foresta. I Masnadieri: Dall'infame . . . Tu del mio Carlo. Otello: Willow song; Ave Maria. Simon Boccanegra: Come in quest'ora. I Vespri siciliani: Marcè, diletti.*

*** Decca SXL 6605. Maria Chiara (soprano), John Alldis Choir, Royal Opera House, Covent Garden, Orchestra, Nello Santi.

The natural creamy beauty of Maria Chiara's voice, used intelligently in an imaginatively chosen sequence of arias, some of them rare, makes for a wonderfully enjoyable disc. Chiara's intonation in the *Otello* is not quite above suspicion, but it is rare that a voice can caress the ear so seductively. Particularly fine is Joan of Arc's Cavatina. In many ways this is the finest available single-disc recital of Verdi arias. With singing often of ravishing quality and with excellent recording, this fine collection matches Chiara's outstanding earlier miscellaneous recital disc (SXL 6548), discussed in our *Treasury* volume and worthy of a rosette.

Arias: *Alzira: Da Gusman su fragil barca. Aroldo: Ah! dagli scanni eterei. Attila: Oh! nel fuggente nuvolo. Il Corsaro: Non so le tetre immagini. I Due Foscari: Tu al cui sguardo. Un Giorno di regno: Grave a core innamorato. I Lombardi: Non fu sogno!*
*** RCA SB 6748. Montserrat Caballé (soprano), RCA Italiana Opera Orchestra, Anton Guadagno.

These 'Verdi rarities', taken from operas of the early years, make up a commandingly brilliant disc when sung with such assurance as by Caballé. She is here at her finest, challenged by the technical difficulties as well as the need to convey the drama. She makes one forget that in between the big memorable tunes there are often less-than-inspired passages. Fine accompaniment and first-rate recording.

Arias: *Attila: Santo di patria . . . Allor che . . . Da te questo. Ernani: Surta è la notte . . . Ernani, involami. Luisa Miller: Lo speri invano . . . Tu puniscimi. I Masnadieri: Dall'infame . . . Tu del mio Carlo. Rigoletto: Caro nome. La Traviata: E strano . . . Ah, fors'è lui . . . Sempre libera; Addio del passato. I Vespri siciliani: Marcè, diletti.*
*** Decca SXL 6190. Joan Sutherland (soprano), various artists.

It was shrewd of Decca to reshuffle some of Sutherland's available records

under the headings of various composers. This Verdi disc runs parallel with a comparable Bellini recital, and the choice is generally good. It is specially welcome to have the arias from *I Masnadieri, Luisa Miller* and *Attila*, all showing Sutherland at her best, and the preference of recital version over complete-set version in *Caro nome* and vice versa in *Ah fors'è lui* is on the whole justifiable. The varied recording qualities are quite well matched.

Arias: *Un Ballo in maschera: Ecco l'orrido; La Forza del destino: Pace, pace, mio Dio.*
* (*) Decca SET 343/4. Elena Suliotis (soprano), Rome Opera Chorus and Orchestra, Silvio Varviso – MASCAGNI: *Cavalleria Rusticana* ** (also PONCHIELLI: *Aria*).

Suliotis, though an exciting singer, has a technique that lets her down in the recording studio, where the microphone tends to exaggerate faults normally ignored in the thrill of the moment. If anything even more than in the Mascagni opera with which these arias are coupled, Suliotis fails to surmount Verdi's technical challenge, and the result is often rather sour. But the personality is still strong and vivid, and the recording is very good indeed.

Arias: *Il Corsaro: Egli non riede ancora! Don Carlo: Non piangere. Giovanna d'Arco: O fatidica foresta. I Lombardi: Ave Maria. I Masnadieri: Dall'infame . . . Tu del mio Carlo. Otello: Ave Maria. Il Trovatore: Timor di me? . . . D'amor sull'ali rosee; Tu vedrai che amore. I Vespri siciliani: Arrigo! Ah parli.*
** (*) RCA SB 6863. Katia Ricciarelli (soprano), Rome Philharmonic Orchestra, Gianandrea Gavazzeni.

In her first record Katia Ricciarelli, newly enthroned as the toast of Italy, chose a formidably demanding sequence of arias. It is remarkable that so rich and characterful a voice can cope so effortlessly with florid divisions; but next to the great singers who have already put these arias on record, there are clear signs of immaturity. Well worth hearing nonetheless. This singer obviously has flair and that is worth a lot. The voice is balanced too close.

Arias: *Ernani: Surta è la notte* ... *Ernani, involami. I Vespri siciliani: Marcè, diletti.*

> (M) *** Decca Ace of Diamonds SDD 146. Joan Sutherland (soprano), Paris Conservatoire Orchestra, Nello Santi – DONIZETTI: *Linda di Chamounix; Lucia: arias.*⊛ ***

If it is primarily for the Donizetti items that this magnificent recital is famous, these two Verdi arias show a comparable level of memorability, with superb singing throughout.

'Great scenes': Macbeth: Chi v'impose unirvi a noi? . . . Come dal ciel precipita. Nabucco: Gli arredi festivi . . . Sperate, o figli!; Va pensiero . . . Oh chi piange? I Vespri siciliani: O patria . . . O tu, Palermo. Simon Boccanegra: A te l'estremo addio . . . Il lacerato spirito.

> *** Decca SXL 6443. Nicolai Ghiaurov (bass), Ambrosian Singers, London Symphony Orchestra, Claudio Abbado.

These substantial items make an impressive recital, the more so when *Nabucco* is so generously represented. These are not simply arias taken out of context as in the days of 78, but big solos placed in context, and Ghiaurov, always a thoughtful singer, produces marvellous tone and stylish phrasing. Excellent accompaniment and outstanding recording quality.

Victoria, Tomás Luis de (*c.* 1548–1611)

Motets: *Ascendens Christus; Ave Maria; Gaudent in coelis; O Magnum mysterium. Requiem Mass* (sex vocibus).

> * (*) Argo ZRG 570. St John's College, Cambridge, Choir, George Guest.

In spite of the great music featured on this disc, it does not really display the composer's inimitable genius in the way that, for instance, some of George Malcolm's performances do. The St John's Choir sing well in tune, but their whole approach is too 'Anglican' for this passionate Spanish music. The choirboys sound too flabby in tone (especially in the very dull singing of the plainchant), while the men have big vibratos, and these two elements never really mix. The motets fare slightly better than the *Requiem*, but this is not really a disc that can be recommended unreservedly.

Ave Maria (motet); *Jesu dolcis memoria* (hymn); *Magnificat primi toni; Anima mea; Lauda Sion Salvatorum* (sequence).

> (M) *** Oiseau-Lyre SOL 283. Choir of the Carmelite Priory, London, John McCarthy – PALESTRINA: *Collection.****

This outstandingly beautiful disc is discussed under its coupling.

Estote fortes in bello (motet); *Hic vir despiciens mundum* (motet); *Iste sanc-*

tus pro lege Dei (motet); *Litaniae de Beata Virgine; Magnificat primi toni; O quam gloriosum est regnum* (motet and mass); *Veni sponsa Christi* (motet).

   *** Argo ZRG 620. St John's College, Cambridge, Choir, George Guest.

These motets must be numbered among the finest Victoria gave us. The performances are admirably done, and if one accepts the fact that English choirs lack the harsh lines drawn by the firmer-toned Spanish bodies, there is little at which one can cavil. Indeed one is tempted to suggest that this is probably the best record currently available for a collector who wants to sample this composer or this period, and it forms a useful starting point for any library. The recording is clear and well-focused.

Choral music for Holy Week: *Lamentations of Jeremiah; Benedictus; Improperia: Popule meus; O Domine Jesu Christe* (motet); *Pueri Hebraeorum* (antiphon); *Tantum ergo* (motet); *Vere languores nostros* (motet).

   (M) *** Pye Virtuoso TPLS 13007. Scuola di Chiesa, John Hoban.

This admirably planned record gathers together some of Victoria's settings for Holy Week, for which the great Spanish composer created some of his most deeply felt music. The harmonic basis seems deceptively simple (the *Improperia* is a glorious example), yet there is a sense of internal tension in the writing which is often achingly beautiful. Where there is a polyphonic overlay, the answering voices seem to melt into each other with total liquidity of form. This is perfectly captured not only by the wonderful singing on this record and the conductor's feeling for tempo and line, but also by the recording, which achieves a perfect ecclesiastical acoustic in which Victoria's melismas can float, yet does not muffle

the words. This is one of the finest choral records in the catalogue.

Masses and motets: *O quam gloriosum; O magnum mysterium.*

   (M) *** Oiseau-Lyre SOL 270. Mary Thomas (soprano), Jean Allister (contralto), Edgar Fleet (tenor), Christopher Keyte (bass), Choir of the Carmelite Priory, London, John McCarthy.

These are exceptionally fine performances and they are made the more attractive by this ideal recorded presentation, which couples the motet which is musically connected with each mass. The recording is equally outstanding and the microphone placing has been well calculated to the acoustic so that, while the part-writing can be heard clearly, the overall blend is tonally beautiful.

Tenebrae responsories for Holy Week (complete).

   (B) *** Argo Eclipse ECS 747. Westminster Cathedral Choir, George Malcolm.

   (M) *** Pye Virtuoso TPLS 13015. Scuola di Chiesa, John Hoban.

The *Tenebrae responsories* are so called because of the tradition of performing them in the evening in increasing darkness as the candles were extinguished one by one. The music here offers Victoria's settings for Maundy Thursday, Good Friday and Holy Saturday. The three sections between them tell the story of the Crucifixion from Judas's betrayal through to the burial of Jesus. Victoria's magnificent but austere music finds this choir at their best; indeed the record is even more successful than their account of the *Lamentations of Jeremiah* (see above). Admittedly this singing is very different from the kind one encounters in Spain itself but given this absence of harshness and the necessarily dark mood of the music itself, this cannot fail to give satisfaction. The recording has the same finely judged acoustic and atmosphere as the companion disc.

The Argo Eclipse reissue dates from 1960, a period when the Westminster Cathedral Choir under George Malcolm was at its peak. The performance has fine vigour and eloquence, and the recording is excellent. At bargain price this is on balance preferable to the Virtuoso disc, particularly as the Decca pressings are of high quality and free from background interference.

Villa-Lobos, Heitor
(1887–1959)

Bachianas Brasileiras No. 1: excerpt: *Modinha. Uirapurú.*
(M) ** Everest SDBR 3016. New York Stadium Orchestra, Leopold Stokowski – PROKOFIEV: *Cinderella.***

Uirapurú, which takes up the greater part of this side, was the first important orchestral work that Villa-Lobos wrote. The ambitious young composer was determined to rival even the heaviest competition in sheer brilliance of orchestration, using in this programme piece based on a Brazilian folktale an amazing range of percussion instruments. It is just the sort of music to inspire the old magician Stokowski, and he responds with a fine performance, beautifully recorded. *Modinha* is well done too, if with Stokowski's habitual layer of emotion. The Prokofiev coupling is not very apt, but attractive enough.

Bachianas Brasileiras No. 2: The Little Train of the Caipira.
(M) ** Everest SDBR 3041. London Symphony Orchestra, Sir Eugene

Goossens – GINASTERA: *Estancia.***

The Little Train was the result of a journey Villa-Lobos made in Sao Paolo, Brazil, in 1931. The orchestration is imitative, but like Lumbye's *Copenhagen Steam Railway* galop the descriptive writing has considerable melodic charm. The local colour is provided by the use of Latin percussive effects. Excellent performance and recording.

Bachianas Brasileiras: No. 2 (includes *The Little Train of the Caipira*); (i) *No. 5* (for soprano and 8 cellos); *No. 6* (for flute and bassoon); *No. 9.*
** (*) HMV ASD 2994. Orchestre de Paris, Paul Capolongo, (i) with Mady Mesplé (soprano).

A good selection of Villa-Lobos's most colourful (and most popular) works, vigorously directed and well recorded. Mady Mesplé's very French timbre does not ideally suit the lovely *Bachianas Brasileiras No. 5.*

Bachianas Brasileiras: No. 2: The Little Train of the Caipira; (i) *No. 4: Prelude (Introduction); No. 5* (arr. for orchestra); *Magdalena* (musical play): *suite; Modinha preludio.*
(M) * (*) CBS Classics 61564. Orchestra, André Kostelanetz, (i) with André Kostelanetz (piano).

Kostelanetz's treatment of Villa-Lobos underlines the sweetness, and the coarse recording goes further in turning these pieces into pop numbers, not least the *Suite* from *Magdalena* – eight genre pieces like Hollywood film-music of the forties, with church-bell effects and surging violins. The melody of the *Bachianas Brasileiras No. 5* becomes sickly when transferred from voice to strings.

Guitar concerto.
*** CBS 76369. John Williams (guitar), English Chamber Orchestra, Daniel Barenboim – RODRIGO: Concierto de Aranjuez.***

The invention of this Concerto is rather thin, but John Williams's compulsive performance makes the very most of its finer points and especially the rhapsodic quality of the Andantino. The CBS recording is bright and fresh, the guitar recorded characteristically close. The coupling is perhaps the finest available account of Rodrigo's famous Concierto de Aranjuez.

(i) Guitar concerto. Étude in C sharp minor; Preludes Nos. 1 in E minor; 2 in E major; 3 in A minor; 4 in E minor; 5 in D major; Suite populaire brasilienne: Schottisch-Chôro.
** (*) RCA SB 6852. Julian Bream (guitar), (i) with London Symphony Orchestra, André Previn.

Julian Bream is well supported by Previn, although the orchestral contribution is designed by the composer to be comparatively discreet. Bream plays with his usual subtlety and the recording, although rather forward, is otherwise first-rate. The Concerto is short – it does not take up a whole side – and the rest of the programme is more likely to appeal to the guitar enthusiast than the ordinary collector. Even so, several of the Preludes are hauntingly memorable, especially when the concentration of the playing is so readily communicated.

12 Études for guitar; 5 Preludes for guitar.
*** DGG 2530 140. Narciso Yepes (guitar).

Ideal late-night listening, with marvellously aristocratic playing, excellently recorded. Some of the Preludes have a dark intensity quite different from Julian Bream's, though in their way no less poetic. Yepes's technique is impeccable and there is a total absence of fingerboard squeaks, thanks to this and a judicious balance. At times in the Études (not all of which are of equal interest) he sounds a little detached, almost prosaic. But this reservation, which applies to only a handful of the studies, should not prevent recommendation of playing of such distinction and artistry.

5 Preludes for guitar.
** (*) CBS 73350. John Williams (guitar) – GOWERS: Rhapsody.** (*)

The excellent John Williams is very much in the foreground here, for the CBS engineers do not much favour a natural concert-hall acoustic. Apart from the balance, which must be laid firmly at the door of the engineers, these are as perfect and as finely turned as any performances in the catalogue, and readers should allow themselves to follow their own personal allegiances here between Bream, Yepes and John Williams.

Piano pieces: As tres Marias; Bachianas Brasileiras No. 4: Preludio; Prole do bêbe (The Child's Doll) (suite); Rudepoêma.
*** Telefunken SAT 22547. Nelson Freire (piano).

Excellent playing and eminently satisfactory recording of some delightfully colourful piano music, not otherwise represented in the current catalogue.

Viotti, Giovanni
(1755–1824)

Piano concerto in G minor.
(B) ** Turnabout TV 34284S. Felicja
    Blumenthal (piano), Torino Orch-
    estra, Alberto Zedda – PLATTI:
    *Piano concerto No. 1.***

Viotti is best known for his violin
concertos, but this keyboard concerto is
an ambitious piece, spreading to one and
a half LP sides. The first movement is
pleasantly fluent but without really
memorable thematic material. The *Adagio*
is rather more expressive, and the best
movement is the comparatively long final
rondo, which has an attractive flowing
principal tune. The performance here is
smiling and competent, and the recording is one of the best of this enterprising
Vox series.

(i) *Double concerto for piano, violin and
strings in A major; Violin concerto No.
22 in A minor.*
(B) ** Turnabout TV 34229S. Sus-
    anne Lautenbacher (violin), Ber-
    lin Symphony Orchestra, C. A.
    Bünte, (i) with Martin Galling
    (piano).

The most striking of the *Violin concerto*'s three movements is the finale, with
its repeated triplet figure. The *Adagio*
is gracious enough, and the first movement has a pleasant second subject, but it
seems the ideal sort of work to show off
the virtuosity of a soloist and then be
forgotten. It is certainly well played here.
The *Double concerto* is hardly more
memorable, although it has an attractive
galant flavour in the central rondo. The
recording is acceptable, with a touch of
the characteristic Vox astringent quality.

Vivaldi, Antonio
(1675–1741)

L'Estro armonico (12 concertos), *Op.
3*: complete recording.
*** Argo ZRG 733/4. Christopher
    Hogwood, Colin Tilney (harpsi-
    chords and organ), Robert Spen-
    cer (chitarrone), Academy of St
    Martin-in-the-Fields, Neville Mar-
    riner.
(M) ** Vanguard HM 37SD (3 discs).
    Vienna State Opera Chamber Or-
    chestra, Mario Rossi.

As so often, Marriner directs the
Academy in radiant and imaginative performances of baroque music and yet
observes scholarly good manners. The
delightful use of continuo – lute and
organ as well as harpsichord – the sharing
of solo honours, and the consistently
resilient string-playing of the ensemble
make for compelling listening. The
recording is immaculate, with no
deterioration on long sides. Fitting the
twelve concertos on to four sides is a
positive not merely an economic advantage, since the composer groups them in
effect in four sets of three.

Rossi and the Chamber Orchestra of
the Vienna State Opera offer larger-scale
performances, less sprightly but still
stylish. However, the use of three records
instead of two minimizes the economy
of a medium-priced issue. Also the works
are mislabelled: the records are auto-
coupled (sides one and six on the first
disc) but the labels imply a straightforward manual sequence.

*L'Estro armonico: Violin concerto in A
minor, Op. 3/6.*
** (*) Philips 6500 119. Arthur
    Grumiaux (violin), New Philhar-
    monia Orchestra, Edo de Waart –
    BACH: *Double concertos.** (*)

This, the shortest of the three works on this disc, is split between the two sides. It is a concerto notable for a slow movement as heavenly as anything the composer wrote. The playing is warmly expressive and the recording finely balanced.

L'Estro armonico: (i) *Double violin concerto in A minor, Op. 3/8;* (ii) *Double violin concerto in A major (Echo concerto), P.222.*

> (M) *** DGG Privilege 135082. (i) David and Igor Oistrakh (violins), Royal Philharmonic Orchestra; (ii) Soloists, Lucerne Festival Strings, Rudolf Baumgartner – BACH: *Double concertos.*** (*)

L'Estro armonico: Double violin concerto in A minor, Op. 3/8.

> (M) *** DGG Privilege 2726 008 (same performance as above) – BACH and BRAHMS: *Double concertos;* BEETHOVEN: *Triple concerto.*** (*)

The *Double concerto in A minor* (one of the finest of *L'Estro armonico*) sounds splendidly fresh here in this delightfully planned disc of baroque double concertos. The recording too is smoother than in the Bach couplings, while in the *Echo concerto* it is very fine indeed. Here stereo and a cleverly managed reverberant acoustic re-create the novelty which must have intrigued Vivaldi's original audiences. The performance is excellent, and the work not too long to outlast its originality of conception. The *A minor Concerto* is also available in a two-disc anthology.

L'Estro armonico: Violin concertos Nos. 10 in B minor; 11 in D minor.

> (M) ** Decca Ace of Diamonds SDD 417. Moscow Chamber Orchestra, Rudolf Barshai – BARTÓK: *Divertimento.****

The playing of the Moscow Chamber Orchestra is fresh and brilliant (technically it is impeccable), but the lift is sometimes achieved at the expense of limpidity and warmth of phrasing. The bright recording is admirably clear and lets the harpsichord continuo through adequately.

La Stravaganza (12 violin concertos), *Op. 4*: complete recording.

> ⊛ *** Argo ZRG 800/1. Carmel Kaine, Alan Loveday (violins), Academy of St Martin-in-the-Fields, Neville Marriner; Christopher Hogwood, Colin Tilney (harpsichord and organ), Robert Spencer, Anthony Rooley, James Tyler (theorbos).

It has been held that, like *La Cetra*, the invention of *La Stravaganza* does not match that of *L'Estro armonico*, but if the quality of the earlier concertos of the set does not always show Vivaldi at his very best, from about halfway (i.e. from No. 6 onwards) one is constantly astonished at the music's vitality. Even earlier, in the finale of No. 3, or the poetic slow movement of No. 4, Vivaldi provides some marvellously imaginative music, but the later works have a consistency and show the composer at his most enticing. Marriner's performances make the music irresistible. The solo playing of Carmel Kaine and Alan Loveday is superb, and when the Academy's rhythms have such splendid buoyancy and lift it is easy enough to accept Marriner's preference for a relatively sweet style in the often heavenly slow movements. The recording is of the highest quality and as usual the contribution of an imaginatively varied continuo (which includes cello and bassoon in addition to the instruments credited) adds much to the colour of Vivaldi's score. Very highly recommended.

Trial between Harmony and Invention (12 violin concertos), *Op. 8*: complete recording.

** (*) CBS 78225 (3 discs). Pinchas Zukerman (violin), Neil Black (oboe), English Chamber Orchestra.

The first four concertos of Op. 8 are a set within a set, forming what is (deservedly) Vivaldi's most popular work, *The Four Seasons*. Their imaginative force and their eloquence and tunefulness tend to dwarf the remaining eight concertos, but there is some splendid music throughout the complete work, well worth exploring. CBS have squeezed *Spring*, *Summer* and *Autumn* on to the first side, making room on side two for Nos. 5 and 6 besides *Winter*; in this way the whole set has been accommodated on two LPs with no apparent loss of quality. Zukerman's solo playing is distinguished throughout, and the ECO provide unfailingly alert and resilient accompaniments. In *Concerto No. 9 in D minor* Neil Black (oboe) takes the solo position and provides a welcome contrast of timbre. Vivaldi designated this concerto as optionally for violin or oboe but it probably sounds more effective on the wind instrument. The recording throughout is lively, with close balance for the soloists. The sound is attractive but perhaps marginally too bright to be completely natural.

The Four Seasons, Op. 8/1–4 (from *Trial between Harmony and Invention*).

⊛ *** Argo ZRG 654. Alan Loveday (violin), Academy of St Martin-in-the-Fields, Neville Marriner.

(M) *** Philips Universo 6580 002. Henryk Szeryng (violin), English Chamber Orchestra.

*** DGG 2530 296. Michel Schwalbé (violin), Berlin Philharmonic Orchestra, Herbert von Karajan.

*** Decca SXL 6557. Konstanty Kulka (violin), Stuttgart Chamber Orchestra, Karl Münchinger.

** (*) Philips 6500 017. Roberto Michelucci (violin), I Musici.

** (*) CBS Quadraphonic MQ31798; Stereo 73097. Pinchas Zukerman (violin), English Chamber Orchestra.

(B) ** (*) Classics for Pleasure CFP 40016. Kenneth Sillito (violin), Virtuosi of England, Arthur Davison.

(B) * (**) RCA Victrola VICS 1469. Salvatore Accardo (violin), Italian Orchestra da Camera.

(B) ** Decca SPA 201. Werner Krotzinger (violin), Stuttgart Chamber Orchestra, Karl Münchinger.

(B) ** Turnabout TV 34040S. Susanne Lautenbacher (violin), Württemberg Chamber Orchestra, Joerg Faerber.

The Four Seasons, Op. 8/1–4; L'Estro armonico: Violin concerto in D minor, Op. 3/11.

(M) ** (*) DGG Privilege 135024. Wolfgang Schneiderhan (violin), Lucerne Festival Strings, Rudolf Baumgartner.

The Academy of St Martin's gives a magical performance of Vivaldi's four most frequently heard concertos, with an element of fantasy that makes the music sound utterly new. The continuo, for example (beautifully played by Simon Preston), uses a wide variety of tone-colour, and for the slow movement of *Winter*, with its pizzicato accompaniment under a rich violin arioso, Preston switches to the organ and avoids confusion of texture. The opulence of string tone – helped by the acoustic of St John's, Smith Square, where the recording was made – will be too romantic for some, but there is no self-indulgence in this interpretation, no sentimentality, for the contrasts are made sharper and fresher, not smoothed over. The rustic dance which ends *Spring*, for example, has rarely if ever sounded so light and pointed. A demonstration disc.

The Universo makes a fine middle-priced recommendation, and the only reservation is that the very soft-grained tone of the harpsichord in the continuo does not come through to the listener readily. But Szeryng's performances are eloquent and beautifully played, and the alert, resilient accompaniments are stylish. The sound is atmospheric, naturally balanced (although the violin is forward) and pleasingly resonant. Perhaps there is a degree too much reverberation, but the chamber proportions of the performance are retained.

Michel Schwalbé is a truly memorable soloist. His playing is neat, precise and wonderfully musical, with a touch of Italian sunshine in the tone. His sparkling playing is set against radiant Berlin Philharmonic string textures, and the engineers appear to have damped down the bass end of the audio spectrum to prevent too cushioned a sound. The tonal beauty of Karajan's conception is not achieved at the expense of vitality, and although the harpsichord hardly comes through, the overall scale is acceptable. Not a conventional account, then, but very rewarding of its kind.

Münchinger and the Stuttgart Chamber Orchestra, whose early LPs did so much to reawaken interest in Vivaldi, here show that their stylish and lively manner is as compelling as ever, helped by vivid recording. Though this is plainer than many versions, it stands as one of the most satisfying.

I Musici must have played this work countless times and probably find it more difficult than most groups to bring freshness to each new recording. Here Roberto Michelucci is a first-class soloist, displaying bursts of bravura in the outer movements but often musingly thought-

ful in the slower ones. His expressiveness is finely judged, and the group are naturally balanced with the harpsichord coming through in the right way, without exaggeration. The last degree of spontaneity is sometimes missing, but this is an enjoyable disc.

Schneiderhan's fine performance is very competitive at medium price, especially as, because of fast tempi, it is the only version that can make room for a bonus. The snag is the recorded quality, which is somewhat insubstantial and lacking in bass. Otherwise it is clean and clear. Surprisingly the bass returns in the bonus item (which indeed sounds a little plummy in tone), and then one is made aware what was missing in the *Seasons*.

Zukerman's performances come from his complete set (see above). The playing brings out all the drama, and although its expressive qualities are in no doubt and the slow movements offer thoughtful, often searching playing, this is not as imaginative as Marriner's disc. The acoustic has a faintly hollow resonance, and the quadraphonic disc emphasizes this, adding marginal extra atmosphere, although with forward balance of the soloists.

An enjoyable forthright performance from Arthur Davison and the Virtuosi of England, marked by assured violin-playing from Sillito. The soloist is balanced too far forward, which detracts from gentler expressiveness, but otherwise the sound is vivid and firm.

The RCA recording has an excess of fizzy, high treble, which is a great pity for it is potentially the finest bargain version. The solo playing is vital and the soloist's tone has the proper gleaming sparkle. Salvatore Accardo is an excellent player and an individual one. There are some minor distortions of tempi (in the solo passage towards the end of the first concerto, for instance), but they are spontaneously done and this is a comparatively small blemish, if blemish it is. The accompanying chamber orchestra are alert and they miss none of the incidental points of Vivaldi's score: the barking dog effect (in the slow movement of No. 1) is nicely managed.

Münchinger was the first to bring out the *Four Seasons* and his justly famous mono disc is still available, a distinguished Eclipse record (ECS 506) with Barchet a first-class soloist. The playing has more sparkle and imagination, although the sound has less body, than in the early stereo remake with Krotzinger. This is a straightforward, rather Germanic account, somewhat phlegmatic in the familiar Münchinger way. The recording is good, though the treble is somewhat over-bright. Münchinger's more recent record with Kulka is a great improvement on this and well worth the extra money, on recording grounds alone.

Lautenbacher plays with assurance and fine tone. She is beautifully recorded and this is certainly enjoyable, if it misses the Italianate fire of the Victrola record in the same price-range.

La Cetra (12 violin concertos), *Op. 9*: complete recording.
  ** (*) Philips 6703 012 (3 discs). Felix Ayo (violin), I Musici.

Even if *La Cetra* is not as richly inventive as the Op. 3 set, it nonetheless offers some magnificent and rewarding music during its course, and it would be difficult to find more persuasive or characterful accounts. Felix Ayo and I Musici play with tremendous spirit and full-blooded tone, and the recording is both opulent in tone and well-balanced. Readers should sample the fine *Concerto No. 3 in G minor*, and their enthusiasm will be ignited. One drawback: the solo passages are given no continuo support, though there is an organ continuo for the ripieno concertino sections.

Concertos for two orchestras: *Concerto in C major in due Cori; Concerto in B*

flat major in due Cori (con violino scordato); *Concerto in A major in due Cori* (con flauti obligati); *Concerto in D major in due Cori.*
  ** (*) Telefunken SAWT 9600. Les Solistes de Bruxelles (1st orchestra), I Solisti di Milano (2nd orchestra).

These works are the very epitome of the baroque tradition, and they were probably written for performance in the San Marco Basilica, where the architectural design not only allowed antiphonal choral and vocal groups but even provided a pair of organs to go with them. In this recording the continuo is happily contrasted, with a harpsichord for one orchestra and an organ for the other. All four works are attractively inventive. The opening of the *A major Concerto* where the organ answers the flutes is delightful, and the finale of the *D major* is memorable in its harmonic richness. Excellent performances, but a rather dry acoustic. These performances were originally issued on HMV mid-priced label. The Telefunken replacement does not sound quite so sweet in tone and costs much more, but it remains a valuable issue. In some copies the channels on side two are reversed.

Flute concertos, Op. 10, Nos 1 in F major (La Tempesta di mare), P.261; 2 in G minor (La Notte), P.342; 3 in D major (Il Cardellino), P.155; 4 in G major, P.104; 5 in F major, P.262; 6 in G major, P.105.
  *** Philips SAL 3705. Severino Gazzelloni (flute), I Musici.
  (B) * (*) Turnabout TV 34023S. Jean-Pierre Rampal (flute), Robert Veyron-Lacroix (harpsichord continuo), Louis de Froment Chamber Ensemble.

A recital of flute concertos is a rather daunting prospect in the ordinary course of events, but Gazzelloni is an artist of such quality and poetry that any doubts are banished. And it must be added that these concertos show Vivaldi in the best light. *La Notte* is little short of a masterpiece by any standards. Gazzelloni's tone is admirably fresh and clean, and I Musici give him splendid support. An outstanding disc in every way.

Jean-Pierre Rampal plays well but the recording of his accompanying ensemble is dry and rather meagre, with the continuo (an imaginative one, as it happens) also recorded too close to the microphones. The Philips disc is the one to have.

Flute concertos in A minor, P.80; in G major, P.140; in D major, P.203; in D major, P.205; Concerto for flute, with bassoon, in G minor (La Notte), Op. 10/2, P. 342.

** (*) Philips 6500 707. Severino Gazzelloni (flute), I Musici.

With five flute concertos in a row this may not be a record to play all at once; but Gazzelloni's playing is masterly, the accompaniments have splendid life and detail, and the balance and quality of the recording are of the highest order. The bassoonist (Jiri Staviček) offers a welcome change of colour in *La Notte*, although he has not a great deal to contribute. A fine disc of its kind, but not as attractive as some other collections where the instrumentation is more varied.

Guitar concertos in A major; in D major, P.209.

** (*) CBS 72798. John Williams (guitar), English Chamber Orchestra; Colin Tilney (harpsichord) – GIULIANI: *Guitar concerto.****

These are delightful and pleasing works played with predictable liveliness and artistry. They are not helped by a balance that places the soloist too far forward and

the sound is a bit unnatural and overnourished.

Guitar concerto in D major, P.209; Double concerto in D minor for lute and viola d'amore, P.266.

(B) ** Pye GSGC 14041. Herman Leeb (guitar or lute), Rosemary Green (viola d'amore), Anglian Ensemble, John Snashall – PERGOLESI: *Violin concerto etc.****

This record looks more attractive than it is, for the musical material of which the D minor work is constructed is seldom memorable. There are few flashes of the imaginative Vivaldi, and mostly it is the novelty of timbre which is left to make the contrasts possible with two such diverse soloists. Both performances here are good; the recording puts the soloists rather close.

Double horn concerto in F major, P.320.

(B) ** Turnabout TV 34078S. Alois Spach, Gottfried Roth (horns), Mainz Chamber Orchestra, Günter Kehr – ROSETTI: *Concerto*; TELEMANN: *Suite.*****

The *Double horn concerto* is characteristic, with an imaginative and very striking finale. It receives here an excellent performance and good recording.

Lute concerto in D major, P.209.

** RCA SB 6635. Julian Bream (lute), Julian Bream Consort – BRITTEN: *Courtly Dances ***; RODRIGO: *Concerto.** (*)

This is not one of Vivaldi's most memorable concertos, but it is brilliantly played. The actual arrangement and the close placing of the small chamber group give the music-making a curiously modern sound.

*Double mandolin concerto in G major,
P.133; Mandolin concerto in C major,
P.134; Lute concerto in D major, P.209;
Trio in G minor for violin, lute and
continuo.*

> (B) ** Turnabout TV 34153S. Paul
> Grund, Artur Rumentsch (man-
> dolins), Anton Stingl (lute), Ru-
> dolf Breitschmid (violin), Würt-
> temberg Chamber Orchestra,
> Joerg Faerber.

A lively, bright-toned collection of
music for lute and mandolin. Vivaldi's
invention is not always at its most
imaginative here, but the diverse effects
of timbre and the lively playing and
recording make a good effect. The
accompaniment is stylish and the recording has a sense of space, although the
soloists are placed well forward. An
enjoyable disc, but not to be taken all at
once.

*Oboe concertos in D minor; in A
minor.*

> (B) ** Classics for Pleasure CFP 163.
> Sidney Sutcliffe (oboe), Virtuosi
> of England, Arthur Davison –
> ALBINONI: *Oboe concertos.***

As with the coupling, these performances are admirably alive and sensitive
to matters of style. The disc is most
enjoyable, but a little more unbending
from the participants, especially in the
slow movements, would have made it
even more beguiling.

*Concertos for strings: in D minor
(Madrigalesco), P.86; in G major
(Alla rustica), P.143; Violin concertos:
in D major (L'Inquietudine), P.208; in
E major (L'Amoroso), P.246; Double
violin concerto in A major, P.28;
Sinfonia in B minor (Al Santo Sepol-
cro), P.21.*

> ** (*) DGG 2530 094. Soloists,

Berlin Philharmonic Orchestra,
Herbert von Karajan.

Karajan relaxes with members of his
Berlin orchestra far away from the city
on an annual working holiday. The relaxation and enjoyment, coupled with extraordinary refinement of execution, make
this a record which stands out among
most Vivaldi offerings, but there is an
element of self-indulgence in Karajan's
interpretations which makes the result
too sweet for frequent repetition, quite
apart from scholarly considerations of
style. Refined recording to match the
performances, which include four
memorable nicknamed concertos. The
Sinfonia is an amazing piece, considering
the date of composition.

*Concertos for strings: in A major, P.235;
in G major (Alla rustica), P.143;
Double violin concerto in B flat major,
P.390; Triple violin concerto in F
major, P.278; Double violoncello concerto in G minor, P.411; Sinfonia in B
minor (Al Santo Sepolcro), P.21.*

> *** Decca SXL 6628. Lucerne Festi-
> val Strings, Rudolf Baumgartner.

Although these works are well represented in the catalogue, readers coming
fresh to Vivaldi could do worse than
attack this disc. The playing is splendidly
alert and vigorous, and the overall
impression is enormously fresh. Baumgartner is not always the most sensitive
of conductors, but the Lucerne orchestra
play well for him on this occasion and
they are admirably recorded.

*Violin concertos: in E minor (Il
Favorito), P.106; in D major (L'In-
quietudine), P.208; in E major
(L'Amoroso), P.246; in E major (Il
Riposo), P.248; in C minor (Il Sos-
petto), P.419.*

> (M) *** Philips Universo 6580 007.
> I Musici.

The original full-priced stereo issue missed out *Il Favorito* (although it was present on the mono equivalent). Here it is restored, and at the same time the price is reduced. The lyrical fervour of I Musici is heard at its most attractive in this fine collection, and all the works show Vivaldi on top form. With warm yet not undetailed recording, this can be highly recommended.

Violin concertos: in A minor, Op. 9/5, P.10; in E minor (Il Favorito), P.106; in E major (L'Amoroso), P.246; in G minor, Op. 12/1, P.343.

⊛ *** Philips 6500 690. Arthur Grumiaux (violin), Dresden State Orchestra, Vittorio Negri.

Absolutely marvellous playing here, wonderfully poised and aristocratic yet illuminated in every bar by Grumiaux's imaginative feeling for what are four of Vivaldi's finest concertos. The accompaniment too has splendid life and vigour and is most sympathetic to Grumiaux's expressive, unmannered way with the slow movements. With first-class sound this is one of the most desirable of all Vivaldi collections.

Double violin concertos: in A minor, P.2; in D minor, P.250; Triple violin concerto in F major, P.278; Concerto in B minor for 4 violins, Op. 3/10.

*** CBS Quadraphonic MQ 32230; Stereo 73201. Kenneth Sillito, José-Luis Garcia, John Tunnell (violins), English Chamber Orchestra, dir. Pinchas Zukerman (violin); Philip Ledger (harpsichord).

Zukerman, directing as well as leading the soloists, presents a delightful coupling of multiple concertos, stylishly performed, with fine contributions from Philip Ledger as continuo player – what you can hear of him. The recording is very forward and the quadraphonic version,

which provides some very beautiful sound, is unable to give a natural relationship between soloists and orchestra because of this artificial balance. But the ear quickly adjusts and this is a highly desirable collection.

MISCELLANEOUS COLLECTIONS

Bassoon concerto in A minor, P.70; Concerto in C major for 2 oboes and 2 clarinets, P.73; Concerto in G major for oboe and bassoon, P.129; Oboe concerto in C major, P.41.

(B) * (*) Turnabout TV 34025S. Soloists, Gli Accademici di Milano.

There is some attractive music here. The concerto for two oboes and two clarinets is charming and anticipates the Handel of the *Arrival of the Queen of Sheba*; the oboe concerto is also attractive and nicely played. The oboe and bassoon concerto has a gay first movement, but the recording (variable throughout) is rather subfusc for the somewhat lugubrious bassoon concerto. In general the quick movements come off best: the slow movements plod a little, with an unimaginatively realized continuo.

Bassoon concerto in E minor, P.137; Double oboe concerto, P.302; Concerto for oboe and bassoon, P.129; Piccolo concerto in A minor, P.83.

(M) ** Supraphon SUAST 50967. Soloists, Ars Rediviva Orchestra, Milan Munclinger.

An excellent companion for Munclinger's other disc of wind concertos (see below), if perhaps the music itself is not quite so winning. But performances and recording are both good.

Bassoon concerto in G minor, P.342; Flute concerto in G minor (La Notte),

Op. 10/2; Double mandolin concerto in G major, P.133; Concerto in A major for strings, P.235; Violin concerto in C major (for violin, strings a due cori, and 2 harpsichords), *P.14.*

(M) ** (*) Vanguard HM 16SD. Julius Baker (flute), Rudolf Klepac (bassoon), soloists, I Solisti di Zagreb, Antonio Janigro.

There are some marvellous works here; in fact the disc could well be addressed to the collector tired of Vivaldi for one leaves it refreshed and with one's enthusiasm rekindled. *La Notte* is superb and so too is the *G minor Bassoon concerto.* The performances are good, and although the recording is not of the most recent provenance it is perfectly acceptable.

Flute concerto in G minor (La Notte), Op. 10/2; Mandolin concerto in C major, P.134; Double mandolin concerto in G major, P.133; Recorder concerto in C major, P.78; Concerto in B minor for 4 violins, Op. 3/10.

(M) *** HMV SXLP 30144. Soloists, Toulouse Chamber Orchestra, Louis Auriacombe.

A lively clutch of six very agreeable concertos (those for mandolin being piquant in timbre rather than memorable in invention), vividly played and excellently recorded. Several of the works here are available in at least one other collection, but this anthology makes a rather satisfying whole, diverse in colour and substance.

Concertos in C major and G minor for flute, oboe, violin and bassoon; Concerto in G minor for flute, violin and cello; Concerto in F major for flute, oboe and violin; Concerto in G minor for flute and oboe.

(M) *** Supraphon SUAST 50671. Ars Rediviva Ensemble, Milan Munclinger.

This fine collection is expertly played and beautifully recorded. It shows Vivaldi at his most imaginative in his feeling for the blend and contrast of wind colours. The *Concerto in C major for flute, oboe, violin and bassoon* offers some delicious sounds, and this disc as a whole abounds in sprightly rhythms. There is no lack of melodic charm, and the sad little *Largo cantabile* of the *F major Concerto* and the *Largo* of the *G minor* (*for flute, violin and cello*) are both delightful.

Concerto in C major for 2 flutes, 2 salmò, 2 violins 'in tromba marina', 2 mandolins, 2 theorbos, cello and strings, P.16; Mandolin concerto in C major, P.134; Double mandolin concerto in G major, P.133; Concerto in D minor for viola d'amore and guitar, P.266; Concerto for 2 violins and guitar, P.209.

** DGG 2530 211. Soloists, Paul Kuentz Chamber Orchestra.

An intimate programme, for late-evening listening, with a mellow recording to match. The *Mandolin concertos* are beautifully recorded, the miniature sound of the solo mandolins truthfully captured, the duet concerto having a gentle charm. P.266 and P.209 were intended for the lute rather than the guitar, but Yepes is persuasive here, particularly in the slow movements. The concertante work, P.16, rounds off the programme effectively. A pleasant rather than a distinctive concert.

Concerto in F major for flute, oboe and bassoon (La Tempesta di mare), Op. 10/1, P.261; Double horn concertos: in F major, P.320; in F major, P.321; Concerto in C major for 2 oboes and 2 clarinets, P.74; Concerto in G minor for violin, 2 flutes, 2 oboes and 2 bassoons, P.383.

(*) DGG Archive 2533 044. Soloists, Munich Chamber Orchestra, Hans Stadlmair.

If you fancy a collection of Vivaldi's wind concertos, this well planned disc would be hard to beat. The piquant sounds of the *G minor Concerto* are delightful, and it is a pity that the recording has a slight edge on it here. But throughout the rest of the disc it is of best Archive standard, as is the playing. Indeed the performance of the *Concerto for two horns*, P.321, is masterly, wonderfully confident and assured. Here Vivaldi keeps his soloists on tip-toes, even in the slow movement, whereas in the other *Double horn concerto* he gives them a rest in the gracious *Largo*. But the outer movements are ingeniously contrived out of open-note arpeggios and scalic devices. The effect is brilliant, and the robust style of the playing brings a smile of pleasure. The *Tempesta di mare concerto* again shows the composer in highly imaginative form, and the solo playing is splendid, bursting with life and colour.

Sopranino recorder concertos: in C major, P.78; in A minor, P.83; Concerto in D minor for viola d'amore and lute, P.266; Viola d'amore concerto in D minor.

(B) ** Turnabout TV 34009S. Soloists, Württemberg Chamber Orchestra, Joerg Faerber.

An enjoyable collection of Vivaldi concertos, featuring two bright little works for piccolo, in which Hans-Martin Linde proves an admirable soloist. The less robust sounds of lute and viola d'amore offer a complete contrast to the piccolo, and both these *D minor Concertos* are attractive. The chamber orchestra, like the soloists, is well recorded.

Double concertos: in B flat major for 2 violins, P.365; in F major for violin and and organ, P.274; in G minor for 2 violoncellos, P.411. Concertos for strings: in E minor, P.127; in A major, P.235; in G minor, P.394.

*** Philips 6500 322. I Musici.

These are all admirably inventive pieces and the performances have great sparkle and *élan*. The disc would make an excellent introduction to Vivaldi's work outside the famous *L'Estro armonico*, and the recording has excellent perspective and sonority.

CHAMBER MUSIC

6 Sonatas (Il Pastor fido), Op. 13.

*** DGG Archive 2533 117. Hans-Martin Linde (flute and recorder), Eduard Melkus (violin), Alfred Sous (oboe), René Zosso (hurdy-gurdy), Garo Atmacayan (cello), Walter Stiftner (bassoon), Huguette Dreyfus (harpsichord).

A much more persuasive account of *Il Pastor fido* than any previous rival. Played like this, in such lively and radiant performances, the music is quite captivating. Strongly recommended.

VOCAL MUSIC

Al Santo Sepulcro: Sinfonia and Sonata; (i) 2 Introductions for the Miserere; Stabat Mater.

*** Telefunken SAWT 9590. I Solisti di Milano, Angelo Ephrikian, (i) with Aafje Heynis (contralto).

A superbly played and recorded disc that opens more doors into the range and scope of Vivaldi's imaginative genius. All this music was written for Lenten performance and the *Sinfonia and Sonata*

'At the Holy Sepulchre' show a much more searching expressiveness than is normally found in the concertos. The comparatively concise *Stabat Mater* too shows the composer's powers at full stretch with an eloquent setting for contralto with strings. It was written for female voice, and Aafje Heynis sings it with just the right degree of restraint yet no lack of expressive feeling. The *Introductions for the Miserere* are each in the form of an aria, with recitatives; unfortunately the work which they are intended to preface is not known. A first-class issue, recorded in a most convincing acoustic.

Gloria in D major.
> ** (*) Argo ZRG 505. Elizabeth Vaughan (soprano), Janet Baker (contralto), Ian Partridge (tenor), Christopher Keyte (bass), King's College, Cambridge, Choir, Academy of St Martin-in-the-Fields, David Willcocks – PERGOLESI: *Magnificat.** (*)

This version uses comparatively small forces, and save for the occasional trace of preciosity it is very stylish indeed. It has an excellent team of soloists and is very well recorded. Some might feel the exaggerated consonants are tiresome, but this is unquestionably a most acceptable performance.

COLLECTION

'Greatest hits': (i; ii) *The Four Seasons: Spring, Op. 8/1;* (iii) *Concerto in G major for diverse instruments with mandolins* (arr. Casella); (iv) *(ii) Guitar concerto in D major;* (v) *Double mandolin concerto in G major, P.133;* (vi) *Double violin concerto in D major;* (i; ii; vii) *L'Estro armonico: Concerto in B minor for 4 violins, Op. 3/10.*
> (B) *** CBS Harmony 30054. (i)

Pinchas Zukerman (violin and dir.); (ii) English Chamber Orchestra; (iii) Soloists, New York Philharmonic Orchestra, Leonard Bernstein; (iv) John Williams (guitar); (v) Sol Golchberg, Mary Zelnicki (mandolins), New York Sinfonietta, Max Gobermann; (vi) David Oistrakh, Isaac Stern (violins), Philadelphia Orchestra, Eugene Ormandy; (vii) Kenneth Sillito, José-Luis Garcia, John Tunnell (violins).

This is an almost ideal sampler disc, guaranteed to delight not only the newcomer to Vivaldi but the enthusiast too, with excellent, imaginative performances of complete concertos. An outstanding bargain.

Volkmann, Friedrich Robert
(1815–83)

Serenade No. 2 in F major, Op. 63.
> (B) * Turnabout TV 34370S. Hungarian Chamber Orchestra, Vilmos Tátrai – TCHAIKOVSKY: *Souvenir de Florence.**

Volkmann's *Serenade* is short but attractive. It is quite well played, but the aggressive-sounding close-balanced recording robs it of any charm.

Vořišek, Jan
(1791–1825)

Symphony in D major.
> ** Philips 6500 203. English Chamber Orchestra, Charles Mackerras – DVOŘÁK: *Czech suite.**

* Unicorn RHS 309. New Philharmonia Orchestra, Michael Bialoguski – MARTINŮ: *Symphony No. 6*.*

Voříšek is the nearest the Czechs got to producing a Beethoven. This remarkably powerful work has fingerprints of the great German composer everywhere, yet manages to retain its own individuality. The slow movement is especially fine, and after an attractive scherzo, the finale has something in common with that of Beethoven's *Fourth Symphony*. But the music is nothing like a carbon copy, and one feels that Voříšek had much temperamentally in common with Beethoven to be able to write so convincingly in such a similar idiom. There used to be a splendid performance of the work on Supraphon by the Prague Chamber Orchestra, and the newer version by Mackerras, by comparison, is rather lightweight. It is a neat, small-scale performance, with characteristically lively tempi, and Philips provide good, clean sound. The playing of the New Philharmonia under Dr Bialoguski does not challenge it.

Wagenseil, Georg
(1715–77)

Harp concerto in G major.
(M) ** DGG Privilege 135093. Nicanor Zabaleta (harp), Chamber Orchestra, Paul Kuentz – HANDEL: *Harp concerto*; MOZART: *Flute and harp concerto*.***

Wagenseil was a Viennese piano virtuoso, much admired by Schubert. His *Harp concerto*, written about 1750, is a pleasant example of the *galant* style; the felicity of the writing in the first two movements is capped by a very jolly finale. Both performance and recording here can be commended.

Wagner, Richard
(1813–83)

A Faust overture; Der fliegende Holländer (The Flying Dutchman): overture; Lohengrin: Prelude to Act 1; Die Meistersinger von Nürnberg (The Mastersingers): Prelude to Act 1; Rienzi: overture.
(M) *** CBS Classics 61263. Cleveland Orchestra, George Szell.

Szell's collection of Wagner overtures stands out for superbly polished playing and for including what has become a rarity on record, *A Faust overture*. Hearing this searingly dramatic and intense work, one wonders why it has not become a repertory piece. The *Meistersinger prelude* starts rather stiffly, but it works up to full intensity, and otherwise these are all magnificent performances, well recorded in a clear, forward Cleveland manner. On a mid-price label an excellent bargain.

A Faust overture; Der fliegende Holländer: overture; Das Rheingold: Entry of the gods into Valhalla; Rienzi: overture; Tannhäuser: Grand march.
** (*) HMV ASD 3071. London Philharmonic Orchestra, Sir Adrian Boult.

Although listed first, this was the last to be issued of Boult's four Wagner orchestral anthologies. Its merits and limitations summarize the quality of the complete series. The orchestral playing is good rather than outstandingly incisive; the recordings are rich and often spectacular, although sometimes the resonance masks inner detail, notably here in *The Flying Dutchman overture*. Boult is at his best in the unforced dignity of the *Entry of the gods into Valhalla*, or in the glowing colours of the *Tannhäuser march*, which is done with spirited affection. The opening tune of *Rienzi* is warmly phrased, but the overall performance lacks sheer gusto, and the account of the *Faust overture* has not the concentration of Szell's performance.

A Faust overture; Die Meistersinger: Prelude to Act 1; Tannhäuser: overture; Tristan und Isolde: Prelude and Liebestod.
> ** CBS 73215. New York Philharmonic Orchestra, Pierre Boulez.

There is little or no mystery in Boulez's view of Wagner. The most completely successful item here is the *Meistersinger prelude*, spacious and well pointed, and the *Faust overture*, after a matter-of-fact introduction, brings out the dark, biting quality in Boulez's conducting; but *Tannhäuser* is made to sound like Meyerbeer and *Tristan* lacks tension. Good recording of improved New York vintage.

Marches: Grosser Festmarsch; Huldigungsmarsch; Kaisermarsch; Overtures: Die Feen; Liebesverbot.
> *** HMV ASD 2837. London Symphony Orchestra, Marek Janowski.

A fascinating collection of Wagner rarities, well performed and recorded. This may not be great music, but it is good to remind ourselves that in *Liebesverbot* even Wagner could relax in music that echoes Donizetti.

Siegfried idyll (original scoring).
> *** Decca SET 323/4. Vienna Philharmonic Orchestra, Sir Georg Solti – BRUCKNER: *Symphony No. 7.***
> ** (*) Columbia SAX 2454/5. Philharmonia Orchestra, Otto Klemperer – BRUCKNER: *Symphony No. 7.* (*)

So rich is the sound Decca provide for Solti that one is never conscious of any asceticism and the playing is similarly warm and committed. Only in the central climax does one sense the need for a larger body of strings, but the reading as a whole is so compelling that criticism is confounded. Klemperer too gives a noble reading and is finely recorded, but here one is more conscious of the small number of strings.

Siegfried idyll; (i) *Adagio for clarinet and strings.*
> ** (*) Argo ZRG 604. Academy of St Martin-in-the-Fields, Neville Marriner, (i) with Jack Brymer (clarinet) – R. STRAUSS: *Metamorphosen.****

A good performance of the *Siegfried idyll* in the chamber form that comes close to the one Cosima would have heard. It will not appeal to everyone, particularly in the passages for single strings. The middle section will also strike some listeners as a bit on the fast side. Of course, there are sensitive touches, and the engineers produce a good sound picture. The *Adagio for clarinet and strings* (see also below) is a useful fill-up and incidentally an excellent piece for a quiz.

Siegfried idyll; Der fliegende Holländer: overture; Rienzi: overture; Tannhäuser: Venusberg music (Paris version).
> (M) ** Philips Universo 6580 063. Vienna Symphony Orchestra, Wolfgang Sawallisch.

Sawallisch provides exciting readings of the *Dutchman* and *Rienzi* (especially) and a very good *Venusberg music* too. The *Siegfried idyll* is well played but lacks something in both tension and sense of repose. All the same, with vivid recording this is good value at medium price.

Siegfried idyll; Parsifal, Act 1: *Prelude and Transformation music;* Act 3: *Pre-*

1073

lude; *Good Friday music; Transformation music.*

> ** HMV ASD 3000. London Symphony Orchestra, Sir Adrian Boult.

There is some fine orchestral playing here, but it is not immaculate, and on side two, which is devoted to the *Parsifal* excerpts starting with the Act 1 *Transformation music*, the concentration is not always held at the highest level. The performance of the *Siegfried idyll* is gentle and persuasive, if lacking something in lyrical fervour; the *Prelude to Act 1* of *Parsifal* offers some superb brass sounds, but has a certain episodic quality. The recording is generally good, but this is not first choice among Boult's Wagner records.

Siegfried idyll; Lohengrin: Prelude to Act 1; Die Meistersinger: Prelude to Act 1; Tristan und Isolde: Prelude and Liebestod.

> ** (*) DGG 2536 019. Berlin Philharmonic Orchestra, Rafael Kubelik.

This is a reissue (with no price reduction) of a fine collection. There is some marvellous playing here from the Berlin Philharmonic, and the recording is suitably spacious. Kubelik's readings are expansive and relaxed rather than gripping, but this is still a very enjoyable anthology.

Der fliegende Holländer: overture; Lohengrin: Preludes to Acts 1 and 3; Die Meistersinger: Prelude to Act 1; Tristan und Isolde: Prelude and Liebestod.

> ** (*) Decca SXL 6656. Vienna Philharmonic Orchestra, Horst Stein.

Anyone looking for a superbly recorded and generous collection of favourite Wagner orchestral pieces, given that special sheen which is the prerogative of the Vienna Phil., could do a great deal worse than try this excellent disc. It offers sumptuous yet clear recording within a finely judged resonance, and the *Meistersinger prelude*, in a richly spacious reading, is particularly satisfying. The other overture, *The Flying Dutchman*, is given a similarly broad reading and there is some lack of electricity here. The *Third act Lohengrin prelude* too is less than ideal: having presented it with great brilliance and *élan*, the conductor opts for the original opera-house conclusion, which means he goes on into the first two bars of the *Wedding march* and then stops. This is silly when there is a perfectly good concert ending available. But this is a small blemish, when the *Tristan Prelude and Liebestod* is so finely moulded and the *Lohengrin Prelude to Act 1* (an elusive piece on disc) played so radiantly, its great climax so well placed.

Der fliegende Holländer: overture; Die Meistersinger: Prelude to Act 1; Tristan und Isolde: Prelude and Liebestod.

> ** Decca Phase 4 PFS 4158. New Philharmonia Orchestra, Carlos Paita.

Not a very generous offering of Wagner overtures conducted by a talented youngster, but Phase 4 technique works best with wide-spaced grooves. This is designed to please those who want their Wagner souped up, but otherwise there are far more recommendable collections. It seems strange nowadays to return to a purely orchestral version of the *Liebestod*.

Der fliegende Holländer: overture; Rienzi: overture; Tannhäuser: overture; Bacchanale.

> (**) Decca SET 227. Vienna Philharmonic Orchestra and Singverein, Sir Georg Solti.

The Vienna Philharmonic are very hard-driven, and the result sounds unnecessarily frenetic. *Rienzi* is best: the big opening string tune is played gloriously. Unfortunately the Decca recording is toppy and edgy, and on wide-range equipment one has to filter strongly to get a smooth sound.

Overtures: Der fliegende Holländer; Rienzi; Tannhäuser; Lohengrin: Prelude to Act 1.
  ** (*) HMV ASD 2695. Philharmonia Orchestra, Otto Klemperer.
Götterdämmerung: Siegfried's Rhine journey; Parsifal: Prelude to Act 1; Das Rheingold: Entry of the gods into Valhalla; Siegfried: Forest murmurs; Tannhäuser: Prelude to Act 3; Die Walküre: Ride of the Valkyries.
  ** (*) HMV ASD 2697. Philharmonia Orchestra, Otto Klemperer.
Lohengrin: Prelude to Act 3; Die Meistersinger: Prelude to Act 1; Dance of the apprentices and Entry of the masters; Tristan und Isolde: Prelude and Liebestod; Götterdämmerung: Siegfried's funeral march.
  ** (*) HMV ASD 2696. Philharmonia Orchestra, Otto Klemperer.

It is good to have Klemperer's view of Wagner. Most of these performances have the sort of incandescent glow one finds only in the interpretations of really great conductors, and the Philharmonia plays immaculately. But judged by the highest standards Klemperer falls just a degree short. These plodding Mastersingers are just a little too full of German pudding, and the *Tristan Prelude and Liebestod* does not have the sense of wonder that Toscanini, for one, brought. The recordings have been remastered and successfully freshened, but they originally date from 1960 and one would have thought EMI could have found a way to reduce the price.

Götterdämmerung: Siegfried's Rhine journey; Siegfried's funeral march;

Final scene; Das Rheingold: Entry of the gods into Valhalla; Siegfried: Forest murmurs; Die Walküre: Ride of the Valkyries; Magic fire music.
  (M) ** CBS Classics 61114. Cleveland Orchestra, George Szell.

These are brilliantly played performances, and there are certainly some spectacular moments, but the recording has achieved its brilliance at the expense of weight at the bass end, which needs boosting.

Götterdämmerung: Dawn and Siegfried's Rhine journey; Siegfried's funeral march; Siegfried: Forest murmurs; Tannhäuser: Prelude to Act 3; Tristan und Isolde: Prelude to Act 3; Die Walküre: Ride of the Valkyries.
  ** HMV ASD 2934. London Philharmonic Orchestra, Sir Adrian Boult.

In the last resort this is a disappointing collection. It is for the most part finely played, but too often the electricity is missing, and even *Forest murmurs* lacks atmosphere. The most striking performance is the beautiful original version of Wagner's *Prelude to Act 3, Tannhäuser.* This is a comparatively extended synthesis of the motifs associated with Elisabeth; the orchestration is gentle and evocative, and Boult presents it with a simple eloquence which is extremely effective. However, the characterization elsewhere is less sure and *Siegfried's funeral march* has not the breadth that some other conductors find. The recording is generally of first-class quality although the first climax of the opening item (*Dawn*) is slightly muddled by the resonance.

Götterdämmerung: Dawn and Siegfried's Rhine journey; Siegfried's funeral march; Immolation scene; Das Rheingold: Invocation of Alberich;

Entry of the gods into Valhalla; Siegfried: Forest murmurs; Die Walküre: Ride of the Valkyries; Magic fire music.

(M) * (*) R C A LSB 4062. Philadelphia Orchestra, Eugene Ormandy.

This medium-priced collection offers a generous measure for those who prefer their Wagner without voices. For the most part the performances are well paced, although Ormandy often chooses fairly fast tempi. The manner is broad rather than conveying a special degree of excitement, and although the orchestral playing is assured, the rather dry recording does not produce any very spectacular sounds. The *Immolation scene* from *Götterdämmerung* (which closes the concert) is the most successful item.

Lohengrin: Preludes to Acts 1 and 3; Die Meistersinger: Prelude to Act 1; Parsifal: Prelude to Act 1.

** Decca SXL 6298. Vienna Philharmonic Orchestra, Zubin Mehta − LISZT: *Les Préludes.***

Unquestionably the Decca recording here offers very fine sound, and the playing of the Vienna Philharmonic is superb. Yet Mehta, who is always competent, does not add any personal magic. The climax of the *Act 1 Lohengrin prelude* is well prepared, yet the moment of culmination, with the great cymbal clashes, is not overwhelming; the *Parsifal prelude* is beautiful, yet lacks the final glow, and the *Meistersinger prelude* has no rich, expansive quality.

Lohengrin: Preludes to Acts 1 and 3; Die Meistersinger: Preludes to Acts 1 and 3; Tannhäuser: overture; Tristan und Isolde: Prelude to Act 1.

** (*) H M V Quadraphonic Q4- ASD 2812; Stereo ASD 2812. New Philharmonia Orchestra, Sir Adrian Boult.

Although the orchestral playing is not absolutely immaculate this is the most satisfying of Sir Adrian Boult's four Wagner collections. The quadraphonic version is predictably sumptuous, although it is not too clear in internal focus (the stereo version has more edge, but is also somewhat more refined). The highlights are the *Third act Prelude* to *Die Meistersinger*, which is finely moulded and offers some superbly rich brass sonority, and the *Tannhäuser overture*.

Lohengrin: Prelude to Act 3; Die Meistersinger: Dance of the apprentices; Entry of the Masters; Tannhäuser: Grand march; Tristan und Isolde: Liebestod; Die Walküre: Ride of the Valkyries; Magic fire music.

(M) * (*) CBS Classics 61196. New York Philharmonic Orchestra, Leonard Bernstein.

These performances are brilliant enough. The violins in the *Tannhäuser overture*, for instance, certainly show a sense of bravura, but one needs more depth both to the approach and to the sound − which is top-heavy − to bring out the majesty of the *Meistersinger* excerpts.

Parsifal: Prelude and Good Friday music.

(M) ** (*) DGG Privilege 2726 054 (2 discs). Bavarian Radio Orchestra, Eugen Jochum − BRUCKNER: *Symphony No. 7.***

Splendid playing and first-class recording, which although it comes from the early days of stereo does not show its age. There is the most beautiful string and brass tone here. Perhaps the last degree of mystery is missing from the *Prelude*, but the *Good Friday music* has a moving serenity, especially in the closing pages. A good coupling for a highly recommendable Bruckner *Seventh*.

Tristan und Isolde: Love music from Acts 2 and 3 (arr. Stokowski).

(M) ** (*) CBS Classics 61288. Philadelphia Orchestra, Leopold Stokowski – FALLA: *El amor brujo.****

Stokowski's orchestral synthesis of the Act 2 love music and the Act 3 *Liebestod* is 'an attempt to capture in a much smaller compass the emotional and sensual impact of the opera itself'. Certainly the off-stage horns from the start of Act 2 are as evocative here as in any opera-house, and Stokowski's combination of urgency and the richest possible sense of line makes for a compelling experience, if one that is related more to Stokowski than to Wagner. A strange coupling for the Falla ballet, but a worthwhile one.

CHAMBER MUSIC

Adagio for clarinet and strings.

(M) *** Decca Ace of Diamonds SDD 249. Alfred Boskovsky (clarinet), members of the Vienna Octet – BRAHMS: *Clarinet quintet.** (*)

This may or may not be by Wagner: the evidence is not conclusive. But, stylistically at least, this attractive Weberian music is quite in keeping with what we know Wagner was writing in his early years, and it makes an attractive fill-up.

VOCAL MUSIC

Wesendonk Lieder (Der Engel; Stehe still; Im Treibhaus; Schmerzen; Träume).

* (*) Decca SXL 6446. Marilyn Horne (soprano), Royal Philharmonic Orchestra, Henry Lewis – MAHLER: *Kindertotenlieder.** (*)

Marilyn Horne's singing is tonally beautiful, but lacking in emotional warmth. As in the Mahler on the reverse there is much to admire, but in these lovely songs that is not enough.

Wesendonk Lieder (complete); Der fliegende Holländer: Senta's ballad. Rienzi: Gerechter Gott . . . In seiner Blüte. Die Feen: Weh mir, so nah' . . . Ich haufe selbst die.

** (*) Philips 6500 294. Birgit Nilsson (soprano), John Alldis Choir, London Symphony Orchestra, Colin Davis.

Nilsson gives a somewhat restrained performance of the *Wesendonk Lieder*, matching the refined playing of the LSO under Davis. The disc is chiefly valuable for the rarities from *Rienzi* and *Die Feen*. The *Rienzi* aria – for Adriano, a breeches role – has a Weberian cabaletta, introduced over dramatic chimes. The aria from *Die Feen* is even more obviously like Weber, but refreshingly direct, with another cabaletta which similarly taxes the soprano. Good recording.

Wesendonk Lieder (complete); Lohengrin: Einsam in trüben Tagen (Elsa's dream).Parsifal: Ich sah' das Kind. Die Walküre: Der Männer Sippe; Du bist der Lenz.

(M) ** (*) Decca Ace of Diamonds SDD 212. Kirsten Flagstad (soprano), Vienna Philharmonic Orchestra, Hans Knappertsbusch.

Flagstad's glorious voice is perfectly suited to the rich inspiration of the *Wesendonk Lieder*. *Im Treibhaus* is particularly beautiful. Sieglinde's solo too is magnificent – and interesting to contrast with Flagstad's later version in the complete Act 1 (see below) – but the scale of voice makes *Elsa's dream* sound a little unwieldy, and, fine as it is vocally,

Kundry's *Herzeleide* sounds rather staid for a seductress. Fine accompaniment and excellent recording for its 1956 vintage.

OPERA

Der fliegende Holländer (The Flying Dutchman; opera in 3 acts): complete recording.

(M) ** (*) Decca 2 BB 109/11. George London (baritone), Leonie Rysanek (soprano), Giorgio Tozzi (bass), Karl Liebl, Richard Lewis (tenors), Rosalind Elias (mezzo-soprano), Chorus and Orchestra of Royal Opera House, Covent Garden, Antal Dorati.

(B) ** (*) Decca Eclipse ECS 665/7. Bayreuth Festival 1955 performance: Hermann Uhde (baritone), Astrid Varnay (soprano), Ludwig Weber (bass), Rudolf Lustig, Josef Traxel (tenors), Elisabeth Schaertel (mezzo-soprano), Bayreuth Festival Chorus and Orchestra, Joseph Keilberth.

** (*) HMV SLS 934 (3 discs). Theo Adam (bass-baritone), Anja Silja (soprano), Martti Talvela (bass), Ernst Kozub, Gerhard Unger (tenors), Annelies Burmeister (mezzo-soprano), BBC Chorus, New Philharmonia Orchestra, Otto Klemperer.

** DGG 2709 040 (3 discs). Bayreuth Festival 1971 performance: Thomas Stewart (baritone), Gwyneth Jones (soprano), Karl Ridderbusch (bass), Herman Esser, Harald Elk (tenors), Sieglinde Wagner (contralto), Bayreuth Festival Chorus and Orchestra, Karl Boehm.

The outstanding quality of the Dorati set is the conducting and general sense of teamwork. The Covent Garden Orchestra is on top form, with the forcefulness of Dorati making up for any marginal lack of polish. The chorus too is splendid and the recording is gloriously clear and real. In this opera all these points are of great importance, and for many they will be decisive, when the set is reissued at medium price. George London's Dutchman is the drawback; the voice is comparatively ill-defined, the phrasing sometimes clumsy. Rysanek is not always the steadiest of Sentas, but she sings with character, and the rest of the cast is vocally reliable. With all one's reservations there is a great deal to enjoy here.

Decca went experimentally to Bayreuth in 1955, and there produced the very impressive Keilberth set, still satisfyingly atmospheric in sound. Keilberth's direction is urgently dramatic, and the chorus sings consistently well. Uhde is a fine Dutchman and Varnay an impressive Senta. An outstanding bargain on Decca's cheapest label, even if no libretto is provided.

To have Klemperer conducting a complete Wagner opera provides a historic document, a great musician thinking aloud through a score which is always in danger of being underestimated. Predictably the reading is spacious in its tempi: the drama hardly grips you by the throat. But the intensity is irresistible. It may be hard to recommend this as a first choice to any but a committed devotee of the conductor, but all Wagnerians should try and hear it. It is a pity that Anja Silja was chosen as Senta, even though she is not as squally in tone as she can be. Otherwise a strong vocal cast, much beautiful playing (particularly from the wind soloists) and a vivid if not particularly atmospheric recording.

The fact that Boehm's 1971 Bayreuth recording is from a live performance detracts from its appeal, for the chorus, poorly disciplined in their singing, are noisy on the stage and this is distracting. Gwyneth Jones sings beautifully in pianissimo passages but develops a wobble which worsens as she puts pressure on the voice. Thomas Stewart is better focused in tone than he sometimes is. Boehm's searching interpretation is well worth hearing, but on balance this is a disappointing set.

Götterdämmerung (opera in Prologue and 3 acts): complete recording.

*** Decca SET 292/7. Birgit Nilsson (soprano), Wolfgang Windgassen (tenor), Dietrich Fischer-Dieskau (baritone), Gottlob Frick, Gustav Neidlinger (basses), Claire Watson (soprano), Christa Ludwig (mezzo-soprano), Vienna State Opera Chorus, Vienna Philharmonic Orchestra, Sir Georg Solti.

*** DGG 2716 001 (6 discs). Helga Dernesch (soprano), Helge Brilioth (tenor), Thomas Stewart (baritone), Karl Ridderbusch, Zoltan Keleman (basses), Gundula Janowitz (soprano), Christa Ludwig (mezzo-soprano), German Opera Chorus, Berlin Philharmonic Orchestra, Herbert von Karajan.

In Decca's formidable task of recording the whole *Ring* cycle under Solti, *Götterdämmerung* provided the most daunting challenge of all; but characteristically Solti, and with him the Vienna Philharmonic and the Decca recording team under John Culshaw were inspired to heights even beyond earlier achievements. Even the trifling objections raised on earlier issues have been eliminated here. The balance between voices and orchestra has by some magic been made perfect, with voices clear but orchestra still rich and near-sounding. Above all Solti seems to have matured into a warmer and wiser director. He drives hard still, but no longer is there any feeling of over-driving, and even the *Funeral march*, which in his early Covent Garden performances was brutal in its power, is made into a natural not a forced climax. There is not a single weak link in the cast. Nilsson surpasses herself in the magnificence of her singing: even Flagstad in her prime would not have been more masterful as Brünnhilde. As in *Siegfried*, Windgassen is in superb voice; Frick is a vivid Hagen, and Fischer-Dieskau achieves the near-impossible in making Gunther an interesting and even sympathetic character. As for the recording quality, it surpasses even Decca's earlier achievement. No more magnificent set has appeared in the whole history of the gramophone.

Karajan like Solti before him reserved for the concluding *Ring* opera his finest achievement. His singing cast is marginally even finer than Solti's, and his performance conveys the steady flow of recording sessions prepared in relation to live performances. But ultimately he falls short of Solti's achievement in the orgasmic quality of the music, the quality which finds an emotional culmination in such moments as the end of Brünnhilde's and Siegfried's love scene, the climax of the *Funeral march* and the culmination of the *Immolation*. At each of these points Karajan is a degree less committed, beautifully as the players respond, and warm as his overall approach is. Dernesch's Brünnhilde is warmer than Nilsson's, with a glorious range of tone. Brilioth as Siegfried is fresh and young-sounding, while the Gutrune of Gundula Janowitz is far preferable to that of Claire Watson on Decca. The matching is otherwise very even. The balance of voices in the recording may for some dictate a choice: DGG brings the singers closer, gives less brilliance to the orchestral texture.

Götterdämmerung: excerpts: Act 3, Scenes 2 and 3 (sung in English).

(M) *** Unicorn UNS 245/6. Rita Hunter (soprano), Alberto Remedios (tenor), Clifford Grant (bass), Norman Bailey (bass-baritone), Sadler's Wells Chorus and Orchestra, Reginald Goodall.

Like the HMV complete *Siegfried* this will delight the lover of opera in English. Unlike the CFP disc with the same two principals (see below) this one concentrates on the end of the opera, giving the last hour of Act 3. Goodall draws full shining tone from the Sadler's Wells Orchestra to give a superb sense of continuity, just as in the opera-house. The singers are impressively consistent, with Hunter rising to the climax of the *Immolation* scene with firm, unswerving tone. Vivid recording.

Götterdämmerung: highlights.
*** Decca SXL 6220 (from above recording cond. Solti).

The recording of the Decca *Götterdämmerung* was celebrated by one of the classics of television film, Humphrey Burton's *The Golden Ring*. This selection from the complete recording was timed to appear for one of the film's presentations, and it makes an excellent reminder not only for nostalgic viewers but for anyone daunted by the six discs of the complete set. The items could hardly be better chosen, with the rallying chorus of Act 2 a welcome addition to the obvious, predictable items. Stunning recording quality.

Götterdämmerung: scenes (sung in German): *Dawn; Brünnhilde and Siegfried's entrance; Siegfried's Rhine journey; Siegfried's funeral march; Brünnhilde's immolation.*
(B) *** Classics for Pleasure CFP 40008. Rita Hunter (soprano), Alberto Remedios (tenor), London Philharmonic Orchestra, Charles Mackerras.

Vocally what stands out from Hunter's performance is the pinging precision of even the most formidable exposed notes. Here she reveals herself as a natural competitor in the international league, and her simple, fresh manner in the most intense moment of the *Immolation*, the hushed farewell of *Ruhe, du Gott*, is most affectingly caught. Remedios is also in splendid form, and Mackerras draws dedicated and dramatic playing from the LPO. An outstanding bargain disc of Wagner.

Lohengrin (opera in 3 acts): complete recording.
** DGG 2713 005 (5 discs). James King (tenor), Gundula Janowitz (soprano), Thomas Stewart (baritone), Gwyneth Jones (soprano), Karl Ridderbusch (bass), Bavarian Radio Chorus and Orchestra, Rafael Kubelik.
Lohengrin: scenes.
** DGG 2536 028 (from above recording).

The performance of Janowitz as Elsa is ravishing, with a constant stream of glorious tone over the widest range, and deeply expressive phrasing. For her alone this set is one for Wagnerians to hear. James King is an imaginative Lohengrin, but Thomas Stewart's Telramund has nothing like the dramatic intensity one ideally requires. Gwyneth Jones as the wicked Ortrud provides a sad showing. The pain of her performance, with many passages completely out of control, would be enough to turn most collectors away, and though Kubelik's interpretation is dedicated and thoughtful, it cannot compare with Kempe's, which glowed with expressive conviction and was the finest recorded memorial yet to one of the greatest Wagner conductors. Under the circumstances *Lohengrin* enthusiasts might do better to invest in DGG's single-disc selection (sensibly featuring key scenes from the opera) until the Kempe set returns to the catalogue.

Die Meistersinger von Nürnberg (The Mastersingers of Nuremberg; opera in 3 acts): complete recording.

** (*) HMV SLS 957 (5 discs). Theo Adam (bass), Helen Donath (soprano), Geraint Evans (baritone), Ruth Hess (mezzo-soprano), Zoltan Kelemen, Karl Ridderbusch (basses), René Kollo, Peter Schreier (tenors), Leipzig Radio Chorus, Dresden State Opera and Orchestra, Herbert von Karajan.

The absence of a really viable version of *Meistersinger* in stereo was one of the most serious gaps in the catalogue until this generally fine Karajan set came along. What had held up at least four record companies was the difficulty of finding a truly adequate Sachs (Fischer-Dieskau resisting all advances). The irony is that HMV, having set up this star-studded version, fell down badly in the choice of Sachs. Theo Adam, promising in many ways, has quite the wrong voice for the part, in one way too young-sounding, in another too grating, not focused enough. After that keen disappointment there is much to enjoy, for in a modestly reverberant acoustic (a smallish church was used) Karajan draws from the Dresden players and chorus a rich performance which retains a degree of bourgeois intimacy. Anyone wanting an expansive sound may be disappointed, but Karajan's thoughtful approach and sure command of phrasing are most enjoyable. Donath is a touching, sweet-toned Eva, Kollo as true and ringing a Walther as one could find today, Geraint Evans an incomparably vivid Backmesser, and Ridderbusch a glorious-toned Pogner who really should have been singing Sachs.

Parsifal (opera in 3 acts): complete recording.

*** Decca SET 550/4. René Kollo (tenor), Christa Ludwig (mezzo-soprano), Dietrich Fischer-Dieskau, Hans Hotter, Zoltan Kelemen (baritones), Gottlob Frick (bass), Vienna Boys' Choir, Vienna Opera Chorus, Vienna Philharmonic Orchestra, Sir Georg Solti.

(M) *** Philips 6729 002 (5 discs). Jess Thomas (tenor), Irene Dallis (soprano), George London (baritone), Martti Talvela, Gustav Neidlinger (basses), Hans Hotter (baritone), Bayreuth Festival (1963) Chorus and Orchestra, Hans Knappertsbusch.

** (*) DGG 2713 004 (5 discs). James King (tenor), Gwyneth Jones (soprano), Thomas Stewart (baritone), Karl Ridderbusch, Donald McIntyre, Franz Crass (basses), Bayreuth Festival (1970) Chorus and Orchestra, Pierre Boulez.

It was natural that after Solti's other magnificent Wagner recordings for Decca, he should want to go on to this last of the operas. In almost every way it is just as powerful an achievement as any of his previous Wagner recordings in Vienna, with the Decca engineers surpassing themselves in vividness of sound and the Vienna Philharmonic in radiant form. The singing cast could hardly be stronger, every one of them pointing words with fine, illuminating care for detail. The complex balances of sound, not least in the *Good Friday music*, are beautifully caught, and throughout Solti shows his sustained intensity in Wagner. There remains just one doubt, but that rather serious – the lack of the spiritual quality which makes Knappertsbusch's live

1081

version so involving. Maybe it is better after all not to record this opera in the studio.

Knappertsbusch's expansive and dedicated reading is superbly caught in the Philips set, arguably the finest live recording ever made in the Festspielhaus at Bayreuth, with outstanding singing from Jess Thomas as Parsifal and Hans Hotter as Gurnemanz. Though Knappertsbusch chooses consistently slow tempi, there is no sense of excessive squareness or length, so intense is the concentration of the performance, its spiritual quality. This of all operas is one that seems to gain from being recorded live, and stage noises and coughs here are very few and far between.

Like two earlier recordings of *Parsifal* (one Decca, one Philips, both with Knappertsbusch) the D G G set was also taken from live performances at the Festspielhaus in 1970. Boulez's approach to this expansive score could hardly be more sharply in contrast with Knappertsbusch's. By traditional standards his tempi are consistently fast, yet to the unprejudiced ear they rarely sound rushed, merely urgent in a way that is very rare in this opera. With the textures clarified in a way characteristic of Boulez the result is a fresh and compelling experience lacking perhaps in devotional gentleness but little the worse for that. Even the Flower-maidens sing like young apprentices rather than seductive beauties. James King makes a firm, strong, rather baritonal hero, Thomas Stewart a fine, tense Amfortas, and Gwyneth Jones is in strong voice, only occasionally shrill in tone and aptly so. A strong cast, helped by atmospheric recording. Traditionalists will still go to the Philips set or the Solti, but the D G G set certainly offers a thrilling new look.

Parsifal: highlights.
** (*) Decca SET 574 (from above recording cond. Solti).

If you cut chunks from *Parsifal* they bleed even more disturbingly than with most Wagner operas, and most of these items end in mid-air. Though they are well chosen, inevitably the result gives only an imperfect idea of Solti's fine overall control. Outstanding performance and recording as in the complete set.

Parsifal, Act 2: *Dies alles . . . Erlösung, Frevlerin, biet'ich auch dir . . .* (to end of act); *Die Walküre,* Act 1: *Schläfst du, Gast* (to end of act).
** (*) Philips 6500 661. Birgit Nilsson (soprano), Helge Brilioth (tenor), Norman Bailey (bass), Royal Opera House, Covent Garden, Orchestra, Leif Segerstam.

This disc is chiefly valuable for presenting Birgit Nilsson's searching and intense assumption of the role of Kundry in *Parsifal*, marvellous in its range of tone and expression. In both *Parsifal* and *Walküre* Brilioth, though one of the finest of latterday Heldentenors, finds himself hard-pressed to match the searing power of Nilsson. Fine playing and recording.

Das Rheingold (opera in 1 act, 4 scenes): complete recording.
*** Decca SET 382/4. George London (baritone), Kirsten Flagstad (soprano), Set Svanholm (tenor), Gustav Neidlinger (bass), Vienna Philharmonic Orchestra, Sir Georg Solti.
*** D G G 2709 023 (3 discs). Dietrich Fischer-Dieskau (baritone), Josephine Veasey (mezzo-soprano), Gerhard Stolze (tenor), Zoltan Kelemen (bass), Berlin Philharmonic Orchestra, Herbert von Karajan.

The Decca set was the first recording ever issued commercially of the opening drama in the *Ring* cycle. Solti gives a magnificent reading of the score, crisp, dramatic and direct. He somehow brings a freshness to the music without ever overdriving or losing an underlying sympathy. Vocally the set is held together by the unforgettable singing of Neidlinger as Alberich. Too often the part – admittedly ungrateful on the voice – is spoken rather than sung, but Neidlinger vocalizes with wonderful precision and makes the character of the dwarf develop from the comic creature of the opening scene to the demented monster of the last. Flagstad specially learnt the part of Fricka for this recording, and her singing makes one regret that she never took the part on the stage. But regret is small when a singer of the greatness of Flagstad found the opportunity during so-called retirement to extend her reputation with performances such as this. Only the slightest trace of hardness in the upper register occasionally betrays her, and the golden power and richness of her singing are for the rest unimpaired – enhanced even, when the recorded quality is as true as this. As Wotan, George London is sometimes a little rough – a less brilliant recording might not betray him – but this is a dramatic portrayal of the young Wotan. Svanholm could be more characterful as Loge, but again it is a relief to hear the part really sung. Much has been written on the quality of the recording, and without any doubt it deserves the highest star rating. Decca went to special trouble to produce the recording as for a stage performance and to follow Wagner's intentions as closely as possible. They certainly succeeded. Even those who are sometimes troubled by the almost excessive sharpness of definition Decca provides in complex scores – the 'Festival Hall' effect – will find that here the clarity does not prevent Wagner's orchestral effects from coming over in their full bloom of richness. An outstanding achievement.

Karajan's account is more reflective than Solti's. The very measured pace of the *Prelude* indicates this at the start, and there is often an extra bloom on the Berlin Philharmonic playing. But Karajan's very reflectiveness has its less welcome side, for the tension rarely varies. One finds such incidents as Alberich's stealing of the gold or Donner's hammer-blow passing by without one's pulse quickening as it should. Unexpectedly, Karajan is not so subtle as Solti in shaping phrases and rhythms. There is also no doubt that the D G G recording managers were not so painstaking as John Culshaw's Decca team, and that too makes the end-result less compellingly dramatic. But on the credit side the singing cast has hardly any flaw at all, and Fischer-Dieskau's Wotan is a brilliant, memorable creation, virile and expressive. Among the others Veasey is excellent, though obviously she cannot efface memories of Flagstad; Gerhard Stolze, with his flickering, almost *Sprechstimme* as Loge, gives an intensely vivid if, for some, controversial interpretation. The recording is excellent but does not outshine the Decca.

Das Rheingold: highlights.
*** Decca SET 482 (from above recording cond. Solti).

It is almost impossible to choose 'highlights' from this opera, but Decca provide a generous and intelligently chosen set of excerpts, culminating in the whole of the climactic last scene, superbly performed here, with Flagstad dominant as Fricka in her brief solos. Although the complete recording was made as early as 1958, the sound is still splendid in this transfer.

Der Ring des Nibelungen: an introduction to the 4 operas of *The Ring* by Deryck Cooke, with 193 music examples; *Siegfried idyll; Kinderkatechismus.*

*** Decca SET 406/8. Vienna Boys' Choir, Vienna Philharmonic Orchestra, Sir Georg Solti.

Deryck Cooke's fascinating and scholarly lecture is included in Decca's bumper box of Solti's complete *Ring* cycle. Its separate issue is welcome, particularly when it also brings on side six two supplements related to the great tetralogy, the well-known *Siegfried idyll* and the charming, tongue-in-cheek *Kinderkatechismus*, another birthday tribute for Cosima, this time for boys' voices. Deryck Cooke's lecture (the text is given in print as well as on disc) demonstrates how the many leading motives in the *Ring* develop from one another, springing from an initial germ. It is riveting, though even dedicated Wagnerians may not want to hear it many times over. The music examples – many of them specially prepared – are not always inserted with the skill one is accustomed to on BBC Radio 3.

Der Ring des Nibelungen (*Das Rheingold; Die Walküre; Siegfried; Götterdämmerung*): complete recording.

⊛ *** Decca RING 1–22. Sir Georg Solti (for cast lists see under each opera).

** (*) Philips 6747 037 (16 discs). Wolfgang Windgassen (tenor), Birgit Nilsson (soprano), Leonie Rysanek (mezzo-soprano), James King (tenor), Gustav Neidlinger, Theo Adam (basses), Bayreuth Festival casts 1966/7, Bayreuth Festival Orchestra, Karl Boehm.

The Decca set – one of the great achievements of the gramophone – is issued in a special box-album with the Deryck Cooke supplement (see above).

Boehm's set of *The Ring* is taken from live performances given at Bayreuth in 1966 and 1967. Inevitably it is flawed, when compared with the two studio-made versions by Solti and Karajan, and the sound, though it conveys the atmosphere of the Festspielhaus well enough, gives an imperfect idea of Wagnerian richness. The singing too is variable, with Windgassen as Siegfried markedly less impressive than in Solti's Decca set, and Birgit Nilsson, as Brünnhilde in the last two operas, less immaculate than before. Martha Mödl is the less reliable Brünnhilde in *Walküre*. Boehm characteristically favours rather fast tempi, but none of these factors need worry overmuch a Wagnerian who above all wants the flavour of a live performance, its tensions and resolutions. This has its place alongside the other cycles on record.

Siegfried (opera in 3 acts): complete recording.

*** Decca SET 242/6. Wolfgang Windgassen (tenor), Birgit Nilsson (soprano), Hans Hotter (baritone), Gerhard Stolze (tenor), Gustav Neidlinger, Kurt Böhme (basses), Marga Höffgen (contralto), Joan Sutherland (soprano), Vienna Philharmonic Orchestra, Sir Georg Solti.

** DGG 2713 003 (5 discs). Jess Thomas (tenor), Helga Dernesch (soprano), Thomas Stewart (baritone), Gerhard Stolze (tenor), Zoltan Kelemen, Karl Ridderbusch (basses), Oralia Dominguez (mezzo-soprano), Berlin Philharmonic Orchestra, Herbert von Karajan.

Siegfried has too long been thought of as the grimmest of the *Ring* cycle, with dark colours predominating. It is true that the predominance of male voices till the very end, and Wagner's deliberate matching of this in his orchestration, give a special colour to the opera, but a performance as buoyant as Solti's reveals that more than in most Wagner the message is one of optimism. Each of the three acts ends with a scene of triumphant optimism – the first act in Siegfried's forging song, the second with him hot in pursuit of the woodbird, and the third with the most opulent of love duets.

Solti's array of singers could hardly be bettered. Windgassen is at the very peak of his form, lyrical as well as heroic. Hotter has never been more impressive on records, his Wotan at last captured adequately. Stolze, Neidlinger and Böhme are all exemplary, and predictably Joan Sutherland makes the most seductive of woodbirds. Only the conducting of Solti leaves a tiny margin of doubt. In the dramatic moments he could hardly be more impressive, but that very woodbird scene shows up the shortcomings. The bird's melismatic carolling is plainly intended to have a degree of freedom, whereas Solti allows little or no lilt in the music at all. But it is a minute flaw in a supreme achievement. With singing finer than any opera-house could normally provide, with masterly playing from the Vienna Philharmonic, and Decca's most opulent recording this is a set likely to stand comparison with anything the rest of the century may provide.

When Siegfried is outsung by Mime, it is time to complain, and though the DGG set has many fine qualities – not least the Brünnhilde of Helga Dernesch – it hardly rivals the Solti version. Windgassen on Decca gave a classic performance, and any comparison highlights the serious shortcomings of Jess Thomas. It only makes matters worse that DGG balance favours the voices more than the Decca. Otherwise the vocal cast is strong, and Karajan provides the seamless playing which characterizes his cycle. Recommended only to those irrevocably committed to the Karajan cycle.

Siegfried: Forging scene; Final duet.
   *** Decca SXL 6142 (from above recording cond. Solti).

Wisely, instead of providing a highlights disc Decca concentrated on the closing scenes of Acts 1 and 3. It is a pity, perhaps, that another short band could not have been included to give a taste of the Act 2 finale, with the woodbird too, but as it is the sides are very long. Though the final duet is much more closely packed on this disc than in the complete set, the quality of sound has been very well maintained.

Siegfried: complete recording (sung in English).
   (M) *** HMV SLS 875 (5 discs). Alberto Remedios (tenor), Rita Hunter (soprano), Norman Bailey (baritone), Gregory Dempsey (tenor), Derek Hammond Stroud (baritone), Clifford Grant (bass), Anne Collins (mezzo-soprano), Sadler's Wells Orchestra, Reginald Goodall.

Compounded from three live performances at the Coliseum, this magnificent set gives a superb sense of dramatic realism. More tellingly than in almost any other Wagner opera recording, Goodall's spacious direction here conveys the genuine dramatic crunch that gives the experience of hearing Wagner in the opera-house its unique power, its overwhelming force. In the *Prelude* there are intrusive audience noises, and towards the end the Sadler's Wells violins have one or two shaky moments, but this is unmistakably a great interpretation caught on the wing. Remedios, more than any rival on record, conveys not only heroic strength but clear-ringing youthfulness, caressing the ear as well as exciting it. Norman Bailey makes a magnificently noble Wanderer, steady of tone, and Gregory Dempsey is a characterful Mime, even if his deliberate whining tone is not well caught on record. The sound is superbly realistic even making no allowances for the conditions. Lovers of opera in English should grasp the opportunity of hearing this unique set.

Tannhäuser (opera in 3 acts; Paris version): complete recording.

> *** Decca SET 506/9. René Kollo (tenor), Helga Dernesch (soprano), Christa Ludwig (mezzo-soprano), Hans Sotin (bass), Victor Braun (baritone), Werner Hollweg (tenor), Vienna State Opera Chorus, Vienna Philharmonic Orchestra, Sir Georg Solti.

Solti provides an electrifying experience, demonstrating beyond a shadow of doubt how much more effective the Paris revision of *Tannhäuser* is compared with the usual Dresden version. The differences lie mainly – though not entirely – in the first act in the scene between Tannhäuser and Venus. Wagner rewrote most of the scene at a time when his style had developed enormously. The love music here is closer to *Walküre* and *Tristan* than to the rest of *Tannhäuser*. The hero's harp song enters each time in its straight diatonic style with a jolt, but that is only apt, and the richness of inspiration, the musical intensification – beautifully conveyed here – transform the opera. The Paris version has never been recorded before, and that alone should dictate choice. But quite apart from that Solti gives one of his very finest Wagner performances to date, helped by superb playing from the Vienna Philharmonic and an outstanding cast, superlatively recorded. Dernesch as Elisabeth and Ludwig as Venus outshine all rivalry, and Kollo, though not ideal, makes as fine a Heldentenor as we are currently likely to hear.

Tannhäuser (Paris version): highlights.

> *** Decca SET 556 (from above recording).

Solti's set of *Tannhäuser*, by a fair margin the most compelling version ever recorded, should be sampled whole, but this is a reasonable enough selection, even if there are one or two chunks which defy neatness in the editing. Excellent recording.

Tannhäuser: Overture and Venusberg music.

> ** Decca Phase 4 PFS 4187. London Symphony Orchestra with chorus, Erich Leinsdorf – R. STRAUSS: *Rosenkavalier suite.***

Leinsdorf's performance of the *Tannhäuser overture and Venusberg music* has two obvious merits quite apart from the quality of the LSO's playing. The version of the score is used which links the two together, and in the Venusberg passages Phase 4 sumptuously lays on a heavenly (or should one say infernal?) choir. Two extrovert items recorded with opulent sound in multi-channel technique. The coupling makes excellent sense.

Tristan und Isolde (opera in 3 acts): complete recording.

> *** HMV SLS 963 (5 discs). Jon Vickers (tenor), Helga Dernesch (soprano), Christa Ludwig (mezzo-soprano), Walter Berry, Karl Ridderbusch (basses), Berlin Philharmonic Orchestra, Herbert von Karajan.

> ** (*) Decca SET 204/8. Fritz Uhl (tenor), Birgit Nilsson (soprano), Regina Resnik (contralto), Arnold van Mill (bass), Tom Krause (baritone), Vienna Philharmonic Orchestra, Sir Georg Solti.

> ** (*) DGG 2713 001 (5 discs). Wolfgang Windgassen (tenor), Birgit Nilsson (soprano), Christa Ludwig (mezzo-soprano), Martti Talvela (bass), Eberhard Waechter (baritone), Bayreuth Festival 1966 Orchestra, Karl Boehm.

Karajan's is a sensual performance of Wagner's masterpiece, caressingly beautiful and with superbly refined playing from the Berlin Philharmonic. At the climactic points of each act Karajan is a tantalizing deceiver, leading you to expect that the moment of resolution will not be fully achieved, but then punching home with a final crescendo of supreme force. He is helped by a recording (not ideally balanced, but warmly atmospheric) which copes with an enormous dynamic range. Dernesch as Isolde is seductively feminine, not so noble as Flagstad, not so tough and unflinching as Nilsson, but the human quality makes this account if anything more moving still, helped by glorious tone-colour through every range. Jon Vickers matches her, in what is arguably his finest performance on record, allowing himself true pianissimo shading. The rest of the cast is excellent too. A radiantly compelling set.

Solti's performance is less flexible and sensuous than Karajan's, but he shows himself ready to relax in Wagner's more expansive periods. On the other hand the end of Act 1 and the opening of the *Love duet* have a knife-edged dramatic tension. Birgit Nilsson responds superbly to his direction. There are moments when the great intensity that Flagstad brought to the part is not equalled, but more often than not Nilsson is masterly in her conviction, and – it cannot be emphasized too strongly – she never attacks below the note as Flagstad did, so that miraculously at the opening of the *Love duet* the impossibly difficult top Cs come out and hit the listener crisply and cleanly, dead on the note, and the *Liebestod* is all the more moving for having no soupy swerves at the climax.

Fritz Uhl is a really musical Heldentenor who also has the power needed for the part. Only during one passage of the *Love duet* (*O Sink' Hernieder'*) does he sound tired, and for the most part this is a superbly focused voice. Dramatically he leaves the centre of the stage to

Isolde, but his long solo passages in Act 3 are superb and make that sometimes tedious act into something genuinely gripping. The Kurwenal of Tom Krause and the King Mark of Arnold van Mill are both excellent, and it is only Regina Resnik as Brangaene who gives any disappointment. The production has the usual Decca/Culshaw imaginative touch, and the recording matches brilliance and clarity with satisfying co-ordination and richness of sound.

Boehm's account was taken from a live performance at Bayreuth, but apart from such passages as the *Prelude* and concluding *Liebestod*, where the experience is vivid, the performance too often acquires tension of the wrong sort, and Boehm's speeds are surprisingly fast. Nilsson is here more expressive but less bright-toned than in the Decca set, and Windgassen – in his time an incomparable Tristan – begins to show signs of wear in the voice. The other two male principals are first-rate, but Christa Ludwig's Brangaene is unexpectedly marred by a pronounced vibrato in the great warning solos that punctuate the *Love duet*. The recording favours the voices, suffering inevitably from live recording conditions.

Tristan und Isolde: highlights.
  ** (*) DGG slpem 136433 (from above recording cond. Boehm).

Boehm's reading of *Tristan* lacks – in the love music at least – the glowing expansive warmth one ideally needs. But a one-disc selection covering the obvious high points of the opera is welcome, and though the recording – made live in the Festspielhaus – has dated a little, this can be safely recommended.

Die Walküre (opera in 3 acts): complete recording.
  *** Decca set 321/6. Birgit Nilsson (soprano), Régine Crespin, Christa Ludwig (mezzo-sopranos), James

King (tenor), Hans Hotter (baritone), Gottlob Frick (bass), Vienna Philharmonic Orchestra, Sir Georg Solti.

** (*) DGG 2713 002 (5 discs). Régine Crespin (mezzo-soprano), Gundula Janowitz (soprano), Josephine Veasey (mezzo-soprano), Jon Vickers (tenor), Thomas Stewart (baritone), Martti Talvela (bass), Berlin Philharmonic Orchestra, Herbert von Karajan.

(M) ** (*) Decca 7BB 125/9. Birgit Nilsson (soprano), Gré Brouwenstijn (soprano), Jon Vickers (tenor), George London (baritone), David Ward (bass), London Symphony Orchestra, Erich Leinsdorf.

Solti's conception of *Die Walküre* is more lyrical than one would have expected from his recordings of the three other *Ring* operas. He sees Act 2 as the kernel of the work, perhaps even of the whole cycle. Acts 1 and 3 have their supremely attractive set-pieces, which must inevitably make them more popular as entertainment, but here one appreciates that in Act 2 the conflict of wills between Wotan and Fricka makes for one of Wagner's most deeply searching scenes. That is the more apparent when the greatest of latterday Wotans, Hans Hotter, takes the role, and Christa Ludwig sings with searing dramatic sense as his wife. Before that Act 1 seems a little underplayed, not nearly so sharp-edged as in Decca's rival version with Leinsdorf. This is partly because of Solti's deliberate lyricism – apt enough when love and spring greetings are in the air – but also (on the debit side) because James King fails to project the character of Siegmund, fails to delve into the word-meanings, as all the other members of the cast consistently do. Crespin has never sung more beautifully on record, but even

that cannot cancel out the shortcoming. As for Nilsson's Brünnhilde it has grown mellower since she made the earlier Decca recording, the emotions are clearer, and under-the-note attack is almost eliminated. Some may hesitate in the face of Hotter's obvious vocal trials but the unsteadiness is if anything less marked than in his EMI recordings of items done many years ago. Superlative recording.

The great merits of Karajan's version in competition with Solti's are the refinement of the orchestral playing and the heroic strength of Jon Vickers as Siegmund. With that underlined, one cannot but note that the vocal shortcomings here are generally more marked, and the total result does not add up to quite so compelling a dramatic experience; one is less involved. Thomas Stewart may have a younger, firmer voice than Hotter, but the character of Wotan emerges only partially. It is not just that he misses some of the word-meaning, but that on occasion – as in the kissing away of Brünnhilde's godhead – he underlines too crudely. A fine performance nonetheless, and Josephine Veasey as Fricka matches her rival Ludwig in conveying the biting intensity of the part. Gundula Janowitz's Sieglinde has its beautiful moments, but the singing is ultimately a little static. Crespin's Brünnhilde is impressive, but nothing like so satisfying as her study of Sieglinde on the Decca set. The voice is at times strained into unsteadiness, which the microphone seems to exaggerate. The DGG recording is good, but not quite in the same class as the Decca – though some machines may favour things the other way round.

In the earlier Decca set the playing of the LSO is splendid, and the sound is first-class. Leinsdorf, as in many RCA opera sets, is one of the major snags. He is vigorous and efficient, and the result is always exciting; but there is a monotony about his continual hard-driving. When one goes back to the old Furtwängler set (mono) the variation of tension, the sense of forward movement, make for something far more compelling. Leinsdorf affects the singers. Vickers misses the point of the spring greeting in a strangely ham-fisted piece of singing. Fortunately, this is very much an exception with him: most of his performance is superbly rich and heroic. Gré Brouwenstijn is even finer as Sieglinde. Her voice is purer-sounding and more radiant than ever before on record. David Ward is a resonant Hunding, Rita Gorr a strong Fricka. Nilsson is predictably excellent as Brünnhilde but not impeccable. It is the Wotan of George London that is the most serious blot on the set. The voice sounds coarse-grained and throaty, and since the recording is otherwise so superb one can hardly blame the technicians.

Die Walküre: highlights.
*** Decca SET 390 (from above recording cond. Solti).
(M) ** (*) Decca Ace of Diamonds SDD 430 (from above recording cond. Leinsdorf).

The Solti highlights disc is generously full and spectacularly well recorded. The items chosen make a particularly satisfying reminder of some of the finest moments in the set. Highly recommended to those for whom five records at premium price is not practicable. The Ace of Diamonds selection also concentrates some of the more outstanding moments of the complete recording: in excerpts the Leinsdorf performance seems more impressive. The quality of the singing is emphasized and the overforcefulness of the conducting is less noticeable when heard over a shorter span. Excellent recording.

Die Walküre: Act 1 (complete); *Götterdämmerung: Dawn and Siegfried's Rhine journey; Siegfried's funeral march.*

(M) *** Decca Ace of Diamonds GOS 581/2. Kirsten Flagstad (soprano), Set Svanholm (tenor), Arnold van Mill (bass), Vienna Philharmonic Orchestra, Hans Knappertsbusch.

This was a worthy companion to the Decca set of Act 3 (see below). Flagstad's voice is not so naturally suited to Sieglinde as to Brünnhilde, but although she cannot alter the essentially noble tone-colour of her voice this artist sings with wonderful gentleness to bring out Sieglinde's inner character. The meaning of the words is expressed in a manner almost reminiscent of Lieder-singing. Svanholm no longer has a really grateful-sounding voice but he sings intelligently. Arnold van Mill, when he rids himself of the habit of swerving up to notes, sings with great incisiveness – as in his challenge to Siegmund – and on occasion sounds almost too heroic for so grim a character as Hunding. Knappertsbusch is not so clean-edged and vital as Solti, but this is a dramatic reading with plenty of atmosphere – the sword theme shines out gloriously on the trumpet when Siegmund sees it gleaming in the tree. For the orchestral extracts from *Götterdämmerung* Knappertsbusch returns to his usual duller style, but the stereo ensures that unexceptional playing is still enjoyable.

Die Walküre: Act 1 (complete); Act 3: *Wotan's farewell.*
** (*) HMV SLS 968 (2 discs). Helga Dernesch (soprano), William Cochran (tenor), Norman Bailey (baritone), Hans Sotin (bass), New Philharmonia Orchestra, Otto Klemperer.

In places in *Wotan's farewell* there is almost a hint of self-parody in Klemperer's reading with its measured tempi and gruff manner. That final side from

Act 3 is by far the least impressive here, despite fine singing from Norman Bailey. Act 1 is quite different, concentrated and intense, showing a great musician meditating and rethinking, never merely plodding. In the pauseful exchanges Klemperer's care for phrasing, his ability to lead the ear on with what for him is a surprisingly expressive style, make this an unforgettable experience, a fine souvenir of Klemperer's very last period in the recording studio. Dernesch, Cochran and Sotin make a fine trio of soloists, and the recording is outstanding.

Die Walküre: Act 2: *Todesverkündigung (Death announcement scene);* Act 3 (complete).

> (M) *** Decca Ace of Diamonds GOS 577/8. Kirsten Flagstad (soprano), Set Svanholm (tenor), Otto Edelmann (bass), Vienna Philharmonic Orchestra, Sir Georg Solti.

One remembers well the excitement of this as an original full-priced issue. Just when we thought there was no chance of the finest Brünnhilde of her time recording the part, Decca put us eternally in their debt by issuing this set. The reissue is no less valuable, even though we now have the complete *Ring* with Nilsson. Flagstad sings radiantly. During her period of retirement, before these records were made, she seemed to have acquired an extra wisdom and an extra maturity in interpretation. The meticulousness needed in the recording studio obviously brought out all her finest qualities, and there is no more than a touch of hardness on some of the top notes to show that the voice is no longer as young as it was. Edelmann is not the ideal Wotan. He has a particularly well-focused voice and when he sings straight, without sliding up or sitting under the note, the result is superb. It is perhaps a tribute to the quality of his voice that one can tell so clearly when

he is singing under the note. So many Wotans are wobbly, and that Edelmann never is. Svanholm in the *Death announcement scene* sings intelligently if not always with grateful tone-colour, but it is Solti's conducting that prevents any slight blemishes from mattering. His rethinking of the score means that time and time again at particularly dramatic points one finds that the increased excitement engendered is merely the result of a literal following of all Wagner's markings. The recording too is remarkably vivid, anticipating the excellence of the great *Ring* project which was to follow.

COLLECTIONS

'Great moments': Lohengrin: *Preludes to Acts 1 and 3;* Rienzi: *overture;* (i) Die Walküre: *Wotan's farewell and Magic fire music.*

> ** Decca Phase 4 PFS 4205. New Philharmonia Orchestra, George Hurst, (i) with David Ward (bass).

It was time that record-collectors had a chance to sample the fine impersonation of Wotan by David Ward, even if this account of *Wotan's farewell* falls short of the ideal. The microphone shows up a certain fuzziness in the tone, but those who have enjoyed Ward's performances at Covent Garden – and for that matter all over the world – here have a fair reminder of his artistry. Hurst's interpretations of this and the other 'great moments' are strong and straightforward, recorded with exaggerated echo in the rather spectacular manner of Phase 4.

'The "Golden" Ring': Das Rheingold: *Entry of the gods into Valhalla;* Die Walküre: *Ride of the Valkyries;* Siegfried: *Forest murmurs;* Götterdämmerung: *Prelude; Siegfried's Rhine journey; Rhinemaidens' song; Siegfried's funeral march.* Siegfried idyll.

*** Decca SXL 6421. Birgit Nilsson (soprano), Wolfgang Windgassen (tenor), Vienna Philharmonic Orchestra, Sir Georg Solti.

This collection of 'pops' from the *Ring* plus the *Siegfried idyll* (also available on Deryck Cooke's *Ring* lecture disc; see above), makes a generous disc, highly recommendable to anyone just setting out on the path of Wagner-worship. Fine performances from the complete cycle, and brilliant recording.

'*Greatest hits*': *Lohengrin:* (i) *Prelude to Act 3;* (i; ii) *Bridal chorus;* (iii) *Die Meistersinger: Prelude to Act 1; Tannhäuser:* (iv) *Grand march;* (i; ii) *Pilgrims' chorus;* (i) *Tristan und Isolde: Liebestod;* (iv) *Die Walküre: Ride of the Valkyries.*

> (B) ** CBS Harmony 30008. (i) Philadelphia Orchestra, Eugene Ormandy; (ii) Mormon Tabernacle Choir; (iii) Cleveland Orchestra, George Szell; (iv) New York Philharmonic Orchestra, Leonard Bernstein.

Szell opens this collection with a fine performance of the *Meistersinger prelude.* The only vocal items are the two choruses, sonorously presented by the Mormons. Bernstein's *Ride of the Valkyries* is characteristically brilliant but lacks weight in the bass, and in the *March* from *Tannhäuser* the recording could use more richness in the middle frequencies. But on the whole this is an acceptable collection.

'*Greatest hits, Vol. 2*': (i) *Siegfried idyll;* (ii) *Götterdämmerung: Dawn and Siegfried's Rhine journey;* (i) *Lohengrin: Prelude to Act 1;* (ii) *Das Rheingold: Entry of the gods into Valhalla; Tannhäuser: Overture.*

> (B) * (*) CBS Harmony 30038. (i)

Columbia Symphony Orchestra, Bruno Walter; (ii) Cleveland Orchestra, George Szell.

This opens with a thrilling performance of the *Entry of the gods into Valhalla.* It is vividly recorded, but the sound is less refined in the scene from *Götterdämmerung*, although the concentration of the playing here is impressive. The *Tannhäuser overture* is much cooler, and both here and in Walter's *Lohengrin prelude*, which is disappointingly unexpansive, the dry recorded sound detracts from the effect of the performances. Walter's *Siegfried idyll* is not wanting in atmosphere (although the quality is acceptable rather than outstanding), and this performance has a certain distinction, although it too is restrained.

'*The world of Wagner*': (i; ii) *Götterdämmerung: Siegfried's Rhine journey; Siegfried's funeral march; Tannhäuser: Overture;* (iii) *Elisabeth's greeting;* (iv) *O star of eve; Tristan und Isolde:* (i) *Liebestod; Die Walküre: Ride of the Valkyries;* (v) *Magic fire music.*

> (B) (**) Decca SPA 317. (i) Birgit Nilsson (soprano); (ii) Wolfgang Windgassen (tenor); (iii) Helga Dernesch (soprano); (iv) Victor Braun (baritone); (v) Hans Hotter (baritone); all with Vienna Philharmonic Orchestra, Sir Georg Solti.

These 'bleeding chunks' let blood sometimes at both ends, with fades-in as well as fades-out. Wagner is virtually impossible to summarize in this way (if the excerpts are taken from complete versions), for his music seldom produces a suitable cadence where it might be wanted. Of course, the performances are of the highest quality, but this is a most unsatisfying set of excerpts, and it would certainly have been better to have chosen Hotter's *Magic fire music* scene to end the disc (as it comes to a proper finish) than leaving us in mid-air at the end of *Siegfried's funeral march*. The transfers are almost too brilliant, with a hint of shrillness, and the heavy modulation at the climax of the *Liebestod* right at the end of side one will offer problems to all but the finest pick-ups.

Wallace, Vincent
(1812–65)

Maritana (opera in 3 acts): *Overture; In happy moments; Yes, let me like a soldier fall; Scenes that are brightest*.

** H M V CSD 3651. Veronica Dunne (soprano), Uel Deane (tenor), Eric Hinds (baritone), Orchestra, Havelock Nelson – BALFE: *Bohemian Girl*; BENEDICT: *Lily of Killarney*.**

Maritana was first produced at the Drury Lane Theatre in 1845. Rightly, even though the selection is short, the overture is included, for it is a marvellously typical piece in the melodramatic pot-pourri style. It is carried along splendidly by an inherently vulgar vitality and features as its centrepiece the memorable *Scenes that are brightest*, which is also sung here, a little gustily, by Veronica Dunne. But Miss Dunne has an ample voice and better this than a soubrette style. The baritone, Eric Hinds, has a warm voice and fatherly manner (he would do Germont in *Traviata* well) and he sings *In happy moments* with the proper degree of maudlin cheerfulness. This is irresistible. The tenor is less characterful in *Yes, let me like a soldier fall* – there is no rattle of drums and cannon in his delivery – but he has a pleasant voice and this is enjoyable enough. The conductor really has the feel for Wallace's scoring, and the recording balance is equally happy, so that the

orchestral colour with its flavour of the bandstand comes over well. Most enjoyable.

Walton, William
(born 1902)

Capriccio burlesco; Crown Imperial (coronation march, 1937); *Johannesburg Festival overture; Orb and Sceptre* (coronation march, 1953); *Scapino overture; The Spitfire: Prelude and fugue* (incidental music for the film *The First of the Few*).

** (*) Columbia Studio 2 TWO 272. Royal Liverpool Philharmonic Orchestra, Sir Charles Groves.

An attractive collection of Walton's popular shorter orchestral pieces. The orchestral playing is excellent, and if Groves is a little phlegmatic in the two marches, the *nobilmente* concept tending to minimize the bite, the *Johannesburg Festival overture* has a sparkling scherzando quality. The stirring music for *The First of the Few* is also very effective, helped by the splendid recording, resonant and sonorous, yet bright and clear.

Capriccio burlesco; Façade (ballet): *Suite No. 1; Johannesburg Festival overture*.

(M) ** (*) CBS Classics 61365. Orchestra, André Kostelanetz – BRITTEN: *Soirées musicales*.**

Walton wrote his *Capriccio burlesco* on a commission from Kostelanetz, who conducted the first performance in New York. This characteristic bustling piece is here given a performance of tremendous brio, and so are the other two items, the everdelectable *Façade* pieces and the most lovable and exuberant of Walton's three witty overtures. Forward, larger-than-life recording.

Capriccio burlesco; The Quest (ballet suite)*; Scapino overture;* (i) *Sinfonia concertante for orchestra with piano.*

*** Lyrita SRCS 49. London Symphony Orchestra, the composer, (i) with Peter Katin (piano).

We have needed a new recording of the *Sinfonia concertante* for a long time, though this admittedly has not the bite and dash of the post-war recording briefly available again on World Record Club (SH 128). But what is even more valuable is *The Quest*, an attractive score not otherwise represented on record, so that this disc will be eagerly sought by admirers of Walton's music. The performances have the composer's authority, though there are the odd untidinesses here and there. On the whole, though, good playing and truthful recording.

(i) *Viola concerto;* (ii) *Violin concerto.*
** (*) HMV ASD 2542. Yehudi Menuhin (i) (viola), New Philharmonia Orchestra; (ii) (violin), London Symphony Orchestra; both cond. the composer.
(M) ** (*) CBS Classics 61584. (i) Paul Doktor (viola), London Philharmonic Orchestra, Edward Downes; (ii) Zino Francescatti (violin), Philadelphia Orchestra, Eugene Ormandy.

Fine performances of both works from Menuhin, who is in reasonably good form in the *Violin concerto* and makes a very good showing in the masterly *Viola concerto.* Walton himself is at the helm and secures expert playing from the New Philharmonia and the LSO. HMV provide a musically satisfying balance and excellent sound. But many Waltonians will not approve the extremely slow account of the *Viola concerto* first movement.

Both Doktor and Francescatti give urgent and passionate readings of two of the greatest romantic concertos of the century. Doktor's recording is particularly valuable, since this work has been comparatively unlucky on record. The balance favours the soloist, but not so as to mar enjoyment. The *Violin concerto*, an older recording, still sounds well, with good atmospheric sound. Francescatti may not always convey the finer shadings of the music, but the assurance of his playing is consistently compelling.

Violin concerto.
⊛ *** Decca SXL 6601. Kyung-Wha Chung (violin), London Symphony Orchestra, André Previn – STRAVINSKY: *Violin concerto.***

The *Violin concerto*, written for Heifetz in 1939, shows Walton at his most distinctively compelling. Even he has rarely written melodies so ravishingly beautiful, so hauntedly romantic, yet his equally personal brand of spikiness has rarely if ever been presented with more power. Kyung-Wha Chung recorded this rich work immediately after playing a long sequence of live performances, and the brooding intensity of the opening presents the first melody with a depth of expressiveness, tender and hushed, that has never been matched on record, not even by Heifetz himself. With Previn as guide, and with the composer himself as a sympathetic observer at the recording sessions, Chung then builds up a performance which must remain a classic, showing the concerto as one of the greatest of the century in this genre. Outstandingly fine recording.

Violoncello concerto.
*** HMV ASD 2924. Paul Tortelier (cello), Bournemouth Symphony Orchestra, Paavo Berglund – SHOSTAKOVICH: *Cello concerto.***
(M) ** RCA LSB 4101. Gregor Piatigorsky (cello), Boston Symphony

Orchestra, Charles Munch –
BLOCH: *Schelomo.*** (*)

The *Cello concerto*, written for Piatigorsky soon after Walton had completed his opera *Troilus and Cressida*, is a
work that has often seemed rather cool
in comparison with his two earlier string
concertos, but here Tortelier with characteristically passionate playing shows the
composer's consistency. After the haunting melancholy of the first movement,
the central scherzo emerges as a far
weightier piece than most such movements, while the final variations have
never before on record developed with
such sense of compulsion. More than
ever one senses the direct link with the
moods and emotions of *Troilus and
Cressida*, different from early Walton but
just as seductive. Excellent playing and
rich, warm recording.

Piatigorsky's version will always
remain a classic of its kind, and some will
prefer its chillier, more austere approach,
coupled with immaculate playing of
bravura. Good recording of its period.

Façade (an entertainment with words
by Edith Sitwell): complete recording.
** (*) HMV ASD 2786. Fenella
Fielding, Michael Flanders (speak-
ers), Academy of St Martin-in-
the-Fields, Neville Marriner.
(M) ** (*) Philips International 6832
037. Cleo Laine, Annie Ross
(speakers), Ensemble, Johnny
Dankworth.
* Argo ZRG 649. Peggy Ashcroft,
Paul Scofield (speakers), London
Sinfonietta, the composer.

Fenella Fielding and Michael Flanders
make a characterful pair of reciters for
Edith Sitwell's *Façade* poems, the one
relishing in echo the *grande dame* quality
of the poetess, the other wonderfully fleet
of tongue, if not so miraculously deft as
the late Constant Lambert, or even Peter

Pears, who with Edith Sitwell herself still
provides the finest available performance
of the complete entertainment on Decca
Eclipse (ECS 560); this is not real stereo
but the transcription is astonishingly
successful, clear and atmospheric. The
HMV stereo is naturally cleaner,
more brilliant, but the balance favours
the reciters against Neville Marriner's
wittily pointed accompaniment.

The Cleo Laine/Annie Ross performance is controversial. With its distinct
jazz overtones, this is a version you will
either enjoy very much (as does I.M.) or
find slightly self-conscious (as does E.G.).
Certainly at medium price it is worth
trying.

Walton's own recording on Argo is a
near-disaster, not for the musical side
(which sadly can barely be heard behind
the speakers) but for the utter miscasting
of Paul Scofield, the slowest and least
rhythmic of reciters. Peggy Ashcroft is
more aptly characterful, but also lags
behind the beat. She is recorded so close
her breath is constantly in one's ear.

*Façade: Ballet suites Nos. 1 and 2
(Scotch rhapsody; Valse; Tango-paso-
doblé; Swiss yodelling song; Country
dance; Polka; Noche espagnole; Popular song; Old Sir Faulk; Tarantella
sevilla.)*
(B) *** Decca Eclipse ECS 586. Orchestra of the Royal Opera House,
Covent Garden, Anatole Fistoulari – LECOCQ: *Mam'zelle Angot.****

Fistoulari includes all the music from
both suites but with the numbers
rearranged, presumably in ballet order.
His account is brilliant and witty. The
best numbers are the delightfully delicate
Country dance and a superb *Old Sir
Faulk*, where the foxtrot style of the
twenties is perfectly parodied. The recording is first-class.

Façade: Suite No. 1 (complete); *Suite No. 2: Scotch rhapsody; Popular song; Old Sir Faulk* (only).

(M) ** HMV sxlp 30114. Royal Philharmonic Orchestra, Sir Malcolm Sargent – BRITTEN: *Simple symphony; Young Person's Guide.***

Sir Malcolm's musical personality is strong here. A lighter touch might have found more wit in some of the numbers, but the conductor's rather bland approach suits *Old Sir Faulk* especially well. The recording was always warm and spacious; now it has an extra touch of brightness, which is apt.

Film scores: *The First of the Few: Spitfire prelude and fugue; Hamlet: Funeral march; Henry V: suite (Passacaglia – Death of Falstaff; Charge and battle; Touch her soft lips and part; Agincourt song); Richard III: Prelude and suite.*

(M) ** (*) HMV sxlp 30139. Philharmonia Orchestra, the composer.

It has been said of film music that it is only good film music if it is not noticed. This is, of course, only partly true, and in recent years a striking 'theme' associated with a famous movie has often had the effect of bringing audiences into the cinema to see the action associated with it. But Walton's film scores mostly date from an earlier period, when the writing followed a long-established tradition of incidental music for the theatre. The score for *Richard III* is a good example of this. The inspiration is direct, and the individual pieces are sufficiently varied in style to make up a good suite. The score for *Henry V* is rather less striking, although the music for the *Death of Falstaff* is touching. But easily the most memorable piece here is the stirring and eloquent *Prelude and fugue* Walton put together from his music for the bio-

graphical film about R. J. Mitchell, the designer of the Spitfire. The performances on this disc have atmosphere and intensity, and if the recording is not as brilliant and clearly defined as it might be, it has plenty of warmth and colour.

Sonata for strings.

*** Argo zrg 711. Iona Brown, Trevor Connah (violins), Stephen Shingles (viola), Kenneth Heath (cello), Academy of St Martin-in-the-Fields, Neville Marriner – PROKOFIEV: *Visions fugitives.****

Walton made this transcription of his *String quartet* of 1947 at the express suggestion of Neville Marriner. For the bigger ensemble Walton tautened the argument, while expanding the richness of texture, frequently relating the full band to the sound of four solo instruments. Though something of the acerbity of the original is lost, the result is another in the sequence of great British string works, warmly romantic in lyricism in the first and third movements, spikily brilliant in the scherzo and finale. Superb performance and recording.

Symphony No. 1 in B flat minor.

(M) *** RCA lsb 4100. London Symphony Orchestra, André Previn.

(M) ** (*) HMV sxlp 30138. New Philharmonia Orchestra, Sir Malcolm Sargent.

(B) * (*) Pye gsgc 14008. London Philharmonic Orchestra, Sir Adrian Boult.

Previn gives a marvellously biting account of this magnificent symphony. His fast tempi may initially make one feel that he is pressing too hard, but his ability to screw the dramatic tension tighter and tighter until the final resolution is most assured, and certainly reflects the tense mood of the mid-thirties, as well as the youthful Walton's own dynamism. '*Presto con malizia*' says the score for the scherzo, and malice is exactly what Previn conveys, with the hints of vulgarity and humour securely placed. In the slow movement Previn finds real warmth, giving some of the melodies an Elgarian richness, and the finale's tension here helps to overcome any feeling that it is too facile, too easily happy a conclusion. The valedictory trumpet solo in the final section is not so hushed as it might be, but the surge on to the end is richly convincing. The bright recording quality matches Previn's youthful approach.

Sargent's is a less urgent performance of this highly dramatic symphony. The playing of the New Philharmonia is a degree more polished, the phrasing more consciously lyrical, and anyone wanting a reflective view of the work would plainly prefer it. But the comparative absence of fire in the scherzo is a serious shortcoming, and there is little doubt that Previn's view reflects the period more convincingly. The EMI recording, not so brilliant as the RCA, lets through rather more beauty of detail, and is richer in the matter of string tone.

Boult's performance too is a fine one, ringing with power and conviction, and it seems a pity that Pye in their – admittedly partly successful – efforts to modernize the sound have added extra reverberation. This clouds the detail objectionably, and the bold brass climaxes of the first movement have an overhang. The scherzo too loses much of its pointed impact, and in the finale the strings lack focus.

Symphony No. 2; Portsmouth Point overture; Scapino overture.
> *** HMV ASD 2990. London Symphony Orchestra, André Previn – LAMBERT: *The Rio Grande.*** (*)

If Walton's *Second Symphony* prompted George Szell to direct the Cleveland Orchestra in one of its most spectacular

performances on record (see below), André Previn and the LSO give another brilliant performance, which in some ways gets closer to the heart of the music, with its overtones of the romantic opera *Troilus and Cressida*. Previn is less literal than Szell, more sparkling in the outer movements, more warmly romantic in the central slow movement. In the two overtures Previn, the shrewdest and most perceptive of Waltonians, finds more light and shade than usual. The recording is outstandingly good.

Symphony No. 2; Variations on a theme of Hindemith.
> (M) *** CBS Classics 61087. Cleveland Orchestra, George Szell.

In a letter to the conductor Walton expressed himself greatly pleased with this performance of the symphony. 'It is a quite fantastic and stupendous performance from every point of view. Firstly, it is absolutely right musically speaking, and the virtuosity is quite staggering, especially the Fugato; but everything is phrased and balanced in an unbelievable way.' Szell's performance of the *Hindemith variations* is no less praiseworthy. Again the music is immaculate technically, but lacking, in most performances, the sense of urgency which marked all Walton's pre-war music. Under Szell, however, there is far less room for doubt, and each chiselled fragment is perfectly set in place, brightly and memorably. With such a coupling and clear, brilliant recording, the Cleveland Orchestra could hardly be displayed to better advantage.

String quartet in A minor.
> ** Argo ZRG 5329. Allegri Quartet – MACONCHY: *Quartet No. 5.****

Walton's *Quartet* (1947) was the first major work to appear after his long period of lying fallow during the war (save for writing film scores). To some it seemed a comparatively slight work, and its neatly chiselled pattern of two brief and brilliant scherzos acting as epilogues to two longer and more serious movements was the opposite of portentous. But the material is all most memorable, very much of the vintage that is displayed in the pre-war works rather than the later works when Walton's inspiration lost some of its vitality. There was a magnificent first recording on an early LP by the Hollywood Quartet, and by comparison with that this one runs at rather a low voltage. But it is so compelling a work that any version is most welcome, and as ever the Allegri Quartet make up for lack of brilliance with understanding and sympathy. Excellent recording quality.

Violin sonata.

(B) * (*) Pye GSGC 14111. Mary Nemet (violin), Roxanne Wruble (piano) – BRITTEN: *Suite.***

Walton's *Violin sonata* was written soon after the war, with Yehudi Menuhin's vibrant playing in mind. Mary Nemet brings to it the romantic style and warmth of phrasing which its leisurely paragraphs call for, but the tone is not always rich enough or the intonation clean enough. Of all Walton's works this is formally one of the least satisfactory, with its two longish movements neither fast nor slow, and one really needs more positive playing if its weaknesses are to be disguised. Very welcome all the same, with so apt a coupling. Clean, atmospheric recording.

Belshazzar's Feast (oratorio).

(B) ** (*) Classics for Pleasure CFP 40063. Michael Rippon (baritone), Hallé Choir, Hallé Orchestra, James Loughran.

(M) ** Vox STGBY 658. Robert Peterson (baritone), Utah University Civic Chorale, Utah Symphony Orchestra, Maurice Abra-

vanel – VAUGHAN WILLIAMS: *The Lark ascending.** (*)

(i) *Belshazzar's Feast. Improvisations on an impromptu of Benjamin Britten.*

*** HMV SAN 324. London Symphony Orchestra, André Previn, (i) with John Shirley-Quirk (baritone), LSO Chorus.

(i) *Belshazzar's Feast;* (ii) *Partita for orchestra.*

(M) ** CBS Classics 61264. (i) Walter Cassell (baritone), Rutgers University Choir, Philadelphia Orchestra, Eugene Ormandy; (ii) Cleveland Orchestra, George Szell.

Previn's is the richest and most spectacular version of *Belshazzar's Feast* yet recorded. As a Waltonian he seems to have taken on the mantle of the composer himself as interpreter. This fine performance was recorded with Walton present on his seventieth birthday, and though Previn's tempi are occasionally slower than those set by Walton himself in his two recordings, the authenticity is clear, with consistently sharp attack and with dynamic markings meticulously observed down to the tiniest hairpin markings. Chorus and orchestra are challenged to their finest standards, and Shirley-Quirk proves a searching and imaginative soloist. Fine vivid sound. The *Improvisations*, given a first recording, make a generous fill-up.

Loughran's version is forthright and dramatic, helped by splendid brilliant recording quality. The orchestra is particularly well caught, and so is the excellent soloist, firm and clear in attack. The snag is the work of the chorus, relatively small and placed rather close to the microphones, so that details of imperfect ensemble and intonation tend to be exaggerated. The result is still a fine, convincing account of a gripping masterpiece, outstanding at the price.

Ormandy's performance is characteristically bold and spacious in conception.

1097

The chorus are enthusiastic, and even though the singing itself is not too sophisticated, the overall effect carries conviction. The soloist is forthright and his words are clear. The recording is very good. Szell's performance of the *Partita* makes an excellent bonus, brilliantly played and extremely brilliantly recorded.

Abravanel directs a strong and colourful performance, not ideally polished, but with a good firm baritone soloist and enthusiastic choral singing. Good recording.

3 Carols; Jubilate; Litany; Missa brevis; Set me a seal; The Twelve; Where does the uttered music go?
*** Argo ZRG 725. Christ Church Cathedral Choir, Oxford, Simon Preston; Stephen Darlington (organ).

This delightful disc, superbly performed and recorded, gives an excellent survey of Walton's choral development over five decades, from the work of the chorister at Christ Church Cathedral to the *Jubilate* given first at the Cathedral in 1972. In *The Twelve*, another late work, Walton sets the words of Auden, also from the same college. The *Missa brevis* is uncharacteristically austere – it was originally written for Coventry Cathedral – but in everything the distinctive Walton touch can be detected, the magic ingredient that gives life to any of his music, however simple.

A Song for the Lord Mayor's Table (song cycle). Songs: *Daphne; Façade: Through gilded trellises; Old Sir Faulk.*
(M) ** (*) Oiseau-Lyre SOL 331. Heather Harper (soprano), English Chamber Orchestra, Raymond Leppard; Paul Hamburger (piano) – MACONCHY: *Ariadne.*** (*)

Walton wrote his delightful song cycle for Schwarzkopf to sing at the first City of London Festival, and though Heather Harper is not quite so imaginative as the original performer, she makes much of these vigorous and memorable little songs, including the unexpected setting of *Oranges and lemons*. The offshoots from *Façade* are also most welcome to the catalogue. Good recording.

Warlock, Peter
(1894–1930)

Capriol suite for strings.
(M) ** HMV SXLP 30126. Royal Philharmonic Orchestra, Sir Malcolm Sargent – HOLST: *Beni Mora etc.;* ELGAR: *Serenade.***

Sargent's tempi are broad and he brings out the richness of harmony and the music's dignified sonority rather than investing the score with any special vitality; but with such excellent string-playing and a warm recording, this is very enjoyable.

The Curlew (song cycle for tenor, flute, cor anglais and strings).
(M) *** HMV HQS 1325. Ian Partridge (tenor), Music Group of London – VAUGHAN WILLIAMS: *4 Hymns etc.****

The Curlew is Warlock's most striking and ambitious work, a continuous setting of a sequence of poems by Yeats, which reflect the darker side of the composer's complex personality. Ian Partridge, with the subtlest shading of tone-colour and the most sensitive response to word-meaning, gives an intensely poetic performance, beautifully recorded.

The Curlew (song cycle). Songs: *The Birds; Chopcherry; The fairest May;*

Mourne no more; My ghostly fader; Nursery jingles (How many miles to Babylon?; O, my kitten; Little Jack Jingle; Suky, you shall be my wife; Jenney Gray); Sleep; The Water Lily.

** (*) Pearl SHE 510. James Griffett (tenor), Haffner String Quartet, Mary Murdoch (cor anglais), Mary Ryan (flute).

Though this performance of The Curlew is not so beautiful or quite so imaginative as Ian Partridge's, it is good to have a whole record of songs by a composer with a strikingly distinctive feeling for English verse. Each one of these songs is a miniature of fine sensitivity, and James Griffett sings them with keen insight, pointing the words admirably. Good recording.

'Merry-go-down' (anthology): Capriol: Tordion; Mattachins. Hey troly loly lo; Fill the cup; In an arbour green; Sweet content; Prosdocimus de Beldamandis Snr. Cod-pieces: Beethoven's binge; The old codger. Peter Warlock's fancy; I asked a thief to steal me a peach; Jillian of Berry; My ghostly fader; Away to Twiver; Mother's ruin; Drunken song in the Saurian mode. E. J. MOERAN and WARLOCK: Maltworms. OINOPHILUS: In good company. ARISTOTLE: An observation on beer-drinkers. NASHE: Eight kinds of drunkenness. WHYTHORNE: As thy shadow itself apply'th. DOWLAND: My Lady Hunsdon's puffe; Mrs White's nothinge. BLUNT: The drunken wizard. BEAUMONT and FLETCHER: The Knight of the Burning Pestle (excerpts). ROSSETER: When Laura smiles. RAVENSCROFT: Malt's come down; The maid she went a-milking; By a bank as I lay; Jinkin the Jester; What hap had I to marry a shrew; He that will an alehouse keep. ANON., ed. WARLOCK:

Have you seen but a white lily grow?; One more river; Wine v. women; The lady's birthday. WARLOCK, arr. TOMLINSON: Piggesnie.

(M) *** Unicorn UNS 249. Ian Partridge (tenor), Neilson Taylor (baritone), Jennifer Partridge (piano and soprano), Peter Gray (speaker), Jennifer Partridge, Fred Tomlinson (piano duet).

Songs, partsongs, rounds and readings from a Warlock anthology – a delightful collection, with specially fine singing from Ian Partridge. Fascinating too are the piano duets, including parodies of Beethoven and Franck. An oddity worth investigating, well recorded.

Weber, Carl Maria von (1786–1826)

Overtures: Abu Hassan; Beherrscher der Geister (The Ruler of the Spirits); Der Freischütz; Euryanthe; Jubel; Oberon; Preciosa.

(B) ** Decca Eclipse ECS 645. Suisse Romande Orchestra, Ernest Ansermet.

This is an early Ansermet record. The orchestral playing is robust and not comparable in refinement with Karajan's Berlin Philharmonic disc (see below). The sound is atmospheric and quite vivid, the balance not always perfect: the muted string passage in Euryanthe seems too near and fails to achieve a real pianissimo. Jubel, not included when the disc was first issued, is notable mainly for including God Save the Queen. A good bargain issue.

Overtures: Abu Hassan; Beherrscher der Geister; Euryanthe; Der Freischütz; Oberon; Peter Schmoll.

*** DGG 2530 315. Berlin Philharmonic Orchestra, Herbert von Karajan.

An outstanding disc of Weber overtures performed with great style and refinement. Warm recording.

Andante and Hungarian rondo (for bassoon and orchestra), *Op. 35; Bassoon concerto in F major, Op. 75.*

(B) ** Turnabout TV 34039S. George Zukerman (bassoon), Württemberg Chamber Orchestra, Joerg Faerber – MOZART: *Bassoon concerto.***

The *Bassoon concerto* is somewhat insubstantial, without much orchestral interest, but the *Andante and Hungarian rondo* (originally written for viola and rescored for bassoon by the composer) is more characteristic of Weber's usual instrumental and melodic facility. Both performances are excellent.

(i) *Andante and Hungarian rondo in C minor for viola and orchestra;* (ii) *Horn concerto in E minor, Op. 45;* (iii) *Piano concerto No. 2 in E flat major, Op. 32;* (iv) *Romanza siciliana in G minor for flute and small orchestra.*

(B) * (*) Turnabout TV 34488S. (i) Ulrich Koch (viola); (ii) Francis Orval (horn); (iii) Akiko Sagara (piano); (iv) Peter Thalheimer (flute); all with Hamburg Symphony Orchestra, Günter Neidlinger.

A serviceable collection of works that, with one exception, are not otherwise available in stereo. The recording is characteristically dry, like the other records in this Turnabout series, and it must be admitted that there is a serious lack of charm, especially in the *Piano concerto No. 2*, which is rather clattery.

The *Andante and Hungarian rondo* is given in the original version, and Zukerman's companion Turnabout performance (see above) proves that Weber's second thoughts were best: it sounds somewhat lugubrious here. The *Horn concerto* is written to encompass the horn's extreme limits of bravura. Orval plays it with impressive assurance, but the horn chords which are its special feature (the soloist sings one note, plays another and sets the instrument's natural harmonics resounding) sound rather comic here. There is a superb performance of this work by Hermann Baumann on BASF (BAC 3037) within a collection discussed in our *Treasury* volume.

Clarinet concerto No. 1 in F minor, Op. 73; Clarinet concertino in C minor, Op. 26.

*** HMV ASD 2455. Gervase de Peyer (clarinet), New Philharmonia Orchestra, Rafael Frühbeck de Burgos.

These are charming pieces that require, and here receive, great elegance in performance. Gervase de Peyer plays the virtuoso solo parts with studied ease, and the orchestral support is as alert and lively as one could ask for. The recordings are reasonably wide in range and produce an agreeably warm sound.

(i) *Clarinet concerto No. 1 in F minor, Op. 73;* (ii) *Clarinet concertino in C minor, Op. 26;* (iii) *Clarinet quintet in B flat major, Op. 34.*

(B) ** Turnabout TV 34151S. David Glazer (clarinet), with (i) Württemberg Chamber Orchestra, Joerg Faerber; (ii) Innsbruck Symphony Orchestra, Robert Wagner; (iii) Kohon Quartet.

A valuable anthology, reasonably priced. The performances of both the concertante works are on the dry side (the recording is partly at fault); the *Quintet* is warmer, if at the expense of clarity of texture. But on the whole this is a useful disc.

(i) *Clarinet concerto No. 1 in F minor, Op. 73;* (ii) *Invitation to the Dance* (orch. Berlioz); (ii; iii) *Konzertstück in F minor* (for piano and orchestra), *Op. 79.*

    (M) *** DGG Privilege 2538 087. (i) Karl Leister (clarinet), Berlin Philharmonic Orchestra, Rafael Kubelik; (ii) Berlin Radio Symphony Orchestra, Ferenc Fricsay; (iii) Margrit Weber (piano).

This is an attractive collection, offering an altogether higher degree of sophistication of both performance and recording than the Turnabout series of Weber concertante discs. At less than full price Karl Leister's excellent, if slightly reticent musicianship is fully acceptable (the performance of the *Clarinet concerto* is also available coupled with the Mozart at full price: SLPEM 136550). Margrit Weber's reading of the *Konzertstück* is first-class. Her approach is classical in style, but she clearly sympathizes with the operatic element in the music, and she is well supported by Fricsay, who also gives an enjoyable account of *Invitation to the Dance*. This is possibly the best single investment in this section of Weber's output.

Clarinet concerto No. 2 in E flat major, Op. 74.

    (M) ** Oiseau-Lyre SOL 60035. Gervase de Peyer (clarinet), London Symphony Orchestra, Colin Davis – SPOHR: *Clarinet concerto No. 1.***

The *Second Clarinet concerto* is full of character. The second subject of the first

movement – a real singer's tune – is especially memorable, as is the infectious finale, packed with fireworks. Only the central *Andante* is disappointing, being devoid of melodic distinction. The piece makes an excellent foil to its Spohr coupling, and Gervase de Peyer is fully up to the considerable virtuosity demanded in the soloist. The recording is dry, and the clarinet suffers slightly in the upper register from exaggeration by the microphone of its upper partials. However, a treble reduction can correct this to a considerable extent.

Piano concerto No. 1 in C major, Op. 11; Konzertstück in F minor (for piano and orchestra), *Op. 79; Polacca brillante (L'Hilarité) in E major, Op. 72* (arr. for piano and orchestra by Liszt).

    (B) * (*) Turnabout TV 34406S. Maria Littauer (piano), Hamburg Symphony Orchestra, Siegfried Köhler.

The recording here is shallow and the orchestral sound thin and undistinguished. The piano tone is acceptable and these performances have plenty of life; but Margrit Weber's account of the *Konzertstück* on Privilege (see above) has more substance.

Grand pot-pourri for violoncello and orchestra.

    (B) ** Turnabout TV 34306S. Thomas Blees (violoncello), Berlin Symphony Orchestra, C. A. Bünte – DANZI: *Cello concerto.*** (*)

Weber's *Grand pot-pourri* (strange title) is in fact an attractive cello concerto in all but name, not so vital a novelty as the fine Danzi work on the reverse, but an interesting addition to the Weber catalogue. The four comparatively brief sections display the cello well, and Thomas Blees confirms the good opinions inspired by the Danzi concerto. Warm, committed playing from the orchestra, and good vivid stereo. An excellent bargain.

Symphony No. 1 in C major.
*** Philips 6500 154. New Philharmonia Orchestra, Wilfried Boettcher — CHERUBINI: *Symphony.****

This delightful symphony is well served both by the New Philharmonia under Boettcher and by the Philips engineers, who produce a most musical sound. Since the deletion of Kleiber's mono version, there is no alternative, and the attractions of the record are enhanced by its coupling, the fine Cherubini *Symphony*, also not otherwise available.

Clarinet quintet in B flat major, Op. 34.
(M) ** Oiseau-Lyre SOL 60020. Gervase de Peyer (clarinet), Melos Ensemble — MOZART: *Clarinet trio.****

This record of the *Clarinet quintet*, with its extrovert dotted rhythms in the first movement, and an almost bucolic scherzo, projects the music well. Gervase de Peyer is an excellent soloist and he is well supported by the string group. Good if not outstanding sound.

Flute trio in G minor (for flute, cello and piano), *Op. 63.*
(M) *** Oiseau-Lyre SOL 284. Melos Ensemble — BEETHOVEN: *Serenade.****
(B) *** Turnabout TV 34329S. Bernard Goldberg (flute), Theo Salzman (cello), Harry Franklin (piano) — DUSSEK: *Trio.****

This attractive *Trio* makes an excellent partner for Beethoven's miniature masterpiece, and on the Oiseau-Lyre disc, with felicitous playing and excellent recording, it is most enjoyable. On Turnabout too it is played with attractive spontaneity

and elegance, and the recording here is better focused than on the coupling.

OPERA

Der Freischütz (opera in 3 acts): complete recording.
*** DGG 2720 071 (3 discs). Gundula Janowitz, Edith Mathis (sopranos), Peter Schreier (tenor), Theo Adam (baritone), Siegfried Vogel, Franz Crass (basses), Leipzig Radio Chorus, Dresden State Orchestra, Carlos Kleiber.

This marked Carlos Kleiber's first major recording venture. The young conductor, son of a famous father, had already won himself a reputation for inspiration and unpredictability, and this fine, incisive account of Weber's atmospheric and adventurous score bears out all the good reports. With the help of an outstanding singing cast, excellent work by the recording producer, and electrically clear recording, this is a most compelling version of an opera which transfers well to the gramophone. Only occasionally does Kleiber betray a fractional lack of warmth.

Oberon (opera in 3 acts): complete recording.
*** DGG 2709 035 (3 discs). Donald Grobe (tenor), Birgit Nilsson (soprano), Placido Domingo (tenor), Hermann Prey (baritone), Julia Hamari (mezzo-soprano), Marga Schiml (soprano), Bavarian Radio Chorus and Symphony Orchestra, Rafael Kubelik.

Rarely has operatic inspiration been squandered so cruelly on impossible material as in Weber's *Oberon*. We owe it to Covent Garden's strange ideas in the mid-1820s of what 'English opera' should be that Weber's delicately conceived score is a sequence of illogical arias, scenas and ensembles strung together by an absurd pantomime plot. Though even on record the result is slacker because of that loose construction, one can appreciate, in a performance as stylish and refined as this, the contribution of Weber. The set numbers are separated by a sprinkling of dialogue (German not English) with help from a narration by one of Oberon's fairy characters. Birgit Nilsson is commanding in *Ocean, thou mighty monster*, and there is excellent singing too from the other principals, helped by Kubelik's ethereally light handling of the orchestra. Excellent recording.

Webern, Anton
(1883–1945)

5 Movements, Op. 5.
    ** (*) Argo ZRG 763. Academy of St Martin-in-the-Fields, Neville Marriner – HINDEMITH: *5 pieces*; SCHOENBERG: *Verklaerte Nacht.****

Where with *Verklaerte Nacht* Marriner has the best of both worlds, here, with more sharply etched writing, he cannot hope to match the original string-quartet medium in clarity and bite. The music is inevitably made more romantic, but with dedicated playing the result is deeply satisfying. Excellent recording.

5 Movements, Op. 5; Passacaglia, Op. 1; 6 Pieces for orchestra, Op. 6; Symphony, Op. 21.
    *** DGG 2711 014 (4 discs). Berlin Philharmonic Orchestra, Herbert von Karajan – BERG: *Lyric suite; 3 Pieces;* SCHOENBERG: *Pelleas and Melisande; Variations; Verklaerte Nacht.****

In the four-disc collection of music of the Second Viennese School, this last disc, devoted to four compact and chiselled Webern works, is in many ways the most remarkable of all. Karajan's expressive refinement reveals the emotional undertones behind this seemingly austere music, and the results are riveting – as for example in the dramatic and intense *Funeral march* of Op. 6. Op. 21 is altogether more difficult to grasp, but Karajan still conveys the intensity of argument even to the unskilled ear. Outstanding recording quality.

5 Pieces for orchestra, Op. 10.
    *** Philips SAL 3539. London Symphony Orchestra, Antal Dorati – BERG and SCHOENBERG: *Pieces.****

Webern's *Five pieces*, Op. 10, written between 1911 and 1913, mark an extreme point in his early development. Their compression is extreme, and their play with almost inaudible fragments may make the unsympathetic listener lose patience too quickly. What we are now gradually coming to appreciate, thanks to such performances as this, is that, like so much of Berg and Schoenberg, they have their emotional point. The coupling could hardly be more fitting, and the whole record can be strongly recommended to anyone genuinely wanting to explore the early work of Schoenberg and his followers before they formalized their ideas in twelve-note technique. Brighter recording quality than is common from this source, to match the precision of the writing.

6 Bagatelles for string quartet, Op. 9; 5 Movements for string quartet, Op. 5; Slow movement for string quartet (1905); String quartet (1905); String quartet, Op. 28.
    *** Philips 6500 105. Quartetto Italiano.

Readers who quail at the name of Webern need not tremble at the prospect of hearing this record. The early music in particular is most accessible, and all of it is played with such conviction and beauty of tone that its difficulties melt away or at least become manageable. The recording is of outstanding vividness and presence, and it is difficult to imagine a more eloquent or persuasive introduction to Webern's chamber music than this.

4 Pieces (for violin and piano), *Op. 7*.
(M) ** Supraphon SUAST 50693. Petr Messiereur (violin), Jarmila Kozderková (piano) – HINDEMITH: *Sonata;* SCHOENBERG: *Fantasy;* STRAVINSKY: *Duo concertante.***

These pieces were written some twenty years before anything else on the record, but even in this adventurous company they sound much more modern than their date of composition (1910) would suggest. They reflect Webern's first period of experiment with atonality, and though they hardly make engaging listening, their pithy argument repays close study. As in the other works on the disc, the Czech duo plays most strongly and sensitively.

Quartet for violin, clarinet, tenor saxophone and piano, Op. 22; String trio, Op. 20.
(M) ** Supraphon SUAST 50819. Musica Viva Pragensis, Zbynek Vostrak – SCHOENBERG: *Suite.** (*).

The *String trio,* Webern's first attempt at serial instrumental writing, dates from 1927 and the *Quartet* from 1930. Of the two the *Trio* is the more approachable; the *Quartet,* with its curious choice of instrumentation, shows Webernian fragmentation in extreme form. The performances bring the music to life (as far as Webern's writing can be said to be alive, using the term in its human sense), and the recording is quite good.

Weelkes, Thomas
(*c.* 1575–1623)

Alleluia; Give ear, O Lord; Hosanna to the son of David; I heard a voice; Nunc dimittis (in 5 parts); *When David heard; Organ voluntary.*
(B) ** Argo Eclipse ECS 683. Choir of St John's College, Cambridge, George Guest; Peter White (organ) – TALLIS: *Collection.***

There is some beautiful music here, and the programme provides plenty of contrast. The two anthems, *Alleluia* and *Hosanna,* are forthright and full of conviction, while *Give ear, O Lord* is appropriately more withdrawn in style. The reconstructed *Nunc dimittis* and the moving lament, *When David heard,* both show the composer at his most imaginative. The singing here is more consistently satisfying than on the Tallis side of the disc, although the anthems might have sounded more joyous. The recording has plenty of atmosphere.

Madrigals: *As Vesta was; Ay me, alas, hey ho; Cease now delight; Cease sorrows now; Hark, all ye lovely saints; Lady, the birds right fairly; Like two proud armies; My Phyllis bids me pack away; O care, thou wilt dispatch me – Hence care thou art too cruel; On the plains, fairy trains; Say, dear, when will your frowning leave; Sing we at pleasure; Strike it up tabor; Sweet love, I will no more abuse thee; Tan ta ra cries Mars; Those sweet delightful lilies; Though my carriage be but careless; Thule, the period of Cosmography – The Andalusian merchant; Why are you ladies – Hark, I hear some dancing.*
*** Decca SXL 6384. Wilbye Consort, dir. Peter Pears.

This record contains a number of Weelkes's most masterly madrigals, including *Thule, the period of Cosmography* and the famous *As Vesta was*. It serves as an admirable introduction to his work and can be safely recommended to all serious collectors. The performances are done with great style, as one would expect, and there is a splendid flow and sense of line here, even if occasionally some of the words are not so expressively treated. The recording is detailed and clear.

Weill, Kurt
(1900–1950)

Symphonies Nos. 1 and 2.
** (*) Argo ZRG 755. BBC Symphony Orchestra, Gary Bertini.

Both of these symphonies are fascinating works. The *Symphony No. 1* was a student piece, written in Berlin in 1921 when Weill was still a Busoni pupil. Fortunately the influences were mainly from Mahler and Schoenberg rather than Busoni (hence the master's disapproval), and though the thickness of texture has its dangers, the youthful urgency and imagination of the argument in a complex interlinked form carries the work off most successfully. The *Symphony No. 2* of 1933–4 is an obviously more mature work, with three colourful and effective moments that have much in common with the Soviet symphonies that Shostakovich, Kabalevsky and others were beginning to write at the time. Behind the characteristic ostinatos and near-vulgar melodies, there is a lurking seriousness – reflection of Weill's personal trials as he left Germany for American exile – and some assess this as the first really important symphony in the Austro-German tradition after the death of Mahler. The performances are committed, but could be better-disciplined. Good recording.

(i) *Der Dreigroschenoper (The Threepenny Opera):* complete recording; (ii) Songs: *Das Berliner Requiem: Ballade vom ertrunken Mädchen. Happy End: Bilbao song; Surabaya Johnny; Matrosen Tango; Mahagonny: Havanna Lied; Alabama song; Wie mann sich bettet. Der Silbersee: Lied der Fennimore.*
(M) ***** CBS 78279 (2 discs). (i)** Lotte Lenya, Wolfgang Neuss, Willy Trenk-Trebisch, Trude Hesterberg, Erich Schellow, Johanna Koczian, Wolfgang Grunert, Chorus and Dance Orchestra of Radio Free Berlin, Wilhelm Bruckner-Ruggeberg; (ii) Lotte Lenya with Orchestra, Roger Bean.

This is a vividly authentic recording of *The Threepenny Opera*, Weill's most famous score, darkly incisive and atmospheric, with Lotte Lenya giving an incomparable performance as Jenny. All the wrong associations built up round the music from indifferent performances melt away in the face of a reading as sharp and intense as this. Bright, immediate, real stereo recording. The songs make a marvellous filler on the fourth side, and although here the stereo is simulated the sound has plenty of atmosphere.

Weinberger, Jaromir
(1896–1967)

Schwanda the Bagpiper: Polka and fugue.
(M) *** (*) HMV SXLP 30125. Royal Philharmonic Orchestra, Rudolf Kempe – SMETANA: *Bartered Bride: overture etc.*; DVOŘÁK: *Scherzo capriccioso*.****

Kempe does the *Polka* stylishly and builds up the *Fugue* to an impressive climax. The recording, however, produces a touch of coarseness at the final climax because of the reverberation.

Weiss, Silvius
(1686–1750)

Fantasia in E minor; Suite in E flat major (for guitar).

*** DGG 2530 096. Narciso Yepes (guitar) – BACH: *Guitar music.****

The *Suite in E flat* is an attractive work, making a good coupling for some fine Bach performances.

Wellesz, Egon
(1885–1974)

Octet, Op. 67.

(M) *** Decca Ace of Diamonds SDD 316. Vienna Octet – BADINGS: *Octet.****

This great Austrian scholar and composer settled in Oxford in 1938 and played an important role in the musical life of the university. His work as a scholar in the field of Byzantine music was internationally renowned and his music was widely performed in post-war Austria. This *Octet* was commissioned by the Vienna Octet for performance at Salzburg, and it has both warmth and charm to commend it. Although Wellesz was the first biographer of Schoenberg and an early protagonist of the twelve-note discipline, he later rejected it and his early symphonies, written after he came to this country, and this *Octet* are wholly diatonic. The performance could hardly be more sympathetic and the score is beautifully recorded.

Whyte, Robert
(died 1574)

The Lamentations of Jeremiah (for five voices); *Magnificat on the first tone* (for six voices); Hymn: *Christe qui lux es et dies* (for five voices).

(M) ** (*) Pye Virtuoso TPLS 13008. Scuola di Chiesa, John Hoban.

Robert Whyte is a name known to very few people in this country: yet he is one of the finest composers of the Renaissance from these shores and his name deserves to rank among the most honoured of our musical figures. This record should do much to further his cause, for these fine works including the *Jeremiah Lamentations* are stylishly performed under the expert direction of John Hoban. Unfortunately the recording is not of comparable quality, but it would be wrong to dwell on its shortcomings when the interest of the music and the merits of the performance are so strong.

Widor, Charles-Marie
(1844–1937)

Organ symphony No. 5 in F minor, Op. 42/1.

(M) ** Nonesuch H 71210. Richard Ellsasser (organ of Hammond Museum, Gloucester, Mass.).

A recording of the complete *Organ symphony No. 5* is welcome, if only to show that the extraction of the famous *Toccata* finale for separate performance is entirely justified; the writing in the rest of the work is comparatively conventional and in no way equal to this famous piece. Richard Ellsasser is an eloquent and musical advocate, but he seems reluctant to draw on his big guns even in the *Toccata* itself, which here is comparatively restrained. The organ in use is a large-scale one (10,000 pipes, four manuals and 144 stops), built by John Hays Hammond in a stone tower of his castle home. The recording is admirable, faithful and easy to reproduce.

Organ symphony No. 5 in F minor, Op. 42/1: Toccata.
  (B) ** (*) Pye GSGC 14024. Ralph Downes (organ of the Royal Festival Hall, London) – BACH: *Recital.****

A brilliant performance of the famous *Toccata*, and the recording faithfully conveys the wide spatial placement of the organ in the Festival Hall. Unfortunately, in current pressings the sound is too highly modulated in the grooves, and the result is somewhat rough in the spectacular moments.

Organ symphony No. 5 in F minor, Op. 42/1: Toccata; Organ symphony No. 6, Op. 42/2: Allegro; Intermezzo.
  (B) * (*) Turnabout TV 34238S. Xavier Darasse (organ of St Sernin, Toulouse) – FRANCK and SAINT-SAËNS: *Pieces.* (*)

The famous *Toccata* emerges vividly, and the excerpts from the less well-known *Sixth Symphony* are also welcome, although the recording is somewhat harsh. Neither record label nor sleeve makes the contents of this disc very clear so far as the Widor is concerned.

Wieniawski, Henryk
(1835–80)

Violin concertos Nos. 1 in F sharp minor, Op. 14; 2 in D minor, Op. 22.
  *** HMV ASD 2870. Itzhak Perlman

(violin), London Philharmonic Orchestra, Seiji Ozawa.

Those who have enjoyed the relatively well-known *Second Concerto* of this contemporary of Tchaikovsky's should investigate this coupling of his two concertos. The *First* may not be so consistently memorable as the *Second*, but the central *Preghiera* is darkly intense, and the finale is full of the showmanship that was the mark of the composer's own virtuosity on the violin. Perlman gives scintillating performances, full of flair, and is excellently accompanied. First-rate recording.

Violin concerto No. 2 in D minor, Op. 22.
  *** Philips 6500 421. Henryk Szeryng (violin), Bamberg Symphony Orchestra, Jan Krenz – SZYMANOWSKI: *Violin concerto No. 2.****
  ** (*) CBS 72942. Pinchas Zukerman (violin), Royal Philharmonic Orchestra, Lawrence Foster – BLOCH: *Baal Shem ***; KABALEVSKY: *Concerto.** (*)
  (M) * (*) Supraphon SUAST 50687. Ida Haendel (violin), Prague Symphony Orchestra, Václav Smetáček – GLAZOUNOV: *Concerto.* (*)

A fine performance from Szeryng, a good alternative to the Perlman (see above), even though the latter probably surpasses Szeryng in sheer pyrotechnics. However, the Szymanowski *Concerto* with which the Szeryng is coupled balances the choice in his favour.

Zukerman's performance is a first-rate one too, with a beautiful account of the second movement, *Romance*. The bravura in the outer movements sparkles but is always tempered with musicianship. Close-up CBS recording and good couplings.

Miss Haendel is rather cagey about the show-off bits, but makes the most of the lyrical tunes. She is attentively accompanied, and the recording brings out plenty of orchestral detail but gives the soloist a rather wiry tone.

Légende, Op. 17.
> (B) ** Decca Eclipse ECS 663. Alfredo Campoli (violin), London Philharmonic Orchestra, Pierino Gamba – SAINT-SAËNS: *Violin concerto No. 3***; SARASATE: *Zigeunerweisen.****

The *Légende* opens atmospherically but its main theme is not really distinctive. Campoli's performance is sympathetic and the recording more than adequate.

Wilbye, John
(1574–1638)

Madrigals: *All pleasure is of this condition; As fair as morn; Come shepherd swains; Down in a valley; Draw on sweet night; Happy, oh happy he; Hard destinies are love and beauty; Softly, O softly drop my eyes; Stay, Corydon thou swain; Sweet honey sucking bees; There where I saw; Weep, weep mine eyes; Ye that do live in pleasures; Yet sweet, take heed.*
> (M) ** (*) Decca Ace of Diamonds SDD 275. Wilbye Consort, dir. Peter Pears.

Wilbye is one of the greatest of all madrigal composers and probably the greatest English madrigalist. As is to be expected, these artists give performances of the utmost technical aplomb, with superlatively true intonation and excellent tone. Unfortunately they are a trifle mannered, and many readers will feel that they sacrifice the earthier, robust qualities of the music to beauty of vocal tone. However this may be, there is such

a wealth of fine music on this record that reservations concerning the performance should not deter the reader. The recording is admirable and extremely clear.

Williams, Grace
(born 1906)

(i) *Carillons for oboe and orchestra.* (ii) *Trumpet concerto. Fantasia on Welsh nursery rhymes.* (iii) *Fairest of Stars.*
> *** HMV ASD 3006. (i) Anthony Camden (oboe); (ii) Howard Snell (trumpet); (iii) Janet Price (soprano); all with London Symphony Orchestra, Sir Charles Groves.

It is good to come across a composer who so glowingly shows that she believes in pleasing the listener's ear. The works here range attractively from the simple, well-known *Fantasia* (rather more than a colourfully orchestrated pot-pourri) through two crisply conceived concertante pieces to the relatively tough setting of Milton for soprano and orchestra, *Fairest of Stars.* The trumpet and oboe works – superbly played by soloists from the LSO – both show the affection and understanding of individual instrumental timbre which mark Grace Williams's work. A credit to the Welsh Arts Council that such a record can be produced. First-rate recording.

Penillion for orchestra.
> *** HMV ASD 2739. Royal Philharmonic Orchestra, Sir Charles Groves – HODDINOTT: *Welsh dances;* JONES: *The Country beyond the Stars.****

Penillion, written for the National Youth Orchestra of Wales, is a set of four colourful, imaginative pieces, easy on the ear but full of individual touches. 'Penillion' is the Welsh word for stanza, and though Grace Williams does not use any folk material, she retains the idea of a central melodic line (on the trumpet in the first two pieces) in stanza form. Excellent performance and recording.

Williamson, Malcolm
(born 1931)

(i) *Piano concerto No. 2;* (i; ii) *Concerto for 2 pianos and strings; Epitaphs for Edith Sitwell.*
*** EMI EMD 5520. (i) Gwenneth Pryor (piano); (ii) the composer (piano); strings of the English Chamber Orchestra, Yuval Zaliouk.

This is music designed to be enjoyed. Williamson wrote his *Piano concerto No. 2* at high speed, and its generous mixture of flavours makes up a disc that has far more to it than you might think at first from its jazzy syncopations. The *Two-piano concerto* is altogether tougher, though unmistakably from the same hand, while the *Epitaphs for Edith Sitwell* (originally for organ solo) show the composer at his most searching in tribute to the poet who inspired his second opera, *English Eccentrics*. Excellent performances and recording.

Violin concerto.
*** HMV ASD 2759. Yehudi Menuhin (violin), London Philharmonic Orchestra, Sir Adrian Boult – BERKELEY: *Concerto.****

An eloquent work with much greater expressive power and depth than one usually associates with this sometimes facile Australian composer. Menuhin plays it beautifully, and the LPO under Boult give generous support. The EMI recording is admirably clear and detailed,

and readers are urged to sample this satisfying and thoughtful concerto.

(i; ii) *Pas de quatre;* (i; iii) *Piano quintet;* (i) *5 Preludes for piano;* (iv; i) *From a Child's Garden* (song cycle).
*** Argo ZRG 682. (i) the composer (piano); (ii) Nash Ensemble; (iii) Gabrieli String Quartet; (iv) April Cantelo (soprano).

The *Piano quintet*, taking up barely a quarter of this disc, is a work which in its biting intensity gives a new perspective to Williamson's genius. Two comparatively brief meditative slow movements frame a central sonata-form movement which compresses into its energetic span an unusually powerful argument. This is music which invites eager repetition on the gramophone, particularly when the performance – with the composer at the piano – is fittingly intense. The rest of the disc is taken up with less taxing but equally repeat-worthy music, a setting of Stevenson poems for children, utterly fresh and simple; a brief and colourful ballet score; a set of deceptively simple preludes, innocently but vividly descriptive. Excellent recording. A record of modern music that challenges as well as delights.

The Happy Prince (children's opera in 1 act): complete recording.
*** Argo ZNF 5. Pauline Stevens, April Cantelo, Maureen Lehane, Iris Kells, Sheila Rex, Jean Allister, Guildhall Chamber Choir, Marriner String Quintet, the composer and Richard Rodney Bennett (piano duet), percussion, Marcus Dods.

Williamson's first opera for children takes the Oscar Wilde fairy story about the statue and the swallow, and with utmost simplicity turns it into a magical entertainment. Williamson's method is so direct it may initially strike the grown-up listener as embarrassingly naïf, but a crisp, professional performance like this brings home the emotional point of the story with a Puccini-like sureness. The impact is the more powerful for being achieved after a fairly close shave with cloying sentimentality. Inevitably the parallel with Britten will be drawn, but Williamson's sweet, rather thick textures and climbing melodies give the music a strong character of its own. The part of the Prince (the statue that is gradually robbed of his glory) is taken by the dedicatee, Pauline Stevens, and April Cantelo sings sweetly as the Swallow. The sleeve includes a complete libretto and notes.

Julius Caesar Jones (opera for children in 2 acts): complete recording.
** ** (*) Argo ZRG 529. April Cantelo, Norma Proctor, Michael Maurel, Finchley Children's Music Group, John Andrewes.

Julius Caesar Jones is a larger-scale work than *The Happy Prince* – its two acts spreading over a whole evening's entertainment. It is based on children's games of make-believe, with the children of an ordinary suburban family finding a world of their own in the Fortunate Isles which they create at the end of their garden. The exotic, tropical atmosphere of this child-created world releases a rich vein of inspiration in Williamson, and though the moral at the end – when the children become the practical actors and the grown-ups the dreamers – seems rather too facile, the whole entertainment is most memorable, and transfers well to the medium of the gramophone. Unlike the Argo recording of *The Happy Prince* this one employs the original company of children for all the parts except those of the three grown-ups. The results are – if one is honest – musically variable, but the performance has still

caught the right, fresh flavour. The recording quality is very good indeed, despite very long sides. A libretto is included with the record.

Wolf, Hugo
(1860–1903)

Italian serenade in G major.
*** Philips SAL 3640. I Musici – MENDELSSOHN: *Octet;* ROSSINI: *Sonata.****
** Decca SXL 6533. Stuttgart Chamber Orchestra, Karl Münchinger – SUK: *Serenade;* R. STRAUSS: *Capriccio introduction.***

The *Italian serenade* is an infectiously gay and high-spirited piece, a masterpiece without doubt and one whose popularity is by no means as great as it should be. I Musici play it extremely well, even if they do not do full justice to its effervescent spirits and sheer *joie de vivre.* They are well recorded and reproduced vividly. Münchinger's performance is good, but could be outstanding if it had a shade more sparkle. Well recorded.

String quartet in D minor.
(B) ** Oryx 1820. Keller Quartet.

The *String quartet* was written when Wolf was only twenty, the finale added later. The music has all the direct passion of youth, and the Keller Quartet match the work with the ardent eloquence of their performance. The virile style means that there is very little relaxation, but the intensity offers its own spontaneity. The recording is forward but truthful. Incidentally the performance reverses the order of the slow movement and scherzo.

Lieder: *Auch kleine Dinge; Heiss mich nicht Reden; Kennst du das Land;*

Mausfallen spruchlein; Nur wer die Sehnsucht kennt; So lasst mich scheinen.
(M) ** Oiseau-Lyre SOL 293. Helen Watts (contralto), Geoffrey Parsons (piano) – SCHUMANN: *Frauenliebe und Leben.***

Helen Watts is a fine artist, and her singing will surely give much pleasure here. The performances tend to be just a little too undercharacterized to be comparable with those of the greatest Wolf interpreters. Geoffrey Parsons accompanies sensitively, and the recording is of very good quality.

Italienisches Liederbuch: complete recording.
*** Philips 6700 041 (2 discs). Elly Ameling (soprano), Gérard Souzay (baritone), Dalton Baldwin (piano).

Elly Ameling, delicately sweet and precise, contrasts well with Souzay with his fine-drawn sense of line. The charm and point of these brief but intensely imaginative songs are well presented, with perceptive accompaniment from Dalton Baldwin. It is sad that the unforgettable version of Schwarzkopf and Fischer-Dieskau with Gerald Moore has been deleted, but this Philips set is welcome as a fair substitute. Good recording.

Mörike Lieder: complete recording.
*** DGG 2740 113 (3 discs). Dietrich Fischer-Dieskau (baritone), Daniel Barenboim (piano).
(M) ** (*) Argo 3BBA 1008/10. Benjamin Luxon (baritone), David Willison (piano).

Fischer-Dieskau and Barenboim give a performance of this formidable collection of some of Wolf's most inspired songs which consistently reveals an ability to spark off each other's imagination. In song after song Fischer-Dieskau is masterly in scene-setting, in story-telling, in pointing gaiety, as in *Er ist's*, or drawing out expressive legato, as in *Verborgenheit*. The recording is excellent. This set includes two songs not in the Argo version.

Benjamin Luxon and David Willison give thoughtful, finely conceived performances, lacking not detail but the sense of spontaneous imagination which illuminates the version of Fischer-Dieskau. Luxon's voice is not always well treated by the microphone, sounding gritty at times.

Mörike Lieder: *An eine Aeolsharfe; Auf eine Christblume I and II; Begegnung; Bei einer Trauung; Elfenlied; Er ist's; Gebet; Die Geister am Mummelsee; In der Frühe; Der Knabe und das Immlein; Lebe wohl; Lied vom Winde; Nimmersatte Liebe; Nixe Binsefuss; Rat einer Alten; Schlafendes Jesuskind; Selbstgeständnis; Ein Stündlein wohl vor Tag; Das verlassene Mägdlein.*
** Philips 6500 128. Elly Ameling (soprano), Dalton Baldwin (piano).

Elly Ameling possesses a voice of great charm, and her readings here are unfailingly musical. Her diction is clean and her interpretations intelligent. Yet there is a certain uniformity of colour and mood that makes listening to the recital as a whole less satisfying than choosing individual songs. There is, needless to say, much to enjoy, and the recording cannot be flawed. Dalton Baldwin is a bit prosaic at times but against this must be balanced some highly musical and carefully thought-out details. There is some marvellous music in this recital and it is on this count that it must be recommended.

Das Spanische Liederbuch (complete): *Geistliche Lieder (Sacred songs) 1–10;*

Weltliche Lieder (Secular songs) 1–34.
** (*) DGG 2707 035 (2 discs). Elisabeth Schwarzkopf (soprano), Dietrich Fischer-Dieskau (baritone), Gerald Moore (piano).

The advantage of this set is its variety. The *Spanische Liederbuch* was not intended as a cycle, and there are few people, one imagines, who would wish to hear it from end to end at one sitting. However, the set, with its ten sacred and thirty-four secular songs, naturally gains from the variety of vocal timbre, and both Schwarzkopf and Fischer-Dieskau are in excellent form here, even if the former will disappoint some of her admirers as sounding just a little mannered, even arch, at times. The recording is very good, and Gerald Moore's accompanying is predictably perceptive in its musicianship.

Wolf-Ferrari, Ermanno
(1876–1948)

Il Campiello: Intermezzo (The Little Field); Ritornello. La Dama Bomba: overture. I quattro rusteghi: Prelude to Act 2. The Jewels of the Madonna: suite. Susanna's Secret: overture.
(M) ** (*) Decca Ace of Diamonds SDD 452. Paris Conservatoire Orchestra, Nello Santi.

The performances here are not of the most subtle, but they are crisp, clean and lively. Santi would not be himself if he did not tighten up in many places which call for warmer, freer treatment. But the recording is first-rate and the playing itself is good enough to outweigh such shortcomings – and what delightful music it all is, unashamedly frothy and lightweight.

Wood, Hugh
(born 1932)

String quartet No. 1, Op. 4.
*** Argo ZRG 565. Aeolian Quartet – MAW: *Quartet.****

A shorter, less luxuriant work than the fine quartet by Nicholas Maw on the reverse, but one which shares with it a natural, unforced seriousness of utterance. Wood's idiom is not always easy on the ear, but with a fine performance from the Aeolian Quartet, naturally committed players, this is a work which rewards repetition on the gramophone. First-rate recording.

(i) *String quartets Nos. 1, Op. 4; 2, Op. 13;* (ii) *The Horses* (3 songs of poems by Ted Hughes), *Op. 10; The Rider Victory* (4 songs of poems by Edwin Muir).
*** Argo ZRG 750. (i) Dartington String Quartet; (ii) April Cantelo (soprano), Paul Hamburger (piano).

Hugh Wood's thoughtful music deserves representation on record, particularly in performances as strong and effective as these. The *First Quartet*, dating from the early 1960s, reveals a continuing debt to Berg, but with the *Second Quartet* Wood develops his own more concentrated style in a formidably argued single movement of 39 sections. The two sets of songs, also atonal in idiom, yet reveal a sympathetic reliance on conventional values. Excellent recording.

Ysaÿe, Eugène
(1858–1931)

Au rouet, Op. 13; Fantaisie, Op. 32 (both for violin and piano).
- (M) * Supraphon SUAST 50580. Karel Sroubek (violin), Josef Hála (piano) — SZYMANOWSKI: *Mythes.***

Ysaÿe's solo sonatas are exploratory and full of character, but the two pieces here are conventional essays in romantic rhetoric that greatly outstay their welcome.

Zandonai, Riccardo
(1883–1944)

Francesca da Rimini (opera in 4 acts): excerpts.
- ** (*) Decca SET 422. Magda Olivero (soprano), Mario del Monaco (tenor), Monte Carlo Opera Orchestra, Nicola Rescigno.

Magda Olivero is a fine artist who has not been represented nearly enough on record, and this Zandonai disc – like the complete set of Giordano's *Fedora*, also on Decca – does some belated justice. It would have been preferable to have a complete version of this ambitious opera – the publisher Tito Ricordi tended to think more highly of it than of the operas of his other more famous client, Puccini – but these selections give a fair flavour. Decca opted to record three substantial scenes rather than snippets, and though Mario del Monaco as Paolo is predictably coarse in style, his tone is rich and strong, and he does not detract from the achievement, unfailingly perceptive and musicianly, of Olivero as Francesca herself. Good recording.

Zelenka, Jan Dismas
(1679–1745)

Sonatas Nos. 1 in F major; 2 in G minor; 3 in B flat major; 4 in G minor; 5 in F major; 6 in C minor.
- ⊛ *** DGG Archive 2708 027 (2 discs). Heinz Holliger, Maurice Bourgue (oboes), Saschko Gawriloff (violin), Klaus Thunemann (bassoon), Lucio Buccarella (double-bass), Christiane Jaccottet (harpsichord).

Zelenka, a contemporary of Bach born in Bohemia, worked for most of his life in Dresden – another dull German Kapellmeister, you might think. But thanks to the urgent advocacy of the oboist Heinz Holliger, we can now appreciate just how vital and original Zelenka's admittedly limited genius was. In these *Trio sonatas* it is almost as though Bach had had a touch of Ives in him, so unexpected are some of the developments and turns of argument. The tone of voice is often dark and intense, directly comparable to Bach at his finest, and all through these superb performances the electricity of the original inspiration comes over with exhilarating immediacy. Fine recording. A set to recommend urgently to any lover of baroque music.

Zeller, Karl
(1842–98)

Der Vogelhändler (operetta): abridged recording.
- (M) ** (*) Telefunken NT 600. Hilde Gueden (soprano), Peter Minch (tenor), Benno Kusche, Heinz-Maria Lins, Lotte Schädle, Karl

Terkal, Martha Mödl, Grand Operetta Chorus and Orchestra, Carl Michalski.

Zeller's score for *Der Vogelhändler (The Bird-catcher)*, dating from 1882, is more consistently inspired than that for the more famous *Dubarry*, although it does not have one single item like *I give my heart* (from the latter piece) with a melodic contour to be instantly memorable. This infectious performance offers a generally high standard and by the finale of Act 1 Zeller is pouring out a virtually continuous stream of attractive invention, which the cast here put over with idiomatic verve. Hilde Gueden has some fine moments in the latter part of the operetta and all the soloists are excellent. The bright Telefunken sound places everything in a forward balance, but the acoustic is not wanting in atmosphere. Admirers of Lehár should find this disc well worth investigating, but it is a pity that no synopsis or details of the contents in English are provided on the sleeve.

More about Penguins
and Pelicans

Penguinews, which appears every month, contains details of all the new books issued by Penguins as they are published. From time to time it is supplemented by *Penguins in Print*, which is a complete list of all titles available. (There are some five thousand of these.)

A specimen copy of *Penguinews* will be sent to you free on request. For a year's issues (including the complete lists) please send 50p if you live in the British Isles, or 75p if you live elsewhere. Just write to Dept EP, Penguin Books Ltd, Harmondsworth, Middlesex, enclosing a cheque or postal order, and your name will be added to the mailing list.

In the U.S.A.: For a complete list of books available from Penguins in the United States write to Dept CS, Penguin Books Inc., 7110 Ambassador Road, Baltimore, Maryland 21207.

In Canada: For a complete list of books available from Penguin in Canada write to Penguin Books Canada Ltd, 41 Steelcase Road West, Markham, Ontario.